W9-BCI-457

A DOONESBURY
RETROSPECTIVE

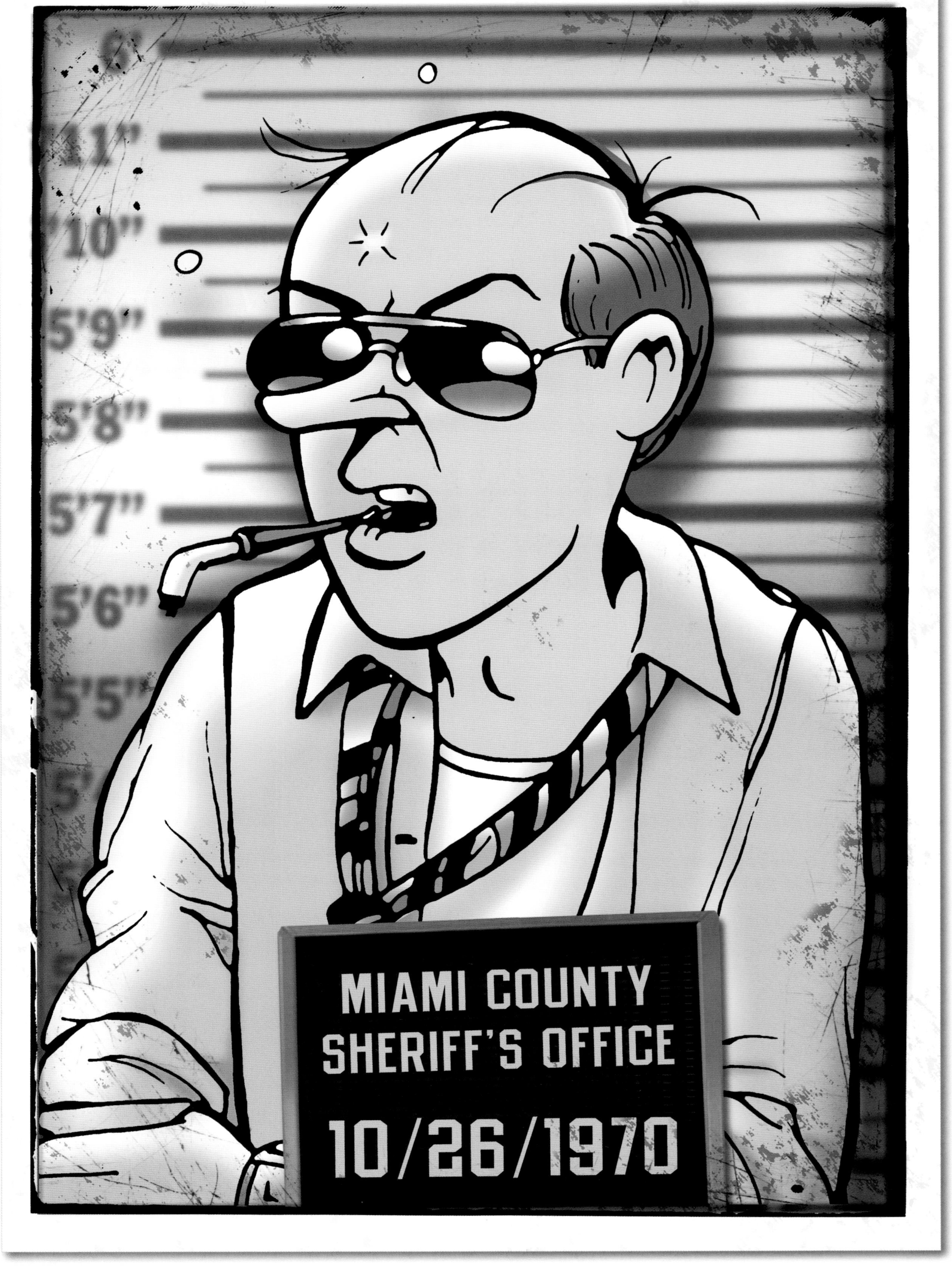
10"
5'9"
5'8"
5'7"
5'6"
5'5"
MIAMI COUNTY
SHERIFF'S OFFICE
10/26/1970

A DOONESBURY RETROSPECTIVE

GB Trudeau

Andrews McMeel
Publishing, LLC

Kansas City • Sydney • London

DOONESBURY is distributed internationally by Universal Uclick.

40: A Doonesbury Retrospective copyright © 2010 by G. B. Trudeau.
All rights reserved. Printed in China. No part of this book may be used
or reproduced in any manner whatsoever without written permission except
in the case of reprints in the context of reviews. For information, write
Andrews McMeel Publishing, LLC, an Andrews McMeel Universal company,
1130 Walnut Street, Kansas City, Missouri 64106.

10 11 12 13 14 POA 10 9 8 7 6 5 4 3 2 1

ISBN: 978-0-7407-9735-4

Library of Congress Control Number: 2010924501
www.andrewsmcmeel.com

DOONESBURY may be viewed on the Internet at:
www.doonesbury.com and www.GoComics.com

ATTENTION: SCHOOLS AND BUSINESSES

Andrews McMeel books are available at quantity discounts with bulk purchase for
educational, business, or sales promotional use. For information, please write to:
Special Sales Department, Andrews McMeel Publishing, LLC,
1130 Walnut Street, Kansas City, Missouri 64106.

Produced by Lionheart Books Ltd.
5200 Peachtree Road*
Atlanta, Georgia 30341

Cover, slipcase, essay spreads and character map designed by
George Corsillo, Design Monsters

Printed in China through Asia Pacific Offset

For Jane

"In 1970, there were so many banners afield,
so many movements afire."

Contents

Introduction

A few words about what this collection is not.

It's not about Watergate, gas lines, cardigans, Reaganomics, a thousand points of light, Monica, New Orleans, or even Dubya. None of that.

Admit it, you're relieved.

You've either forgotten much of the historical detritus referenced in *Doonesbury* through the years, or, even more understandable, you'd like to. Or—and there's no shame in this, either—you weren't alive when much of it went down. In any event, it's tough decoding long-expired topical material, and there's little pleasure in humor that requires explanation.

So this anthology isn't about the defining events of the last four decades. It is instead about how it felt to live through those years—a loosely organized chronicle of modern times, as crowdsourced by what was once called "the *Doonesbury* gang."

That gang is now a mob, but it all began with a single character—B.D., a knuckleheaded college quarterback who presided over a huddle of talented but infantile subordinates.

"Most humor strips do just fine with a half-dozen or so players. . . . By the late '80s, *Doonesbury* had almost forty."

The strip, then called *Bull Tales*, was strictly a campus one-off, a coattail creation. It was inspired by a local phenom named Brian Dowling, who in real life was as smart and modest as his comic strip counterpart was obtuse and arrogant. (Hence the humor, I hoped.) There was no reason Dowling should have enjoyed his shabby portrayal in the strip, but it seems he did, adding to his aura of imperturbability.

Then came syndication. The narrow focus had worked fine for a local sports strip, but to court the attention of a national audience, a more diverse cast had to be assembled. And so I added eponymous everyman Mike Doonesbury and snarky activist Mark Slackmeyer—sturdy, recognizable archetypes to join B.D. as the strip's tent-pole characters. It was my first and last concession to editorial balance, and I quickly subverted it. As *Doonesbury* opened wide and gained momentum, a supporting cast converged from all directions: Zonker, avatar of high hippie slackness; Joanie, accidental feminist; Ginny, post-civil rights era black striver; and Rev. Scot Sloan, social justice warrior.

In 1970, there were so many banners afield, so many movements afire. And since the action was predominantly playing out on college campuses, I decided to stick with the undergraduate scene I knew. For the next twelve years, the core characters in *Doonesbury* stayed put, happily hunkered down at Walden, the cozy commune that housed them as they faithfully failed to age out of college. Finally, in 1984, I took a sabbatical and hit the reset button. The strip's static universe lurched into real time, dislodging the cast from their bucolic surroundings and sending them to join secondary characters such as Duke, Lacey, J.J., and Zeke, who had been growing up in a parallel universe more responsive to the passage of time.

Thus realigned, the tribe fanned out across the country, alighting in new venues such as the East Village and Georgetown and Malibu, where their lives were of necessity repopulated with mates, friends, associates, and (whoa!) children. A profusion of new supporting characters popped up everywhere.

Most humor strips do just fine with a half-dozen or so players. *Calvin and Hobbes* had only two essential characters, and one of them was imaginary. By the late '80s, *Doonesbury* had almost forty. The clutter became challenging for longtime readers

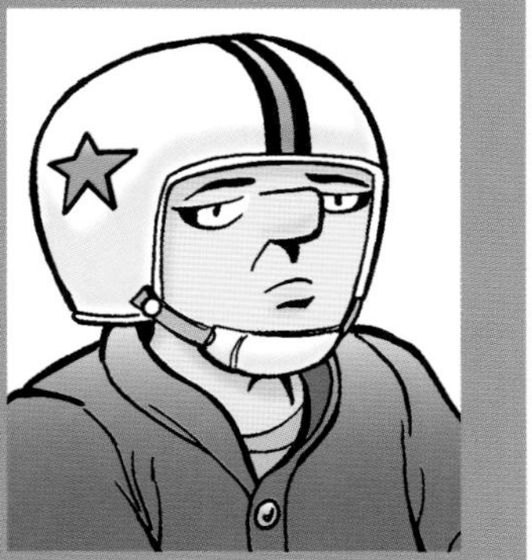

FIRST WAVE
1970–1974

B.D.
Mike Doonesbury
Mark Slackmeyer
Phil Slackmeyer
Zonker Harris
Barbara Ann Boopstein
Nguyen Van Phred
Bernie
Rufus Jackson
Rev. Scot Sloan
Joanie Caucus
Jim Andrews
President King
Roland Burton Hedley, Jr.

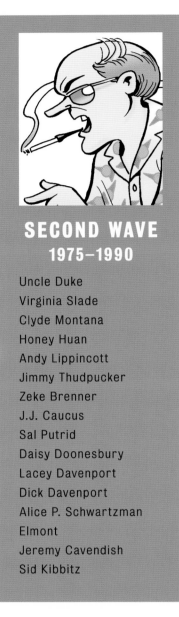

SECOND WAVE
1975–1990

Uncle Duke
Virginia Slade
Clyde Montana
Honey Huan
Andy Lippincott
Jimmy Thudpucker
Zeke Brenner
J.J. Caucus
Sal Putrid
Daisy Doonesbury
Lacey Davenport
Dick Davenport
Alice P. Schwartzman
Elmont
Jeremy Cavendish
Sid Kibbitz

intimidating for latecomers—like opening a Russian novel in the middle. But the matrix of relationships at the heart of *Doonesbury* yielded endless narrative possibilities. I didn't have to find a new twist on old themes as most legacy strips do—or rethread the needle every day like a gag cartoonist. I simply followed the characters into their quotidian lives, played out against a scrim of cultural and political context, and occasionally bumped them into that thicket of coincidence that only fictional characters must endure. Honey reencounters her old roommate J.J. on Donald Trump's yacht! Mike marries Kim, introduced twenty years earlier as a Vietnamese orphan! Alex and Toggle find each other on Facebook! Think of the odds! All storytellers stand on the shoulders of Dickens.

So the midlife sprawl, the unceasing procreation, helped to keep the strip relevant and on its feet. And in recent years, a third wave of dramatis personae has been dispatched to rejuvenate the strip, adding to its social complexity: Zipper, the Gen-Xer who goes into a controlled stall long enough to join the Millennials; Alex, the brilliant girl geek with untethered dreams; the young wounded veteran Toggle, struggling to find a New Normal; Melissa, the Army mechanic who battles invisible demons while getting broken choppers back up into the thin air over Afghanistan.

And since we all need someone to lean on, most of these newbies arrived with support. Wingmen such as Jeff, Drew, Roz, and Dr. Shipley. Caregivers such as Elias, Cora, and Mrs. DeLuca. Even B.D.'s daughter Sam has someone to inspire and motivate her. Unfortunately, it's Sarah Palin, but I live to serve my characters, and to Sam, the feisty former pageant queen is catnip.

New characters always arrive flush with possibility, especially the younger ones. Teenagers and twentysomethings are in the act of becoming, they're at their most dynamic, unlike their elders, who've pretty much become what they're going to be. With an established character such as Mike, readers can generally predict how he will react to a new plot development; with Alex, not so much. So which of the two do you suppose is more fun to write for? Hint: You've been seeing a lot of her lately.

A reader recently noted that Alex has become the new center of gravity in the strip, that *Doonesbury's* auspices have passed from Mike to his daughter. What a concept. Alex was only born in 1988, but now, from her shaky perch as an insecure undergraduate, she rules. The strip's original animating idea—that it's inherently interesting to watch a generation come of age—repeats itself.

Of course, not all the newer characters are young—Elias, the Vet Center counselor; Cora, the sexual trauma specialist; Sherm, the studio owner; and Dr. Shipley, the community college prof, are all grizzled veterans, but with those characters, the fun is in the reverse engineering. The reveal lies not in what they become, but in how they became what they are. The backstory is rarely worked out in advance, so I get to go on the same journey as the readers, preceding them by mere days, narrating over my shoulder: "Aha! *This* explains a lot!"

None of which is to say that the old, established characters aren't essential. Without them, *Doonesbury* would flap around, unfocused and flimsy. Mike and B.D. and Joanie and their long histories give the strip ballast, a sense of cumulative weight and purpose. When I return to them, it's not out of laziness or habit—I'm simply reconnecting with my roots. Respect must be paid to the founding dudes.

But only, I should add, on the clock. I refuse to fraternize with any of the crew during off-hours. It's challenging enough to find time for real-life loved ones without competition from my little imaginary pals. So they always recede from thought when I'm away from my drawing board. Both they and I need alone time.

So, here, feel free to borrow them for a while. Get reacquainted with some old buds and let them take you back to times that weren't necessarily better or worse, just different. Don't be sore if an old favorite is missing; this volume, as massive as it may appear, contains only 13 percent of the over 14,000 published strips. For those of you new to *Doonesbury*, and those who have been away for a while, I've provided some running commentary on the characters, as well as a clarifying, if vertiginous, relationship chart at the centerfold. Other than that, you're on your own.

Hope you enjoy the trip.

Garry Trudeau

New York City
March 3, 2010

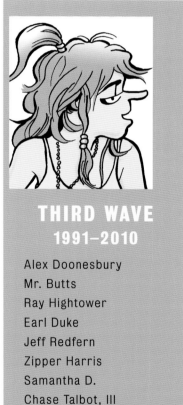

THIRD WAVE
1991–2010

Alex Doonesbury
Mr. Butts
Ray Hightower
Earl Duke
Jeff Redfern
Zipper Harris
Samantha D.
Chase Talbot, III
Kim Rosenthal
Drew
Elias
Melissa Wheeler
President Trff Bmzklfrpz
Leo DeLuca

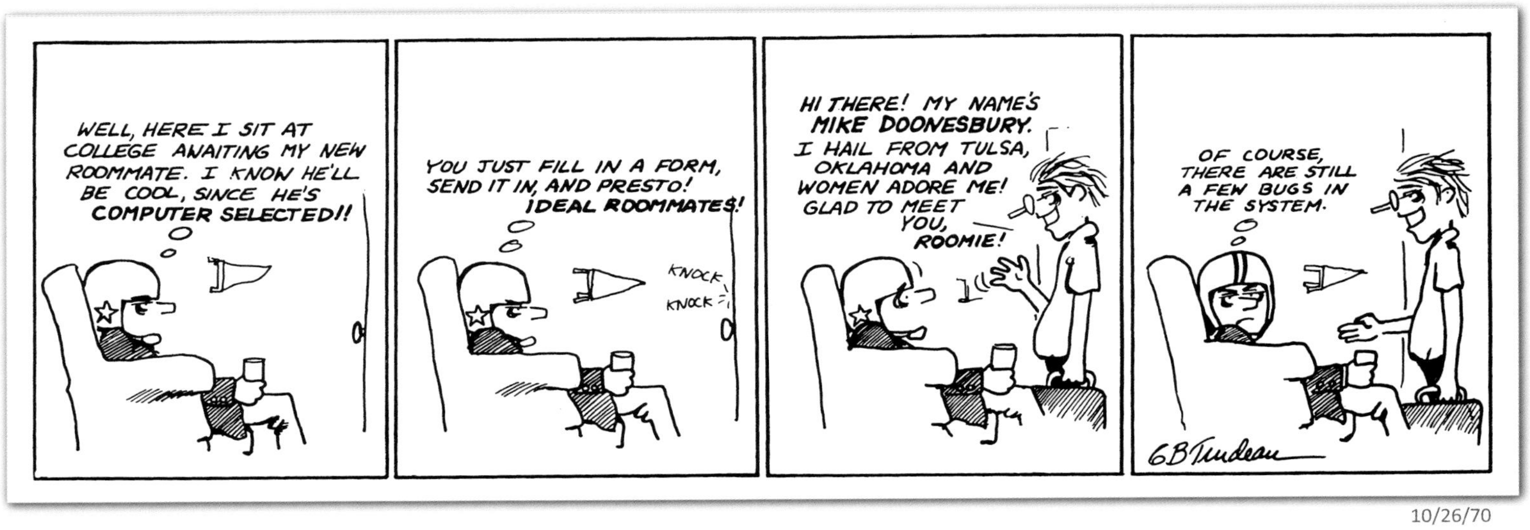
WELL, HERE I SIT AT COLLEGE AWAITING MY NEW ROOMMATE. I KNOW HE'LL BE COOL, SINCE HE'S COMPUTER SELECTED!!
YOU JUST FILL IN A FORM, SEND IT IN, AND PRESTO! IDEAL ROOMMATES!
KNOCK KNOCK
HI THERE! MY NAME'S MIKE DOONESBURY. I HAIL FROM TULSA, OKLAHOMA AND WOMEN ADORE ME! GLAD TO MEET YOU, ROOMIE!
OF COURSE, THERE ARE STILL A FEW BUGS IN THE SYSTEM.

10/26/70

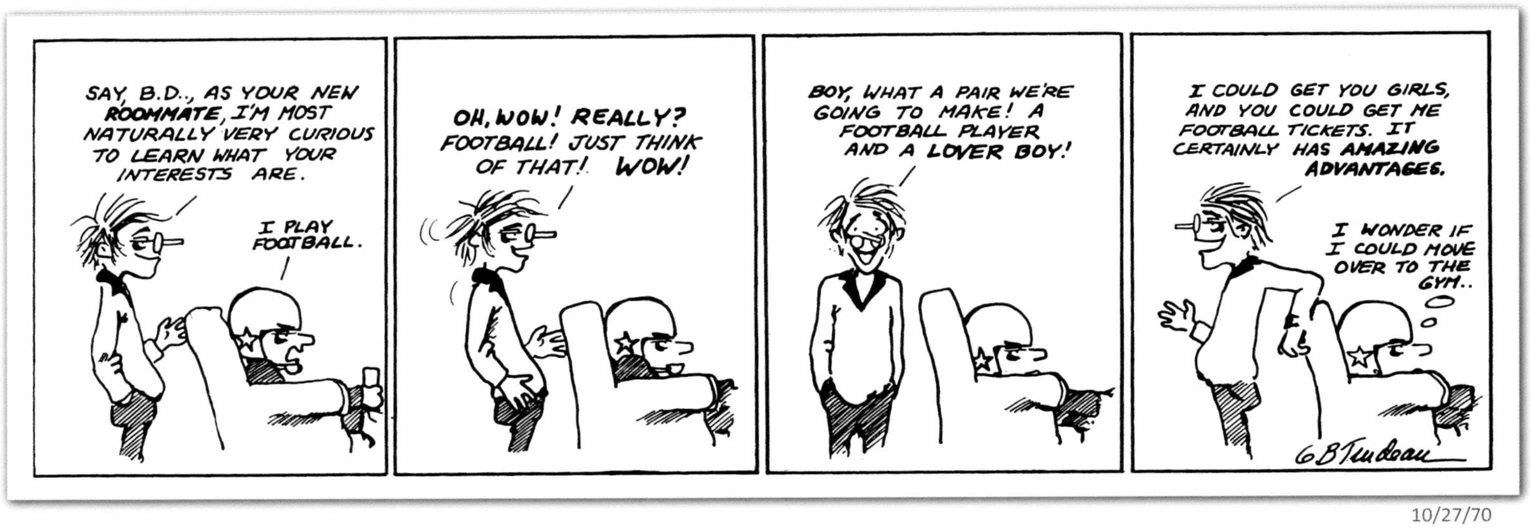
SAY, B.D., AS YOUR NEW ROOMMATE, I'M MOST NATURALLY VERY CURIOUS TO LEARN WHAT YOUR INTERESTS ARE.
I PLAY FOOTBALL.
OH, WOW! REALLY? FOOTBALL! JUST THINK OF THAT! WOW!
BOY, WHAT A PAIR WE'RE GOING TO MAKE! A FOOTBALL PLAYER AND A LOVER BOY!
I COULD GET YOU GIRLS, AND YOU COULD GET ME FOOTBALL TICKETS. IT CERTAINLY HAS AMAZING ADVANTAGES.
I WONDER IF I COULD MOVE OVER TO THE GYM..

10/27/70

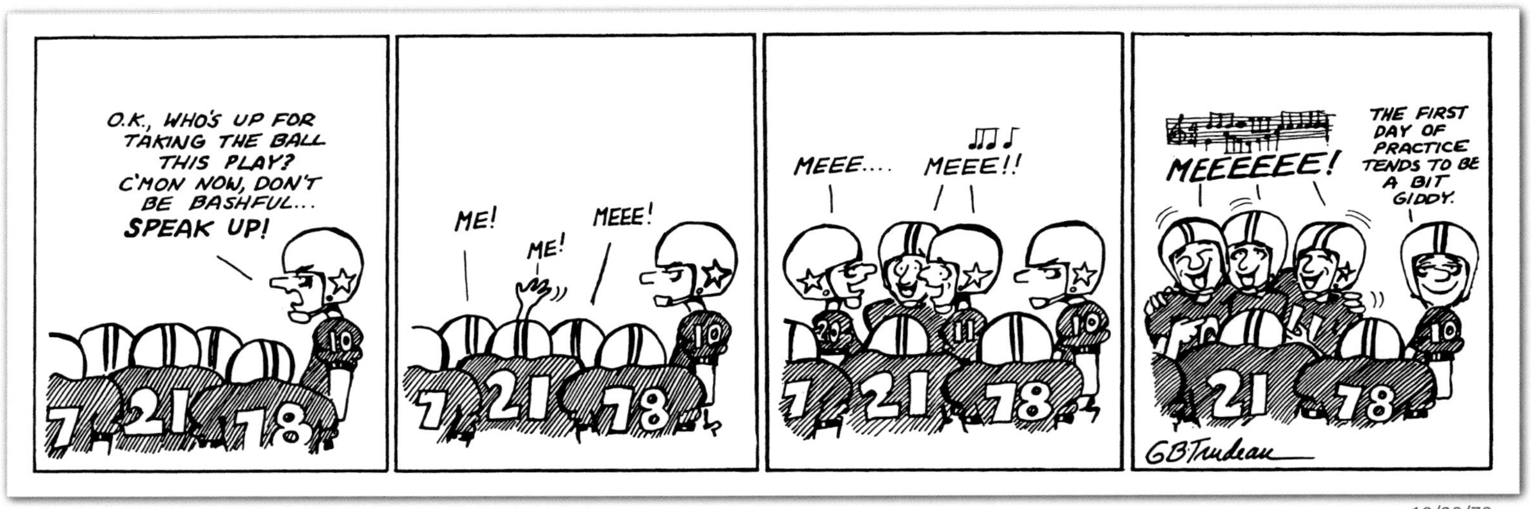
O.K., WHO'S UP FOR TAKING THE BALL THIS PLAY? C'MON NOW, DON'T BE BASHFUL... SPEAK UP!
ME!
ME!
MEEE!
MEEE....
MEEE!!
MEEEEEE!
THE FIRST DAY OF PRACTICE TENDS TO BE A BIT GIDDY.

10/30/70

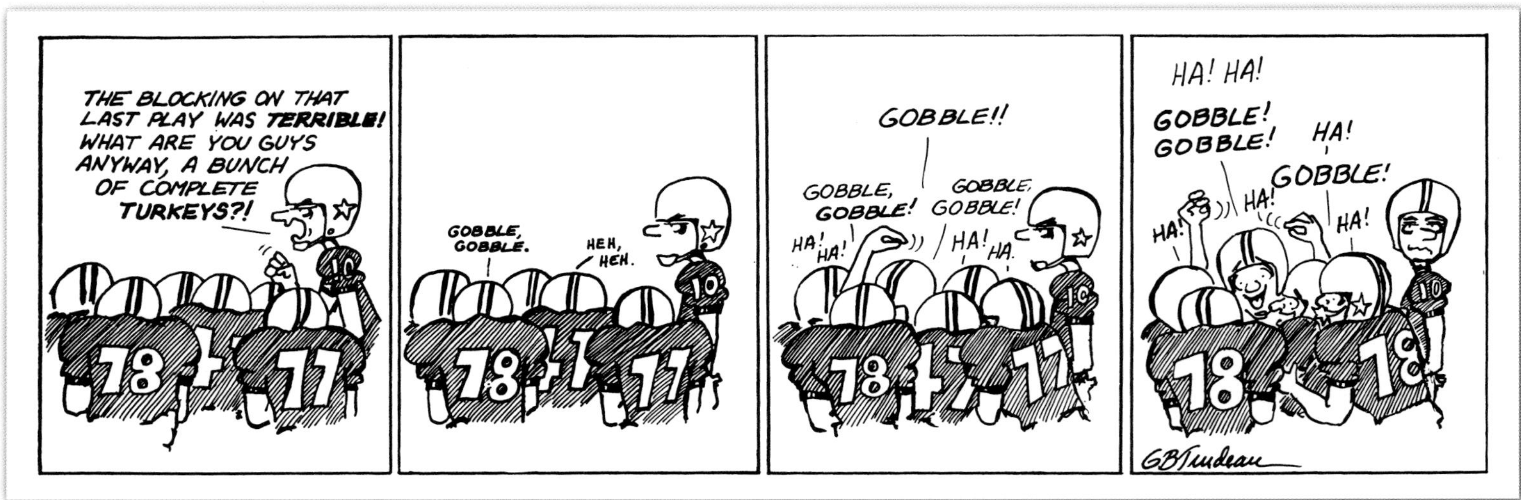
THE BLOCKING ON THAT LAST PLAY WAS TERRIBLE! WHAT ARE YOU GUYS ANYWAY, A BUNCH OF COMPLETE TURKEYS?!
GOBBLE, GOBBLE.
HEH, HEH.
GOBBLE!!
GOBBLE, GOBBLE!
GOBBLE, GOBBLE!
HA! HA!
HA! HA.
HA! HA!
GOBBLE! GOBBLE!
HA!
GOBBLE!
HA!
HA!
HA!

11/3/70

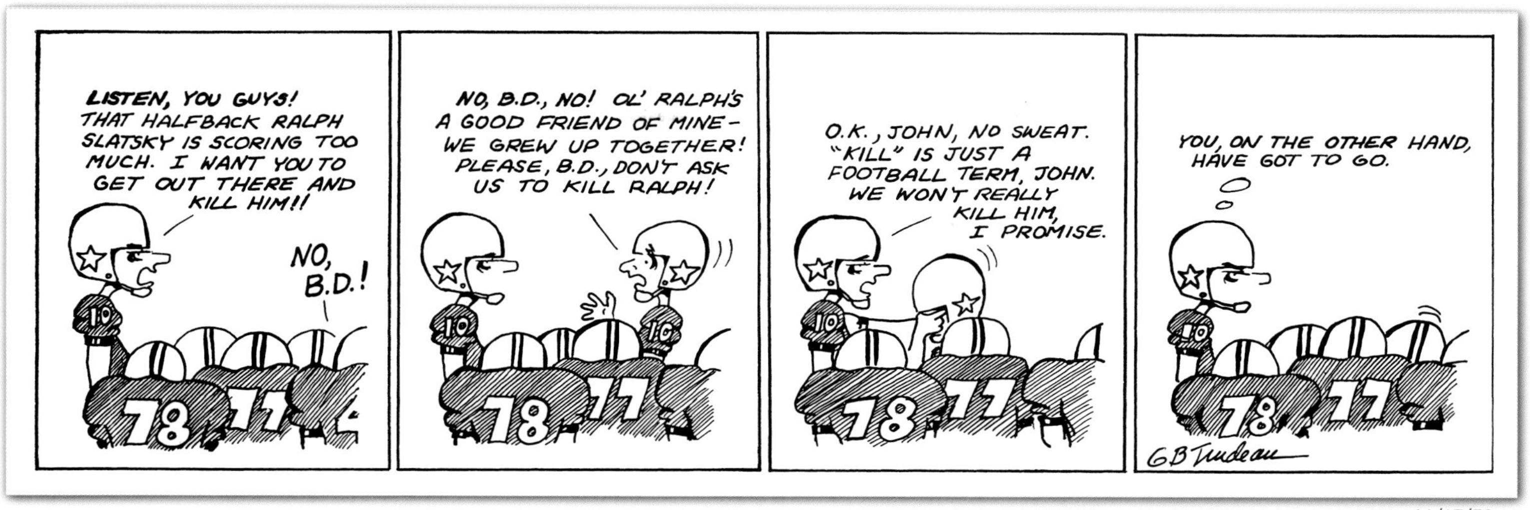
LISTEN, YOU GUYS! THAT HALFBACK RALPH SLATSKY IS SCORING TOO MUCH. I WANT YOU TO GET OUT THERE AND KILL HIM!!
NO, B.D.!
NO, B.D., NO! OL' RALPH'S A GOOD FRIEND OF MINE- WE GREW UP TOGETHER! PLEASE, B.D., DON'T ASK US TO KILL RALPH!
O.K., JOHN, NO SWEAT. "KILL" IS JUST A FOOTBALL TERM, JOHN. WE WON'T REALLY KILL HIM, I PROMISE.
YOU, ON THE OTHER HAND, HAVE GOT TO GO.
GBTrudeau
11/17/70

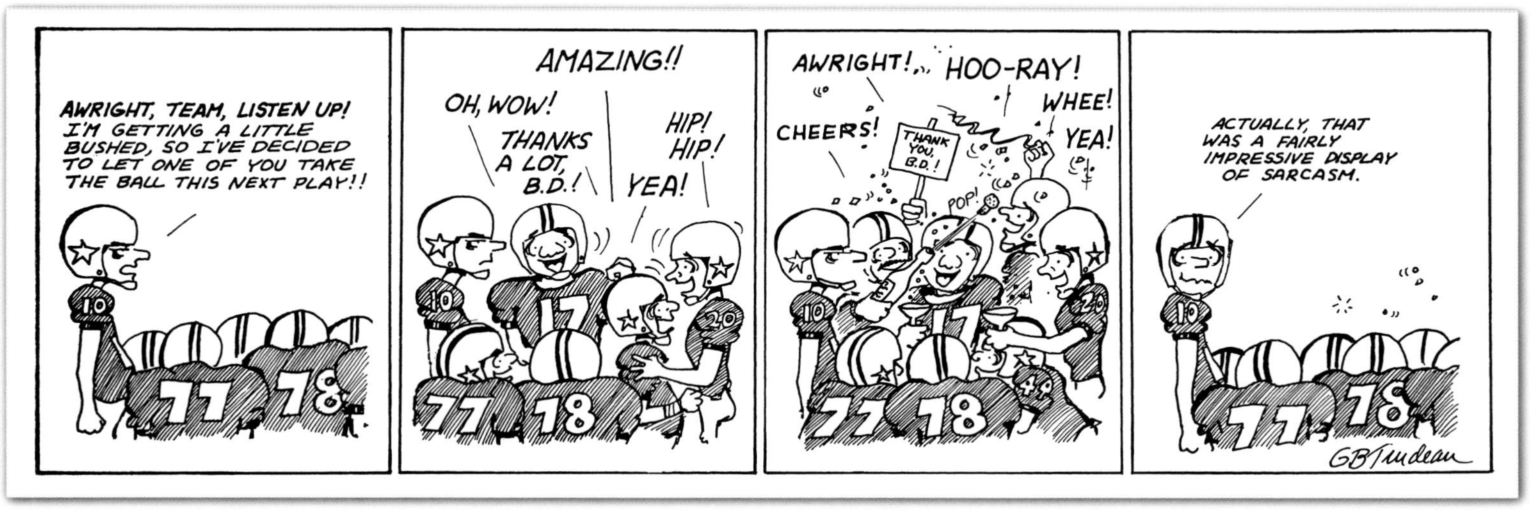
AWRIGHT, TEAM, LISTEN UP! I'M GETTING A LITTLE BUSHED, SO I'VE DECIDED TO LET ONE OF YOU TAKE THE BALL THIS NEXT PLAY!!
AMAZING!!
OH, WOW!
THANKS A LOT, B.D.!
HIP! HIP!
YEA!
AWRIGHT!
HOO-RAY!
WHEE!
CHEERS!
YEA!
THANK YOU, B.D.!
POP!
ACTUALLY, THAT WAS A FAIRLY IMPRESSIVE DISPLAY OF SARCASM.
GBTrudeau
11/16/70

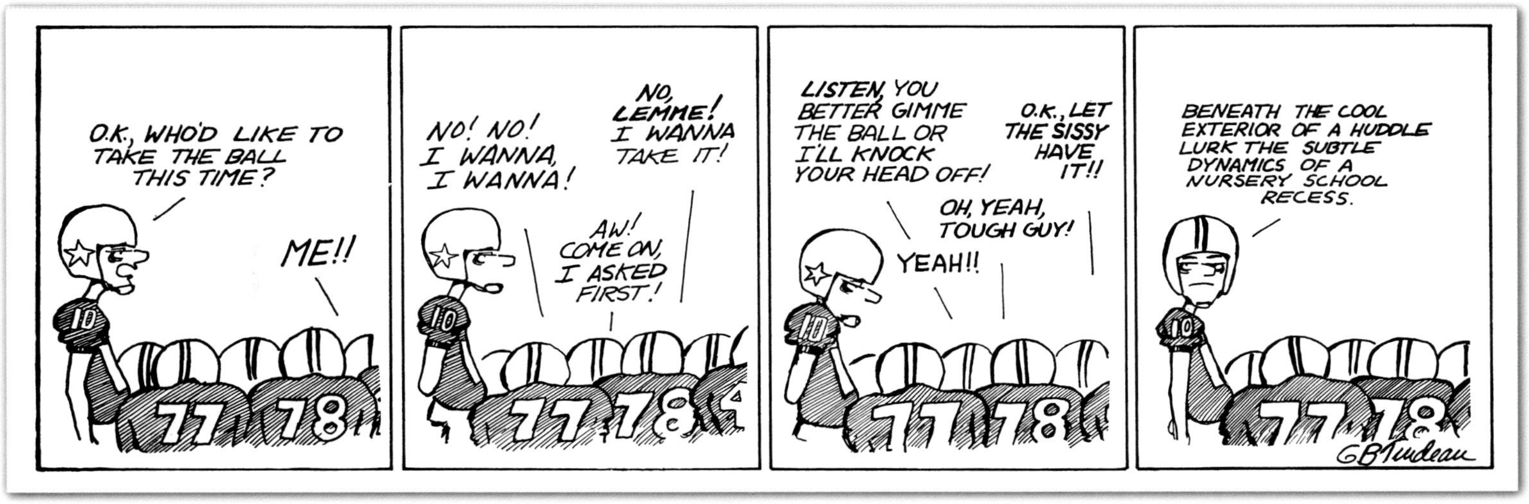
O.K., WHO'D LIKE TO TAKE THE BALL THIS TIME?
ME!!
NO! NO! I WANNA, I WANNA!
NO, LEMME! I WANNA TAKE IT!
AW! COME ON, I ASKED FIRST!
LISTEN, YOU BETTER GIMME THE BALL OR I'LL KNOCK YOUR HEAD OFF!
O.K., LET THE SISSY HAVE IT!!
OH, YEAH, TOUGH GUY!
YEAH!!
BENEATH THE COOL EXTERIOR OF A HUDDLE LURK THE SUBTLE DYNAMICS OF A NURSERY SCHOOL RECESS.
GBTrudeau
11/28/70

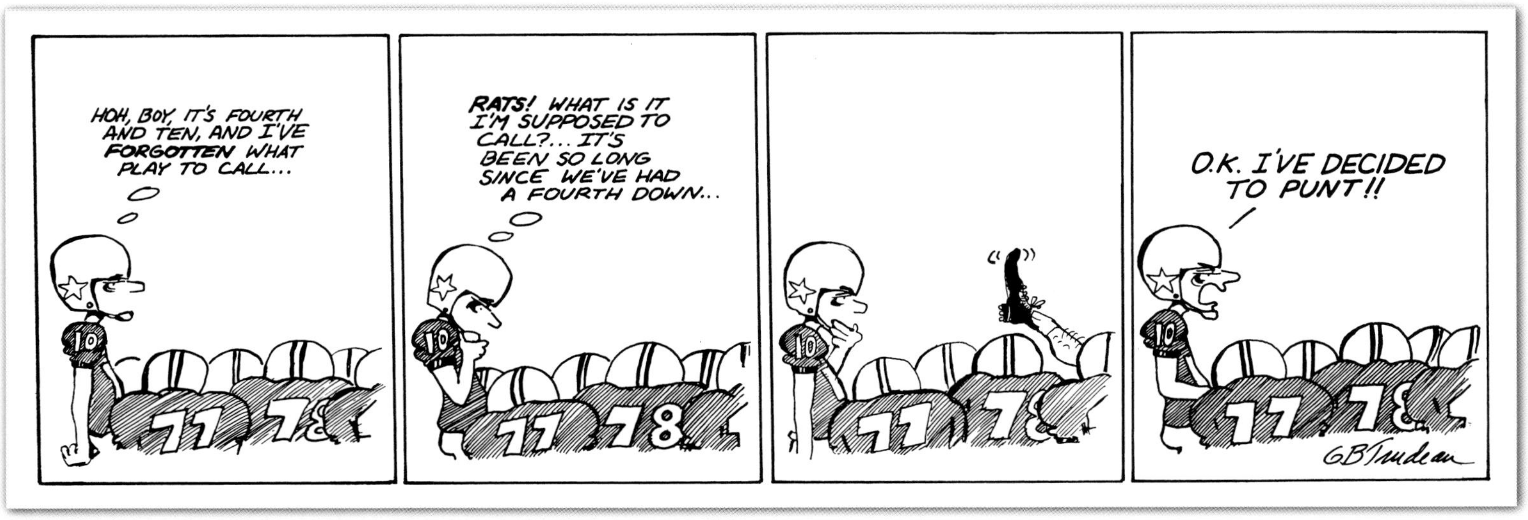
HOH, BOY, IT'S FOURTH AND TEN, AND I'VE FORGOTTEN WHAT PLAY TO CALL...
RATS! WHAT IS IT I'M SUPPOSED TO CALL?... IT'S BEEN SO LONG SINCE WE'VE HAD A FOURTH DOWN...
O.K. I'VE DECIDED TO PUNT!!
GBTrudeau
11/5/70

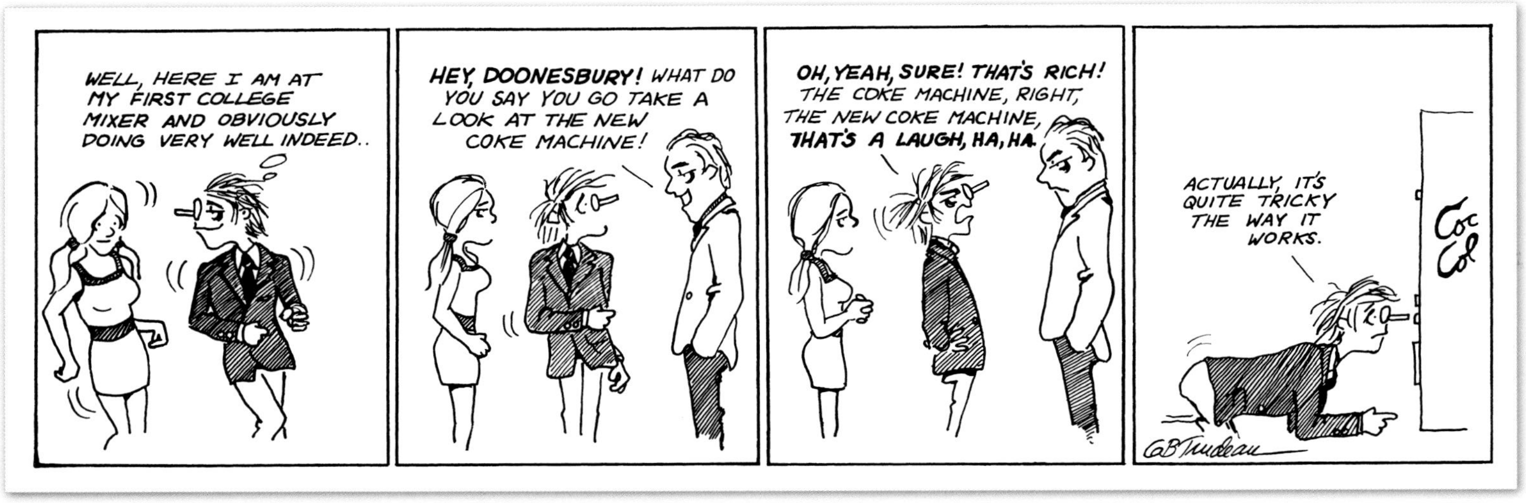
WELL, HERE I AM AT MY FIRST COLLEGE MIXER AND OBVIOUSLY DOING VERY WELL INDEED..
HEY, DOONESBURY! WHAT DO YOU SAY YOU GO TAKE A LOOK AT THE NEW COKE MACHINE!
OH, YEAH, SURE! THAT'S RICH! THE COKE MACHINE, RIGHT, THE NEW COKE MACHINE, THAT'S A LAUGH, HA, HA.
ACTUALLY, IT'S QUITE TRICKY THE WAY IT WORKS.

11/23/70

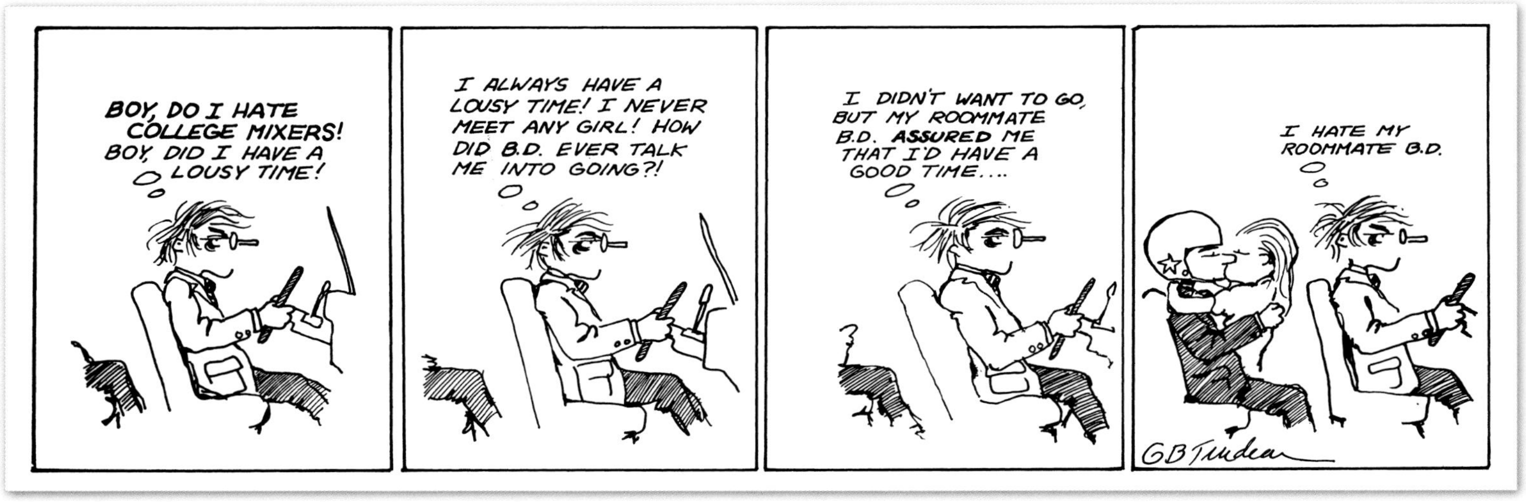
BOY, DO I HATE COLLEGE MIXERS! BOY, DID I HAVE A LOUSY TIME!
I ALWAYS HAVE A LOUSY TIME! I NEVER MEET ANY GIRL! HOW DID B.D. EVER TALK ME INTO GOING?!
I DIDN'T WANT TO GO, BUT MY ROOMMATE B.D. ASSURED ME THAT I'D HAVE A GOOD TIME....
I HATE MY ROOMMATE B.D.

11/24/70

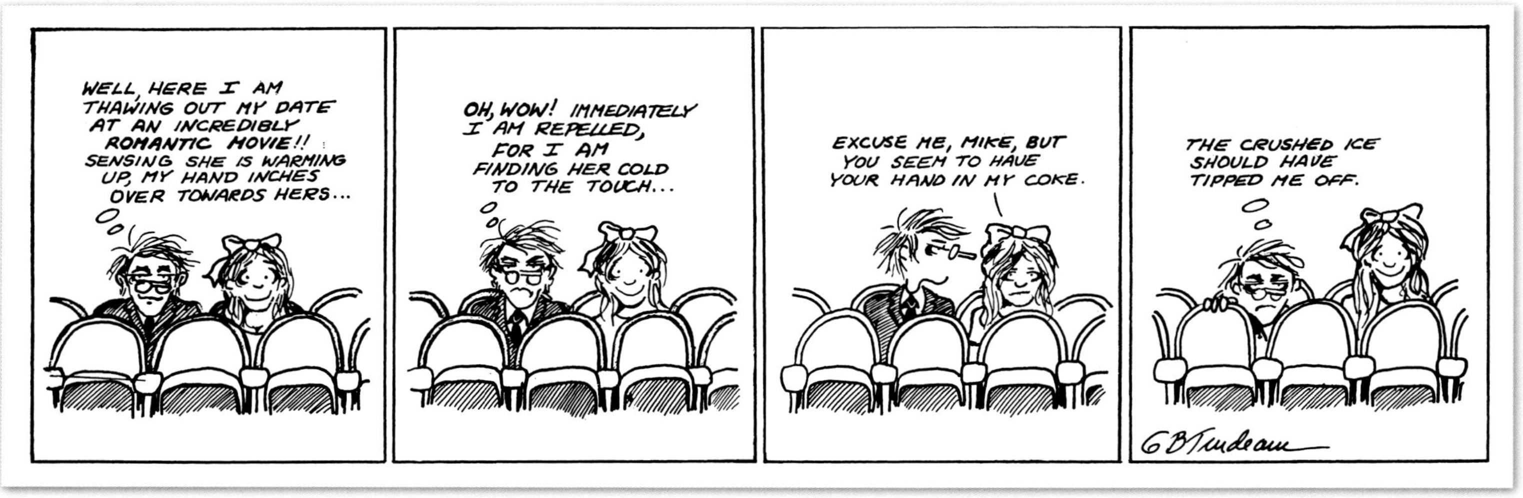
WELL, HERE I AM THAWING OUT MY DATE AT AN INCREDIBLY ROMANTIC MOVIE!! SENSING SHE IS WARMING UP, MY HAND INCHES OVER TOWARDS HERS...
OH, WOW! IMMEDIATELY I AM REPELLED, FOR I AM FINDING HER COLD TO THE TOUCH...
EXCUSE ME, MIKE, BUT YOU SEEM TO HAVE YOUR HAND IN MY COKE.
THE CRUSHED ICE SHOULD HAVE TIPPED ME OFF.

11/10/70

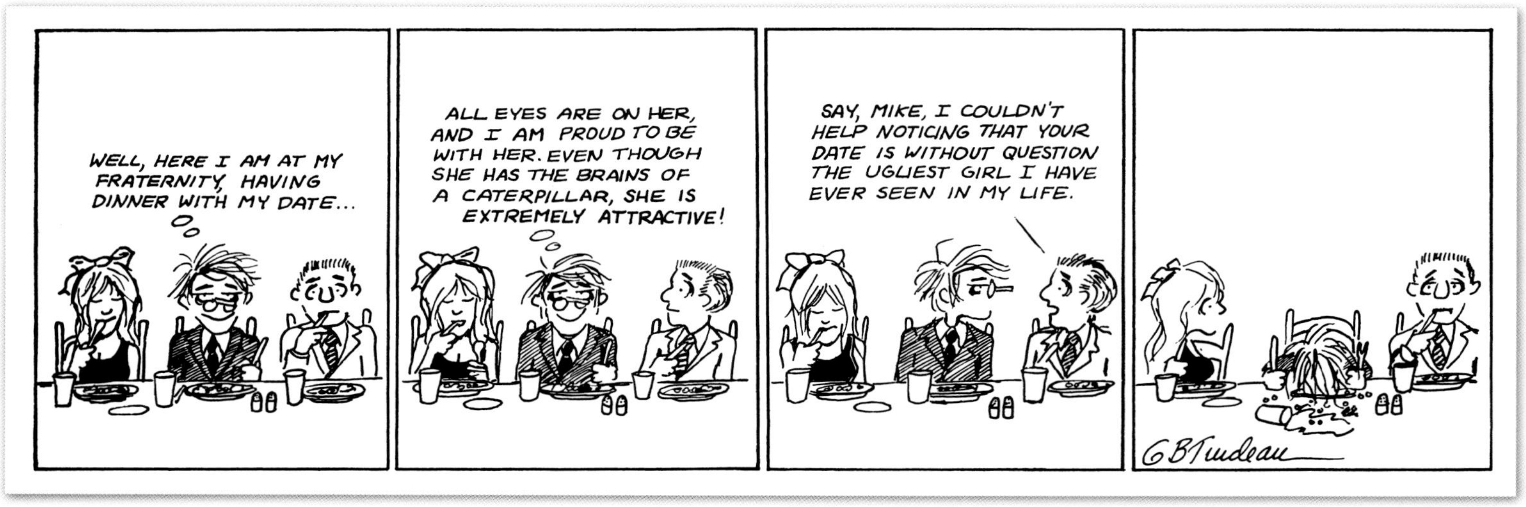
WELL, HERE I AM AT MY FRATERNITY, HAVING DINNER WITH MY DATE...
ALL EYES ARE ON HER, AND I AM PROUD TO BE WITH HER. EVEN THOUGH SHE HAS THE BRAINS OF A CATERPILLAR, SHE IS EXTREMELY ATTRACTIVE!
SAY, MIKE, I COULDN'T HELP NOTICING THAT YOUR DATE IS WITHOUT QUESTION THE UGLIEST GIRL I HAVE EVER SEEN IN MY LIFE.

11/27/70

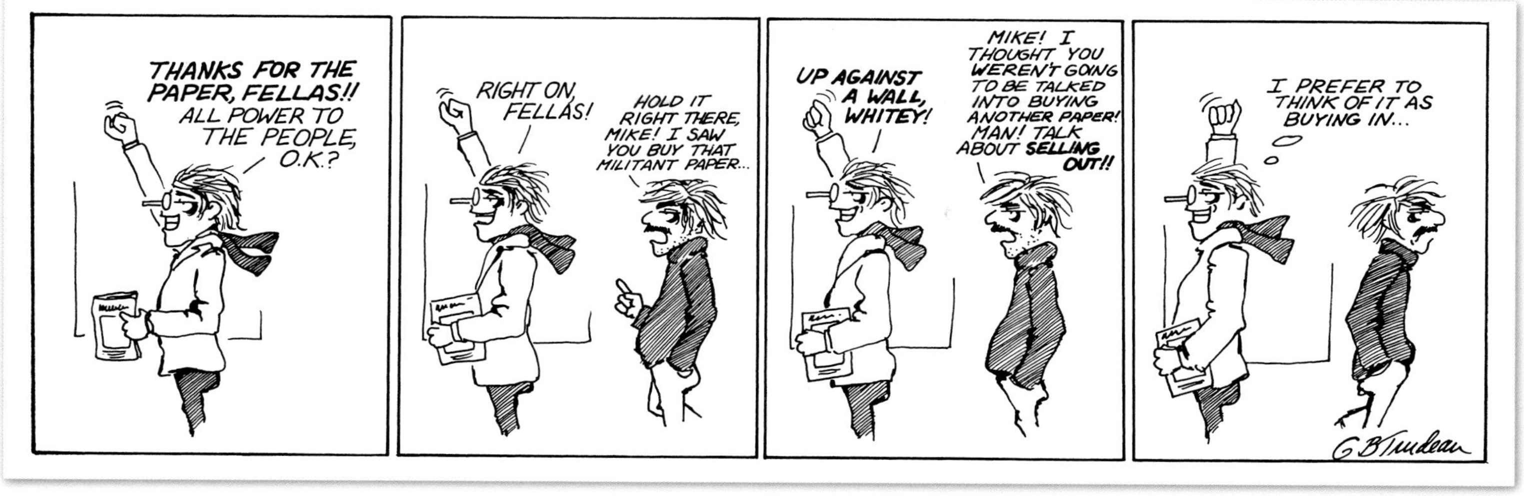
THANKS FOR THE PAPER, FELLAS!! ALL POWER TO THE PEOPLE, O.K.?
RIGHT ON, FELLAS!
HOLD IT RIGHT THERE, MIKE! I SAW YOU BUY THAT MILITANT PAPER...
UP AGAINST A WALL, WHITEY!
MIKE! I THOUGHT YOU WEREN'T GOING TO BE TALKED INTO BUYING ANOTHER PAPER! MAN! TALK ABOUT SELLING OUT!!
I PREFER TO THINK OF IT AS BUYING IN...
GBTrudeau

11/19/70

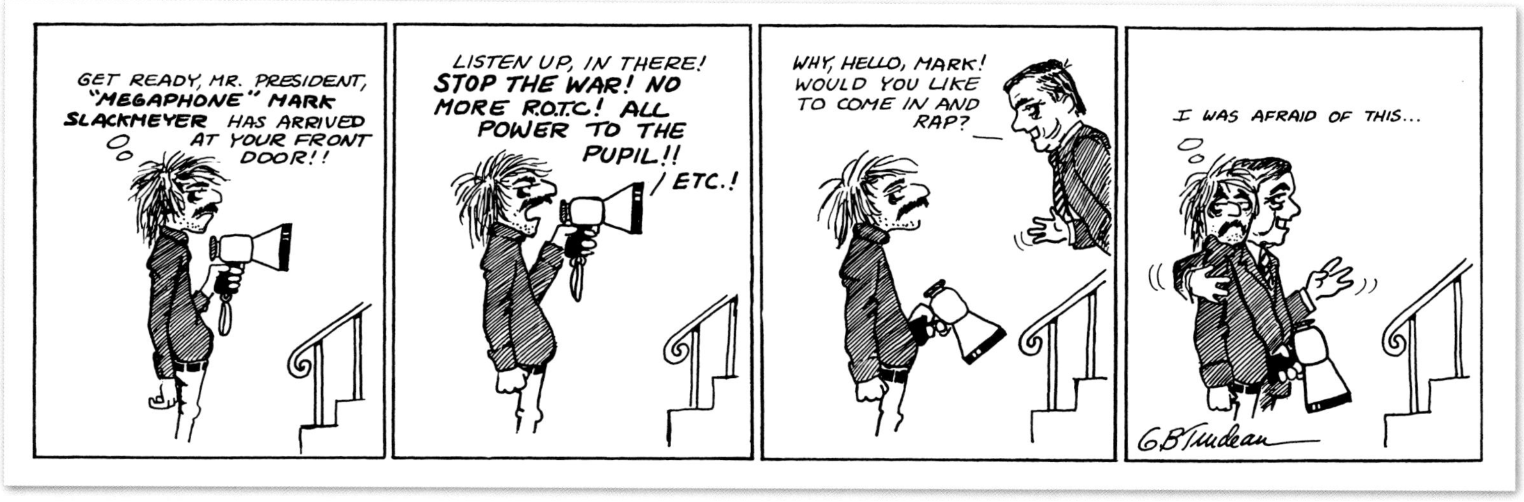
GET READY, MR. PRESIDENT, "MEGAPHONE" MARK SLACKMEYER HAS ARRIVED AT YOUR FRONT DOOR!!
LISTEN UP, IN THERE! STOP THE WAR! NO MORE R.O.T.C! ALL POWER TO THE PUPIL!!
ETC.!
WHY, HELLO, MARK! WOULD YOU LIKE TO COME IN AND RAP?
I WAS AFRAID OF THIS...
GBTrudeau

11/30/70

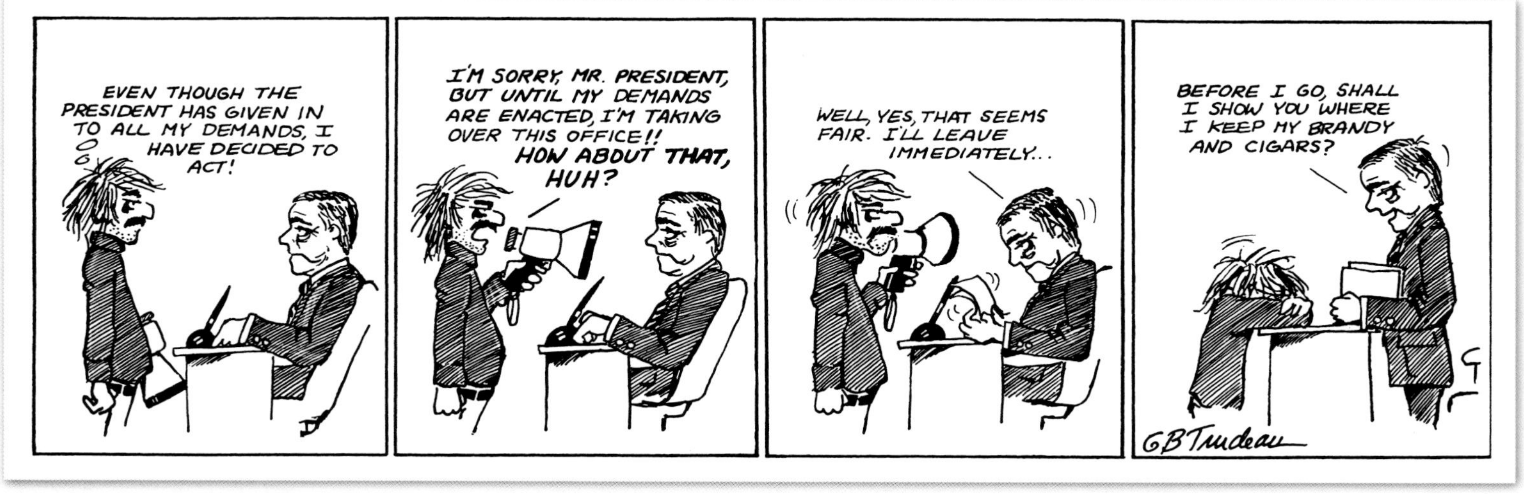
EVEN THOUGH THE PRESIDENT HAS GIVEN IN TO ALL MY DEMANDS, I HAVE DECIDED TO ACT!
I'M SORRY, MR. PRESIDENT, BUT UNTIL MY DEMANDS ARE ENACTED, I'M TAKING OVER THIS OFFICE!! HOW ABOUT THAT, HUH?
WELL, YES, THAT SEEMS FAIR. I'LL LEAVE IMMEDIATELY...
BEFORE I GO, SHALL I SHOW YOU WHERE I KEEP MY BRANDY AND CIGARS?
GBTrudeau

12/1/70

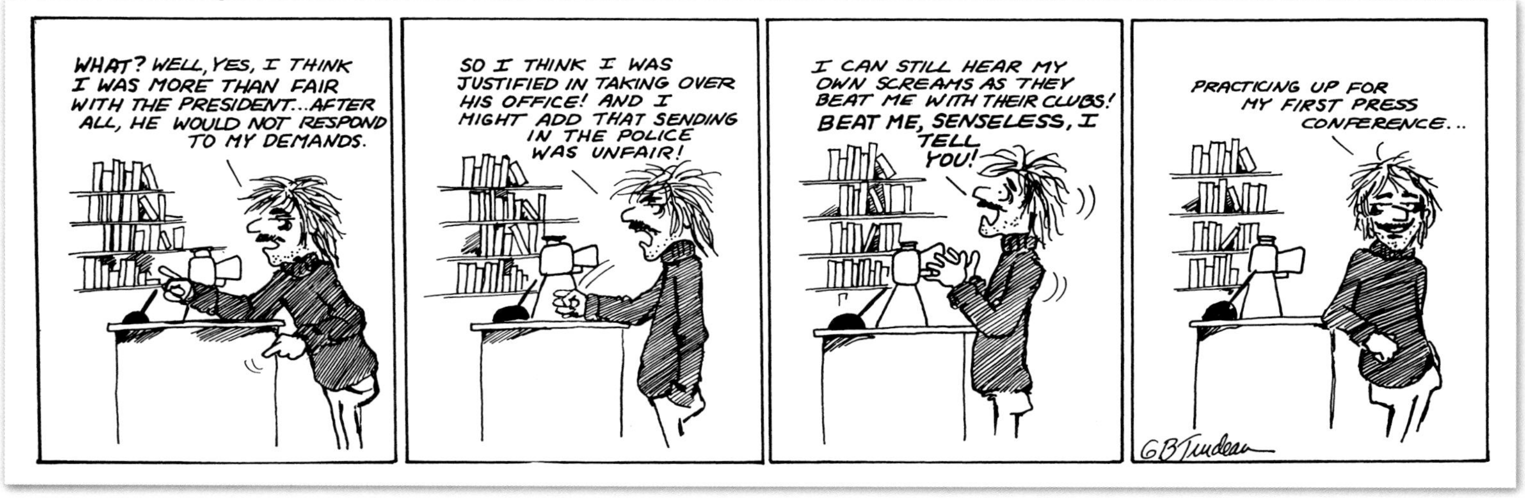
WHAT? WELL, YES, I THINK I WAS MORE THAN FAIR WITH THE PRESIDENT... AFTER ALL, HE WOULD NOT RESPOND TO MY DEMANDS.
SO I THINK I WAS JUSTIFIED IN TAKING OVER HIS OFFICE! AND I MIGHT ADD THAT SENDING IN THE POLICE WAS UNFAIR!
I CAN STILL HEAR MY OWN SCREAMS AS THEY BEAT ME WITH THEIR CLUBS! BEAT ME, SENSELESS, I TELL YOU!
PRACTICING UP FOR MY FIRST PRESS CONFERENCE...
GBTrudeau

11/2/70

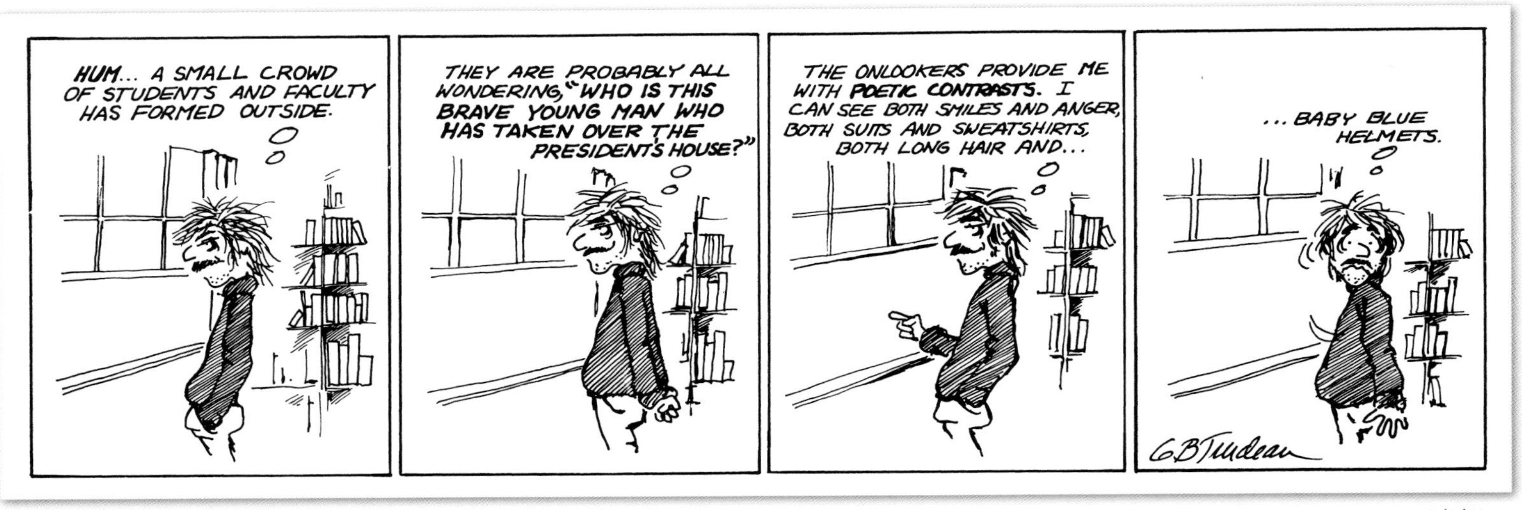
HUM... A SMALL CROWD OF STUDENTS AND FACULTY HAS FORMED OUTSIDE.
THEY ARE PROBABLY ALL WONDERING, "WHO IS THIS BRAVE YOUNG MAN WHO HAS TAKEN OVER THE PRESIDENT'S HOUSE?"
THE ONLOOKERS PROVIDE ME WITH POETIC CONTRASTS. I CAN SEE BOTH SMILES AND ANGER, BOTH SUITS AND SWEATSHIRTS, BOTH LONG HAIR AND...
... BABY BLUE HELMETS.
GBTrudeau

12/3/70

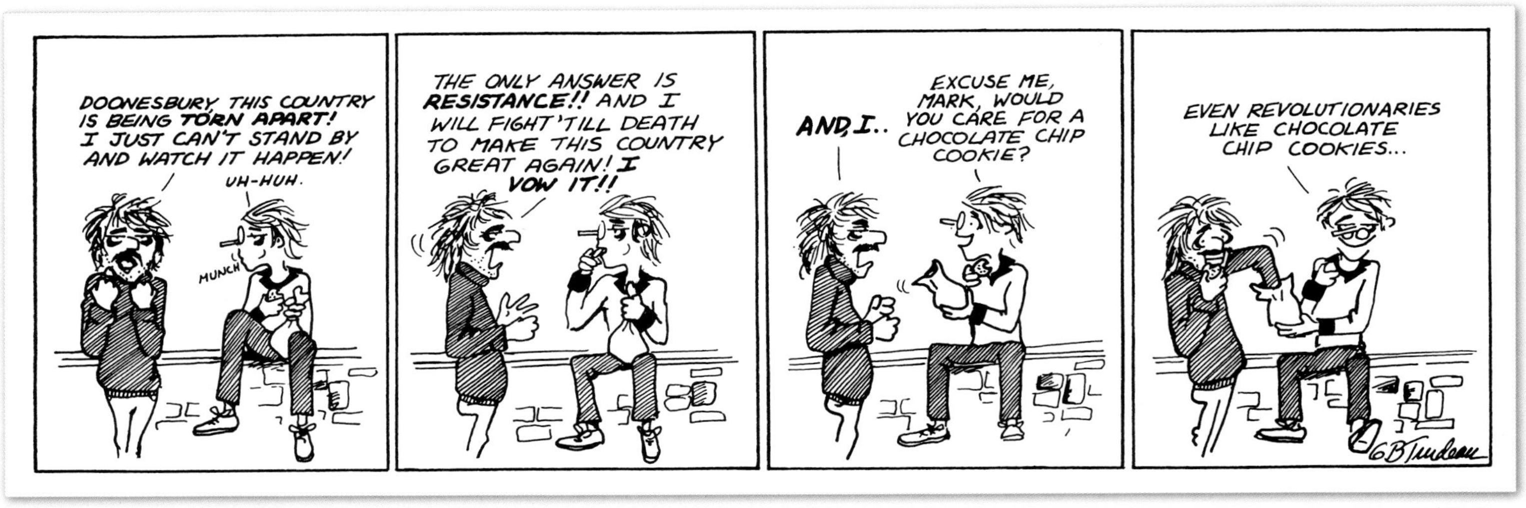
DOONESBURY, THIS COUNTRY IS BEING TORN APART! I JUST CAN'T STAND BY AND WATCH IT HAPPEN!
UH-HUH.
MUNCH
THE ONLY ANSWER IS RESISTANCE!! AND I WILL FIGHT 'TILL DEATH TO MAKE THIS COUNTRY GREAT AGAIN! I VOW IT!!
AND, I..
EXCUSE ME, MARK, WOULD YOU CARE FOR A CHOCOLATE CHIP COOKIE?
EVEN REVOLUTIONARIES LIKE CHOCOLATE CHIP COOKIES...
GBTrudeau

12/22/70

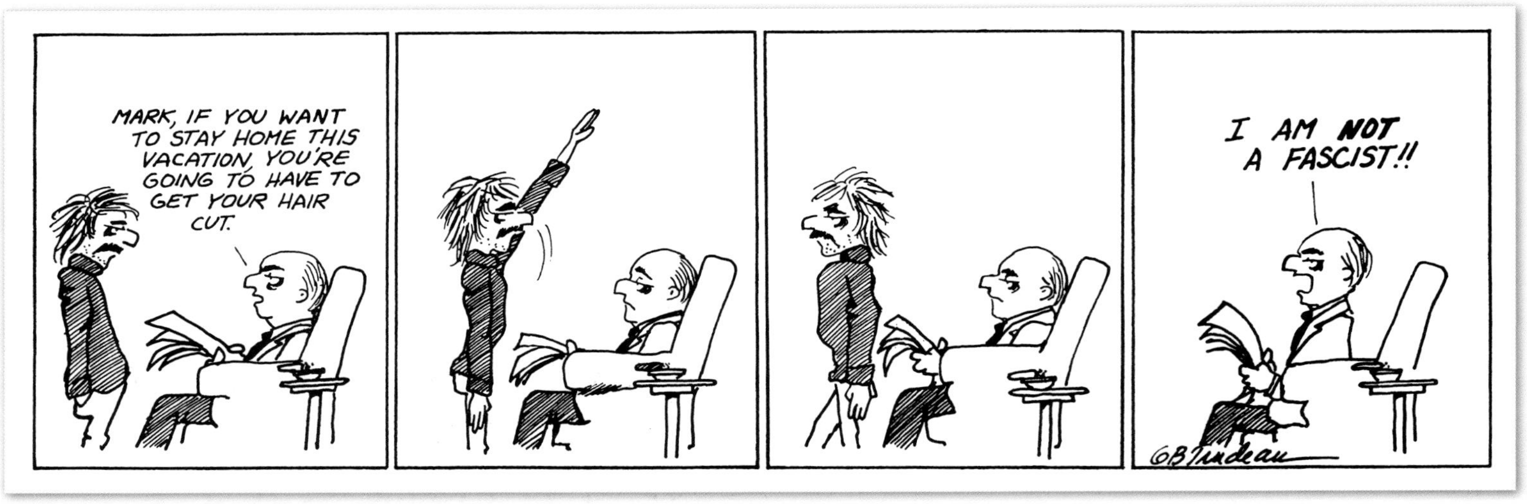
MARK, IF YOU WANT TO STAY HOME THIS VACATION, YOU'RE GOING TO HAVE TO GET YOUR HAIR CUT.
I AM NOT A FASCIST!!
GBTrudeau

12/23/70

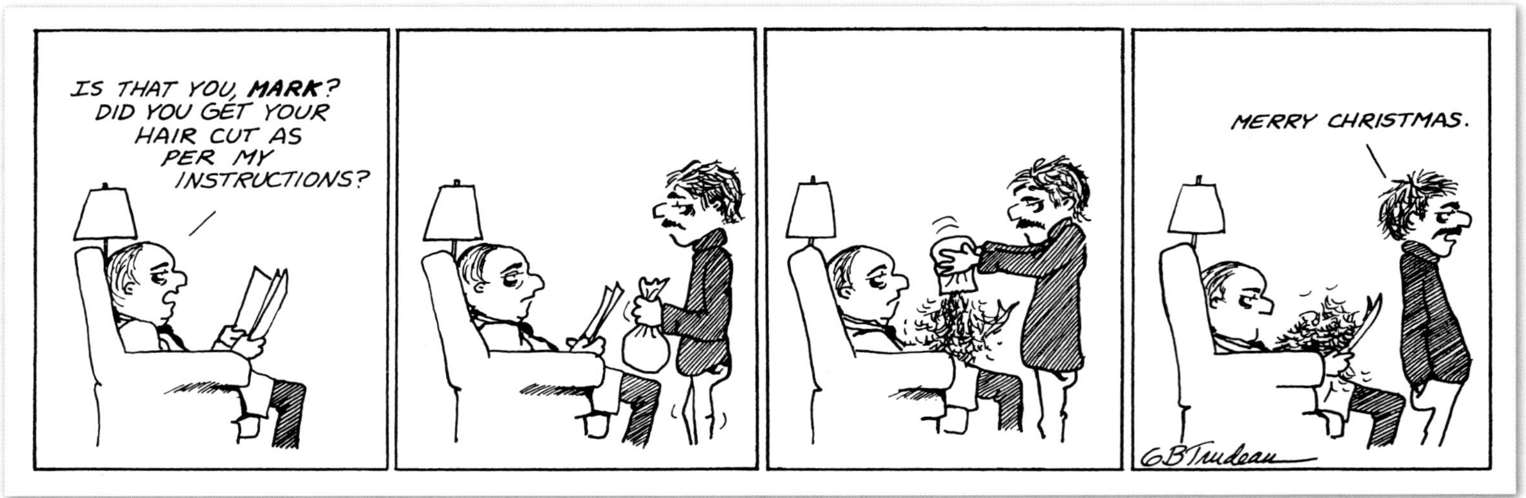
IS THAT YOU, MARK? DID YOU GET YOUR HAIR CUT AS PER MY INSTRUCTIONS?
MERRY CHRISTMAS.
GBTrudeau

12/25/70

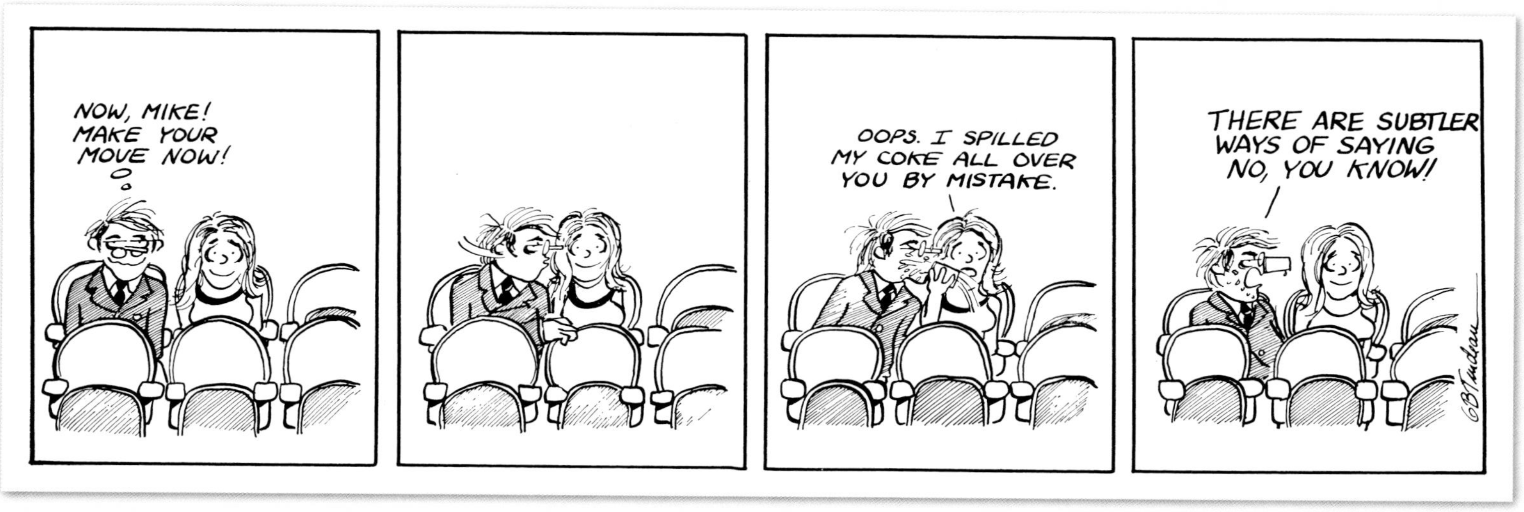
NOW, MIKE! MAKE YOUR MOVE NOW!
OOPS. I SPILLED MY COKE ALL OVER YOU BY MISTAKE.
THERE ARE SUBTLER WAYS OF SAYING NO, YOU KNOW!

2/26/71

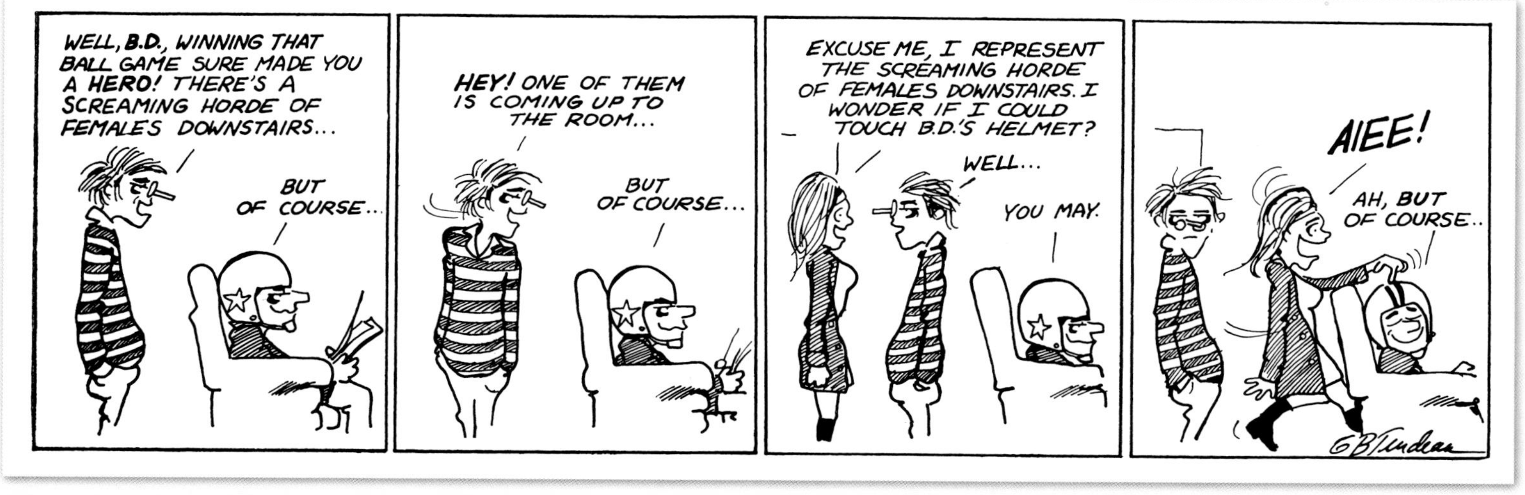
WELL, B.D., WINNING THAT BALL GAME SURE MADE YOU A HERO! THERE'S A SCREAMING HORDE OF FEMALES DOWNSTAIRS...
BUT OF COURSE...
HEY! ONE OF THEM IS COMING UP TO THE ROOM...
BUT OF COURSE...
EXCUSE ME, I REPRESENT THE SCREAMING HORDE OF FEMALES DOWNSTAIRS. I WONDER IF I COULD TOUCH B.D.'S HELMET?
WELL...
YOU MAY.
AIEE!
AH, BUT OF COURSE..

1/2/71

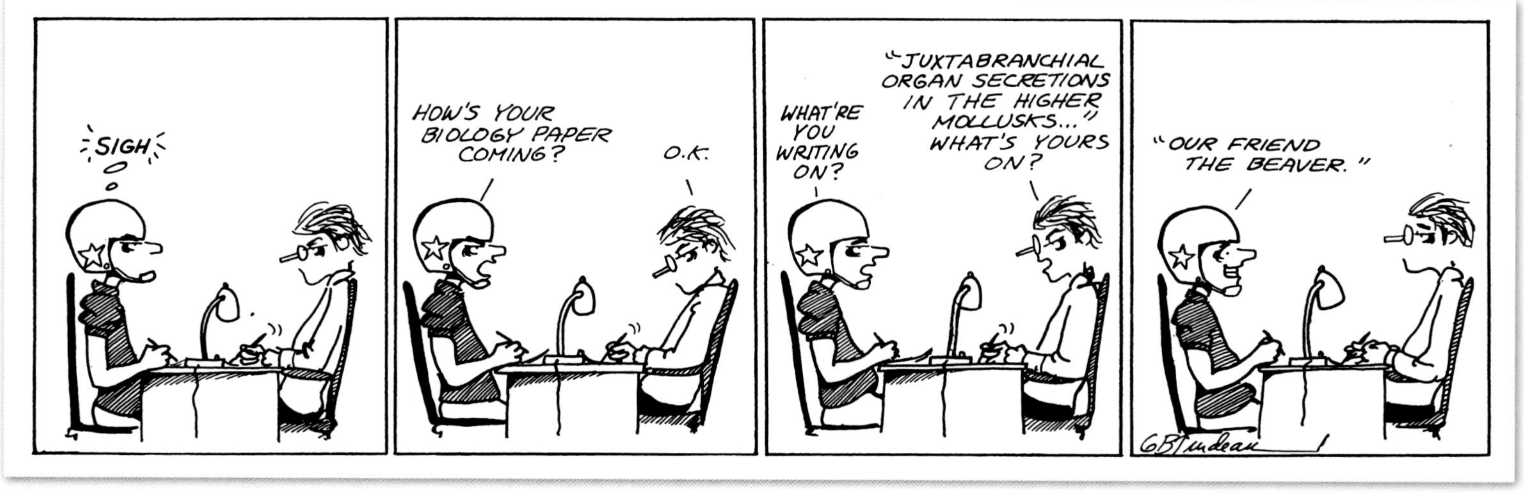
SIGH
HOW'S YOUR BIOLOGY PAPER COMING?
O.K.
WHAT'RE YOU WRITING ON?
"JUXTABRANCHIAL ORGAN SECRETIONS IN THE HIGHER MOLLUSKS..." WHAT'S YOURS ON?
"OUR FRIEND THE BEAVER."

12/8/70

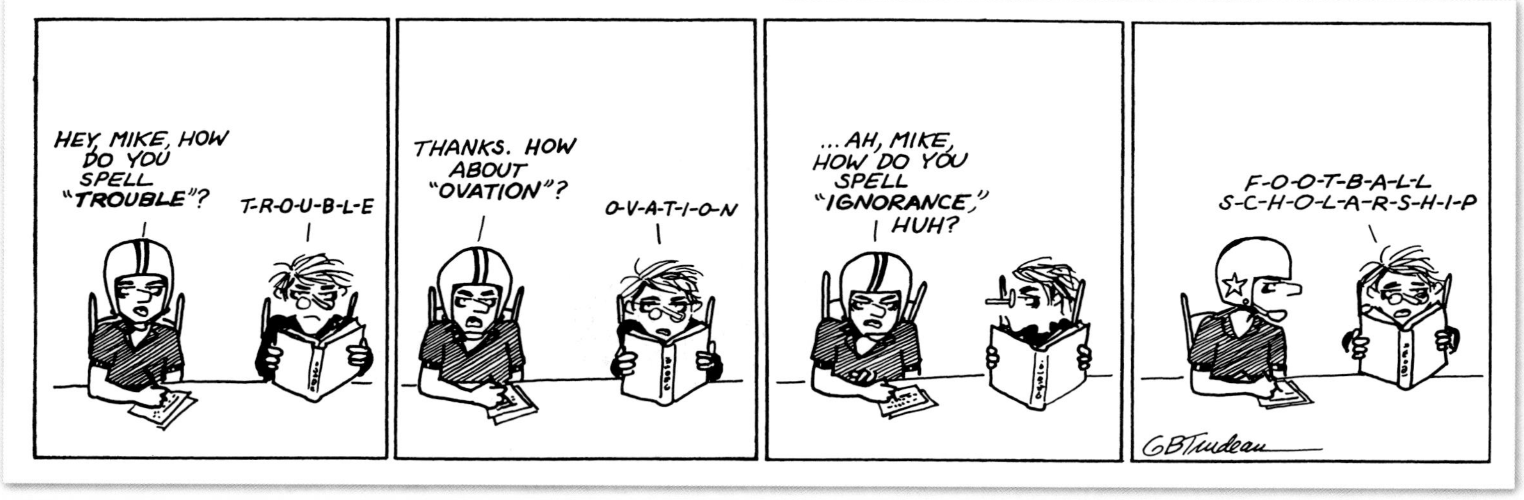
HEY, MIKE, HOW DO YOU SPELL "TROUBLE"?
T-R-O-U-B-L-E
THANKS. HOW ABOUT "OVATION"?
O-V-A-T-I-O-N
...AH, MIKE, HOW DO YOU SPELL "IGNORANCE," HUH?
F-O-O-T-B-A-L-L S-C-H-O-L-A-R-S-H-I-P

1/7/71

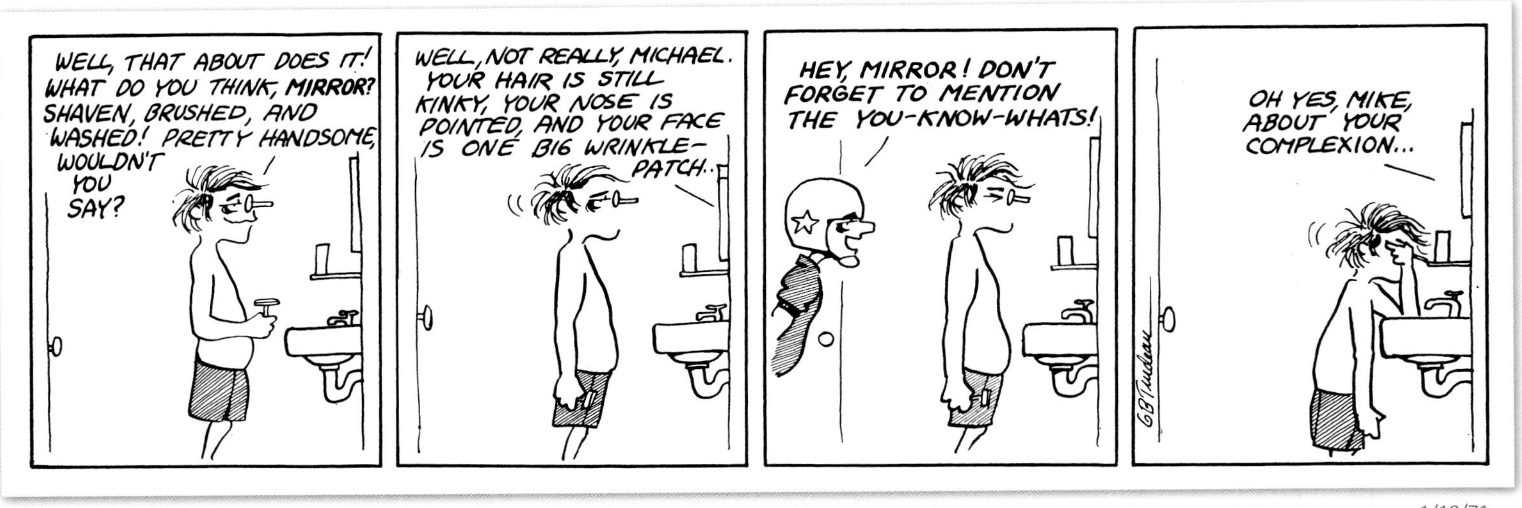
WELL, THAT ABOUT DOES IT! WHAT DO YOU THINK, MIRROR? SHAVEN, BRUSHED, AND WASHED! PRETTY HANDSOME, WOULDN'T YOU SAY?
WELL, NOT REALLY, MICHAEL. YOUR HAIR IS STILL KINKY, YOUR NOSE IS POINTED, AND YOUR FACE IS ONE BIG WRINKLE-PATCH..
HEY, MIRROR! DON'T FORGET TO MENTION THE YOU-KNOW-WHATS!
OH YES, MIKE, ABOUT YOUR COMPLEXION...
GBTrudeau

1/18/71

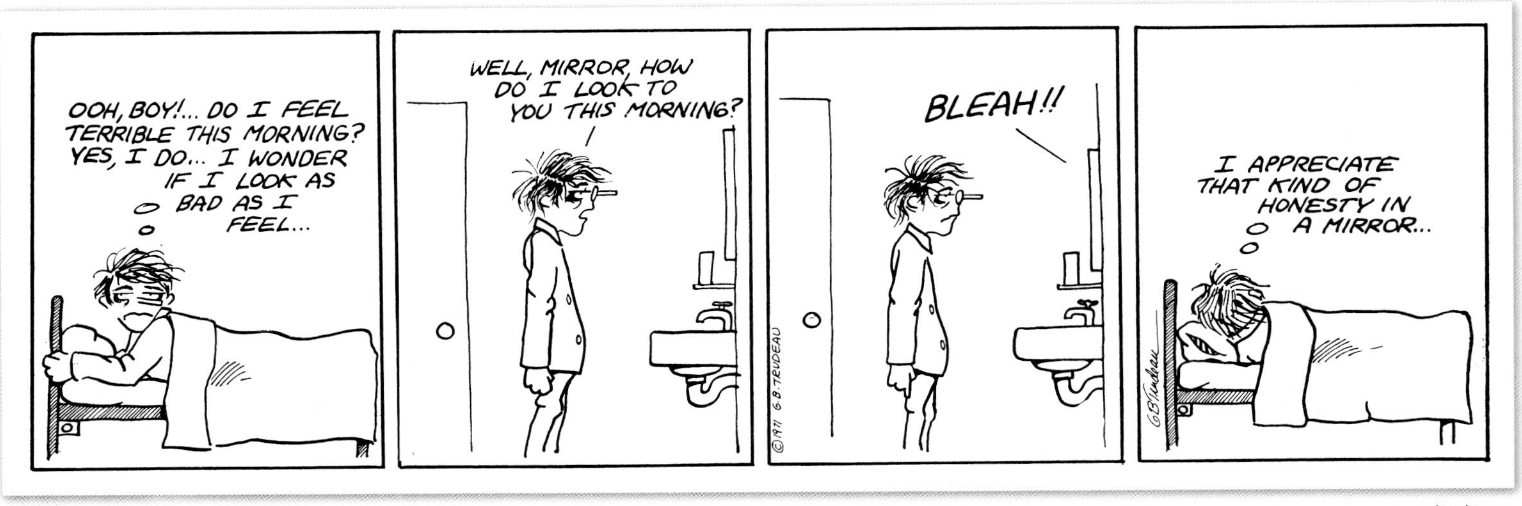
OOH, BOY!... DO I FEEL TERRIBLE THIS MORNING? YES, I DO... I WONDER IF I LOOK AS BAD AS I FEEL...
WELL, MIRROR, HOW DO I LOOK TO YOU THIS MORNING?
BLEAH!!
©1971 G.B. TRUDEAU
I APPRECIATE THAT KIND OF HONESTY IN A MIRROR...
GBTrudeau

1/21/71

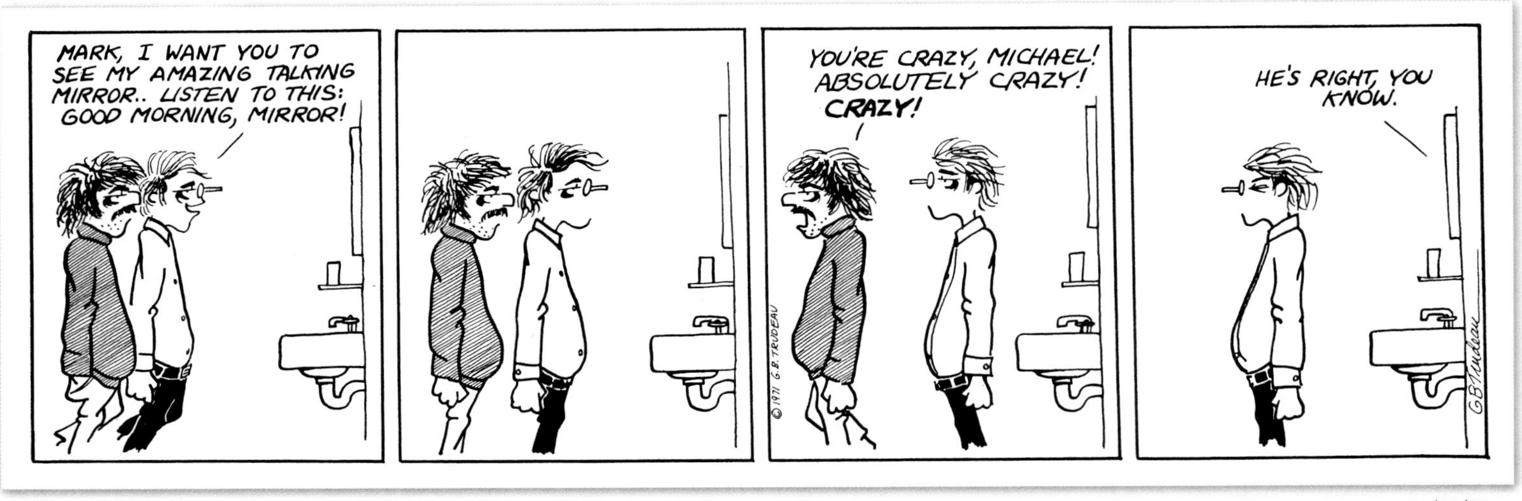
MARK, I WANT YOU TO SEE MY AMAZING TALKING MIRROR.. LISTEN TO THIS: GOOD MORNING, MIRROR!
YOU'RE CRAZY, MICHAEL! ABSOLUTELY CRAZY! CRAZY!
©1971 G.B. TRUDEAU
HE'S RIGHT, YOU KNOW.
GBTrudeau

1/22/71

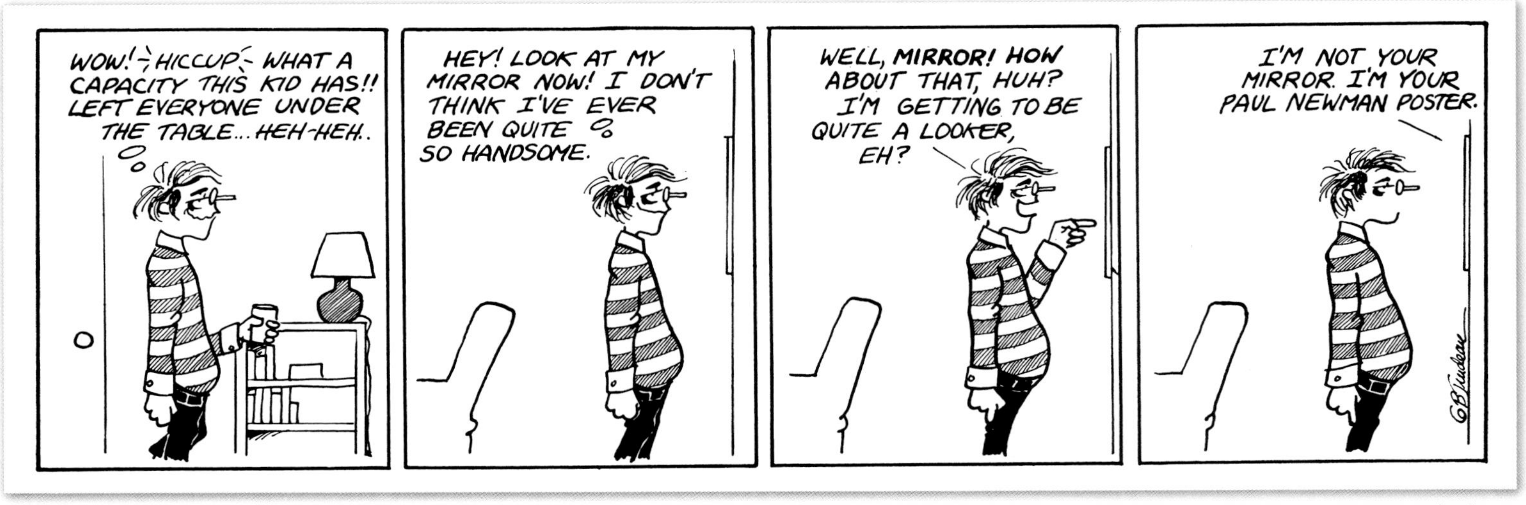
WOW! -HICCUP- WHAT A CAPACITY THIS KID HAS!! LEFT EVERYONE UNDER THE TABLE... HEH-HEH..
HEY! LOOK AT MY MIRROR NOW! I DON'T THINK I'VE EVER BEEN QUITE SO HANDSOME.
WELL, MIRROR! HOW ABOUT THAT, HUH? I'M GETTING TO BE QUITE A LOOKER, EH?
I'M NOT YOUR MIRROR. I'M YOUR PAUL NEWMAN POSTER.
GBTrudeau

1/23/71

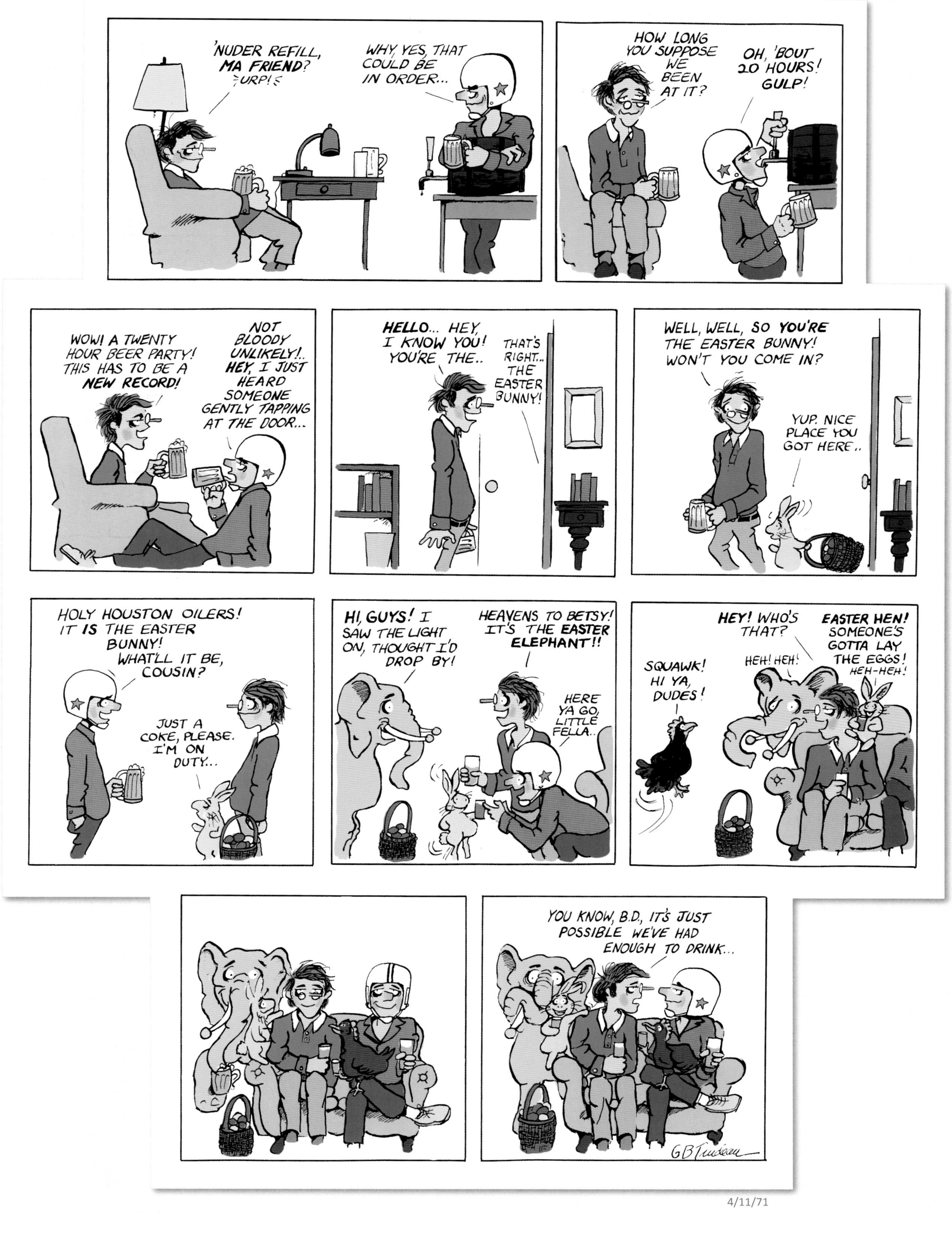
'NUDER REFILL, MA FRIEND?
URP!
WHY, YES, THAT COULD BE IN ORDER...
HOW LONG YOU SUPPOSE WE BEEN AT IT?
OH, 'BOUT 20 HOURS! GULP!
WOW! A TWENTY HOUR BEER PARTY! THIS HAS TO BE A NEW RECORD!
NOT BLOODY UNLIKELY!.. HEY, I JUST HEARD SOMEONE GENTLY TAPPING AT THE DOOR...
HELLO... HEY, I KNOW YOU! YOU'RE THE..
THAT'S RIGHT... THE EASTER BUNNY!
WELL, WELL, SO YOU'RE THE EASTER BUNNY! WON'T YOU COME IN?
YUP. NICE PLACE YOU GOT HERE..
HOLY HOUSTON OILERS! IT IS THE EASTER BUNNY!
WHAT'LL IT BE, COUSIN?
JUST A COKE, PLEASE. I'M ON DUTY...
HI, GUYS! I SAW THE LIGHT ON, THOUGHT I'D DROP BY!
HEAVENS TO BETSY! IT'S THE EASTER ELEPHANT!!
HERE YA GO, LITTLE FELLA..
HEY! WHO'S THAT?
EASTER HEN! SOMEONE'S GOTTA LAY THE EGGS!
HEH! HEH!
HEH-HEH!
SQUAWK! HI YA, DUDES!
YOU KNOW, B.D., IT'S JUST POSSIBLE WE'VE HAD ENOUGH TO DRINK...
GBTrudeau

4/11/71

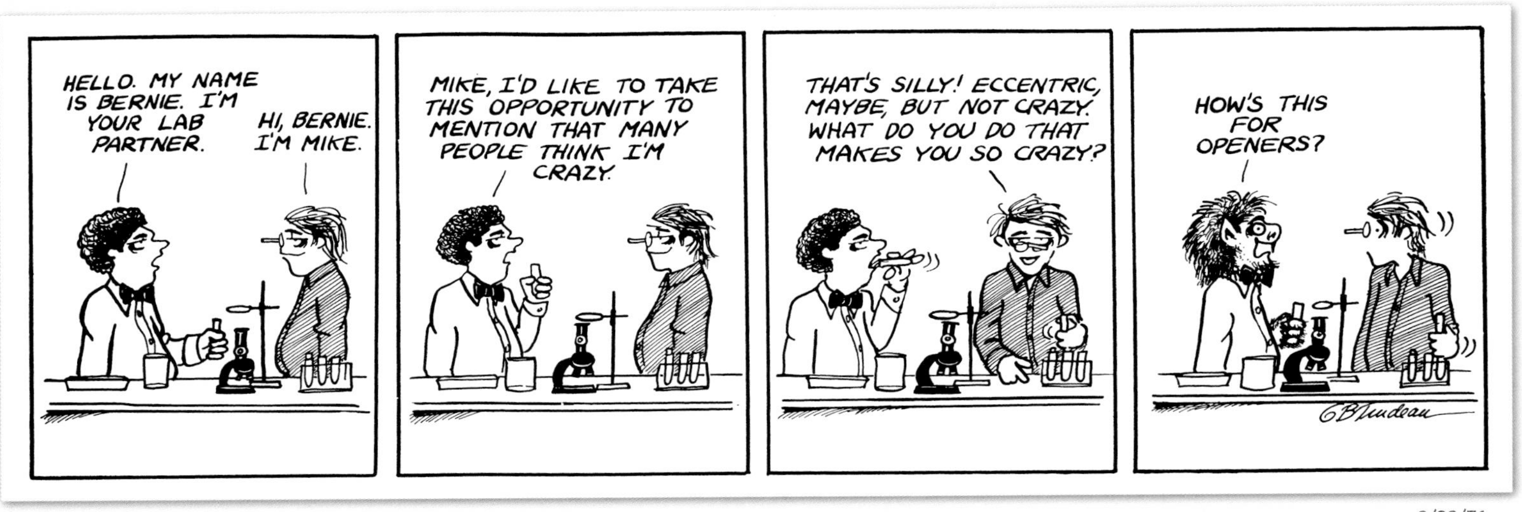
HELLO. MY NAME IS BERNIE. I'M YOUR LAB PARTNER.
HI, BERNIE. I'M MIKE.
MIKE, I'D LIKE TO TAKE THIS OPPORTUNITY TO MENTION THAT MANY PEOPLE THINK I'M CRAZY.
THAT'S SILLY! ECCENTRIC, MAYBE, BUT NOT CRAZY. WHAT DO YOU DO THAT MAKES YOU SO CRAZY?
HOW'S THIS FOR OPENERS?

2/22/71

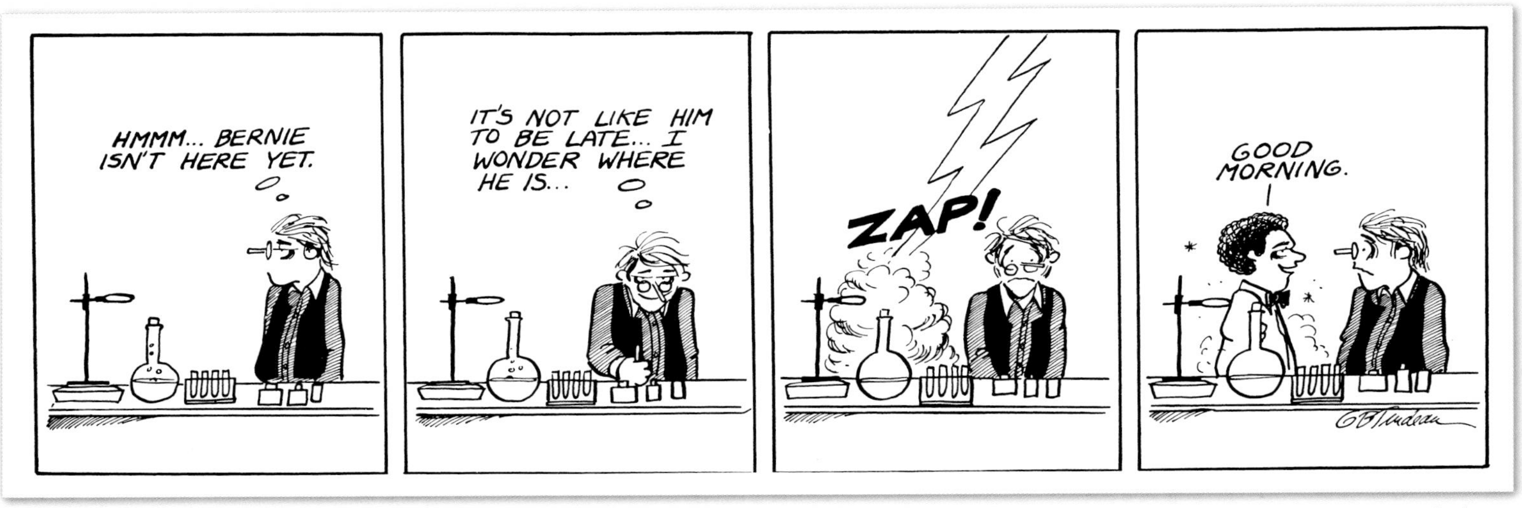
HMMM... BERNIE ISN'T HERE YET.
IT'S NOT LIKE HIM TO BE LATE... I WONDER WHERE HE IS...
ZAP!
GOOD MORNING.

2/23/71

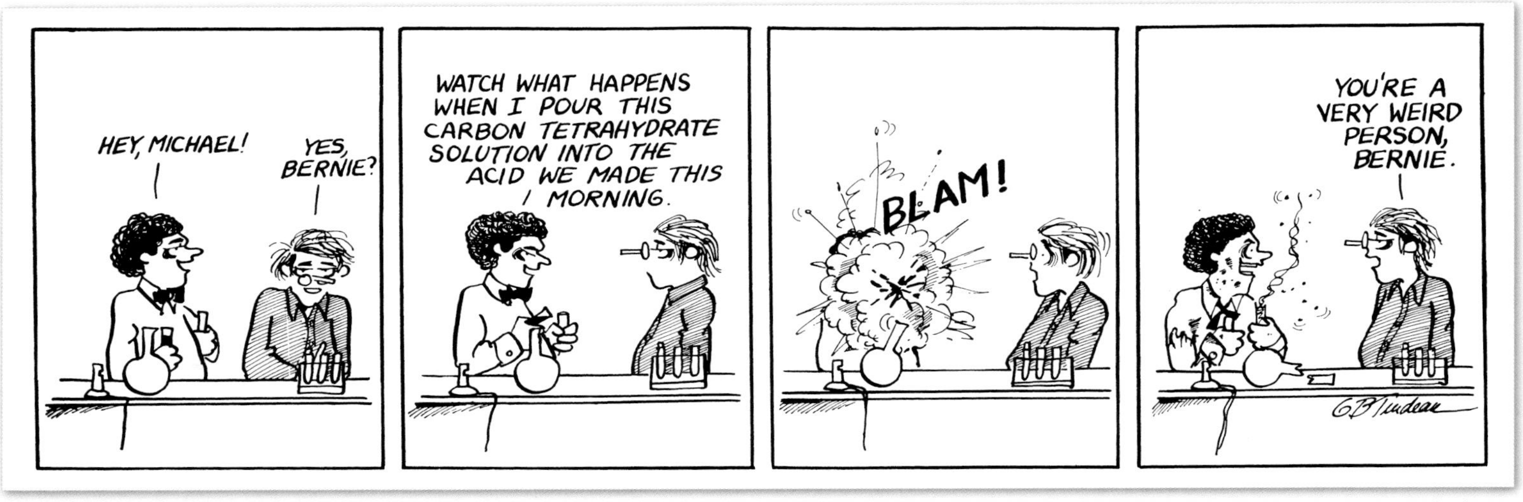
HEY, MICHAEL!
YES, BERNIE?
WATCH WHAT HAPPENS WHEN I POUR THIS CARBON TETRAHYDRATE SOLUTION INTO THE ACID WE MADE THIS MORNING.
BLAM!
YOU'RE A VERY WEIRD PERSON, BERNIE.

2/24/71

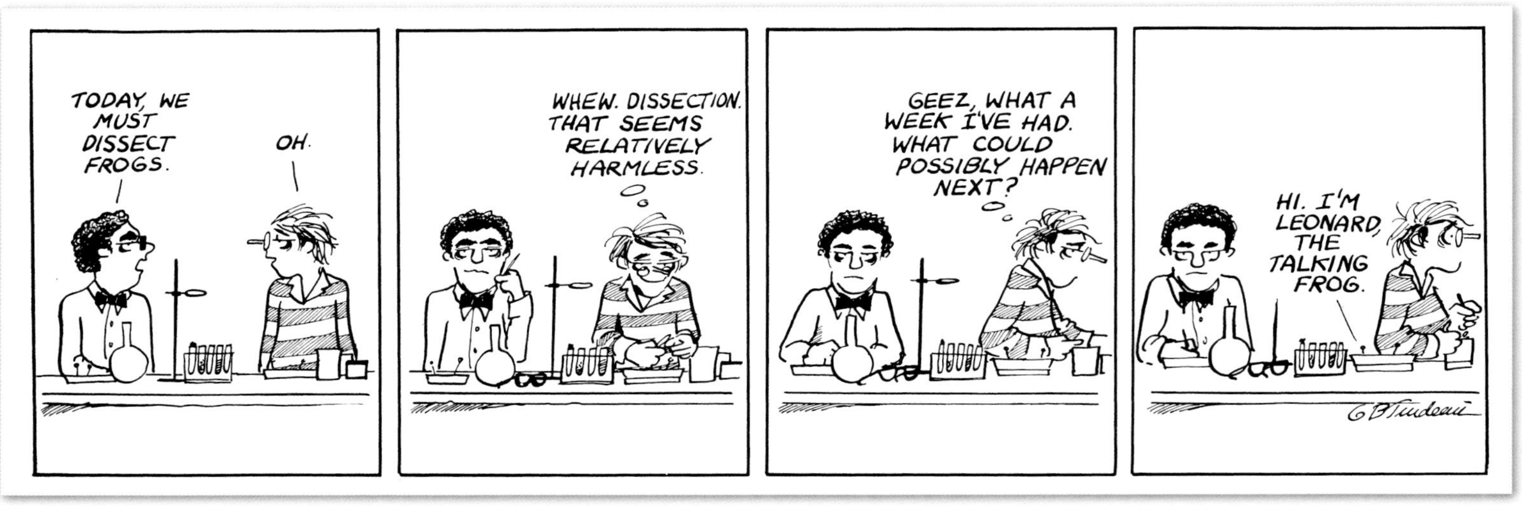
TODAY, WE MUST DISSECT FROGS.
OH.
WHEW. DISSECTION. THAT SEEMS RELATIVELY HARMLESS.
GEEZ, WHAT A WEEK I'VE HAD. WHAT COULD POSSIBLY HAPPEN NEXT?
HI. I'M LEONARD, THE TALKING FROG.

2/25/71

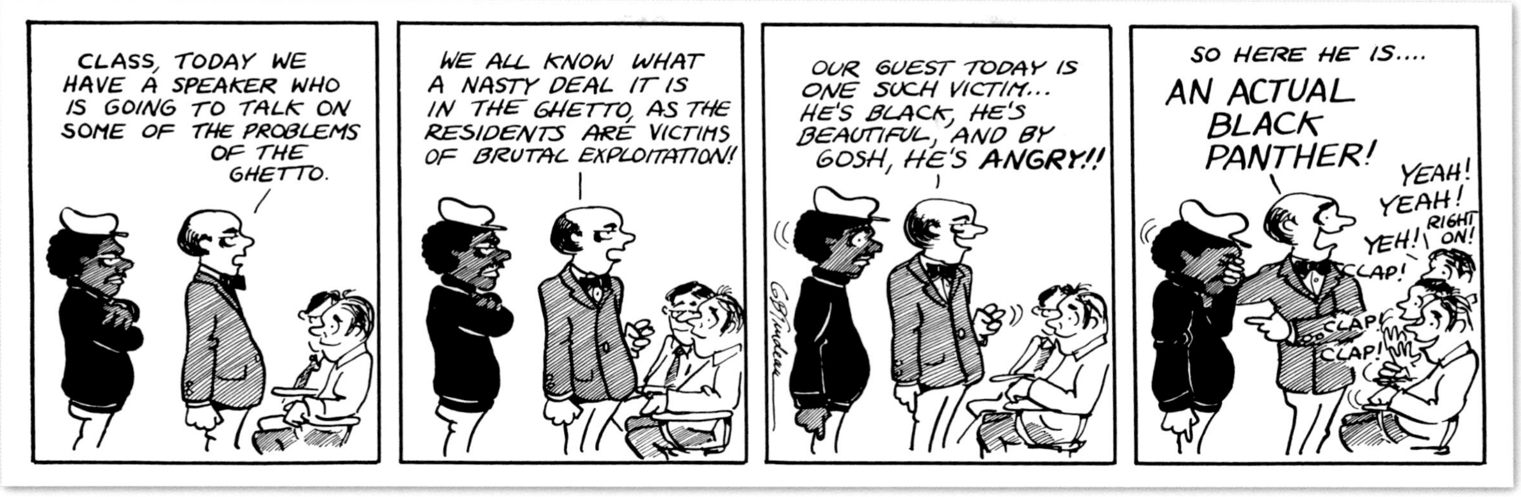
CLASS, TODAY WE HAVE A SPEAKER WHO IS GOING TO TALK ON SOME OF THE PROBLEMS OF THE GHETTO.
WE ALL KNOW WHAT A NASTY DEAL IT IS IN THE GHETTO, AS THE RESIDENTS ARE VICTIMS OF BRUTAL EXPLOITATION!
OUR GUEST TODAY IS ONE SUCH VICTIM... HE'S BLACK, HE'S BEAUTIFUL, AND BY GOSH, HE'S ANGRY!!
SO HERE HE IS....
AN ACTUAL BLACK PANTHER!
YEAH! YEAH!
YEH!
RIGHT ON!
CLAP!
CLAP!
CLAP!
G.B. Trudeau

3/11/71

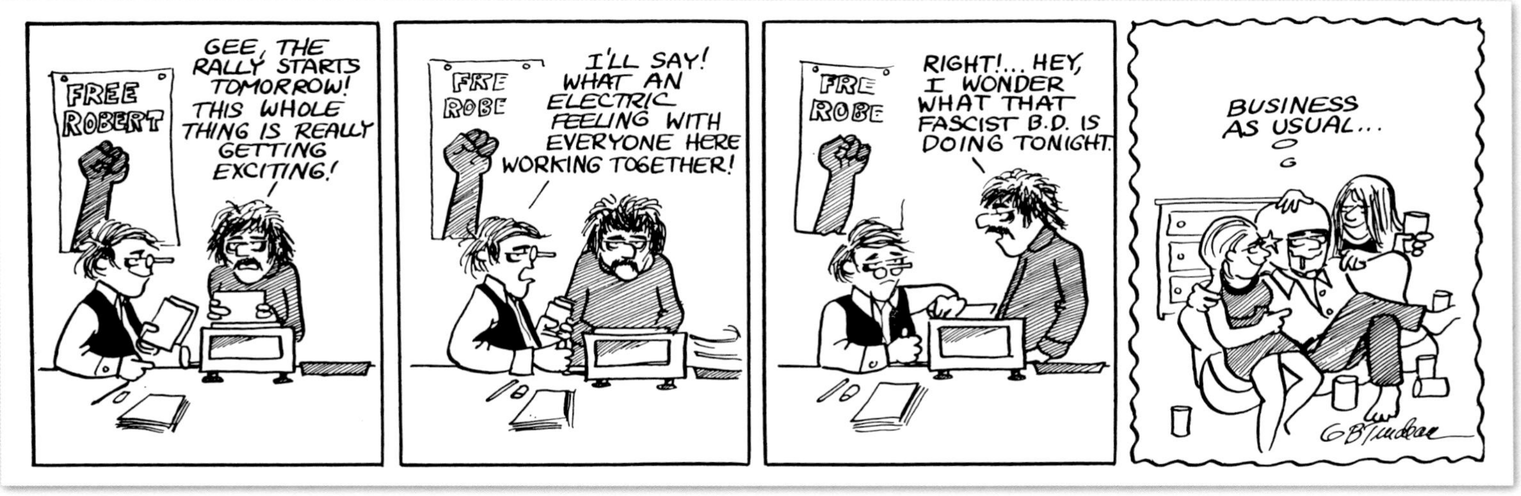
FREE ROBERT
GEE, THE RALLY STARTS TOMORROW! THIS WHOLE THING IS REALLY GETTING EXCITING!
I'LL SAY! WHAT AN ELECTRIC FEELING WITH EVERYONE HERE WORKING TOGETHER!
RIGHT!... HEY, I WONDER WHAT THAT FASCIST B.D. IS DOING TONIGHT.
BUSINESS AS USUAL...
G.B. Trudeau

3/16/71

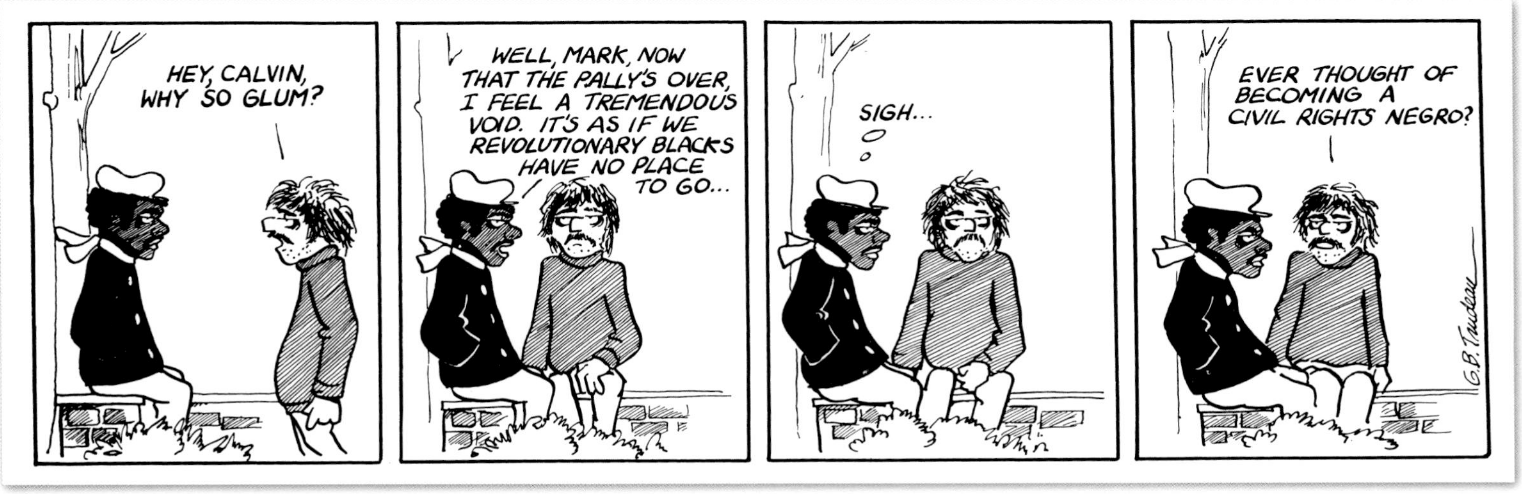
HEY, CALVIN, WHY SO GLUM?
WELL, MARK, NOW THAT THE PALLY'S OVER, I FEEL A TREMENDOUS VOID. IT'S AS IF WE REVOLUTIONARY BLACKS HAVE NO PLACE TO GO...
SIGH...
EVER THOUGHT OF BECOMING A CIVIL RIGHTS NEGRO?
G.B. Trudeau

3/19/71

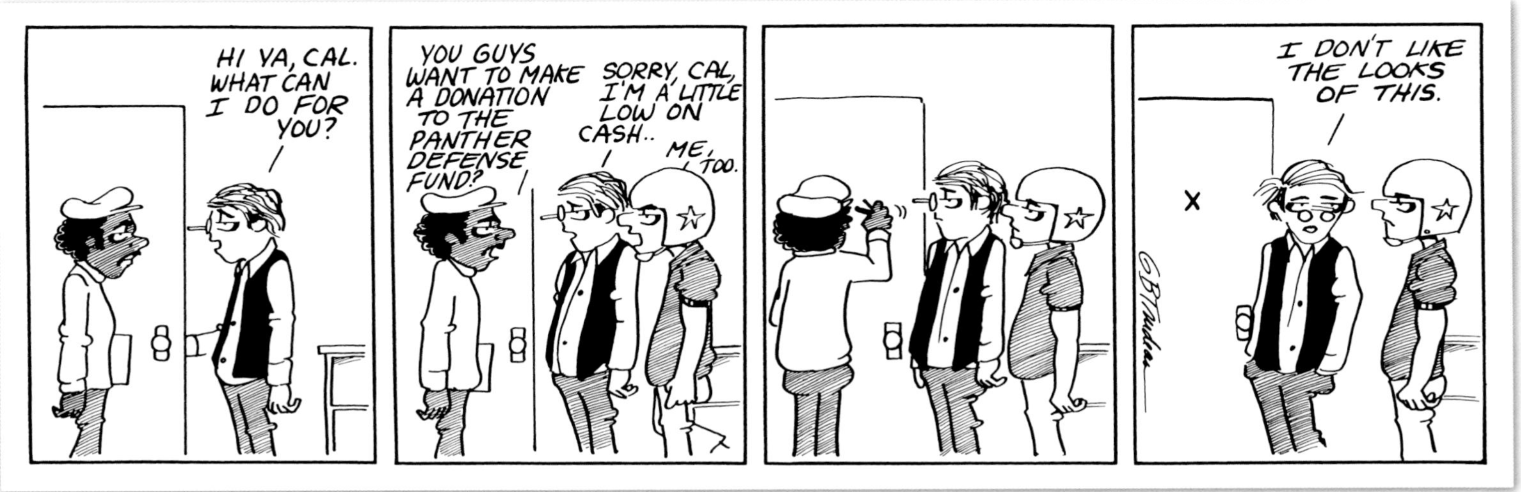
HI YA, CAL. WHAT CAN I DO FOR YOU?
YOU GUYS WANT TO MAKE A DONATION TO THE PANTHER DEFENSE FUND?
SORRY, CAL, I'M A LITTLE LOW ON CASH..
ME, TOO.
X
I DON'T LIKE THE LOOKS OF THIS.
G.B. Trudeau

10/28/71

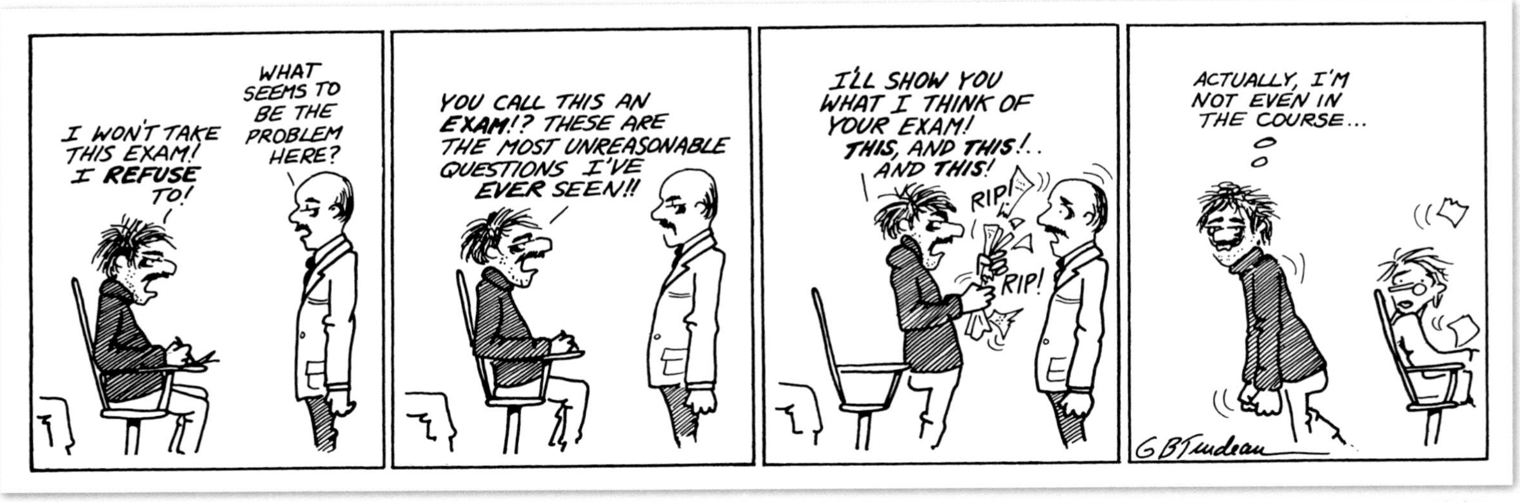
I WON'T TAKE THIS EXAM! I REFUSE TO!
WHAT SEEMS TO BE THE PROBLEM HERE?
YOU CALL THIS AN EXAM!? THESE ARE THE MOST UNREASONABLE QUESTIONS I'VE EVER SEEN!!
I'LL SHOW YOU WHAT I THINK OF YOUR EXAM! THIS, AND THIS!.. AND THIS!
RIP!
RIP!
ACTUALLY, I'M NOT EVEN IN THE COURSE...
G.B.Trudeau

1/8/71

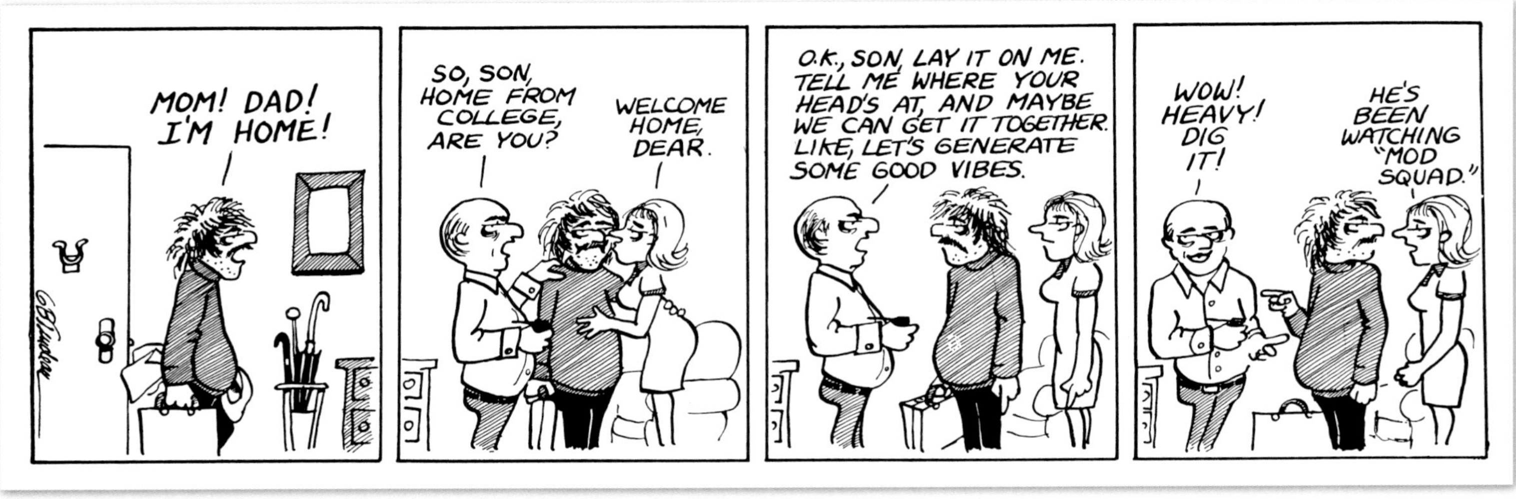
MOM! DAD! I'M HOME!
G.B.Trudeau
SO, SON, HOME FROM COLLEGE, ARE YOU?
WELCOME HOME, DEAR.
O.K., SON, LAY IT ON ME. TELL ME WHERE YOUR HEAD'S AT, AND MAYBE WE CAN GET IT TOGETHER. LIKE, LET'S GENERATE SOME GOOD VIBES.
WOW! HEAVY! DIG IT!
HE'S BEEN WATCHING "MOD SQUAD."

3/30/71

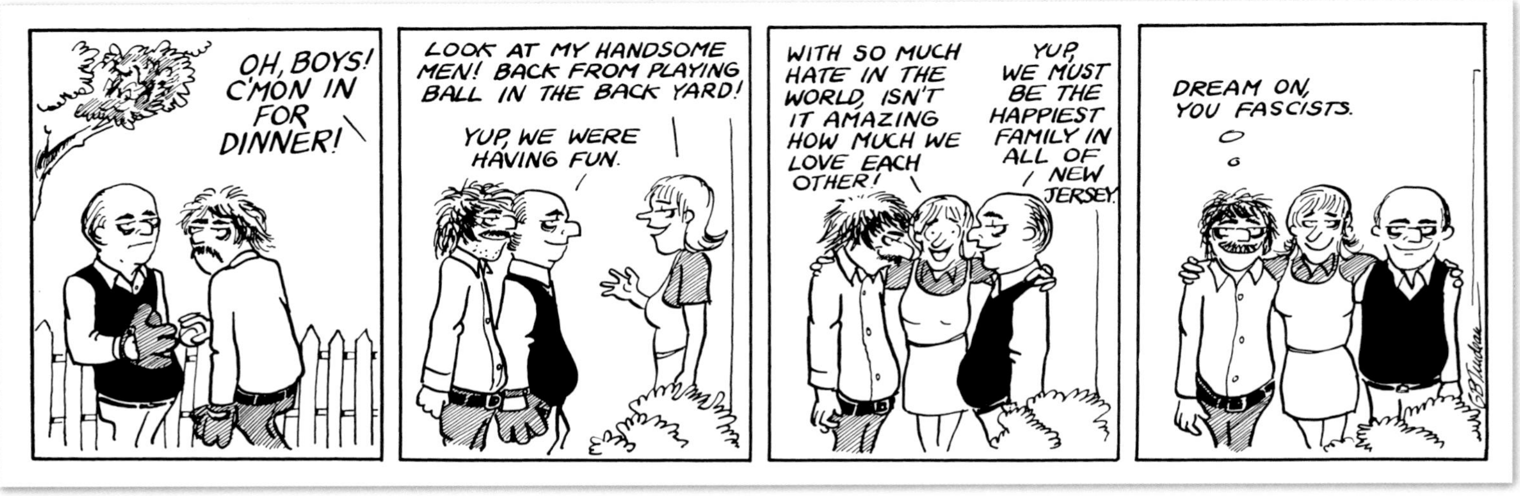
OH, BOYS! C'MON IN FOR DINNER!
LOOK AT MY HANDSOME MEN! BACK FROM PLAYING BALL IN THE BACK YARD!
YUP, WE WERE HAVING FUN.
WITH SO MUCH HATE IN THE WORLD, ISN'T IT AMAZING HOW MUCH WE LOVE EACH OTHER!
YUP, WE MUST BE THE HAPPIEST FAMILY IN ALL OF NEW JERSEY.
DREAM ON, YOU FASCISTS.
G.B.Trudeau

3/31/71

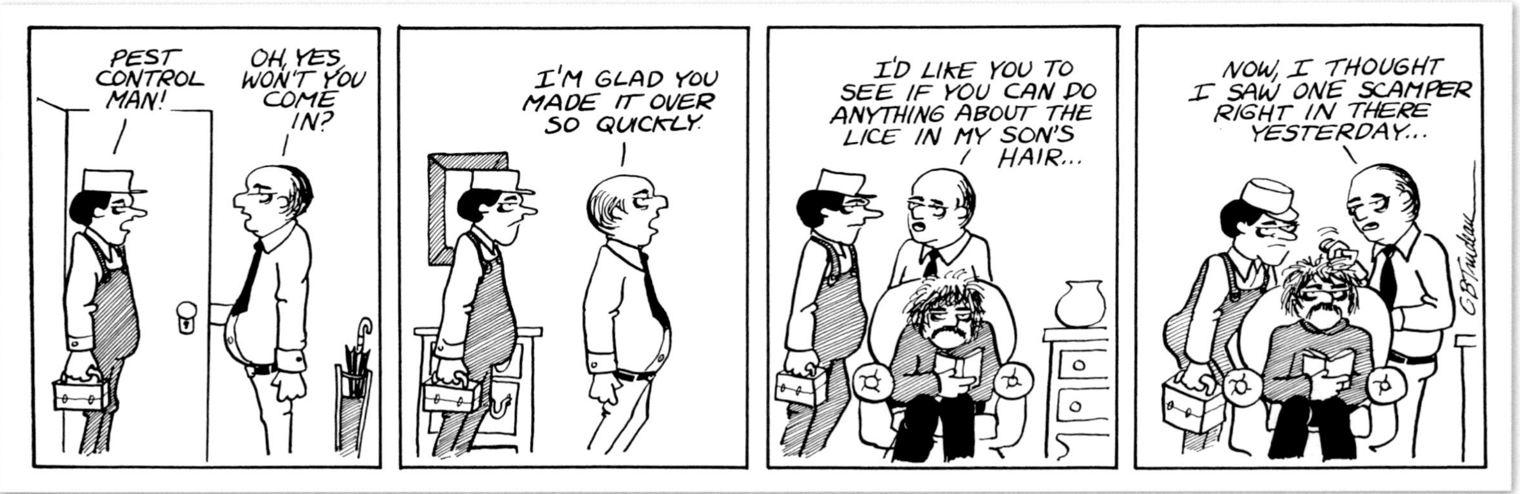
PEST CONTROL MAN!
OH, YES, WON'T YOU COME IN?
I'M GLAD YOU MADE IT OVER SO QUICKLY.
I'D LIKE YOU TO SEE IF YOU CAN DO ANYTHING ABOUT THE LICE IN MY SON'S HAIR...
NOW, I THOUGHT I SAW ONE SCAMPER RIGHT IN THERE YESTERDAY...
G.B.Trudeau

4/2/71

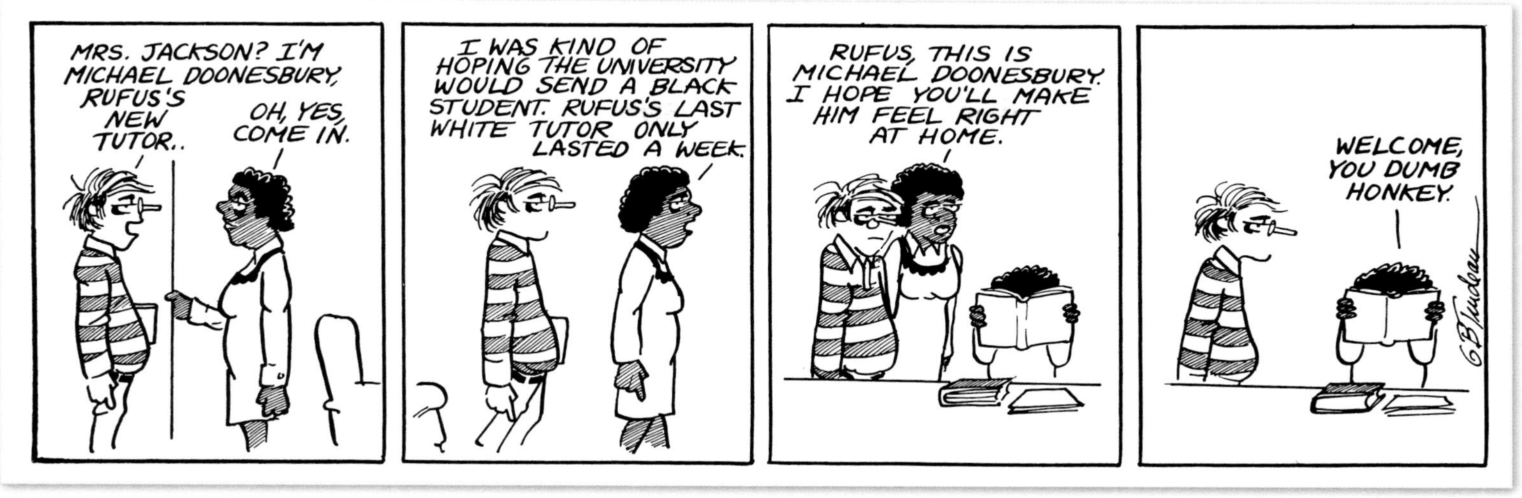
MRS. JACKSON? I'M MICHAEL DOONESBURY, RUFUS'S NEW TUTOR..
OH, YES, COME IN.
I WAS KIND OF HOPING THE UNIVERSITY WOULD SEND A BLACK STUDENT. RUFUS'S LAST WHITE TUTOR ONLY LASTED A WEEK.
RUFUS, THIS IS MICHAEL DOONESBURY. I HOPE YOU'LL MAKE HIM FEEL RIGHT AT HOME.
WELCOME, YOU DUMB HONKEY.

4/5/71

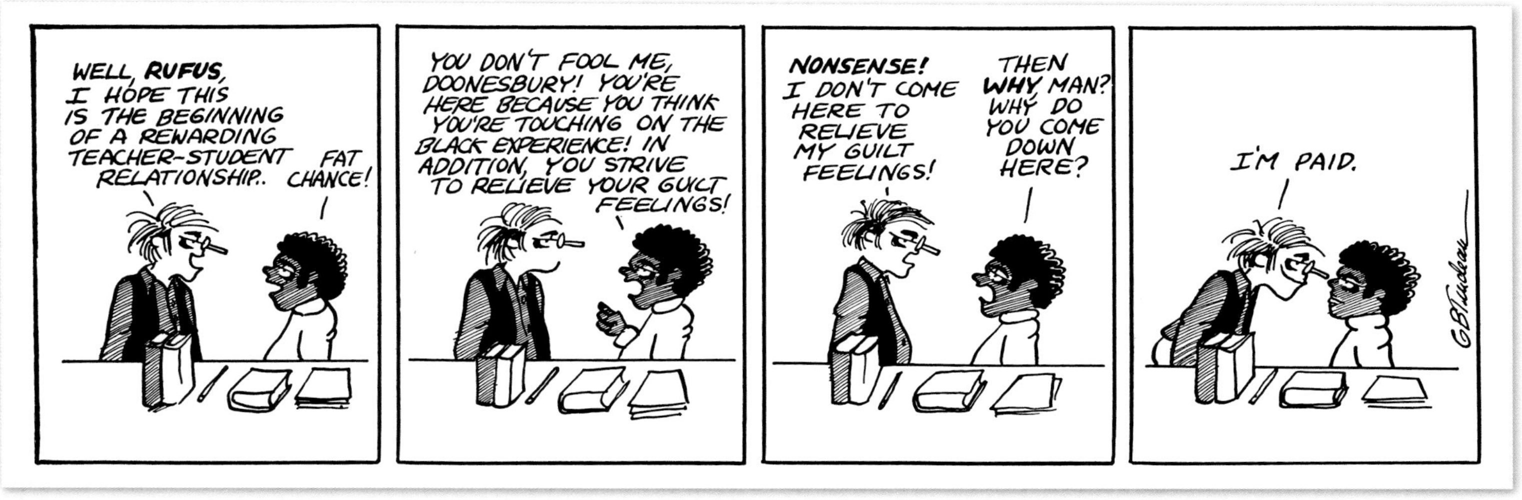
WELL, RUFUS, I HOPE THIS IS THE BEGINNING OF A REWARDING TEACHER-STUDENT RELATIONSHIP..
FAT CHANCE!
YOU DON'T FOOL ME, DOONESBURY! YOU'RE HERE BECAUSE YOU THINK YOU'RE TOUCHING ON THE BLACK EXPERIENCE! IN ADDITION, YOU STRIVE TO RELIEVE YOUR GUILT FEELINGS!
NONSENSE! I DON'T COME HERE TO RELIEVE MY GUILT FEELINGS!
THEN WHY, MAN? WHY DO YOU COME DOWN HERE?
I'M PAID.

4/6/71

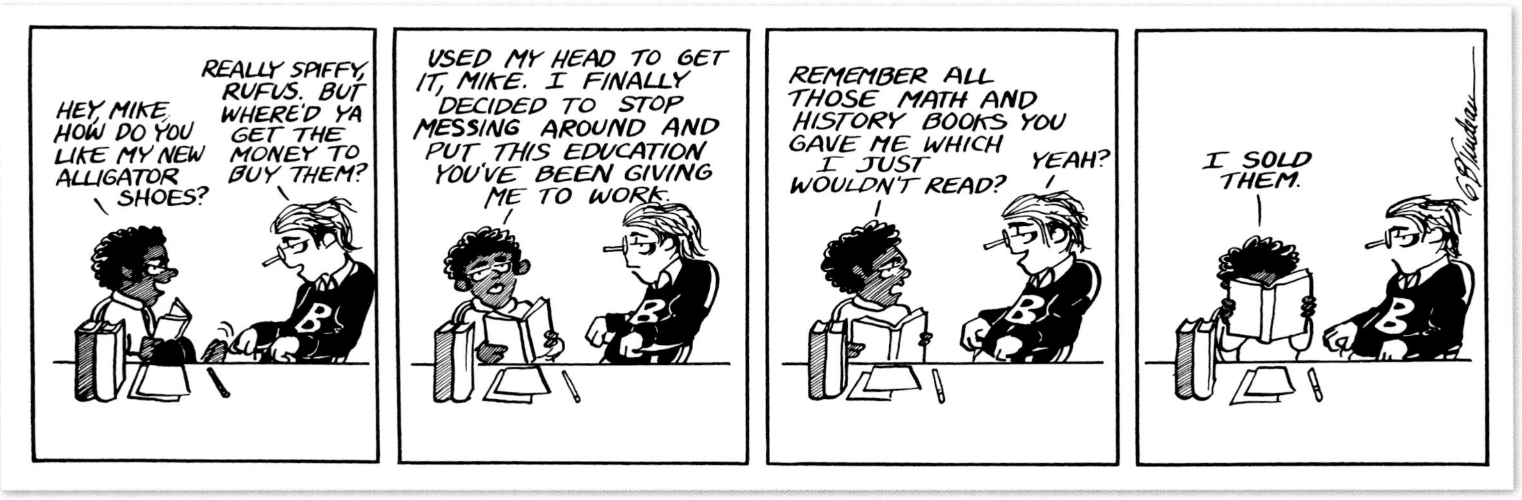
HEY, MIKE, HOW DO YOU LIKE MY NEW ALLIGATOR SHOES?
REALLY SPIFFY, RUFUS. BUT WHERE'D YA GET THE MONEY TO BUY THEM?
USED MY HEAD TO GET IT, MIKE. I FINALLY DECIDED TO STOP MESSING AROUND AND PUT THIS EDUCATION YOU'VE BEEN GIVING ME TO WORK.
REMEMBER ALL THOSE MATH AND HISTORY BOOKS YOU GAVE ME WHICH I JUST WOULDN'T READ?
YEAH?
I SOLD THEM.

5/21/71

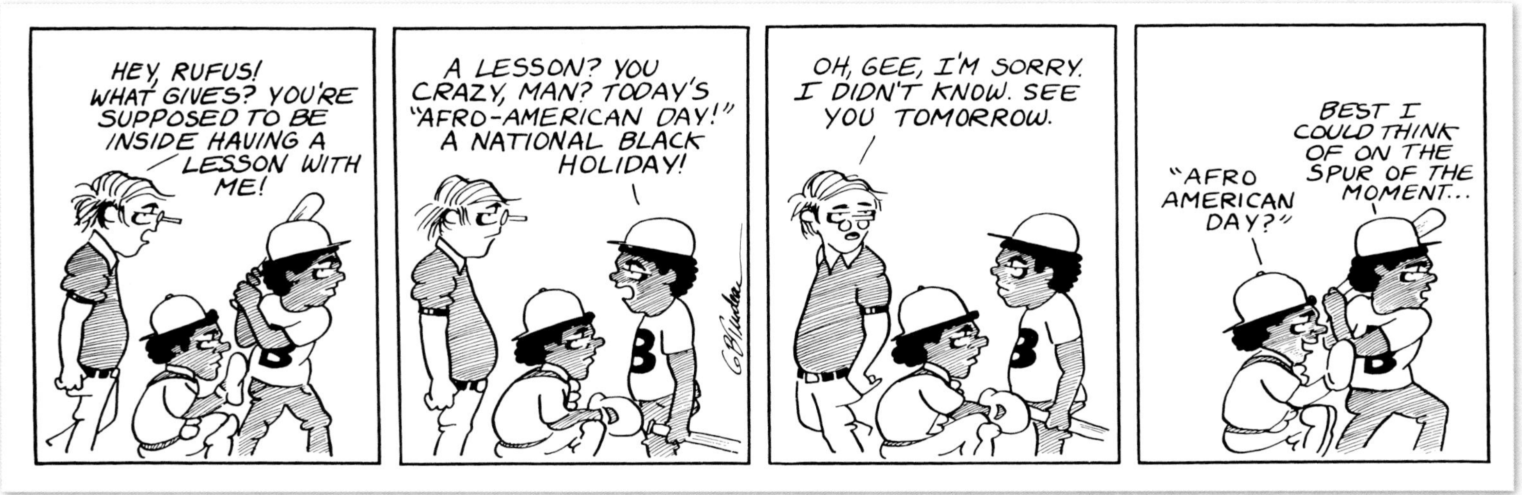
HEY, RUFUS! WHAT GIVES? YOU'RE SUPPOSED TO BE INSIDE HAVING A LESSON WITH ME!
A LESSON? YOU CRAZY, MAN? TODAY'S "AFRO-AMERICAN DAY!" A NATIONAL BLACK HOLIDAY!
OH, GEE, I'M SORRY. I DIDN'T KNOW. SEE YOU TOMORROW.
"AFRO AMERICAN DAY?"
BEST I COULD THINK OF ON THE SPUR OF THE MOMENT...

9/9/71

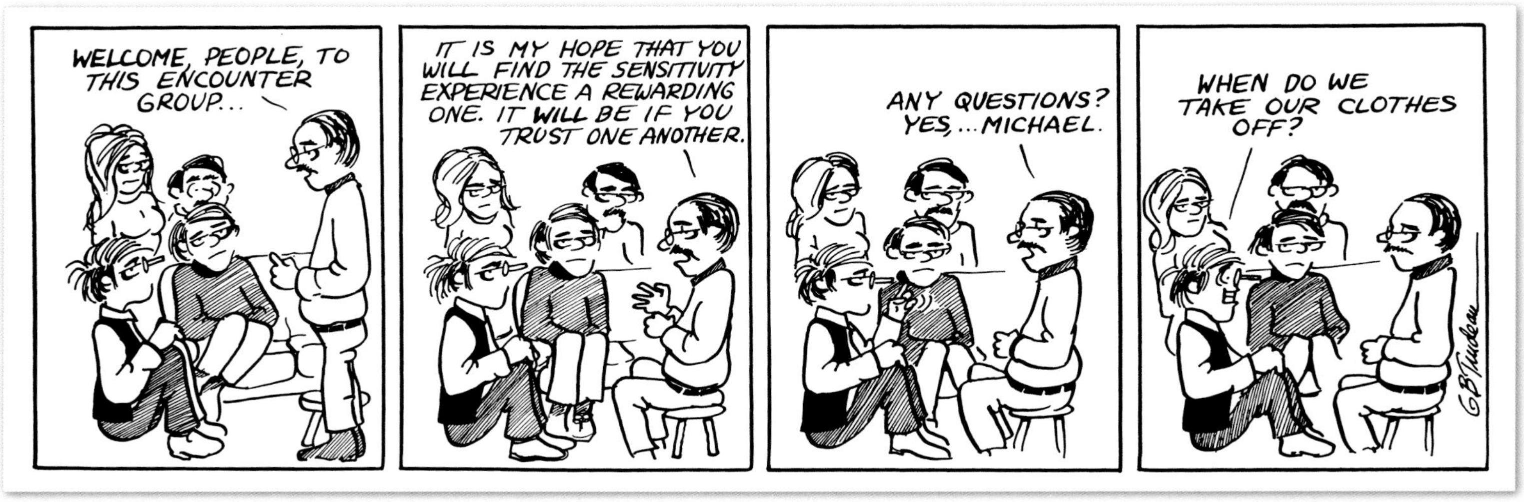
WELCOME, PEOPLE, TO THIS ENCOUNTER GROUP...
IT IS MY HOPE THAT YOU WILL FIND THE SENSITIVITY EXPERIENCE A REWARDING ONE. IT WILL BE IF YOU TRUST ONE ANOTHER.
ANY QUESTIONS? YES, ...MICHAEL.
WHEN DO WE TAKE OUR CLOTHES OFF?
GBTrudeau

4/20/71

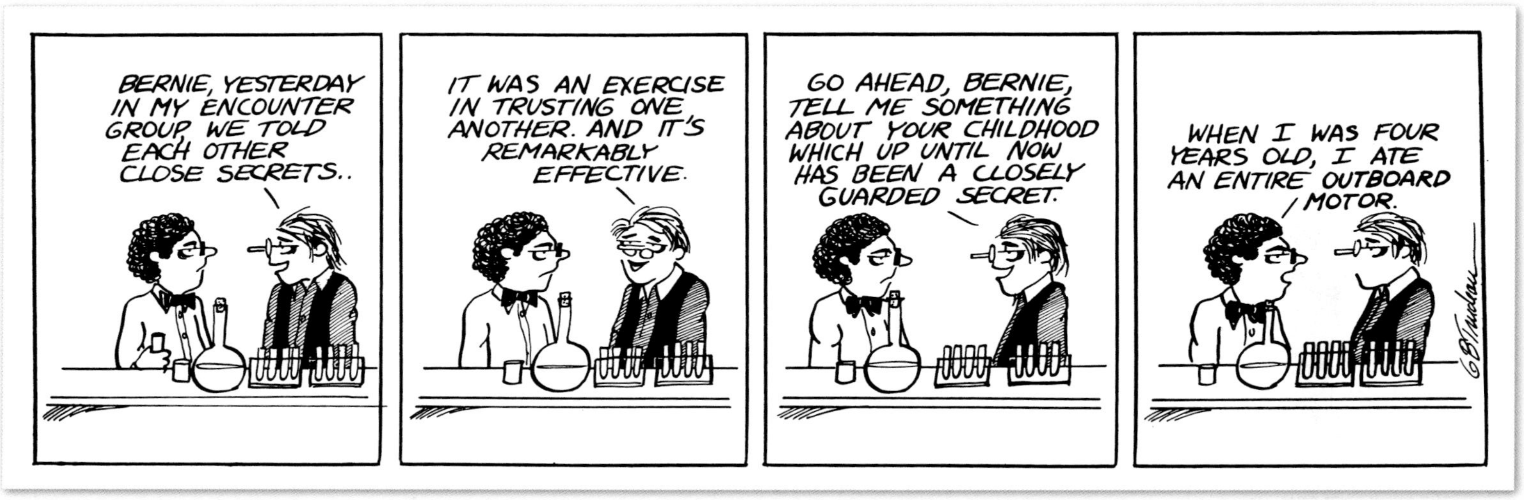
BERNIE, YESTERDAY IN MY ENCOUNTER GROUP WE TOLD EACH OTHER CLOSE SECRETS..
IT WAS AN EXERCISE IN TRUSTING ONE ANOTHER. AND IT'S REMARKABLY EFFECTIVE.
GO AHEAD, BERNIE, TELL ME SOMETHING ABOUT YOUR CHILDHOOD WHICH UP UNTIL NOW HAS BEEN A CLOSELY GUARDED SECRET.
WHEN I WAS FOUR YEARS OLD, I ATE AN ENTIRE OUTBOARD MOTOR.
GBTrudeau

4/21/71

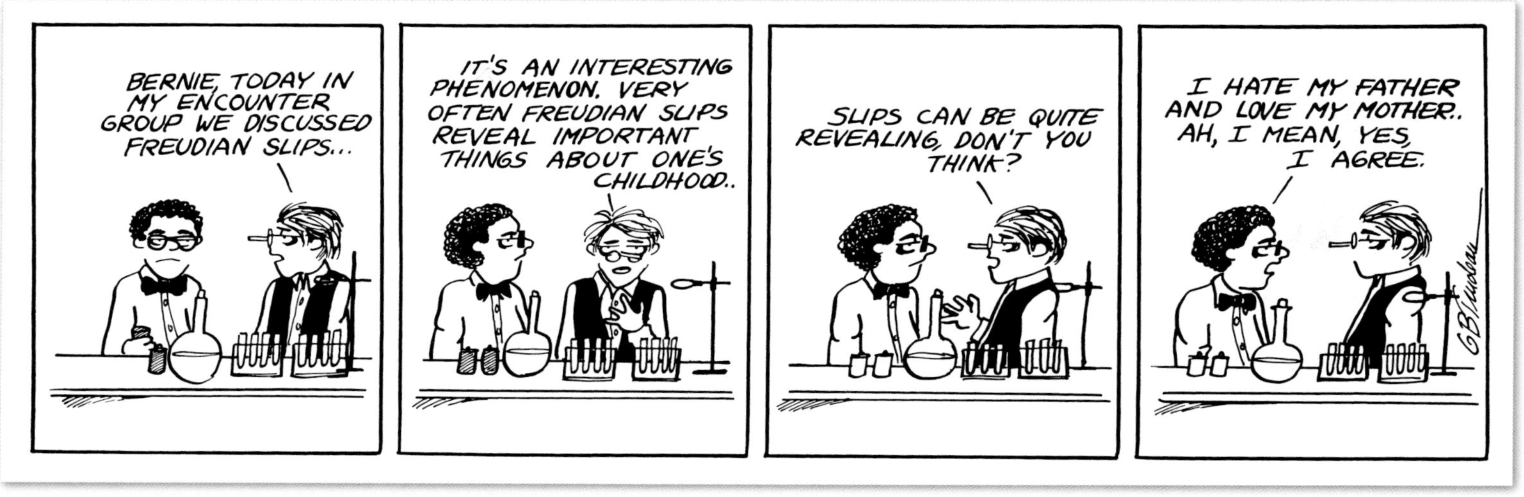
BERNIE, TODAY IN MY ENCOUNTER GROUP WE DISCUSSED FREUDIAN SLIPS...
IT'S AN INTERESTING PHENOMENON. VERY OFTEN FREUDIAN SLIPS REVEAL IMPORTANT THINGS ABOUT ONE'S CHILDHOOD..
SLIPS CAN BE QUITE REVEALING, DON'T YOU THINK?
I HATE MY FATHER AND LOVE MY MOTHER.. AH, I MEAN, YES, I AGREE.
GBTrudeau

4/22/71

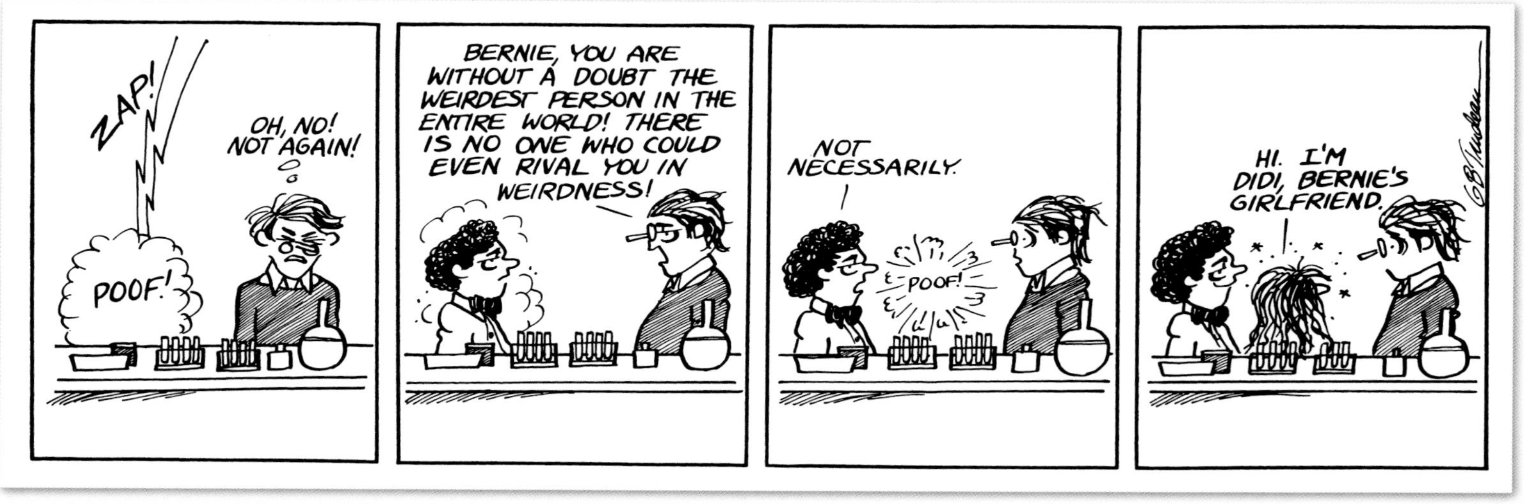
ZAP!
OH, NO! NOT AGAIN!
POOF!
BERNIE, YOU ARE WITHOUT A DOUBT THE WEIRDEST PERSON IN THE ENTIRE WORLD! THERE IS NO ONE WHO COULD EVEN RIVAL YOU IN WEIRDNESS!
NOT NECESSARILY.
POOF!
HI. I'M DIDI, BERNIE'S GIRLFRIEND.
GBTrudeau

5/18/71

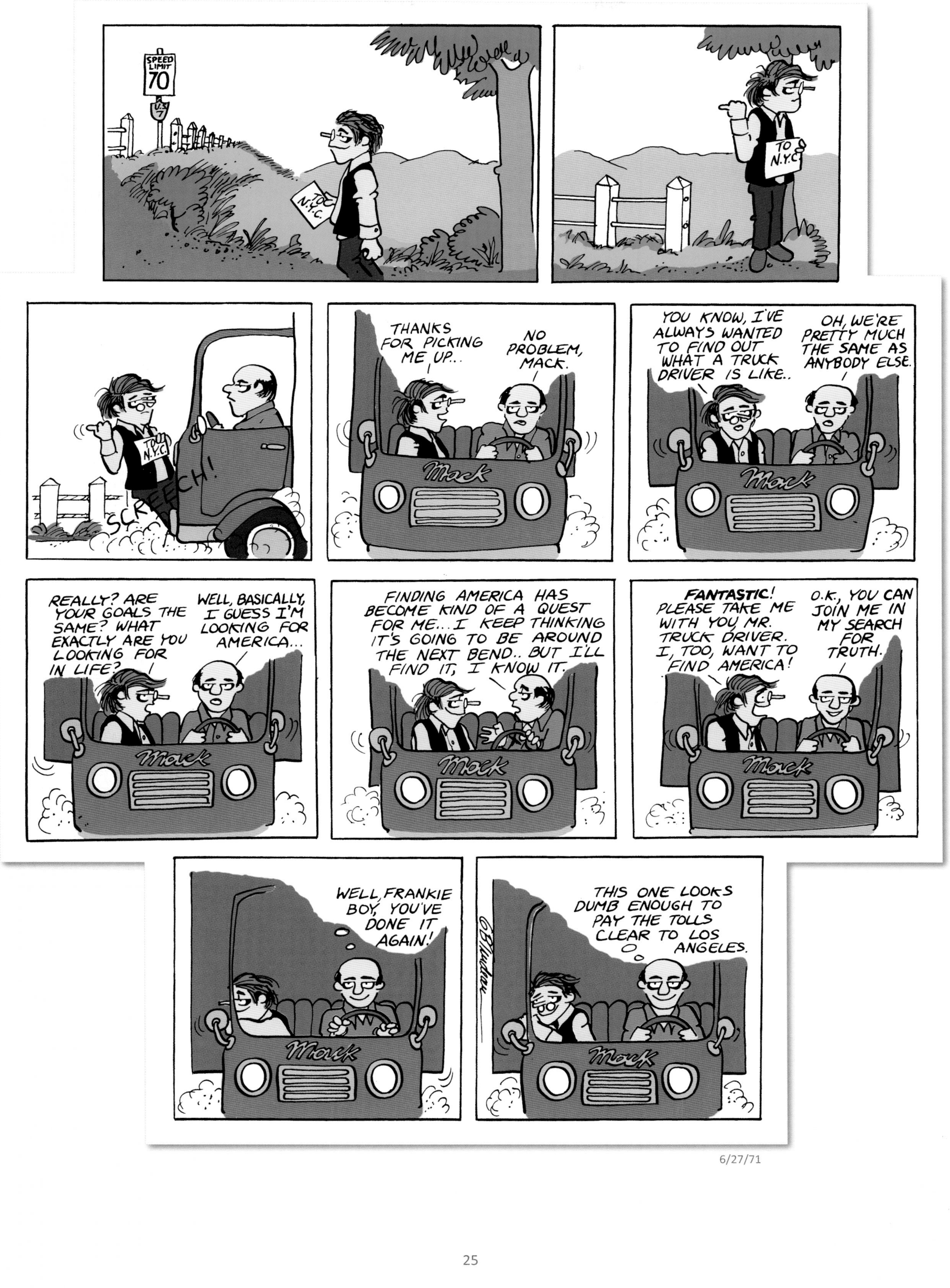
SPEED LIMIT 70
U.S. 7
TO N.Y.C.
TO N.Y.C.
TO N.Y.C.
SCREECH!
THANKS FOR PICKING ME UP..
NO PROBLEM, MACK.
Mack
YOU KNOW, I'VE ALWAYS WANTED TO FIND OUT WHAT A TRUCK DRIVER IS LIKE..
OH, WE'RE PRETTY MUCH THE SAME AS ANYBODY ELSE.
REALLY? ARE YOUR GOALS THE SAME? WHAT EXACTLY ARE YOU LOOKING FOR IN LIFE?
WELL, BASICALLY, I GUESS I'M LOOKING FOR AMERICA...
FINDING AMERICA HAS BECOME KIND OF A QUEST FOR ME... I KEEP THINKING IT'S GOING TO BE AROUND THE NEXT BEND.. BUT I'LL FIND IT, I KNOW IT.
FANTASTIC! PLEASE TAKE ME WITH YOU MR. TRUCK DRIVER. I, TOO, WANT TO FIND AMERICA!
O.K., YOU CAN JOIN ME IN MY SEARCH FOR TRUTH.
WELL, FRANKIE BOY, YOU'VE DONE IT AGAIN!
THIS ONE LOOKS DUMB ENOUGH TO PAY THE TOLLS CLEAR TO LOS ANGELES.

6/27/71

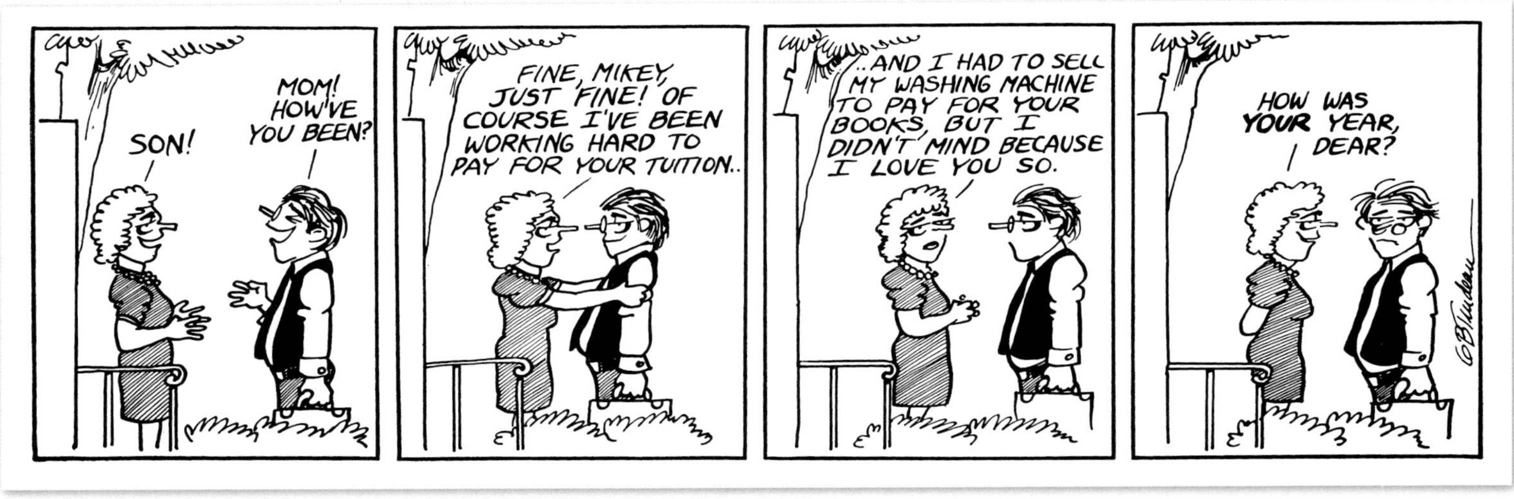
SON!
MOM! HOW'VE YOU BEEN?
FINE, MIKEY, JUST FINE! OF COURSE I'VE BEEN WORKING HARD TO PAY FOR YOUR TUITION..
..AND I HAD TO SELL MY WASHING MACHINE TO PAY FOR YOUR BOOKS, BUT I DIDN'T MIND BECAUSE I LOVE YOU SO.
HOW WAS **YOUR** YEAR, DEAR?

6/5/71

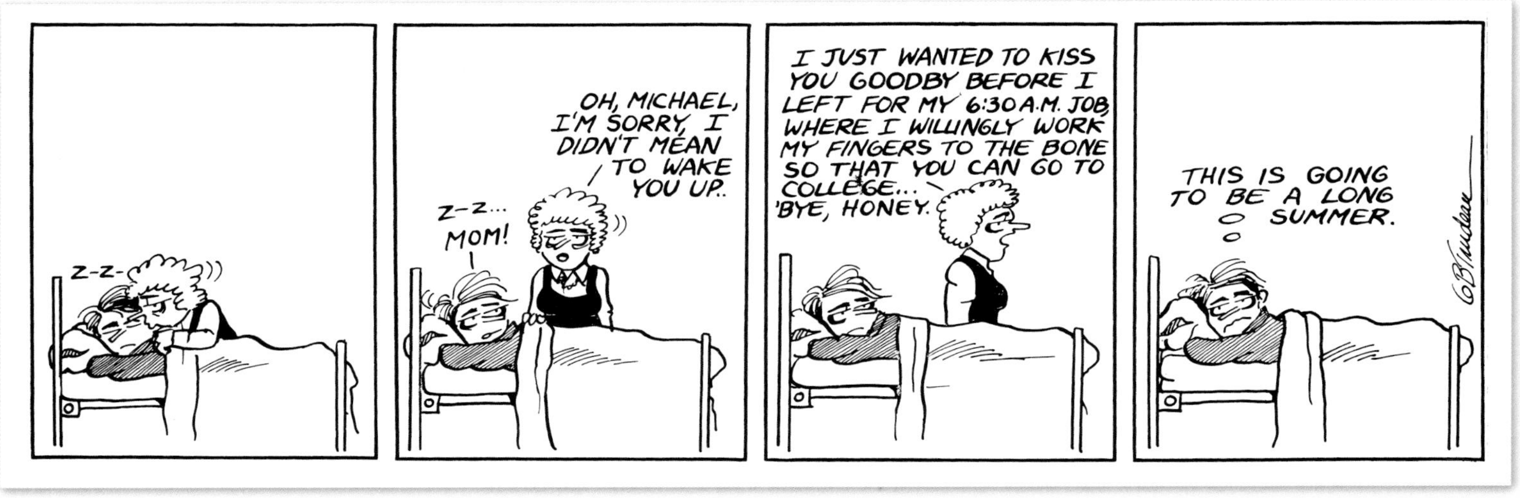
Z-Z-
Z-Z...
MOM!
OH, MICHAEL, I'M SORRY, I DIDN'T MEAN TO WAKE YOU UP..
I JUST WANTED TO KISS YOU GOODBY BEFORE I LEFT FOR MY 6:30 A.M. JOB, WHERE I WILLINGLY WORK MY FINGERS TO THE BONE SO THAT YOU CAN GO TO COLLEGE... 'BYE, HONEY.
THIS IS GOING TO BE A LONG SUMMER.

6/9/71

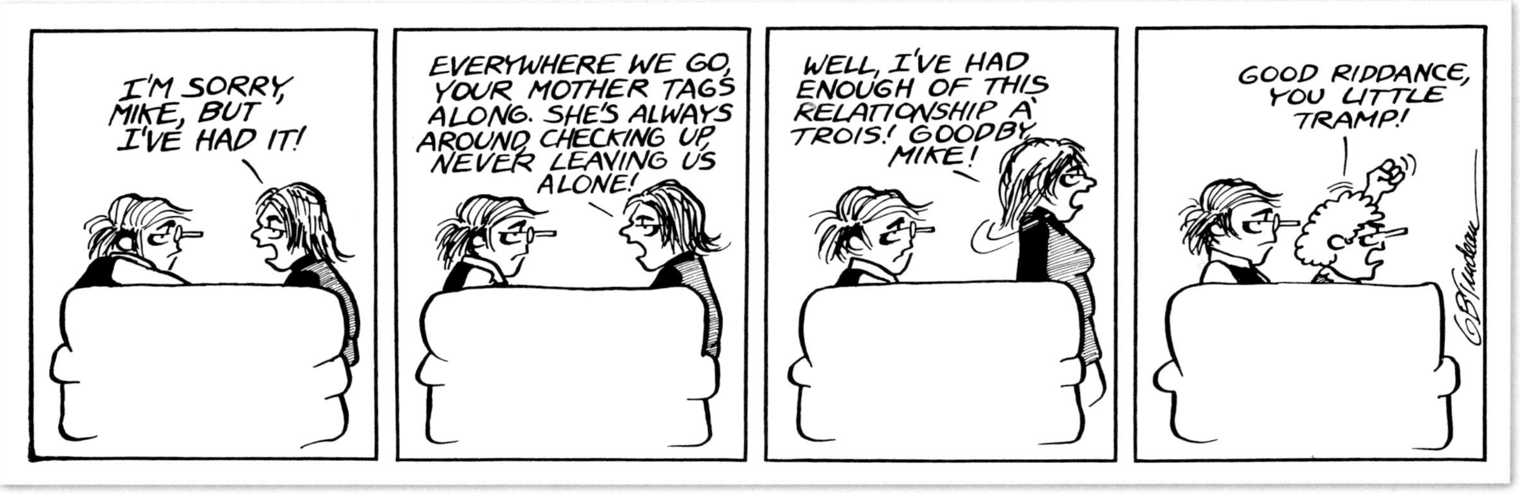
I'M SORRY, MIKE, BUT I'VE HAD IT!
EVERYWHERE WE GO, YOUR MOTHER TAGS ALONG. SHE'S ALWAYS AROUND CHECKING UP, NEVER LEAVING US ALONE!
WELL, I'VE HAD ENOUGH OF THIS RELATIONSHIP À TROIS! GOODBY, MIKE!
GOOD RIDDANCE, YOU LITTLE TRAMP!

6/28/71

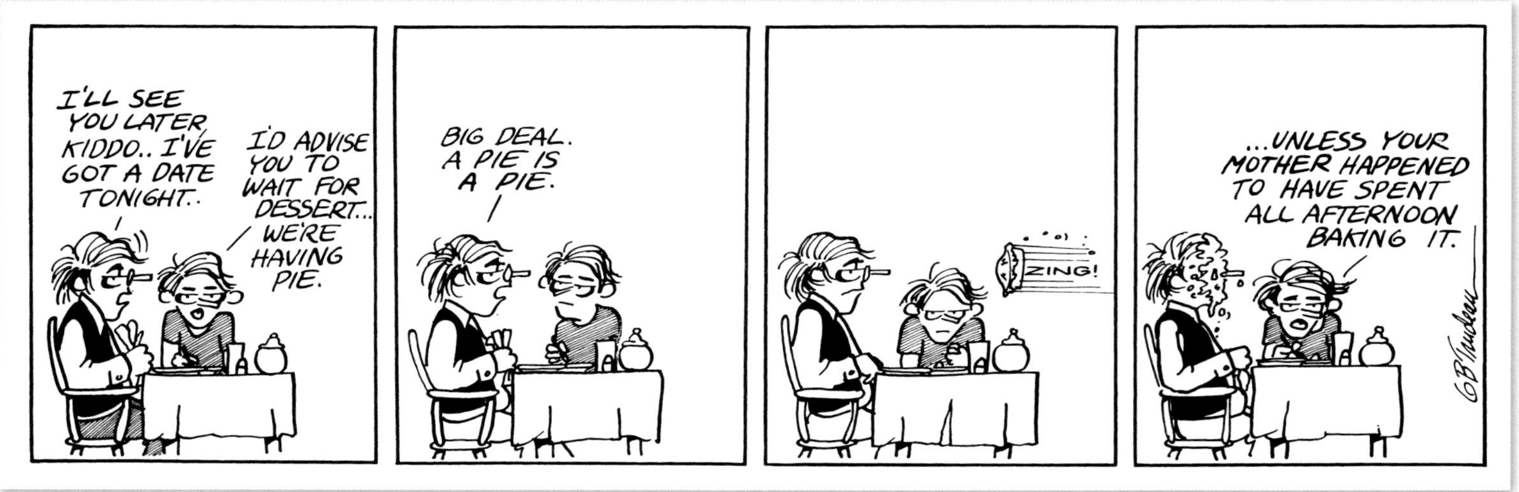
I'LL SEE YOU LATER, KIDDO.. I'VE GOT A DATE TONIGHT..
I'D ADVISE YOU TO WAIT FOR DESSERT... WE'RE HAVING PIE.
BIG DEAL. A PIE IS A PIE.
ZING!
...UNLESS YOUR MOTHER HAPPENED TO HAVE SPENT ALL AFTERNOON BAKING IT.

7/2/71

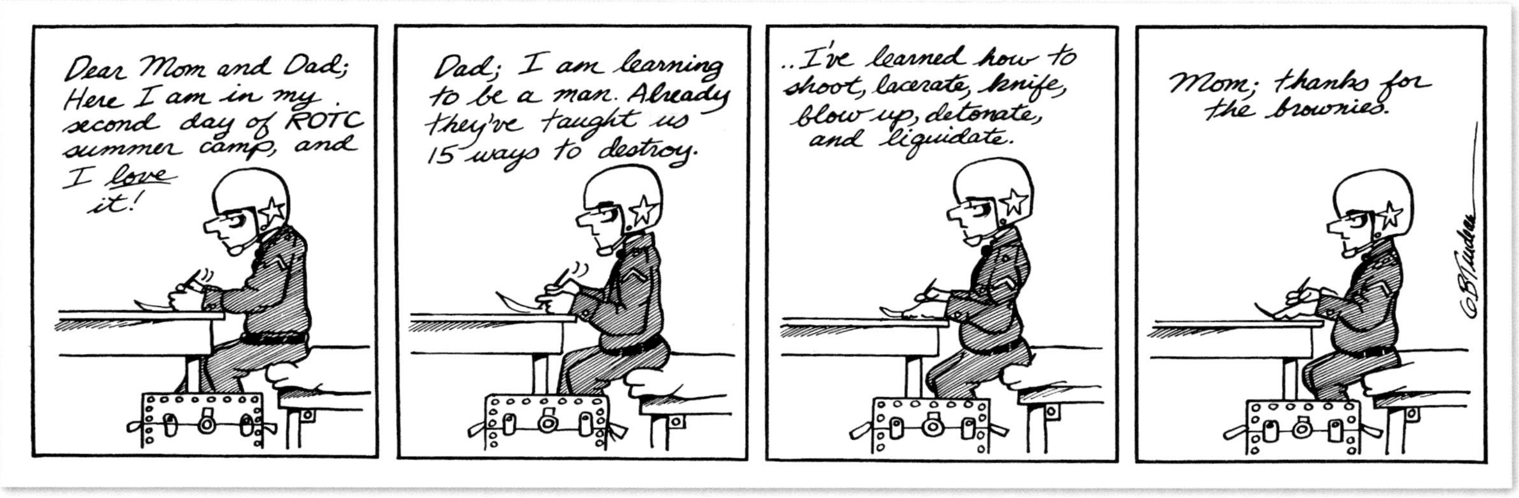
Dear Mom and Dad; Here I am in my second day of ROTC summer camp, and I love it!
Dad; I am learning to be a man. Already they've taught us 15 ways to destroy.
..I've learned how to shoot, lacerate, knife, blow up, detonate, and liquidate.
Mom; thanks for the brownies.

6/14/71

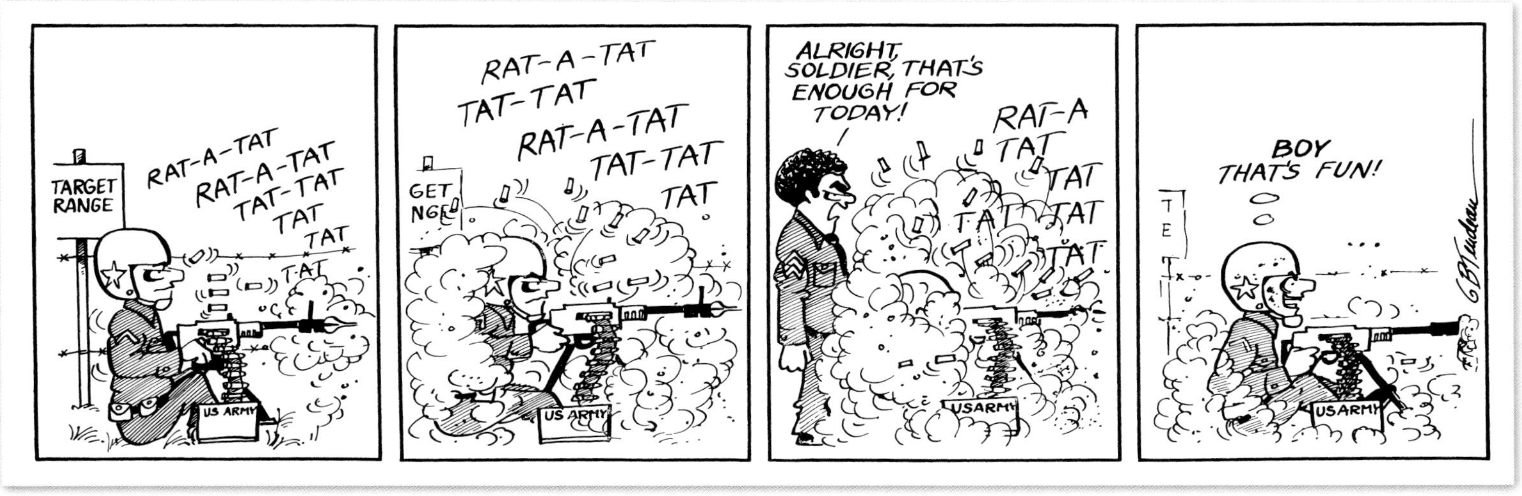
TARGET RANGE
RAT-A-TAT RAT-A-TAT TAT-TAT TAT TAT T-AT
US ARMY
RAT-A-TAT TAT-TAT RAT-A-TAT TAT-TAT TAT
US ARMY
ALRIGHT, SOLDIER, THAT'S ENOUGH FOR TODAY!
RAT-A TAT TAT TAT TAT TAT TAT
USARMY
BOY THAT'S FUN!
USARMY

6/16/71

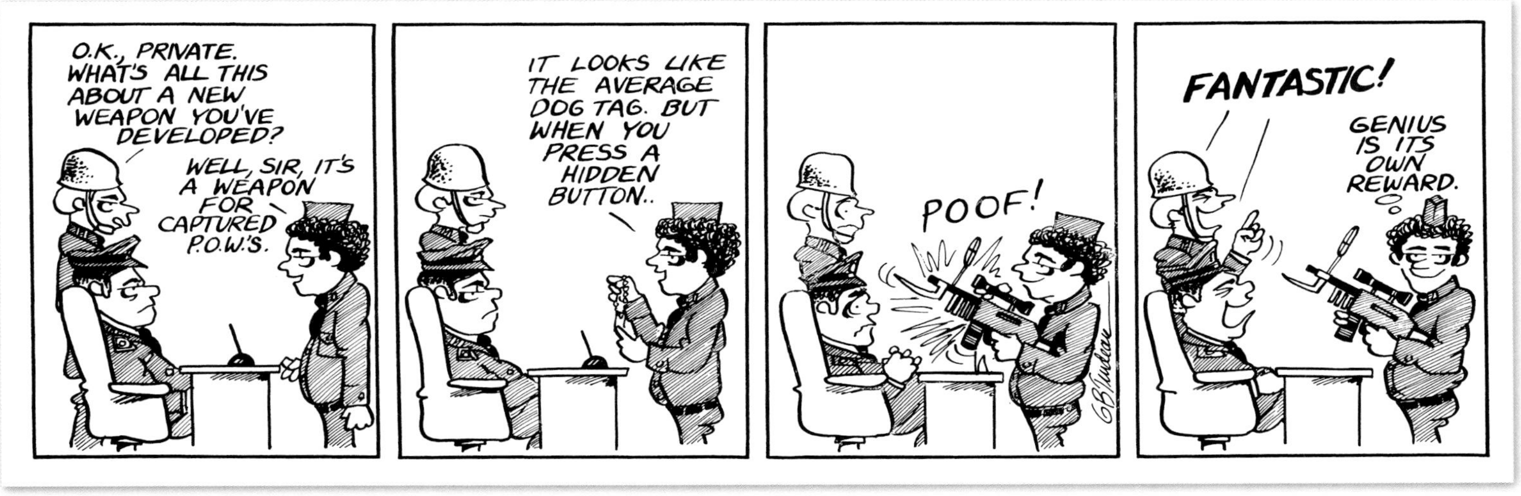
O.K., PRIVATE. WHAT'S ALL THIS ABOUT A NEW WEAPON YOU'VE DEVELOPED?
WELL, SIR, IT'S A WEAPON FOR CAPTURED P.O.W.'S.
IT LOOKS LIKE THE AVERAGE DOG TAG. BUT WHEN YOU PRESS A HIDDEN BUTTON..
POOF!
FANTASTIC!
GENIUS IS ITS OWN REWARD.

6/17/71

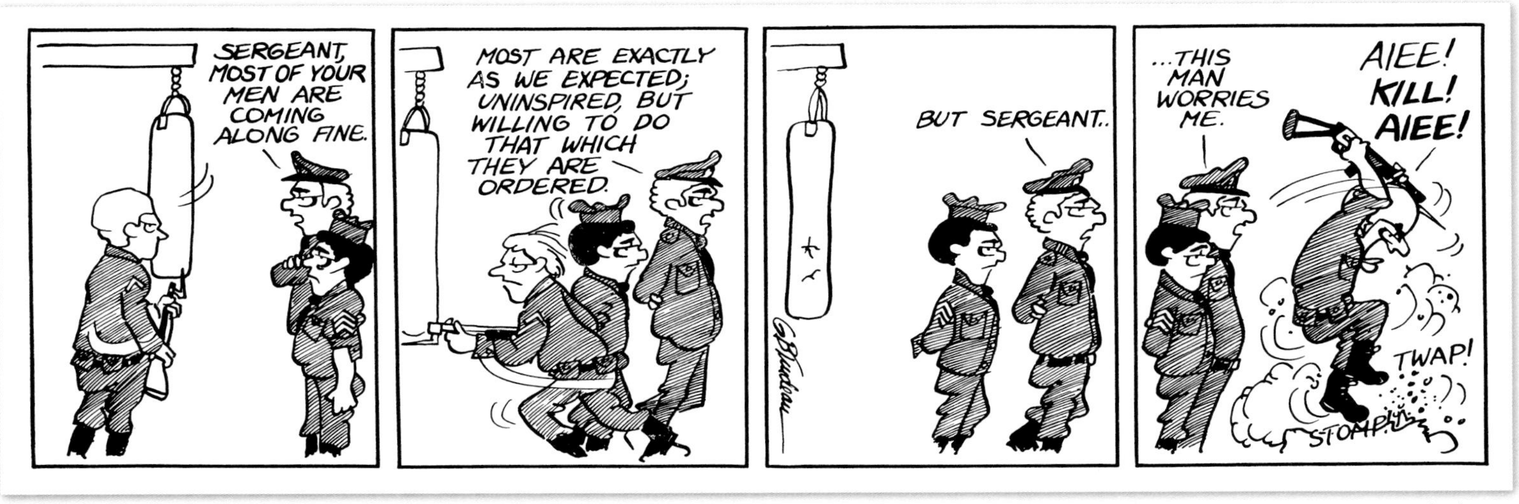
SERGEANT, MOST OF YOUR MEN ARE COMING ALONG FINE.
MOST ARE EXACTLY AS WE EXPECTED; UNINSPIRED, BUT WILLING TO DO THAT WHICH THEY ARE ORDERED.
BUT SERGEANT..
...THIS MAN WORRIES ME.
AIEE! KILL! AIEE!
TWAP!
STOMP!

6/18/71

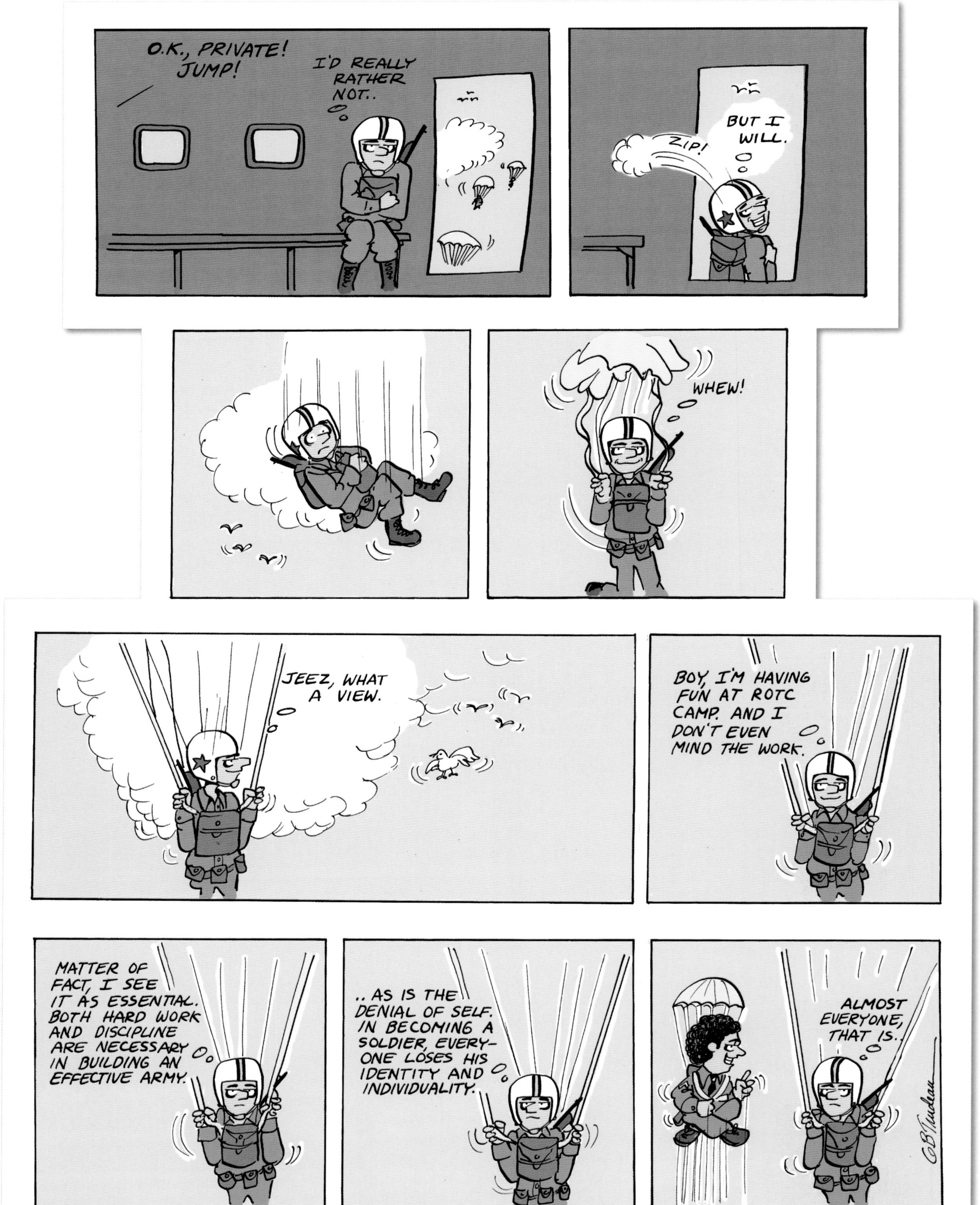
O.K., PRIVATE! JUMP!
I'D REALLY RATHER NOT..
ZIP!
BUT I WILL.
WHEW!
JEEZ, WHAT A VIEW.
BOY, I'M HAVING FUN AT ROTC CAMP. AND I DON'T EVEN MIND THE WORK.
MATTER OF FACT, I SEE IT AS ESSENTIAL. BOTH HARD WORK AND DISCIPLINE ARE NECESSARY IN BUILDING AN EFFECTIVE ARMY.
.. AS IS THE DENIAL OF SELF. IN BECOMING A SOLDIER, EVERY-ONE LOSES HIS IDENTITY AND INDIVIDUALITY.
ALMOST EVERYONE, THAT IS..
GBTrudeau

6/20/71

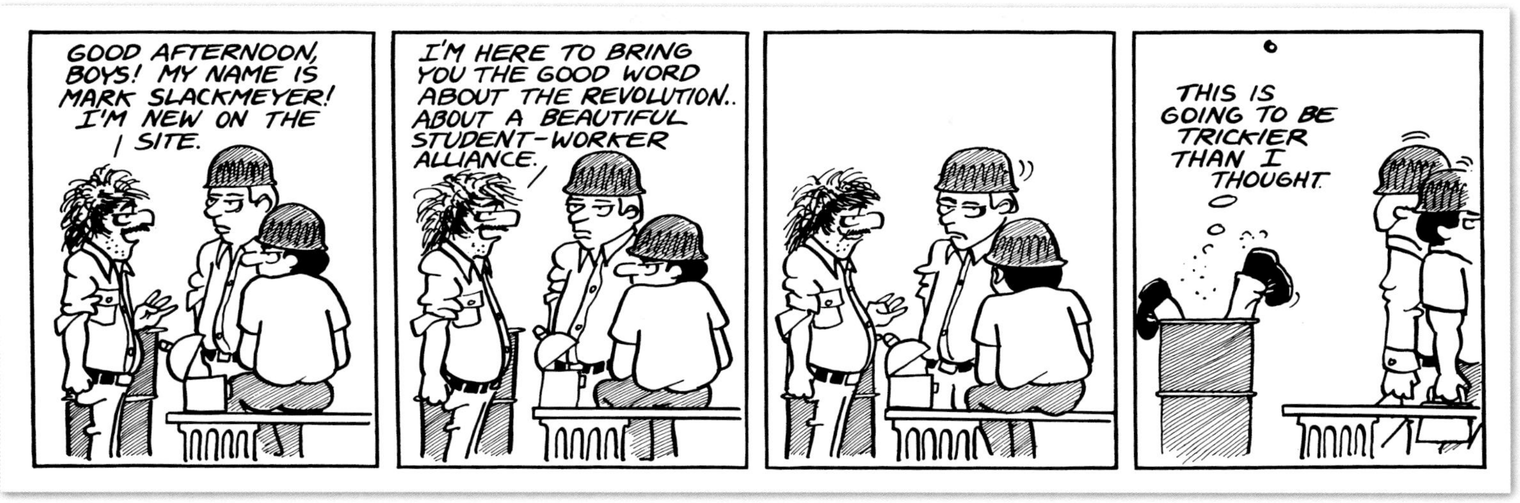
GOOD AFTERNOON, BOYS! MY NAME IS MARK SLACKMEYER! I'M NEW ON THE SITE.
I'M HERE TO BRING YOU THE GOOD WORD ABOUT THE REVOLUTION.. ABOUT A BEAUTIFUL STUDENT-WORKER ALLIANCE.
THIS IS GOING TO BE TRICKIER THAN I THOUGHT.

7/6/71

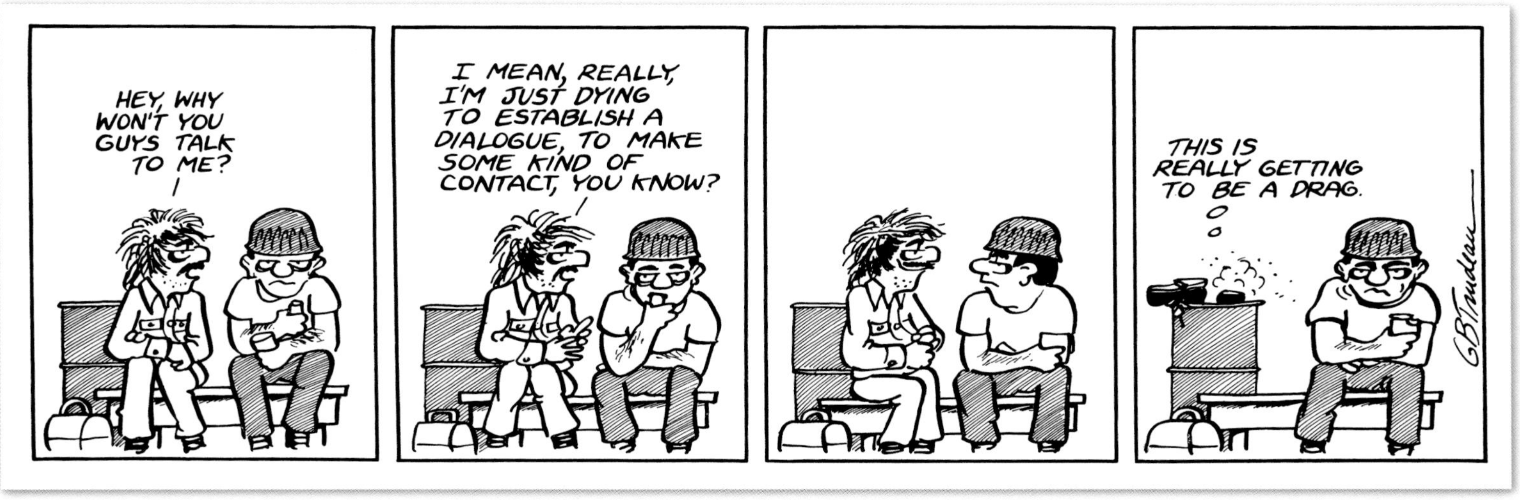
HEY, WHY WON'T YOU GUYS TALK TO ME?
I MEAN, REALLY, I'M JUST DYING TO ESTABLISH A DIALOGUE, TO MAKE SOME KIND OF CONTACT, YOU KNOW?
THIS IS REALLY GETTING TO BE A DRAG.

7/8/71

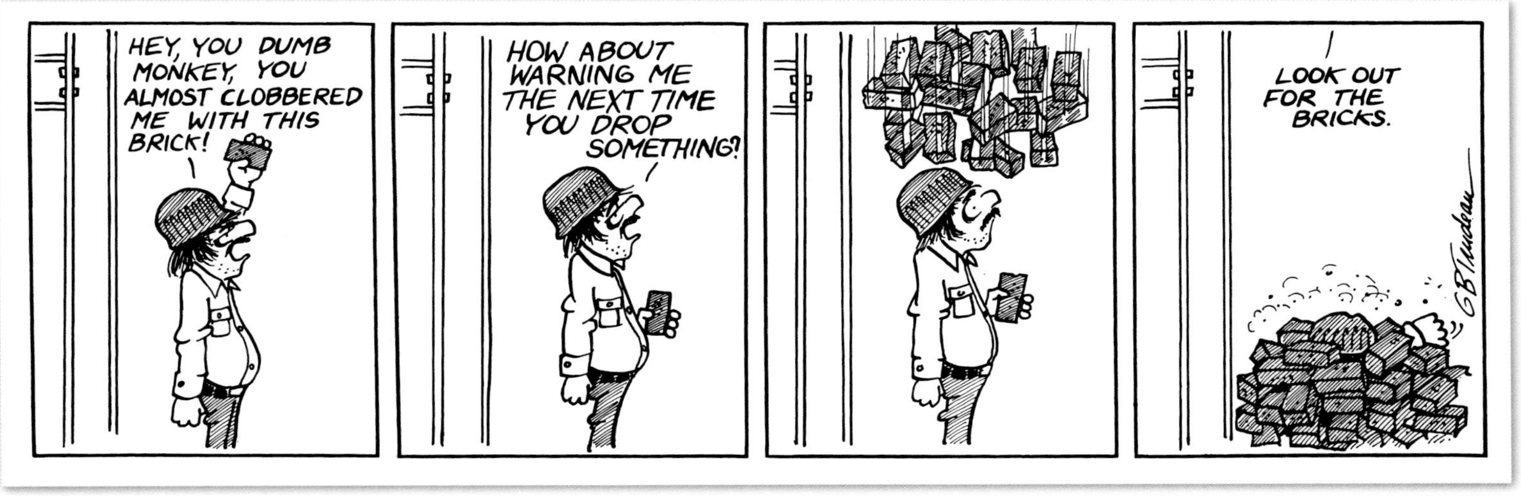
HEY, YOU DUMB MONKEY, YOU ALMOST CLOBBERED ME WITH THIS BRICK!
HOW ABOUT WARNING ME THE NEXT TIME YOU DROP SOMETHING?
LOOK OUT FOR THE BRICKS.

7/9/71

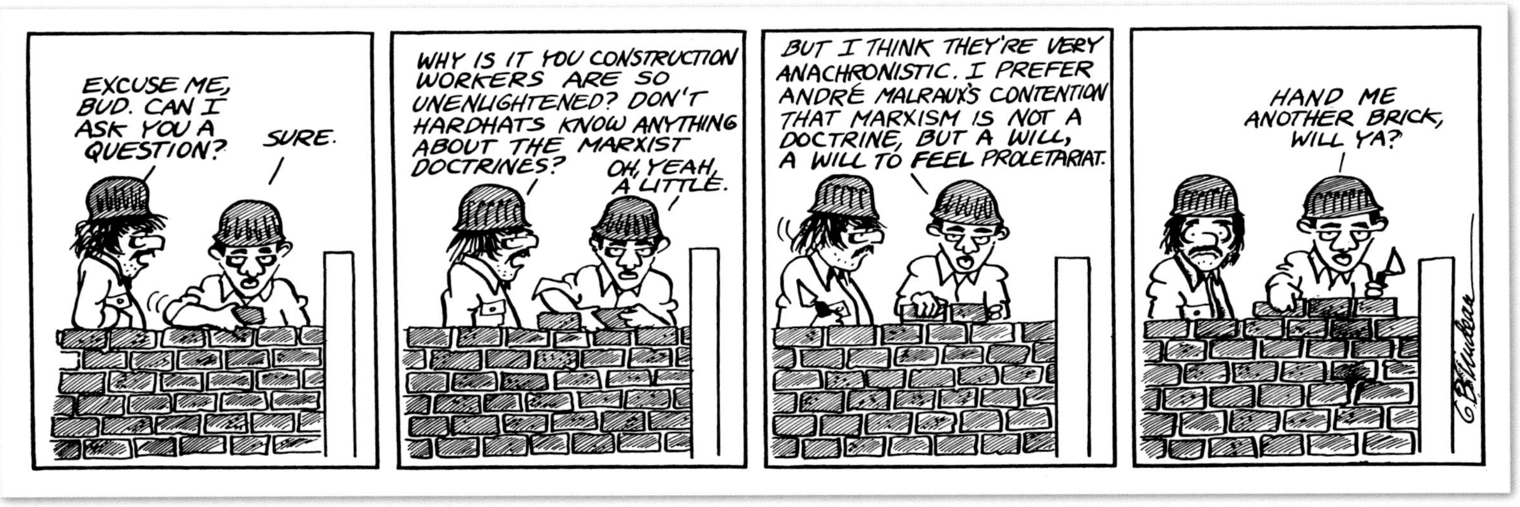
EXCUSE ME, BUD. CAN I ASK YOU A QUESTION?
SURE.
WHY IS IT YOU CONSTRUCTION WORKERS ARE SO UNENLIGHTENED? DON'T HARDHATS KNOW ANYTHING ABOUT THE MARXIST DOCTRINES?
OH, YEAH, A LITTLE.
BUT I THINK THEY'RE VERY ANACHRONISTIC. I PREFER ANDRÉ MALRAUX'S CONTENTION THAT MARXISM IS NOT A DOCTRINE, BUT A WILL, A WILL TO FEEL PROLETARIAT.
HAND ME ANOTHER BRICK, WILL YA?

7/17/71

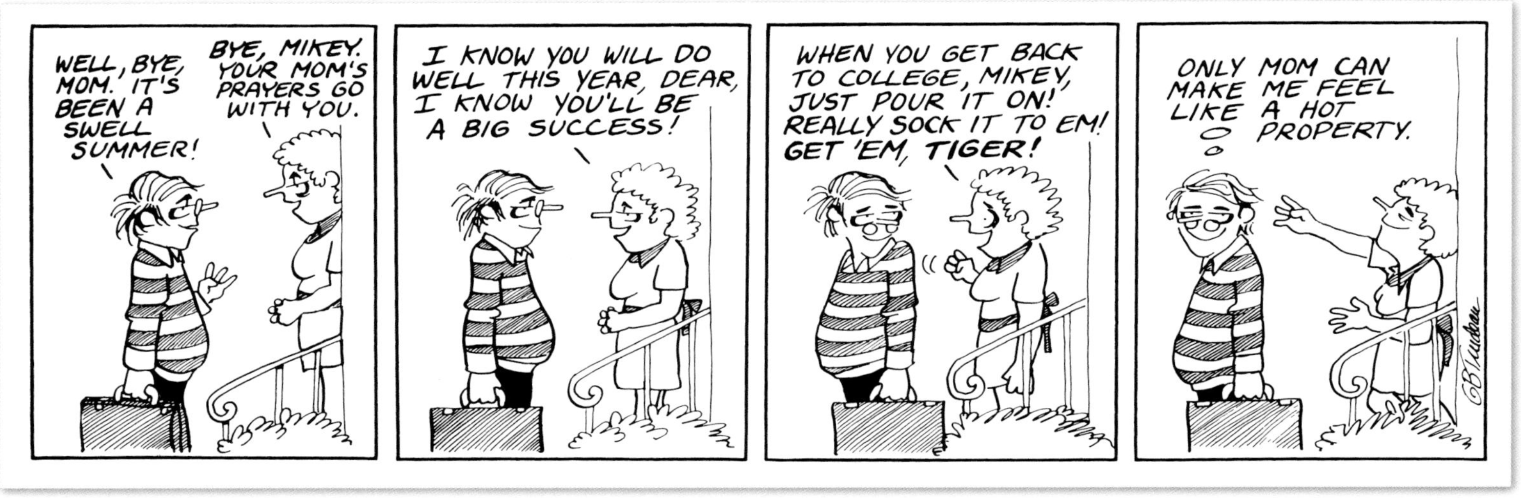
WELL, BYE, MOM. IT'S BEEN A SWELL SUMMER!
BYE, MIKEY. YOUR MOM'S PRAYERS GO WITH YOU.
I KNOW YOU WILL DO WELL THIS YEAR, DEAR, I KNOW YOU'LL BE A BIG SUCCESS!
WHEN YOU GET BACK TO COLLEGE, MIKEY, JUST POUR IT ON! REALLY SOCK IT TO EM! GET 'EM, TIGER!
ONLY MOM CAN MAKE ME FEEL LIKE A HOT PROPERTY.
GBTrudeau

8/31/71

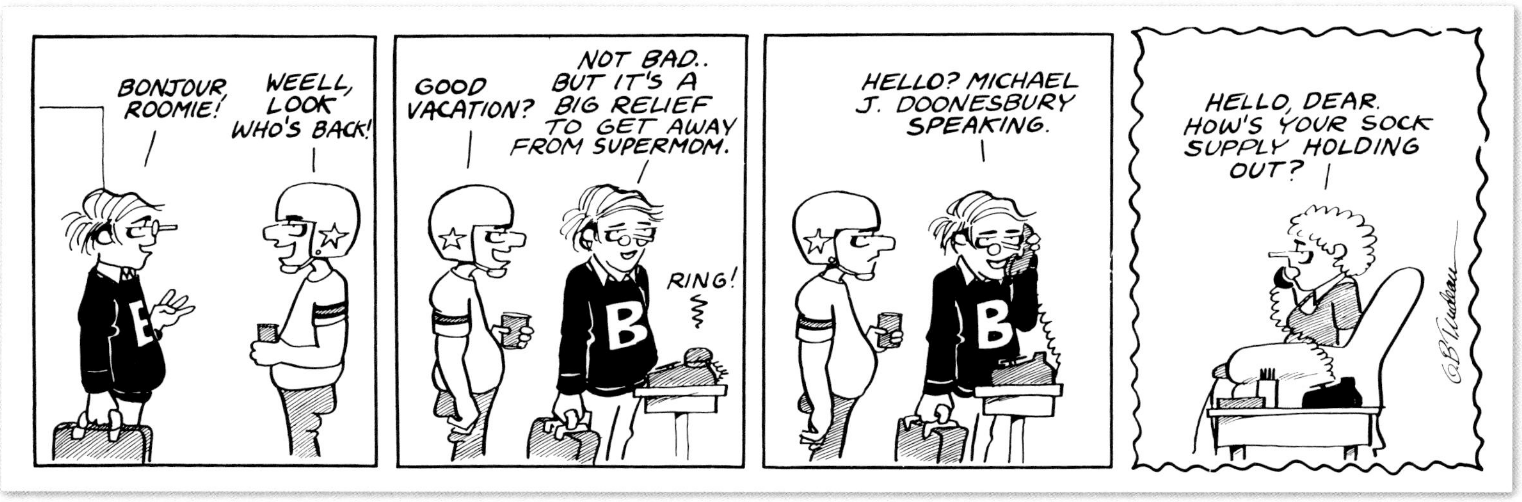
BONJOUR, ROOMIE!
WEELL, LOOK WHO'S BACK!
GOOD VACATION?
NOT BAD.. BUT IT'S A BIG RELIEF TO GET AWAY FROM SUPERMOM.
RING!
HELLO? MICHAEL J. DOONESBURY SPEAKING.
HELLO, DEAR. HOW'S YOUR SOCK SUPPLY HOLDING OUT?
GBTrudeau

9/1/71

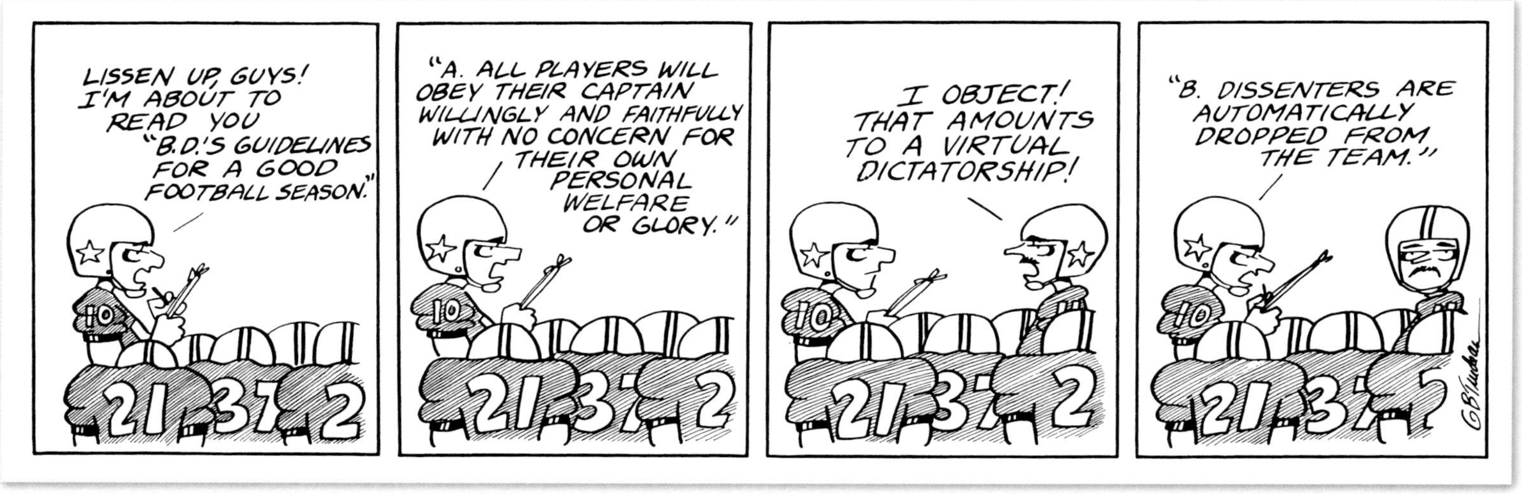
LISSEN UP, GUYS! I'M ABOUT TO READ YOU "B.D.'S GUIDELINES FOR A GOOD FOOTBALL SEASON."
"A. ALL PLAYERS WILL OBEY THEIR CAPTAIN WILLINGLY AND FAITHFULLY WITH NO CONCERN FOR THEIR OWN PERSONAL WELFARE OR GLORY."
I OBJECT! THAT AMOUNTS TO A VIRTUAL DICTATORSHIP!
"B. DISSENTERS ARE AUTOMATICALLY DROPPED FROM THE TEAM."
GBTrudeau

9/3/71

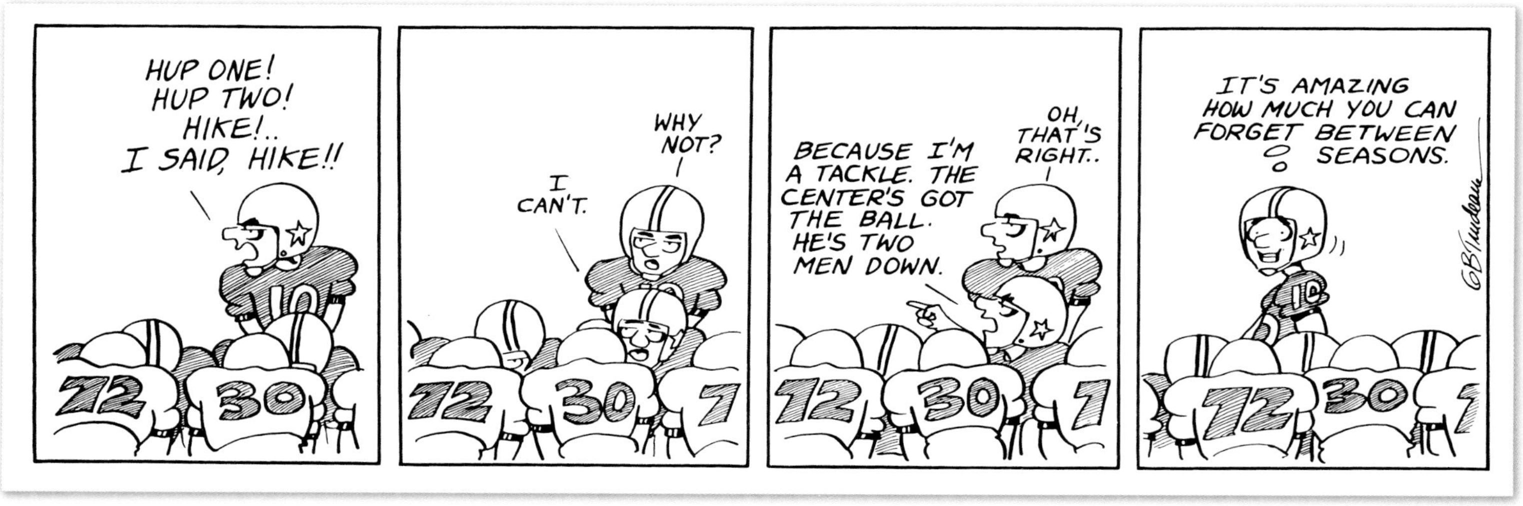
HUP ONE! HUP TWO! HIKE!.. I SAID, HIKE!!
WHY NOT?
I CAN'T.
BECAUSE I'M A TACKLE. THE CENTER'S GOT THE BALL. HE'S TWO MEN DOWN.
OH, THAT'S RIGHT..
IT'S AMAZING HOW MUCH YOU CAN FORGET BETWEEN SEASONS.
GBTrudeau

9/4/71

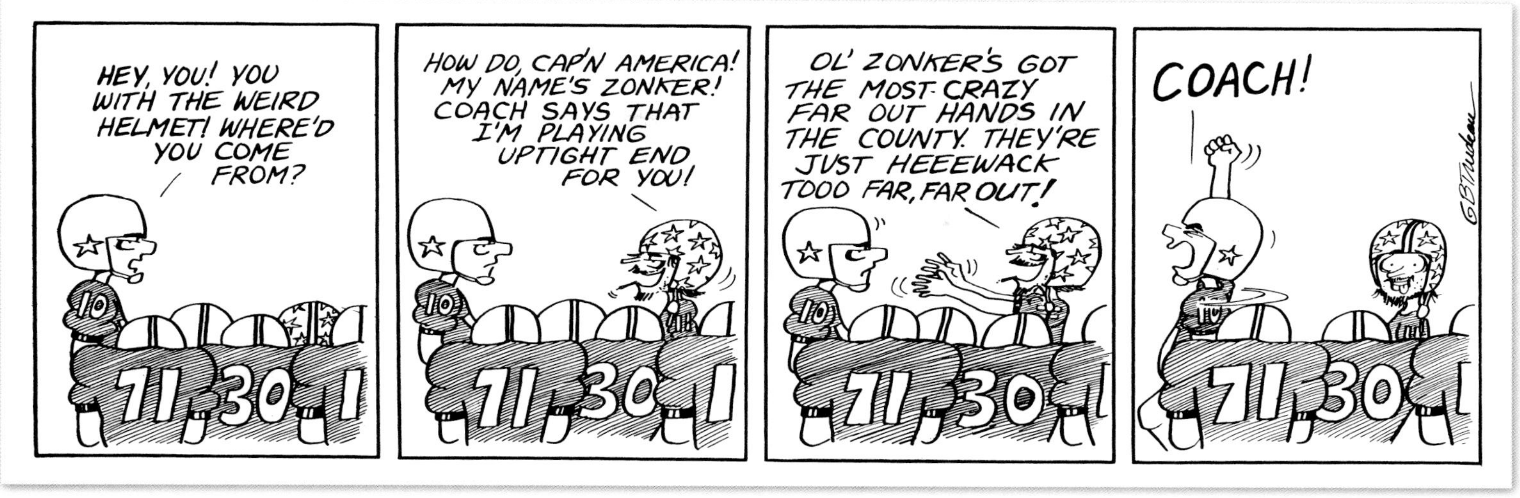
HEY, YOU! YOU WITH THE WEIRD HELMET! WHERE'D YOU COME FROM?
HOW DO, CAP'N AMERICA! MY NAME'S ZONKER! COACH SAYS THAT I'M PLAYING UPTIGHT END FOR YOU!
OL' ZONKER'S GOT THE MOST CRAZY FAR OUT HANDS IN THE COUNTY. THEY'RE JUST HEEEWACK TOOO FAR, FAR OUT!
COACH!
GBTrudeau

9/21/71

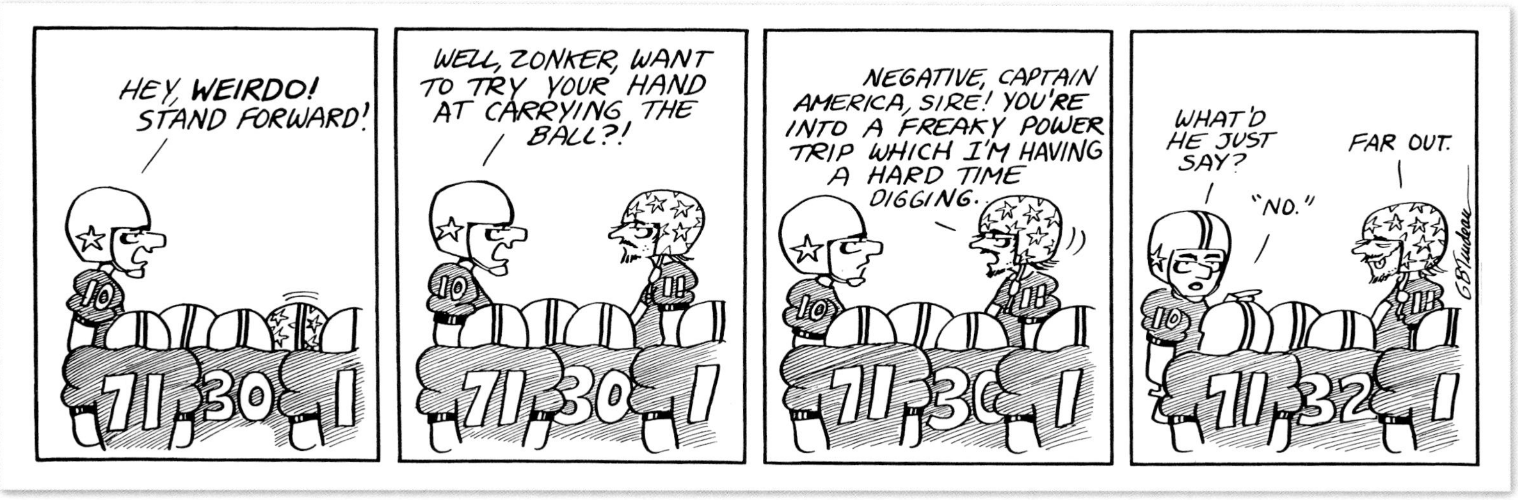
HEY, WEIRDO! STAND FORWARD!
WELL, ZONKER, WANT TO TRY YOUR HAND AT CARRYING THE BALL?!
NEGATIVE, CAPTAIN AMERICA, SIRE! YOU'RE INTO A FREAKY POWER TRIP WHICH I'M HAVING A HARD TIME DIGGING.
WHAT'D HE JUST SAY?
"NO."
FAR OUT.
GBTrudeau

9/22/71

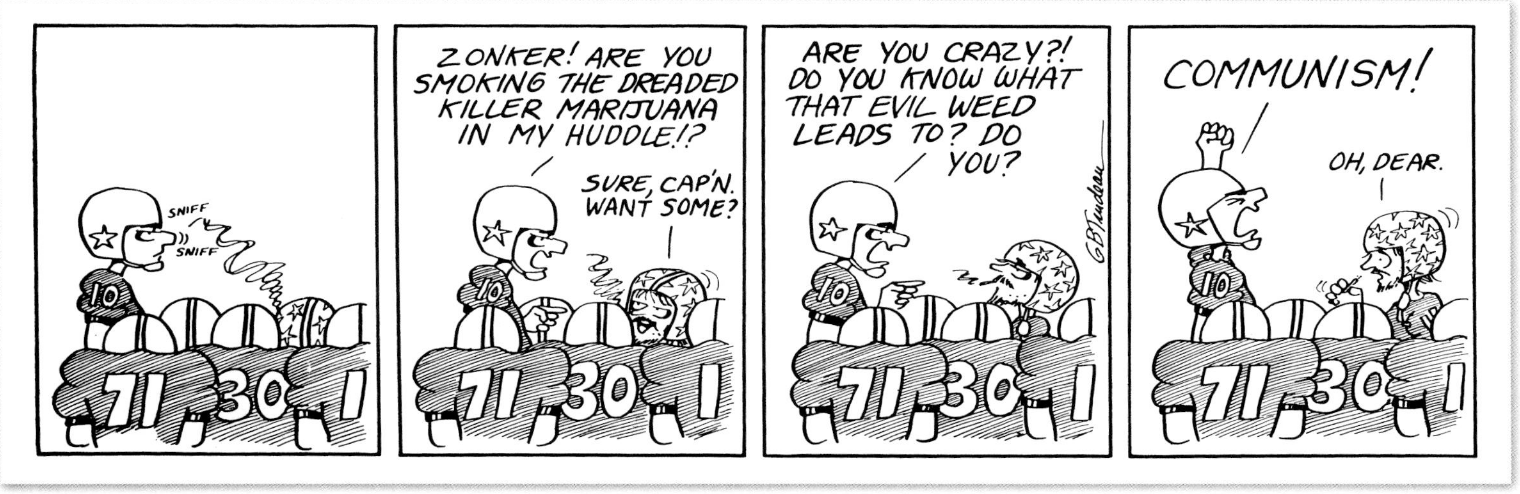
SNIFF
SNIFF
ZONKER! ARE YOU SMOKING THE DREADED KILLER MARIJUANA IN MY HUDDLE!?
SURE, CAP'N. WANT SOME?
ARE YOU CRAZY?! DO YOU KNOW WHAT THAT EVIL WEED LEADS TO? DO YOU?
GBTrudeau
COMMUNISM!
OH, DEAR.

9/23/71

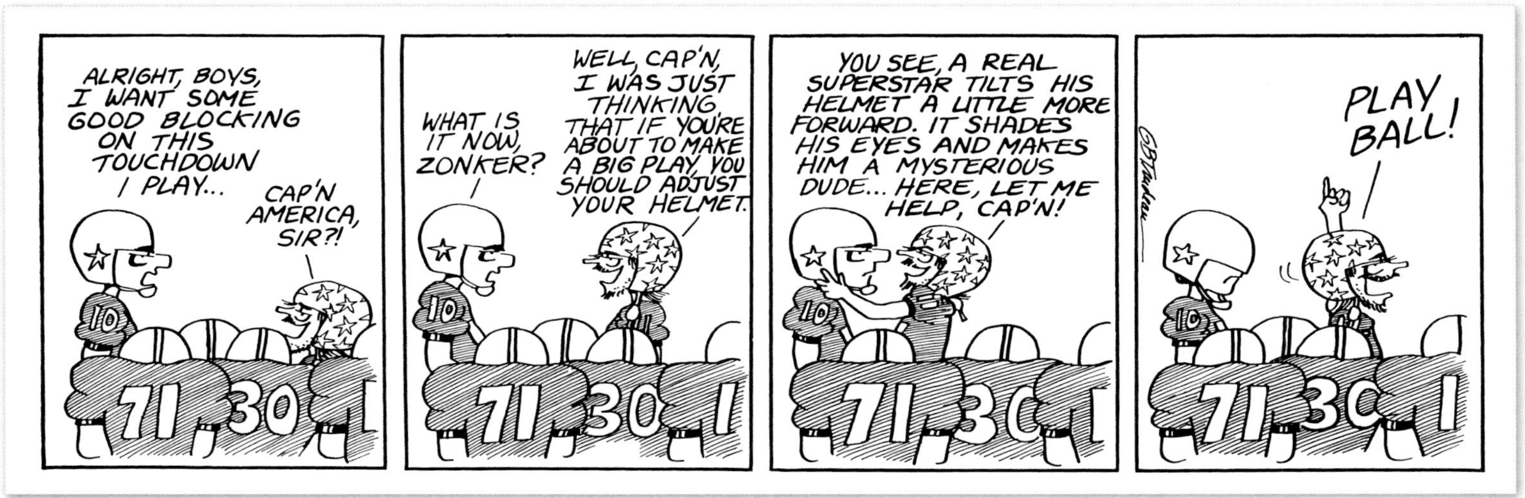
ALRIGHT, BOYS, I WANT SOME GOOD BLOCKING ON THIS TOUCHDOWN PLAY...
CAP'N AMERICA, SIR?!
WHAT IS IT NOW, ZONKER?
WELL, CAP'N, I WAS JUST THINKING THAT IF YOU'RE ABOUT TO MAKE A BIG PLAY, YOU SHOULD ADJUST YOUR HELMET.
YOU SEE, A REAL SUPERSTAR TILTS HIS HELMET A LITTLE MORE FORWARD. IT SHADES HIS EYES AND MAKES HIM A MYSTERIOUS DUDE... HERE, LET ME HELP, CAP'N!
GBTrudeau
PLAY BALL!

10/12/71

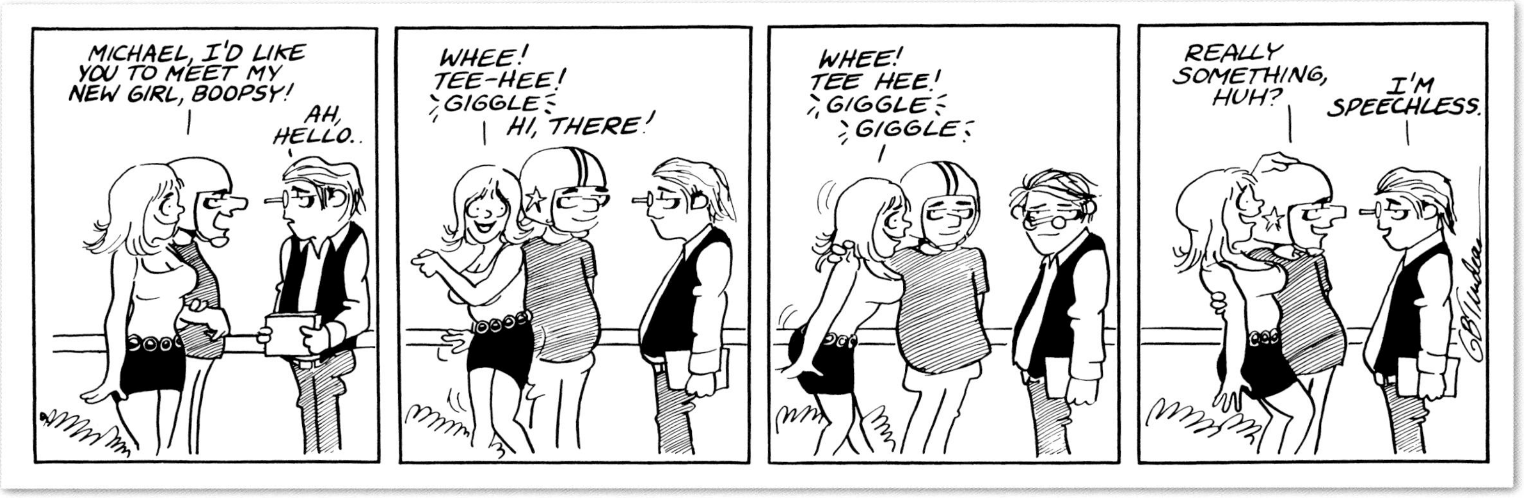
MICHAEL, I'D LIKE YOU TO MEET MY NEW GIRL, BOOPSY!
AH, HELLO..
WHEE! TEE-HEE! GIGGLE
HI, THERE!
WHEE! TEE HEE! GIGGLE GIGGLE
REALLY SOMETHING, HUH?
I'M SPEECHLESS.

9/15/71

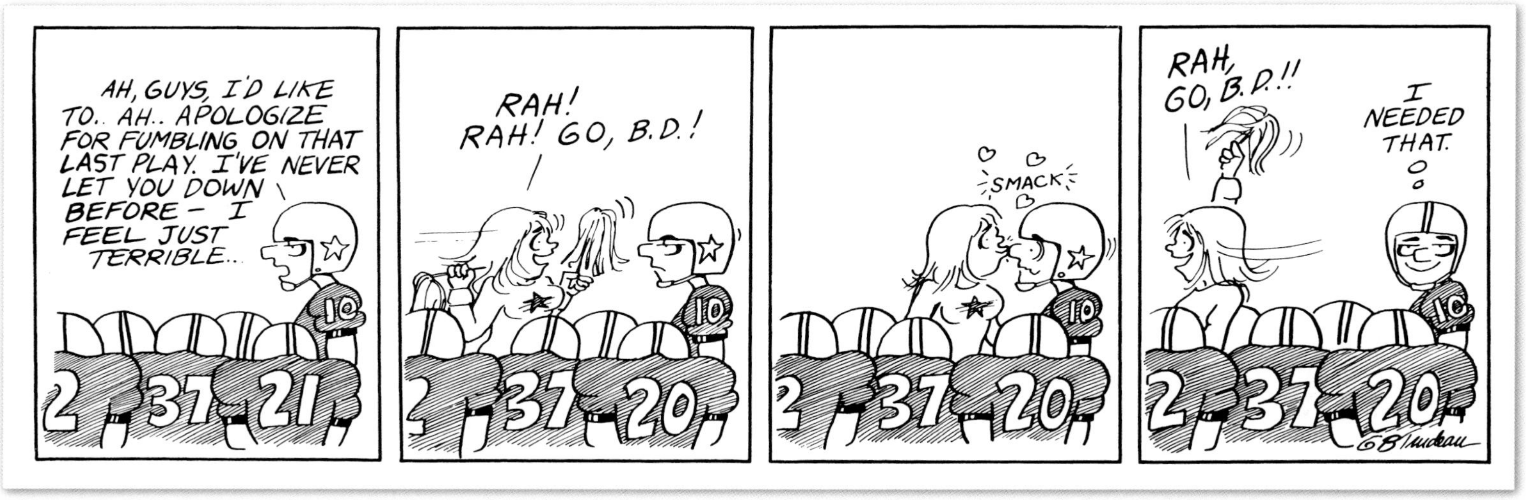
AH, GUYS, I'D LIKE TO.. AH.. APOLOGIZE FOR FUMBLING ON THAT LAST PLAY. I'VE NEVER LET YOU DOWN BEFORE – I FEEL JUST TERRIBLE...
RAH! RAH! GO, B.D.!
SMACK
RAH, GO, B.D.!!
I NEEDED THAT.

9/17/71

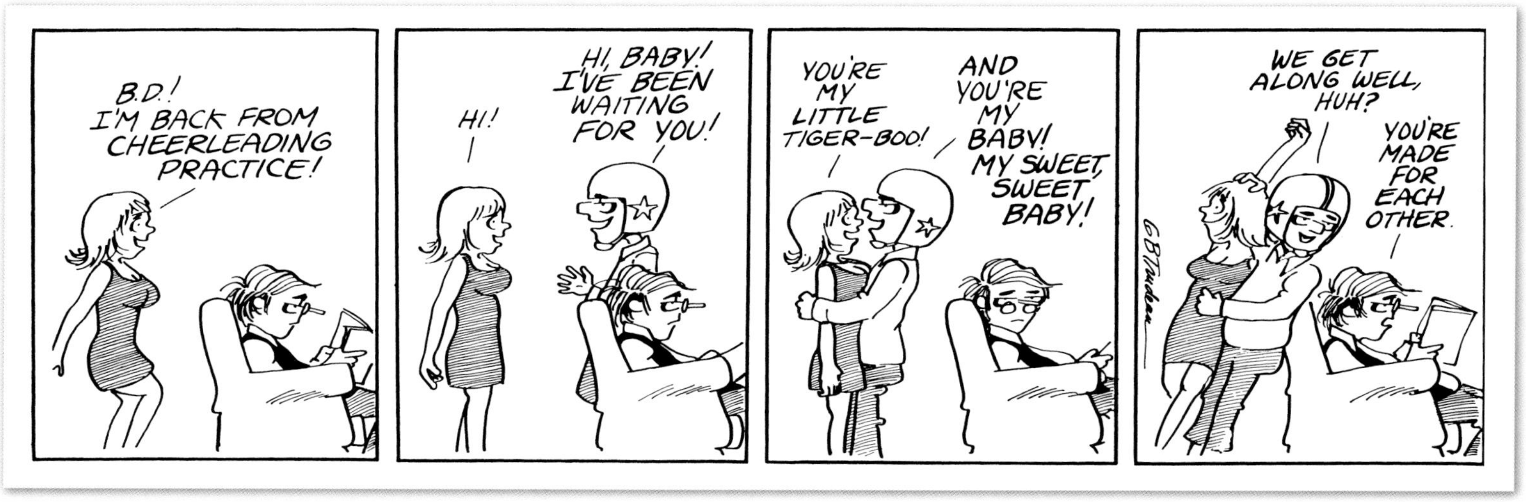
B.D.! I'M BACK FROM CHEERLEADING PRACTICE!
HI!
HI, BABY! I'VE BEEN WAITING FOR YOU!
YOU'RE MY LITTLE TIGER-BOO!
AND YOU'RE MY BABY! MY SWEET, SWEET BABY!
WE GET ALONG WELL, HUH?
YOU'RE MADE FOR EACH OTHER.

9/27/71

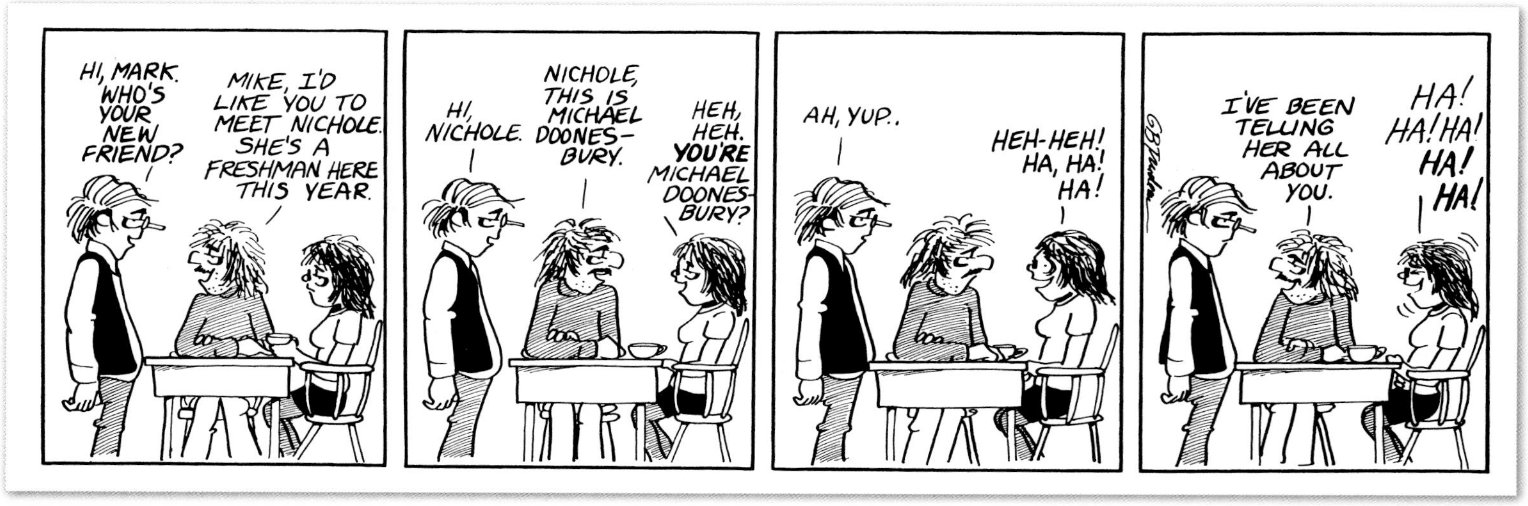
HI, MARK. WHO'S YOUR NEW FRIEND?
MIKE, I'D LIKE YOU TO MEET NICHOLE. SHE'S A FRESHMAN HERE THIS YEAR.
HI, NICHOLE.
NICHOLE, THIS IS MICHAEL DOONESBURY.
HEH, HEH. YOU'RE MICHAEL DOONESBURY?
AH, YUP..
HEH-HEH! HA, HA! HA!
I'VE BEEN TELLING HER ALL ABOUT YOU.
HA! HA! HA! HA! HA!

9/29/71

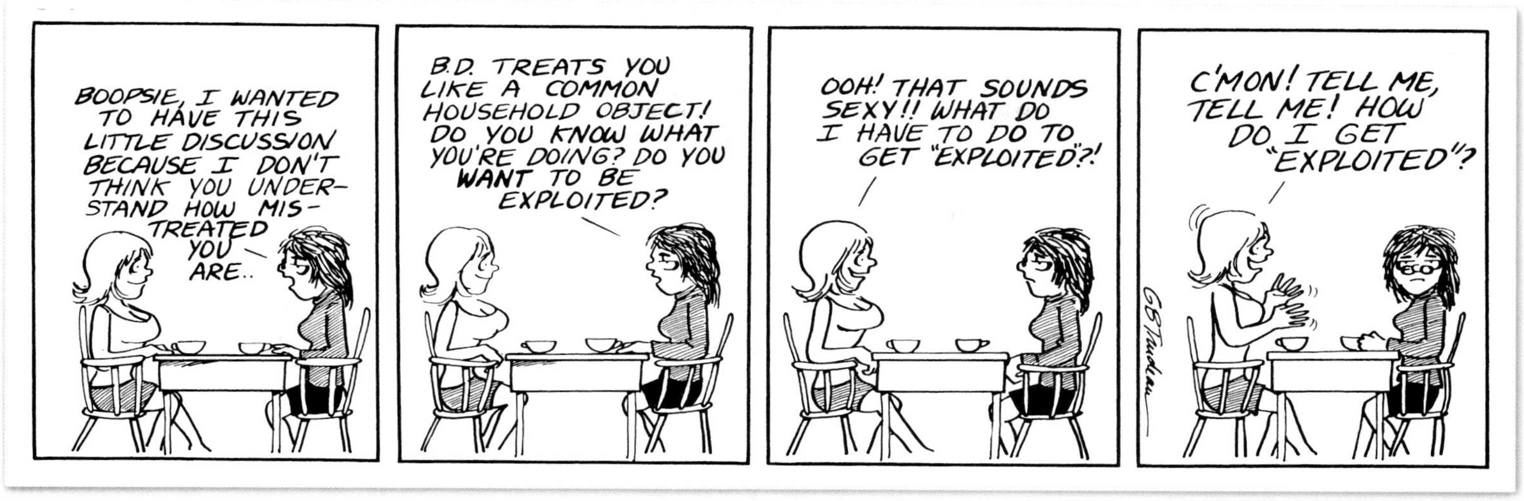
BOOPSIE, I WANTED TO HAVE THIS LITTLE DISCUSSION BECAUSE I DON'T THINK YOU UNDERSTAND HOW MISTREATED YOU ARE..
B.D. TREATS YOU LIKE A COMMON HOUSEHOLD OBJECT! DO YOU KNOW WHAT YOU'RE DOING? DO YOU WANT TO BE EXPLOITED?
OOH! THAT SOUNDS SEXY!! WHAT DO I HAVE TO DO TO GET "EXPLOITED"?!
C'MON! TELL ME, TELL ME! HOW DO I GET "EXPLOITED"?

10/1/71

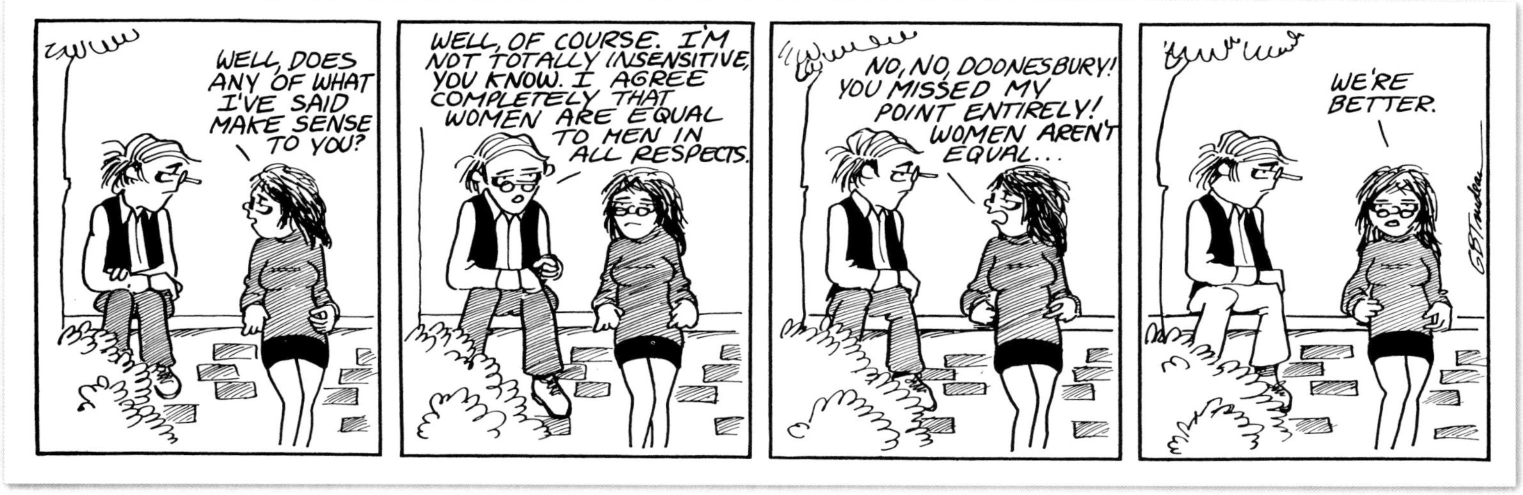
WELL, DOES ANY OF WHAT I'VE SAID MAKE SENSE TO YOU?
WELL, OF COURSE. I'M NOT TOTALLY INSENSITIVE, YOU KNOW. I AGREE COMPLETELY THAT WOMEN ARE EQUAL TO MEN IN ALL RESPECTS.
NO, NO, DOONESBURY! YOU MISSED MY POINT ENTIRELY! WOMEN AREN'T EQUAL...
WE'RE BETTER.

10/4/71

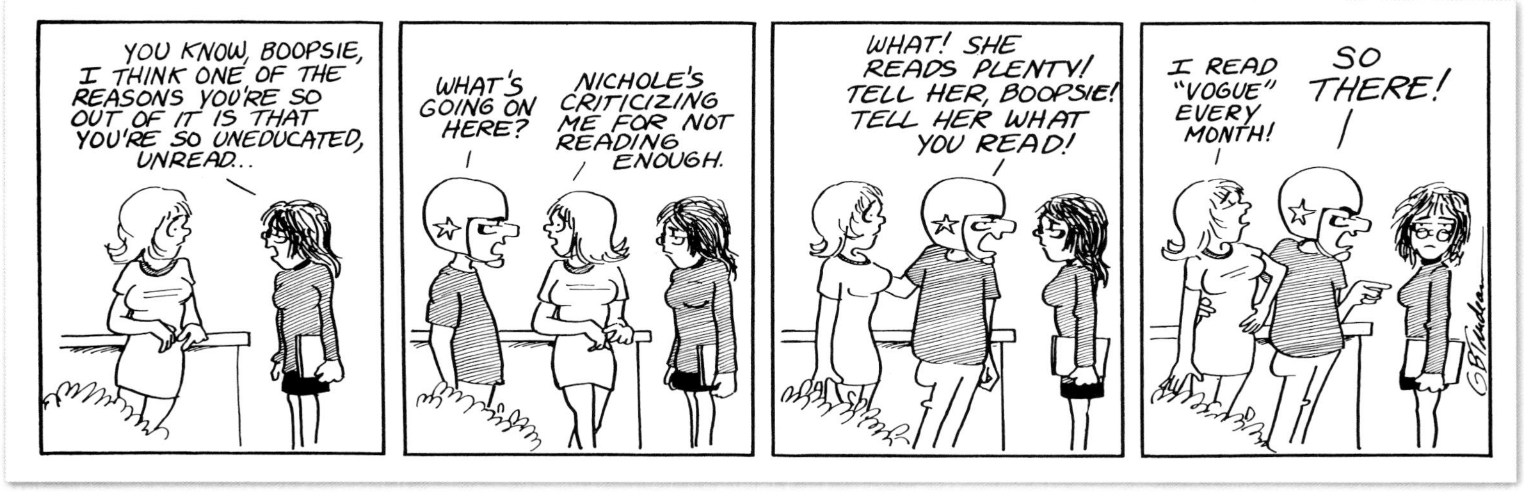
YOU KNOW, BOOPSIE, I THINK ONE OF THE REASONS YOU'RE SO OUT OF IT IS THAT YOU'RE SO UNEDUCATED, UNREAD...
WHAT'S GOING ON HERE?
NICHOLE'S CRITICIZING ME FOR NOT READING ENOUGH.
WHAT! SHE READS PLENTY! TELL HER, BOOPSIE! TELL HER WHAT YOU READ!
I READ "VOGUE" EVERY MONTH!
SO THERE!

10/5/71

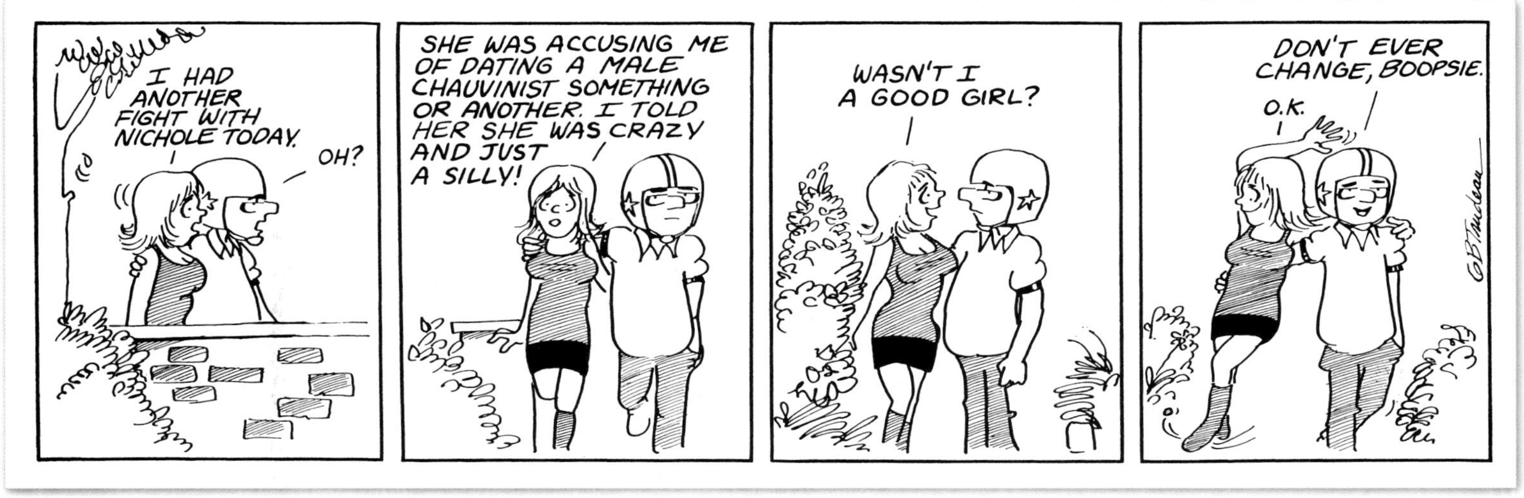
I HAD ANOTHER FIGHT WITH NICHOLE TODAY.
OH?
SHE WAS ACCUSING ME OF DATING A MALE CHAUVINIST SOMETHING OR ANOTHER. I TOLD HER SHE WAS CRAZY AND JUST A SILLY!
WASN'T I A GOOD GIRL?
DON'T EVER CHANGE, BOOPSIE.
O.K.

10/6/71

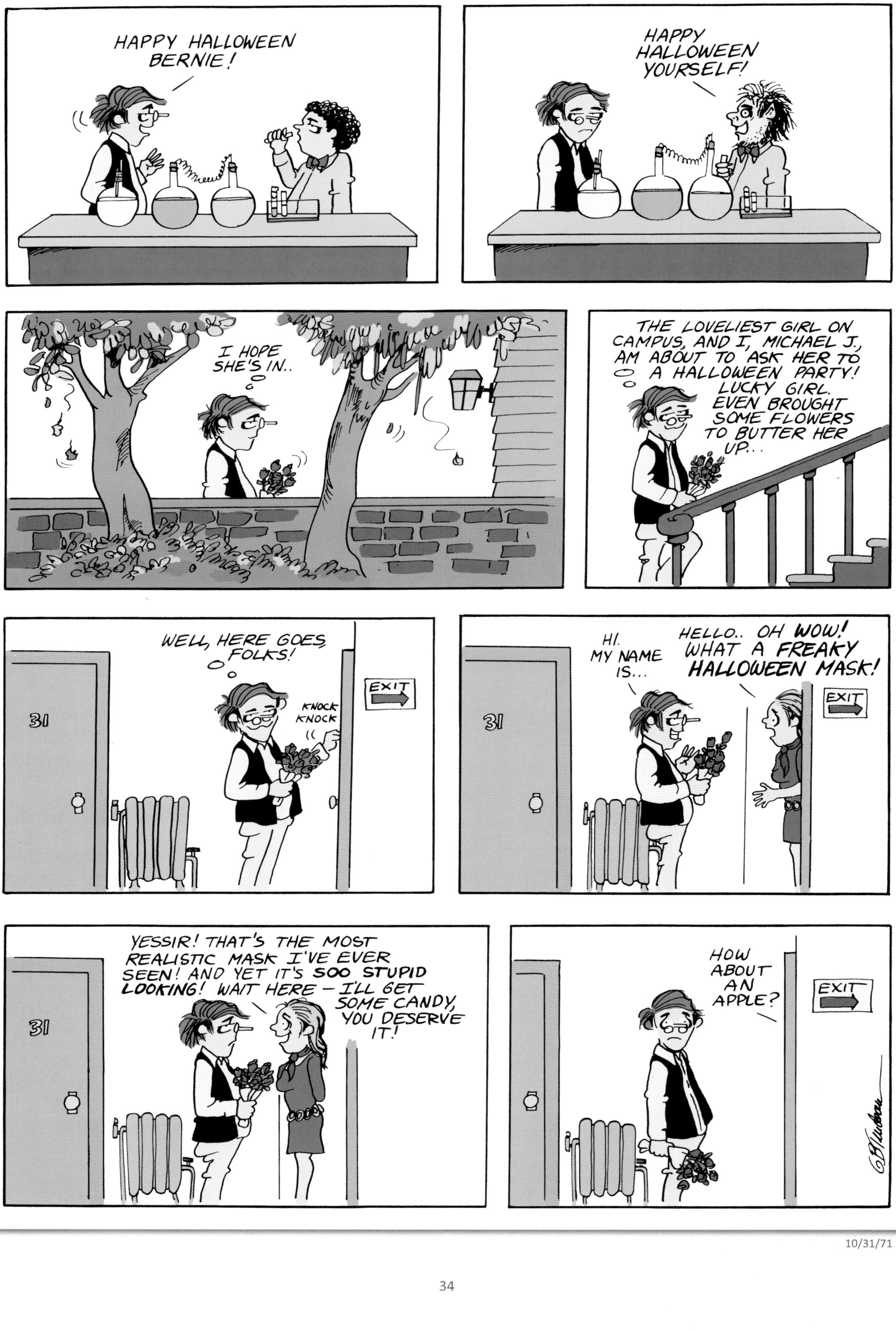
HAPPY HALLOWEEN BERNIE!
HAPPY HALLOWEEN YOURSELF!
I HOPE SHE'S IN..
THE LOVELIEST GIRL ON CAMPUS, AND I, MICHAEL J., AM ABOUT TO ASK HER TO A HALLOWEEN PARTY! LUCKY GIRL. EVEN BROUGHT SOME FLOWERS TO BUTTER HER UP...
WELL, HERE GOES, FOLKS!
KNOCK KNOCK
EXIT
31
HI. MY NAME IS...
HELLO.. OH WOW! WHAT A FREAKY HALLOWEEN MASK!
YESSIR! THAT'S THE MOST REALISTIC MASK I'VE EVER SEEN! AND YET IT'S SOO STUPID LOOKING! WAIT HERE – I'LL GET SOME CANDY, YOU DESERVE IT!
HOW ABOUT AN APPLE?

10/31/71

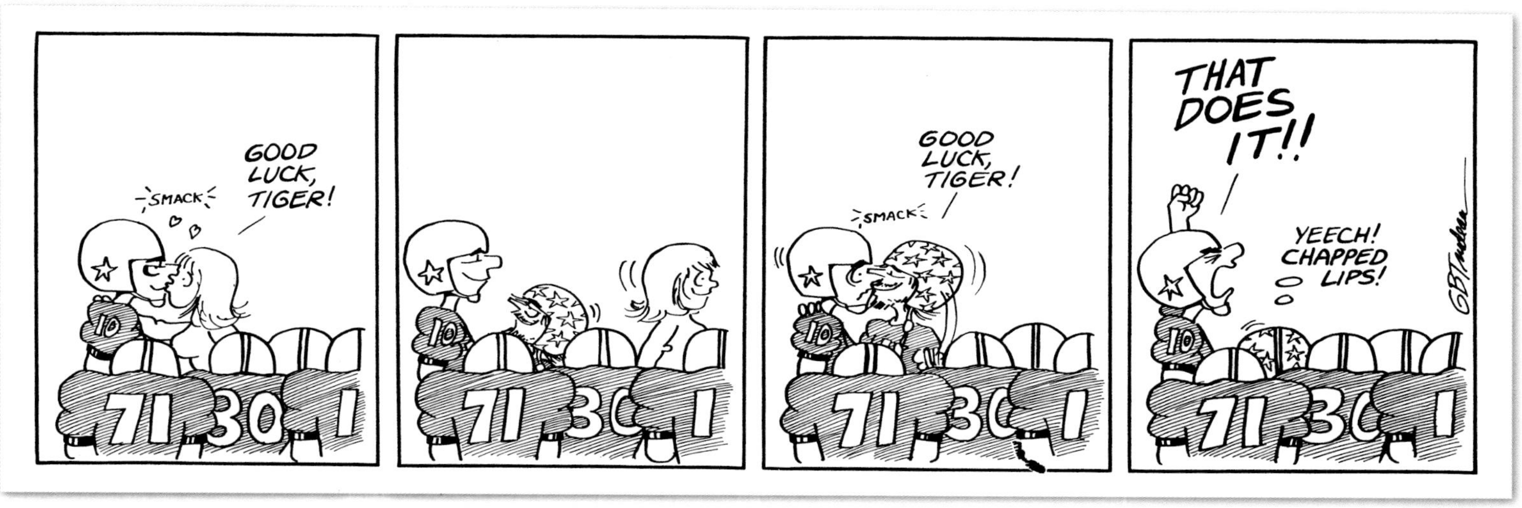
SMACK
GOOD LUCK, TIGER!
SMACK
GOOD LUCK, TIGER!
THAT DOES IT!!
YEECH! CHAPPED LIPS!
GBTrudeau

10/18/71

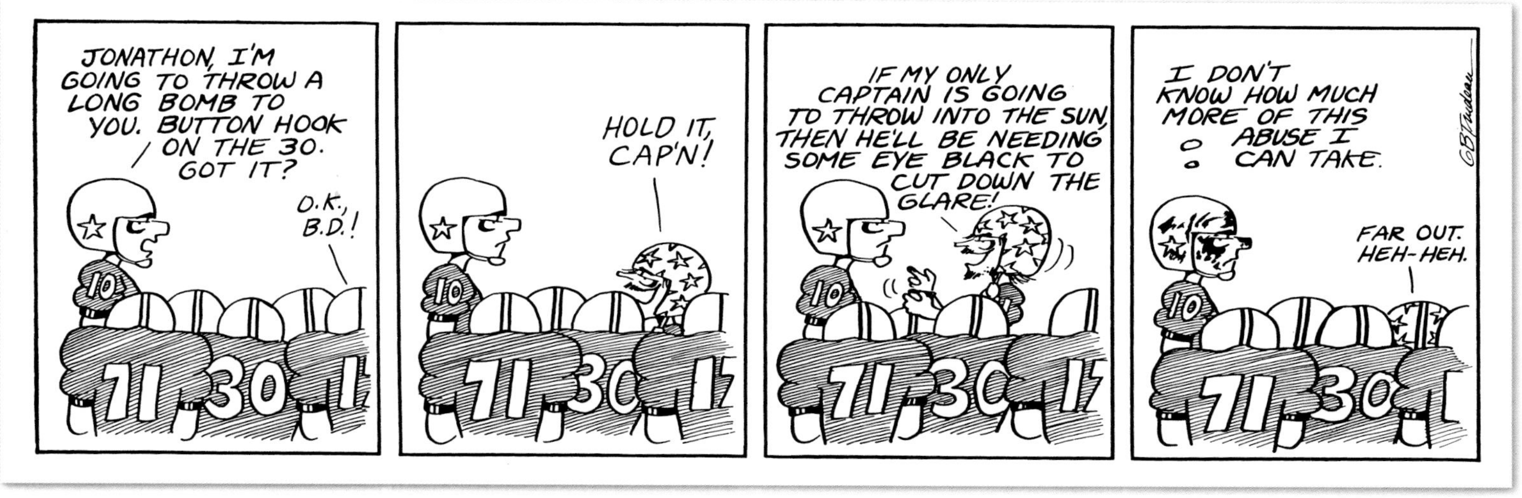
JONATHON, I'M GOING TO THROW A LONG BOMB TO YOU. BUTTON HOOK ON THE 30. GOT IT?
O.K., B.D.!
HOLD IT, CAP'N!
IF MY ONLY CAPTAIN IS GOING TO THROW INTO THE SUN, THEN HE'LL BE NEEDING SOME EYE BLACK TO CUT DOWN THE GLARE!
I DON'T KNOW HOW MUCH MORE OF THIS ABUSE I CAN TAKE.
FAR OUT. HEH-HEH.

10/15/71

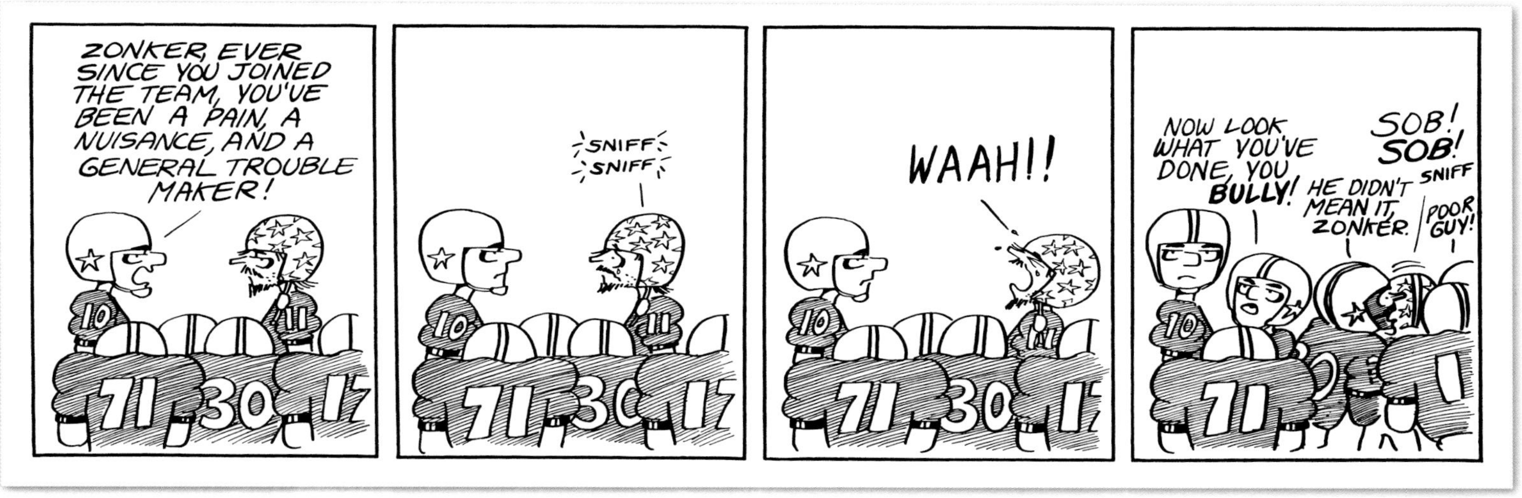
ZONKER, EVER SINCE YOU JOINED THE TEAM, YOU'VE BEEN A PAIN, A NUISANCE, AND A GENERAL TROUBLE MAKER!
SNIFF SNIFF
WAAH!!
NOW LOOK WHAT YOU'VE DONE, YOU BULLY!
HE DIDN'T MEAN IT, ZONKER.
SOB! SOB!
SNIFF
POOR GUY!

10/19/71

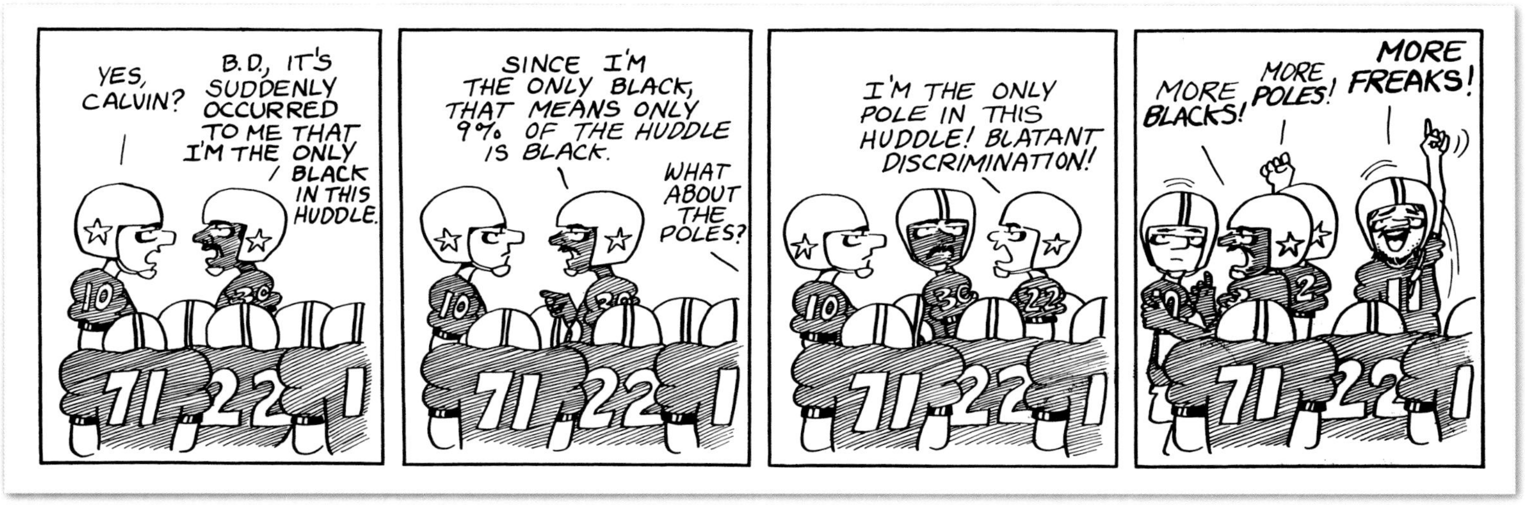
YES, CALVIN?
B.D., IT'S SUDDENLY OCCURRED TO ME THAT I'M THE ONLY BLACK IN THIS HUDDLE.
SINCE I'M THE ONLY BLACK, THAT MEANS ONLY 9% OF THE HUDDLE IS BLACK.
WHAT ABOUT THE POLES?
I'M THE ONLY POLE IN THIS HUDDLE! BLATANT DISCRIMINATION!
MORE BLACKS!
MORE POLES!
MORE FREAKS!

10/20/71

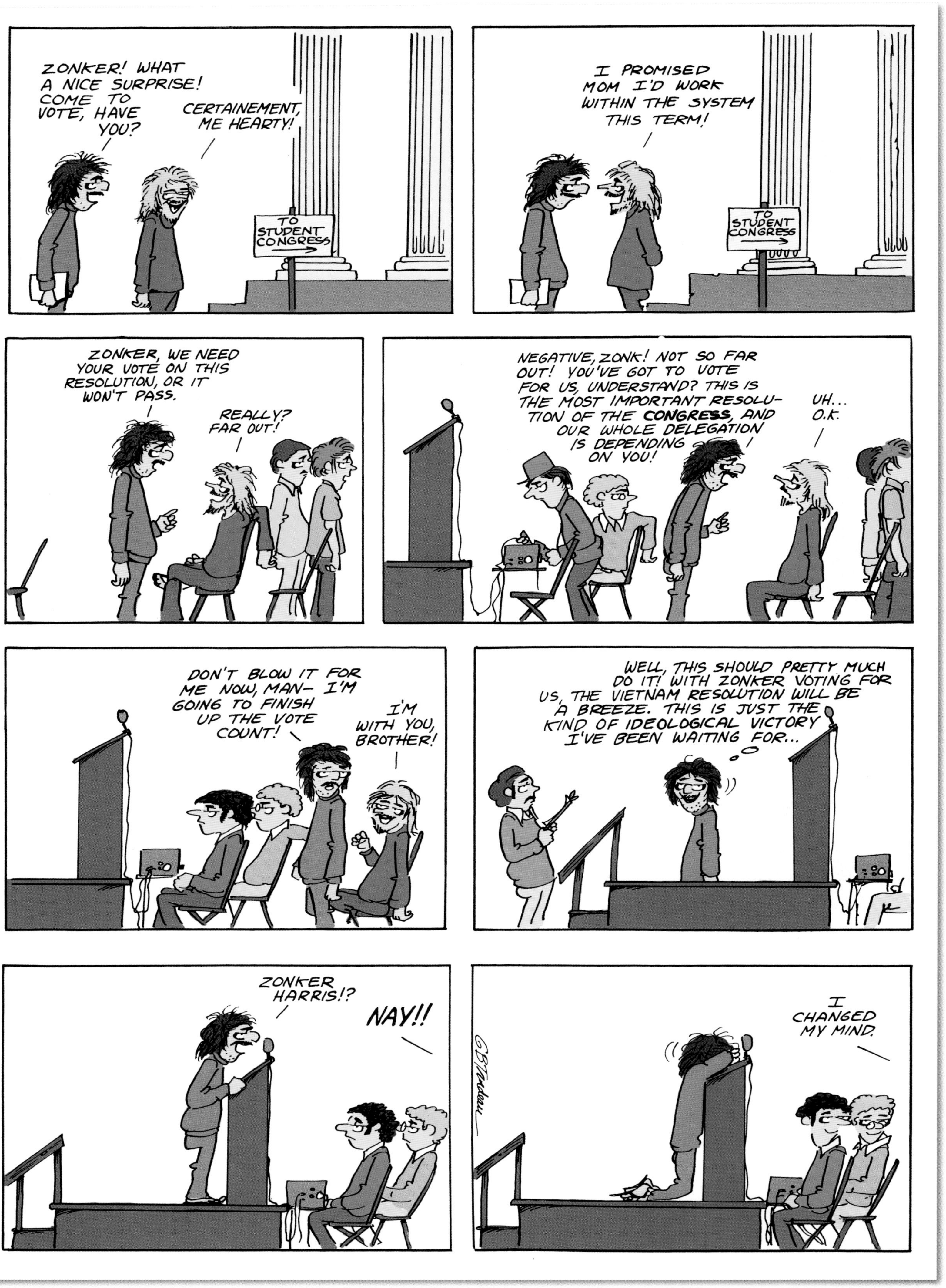
ZONKER! WHAT A NICE SURPRISE! COME TO VOTE, HAVE YOU?
CERTAINEMENT, ME HEARTY!
TO STUDENT CONGRESS
I PROMISED MOM I'D WORK WITHIN THE SYSTEM THIS TERM!
TO STUDENT CONGRESS
ZONKER, WE NEED YOUR VOTE ON THIS RESOLUTION, OR IT WON'T PASS.
REALLY? FAR OUT!
NEGATIVE, ZONK! NOT SO FAR OUT! YOU'VE GOT TO VOTE FOR US, UNDERSTAND? THIS IS THE MOST IMPORTANT RESOLUTION OF THE CONGRESS, AND OUR WHOLE DELEGATION IS DEPENDING ON YOU!
UH... O.K.
DON'T BLOW IT FOR ME NOW, MAN– I'M GOING TO FINISH UP THE VOTE COUNT!
I'M WITH YOU, BROTHER!
WELL, THIS SHOULD PRETTY MUCH DO IT! WITH ZONKER VOTING FOR US, THE VIETNAM RESOLUTION WILL BE A BREEZE. THIS IS JUST THE KIND OF IDEOLOGICAL VICTORY I'VE BEEN WAITING FOR...
ZONKER HARRIS!?
NAY!!
I CHANGED MY MIND.

12/5/71

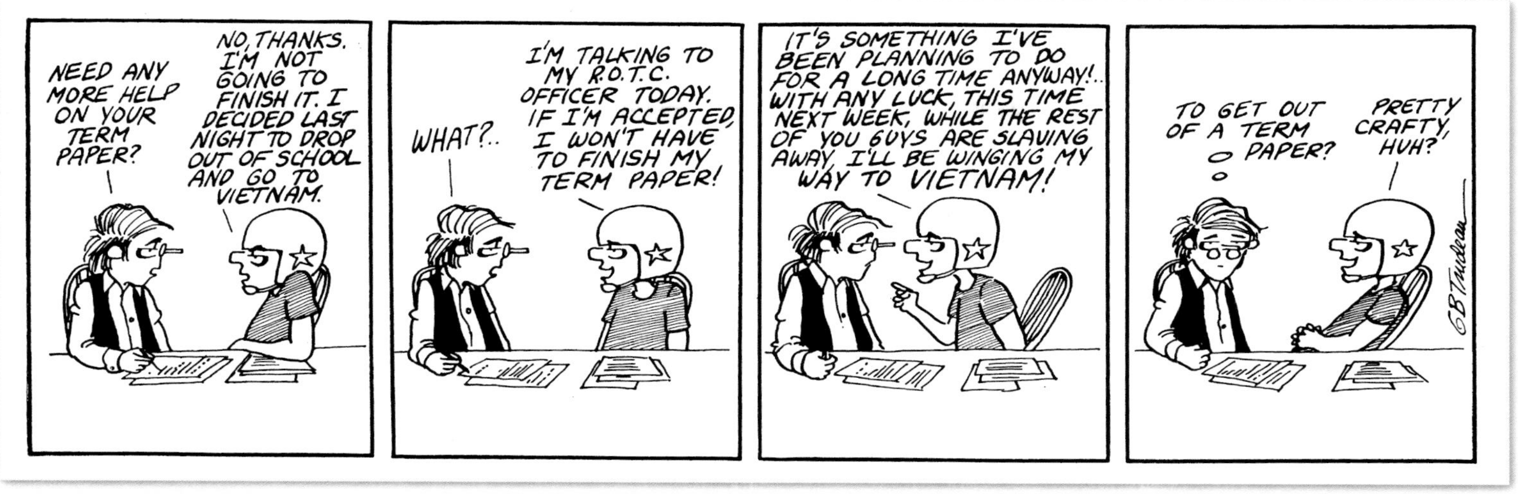
NEED ANY MORE HELP ON YOUR TERM PAPER?
NO, THANKS. I'M NOT GOING TO FINISH IT. I DECIDED LAST NIGHT TO DROP OUT OF SCHOOL AND GO TO VIETNAM.
WHAT?..
I'M TALKING TO MY R.O.T.C. OFFICER TODAY. IF I'M ACCEPTED, I WON'T HAVE TO FINISH MY TERM PAPER!
IT'S SOMETHING I'VE BEEN PLANNING TO DO FOR A LONG TIME ANYWAY!.. WITH ANY LUCK, THIS TIME NEXT WEEK, WHILE THE REST OF YOU GUYS ARE SLAVING AWAY, I'LL BE WINGING MY WAY TO VIETNAM!
TO GET OUT OF A TERM PAPER?
PRETTY CRAFTY, HUH?

1/31/72

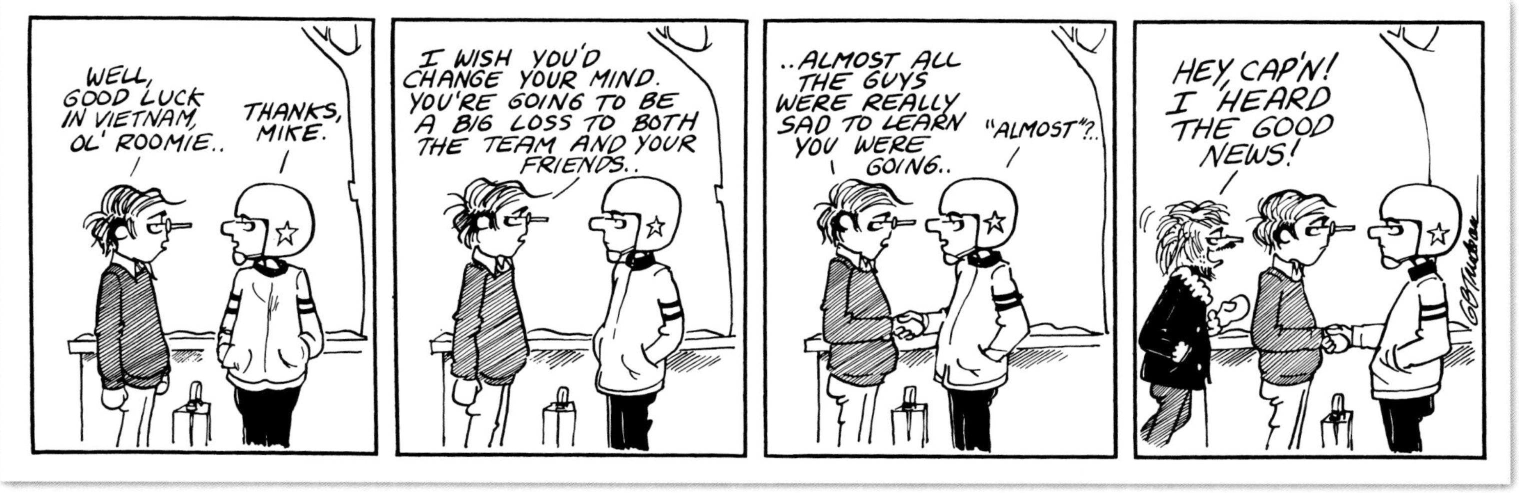
WELL, GOOD LUCK IN VIETNAM, OL' ROOMIE..
THANKS, MIKE.
I WISH YOU'D CHANGE YOUR MIND. YOU'RE GOING TO BE A BIG LOSS TO BOTH THE TEAM AND YOUR FRIENDS..
..ALMOST ALL THE GUYS WERE REALLY SAD TO LEARN YOU WERE GOING..
"ALMOST"?..
HEY, CAP'N! I HEARD THE GOOD NEWS!

2/4/72

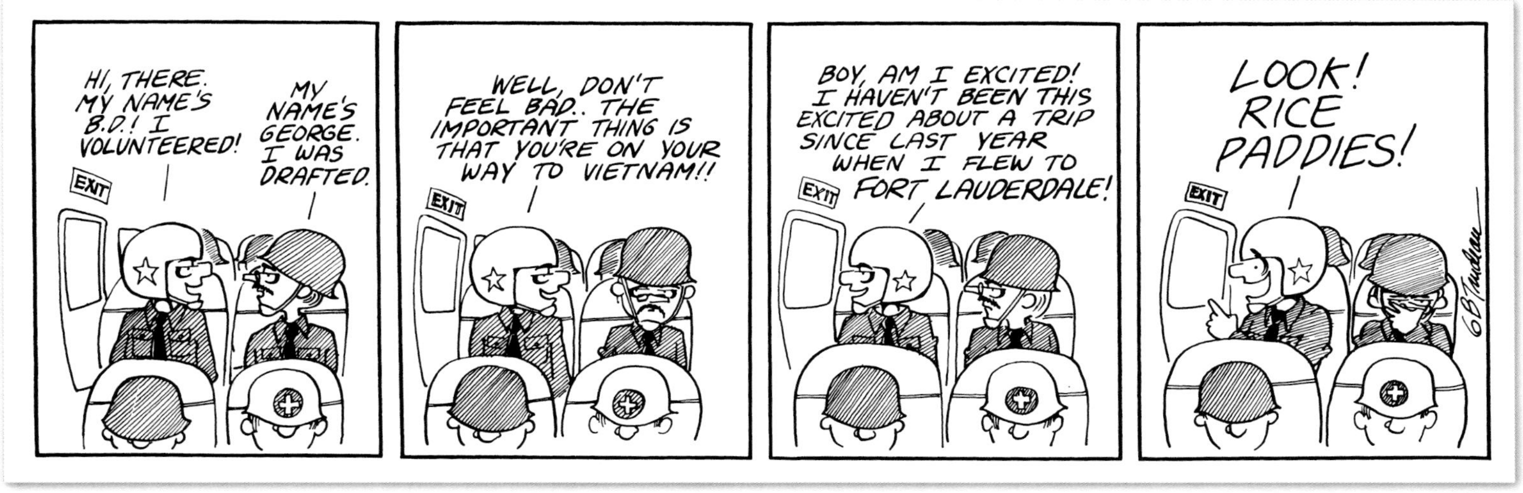
HI, THERE. MY NAME'S B.D.! I VOLUNTEERED!
MY NAME'S GEORGE. I WAS DRAFTED.
EXIT
WELL, DON'T FEEL BAD.. THE IMPORTANT THING IS THAT YOU'RE ON YOUR WAY TO VIETNAM!!
BOY, AM I EXCITED! I HAVEN'T BEEN THIS EXCITED ABOUT A TRIP SINCE LAST YEAR WHEN I FLEW TO FORT LAUDERDALE!
LOOK! RICE PADDIES!

2/7/72

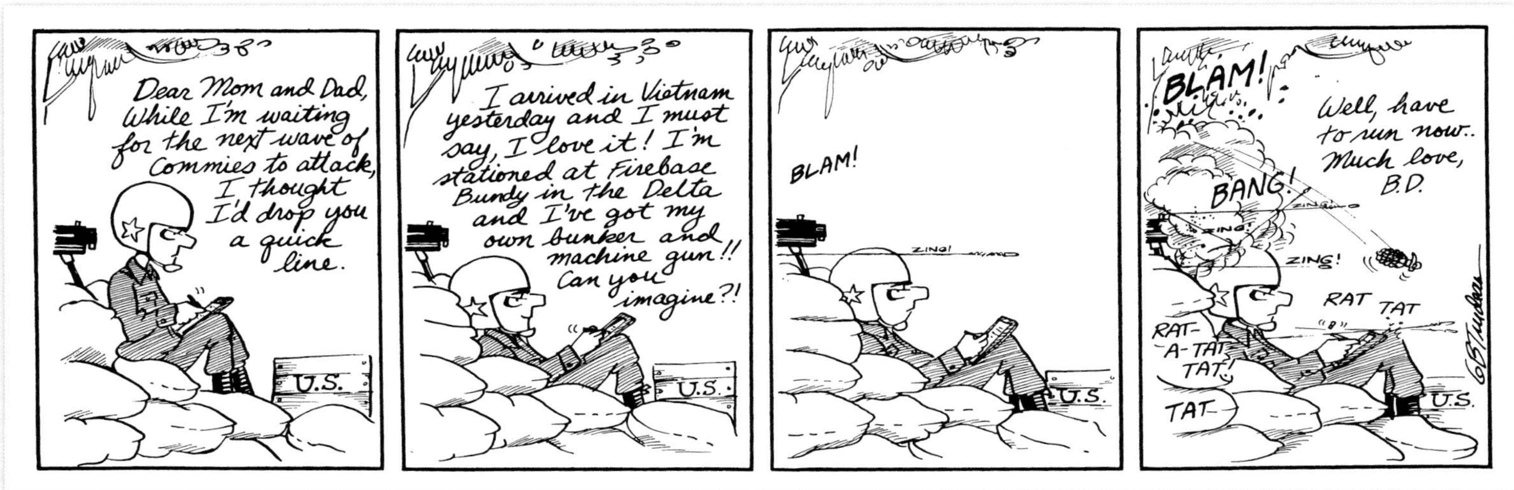
Dear Mom and Dad, While I'm waiting for the next wave of Commies to attack, I thought I'd drop you a quick line.
U.S.
I arrived in Vietnam yesterday and I must say, I love it! I'm stationed at Firebase Bundy in the Delta and I've got my own bunker and machine gun!! Can you imagine?!
BLAM!
ZING!
BLAM!
BANG!
ZING!
Well, have to run now.. Much love, B.D.
RAT TAT
RAT-A-TAT! TAT!
TAT

2/8/72

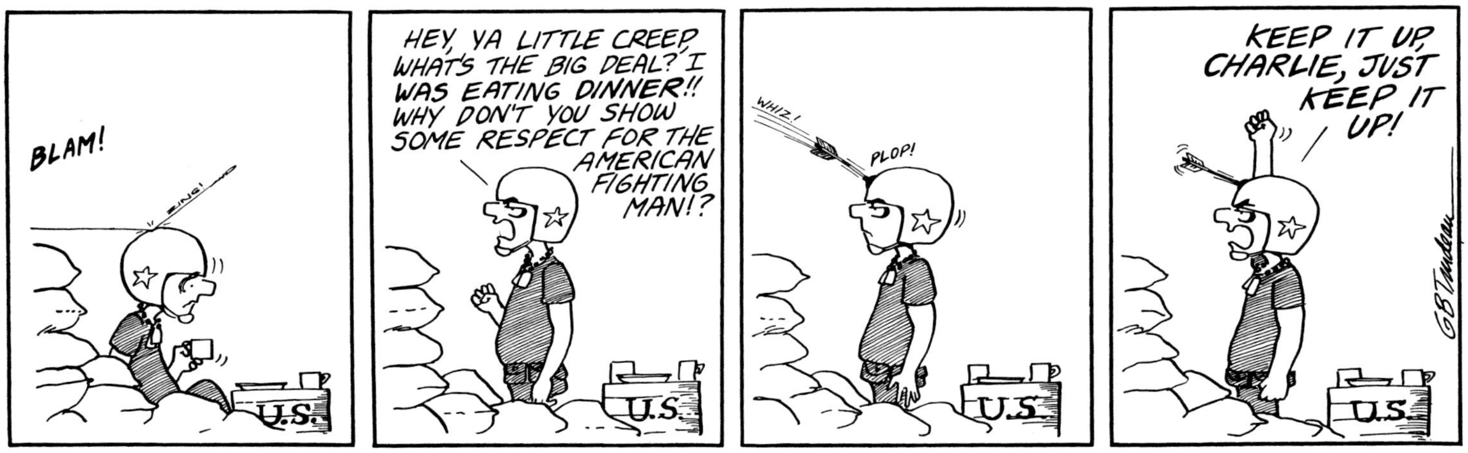
BLAM!
ZING!
HEY, YA LITTLE CREEP, WHAT'S THE BIG DEAL? I WAS EATING DINNER!! WHY DON'T YOU SHOW SOME RESPECT FOR THE AMERICAN FIGHTING MAN!?
WHIZ!
PLOP!
KEEP IT UP, CHARLIE, JUST KEEP IT UP!
U.S.
GBTrudeau

2/11/72

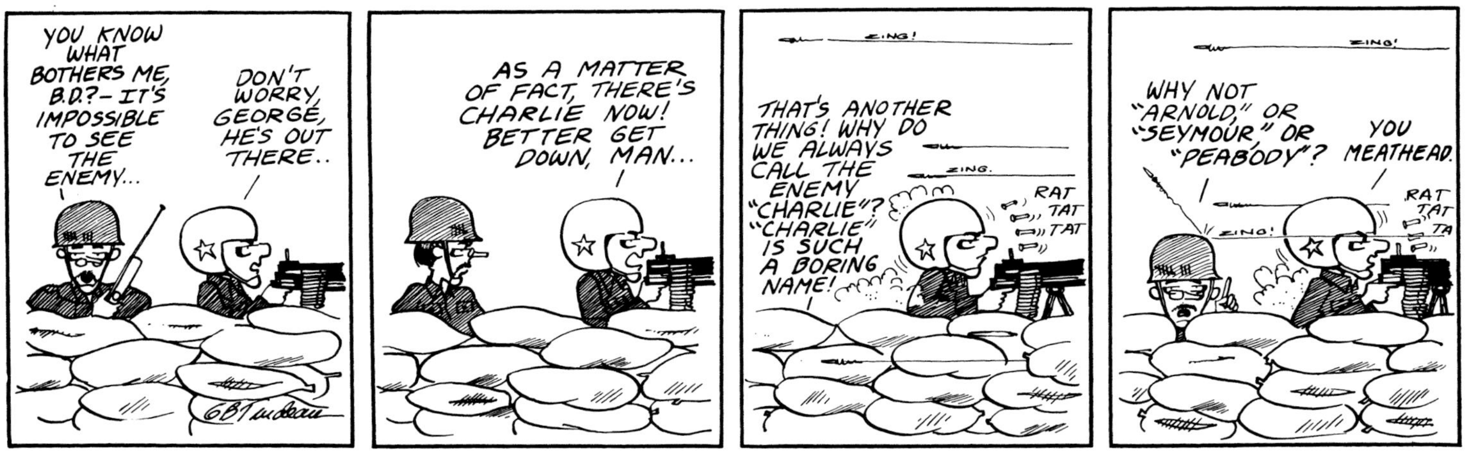
YOU KNOW WHAT BOTHERS ME, B.D.?– IT'S IMPOSSIBLE TO SEE THE ENEMY...
DON'T WORRY, GEORGE, HE'S OUT THERE..
AS A MATTER OF FACT, THERE'S CHARLIE NOW! BETTER GET DOWN, MAN...
ZING!
THAT'S ANOTHER THING! WHY DO WE ALWAYS CALL THE ENEMY "CHARLIE"? "CHARLIE" IS SUCH A BORING NAME!
ZING.
RAT TAT TAT
ZING!
WHY NOT "ARNOLD," OR "SEYMOUR" OR "PEABODY"?
YOU MEATHEAD.
ZING!
RAT TAT TA
GBTrudeau

2/10/72

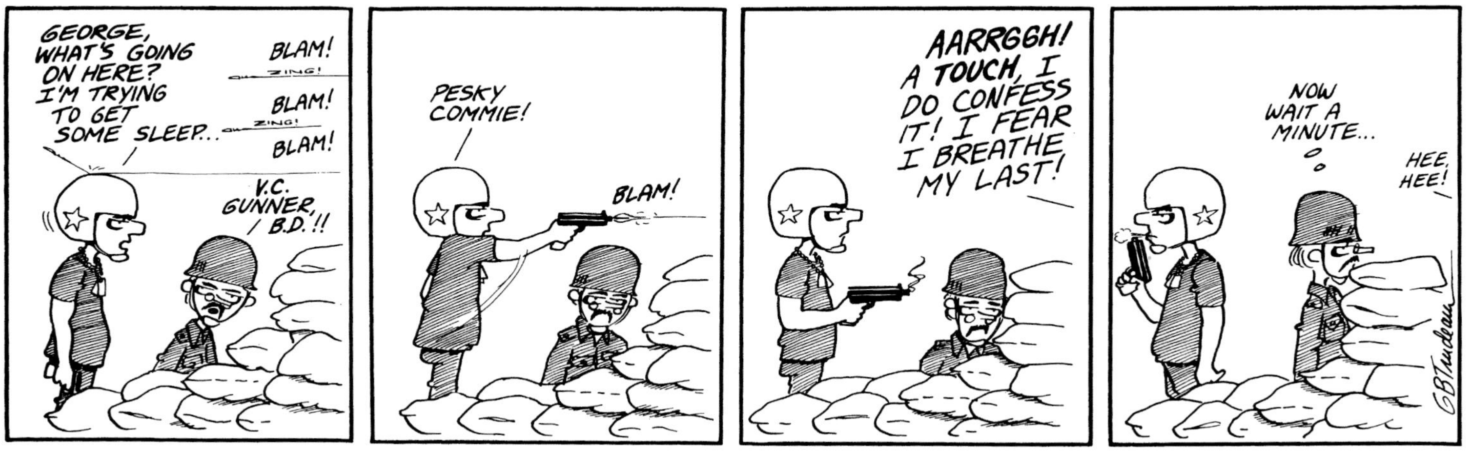
GEORGE, WHAT'S GOING ON HERE? I'M TRYING TO GET SOME SLEEP...
BLAM!
ZING!
BLAM!
ZING!
BLAM!
V.C. GUNNER, B.D.!!
PESKY COMMIE!
BLAM!
AARRGGH! A TOUCH, I DO CONFESS IT! I FEAR I BREATHE MY LAST!
NOW WAIT A MINUTE...
HEE, HEE!
GBTrudeau

2/14/72

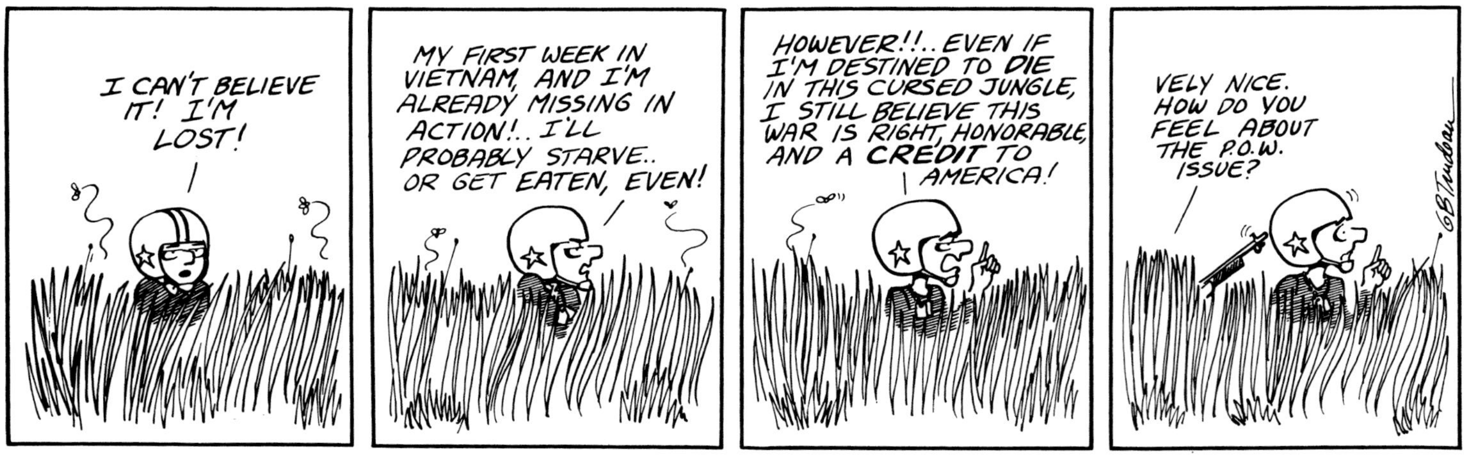
I CAN'T BELIEVE IT! I'M LOST!
MY FIRST WEEK IN VIETNAM, AND I'M ALREADY MISSING IN ACTION!.. I'LL PROBABLY STARVE.. OR GET EATEN, EVEN!
HOWEVER!!.. EVEN IF I'M DESTINED TO DIE IN THIS CURSED JUNGLE, I STILL BELIEVE THIS WAR IS RIGHT, HONORABLE, AND A CREDIT TO AMERICA!
VELY NICE. HOW DO YOU FEEL ABOUT THE P.O.W. ISSUE?
GBTrudeau

2/16/72

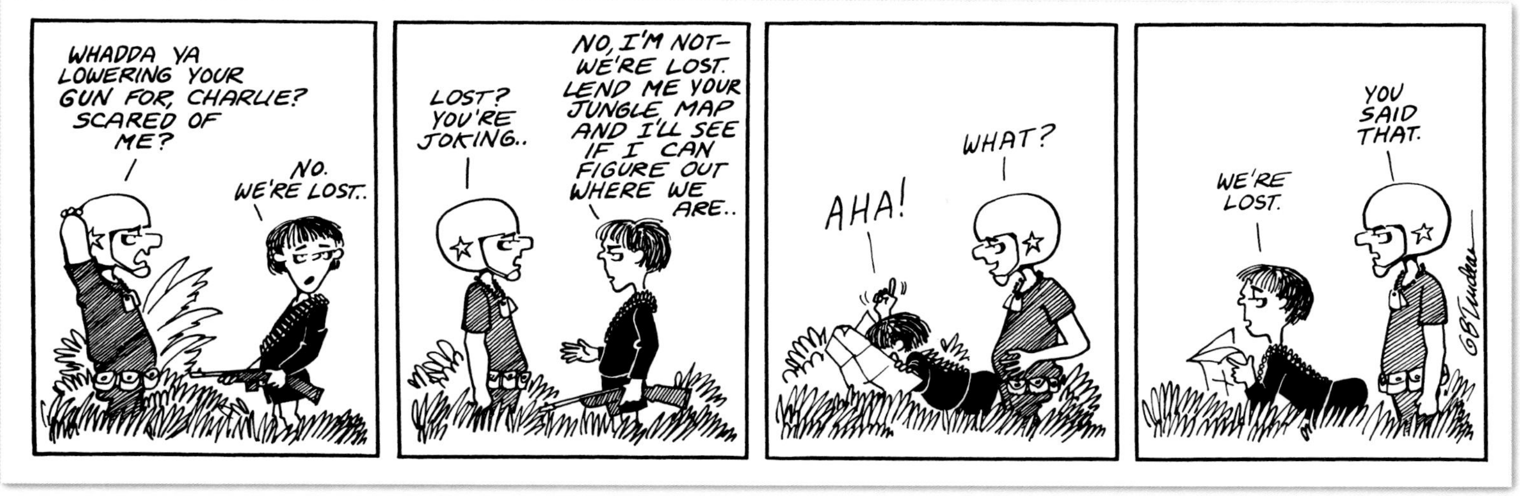
WHADDA YA LOWERING YOUR GUN FOR, CHARLIE? SCARED OF ME?
NO. WE'RE LOST..
LOST? YOU'RE JOKING..
NO, I'M NOT—WE'RE LOST. LEND ME YOUR JUNGLE MAP AND I'LL SEE IF I CAN FIGURE OUT WHERE WE ARE..
AHA!
WHAT?
WE'RE LOST.
YOU SAID THAT.

2/17/72

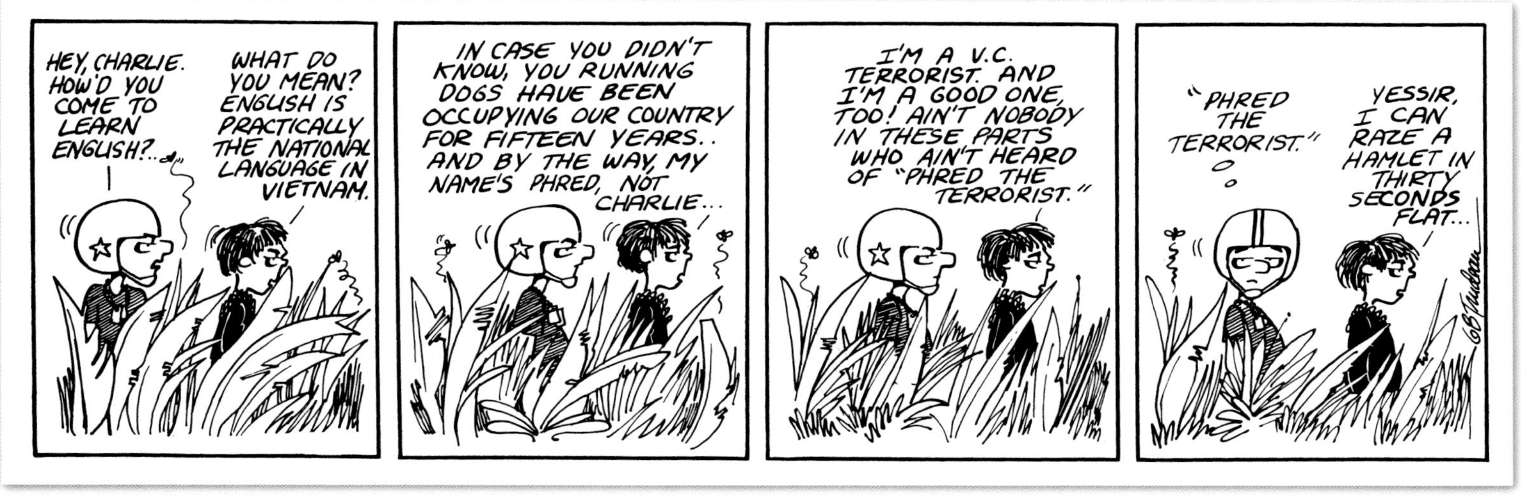
HEY, CHARLIE. HOW'D YOU COME TO LEARN ENGLISH?...
WHAT DO YOU MEAN? ENGLISH IS PRACTICALLY THE NATIONAL LANGUAGE IN VIETNAM.
IN CASE YOU DIDN'T KNOW, YOU RUNNING DOGS HAVE BEEN OCCUPYING OUR COUNTRY FOR FIFTEEN YEARS.. AND BY THE WAY, MY NAME'S PHRED, NOT CHARLIE...
I'M A V.C. TERRORIST. AND I'M A GOOD ONE, TOO! AIN'T NOBODY IN THESE PARTS WHO AIN'T HEARD OF "PHRED THE TERRORIST."
"PHRED THE TERRORIST."
YESSIR, I CAN RAZE A HAMLET IN THIRTY SECONDS FLAT...

2/18/72

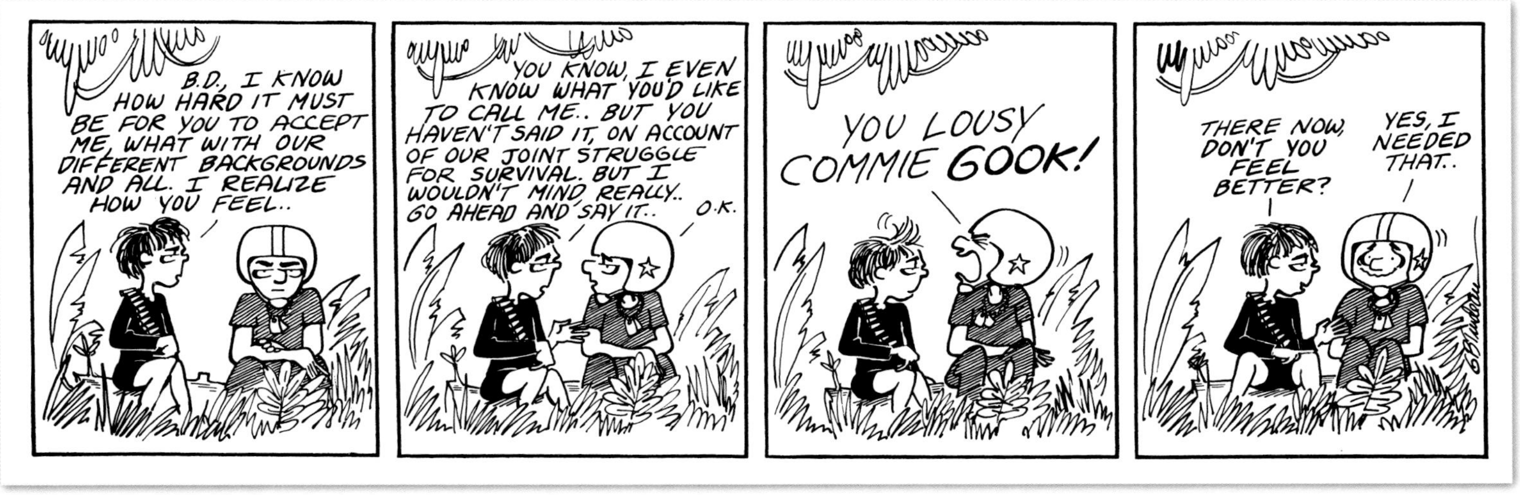
B.D., I KNOW HOW HARD IT MUST BE FOR YOU TO ACCEPT ME, WHAT WITH OUR DIFFERENT BACKGROUNDS AND ALL. I REALIZE HOW YOU FEEL..
YOU KNOW, I EVEN KNOW WHAT YOU'D LIKE TO CALL ME.. BUT YOU HAVEN'T SAID IT, ON ACCOUNT OF OUR JOINT STRUGGLE FOR SURVIVAL. BUT I WOULDN'T MIND REALLY.. GO AHEAD AND SAY IT..
O.K.
YOU LOUSY COMMIE GOOK!
THERE NOW, DON'T YOU FEEL BETTER?
YES, I NEEDED THAT..

2/25/72

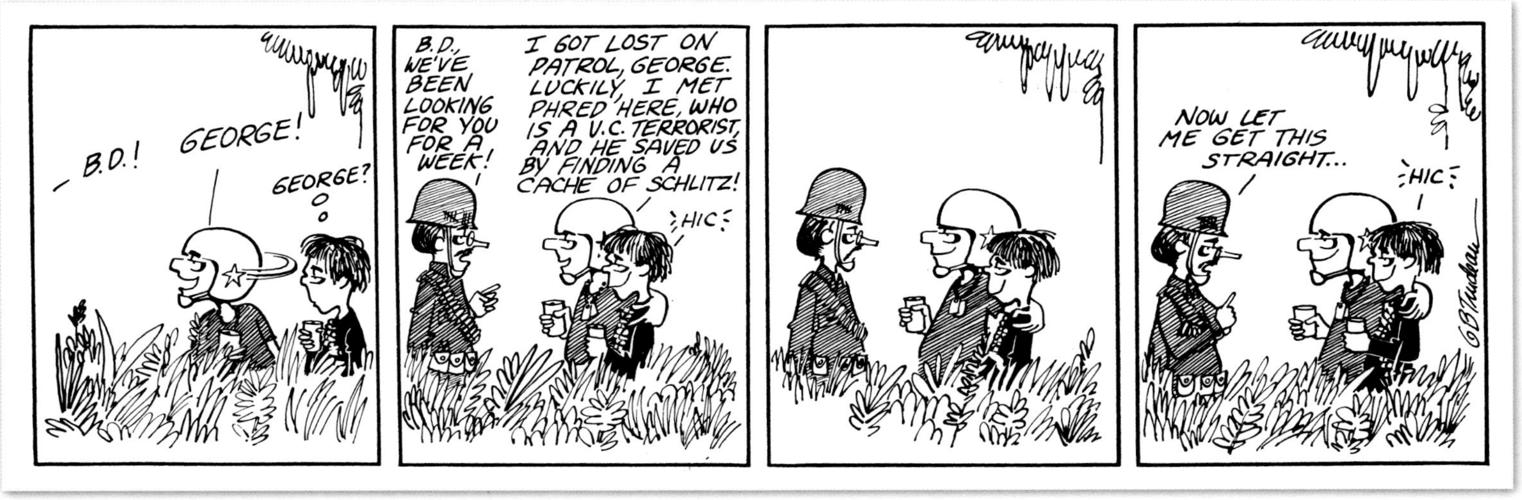
B.D.!
GEORGE!
GEORGE?
B.D., WE'VE BEEN LOOKING FOR YOU FOR A WEEK!
I GOT LOST ON PATROL, GEORGE. LUCKILY, I MET PHRED HERE, WHO IS A V.C. TERRORIST, AND HE SAVED US BY FINDING A CACHE OF SCHLITZ!
HIC
NOW LET ME GET THIS STRAIGHT...
HIC

3/1/72

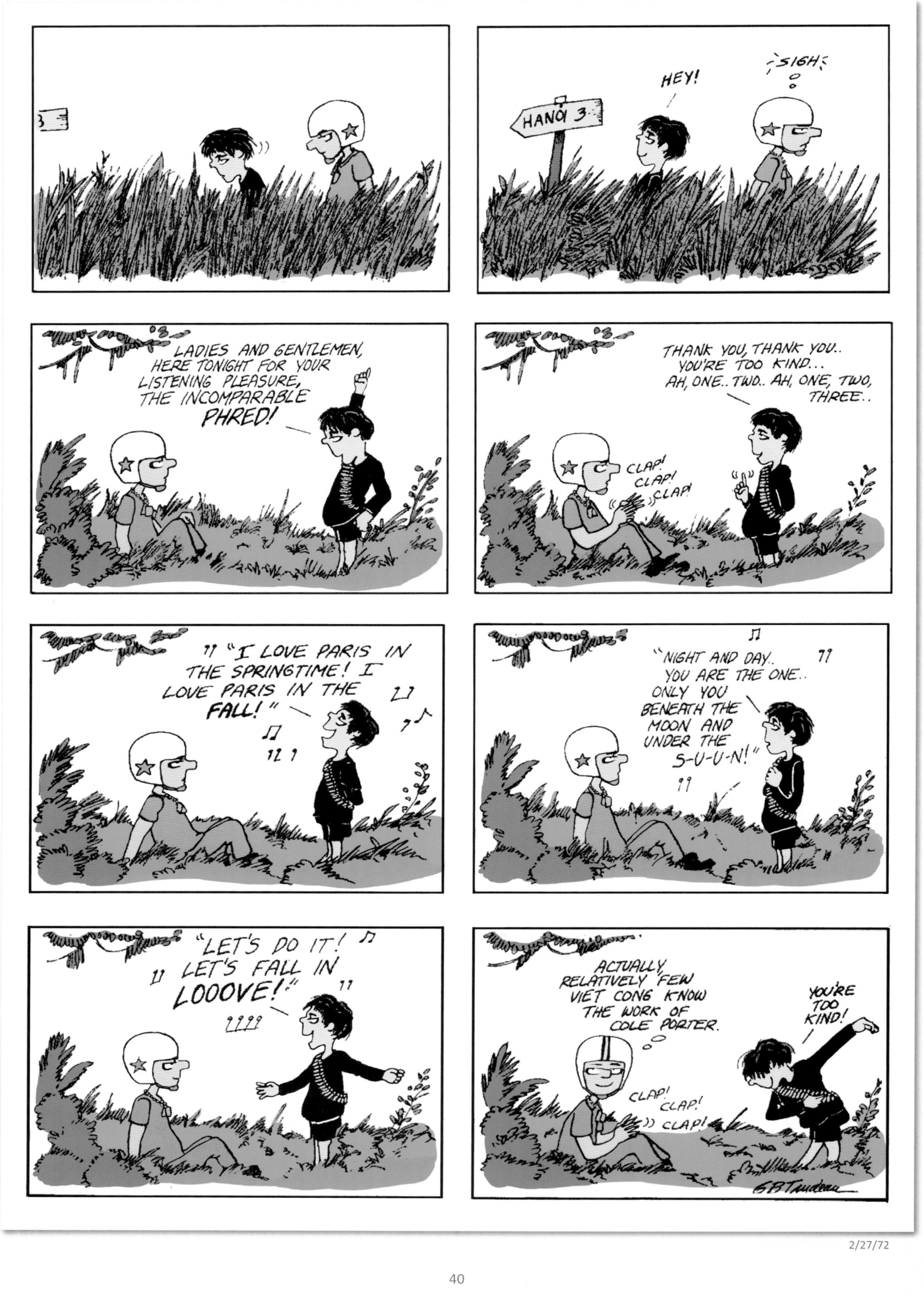

HANOI 3
HEY!
SIGH
LADIES AND GENTLEMEN, HERE TONIGHT FOR YOUR LISTENING PLEASURE, THE INCOMPARABLE PHRED!
THANK YOU, THANK YOU.. YOU'RE TOO KIND... AH, ONE..TWO.. AH, ONE, TWO, THREE..
CLAP! CLAP! CLAP!
"I LOVE PARIS IN THE SPRINGTIME! I LOVE PARIS IN THE FALL!"
"NIGHT AND DAY.. YOU ARE THE ONE.. ONLY YOU BENEATH THE MOON AND UNDER THE S-U-U-N!"
"LET'S DO IT! LET'S FALL IN LOOOVE!"
ACTUALLY, RELATIVELY FEW VIET CONG KNOW THE WORK OF COLE PORTER.
YOU'RE TOO KIND!
CLAP! CLAP! CLAP!
GBTrudeau

2/27/72

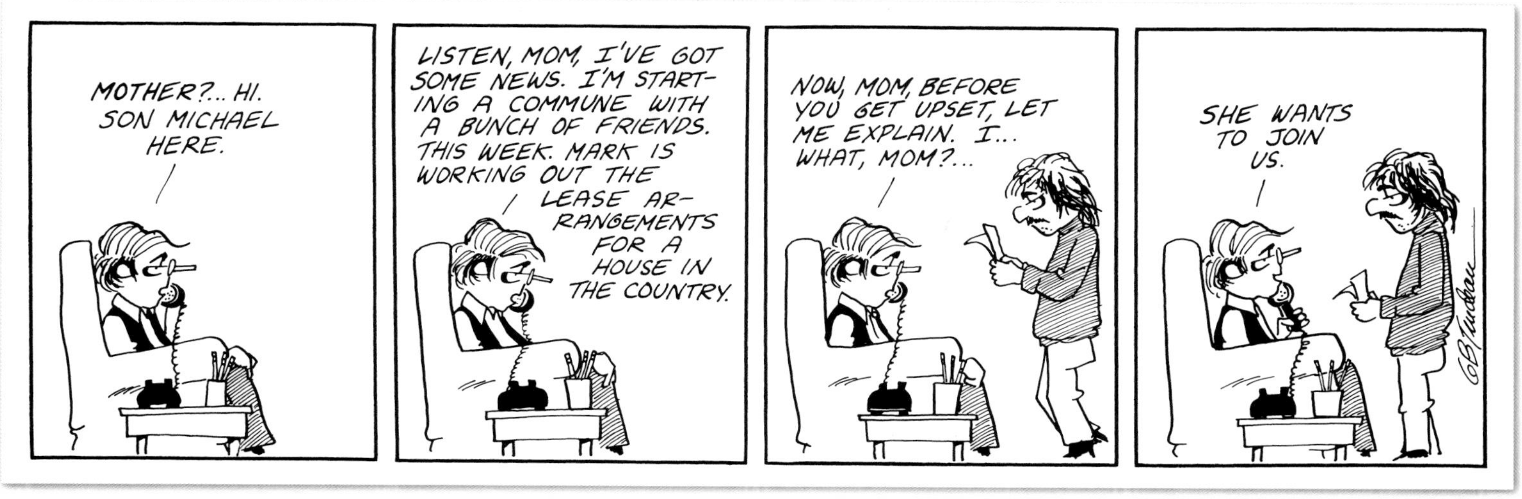
MOTHER?... HI. SON MICHAEL HERE.
LISTEN, MOM, I'VE GOT SOME NEWS. I'M STARTING A COMMUNE WITH A BUNCH OF FRIENDS. THIS WEEK. MARK IS WORKING OUT THE LEASE ARRANGEMENTS FOR A HOUSE IN THE COUNTRY.
NOW, MOM, BEFORE YOU GET UPSET, LET ME EXPLAIN. I... WHAT, MOM?...
SHE WANTS TO JOIN US.

4/18/72

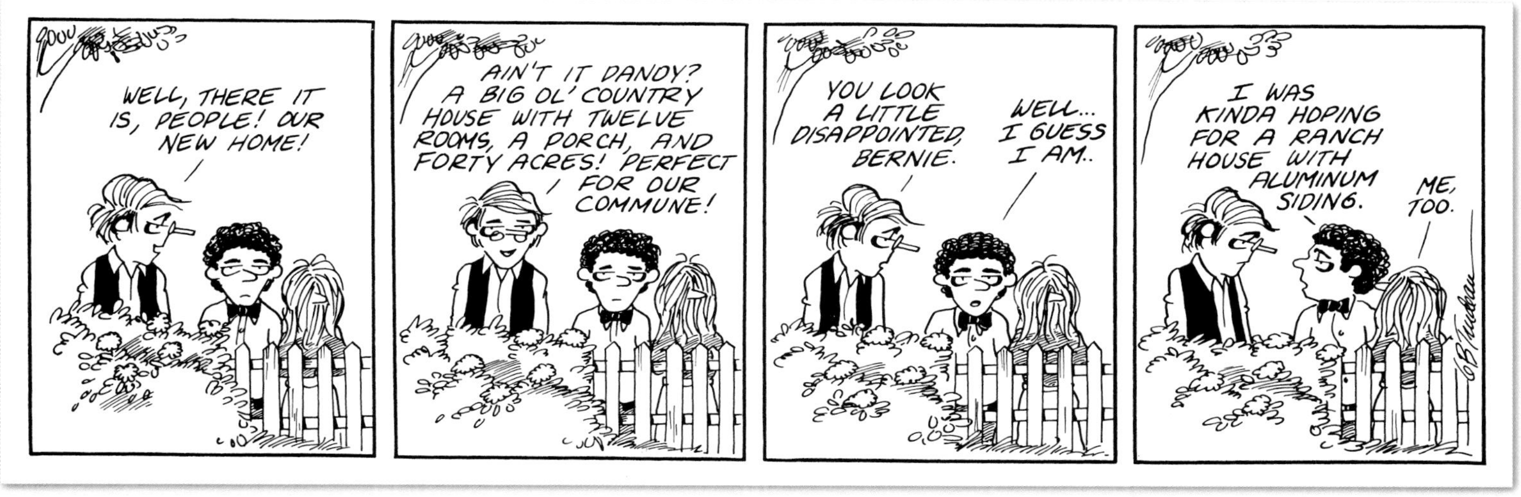
WELL, THERE IT IS, PEOPLE! OUR NEW HOME!
AIN'T IT DANDY? A BIG OL' COUNTRY HOUSE WITH TWELVE ROOMS, A PORCH, AND FORTY ACRES! PERFECT FOR OUR COMMUNE!
YOU LOOK A LITTLE DISAPPOINTED, BERNIE.
WELL... I GUESS I AM..
I WAS KINDA HOPING FOR A RANCH HOUSE WITH ALUMINUM SIDING.
ME, TOO.

4/19/72

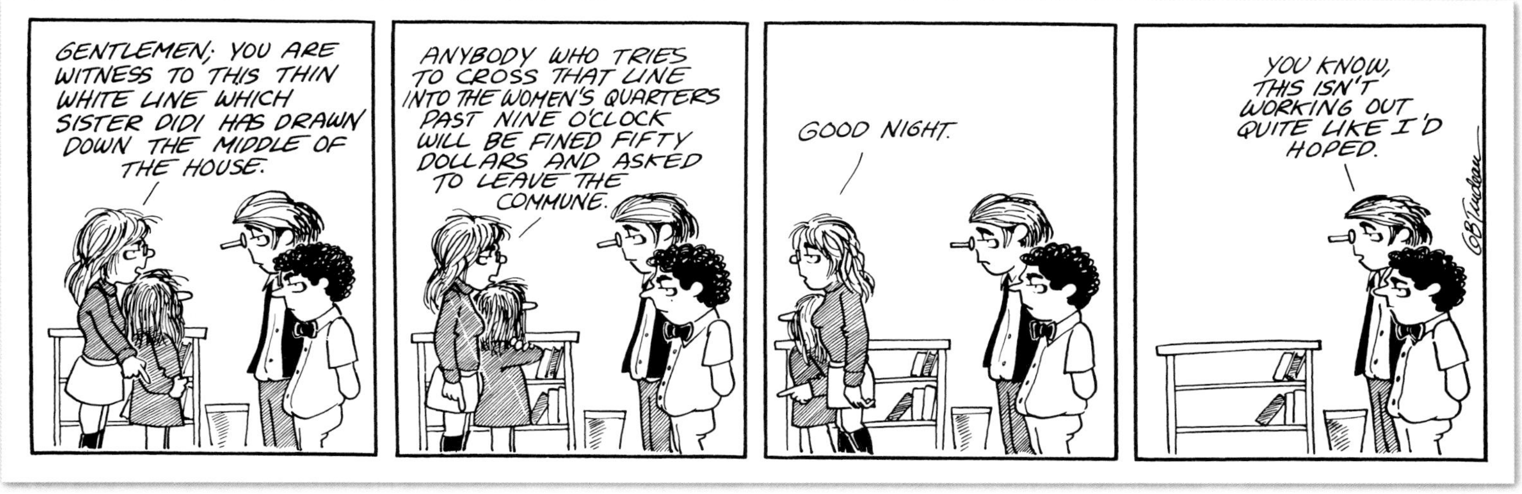
GENTLEMEN: YOU ARE WITNESS TO THIS THIN WHITE LINE WHICH SISTER DIDI HAS DRAWN DOWN THE MIDDLE OF THE HOUSE.
ANYBODY WHO TRIES TO CROSS THAT LINE INTO THE WOMEN'S QUARTERS PAST NINE O'CLOCK WILL BE FINED FIFTY DOLLARS AND ASKED TO LEAVE THE COMMUNE.
GOOD NIGHT.
YOU KNOW, THIS ISN'T WORKING OUT QUITE LIKE I'D HOPED.

4/20/72

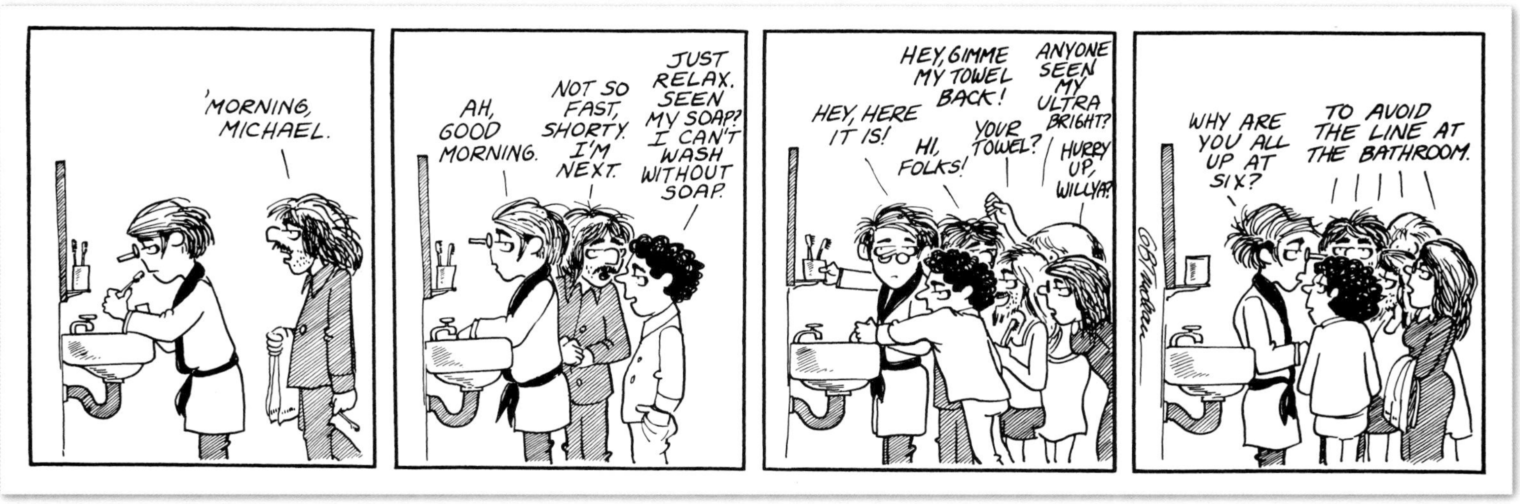
'MORNING, MICHAEL.
AH, GOOD MORNING.
NOT SO FAST, SHORTY. I'M NEXT.
JUST RELAX. SEEN MY SOAP? I CAN'T WASH WITHOUT SOAP.
HEY, HERE IT IS!
HEY, GIMME MY TOWEL BACK!
HI, FOLKS!
YOUR TOWEL?
ANYONE SEEN MY ULTRA BRIGHT?
HURRY UP, WILLYA?
WHY ARE YOU ALL UP AT SIX?
TO AVOID THE LINE AT THE BATHROOM.

4/21/72

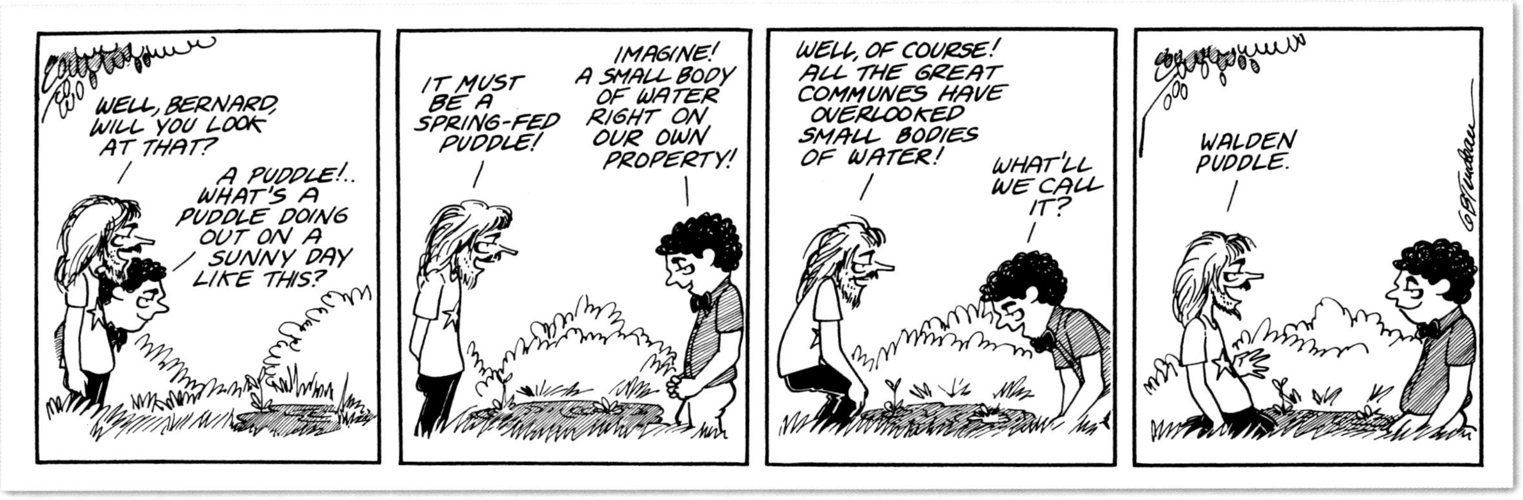
WELL, BERNARD, WILL YOU LOOK AT THAT?
A PUDDLE!.. WHAT'S A PUDDLE DOING OUT ON A SUNNY DAY LIKE THIS?
IT MUST BE A SPRING-FED PUDDLE!
IMAGINE! A SMALL BODY OF WATER RIGHT ON OUR OWN PROPERTY!
WELL, OF COURSE! ALL THE GREAT COMMUNES HAVE OVERLOOKED SMALL BODIES OF WATER!
WHAT'LL WE CALL IT?
WALDEN PUDDLE.

4/24/72

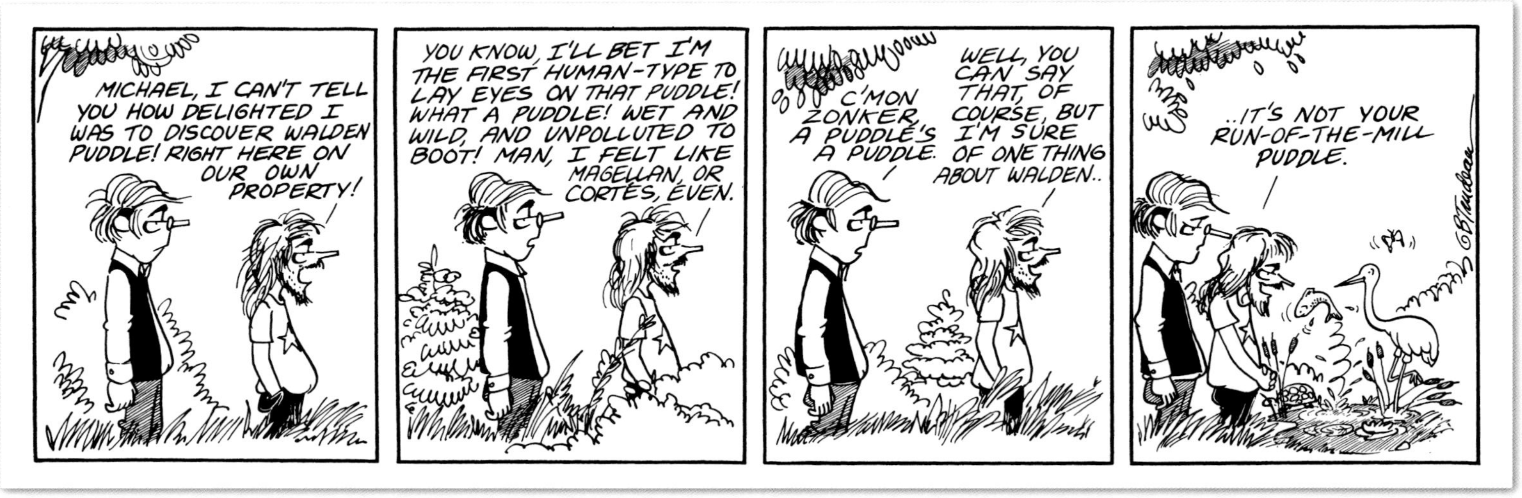
MICHAEL, I CAN'T TELL YOU HOW DELIGHTED I WAS TO DISCOVER WALDEN PUDDLE! RIGHT HERE ON OUR OWN PROPERTY!
YOU KNOW, I'LL BET I'M THE FIRST HUMAN-TYPE TO LAY EYES ON THAT PUDDLE! WHAT A PUDDLE! WET AND WILD, AND UNPOLLUTED TO BOOT! MAN, I FELT LIKE MAGELLAN, OR CORTES, EVEN.
C'MON ZONKER, A PUDDLE'S A PUDDLE.
WELL, YOU CAN SAY THAT, OF COURSE, BUT I'M SURE OF ONE THING ABOUT WALDEN..
..IT'S NOT YOUR RUN-OF-THE-MILL PUDDLE.

4/25/72

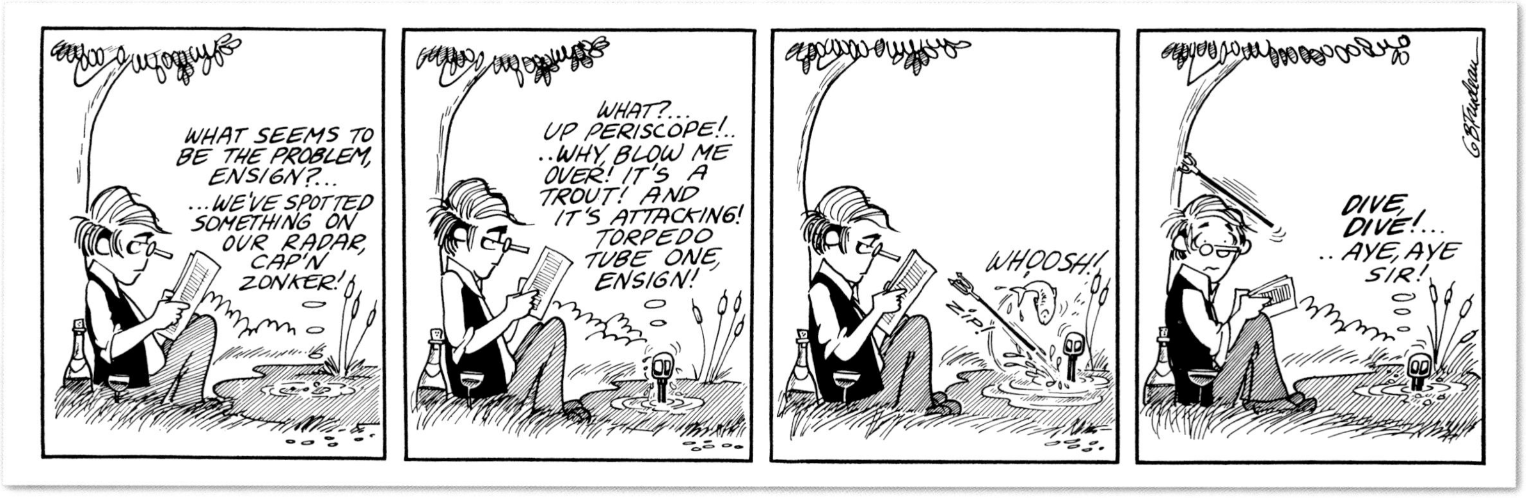
WHAT SEEMS TO BE THE PROBLEM, ENSIGN?... ...WE'VE SPOTTED SOMETHING ON OUR RADAR, CAP'N ZONKER!
WHAT?... UP PERISCOPE!.. ..WHY, BLOW ME OVER! IT'S A TROUT! AND IT'S ATTACKING! TORPEDO TUBE ONE, ENSIGN!
WHOOSH!
DIVE, DIVE!... ..AYE, AYE SIR!

4/27/72

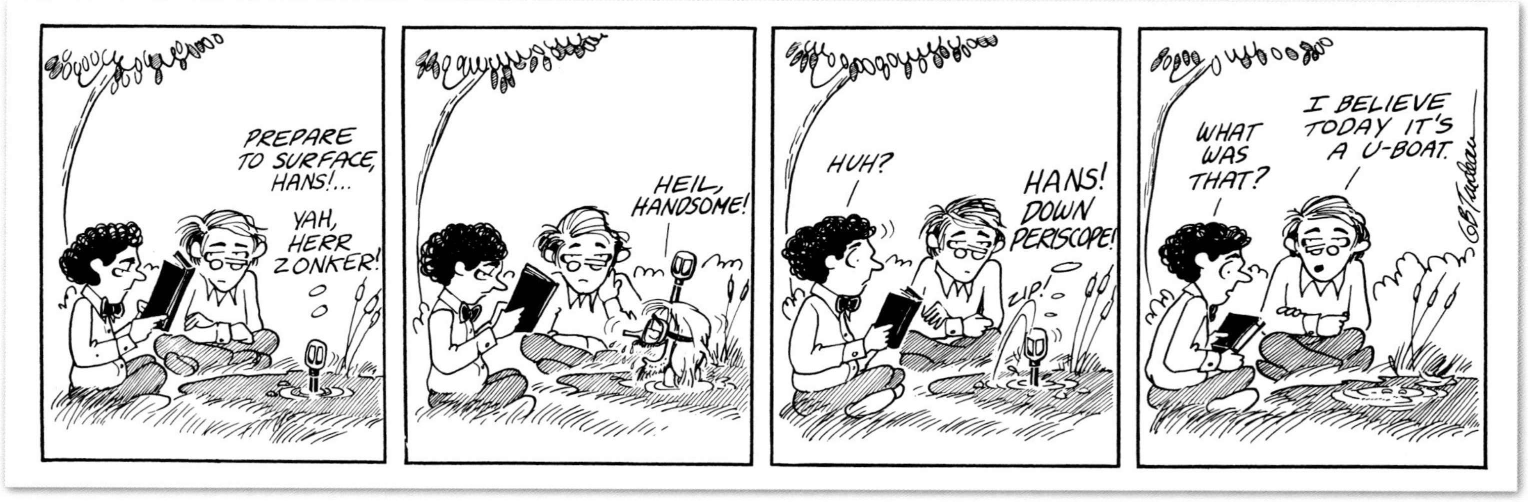
PREPARE TO SURFACE, HANS!...
YAH, HERR ZONKER!
HEIL, HANDSOME!
HUH?
HANS! DOWN PERISCOPE!
ZIP!
WHAT WAS THAT?
I BELIEVE TODAY IT'S A U-BOAT.

4/28/72

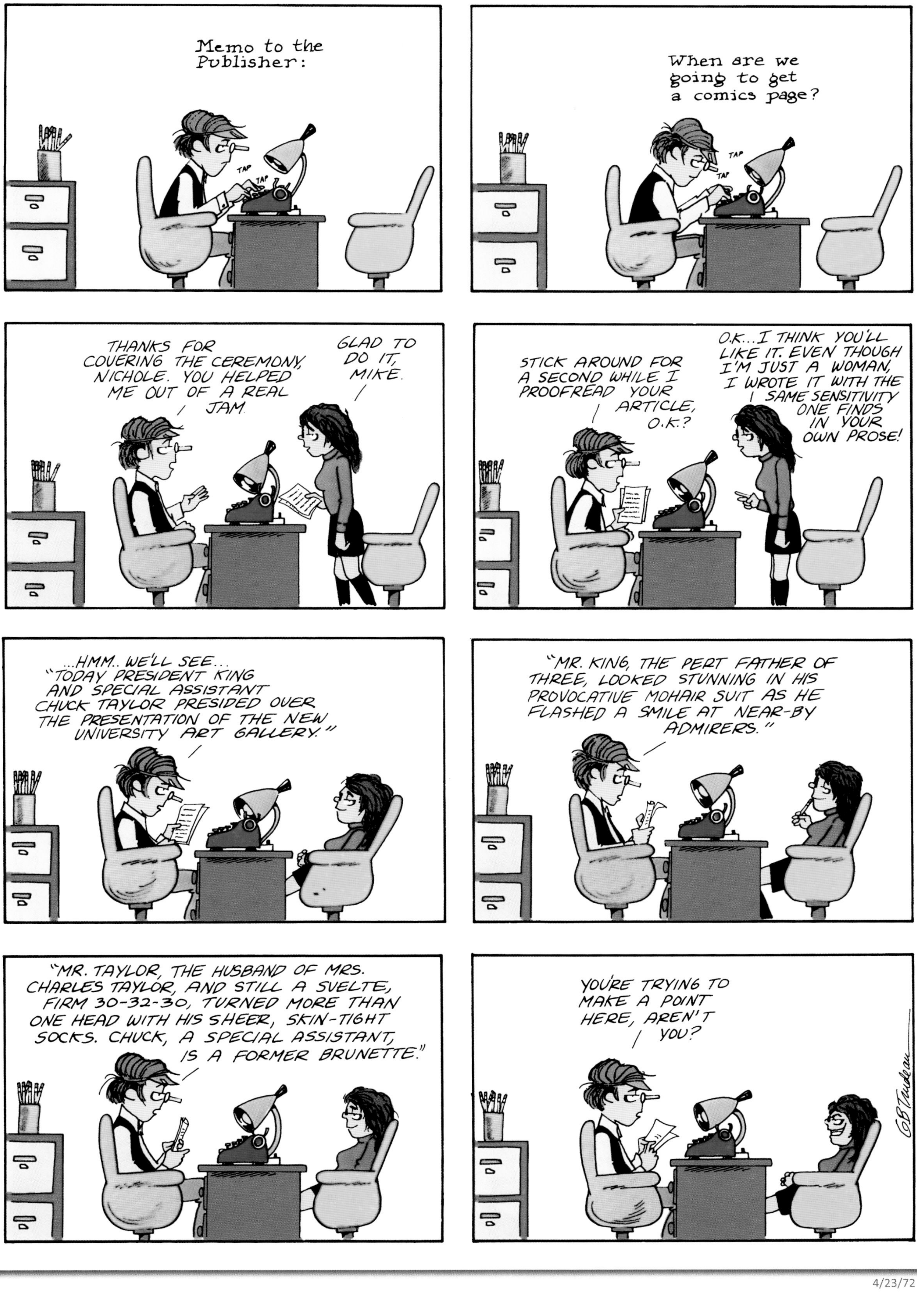
Memo to the Publisher:
TAP TAP
When are we going to get a comics page?
TAP TAP
THANKS FOR COVERING THE CEREMONY, NICHOLE. YOU HELPED ME OUT OF A REAL JAM.
GLAD TO DO IT, MIKE.
STICK AROUND FOR A SECOND WHILE I PROOFREAD YOUR ARTICLE, O.K.?
O.K...I THINK YOU'LL LIKE IT. EVEN THOUGH I'M JUST A WOMAN, I WROTE IT WITH THE SAME SENSITIVITY ONE FINDS IN YOUR OWN PROSE!
...HMM.. WE'LL SEE... "TODAY PRESIDENT KING AND SPECIAL ASSISTANT CHUCK TAYLOR PRESIDED OVER THE PRESENTATION OF THE NEW UNIVERSITY ART GALLERY."
"MR. KING, THE PERT FATHER OF THREE, LOOKED STUNNING IN HIS PROVOCATIVE MOHAIR SUIT AS HE FLASHED A SMILE AT NEAR-BY ADMIRERS."
"MR. TAYLOR, THE HUSBAND OF MRS. CHARLES TAYLOR, AND STILL A SVELTE, FIRM 30-32-30, TURNED MORE THAN ONE HEAD WITH HIS SHEER, SKIN-TIGHT SOCKS. CHUCK, A SPECIAL ASSISTANT, IS A FORMER BRUNETTE."
YOU'RE TRYING TO MAKE A POINT HERE, AREN'T YOU?
GBTrudeau

4/23/72

Michael Doonesbury

At my high school, which for many was not a pleasant place, "doone" was one of the more benign pejoratives. A doone was akin to a doofus—a clueless sort, but without any mean to him. His innocence conveyed a kind of grace, so the doone was often held in some affection by his posse.

At least ours was. My friend Charles Pillsbury didn't ask for comic strip immortality, but he also didn't seem to mind much when I conflated his good nature and his good name to produce *Doonesbury*'s title. Which proved he was a doone. Seriously, case closed. A pencil-nosed cartoon avatar has followed him around his entire adult life, and he's never once complained. Who could be that good natured? Only a doone.

There were other inspirations for Mike Doonesbury—some of them autobiographical—but Charlie furnished the hard kernel of decency that allowed Mike to survive a lifetime of moral hazard. Not that his decency was always conspicuous. Mike's early emotional development wasn't just arrested; it sometimes appeared to reverse course. Humiliation piled upon humiliation, always triggered by a puzzling grandiosity. (His opening lines in the strip: "Hi, there! My name's Mike Doonesbury! I hail from Tulsa, Oklahoma, and women adore me!")

"Boy, what a pair we're going to make! A football player and a lover boy!"

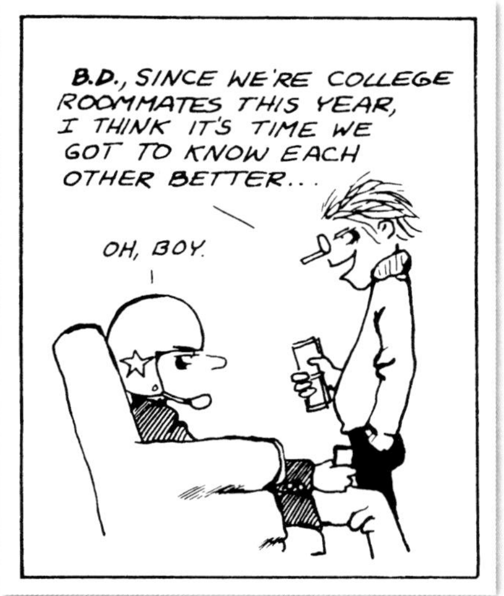
B.D., SINCE WE'RE COLLEGE ROOMMATES THIS YEAR, I THINK IT'S TIME WE GOT TO KNOW EACH OTHER BETTER...
OH, BOY.

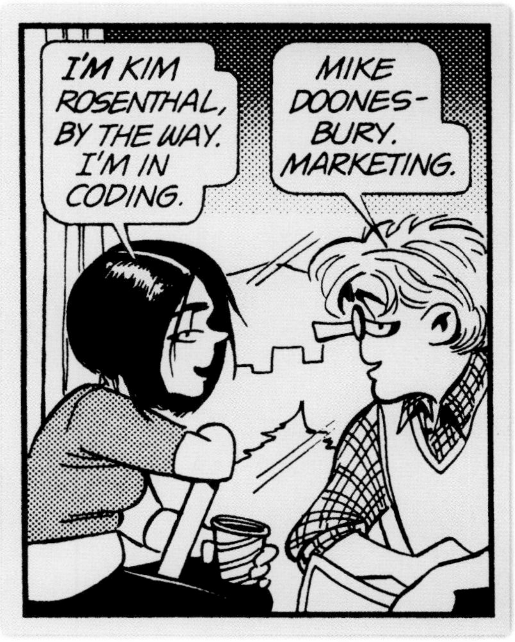
I'M KIM ROSENTHAL, BY THE WAY. I'M IN CODING.
MIKE DOONESBURY. MARKETING.

With that tragically inept start, who could have foreseen that Mike was destined to become the Richie Cunningham of the strip, all common sense and groundedness? True, it took years for him to completely free himself of the poor choices and wild course corrections of youth, but for the most part he evolved into the group's designated grown-up. His main job was to provide contrast, to play magnetic north as everyone around him headed south. When, during the summer of 1986, a half-dozen converging story lines dumped all the principal characters on Mike's doorstep simultaneously, he alone was qualified to cope, to keep the place from burning down until I could contrive a loft-clearing police bust.

If this makes Mike less interesting as a dramatic character, it's the kind of trade-off most storytellers seem willing to suffer. Generally speaking, readers prefer their chaos served up in the presence of some kind of order. Without pushback, anarchy can become tedious—a lesson I relearn every time I separate Duke from Honey. Likewise, in order to truly savor J.J.'s inanities or Alex's flights of self-delusion, Mike's sensible, contrapuntal utterances are indispensable, even if we watch them go ignored.

Years ago, during a workshop for the Broadway version of *Doonesbury*, Ralph Bruneau, the actor playing Mike, sang to perfection a new solo he'd just been handed by the composer. Our Boopsie scowled at him, resentful that he'd been assigned such a lovely piece. Ralph smiled back at her serenely and said, "And what's the strip called? *Boopsie*? I don't think so."

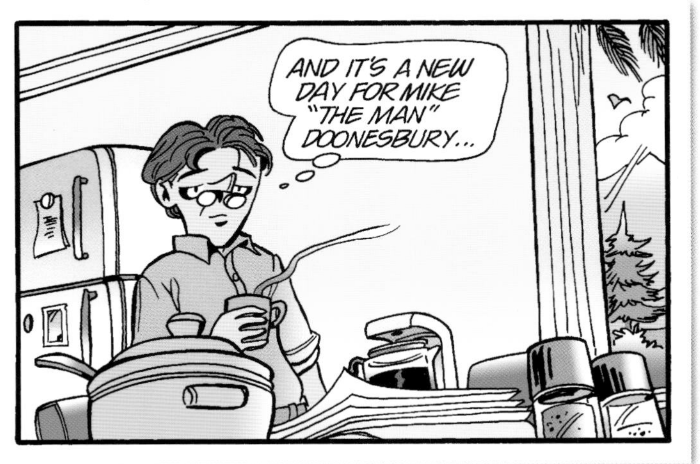
AND IT'S A NEW DAY FOR MIKE "THE MAN" DOONESBURY...

Nope, it's Mike's strip. Every zoo needs a keeper.

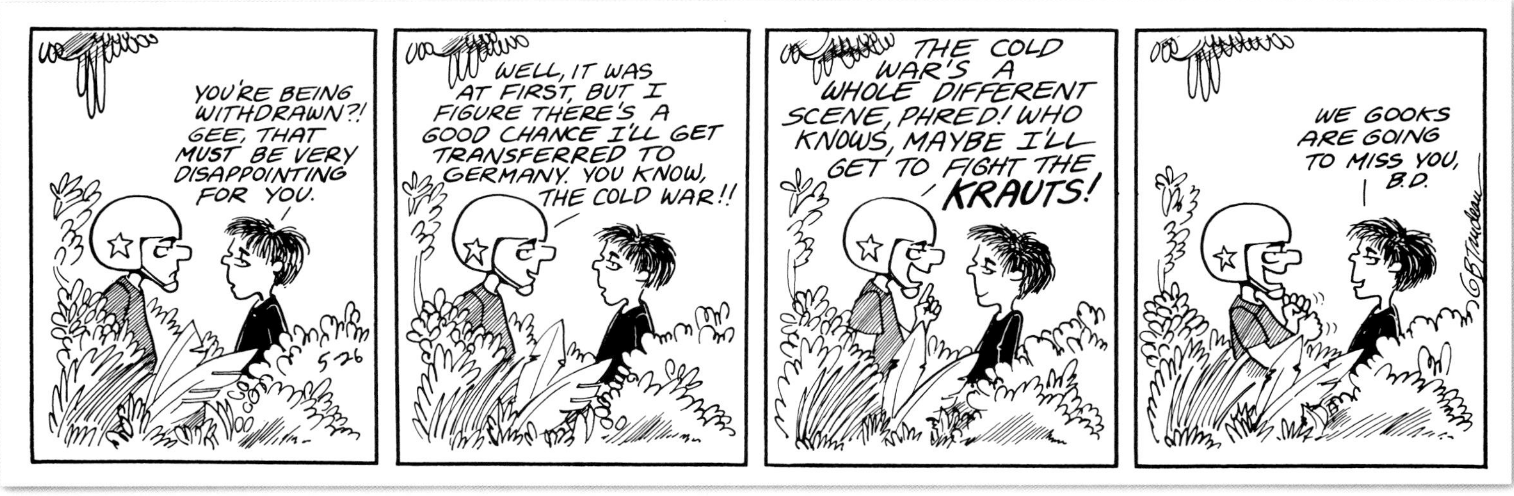
YOU'RE BEING WITHDRAWN?! GEE, THAT MUST BE VERY DISAPPOINTING FOR YOU.
5-26
WELL, IT WAS AT FIRST, BUT I FIGURE THERE'S A GOOD CHANCE I'LL GET TRANSFERRED TO GERMANY. YOU KNOW, THE COLD WAR!!
THE COLD WAR'S A WHOLE DIFFERENT SCENE, PHRED! WHO KNOWS, MAYBE I'LL GET TO FIGHT THE KRAUTS!
WE GOOKS ARE GOING TO MISS YOU, B.D.

5/26/72

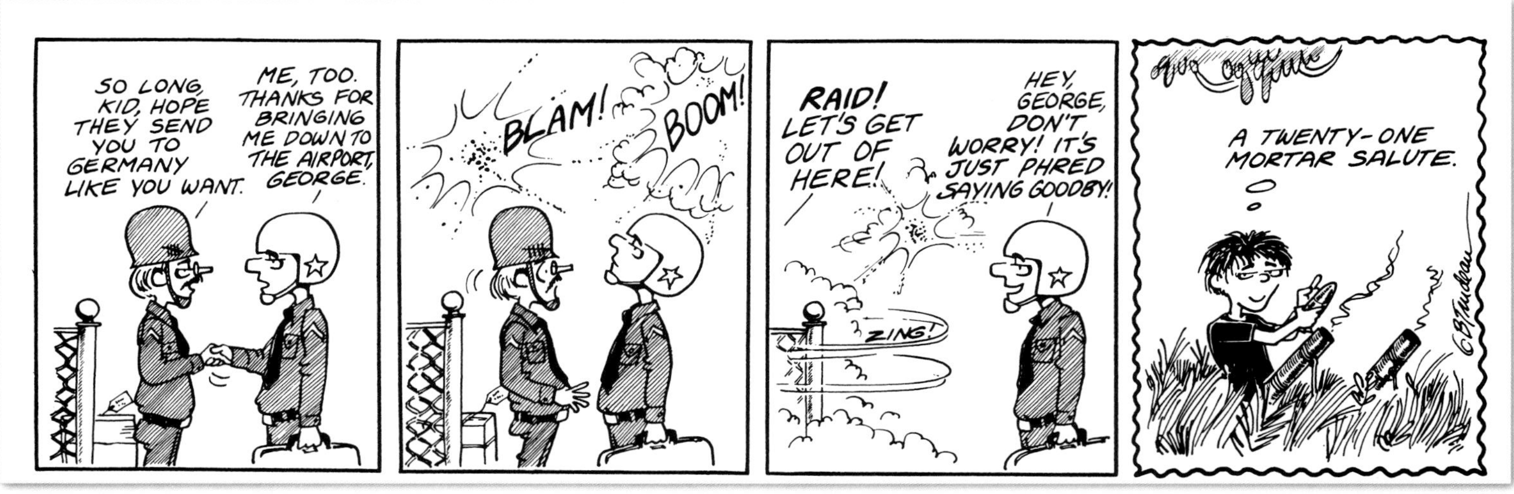
SO LONG, KID, HOPE THEY SEND YOU TO GERMANY LIKE YOU WANT.
ME, TOO. THANKS FOR BRINGING ME DOWN TO THE AIRPORT, GEORGE.
BLAM!
BOOM!
RAID! LET'S GET OUT OF HERE!
HEY, GEORGE, DON'T WORRY! IT'S JUST PHRED SAYING GOODBY!
ZING!
A TWENTY-ONE MORTAR SALUTE.

5/27/72

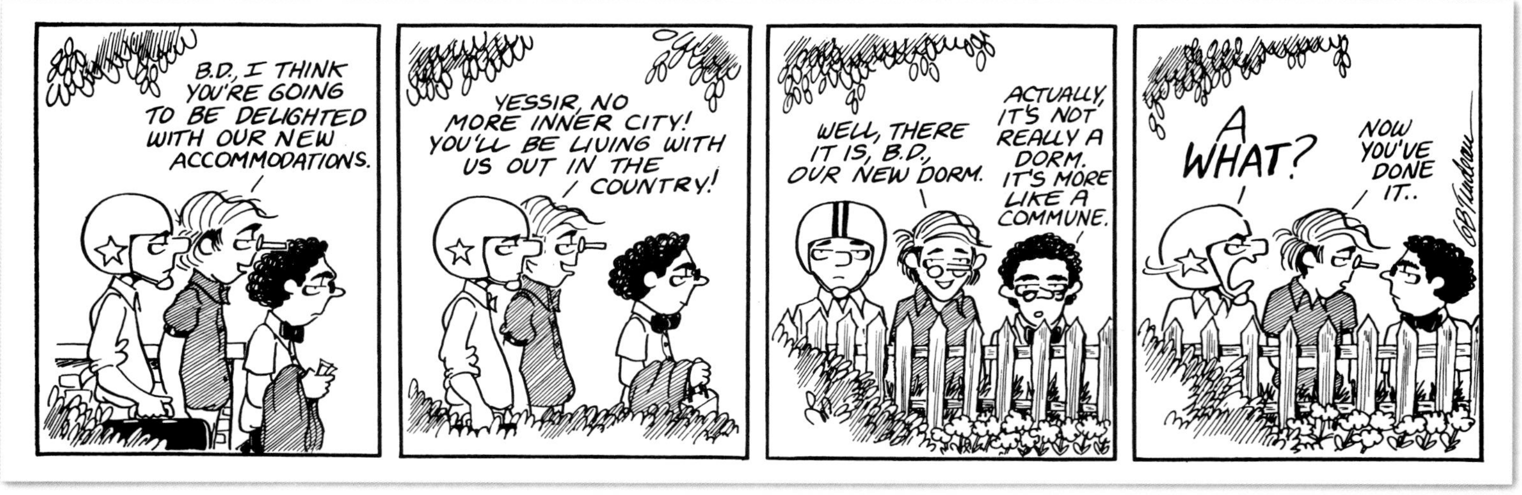
B.D., I THINK YOU'RE GOING TO BE DELIGHTED WITH OUR NEW ACCOMMODATIONS.
YESSIR, NO MORE INNER CITY! YOU'LL BE LIVING WITH US OUT IN THE COUNTRY!
WELL, THERE IT IS, B.D, OUR NEW DORM.
ACTUALLY, IT'S NOT REALLY A DORM. IT'S MORE LIKE A COMMUNE.
A WHAT?
NOW YOU'VE DONE IT..

5/30/72

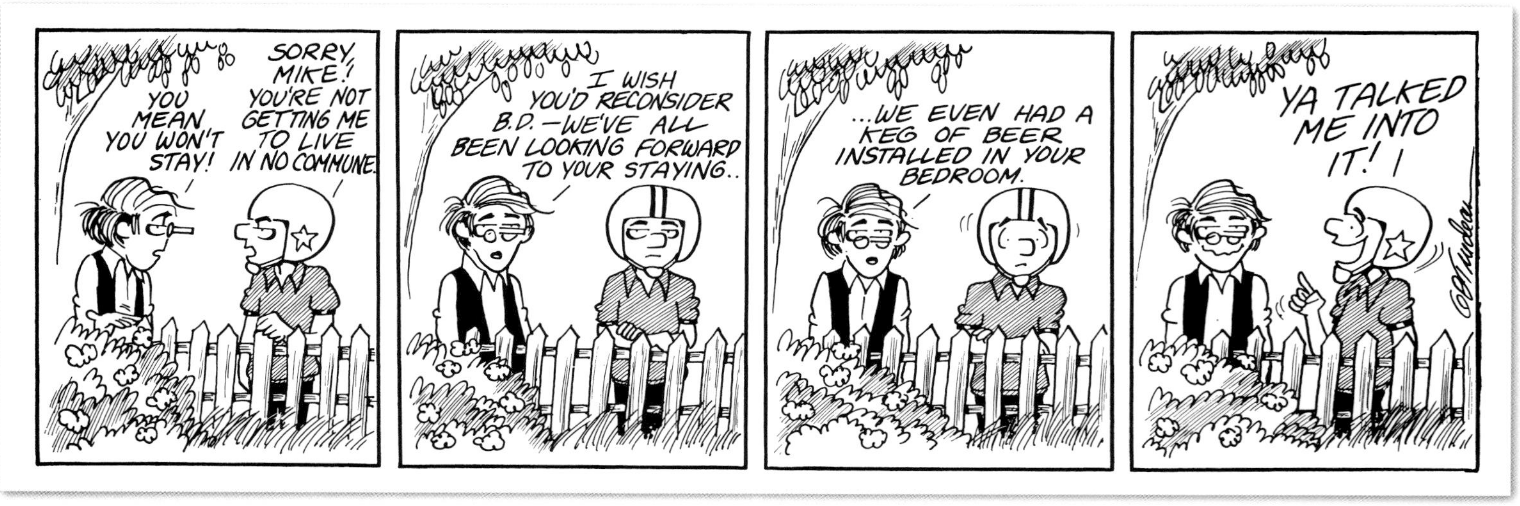
YOU MEAN YOU WON'T STAY!
SORRY, MIKE! YOU'RE NOT GETTING ME TO LIVE IN NO COMMUNE!
I WISH YOU'D RECONSIDER B.D.—WE'VE ALL BEEN LOOKING FORWARD TO YOUR STAYING..
...WE EVEN HAD A KEG OF BEER INSTALLED IN YOUR BEDROOM.
YA TALKED ME INTO IT!

5/31/72

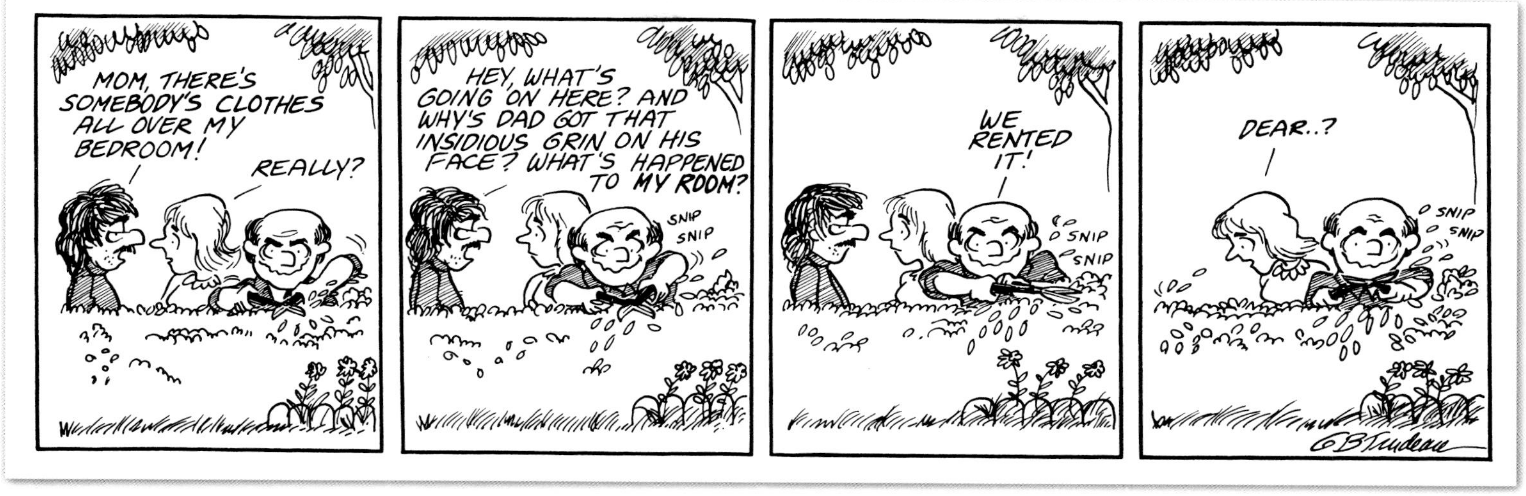
MOM, THERE'S SOMEBODY'S CLOTHES ALL OVER MY BEDROOM!
REALLY?
HEY, WHAT'S GOING ON HERE? AND WHY'S DAD GOT THAT INSIDIOUS GRIN ON HIS FACE? WHAT'S HAPPENED TO **MY ROOM?**
SNIP SNIP
WE RENTED IT!
SNIP SNIP
DEAR..?
SNIP SNIP

6/29/72

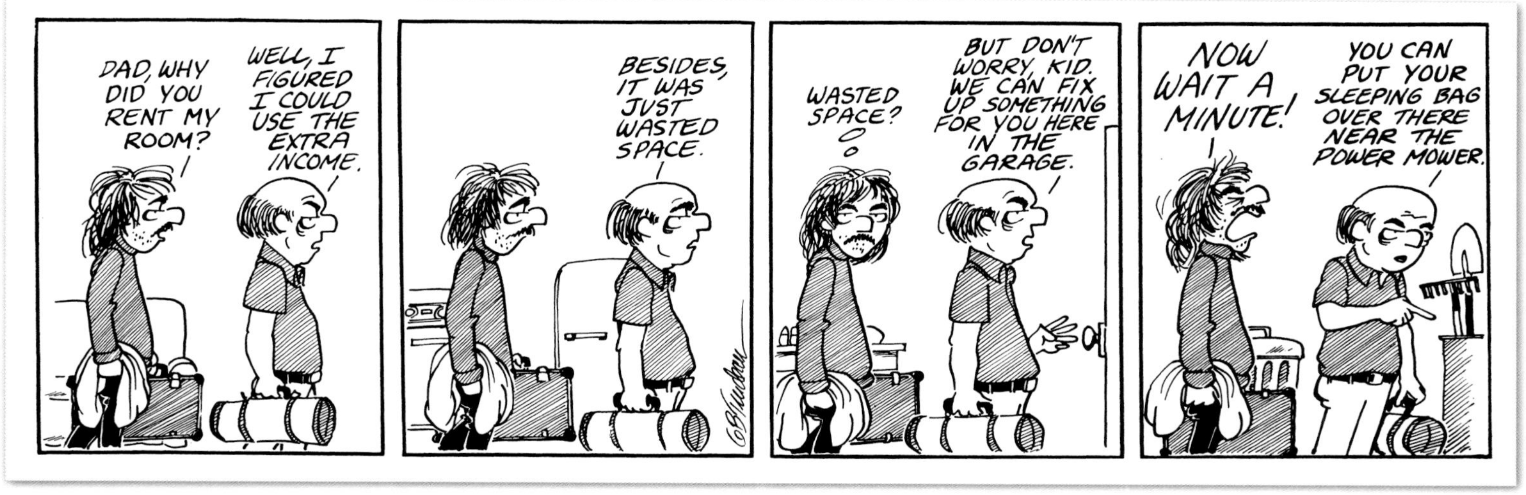
DAD, WHY DID YOU RENT MY ROOM?
WELL, I FIGURED I COULD USE THE EXTRA INCOME.
BESIDES, IT WAS JUST WASTED SPACE.
WASTED SPACE?
BUT DON'T WORRY, KID. WE CAN FIX UP SOMETHING FOR YOU HERE IN THE GARAGE.
NOW WAIT A MINUTE!
YOU CAN PUT YOUR SLEEPING BAG OVER THERE NEAR THE POWER MOWER.

6/30/72

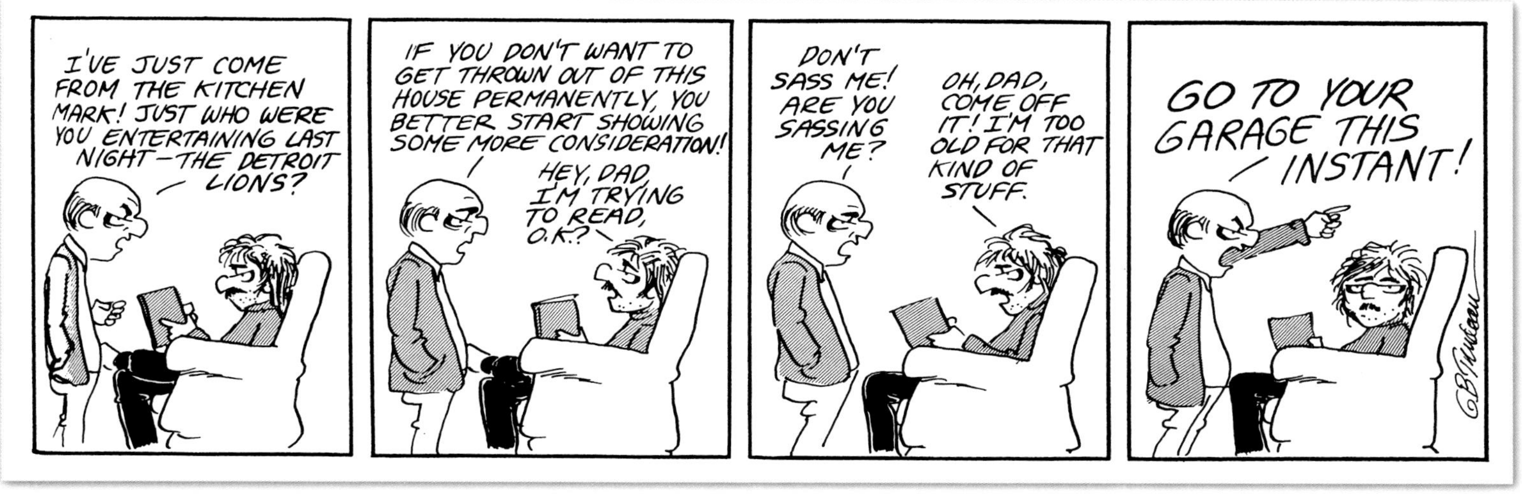
I'VE JUST COME FROM THE KITCHEN MARK! JUST WHO WERE YOU ENTERTAINING LAST NIGHT—THE DETROIT LIONS?
IF YOU DON'T WANT TO GET THROWN OUT OF THIS HOUSE PERMANENTLY, YOU BETTER START SHOWING SOME MORE CONSIDERATION!
HEY, DAD, I'M TRYING TO READ, O.K.?
DON'T SASS ME! ARE YOU SASSING ME?
OH, DAD, COME OFF IT! I'M TOO OLD FOR THAT KIND OF STUFF.
GO TO YOUR GARAGE THIS INSTANT!

7/21/72

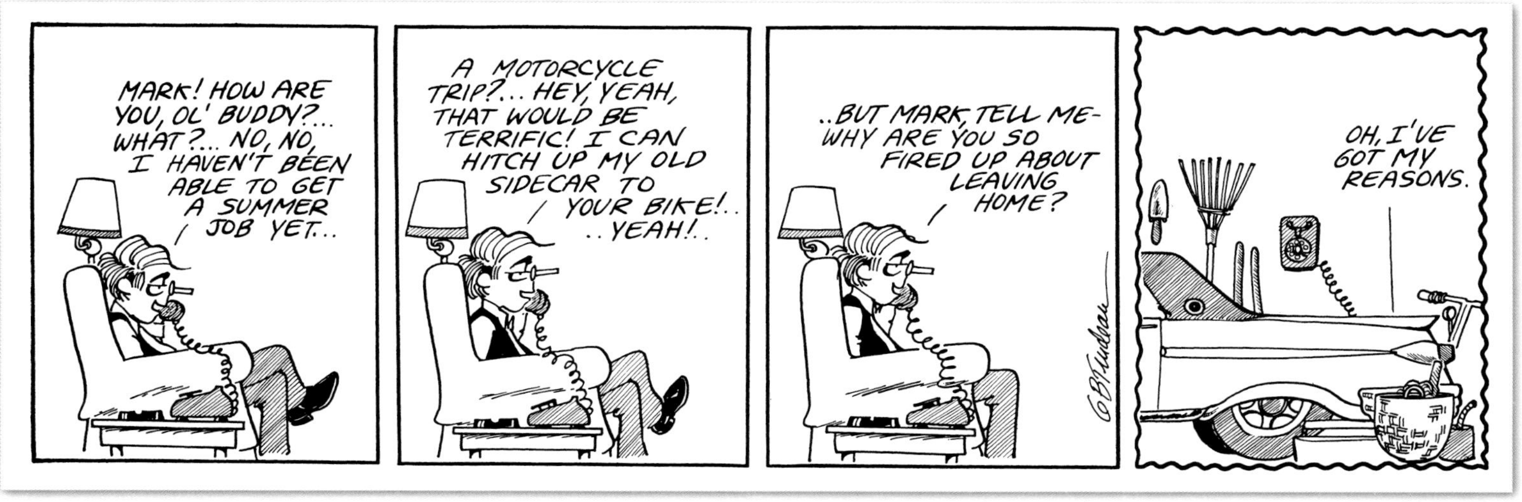
MARK! HOW ARE YOU, OL' BUDDY?... WHAT?... NO, NO, I HAVEN'T BEEN ABLE TO GET A SUMMER JOB YET...
A MOTORCYCLE TRIP?... HEY, YEAH, THAT WOULD BE TERRIFIC! I CAN HITCH UP MY OLD SIDECAR TO YOUR BIKE!.. ..YEAH!..
..BUT MARK, TELL ME— WHY ARE YOU SO FIRED UP ABOUT LEAVING HOME?
OH, I'VE GOT MY REASONS.

7/27/72

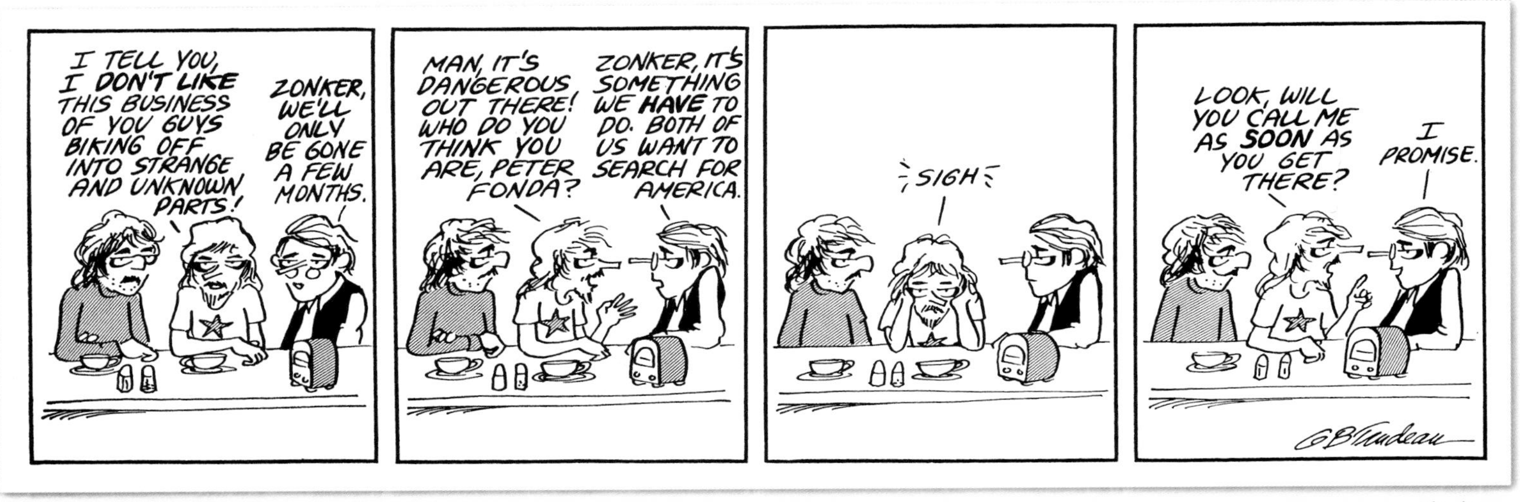
I TELL YOU, I **DON'T LIKE** THIS BUSINESS OF YOU GUYS BIKING OFF INTO STRANGE AND UNKNOWN **PARTS!**
ZONKER, WE'LL ONLY BE GONE A FEW MONTHS.
MAN, IT'S DANGEROUS OUT THERE! WHO DO YOU **THINK YOU** ARE, PETER FONDA?
ZONKER, IT'S SOMETHING WE **HAVE** TO DO. BOTH OF US WANT TO SEARCH FOR **AMERICA.**
SIGH
LOOK, WILL YOU **CALL** ME AS **SOON** AS YOU GET THERE?
I PROMISE.

7/31/72

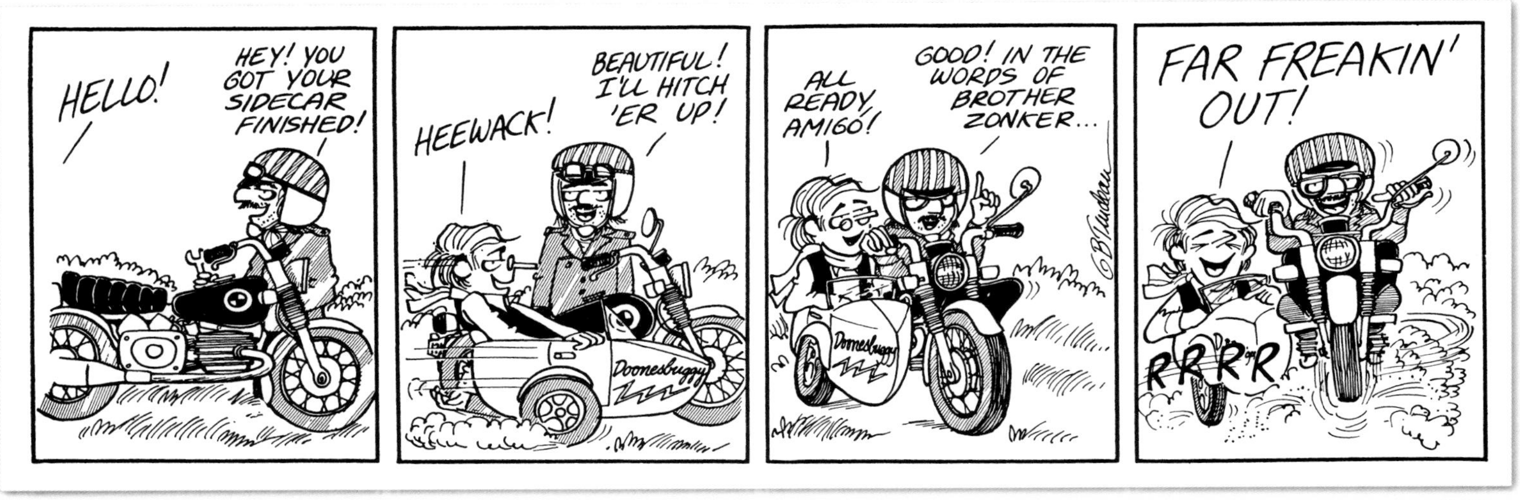
HELLO!
HEY! YOU GOT YOUR SIDECAR FINISHED!
HEEWACK!
BEAUTIFUL! I'LL HITCH 'ER UP!
Doonesbuggy
ALL READY AMIGO!
GOOD! IN THE WORDS OF BROTHER ZONKER...
FAR FREAKIN' OUT!
RRRR

8/1/72

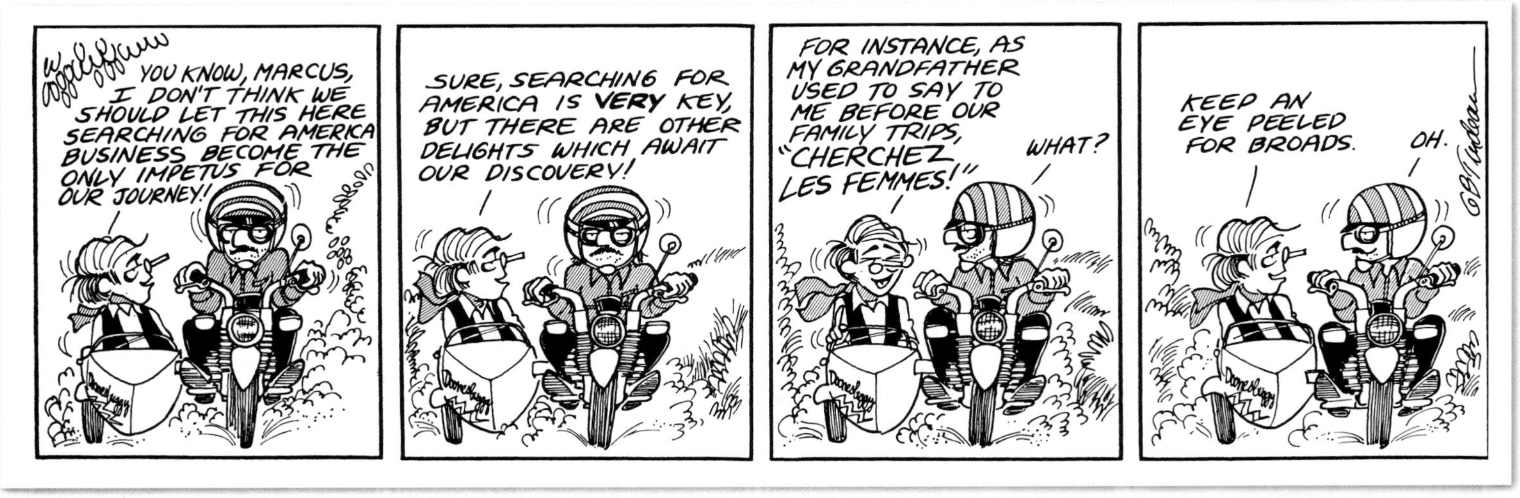
YOU KNOW, MARCUS, I DON'T THINK WE SHOULD LET THIS HERE SEARCHING FOR AMERICA BUSINESS BECOME THE ONLY IMPETUS FOR OUR JOURNEY!
SURE, SEARCHING FOR AMERICA IS **VERY** KEY, BUT THERE ARE OTHER DELIGHTS WHICH AWAIT OUR DISCOVERY!
FOR INSTANCE, AS MY GRANDFATHER USED TO SAY TO ME BEFORE OUR FAMILY TRIPS, "CHERCHEZ LES FEMMES!"
WHAT?
KEEP AN EYE PEELED FOR BROADS.
OH.

8/2/72

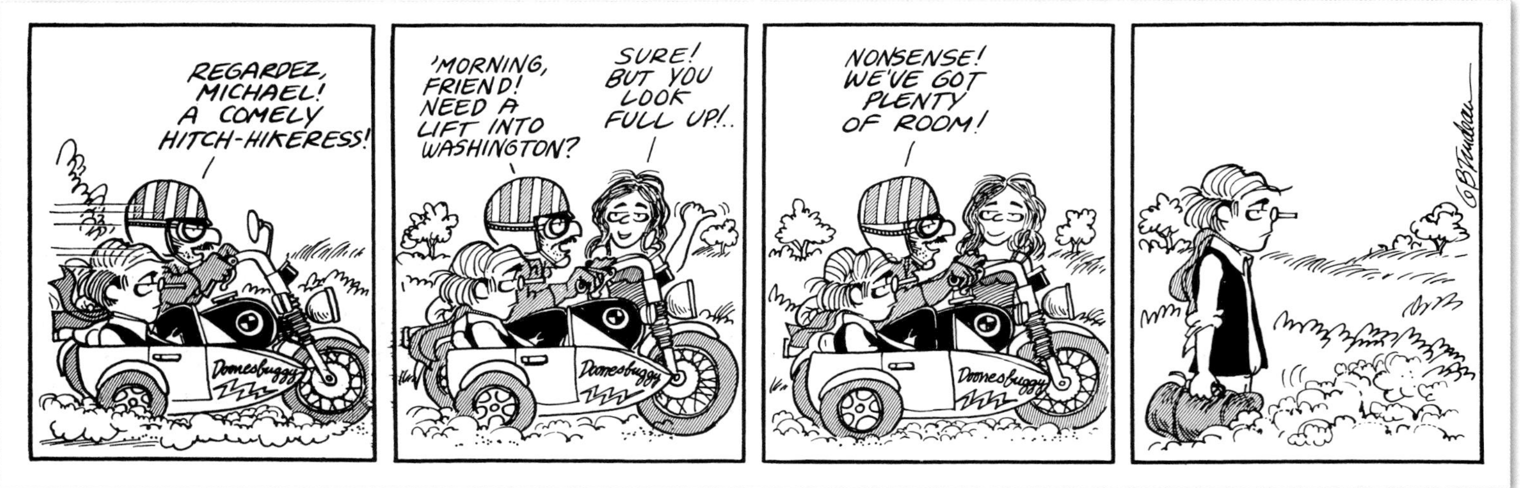
REGARDEZ, MICHAEL! A COMELY HITCH-HIKERESS!
Doonesbuggy
'MORNING, FRIEND! NEED A LIFT INTO WASHINGTON?
SURE! BUT YOU LOOK FULL UP!..
NONSENSE! WE'VE GOT PLENTY OF ROOM!

8/10/72

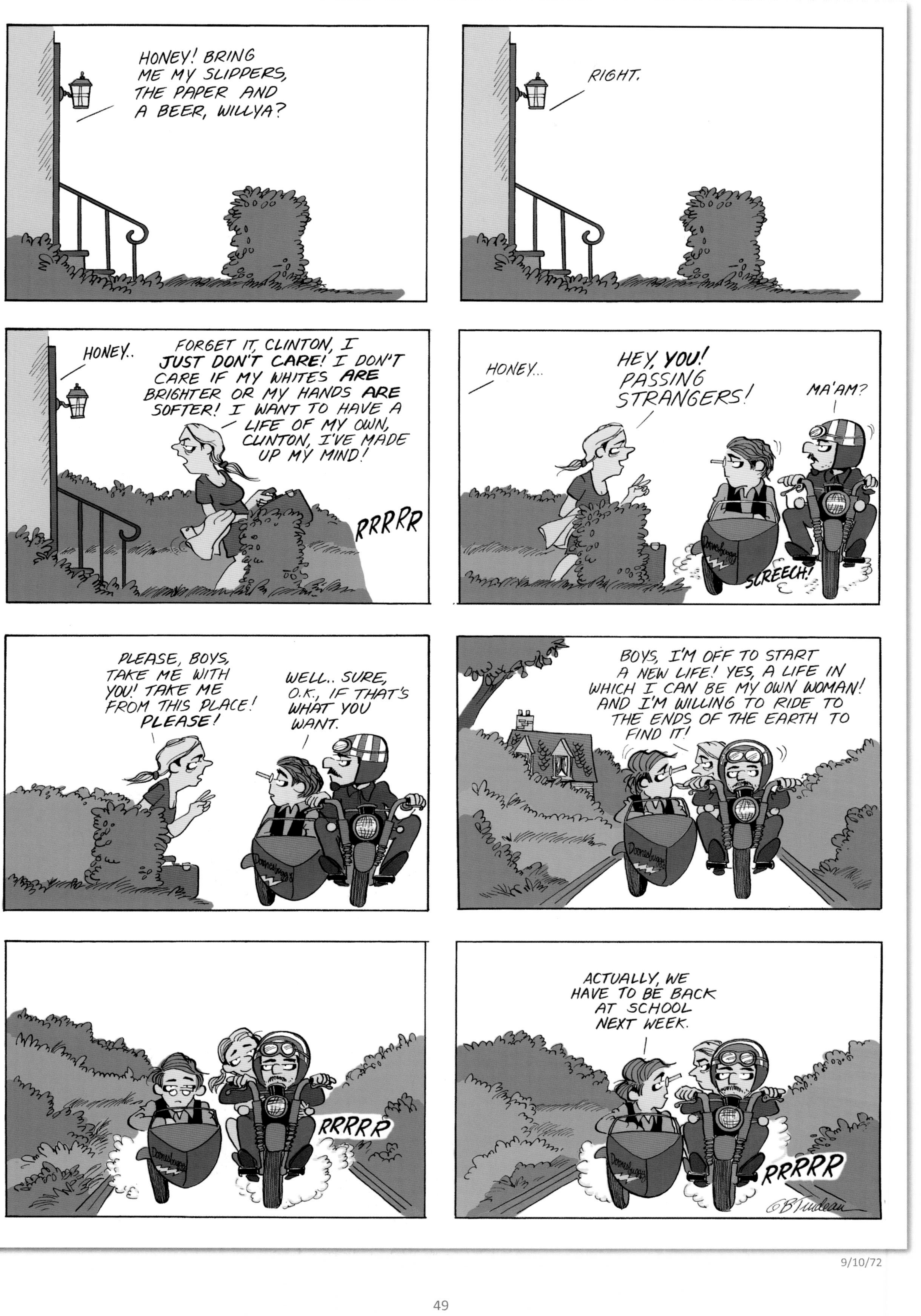
HONEY! BRING ME MY SLIPPERS, THE PAPER AND A BEER, WILLYA?
RIGHT.
HONEY..
FORGET IT, CLINTON, I JUST DON'T CARE! I DON'T CARE IF MY WHITES ARE BRIGHTER OR MY HANDS ARE SOFTER! I WANT TO HAVE A LIFE OF MY OWN, CLINTON, I'VE MADE UP MY MIND!
RRRRR
HONEY...
HEY, YOU! PASSING STRANGERS!
MA'AM?
SCREECH!
PLEASE, BOYS, TAKE ME WITH YOU! TAKE ME FROM THIS PLACE! PLEASE!
WELL.. SURE, O.K., IF THAT'S WHAT YOU WANT.
BOYS, I'M OFF TO START A NEW LIFE! YES, A LIFE IN WHICH I CAN BE MY OWN WOMAN! AND I'M WILLING TO RIDE TO THE ENDS OF THE EARTH TO FIND IT!
RRRRR
ACTUALLY, WE HAVE TO BE BACK AT SCHOOL NEXT WEEK.
RRRRR
©BTrudeau

9/10/72

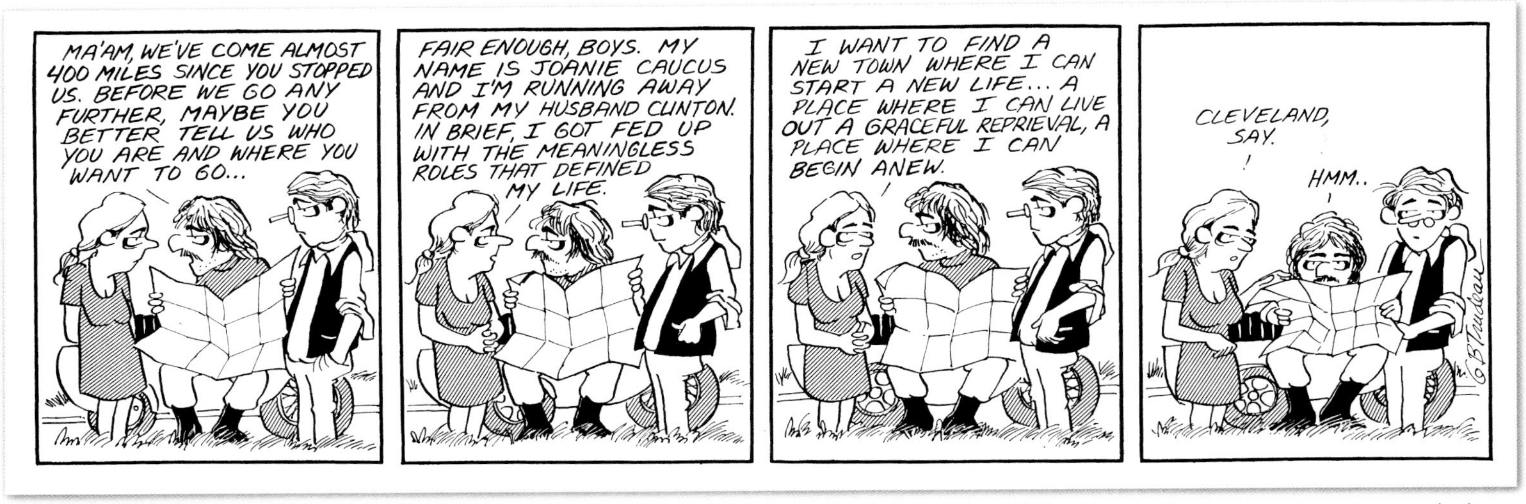
MA'AM, WE'VE COME ALMOST 400 MILES SINCE YOU STOPPED US. BEFORE WE GO ANY FURTHER, MAYBE YOU BETTER TELL US WHO YOU ARE AND WHERE YOU WANT TO GO...
FAIR ENOUGH, BOYS. MY NAME IS JOANIE CAUCUS AND I'M RUNNING AWAY FROM MY HUSBAND CLINTON. IN BRIEF, I GOT FED UP WITH THE MEANINGLESS ROLES THAT DEFINED MY LIFE.
I WANT TO FIND A NEW TOWN WHERE I CAN START A NEW LIFE... A PLACE WHERE I CAN LIVE OUT A GRACEFUL REPRIEVAL, A PLACE WHERE I CAN BEGIN ANEW.
CLEVELAND, SAY.
HMM..

9/11/72

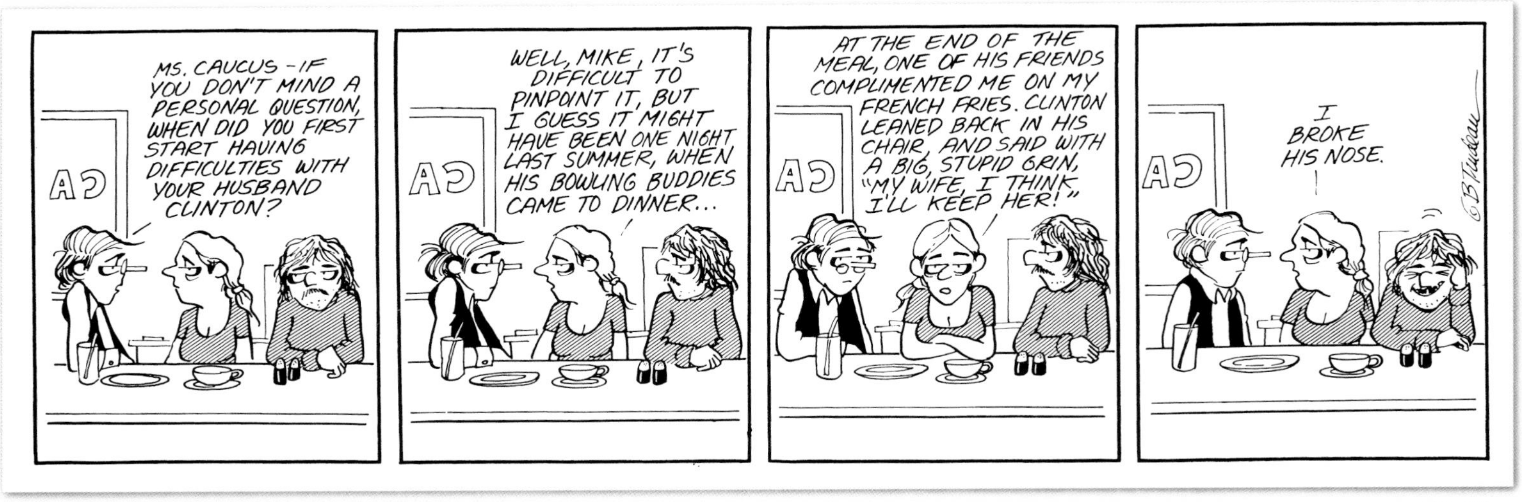
MS. CAUCUS - IF YOU DON'T MIND A PERSONAL QUESTION, WHEN DID YOU FIRST START HAVING DIFFICULTIES WITH YOUR HUSBAND CLINTON?
WELL, MIKE, IT'S DIFFICULT TO PINPOINT IT, BUT I GUESS IT MIGHT HAVE BEEN ONE NIGHT LAST SUMMER, WHEN HIS BOWLING BUDDIES CAME TO DINNER...
AT THE END OF THE MEAL, ONE OF HIS FRIENDS COMPLIMENTED ME ON MY FRENCH FRIES. CLINTON LEANED BACK IN HIS CHAIR, AND SAID WITH A BIG, STUPID GRIN, "MY WIFE, I THINK I'LL KEEP HER!"
I BROKE HIS NOSE.

9/12/72

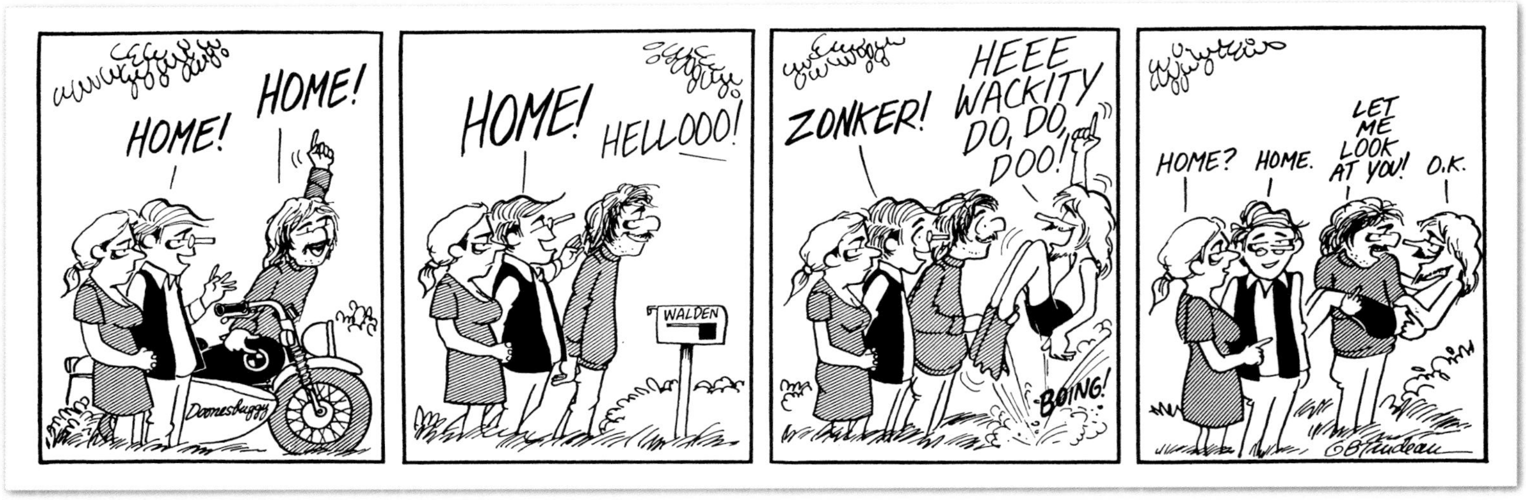
HOME!
HOME!
Doonesbuggy
HOME!
HELLOOO!
WALDEN
ZONKER!
HEEE WACKITY DO, DO, DOO!
BOING!
HOME?
HOME.
LET ME LOOK AT YOU!
O.K.

9/18/72

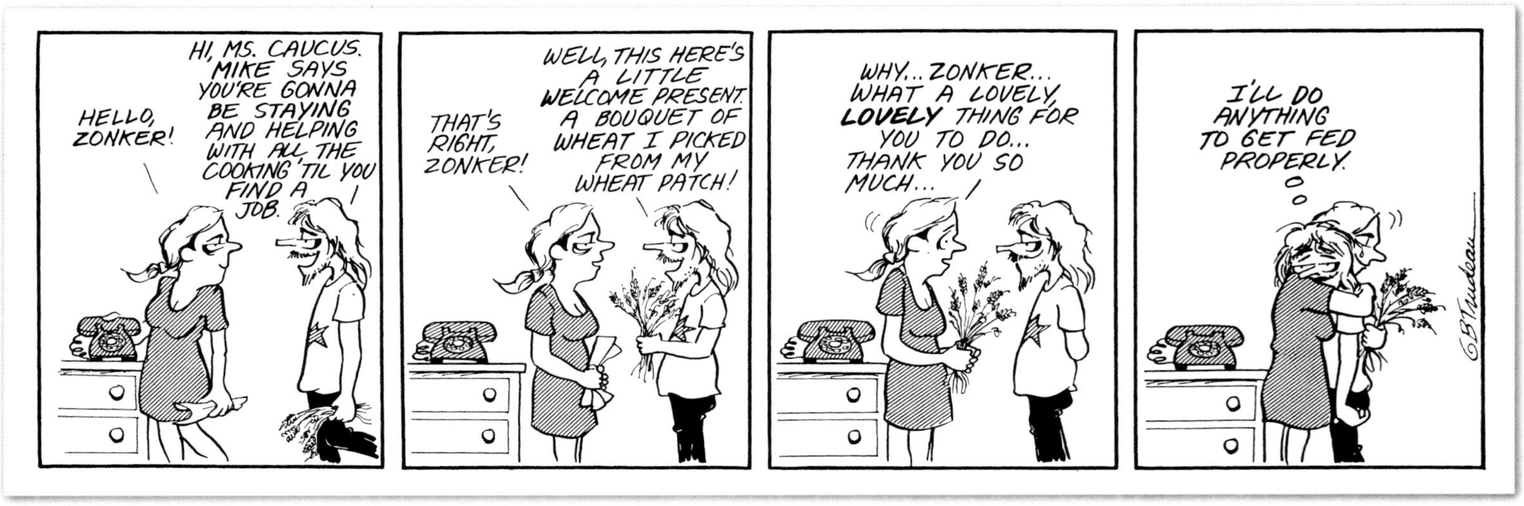
HELLO, ZONKER!
HI, MS. CAUCUS. MIKE SAYS YOU'RE GONNA BE STAYING AND HELPING WITH ALL THE COOKING 'TIL YOU FIND A JOB.
THAT'S RIGHT, ZONKER!
WELL, THIS HERE'S A LITTLE WELCOME PRESENT. A BOUQUET OF WHEAT I PICKED FROM MY WHEAT PATCH!
WHY... ZONKER... WHAT A LOVELY, LOVELY THING FOR YOU TO DO... THANK YOU SO MUCH...
I'LL DO ANYTHING TO GET FED PROPERLY.

9/21/72

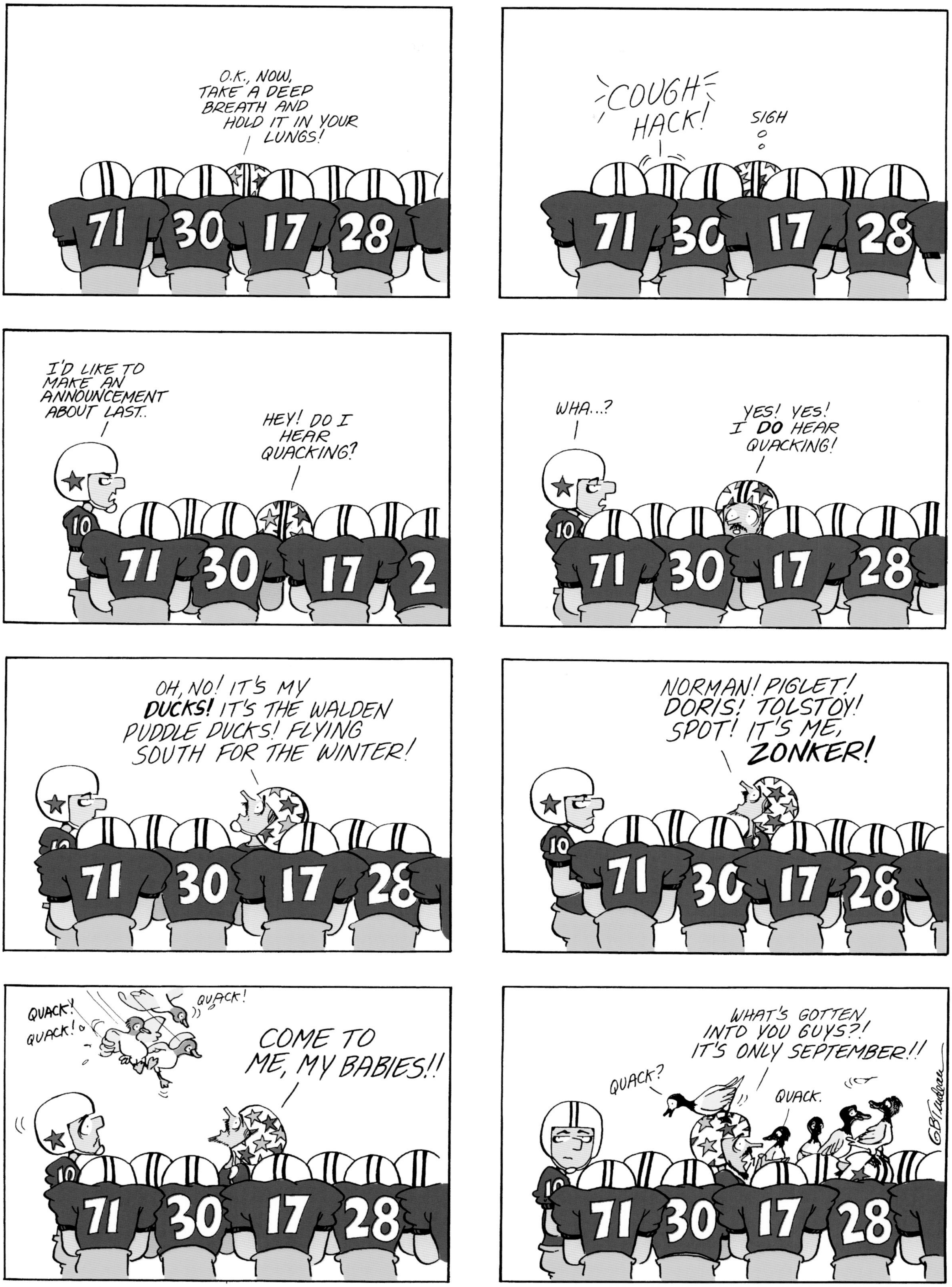
O.K., NOW, TAKE A DEEP BREATH AND HOLD IT IN YOUR LUNGS!
71 30 17 28
COUGH HACK!
SIGH
71 30 17 28
I'D LIKE TO MAKE AN ANNOUNCEMENT ABOUT LAST..
HEY! DO I HEAR QUACKING?
10 71 30 17 2
WHA...?
YES! YES! I DO HEAR QUACKING!
10 71 30 17 28
OH, NO! IT'S MY DUCKS! IT'S THE WALDEN PUDDLE DUCKS! FLYING SOUTH FOR THE WINTER!
71 30 17 28
NORMAN! PIGLET! DORIS! TOLSTOY! SPOT! IT'S ME, ZONKER!
10 71 30 17 28
QUACK! QUACK!
QUACK!
COME TO ME, MY BABIES!!
10 71 30 17 28
WHAT'S GOTTEN INTO YOU GUYS?! IT'S ONLY SEPTEMBER!!
QUACK?
QUACK.
GBTrudeau
71 30 17 28

9/24/72

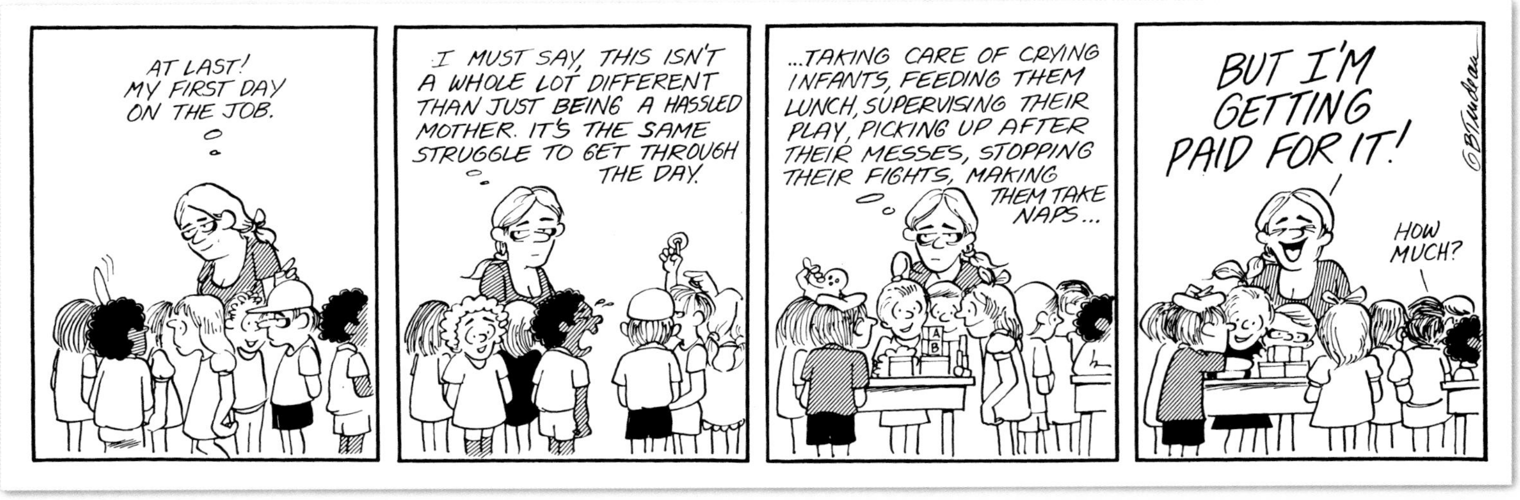
AT LAST! MY FIRST DAY ON THE JOB.
I MUST SAY, THIS ISN'T A WHOLE LOT DIFFERENT THAN JUST BEING A HASSLED MOTHER. IT'S THE SAME STRUGGLE TO GET THROUGH THE DAY.
...TAKING CARE OF CRYING INFANTS, FEEDING THEM LUNCH, SUPERVISING THEIR PLAY, PICKING UP AFTER THEIR MESSES, STOPPING THEIR FIGHTS, MAKING THEM TAKE NAPS...
BUT I'M GETTING PAID FOR IT!
HOW MUCH?

10/10/72

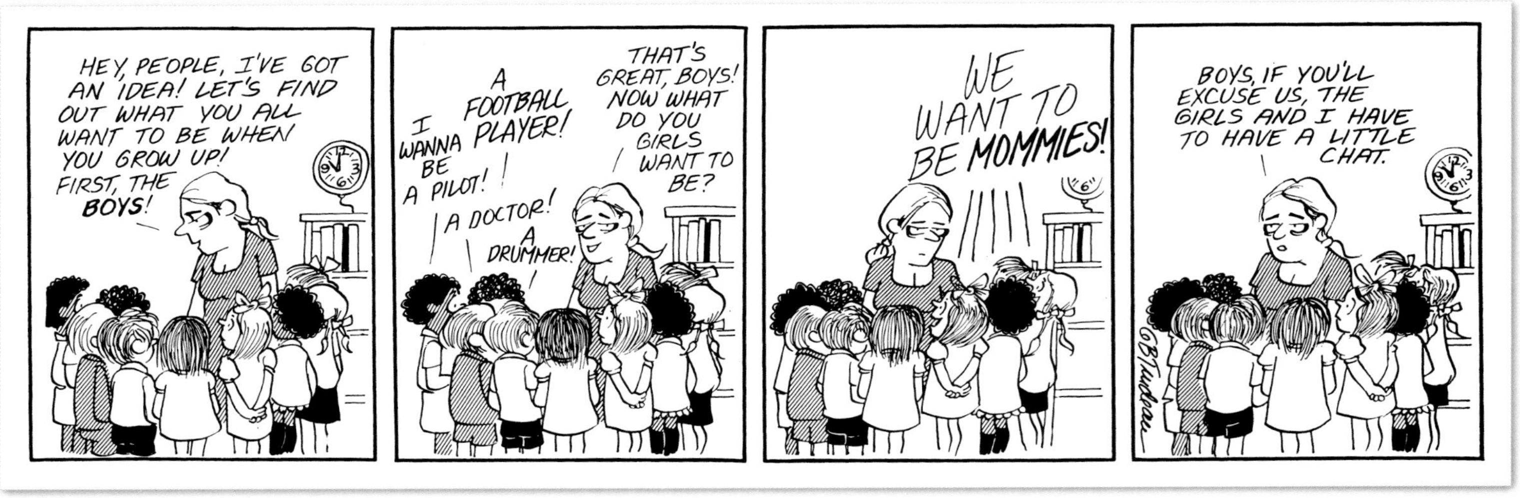
HEY, PEOPLE, I'VE GOT AN IDEA! LET'S FIND OUT WHAT YOU ALL WANT TO BE WHEN YOU GROW UP! FIRST, THE BOYS!
I WANNA BE A PILOT!
A FOOTBALL PLAYER!
A DOCTOR!
A DRUMMER!
THAT'S GREAT, BOYS! NOW WHAT DO YOU GIRLS WANT TO BE?
WE WANT TO BE MOMMIES!
BOYS, IF YOU'LL EXCUSE US, THE GIRLS AND I HAVE TO HAVE A LITTLE CHAT.

10/11/72

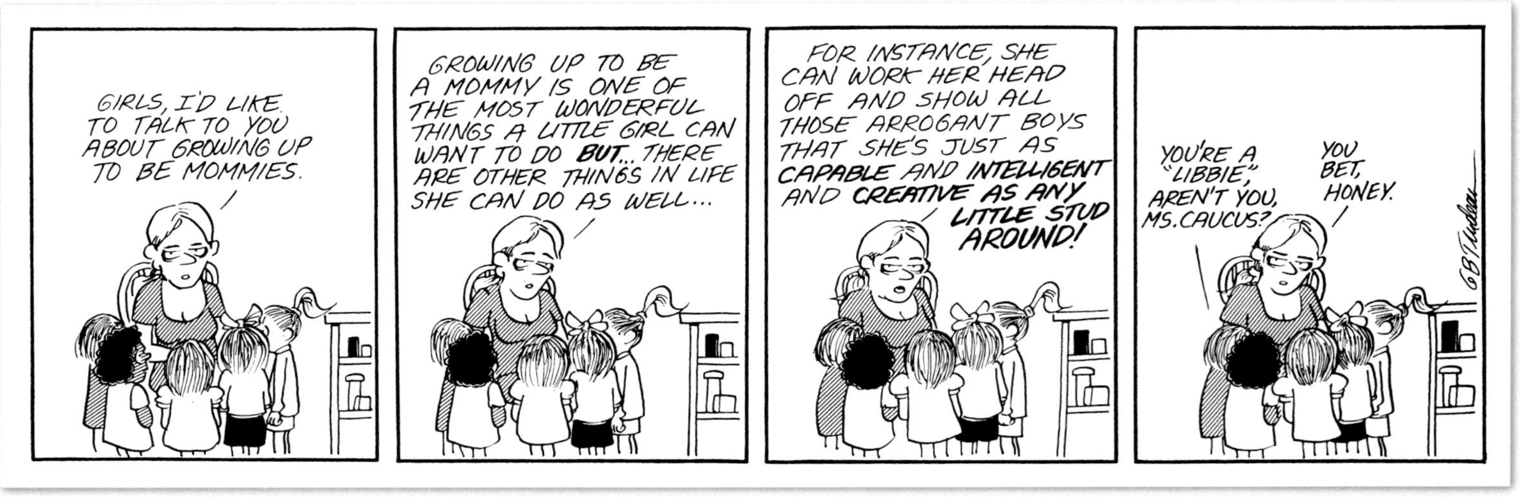
GIRLS, I'D LIKE TO TALK TO YOU ABOUT GROWING UP TO BE MOMMIES.
GROWING UP TO BE A MOMMY IS ONE OF THE MOST WONDERFUL THINGS A LITTLE GIRL CAN WANT TO DO BUT... THERE ARE OTHER THINGS IN LIFE SHE CAN DO AS WELL...
FOR INSTANCE, SHE CAN WORK HER HEAD OFF AND SHOW ALL THOSE ARROGANT BOYS THAT SHE'S JUST AS CAPABLE AND INTELLIGENT AND CREATIVE AS ANY LITTLE STUD AROUND!
YOU'RE A "LIBBIE," AREN'T YOU, MS. CAUCUS?
YOU BET, HONEY.

10/12/72

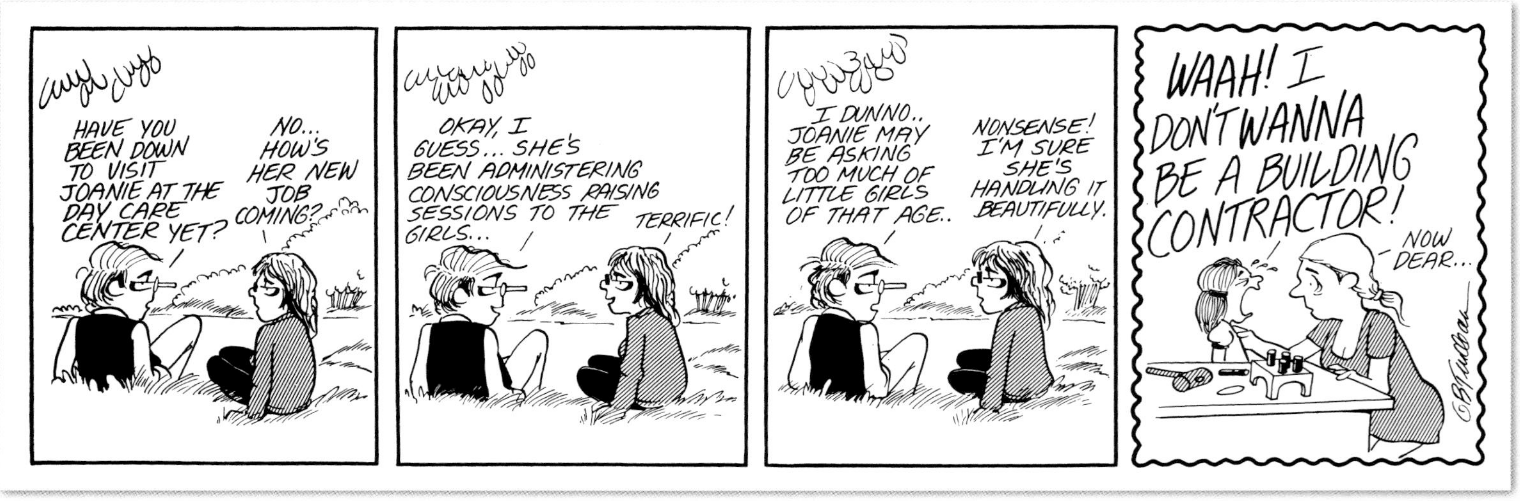
HAVE YOU BEEN DOWN TO VISIT JOANIE AT THE DAY CARE CENTER YET?
NO... HOW'S HER NEW JOB COMING?
OKAY, I GUESS... SHE'S BEEN ADMINISTERING CONSCIOUSNESS RAISING SESSIONS TO THE GIRLS...
TERRIFIC!
I DUNNO.. JOANIE MAY BE ASKING TOO MUCH OF LITTLE GIRLS OF THAT AGE..
NONSENSE! I'M SURE SHE'S HANDLING IT BEAUTIFULLY.
WAAH! I DON'T WANNA BE A BUILDING CONTRACTOR!
NOW DEAR...

10/16/72

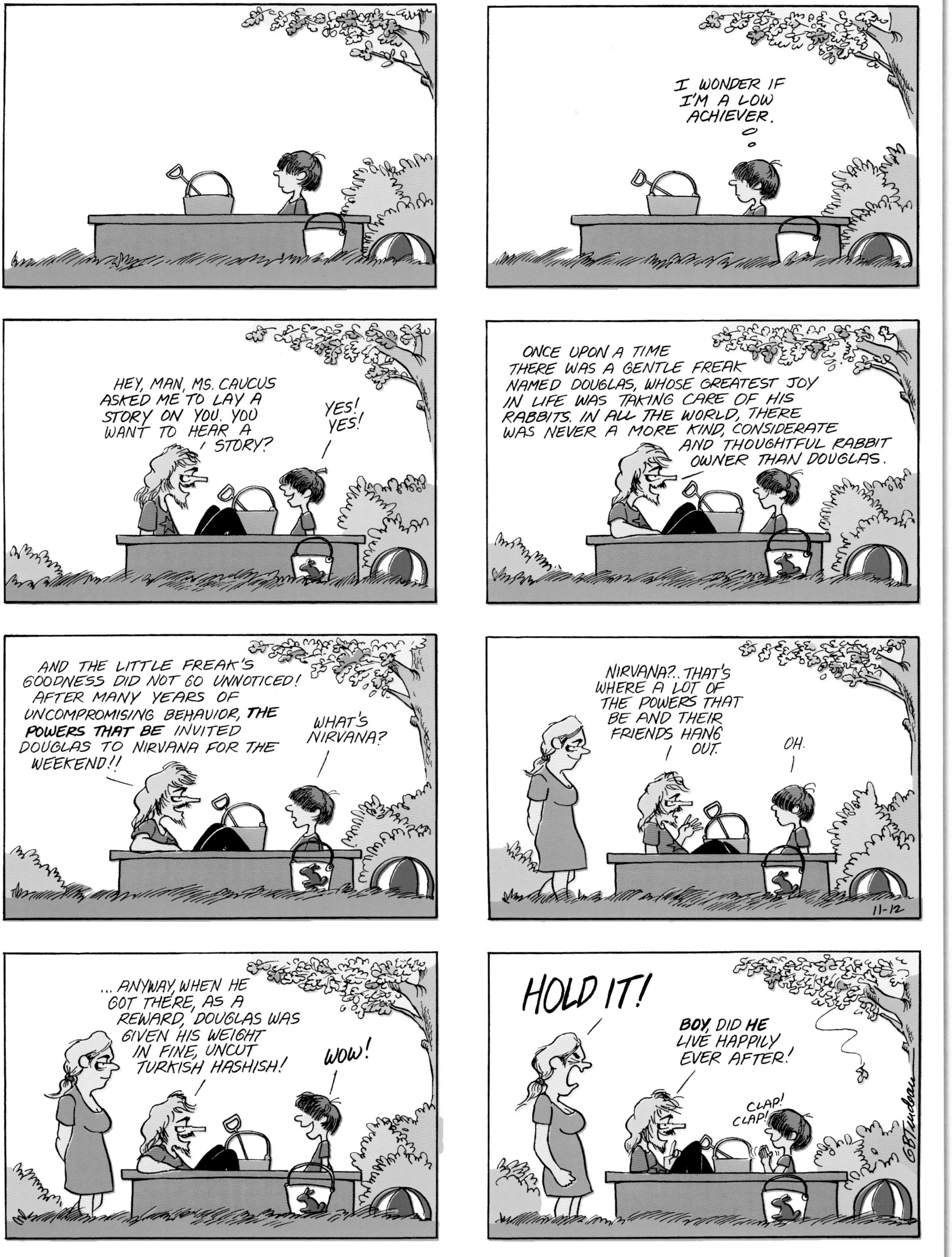

I WONDER IF I'M A LOW ACHIEVER.
HEY, MAN, MS. CAUCUS ASKED ME TO LAY A STORY ON YOU. YOU WANT TO HEAR A STORY?
YES! YES!
ONCE UPON A TIME THERE WAS A GENTLE FREAK NAMED DOUGLAS, WHOSE GREATEST JOY IN LIFE WAS TAKING CARE OF HIS RABBITS. IN ALL THE WORLD, THERE WAS NEVER A MORE KIND, CONSIDERATE AND THOUGHTFUL RABBIT OWNER THAN DOUGLAS.
AND THE LITTLE FREAK'S GOODNESS DID NOT GO UNNOTICED! AFTER MANY YEARS OF UNCOMPROMISING BEHAVIOR, THE POWERS THAT BE INVITED DOUGLAS TO NIRVANA FOR THE WEEKEND!!
WHAT'S NIRVANA?
NIRVANA?.. THAT'S WHERE A LOT OF THE POWERS THAT BE AND THEIR FRIENDS HANG OUT.
OH.
11-12
...ANYWAY, WHEN HE GOT THERE, AS A REWARD, DOUGLAS WAS GIVEN HIS WEIGHT IN FINE, UNCUT TURKISH HASHISH!
WOW!
HOLD IT!
BOY, DID HE LIVE HAPPILY EVER AFTER!
CLAP! CLAP!
GBTrudeau

11/12/72

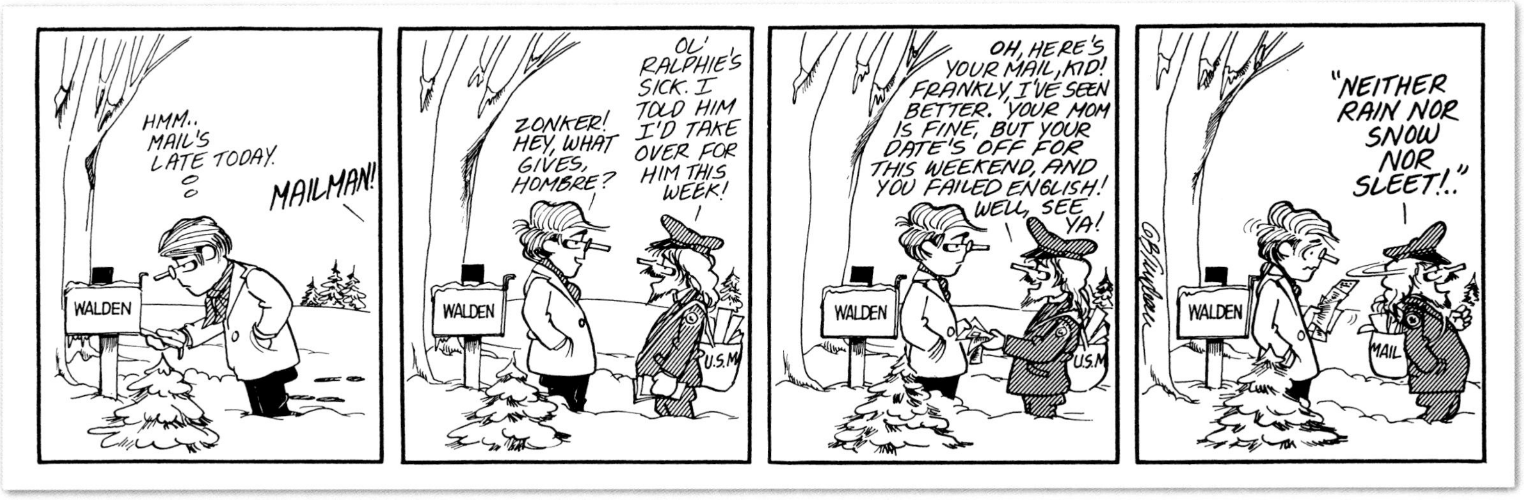
HMM.. MAIL'S LATE TODAY.
MAILMAN!
ZONKER! HEY, WHAT GIVES, HOMBRE?
OL' RALPHIE'S SICK. I TOLD HIM I'D TAKE OVER FOR HIM THIS WEEK!
WALDEN
U.S.M
OH, HERE'S YOUR MAIL, KID! FRANKLY, I'VE SEEN BETTER. YOUR MOM IS FINE, BUT YOUR DATE'S OFF FOR THIS WEEKEND, AND YOU FAILED ENGLISH! WELL, SEE YA!
"NEITHER RAIN NOR SNOW NOR SLEET!.."
MAIL

1/16/73

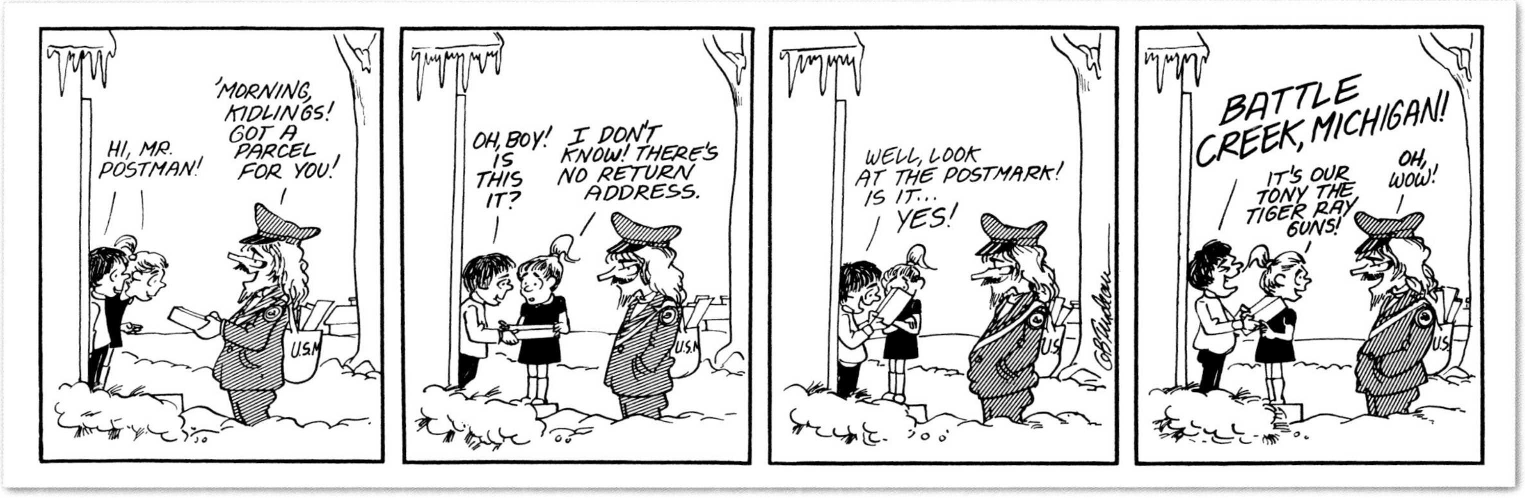
HI, MR. POSTMAN!
'MORNING, KIDLINGS! GOT A PARCEL FOR YOU!
OH, BOY! IS THIS IT?
I DON'T KNOW! THERE'S NO RETURN ADDRESS.
WELL, LOOK AT THE POSTMARK! IS IT...
YES!
BATTLE CREEK, MICHIGAN!
IT'S OUR TONY THE TIGER RAY GUNS!
OH, WOW!

1/17/73

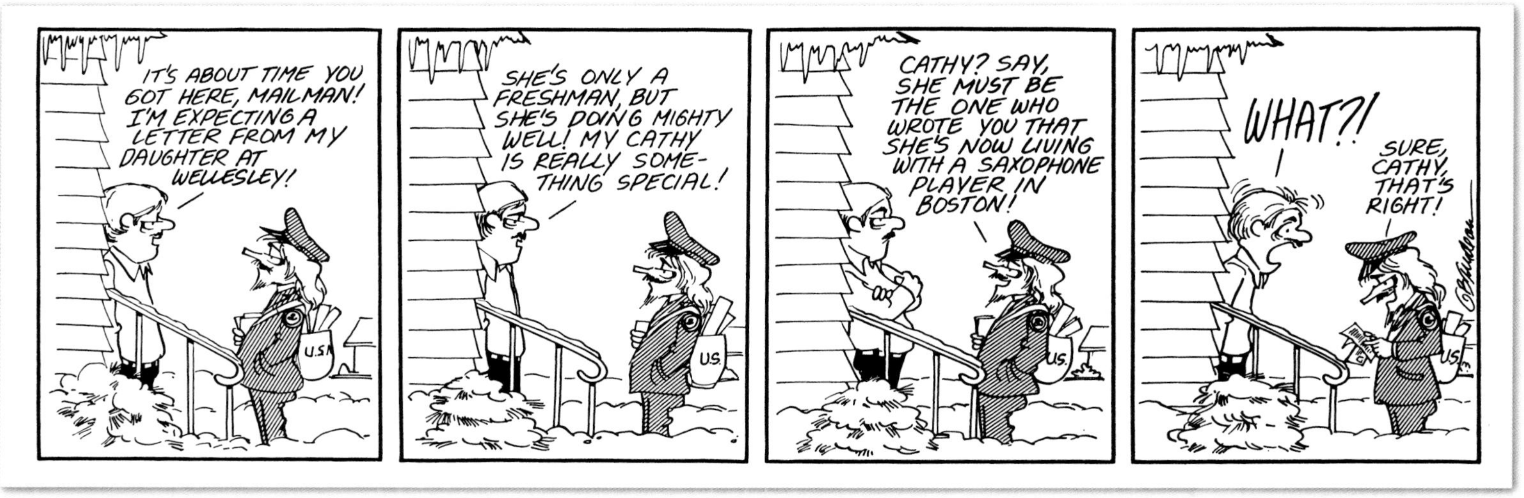
IT'S ABOUT TIME YOU GOT HERE, MAILMAN! I'M EXPECTING A LETTER FROM MY DAUGHTER AT WELLESLEY!
SHE'S ONLY A FRESHMAN, BUT SHE'S DOING MIGHTY WELL! MY CATHY IS REALLY SOMETHING SPECIAL!
CATHY? SAY, SHE MUST BE THE ONE WHO WROTE YOU THAT SHE'S NOW LIVING WITH A SAXOPHONE PLAYER IN BOSTON!
WHAT?!
SURE, CATHY, THAT'S RIGHT!

1/18/73

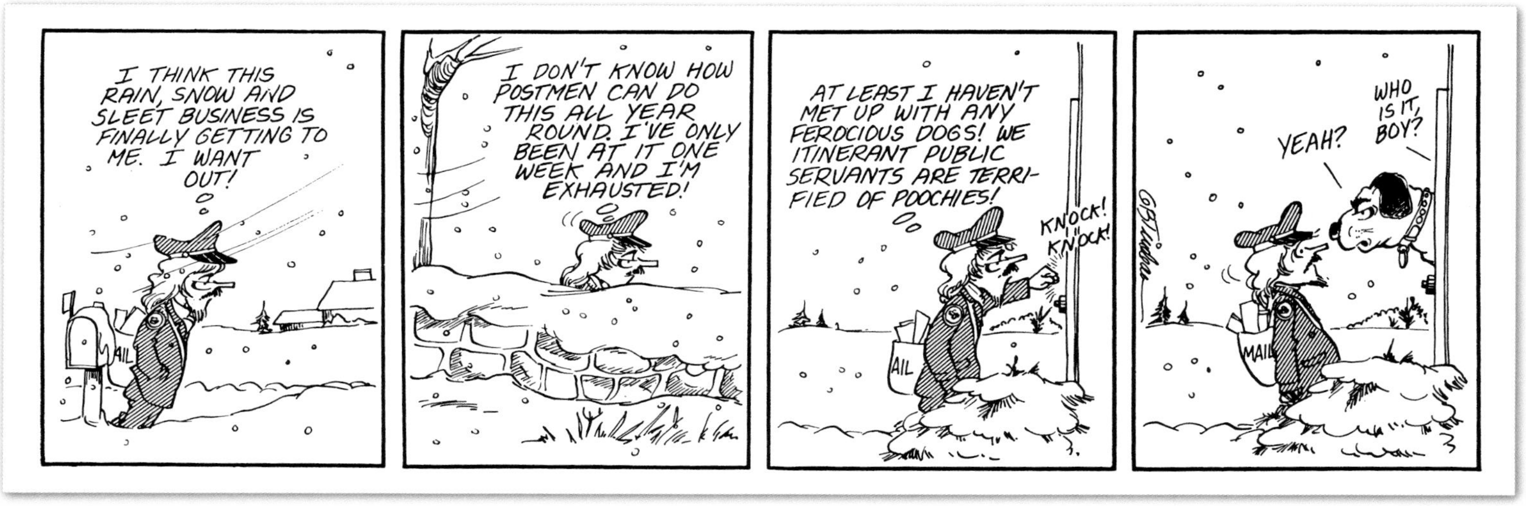
I THINK THIS RAIN, SNOW AND SLEET BUSINESS IS FINALLY GETTING TO ME. I WANT OUT!
I DON'T KNOW HOW POSTMEN CAN DO THIS ALL YEAR ROUND. I'VE ONLY BEEN AT IT ONE WEEK AND I'M EXHAUSTED!
AT LEAST I HAVEN'T MET UP WITH ANY FEROCIOUS DOGS! WE ITINERANT PUBLIC SERVANTS ARE TERRIFIED OF POOCHIES!
KNOCK! KNOCK!
YEAH?
WHO IS IT, BOY?

1/19/73

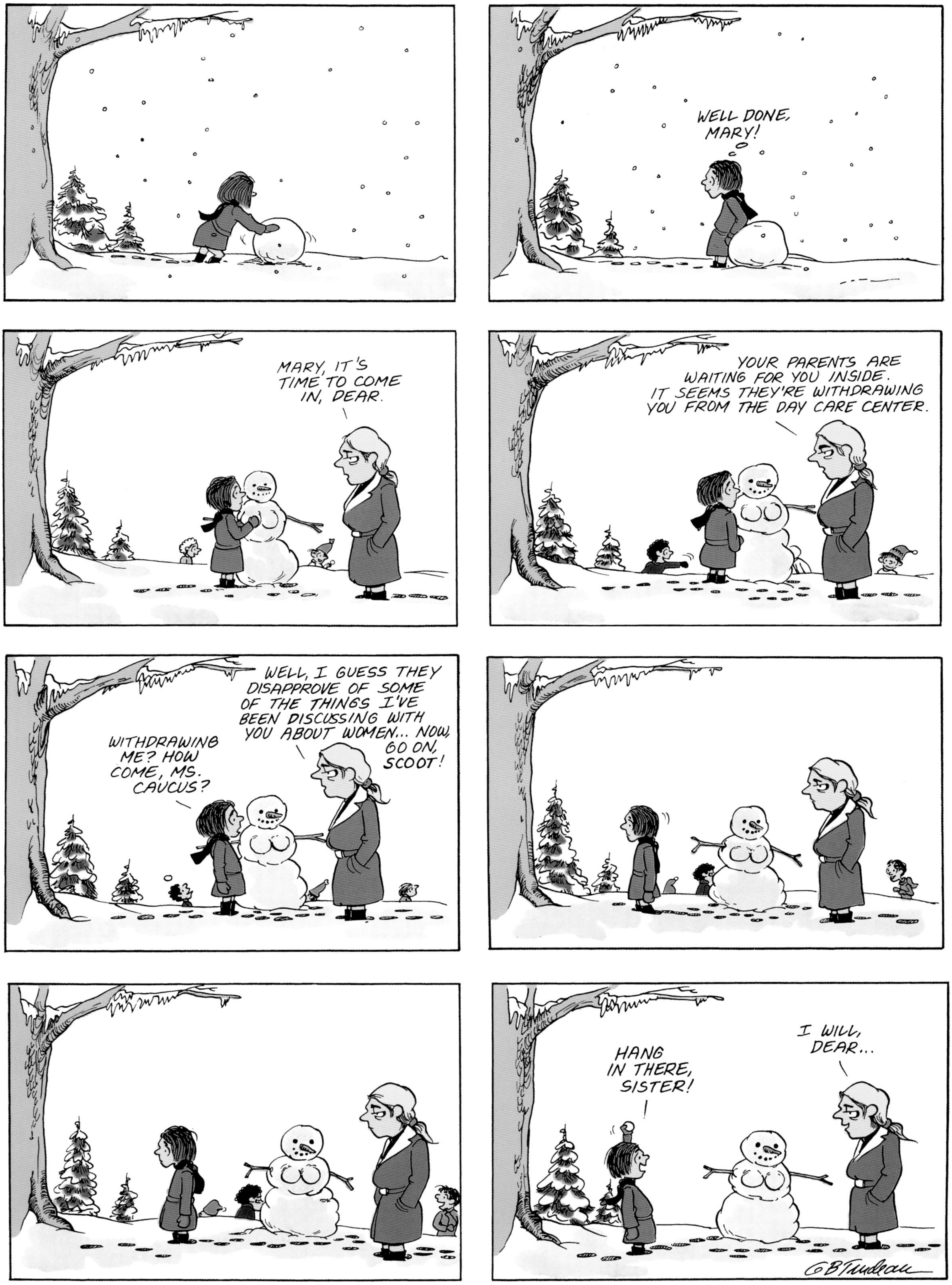
WELL DONE, MARY!
MARY, IT'S TIME TO COME IN, DEAR.
YOUR PARENTS ARE WAITING FOR YOU INSIDE. IT SEEMS THEY'RE WITHDRAWING YOU FROM THE DAY CARE CENTER.
WITHDRAWING ME? HOW COME, MS. CAUCUS?
WELL, I GUESS THEY DISAPPROVE OF SOME OF THE THINGS I'VE BEEN DISCUSSING WITH YOU ABOUT WOMEN... NOW, GO ON, SCOOT!
HANG IN THERE, SISTER!
I WILL, DEAR...
©BTrudeau

1/14/73

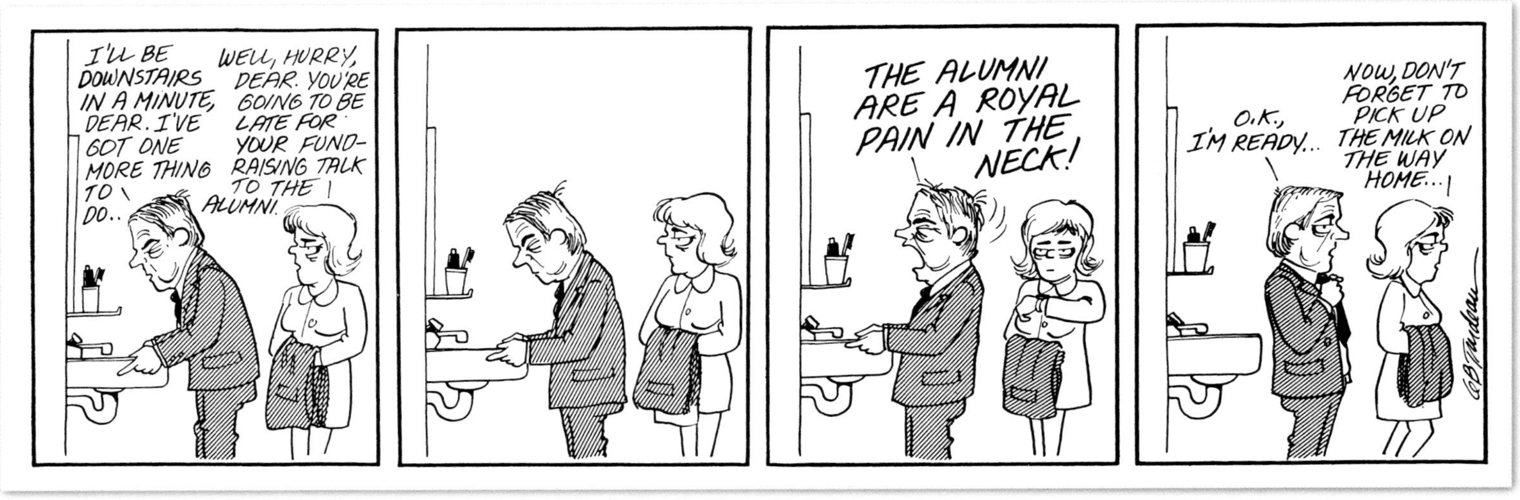
I'LL BE DOWNSTAIRS IN A MINUTE, DEAR. I'VE GOT ONE MORE THING TO DO..
WELL, HURRY, DEAR. YOU'RE GOING TO BE LATE FOR YOUR FUND-RAISING TALK TO THE ALUMNI!
THE ALUMNI ARE A ROYAL PAIN IN THE NECK!
O.K., I'M READY...
NOW, DON'T FORGET TO PICK UP THE MILK ON THE WAY HOME...!

3/12/73

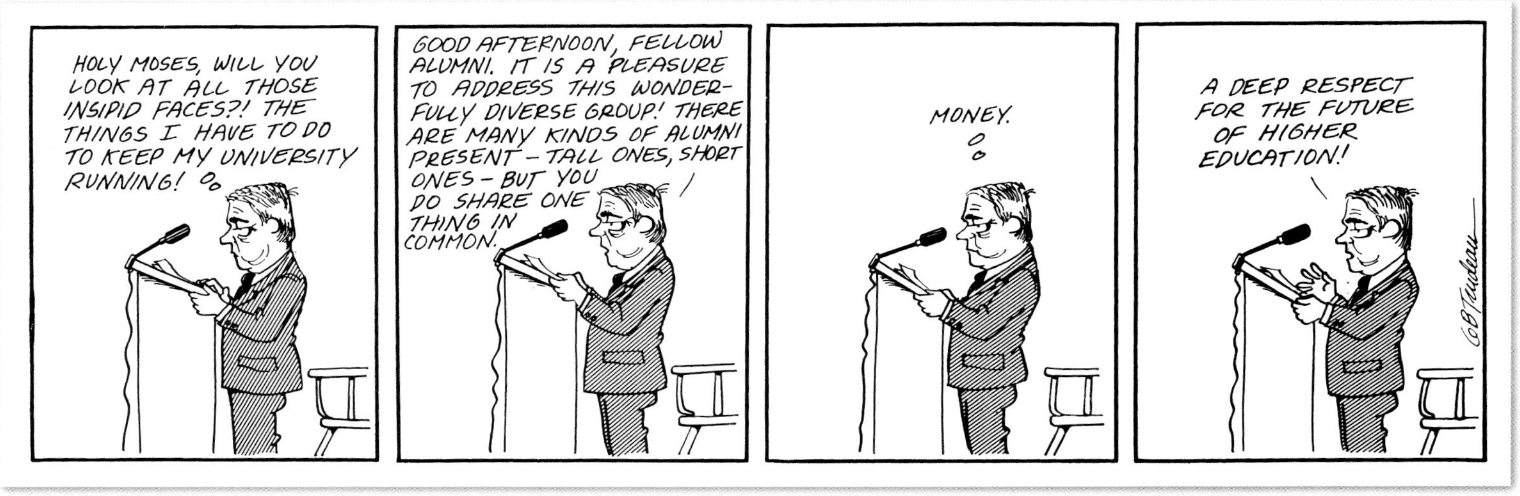
HOLY MOSES, WILL YOU LOOK AT ALL THOSE INSIPID FACES?! THE THINGS I HAVE TO DO TO KEEP MY UNIVERSITY RUNNING!
GOOD AFTERNOON, FELLOW ALUMNI. IT IS A PLEASURE TO ADDRESS THIS WONDERFULLY DIVERSE GROUP! THERE ARE MANY KINDS OF ALUMNI PRESENT - TALL ONES, SHORT ONES - BUT YOU DO SHARE ONE THING IN COMMON.
MONEY.
A DEEP RESPECT FOR THE FUTURE OF HIGHER EDUCATION!

3/13/73

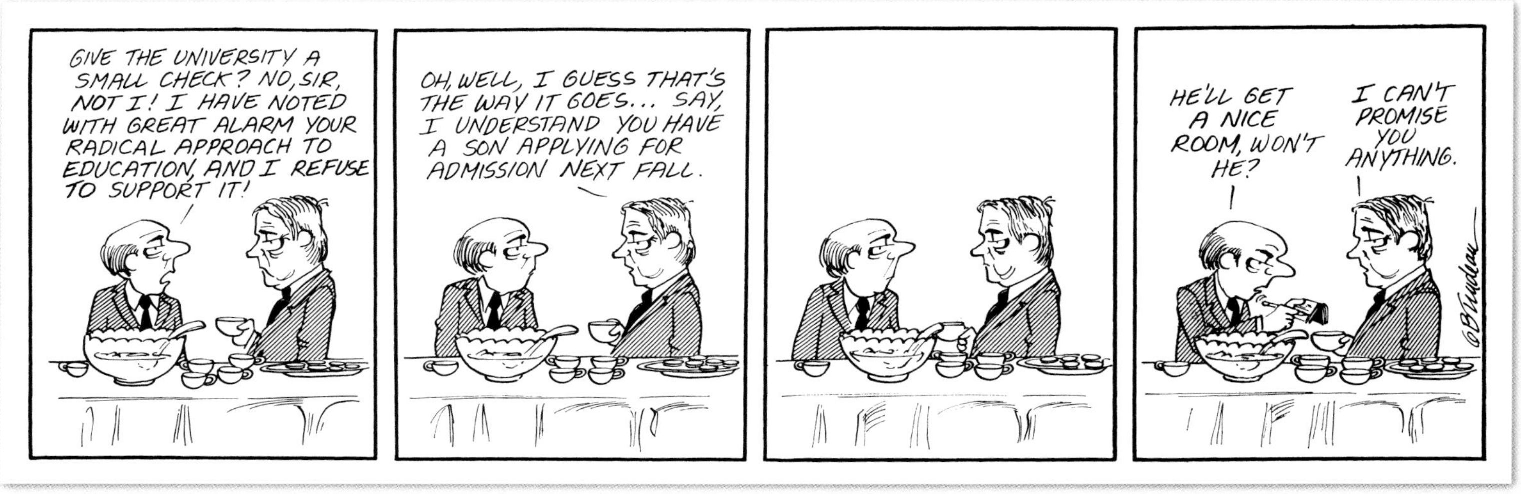
GIVE THE UNIVERSITY A SMALL CHECK? NO, SIR, NOT I! I HAVE NOTED WITH GREAT ALARM YOUR RADICAL APPROACH TO EDUCATION, AND I REFUSE TO SUPPORT IT!
OH, WELL, I GUESS THAT'S THE WAY IT GOES... SAY, I UNDERSTAND YOU HAVE A SON APPLYING FOR ADMISSION NEXT FALL.
HE'LL GET A NICE ROOM, WON'T HE?
I CAN'T PROMISE YOU ANYTHING.

3/15/73

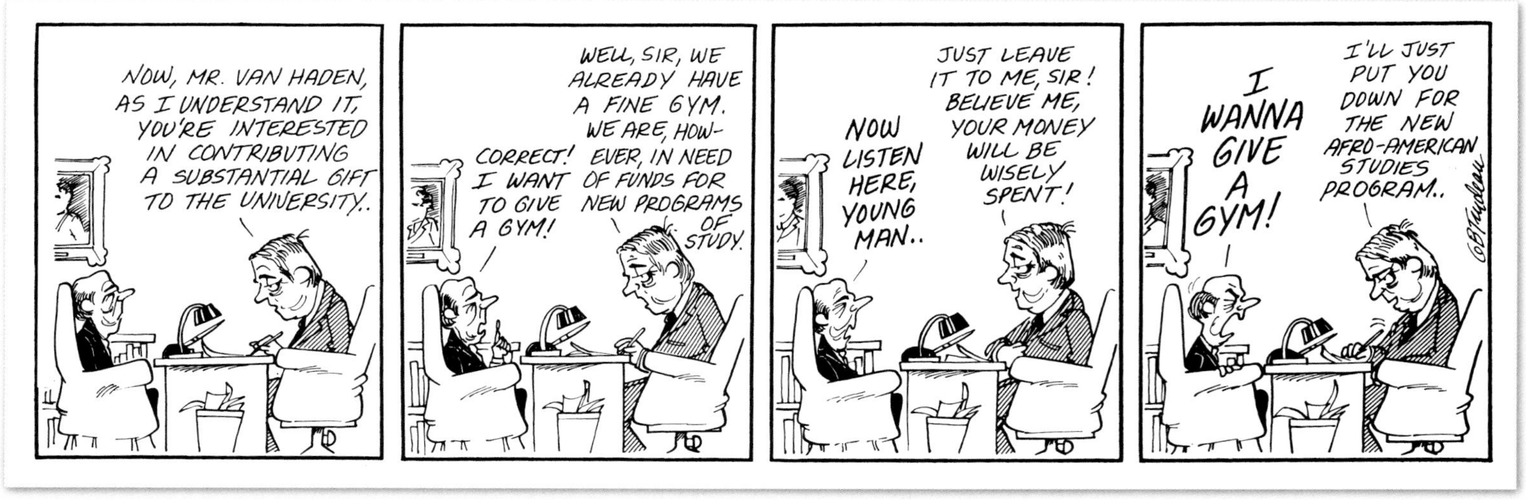
NOW, MR. VAN HADEN, AS I UNDERSTAND IT, YOU'RE INTERESTED IN CONTRIBUTING A SUBSTANTIAL GIFT TO THE UNIVERSITY..
CORRECT! I WANT TO GIVE A GYM!
WELL, SIR, WE ALREADY HAVE A FINE GYM. WE ARE, HOWEVER, IN NEED OF FUNDS FOR NEW PROGRAMS OF STUDY.
NOW LISTEN HERE, YOUNG MAN..
JUST LEAVE IT TO ME, SIR! BELIEVE ME, YOUR MONEY WILL BE WISELY SPENT!
I WANNA GIVE A GYM!
I'LL JUST PUT YOU DOWN FOR THE NEW AFRO-AMERICAN STUDIES PROGRAM..

3/16/73

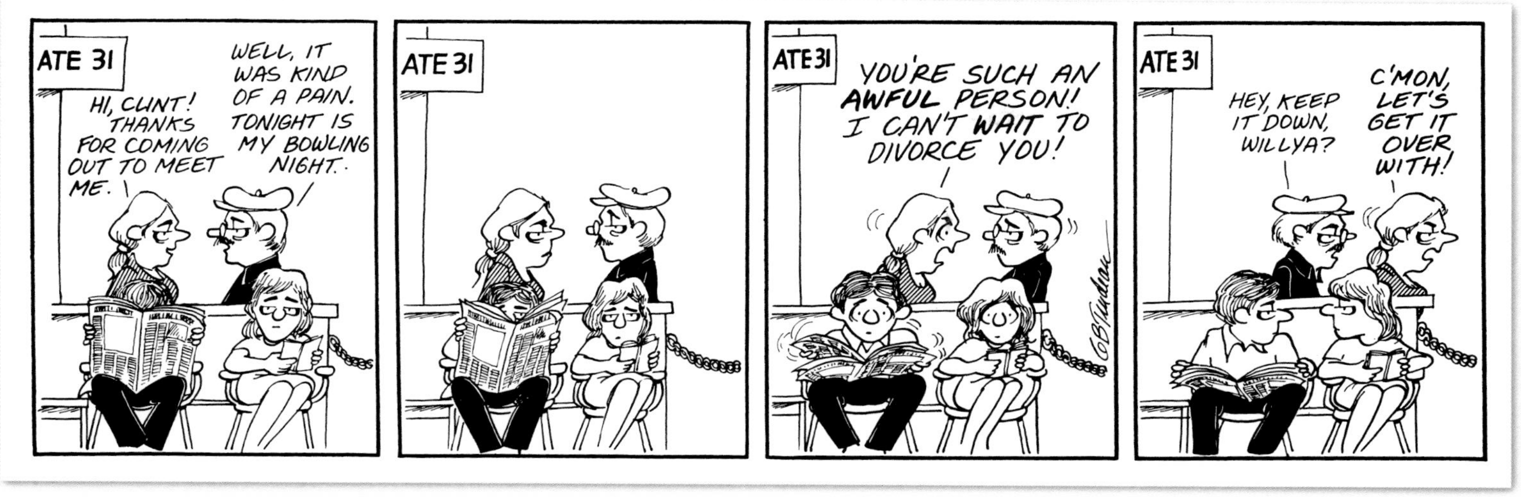
ATE 31
HI, CLINT! THANKS FOR COMING OUT TO MEET ME.
WELL, IT WAS KIND OF A PAIN. TONIGHT IS MY BOWLING NIGHT..
ATE 31
ATE 31
YOU'RE SUCH AN AWFUL PERSON! I CAN'T WAIT TO DIVORCE YOU!
ATE 31
HEY, KEEP IT DOWN, WILLYA?
C'MON, LET'S GET IT OVER WITH!

4/18/73

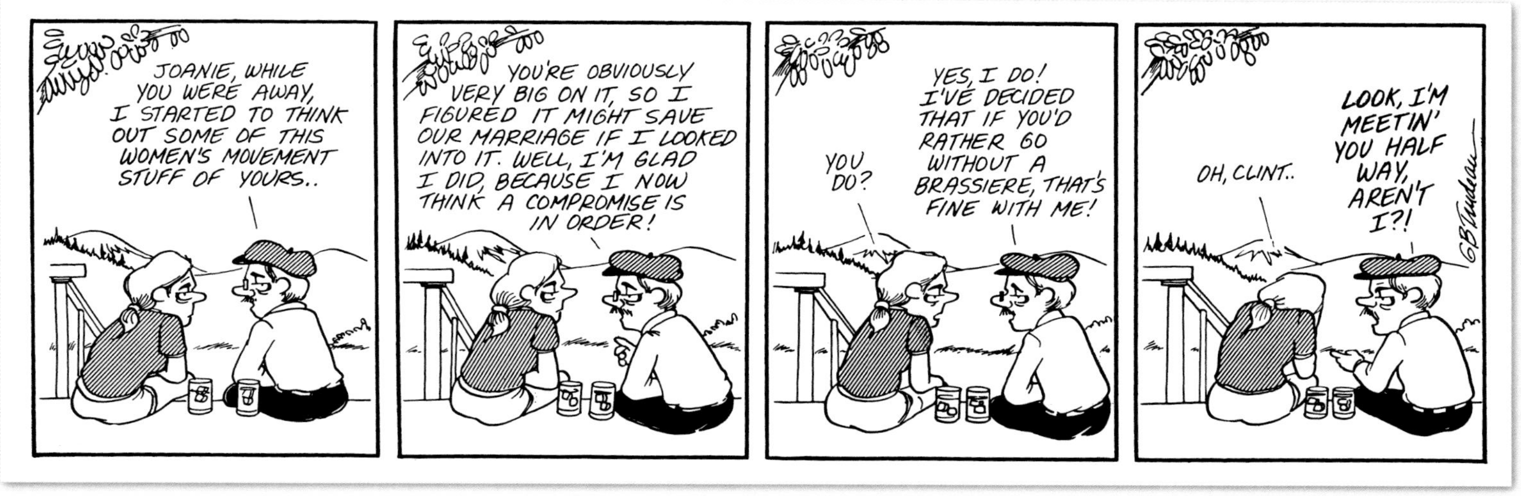
JOANIE, WHILE YOU WERE AWAY, I STARTED TO THINK OUT SOME OF THIS WOMEN'S MOVEMENT STUFF OF YOURS..
YOU'RE OBVIOUSLY VERY BIG ON IT, SO I FIGURED IT MIGHT SAVE OUR MARRIAGE IF I LOOKED INTO IT. WELL, I'M GLAD I DID, BECAUSE I NOW THINK A COMPROMISE IS IN ORDER!
YOU DO?
YES, I DO! I'VE DECIDED THAT IF YOU'D RATHER GO WITHOUT A BRASSIERE, THAT'S FINE WITH ME!
OH, CLINT..
LOOK, I'M MEETIN' YOU HALF WAY, AREN'T I?!

4/20/73

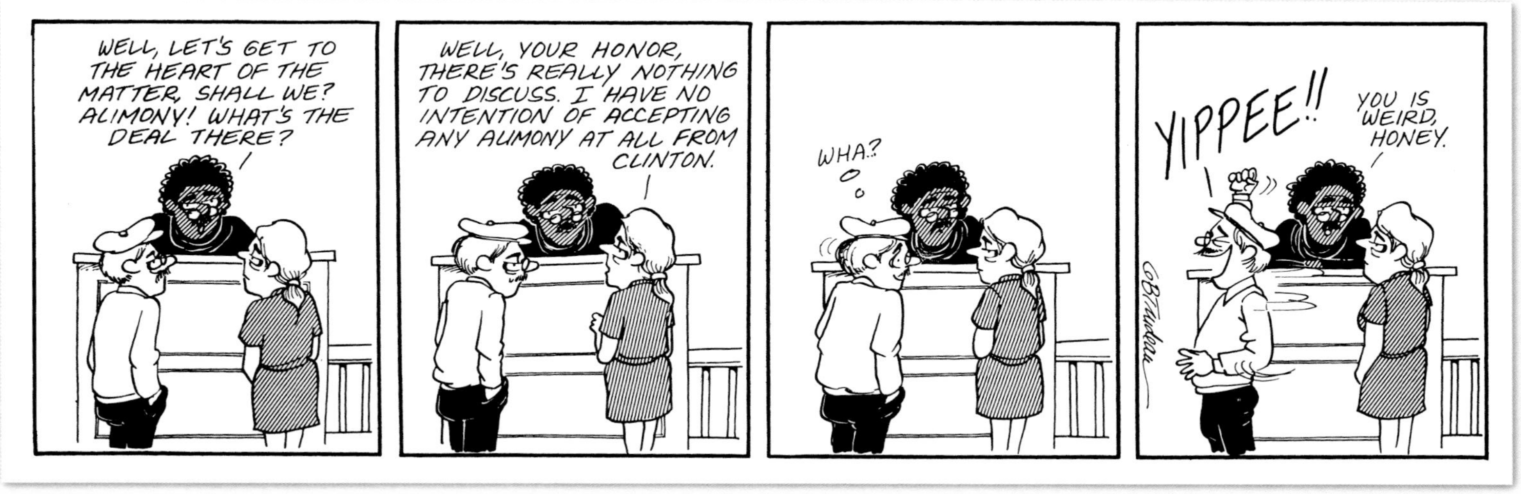
WELL, LET'S GET TO THE HEART OF THE MATTER, SHALL WE? ALIMONY! WHAT'S THE DEAL THERE?
WELL, YOUR HONOR, THERE'S REALLY NOTHING TO DISCUSS. I HAVE NO INTENTION OF ACCEPTING ANY ALIMONY AT ALL FROM CLINTON.
WHA?
YIPPEE!!
YOU IS WEIRD, HONEY.

4/24/73

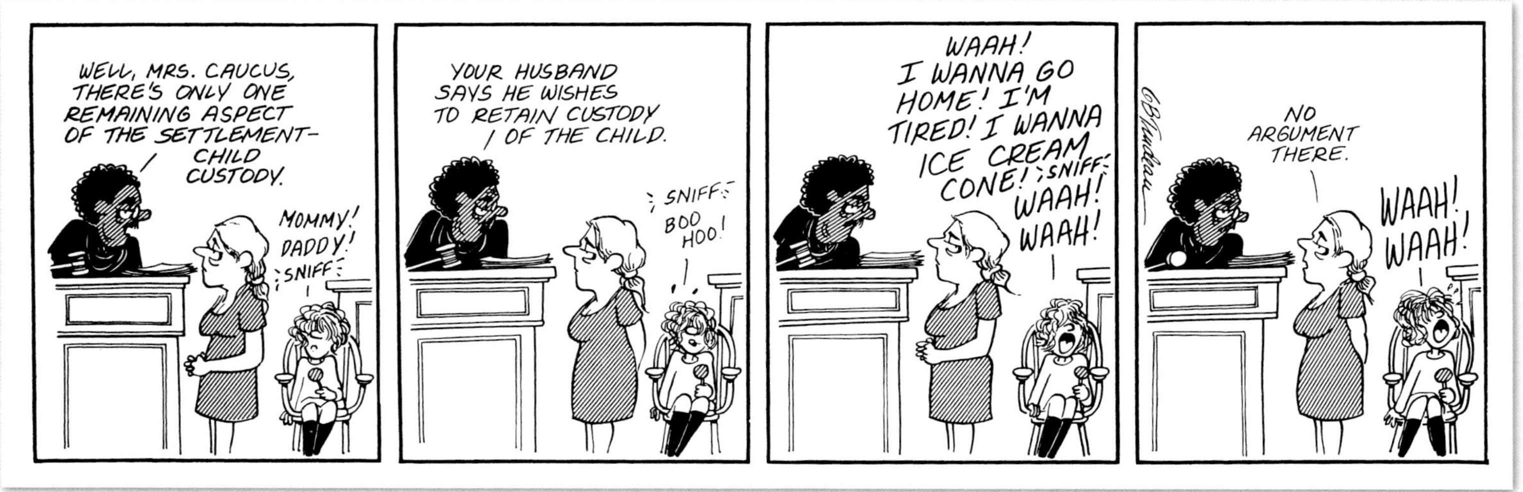
WELL, MRS. CAUCUS, THERE'S ONLY ONE REMAINING ASPECT OF THE SETTLEMENT— CHILD CUSTODY.
MOMMY! DADDY! SNIFF
YOUR HUSBAND SAYS HE WISHES TO RETAIN CUSTODY OF THE CHILD.
SNIFF BOO HOO!
WAAH! I WANNA GO HOME! I'M TIRED! I WANNA ICE CREAM CONE! SNIFF WAAH! WAAH!
NO ARGUMENT THERE.
WAAH! WAAH!

4/25/73

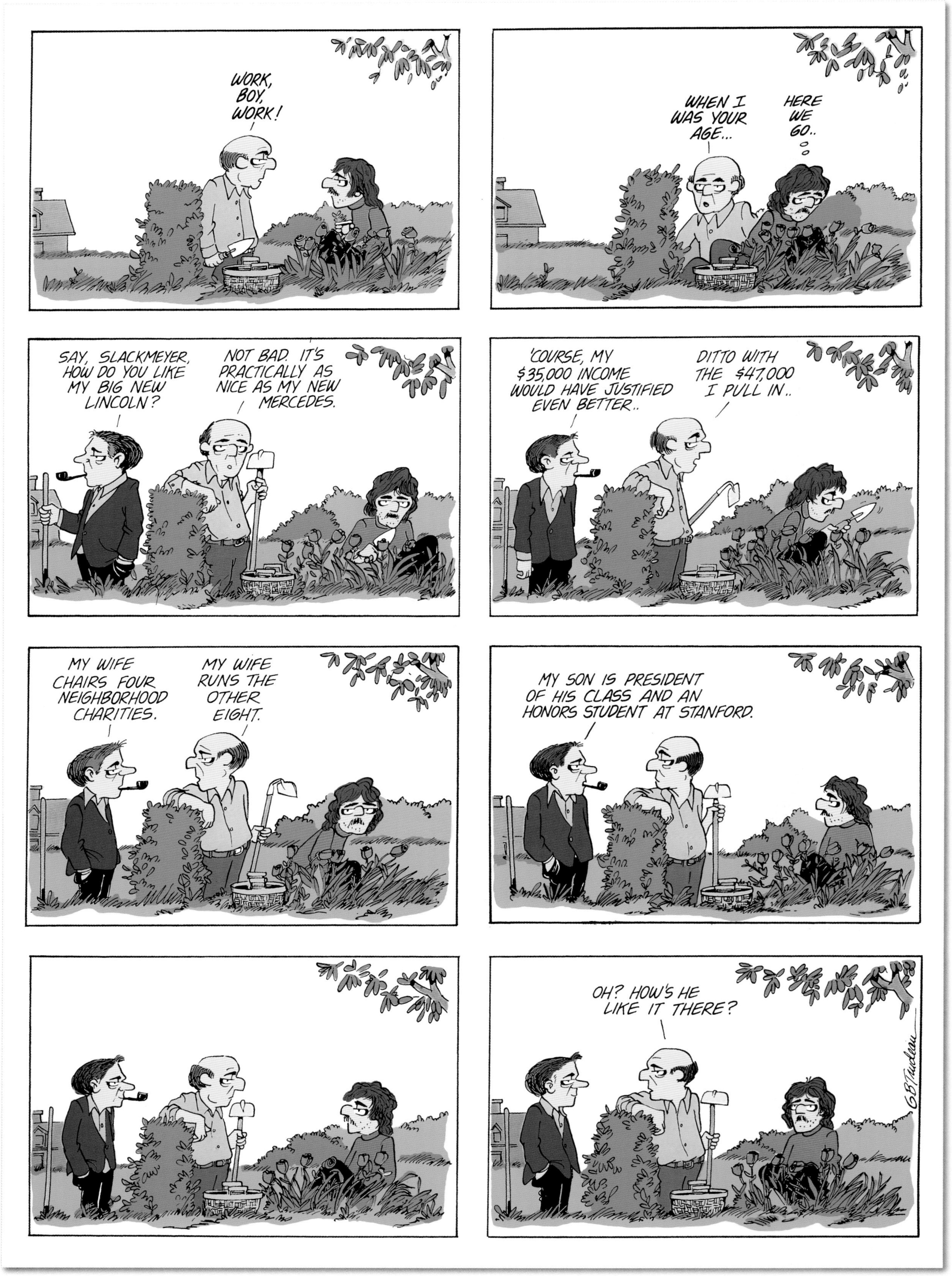
WORK, BOY, WORK!
WHEN I WAS YOUR AGE...
HERE WE GO..
SAY, SLACKMEYER, HOW DO YOU LIKE MY BIG NEW LINCOLN?
NOT BAD. IT'S PRACTICALLY AS NICE AS MY NEW MERCEDES.
'COURSE, MY $35,000 INCOME WOULD HAVE JUSTIFIED EVEN BETTER..
DITTO WITH THE $47,000 I PULL IN..
MY WIFE CHAIRS FOUR NEIGHBORHOOD CHARITIES.
MY WIFE RUNS THE OTHER EIGHT.
MY SON IS PRESIDENT OF HIS CLASS AND AN HONORS STUDENT AT STANFORD.
OH? HOW'S HE LIKE IT THERE?
GBTrudeau

8/12/73

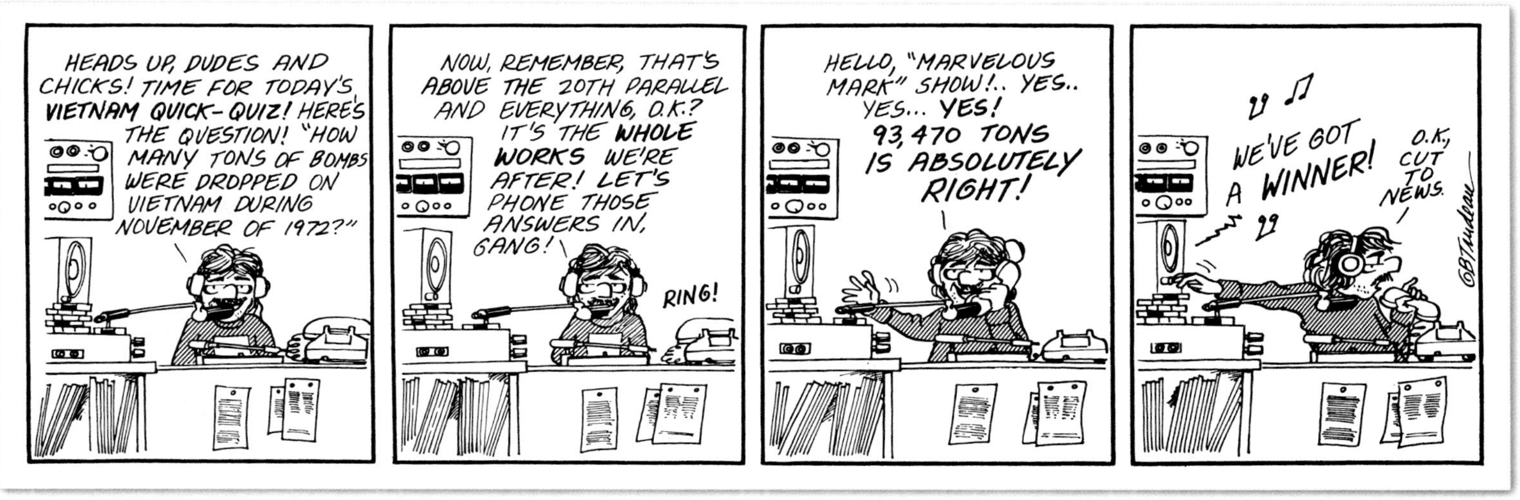
HEADS UP, DUDES AND CHICKS! TIME FOR TODAY'S VIETNAM QUICK-QUIZ! HERE'S THE QUESTION! "HOW MANY TONS OF BOMBS WERE DROPPED ON VIETNAM DURING NOVEMBER OF 1972?"
NOW, REMEMBER, THAT'S ABOVE THE 20TH PARALLEL AND EVERYTHING, O.K.? IT'S THE WHOLE WORKS WE'RE AFTER! LET'S PHONE THOSE ANSWERS IN, GANG!
RING!
HELLO, "MARVELOUS MARK" SHOW!.. YES.. YES... YES! 93,470 TONS IS ABSOLUTELY RIGHT!
WE'VE GOT A WINNER!
O.K., CUT TO NEWS.

2/15/73

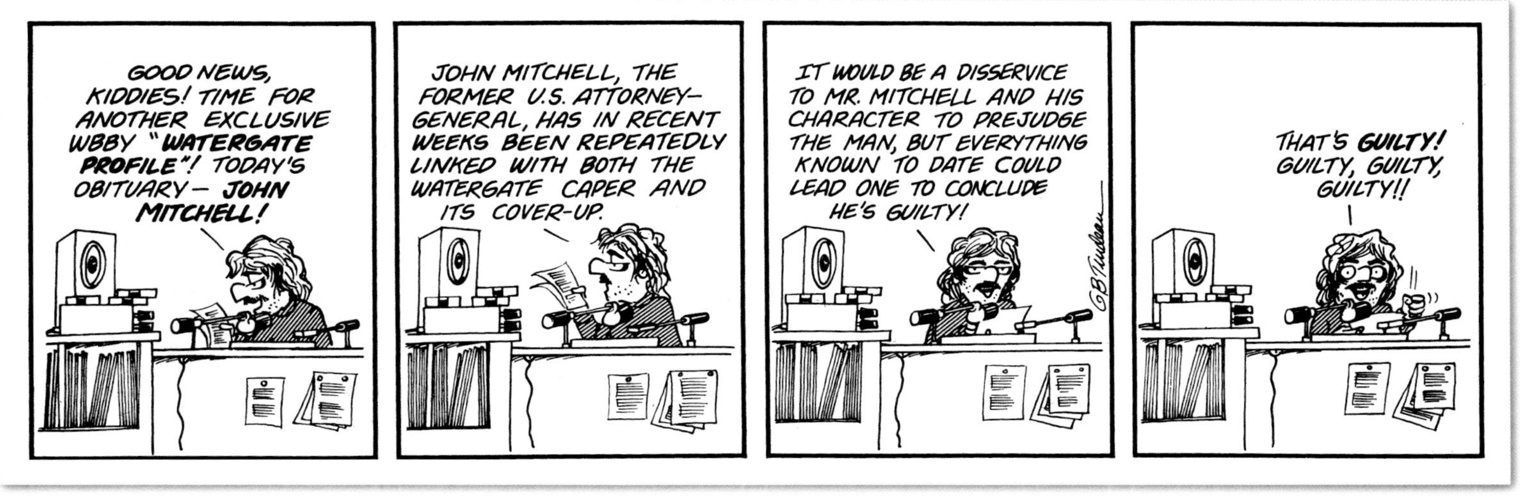
GOOD NEWS, KIDDIES! TIME FOR ANOTHER EXCLUSIVE WBBY "WATERGATE PROFILE"! TODAY'S OBITUARY— JOHN MITCHELL!
JOHN MITCHELL, THE FORMER U.S. ATTORNEY-GENERAL, HAS IN RECENT WEEKS BEEN REPEATEDLY LINKED WITH BOTH THE WATERGATE CAPER AND ITS COVER-UP.
IT WOULD BE A DISSERVICE TO MR. MITCHELL AND HIS CHARACTER TO PREJUDGE THE MAN, BUT EVERYTHING KNOWN TO DATE COULD LEAD ONE TO CONCLUDE HE'S GUILTY!
THAT'S GUILTY! GUILTY, GUILTY, GUILTY!!

5/29/73

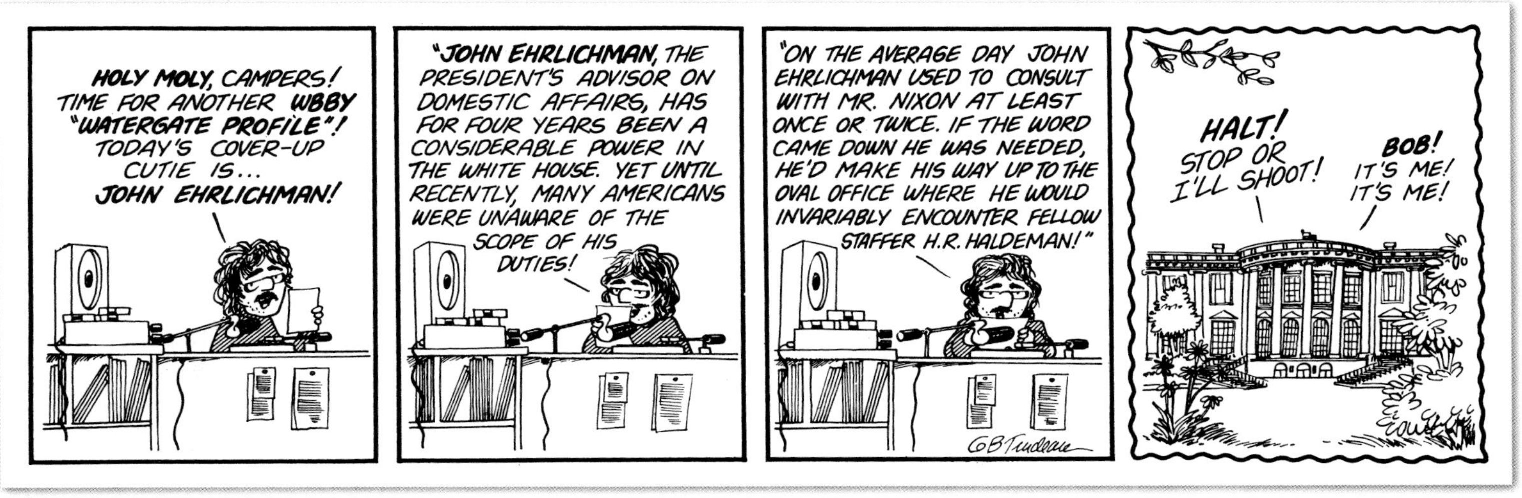
HOLY MOLY, CAMPERS! TIME FOR ANOTHER WBBY "WATERGATE PROFILE"! TODAY'S COVER-UP CUTIE IS... JOHN EHRLICHMAN!
"JOHN EHRLICHMAN, THE PRESIDENT'S ADVISOR ON DOMESTIC AFFAIRS, HAS FOR FOUR YEARS BEEN A CONSIDERABLE POWER IN THE WHITE HOUSE. YET UNTIL RECENTLY, MANY AMERICANS WERE UNAWARE OF THE SCOPE OF HIS DUTIES!
"ON THE AVERAGE DAY JOHN EHRLICHMAN USED TO CONSULT WITH MR. NIXON AT LEAST ONCE OR TWICE. IF THE WORD CAME DOWN HE WAS NEEDED, HE'D MAKE HIS WAY UP TO THE OVAL OFFICE WHERE HE WOULD INVARIABLY ENCOUNTER FELLOW STAFFER H.R. HALDEMAN!"
HALT! STOP OR I'LL SHOOT!
BOB! IT'S ME! IT'S ME!

5/31/73

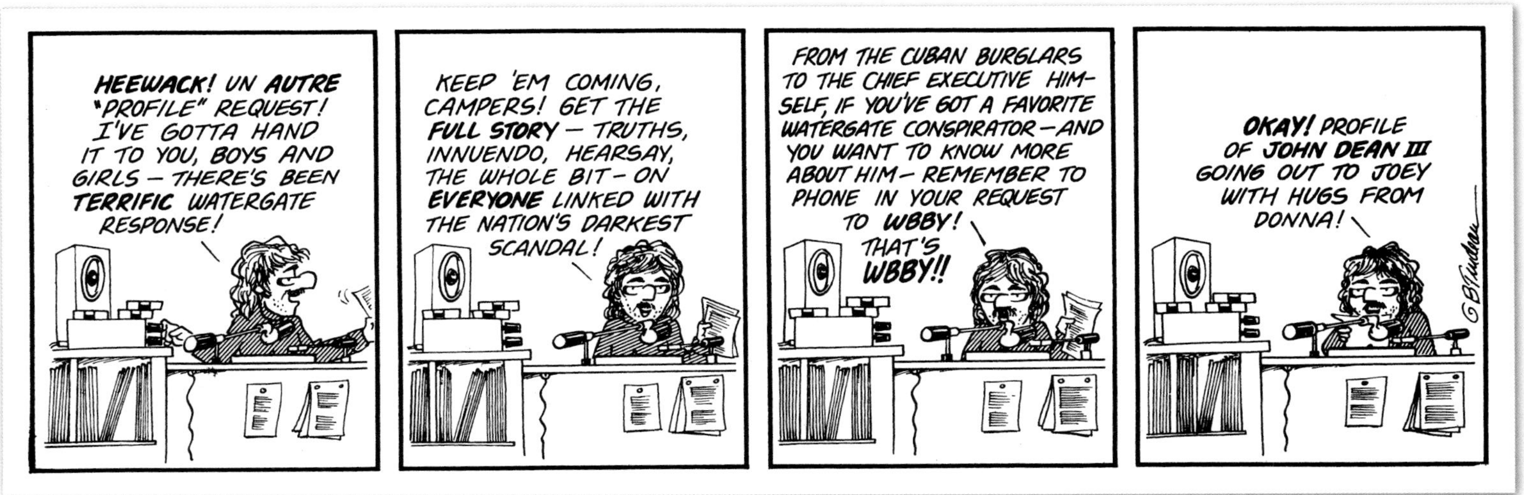
HEEWACK! UN AUTRE "PROFILE" REQUEST! I'VE GOTTA HAND IT TO YOU, BOYS AND GIRLS — THERE'S BEEN TERRIFIC WATERGATE RESPONSE!
KEEP 'EM COMING, CAMPERS! GET THE FULL STORY — TRUTHS, INNUENDO, HEARSAY, THE WHOLE BIT — ON EVERYONE LINKED WITH THE NATION'S DARKEST SCANDAL!
FROM THE CUBAN BURGLARS TO THE CHIEF EXECUTIVE HIMSELF, IF YOU'VE GOT A FAVORITE WATERGATE CONSPIRATOR — AND YOU WANT TO KNOW MORE ABOUT HIM — REMEMBER TO PHONE IN YOUR REQUEST TO WBBY!
THAT'S WBBY!!
OKAY! PROFILE OF JOHN DEAN III GOING OUT TO JOEY WITH HUGS FROM DONNA!

6/1/73

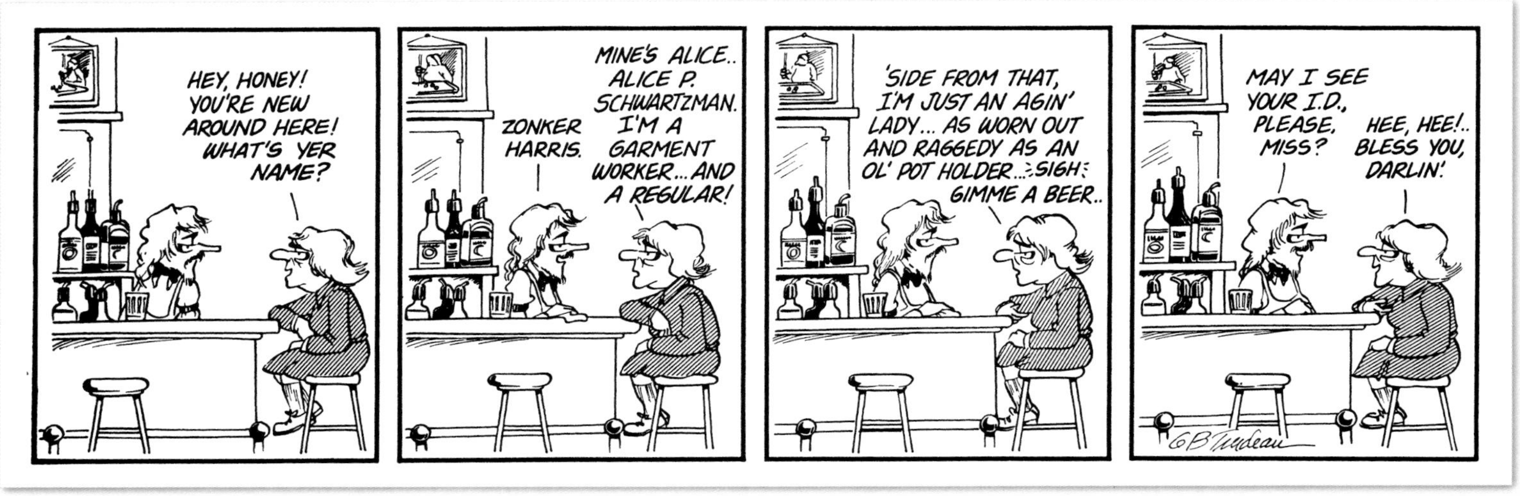
HEY, HONEY! YOU'RE NEW AROUND HERE! WHAT'S YER NAME?
ZONKER HARRIS.
MINE'S ALICE.. ALICE P. SCHWARTZMAN. I'M A GARMENT WORKER... AND A REGULAR!
'SIDE FROM THAT, I'M JUST AN AGIN' LADY... AS WORN OUT AND RAGGEDY AS AN OL' POT HOLDER... :SIGH: GIMME A BEER..
MAY I SEE YOUR I.D., PLEASE, MISS?
HEE, HEE!.. BLESS YOU, DARLIN'.

8/24/73

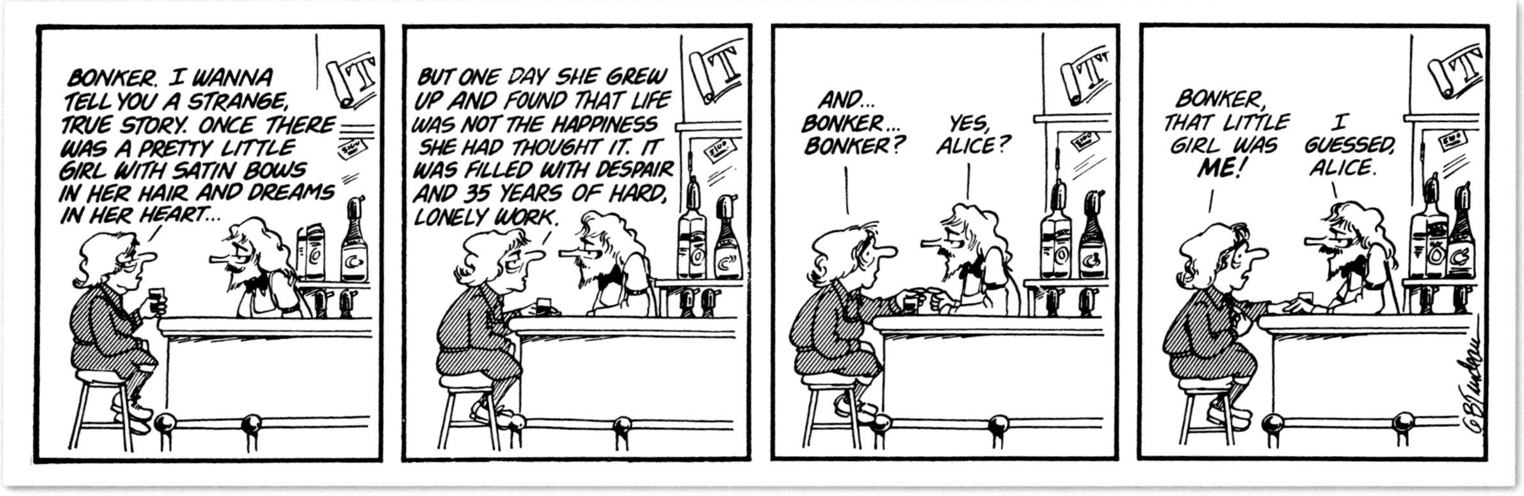
BONKER. I WANNA TELL YOU A STRANGE, TRUE STORY. ONCE THERE WAS A PRETTY LITTLE GIRL WITH SATIN BOWS IN HER HAIR AND DREAMS IN HER HEART...
BUT ONE DAY SHE GREW UP AND FOUND THAT LIFE WAS NOT THE HAPPINESS SHE HAD THOUGHT IT. IT WAS FILLED WITH DESPAIR AND 35 YEARS OF HARD, LONELY WORK.
AND... BONKER... BONKER?
YES, ALICE?
BONKER, THAT LITTLE GIRL WAS ME!
I GUESSED, ALICE.

8/25/73

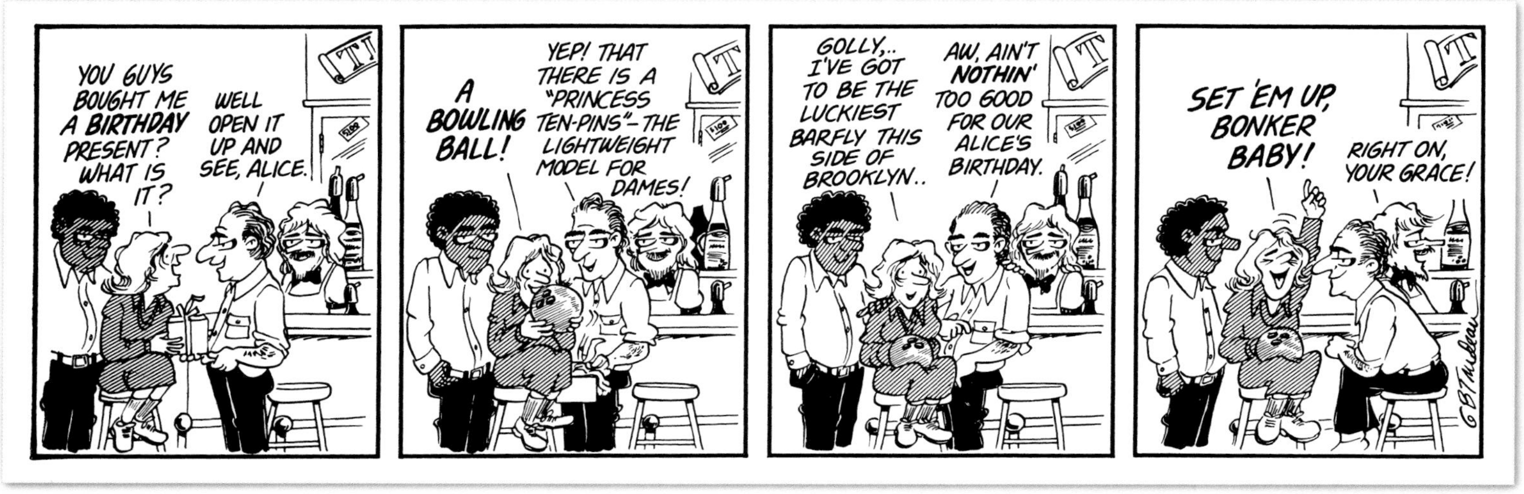
YOU GUYS BOUGHT ME A BIRTHDAY PRESENT? WHAT IS IT?
WELL OPEN IT UP AND SEE, ALICE.
A BOWLING BALL!
YEP! THAT THERE IS A "PRINCESS TEN-PINS"– THE LIGHTWEIGHT MODEL FOR DAMES!
GOLLY,.. I'VE GOT TO BE THE LUCKIEST BARFLY THIS SIDE OF BROOKLYN..
AW, AIN'T NOTHIN' TOO GOOD FOR OUR ALICE'S BIRTHDAY.
SET 'EM UP, BONKER BABY!
RIGHT ON, YOUR GRACE!

8/30/73

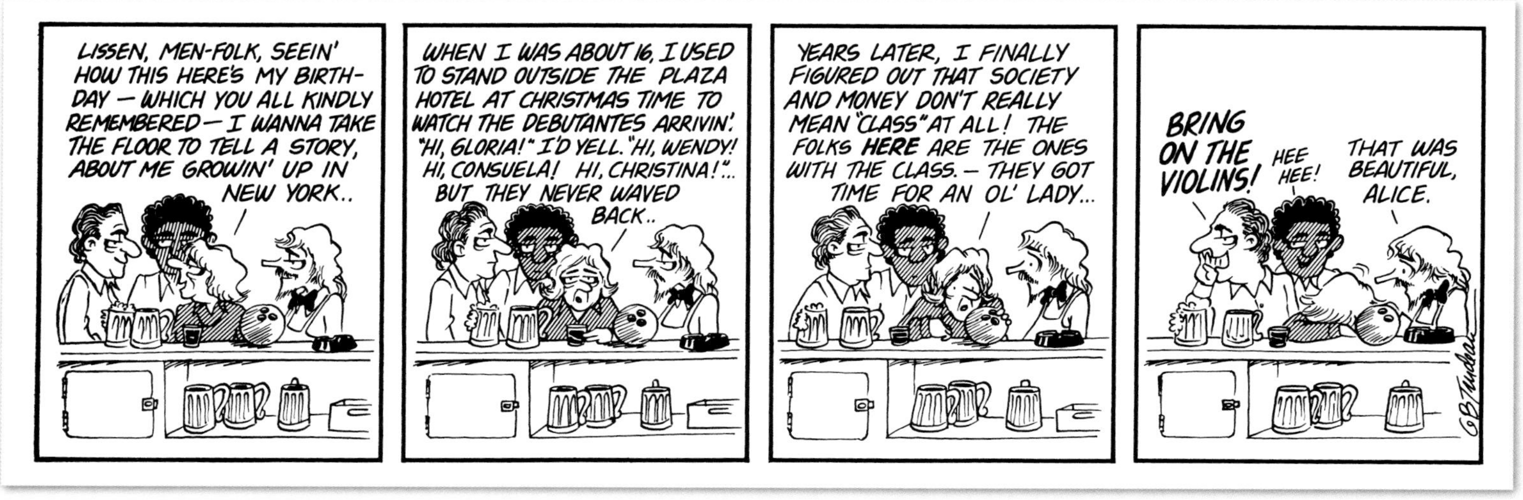
LISSEN, MEN-FOLK, SEEIN' HOW THIS HERE'S MY BIRTH-DAY – WHICH YOU ALL KINDLY REMEMBERED – I WANNA TAKE THE FLOOR TO TELL A STORY, ABOUT ME GROWIN' UP IN NEW YORK..
WHEN I WAS ABOUT 16, I USED TO STAND OUTSIDE THE PLAZA HOTEL AT CHRISTMAS TIME TO WATCH THE DEBUTANTES ARRIVIN'. "HI, GLORIA!" I'D YELL. "HI, WENDY! HI, CONSUELA! HI, CHRISTINA!"... BUT THEY NEVER WAVED BACK..
YEARS LATER, I FINALLY FIGURED OUT THAT SOCIETY AND MONEY DON'T REALLY MEAN "CLASS" AT ALL! THE FOLKS HERE ARE THE ONES WITH THE CLASS. – THEY GOT TIME FOR AN OL' LADY...
BRING ON THE VIOLINS!
HEE HEE!
THAT WAS BEAUTIFUL, ALICE.

8/31/73

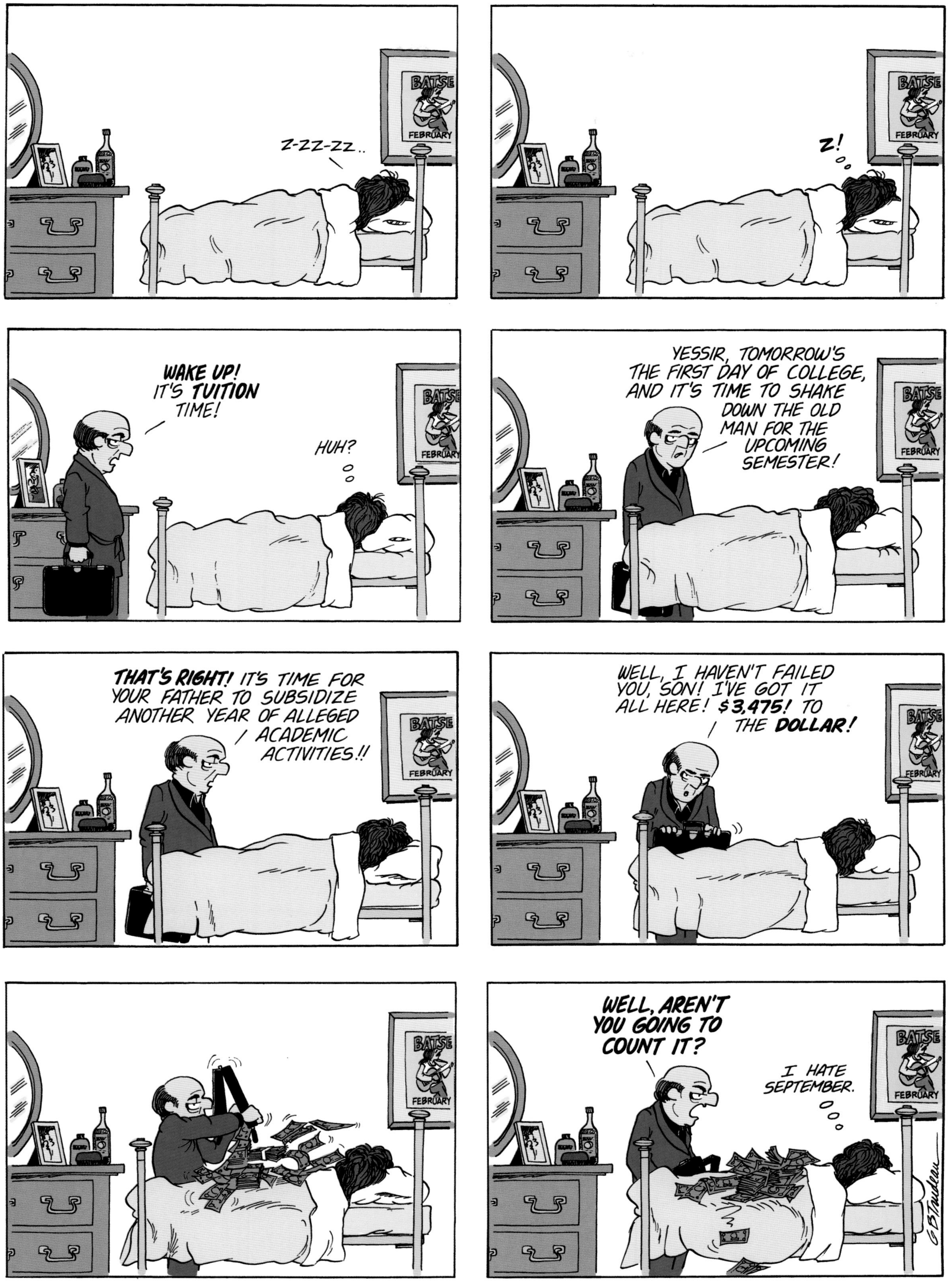
Z-ZZ-ZZ..
Z!
WAKE UP! IT'S TUITION TIME!
HUH?
YESSIR, TOMORROW'S THE FIRST DAY OF COLLEGE, AND IT'S TIME TO SHAKE DOWN THE OLD MAN FOR THE UPCOMING SEMESTER!
THAT'S RIGHT! IT'S TIME FOR YOUR FATHER TO SUBSIDIZE ANOTHER YEAR OF ALLEGED ACADEMIC ACTIVITIES!!
WELL, I HAVEN'T FAILED YOU, SON! I'VE GOT IT ALL HERE! $3,475! TO THE DOLLAR!
WELL, AREN'T YOU GOING TO COUNT IT?
I HATE SEPTEMBER.
BATSE
FEBRUARY
G.B. Trudeau

9/2/73

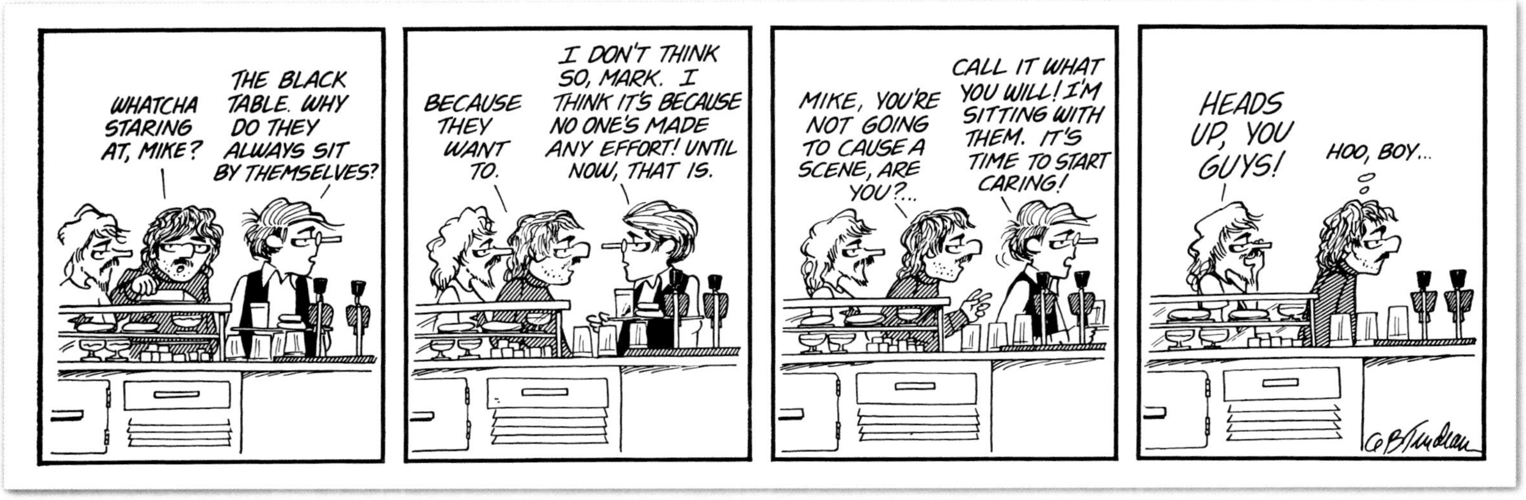
WHATCHA STARING AT, MIKE?
THE BLACK TABLE. WHY DO THEY ALWAYS SIT BY THEMSELVES?
BECAUSE THEY WANT TO.
I DON'T THINK SO, MARK. I THINK IT'S BECAUSE NO ONE'S MADE ANY EFFORT! UNTIL NOW, THAT IS.
MIKE, YOU'RE NOT GOING TO CAUSE A SCENE, ARE YOU?...
CALL IT WHAT YOU WILL! I'M SITTING WITH THEM. IT'S TIME TO START CARING!
HEADS UP, YOU GUYS!
HOO, BOY...

9/11/73

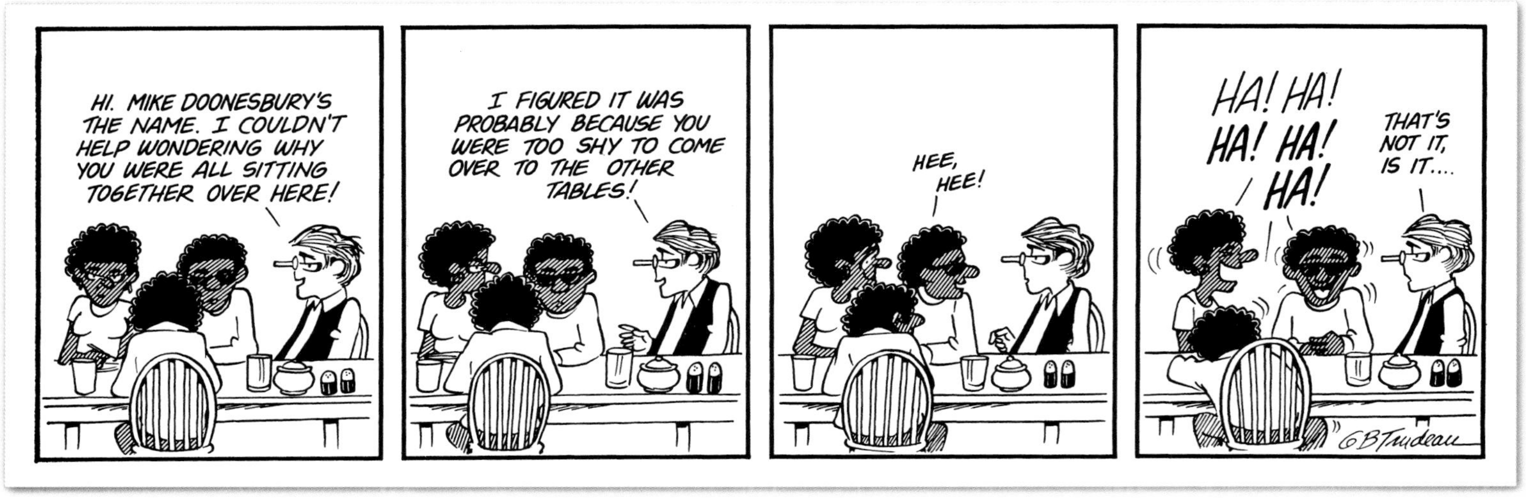
HI. MIKE DOONESBURY'S THE NAME. I COULDN'T HELP WONDERING WHY YOU WERE ALL SITTING TOGETHER OVER HERE!
I FIGURED IT WAS PROBABLY BECAUSE YOU WERE TOO SHY TO COME OVER TO THE OTHER TABLES!
HEE, HEE!
HA! HA! HA! HA! HA!
THAT'S NOT IT, IS IT....

9/12/73

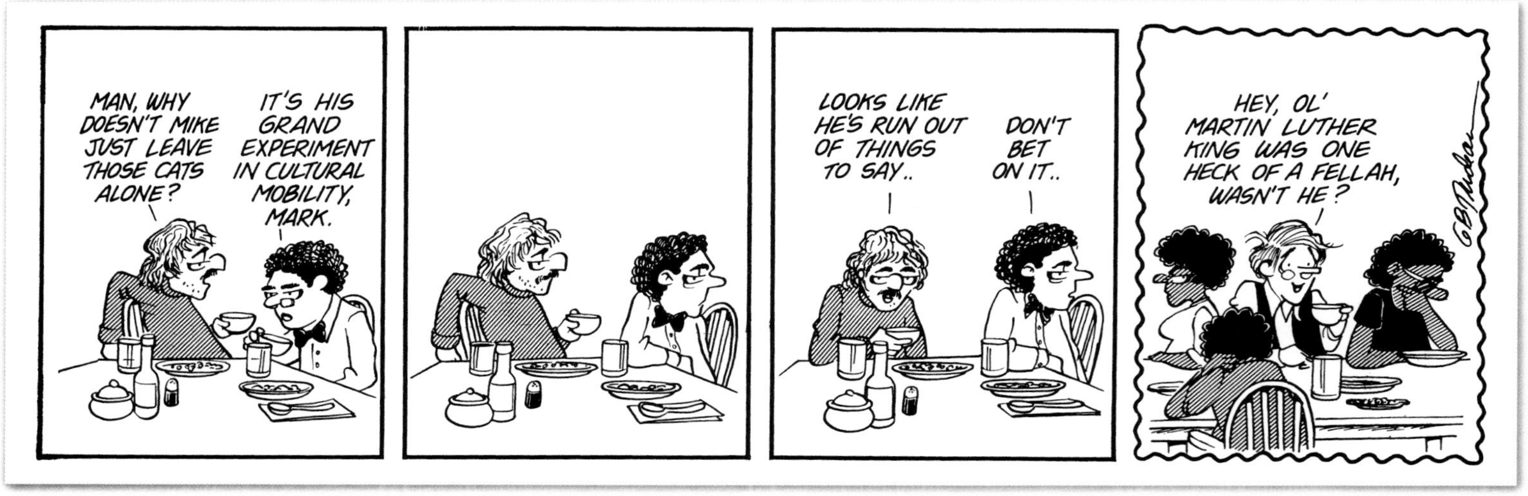
MAN, WHY DOESN'T MIKE JUST LEAVE THOSE CATS ALONE?
IT'S HIS GRAND EXPERIMENT IN CULTURAL MOBILITY, MARK.
LOOKS LIKE HE'S RUN OUT OF THINGS TO SAY..
DON'T BET ON IT..
HEY, OL' MARTIN LUTHER KING WAS ONE HECK OF A FELLAH, WASN'T HE?

9/13/73

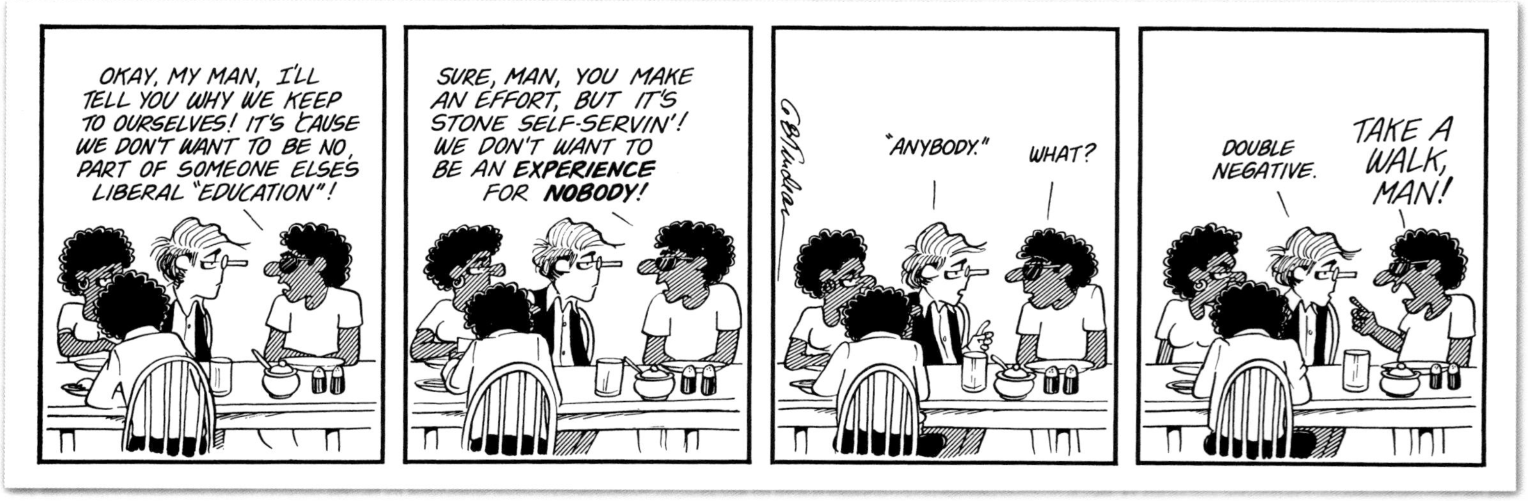
OKAY, MY MAN, I'LL TELL YOU WHY WE KEEP TO OURSELVES! IT'S 'CAUSE WE DON'T WANT TO BE NO PART OF SOMEONE ELSE'S LIBERAL "EDUCATION"!
SURE, MAN, YOU MAKE AN EFFORT, BUT IT'S STONE SELF-SERVIN'! WE DON'T WANT TO BE AN EXPERIENCE FOR NOBODY!
"ANYBODY."
WHAT?
DOUBLE NEGATIVE.
TAKE A WALK, MAN!

9/14/73

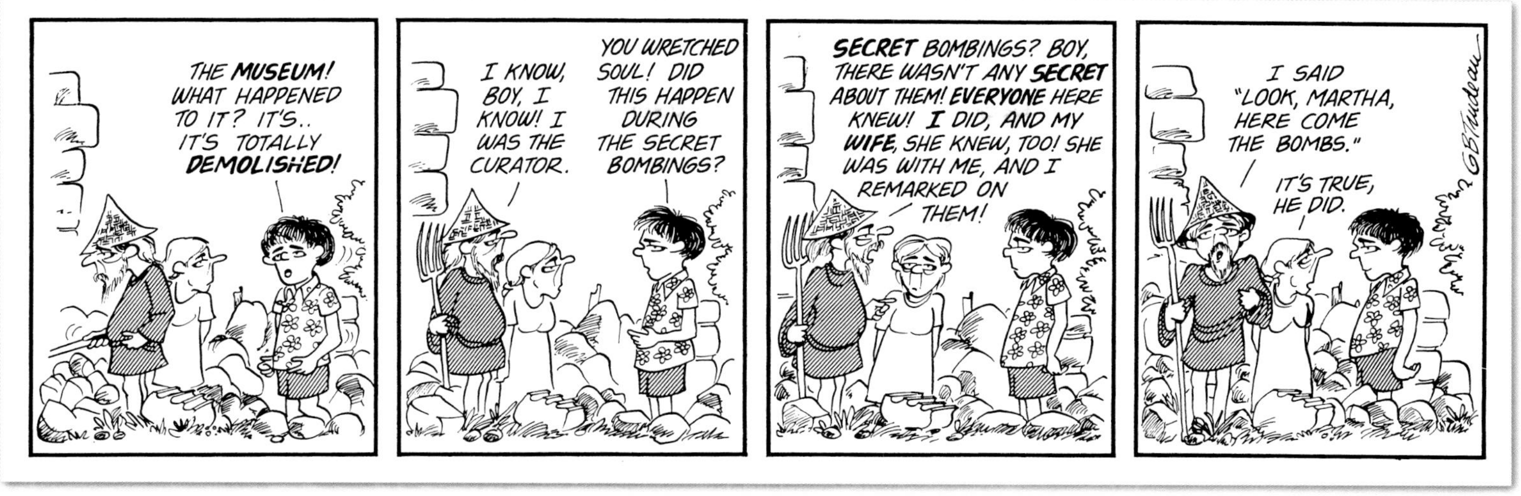
THE MUSEUM! WHAT HAPPENED TO IT? IT'S.. IT'S TOTALLY DEMOLISHED!
I KNOW, BOY, I KNOW! I WAS THE CURATOR.
YOU WRETCHED SOUL! DID THIS HAPPEN DURING THE SECRET BOMBINGS?
SECRET BOMBINGS? BOY, THERE WASN'T ANY SECRET ABOUT THEM! EVERYONE HERE KNEW! I DID, AND MY WIFE, SHE KNEW, TOO! SHE WAS WITH ME, AND I REMARKED ON THEM!
I SAID "LOOK, MARTHA, HERE COME THE BOMBS."
IT'S TRUE, HE DID.
GBTrudeau

11/10/73

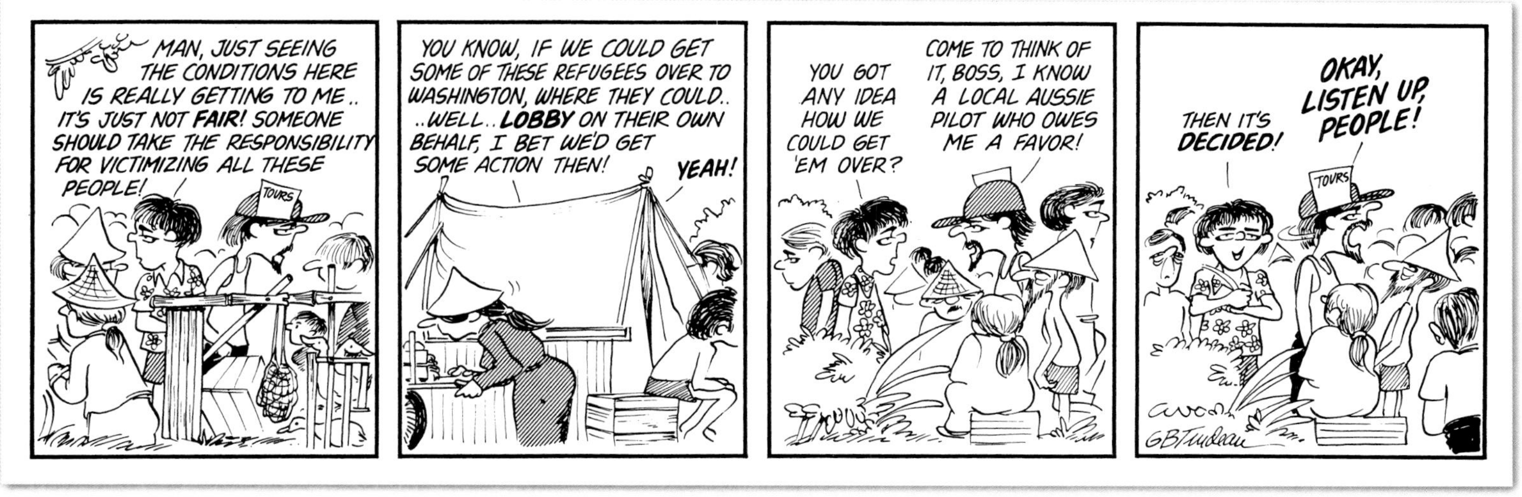
MAN, JUST SEEING THE CONDITIONS HERE IS REALLY GETTING TO ME.. IT'S JUST NOT FAIR! SOMEONE SHOULD TAKE THE RESPONSIBILITY FOR VICTIMIZING ALL THESE PEOPLE!
TOURS
YOU KNOW, IF WE COULD GET SOME OF THESE REFUGEES OVER TO WASHINGTON, WHERE THEY COULD.. ..WELL.. LOBBY ON THEIR OWN BEHALF, I BET WE'D GET SOME ACTION THEN!
YEAH!
YOU GOT ANY IDEA HOW WE COULD GET 'EM OVER?
COME TO THINK OF IT, BOSS, I KNOW A LOCAL AUSSIE PILOT WHO OWES ME A FAVOR!
THEN IT'S DECIDED!
OKAY, LISTEN UP, PEOPLE!
TOURS
GBTrudeau

11/15/73

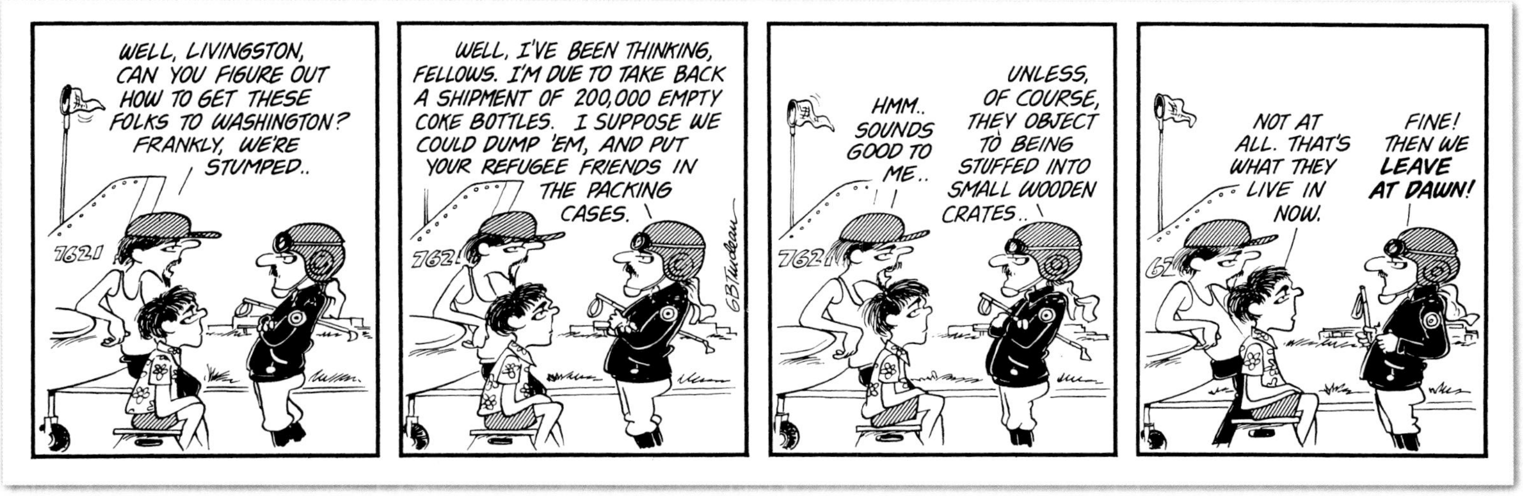
WELL, LIVINGSTON, CAN YOU FIGURE OUT HOW TO GET THESE FOLKS TO WASHINGTON? FRANKLY, WE'RE STUMPED..
7621
WELL, I'VE BEEN THINKING, FELLOWS. I'M DUE TO TAKE BACK A SHIPMENT OF 200,000 EMPTY COKE BOTTLES. I SUPPOSE WE COULD DUMP 'EM, AND PUT YOUR REFUGEE FRIENDS IN THE PACKING CASES.
GBTrudeau
HMM.. SOUNDS GOOD TO ME..
UNLESS, OF COURSE, THEY OBJECT TO BEING STUFFED INTO SMALL WOODEN CRATES..
NOT AT ALL. THAT'S WHAT THEY LIVE IN NOW.
FINE! THEN WE LEAVE AT DAWN!

11/17/73

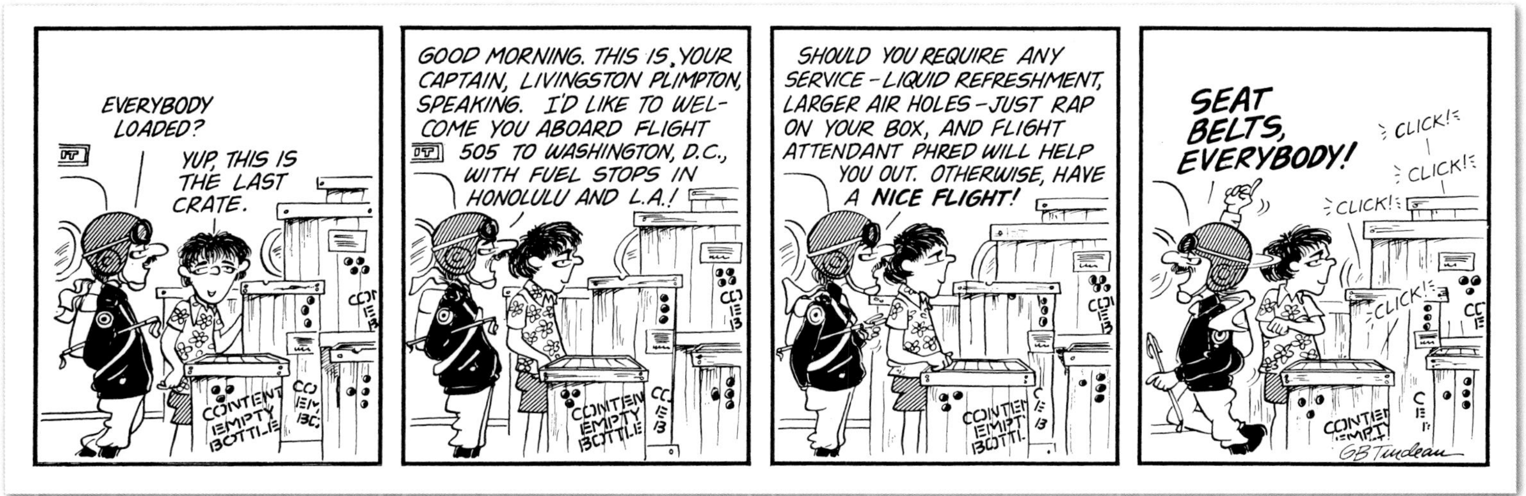
EVERYBODY LOADED?
YUP, THIS IS THE LAST CRATE.
CONTENT EMPTY BOTTLE
GOOD MORNING. THIS IS YOUR CAPTAIN, LIVINGSTON PLIMPTON, SPEAKING. I'D LIKE TO WELCOME YOU ABOARD FLIGHT 505 TO WASHINGTON, D.C., WITH FUEL STOPS IN HONOLULU AND L.A.!
SHOULD YOU REQUIRE ANY SERVICE - LIQUID REFRESHMENT, LARGER AIR HOLES - JUST RAP ON YOUR BOX, AND FLIGHT ATTENDANT PHRED WILL HELP YOU OUT. OTHERWISE, HAVE A NICE FLIGHT!
SEAT BELTS, EVERYBODY!
CLICK!
CLICK!
CLICK!
CLICK!
GBTrudeau

11/19/73

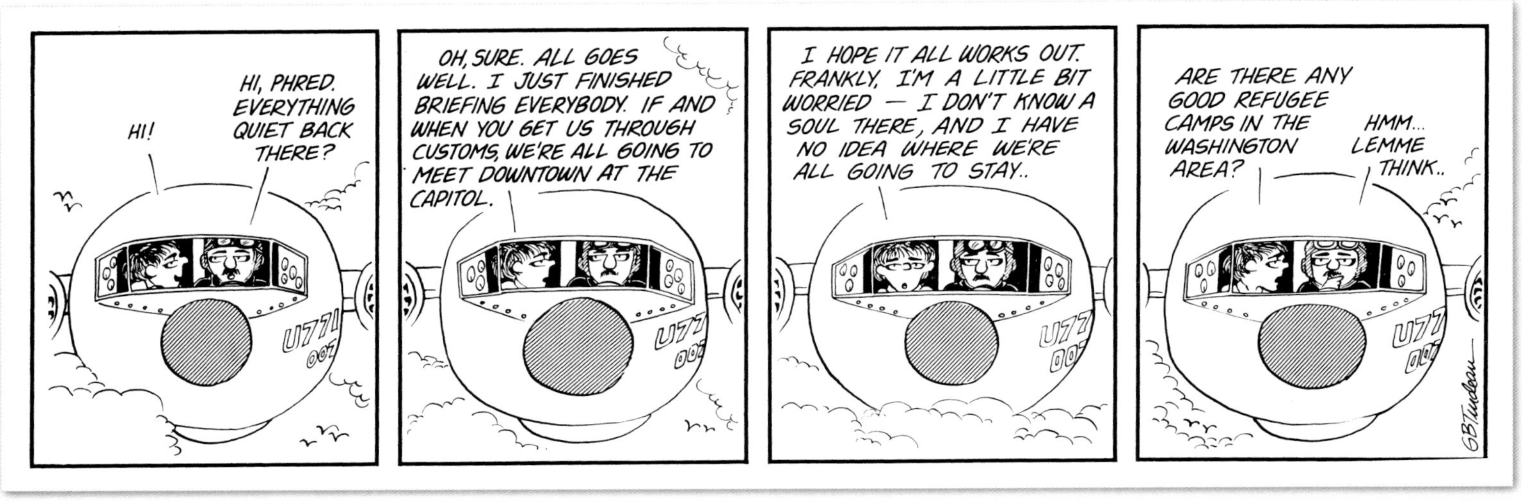
HI!
HI, PHRED. EVERYTHING QUIET BACK THERE?
OH, SURE. ALL GOES WELL. I JUST FINISHED BRIEFING EVERYBODY. IF AND WHEN YOU GET US THROUGH CUSTOMS, WE'RE ALL GOING TO MEET DOWNTOWN AT THE CAPITOL.
I HOPE IT ALL WORKS OUT. FRANKLY, I'M A LITTLE BIT WORRIED — I DON'T KNOW A SOUL THERE, AND I HAVE NO IDEA WHERE WE'RE ALL GOING TO STAY..
ARE THERE ANY GOOD REFUGEE CAMPS IN THE WASHINGTON AREA?
HMM... LEMME THINK..
U771
GBTrudeau

11/21/73

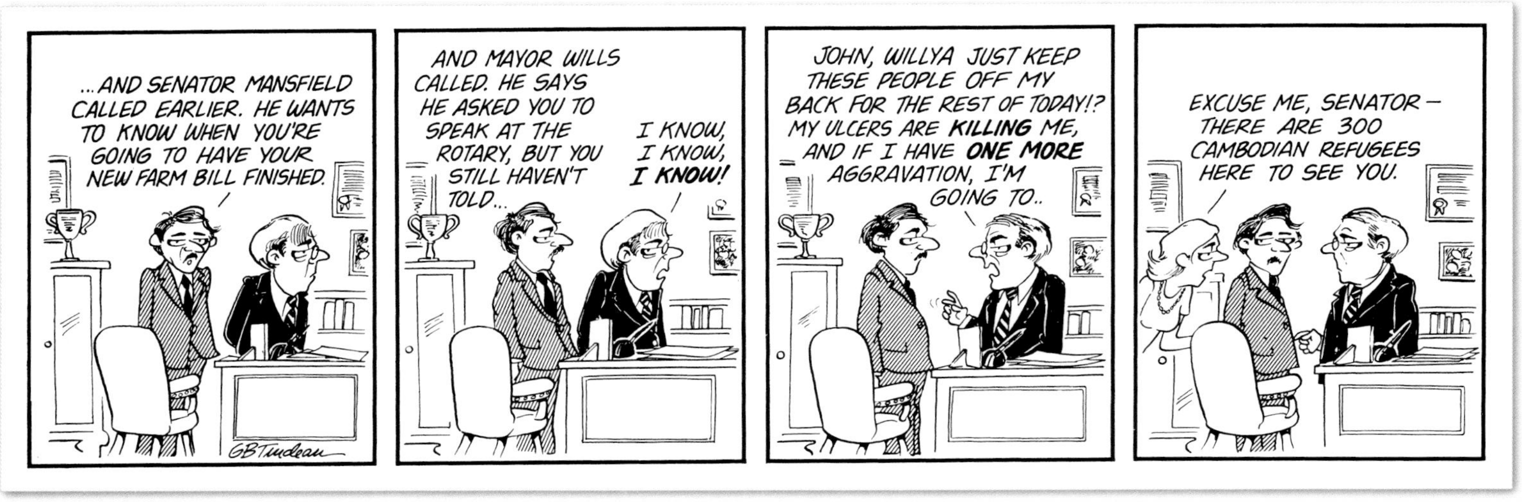
...AND SENATOR MANSFIELD CALLED EARLIER. HE WANTS TO KNOW WHEN YOU'RE GOING TO HAVE YOUR NEW FARM BILL FINISHED.
GBTrudeau
AND MAYOR WILLS CALLED. HE SAYS HE ASKED YOU TO SPEAK AT THE ROTARY, BUT YOU STILL HAVEN'T TOLD...
I KNOW, I KNOW, I KNOW!
JOHN, WILLYA JUST KEEP THESE PEOPLE OFF MY BACK FOR THE REST OF TODAY!? MY ULCERS ARE KILLING ME, AND IF I HAVE ONE MORE AGGRAVATION, I'M GOING TO..
EXCUSE ME, SENATOR — THERE ARE 300 CAMBODIAN REFUGEES HERE TO SEE YOU.

11/23/73

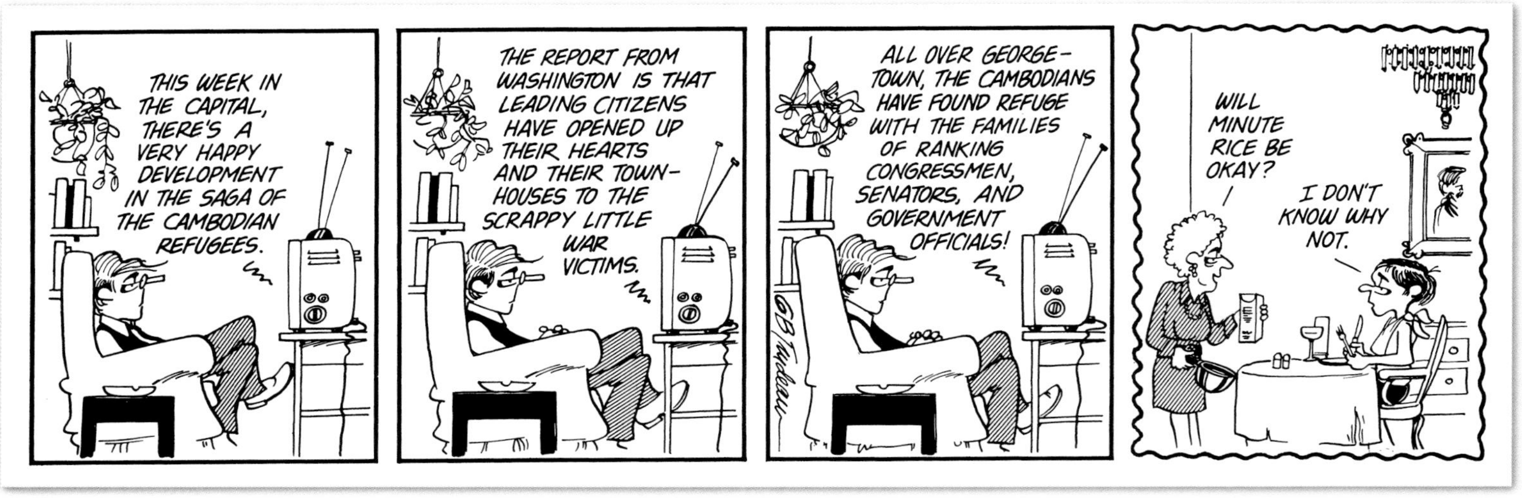
THIS WEEK IN THE CAPITAL, THERE'S A VERY HAPPY DEVELOPMENT IN THE SAGA OF THE CAMBODIAN REFUGEES.
THE REPORT FROM WASHINGTON IS THAT LEADING CITIZENS HAVE OPENED UP THEIR HEARTS AND THEIR TOWN-HOUSES TO THE SCRAPPY LITTLE WAR VICTIMS.
ALL OVER GEORGE-TOWN, THE CAMBODIANS HAVE FOUND REFUGE WITH THE FAMILIES OF RANKING CONGRESSMEN, SENATORS, AND GOVERNMENT OFFICIALS!
GBTrudeau
WILL MINUTE RICE BE OKAY?
I DON'T KNOW WHY NOT.

11/26/73

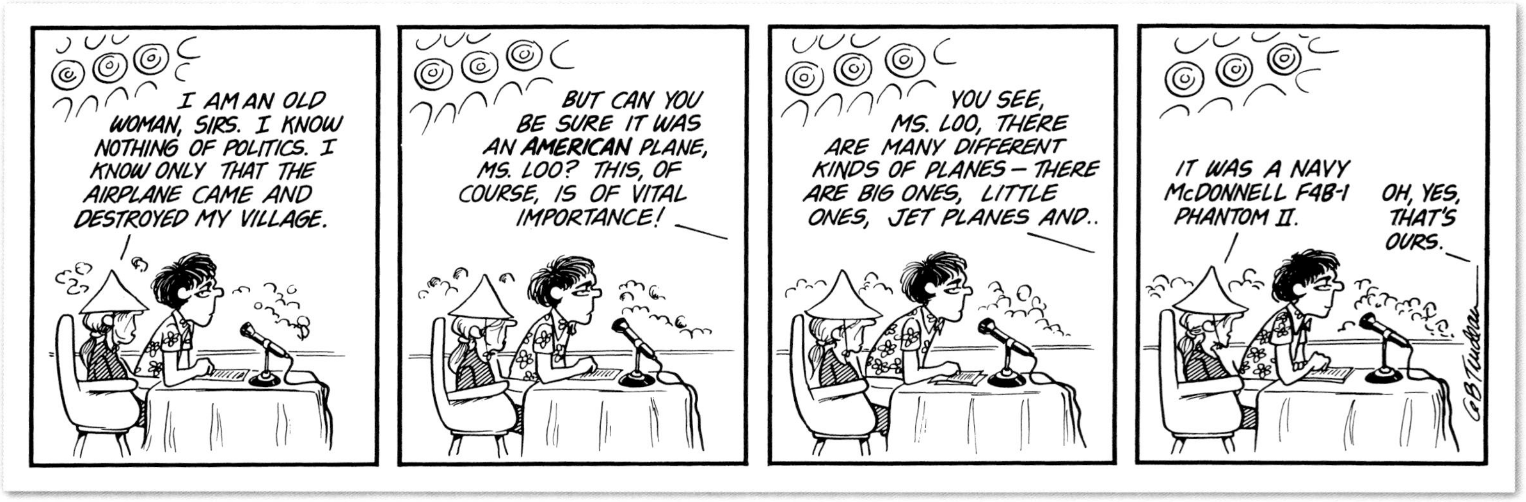
I AM AN OLD WOMAN, SIRS. I KNOW NOTHING OF POLITICS. I KNOW ONLY THAT THE AIRPLANE CAME AND DESTROYED MY VILLAGE.
BUT CAN YOU BE SURE IT WAS AN AMERICAN PLANE, MS. LOO? THIS, OF COURSE, IS OF VITAL IMPORTANCE!
YOU SEE, MS. LOO, THERE ARE MANY DIFFERENT KINDS OF PLANES — THERE ARE BIG ONES, LITTLE ONES, JET PLANES AND..
IT WAS A NAVY McDONNELL F4B-I PHANTOM II.
OH, YES, THAT'S OURS.
GBTrudeau

12/5/73

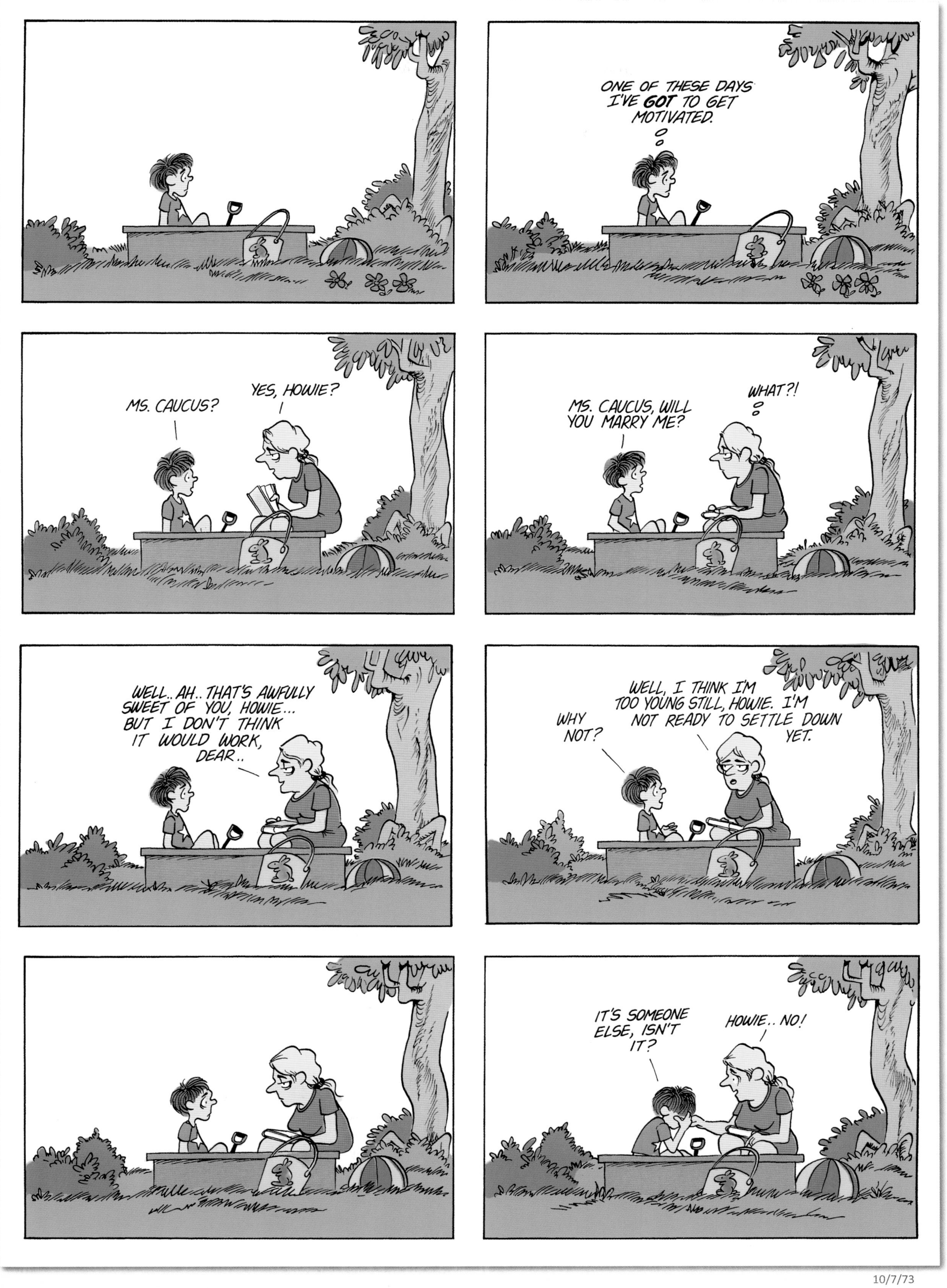
ONE OF THESE DAYS I'VE GOT TO GET MOTIVATED.
MS. CAUCUS?
YES, HOWIE?
MS. CAUCUS, WILL YOU MARRY ME?
WHAT?!
WELL.. AH.. THAT'S AWFULLY SWEET OF YOU, HOWIE... BUT I DON'T THINK IT WOULD WORK, DEAR..
WHY NOT?
WELL, I THINK I'M TOO YOUNG STILL, HOWIE. I'M NOT READY TO SETTLE DOWN YET.
IT'S SOMEONE ELSE, ISN'T IT?
HOWIE.. NO!

10/7/73

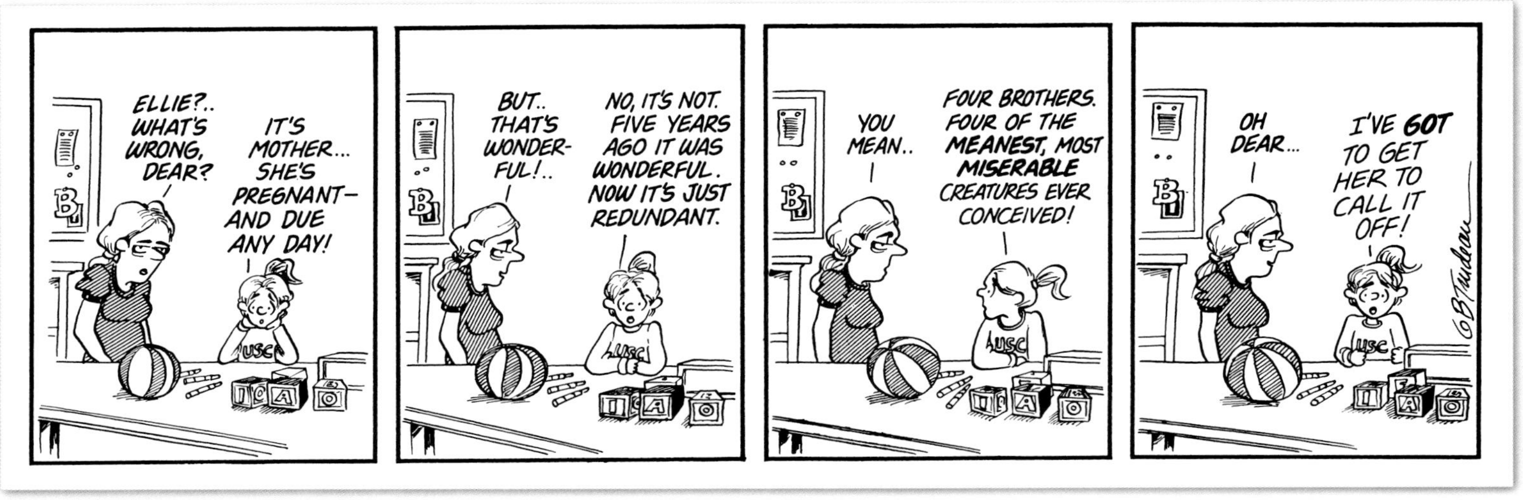
ELLIE?.. WHAT'S WRONG, DEAR?
IT'S MOTHER... SHE'S PREGNANT— AND DUE ANY DAY!
BUT.. THAT'S WONDER-FUL!..
NO, IT'S NOT. FIVE YEARS AGO IT WAS WONDERFUL. NOW IT'S JUST REDUNDANT.
YOU MEAN..
FOUR BROTHERS. FOUR OF THE **MEANEST**, MOST **MISERABLE** CREATURES EVER CONCEIVED!
OH DEAR...
I'VE **GOT** TO GET HER TO CALL IT OFF!

12/10/73

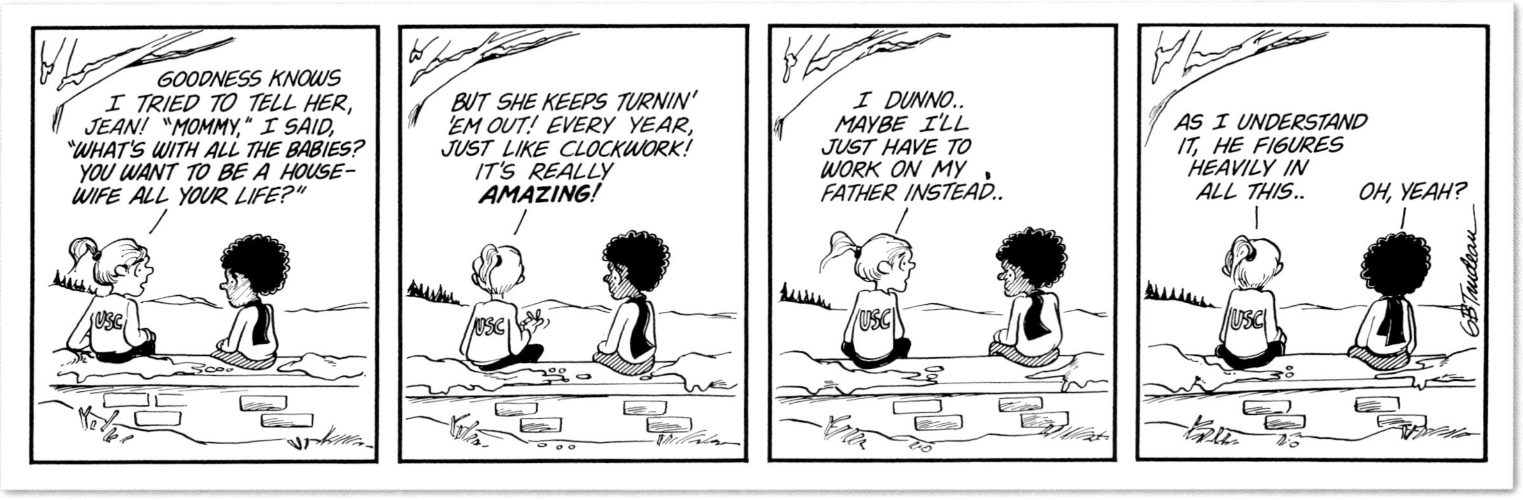
GOODNESS KNOWS I TRIED TO TELL HER, JEAN! "MOMMY," I SAID, "WHAT'S WITH ALL THE BABIES? YOU WANT TO BE A HOUSE-WIFE ALL YOUR LIFE?"
BUT SHE KEEPS TURNIN' 'EM OUT! EVERY YEAR, JUST LIKE CLOCKWORK! IT'S REALLY **AMAZING!**
I DUNNO.. MAYBE I'LL JUST HAVE TO WORK ON MY FATHER INSTEAD..
AS I UNDERSTAND IT, HE FIGURES HEAVILY IN ALL THIS..
OH, YEAH?

12/11/73

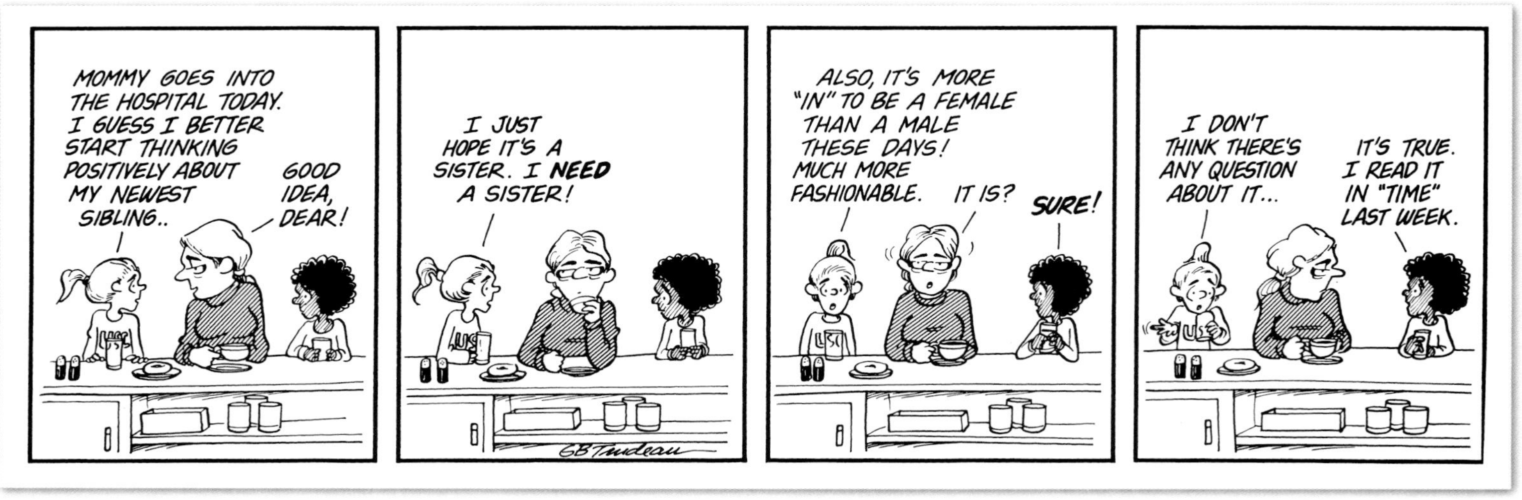
MOMMY GOES INTO THE HOSPITAL TODAY. I GUESS I BETTER START THINKING POSITIVELY ABOUT MY NEWEST SIBLING..
GOOD IDEA, DEAR!
I JUST HOPE IT'S A SISTER. I **NEED** A SISTER!
ALSO, IT'S MORE "IN" TO BE A FEMALE THAN A MALE THESE DAYS! MUCH MORE FASHIONABLE.
IT IS?
SURE!
I DON'T THINK THERE'S ANY QUESTION ABOUT IT...
IT'S TRUE. I READ IT IN "TIME" LAST WEEK.

12/12/73

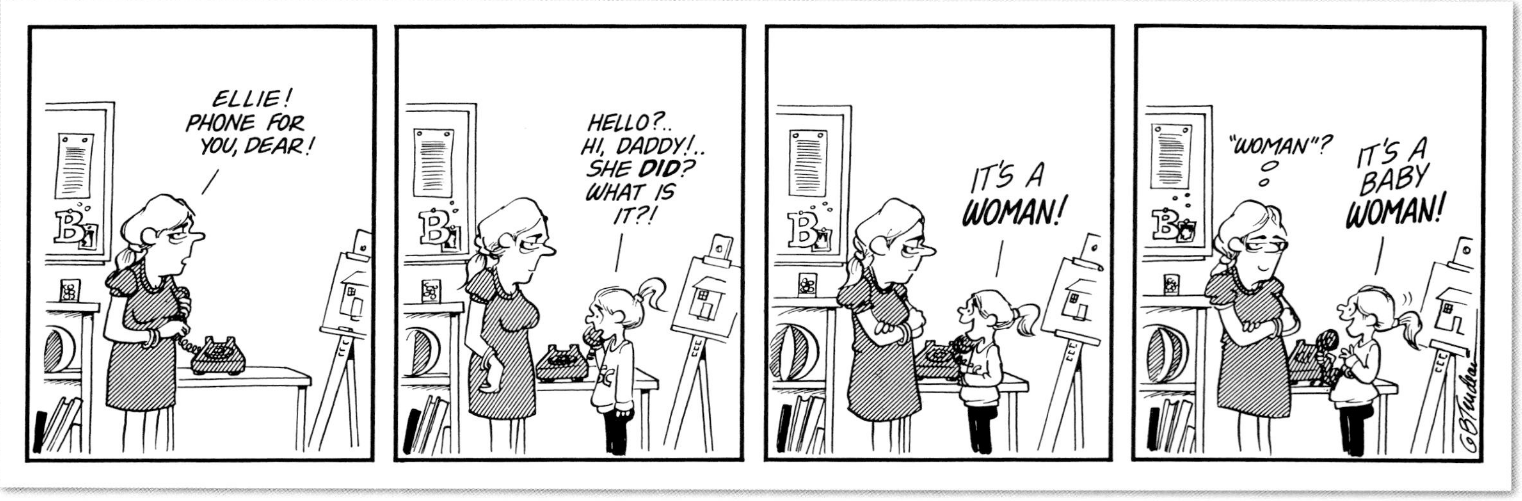
ELLIE! PHONE FOR YOU, DEAR!
HELLO?.. HI, DADDY!.. SHE **DID**? WHAT IS IT?!
IT'S A **WOMAN!**
"WOMAN"?
IT'S A BABY **WOMAN!**

12/13/73

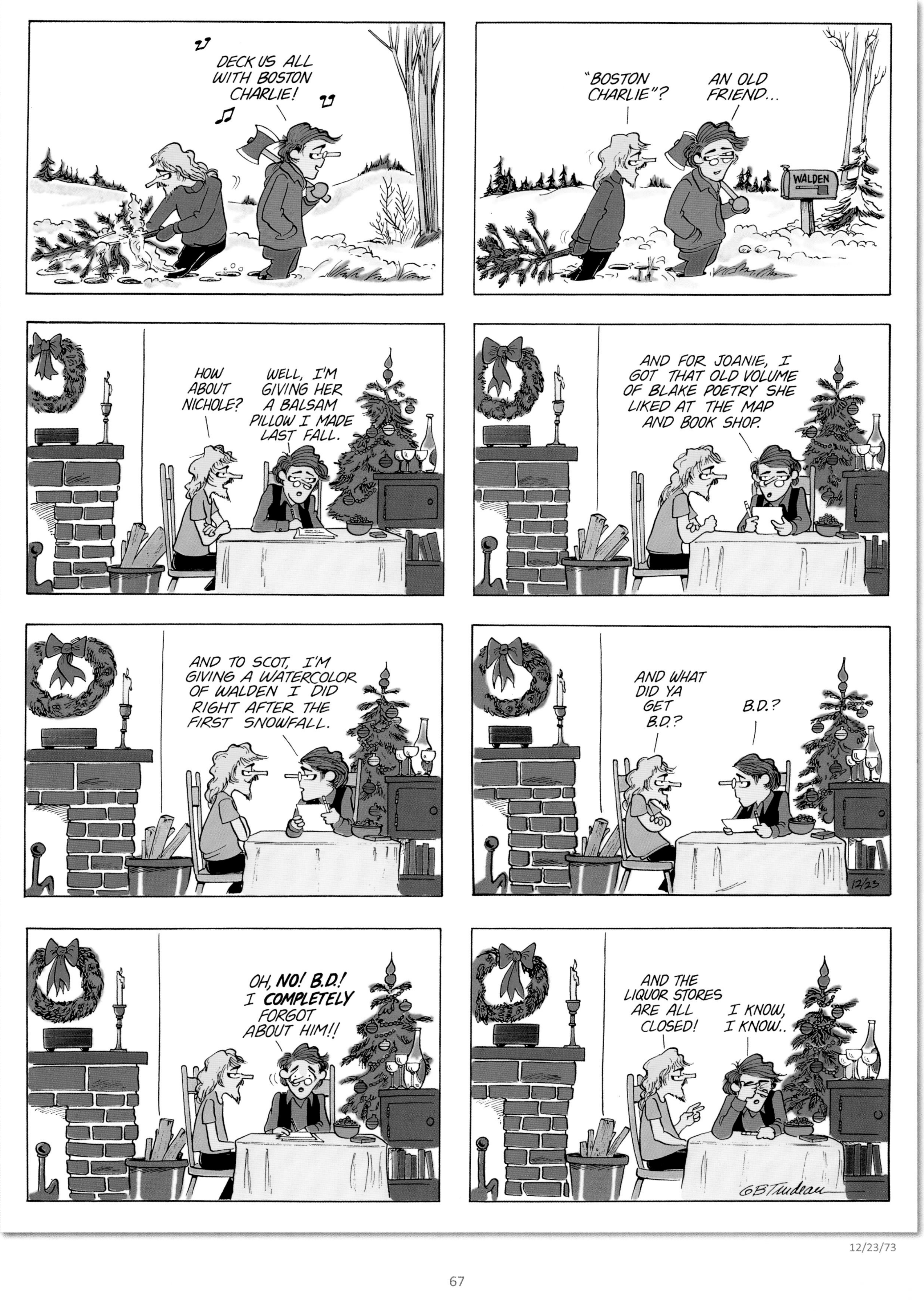
DECK US ALL WITH BOSTON CHARLIE!
"BOSTON CHARLIE"?
AN OLD FRIEND...
WALDEN
HOW ABOUT NICHOLE?
WELL, I'M GIVING HER A BALSAM PILLOW I MADE LAST FALL.
AND FOR JOANIE, I GOT THAT OLD VOLUME OF BLAKE POETRY SHE LIKED AT THE MAP AND BOOK SHOP.
AND TO SCOT, I'M GIVING A WATERCOLOR OF WALDEN I DID RIGHT AFTER THE FIRST SNOWFALL.
AND WHAT DID YA GET B.D.?
B.D.?
12/23
OH, **NO! B.D.!** I **COMPLETELY** FORGOT ABOUT HIM!!
AND THE LIQUOR STORES ARE ALL CLOSED!
I KNOW, I KNOW..
GBTrudeau

12/23/73

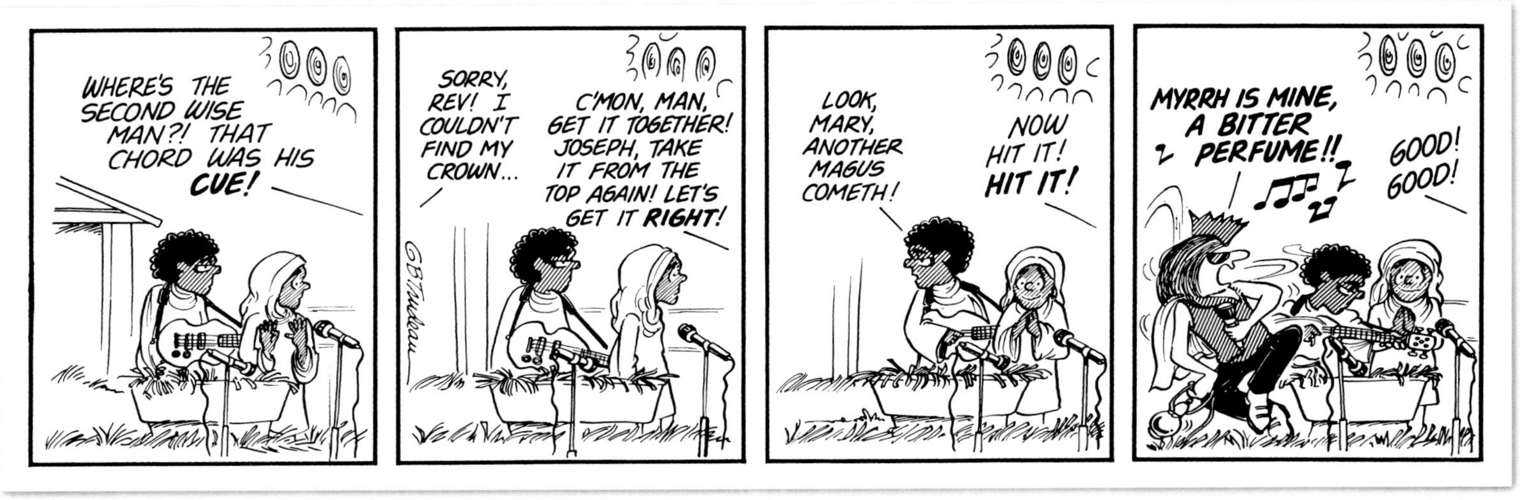
WHERE'S THE SECOND WISE MAN?! THAT CHORD WAS HIS **CUE!**
SORRY, REV! I COULDN'T FIND MY CROWN...
C'MON, MAN, GET IT TOGETHER! JOSEPH, TAKE IT FROM THE TOP AGAIN! LET'S GET IT **RIGHT!**
LOOK, MARY, ANOTHER MAGUS COMETH!
NOW HIT IT! **HIT IT!**
MYRRH IS MINE, A BITTER PERFUME!!
GOOD! GOOD!

12/18/73

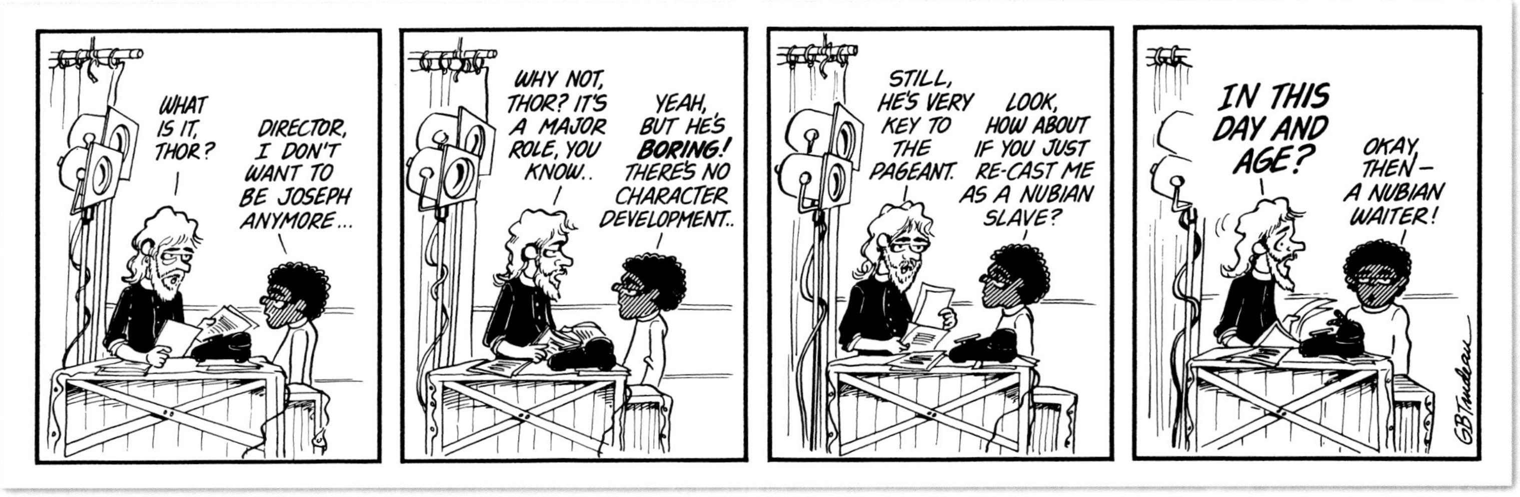
WHAT IS IT, THOR?
DIRECTOR, I DON'T WANT TO BE JOSEPH ANYMORE...
WHY NOT, THOR? IT'S A MAJOR ROLE, YOU KNOW..
YEAH, BUT HE'S **BORING!** THERE'S NO CHARACTER DEVELOPMENT..
STILL, HE'S VERY KEY TO THE PAGEANT.
LOOK, HOW ABOUT IF YOU JUST RE-CAST ME AS A NUBIAN SLAVE?
IN THIS DAY AND AGE?
OKAY, THEN— A NUBIAN WAITER!

12/19/73

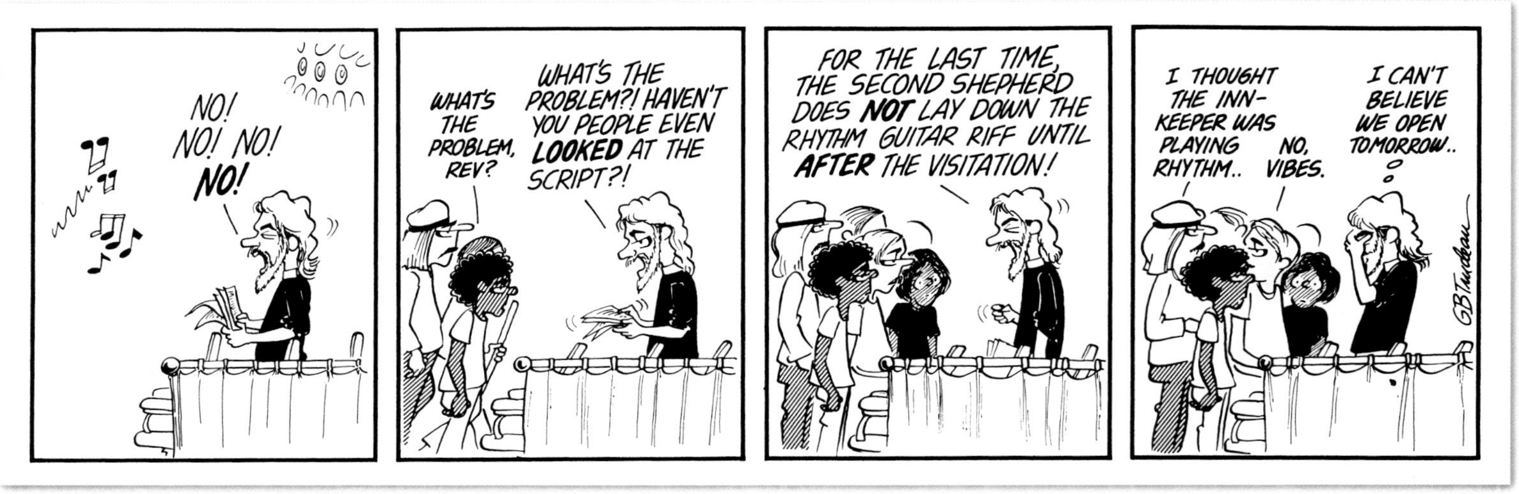
NO! NO! NO! **NO!**
WHAT'S THE PROBLEM, REV?
WHAT'S THE PROBLEM?! HAVEN'T YOU PEOPLE EVEN **LOOKED** AT THE SCRIPT?!
FOR THE LAST TIME, THE SECOND SHEPHERD DOES **NOT** LAY DOWN THE RHYTHM GUITAR RIFF UNTIL **AFTER** THE VISITATION!
I THOUGHT THE INN-KEEPER WAS PLAYING RHYTHM..
NO, VIBES.
I CAN'T BELIEVE WE OPEN TOMORROW..

12/20/73

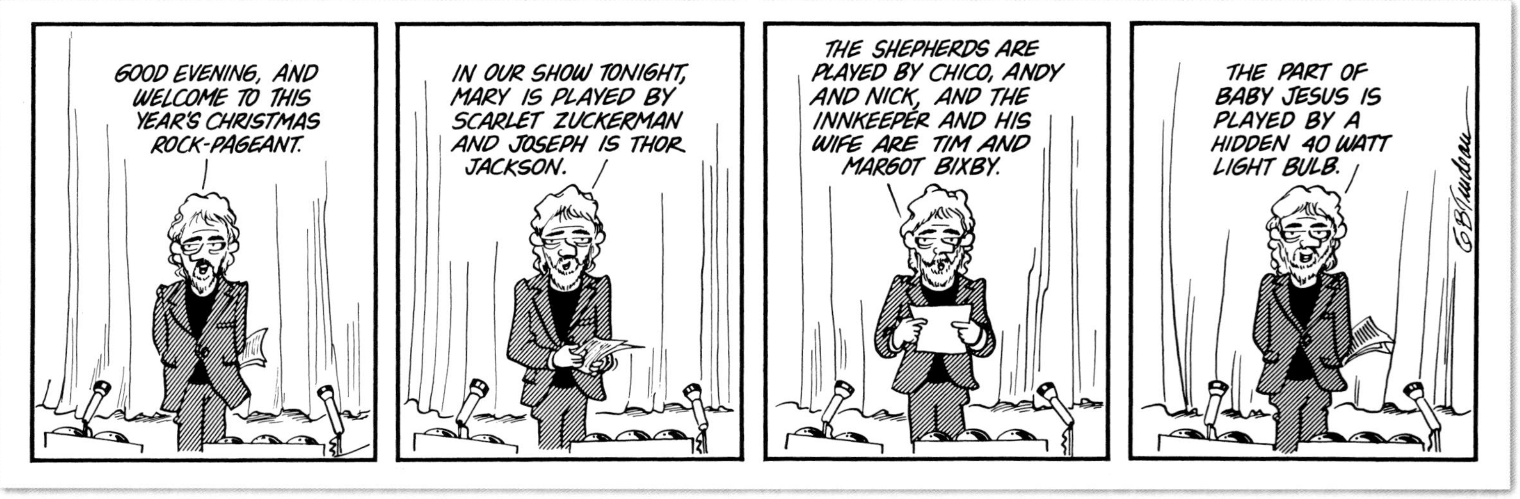
GOOD EVENING, AND WELCOME TO THIS YEAR'S CHRISTMAS ROCK-PAGEANT.
IN OUR SHOW TONIGHT, MARY IS PLAYED BY SCARLET ZUCKERMAN AND JOSEPH IS THOR JACKSON.
THE SHEPHERDS ARE PLAYED BY CHICO, ANDY AND NICK, AND THE INNKEEPER AND HIS WIFE ARE TIM AND MARGOT BIXBY.
THE PART OF BABY JESUS IS PLAYED BY A HIDDEN 40 WATT LIGHT BULB.

12/21/73

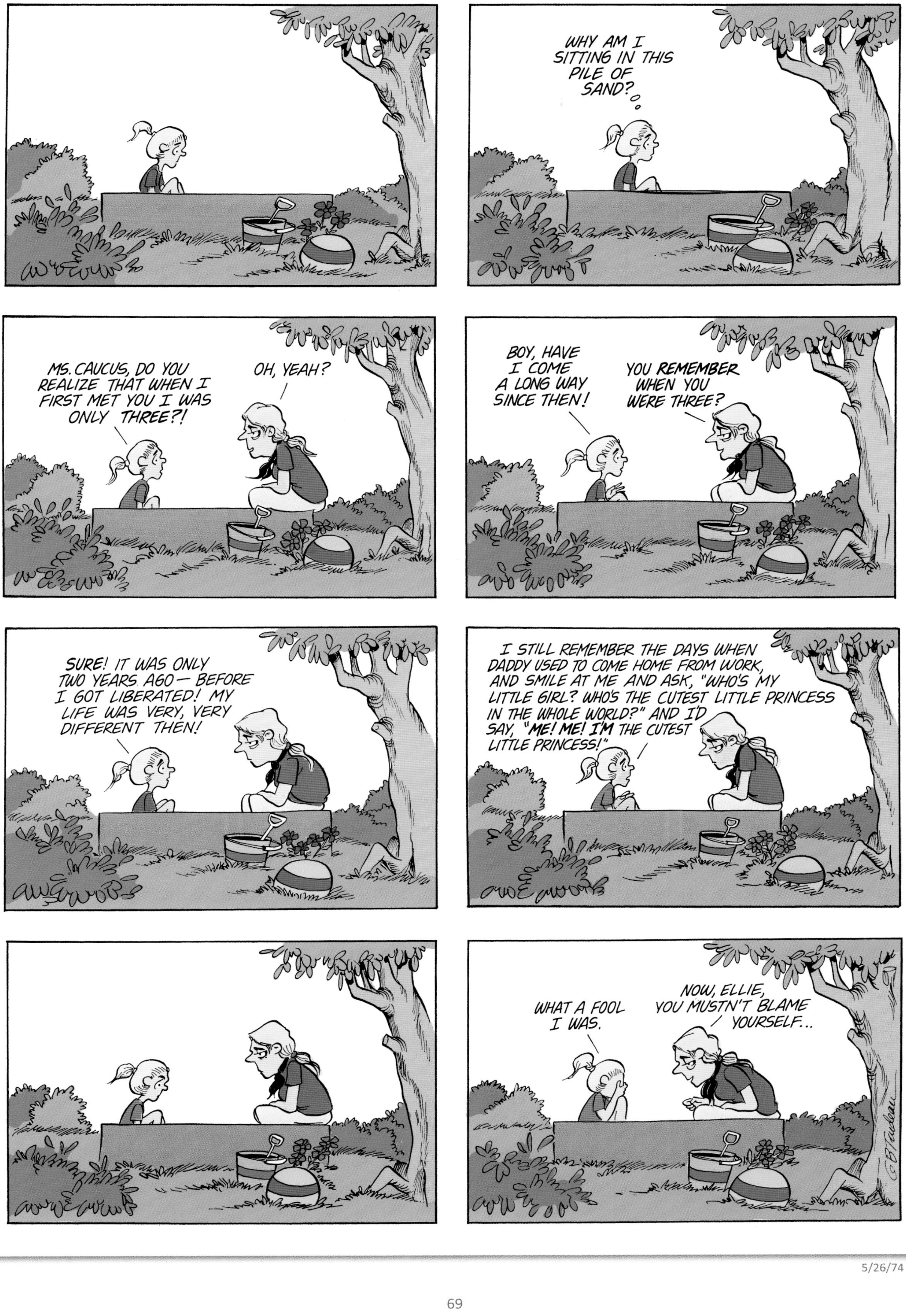

WHY AM I SITTING IN THIS PILE OF SAND?
MS. CAUCUS, DO YOU REALIZE THAT WHEN I FIRST MET YOU I WAS ONLY THREE?!
OH, YEAH?
BOY, HAVE I COME A LONG WAY SINCE THEN!
YOU REMEMBER WHEN YOU WERE THREE?
SURE! IT WAS ONLY TWO YEARS AGO— BEFORE I GOT LIBERATED! MY LIFE WAS VERY, VERY DIFFERENT THEN!
I STILL REMEMBER THE DAYS WHEN DADDY USED TO COME HOME FROM WORK, AND SMILE AT ME AND ASK, "WHO'S MY LITTLE GIRL? WHO'S THE CUTEST LITTLE PRINCESS IN THE WHOLE WORLD?" AND I'D SAY, "ME! ME! I'M THE CUTEST LITTLE PRINCESS!"
WHAT A FOOL I WAS.
NOW, ELLIE, YOU MUSTN'T BLAME YOURSELF...

5/26/74

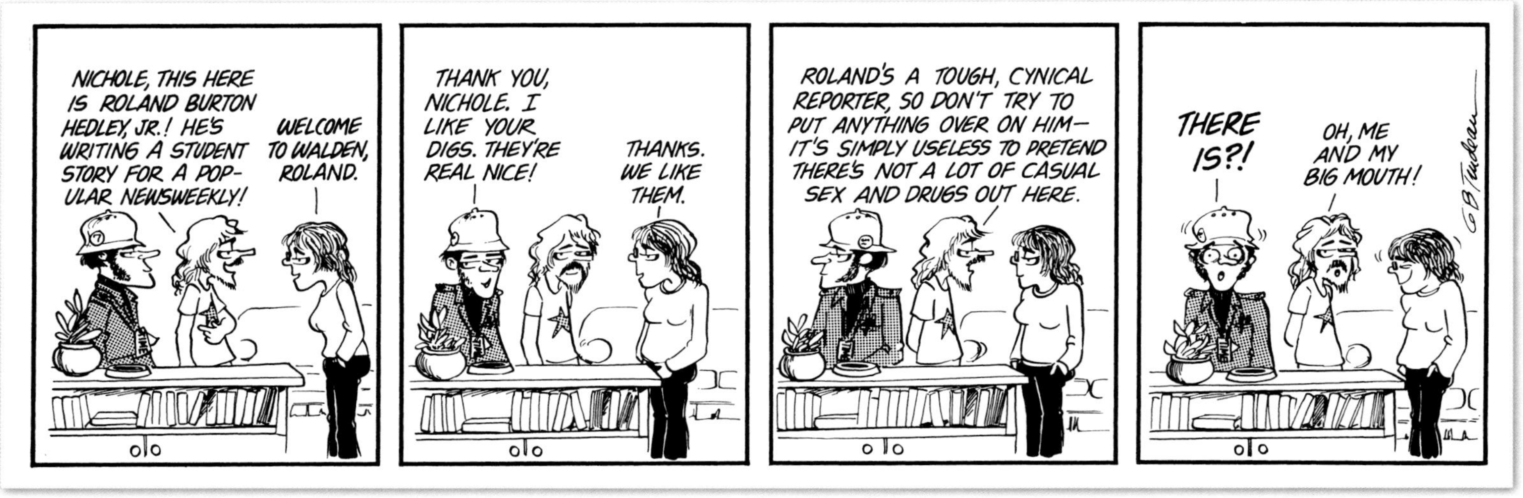
NICHOLE, THIS HERE IS ROLAND BURTON HEDLEY, JR.! HE'S WRITING A STUDENT STORY FOR A POPULAR NEWSWEEKLY!
WELCOME TO WALDEN, ROLAND.
THANK YOU, NICHOLE. I LIKE YOUR DIGS. THEY'RE REAL NICE!
THANKS. WE LIKE THEM.
ROLAND'S A TOUGH, CYNICAL REPORTER, SO DON'T TRY TO PUT ANYTHING OVER ON HIM— IT'S SIMPLY USELESS TO PRETEND THERE'S NOT A LOT OF CASUAL SEX AND DRUGS OUT HERE.
THERE IS?!
OH, ME AND MY BIG MOUTH!

3/7/74

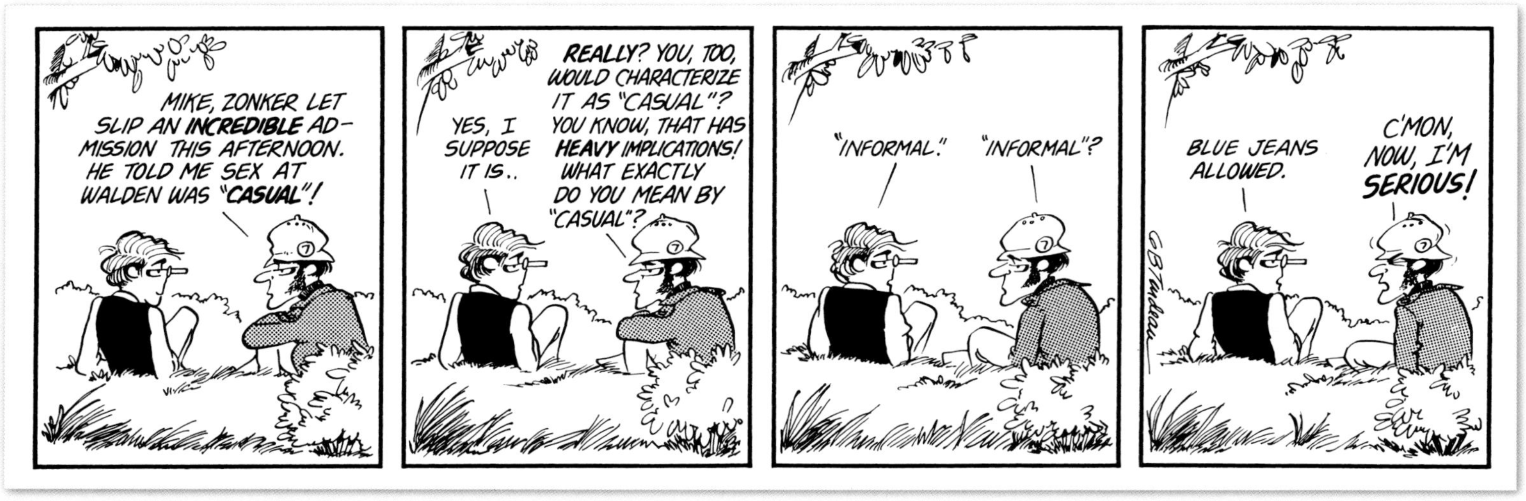
MIKE, ZONKER LET SLIP AN **INCREDIBLE** ADMISSION THIS AFTERNOON. HE TOLD ME SEX AT WALDEN WAS "**CASUAL**"!
YES, I SUPPOSE IT IS..
REALLY? YOU, TOO, WOULD CHARACTERIZE IT AS "CASUAL"? YOU KNOW, THAT HAS **HEAVY** IMPLICATIONS! WHAT EXACTLY DO YOU MEAN BY "CASUAL"?
"INFORMAL."
"INFORMAL"?
BLUE JEANS ALLOWED.
C'MON, NOW, I'M **SERIOUS**!

3/8/74

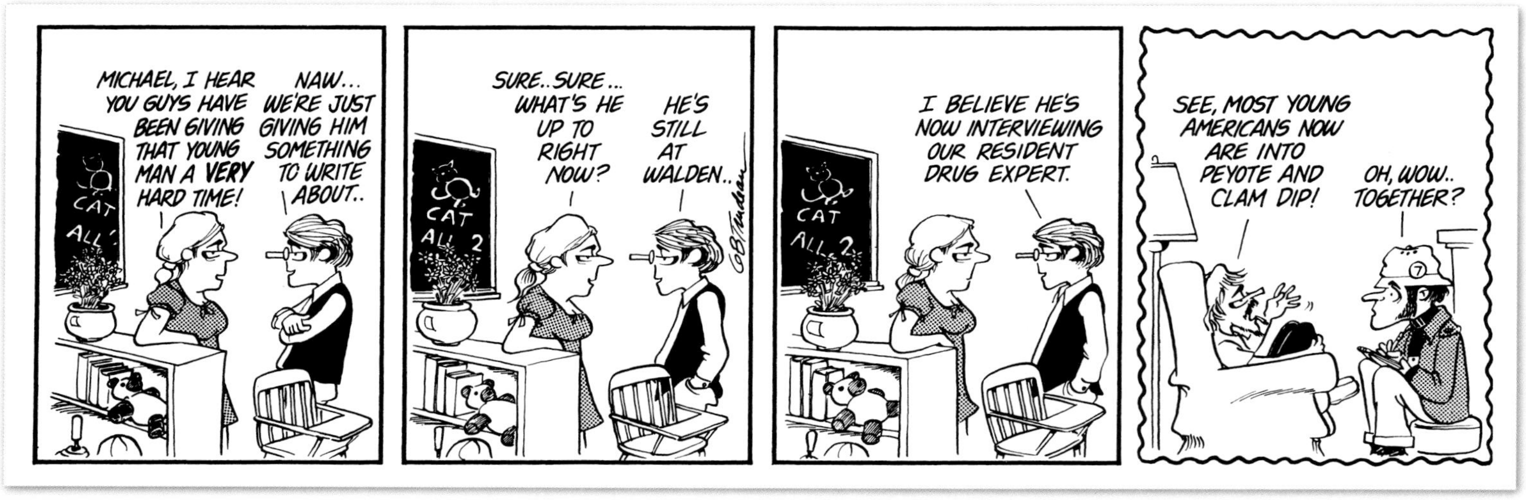
MICHAEL, I HEAR YOU GUYS HAVE BEEN GIVING THAT YOUNG MAN A **VERY** HARD TIME!
NAW... WE'RE JUST GIVING HIM SOMETHING TO WRITE ABOUT..
SURE..SURE... WHAT'S HE UP TO RIGHT NOW?
HE'S STILL AT WALDEN..
I BELIEVE HE'S NOW INTERVIEWING OUR RESIDENT DRUG EXPERT.
SEE, MOST YOUNG AMERICANS NOW ARE INTO PEYOTE AND CLAM DIP!
OH, WOW.. TOGETHER?

3/9/74

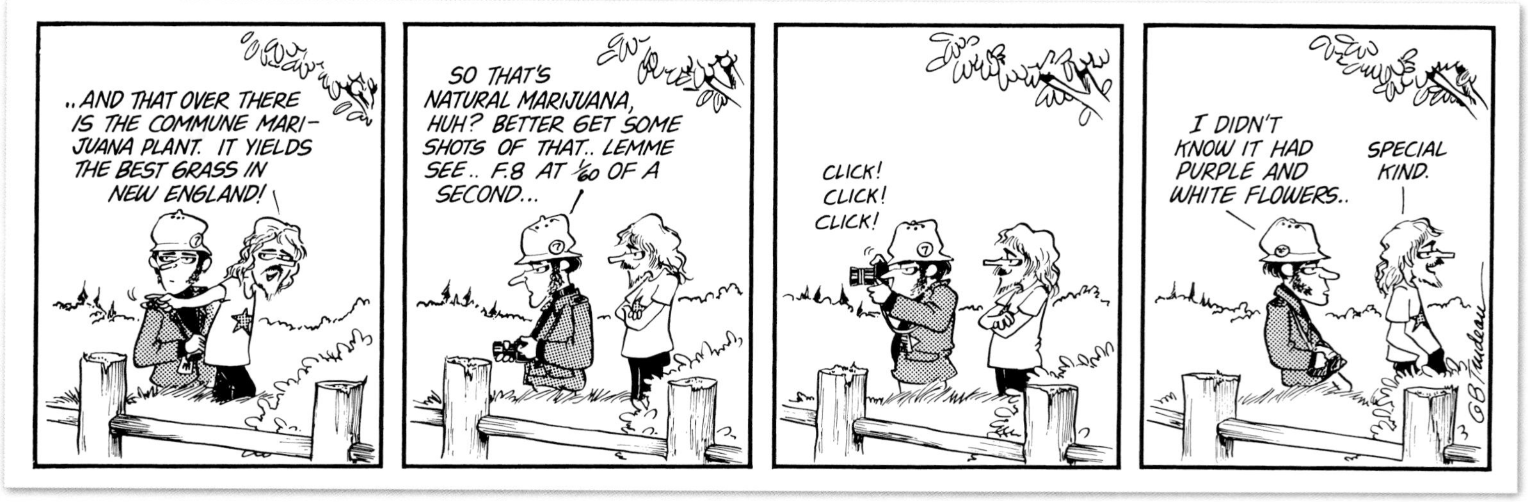
..AND THAT OVER THERE IS THE COMMUNE MARIJUANA PLANT. IT YIELDS THE BEST GRASS IN NEW ENGLAND!
SO THAT'S NATURAL MARIJUANA, HUH? BETTER GET SOME SHOTS OF THAT.. LEMME SEE.. F.8 AT 1/60 OF A SECOND...
CLICK! CLICK! CLICK!
I DIDN'T KNOW IT HAD PURPLE AND WHITE FLOWERS..
SPECIAL KIND.

3/12/74

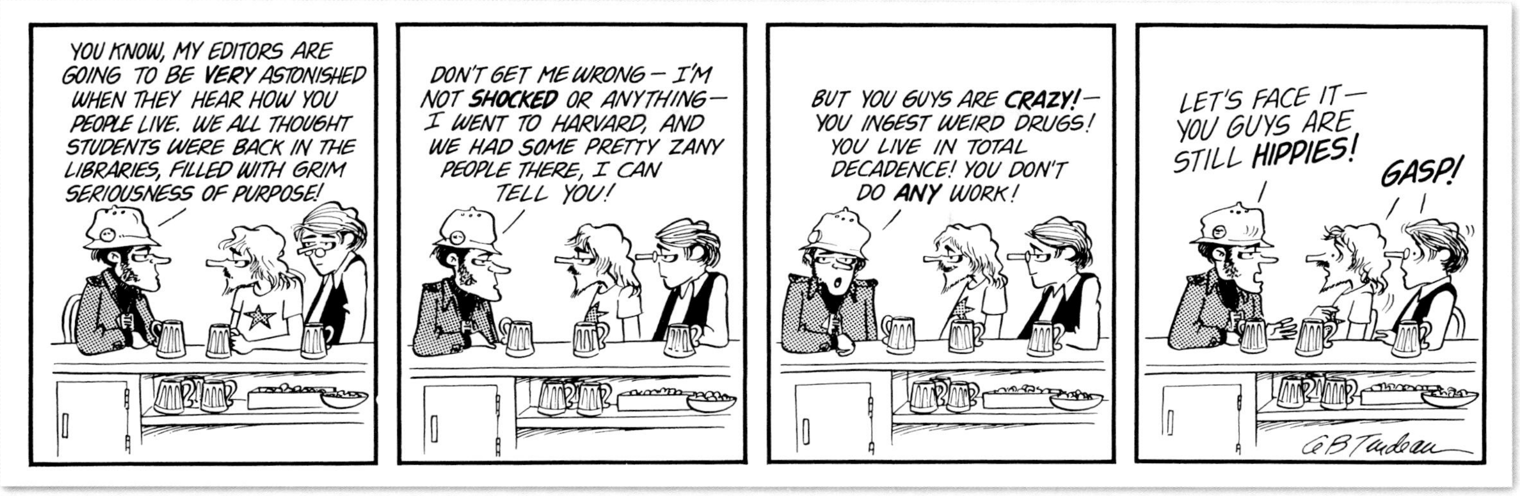
YOU KNOW, MY EDITORS ARE GOING TO BE VERY ASTONISHED WHEN THEY HEAR HOW YOU PEOPLE LIVE. WE ALL THOUGHT STUDENTS WERE BACK IN THE LIBRARIES, FILLED WITH GRIM SERIOUSNESS OF PURPOSE!
DON'T GET ME WRONG — I'M NOT SHOCKED OR ANYTHING — I WENT TO HARVARD, AND WE HAD SOME PRETTY ZANY PEOPLE THERE, I CAN TELL YOU!
BUT YOU GUYS ARE CRAZY! — YOU INGEST WEIRD DRUGS! YOU LIVE IN TOTAL DECADENCE! YOU DON'T DO ANY WORK!
LET'S FACE IT — YOU GUYS ARE STILL HIPPIES!
GASP!
GBTrudeau

3/13/74

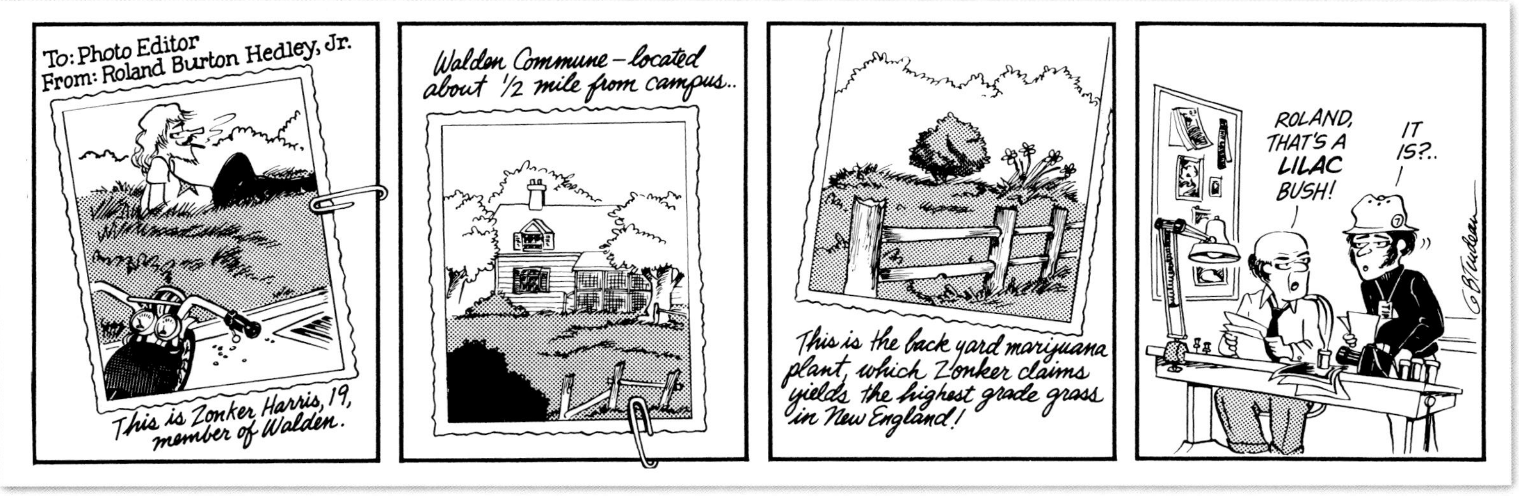
To: Photo Editor
From: Roland Burton Hedley, Jr.
This is Zonker Harris, 19, member of Walden.
Walden Commune — located about 1/2 mile from campus..
This is the back yard marijuana plant, which Zonker claims yields the highest grade grass in New England!
ROLAND, THAT'S A LILAC BUSH!
IT IS?..
GBTrudeau

3/16/74

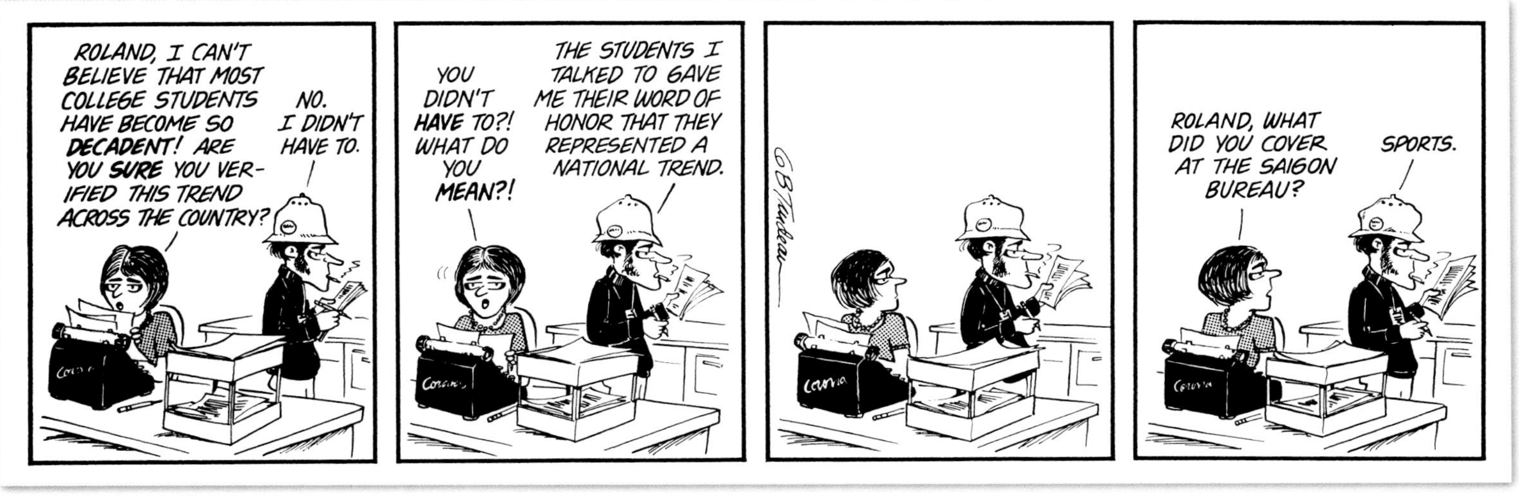
ROLAND, I CAN'T BELIEVE THAT MOST COLLEGE STUDENTS HAVE BECOME SO DECADENT! ARE YOU SURE YOU VERIFIED THIS TREND ACROSS THE COUNTRY?
NO. I DIDN'T HAVE TO.
YOU DIDN'T HAVE TO?! WHAT DO YOU MEAN?!
THE STUDENTS I TALKED TO GAVE ME THEIR WORD OF HONOR THAT THEY REPRESENTED A NATIONAL TREND.
GBTrudeau
ROLAND, WHAT DID YOU COVER AT THE SAIGON BUREAU?
SPORTS.

3/18/74

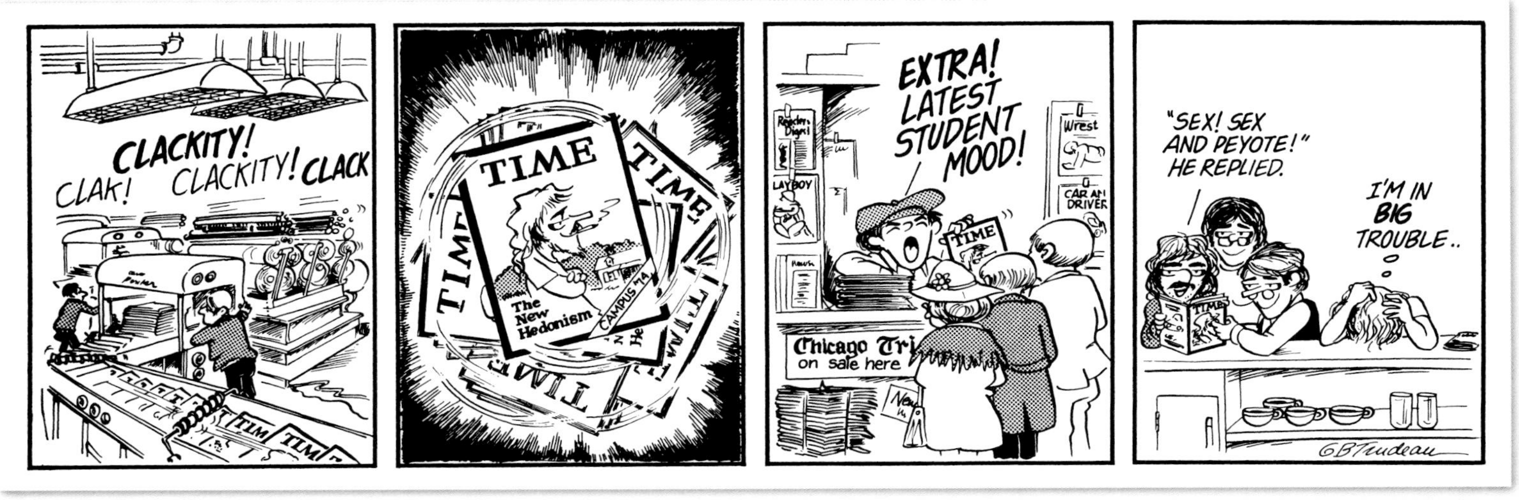
CLACKITY!
CLAK! CLACKITY! CLACK
TIME
The New Hedonism
CAMPUS '74
EXTRA! LATEST STUDENT MOOD!
Chicago Tri
on sale here
"SEX! SEX AND PEYOTE!" HE REPLIED.
I'M IN BIG TROUBLE..
GBTrudeau

3/19/74

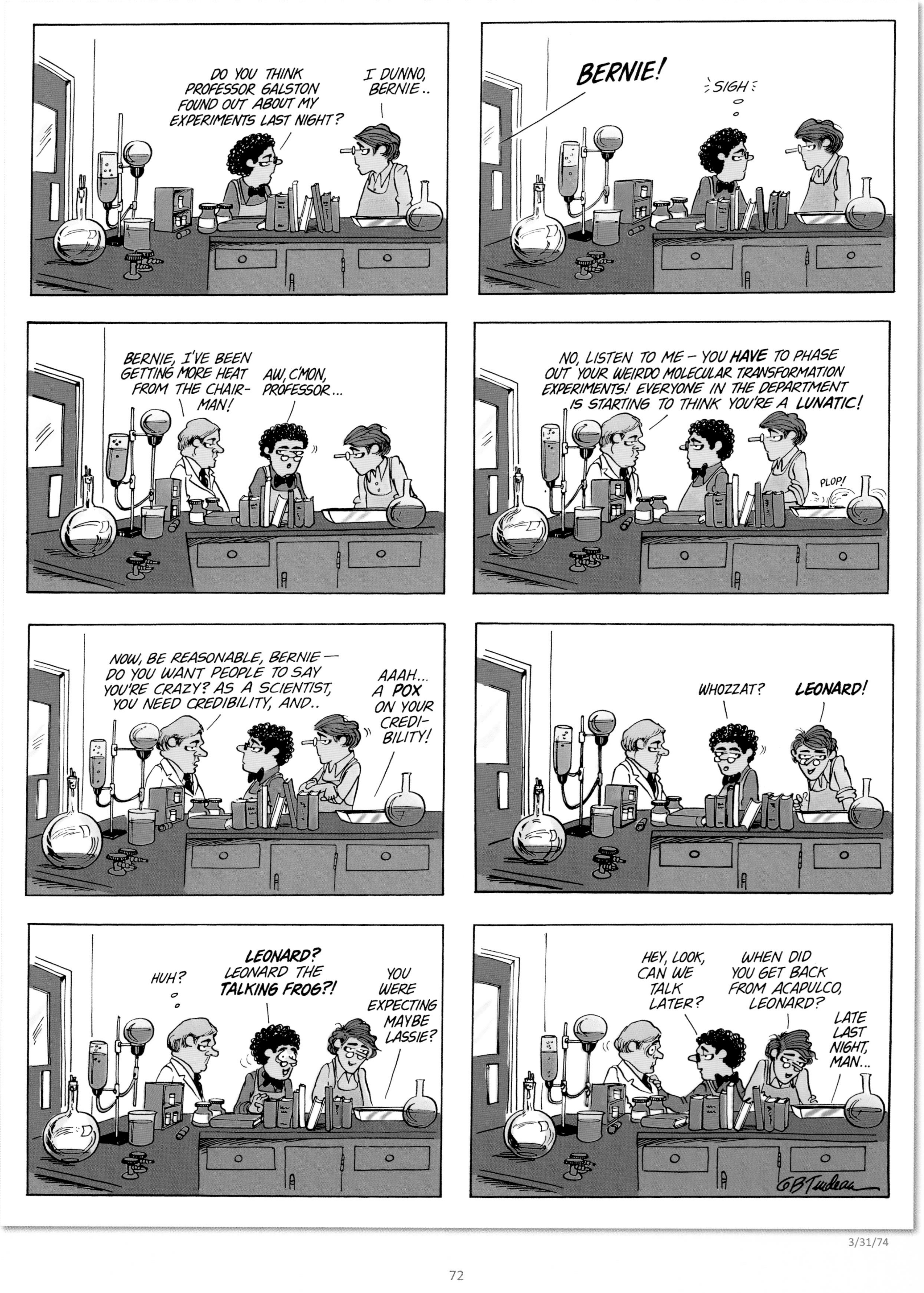
DO YOU THINK PROFESSOR GALSTON FOUND OUT ABOUT MY EXPERIMENTS LAST NIGHT?
I DUNNO, BERNIE..
BERNIE!
SIGH
BERNIE, I'VE BEEN GETTING MORE HEAT FROM THE CHAIRMAN!
AW, C'MON, PROFESSOR...
NO, LISTEN TO ME – YOU HAVE TO PHASE OUT YOUR WEIRDO MOLECULAR TRANSFORMATION EXPERIMENTS! EVERYONE IN THE DEPARTMENT IS STARTING TO THINK YOU'RE A LUNATIC!
PLOP!
NOW, BE REASONABLE, BERNIE – DO YOU WANT PEOPLE TO SAY YOU'RE CRAZY? AS A SCIENTIST, YOU NEED CREDIBILITY, AND..
AAAH... A POX ON YOUR CREDIBILITY!
WHOZZAT?
LEONARD!
HUH?
LEONARD? LEONARD THE TALKING FROG?!
YOU WERE EXPECTING MAYBE LASSIE?
HEY, LOOK, CAN WE TALK LATER?
WHEN DID YOU GET BACK FROM ACAPULCO, LEONARD?
LATE LAST NIGHT, MAN...
GBTrudeau

3/31/74

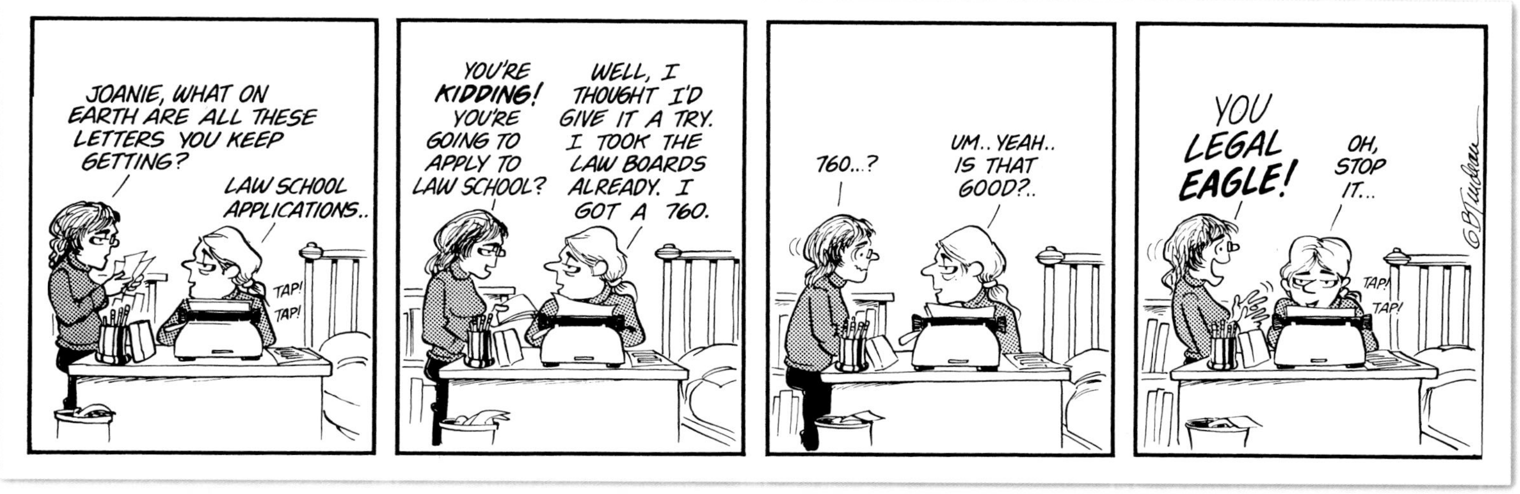
JOANIE, WHAT ON EARTH ARE ALL THESE LETTERS YOU KEEP GETTING?
LAW SCHOOL APPLICATIONS..
TAP! TAP!
YOU'RE KIDDING! YOU'RE GOING TO APPLY TO LAW SCHOOL?
WELL, I THOUGHT I'D GIVE IT A TRY. I TOOK THE LAW BOARDS ALREADY. I GOT A 760.
760...?
UM.. YEAH.. IS THAT GOOD?..
YOU LEGAL EAGLE!
OH, STOP IT...
TAP! TAP!

2/20/74

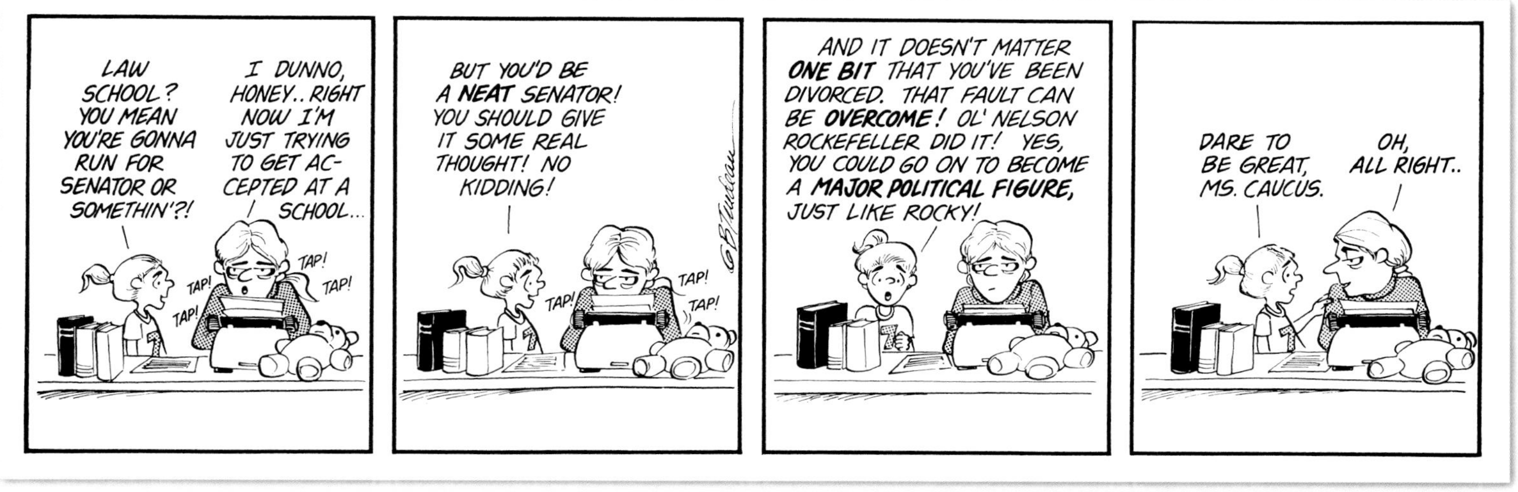
LAW SCHOOL? YOU MEAN YOU'RE GONNA RUN FOR SENATOR OR SOMETHIN'?!
I DUNNO, HONEY.. RIGHT NOW I'M JUST TRYING TO GET ACCEPTED AT A SCHOOL...
TAP! TAP! TAP! TAP!
BUT YOU'D BE A NEAT SENATOR! YOU SHOULD GIVE IT SOME REAL THOUGHT! NO KIDDING!
TAP! TAP! TAP!
AND IT DOESN'T MATTER ONE BIT THAT YOU'VE BEEN DIVORCED. THAT FAULT CAN BE OVERCOME! OL' NELSON ROCKEFELLER DID IT! YES, YOU COULD GO ON TO BECOME A MAJOR POLITICAL FIGURE, JUST LIKE ROCKY!
DARE TO BE GREAT, MS. CAUCUS.
OH, ALL RIGHT..

2/21/74

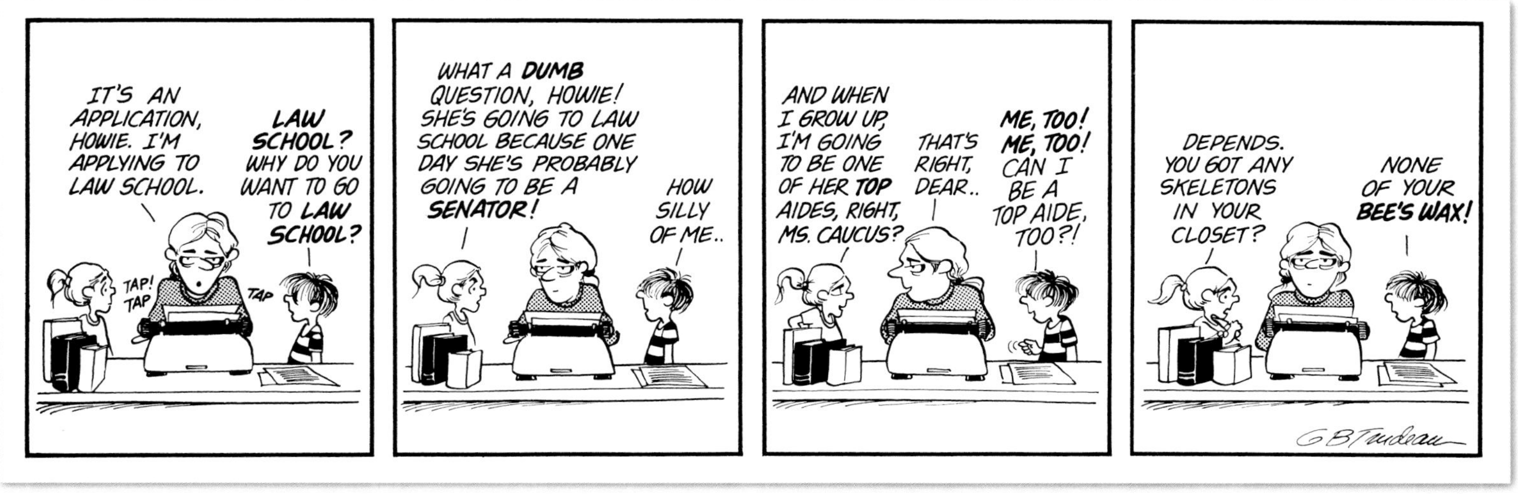
IT'S AN APPLICATION, HOWIE. I'M APPLYING TO LAW SCHOOL.
LAW SCHOOL? WHY DO YOU WANT TO GO TO LAW SCHOOL?
TAP! TAP TAP
WHAT A DUMB QUESTION, HOWIE! SHE'S GOING TO LAW SCHOOL BECAUSE ONE DAY SHE'S PROBABLY GOING TO BE A SENATOR!
HOW SILLY OF ME..
AND WHEN I GROW UP, I'M GOING TO BE ONE OF HER TOP AIDES, RIGHT, MS. CAUCUS?
THAT'S RIGHT, DEAR..
ME, TOO! ME, TOO! CAN I BE A TOP AIDE, TOO?!
DEPENDS. YOU GOT ANY SKELETONS IN YOUR CLOSET?
NONE OF YOUR BEE'S WAX!

2/22/74

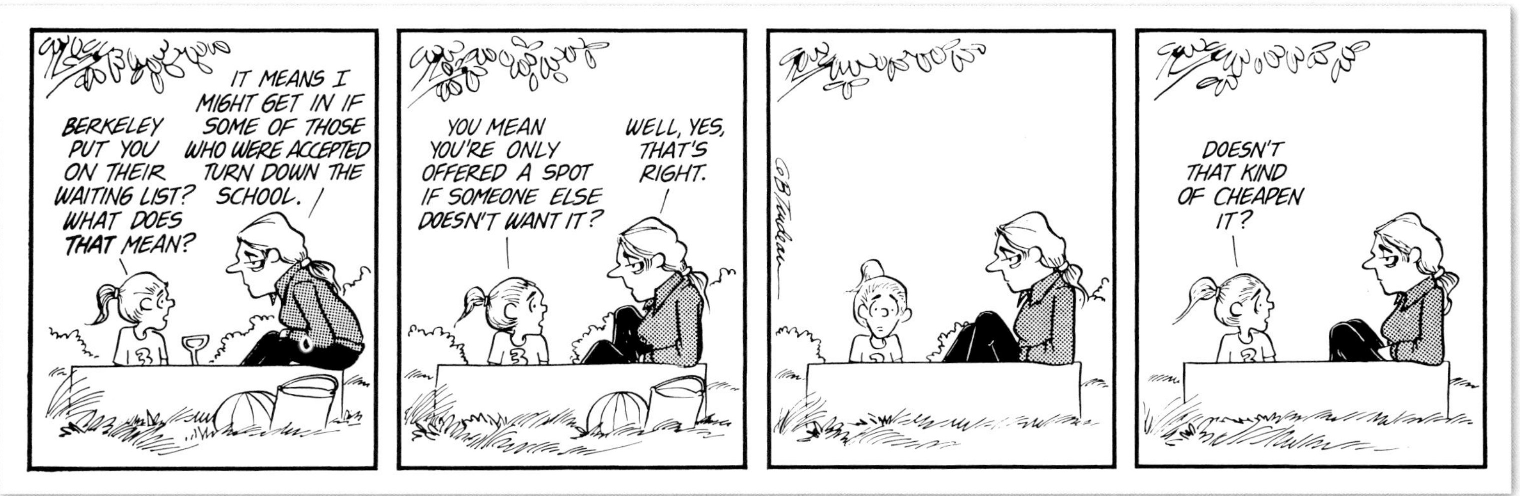
BERKELEY PUT YOU ON THEIR WAITING LIST? WHAT DOES THAT MEAN?
IT MEANS I MIGHT GET IN IF SOME OF THOSE WHO WERE ACCEPTED TURN DOWN THE SCHOOL.
YOU MEAN YOU'RE ONLY OFFERED A SPOT IF SOMEONE ELSE DOESN'T WANT IT?
WELL, YES, THAT'S RIGHT.
DOESN'T THAT KIND OF CHEAPEN IT?

4/12/74

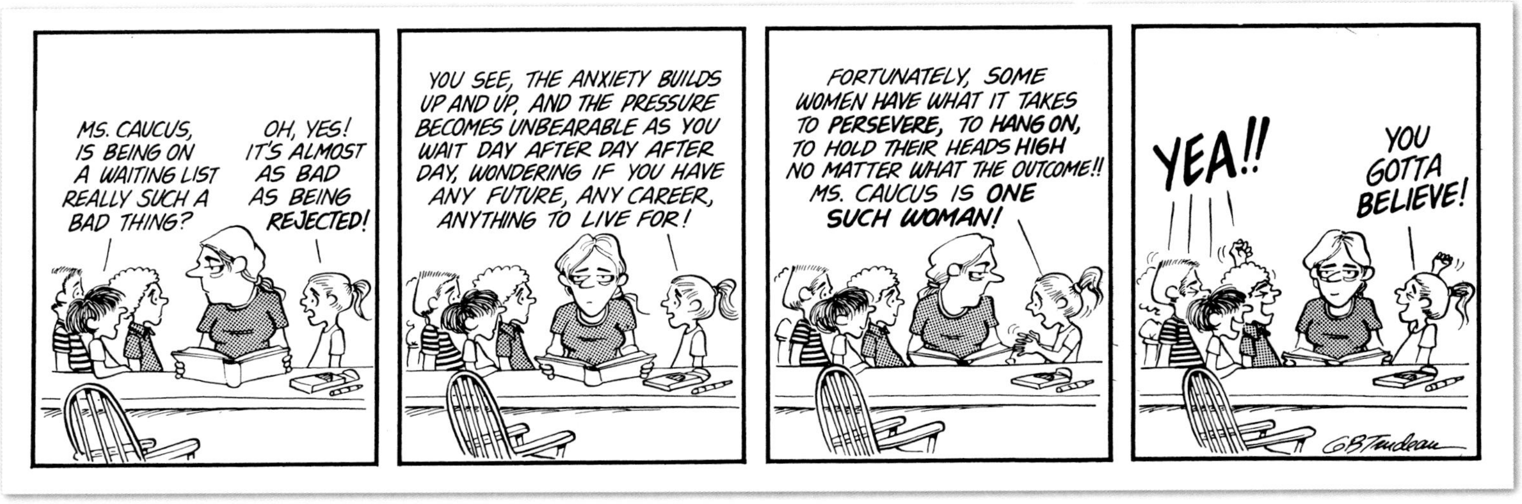
MS. CAUCUS, IS BEING ON A WAITING LIST REALLY SUCH A BAD THING?
OH, YES! IT'S ALMOST AS BAD AS BEING REJECTED!
YOU SEE, THE ANXIETY BUILDS UP AND UP, AND THE PRESSURE BECOMES UNBEARABLE AS YOU WAIT DAY AFTER DAY AFTER DAY, WONDERING IF YOU HAVE ANY FUTURE, ANY CAREER, ANYTHING TO LIVE FOR!
FORTUNATELY, SOME WOMEN HAVE WHAT IT TAKES TO PERSEVERE, TO HANG ON, TO HOLD THEIR HEADS HIGH NO MATTER WHAT THE OUTCOME!! MS. CAUCUS IS ONE SUCH WOMAN!
YEA!!
YOU GOTTA BELIEVE!
GBTrudeau

4/18/74

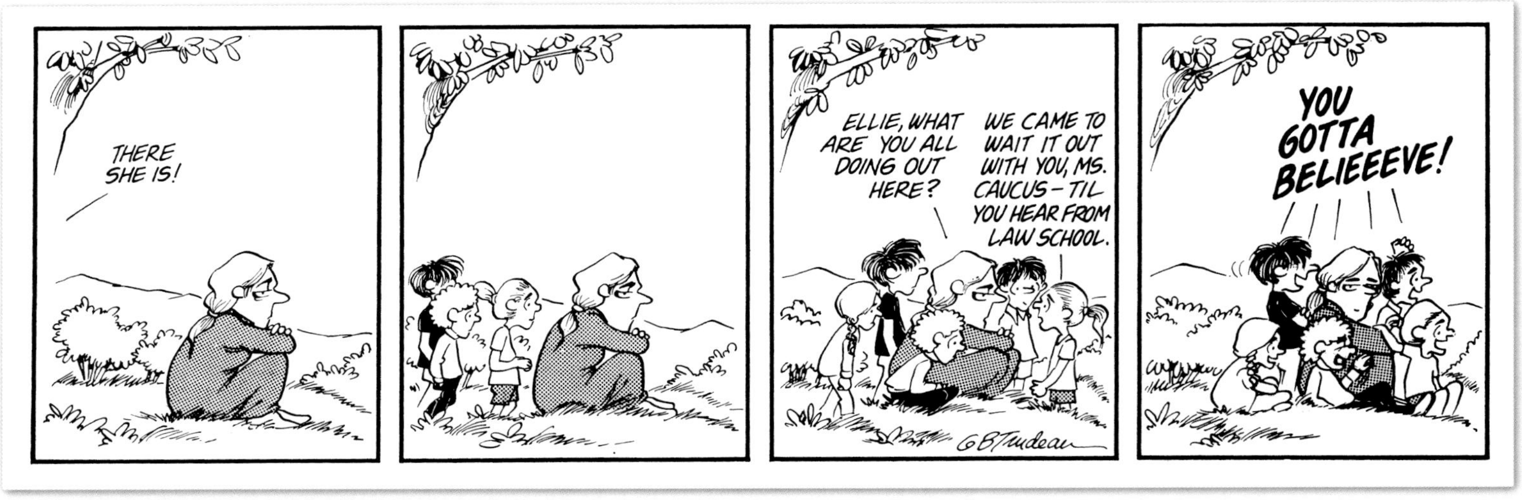
THERE SHE IS!
ELLIE, WHAT ARE YOU ALL DOING OUT HERE?
WE CAME TO WAIT IT OUT WITH YOU, MS. CAUCUS–TIL YOU HEAR FROM LAW SCHOOL.
YOU GOTTA BELIEEEVE!
GBTrudeau

4/19/74

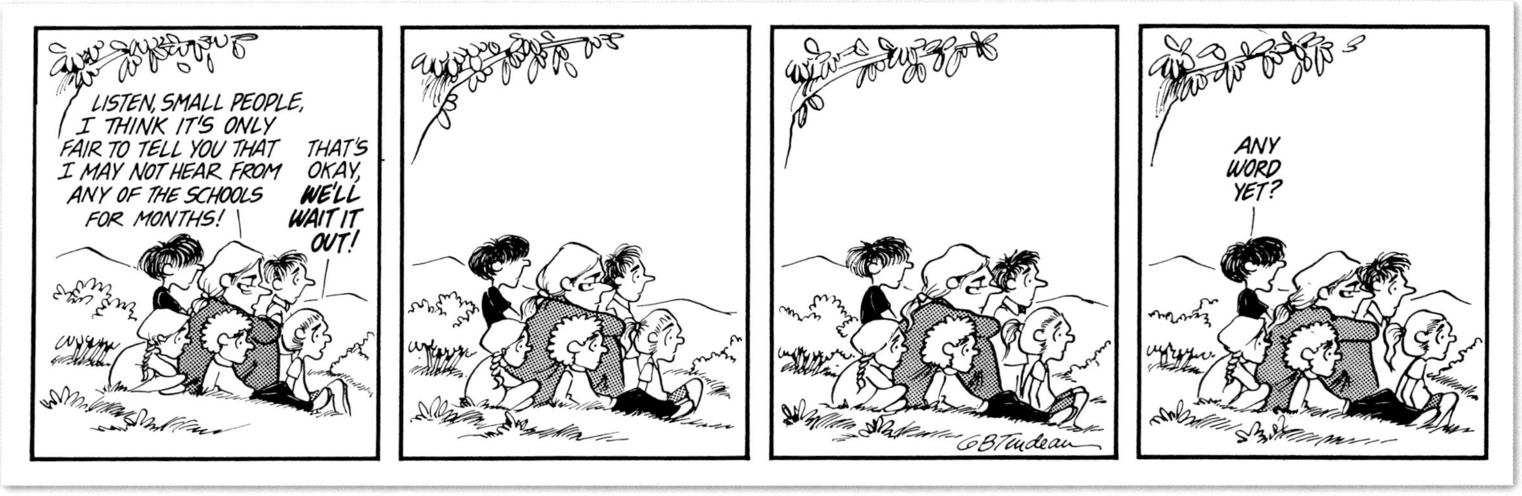
LISTEN, SMALL PEOPLE, I THINK IT'S ONLY FAIR TO TELL YOU THAT I MAY NOT HEAR FROM ANY OF THE SCHOOLS FOR MONTHS!
THAT'S OKAY, WE'LL WAIT IT OUT!
ANY WORD YET?
GBTrudeau

4/20/74

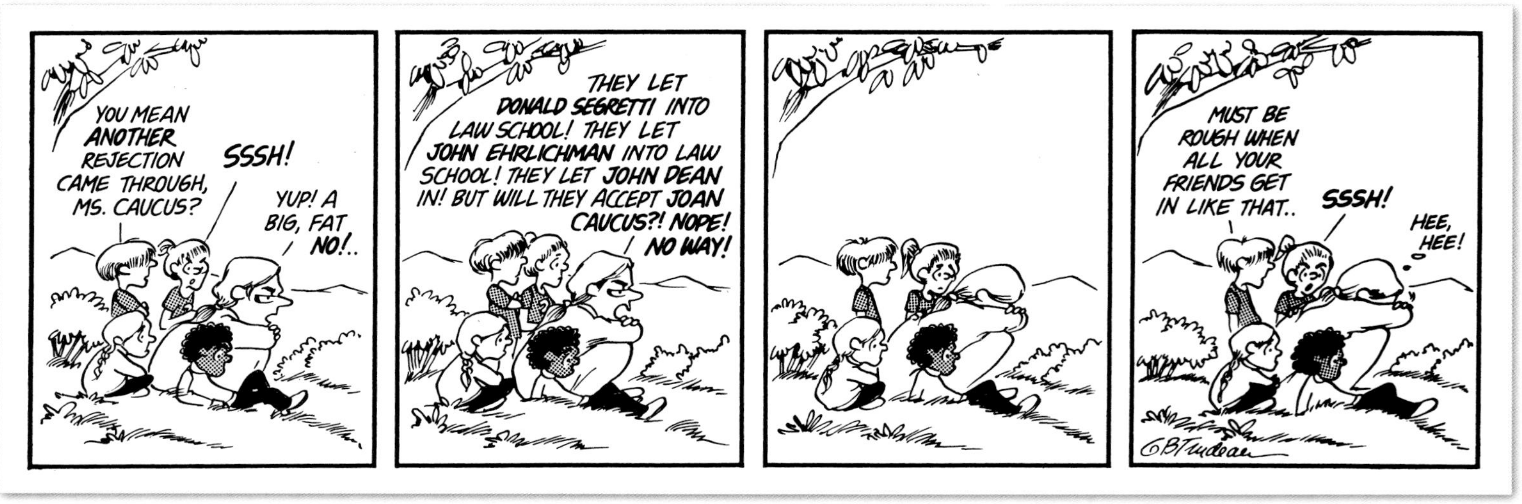
YOU MEAN ANOTHER REJECTION CAME THROUGH, MS. CAUCUS?
SSSH!
YUP! A BIG, FAT NO!..
THEY LET DONALD SEGRETTI INTO LAW SCHOOL! THEY LET JOHN EHRLICHMAN INTO LAW SCHOOL! THEY LET JOHN DEAN IN! BUT WILL THEY ACCEPT JOAN CAUCUS?! NOPE! NO WAY!
MUST BE ROUGH WHEN ALL YOUR FRIENDS GET IN LIKE THAT..
SSSH!
HEE, HEE!
GBTrudeau

5/10/74

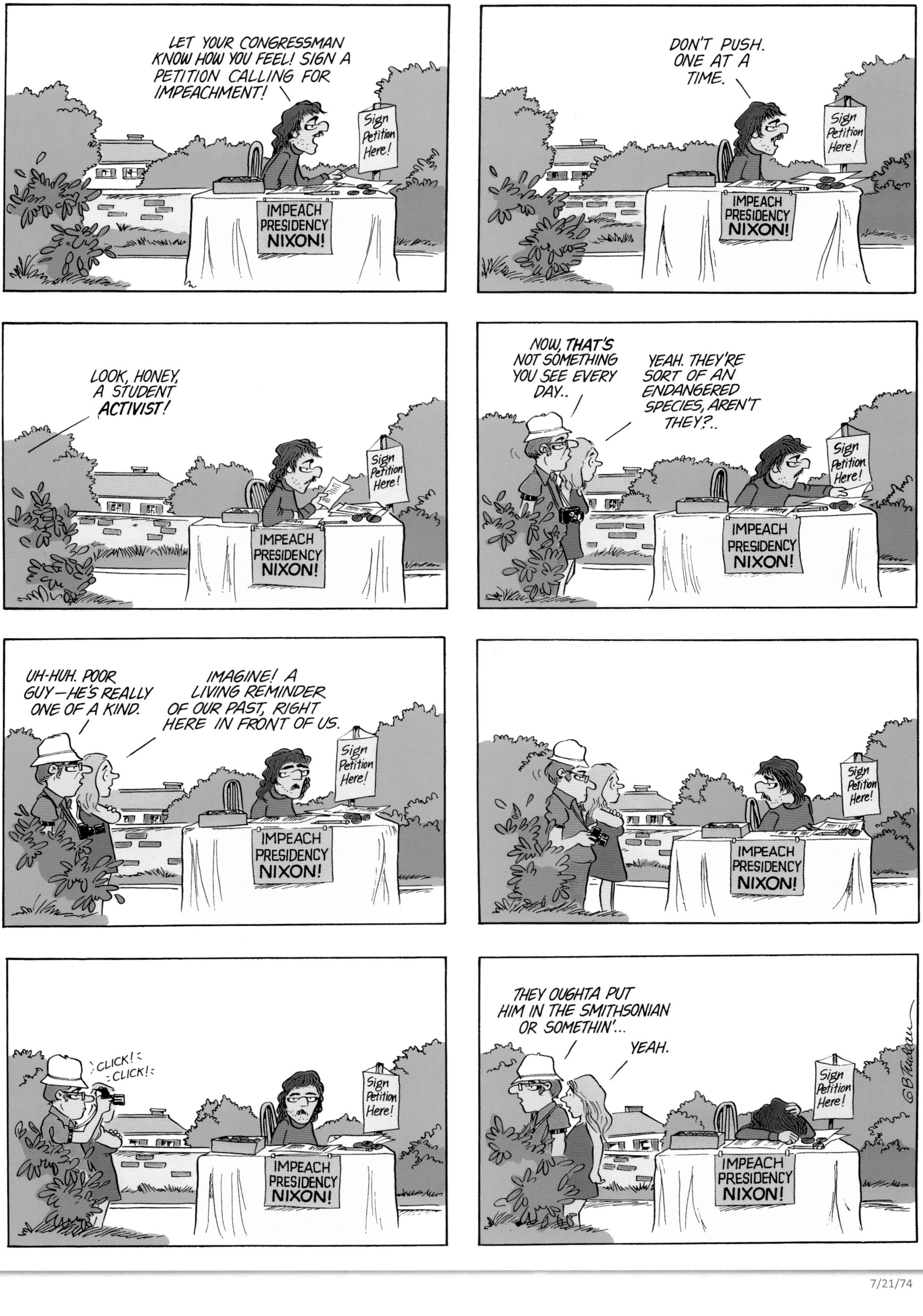
LET YOUR CONGRESSMAN KNOW HOW YOU FEEL! SIGN A PETITION CALLING FOR IMPEACHMENT!
Sign Petition Here!
IMPEACH PRESIDENCY NIXON!
DON'T PUSH. ONE AT A TIME.
LOOK, HONEY, A STUDENT ACTIVIST!
NOW, THAT'S NOT SOMETHING YOU SEE EVERY DAY..
YEAH. THEY'RE SORT OF AN ENDANGERED SPECIES, AREN'T THEY?..
UH-HUH. POOR GUY—HE'S REALLY ONE OF A KIND.
IMAGINE! A LIVING REMINDER OF OUR PAST, RIGHT HERE IN FRONT OF US.
CLICK! CLICK!
THEY OUGHTA PUT HIM IN THE SMITHSONIAN OR SOMETHIN'...
YEAH.
©B Trudeau

7/21/74

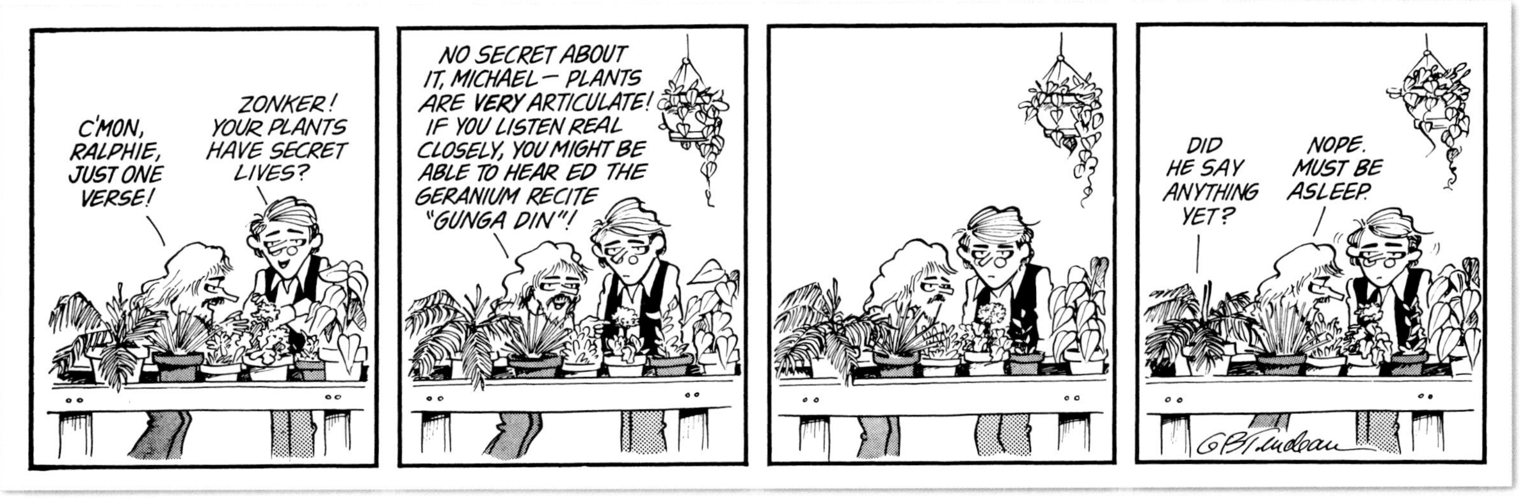
C'MON, RALPHIE, JUST ONE VERSE!
ZONKER! YOUR PLANTS HAVE SECRET LIVES?
NO SECRET ABOUT IT, MICHAEL— PLANTS ARE VERY ARTICULATE! IF YOU LISTEN REAL CLOSELY, YOU MIGHT BE ABLE TO HEAR ED THE GERANIUM RECITE "GUNGA DIN"!
DID HE SAY ANYTHING YET?
NOPE. MUST BE ASLEEP.

10/21/74

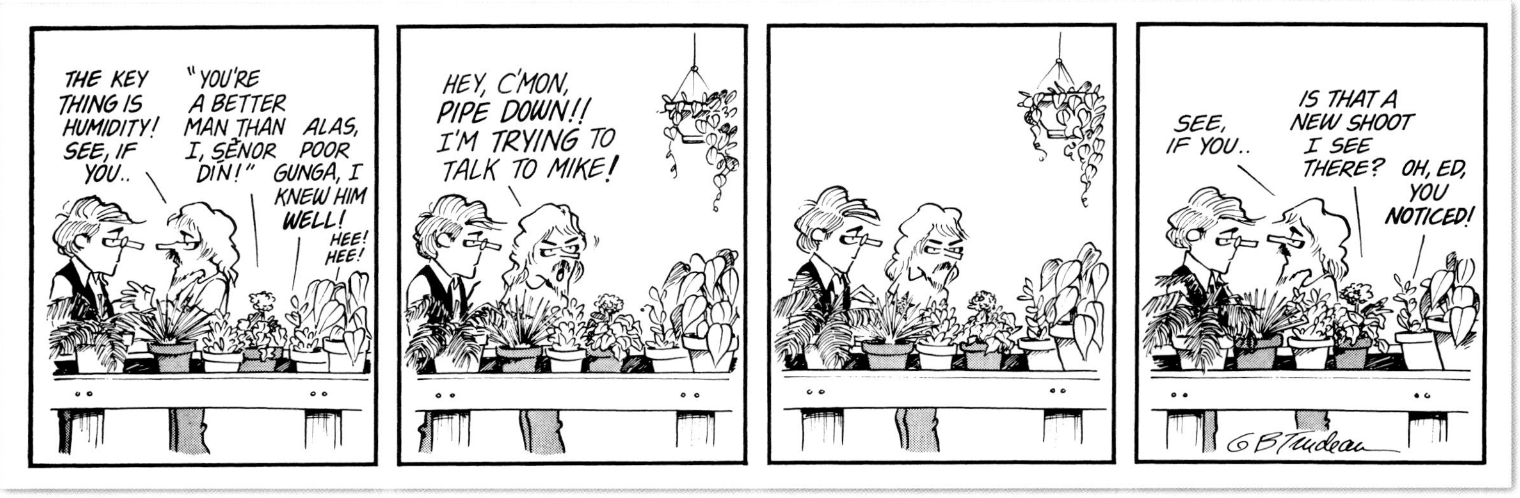
THE KEY THING IS HUMIDITY! SEE, IF YOU..
"YOU'RE A BETTER MAN THAN I, SEÑOR DIN!"
ALAS, POOR GUNGA, I KNEW HIM WELL! HEE! HEE!
HEY, C'MON, PIPE DOWN!! I'M TRYING TO TALK TO MIKE!
SEE, IF YOU..
IS THAT A NEW SHOOT I SEE THERE?
OH, ED, YOU NOTICED!

10/22/74

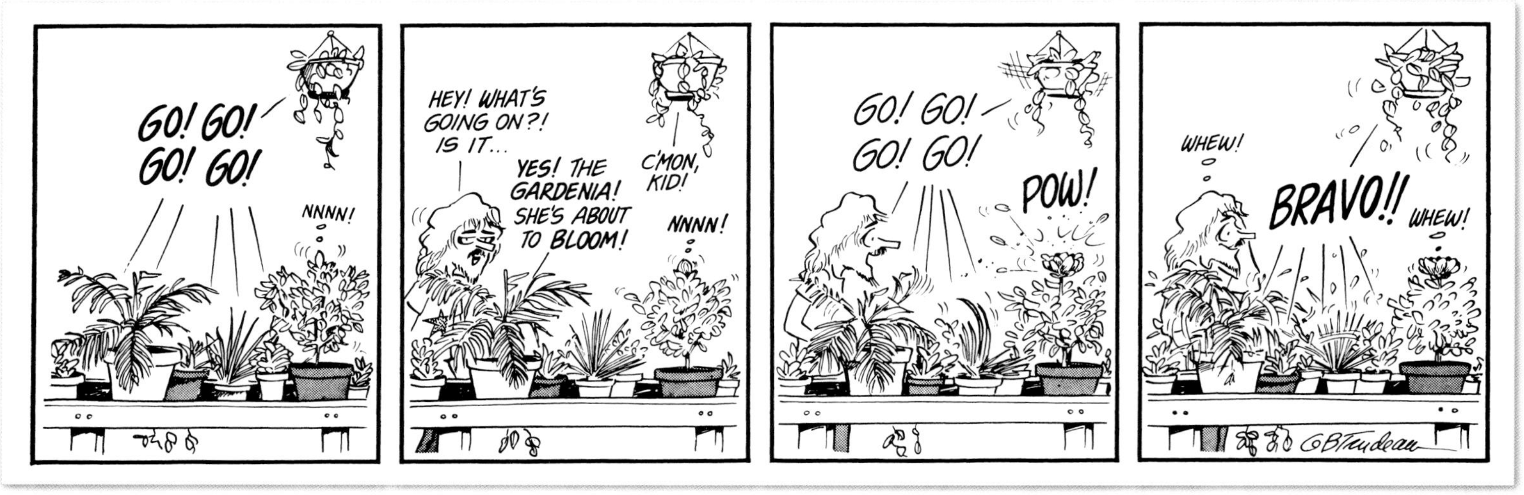
GO! GO! GO! GO!
NNNN!
HEY! WHAT'S GOING ON?! IS IT...
YES! THE GARDENIA! SHE'S ABOUT TO BLOOM!
C'MON, KID!
NNNN!
GO! GO! GO! GO!
POW!
WHEW!
BRAVO!!
WHEW!

10/24/74

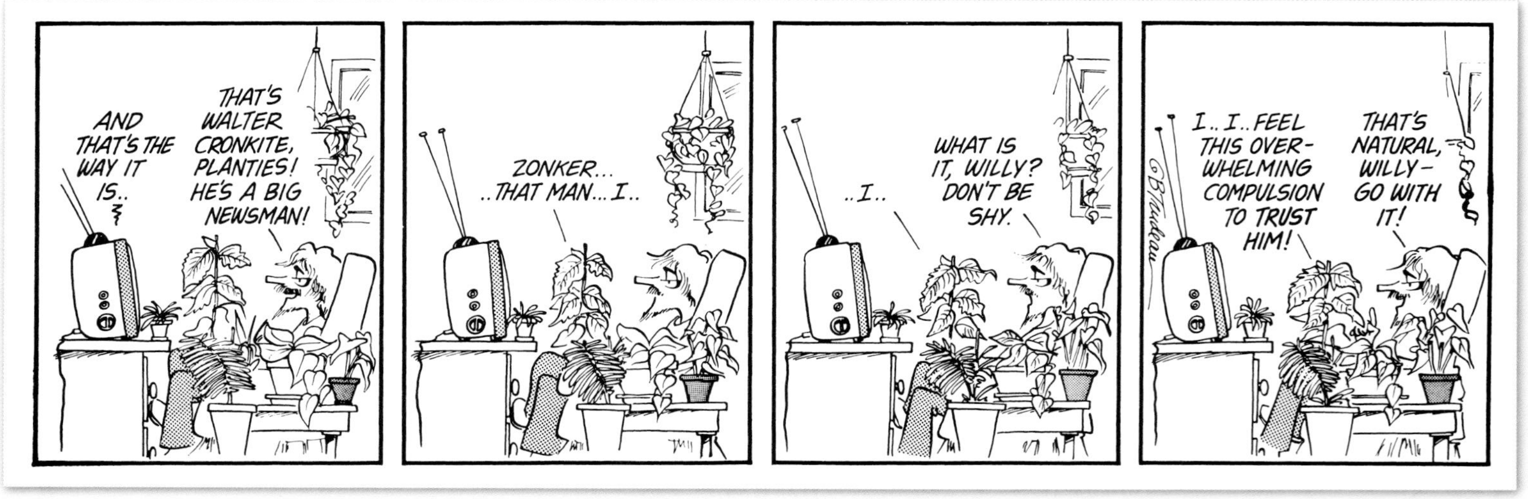
AND THAT'S THE WAY IT IS..
THAT'S WALTER CRONKITE, PLANTIES! HE'S A BIG NEWSMAN!
ZONKER... ..THAT MAN... I..
..I..
WHAT IS IT, WILLY? DON'T BE SHY.
I.. I.. FEEL THIS OVER-WHELMING COMPULSION TO TRUST HIM!
THAT'S NATURAL, WILLY— GO WITH IT!

10/25/74

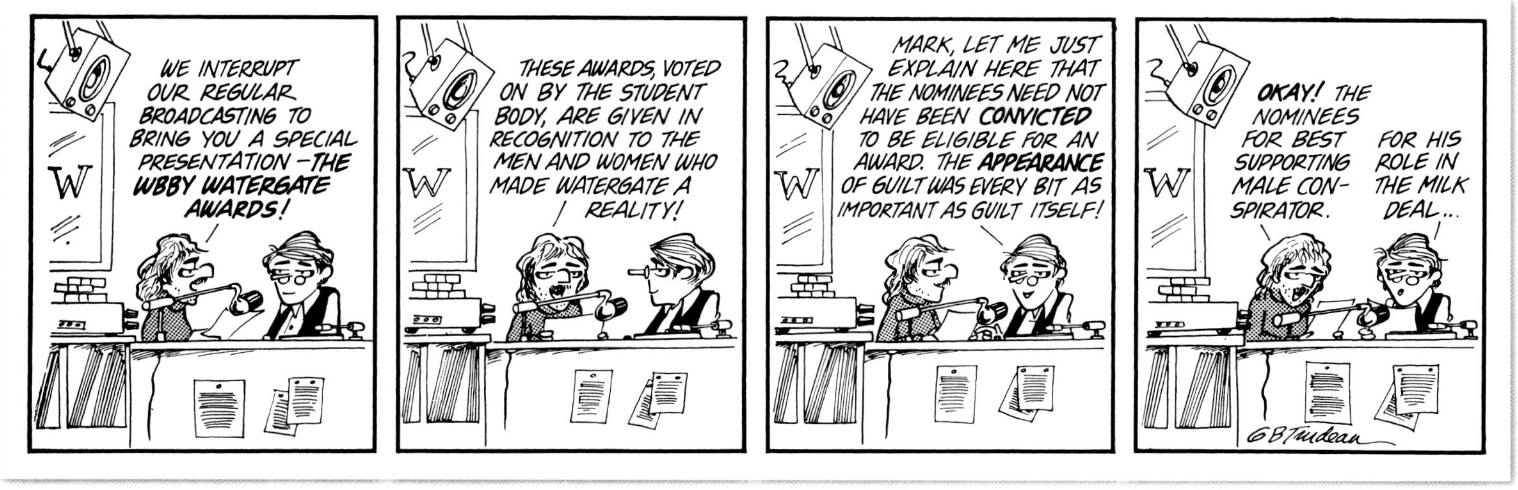
WE INTERRUPT OUR REGULAR BROADCASTING TO BRING YOU A SPECIAL PRESENTATION — THE WBBY WATERGATE AWARDS!
THESE AWARDS, VOTED ON BY THE STUDENT BODY, ARE GIVEN IN RECOGNITION TO THE MEN AND WOMEN WHO MADE WATERGATE A REALITY!
MARK, LET ME JUST EXPLAIN HERE THAT THE NOMINEES NEED NOT HAVE BEEN CONVICTED TO BE ELIGIBLE FOR AN AWARD. THE APPEARANCE OF GUILT WAS EVERY BIT AS IMPORTANT AS GUILT ITSELF!
OKAY! THE NOMINEES FOR BEST SUPPORTING MALE CONSPIRATOR.
FOR HIS ROLE IN THE MILK DEAL...
GBTrudeau

4/23/74

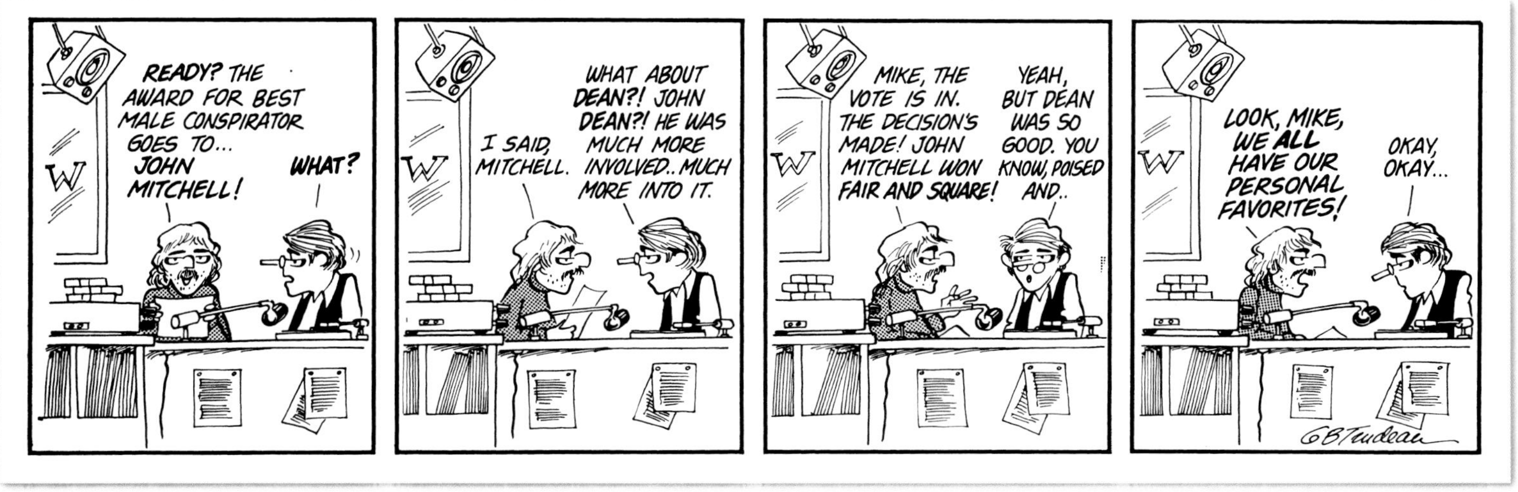
READY? THE AWARD FOR BEST MALE CONSPIRATOR GOES TO... JOHN MITCHELL!
WHAT?
I SAID, MITCHELL.
WHAT ABOUT DEAN?! JOHN DEAN?! HE WAS MUCH MORE INVOLVED.. MUCH MORE INTO IT.
MIKE, THE VOTE IS IN. THE DECISION'S MADE! JOHN MITCHELL WON FAIR AND SQUARE!
YEAH, BUT DEAN WAS SO GOOD. YOU KNOW, POISED AND..
LOOK, MIKE, WE ALL HAVE OUR PERSONAL FAVORITES!
OKAY, OKAY...
GBTrudeau

4/24/74

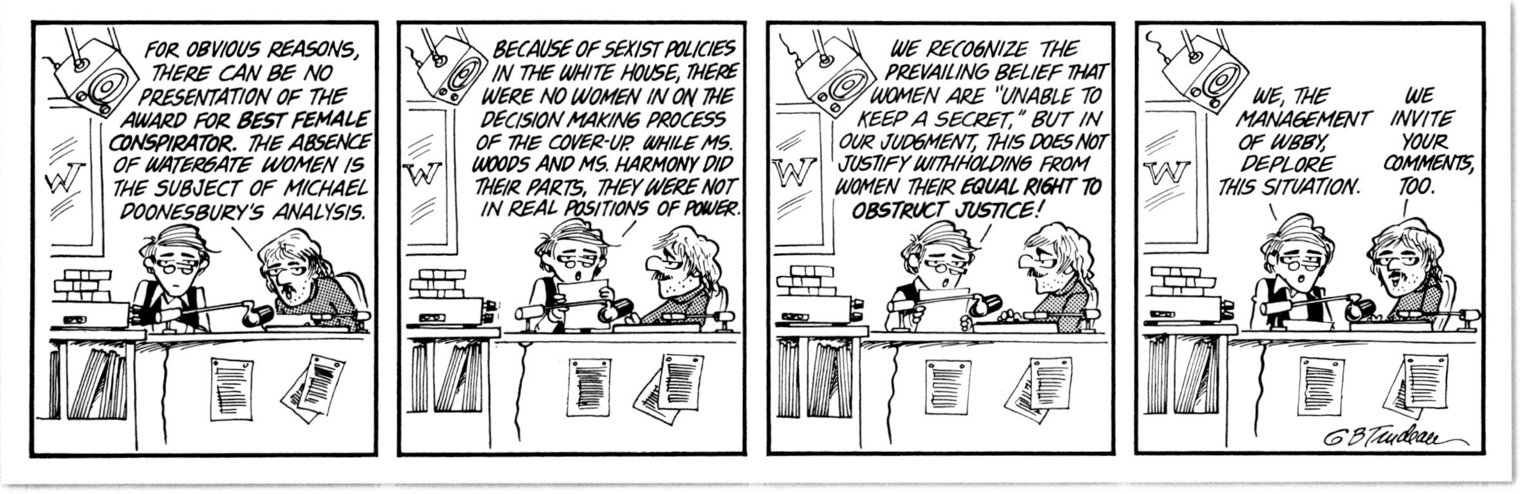
FOR OBVIOUS REASONS, THERE CAN BE NO PRESENTATION OF THE AWARD FOR BEST FEMALE CONSPIRATOR. THE ABSENCE OF WATERGATE WOMEN IS THE SUBJECT OF MICHAEL DOONESBURY'S ANALYSIS.
BECAUSE OF SEXIST POLICIES IN THE WHITE HOUSE, THERE WERE NO WOMEN IN ON THE DECISION MAKING PROCESS OF THE COVER-UP. WHILE MS. WOODS AND MS. HARMONY DID THEIR PARTS, THEY WERE NOT IN REAL POSITIONS OF POWER.
WE RECOGNIZE THE PREVAILING BELIEF THAT WOMEN ARE "UNABLE TO KEEP A SECRET," BUT IN OUR JUDGMENT, THIS DOES NOT JUSTIFY WITHHOLDING FROM WOMEN THEIR EQUAL RIGHT TO OBSTRUCT JUSTICE!
WE, THE MANAGEMENT OF WBBY, DEPLORE THIS SITUATION.
WE INVITE YOUR COMMENTS, TOO.
GBTrudeau

4/25/74

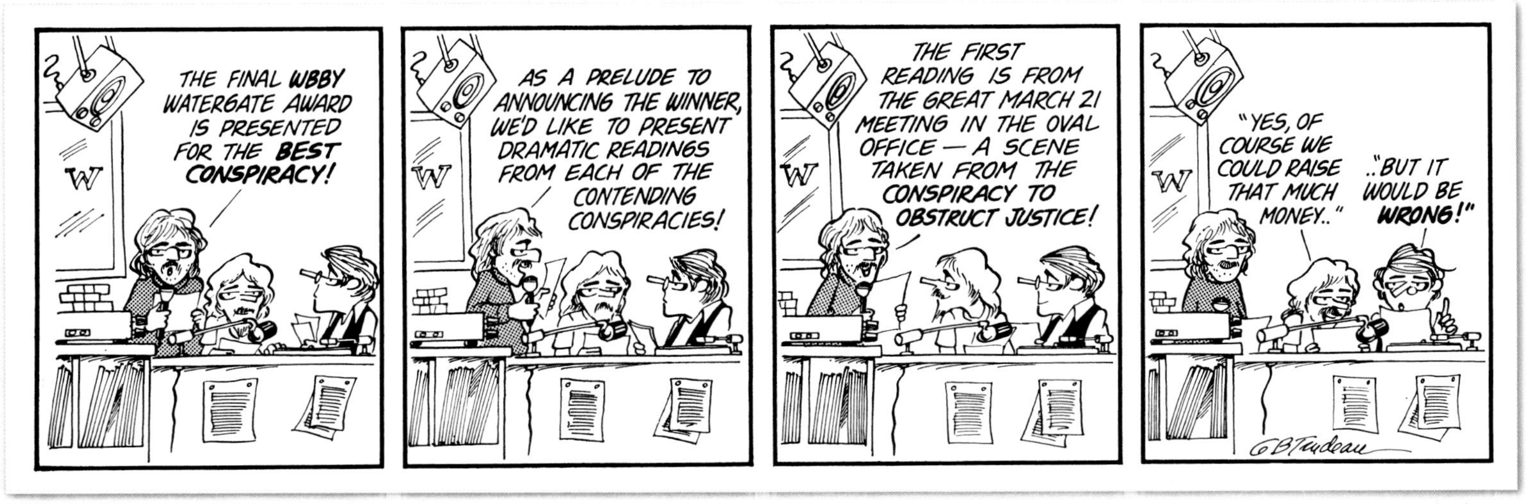
THE FINAL WBBY WATERGATE AWARD IS PRESENTED FOR THE BEST CONSPIRACY!
AS A PRELUDE TO ANNOUNCING THE WINNER, WE'D LIKE TO PRESENT DRAMATIC READINGS FROM EACH OF THE CONTENDING CONSPIRACIES!
THE FIRST READING IS FROM THE GREAT MARCH 21 MEETING IN THE OVAL OFFICE — A SCENE TAKEN FROM THE CONSPIRACY TO OBSTRUCT JUSTICE!
"YES, OF COURSE WE COULD RAISE THAT MUCH MONEY.."
.."BUT IT WOULD BE WRONG!"
GBTrudeau

4/26/74

B.D.

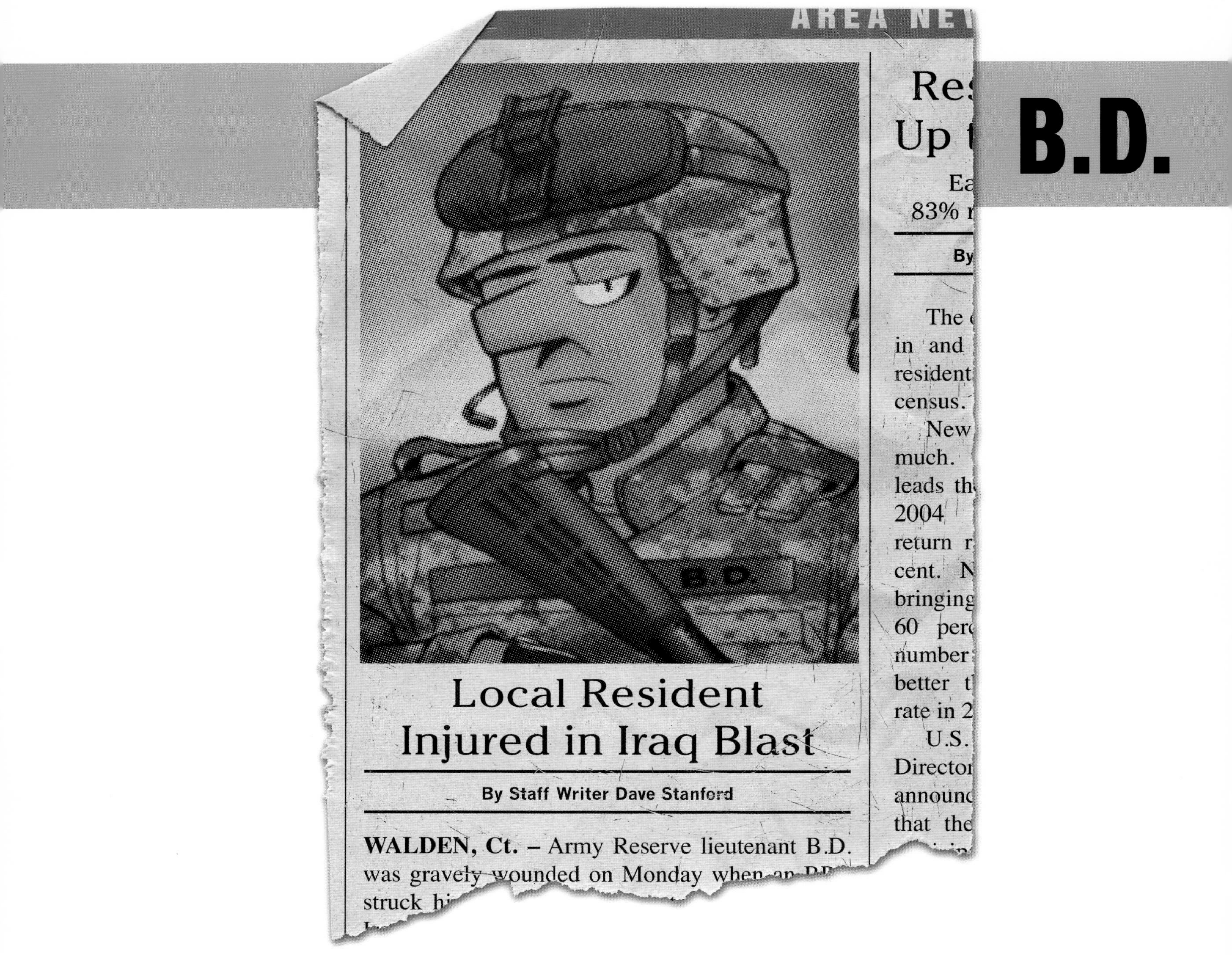
B.D.

AREA NE

Res
Up t
Ea
83% r
By
The
in and
resident
census.
New
much.
leads th
2004
return r
cent. N
bringing
60 perc
number
better t
rate in 2
U.S.
Director
announc
that the

Local Resident
Injured in Iraq Blast

By Staff Writer Dave Stanford

WALDEN, Ct. – Army Reserve lieutenant B.D. was gravely wounded on Monday when an RP
struck hi

From the first day, B.D. was a hard case, a knucklehead's knucklehead. He couldn't have been less like his inspiration, Yale quarterback Brian Dowling, the nicest guy I'd never met. And that was the joke. Dowling was famously self-effacing, his campus nickname ("God") not withstanding. He fell all over himself crediting his teammates for the long, unbroken string of victories he engineered as a collegian. B.D., by contrast, was a gridiron diva, imperious and demanding, smoldering with contempt for supporting players he considered mediocre and unserious.

The alternative universe thing worked pretty well as long as the team won, which under Dowling's leadership it always did. You can mock a divinity during the good times; the hilarity only vanishes when he comes up mortal. Or, in this case, when the season ends.

When a warrior retires from the field, he usually hangs up his helmet. B.D. kept his in place, and not just as a way to draw attention at mixers. The underlying vulnerability had been obvious from the start—his fellow players, after all, had had some success getting into his head. Indeed, one teammate in particular, Zonker, had no other on-field ambition.

"If you're going to fight commies, you need eleven men on the field!"

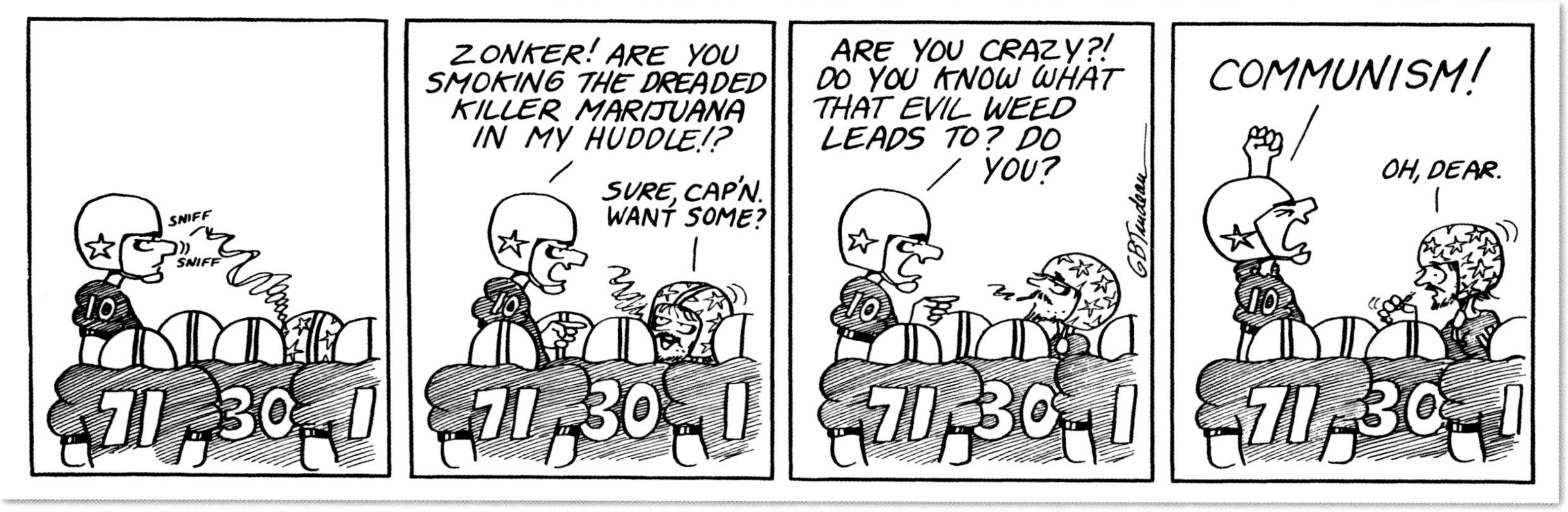
SNIFF
SNIFF
ZONKER! ARE YOU SMOKING THE DREADED KILLER MARIJUANA IN MY HUDDLE!?
SURE, CAP'N. WANT SOME?
ARE YOU CRAZY?! DO YOU KNOW WHAT THAT EVIL WEED LEADS TO? DO YOU?
COMMUNISM!
OH, DEAR.
71
30
1
10

So B.D. moved out into life with a protective shell, shielded from doubt or insight, impervious to slight, firmly resistant to the disturbing new world of personal growth and male hugs. (*Seinfeld* was B.D.'s kind of show.) And the barrier proved impermeable in both directions; not only did it keep unwelcome challenges out, it kept comforting shibboleths in. Despite the tumult around him, B.D.'s bedrock conservatism went unexamined, his relationship with Boopsie his only link to the governing progressive ethos of his fellow communards.

With the *Doonesbury* diaspora in 1984, B.D. set off on his own, and at each bend of the path he was refitted for headgear. A benchwarming career with the Los Angeles Rams turned into a tour of duty in the National Guard, which segued into a stint with the California Highway Patrol. A subsequent job as coach for the Walden Fighting Swooshes was upended by a tour of duty at Ground Zero, followed by deployment to Iraq. With each reinvention, helmets were swapped out, but always offstage, so B.D.'s bare noggin went unglimpsed for thirty-six years.

Until Fallujah. A rocket attack on B.D.'s Humvee removed his leg, but it was the loss of his helmet that startled and moved readers the most. Revealed at last was B.D.'s matted, graying hair, but more significantly, his badly battered soul. Incapacitated officers often suffer deeply over the loss of personal control, and the aging reservist was not spared. Reeling from his wounds, B.D. sank into the miasma of stress trauma, and turned to kindred spirits to help him map out a New Normal. It was that journey which revealed layers of courage and humanity that even his creator had never thought to look for.

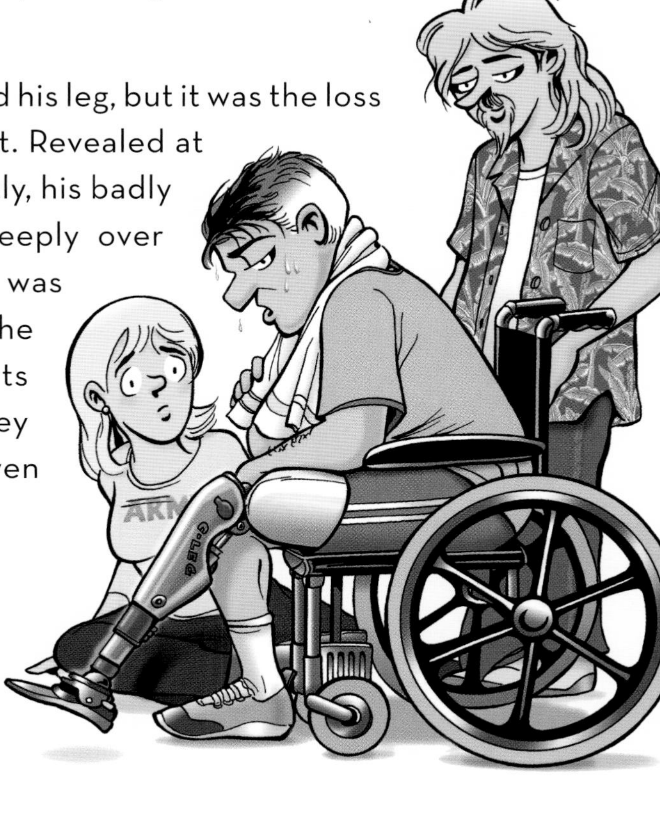

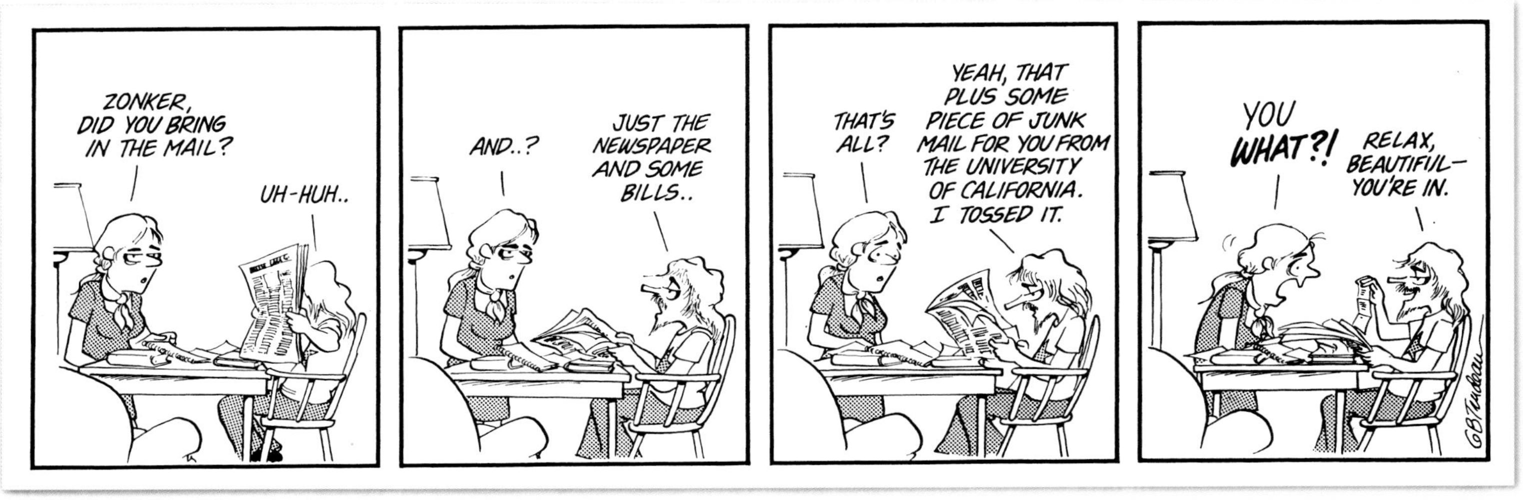
ZONKER, DID YOU BRING IN THE MAIL?
UH-HUH..
AND..?
JUST THE NEWSPAPER AND SOME BILLS..
THAT'S ALL?
YEAH, THAT PLUS SOME PIECE OF JUNK MAIL FOR YOU FROM THE UNIVERSITY OF CALIFORNIA. I TOSSED IT.
YOU WHAT?!
RELAX, BEAUTIFUL— YOU'RE IN.

5/30/74

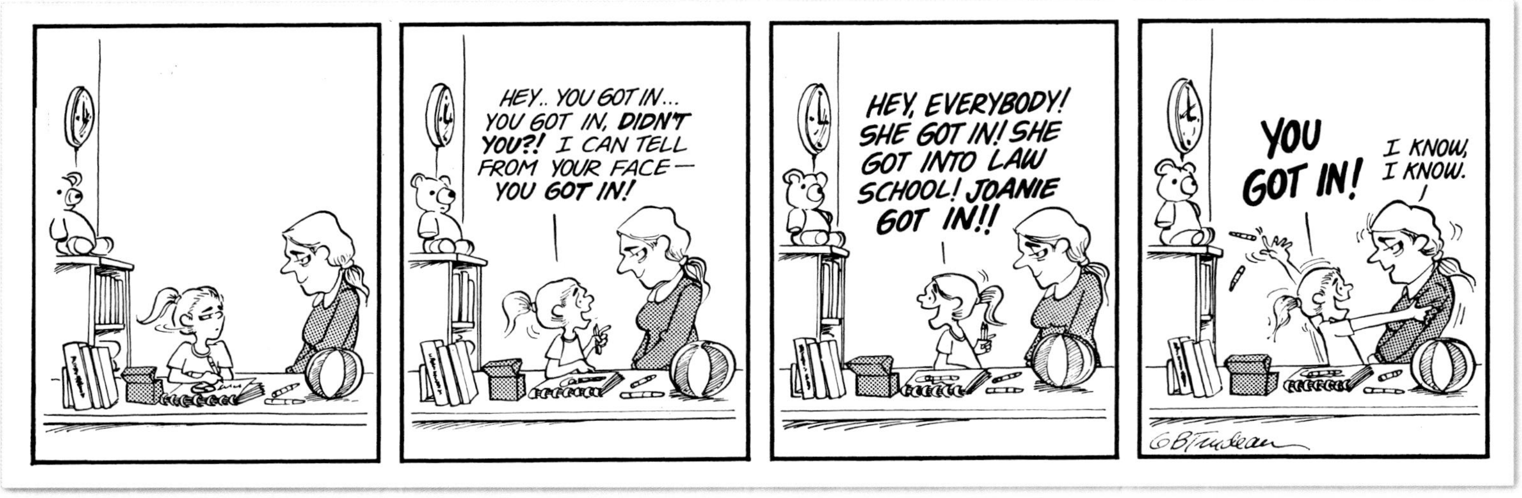
HEY.. YOU GOT IN... YOU GOT IN, DIDN'T YOU?! I CAN TELL FROM YOUR FACE— YOU GOT IN!
HEY, EVERYBODY! SHE GOT IN! SHE GOT INTO LAW SCHOOL! JOANIE GOT IN!!
YOU GOT IN!
I KNOW, I KNOW.

5/31/74

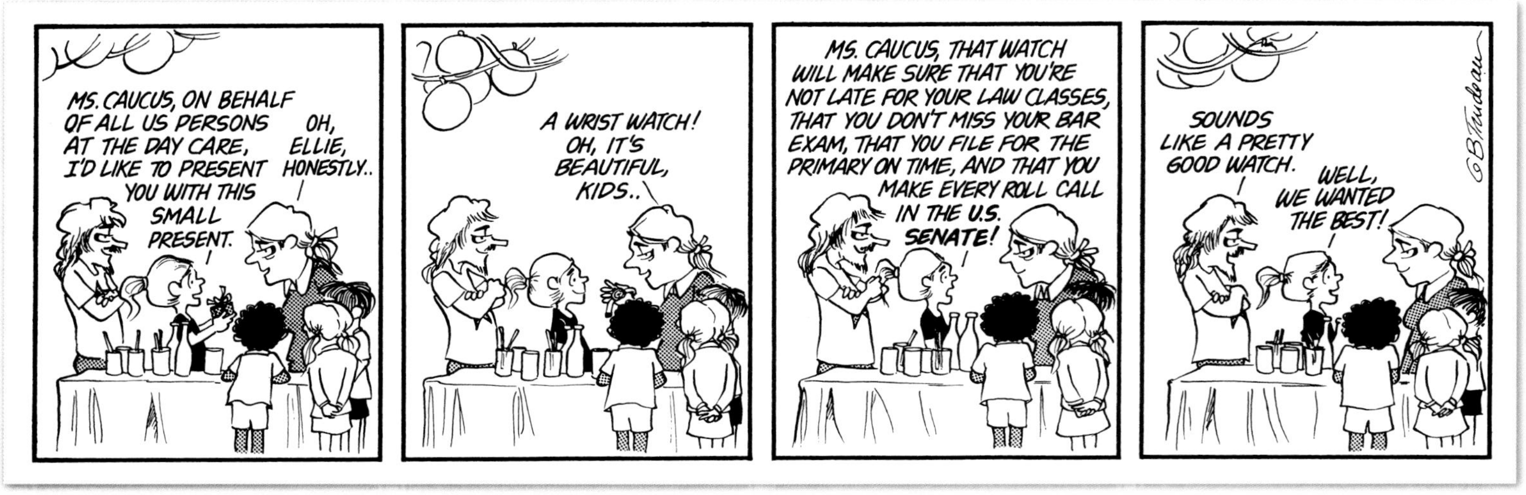
MS. CAUCUS, ON BEHALF OF ALL US PERSONS AT THE DAY CARE, I'D LIKE TO PRESENT YOU WITH THIS SMALL PRESENT.
OH, ELLIE, HONESTLY..
A WRIST WATCH! OH, IT'S BEAUTIFUL, KIDS..
MS. CAUCUS, THAT WATCH WILL MAKE SURE THAT YOU'RE NOT LATE FOR YOUR LAW CLASSES, THAT YOU DON'T MISS YOUR BAR EXAM, THAT YOU FILE FOR THE PRIMARY ON TIME, AND THAT YOU MAKE EVERY ROLL CALL IN THE U.S. SENATE!
SOUNDS LIKE A PRETTY GOOD WATCH.
WELL, WE WANTED THE BEST!

7/2/74

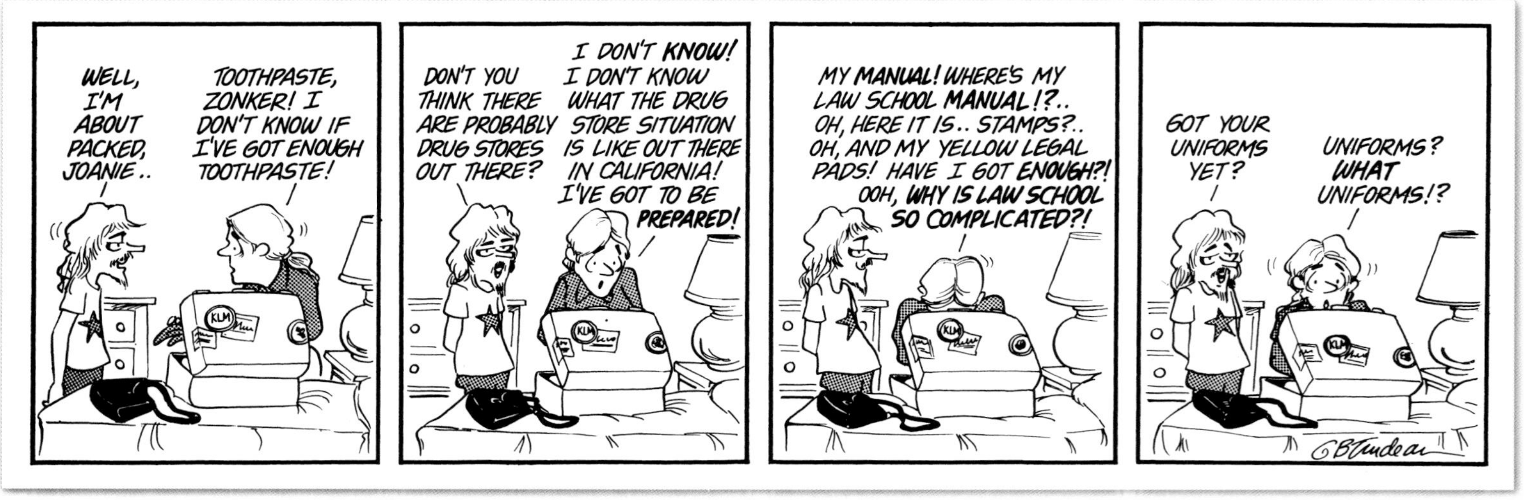
WELL, I'M ABOUT PACKED, JOANIE..
TOOTHPASTE, ZONKER! I DON'T KNOW IF I'VE GOT ENOUGH TOOTHPASTE!
DON'T YOU THINK THERE ARE PROBABLY DRUG STORES OUT THERE?
I DON'T KNOW! I DON'T KNOW WHAT THE DRUG STORE SITUATION IS LIKE OUT THERE IN CALIFORNIA! I'VE GOT TO BE PREPARED!
MY MANUAL! WHERE'S MY LAW SCHOOL MANUAL!?.. OH, HERE IT IS.. STAMPS?.. OH, AND MY YELLOW LEGAL PADS! HAVE I GOT ENOUGH?! OOH, WHY IS LAW SCHOOL SO COMPLICATED?!
GOT YOUR UNIFORMS YET?
UNIFORMS? WHAT UNIFORMS!?

7/3/74

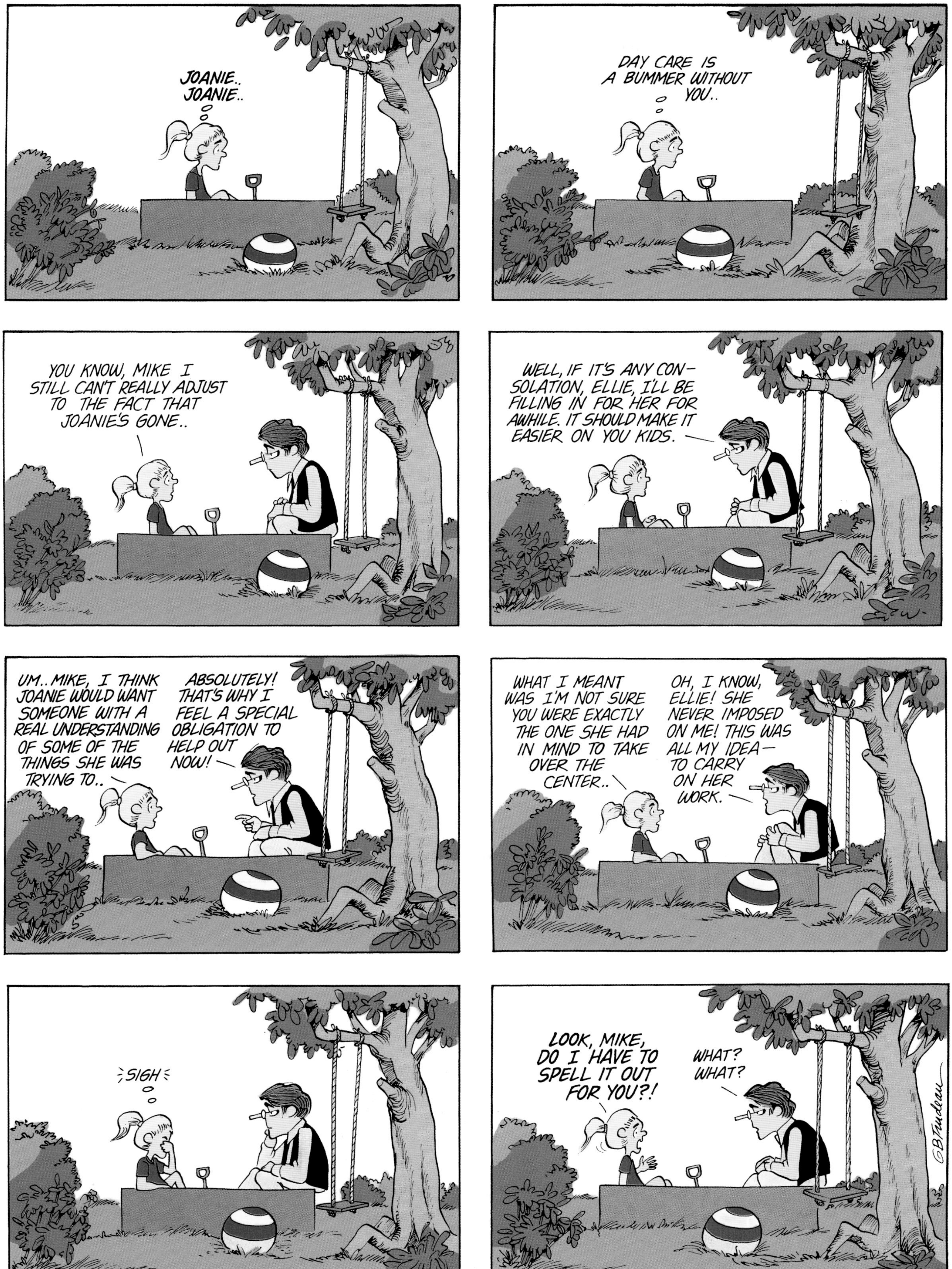
JOANIE.. JOANIE..
DAY CARE IS A BUMMER WITHOUT YOU..
YOU KNOW, MIKE I STILL CAN'T REALLY ADJUST TO THE FACT THAT JOANIE'S GONE..
WELL, IF IT'S ANY CONSOLATION, ELLIE, I'LL BE FILLING IN FOR HER FOR AWHILE. IT SHOULD MAKE IT EASIER ON YOU KIDS.
UM.. MIKE, I THINK JOANIE WOULD WANT SOMEONE WITH A REAL UNDERSTANDING OF SOME OF THE THINGS SHE WAS TRYING TO..
ABSOLUTELY! THAT'S WHY I FEEL A SPECIAL OBLIGATION TO HELP OUT NOW!
WHAT I MEANT WAS I'M NOT SURE YOU WERE EXACTLY THE ONE SHE HAD IN MIND TO TAKE OVER THE CENTER..
OH, I KNOW, ELLIE! SHE NEVER IMPOSED ON ME! THIS WAS ALL MY IDEA— TO CARRY ON HER WORK.
SIGH
LOOK, MIKE, DO I HAVE TO SPELL IT OUT FOR YOU?!
WHAT? WHAT?
GBTrudeau

8/4/74

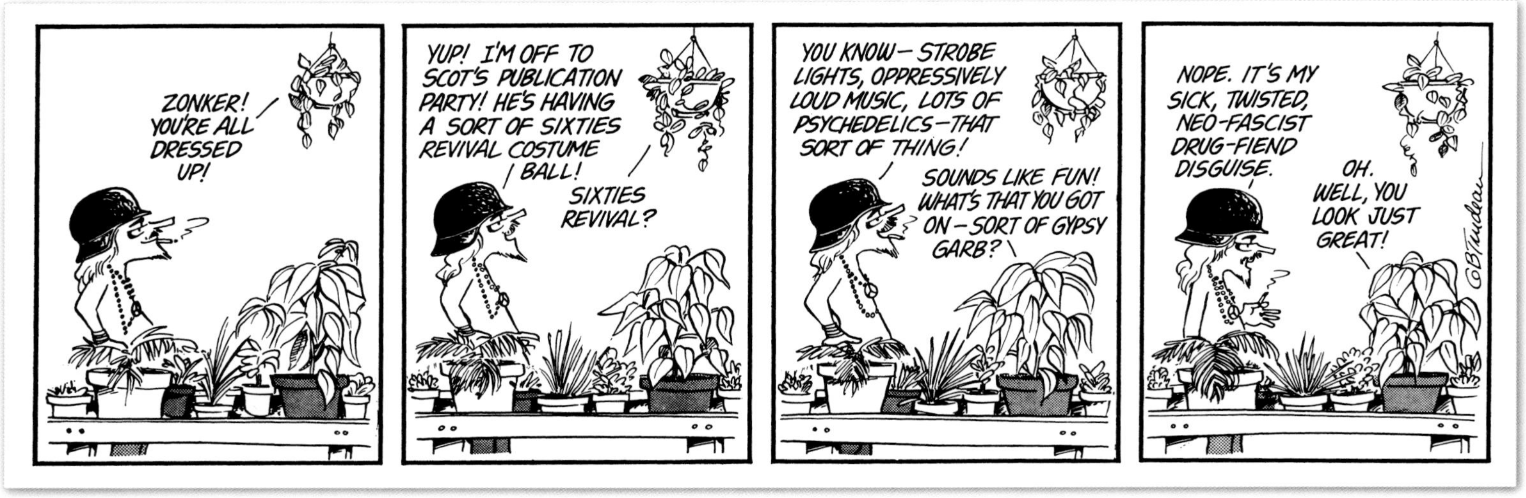
ZONKER! YOU'RE ALL DRESSED UP!
YUP! I'M OFF TO SCOT'S PUBLICATION PARTY! HE'S HAVING A SORT OF SIXTIES REVIVAL COSTUME BALL!
SIXTIES REVIVAL?
YOU KNOW—STROBE LIGHTS, OPPRESSIVELY LOUD MUSIC, LOTS OF PSYCHEDELICS—THAT SORT OF THING!
SOUNDS LIKE FUN! WHAT'S THAT YOU GOT ON—SORT OF GYPSY GARB?
NOPE. IT'S MY SICK, TWISTED, NEO-FASCIST DRUG-FIEND DISGUISE.
OH. WELL, YOU LOOK JUST GREAT!
GBTrudeau

12/9/74

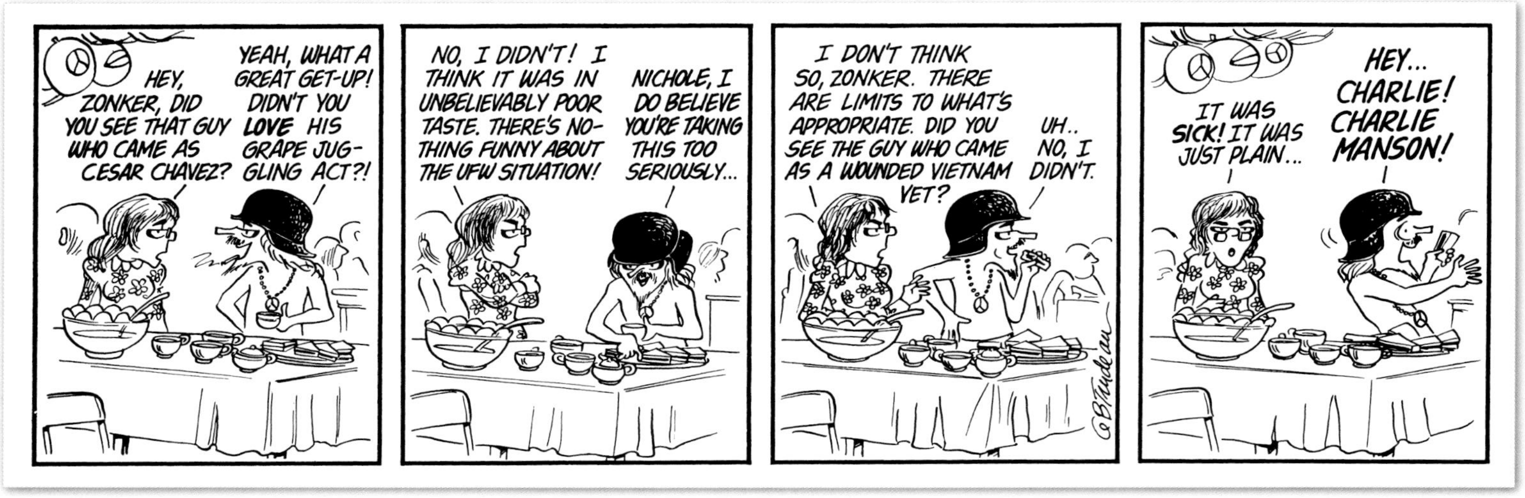
HEY, ZONKER, DID YOU SEE THAT GUY WHO CAME AS CESAR CHAVEZ?
YEAH, WHAT A GREAT GET-UP! DIDN'T YOU LOVE HIS GRAPE JUGGLING ACT?!
NO, I DIDN'T! I THINK IT WAS IN UNBELIEVABLY POOR TASTE. THERE'S NOTHING FUNNY ABOUT THE UFW SITUATION!
NICHOLE, I DO BELIEVE YOU'RE TAKING THIS TOO SERIOUSLY...
I DON'T THINK SO, ZONKER. THERE ARE LIMITS TO WHAT'S APPROPRIATE. DID YOU SEE THE GUY WHO CAME AS A WOUNDED VIETNAM VET?
UH.. NO, I DIDN'T.
GBTrudeau
IT WAS SICK! IT WAS JUST PLAIN...
HEY... CHARLIE! CHARLIE MANSON!

12/10/74

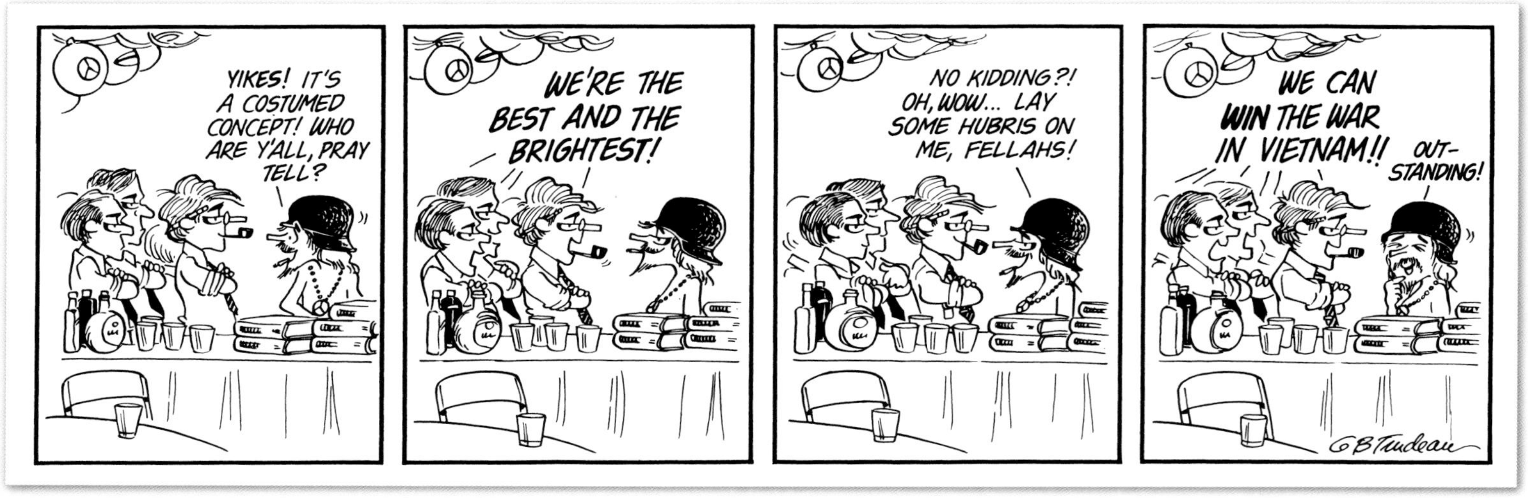
YIKES! IT'S A COSTUMED CONCEPT! WHO ARE Y'ALL, PRAY TELL?
WE'RE THE BEST AND THE BRIGHTEST!
NO KIDDING?! OH, WOW... LAY SOME HUBRIS ON ME, FELLAHS!
WE CAN WIN THE WAR IN VIETNAM!!
OUT-STANDING!
GBTrudeau

12/12/74

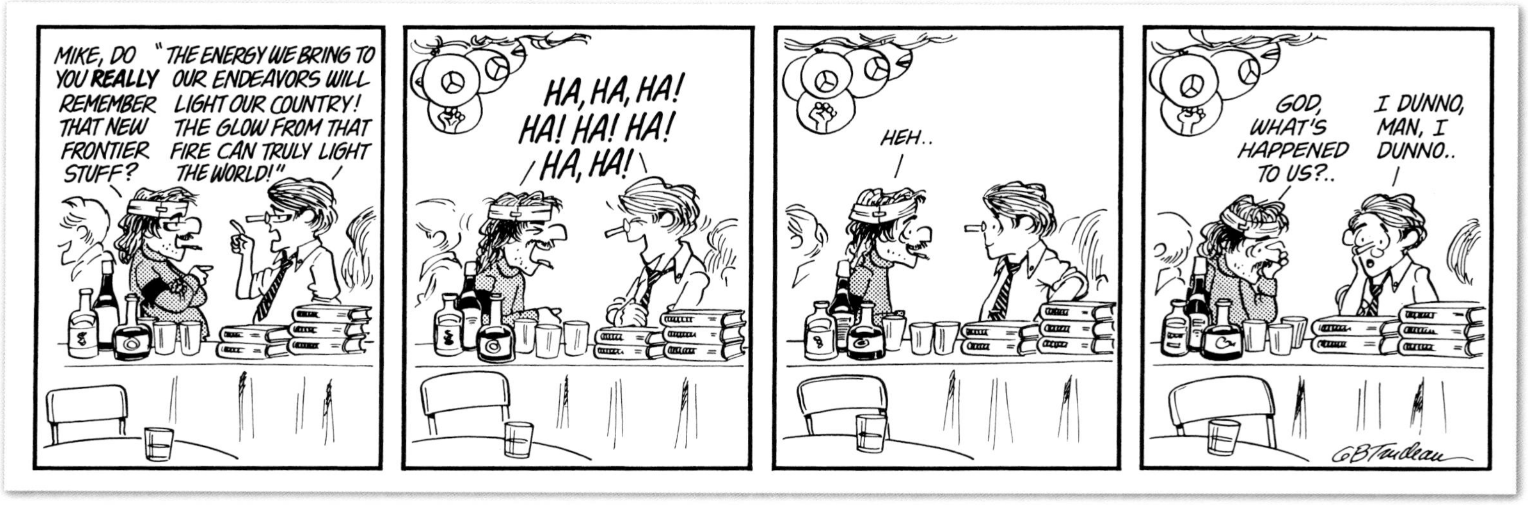
MIKE, DO YOU REALLY REMEMBER THAT NEW FRONTIER STUFF?
"THE ENERGY WE BRING TO OUR ENDEAVORS WILL LIGHT OUR COUNTRY! THE GLOW FROM THAT FIRE CAN TRULY LIGHT THE WORLD!"
HA, HA, HA! HA! HA! HA! HA, HA!
HEH..
GOD, WHAT'S HAPPENED TO US?..
I DUNNO, MAN, I DUNNO..
GBTrudeau

12/13/74

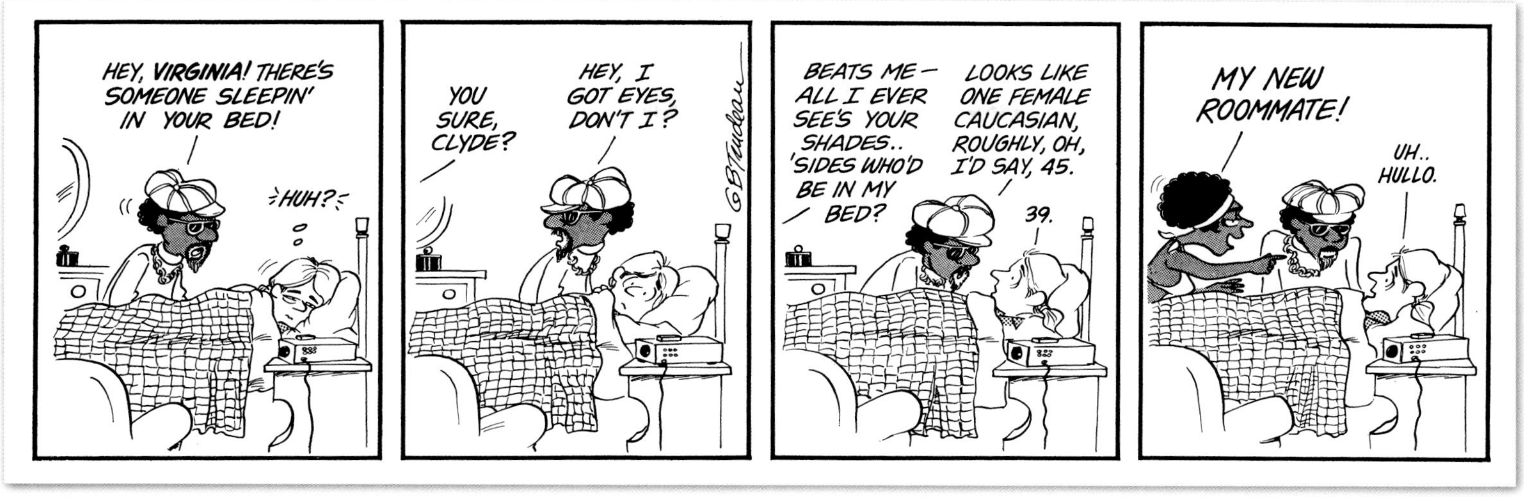
HEY, VIRGINIA! THERE'S SOMEONE SLEEPIN' IN YOUR BED!
HUH?
YOU SURE, CLYDE?
HEY, I GOT EYES, DON'T I?
BEATS ME— ALL I EVER SEE'S YOUR SHADES.. 'SIDES WHO'D BE IN MY BED?
LOOKS LIKE ONE FEMALE CAUCASIAN, ROUGHLY, OH, I'D SAY, 45.
39.
MY NEW ROOMMATE!
UH.. HULLO.

8/19/74

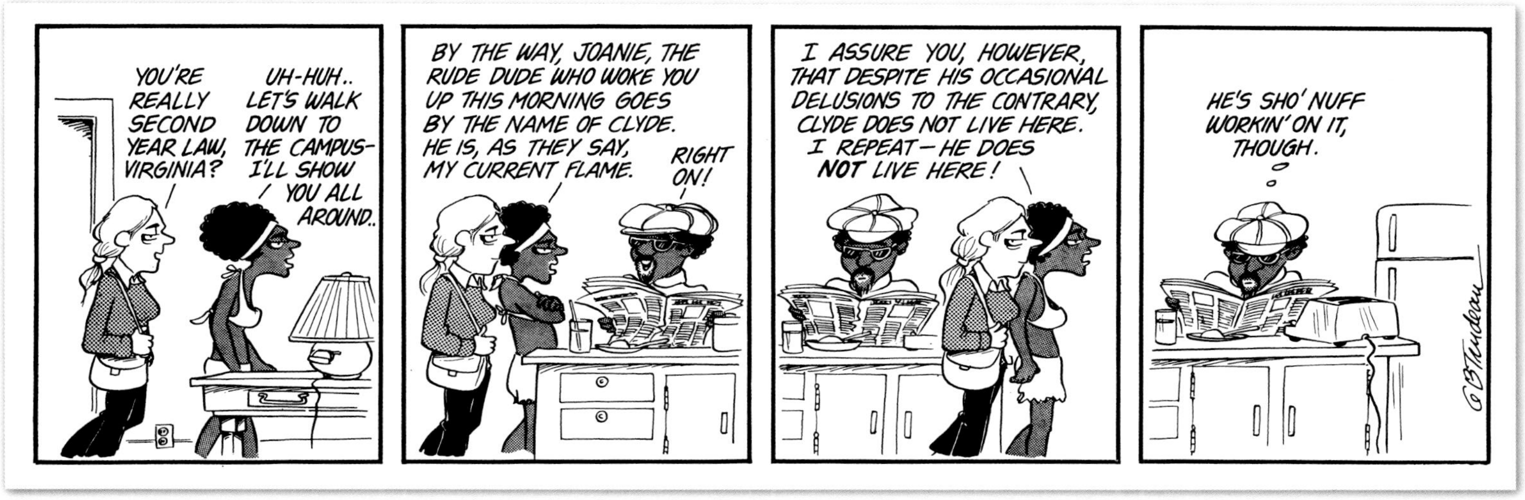
YOU'RE REALLY SECOND YEAR LAW, VIRGINIA?
UH-HUH.. LET'S WALK DOWN TO THE CAMPUS- I'LL SHOW YOU ALL AROUND..
BY THE WAY, JOANIE, THE RUDE DUDE WHO WOKE YOU UP THIS MORNING GOES BY THE NAME OF CLYDE. HE IS, AS THEY SAY, MY CURRENT FLAME.
RIGHT ON!
I ASSURE YOU, HOWEVER, THAT DESPITE HIS OCCASIONAL DELUSIONS TO THE CONTRARY, CLYDE DOES NOT LIVE HERE. I REPEAT—HE DOES NOT LIVE HERE!
HE'S SHO' NUFF WORKIN' ON IT, THOUGH.

8/20/74

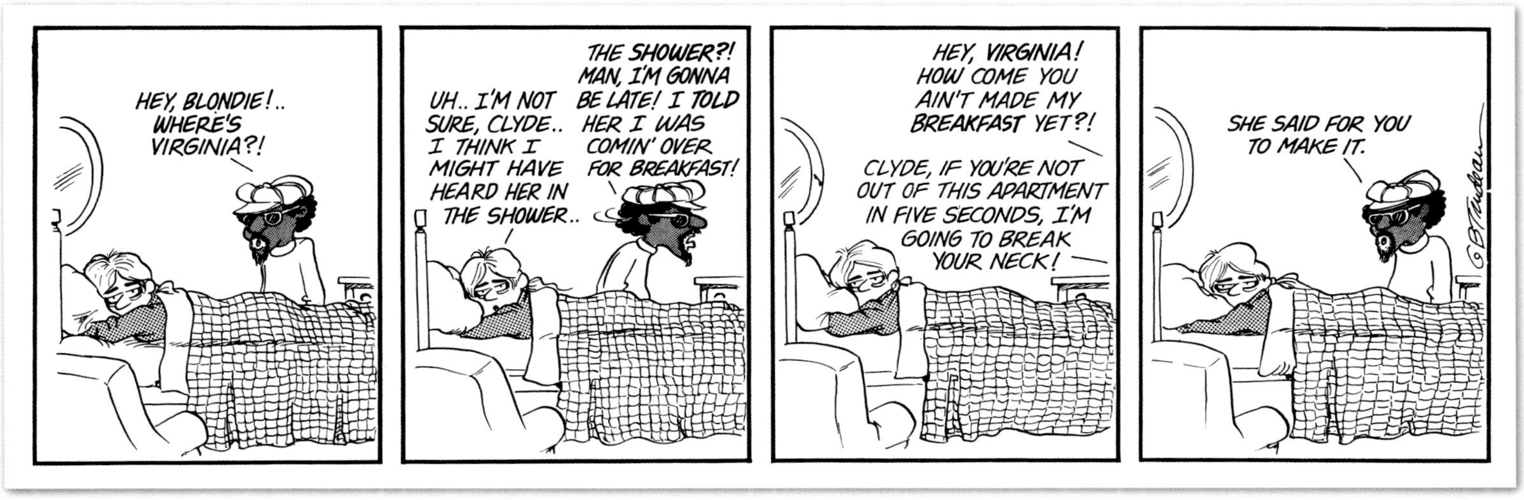
HEY, BLONDIE!.. WHERE'S VIRGINIA?!
UH.. I'M NOT SURE, CLYDE.. I THINK I MIGHT HAVE HEARD HER IN THE SHOWER..
THE SHOWER?! MAN, I'M GONNA BE LATE! I TOLD HER I WAS COMIN' OVER FOR BREAKFAST!
HEY, VIRGINIA! HOW COME YOU AIN'T MADE MY BREAKFAST YET?!
CLYDE, IF YOU'RE NOT OUT OF THIS APARTMENT IN FIVE SECONDS, I'M GOING TO BREAK YOUR NECK!
SHE SAID FOR YOU TO MAKE IT.

8/21/74

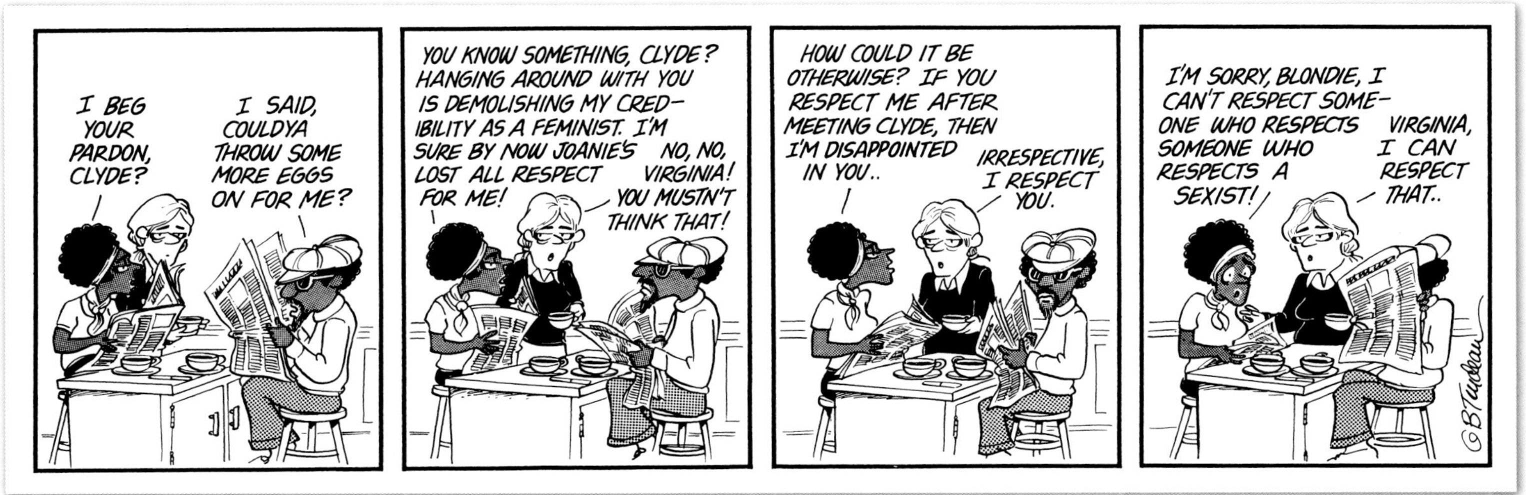
I BEG YOUR PARDON, CLYDE?
I SAID, COULDYA THROW SOME MORE EGGS ON FOR ME?
YOU KNOW SOMETHING, CLYDE? HANGING AROUND WITH YOU IS DEMOLISHING MY CREDIBILITY AS A FEMINIST. I'M SURE BY NOW JOANIE'S LOST ALL RESPECT FOR ME!
NO, NO, VIRGINIA! YOU MUSTN'T THINK THAT!
HOW COULD IT BE OTHERWISE? IF YOU RESPECT ME AFTER MEETING CLYDE, THEN I'M DISAPPOINTED IN YOU..
IRRESPECTIVE, I RESPECT YOU.
I'M SORRY, BLONDIE, I CAN'T RESPECT SOMEONE WHO RESPECTS SOMEONE WHO RESPECTS A SEXIST!
VIRGINIA, I CAN RESPECT THAT..

8/22/74

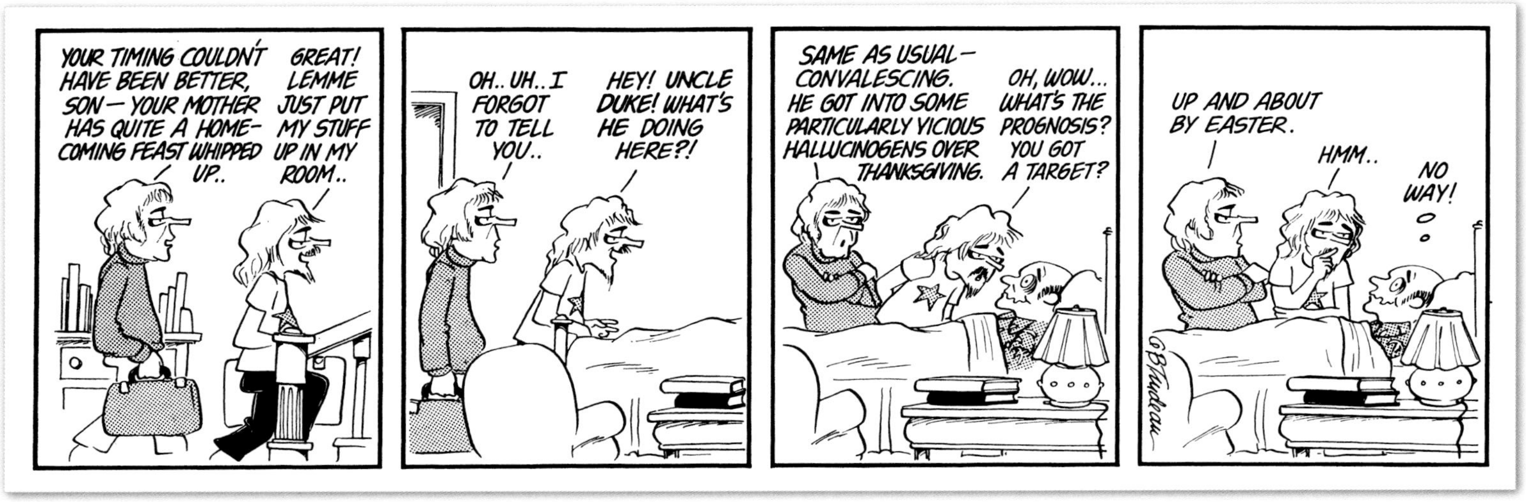
YOUR TIMING COULDN'T HAVE BEEN BETTER, SON— YOUR MOTHER HAS QUITE A HOME-COMING FEAST WHIPPED UP..
GREAT! LEMME JUST PUT MY STUFF UP IN MY ROOM..
OH.. UH.. I FORGOT TO TELL YOU..
HEY! UNCLE DUKE! WHAT'S HE DOING HERE?!
SAME AS USUAL— CONVALESCING. HE GOT INTO SOME PARTICULARLY VICIOUS HALLUCINOGENS OVER THANKSGIVING.
OH, WOW... WHAT'S THE PROGNOSIS? YOU GOT A TARGET?
UP AND ABOUT BY EASTER.
HMM..
NO WAY!

12/23/74

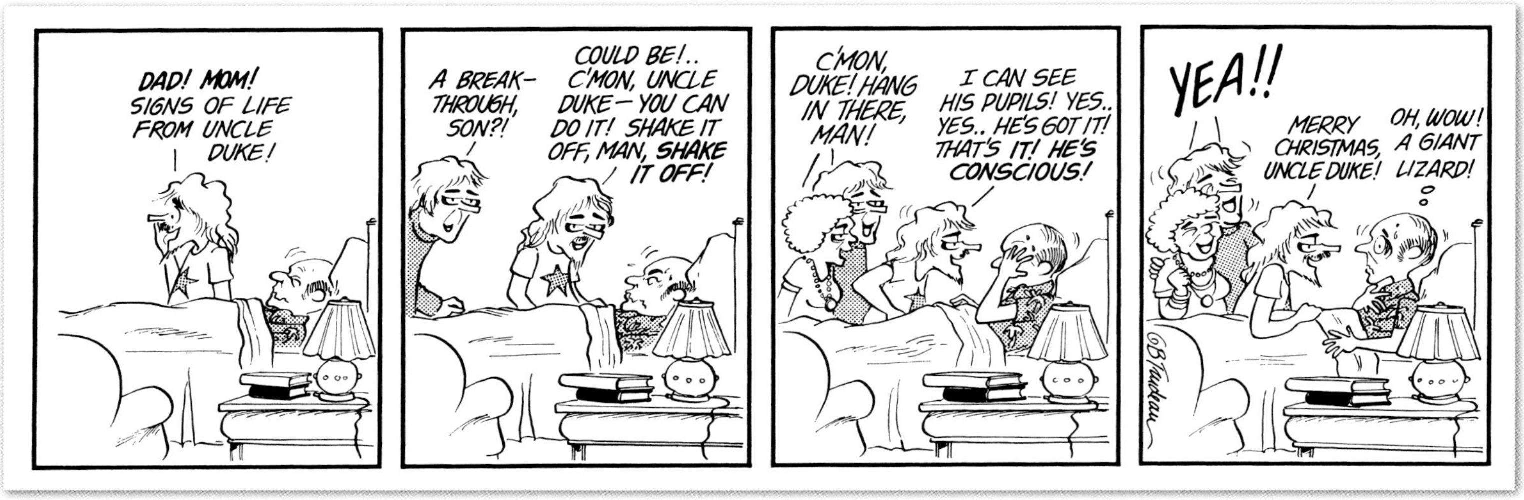
DAD! MOM! SIGNS OF LIFE FROM UNCLE DUKE!
A BREAK-THROUGH, SON?!
COULD BE!.. C'MON, UNCLE DUKE— YOU CAN DO IT! SHAKE IT OFF, MAN, SHAKE IT OFF!
C'MON, DUKE! HANG IN THERE, MAN!
I CAN SEE HIS PUPILS! YES.. YES.. HE'S GOT IT! THAT'S IT! HE'S CONSCIOUS!
YEA!!
MERRY CHRISTMAS, UNCLE DUKE!
OH, WOW! A GIANT LIZARD!

12/24/74

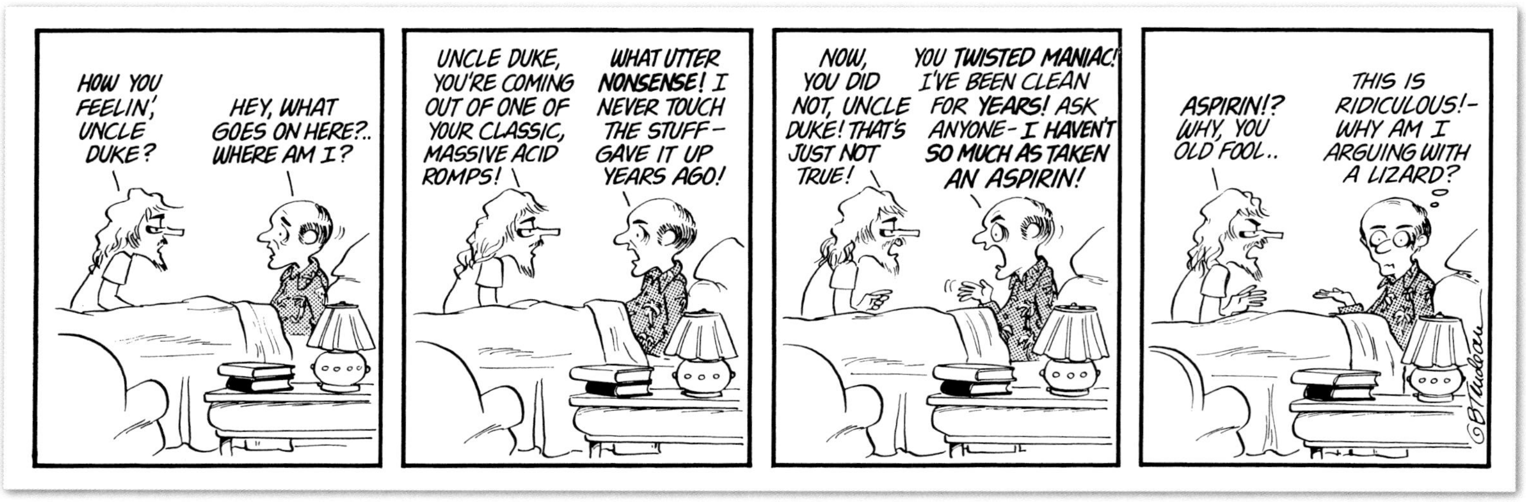
HOW YOU FEELIN', UNCLE DUKE?
HEY, WHAT GOES ON HERE?.. WHERE AM I?
UNCLE DUKE, YOU'RE COMING OUT OF ONE OF YOUR CLASSIC, MASSIVE ACID ROMPS!
WHAT UTTER NONSENSE! I NEVER TOUCH THE STUFF— GAVE IT UP YEARS AGO!
NOW, YOU DID NOT, UNCLE DUKE! THAT'S JUST NOT TRUE!
YOU TWISTED MANIAC! I'VE BEEN CLEAN FOR YEARS! ASK ANYONE— I HAVEN'T SO MUCH AS TAKEN AN ASPIRIN!
ASPIRIN!? WHY, YOU OLD FOOL..
THIS IS RIDICULOUS!— WHY AM I ARGUING WITH A LIZARD?

12/25/74

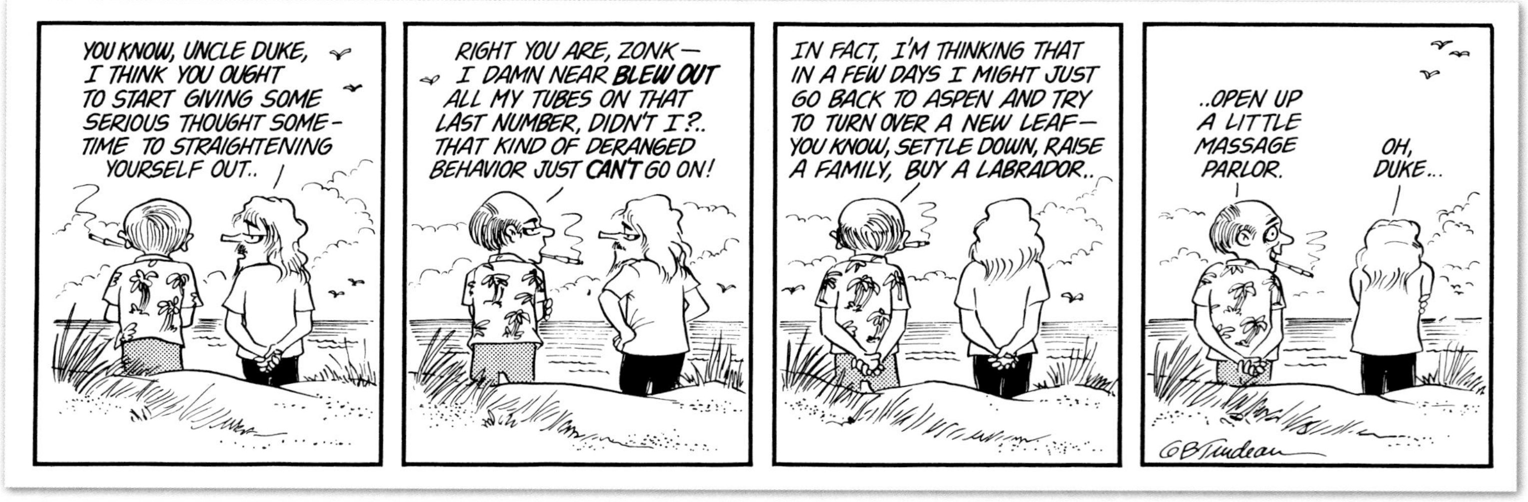
YOU KNOW, UNCLE DUKE, I THINK YOU OUGHT TO START GIVING SOME SERIOUS THOUGHT SOME-TIME TO STRAIGHTENING YOURSELF OUT..
RIGHT YOU ARE, ZONK— I DAMN NEAR BLEW OUT ALL MY TUBES ON THAT LAST NUMBER, DIDN'T I?.. THAT KIND OF DERANGED BEHAVIOR JUST CAN'T GO ON!
IN FACT, I'M THINKING THAT IN A FEW DAYS I MIGHT JUST GO BACK TO ASPEN AND TRY TO TURN OVER A NEW LEAF— YOU KNOW, SETTLE DOWN, RAISE A FAMILY, BUY A LABRADOR..
..OPEN UP A LITTLE MASSAGE PARLOR.
OH, DUKE...

12/28/74

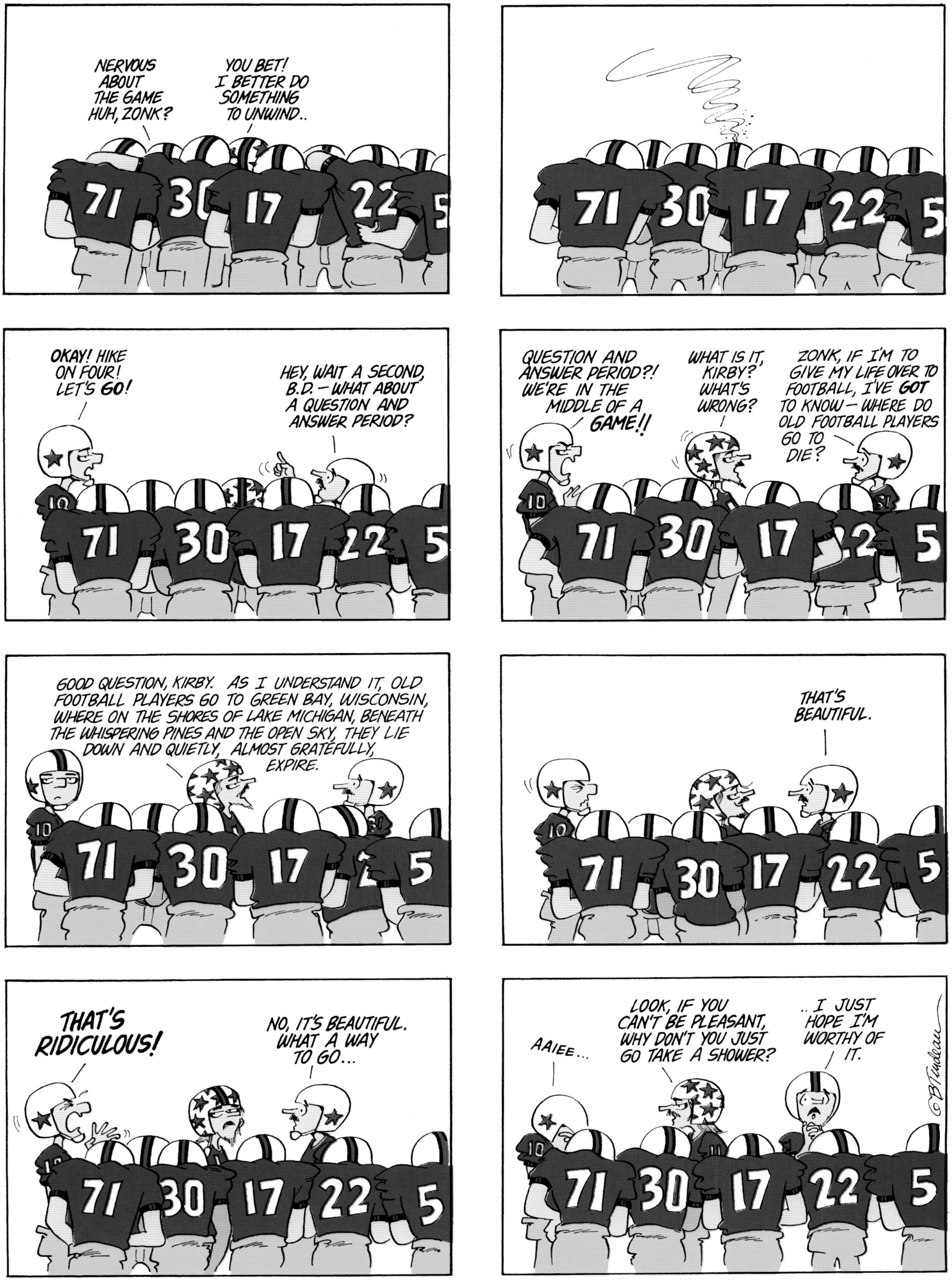
NERVOUS ABOUT THE GAME HUH, ZONK?
YOU BET! I BETTER DO SOMETHING TO UNWIND..
OKAY! HIKE ON FOUR! LET'S GO!
HEY, WAIT A SECOND, B.D.—WHAT ABOUT A QUESTION AND ANSWER PERIOD?
QUESTION AND ANSWER PERIOD?! WE'RE IN THE MIDDLE OF A GAME!!
WHAT IS IT, KIRBY? WHAT'S WRONG?
ZONK, IF I'M TO GIVE MY LIFE OVER TO FOOTBALL, I'VE GOT TO KNOW—WHERE DO OLD FOOTBALL PLAYERS GO TO DIE?
GOOD QUESTION, KIRBY. AS I UNDERSTAND IT, OLD FOOTBALL PLAYERS GO TO GREEN BAY, WISCONSIN, WHERE ON THE SHORES OF LAKE MICHIGAN, BENEATH THE WHISPERING PINES AND THE OPEN SKY, THEY LIE DOWN AND QUIETLY, ALMOST GRATEFULLY, EXPIRE.
THAT'S BEAUTIFUL.
THAT'S RIDICULOUS!
NO, IT'S BEAUTIFUL. WHAT A WAY TO GO...
AAIEE...
LOOK, IF YOU CAN'T BE PLEASANT, WHY DON'T YOU JUST GO TAKE A SHOWER?
..I JUST HOPE I'M WORTHY OF IT.
©BTrudeau

9/1/74

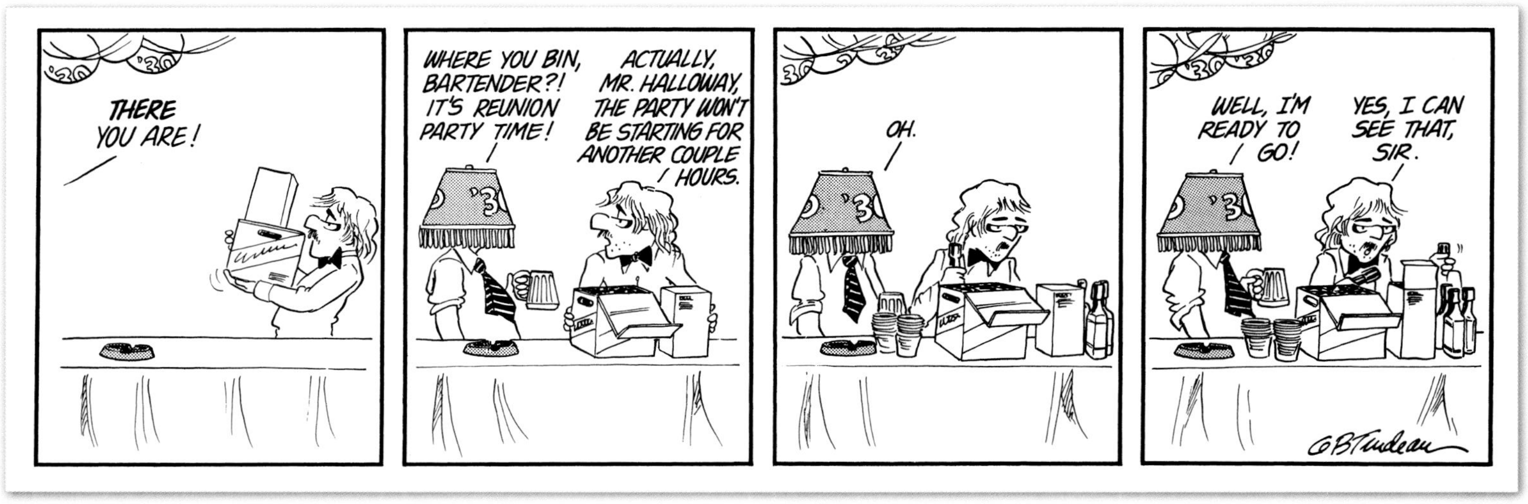
THERE YOU ARE!
WHERE YOU BIN, BARTENDER?! IT'S REUNION PARTY TIME!
ACTUALLY, MR. HALLOWAY, THE PARTY WON'T BE STARTING FOR ANOTHER COUPLE HOURS.
OH.
WELL, I'M READY TO GO!
YES, I CAN SEE THAT, SIR.
GBTrudeau

4/28/75

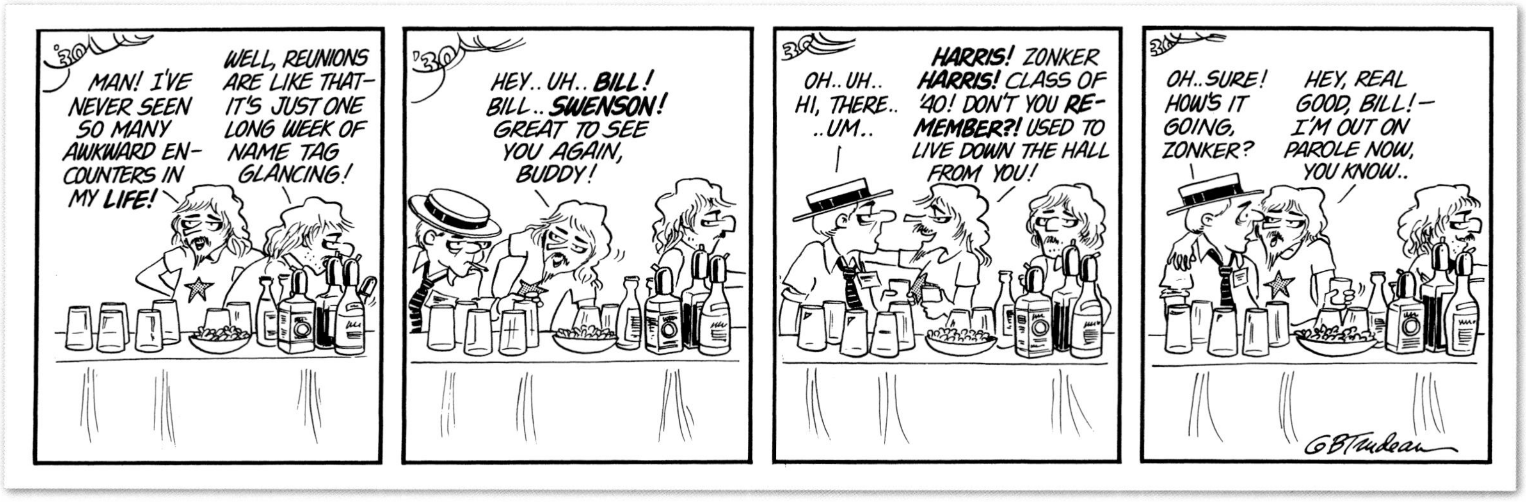
MAN! I'VE NEVER SEEN SO MANY AWKWARD ENCOUNTERS IN MY LIFE!
WELL, REUNIONS ARE LIKE THAT–IT'S JUST ONE LONG WEEK OF NAME TAG GLANCING!
HEY.. UH.. BILL! BILL.. SWENSON! GREAT TO SEE YOU AGAIN, BUDDY!
OH.. UH.. HI, THERE.. ..UM..
HARRIS! ZONKER HARRIS! CLASS OF '40! DON'T YOU REMEMBER?! USED TO LIVE DOWN THE HALL FROM YOU!
OH.. SURE! HOW'S IT GOING, ZONKER?
HEY, REAL GOOD, BILL!–I'M OUT ON PAROLE NOW, YOU KNOW..
GBTrudeau

4/29/75

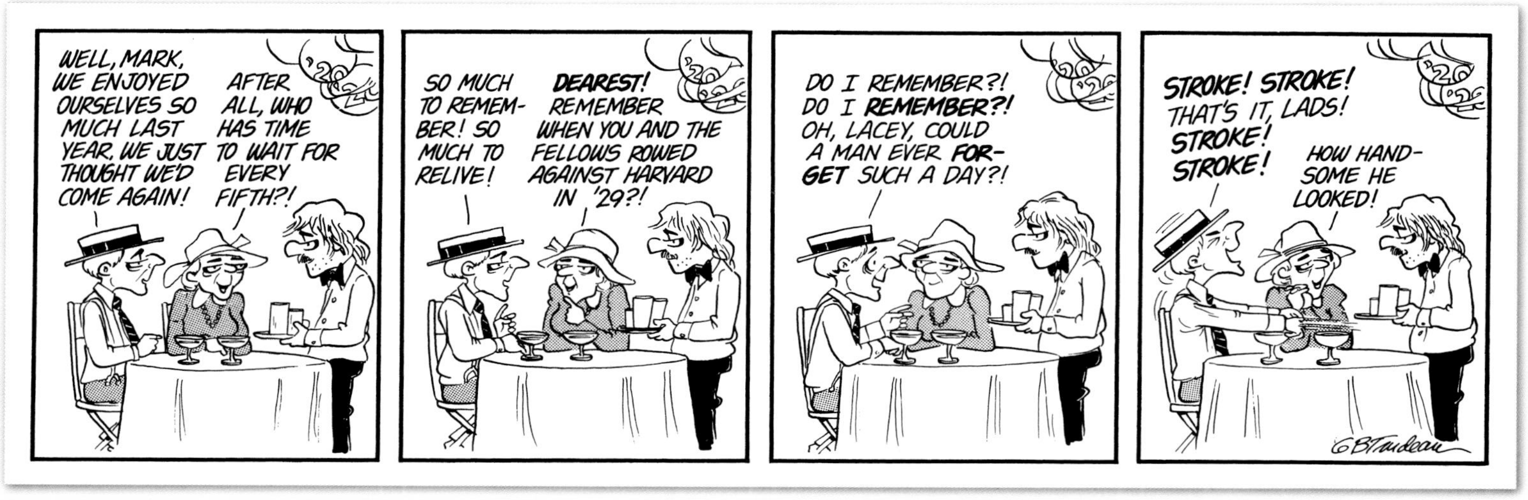
WELL, MARK, WE ENJOYED OURSELVES SO MUCH LAST YEAR, WE JUST THOUGHT WE'D COME AGAIN!
AFTER ALL, WHO HAS TIME TO WAIT FOR EVERY FIFTH?!
SO MUCH TO REMEMBER! SO MUCH TO RELIVE!
DEAREST! REMEMBER WHEN YOU AND THE FELLOWS ROWED AGAINST HARVARD IN '29?!
DO I REMEMBER?! DO I REMEMBER?! OH, LACEY, COULD A MAN EVER FORGET SUCH A DAY?!
STROKE! STROKE! THAT'S IT, LADS! STROKE! STROKE!
HOW HANDSOME HE LOOKED!
GBTrudeau

5/1/75

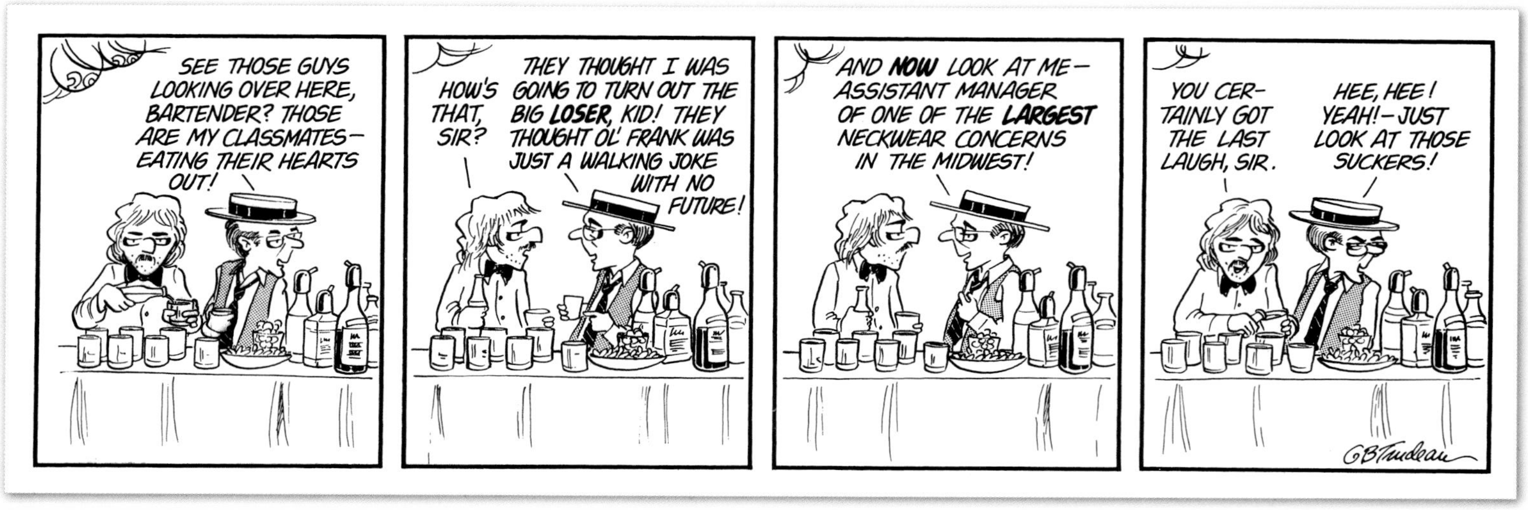
SEE THOSE GUYS LOOKING OVER HERE, BARTENDER? THOSE ARE MY CLASSMATES–EATING THEIR HEARTS OUT!
HOW'S THAT, SIR?
THEY THOUGHT I WAS GOING TO TURN OUT THE BIG LOSER, KID! THEY THOUGHT OL' FRANK WAS JUST A WALKING JOKE WITH NO FUTURE!
AND NOW LOOK AT ME–ASSISTANT MANAGER OF ONE OF THE LARGEST NECKWEAR CONCERNS IN THE MIDWEST!
YOU CERTAINLY GOT THE LAST LAUGH, SIR.
HEE, HEE! YEAH!–JUST LOOK AT THOSE SUCKERS!
GBTrudeau

5/3/75

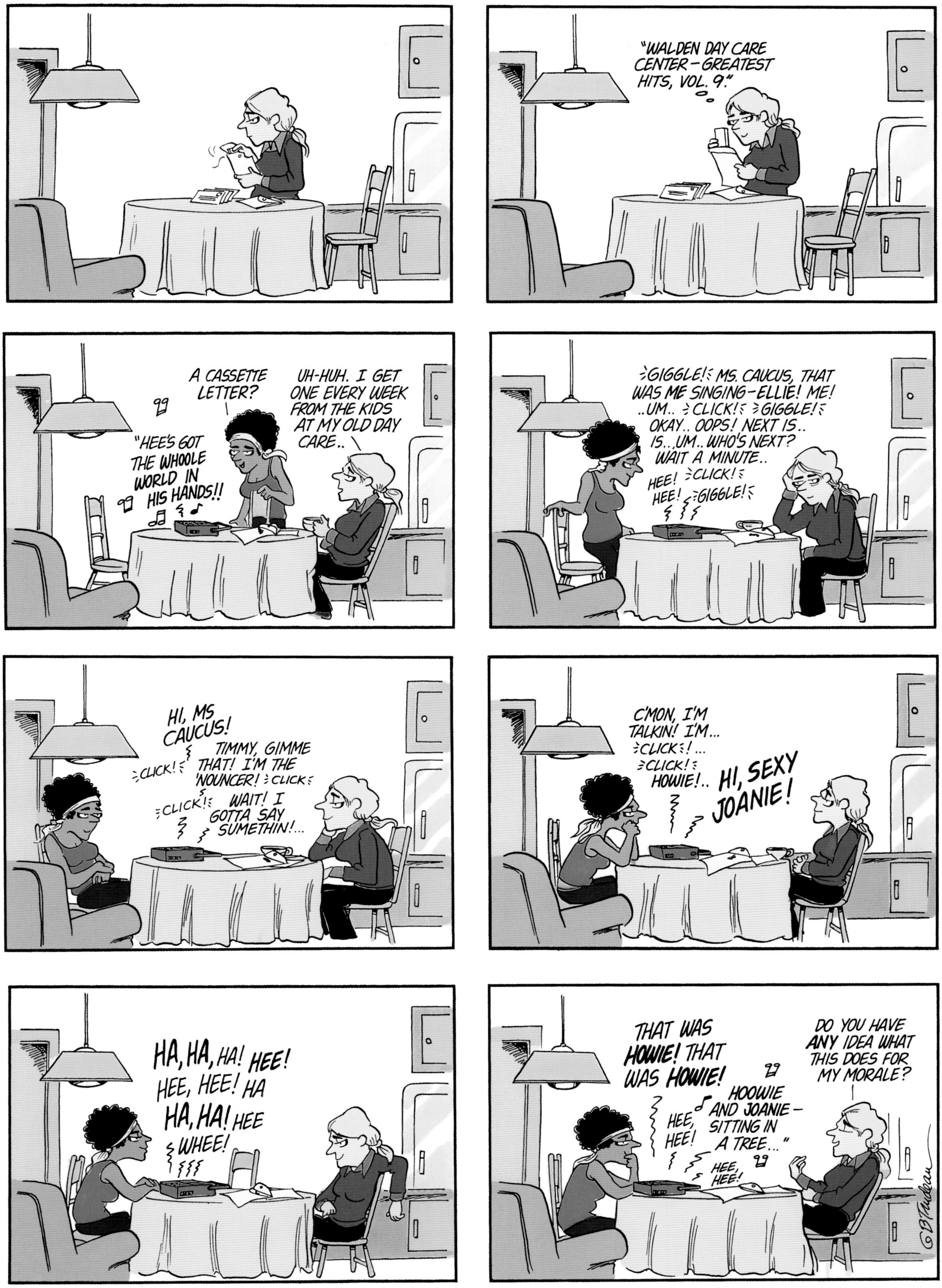
"WALDEN DAY CARE CENTER—GREATEST HITS, VOL. 9."
A CASSETTE LETTER?
UH-HUH. I GET ONE EVERY WEEK FROM THE KIDS AT MY OLD DAY CARE..
"HEE'S GOT THE WHOOLE WORLD IN HIS HANDS!!
GIGGLE! MS. CAUCUS, THAT WAS ME SINGING—ELLIE! ME! ..UM.. CLICK! GIGGLE! OKAY.. OOPS! NEXT IS.. IS...UM.. WHO'S NEXT? WAIT A MINUTE..
HEE! HEE! CLICK! GIGGLE!
HI, MS CAUCUS!
CLICK!
TIMMY, GIMME THAT! I'M THE 'NOUNCER! CLICK
CLICK!
WAIT! I GOTTA SAY SUMETHIN!...
C'MON, I'M TALKIN! I'M... CLICK!... CLICK! HOWIE!..
HI, SEXY JOANIE!
HA, HA, HA! HEE! HEE, HEE! HA HA, HA! HEE WHEE!
THAT WAS HOWIE! THAT WAS HOWIE!
HEE, HEE!
HOOWIE AND JOANIE—SITTING IN A TREE..."
HEE, HEE!
DO YOU HAVE ANY IDEA WHAT THIS DOES FOR MY MORALE?
©GBTrudeau

3/30/75

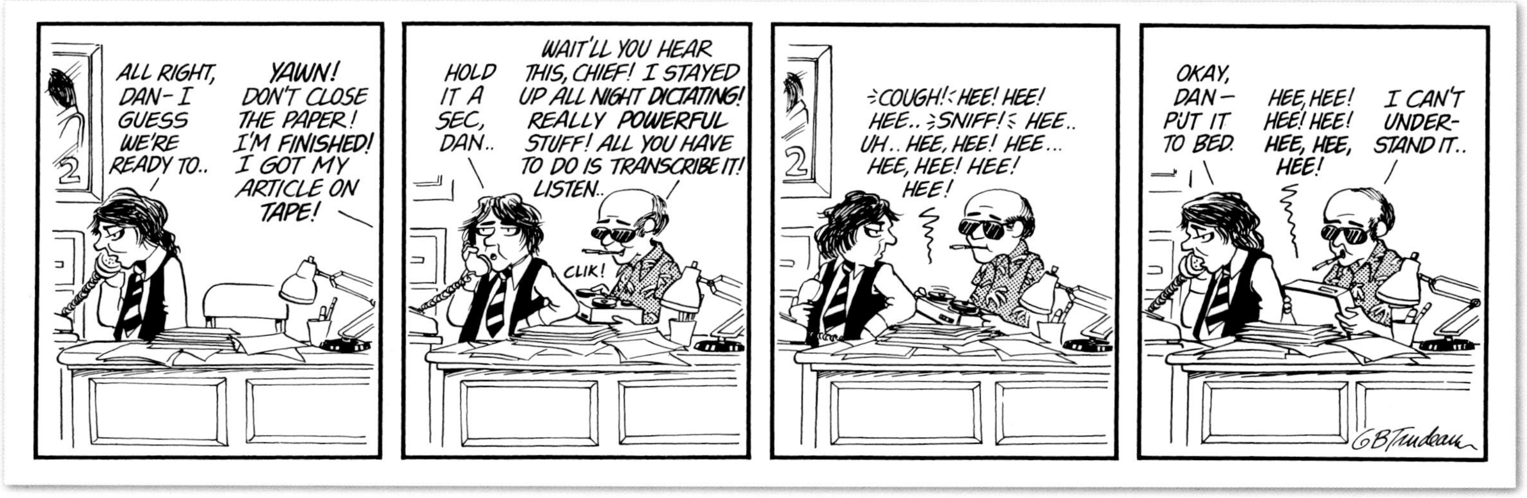
ALL RIGHT, DAN– I GUESS WE'RE READY TO..
YAWN! DON'T CLOSE THE PAPER! I'M FINISHED! I GOT MY ARTICLE ON TAPE!
HOLD IT A SEC, DAN..
WAIT'LL YOU HEAR THIS, CHIEF! I STAYED UP ALL NIGHT DICTATING! REALLY POWERFUL STUFF! ALL YOU HAVE TO DO IS TRANSCRIBE IT! LISTEN..
CLIK!
COUGH! HEE! HEE! HEE.. SNIFF! HEE.. UH.. HEE, HEE! HEE... HEE, HEE! HEE! HEE!
OKAY, DAN– PUT IT TO BED.
HEE, HEE! HEE! HEE! HEE, HEE, HEE!
I CAN'T UNDER-STAND IT..
GB Trudeau

1/9/75

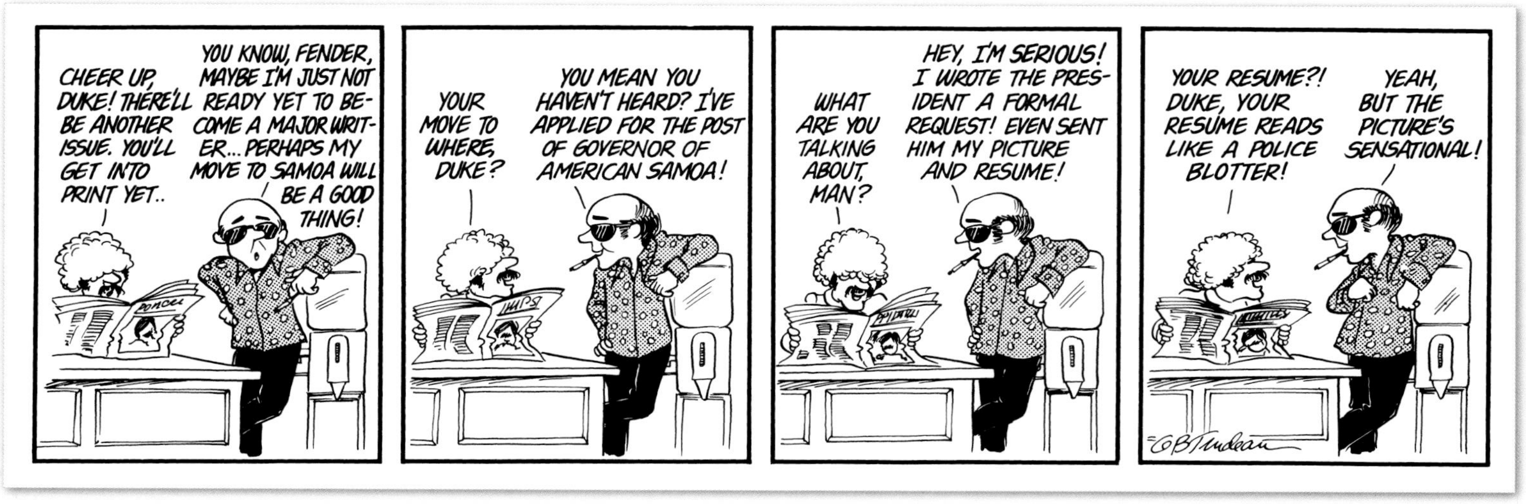
CHEER UP, DUKE! THERE'LL BE ANOTHER ISSUE. YOU'LL GET INTO PRINT YET..
YOU KNOW, FENDER, MAYBE I'M JUST NOT READY YET TO BE-COME A MAJOR WRIT-ER... PERHAPS MY MOVE TO SAMOA WILL BE A GOOD THING!
YOUR MOVE TO WHERE, DUKE?
YOU MEAN YOU HAVEN'T HEARD? I'VE APPLIED FOR THE POST OF GOVERNOR OF AMERICAN SAMOA!
WHAT ARE YOU TALKING ABOUT, MAN?
HEY, I'M SERIOUS! I WROTE THE PRES-IDENT A FORMAL REQUEST! EVEN SENT HIM MY PICTURE AND RESUME!
YOUR RESUME?! DUKE, YOUR RESUME READS LIKE A POLICE BLOTTER!
YEAH, BUT THE PICTURE'S SENSATIONAL!
GB Trudeau

1/10/75

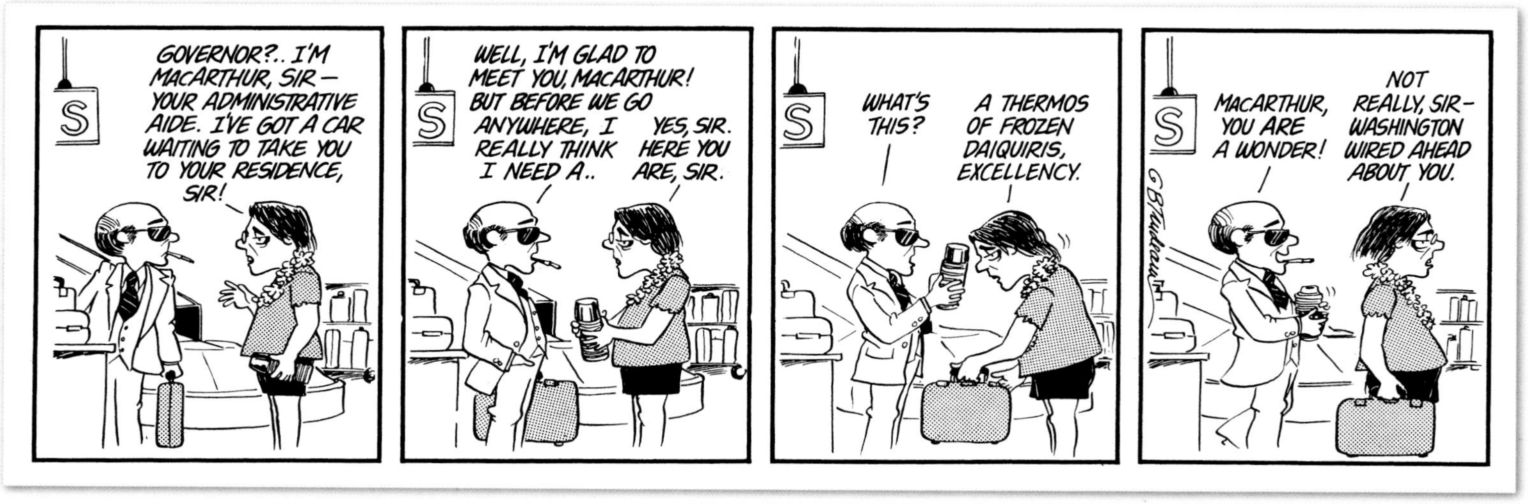
GOVERNOR?.. I'M MacARTHUR, SIR– YOUR ADMINISTRATIVE AIDE. I'VE GOT A CAR WAITING TO TAKE YOU TO YOUR RESIDENCE, SIR!
WELL, I'M GLAD TO MEET YOU, MacARTHUR! BUT BEFORE WE GO ANYWHERE, I REALLY THINK I NEED A..
YES, SIR. HERE YOU ARE, SIR.
WHAT'S THIS?
A THERMOS OF FROZEN DAIQUIRIS, EXCELLENCY.
MacARTHUR, YOU ARE A WONDER!
NOT REALLY, SIR– WASHINGTON WIRED AHEAD ABOUT YOU.
GB Trudeau

1/16/75

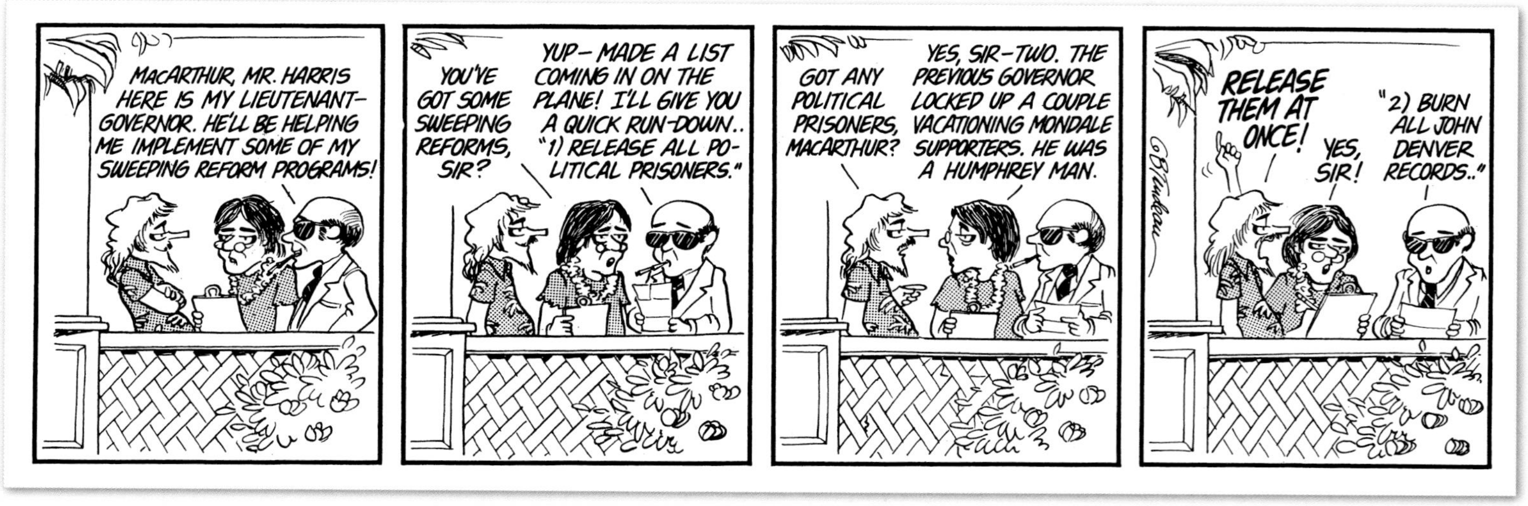
MacARTHUR, MR. HARRIS HERE IS MY LIEUTENANT-GOVERNOR. HE'LL BE HELPING ME IMPLEMENT SOME OF MY SWEEPING REFORM PROGRAMS!
YOU'VE GOT SOME SWEEPING REFORMS, SIR?
YUP– MADE A LIST COMING IN ON THE PLANE! I'LL GIVE YOU A QUICK RUN-DOWN.. "1) RELEASE ALL PO-LITICAL PRISONERS."
GOT ANY POLITICAL PRISONERS, MacARTHUR?
YES, SIR–TWO. THE PREVIOUS GOVERNOR LOCKED UP A COUPLE VACATIONING MONDALE SUPPORTERS. HE WAS A HUMPHREY MAN.
RELEASE THEM AT ONCE!
YES, SIR!
"2) BURN ALL JOHN DENVER RECORDS.."
GB Trudeau

1/17/75

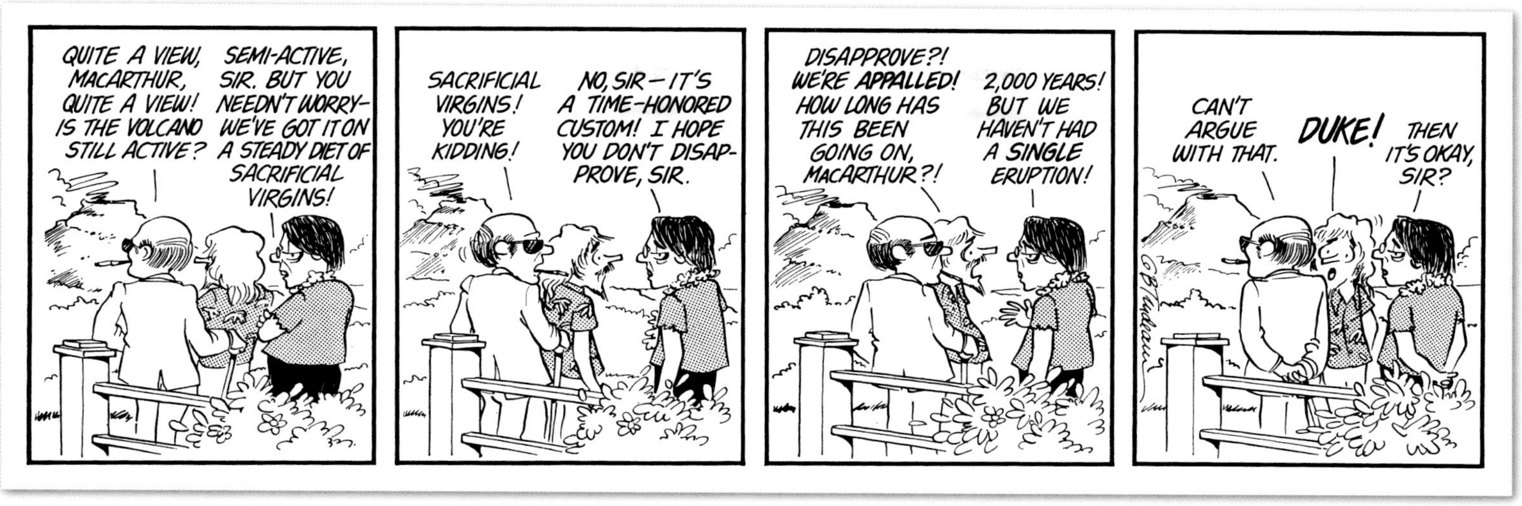
QUITE A VIEW, MACARTHUR, QUITE A VIEW! IS THE VOLCANO STILL ACTIVE?
SEMI-ACTIVE, SIR. BUT YOU NEEDN'T WORRY– WE'VE GOT IT ON A STEADY DIET OF SACRIFICIAL VIRGINS!
SACRIFICIAL VIRGINS! YOU'RE KIDDING!
NO, SIR– IT'S A TIME-HONORED CUSTOM! I HOPE YOU DON'T DISAPPROVE, SIR.
DISAPPROVE?! WE'RE APPALLED! HOW LONG HAS THIS BEEN GOING ON, MACARTHUR?!
2,000 YEARS! BUT WE HAVEN'T HAD A SINGLE ERUPTION!
CAN'T ARGUE WITH THAT.
DUKE!
THEN IT'S OKAY, SIR?

1/20/75

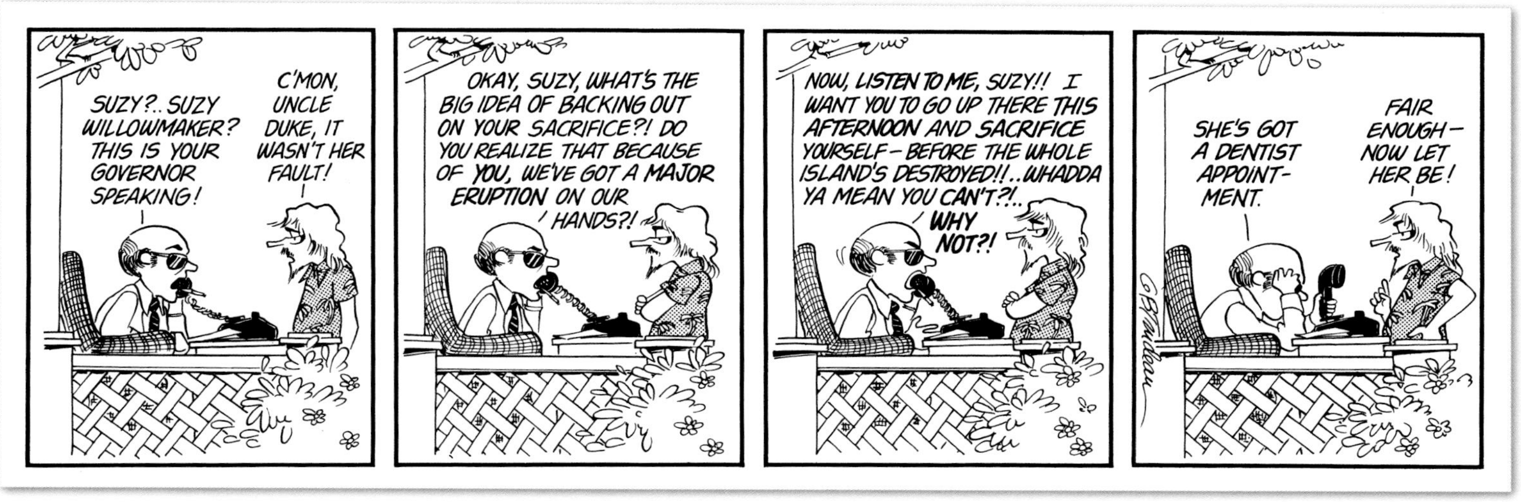
SUZY?.. SUZY WILLOWMAKER? THIS IS YOUR GOVERNOR SPEAKING!
C'MON, UNCLE DUKE, IT WASN'T HER FAULT!
OKAY, SUZY, WHAT'S THE BIG IDEA OF BACKING OUT ON YOUR SACRIFICE?! DO YOU REALIZE THAT BECAUSE OF YOU, WE'VE GOT A MAJOR ERUPTION ON OUR HANDS?!
NOW, LISTEN TO ME, SUZY!! I WANT YOU TO GO UP THERE THIS AFTERNOON AND SACRIFICE YOURSELF– BEFORE THE WHOLE ISLAND'S DESTROYED!!.. WHADDA YA MEAN YOU CAN'T?!..
WHY NOT?!
SHE'S GOT A DENTIST APPOINTMENT.
FAIR ENOUGH– NOW LET HER BE!

2/4/75

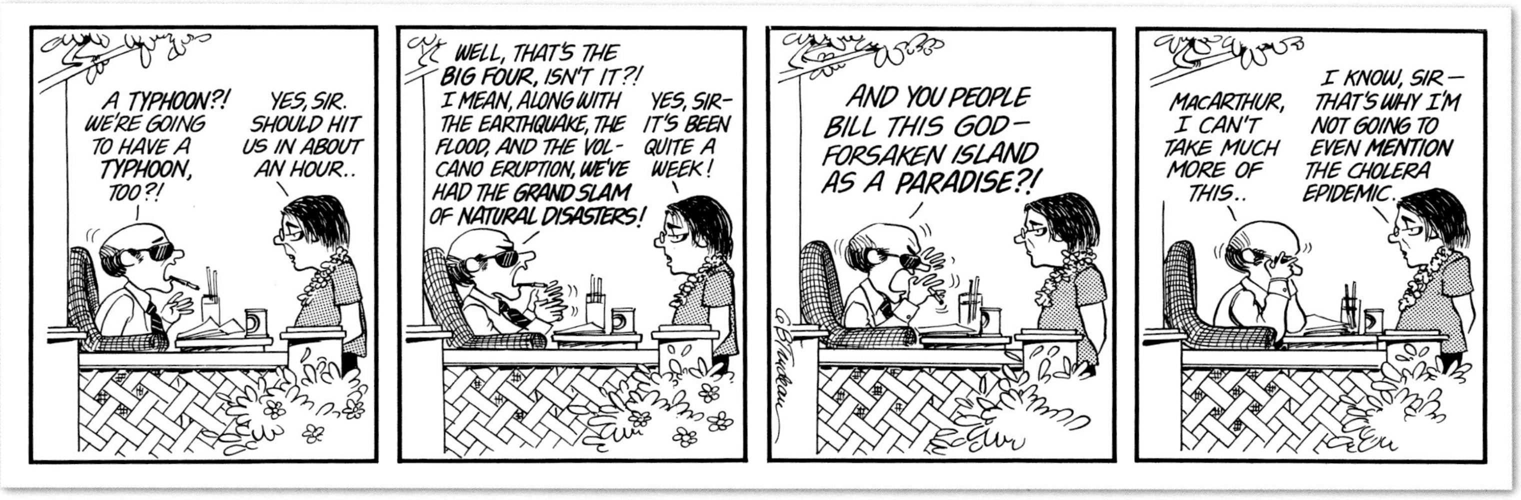
A TYPHOON?! WE'RE GOING TO HAVE A TYPHOON, TOO?!
YES, SIR. SHOULD HIT US IN ABOUT AN HOUR..
WELL, THAT'S THE BIG FOUR, ISN'T IT?! I MEAN, ALONG WITH THE EARTHQUAKE, THE FLOOD, AND THE VOLCANO ERUPTION, WE'VE HAD THE GRAND SLAM OF NATURAL DISASTERS!
YES, SIR– IT'S BEEN QUITE A WEEK!
AND YOU PEOPLE BILL THIS GOD-FORSAKEN ISLAND AS A PARADISE?!
MACARTHUR, I CAN'T TAKE MUCH MORE OF THIS..
I KNOW, SIR– THAT'S WHY I'M NOT GOING TO EVEN MENTION THE CHOLERA EPIDEMIC.

2/5/75

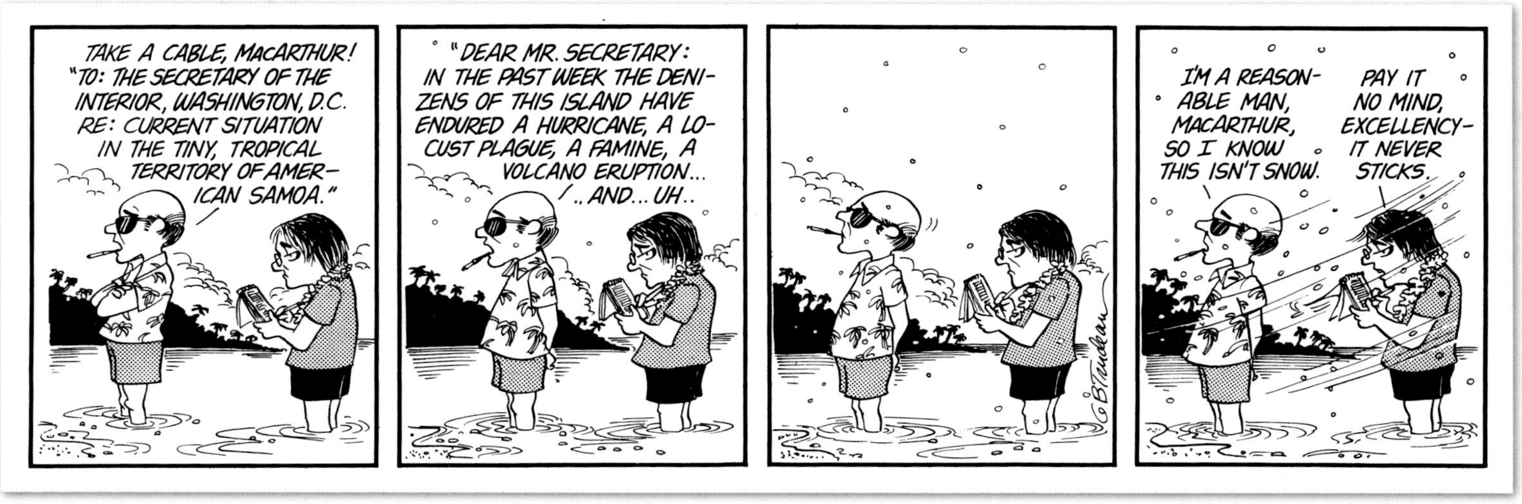
TAKE A CABLE, MACARTHUR! "TO: THE SECRETARY OF THE INTERIOR, WASHINGTON, D.C. RE: CURRENT SITUATION IN THE TINY, TROPICAL TERRITORY OF AMERICAN SAMOA."
" "DEAR MR. SECRETARY: IN THE PAST WEEK THE DENIZENS OF THIS ISLAND HAVE ENDURED A HURRICANE, A LOCUST PLAGUE, A FAMINE, A VOLCANO ERUPTION... .. AND... UH..
I'M A REASONABLE MAN, MACARTHUR, SO I KNOW THIS ISN'T SNOW.
PAY IT NO MIND, EXCELLENCY– IT NEVER STICKS.

2/6/75

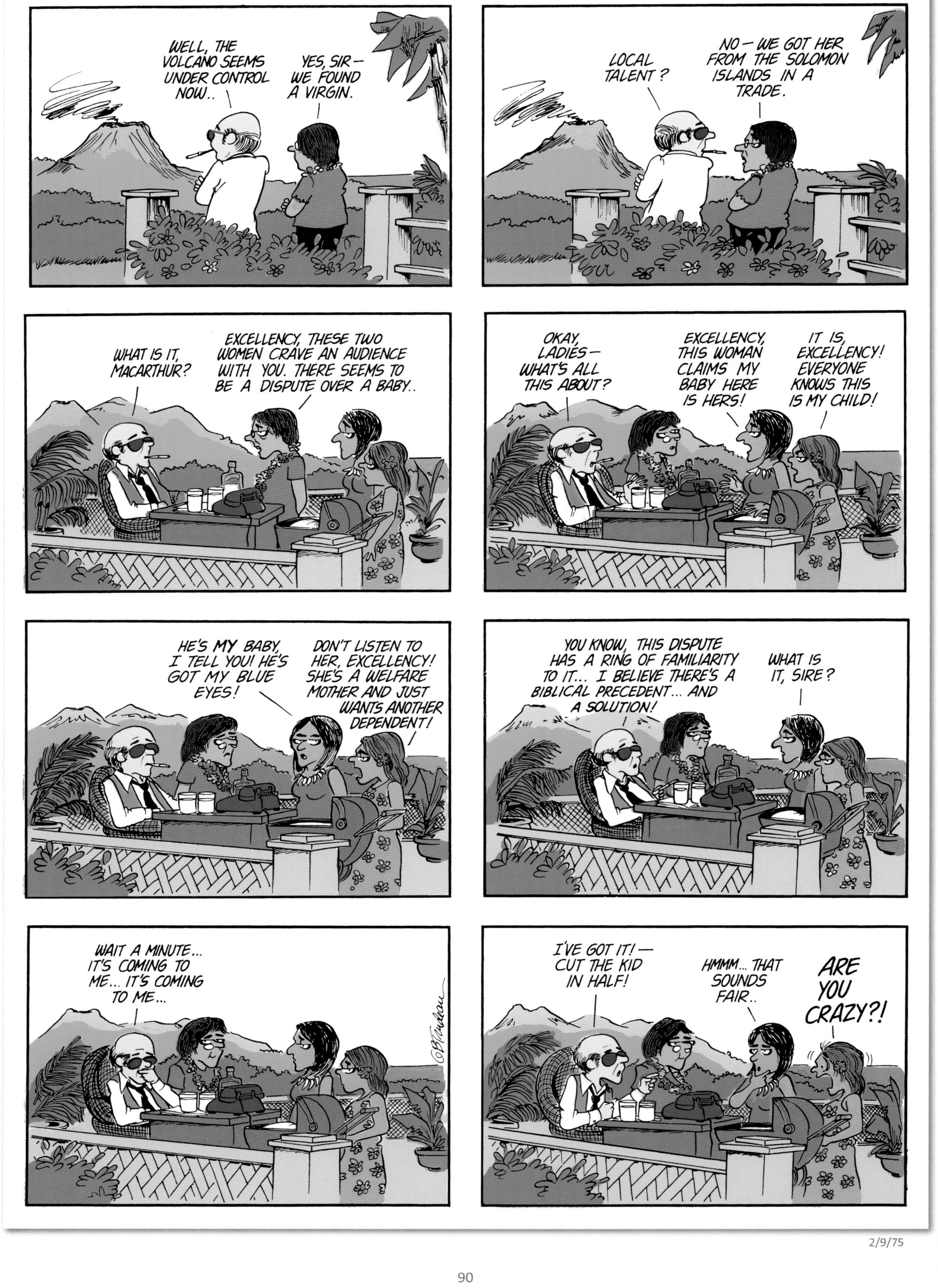

WELL, THE VOLCANO SEEMS UNDER CONTROL NOW..
YES, SIR— WE FOUND A VIRGIN.
LOCAL TALENT?
NO— WE GOT HER FROM THE SOLOMON ISLANDS IN A TRADE.
WHAT IS IT, MACARTHUR?
EXCELLENCY, THESE TWO WOMEN CRAVE AN AUDIENCE WITH YOU. THERE SEEMS TO BE A DISPUTE OVER A BABY..
OKAY, LADIES— WHAT'S ALL THIS ABOUT?
EXCELLENCY, THIS WOMAN CLAIMS MY BABY HERE IS HERS!
IT IS, EXCELLENCY! EVERYONE KNOWS THIS IS MY CHILD!
HE'S MY BABY, I TELL YOU! HE'S GOT MY BLUE EYES!
DON'T LISTEN TO HER, EXCELLENCY! SHE'S A WELFARE MOTHER AND JUST WANTS ANOTHER DEPENDENT!
YOU KNOW, THIS DISPUTE HAS A RING OF FAMILIARITY TO IT... I BELIEVE THERE'S A BIBLICAL PRECEDENT... AND A SOLUTION!
WHAT IS IT, SIRE?
WAIT A MINUTE... IT'S COMING TO ME... IT'S COMING TO ME...
I'VE GOT IT!— CUT THE KID IN HALF!
HMMM... THAT SOUNDS FAIR..
ARE YOU CRAZY?!

2/9/75

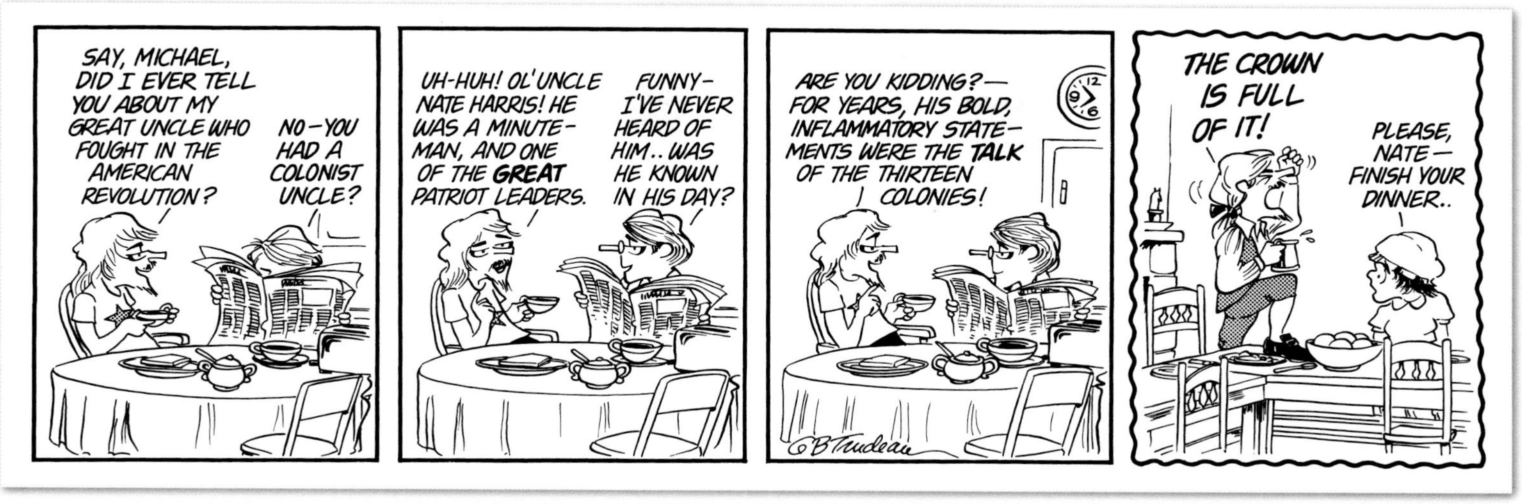
SAY, MICHAEL, DID I EVER TELL YOU ABOUT MY GREAT UNCLE WHO FOUGHT IN THE AMERICAN REVOLUTION?
NO—YOU HAD A COLONIST UNCLE?
UH-HUH! OL' UNCLE NATE HARRIS! HE WAS A MINUTE-MAN, AND ONE OF THE GREAT PATRIOT LEADERS.
FUNNY—I'VE NEVER HEARD OF HIM.. WAS HE KNOWN IN HIS DAY?
ARE YOU KIDDING?—FOR YEARS, HIS BOLD, INFLAMMATORY STATE-MENTS WERE THE TALK OF THE THIRTEEN COLONIES!
THE CROWN IS FULL OF IT!
PLEASE, NATE—FINISH YOUR DINNER..
G.B. Trudeau

7/21/75

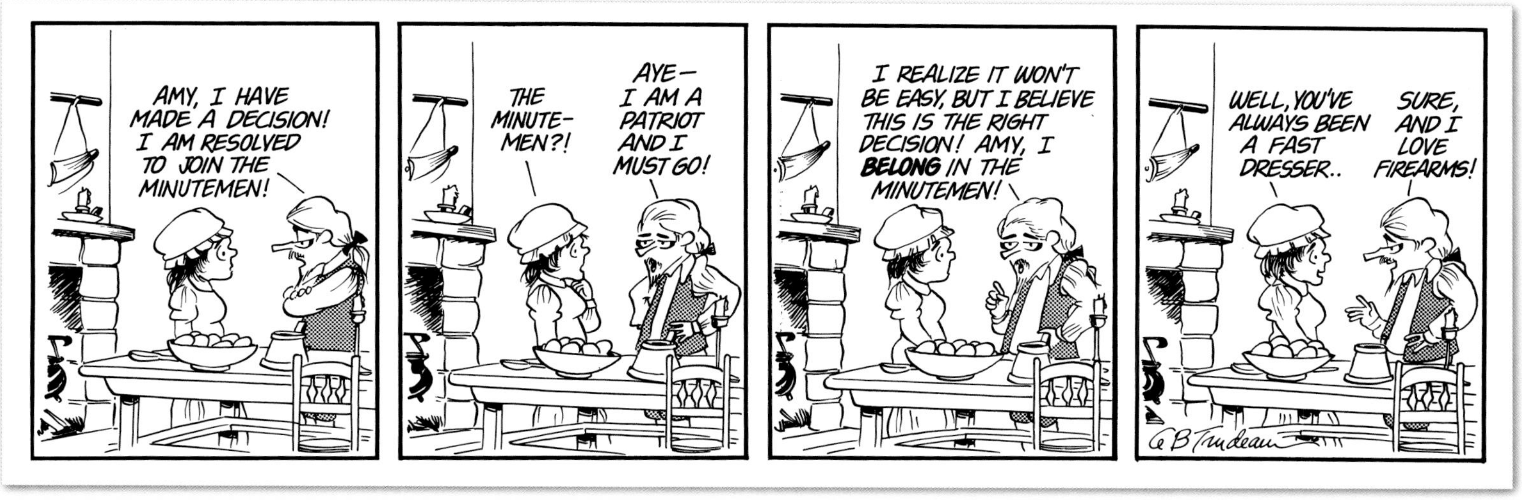
AMY, I HAVE MADE A DECISION! I AM RESOLVED TO JOIN THE MINUTEMEN!
THE MINUTE-MEN?!
AYE—I AM A PATRIOT AND I MUST GO!
I REALIZE IT WON'T BE EASY, BUT I BELIEVE THIS IS THE RIGHT DECISION! AMY, I BELONG IN THE MINUTEMEN!
WELL, YOU'VE ALWAYS BEEN A FAST DRESSER..
SURE, AND I LOVE FIREARMS!
G.B. Trudeau

7/23/75

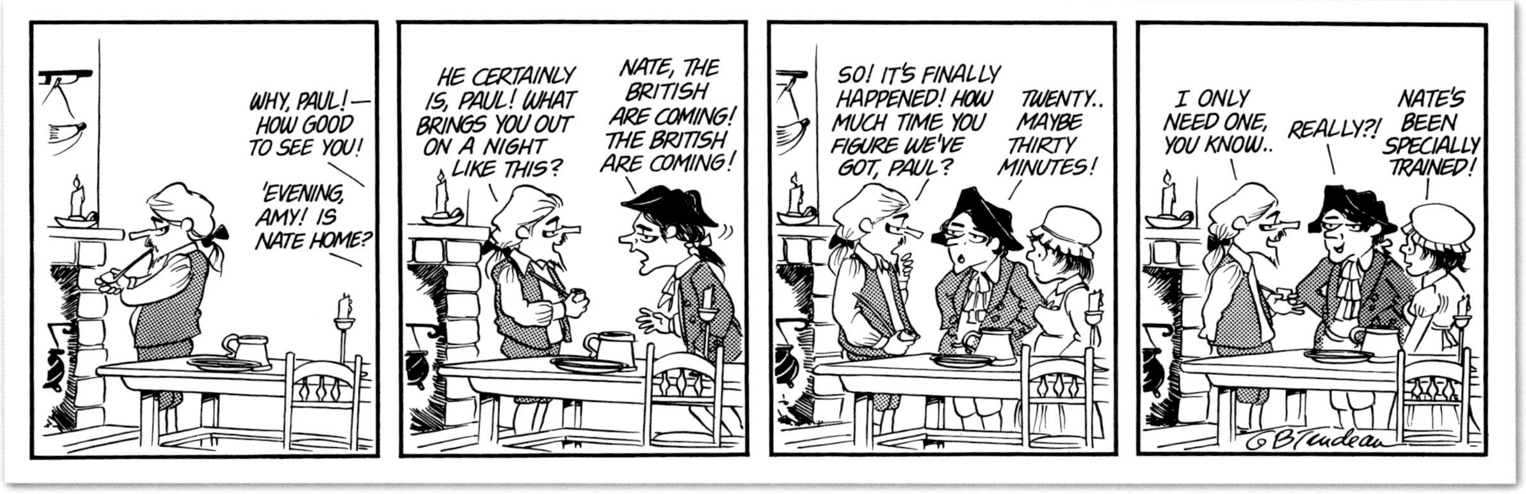
WHY, PAUL!—HOW GOOD TO SEE YOU!
'EVENING, AMY! IS NATE HOME?
HE CERTAINLY IS, PAUL! WHAT BRINGS YOU OUT ON A NIGHT LIKE THIS?
NATE, THE BRITISH ARE COMING! THE BRITISH ARE COMING!
SO! IT'S FINALLY HAPPENED! HOW MUCH TIME YOU FIGURE WE'VE GOT, PAUL?
TWENTY.. MAYBE THIRTY MINUTES!
I ONLY NEED ONE, YOU KNOW..
REALLY?!
NATE'S BEEN SPECIALLY TRAINED!
G.B. Trudeau

7/24/75

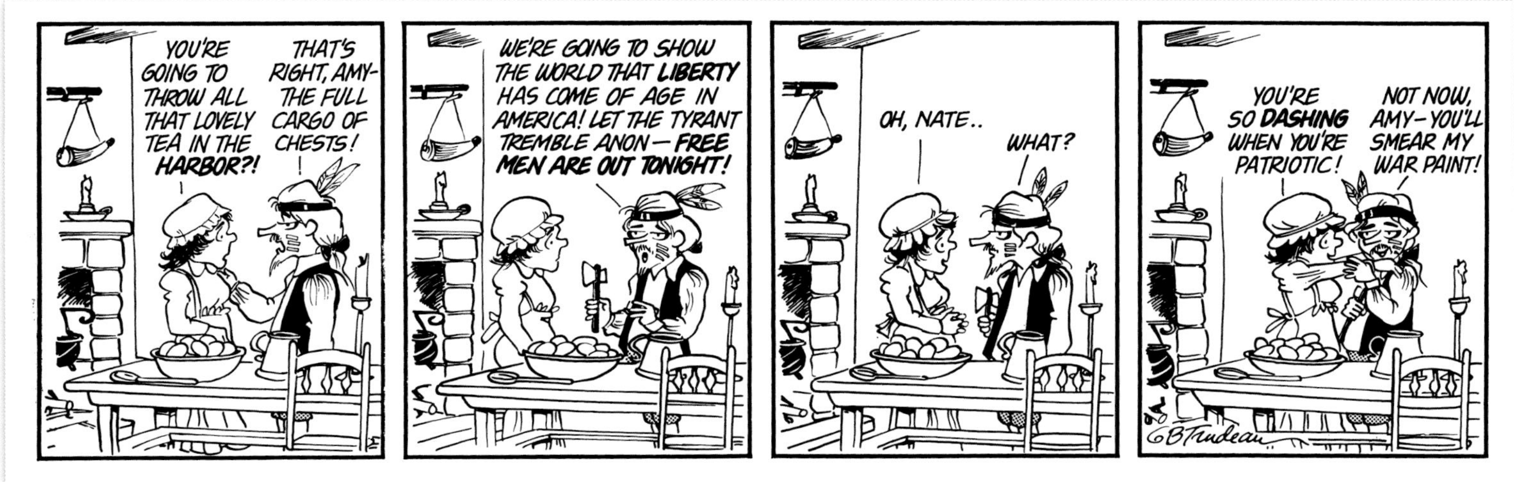
YOU'RE GOING TO THROW ALL THAT LOVELY TEA IN THE HARBOR?!
THAT'S RIGHT, AMY—THE FULL CARGO OF CHESTS!
WE'RE GOING TO SHOW THE WORLD THAT LIBERTY HAS COME OF AGE IN AMERICA! LET THE TYRANT TREMBLE ANON—FREE MEN ARE OUT TONIGHT!
OH, NATE..
WHAT?
YOU'RE SO DASHING WHEN YOU'RE PATRIOTIC!
NOT NOW, AMY—YOU'LL SMEAR MY WAR PAINT!
G.B. Trudeau

7/28/75

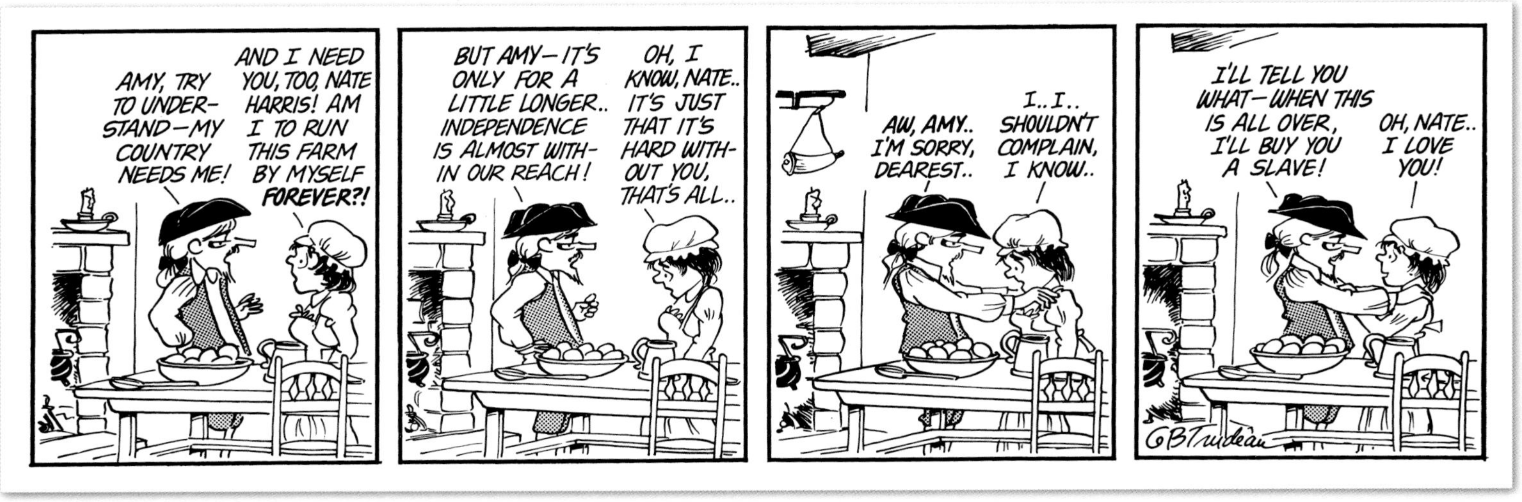
AMY, TRY TO UNDER-STAND—MY COUNTRY NEEDS ME!
AND I NEED YOU, TOO, NATE HARRIS! AM I TO RUN THIS FARM BY MYSELF FOREVER?!
BUT AMY—IT'S ONLY FOR A LITTLE LONGER.. INDEPENDENCE IS ALMOST WITH-IN OUR REACH!
OH, I KNOW, NATE.. IT'S JUST THAT IT'S HARD WITH-OUT YOU, THAT'S ALL..
AW, AMY.. I'M SORRY, DEAREST..
I..I.. SHOULDN'T COMPLAIN, I KNOW..
I'LL TELL YOU WHAT—WHEN THIS IS ALL OVER, I'LL BUY YOU A SLAVE!
OH, NATE.. I LOVE YOU!
GBTrudeau

7/29/75

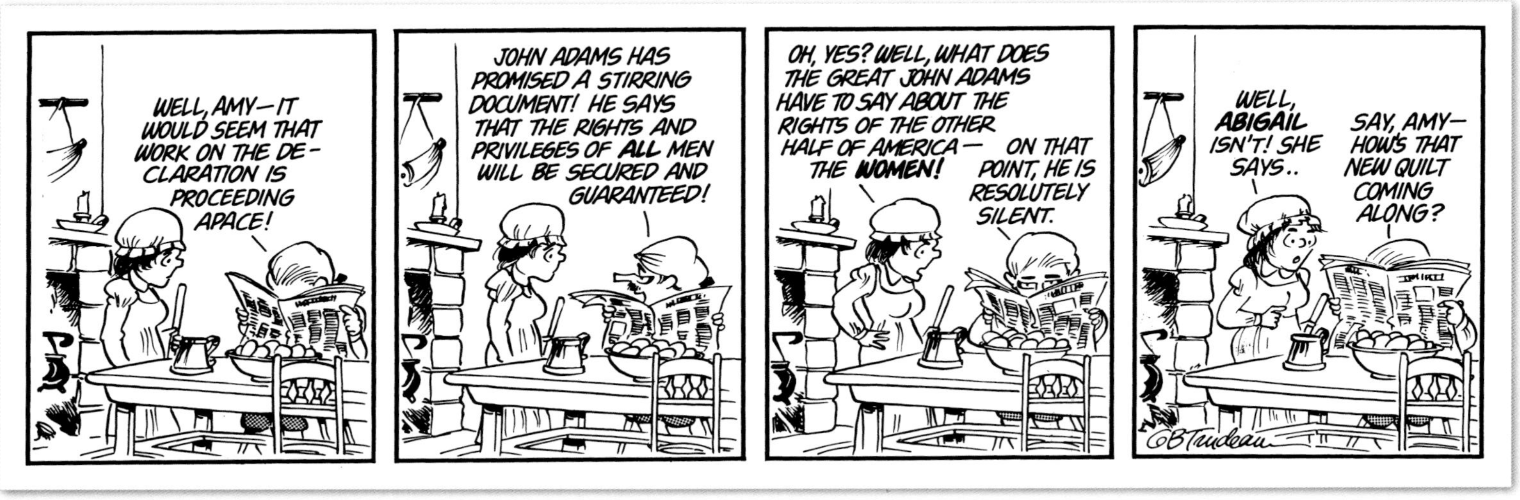
WELL, AMY—IT WOULD SEEM THAT WORK ON THE DE-CLARATION IS PROCEEDING APACE!
JOHN ADAMS HAS PROMISED A STIRRING DOCUMENT! HE SAYS THAT THE RIGHTS AND PRIVILEGES OF ALL MEN WILL BE SECURED AND GUARANTEED!
OH, YES? WELL, WHAT DOES THE GREAT JOHN ADAMS HAVE TO SAY ABOUT THE RIGHTS OF THE OTHER HALF OF AMERICA—THE WOMEN!
ON THAT POINT, HE IS RESOLUTELY SILENT.
WELL, ABIGAIL ISN'T! SHE SAYS..
SAY, AMY—HOW'S THAT NEW QUILT COMING ALONG?
GBTrudeau

7/31/75

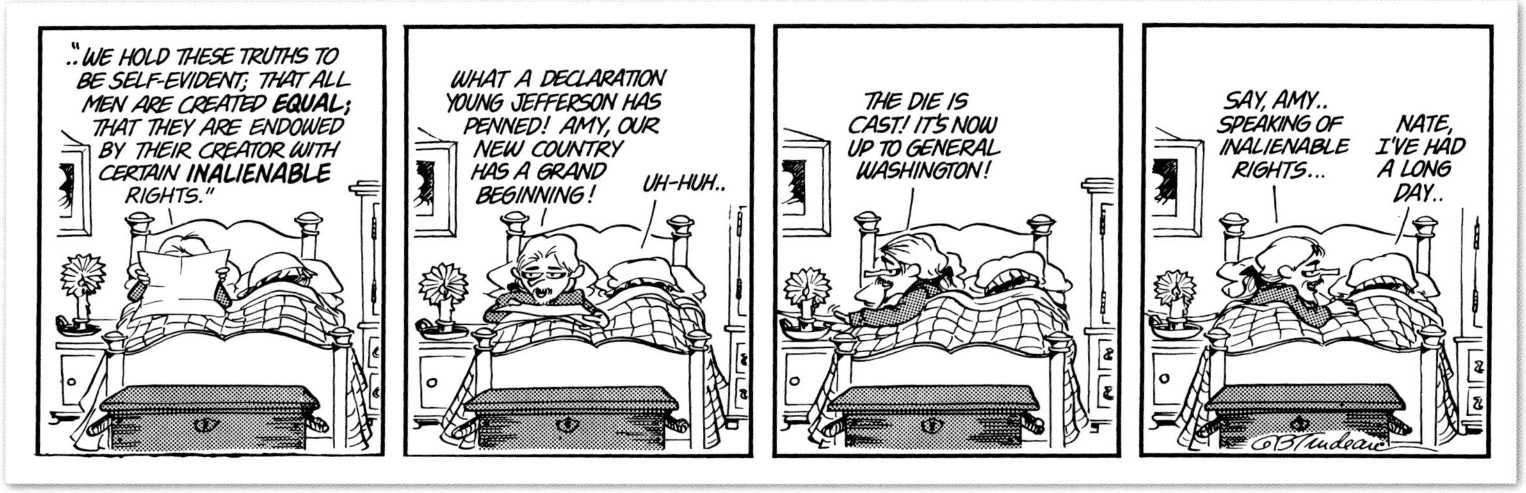
"..WE HOLD THESE TRUTHS TO BE SELF-EVIDENT; THAT ALL MEN ARE CREATED EQUAL; THAT THEY ARE ENDOWED BY THEIR CREATOR WITH CERTAIN INALIENABLE RIGHTS."
WHAT A DECLARATION YOUNG JEFFERSON HAS PENNED! AMY, OUR NEW COUNTRY HAS A GRAND BEGINNING!
UH-HUH..
THE DIE IS CAST! IT'S NOW UP TO GENERAL WASHINGTON!
SAY, AMY.. SPEAKING OF INALIENABLE RIGHTS...
NATE, I'VE HAD A LONG DAY..
GBTrudeau

8/1/75

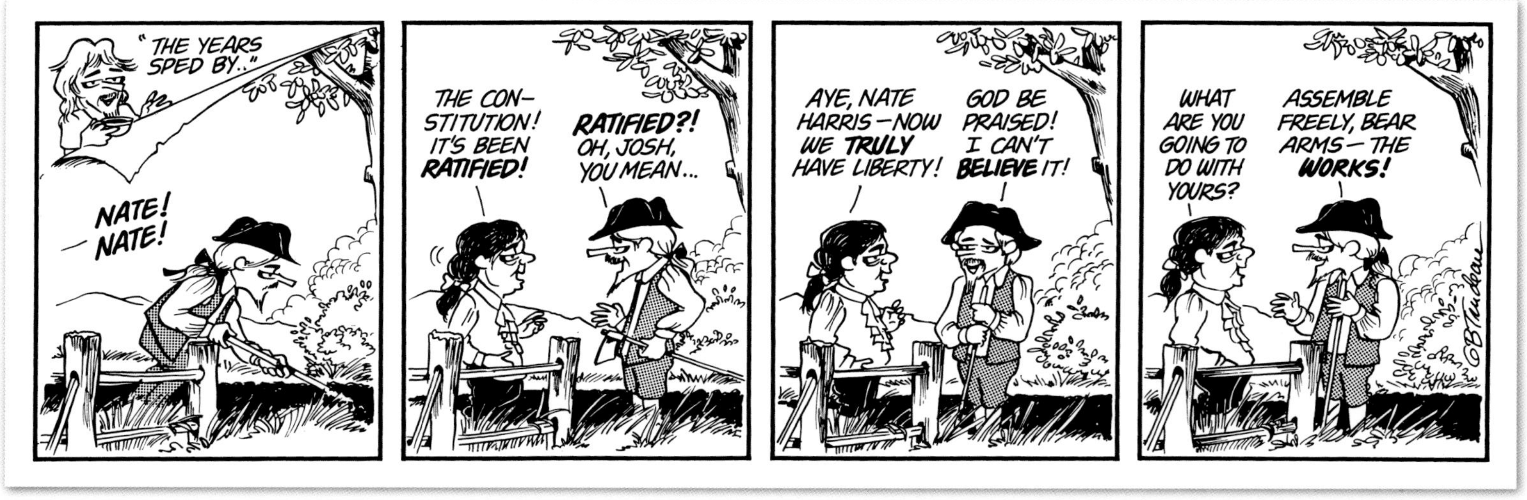
"THE YEARS SPED BY.."
NATE! NATE!
THE CON-STITUTION! IT'S BEEN RATIFIED!
RATIFIED?! OH, JOSH, YOU MEAN...
AYE, NATE HARRIS—NOW WE TRULY HAVE LIBERTY!
GOD BE PRAISED! I CAN'T BELIEVE IT!
WHAT ARE YOU GOING TO DO WITH YOURS?
ASSEMBLE FREELY, BEAR ARMS—THE WORKS!
GBTrudeau

8/2/75

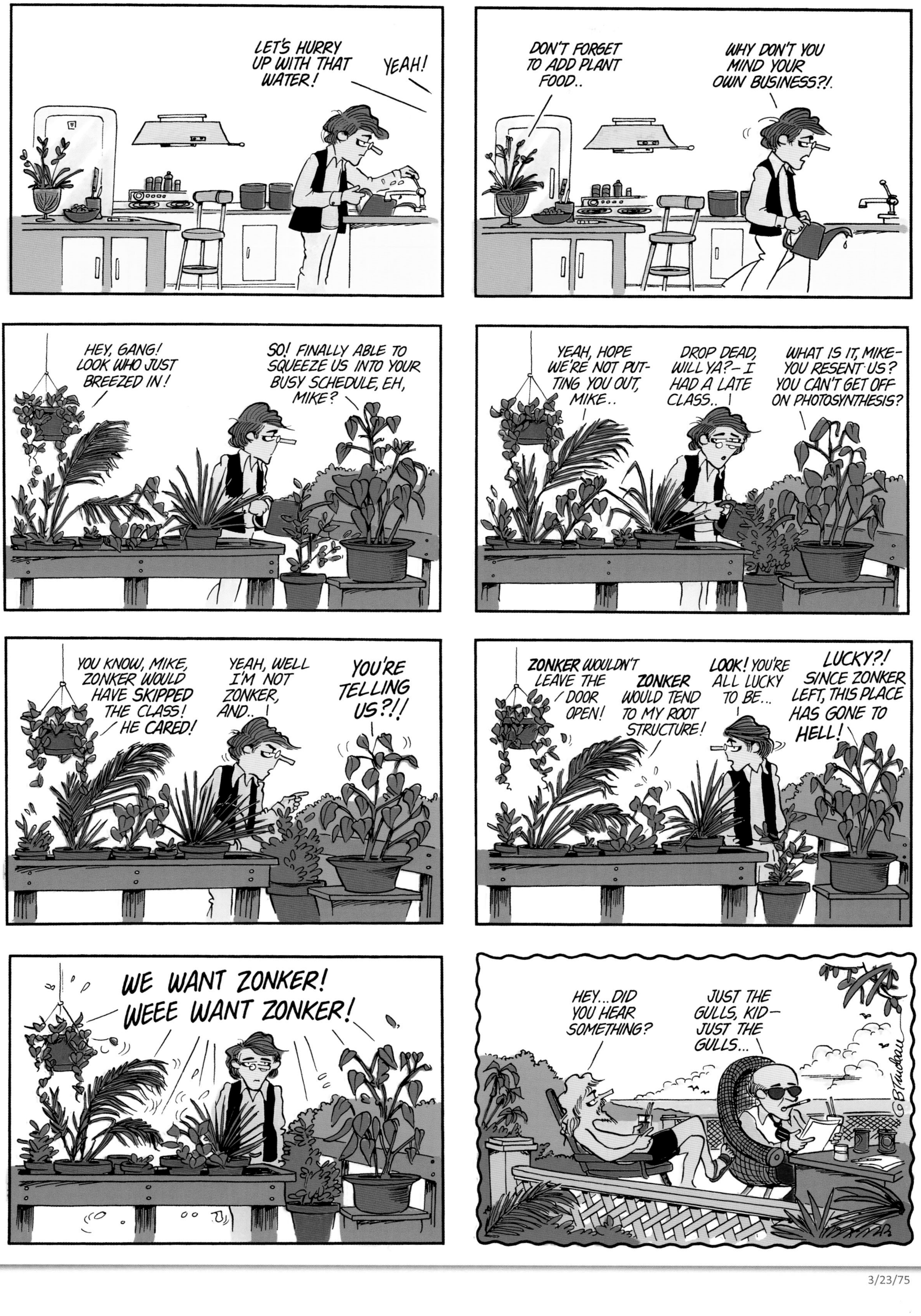
LET'S HURRY UP WITH THAT WATER!
YEAH!
DON'T FORGET TO ADD PLANT FOOD..
WHY DON'T YOU MIND YOUR OWN BUSINESS?!.
HEY, GANG! LOOK WHO JUST BREEZED IN!
SO! FINALLY ABLE TO SQUEEZE US INTO YOUR BUSY SCHEDULE, EH, MIKE?
YEAH, HOPE WE'RE NOT PUTTING YOU OUT, MIKE..
DROP DEAD, WILL YA?— I HAD A LATE CLASS..
WHAT IS IT, MIKE— YOU RESENT US? YOU CAN'T GET OFF ON PHOTOSYNTHESIS?
YOU KNOW, MIKE, ZONKER WOULD HAVE SKIPPED THE CLASS! HE CARED!
YEAH, WELL I'M NOT ZONKER, AND..
YOU'RE TELLING US?!!
ZONKER WOULDN'T LEAVE THE DOOR OPEN!
ZONKER WOULD TEND TO MY ROOT STRUCTURE!
LOOK! YOU'RE ALL LUCKY TO BE...
LUCKY?! SINCE ZONKER LEFT, THIS PLACE HAS GONE TO HELL!
WE WANT ZONKER! WEEE WANT ZONKER!
HEY... DID YOU HEAR SOMETHING?
JUST THE GULLS, KID— JUST THE GULLS...
©GBTrudeau

3/23/75

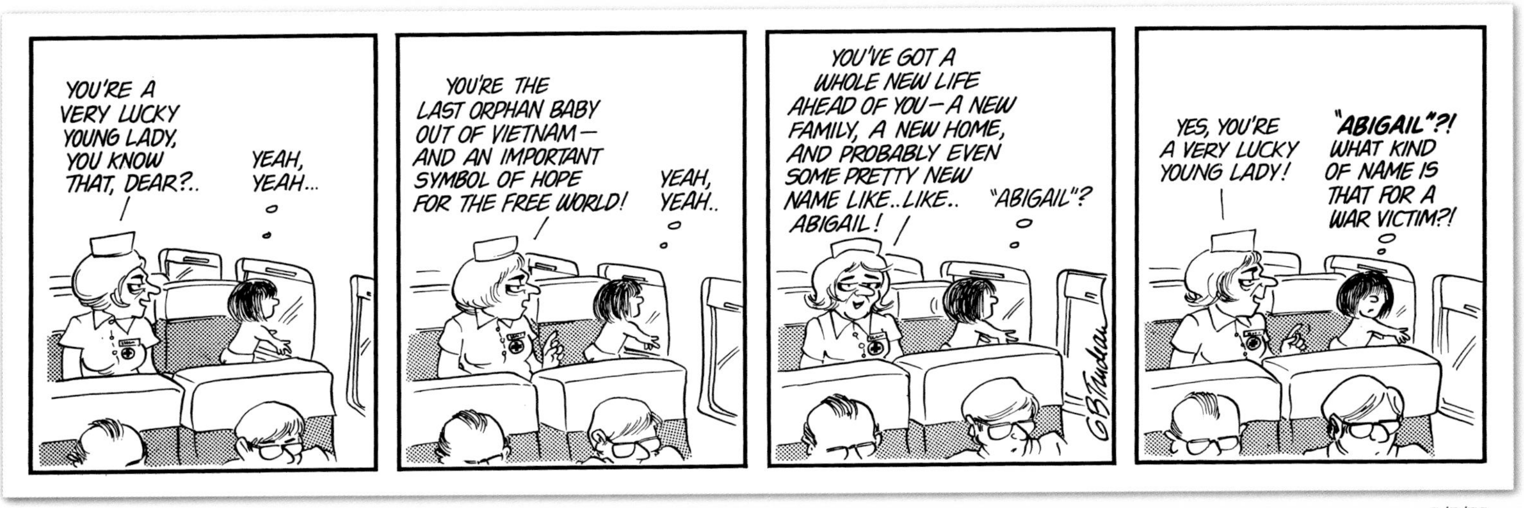
YOU'RE A VERY LUCKY YOUNG LADY, YOU KNOW THAT, DEAR?..
YEAH, YEAH...
YOU'RE THE LAST ORPHAN BABY OUT OF VIETNAM — AND AN IMPORTANT SYMBOL OF HOPE FOR THE FREE WORLD!
YEAH, YEAH..
YOU'VE GOT A WHOLE NEW LIFE AHEAD OF YOU — A NEW FAMILY, A NEW HOME, AND PROBABLY EVEN SOME PRETTY NEW NAME LIKE..LIKE.. ABIGAIL!
"ABIGAIL"?
YES, YOU'RE A VERY LUCKY YOUNG LADY!
"ABIGAIL"?! WHAT KIND OF NAME IS THAT FOR A WAR VICTIM?!
GBTrudeau

5/5/75

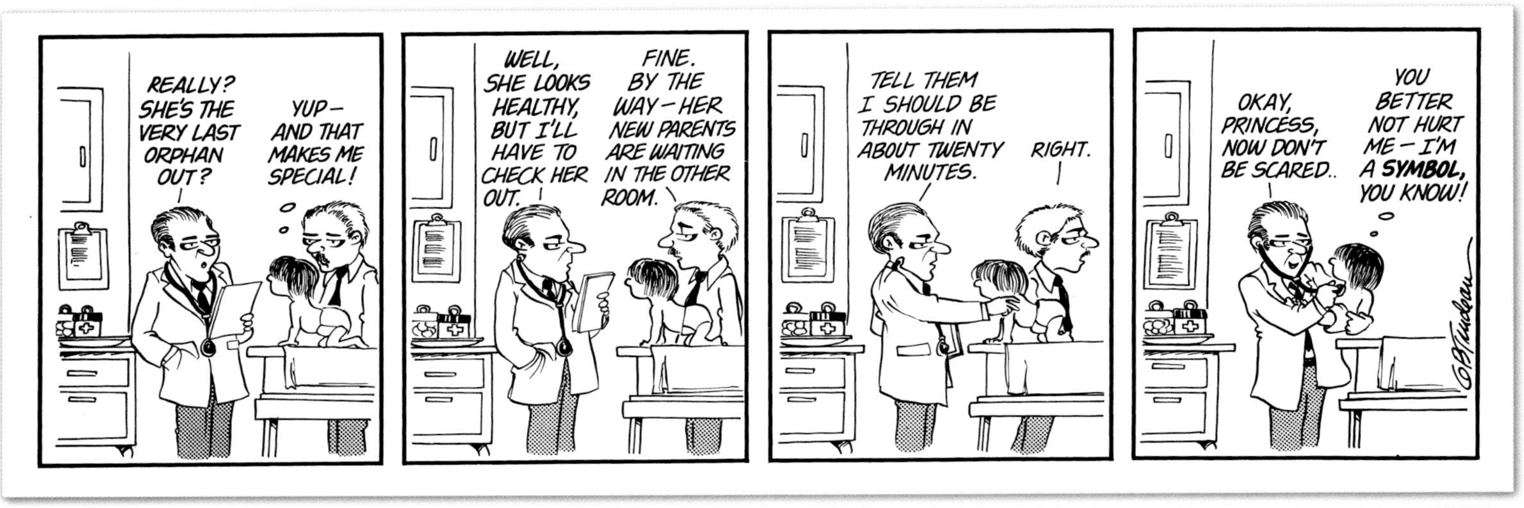
REALLY? SHE'S THE VERY LAST ORPHAN OUT?
YUP — AND THAT MAKES ME SPECIAL!
WELL, SHE LOOKS HEALTHY, BUT I'LL HAVE TO CHECK HER OUT.
FINE. BY THE WAY — HER NEW PARENTS ARE WAITING IN THE OTHER ROOM.
TELL THEM I SHOULD BE THROUGH IN ABOUT TWENTY MINUTES.
RIGHT.
OKAY, PRINCESS, NOW DON'T BE SCARED..
YOU BETTER NOT HURT ME — I'M A SYMBOL, YOU KNOW!
GBTrudeau

5/6/75

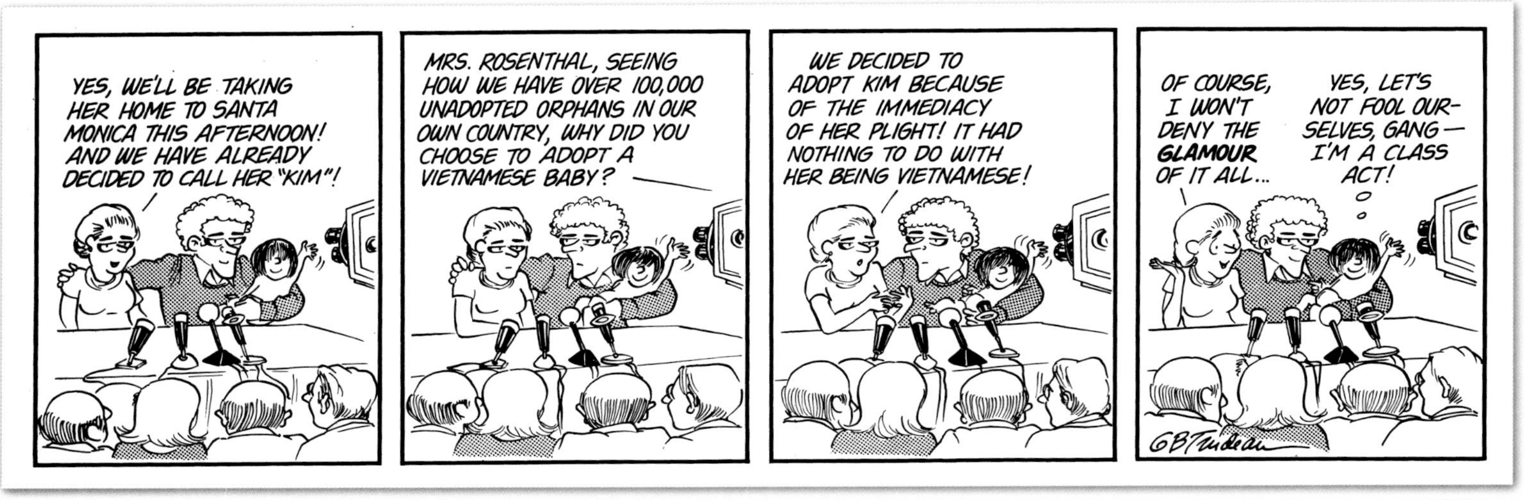
YES, WE'LL BE TAKING HER HOME TO SANTA MONICA THIS AFTERNOON! AND WE HAVE ALREADY DECIDED TO CALL HER "KIM"!
MRS. ROSENTHAL, SEEING HOW WE HAVE OVER 100,000 UNADOPTED ORPHANS IN OUR OWN COUNTRY, WHY DID YOU CHOOSE TO ADOPT A VIETNAMESE BABY?
WE DECIDED TO ADOPT KIM BECAUSE OF THE IMMEDIACY OF HER PLIGHT! IT HAD NOTHING TO DO WITH HER BEING VIETNAMESE!
OF COURSE, I WON'T DENY THE GLAMOUR OF IT ALL...
YES, LET'S NOT FOOL OURSELVES, GANG — I'M A CLASS ACT!
GBTrudeau

5/7/75

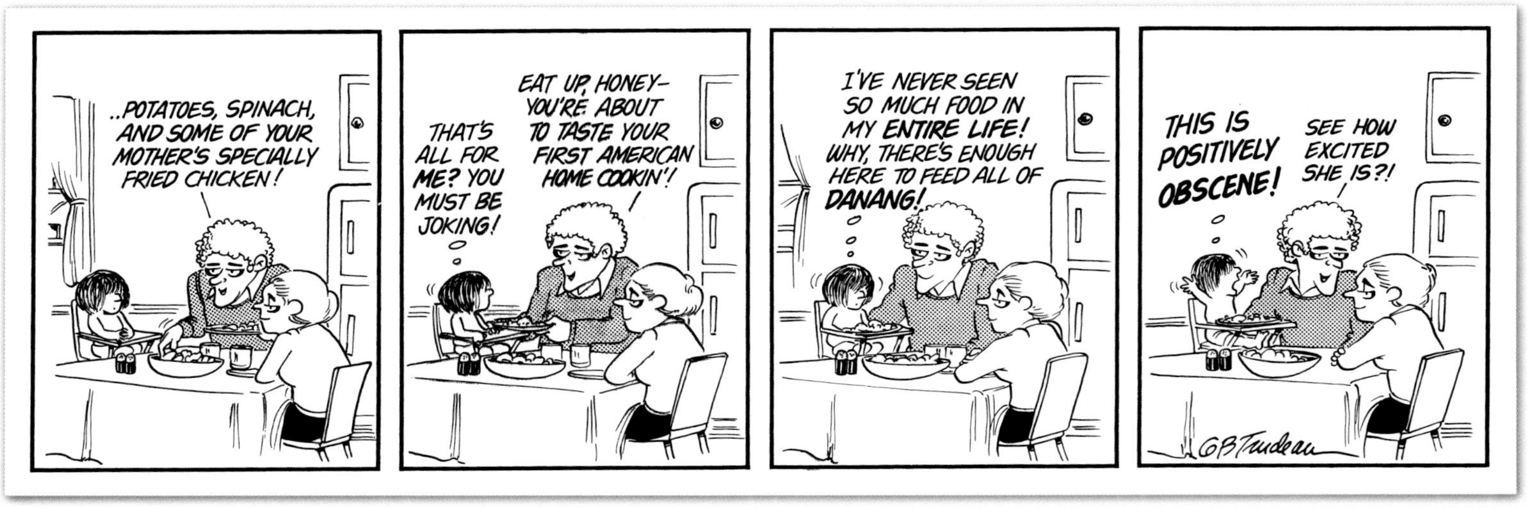
..POTATOES, SPINACH, AND SOME OF YOUR MOTHER'S SPECIALLY FRIED CHICKEN!
THAT'S ALL FOR ME? YOU MUST BE JOKING!
EAT UP, HONEY — YOU'RE ABOUT TO TASTE YOUR FIRST AMERICAN HOME COOKIN'!
I'VE NEVER SEEN SO MUCH FOOD IN MY ENTIRE LIFE! WHY, THERE'S ENOUGH HERE TO FEED ALL OF DANANG!
THIS IS POSITIVELY OBSCENE!
SEE HOW EXCITED SHE IS?!
GBTrudeau

5/9/75

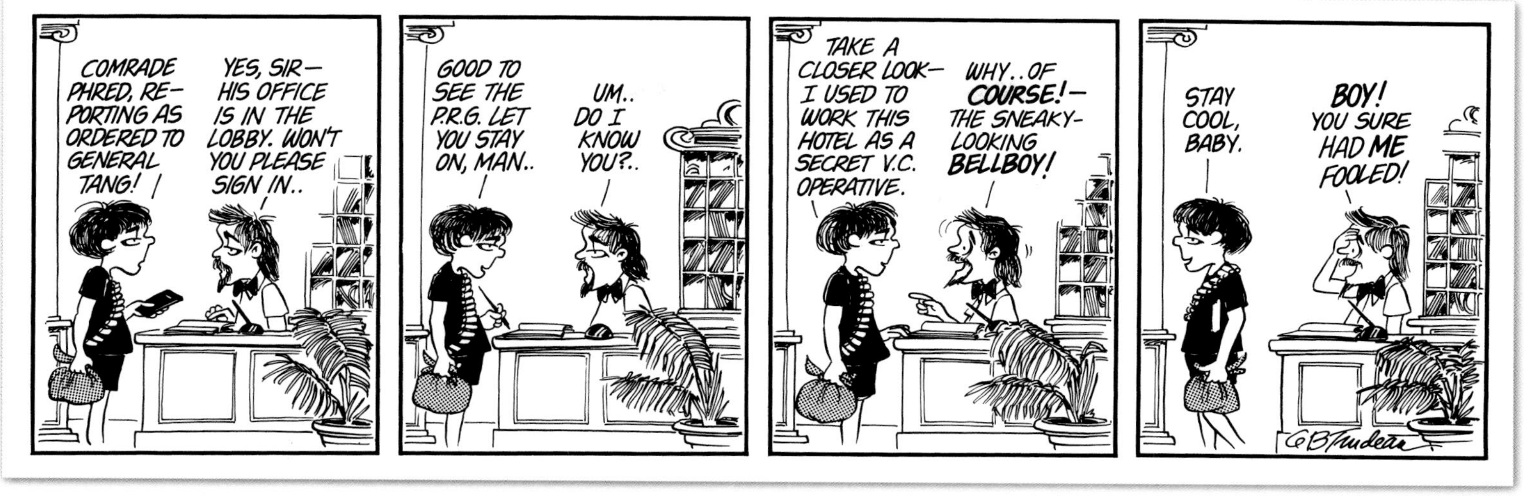
COMRADE PHRED, REPORTING AS ORDERED TO GENERAL TANG!
YES, SIR— HIS OFFICE IS IN THE LOBBY. WON'T YOU PLEASE SIGN IN..
GOOD TO SEE THE P.R.G. LET YOU STAY ON, MAN..
UM.. DO I KNOW YOU?..
TAKE A CLOSER LOOK— I USED TO WORK THIS HOTEL AS A SECRET V.C. OPERATIVE.
WHY..OF COURSE!— THE SNEAKY-LOOKING BELLBOY!
STAY COOL, BABY.
BOY! YOU SURE HAD ME FOOLED!
GBTrudeau

5/27/75

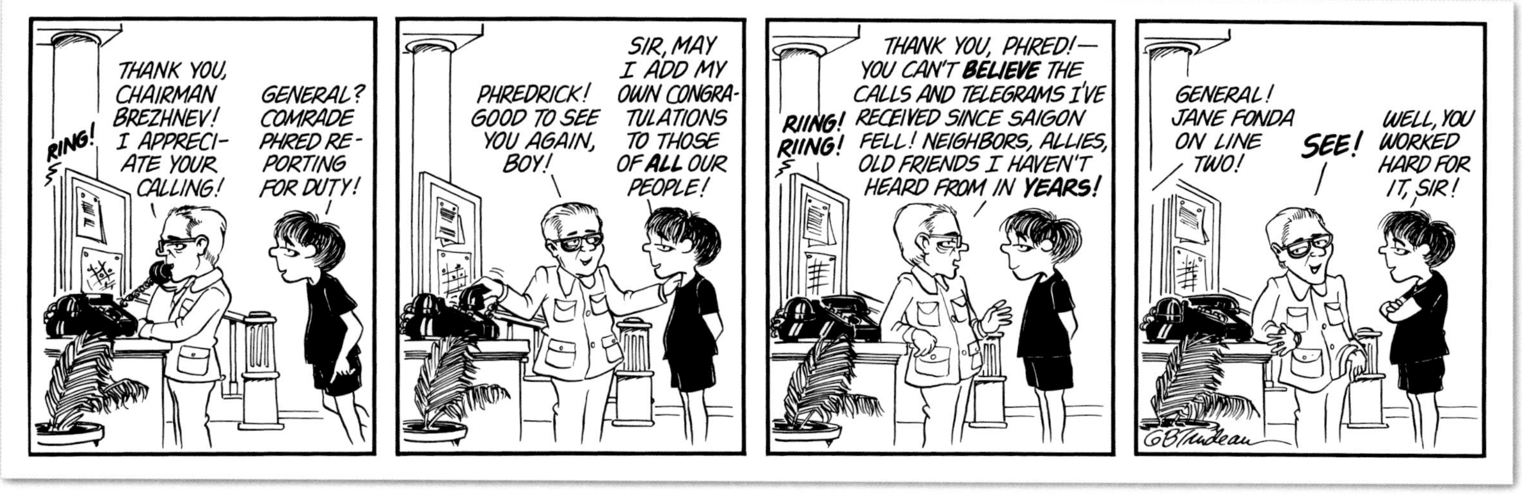
RING!
THANK YOU, CHAIRMAN BREZHNEV! I APPRECIATE YOUR CALLING!
GENERAL? COMRADE PHRED REPORTING FOR DUTY!
PHREDRICK! GOOD TO SEE YOU AGAIN, BOY!
SIR, MAY I ADD MY OWN CONGRATULATIONS TO THOSE OF ALL OUR PEOPLE!
RIING! RIING!
THANK YOU, PHRED!— YOU CAN'T BELIEVE THE CALLS AND TELEGRAMS I'VE RECEIVED SINCE SAIGON FELL! NEIGHBORS, ALLIES, OLD FRIENDS I HAVEN'T HEARD FROM IN YEARS!
GENERAL! JANE FONDA ON LINE TWO!
SEE!
WELL, YOU WORKED HARD FOR IT, SIR!
GBTrudeau

5/28/75

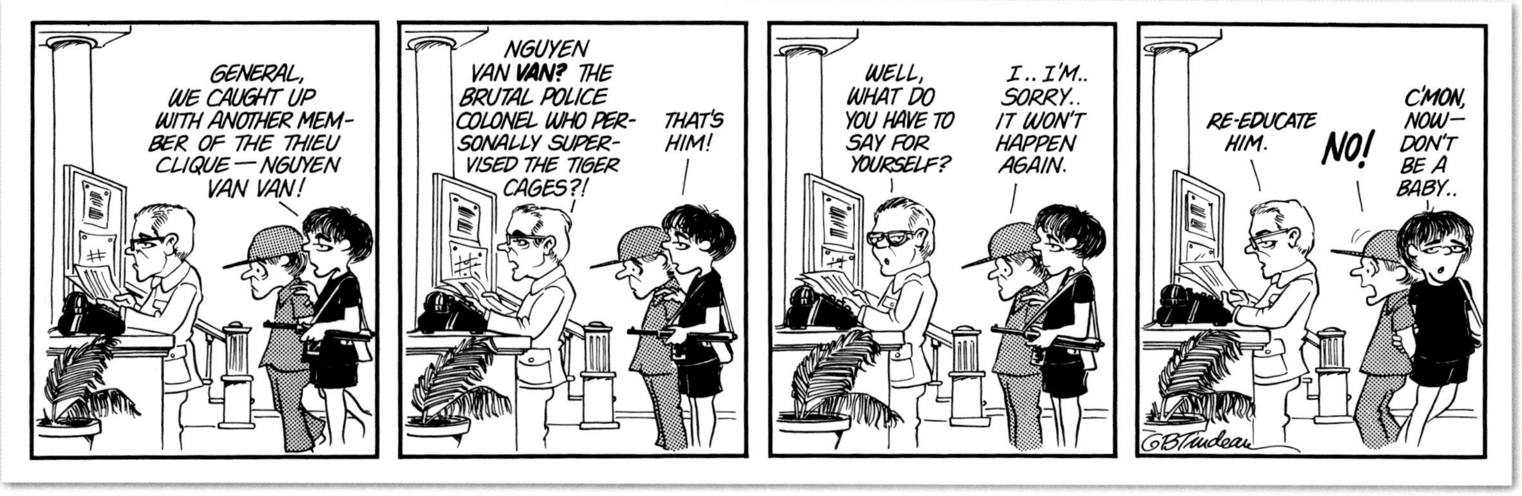
GENERAL, WE CAUGHT UP WITH ANOTHER MEMBER OF THE THIEU CLIQUE— NGUYEN VAN VAN!
NGUYEN VAN VAN? THE BRUTAL POLICE COLONEL WHO PERSONALLY SUPERVISED THE TIGER CAGES?!
THAT'S HIM!
WELL, WHAT DO YOU HAVE TO SAY FOR YOURSELF?
I.. I'M.. SORRY.. IT WON'T HAPPEN AGAIN.
RE-EDUCATE HIM.
NO!
C'MON, NOW— DON'T BE A BABY..
GBTrudeau

5/30/75

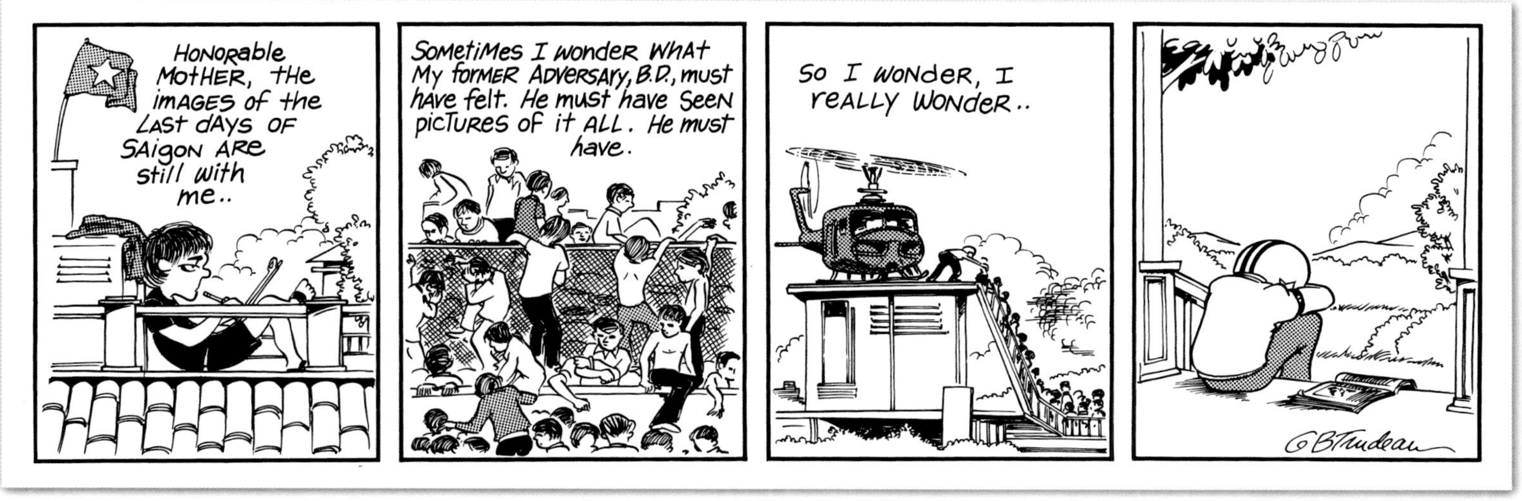
Honorable Mother, the images of the Last days of Saigon are still with me..
Sometimes I wonder what my former adversary, B.D., must have felt. He must have seen pictures of it ALL. He must have.
So I wonder, I really wonder..
GBTrudeau

5/31/75

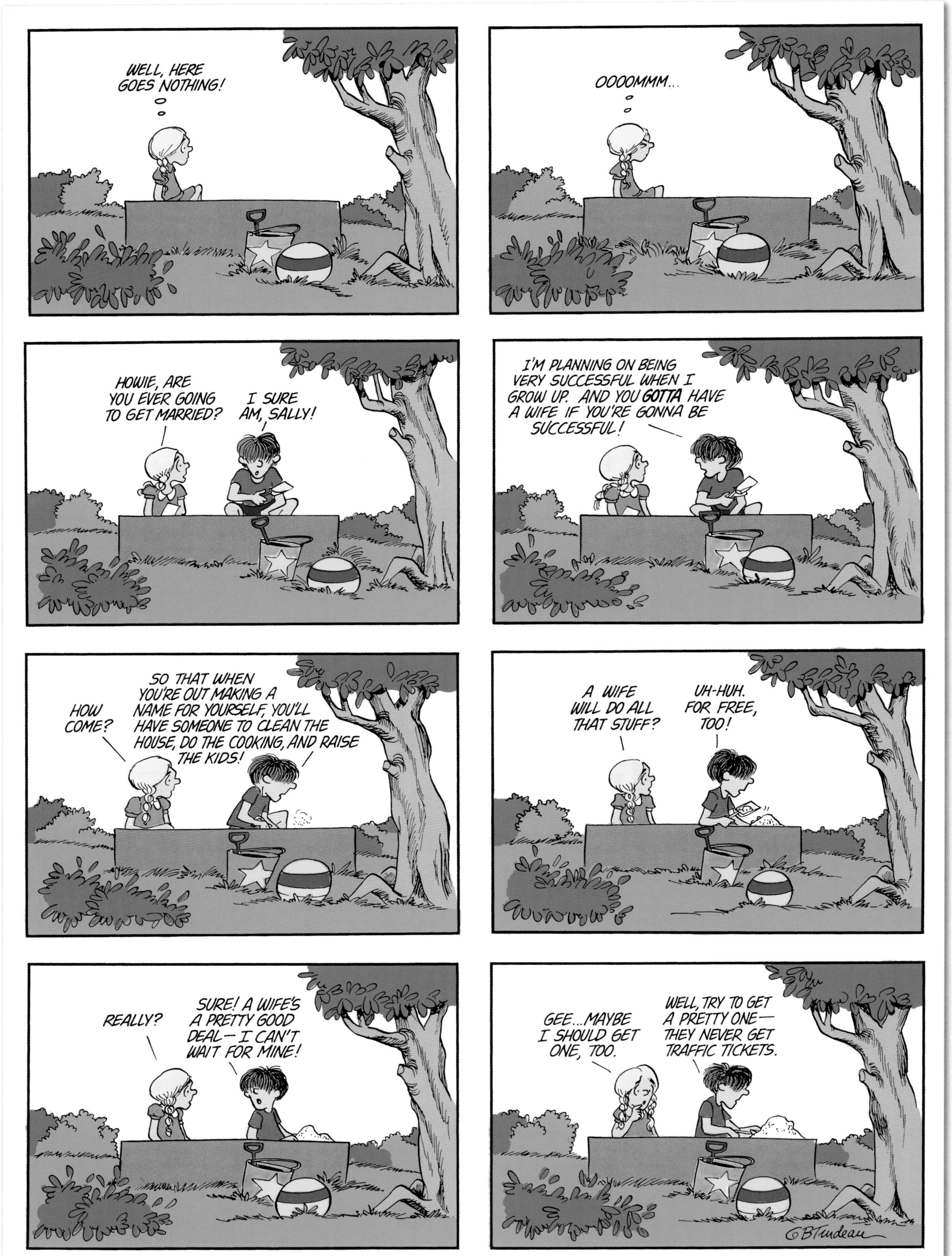
WELL, HERE GOES NOTHING!
OOOOMMM...
HOWIE, ARE YOU EVER GOING TO GET MARRIED?
I SURE AM, SALLY!
I'M PLANNING ON BEING VERY SUCCESSFUL WHEN I GROW UP. AND YOU GOTTA HAVE A WIFE IF YOU'RE GONNA BE SUCCESSFUL!
HOW COME?
SO THAT WHEN YOU'RE OUT MAKING A NAME FOR YOURSELF, YOU'LL HAVE SOMEONE TO CLEAN THE HOUSE, DO THE COOKING, AND RAISE THE KIDS!
A WIFE WILL DO ALL THAT STUFF?
UH-HUH. FOR FREE, TOO!
REALLY?
SURE! A WIFE'S A PRETTY GOOD DEAL— I CAN'T WAIT FOR MINE!
GEE...MAYBE I SHOULD GET ONE, TOO.
WELL, TRY TO GET A PRETTY ONE— THEY NEVER GET TRAFFIC TICKETS.
GBTrudeau

4/27/75

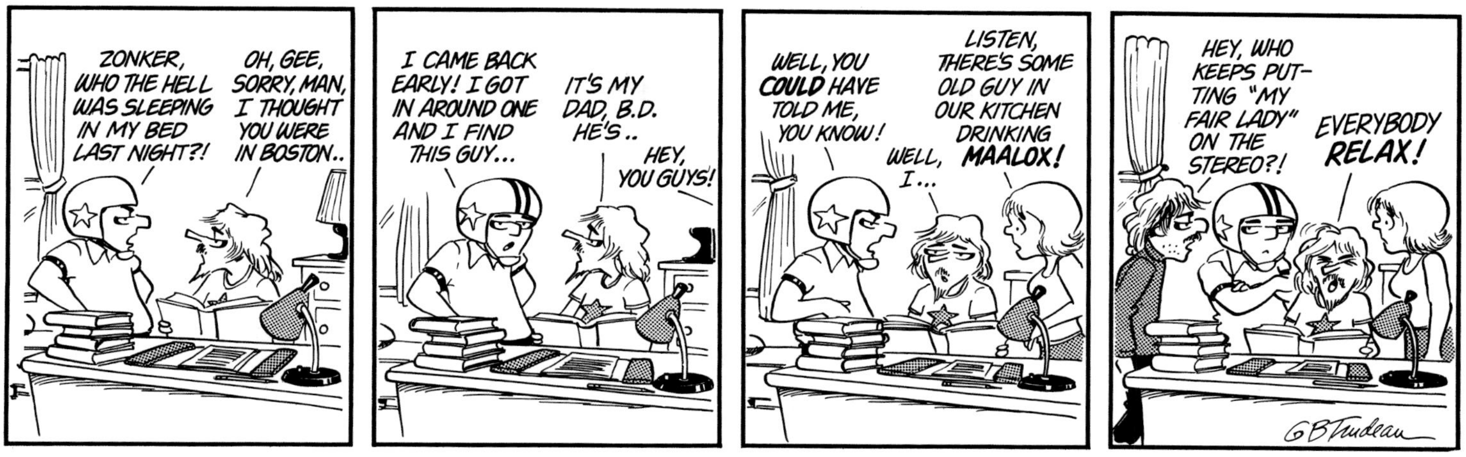
ZONKER, WHO THE HELL WAS SLEEPING IN MY BED LAST NIGHT?!
OH, GEE, SORRY, MAN, I THOUGHT YOU WERE IN BOSTON..
I CAME BACK EARLY! I GOT IN AROUND ONE AND I FIND THIS GUY...
IT'S MY DAD, B.D. HE'S..
HEY, YOU GUYS!
WELL, YOU COULD HAVE TOLD ME, YOU KNOW!
WELL, I...
LISTEN, THERE'S SOME OLD GUY IN OUR KITCHEN DRINKING MAALOX!
HEY, WHO KEEPS PUTTING "MY FAIR LADY" ON THE STEREO?!
EVERYBODY RELAX!
GBTrudeau

10/31/75

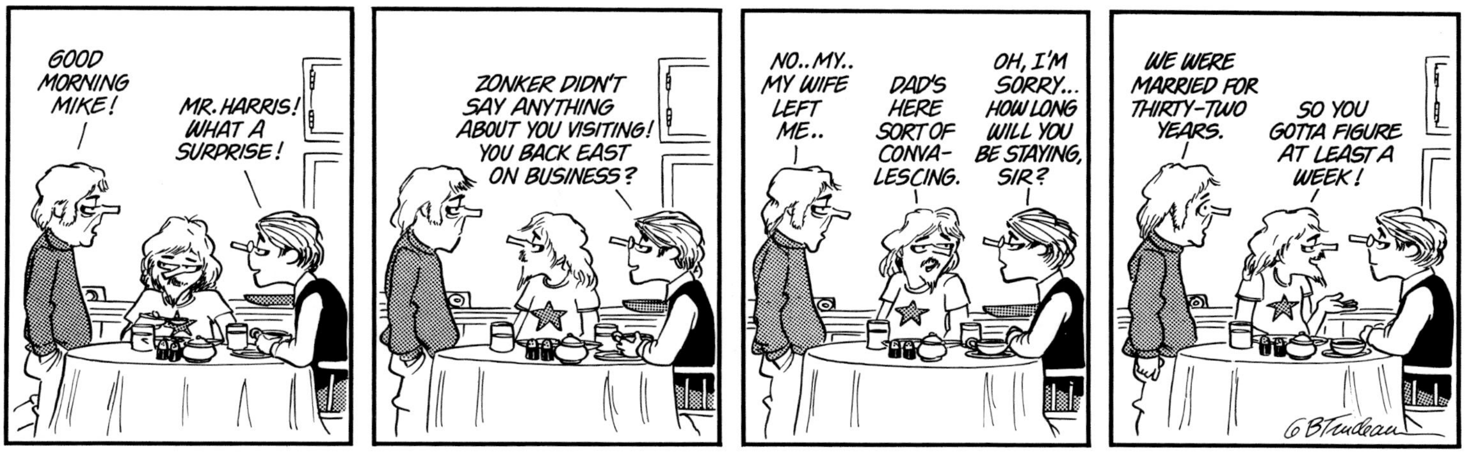
GOOD MORNING MIKE!
MR. HARRIS! WHAT A SURPRISE!
ZONKER DIDN'T SAY ANYTHING ABOUT YOU VISITING! YOU BACK EAST ON BUSINESS?
NO..MY.. MY WIFE LEFT ME..
DAD'S HERE SORT OF CONVALESCING.
OH, I'M SORRY... HOW LONG WILL YOU BE STAYING, SIR?
WE WERE MARRIED FOR THIRTY-TWO YEARS.
SO YOU GOTTA FIGURE AT LEAST A WEEK!
GBTrudeau

11/1/75

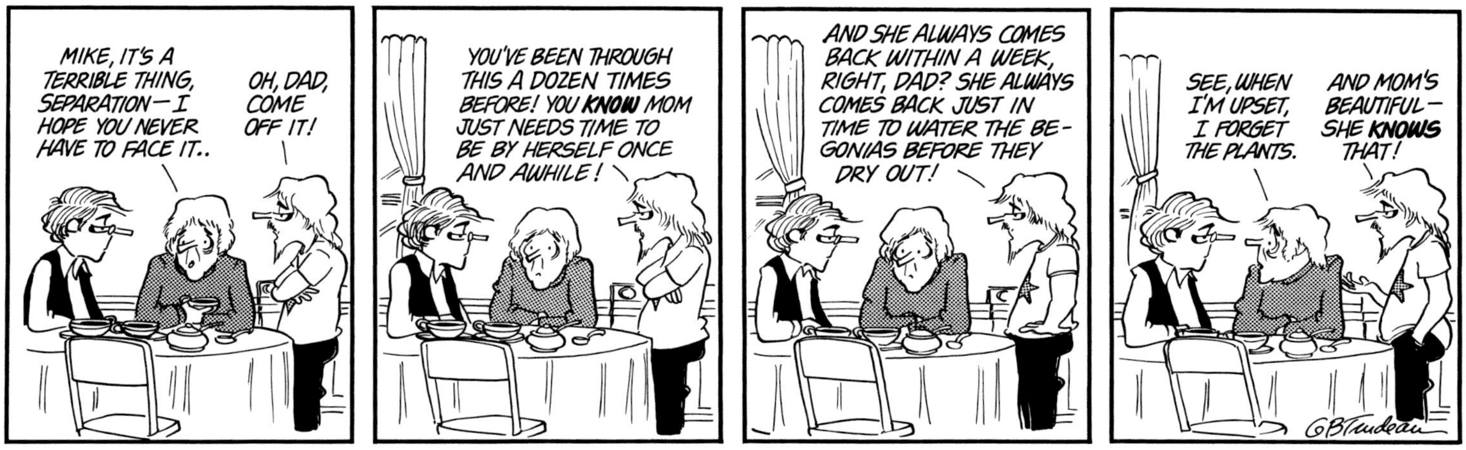
MIKE, IT'S A TERRIBLE THING, SEPARATION—I HOPE YOU NEVER HAVE TO FACE IT..
OH, DAD, COME OFF IT!
YOU'VE BEEN THROUGH THIS A DOZEN TIMES BEFORE! YOU KNOW MOM JUST NEEDS TIME TO BE BY HERSELF ONCE AND AWHILE!
AND SHE ALWAYS COMES BACK WITHIN A WEEK, RIGHT, DAD? SHE ALWAYS COMES BACK JUST IN TIME TO WATER THE BEGONIAS BEFORE THEY DRY OUT!
SEE, WHEN I'M UPSET, I FORGET THE PLANTS.
AND MOM'S BEAUTIFUL—SHE KNOWS THAT!
GBTrudeau

11/3/75

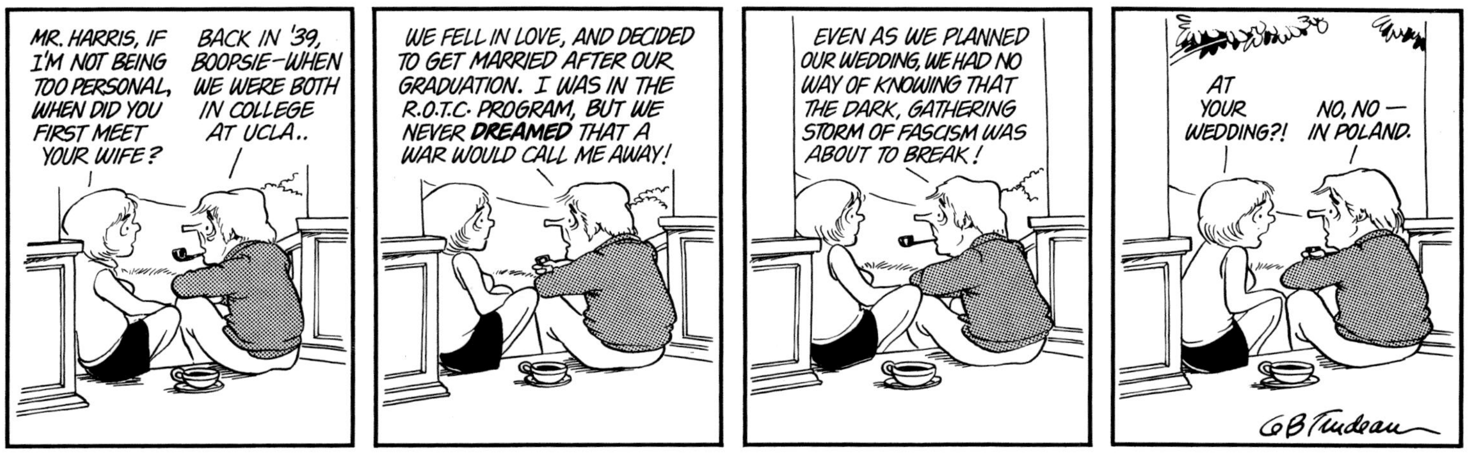
MR. HARRIS, IF I'M NOT BEING TOO PERSONAL, WHEN DID YOU FIRST MEET YOUR WIFE?
BACK IN '39, BOORSIE—WHEN WE WERE BOTH IN COLLEGE AT UCLA..
WE FELL IN LOVE, AND DECIDED TO GET MARRIED AFTER OUR GRADUATION. I WAS IN THE R.O.T.C. PROGRAM, BUT WE NEVER DREAMED THAT A WAR WOULD CALL ME AWAY!
EVEN AS WE PLANNED OUR WEDDING, WE HAD NO WAY OF KNOWING THAT THE DARK, GATHERING STORM OF FASCISM WAS ABOUT TO BREAK!
AT YOUR WEDDING?!
NO, NO—IN POLAND.
GBTrudeau

11/28/75

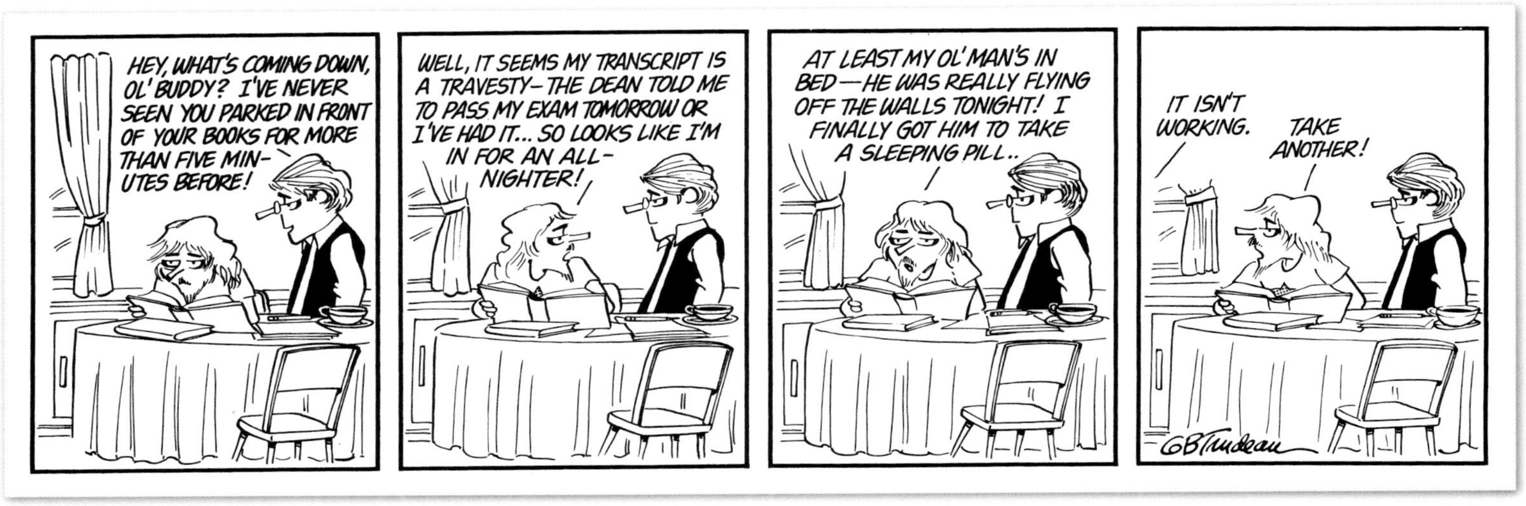
HEY, WHAT'S COMING DOWN, OL' BUDDY? I'VE NEVER SEEN YOU PARKED IN FRONT OF YOUR BOOKS FOR MORE THAN FIVE MIN-UTES BEFORE!
WELL, IT SEEMS MY TRANSCRIPT IS A TRAVESTY—THE DEAN TOLD ME TO PASS MY EXAM TOMORROW OR I'VE HAD IT... SO LOOKS LIKE I'M IN FOR AN ALL-NIGHTER!
AT LEAST MY OL' MAN'S IN BED—HE WAS REALLY FLYING OFF THE WALLS TONIGHT! I FINALLY GOT HIM TO TAKE A SLEEPING PILL..
IT ISN'T WORKING.
TAKE ANOTHER!
GBTrudeau

12/1/75

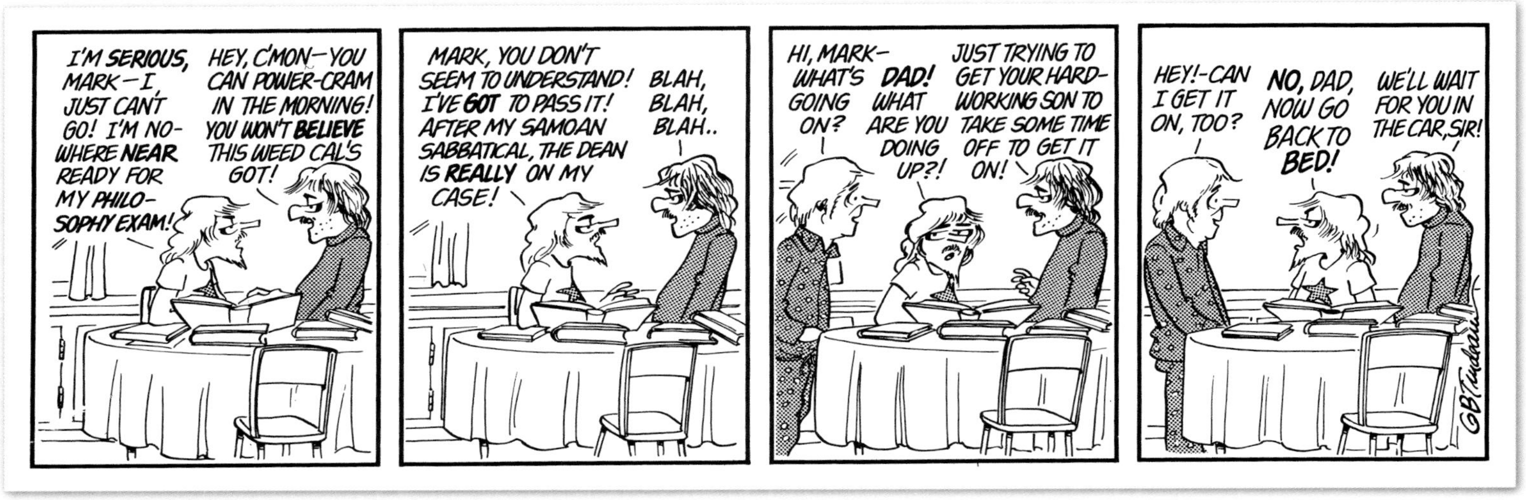
I'M SERIOUS, MARK—I JUST CAN'T GO! I'M NOWHERE NEAR READY FOR MY PHILOSOPHY EXAM!
HEY, C'MON—YOU CAN POWER-CRAM IN THE MORNING! YOU WON'T BELIEVE THIS WEED CAL'S GOT!
MARK, YOU DON'T SEEM TO UNDERSTAND! I'VE GOT TO PASS IT! AFTER MY SAMOAN SABBATICAL, THE DEAN IS REALLY ON MY CASE!
BLAH, BLAH, BLAH..
HI, MARK—WHAT'S GOING ON?
DAD! WHAT ARE YOU DOING UP?!
JUST TRYING TO GET YOUR HARD-WORKING SON TO TAKE SOME TIME OFF TO GET IT ON!
HEY!—CAN I GET IT ON, TOO?
NO, DAD, NOW GO BACK TO BED!
WE'LL WAIT FOR YOU IN THE CAR, SIR!
GBTrudeau

12/2/75

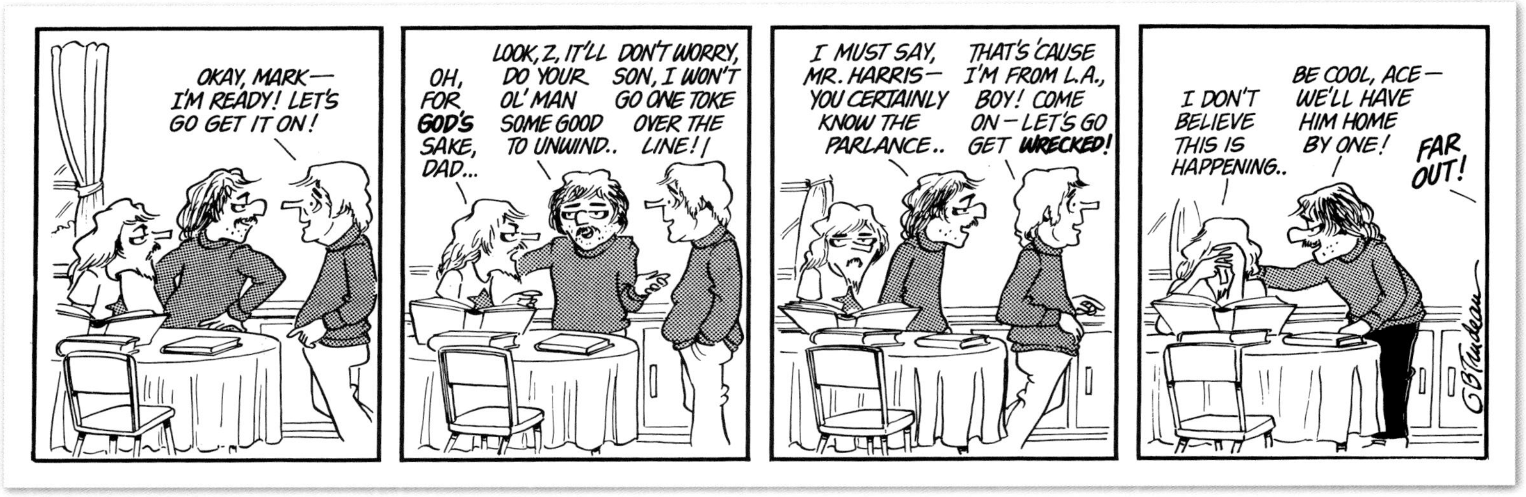
OKAY, MARK—I'M READY! LET'S GO GET IT ON!
OH, FOR GOD'S SAKE, DAD...
LOOK, Z, IT'LL DO YOUR OL' MAN SOME GOOD TO UNWIND..
DON'T WORRY, SON, I WON'T GO ONE TOKE OVER THE LINE!!
I MUST SAY, MR. HARRIS—YOU CERTAINLY KNOW THE PARLANCE..
THAT'S 'CAUSE I'M FROM L.A., BOY! COME ON—LET'S GO GET WRECKED!
I DON'T BELIEVE THIS IS HAPPENING..
BE COOL, ACE—WE'LL HAVE HIM HOME BY ONE!
FAR OUT!
GBTrudeau

12/3/75

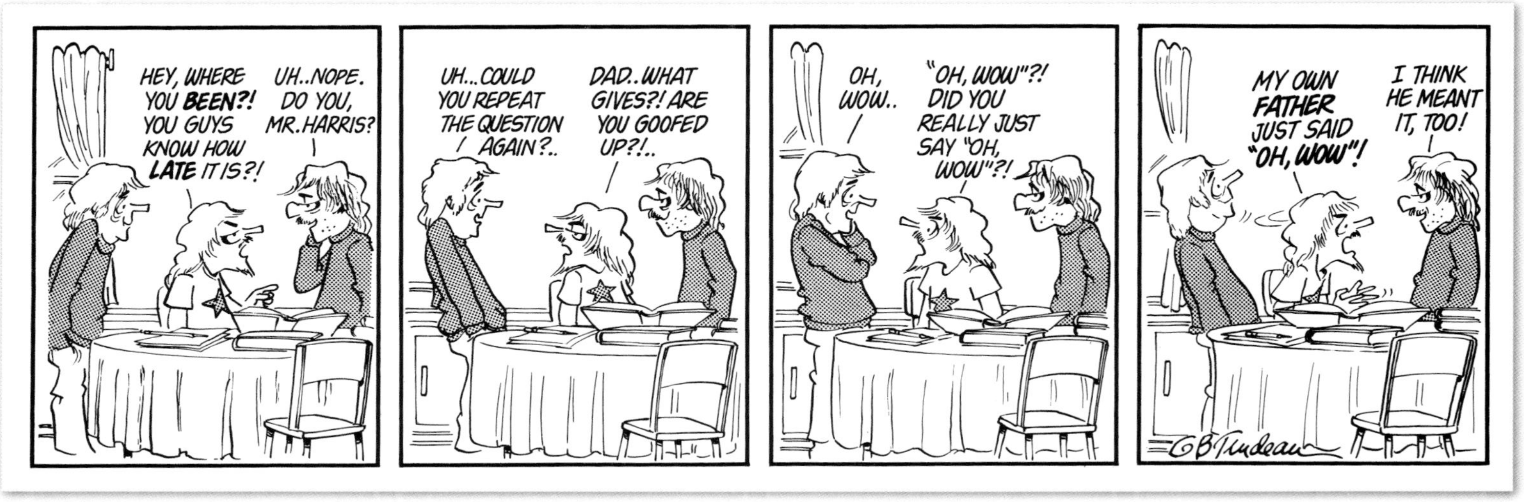
HEY, WHERE YOU BEEN?! YOU GUYS KNOW HOW LATE IT IS?!
UH..NOPE. DO YOU, MR. HARRIS?
UH...COULD YOU REPEAT THE QUESTION AGAIN?..
DAD..WHAT GIVES?! ARE YOU GOOFED UP?!..
OH, WOW..
"OH, WOW"?! DID YOU REALLY JUST SAY "OH, WOW"?!
MY OWN FATHER JUST SAID "OH, WOW"!
I THINK HE MEANT IT, TOO!
GBTrudeau

12/4/75

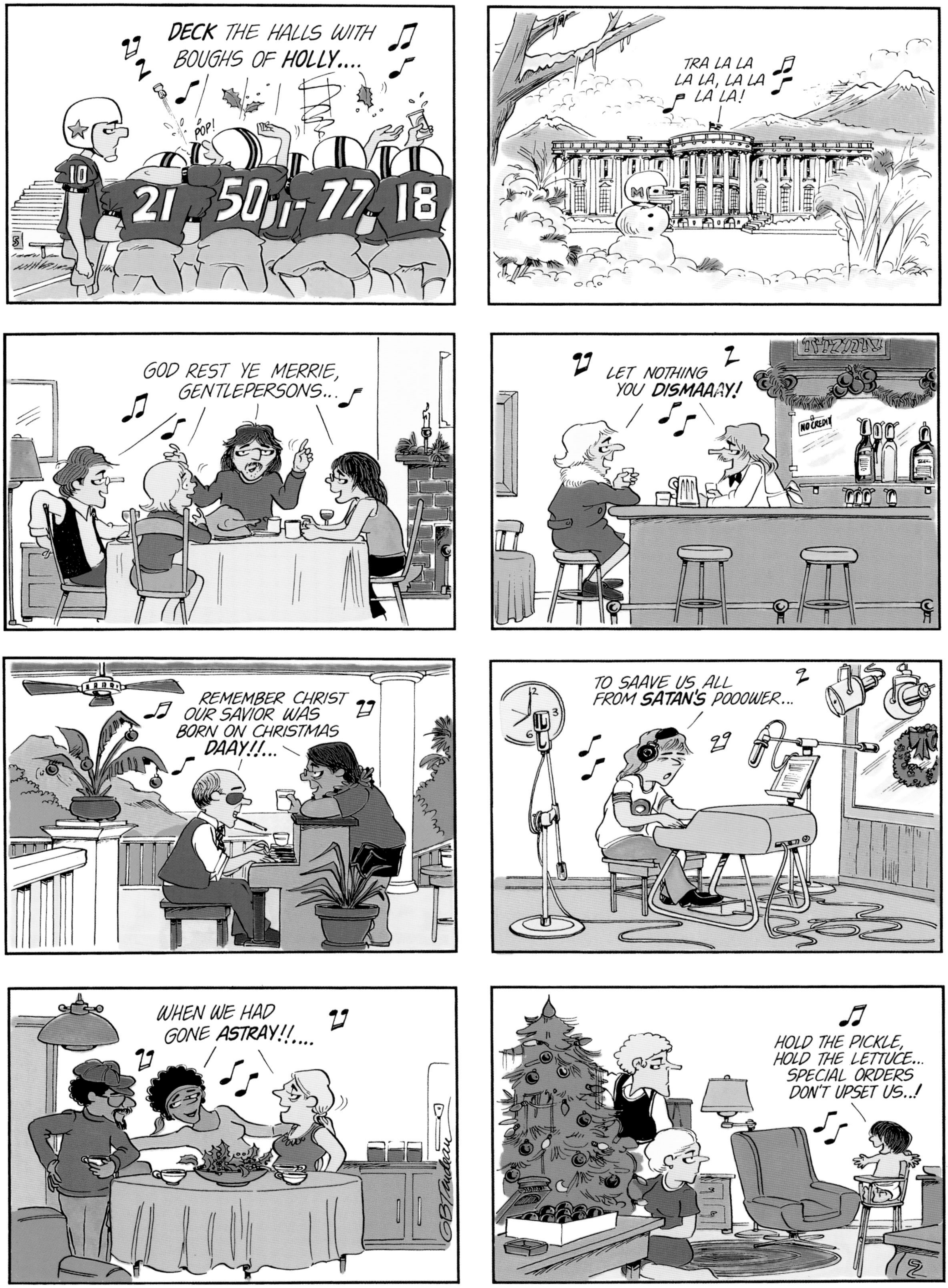
DECK THE HALLS WITH BOUGHS OF HOLLY....
POP!
TRA LA LA LA LA, LA LA LA LA!
GOD REST YE MERRIE, GENTLEPERSONS...
LET NOTHING YOU DISMAAAY!
NO CREDIT
REMEMBER CHRIST OUR SAVIOR WAS BORN ON CHRISTMAS DAAY!!...
TO SAAVE US ALL FROM SATAN'S POOOWER...
WHEN WE HAD GONE ASTRAY!!....
HOLD THE PICKLE, HOLD THE LETTUCE... SPECIAL ORDERS DON'T UPSET US..!

12/21/75

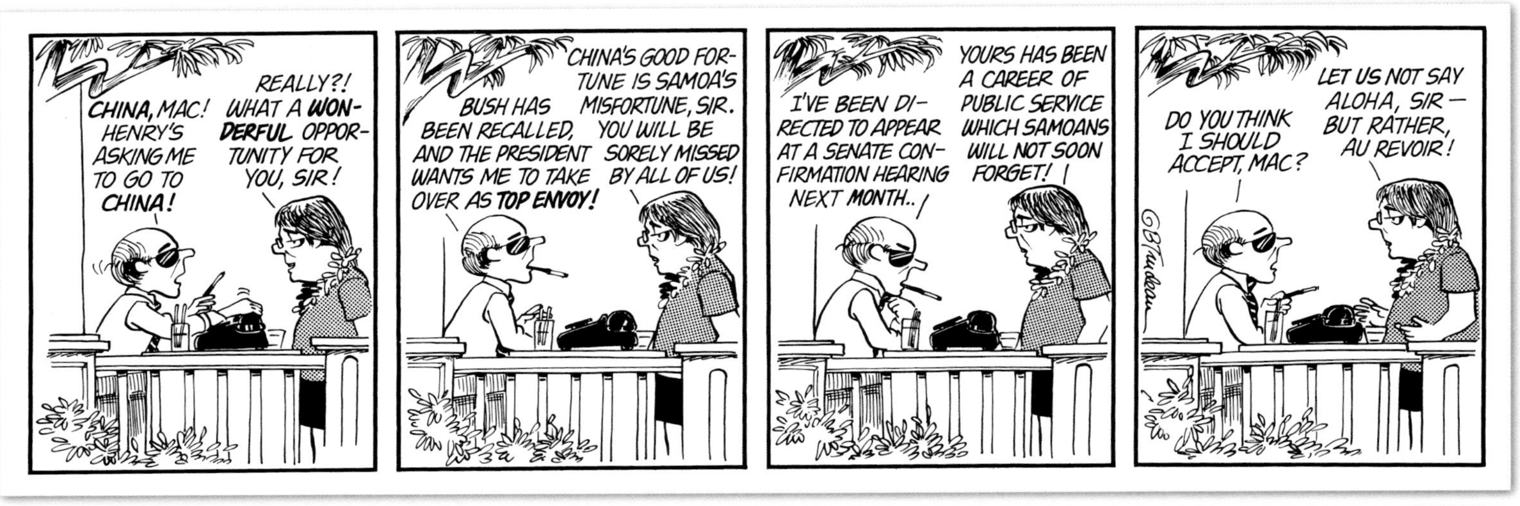
CHINA, MAC! HENRY'S ASKING ME TO GO TO CHINA!
REALLY?! WHAT A WONDERFUL OPPORTUNITY FOR YOU, SIR!
BUSH HAS BEEN RECALLED, AND THE PRESIDENT WANTS ME TO TAKE OVER AS TOP ENVOY!
CHINA'S GOOD FORTUNE IS SAMOA'S MISFORTUNE, SIR. YOU WILL BE SORELY MISSED BY ALL OF US!
I'VE BEEN DIRECTED TO APPEAR AT A SENATE CONFIRMATION HEARING NEXT MONTH..
YOURS HAS BEEN A CAREER OF PUBLIC SERVICE WHICH SAMOANS WILL NOT SOON FORGET!
DO YOU THINK I SHOULD ACCEPT, MAC?
LET US NOT SAY ALOHA, SIR – BUT RATHER, AU REVOIR!
GBTrudeau

12/23/75

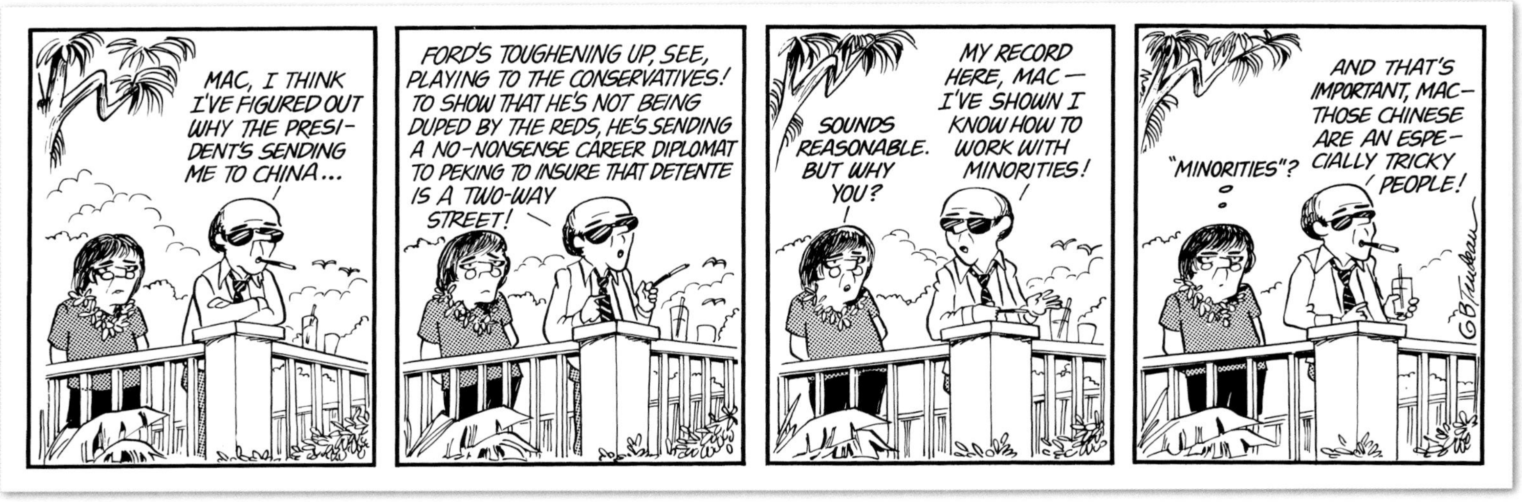
MAC, I THINK I'VE FIGURED OUT WHY THE PRESIDENT'S SENDING ME TO CHINA...
FORD'S TOUGHENING UP, SEE, PLAYING TO THE CONSERVATIVES! TO SHOW THAT HE'S NOT BEING DUPED BY THE REDS, HE'S SENDING A NO-NONSENSE CAREER DIPLOMAT TO PEKING TO INSURE THAT DETENTE IS A TWO-WAY STREET!
SOUNDS REASONABLE. BUT WHY YOU?
MY RECORD HERE, MAC – I'VE SHOWN I KNOW HOW TO WORK WITH MINORITIES!
"MINORITIES"?
AND THAT'S IMPORTANT, MAC – THOSE CHINESE ARE AN ESPECIALLY TRICKY PEOPLE!
GBTrudeau

12/24/75

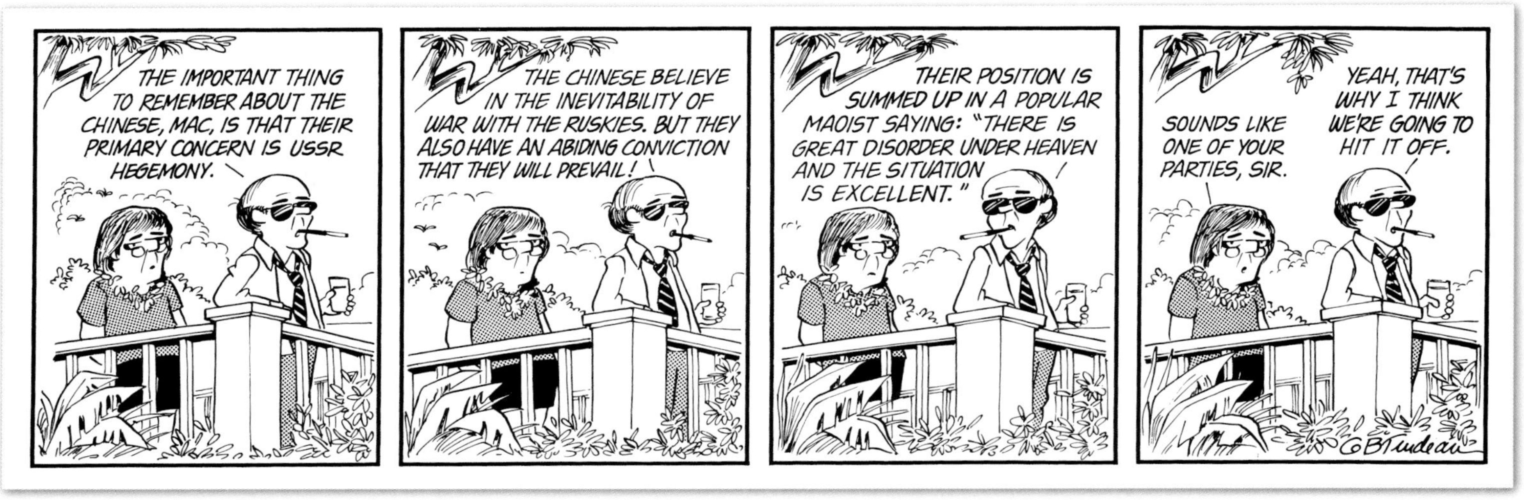
THE IMPORTANT THING TO REMEMBER ABOUT THE CHINESE, MAC, IS THAT THEIR PRIMARY CONCERN IS USSR HEGEMONY.
THE CHINESE BELIEVE IN THE INEVITABILITY OF WAR WITH THE RUSKIES. BUT THEY ALSO HAVE AN ABIDING CONVICTION THAT THEY WILL PREVAIL!
THEIR POSITION IS SUMMED UP IN A POPULAR MAOIST SAYING: "THERE IS GREAT DISORDER UNDER HEAVEN AND THE SITUATION IS EXCELLENT."
SOUNDS LIKE ONE OF YOUR PARTIES, SIR.
YEAH, THAT'S WHY I THINK WE'RE GOING TO HIT IT OFF.
GBTrudeau

12/25/75

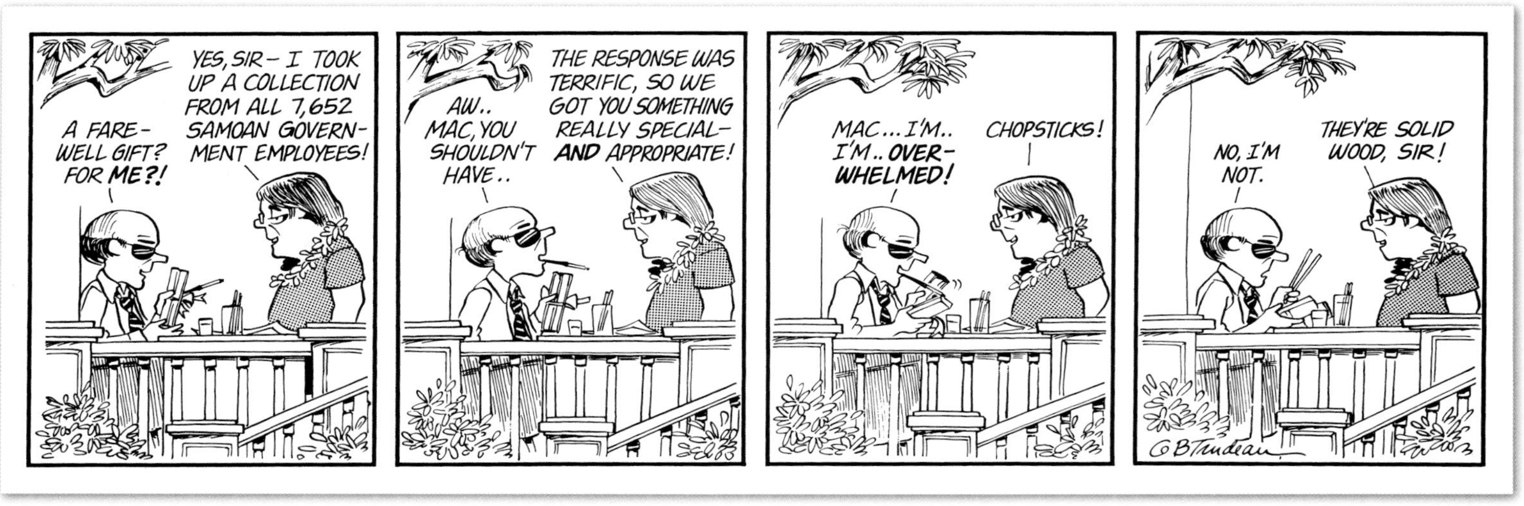
A FAREWELL GIFT? FOR ME?!
YES, SIR – I TOOK UP A COLLECTION FROM ALL 7,652 SAMOAN GOVERNMENT EMPLOYEES!
AW.. MAC, YOU SHOULDN'T HAVE..
THE RESPONSE WAS TERRIFIC, SO WE GOT YOU SOMETHING REALLY SPECIAL – AND APPROPRIATE!
MAC... I'M.. I'M.. OVERWHELMED!
CHOPSTICKS!
NO, I'M NOT.
THEY'RE SOLID WOOD, SIR!
GBTrudeau

12/26/75

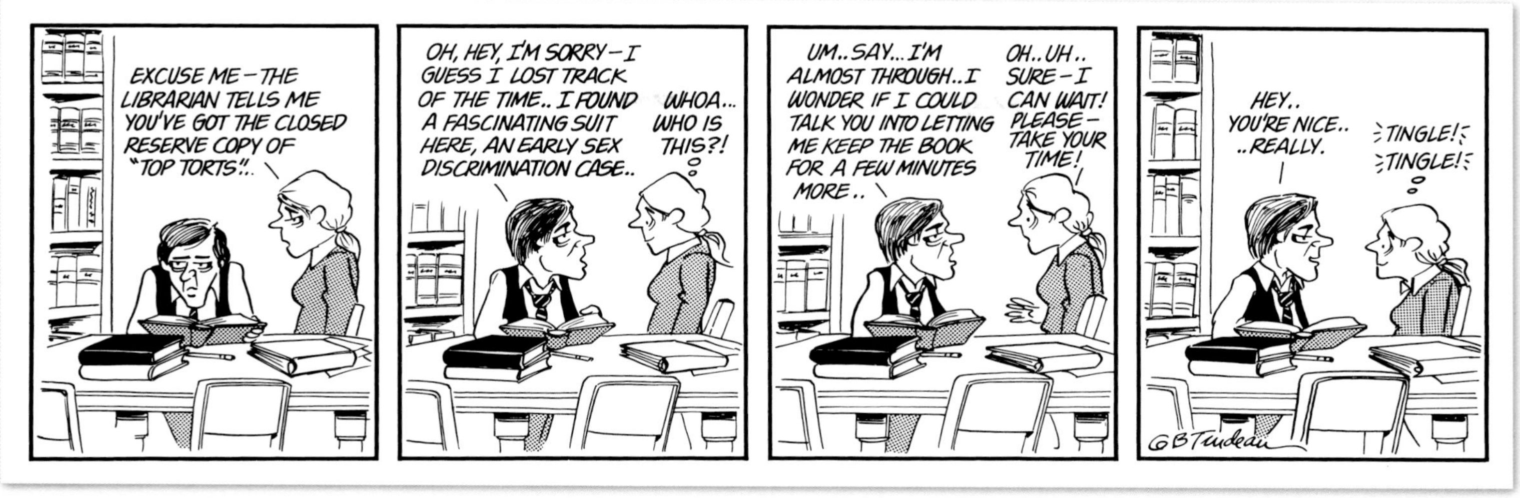
EXCUSE ME—THE LIBRARIAN TELLS ME YOU'VE GOT THE CLOSED RESERVE COPY OF "TOP TORTS"..
OH, HEY, I'M SORRY—I GUESS I LOST TRACK OF THE TIME.. I FOUND A FASCINATING SUIT HERE, AN EARLY SEX DISCRIMINATION CASE..
WHOA... WHO IS THIS?!
UM.. SAY... I'M ALMOST THROUGH.. I WONDER IF I COULD TALK YOU INTO LETTING ME KEEP THE BOOK FOR A FEW MINUTES MORE..
OH.. UH.. SURE—I CAN WAIT! PLEASE—TAKE YOUR TIME!
HEY.. YOU'RE NICE.. ..REALLY.
TINGLE! TINGLE!
GBTrudeau

1/27/76

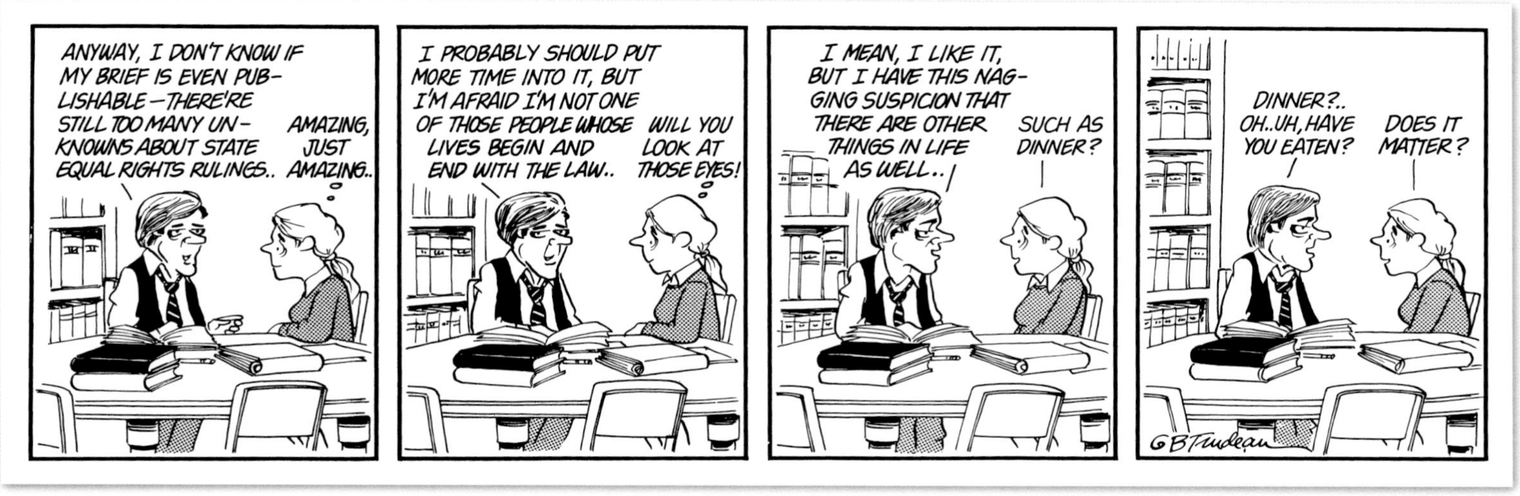
ANYWAY, I DON'T KNOW IF MY BRIEF IS EVEN PUBLISHABLE—THERE'RE STILL TOO MANY UNKNOWNS ABOUT STATE EQUAL RIGHTS RULINGS..
AMAZING, JUST AMAZING..
I PROBABLY SHOULD PUT MORE TIME INTO IT, BUT I'M AFRAID I'M NOT ONE OF THOSE PEOPLE WHOSE LIVES BEGIN AND END WITH THE LAW..
WILL YOU LOOK AT THOSE EYES!
I MEAN, I LIKE IT, BUT I HAVE THIS NAGGING SUSPICION THAT THERE ARE OTHER THINGS IN LIFE AS WELL..
SUCH AS DINNER?
DINNER?.. OH..UH, HAVE YOU EATEN?
DOES IT MATTER?
GBTrudeau

1/29/76

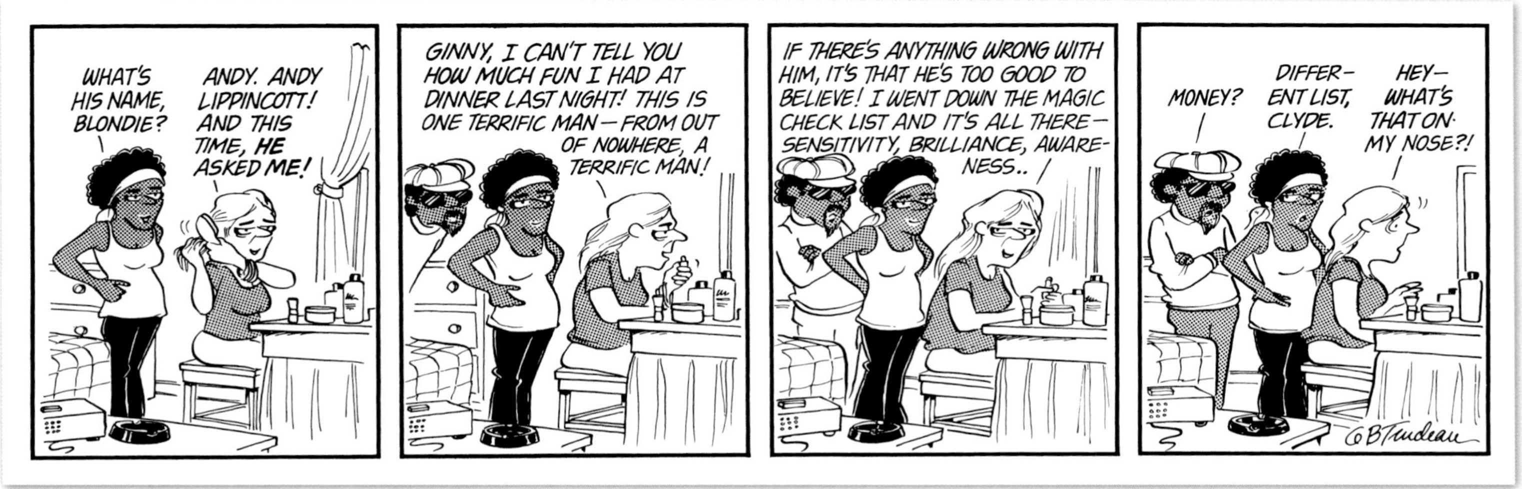
WHAT'S HIS NAME, BLONDIE?
ANDY. ANDY LIPPINCOTT! AND THIS TIME, HE ASKED ME!
GINNY, I CAN'T TELL YOU HOW MUCH FUN I HAD AT DINNER LAST NIGHT! THIS IS ONE TERRIFIC MAN—FROM OUT OF NOWHERE, A TERRIFIC MAN!
IF THERE'S ANYTHING WRONG WITH HIM, IT'S THAT HE'S TOO GOOD TO BELIEVE! I WENT DOWN THE MAGIC CHECK LIST AND IT'S ALL THERE—SENSITIVITY, BRILLIANCE, AWARENESS..
MONEY?
DIFFERENT LIST, CLYDE.
HEY—WHAT'S THAT ON MY NOSE?!
GBTrudeau

1/30/76

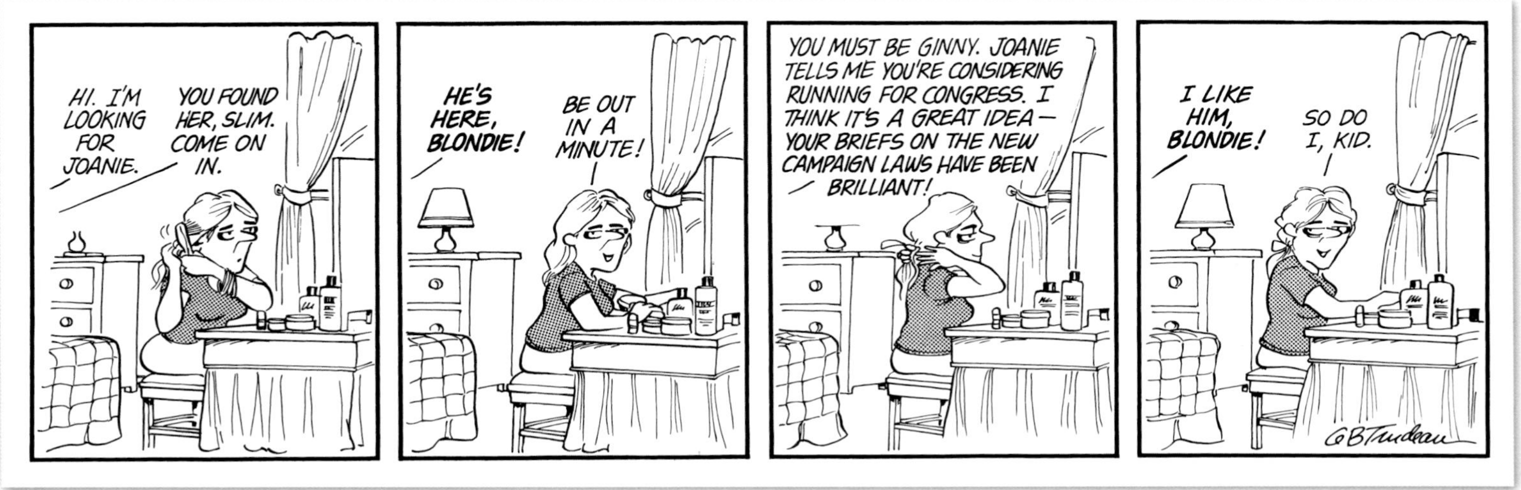
HI. I'M LOOKING FOR JOANIE.
YOU FOUND HER, SLIM. COME ON IN.
HE'S HERE, BLONDIE!
BE OUT IN A MINUTE!
YOU MUST BE GINNY. JOANIE TELLS ME YOU'RE CONSIDERING RUNNING FOR CONGRESS. I THINK IT'S A GREAT IDEA—YOUR BRIEFS ON THE NEW CAMPAIGN LAWS HAVE BEEN BRILLIANT!
I LIKE HIM, BLONDIE!
SO DO I, KID.
GBTrudeau

1/31/76

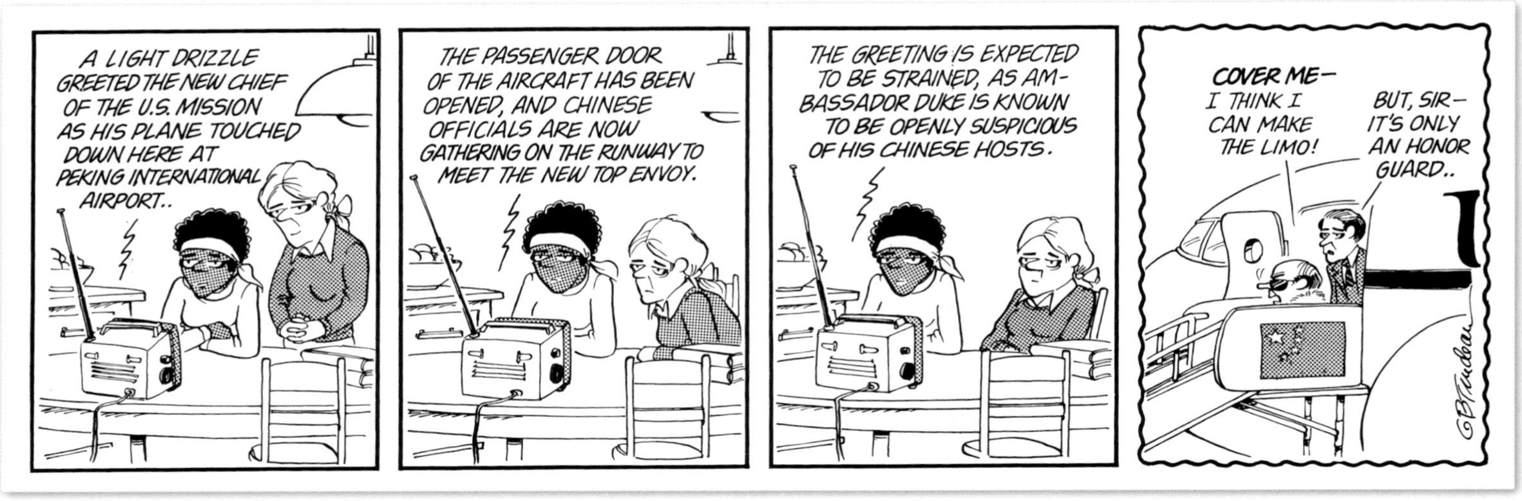
A LIGHT DRIZZLE GREETED THE NEW CHIEF OF THE U.S. MISSION AS HIS PLANE TOUCHED DOWN HERE AT PEKING INTERNATIONAL AIRPORT..
THE PASSENGER DOOR OF THE AIRCRAFT HAS BEEN OPENED, AND CHINESE OFFICIALS ARE NOW GATHERING ON THE RUNWAY TO MEET THE NEW TOP ENVOY.
THE GREETING IS EXPECTED TO BE STRAINED, AS AMBASSADOR DUKE IS KNOWN TO BE OPENLY SUSPICIOUS OF HIS CHINESE HOSTS.
COVER ME— I THINK I CAN MAKE THE LIMO!
BUT, SIR— IT'S ONLY AN HONOR GUARD..
GBTrudeau

1/21/76

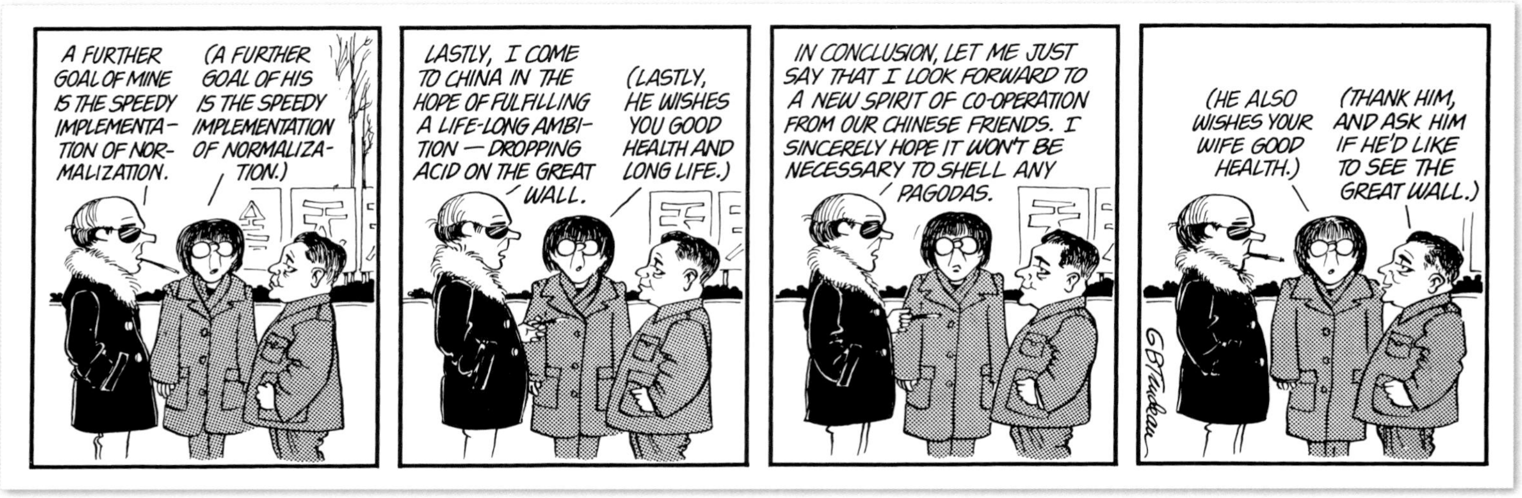
A FURTHER GOAL OF MINE IS THE SPEEDY IMPLEMENTATION OF NORMALIZATION.
(A FURTHER GOAL OF HIS IS THE SPEEDY IMPLEMENTATION OF NORMALIZATION.)
LASTLY, I COME TO CHINA IN THE HOPE OF FULFILLING A LIFE-LONG AMBITION — DROPPING ACID ON THE GREAT WALL.
(LASTLY, HE WISHES YOU GOOD HEALTH AND LONG LIFE.)
IN CONCLUSION, LET ME JUST SAY THAT I LOOK FORWARD TO A NEW SPIRIT OF CO-OPERATION FROM OUR CHINESE FRIENDS. I SINCERELY HOPE IT WON'T BE NECESSARY TO SHELL ANY PAGODAS.
(HE ALSO WISHES YOUR WIFE GOOD HEALTH.)
(THANK HIM, AND ASK HIM IF HE'D LIKE TO SEE THE GREAT WALL.)
GBTrudeau

1/22/76

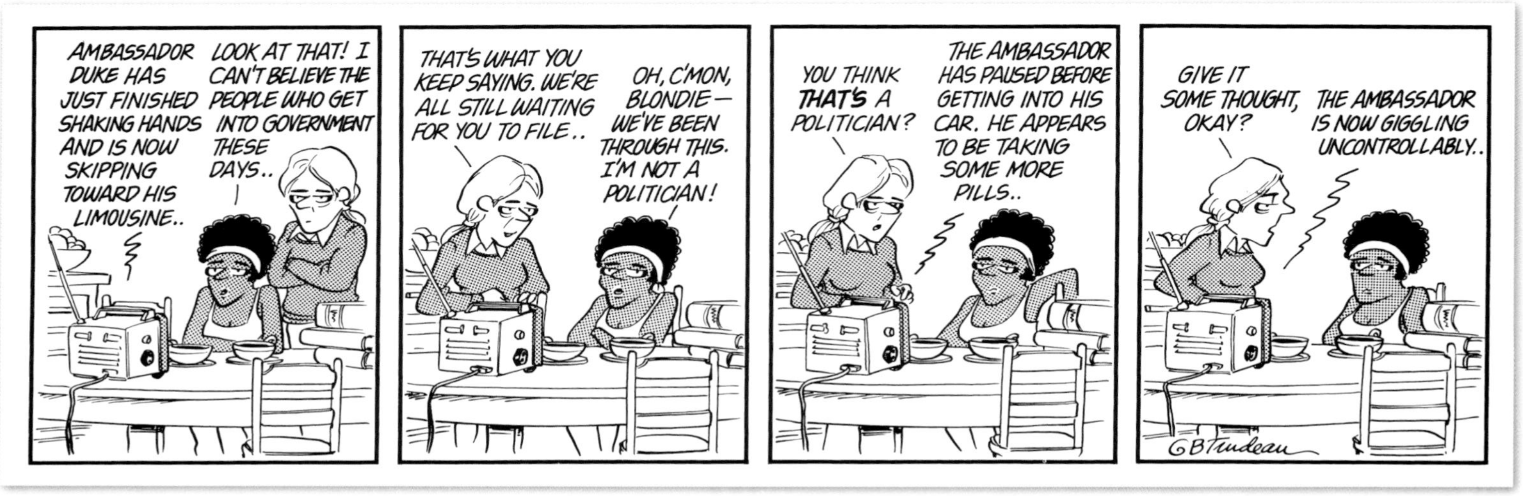
AMBASSADOR DUKE HAS JUST FINISHED SHAKING HANDS AND IS NOW SKIPPING TOWARD HIS LIMOUSINE..
LOOK AT THAT! I CAN'T BELIEVE THE PEOPLE WHO GET INTO GOVERNMENT THESE DAYS..
THAT'S WHAT YOU KEEP SAYING. WE'RE ALL STILL WAITING FOR YOU TO FILE..
OH, C'MON, BLONDIE— WE'VE BEEN THROUGH THIS. I'M NOT A POLITICIAN!
YOU THINK THAT'S A POLITICIAN?
THE AMBASSADOR HAS PAUSED BEFORE GETTING INTO HIS CAR. HE APPEARS TO BE TAKING SOME MORE PILLS..
GIVE IT SOME THOUGHT, OKAY?
THE AMBASSADOR IS NOW GIGGLING UNCONTROLLABLY..
GBTrudeau

1/23/76

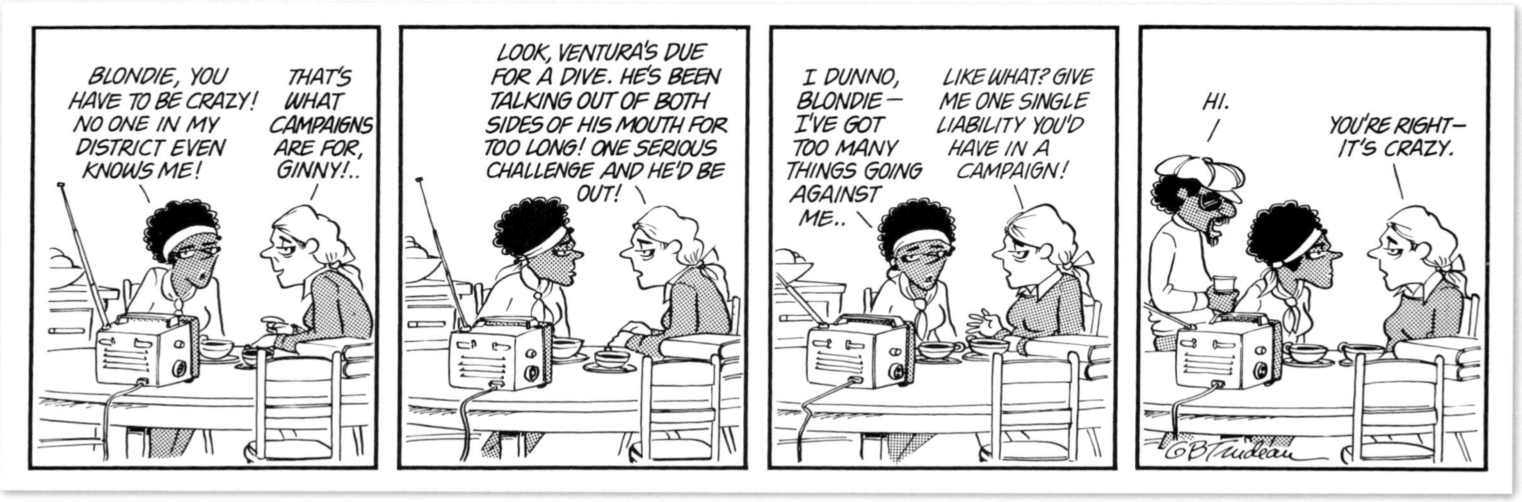
BLONDIE, YOU HAVE TO BE CRAZY! NO ONE IN MY DISTRICT EVEN KNOWS ME!
THAT'S WHAT CAMPAIGNS ARE FOR, GINNY!..
LOOK, VENTURA'S DUE FOR A DIVE. HE'S BEEN TALKING OUT OF BOTH SIDES OF HIS MOUTH FOR TOO LONG! ONE SERIOUS CHALLENGE AND HE'D BE OUT!
I DUNNO, BLONDIE— I'VE GOT TOO MANY THINGS GOING AGAINST ME..
LIKE WHAT? GIVE ME ONE SINGLE LIABILITY YOU'D HAVE IN A CAMPAIGN!
HI.
YOU'RE RIGHT— IT'S CRAZY.
GBTrudeau

1/24/76

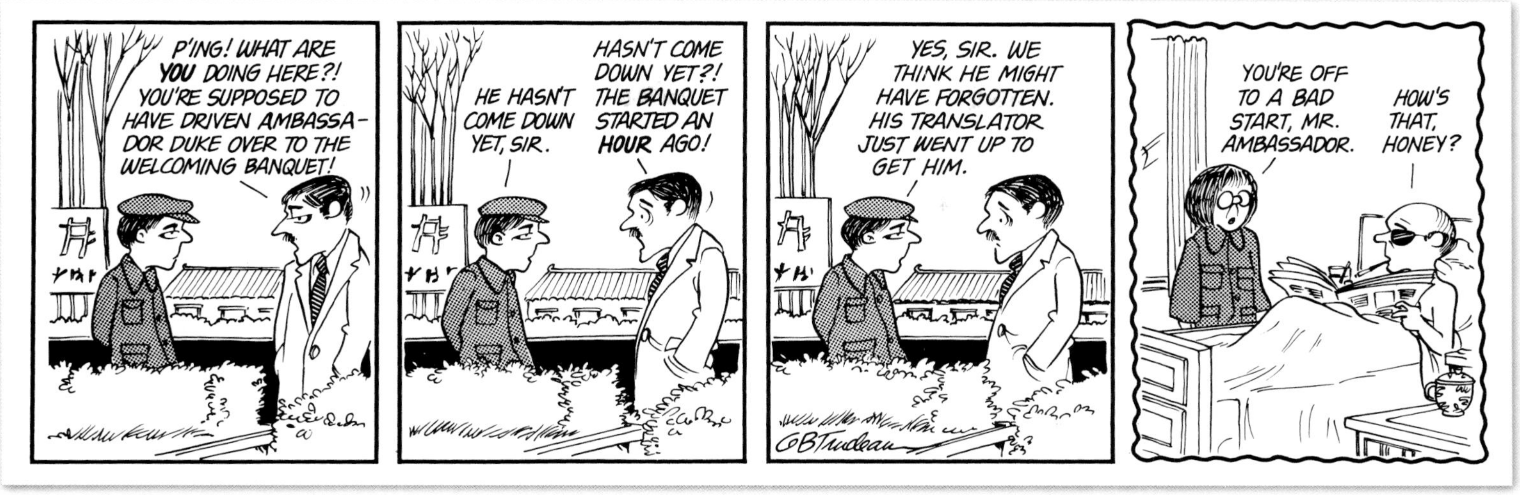
P'ING! WHAT ARE YOU DOING HERE?! YOU'RE SUPPOSED TO HAVE DRIVEN AMBASSADOR DUKE OVER TO THE WELCOMING BANQUET!
HE HASN'T COME DOWN YET, SIR.
HASN'T COME DOWN YET?! THE BANQUET STARTED AN HOUR AGO!
YES, SIR. WE THINK HE MIGHT HAVE FORGOTTEN. HIS TRANSLATOR JUST WENT UP TO GET HIM.
YOU'RE OFF TO A BAD START, MR. AMBASSADOR.
HOW'S THAT, HONEY?

2/16/76

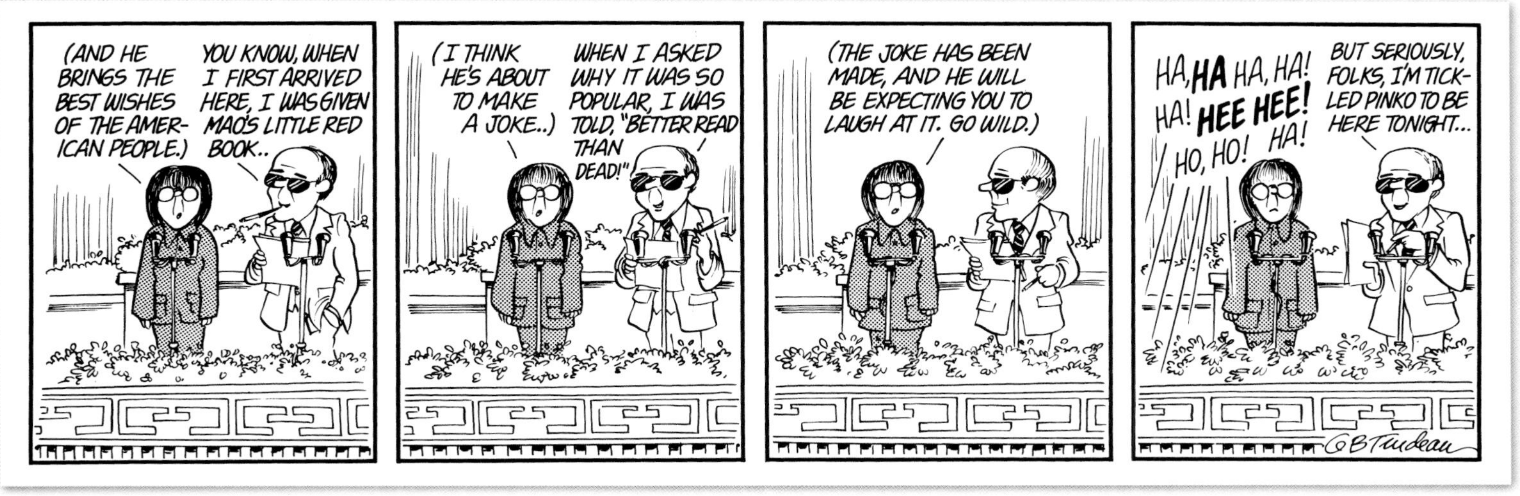
(AND HE BRINGS THE BEST WISHES OF THE AMERICAN PEOPLE.)
YOU KNOW, WHEN I FIRST ARRIVED HERE, I WAS GIVEN MAO'S LITTLE RED BOOK..
(I THINK HE'S ABOUT TO MAKE A JOKE..)
WHEN I ASKED WHY IT WAS SO POPULAR, I WAS TOLD, "BETTER READ THAN DEAD!"
(THE JOKE HAS BEEN MADE, AND HE WILL BE EXPECTING YOU TO LAUGH AT IT. GO WILD.)
HA, HA HA, HA! HA! HEE HEE! HO, HO! HA!
BUT SERIOUSLY, FOLKS, I'M TICKLED PINKO TO BE HERE TONIGHT...

2/18/76

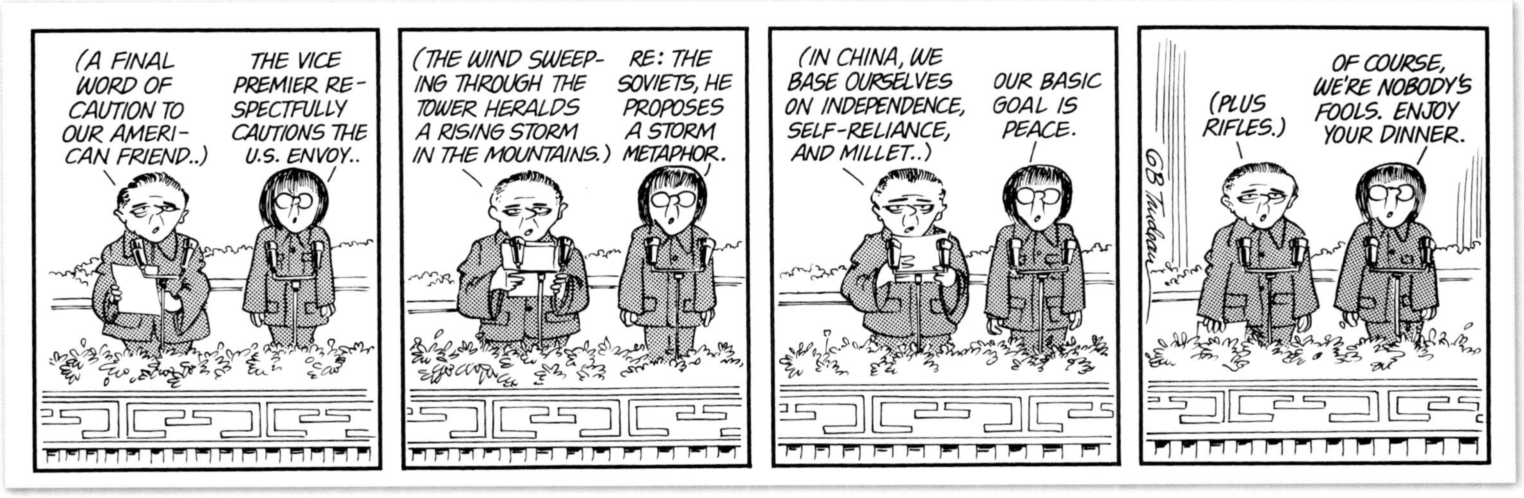
(A FINAL WORD OF CAUTION TO OUR AMERICAN FRIEND..)
THE VICE PREMIER RESPECTFULLY CAUTIONS THE U.S. ENVOY..
(THE WIND SWEEPING THROUGH THE TOWER HERALDS A RISING STORM IN THE MOUNTAINS.)
RE: THE SOVIETS, HE PROPOSES A STORM METAPHOR.
(IN CHINA, WE BASE OURSELVES ON INDEPENDENCE, SELF-RELIANCE, AND MILLET..)
OUR BASIC GOAL IS PEACE.
(PLUS RIFLES.)
OF COURSE, WE'RE NOBODY'S FOOLS. ENJOY YOUR DINNER.

2/19/76

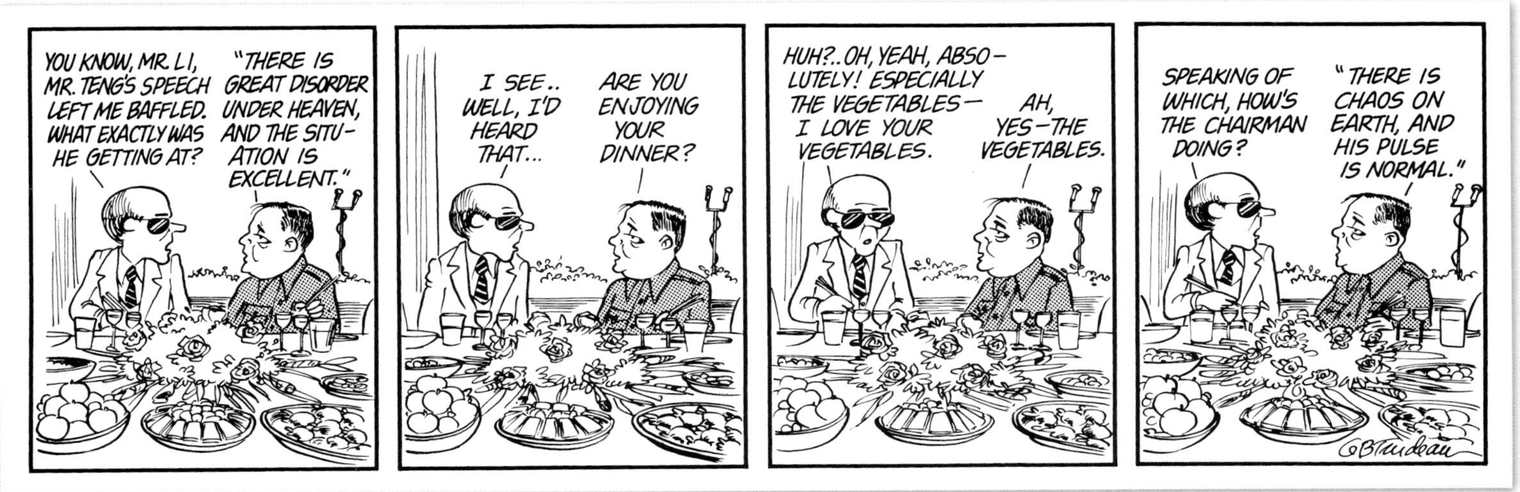
YOU KNOW, MR. LI, MR. TENG'S SPEECH LEFT ME BAFFLED. WHAT EXACTLY WAS HE GETTING AT?
"THERE IS GREAT DISORDER UNDER HEAVEN, AND THE SITUATION IS EXCELLENT."
I SEE.. WELL, I'D HEARD THAT...
ARE YOU ENJOYING YOUR DINNER?
HUH?..OH, YEAH, ABSOLUTELY! ESPECIALLY THE VEGETABLES— I LOVE YOUR VEGETABLES.
AH, YES—THE VEGETABLES.
SPEAKING OF WHICH, HOW'S THE CHAIRMAN DOING?
"THERE IS CHAOS ON EARTH, AND HIS PULSE IS NORMAL."

2/20/76

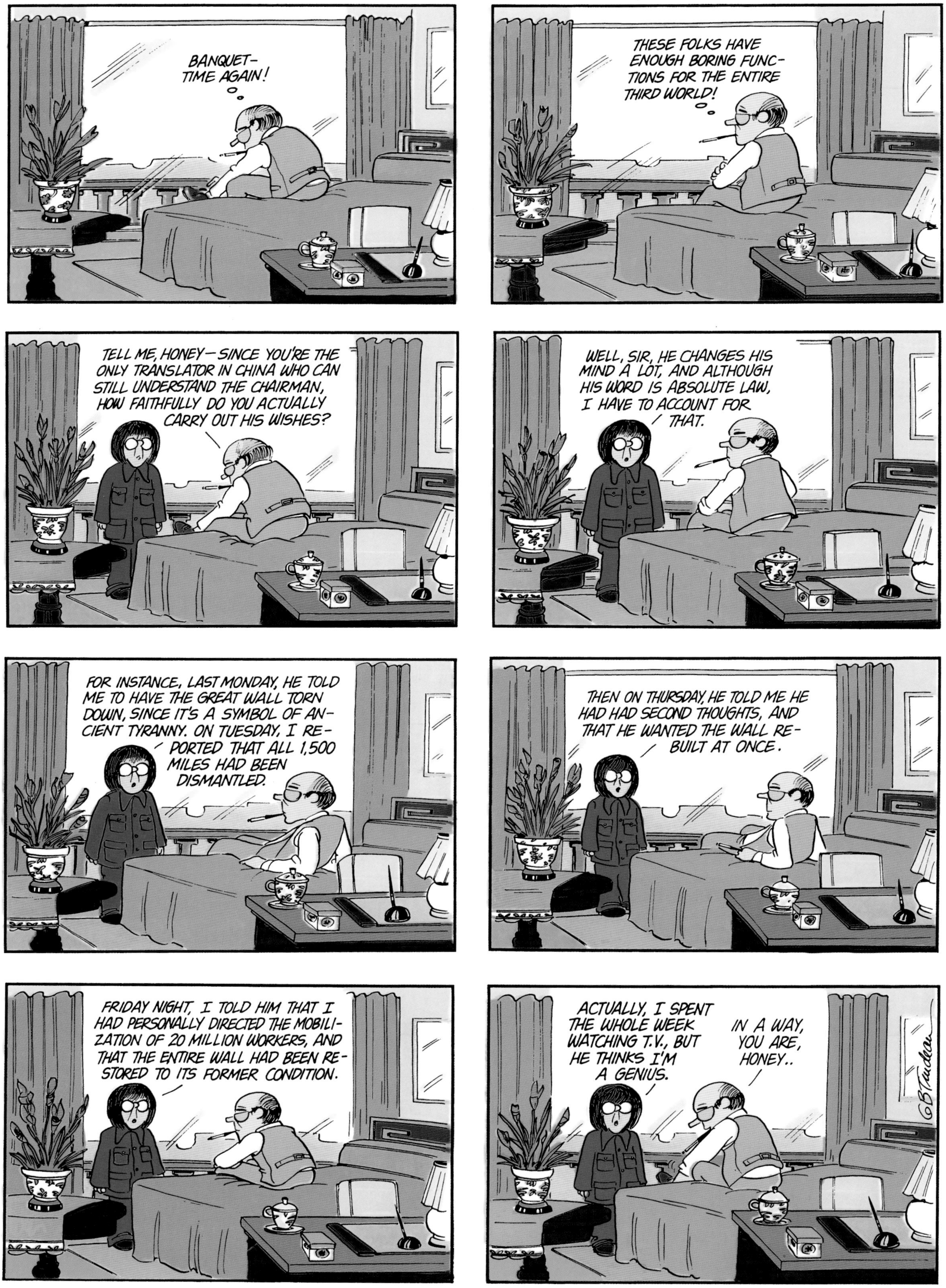
BANQUET-TIME AGAIN!
THESE FOLKS HAVE ENOUGH BORING FUNCTIONS FOR THE ENTIRE THIRD WORLD!
TELL ME, HONEY—SINCE YOU'RE THE ONLY TRANSLATOR IN CHINA WHO CAN STILL UNDERSTAND THE CHAIRMAN, HOW FAITHFULLY DO YOU ACTUALLY CARRY OUT HIS WISHES?
WELL, SIR, HE CHANGES HIS MIND A LOT, AND ALTHOUGH HIS WORD IS ABSOLUTE LAW, I HAVE TO ACCOUNT FOR THAT.
FOR INSTANCE, LAST MONDAY, HE TOLD ME TO HAVE THE GREAT WALL TORN DOWN, SINCE IT'S A SYMBOL OF ANCIENT TYRANNY. ON TUESDAY, I REPORTED THAT ALL 1,500 MILES HAD BEEN DISMANTLED.
THEN ON THURSDAY, HE TOLD ME HE HAD HAD SECOND THOUGHTS, AND THAT HE WANTED THE WALL REBUILT AT ONCE.
FRIDAY NIGHT, I TOLD HIM THAT I HAD PERSONALLY DIRECTED THE MOBILIZATION OF 20 MILLION WORKERS, AND THAT THE ENTIRE WALL HAD BEEN RESTORED TO ITS FORMER CONDITION.
ACTUALLY, I SPENT THE WHOLE WEEK WATCHING T.V., BUT HE THINKS I'M A GENIUS.
IN A WAY, YOU ARE, HONEY..
GBTrudeau

5/9/76

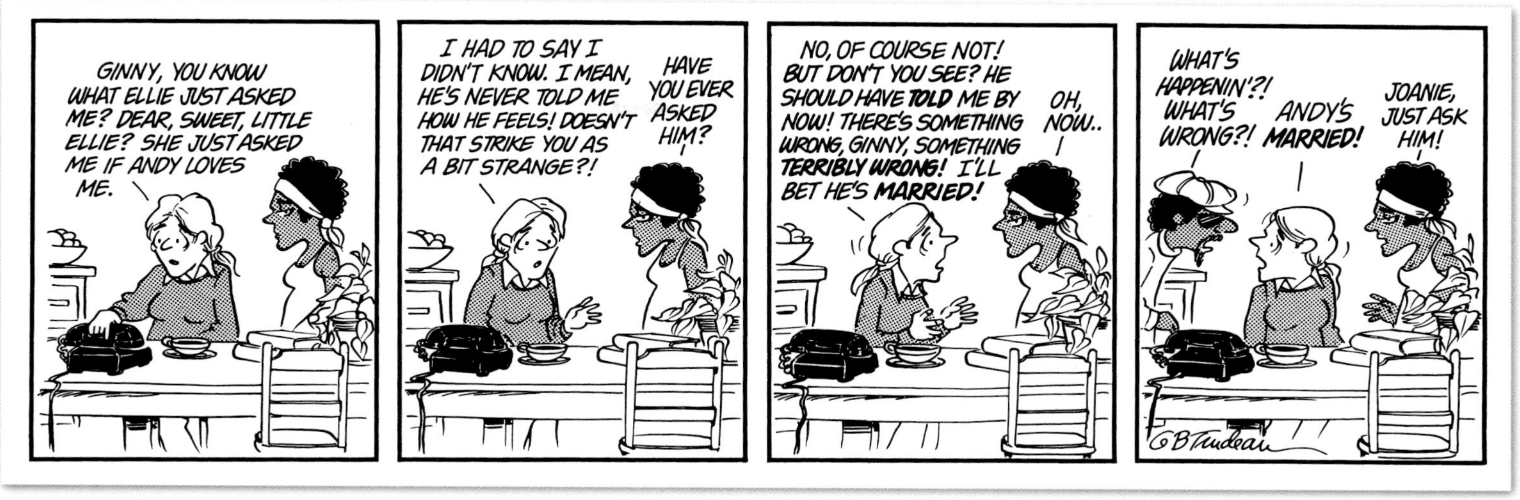
GINNY, YOU KNOW WHAT ELLIE JUST ASKED ME? DEAR, SWEET, LITTLE ELLIE? SHE JUST ASKED ME IF ANDY LOVES ME.
I HAD TO SAY I DIDN'T KNOW. I MEAN, HE'S NEVER TOLD ME HOW HE FEELS! DOESN'T THAT STRIKE YOU AS A BIT STRANGE?!
HAVE YOU EVER ASKED HIM?
NO, OF COURSE NOT! BUT DON'T YOU SEE? HE SHOULD HAVE TOLD ME BY NOW! THERE'S SOMETHING WRONG, GINNY, SOMETHING TERRIBLY WRONG! I'LL BET HE'S MARRIED!
OH, NOW..
WHAT'S HAPPENIN'?! WHAT'S WRONG?!
ANDY'S MARRIED!
JOANIE, JUST ASK HIM!

2/7/76

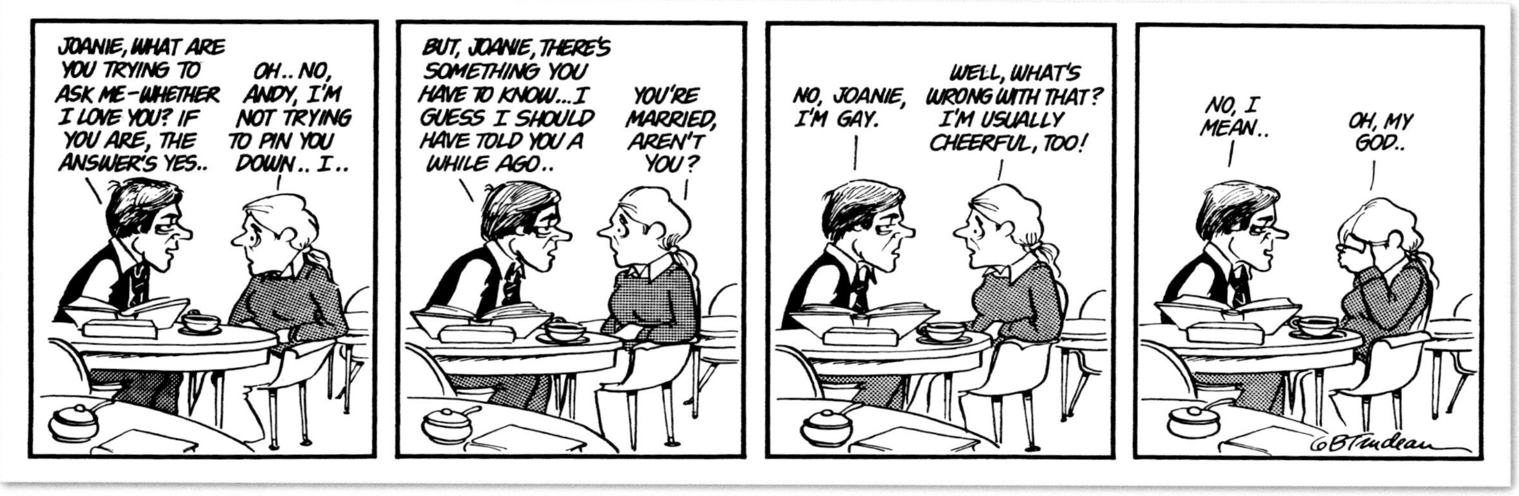
JOANIE, WHAT ARE YOU TRYING TO ASK ME–WHETHER I LOVE YOU? IF YOU ARE, THE ANSWER'S YES..
OH.. NO, ANDY, I'M NOT TRYING TO PIN YOU DOWN.. I..
BUT, JOANIE, THERE'S SOMETHING YOU HAVE TO KNOW... I GUESS I SHOULD HAVE TOLD YOU A WHILE AGO..
YOU'RE MARRIED, AREN'T YOU?
NO, JOANIE, I'M GAY.
WELL, WHAT'S WRONG WITH THAT? I'M USUALLY CHEERFUL, TOO!
NO, I MEAN..
OH, MY GOD..

2/10/76

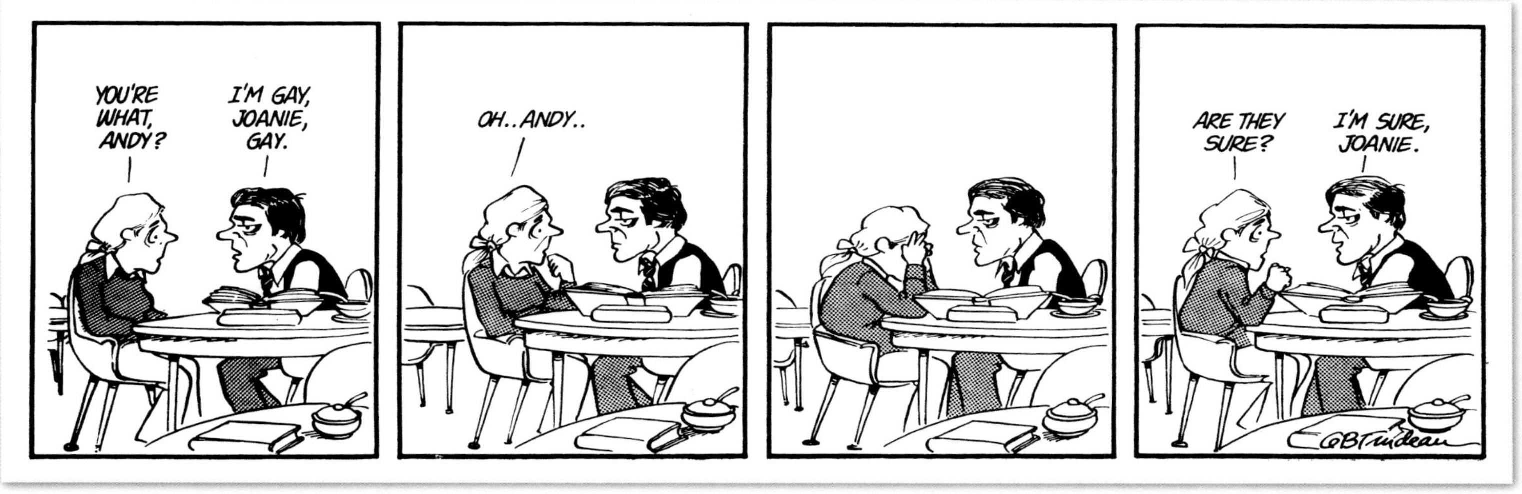
YOU'RE WHAT, ANDY?
I'M GAY, JOANIE, GAY.
OH.. ANDY..
ARE THEY SURE?
I'M SURE, JOANIE.

2/11/76

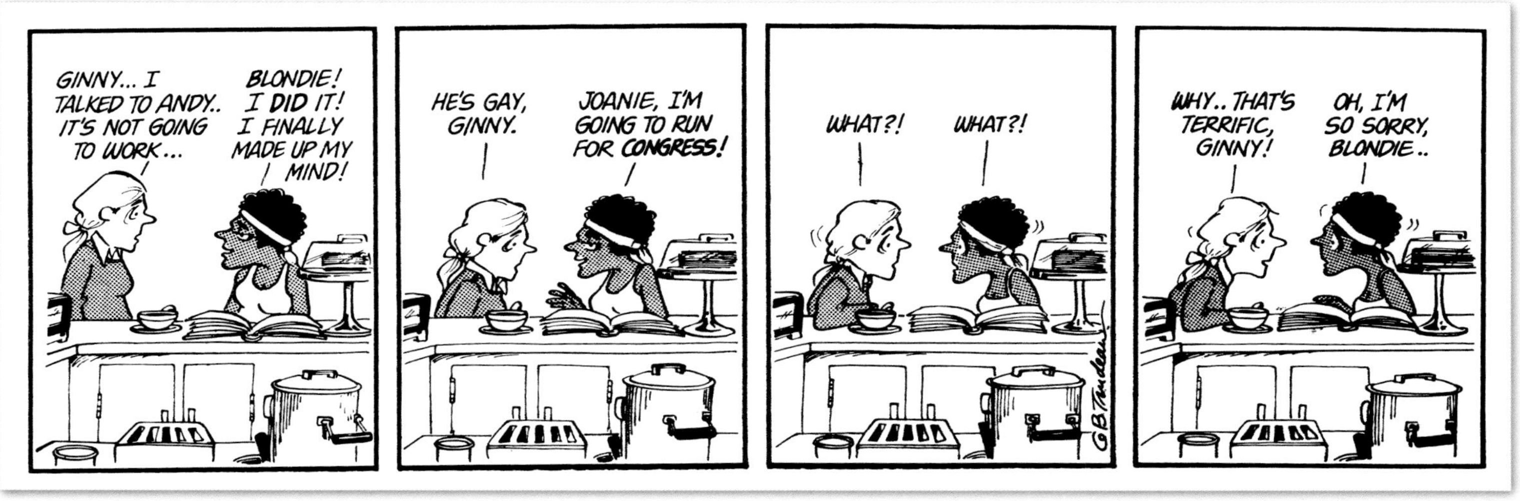
GINNY... I TALKED TO ANDY.. IT'S NOT GOING TO WORK...
BLONDIE! I DID IT! I FINALLY MADE UP MY MIND!
HE'S GAY, GINNY.
JOANIE, I'M GOING TO RUN FOR CONGRESS!
WHAT?!
WHAT?!
WHY.. THAT'S TERRIFIC, GINNY!
OH, I'M SO SORRY, BLONDIE..

2/12/76

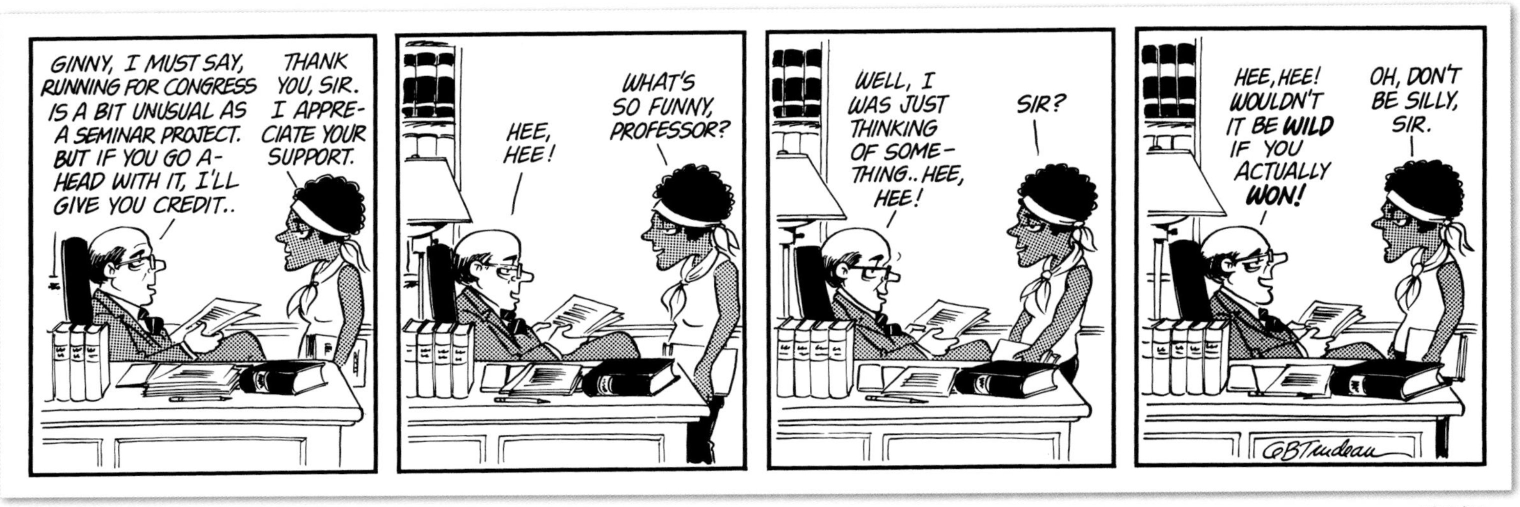
GINNY, I MUST SAY, RUNNING FOR CONGRESS IS A BIT UNUSUAL AS A SEMINAR PROJECT. BUT IF YOU GO AHEAD WITH IT, I'LL GIVE YOU CREDIT..
THANK YOU, SIR. I APPRECIATE YOUR SUPPORT.
HEE, HEE!
WHAT'S SO FUNNY, PROFESSOR?
WELL, I WAS JUST THINKING OF SOMETHING.. HEE, HEE!
SIR?
HEE, HEE! WOULDN'T IT BE WILD IF YOU ACTUALLY WON!
OH, DON'T BE SILLY, SIR.
©BTrudeau

3/15/76

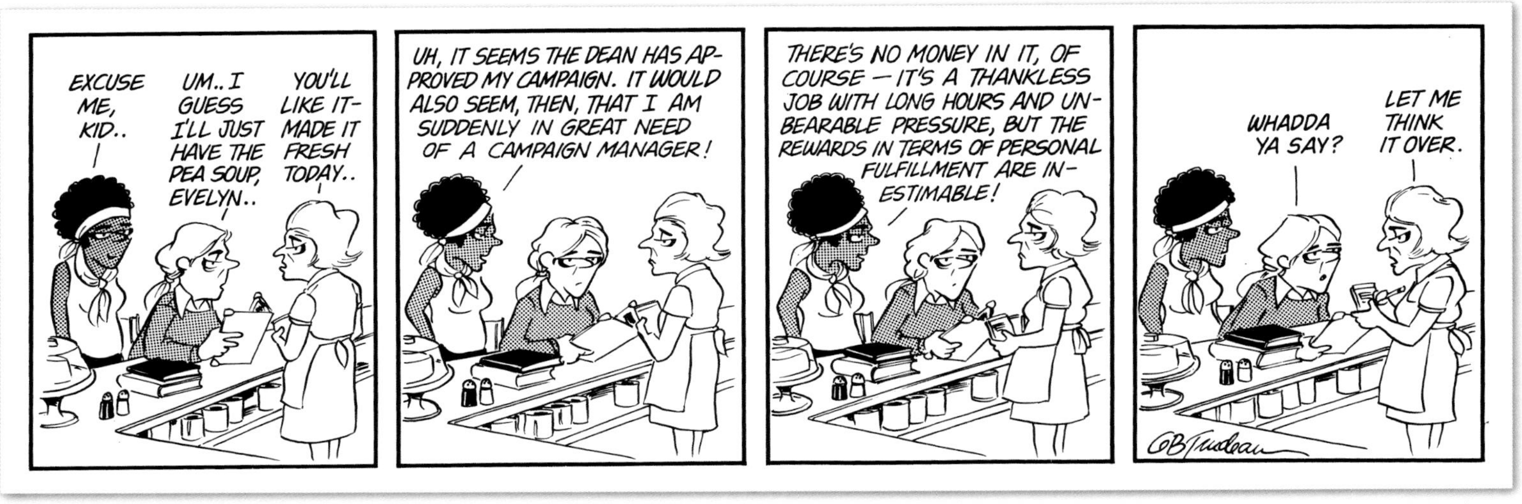
EXCUSE ME, KID..
UM.. I GUESS I'LL JUST HAVE THE PEA SOUP, EVELYN..
YOU'LL LIKE IT-MADE IT FRESH TODAY..
UH, IT SEEMS THE DEAN HAS APPROVED MY CAMPAIGN. IT WOULD ALSO SEEM, THEN, THAT I AM SUDDENLY IN GREAT NEED OF A CAMPAIGN MANAGER!
THERE'S NO MONEY IN IT, OF COURSE — IT'S A THANKLESS JOB WITH LONG HOURS AND UNBEARABLE PRESSURE, BUT THE REWARDS IN TERMS OF PERSONAL FULFILLMENT ARE INESTIMABLE!
WHADDA YA SAY?
LET ME THINK IT OVER.
©BTrudeau

3/16/76

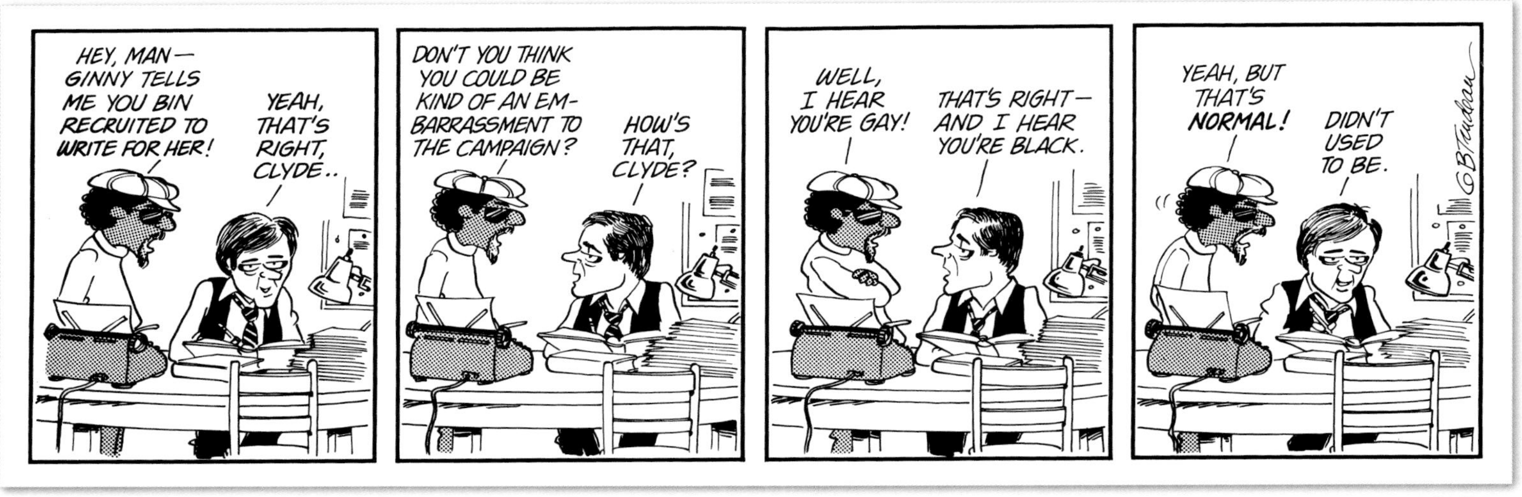
HEY, MAN— GINNY TELLS ME YOU BIN RECRUITED TO WRITE FOR HER!
YEAH, THAT'S RIGHT, CLYDE..
DON'T YOU THINK YOU COULD BE KIND OF AN EMBARRASSMENT TO THE CAMPAIGN?
HOW'S THAT, CLYDE?
WELL, I HEAR YOU'RE GAY!
THAT'S RIGHT— AND I HEAR YOU'RE BLACK.
YEAH, BUT THAT'S NORMAL!
DIDN'T USED TO BE.
©BTrudeau

3/20/76

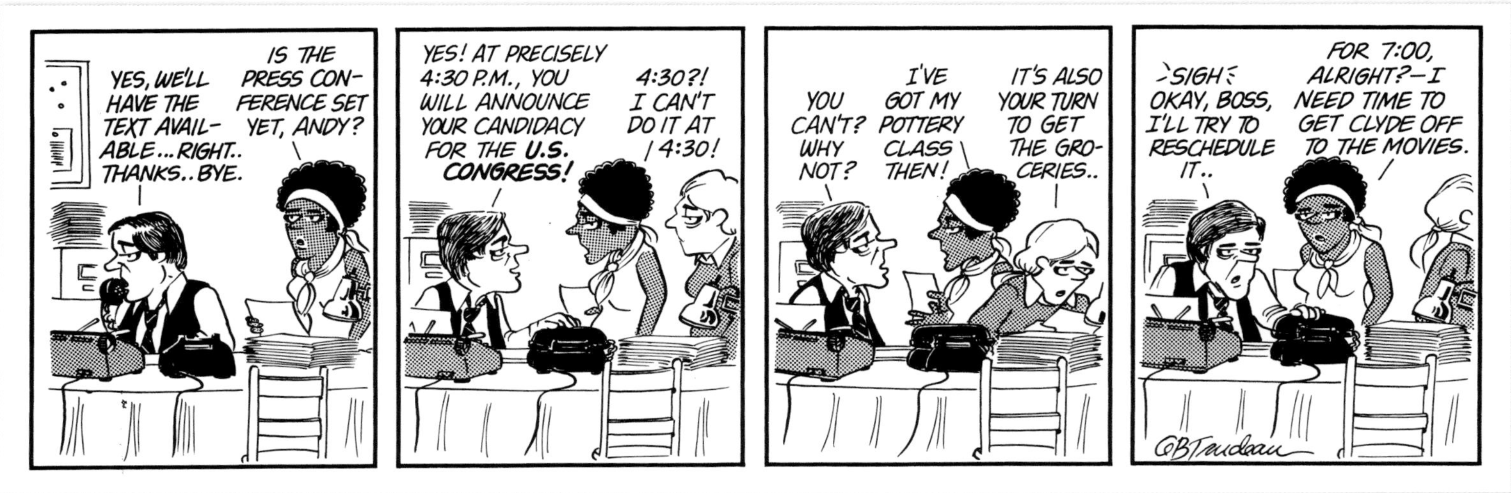
YES, WE'LL HAVE THE TEXT AVAILABLE... RIGHT.. THANKS.. BYE.
IS THE PRESS CONFERENCE SET YET, ANDY?
YES! AT PRECISELY 4:30 P.M., YOU WILL ANNOUNCE YOUR CANDIDACY FOR THE U.S. CONGRESS!
4:30?! I CAN'T DO IT AT 4:30!
YOU CAN'T? WHY NOT?
I'VE GOT MY POTTERY CLASS THEN!
IT'S ALSO YOUR TURN TO GET THE GROCERIES..
SIGH
OKAY, BOSS, I'LL TRY TO RESCHEDULE IT..
FOR 7:00, ALRIGHT?—I NEED TIME TO GET CLYDE OFF TO THE MOVIES.
©BTrudeau

3/21/76

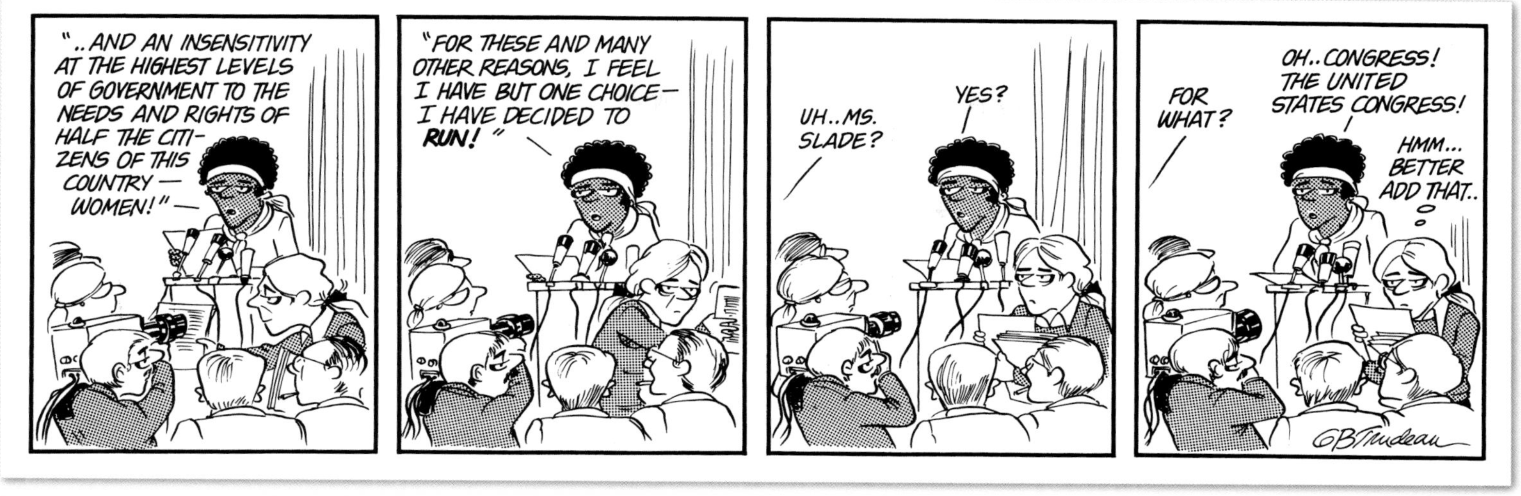
"..AND AN INSENSITIVITY AT THE HIGHEST LEVELS OF GOVERNMENT TO THE NEEDS AND RIGHTS OF HALF THE CITIZENS OF THIS COUNTRY — WOMEN!" —
"FOR THESE AND MANY OTHER REASONS, I FEEL I HAVE BUT ONE CHOICE — I HAVE DECIDED TO RUN!"
UH..MS. SLADE?
YES?
FOR WHAT?
OH..CONGRESS! THE UNITED STATES CONGRESS!
HMM... BETTER ADD THAT..

3/24/76

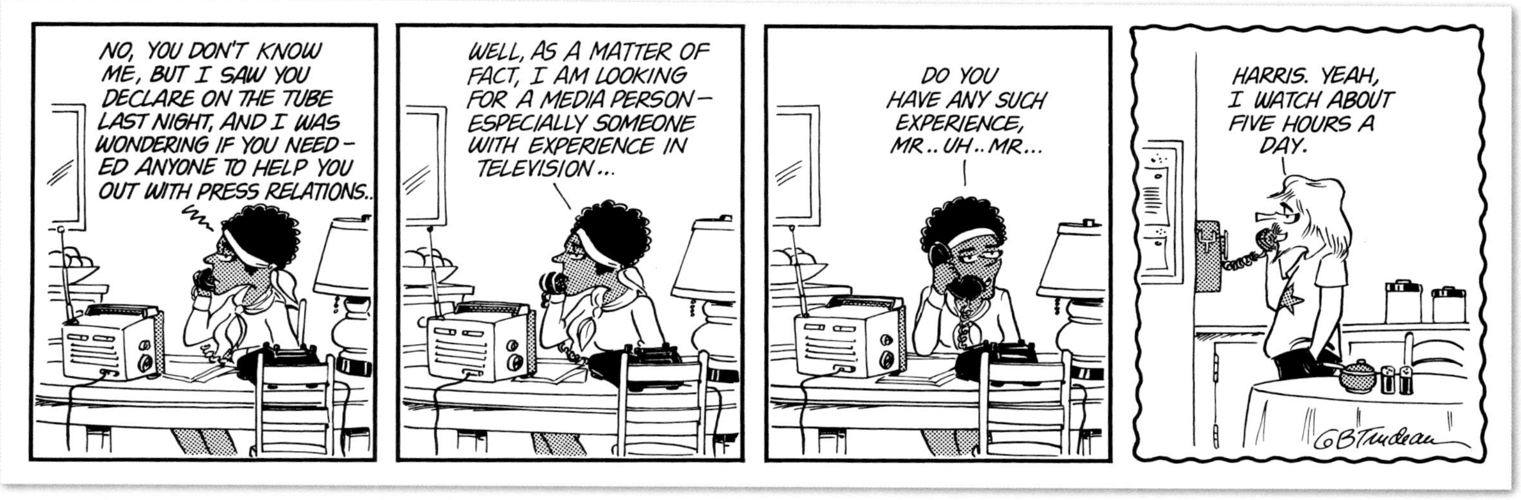
NO, YOU DON'T KNOW ME, BUT I SAW YOU DECLARE ON THE TUBE LAST NIGHT, AND I WAS WONDERING IF YOU NEEDED ANYONE TO HELP YOU OUT WITH PRESS RELATIONS..
WELL, AS A MATTER OF FACT, I AM LOOKING FOR A MEDIA PERSON — ESPECIALLY SOMEONE WITH EXPERIENCE IN TELEVISION...
DO YOU HAVE ANY SUCH EXPERIENCE, MR..UH..MR...
HARRIS. YEAH, I WATCH ABOUT FIVE HOURS A DAY.

3/26/76

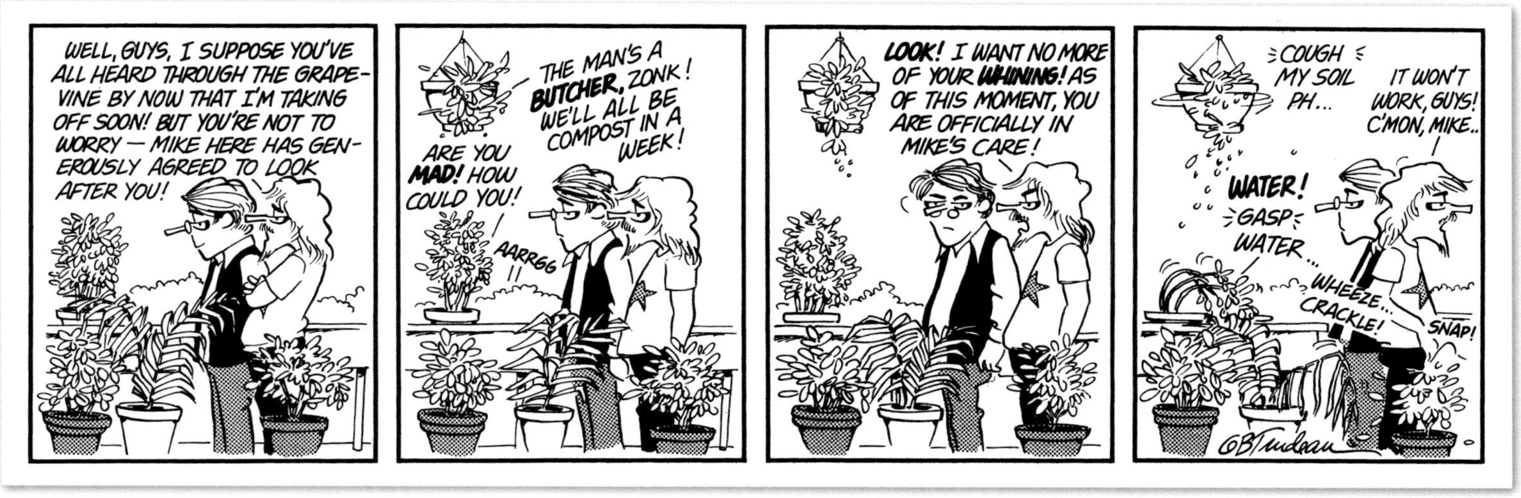
WELL, GUYS, I SUPPOSE YOU'VE ALL HEARD THROUGH THE GRAPEVINE BY NOW THAT I'M TAKING OFF SOON! BUT YOU'RE NOT TO WORRY — MIKE HERE HAS GENEROUSLY AGREED TO LOOK AFTER YOU!
THE MAN'S A BUTCHER, ZONK! WE'LL ALL BE COMPOST IN A WEEK!
ARE YOU MAD! HOW COULD YOU!
AARRGG!!
LOOK! I WANT NO MORE OF YOUR WHINING! AS OF THIS MOMENT, YOU ARE OFFICIALLY IN MIKE'S CARE!
COUGH MY SOIL PH...
IT WON'T WORK, GUYS! C'MON, MIKE..
WATER!
GASP WATER...
WHEEZE..
CRACKLE!
SNAP!

3/29/76

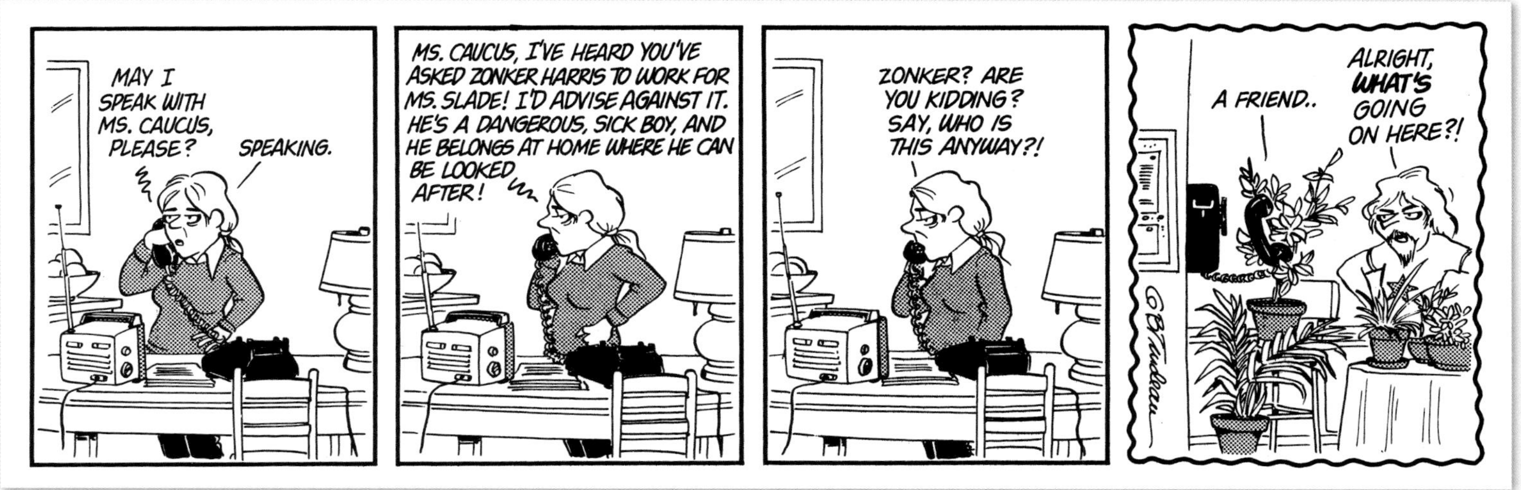
MAY I SPEAK WITH MS. CAUCUS, PLEASE?
SPEAKING.
MS. CAUCUS, I'VE HEARD YOU'VE ASKED ZONKER HARRIS TO WORK FOR MS. SLADE! I'D ADVISE AGAINST IT. HE'S A DANGEROUS, SICK BOY, AND HE BELONGS AT HOME WHERE HE CAN BE LOOKED AFTER!
ZONKER? ARE YOU KIDDING? SAY, WHO IS THIS ANYWAY?!
A FRIEND..
ALRIGHT, WHAT'S GOING ON HERE?!

3/31/76

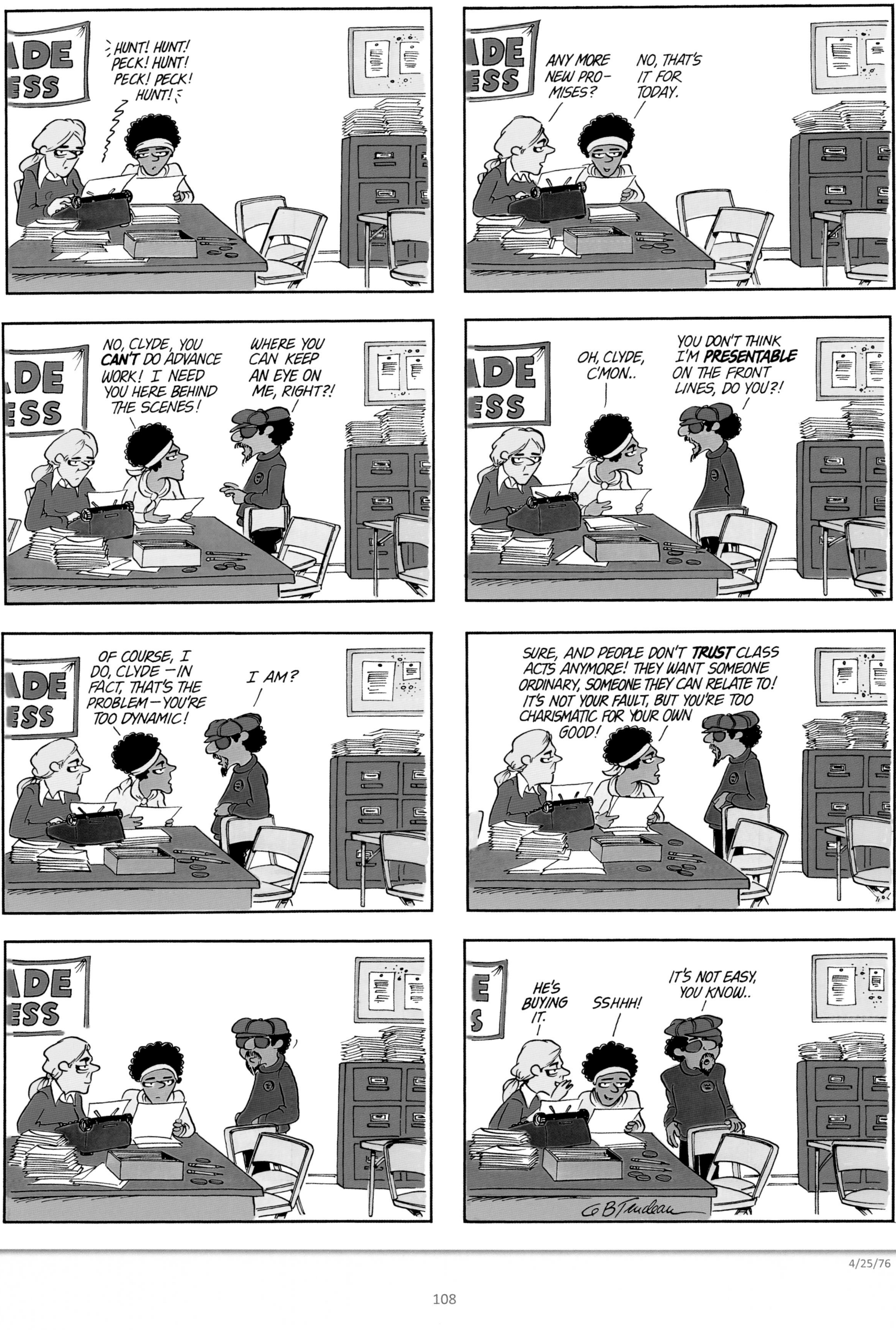
HUNT! HUNT! PECK! HUNT! PECK! PECK! HUNT!
ANY MORE NEW PRO-MISES?
NO, THAT'S IT FOR TODAY.
NO, CLYDE, YOU **CAN'T** DO ADVANCE WORK! I NEED YOU HERE BEHIND THE SCENES!
WHERE YOU CAN KEEP AN EYE ON ME, RIGHT?!
OH, CLYDE, C'MON..
YOU DON'T THINK I'M **PRESENTABLE** ON THE FRONT LINES, DO YOU?!
OF COURSE, I DO, CLYDE—IN FACT, THAT'S THE PROBLEM—YOU'RE TOO DYNAMIC!
I AM?
SURE, AND PEOPLE DON'T **TRUST** CLASS ACTS ANYMORE! THEY WANT SOMEONE ORDINARY, SOMEONE THEY CAN RELATE TO! IT'S NOT YOUR FAULT, BUT YOU'RE TOO CHARISMATIC FOR YOUR OWN GOOD!
HE'S BUYING IT.
SSHHH!
IT'S NOT EASY, YOU KNOW..
G.B.Trudeau

4/25/76

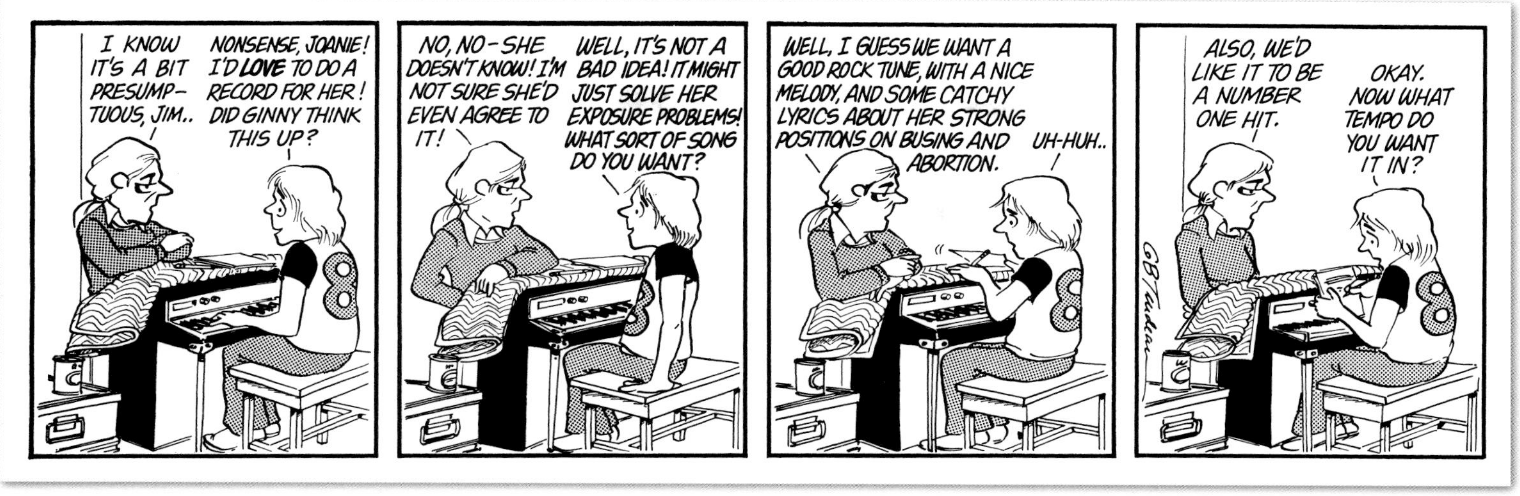
I KNOW IT'S A BIT PRESUMP-TUOUS, JIM..
NONSENSE, JOANIE! I'D **LOVE** TO DO A RECORD FOR HER! DID GINNY THINK THIS UP?
NO, NO - SHE DOESN'T KNOW! I'M NOT SURE SHE'D EVEN AGREE TO IT!
WELL, IT'S NOT A BAD IDEA! IT MIGHT JUST SOLVE HER EXPOSURE PROBLEMS! WHAT SORT OF SONG DO YOU WANT?
WELL, I GUESS WE WANT A GOOD ROCK TUNE, WITH A NICE MELODY, AND SOME CATCHY LYRICS ABOUT HER STRONG POSITIONS ON BUSING AND ABORTION.
UH-HUH..
ALSO, WE'D LIKE IT TO BE A NUMBER ONE HIT.
OKAY. NOW WHAT TEMPO DO YOU WANT IT IN?

8/2/76

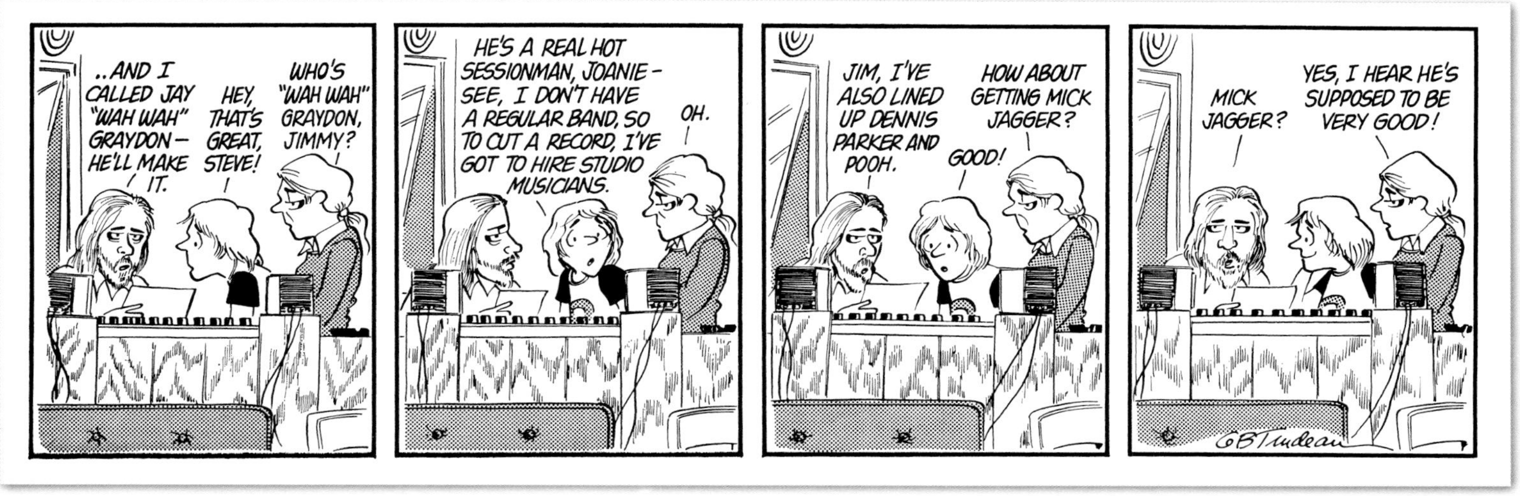
..AND I CALLED JAY "WAH WAH" GRAYDON - HE'LL MAKE IT.
HEY, THAT'S GREAT, STEVE!
WHO'S "WAH WAH" GRAYDON, JIMMY?
HE'S A REAL HOT SESSIONMAN, JOANIE - SEE, I DON'T HAVE A REGULAR BAND, SO TO CUT A RECORD, I'VE GOT TO HIRE STUDIO MUSICIANS.
OH.
JIM, I'VE ALSO LINED UP DENNIS PARKER AND POOH.
GOOD!
HOW ABOUT GETTING MICK JAGGER?
MICK JAGGER?
YES, I HEAR HE'S SUPPOSED TO BE VERY GOOD!

8/4/76

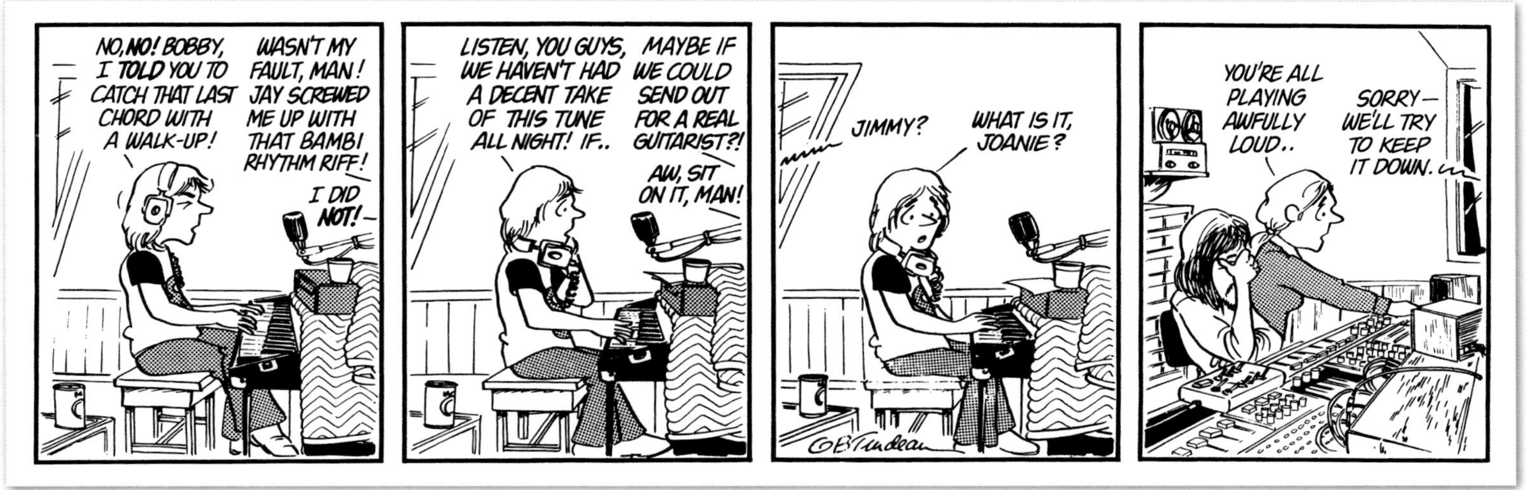
NO, **NO!** BOBBY, I **TOLD** YOU TO CATCH THAT LAST CHORD WITH A WALK-UP!
WASN'T MY FAULT, MAN! JAY SCREWED ME UP WITH THAT BAMBI RHYTHM RIFF!
I DID **NOT!**
LISTEN, YOU GUYS, WE HAVEN'T HAD A DECENT TAKE OF THIS TUNE ALL NIGHT! IF..
MAYBE IF WE COULD SEND OUT FOR A REAL GUITARIST?!
AW, SIT ON IT, MAN!
JIMMY?
WHAT IS IT, JOANIE?
YOU'RE ALL PLAYING AWFULLY LOUD..
SORRY - WE'LL TRY TO KEEP IT DOWN.

8/10/76

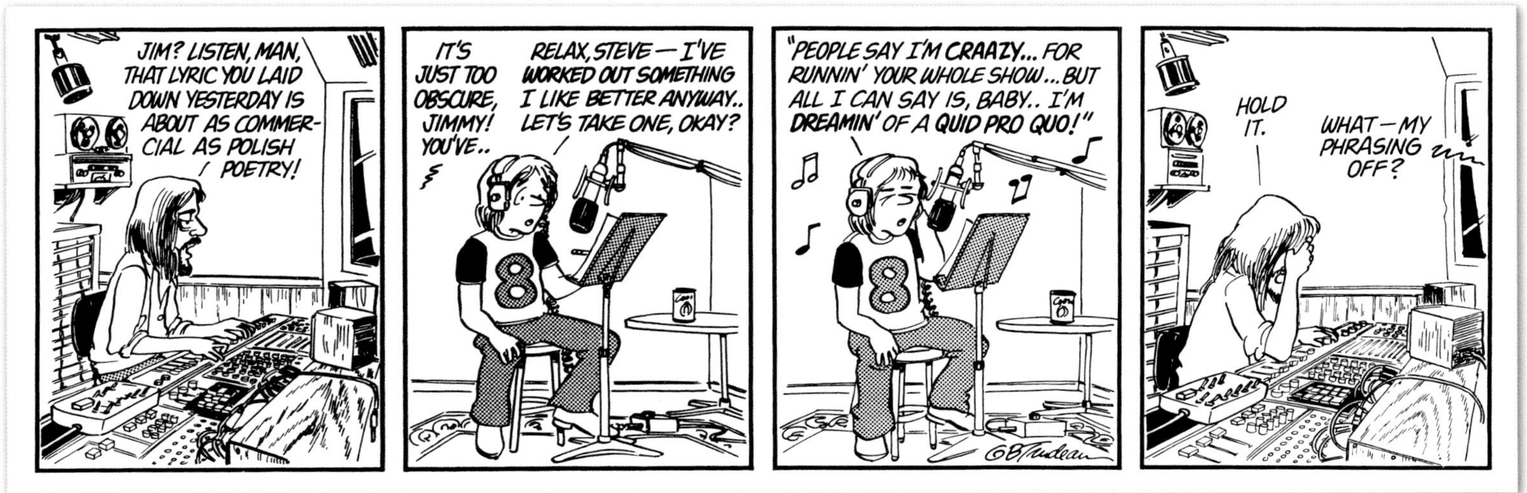
JIM? LISTEN, MAN, THAT LYRIC YOU LAID DOWN YESTERDAY IS ABOUT AS COMMER-CIAL AS POLISH POETRY!
IT'S JUST TOO OBSCURE, JIMMY! YOU'VE..
RELAX, STEVE — I'VE **WORKED OUT SOMETHING** I LIKE **BETTER ANYWAY..** LET'S TAKE ONE, OKAY?
"PEOPLE SAY I'M **CRAAZY...** FOR RUNNIN' YOUR WHOLE SHOW... BUT ALL I CAN SAY IS, BABY.. I'M **DREAMIN'** OF A **QUID PRO QUO!**"
HOLD IT.
WHAT — MY PHRASING OFF?

8/13/76

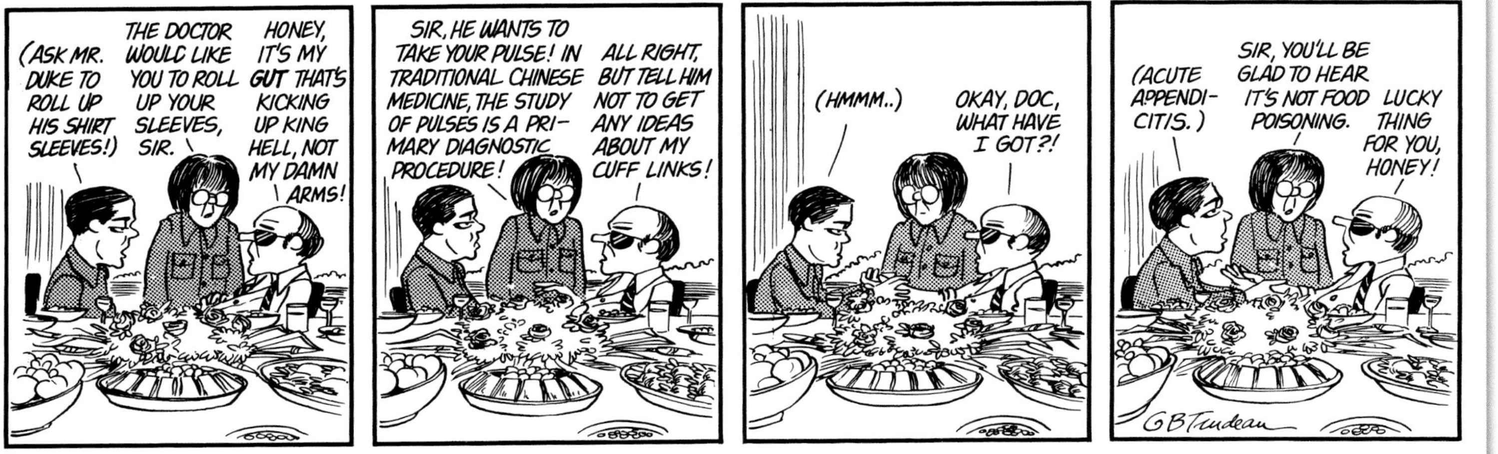
(ASK MR. DUKE TO ROLL UP HIS SHIRT SLEEVES!)
THE DOCTOR WOULD LIKE YOU TO ROLL UP YOUR SLEEVES, SIR.
HONEY, IT'S MY GUT THAT'S KICKING UP KING HELL, NOT MY DAMN ARMS!
SIR, HE WANTS TO TAKE YOUR PULSE! IN TRADITIONAL CHINESE MEDICINE, THE STUDY OF PULSES IS A PRIMARY DIAGNOSTIC PROCEDURE!
ALL RIGHT, BUT TELL HIM NOT TO GET ANY IDEAS ABOUT MY CUFF LINKS!
(HMMM..)
OKAY, DOC, WHAT HAVE I GOT?!
(ACUTE APPENDICITIS.)
SIR, YOU'LL BE GLAD TO HEAR IT'S NOT FOOD POISONING.
LUCKY THING FOR YOU, HONEY!
GBTrudeau

8/25/76

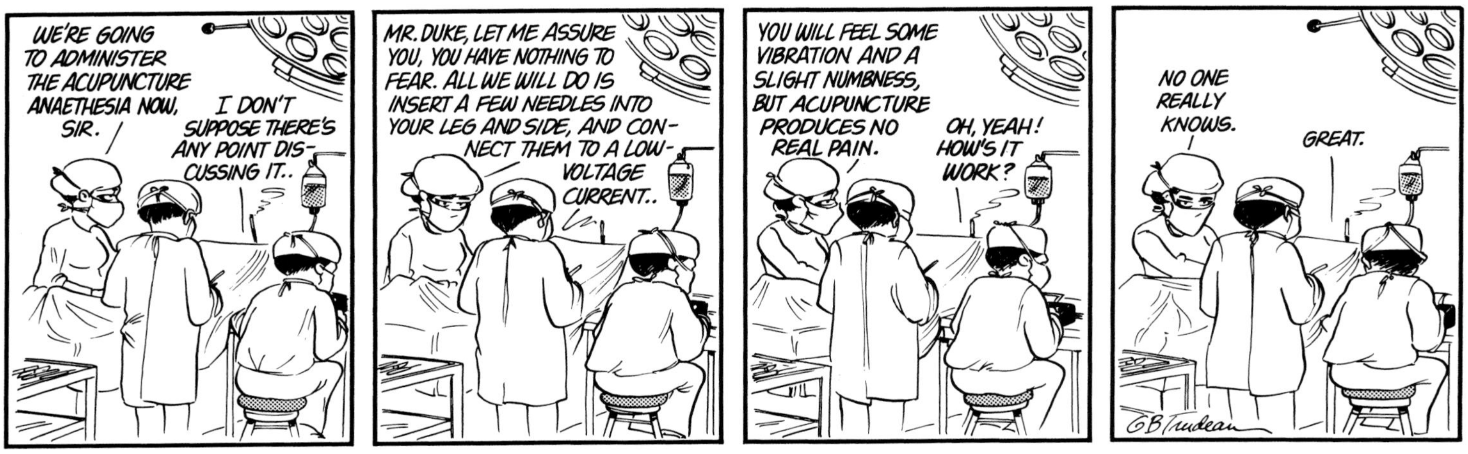
WE'RE GOING TO ADMINISTER THE ACUPUNCTURE ANAETHESIA NOW, SIR.
I DON'T SUPPOSE THERE'S ANY POINT DISCUSSING IT..
MR. DUKE, LET ME ASSURE YOU, YOU HAVE NOTHING TO FEAR. ALL WE WILL DO IS INSERT A FEW NEEDLES INTO YOUR LEG AND SIDE, AND CONNECT THEM TO A LOW-VOLTAGE CURRENT..
YOU WILL FEEL SOME VIBRATION AND A SLIGHT NUMBNESS, BUT ACUPUNCTURE PRODUCES NO REAL PAIN.
OH, YEAH! HOW'S IT WORK?
NO ONE REALLY KNOWS.
GREAT.
GBTrudeau

8/31/76

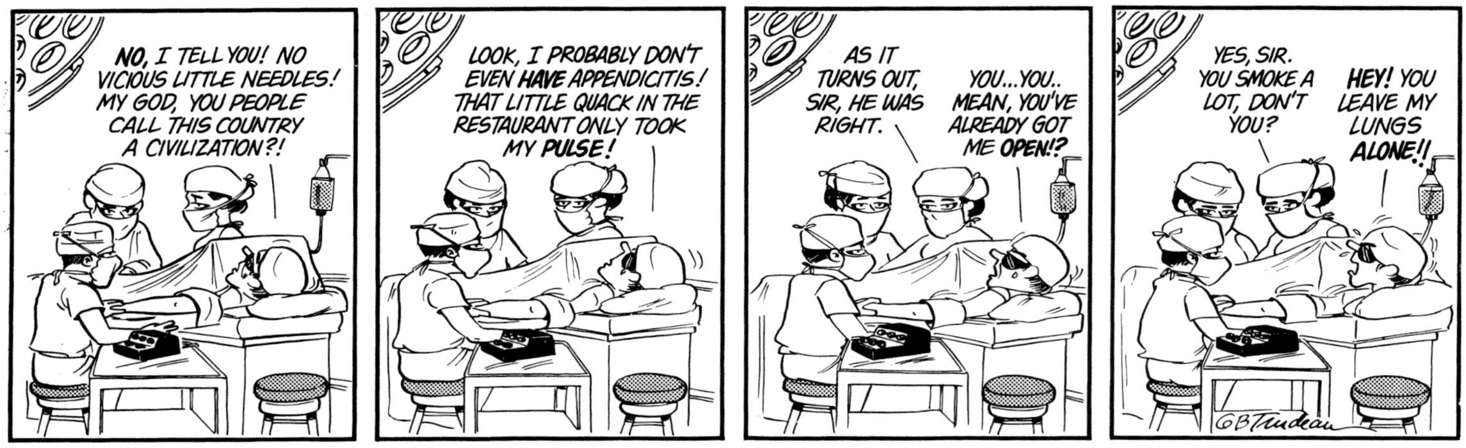
NO, I TELL YOU! NO VICIOUS LITTLE NEEDLES! MY GOD, YOU PEOPLE CALL THIS COUNTRY A CIVILIZATION?!
LOOK, I PROBABLY DON'T EVEN HAVE APPENDICITIS! THAT LITTLE QUACK IN THE RESTAURANT ONLY TOOK MY PULSE!
AS IT TURNS OUT, SIR, HE WAS RIGHT.
YOU...YOU.. MEAN, YOU'VE ALREADY GOT ME OPEN!?
YES, SIR. YOU SMOKE A LOT, DON'T YOU?
HEY! YOU LEAVE MY LUNGS ALONE!!
GBTrudeau

9/1/76

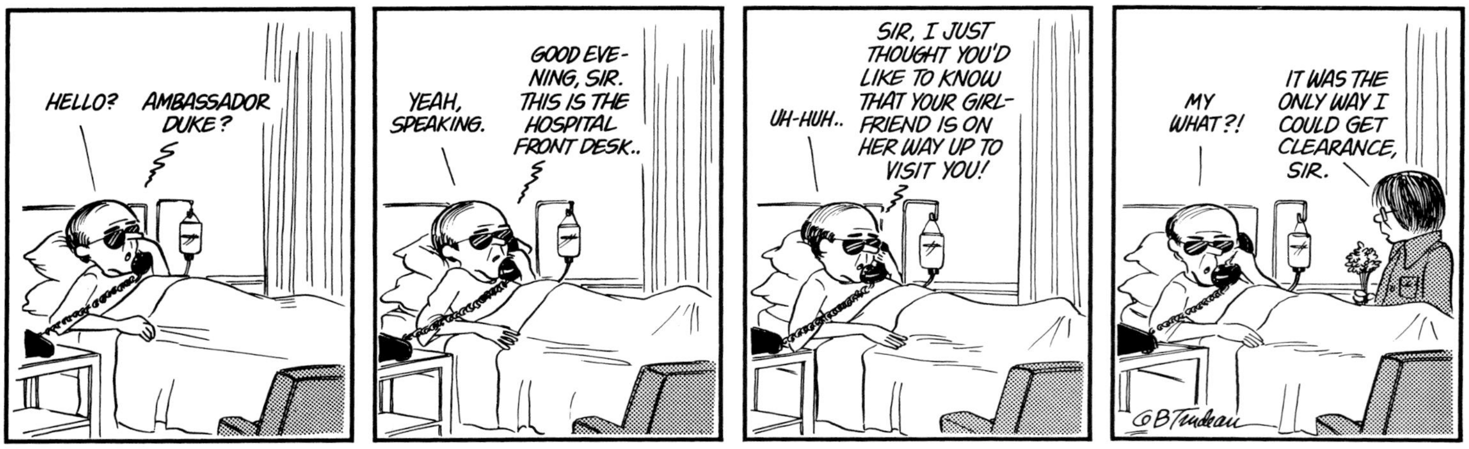
HELLO?
AMBASSADOR DUKE?
YEAH, SPEAKING.
GOOD EVENING, SIR. THIS IS THE HOSPITAL FRONT DESK..
UH-HUH..
SIR, I JUST THOUGHT YOU'D LIKE TO KNOW THAT YOUR GIRLFRIEND IS ON HER WAY UP TO VISIT YOU!
MY WHAT?!
IT WAS THE ONLY WAY I COULD GET CLEARANCE, SIR.
GBTrudeau

9/4/76

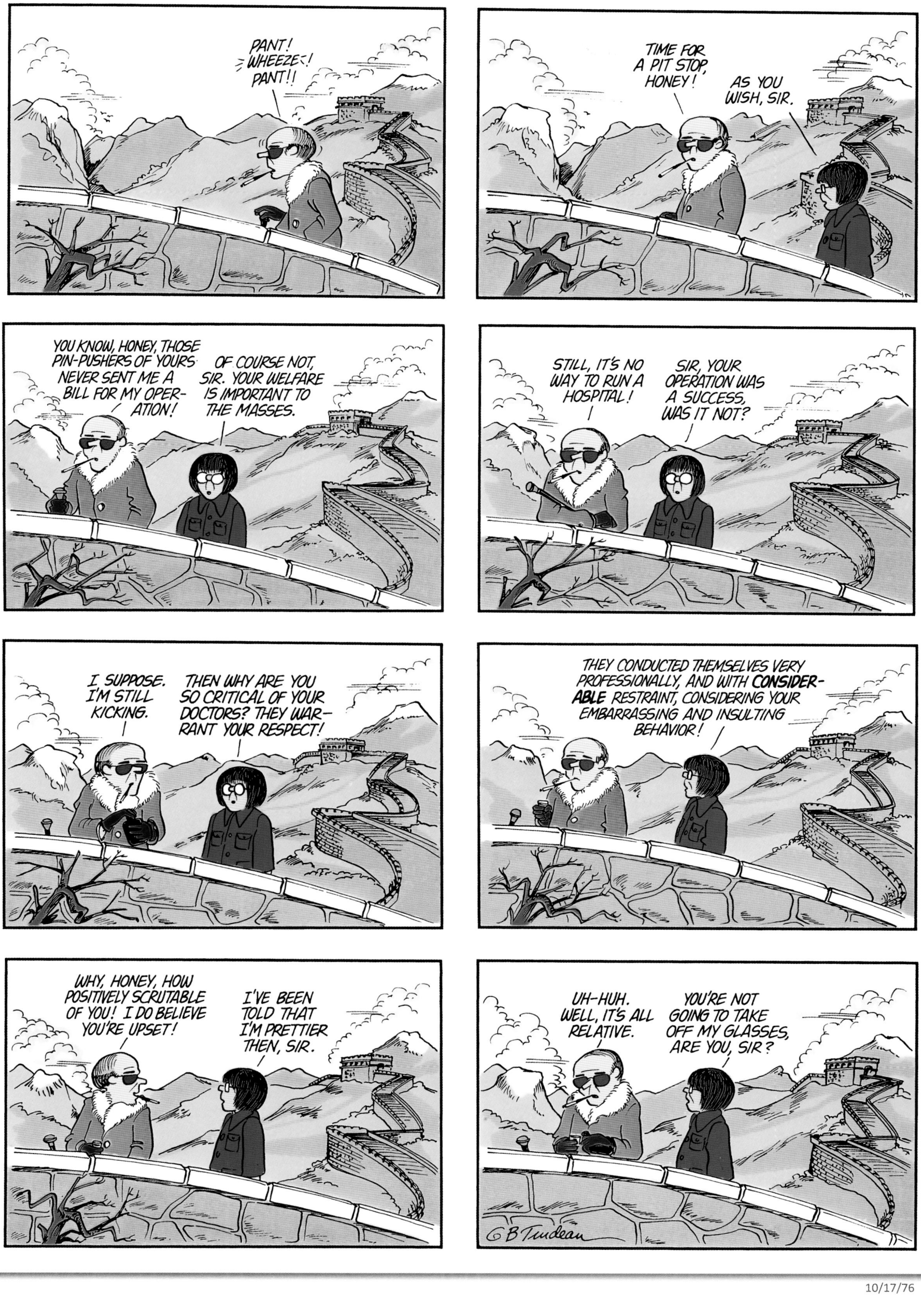
PANT! WHEEZE! PANT!!
TIME FOR A PIT STOP, HONEY!
AS YOU WISH, SIR.
YOU KNOW, HONEY, THOSE PIN-PUSHERS OF YOURS NEVER SENT ME A BILL FOR MY OPERATION!
OF COURSE NOT, SIR. YOUR WELFARE IS IMPORTANT TO THE MASSES.
STILL, IT'S NO WAY TO RUN A HOSPITAL!
SIR, YOUR OPERATION WAS A SUCCESS, WAS IT NOT?
I SUPPOSE. I'M STILL KICKING.
THEN WHY ARE YOU SO CRITICAL OF YOUR DOCTORS? THEY WARRANT YOUR RESPECT!
THEY CONDUCTED THEMSELVES VERY PROFESSIONALLY, AND WITH CONSIDERABLE RESTRAINT, CONSIDERING YOUR EMBARRASSING AND INSULTING BEHAVIOR!
WHY, HONEY, HOW POSITIVELY SCRUTABLE OF YOU! I DO BELIEVE YOU'RE UPSET!
I'VE BEEN TOLD THAT I'M PRETTIER THEN, SIR.
UH-HUH. WELL, IT'S ALL RELATIVE.
YOU'RE NOT GOING TO TAKE OFF MY GLASSES, ARE YOU, SIR?
GB Trudeau

10/17/76

Mark Slackmeyer

PRESS
WHITE HOUSE PRESS CORPS

RADIO-TELEVISION

npr
NPR Corres-
pondent
Access
Exp. 10/26/10

Name: MARK SLACKMEYER
Signature: *Mark Slackmeyer*
No. 0022350

THE WHITE HOUSE
WASHINGTON

Back when the strip was more akin to puppetry than commentary, the third archetype I taped to a stick was the Student Radical. Naming him Mark was a bit obvious (Columbia activist Mark Rudd was much in the news those days), but so was the rest of my conception. Mark was cut from stiff cardboard, and I made no apologies for it. While I was committed to the antiwar cause, I found much of its leadership clownish.

Part of the problem was I just didn't understand what made for effective political theater. The public rant, then as now, left me unmoved, as did its reductionist offshoot, the slogan. It didn't help that I was easily the most self-conscious activist at any rally. Even in the safety of a crowd, I couldn't get myself to contribute a single "Power to the people!" or "Up against the wall!" without cringing, or worse, giggling. The rhetoric seemed ridiculous, and I couldn't understand why otherwise thoughtful people were so happy to repeat everything that was shouted at them through a bullhorn.

"That's guilty! Guilty, guilty, guilty!"

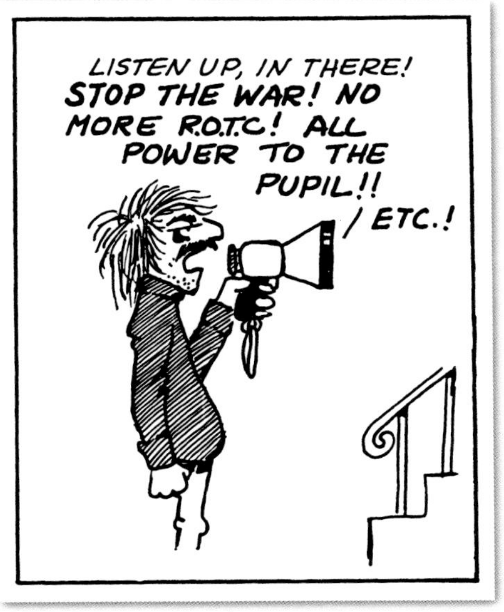
LISTEN UP, IN THERE! STOP THE WAR! NO MORE R.O.T.C.! ALL POWER TO THE PUPIL!! / ETC.!

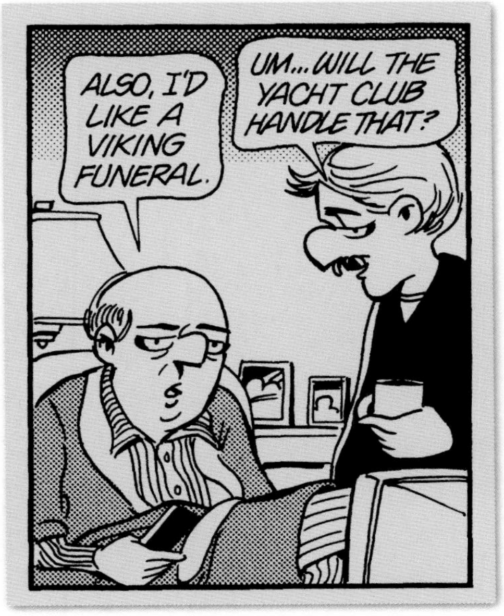
ALSO, I'D LIKE A VIKING FUNERAL.
UM... WILL THE YACHT CLUB HANDLE THAT?

As the antiwar movement matured, my position on the matter mellowed, largely for practical reasons. If you're going to gather 100,000 people in one place, you do need *something* for them to chant, and the catchier the better. The wildly popular "Hey, hey, LBJ! How many kids did you kill today?" may have been unfairly premised, but it was easy to learn, scanned well, and drove the president crazy. So coherence isn't everything.

It's a little embarrassing when a writer has to catch up with his own creation, but it's almost as if Mark understood all this before I did. As a born provocateur, he intuitively knew that it's not about the stunts you pull—it's the buttons you push. When he took to the airwaves and declared Watergate conspirator John Mitchell "Guilty! Guilty! Guilty!" before he'd even been indicted, the manic grin he wore for the occasion told the tale; he was looking for blowback, just as surely as Rush Limbaugh does when he calls Obama a racist.

In subsequent years, Mark shed some of the merry prankster perversity, but he still lives to mix it up. That he would be allowed to do so at staid NPR pushes credulity, but without its moderating culture, Mark might well have evolved into just another shock jock. Instead, he anguishes over the liberal contradiction—its tolerance for all viewpoints, including conservative contempt for tolerance. It is, to say the least, his Achilles' heel, and one that former debate partner Chase was happy to gnaw on. It might have been easier to keep Mark the doctrinaire marionette he was in 1970, but then he couldn't have shared his creator's raging ambivalence about what kind of people we are meant to be.

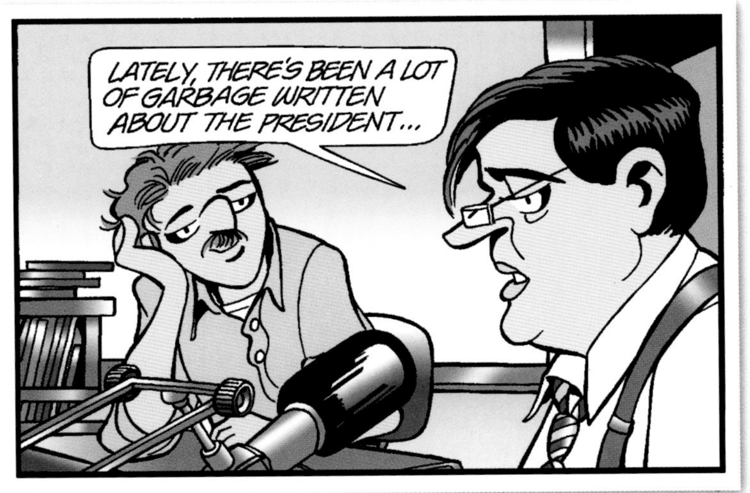
LATELY, THERE'S BEEN A LOT OF GARBAGE WRITTEN ABOUT THE PRESIDENT...

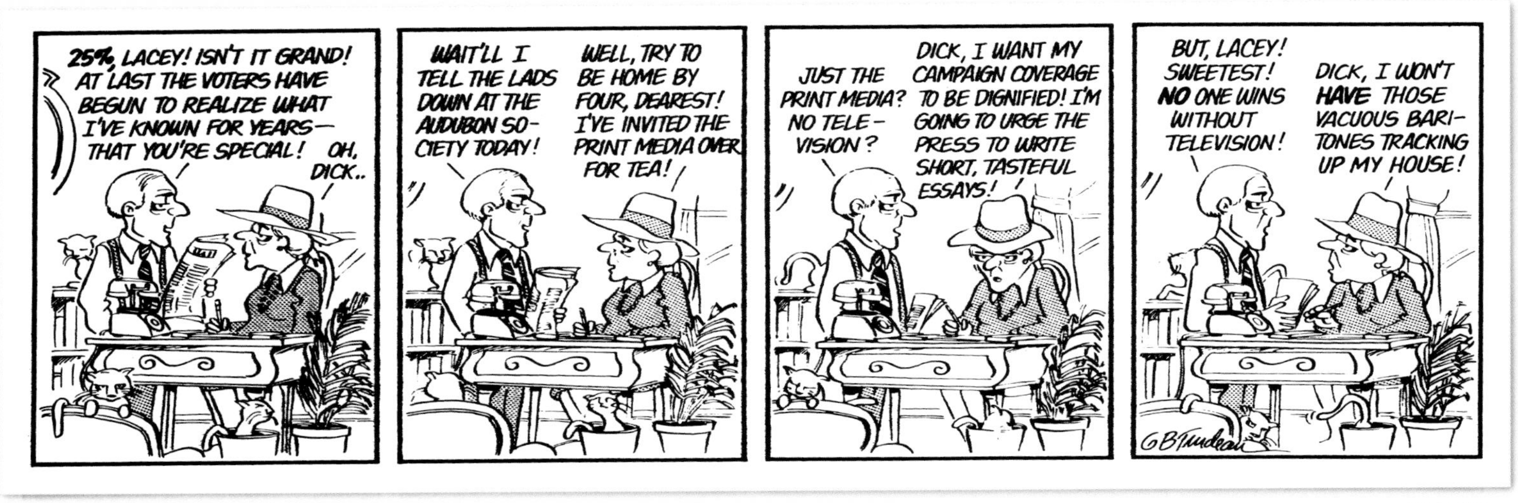
25%, LACEY! ISN'T IT GRAND! AT LAST THE VOTERS HAVE BEGUN TO REALIZE WHAT I'VE KNOWN FOR YEARS— THAT YOU'RE SPECIAL!
OH, DICK..
WAIT'LL I TELL THE LADS DOWN AT THE AUDUBON SOCIETY TODAY!
WELL, TRY TO BE HOME BY FOUR, DEAREST! I'VE INVITED THE PRINT MEDIA OVER FOR TEA!
JUST THE PRINT MEDIA? NO TELEVISION?
DICK, I WANT MY CAMPAIGN COVERAGE TO BE DIGNIFIED! I'M GOING TO URGE THE PRESS TO WRITE SHORT, TASTEFUL ESSAYS!
BUT, LACEY! SWEETEST! NO ONE WINS WITHOUT TELEVISION!
DICK, I WON'T HAVE THOSE VACUOUS BARITONES TRACKING UP MY HOUSE!
GBTrudeau

10/11/76

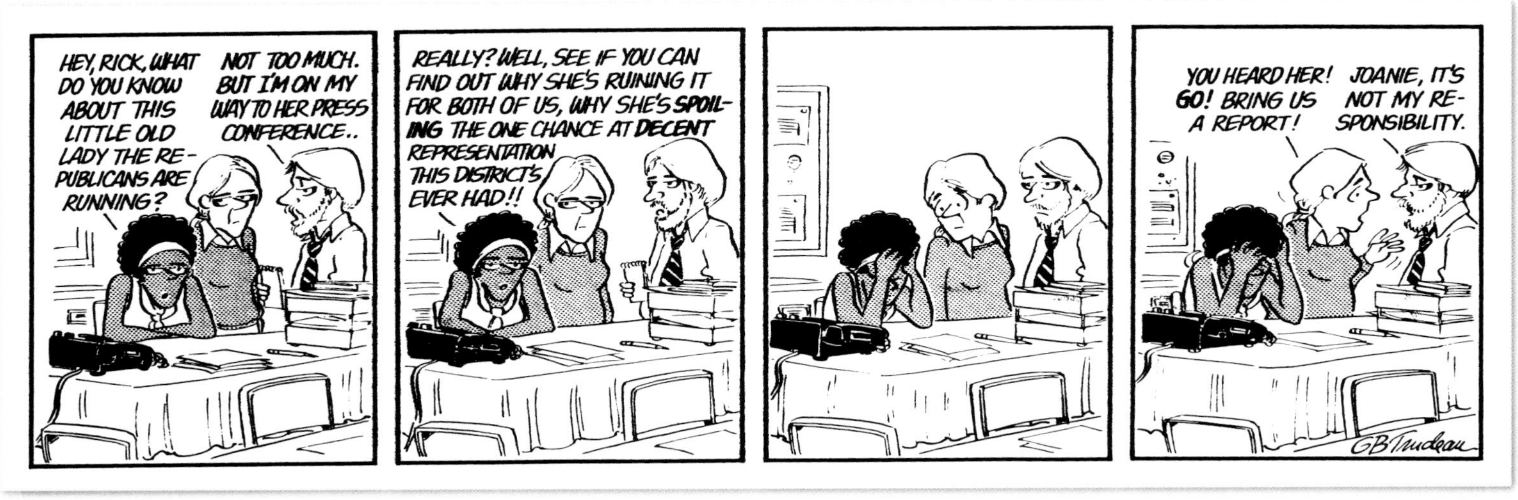
HEY, RICK, WHAT DO YOU KNOW ABOUT THIS LITTLE OLD LADY THE REPUBLICANS ARE RUNNING?
NOT TOO MUCH. BUT I'M ON MY WAY TO HER PRESS CONFERENCE..
REALLY? WELL, SEE IF YOU CAN FIND OUT WHY SHE'S RUINING IT FOR BOTH OF US, WHY SHE'S SPOILING THE ONE CHANCE AT DECENT REPRESENTATION THIS DISTRICT'S EVER HAD!!
YOU HEARD HER! GO! BRING US A REPORT!
JOANIE, IT'S NOT MY RESPONSIBILITY.
GBTrudeau

10/12/76

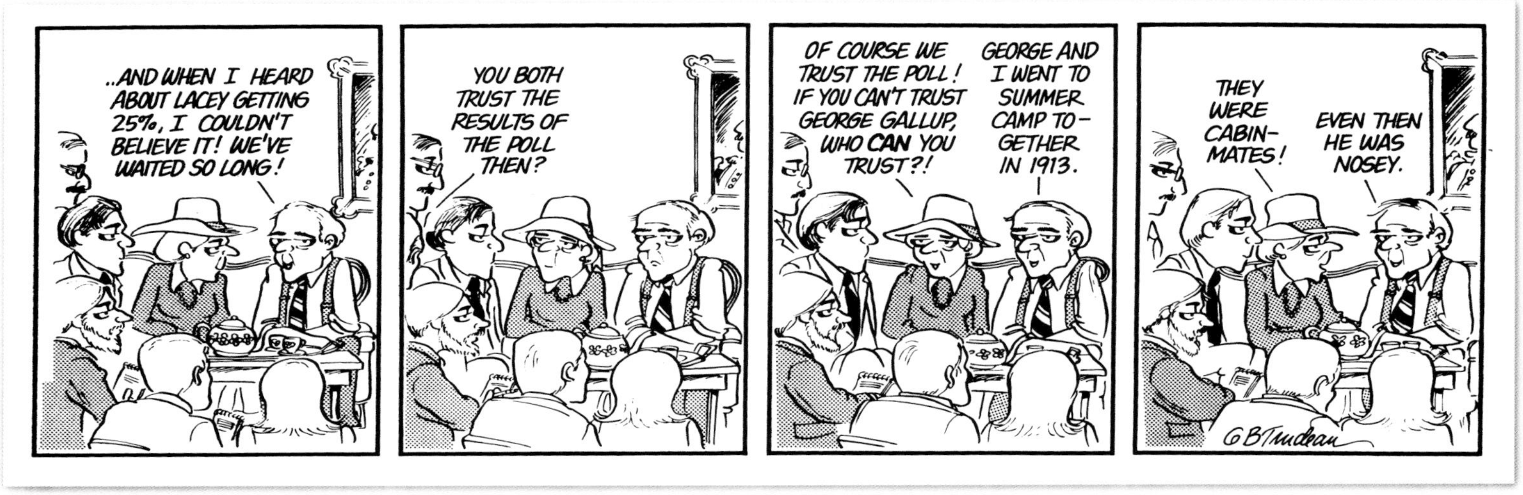
..AND WHEN I HEARD ABOUT LACEY GETTING 25%, I COULDN'T BELIEVE IT! WE'VE WAITED SO LONG!
YOU BOTH TRUST THE RESULTS OF THE POLL THEN?
OF COURSE WE TRUST THE POLL! IF YOU CAN'T TRUST GEORGE GALLUP, WHO CAN YOU TRUST?!
GEORGE AND I WENT TO SUMMER CAMP TOGETHER IN 1913.
THEY WERE CABINMATES!
EVEN THEN HE WAS NOSEY.
GBTrudeau

10/14/76

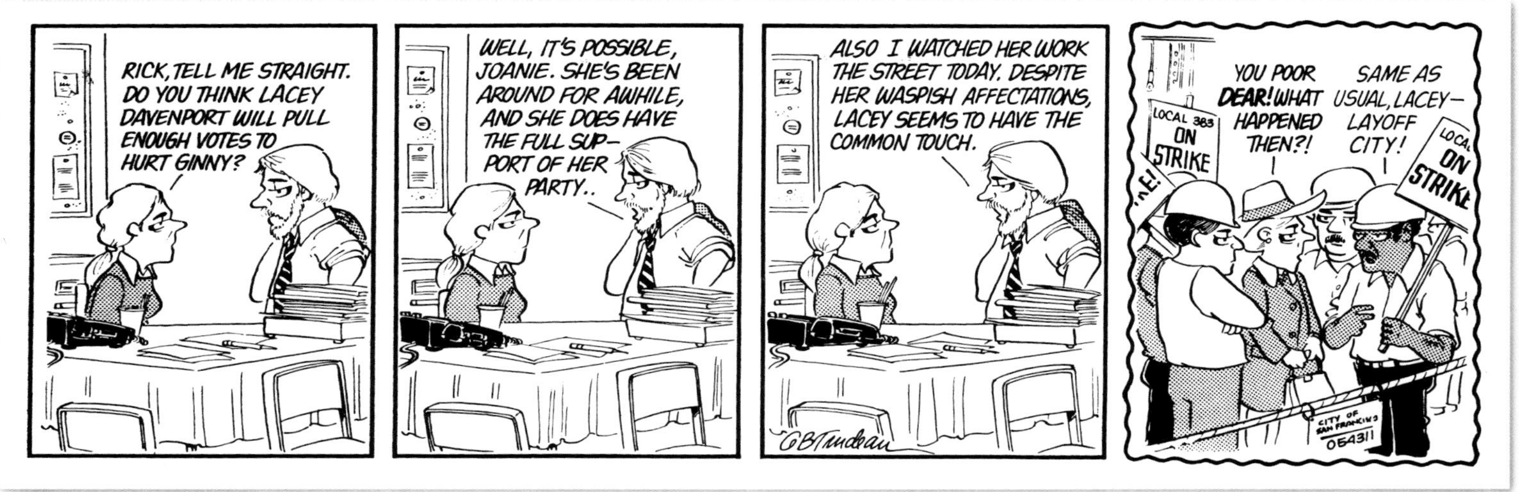
RICK, TELL ME STRAIGHT. DO YOU THINK LACEY DAVENPORT WILL PULL ENOUGH VOTES TO HURT GINNY?
WELL, IT'S POSSIBLE, JOANIE. SHE'S BEEN AROUND FOR AWHILE, AND SHE DOES HAVE THE FULL SUPPORT OF HER PARTY..
ALSO I WATCHED HER WORK THE STREET TODAY. DESPITE HER WASPISH AFFECTATIONS, LACEY SEEMS TO HAVE THE COMMON TOUCH.
GBTrudeau
LOCAL 383 ON STRIKE
YOU POOR DEAR! WHAT HAPPENED THEN?!
SAME AS USUAL, LACEY— LAYOFF CITY!
ON STRIKE

10/16/76

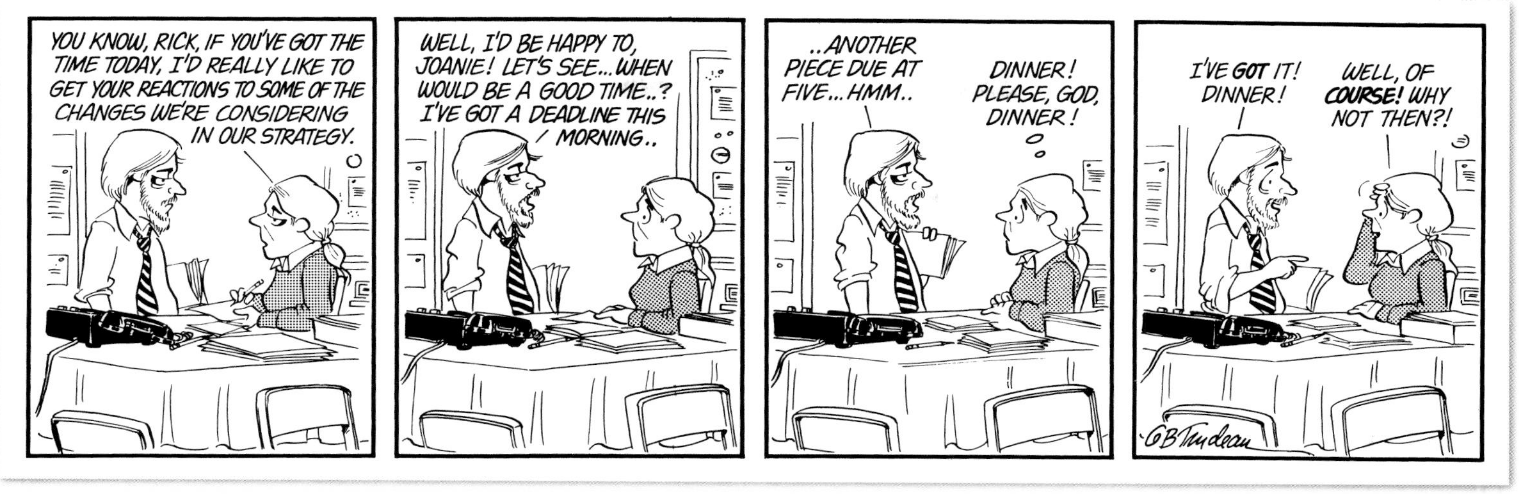
YOU KNOW, RICK, IF YOU'VE GOT THE TIME TODAY, I'D REALLY LIKE TO GET YOUR REACTIONS TO SOME OF THE CHANGES WE'RE CONSIDERING IN OUR STRATEGY.
WELL, I'D BE HAPPY TO, JOANIE! LET'S SEE... WHEN WOULD BE A GOOD TIME..? I'VE GOT A DEADLINE THIS MORNING..
..ANOTHER PIECE DUE AT FIVE... HMM..
DINNER! PLEASE, GOD, DINNER!
I'VE GOT IT! DINNER!
WELL, OF COURSE! WHY NOT THEN?!
GBTrudeau

10/21/76

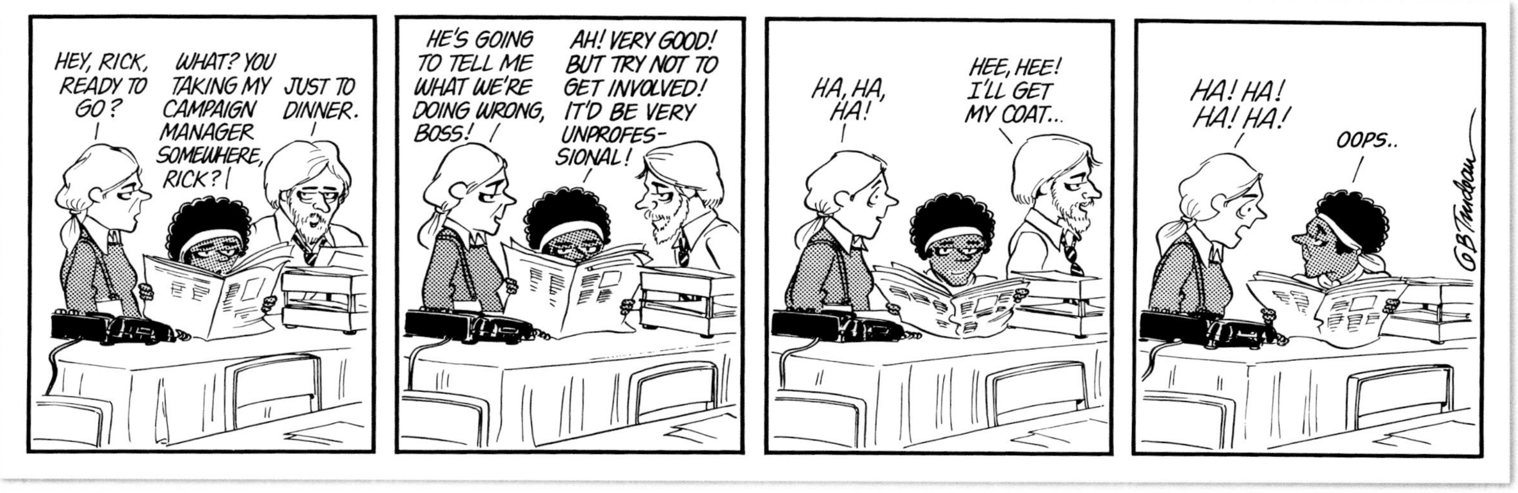
HEY, RICK, READY TO GO?
WHAT? YOU TAKING MY CAMPAIGN MANAGER SOMEWHERE, RICK?
JUST TO DINNER.
HE'S GOING TO TELL ME WHAT WE'RE DOING WRONG, BOSS!
AH! VERY GOOD! BUT TRY NOT TO GET INVOLVED! IT'D BE VERY UNPROFESSIONAL!
HA, HA, HA!
HEE, HEE! I'LL GET MY COAT...
HA! HA! HA! HA!
OOPS..
GBTrudeau

10/22/76

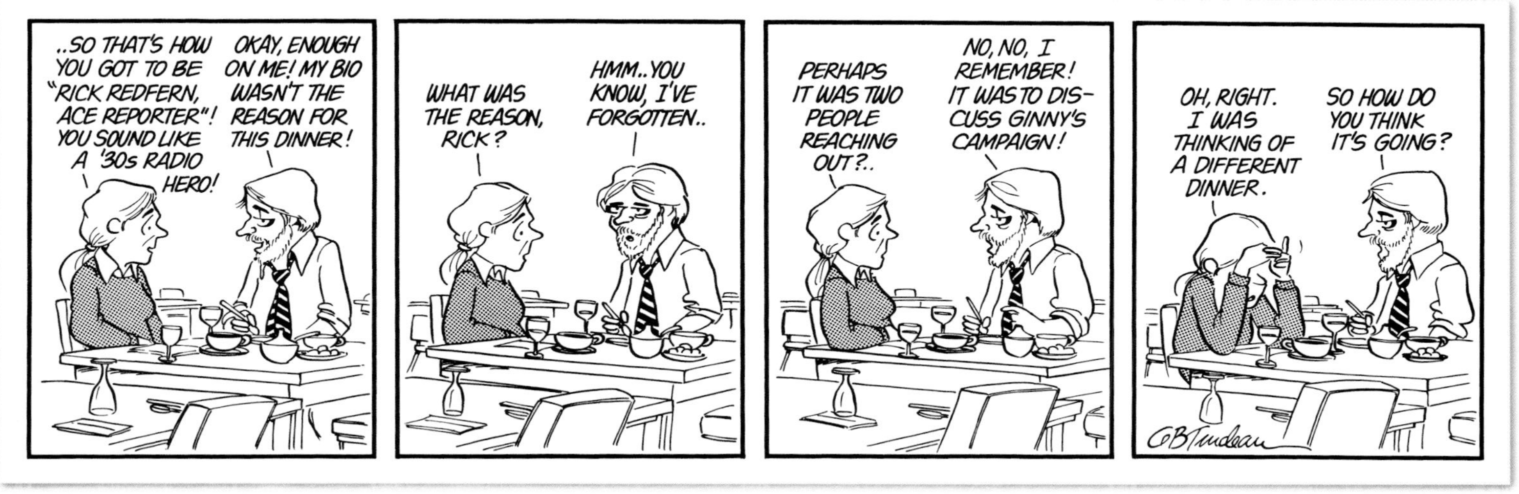
..SO THAT'S HOW YOU GOT TO BE "RICK REDFERN, ACE REPORTER"! YOU SOUND LIKE A '30s RADIO HERO!
OKAY, ENOUGH ON ME! MY BIO WASN'T THE REASON FOR THIS DINNER!
WHAT WAS THE REASON, RICK?
HMM.. YOU KNOW, I'VE FORGOTTEN..
PERHAPS IT WAS TWO PEOPLE REACHING OUT?..
NO, NO, I REMEMBER! IT WAS TO DISCUSS GINNY'S CAMPAIGN!
OH, RIGHT. I WAS THINKING OF A DIFFERENT DINNER.
SO HOW DO YOU THINK IT'S GOING?
GBTrudeau

10/23/76

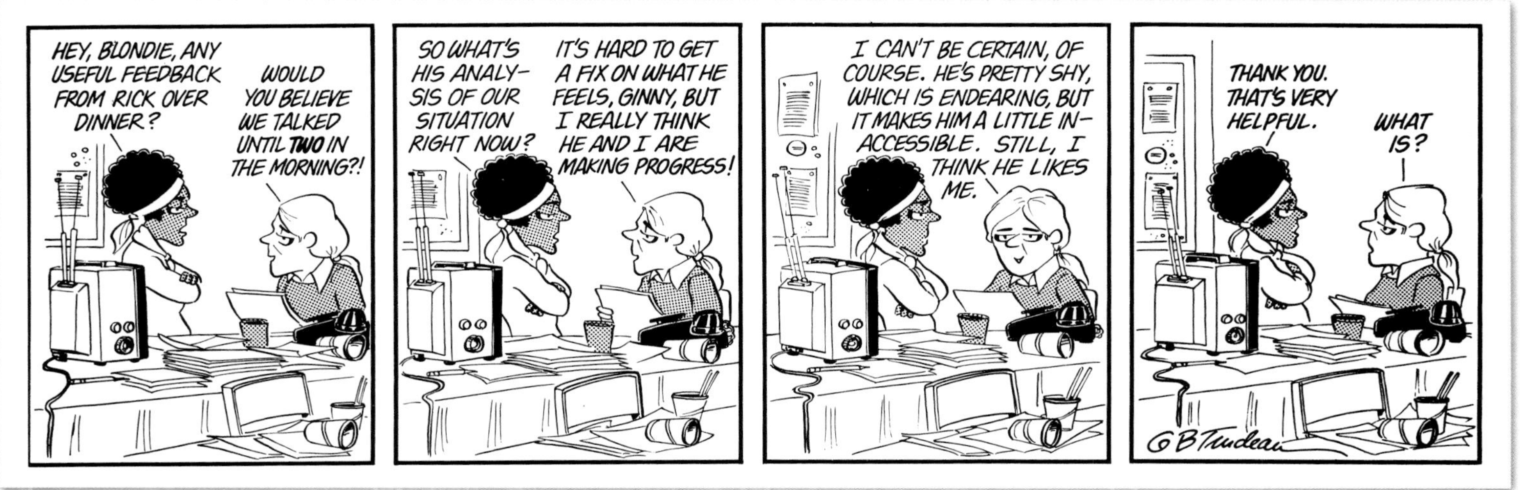
HEY, BLONDIE, ANY USEFUL FEEDBACK FROM RICK OVER DINNER?
WOULD YOU BELIEVE WE TALKED UNTIL TWO IN THE MORNING?!
SO WHAT'S HIS ANALYSIS OF OUR SITUATION RIGHT NOW?
IT'S HARD TO GET A FIX ON WHAT HE FEELS, GINNY, BUT I REALLY THINK HE AND I ARE MAKING PROGRESS!
I CAN'T BE CERTAIN, OF COURSE. HE'S PRETTY SHY, WHICH IS ENDEARING, BUT IT MAKES HIM A LITTLE INACCESSIBLE. STILL, I THINK HE LIKES ME.
THANK YOU. THAT'S VERY HELPFUL.
WHAT IS?
GBTrudeau

10/25/76

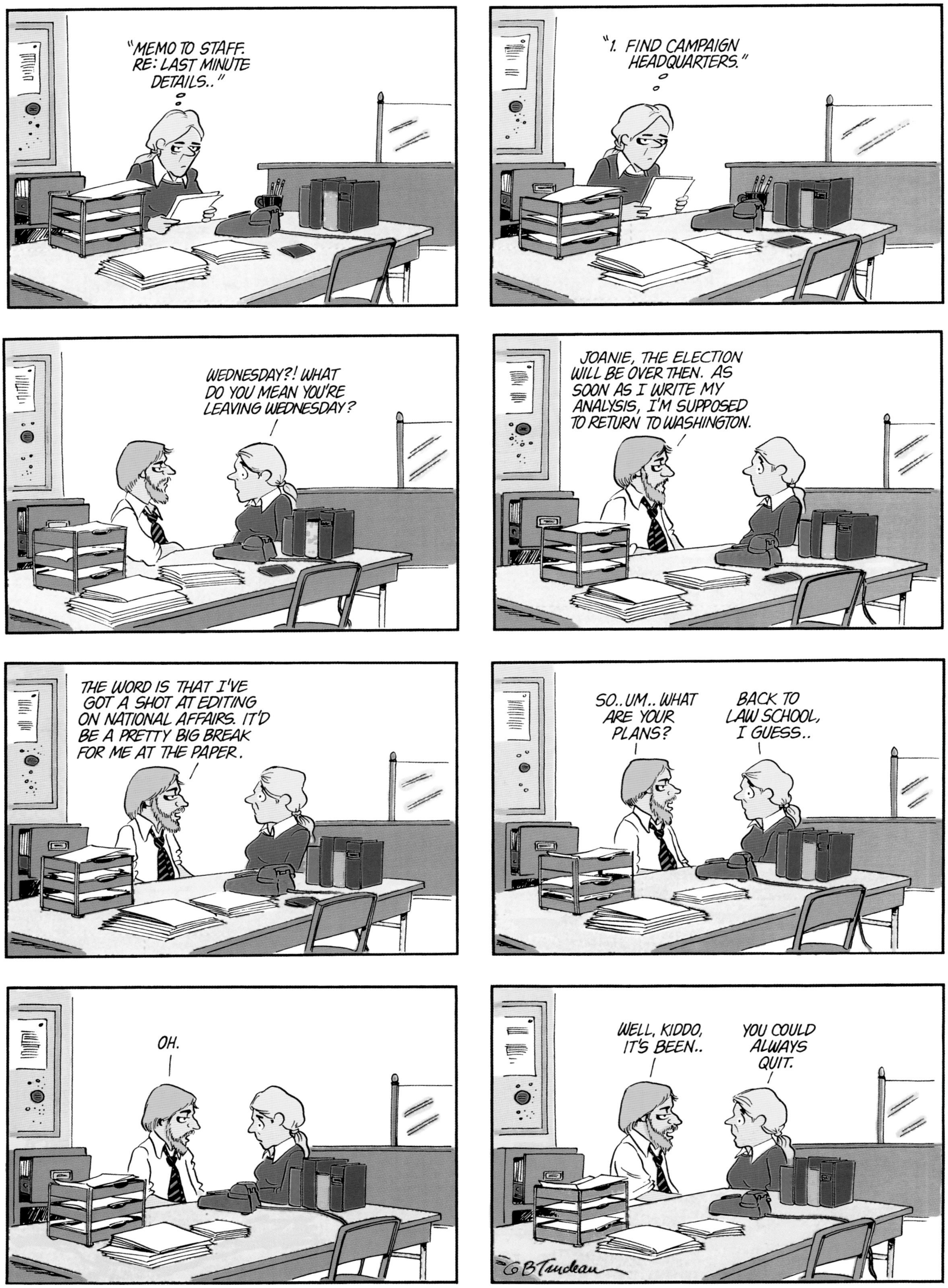
"MEMO TO STAFF. RE: LAST MINUTE DETAILS.."
"1. FIND CAMPAIGN HEADQUARTERS."
WEDNESDAY?! WHAT DO YOU MEAN YOU'RE LEAVING WEDNESDAY?
JOANIE, THE ELECTION WILL BE OVER THEN. AS SOON AS I WRITE MY ANALYSIS, I'M SUPPOSED TO RETURN TO WASHINGTON.
THE WORD IS THAT I'VE GOT A SHOT AT EDITING ON NATIONAL AFFAIRS. IT'D BE A PRETTY BIG BREAK FOR ME AT THE PAPER.
SO.. UM.. WHAT ARE YOUR PLANS?
BACK TO LAW SCHOOL, I GUESS..
OH.
WELL, KIDDO, IT'S BEEN..
YOU COULD ALWAYS QUIT.
G B Trudeau

10/31/76

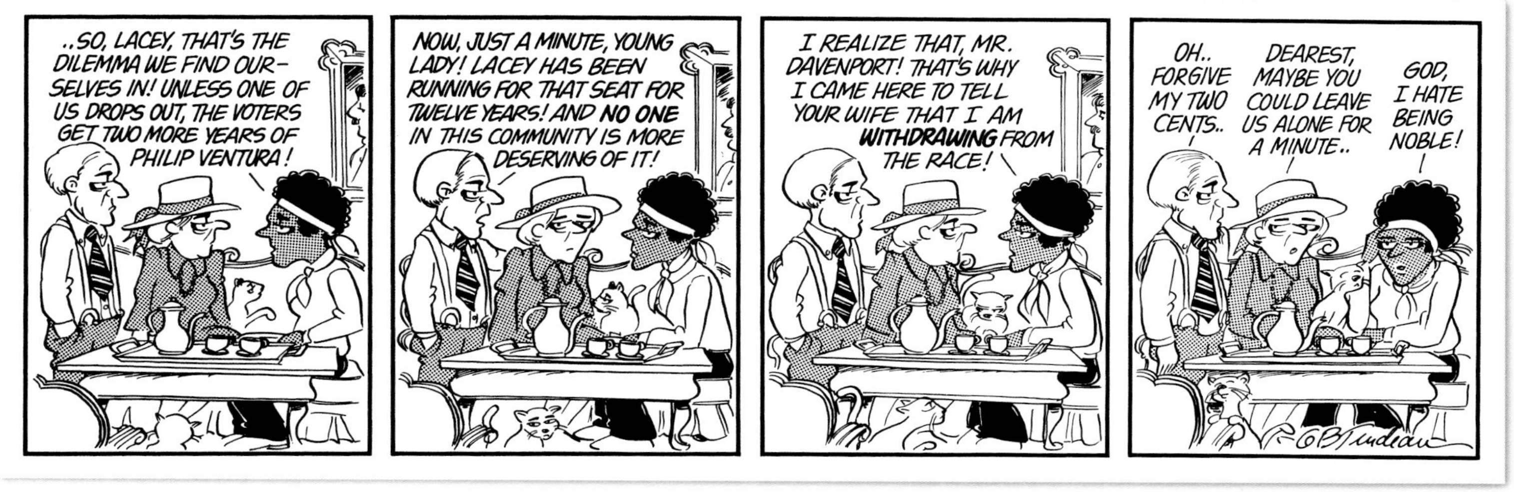
..SO, LACEY, THAT'S THE DILEMMA WE FIND OURSELVES IN! UNLESS ONE OF US DROPS OUT, THE VOTERS GET TWO MORE YEARS OF PHILIP VENTURA!
NOW, JUST A MINUTE, YOUNG LADY! LACEY HAS BEEN RUNNING FOR THAT SEAT FOR TWELVE YEARS! AND NO ONE IN THIS COMMUNITY IS MORE DESERVING OF IT!
I REALIZE THAT, MR. DAVENPORT! THAT'S WHY I CAME HERE TO TELL YOUR WIFE THAT I AM WITHDRAWING FROM THE RACE!
OH.. FORGIVE MY TWO CENTS..
DEAREST, MAYBE YOU COULD LEAVE US ALONE FOR A MINUTE..
GOD, I HATE BEING NOBLE!

10/30/76

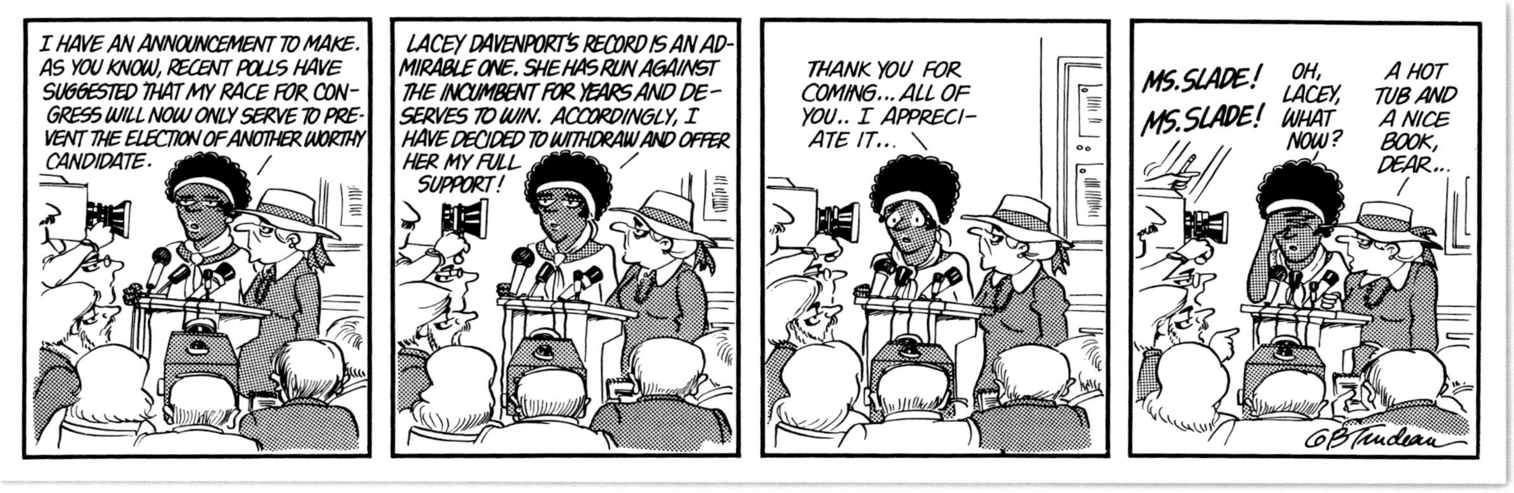
I HAVE AN ANNOUNCEMENT TO MAKE. AS YOU KNOW, RECENT POLLS HAVE SUGGESTED THAT MY RACE FOR CONGRESS WILL NOW ONLY SERVE TO PREVENT THE ELECTION OF ANOTHER WORTHY CANDIDATE.
LACEY DAVENPORT'S RECORD IS AN ADMIRABLE ONE. SHE HAS RUN AGAINST THE INCUMBENT FOR YEARS AND DESERVES TO WIN. ACCORDINGLY, I HAVE DECIDED TO WITHDRAW AND OFFER HER MY FULL SUPPORT!
THANK YOU FOR COMING... ALL OF YOU.. I APPRECIATE IT...
MS. SLADE! MS. SLADE!
OH, LACEY, WHAT NOW?
A HOT TUB AND A NICE BOOK, DEAR...

11/1/76

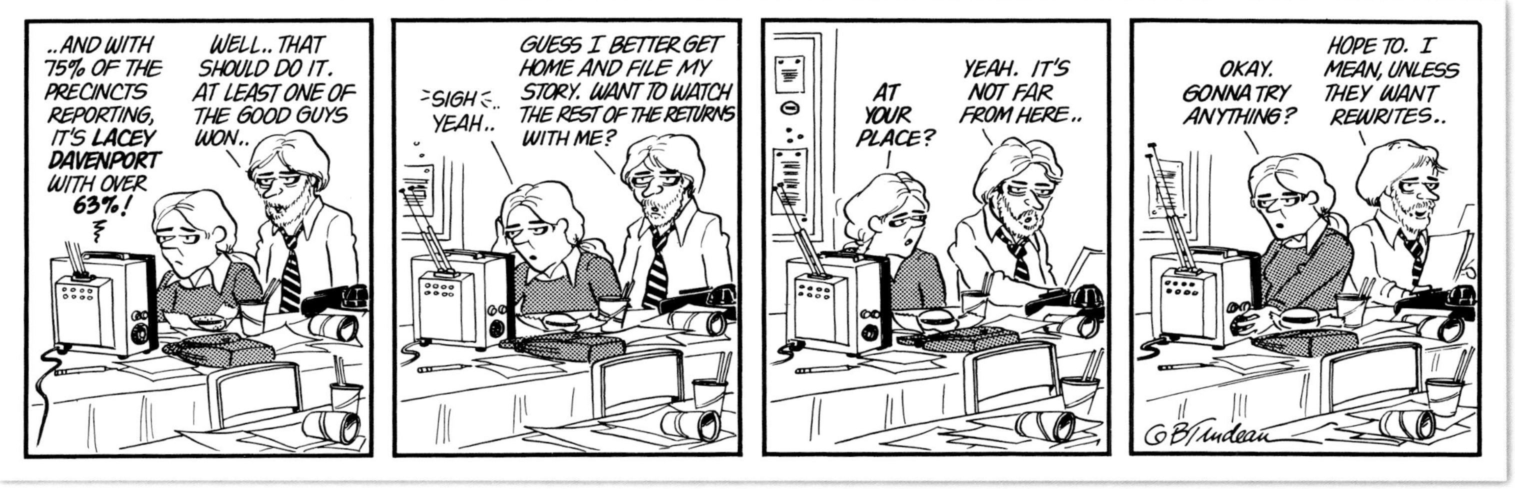
..AND WITH 75% OF THE PRECINCTS REPORTING, IT'S LACEY DAVENPORT WITH OVER 63%!
WELL.. THAT SHOULD DO IT. AT LEAST ONE OF THE GOOD GUYS WON..
SIGH YEAH..
GUESS I BETTER GET HOME AND FILE MY STORY. WANT TO WATCH THE REST OF THE RETURNS WITH ME?
AT YOUR PLACE?
YEAH. IT'S NOT FAR FROM HERE..
OKAY. GONNA TRY ANYTHING?
HOPE TO. I MEAN, UNLESS THEY WANT REWRITES..

11/2/76

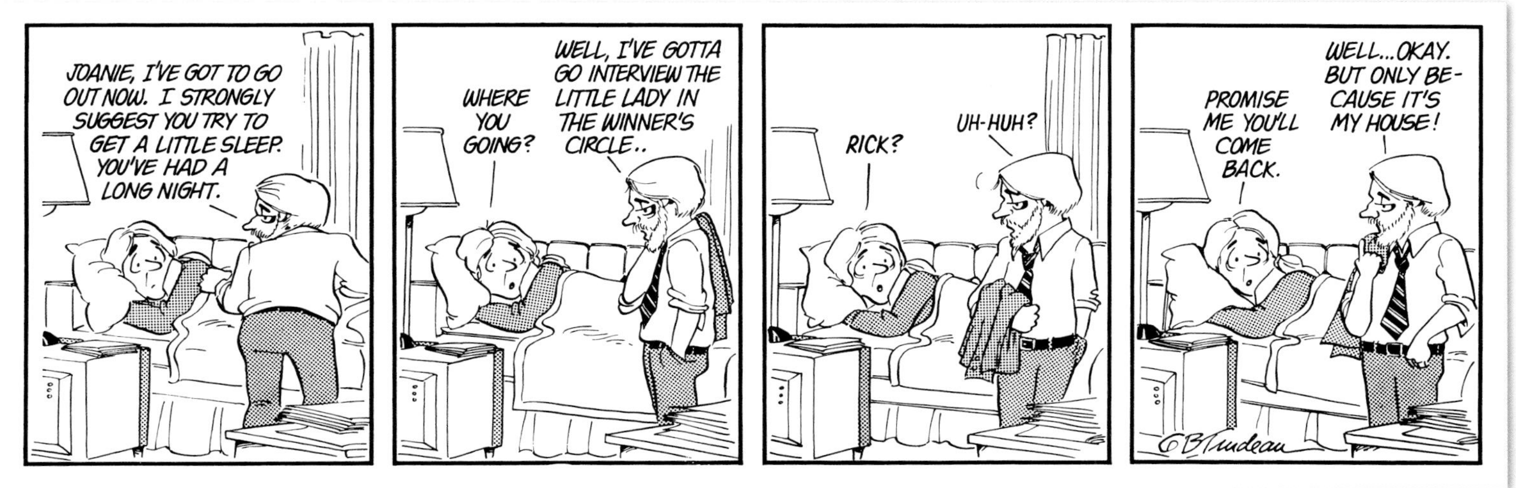
JOANIE, I'VE GOT TO GO OUT NOW. I STRONGLY SUGGEST YOU TRY TO GET A LITTLE SLEEP. YOU'VE HAD A LONG NIGHT.
WHERE YOU GOING?
WELL, I'VE GOTTA GO INTERVIEW THE LITTLE LADY IN THE WINNER'S CIRCLE..
RICK?
UH-HUH?
PROMISE ME YOU'LL COME BACK.
WELL...OKAY. BUT ONLY BECAUSE IT'S MY HOUSE!

11/5/76

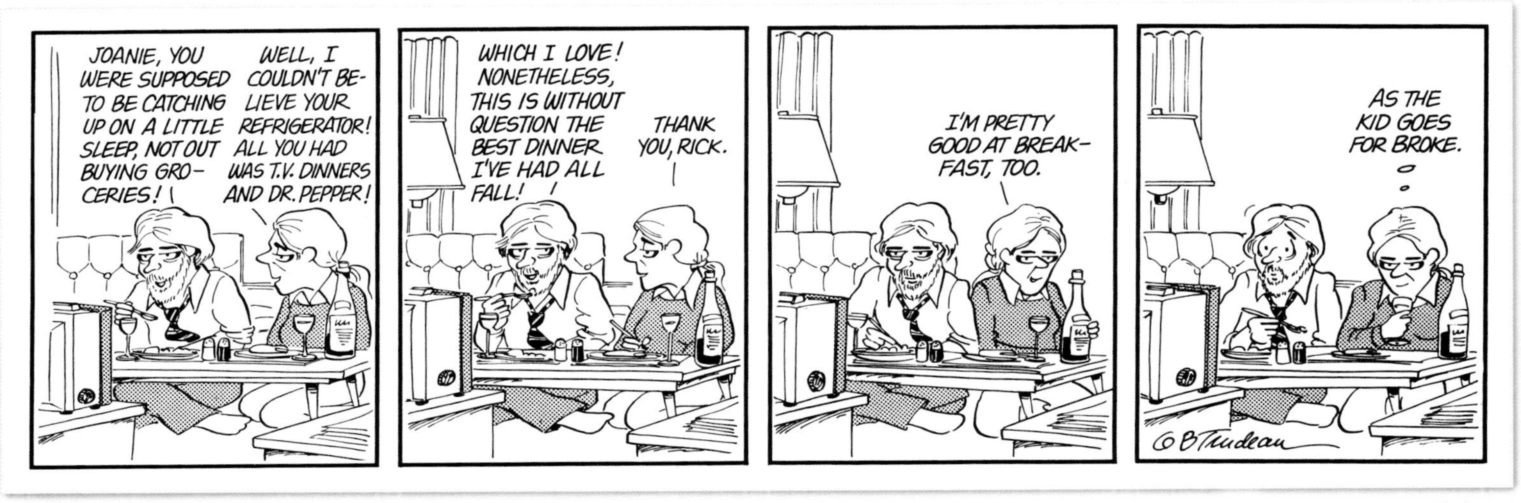
JOANIE, YOU WERE SUPPOSED TO BE CATCHING UP ON A LITTLE SLEEP, NOT OUT BUYING GROCERIES!
WELL, I COULDN'T BELIEVE YOUR REFRIGERATOR! ALL YOU HAD WAS T.V. DINNERS AND DR. PEPPER!
WHICH I LOVE! NONETHELESS, THIS IS WITHOUT QUESTION THE BEST DINNER I'VE HAD ALL FALL!
THANK YOU, RICK.
I'M PRETTY GOOD AT BREAKFAST, TOO.
AS THE KID GOES FOR BROKE.

11/9/76

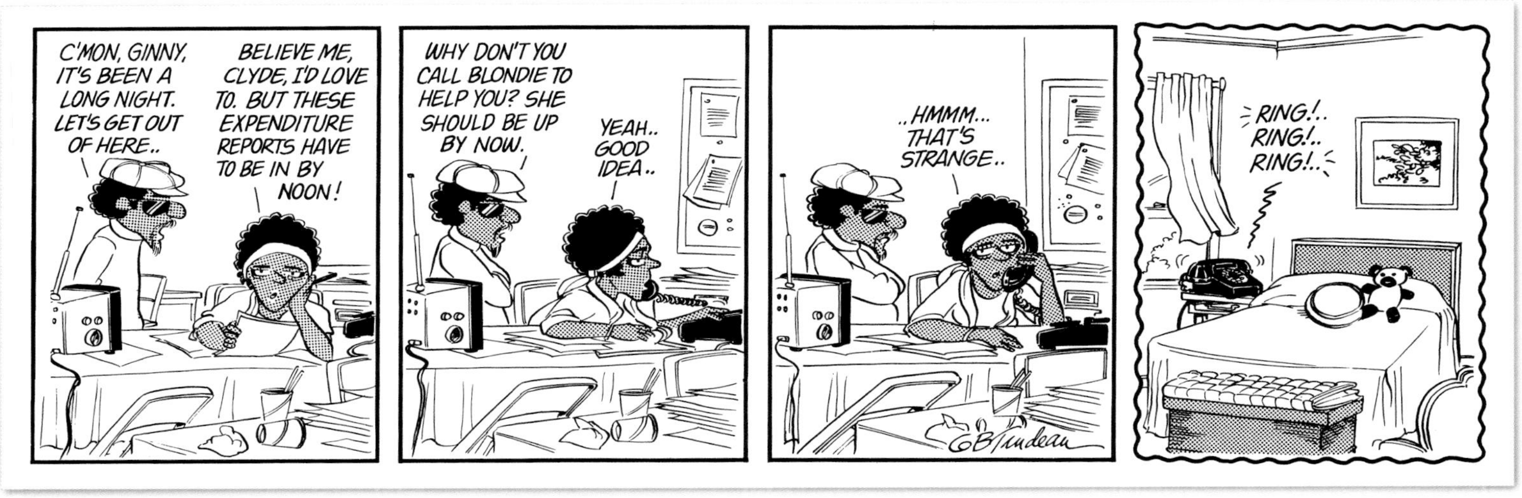
C'MON, GINNY, IT'S BEEN A LONG NIGHT. LET'S GET OUT OF HERE..
BELIEVE ME, CLYDE, I'D LOVE TO. BUT THESE EXPENDITURE REPORTS HAVE TO BE IN BY NOON!
WHY DON'T YOU CALL BLONDIE TO HELP YOU? SHE SHOULD BE UP BY NOW.
YEAH.. GOOD IDEA..
..HMMM.. THAT'S STRANGE..
RING!.. RING!.. RING!..

11/10/76

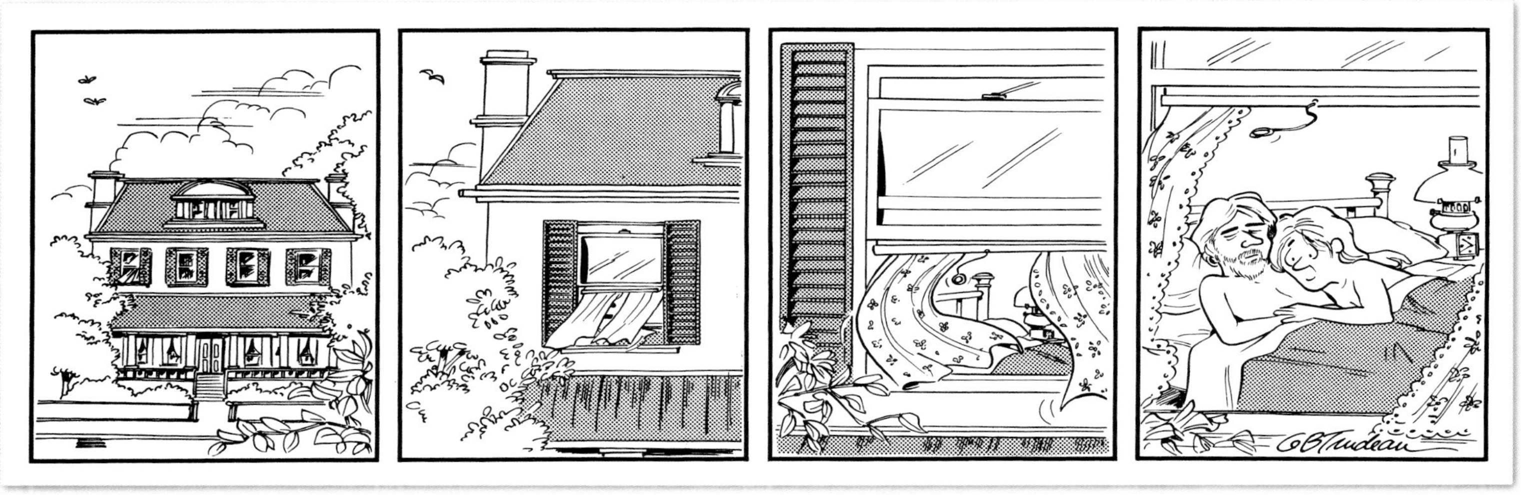

11/13/76

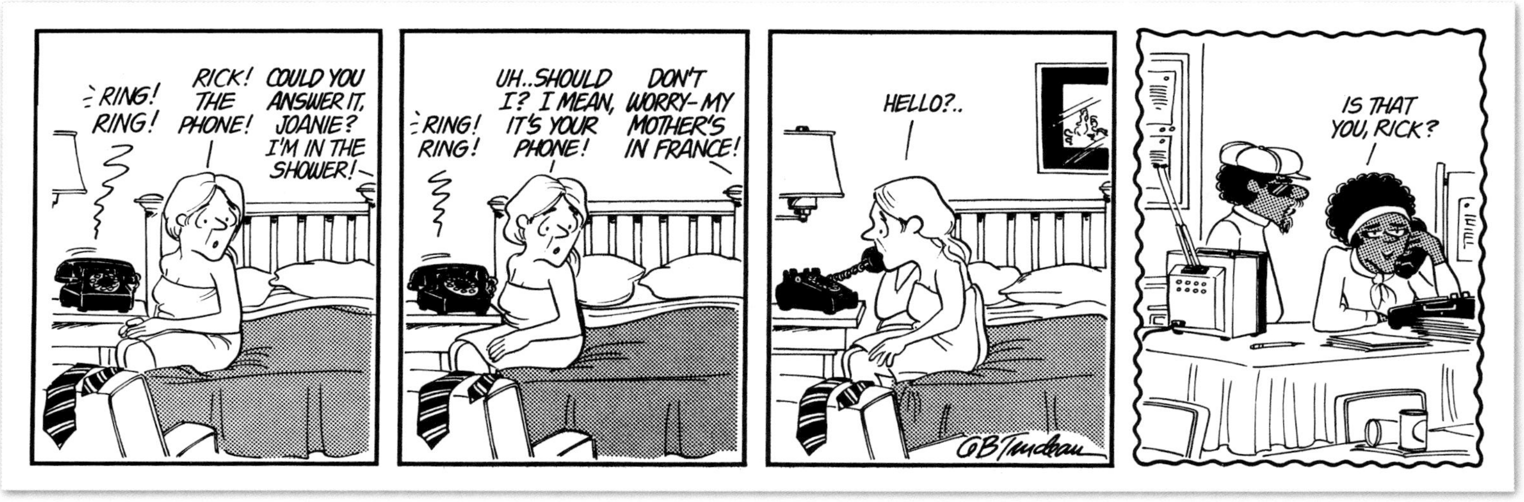
RING! RING!
RICK! THE PHONE!
COULD YOU ANSWER IT, JOANIE? I'M IN THE SHOWER!
RING! RING!
UH..SHOULD I? I MEAN, IT'S YOUR PHONE!
DON'T WORRY- MY MOTHER'S IN FRANCE!
HELLO?..
IS THAT YOU, RICK?

11/16/76

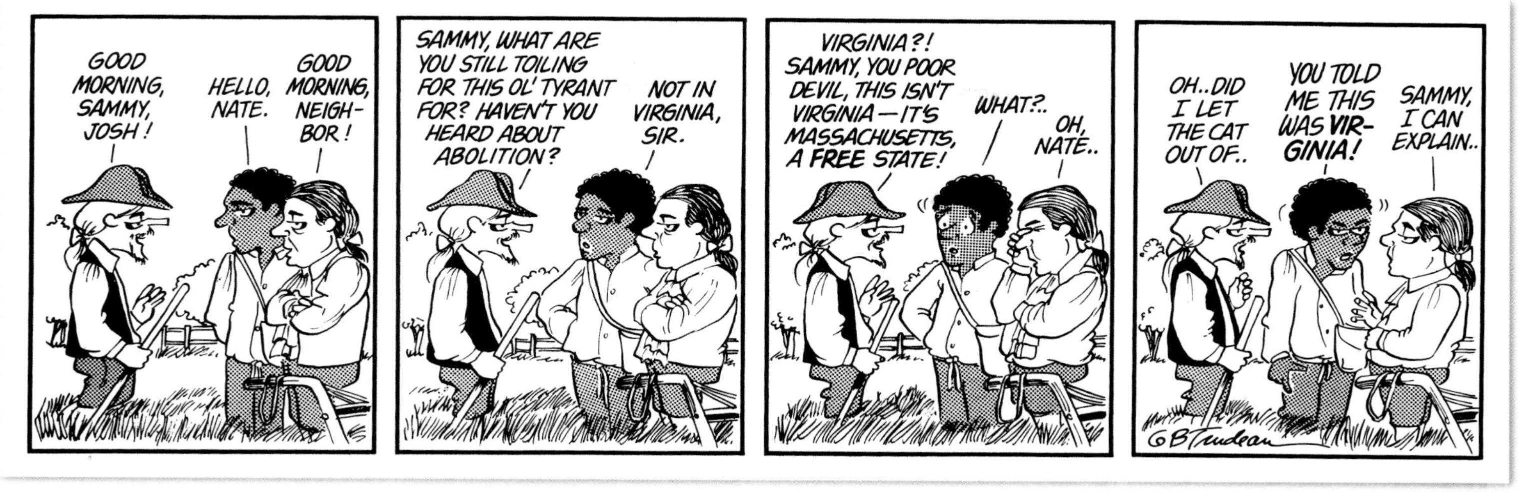
GOOD MORNING, SAMMY, JOSH!
HELLO, NATE.
GOOD MORNING, NEIGH-BOR!
SAMMY, WHAT ARE YOU STILL TOILING FOR THIS OL' TYRANT FOR? HAVEN'T YOU HEARD ABOUT ABOLITION?
NOT IN VIRGINIA, SIR.
VIRGINIA?! SAMMY, YOU POOR DEVIL, THIS ISN'T VIRGINIA—IT'S MASSACHUSETTS, A FREE STATE!
WHAT?..
OH, NATE..
OH..DID I LET THE CAT OUT OF..
YOU TOLD ME THIS WAS VIR-GINIA!
SAMMY, I CAN EXPLAIN..
G B Trudeau

9/28/76

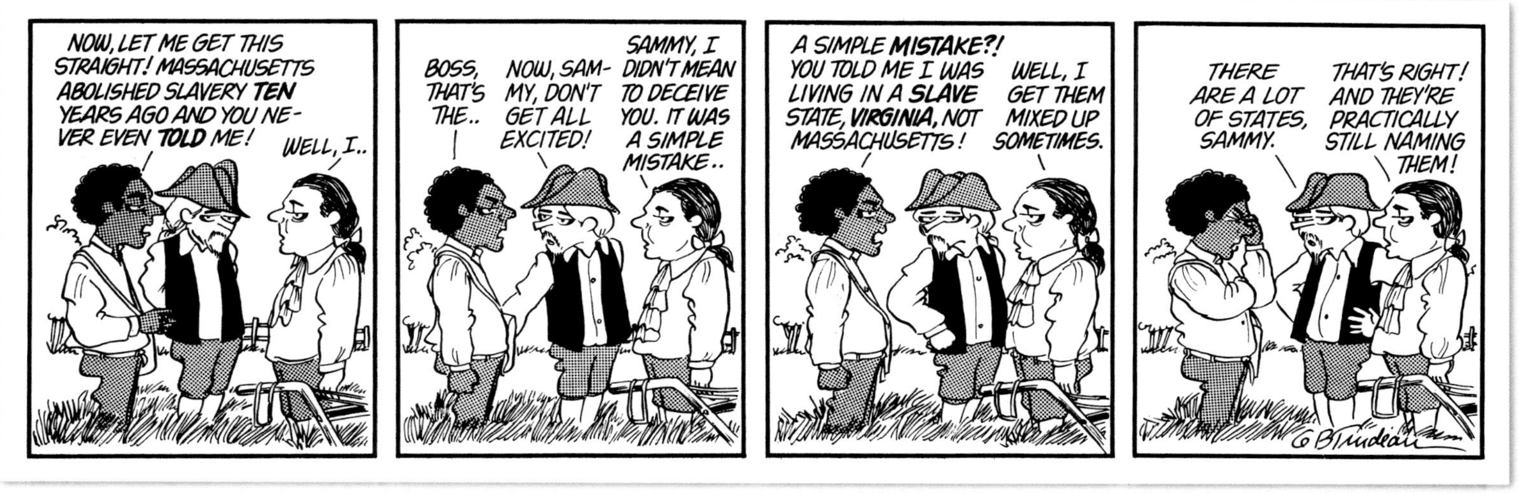
NOW, LET ME GET THIS STRAIGHT! MASSACHUSETTS ABOLISHED SLAVERY TEN YEARS AGO AND YOU NE-VER EVEN TOLD ME!
WELL, I..
BOSS, THAT'S THE..
NOW, SAM-MY, DON'T GET ALL EXCITED!
SAMMY, I DIDN'T MEAN TO DECEIVE YOU. IT WAS A SIMPLE MISTAKE..
A SIMPLE MISTAKE?! YOU TOLD ME I WAS LIVING IN A SLAVE STATE, VIRGINIA, NOT MASSACHUSETTS!
WELL, I GET THEM MIXED UP SOMETIMES.
THERE ARE A LOT OF STATES, SAMMY.
THAT'S RIGHT! AND THEY'RE PRACTICALLY STILL NAMING THEM!
G B Trudeau

9/29/76

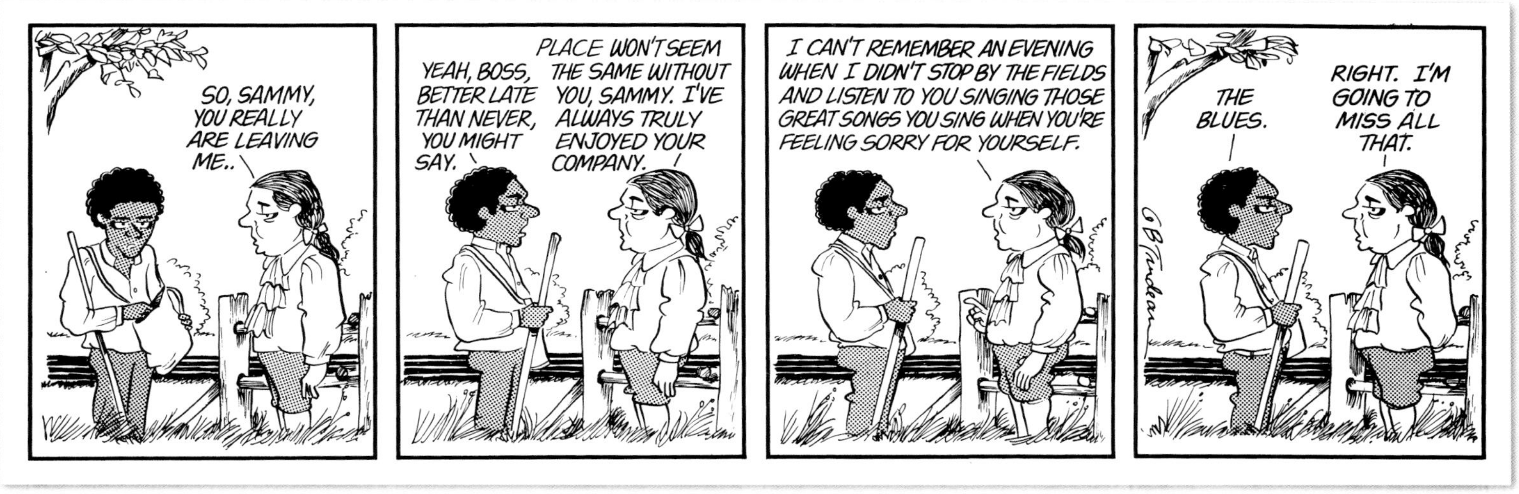
SO, SAMMY, YOU REALLY ARE LEAVING ME..
YEAH, BOSS, BETTER LATE THAN NEVER, YOU MIGHT SAY.
PLACE WON'T SEEM THE SAME WITHOUT YOU, SAMMY. I'VE ALWAYS TRULY ENJOYED YOUR COMPANY.
I CAN'T REMEMBER AN EVENING WHEN I DIDN'T STOP BY THE FIELDS AND LISTEN TO YOU SINGING THOSE GREAT SONGS YOU SING WHEN YOU'RE FEELING SORRY FOR YOURSELF.
THE BLUES.
RIGHT. I'M GOING TO MISS ALL THAT.
G B Trudeau

9/30/76

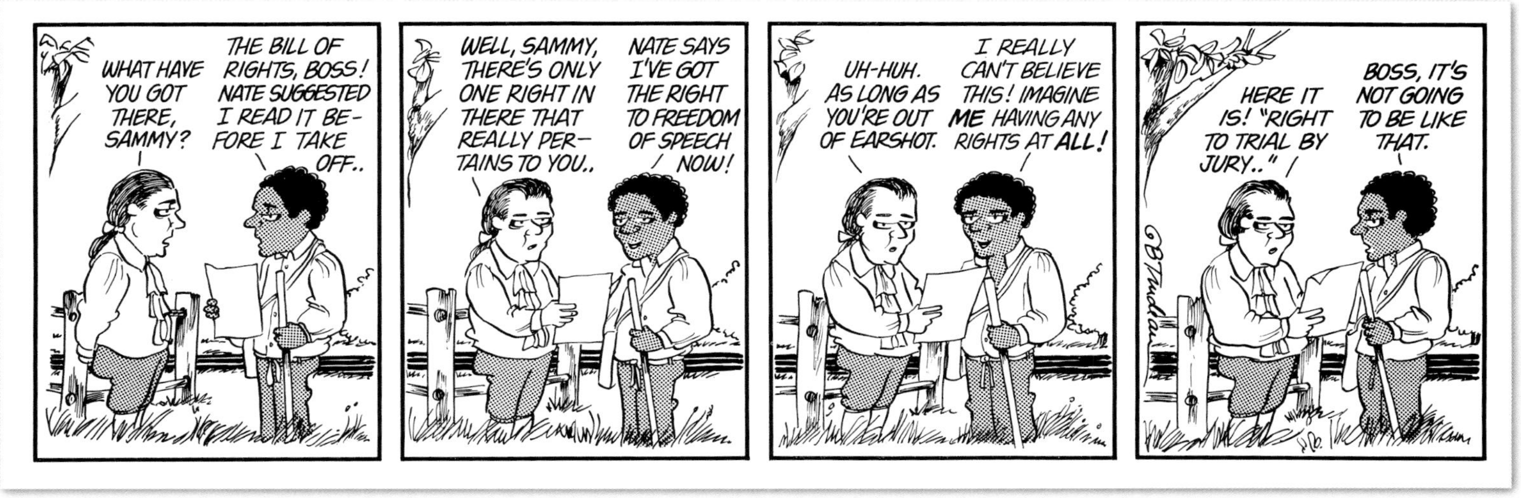
WHAT HAVE YOU GOT THERE, SAMMY?
THE BILL OF RIGHTS, BOSS! NATE SUGGESTED I READ IT BE-FORE I TAKE OFF..
WELL, SAMMY, THERE'S ONLY ONE RIGHT IN THERE THAT REALLY PER-TAINS TO YOU..
NATE SAYS I'VE GOT THE RIGHT TO FREEDOM OF SPEECH NOW!
UH-HUH. AS LONG AS YOU'RE OUT OF EARSHOT.
I REALLY CAN'T BELIEVE THIS! IMAGINE ME HAVING ANY RIGHTS AT ALL!
HERE IT IS! "RIGHT TO TRIAL BY JURY.."
BOSS, IT'S NOT GOING TO BE LIKE THAT.
G B Trudeau

10/1/76

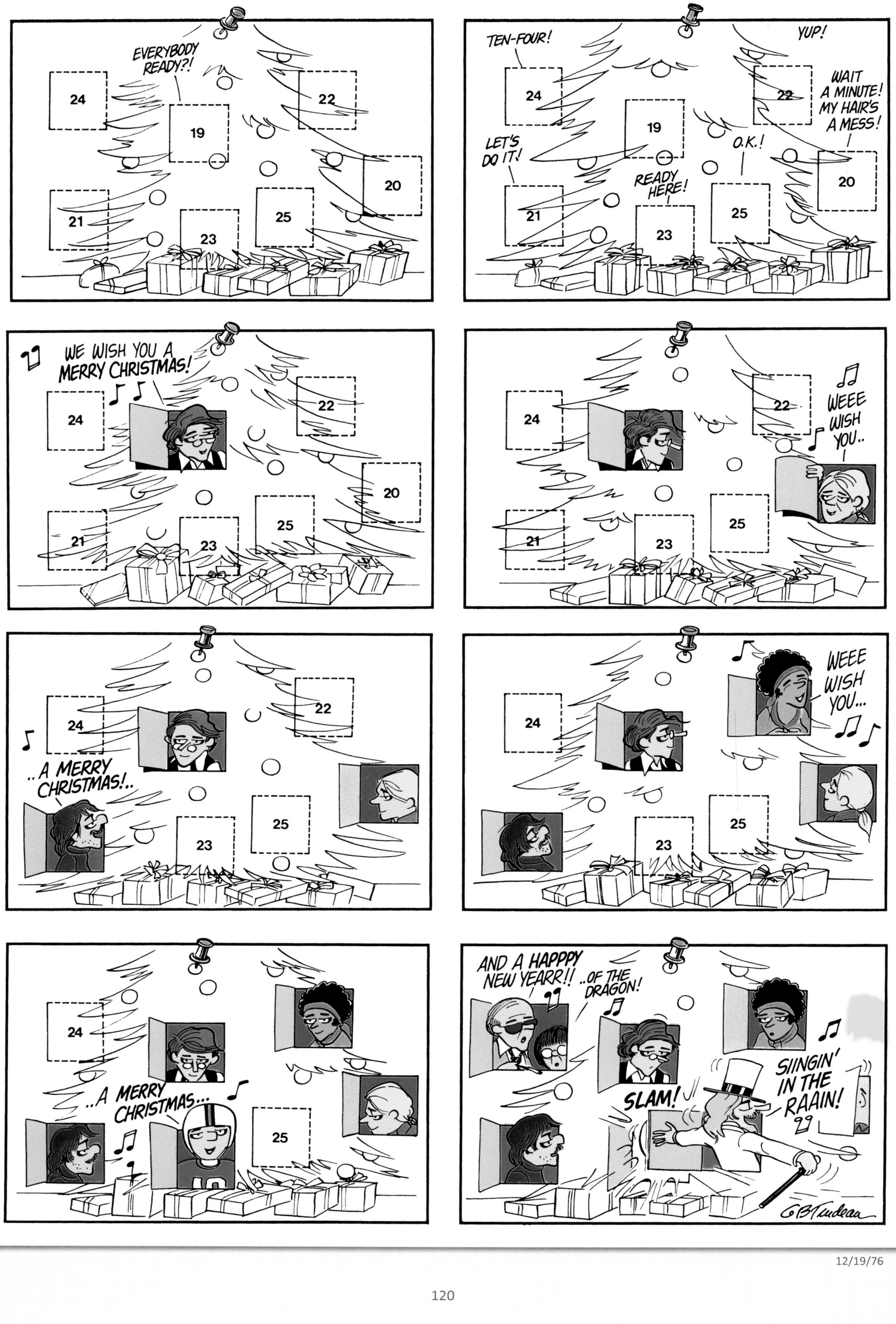
EVERYBODY READY?!
24
19
22
20
21
23
25
TEN-FOUR!
YUP!
WAIT A MINUTE! MY HAIR'S A MESS!
LET'S DO IT!
READY HERE!
O.K.!
WE WISH YOU A MERRY CHRISTMAS!
WEEE WISH YOU..
..A MERRY CHRISTMAS!..
WEEE WISH YOU...
..A MERRY CHRISTMAS...
AND A HAPPPY NEW YEARR!!
..OF THE DRAGON!
SLAM!
SIINGIN' IN THE RAAIN!
GBTrudeau

12/19/76

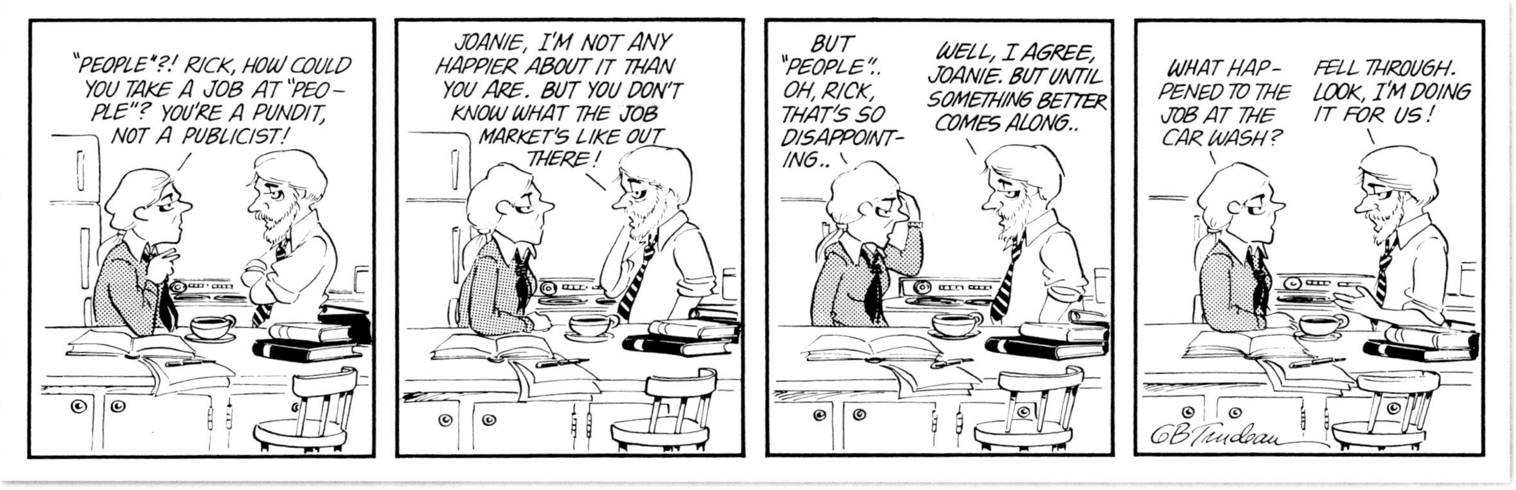
"PEOPLE"?! RICK, HOW COULD YOU TAKE A JOB AT "PEOPLE"? YOU'RE A PUNDIT, NOT A PUBLICIST!
JOANIE, I'M NOT ANY HAPPIER ABOUT IT THAN YOU ARE. BUT YOU DON'T KNOW WHAT THE JOB MARKET'S LIKE OUT THERE!
BUT "PEOPLE".. OH, RICK, THAT'S SO DISAPPOINTING..
WELL, I AGREE, JOANIE. BUT UNTIL SOMETHING BETTER COMES ALONG..
WHAT HAPPENED TO THE JOB AT THE CAR WASH?
FELL THROUGH. LOOK, I'M DOING IT FOR US!
GB Trudeau

1/13/77

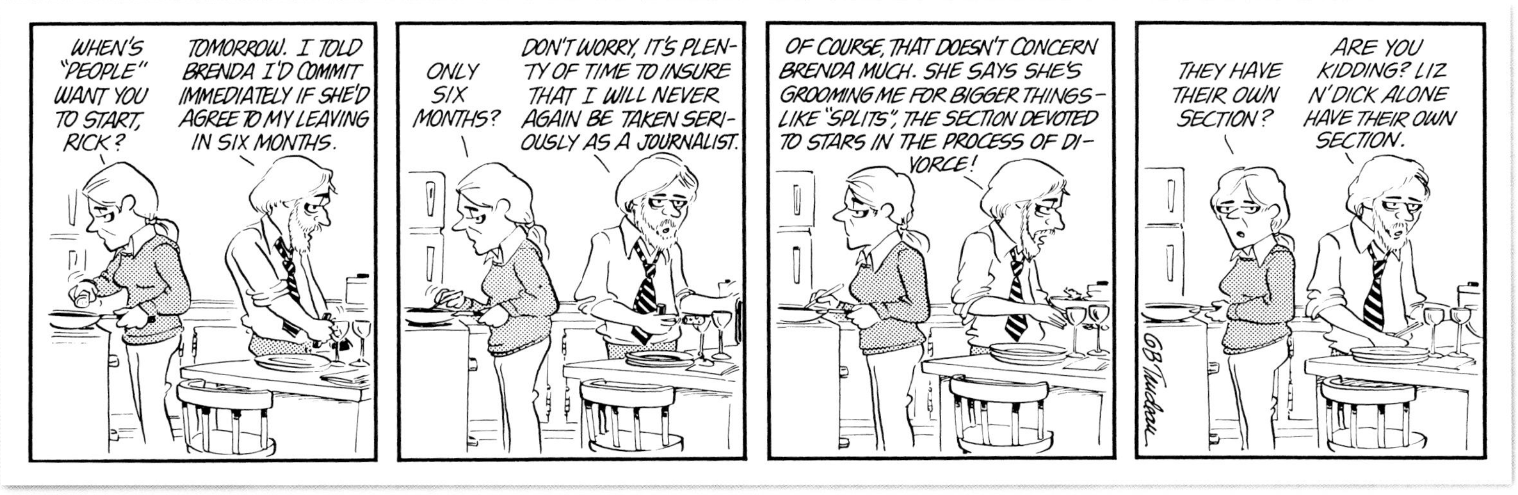
WHEN'S "PEOPLE" WANT YOU TO START, RICK?
TOMORROW. I TOLD BRENDA I'D COMMIT IMMEDIATELY IF SHE'D AGREE TO MY LEAVING IN SIX MONTHS.
ONLY SIX MONTHS?
DON'T WORRY, IT'S PLENTY OF TIME TO INSURE THAT I WILL NEVER AGAIN BE TAKEN SERIOUSLY AS A JOURNALIST.
OF COURSE, THAT DOESN'T CONCERN BRENDA MUCH. SHE SAYS SHE'S GROOMING ME FOR BIGGER THINGS—LIKE "SPLITS", THE SECTION DEVOTED TO STARS IN THE PROCESS OF DIVORCE!
THEY HAVE THEIR OWN SECTION?
ARE YOU KIDDING? LIZ N' DICK ALONE HAVE THEIR OWN SECTION.
GB Trudeau

1/14/77

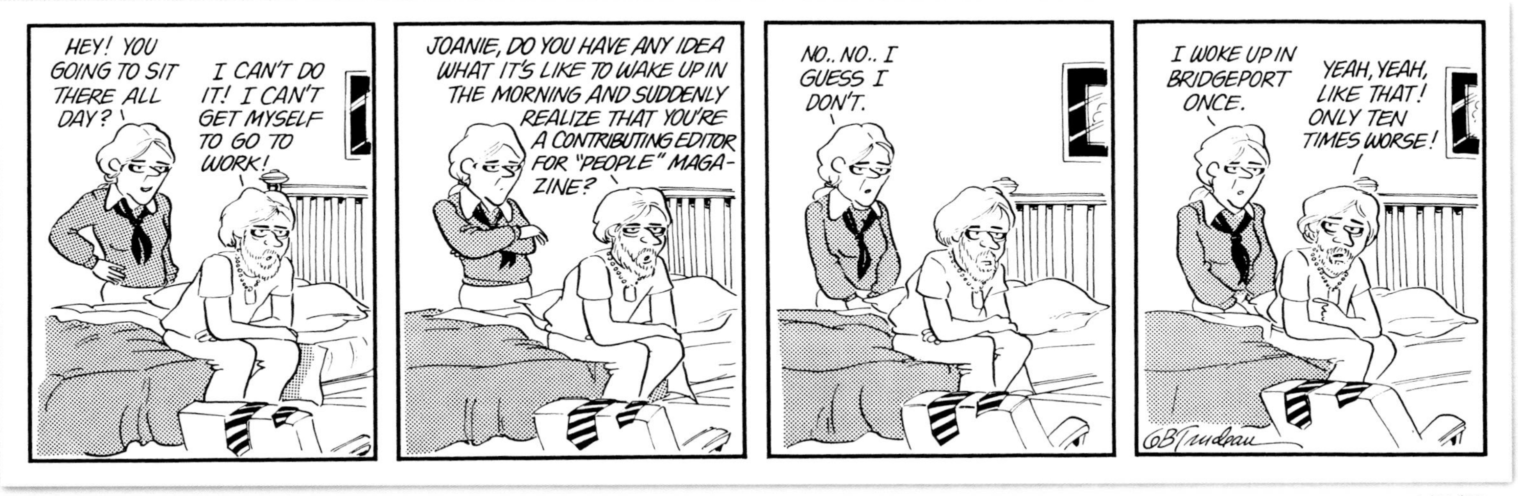
HEY! YOU GOING TO SIT THERE ALL DAY?
I CAN'T DO IT! I CAN'T GET MYSELF TO GO TO WORK!
JOANIE, DO YOU HAVE ANY IDEA WHAT IT'S LIKE TO WAKE UP IN THE MORNING AND SUDDENLY REALIZE THAT YOU'RE A CONTRIBUTING EDITOR FOR "PEOPLE" MAGAZINE?
NO.. NO.. I GUESS I DON'T.
I WOKE UP IN BRIDGEPORT ONCE.
YEAH, YEAH, LIKE THAT! ONLY TEN TIMES WORSE!
GB Trudeau

1/15/77

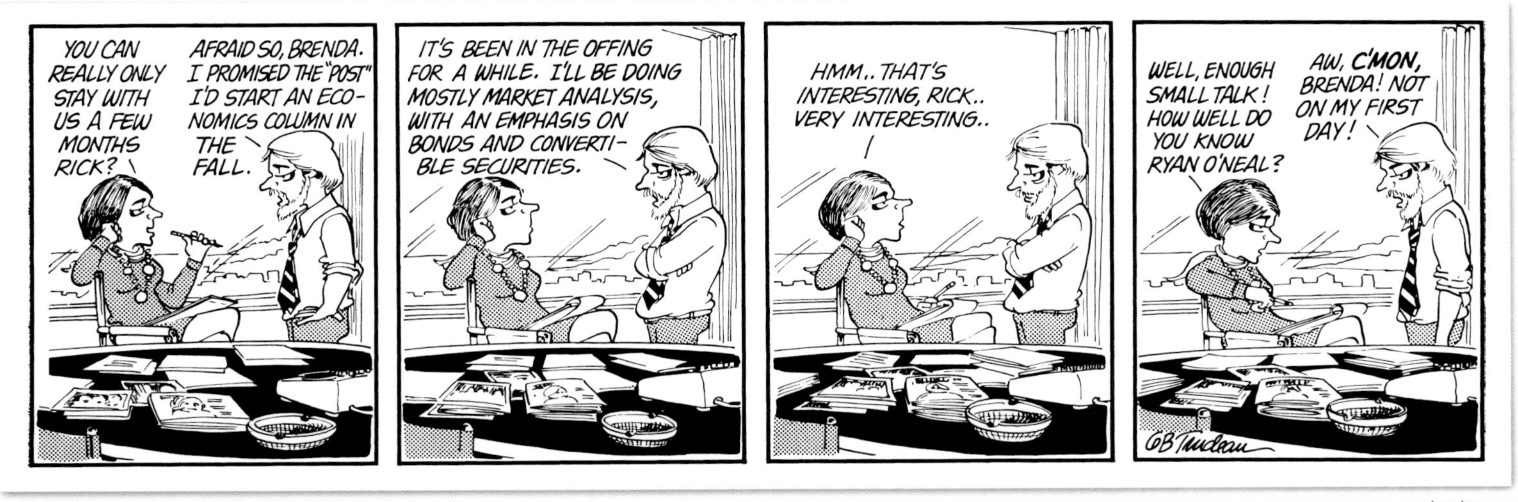
YOU CAN REALLY ONLY STAY WITH US A FEW MONTHS RICK?
AFRAID SO, BRENDA. I PROMISED THE "POST" I'D START AN ECONOMICS COLUMN IN THE FALL.
IT'S BEEN IN THE OFFING FOR A WHILE. I'LL BE DOING MOSTLY MARKET ANALYSIS, WITH AN EMPHASIS ON BONDS AND CONVERTIBLE SECURITIES.
HMM.. THAT'S INTERESTING, RICK.. VERY INTERESTING..
WELL, ENOUGH SMALL TALK! HOW WELL DO YOU KNOW RYAN O'NEAL?
AW, C'MON, BRENDA! NOT ON MY FIRST DAY!
GB Trudeau

1/17/77

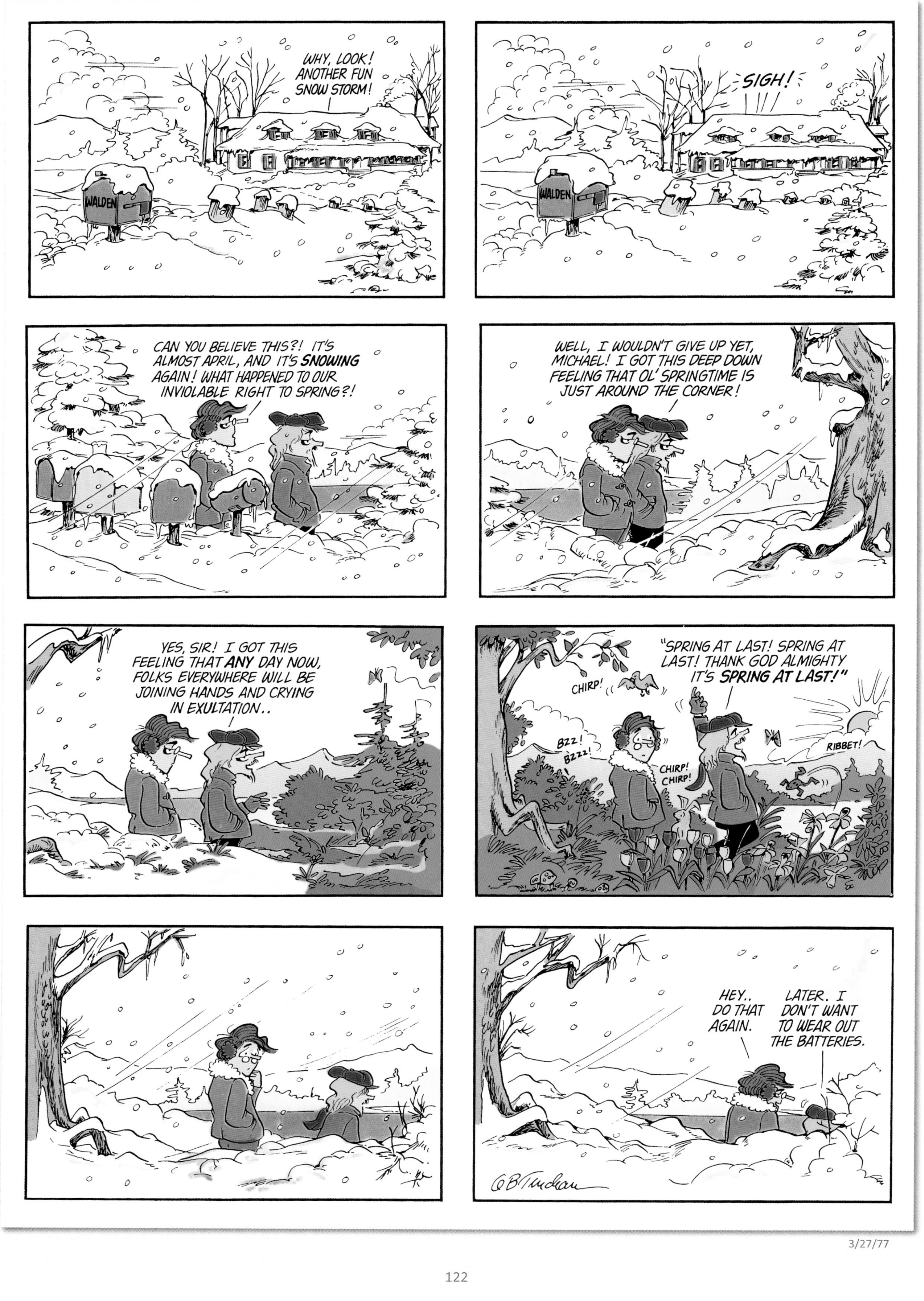

WHY, LOOK! ANOTHER FUN SNOW STORM!
WALDEN
SIGH!
WALDEN
CAN YOU BELIEVE THIS?! IT'S ALMOST APRIL, AND IT'S **SNOWING** AGAIN! WHAT HAPPENED TO OUR INVIOLABLE RIGHT TO SPRING?!
WELL, I WOULDN'T GIVE UP YET, MICHAEL! I GOT THIS DEEP DOWN FEELING THAT OL' SPRINGTIME IS JUST AROUND THE CORNER!
YES, SIR! I GOT THIS FEELING THAT **ANY** DAY NOW, FOLKS EVERYWHERE WILL BE JOINING HANDS AND CRYING IN EXULTATION..
"SPRING AT LAST! SPRING AT LAST! THANK GOD ALMIGHTY IT'S **SPRING AT LAST!**"
CHIRP!
BZZ! BZZZ!
CHIRP! CHIRP!
RIBBET!
HEY.. DO THAT AGAIN.
LATER. I DON'T WANT TO WEAR OUT THE BATTERIES.
GBTrudeau

3/27/77

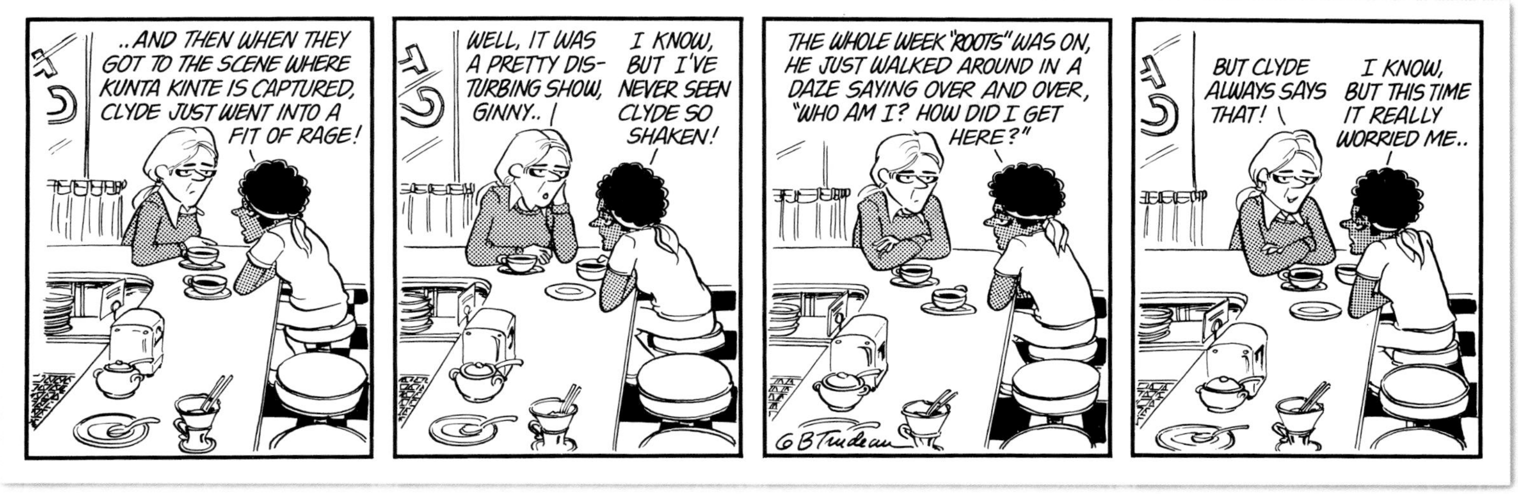
..AND THEN WHEN THEY GOT TO THE SCENE WHERE KUNTA KINTE IS CAPTURED, CLYDE JUST WENT INTO A FIT OF RAGE!
WELL, IT WAS A PRETTY DISTURBING SHOW, GINNY..
I KNOW, BUT I'VE NEVER SEEN CLYDE SO SHAKEN!
THE WHOLE WEEK "ROOTS" WAS ON, HE JUST WALKED AROUND IN A DAZE SAYING OVER AND OVER, "WHO AM I? HOW DID I GET HERE?"
BUT CLYDE ALWAYS SAYS THAT!
I KNOW, BUT THIS TIME IT REALLY WORRIED ME..

3/7/77

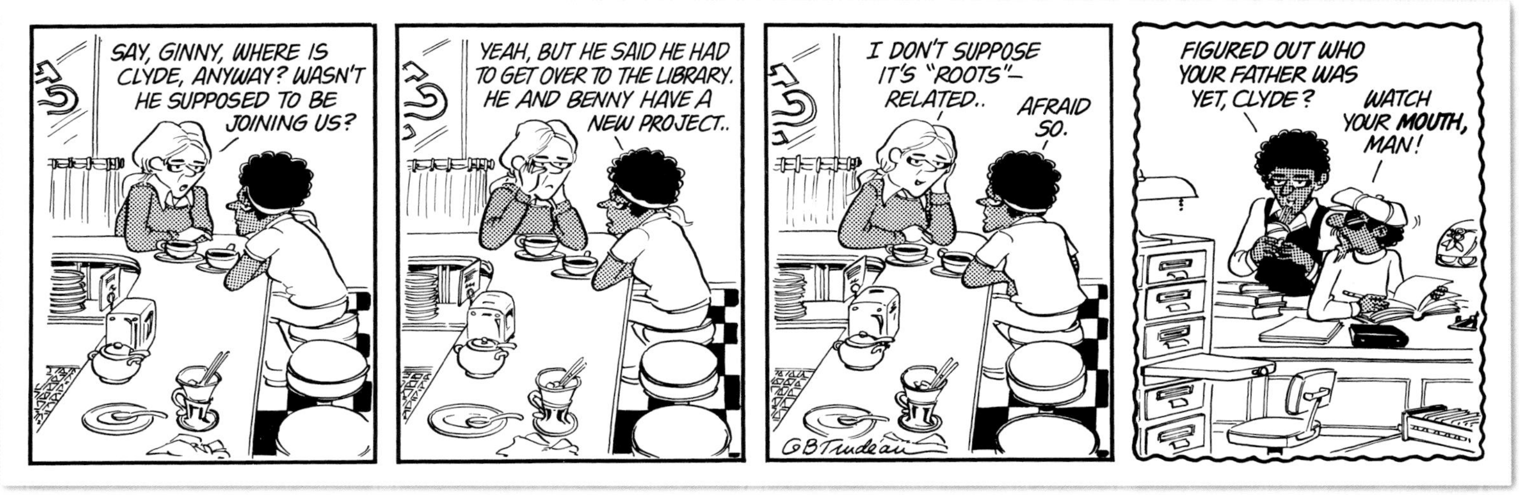
SAY, GINNY, WHERE IS CLYDE, ANYWAY? WASN'T HE SUPPOSED TO BE JOINING US?
YEAH, BUT HE SAID HE HAD TO GET OVER TO THE LIBRARY. HE AND BENNY HAVE A NEW PROJECT..
I DON'T SUPPOSE IT'S "ROOTS"-RELATED..
AFRAID SO.
FIGURED OUT WHO YOUR FATHER WAS YET, CLYDE?
WATCH YOUR MOUTH, MAN!

3/8/77

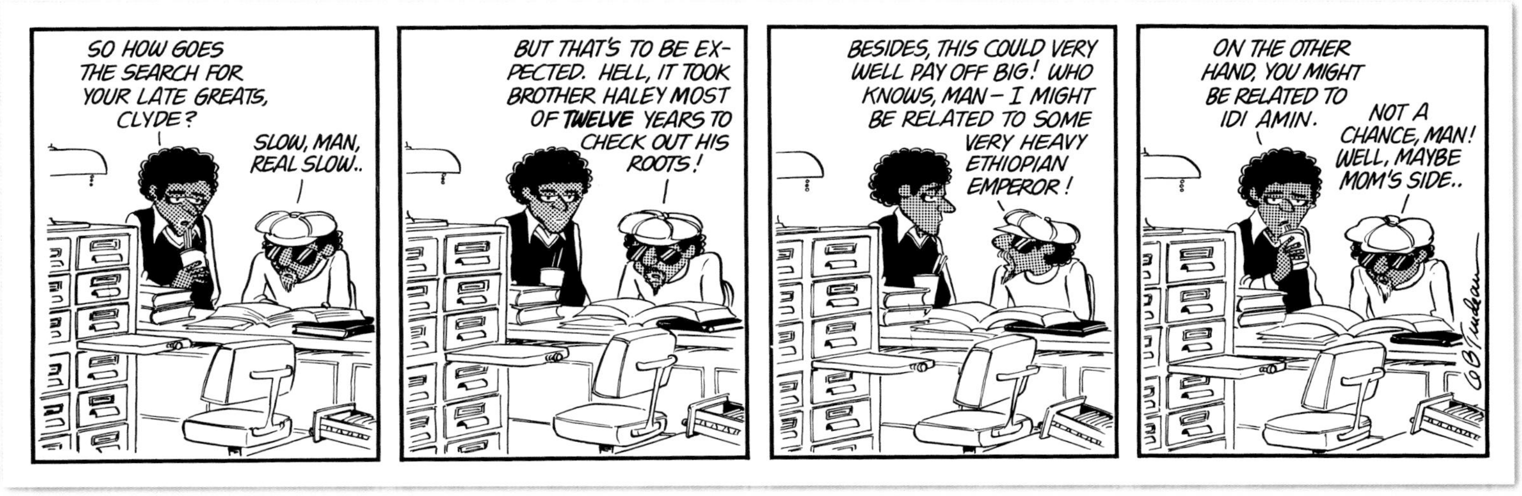
SO HOW GOES THE SEARCH FOR YOUR LATE GREATS, CLYDE?
SLOW, MAN, REAL SLOW..
BUT THAT'S TO BE EXPECTED. HELL, IT TOOK BROTHER HALEY MOST OF TWELVE YEARS TO CHECK OUT HIS ROOTS!
BESIDES, THIS COULD VERY WELL PAY OFF BIG! WHO KNOWS, MAN – I MIGHT BE RELATED TO SOME VERY HEAVY ETHIOPIAN EMPEROR!
ON THE OTHER HAND, YOU MIGHT BE RELATED TO IDI AMIN.
NOT A CHANCE, MAN! WELL, MAYBE MOM'S SIDE..

3/9/77

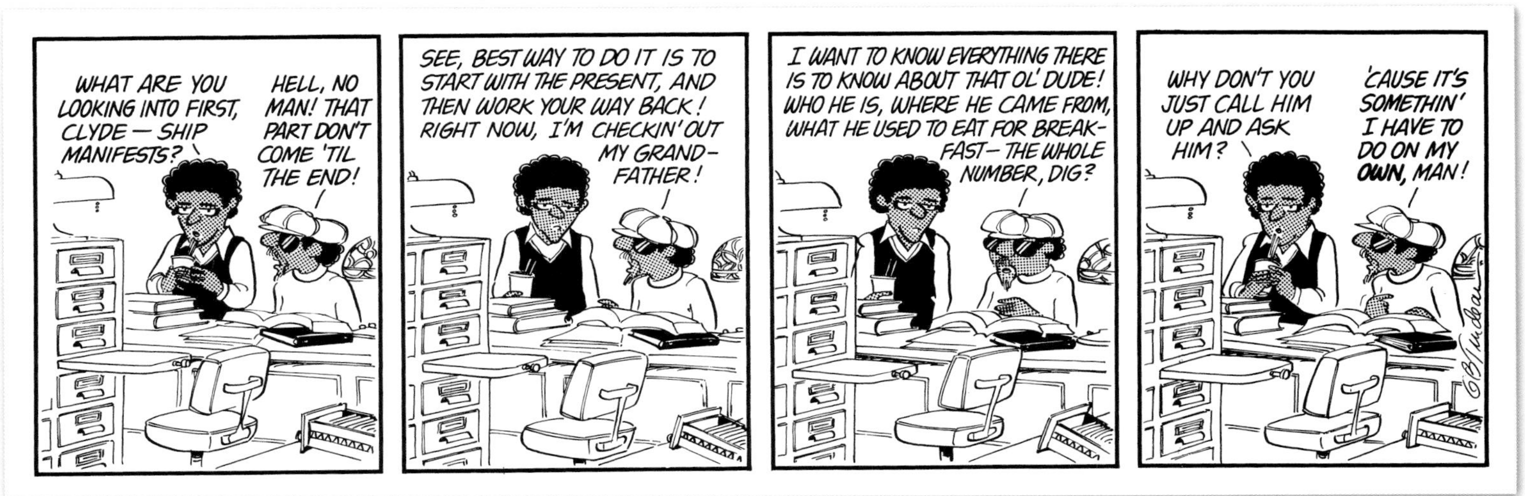
WHAT ARE YOU LOOKING INTO FIRST, CLYDE – SHIP MANIFESTS?
HELL, NO MAN! THAT PART DON'T COME 'TIL THE END!
SEE, BEST WAY TO DO IT IS TO START WITH THE PRESENT, AND THEN WORK YOUR WAY BACK! RIGHT NOW, I'M CHECKIN' OUT MY GRANDFATHER!
I WANT TO KNOW EVERYTHING THERE IS TO KNOW ABOUT THAT OL' DUDE! WHO HE IS, WHERE HE CAME FROM, WHAT HE USED TO EAT FOR BREAKFAST– THE WHOLE NUMBER, DIG?
WHY DON'T YOU JUST CALL HIM UP AND ASK HIM?
'CAUSE IT'S SOMETHIN' I HAVE TO DO ON MY OWN, MAN!

3/10/77

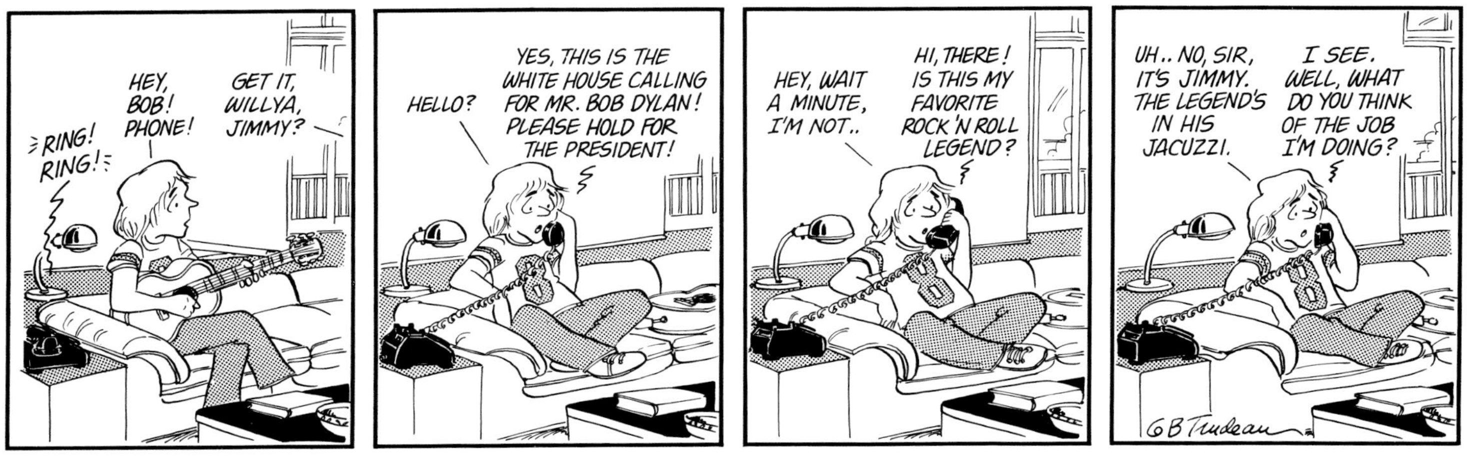
RING! RING!
HEY, BOB! PHONE!
GET IT, WILLYA, JIMMY?
HELLO?
YES, THIS IS THE WHITE HOUSE CALLING FOR MR. BOB DYLAN! PLEASE HOLD FOR THE PRESIDENT!
HEY, WAIT A MINUTE, I'M NOT..
HI, THERE! IS THIS MY FAVORITE ROCK 'N ROLL LEGEND?
UH.. NO, SIR, IT'S JIMMY. THE LEGEND'S IN HIS JACUZZI.
I SEE. WELL, WHAT DO YOU THINK OF THE JOB I'M DOING?
GB Trudeau

2/15/77

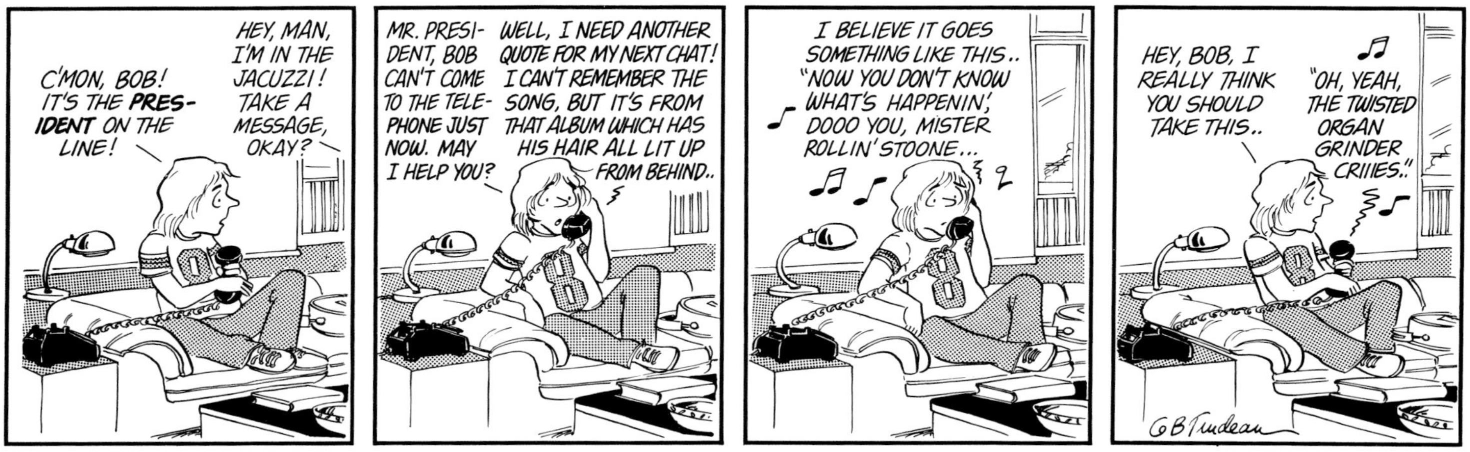
C'MON, BOB! IT'S THE PRESIDENT ON THE LINE!
HEY, MAN, I'M IN THE JACUZZI! TAKE A MESSAGE, OKAY?
MR. PRESIDENT, BOB CAN'T COME TO THE TELEPHONE JUST NOW. MAY I HELP YOU?
WELL, I NEED ANOTHER QUOTE FOR MY NEXT CHAT! I CAN'T REMEMBER THE SONG, BUT IT'S FROM THAT ALBUM WHICH HAS HIS HAIR ALL LIT UP FROM BEHIND..
I BELIEVE IT GOES SOMETHING LIKE THIS.. "NOW YOU DON'T KNOW WHAT'S HAPPENIN', DOOO YOU, MISTER ROLLIN' STOONE..."
HEY, BOB, I REALLY THINK YOU SHOULD TAKE THIS..
"OH, YEAH, THE TWISTED ORGAN GRINDER CRIIES.."
GB Trudeau

2/16/77

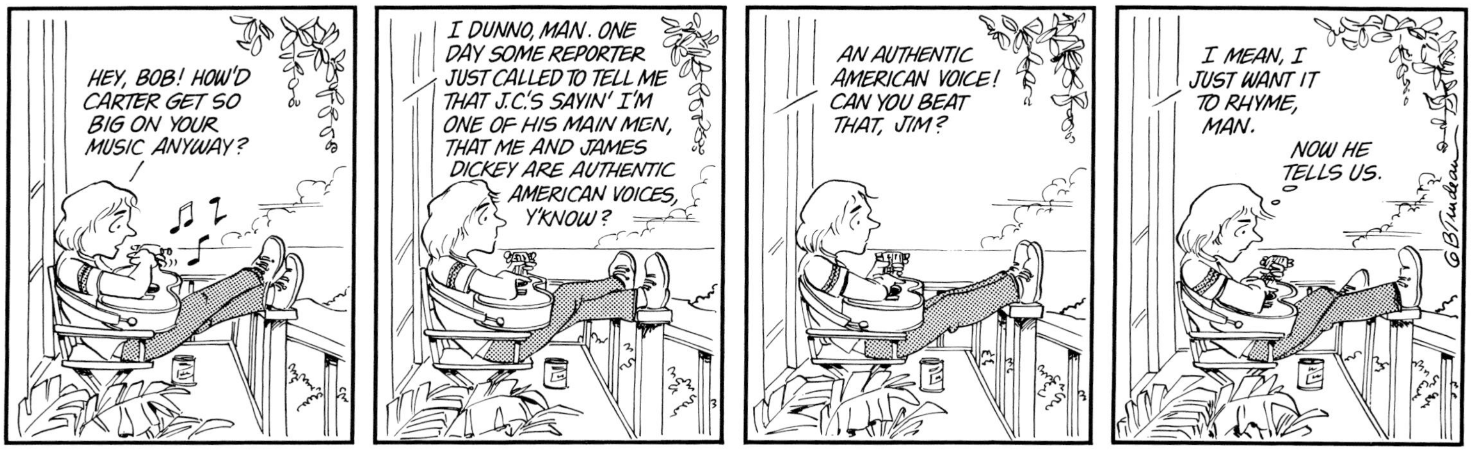
HEY, BOB! HOW'D CARTER GET SO BIG ON YOUR MUSIC ANYWAY?
I DUNNO, MAN. ONE DAY SOME REPORTER JUST CALLED TO TELL ME THAT J.C.'S SAYIN' I'M ONE OF HIS MAIN MEN, THAT ME AND JAMES DICKEY ARE AUTHENTIC AMERICAN VOICES, Y'KNOW?
AN AUTHENTIC AMERICAN VOICE! CAN YOU BEAT THAT, JIM?
I MEAN, I JUST WANT IT TO RHYME, MAN.
NOW HE TELLS US.
GB Trudeau

2/18/77

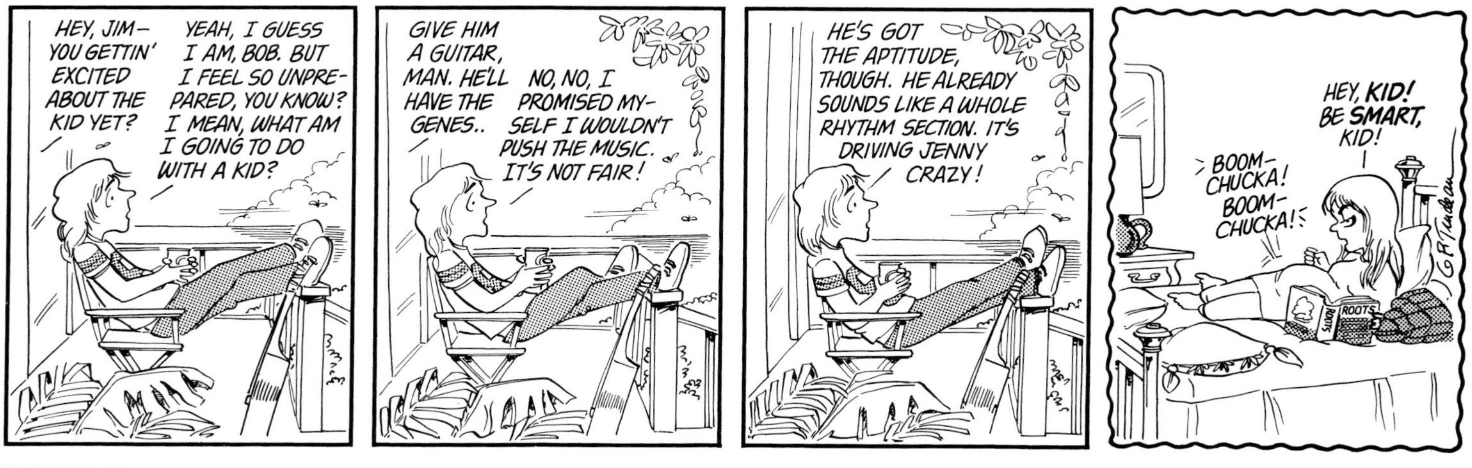
HEY, JIM— YOU GETTIN' EXCITED ABOUT THE KID YET?
YEAH, I GUESS I AM, BOB. BUT I FEEL SO UNPREPARED, YOU KNOW? I MEAN, WHAT AM I GOING TO DO WITH A KID?
GIVE HIM A GUITAR, MAN. HE'LL HAVE THE GENES..
NO, NO, I PROMISED MYSELF I WOULDN'T PUSH THE MUSIC. IT'S NOT FAIR!
HE'S GOT THE APTITUDE, THOUGH. HE ALREADY SOUNDS LIKE A WHOLE RHYTHM SECTION. IT'S DRIVING JENNY CRAZY!
BOOM-CHUCKA! BOOM-CHUCKA!
HEY, KID! BE SMART, KID!
ROOTS
GB Trudeau

2/22/77

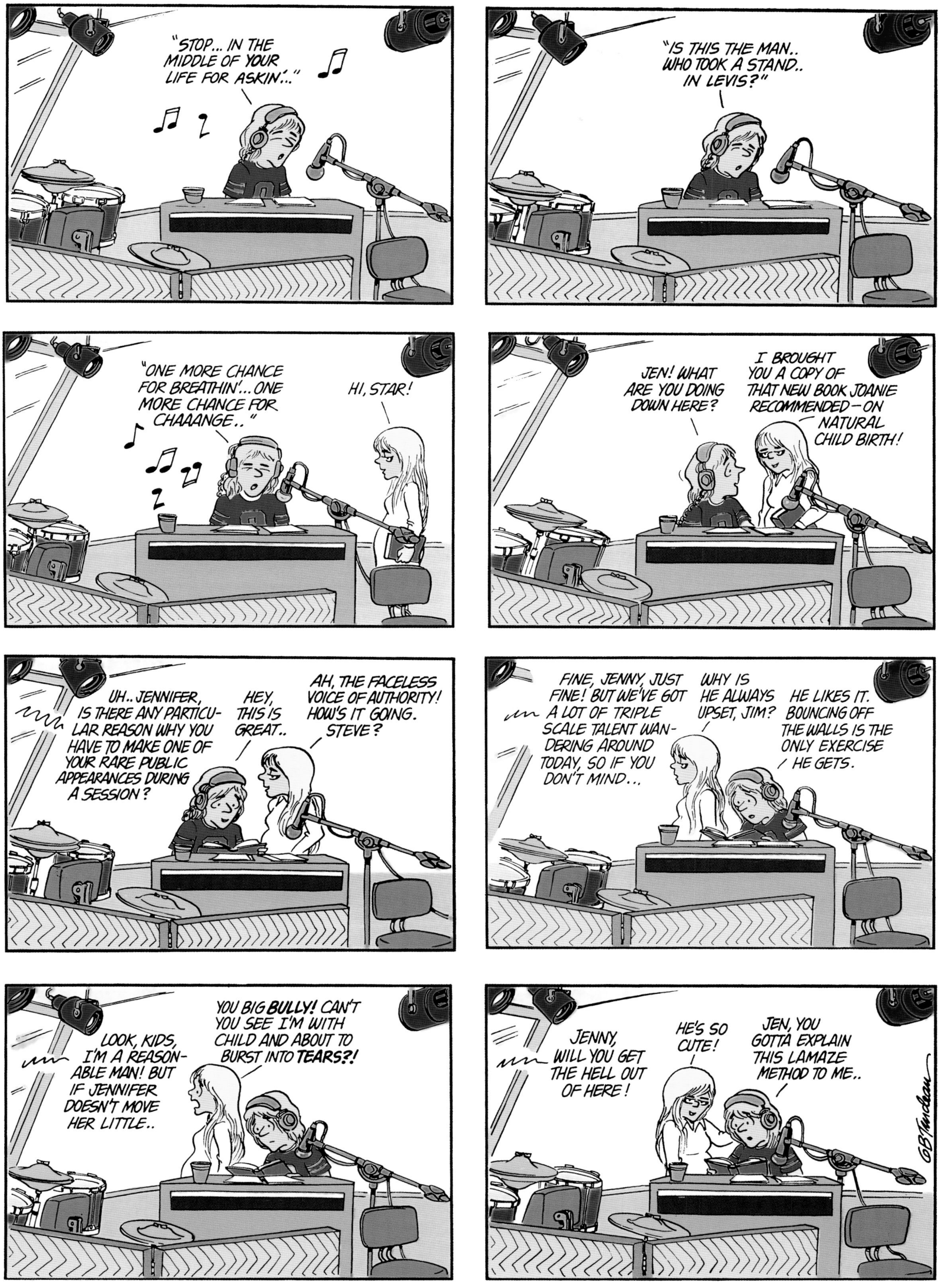
"STOP... IN THE MIDDLE OF YOUR LIFE FOR ASKIN'..."
"IS THIS THE MAN.. WHO TOOK A STAND.. IN LEVIS?"
"ONE MORE CHANCE FOR BREATHIN'... ONE MORE CHANCE FOR CHAAANGE.."
HI, STAR!
JEN! WHAT ARE YOU DOING DOWN HERE?
I BROUGHT YOU A COPY OF THAT NEW BOOK JOANIE RECOMMENDED—ON NATURAL CHILD BIRTH!
UH.. JENNIFER, IS THERE ANY PARTICULAR REASON WHY YOU HAVE TO MAKE ONE OF YOUR RARE PUBLIC APPEARANCES DURING A SESSION?
HEY, THIS IS GREAT..
AH, THE FACELESS VOICE OF AUTHORITY! HOW'S IT GOING, STEVE?
FINE, JENNY, JUST FINE! BUT WE'VE GOT A LOT OF TRIPLE SCALE TALENT WANDERING AROUND TODAY, SO IF YOU DON'T MIND...
WHY IS HE ALWAYS UPSET, JIM?
HE LIKES IT. BOUNCING OFF THE WALLS IS THE ONLY EXERCISE HE GETS.
LOOK, KIDS, I'M A REASONABLE MAN! BUT IF JENNIFER DOESN'T MOVE HER LITTLE..
YOU BIG BULLY! CAN'T YOU SEE I'M WITH CHILD AND ABOUT TO BURST INTO TEARS?!
JENNY, WILL YOU GET THE HELL OUT OF HERE!
HE'S SO CUTE!
JEN, YOU GOTTA EXPLAIN THIS LAMAZE METHOD TO ME..
GBTrudeau

2/27/77

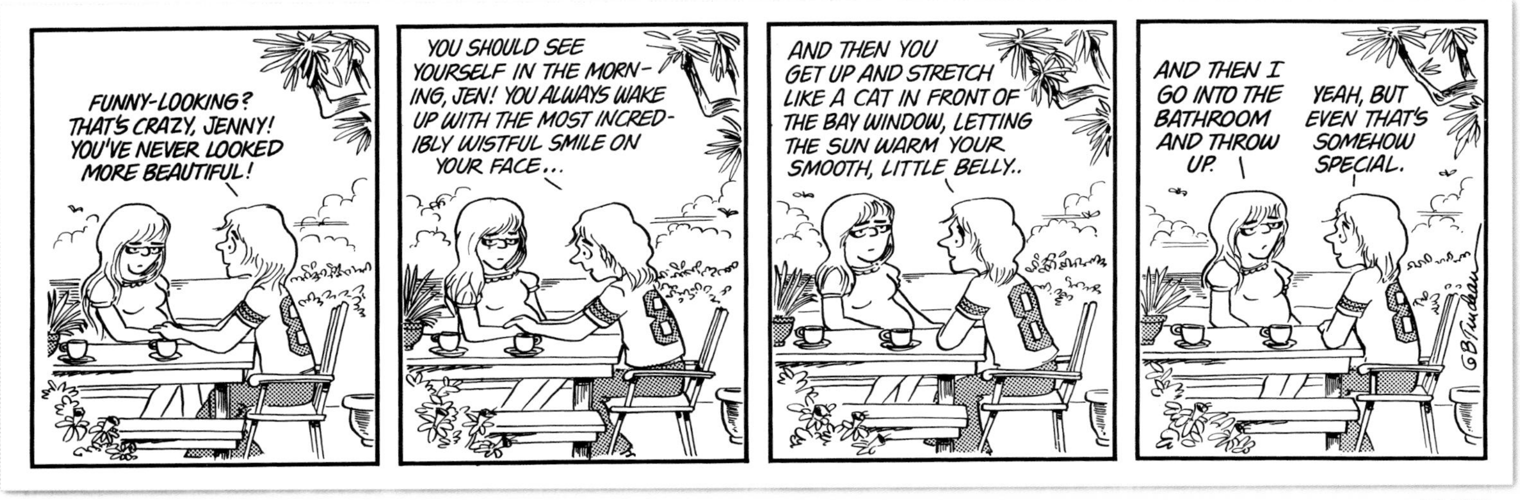
FUNNY-LOOKING? THAT'S CRAZY, JENNY! YOU'VE NEVER LOOKED MORE BEAUTIFUL!
YOU SHOULD SEE YOURSELF IN THE MORNING, JEN! YOU ALWAYS WAKE UP WITH THE MOST INCREDIBLY WISTFUL SMILE ON YOUR FACE...
AND THEN YOU GET UP AND STRETCH LIKE A CAT IN FRONT OF THE BAY WINDOW, LETTING THE SUN WARM YOUR SMOOTH, LITTLE BELLY..
AND THEN I GO INTO THE BATHROOM AND THROW UP.
YEAH, BUT EVEN THAT'S SOMEHOW SPECIAL.
GBTrudeau

2/26/77

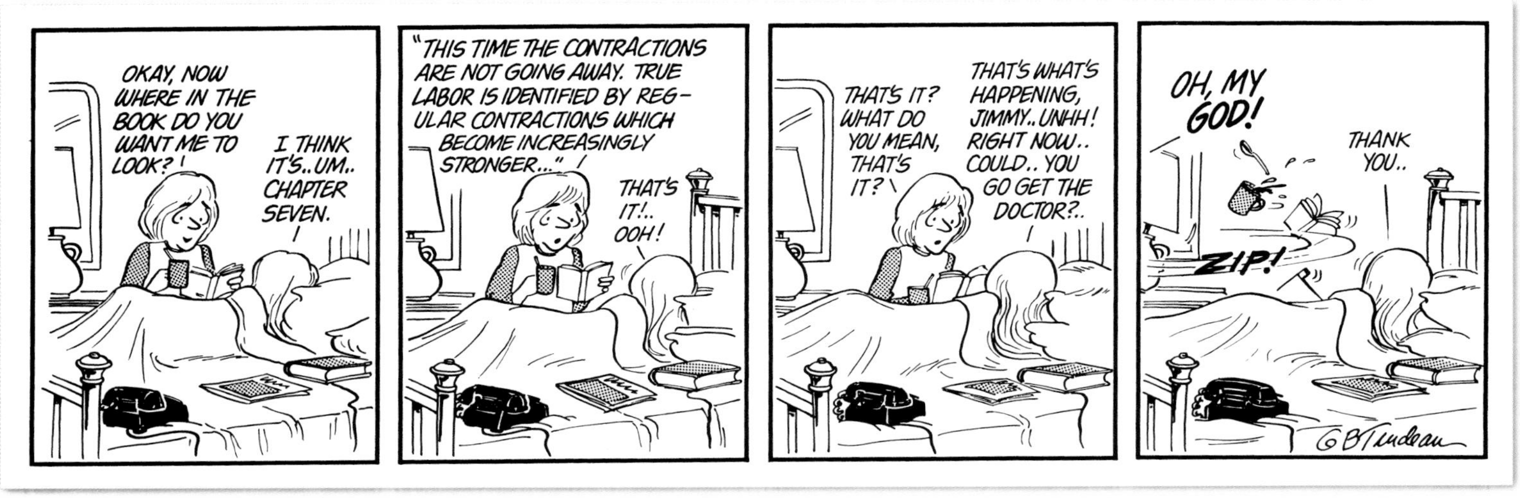
OKAY, NOW WHERE IN THE BOOK DO YOU WANT ME TO LOOK?
I THINK IT'S..UM.. CHAPTER SEVEN.
"THIS TIME THE CONTRACTIONS ARE NOT GOING AWAY. TRUE LABOR IS IDENTIFIED BY REGULAR CONTRACTIONS WHICH BECOME INCREASINGLY STRONGER..."
THAT'S IT!.. OOH!
THAT'S IT? WHAT DO YOU MEAN, THAT'S IT?
THAT'S WHAT'S HAPPENING, JIMMY.. UNHH! RIGHT NOW.. COULD.. YOU GO GET THE DOCTOR?..
OH, MY GOD!
ZIP!
THANK YOU..
GBTrudeau

3/14/77

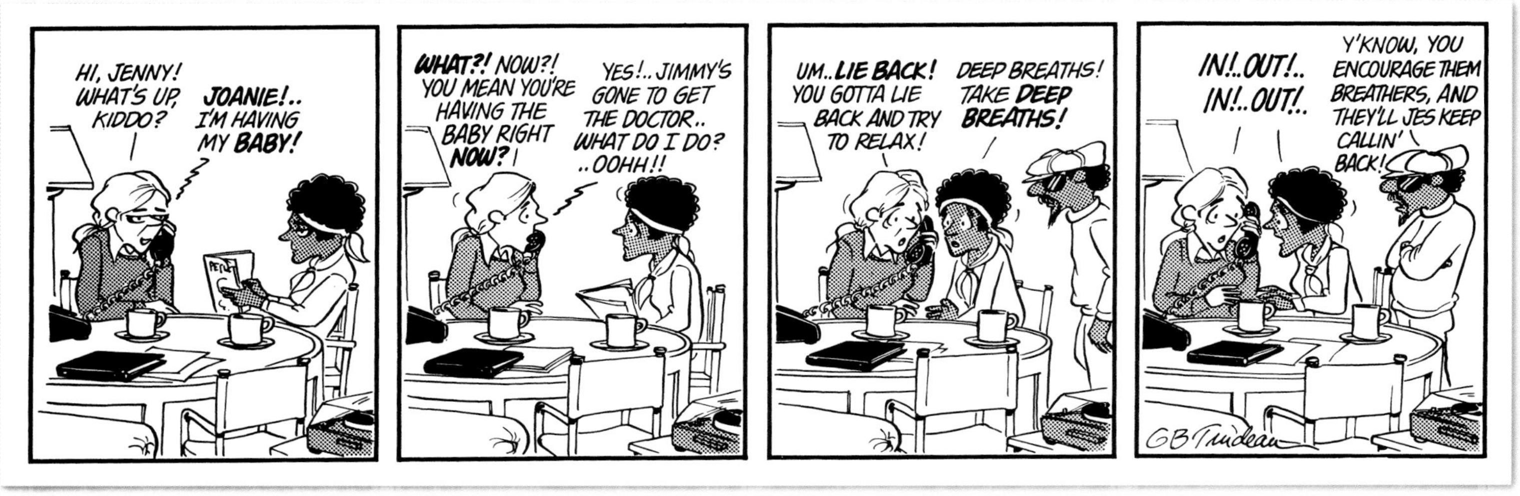
HI, JENNY! WHAT'S UP, KIDDO?
JOANIE!.. I'M HAVING MY BABY!
WHAT?! NOW?! YOU MEAN YOU'RE HAVING THE BABY RIGHT NOW?!
YES!.. JIMMY'S GONE TO GET THE DOCTOR.. WHAT DO I DO? ..OOHH!!
UM.. LIE BACK! YOU GOTTA LIE BACK AND TRY TO RELAX!
DEEP BREATHS! TAKE DEEP BREATHS!
IN!..OUT!.. IN!..OUT!..
Y'KNOW, YOU ENCOURAGE THEM BREATHERS, AND THEY'LL JES KEEP CALLIN' BACK!
GBTrudeau

3/15/77

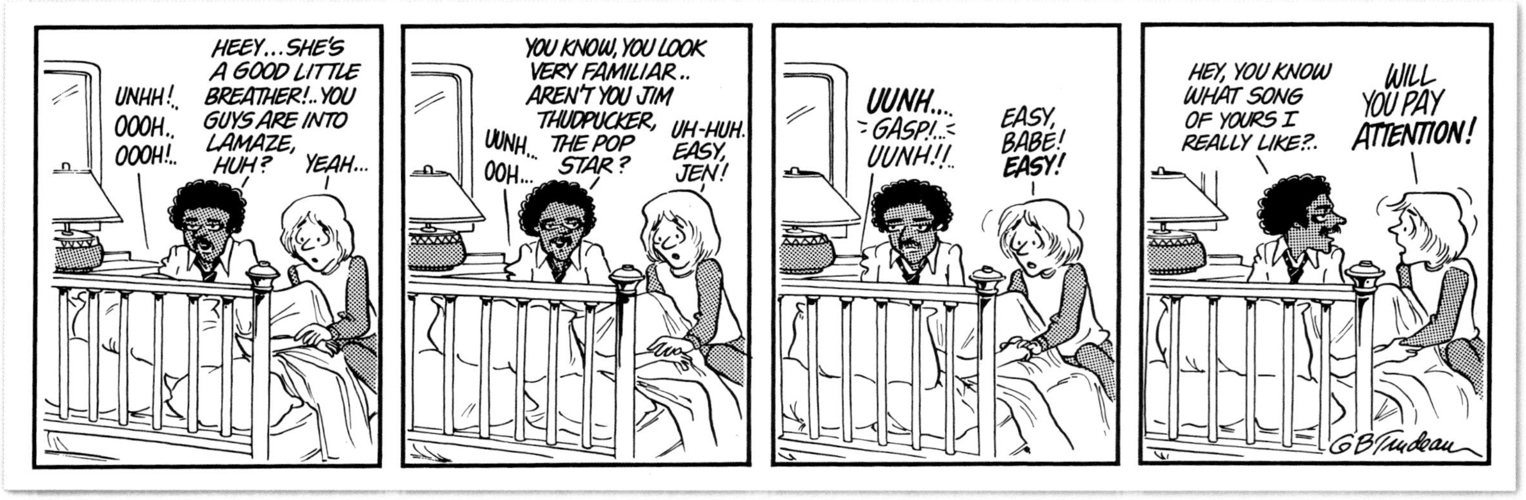
UNHH!.. OOOH!.. OOOH!..
HEEY... SHE'S A GOOD LITTLE BREATHER!.. YOU GUYS ARE INTO LAMAZE, HUH?
YEAH...
YOU KNOW, YOU LOOK VERY FAMILIAR.. AREN'T YOU JIM THUDPUCKER, THE POP STAR?
UNNH.. OOH...
UH-HUH. EASY, JEN!
UUNH... GASP!.. UUNH!!..
EASY, BABE! EASY!
HEY, YOU KNOW WHAT SONG OF YOURS I REALLY LIKE?..
WILL YOU PAY ATTENTION!
GBTrudeau

3/17/77

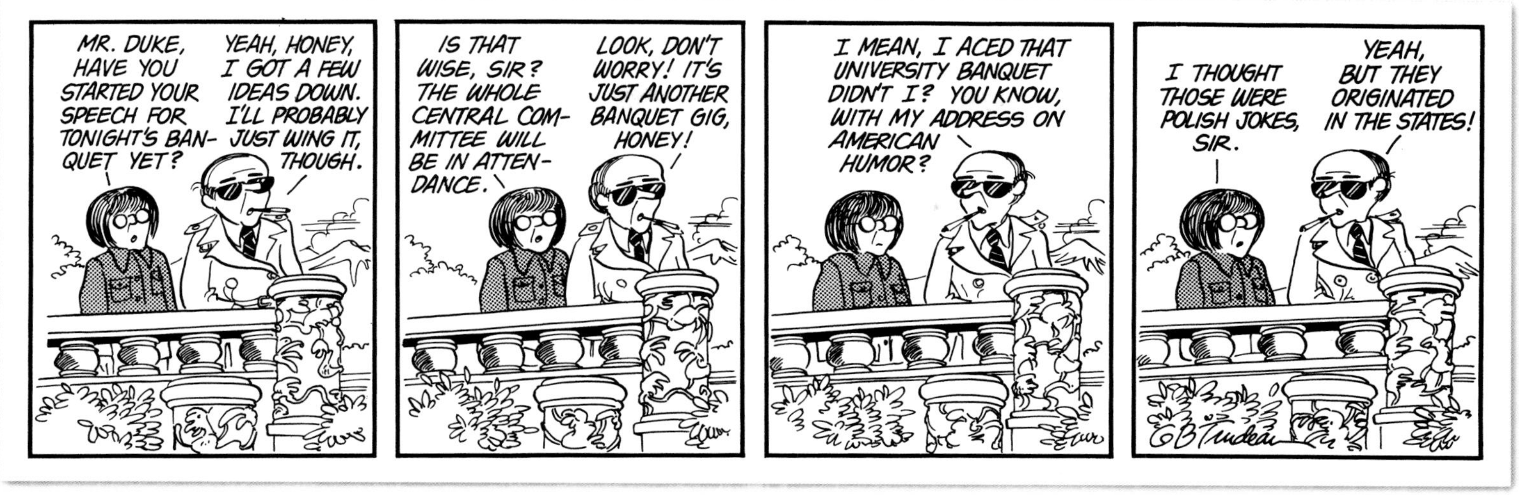
MR. DUKE, HAVE YOU STARTED YOUR SPEECH FOR TONIGHT'S BANQUET YET?
YEAH, HONEY, I GOT A FEW IDEAS DOWN. I'LL PROBABLY JUST WING IT, THOUGH.
IS THAT WISE, SIR? THE WHOLE CENTRAL COMMITTEE WILL BE IN ATTENDANCE.
LOOK, DON'T WORRY! IT'S JUST ANOTHER BANQUET GIG, HONEY!
I MEAN, I ACED THAT UNIVERSITY BANQUET DIDN'T I? YOU KNOW, WITH MY ADDRESS ON AMERICAN HUMOR?
I THOUGHT THOSE WERE POLISH JOKES, SIR.
YEAH, BUT THEY ORIGINATED IN THE STATES!
GBTrudeau

6/13/77

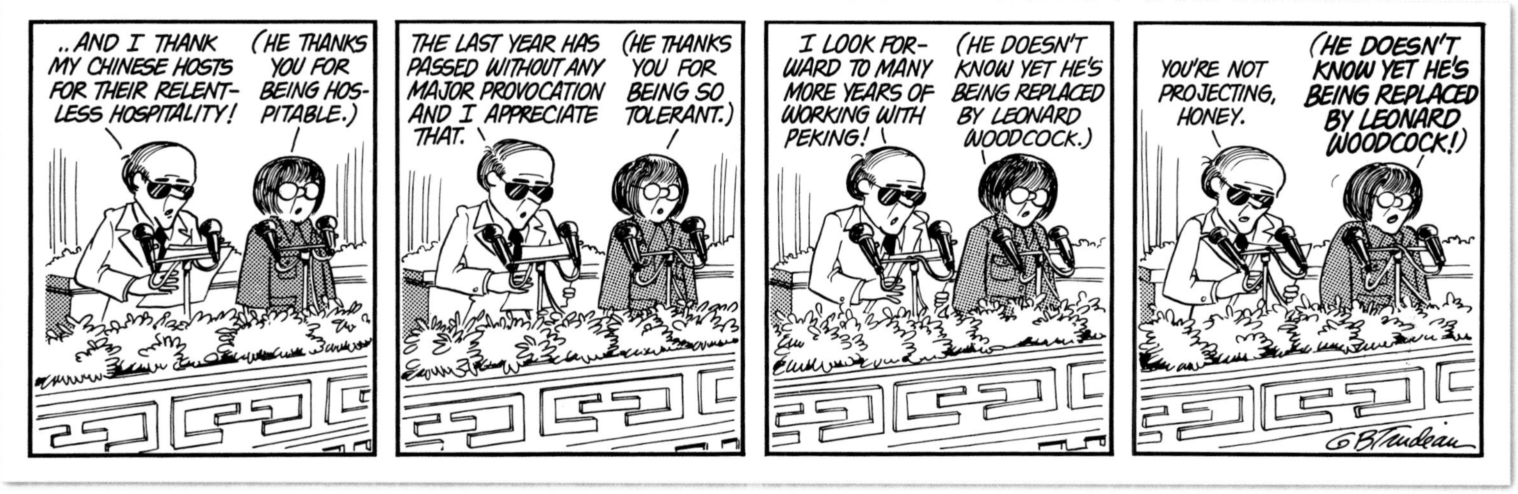
..AND I THANK MY CHINESE HOSTS FOR THEIR RELENTLESS HOSPITALITY!
(HE THANKS YOU FOR BEING HOSPITABLE.)
THE LAST YEAR HAS PASSED WITHOUT ANY MAJOR PROVOCATION AND I APPRECIATE THAT.
(HE THANKS YOU FOR BEING SO TOLERANT.)
I LOOK FORWARD TO MANY MORE YEARS OF WORKING WITH PEKING!
(HE DOESN'T KNOW YET HE'S BEING REPLACED BY LEONARD WOODCOCK.)
YOU'RE NOT PROJECTING, HONEY.
(HE DOESN'T KNOW YET HE'S BEING REPLACED BY LEONARD WOODCOCK!)
GBTrudeau

6/16/77

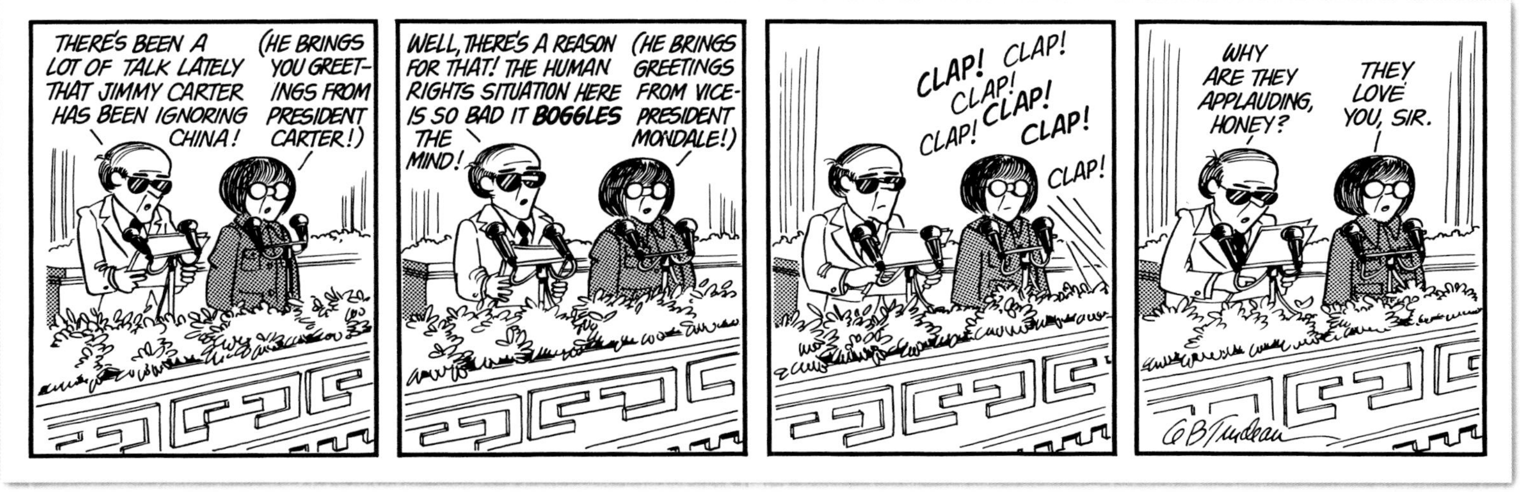
THERE'S BEEN A LOT OF TALK LATELY THAT JIMMY CARTER HAS BEEN IGNORING CHINA!
(HE BRINGS YOU GREETINGS FROM PRESIDENT CARTER!)
WELL, THERE'S A REASON FOR THAT! THE HUMAN RIGHTS SITUATION HERE IS SO BAD IT BOGGLES THE MIND!
(HE BRINGS GREETINGS FROM VICE-PRESIDENT MONDALE!)
CLAP! CLAP! CLAP! CLAP! CLAP! CLAP! CLAP!
WHY ARE THEY APPLAUDING, HONEY?
THEY LOVE YOU, SIR.
GBTrudeau

6/17/77

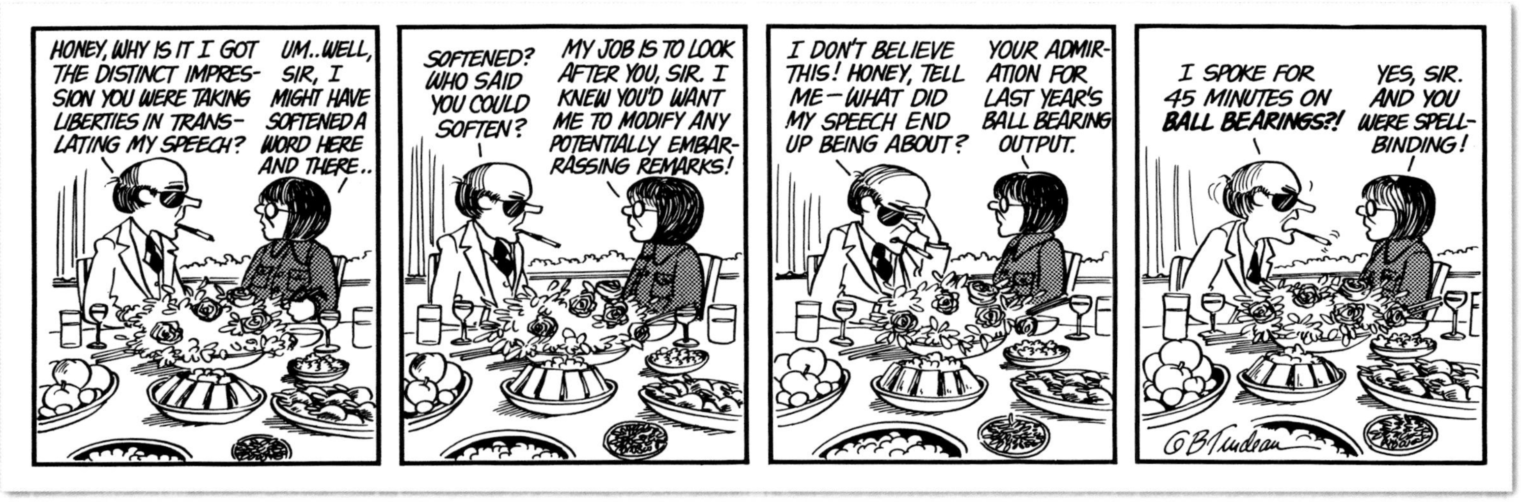
HONEY, WHY IS IT I GOT THE DISTINCT IMPRESSION YOU WERE TAKING LIBERTIES IN TRANSLATING MY SPEECH?
UM..WELL, SIR, I MIGHT HAVE SOFTENED A WORD HERE AND THERE..
SOFTENED? WHO SAID YOU COULD SOFTEN?
MY JOB IS TO LOOK AFTER YOU, SIR. I KNEW YOU'D WANT ME TO MODIFY ANY POTENTIALLY EMBARRASSING REMARKS!
I DON'T BELIEVE THIS! HONEY, TELL ME—WHAT DID MY SPEECH END UP BEING ABOUT?
YOUR ADMIRATION FOR LAST YEAR'S BALL BEARING OUTPUT.
I SPOKE FOR 45 MINUTES ON BALL BEARINGS?!
YES, SIR. AND YOU WERE SPELLBINDING!
GBTrudeau

6/18/77

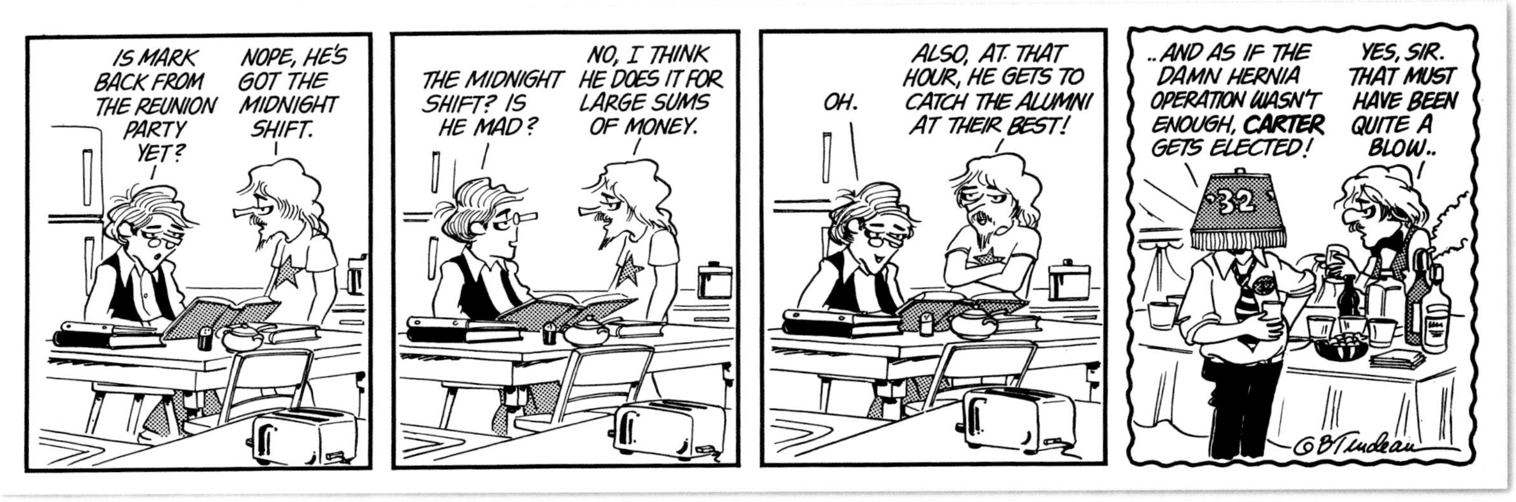
IS MARK BACK FROM THE REUNION PARTY YET?
NOPE, HE'S GOT THE MIDNIGHT SHIFT.
THE MIDNIGHT SHIFT? IS HE MAD?
NO, I THINK HE DOES IT FOR LARGE SUMS OF MONEY.
OH.
ALSO, AT THAT HOUR, HE GETS TO CATCH THE ALUMNI AT THEIR BEST!
..AND AS IF THE DAMN HERNIA OPERATION WASN'T ENOUGH, CARTER GETS ELECTED!
YES, SIR. THAT MUST HAVE BEEN QUITE A BLOW..
32
©BTrudeau

5/2/77

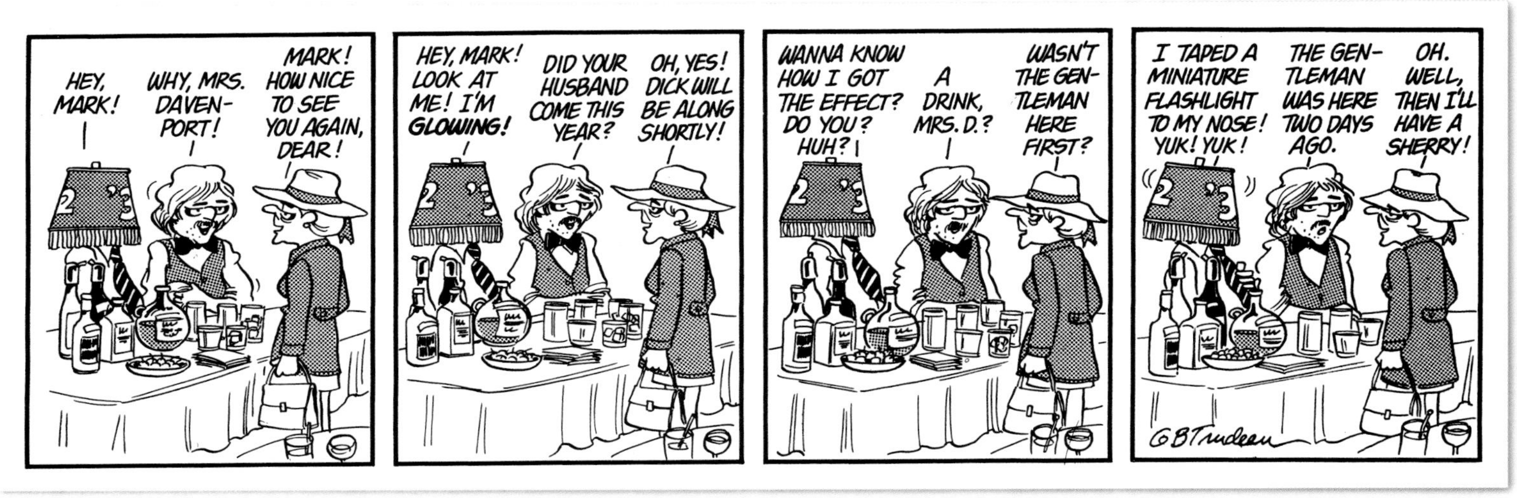
HEY, MARK!
WHY, MRS. DAVENPORT!
MARK! HOW NICE TO SEE YOU AGAIN, DEAR!
HEY, MARK! LOOK AT ME! I'M GLOWING!
DID YOUR HUSBAND COME THIS YEAR?
OH, YES! DICK WILL BE ALONG SHORTLY!
WANNA KNOW HOW I GOT THE EFFECT? DO YOU? HUH?
A DRINK, MRS. D.?
WASN'T THE GENTLEMAN HERE FIRST?
I TAPED A MINIATURE FLASHLIGHT TO MY NOSE! YUK! YUK!
THE GENTLEMAN WAS HERE TWO DAYS AGO.
OH. WELL, THEN I'LL HAVE A SHERRY!
©BTrudeau

5/4/77

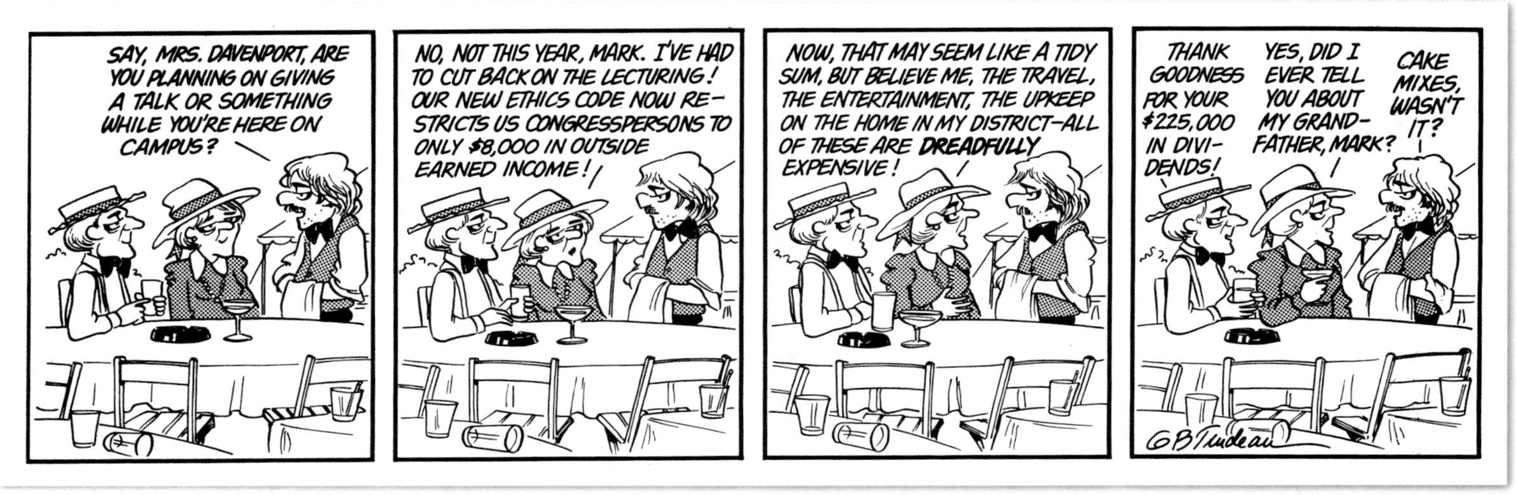
SAY, MRS. DAVENPORT, ARE YOU PLANNING ON GIVING A TALK OR SOMETHING WHILE YOU'RE HERE ON CAMPUS?
NO, NOT THIS YEAR, MARK. I'VE HAD TO CUT BACK ON THE LECTURING! OUR NEW ETHICS CODE NOW RESTRICTS US CONGRESSPERSONS TO ONLY $8,000 IN OUTSIDE EARNED INCOME!
NOW, THAT MAY SEEM LIKE A TIDY SUM, BUT BELIEVE ME, THE TRAVEL, THE ENTERTAINMENT, THE UPKEEP ON THE HOME IN MY DISTRICT—ALL OF THESE ARE DREADFULLY EXPENSIVE!
THANK GOODNESS FOR YOUR $225,000 IN DIVIDENDS!
YES, DID I EVER TELL YOU ABOUT MY GRANDFATHER, MARK?
CAKE MIXES, WASN'T IT?
©BTrudeau

5/5/77

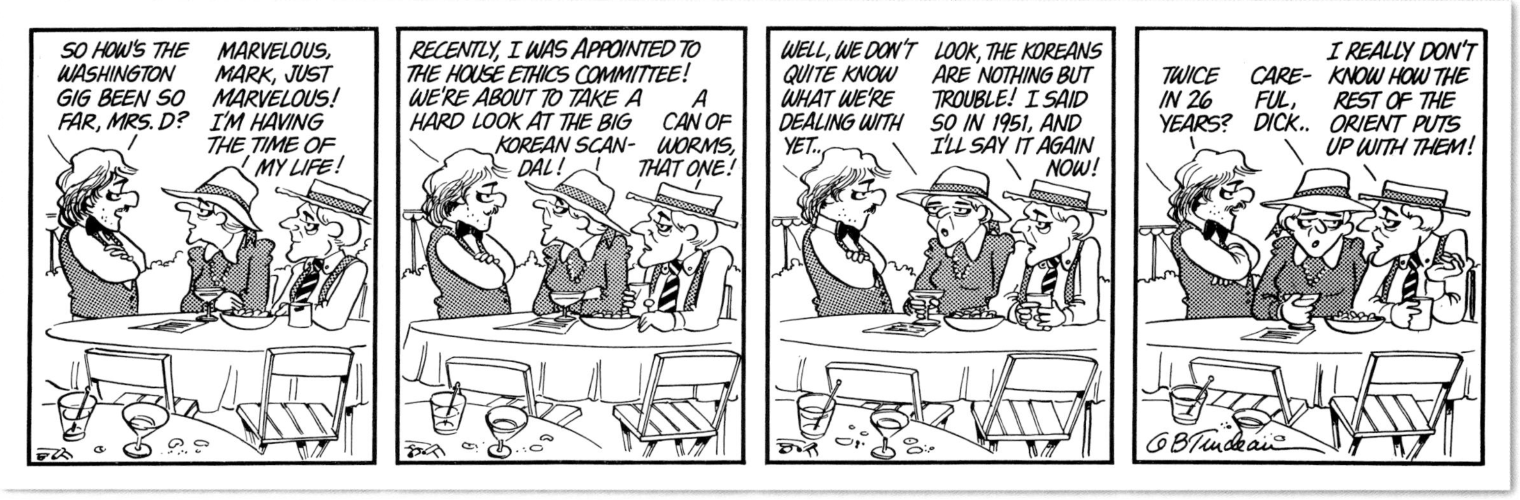
SO HOW'S THE WASHINGTON GIG BEEN SO FAR, MRS. D?
MARVELOUS, MARK, JUST MARVELOUS! I'M HAVING THE TIME OF MY LIFE!
RECENTLY, I WAS APPOINTED TO THE HOUSE ETHICS COMMITTEE! WE'RE ABOUT TO TAKE A HARD LOOK AT THE BIG KOREAN SCANDAL!
A CAN OF WORMS, THAT ONE!
WELL, WE DON'T QUITE KNOW WHAT WE'RE DEALING WITH YET..
LOOK, THE KOREANS ARE NOTHING BUT TROUBLE! I SAID SO IN 1951, AND I'LL SAY IT AGAIN NOW!
TWICE IN 26 YEARS?
CAREFUL, DICK..
I REALLY DON'T KNOW HOW THE REST OF THE ORIENT PUTS UP WITH THEM!
©BTrudeau

5/11/77

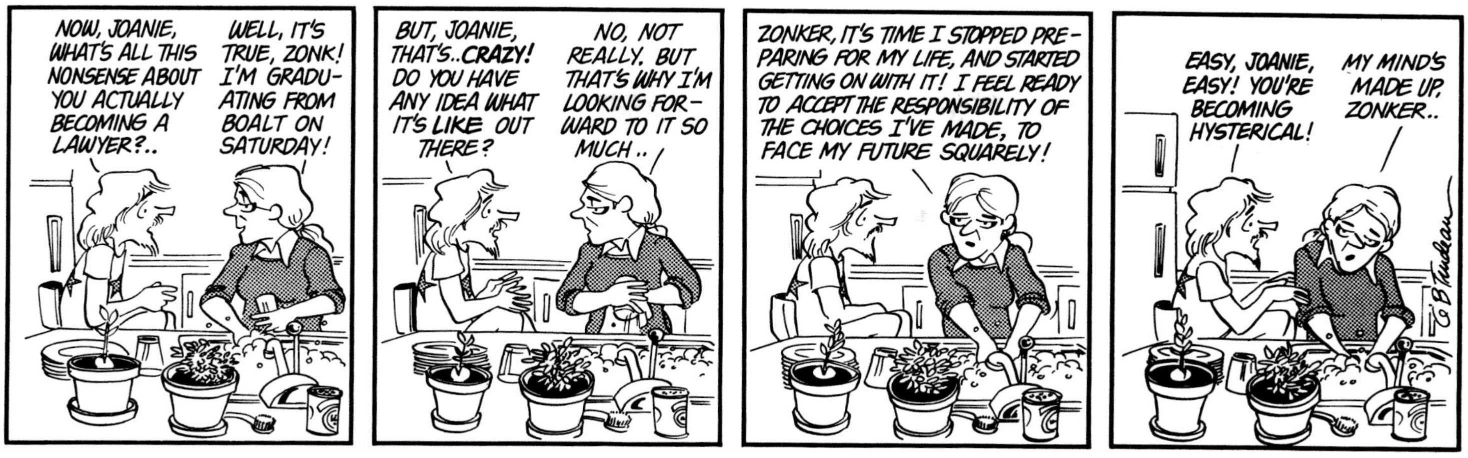
NOW, JOANIE, WHAT'S ALL THIS NONSENSE ABOUT YOU ACTUALLY BECOMING A LAWYER?..
WELL, IT'S TRUE, ZONK! I'M GRADUATING FROM BOALT ON SATURDAY!
BUT, JOANIE, THAT'S..CRAZY! DO YOU HAVE ANY IDEA WHAT IT'S LIKE OUT THERE?
NO, NOT REALLY. BUT THAT'S WHY I'M LOOKING FORWARD TO IT SO MUCH..
ZONKER, IT'S TIME I STOPPED PREPARING FOR MY LIFE, AND STARTED GETTING ON WITH IT! I FEEL READY TO ACCEPT THE RESPONSIBILITY OF THE CHOICES I'VE MADE, TO FACE MY FUTURE SQUARELY!
EASY, JOANIE, EASY! YOU'RE BECOMING HYSTERICAL!
MY MIND'S MADE UP, ZONKER..
GB Trudeau

5/17/77

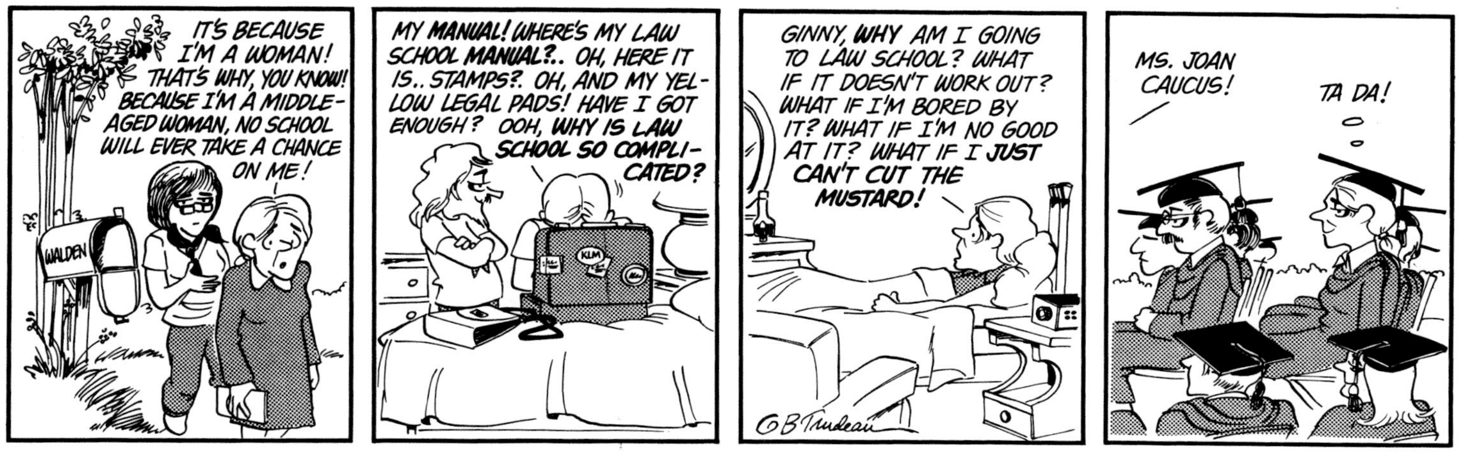
IT'S BECAUSE I'M A WOMAN! THAT'S WHY, YOU KNOW! BECAUSE I'M A MIDDLE-AGED WOMAN, NO SCHOOL WILL EVER TAKE A CHANCE ON ME!
WALDEN
MY MANUAL! WHERE'S MY LAW SCHOOL MANUAL?.. OH, HERE IT IS.. STAMPS?. OH, AND MY YELLOW LEGAL PADS! HAVE I GOT ENOUGH? OOH, WHY IS LAW SCHOOL SO COMPLICATED?
GINNY, WHY AM I GOING TO LAW SCHOOL? WHAT IF IT DOESN'T WORK OUT? WHAT IF I'M BORED BY IT? WHAT IF I'M NO GOOD AT IT? WHAT IF I JUST CAN'T CUT THE MUSTARD!
GB Trudeau
MS. JOAN CAUCUS!
TA DA!

5/21/77

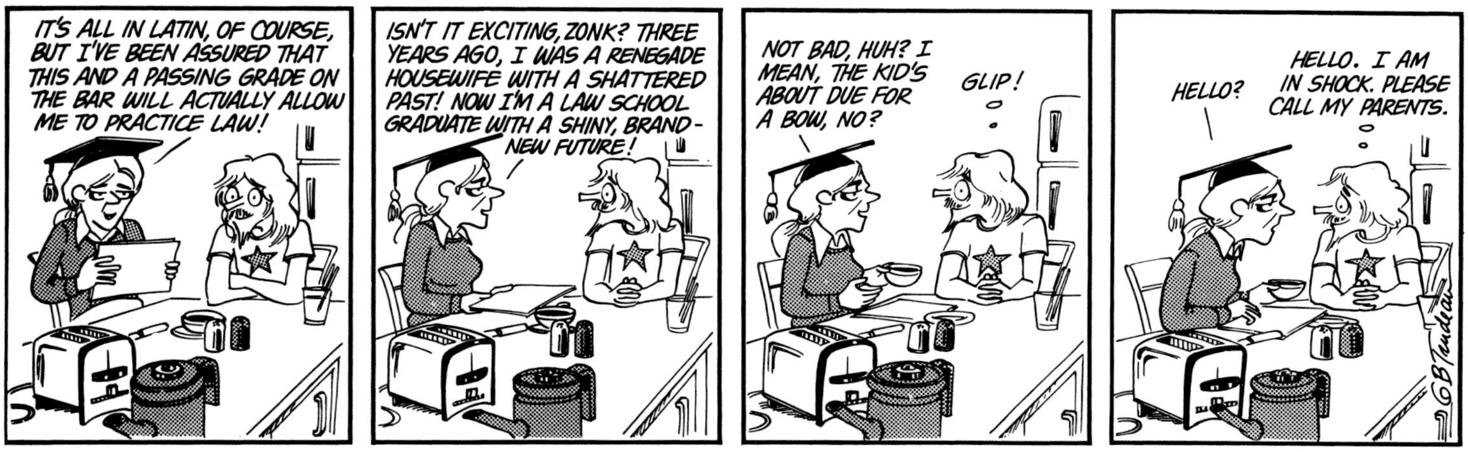
IT'S ALL IN LATIN, OF COURSE, BUT I'VE BEEN ASSURED THAT THIS AND A PASSING GRADE ON THE BAR WILL ACTUALLY ALLOW ME TO PRACTICE LAW!
ISN'T IT EXCITING, ZONK? THREE YEARS AGO, I WAS A RENEGADE HOUSEWIFE WITH A SHATTERED PAST! NOW I'M A LAW SCHOOL GRADUATE WITH A SHINY, BRAND-NEW FUTURE!
NOT BAD, HUH? I MEAN, THE KID'S ABOUT DUE FOR A BOW, NO?
GLIP!
HELLO?
HELLO. I AM IN SHOCK. PLEASE CALL MY PARENTS.
GB Trudeau

5/23/77

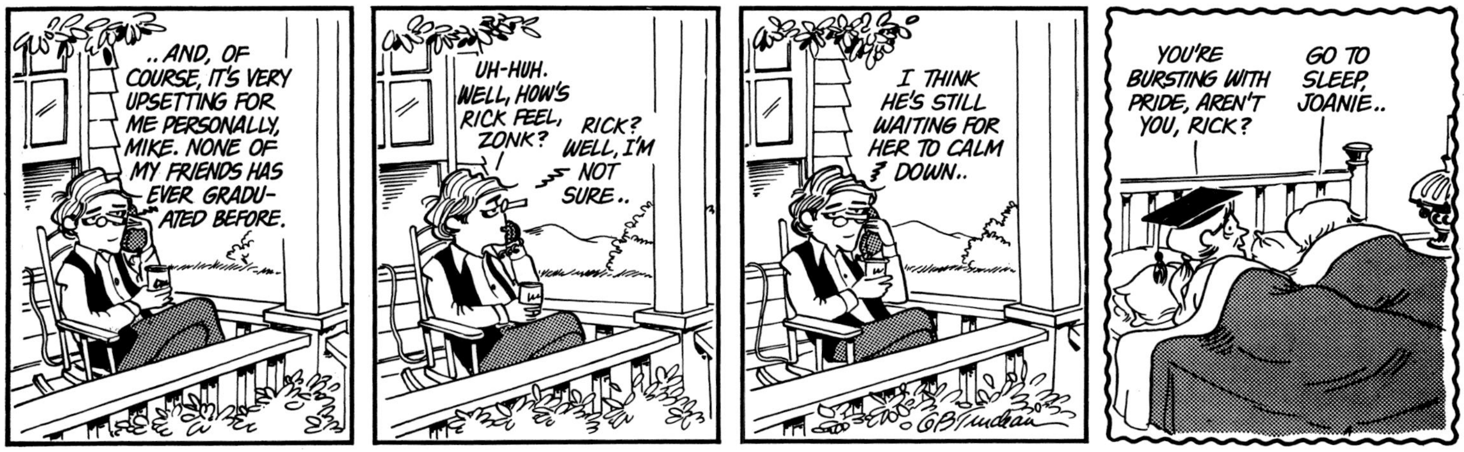
..AND, OF COURSE, IT'S VERY UPSETTING FOR ME PERSONALLY, MIKE. NONE OF MY FRIENDS HAS EVER GRADUATED BEFORE.
UH-HUH. WELL, HOW'S RICK FEEL, ZONK?
RICK? WELL, I'M NOT SURE..
I THINK HE'S STILL WAITING FOR HER TO CALM DOWN..
GB Trudeau
YOU'RE BURSTING WITH PRIDE, AREN'T YOU, RICK?
GO TO SLEEP, JOANIE..

5/24/77

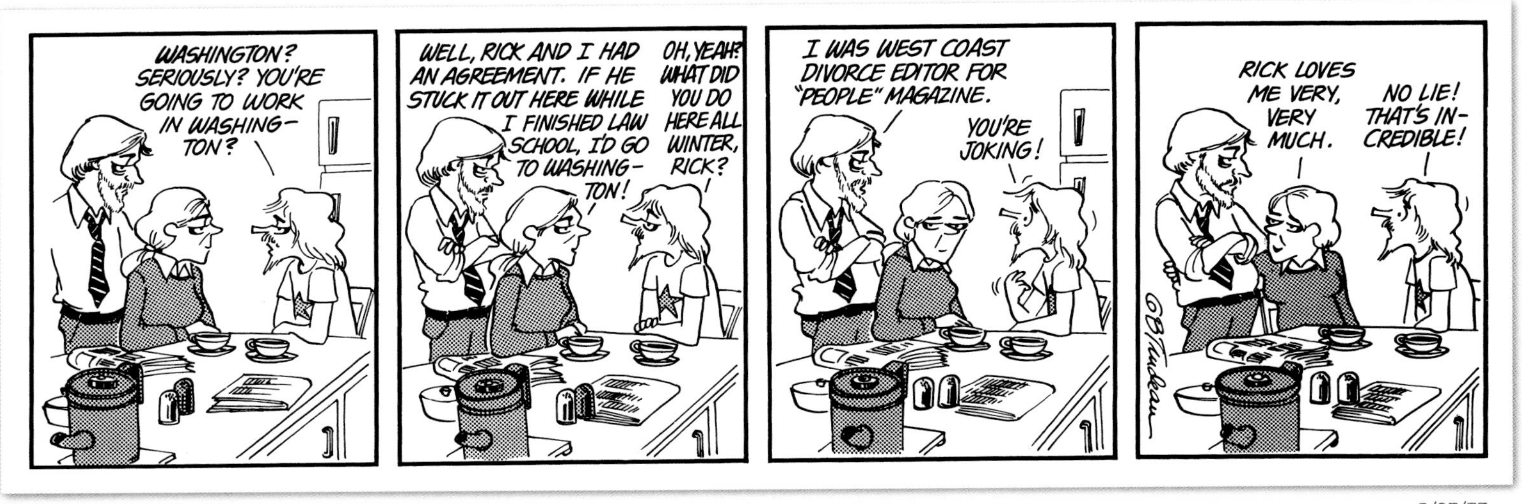
WASHINGTON? SERIOUSLY? YOU'RE GOING TO WORK IN WASHINGTON?
WELL, RICK AND I HAD AN AGREEMENT. IF HE STUCK IT OUT HERE WHILE I FINISHED LAW SCHOOL, I'D GO TO WASHINGTON!
OH, YEAH? WHAT DID YOU DO HERE ALL WINTER, RICK?
I WAS WEST COAST DIVORCE EDITOR FOR "PEOPLE" MAGAZINE.
YOU'RE JOKING!
RICK LOVES ME VERY, VERY MUCH.
NO LIE! THAT'S INCREDIBLE!

5/27/77

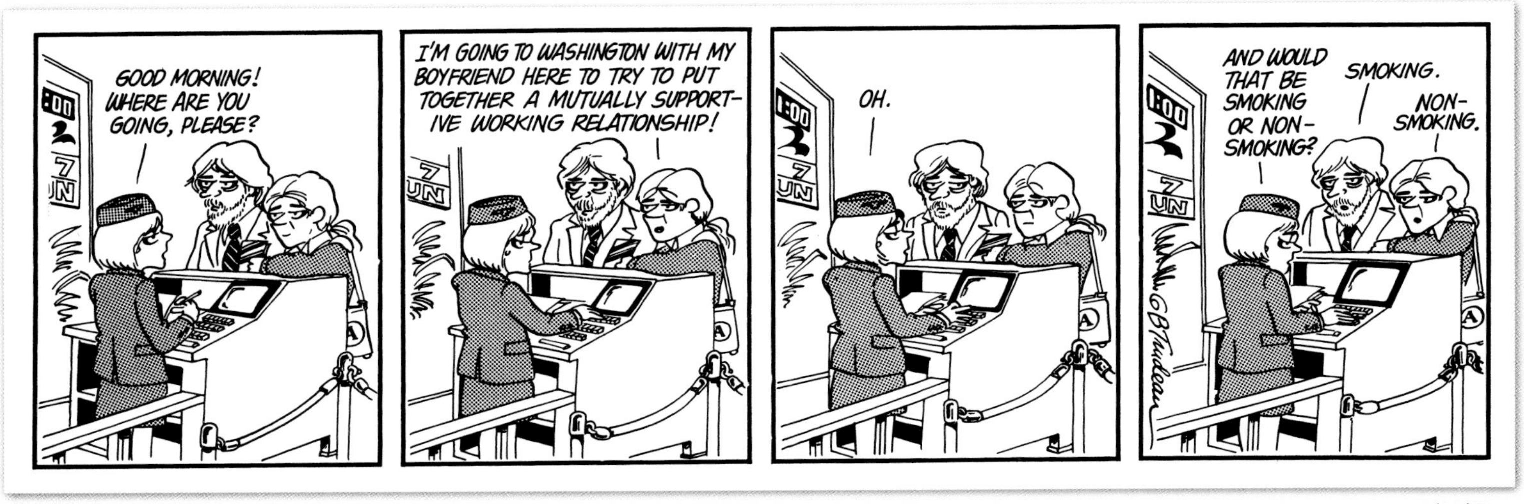
GOOD MORNING! WHERE ARE YOU GOING, PLEASE?
I'M GOING TO WASHINGTON WITH MY BOYFRIEND HERE TO TRY TO PUT TOGETHER A MUTUALLY SUPPORTIVE WORKING RELATIONSHIP!
OH.
AND WOULD THAT BE SMOKING OR NON-SMOKING?
SMOKING.
NON-SMOKING.

5/28/77

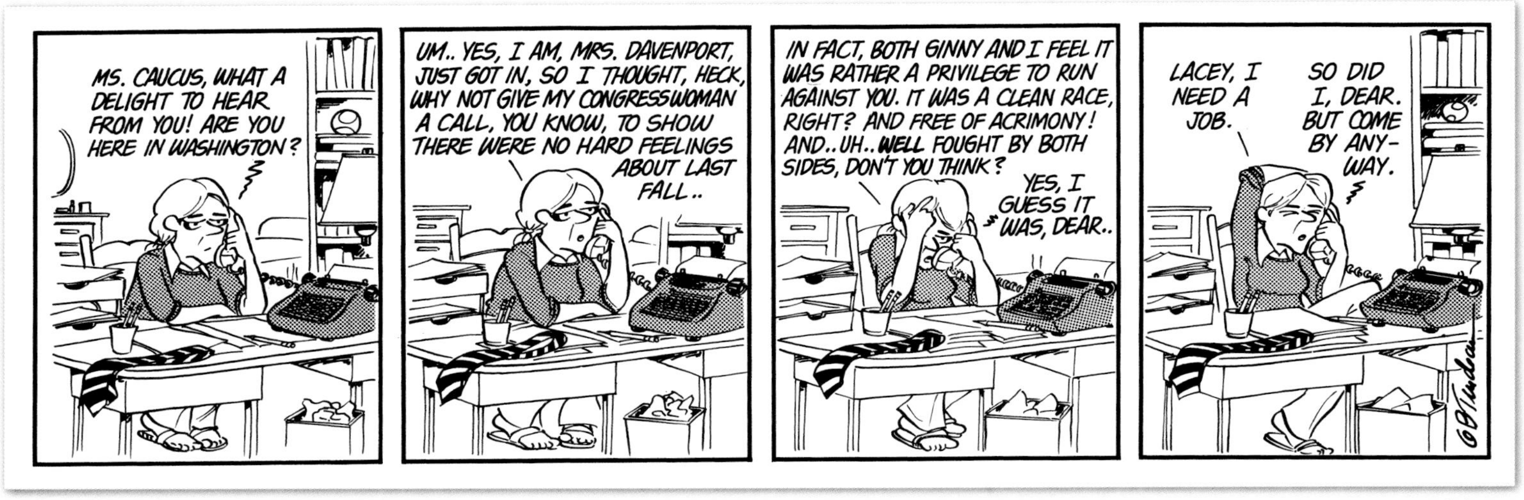
MS. CAUCUS, WHAT A DELIGHT TO HEAR FROM YOU! ARE YOU HERE IN WASHINGTON?
UM.. YES, I AM, MRS. DAVENPORT, JUST GOT IN, SO I THOUGHT, HECK, WHY NOT GIVE MY CONGRESSWOMAN A CALL, YOU KNOW, TO SHOW THERE WERE NO HARD FEELINGS ABOUT LAST FALL..
IN FACT, BOTH GINNY AND I FEEL IT WAS RATHER A PRIVILEGE TO RUN AGAINST YOU. IT WAS A CLEAN RACE, RIGHT? AND FREE OF ACRIMONY! AND..UH..WELL FOUGHT BY BOTH SIDES, DON'T YOU THINK?
YES, I GUESS IT WAS, DEAR..
LACEY, I NEED A JOB.
SO DID I, DEAR. BUT COME BY ANYWAY.

6/1/77

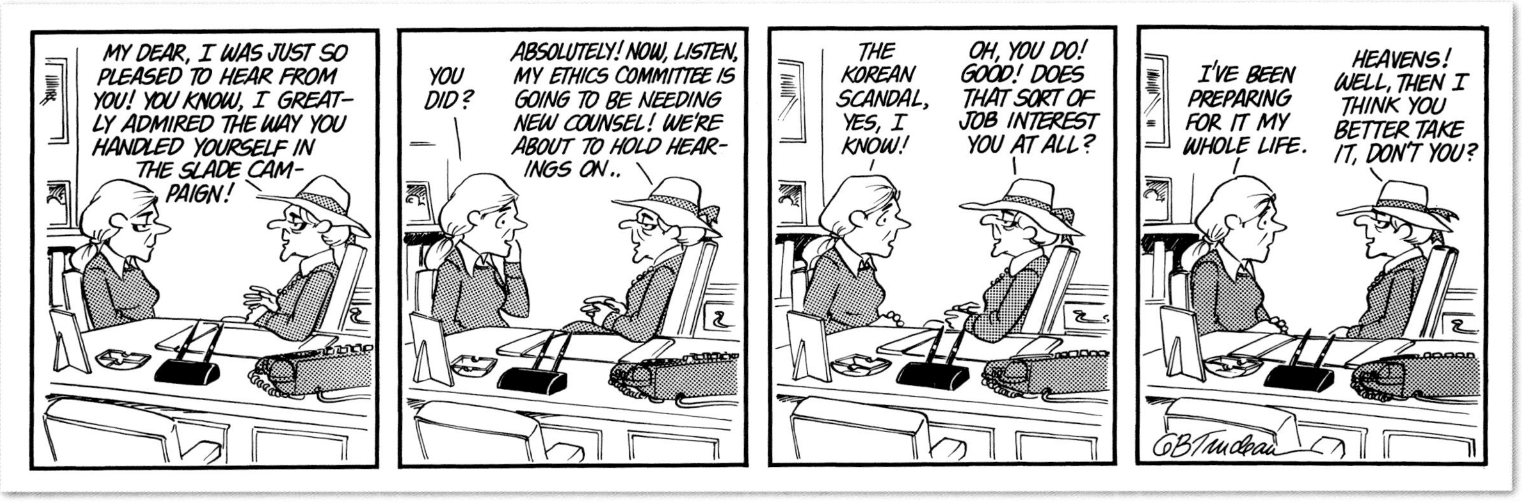
MY DEAR, I WAS JUST SO PLEASED TO HEAR FROM YOU! YOU KNOW, I GREATLY ADMIRED THE WAY YOU HANDLED YOURSELF IN THE SLADE CAMPAIGN!
YOU DID?
ABSOLUTELY! NOW, LISTEN, MY ETHICS COMMITTEE IS GOING TO BE NEEDING NEW COUNSEL! WE'RE ABOUT TO HOLD HEARINGS ON..
THE KOREAN SCANDAL, YES, I KNOW!
OH, YOU DO! GOOD! DOES THAT SORT OF JOB INTEREST YOU AT ALL?
I'VE BEEN PREPARING FOR IT MY WHOLE LIFE.
HEAVENS! WELL, THEN I THINK YOU BETTER TAKE IT, DON'T YOU?

6/2/77

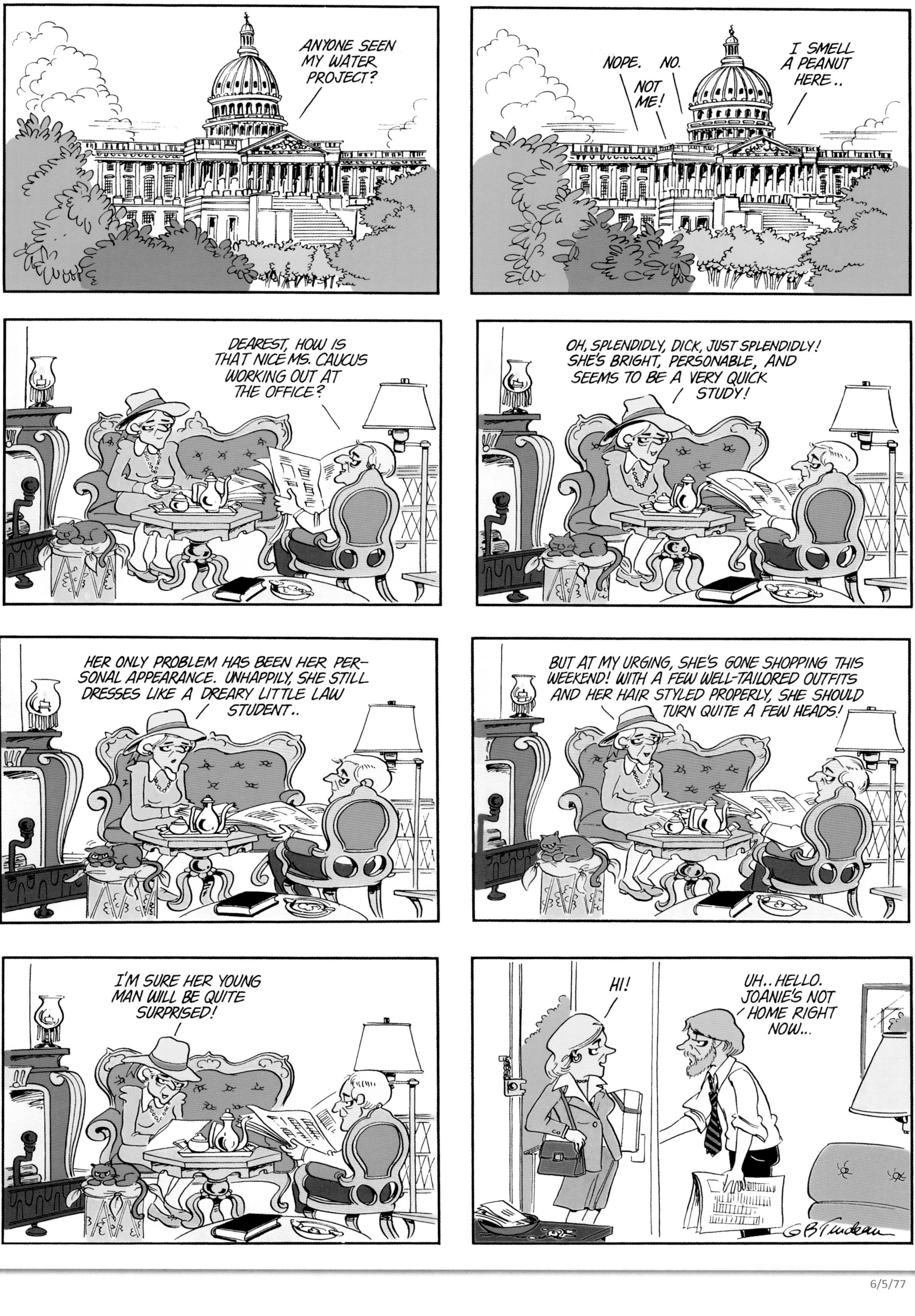
ANYONE SEEN MY WATER PROJECT?
NOPE.
NO.
NOT ME!
I SMELL A PEANUT HERE..
DEAREST, HOW IS THAT NICE MS. CAUCUS WORKING OUT AT THE OFFICE?
OH, SPLENDIDLY, DICK, JUST SPLENDIDLY! SHE'S BRIGHT, PERSONABLE, AND SEEMS TO BE A VERY QUICK STUDY!
HER ONLY PROBLEM HAS BEEN HER PERSONAL APPEARANCE. UNHAPPILY, SHE STILL DRESSES LIKE A DREARY LITTLE LAW STUDENT..
BUT AT MY URGING, SHE'S GONE SHOPPING THIS WEEKEND! WITH A FEW WELL-TAILORED OUTFITS AND HER HAIR STYLED PROPERLY, SHE SHOULD TURN QUITE A FEW HEADS!
I'M SURE HER YOUNG MAN WILL BE QUITE SURPRISED!
HI!
UH.. HELLO. JOANIE'S NOT HOME RIGHT NOW...
G B Trudeau

6/5/77

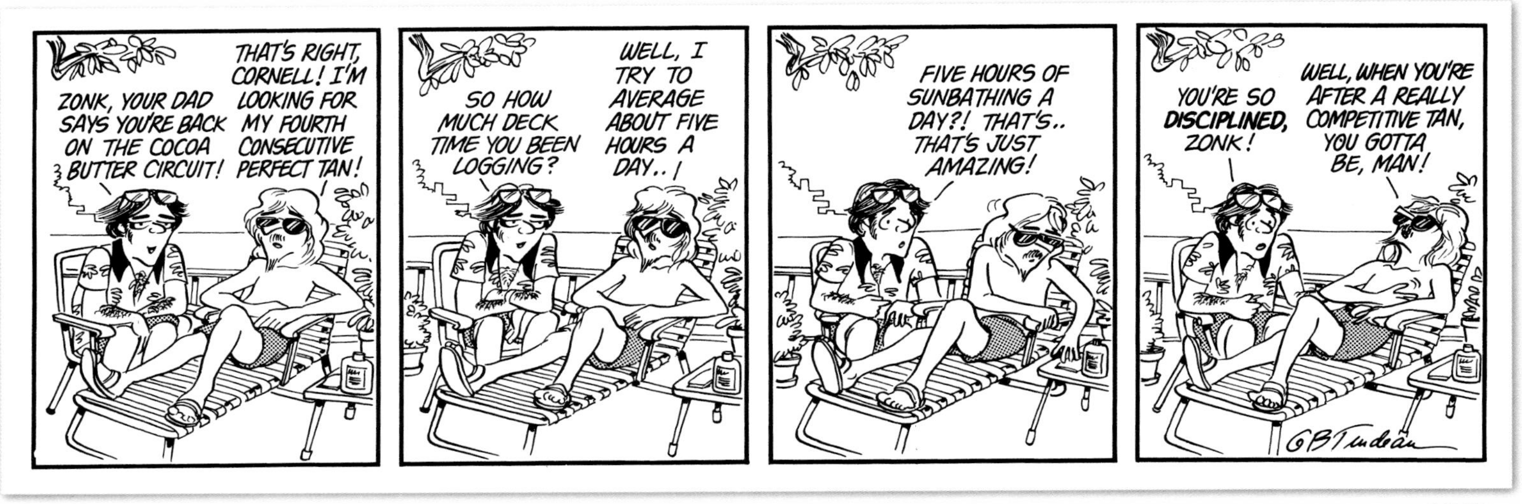
ZONK, YOUR DAD SAYS YOU'RE BACK ON THE COCOA BUTTER CIRCUIT!
THAT'S RIGHT, CORNELL! I'M LOOKING FOR MY FOURTH CONSECUTIVE PERFECT TAN!
SO HOW MUCH DECK TIME YOU BEEN LOGGING?
WELL, I TRY TO AVERAGE ABOUT FIVE HOURS A DAY..
FIVE HOURS OF SUNBATHING A DAY?! THAT'S.. THAT'S JUST AMAZING!
YOU'RE SO DISCIPLINED, ZONK!
WELL, WHEN YOU'RE AFTER A REALLY COMPETITIVE TAN, YOU GOTTA BE, MAN!
GBTrudeau

6/7/77

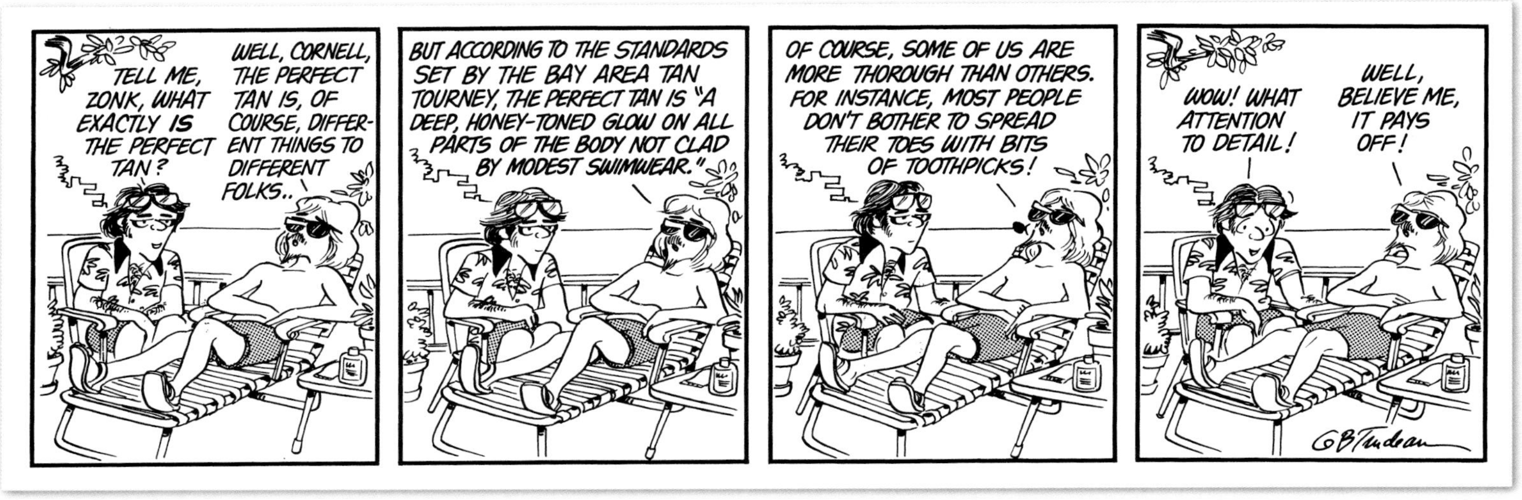
TELL ME, ZONK, WHAT EXACTLY IS THE PERFECT TAN?
WELL, CORNELL, THE PERFECT TAN IS, OF COURSE, DIFFERENT THINGS TO DIFFERENT FOLKS..
BUT ACCORDING TO THE STANDARDS SET BY THE BAY AREA TAN TOURNEY, THE PERFECT TAN IS "A DEEP, HONEY-TONED GLOW ON ALL PARTS OF THE BODY NOT CLAD BY MODEST SWIMWEAR."
OF COURSE, SOME OF US ARE MORE THOROUGH THAN OTHERS. FOR INSTANCE, MOST PEOPLE DON'T BOTHER TO SPREAD THEIR TOES WITH BITS OF TOOTHPICKS!
WOW! WHAT ATTENTION TO DETAIL!
WELL, BELIEVE ME, IT PAYS OFF!
GBTrudeau

6/8/77

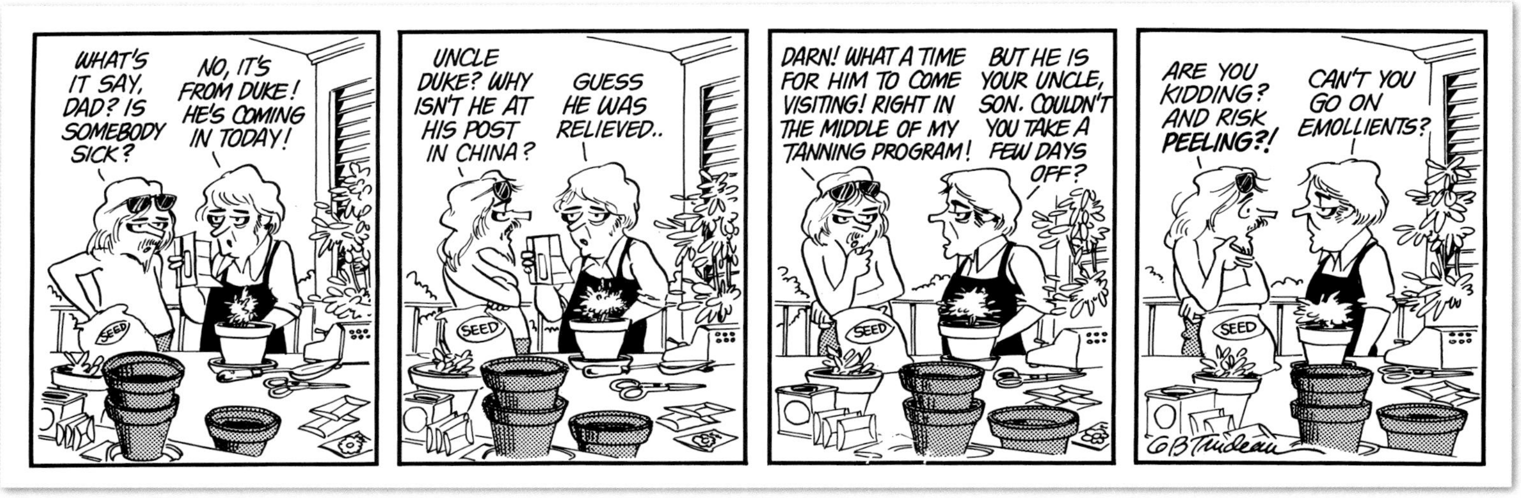
WHAT'S IT SAY, DAD? IS SOMEBODY SICK?
NO, IT'S FROM DUKE! HE'S COMING IN TODAY!
SEED
UNCLE DUKE? WHY ISN'T HE AT HIS POST IN CHINA?
GUESS HE WAS RELIEVED..
SEED
DARN! WHAT A TIME FOR HIM TO COME VISITING! RIGHT IN THE MIDDLE OF MY TANNING PROGRAM!
BUT HE IS YOUR UNCLE, SON. COULDN'T YOU TAKE A FEW DAYS OFF?
SEED
ARE YOU KIDDING? AND RISK PEELING?!
CAN'T YOU GO ON EMOLLIENTS?
SEED
GBTrudeau

6/29/77

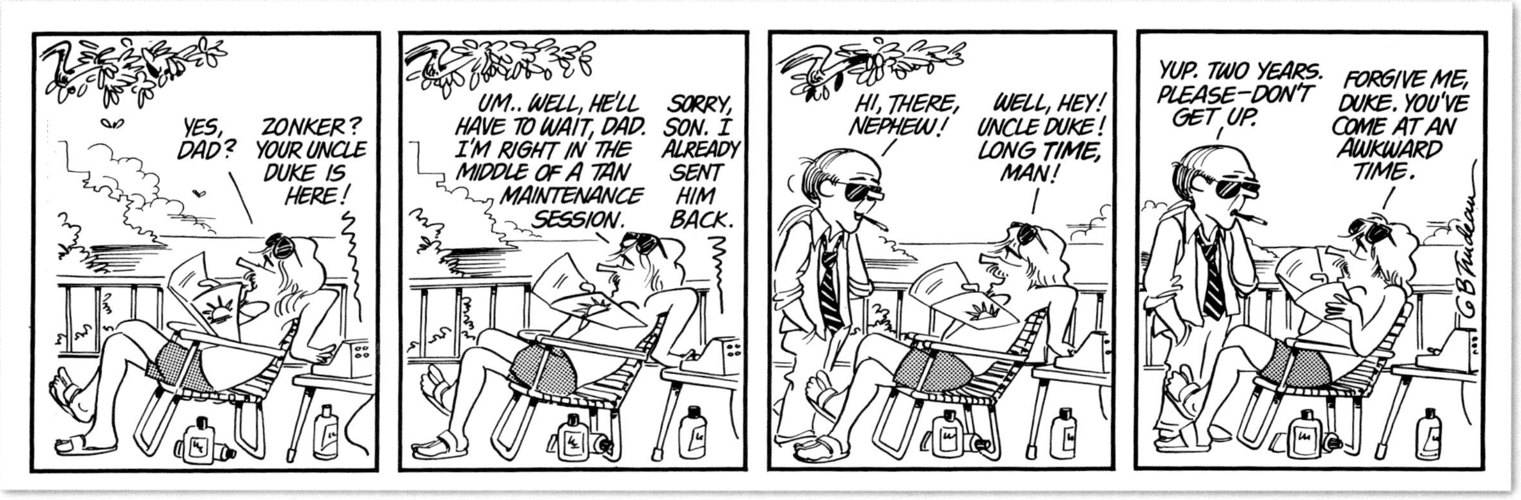
ZONKER? YOUR UNCLE DUKE IS HERE!
YES, DAD?
UM.. WELL, HE'LL HAVE TO WAIT, DAD. I'M RIGHT IN THE MIDDLE OF A TAN MAINTENANCE SESSION.
SORRY, SON. I ALREADY SENT HIM BACK.
HI, THERE, NEPHEW!
WELL, HEY! UNCLE DUKE! LONG TIME, MAN!
YUP. TWO YEARS. PLEASE—DON'T GET UP.
FORGIVE ME, DUKE. YOU'VE COME AT AN AWKWARD TIME.
GBTrudeau

6/30/77

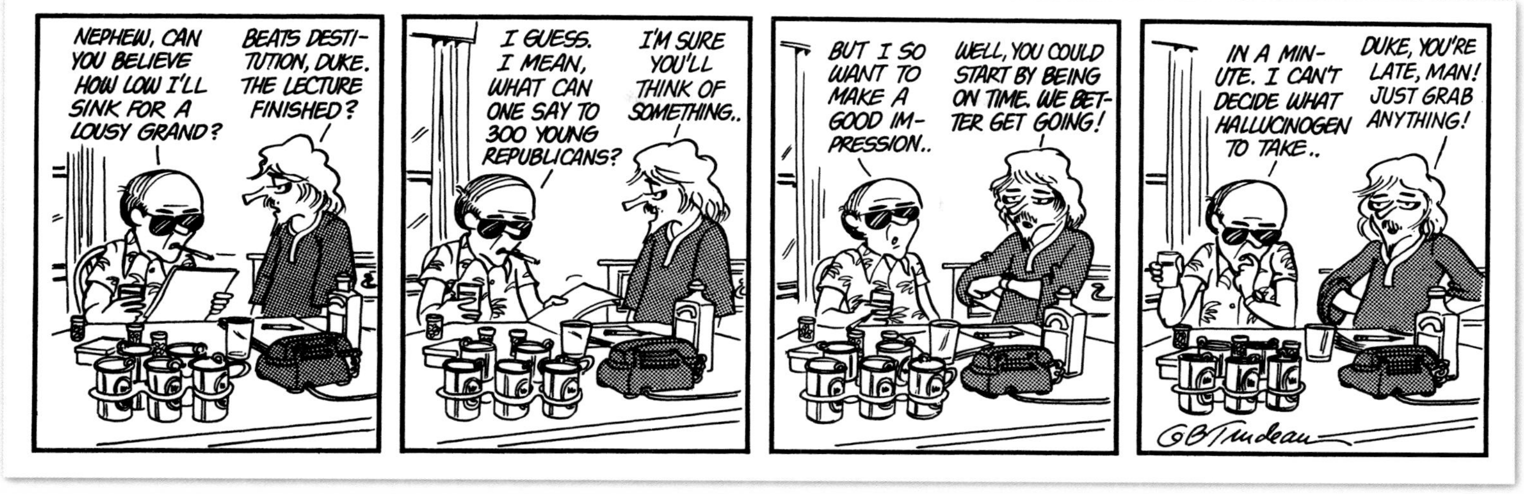
NEPHEW, CAN YOU BELIEVE HOW LOW I'LL SINK FOR A LOUSY GRAND?
BEATS DESTITUTION, DUKE. THE LECTURE FINISHED?
I GUESS. I MEAN, WHAT CAN ONE SAY TO 300 YOUNG REPUBLICANS?
I'M SURE YOU'LL THINK OF SOMETHING..
BUT I SO WANT TO MAKE A GOOD IMPRESSION..
WELL, YOU COULD START BY BEING ON TIME. WE BETTER GET GOING!
IN A MINUTE. I CAN'T DECIDE WHAT HALLUCINOGEN TO TAKE..
DUKE, YOU'RE LATE, MAN! JUST GRAB ANYTHING!
GBTrudeau

8/15/77

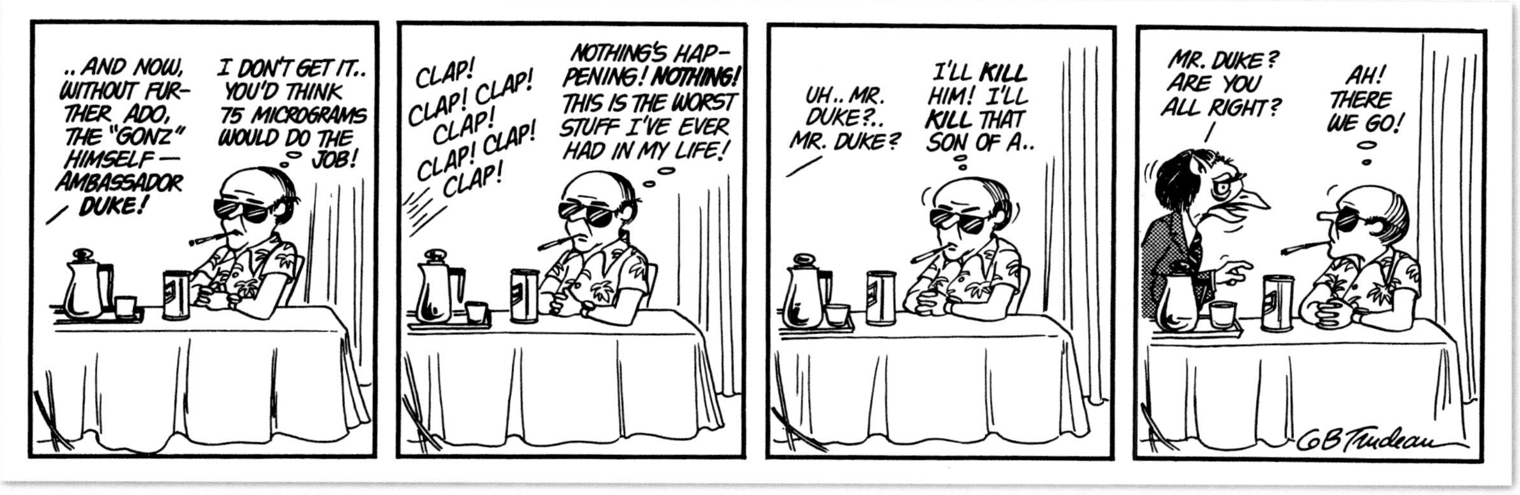
..AND NOW, WITHOUT FURTHER ADO, THE "GONZ" HIMSELF— AMBASSADOR DUKE!
I DON'T GET IT.. YOU'D THINK 75 MICROGRAMS WOULD DO THE JOB!
CLAP! CLAP! CLAP! CLAP! CLAP! CLAP! CLAP!
NOTHING'S HAPPENING! NOTHING! THIS IS THE WORST STUFF I'VE EVER HAD IN MY LIFE!
UH.. MR. DUKE?.. MR. DUKE?
I'LL KILL HIM! I'LL KILL THAT SON OF A..
MR. DUKE? ARE YOU ALL RIGHT?
AH! THERE WE GO!
GBTrudeau

8/17/77

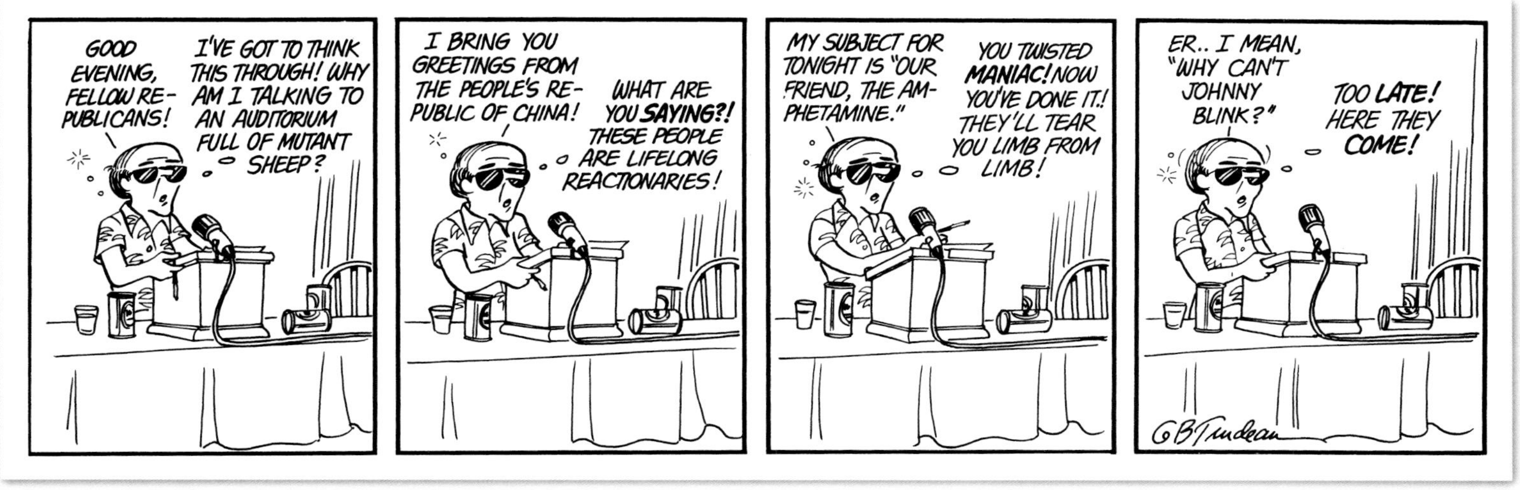
GOOD EVENING, FELLOW REPUBLICANS!
I'VE GOT TO THINK THIS THROUGH! WHY AM I TALKING TO AN AUDITORIUM FULL OF MUTANT SHEEP?
I BRING YOU GREETINGS FROM THE PEOPLE'S REPUBLIC OF CHINA!
WHAT ARE YOU SAYING?! THESE PEOPLE ARE LIFELONG REACTIONARIES!
MY SUBJECT FOR TONIGHT IS "OUR FRIEND, THE AMPHETAMINE."
YOU TWISTED MANIAC! NOW YOU'VE DONE IT! THEY'LL TEAR YOU LIMB FROM LIMB!
ER.. I MEAN, "WHY CAN'T JOHNNY BLINK?"
TOO LATE! HERE THEY COME!
GBTrudeau

8/19/77

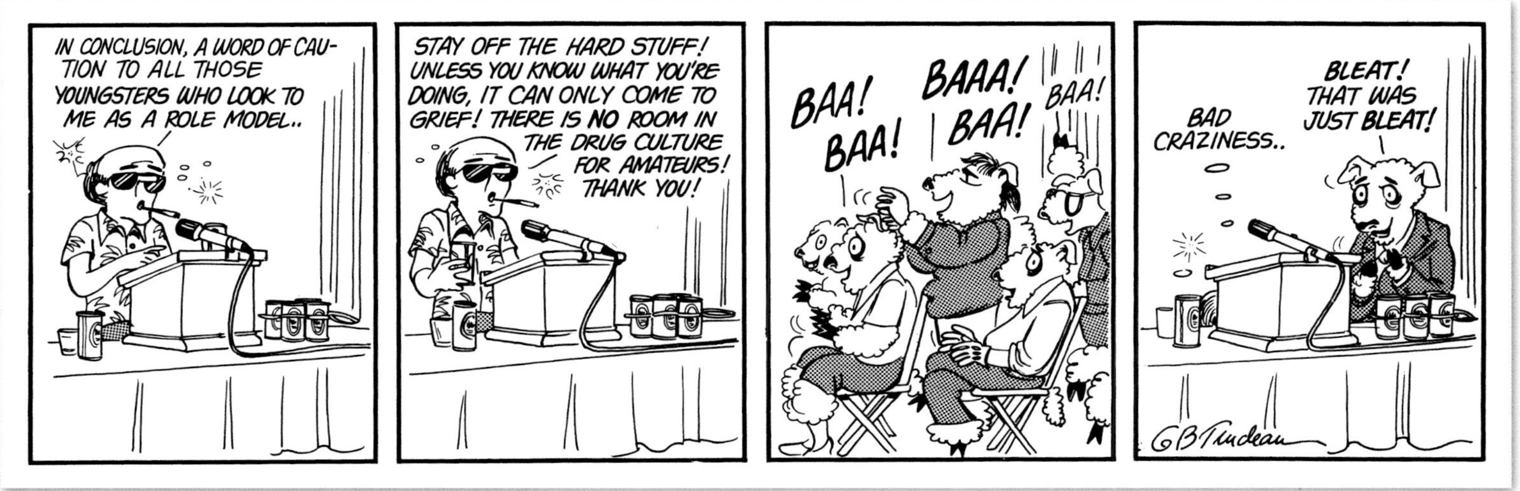
IN CONCLUSION, A WORD OF CAUTION TO ALL THOSE YOUNGSTERS WHO LOOK TO ME AS A ROLE MODEL..
STAY OFF THE HARD STUFF! UNLESS YOU KNOW WHAT YOU'RE DOING, IT CAN ONLY COME TO GRIEF! THERE IS NO ROOM IN THE DRUG CULTURE FOR AMATEURS! THANK YOU!
BAA! BAA!
BAAA! BAA!
BAA!
BAD CRAZINESS..
BLEAT! THAT WAS JUST BLEAT!
GBTrudeau

8/20/77

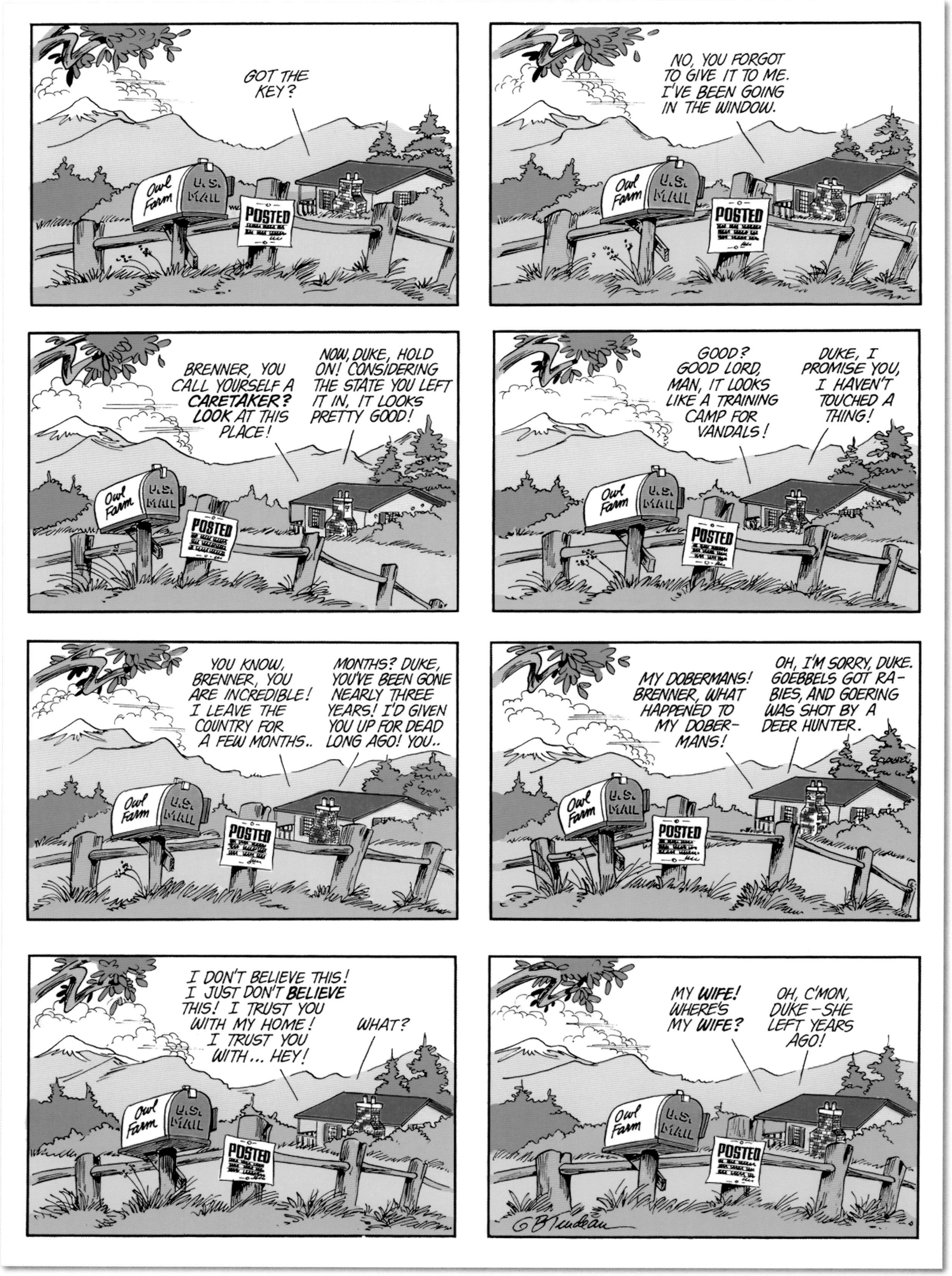
GOT THE KEY?
NO, YOU FORGOT TO GIVE IT TO ME. I'VE BEEN GOING IN THE WINDOW.
BRENNER, YOU CALL YOURSELF A CARETAKER? LOOK AT THIS PLACE!
NOW, DUKE, HOLD ON! CONSIDERING THE STATE YOU LEFT IT IN, IT LOOKS PRETTY GOOD!
GOOD? GOOD LORD, MAN, IT LOOKS LIKE A TRAINING CAMP FOR VANDALS!
DUKE, I PROMISE YOU, I HAVEN'T TOUCHED A THING!
YOU KNOW, BRENNER, YOU ARE INCREDIBLE! I LEAVE THE COUNTRY FOR A FEW MONTHS..
MONTHS? DUKE, YOU'VE BEEN GONE NEARLY THREE YEARS! I'D GIVEN YOU UP FOR DEAD LONG AGO! YOU..
MY DOBERMANS! BRENNER, WHAT HAPPENED TO MY DOBERMANS!
OH, I'M SORRY, DUKE. GOEBBELS GOT RABIES, AND GOERING WAS SHOT BY A DEER HUNTER.
I DON'T BELIEVE THIS! I JUST DON'T BELIEVE THIS! I TRUST YOU WITH MY HOME! I TRUST YOU WITH... HEY!
WHAT?
MY WIFE! WHERE'S MY WIFE?
OH, C'MON, DUKE—SHE LEFT YEARS AGO!
Owl Farm
U.S. MAIL
POSTED
G B Trudeau

7/24/77

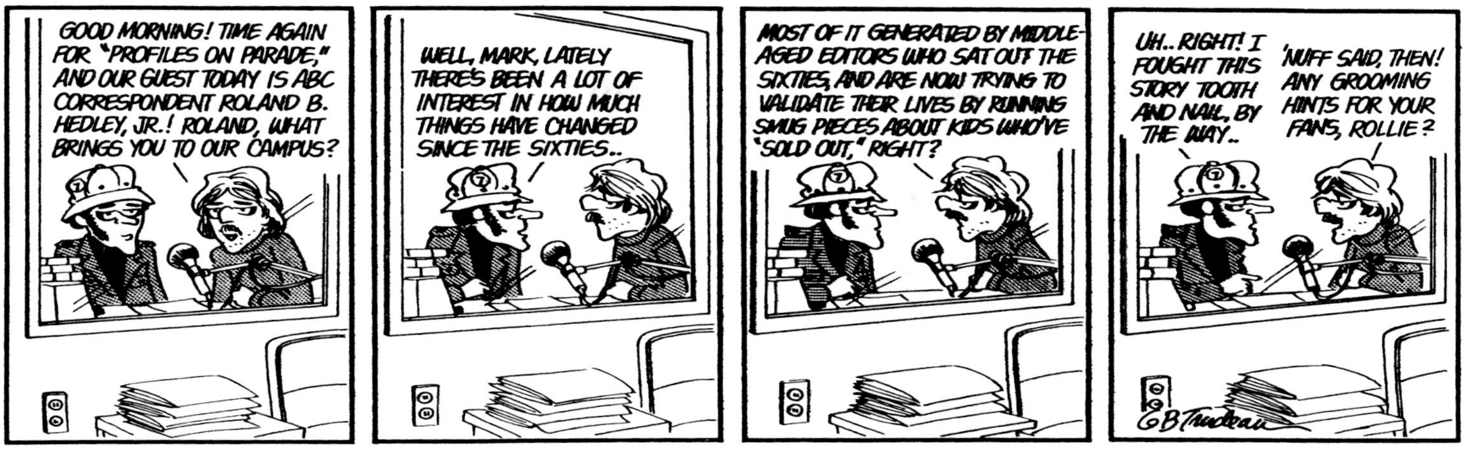
GOOD MORNING! TIME AGAIN FOR "PROFILES ON PARADE," AND OUR GUEST TODAY IS ABC CORRESPONDENT ROLAND B. HEDLEY, JR.! ROLAND, WHAT BRINGS YOU TO OUR CAMPUS?
WELL, MARK, LATELY THERE'S BEEN A LOT OF INTEREST IN HOW MUCH THINGS HAVE CHANGED SINCE THE SIXTIES..
MOST OF IT GENERATED BY MIDDLE-AGED EDITORS WHO SAT OUT THE SIXTIES, AND ARE NOW TRYING TO VALIDATE THEIR LIVES BY RUNNING SMUG PIECES ABOUT KIDS WHO'VE "SOLD OUT," RIGHT?
UH.. RIGHT! I FOUGHT THIS STORY TOOTH AND NAIL, BY THE WAY..
'NUFF SAID, THEN! ANY GROOMING HINTS FOR YOUR FANS, ROLLIE?
GB Trudeau

11/5/77

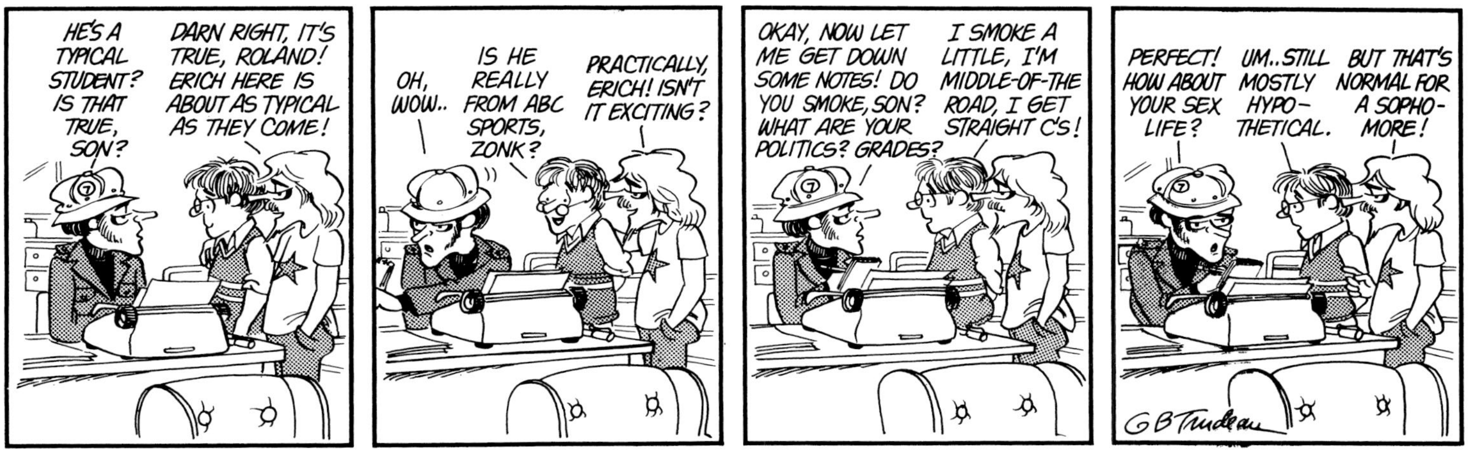
HE'S A TYPICAL STUDENT? IS THAT TRUE, SON?
DARN RIGHT, IT'S TRUE, ROLAND! ERICH HERE IS ABOUT AS TYPICAL AS THEY COME!
OH, WOW..
IS HE REALLY FROM ABC SPORTS, ZONK?
PRACTICALLY, ERICH! ISN'T IT EXCITING?
OKAY, NOW LET ME GET DOWN SOME NOTES! DO YOU SMOKE, SON? WHAT ARE YOUR POLITICS? GRADES?
I SMOKE A LITTLE, I'M MIDDLE-OF-THE ROAD, I GET STRAIGHT C'S!
PERFECT! HOW ABOUT YOUR SEX LIFE?
UM.. STILL MOSTLY HYPO-THETICAL.
BUT THAT'S NORMAL FOR A SOPHO-MORE!
GB Trudeau

11/8/77

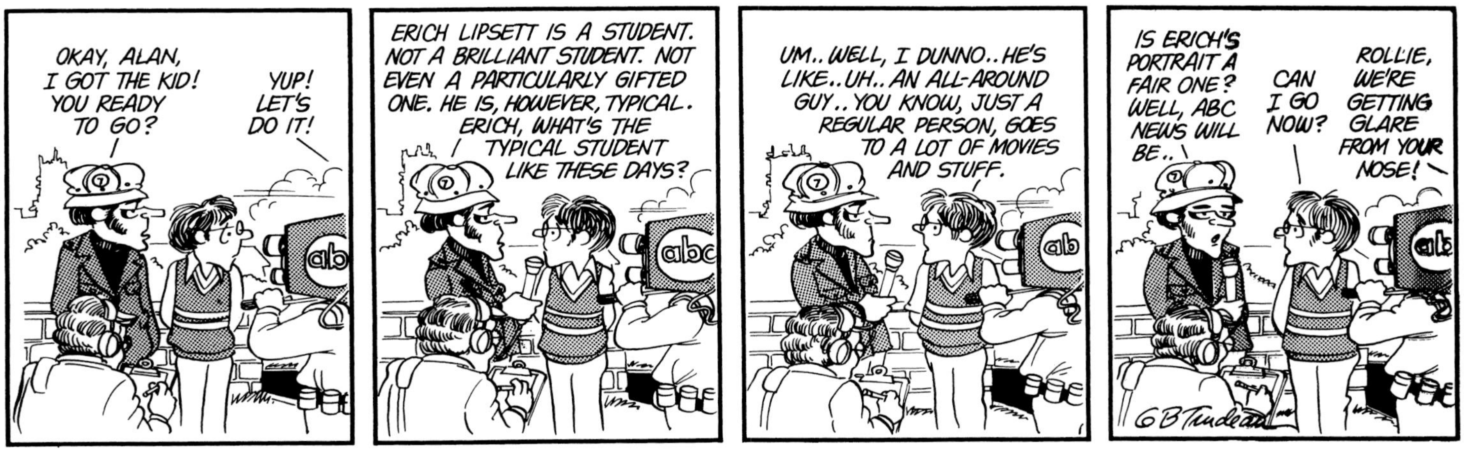
OKAY, ALAN, I GOT THE KID! YOU READY TO GO?
YUP! LET'S DO IT!
ERICH LIPSETT IS A STUDENT. NOT A BRILLIANT STUDENT. NOT EVEN A PARTICULARLY GIFTED ONE. HE IS, HOWEVER, TYPICAL. ERICH, WHAT'S THE TYPICAL STUDENT LIKE THESE DAYS?
UM.. WELL, I DUNNO.. HE'S LIKE.. UH.. AN ALL-AROUND GUY.. YOU KNOW, JUST A REGULAR PERSON, GOES TO A LOT OF MOVIES AND STUFF.
IS ERICH'S PORTRAIT A FAIR ONE? WELL, ABC NEWS WILL BE..
CAN I GO NOW?
ROLLIE, WE'RE GETTING GLARE FROM YOUR NOSE!
GB Trudeau

11/9/77

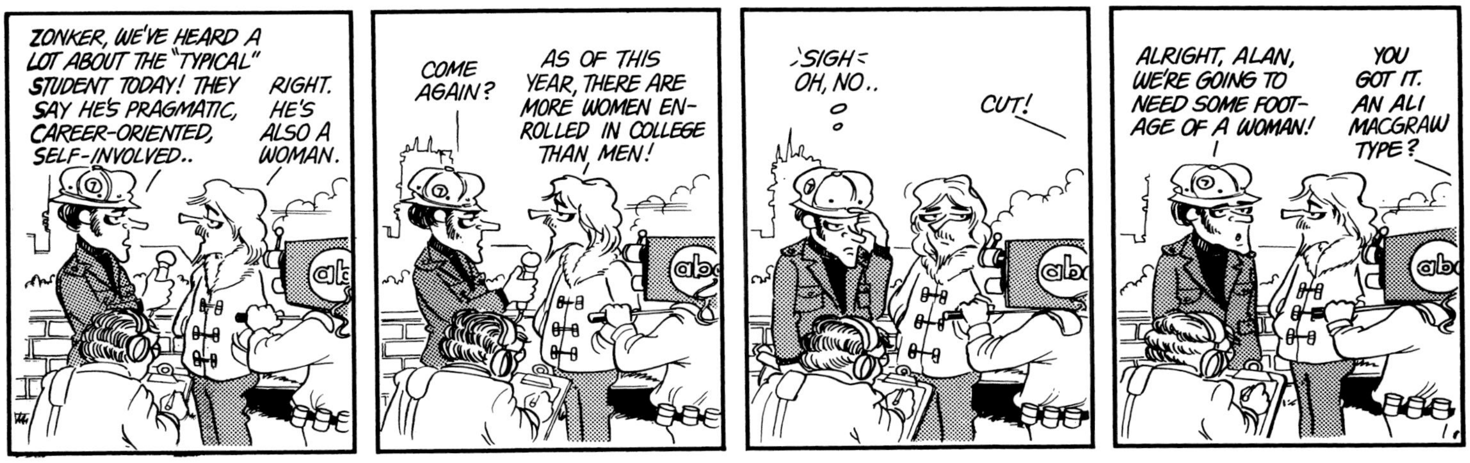
ZONKER, WE'VE HEARD A LOT ABOUT THE "TYPICAL" STUDENT TODAY! THEY SAY HE'S PRAGMATIC, CAREER-ORIENTED, SELF-INVOLVED..
RIGHT. HE'S ALSO A WOMAN.
COME AGAIN?
AS OF THIS YEAR, THERE ARE MORE WOMEN ENROLLED IN COLLEGE THAN MEN!
SIGH OH, NO..
CUT!
ALRIGHT, ALAN, WE'RE GOING TO NEED SOME FOOT-AGE OF A WOMAN!
YOU GOT IT. AN ALI MACGRAW TYPE?

11/12/77

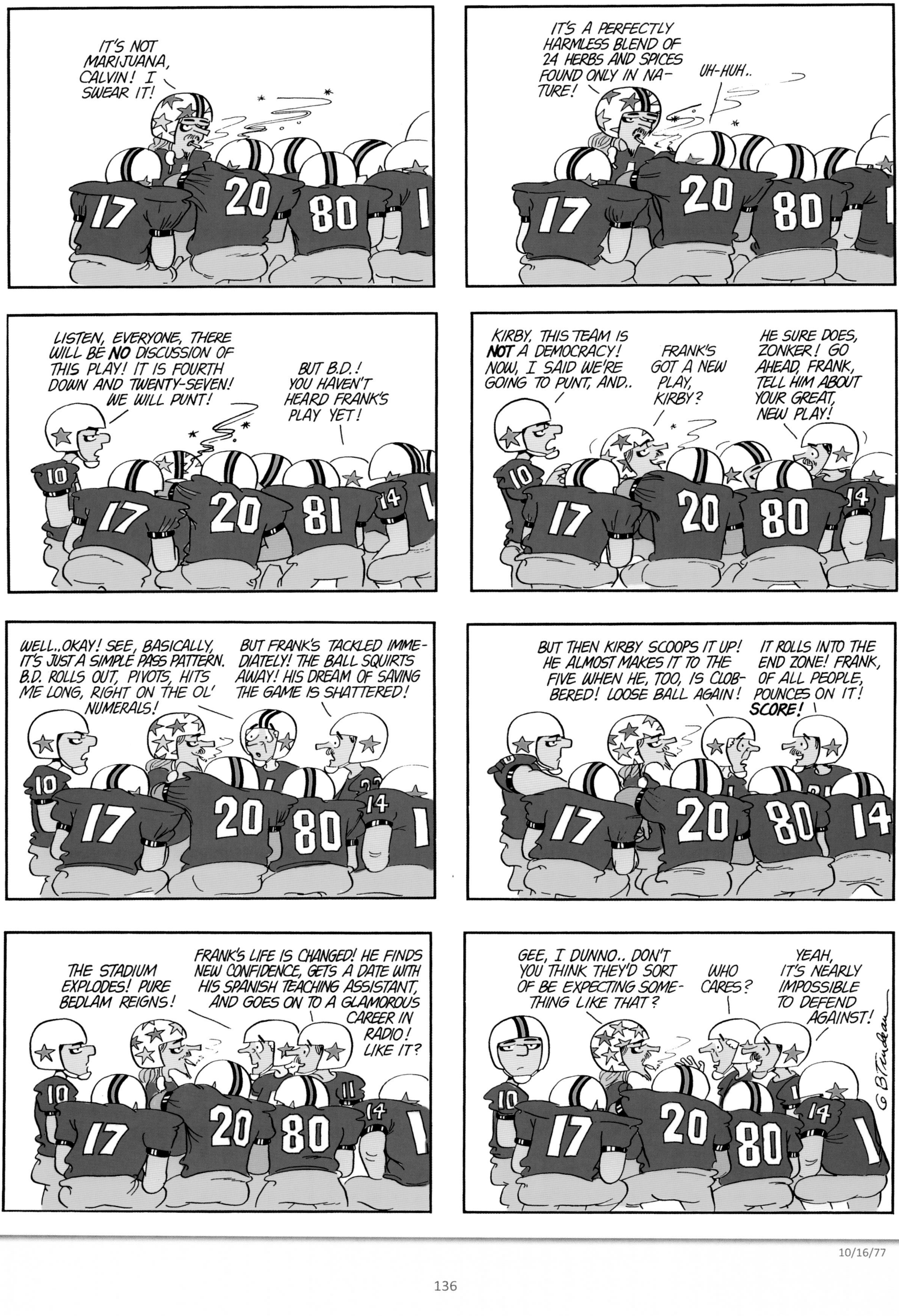
IT'S NOT MARIJUANA, CALVIN! I SWEAR IT!
IT'S A PERFECTLY HARMLESS BLEND OF 24 HERBS AND SPICES FOUND ONLY IN NATURE!
UH-HUH..
LISTEN, EVERYONE, THERE WILL BE NO DISCUSSION OF THIS PLAY! IT IS FOURTH DOWN AND TWENTY-SEVEN! WE WILL PUNT!
BUT B.D.! YOU HAVEN'T HEARD FRANK'S PLAY YET!
KIRBY, THIS TEAM IS NOT A DEMOCRACY! NOW, I SAID WE'RE GOING TO PUNT, AND..
FRANK'S GOT A NEW PLAY, KIRBY?
HE SURE DOES, ZONKER! GO AHEAD, FRANK, TELL HIM ABOUT YOUR GREAT, NEW PLAY!
WELL..OKAY! SEE, BASICALLY, IT'S JUST A SIMPLE PASS PATTERN. B.D. ROLLS OUT, PIVOTS, HITS ME LONG, RIGHT ON THE OL' NUMERALS!
BUT FRANK'S TACKLED IMMEDIATELY! THE BALL SQUIRTS AWAY! HIS DREAM OF SAVING THE GAME IS SHATTERED!
BUT THEN KIRBY SCOOPS IT UP! HE ALMOST MAKES IT TO THE FIVE WHEN HE, TOO, IS CLOBBERED! LOOSE BALL AGAIN!
IT ROLLS INTO THE END ZONE! FRANK, OF ALL PEOPLE, POUNCES ON IT! SCORE!
THE STADIUM EXPLODES! PURE BEDLAM REIGNS!
FRANK'S LIFE IS CHANGED! HE FINDS NEW CONFIDENCE, GETS A DATE WITH HIS SPANISH TEACHING ASSISTANT, AND GOES ON TO A GLAMOROUS CAREER IN RADIO! LIKE IT?
GEE, I DUNNO.. DON'T YOU THINK THEY'D SORT OF BE EXPECTING SOMETHING LIKE THAT?
WHO CARES?
YEAH, IT'S NEARLY IMPOSSIBLE TO DEFEND AGAINST!
© GBTrudeau

10/16/77

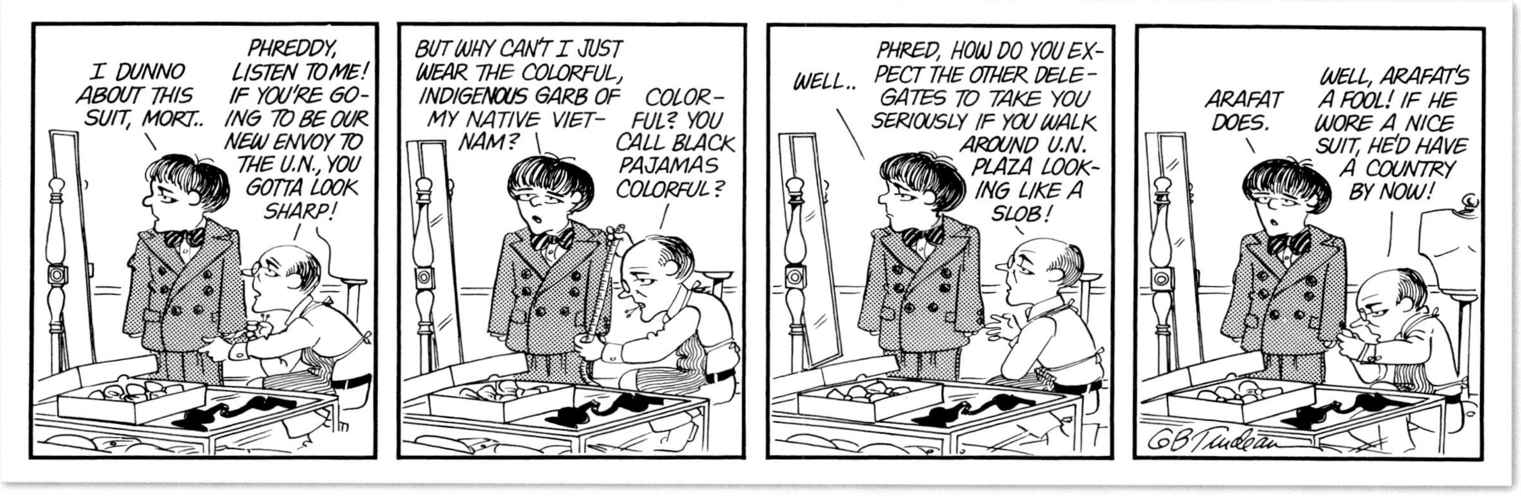
I DUNNO ABOUT THIS SUIT, MORT..
PHREDDY, LISTEN TO ME! IF YOU'RE GOING TO BE OUR NEW ENVOY TO THE U.N., YOU GOTTA LOOK SHARP!
BUT WHY CAN'T I JUST WEAR THE COLORFUL, INDIGENOUS GARB OF MY NATIVE VIETNAM?
COLORFUL? YOU CALL BLACK PAJAMAS COLORFUL?
WELL..
PHRED, HOW DO YOU EXPECT THE OTHER DELEGATES TO TAKE YOU SERIOUSLY IF YOU WALK AROUND U.N. PLAZA LOOKING LIKE A SLOB!
ARAFAT DOES.
WELL, ARAFAT'S A FOOL! IF HE WORE A NICE SUIT, HE'D HAVE A COUNTRY BY NOW!
GBTrudeau

2/28/78

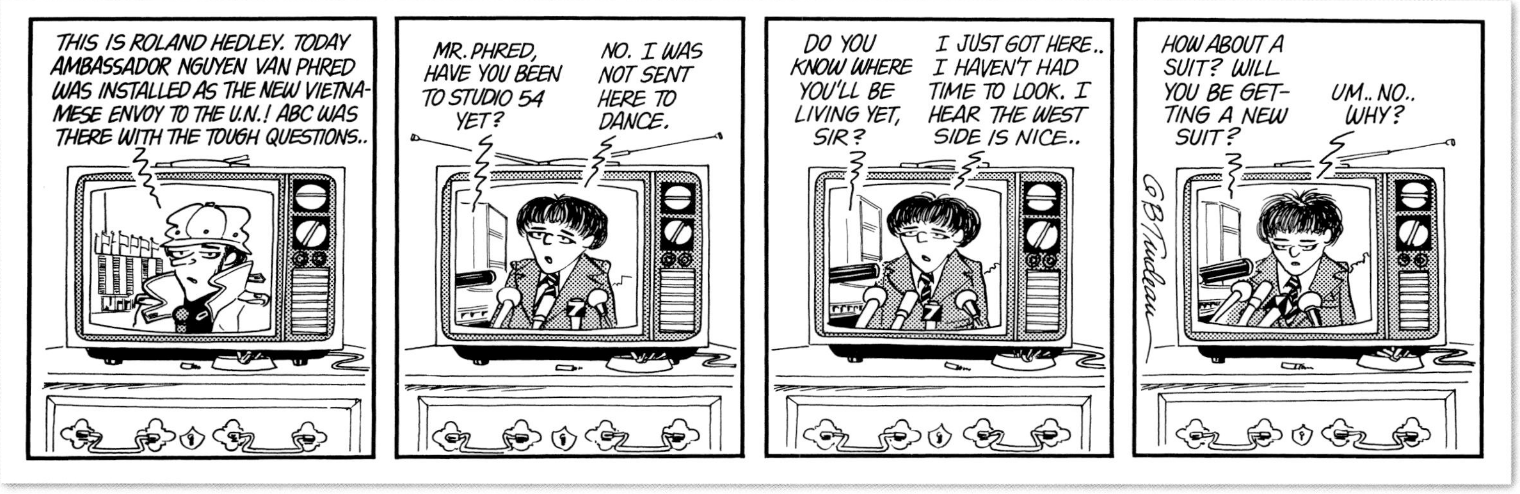
THIS IS ROLAND HEDLEY. TODAY AMBASSADOR NGUYEN VAN PHRED WAS INSTALLED AS THE NEW VIETNAMESE ENVOY TO THE U.N.! ABC WAS THERE WITH THE TOUGH QUESTIONS..
MR. PHRED, HAVE YOU BEEN TO STUDIO 54 YET?
NO. I WAS NOT SENT HERE TO DANCE.
DO YOU KNOW WHERE YOU'LL BE LIVING YET, SIR?
I JUST GOT HERE.. I HAVEN'T HAD TIME TO LOOK. I HEAR THE WEST SIDE IS NICE..
HOW ABOUT A SUIT? WILL YOU BE GETTING A NEW SUIT?
UM.. NO.. WHY?
GBTrudeau

3/6/78

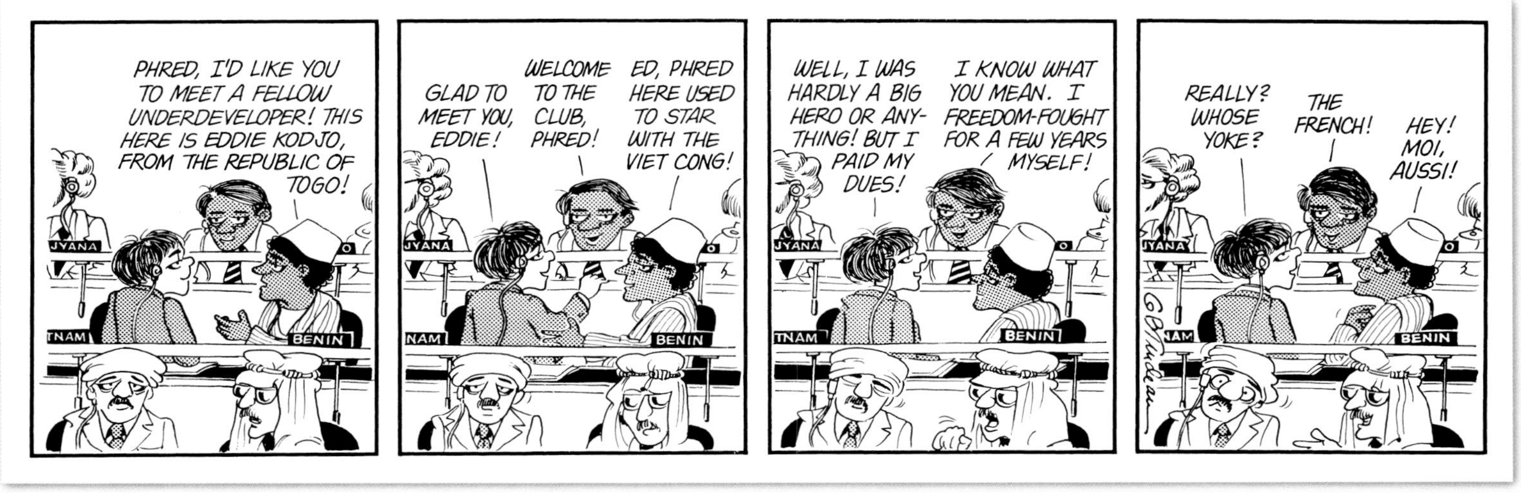
PHRED, I'D LIKE YOU TO MEET A FELLOW UNDERDEVELOPER! THIS HERE IS EDDIE KODJO, FROM THE REPUBLIC OF TOGO!
GLAD TO MEET YOU, EDDIE!
WELCOME TO THE CLUB, PHRED!
ED, PHRED HERE USED TO STAR WITH THE VIET CONG!
WELL, I WAS HARDLY A BIG HERO OR ANYTHING! BUT I PAID MY DUES!
I KNOW WHAT YOU MEAN. I FREEDOM-FOUGHT FOR A FEW YEARS MYSELF!
REALLY? WHOSE YOKE?
THE FRENCH!
HEY! MOI, AUSSI!
GBTrudeau

3/13/78

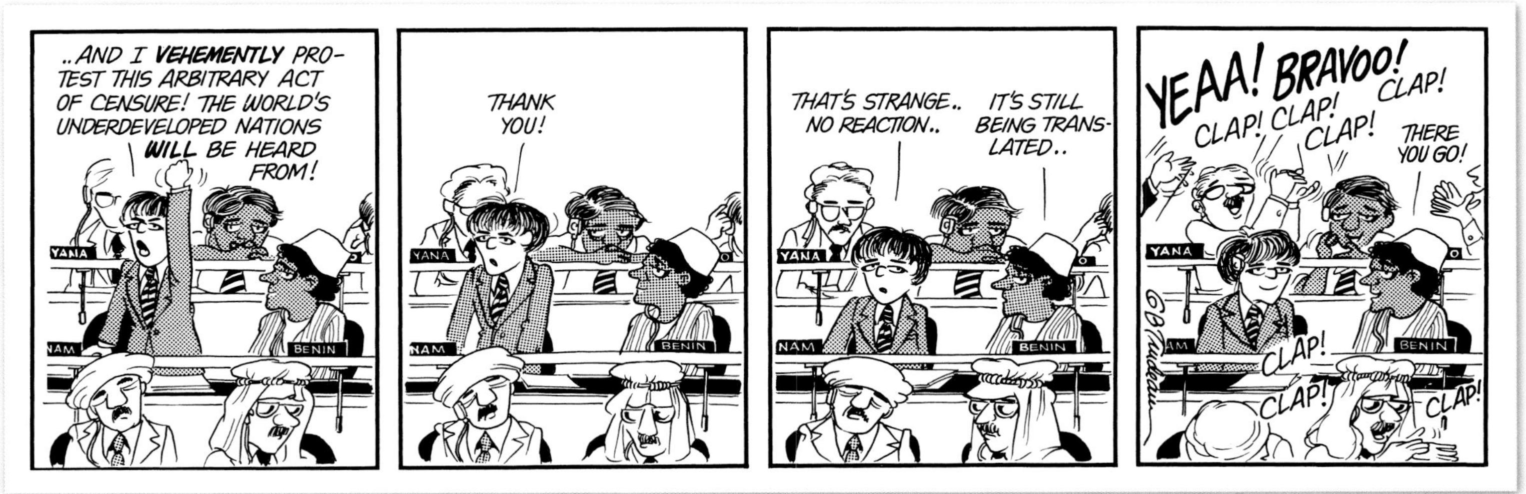
..AND I **VEHEMENTLY** PROTEST THIS ARBITRARY ACT OF CENSURE! THE WORLD'S UNDERDEVELOPED NATIONS **WILL** BE HEARD FROM!
THANK YOU!
THAT'S STRANGE.. NO REACTION..
IT'S STILL BEING TRANSLATED..
YEAA! BRAVOO!
CLAP! CLAP! CLAP! CLAP!
THERE YOU GO!
CLAP! CLAP! CLAP!
GBTrudeau

3/17/78

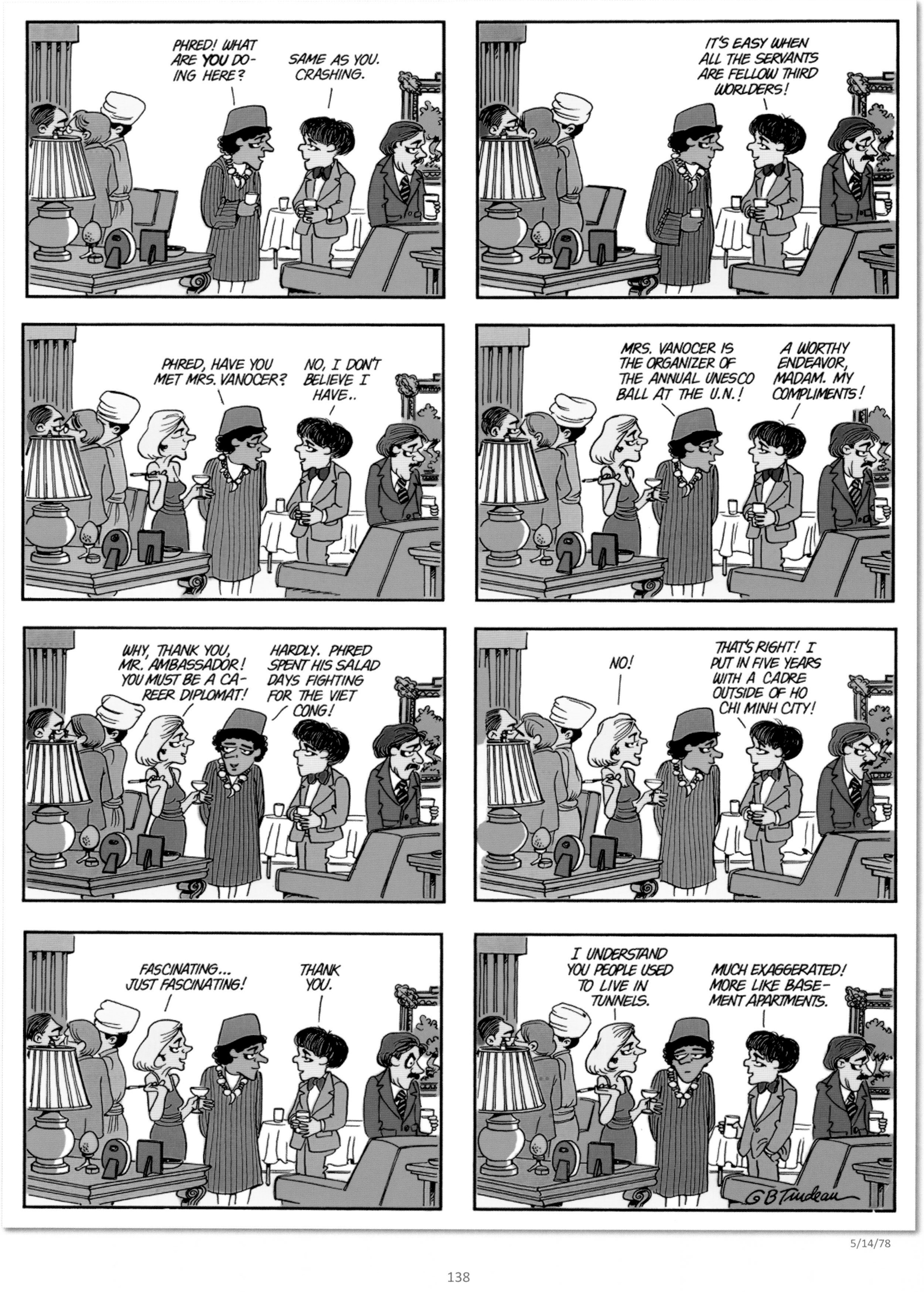
PHRED! WHAT ARE YOU DOING HERE?
SAME AS YOU. CRASHING.
IT'S EASY WHEN ALL THE SERVANTS ARE FELLOW THIRD WORLDERS!
PHRED, HAVE YOU MET MRS. VANOCER?
NO, I DON'T BELIEVE I HAVE..
MRS. VANOCER IS THE ORGANIZER OF THE ANNUAL UNESCO BALL AT THE U.N.!
A WORTHY ENDEAVOR, MADAM. MY COMPLIMENTS!
WHY, THANK YOU, MR. AMBASSADOR! YOU MUST BE A CAREER DIPLOMAT!
HARDLY. PHRED SPENT HIS SALAD DAYS FIGHTING FOR THE VIET CONG!
NO!
THAT'S RIGHT! I PUT IN FIVE YEARS WITH A CADRE OUTSIDE OF HO CHI MINH CITY!
FASCINATING... JUST FASCINATING!
THANK YOU.
I UNDERSTAND YOU PEOPLE USED TO LIVE IN TUNNELS.
MUCH EXAGGERATED! MORE LIKE BASEMENT APARTMENTS.
GB Trudeau

5/14/78

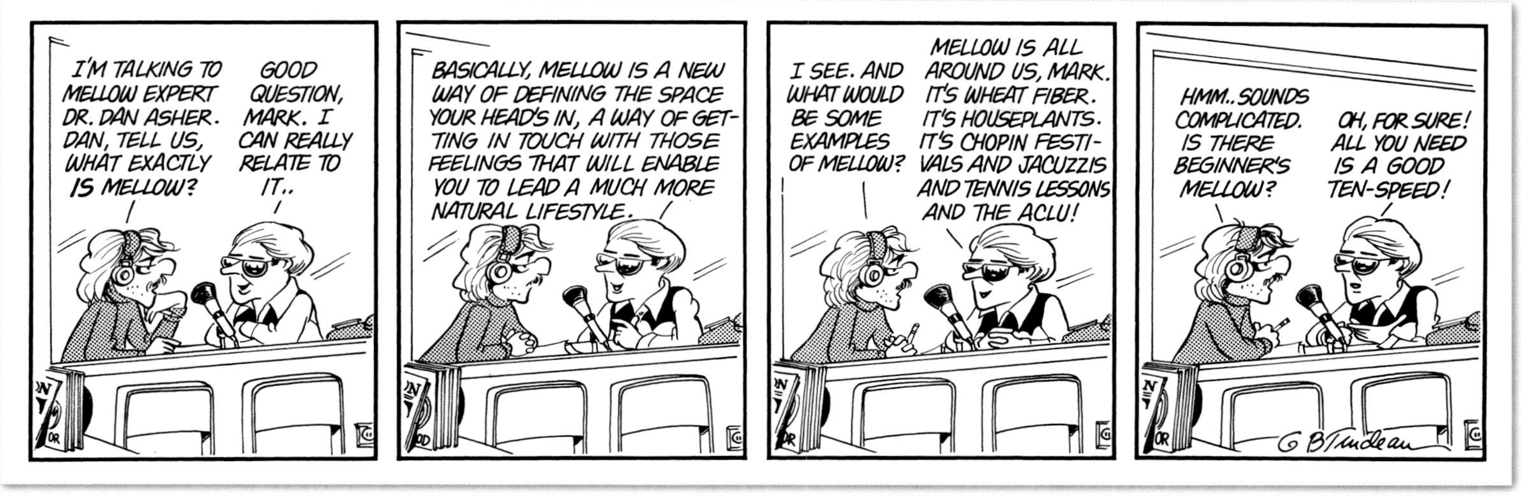
I'M TALKING TO MELLOW EXPERT DR. DAN ASHER. DAN, TELL US, WHAT EXACTLY IS MELLOW?
GOOD QUESTION, MARK. I CAN REALLY RELATE TO IT..
BASICALLY, MELLOW IS A NEW WAY OF DEFINING THE SPACE YOUR HEAD'S IN, A WAY OF GETTING IN TOUCH WITH THOSE FEELINGS THAT WILL ENABLE YOU TO LEAD A MUCH MORE NATURAL LIFESTYLE.
I SEE. AND WHAT WOULD BE SOME EXAMPLES OF MELLOW?
MELLOW IS ALL AROUND US, MARK. IT'S WHEAT FIBER. IT'S HOUSEPLANTS. IT'S CHOPIN FESTIVALS AND JACUZZIS AND TENNIS LESSONS AND THE ACLU!
HMM.. SOUNDS COMPLICATED. IS THERE BEGINNER'S MELLOW?
OH, FOR SURE! ALL YOU NEED IS A GOOD TEN-SPEED!

4/18/78

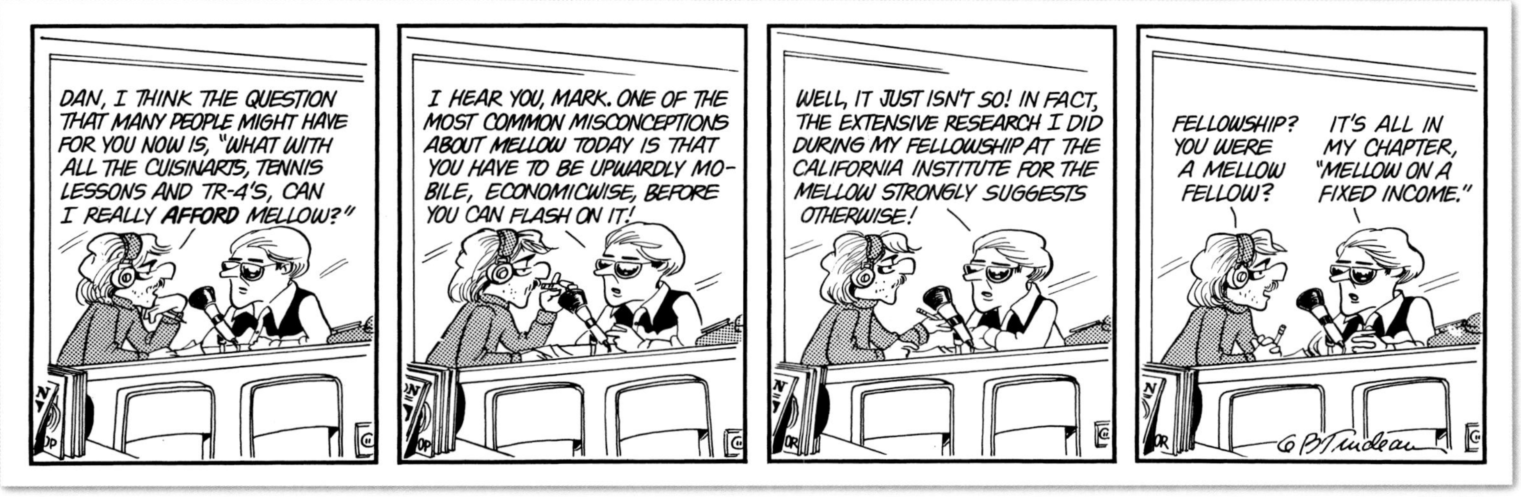
DAN, I THINK THE QUESTION THAT MANY PEOPLE MIGHT HAVE FOR YOU NOW IS, "WHAT WITH ALL THE CUISINARTS, TENNIS LESSONS AND TR-4'S, CAN I REALLY AFFORD MELLOW?"
I HEAR YOU, MARK. ONE OF THE MOST COMMON MISCONCEPTIONS ABOUT MELLOW TODAY IS THAT YOU HAVE TO BE UPWARDLY MOBILE, ECONOMICWISE, BEFORE YOU CAN FLASH ON IT!
WELL, IT JUST ISN'T SO! IN FACT, THE EXTENSIVE RESEARCH I DID DURING MY FELLOWSHIP AT THE CALIFORNIA INSTITUTE FOR THE MELLOW STRONGLY SUGGESTS OTHERWISE!
FELLOWSHIP? YOU WERE A MELLOW FELLOW?
IT'S ALL IN MY CHAPTER, "MELLOW ON A FIXED INCOME."

4/19/78

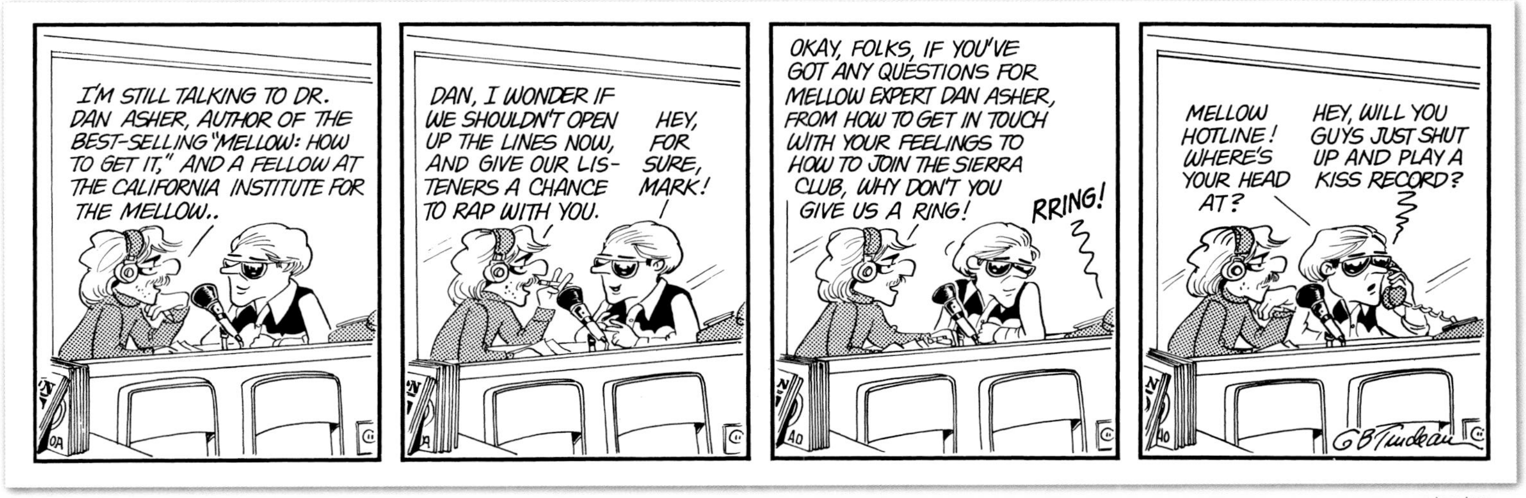
I'M STILL TALKING TO DR. DAN ASHER, AUTHOR OF THE BEST-SELLING "MELLOW: HOW TO GET IT," AND A FELLOW AT THE CALIFORNIA INSTITUTE FOR THE MELLOW..
DAN, I WONDER IF WE SHOULDN'T OPEN UP THE LINES NOW, AND GIVE OUR LISTENERS A CHANCE TO RAP WITH YOU.
HEY, FOR SURE, MARK!
OKAY, FOLKS, IF YOU'VE GOT ANY QUESTIONS FOR MELLOW EXPERT DAN ASHER, FROM HOW TO GET IN TOUCH WITH YOUR FEELINGS TO HOW TO JOIN THE SIERRA CLUB, WHY DON'T YOU GIVE US A RING!
RRING!
MELLOW HOTLINE! WHERE'S YOUR HEAD AT?
HEY, WILL YOU GUYS JUST SHUT UP AND PLAY A KISS RECORD?

4/20/78

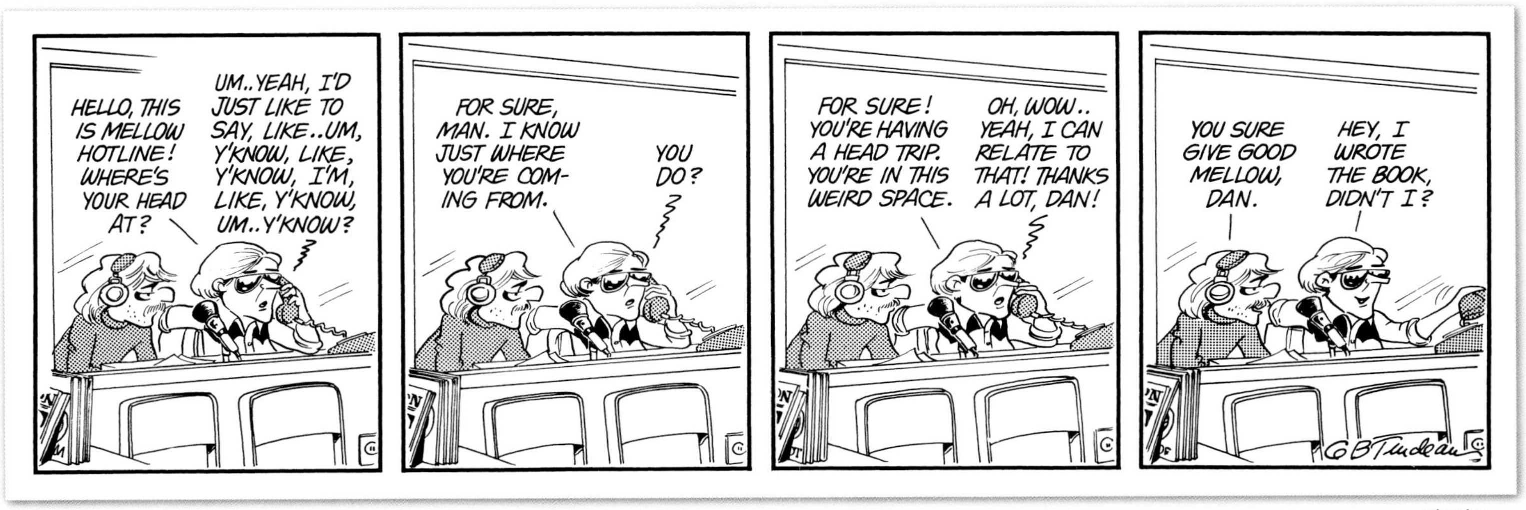
HELLO, THIS IS MELLOW HOTLINE! WHERE'S YOUR HEAD AT?
UM.. YEAH, I'D JUST LIKE TO SAY, LIKE.. UM, Y'KNOW, LIKE, Y'KNOW, I'M, LIKE, Y'KNOW, UM.. Y'KNOW?
FOR SURE, MAN. I KNOW JUST WHERE YOU'RE COMING FROM.
YOU DO?
FOR SURE! YOU'RE HAVING A HEAD TRIP. YOU'RE IN THIS WEIRD SPACE.
OH, WOW.. YEAH, I CAN RELATE TO THAT! THANKS A LOT, DAN!
YOU SURE GIVE GOOD MELLOW, DAN.
HEY, I WROTE THE BOOK, DIDN'T I?

4/22/78

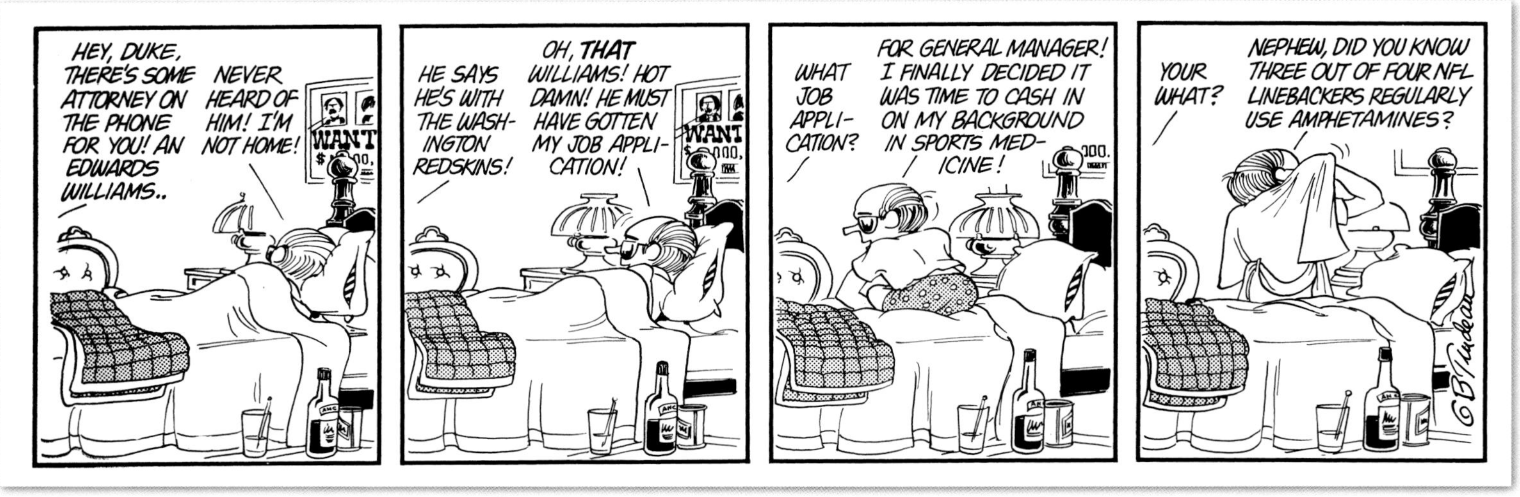
HEY, DUKE, THERE'S SOME ATTORNEY ON THE PHONE FOR YOU! AN EDWARDS WILLIAMS..
NEVER HEARD OF HIM! I'M NOT HOME!
HE SAYS HE'S WITH THE WASHINGTON REDSKINS!
OH, THAT WILLIAMS! HOT DAMN! HE MUST HAVE GOTTEN MY JOB APPLICATION!
WHAT JOB APPLICATION?
FOR GENERAL MANAGER! I FINALLY DECIDED IT WAS TIME TO CASH IN ON MY BACKGROUND IN SPORTS MEDICINE!
YOUR WHAT?
NEPHEW, DID YOU KNOW THREE OUT OF FOUR NFL LINEBACKERS REGULARLY USE AMPHETAMINES?
GBTrudeau

2/15/78

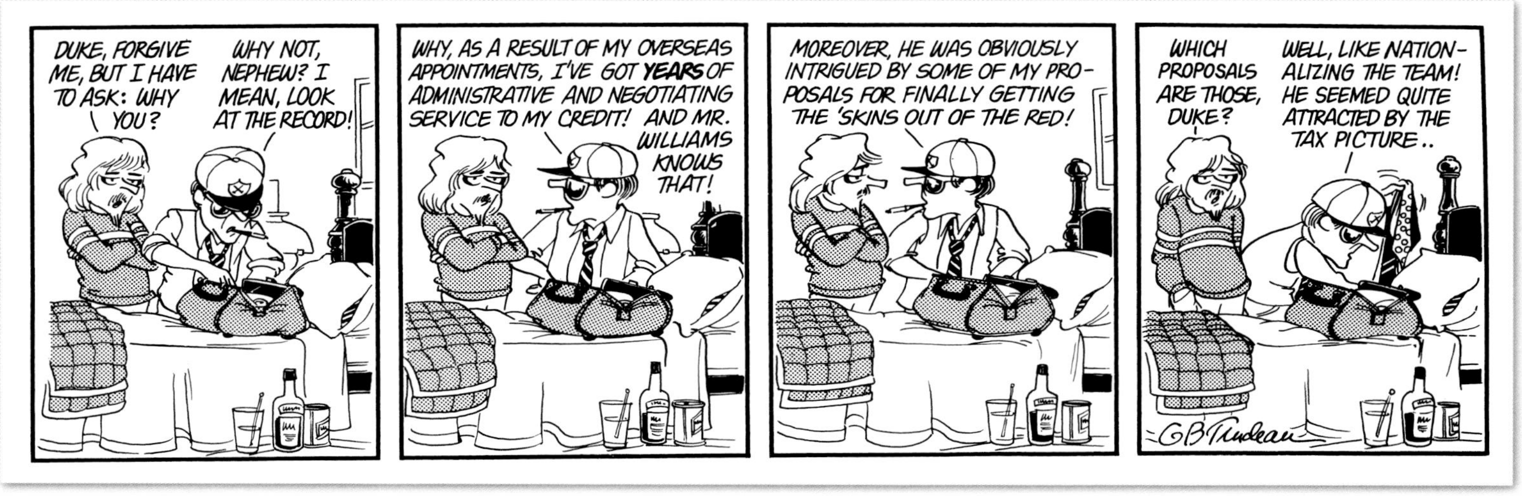
DUKE, FORGIVE ME, BUT I HAVE TO ASK: WHY YOU?
WHY NOT, NEPHEW? I MEAN, LOOK AT THE RECORD!
WHY, AS A RESULT OF MY OVERSEAS APPOINTMENTS, I'VE GOT YEARS OF ADMINISTRATIVE AND NEGOTIATING SERVICE TO MY CREDIT! AND MR. WILLIAMS KNOWS THAT!
MOREOVER, HE WAS OBVIOUSLY INTRIGUED BY SOME OF MY PROPOSALS FOR FINALLY GETTING THE 'SKINS OUT OF THE RED!
WHICH PROPOSALS ARE THOSE, DUKE?
WELL, LIKE NATIONALIZING THE TEAM! HE SEEMED QUITE ATTRACTED BY THE TAX PICTURE..
GBTrudeau

2/18/78

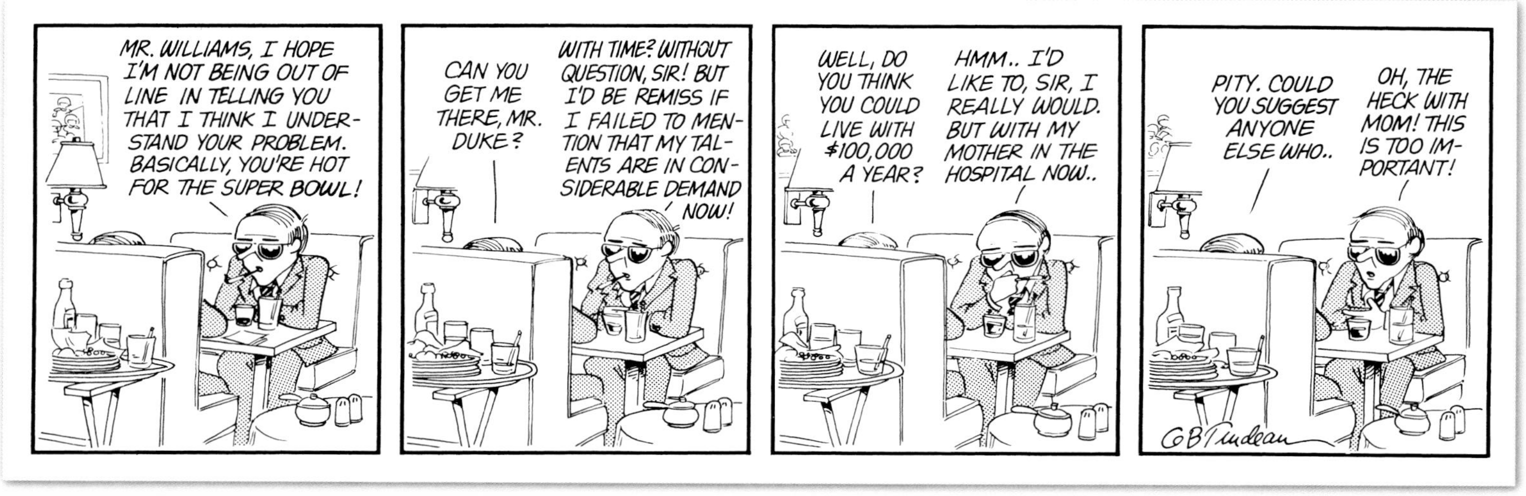
MR. WILLIAMS, I HOPE I'M NOT BEING OUT OF LINE IN TELLING YOU THAT I THINK I UNDERSTAND YOUR PROBLEM. BASICALLY, YOU'RE HOT FOR THE SUPER BOWL!
CAN YOU GET ME THERE, MR. DUKE?
WITH TIME? WITHOUT QUESTION, SIR! BUT I'D BE REMISS IF I FAILED TO MENTION THAT MY TALENTS ARE IN CONSIDERABLE DEMAND NOW!
WELL, DO YOU THINK YOU COULD LIVE WITH $100,000 A YEAR?
HMM.. I'D LIKE TO, SIR, I REALLY WOULD. BUT WITH MY MOTHER IN THE HOSPITAL NOW..
PITY. COULD YOU SUGGEST ANYONE ELSE WHO..
OH, THE HECK WITH MOM! THIS IS TOO IMPORTANT!
GBTrudeau

2/23/78

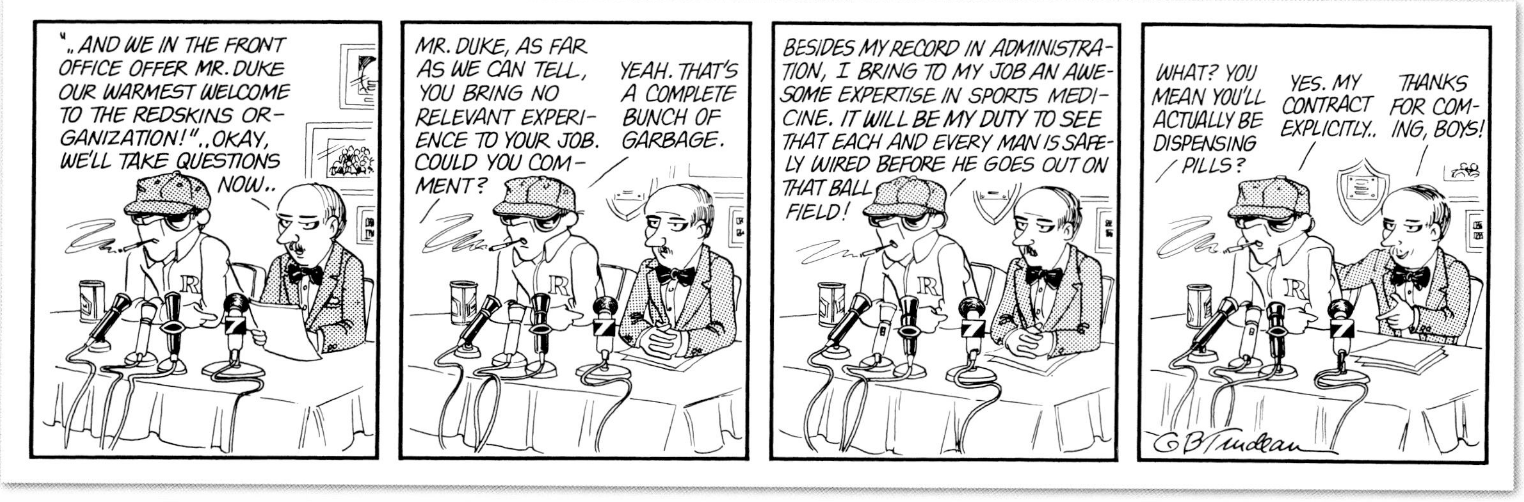
".. AND WE IN THE FRONT OFFICE OFFER MR. DUKE OUR WARMEST WELCOME TO THE REDSKINS ORGANIZATION!".. OKAY, WE'LL TAKE QUESTIONS NOW..
MR. DUKE, AS FAR AS WE CAN TELL, YOU BRING NO RELEVANT EXPERIENCE TO YOUR JOB. COULD YOU COMMENT?
YEAH. THAT'S A COMPLETE BUNCH OF GARBAGE.
BESIDES MY RECORD IN ADMINISTRATION, I BRING TO MY JOB AN AWESOME EXPERTISE IN SPORTS MEDICINE. IT WILL BE MY DUTY TO SEE THAT EACH AND EVERY MAN IS SAFELY WIRED BEFORE HE GOES OUT ON THAT BALL FIELD!
WHAT? YOU MEAN YOU'LL ACTUALLY BE DISPENSING PILLS?
YES. MY CONTRACT EXPLICITLY..
THANKS FOR COMING, BOYS!
GBTrudeau

2/24/78

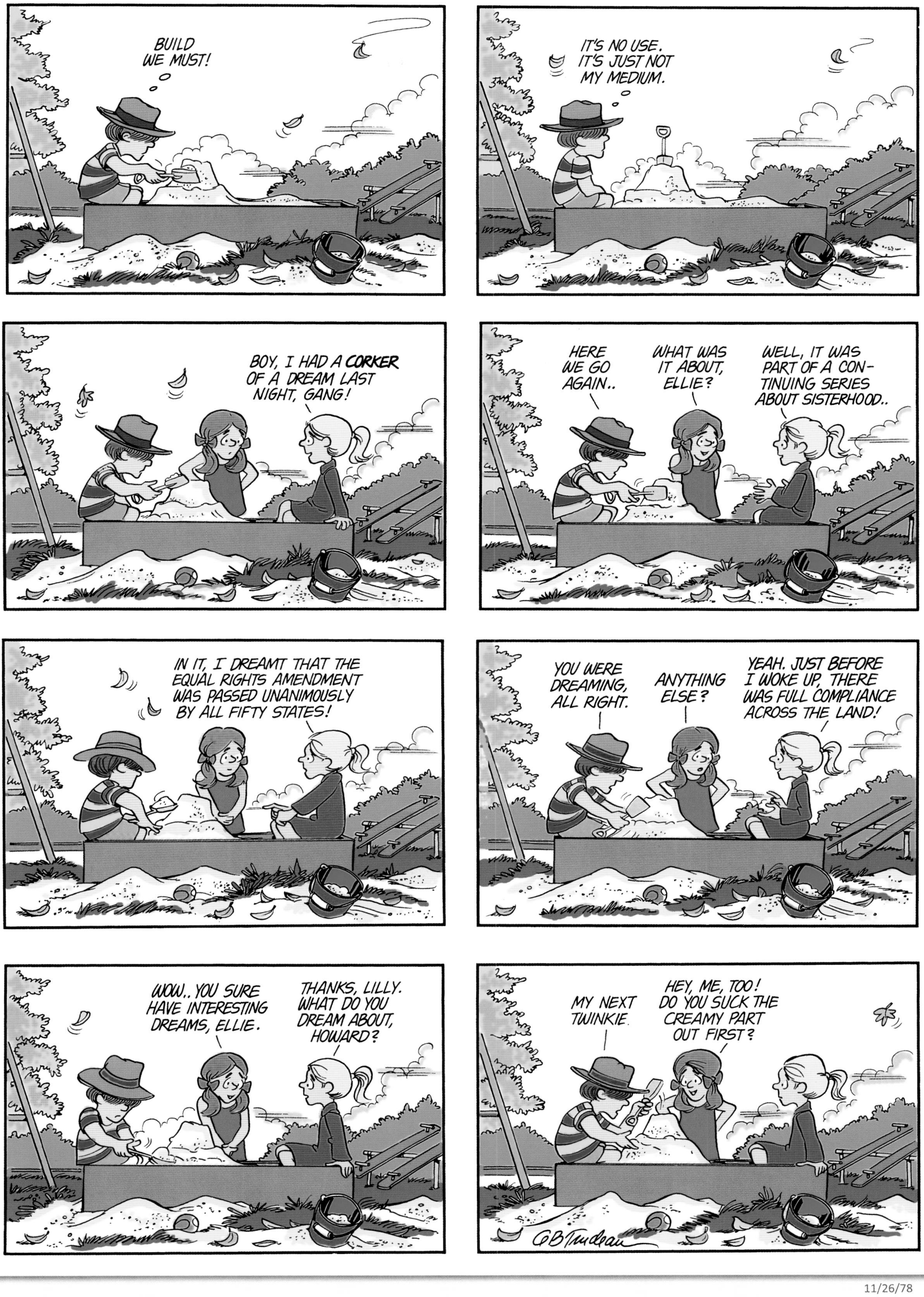
BUILD WE MUST!
IT'S NO USE. IT'S JUST NOT MY MEDIUM.
BOY, I HAD A **CORKER** OF A DREAM LAST NIGHT, GANG!
HERE WE GO AGAIN..
WHAT WAS IT ABOUT, ELLIE?
WELL, IT WAS PART OF A CONTINUING SERIES ABOUT SISTERHOOD..
IN IT, I DREAMT THAT THE EQUAL RIGHTS AMENDMENT WAS PASSED UNANIMOUSLY BY ALL FIFTY STATES!
YOU WERE DREAMING, ALL RIGHT.
ANYTHING ELSE?
YEAH. JUST BEFORE I WOKE UP, THERE WAS FULL COMPLIANCE ACROSS THE LAND!
WOW.. YOU SURE HAVE INTERESTING DREAMS, ELLIE.
THANKS, LILLY. WHAT DO YOU DREAM ABOUT, HOWARD?
MY NEXT TWINKIE.
HEY, ME, TOO! DO YOU SUCK THE CREAMY PART OUT FIRST?
GBTrudeau

11/26/78

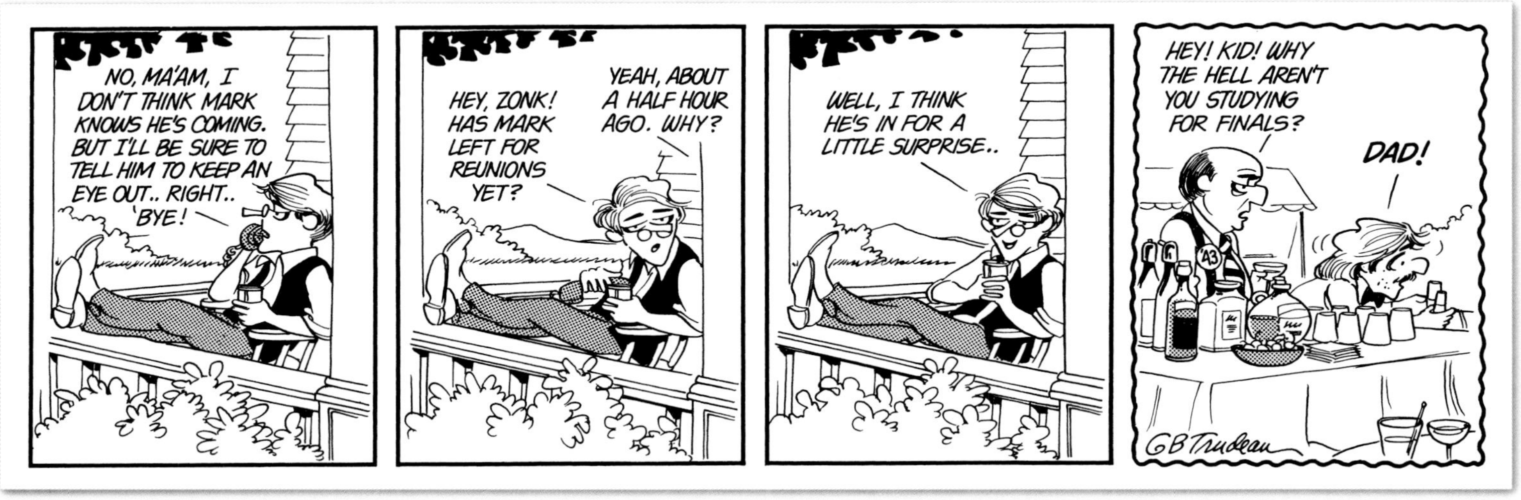
NO, MA'AM, I DON'T THINK MARK KNOWS HE'S COMING. BUT I'LL BE SURE TO TELL HIM TO KEEP AN EYE OUT.. RIGHT.. 'BYE!
HEY, ZONK! HAS MARK LEFT FOR REUNIONS YET?
YEAH, ABOUT A HALF HOUR AGO. WHY?
WELL, I THINK HE'S IN FOR A LITTLE SURPRISE..
HEY! KID! WHY THE HELL AREN'T YOU STUDYING FOR FINALS?
DAD!
GBTrudeau

5/9/78

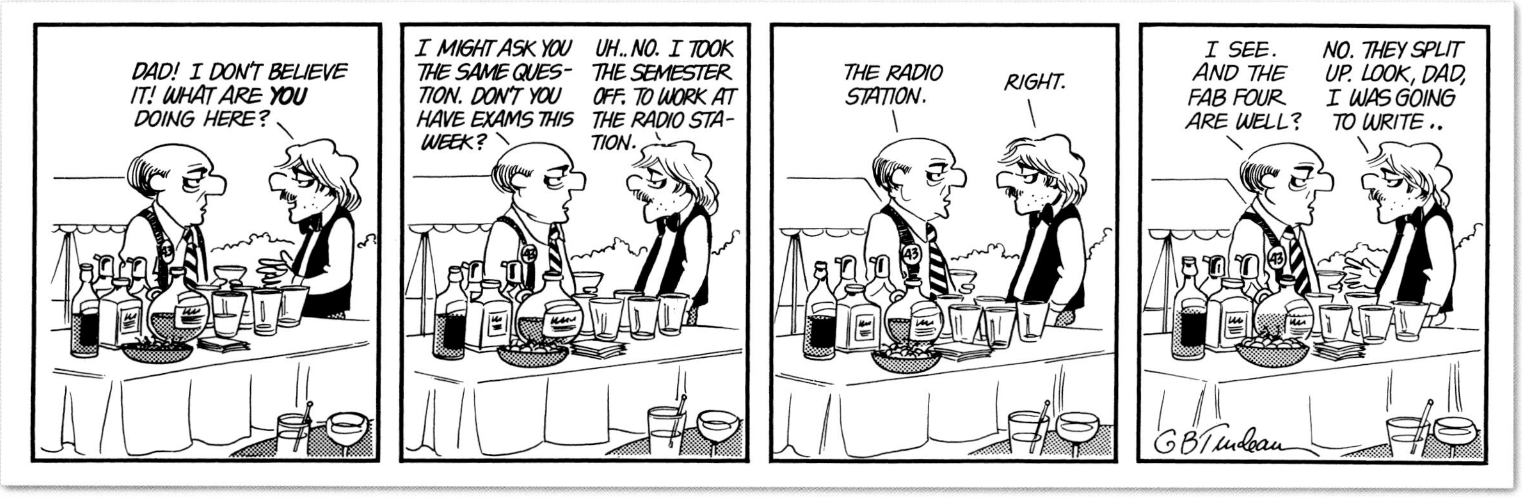
DAD! I DON'T BELIEVE IT! WHAT ARE YOU DOING HERE?
I MIGHT ASK YOU THE SAME QUESTION. DON'T YOU HAVE EXAMS THIS WEEK?
UH.. NO. I TOOK THE SEMESTER OFF. TO WORK AT THE RADIO STATION.
THE RADIO STATION.
RIGHT.
I SEE. AND THE FAB FOUR ARE WELL?
NO. THEY SPLIT UP. LOOK, DAD, I WAS GOING TO WRITE..
GBTrudeau

5/10/78

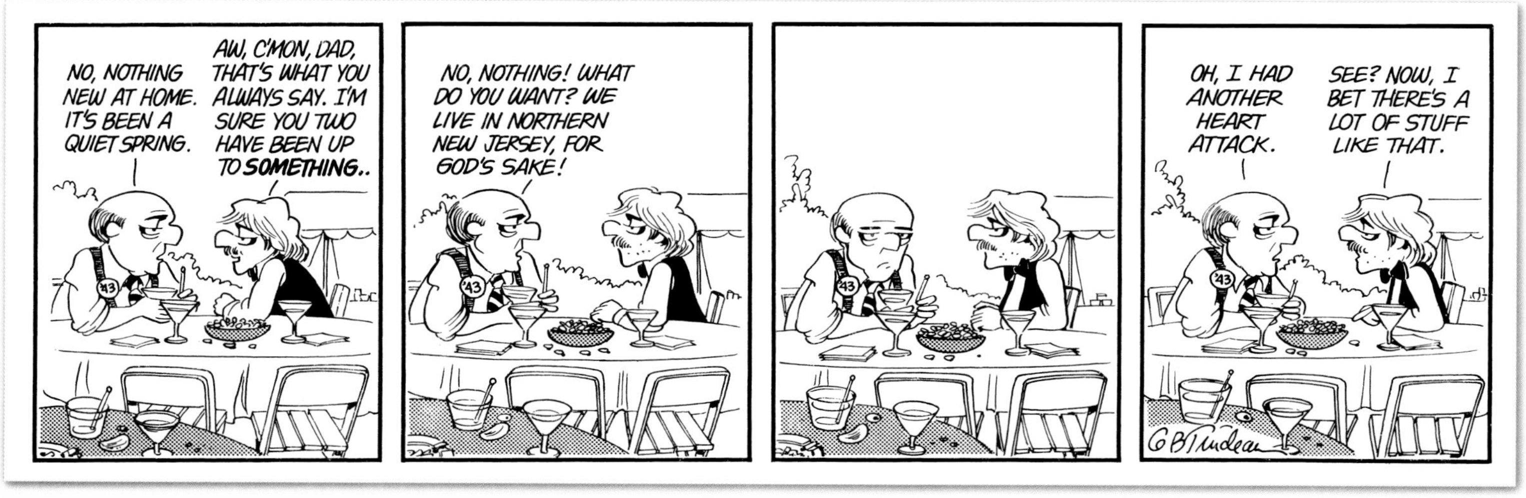
NO, NOTHING NEW AT HOME. IT'S BEEN A QUIET SPRING.
AW, C'MON, DAD, THAT'S WHAT YOU ALWAYS SAY. I'M SURE YOU TWO HAVE BEEN UP TO SOMETHING..
NO, NOTHING! WHAT DO YOU WANT? WE LIVE IN NORTHERN NEW JERSEY, FOR GOD'S SAKE!
OH, I HAD ANOTHER HEART ATTACK.
SEE? NOW, I BET THERE'S A LOT OF STUFF LIKE THAT.
GBTrudeau

5/11/78

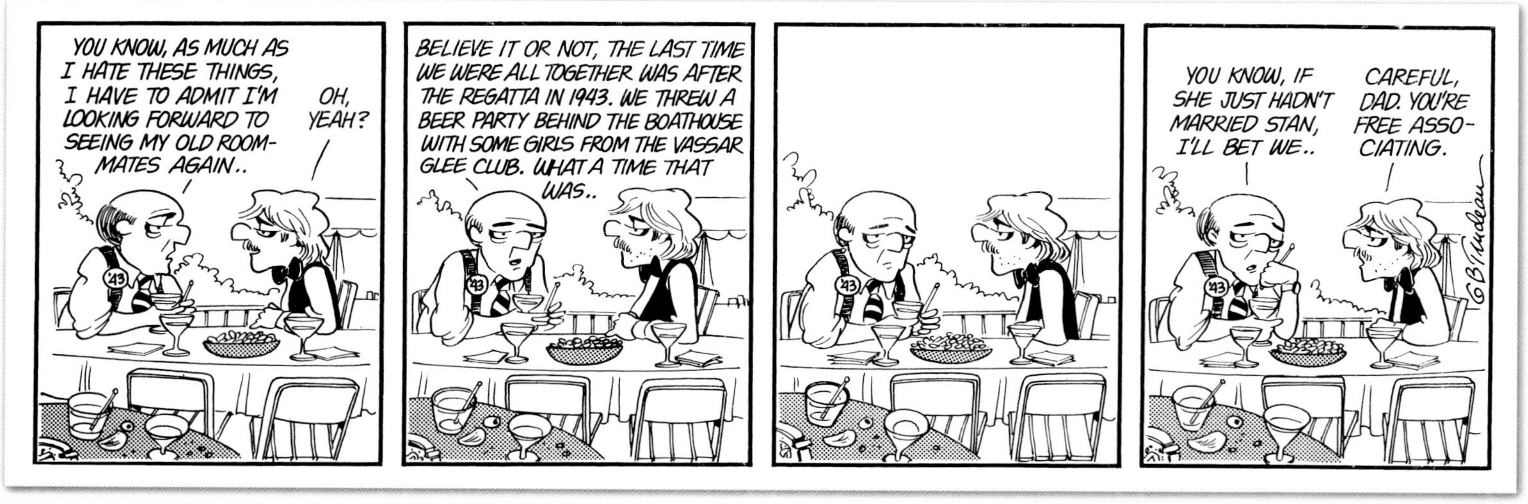
YOU KNOW, AS MUCH AS I HATE THESE THINGS, I HAVE TO ADMIT I'M LOOKING FORWARD TO SEEING MY OLD ROOMMATES AGAIN..
OH, YEAH?
BELIEVE IT OR NOT, THE LAST TIME WE WERE ALL TOGETHER WAS AFTER THE REGATTA IN 1943. WE THREW A BEER PARTY BEHIND THE BOATHOUSE WITH SOME GIRLS FROM THE VASSAR GLEE CLUB. WHAT A TIME THAT WAS..
YOU KNOW, IF SHE JUST HADN'T MARRIED STAN, I'LL BET WE..
CAREFUL, DAD. YOU'RE FREE ASSOCIATING.
GBTrudeau

5/12/78

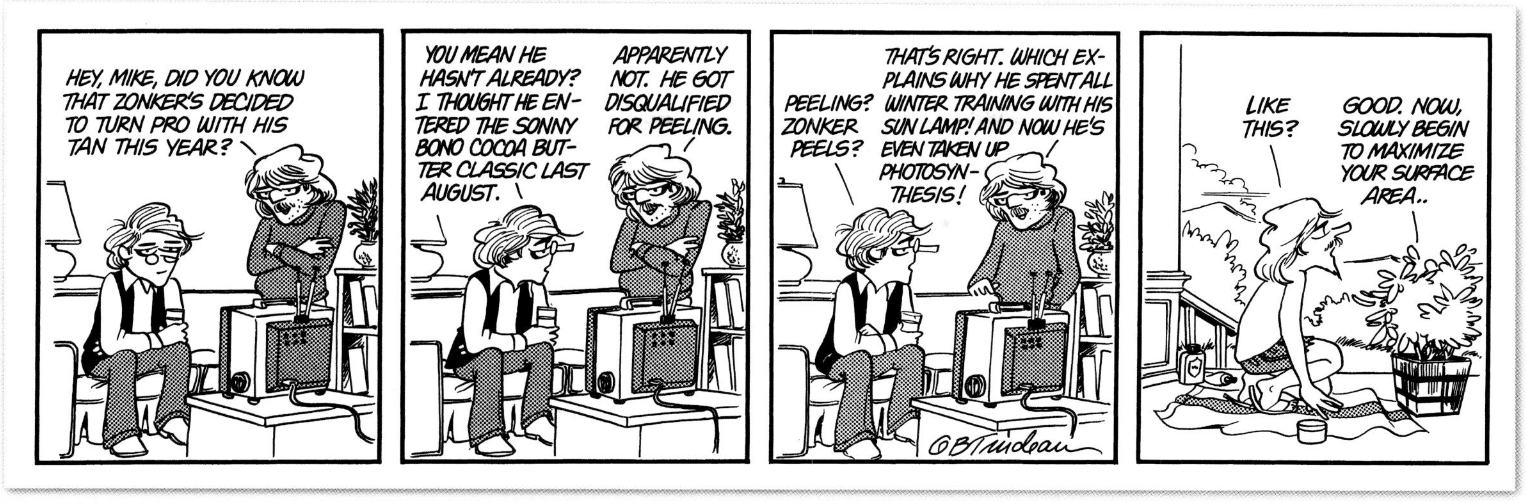
HEY, MIKE, DID YOU KNOW THAT ZONKER'S DECIDED TO TURN PRO WITH HIS TAN THIS YEAR?
YOU MEAN HE HASN'T ALREADY? I THOUGHT HE ENTERED THE SONNY BONO COCOA BUTTER CLASSIC LAST AUGUST.
APPARENTLY NOT. HE GOT DISQUALIFIED FOR PEELING.
PEELING? ZONKER PEELS?
THAT'S RIGHT. WHICH EXPLAINS WHY HE SPENT ALL WINTER TRAINING WITH HIS SUN LAMP! AND NOW HE'S EVEN TAKEN UP PHOTOSYNTHESIS!
G.B. Trudeau
LIKE THIS?
GOOD. NOW, SLOWLY BEGIN TO MAXIMIZE YOUR SURFACE AREA..

6/26/78

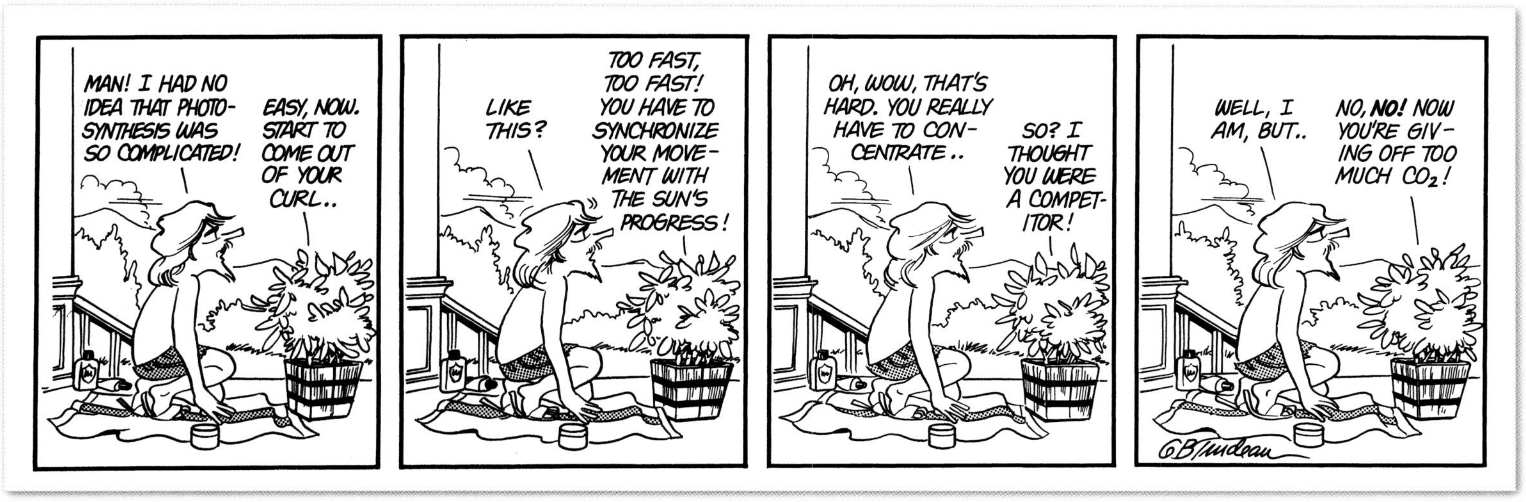
MAN! I HAD NO IDEA THAT PHOTOSYNTHESIS WAS SO COMPLICATED!
EASY, NOW. START TO COME OUT OF YOUR CURL..
LIKE THIS?
TOO FAST, TOO FAST! YOU HAVE TO SYNCHRONIZE YOUR MOVEMENT WITH THE SUN'S PROGRESS!
OH, WOW, THAT'S HARD. YOU REALLY HAVE TO CONCENTRATE..
SO? I THOUGHT YOU WERE A COMPETITOR!
WELL, I AM, BUT..
NO, NO! NOW YOU'RE GIVING OFF TOO MUCH CO_2!
G.B. Trudeau

6/27/78

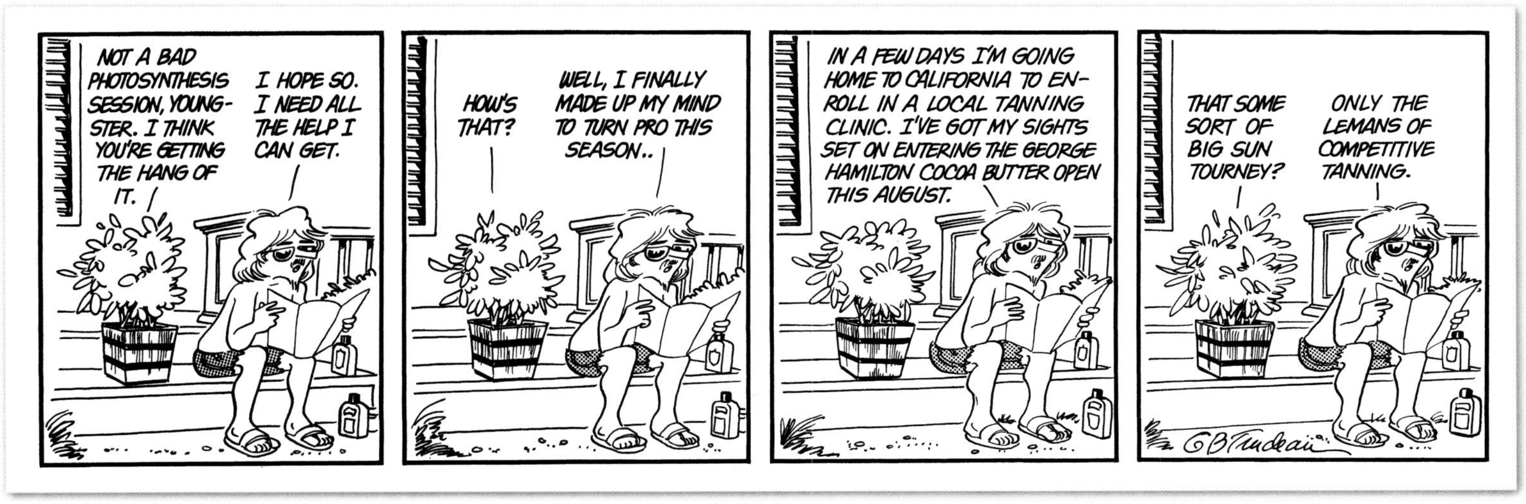
NOT A BAD PHOTOSYNTHESIS SESSION, YOUNGSTER. I THINK YOU'RE GETTING THE HANG OF IT.
I HOPE SO. I NEED ALL THE HELP I CAN GET.
HOW'S THAT?
WELL, I FINALLY MADE UP MY MIND TO TURN PRO THIS SEASON..
IN A FEW DAYS I'M GOING HOME TO CALIFORNIA TO ENROLL IN A LOCAL TANNING CLINIC. I'VE GOT MY SIGHTS SET ON ENTERING THE GEORGE HAMILTON COCOA BUTTER OPEN THIS AUGUST.
THAT SOME SORT OF BIG SUN TOURNEY?
ONLY THE LEMANS OF COMPETITIVE TANNING.
G.B. Trudeau

6/28/78

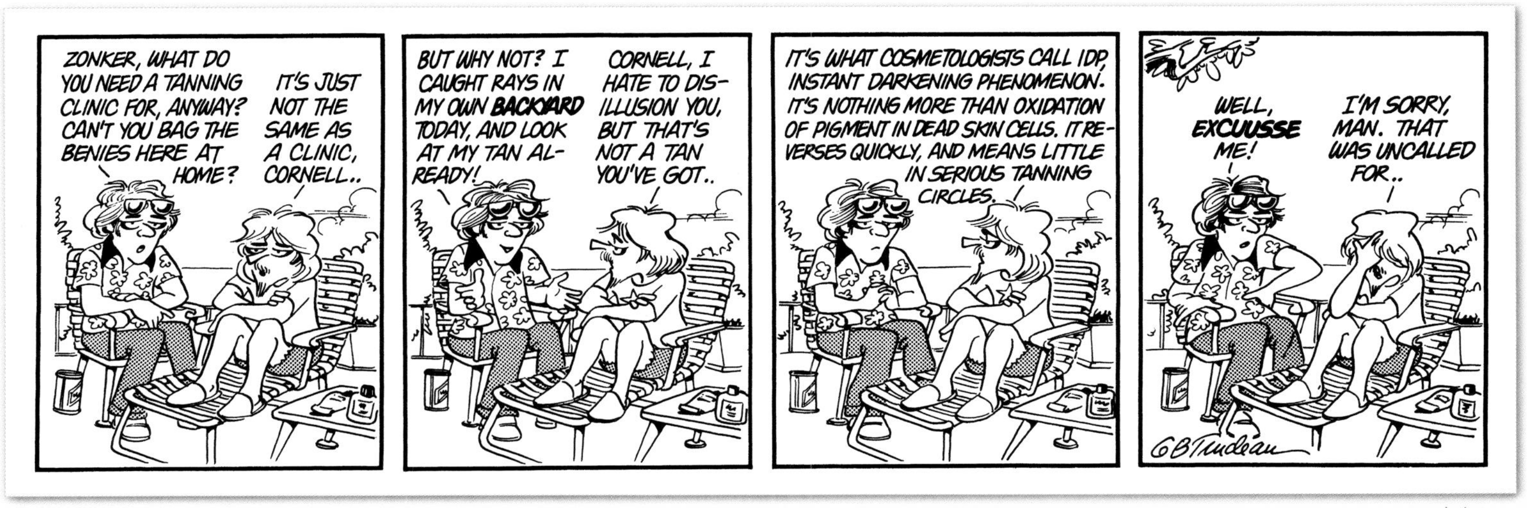
ZONKER, WHAT DO YOU NEED A TANNING CLINIC FOR, ANYWAY? CAN'T YOU BAG THE BENIES HERE AT HOME?
IT'S JUST NOT THE SAME AS A CLINIC, CORNELL..
BUT WHY NOT? I CAUGHT RAYS IN MY OWN BACKYARD TODAY, AND LOOK AT MY TAN ALREADY!
CORNELL, I HATE TO DISILLUSION YOU, BUT THAT'S NOT A TAN YOU'VE GOT..
IT'S WHAT COSMETOLOGISTS CALL IDP, INSTANT DARKENING PHENOMENON. IT'S NOTHING MORE THAN OXIDATION OF PIGMENT IN DEAD SKIN CELLS. IT REVERSES QUICKLY, AND MEANS LITTLE IN SERIOUS TANNING CIRCLES.
WELL, EXCUUSSE ME!
I'M SORRY, MAN. THAT WAS UNCALLED FOR..
G.B. Trudeau

7/8/78

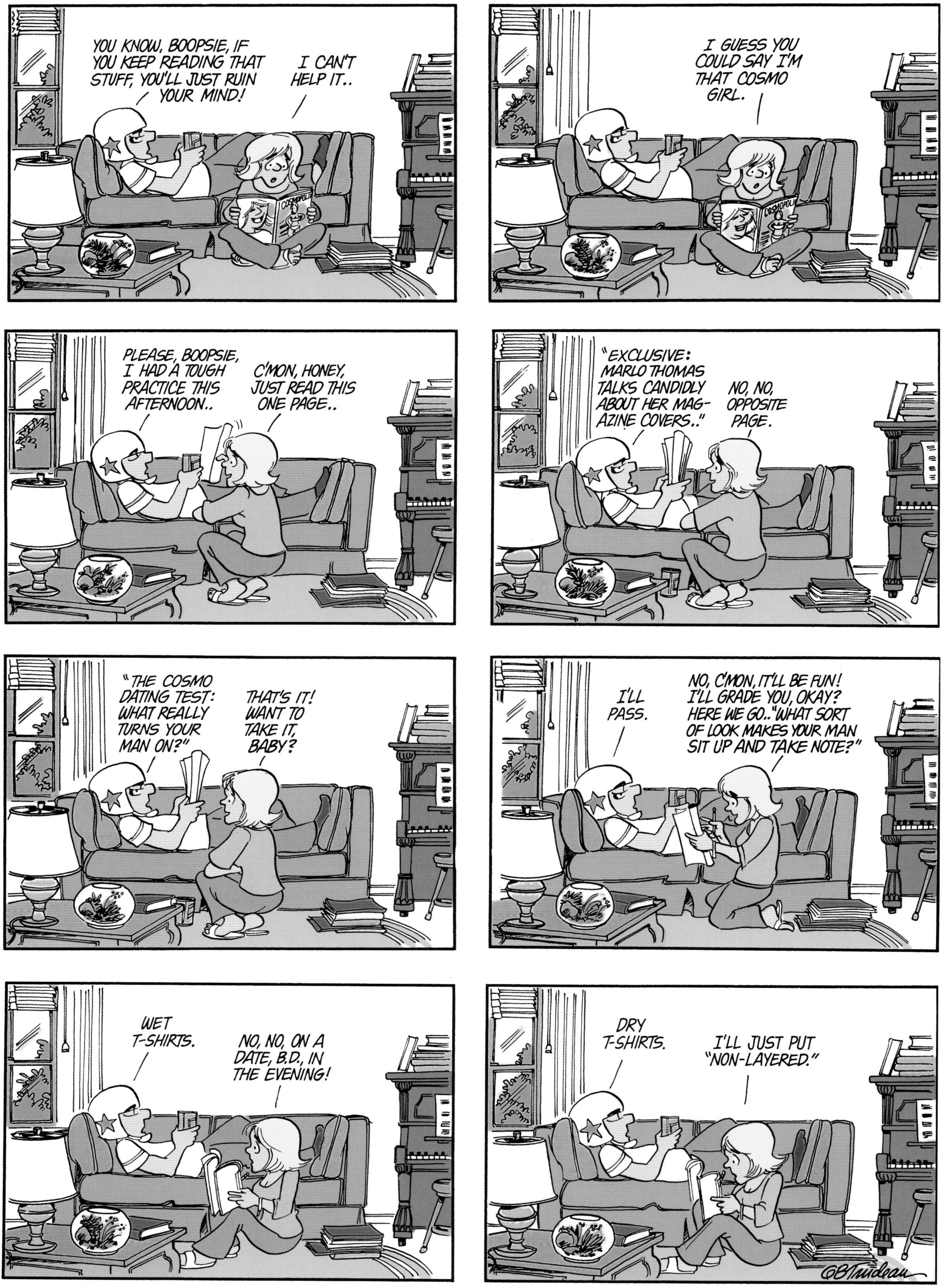
YOU KNOW, BOOPSIE, IF YOU KEEP READING THAT STUFF, YOU'LL JUST RUIN YOUR MIND!
I CAN'T HELP IT..
COSMOPOLI
I GUESS YOU COULD SAY I'M THAT COSMO GIRL.
COSMOPOLI
PLEASE, BOOPSIE, I HAD A TOUGH PRACTICE THIS AFTERNOON..
C'MON, HONEY, JUST READ THIS ONE PAGE..
"EXCLUSIVE: MARLO THOMAS TALKS CANDIDLY ABOUT HER MAGAZINE COVERS.."
NO, NO, OPPOSITE PAGE.
"THE COSMO DATING TEST: WHAT REALLY TURNS YOUR MAN ON?"
THAT'S IT! WANT TO TAKE IT, BABY?
I'LL PASS.
NO, C'MON, IT'LL BE FUN! I'LL GRADE YOU, OKAY? HERE WE GO.."WHAT SORT OF LOOK MAKES YOUR MAN SIT UP AND TAKE NOTE?"
WET T-SHIRTS.
NO, NO, ON A DATE, B.D., IN THE EVENING!
DRY T-SHIRTS.
I'LL JUST PUT "NON-LAYERED."
GBTrudeau

9/10/78

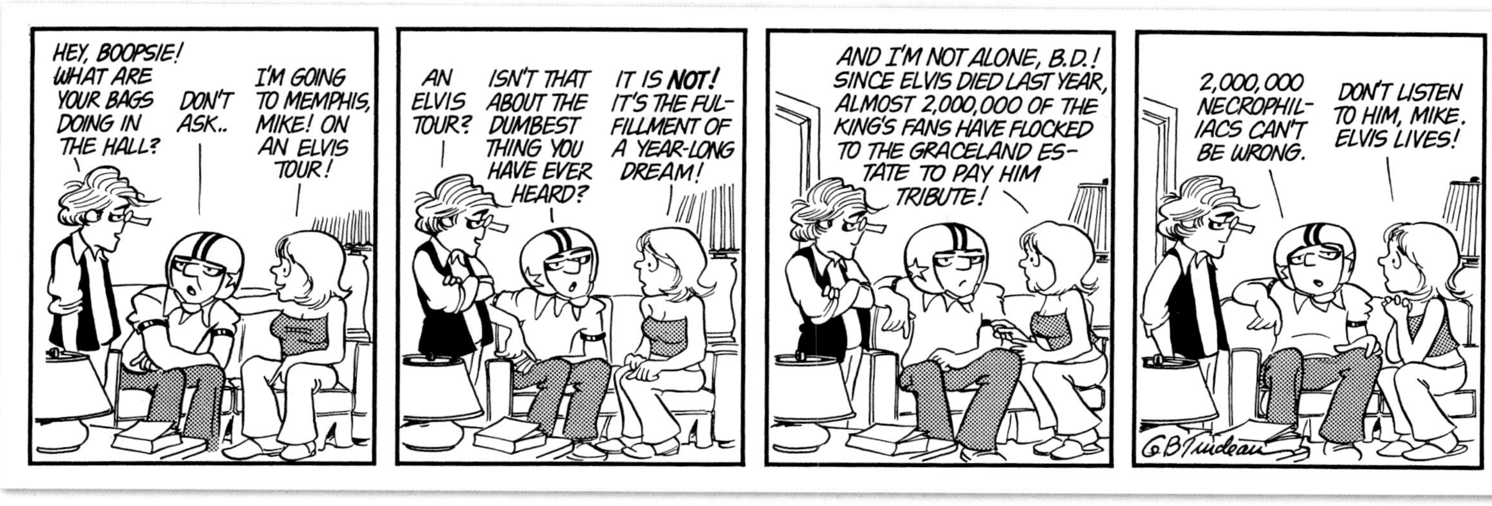
HEY, BOOPSIE! WHAT ARE YOUR BAGS DOING IN THE HALL?
DON'T ASK..
I'M GOING TO MEMPHIS, MIKE! ON AN ELVIS TOUR!
AN ELVIS TOUR?
ISN'T THAT ABOUT THE DUMBEST THING YOU HAVE EVER HEARD?
IT IS NOT! IT'S THE FULFILLMENT OF A YEAR-LONG DREAM!
AND I'M NOT ALONE, B.D.! SINCE ELVIS DIED LAST YEAR, ALMOST 2,000,000 OF THE KING'S FANS HAVE FLOCKED TO THE GRACELAND ESTATE TO PAY HIM TRIBUTE!
2,000,000 NECROPHILIACS CAN'T BE WRONG.
DON'T LISTEN TO HIM, MIKE. ELVIS LIVES!

8/28/78

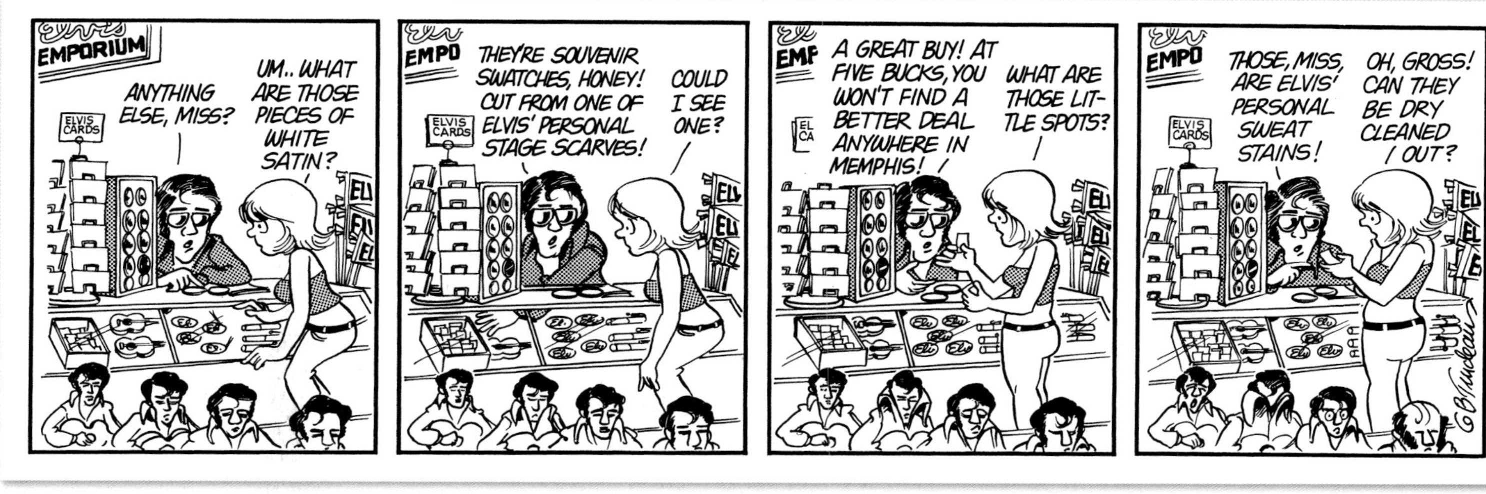
EMPORIUM
ELVIS CARDS
ANYTHING ELSE, MISS?
UM.. WHAT ARE THOSE PIECES OF WHITE SATIN?
THEY'RE SOUVENIR SWATCHES, HONEY! CUT FROM ONE OF ELVIS' PERSONAL STAGE SCARVES!
COULD I SEE ONE?
A GREAT BUY! AT FIVE BUCKS, YOU WON'T FIND A BETTER DEAL ANYWHERE IN MEMPHIS!
WHAT ARE THOSE LITTLE SPOTS?
THOSE, MISS, ARE ELVIS' PERSONAL SWEAT STAINS!
OH, GROSS! CAN THEY BE DRY CLEANED OUT?

9/1/78

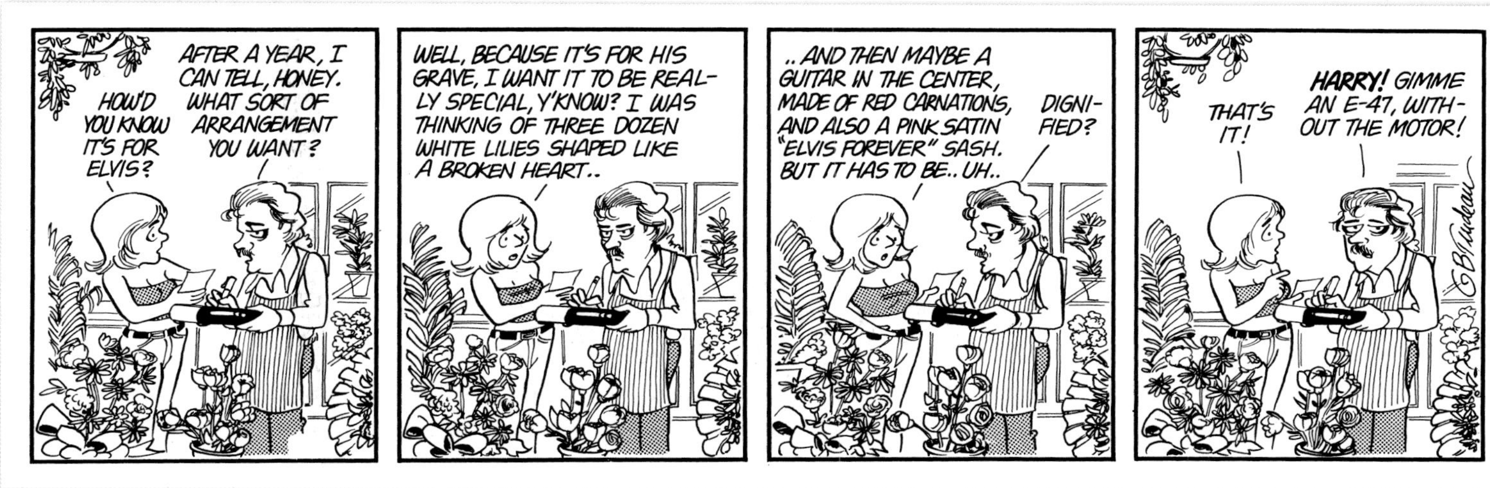
HOW'D YOU KNOW IT'S FOR ELVIS?
AFTER A YEAR, I CAN TELL, HONEY. WHAT SORT OF ARRANGEMENT YOU WANT?
WELL, BECAUSE IT'S FOR HIS GRAVE, I WANT IT TO BE REALLY SPECIAL, Y'KNOW? I WAS THINKING OF THREE DOZEN WHITE LILIES SHAPED LIKE A BROKEN HEART..
..AND THEN MAYBE A GUITAR IN THE CENTER, MADE OF RED CARNATIONS, AND ALSO A PINK SATIN "ELVIS FOREVER" SASH. BUT IT HAS TO BE.. UH..
DIGNIFIED?
THAT'S IT!
HARRY! GIMME AN E-47, WITHOUT THE MOTOR!

9/2/78

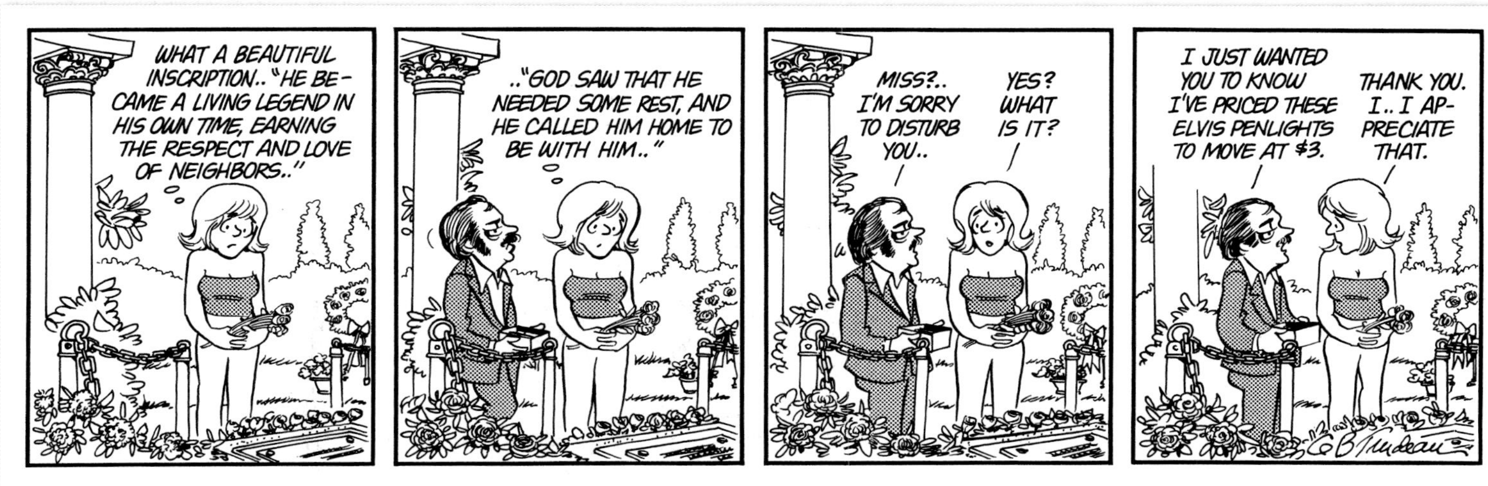
WHAT A BEAUTIFUL INSCRIPTION.. "HE BECAME A LIVING LEGEND IN HIS OWN TIME, EARNING THE RESPECT AND LOVE OF NEIGHBORS.."
.."GOD SAW THAT HE NEEDED SOME REST, AND HE CALLED HIM HOME TO BE WITH HIM.."
MISS?.. I'M SORRY TO DISTURB YOU..
YES? WHAT IS IT?
I JUST WANTED YOU TO KNOW I'VE PRICED THESE ELVIS PENLIGHTS TO MOVE AT $3.
THANK YOU. I.. I APPRECIATE THAT.

9/6/78

ZONKER HARRIS

With a little help from Bob Dylan, my generation—the baby boomers—pretty much invented the whole idea of "forever young." In fact, the worst thing we can say about anything is that it is "old." Old paradigms, old thinking, but particularly old age. When baby boomers are asked in polls when old age begins, the average response is 80—two full years past life expectancy.

So the New Old is death. When a baby boomer passes on, it will be said that he died of late middle age.

We were not always this way. It's hard to believe now, but there actually was a time within living memory when childhood was viewed as an interminable burden. The British novelist Ian McEwan dates the cultural pivot point to the early '60s. Prior to that, he wrote in *On Chesil Beach*, "To be young was a social encumbrance, a mark of irrelevance, a faintly embarrassing condition for which marriage was the beginning of a cure."

How quickly the "embarrassing condition" became adulthood, for which, of course, there is no cure at all. Thanks to the Kennedys, the Beatles, the pill, the war, and a myriad of other co-factors, young people hijacked the culture and never gave it back. If youth was once regarded as unserious, no one seems to remember. We are now three generations deep into rock, jeans, and dope; there's no turning back.

"Who'd have guessed I'd grow up to be a powerful, respected babysitter?"

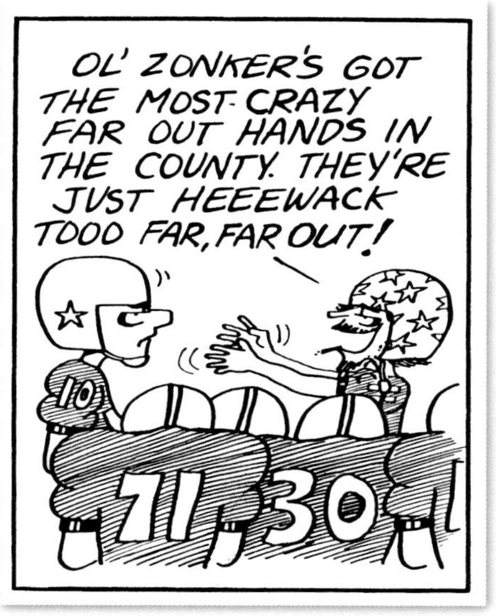
OL' ZONKER'S GOT THE MOST-CRAZY FAR OUT HANDS IN THE COUNTY. THEY'RE JUST HEEEWACK TOOD FAR, FAR OUT!
10
11,30

Which is just fine with Zonk, who is and always has been fully vested. Ever since he came aboard as Walden's resident chillhead, Zonker has stood for standing still. He's lived in the present moment, heedful of John Lennon's warning that life is what happens to you when you're busy making other plans. He was abetted, of course, by a charming cartoon convention—the suspension of the aging process—but even after the ban on real time was lifted in 1984, Zonker remained the strip's perennial man-child. Whatever gains he made in sophistication, he seemed to surrender in maturity, maintaining equilibrium but also paralysis. Thus, a life of odd jobs, sponging off buds, getting baked, and never, ever going on a second date.

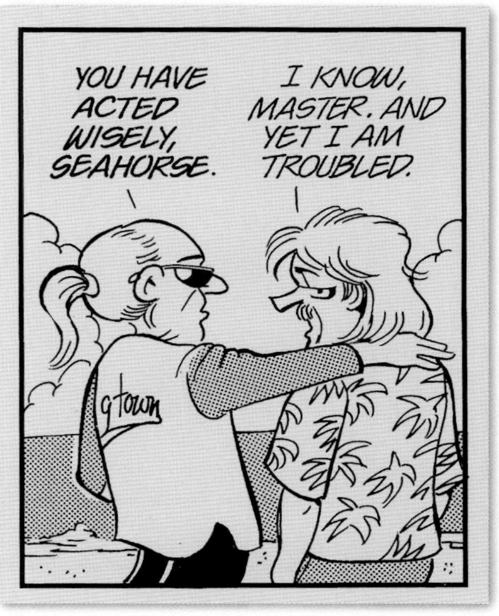
YOU HAVE ACTED WISELY, SEAHORSE.
I KNOW, MASTER. AND YET I AM TROUBLED.
G'town

Zonker took his name from a proto-hippie named Steve "Zonker" Lambrecht, one of the Merry Pranksters immortalized in Tom Wolfe's *The Electric Kool-Aid Acid Test*. But his earliest antecedent was probably TV's Maynard G. Krebs, Dobie Gillis's beatnik sidekick whose voice cracked whenever he said the word "work." In the late '50s, the notion that life had more to offer than work was deeply subversive, even dangerous, so Maynard drew a lot of nervous laughter from the squares. And they were right to be worried; within five years, the counterculture was in full flower.

Like Maynard, Zonker was created as a foil. I dropped him into B.D.'s huddle as pushback to the deeply straight quarterback, who was ill-equipped to cope with Zonker's gleeful assault on his authority. For several years the little freak had the upper hand, but as the tide turned, and hippies gave way to yuppies, it was B.D. who regained standing and Zonker who became disenfranchised. He is still in the grip of "forever young," but the dream of it leading to Nirvana has gotten old. He seems to have finally grasped that life is also what happens to you when you're busy making no plans at all.

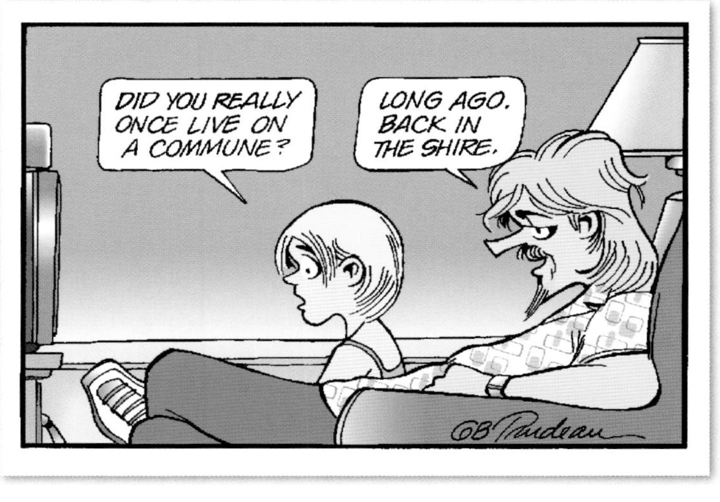
DID YOU REALLY ONCE LIVE ON A COMMUNE?
LONG AGO. BACK IN THE SHIRE.
GBTrudeau

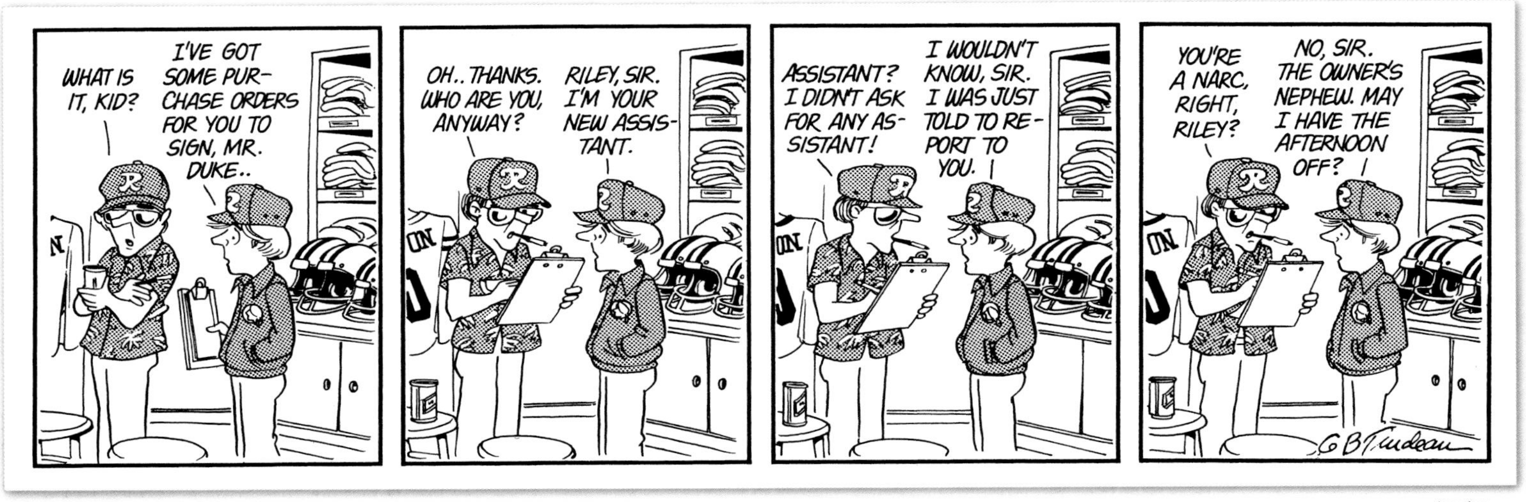
WHAT IS IT, KID?
I'VE GOT SOME PURCHASE ORDERS FOR YOU TO SIGN, MR. DUKE..
OH.. THANKS. WHO ARE YOU, ANYWAY?
RILEY, SIR. I'M YOUR NEW ASSISTANT.
ASSISTANT? I DIDN'T ASK FOR ANY ASSISTANT!
I WOULDN'T KNOW, SIR. I WAS JUST TOLD TO REPORT TO YOU.
YOU'RE A NARC, RIGHT, RILEY?
NO, SIR. THE OWNER'S NEPHEW. MAY I HAVE THE AFTERNOON OFF?
G.B. Trudeau

7/17/78

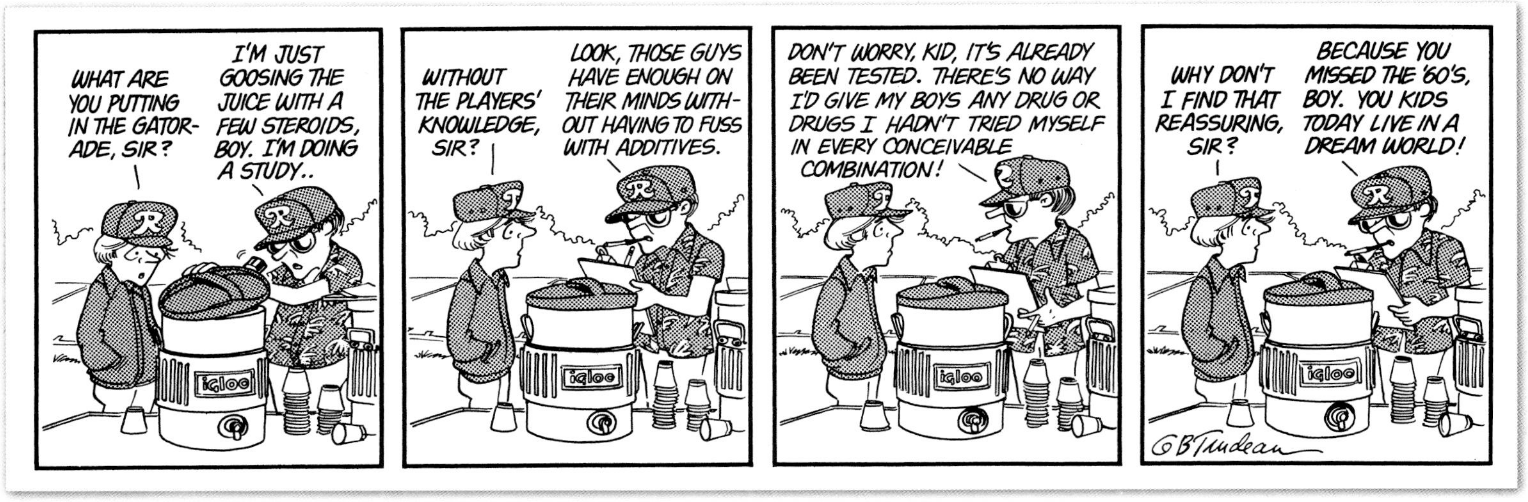
WHAT ARE YOU PUTTING IN THE GATORADE, SIR?
I'M JUST GOOSING THE JUICE WITH A FEW STEROIDS, BOY. I'M DOING A STUDY..
WITHOUT THE PLAYERS' KNOWLEDGE, SIR?
LOOK, THOSE GUYS HAVE ENOUGH ON THEIR MINDS WITHOUT HAVING TO FUSS WITH ADDITIVES.
DON'T WORRY, KID, IT'S ALREADY BEEN TESTED. THERE'S NO WAY I'D GIVE MY BOYS ANY DRUG OR DRUGS I HADN'T TRIED MYSELF IN EVERY CONCEIVABLE COMBINATION!
WHY DON'T I FIND THAT REASSURING, SIR?
BECAUSE YOU MISSED THE '60'S, BOY. YOU KIDS TODAY LIVE IN A DREAM WORLD!
igloo
G.B. Trudeau

7/20/78

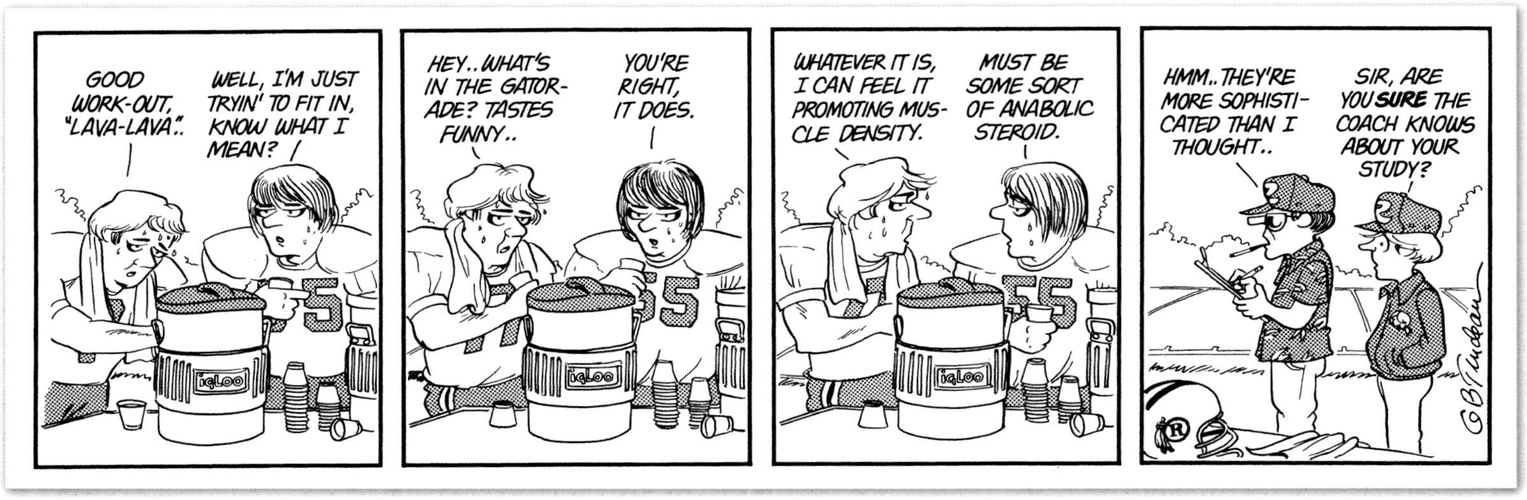
GOOD WORK-OUT, "LAVA-LAVA".
WELL, I'M JUST TRYIN' TO FIT IN, KNOW WHAT I MEAN?
HEY.. WHAT'S IN THE GATORADE? TASTES FUNNY..
YOU'RE RIGHT, IT DOES.
WHATEVER IT IS, I CAN FEEL IT PROMOTING MUSCLE DENSITY.
MUST BE SOME SORT OF ANABOLIC STEROID.
HMM.. THEY'RE MORE SOPHISTICATED THAN I THOUGHT..
SIR, ARE YOU SURE THE COACH KNOWS ABOUT YOUR STUDY?
igloo
G.B. Trudeau

7/21/78

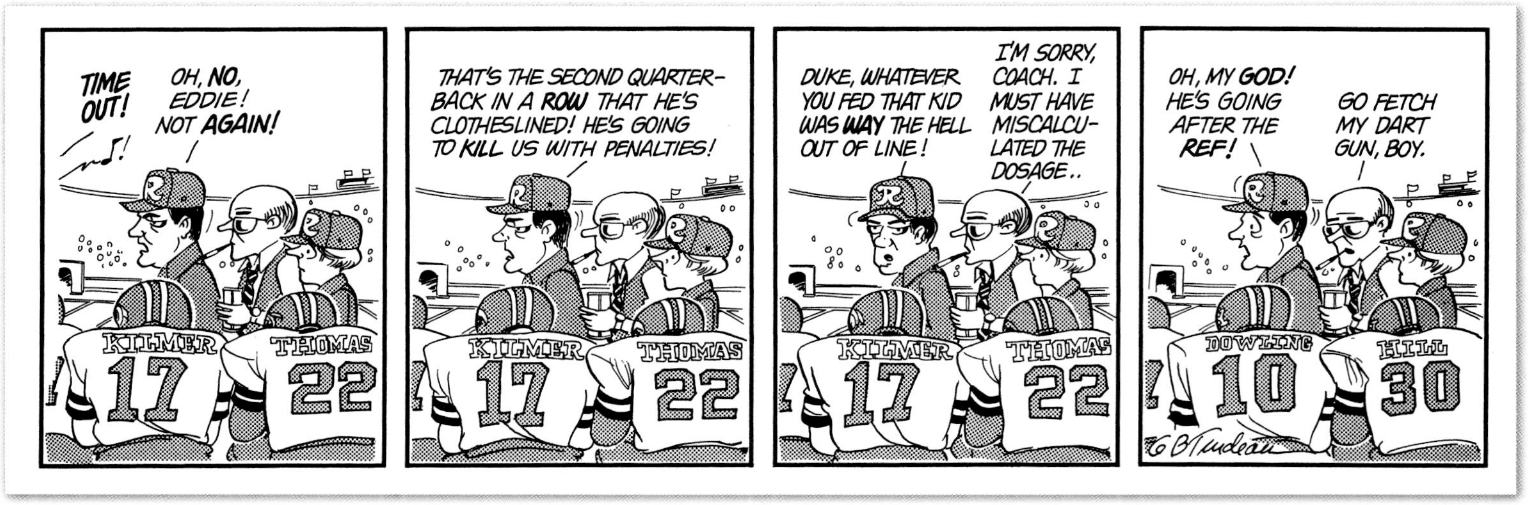
TIME OUT!
OH, NO, EDDIE! NOT AGAIN!
THAT'S THE SECOND QUARTERBACK IN A ROW THAT HE'S CLOTHESLINED! HE'S GOING TO KILL US WITH PENALTIES!
DUKE, WHATEVER YOU FED THAT KID WAS WAY THE HELL OUT OF LINE!
I'M SORRY, COACH. I MUST HAVE MISCALCULATED THE DOSAGE..
OH, MY GOD! HE'S GOING AFTER THE REF!
GO FETCH MY DART GUN, BOY.
KILMER 17
THOMAS 22
DOWLING 10
HILL 30
G.B. Trudeau

9/15/78

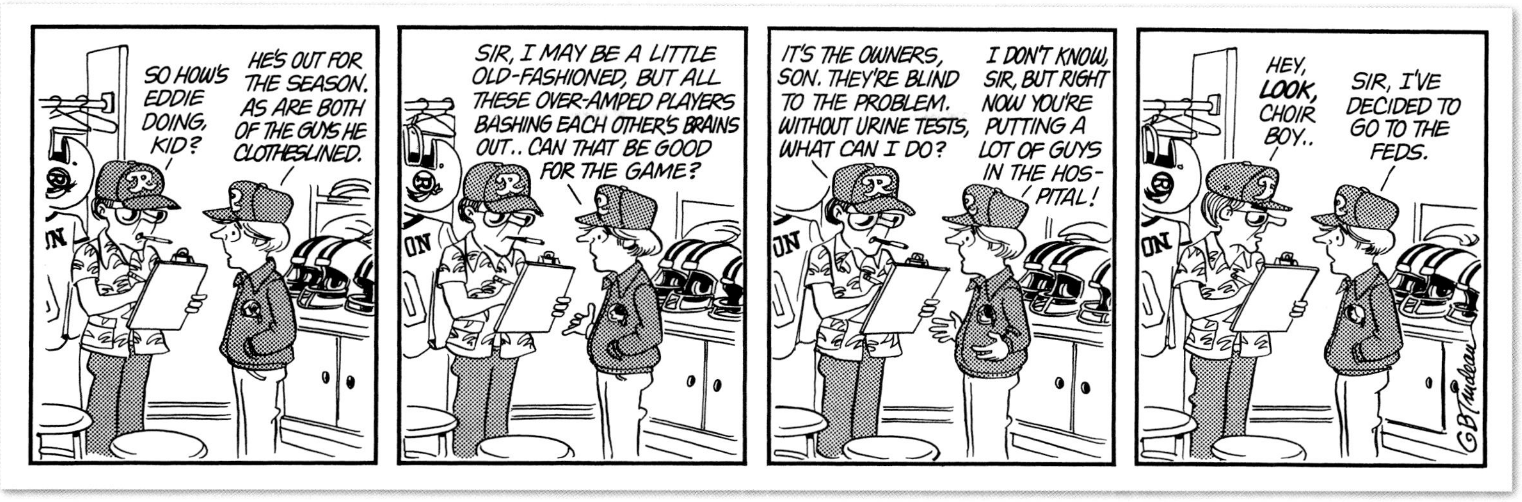
SO HOW'S EDDIE DOING, KID?
HE'S OUT FOR THE SEASON. AS ARE BOTH OF THE GUYS HE CLOTHESLINED.
SIR, I MAY BE A LITTLE OLD-FASHIONED, BUT ALL THESE OVER-AMPED PLAYERS BASHING EACH OTHER'S BRAINS OUT.. CAN THAT BE GOOD FOR THE GAME?
IT'S THE OWNERS, SON. THEY'RE BLIND TO THE PROBLEM. WITHOUT URINE TESTS, WHAT CAN I DO?
I DON'T KNOW, SIR, BUT RIGHT NOW YOU'RE PUTTING A LOT OF GUYS IN THE HOSPITAL!
HEY, LOOK, CHOIR BOY..
SIR, I'VE DECIDED TO GO TO THE FEDS.
GBTrudeau

9/16/78

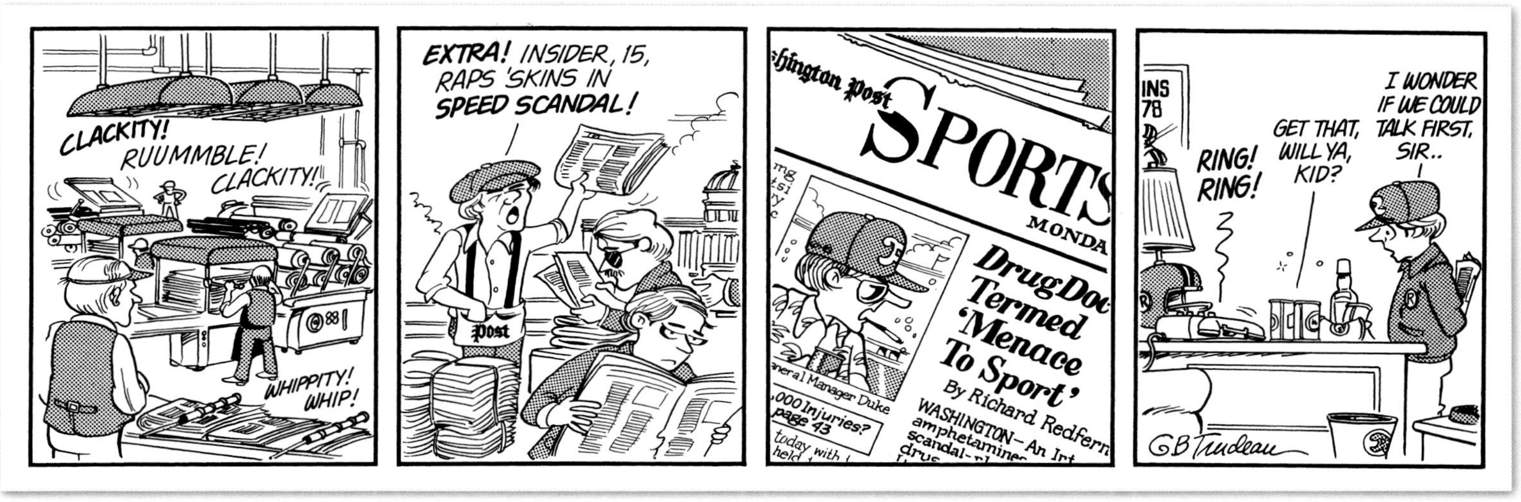
CLACKITY! RUUMMBLE! CLACKITY!
WHIPPITY! WHIP!
EXTRA! INSIDER, 15, RAPS 'SKINS IN SPEED SCANDAL!
Post
SPORTS
Drug Doc Termed 'Menace To Sport'
By Richard Redfern
RING! RING!
GET THAT, WILL YA, KID?
I WONDER IF WE COULD TALK FIRST, SIR..
GBTrudeau

9/25/78

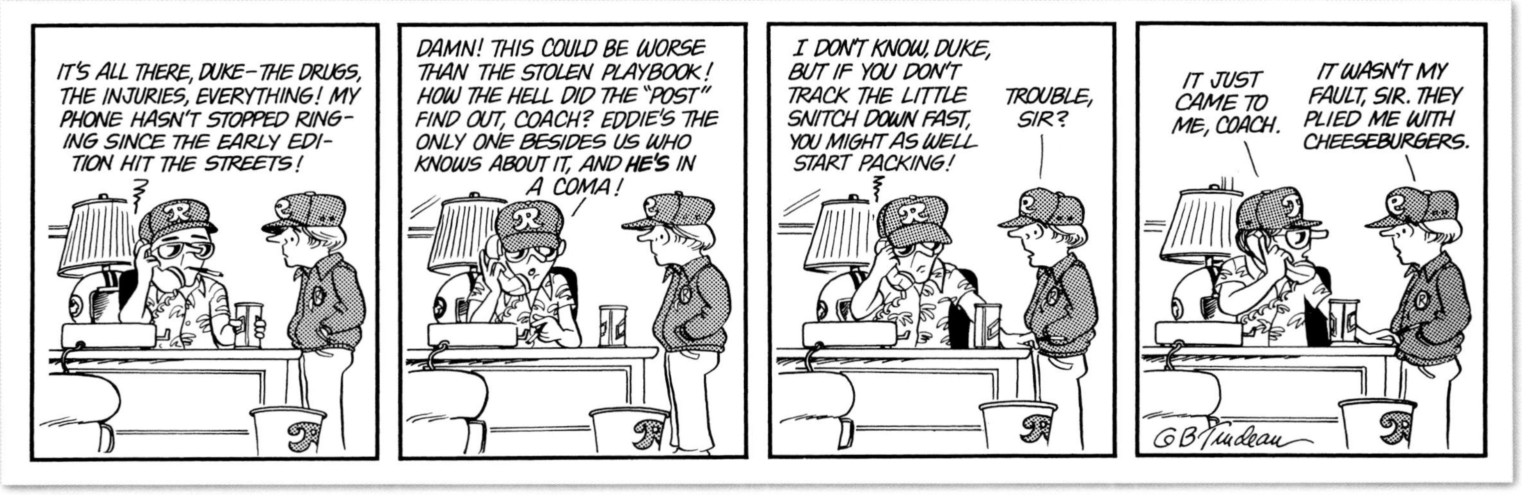
IT'S ALL THERE, DUKE—THE DRUGS, THE INJURIES, EVERYTHING! MY PHONE HASN'T STOPPED RINGING SINCE THE EARLY EDITION HIT THE STREETS!
DAMN! THIS COULD BE WORSE THAN THE STOLEN PLAYBOOK! HOW THE HELL DID THE "POST" FIND OUT, COACH? EDDIE'S THE ONLY ONE BESIDES US WHO KNOWS ABOUT IT, AND HE'S IN A COMA!
I DON'T KNOW, DUKE, BUT IF YOU DON'T TRACK THE LITTLE SNITCH DOWN FAST, YOU MIGHT AS WELL START PACKING!
TROUBLE, SIR?
IT JUST CAME TO ME, COACH.
IT WASN'T MY FAULT, SIR. THEY PLIED ME WITH CHEESEBURGERS.
GBTrudeau

9/26/78

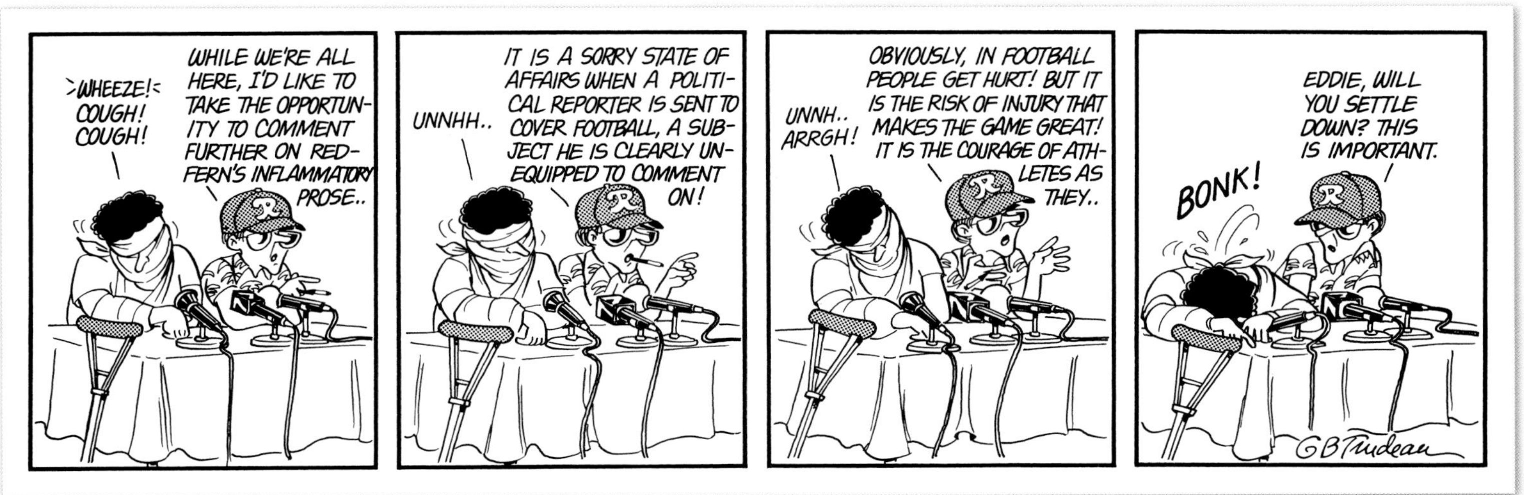
>WHEEZE!< COUGH! COUGH!
WHILE WE'RE ALL HERE, I'D LIKE TO TAKE THE OPPORTUNITY TO COMMENT FURTHER ON REDFERN'S INFLAMMATORY PROSE..
UNNHH..
IT IS A SORRY STATE OF AFFAIRS WHEN A POLITICAL REPORTER IS SENT TO COVER FOOTBALL, A SUBJECT HE IS CLEARLY UNEQUIPPED TO COMMENT ON!
UNNH.. ARRGH!
OBVIOUSLY, IN FOOTBALL PEOPLE GET HURT! BUT IT IS THE RISK OF INJURY THAT MAKES THE GAME GREAT! IT IS THE COURAGE OF ATHLETES AS THEY..
BONK!
EDDIE, WILL YOU SETTLE DOWN? THIS IS IMPORTANT.
GBTrudeau

9/30/78

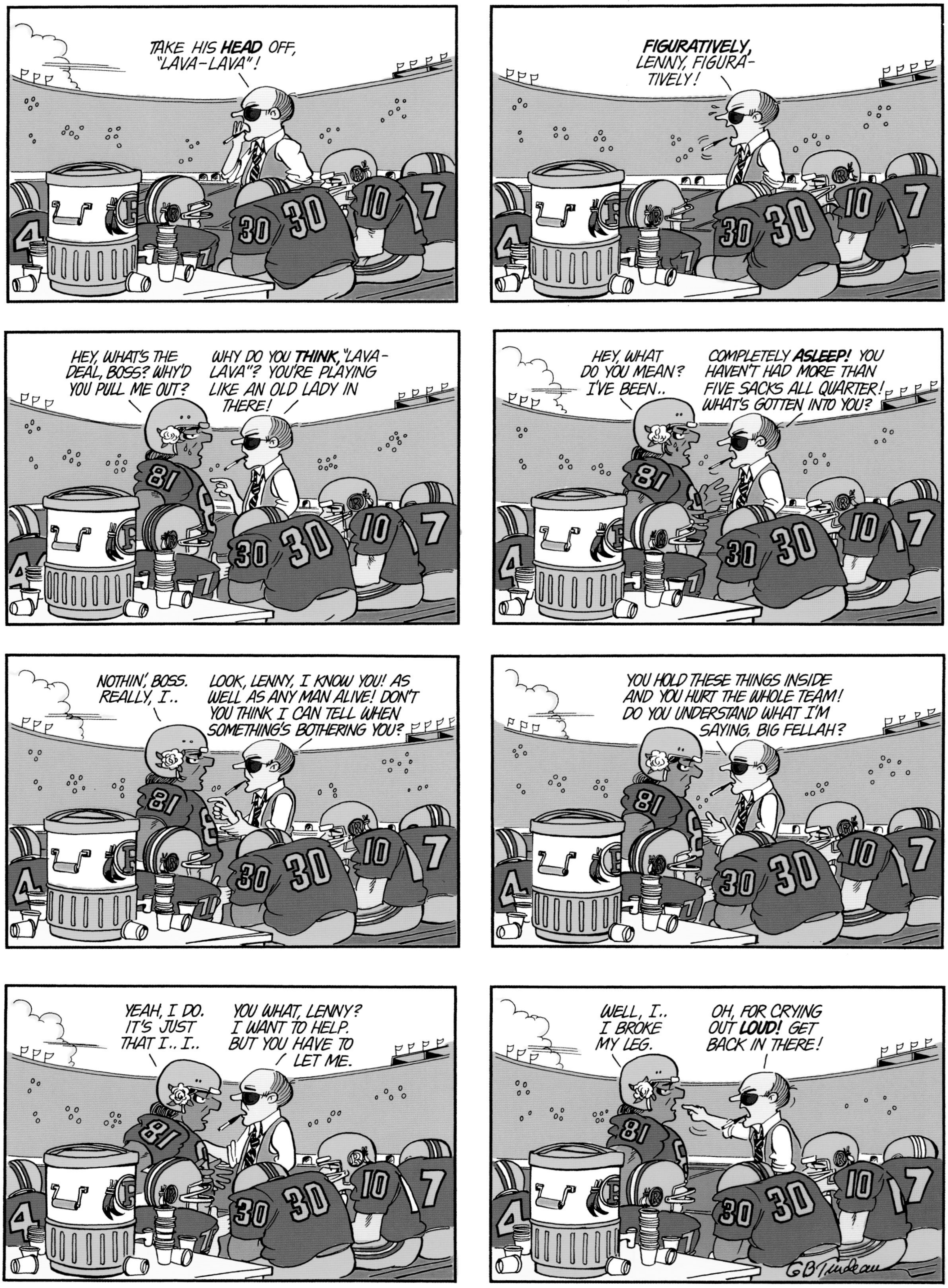

TAKE HIS **HEAD** OFF, "LAVA-LAVA"!
FIGURATIVELY, LENNY, FIGURATIVELY!
HEY, WHAT'S THE DEAL, BOSS? WHY'D YOU PULL ME OUT?
WHY DO YOU **THINK,** "LAVA-LAVA"? YOU'RE PLAYING LIKE AN OLD LADY IN THERE!
HEY, WHAT DO YOU MEAN? I'VE BEEN..
COMPLETELY **ASLEEP!** YOU HAVEN'T HAD MORE THAN FIVE SACKS ALL QUARTER! WHAT'S GOTTEN INTO YOU?
NOTHIN', BOSS. REALLY, I..
LOOK, LENNY, I KNOW YOU! AS WELL AS ANY MAN ALIVE! DON'T YOU THINK I CAN TELL WHEN SOMETHING'S BOTHERING YOU?
YOU HOLD THESE THINGS INSIDE AND YOU HURT THE WHOLE TEAM! DO YOU UNDERSTAND WHAT I'M SAYING, BIG FELLAH?
YEAH, I DO. IT'S JUST THAT I.. I..
YOU WHAT, LENNY? I WANT TO HELP. BUT YOU HAVE TO LET ME.
WELL, I.. I BROKE MY LEG.
OH, FOR CRYING OUT **LOUD!** GET BACK IN THERE!
GBTrudeau

10/22/78

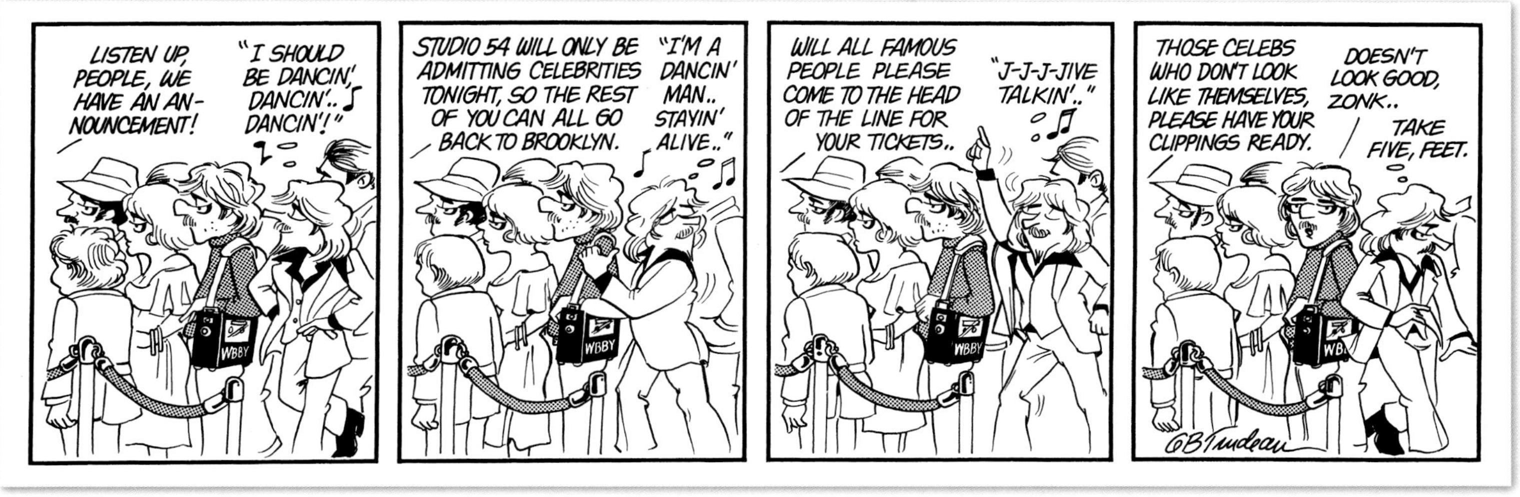
LISTEN UP, PEOPLE, WE HAVE AN ANNOUNCEMENT!
"I SHOULD BE DANCIN', DANCIN'.. DANCIN'!"
STUDIO 54 WILL ONLY BE ADMITTING CELEBRITIES TONIGHT, SO THE REST OF YOU CAN ALL GO BACK TO BROOKLYN.
"I'M A DANCIN' MAN.. STAYIN' ALIVE.."
WILL ALL FAMOUS PEOPLE PLEASE COME TO THE HEAD OF THE LINE FOR YOUR TICKETS..
"J-J-J-JIVE TALKIN'.."
THOSE CELEBS WHO DON'T LOOK LIKE THEMSELVES, PLEASE HAVE YOUR CLIPPINGS READY.
DOESN'T LOOK GOOD, ZONK..
TAKE FIVE, FEET.
WBBY

7/28/78

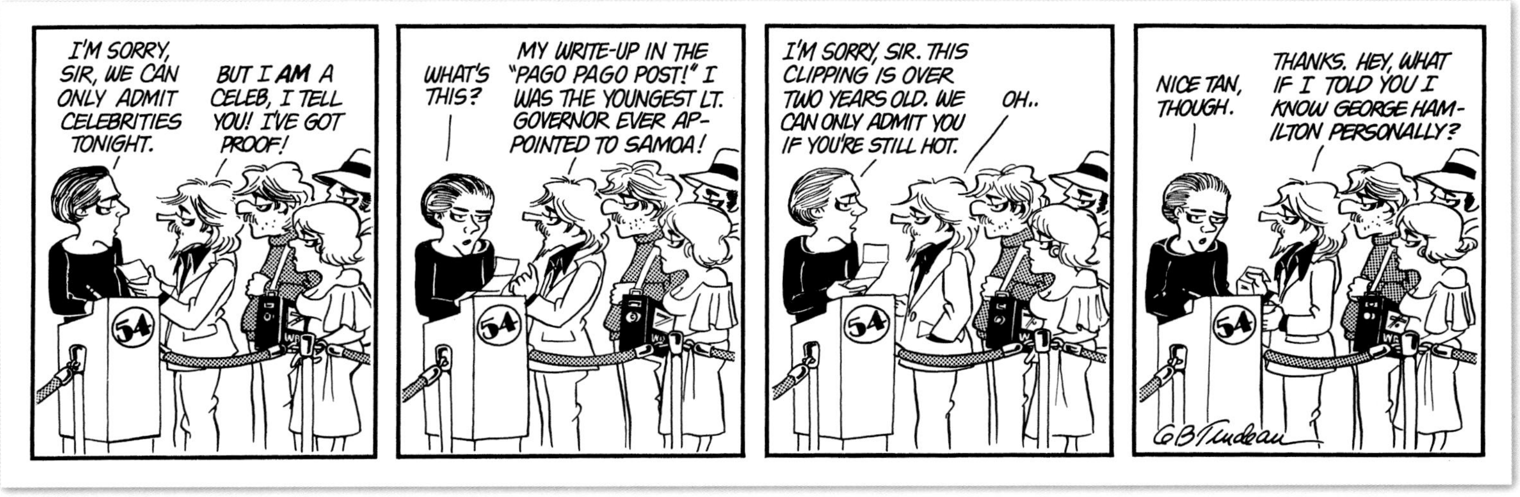
I'M SORRY, SIR, WE CAN ONLY ADMIT CELEBRITIES TONIGHT.
BUT I AM A CELEB, I TELL YOU! I'VE GOT PROOF!
WHAT'S THIS?
MY WRITE-UP IN THE "PAGO PAGO POST!" I WAS THE YOUNGEST LT. GOVERNOR EVER APPOINTED TO SAMOA!
I'M SORRY, SIR. THIS CLIPPING IS OVER TWO YEARS OLD. WE CAN ONLY ADMIT YOU IF YOU'RE STILL HOT.
OH..
NICE TAN, THOUGH.
THANKS. HEY, WHAT IF I TOLD YOU I KNOW GEORGE HAMILTON PERSONALLY?
54

7/31/78

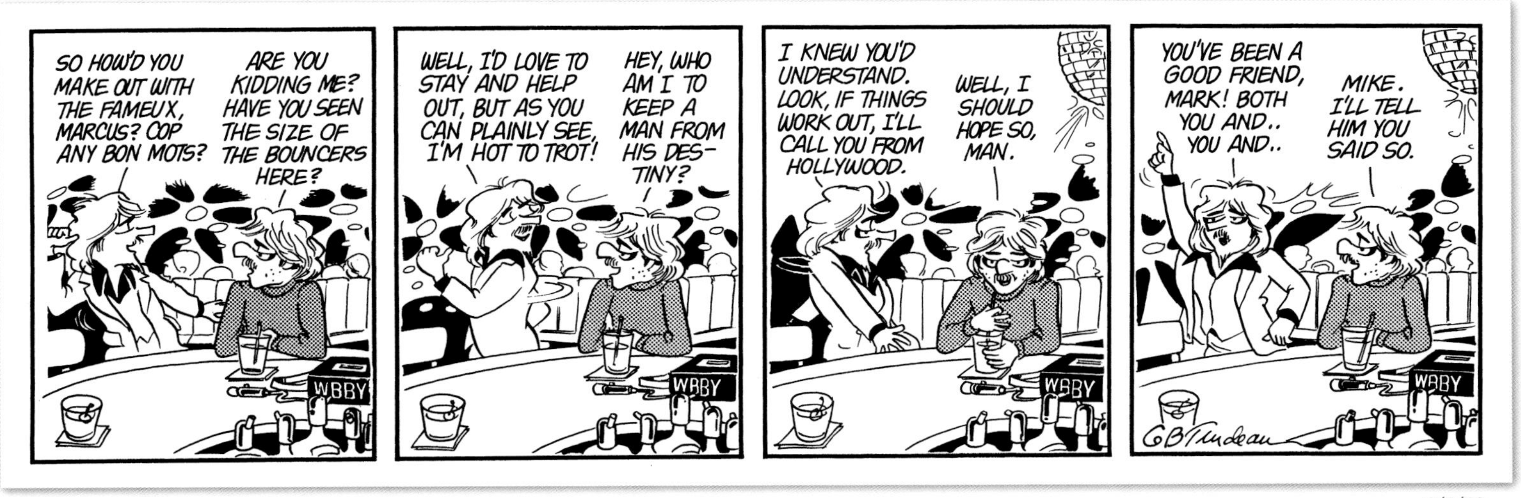
SO HOW'D YOU MAKE OUT WITH THE FAMEUX, MARCUS? COP ANY BON MOTS?
ARE YOU KIDDING ME? HAVE YOU SEEN THE SIZE OF THE BOUNCERS HERE?
WELL, I'D LOVE TO STAY AND HELP OUT, BUT AS YOU CAN PLAINLY SEE, I'M HOT TO TROT!
HEY, WHO AM I TO KEEP A MAN FROM HIS DESTINY?
I KNEW YOU'D UNDERSTAND. LOOK, IF THINGS WORK OUT, I'LL CALL YOU FROM HOLLYWOOD.
WELL, I SHOULD HOPE SO, MAN.
YOU'VE BEEN A GOOD FRIEND, MARK! BOTH YOU AND.. YOU AND..
MIKE. I'LL TELL HIM YOU SAID SO.
WBBY

8/2/78

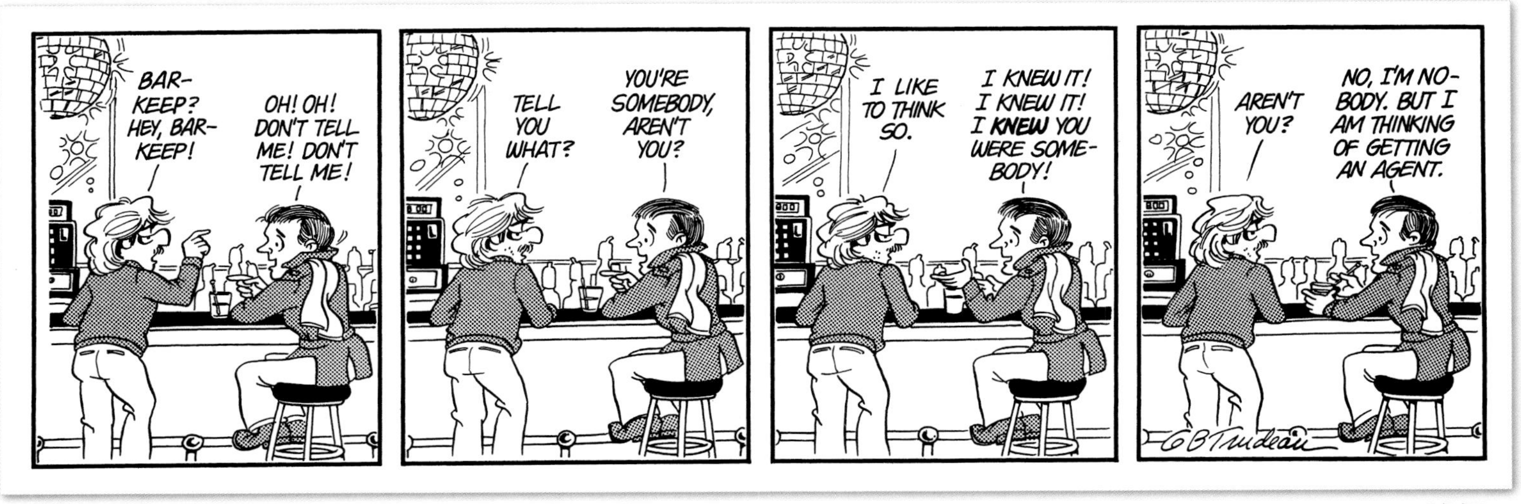
BARKEEP? HEY, BARKEEP!
OH! OH! DON'T TELL ME! DON'T TELL ME!
TELL YOU WHAT?
YOU'RE SOMEBODY, AREN'T YOU?
I LIKE TO THINK SO.
I KNEW IT! I KNEW IT! I KNEW YOU WERE SOMEBODY!
AREN'T YOU?
NO, I'M NOBODY. BUT I AM THINKING OF GETTING AN AGENT.

8/3/78

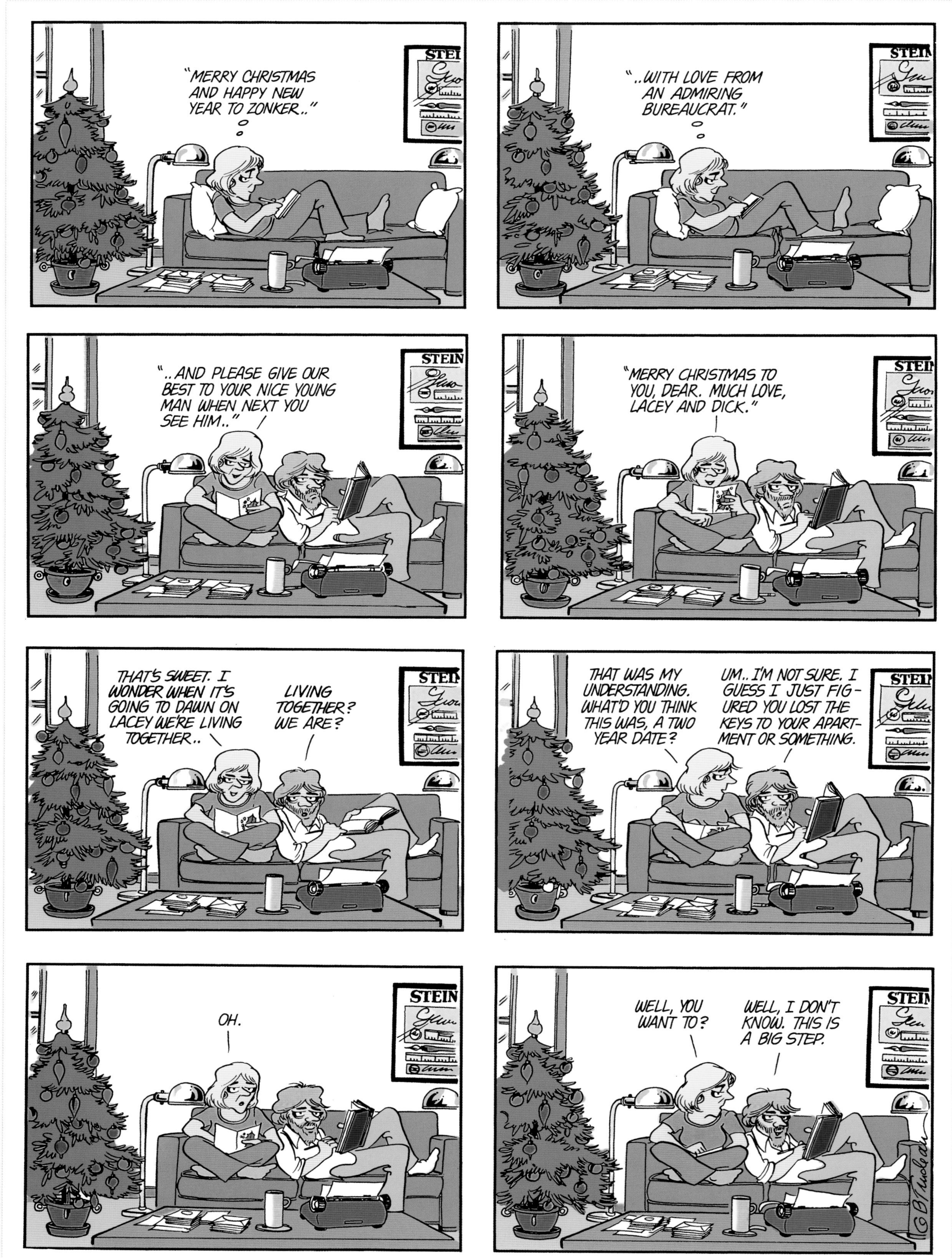
"MERRY CHRISTMAS AND HAPPY NEW YEAR TO ZONKER.."
"..WITH LOVE FROM AN ADMIRING BUREAUCRAT."
"..AND PLEASE GIVE OUR BEST TO YOUR NICE YOUNG MAN WHEN NEXT YOU SEE HIM.."
"MERRY CHRISTMAS TO YOU, DEAR. MUCH LOVE, LACEY AND DICK."
THAT'S SWEET. I WONDER WHEN IT'S GOING TO DAWN ON LACEY WE'RE LIVING TOGETHER..
LIVING TOGETHER? WE ARE?
THAT WAS MY UNDERSTANDING. WHAT'D YOU THINK THIS WAS, A TWO YEAR DATE?
UM.. I'M NOT SURE. I GUESS I JUST FIGURED YOU LOST THE KEYS TO YOUR APARTMENT OR SOMETHING.
OH.
WELL, YOU WANT TO?
WELL, I DON'T KNOW. THIS IS A BIG STEP.

12/17/78

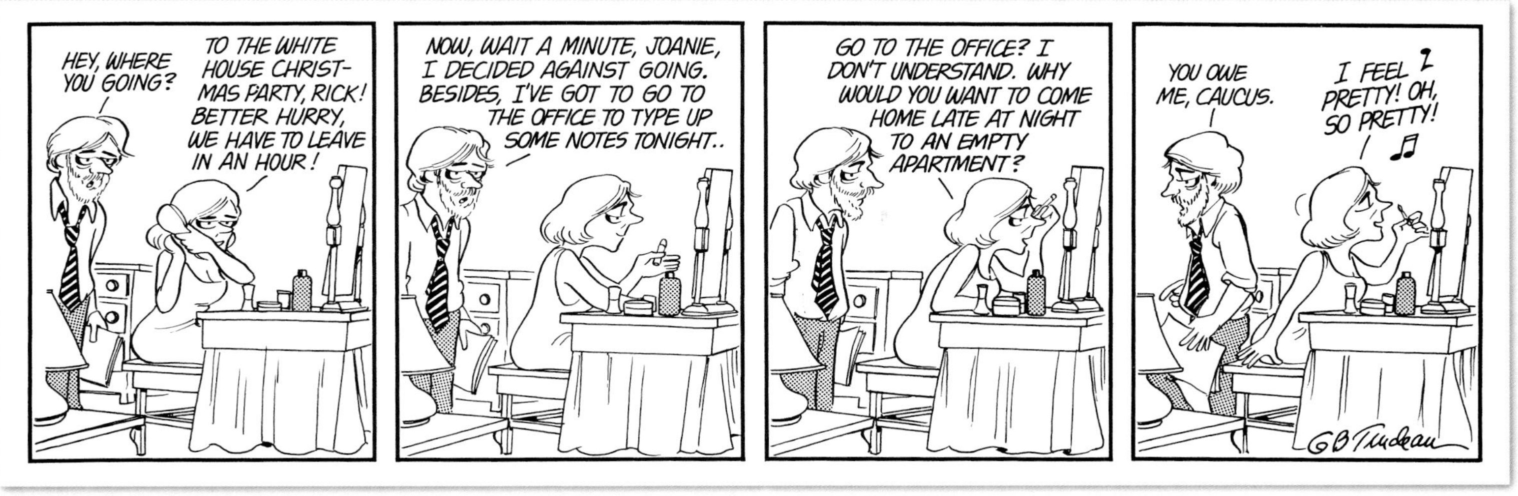
HEY, WHERE YOU GOING?
TO THE WHITE HOUSE CHRISTMAS PARTY, RICK! BETTER HURRY, WE HAVE TO LEAVE IN AN HOUR!
NOW, WAIT A MINUTE, JOANIE, I DECIDED AGAINST GOING. BESIDES, I'VE GOT TO GO TO THE OFFICE TO TYPE UP SOME NOTES TONIGHT..
GO TO THE OFFICE? I DON'T UNDERSTAND. WHY WOULD YOU WANT TO COME HOME LATE AT NIGHT TO AN EMPTY APARTMENT?
YOU OWE ME, CAUCUS.
I FEEL PRETTY! OH, SO PRETTY!
GB Trudeau

12/20/78

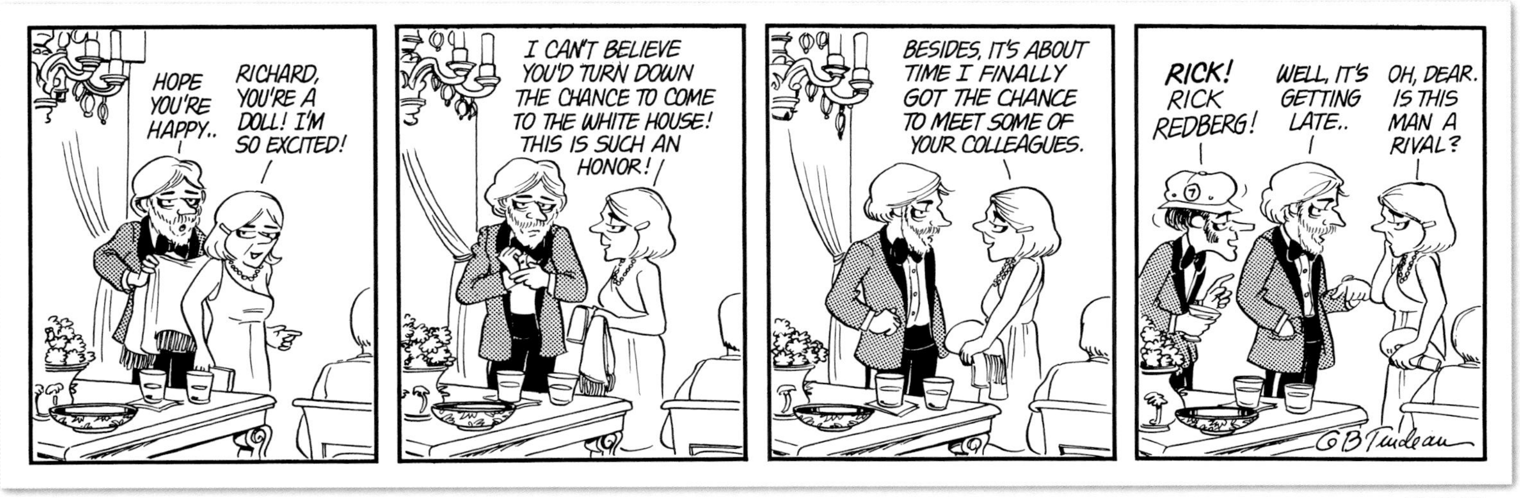
HOPE YOU'RE HAPPY..
RICHARD, YOU'RE A DOLL! I'M SO EXCITED!
I CAN'T BELIEVE YOU'D TURN DOWN THE CHANCE TO COME TO THE WHITE HOUSE! THIS IS SUCH AN HONOR!
BESIDES, IT'S ABOUT TIME I FINALLY GOT THE CHANCE TO MEET SOME OF YOUR COLLEAGUES.
RICK! RICK REDBERG!
WELL, IT'S GETTING LATE..
OH, DEAR. IS THIS MAN A RIVAL?
GB Trudeau

12/21/78

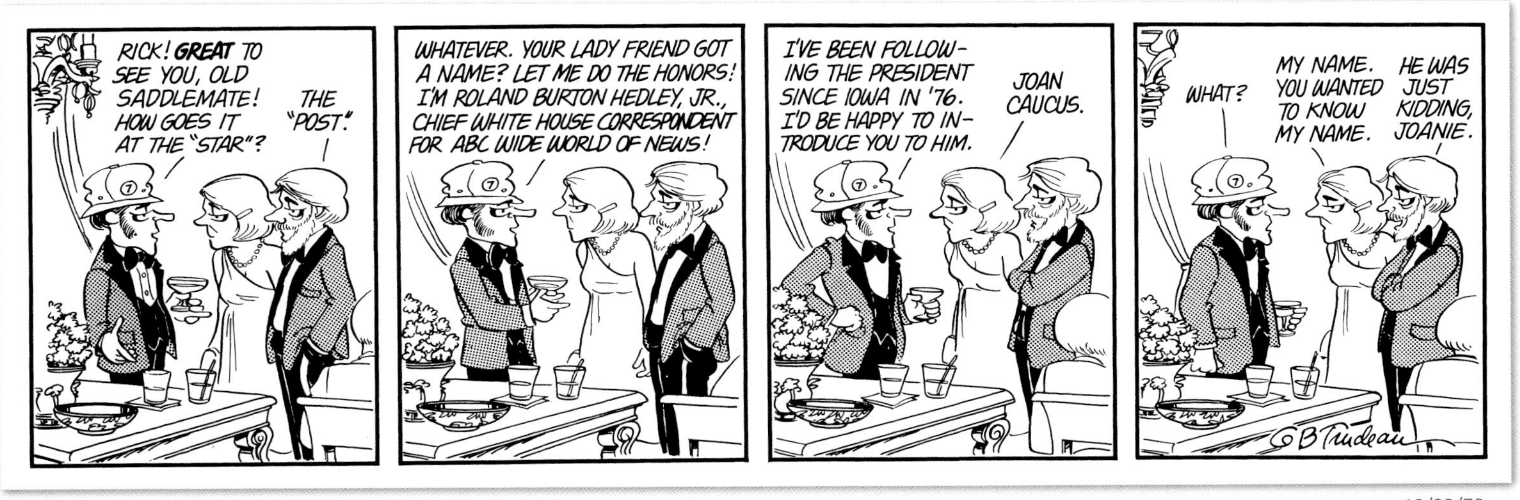
RICK! GREAT TO SEE YOU, OLD SADDLEMATE! HOW GOES IT AT THE "STAR"?
THE "POST."
WHATEVER. YOUR LADY FRIEND GOT A NAME? LET ME DO THE HONORS! I'M ROLAND BURTON HEDLEY, JR., CHIEF WHITE HOUSE CORRESPONDENT FOR ABC WIDE WORLD OF NEWS!
I'VE BEEN FOLLOWING THE PRESIDENT SINCE IOWA IN '76. I'D BE HAPPY TO INTRODUCE YOU TO HIM.
JOAN CAUCUS.
WHAT?
MY NAME. YOU WANTED TO KNOW MY NAME.
HE WAS JUST KIDDING, JOANIE.
GB Trudeau

12/22/78

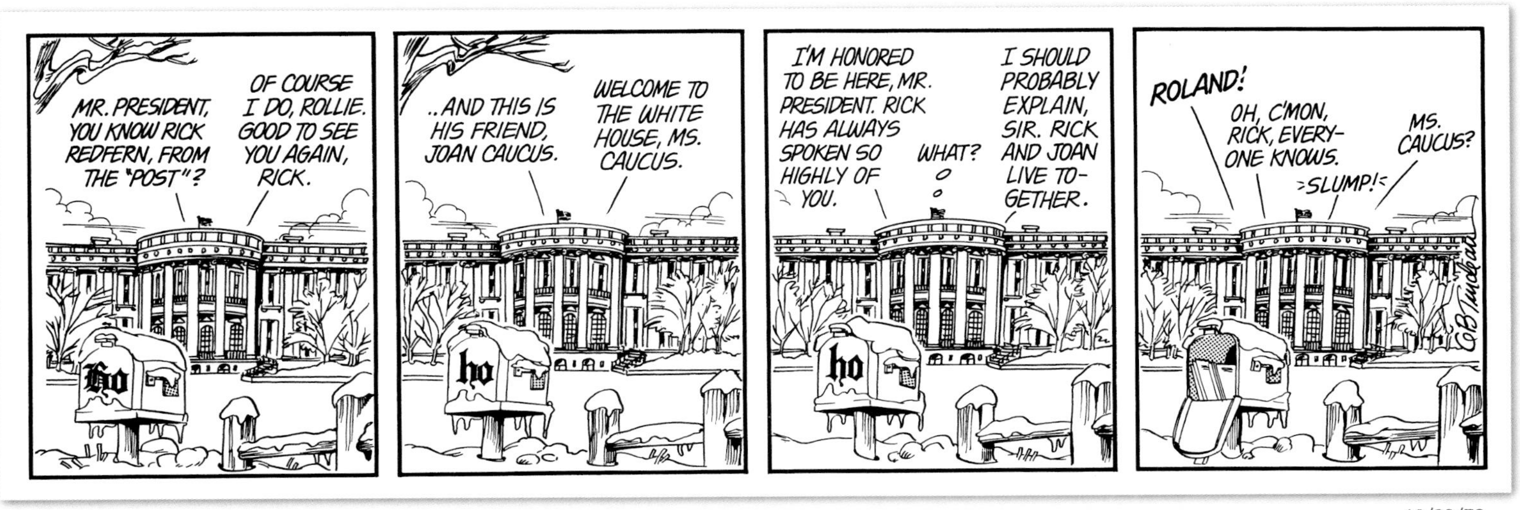
MR. PRESIDENT, YOU KNOW RICK REDFERN, FROM THE "POST"?
OF COURSE I DO, ROLLIE. GOOD TO SEE YOU AGAIN, RICK.
..AND THIS IS HIS FRIEND, JOAN CAUCUS.
WELCOME TO THE WHITE HOUSE, MS. CAUCUS.
I'M HONORED TO BE HERE, MR. PRESIDENT. RICK HAS ALWAYS SPOKEN SO HIGHLY OF YOU.
WHAT?
I SHOULD PROBABLY EXPLAIN, SIR. RICK AND JOAN LIVE TOGETHER.
ROLAND!
OH, C'MON, RICK, EVERYONE KNOWS.
SLUMP!
MS. CAUCUS?
GB Trudeau

12/23/78

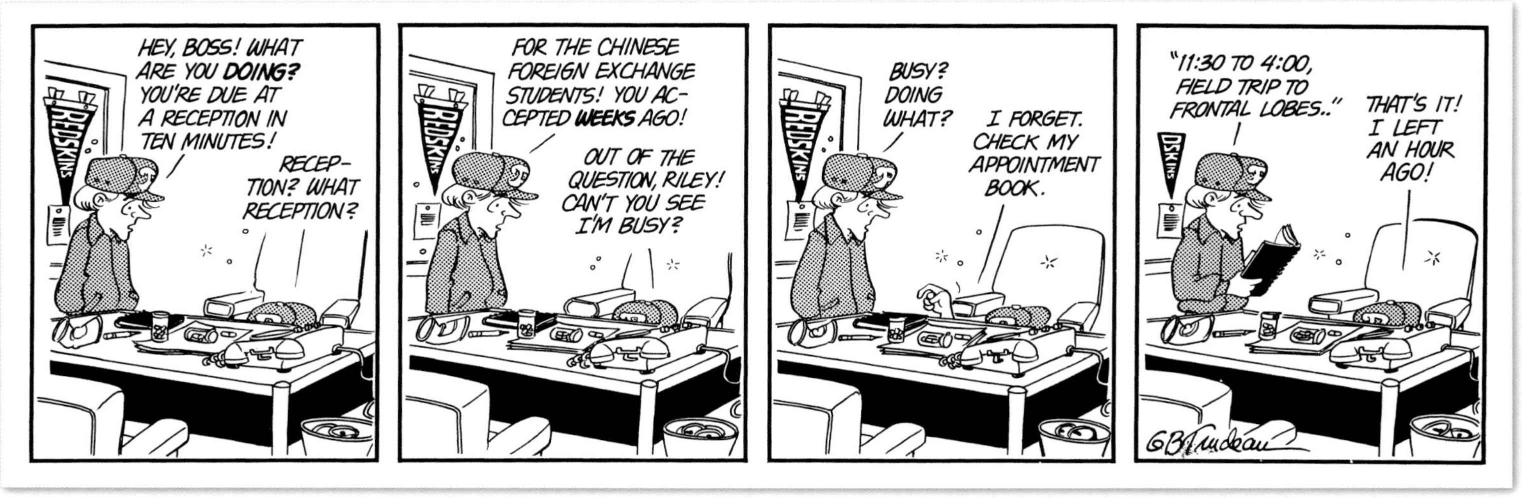
HEY, BOSS! WHAT ARE YOU **DOING?** YOU'RE DUE AT A RECEPTION IN TEN MINUTES!
RECEPTION? WHAT RECEPTION?
FOR THE CHINESE FOREIGN EXCHANGE STUDENTS! YOU ACCEPTED **WEEKS** AGO!
OUT OF THE QUESTION, RILEY! CAN'T YOU SEE I'M BUSY?
BUSY? DOING WHAT?
I FORGET. CHECK MY APPOINTMENT BOOK.
"11:30 TO 4:00, FIELD TRIP TO FRONTAL LOBES.."
THAT'S IT! I LEFT AN HOUR AGO!
GB Trudeau

11/6/78

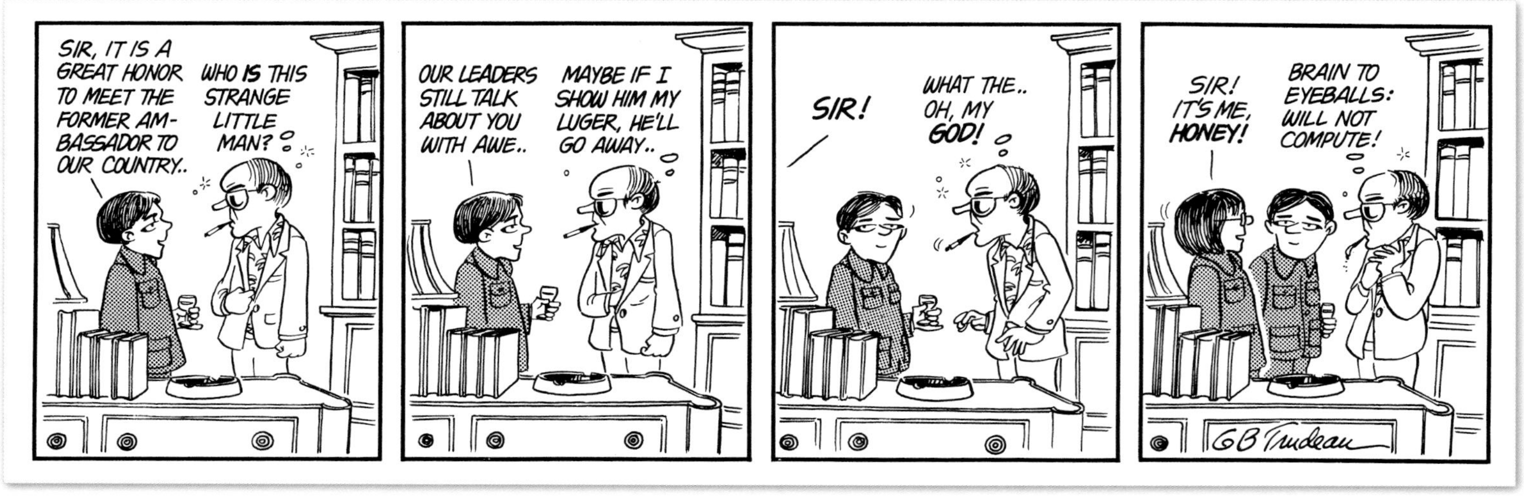
SIR, IT IS A GREAT HONOR TO MEET THE FORMER AMBASSADOR TO OUR COUNTRY..
WHO **IS** THIS STRANGE LITTLE MAN?
OUR LEADERS STILL TALK ABOUT YOU WITH AWE..
MAYBE IF I SHOW HIM MY LUGER, HE'LL GO AWAY..
SIR!
WHAT THE.. OH, MY **GOD!**
SIR! IT'S ME, **HONEY!**
BRAIN TO EYEBALLS: WILL NOT COMPUTE!
GB Trudeau

11/9/78

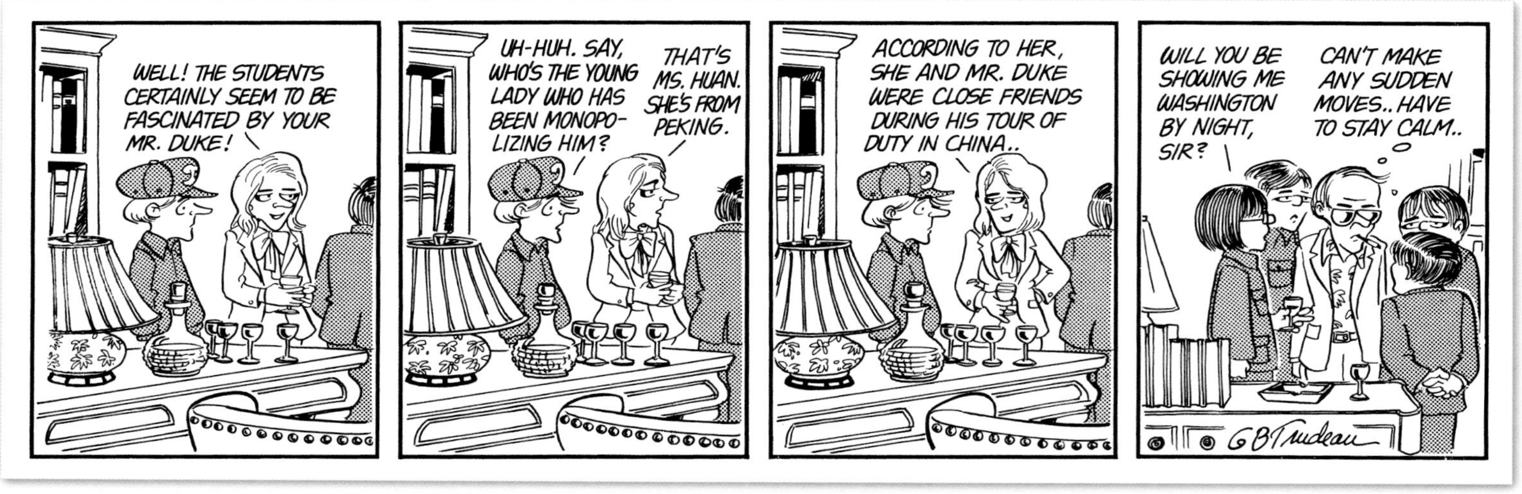
WELL! THE STUDENTS CERTAINLY SEEM TO BE FASCINATED BY YOUR MR. DUKE!
UH-HUH. SAY, WHO'S THE YOUNG LADY WHO HAS BEEN MONOPOLIZING HIM?
THAT'S MS. HUAN. SHE'S FROM PEKING.
ACCORDING TO HER, SHE AND MR. DUKE WERE CLOSE FRIENDS DURING HIS TOUR OF DUTY IN CHINA..
WILL YOU BE SHOWING ME WASHINGTON BY NIGHT, SIR?
CAN'T MAKE ANY SUDDEN MOVES.. HAVE TO STAY CALM..
GB Trudeau

11/11/78

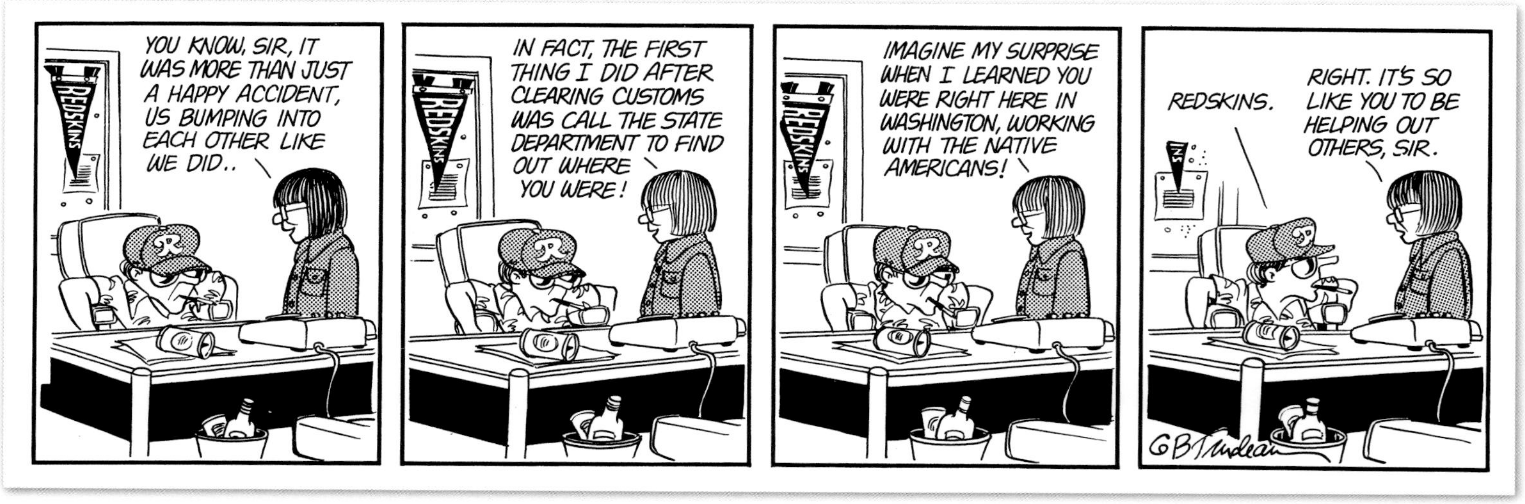
YOU KNOW, SIR, IT WAS MORE THAN JUST A HAPPY ACCIDENT, US BUMPING INTO EACH OTHER LIKE WE DID..
IN FACT, THE FIRST THING I DID AFTER CLEARING CUSTOMS WAS CALL THE STATE DEPARTMENT TO FIND OUT WHERE YOU WERE!
IMAGINE MY SURPRISE WHEN I LEARNED YOU WERE RIGHT HERE IN WASHINGTON, WORKING WITH THE NATIVE AMERICANS!
REDSKINS.
RIGHT. IT'S SO LIKE YOU TO BE HELPING OUT OTHERS, SIR.
GB Trudeau

11/21/78

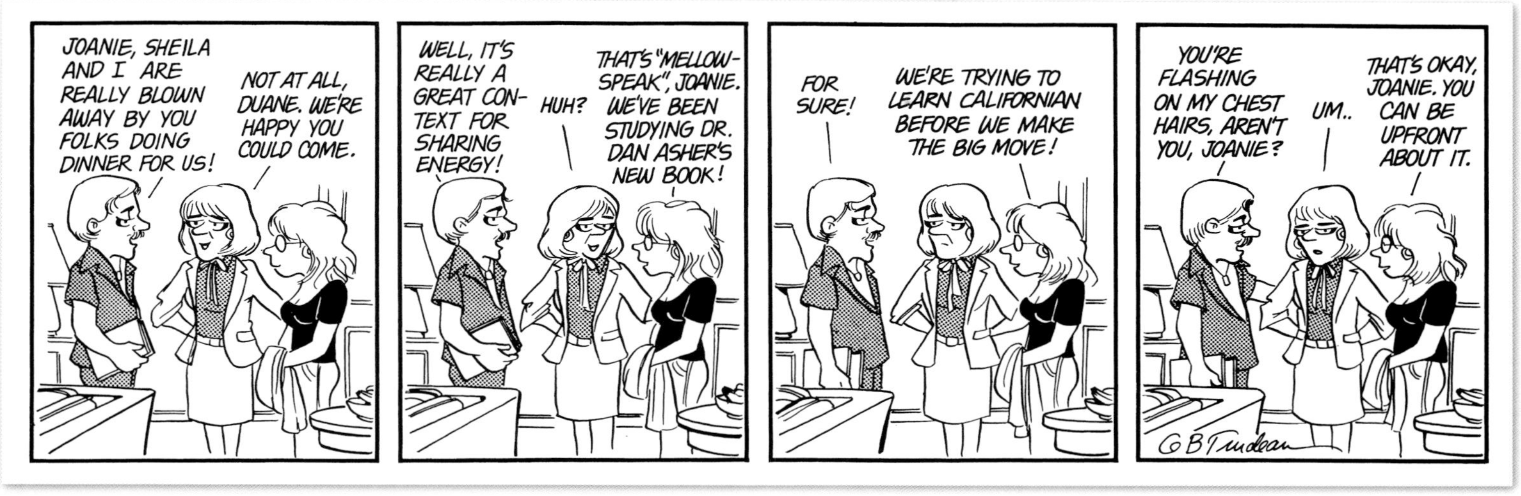
JOANIE, SHEILA AND I ARE REALLY BLOWN AWAY BY YOU FOLKS DOING DINNER FOR US!
NOT AT ALL, DUANE. WE'RE HAPPY YOU COULD COME.
WELL, IT'S REALLY A GREAT CONTEXT FOR SHARING ENERGY!
HUH?
THAT'S "MELLOW-SPEAK", JOANIE. WE'VE BEEN STUDYING DR. DAN ASHER'S NEW BOOK!
FOR SURE!
WE'RE TRYING TO LEARN CALIFORNIAN BEFORE WE MAKE THE BIG MOVE!
YOU'RE FLASHING ON MY CHEST HAIRS, AREN'T YOU, JOANIE?
UM..
THAT'S OKAY, JOANIE. YOU CAN BE UPFRONT ABOUT IT.
GBTrudeau

5/14/79

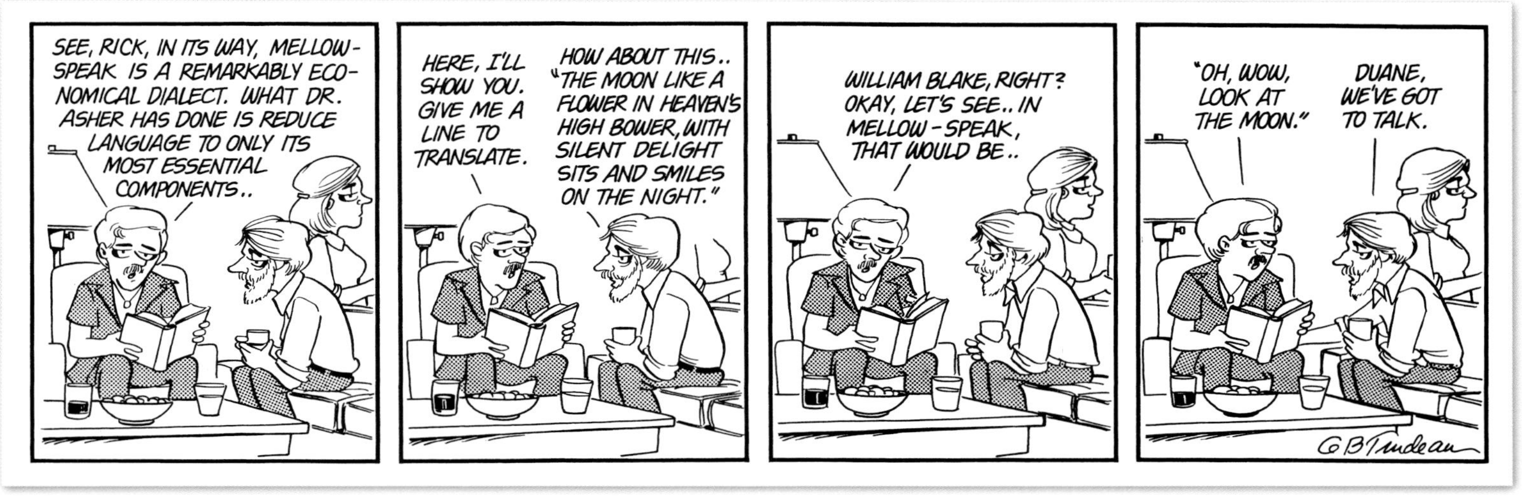
SEE, RICK, IN ITS WAY, MELLOW-SPEAK IS A REMARKABLY ECONOMICAL DIALECT. WHAT DR. ASHER HAS DONE IS REDUCE LANGUAGE TO ONLY ITS MOST ESSENTIAL COMPONENTS..
HERE, I'LL SHOW YOU. GIVE ME A LINE TO TRANSLATE.
HOW ABOUT THIS.. "THE MOON LIKE A FLOWER IN HEAVEN'S HIGH BOWER, WITH SILENT DELIGHT SITS AND SMILES ON THE NIGHT."
WILLIAM BLAKE, RIGHT? OKAY, LET'S SEE.. IN MELLOW-SPEAK, THAT WOULD BE..
"OH, WOW, LOOK AT THE MOON."
DUANE, WE'VE GOT TO TALK.
GBTrudeau

5/16/79

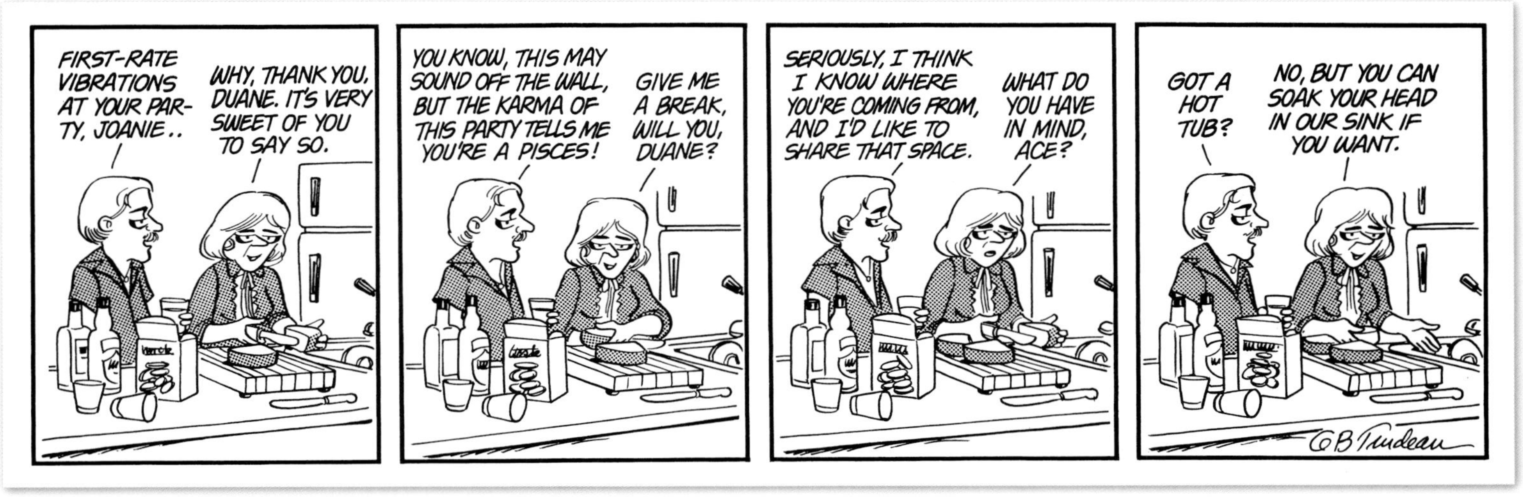
FIRST-RATE VIBRATIONS AT YOUR PARTY, JOANIE..
WHY, THANK YOU, DUANE. IT'S VERY SWEET OF YOU TO SAY SO.
YOU KNOW, THIS MAY SOUND OFF THE WALL, BUT THE KARMA OF THIS PARTY TELLS ME YOU'RE A PISCES!
GIVE ME A BREAK, WILL YOU, DUANE?
SERIOUSLY, I THINK I KNOW WHERE YOU'RE COMING FROM, AND I'D LIKE TO SHARE THAT SPACE.
WHAT DO YOU HAVE IN MIND, ACE?
GOT A HOT TUB?
NO, BUT YOU CAN SOAK YOUR HEAD IN OUR SINK IF YOU WANT.
GBTrudeau

5/17/79

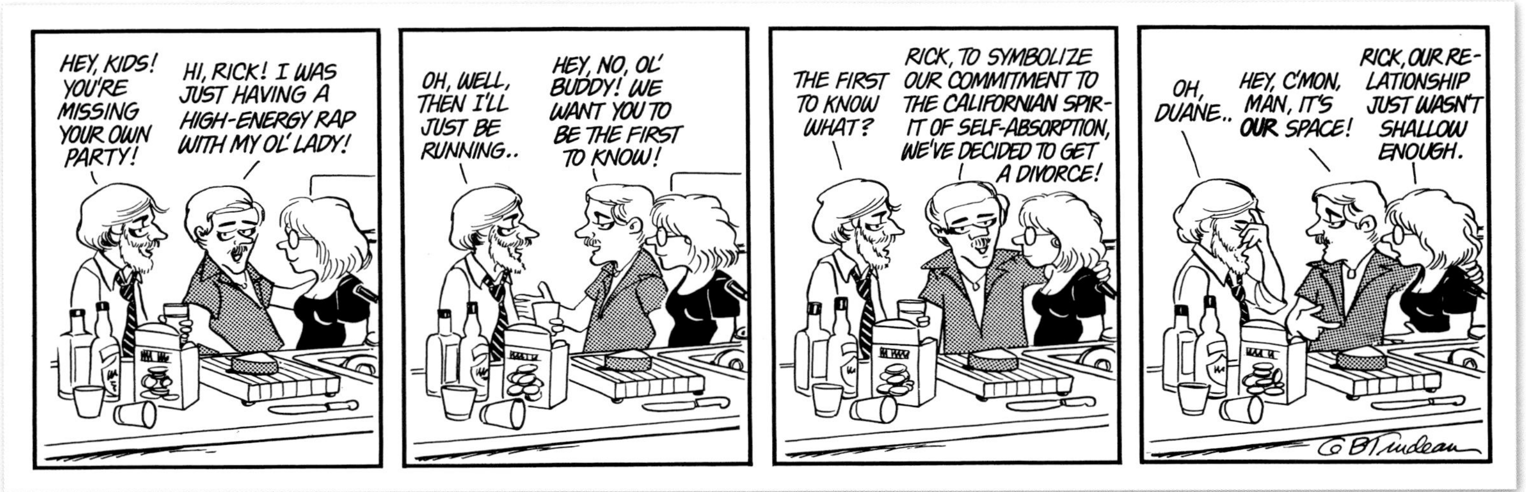
HEY, KIDS! YOU'RE MISSING YOUR OWN PARTY!
HI, RICK! I WAS JUST HAVING A HIGH-ENERGY RAP WITH MY OL' LADY!
OH, WELL, THEN I'LL JUST BE RUNNING..
HEY, NO, OL' BUDDY! WE WANT YOU TO BE THE FIRST TO KNOW!
THE FIRST TO KNOW WHAT?
RICK, TO SYMBOLIZE OUR COMMITMENT TO THE CALIFORNIAN SPIRIT OF SELF-ABSORPTION, WE'VE DECIDED TO GET A DIVORCE!
OH, DUANE..
HEY, C'MON, MAN, IT'S OUR SPACE!
RICK, OUR RELATIONSHIP JUST WASN'T SHALLOW ENOUGH.
GBTrudeau

5/18/79

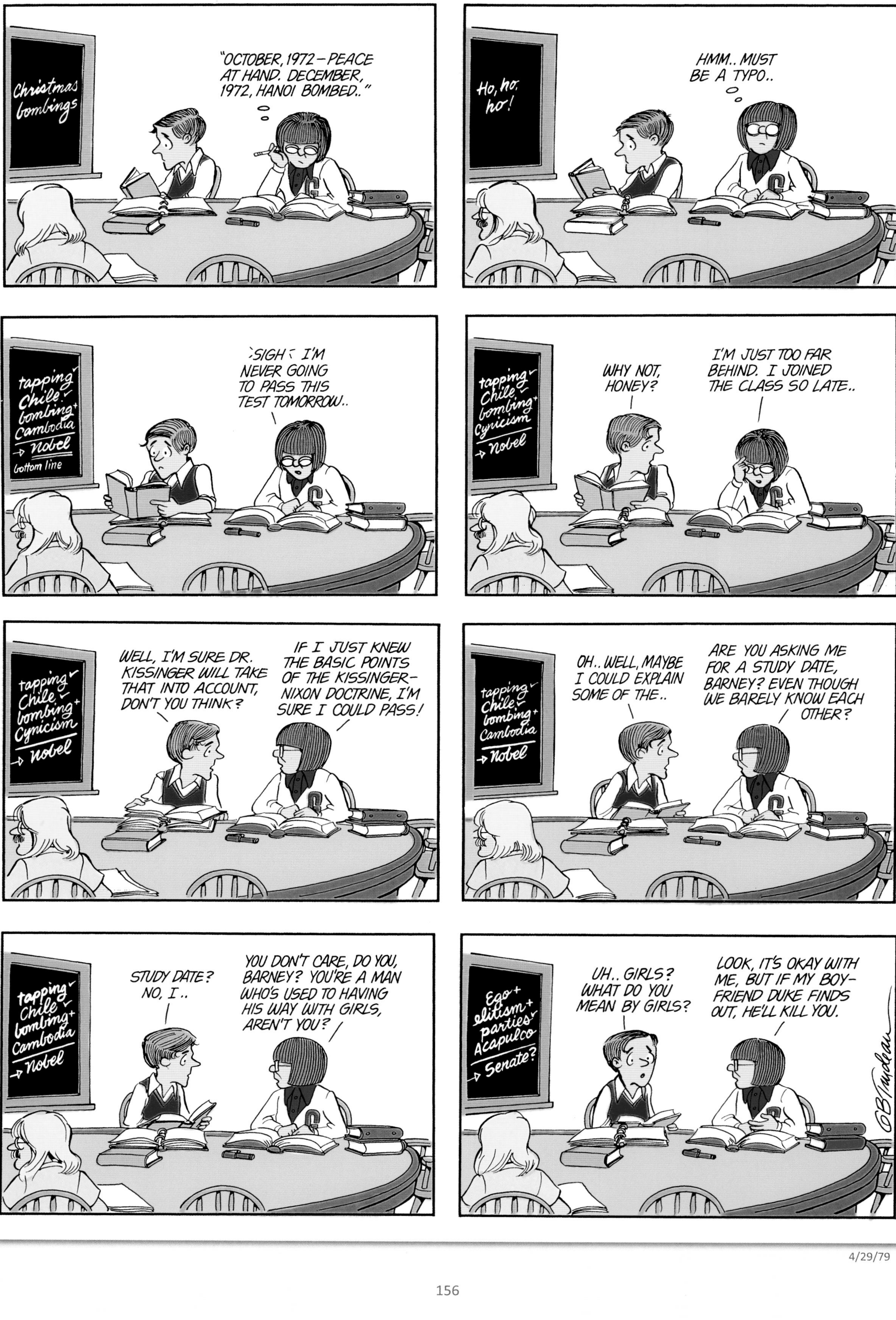
Christmas bombings
"OCTOBER, 1972—PEACE AT HAND. DECEMBER, 1972, HANOI BOMBED.."
Ho, ho, ho!
HMM.. MUST BE A TYPO..
tapping Chile bombing+ Cambodia → Nobel bottom line
·SIGH· I'M NEVER GOING TO PASS THIS TEST TOMORROW..
tapping Chile bombing+ Cynicism → Nobel
WHY NOT, HONEY?
I'M JUST TOO FAR BEHIND. I JOINED THE CLASS SO LATE..
tapping Chile bombing+ Cynicism → Nobel
WELL, I'M SURE DR. KISSINGER WILL TAKE THAT INTO ACCOUNT, DON'T YOU THINK?
IF I JUST KNEW THE BASIC POINTS OF THE KISSINGER-NIXON DOCTRINE, I'M SURE I COULD PASS!
tapping Chile bombing+ Cambodia → Nobel
OH.. WELL, MAYBE I COULD EXPLAIN SOME OF THE..
ARE YOU ASKING ME FOR A STUDY DATE, BARNEY? EVEN THOUGH WE BARELY KNOW EACH OTHER?
tapping Chile bombing+ Cambodia → Nobel
STUDY DATE? NO, I..
YOU DON'T CARE, DO YOU, BARNEY? YOU'RE A MAN WHO'S USED TO HAVING HIS WAY WITH GIRLS, AREN'T YOU?
Ego+ elitism+ parties+ Acapulco → Senate?
UH.. GIRLS? WHAT DO YOU MEAN BY GIRLS?
LOOK, IT'S OKAY WITH ME, BUT IF MY BOY-FRIEND DUKE FINDS OUT, HE'LL KILL YOU.
GBTrudeau

4/29/79

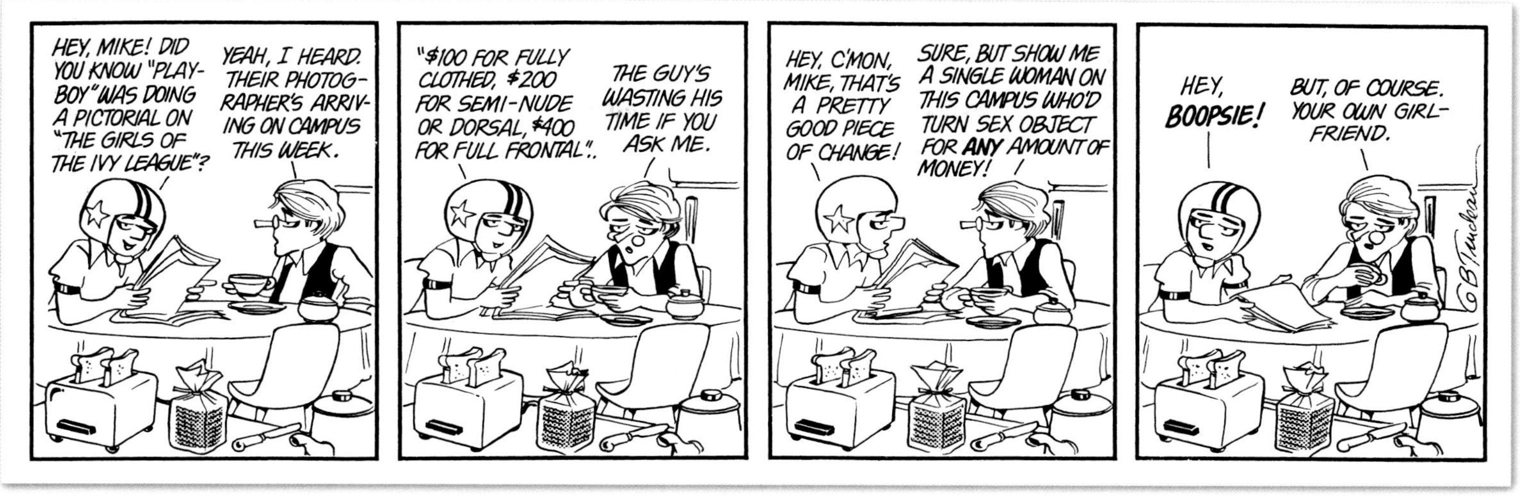
HEY, MIKE! DID YOU KNOW "PLAYBOY" WAS DOING A PICTORIAL ON "THE GIRLS OF THE IVY LEAGUE"?
YEAH, I HEARD. THEIR PHOTOGRAPHER'S ARRIVING ON CAMPUS THIS WEEK.
"$100 FOR FULLY CLOTHED, $200 FOR SEMI-NUDE OR DORSAL, $400 FOR FULL FRONTAL"..
THE GUY'S WASTING HIS TIME IF YOU ASK ME.
HEY, C'MON, MIKE, THAT'S A PRETTY GOOD PIECE OF CHANGE!
SURE, BUT SHOW ME A SINGLE WOMAN ON THIS CAMPUS WHO'D TURN SEX OBJECT FOR ANY AMOUNT OF MONEY!
HEY, BOOPSIE!
BUT, OF COURSE. YOUR OWN GIRLFRIEND.

5/21/79

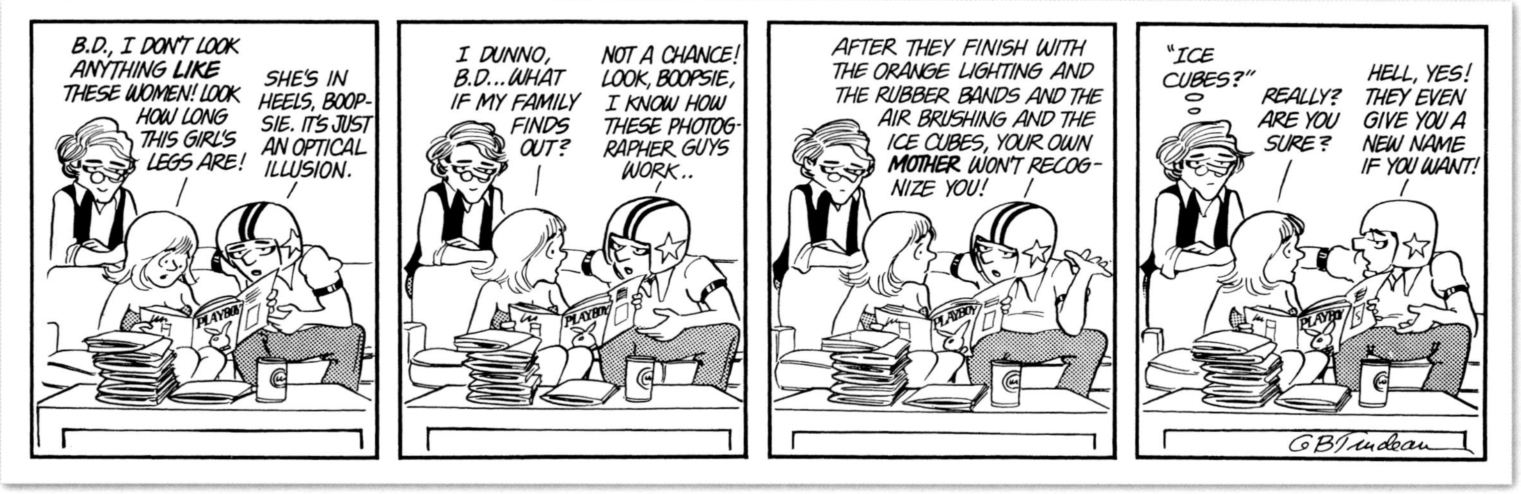
B.D., I DON'T LOOK ANYTHING LIKE THESE WOMEN! LOOK HOW LONG THIS GIRL'S LEGS ARE!
SHE'S IN HEELS, BOOPSIE. IT'S JUST AN OPTICAL ILLUSION.
I DUNNO, B.D.... WHAT IF MY FAMILY FINDS OUT?
NOT A CHANCE! LOOK, BOOPSIE, I KNOW HOW THESE PHOTOGRAPHER GUYS WORK..
AFTER THEY FINISH WITH THE ORANGE LIGHTING AND THE RUBBER BANDS AND THE AIR BRUSHING AND THE ICE CUBES, YOUR OWN MOTHER WON'T RECOGNIZE YOU!
"ICE CUBES?"
REALLY? ARE YOU SURE?
HELL, YES! THEY EVEN GIVE YOU A NEW NAME IF YOU WANT!

5/23/79

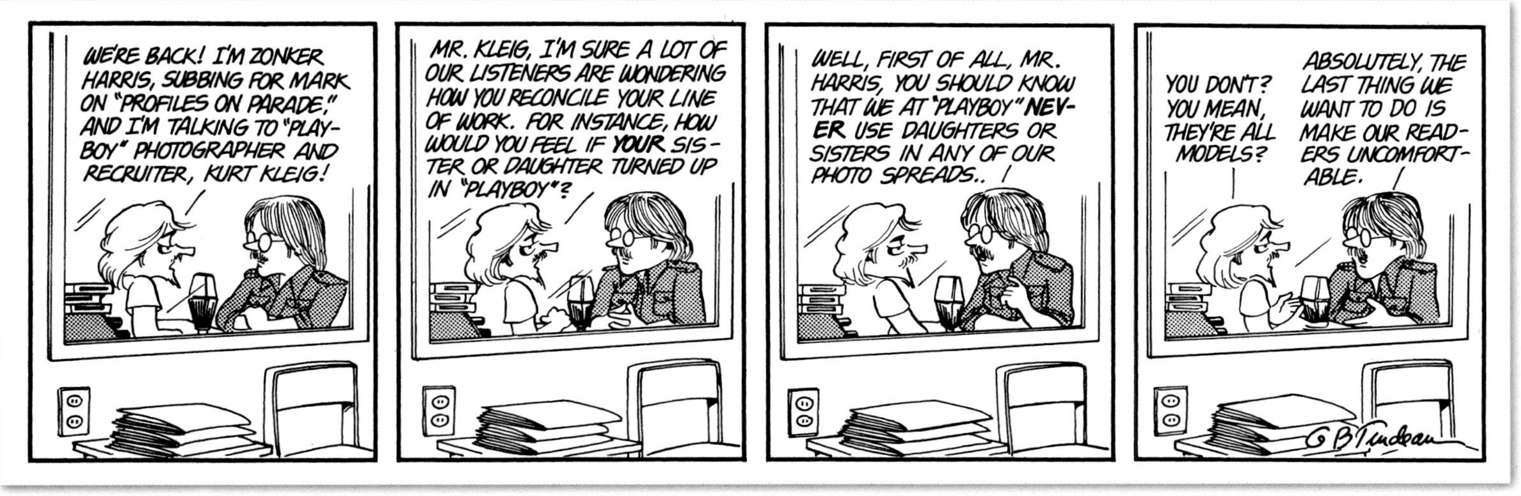
WE'RE BACK! I'M ZONKER HARRIS, SUBBING FOR MARK ON "PROFILES ON PARADE," AND I'M TALKING TO "PLAYBOY" PHOTOGRAPHER AND RECRUITER, KURT KLEIG!
MR. KLEIG, I'M SURE A LOT OF OUR LISTENERS ARE WONDERING HOW YOU RECONCILE YOUR LINE OF WORK. FOR INSTANCE, HOW WOULD YOU FEEL IF YOUR SISTER OR DAUGHTER TURNED UP IN "PLAYBOY"?
WELL, FIRST OF ALL, MR. HARRIS, YOU SHOULD KNOW THAT WE AT "PLAYBOY" NEVER USE DAUGHTERS OR SISTERS IN ANY OF OUR PHOTO SPREADS..
YOU DON'T? YOU MEAN, THEY'RE ALL MODELS?
ABSOLUTELY, THE LAST THING WE WANT TO DO IS MAKE OUR READERS UNCOMFORTABLE.

5/25/79

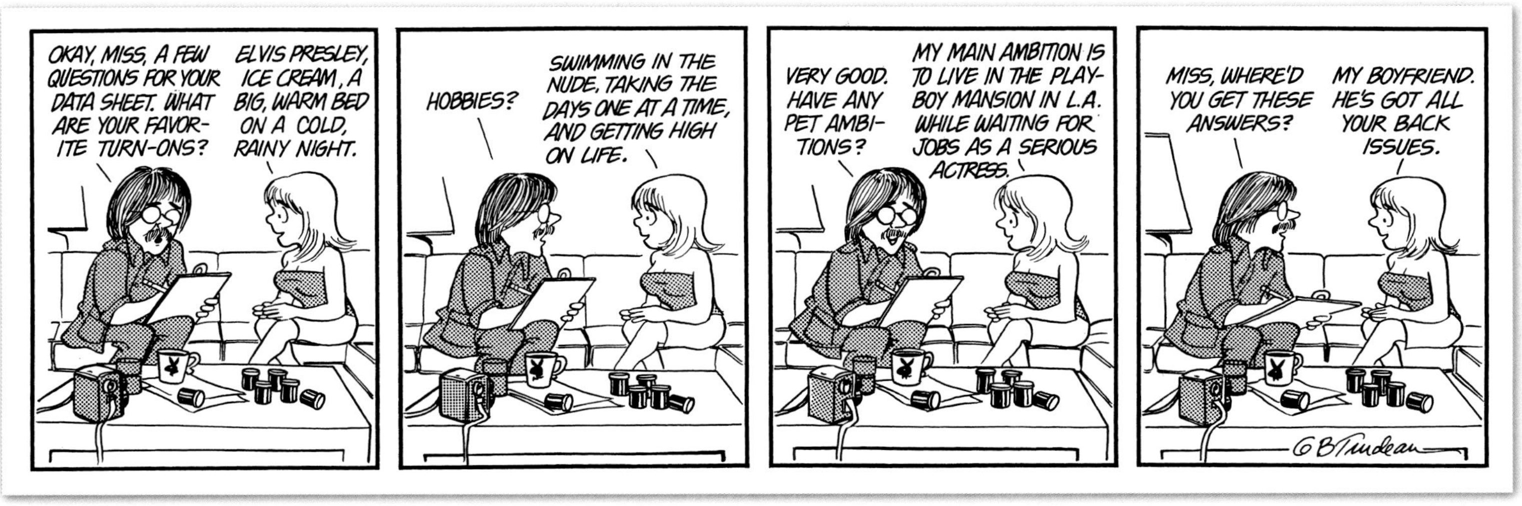
OKAY, MISS, A FEW QUESTIONS FOR YOUR DATA SHEET. WHAT ARE YOUR FAVORITE TURN-ONS?
ELVIS PRESLEY, ICE CREAM, A BIG, WARM BED ON A COLD, RAINY NIGHT.
HOBBIES?
SWIMMING IN THE NUDE, TAKING THE DAYS ONE AT A TIME, AND GETTING HIGH ON LIFE.
VERY GOOD. HAVE ANY PET AMBITIONS?
MY MAIN AMBITION IS TO LIVE IN THE PLAYBOY MANSION IN L.A. WHILE WAITING FOR JOBS AS A SERIOUS ACTRESS.
MISS, WHERE'D YOU GET THESE ANSWERS?
MY BOYFRIEND. HE'S GOT ALL YOUR BACK ISSUES.

5/28/79

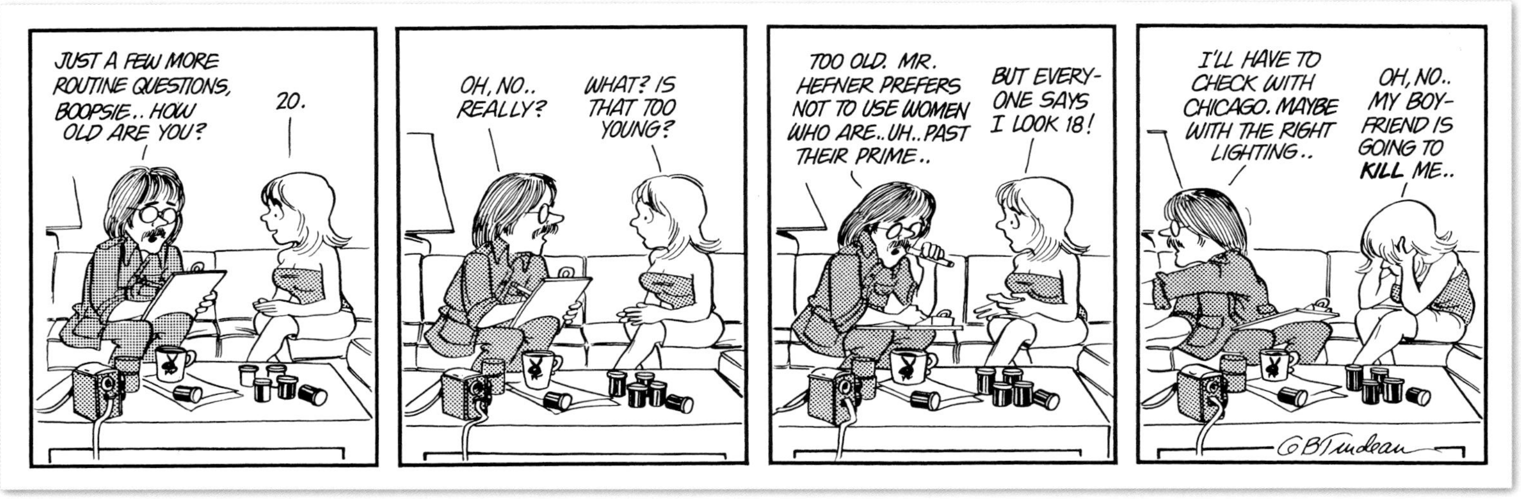
JUST A FEW MORE ROUTINE QUESTIONS, BOOPSIE.. HOW OLD ARE YOU?
20.
OH, NO.. REALLY?
WHAT? IS THAT TOO YOUNG?
TOO OLD. MR. HEFNER PREFERS NOT TO USE WOMEN WHO ARE..UH..PAST THEIR PRIME..
BUT EVERY-ONE SAYS I LOOK 18!
I'LL HAVE TO CHECK WITH CHICAGO. MAYBE WITH THE RIGHT LIGHTING..
OH, NO.. MY BOY-FRIEND IS GOING TO **KILL** ME..
GBTrudeau

5/29/79

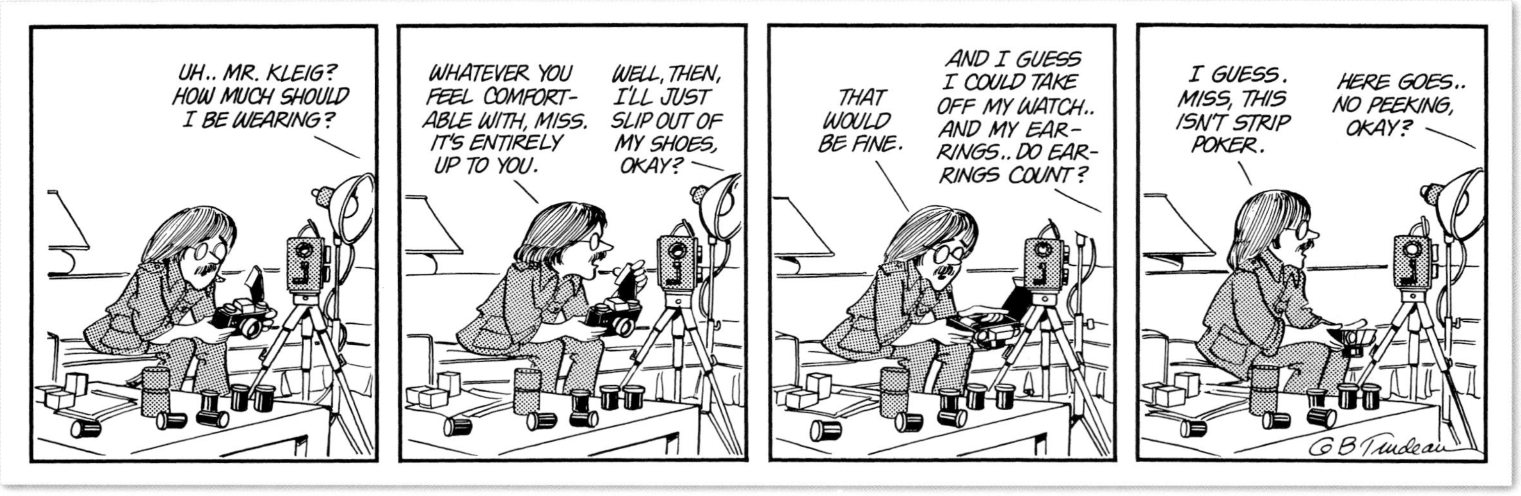
UH.. MR. KLEIG? HOW MUCH SHOULD I BE WEARING?
WHATEVER YOU FEEL COMFORT-ABLE WITH, MISS. IT'S ENTIRELY UP TO YOU.
WELL, THEN, I'LL JUST SLIP OUT OF MY SHOES, OKAY?
THAT WOULD BE FINE.
AND I GUESS I COULD TAKE OFF MY WATCH.. AND MY EAR-RINGS.. DO EAR-RINGS COUNT?
I GUESS. MISS, THIS ISN'T STRIP POKER.
HERE GOES.. NO PEEKING, OKAY?
GBTrudeau

5/31/79

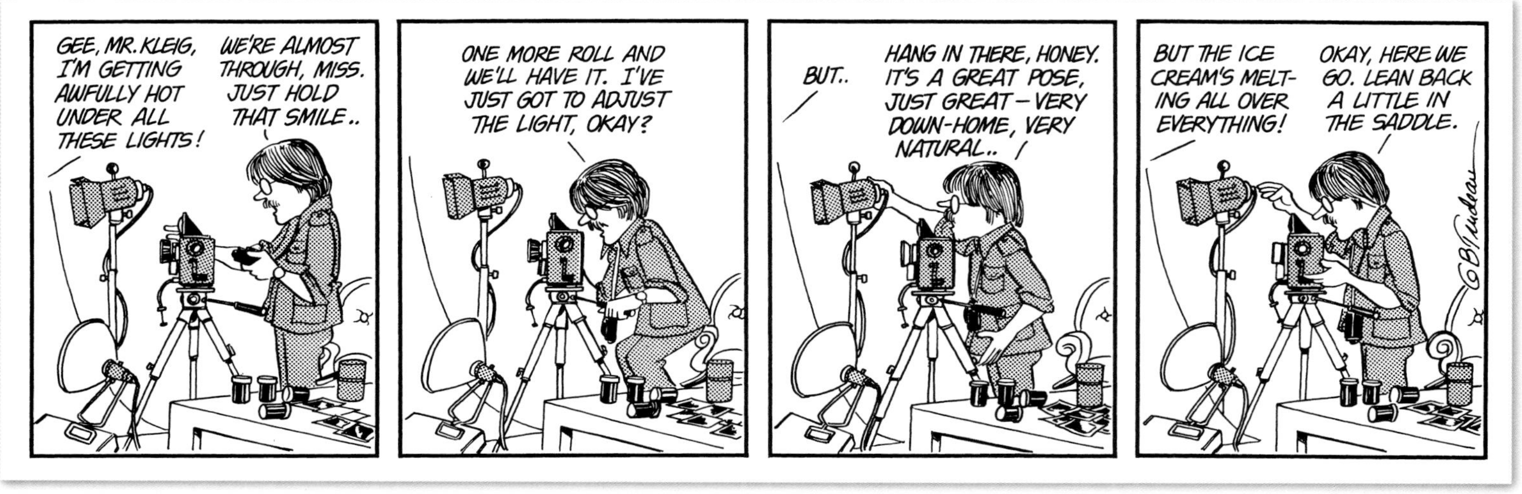
GEE, MR. KLEIG, I'M GETTING AWFULLY HOT UNDER ALL THESE LIGHTS!
WE'RE ALMOST THROUGH, MISS. JUST HOLD THAT SMILE..
ONE MORE ROLL AND WE'LL HAVE IT. I'VE JUST GOT TO ADJUST THE LIGHT, OKAY?
BUT..
HANG IN THERE, HONEY. IT'S A GREAT POSE, JUST GREAT—VERY DOWN-HOME, VERY NATURAL..
BUT THE ICE CREAM'S MELT-ING ALL OVER EVERYTHING!
OKAY, HERE WE GO. LEAN BACK A LITTLE IN THE SADDLE.
GBTrudeau

6/1/79

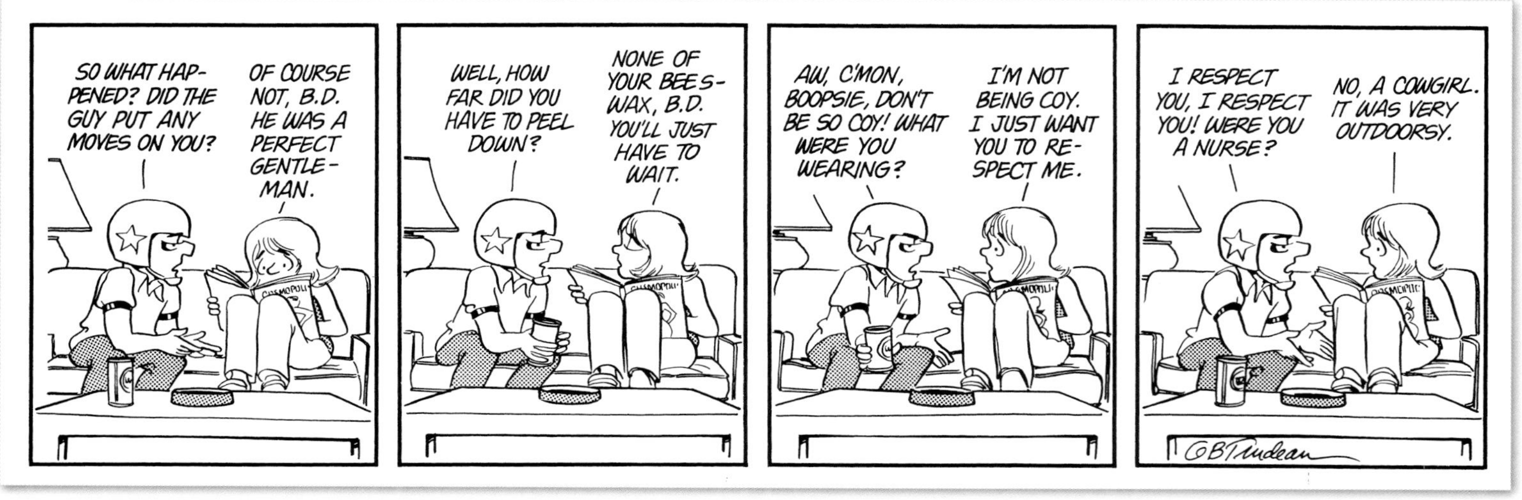
SO WHAT HAP-PENED? DID THE GUY PUT ANY MOVES ON YOU?
OF COURSE NOT, B.D. HE WAS A PERFECT GENTLE-MAN.
WELL, HOW FAR DID YOU HAVE TO PEEL DOWN?
NONE OF YOUR BEES-WAX, B.D. YOU'LL JUST HAVE TO WAIT.
AW, C'MON, BOOPSIE, DON'T BE SO COY! WHAT WERE YOU WEARING?
I'M NOT BEING COY. I JUST WANT YOU TO RE-SPECT ME.
I RESPECT YOU, I RESPECT YOU! WERE YOU A NURSE?
NO, A COWGIRL. IT WAS VERY OUTDOORSY.
GBTrudeau

6/2/79

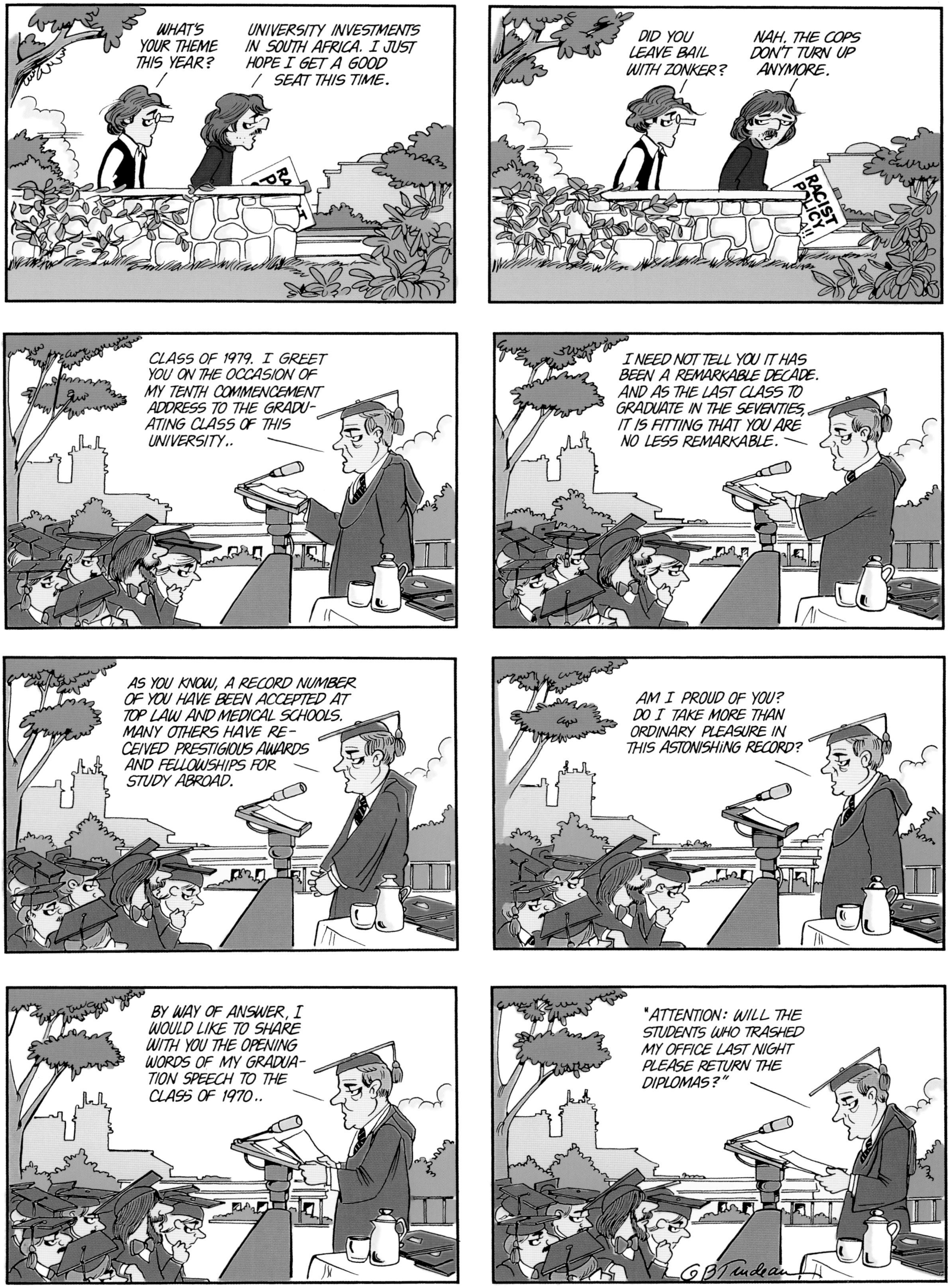
WHAT'S YOUR THEME THIS YEAR?
UNIVERSITY INVESTMENTS IN SOUTH AFRICA. I JUST HOPE I GET A GOOD SEAT THIS TIME.
DID YOU LEAVE BAIL WITH ZONKER?
NAH. THE COPS DON'T TURN UP ANYMORE.
RACIST POLICY!!
CLASS OF 1979. I GREET YOU ON THE OCCASION OF MY TENTH COMMENCEMENT ADDRESS TO THE GRADUATING CLASS OF THIS UNIVERSITY..
I NEED NOT TELL YOU IT HAS BEEN A REMARKABLE DECADE. AND AS THE LAST CLASS TO GRADUATE IN THE SEVENTIES, IT IS FITTING THAT YOU ARE NO LESS REMARKABLE.
AS YOU KNOW, A RECORD NUMBER OF YOU HAVE BEEN ACCEPTED AT TOP LAW AND MEDICAL SCHOOLS. MANY OTHERS HAVE RECEIVED PRESTIGIOUS AWARDS AND FELLOWSHIPS FOR STUDY ABROAD.
AM I PROUD OF YOU? DO I TAKE MORE THAN ORDINARY PLEASURE IN THIS ASTONISHING RECORD?
BY WAY OF ANSWER, I WOULD LIKE TO SHARE WITH YOU THE OPENING WORDS OF MY GRADUATION SPEECH TO THE CLASS OF 1970..
"ATTENTION: WILL THE STUDENTS WHO TRASHED MY OFFICE LAST NIGHT PLEASE RETURN THE DIPLOMAS?"
© GB Trudeau

5/27/79

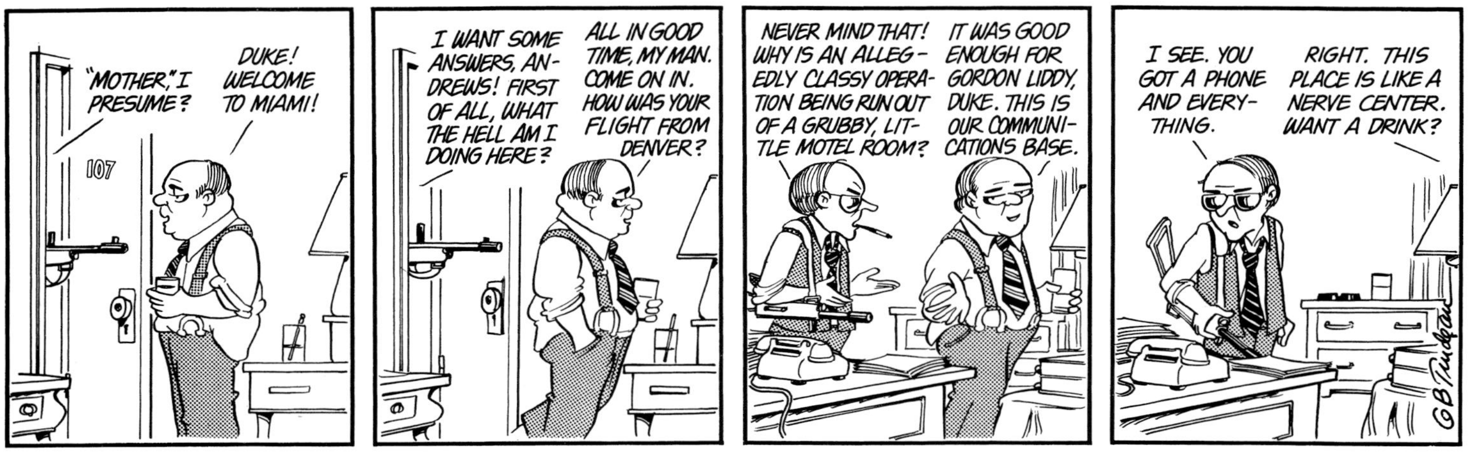
"MOTHER," I PRESUME?
DUKE! WELCOME TO MIAMI!
107
I WANT SOME ANSWERS, ANDREWS! FIRST OF ALL, WHAT THE HELL AM I DOING HERE?
ALL IN GOOD TIME, MY MAN. COME ON IN. HOW WAS YOUR FLIGHT FROM DENVER?
NEVER MIND THAT! WHY IS AN ALLEGEDLY CLASSY OPERATION BEING RUN OUT OF A GRUBBY, LITTLE MOTEL ROOM?
IT WAS GOOD ENOUGH FOR GORDON LIDDY, DUKE. THIS IS OUR COMMUNICATIONS BASE.
I SEE. YOU GOT A PHONE AND EVERYTHING.
RIGHT. THIS PLACE IS LIKE A NERVE CENTER. WANT A DRINK?
GBTrudeau

7/2/79

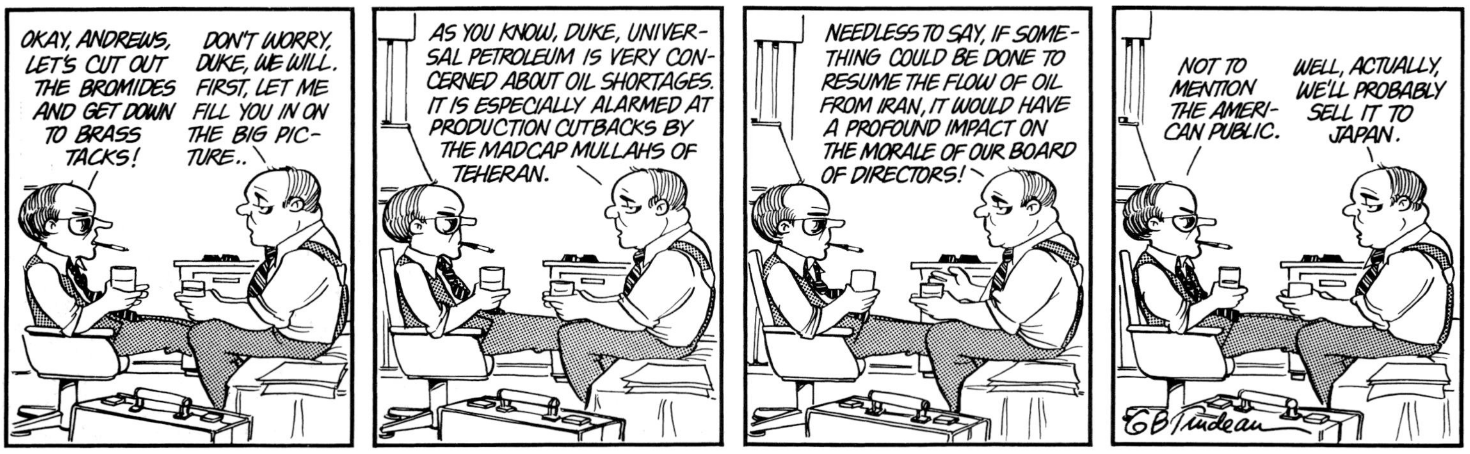
OKAY, ANDREWS, LET'S CUT OUT THE BROMIDES AND GET DOWN TO BRASS TACKS!
DON'T WORRY, DUKE, WE WILL. FIRST, LET ME FILL YOU IN ON THE BIG PICTURE..
AS YOU KNOW, DUKE, UNIVERSAL PETROLEUM IS VERY CONCERNED ABOUT OIL SHORTAGES. IT IS ESPECIALLY ALARMED AT PRODUCTION CUTBACKS BY THE MADCAP MULLAHS OF TEHERAN.
NEEDLESS TO SAY, IF SOMETHING COULD BE DONE TO RESUME THE FLOW OF OIL FROM IRAN, IT WOULD HAVE A PROFOUND IMPACT ON THE MORALE OF OUR BOARD OF DIRECTORS!
NOT TO MENTION THE AMERICAN PUBLIC.
WELL, ACTUALLY, WE'LL PROBABLY SELL IT TO JAPAN.
GBTrudeau

7/3/79

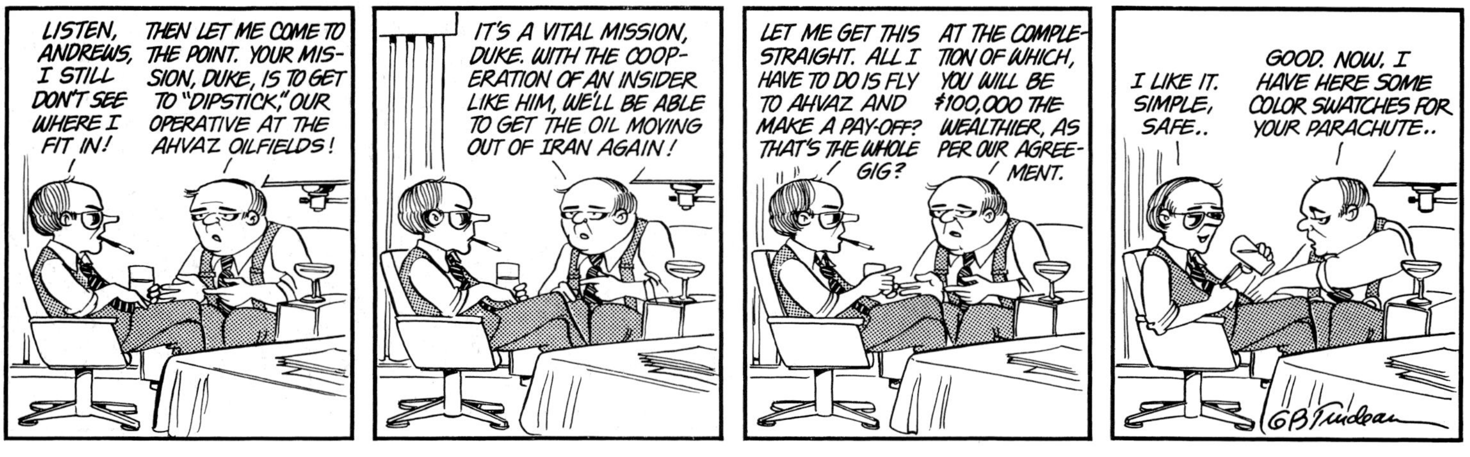
LISTEN, ANDREWS, I STILL DON'T SEE WHERE I FIT IN!
THEN LET ME COME TO THE POINT. YOUR MISSION, DUKE, IS TO GET TO "DIPSTICK," OUR OPERATIVE AT THE AHVAZ OILFIELDS!
IT'S A VITAL MISSION, DUKE. WITH THE COOPERATION OF AN INSIDER LIKE HIM, WE'LL BE ABLE TO GET THE OIL MOVING OUT OF IRAN AGAIN!
LET ME GET THIS STRAIGHT. ALL I HAVE TO DO IS FLY TO AHVAZ AND MAKE A PAY-OFF? THAT'S THE WHOLE GIG?
AT THE COMPLETION OF WHICH, YOU WILL BE $100,000 THE WEALTHIER, AS PER OUR AGREEMENT.
I LIKE IT. SIMPLE, SAFE..
GOOD. NOW, I HAVE HERE SOME COLOR SWATCHES FOR YOUR PARACHUTE..
GBTrudeau

7/5/79

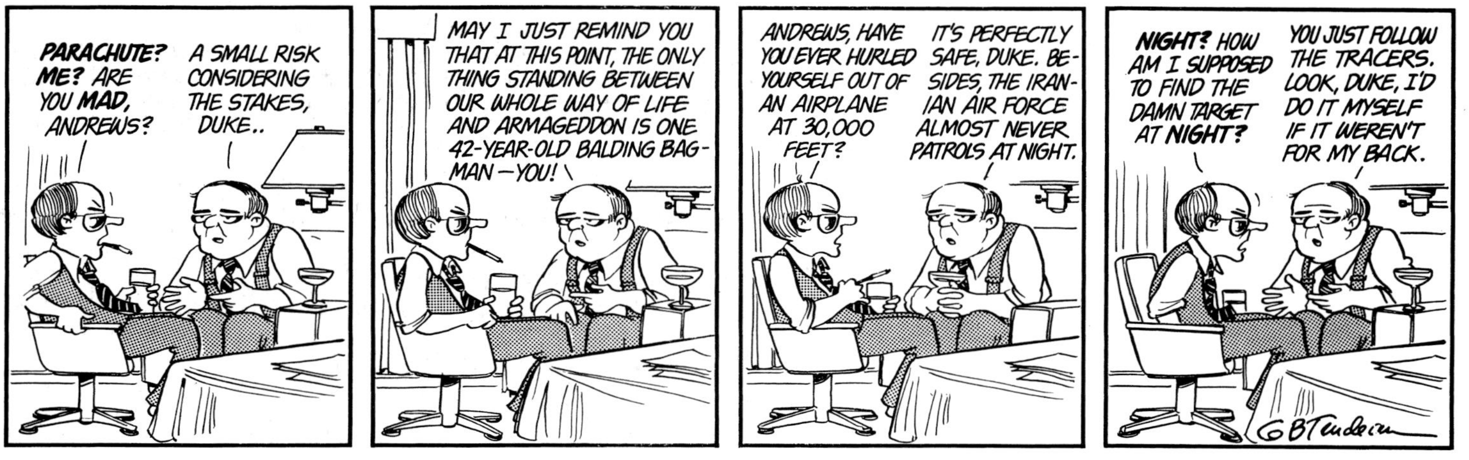
PARACHUTE? ME? ARE YOU MAD, ANDREWS?
A SMALL RISK CONSIDERING THE STAKES, DUKE..
MAY I JUST REMIND YOU THAT AT THIS POINT, THE ONLY THING STANDING BETWEEN OUR WHOLE WAY OF LIFE AND ARMAGEDDON IS ONE 42-YEAR-OLD BALDING BAGMAN—YOU!
ANDREWS, HAVE YOU EVER HURLED YOURSELF OUT OF AN AIRPLANE AT 30,000 FEET?
IT'S PERFECTLY SAFE, DUKE. BESIDES, THE IRANIAN AIR FORCE ALMOST NEVER PATROLS AT NIGHT.
NIGHT? HOW AM I SUPPOSED TO FIND THE DAMN TARGET AT NIGHT?
YOU JUST FOLLOW THE TRACERS. LOOK, DUKE, I'D DO IT MYSELF IF IT WEREN'T FOR MY BACK.
GBTrudeau

7/6/79

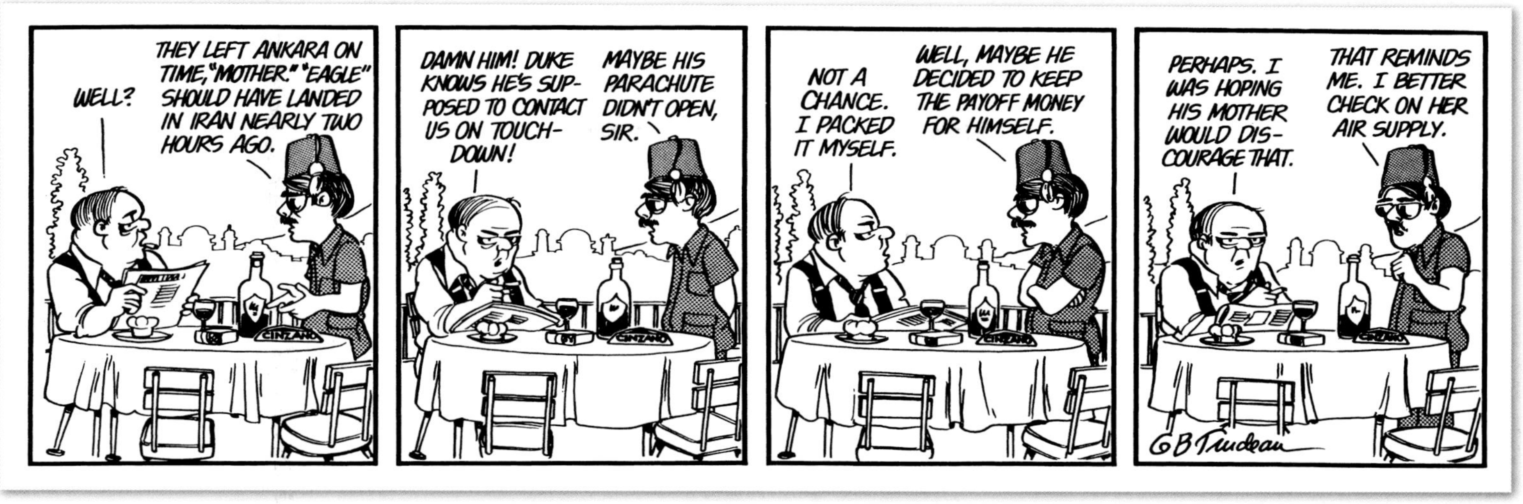
WELL?
THEY LEFT ANKARA ON TIME, "MOTHER." "EAGLE" SHOULD HAVE LANDED IN IRAN NEARLY TWO HOURS AGO.
DAMN HIM! DUKE KNOWS HE'S SUPPOSED TO CONTACT US ON TOUCH-DOWN!
MAYBE HIS PARACHUTE DIDN'T OPEN, SIR.
NOT A CHANCE. I PACKED IT MYSELF.
WELL, MAYBE HE DECIDED TO KEEP THE PAYOFF MONEY FOR HIMSELF.
PERHAPS. I WAS HOPING HIS MOTHER WOULD DISCOURAGE THAT.
THAT REMINDS ME. I BETTER CHECK ON HER AIR SUPPLY.
GB Trudeau

8/27/79

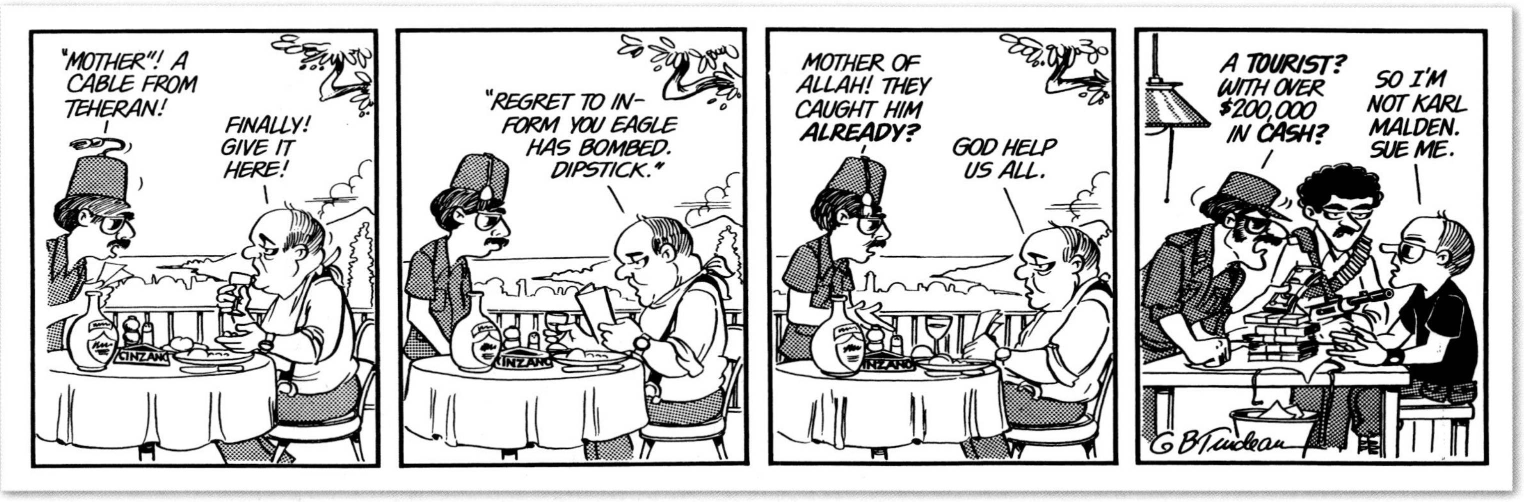
"MOTHER"! A CABLE FROM TEHERAN!
FINALLY! GIVE IT HERE!
"REGRET TO INFORM YOU EAGLE HAS BOMBED. DIPSTICK."
MOTHER OF ALLAH! THEY CAUGHT HIM ALREADY?
GOD HELP US ALL.
A TOURIST? WITH OVER $200,000 IN CASH?
SO I'M NOT KARL MALDEN. SUE ME.
GB Trudeau

8/29/79

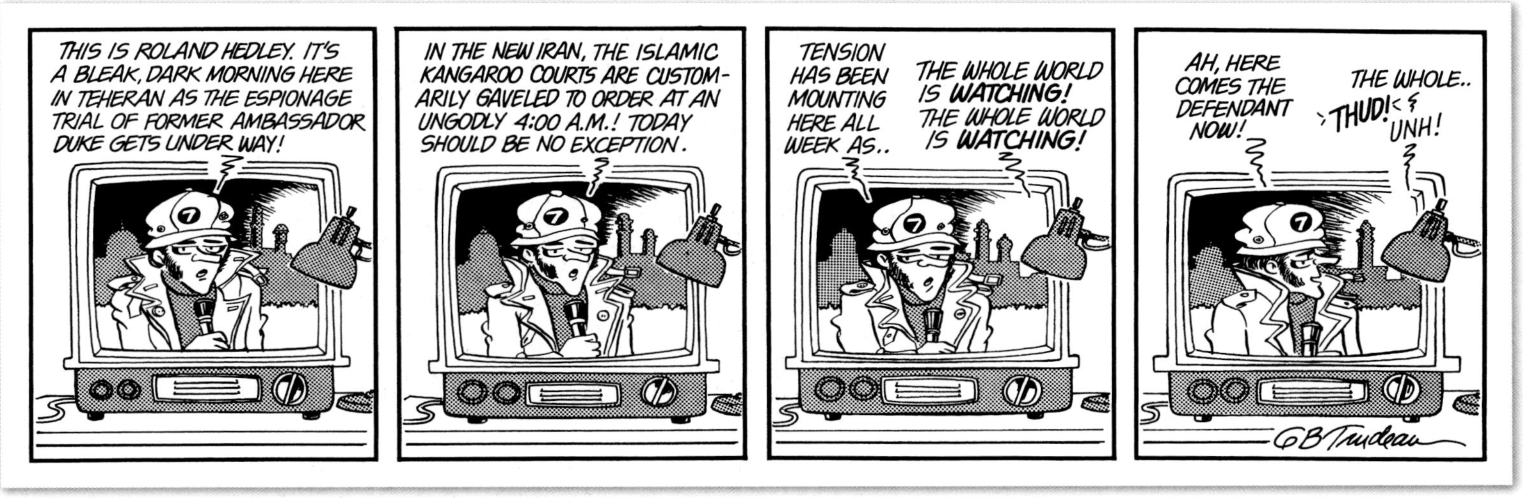
THIS IS ROLAND HEDLEY. IT'S A BLEAK, DARK MORNING HERE IN TEHERAN AS THE ESPIONAGE TRIAL OF FORMER AMBASSADOR DUKE GETS UNDER WAY!
IN THE NEW IRAN, THE ISLAMIC KANGAROO COURTS ARE CUSTOMARILY GAVELED TO ORDER AT AN UNGODLY 4:00 A.M.! TODAY SHOULD BE NO EXCEPTION.
TENSION HAS BEEN MOUNTING HERE ALL WEEK AS..
THE WHOLE WORLD IS WATCHING! THE WHOLE WORLD IS WATCHING!
AH, HERE COMES THE DEFENDANT NOW!
THE WHOLE..
THUD!
UNH!
GB Trudeau

9/3/79

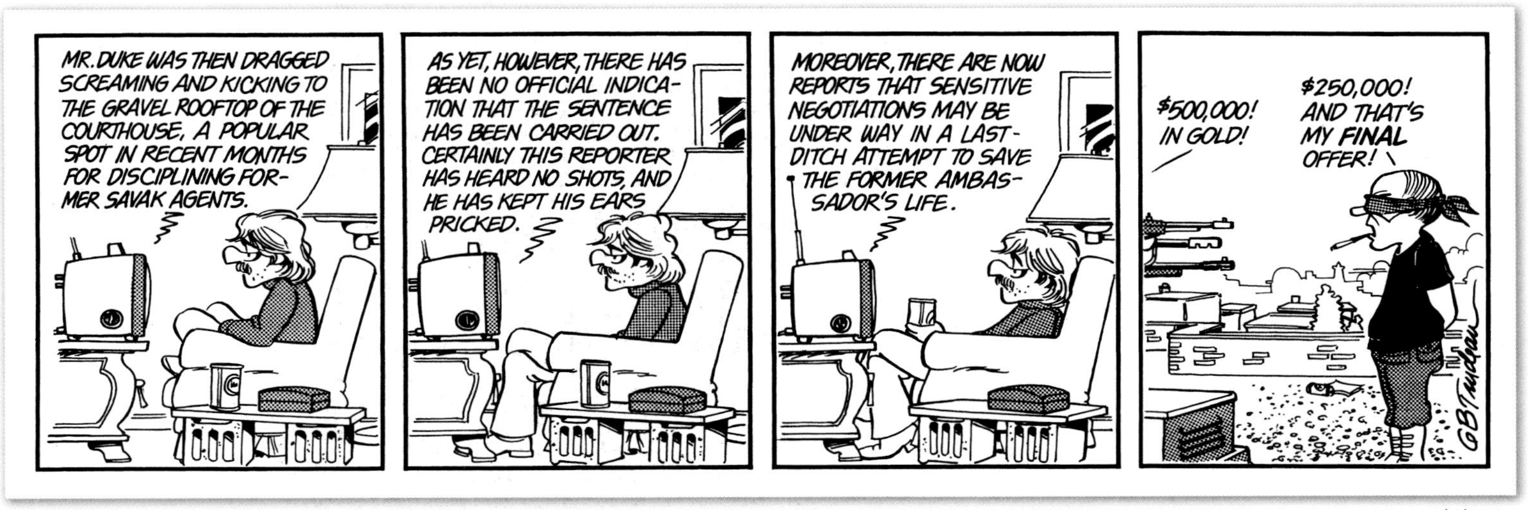
MR. DUKE WAS THEN DRAGGED SCREAMING AND KICKING TO THE GRAVEL ROOFTOP OF THE COURTHOUSE, A POPULAR SPOT IN RECENT MONTHS FOR DISCIPLINING FORMER SAVAK AGENTS.
AS YET, HOWEVER, THERE HAS BEEN NO OFFICIAL INDICATION THAT THE SENTENCE HAS BEEN CARRIED OUT. CERTAINLY THIS REPORTER HAS HEARD NO SHOTS, AND HE HAS KEPT HIS EARS PRICKED.
MOREOVER, THERE ARE NOW REPORTS THAT SENSITIVE NEGOTIATIONS MAY BE UNDER WAY IN A LAST-DITCH ATTEMPT TO SAVE THE FORMER AMBASSADOR'S LIFE.
$500,000! IN GOLD!
$250,000! AND THAT'S MY FINAL OFFER!
GB Trudeau

9/7/79

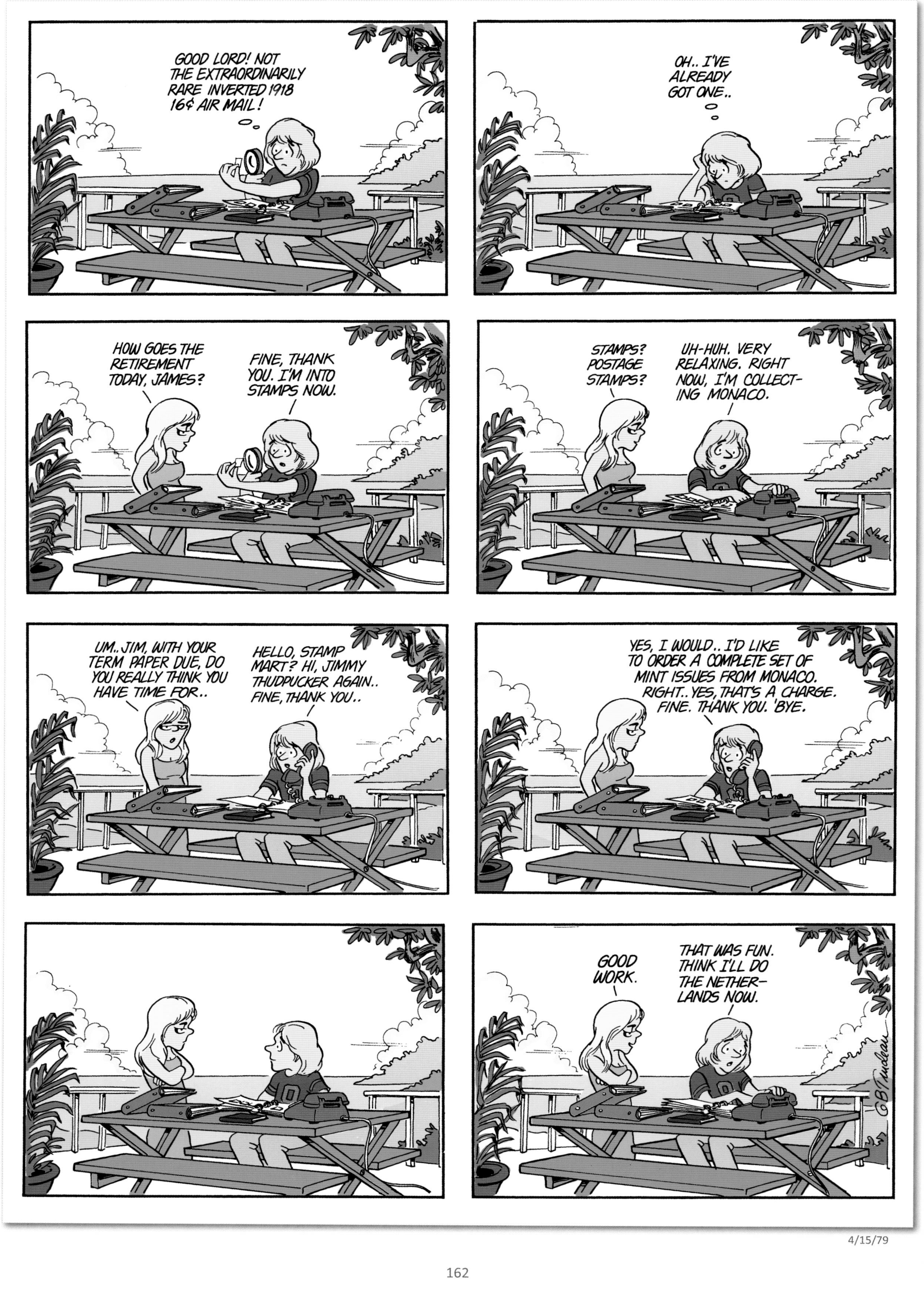
GOOD LORD! NOT THE EXTRAORDINARILY RARE INVERTED 1918 16¢ AIR MAIL!
OH.. I'VE ALREADY GOT ONE..
HOW GOES THE RETIREMENT TODAY, JAMES?
FINE, THANK YOU. I'M INTO STAMPS NOW.
STAMPS? POSTAGE STAMPS?
UH-HUH. VERY RELAXING. RIGHT NOW, I'M COLLECTING MONACO.
UM.. JIM, WITH YOUR TERM PAPER DUE, DO YOU REALLY THINK YOU HAVE TIME FOR..
HELLO, STAMP MART? HI, JIMMY THUDPUCKER AGAIN.. FINE, THANK YOU..
YES, I WOULD.. I'D LIKE TO ORDER A COMPLETE SET OF MINT ISSUES FROM MONACO. RIGHT.. YES, THAT'S A CHARGE. FINE. THANK YOU. 'BYE.
GOOD WORK.
THAT WAS FUN. THINK I'LL DO THE NETHER-LANDS NOW.
©BTrudeau

4/15/79

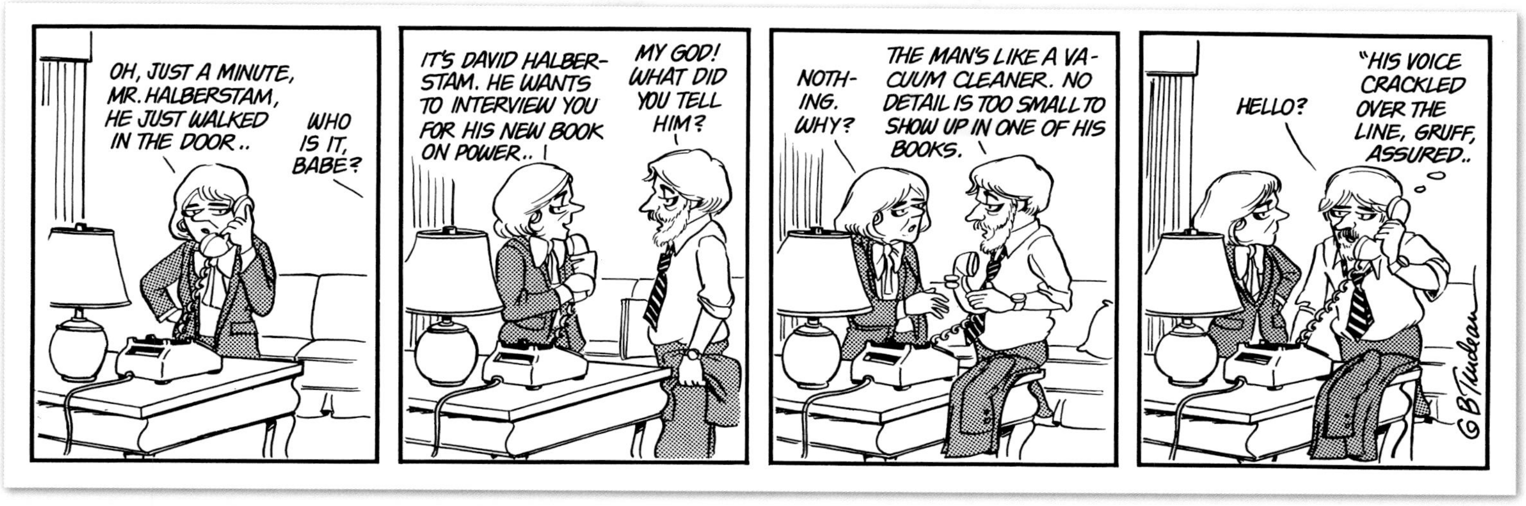
OH, JUST A MINUTE, MR. HALBERSTAM, HE JUST WALKED IN THE DOOR..
WHO IS IT, BABE?
IT'S DAVID HALBERSTAM. HE WANTS TO INTERVIEW YOU FOR HIS NEW BOOK ON POWER..
MY GOD! WHAT DID YOU TELL HIM?
NOTHING. WHY?
THE MAN'S LIKE A VACUUM CLEANER. NO DETAIL IS TOO SMALL TO SHOW UP IN ONE OF HIS BOOKS.
HELLO?
"HIS VOICE CRACKLED OVER THE LINE, GRUFF, ASSURED..
GB Trudeau

7/24/79

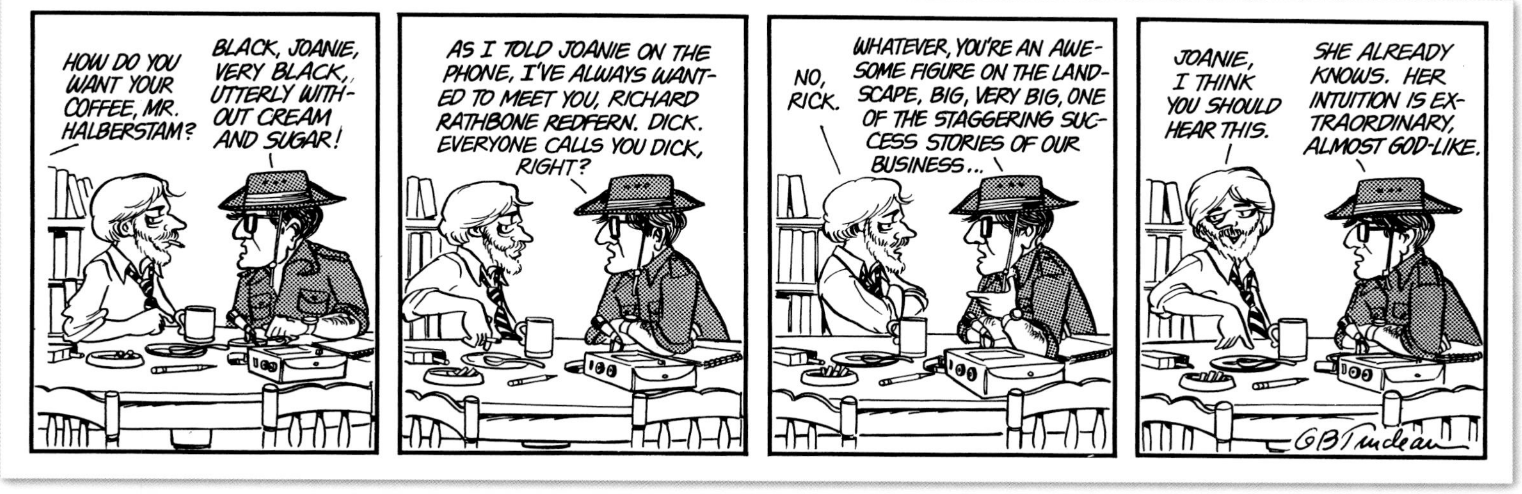
HOW DO YOU WANT YOUR COFFEE, MR. HALBERSTAM?
BLACK, JOANIE, VERY BLACK, UTTERLY WITHOUT CREAM AND SUGAR!
AS I TOLD JOANIE ON THE PHONE, I'VE ALWAYS WANTED TO MEET YOU, RICHARD RATHBONE REDFERN. DICK. EVERYONE CALLS YOU DICK, RIGHT?
NO, RICK.
WHATEVER, YOU'RE AN AWESOME FIGURE ON THE LANDSCAPE, BIG, VERY BIG, ONE OF THE STAGGERING SUCCESS STORIES OF OUR BUSINESS...
JOANIE, I THINK YOU SHOULD HEAR THIS.
SHE ALREADY KNOWS. HER INTUITION IS EXTRAORDINARY, ALMOST GOD-LIKE.
GB Trudeau

7/27/79

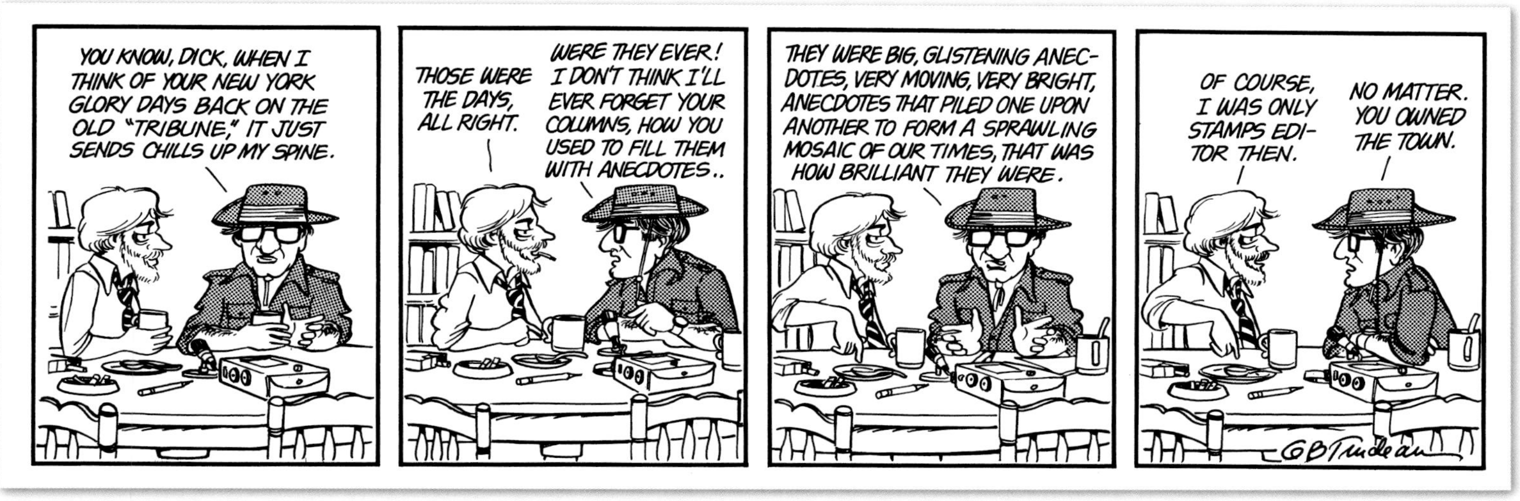
YOU KNOW, DICK, WHEN I THINK OF YOUR NEW YORK GLORY DAYS BACK ON THE OLD "TRIBUNE," IT JUST SENDS CHILLS UP MY SPINE.
THOSE WERE THE DAYS, ALL RIGHT.
WERE THEY EVER! I DON'T THINK I'LL EVER FORGET YOUR COLUMNS, HOW YOU USED TO FILL THEM WITH ANECDOTES..
THEY WERE BIG, GLISTENING ANECDOTES, VERY MOVING, VERY BRIGHT, ANECDOTES THAT PILED ONE UPON ANOTHER TO FORM A SPRAWLING MOSAIC OF OUR TIMES, THAT WAS HOW BRILLIANT THEY WERE.
OF COURSE, I WAS ONLY STAMPS EDITOR THEN.
NO MATTER. YOU OWNED THE TOWN.
GB Trudeau

7/28/79

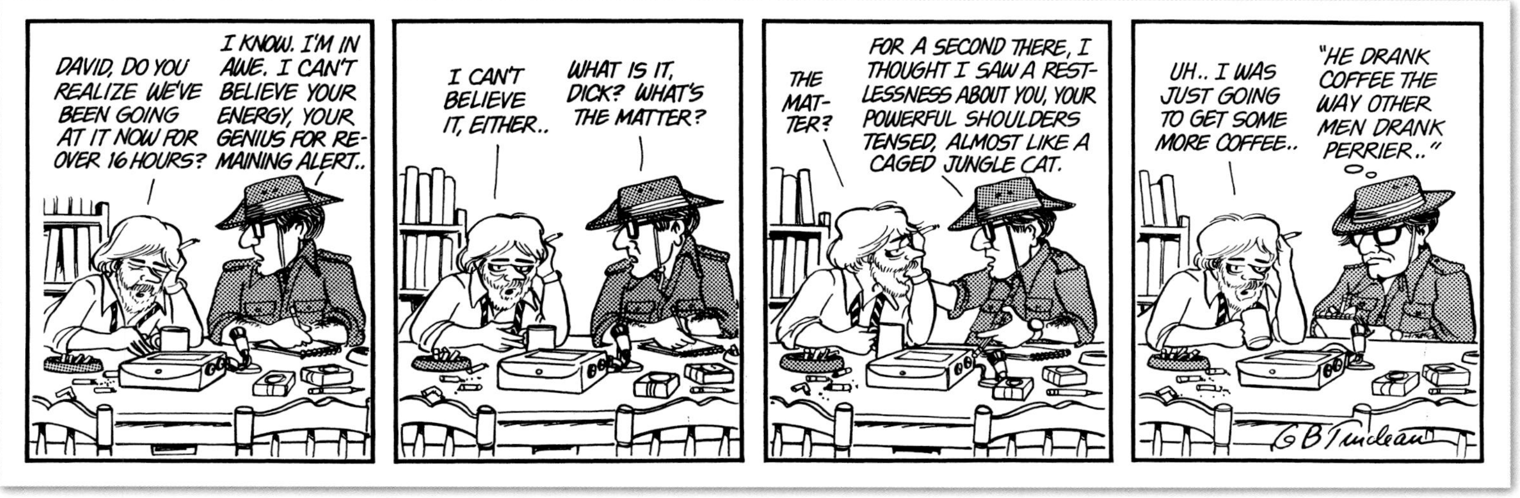
DAVID, DO YOU REALIZE WE'VE BEEN GOING AT IT NOW FOR OVER 16 HOURS?
I KNOW. I'M IN AWE. I CAN'T BELIEVE YOUR ENERGY, YOUR GENIUS FOR REMAINING ALERT..
I CAN'T BELIEVE IT, EITHER..
WHAT IS IT, DICK? WHAT'S THE MATTER?
THE MATTER?
FOR A SECOND THERE, I THOUGHT I SAW A RESTLESSNESS ABOUT YOU, YOUR POWERFUL SHOULDERS TENSED, ALMOST LIKE A CAGED JUNGLE CAT.
UH.. I WAS JUST GOING TO GET SOME MORE COFFEE..
"HE DRANK COFFEE THE WAY OTHER MEN DRANK PERRIER.."
GB Trudeau

8/1/79

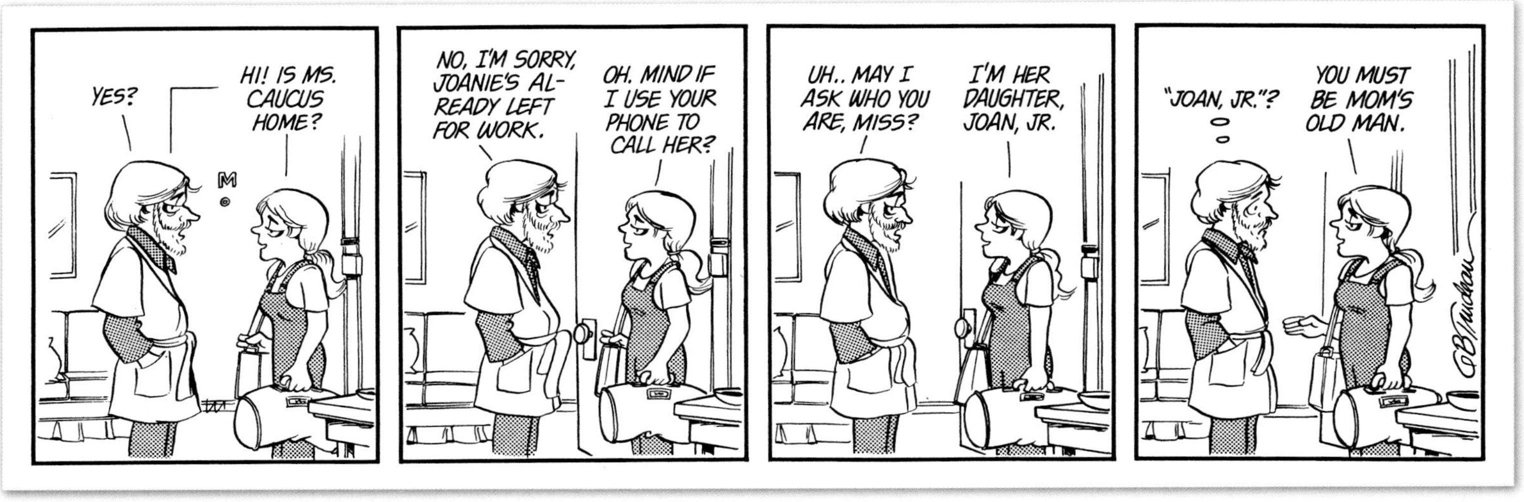
YES?
HI! IS MS. CAUCUS HOME?
M
NO, I'M SORRY, JOANIE'S ALREADY LEFT FOR WORK.
OH. MIND IF I USE YOUR PHONE TO CALL HER?
UH.. MAY I ASK WHO YOU ARE, MISS?
I'M HER DAUGHTER, JOAN, JR.
"JOAN, JR."?
YOU MUST BE MOM'S OLD MAN.
GBTrudeau

9/10/79

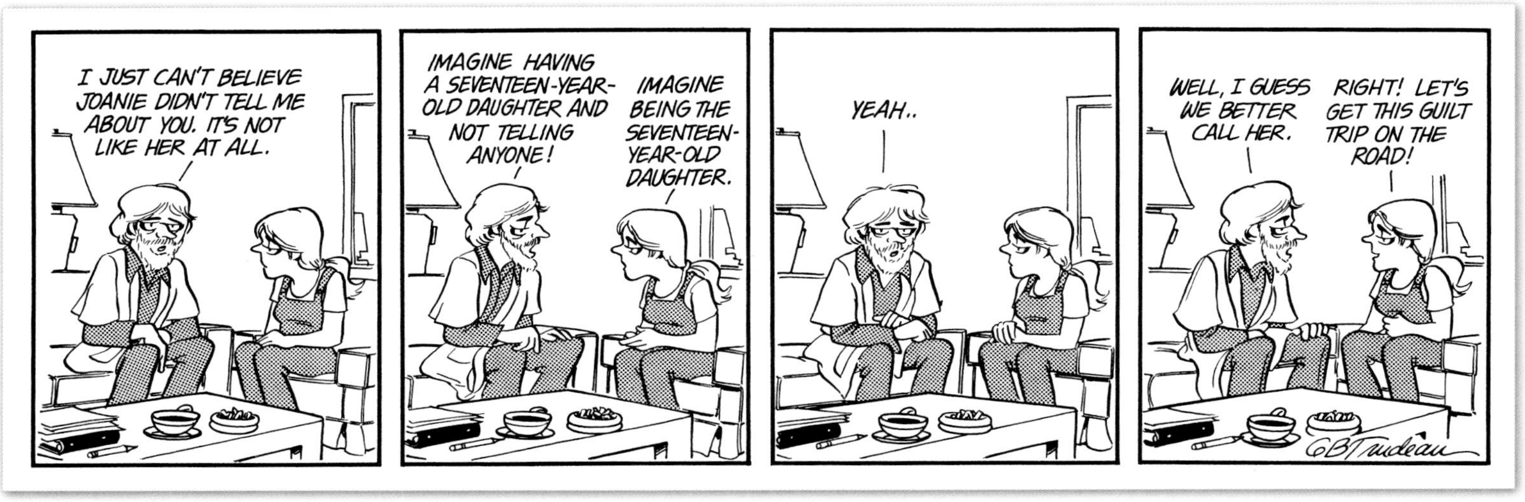
I JUST CAN'T BELIEVE JOANIE DIDN'T TELL ME ABOUT YOU. IT'S NOT LIKE HER AT ALL.
IMAGINE HAVING A SEVENTEEN-YEAR-OLD DAUGHTER AND NOT TELLING ANYONE!
IMAGINE BEING THE SEVENTEEN-YEAR-OLD DAUGHTER.
YEAH..
WELL, I GUESS WE BETTER CALL HER.
RIGHT! LET'S GET THIS GUILT TRIP ON THE ROAD!
GBTrudeau

9/13/79

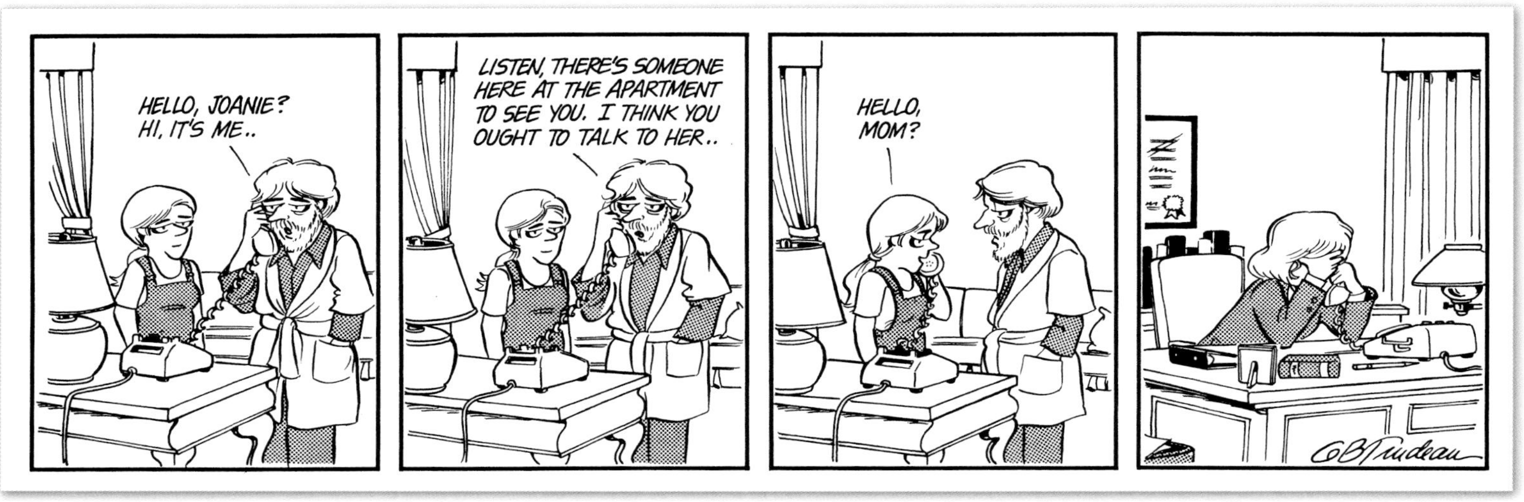
HELLO, JOANIE? HI, IT'S ME..
LISTEN, THERE'S SOMEONE HERE AT THE APARTMENT TO SEE YOU. I THINK YOU OUGHT TO TALK TO HER..
HELLO, MOM?
GBTrudeau

9/14/79

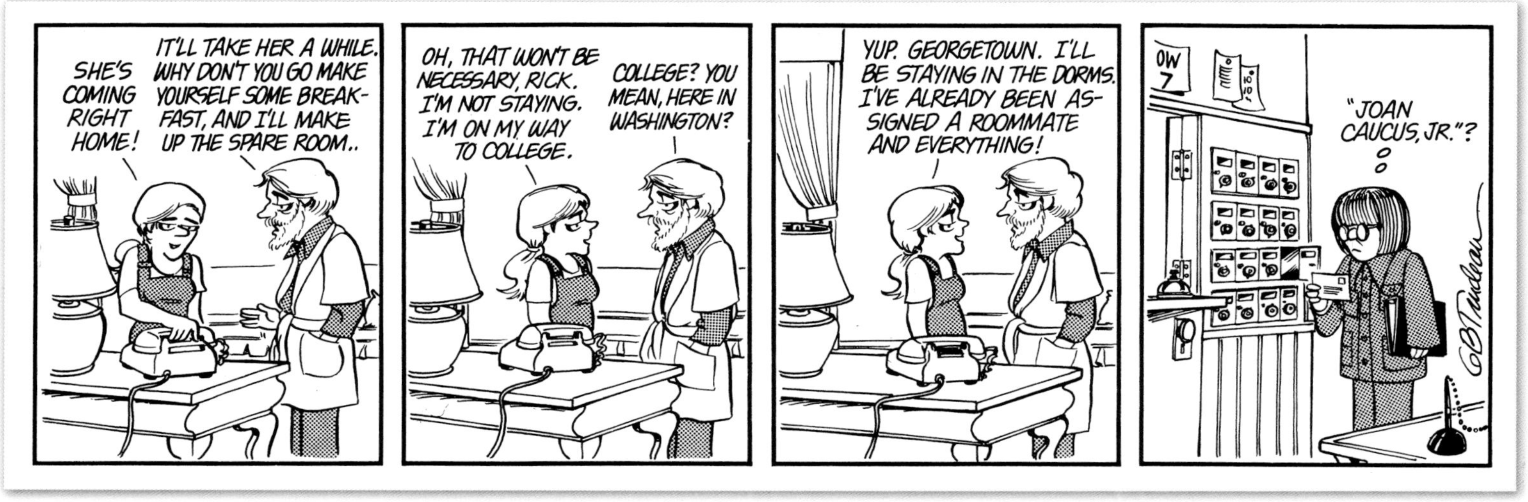
SHE'S COMING RIGHT HOME!
IT'LL TAKE HER A WHILE. WHY DON'T YOU GO MAKE YOURSELF SOME BREAKFAST, AND I'LL MAKE UP THE SPARE ROOM..
OH, THAT WON'T BE NECESSARY, RICK. I'M NOT STAYING. I'M ON MY WAY TO COLLEGE.
COLLEGE? YOU MEAN, HERE IN WASHINGTON?
YUP. GEORGETOWN. I'LL BE STAYING IN THE DORMS. I'VE ALREADY BEEN ASSIGNED A ROOMMATE AND EVERYTHING!
"JOAN CAUCUS, JR."?
GBTrudeau

9/15/79

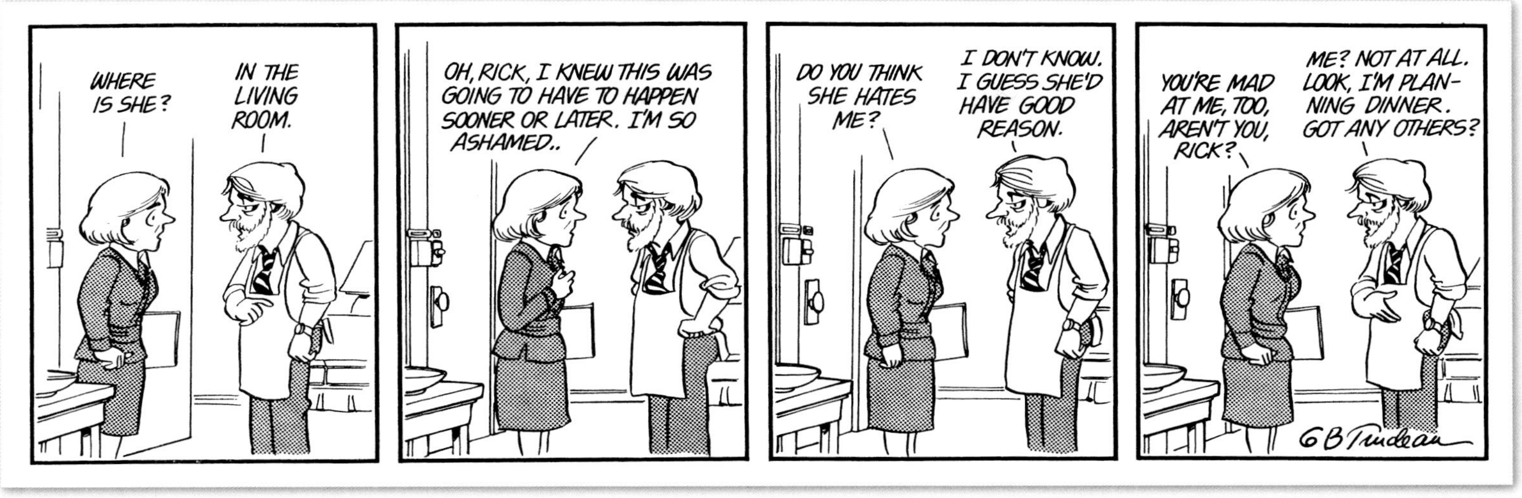
WHERE IS SHE?
IN THE LIVING ROOM.
OH, RICK, I KNEW THIS WAS GOING TO HAVE TO HAPPEN SOONER OR LATER. I'M SO ASHAMED..
DO YOU THINK SHE HATES ME?
I DON'T KNOW. I GUESS SHE'D HAVE GOOD REASON.
YOU'RE MAD AT ME, TOO, AREN'T YOU, RICK?
ME? NOT AT ALL. LOOK, I'M PLANNING DINNER. GOT ANY OTHERS?
G B Trudeau

9/17/79

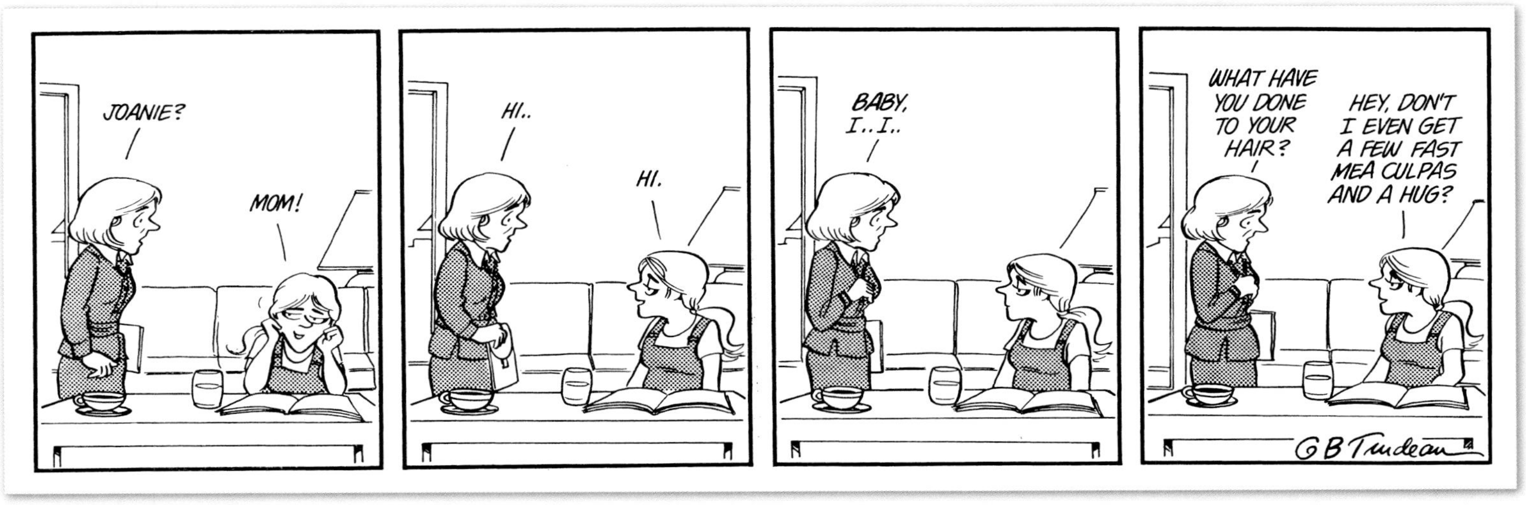
JOANIE?
MOM!
HI..
HI.
BABY. I.. I..
WHAT HAVE YOU DONE TO YOUR HAIR?
HEY, DON'T I EVEN GET A FEW FAST MEA CULPAS AND A HUG?
G B Trudeau

9/18/79

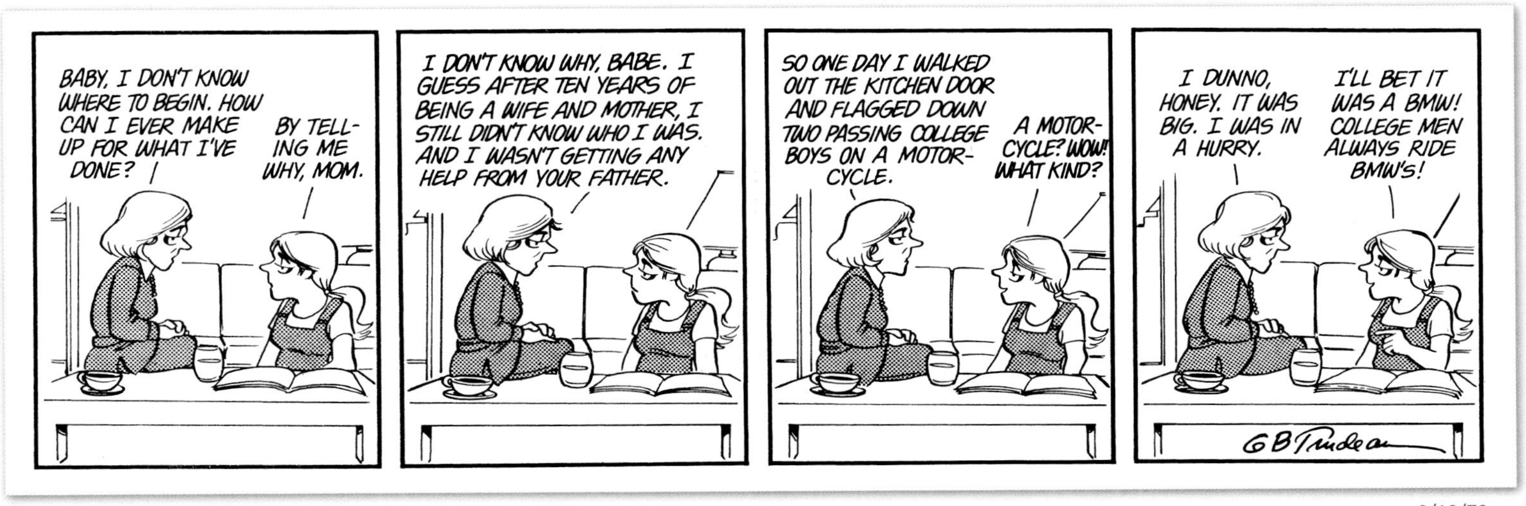
BABY, I DON'T KNOW WHERE TO BEGIN. HOW CAN I EVER MAKE UP FOR WHAT I'VE DONE?
BY TELLING ME WHY, MOM.
I DON'T KNOW WHY, BABE. I GUESS AFTER TEN YEARS OF BEING A WIFE AND MOTHER, I STILL DIDN'T KNOW WHO I WAS. AND I WASN'T GETTING ANY HELP FROM YOUR FATHER.
SO ONE DAY I WALKED OUT THE KITCHEN DOOR AND FLAGGED DOWN TWO PASSING COLLEGE BOYS ON A MOTORCYCLE.
A MOTORCYCLE? WOW! WHAT KIND?
I DUNNO, HONEY. IT WAS BIG. I WAS IN A HURRY.
I'LL BET IT WAS A BMW! COLLEGE MEN ALWAYS RIDE BMW'S!
G B Trudeau

9/19/79

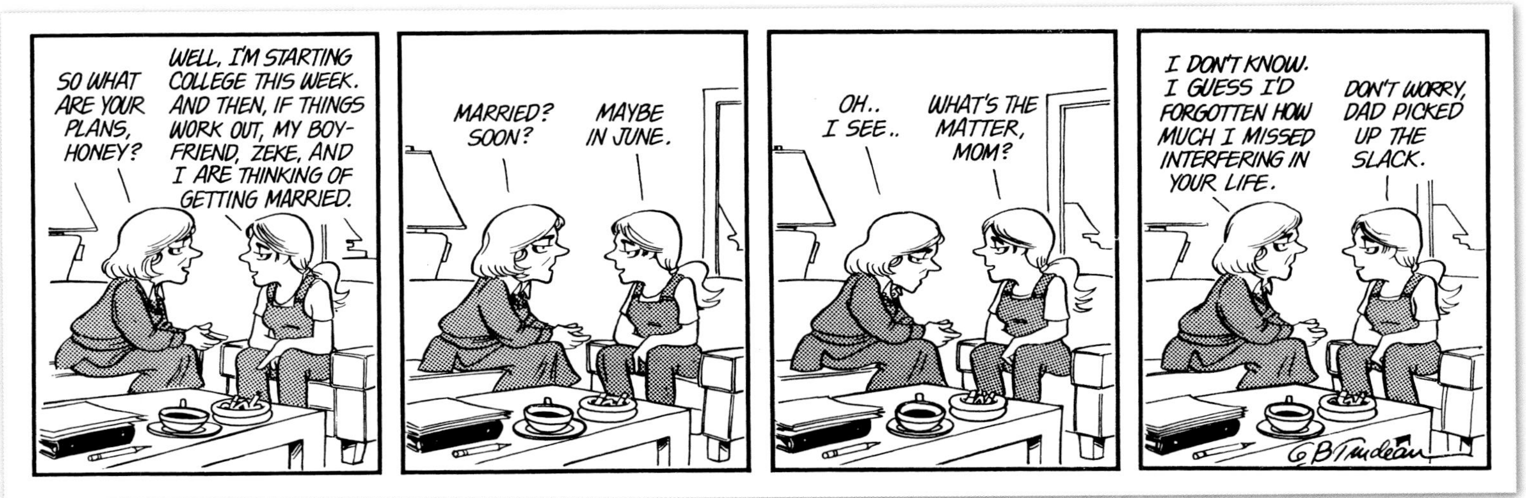
SO WHAT ARE YOUR PLANS, HONEY?
WELL, I'M STARTING COLLEGE THIS WEEK. AND THEN, IF THINGS WORK OUT, MY BOYFRIEND, ZEKE, AND I ARE THINKING OF GETTING MARRIED.
MARRIED? SOON?
MAYBE IN JUNE.
OH.. I SEE..
WHAT'S THE MATTER, MOM?
I DON'T KNOW. I GUESS I'D FORGOTTEN HOW MUCH I MISSED INTERFERING IN YOUR LIFE.
DON'T WORRY, DAD PICKED UP THE SLACK.
G B Trudeau

9/21/79

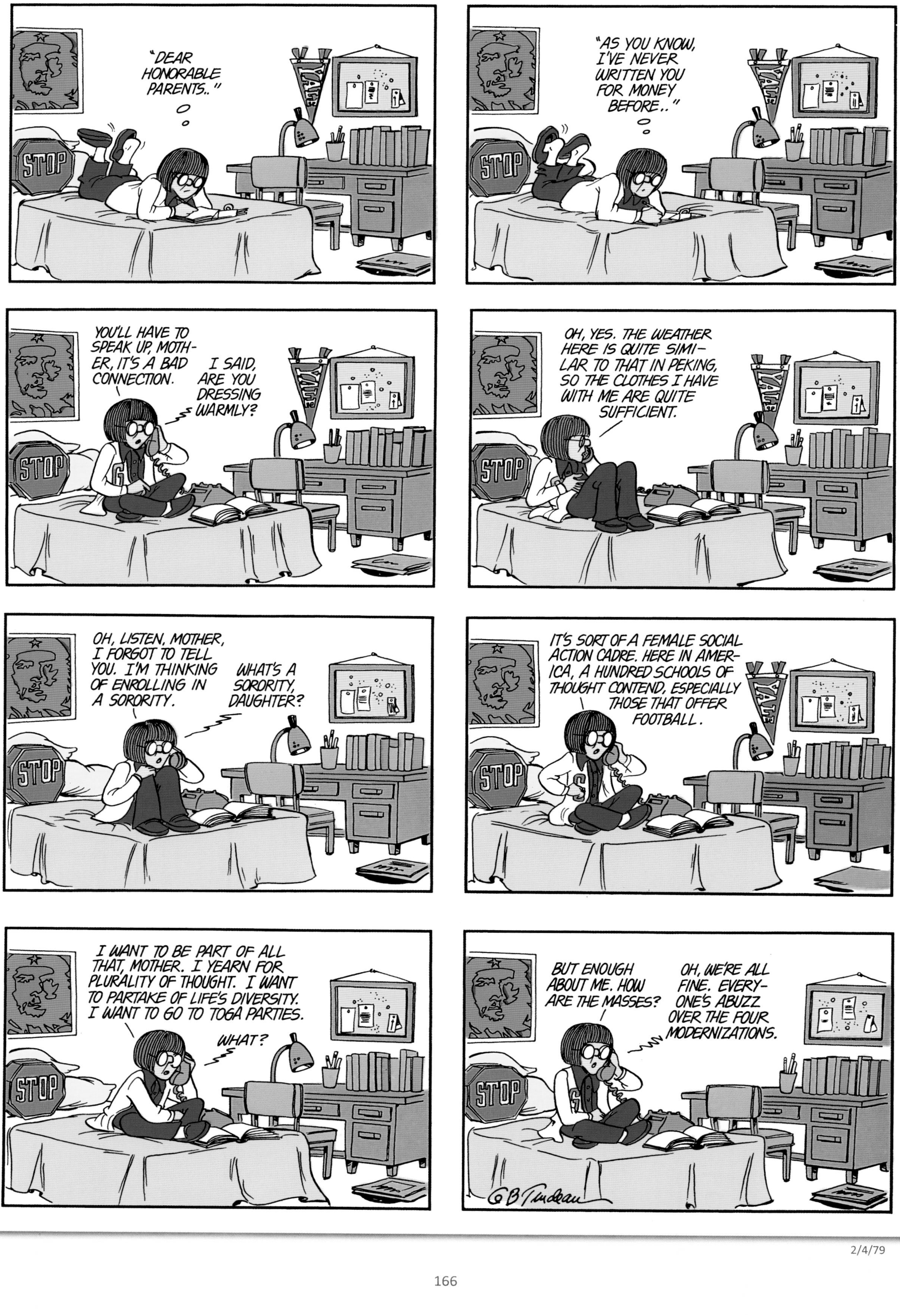
"DEAR HONORABLE PARENTS.."
STOP
YALE
"AS YOU KNOW, I'VE NEVER WRITTEN YOU FOR MONEY BEFORE.."
STOP
YALE
YOU'LL HAVE TO SPEAK UP, MOTHER, IT'S A BAD CONNECTION.
I SAID, ARE YOU DRESSING WARMLY?
STOP
YALE
OH, YES. THE WEATHER HERE IS QUITE SIMILAR TO THAT IN PEKING, SO THE CLOTHES I HAVE WITH ME ARE QUITE SUFFICIENT.
STOP
YALE
OH, LISTEN, MOTHER, I FORGOT TO TELL YOU. I'M THINKING OF ENROLLING IN A SORORITY.
WHAT'S A SORORITY, DAUGHTER?
STOP
IT'S SORT OF A FEMALE SOCIAL ACTION CADRE. HERE IN AMERICA, A HUNDRED SCHOOLS OF THOUGHT CONTEND, ESPECIALLY THOSE THAT OFFER FOOTBALL.
STOP
YALE
I WANT TO BE PART OF ALL THAT, MOTHER. I YEARN FOR PLURALITY OF THOUGHT. I WANT TO PARTAKE OF LIFE'S DIVERSITY. I WANT TO GO TO TOGA PARTIES.
WHAT?
STOP
BUT ENOUGH ABOUT ME. HOW ARE THE MASSES?
OH, WE'RE ALL FINE. EVERYONE'S ABUZZ OVER THE FOUR MODERNIZATIONS.
STOP
GB Trudeau

2/4/79

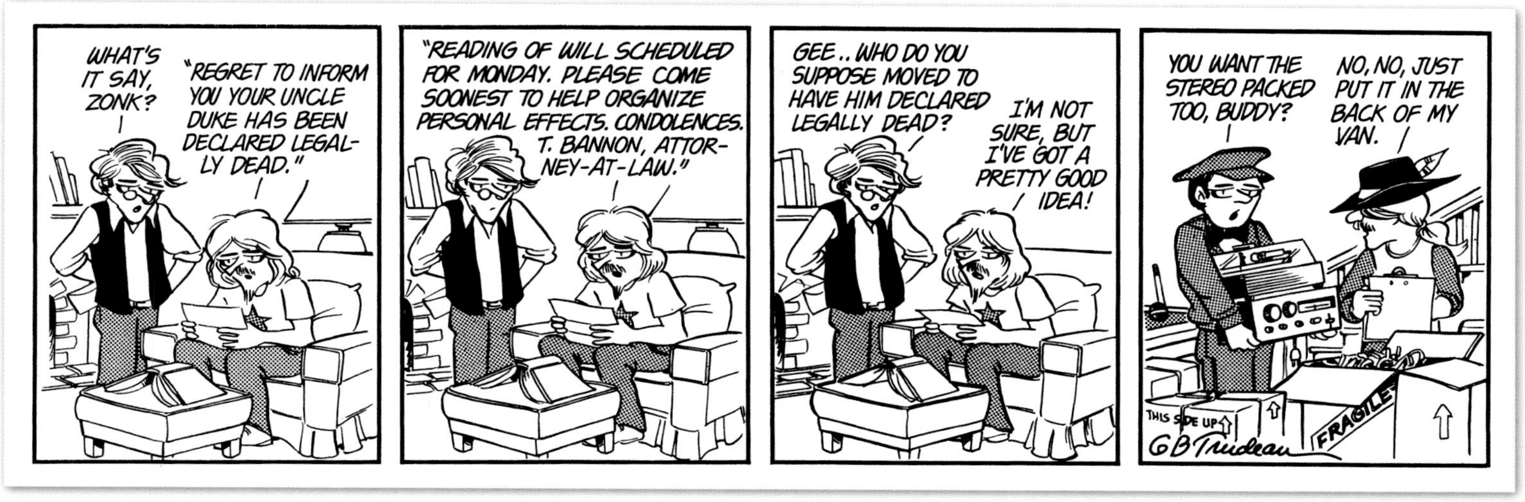
WHAT'S IT SAY, ZONK?
"REGRET TO INFORM YOU YOUR UNCLE DUKE HAS BEEN DECLARED LEGALLY DEAD."
"READING OF WILL SCHEDULED FOR MONDAY. PLEASE COME SOONEST TO HELP ORGANIZE PERSONAL EFFECTS. CONDOLENCES. T. BANNON, ATTORNEY-AT-LAW."
GEE.. WHO DO YOU SUPPOSE MOVED TO HAVE HIM DECLARED LEGALLY DEAD?
I'M NOT SURE, BUT I'VE GOT A PRETTY GOOD IDEA!
YOU WANT THE STEREO PACKED TOO, BUDDY?
NO, NO, JUST PUT IT IN THE BACK OF MY VAN.
THIS SIDE UP
FRAGILE
GBTrudeau

11/5/79

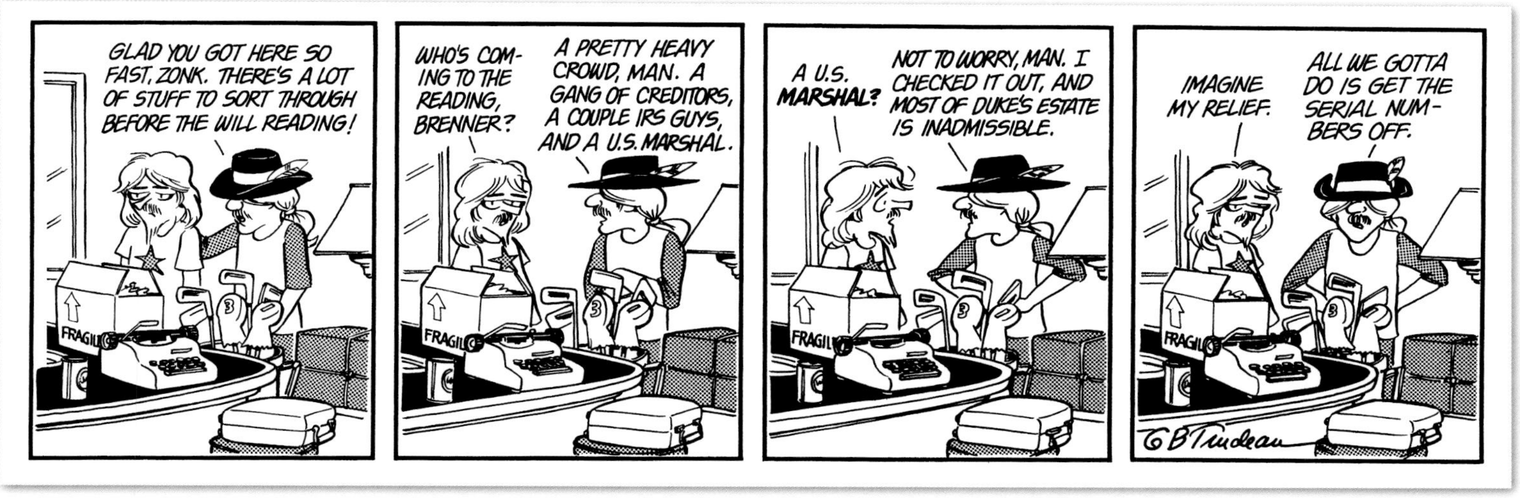
GLAD YOU GOT HERE SO FAST, ZONK. THERE'S A LOT OF STUFF TO SORT THROUGH BEFORE THE WILL READING!
WHO'S COMING TO THE READING, BRENNER?
A PRETTY HEAVY CROWD, MAN. A GANG OF CREDITORS, A COUPLE IRS GUYS, AND A U.S. MARSHAL.
A U.S. MARSHAL?
NOT TO WORRY, MAN. I CHECKED IT OUT, AND MOST OF DUKE'S ESTATE IS INADMISSIBLE.
IMAGINE MY RELIEF.
ALL WE GOTTA DO IS GET THE SERIAL NUMBERS OFF.
FRAGILE
GBTrudeau

11/7/79

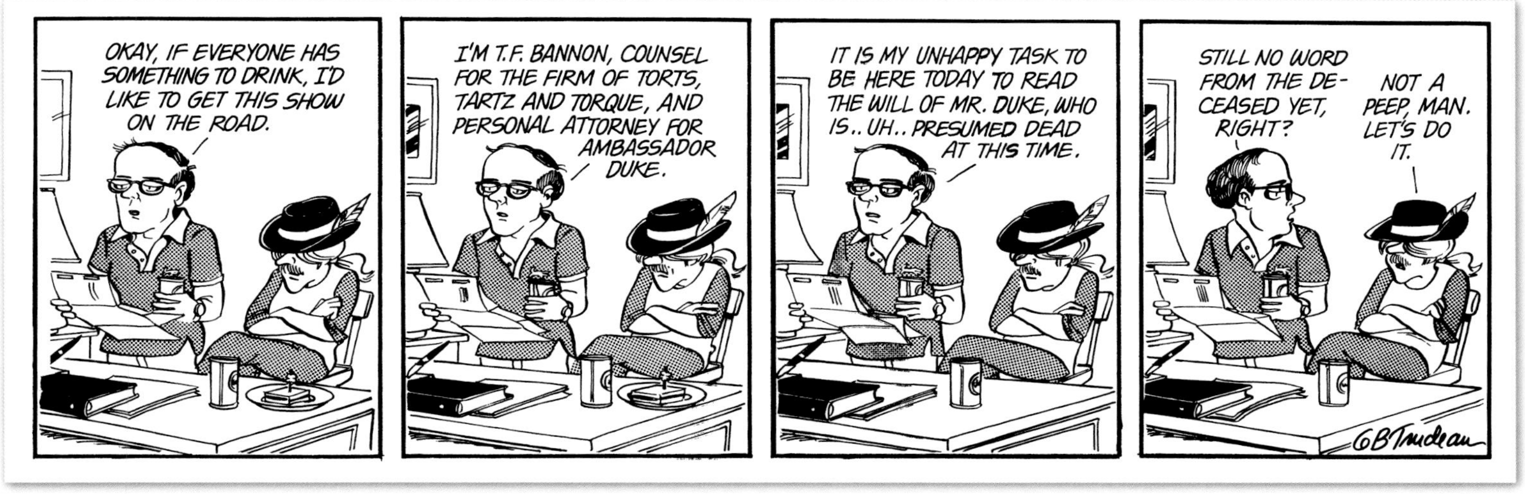
OKAY, IF EVERYONE HAS SOMETHING TO DRINK, I'D LIKE TO GET THIS SHOW ON THE ROAD.
I'M T.F. BANNON, COUNSEL FOR THE FIRM OF TORTS, TARTZ AND TORQUE, AND PERSONAL ATTORNEY FOR AMBASSADOR DUKE.
IT IS MY UNHAPPY TASK TO BE HERE TODAY TO READ THE WILL OF MR. DUKE, WHO IS.. UH.. PRESUMED DEAD AT THIS TIME.
STILL NO WORD FROM THE DECEASED YET, RIGHT?
NOT A PEEP, MAN. LET'S DO IT.
GBTrudeau

11/27/79

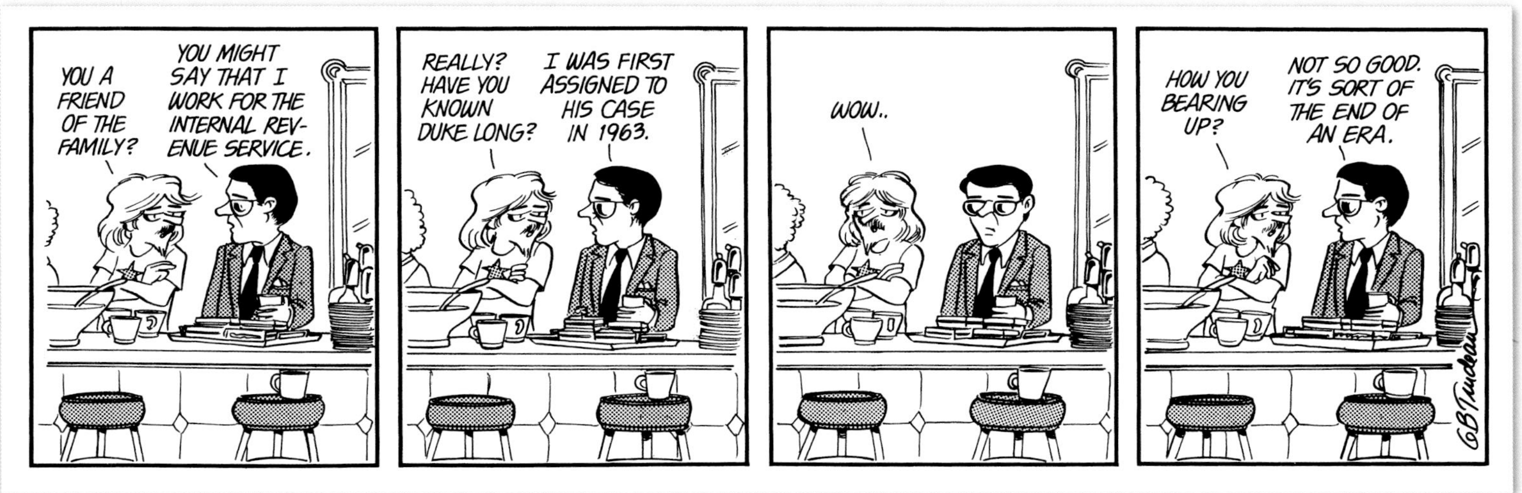
YOU A FRIEND OF THE FAMILY?
YOU MIGHT SAY THAT I WORK FOR THE INTERNAL REVENUE SERVICE.
REALLY? HAVE YOU KNOWN DUKE LONG?
I WAS FIRST ASSIGNED TO HIS CASE IN 1963.
WOW..
HOW YOU BEARING UP?
NOT SO GOOD. IT'S SORT OF THE END OF AN ERA.
GBTrudeau

11/28/79

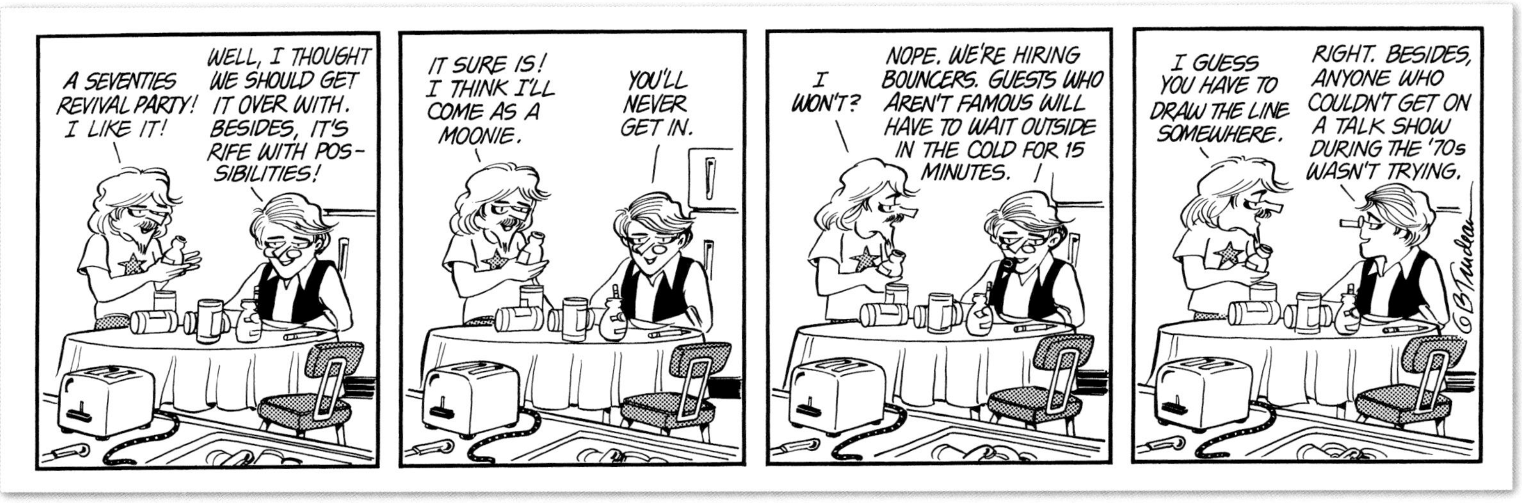
A SEVENTIES REVIVAL PARTY! I LIKE IT!
WELL, I THOUGHT WE SHOULD GET IT OVER WITH. BESIDES, IT'S RIFE WITH POSSIBILITIES!
IT SURE IS! I THINK I'LL COME AS A MOONIE.
YOU'LL NEVER GET IN.
I WON'T?
NOPE. WE'RE HIRING BOUNCERS. GUESTS WHO AREN'T FAMOUS WILL HAVE TO WAIT OUTSIDE IN THE COLD FOR 15 MINUTES.
I GUESS YOU HAVE TO DRAW THE LINE SOMEWHERE.
RIGHT. BESIDES, ANYONE WHO COULDN'T GET ON A TALK SHOW DURING THE '70s WASN'T TRYING.
GB Trudeau

12/4/79

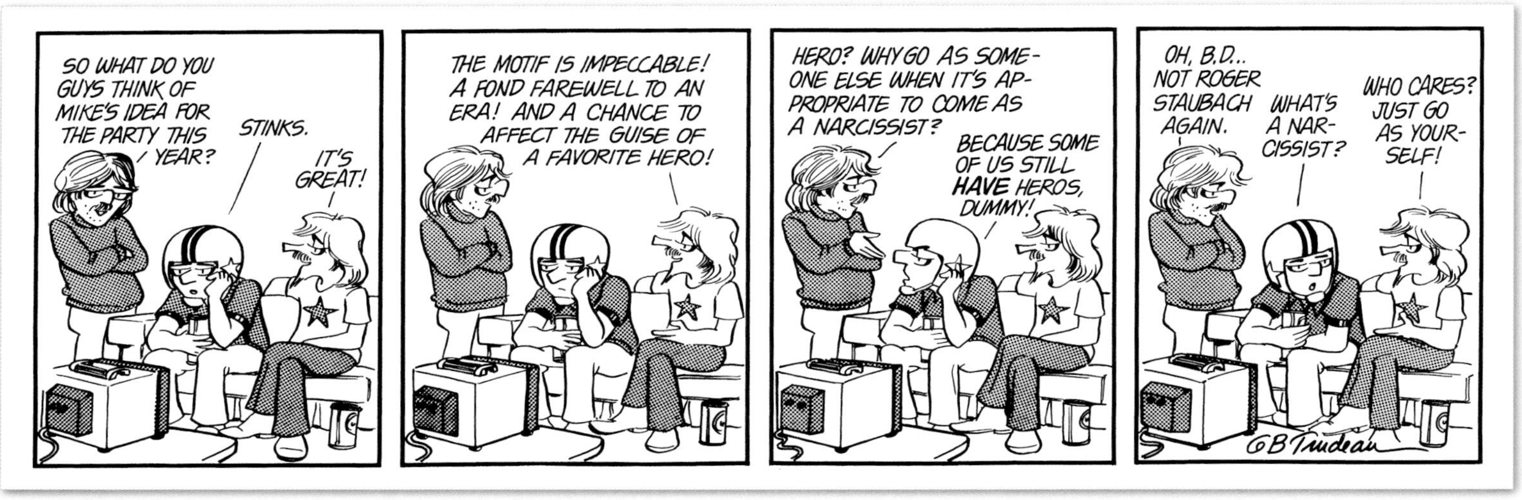
SO WHAT DO YOU GUYS THINK OF MIKE'S IDEA FOR THE PARTY THIS YEAR?
STINKS.
IT'S GREAT!
THE MOTIF IS IMPECCABLE! A FOND FAREWELL TO AN ERA! AND A CHANCE TO AFFECT THE GUISE OF A FAVORITE HERO!
HERO? WHY GO AS SOMEONE ELSE WHEN IT'S APPROPRIATE TO COME AS A NARCISSIST?
BECAUSE SOME OF US STILL HAVE HEROS, DUMMY!
OH, B.D.. NOT ROGER STAUBACH AGAIN.
WHAT'S A NARCISSIST?
WHO CARES? JUST GO AS YOURSELF!
GB Trudeau

12/8/79

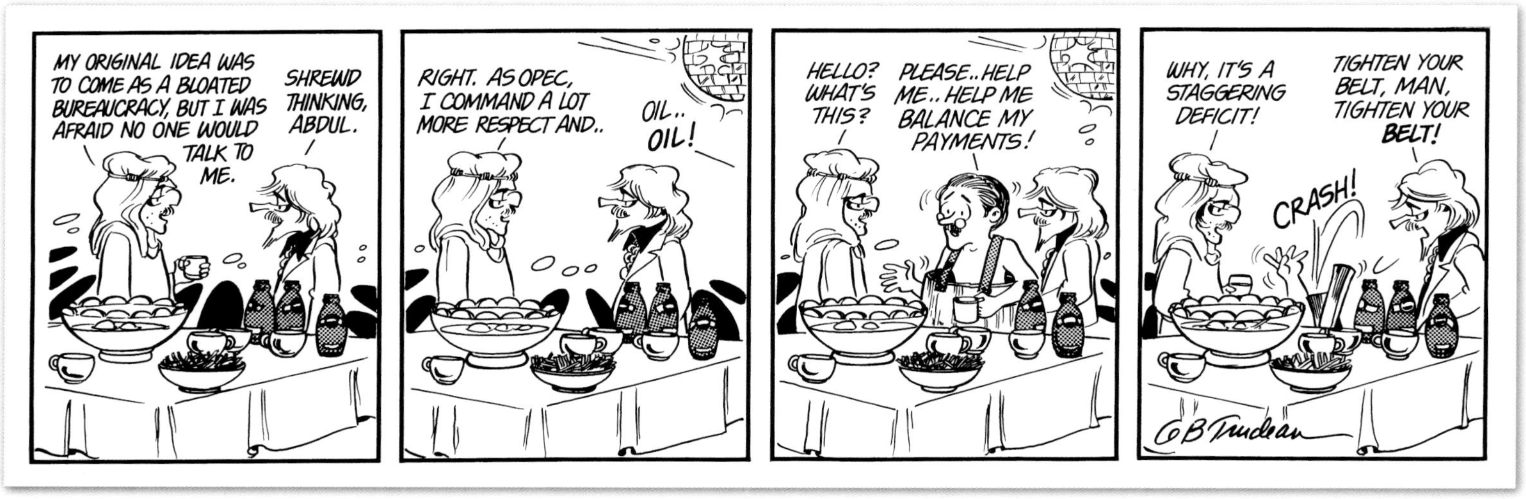
MY ORIGINAL IDEA WAS TO COME AS A BLOATED BUREAUCRACY, BUT I WAS AFRAID NO ONE WOULD TALK TO ME.
SHREWD THINKING, ABDUL.
RIGHT. AS OPEC, I COMMAND A LOT MORE RESPECT AND..
OIL.. OIL!
HELLO? WHAT'S THIS?
PLEASE.. HELP ME.. HELP ME BALANCE MY PAYMENTS!
WHY, IT'S A STAGGERING DEFICIT!
TIGHTEN YOUR BELT, MAN, TIGHTEN YOUR BELT!
CRASH!
GB Trudeau

12/15/79

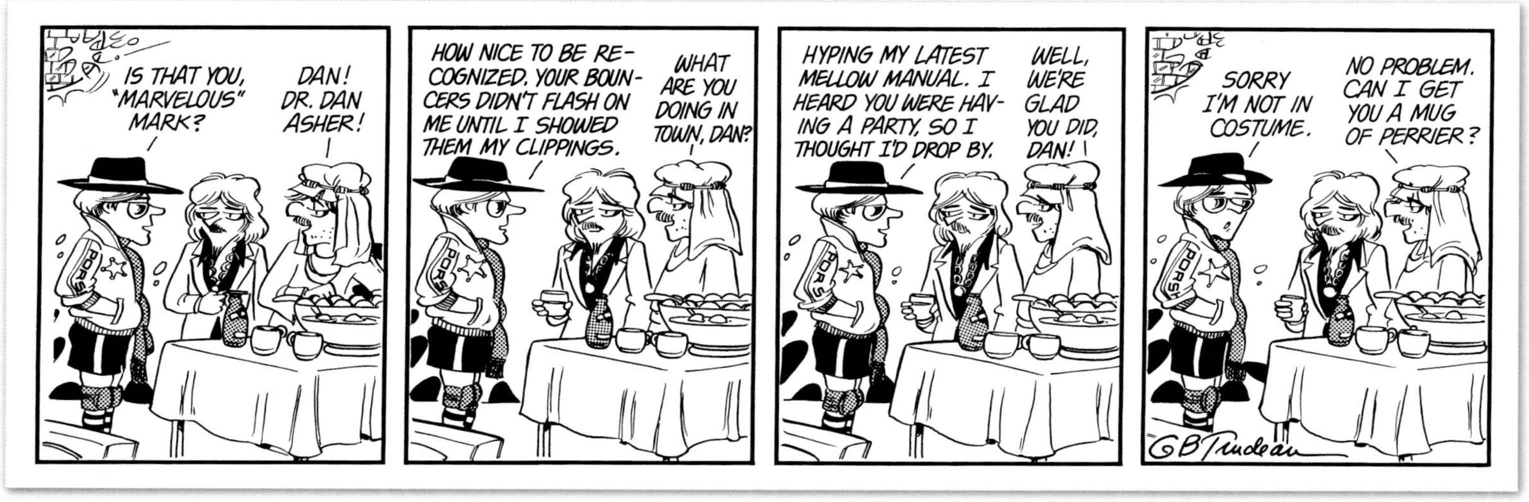
IS THAT YOU, "MARVELOUS" MARK?
DAN! DR. DAN ASHER!
HOW NICE TO BE RECOGNIZED. YOUR BOUNCERS DIDN'T FLASH ON ME UNTIL I SHOWED THEM MY CLIPPINGS.
WHAT ARE YOU DOING IN TOWN, DAN?
HYPING MY LATEST MELLOW MANUAL. I HEARD YOU WERE HAVING A PARTY, SO I THOUGHT I'D DROP BY.
WELL, WE'RE GLAD YOU DID, DAN!
SORRY I'M NOT IN COSTUME.
NO PROBLEM. CAN I GET YOU A MUG OF PERRIER?
GB Trudeau

12/14/79

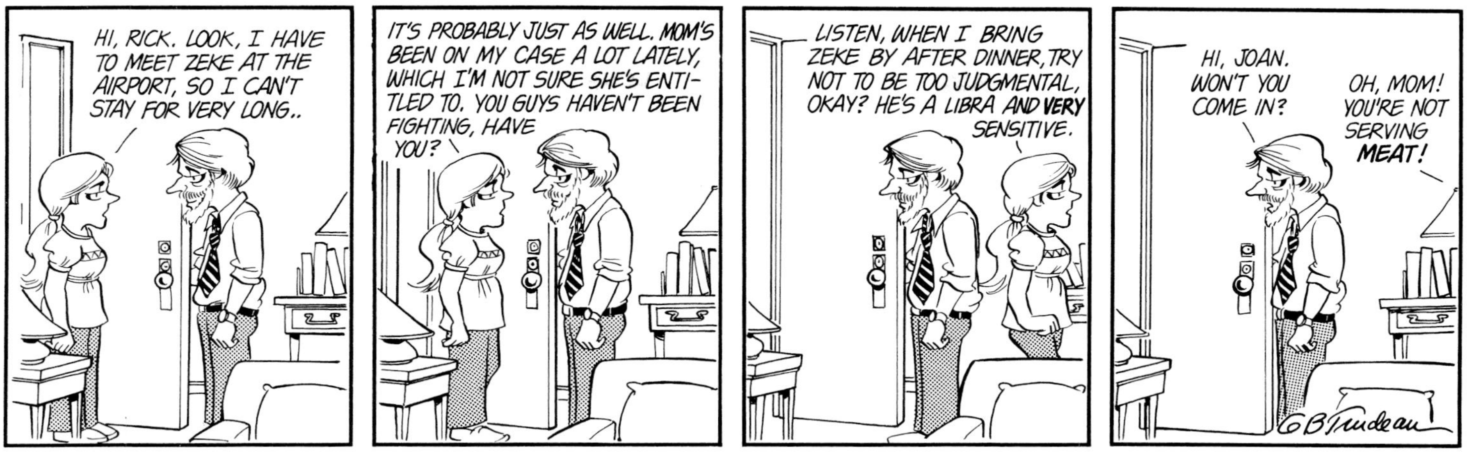
HI, RICK. LOOK, I HAVE TO MEET ZEKE AT THE AIRPORT, SO I CAN'T STAY FOR VERY LONG..
IT'S PROBABLY JUST AS WELL. MOM'S BEEN ON MY CASE A LOT LATELY, WHICH I'M NOT SURE SHE'S ENTITLED TO. YOU GUYS HAVEN'T BEEN FIGHTING, HAVE YOU?
LISTEN, WHEN I BRING ZEKE BY AFTER DINNER, TRY NOT TO BE TOO JUDGMENTAL, OKAY? HE'S A LIBRA AND VERY SENSITIVE.
HI, JOAN. WON'T YOU COME IN?
OH, MOM! YOU'RE NOT SERVING MEAT!
GBTrudeau

12/18/79

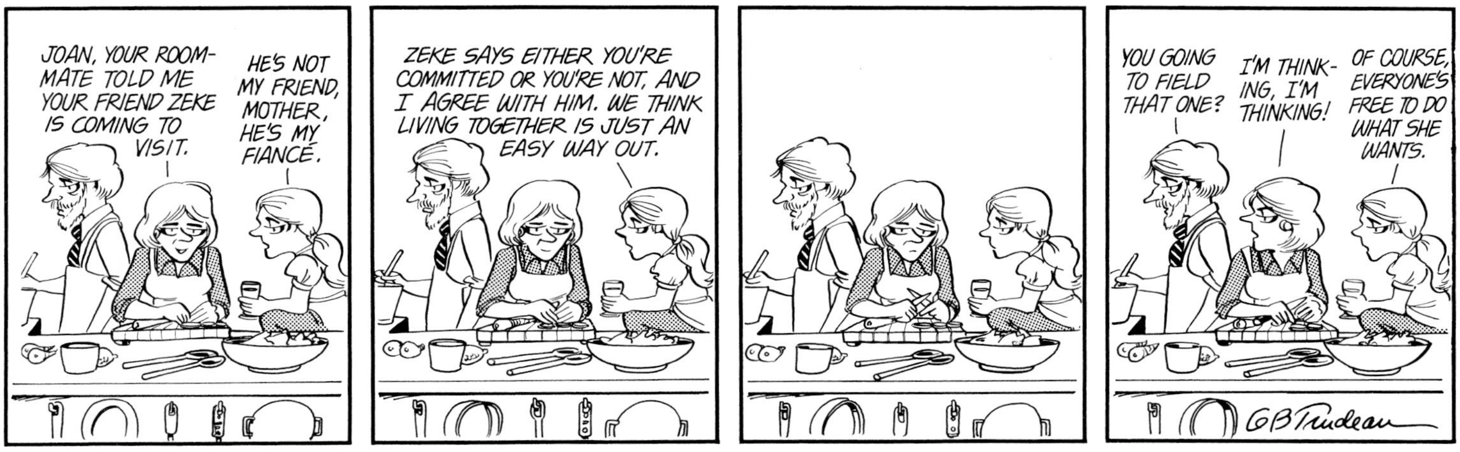
JOAN, YOUR ROOMMATE TOLD ME YOUR FRIEND ZEKE IS COMING TO VISIT.
HE'S NOT MY FRIEND, MOTHER, HE'S MY FIANCÉ.
ZEKE SAYS EITHER YOU'RE COMMITTED OR YOU'RE NOT, AND I AGREE WITH HIM. WE THINK LIVING TOGETHER IS JUST AN EASY WAY OUT.
YOU GOING TO FIELD THAT ONE?
I'M THINKING, I'M THINKING!
OF COURSE, EVERYONE'S FREE TO DO WHAT SHE WANTS.
GBTrudeau

12/19/79

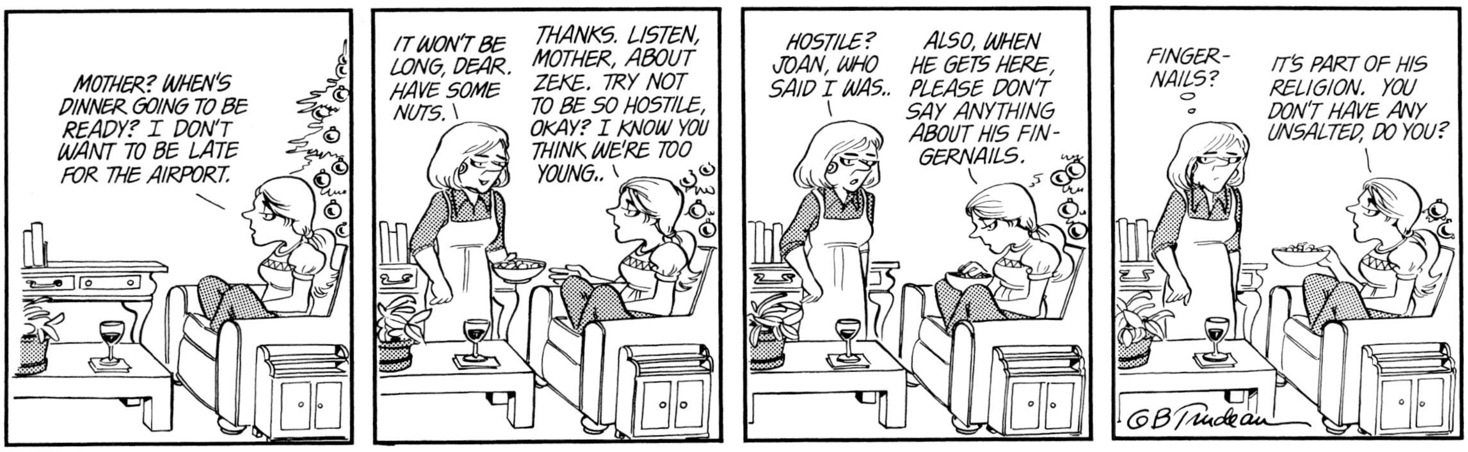
MOTHER? WHEN'S DINNER GOING TO BE READY? I DON'T WANT TO BE LATE FOR THE AIRPORT.
IT WON'T BE LONG, DEAR. HAVE SOME NUTS.
THANKS. LISTEN, MOTHER, ABOUT ZEKE. TRY NOT TO BE SO HOSTILE, OKAY? I KNOW YOU THINK WE'RE TOO YOUNG..
HOSTILE? JOAN, WHO SAID I WAS..
ALSO, WHEN HE GETS HERE, PLEASE DON'T SAY ANYTHING ABOUT HIS FINGERNAILS.
FINGERNAILS?
IT'S PART OF HIS RELIGION. YOU DON'T HAVE ANY UNSALTED, DO YOU?
GBTrudeau

12/20/79

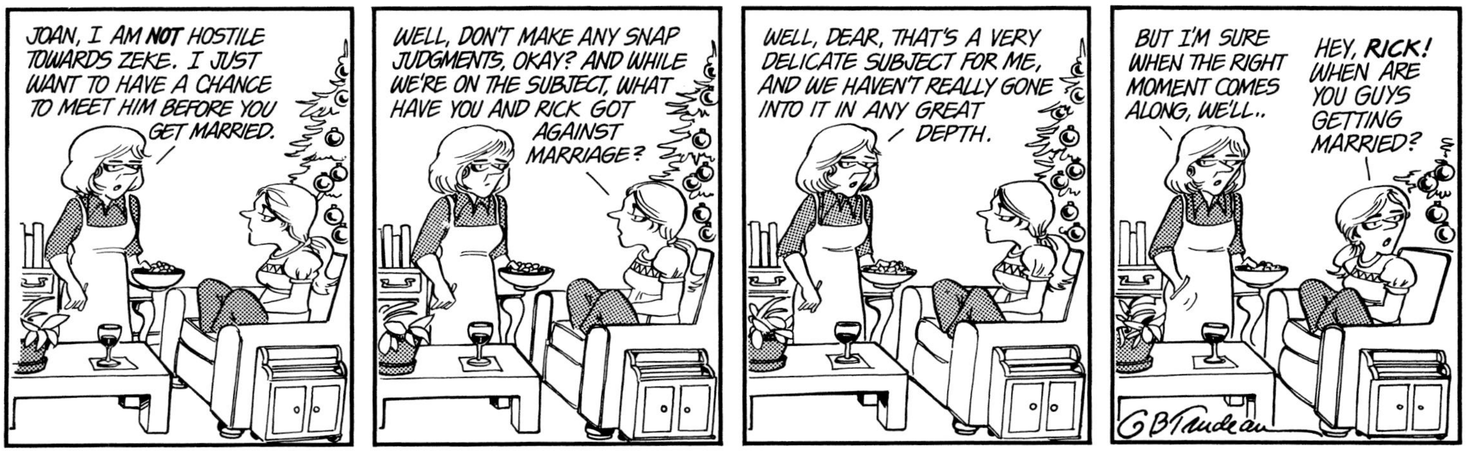
JOAN, I AM NOT HOSTILE TOWARDS ZEKE. I JUST WANT TO HAVE A CHANCE TO MEET HIM BEFORE YOU GET MARRIED.
WELL, DON'T MAKE ANY SNAP JUDGMENTS, OKAY? AND WHILE WE'RE ON THE SUBJECT, WHAT HAVE YOU AND RICK GOT AGAINST MARRIAGE?
WELL, DEAR, THAT'S A VERY DELICATE SUBJECT FOR ME, AND WE HAVEN'T REALLY GONE INTO IT IN ANY GREAT DEPTH.
BUT I'M SURE WHEN THE RIGHT MOMENT COMES ALONG, WE'LL..
HEY, RICK! WHEN ARE YOU GUYS GETTING MARRIED?
GBTrudeau

12/21/79

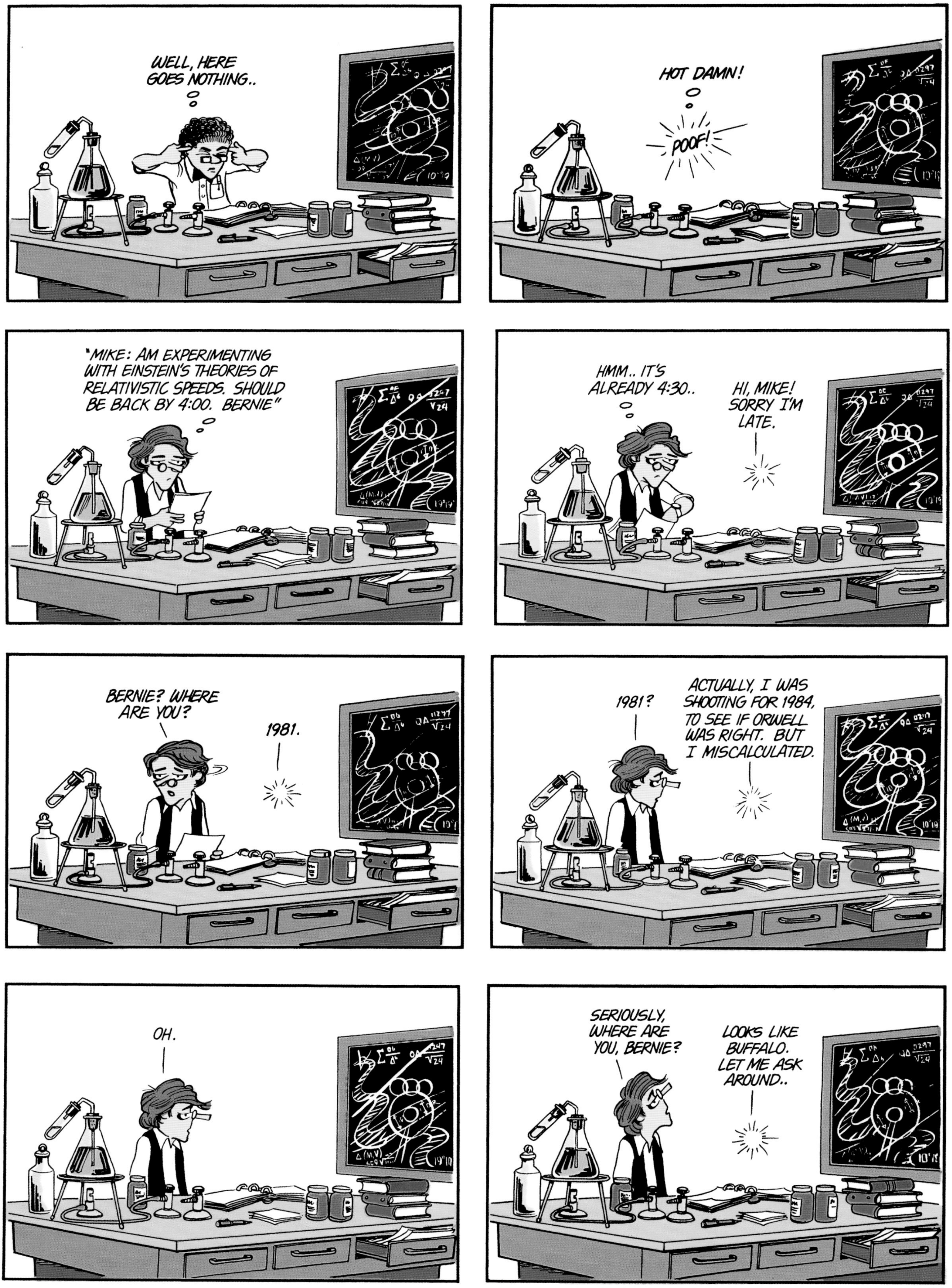
WELL, HERE GOES NOTHING..
HOT DAMN!
POOF!
"MIKE: AM EXPERIMENTING WITH EINSTEIN'S THEORIES OF RELATIVISTIC SPEEDS. SHOULD BE BACK BY 4:00. BERNIE"
HMM.. IT'S ALREADY 4:30..
HI, MIKE! SORRY I'M LATE.
BERNIE? WHERE ARE YOU?
1981.
1981?
ACTUALLY, I WAS SHOOTING FOR 1984, TO SEE IF ORWELL WAS RIGHT. BUT I MISCALCULATED.
OH.
SERIOUSLY, WHERE ARE YOU, BERNIE?
LOOKS LIKE BUFFALO. LET ME ASK AROUND..

5/13/79

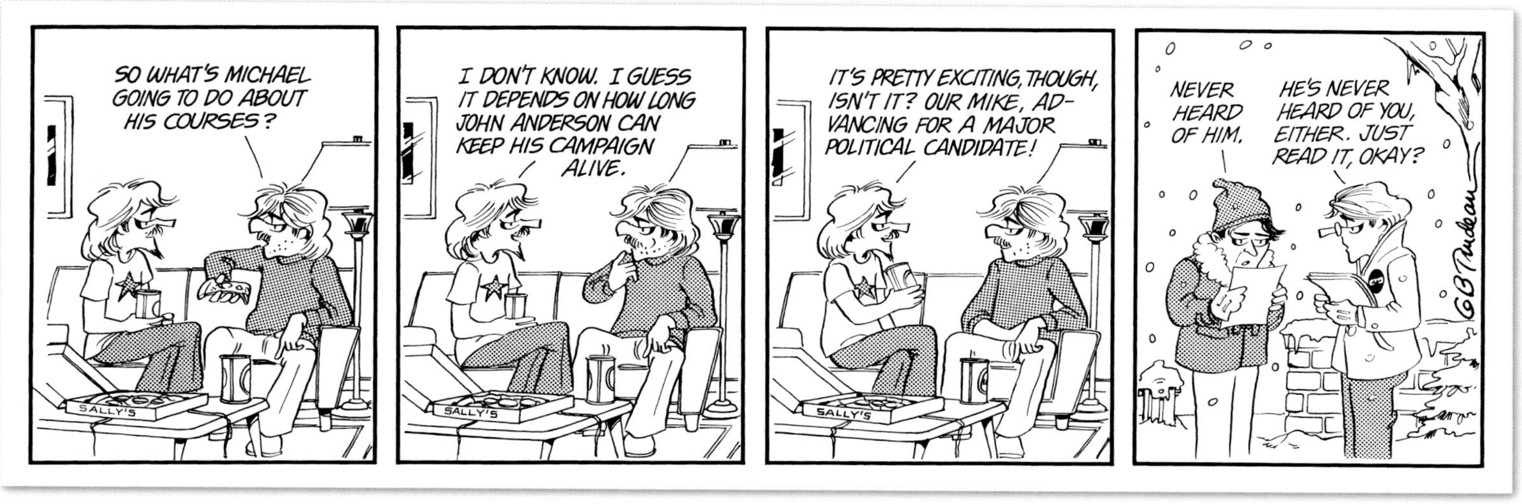
SO WHAT'S MICHAEL GOING TO DO ABOUT HIS COURSES?
I DON'T KNOW. I GUESS IT DEPENDS ON HOW LONG JOHN ANDERSON CAN KEEP HIS CAMPAIGN ALIVE.
IT'S PRETTY EXCITING, THOUGH, ISN'T IT? OUR MIKE, ADVANCING FOR A MAJOR POLITICAL CANDIDATE!
NEVER HEARD OF HIM.
HE'S NEVER HEARD OF YOU, EITHER. JUST READ IT, OKAY?
SALLY'S

2/18/80

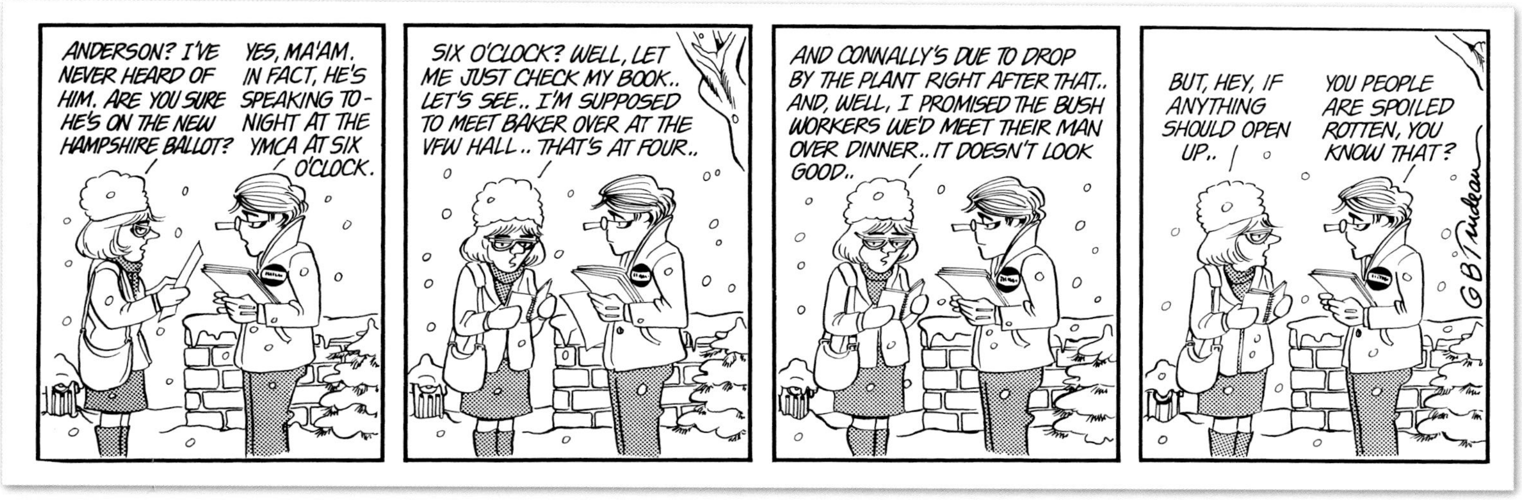
ANDERSON? I'VE NEVER HEARD OF HIM. ARE YOU SURE HE'S ON THE NEW HAMPSHIRE BALLOT?
YES, MA'AM. IN FACT, HE'S SPEAKING TONIGHT AT THE YMCA AT SIX O'CLOCK.
SIX O'CLOCK? WELL, LET ME JUST CHECK MY BOOK.. LET'S SEE.. I'M SUPPOSED TO MEET BAKER OVER AT THE VFW HALL.. THAT'S AT FOUR..
AND CONNALLY'S DUE TO DROP BY THE PLANT RIGHT AFTER THAT.. AND, WELL, I PROMISED THE BUSH WORKERS WE'D MEET THEIR MAN OVER DINNER.. IT DOESN'T LOOK GOOD..
BUT, HEY, IF ANYTHING SHOULD OPEN UP..
YOU PEOPLE ARE SPOILED ROTTEN, YOU KNOW THAT?

2/19/80

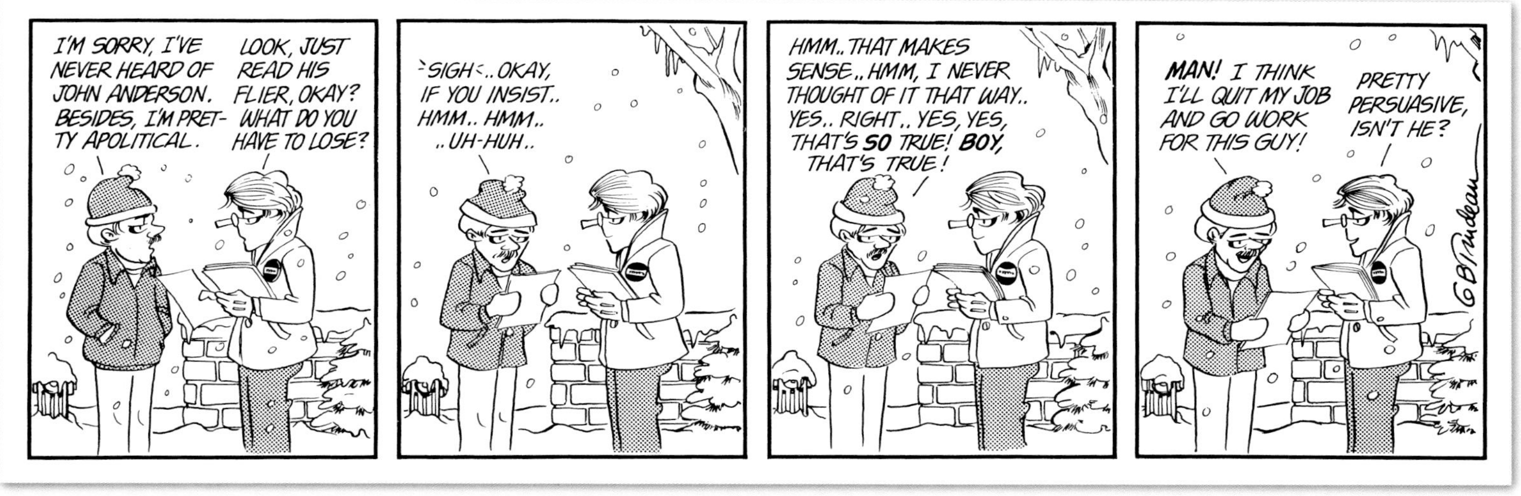
I'M SORRY, I'VE NEVER HEARD OF JOHN ANDERSON. BESIDES, I'M PRETTY APOLITICAL.
LOOK, JUST READ HIS FLIER, OKAY? WHAT DO YOU HAVE TO LOSE?
>SIGH<.. OKAY, IF YOU INSIST.. HMM.. HMM.. ..UH-HUH..
HMM.. THAT MAKES SENSE.. HMM, I NEVER THOUGHT OF IT THAT WAY.. YES.. RIGHT.. YES, YES, THAT'S SO TRUE! BOY, THAT'S TRUE!
MAN! I THINK I'LL QUIT MY JOB AND GO WORK FOR THIS GUY!
PRETTY PERSUASIVE, ISN'T HE?

2/20/80

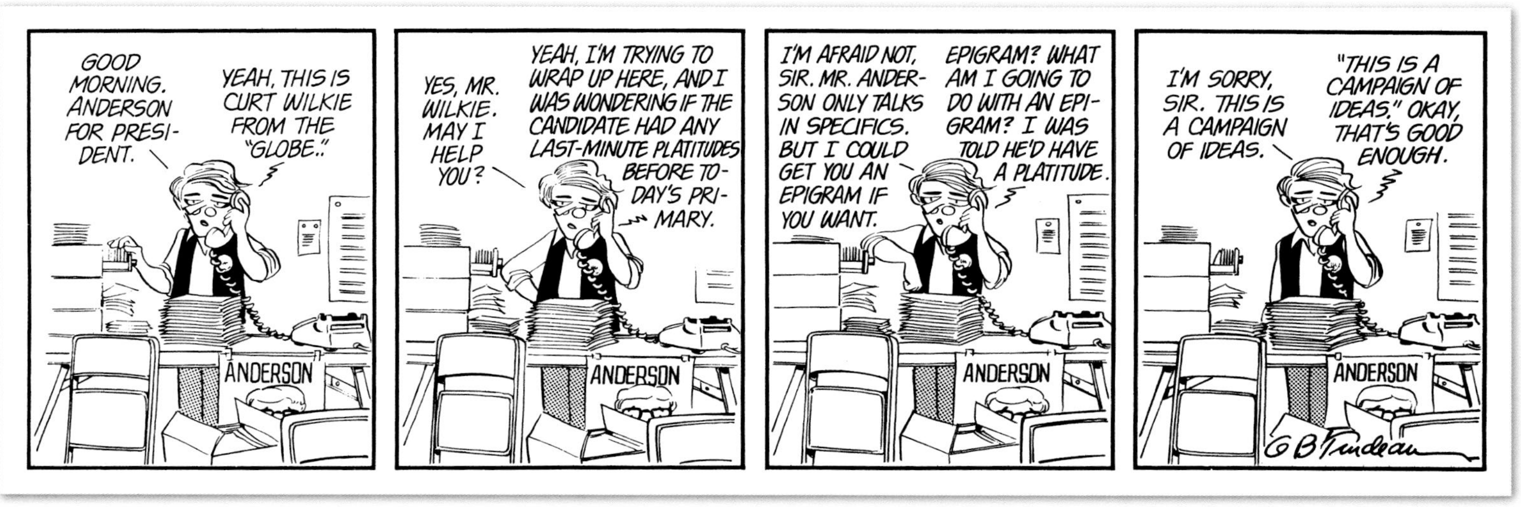
GOOD MORNING. ANDERSON FOR PRESIDENT.
YEAH, THIS IS CURT WILKIE FROM THE "GLOBE."
YES, MR. WILKIE. MAY I HELP YOU?
YEAH, I'M TRYING TO WRAP UP HERE, AND I WAS WONDERING IF THE CANDIDATE HAD ANY LAST-MINUTE PLATITUDES BEFORE TODAY'S PRIMARY.
I'M AFRAID NOT, SIR. MR. ANDERSON ONLY TALKS IN SPECIFICS. BUT I COULD GET YOU AN EPIGRAM IF YOU WANT.
EPIGRAM? WHAT AM I GOING TO DO WITH AN EPIGRAM? I WAS TOLD HE'D HAVE A PLATITUDE.
I'M SORRY, SIR. THIS IS A CAMPAIGN OF IDEAS.
"THIS IS A CAMPAIGN OF IDEAS." OKAY, THAT'S GOOD ENOUGH.
ANDERSON

3/18/80

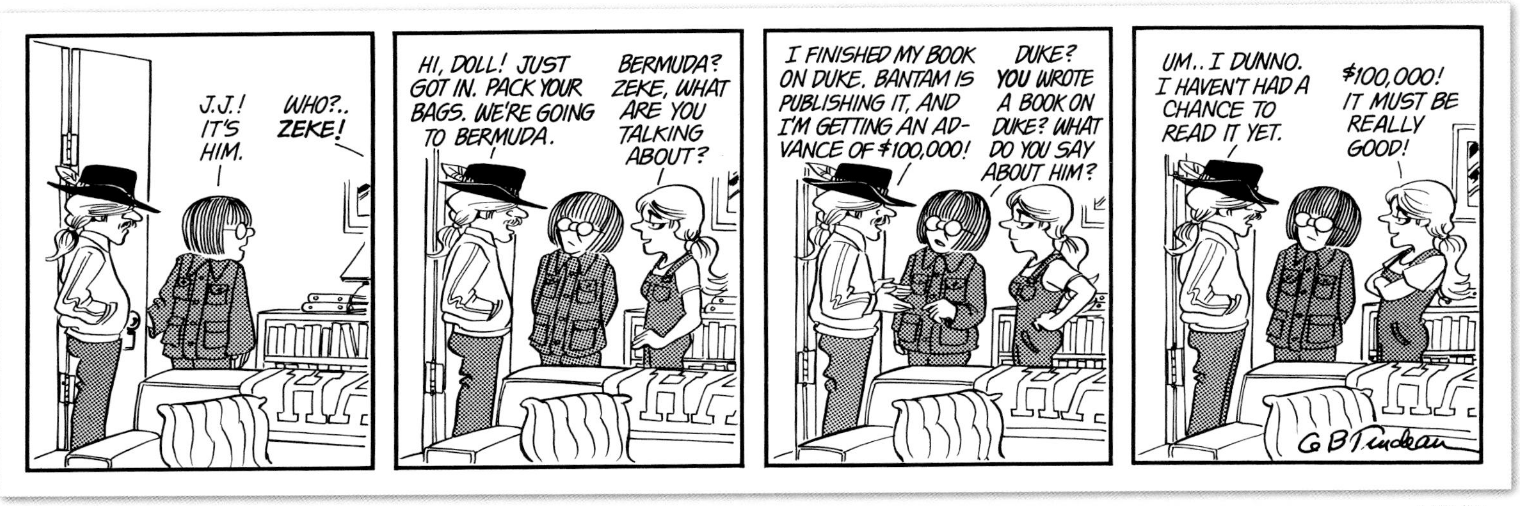
J.J.! IT'S HIM.
WHO?.. ZEKE!
HI, DOLL! JUST GOT IN. PACK YOUR BAGS. WE'RE GOING TO BERMUDA.
BERMUDA? ZEKE, WHAT ARE YOU TALKING ABOUT?
I FINISHED MY BOOK ON DUKE. BANTAM IS PUBLISHING IT, AND I'M GETTING AN ADVANCE OF $100,000!
DUKE? **YOU** WROTE A BOOK ON DUKE? WHAT DO YOU SAY ABOUT HIM?
UM.. I DUNNO. I HAVEN'T HAD A CHANCE TO READ IT YET.
$100,000! IT MUST BE REALLY GOOD!
G B Trudeau

3/10/80

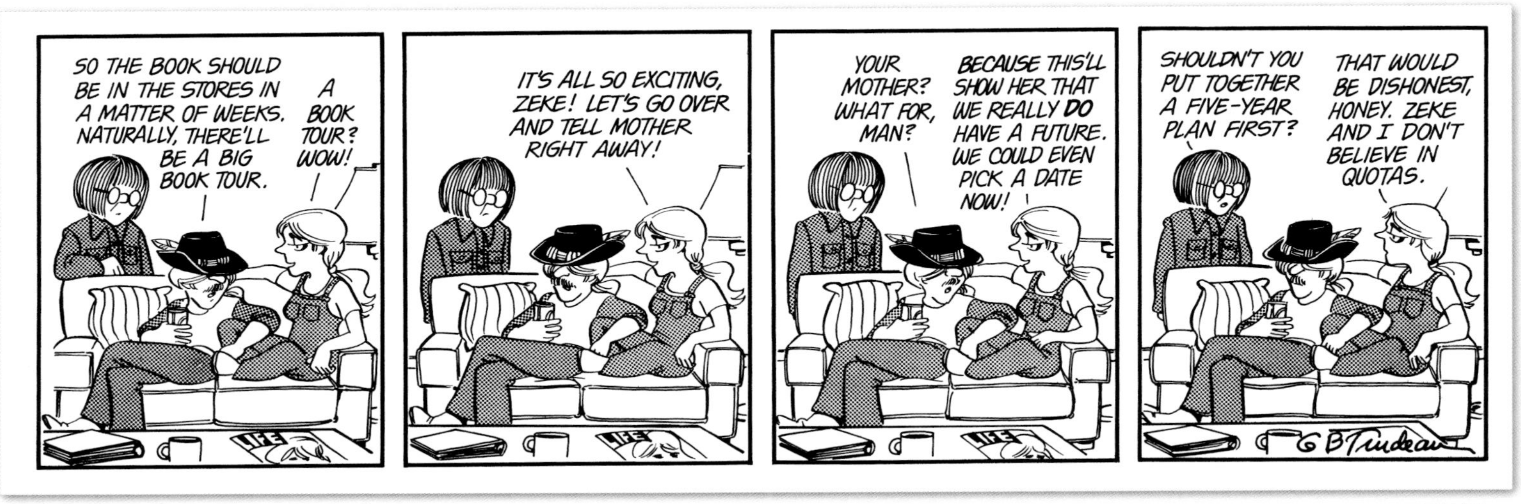
SO THE BOOK SHOULD BE IN THE STORES IN A MATTER OF WEEKS. NATURALLY, THERE'LL BE A BIG BOOK TOUR.
A BOOK TOUR? WOW!
IT'S ALL SO EXCITING, ZEKE! LET'S GO OVER AND TELL MOTHER RIGHT AWAY!
YOUR MOTHER? WHAT FOR, MAN?
BECAUSE THIS'LL SHOW HER THAT WE REALLY **DO** HAVE A FUTURE. WE COULD EVEN PICK A DATE NOW!
SHOULDN'T YOU PUT TOGETHER A FIVE-YEAR PLAN FIRST?
THAT WOULD BE DISHONEST, HONEY. ZEKE AND I DON'T BELIEVE IN QUOTAS.
G B Trudeau

3/11/80

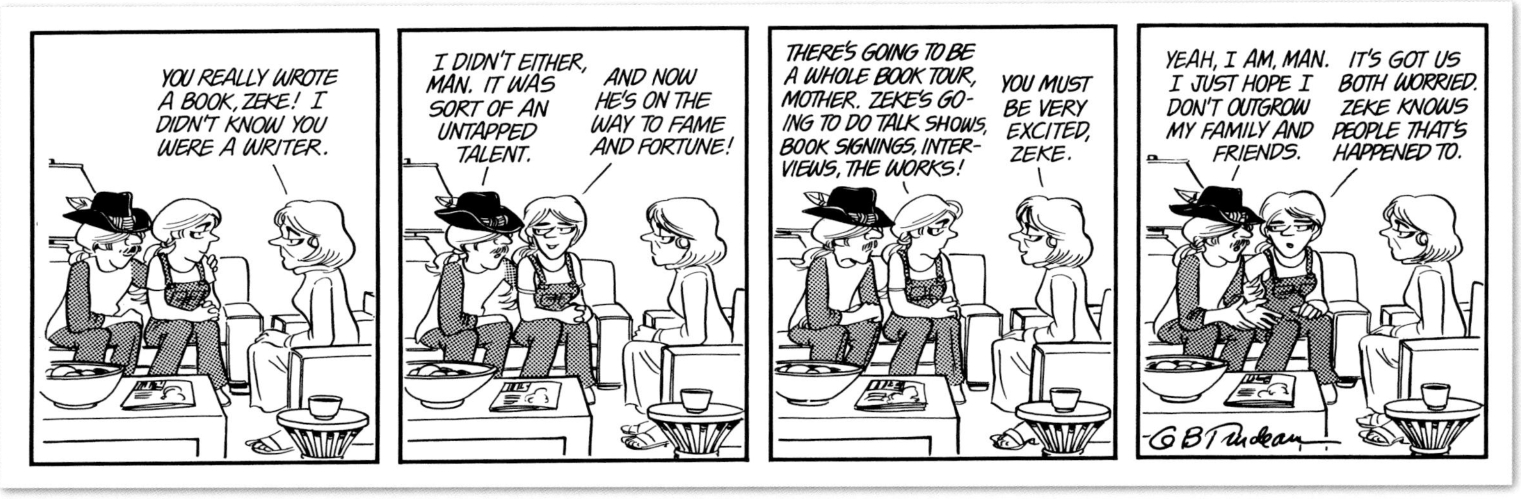
YOU REALLY WROTE A BOOK, ZEKE! I DIDN'T KNOW YOU WERE A WRITER.
I DIDN'T EITHER, MAN. IT WAS SORT OF AN UNTAPPED TALENT.
AND NOW HE'S ON THE WAY TO FAME AND FORTUNE!
THERE'S GOING TO BE A WHOLE BOOK TOUR, MOTHER. ZEKE'S GOING TO DO TALK SHOWS, BOOK SIGNINGS, INTERVIEWS, THE WORKS!
YOU MUST BE VERY EXCITED, ZEKE.
YEAH, I AM, MAN. I JUST HOPE I DON'T OUTGROW MY FAMILY AND FRIENDS.
IT'S GOT US BOTH WORRIED. ZEKE KNOWS PEOPLE THAT'S HAPPENED TO.
G B Trudeau

3/12/80

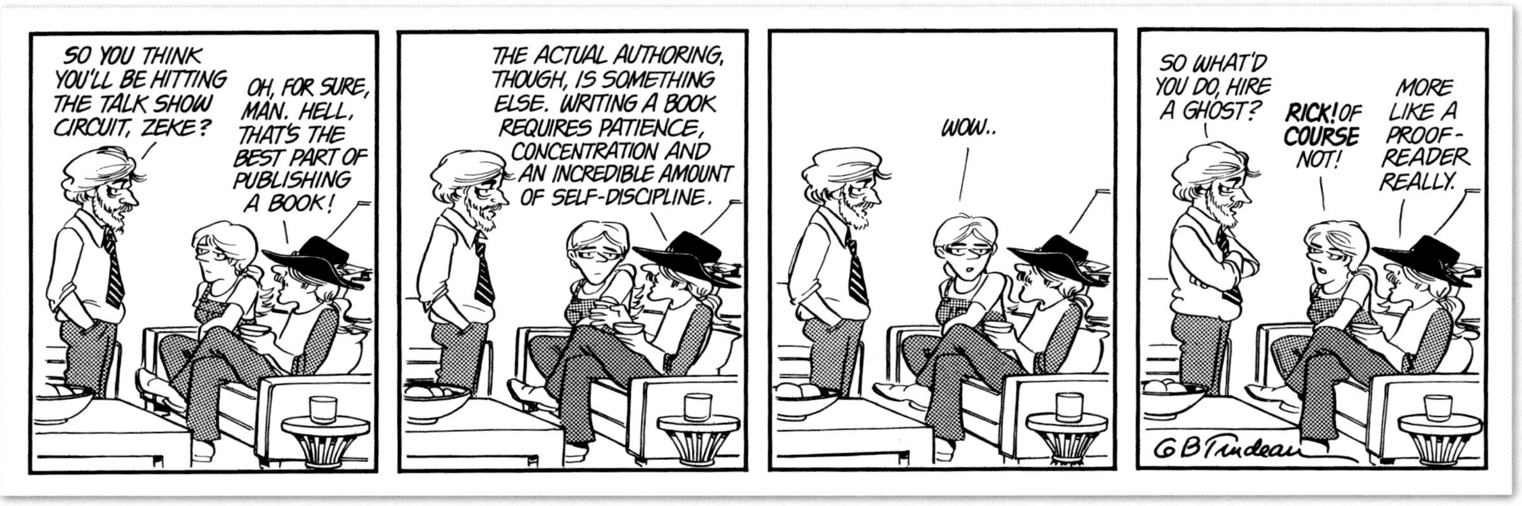
SO YOU THINK YOU'LL BE HITTING THE TALK SHOW CIRCUIT, ZEKE?
OH, FOR SURE, MAN. HELL, THAT'S THE BEST PART OF PUBLISHING A BOOK!
THE ACTUAL AUTHORING, THOUGH, IS SOMETHING ELSE. WRITING A BOOK REQUIRES PATIENCE, CONCENTRATION AND AN INCREDIBLE AMOUNT OF SELF-DISCIPLINE.
WOW..
SO WHAT'D YOU DO, HIRE A GHOST?
RICK! OF **COURSE** NOT!
MORE LIKE A PROOF-READER REALLY.
G B Trudeau

3/14/80

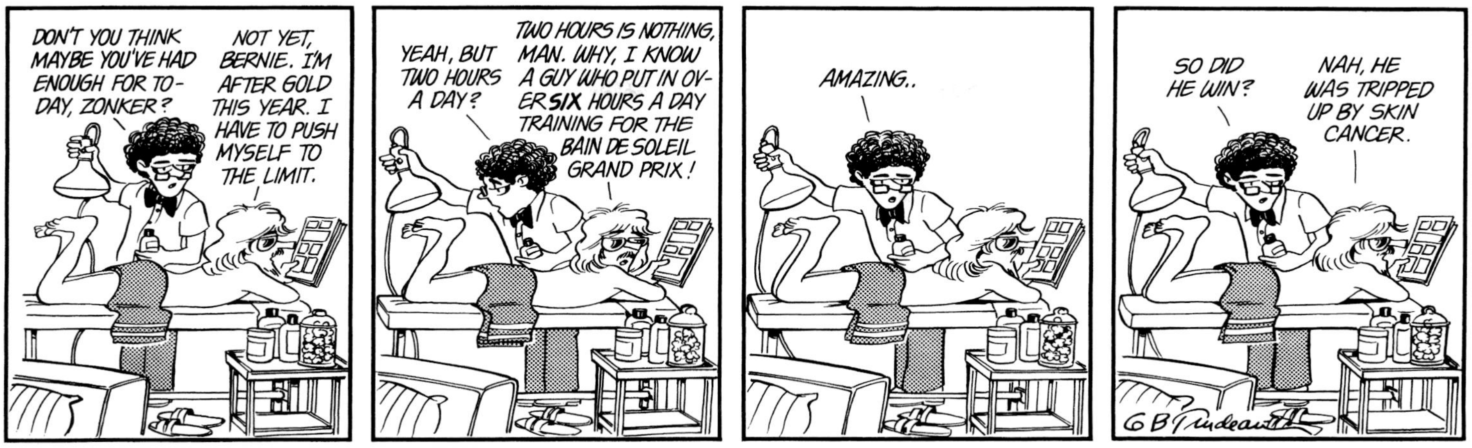
DON'T YOU THINK MAYBE YOU'VE HAD ENOUGH FOR TO-DAY, ZONKER?
NOT YET, BERNIE. I'M AFTER GOLD THIS YEAR. I HAVE TO PUSH MYSELF TO THE LIMIT.
YEAH, BUT TWO HOURS A DAY?
TWO HOURS IS NOTHING, MAN. WHY, I KNOW A GUY WHO PUT IN OV-ER SIX HOURS A DAY TRAINING FOR THE BAIN DE SOLEIL GRAND PRIX!
AMAZING..
SO DID HE WIN?
NAH, HE WAS TRIPPED UP BY SKIN CANCER.
G B Trudeau

3/25/80

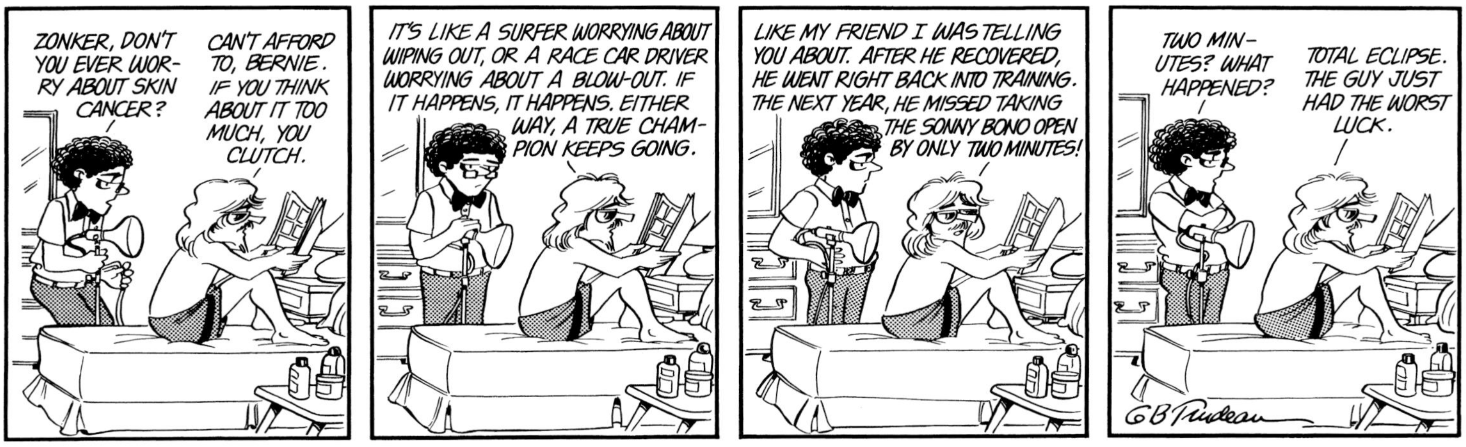
ZONKER, DON'T YOU EVER WOR-RY ABOUT SKIN CANCER?
CAN'T AFFORD TO, BERNIE. IF YOU THINK ABOUT IT TOO MUCH, YOU CLUTCH.
IT'S LIKE A SURFER WORRYING ABOUT WIPING OUT, OR A RACE CAR DRIVER WORRYING ABOUT A BLOW-OUT. IF IT HAPPENS, IT HAPPENS. EITHER WAY, A TRUE CHAM-PION KEEPS GOING.
LIKE MY FRIEND I WAS TELLING YOU ABOUT. AFTER HE RECOVERED, HE WENT RIGHT BACK INTO TRAINING. THE NEXT YEAR, HE MISSED TAKING THE SONNY BONO OPEN BY ONLY TWO MINUTES!
TWO MIN-UTES? WHAT HAPPENED?
TOTAL ECLIPSE. THE GUY JUST HAD THE WORST LUCK.
G B Trudeau

3/26/80

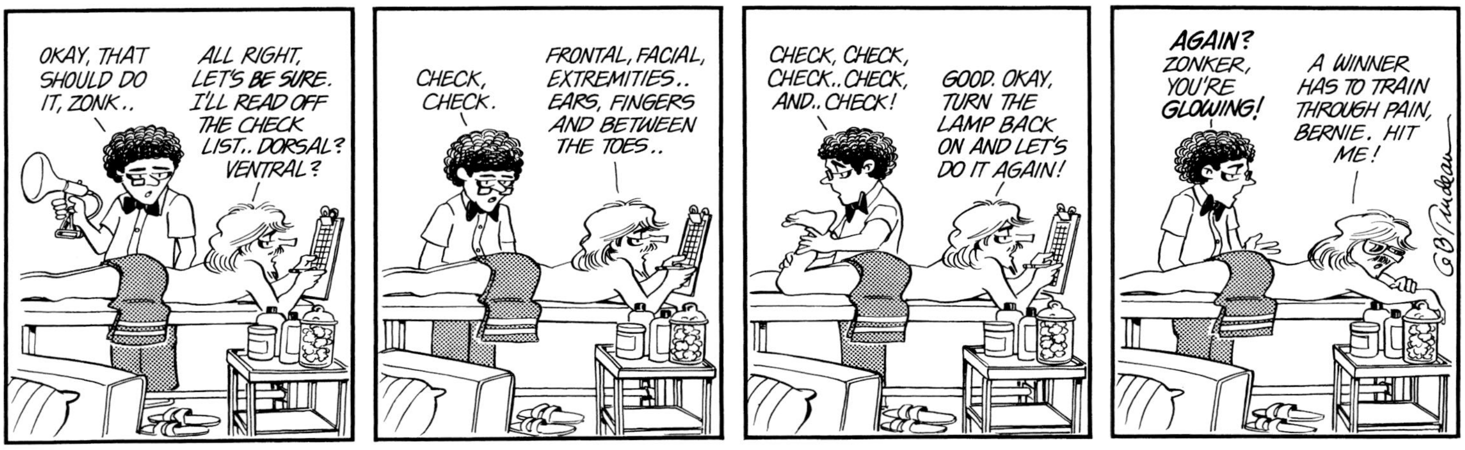
OKAY, THAT SHOULD DO IT, ZONK..
ALL RIGHT, LET'S BE SURE. I'LL READ OFF THE CHECK LIST.. DORSAL? VENTRAL?
CHECK, CHECK.
FRONTAL, FACIAL, EXTREMITIES.. EARS, FINGERS AND BETWEEN THE TOES..
CHECK, CHECK, CHECK..CHECK, AND..CHECK!
GOOD. OKAY, TURN THE LAMP BACK ON AND LET'S DO IT AGAIN!
AGAIN? ZONKER, YOU'RE GLOWING!
A WINNER HAS TO TRAIN THROUGH PAIN, BERNIE. HIT ME!
G B Trudeau

3/27/80

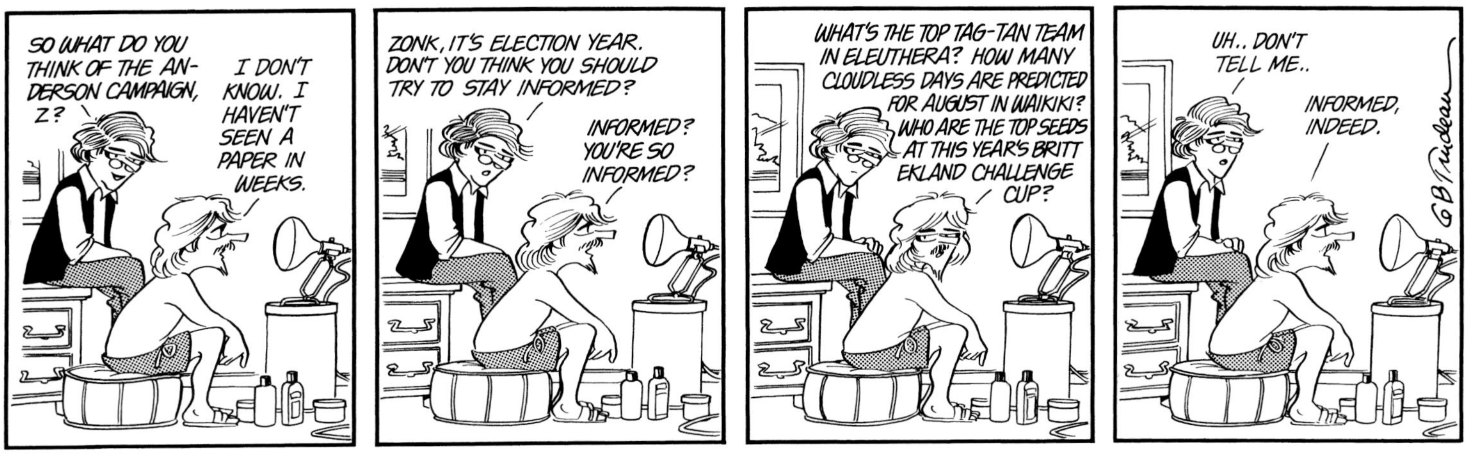
SO WHAT DO YOU THINK OF THE AN-DERSON CAMPAIGN, Z?
I DON'T KNOW. I HAVEN'T SEEN A PAPER IN WEEKS.
ZONK, IT'S ELECTION YEAR. DON'T YOU THINK YOU SHOULD TRY TO STAY INFORMED?
INFORMED? YOU'RE SO INFORMED?
WHAT'S THE TOP TAG-TAN TEAM IN ELEUTHERA? HOW MANY CLOUDLESS DAYS ARE PREDICTED FOR AUGUST IN WAIKIKI? WHO ARE THE TOP SEEDS AT THIS YEAR'S BRITT EKLAND CHALLENGE CUP?
UH.. DON'T TELL ME..
INFORMED, INDEED.
G B Trudeau

3/28/80

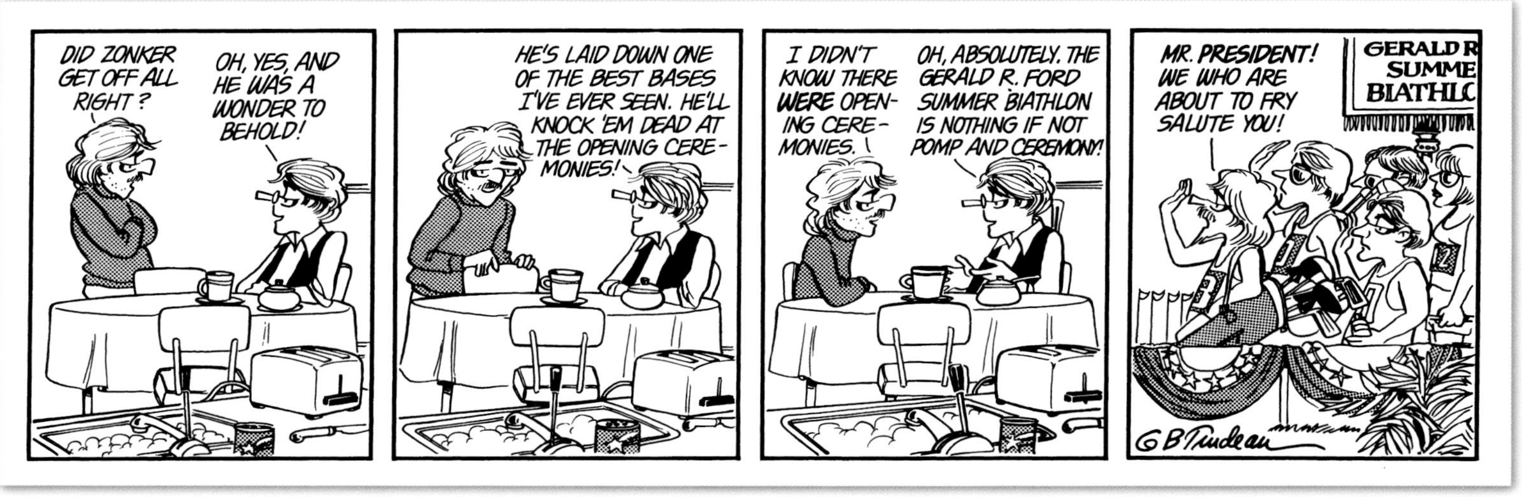
DID ZONKER GET OFF ALL RIGHT?
OH, YES, AND HE WAS A WONDER TO BEHOLD!
HE'S LAID DOWN ONE OF THE BEST BASES I'VE EVER SEEN. HE'LL KNOCK 'EM DEAD AT THE OPENING CERE-MONIES!
I DIDN'T KNOW THERE WERE OPEN-ING CERE-MONIES.
OH, ABSOLUTELY. THE GERALD R. FORD SUMMER BIATHLON IS NOTHING IF NOT POMP AND CEREMONY!
GERALD R SUMME BIATHLO
MR. PRESIDENT! WE WHO ARE ABOUT TO FRY SALUTE YOU!
GB Trudeau

7/7/80

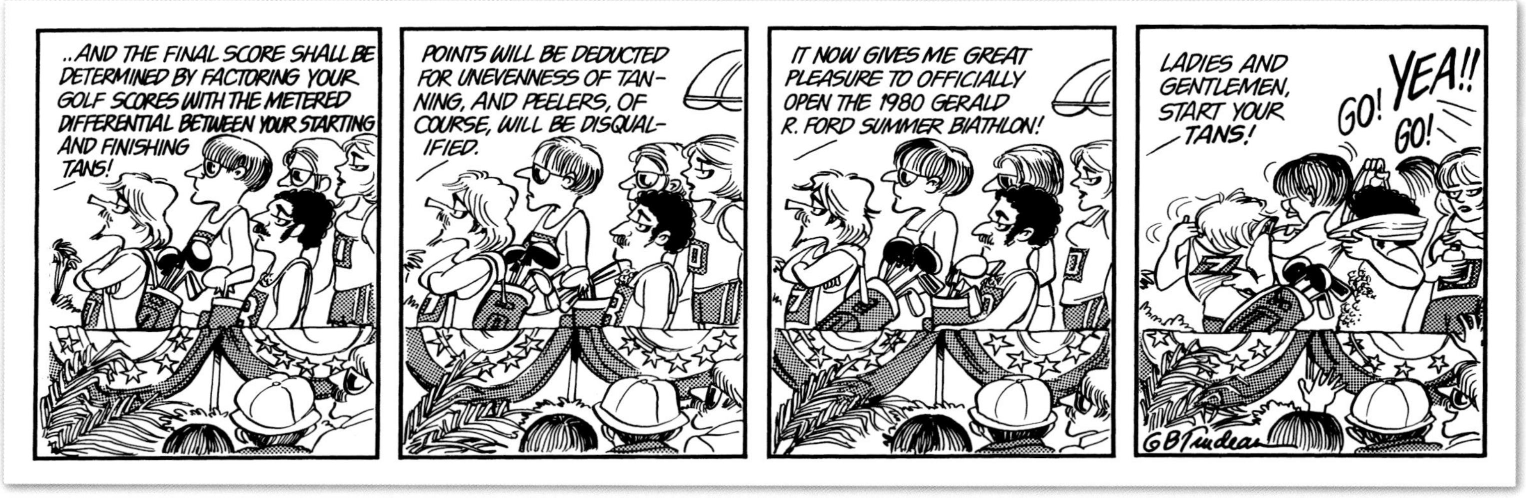
..AND THE FINAL SCORE SHALL BE DETERMINED BY FACTORING YOUR GOLF SCORES WITH THE METERED DIFFERENTIAL BETWEEN YOUR STARTING AND FINISHING TANS!
POINTS WILL BE DEDUCTED FOR UNEVENNESS OF TAN-NING, AND PEELERS, OF COURSE, WILL BE DISQUAL-IFIED.
IT NOW GIVES ME GREAT PLEASURE TO OFFICIALLY OPEN THE 1980 GERALD R. FORD SUMMER BIATHLON!
LADIES AND GENTLEMEN, START YOUR TANS!
GO! YEA!! GO!
GB Trudeau

7/8/80

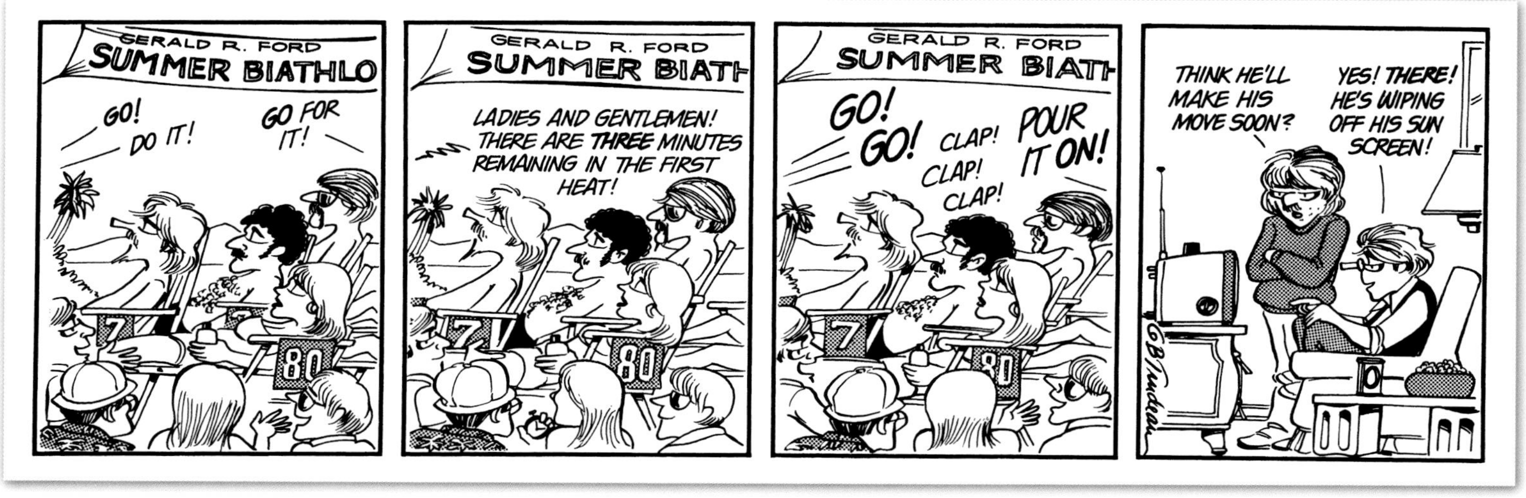
GERALD R. FORD SUMMER BIATHLO
GO! DO IT! GO FOR IT!
GERALD R. FORD SUMMER BIATH
LADIES AND GENTLEMEN! THERE ARE THREE MINUTES REMAINING IN THE FIRST HEAT!
GERALD R. FORD SUMMER BIATH
GO! GO! CLAP! CLAP! CLAP! POUR IT ON!
THINK HE'LL MAKE HIS MOVE SOON?
YES! THERE! HE'S WIPING OFF HIS SUN SCREEN!
GB Trudeau

7/10/80

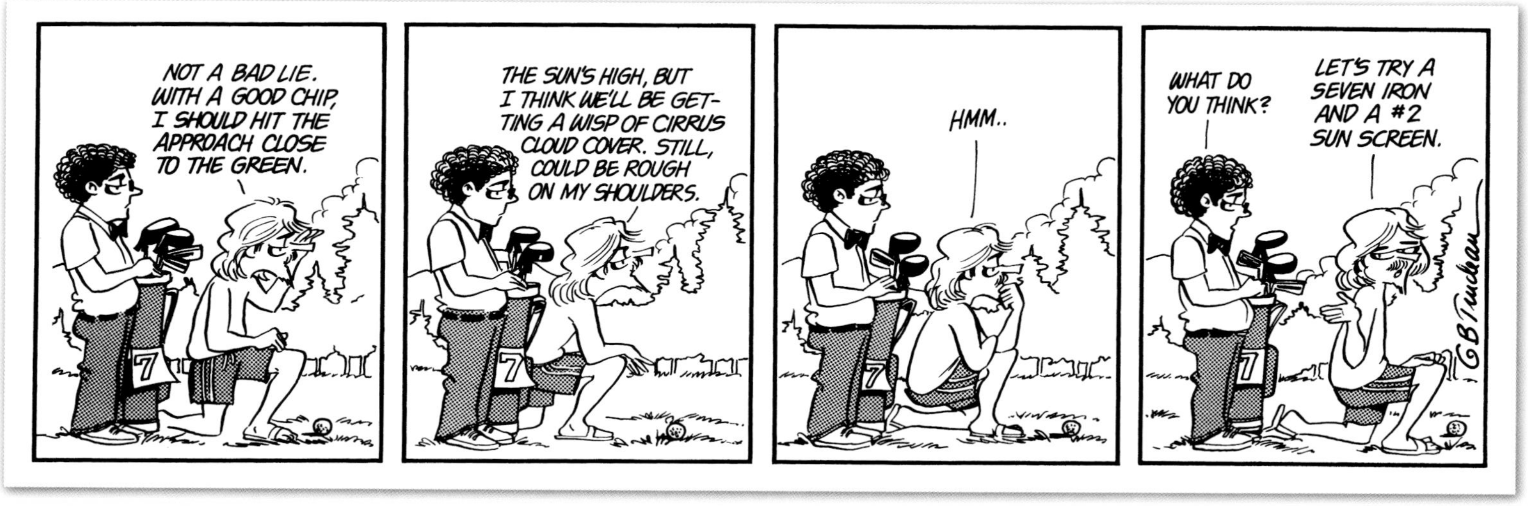
NOT A BAD LIE. WITH A GOOD CHIP, I SHOULD HIT THE APPROACH CLOSE TO THE GREEN.
THE SUN'S HIGH, BUT I THINK WE'LL BE GET-TING A WISP OF CIRRUS CLOUD COVER. STILL, COULD BE ROUGH ON MY SHOULDERS.
HMM..
WHAT DO YOU THINK?
LET'S TRY A SEVEN IRON AND A #2 SUN SCREEN.
GB Trudeau

7/12/80

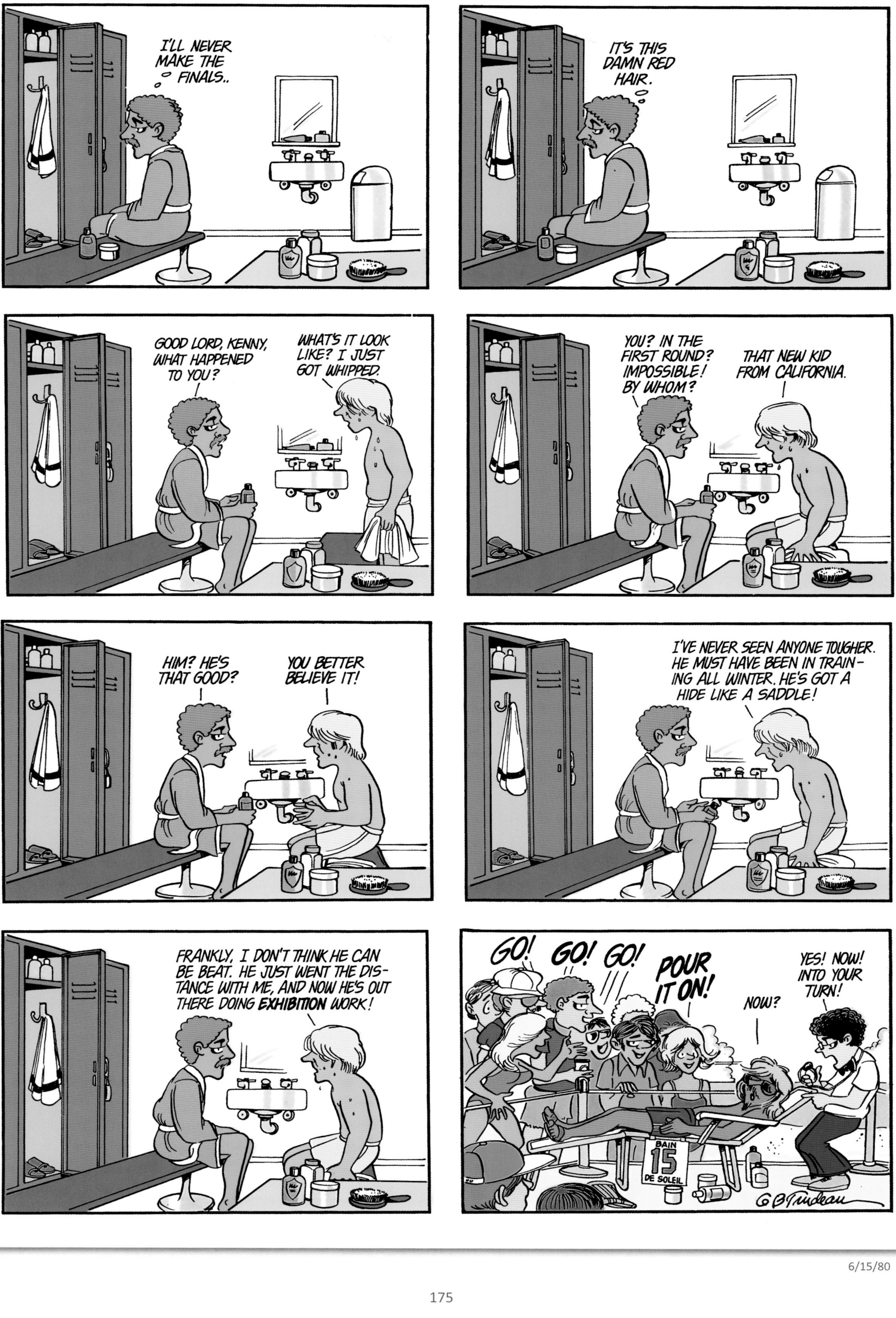
I'LL NEVER MAKE THE FINALS..
IT'S THIS DAMN RED HAIR.
GOOD LORD, KENNY, WHAT HAPPENED TO YOU?
WHAT'S IT LOOK LIKE? I JUST GOT WHIPPED.
YOU? IN THE FIRST ROUND? IMPOSSIBLE! BY WHOM?
THAT NEW KID FROM CALIFORNIA.
HIM? HE'S THAT GOOD?
YOU BETTER BELIEVE IT!
I'VE NEVER SEEN ANYONE TOUGHER. HE MUST HAVE BEEN IN TRAINING ALL WINTER. HE'S GOT A HIDE LIKE A SADDLE!
FRANKLY, I DON'T THINK HE CAN BE BEAT. HE JUST WENT THE DISTANCE WITH ME, AND NOW HE'S OUT THERE DOING EXHIBITION WORK!
GO!
GO!
GO!
POUR IT ON!
NOW?
YES! NOW! INTO YOUR TURN!
BAIN 15 DE SOLEIL
G.B.Trudeau

6/15/80

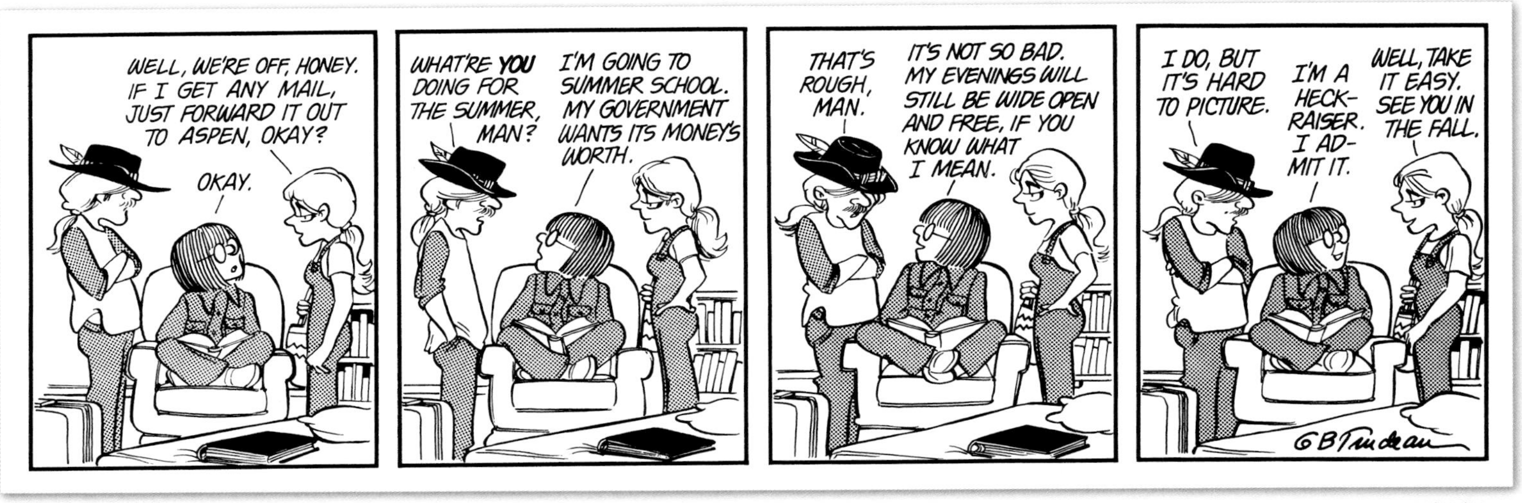
WELL, WE'RE OFF, HONEY. IF I GET ANY MAIL, JUST FORWARD IT OUT TO ASPEN, OKAY?
OKAY.
WHAT'RE **YOU** DOING FOR THE SUMMER, MAN?
I'M GOING TO SUMMER SCHOOL. MY GOVERNMENT WANTS ITS MONEY'S WORTH.
THAT'S ROUGH, MAN.
IT'S NOT SO BAD. MY EVENINGS WILL STILL BE WIDE OPEN AND FREE, IF YOU KNOW WHAT I MEAN.
I DO, BUT IT'S HARD TO PICTURE.
I'M A HECK-RAISER. I ADMIT IT.
WELL, TAKE IT EASY. SEE YOU IN THE FALL.
GBTrudeau

6/23/80

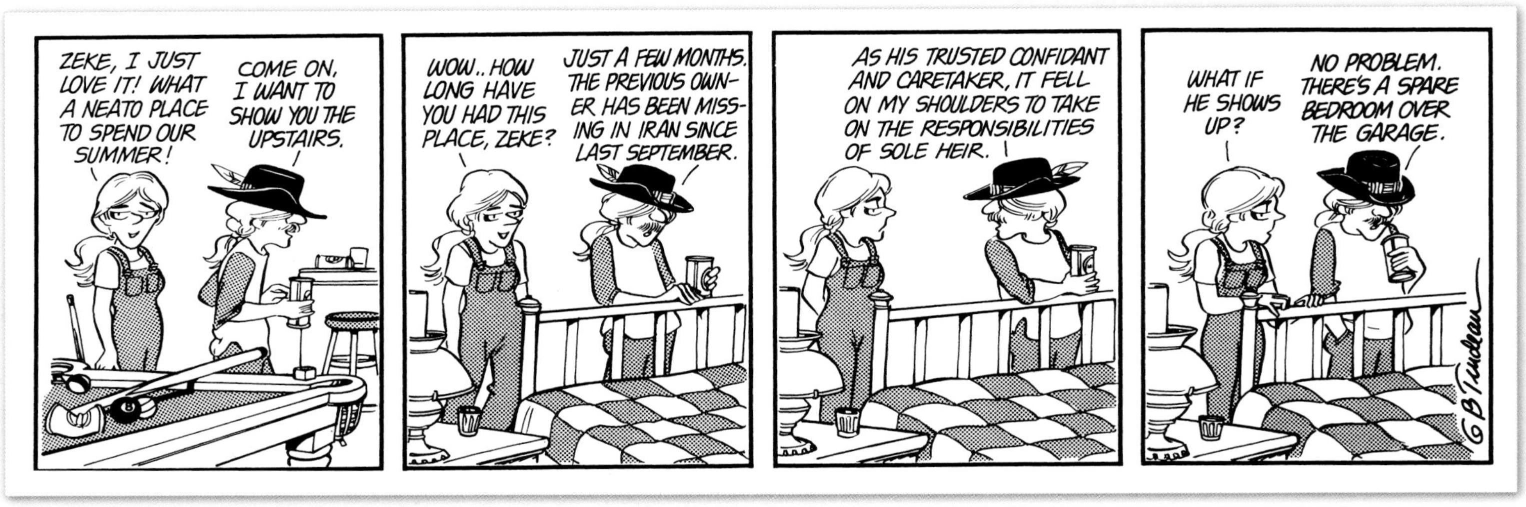
ZEKE, I JUST LOVE IT! WHAT A NEATO PLACE TO SPEND OUR SUMMER!
COME ON, I WANT TO SHOW YOU THE UPSTAIRS.
WOW.. HOW LONG HAVE YOU HAD THIS PLACE, ZEKE?
JUST A FEW MONTHS. THE PREVIOUS OWNER HAS BEEN MISSING IN IRAN SINCE LAST SEPTEMBER.
AS HIS TRUSTED CONFIDANT AND CARETAKER, IT FELL ON MY SHOULDERS TO TAKE ON THE RESPONSIBILITIES OF SOLE HEIR.
WHAT IF HE SHOWS UP?
NO PROBLEM. THERE'S A SPARE BEDROOM OVER THE GARAGE.
GBTrudeau

6/25/80

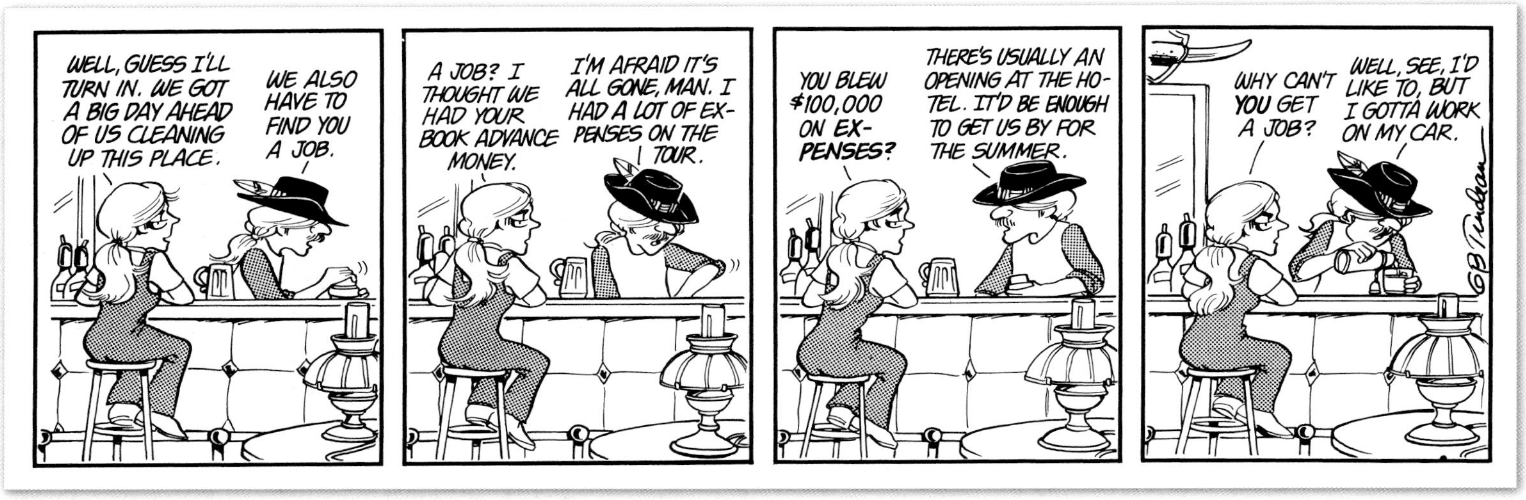
WELL, GUESS I'LL TURN IN. WE GOT A BIG DAY AHEAD OF US CLEANING UP THIS PLACE.
WE ALSO HAVE TO FIND YOU A JOB.
A JOB? I THOUGHT WE HAD YOUR BOOK ADVANCE MONEY.
I'M AFRAID IT'S ALL GONE, MAN. I HAD A LOT OF EXPENSES ON THE TOUR.
YOU BLEW $100,000 ON **EXPENSES?**
THERE'S USUALLY AN OPENING AT THE HOTEL. IT'D BE ENOUGH TO GET US BY FOR THE SUMMER.
WHY CAN'T **YOU** GET A JOB?
WELL, SEE, I'D LIKE TO, BUT I GOTTA WORK ON MY CAR.
GBTrudeau

6/27/80

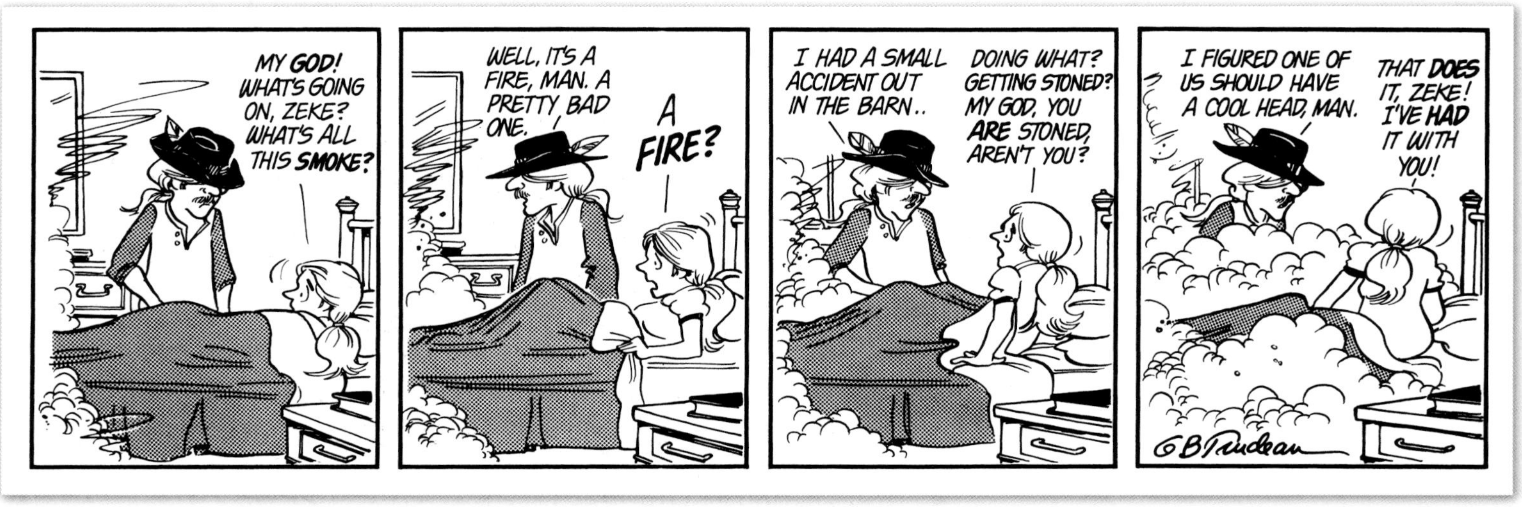
MY **GOD!** WHAT'S GOING ON, ZEKE? WHAT'S ALL THIS **SMOKE?**
WELL, IT'S A FIRE, MAN. A PRETTY BAD ONE.
A **FIRE?**
I HAD A SMALL ACCIDENT OUT IN THE BARN..
DOING WHAT? GETTING STONED? MY GOD, YOU **ARE** STONED, AREN'T YOU?
I FIGURED ONE OF US SHOULD HAVE A COOL HEAD, MAN.
THAT **DOES** IT, ZEKE! I'VE **HAD** IT WITH YOU!
GBTrudeau

7/1/80

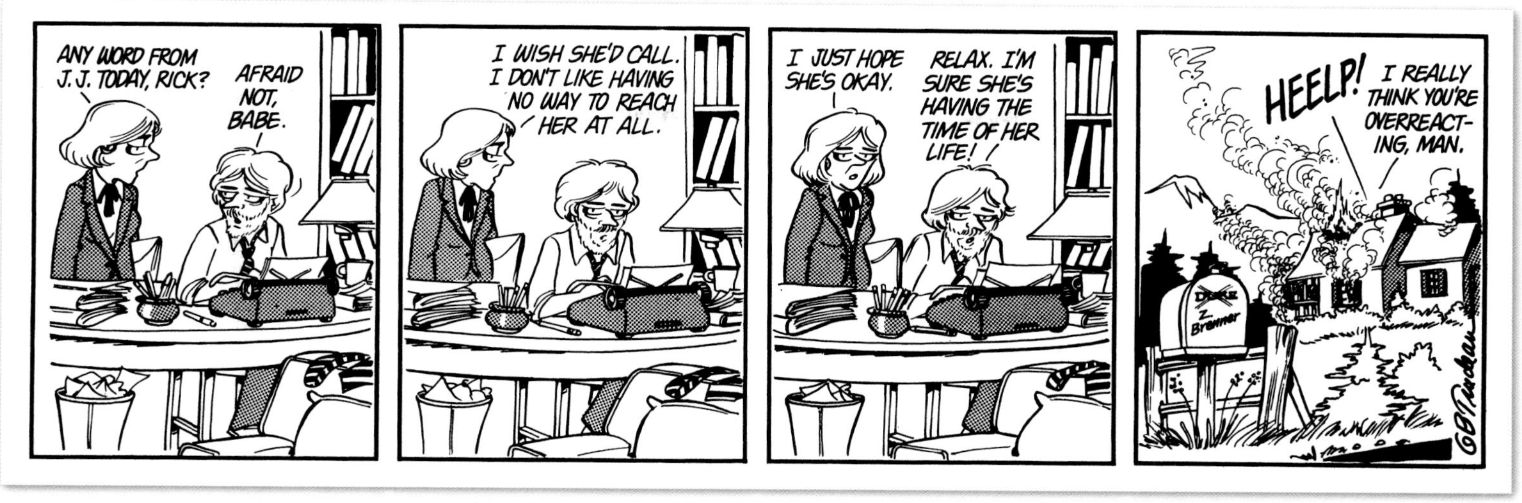
ANY WORD FROM J. J. TODAY, RICK?
AFRAID NOT, BABE.
I WISH SHE'D CALL. I DON'T LIKE HAVING NO WAY TO REACH HER AT ALL.
I JUST HOPE SHE'S OKAY.
RELAX. I'M SURE SHE'S HAVING THE TIME OF HER LIFE!
HEELP!
I REALLY THINK YOU'RE OVERREACTING, MAN.
GB Trudeau

7/2/80

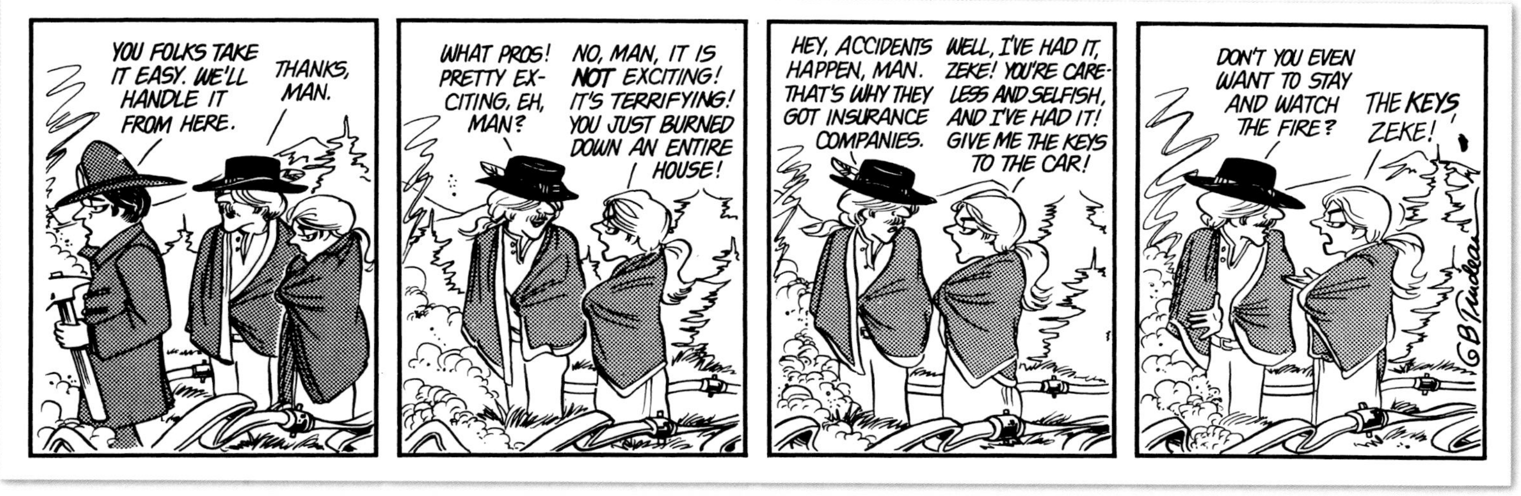
YOU FOLKS TAKE IT EASY. WE'LL HANDLE IT FROM HERE.
THANKS, MAN.
WHAT PROS! PRETTY EXCITING, EH, MAN?
NO, MAN, IT IS **NOT** EXCITING! IT'S TERRIFYING! YOU JUST BURNED DOWN AN ENTIRE HOUSE!
HEY, ACCIDENTS HAPPEN, MAN. THAT'S WHY THEY GOT INSURANCE COMPANIES.
WELL, I'VE HAD IT, ZEKE! YOU'RE CARELESS AND SELFISH, AND I'VE HAD IT! GIVE ME THE KEYS TO THE CAR!
DON'T YOU EVEN WANT TO STAY AND WATCH THE FIRE?
THE **KEYS** ZEKE!
GB Trudeau

7/3/80

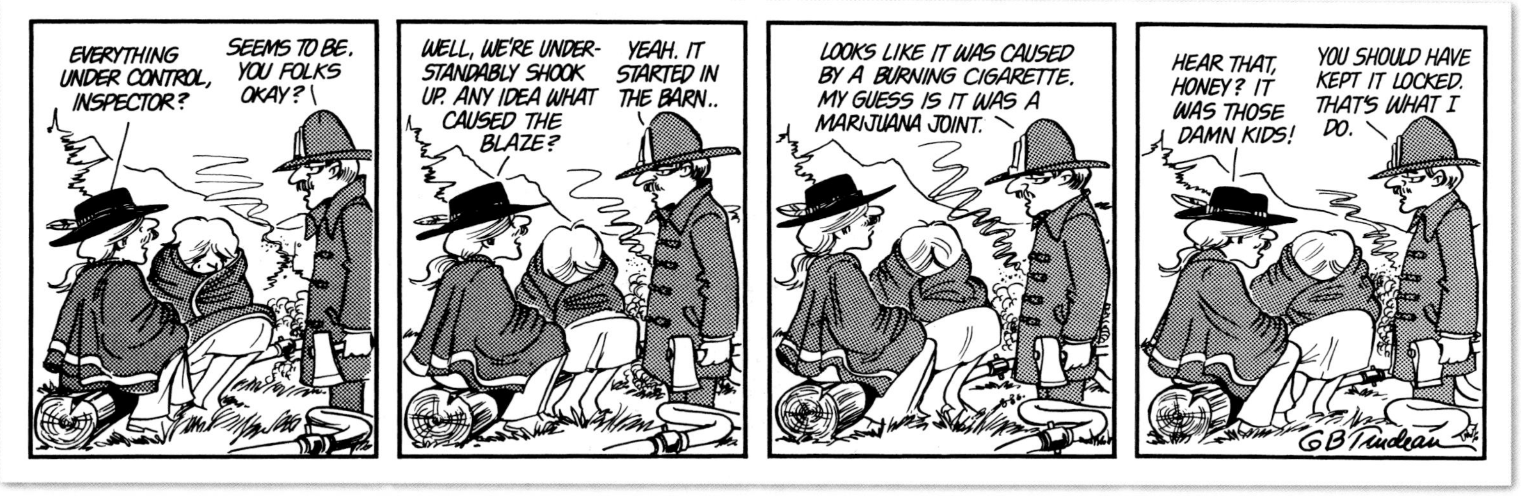
EVERYTHING UNDER CONTROL, INSPECTOR?
SEEMS TO BE. YOU FOLKS OKAY?
WELL, WE'RE UNDERSTANDABLY SHOOK UP. ANY IDEA WHAT CAUSED THE BLAZE?
YEAH. IT STARTED IN THE BARN..
LOOKS LIKE IT WAS CAUSED BY A BURNING CIGARETTE. MY GUESS IS IT WAS A MARIJUANA JOINT.
HEAR THAT, HONEY? IT WAS THOSE DAMN KIDS!
YOU SHOULD HAVE KEPT IT LOCKED. THAT'S WHAT I DO.
GB Trudeau

7/4/80

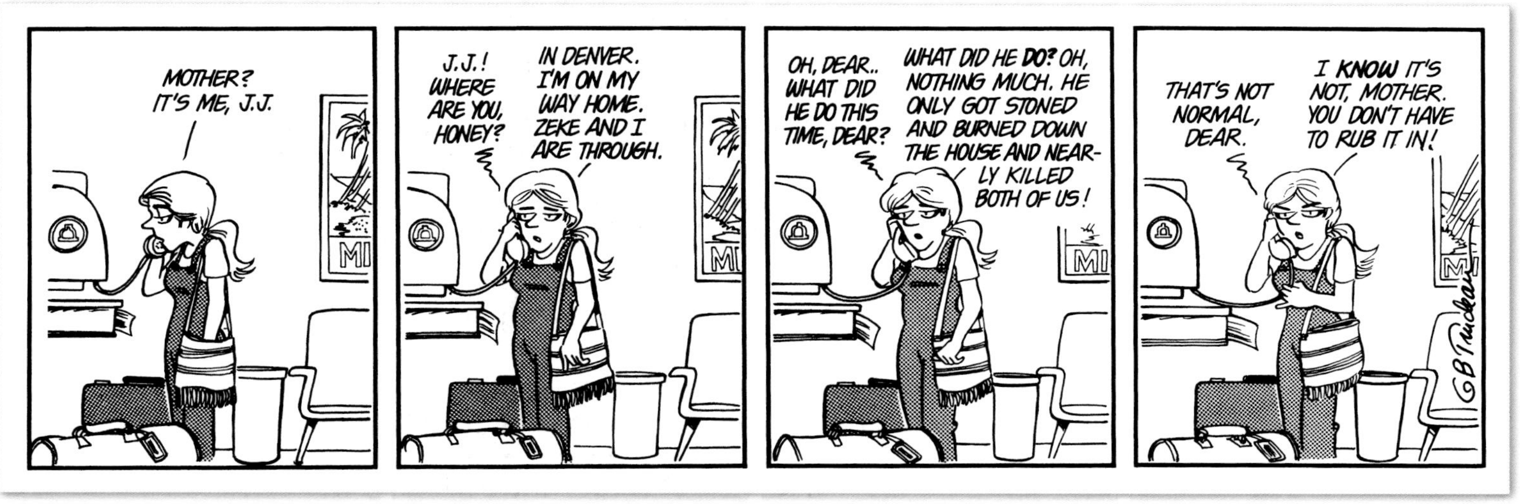
MOTHER? IT'S ME, J.J.
J.J.! WHERE ARE YOU, HONEY?
IN DENVER. I'M ON MY WAY HOME. ZEKE AND I ARE THROUGH.
OH, DEAR.. WHAT DID HE DO THIS TIME, DEAR?
WHAT DID HE **DO?** OH, NOTHING MUCH. HE ONLY GOT STONED AND BURNED DOWN THE HOUSE AND NEARLY KILLED BOTH OF US!
THAT'S NOT NORMAL, DEAR.
I **KNOW** IT'S NOT, MOTHER. YOU DON'T HAVE TO RUB IT IN!
GB Trudeau

7/5/80

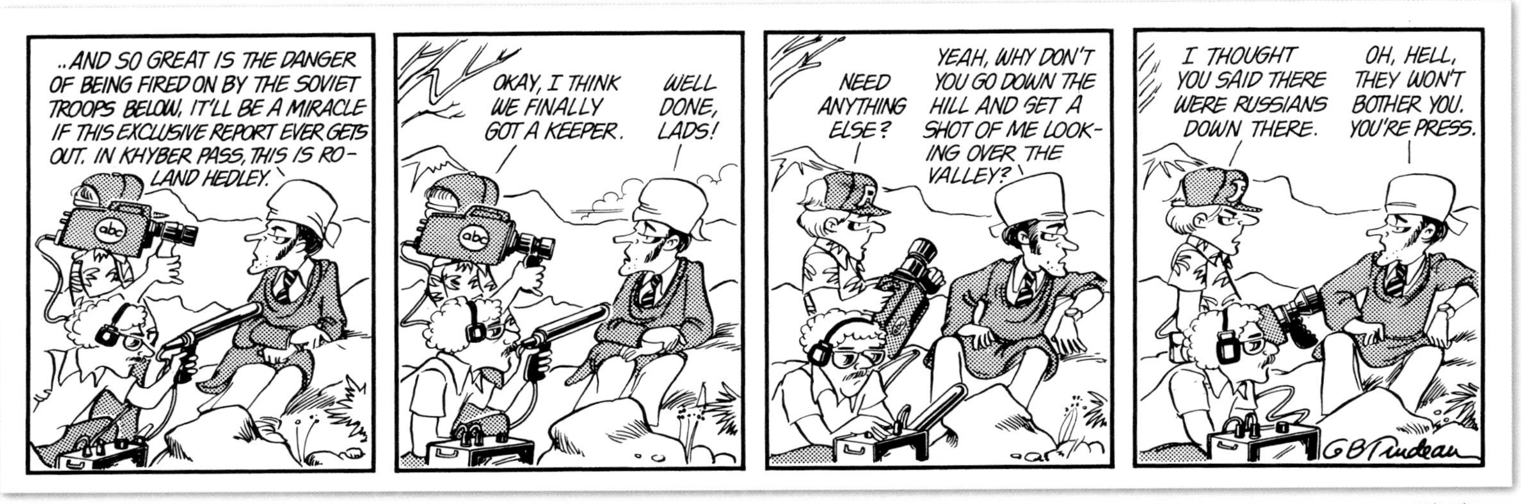
..AND SO GREAT IS THE DANGER OF BEING FIRED ON BY THE SOVIET TROOPS BELOW, IT'LL BE A MIRACLE IF THIS EXCLUSIVE REPORT EVER GETS OUT. IN KHYBER PASS, THIS IS ROLAND HEDLEY.
OKAY, I THINK WE FINALLY GOT A KEEPER.
WELL DONE, LADS!
NEED ANYTHING ELSE?
YEAH, WHY DON'T YOU GO DOWN THE HILL AND GET A SHOT OF ME LOOKING OVER THE VALLEY?
I THOUGHT YOU SAID THERE WERE RUSSIANS DOWN THERE.
OH, HELL, THEY WON'T BOTHER YOU. YOU'RE PRESS.
GBTrudeau

7/29/80

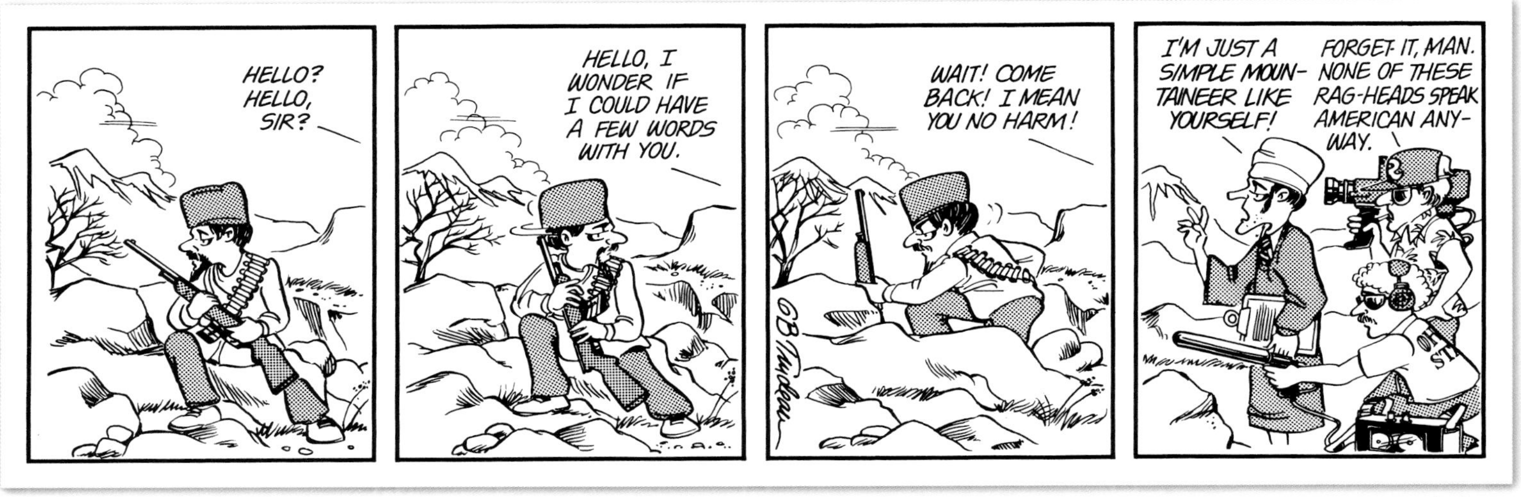
HELLO? HELLO, SIR?
HELLO, I WONDER IF I COULD HAVE A FEW WORDS WITH YOU.
WAIT! COME BACK! I MEAN YOU NO HARM!
GBTrudeau
I'M JUST A SIMPLE MOUNTAINEER LIKE YOURSELF!
FORGET IT, MAN. NONE OF THESE RAG-HEADS SPEAK AMERICAN ANYWAY.

7/30/80

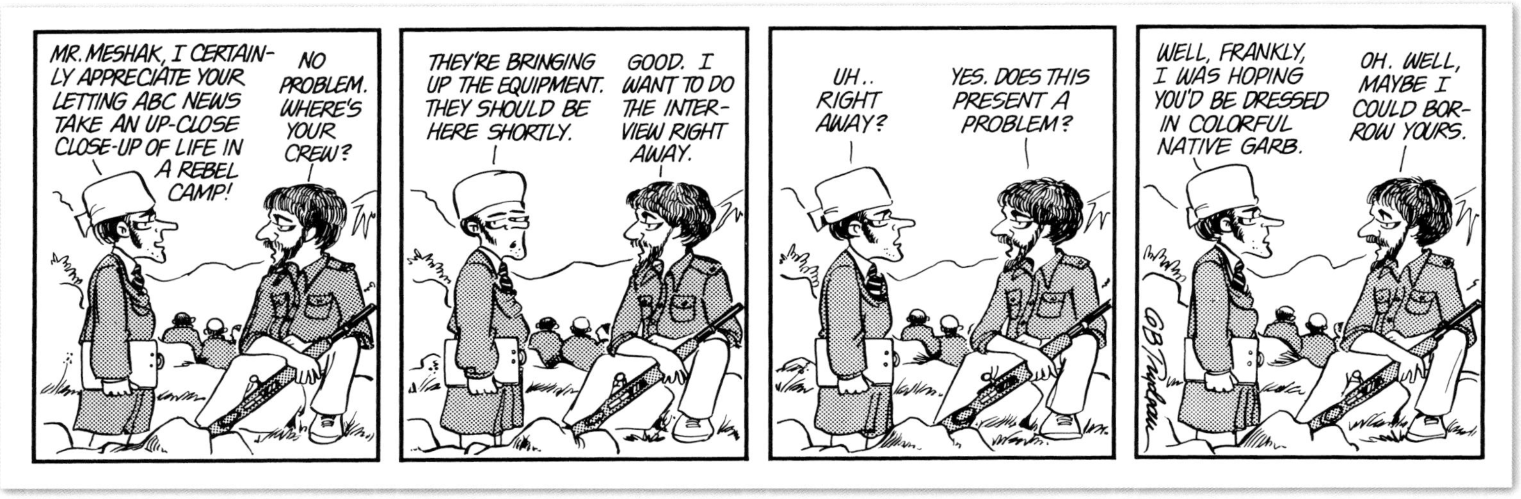
MR. MESHAK, I CERTAINLY APPRECIATE YOUR LETTING ABC NEWS TAKE AN UP-CLOSE CLOSE-UP OF LIFE IN A REBEL CAMP!
NO PROBLEM. WHERE'S YOUR CREW?
THEY'RE BRINGING UP THE EQUIPMENT. THEY SHOULD BE HERE SHORTLY.
GOOD. I WANT TO DO THE INTERVIEW RIGHT AWAY.
UH.. RIGHT AWAY?
YES. DOES THIS PRESENT A PROBLEM?
GBTrudeau
WELL, FRANKLY, I WAS HOPING YOU'D BE DRESSED IN COLORFUL NATIVE GARB.
OH. WELL, MAYBE I COULD BORROW YOURS.

8/1/80

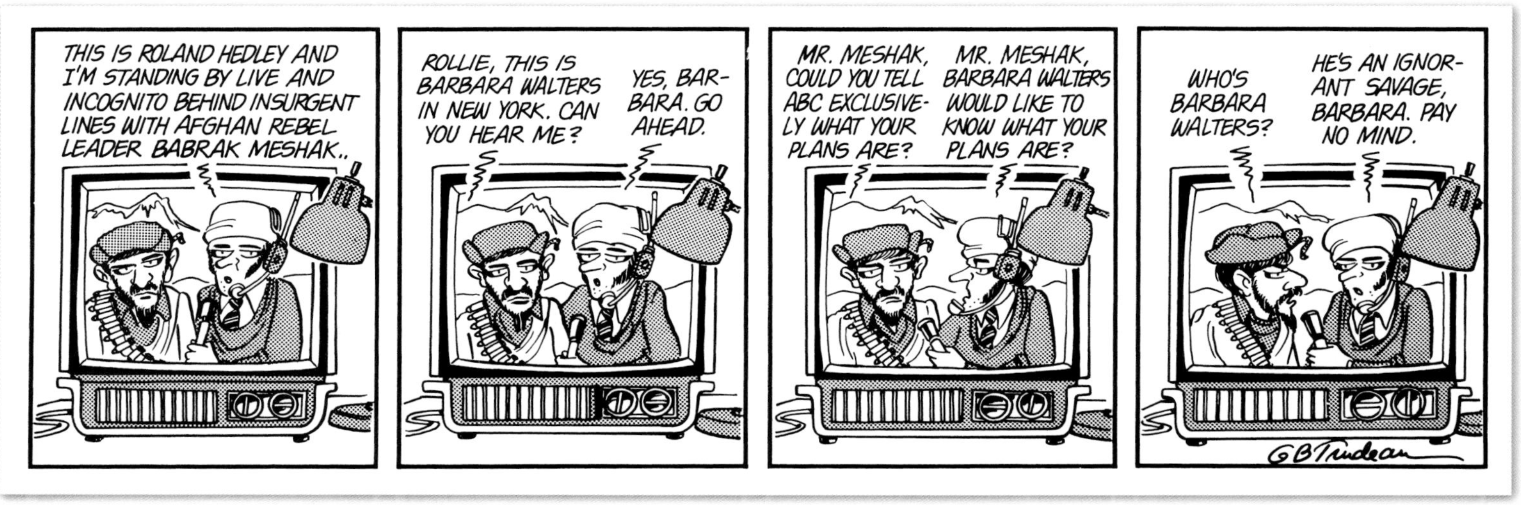
THIS IS ROLAND HEDLEY AND I'M STANDING BY LIVE AND INCOGNITO BEHIND INSURGENT LINES WITH AFGHAN REBEL LEADER BABRAK MESHAK..
ROLLIE, THIS IS BARBARA WALTERS IN NEW YORK. CAN YOU HEAR ME?
YES, BARBARA. GO AHEAD.
MR. MESHAK, COULD YOU TELL ABC EXCLUSIVELY WHAT YOUR PLANS ARE?
MR. MESHAK, BARBARA WALTERS WOULD LIKE TO KNOW WHAT YOUR PLANS ARE?
WHO'S BARBARA WALTERS?
HE'S AN IGNORANT SAVAGE, BARBARA. PAY NO MIND.
GBTrudeau

8/2/80

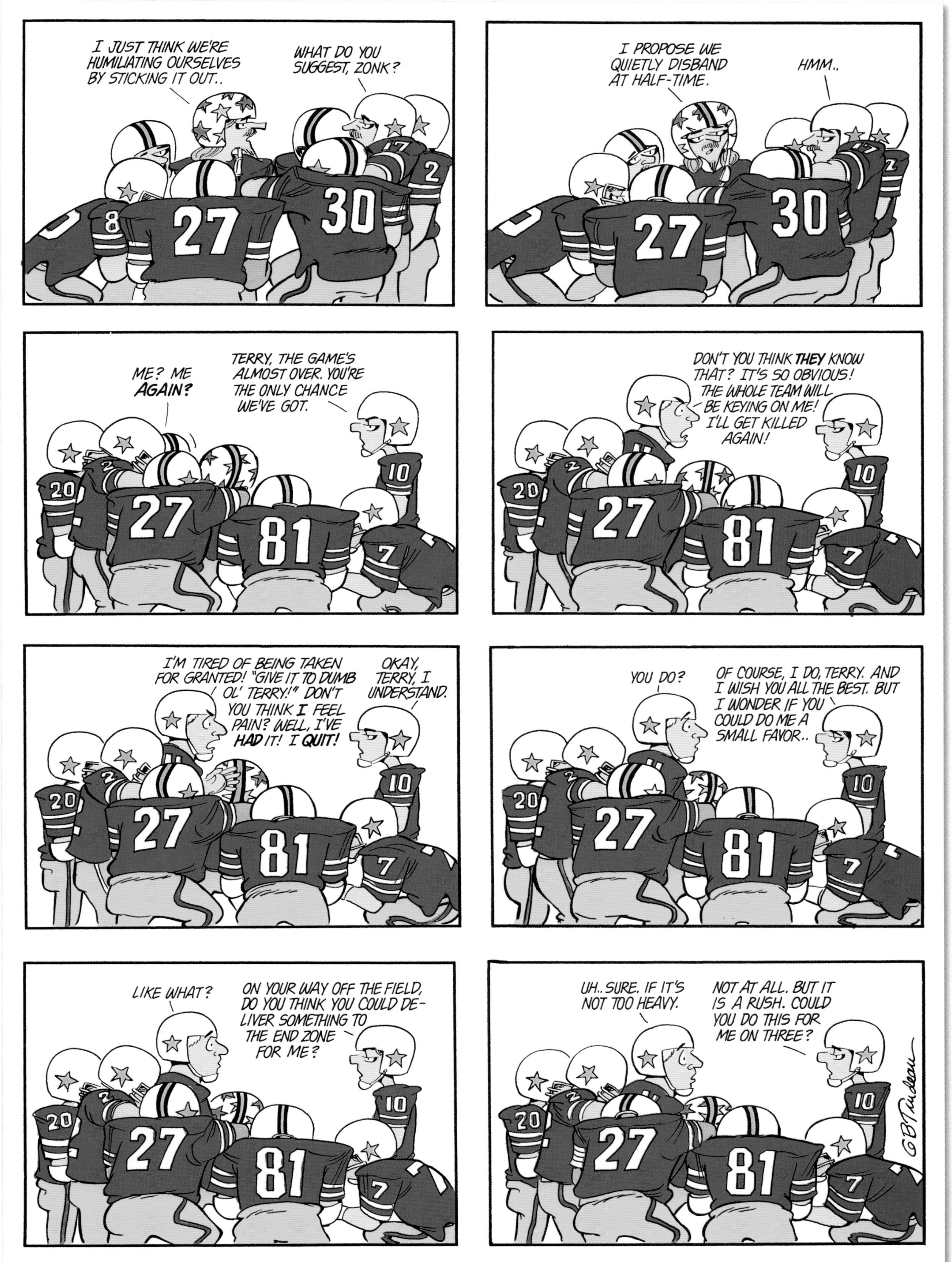
I JUST THINK WE'RE HUMILIATING OURSELVES BY STICKING IT OUT..
WHAT DO YOU SUGGEST, ZONK?
I PROPOSE WE QUIETLY DISBAND AT HALF-TIME.
HMM..
ME? ME AGAIN?
TERRY, THE GAME'S ALMOST OVER. YOU'RE THE ONLY CHANCE WE'VE GOT.
DON'T YOU THINK THEY KNOW THAT? IT'S SO OBVIOUS! THE WHOLE TEAM WILL BE KEYING ON ME! I'LL GET KILLED AGAIN!
I'M TIRED OF BEING TAKEN FOR GRANTED! "GIVE IT TO DUMB OL' TERRY!" DON'T YOU THINK I FEEL PAIN? WELL, I'VE HAD IT! I QUIT!
OKAY, TERRY, I UNDERSTAND.
YOU DO?
OF COURSE, I DO, TERRY. AND I WISH YOU ALL THE BEST. BUT I WONDER IF YOU COULD DO ME A SMALL FAVOR..
LIKE WHAT?
ON YOUR WAY OFF THE FIELD, DO YOU THINK YOU COULD DELIVER SOMETHING TO THE END ZONE FOR ME?
UH.. SURE. IF IT'S NOT TOO HEAVY.
NOT AT ALL. BUT IT IS A RUSH. COULD YOU DO THIS FOR ME ON THREE?
GBTrudeau

10/26/80

BOOPSIE

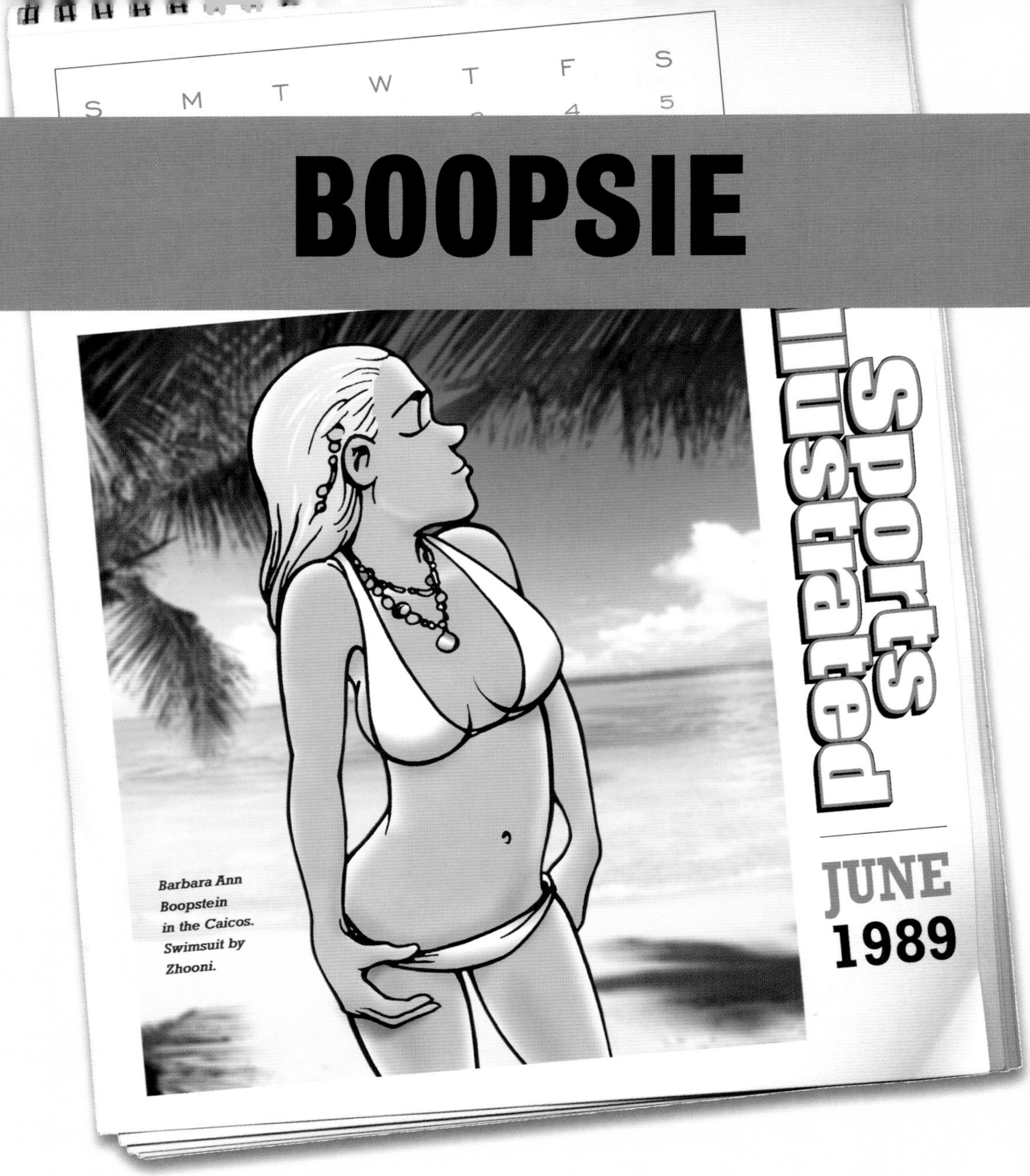
S M T W T F S
5
Sports Illustrated
JUNE
1989
Barbara Ann Boopstein in the Caicos. Swimsuit by Zhooni.

Of all the graphic notations that cartoonists have devised over the years, perhaps the most versatile is the arc-and-dot combination used for representing eyes. Jules Feiffer used it to convey emotions as varied as anger, astonishment, and despair. Charles Schulz, with a stubbier curve, rendered it to imbue his creations with wonder or apprehension or disappointment.

For me, the semicircled eye was mainly about innocence. It was an alternative to the world-weary, hooded version that I'd issued to the founding characters. When Boopsie joined the gang, she was a naïve, prefeminist bubblehead, and the iconic *Doonesbury* eye, with its hint of sophistication and detachment, looked all wrong on her. It undercut her utter lack of guile. The elegant little arc and dot seemed the way to go.

As the cast grew, so did the need to differentiate. The innocent eyes showed up again at the day care center, where all the children had them (except for Howie, whose eyes were concealed, reflecting his blinkered attitude toward girls). Thereafter, the style was used almost exclusively to convey youth or immaturity, meaning that some characters eventually outgrew it, graduating to the more ubiquitous slash eyes. Alex did so in the course of a single strip.

"B.D., I served in the Punic wars, so don't patronize me."

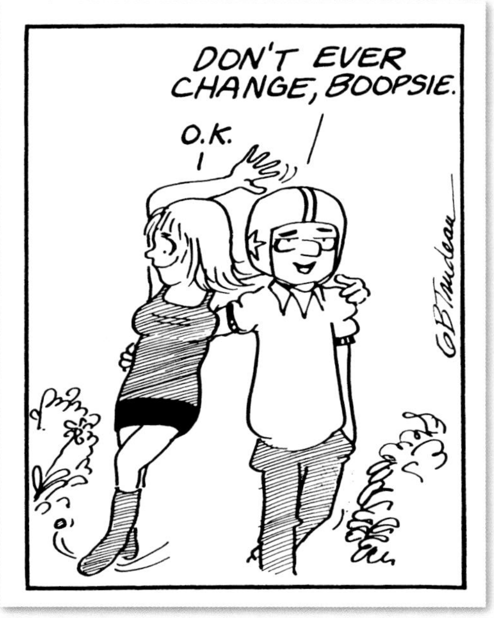
DON'T EVER CHANGE, BOOPSIE.
O.K.
GBTrudeau

Boopsie's eyes, of course, have remained unchanged, a sort of tribute to her enduring lack of cynicism. Not that the rest of her hasn't evolved. The spacey beach babe is gone, replaced by a fierce mama bear with sturdy values and abundant good sense. Even her self-esteem has deepened. Old Boopsie would have forgiven B.D. his infidelity during the Gulf War; New Boopsie insisted that he redate her and build trust back up from scratch.

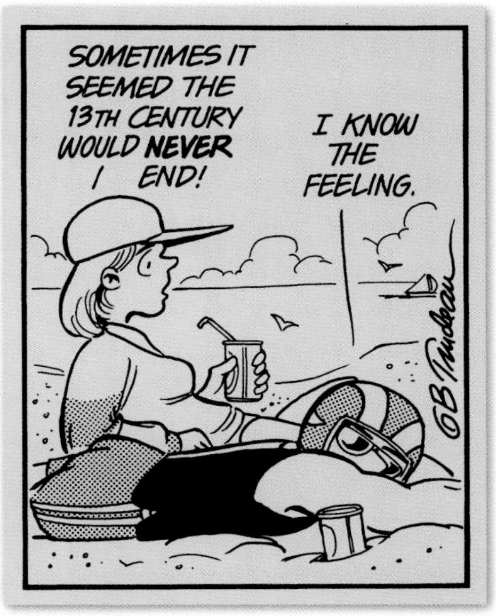
SOMETIMES IT SEEMED THE 13TH CENTURY WOULD **NEVER** END!
I KNOW THE FEELING.
GBTrudeau

I have a longtime friend named Barbara who sometimes calls herself "Boopsie." I myself would never address her that way, as Barbara is formidable in a way Boopsie is not. She's a successful New Age writer and publisher, and it was one of her company's books that transformed astrology's Harmonic Convergence of August 16–17, 1987, into a genuine media phenomenon. For Boopsie, the Convergence, which promised to usher in a new era of intergalactic peace, was the culmination of her long search for meaning along Malibu Colony's golden coastline. It had been an arduous journey, often disrupted by the appearance of Hunk-Ra, the good-looking 21,000-year-old warrior whom she channeled, so readers surely felt her pain when a long night of skywatching from her car sparked no feelings of transformation beyond a familiar urge to go shopping. Barbara, in contrast, reported that her night spent on the pyramids of Teotihuacan yielded multiple sightings of dazzling extraterrestrial vehicles streaking across the heavens.

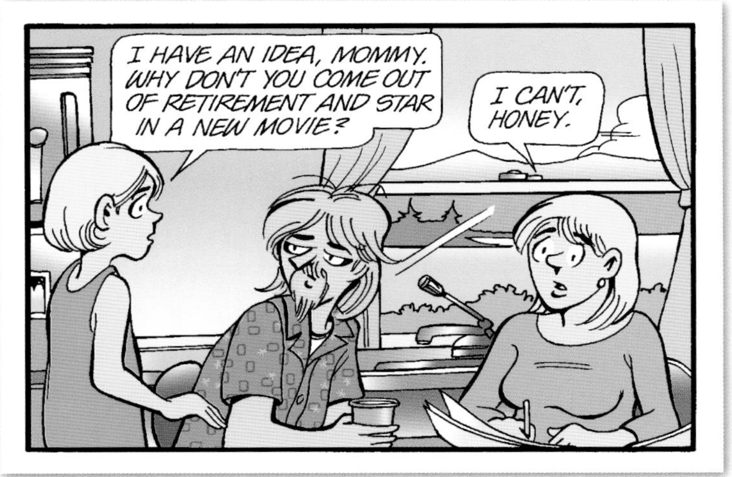
I HAVE AN IDEA, MOMMY. WHY DON'T YOU COME OUT OF RETIREMENT AND STAR IN A NEW MOVIE?
I CAN'T, HONEY.

As Louis Pasteur liked to say, fortune favors the prepared mind. Boopsie might be better primed by the time we arrive at the Mayan Long Count (a.k.a. the End of History) scheduled for December 21, 2012, but whatever the outcome, it's a safe bet she'll witness it with eyes wide open.

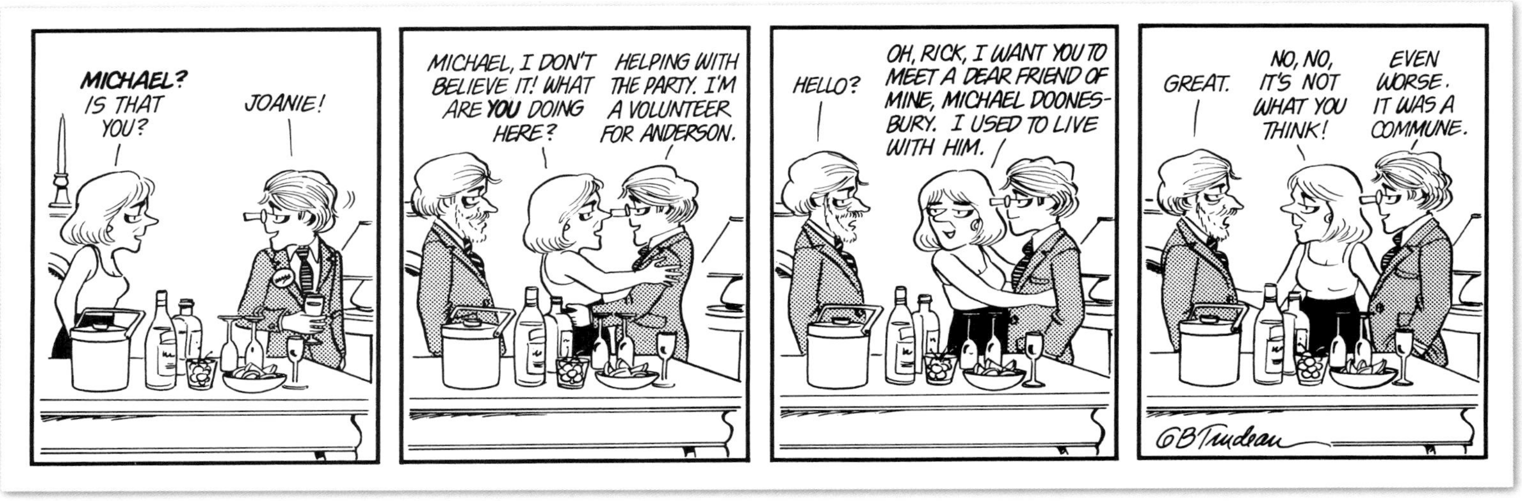
MICHAEL? IS THAT YOU?
JOANIE!
MICHAEL, I DON'T BELIEVE IT! WHAT ARE YOU DOING HERE?
HELPING WITH THE PARTY. I'M A VOLUNTEER FOR ANDERSON.
HELLO?
OH, RICK, I WANT YOU TO MEET A DEAR FRIEND OF MINE, MICHAEL DOONESBURY. I USED TO LIVE WITH HIM.
GREAT.
NO, NO, IT'S NOT WHAT YOU THINK!
EVEN WORSE. IT WAS A COMMUNE.
GBTrudeau

9/9/80

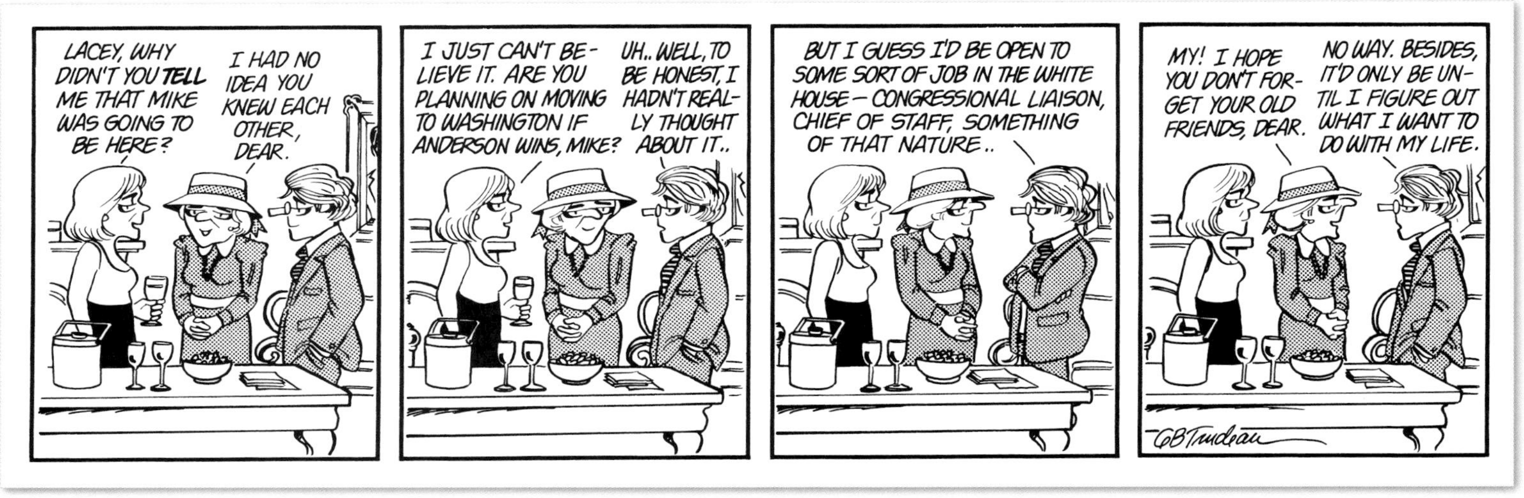
LACEY, WHY DIDN'T YOU TELL ME THAT MIKE WAS GOING TO BE HERE?
I HAD NO IDEA YOU KNEW EACH OTHER, DEAR.
I JUST CAN'T BELIEVE IT. ARE YOU PLANNING ON MOVING TO WASHINGTON IF ANDERSON WINS, MIKE?
UH.. WELL, TO BE HONEST, I HADN'T REALLY THOUGHT ABOUT IT..
BUT I GUESS I'D BE OPEN TO SOME SORT OF JOB IN THE WHITE HOUSE—CONGRESSIONAL LIAISON, CHIEF OF STAFF, SOMETHING OF THAT NATURE..
MY! I HOPE YOU DON'T FORGET YOUR OLD FRIENDS, DEAR.
NO WAY. BESIDES, IT'D ONLY BE UNTIL I FIGURE OUT WHAT I WANT TO DO WITH MY LIFE.
GBTrudeau

9/10/80

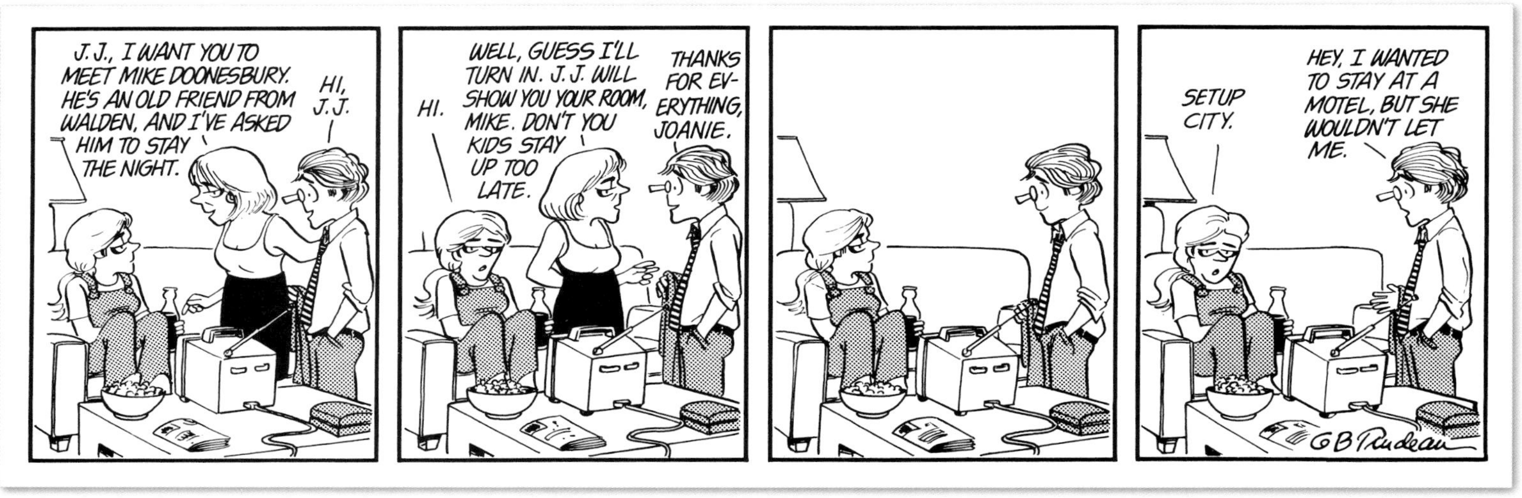
J.J., I WANT YOU TO MEET MIKE DOONESBURY. HE'S AN OLD FRIEND FROM WALDEN, AND I'VE ASKED HIM TO STAY THE NIGHT.
HI, J.J.
HI.
WELL, GUESS I'LL TURN IN. J.J. WILL SHOW YOU YOUR ROOM, MIKE. DON'T YOU KIDS STAY UP TOO LATE.
THANKS FOR EVERYTHING, JOANIE.
SETUP CITY.
HEY, I WANTED TO STAY AT A MOTEL, BUT SHE WOULDN'T LET ME.
GBTrudeau

9/15/80

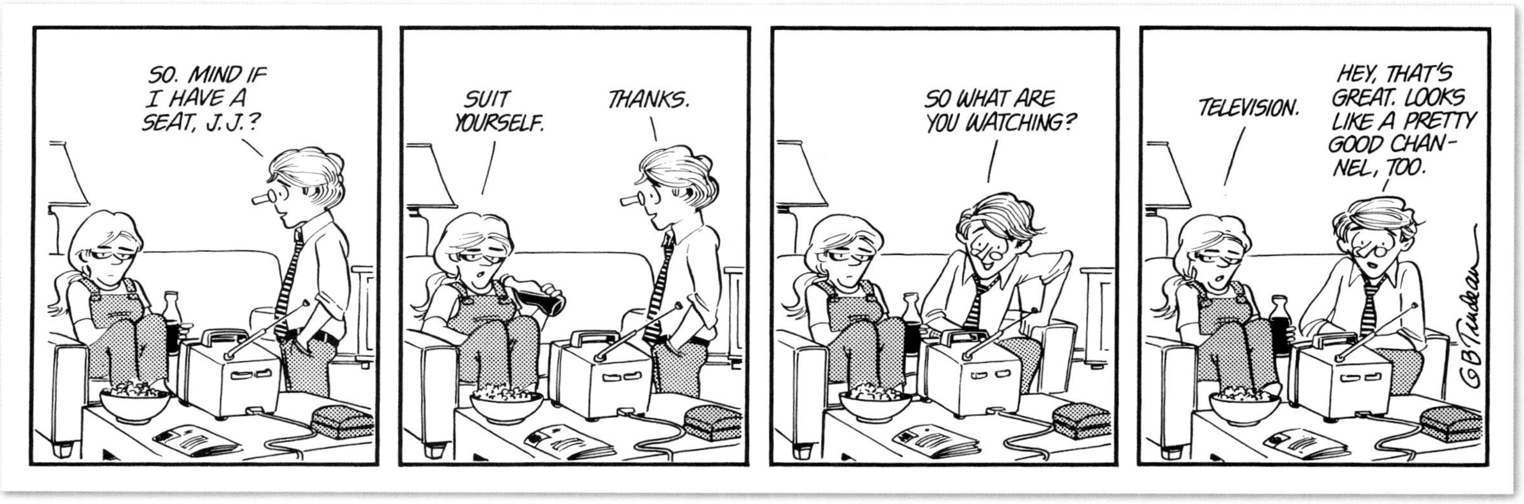
SO. MIND IF I HAVE A SEAT, J.J.?
SUIT YOURSELF.
THANKS.
SO WHAT ARE YOU WATCHING?
TELEVISION.
HEY, THAT'S GREAT. LOOKS LIKE A PRETTY GOOD CHANNEL, TOO.
GBTrudeau

9/16/80

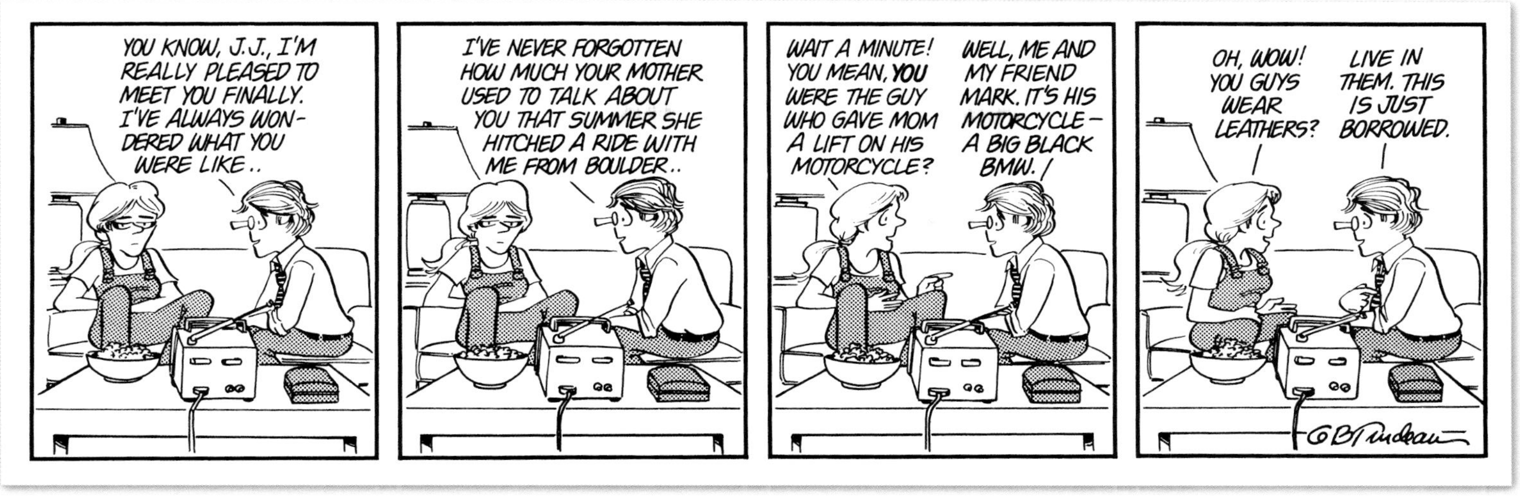
YOU KNOW, J.J., I'M REALLY PLEASED TO MEET YOU FINALLY. I'VE ALWAYS WONDERED WHAT YOU WERE LIKE..
I'VE NEVER FORGOTTEN HOW MUCH YOUR MOTHER USED TO TALK ABOUT YOU THAT SUMMER SHE HITCHED A RIDE WITH ME FROM BOULDER..
WAIT A MINUTE! YOU MEAN, YOU WERE THE GUY WHO GAVE MOM A LIFT ON HIS MOTORCYCLE?
WELL, ME AND MY FRIEND MARK. IT'S HIS MOTORCYCLE – A BIG BLACK BMW. !
OH, WOW! YOU GUYS WEAR LEATHERS?
LIVE IN THEM. THIS IS JUST BORROWED.
G B Trudeau

9/17/80

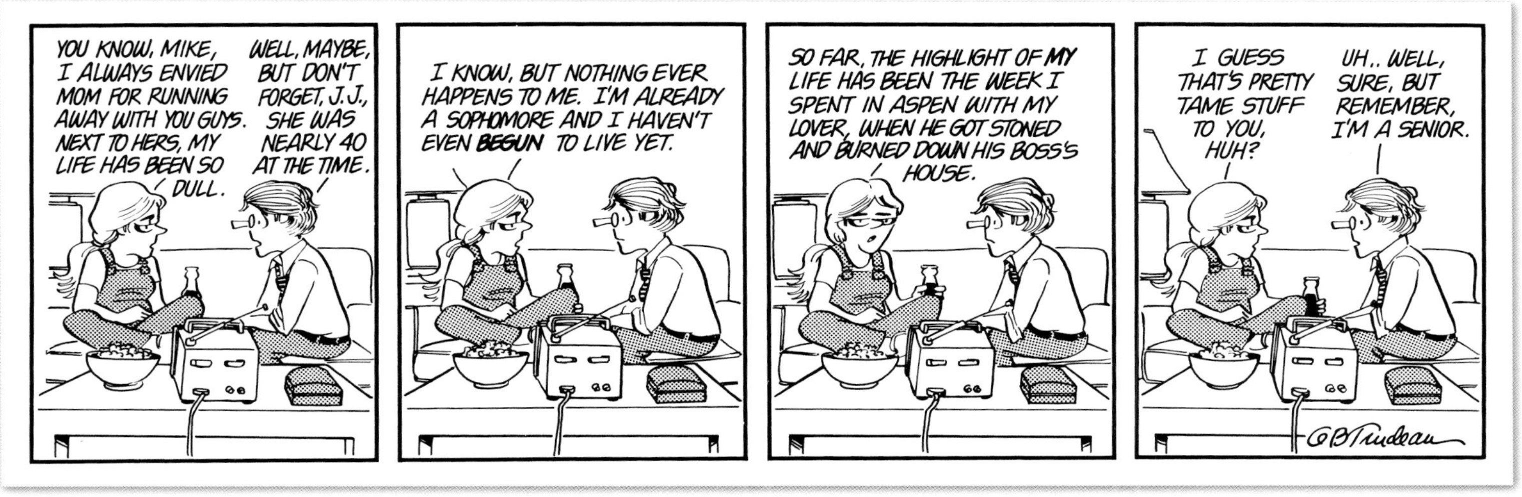
YOU KNOW, MIKE, I ALWAYS ENVIED MOM FOR RUNNING AWAY WITH YOU GUYS. NEXT TO HERS, MY LIFE HAS BEEN SO DULL.
WELL, MAYBE, BUT DON'T FORGET, J.J., SHE WAS NEARLY 40 AT THE TIME.
I KNOW, BUT NOTHING EVER HAPPENS TO ME. I'M ALREADY A SOPHOMORE AND I HAVEN'T EVEN BEGUN TO LIVE YET.
SO FAR, THE HIGHLIGHT OF MY LIFE HAS BEEN THE WEEK I SPENT IN ASPEN WITH MY LOVER, WHEN HE GOT STONED AND BURNED DOWN HIS BOSS'S HOUSE.
I GUESS THAT'S PRETTY TAME STUFF TO YOU, HUH?
UH.. WELL, SURE, BUT REMEMBER, I'M A SENIOR.
G B Trudeau

9/18/80

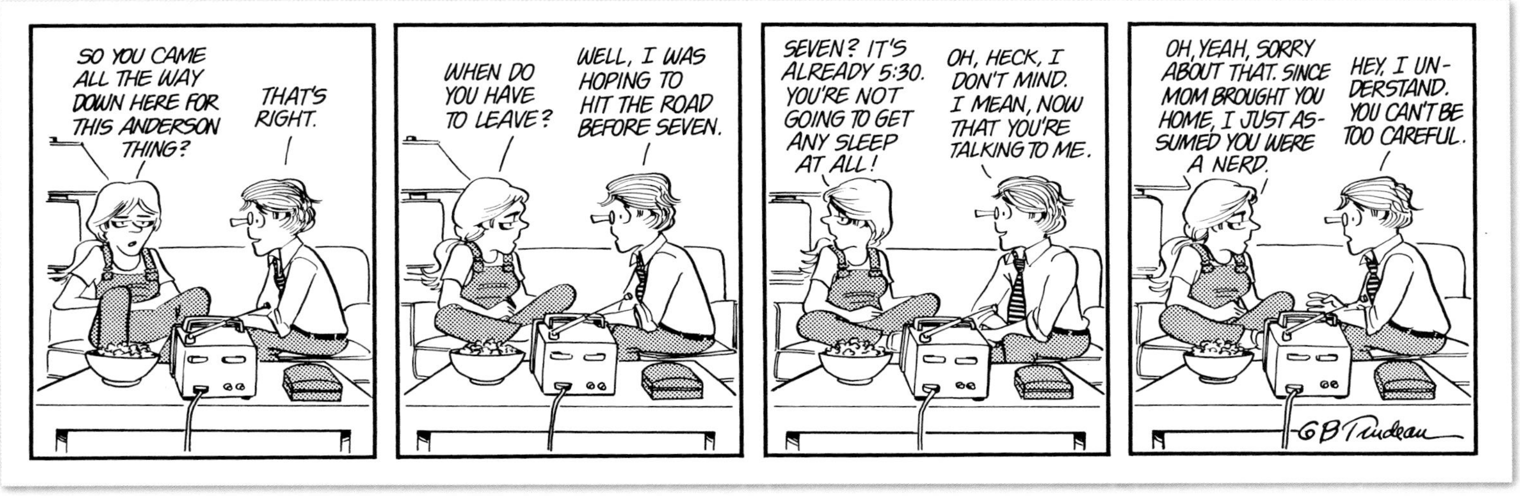
SO YOU CAME ALL THE WAY DOWN HERE FOR THIS ANDERSON THING?
THAT'S RIGHT.
WHEN DO YOU HAVE TO LEAVE?
WELL, I WAS HOPING TO HIT THE ROAD BEFORE SEVEN.
SEVEN? IT'S ALREADY 5:30. YOU'RE NOT GOING TO GET ANY SLEEP AT ALL!
OH, HECK, I DON'T MIND. I MEAN, NOW THAT YOU'RE TALKING TO ME.
OH, YEAH, SORRY ABOUT THAT. SINCE MOM BROUGHT YOU HOME, I JUST ASSUMED YOU WERE A NERD.
HEY, I UNDERSTAND. YOU CAN'T BE TOO CAREFUL.
G B Trudeau

9/19/80

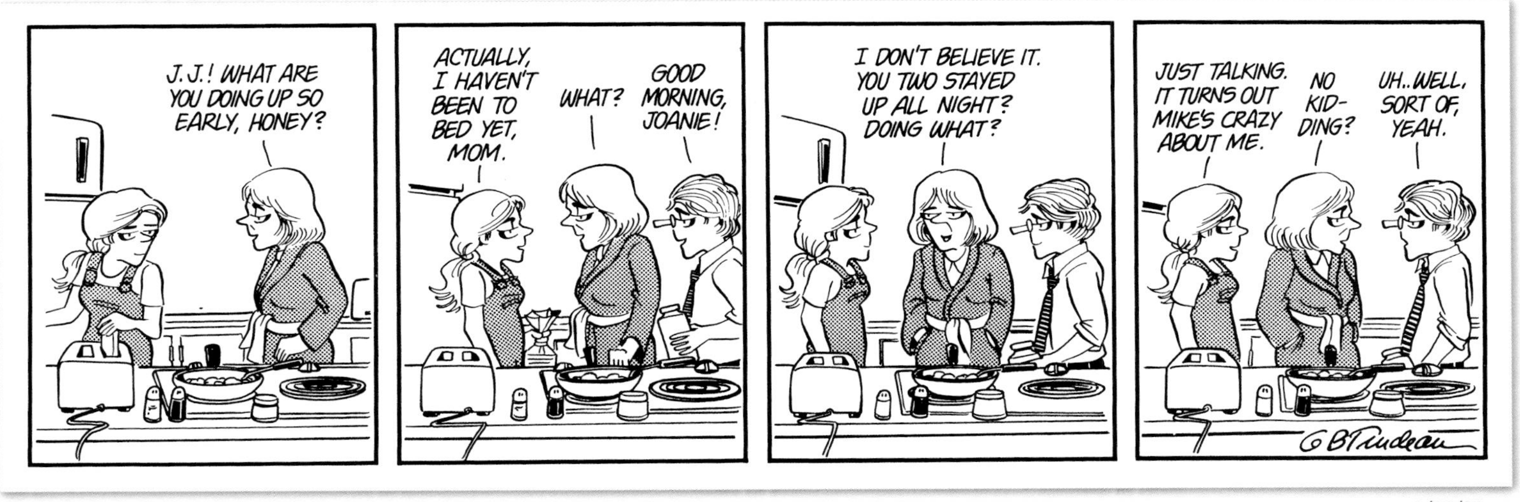
J.J.! WHAT ARE YOU DOING UP SO EARLY, HONEY?
ACTUALLY, I HAVEN'T BEEN TO BED YET, MOM.
WHAT?
GOOD MORNING, JOANIE!
I DON'T BELIEVE IT. YOU TWO STAYED UP ALL NIGHT? DOING WHAT?
JUST TALKING. IT TURNS OUT MIKE'S CRAZY ABOUT ME.
NO KIDDING?
UH.. WELL, SORT OF, YEAH.
G B Trudeau

9/20/80

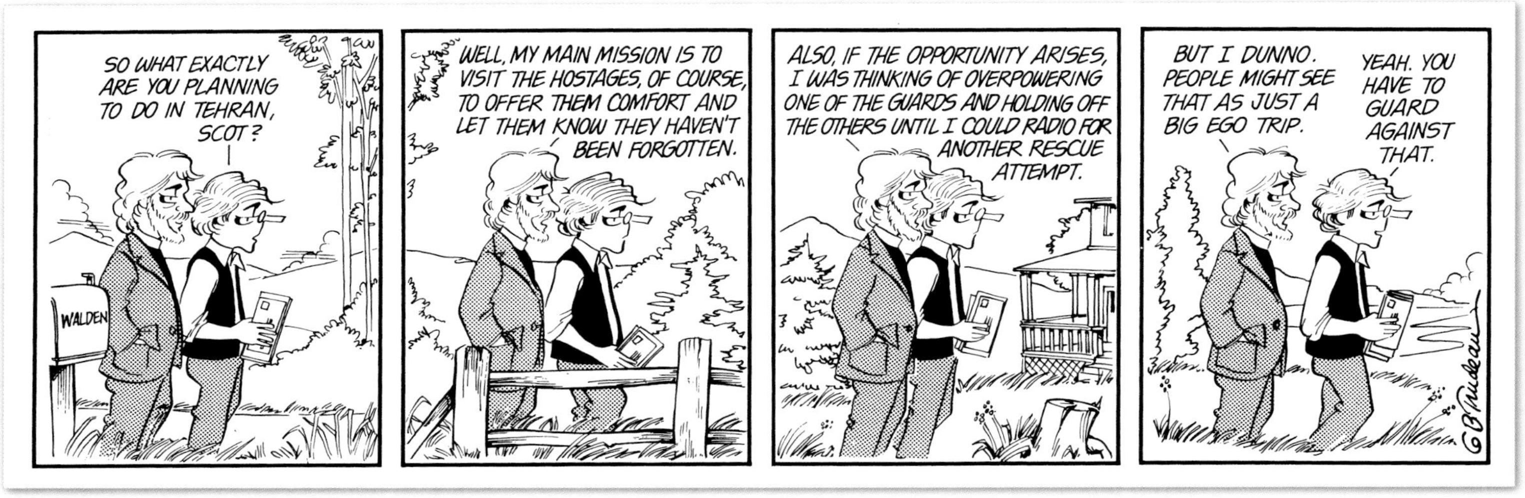
SO WHAT EXACTLY ARE YOU PLANNING TO DO IN TEHRAN, SCOT?
WALDEN
WELL, MY MAIN MISSION IS TO VISIT THE HOSTAGES, OF COURSE, TO OFFER THEM COMFORT AND LET THEM KNOW THEY HAVEN'T BEEN FORGOTTEN.
ALSO, IF THE OPPORTUNITY ARISES, I WAS THINKING OF OVERPOWERING ONE OF THE GUARDS AND HOLDING OFF THE OTHERS UNTIL I COULD RADIO FOR ANOTHER RESCUE ATTEMPT.
BUT I DUNNO. PEOPLE MIGHT SEE THAT AS JUST A BIG EGO TRIP.
YEAH. YOU HAVE TO GUARD AGAINST THAT.
GBTrudeau

5/27/80

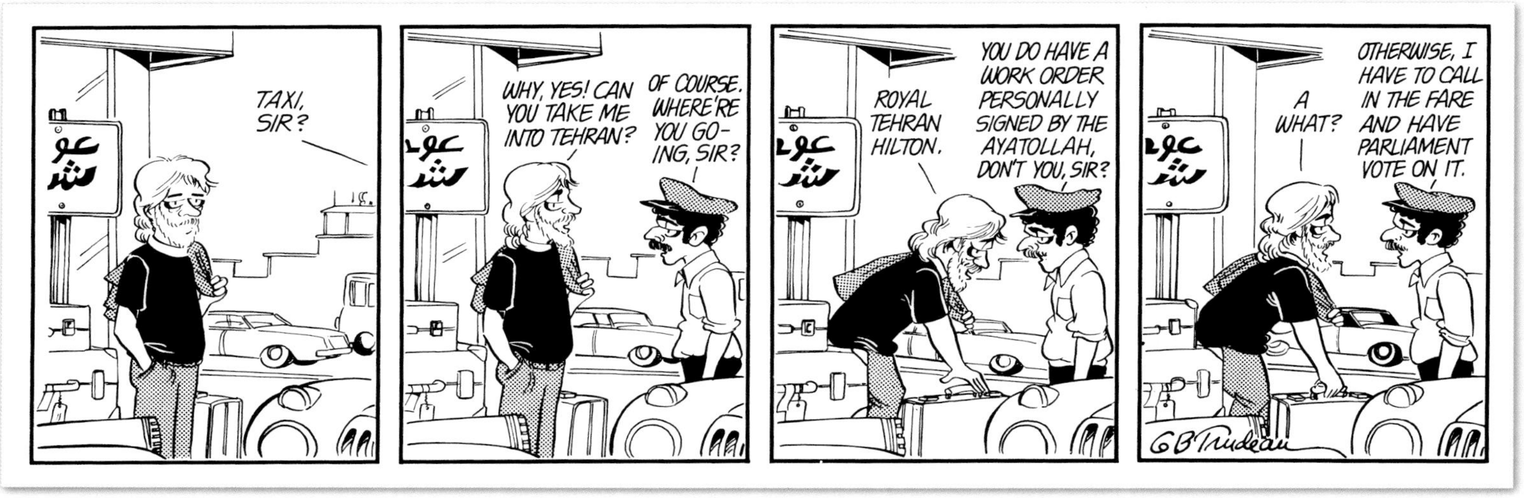
TAXI, SIR?
WHY, YES! CAN YOU TAKE ME INTO TEHRAN?
OF COURSE. WHERE'RE YOU GOING, SIR?
ROYAL TEHRAN HILTON.
YOU DO HAVE A WORK ORDER PERSONALLY SIGNED BY THE AYATOLLAH, DON'T YOU, SIR?
A WHAT?
OTHERWISE, I HAVE TO CALL IN THE FARE AND HAVE PARLIAMENT VOTE ON IT.
GBTrudeau

5/30/80

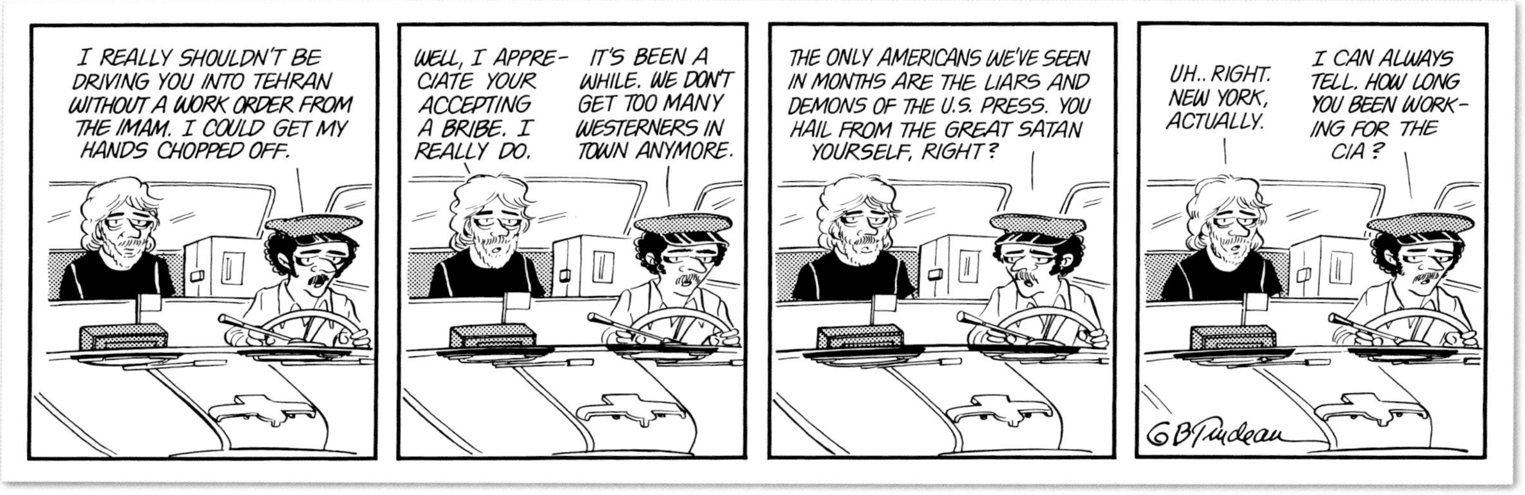
I REALLY SHOULDN'T BE DRIVING YOU INTO TEHRAN WITHOUT A WORK ORDER FROM THE IMAM. I COULD GET MY HANDS CHOPPED OFF.
WELL, I APPRECIATE YOUR ACCEPTING A BRIBE. I REALLY DO.
IT'S BEEN A WHILE. WE DON'T GET TOO MANY WESTERNERS IN TOWN ANYMORE.
THE ONLY AMERICANS WE'VE SEEN IN MONTHS ARE THE LIARS AND DEMONS OF THE U.S. PRESS. YOU HAIL FROM THE GREAT SATAN YOURSELF, RIGHT?
UH.. RIGHT. NEW YORK, ACTUALLY.
I CAN ALWAYS TELL. HOW LONG YOU BEEN WORKING FOR THE CIA?
GBTrudeau

5/31/80

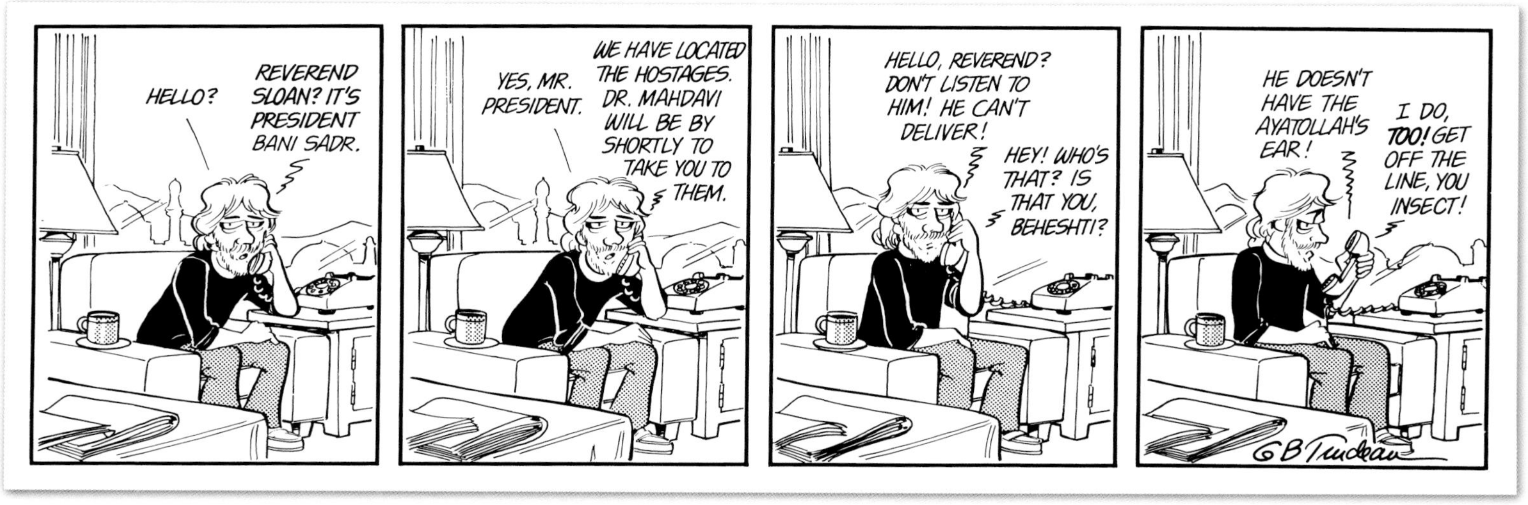
HELLO?
REVEREND SLOAN? IT'S PRESIDENT BANI SADR.
YES, MR. PRESIDENT.
WE HAVE LOCATED THE HOSTAGES. DR. MAHDAVI WILL BE BY SHORTLY TO TAKE YOU TO THEM.
HELLO, REVEREND? DON'T LISTEN TO HIM! HE CAN'T DELIVER!
HEY! WHO'S THAT? IS THAT YOU, BEHESHTI?
HE DOESN'T HAVE THE AYATOLLAH'S EAR!
I DO, TOO! GET OFF THE LINE, YOU INSECT!
GBTrudeau

6/16/80

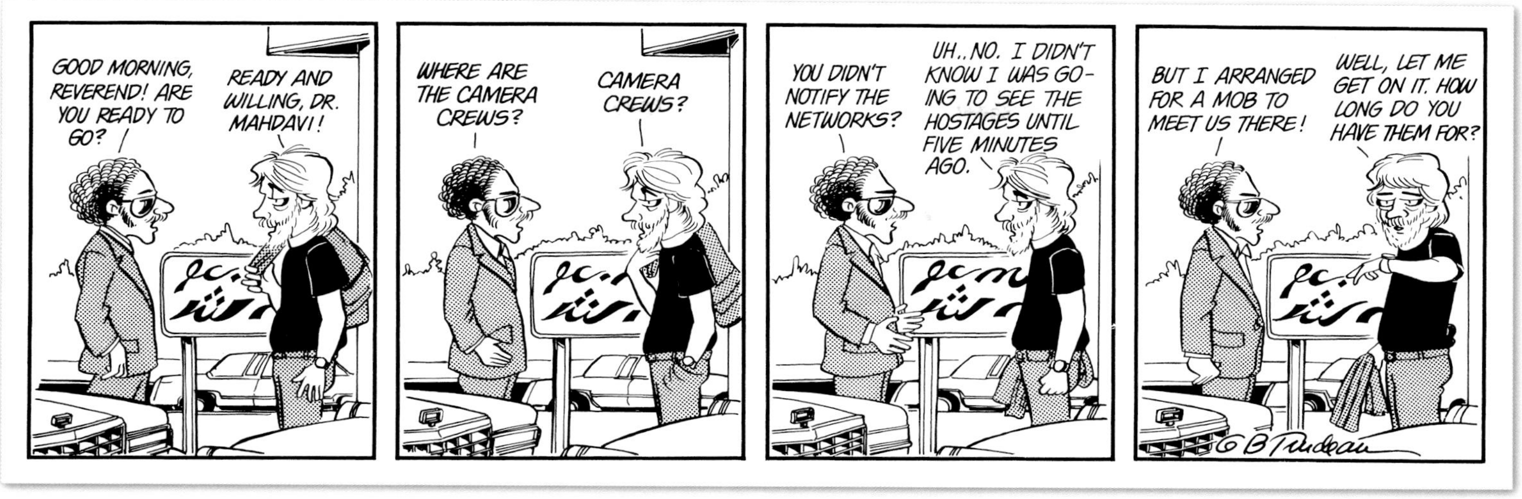
GOOD MORNING, REVEREND! ARE YOU READY TO GO?
READY AND WILLING, DR. MAHDAVI!
WHERE ARE THE CAMERA CREWS?
CAMERA CREWS?
YOU DIDN'T NOTIFY THE NETWORKS?
UH.. NO. I DIDN'T KNOW I WAS GOING TO SEE THE HOSTAGES UNTIL FIVE MINUTES AGO.
BUT I ARRANGED FOR A MOB TO MEET US THERE!
WELL, LET ME GET ON IT. HOW LONG DO YOU HAVE THEM FOR?
GB Trudeau

6/17/80

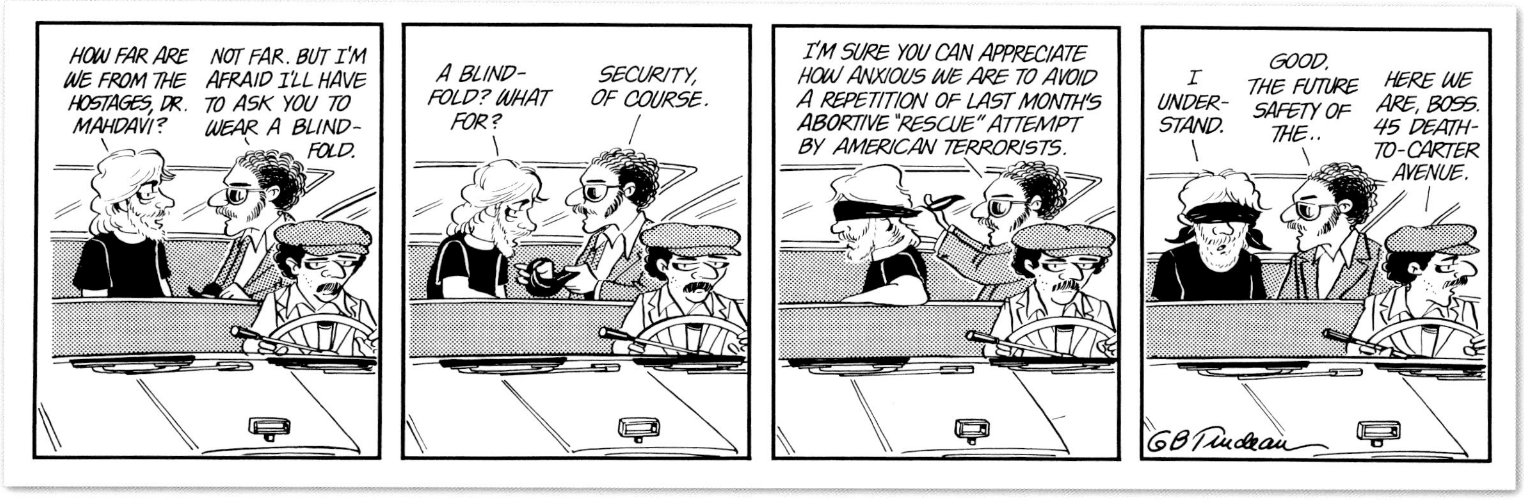
HOW FAR ARE WE FROM THE HOSTAGES, DR. MAHDAVI?
NOT FAR. BUT I'M AFRAID I'LL HAVE TO ASK YOU TO WEAR A BLIND-FOLD.
A BLIND-FOLD? WHAT FOR?
SECURITY, OF COURSE.
I'M SURE YOU CAN APPRECIATE HOW ANXIOUS WE ARE TO AVOID A REPETITION OF LAST MONTH'S ABORTIVE "RESCUE" ATTEMPT BY AMERICAN TERRORISTS.
I UNDER-STAND.
GOOD. THE FUTURE SAFETY OF THE..
HERE WE ARE, BOSS. 45 DEATH-TO-CARTER AVENUE.
GB Trudeau

6/18/80

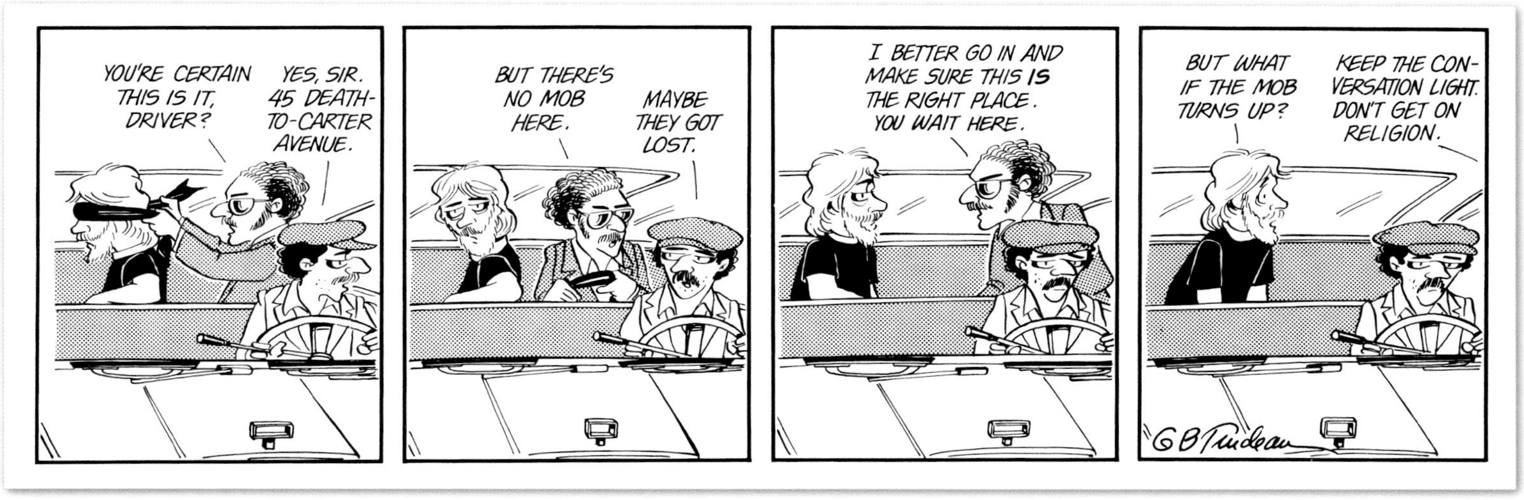
YOU'RE CERTAIN THIS IS IT, DRIVER?
YES, SIR. 45 DEATH-TO-CARTER AVENUE.
BUT THERE'S NO MOB HERE.
MAYBE THEY GOT LOST.
I BETTER GO IN AND MAKE SURE THIS IS THE RIGHT PLACE. YOU WAIT HERE.
BUT WHAT IF THE MOB TURNS UP?
KEEP THE CONVERSATION LIGHT. DON'T GET ON RELIGION.
GB Trudeau

6/19/80

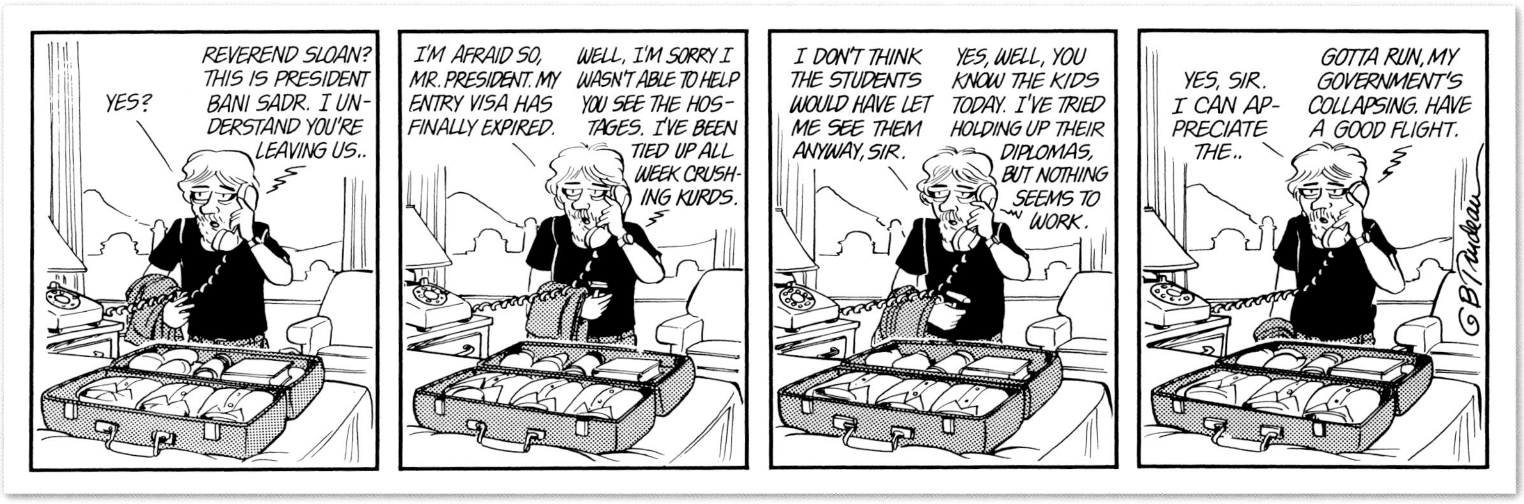
YES?
REVEREND SLOAN? THIS IS PRESIDENT BANI SADR. I UNDERSTAND YOU'RE LEAVING US..
I'M AFRAID SO, MR. PRESIDENT. MY ENTRY VISA HAS FINALLY EXPIRED.
WELL, I'M SORRY I WASN'T ABLE TO HELP YOU SEE THE HOSTAGES. I'VE BEEN TIED UP ALL WEEK CRUSHING KURDS.
I DON'T THINK THE STUDENTS WOULD HAVE LET ME SEE THEM ANYWAY, SIR.
YES, WELL, YOU KNOW THE KIDS TODAY. I'VE TRIED HOLDING UP THEIR DIPLOMAS, BUT NOTHING SEEMS TO WORK.
YES, SIR. I CAN APPRECIATE THE..
GOTTA RUN, MY GOVERNMENT'S COLLAPSING. HAVE A GOOD FLIGHT.
GB Trudeau

6/21/80

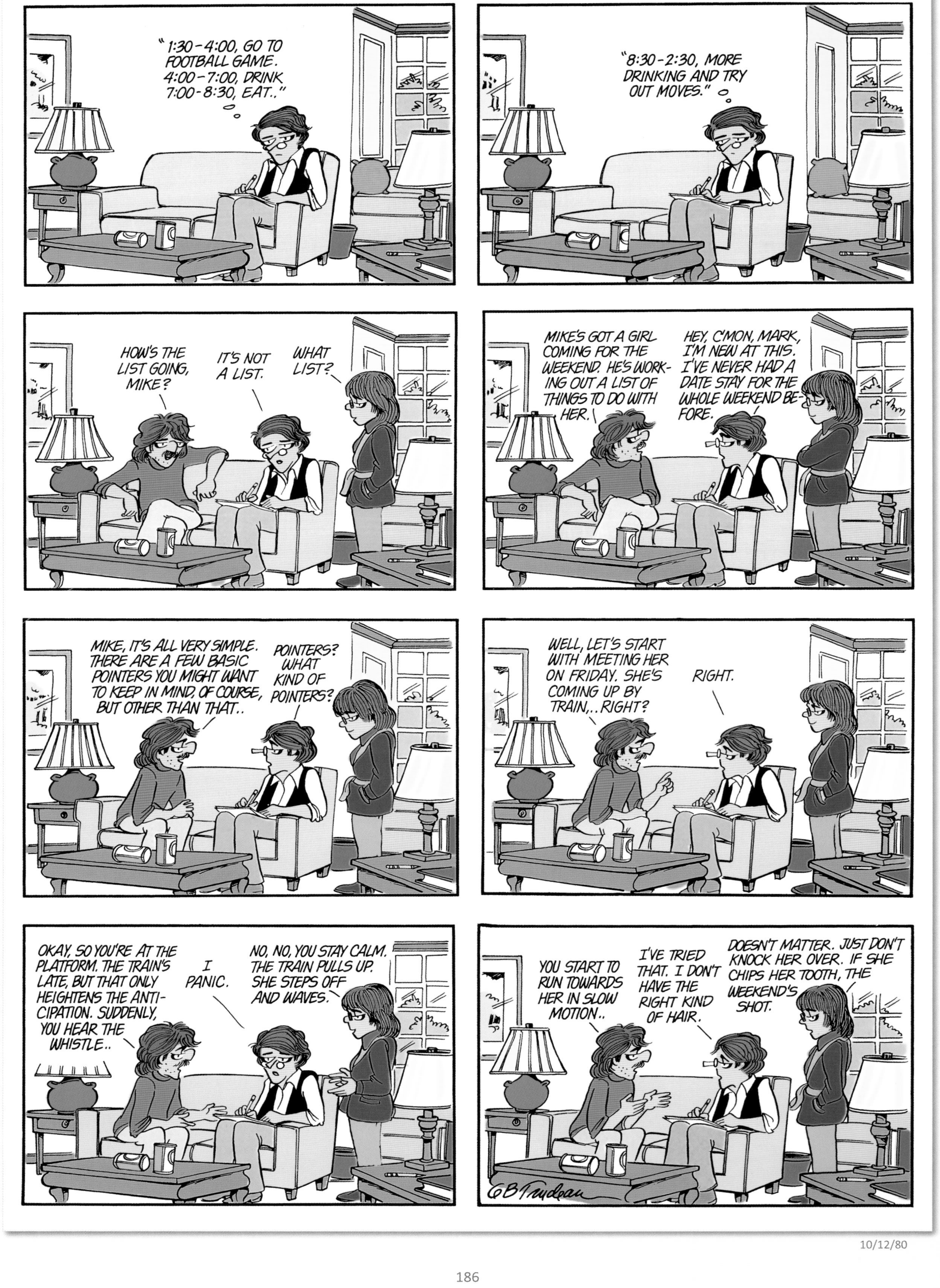
"1:30-4:00, GO TO FOOTBALL GAME. 4:00-7:00, DRINK 7:00-8:30, EAT.."
"8:30-2:30, MORE DRINKING AND TRY OUT MOVES."
HOW'S THE LIST GOING, MIKE?
IT'S NOT A LIST.
WHAT LIST?
MIKE'S GOT A GIRL COMING FOR THE WEEKEND. HE'S WORKING OUT A LIST OF THINGS TO DO WITH HER.
HEY, C'MON, MARK, I'M NEW AT THIS. I'VE NEVER HAD A DATE STAY FOR THE WHOLE WEEKEND BEFORE.
MIKE, IT'S ALL VERY SIMPLE. THERE ARE A FEW BASIC POINTERS YOU MIGHT WANT TO KEEP IN MIND, OF COURSE, BUT OTHER THAN THAT..
POINTERS? WHAT KIND OF POINTERS?
WELL, LET'S START WITH MEETING HER ON FRIDAY. SHE'S COMING UP BY TRAIN,.. RIGHT?
RIGHT.
OKAY, SO YOU'RE AT THE PLATFORM. THE TRAIN'S LATE, BUT THAT ONLY HEIGHTENS THE ANTICIPATION. SUDDENLY, YOU HEAR THE WHISTLE..
I PANIC.
NO, NO, YOU STAY CALM. THE TRAIN PULLS UP. SHE STEPS OFF AND WAVES.
YOU START TO RUN TOWARDS HER IN SLOW MOTION..
I'VE TRIED THAT. I DON'T HAVE THE RIGHT KIND OF HAIR.
DOESN'T MATTER. JUST DON'T KNOCK HER OVER. IF SHE CHIPS HER TOOTH, THE WEEKEND'S SHOT.
GB Trudeau

10/12/80

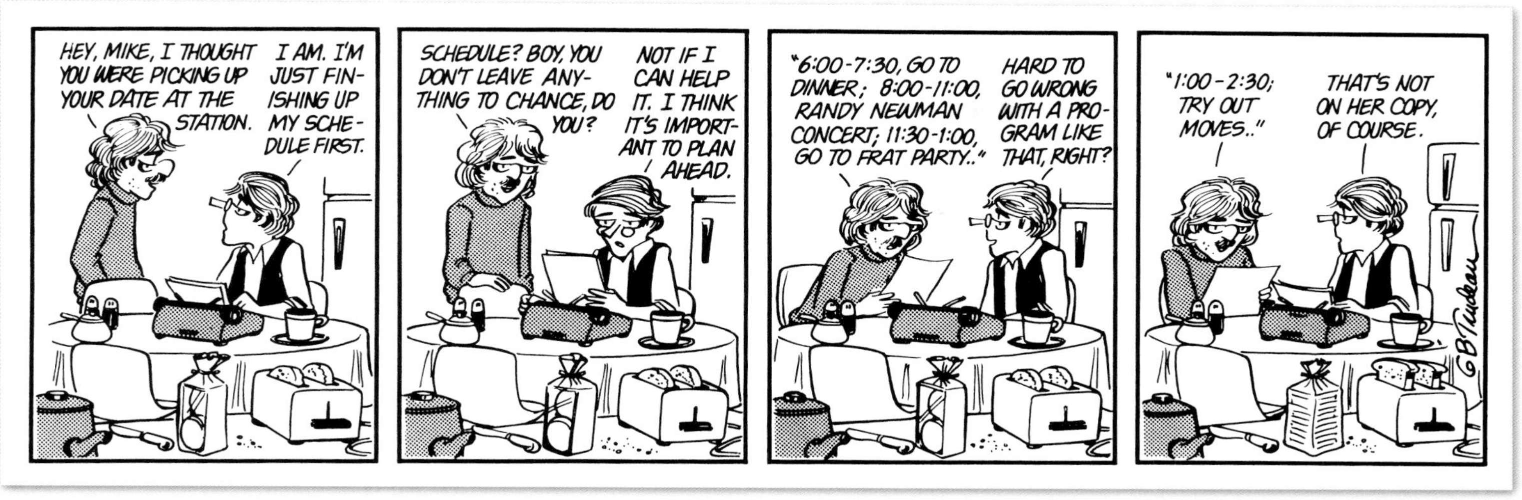
HEY, MIKE, I THOUGHT YOU WERE PICKING UP YOUR DATE AT THE STATION.
I AM. I'M JUST FINISHING UP MY SCHEDULE FIRST.
SCHEDULE? BOY, YOU DON'T LEAVE ANYTHING TO CHANCE, DO YOU?
NOT IF I CAN HELP IT. I THINK IT'S IMPORTANT TO PLAN AHEAD.
"6:00-7:30, GO TO DINNER; 8:00-11:00, RANDY NEWMAN CONCERT; 11:30-1:00, GO TO FRAT PARTY.."
HARD TO GO WRONG WITH A PROGRAM LIKE THAT, RIGHT?
"1:00-2:30; TRY OUT MOVES.."
THAT'S NOT ON HER COPY, OF COURSE.
G B Trudeau

10/13/80

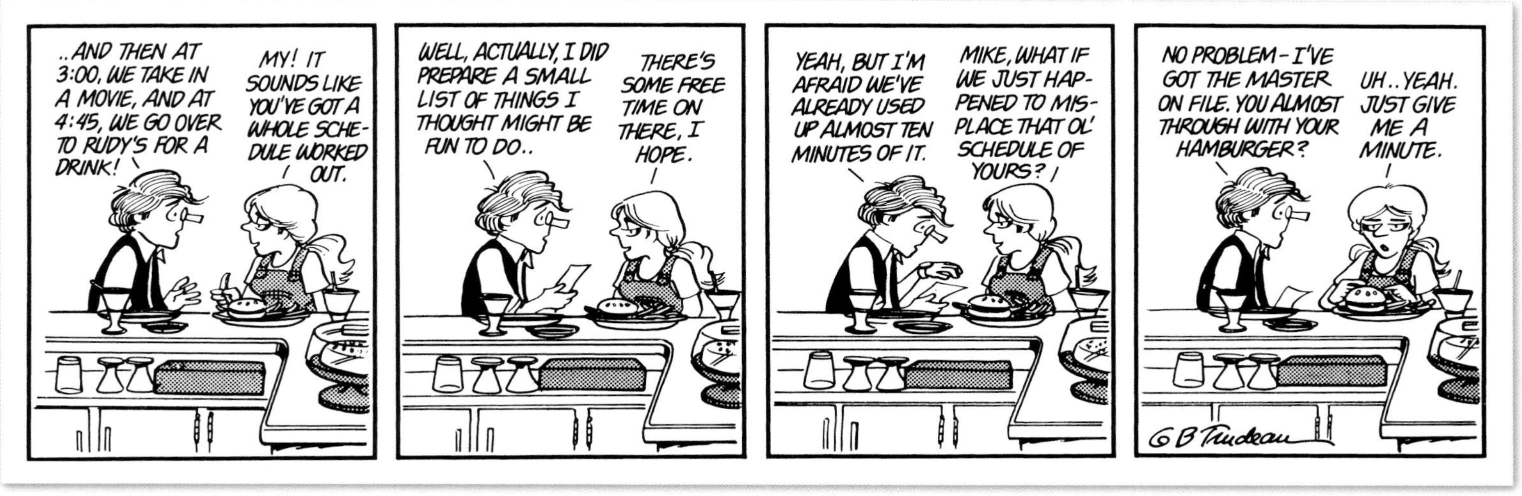
..AND THEN AT 3:00, WE TAKE IN A MOVIE, AND AT 4:45, WE GO OVER TO RUDY'S FOR A DRINK!
MY! IT SOUNDS LIKE YOU'VE GOT A WHOLE SCHEDULE WORKED OUT.
WELL, ACTUALLY, I DID PREPARE A SMALL LIST OF THINGS I THOUGHT MIGHT BE FUN TO DO..
THERE'S SOME FREE TIME ON THERE, I HOPE.
YEAH, BUT I'M AFRAID WE'VE ALREADY USED UP ALMOST TEN MINUTES OF IT.
MIKE, WHAT IF WE JUST HAPPENED TO MISPLACE THAT OL' SCHEDULE OF YOURS?
NO PROBLEM - I'VE GOT THE MASTER ON FILE. YOU ALMOST THROUGH WITH YOUR HAMBURGER?
UH.. YEAH. JUST GIVE ME A MINUTE.
G B Trudeau

10/15/80

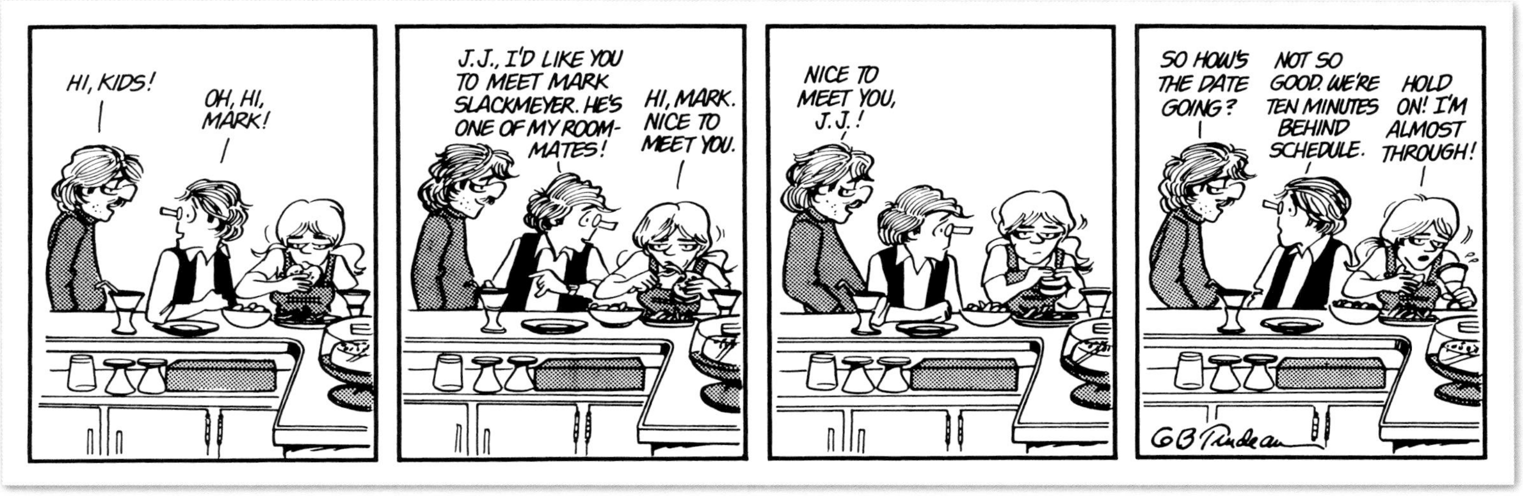
HI, KIDS!
OH, HI, MARK!
J.J., I'D LIKE YOU TO MEET MARK SLACKMEYER. HE'S ONE OF MY ROOMMATES!
HI, MARK. NICE TO MEET YOU.
NICE TO MEET YOU, J.J.!
SO HOW'S THE DATE GOING?
NOT SO GOOD. WE'RE TEN MINUTES BEHIND SCHEDULE.
HOLD ON! I'M ALMOST THROUGH!
G B Trudeau

10/16/80

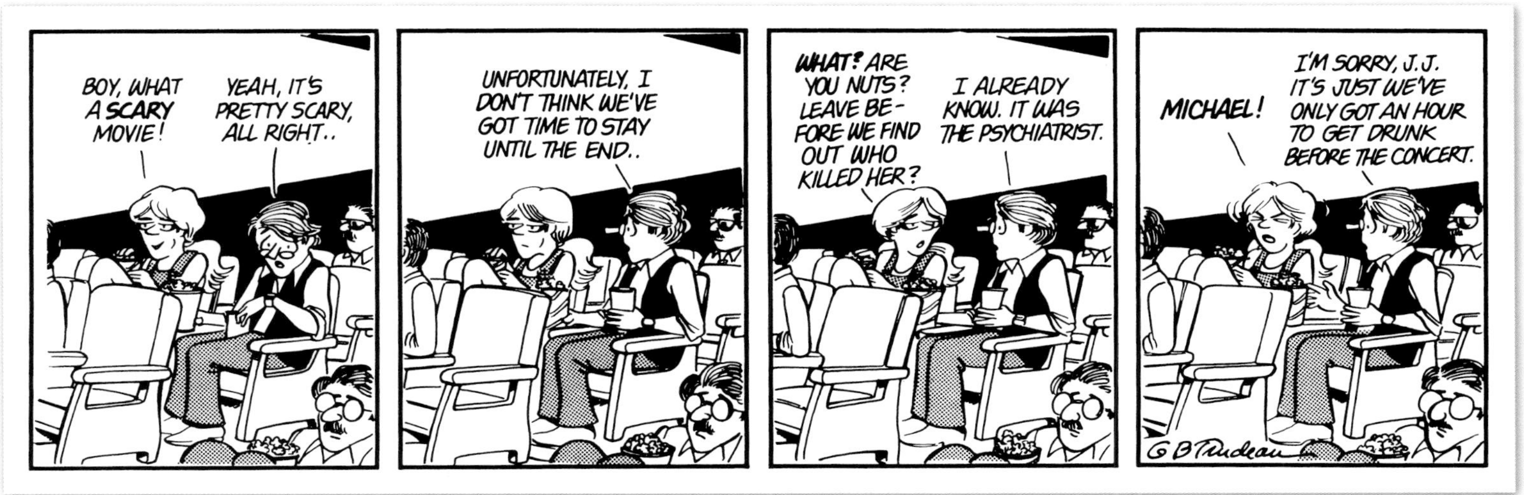
BOY, WHAT A SCARY MOVIE!
YEAH, IT'S PRETTY SCARY, ALL RIGHT..
UNFORTUNATELY, I DON'T THINK WE'VE GOT TIME TO STAY UNTIL THE END..
WHAT? ARE YOU NUTS? LEAVE BEFORE WE FIND OUT WHO KILLED HER?
I ALREADY KNOW. IT WAS THE PSYCHIATRIST.
MICHAEL!
I'M SORRY, J.J. IT'S JUST WE'VE ONLY GOT AN HOUR TO GET DRUNK BEFORE THE CONCERT.
G B Trudeau

10/17/80

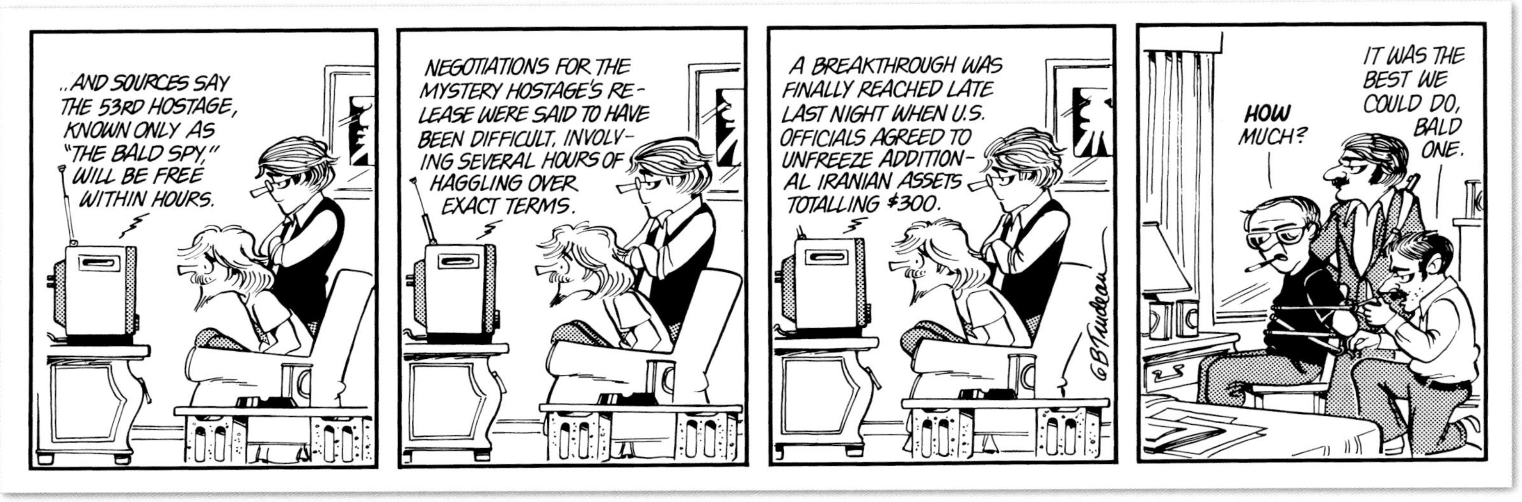
..AND SOURCES SAY THE 53RD HOSTAGE, KNOWN ONLY AS "THE BALD SPY," WILL BE FREE WITHIN HOURS.
NEGOTIATIONS FOR THE MYSTERY HOSTAGE'S RELEASE WERE SAID TO HAVE BEEN DIFFICULT, INVOLVING SEVERAL HOURS OF HAGGLING OVER EXACT TERMS.
A BREAKTHROUGH WAS FINALLY REACHED LATE LAST NIGHT WHEN U.S. OFFICIALS AGREED TO UNFREEZE ADDITIONAL IRANIAN ASSETS TOTALLING $300.
HOW MUCH?
IT WAS THE BEST WE COULD DO, BALD ONE.

1/27/81

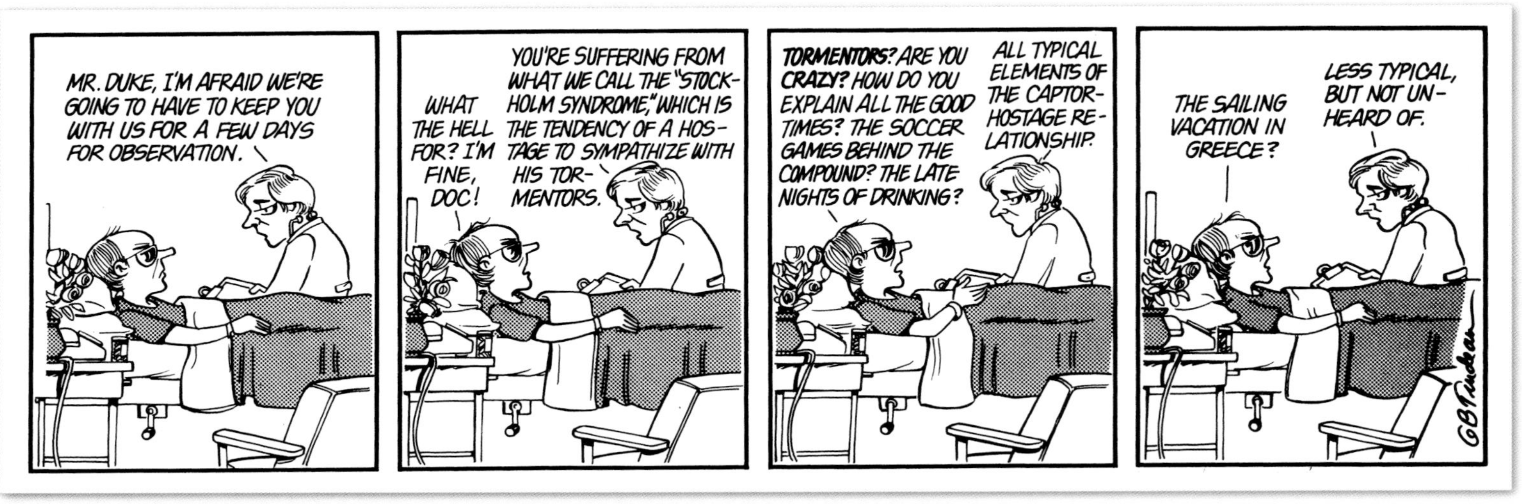
MR. DUKE, I'M AFRAID WE'RE GOING TO HAVE TO KEEP YOU WITH US FOR A FEW DAYS FOR OBSERVATION.
WHAT THE HELL FOR? I'M FINE, DOC!
YOU'RE SUFFERING FROM WHAT WE CALL THE "STOCKHOLM SYNDROME," WHICH IS THE TENDENCY OF A HOSTAGE TO SYMPATHIZE WITH HIS TORMENTORS.
TORMENTORS? ARE YOU CRAZY? HOW DO YOU EXPLAIN ALL THE GOOD TIMES? THE SOCCER GAMES BEHIND THE COMPOUND? THE LATE NIGHTS OF DRINKING?
ALL TYPICAL ELEMENTS OF THE CAPTOR-HOSTAGE RELATIONSHIP.
THE SAILING VACATION IN GREECE?
LESS TYPICAL, BUT NOT UNHEARD OF.

1/31/81

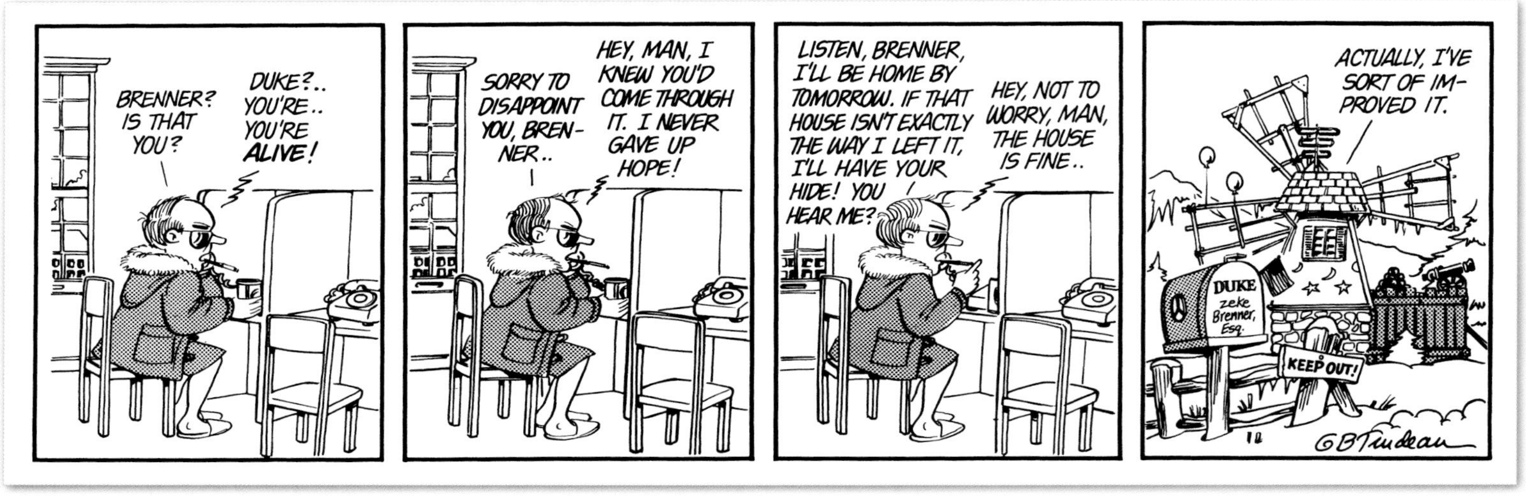
BRENNER? IS THAT YOU?
DUKE?.. YOU'RE.. YOU'RE ALIVE!
SORRY TO DISAPPOINT YOU, BRENNER..
HEY, MAN, I KNEW YOU'D COME THROUGH IT. I NEVER GAVE UP HOPE!
LISTEN, BRENNER, I'LL BE HOME BY TOMORROW. IF THAT HOUSE ISN'T EXACTLY THE WAY I LEFT IT, I'LL HAVE YOUR HIDE! YOU HEAR ME?
HEY, NOT TO WORRY, MAN, THE HOUSE IS FINE..
ACTUALLY, I'VE SORT OF IMPROVED IT.
DUKE
zeke Brenner, Esq.
KEEP OUT!

2/11/81

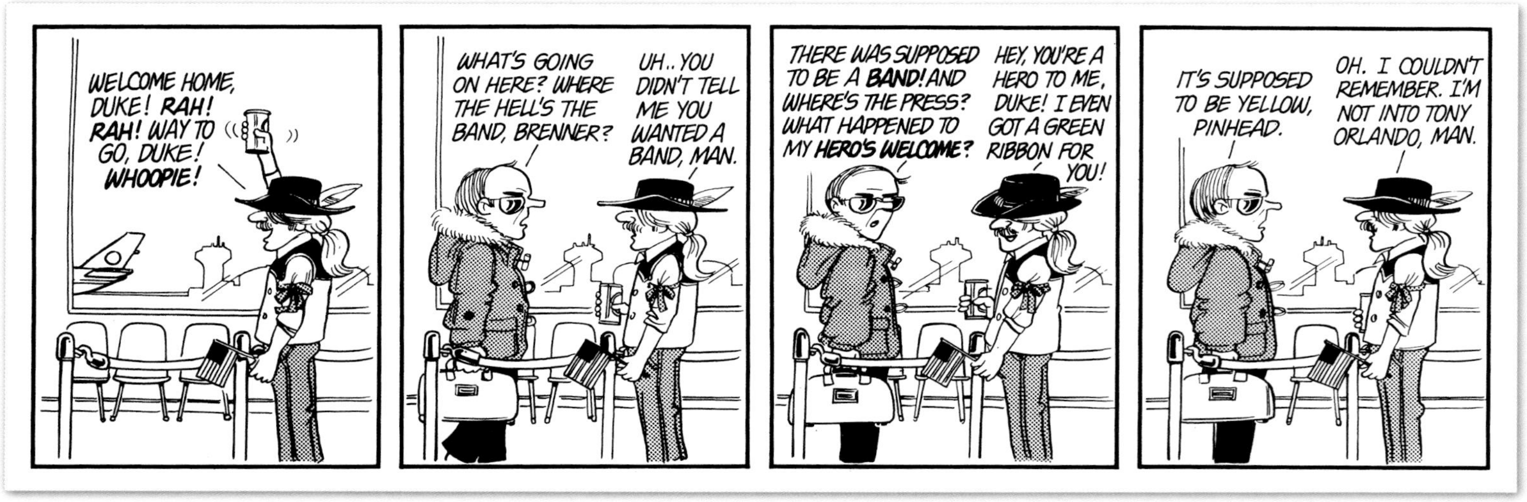
WELCOME HOME, DUKE! RAH! RAH! WAY TO GO, DUKE! WHOOPIE!
WHAT'S GOING ON HERE? WHERE THE HELL'S THE BAND, BRENNER?
UH.. YOU DIDN'T TELL ME YOU WANTED A BAND, MAN.
THERE WAS SUPPOSED TO BE A BAND! AND WHERE'S THE PRESS? WHAT HAPPENED TO MY HERO'S WELCOME?
HEY, YOU'RE A HERO TO ME, DUKE! I EVEN GOT A GREEN RIBBON FOR YOU!
IT'S SUPPOSED TO BE YELLOW, PINHEAD.
OH. I COULDN'T REMEMBER. I'M NOT INTO TONY ORLANDO, MAN.

2/14/81

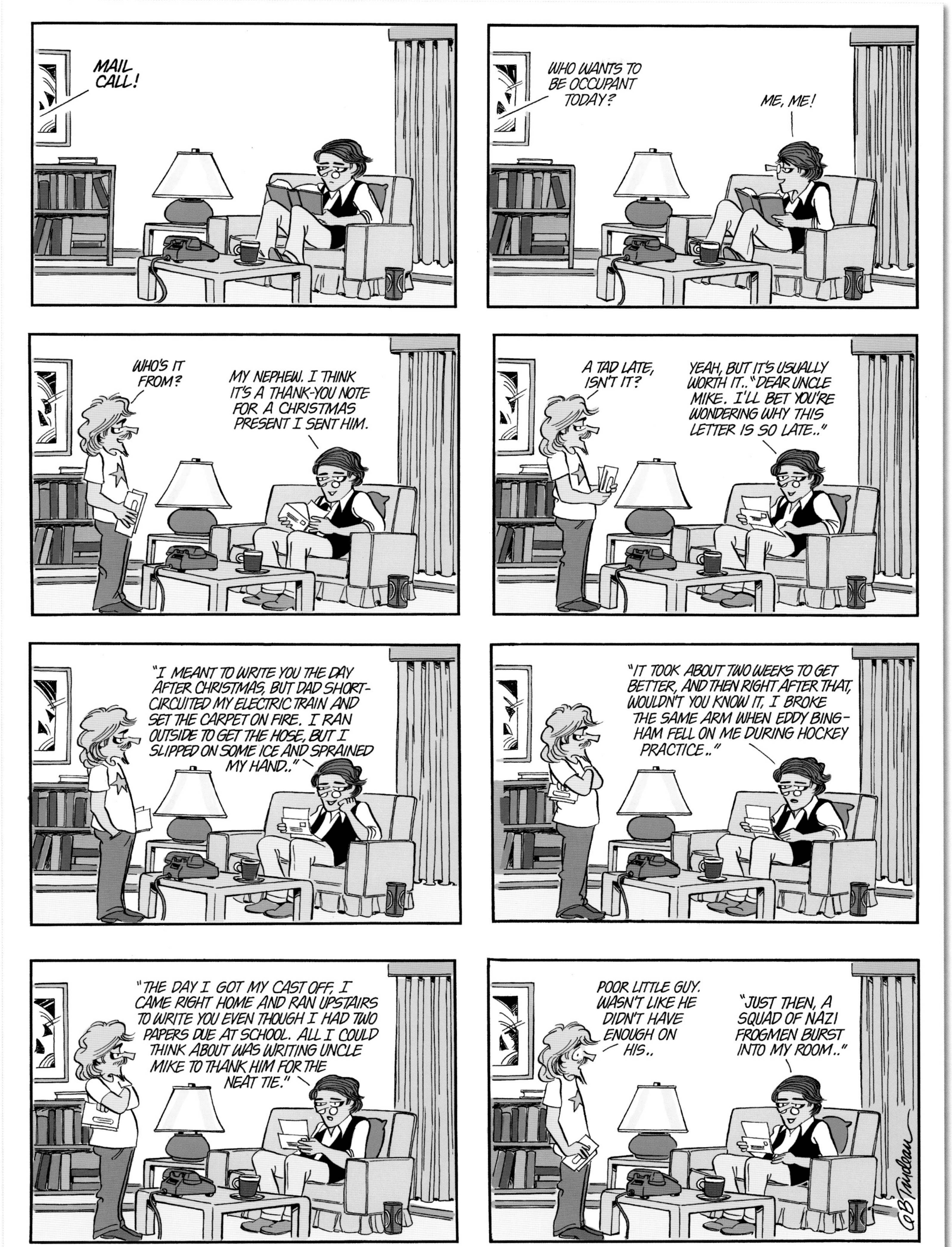
MAIL CALL!
WHO WANTS TO BE OCCUPANT TODAY?
ME, ME!
WHO'S IT FROM?
MY NEPHEW. I THINK IT'S A THANK-YOU NOTE FOR A CHRISTMAS PRESENT I SENT HIM.
A TAD LATE, ISN'T IT?
YEAH, BUT IT'S USUALLY WORTH IT.."DEAR UNCLE MIKE. I'LL BET YOU'RE WONDERING WHY THIS LETTER IS SO LATE.."
"I MEANT TO WRITE YOU THE DAY AFTER CHRISTMAS, BUT DAD SHORT-CIRCUITED MY ELECTRIC TRAIN AND SET THE CARPET ON FIRE. I RAN OUTSIDE TO GET THE HOSE, BUT I SLIPPED ON SOME ICE AND SPRAINED MY HAND.."
"IT TOOK ABOUT TWO WEEKS TO GET BETTER, AND THEN RIGHT AFTER THAT, WOULDN'T YOU KNOW IT, I BROKE THE SAME ARM WHEN EDDY BING-HAM FELL ON ME DURING HOCKEY PRACTICE.."
"THE DAY I GOT MY CAST OFF, I CAME RIGHT HOME AND RAN UPSTAIRS TO WRITE YOU EVEN THOUGH I HAD TWO PAPERS DUE AT SCHOOL. ALL I COULD THINK ABOUT WAS WRITING UNCLE MIKE TO THANK HIM FOR THE NEAT TIE."
POOR LITTLE GUY. WASN'T LIKE HE DIDN'T HAVE ENOUGH ON HIS..
"JUST THEN, A SQUAD OF NAZI FROGMEN BURST INTO MY ROOM.."
GBTrudeau

2/8/81

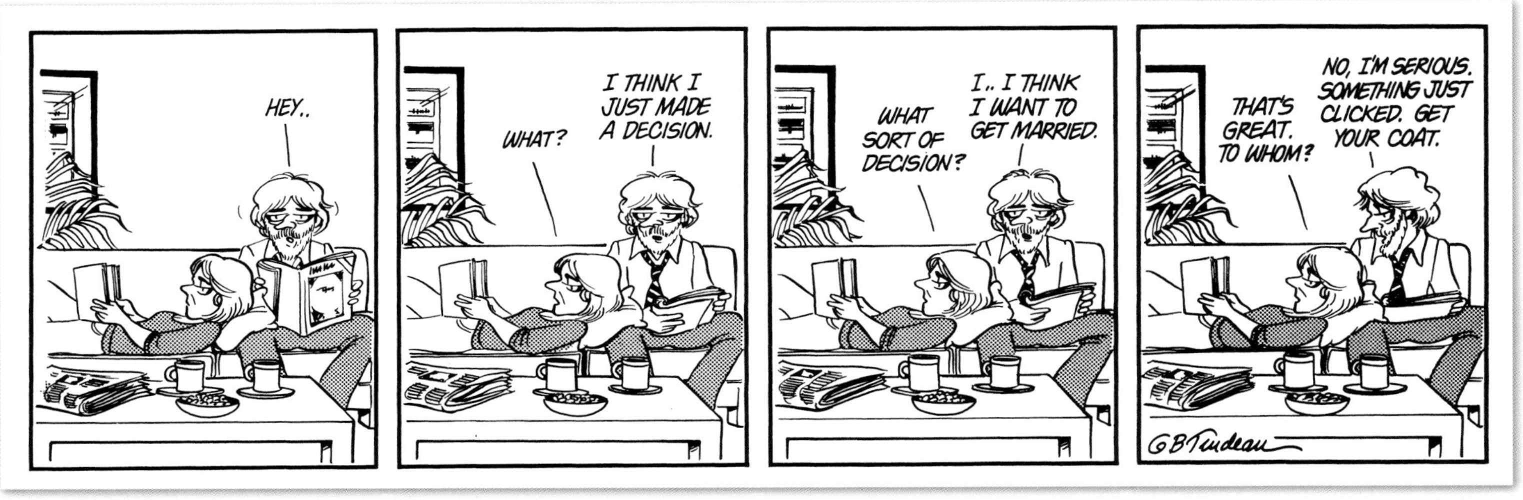
HEY..
WHAT?
I THINK I JUST MADE A DECISION.
WHAT SORT OF DECISION?
I.. I THINK I WANT TO GET MARRIED.
THAT'S GREAT. TO WHOM?
NO, I'M SERIOUS. SOMETHING JUST CLICKED. GET YOUR COAT.

3/30/81

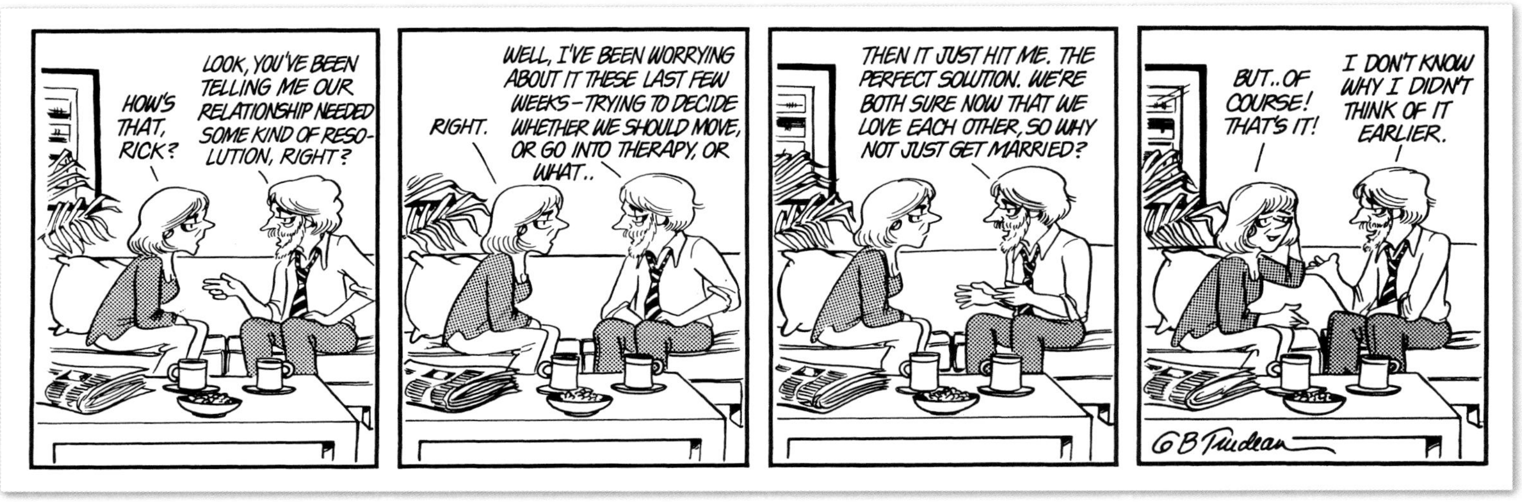
HOW'S THAT, RICK?
LOOK, YOU'VE BEEN TELLING ME OUR RELATIONSHIP NEEDED SOME KIND OF RESOLUTION, RIGHT?
RIGHT.
WELL, I'VE BEEN WORRYING ABOUT IT THESE LAST FEW WEEKS–TRYING TO DECIDE WHETHER WE SHOULD MOVE, OR GO INTO THERAPY, OR WHAT..
THEN IT JUST HIT ME. THE PERFECT SOLUTION. WE'RE BOTH SURE NOW THAT WE LOVE EACH OTHER, SO WHY NOT JUST GET MARRIED?
BUT..OF COURSE! THAT'S IT!
I DON'T KNOW WHY I DIDN'T THINK OF IT EARLIER.

3/31/81

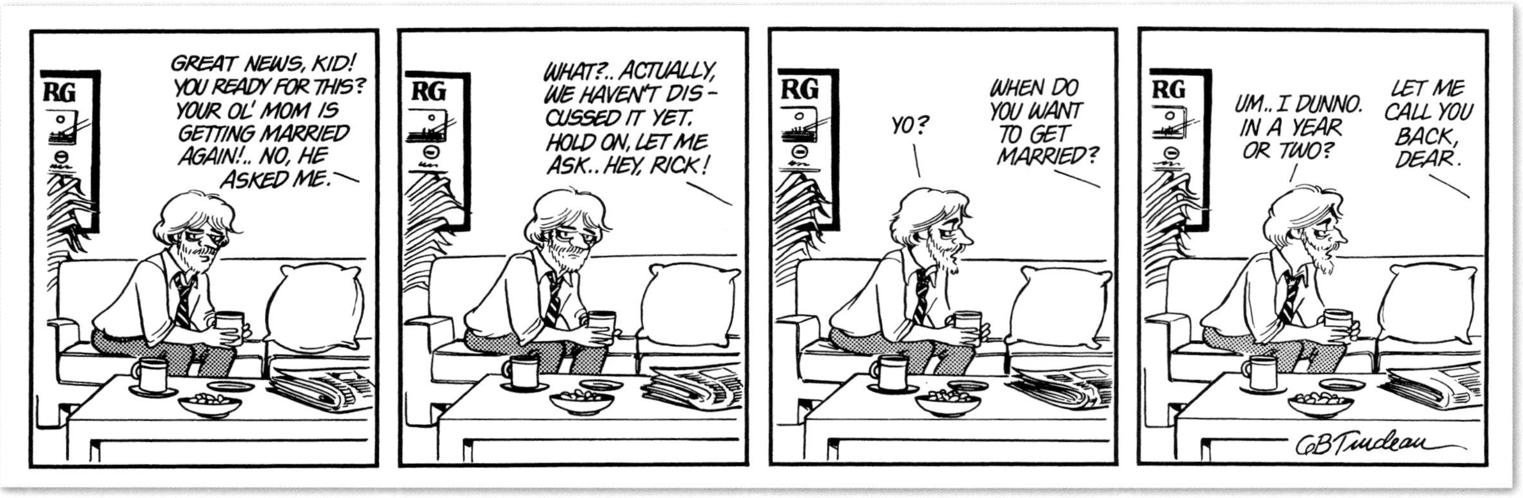
GREAT NEWS, KID! YOU READY FOR THIS? YOUR OL' MOM IS GETTING MARRIED AGAIN!.. NO, HE ASKED ME.
WHAT?.. ACTUALLY, WE HAVEN'T DISCUSSED IT YET. HOLD ON, LET ME ASK.. HEY, RICK!
YO?
WHEN DO YOU WANT TO GET MARRIED?
UM.. I DUNNO. IN A YEAR OR TWO?
LET ME CALL YOU BACK, DEAR.

4/2/81

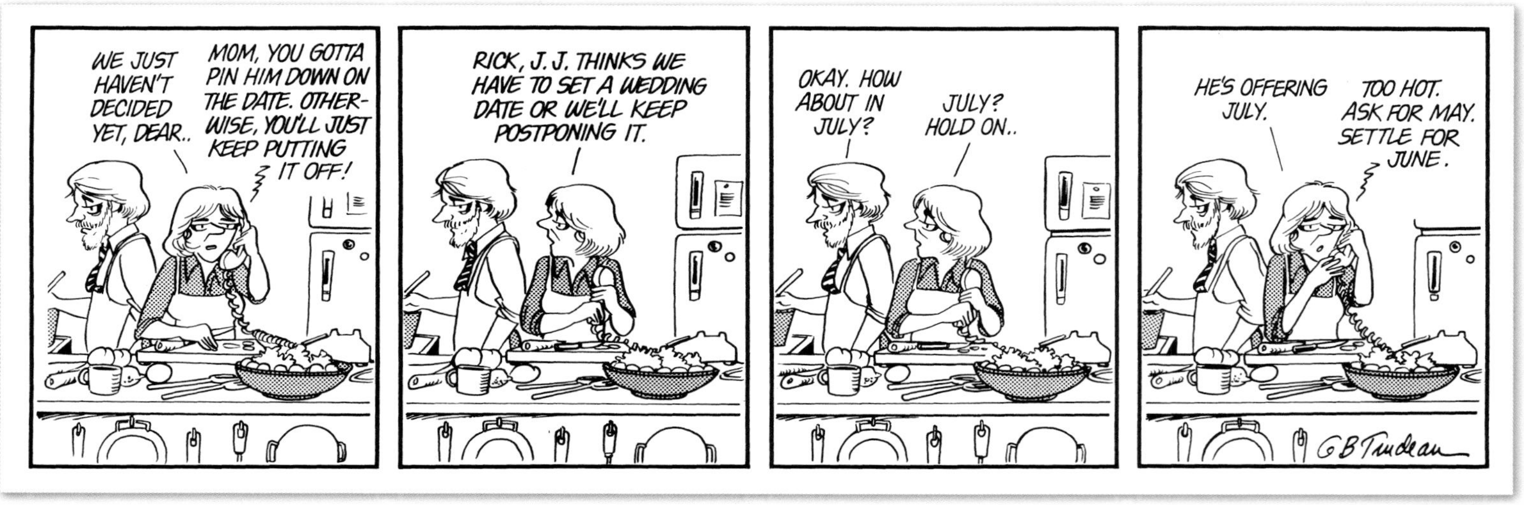
WE JUST HAVEN'T DECIDED YET, DEAR..
MOM, YOU GOTTA PIN HIM DOWN ON THE DATE. OTHERWISE, YOU'LL JUST KEEP PUTTING IT OFF!
RICK, J. J. THINKS WE HAVE TO SET A WEDDING DATE OR WE'LL KEEP POSTPONING IT.
OKAY. HOW ABOUT IN JULY?
JULY? HOLD ON..
HE'S OFFERING JULY.
TOO HOT. ASK FOR MAY. SETTLE FOR JUNE.

4/6/81

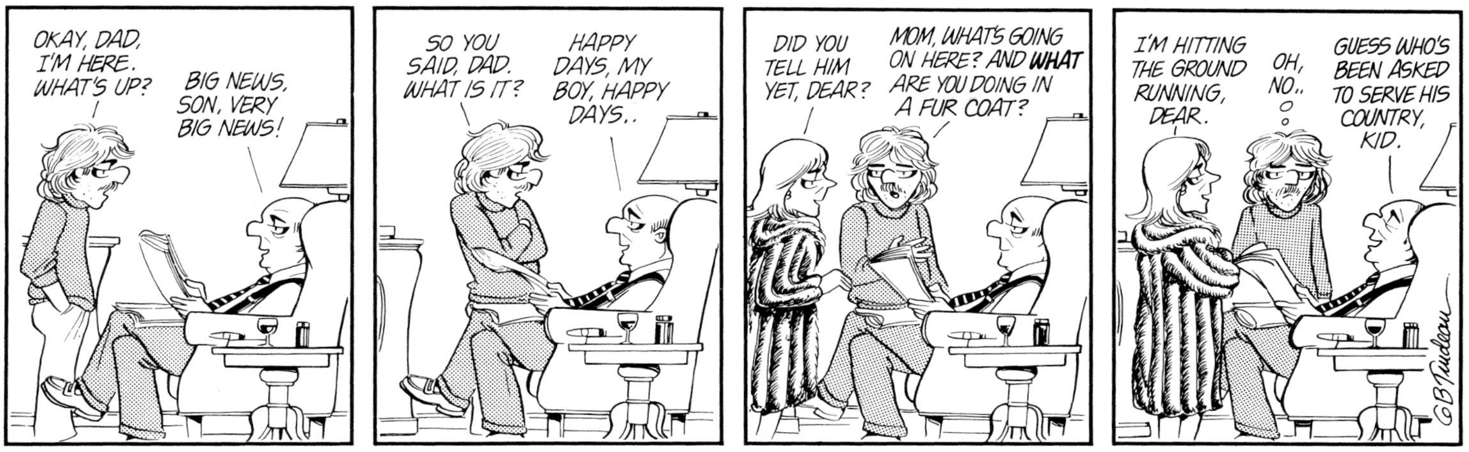
OKAY, DAD, I'M HERE. WHAT'S UP?
BIG NEWS, SON, VERY BIG NEWS!
SO YOU SAID, DAD. WHAT IS IT?
HAPPY DAYS, MY BOY, HAPPY DAYS..
DID YOU TELL HIM YET, DEAR?
MOM, WHAT'S GOING ON HERE? AND **WHAT** ARE YOU DOING IN A FUR COAT?
I'M HITTING THE GROUND RUNNING, DEAR.
OH, NO..
GUESS WHO'S BEEN ASKED TO SERVE HIS COUNTRY, KID.
G B Trudeau

3/10/81

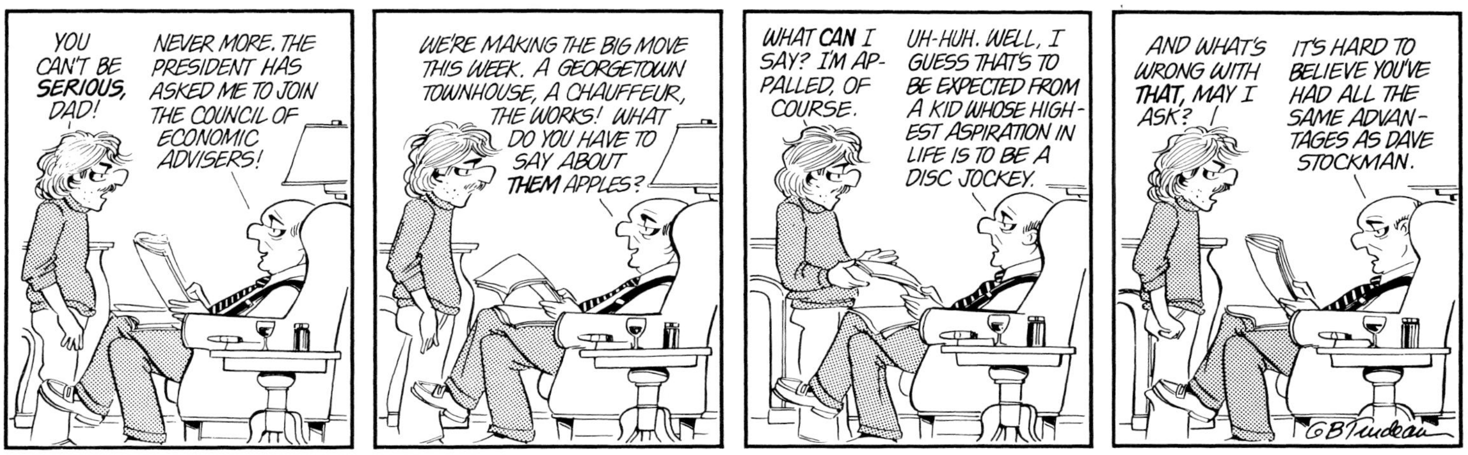
YOU CAN'T BE **SERIOUS,** DAD!
NEVER MORE. THE PRESIDENT HAS ASKED ME TO JOIN THE COUNCIL OF ECONOMIC ADVISERS!
WE'RE MAKING THE BIG MOVE THIS WEEK. A GEORGETOWN TOWNHOUSE, A CHAUFFEUR, THE WORKS! WHAT DO YOU HAVE TO SAY ABOUT **THEM** APPLES?
WHAT **CAN** I SAY? I'M APPALLED, OF COURSE.
UH-HUH. WELL, I GUESS THAT'S TO BE EXPECTED FROM A KID WHOSE HIGHEST ASPIRATION IN LIFE IS TO BE A DISC JOCKEY.
AND WHAT'S WRONG WITH **THAT,** MAY I ASK?
IT'S HARD TO BELIEVE YOU'VE HAD ALL THE SAME ADVANTAGES AS DAVE STOCKMAN.
G B Trudeau

3/11/81

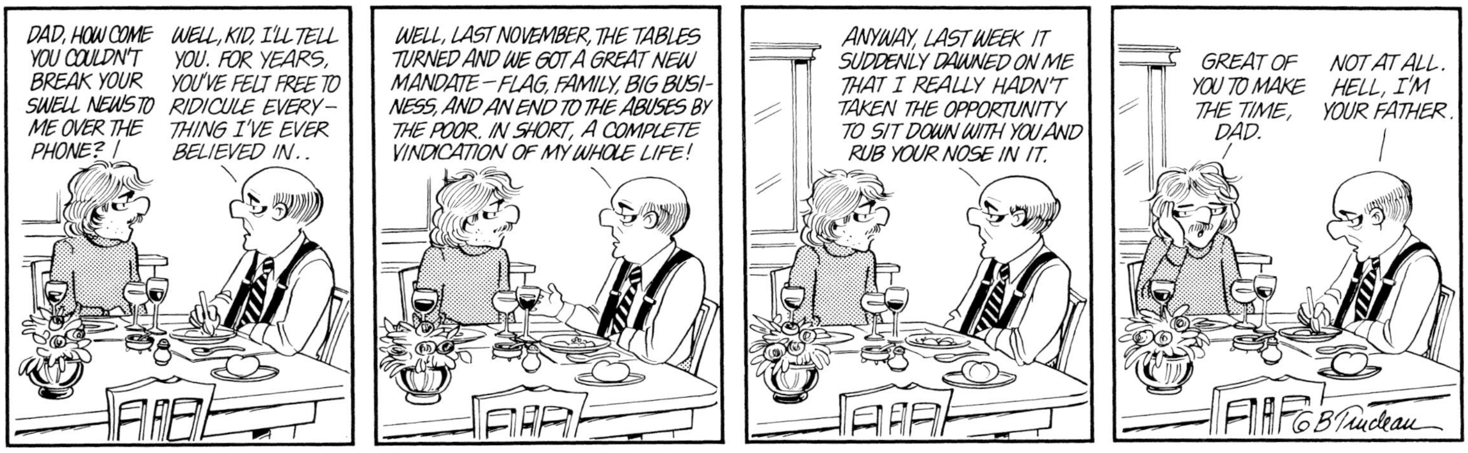
DAD, HOW COME YOU COULDN'T BREAK YOUR SWELL NEWS TO ME OVER THE PHONE?
WELL, KID, I'LL TELL YOU. FOR YEARS, YOU'VE FELT FREE TO RIDICULE EVERYTHING I'VE EVER BELIEVED IN..
WELL, LAST NOVEMBER, THE TABLES TURNED AND WE GOT A GREAT NEW MANDATE—FLAG, FAMILY, BIG BUSINESS, AND AN END TO THE ABUSES BY THE POOR. IN SHORT, A COMPLETE VINDICATION OF MY WHOLE LIFE!
ANYWAY, LAST WEEK IT SUDDENLY DAWNED ON ME THAT I REALLY HADN'T TAKEN THE OPPORTUNITY TO SIT DOWN WITH YOU AND RUB YOUR NOSE IN IT.
GREAT OF YOU TO MAKE THE TIME, DAD.
NOT AT ALL. HELL, I'M YOUR FATHER.
G B Trudeau

3/12/81

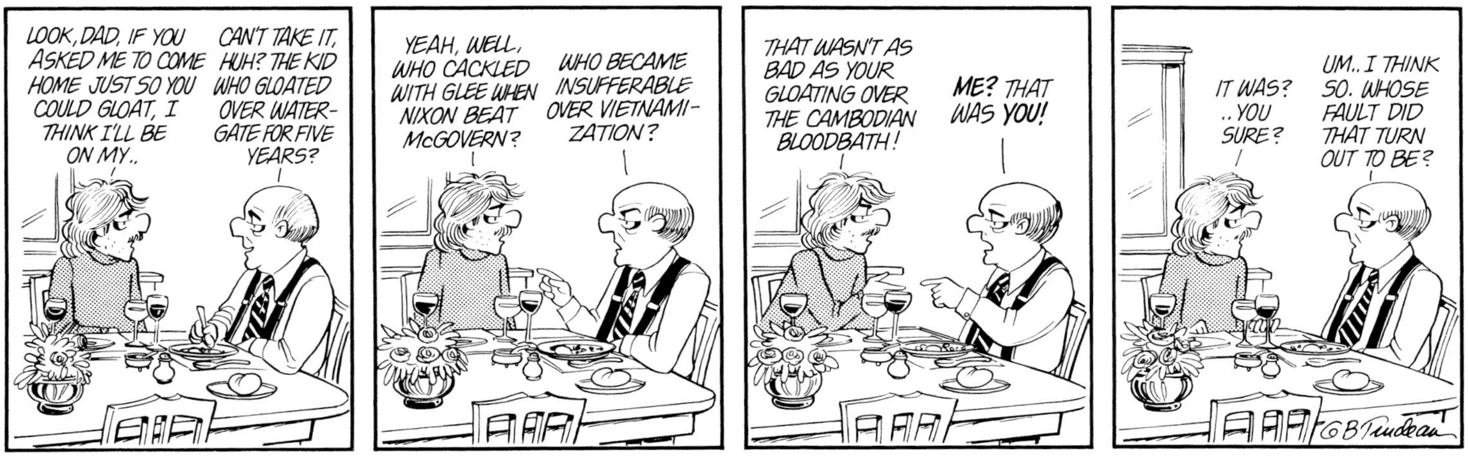
LOOK, DAD, IF YOU ASKED ME TO COME HOME JUST SO YOU COULD GLOAT, I THINK I'LL BE ON MY..
CAN'T TAKE IT, HUH? THE KID WHO GLOATED OVER WATERGATE FOR FIVE YEARS?
YEAH, WELL, WHO CACKLED WITH GLEE WHEN NIXON BEAT McGOVERN?
WHO BECAME INSUFFERABLE OVER VIETNAMIZATION?
THAT WASN'T AS BAD AS YOUR GLOATING OVER THE CAMBODIAN BLOODBATH!
ME? THAT WAS **YOU!**
IT WAS? ..YOU SURE?
UM.. I THINK SO. WHOSE FAULT DID THAT TURN OUT TO BE?
G B Trudeau

3/13/81

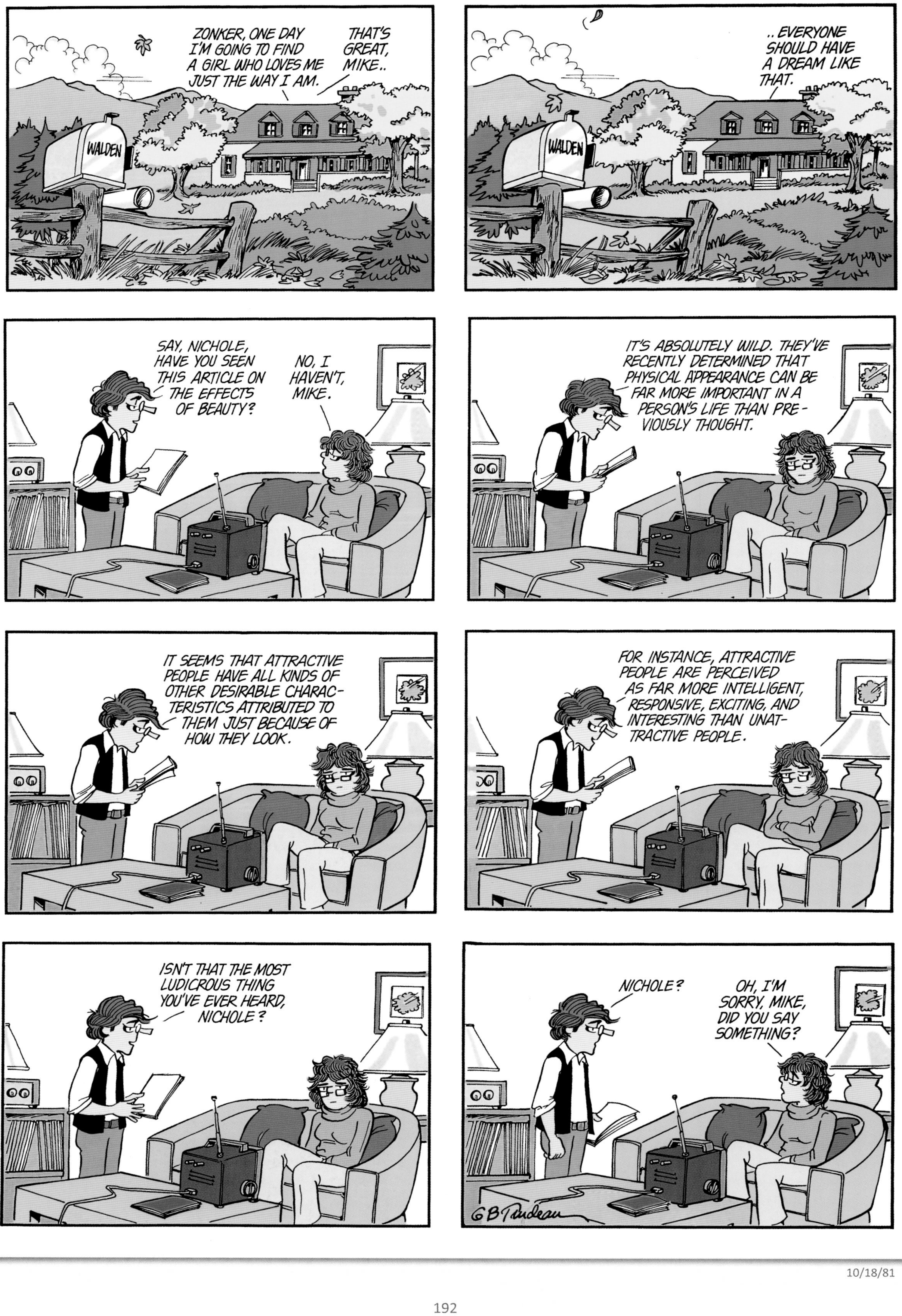
ZONKER, ONE DAY I'M GOING TO FIND A GIRL WHO LOVES ME JUST THE WAY I AM.
THAT'S GREAT, MIKE..
WALDEN
..EVERYONE SHOULD HAVE A DREAM LIKE THAT.
WALDEN
SAY, NICHOLE, HAVE YOU SEEN THIS ARTICLE ON THE EFFECTS OF BEAUTY?
NO, I HAVEN'T, MIKE.
IT'S ABSOLUTELY WILD. THEY'VE RECENTLY DETERMINED THAT PHYSICAL APPEARANCE CAN BE FAR MORE IMPORTANT IN A PERSON'S LIFE THAN PREVIOUSLY THOUGHT.
IT SEEMS THAT ATTRACTIVE PEOPLE HAVE ALL KINDS OF OTHER DESIRABLE CHARACTERISTICS ATTRIBUTED TO THEM JUST BECAUSE OF HOW THEY LOOK.
FOR INSTANCE, ATTRACTIVE PEOPLE ARE PERCEIVED AS FAR MORE INTELLIGENT, RESPONSIVE, EXCITING, AND INTERESTING THAN UNATTRACTIVE PEOPLE.
ISN'T THAT THE MOST LUDICROUS THING YOU'VE EVER HEARD, NICHOLE?
NICHOLE?
OH, I'M SORRY, MIKE, DID YOU SAY SOMETHING?
GBTrudeau

10/18/81

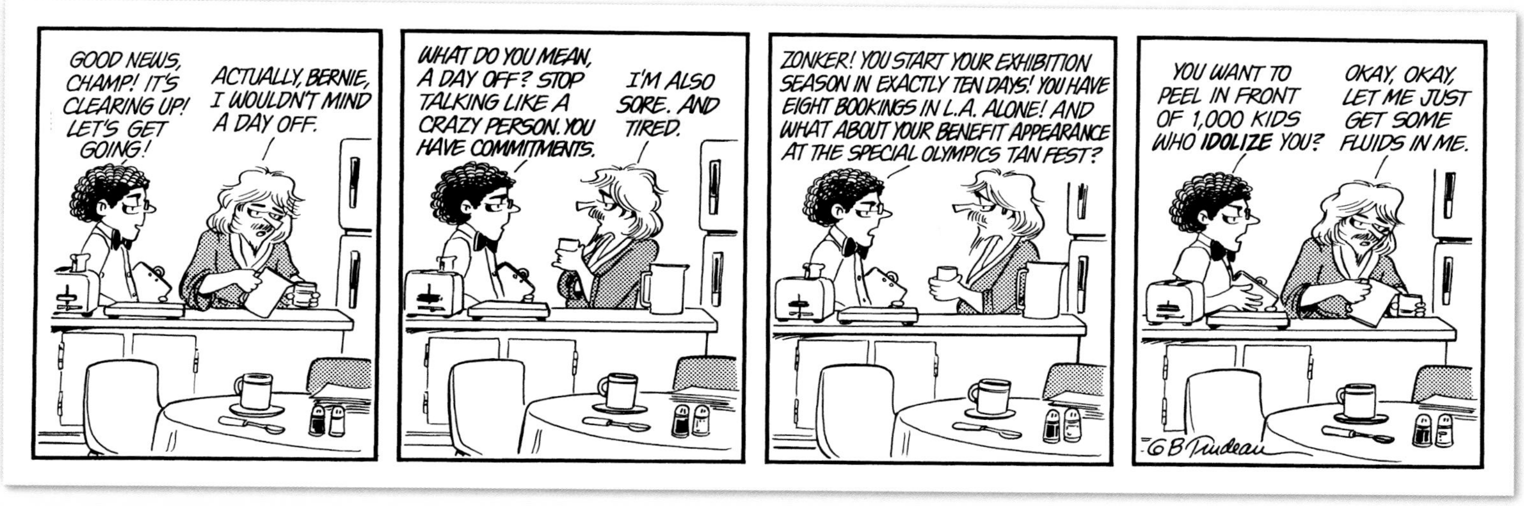
GOOD NEWS, CHAMP! IT'S CLEARING UP! LET'S GET GOING!
ACTUALLY, BERNIE, I WOULDN'T MIND A DAY OFF.
WHAT DO YOU MEAN, A DAY OFF? STOP TALKING LIKE A CRAZY PERSON. YOU HAVE COMMITMENTS.
I'M ALSO SORE. AND TIRED.
ZONKER! YOU START YOUR EXHIBITION SEASON IN EXACTLY TEN DAYS! YOU HAVE EIGHT BOOKINGS IN L.A. ALONE! AND WHAT ABOUT YOUR BENEFIT APPEARANCE AT THE SPECIAL OLYMPICS TAN FEST?
YOU WANT TO PEEL IN FRONT OF 1,000 KIDS WHO IDOLIZE YOU?
OKAY, OKAY, LET ME JUST GET SOME FLUIDS IN ME.
G.B. Trudeau

4/28/81

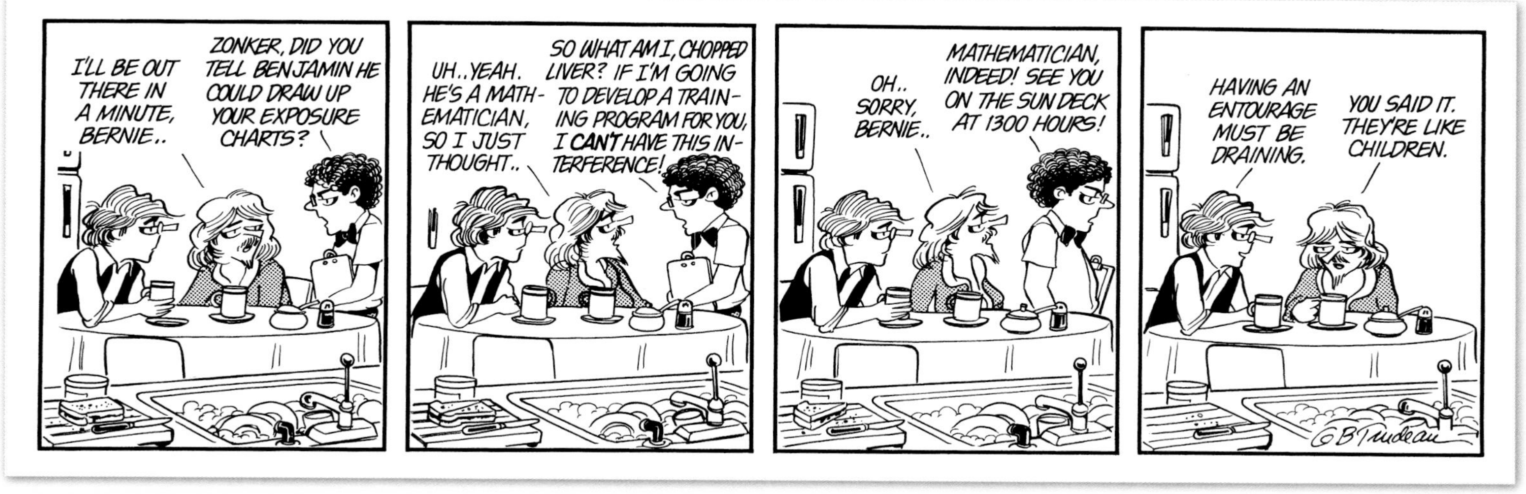
I'LL BE OUT THERE IN A MINUTE, BERNIE..
ZONKER, DID YOU TELL BENJAMIN HE COULD DRAW UP YOUR EXPOSURE CHARTS?
UH..YEAH. HE'S A MATHEMATICIAN, SO I JUST THOUGHT..
SO WHAT AM I, CHOPPED LIVER? IF I'M GOING TO DEVELOP A TRAINING PROGRAM FOR YOU, I CAN'T HAVE THIS INTERFERENCE!
OH.. SORRY, BERNIE..
MATHEMATICIAN, INDEED! SEE YOU ON THE SUN DECK AT 1300 HOURS!
HAVING AN ENTOURAGE MUST BE DRAINING.
YOU SAID IT. THEY'RE LIKE CHILDREN.
G.B. Trudeau

4/30/81

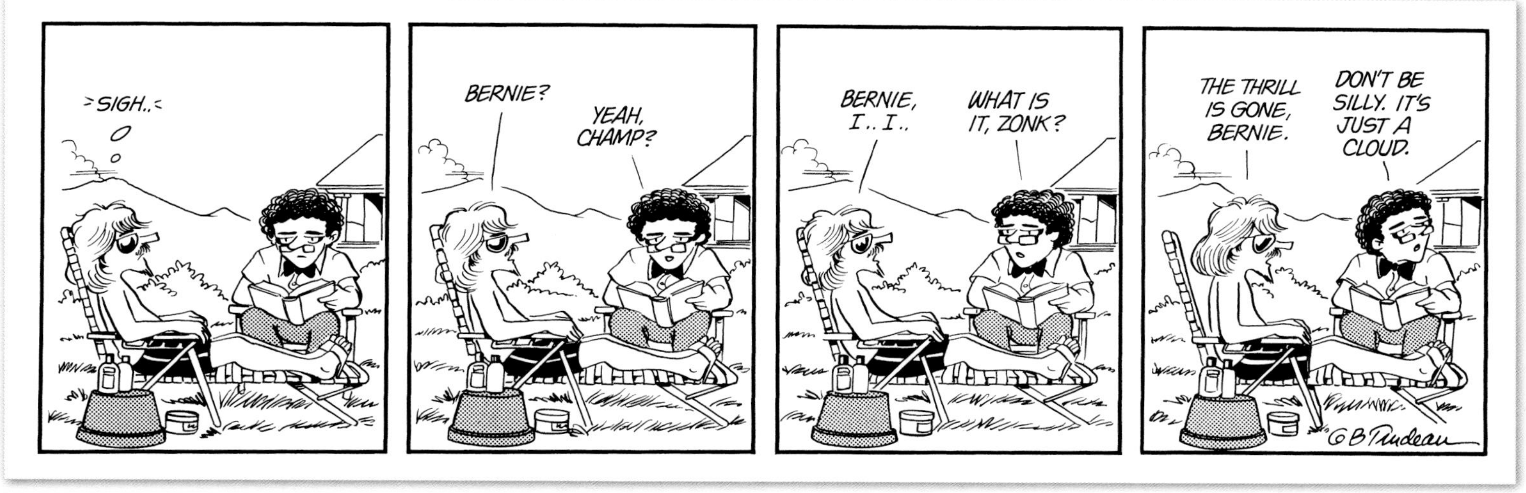
SIGH..
BERNIE?
YEAH, CHAMP?
BERNIE, I.. I..
WHAT IS IT, ZONK?
THE THRILL IS GONE, BERNIE.
DON'T BE SILLY. IT'S JUST A CLOUD.
G.B. Trudeau

5/1/81

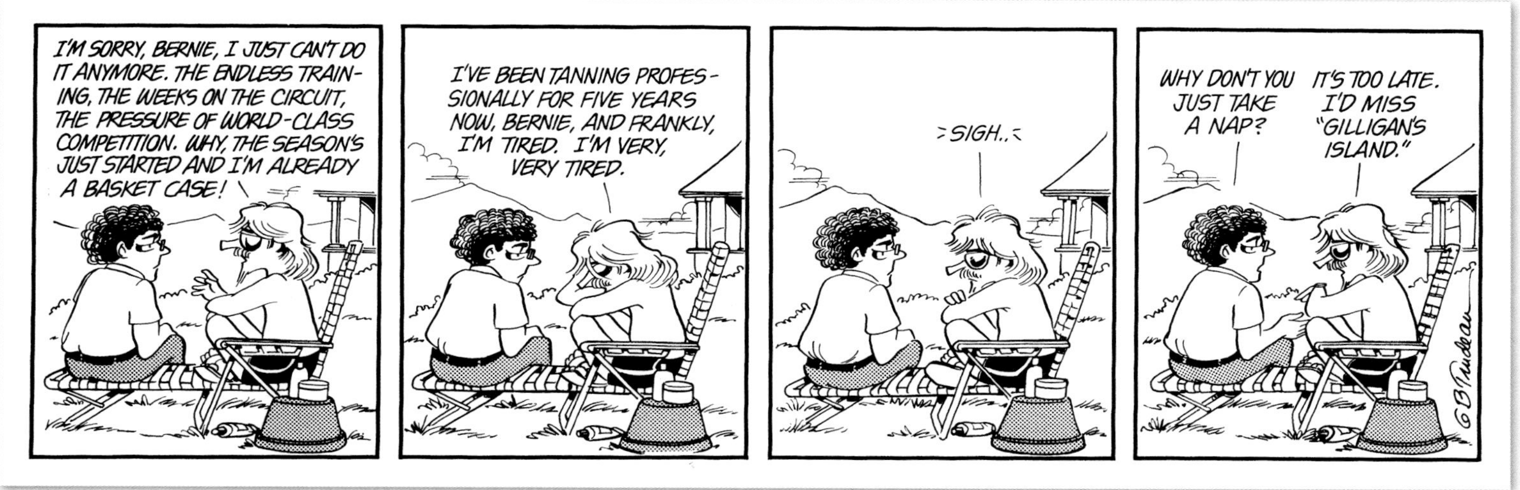
I'M SORRY, BERNIE, I JUST CAN'T DO IT ANYMORE. THE ENDLESS TRAINING, THE WEEKS ON THE CIRCUIT, THE PRESSURE OF WORLD-CLASS COMPETITION. WHY, THE SEASON'S JUST STARTED AND I'M ALREADY A BASKET CASE!
I'VE BEEN TANNING PROFESSIONALLY FOR FIVE YEARS NOW, BERNIE, AND FRANKLY, I'M TIRED. I'M VERY, VERY TIRED.
SIGH..
WHY DON'T YOU JUST TAKE A NAP?
IT'S TOO LATE. I'D MISS "GILLIGAN'S ISLAND."
G.B. Trudeau

5/2/81

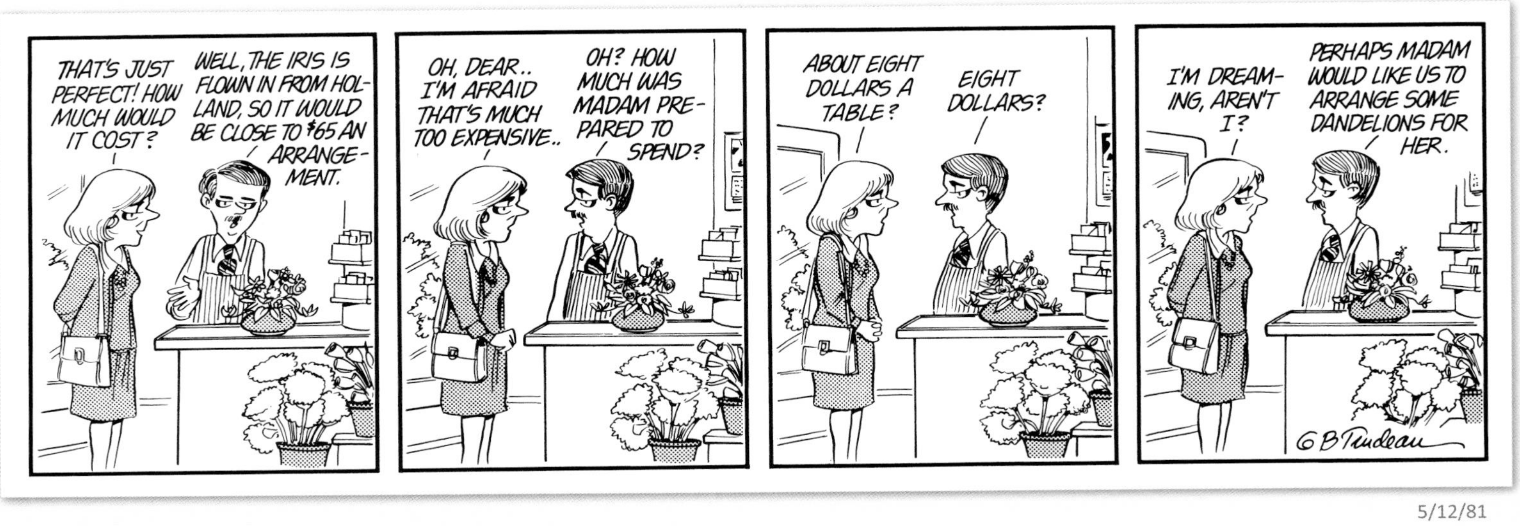
THAT'S JUST PERFECT! HOW MUCH WOULD IT COST?
WELL, THE IRIS IS FLOWN IN FROM HOLLAND, SO IT WOULD BE CLOSE TO $65 AN ARRANGEMENT.
OH, DEAR.. I'M AFRAID THAT'S MUCH TOO EXPENSIVE..
OH? HOW MUCH WAS MADAM PREPARED TO SPEND?
ABOUT EIGHT DOLLARS A TABLE?
EIGHT DOLLARS?
I'M DREAMING, AREN'T I?
PERHAPS MADAM WOULD LIKE US TO ARRANGE SOME DANDELIONS FOR HER.
G B Trudeau

5/12/81

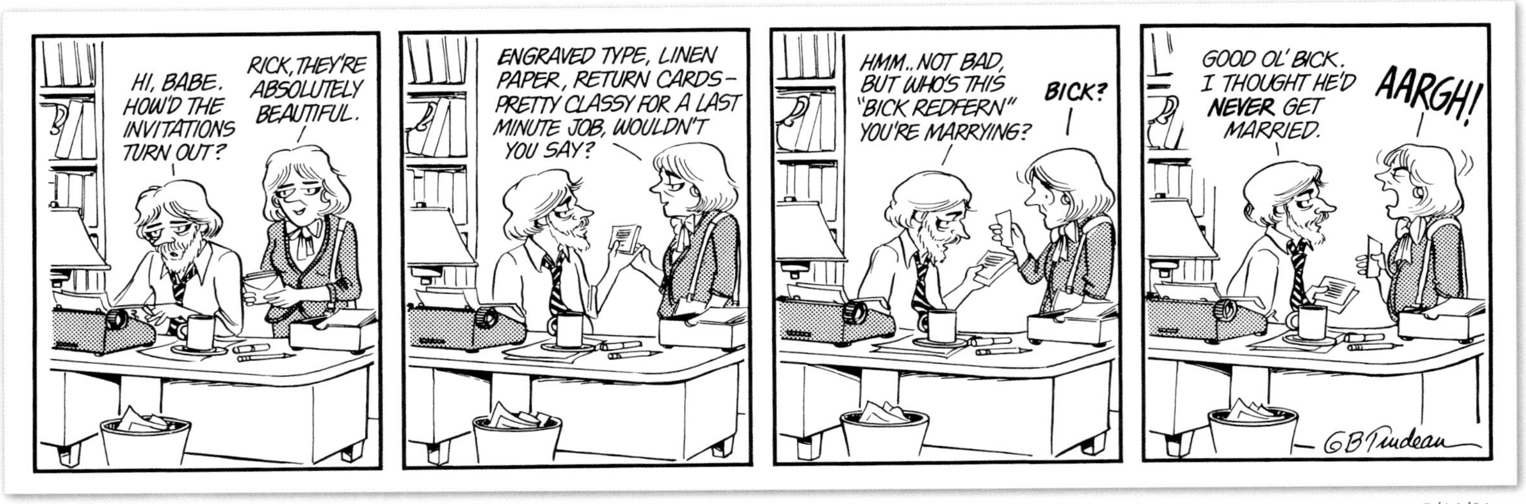
HI, BABE. HOW'D THE INVITATIONS TURN OUT?
RICK, THEY'RE ABSOLUTELY BEAUTIFUL.
ENGRAVED TYPE, LINEN PAPER, RETURN CARDS– PRETTY CLASSY FOR A LAST MINUTE JOB, WOULDN'T YOU SAY?
HMM.. NOT BAD, BUT WHO'S THIS "BICK REDFERN" YOU'RE MARRYING?
BICK?
GOOD OL' BICK. I THOUGHT HE'D NEVER GET MARRIED.
AARGH!
G B Trudeau

5/14/81

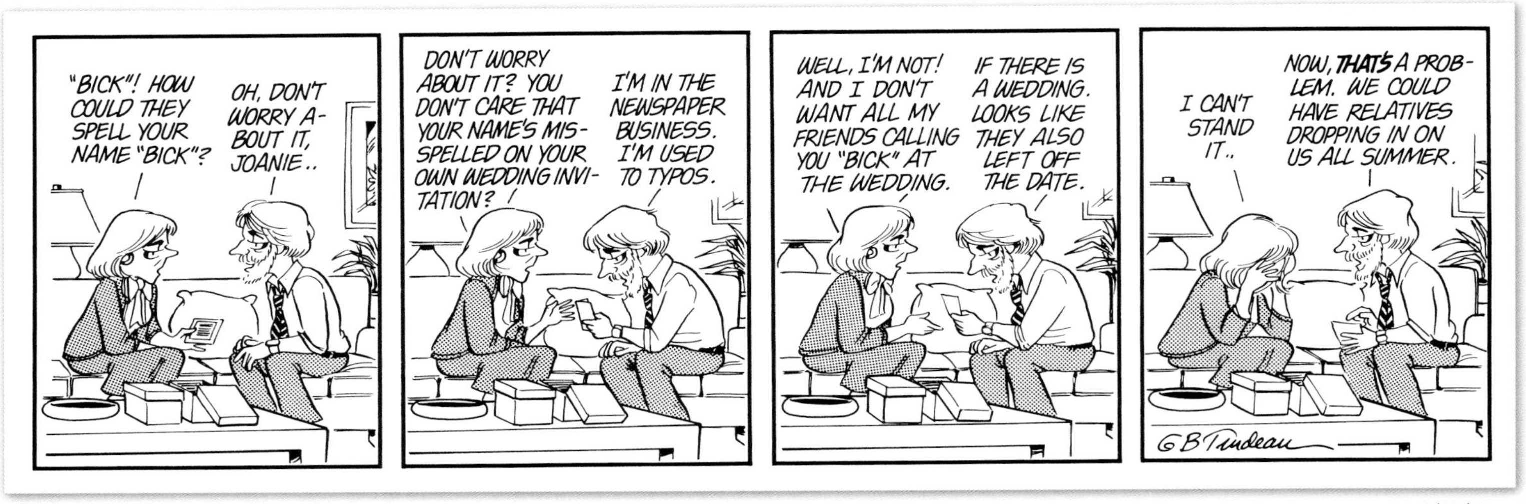
"BICK"! HOW COULD THEY SPELL YOUR NAME "BICK"?
OH, DON'T WORRY ABOUT IT, JOANIE..
DON'T WORRY ABOUT IT? YOU DON'T CARE THAT YOUR NAME'S MISSPELLED ON YOUR OWN WEDDING INVITATION?
I'M IN THE NEWSPAPER BUSINESS. I'M USED TO TYPOS.
WELL, I'M NOT! AND I DON'T WANT ALL MY FRIENDS CALLING YOU "BICK" AT THE WEDDING.
IF THERE IS A WEDDING. LOOKS LIKE THEY ALSO LEFT OFF THE DATE.
I CAN'T STAND IT..
NOW, THAT'S A PROBLEM. WE COULD HAVE RELATIVES DROPPING IN ON US ALL SUMMER.
G B Trudeau

5/15/81

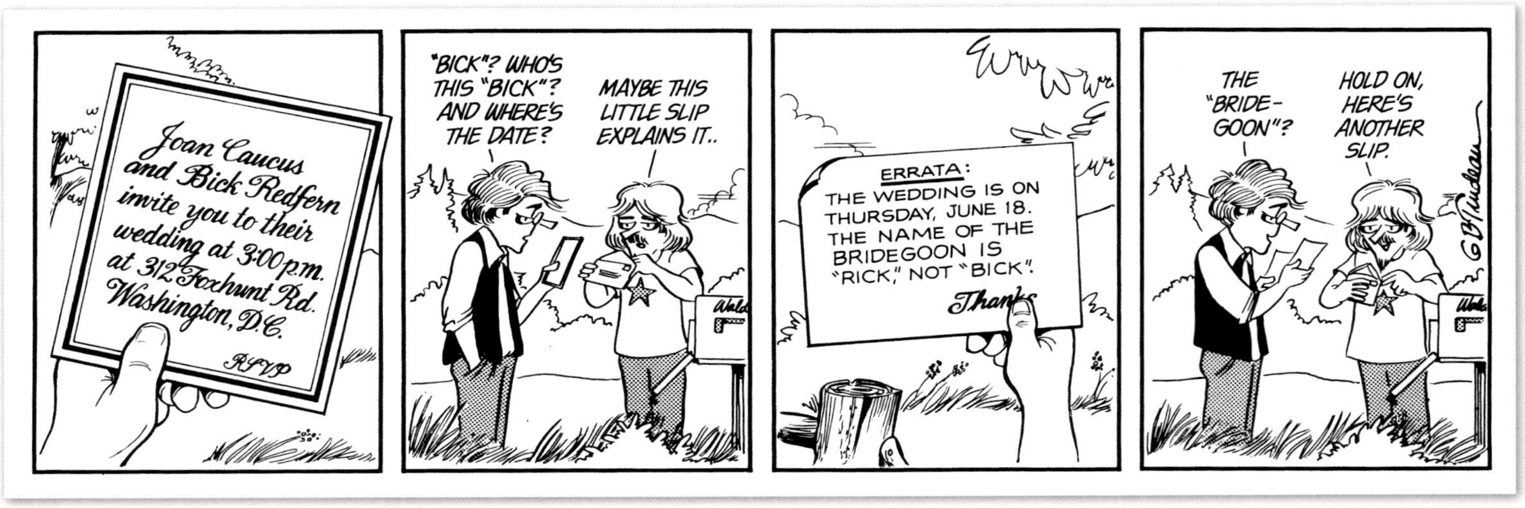
Joan Caucus and Bick Redfern invite you to their wedding at 3:00 p.m. at 312 Foxhunt Rd. Washington, D.C.
RSVP
"BICK"? WHO'S THIS "BICK"? AND WHERE'S THE DATE?
MAYBE THIS LITTLE SLIP EXPLAINS IT..
ERRATA: THE WEDDING IS ON THURSDAY, JUNE 18. THE NAME OF THE BRIDEGOON IS "RICK," NOT "BICK".
Thanks
THE "BRIDE-GOON"?
HOLD ON, HERE'S ANOTHER SLIP.
G B Trudeau

6/1/81

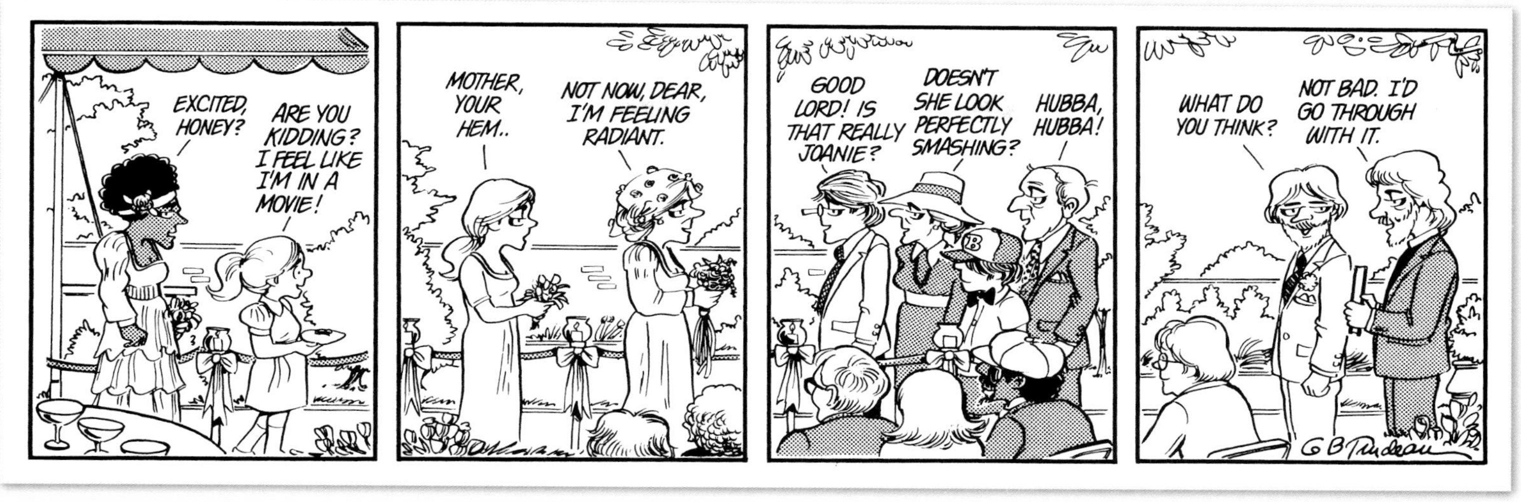
EXCITED, HONEY?
ARE YOU KIDDING? I FEEL LIKE I'M IN A MOVIE!
MOTHER, YOUR HEM..
NOT NOW, DEAR, I'M FEELING RADIANT.
GOOD LORD! IS THAT REALLY JOANIE?
DOESN'T SHE LOOK PERFECTLY SMASHING?
HUBBA, HUBBA!
WHAT DO YOU THINK?
NOT BAD. I'D GO THROUGH WITH IT.
G B Trudeau

6/16/81

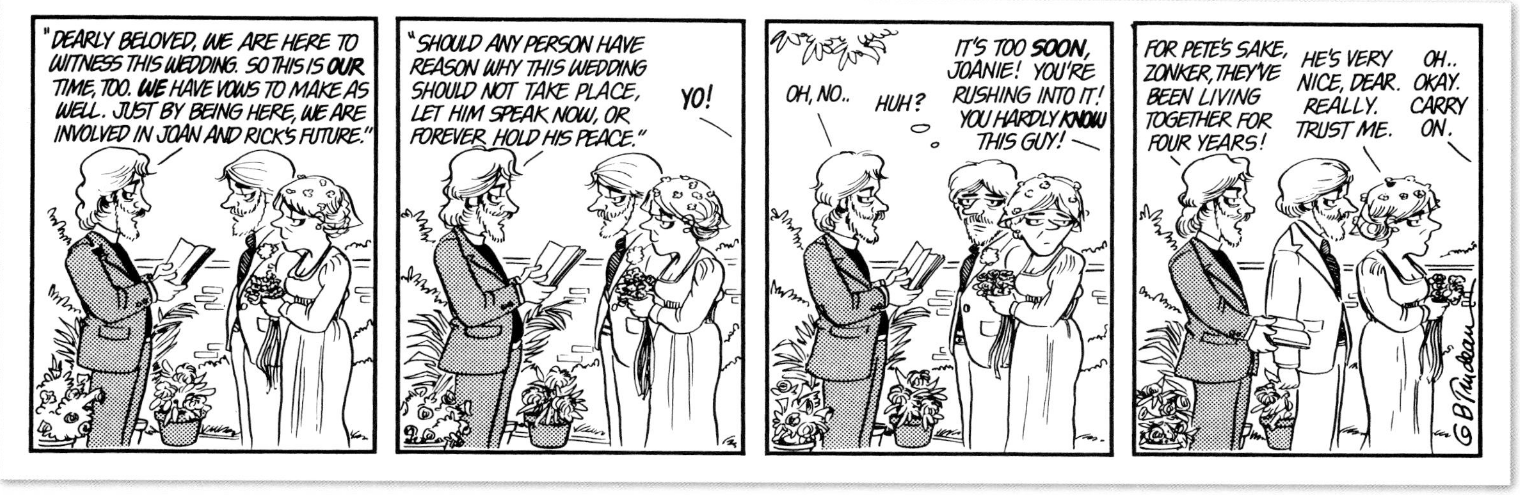
"DEARLY BELOVED, WE ARE HERE TO WITNESS THIS WEDDING. SO THIS IS OUR TIME, TOO. WE HAVE VOWS TO MAKE AS WELL. JUST BY BEING HERE, WE ARE INVOLVED IN JOAN AND RICK'S FUTURE."
"SHOULD ANY PERSON HAVE REASON WHY THIS WEDDING SHOULD NOT TAKE PLACE, LET HIM SPEAK NOW, OR FOREVER HOLD HIS PEACE."
YO!
OH, NO..
HUH?
IT'S TOO SOON, JOANIE! YOU'RE RUSHING INTO IT! YOU HARDLY KNOW THIS GUY!
FOR PETE'S SAKE, ZONKER, THEY'VE BEEN LIVING TOGETHER FOR FOUR YEARS!
HE'S VERY NICE, DEAR. REALLY. TRUST ME.
OH.. OKAY. CARRY ON.
G B Trudeau

6/17/81

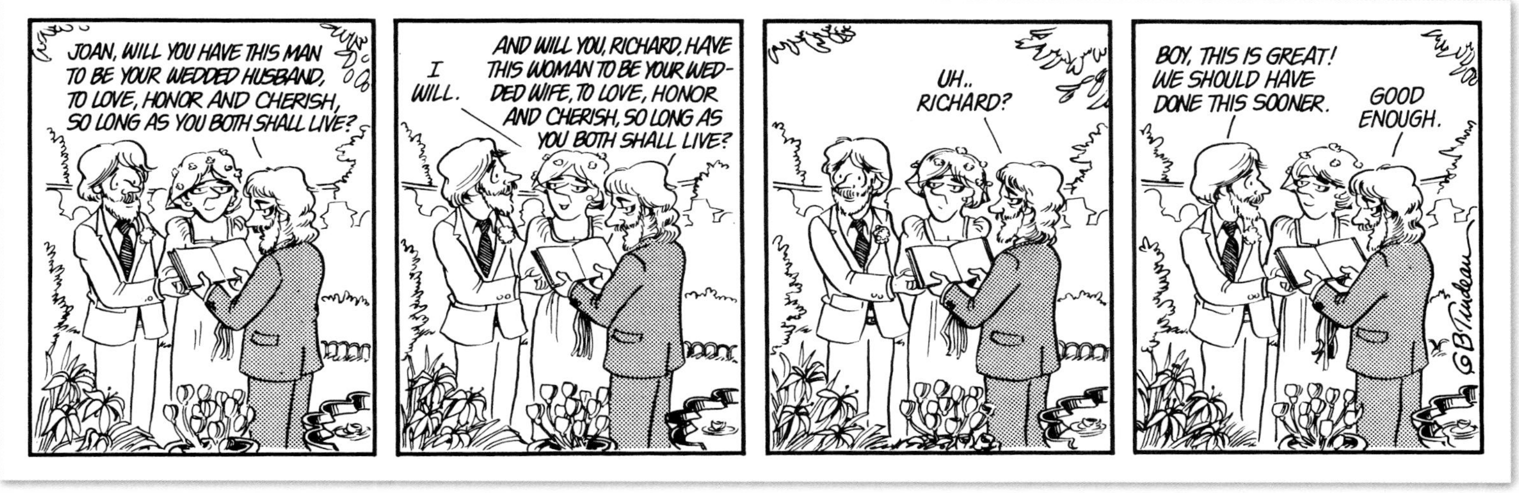
JOAN, WILL YOU HAVE THIS MAN TO BE YOUR WEDDED HUSBAND, TO LOVE, HONOR AND CHERISH, SO LONG AS YOU BOTH SHALL LIVE?
I WILL.
AND WILL YOU, RICHARD, HAVE THIS WOMAN TO BE YOUR WEDDED WIFE, TO LOVE, HONOR AND CHERISH, SO LONG AS YOU BOTH SHALL LIVE?
UH.. RICHARD?
BOY, THIS IS GREAT! WE SHOULD HAVE DONE THIS SOONER.
GOOD ENOUGH.
G B Trudeau

6/18/81

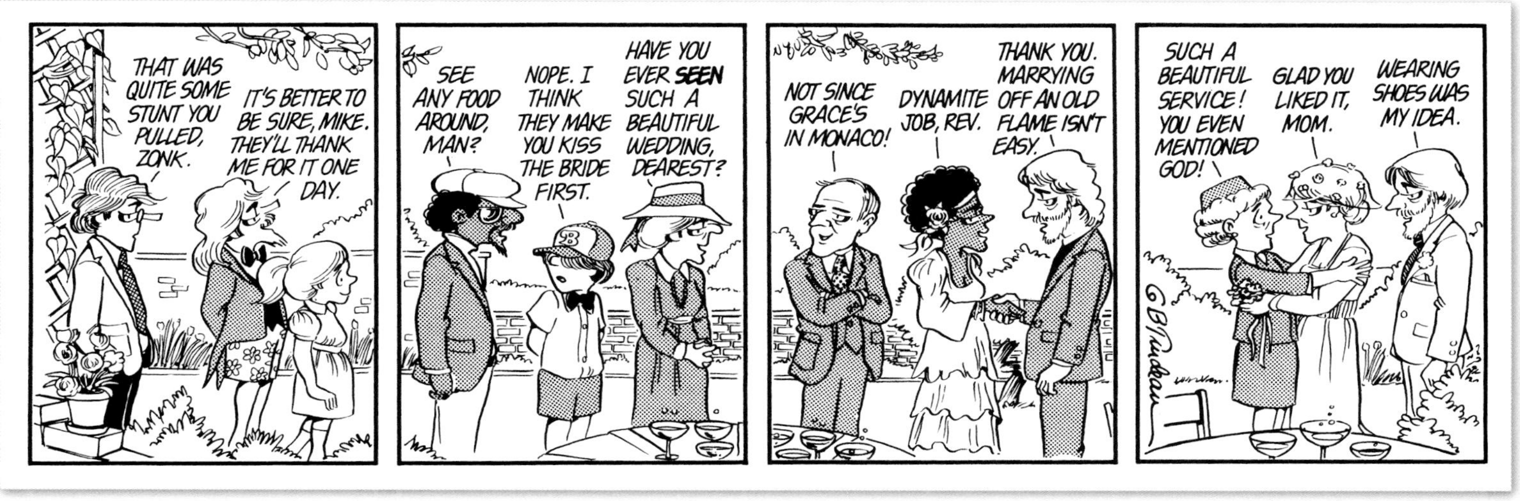
THAT WAS QUITE SOME STUNT YOU PULLED, ZONK.
IT'S BETTER TO BE SURE, MIKE. THEY'LL THANK ME FOR IT ONE DAY.
SEE ANY FOOD AROUND, MAN?
NOPE. I THINK THEY MAKE YOU KISS THE BRIDE FIRST.
HAVE YOU EVER SEEN SUCH A BEAUTIFUL WEDDING, DEAREST?
NOT SINCE GRACE'S IN MONACO!
DYNAMITE JOB, REV.
THANK YOU. MARRYING OFF AN OLD FLAME ISN'T EASY.
SUCH A BEAUTIFUL SERVICE! YOU EVEN MENTIONED GOD!
GLAD YOU LIKED IT, MOM.
WEARING SHOES WAS MY IDEA.
G B Trudeau

6/19/81

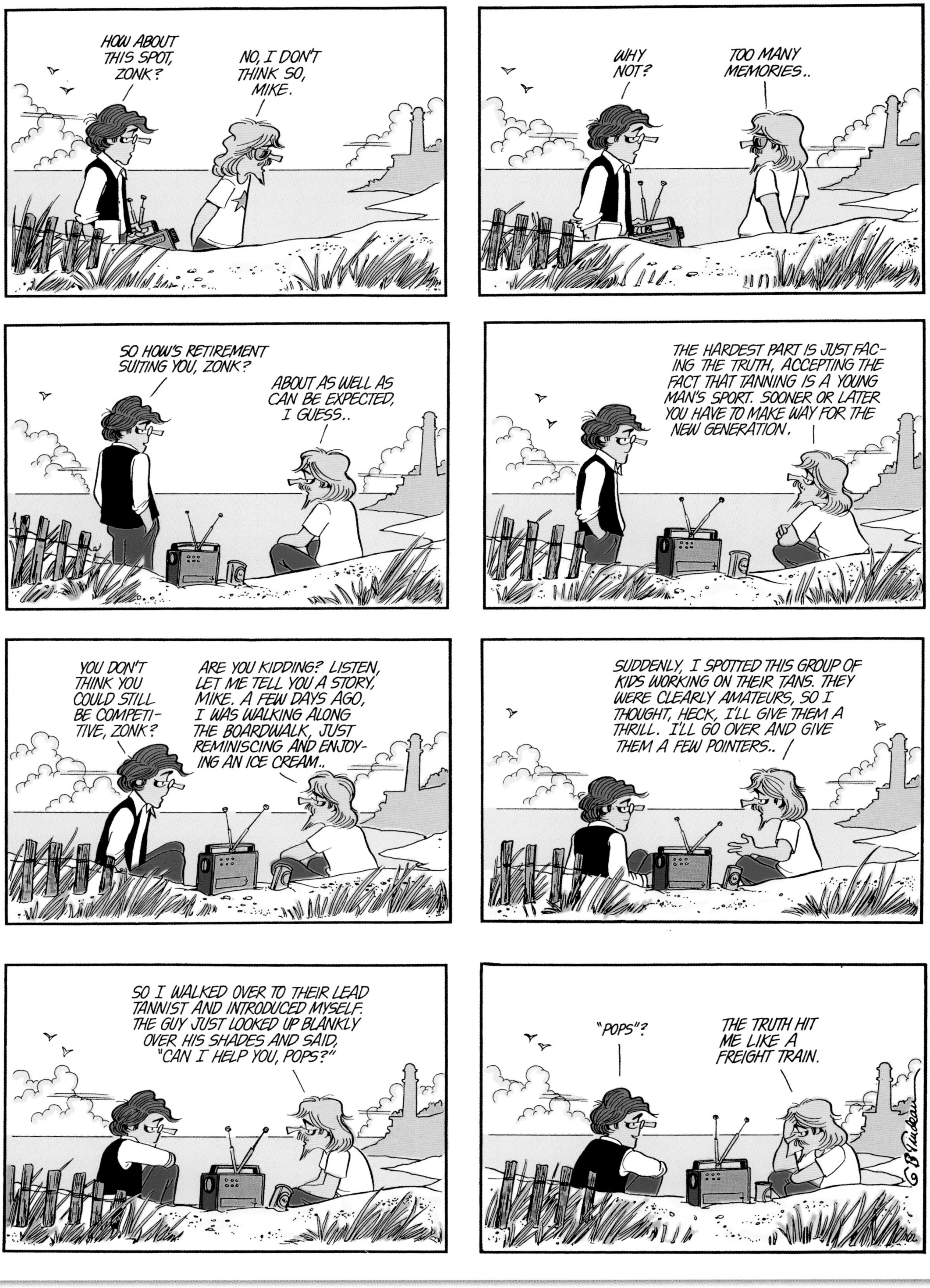

HOW ABOUT THIS SPOT, ZONK?
NO, I DON'T THINK SO, MIKE.
WHY NOT?
TOO MANY MEMORIES..
SO HOW'S RETIREMENT SUITING YOU, ZONK?
ABOUT AS WELL AS CAN BE EXPECTED, I GUESS..
THE HARDEST PART IS JUST FACING THE TRUTH, ACCEPTING THE FACT THAT TANNING IS A YOUNG MAN'S SPORT. SOONER OR LATER YOU HAVE TO MAKE WAY FOR THE NEW GENERATION.
YOU DON'T THINK YOU COULD STILL BE COMPETITIVE, ZONK?
ARE YOU KIDDING? LISTEN, LET ME TELL YOU A STORY, MIKE. A FEW DAYS AGO, I WAS WALKING ALONG THE BOARDWALK, JUST REMINISCING AND ENJOYING AN ICE CREAM..
SUDDENLY, I SPOTTED THIS GROUP OF KIDS WORKING ON THEIR TANS. THEY WERE CLEARLY AMATEURS, SO I THOUGHT, HECK, I'LL GIVE THEM A THRILL. I'LL GO OVER AND GIVE THEM A FEW POINTERS..
SO I WALKED OVER TO THEIR LEAD TANNIST AND INTRODUCED MYSELF. THE GUY JUST LOOKED UP BLANKLY OVER HIS SHADES AND SAID, "CAN I HELP YOU, POPS?"
"POPS"?
THE TRUTH HIT ME LIKE A FREIGHT TRAIN.

7/12/81

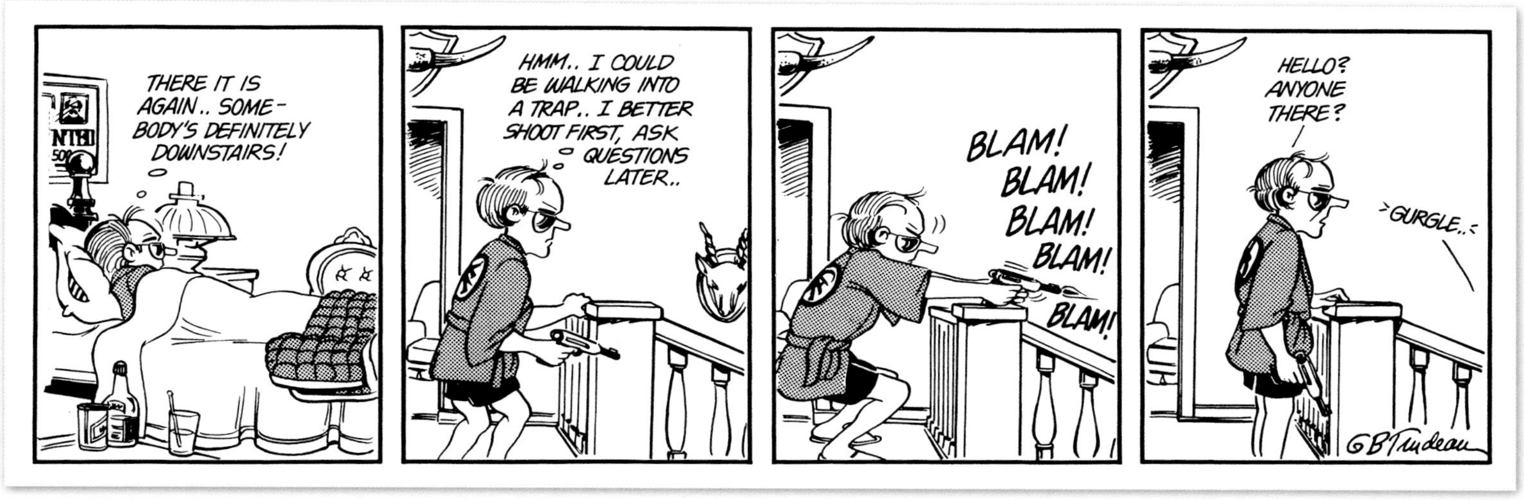
THERE IT IS AGAIN.. SOMEBODY'S DEFINITELY DOWNSTAIRS!
HMM.. I COULD BE WALKING INTO A TRAP.. I BETTER SHOOT FIRST, ASK QUESTIONS LATER..
BLAM! BLAM! BLAM! BLAM! BLAM!
HELLO? ANYONE THERE?
>GURGLE..<
G B Trudeau

8/11/81

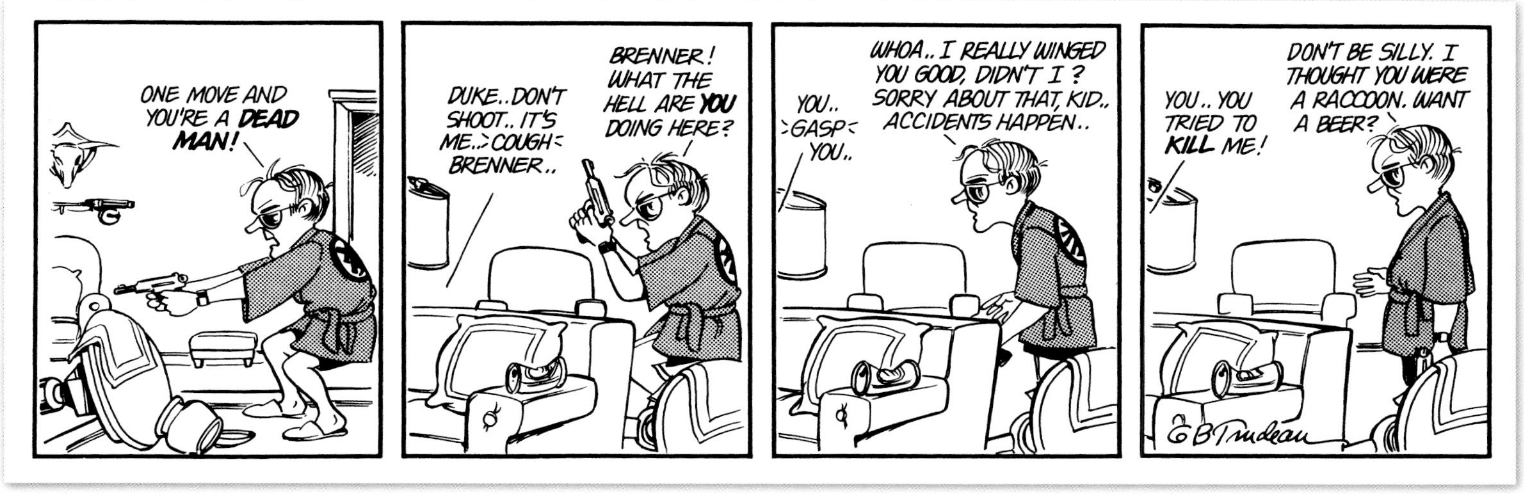
ONE MOVE AND YOU'RE A **DEAD MAN!**
DUKE.. DON'T SHOOT.. IT'S ME.. >COUGH< BRENNER..
BRENNER! WHAT THE HELL ARE **YOU** DOING HERE?
YOU.. >GASP< YOU..
WHOA.. I REALLY WINGED YOU GOOD, DIDN'T I? SORRY ABOUT THAT, KID.. ACCIDENTS HAPPEN..
YOU.. YOU TRIED TO **KILL** ME!
DON'T BE SILLY. I THOUGHT YOU **WERE** A RACCOON. WANT A BEER?
G B Trudeau

8/12/81

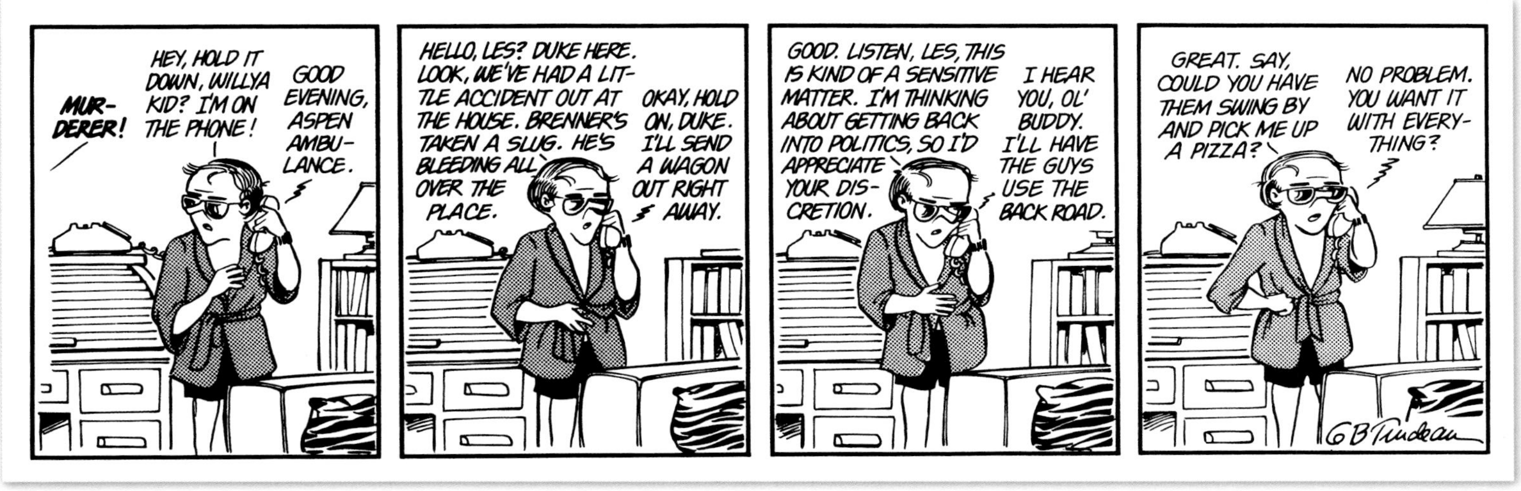
MURDERER!
HEY, HOLD IT DOWN, WILLYA KID? I'M ON THE PHONE!
GOOD EVENING, ASPEN AMBULANCE.
HELLO, LES? DUKE HERE. LOOK, WE'VE HAD A LITTLE ACCIDENT OUT AT THE HOUSE. BRENNER'S TAKEN A SLUG. HE'S BLEEDING ALL OVER THE PLACE.
OKAY, HOLD ON, DUKE. I'LL SEND A WAGON OUT RIGHT AWAY.
GOOD. LISTEN, LES, THIS IS KIND OF A SENSITIVE MATTER. I'M THINKING ABOUT GETTING BACK INTO POLITICS, SO I'D APPRECIATE YOUR DISCRETION.
I HEAR YOU, OL' BUDDY. I'LL HAVE THE GUYS USE THE BACK ROAD.
GREAT. SAY, COULD YOU HAVE THEM SWING BY AND PICK ME UP A PIZZA?
NO PROBLEM. YOU WANT IT WITH EVERYTHING?
G B Trudeau

8/14/81

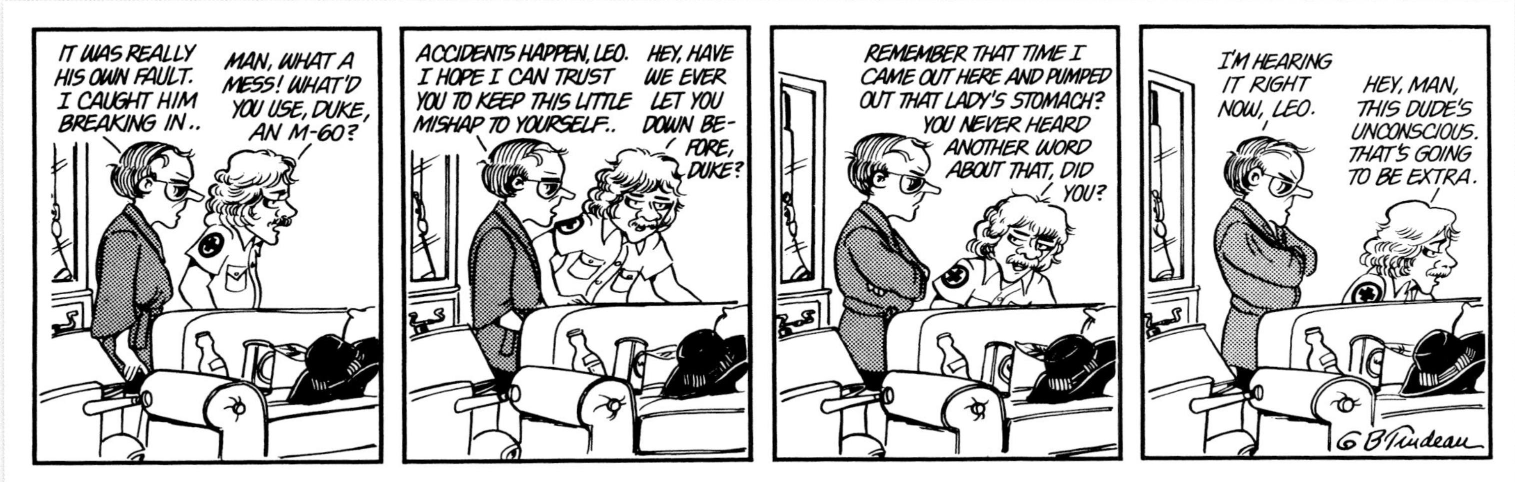
IT WAS REALLY HIS OWN FAULT. I CAUGHT HIM BREAKING IN..
MAN, WHAT A MESS! WHAT'D YOU USE, DUKE, AN M-60?
ACCIDENTS HAPPEN, LEO. I HOPE I CAN TRUST YOU TO KEEP THIS LITTLE MISHAP TO YOURSELF..
HEY, HAVE WE EVER LET YOU DOWN BEFORE, DUKE?
REMEMBER THAT TIME I CAME OUT HERE AND PUMPED OUT THAT LADY'S STOMACH? YOU NEVER HEARD ANOTHER WORD ABOUT THAT, DID YOU?
I'M HEARING IT RIGHT NOW, LEO.
HEY, MAN, THIS DUDE'S UNCONSCIOUS. THAT'S GOING TO BE EXTRA.
G B Trudeau

8/15/81

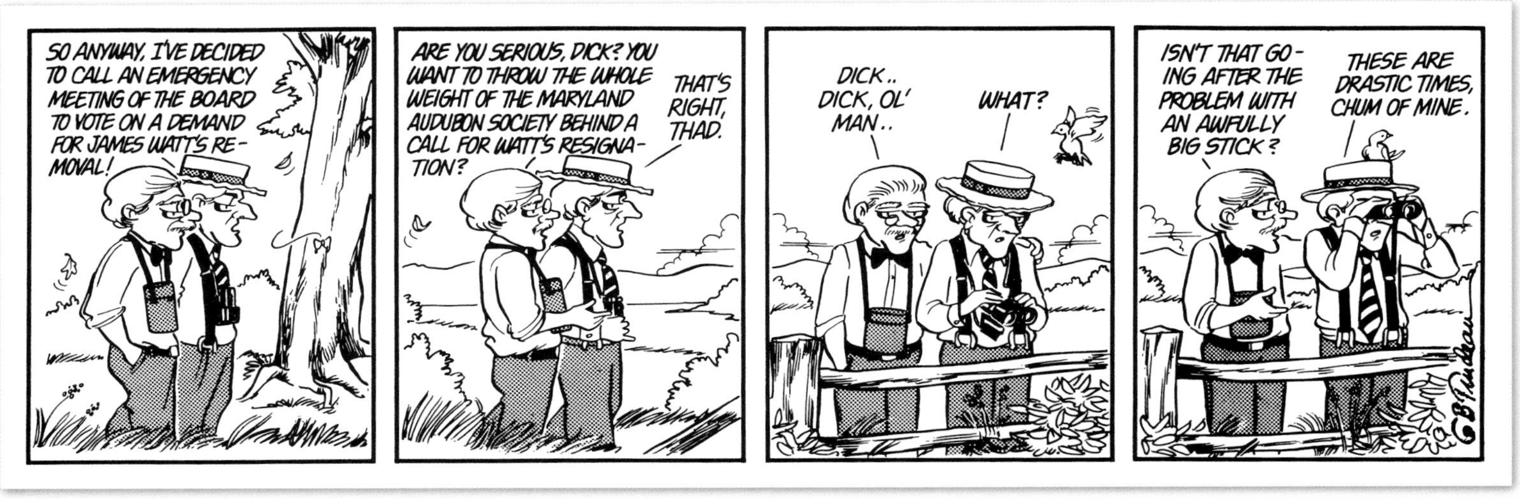
SO ANYWAY, I'VE DECIDED TO CALL AN EMERGENCY MEETING OF THE BOARD TO VOTE ON A DEMAND FOR JAMES WATT'S REMOVAL!
ARE YOU SERIOUS, DICK? YOU WANT TO THROW THE WHOLE WEIGHT OF THE MARYLAND AUDUBON SOCIETY BEHIND A CALL FOR WATT'S RESIGNATION?
THAT'S RIGHT, THAD.
DICK.. DICK, OL' MAN..
WHAT?
ISN'T THAT GOING AFTER THE PROBLEM WITH AN AWFULLY BIG STICK?
THESE ARE DRASTIC TIMES, CHUM OF MINE.
G B Trudeau

9/14/81

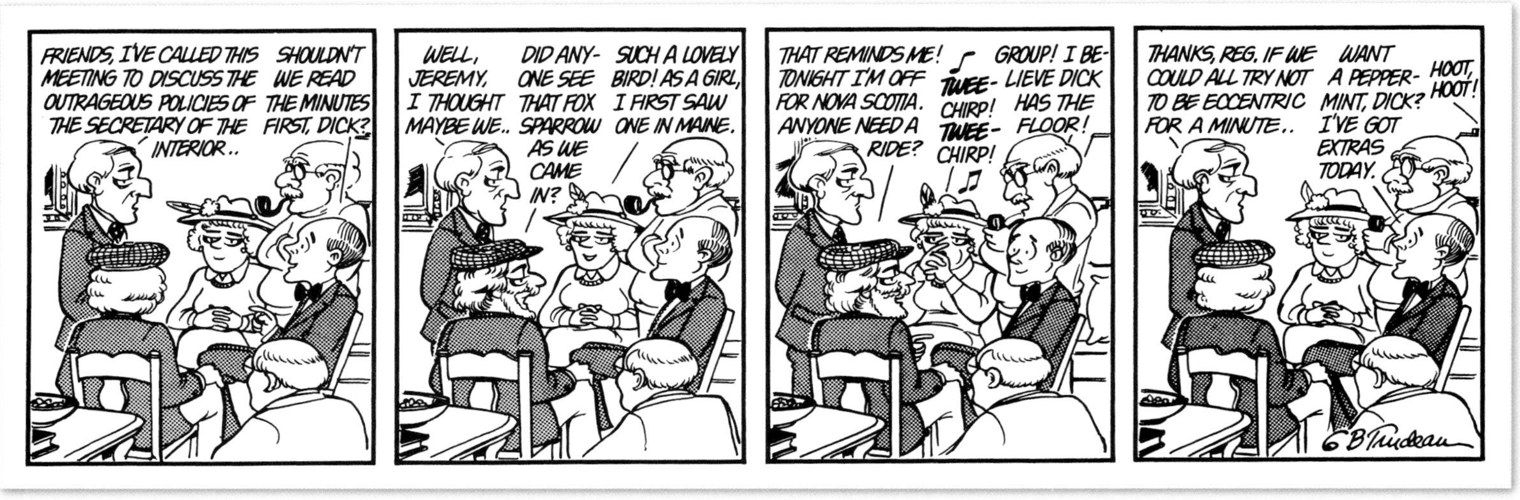
FRIENDS, I'VE CALLED THIS MEETING TO DISCUSS THE OUTRAGEOUS POLICIES OF THE SECRETARY OF THE INTERIOR..
SHOULDN'T WE READ THE MINUTES FIRST, DICK?
WELL, JEREMY, I THOUGHT MAYBE WE..
DID ANYONE SEE THAT FOX SPARROW AS WE CAME IN?
SUCH A LOVELY BIRD! AS A GIRL, I FIRST SAW ONE IN MAINE.
THAT REMINDS ME! TONIGHT I'M OFF FOR NOVA SCOTIA. ANYONE NEED A RIDE?
TWEE-CHIRP! TWEE-CHIRP!
GROUP! I BELIEVE DICK HAS THE FLOOR!
THANKS, REG. IF WE COULD ALL TRY NOT TO BE ECCENTRIC FOR A MINUTE..
WANT A PEPPERMINT, DICK? I'VE GOT EXTRAS TODAY.
HOOT, HOOT!
G B Trudeau

9/16/81

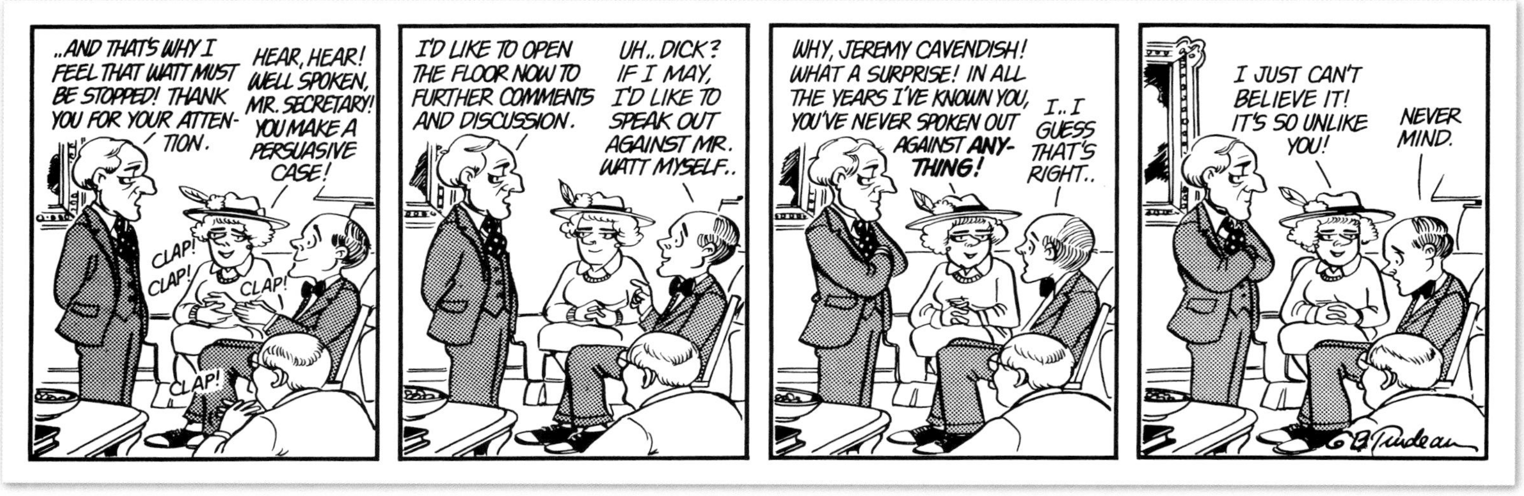
..AND THAT'S WHY I FEEL THAT WATT MUST BE STOPPED! THANK YOU FOR YOUR ATTENTION.
HEAR, HEAR! WELL SPOKEN, MR. SECRETARY! YOU MAKE A PERSUASIVE CASE!
CLAP! CLAP! CLAP! CLAP!
I'D LIKE TO OPEN THE FLOOR NOW TO FURTHER COMMENTS AND DISCUSSION.
UH.. DICK? IF I MAY, I'D LIKE TO SPEAK OUT AGAINST MR. WATT MYSELF..
WHY, JEREMY CAVENDISH! WHAT A SURPRISE! IN ALL THE YEARS I'VE KNOWN YOU, YOU'VE NEVER SPOKEN OUT AGAINST ANYTHING!
I.. I GUESS THAT'S RIGHT..
I JUST CAN'T BELIEVE IT! IT'S SO UNLIKE YOU!
NEVER MIND.
G B Trudeau

9/18/81

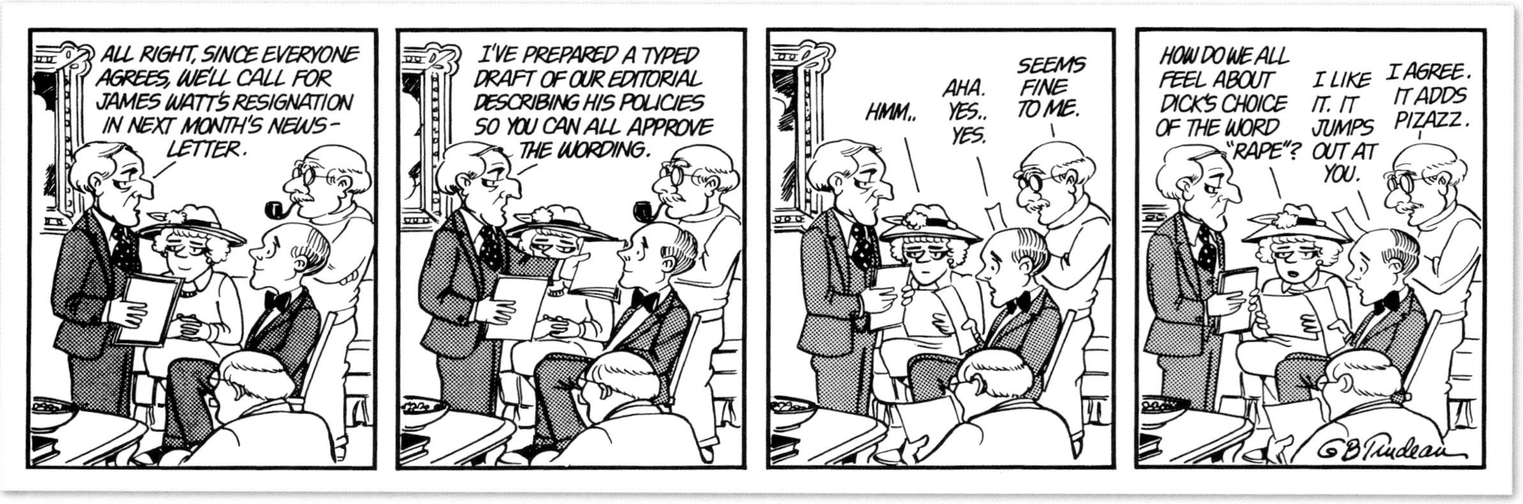
ALL RIGHT, SINCE EVERYONE AGREES, WE'LL CALL FOR JAMES WATT'S RESIGNATION IN NEXT MONTH'S NEWSLETTER.
I'VE PREPARED A TYPED DRAFT OF OUR EDITORIAL DESCRIBING HIS POLICIES SO YOU CAN ALL APPROVE THE WORDING.
HMM..
AHA. YES.. YES.
SEEMS FINE TO ME.
HOW DO WE ALL FEEL ABOUT DICK'S CHOICE OF THE WORD "RAPE"?
I LIKE IT. IT JUMPS OUT AT YOU.
I AGREE. IT ADDS PIZAZZ.
G B Trudeau

9/19/81

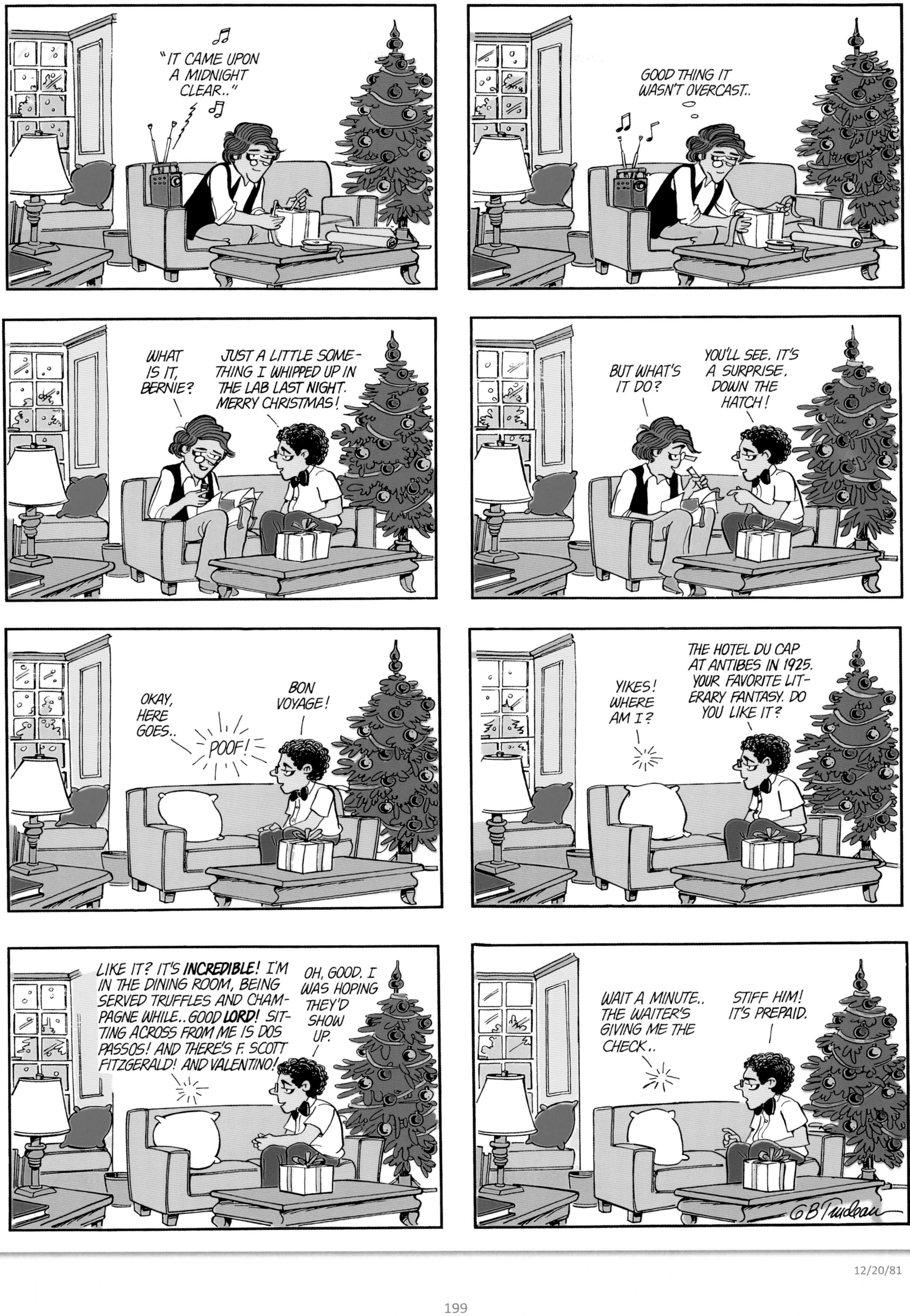
"IT CAME UPON A MIDNIGHT CLEAR.."
GOOD THING IT WASN'T OVERCAST..
WHAT IS IT, BERNIE?
JUST A LITTLE SOMETHING I WHIPPED UP IN THE LAB LAST NIGHT. MERRY CHRISTMAS!
BUT WHAT'S IT DO?
YOU'LL SEE. IT'S A SURPRISE. DOWN THE HATCH!
OKAY, HERE GOES..
POOF!
BON VOYAGE!
YIKES! WHERE AM I?
THE HOTEL DU CAP AT ANTIBES IN 1925. YOUR FAVORITE LITERARY FANTASY. DO YOU LIKE IT?
LIKE IT? IT'S INCREDIBLE! I'M IN THE DINING ROOM, BEING SERVED TRUFFLES AND CHAMPAGNE WHILE..GOOD LORD! SITTING ACROSS FROM ME IS DOS PASSOS! AND THERE'S F. SCOTT FITZGERALD! AND VALENTINO!
OH, GOOD. I WAS HOPING THEY'D SHOW UP.
WAIT A MINUTE.. THE WAITER'S GIVING ME THE CHECK..
STIFF HIM! IT'S PREPAID.
G.B.Trudeau

12/20/81

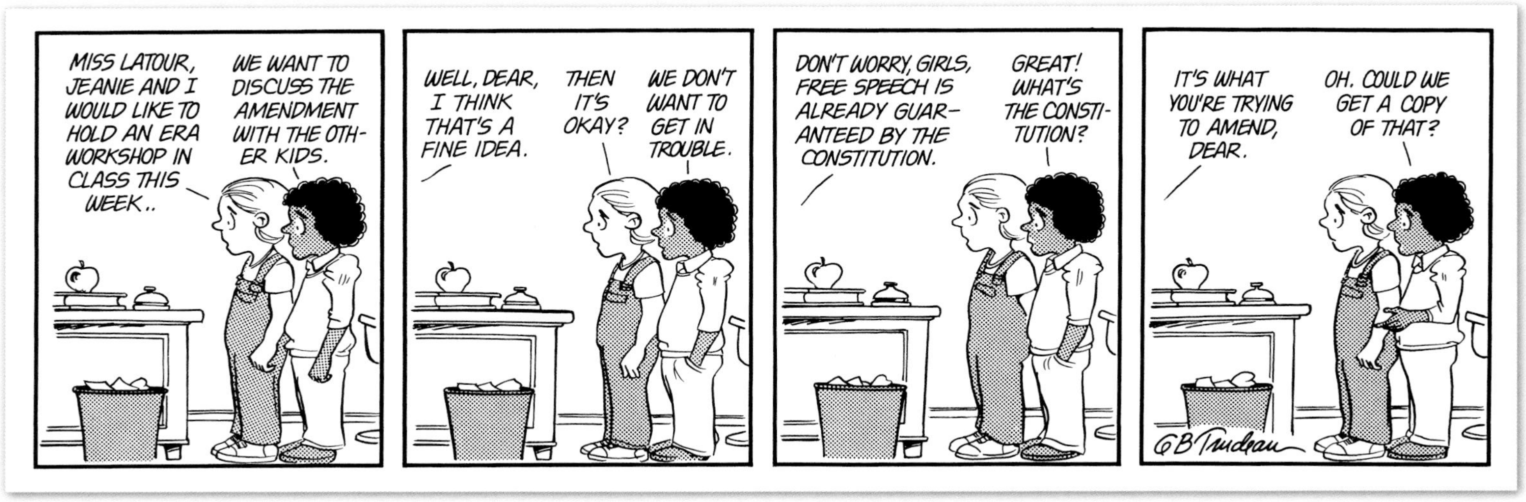
MISS LATOUR, JEANIE AND I WOULD LIKE TO HOLD AN ERA WORKSHOP IN CLASS THIS WEEK..
WE WANT TO DISCUSS THE AMENDMENT WITH THE OTHER KIDS.
WELL, DEAR, I THINK THAT'S A FINE IDEA.
THEN IT'S OKAY?
WE DON'T WANT TO GET IN TROUBLE.
DON'T WORRY, GIRLS, FREE SPEECH IS ALREADY GUARANTEED BY THE CONSTITUTION.
GREAT! WHAT'S THE CONSTITUTION?
IT'S WHAT YOU'RE TRYING TO AMEND, DEAR.
OH. COULD WE GET A COPY OF THAT?
GB Trudeau

12/7/81

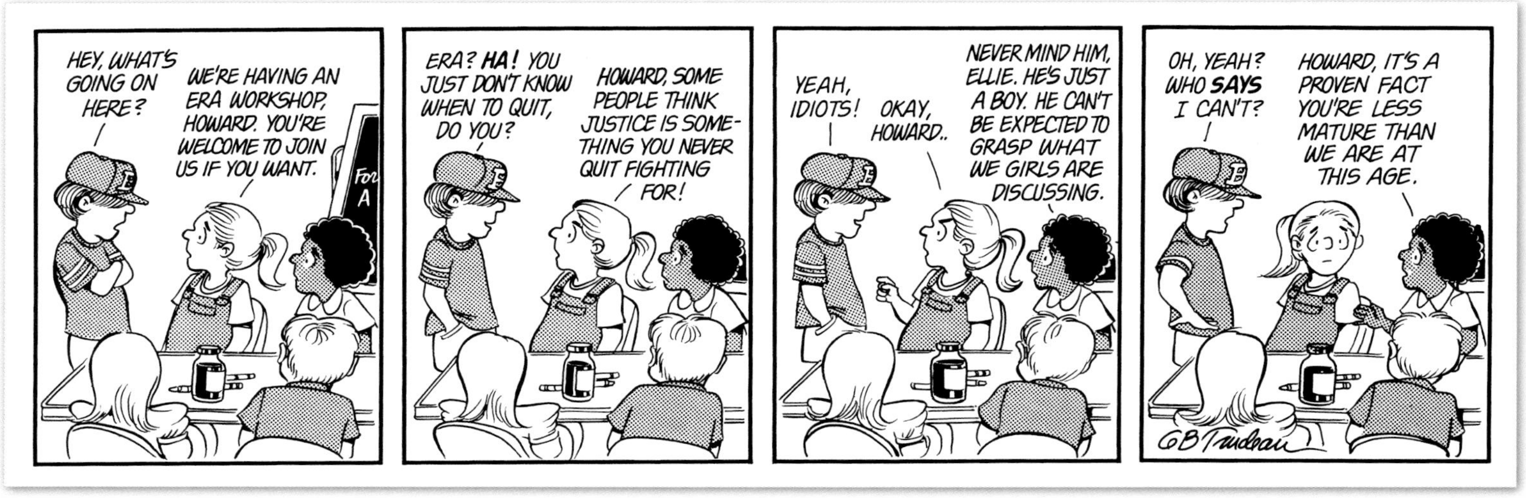
HEY, WHAT'S GOING ON HERE?
WE'RE HAVING AN ERA WORKSHOP, HOWARD. YOU'RE WELCOME TO JOIN US IF YOU WANT.
ERA? HA! YOU JUST DON'T KNOW WHEN TO QUIT, DO YOU?
HOWARD, SOME PEOPLE THINK JUSTICE IS SOMETHING YOU NEVER QUIT FIGHTING FOR!
YEAH, IDIOTS!
OKAY, HOWARD..
NEVER MIND HIM, ELLIE. HE'S JUST A BOY. HE CAN'T BE EXPECTED TO GRASP WHAT WE GIRLS ARE DISCUSSING.
OH, YEAH? WHO SAYS I CAN'T?
HOWARD, IT'S A PROVEN FACT YOU'RE LESS MATURE THAN WE ARE AT THIS AGE.
GB Trudeau

12/8/81

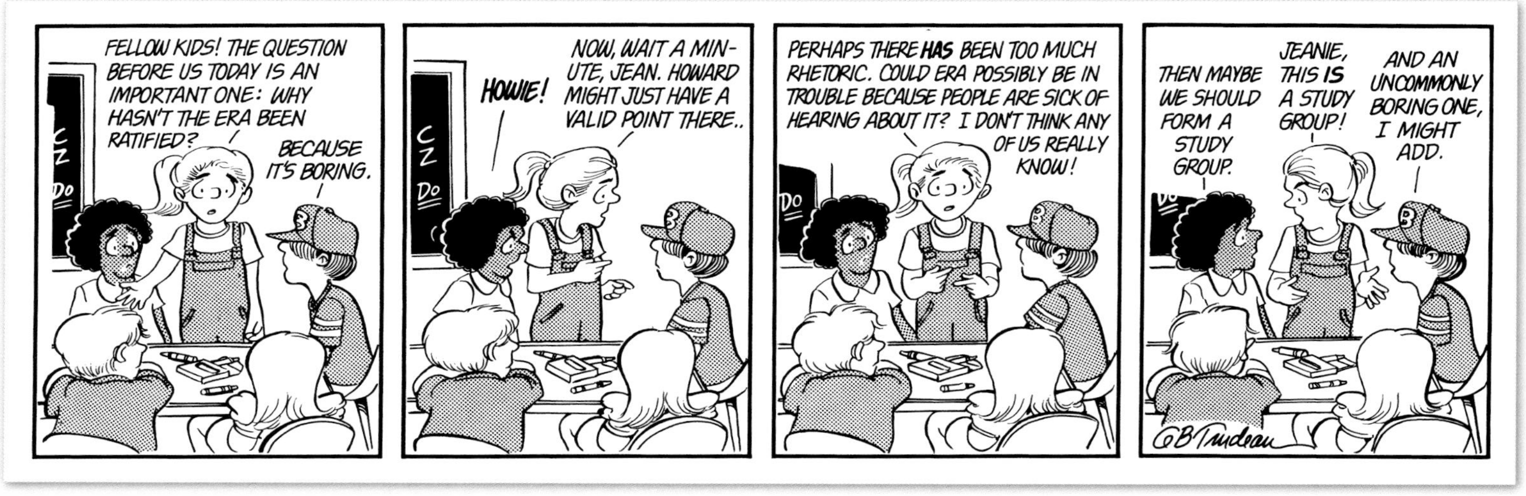
FELLOW KIDS! THE QUESTION BEFORE US TODAY IS AN IMPORTANT ONE: WHY HASN'T THE ERA BEEN RATIFIED?
BECAUSE IT'S BORING.
HOWIE!
NOW, WAIT A MINUTE, JEAN. HOWARD MIGHT JUST HAVE A VALID POINT THERE..
PERHAPS THERE HAS BEEN TOO MUCH RHETORIC. COULD ERA POSSIBLY BE IN TROUBLE BECAUSE PEOPLE ARE SICK OF HEARING ABOUT IT? I DON'T THINK ANY OF US REALLY KNOW!
THEN MAYBE WE SHOULD FORM A STUDY GROUP.
JEANIE, THIS IS A STUDY GROUP!
AND AN UNCOMMONLY BORING ONE, I MIGHT ADD.
GB Trudeau

12/9/81

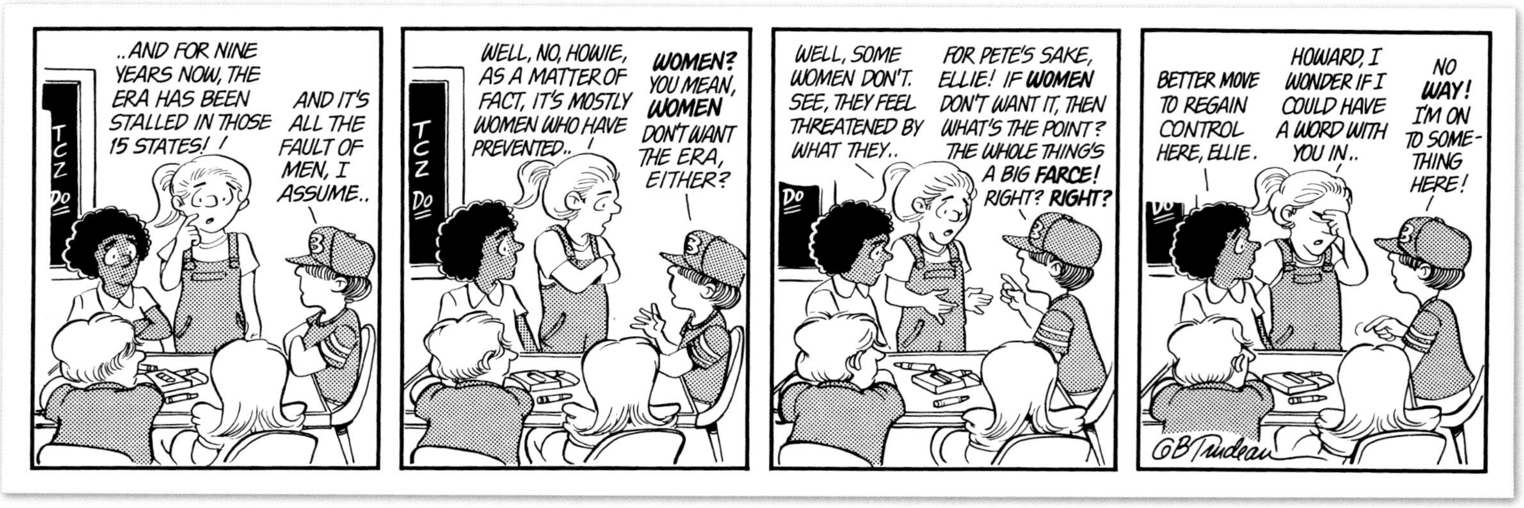
..AND FOR NINE YEARS NOW, THE ERA HAS BEEN STALLED IN THOSE 15 STATES!
AND IT'S ALL THE FAULT OF MEN, I ASSUME..
WELL, NO, HOWIE, AS A MATTER OF FACT, IT'S MOSTLY WOMEN WHO HAVE PREVENTED..
WOMEN? YOU MEAN, WOMEN DON'T WANT THE ERA, EITHER?
WELL, SOME WOMEN DON'T. SEE, THEY FEEL THREATENED BY WHAT THEY..
FOR PETE'S SAKE, ELLIE! IF WOMEN DON'T WANT IT, THEN WHAT'S THE POINT? THE WHOLE THING'S A BIG FARCE! RIGHT? RIGHT?
BETTER MOVE TO REGAIN CONTROL HERE, ELLIE.
HOWARD, I WONDER IF I COULD HAVE A WORD WITH YOU IN..
NO WAY! I'M ON TO SOMETHING HERE!
GB Trudeau

12/10/81

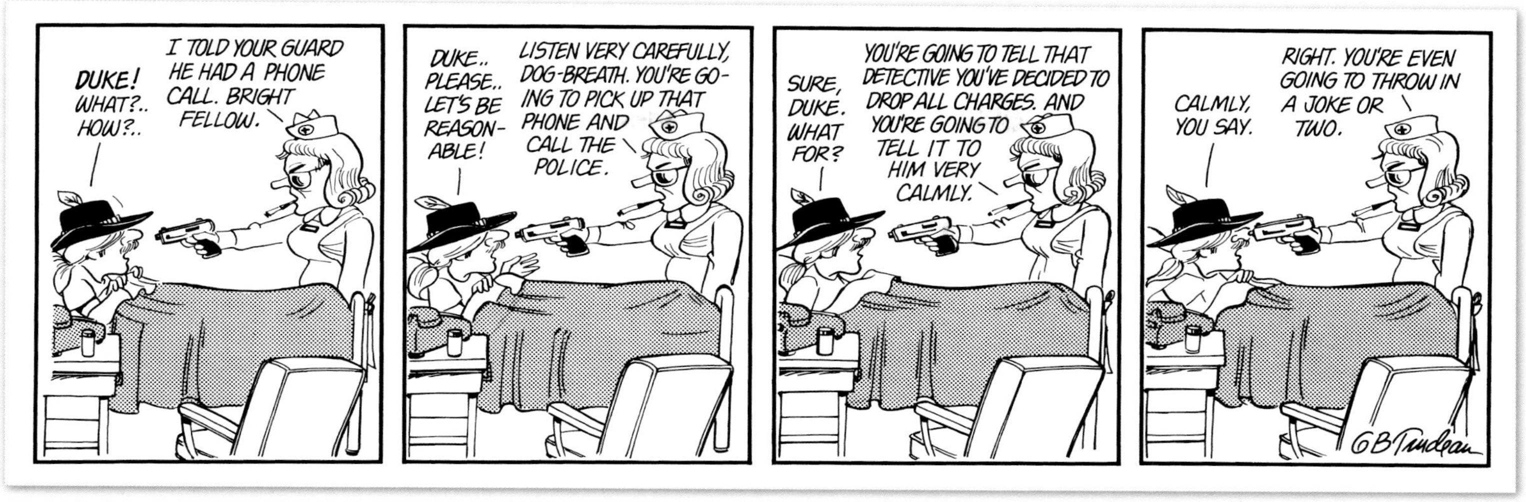
DUKE! WHAT?.. HOW?..
I TOLD YOUR GUARD HE HAD A PHONE CALL. BRIGHT FELLOW.
DUKE.. PLEASE.. LET'S BE REASON-ABLE!
LISTEN VERY CAREFULLY, DOG-BREATH. YOU'RE GO-ING TO PICK UP THAT PHONE AND CALL THE POLICE.
SURE, DUKE. WHAT FOR?
YOU'RE GOING TO TELL THAT DETECTIVE YOU'VE DECIDED TO DROP ALL CHARGES. AND YOU'RE GOING TO TELL IT TO HIM VERY CALMLY.
CALMLY, YOU SAY.
RIGHT. YOU'RE EVEN GOING TO THROW IN A JOKE OR TWO.

11/3/81

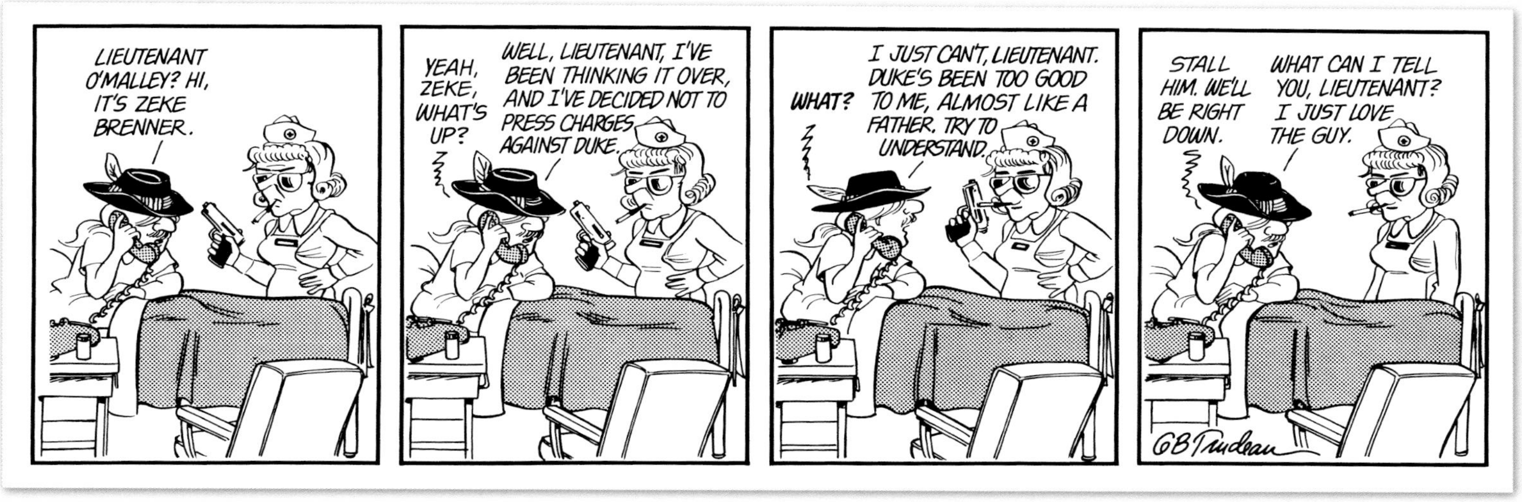
LIEUTENANT O'MALLEY? HI, IT'S ZEKE BRENNER.
YEAH, ZEKE, WHAT'S UP?
WELL, LIEUTENANT, I'VE BEEN THINKING IT OVER, AND I'VE DECIDED NOT TO PRESS CHARGES AGAINST DUKE.
WHAT?
I JUST CAN'T, LIEUTENANT. DUKE'S BEEN TOO GOOD TO ME, ALMOST LIKE A FATHER. TRY TO UNDERSTAND.
STALL HIM. WE'LL BE RIGHT DOWN.
WHAT CAN I TELL YOU, LIEUTENANT? I JUST LOVE THE GUY.

11/4/81

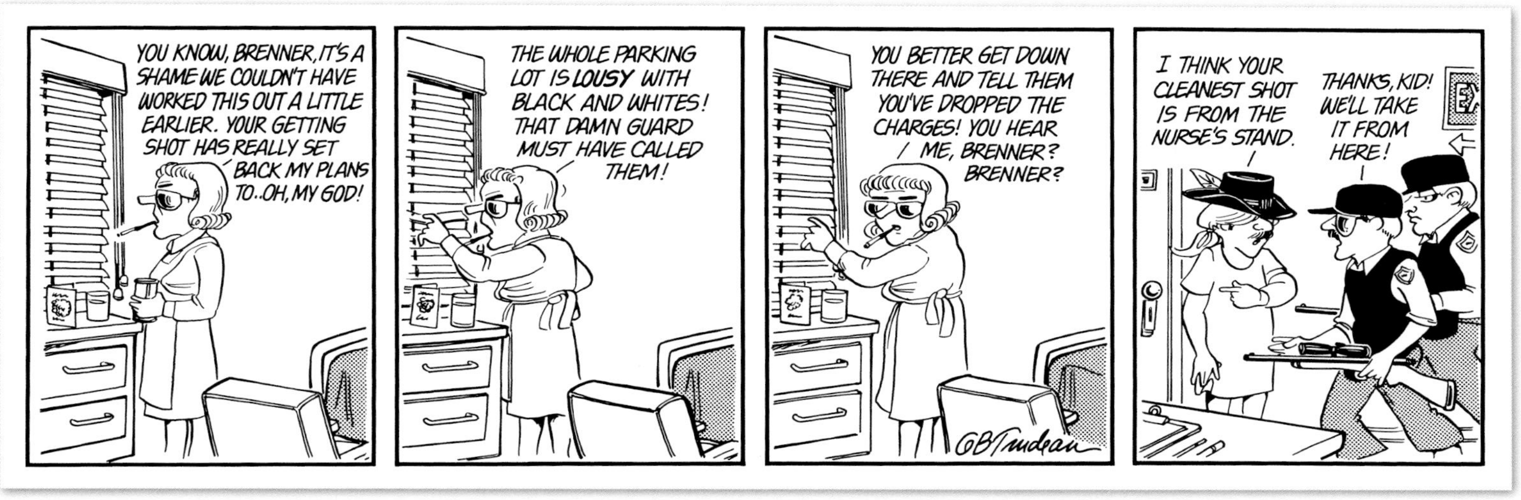
YOU KNOW, BRENNER, IT'S A SHAME WE COULDN'T HAVE WORKED THIS OUT A LITTLE EARLIER. YOUR GETTING SHOT HAS REALLY SET BACK MY PLANS TO..OH, MY GOD!
THE WHOLE PARKING LOT IS LOUSY WITH BLACK AND WHITES! THAT DAMN GUARD MUST HAVE CALLED THEM!
YOU BETTER GET DOWN THERE AND TELL THEM YOU'VE DROPPED THE CHARGES! YOU HEAR ME, BRENNER? BRENNER?
I THINK YOUR CLEANEST SHOT IS FROM THE NURSE'S STAND.
THANKS, KID! WE'LL TAKE IT FROM HERE!

11/6/81

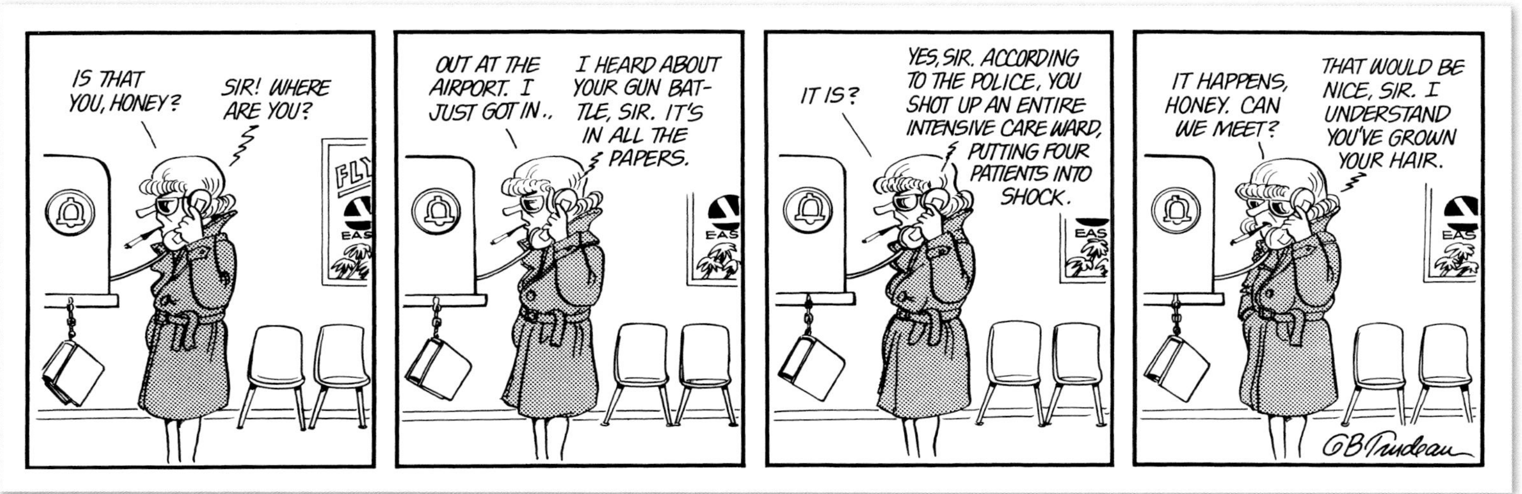
IS THAT YOU, HONEY?
SIR! WHERE ARE YOU?
OUT AT THE AIRPORT. I JUST GOT IN..
I HEARD ABOUT YOUR GUN BAT-TLE, SIR. IT'S IN ALL THE PAPERS.
IT IS?
YES, SIR. ACCORDING TO THE POLICE, YOU SHOT UP AN ENTIRE INTENSIVE CARE WARD, PUTTING FOUR PATIENTS INTO SHOCK.
IT HAPPENS, HONEY. CAN WE MEET?
THAT WOULD BE NICE, SIR. I UNDERSTAND YOU'VE GROWN YOUR HAIR.

11/7/81

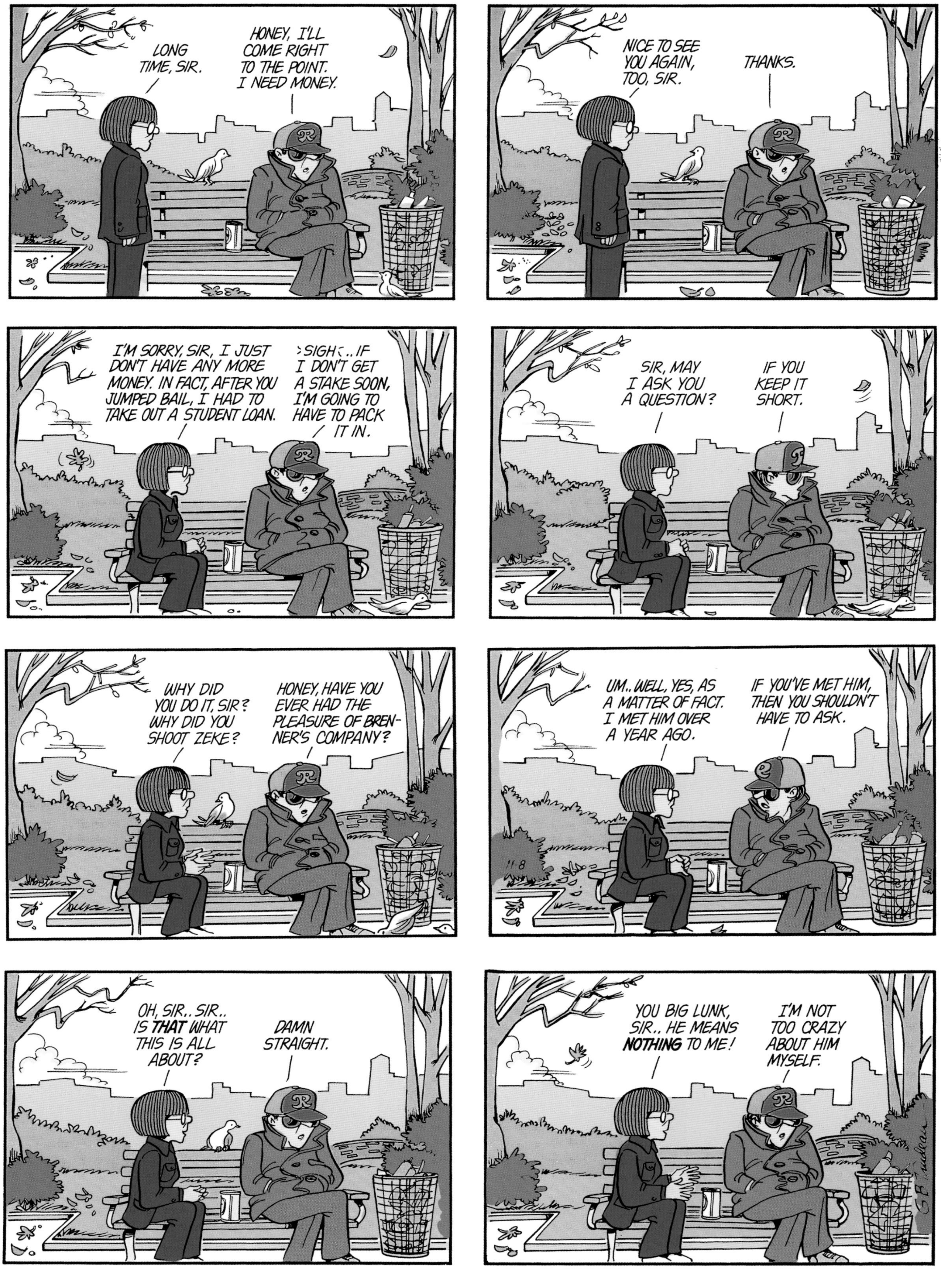
LONG TIME, SIR.
HONEY, I'LL COME RIGHT TO THE POINT. I NEED MONEY.
NICE TO SEE YOU AGAIN, TOO, SIR.
THANKS.
I'M SORRY, SIR, I JUST DON'T HAVE ANY MORE MONEY. IN FACT, AFTER YOU JUMPED BAIL, I HAD TO TAKE OUT A STUDENT LOAN.
›SIGH‹.. IF I DON'T GET A STAKE SOON, I'M GOING TO HAVE TO PACK IT IN.
SIR, MAY I ASK YOU A QUESTION?
IF YOU KEEP IT SHORT.
WHY DID YOU DO IT, SIR? WHY DID YOU SHOOT ZEKE?
HONEY, HAVE YOU EVER HAD THE PLEASURE OF BRENNER'S COMPANY?
UM.. WELL, YES, AS A MATTER OF FACT. I MET HIM OVER A YEAR AGO.
IF YOU'VE MET HIM, THEN YOU SHOULDN'T HAVE TO ASK.
11-8
OH, SIR.. SIR.. IS **THAT** WHAT THIS IS ALL ABOUT?
DAMN STRAIGHT.
YOU BIG LUNK, SIR.. HE MEANS **NOTHING** TO ME!
I'M NOT TOO CRAZY ABOUT HIM MYSELF.
GBTrudeau

11/8/81

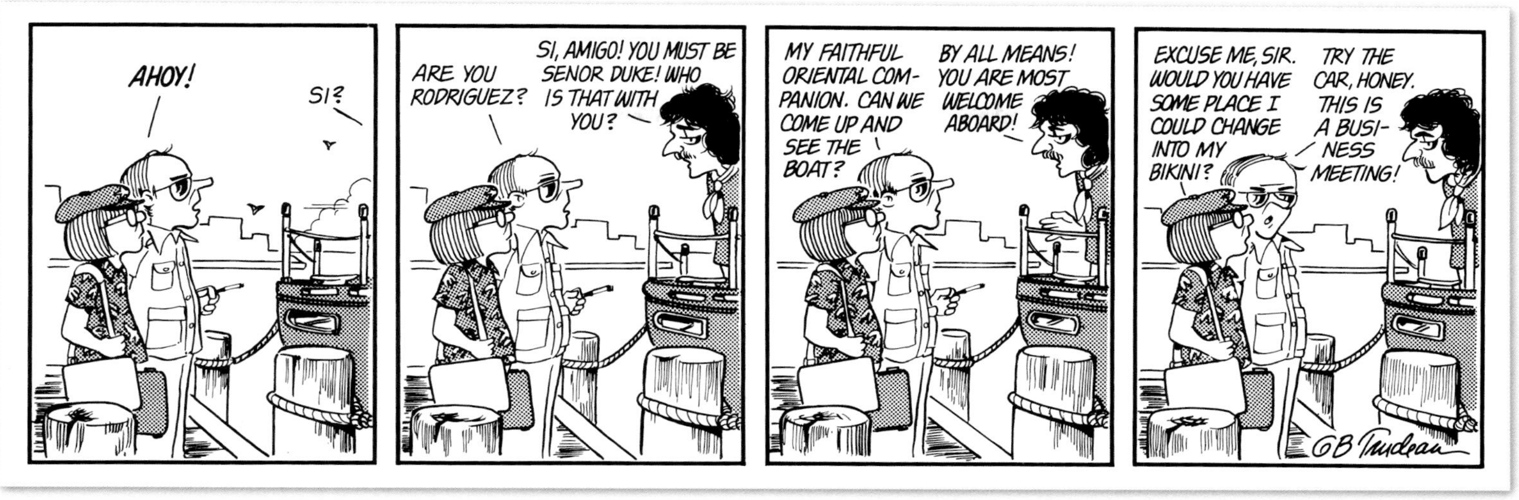
AHOY!
SI?
ARE YOU RODRIGUEZ?
SI, AMIGO! YOU MUST BE SENOR DUKE! WHO IS THAT WITH YOU?
MY FAITHFUL ORIENTAL COMPANION. CAN WE COME UP AND SEE THE BOAT?
BY ALL MEANS! YOU ARE MOST WELCOME ABOARD!
EXCUSE ME, SIR. WOULD YOU HAVE SOME PLACE I COULD CHANGE INTO MY BIKINI?
TRY THE CAR, HONEY. THIS IS A BUSINESS MEETING!
GB Trudeau

12/28/81

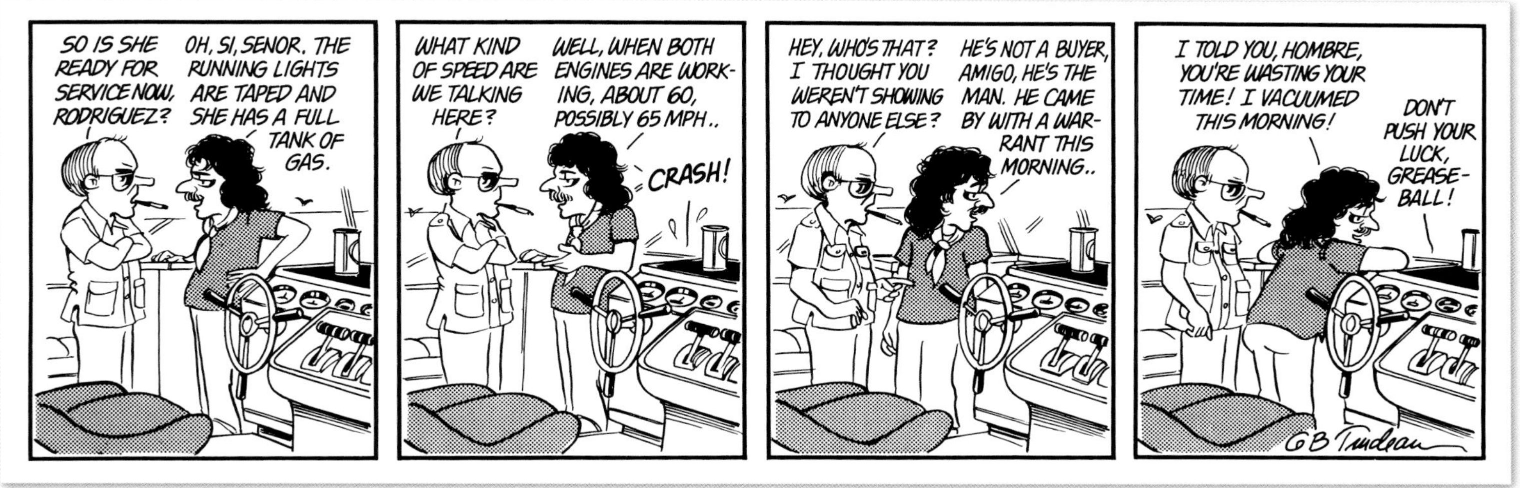
SO IS SHE READY FOR SERVICE NOW, RODRIGUEZ?
OH, SI, SENOR. THE RUNNING LIGHTS ARE TAPED AND SHE HAS A FULL TANK OF GAS.
WHAT KIND OF SPEED ARE WE TALKING HERE?
WELL, WHEN BOTH ENGINES ARE WORKING, ABOUT 60, POSSIBLY 65 MPH..
CRASH!
HEY, WHO'S THAT? I THOUGHT YOU WEREN'T SHOWING TO ANYONE ELSE?
HE'S NOT A BUYER, AMIGO, HE'S THE MAN. HE CAME BY WITH A WARRANT THIS MORNING..
I TOLD YOU, HOMBRE, YOU'RE WASTING YOUR TIME! I VACUUMED THIS MORNING!
DON'T PUSH YOUR LUCK, GREASEBALL!
GB Trudeau

12/29/81

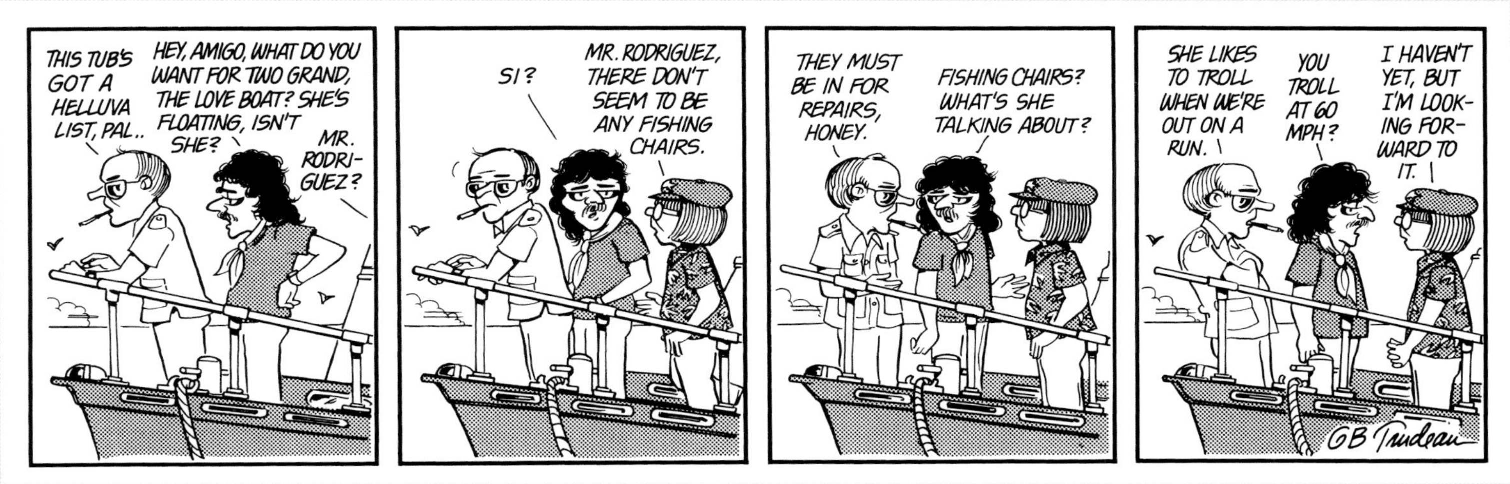
THIS TUB'S GOT A HELLUVA LIST, PAL..
HEY, AMIGO, WHAT DO YOU WANT FOR TWO GRAND, THE LOVE BOAT? SHE'S FLOATING, ISN'T SHE?
MR. RODRIGUEZ?
SI?
MR. RODRIGUEZ, THERE DON'T SEEM TO BE ANY FISHING CHAIRS.
THEY MUST BE IN FOR REPAIRS, HONEY.
FISHING CHAIRS? WHAT'S SHE TALKING ABOUT?
SHE LIKES TO TROLL WHEN WE'RE OUT ON A RUN.
YOU TROLL AT 60 MPH?
I HAVEN'T YET, BUT I'M LOOKING FORWARD TO IT.
GB Trudeau

12/30/81

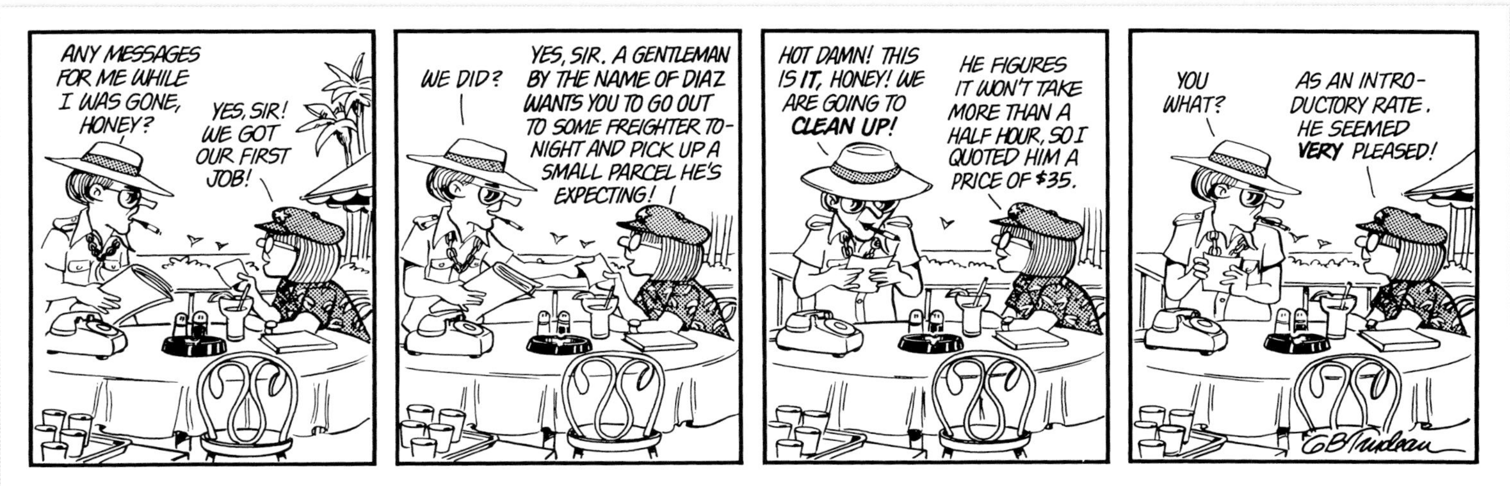
ANY MESSAGES FOR ME WHILE I WAS GONE, HONEY?
YES, SIR! WE GOT OUR FIRST JOB!
WE DID?
YES, SIR. A GENTLEMAN BY THE NAME OF DIAZ WANTS YOU TO GO OUT TO SOME FREIGHTER TONIGHT AND PICK UP A SMALL PARCEL HE'S EXPECTING!
HOT DAMN! THIS IS IT, HONEY! WE ARE GOING TO CLEAN UP!
HE FIGURES IT WON'T TAKE MORE THAN A HALF HOUR, SO I QUOTED HIM A PRICE OF $35.
YOU WHAT?
AS AN INTRODUCTORY RATE. HE SEEMED VERY PLEASED!
GB Trudeau

1/2/82

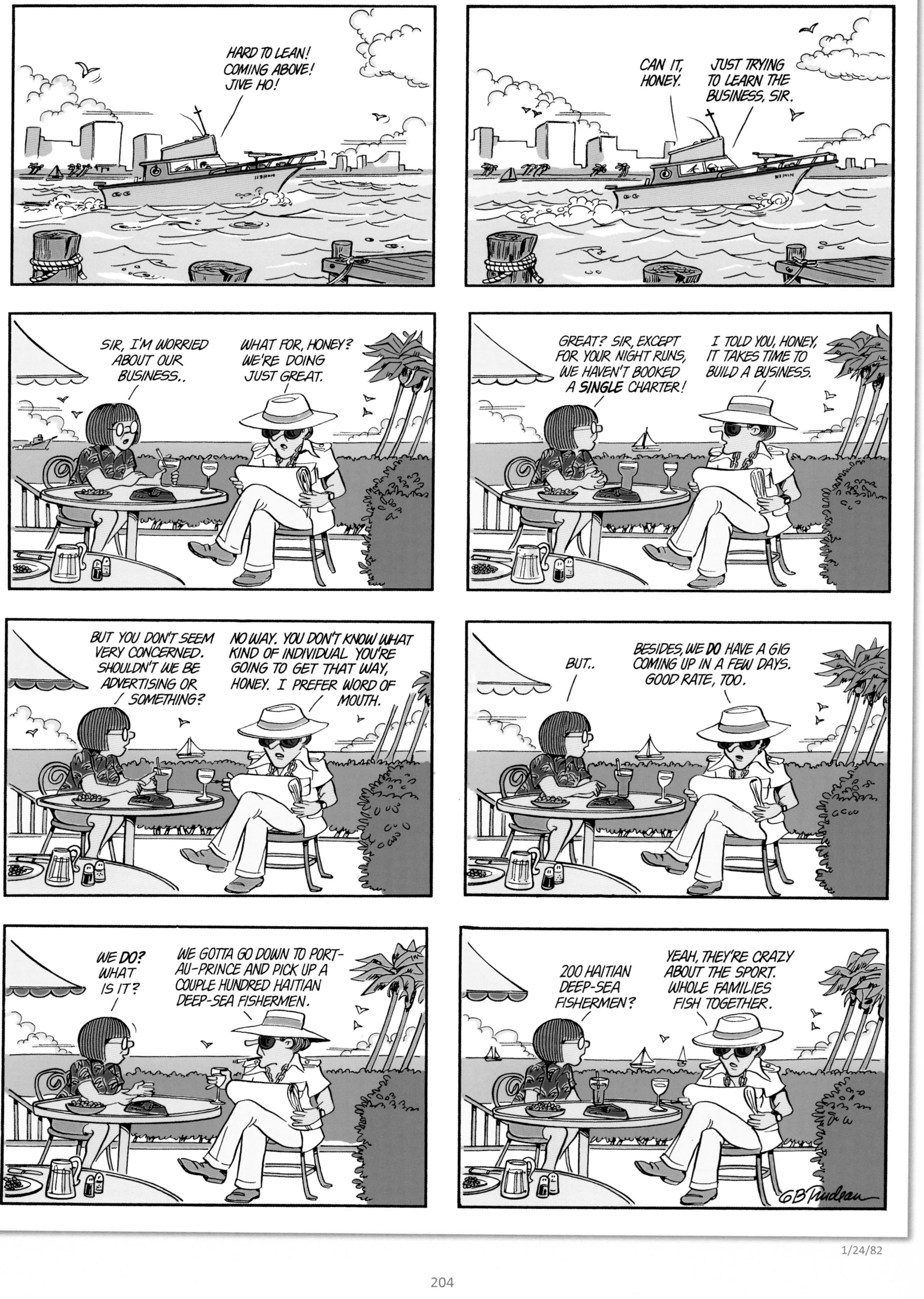
HARD TO LEAN! COMING ABOVE! JIVE HO!
CAN IT, HONEY.
JUST TRYING TO LEARN THE BUSINESS, SIR.
SIR, I'M WORRIED ABOUT OUR BUSINESS..
WHAT FOR, HONEY? WE'RE DOING JUST GREAT.
GREAT? SIR, EXCEPT FOR YOUR NIGHT RUNS, WE HAVEN'T BOOKED A SINGLE CHARTER!
I TOLD YOU, HONEY, IT TAKES TIME TO BUILD A BUSINESS.
BUT YOU DON'T SEEM VERY CONCERNED. SHOULDN'T WE BE ADVERTISING OR SOMETHING?
NO WAY. YOU DON'T KNOW WHAT KIND OF INDIVIDUAL YOU'RE GOING TO GET THAT WAY, HONEY. I PREFER WORD OF MOUTH.
BUT..
BESIDES, WE DO HAVE A GIG COMING UP IN A FEW DAYS. GOOD RATE, TOO.
WE DO? WHAT IS IT?
WE GOTTA GO DOWN TO PORT-AU-PRINCE AND PICK UP A COUPLE HUNDRED HAITIAN DEEP-SEA FISHERMEN.
200 HAITIAN DEEP-SEA FISHERMEN?
YEAH, THEY'RE CRAZY ABOUT THE SPORT. WHOLE FAMILIES FISH TOGETHER.
GB Trudeau

1/24/82

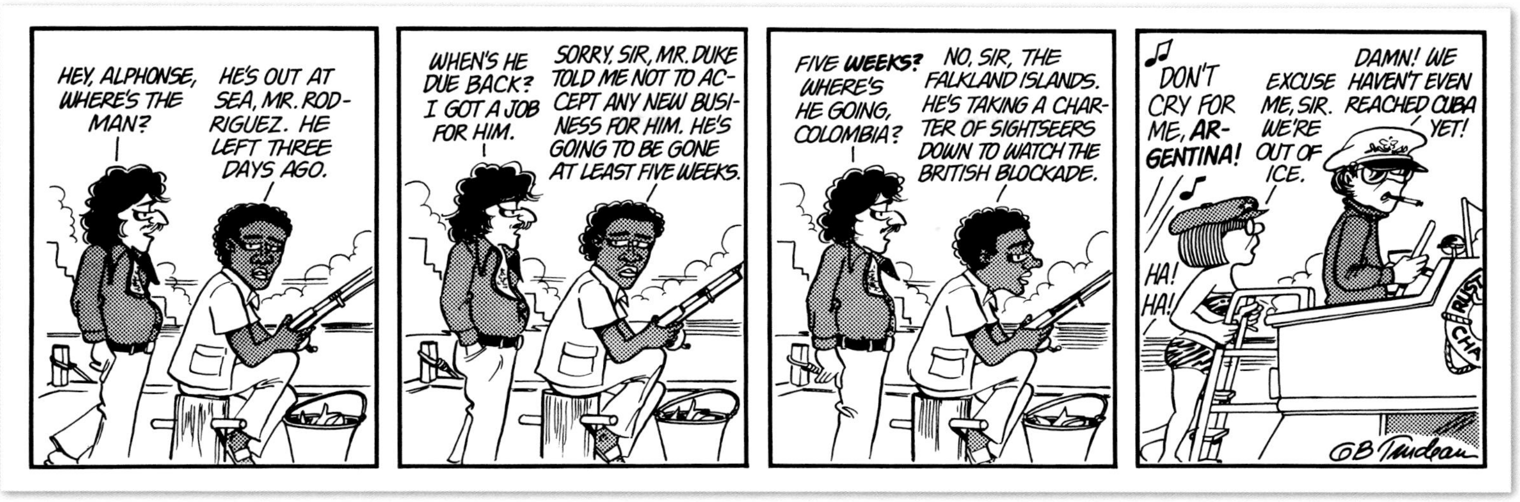
HEY, ALPHONSE, WHERE'S THE MAN?
HE'S OUT AT SEA, MR. RODRIGUEZ. HE LEFT THREE DAYS AGO.
WHEN'S HE DUE BACK? I GOT A JOB FOR HIM.
SORRY, SIR, MR. DUKE TOLD ME NOT TO ACCEPT ANY NEW BUSINESS FOR HIM. HE'S GOING TO BE GONE AT LEAST FIVE WEEKS.
FIVE **WEEKS?** WHERE'S HE GOING, COLOMBIA?
NO, SIR, THE FALKLAND ISLANDS. HE'S TAKING A CHARTER OF SIGHTSEERS DOWN TO WATCH THE BRITISH BLOCKADE.
DON'T CRY FOR ME, **ARGENTINA!**
HA! HA!
EXCUSE ME, SIR. WE'RE OUT OF ICE.
DAMN! WE HAVEN'T EVEN REACHED CUBA YET!
RUSTY
CHA
GBTrudeau

4/19/82

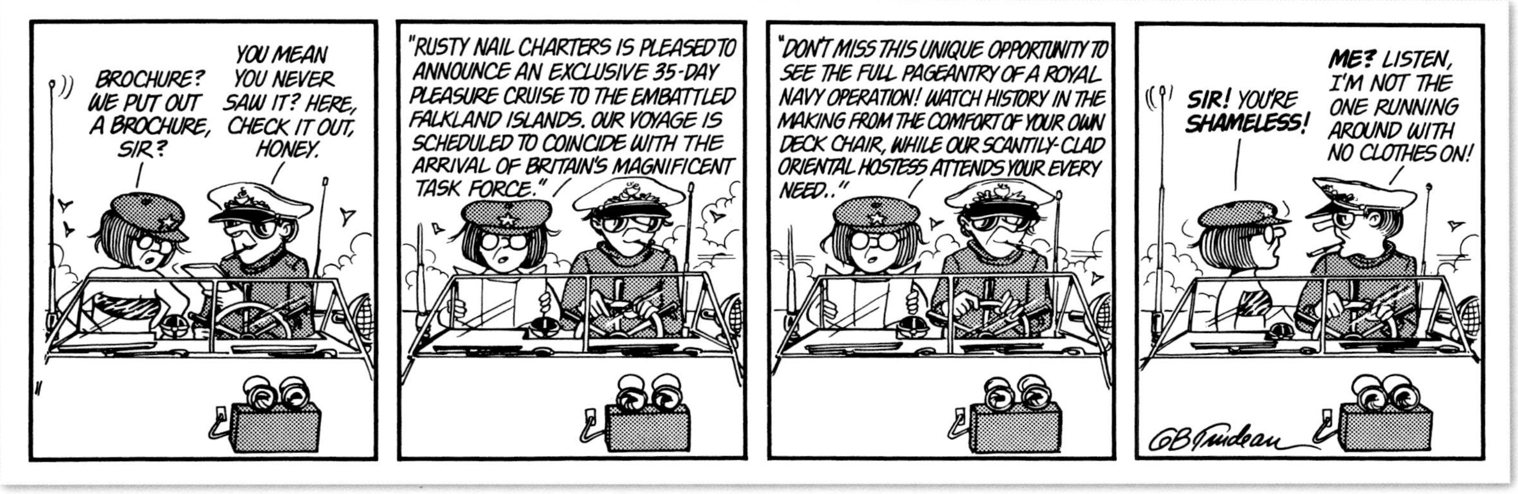
BROCHURE? WE PUT OUT A BROCHURE, SIR?
YOU MEAN YOU NEVER SAW IT? HERE, CHECK IT OUT, HONEY.
"RUSTY NAIL CHARTERS IS PLEASED TO ANNOUNCE AN EXCLUSIVE 35-DAY PLEASURE CRUISE TO THE EMBATTLED FALKLAND ISLANDS. OUR VOYAGE IS SCHEDULED TO COINCIDE WITH THE ARRIVAL OF BRITAIN'S MAGNIFICENT TASK FORCE."
"DON'T MISS THIS UNIQUE OPPORTUNITY TO SEE THE FULL PAGEANTRY OF A ROYAL NAVY OPERATION! WATCH HISTORY IN THE MAKING FROM THE COMFORT OF YOUR OWN DECK CHAIR, WHILE OUR SCANTILY-CLAD ORIENTAL HOSTESS ATTENDS YOUR EVERY NEED.."
SIR! YOU'RE **SHAMELESS!**
ME? LISTEN, I'M NOT THE ONE RUNNING AROUND WITH NO CLOTHES ON!
GBTrudeau

4/21/82

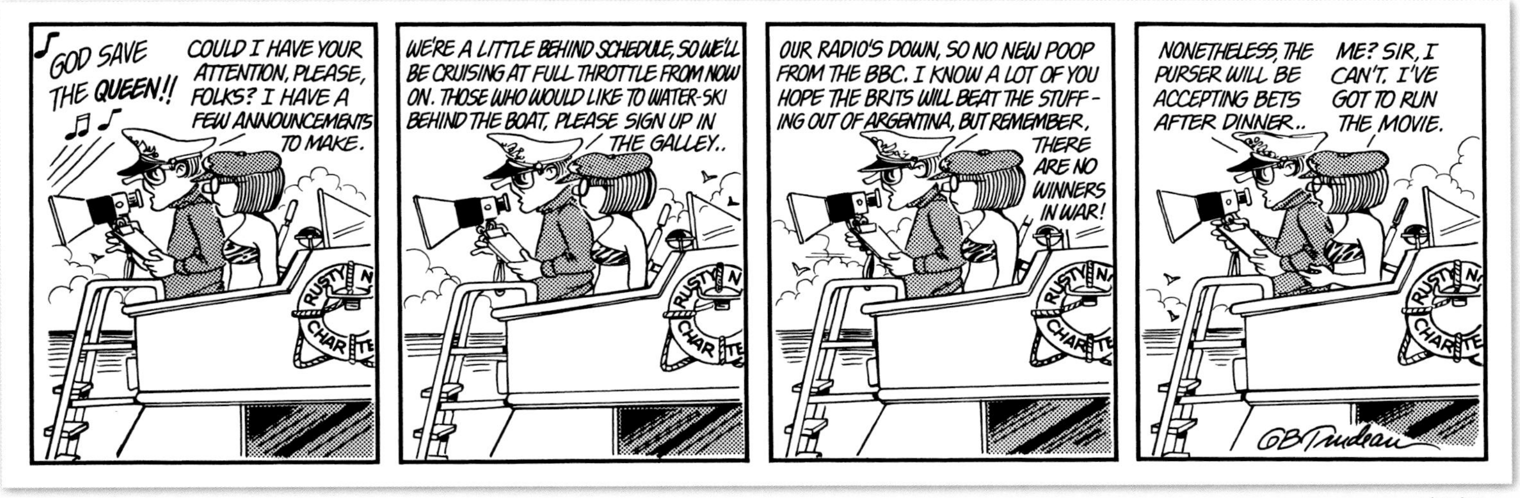
GOD SAVE THE **QUEEN!!**
COULD I HAVE YOUR ATTENTION, PLEASE, FOLKS? I HAVE A FEW ANNOUNCEMENTS TO MAKE.
WE'RE A LITTLE BEHIND SCHEDULE, SO WE'LL BE CRUISING AT FULL THROTTLE FROM NOW ON. THOSE WHO WOULD LIKE TO WATER-SKI BEHIND THE BOAT, PLEASE SIGN UP IN THE GALLEY..
OUR RADIO'S DOWN, SO NO NEW POOP FROM THE BBC. I KNOW A LOT OF YOU HOPE THE BRITS WILL BEAT THE STUFFING OUT OF ARGENTINA, BUT REMEMBER, THERE ARE NO WINNERS IN WAR!
NONETHELESS, THE PURSER WILL BE ACCEPTING BETS AFTER DINNER..
ME? SIR, I CAN'T. I'VE GOT TO RUN THE MOVIE.
GBTrudeau

4/22/82

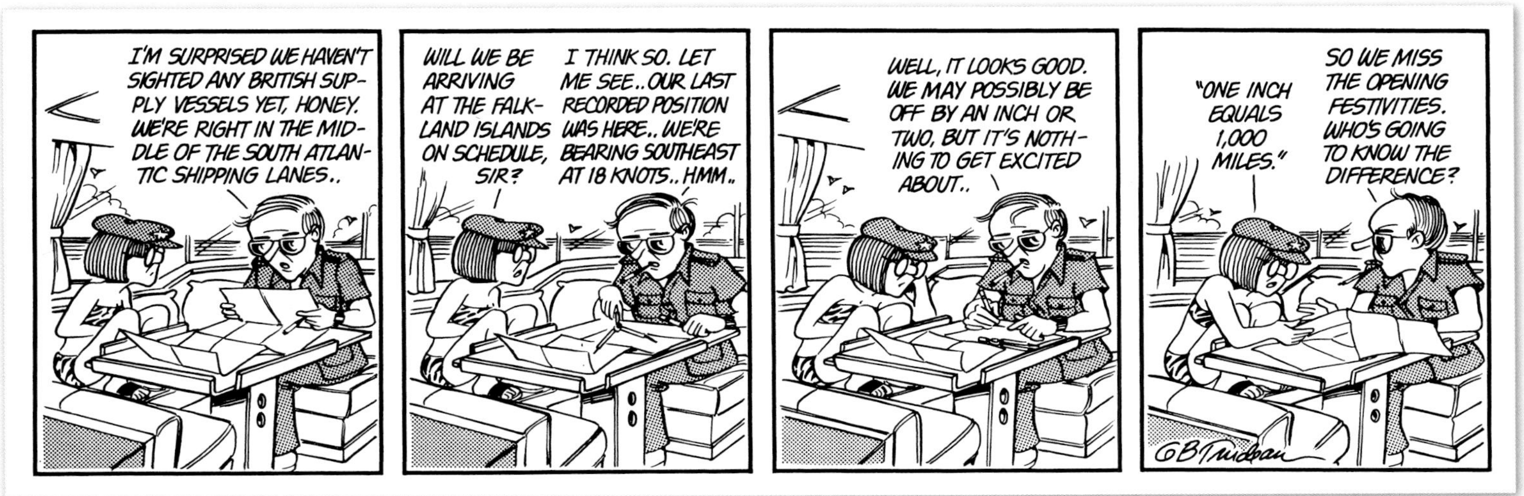
I'M SURPRISED WE HAVEN'T SIGHTED ANY BRITISH SUPPLY VESSELS YET, HONEY. WE'RE RIGHT IN THE MIDDLE OF THE SOUTH ATLANTIC SHIPPING LANES..
WILL WE BE ARRIVING AT THE FALKLAND ISLANDS ON SCHEDULE, SIR?
I THINK SO. LET ME SEE.. OUR LAST RECORDED POSITION WAS HERE.. WE'RE BEARING SOUTHEAST AT 18 KNOTS.. HMM..
WELL, IT LOOKS GOOD. WE MAY POSSIBLY BE OFF BY AN INCH OR TWO, BUT IT'S NOTHING TO GET EXCITED ABOUT..
"ONE INCH EQUALS 1,000 MILES."
SO WE MISS THE OPENING FESTIVITIES. WHO'S GOING TO KNOW THE DIFFERENCE?
GBTrudeau

4/24/82

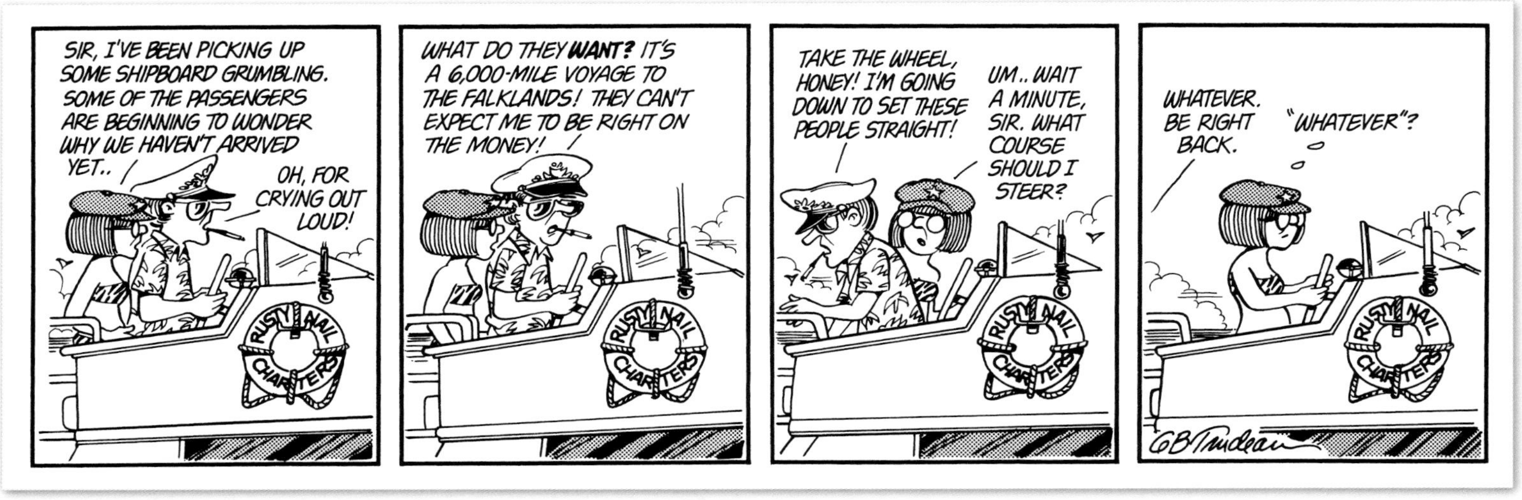
SIR, I'VE BEEN PICKING UP SOME SHIPBOARD GRUMBLING. SOME OF THE PASSENGERS ARE BEGINNING TO WONDER WHY WE HAVEN'T ARRIVED YET..
OH, FOR CRYING OUT LOUD!
WHAT DO THEY WANT? IT'S A 6,000-MILE VOYAGE TO THE FALKLANDS! THEY CAN'T EXPECT ME TO BE RIGHT ON THE MONEY!
TAKE THE WHEEL, HONEY! I'M GOING DOWN TO SET THESE PEOPLE STRAIGHT!
UM.. WAIT A MINUTE, SIR. WHAT COURSE SHOULD I STEER?
WHATEVER. BE RIGHT BACK.
"WHATEVER"?
RUSTY NAIL CHARTERS
GBTrudeau

4/26/82

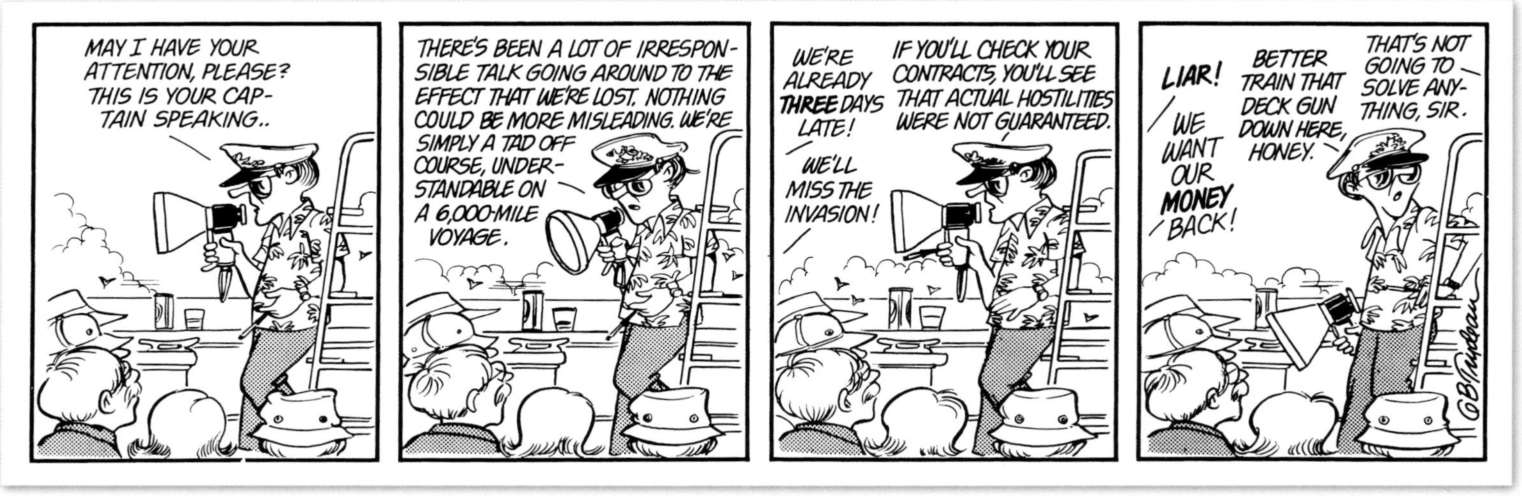
MAY I HAVE YOUR ATTENTION, PLEASE? THIS IS YOUR CAPTAIN SPEAKING..
THERE'S BEEN A LOT OF IRRESPONSIBLE TALK GOING AROUND TO THE EFFECT THAT WE'RE LOST. NOTHING COULD BE MORE MISLEADING. WE'RE SIMPLY A TAD OFF COURSE, UNDERSTANDABLE ON A 6,000-MILE VOYAGE.
WE'RE ALREADY THREE DAYS LATE!
WE'LL MISS THE INVASION!
IF YOU'LL CHECK YOUR CONTRACTS, YOU'LL SEE THAT ACTUAL HOSTILITIES WERE NOT GUARANTEED.
LIAR!
WE WANT OUR MONEY BACK!
BETTER TRAIN THAT DECK GUN DOWN HERE, HONEY.
THAT'S NOT GOING TO SOLVE ANYTHING, SIR.
GBTrudeau

4/27/82

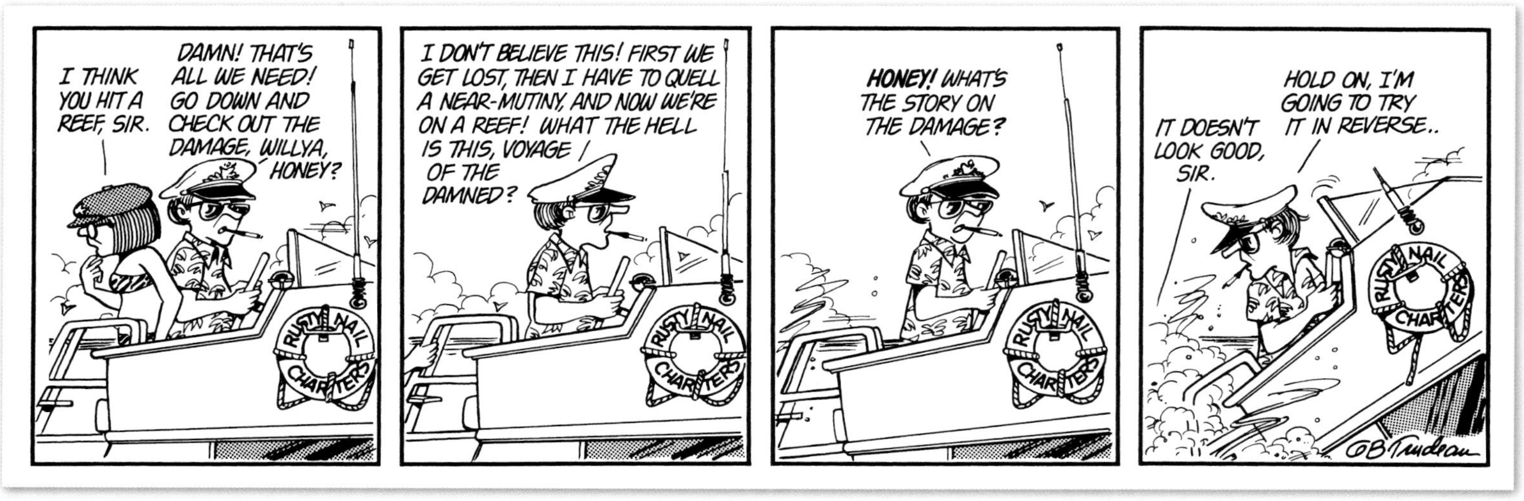
I THINK YOU HIT A REEF, SIR.
DAMN! THAT'S ALL WE NEED! GO DOWN AND CHECK OUT THE DAMAGE, WILLYA, HONEY?
I DON'T BELIEVE THIS! FIRST WE GET LOST, THEN I HAVE TO QUELL A NEAR-MUTINY, AND NOW WE'RE ON A REEF! WHAT THE HELL IS THIS, VOYAGE OF THE DAMNED?
HONEY! WHAT'S THE STORY ON THE DAMAGE?
IT DOESN'T LOOK GOOD, SIR.
HOLD ON, I'M GOING TO TRY IT IN REVERSE..
RUSTY NAIL CHARTERS
GBTrudeau

4/29/82

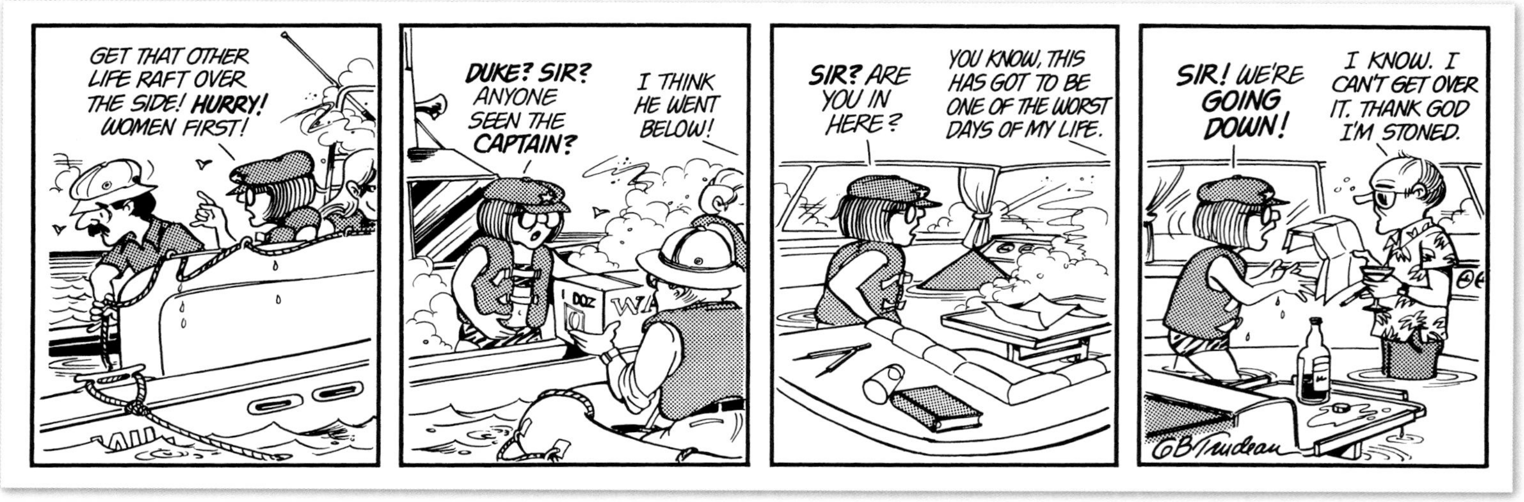
GET THAT OTHER LIFE RAFT OVER THE SIDE! HURRY! WOMEN FIRST!
DUKE? SIR? ANYONE SEEN THE CAPTAIN?
I THINK HE WENT BELOW!
SIR? ARE YOU IN HERE?
YOU KNOW, THIS HAS GOT TO BE ONE OF THE WORST DAYS OF MY LIFE.
SIR! WE'RE GOING DOWN!
I KNOW. I CAN'T GET OVER IT. THANK GOD I'M STONED.
GBTrudeau

4/30/82

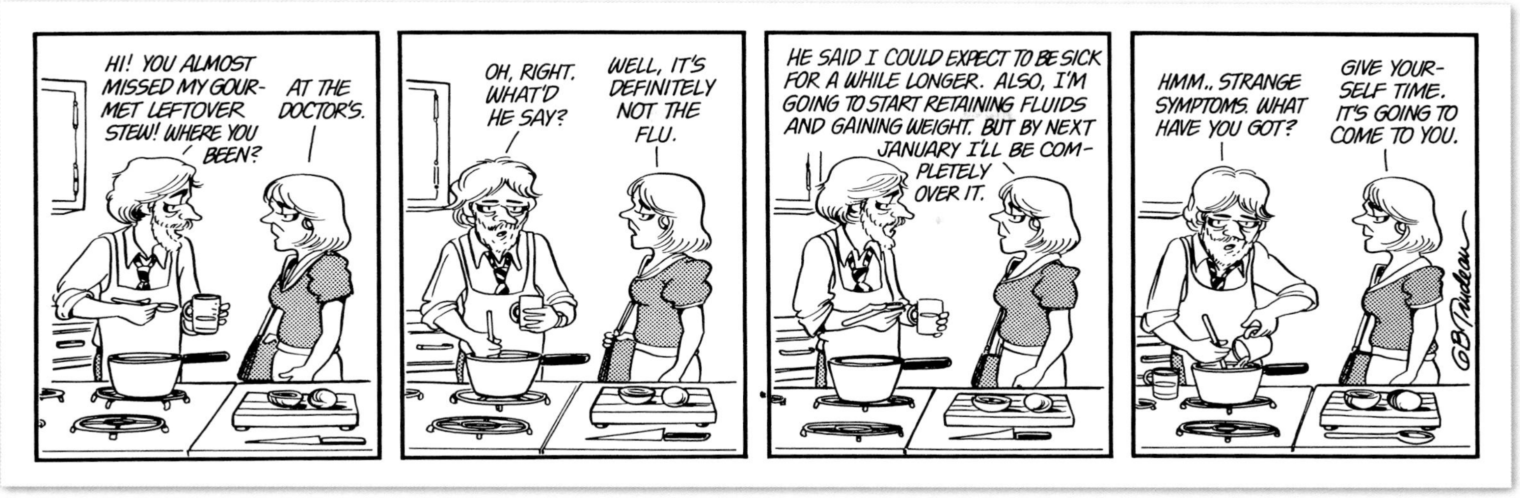
HI! YOU ALMOST MISSED MY GOURMET LEFTOVER STEW! WHERE YOU BEEN?
AT THE DOCTOR'S.
OH, RIGHT. WHAT'D HE SAY?
WELL, IT'S DEFINITELY NOT THE FLU.
HE SAID I COULD EXPECT TO BE SICK FOR A WHILE LONGER. ALSO, I'M GOING TO START RETAINING FLUIDS AND GAINING WEIGHT. BUT BY NEXT JANUARY I'LL BE COMPLETELY OVER IT.
HMM.. STRANGE SYMPTOMS. WHAT HAVE YOU GOT?
GIVE YOURSELF TIME. IT'S GOING TO COME TO YOU.
GB Trudeau

5/17/82

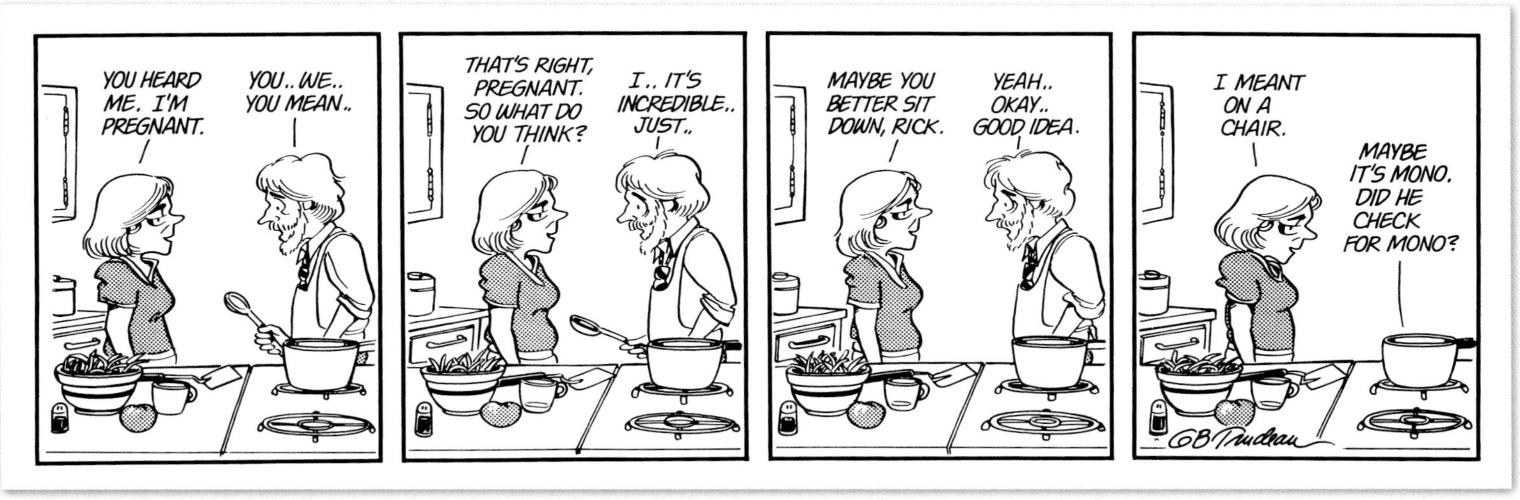
YOU HEARD ME. I'M PREGNANT.
YOU.. WE.. YOU MEAN..
THAT'S RIGHT, PREGNANT. SO WHAT DO YOU THINK?
I.. IT'S INCREDIBLE.. JUST..
MAYBE YOU BETTER SIT DOWN, RICK.
YEAH.. OKAY.. GOOD IDEA.
I MEANT ON A CHAIR.
MAYBE IT'S MONO. DID HE CHECK FOR MONO?
GB Trudeau

5/18/82

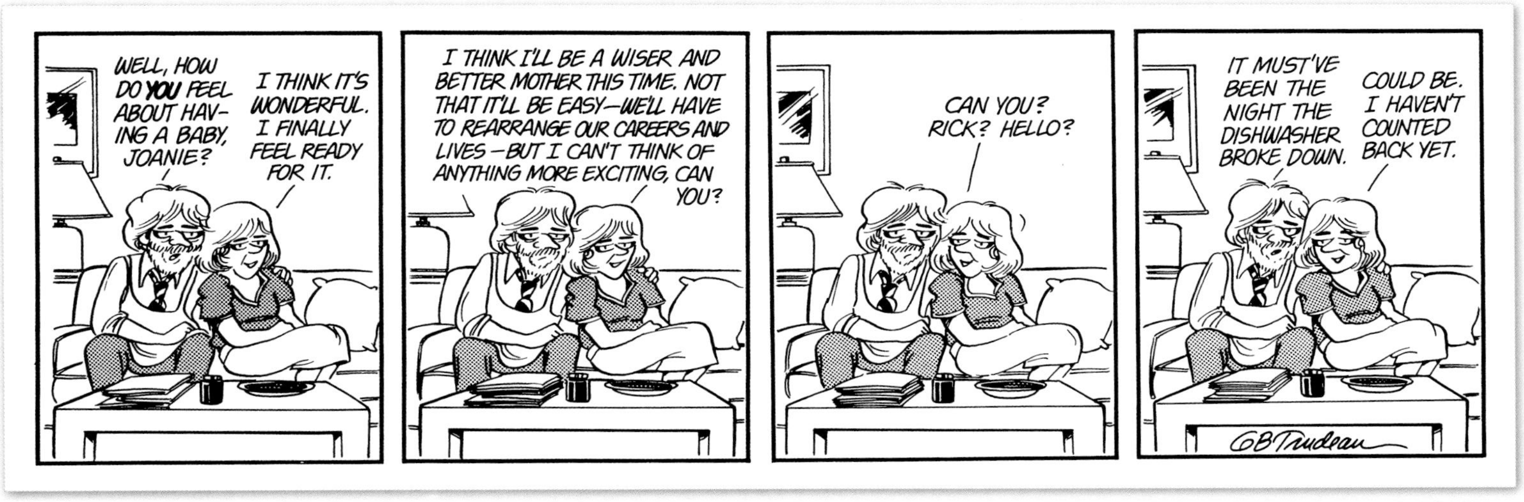
WELL, HOW DO YOU FEEL ABOUT HAVING A BABY, JOANIE?
I THINK IT'S WONDERFUL. I FINALLY FEEL READY FOR IT.
I THINK I'LL BE A WISER AND BETTER MOTHER THIS TIME. NOT THAT IT'LL BE EASY—WE'LL HAVE TO REARRANGE OUR CAREERS AND LIVES—BUT I CAN'T THINK OF ANYTHING MORE EXCITING, CAN YOU?
CAN YOU? RICK? HELLO?
IT MUST'VE BEEN THE NIGHT THE DISHWASHER BROKE DOWN.
COULD BE. I HAVEN'T COUNTED BACK YET.
GB Trudeau

5/21/82

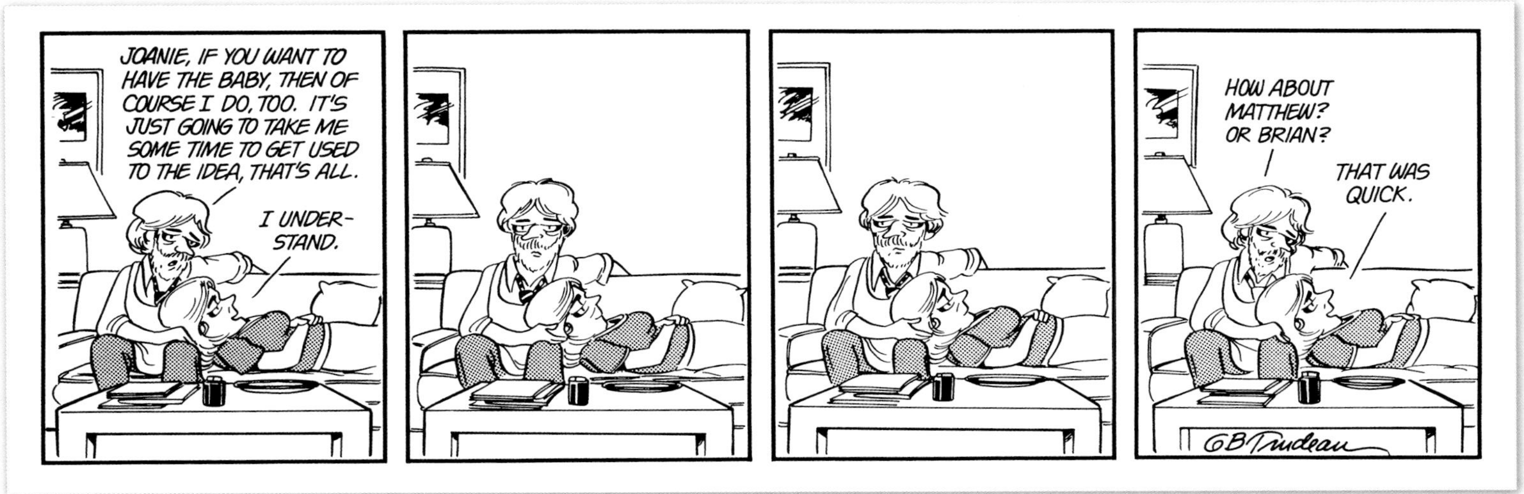
JOANIE, IF YOU WANT TO HAVE THE BABY, THEN OF COURSE I DO, TOO. IT'S JUST GOING TO TAKE ME SOME TIME TO GET USED TO THE IDEA, THAT'S ALL.
I UNDERSTAND.
HOW ABOUT MATTHEW? OR BRIAN?
THAT WAS QUICK.
GB Trudeau

5/22/82

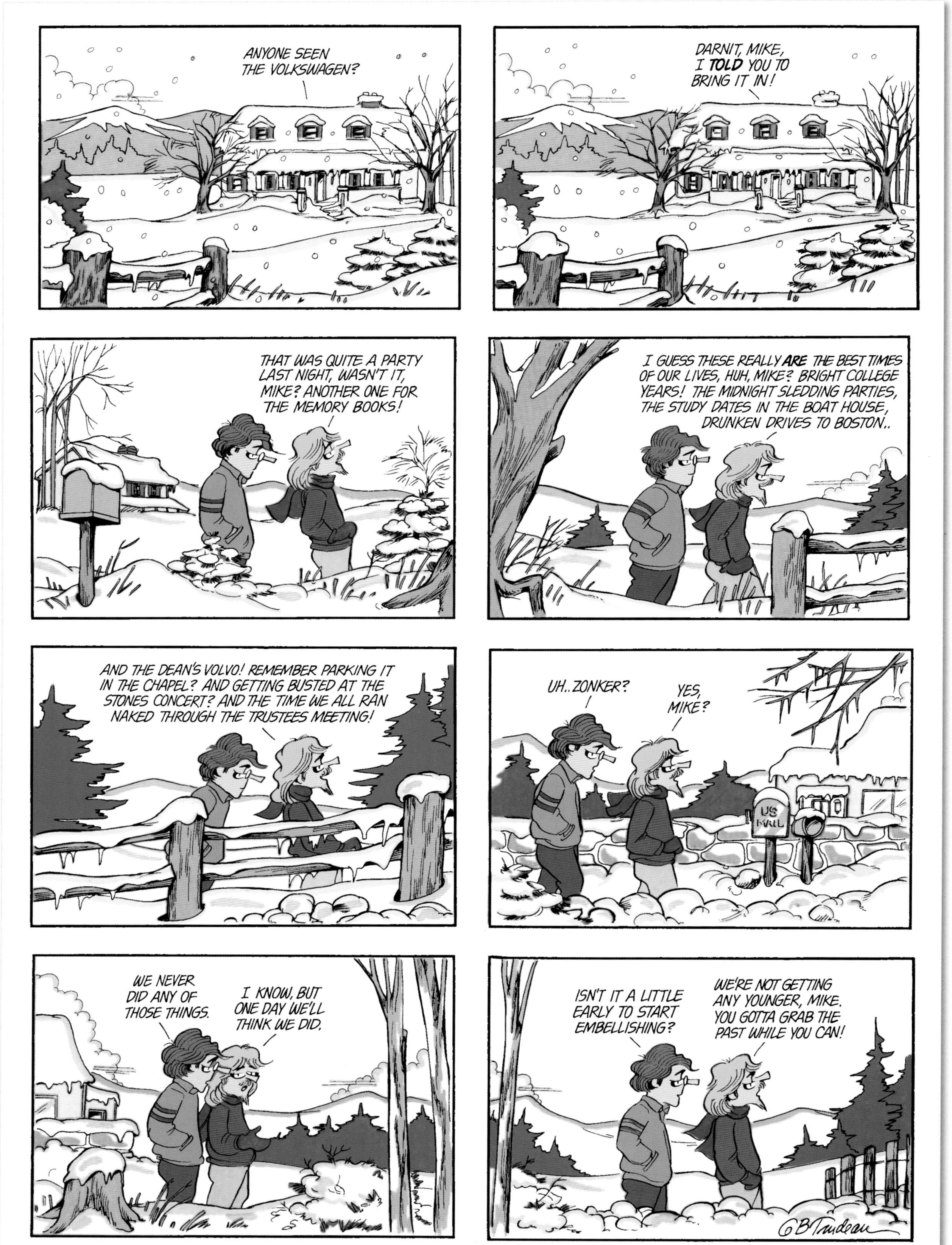
ANYONE SEEN THE VOLKSWAGEN?
DARNIT, MIKE, I TOLD YOU TO BRING IT IN!
THAT WAS QUITE A PARTY LAST NIGHT, WASN'T IT, MIKE? ANOTHER ONE FOR THE MEMORY BOOKS!
I GUESS THESE REALLY ARE THE BEST TIMES OF OUR LIVES, HUH, MIKE? BRIGHT COLLEGE YEARS! THE MIDNIGHT SLEDDING PARTIES, THE STUDY DATES IN THE BOAT HOUSE, DRUNKEN DRIVES TO BOSTON..
AND THE DEAN'S VOLVO! REMEMBER PARKING IT IN THE CHAPEL? AND GETTING BUSTED AT THE STONES CONCERT? AND THE TIME WE ALL RAN NAKED THROUGH THE TRUSTEES MEETING!
UH..ZONKER?
YES, MIKE?
US MAIL
WE NEVER DID ANY OF THOSE THINGS.
I KNOW, BUT ONE DAY WE'LL THINK WE DID.
ISN'T IT A LITTLE EARLY TO START EMBELLISHING?
WE'RE NOT GETTING ANY YOUNGER, MIKE. YOU GOTTA GRAB THE PAST WHILE YOU CAN!
G.B. Trudeau

1/3/82

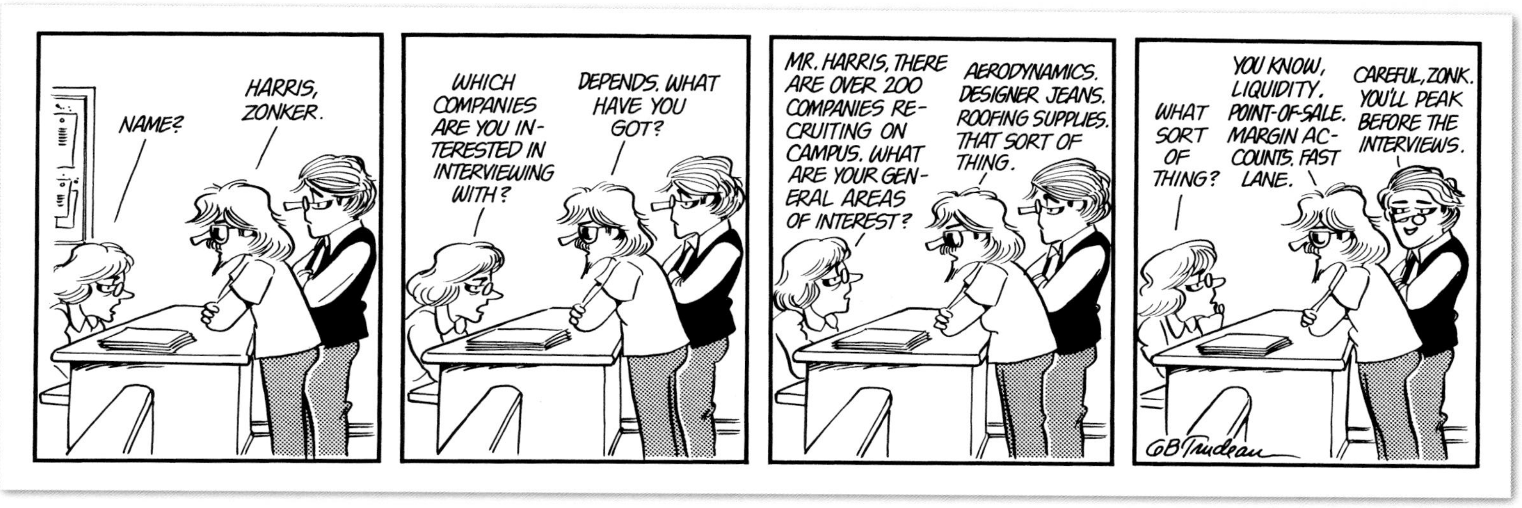
NAME?
HARRIS, ZONKER.
WHICH COMPANIES ARE YOU INTERESTED IN INTERVIEWING WITH?
DEPENDS. WHAT HAVE YOU GOT?
MR. HARRIS, THERE ARE OVER 200 COMPANIES RECRUITING ON CAMPUS. WHAT ARE YOUR GENERAL AREAS OF INTEREST?
AERODYNAMICS. DESIGNER JEANS. ROOFING SUPPLIES. THAT SORT OF THING.
WHAT SORT OF THING?
YOU KNOW, LIQUIDITY. POINT-OF-SALE. MARGIN ACCOUNTS. FAST LANE.
CAREFUL, ZONK. YOU'LL PEAK BEFORE THE INTERVIEWS.
GB Trudeau

9/23/82

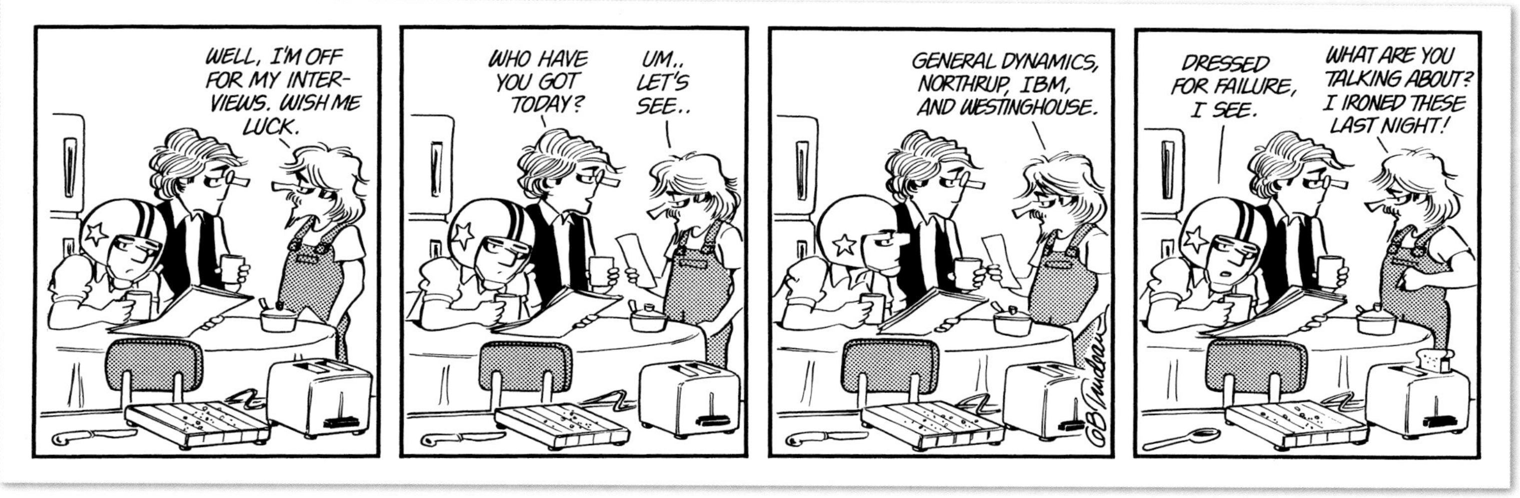
WELL, I'M OFF FOR MY INTERVIEWS. WISH ME LUCK.
WHO HAVE YOU GOT TODAY?
UM.. LET'S SEE..
GENERAL DYNAMICS, NORTHRUP, IBM, AND WESTINGHOUSE.
GB Trudeau
DRESSED FOR FAILURE, I SEE.
WHAT ARE YOU TALKING ABOUT? I IRONED THESE LAST NIGHT!

9/24/82

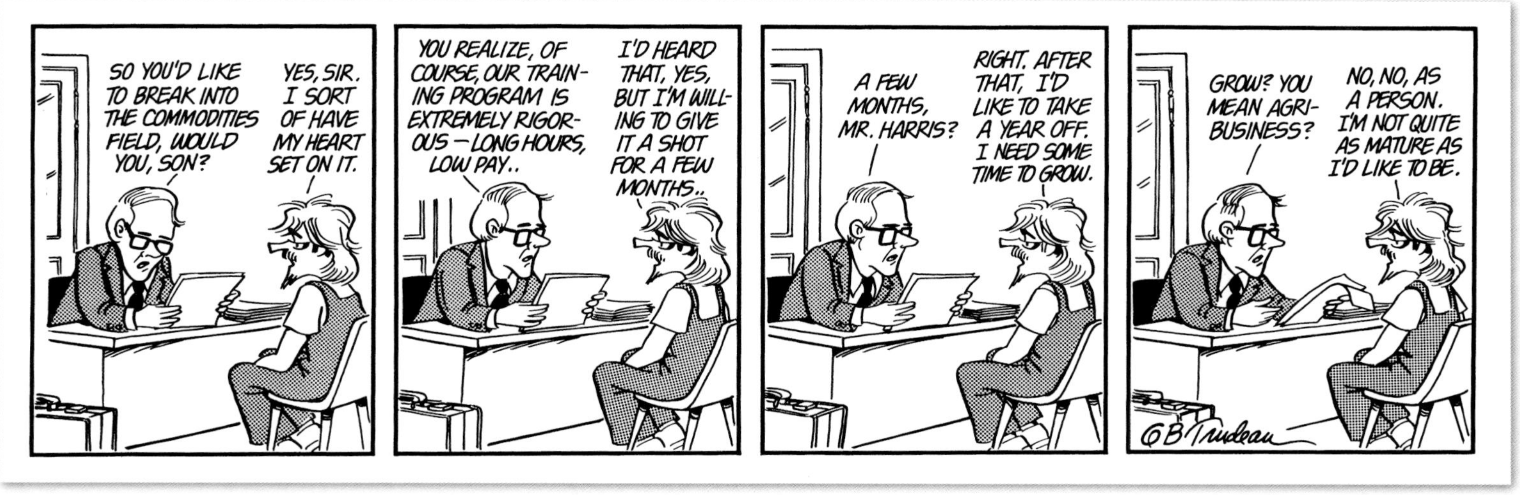
SO YOU'D LIKE TO BREAK INTO THE COMMODITIES FIELD, WOULD YOU, SON?
YES, SIR. I SORT OF HAVE MY HEART SET ON IT.
YOU REALIZE, OF COURSE, OUR TRAINING PROGRAM IS EXTREMELY RIGOROUS — LONG HOURS, LOW PAY..
I'D HEARD THAT, YES, BUT I'M WILLING TO GIVE IT A SHOT FOR A FEW MONTHS..
A FEW MONTHS, MR. HARRIS?
RIGHT. AFTER THAT, I'D LIKE TO TAKE A YEAR OFF. I NEED SOME TIME TO GROW.
GROW? YOU MEAN AGRIBUSINESS?
NO, NO, AS A PERSON. I'M NOT QUITE AS MATURE AS I'D LIKE TO BE.
GB Trudeau

9/29/82

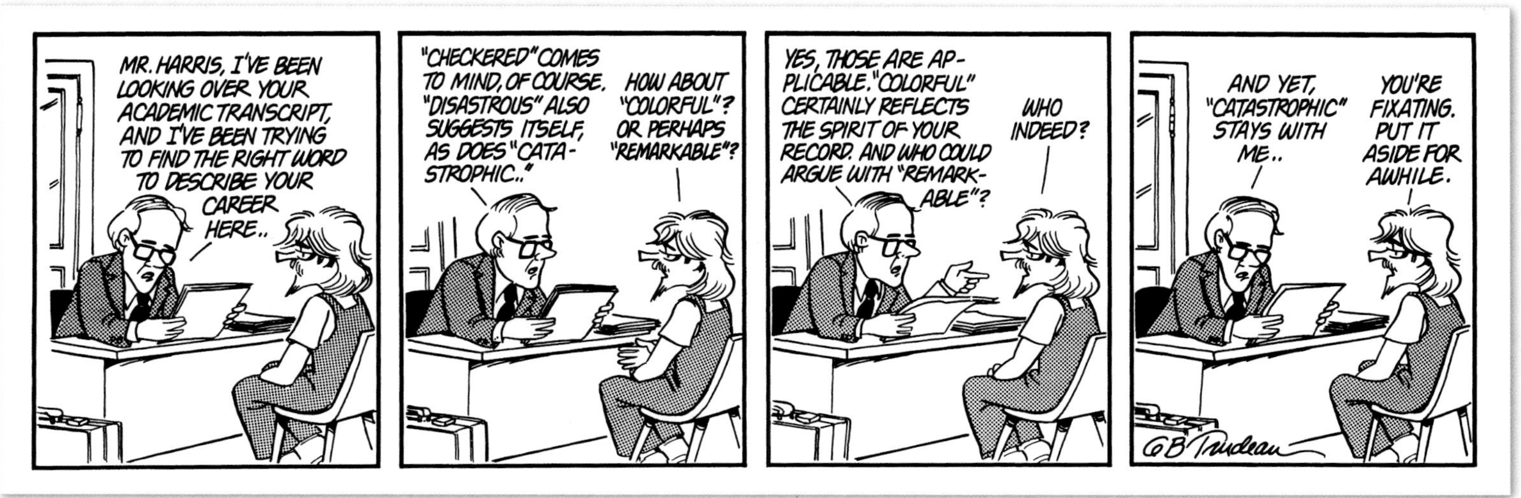
MR. HARRIS, I'VE BEEN LOOKING OVER YOUR ACADEMIC TRANSCRIPT, AND I'VE BEEN TRYING TO FIND THE RIGHT WORD TO DESCRIBE YOUR CAREER HERE..
"CHECKERED" COMES TO MIND, OF COURSE. "DISASTROUS" ALSO SUGGESTS ITSELF, AS DOES "CATASTROPHIC.."
HOW ABOUT "COLORFUL"? OR PERHAPS "REMARKABLE"?
YES, THOSE ARE APPLICABLE. "COLORFUL" CERTAINLY REFLECTS THE SPIRIT OF YOUR RECORD. AND WHO COULD ARGUE WITH "REMARKABLE"?
WHO INDEED?
AND YET, "CATASTROPHIC" STAYS WITH ME..
YOU'RE FIXATING. PUT IT ASIDE FOR AWHILE.
GB Trudeau

9/30/82

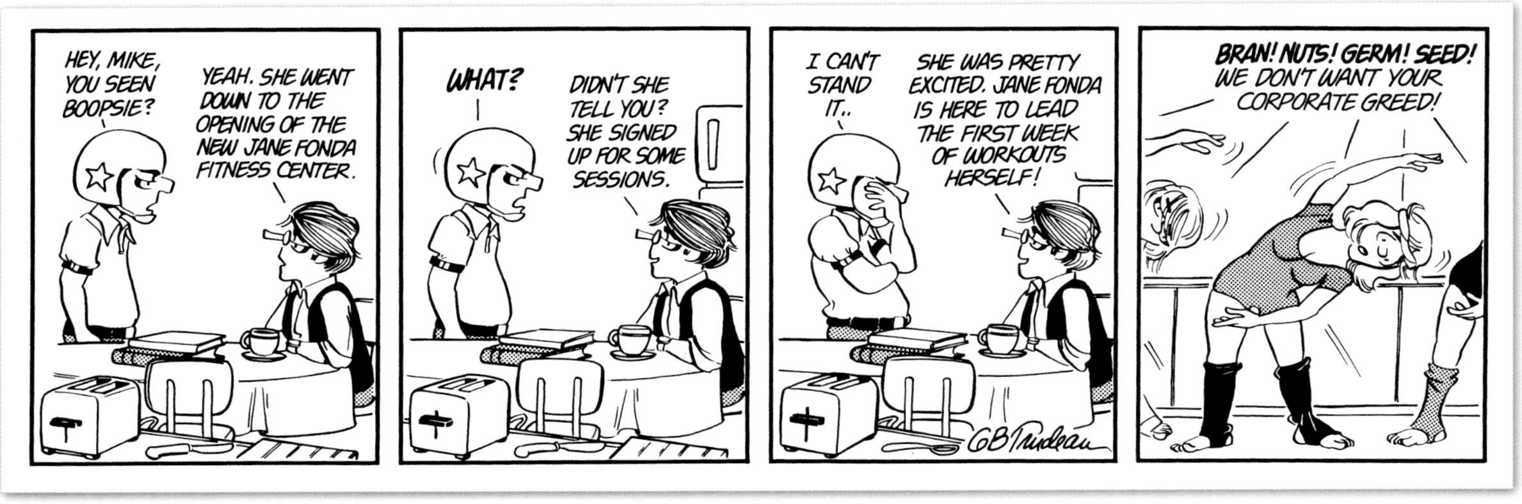
HEY, MIKE, YOU SEEN BOOPSIE?
YEAH. SHE WENT DOWN TO THE OPENING OF THE NEW JANE FONDA FITNESS CENTER.
WHAT?
DIDN'T SHE TELL YOU? SHE SIGNED UP FOR SOME SESSIONS.
I CAN'T STAND IT..
SHE WAS PRETTY EXCITED. JANE FONDA IS HERE TO LEAD THE FIRST WEEK OF WORKOUTS HERSELF!
BRAN! NUTS! GERM! SEED! WE DON'T WANT YOUR CORPORATE GREED!
GBTrudeau

9/13/82

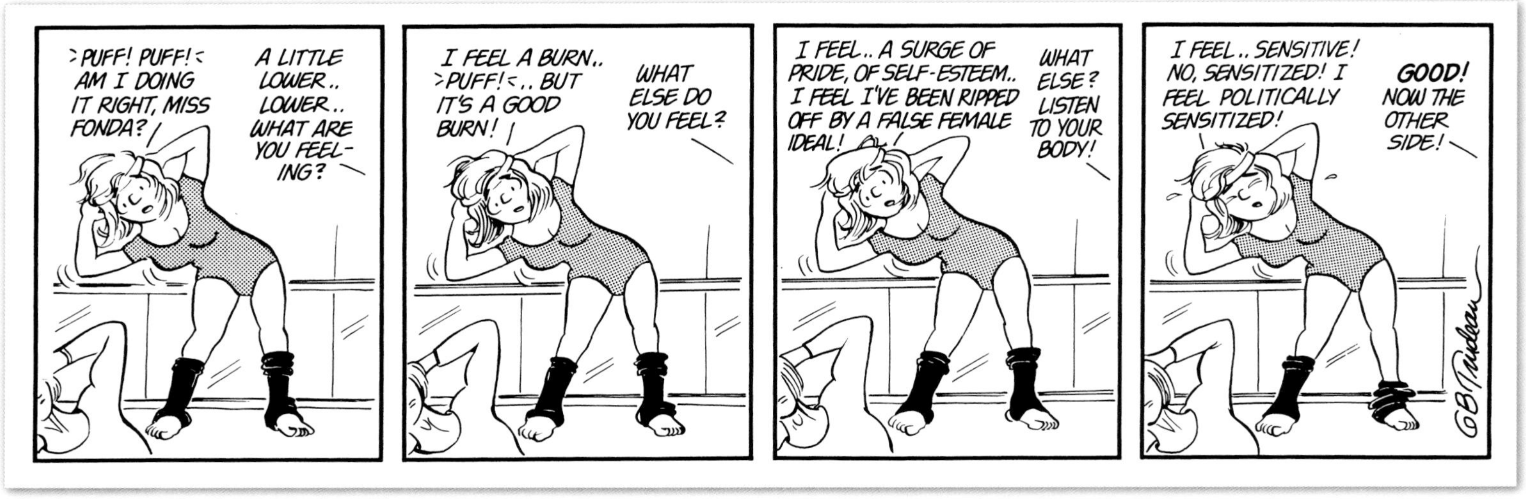
>PUFF! PUFF!< AM I DOING IT RIGHT, MISS FONDA?
A LITTLE LOWER.. LOWER.. WHAT ARE YOU FEELING?
I FEEL A BURN.. >PUFF!<.. BUT IT'S A GOOD BURN!
WHAT ELSE DO YOU FEEL?
I FEEL.. A SURGE OF PRIDE, OF SELF-ESTEEM.. I FEEL I'VE BEEN RIPPED OFF BY A FALSE FEMALE IDEAL!
WHAT ELSE? LISTEN TO YOUR BODY!
I FEEL.. SENSITIVE! NO, SENSITIZED! I FEEL POLITICALLY SENSITIZED!
GOOD! NOW THE OTHER SIDE!
GBTrudeau

9/14/82

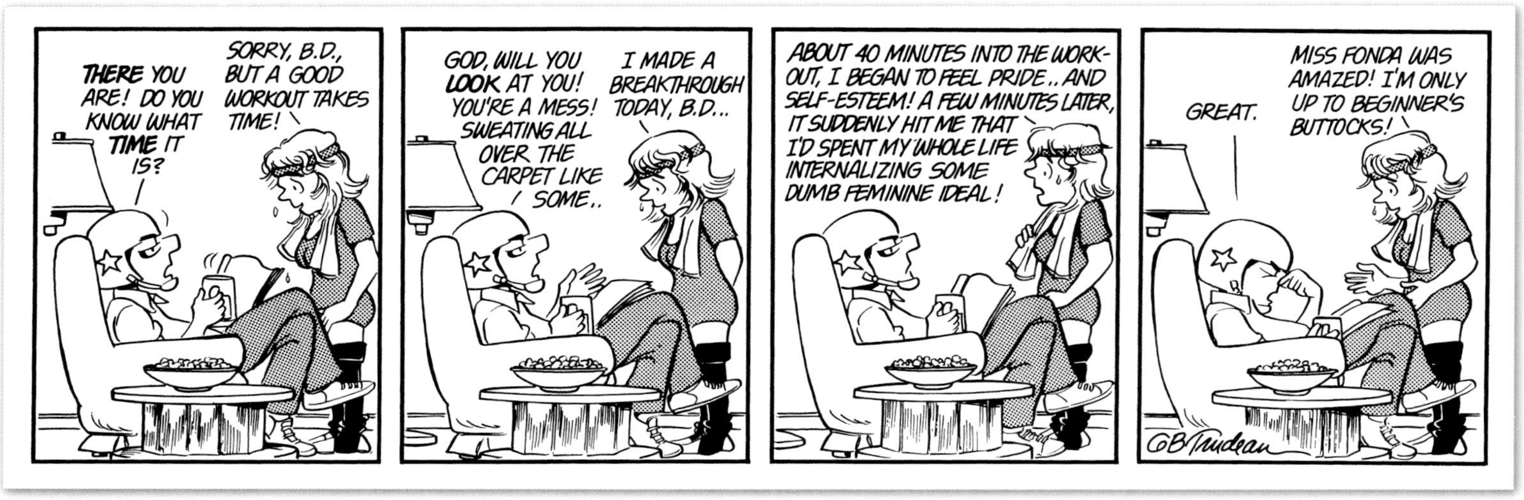
THERE YOU ARE! DO YOU KNOW WHAT TIME IT IS?
SORRY, B.D., BUT A GOOD WORKOUT TAKES TIME!
GOD, WILL YOU LOOK AT YOU! YOU'RE A MESS! SWEATING ALL OVER THE CARPET LIKE SOME..
I MADE A BREAKTHROUGH TODAY, B.D...
ABOUT 40 MINUTES INTO THE WORKOUT, I BEGAN TO FEEL PRIDE.. AND SELF-ESTEEM! A FEW MINUTES LATER, IT SUDDENLY HIT ME THAT I'D SPENT MY WHOLE LIFE INTERNALIZING SOME DUMB FEMININE IDEAL!
GREAT.
MISS FONDA WAS AMAZED! I'M ONLY UP TO BEGINNER'S BUTTOCKS!
GBTrudeau

9/16/82

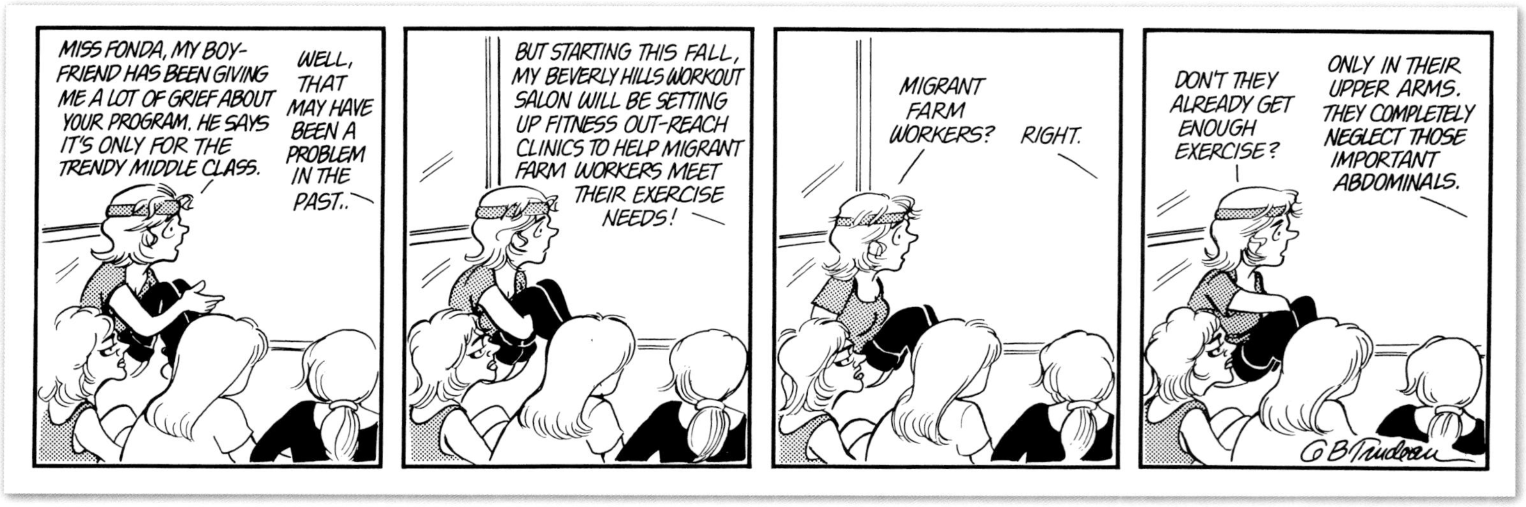
MISS FONDA, MY BOYFRIEND HAS BEEN GIVING ME A LOT OF GRIEF ABOUT YOUR PROGRAM. HE SAYS IT'S ONLY FOR THE TRENDY MIDDLE CLASS.
WELL, THAT MAY HAVE BEEN A PROBLEM IN THE PAST..
BUT STARTING THIS FALL, MY BEVERLY HILLS WORKOUT SALON WILL BE SETTING UP FITNESS OUT-REACH CLINICS TO HELP MIGRANT FARM WORKERS MEET THEIR EXERCISE NEEDS!
MIGRANT FARM WORKERS?
RIGHT.
DON'T THEY ALREADY GET ENOUGH EXERCISE?
ONLY IN THEIR UPPER ARMS. THEY COMPLETELY NEGLECT THOSE IMPORTANT ABDOMINALS.
GBTrudeau

9/18/82

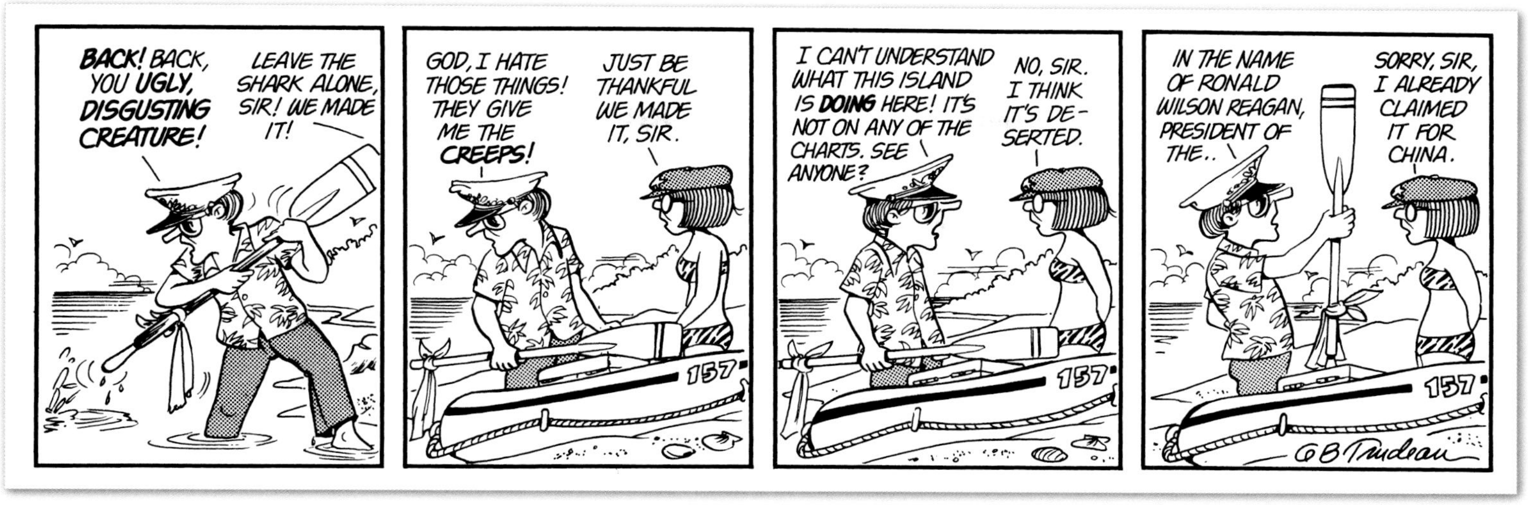
BACK! BACK, YOU UGLY, DISGUSTING CREATURE!
LEAVE THE SHARK ALONE, SIR! WE MADE IT!
GOD, I HATE THOSE THINGS! THEY GIVE ME THE CREEPS!
JUST BE THANKFUL WE MADE IT, SIR.
I CAN'T UNDERSTAND WHAT THIS ISLAND IS DOING HERE! IT'S NOT ON ANY OF THE CHARTS. SEE ANYONE?
NO, SIR. I THINK IT'S DE-SERTED.
IN THE NAME OF RONALD WILSON REAGAN, PRESIDENT OF THE..
SORRY, SIR, I ALREADY CLAIMED IT FOR CHINA.
157
GB Trudeau

5/8/82

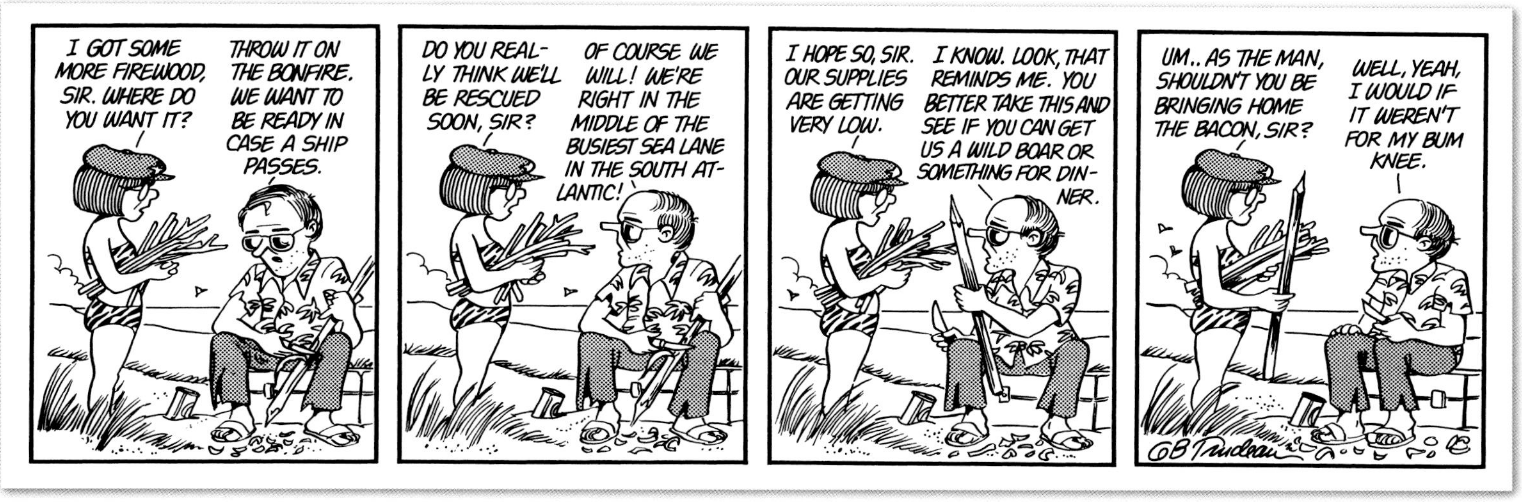
I GOT SOME MORE FIREWOOD, SIR. WHERE DO YOU WANT IT?
THROW IT ON THE BONFIRE. WE WANT TO BE READY IN CASE A SHIP PASSES.
DO YOU REAL-LY THINK WE'LL BE RESCUED SOON, SIR?
OF COURSE WE WILL! WE'RE RIGHT IN THE MIDDLE OF THE BUSIEST SEA LANE IN THE SOUTH AT-LANTIC!
I HOPE SO, SIR. OUR SUPPLIES ARE GETTING VERY LOW.
I KNOW. LOOK, THAT REMINDS ME. YOU BETTER TAKE THIS AND SEE IF YOU CAN GET US A WILD BOAR OR SOMETHING FOR DIN-NER.
UM.. AS THE MAN, SHOULDN'T YOU BE BRINGING HOME THE BACON, SIR?
WELL, YEAH, I WOULD IF IT WEREN'T FOR MY BUM KNEE.
GB Trudeau

5/24/82

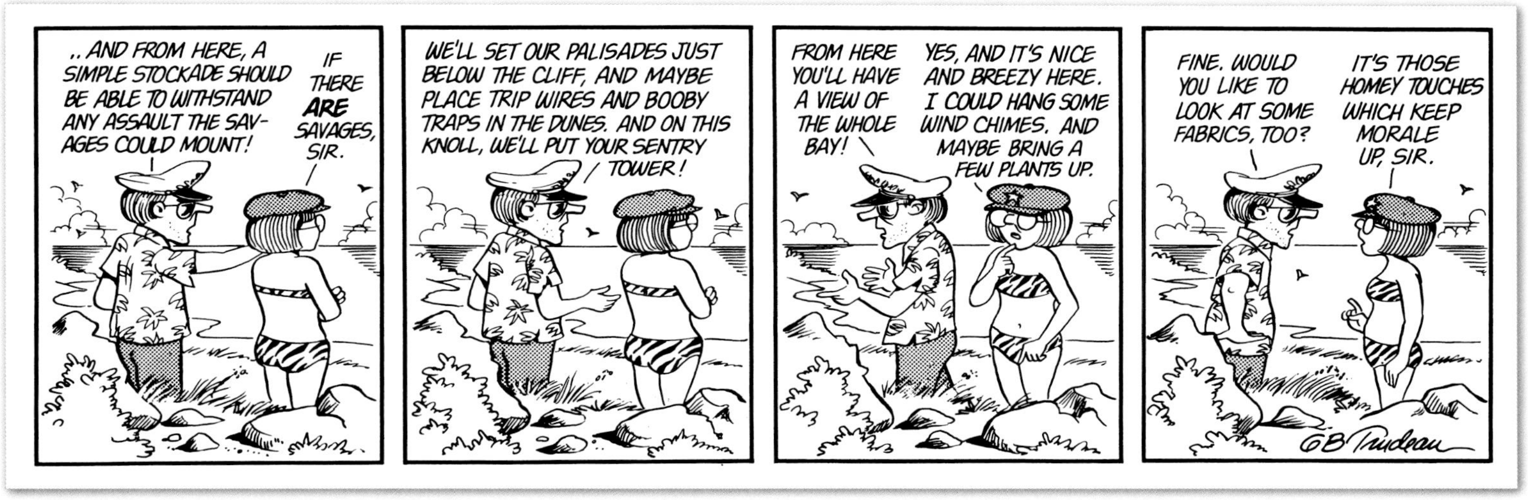
.. AND FROM HERE, A SIMPLE STOCKADE SHOULD BE ABLE TO WITHSTAND ANY ASSAULT THE SAV-AGES COULD MOUNT!
IF THERE ARE SAVAGES, SIR.
WE'LL SET OUR PALISADES JUST BELOW THE CLIFF, AND MAYBE PLACE TRIP WIRES AND BOOBY TRAPS IN THE DUNES. AND ON THIS KNOLL, WE'LL PUT YOUR SENTRY TOWER!
FROM HERE YOU'LL HAVE A VIEW OF THE WHOLE BAY!
YES, AND IT'S NICE AND BREEZY HERE. I COULD HANG SOME WIND CHIMES. AND MAYBE BRING A FEW PLANTS UP.
FINE. WOULD YOU LIKE TO LOOK AT SOME FABRICS, TOO?
IT'S THOSE HOMEY TOUCHES WHICH KEEP MORALE UP, SIR.
GB Trudeau

5/26/82

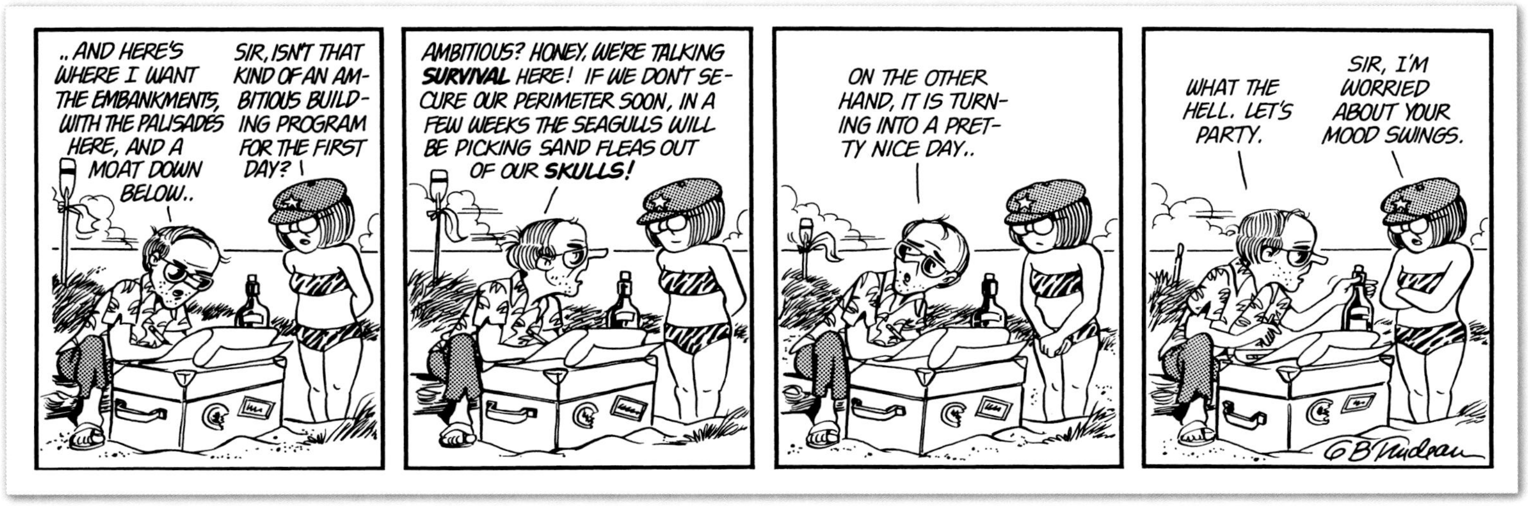
.. AND HERE'S WHERE I WANT THE EMBANKMENTS, WITH THE PALISADES HERE, AND A MOAT DOWN BELOW..
SIR, ISN'T THAT KIND OF AN AM-BITIOUS BUILD-ING PROGRAM FOR THE FIRST DAY?
AMBITIOUS? HONEY, WE'RE TALKING SURVIVAL HERE! IF WE DON'T SE-CURE OUR PERIMETER SOON, IN A FEW WEEKS THE SEAGULLS WILL BE PICKING SAND FLEAS OUT OF OUR SKULLS!
ON THE OTHER HAND, IT IS TURN-ING INTO A PRET-TY NICE DAY..
WHAT THE HELL. LET'S PARTY.
SIR, I'M WORRIED ABOUT YOUR MOOD SWINGS.
GB Trudeau

5/27/82

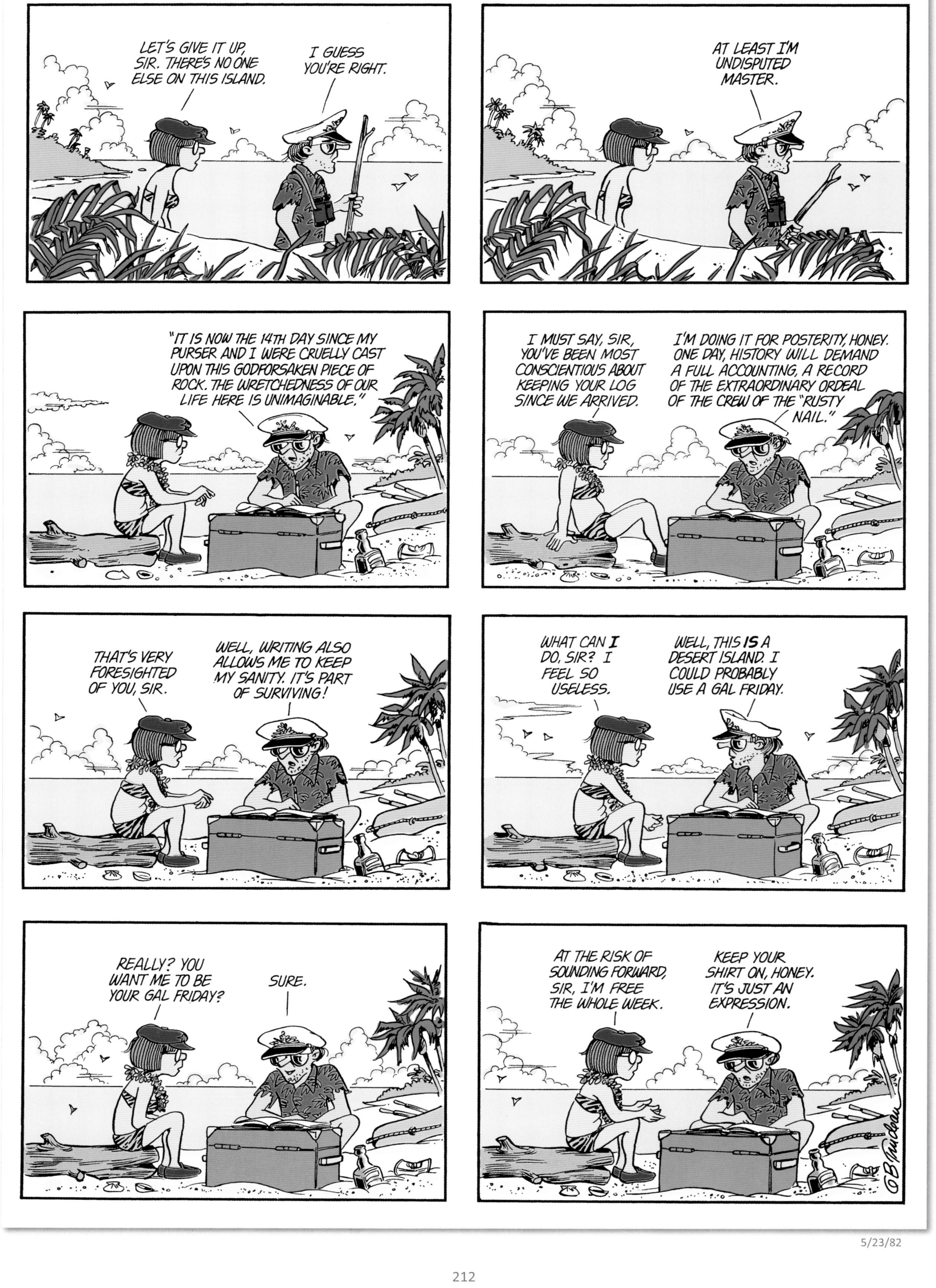
LET'S GIVE IT UP, SIR. THERE'S NO ONE ELSE ON THIS ISLAND.
I GUESS YOU'RE RIGHT.
AT LEAST I'M UNDISPUTED MASTER.
"IT IS NOW THE 14TH DAY SINCE MY PURSER AND I WERE CRUELLY CAST UPON THIS GODFORSAKEN PIECE OF ROCK. THE WRETCHEDNESS OF OUR LIFE HERE IS UNIMAGINABLE."
I MUST SAY, SIR, YOU'VE BEEN MOST CONSCIENTIOUS ABOUT KEEPING YOUR LOG SINCE WE ARRIVED.
I'M DOING IT FOR POSTERITY, HONEY. ONE DAY, HISTORY WILL DEMAND A FULL ACCOUNTING, A RECORD OF THE EXTRAORDINARY ORDEAL OF THE CREW OF THE "RUSTY NAIL."
THAT'S VERY FORESIGHTED OF YOU, SIR.
WELL, WRITING ALSO ALLOWS ME TO KEEP MY SANITY. IT'S PART OF SURVIVING!
WHAT CAN I DO, SIR? I FEEL SO USELESS.
WELL, THIS IS A DESERT ISLAND. I COULD PROBABLY USE A GAL FRIDAY.
REALLY? YOU WANT ME TO BE YOUR GAL FRIDAY?
SURE.
AT THE RISK OF SOUNDING FORWARD, SIR, I'M FREE THE WHOLE WEEK.
KEEP YOUR SHIRT ON, HONEY. IT'S JUST AN EXPRESSION.
©BTrudeau

5/23/82

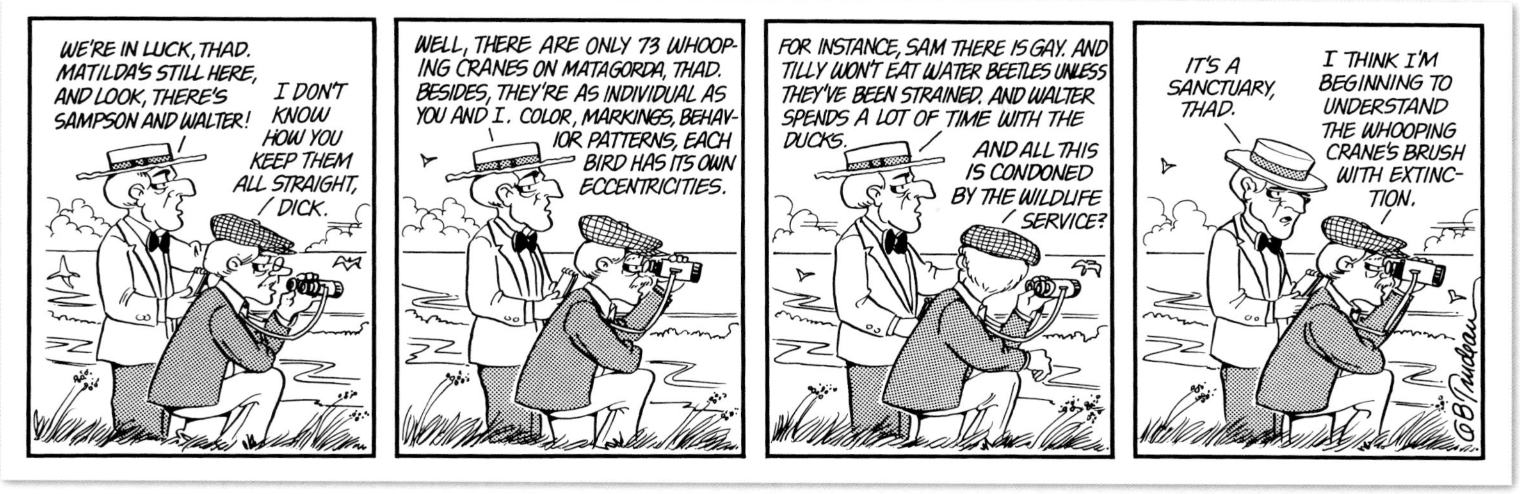
WE'RE IN LUCK, THAD. MATILDA'S STILL HERE, AND LOOK, THERE'S SAMPSON AND WALTER!
I DON'T KNOW HOW YOU KEEP THEM ALL STRAIGHT, DICK.
WELL, THERE ARE ONLY 73 WHOOPING CRANES ON MATAGORDA, THAD. BESIDES, THEY'RE AS INDIVIDUAL AS YOU AND I. COLOR, MARKINGS, BEHAVIOR PATTERNS, EACH BIRD HAS ITS OWN ECCENTRICITIES.
FOR INSTANCE, SAM THERE IS GAY. AND TILLY WON'T EAT WATER BEETLES UNLESS THEY'VE BEEN STRAINED. AND WALTER SPENDS A LOT OF TIME WITH THE DUCKS.
AND ALL THIS IS CONDONED BY THE WILDLIFE SERVICE?
IT'S A SANCTUARY, THAD.
I THINK I'M BEGINNING TO UNDERSTAND THE WHOOPING CRANE'S BRUSH WITH EXTINCTION.
GB Trudeau

6/17/82

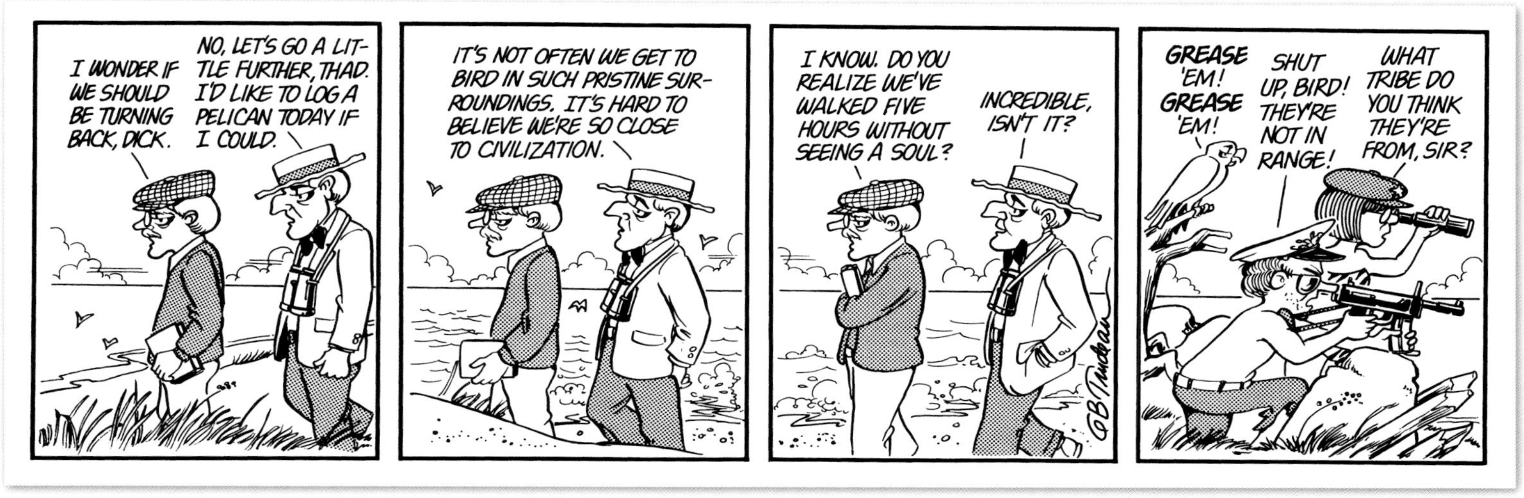
I WONDER IF WE SHOULD BE TURNING BACK, DICK.
NO, LET'S GO A LITTLE FURTHER, THAD. I'D LIKE TO LOG A PELICAN TODAY IF I COULD.
IT'S NOT OFTEN WE GET TO BIRD IN SUCH PRISTINE SURROUNDINGS. IT'S HARD TO BELIEVE WE'RE SO CLOSE TO CIVILIZATION.
I KNOW. DO YOU REALIZE WE'VE WALKED FIVE HOURS WITHOUT SEEING A SOUL?
INCREDIBLE, ISN'T IT?
GB Trudeau
GREASE 'EM! GREASE 'EM!
SHUT UP, BIRD! THEY'RE NOT IN RANGE!
WHAT TRIBE DO YOU THINK THEY'RE FROM, SIR?

6/21/82

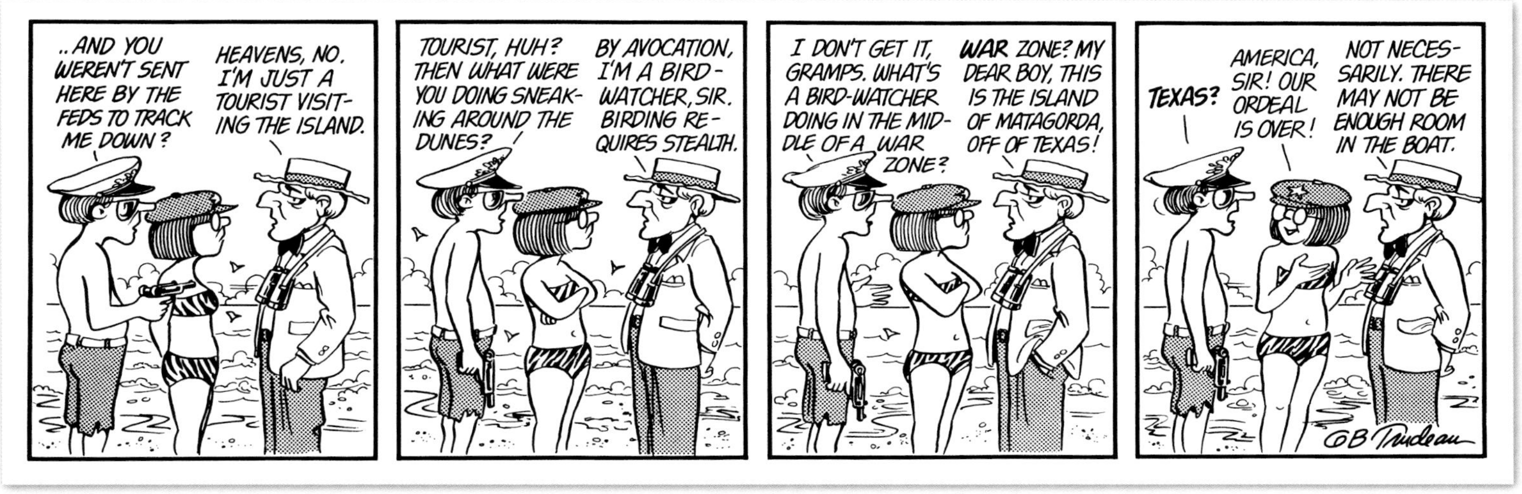
..AND YOU WEREN'T SENT HERE BY THE FEDS TO TRACK ME DOWN?
HEAVENS, NO. I'M JUST A TOURIST VISITING THE ISLAND.
TOURIST, HUH? THEN WHAT WERE YOU DOING SNEAKING AROUND THE DUNES?
BY AVOCATION, I'M A BIRD-WATCHER, SIR. BIRDING REQUIRES STEALTH.
I DON'T GET IT, GRAMPS. WHAT'S A BIRD-WATCHER DOING IN THE MIDDLE OF A WAR ZONE?
WAR ZONE? MY DEAR BOY, THIS IS THE ISLAND OF MATAGORDA, OFF OF TEXAS!
TEXAS?
AMERICA, SIR! OUR ORDEAL IS OVER!
NOT NECESSARILY. THERE MAY NOT BE ENOUGH ROOM IN THE BOAT.
GB Trudeau

6/23/82

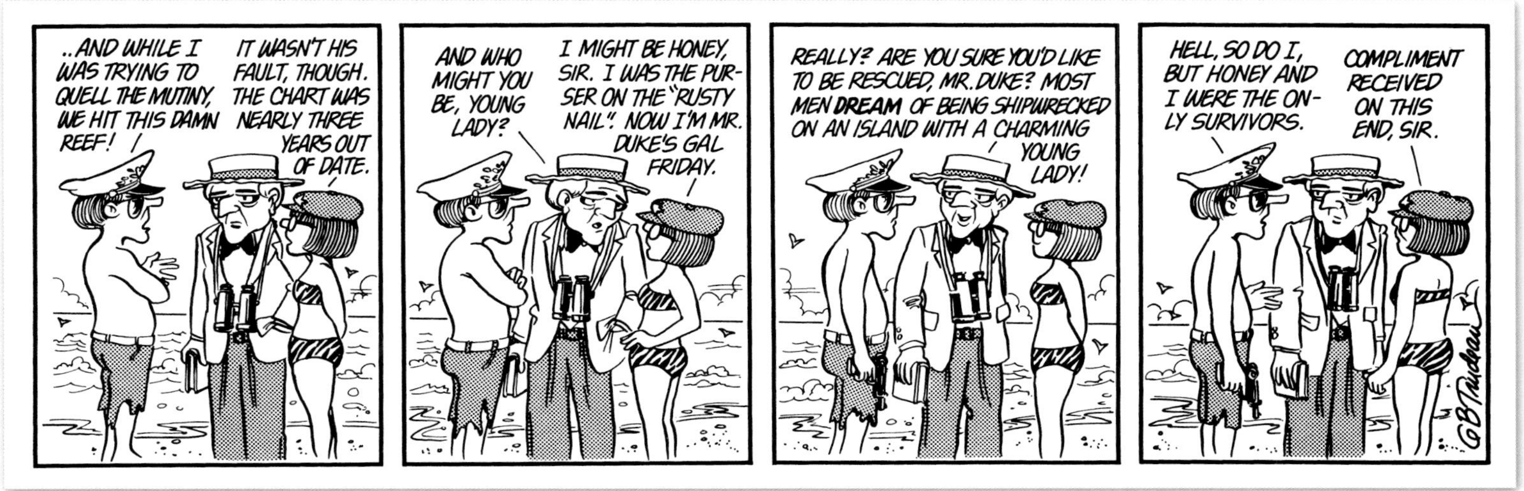
..AND WHILE I WAS TRYING TO QUELL THE MUTINY, WE HIT THIS DAMN REEF!
IT WASN'T HIS FAULT, THOUGH. THE CHART WAS NEARLY THREE YEARS OUT OF DATE.
AND WHO MIGHT YOU BE, YOUNG LADY?
I MIGHT BE HONEY, SIR. I WAS THE PURSER ON THE "RUSTY NAIL". NOW I'M MR. DUKE'S GAL FRIDAY.
REALLY? ARE YOU SURE YOU'D LIKE TO BE RESCUED, MR. DUKE? MOST MEN DREAM OF BEING SHIPWRECKED ON AN ISLAND WITH A CHARMING YOUNG LADY!
HELL, SO DO I, BUT HONEY AND I WERE THE ONLY SURVIVORS.
COMPLIMENT RECEIVED ON THIS END, SIR.
GB Trudeau

6/24/82

Phred

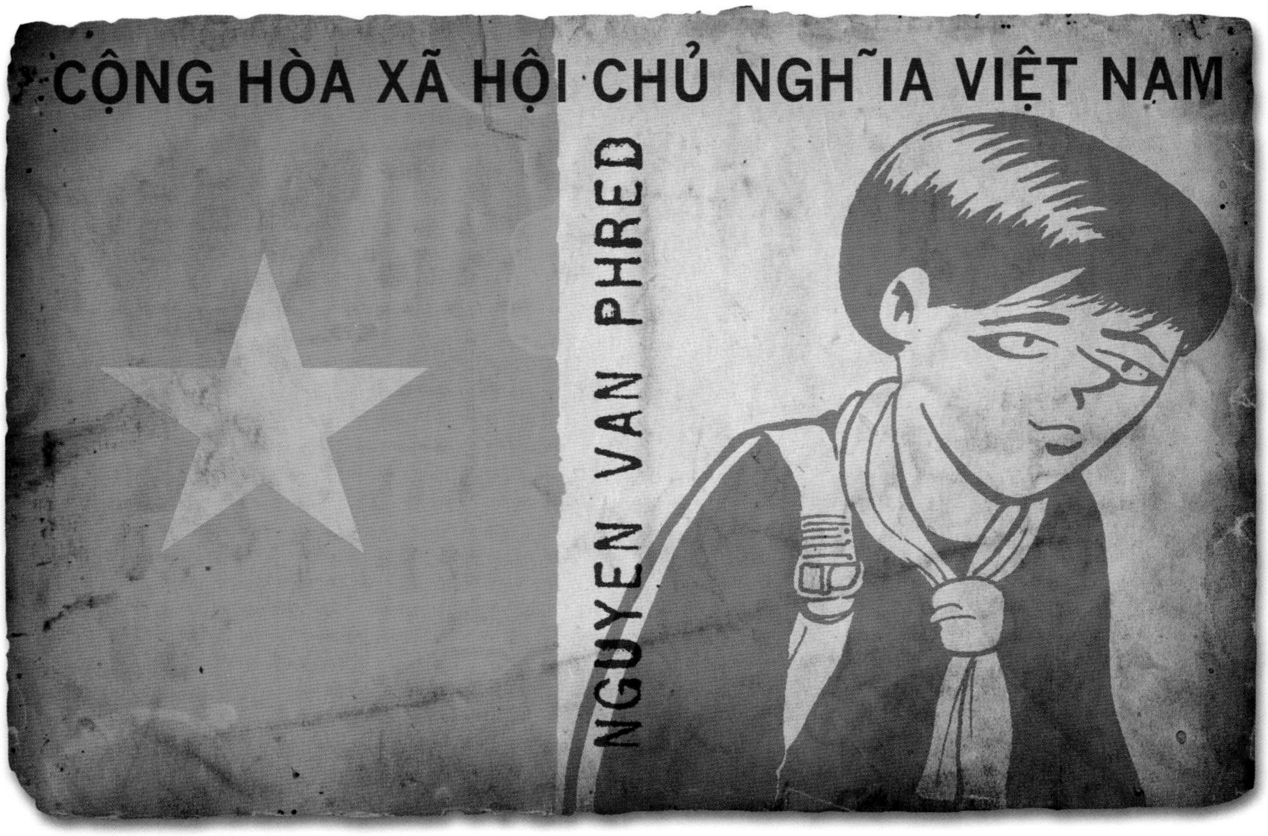
CỘNG HÒA XÃ HỘI CHỦ NGH~IA VIỆT NAM
NGUYEN VAN PHRED

Twenty-five years after the Vietnam War, or what the Vietnamese call the American War, I traveled to Ho Chi Minh City to interview former Viet Cong guerillas. I'd read that many of them had not prospered after Liberation. As southerners, they were widely distrusted by their NVA allies, not just because their loyalties were suspect, but also as a result of a deep cultural gap. The more urbane northerners regarded the Viet Cong as unsophisticated farm boys, Mekong Delta rednecks. But these were Phred's people, and it seemed to me that an effort to look at the war as they had experienced it was long overdue.

The first fighter I talked to had fought from the Cu Chi tunnel complex just north of Saigon. His experiences were filled with every sort of deprivation and horror imaginable. He was the sole survivor of a unit that had been completely wiped out, twice—once through attrition, the second time by a direct hit on their position while he was out foraging. He'd spent the night burying his comrades.

At one point in our discussion, my host described a bombing raid during which he suffered a shrapnel gash so wide that his guts tumbled out of his abdominal cavity. A doctor crawled to his side, and as there was no way to convey him to a field hospital, washed off

"The name's Phred, not Charlie."

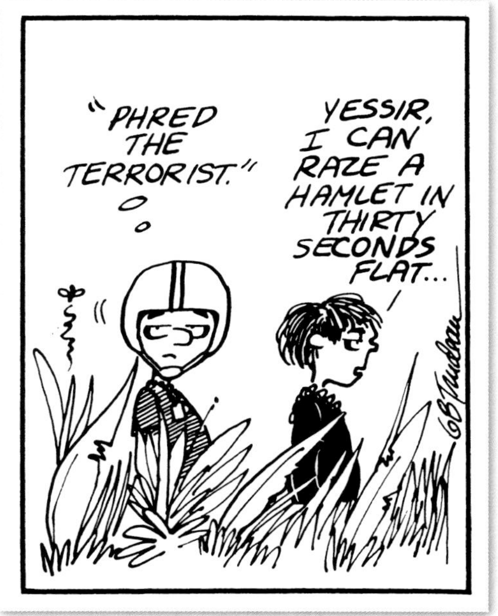
"PHRED THE TERRORIST."
YESSIR, I CAN RAZE A HAMLET IN THIRTY SECONDS FLAT...

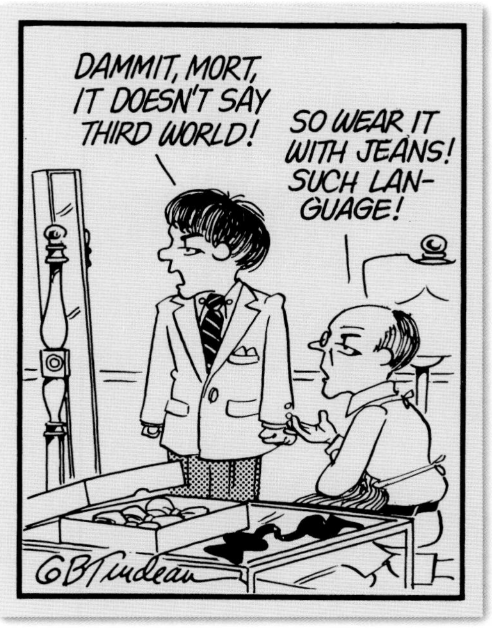
DAMMIT, MORT, IT DOESN'T SAY THIRD WORLD!
SO WEAR IT WITH JEANS! SUCH LANGUAGE!

the fighter's intestines, stuffed them back into his belly, and sewed him up with a long fisherman's needle. As he recalled this story, a flicker of skepticism must have passed over my face, for the man immediately jumped up and unbuttoned his shirt, revealing a long, jagged scar traversing the length of his torso. On either side was a track of widely spaced needle marks.

Needless to say, this tough old veteran bore little similarity to the happy-go-lucky freedom fighter I'd created back in the day. When readers first encountered Nguyen Van Phred in 1972, he was grooving with B.D. in the elephant grass, sharing a stash of purloined brew and belting out Cole Porter songs. The war I'd conjured up was a young man's magical thinking, a hippie fantasia where everyone would get along if just given half a chance. The GIs in the field reading the strip in *Stars and Stripes* knew better, but many of them told me later they were just glad that someone was paying attention to them.

As I left Vietnam, I knew it was time to revisit Phred in the strip. Since diplomatic relations had been normalized in 1994, thousands of American vets had been going back. It was B.D.'s turn. I dispatched him to Ho Chi Minh City where he reconnects with his former foe, now a deputy minister of permitting. Before long, Phred and B.D. are standing in the killing fields of their youth.

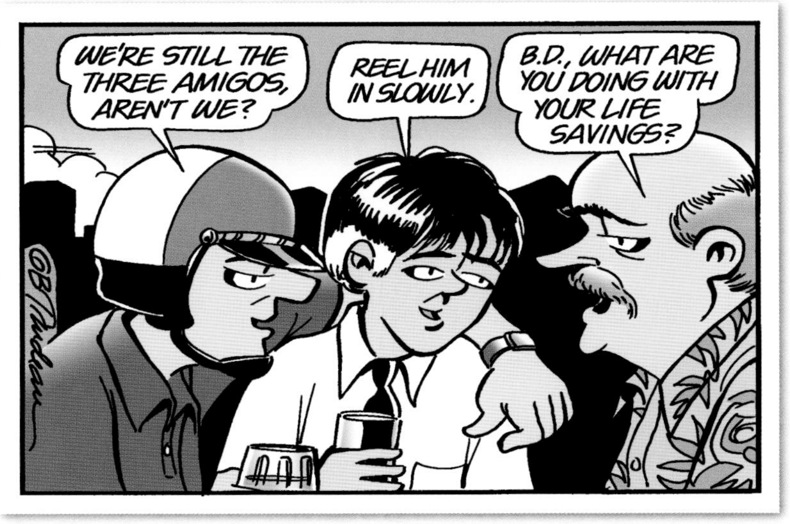
WE'RE STILL THE THREE AMIGOS, AREN'T WE?
REEL HIM IN SLOWLY.
B.D., WHAT ARE YOU DOING WITH YOUR LIFE SAVINGS?

The two men have changed and the world has moved on; but this time, as Phred leads B.D. on an arduous journey through the tunnels B.D. never knew existed, their new connection feels more honestly earned.

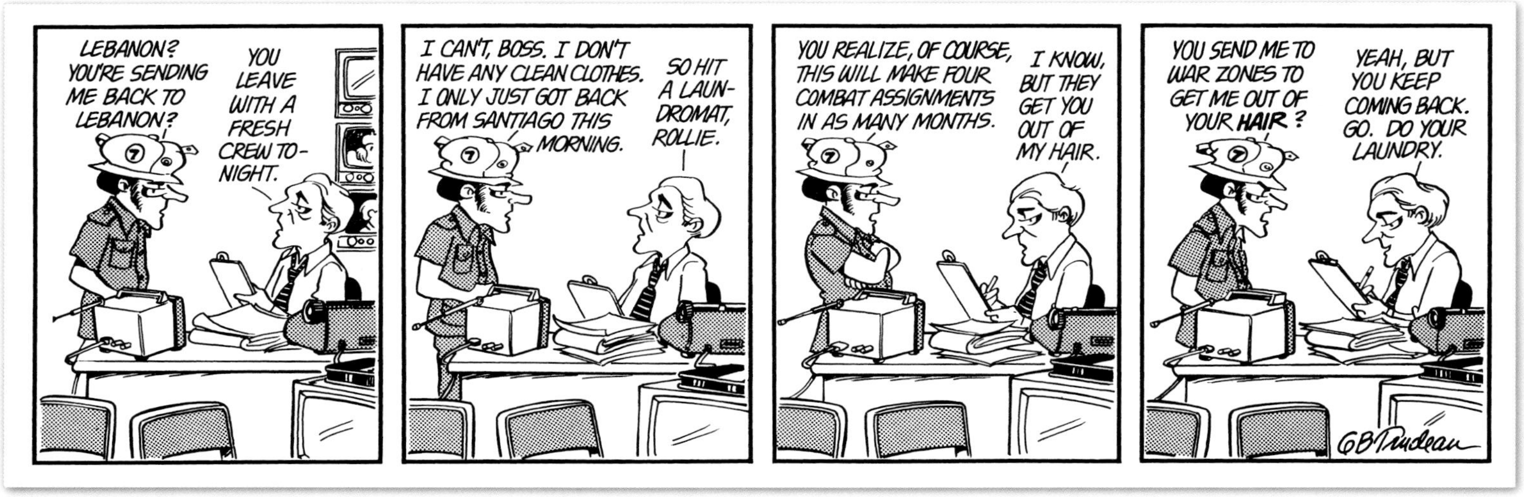
LEBANON? YOU'RE SENDING ME BACK TO LEBANON?
YOU LEAVE WITH A FRESH CREW TO-NIGHT.
I CAN'T, BOSS. I DON'T HAVE ANY CLEAN CLOTHES. I ONLY JUST GOT BACK FROM SANTIAGO THIS MORNING.
SO HIT A LAUN-DROMAT, ROLLIE.
YOU REALIZE, OF COURSE, THIS WILL MAKE FOUR COMBAT ASSIGNMENTS IN AS MANY MONTHS.
I KNOW, BUT THEY GET YOU OUT OF MY HAIR.
YOU SEND ME TO WAR ZONES TO GET ME OUT OF YOUR HAIR?
YEAH, BUT YOU KEEP COMING BACK. GO. DO YOUR LAUNDRY.
GBTrudeau

7/5/82

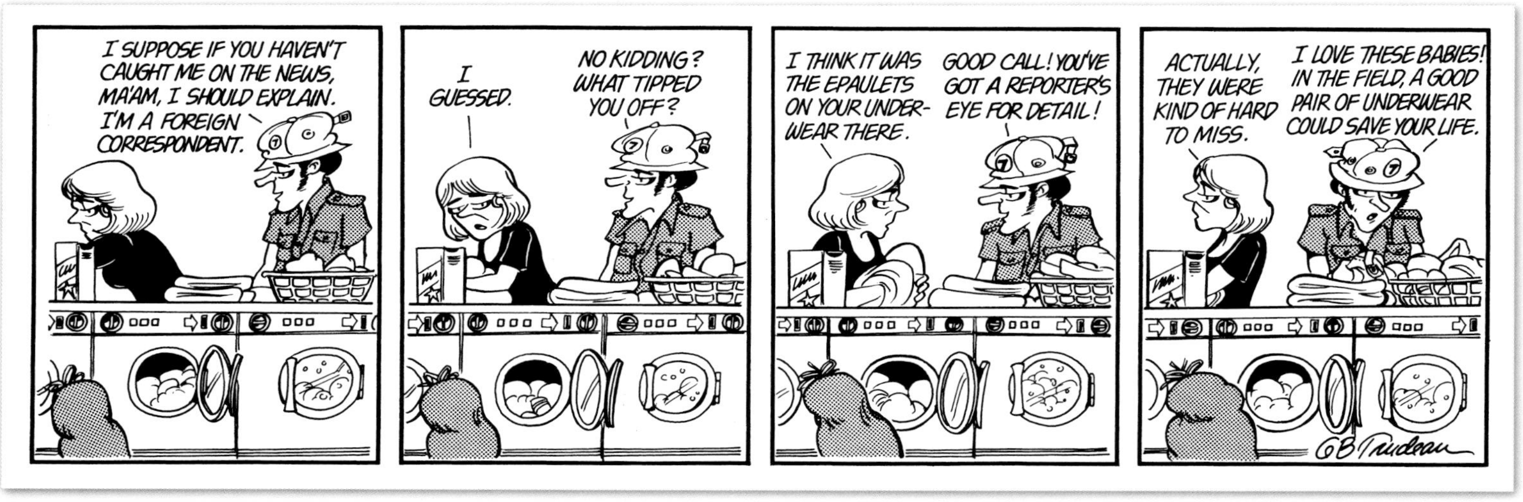
I SUPPOSE IF YOU HAVEN'T CAUGHT ME ON THE NEWS, MA'AM, I SHOULD EXPLAIN. I'M A FOREIGN CORRESPONDENT.
I GUESSED.
NO KIDDING? WHAT TIPPED YOU OFF?
I THINK IT WAS THE EPAULETS ON YOUR UNDER-WEAR THERE.
GOOD CALL! YOU'VE GOT A REPORTER'S EYE FOR DETAIL!
ACTUALLY, THEY WERE KIND OF HARD TO MISS.
I LOVE THESE BABIES! IN THE FIELD, A GOOD PAIR OF UNDERWEAR COULD SAVE YOUR LIFE.
GBTrudeau

7/7/82

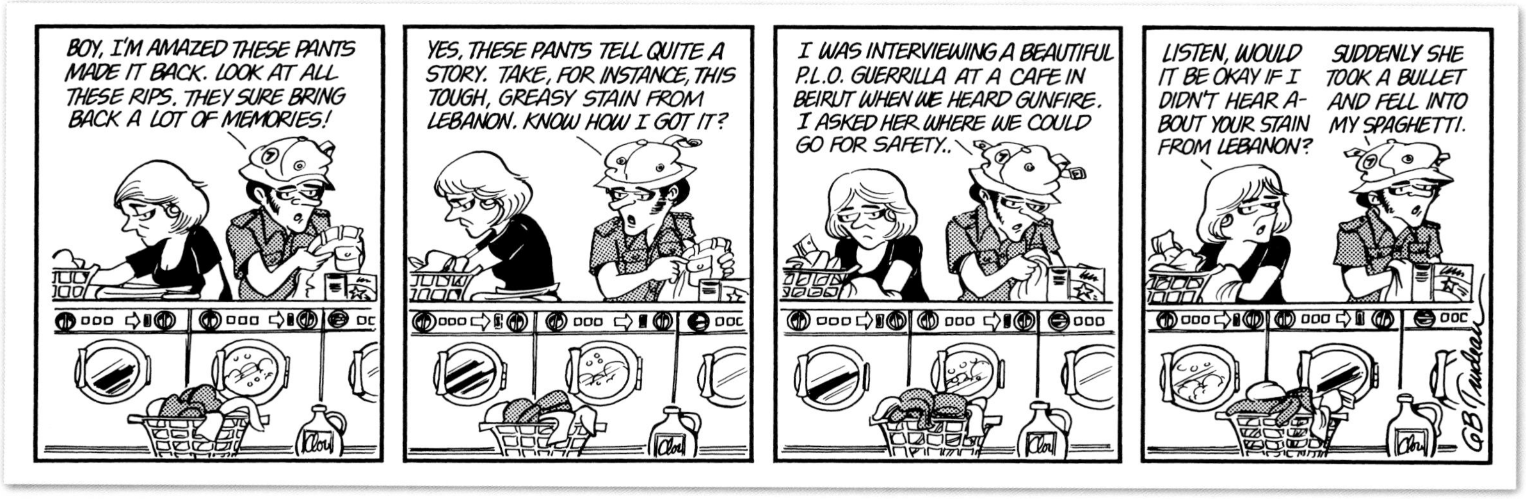
BOY, I'M AMAZED THESE PANTS MADE IT BACK. LOOK AT ALL THESE RIPS. THEY SURE BRING BACK A LOT OF MEMORIES!
YES, THESE PANTS TELL QUITE A STORY. TAKE, FOR INSTANCE, THIS TOUGH, GREASY STAIN FROM LEBANON. KNOW HOW I GOT IT?
I WAS INTERVIEWING A BEAUTIFUL P.L.O. GUERRILLA AT A CAFE IN BEIRUT WHEN WE HEARD GUNFIRE. I ASKED HER WHERE WE COULD GO FOR SAFETY..
LISTEN, WOULD IT BE OKAY IF I DIDN'T HEAR A-BOUT YOUR STAIN FROM LEBANON?
SUDDENLY SHE TOOK A BULLET AND FELL INTO MY SPAGHETTI.
GBTrudeau

7/8/82

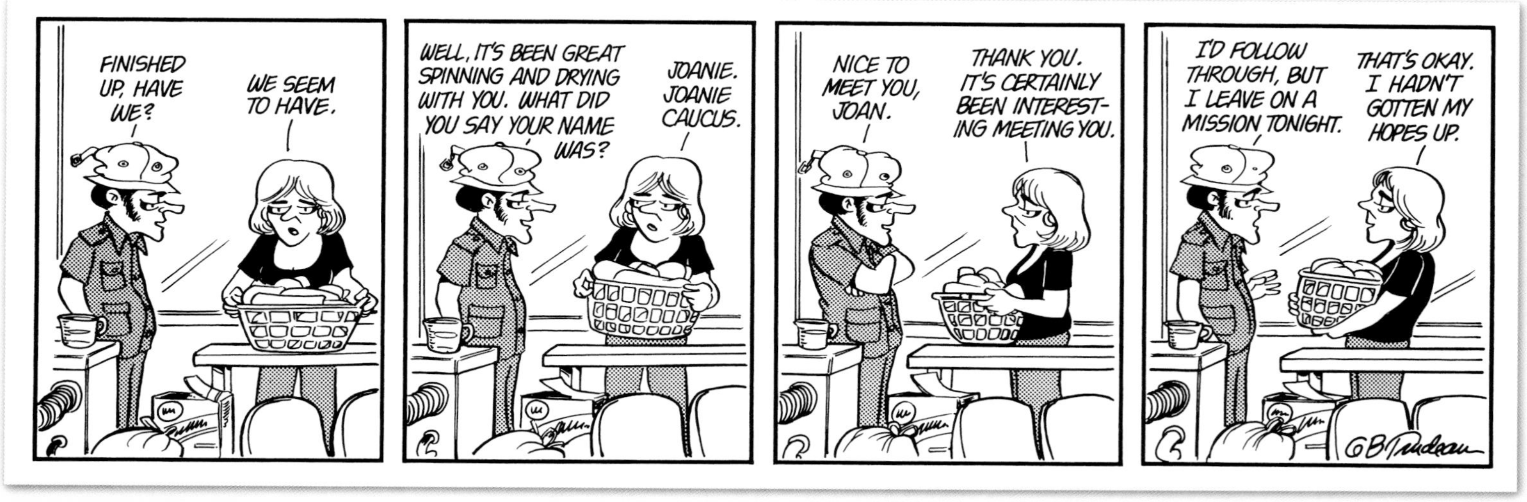
FINISHED UP, HAVE WE?
WE SEEM TO HAVE.
WELL, IT'S BEEN GREAT SPINNING AND DRYING WITH YOU. WHAT DID YOU SAY YOUR NAME WAS?
JOANIE. JOANIE CAUCUS.
NICE TO MEET YOU, JOAN.
THANK YOU. IT'S CERTAINLY BEEN INTEREST-ING MEETING YOU.
I'D FOLLOW THROUGH, BUT I LEAVE ON A MISSION TONIGHT.
THAT'S OKAY. I HADN'T GOTTEN MY HOPES UP.
GBTrudeau

7/10/82

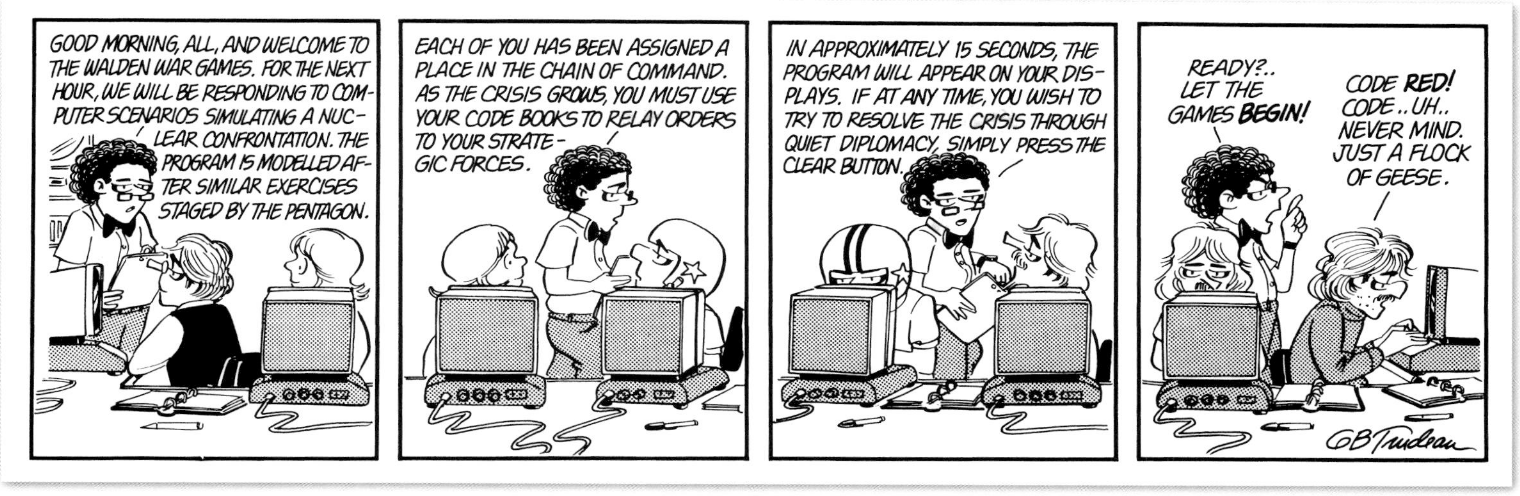
GOOD MORNING, ALL, AND WELCOME TO THE WALDEN WAR GAMES. FOR THE NEXT HOUR, WE WILL BE RESPONDING TO COMPUTER SCENARIOS SIMULATING A NUCLEAR CONFRONTATION. THE PROGRAM IS MODELLED AFTER SIMILAR EXERCISES STAGED BY THE PENTAGON.
EACH OF YOU HAS BEEN ASSIGNED A PLACE IN THE CHAIN OF COMMAND. AS THE CRISIS GROWS, YOU MUST USE YOUR CODE BOOKS TO RELAY ORDERS TO YOUR STRATEGIC FORCES.
IN APPROXIMATELY 15 SECONDS, THE PROGRAM WILL APPEAR ON YOUR DISPLAYS. IF AT ANY TIME, YOU WISH TO TRY TO RESOLVE THE CRISIS THROUGH QUIET DIPLOMACY, SIMPLY PRESS THE CLEAR BUTTON.
READY?.. LET THE GAMES BEGIN!
CODE RED! CODE.. UH.. NEVER MIND. JUST A FLOCK OF GEESE.
GB Trudeau

4/13/82

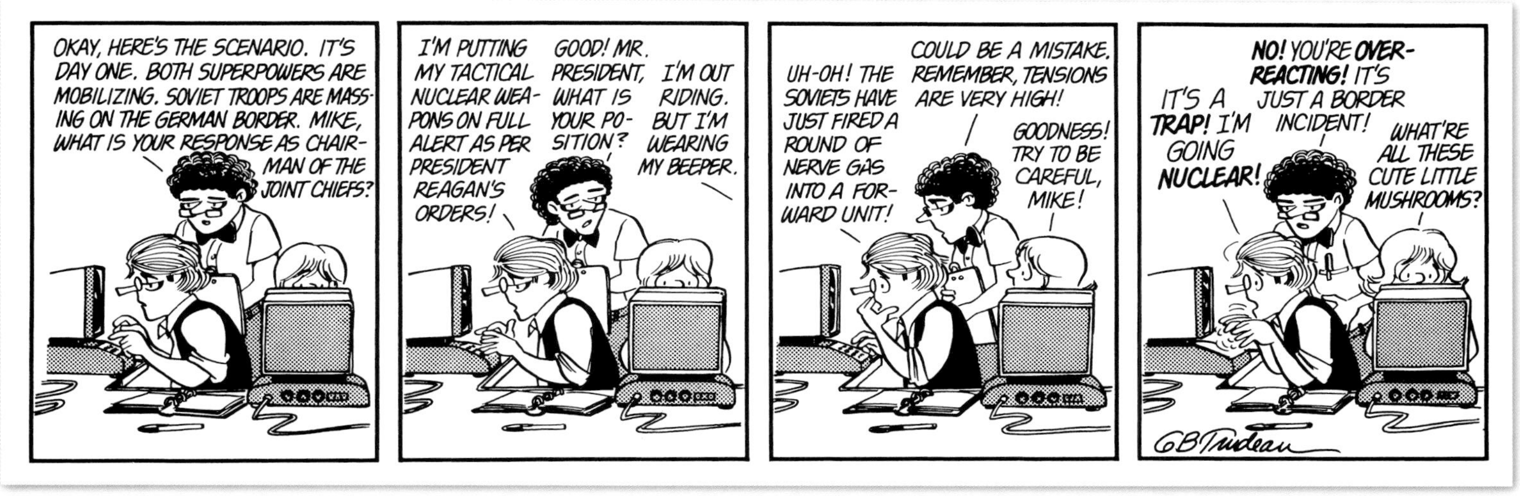
OKAY, HERE'S THE SCENARIO. IT'S DAY ONE. BOTH SUPERPOWERS ARE MOBILIZING. SOVIET TROOPS ARE MASSING ON THE GERMAN BORDER. MIKE, WHAT IS YOUR RESPONSE AS CHAIRMAN OF THE JOINT CHIEFS?
I'M PUTTING MY TACTICAL NUCLEAR WEAPONS ON FULL ALERT AS PER PRESIDENT REAGAN'S ORDERS!
GOOD! MR. PRESIDENT, WHAT IS YOUR POSITION?
I'M OUT RIDING. BUT I'M WEARING MY BEEPER.
UH-OH! THE SOVIETS HAVE JUST FIRED A ROUND OF NERVE GAS INTO A FORWARD UNIT!
COULD BE A MISTAKE. REMEMBER, TENSIONS ARE VERY HIGH!
GOODNESS! TRY TO BE CAREFUL, MIKE!
IT'S A TRAP! I'M GOING NUCLEAR!
NO! YOU'RE OVERREACTING! IT'S JUST A BORDER INCIDENT!
WHAT'RE ALL THESE CUTE LITTLE MUSHROOMS?
GB Trudeau

4/14/82

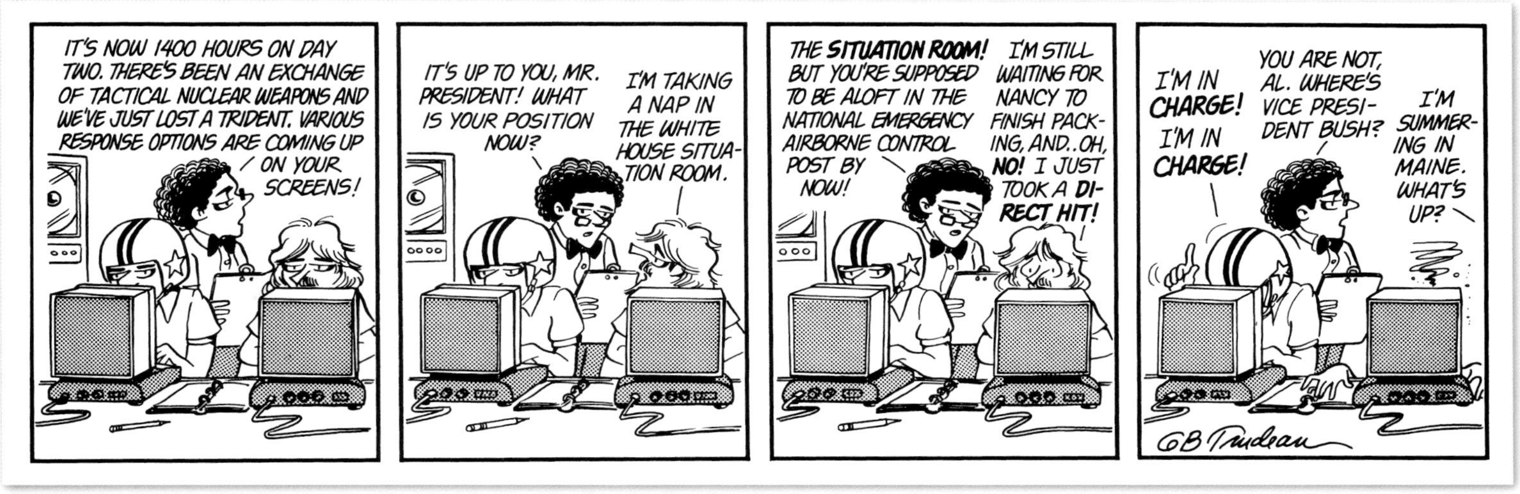
IT'S NOW 1400 HOURS ON DAY TWO. THERE'S BEEN AN EXCHANGE OF TACTICAL NUCLEAR WEAPONS AND WE'VE JUST LOST A TRIDENT. VARIOUS RESPONSE OPTIONS ARE COMING UP ON YOUR SCREENS!
IT'S UP TO YOU, MR. PRESIDENT! WHAT IS YOUR POSITION NOW?
I'M TAKING A NAP IN THE WHITE HOUSE SITUATION ROOM.
THE SITUATION ROOM! BUT YOU'RE SUPPOSED TO BE ALOFT IN THE NATIONAL EMERGENCY AIRBORNE CONTROL POST BY NOW!
I'M STILL WAITING FOR NANCY TO FINISH PACKING, AND.. OH, NO! I JUST TOOK A DIRECT HIT!
I'M IN CHARGE! I'M IN CHARGE!
YOU ARE NOT, AL. WHERE'S VICE PRESIDENT BUSH?
I'M SUMMERING IN MAINE. WHAT'S UP?
GB Trudeau

4/15/82

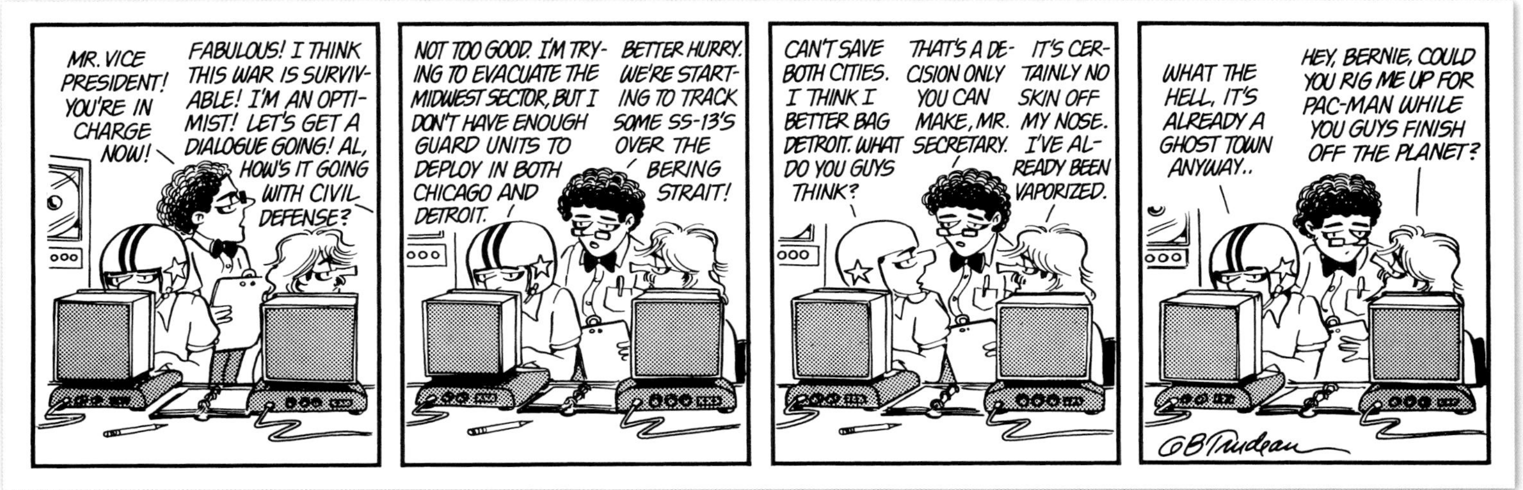
MR. VICE PRESIDENT! YOU'RE IN CHARGE NOW!
FABULOUS! I THINK THIS WAR IS SURVIVABLE! I'M AN OPTIMIST! LET'S GET A DIALOGUE GOING! AL, HOW'S IT GOING WITH CIVIL DEFENSE?
NOT TOO GOOD. I'M TRYING TO EVACUATE THE MIDWEST SECTOR, BUT I DON'T HAVE ENOUGH GUARD UNITS TO DEPLOY IN BOTH CHICAGO AND DETROIT.
BETTER HURRY. WE'RE STARTING TO TRACK SOME SS-13'S OVER THE BERING STRAIT!
CAN'T SAVE BOTH CITIES. I THINK I BETTER BAG DETROIT. WHAT DO YOU GUYS THINK?
THAT'S A DECISION ONLY YOU CAN MAKE, MR. SECRETARY.
IT'S CERTAINLY NO SKIN OFF MY NOSE. I'VE ALREADY BEEN VAPORIZED.
WHAT THE HELL, IT'S ALREADY A GHOST TOWN ANYWAY..
HEY, BERNIE, COULD YOU RIG ME UP FOR PAC-MAN WHILE YOU GUYS FINISH OFF THE PLANET?
GB Trudeau

4/16/82

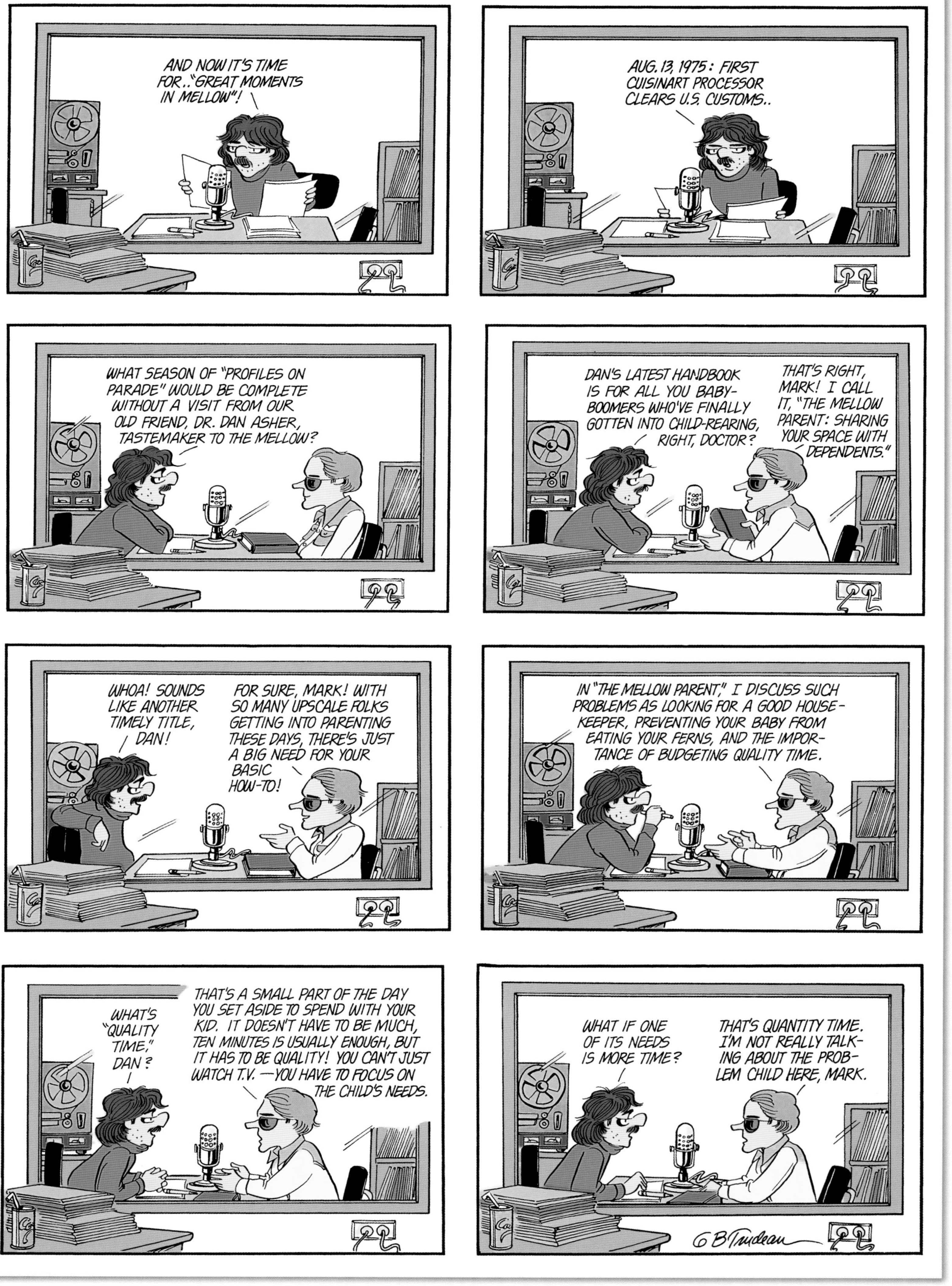
AND NOW IT'S TIME FOR.."GREAT MOMENTS IN MELLOW"!
AUG. 13, 1975: FIRST CUISINART PROCESSOR CLEARS U.S. CUSTOMS..
WHAT SEASON OF "PROFILES ON PARADE" WOULD BE COMPLETE WITHOUT A VISIT FROM OUR OLD FRIEND, DR. DAN ASHER, TASTEMAKER TO THE MELLOW?
DAN'S LATEST HANDBOOK IS FOR ALL YOU BABY-BOOMERS WHO'VE FINALLY GOTTEN INTO CHILD-REARING, RIGHT, DOCTOR?
THAT'S RIGHT, MARK! I CALL IT, "THE MELLOW PARENT: SHARING YOUR SPACE WITH DEPENDENTS."
WHOA! SOUNDS LIKE ANOTHER TIMELY TITLE, DAN!
FOR SURE, MARK! WITH SO MANY UPSCALE FOLKS GETTING INTO PARENTING THESE DAYS, THERE'S JUST A BIG NEED FOR YOUR BASIC HOW-TO!
IN "THE MELLOW PARENT," I DISCUSS SUCH PROBLEMS AS LOOKING FOR A GOOD HOUSE-KEEPER, PREVENTING YOUR BABY FROM EATING YOUR FERNS, AND THE IMPOR-TANCE OF BUDGETING QUALITY TIME.
WHAT'S "QUALITY TIME," DAN?
THAT'S A SMALL PART OF THE DAY YOU SET ASIDE TO SPEND WITH YOUR KID. IT DOESN'T HAVE TO BE MUCH, TEN MINUTES IS USUALLY ENOUGH, BUT IT HAS TO BE QUALITY! YOU CAN'T JUST WATCH T.V. —YOU HAVE TO FOCUS ON THE CHILD'S NEEDS.
WHAT IF ONE OF ITS NEEDS IS MORE TIME?
THAT'S QUANTITY TIME. I'M NOT REALLY TALK-ING ABOUT THE PROB-LEM CHILD HERE, MARK.
G B Trudeau

2/21/82

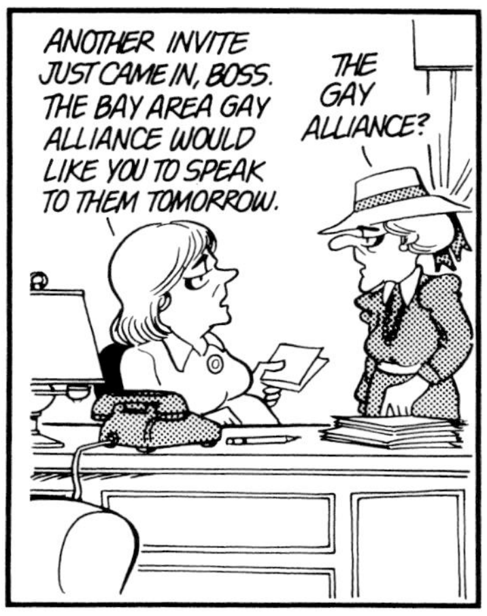
ANOTHER INVITE JUST CAME IN, BOSS. THE BAY AREA GAY ALLIANCE WOULD LIKE YOU TO SPEAK TO THEM TOMORROW.
THE GAY ALLIANCE?
ACTUALLY, YOU MIGHT WANT TO DO THAT ONE. I'VE BEEN LOOKING OVER THE LATEST DEMOGRAPHICS, AND YOUR DISTRICT IS NOW HEAVILY GAY.
GOODNESS! IT IS?
THAT'S RIGHT.
MY, HOW THINGS CHANGE! YES, BY ALL MEANS LET'S GO. I'D LOVE TO HEAR WHAT THEY HAVE TO SAY!
THAT'S VERY OPEN OF YOU, BOSS.
NOT AT ALL. I'VE ALWAYS FOUND CONFIRMED BACHELORS JUST SO FASCINATING!
GB Trudeau

9/6/82

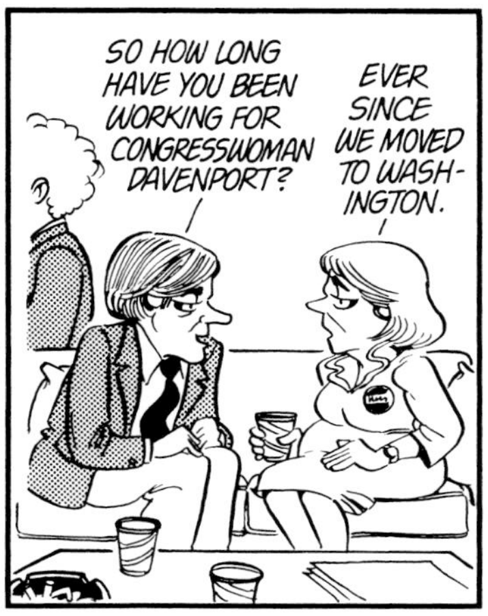
SO HOW LONG HAVE YOU BEEN WORKING FOR CONGRESSWOMAN DAVENPORT?
EVER SINCE WE MOVED TO WASHINGTON.
SHE CERTAINLY SEEMS LIKE A REMARKABLE WOMAN.
OH, SHE IS, ANDY, SHE REALLY IS..
I'M NOT SURE HOW MUCH SHE KNOWS ABOUT HER NEW GAY CONSTITUENCY, BUT SHE'S CERTAINLY WILLING TO LEARN.
GB Trudeau
BUT HAVE YOU TRIED, I MEAN, **REALLY** TRIED, DATING GIRLS YOUR OWN AGE?
IT DOESN'T QUITE WORK THAT WAY, MA'AM.

9/9/82

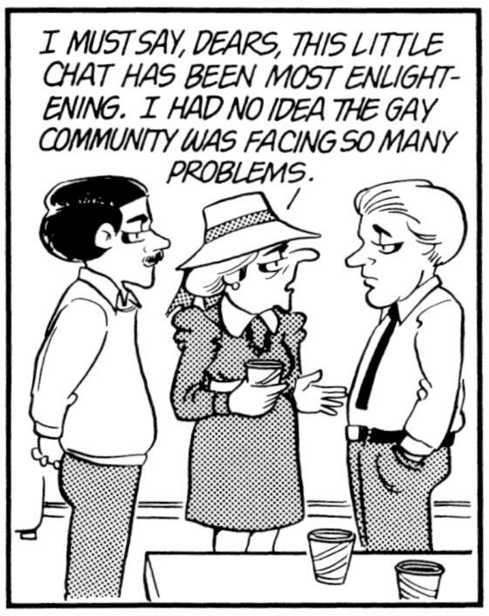
I MUST SAY, DEARS, THIS LITTLE CHAT HAS BEEN MOST ENLIGHTENING. I HAD NO IDEA THE GAY COMMUNITY WAS FACING SO MANY PROBLEMS.
AS YOU CAN IMAGINE, THIS IS ALL NEW GROUND FOR ME. WE NEVER HAD ANY GAYS AMONG OUR FAMILY AND FRIENDS.
WELL, NOW, ACTUALLY, THAT'S NOT TRUE. DICK'S UNCLE ORVILLE CAME OUT OF THE CLOSET LAST YEAR. HE'S A FEDERAL JUDGE IN CHICAGO.
THAT'S GREAT! WHAT MADE HIM DO IT?
HIGH INTEREST RATES. HIS BUTLER TRIED TO BLACKMAIL HIM, AND HE COULDN'T AFFORD IT.
GB Trudeau

9/10/82

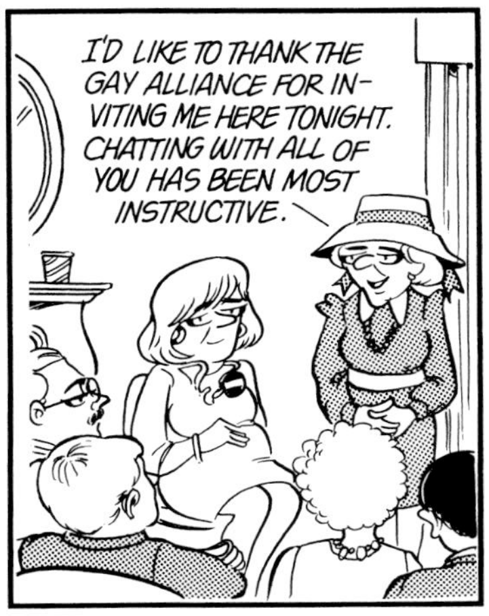
I'D LIKE TO THANK THE GAY ALLIANCE FOR INVITING ME HERE TONIGHT. CHATTING WITH ALL OF YOU HAS BEEN MOST INSTRUCTIVE.
ALSO, I MUST SAY, IT'S REFRESHING TO MEET A GROUP OF CONSTITUENTS WITH SUCH FINE MANNERS. I'M ALSO VERY IMPRESSED WITH HOW NICELY YOU ALL DRESS.
THE ONLY THING I MIGHT QUIBBLE WITH IS YOUR HAIR. SOME OF YOU BOYS HAVE TERRIBLY SHORT HAIRCUTS. HAIR THAT SHORT LOOKS FINE ON NAVY CADETS, BUT OTHERWISE IT MAKES YOU LOOK AWFULLY YOUNG.
UH.. LACEY..
NEVER MIND. MINOR POINT. THANKS AGAIN.
GB Trudeau

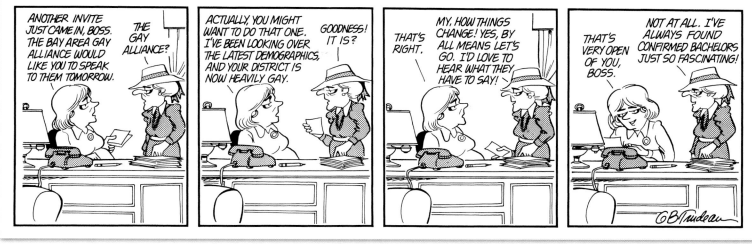

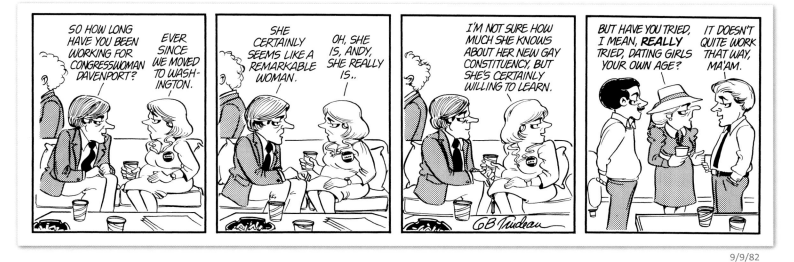

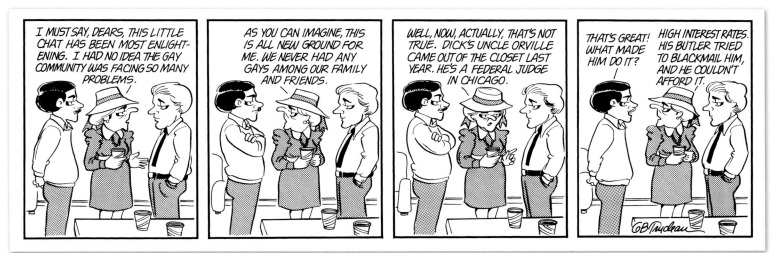

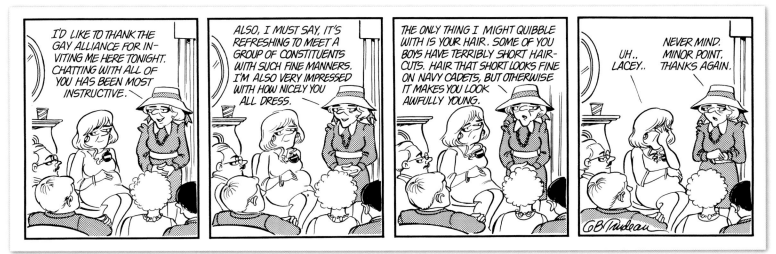

9/11/82

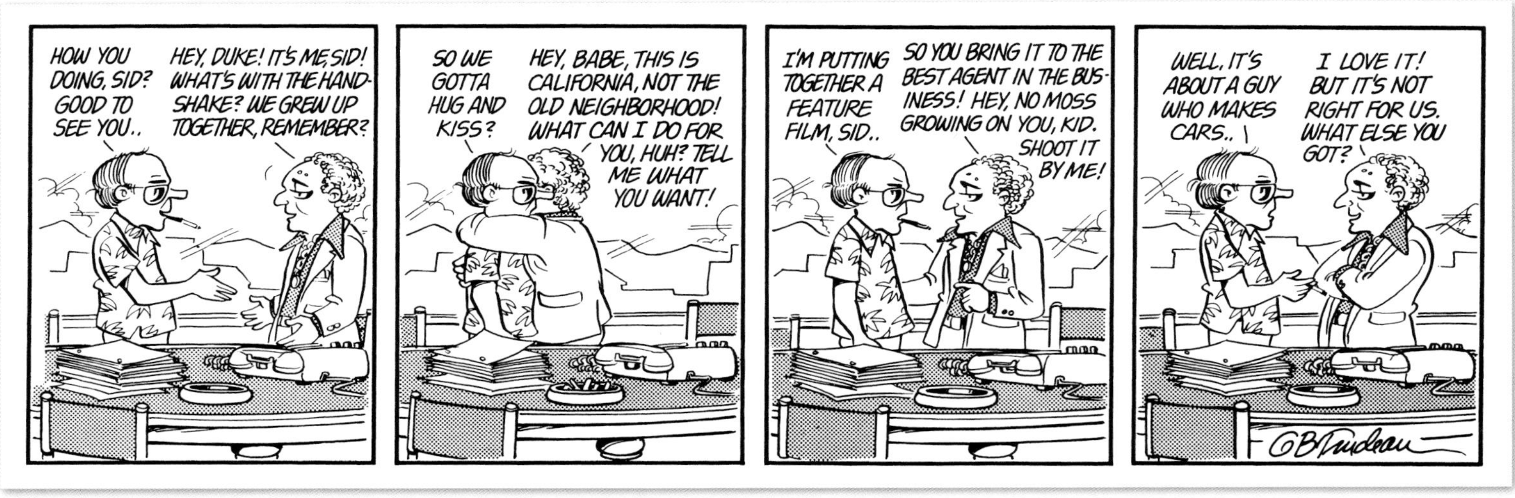
HOW YOU DOING, SID? GOOD TO SEE YOU..
HEY, DUKE! IT'S ME, SID! WHAT'S WITH THE HANDSHAKE? WE GREW UP TOGETHER, REMEMBER?
SO WE GOTTA HUG AND KISS?
HEY, BABE, THIS IS CALIFORNIA, NOT THE OLD NEIGHBORHOOD! WHAT CAN I DO FOR YOU, HUH? TELL ME WHAT YOU WANT!
I'M PUTTING TOGETHER A FEATURE FILM, SID..
SO YOU BRING IT TO THE BEST AGENT IN THE BUSINESS! HEY, NO MOSS GROWING ON YOU, KID. SHOOT IT BY ME!
WELL, IT'S ABOUT A GUY WHO MAKES CARS..
I LOVE IT! BUT IT'S NOT RIGHT FOR US. WHAT ELSE YOU GOT?
GB Trudeau
11/15/82

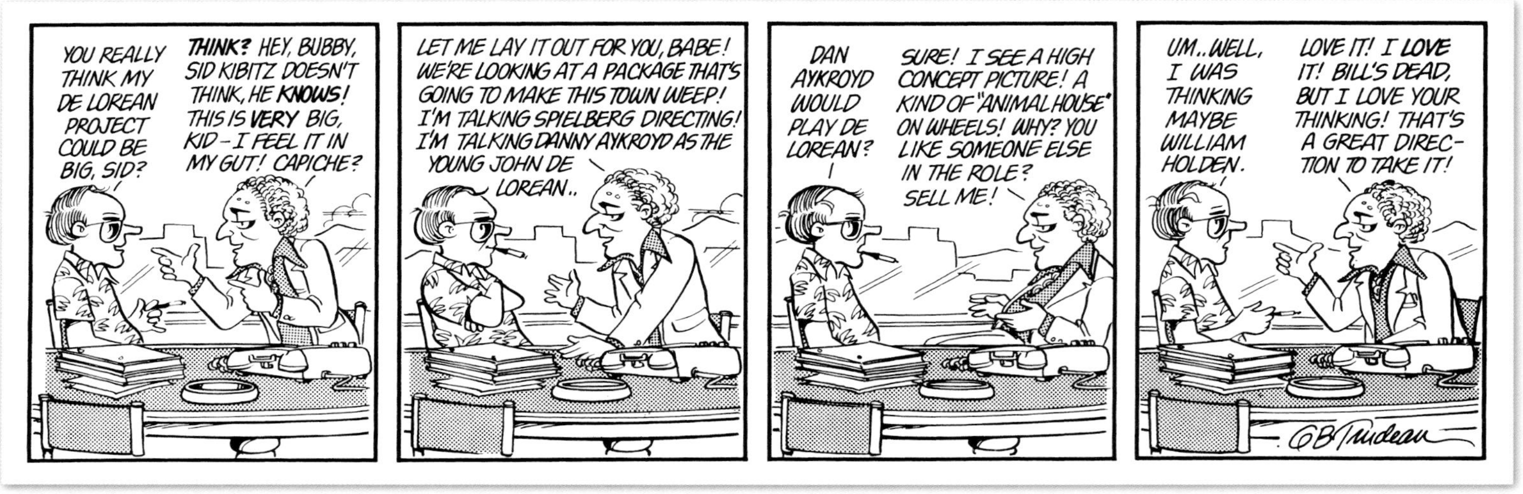
YOU REALLY THINK MY DE LOREAN PROJECT COULD BE BIG, SID?
THINK? HEY, BUBBY, SID KIBITZ DOESN'T THINK, HE KNOWS! THIS IS VERY BIG, KID – I FEEL IT IN MY GUT! CAPICHE?
LET ME LAY IT OUT FOR YOU, BABE! WE'RE LOOKING AT A PACKAGE THAT'S GOING TO MAKE THIS TOWN WEEP! I'M TALKING SPIELBERG DIRECTING! I'M TALKING DANNY AYKROYD AS THE YOUNG JOHN DE LOREAN..
DAN AYKROYD WOULD PLAY DE LOREAN?
SURE! I SEE A HIGH CONCEPT PICTURE! A KIND OF "ANIMAL HOUSE" ON WHEELS! WHY? YOU LIKE SOMEONE ELSE IN THE ROLE? SELL ME!
UM.. WELL, I WAS THINKING MAYBE WILLIAM HOLDEN.
LOVE IT! I LOVE IT! BILL'S DEAD, BUT I LOVE YOUR THINKING! THAT'S A GREAT DIRECTION TO TAKE IT!
GB Trudeau
11/17/82

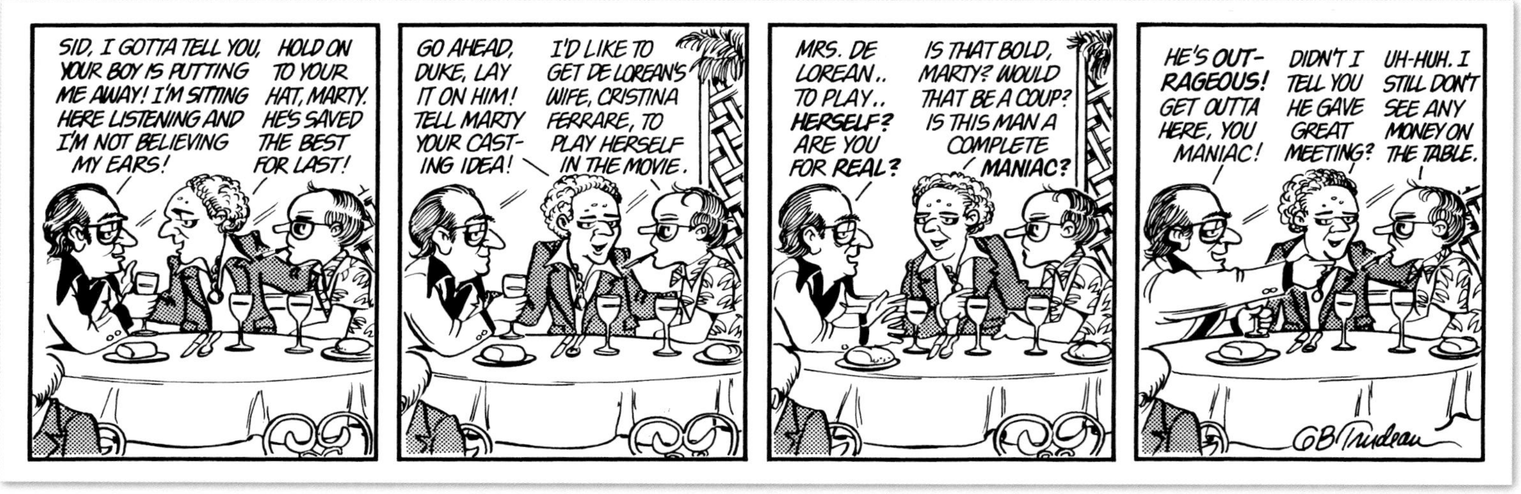
SID, I GOTTA TELL YOU, YOUR BOY IS PUTTING ME AWAY! I'M SITTING HERE LISTENING AND I'M NOT BELIEVING MY EARS!
HOLD ON TO YOUR HAT, MARTY. HE'S SAVED THE BEST FOR LAST!
GO AHEAD, DUKE, LAY IT ON HIM! TELL MARTY YOUR CASTING IDEA!
I'D LIKE TO GET DE LOREAN'S WIFE, CRISTINA FERRARE, TO PLAY HERSELF IN THE MOVIE.
MRS. DE LOREAN.. TO PLAY.. HERSELF? ARE YOU FOR REAL?
IS THAT BOLD, MARTY? WOULD THAT BE A COUP? IS THIS MAN A COMPLETE MANIAC?
HE'S OUTRAGEOUS! GET OUTTA HERE, YOU MANIAC!
DIDN'T I TELL YOU HE GAVE GREAT MEETING?
UH-HUH. I STILL DON'T SEE ANY MONEY ON THE TABLE.
GB Trudeau
11/24/82

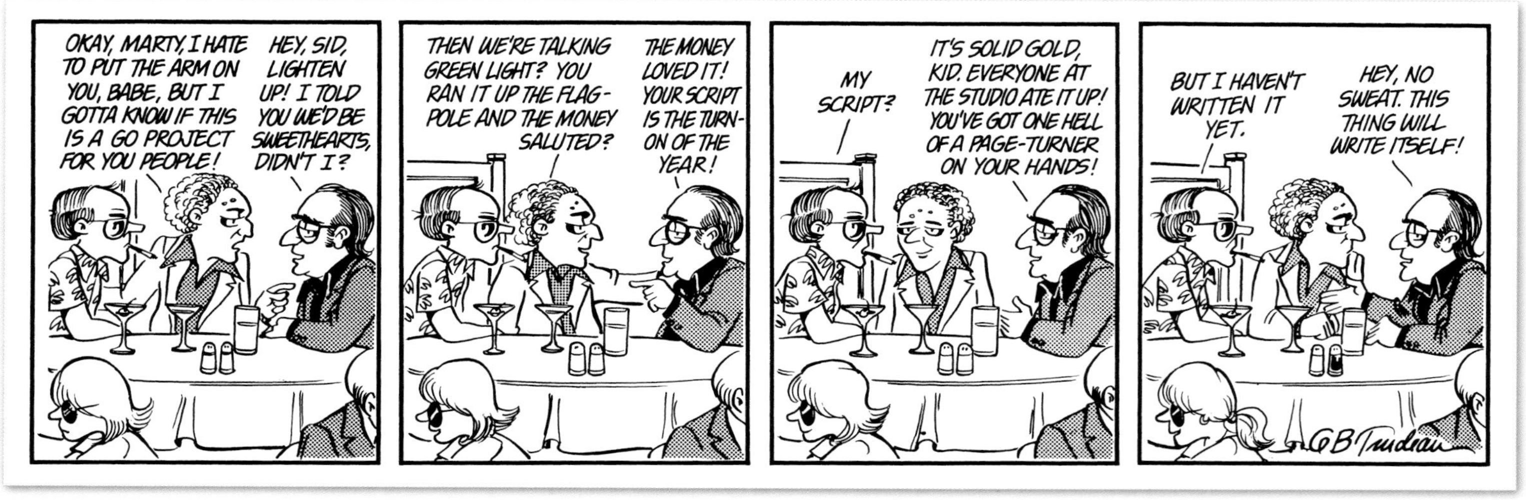
OKAY, MARTY, I HATE TO PUT THE ARM ON YOU, BABE, BUT I GOTTA KNOW IF THIS IS A GO PROJECT FOR YOU PEOPLE!
HEY, SID, LIGHTEN UP! I TOLD YOU WE'D BE SWEETHEARTS, DIDN'T I?
THEN WE'RE TALKING GREEN LIGHT? YOU RAN IT UP THE FLAGPOLE AND THE MONEY SALUTED?
THE MONEY LOVED IT! YOUR SCRIPT IS THE TURN-ON OF THE YEAR!
MY SCRIPT?
IT'S SOLID GOLD, KID. EVERYONE AT THE STUDIO ATE IT UP! YOU'VE GOT ONE HELL OF A PAGE-TURNER ON YOUR HANDS!
BUT I HAVEN'T WRITTEN IT YET.
HEY, NO SWEAT. THIS THING WILL WRITE ITSELF!
GB Trudeau
11/25/82

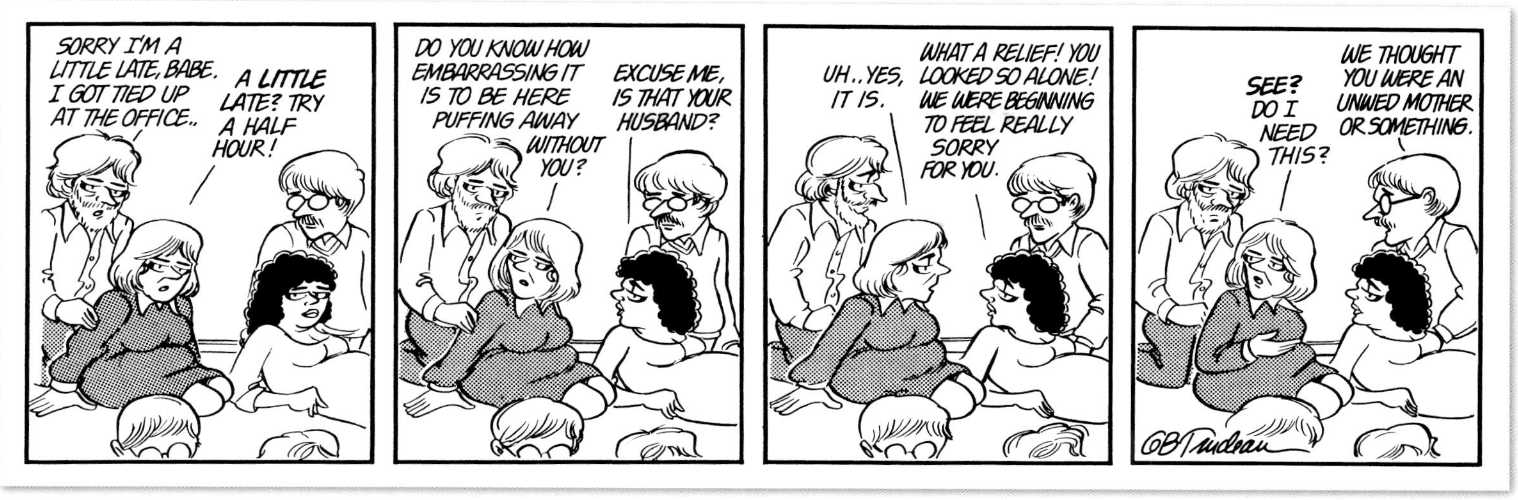
SORRY I'M A LITTLE LATE, BABE. I GOT TIED UP AT THE OFFICE..
A LITTLE LATE? TRY A HALF HOUR!
DO YOU KNOW HOW EMBARRASSING IT IS TO BE HERE PUFFING AWAY WITHOUT YOU?
EXCUSE ME, IS THAT YOUR HUSBAND?
UH..YES, IT IS.
WHAT A RELIEF! YOU LOOKED SO ALONE! WE WERE BEGINNING TO FEEL REALLY SORRY FOR YOU.
SEE? DO I NEED THIS?
WE THOUGHT YOU WERE AN UNWED MOTHER OR SOMETHING.
GB Trudeau

12/7/82

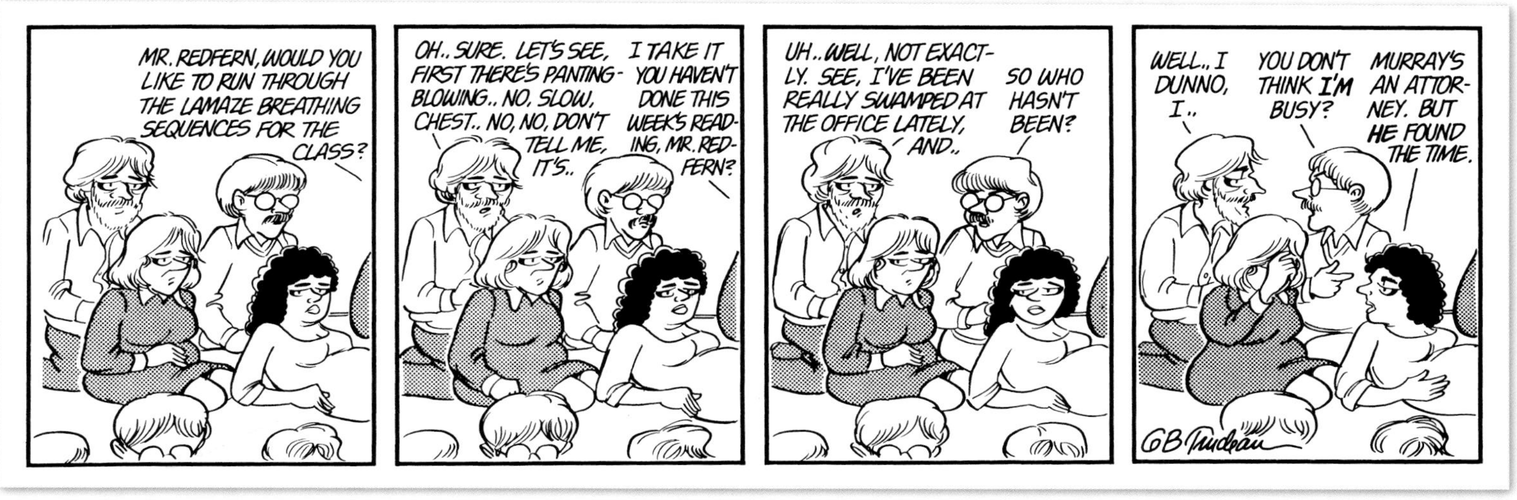
MR. REDFERN, WOULD YOU LIKE TO RUN THROUGH THE LAMAZE BREATHING SEQUENCES FOR THE CLASS?
OH.. SURE. LET'S SEE, FIRST THERE'S PANTING-BLOWING.. NO. SLOW, CHEST.. NO, NO, DON'T TELL ME, IT'S..
I TAKE IT YOU HAVEN'T DONE THIS WEEK'S READING, MR. REDFERN?
UH.. WELL, NOT EXACTLY. SEE, I'VE BEEN REALLY SWAMPED AT THE OFFICE LATELY, AND..
SO WHO HASN'T BEEN?
WELL.. I DUNNO, I..
YOU DON'T THINK I'M BUSY?
MURRAY'S AN ATTORNEY. BUT HE FOUND THE TIME.
GB Trudeau

12/8/82

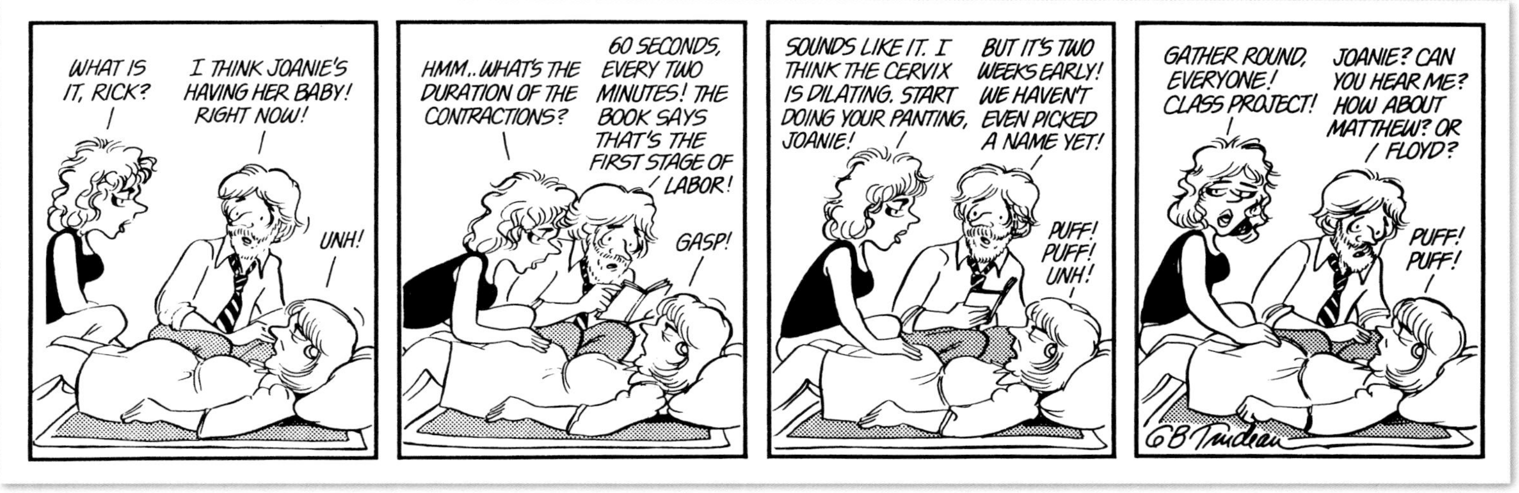
WHAT IS IT, RICK?
I THINK JOANIE'S HAVING HER BABY! RIGHT NOW!
UNH!
HMM.. WHAT'S THE DURATION OF THE CONTRACTIONS?
60 SECONDS, EVERY TWO MINUTES! THE BOOK SAYS THAT'S THE FIRST STAGE OF LABOR!
GASP!
SOUNDS LIKE IT. I THINK THE CERVIX IS DILATING. START DOING YOUR PANTING, JOANIE!
BUT IT'S TWO WEEKS EARLY! WE HAVEN'T EVEN PICKED A NAME YET!
PUFF! PUFF! UNH!
GATHER ROUND, EVERYONE! CLASS PROJECT!
JOANIE? CAN YOU HEAR ME? HOW ABOUT MATTHEW? OR FLOYD?
PUFF! PUFF!
GB Trudeau

12/29/82

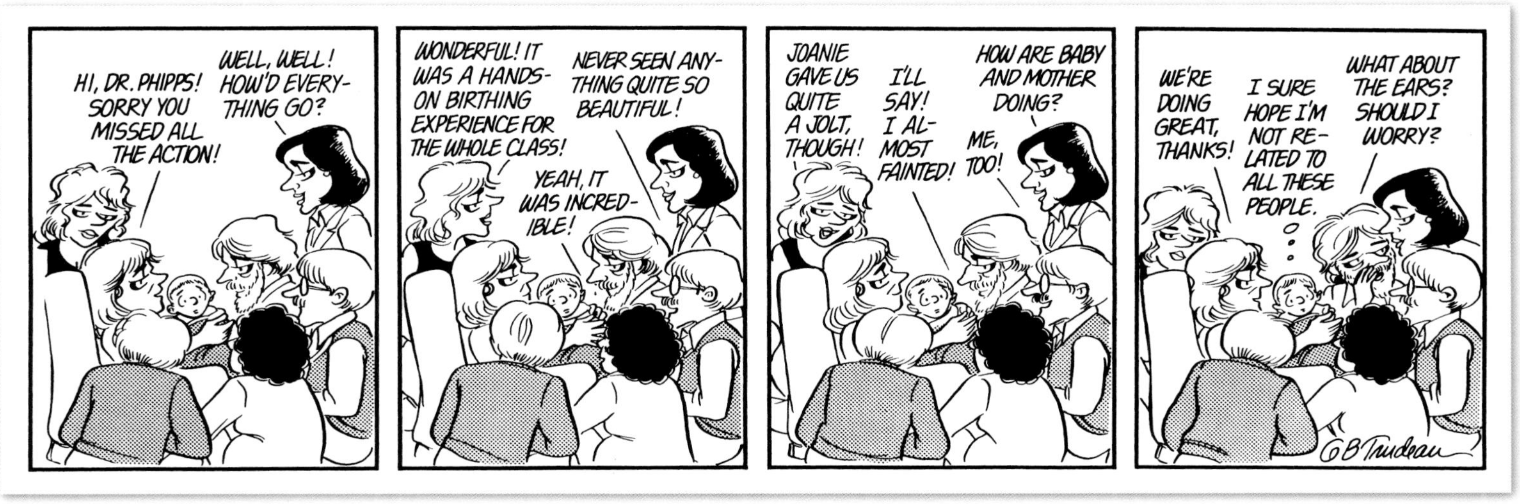
HI, DR. PHIPPS! SORRY YOU MISSED ALL THE ACTION!
WELL, WELL! HOW'D EVERYTHING GO?
WONDERFUL! IT WAS A HANDS-ON BIRTHING EXPERIENCE FOR THE WHOLE CLASS!
NEVER SEEN ANYTHING QUITE SO BEAUTIFUL!
YEAH, IT WAS INCREDIBLE!
JOANIE GAVE US QUITE A JOLT, THOUGH!
I'LL SAY! I ALMOST FAINTED!
HOW ARE BABY AND MOTHER DOING?
ME, TOO!
WE'RE DOING GREAT, THANKS!
I SURE HOPE I'M NOT RELATED TO ALL THESE PEOPLE.
WHAT ABOUT THE EARS? SHOULD I WORRY?
GB Trudeau

1/1/83

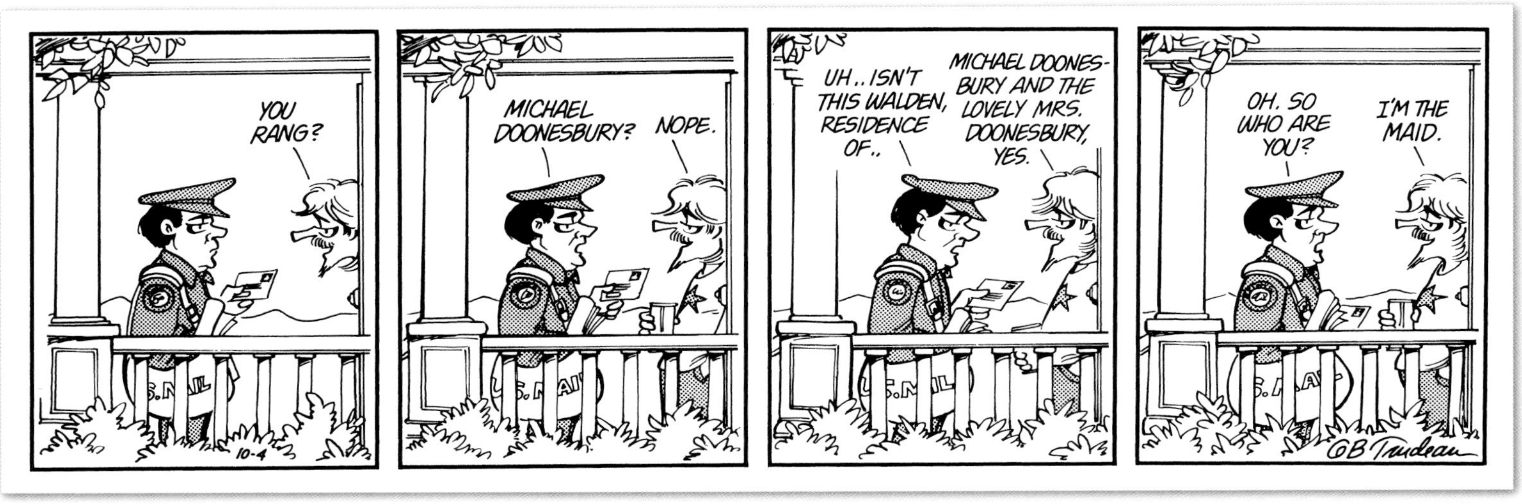
YOU RANG?
MICHAEL DOONESBURY?
NOPE.
UH.. ISN'T THIS WALDEN, RESIDENCE OF..
MICHAEL DOONESBURY AND THE LOVELY MRS. DOONESBURY, YES.
OH. SO WHO ARE YOU?
I'M THE MAID.

10/4/84

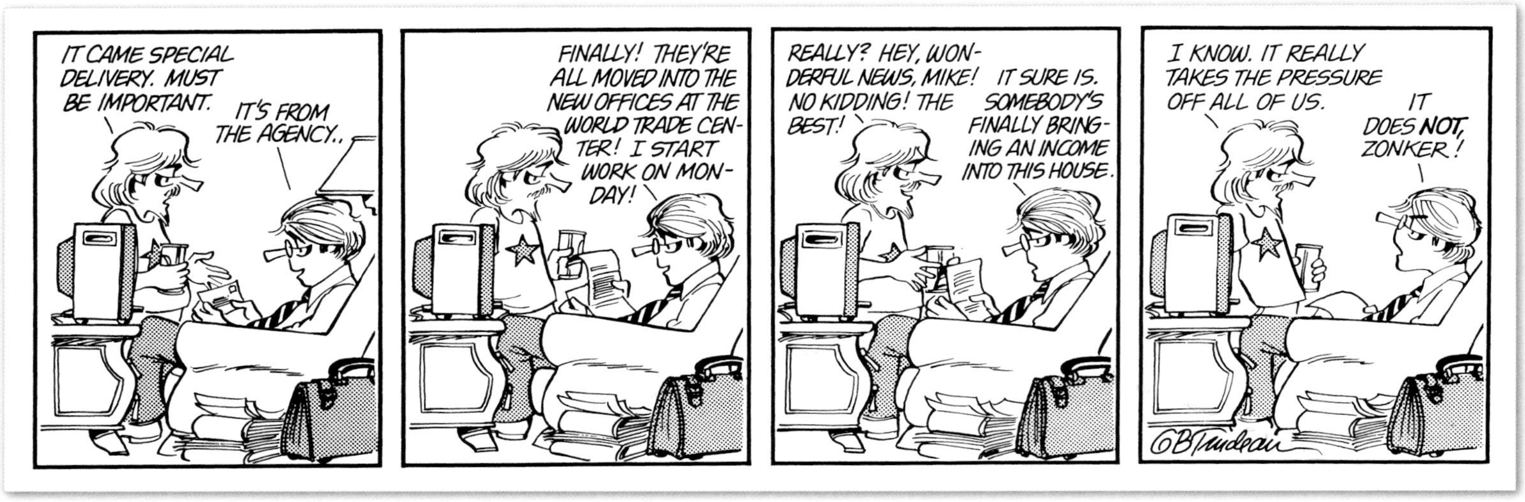
IT CAME SPECIAL DELIVERY. MUST BE IMPORTANT.
IT'S FROM THE AGENCY..
FINALLY! THEY'RE ALL MOVED INTO THE NEW OFFICES AT THE WORLD TRADE CENTER! I START WORK ON MONDAY!
REALLY? HEY, WONDERFUL NEWS, MIKE! NO KIDDING! THE BEST!
IT SURE IS. SOMEBODY'S FINALLY BRINGING AN INCOME INTO THIS HOUSE.
I KNOW. IT REALLY TAKES THE PRESSURE OFF ALL OF US.
IT DOES NOT, ZONKER!

10/5/84

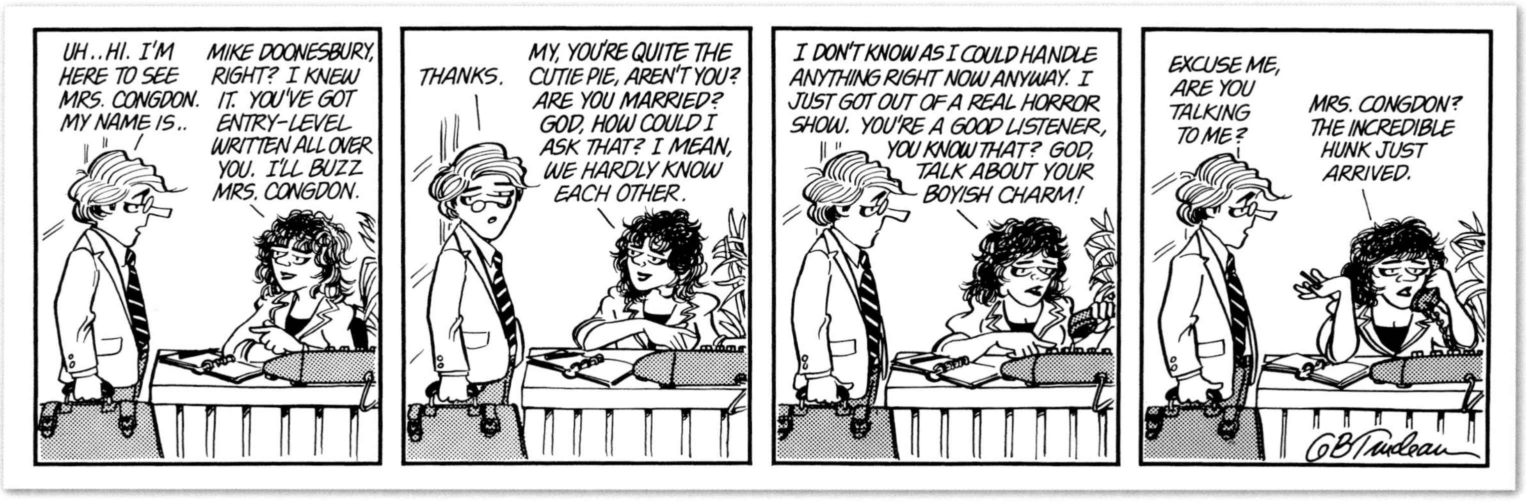
UH.. HI. I'M HERE TO SEE MRS. CONGDON. MY NAME IS..
MIKE DOONESBURY, RIGHT? I KNEW IT. YOU'VE GOT ENTRY-LEVEL WRITTEN ALL OVER YOU. I'LL BUZZ MRS. CONGDON.
THANKS.
MY, YOU'RE QUITE THE CUTIE PIE, AREN'T YOU? ARE YOU MARRIED? GOD, HOW COULD I ASK THAT? I MEAN, WE HARDLY KNOW EACH OTHER.
I DON'T KNOW AS I COULD HANDLE ANYTHING RIGHT NOW ANYWAY. I JUST GOT OUT OF A REAL HORROR SHOW. YOU'RE A GOOD LISTENER, YOU KNOW THAT? GOD, TALK ABOUT YOUR BOYISH CHARM!
EXCUSE ME, ARE YOU TALKING TO ME?
MRS. CONGDON? THE INCREDIBLE HUNK JUST ARRIVED.

10/8/84

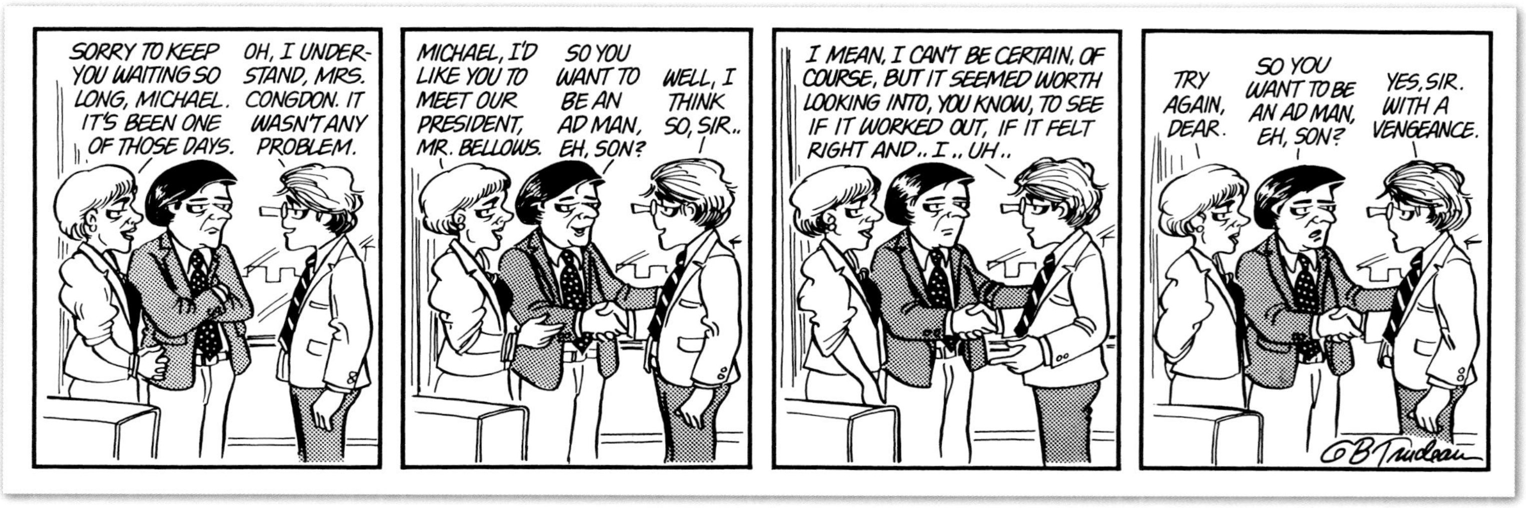
SORRY TO KEEP YOU WAITING SO LONG, MICHAEL. IT'S BEEN ONE OF THOSE DAYS.
OH, I UNDERSTAND, MRS. CONGDON. IT WASN'T ANY PROBLEM.
MICHAEL, I'D LIKE YOU TO MEET OUR PRESIDENT, MR. BELLOWS.
SO YOU WANT TO BE AN AD MAN, EH, SON?
WELL, I THINK SO, SIR..
I MEAN, I CAN'T BE CERTAIN, OF COURSE, BUT IT SEEMED WORTH LOOKING INTO, YOU KNOW, TO SEE IF IT WORKED OUT, IF IT FELT RIGHT AND.. I.. UH..
TRY AGAIN, DEAR.
SO YOU WANT TO BE AN AD MAN, EH, SON?
YES, SIR. WITH A VENGEANCE.

10/10/84

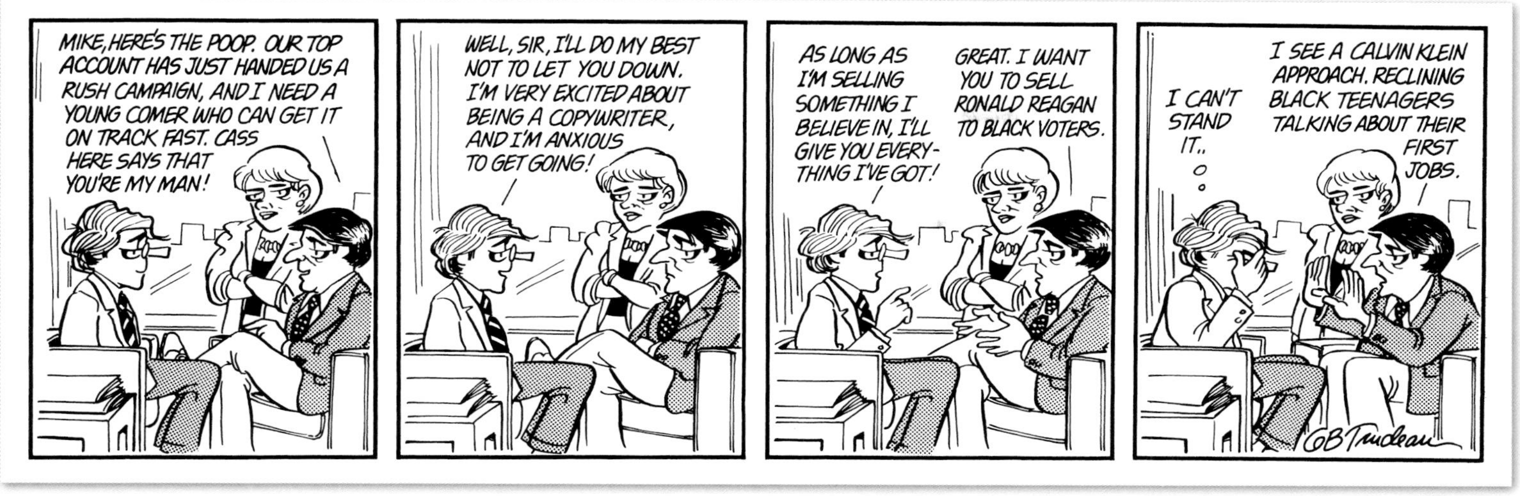
MIKE, HERE'S THE POOP. OUR TOP ACCOUNT HAS JUST HANDED US A RUSH CAMPAIGN, AND I NEED A YOUNG COMER WHO CAN GET IT ON TRACK FAST. CASS HERE SAYS THAT YOU'RE MY MAN!
WELL, SIR, I'LL DO MY BEST NOT TO LET YOU DOWN. I'M VERY EXCITED ABOUT BEING A COPYWRITER, AND I'M ANXIOUS TO GET GOING!
AS LONG AS I'M SELLING SOMETHING I BELIEVE IN, I'LL GIVE YOU EVERYTHING I'VE GOT!
GREAT. I WANT YOU TO SELL RONALD REAGAN TO BLACK VOTERS.
I CAN'T STAND IT..
I SEE A CALVIN KLEIN APPROACH. RECLINING BLACK TEENAGERS TALKING ABOUT THEIR FIRST JOBS.
GB Trudeau
10/11/84

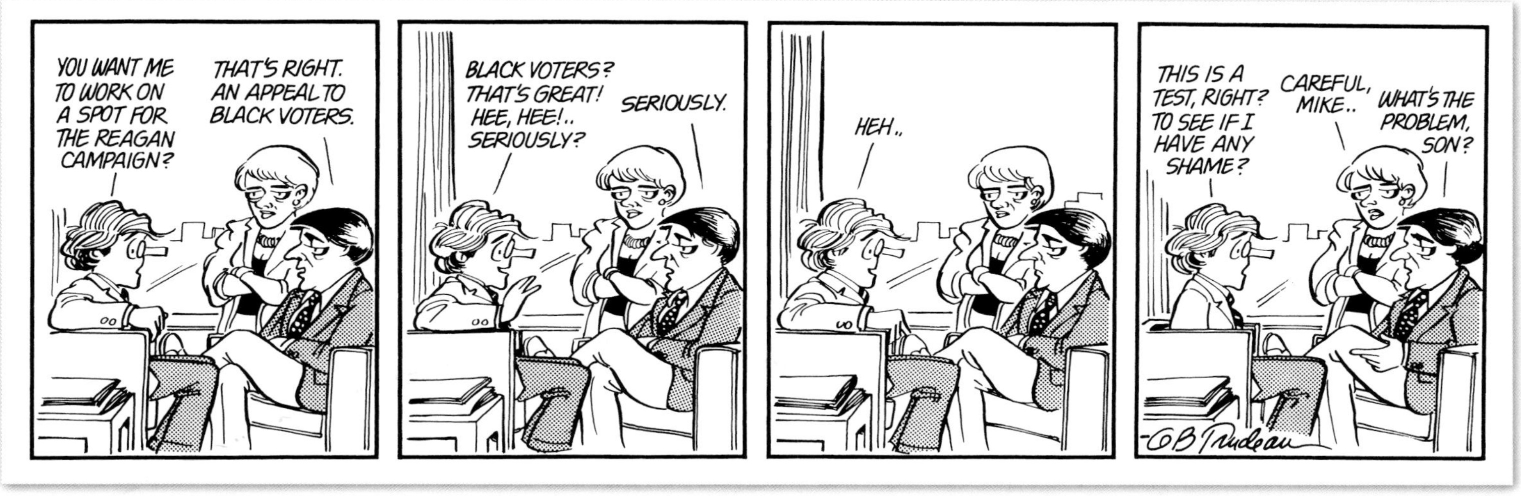
YOU WANT ME TO WORK ON A SPOT FOR THE REAGAN CAMPAIGN?
THAT'S RIGHT. AN APPEAL TO BLACK VOTERS.
BLACK VOTERS? THAT'S GREAT! HEE, HEE!.. SERIOUSLY?
SERIOUSLY.
HEH..
THIS IS A TEST, RIGHT? TO SEE IF I HAVE ANY SHAME?
CAREFUL, MIKE..
WHAT'S THE PROBLEM, SON?
GB Trudeau
10/12/84

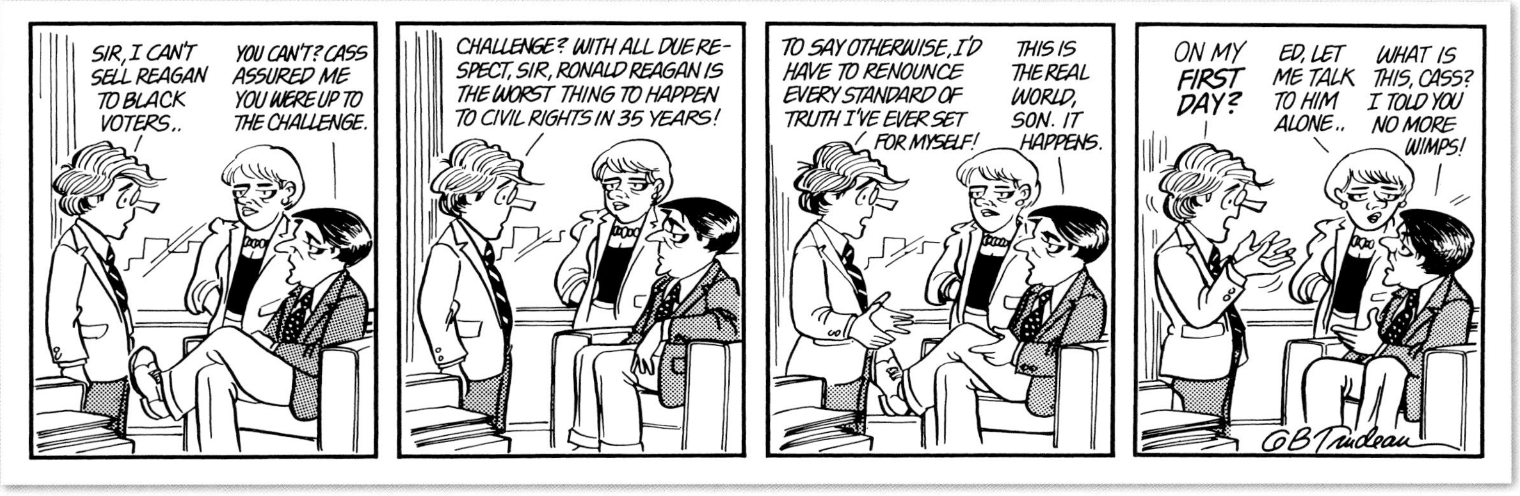
SIR, I CAN'T SELL REAGAN TO BLACK VOTERS..
YOU CAN'T? CASS ASSURED ME YOU WERE UP TO THE CHALLENGE.
CHALLENGE? WITH ALL DUE RESPECT, SIR, RONALD REAGAN IS THE WORST THING TO HAPPEN TO CIVIL RIGHTS IN 35 YEARS!
TO SAY OTHERWISE, I'D HAVE TO RENOUNCE EVERY STANDARD OF TRUTH I'VE EVER SET FOR MYSELF!
THIS IS THE REAL WORLD, SON. IT HAPPENS.
ON MY FIRST DAY?
ED, LET ME TALK TO HIM ALONE..
WHAT IS THIS, CASS? I TOLD YOU NO MORE WIMPS!
GB Trudeau
10/13/84

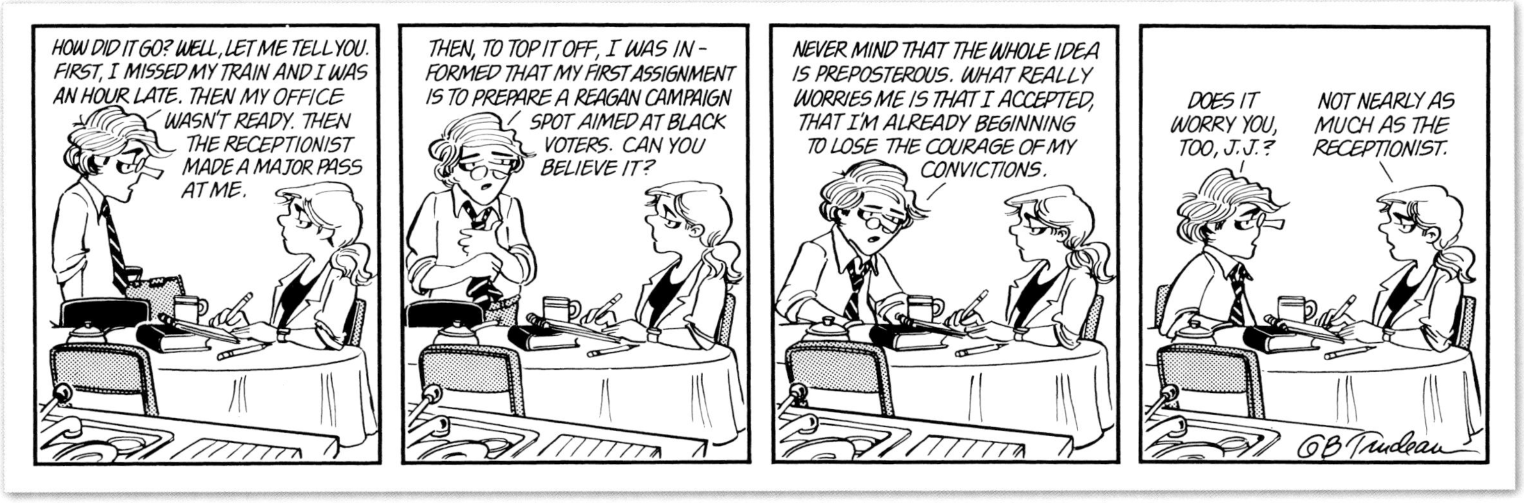
HOW DID IT GO? WELL, LET ME TELL YOU. FIRST, I MISSED MY TRAIN AND I WAS AN HOUR LATE. THEN MY OFFICE WASN'T READY. THEN THE RECEPTIONIST MADE A MAJOR PASS AT ME.
THEN, TO TOP IT OFF, I WAS INFORMED THAT MY FIRST ASSIGNMENT IS TO PREPARE A REAGAN CAMPAIGN SPOT AIMED AT BLACK VOTERS. CAN YOU BELIEVE IT?
NEVER MIND THAT THE WHOLE IDEA IS PREPOSTEROUS. WHAT REALLY WORRIES ME IS THAT I ACCEPTED, THAT I'M ALREADY BEGINNING TO LOSE THE COURAGE OF MY CONVICTIONS.
DOES IT WORRY YOU, TOO, J.J.?
NOT NEARLY AS MUCH AS THE RECEPTIONIST.
GB Trudeau
10/16/84

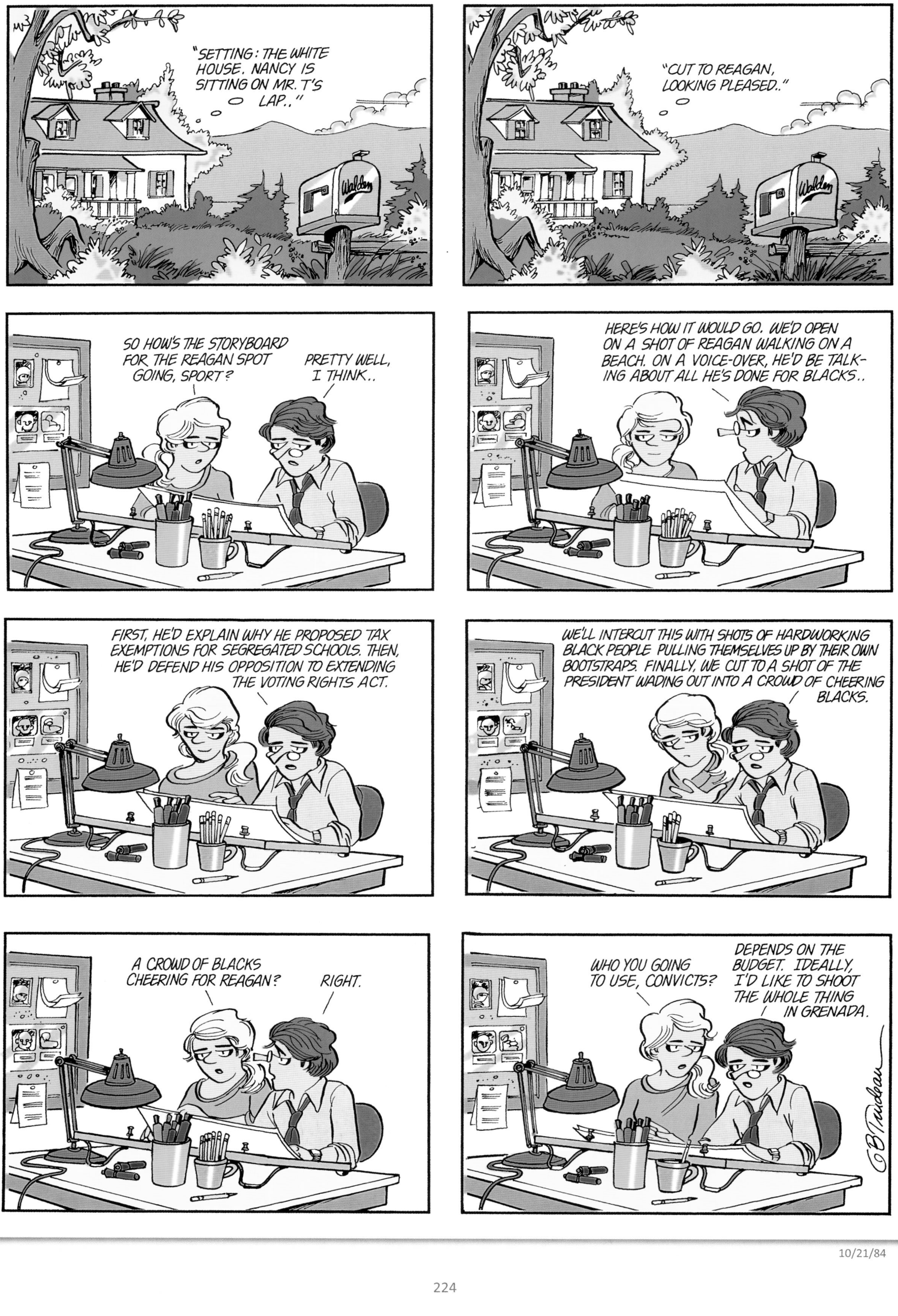
"SETTING: THE WHITE HOUSE. NANCY IS SITTING ON MR. T'S LAP.."
Walden
"CUT TO REAGAN, LOOKING PLEASED.."
Walden
SO HOW'S THE STORYBOARD FOR THE REAGAN SPOT GOING, SPORT?
PRETTY WELL, I THINK..
HERE'S HOW IT WOULD GO. WE'D OPEN ON A SHOT OF REAGAN WALKING ON A BEACH. ON A VOICE-OVER, HE'D BE TALKING ABOUT ALL HE'S DONE FOR BLACKS..
FIRST, HE'D EXPLAIN WHY HE PROPOSED TAX EXEMPTIONS FOR SEGREGATED SCHOOLS. THEN, HE'D DEFEND HIS OPPOSITION TO EXTENDING THE VOTING RIGHTS ACT.
WE'LL INTERCUT THIS WITH SHOTS OF HARDWORKING BLACK PEOPLE PULLING THEMSELVES UP BY THEIR OWN BOOTSTRAPS. FINALLY, WE CUT TO A SHOT OF THE PRESIDENT WADING OUT INTO A CROWD OF CHEERING BLACKS.
A CROWD OF BLACKS CHEERING FOR REAGAN?
RIGHT.
WHO YOU GOING TO USE, CONVICTS?
DEPENDS ON THE BUDGET. IDEALLY, I'D LIKE TO SHOOT THE WHOLE THING IN GRENADA.
GBTrudeau

10/21/84

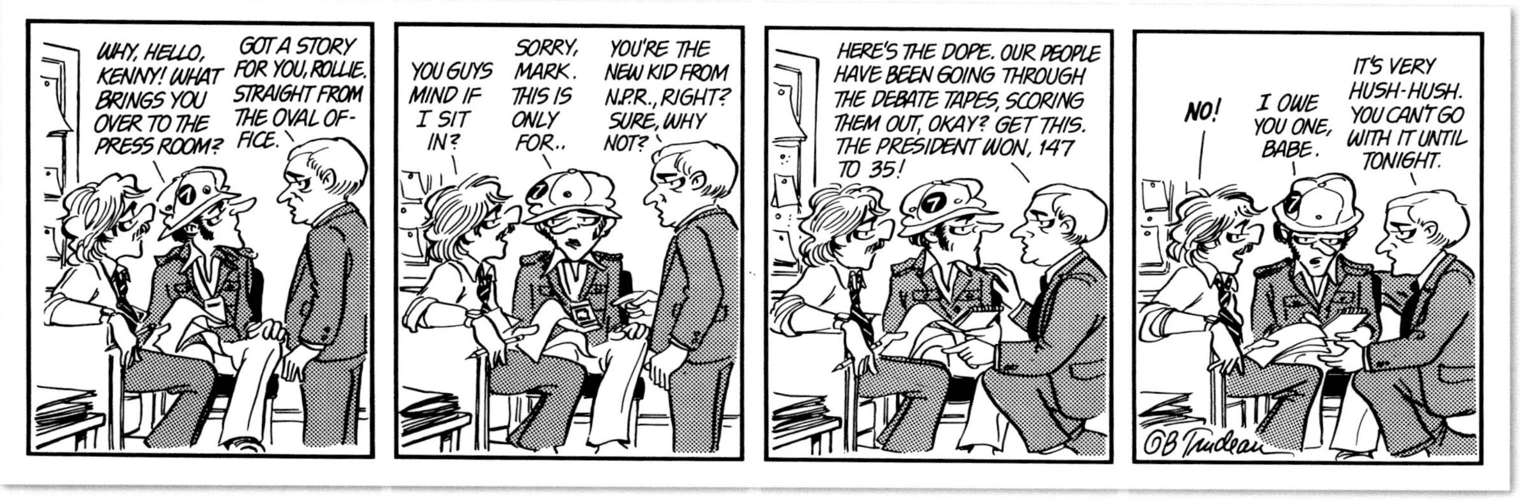
WHY, HELLO, KENNY! WHAT BRINGS YOU OVER TO THE PRESS ROOM?
GOT A STORY FOR YOU, ROLLIE. STRAIGHT FROM THE OVAL OFFICE.
YOU GUYS MIND IF I SIT IN?
SORRY, MARK. THIS IS ONLY FOR..
YOU'RE THE NEW KID FROM N.P.R., RIGHT? SURE, WHY NOT?
HERE'S THE DOPE. OUR PEOPLE HAVE BEEN GOING THROUGH THE DEBATE TAPES, SCORING THEM OUT, OKAY? GET THIS. THE PRESIDENT WON, 147 TO 35!
NO!
I OWE YOU ONE, BABE.
IT'S VERY HUSH-HUSH. YOU CAN'T GO WITH IT UNTIL TONIGHT.
©B Trudeau

10/23/84

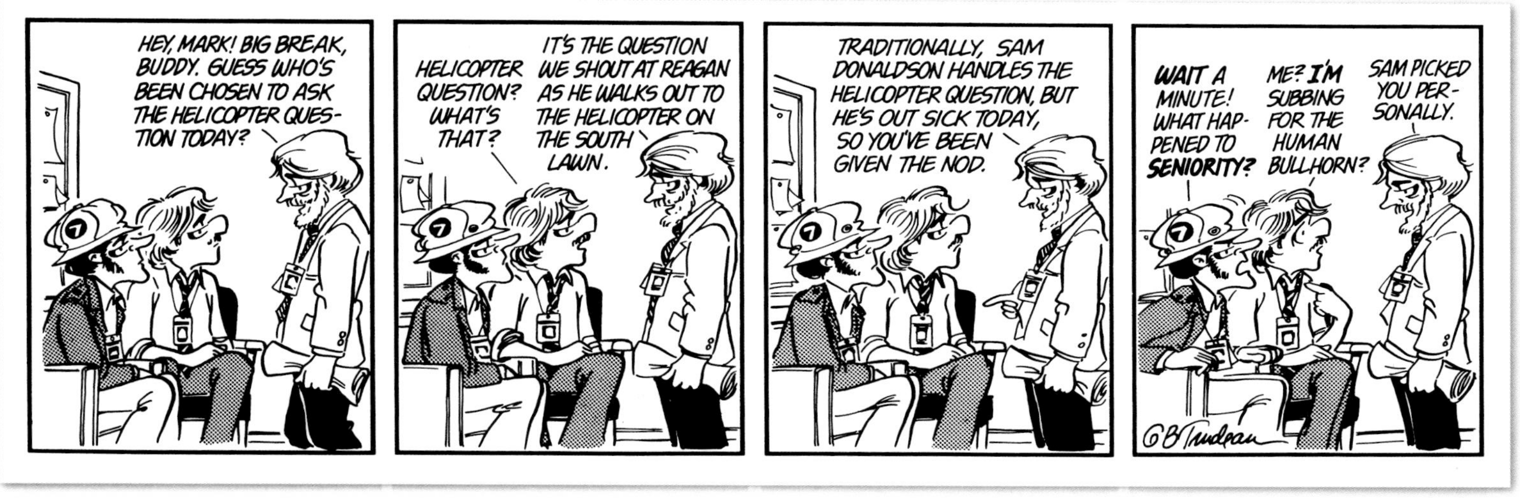
HEY, MARK! BIG BREAK, BUDDY. GUESS WHO'S BEEN CHOSEN TO ASK THE HELICOPTER QUESTION TODAY?
HELICOPTER QUESTION? WHAT'S THAT?
IT'S THE QUESTION WE SHOUT AT REAGAN AS HE WALKS OUT TO THE HELICOPTER ON THE SOUTH LAWN.
TRADITIONALLY, SAM DONALDSON HANDLES THE HELICOPTER QUESTION, BUT HE'S OUT SICK TODAY, SO YOU'VE BEEN GIVEN THE NOD.
WAIT A MINUTE! WHAT HAPPENED TO SENIORITY?
ME? I'M SUBBING FOR THE HUMAN BULLHORN?
SAM PICKED YOU PERSONALLY.
©B Trudeau

10/24/84

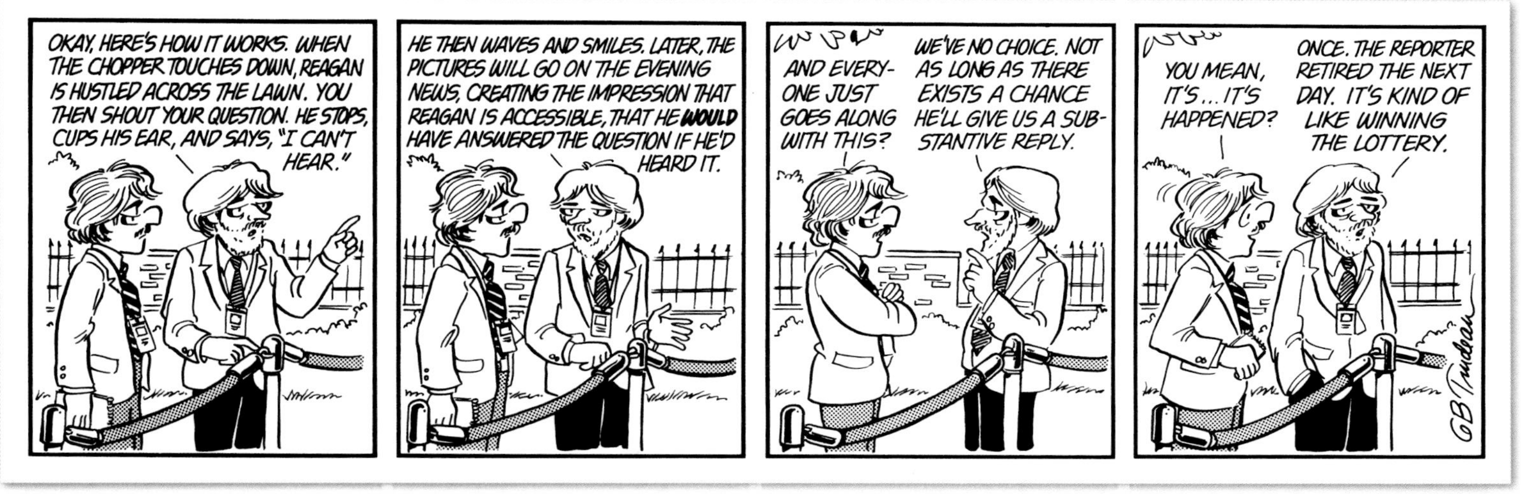
OKAY, HERE'S HOW IT WORKS. WHEN THE CHOPPER TOUCHES DOWN, REAGAN IS HUSTLED ACROSS THE LAWN. YOU THEN SHOUT YOUR QUESTION. HE STOPS, CUPS HIS EAR, AND SAYS, "I CAN'T HEAR."
HE THEN WAVES AND SMILES. LATER, THE PICTURES WILL GO ON THE EVENING NEWS, CREATING THE IMPRESSION THAT REAGAN IS ACCESSIBLE, THAT HE WOULD HAVE ANSWERED THE QUESTION IF HE'D HEARD IT.
AND EVERYONE JUST GOES ALONG WITH THIS?
WE'VE NO CHOICE. NOT AS LONG AS THERE EXISTS A CHANCE HE'LL GIVE US A SUBSTANTIVE REPLY.
YOU MEAN, IT'S... IT'S HAPPENED?
ONCE. THE REPORTER RETIRED THE NEXT DAY. IT'S KIND OF LIKE WINNING THE LOTTERY.
©B Trudeau

10/25/84

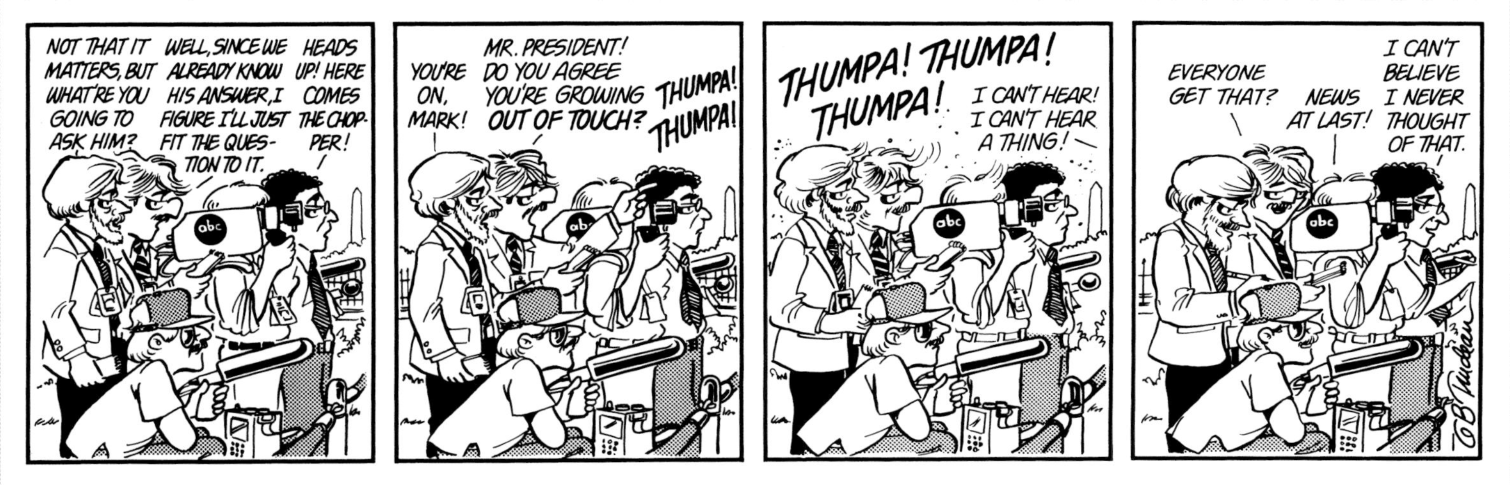
NOT THAT IT MATTERS, BUT WHAT'RE YOU GOING TO ASK HIM?
WELL, SINCE WE ALREADY KNOW HIS ANSWER, I FIGURE I'LL JUST FIT THE QUESTION TO IT.
HEADS UP! HERE COMES THE CHOPPER!
YOU'RE ON, MARK!
MR. PRESIDENT! DO YOU AGREE YOU'RE GROWING OUT OF TOUCH?
THUMPA! THUMPA!
THUMPA! THUMPA! THUMPA!
I CAN'T HEAR! I CAN'T HEAR A THING!
EVERYONE GET THAT?
NEWS AT LAST!
I CAN'T BELIEVE I NEVER THOUGHT OF THAT.
©B Trudeau

10/26/84

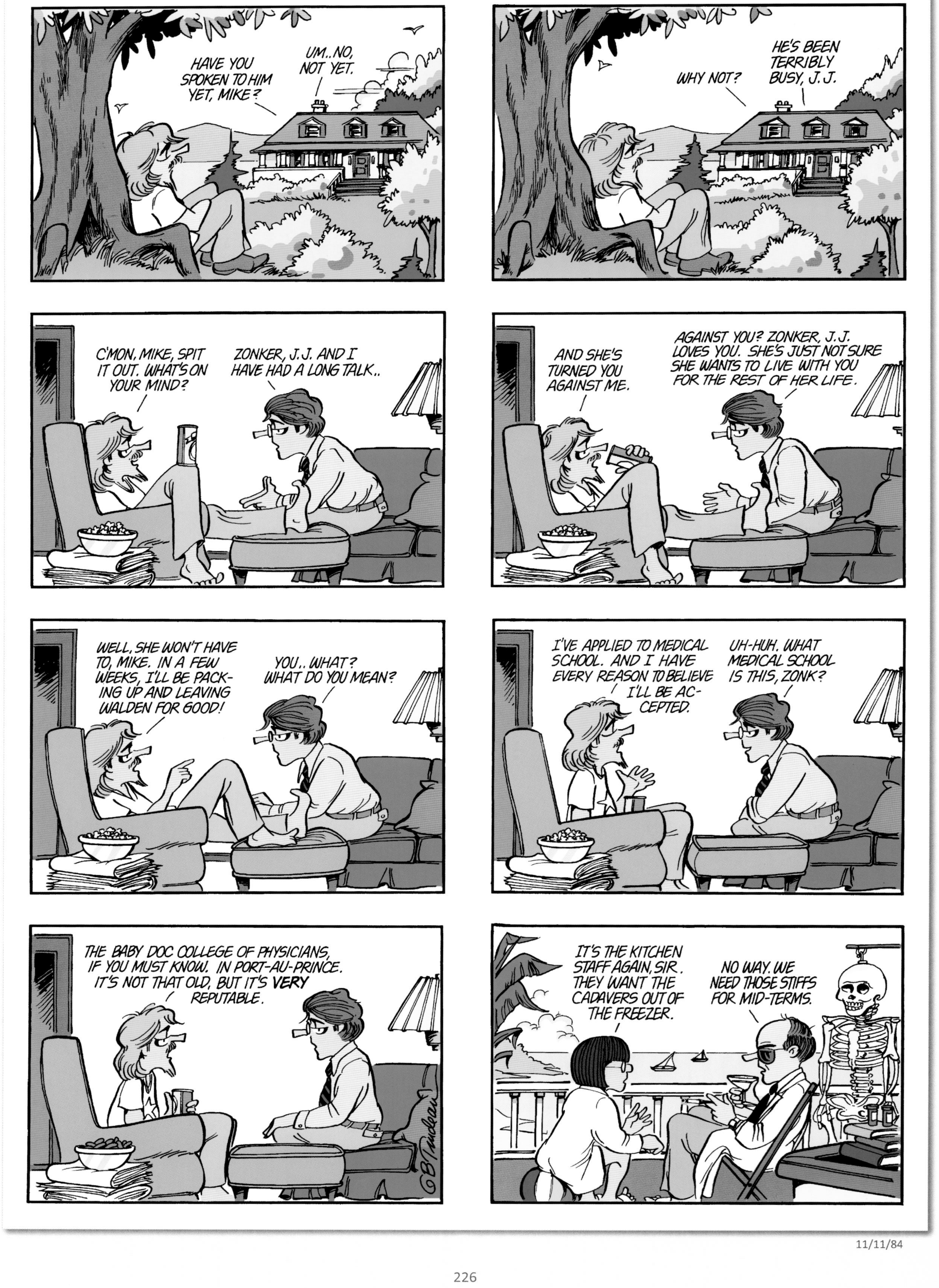
HAVE YOU SPOKEN TO HIM YET, MIKE?
UM.. NO, NOT YET.
WHY NOT?
HE'S BEEN TERRIBLY BUSY, J.J.
C'MON, MIKE, SPIT IT OUT. WHAT'S ON YOUR MIND?
ZONKER, J.J. AND I HAVE HAD A LONG TALK..
AND SHE'S TURNED YOU AGAINST ME.
AGAINST YOU? ZONKER, J.J. LOVES YOU. SHE'S JUST NOT SURE SHE WANTS TO LIVE WITH YOU FOR THE REST OF HER LIFE.
WELL, SHE WON'T HAVE TO, MIKE. IN A FEW WEEKS, I'LL BE PACKING UP AND LEAVING WALDEN FOR GOOD!
YOU.. WHAT? WHAT DO YOU MEAN?
I'VE APPLIED TO MEDICAL SCHOOL. AND I HAVE EVERY REASON TO BELIEVE I'LL BE ACCEPTED.
UH-HUH. WHAT MEDICAL SCHOOL IS THIS, ZONK?
THE BABY DOC COLLEGE OF PHYSICIANS, IF YOU MUST KNOW. IN PORT-AU-PRINCE. IT'S NOT THAT OLD, BUT IT'S VERY REPUTABLE.
IT'S THE KITCHEN STAFF AGAIN, SIR. THEY WANT THE CADAVERS OUT OF THE FREEZER.
NO WAY. WE NEED THOSE STIFFS FOR MID-TERMS.

11/11/84

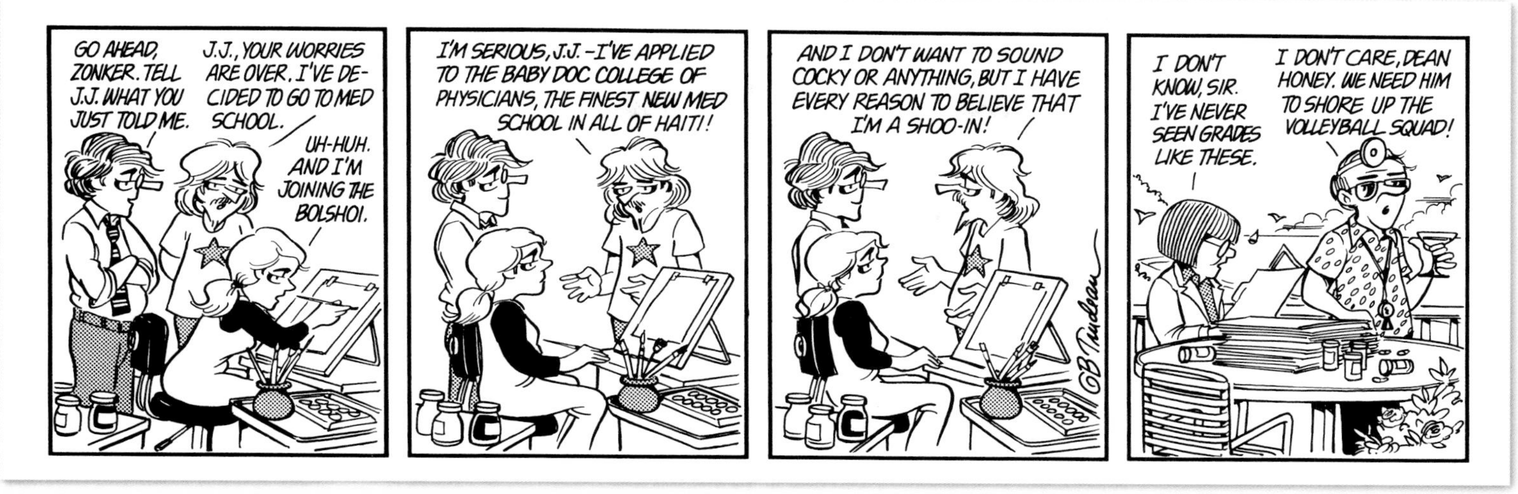
GO AHEAD, ZONKER. TELL J.J. WHAT YOU JUST TOLD ME.
J.J., YOUR WORRIES ARE OVER. I'VE DECIDED TO GO TO MED SCHOOL.
UH-HUH. AND I'M JOINING THE BOLSHOI.
I'M SERIOUS, J.J.–I'VE APPLIED TO THE BABY DOC COLLEGE OF PHYSICIANS, THE FINEST NEW MED SCHOOL IN ALL OF HAITI!
AND I DON'T WANT TO SOUND COCKY OR ANYTHING, BUT I HAVE EVERY REASON TO BELIEVE THAT I'M A SHOO-IN!
I DON'T KNOW, SIR. I'VE NEVER SEEN GRADES LIKE THESE.
I DON'T CARE, DEAN HONEY. WE NEED HIM TO SHORE UP THE VOLLEYBALL SQUAD!
GB Trudeau

11/12/84

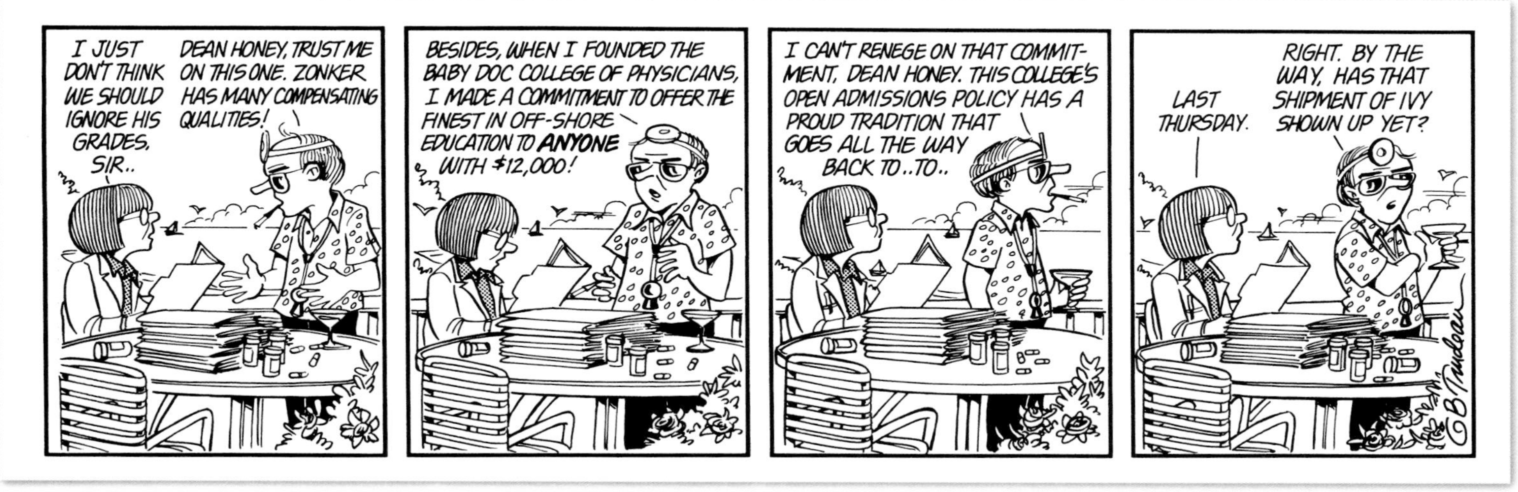
I JUST DON'T THINK WE SHOULD IGNORE HIS GRADES, SIR..
DEAN HONEY, TRUST ME ON THIS ONE. ZONKER HAS MANY COMPENSATING QUALITIES!
BESIDES, WHEN I FOUNDED THE BABY DOC COLLEGE OF PHYSICIANS, I MADE A COMMITMENT TO OFFER THE FINEST IN OFF-SHORE EDUCATION TO ANYONE WITH $12,000!
I CAN'T RENEGE ON THAT COMMITMENT, DEAN HONEY. THIS COLLEGE'S OPEN ADMISSIONS POLICY HAS A PROUD TRADITION THAT GOES ALL THE WAY BACK TO..TO..
LAST THURSDAY.
RIGHT. BY THE WAY, HAS THAT SHIPMENT OF IVY SHOWN UP YET?
GB Trudeau

11/13/84

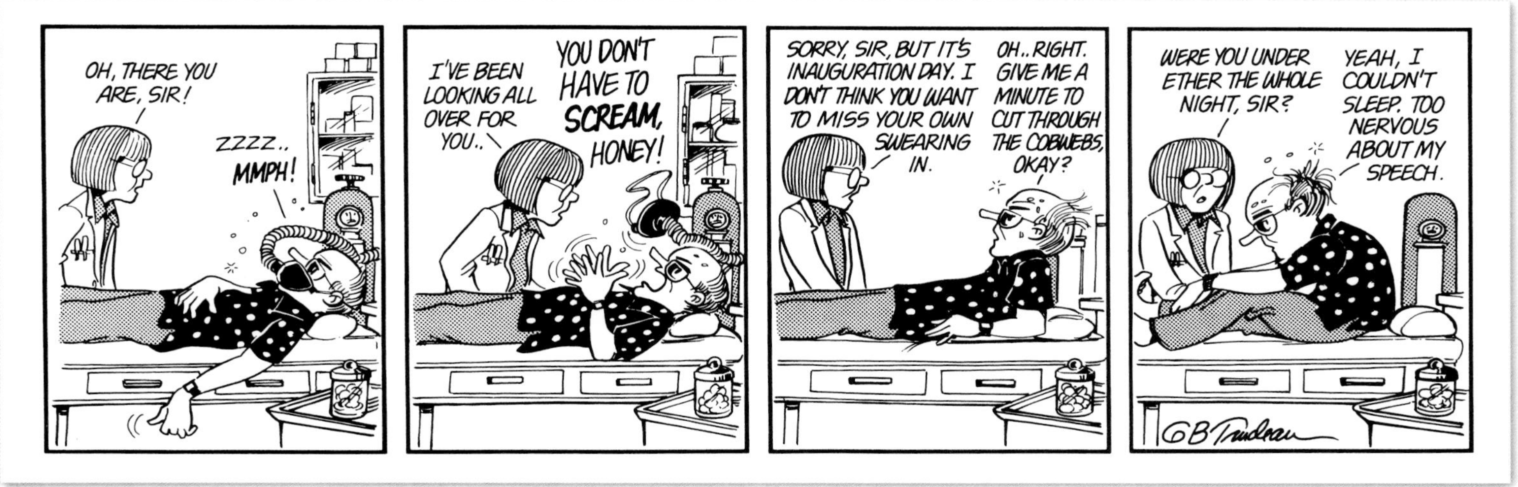
OH, THERE YOU ARE, SIR!
ZZZZ.. MMPH!
I'VE BEEN LOOKING ALL OVER FOR YOU..
YOU DON'T HAVE TO SCREAM, HONEY!
SORRY, SIR, BUT IT'S INAUGURATION DAY. I DON'T THINK YOU WANT TO MISS YOUR OWN SWEARING IN.
OH.. RIGHT. GIVE ME A MINUTE TO CUT THROUGH THE COBWEBS, OKAY?
WERE YOU UNDER ETHER THE WHOLE NIGHT, SIR?
YEAH, I COULDN'T SLEEP. TOO NERVOUS ABOUT MY SPEECH.
GB Trudeau

11/14/84

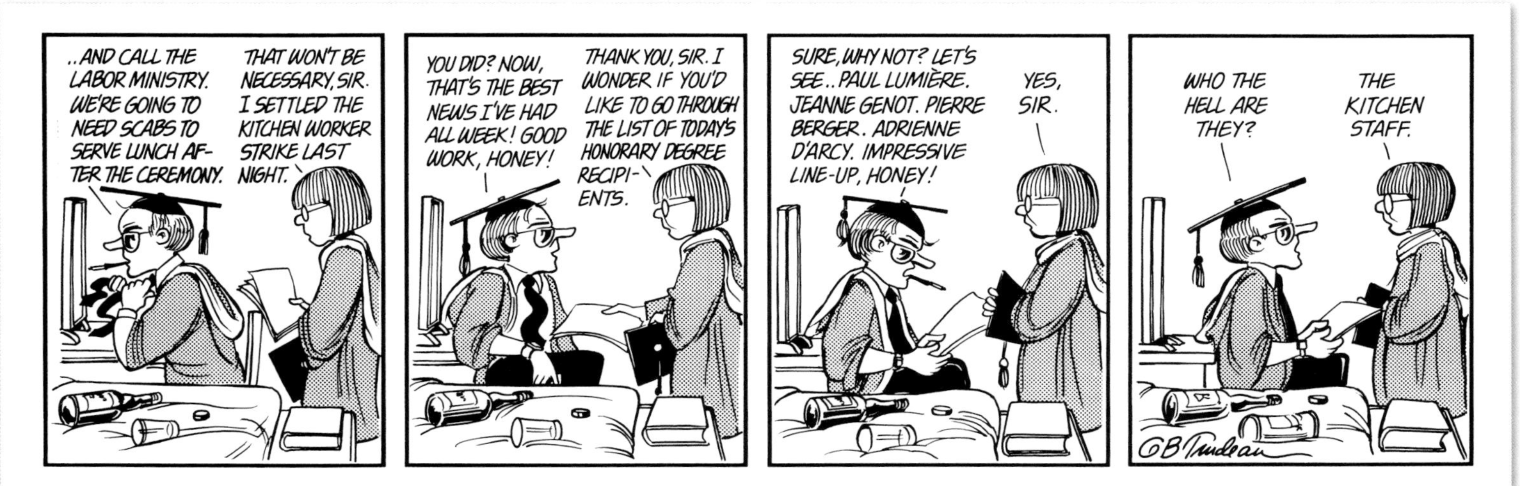
..AND CALL THE LABOR MINISTRY. WE'RE GOING TO NEED SCABS TO SERVE LUNCH AFTER THE CEREMONY.
THAT WON'T BE NECESSARY, SIR. I SETTLED THE KITCHEN WORKER STRIKE LAST NIGHT.
YOU DID? NOW, THAT'S THE BEST NEWS I'VE HAD ALL WEEK! GOOD WORK, HONEY!
THANK YOU, SIR. I WONDER IF YOU'D LIKE TO GO THROUGH THE LIST OF TODAY'S HONORARY DEGREE RECIPIENTS.
SURE, WHY NOT? LET'S SEE.. PAUL LUMIÈRE. JEANNE GENOT. PIERRE BERGER.. ADRIENNE D'ARCY. IMPRESSIVE LINE-UP, HONEY!
YES, SIR.
WHO THE HELL ARE THEY?
THE KITCHEN STAFF.
GB Trudeau

11/16/84

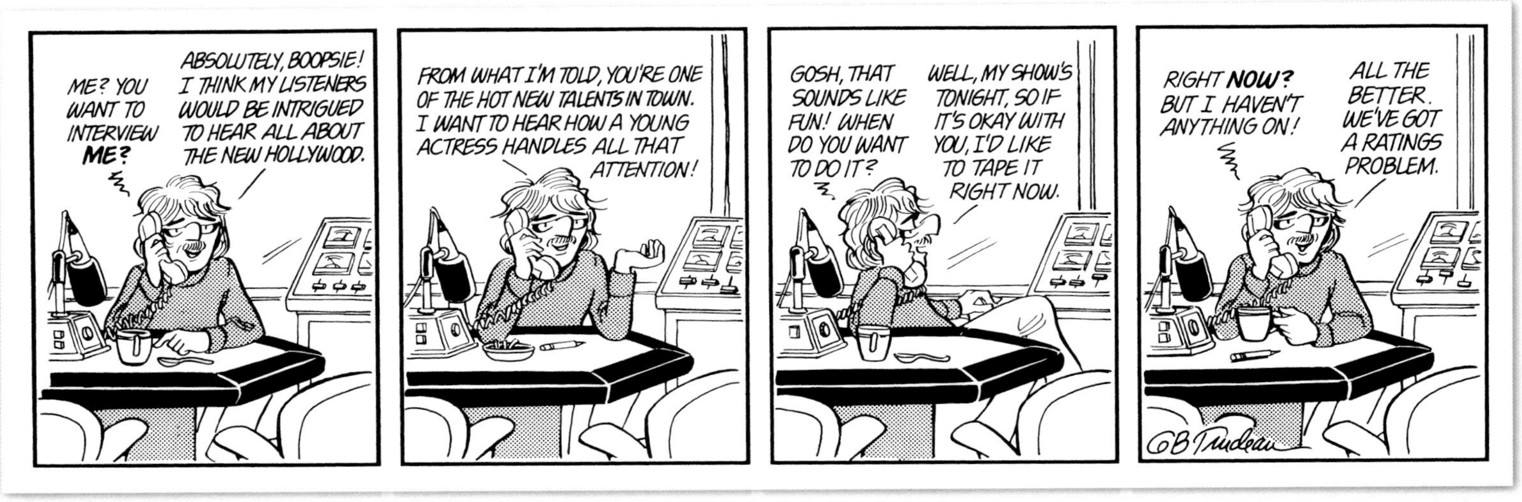
ME? YOU WANT TO INTERVIEW **ME?**
ABSOLUTELY, BOOPSIE! I THINK MY LISTENERS WOULD BE INTRIGUED TO HEAR ALL ABOUT THE NEW HOLLYWOOD.
FROM WHAT I'M TOLD, YOU'RE ONE OF THE HOT NEW TALENTS IN TOWN. I WANT TO HEAR HOW A YOUNG ACTRESS HANDLES ALL THAT ATTENTION!
GOSH, THAT SOUNDS LIKE FUN! WHEN DO YOU WANT TO DO IT?
WELL, MY SHOW'S TONIGHT, SO IF IT'S OKAY WITH YOU, I'D LIKE TO TAPE IT RIGHT NOW.
RIGHT **NOW?** BUT I HAVEN'T ANYTHING ON!
ALL THE BETTER. WE'VE GOT A RATINGS PROBLEM.
GBTrudeau

12/10/84

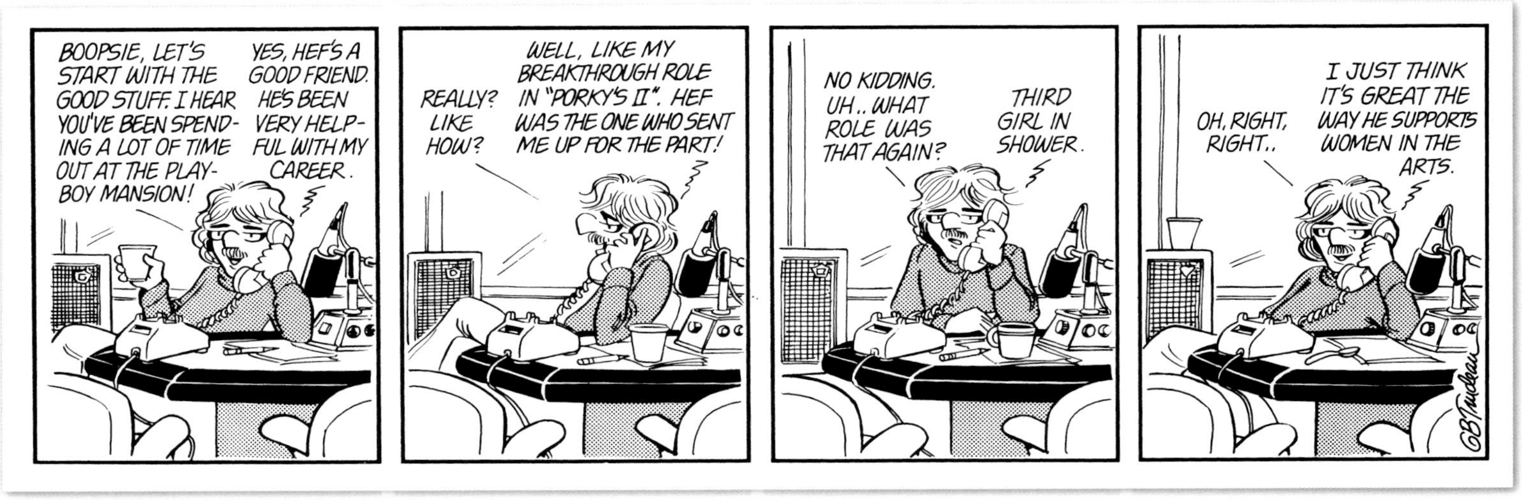
BOOPSIE, LET'S START WITH THE GOOD STUFF. I HEAR YOU'VE BEEN SPENDING A LOT OF TIME OUT AT THE PLAYBOY MANSION!
YES, HEF'S A GOOD FRIEND. HE'S BEEN VERY HELPFUL WITH MY CAREER.
REALLY? LIKE HOW?
WELL, LIKE MY BREAKTHROUGH ROLE IN "PORKY'S II". HEF WAS THE ONE WHO SENT ME UP FOR THE PART!
NO KIDDING. UH.. WHAT ROLE WAS THAT AGAIN?
THIRD GIRL IN SHOWER.
OH, RIGHT, RIGHT..
I JUST THINK IT'S GREAT THE WAY HE SUPPORTS WOMEN IN THE ARTS.
GBTrudeau

12/11/84

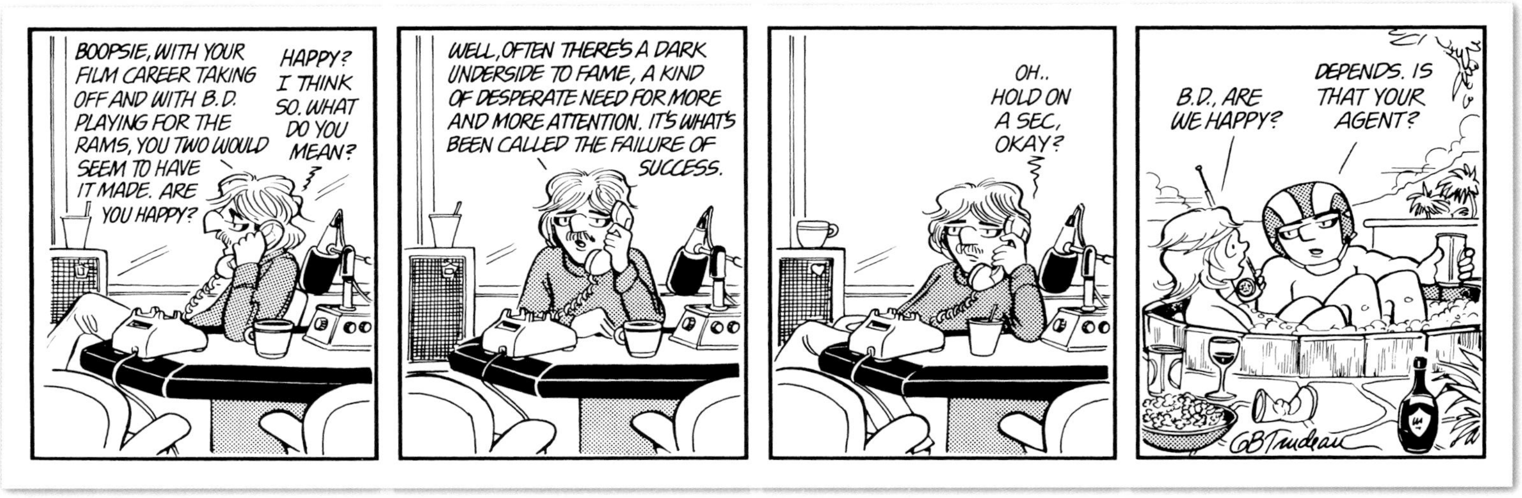
BOOPSIE, WITH YOUR FILM CAREER TAKING OFF AND WITH B.D. PLAYING FOR THE RAMS, YOU TWO WOULD SEEM TO HAVE IT MADE. ARE YOU HAPPY?
HAPPY? I THINK SO. WHAT DO YOU MEAN?
WELL, OFTEN THERE'S A DARK UNDERSIDE TO FAME, A KIND OF DESPERATE NEED FOR MORE AND MORE ATTENTION. IT'S WHAT'S BEEN CALLED THE FAILURE OF SUCCESS.
OH.. HOLD ON A SEC, OKAY?
B.D., ARE WE HAPPY?
DEPENDS. IS THAT YOUR AGENT?
GBTrudeau

12/12/84

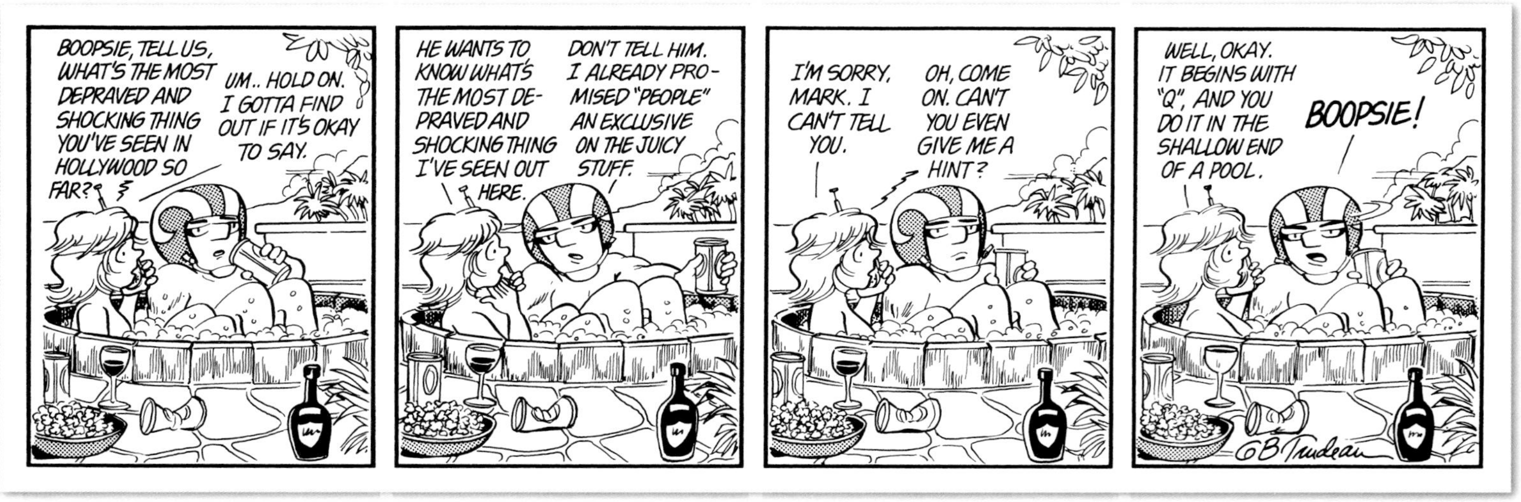
BOOPSIE, TELL US, WHAT'S THE MOST DEPRAVED AND SHOCKING THING YOU'VE SEEN IN HOLLYWOOD SO FAR?
UM.. HOLD ON. I GOTTA FIND OUT IF IT'S OKAY TO SAY.
HE WANTS TO KNOW WHAT'S THE MOST DEPRAVED AND SHOCKING THING I'VE SEEN OUT HERE.
DON'T TELL HIM. I ALREADY PROMISED "PEOPLE" AN EXCLUSIVE ON THE JUICY STUFF.
I'M SORRY, MARK. I CAN'T TELL YOU.
OH, COME ON. CAN'T YOU EVEN GIVE ME A HINT?
WELL, OKAY. IT BEGINS WITH "Q", AND YOU DO IT IN THE SHALLOW END OF A POOL.
BOOPSIE!
GBTrudeau

12/13/84

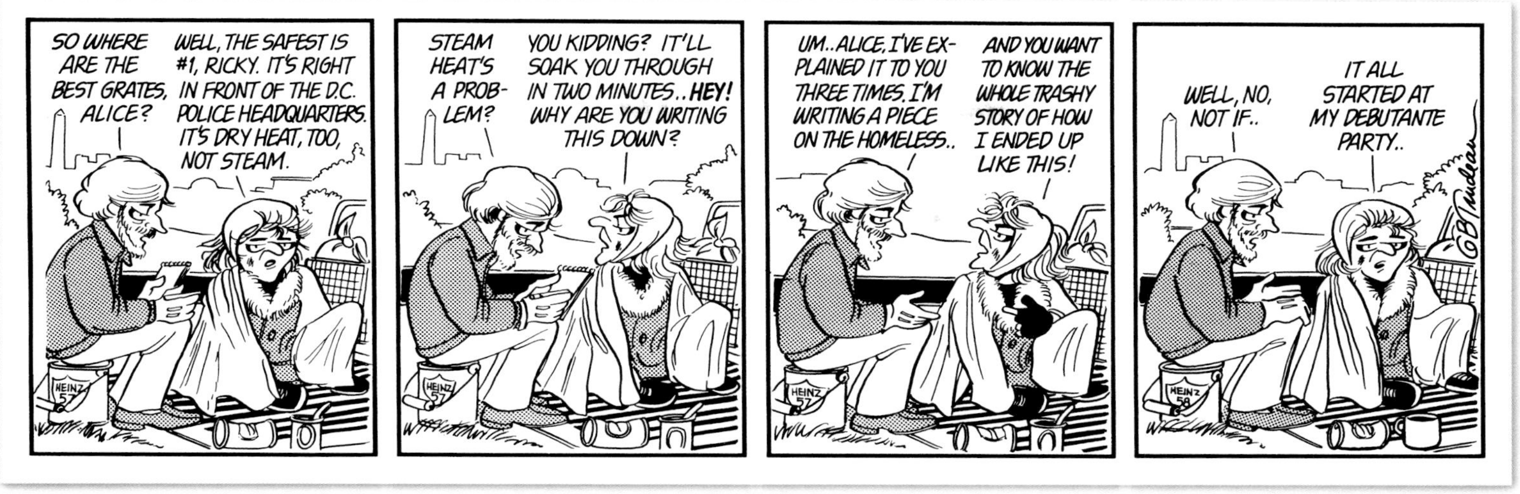
SO WHERE ARE THE BEST GRATES, ALICE?
WELL, THE SAFEST IS #1, RICKY. IT'S RIGHT IN FRONT OF THE D.C. POLICE HEADQUARTERS. IT'S DRY HEAT, TOO, NOT STEAM.
STEAM HEAT'S A PROBLEM?
YOU KIDDING? IT'LL SOAK YOU THROUGH IN TWO MINUTES.. HEY! WHY ARE YOU WRITING THIS DOWN?
UM.. ALICE, I'VE EXPLAINED IT TO YOU THREE TIMES. I'M WRITING A PIECE ON THE HOMELESS..
AND YOU WANT TO KNOW THE WHOLE TRASHY STORY OF HOW I ENDED UP LIKE THIS!
WELL, NO, NOT IF..
IT ALL STARTED AT MY DEBUTANTE PARTY..

12/18/84

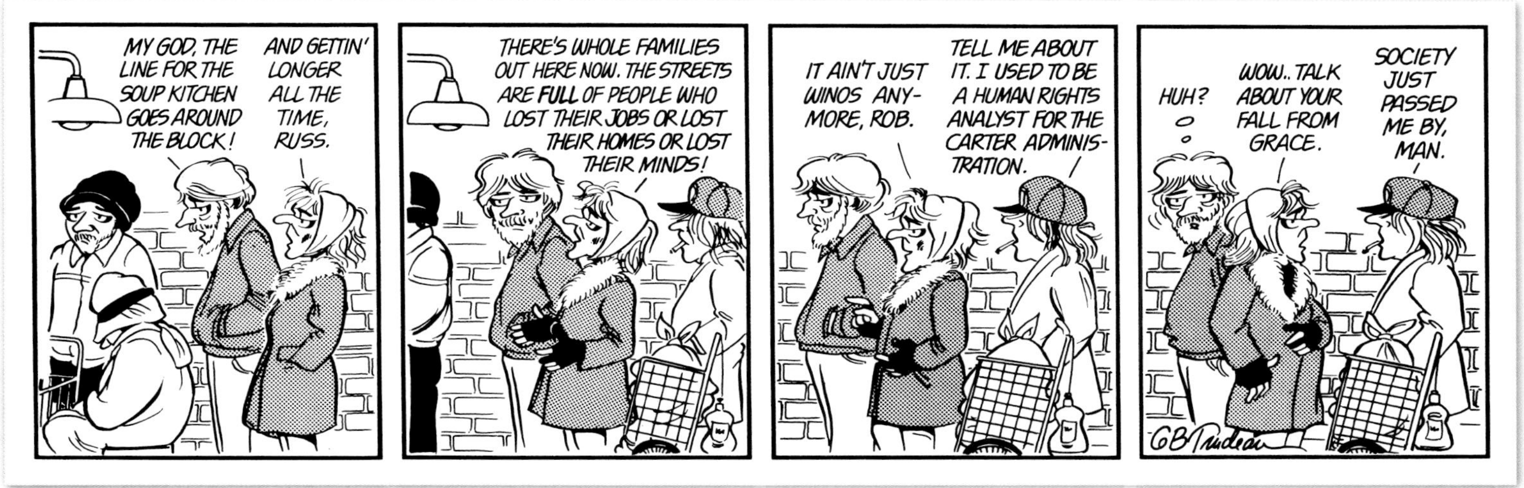
MY GOD, THE LINE FOR THE SOUP KITCHEN GOES AROUND THE BLOCK!
AND GETTIN' LONGER ALL THE TIME, RUSS.
THERE'S WHOLE FAMILIES OUT HERE NOW. THE STREETS ARE FULL OF PEOPLE WHO LOST THEIR JOBS OR LOST THEIR HOMES OR LOST THEIR MINDS!
IT AIN'T JUST WINOS ANYMORE, ROB.
TELL ME ABOUT IT. I USED TO BE A HUMAN RIGHTS ANALYST FOR THE CARTER ADMINISTRATION.
HUH?
WOW.. TALK ABOUT YOUR FALL FROM GRACE.
SOCIETY JUST PASSED ME BY, MAN.

12/19/84

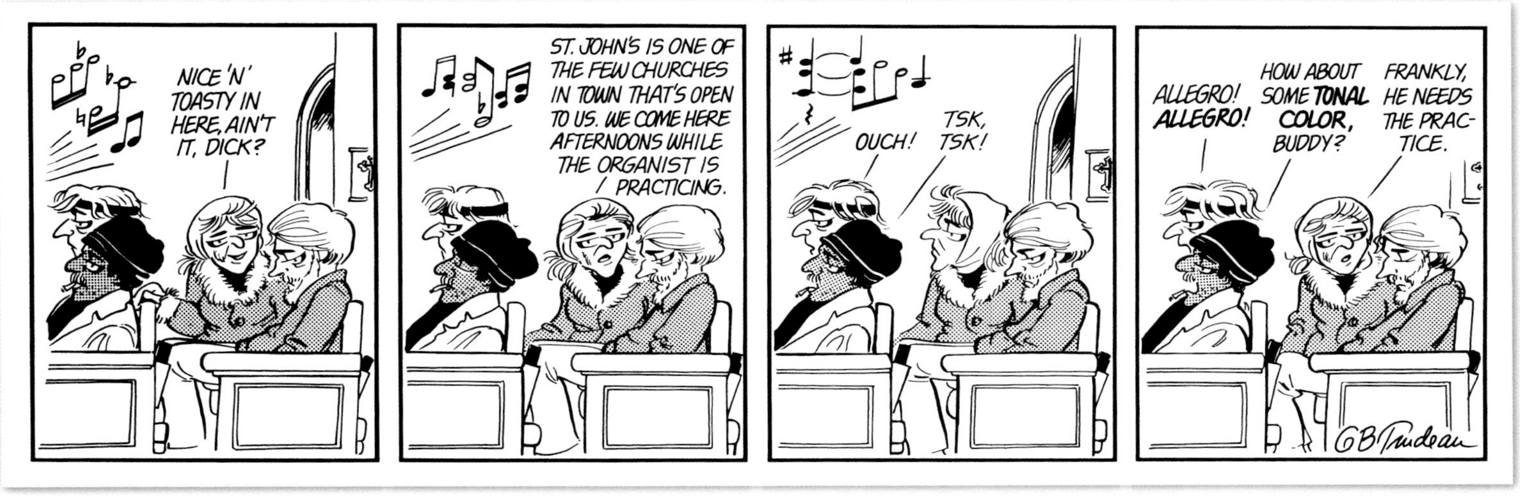
NICE 'N' TOASTY IN HERE, AIN'T IT, DICK?
ST. JOHN'S IS ONE OF THE FEW CHURCHES IN TOWN THAT'S OPEN TO US. WE COME HERE AFTERNOONS WHILE THE ORGANIST IS PRACTICING.
OUCH!
TSK, TSK!
ALLEGRO! ALLEGRO!
HOW ABOUT SOME TONAL COLOR, BUDDY?
FRANKLY, HE NEEDS THE PRACTICE.

12/20/84

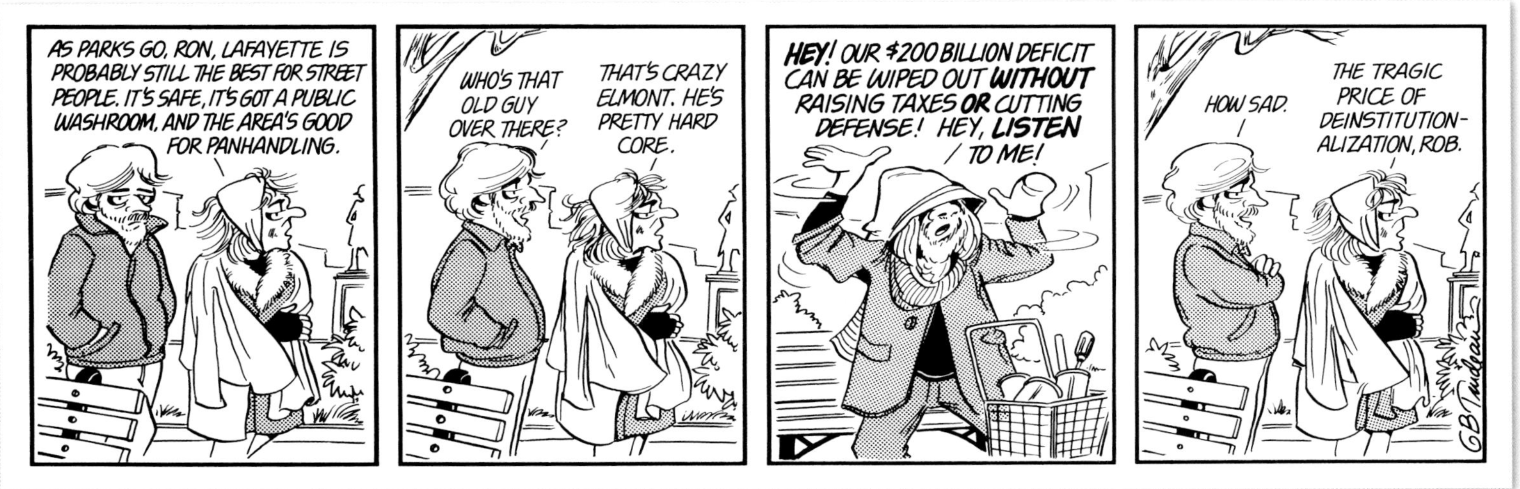
AS PARKS GO, RON, LAFAYETTE IS PROBABLY STILL THE BEST FOR STREET PEOPLE. IT'S SAFE, IT'S GOT A PUBLIC WASHROOM, AND THE AREA'S GOOD FOR PANHANDLING.
WHO'S THAT OLD GUY OVER THERE?
THAT'S CRAZY ELMONT. HE'S PRETTY HARD CORE.
HEY! OUR $200 BILLION DEFICIT CAN BE WIPED OUT WITHOUT RAISING TAXES OR CUTTING DEFENSE! HEY, LISTEN TO ME!
HOW SAD.
THE TRAGIC PRICE OF DEINSTITUTIONALIZATION, ROB.

12/21/84

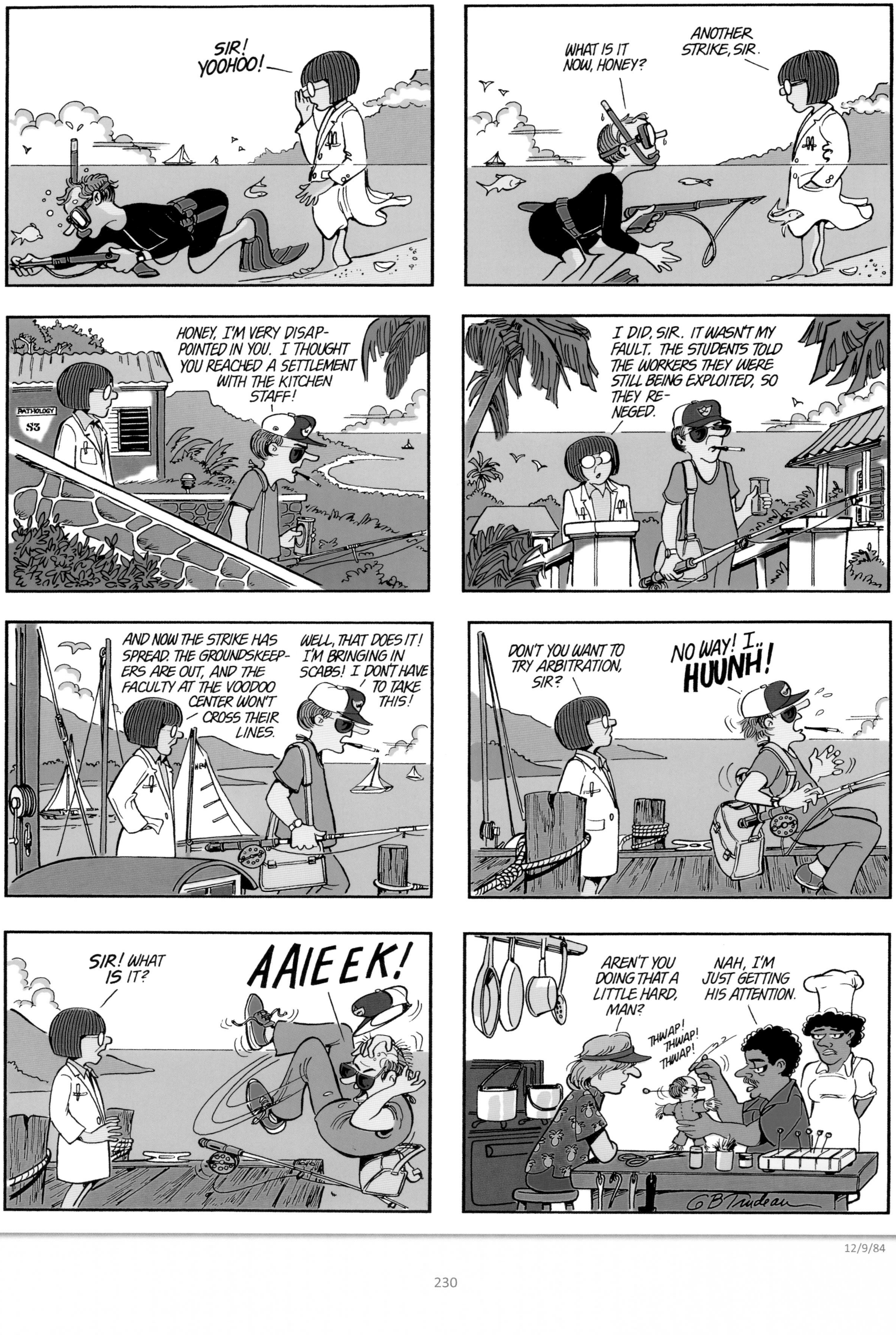

SIR! YOOHOO!
WHAT IS IT NOW, HONEY?
ANOTHER STRIKE, SIR.
HONEY, I'M VERY DISAPPOINTED IN YOU. I THOUGHT YOU REACHED A SETTLEMENT WITH THE KITCHEN STAFF!
PATHOLOGY
S3
I DID, SIR. IT WASN'T MY FAULT. THE STUDENTS TOLD THE WORKERS THEY WERE STILL BEING EXPLOITED, SO THEY RENEGED.
AND NOW THE STRIKE HAS SPREAD. THE GROUNDSKEEPERS ARE OUT, AND THE FACULTY AT THE VOODOO CENTER WON'T CROSS THEIR LINES.
WELL, THAT DOES IT! I'M BRINGING IN SCABS! I DON'T HAVE TO TAKE THIS!
DON'T YOU WANT TO TRY ARBITRATION, SIR?
NO WAY! I.. HUUNH!
SIR! WHAT IS IT?
AAIEEK!
AREN'T YOU DOING THAT A LITTLE HARD, MAN?
NAH, I'M JUST GETTING HIS ATTENTION.
THWAP! THWAP! THWAP!
GBTrudeau

12/9/84

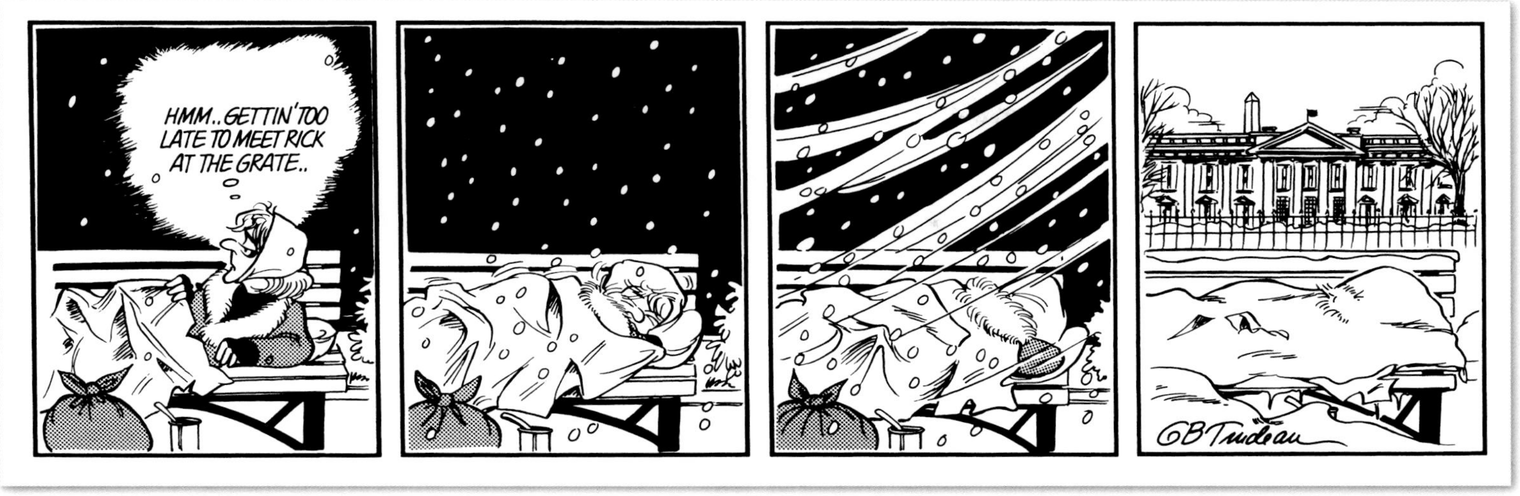
HMM.. GETTIN' TOO LATE TO MEET RICK AT THE GRATE..

1/2/85

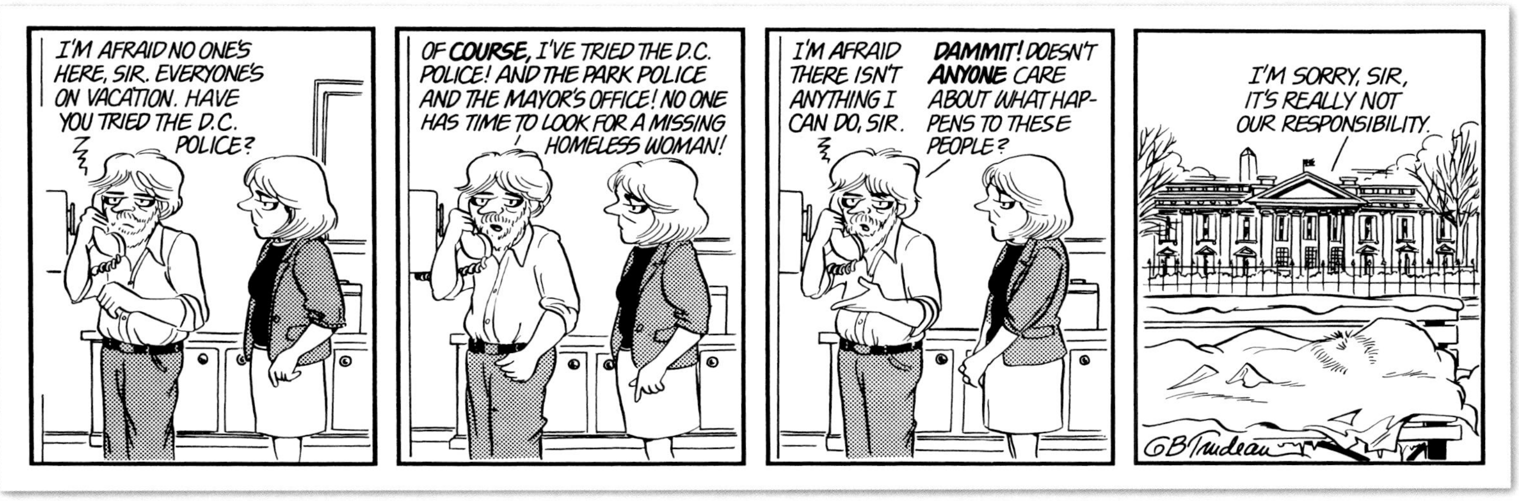
I'M AFRAID NO ONE'S HERE, SIR. EVERYONE'S ON VACATION. HAVE YOU TRIED THE D.C. POLICE?
OF **COURSE**, I'VE TRIED THE D.C. POLICE! AND THE PARK POLICE AND THE MAYOR'S OFFICE! NO ONE HAS TIME TO LOOK FOR A MISSING HOMELESS WOMAN!
I'M AFRAID THERE ISN'T ANYTHING I CAN DO, SIR.
DAMMIT! DOESN'T **ANYONE** CARE ABOUT WHAT HAPPENS TO THESE PEOPLE?
I'M SORRY, SIR, IT'S REALLY NOT OUR RESPONSIBILITY.

1/3/85

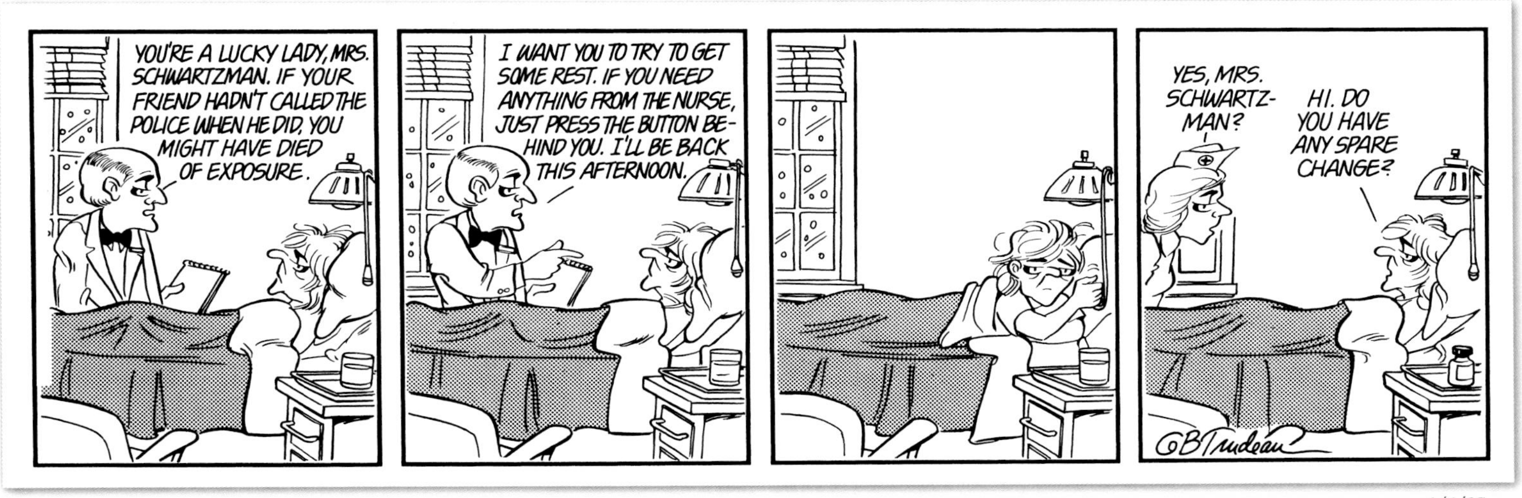
YOU'RE A LUCKY LADY, MRS. SCHWARTZMAN. IF YOUR FRIEND HADN'T CALLED THE POLICE WHEN HE DID, YOU MIGHT HAVE DIED OF EXPOSURE.
I WANT YOU TO TRY TO GET SOME REST. IF YOU NEED ANYTHING FROM THE NURSE, JUST PRESS THE BUTTON BEHIND YOU. I'LL BE BACK THIS AFTERNOON.
YES, MRS. SCHWARTZMAN?
HI. DO YOU HAVE ANY SPARE CHANGE?

1/4/85

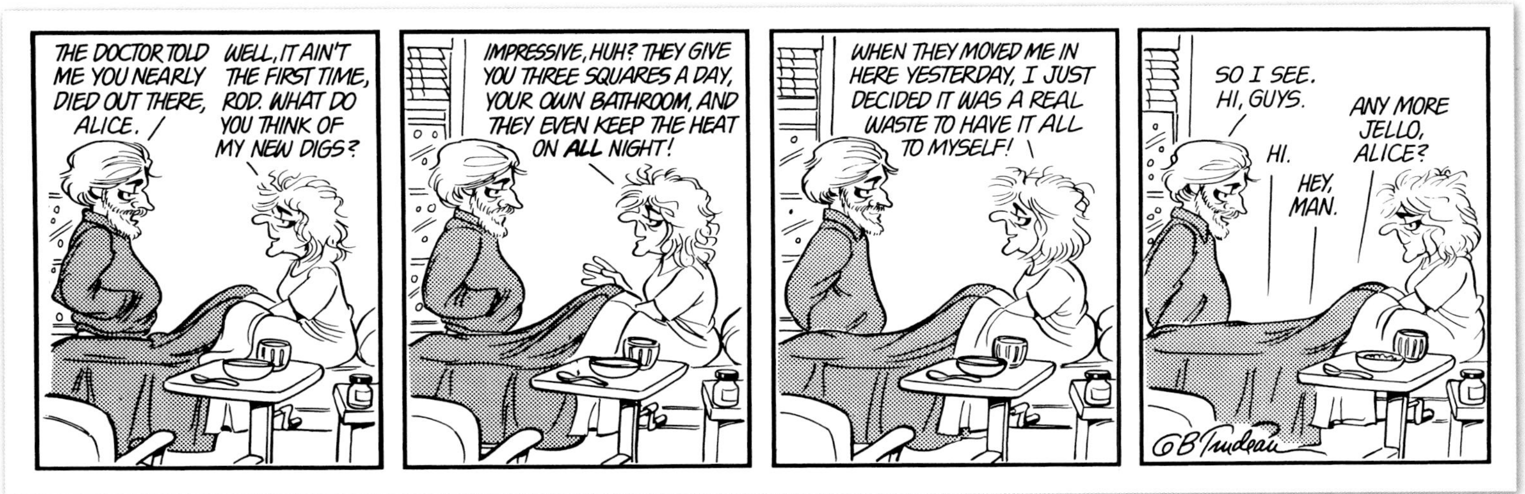
THE DOCTOR TOLD ME YOU NEARLY DIED OUT THERE, ALICE.
WELL, IT AIN'T THE FIRST TIME, ROD. WHAT DO YOU THINK OF MY NEW DIGS?
IMPRESSIVE, HUH? THEY GIVE YOU THREE SQUARES A DAY, YOUR OWN BATHROOM, AND THEY EVEN KEEP THE HEAT ON **ALL** NIGHT!
WHEN THEY MOVED ME IN HERE YESTERDAY, I JUST DECIDED IT WAS A REAL WASTE TO HAVE IT ALL TO MYSELF!
SO I SEE. HI, GUYS.
HI.
HEY, MAN.
ANY MORE JELLO, ALICE?

1/5/85

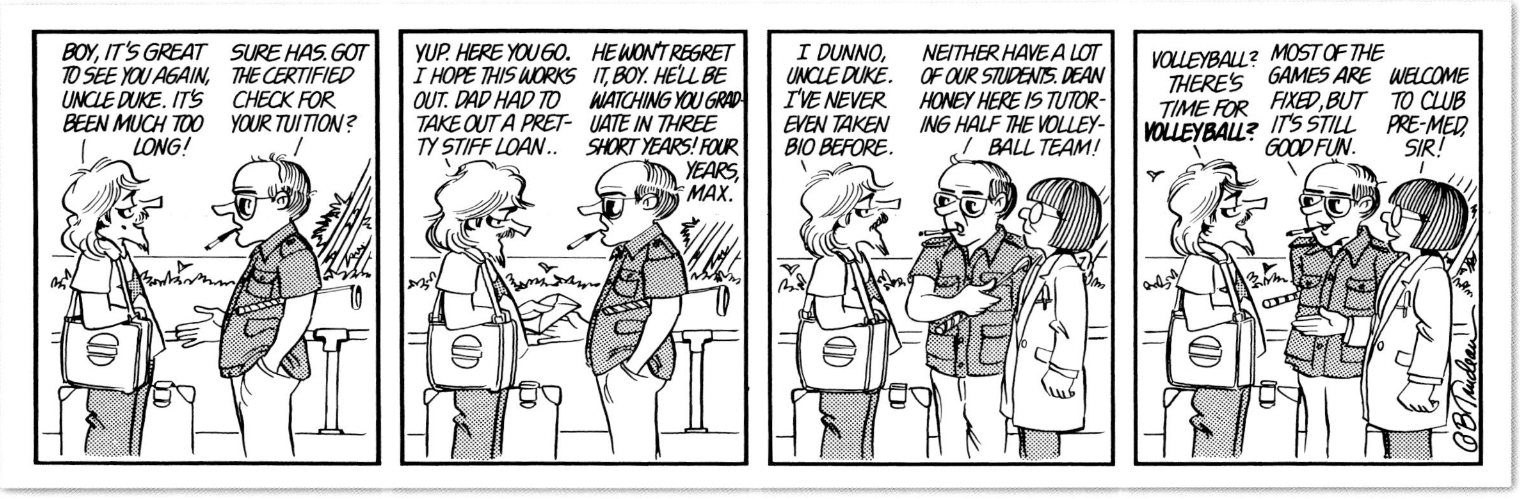
BOY, IT'S GREAT TO SEE YOU AGAIN, UNCLE DUKE. IT'S BEEN MUCH TOO LONG!
SURE HAS. GOT THE CERTIFIED CHECK FOR YOUR TUITION?
YUP. HERE YOU GO. I HOPE THIS WORKS OUT. DAD HAD TO TAKE OUT A PRETTY STIFF LOAN..
HE WON'T REGRET IT, BOY. HE'LL BE WATCHING YOU GRADUATE IN THREE SHORT YEARS! FOUR YEARS, MAX.
I DUNNO, UNCLE DUKE. I'VE NEVER EVEN TAKEN BIO BEFORE.
NEITHER HAVE A LOT OF OUR STUDENTS. DEAN HONEY HERE IS TUTORING HALF THE VOLLEYBALL TEAM!
VOLLEYBALL? THERE'S TIME FOR **VOLLEYBALL?**
MOST OF THE GAMES ARE FIXED, BUT IT'S STILL GOOD FUN.
WELCOME TO CLUB PRE-MED, SIR!

1/7/85

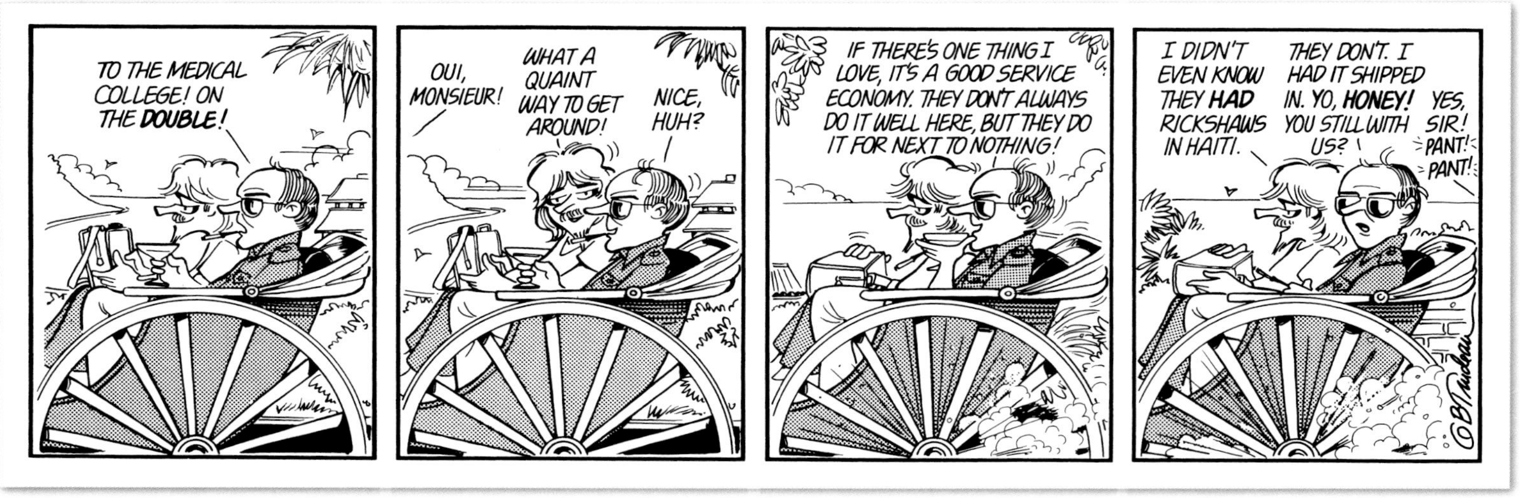
TO THE MEDICAL COLLEGE! ON THE **DOUBLE**!
OUI, MONSIEUR!
WHAT A QUAINT WAY TO GET AROUND!
NICE, HUH?
IF THERE'S ONE THING I LOVE, IT'S A GOOD SERVICE ECONOMY. THEY DON'T ALWAYS DO IT WELL HERE, BUT THEY DO IT FOR NEXT TO NOTHING!
I DIDN'T EVEN KNOW THEY **HAD** RICKSHAWS IN HAITI.
THEY DON'T. I HAD IT SHIPPED IN. YO, **HONEY!** YOU STILL WITH US?
YES, SIR! PANT! PANT!

1/8/85

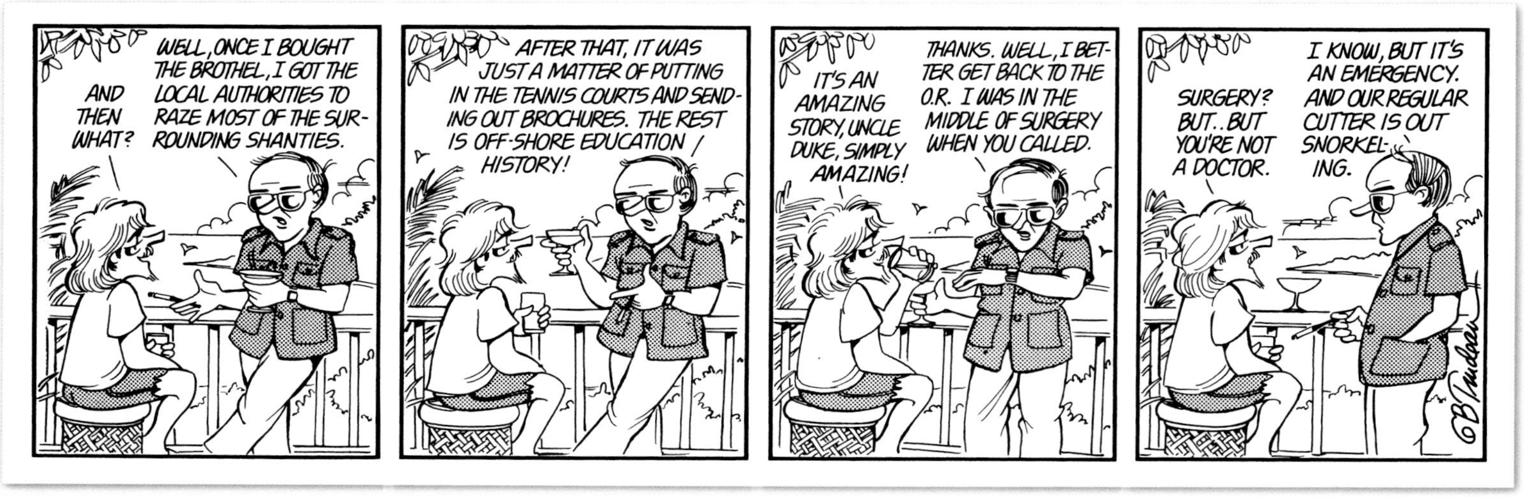
AND THEN WHAT?
WELL, ONCE I BOUGHT THE BROTHEL, I GOT THE LOCAL AUTHORITIES TO RAZE MOST OF THE SURROUNDING SHANTIES.
AFTER THAT, IT WAS JUST A MATTER OF PUTTING IN THE TENNIS COURTS AND SENDING OUT BROCHURES. THE REST IS OFF-SHORE EDUCATION HISTORY!
IT'S AN AMAZING STORY, UNCLE DUKE, SIMPLY AMAZING!
THANKS. WELL, I BETTER GET BACK TO THE O.R. I WAS IN THE MIDDLE OF SURGERY WHEN YOU CALLED.
SURGERY? BUT..BUT YOU'RE NOT A DOCTOR.
I KNOW, BUT IT'S AN EMERGENCY. AND OUR REGULAR CUTTER IS OUT SNORKELING.

1/10/85

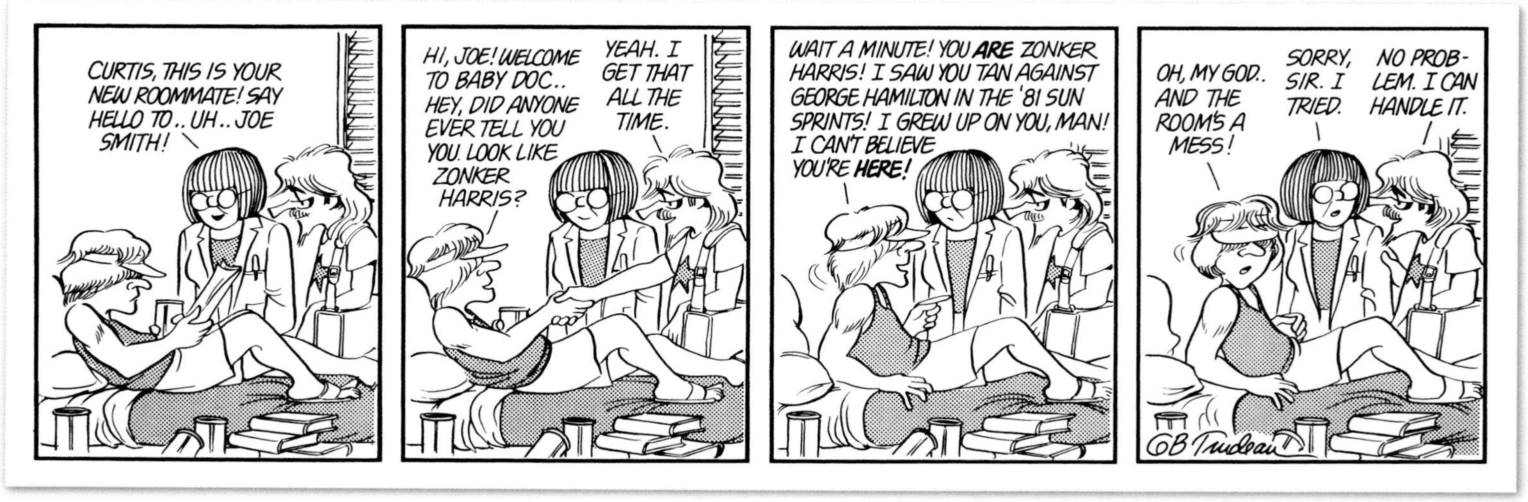
CURTIS, THIS IS YOUR NEW ROOMMATE! SAY HELLO TO..UH..JOE SMITH!
HI, JOE! WELCOME TO BABY DOC.. HEY, DID ANYONE EVER TELL YOU YOU. LOOK LIKE ZONKER HARRIS?
YEAH. I GET THAT ALL THE TIME.
WAIT A MINUTE! YOU **ARE** ZONKER HARRIS! I SAW YOU TAN AGAINST GEORGE HAMILTON IN THE '81 SUN SPRINTS! I GREW UP ON YOU, MAN! I CAN'T BELIEVE YOU'RE **HERE!**
OH, MY GOD.. AND THE ROOM'S A MESS!
SORRY, SIR. I TRIED.
NO PROBLEM. I CAN HANDLE IT.

1/11/85

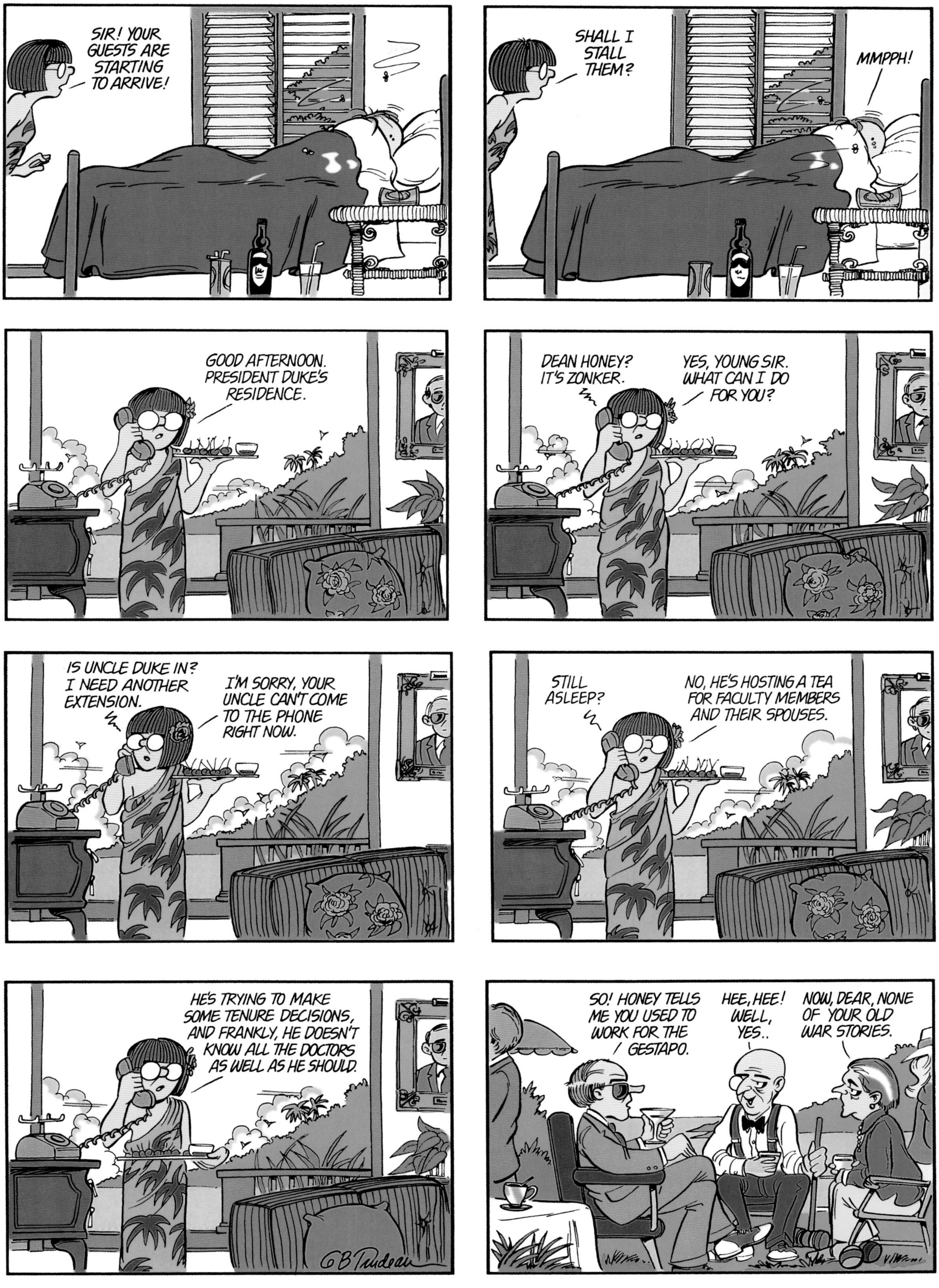
SIR! YOUR GUESTS ARE STARTING TO ARRIVE!
SHALL I STALL THEM?
MMPPH!
GOOD AFTERNOON. PRESIDENT DUKE'S RESIDENCE.
DEAN HONEY? IT'S ZONKER.
YES, YOUNG SIR. WHAT CAN I DO FOR YOU?
IS UNCLE DUKE IN? I NEED ANOTHER EXTENSION.
I'M SORRY, YOUR UNCLE CAN'T COME TO THE PHONE RIGHT NOW.
STILL ASLEEP?
NO, HE'S HOSTING A TEA FOR FACULTY MEMBERS AND THEIR SPOUSES.
HE'S TRYING TO MAKE SOME TENURE DECISIONS, AND FRANKLY, HE DOESN'T KNOW ALL THE DOCTORS AS WELL AS HE SHOULD.
GB Trudeau
SO! HONEY TELLS ME YOU USED TO WORK FOR THE GESTAPO.
HEE, HEE! WELL, YES..
NOW, DEAR, NONE OF YOUR OLD WAR STORIES.

2/24/85

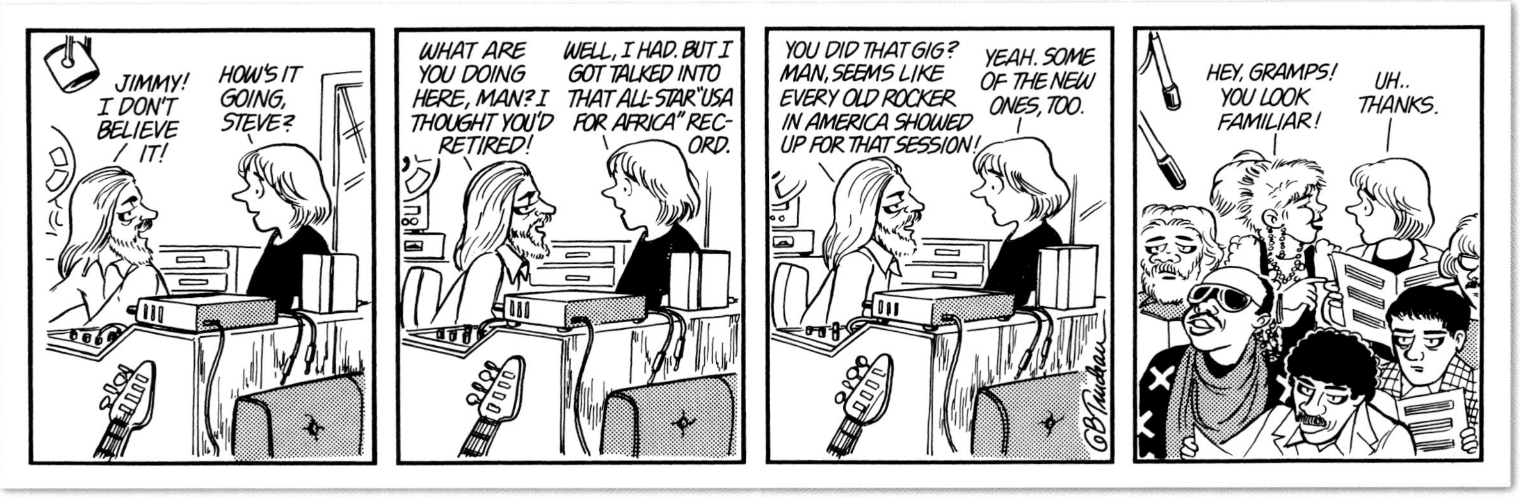
JIMMY! I DON'T BELIEVE IT!
HOW'S IT GOING, STEVE?
WHAT ARE YOU DOING HERE, MAN? I THOUGHT YOU'D RETIRED!
WELL, I HAD. BUT I GOT TALKED INTO THAT ALL-STAR "USA FOR AFRICA" RECORD.
YOU DID THAT GIG? MAN, SEEMS LIKE EVERY OLD ROCKER IN AMERICA SHOWED UP FOR THAT SESSION!
YEAH. SOME OF THE NEW ONES, TOO.
HEY, GRAMPS! YOU LOOK FAMILIAR!
UH.. THANKS.

3/4/85

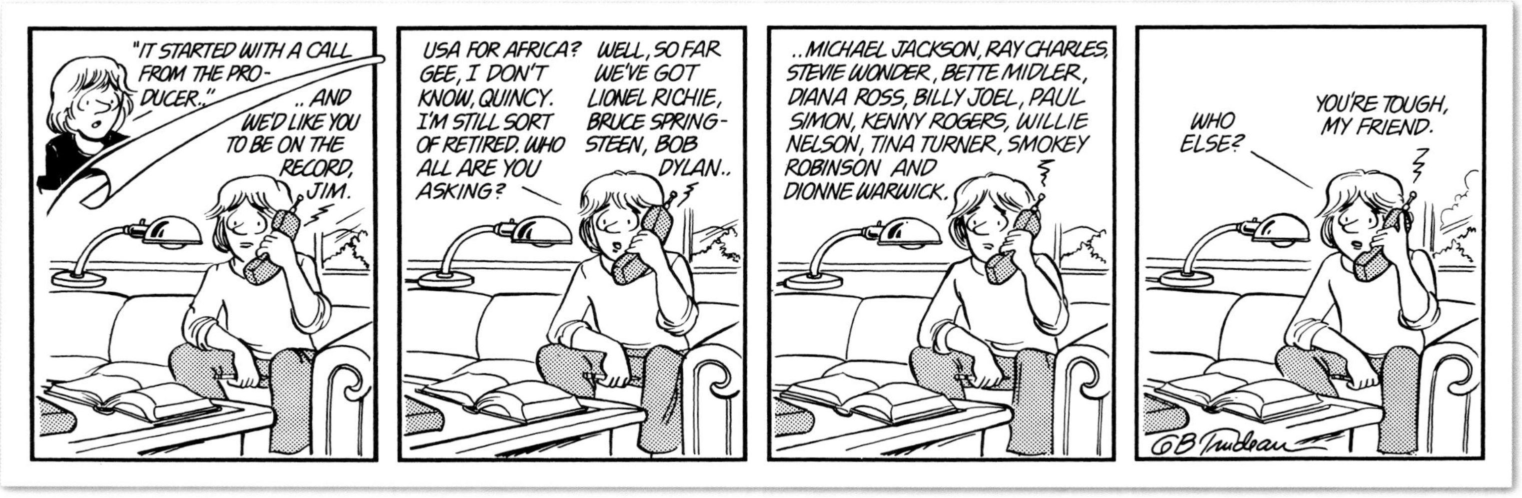
"IT STARTED WITH A CALL FROM THE PRODUCER.."
.. AND WE'D LIKE YOU TO BE ON THE RECORD, JIM.
USA FOR AFRICA? GEE, I DON'T KNOW, QUINCY. I'M STILL SORT OF RETIRED. WHO ALL ARE YOU ASKING?
WELL, SO FAR WE'VE GOT LIONEL RICHIE, BRUCE SPRINGSTEEN, BOB DYLAN..
..MICHAEL JACKSON, RAY CHARLES, STEVIE WONDER, BETTE MIDLER, DIANA ROSS, BILLY JOEL, PAUL SIMON, KENNY ROGERS, WILLIE NELSON, TINA TURNER, SMOKEY ROBINSON AND DIONNE WARWICK.
WHO ELSE?
YOU'RE TOUGH, MY FRIEND.

3/5/85

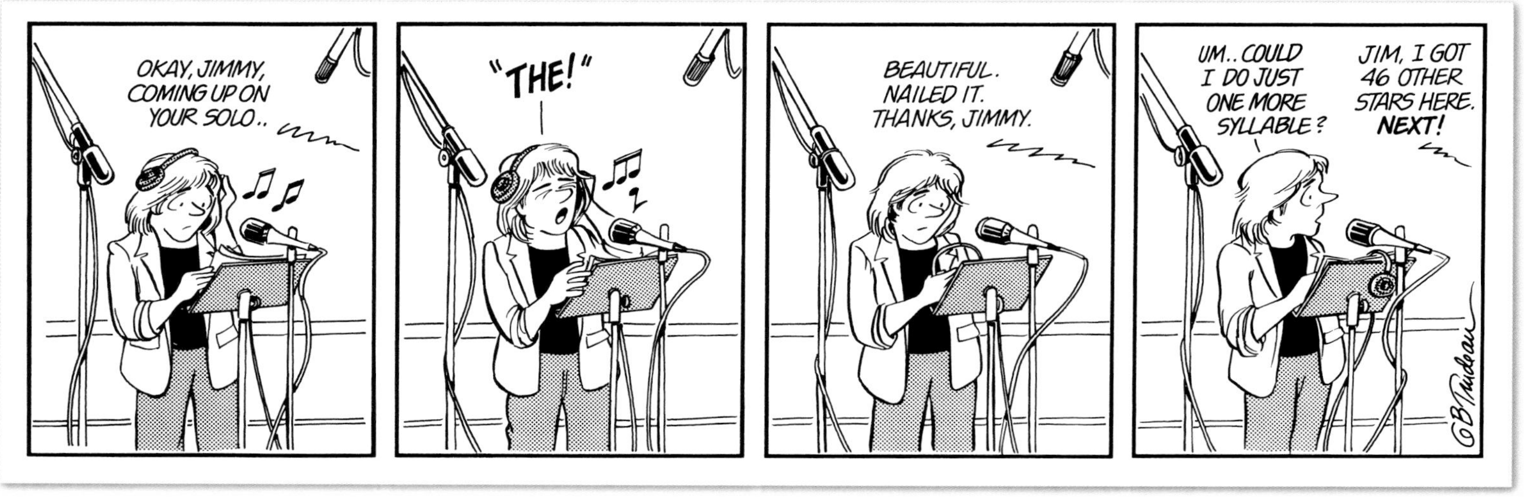
OKAY, JIMMY, COMING UP ON YOUR SOLO..
"THE!"
BEAUTIFUL. NAILED IT. THANKS, JIMMY.
UM.. COULD I DO JUST ONE MORE SYLLABLE?
JIM, I GOT 46 OTHER STARS HERE. NEXT!

3/15/85

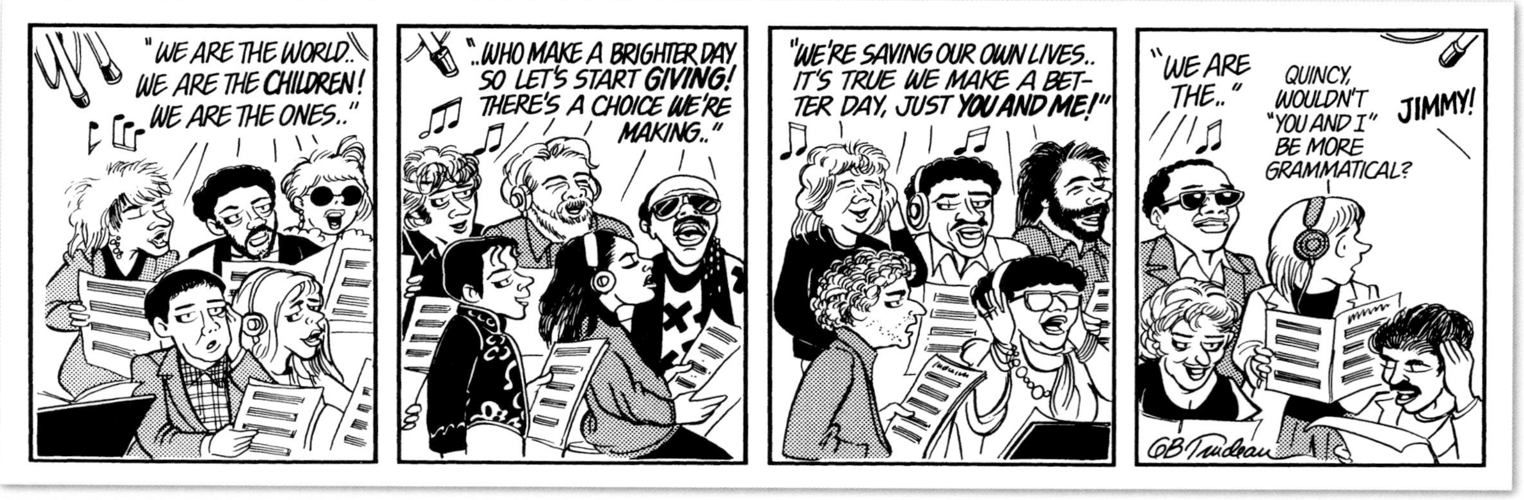
"WE ARE THE WORLD.. WE ARE THE CHILDREN! WE ARE THE ONES.."
"..WHO MAKE A BRIGHTER DAY SO LET'S START GIVING! THERE'S A CHOICE WE'RE MAKING.."
"WE'RE SAVING OUR OWN LIVES.. IT'S TRUE WE MAKE A BETTER DAY, JUST YOU AND ME!"
"WE ARE THE.."
QUINCY, WOULDN'T "YOU AND I" BE MORE GRAMMATICAL?
JIMMY!

3/12/85

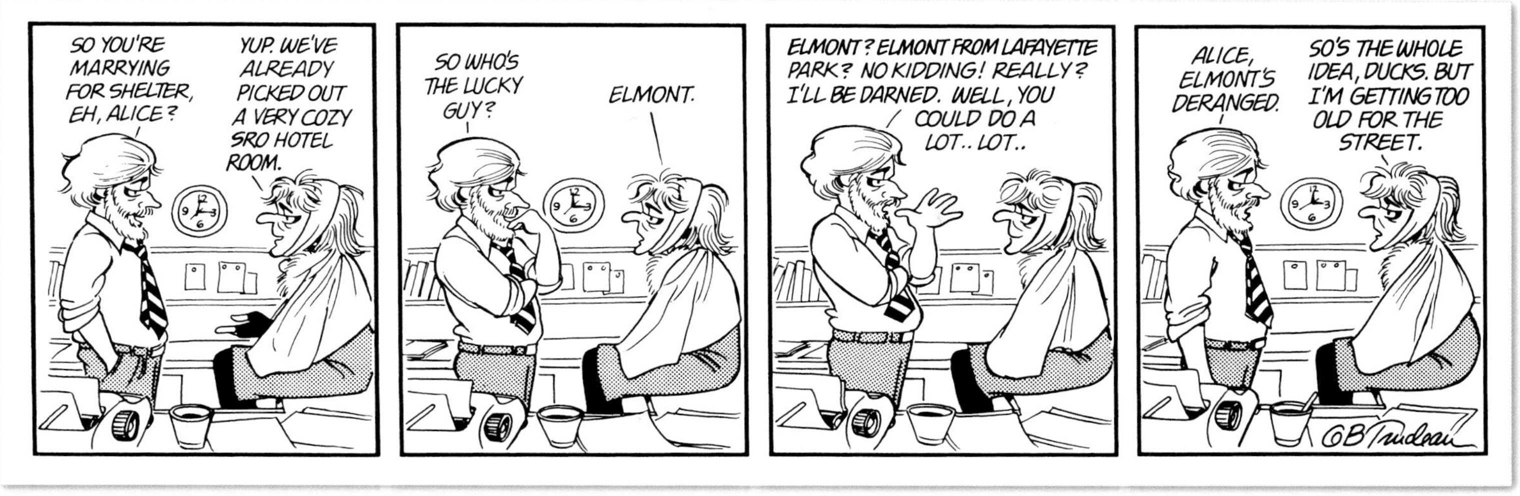
SO YOU'RE MARRYING FOR SHELTER, EH, ALICE?
YUP. WE'VE ALREADY PICKED OUT A VERY COZY SRO HOTEL ROOM.
SO WHO'S THE LUCKY GUY?
ELMONT.
ELMONT? ELMONT FROM LAFAYETTE PARK? NO KIDDING! REALLY? I'LL BE DARNED. WELL, YOU COULD DO A LOT.. LOT..
ALICE, ELMONT'S DERANGED.
SO'S THE WHOLE IDEA, DUCKS. BUT I'M GETTING TOO OLD FOR THE STREET.
©B Trudeau

5/15/85

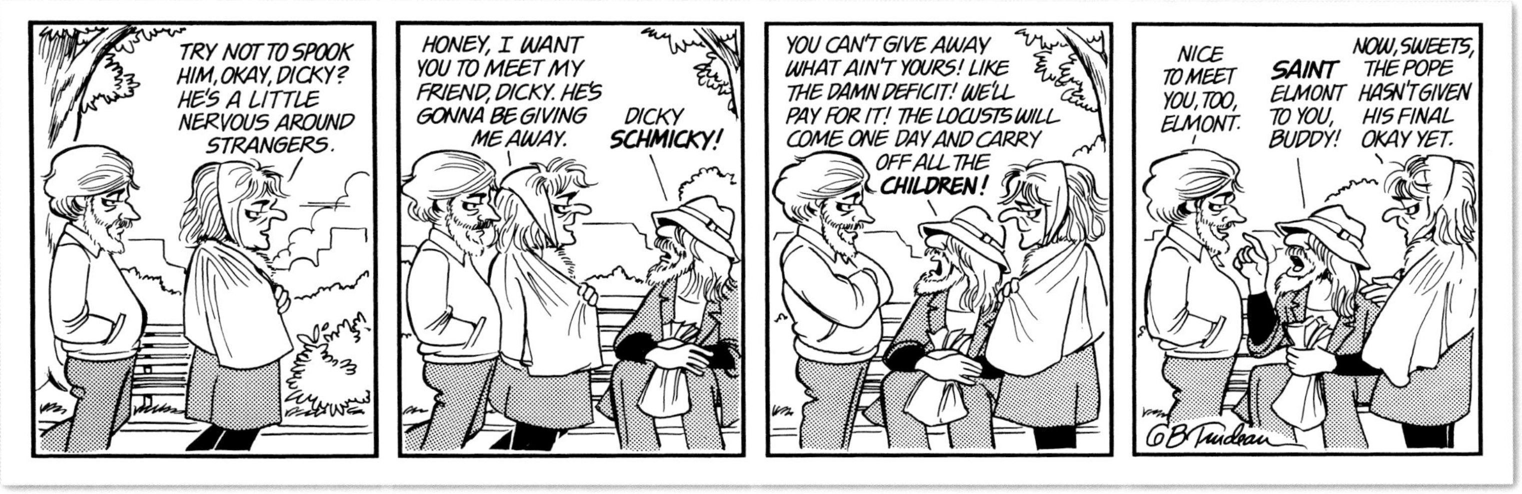
TRY NOT TO SPOOK HIM, OKAY, DICKY? HE'S A LITTLE NERVOUS AROUND STRANGERS.
HONEY, I WANT YOU TO MEET MY FRIEND, DICKY. HE'S GONNA BE GIVING ME AWAY.
DICKY SCHMICKY!
YOU CAN'T GIVE AWAY WHAT AIN'T YOURS! LIKE THE DAMN DEFICIT! WE'LL PAY FOR IT! THE LOCUSTS WILL COME ONE DAY AND CARRY OFF ALL THE CHILDREN!
NICE TO MEET YOU, TOO, ELMONT.
SAINT ELMONT TO YOU, BUDDY!
NOW, SWEETS, THE POPE HASN'T GIVEN HIS FINAL OKAY YET.
©B Trudeau

5/16/85

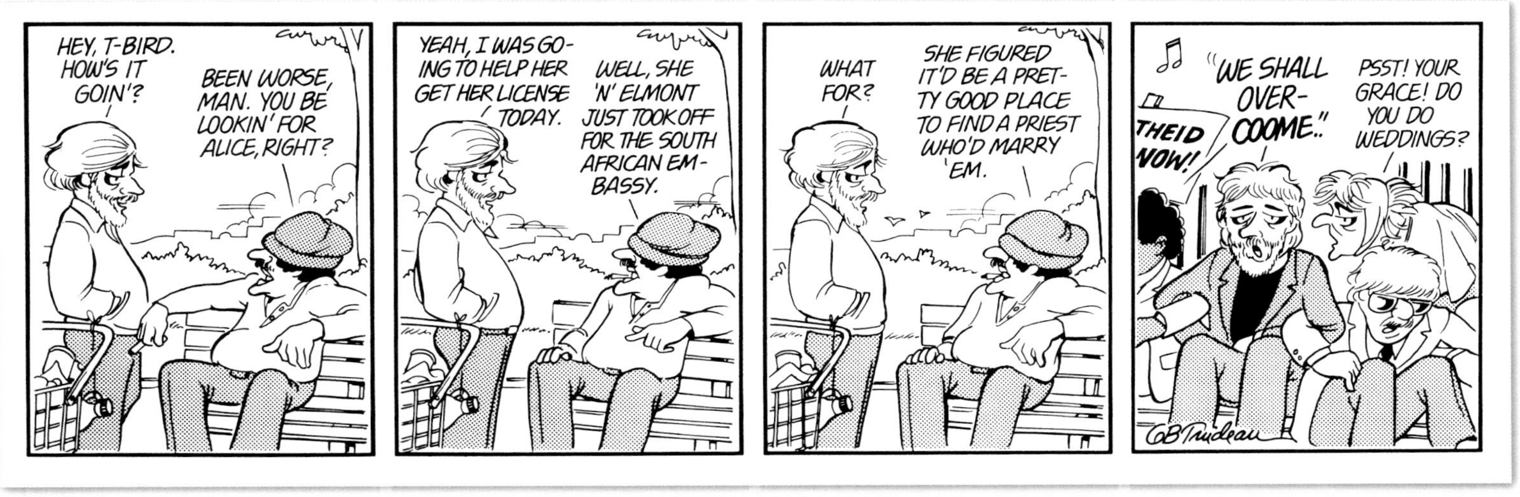
HEY, T-BIRD. HOW'S IT GOIN'?
BEEN WORSE, MAN. YOU BE LOOKIN' FOR ALICE, RIGHT?
YEAH, I WAS GOING TO HELP HER GET HER LICENSE TODAY.
WELL, SHE 'N' ELMONT JUST TOOK OFF FOR THE SOUTH AFRICAN EMBASSY.
WHAT FOR?
SHE FIGURED IT'D BE A PRETTY GOOD PLACE TO FIND A PRIEST WHO'D MARRY 'EM.
"WE SHALL OVERCOOME.."
THEID NOW!
PSST! YOUR GRACE! DO YOU DO WEDDINGS?
©B Trudeau

5/18/85

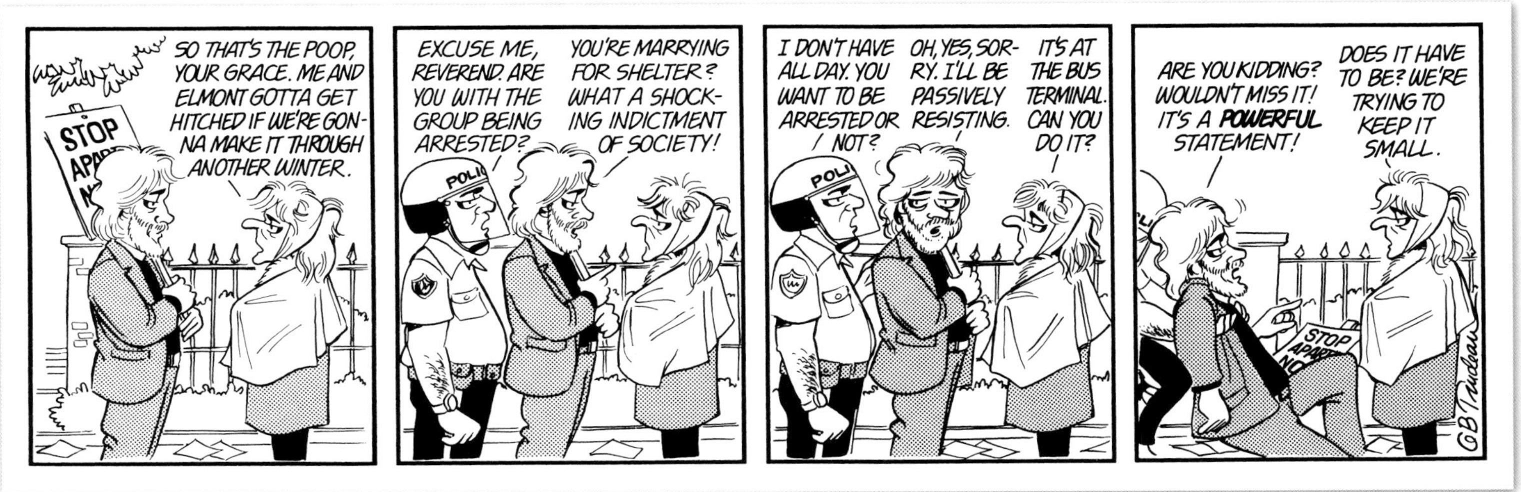
SO THAT'S THE POOP, YOUR GRACE. ME AND ELMONT GOTTA GET HITCHED IF WE'RE GONNA MAKE IT THROUGH ANOTHER WINTER.
STOP
EXCUSE ME, REVEREND. ARE YOU WITH THE GROUP BEING ARRESTED?
YOU'RE MARRYING FOR SHELTER? WHAT A SHOCKING INDICTMENT OF SOCIETY!
I DON'T HAVE ALL DAY. YOU WANT TO BE ARRESTED OR NOT?
OH, YES, SORRY. I'LL BE PASSIVELY RESISTING.
IT'S AT THE BUS TERMINAL. CAN YOU DO IT?
ARE YOU KIDDING? WOULDN'T MISS IT! IT'S A POWERFUL STATEMENT!
DOES IT HAVE TO BE? WE'RE TRYING TO KEEP IT SMALL.
©B Trudeau

5/20/85

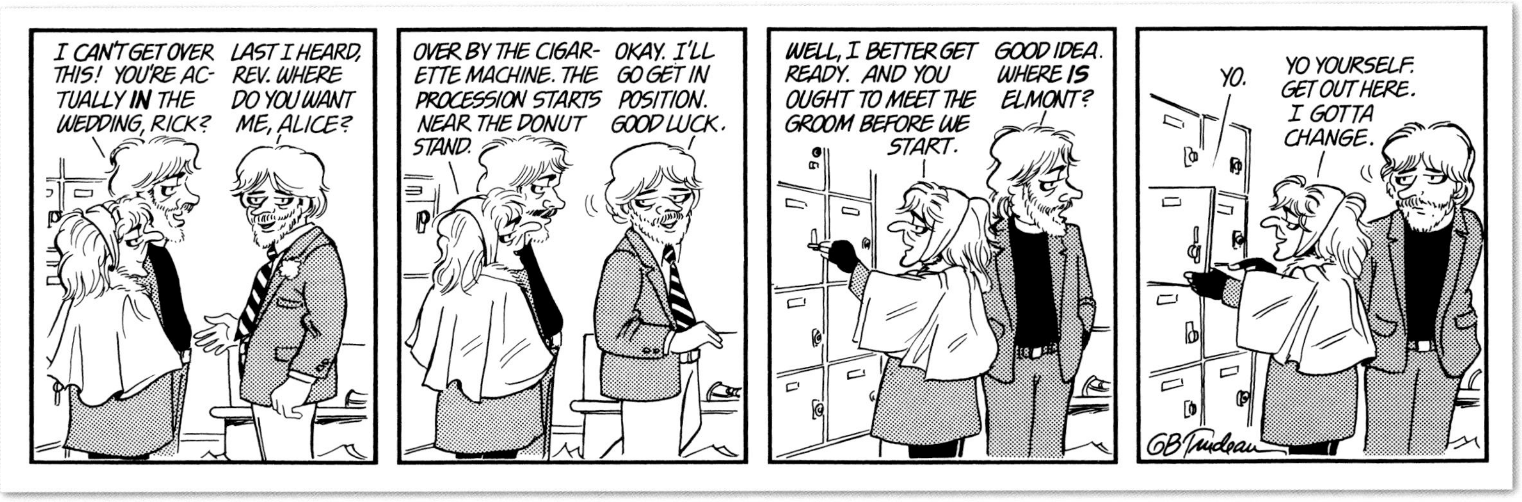
I CAN'T GET OVER THIS! YOU'RE ACTUALLY IN THE WEDDING, RICK?
LAST I HEARD, REV. WHERE DO YOU WANT ME, ALICE?
OVER BY THE CIGARETTE MACHINE. THE PROCESSION STARTS NEAR THE DONUT STAND.
OKAY. I'LL GO GET IN POSITION. GOOD LUCK.
WELL, I BETTER GET READY. AND YOU OUGHT TO MEET THE GROOM BEFORE WE START.
GOOD IDEA. WHERE IS ELMONT?
YO.
YO YOURSELF. GET OUT HERE. I GOTTA CHANGE.
GB Trudeau

5/21/85

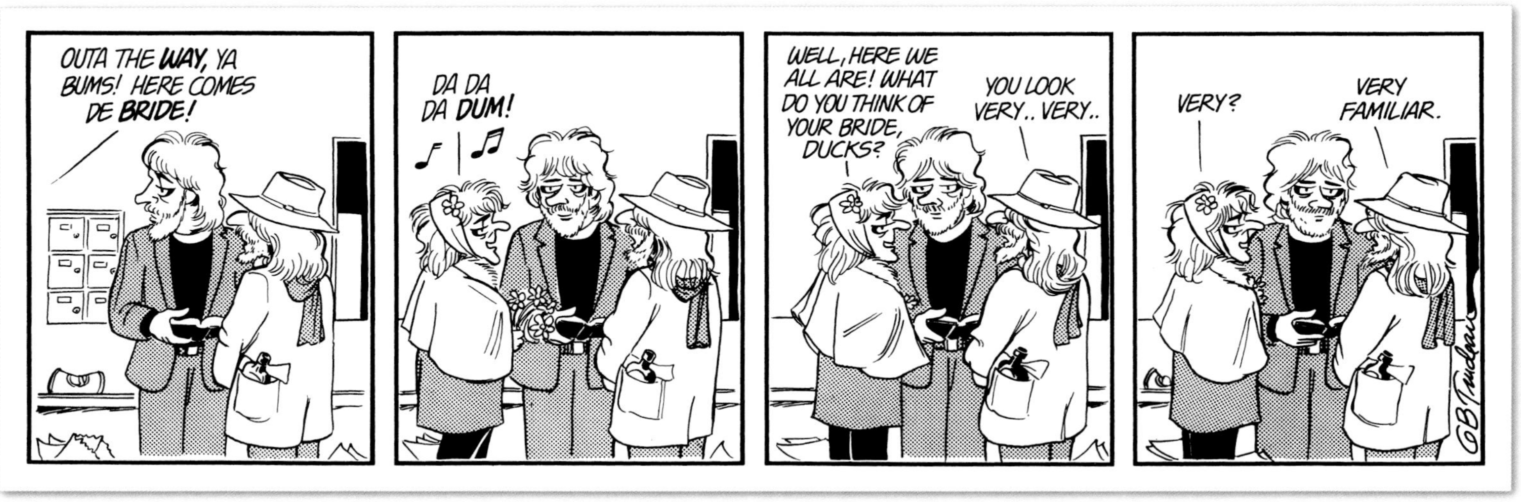
OUTA THE WAY, YA BUMS! HERE COMES DE BRIDE!
DA DA DA DUM!
WELL, HERE WE ALL ARE! WHAT DO YOU THINK OF YOUR BRIDE, DUCKS?
YOU LOOK VERY.. VERY..
VERY?
VERY FAMILIAR.
GB Trudeau

5/22/85

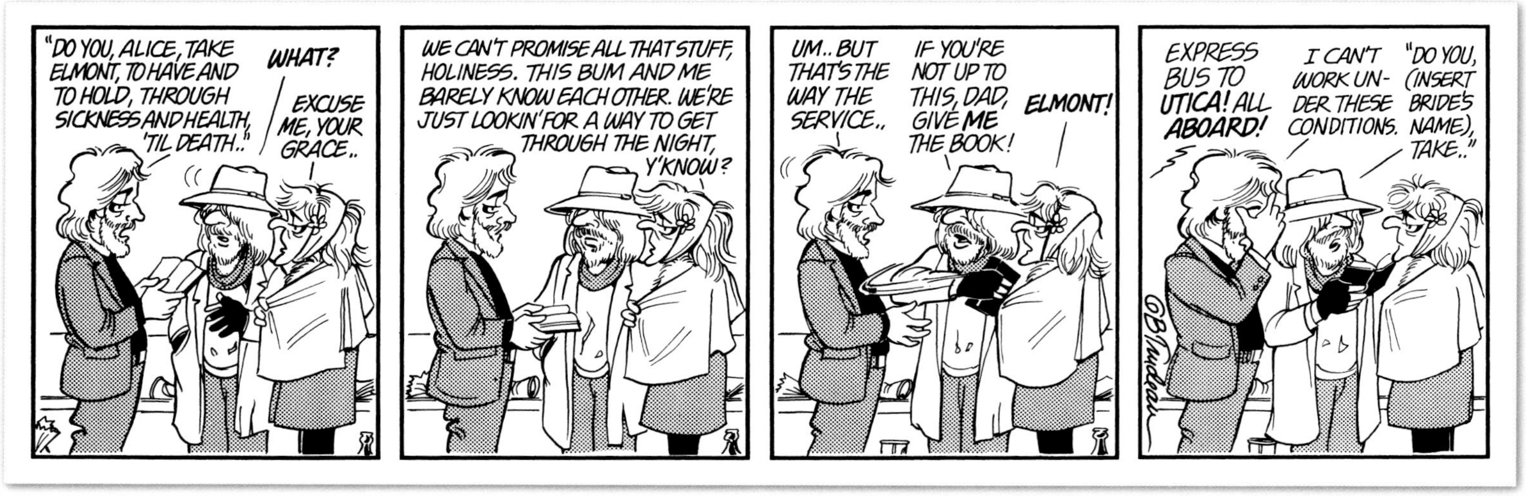
"DO YOU, ALICE, TAKE ELMONT, TO HAVE AND TO HOLD, THROUGH SICKNESS AND HEALTH, 'TIL DEATH.."
WHAT?
EXCUSE ME, YOUR GRACE..
WE CAN'T PROMISE ALL THAT STUFF, HOLINESS. THIS BUM AND ME BARELY KNOW EACH OTHER. WE'RE JUST LOOKIN' FOR A WAY TO GET THROUGH THE NIGHT, Y'KNOW?
UM.. BUT THAT'S THE WAY THE SERVICE..
IF YOU'RE NOT UP TO THIS, DAD, GIVE ME THE BOOK!
ELMONT!
EXPRESS BUS TO UTICA! ALL ABOARD!
I CAN'T WORK UNDER THESE CONDITIONS.
"DO YOU, (INSERT BRIDE'S NAME), TAKE.."
GB Trudeau

5/24/85

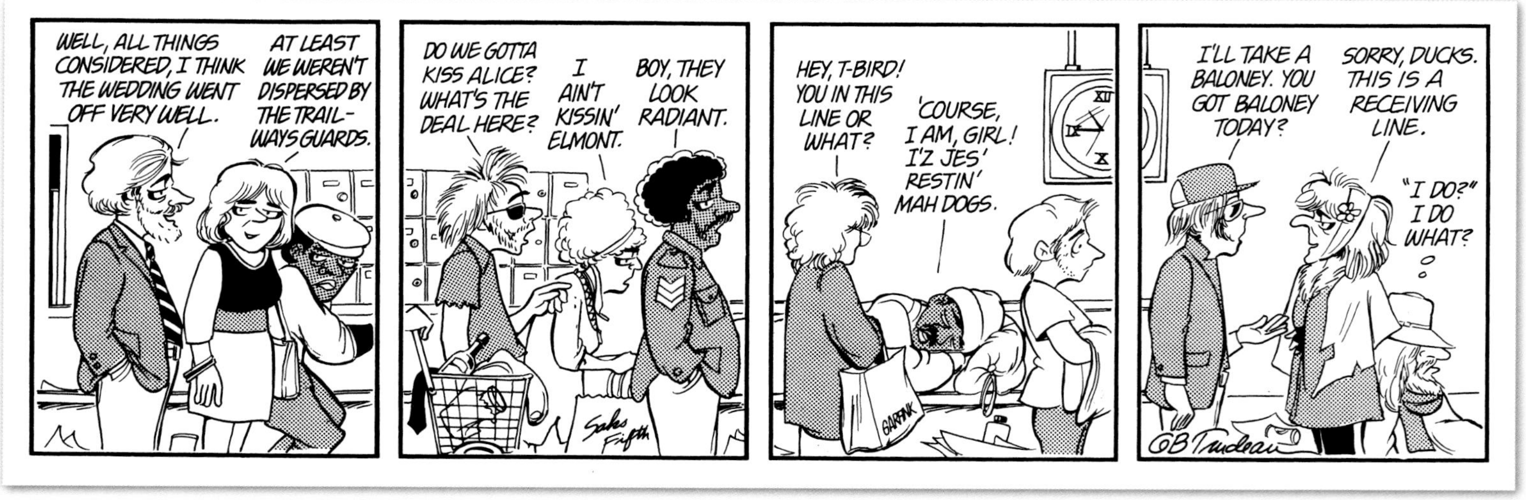
WELL, ALL THINGS CONSIDERED, I THINK THE WEDDING WENT OFF VERY WELL.
AT LEAST WE WEREN'T DISPERSED BY THE TRAILWAYS GUARDS.
DO WE GOTTA KISS ALICE? WHAT'S THE DEAL HERE?
I AIN'T KISSIN' ELMONT.
BOY, THEY LOOK RADIANT.
Saks Fifth
HEY, T-BIRD! YOU IN THIS LINE OR WHAT?
'COURSE, I AM, GIRL! I'Z JES' RESTIN' MAH DOGS.
GARFINK
I'LL TAKE A BALONEY. YOU GOT BALONEY TODAY?
SORRY, DUCKS. THIS IS A RECEIVING LINE.
"I DO?" I DO WHAT?
GB Trudeau

5/25/85

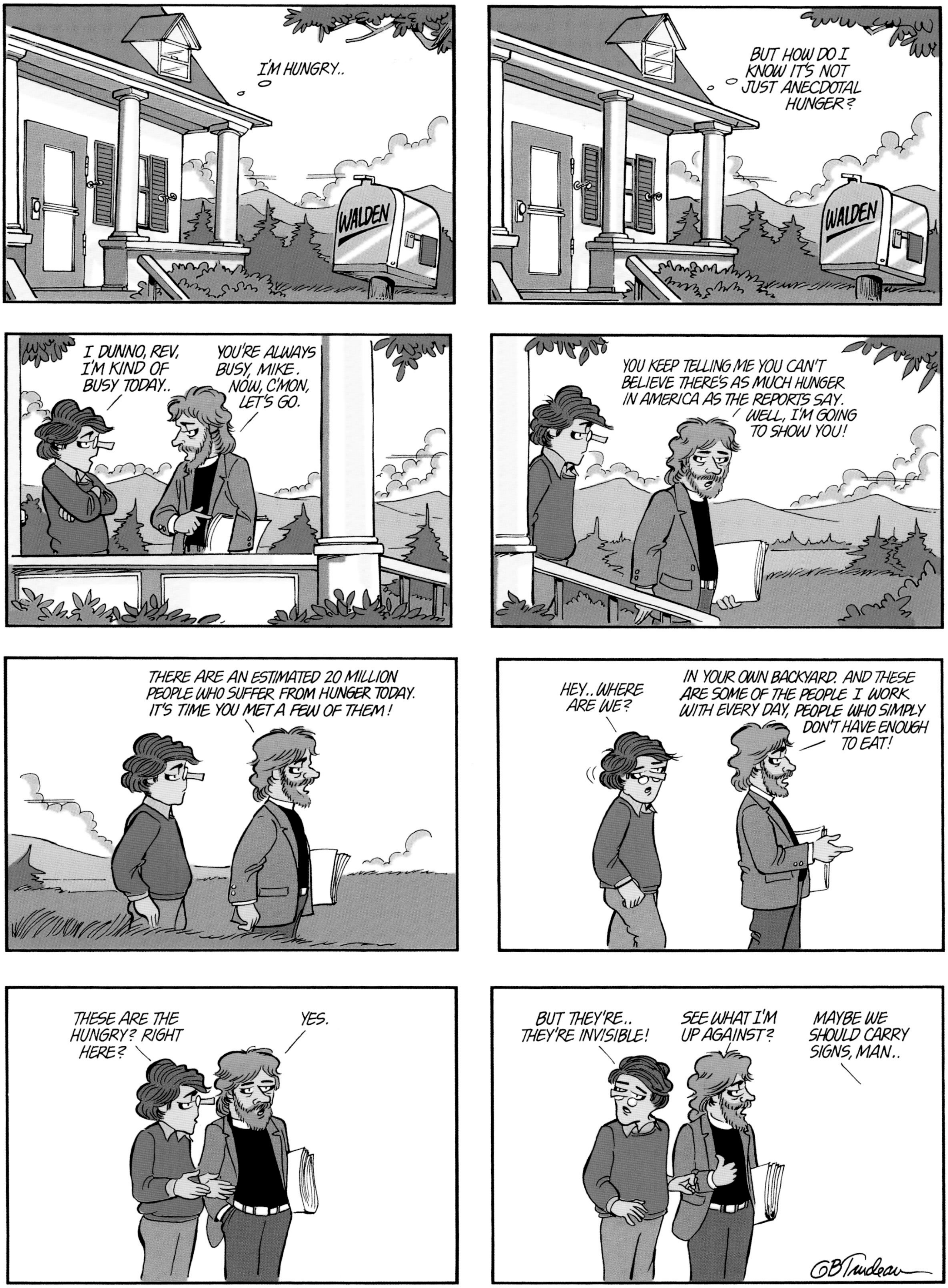
I'M HUNGRY..
BUT HOW DO I KNOW IT'S NOT JUST ANECDOTAL HUNGER?
WALDEN
I DUNNO, REV, I'M KIND OF BUSY TODAY..
YOU'RE ALWAYS BUSY, MIKE. NOW, C'MON, LET'S GO.
YOU KEEP TELLING ME YOU CAN'T BELIEVE THERE'S AS MUCH HUNGER IN AMERICA AS THE REPORTS SAY. WELL, I'M GOING TO SHOW YOU!
THERE ARE AN ESTIMATED 20 MILLION PEOPLE WHO SUFFER FROM HUNGER TODAY. IT'S TIME YOU MET A FEW OF THEM!
HEY.. WHERE ARE WE?
IN YOUR OWN BACKYARD. AND THESE ARE SOME OF THE PEOPLE I WORK WITH EVERY DAY, PEOPLE WHO SIMPLY DON'T HAVE ENOUGH TO EAT!
THESE ARE THE HUNGRY? RIGHT HERE?
YES.
BUT THEY'RE.. THEY'RE INVISIBLE!
SEE WHAT I'M UP AGAINST?
MAYBE WE SHOULD CARRY SIGNS, MAN..
©B Trudeau

4/28/85

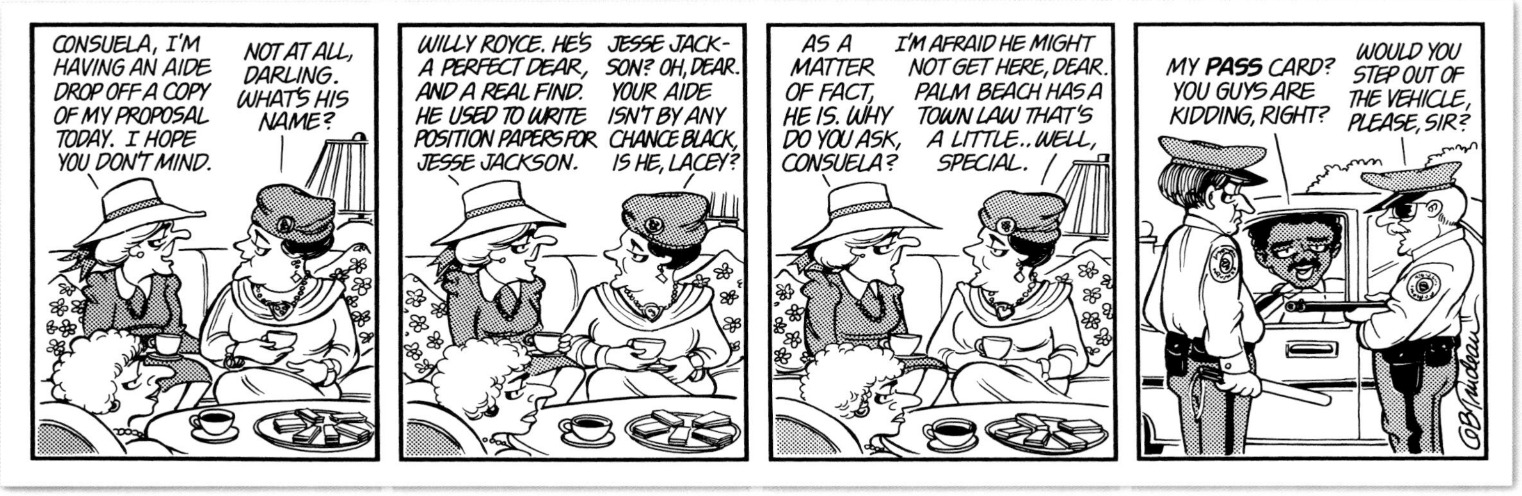
CONSUELA, I'M HAVING AN AIDE DROP OFF A COPY OF MY PROPOSAL TODAY. I HOPE YOU DON'T MIND.
NOT AT ALL, DARLING. WHAT'S HIS NAME?
WILLY ROYCE. HE'S A PERFECT DEAR, AND A REAL FIND. HE USED TO WRITE POSITION PAPERS FOR JESSE JACKSON.
JESSE JACKSON? OH, DEAR. YOUR AIDE ISN'T BY ANY CHANCE BLACK, IS HE, LACEY?
AS A MATTER OF FACT, HE IS. WHY DO YOU ASK, CONSUELA?
I'M AFRAID HE MIGHT NOT GET HERE, DEAR. PALM BEACH HAS A TOWN LAW THAT'S A LITTLE.. WELL, SPECIAL.
MY **PASS** CARD? YOU GUYS ARE KIDDING, RIGHT?
WOULD YOU STEP OUT OF THE VEHICLE, PLEASE, SIR?
GBTrudeau

6/21/85

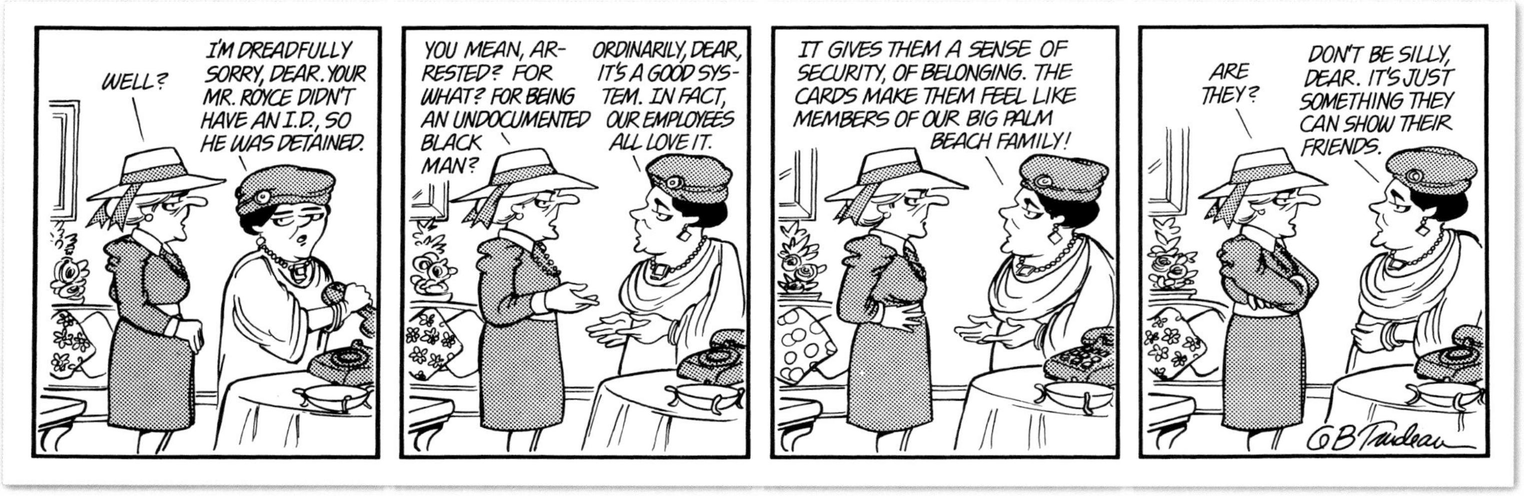
WELL?
I'M DREADFULLY SORRY, DEAR. YOUR MR. ROYCE DIDN'T HAVE AN I.D., SO HE WAS DETAINED.
YOU MEAN, ARRESTED? FOR WHAT? FOR BEING AN UNDOCUMENTED BLACK MAN?
ORDINARILY, DEAR, IT'S A GOOD SYSTEM. IN FACT, OUR EMPLOYEES ALL LOVE IT.
IT GIVES THEM A SENSE OF SECURITY, OF BELONGING. THE CARDS MAKE THEM FEEL LIKE MEMBERS OF OUR BIG PALM BEACH FAMILY!
ARE THEY?
DON'T BE SILLY, DEAR. IT'S JUST SOMETHING THEY CAN SHOW THEIR FRIENDS.
GBTrudeau

6/24/85

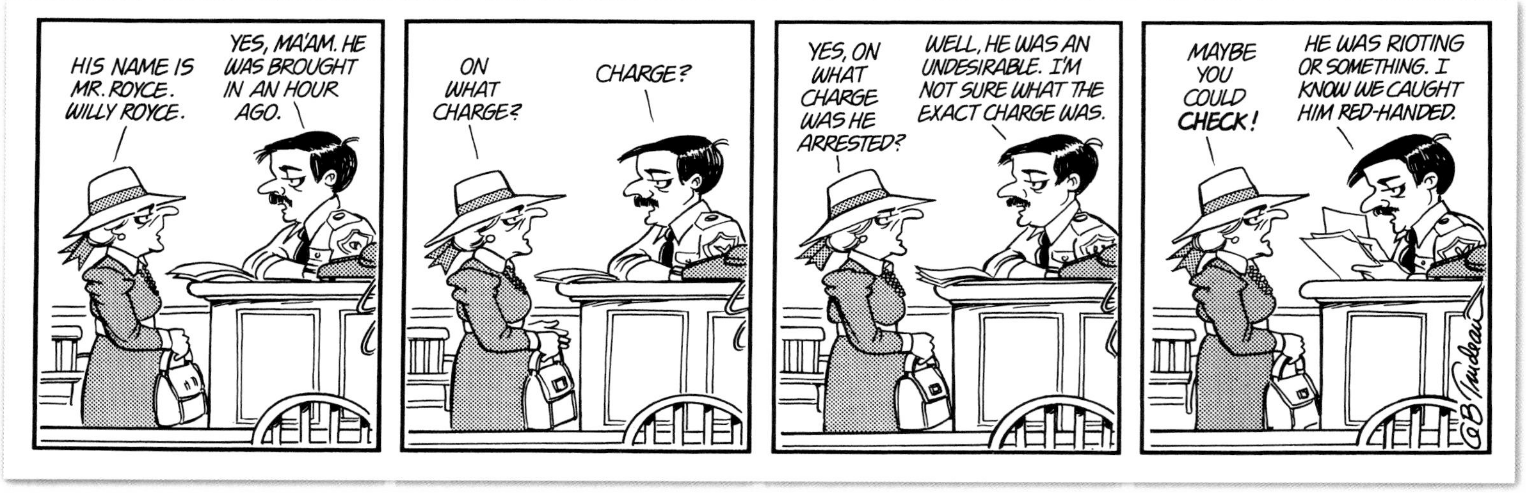
HIS NAME IS MR. ROYCE. WILLY ROYCE.
YES, MA'AM. HE WAS BROUGHT IN AN HOUR AGO.
ON WHAT CHARGE?
CHARGE?
YES, ON WHAT CHARGE WAS HE ARRESTED?
WELL, HE WAS AN UNDESIRABLE. I'M NOT SURE WHAT THE EXACT CHARGE WAS.
MAYBE YOU COULD **CHECK**!
HE WAS RIOTING OR SOMETHING. I KNOW WE CAUGHT HIM RED-HANDED.
GBTrudeau

6/26/85

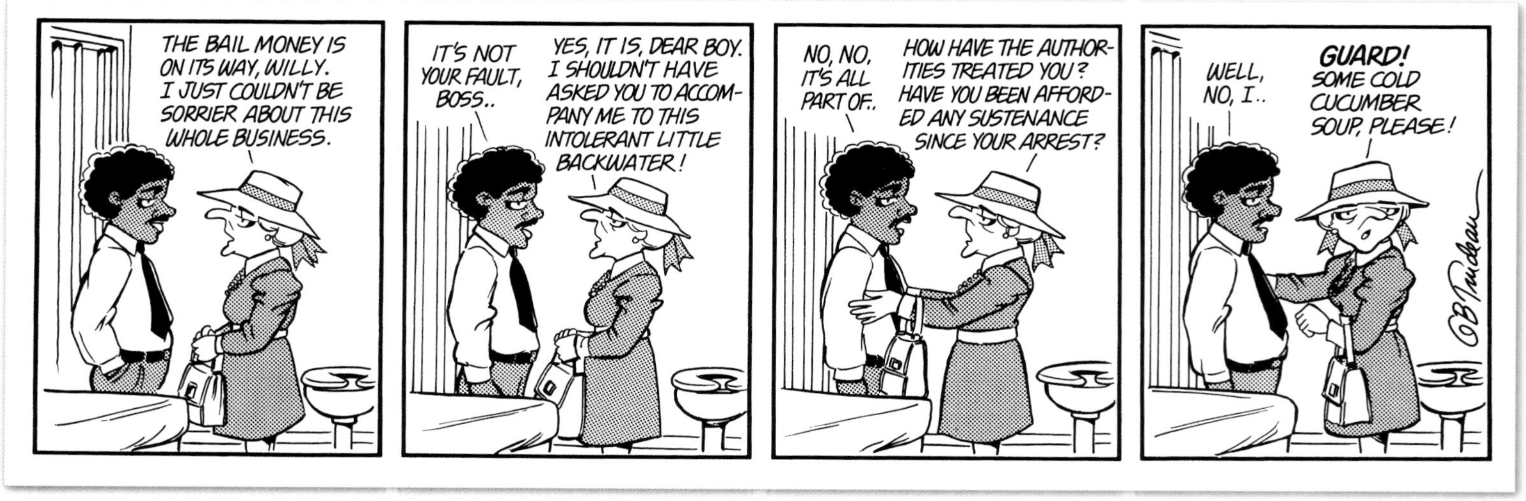
THE BAIL MONEY IS ON ITS WAY, WILLY. I JUST COULDN'T BE SORRIER ABOUT THIS WHOLE BUSINESS.
IT'S NOT YOUR FAULT, BOSS..
YES, IT IS, DEAR BOY. I SHOULDN'T HAVE ASKED YOU TO ACCOMPANY ME TO THIS INTOLERANT LITTLE BACKWATER!
NO, NO, IT'S ALL PART OF..
HOW HAVE THE AUTHORITIES TREATED YOU? HAVE YOU BEEN AFFORDED ANY SUSTENANCE SINCE YOUR ARREST?
WELL, NO, I..
GUARD! SOME COLD CUCUMBER SOUP, PLEASE!
GBTrudeau

6/28/85

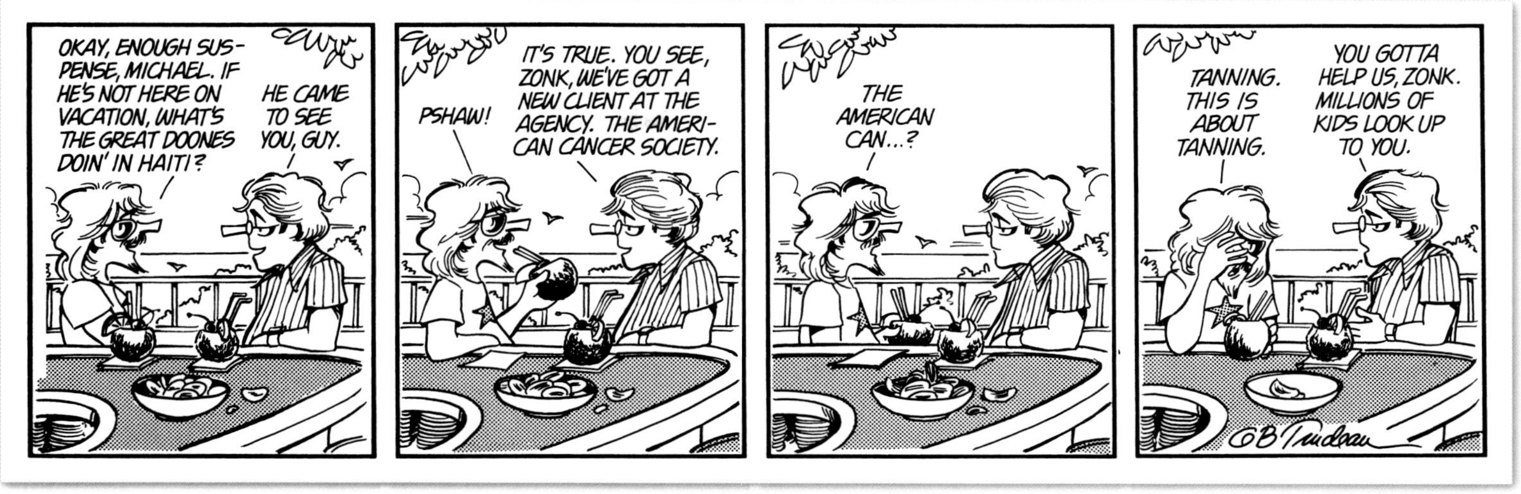
OKAY, ENOUGH SUSPENSE, MICHAEL. IF HE'S NOT HERE ON VACATION, WHAT'S THE GREAT DOONES DOIN' IN HAITI?
HE CAME TO SEE YOU, GUY.
PSHAW!
IT'S TRUE. YOU SEE, ZONK, WE'VE GOT A NEW CLIENT AT THE AGENCY. THE AMERICAN CANCER SOCIETY.
THE AMERICAN CAN...?
TANNING. THIS IS ABOUT TANNING.
YOU GOTTA HELP US, ZONK. MILLIONS OF KIDS LOOK UP TO YOU.
GBTrudeau

7/1/85

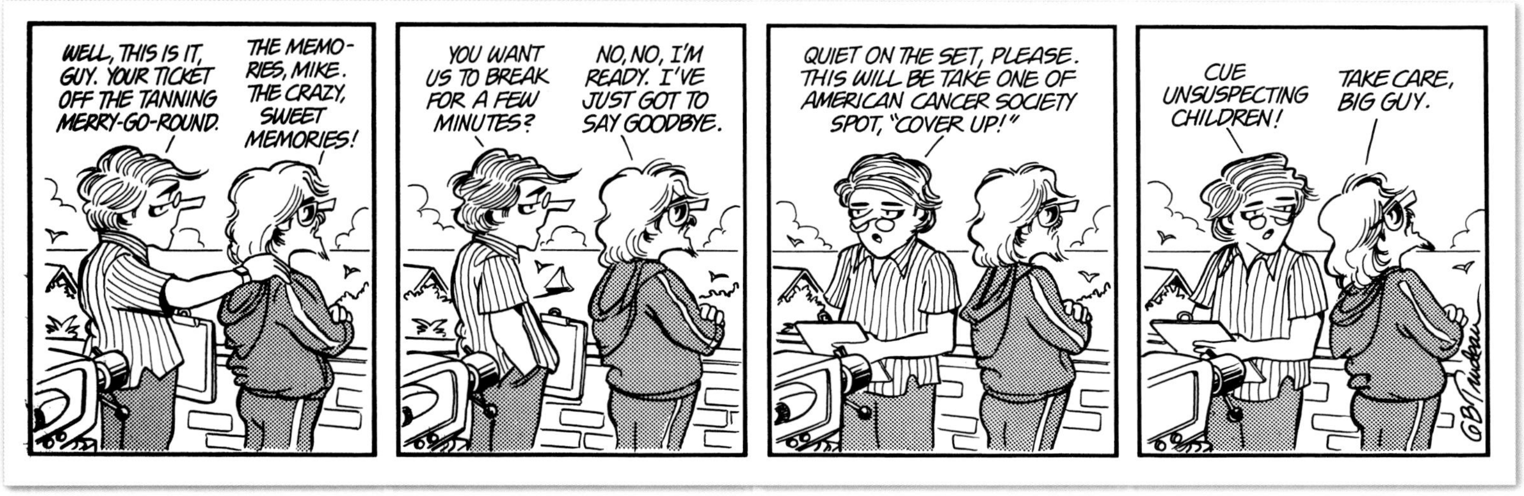
WELL, THIS IS IT, GUY. YOUR TICKET OFF THE TANNING MERRY-GO-ROUND.
THE MEMORIES, MIKE. THE CRAZY, SWEET MEMORIES!
YOU WANT US TO BREAK FOR A FEW MINUTES?
NO, NO, I'M READY. I'VE JUST GOT TO SAY GOODBYE.
QUIET ON THE SET, PLEASE. THIS WILL BE TAKE ONE OF AMERICAN CANCER SOCIETY SPOT, "COVER UP!"
CUE UNSUSPECTING CHILDREN!
TAKE CARE, BIG GUY.
GBTrudeau

7/3/85

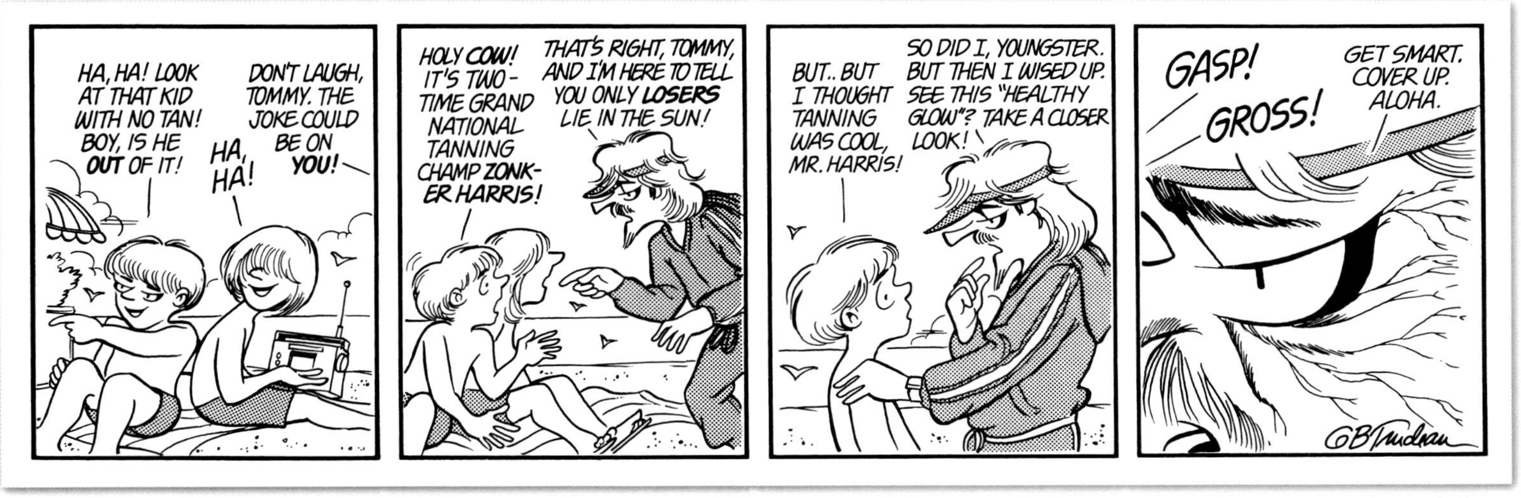
HA, HA! LOOK AT THAT KID WITH NO TAN! BOY, IS HE OUT OF IT!
HA, HA!
DON'T LAUGH, TOMMY. THE JOKE COULD BE ON YOU!
HOLY COW! IT'S TWO-TIME GRAND NATIONAL TANNING CHAMP ZONKER HARRIS!
THAT'S RIGHT, TOMMY, AND I'M HERE TO TELL YOU ONLY LOSERS LIE IN THE SUN!
BUT.. BUT I THOUGHT TANNING WAS COOL, MR. HARRIS!
SO DID I, YOUNGSTER. BUT THEN I WISED UP. SEE THIS "HEALTHY GLOW"? TAKE A CLOSER LOOK!
GASP!
GROSS!
GET SMART. COVER UP. ALOHA.
GBTrudeau

7/4/85

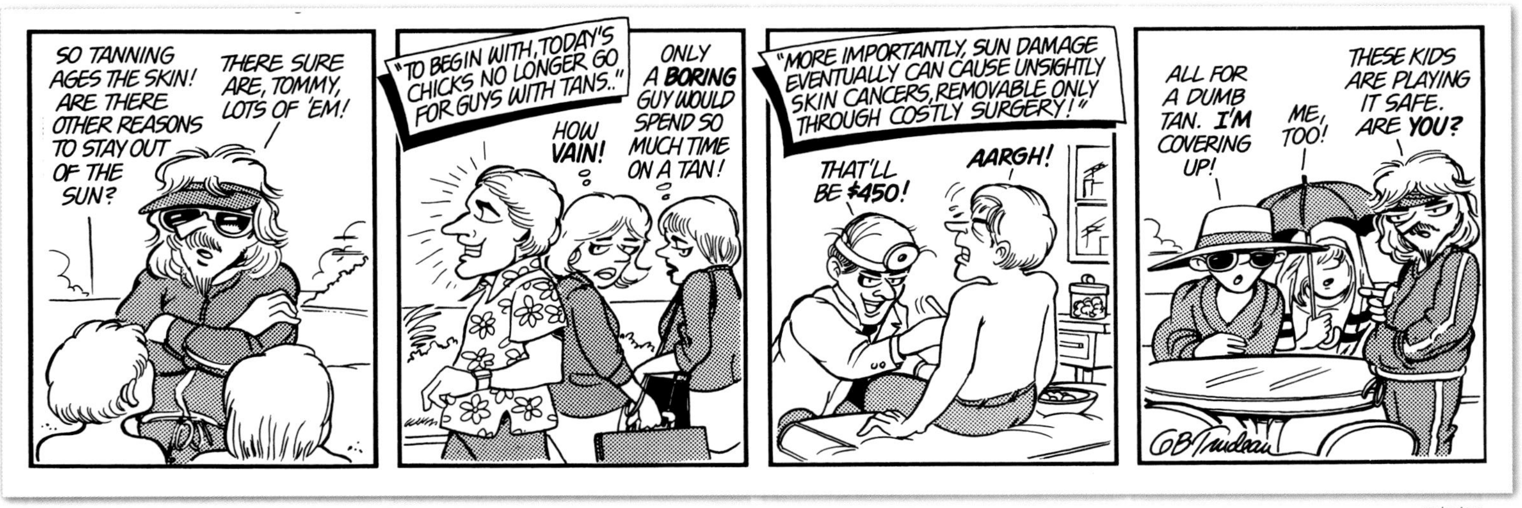
SO TANNING AGES THE SKIN! ARE THERE OTHER REASONS TO STAY OUT OF THE SUN?
THERE SURE ARE, TOMMY, LOTS OF 'EM!
"TO BEGIN WITH, TODAY'S CHICKS NO LONGER GO FOR GUYS WITH TANS.."
HOW VAIN!
ONLY A BORING GUY WOULD SPEND SO MUCH TIME ON A TAN!
"MORE IMPORTANTLY, SUN DAMAGE EVENTUALLY CAN CAUSE UNSIGHTLY SKIN CANCERS, REMOVABLE ONLY THROUGH COSTLY SURGERY!"
THAT'LL BE $450!
AARGH!
ALL FOR A DUMB TAN. I'M COVERING UP!
ME, TOO!
THESE KIDS ARE PLAYING IT SAFE. ARE YOU?
GBTrudeau

7/5/85

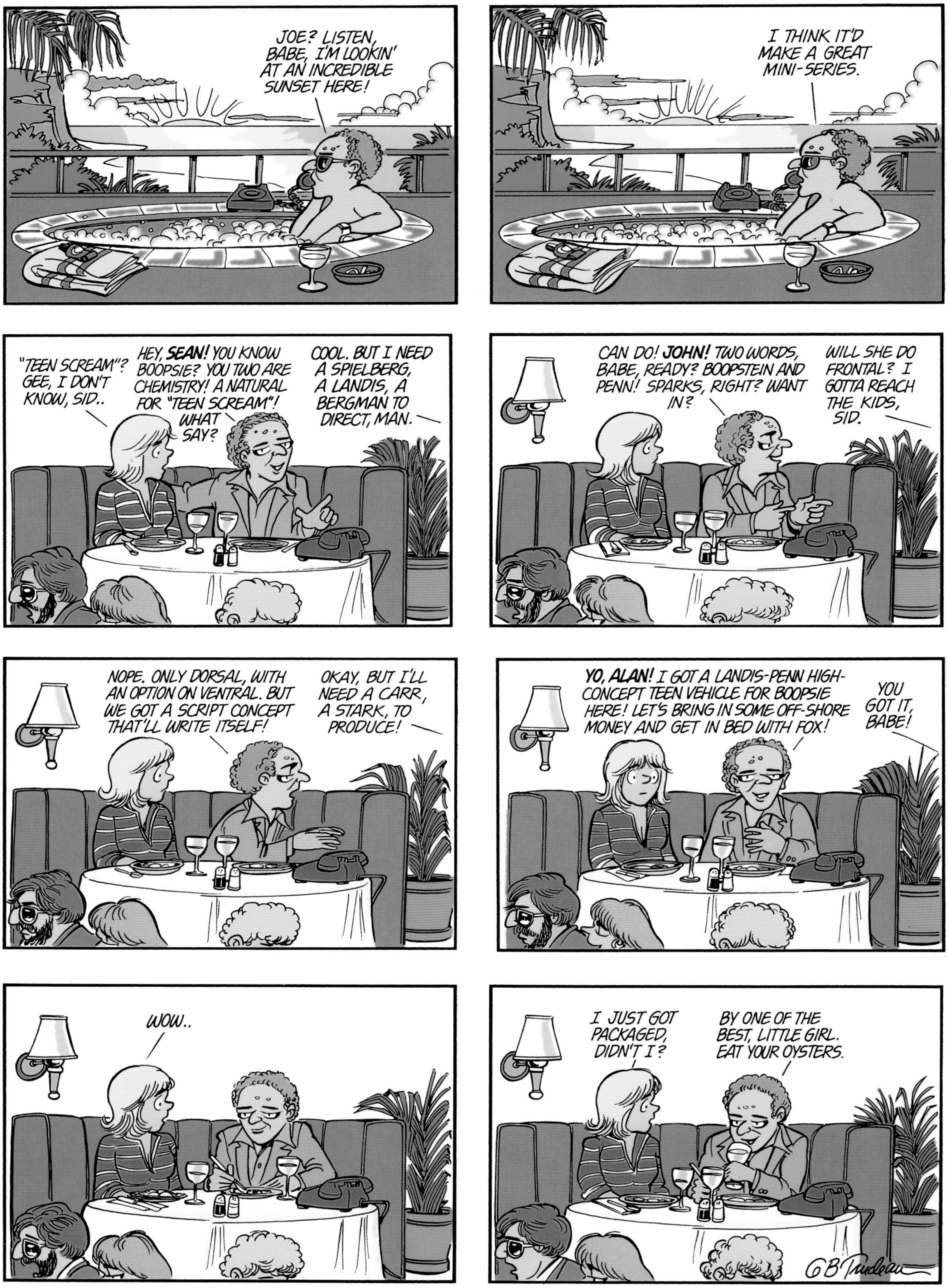
JOE? LISTEN, BABE, I'M LOOKIN' AT AN INCREDIBLE SUNSET HERE!
I THINK IT'D MAKE A GREAT MINI-SERIES.
"TEEN SCREAM"? GEE, I DON'T KNOW, SID..
HEY, SEAN! YOU KNOW BOOPSIE? YOU TWO ARE CHEMISTRY! A NATURAL FOR "TEEN SCREAM"! WHAT SAY?
COOL. BUT I NEED A SPIELBERG, A LANDIS, A BERGMAN TO DIRECT, MAN.
CAN DO! JOHN! TWO WORDS, BABE, READY? BOOPSTEIN AND PENN! SPARKS, RIGHT? WANT IN?
WILL SHE DO FRONTAL? I GOTTA REACH THE KIDS, SID.
NOPE. ONLY DORSAL, WITH AN OPTION ON VENTRAL. BUT WE GOT A SCRIPT CONCEPT THAT'LL WRITE ITSELF!
OKAY, BUT I'LL NEED A CARR, A STARK, TO PRODUCE!
YO, ALAN! I GOT A LANDIS-PENN HIGH-CONCEPT TEEN VEHICLE FOR BOOPSIE HERE! LET'S BRING IN SOME OFF-SHORE MONEY AND GET IN BED WITH FOX!
YOU GOT IT, BABE!
WOW..
I JUST GOT PACKAGED, DIDN'T I?
BY ONE OF THE BEST, LITTLE GIRL. EAT YOUR OYSTERS.
GB Trudeau

4/14/85

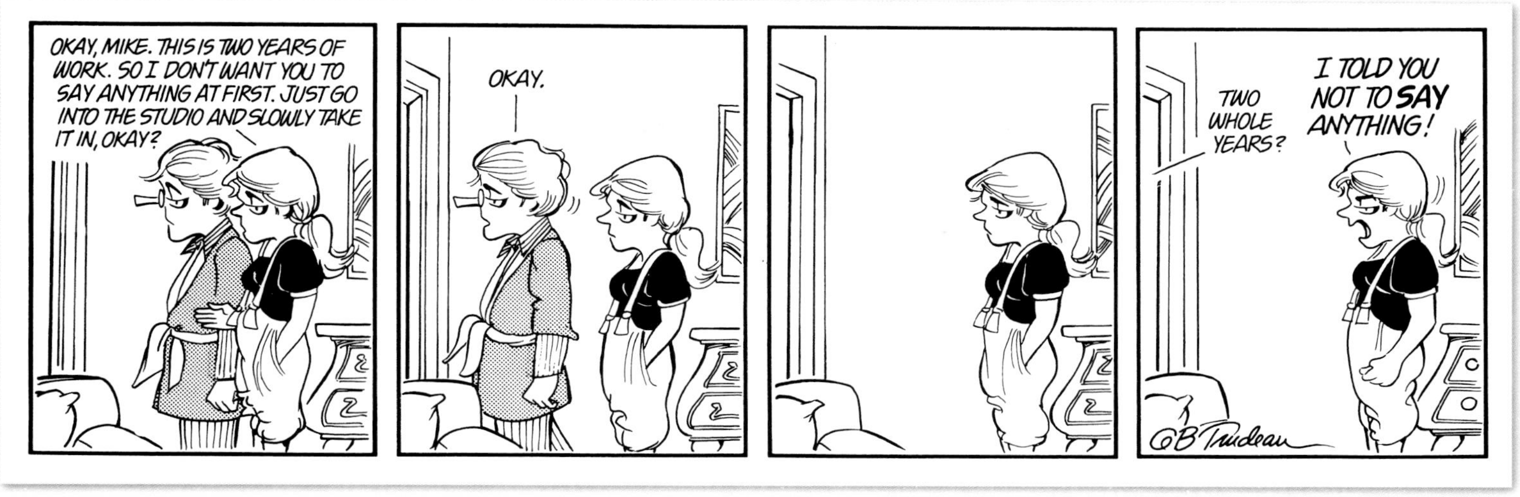
OKAY, MIKE. THIS IS TWO YEARS OF WORK. SO I DON'T WANT YOU TO SAY ANYTHING AT FIRST. JUST GO INTO THE STUDIO AND SLOWLY TAKE IT IN, OKAY?
OKAY.
TWO WHOLE YEARS?
I TOLD YOU NOT TO SAY ANYTHING!

8/27/85

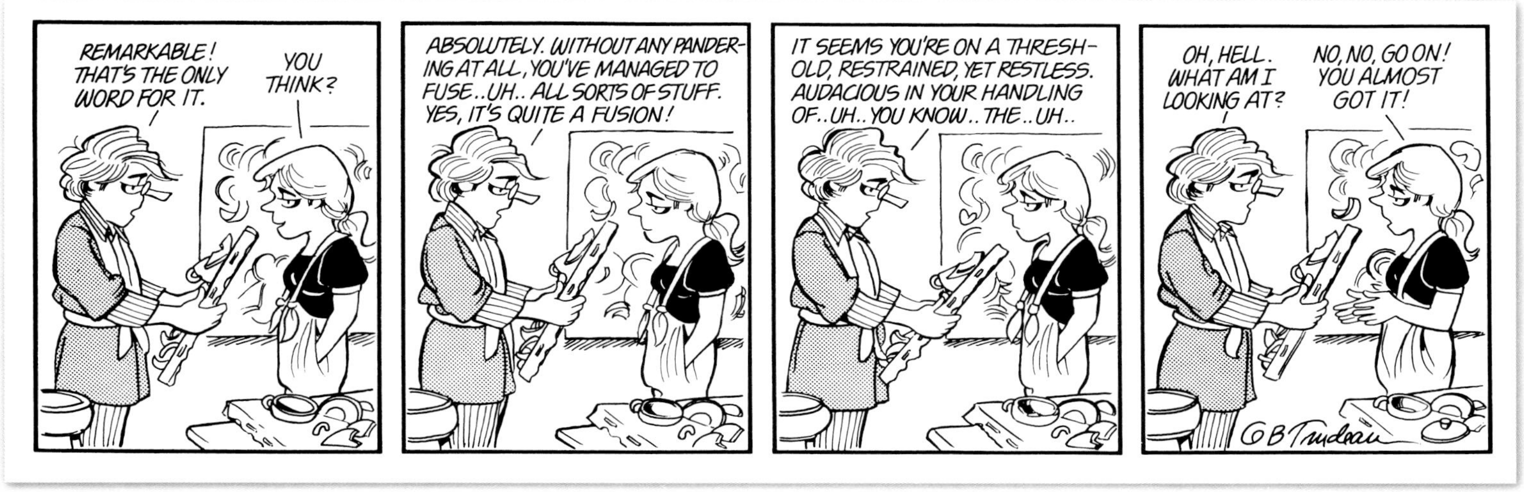
REMARKABLE! THAT'S THE ONLY WORD FOR IT.
YOU THINK?
ABSOLUTELY. WITHOUT ANY PANDERING AT ALL, YOU'VE MANAGED TO FUSE..UH.. ALL SORTS OF STUFF. YES, IT'S QUITE A FUSION!
IT SEEMS YOU'RE ON A THRESHOLD, RESTRAINED, YET RESTLESS. AUDACIOUS IN YOUR HANDLING OF..UH.. YOU KNOW.. THE..UH..
OH, HELL. WHAT AM I LOOKING AT?
NO, NO, GO ON! YOU ALMOST GOT IT!

8/28/85

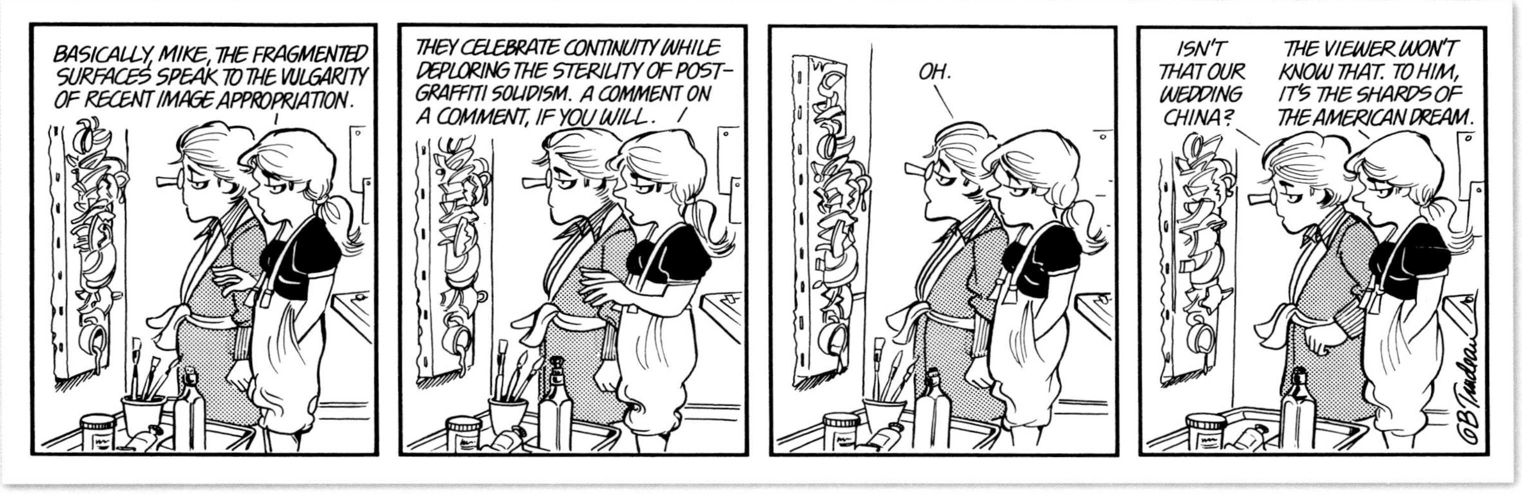
BASICALLY, MIKE, THE FRAGMENTED SURFACES SPEAK TO THE VULGARITY OF RECENT IMAGE APPROPRIATION.
THEY CELEBRATE CONTINUITY WHILE DEPLORING THE STERILITY OF POST-GRAFFITI SOLIDISM. A COMMENT ON A COMMENT, IF YOU WILL.
OH.
ISN'T THAT OUR WEDDING CHINA?
THE VIEWER WON'T KNOW THAT. TO HIM, IT'S THE SHARDS OF THE AMERICAN DREAM.

8/29/85

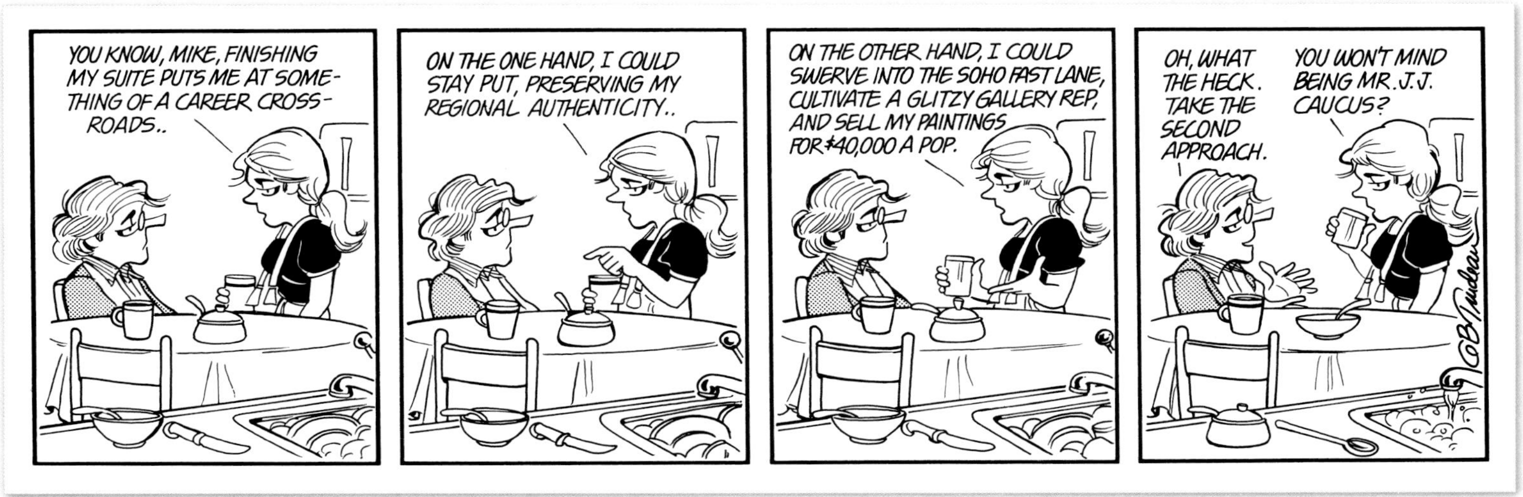
YOU KNOW, MIKE, FINISHING MY SUITE PUTS ME AT SOMETHING OF A CAREER CROSSROADS..
ON THE ONE HAND, I COULD STAY PUT, PRESERVING MY REGIONAL AUTHENTICITY..
ON THE OTHER HAND, I COULD SWERVE INTO THE SOHO FAST LANE, CULTIVATE A GLITZY GALLERY REP, AND SELL MY PAINTINGS FOR $40,000 A POP.
OH, WHAT THE HECK. TAKE THE SECOND APPROACH.
YOU WON'T MIND BEING MR. J.J. CAUCUS?

8/30/85

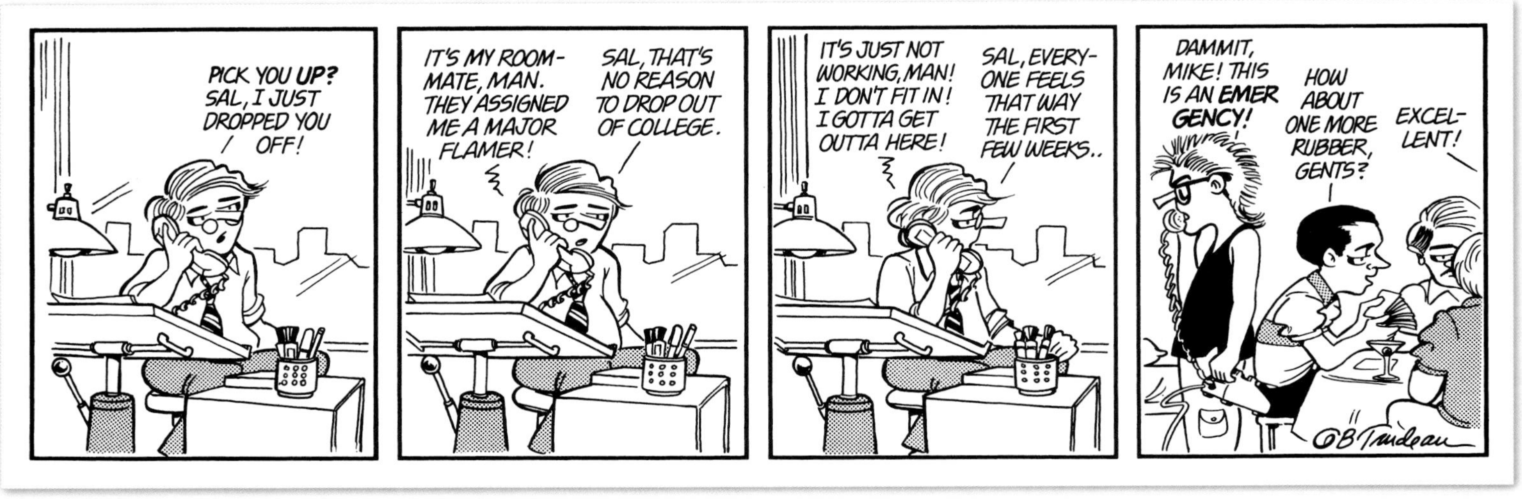
PICK YOU **UP?** SAL, I JUST DROPPED YOU OFF!
IT'S MY ROOMMATE, MAN. THEY ASSIGNED ME A MAJOR FLAMER!
SAL, THAT'S NO REASON TO DROP OUT OF COLLEGE.
IT'S JUST NOT WORKING, MAN! I DON'T FIT IN! I GOTTA GET OUTTA HERE!
SAL, EVERYONE FEELS THAT WAY THE FIRST FEW WEEKS..
DAMMIT, MIKE! THIS IS AN **EMERGENCY!**
HOW ABOUT ONE MORE RUBBER, GENTS?
EXCELLENT!
©B Trudeau

9/23/85

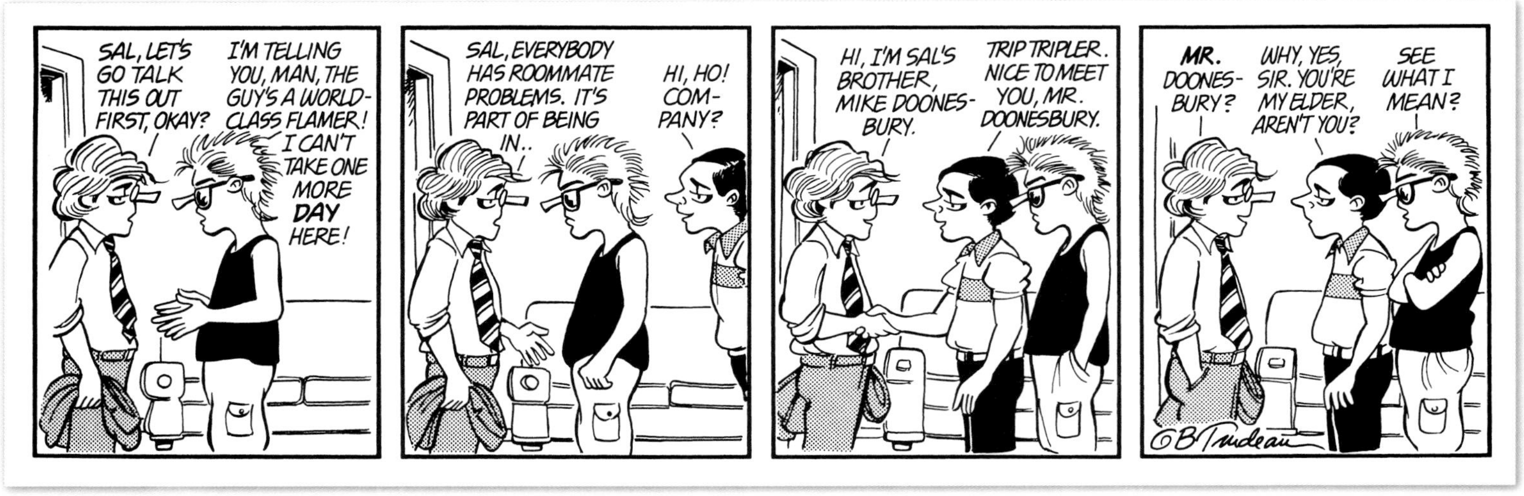
SAL, LET'S GO TALK THIS OUT FIRST, OKAY?
I'M TELLING YOU, MAN, THE GUY'S A WORLD-CLASS FLAMER! I CAN'T TAKE ONE MORE **DAY** HERE!
SAL, EVERYBODY HAS ROOMMATE PROBLEMS. IT'S PART OF BEING IN..
HI, HO! COMPANY?
HI, I'M SAL'S BROTHER, MIKE DOONESBURY.
TRIP TRIPLER. NICE TO MEET YOU, MR. DOONESBURY.
MR. DOONESBURY?
WHY, YES, SIR. YOU'RE MY ELDER, AREN'T YOU?
SEE WHAT I MEAN?
©B Trudeau

9/24/85

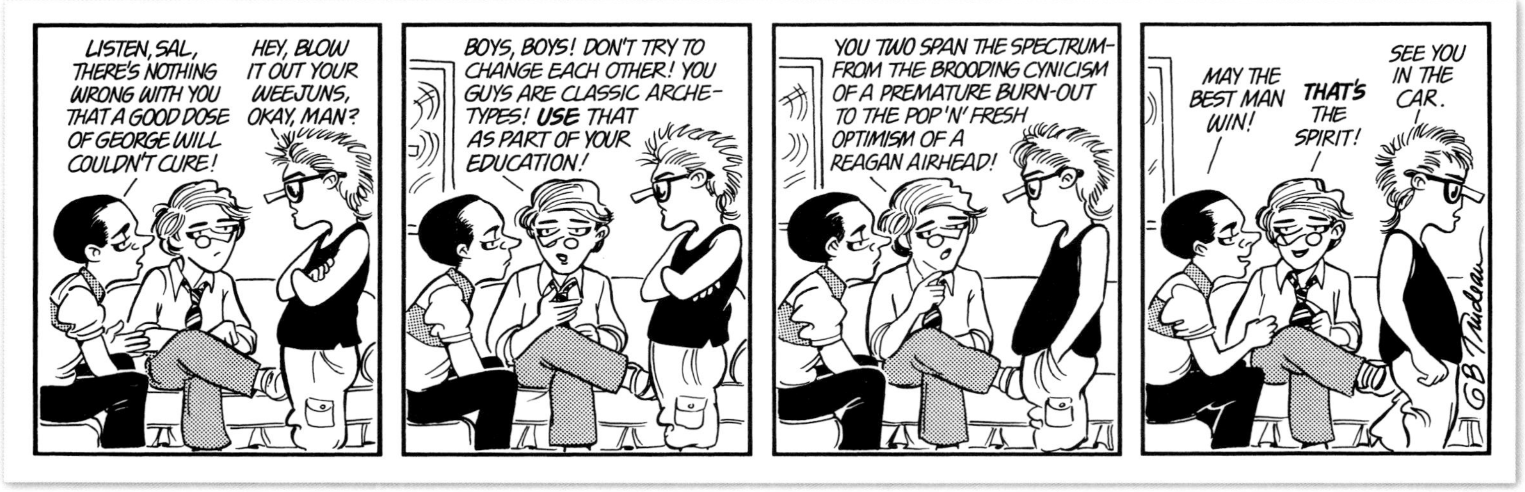
LISTEN, SAL, THERE'S NOTHING WRONG WITH YOU THAT A GOOD DOSE OF GEORGE WILL COULDN'T CURE!
HEY, BLOW IT OUT YOUR WEEJUNS, OKAY, MAN?
BOYS, BOYS! DON'T TRY TO CHANGE EACH OTHER! YOU GUYS ARE CLASSIC ARCHETYPES! **USE** THAT AS PART OF YOUR EDUCATION!
YOU TWO SPAN THE SPECTRUM–FROM THE BROODING CYNICISM OF A PREMATURE BURN-OUT TO THE POP 'N' FRESH OPTIMISM OF A REAGAN AIRHEAD!
MAY THE BEST MAN WIN!
THAT'S THE SPIRIT!
SEE YOU IN THE CAR.
©B Trudeau

9/26/85

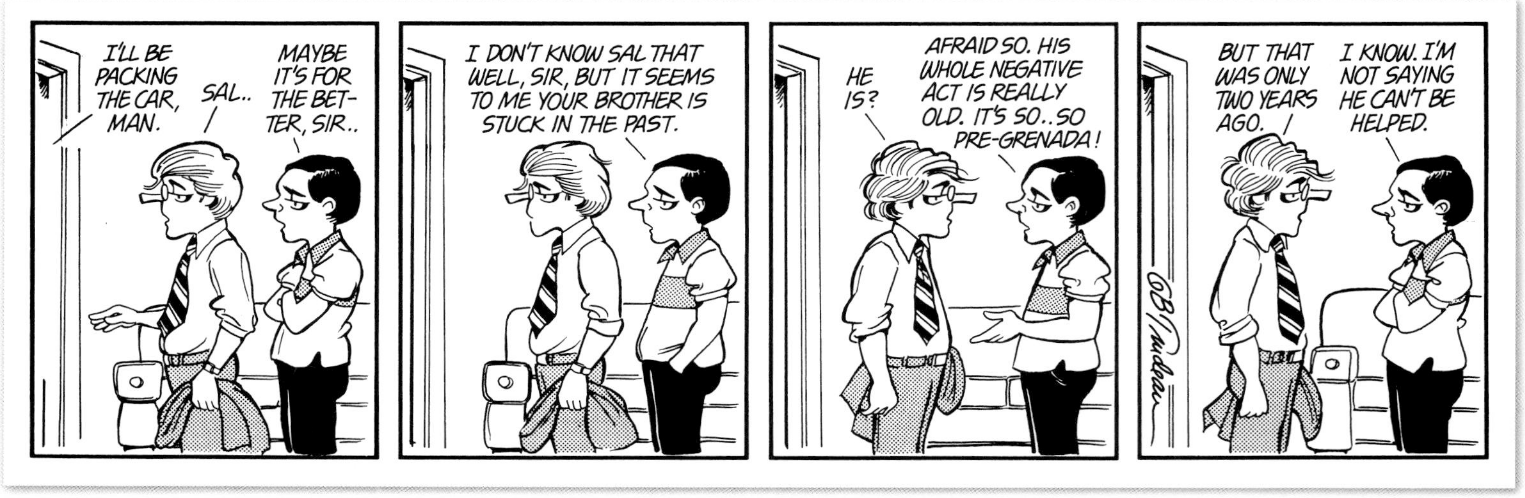
I'LL BE PACKING THE CAR, MAN.
SAL..
MAYBE IT'S FOR THE BETTER, SIR..
I DON'T KNOW SAL THAT WELL, SIR, BUT IT SEEMS TO ME YOUR BROTHER IS STUCK IN THE PAST.
HE IS?
AFRAID SO. HIS WHOLE NEGATIVE ACT IS REALLY OLD. IT'S SO..SO PRE-GRENADA!
BUT THAT WAS ONLY TWO YEARS AGO.
I KNOW. I'M NOT SAYING HE CAN'T BE HELPED.
©B Trudeau

9/27/85

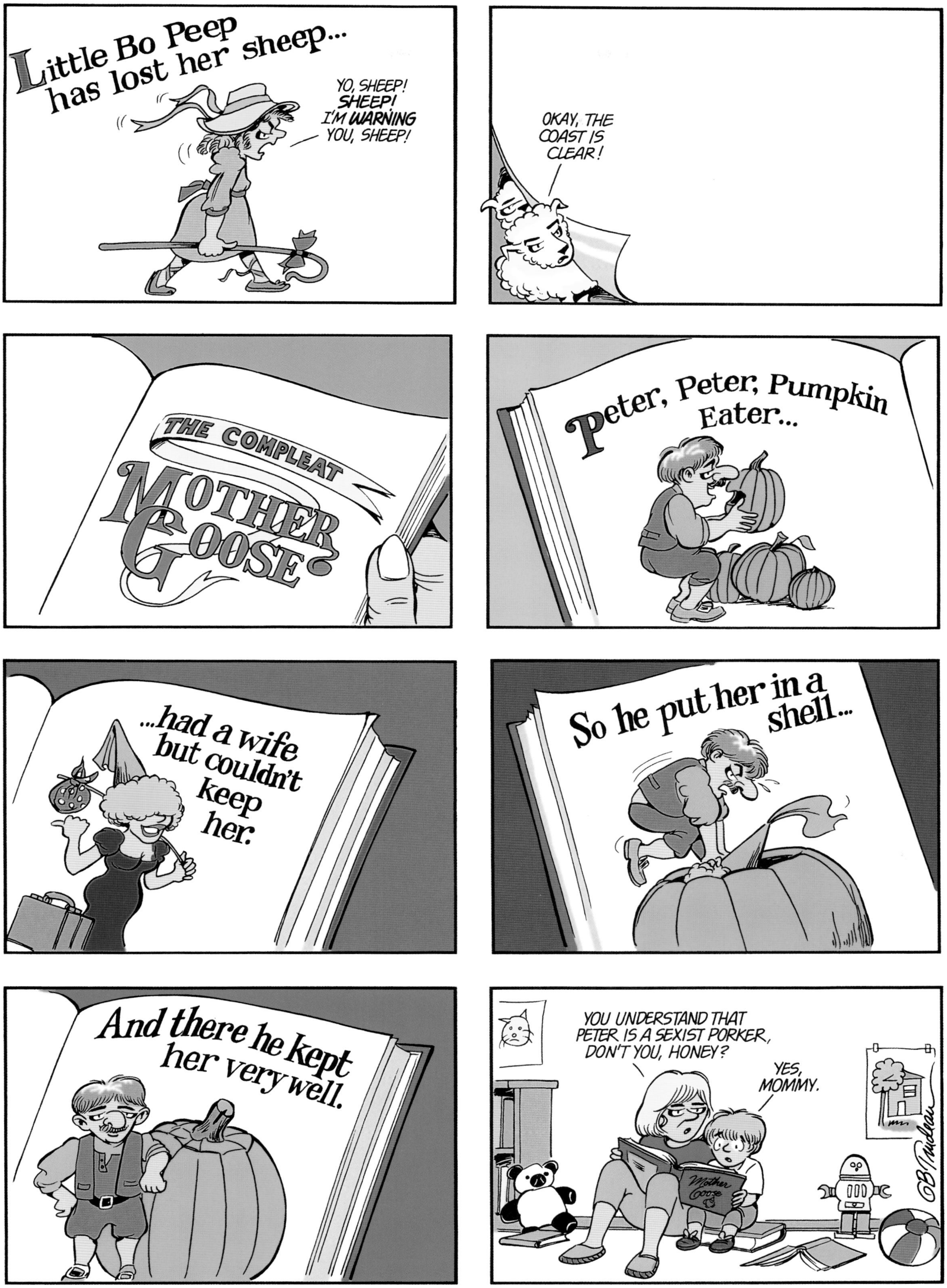
Little Bo Peep has lost her sheep...
YO, SHEEP! SHEEP! I'M WARNING YOU, SHEEP!
OKAY, THE COAST IS CLEAR!
THE COMPLEAT MOTHER GOOSE
Peter, Peter, Pumpkin Eater...
...had a wife but couldn't keep her.
So he put her in a shell...
And there he kept her very well.
YOU UNDERSTAND THAT PETER IS A SEXIST PORKER, DON'T YOU, HONEY?
YES, MOMMY.
Mother Goose
GBTrudeau

11/3/85

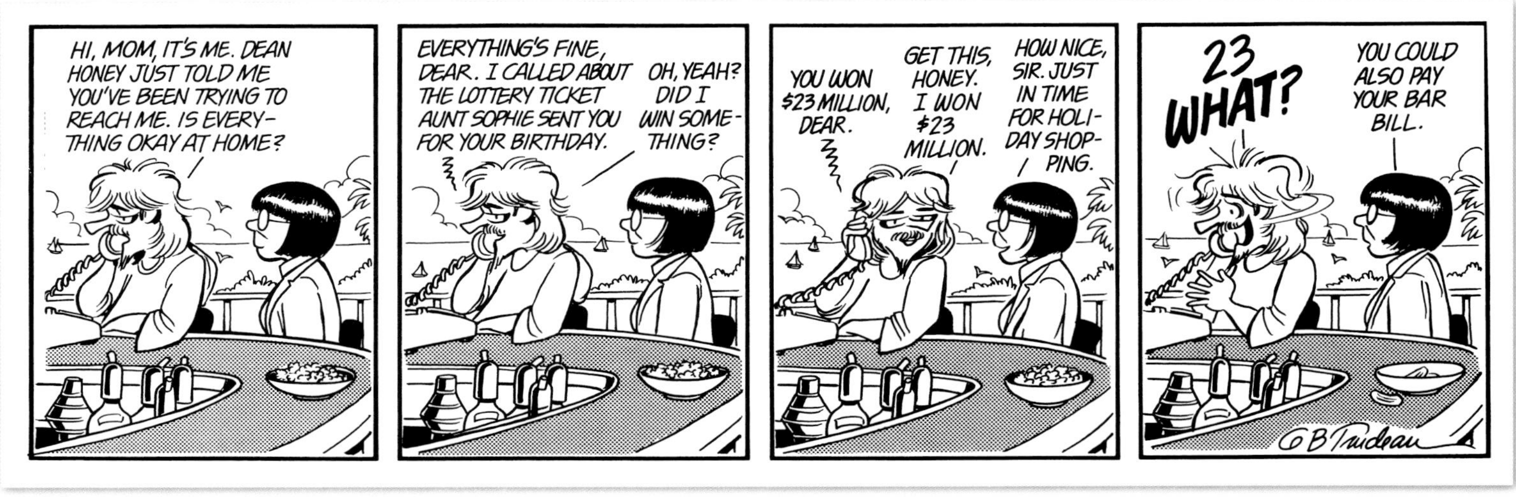
HI, MOM, IT'S ME. DEAN HONEY JUST TOLD ME YOU'VE BEEN TRYING TO REACH ME. IS EVERYTHING OKAY AT HOME?
EVERYTHING'S FINE, DEAR. I CALLED ABOUT THE LOTTERY TICKET AUNT SOPHIE SENT YOU FOR YOUR BIRTHDAY.
OH, YEAH? DID I WIN SOMETHING?
YOU WON $23 MILLION, DEAR.
GET THIS, HONEY. I WON $23 MILLION.
HOW NICE, SIR. JUST IN TIME FOR HOLIDAY SHOPPING.
23 WHAT?
YOU COULD ALSO PAY YOUR BAR BILL.
© B Trudeau

12/2/85

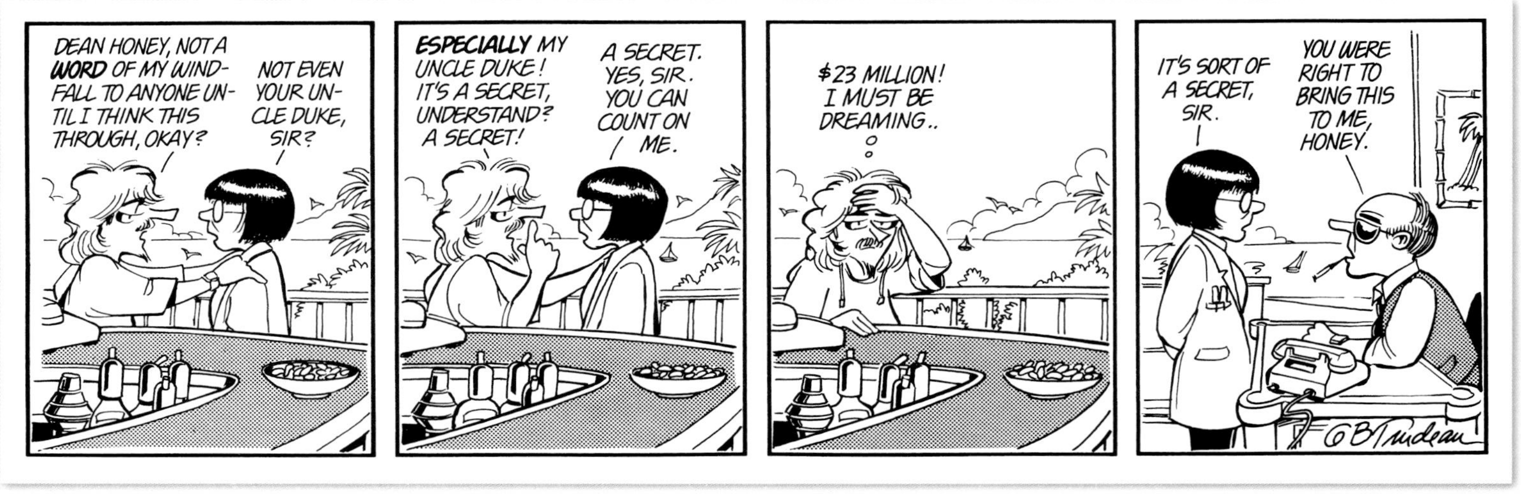
DEAN HONEY, NOT A WORD OF MY WINDFALL TO ANYONE UNTIL I THINK THIS THROUGH, OKAY?
NOT EVEN YOUR UNCLE DUKE, SIR?
ESPECIALLY MY UNCLE DUKE! IT'S A SECRET, UNDERSTAND? A SECRET!
A SECRET. YES, SIR. YOU CAN COUNT ON ME.
$23 MILLION! I MUST BE DREAMING..
IT'S SORT OF A SECRET, SIR.
YOU WERE RIGHT TO BRING THIS TO ME, HONEY.
© B Trudeau

12/4/85

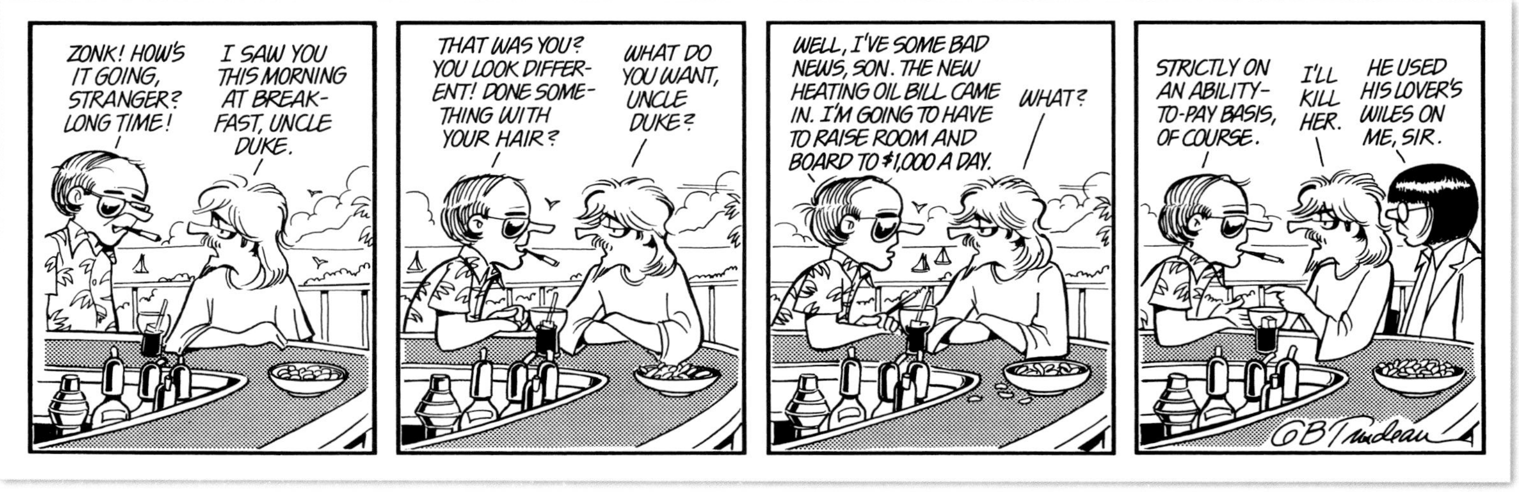
ZONK! HOW'S IT GOING, STRANGER? LONG TIME!
I SAW YOU THIS MORNING AT BREAKFAST, UNCLE DUKE.
THAT WAS YOU? YOU LOOK DIFFERENT! DONE SOMETHING WITH YOUR HAIR?
WHAT DO YOU WANT, UNCLE DUKE?
WELL, I'VE SOME BAD NEWS, SON. THE NEW HEATING OIL BILL CAME IN. I'M GOING TO HAVE TO RAISE ROOM AND BOARD TO $1,000 A DAY.
WHAT?
STRICTLY ON AN ABILITY-TO-PAY BASIS, OF COURSE.
I'LL KILL HER.
HE USED HIS LOVER'S WILES ON ME, SIR.
© B Trudeau

12/5/85

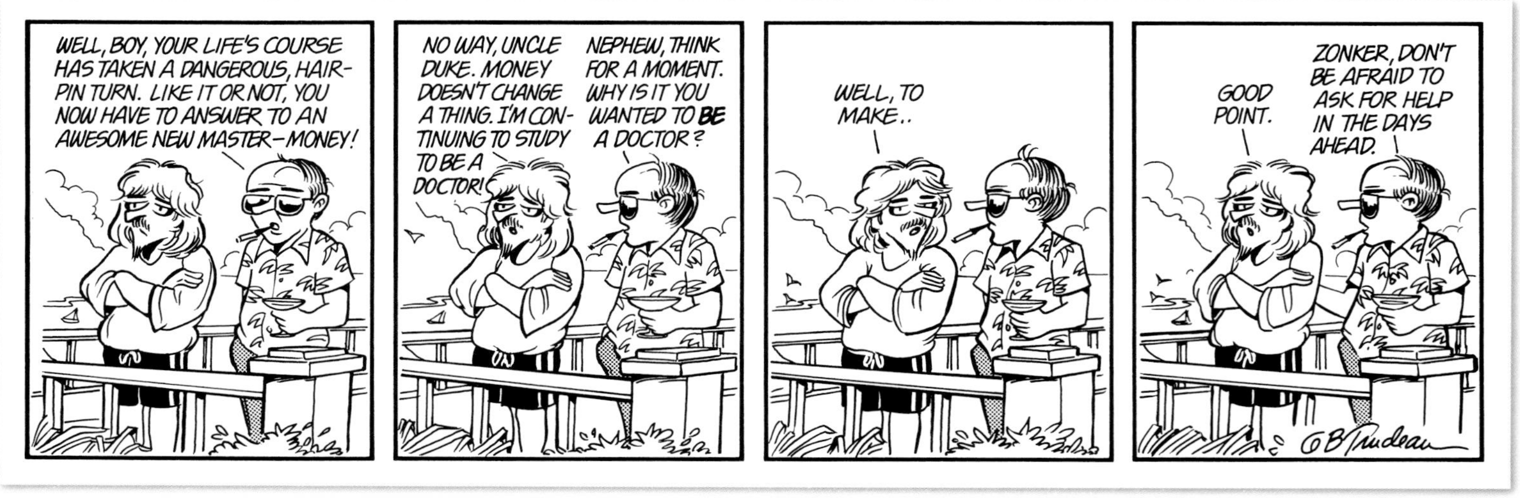
WELL, BOY, YOUR LIFE'S COURSE HAS TAKEN A DANGEROUS, HAIRPIN TURN. LIKE IT OR NOT, YOU NOW HAVE TO ANSWER TO AN AWESOME NEW MASTER—MONEY!
NO WAY, UNCLE DUKE. MONEY DOESN'T CHANGE A THING. I'M CONTINUING TO STUDY TO BE A DOCTOR!
NEPHEW, THINK FOR A MOMENT. WHY IS IT YOU WANTED TO BE A DOCTOR?
WELL, TO MAKE..
GOOD POINT.
ZONKER, DON'T BE AFRAID TO ASK FOR HELP IN THE DAYS AHEAD.
© B Trudeau

12/6/85

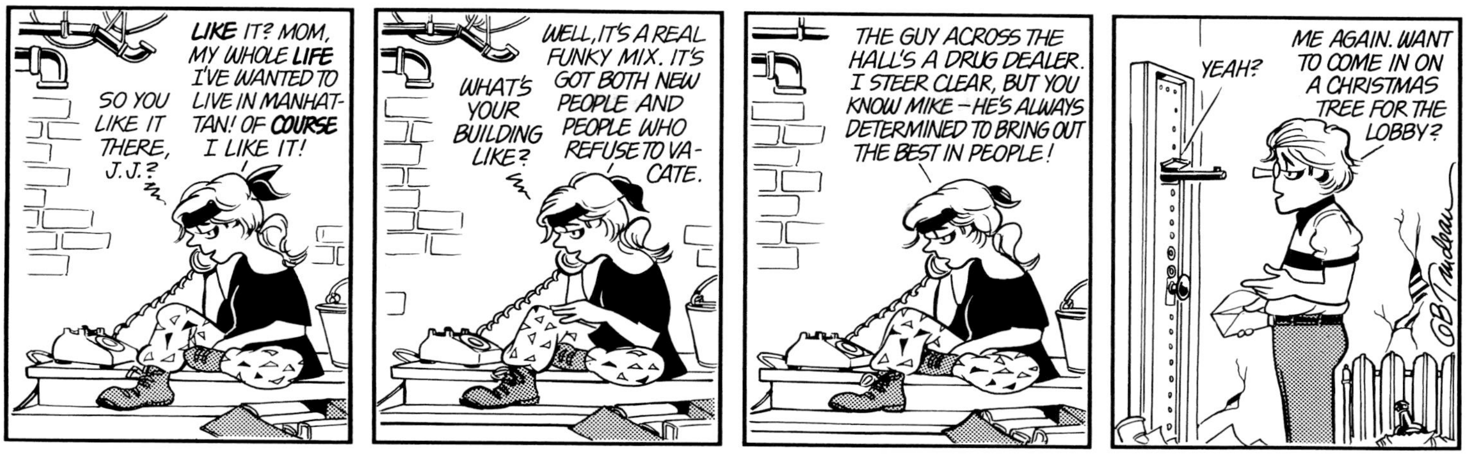
SO YOU LIKE IT THERE, J.J.?
LIKE IT? MOM, MY WHOLE LIFE I'VE WANTED TO LIVE IN MANHATTAN! OF COURSE I LIKE IT!
WHAT'S YOUR BUILDING LIKE?
WELL, IT'S A REAL FUNKY MIX. IT'S GOT BOTH NEW PEOPLE AND PEOPLE WHO REFUSE TO VACATE.
THE GUY ACROSS THE HALL'S A DRUG DEALER. I STEER CLEAR, BUT YOU KNOW MIKE – HE'S ALWAYS DETERMINED TO BRING OUT THE BEST IN PEOPLE!
YEAH?
ME AGAIN. WANT TO COME IN ON A CHRISTMAS TREE FOR THE LOBBY?
GB Trudeau

12/10/85

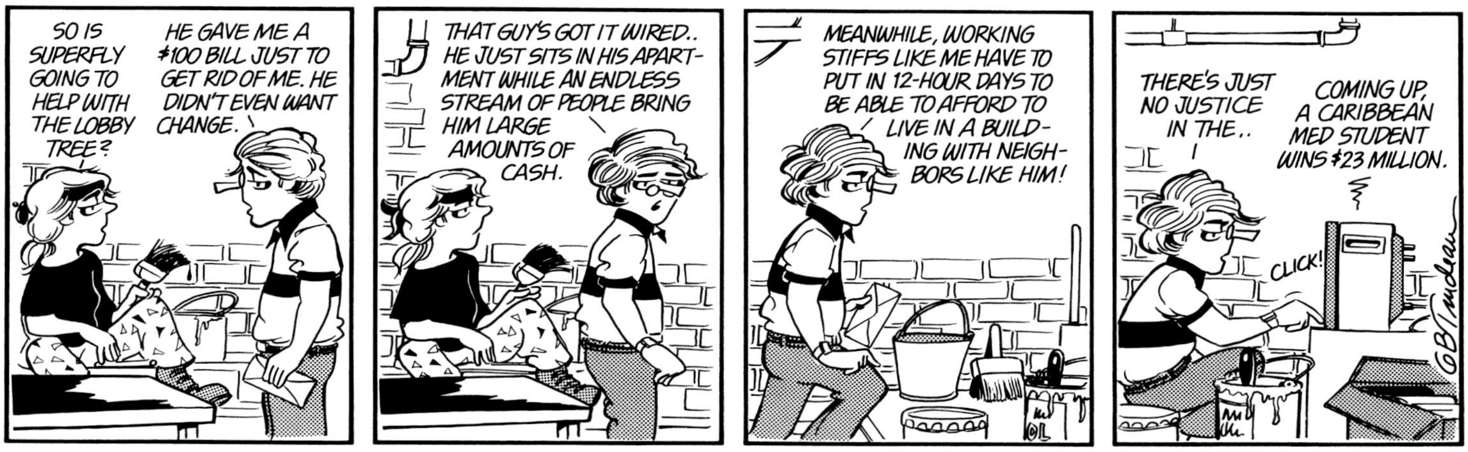
SO IS SUPERFLY GOING TO HELP WITH THE LOBBY TREE?
HE GAVE ME A $100 BILL JUST TO GET RID OF ME. HE DIDN'T EVEN WANT CHANGE.
THAT GUY'S GOT IT WIRED.. HE JUST SITS IN HIS APARTMENT WHILE AN ENDLESS STREAM OF PEOPLE BRING HIM LARGE AMOUNTS OF CASH.
MEANWHILE, WORKING STIFFS LIKE ME HAVE TO PUT IN 12-HOUR DAYS TO BE ABLE TO AFFORD TO LIVE IN A BUILDING WITH NEIGHBORS LIKE HIM!
THERE'S JUST NO JUSTICE IN THE..
COMING UP, A CARIBBEAN MED STUDENT WINS $23 MILLION.
CLICK!
GB Trudeau

12/11/85

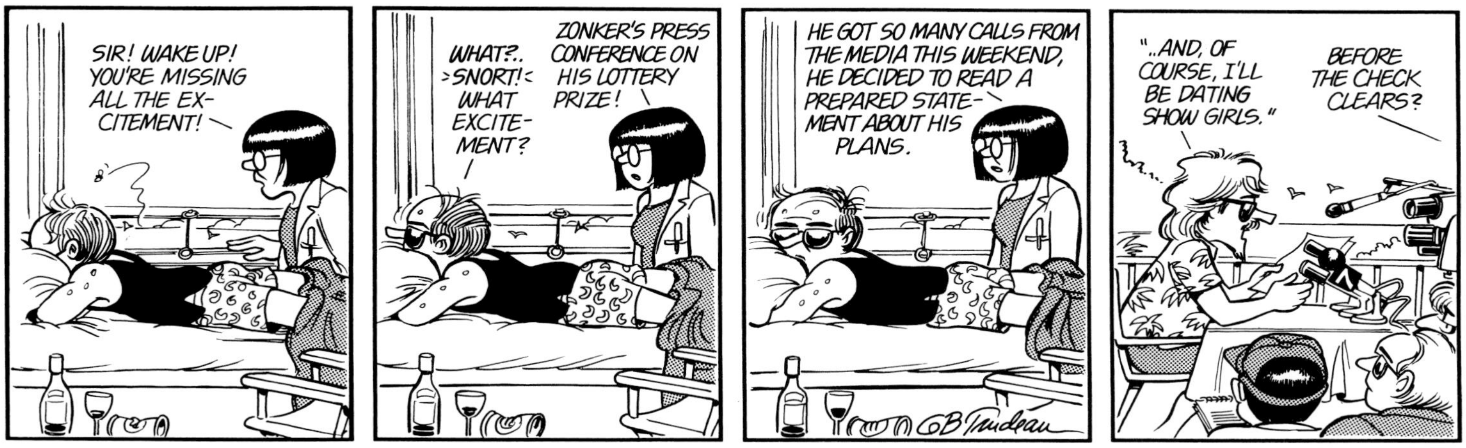
SIR! WAKE UP! YOU'RE MISSING ALL THE EXCITEMENT!
WHAT?.. >SNORT!< WHAT EXCITEMENT?
ZONKER'S PRESS CONFERENCE ON HIS LOTTERY PRIZE!
HE GOT SO MANY CALLS FROM THE MEDIA THIS WEEKEND, HE DECIDED TO READ A PREPARED STATEMENT ABOUT HIS PLANS.
GB Trudeau
"..AND, OF COURSE, I'LL BE DATING SHOW GIRLS."
BEFORE THE CHECK CLEARS?

12/12/85

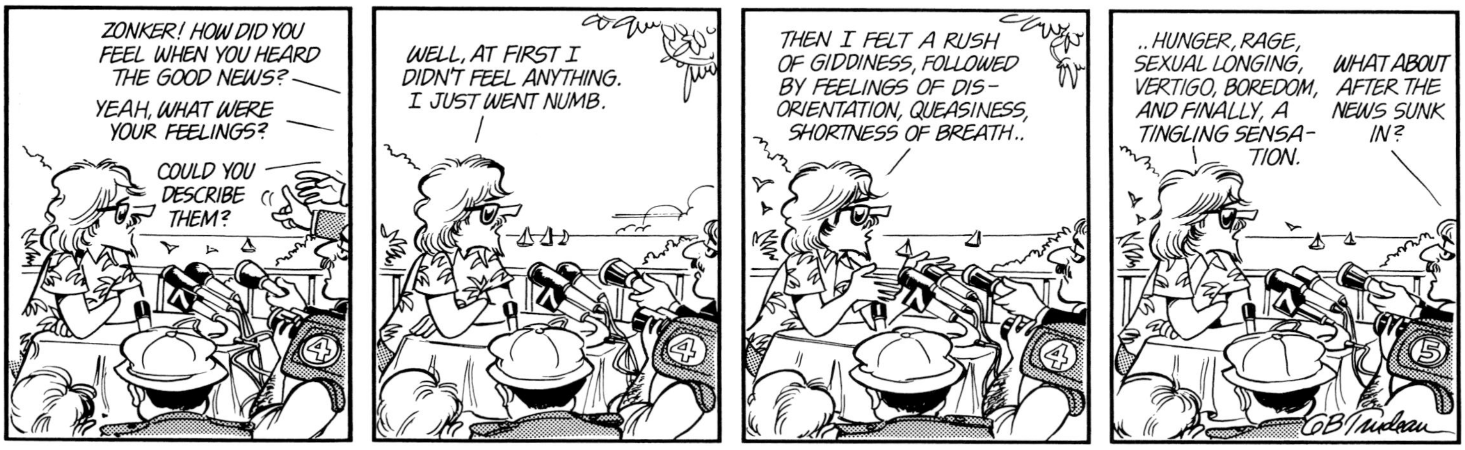
ZONKER! HOW DID YOU FEEL WHEN YOU HEARD THE GOOD NEWS?
YEAH, WHAT WERE YOUR FEELINGS?
COULD YOU DESCRIBE THEM?
WELL, AT FIRST I DIDN'T FEEL ANYTHING. I JUST WENT NUMB.
THEN I FELT A RUSH OF GIDDINESS, FOLLOWED BY FEELINGS OF DISORIENTATION, QUEASINESS, SHORTNESS OF BREATH..
..HUNGER, RAGE, SEXUAL LONGING, VERTIGO, BOREDOM, AND FINALLY, A TINGLING SENSATION.
WHAT ABOUT AFTER THE NEWS SUNK IN?
GB Trudeau

12/13/85

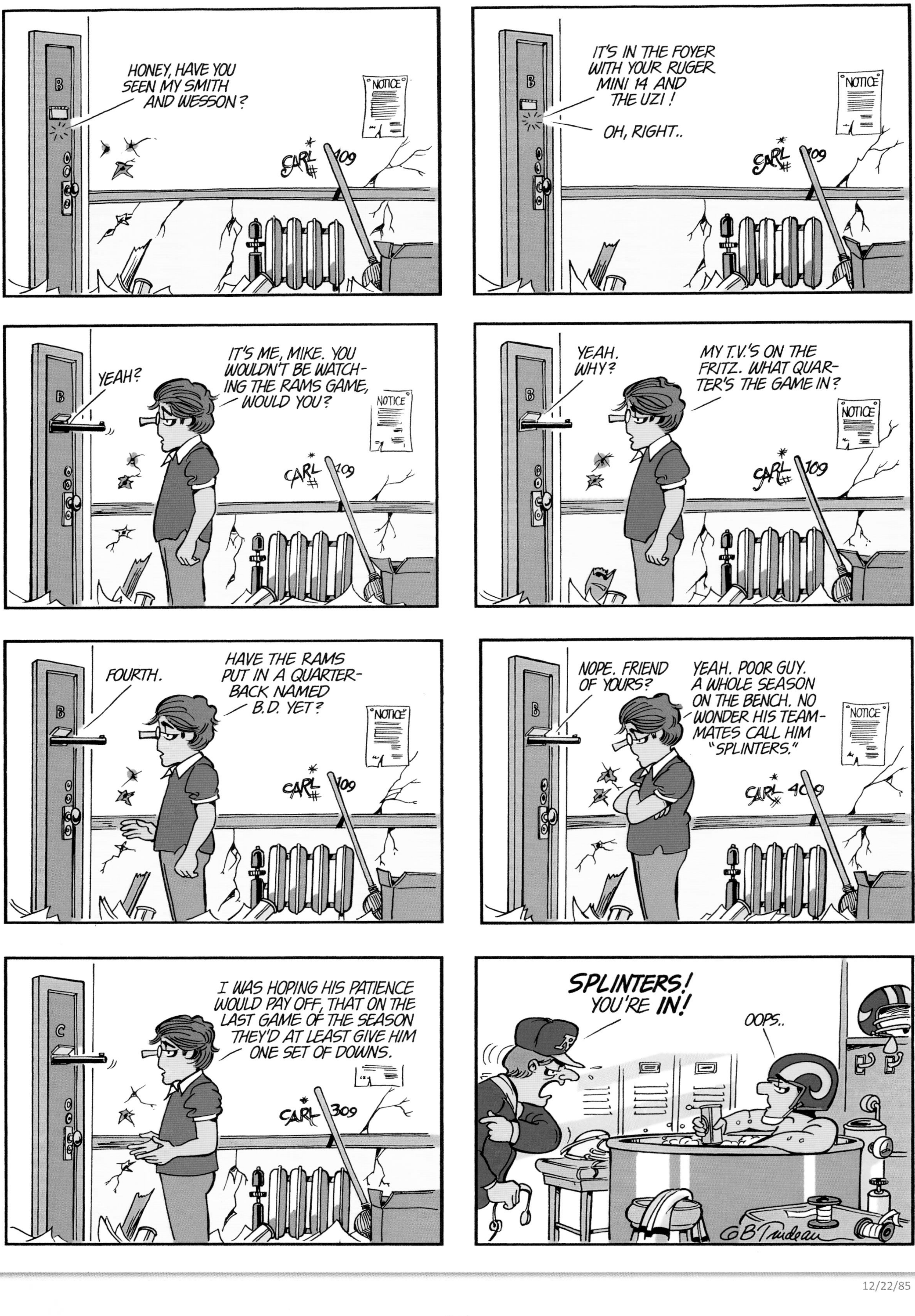
HONEY, HAVE YOU SEEN MY SMITH AND WESSON?
NOTICE
CARL 109
IT'S IN THE FOYER WITH YOUR RUGER MINI 14 AND THE UZI!
OH, RIGHT..
YEAH?
IT'S ME, MIKE. YOU WOULDN'T BE WATCHING THE RAMS GAME, WOULD YOU?
YEAH. WHY?
MY T.V.'S ON THE FRITZ. WHAT QUARTER'S THE GAME IN?
FOURTH.
HAVE THE RAMS PUT IN A QUARTERBACK NAMED B.D. YET?
NOPE. FRIEND OF YOURS?
YEAH. POOR GUY. A WHOLE SEASON ON THE BENCH. NO WONDER HIS TEAMMATES CALL HIM "SPLINTERS."
I WAS HOPING HIS PATIENCE WOULD PAY OFF, THAT ON THE LAST GAME OF THE SEASON THEY'D AT LEAST GIVE HIM ONE SET OF DOWNS.
SPLINTERS! YOU'RE IN!
OOPS..
GB Trudeau

12/22/85

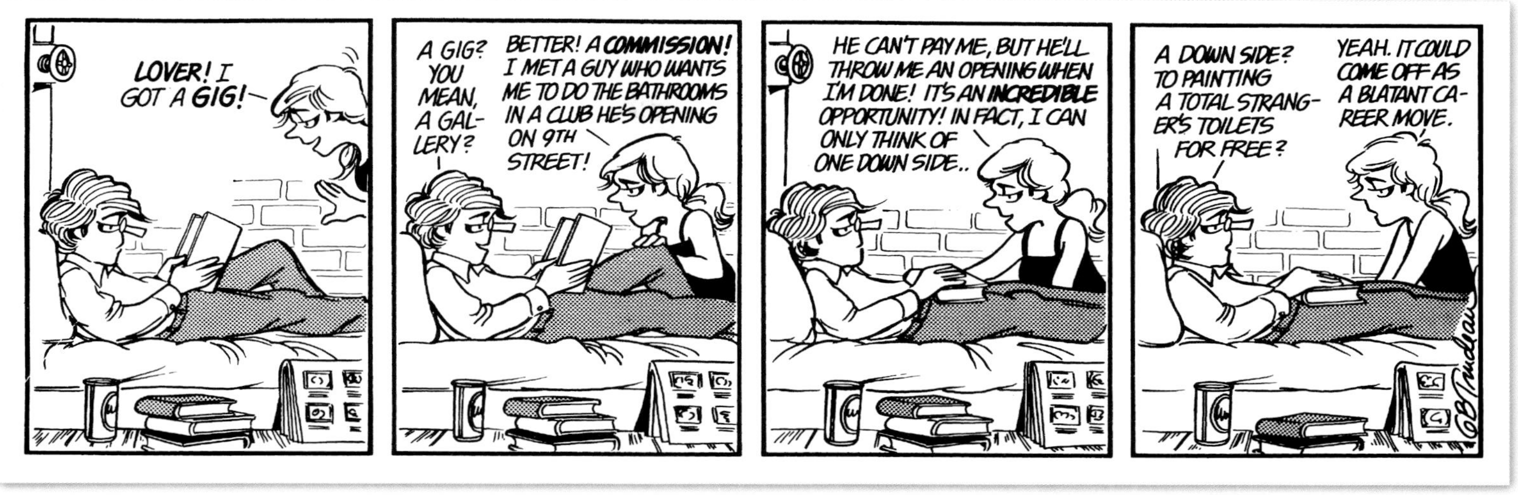
LOVER! I GOT A GIG!
A GIG? YOU MEAN, A GALLERY?
BETTER! A COMMISSION! I MET A GUY WHO WANTS ME TO DO THE BATHROOMS IN A CLUB HE'S OPENING ON 9TH STREET!
HE CAN'T PAY ME, BUT HE'LL THROW ME AN OPENING WHEN I'M DONE! IT'S AN INCREDIBLE OPPORTUNITY! IN FACT, I CAN ONLY THINK OF ONE DOWN SIDE..
A DOWN SIDE? TO PAINTING A TOTAL STRANGER'S TOILETS FOR FREE?
YEAH. IT COULD COME OFF AS A BLATANT CAREER MOVE.
GB Trudeau

1/6/86

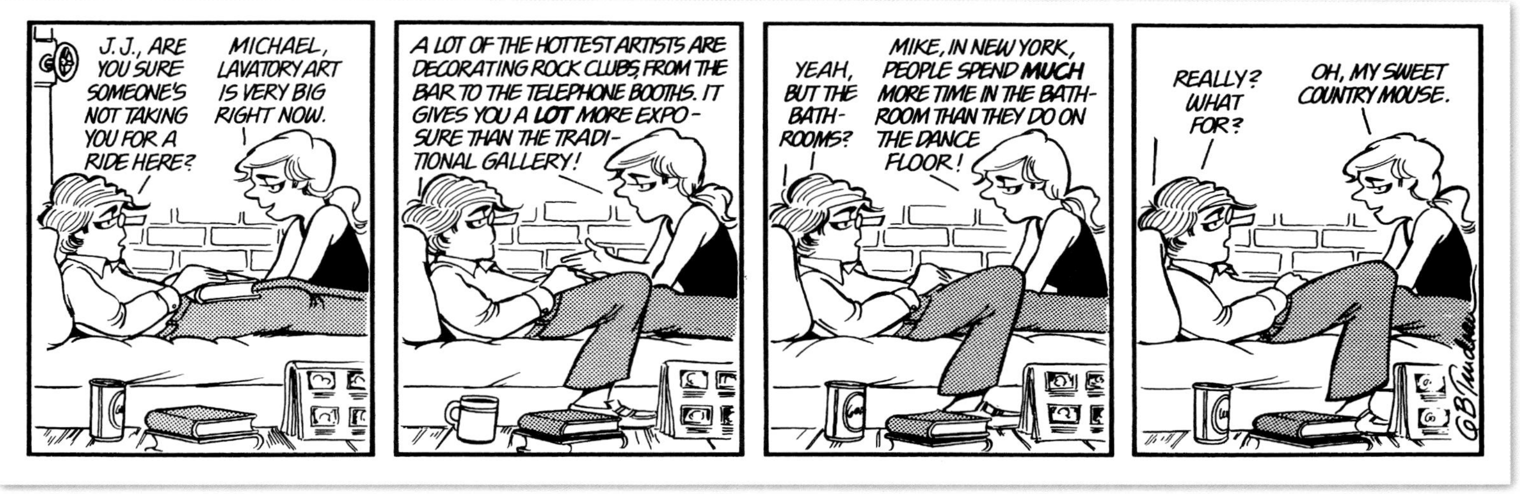
J.J., ARE YOU SURE SOMEONE'S NOT TAKING YOU FOR A RIDE HERE?
MICHAEL, LAVATORY ART IS VERY BIG RIGHT NOW.
A LOT OF THE HOTTEST ARTISTS ARE DECORATING ROCK CLUBS, FROM THE BAR TO THE TELEPHONE BOOTHS. IT GIVES YOU A LOT MORE EXPOSURE THAN THE TRADITIONAL GALLERY!
YEAH, BUT THE BATHROOMS?
MIKE, IN NEW YORK, PEOPLE SPEND MUCH MORE TIME IN THE BATHROOM THAN THEY DO ON THE DANCE FLOOR!
REALLY? WHAT FOR?
OH, MY SWEET COUNTRY MOUSE.
GB Trudeau

1/7/86

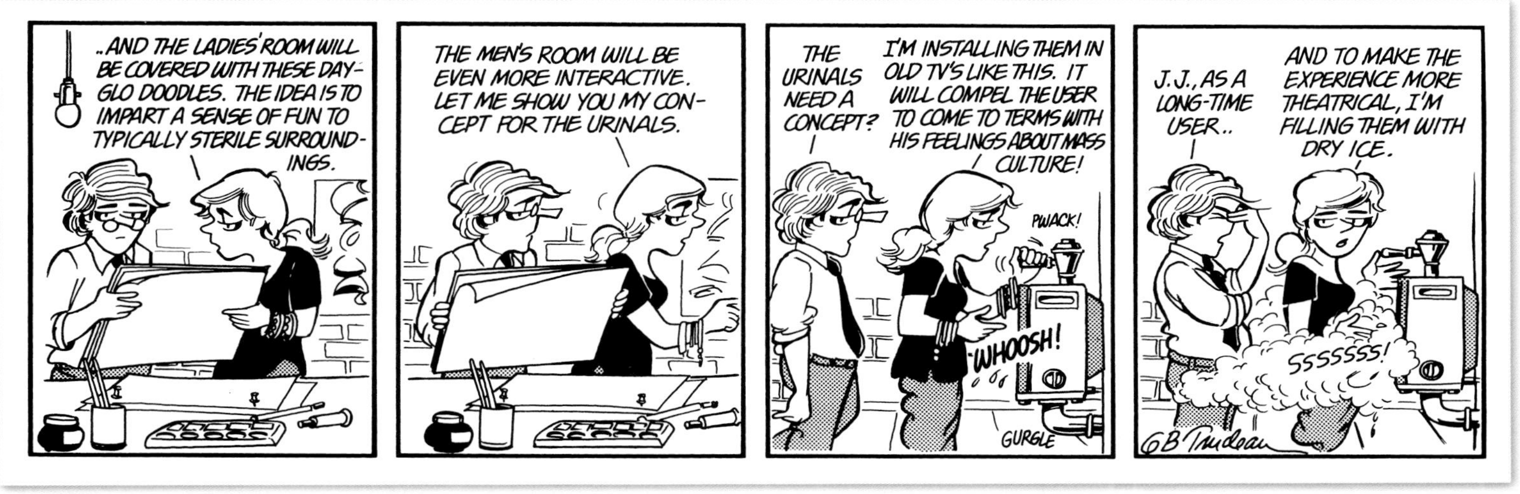
..AND THE LADIES' ROOM WILL BE COVERED WITH THESE DAY-GLO DOODLES. THE IDEA IS TO IMPART A SENSE OF FUN TO TYPICALLY STERILE SURROUNDINGS.
THE MEN'S ROOM WILL BE EVEN MORE INTERACTIVE. LET ME SHOW YOU MY CONCEPT FOR THE URINALS.
THE URINALS NEED A CONCEPT?
I'M INSTALLING THEM IN OLD TV'S LIKE THIS. IT WILL COMPEL THE USER TO COME TO TERMS WITH HIS FEELINGS ABOUT MASS CULTURE!
PWACK!
WHOOSH!
GURGLE
J.J., AS A LONG-TIME USER..
AND TO MAKE THE EXPERIENCE MORE THEATRICAL, I'M FILLING THEM WITH DRY ICE.
SSSSSSS!
GB Trudeau

1/9/86

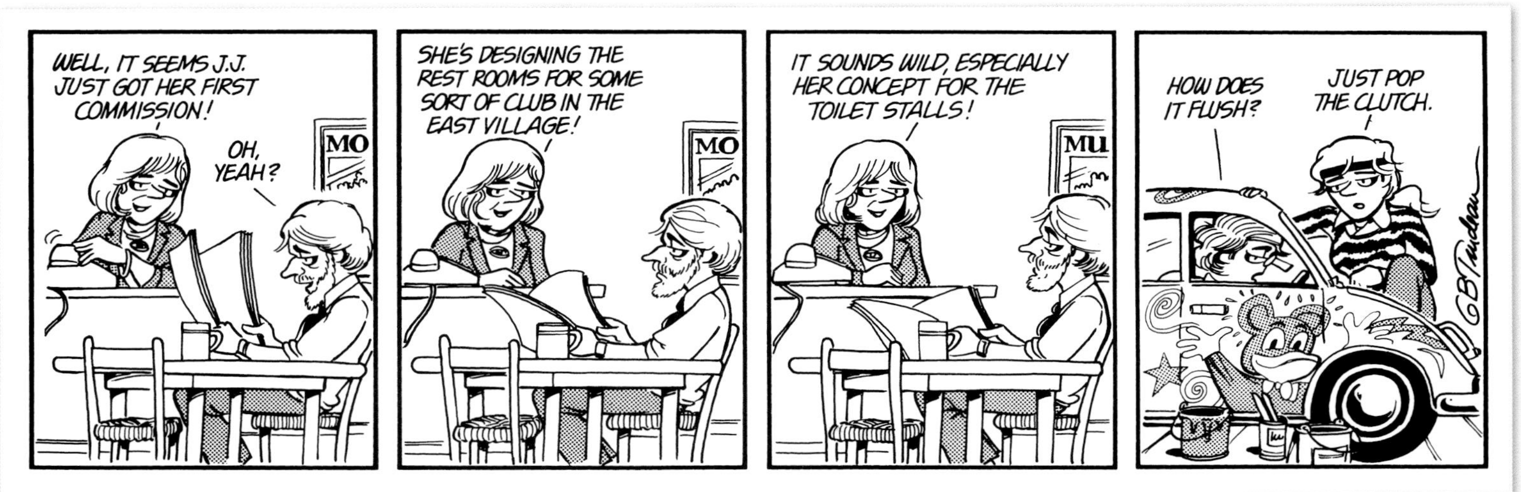
WELL, IT SEEMS J.J. JUST GOT HER FIRST COMMISSION!
OH, YEAH?
SHE'S DESIGNING THE REST ROOMS FOR SOME SORT OF CLUB IN THE EAST VILLAGE!
IT SOUNDS WILD, ESPECIALLY HER CONCEPT FOR THE TOILET STALLS!
HOW DOES IT FLUSH?
JUST POP THE CLUTCH.
GB Trudeau

1/10/86

President King

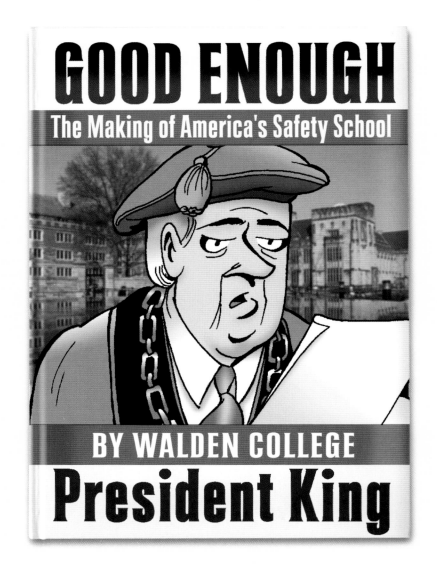

GOOD ENOUGH

The Making of America's Safety School

BY WALDEN COLLEGE

President King

One of my earliest characters bore a striking resemblance to Kingman Brewster Jr., the president of Yale while I was a student there. In my senior year, I invited him to write an introduction to my second collection of strips. I wasn't hopeful—he had a few things on his plate—but a week or so later the introduction arrived, in the form of a long letter berating the author. An excerpt read:

"I would be less than candid and more than fair if I did not tell you that your chances of being well received in any future receiving line are tarnished if not prejudiced."

He signed the letter "Rex." It was a nice bit of foppish foolishness, and quite unexpected because all hell was breaking loose at the time. A Black Panther trial was in progress, there were mass demonstrations on the green, classes had been cancelled, and the National Guard had just rolled onto campus. But Brewster had it all under control; he exuded confidence and cool in the middle of mayhem. He played his various constituencies brilliantly, treating each with respect and disarming humor. He entered into a serious dialogue with the students and never abandoned it. Even as he strode the campus in his

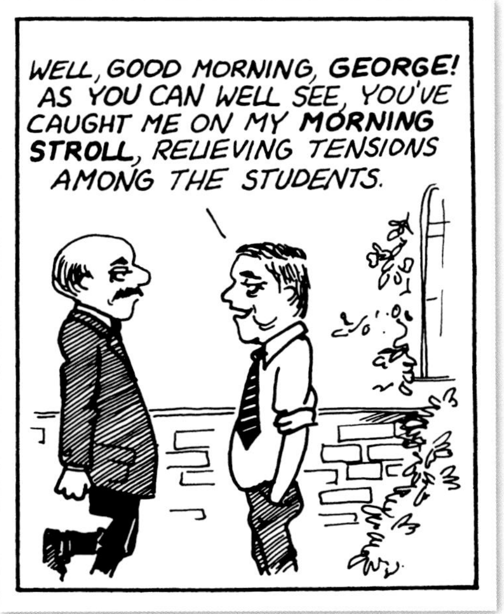
WELL, GOOD MORNING, GEORGE! AS YOU CAN WELL SEE, YOU'VE CAUGHT ME ON MY MORNING STROLL, RELIEVING TENSIONS AMONG THE STUDENTS.

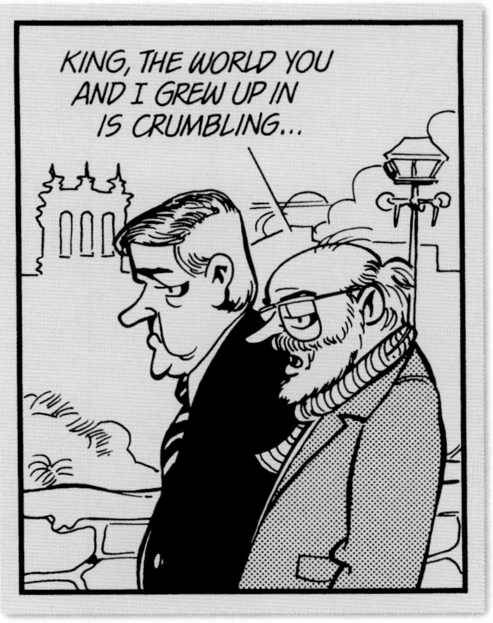
KING, THE WORLD YOU AND I GREW UP IN IS CRUMBLING...

tailored three-piece suit, he was regarded as one of our own. If SDS had tried to take over his office, the rest of us would have thrown them out.

The Revolution was a high-water mark for both Brewster and his cartoon doppelgänger, President King. But while Brewster left Yale in far better shape than he found it, King went on to preside over four decades of steep, uninterrupted decline at Walden. The college's standards slipped so precipitously that it eventually stopped requiring a high school diploma for admission, earning its nickname, "America's Safety School." So ill-prepared were the students drawn by its reputation that Walden in 2006 became the first college in the country to offer a major in Remedial Studies.

King's mistake had been to enter higher education just as its lower reaches were being sacked by a student cohort obsessed with credentials, but not so interested in earning them. There have always been students eager to part with $40,000 a year provided they get nothing in return, and for them, Walden is a dream come true—a place where "stressed" students can begin partying on Wednesday, shop for classes they need not attend, and sue a professor for hurting their feelings. Such colleges exist in abundance. It's not the niche market you might imagine.

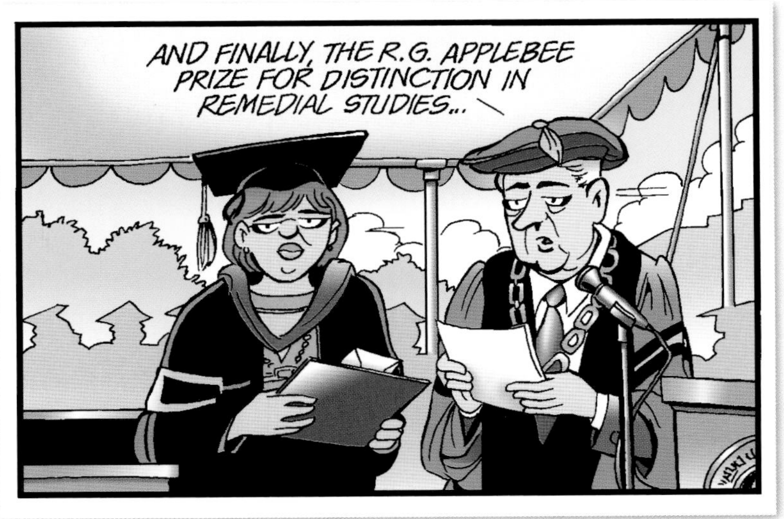
AND FINALLY, THE R.G. APPLEBEE PRIZE FOR DISTINCTION IN REMEDIAL STUDIES...

Sadly, the only thing standing between President King and utter despair is a robust cynicism. His annual graduation speech, delivered in rich tones of sarcasm, is usually cloaked in resignation. King knows that he runs an asylum full of Zippers. That he chooses to remain at his post is a tragedy of inertia.

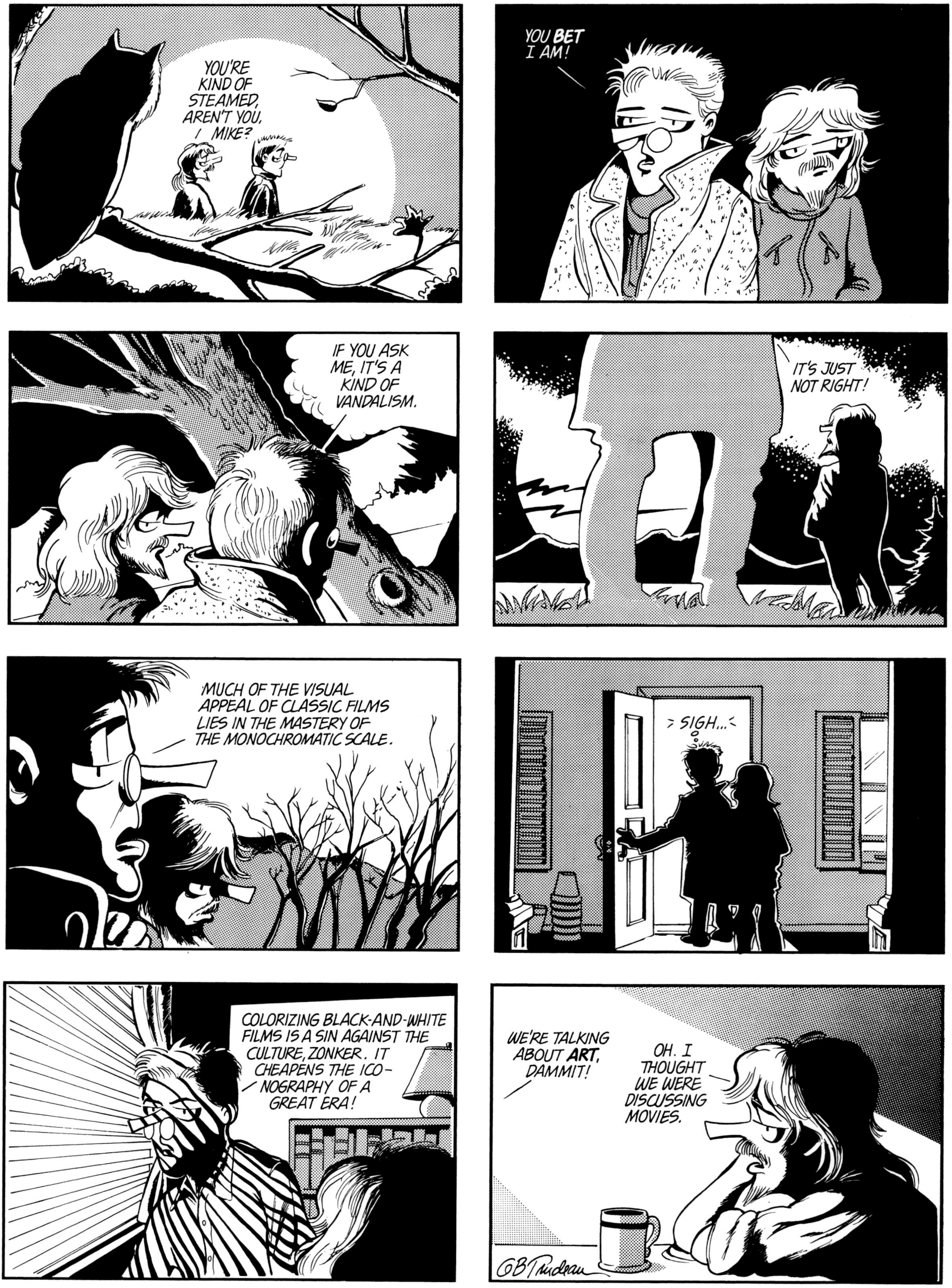
YOU'RE KIND OF STEAMED, AREN'T YOU, MIKE?
YOU BET I AM!
IF YOU ASK ME, IT'S A KIND OF VANDALISM.
IT'S JUST NOT RIGHT!
MUCH OF THE VISUAL APPEAL OF CLASSIC FILMS LIES IN THE MASTERY OF THE MONOCHROMATIC SCALE.
SIGH...
COLORIZING BLACK-AND-WHITE FILMS IS A SIN AGAINST THE CULTURE, ZONKER. IT CHEAPENS THE ICONOGRAPHY OF A GREAT ERA!
WE'RE TALKING ABOUT ART, DAMMIT!
OH. I THOUGHT WE WERE DISCUSSING MOVIES.
GBTrudeau

12/28/86

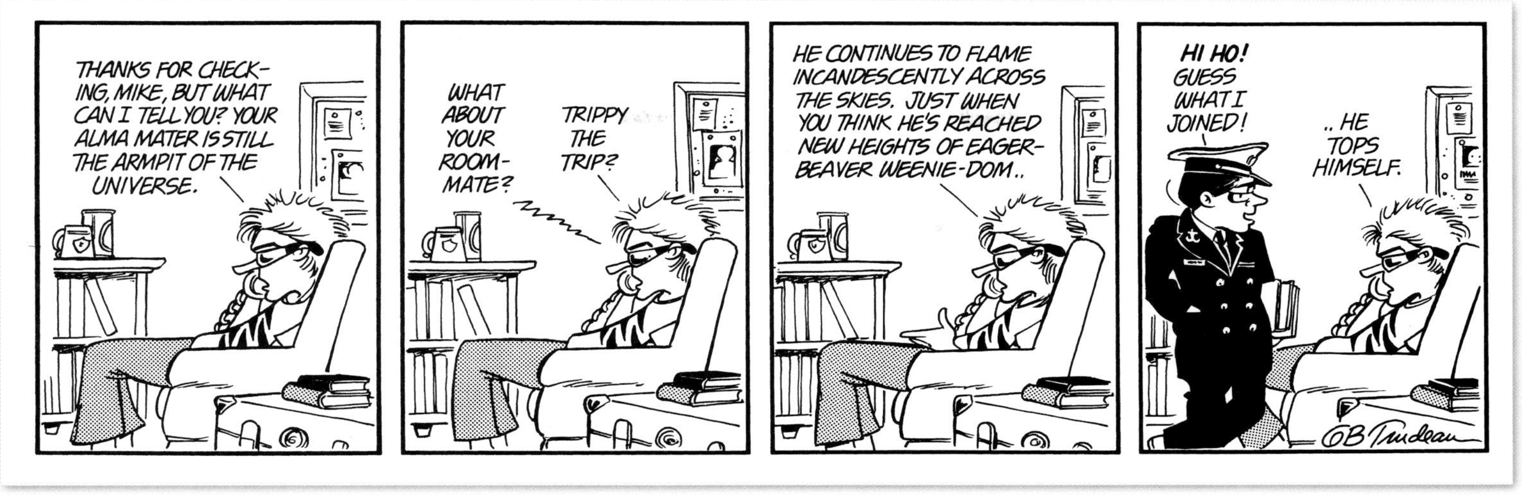
THANKS FOR CHECKING, MIKE, BUT WHAT CAN I TELL YOU? YOUR ALMA MATER IS STILL THE ARMPIT OF THE UNIVERSE.
WHAT ABOUT YOUR ROOMMATE?
TRIPPY THE TRIP?
HE CONTINUES TO FLAME INCANDESCENTLY ACROSS THE SKIES. JUST WHEN YOU THINK HE'S REACHED NEW HEIGHTS OF EAGER-BEAVER WEENIE-DOM..
HI HO! GUESS WHAT I JOINED!
.. HE TOPS HIMSELF.
GB Trudeau

1/14/86

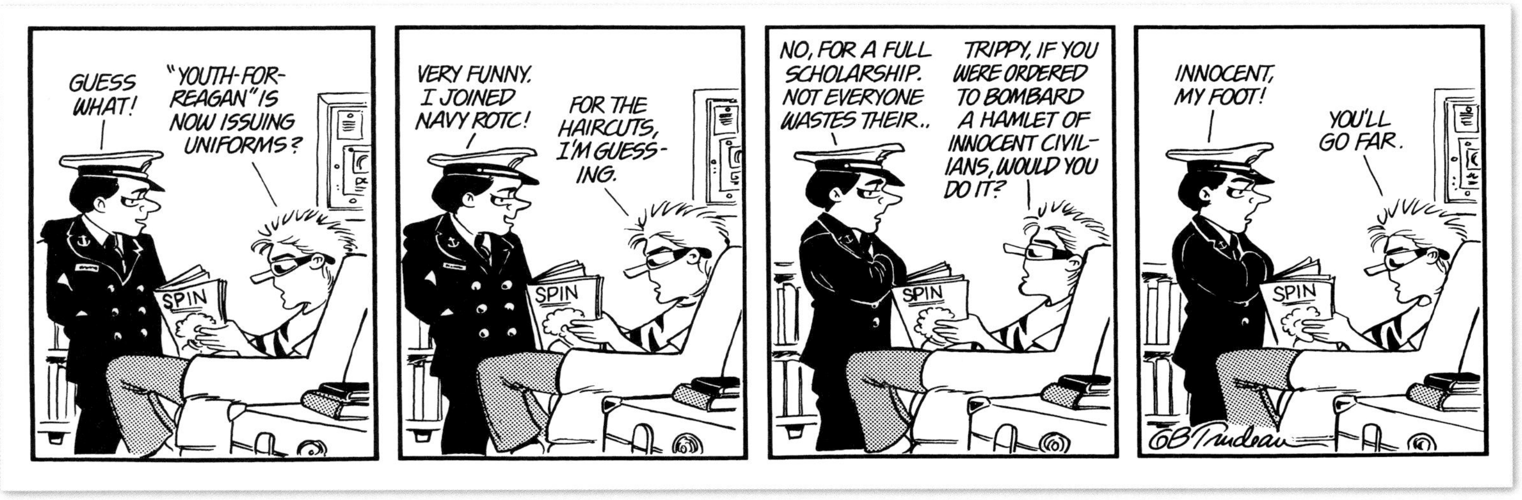
GUESS WHAT!
"YOUTH-FOR-REAGAN" IS NOW ISSUING UNIFORMS?
SPIN
VERY FUNNY. I JOINED NAVY ROTC!
FOR THE HAIRCUTS, I'M GUESSING.
SPIN
NO, FOR A FULL SCHOLARSHIP. NOT EVERYONE WASTES THEIR..
TRIPPY, IF YOU WERE ORDERED TO BOMBARD A HAMLET OF INNOCENT CIVILIANS, WOULD YOU DO IT?
SPIN
INNOCENT, MY FOOT!
YOU'LL GO FAR.
SPIN
GB Trudeau

1/15/86

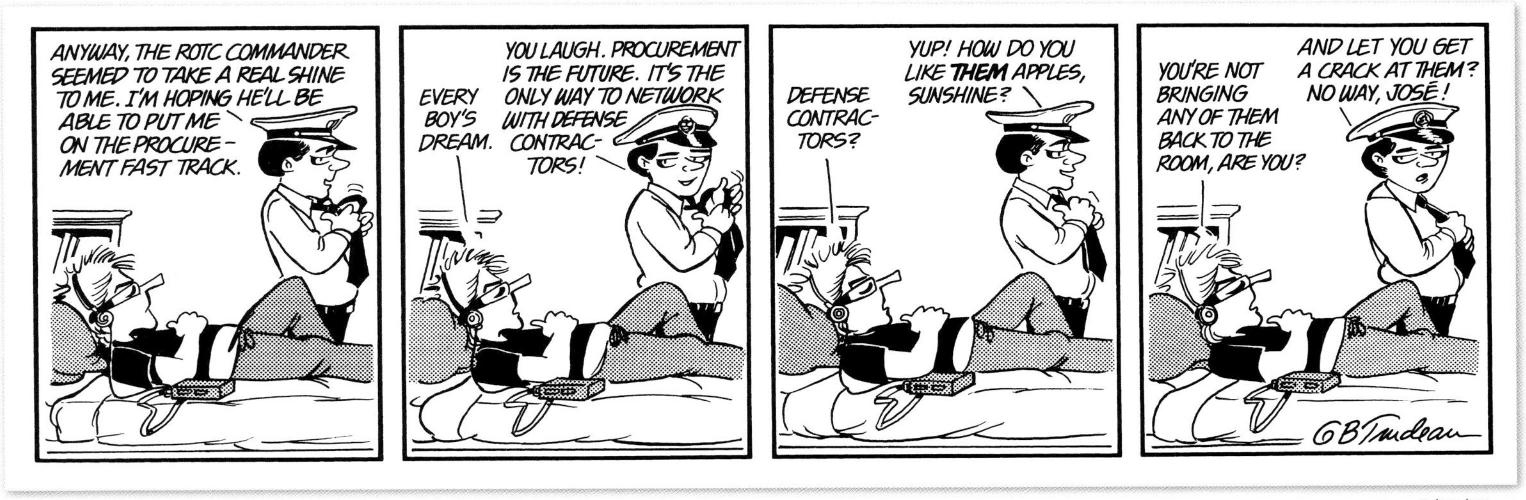
ANYWAY, THE ROTC COMMANDER SEEMED TO TAKE A REAL SHINE TO ME. I'M HOPING HE'LL BE ABLE TO PUT ME ON THE PROCUREMENT FAST TRACK.
EVERY BOY'S DREAM.
YOU LAUGH. PROCUREMENT IS THE FUTURE. IT'S THE ONLY WAY TO NETWORK WITH DEFENSE CONTRACTORS!
DEFENSE CONTRACTORS?
YUP! HOW DO YOU LIKE THEM APPLES, SUNSHINE?
YOU'RE NOT BRINGING ANY OF THEM BACK TO THE ROOM, ARE YOU?
AND LET YOU GET A CRACK AT THEM? NO WAY, JOSÉ!
GB Trudeau

1/16/86

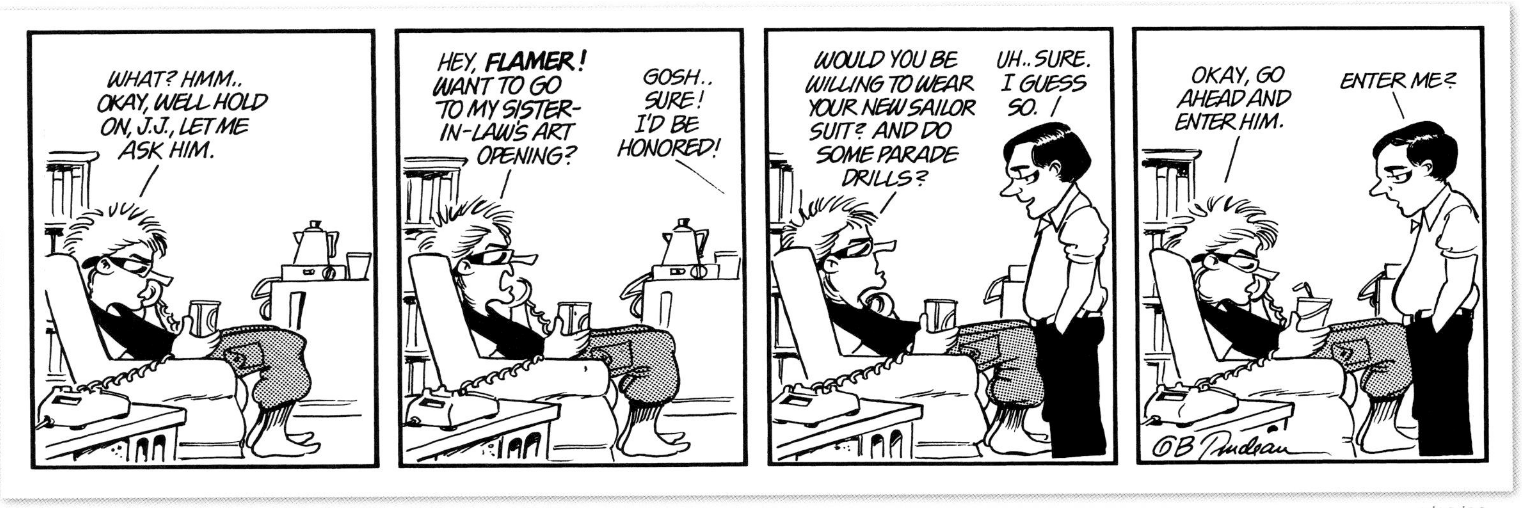
WHAT? HMM.. OKAY, WELL HOLD ON, J.J., LET ME ASK HIM.
HEY, FLAMER! WANT TO GO TO MY SISTER-IN-LAW'S ART OPENING?
GOSH.. SURE! I'D BE HONORED!
WOULD YOU BE WILLING TO WEAR YOUR NEW SAILOR SUIT? AND DO SOME PARADE DRILLS?
UH.. SURE. I GUESS SO.
OKAY, GO AHEAD AND ENTER HIM.
ENTER ME?
GB Trudeau

1/18/86

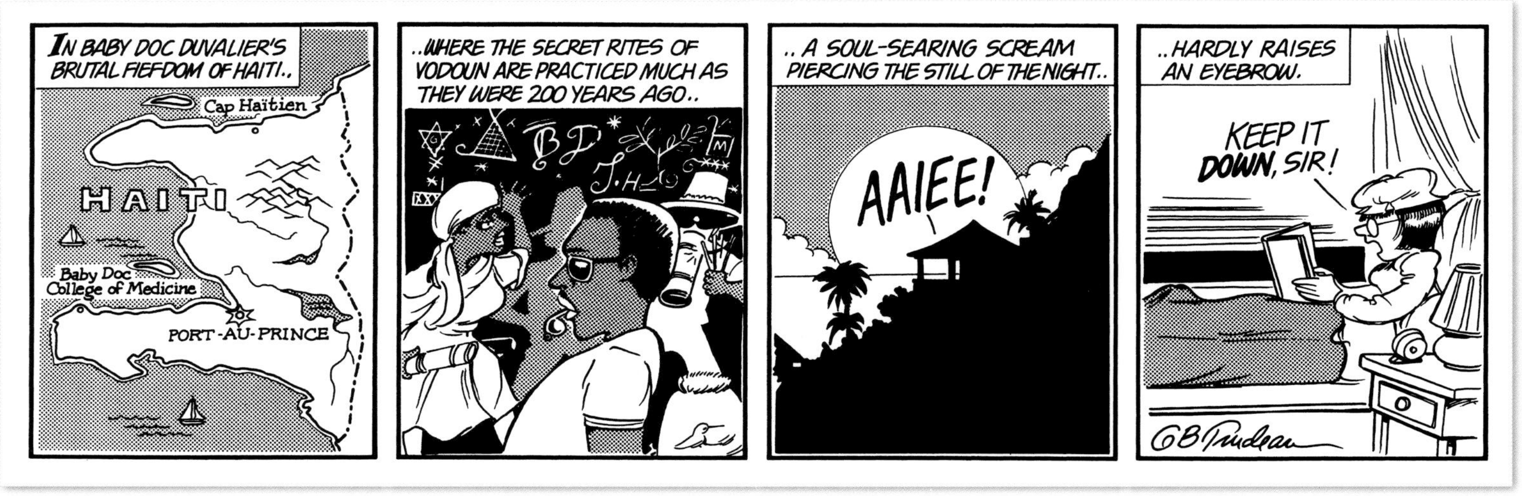
IN BABY DOC DUVALIER'S BRUTAL FIEFDOM OF HAITI..
Cap Haitien
HAITI
Baby Doc College of Medicine
PORT-AU-PRINCE
..WHERE THE SECRET RITES OF VODOUN ARE PRACTICED MUCH AS THEY WERE 200 YEARS AGO..
.. A SOUL-SEARING SCREAM PIERCING THE STILL OF THE NIGHT..
AAIEE!
..HARDLY RAISES AN EYEBROW.
KEEP IT DOWN, SIR!
GB Trudeau

1/20/86

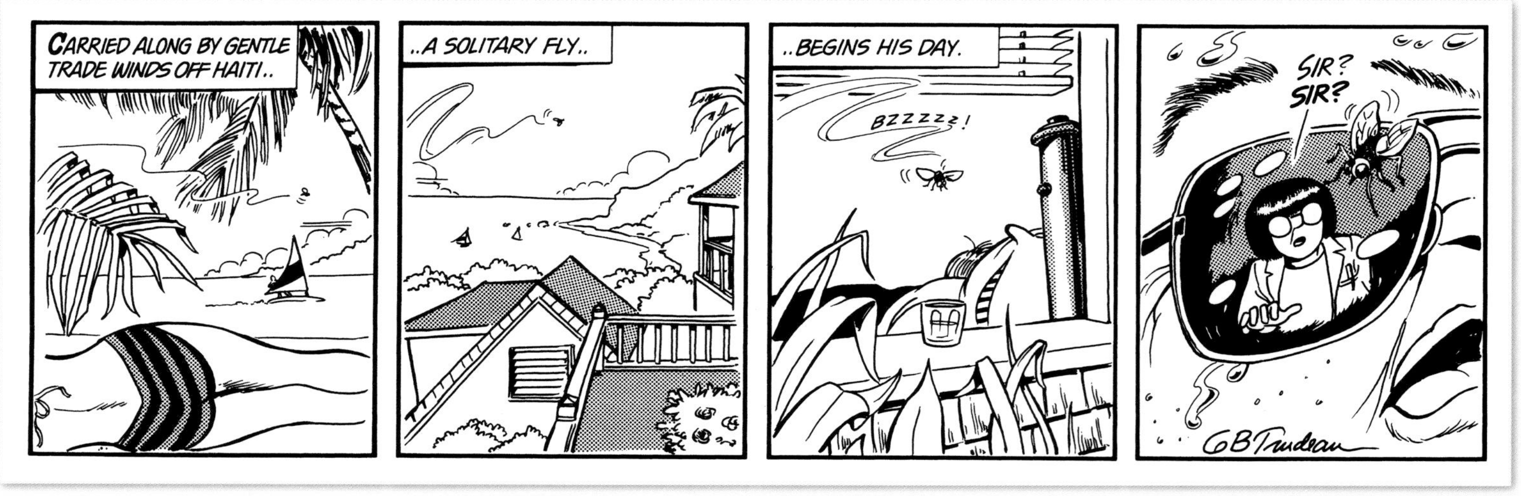
CARRIED ALONG BY GENTLE TRADE WINDS OFF HAITI..
..A SOLITARY FLY..
..BEGINS HIS DAY.
BZZZZZ!
SIR? SIR?
GB Trudeau

1/21/86

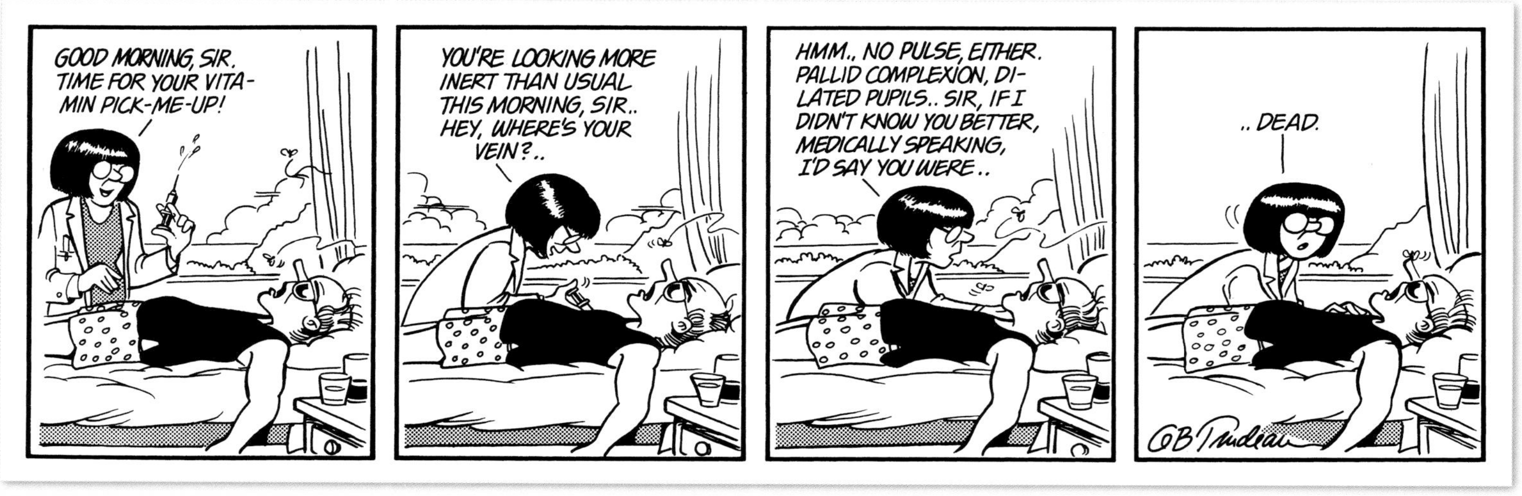
GOOD MORNING, SIR. TIME FOR YOUR VITA-MIN PICK-ME-UP!
YOU'RE LOOKING MORE INERT THAN USUAL THIS MORNING, SIR.. HEY, WHERE'S YOUR VEIN?..
HMM.. NO PULSE, EITHER. PALLID COMPLEXION, DI-LATED PUPILS.. SIR, IF I DIDN'T KNOW YOU BETTER, MEDICALLY SPEAKING, I'D SAY YOU WERE..
..DEAD.
GB Trudeau

1/22/86

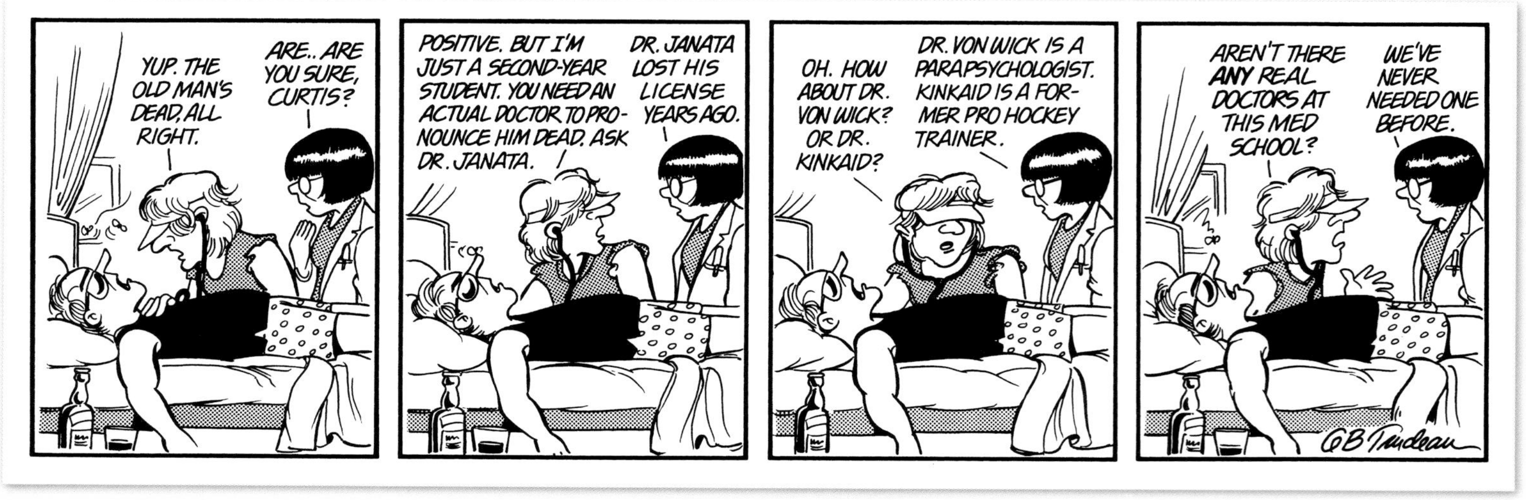
YUP. THE OLD MAN'S DEAD, ALL RIGHT.
ARE.. ARE YOU SURE, CURTIS?
POSITIVE. BUT I'M JUST A SECOND-YEAR STUDENT. YOU NEED AN ACTUAL DOCTOR TO PRO-NOUNCE HIM DEAD. ASK DR. JANATA.
DR. JANATA LOST HIS LICENSE YEARS AGO.
OH. HOW ABOUT DR. VON WICK? OR DR. KINKAID?
DR. VON WICK IS A PARAPSYCHOLOGIST. KINKAID IS A FOR-MER PRO HOCKEY TRAINER.
AREN'T THERE ANY REAL DOCTORS AT THIS MED SCHOOL?
WE'VE NEVER NEEDED ONE BEFORE.
GB Trudeau

1/23/86

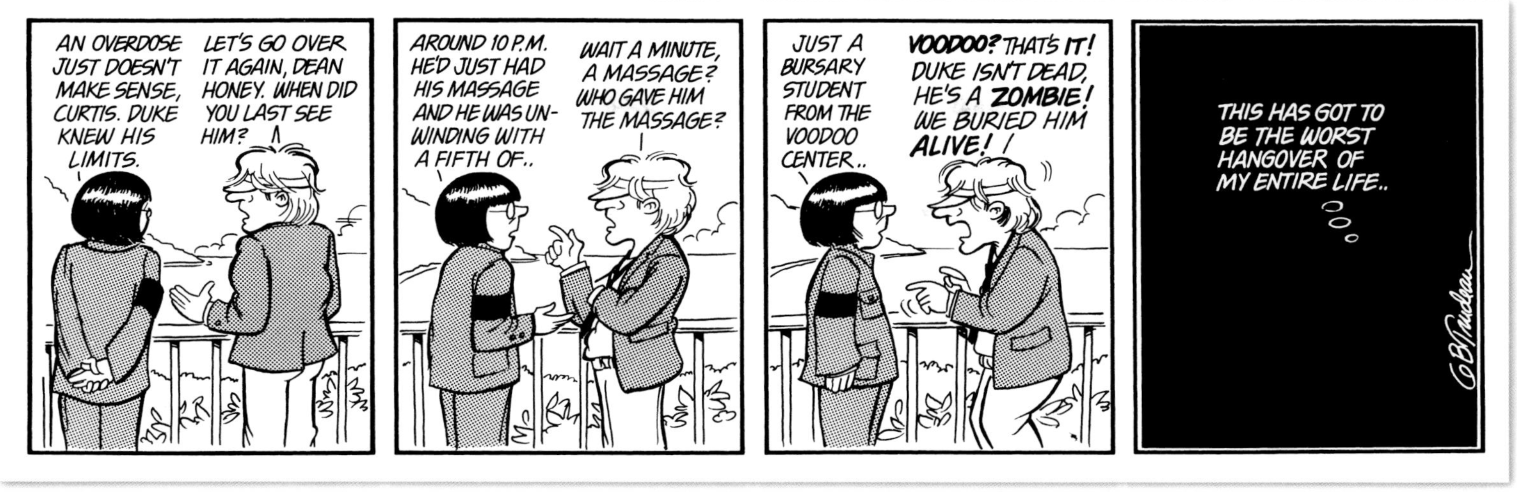
AN OVERDOSE JUST DOESN'T MAKE SENSE, CURTIS. DUKE KNEW HIS LIMITS.
LET'S GO OVER IT AGAIN, DEAN HONEY. WHEN DID YOU LAST SEE HIM?
AROUND 10 P.M. HE'D JUST HAD HIS MASSAGE AND HE WAS UNWINDING WITH A FIFTH OF..
WAIT A MINUTE, A MASSAGE? WHO GAVE HIM THE MASSAGE?
JUST A BURSARY STUDENT FROM THE VOODOO CENTER..
VOODOO? THAT'S IT! DUKE ISN'T DEAD, HE'S A ZOMBIE! WE BURIED HIM ALIVE!
THIS HAS GOT TO BE THE WORST HANGOVER OF MY ENTIRE LIFE..
GB Trudeau

2/3/86

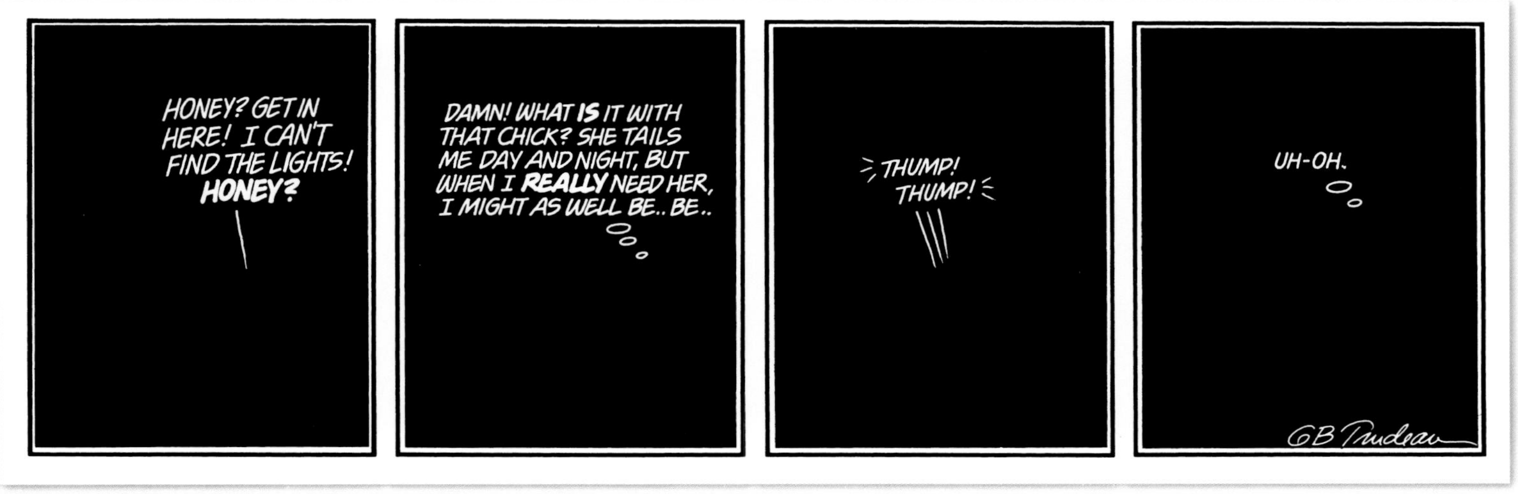
HONEY? GET IN HERE! I CAN'T FIND THE LIGHTS! HONEY?
DAMN! WHAT IS IT WITH THAT CHICK? SHE TAILS ME DAY AND NIGHT, BUT WHEN I REALLY NEED HER, I MIGHT AS WELL BE.. BE..
THUMP! THUMP!
UH-OH.
GB Trudeau

2/6/86

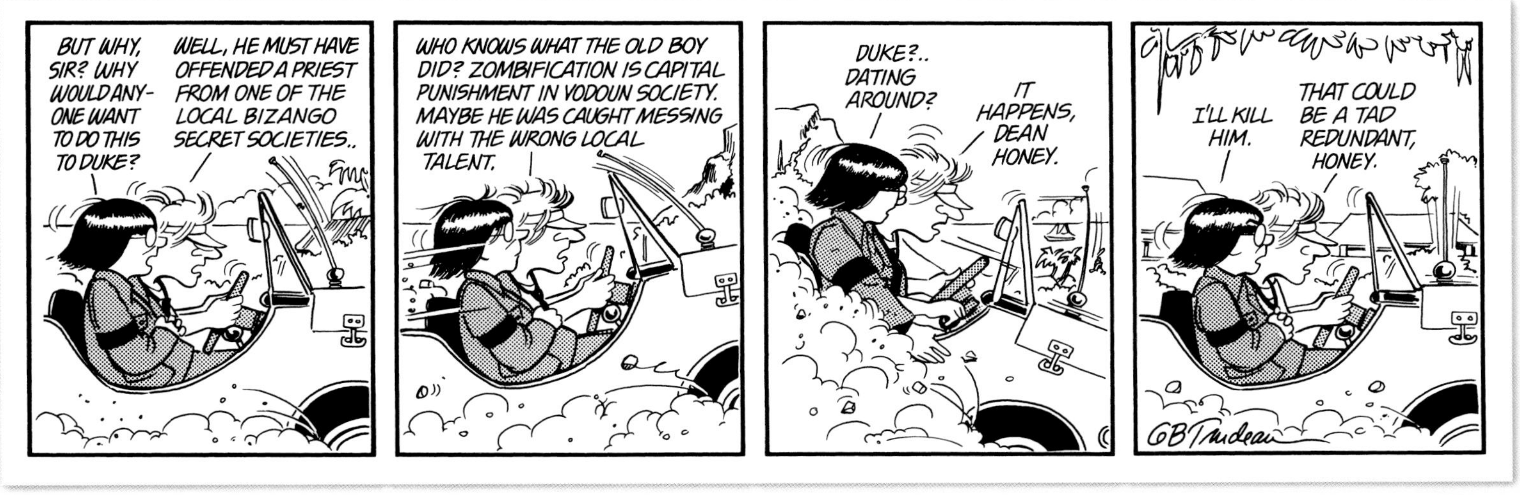
BUT WHY, SIR? WHY WOULD ANYONE WANT TO DO THIS TO DUKE?
WELL, HE MUST HAVE OFFENDED A PRIEST FROM ONE OF THE LOCAL BIZANGO SECRET SOCIETIES..
WHO KNOWS WHAT THE OLD BOY DID? ZOMBIFICATION IS CAPITAL PUNISHMENT IN VODOUN SOCIETY. MAYBE HE WAS CAUGHT MESSING WITH THE WRONG LOCAL TALENT.
DUKE?.. DATING AROUND?
IT HAPPENS, DEAN HONEY.
I'LL KILL HIM.
THAT COULD BE A TAD REDUNDANT, HONEY.
GB Trudeau

2/7/86

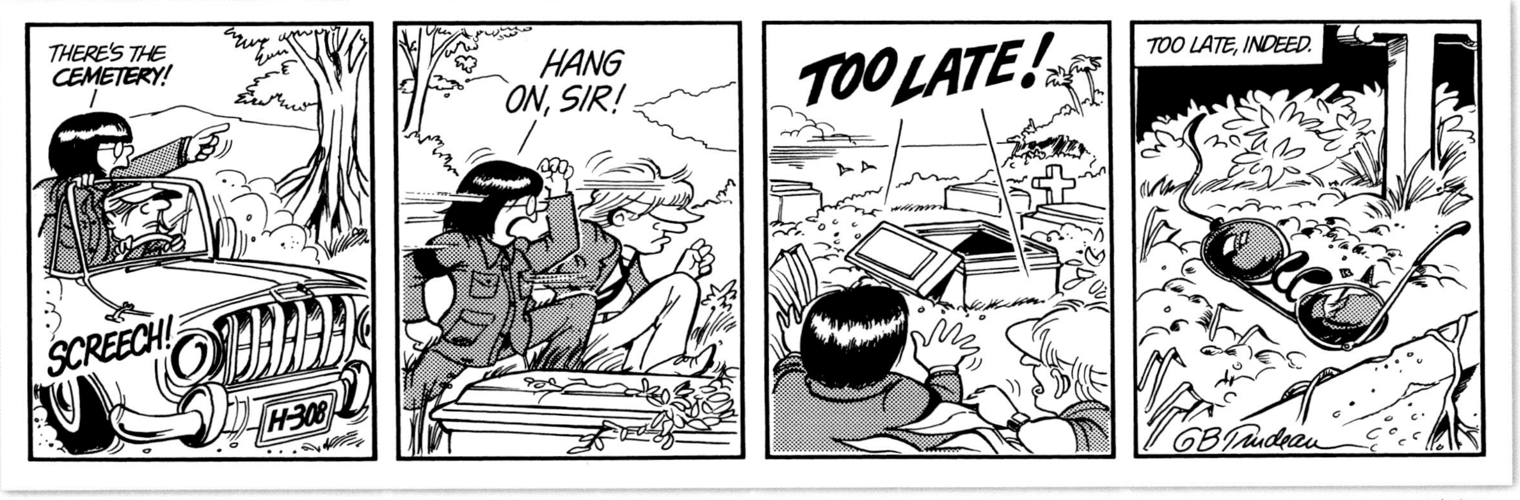
THERE'S THE CEMETERY!
SCREECH!
H-308
HANG ON, SIR!
TOO LATE!
TOO LATE, INDEED.
GB Trudeau

2/8/86

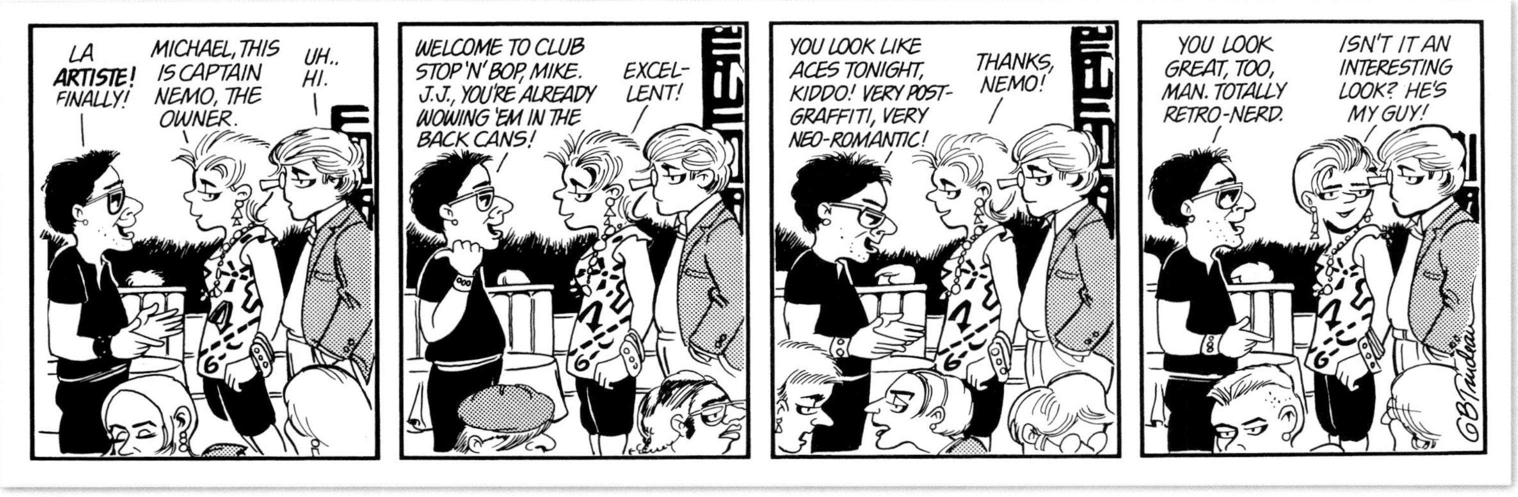
LA ARTISTE! FINALLY!
MICHAEL, THIS IS CAPTAIN NEMO, THE OWNER.
UH.. HI.
WELCOME TO CLUB STOP 'N' BOP, MIKE. J.J., YOU'RE ALREADY WOWING 'EM IN THE BACK CANS!
EXCEL-LENT!
YOU LOOK LIKE ACES TONIGHT, KIDDO! VERY POST-GRAFFITI, VERY NEO-ROMANTIC!
THANKS, NEMO!
YOU LOOK GREAT, TOO, MAN. TOTALLY RETRO-NERD.
ISN'T IT AN INTERESTING LOOK? HE'S MY GUY!

2/14/86

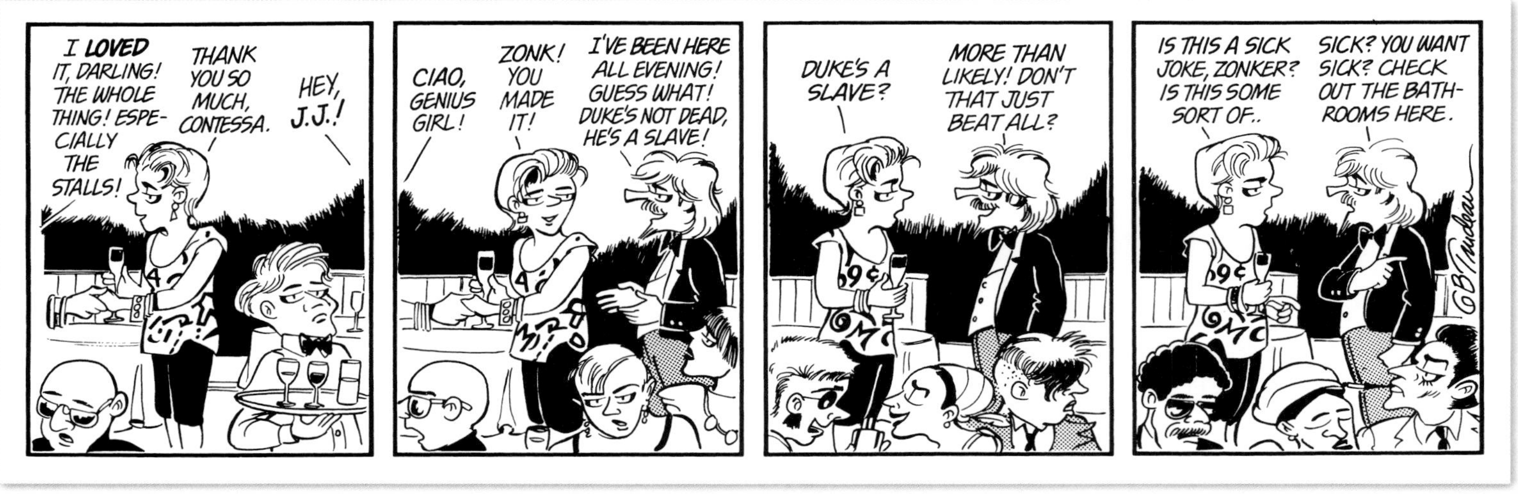
I LOVED IT, DARLING! THE WHOLE THING! ESPE-CIALLY THE STALLS!
THANK YOU SO MUCH, CONTESSA.
HEY, J.J.!
CIAO, GENIUS GIRL!
ZONK! YOU MADE IT!
I'VE BEEN HERE ALL EVENING! GUESS WHAT! DUKE'S NOT DEAD, HE'S A SLAVE!
DUKE'S A SLAVE?
MORE THAN LIKELY! DON'T THAT JUST BEAT ALL?
IS THIS A SICK JOKE, ZONKER? IS THIS SOME SORT OF..
SICK? YOU WANT SICK? CHECK OUT THE BATH-ROOMS HERE.

2/18/86

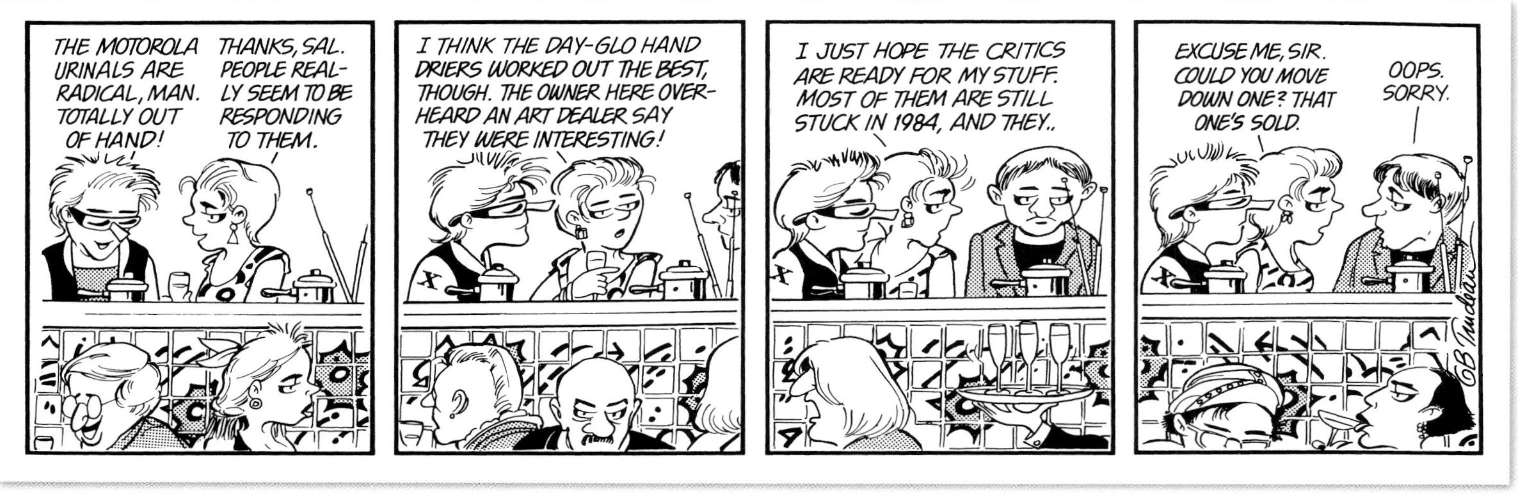
THE MOTOROLA URINALS ARE RADICAL, MAN. TOTALLY OUT OF HAND!
THANKS, SAL. PEOPLE REAL-LY SEEM TO BE RESPONDING TO THEM.
I THINK THE DAY-GLO HAND DRIERS WORKED OUT THE BEST, THOUGH. THE OWNER HERE OVER-HEARD AN ART DEALER SAY THEY WERE INTERESTING!
I JUST HOPE THE CRITICS ARE READY FOR MY STUFF. MOST OF THEM ARE STILL STUCK IN 1984, AND THEY..
EXCUSE ME, SIR. COULD YOU MOVE DOWN ONE? THAT ONE'S SOLD.
OOPS. SORRY.

2/20/86

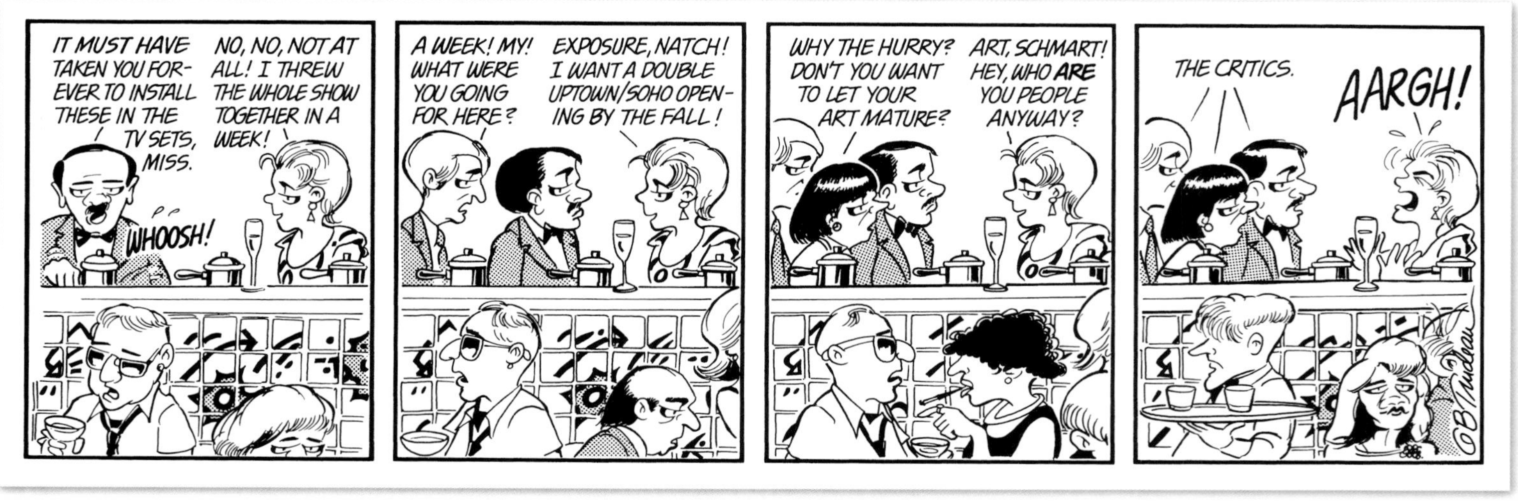
IT MUST HAVE TAKEN YOU FOR-EVER TO INSTALL THESE IN THE TV SETS, MISS.
NO, NO, NOT AT ALL! I THREW THE WHOLE SHOW TOGETHER IN A WEEK!
WHOOSH!
A WEEK! MY! WHAT WERE YOU GOING FOR HERE?
EXPOSURE, NATCH! I WANT A DOUBLE UPTOWN/SOHO OPEN-ING BY THE FALL!
WHY THE HURRY? DON'T YOU WANT TO LET YOUR ART MATURE?
ART, SCHMART! HEY, WHO ARE YOU PEOPLE ANYWAY?
THE CRITICS.
AARGH!

2/21/86

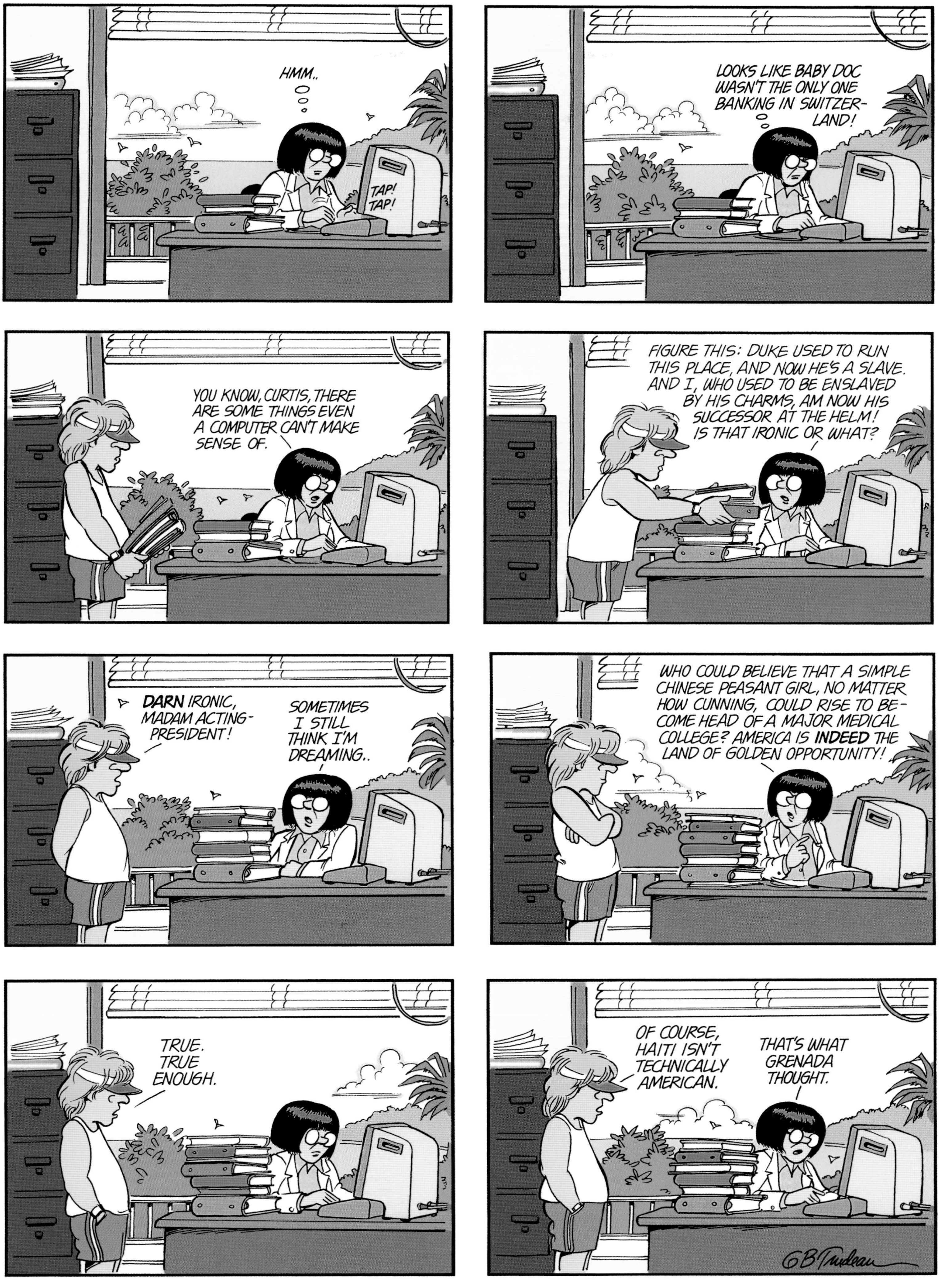
HMM..
TAP! TAP!
LOOKS LIKE BABY DOC WASN'T THE ONLY ONE BANKING IN SWITZER-LAND!
YOU KNOW, CURTIS, THERE ARE SOME THINGS EVEN A COMPUTER CAN'T MAKE SENSE OF.
FIGURE THIS: DUKE USED TO RUN THIS PLACE, AND NOW HE'S A SLAVE. AND I, WHO USED TO BE ENSLAVED BY HIS CHARMS, AM NOW HIS SUCCESSOR AT THE HELM! IS THAT IRONIC OR WHAT?
DARN IRONIC, MADAM ACTING-PRESIDENT!
SOMETIMES I STILL THINK I'M DREAMING..
WHO COULD BELIEVE THAT A SIMPLE CHINESE PEASANT GIRL, NO MATTER HOW CUNNING, COULD RISE TO BE-COME HEAD OF A MAJOR MEDICAL COLLEGE? AMERICA IS INDEED THE LAND OF GOLDEN OPPORTUNITY!
TRUE. TRUE ENOUGH.
OF COURSE, HAITI ISN'T TECHNICALLY AMERICAN.
THAT'S WHAT GRENADA THOUGHT.
GBTrudeau

4/13/86

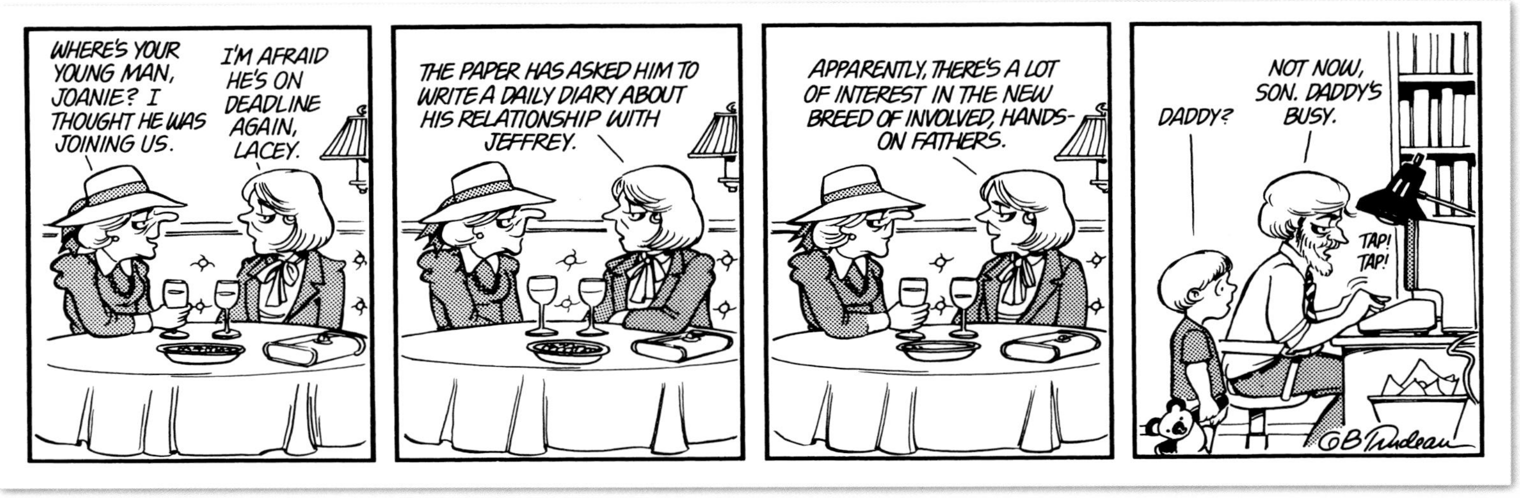
WHERE'S YOUR YOUNG MAN, JOANIE? I THOUGHT HE WAS JOINING US.
I'M AFRAID HE'S ON DEADLINE AGAIN, LACEY.
THE PAPER HAS ASKED HIM TO WRITE A DAILY DIARY ABOUT HIS RELATIONSHIP WITH JEFFREY.
APPARENTLY, THERE'S A LOT OF INTEREST IN THE NEW BREED OF INVOLVED, HANDS-ON FATHERS.
DADDY?
NOT NOW, SON. DADDY'S BUSY.
TAP! TAP!
©B Trudeau

3/25/85

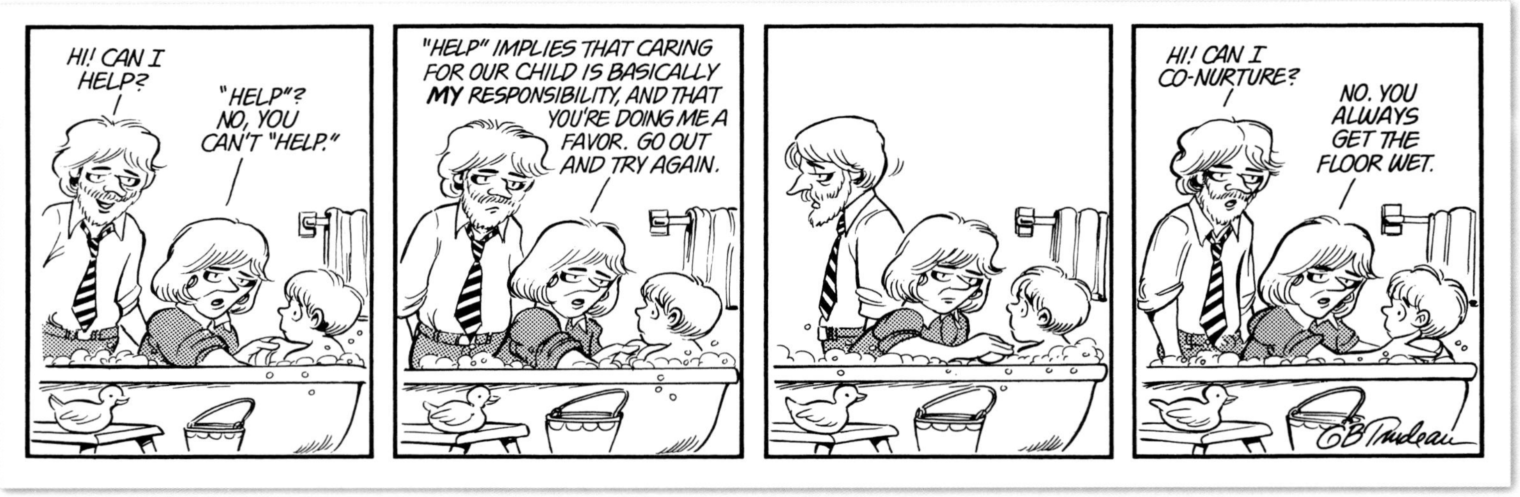
HI! CAN I HELP?
"HELP"? NO, YOU CAN'T "HELP."
"HELP" IMPLIES THAT CARING FOR OUR CHILD IS BASICALLY MY RESPONSIBILITY, AND THAT YOU'RE DOING ME A FAVOR. GO OUT AND TRY AGAIN.
HI! CAN I CO-NURTURE?
NO. YOU ALWAYS GET THE FLOOR WET.
©B Trudeau

8/4/86

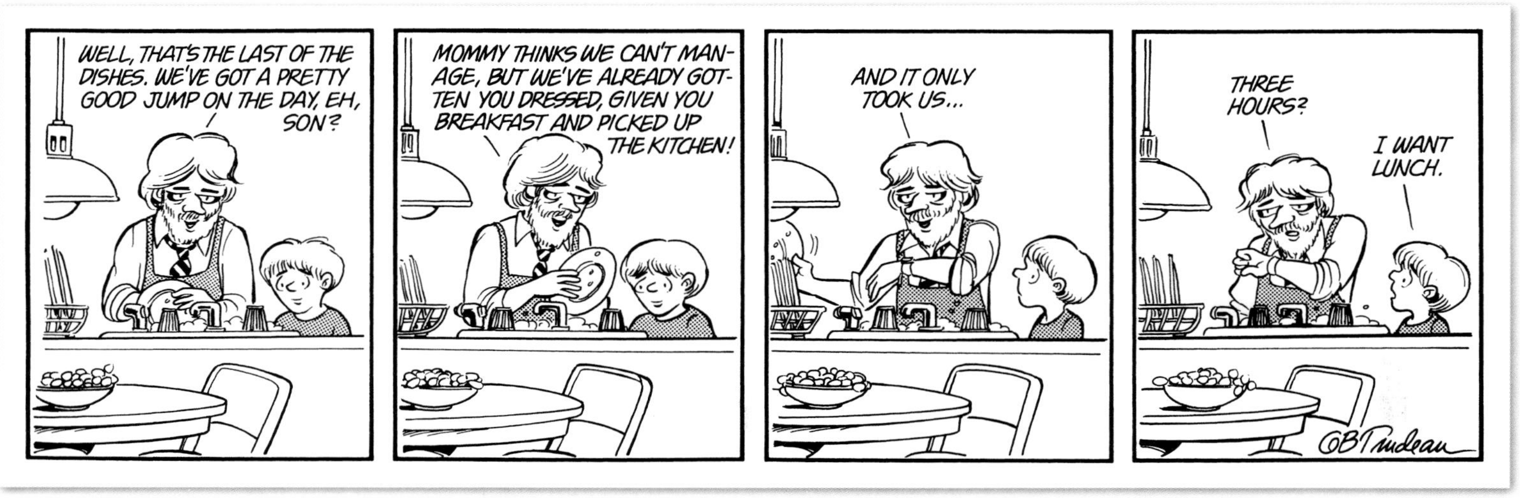
WELL, THAT'S THE LAST OF THE DISHES. WE'VE GOT A PRETTY GOOD JUMP ON THE DAY, EH, SON?
MOMMY THINKS WE CAN'T MANAGE, BUT WE'VE ALREADY GOTTEN YOU DRESSED, GIVEN YOU BREAKFAST AND PICKED UP THE KITCHEN!
AND IT ONLY TOOK US...
THREE HOURS?
I WANT LUNCH.
©B Trudeau

8/6/86

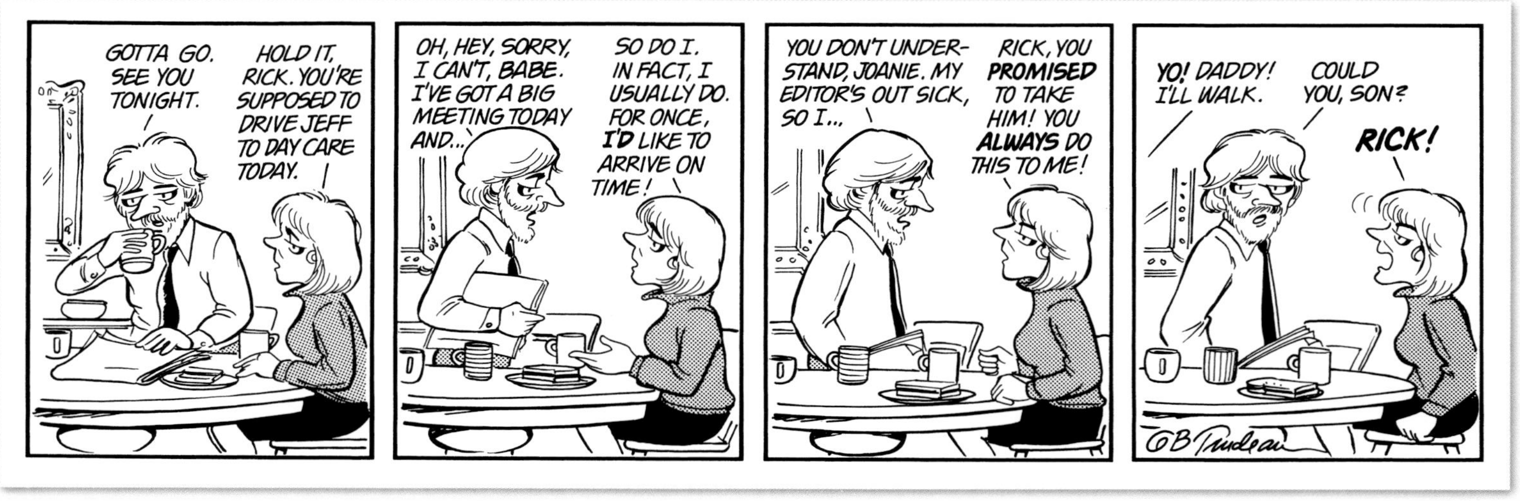
GOTTA GO. SEE YOU TONIGHT.
HOLD IT, RICK. YOU'RE SUPPOSED TO DRIVE JEFF TO DAY CARE TODAY.
OH, HEY, SORRY, I CAN'T, BABE. I'VE GOT A BIG MEETING TODAY AND...
SO DO I. IN FACT, I USUALLY DO. FOR ONCE, I'D LIKE TO ARRIVE ON TIME!
YOU DON'T UNDERSTAND, JOANIE. MY EDITOR'S OUT SICK, SO I...
RICK, YOU PROMISED TO TAKE HIM! YOU ALWAYS DO THIS TO ME!
YO! DADDY! I'LL WALK.
COULD YOU, SON?
RICK!
©B Trudeau

1/19/87

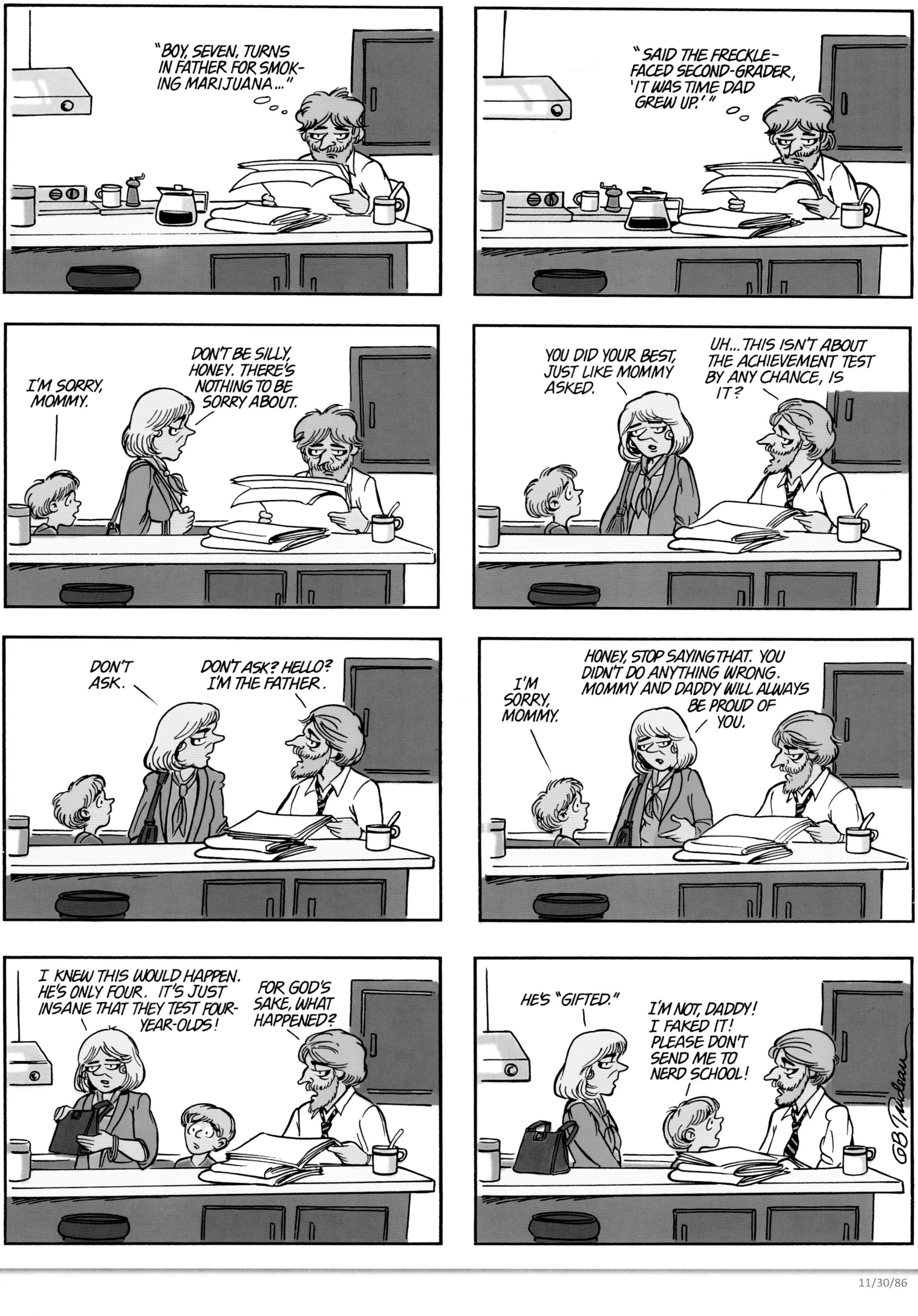
"BOY, SEVEN, TURNS IN FATHER FOR SMOKING MARIJUANA..."
"SAID THE FRECKLE-FACED SECOND-GRADER, 'IT WAS TIME DAD GREW UP.' "
I'M SORRY, MOMMY.
DON'T BE SILLY, HONEY. THERE'S NOTHING TO BE SORRY ABOUT.
YOU DID YOUR BEST, JUST LIKE MOMMY ASKED.
UH... THIS ISN'T ABOUT THE ACHIEVEMENT TEST BY ANY CHANCE, IS IT?
DON'T ASK.
DON'T ASK? HELLO? I'M THE FATHER.
I'M SORRY, MOMMY.
HONEY, STOP SAYING THAT. YOU DIDN'T DO ANYTHING WRONG. MOMMY AND DADDY WILL ALWAYS BE PROUD OF YOU.
I KNEW THIS WOULD HAPPEN. HE'S ONLY FOUR. IT'S JUST INSANE THAT THEY TEST FOUR-YEAR-OLDS!
FOR GOD'S SAKE, WHAT HAPPENED?
HE'S "GIFTED."
I'M NOT, DADDY! I FAKED IT! PLEASE DON'T SEND ME TO NERD SCHOOL!
GB Trudeau

11/30/86

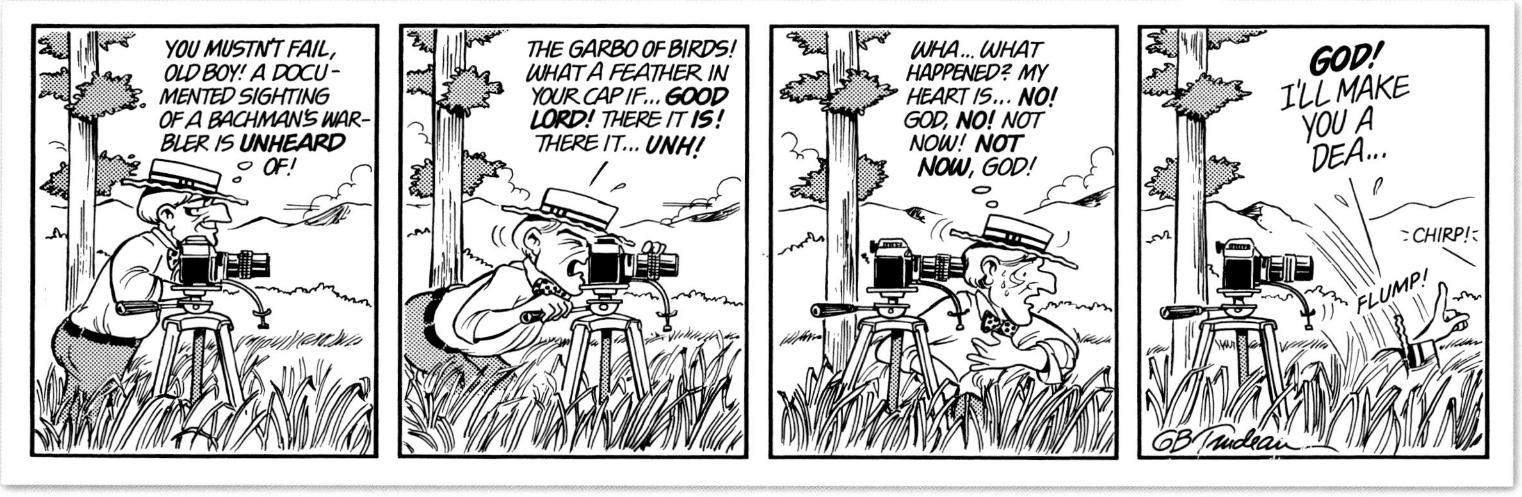
YOU MUSTN'T FAIL, OLD BOY! A DOCU-MENTED SIGHTING OF A BACHMAN'S WAR-BLER IS **UNHEARD** OF!
THE GARBO OF BIRDS! WHAT A FEATHER IN YOUR CAP IF... **GOOD LORD!** THERE IT **IS!** THERE IT... **UNH!**
WHA... WHAT HAPPENED? MY HEART IS... **NO!** GOD, **NO!** NOT NOW! **NOT NOW**, GOD!
GOD! I'LL MAKE YOU A DEA...
CHIRP!
FLUMP!
GB Trudeau

11/4/86

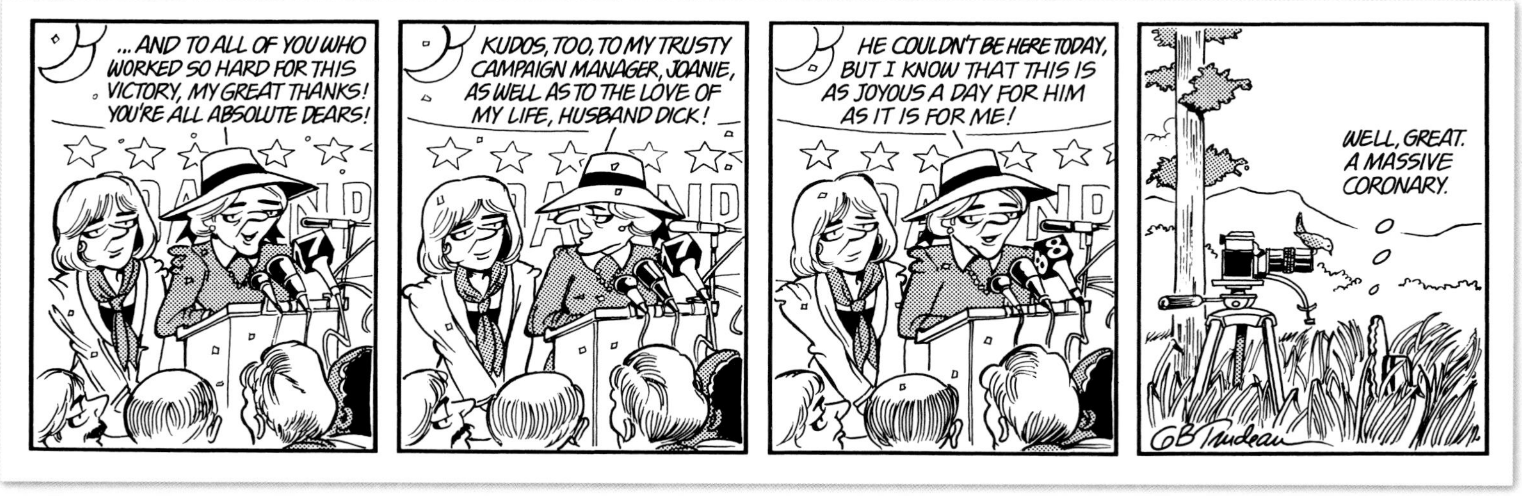
... AND TO ALL OF YOU WHO WORKED SO HARD FOR THIS VICTORY, MY GREAT THANKS! YOU'RE ALL ABSOLUTE DEARS!
KUDOS, TOO, TO MY TRUSTY CAMPAIGN MANAGER, JOANIE, AS WELL AS TO THE LOVE OF MY LIFE, HUSBAND DICK!
HE COULDN'T BE HERE TODAY, BUT I KNOW THAT THIS IS AS JOYOUS A DAY FOR HIM AS IT IS FOR ME!
WELL, GREAT. A MASSIVE CORONARY.
GB Trudeau

11/5/86

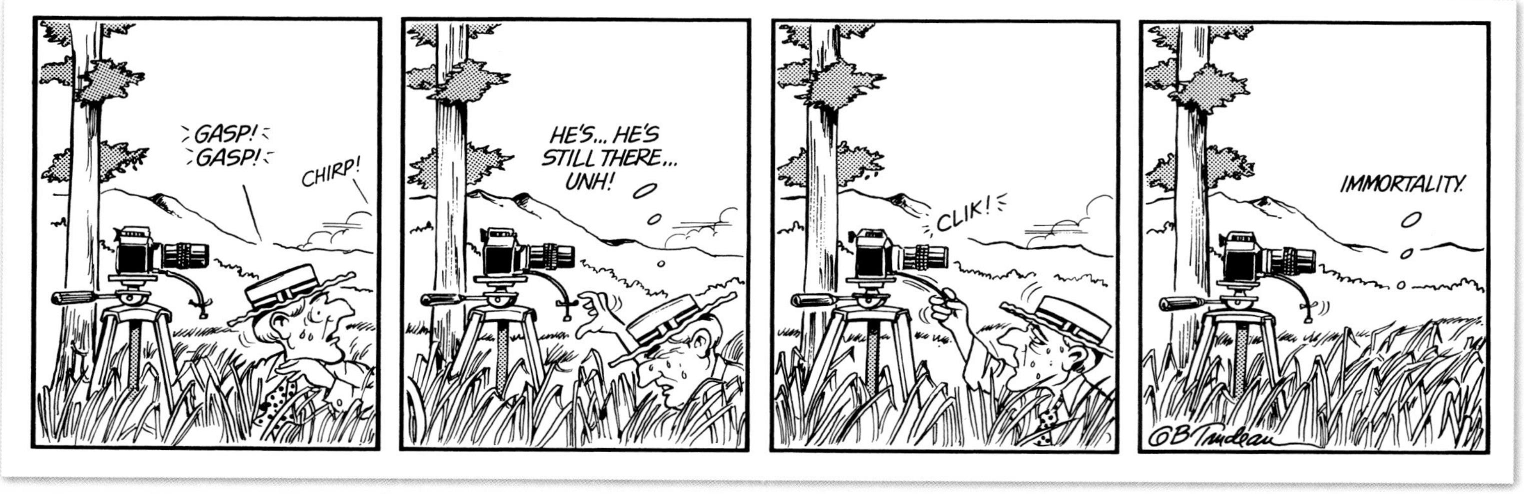
GASP! GASP!
CHIRP!
HE'S... HE'S STILL THERE... UNH!
CLIK!
IMMORTALITY.
GB Trudeau

11/6/86

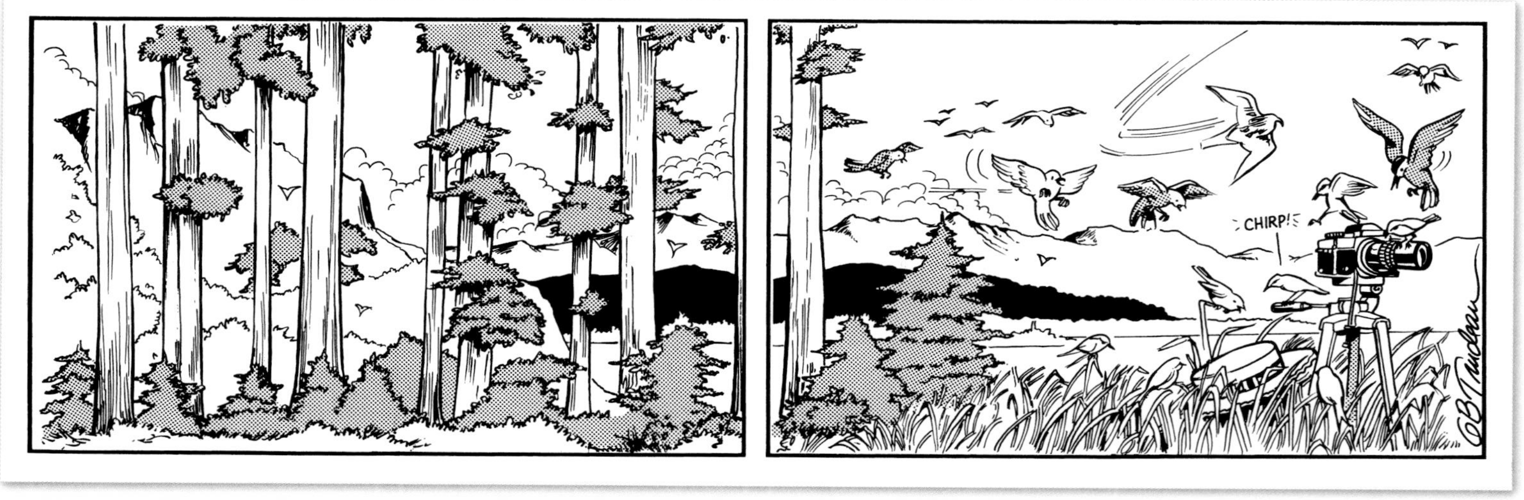
CHIRP!
GB Trudeau

11/7/86

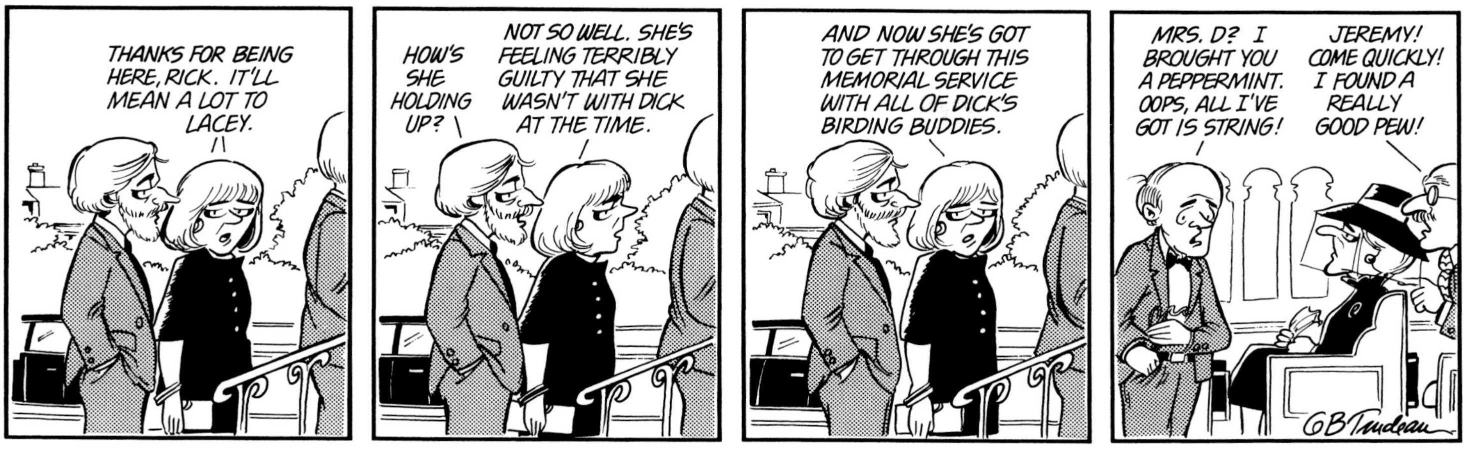
THANKS FOR BEING HERE, RICK. IT'LL MEAN A LOT TO LACEY.
HOW'S SHE HOLDING UP?
NOT SO WELL. SHE'S FEELING TERRIBLY GUILTY THAT SHE WASN'T WITH DICK AT THE TIME.
AND NOW SHE'S GOT TO GET THROUGH THIS MEMORIAL SERVICE WITH ALL OF DICK'S BIRDING BUDDIES.
MRS. D? I BROUGHT YOU A PEPPERMINT. OOPS, ALL I'VE GOT IS STRING!
JEREMY! COME QUICKLY! I FOUND A REALLY GOOD PEW!
GB Trudeau

11/10/86

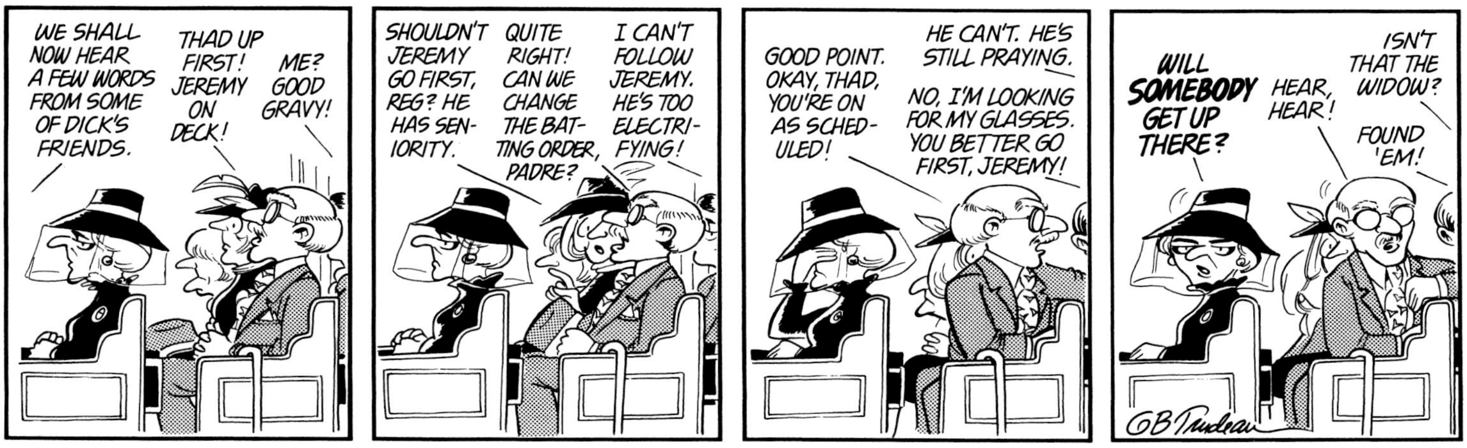
WE SHALL NOW HEAR A FEW WORDS FROM SOME OF DICK'S FRIENDS.
THAD UP FIRST! JEREMY ON DECK!
ME? GOOD GRAVY!
SHOULDN'T JEREMY GO FIRST, REG? HE HAS SENIORITY.
QUITE RIGHT! CAN WE CHANGE THE BATTING ORDER, PADRE?
I CAN'T FOLLOW JEREMY. HE'S TOO ELECTRIFYING!
GOOD POINT. OKAY, THAD, YOU'RE ON AS SCHEDULED!
HE CAN'T. HE'S STILL PRAYING.
NO, I'M LOOKING FOR MY GLASSES. YOU BETTER GO FIRST, JEREMY!
WILL SOMEBODY GET UP THERE?
HEAR, HEAR!
ISN'T THAT THE WIDOW?
FOUND 'EM!
GB Trudeau

11/11/86

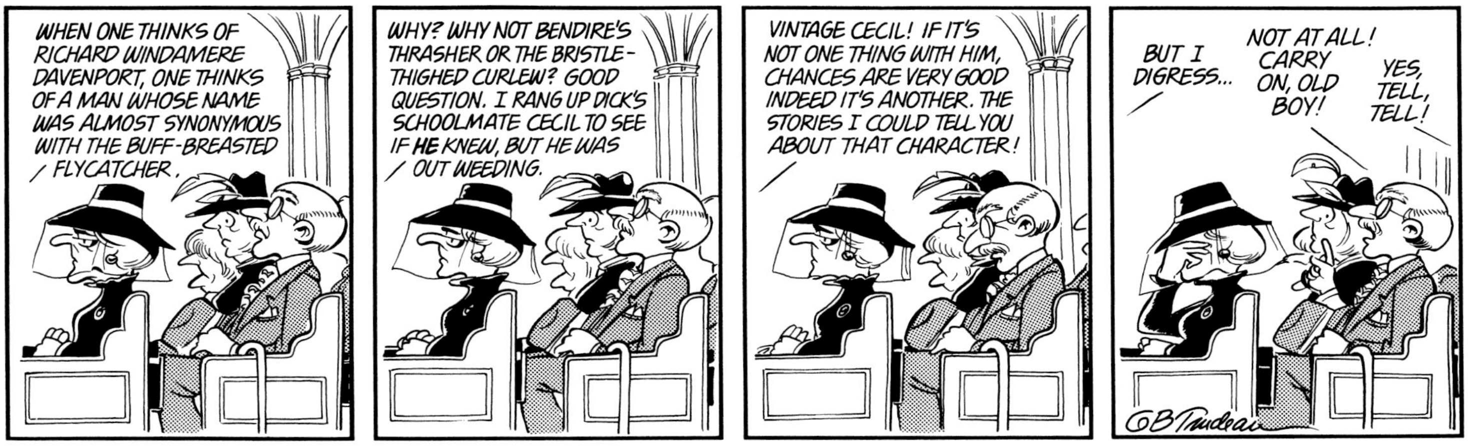
WHEN ONE THINKS OF RICHARD WINDAMERE DAVENPORT, ONE THINKS OF A MAN WHOSE NAME WAS ALMOST SYNONYMOUS WITH THE BUFF-BREASTED FLYCATCHER.
WHY? WHY NOT BENDIRE'S THRASHER OR THE BRISTLE-THIGHED CURLEW? GOOD QUESTION. I RANG UP DICK'S SCHOOLMATE CECIL TO SEE IF HE KNEW, BUT HE WAS OUT WEEDING.
VINTAGE CECIL! IF IT'S NOT ONE THING WITH HIM, CHANCES ARE VERY GOOD INDEED IT'S ANOTHER. THE STORIES I COULD TELL YOU ABOUT THAT CHARACTER!
BUT I DIGRESS...
NOT AT ALL! CARRY ON, OLD BOY!
YES, TELL, TELL!
GB Trudeau

11/13/86

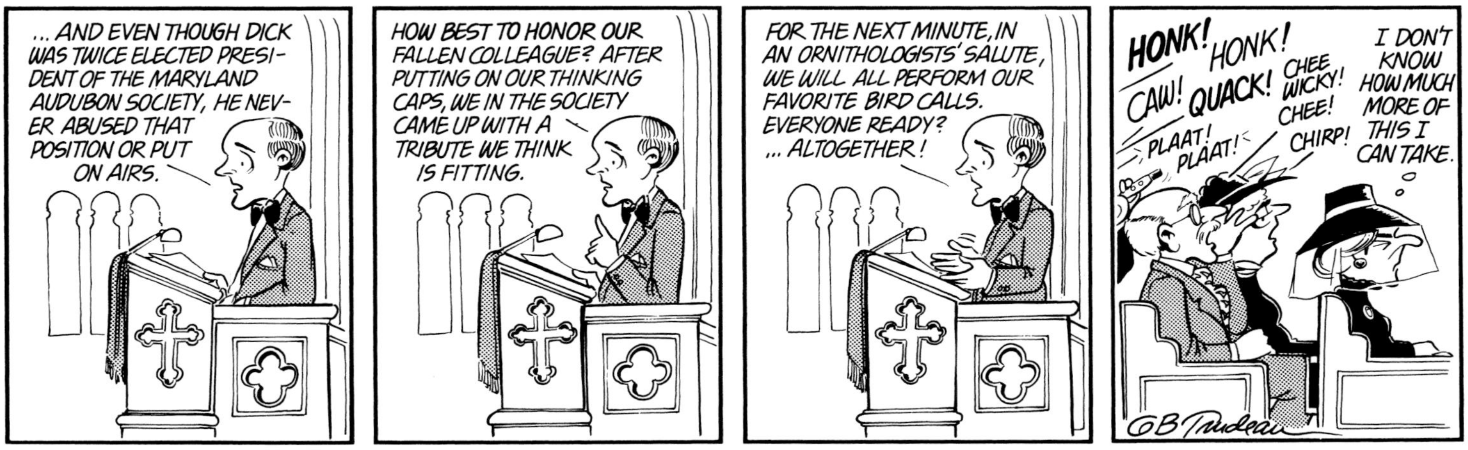
...AND EVEN THOUGH DICK WAS TWICE ELECTED PRESIDENT OF THE MARYLAND AUDUBON SOCIETY, HE NEVER ABUSED THAT POSITION OR PUT ON AIRS.
HOW BEST TO HONOR OUR FALLEN COLLEAGUE? AFTER PUTTING ON OUR THINKING CAPS, WE IN THE SOCIETY CAME UP WITH A TRIBUTE WE THINK IS FITTING.
FOR THE NEXT MINUTE, IN AN ORNITHOLOGISTS' SALUTE, WE WILL ALL PERFORM OUR FAVORITE BIRD CALLS. EVERYONE READY? ...ALTOGETHER!
HONK! HONK!
CAW! QUACK!
PLAAT! PLAAT!
CHEE WICKY! CHEE!
CHIRP!
I DON'T KNOW HOW MUCH MORE OF THIS I CAN TAKE.
GB Trudeau

11/14/86

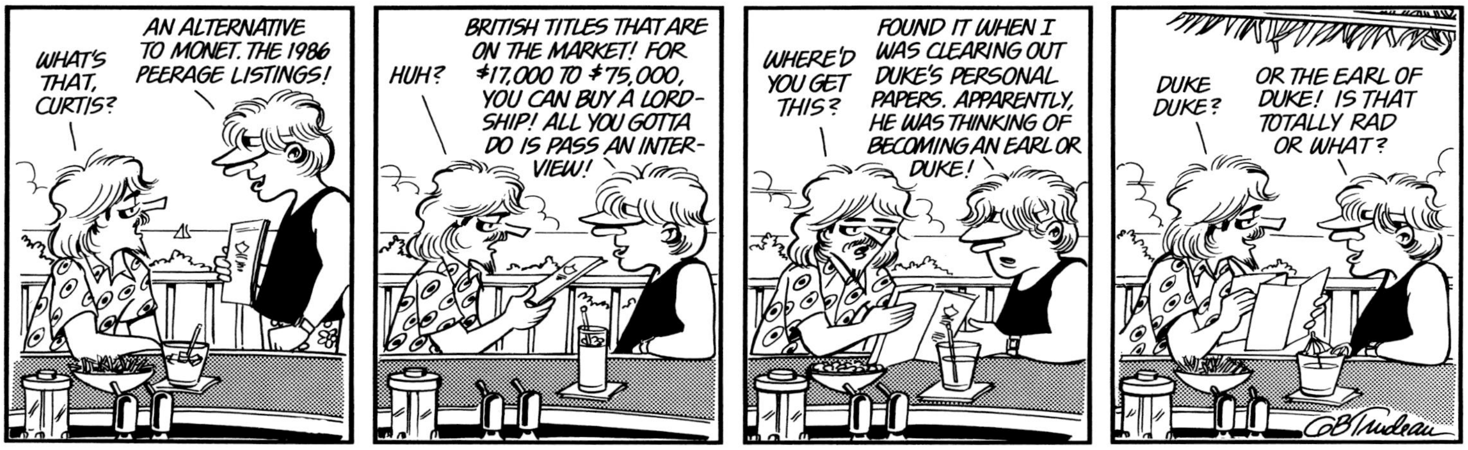
WHAT'S THAT, CURTIS?
AN ALTERNATIVE TO MONET. THE 1986 PEERAGE LISTINGS!
HUH?
BRITISH TITLES THAT ARE ON THE MARKET! FOR $17,000 TO $75,000, YOU CAN BUY A LORDSHIP! ALL YOU GOTTA DO IS PASS AN INTERVIEW!
WHERE'D YOU GET THIS?
FOUND IT WHEN I WAS CLEARING OUT DUKE'S PERSONAL PAPERS. APPARENTLY, HE WAS THINKING OF BECOMING AN EARL OR DUKE!
DUKE DUKE?
OR THE EARL OF DUKE! IS THAT TOTALLY RAD OR WHAT?
GBTrudeau

5/29/86

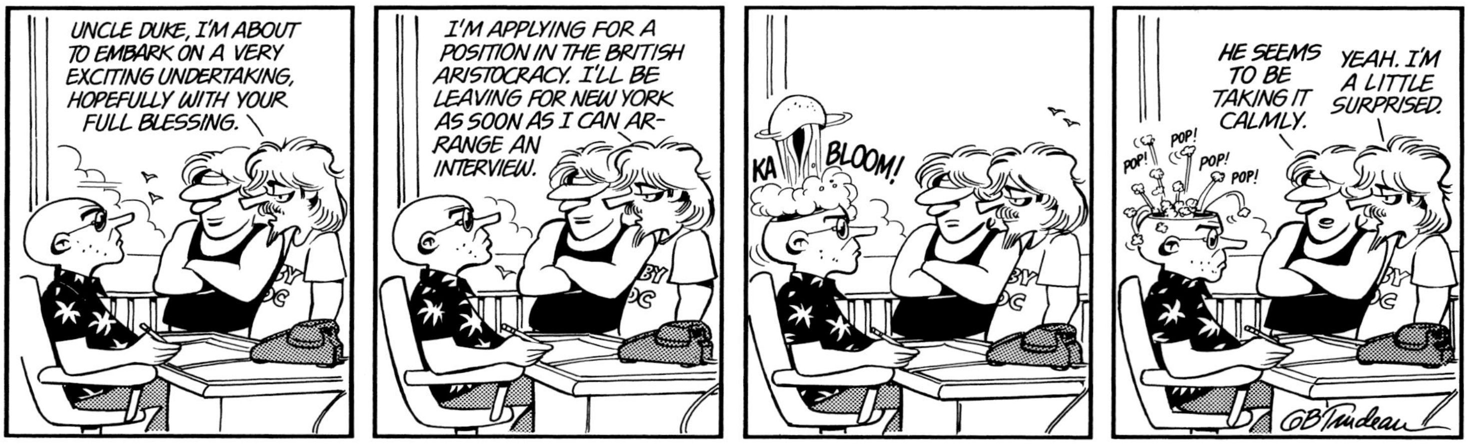
UNCLE DUKE, I'M ABOUT TO EMBARK ON A VERY EXCITING UNDERTAKING, HOPEFULLY WITH YOUR FULL BLESSING.
I'M APPLYING FOR A POSITION IN THE BRITISH ARISTOCRACY. I'LL BE LEAVING FOR NEW YORK AS SOON AS I CAN ARRANGE AN INTERVIEW.
KA BLOOM!
POP! POP! POP! POP!
HE SEEMS TO BE TAKING IT CALMLY.
YEAH. I'M A LITTLE SURPRISED.
GBTrudeau

6/2/86

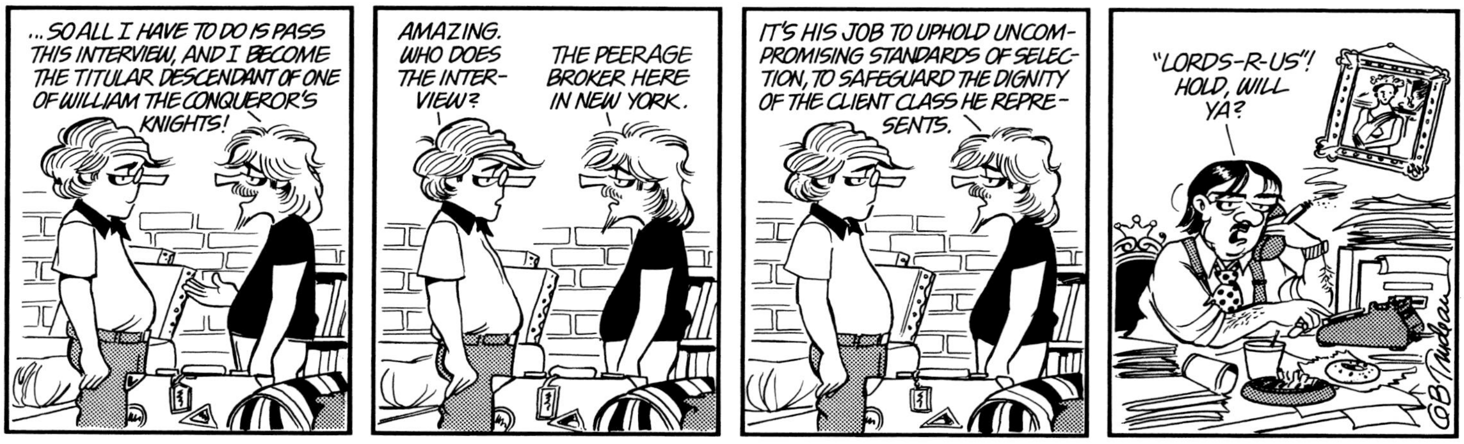
...SO ALL I HAVE TO DO IS PASS THIS INTERVIEW, AND I BECOME THE TITULAR DESCENDANT OF ONE OF WILLIAM THE CONQUEROR'S KNIGHTS!
AMAZING. WHO DOES THE INTERVIEW?
THE PEERAGE BROKER HERE IN NEW YORK.
IT'S HIS JOB TO UPHOLD UNCOMPROMISING STANDARDS OF SELECTION, TO SAFEGUARD THE DIGNITY OF THE CLIENT CLASS HE REPRESENTS.
"LORDS-R-US"! HOLD, WILL YA?
GBTrudeau

6/10/86

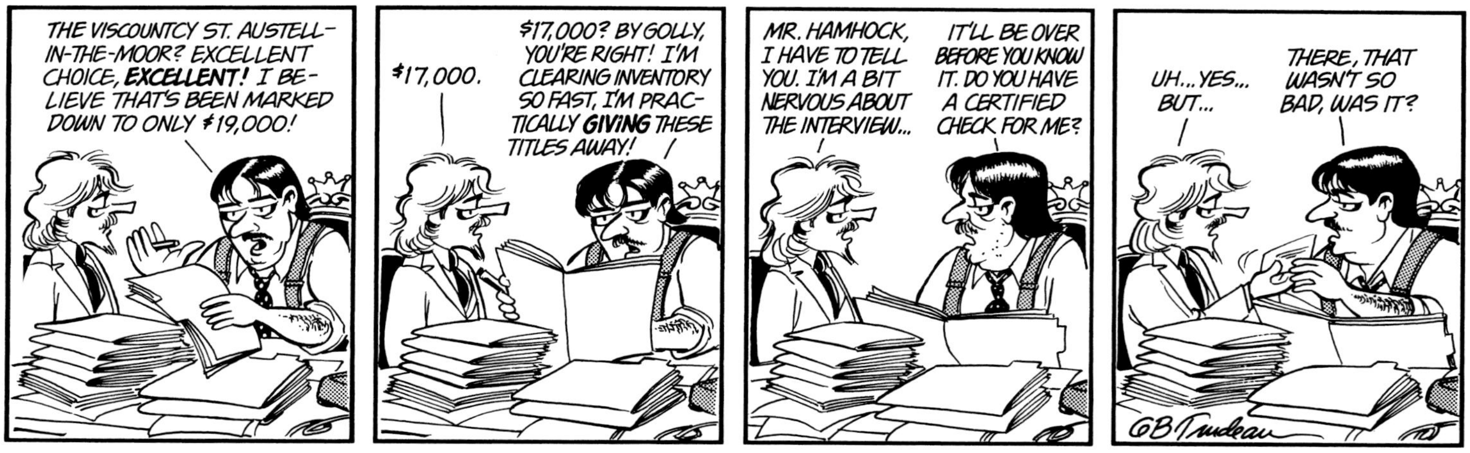
THE VISCOUNTCY ST. AUSTELL-IN-THE-MOOR? EXCELLENT CHOICE, EXCELLENT! I BELIEVE THAT'S BEEN MARKED DOWN TO ONLY $19,000!
$17,000.
$17,000? BY GOLLY, YOU'RE RIGHT! I'M CLEARING INVENTORY SO FAST, I'M PRACTICALLY GIVING THESE TITLES AWAY!
MR. HAMHOCK, I HAVE TO TELL YOU. I'M A BIT NERVOUS ABOUT THE INTERVIEW...
IT'LL BE OVER BEFORE YOU KNOW IT. DO YOU HAVE A CERTIFIED CHECK FOR ME?
UH...YES... BUT...
THERE, THAT WASN'T SO BAD, WAS IT?
GBTrudeau

6/17/86

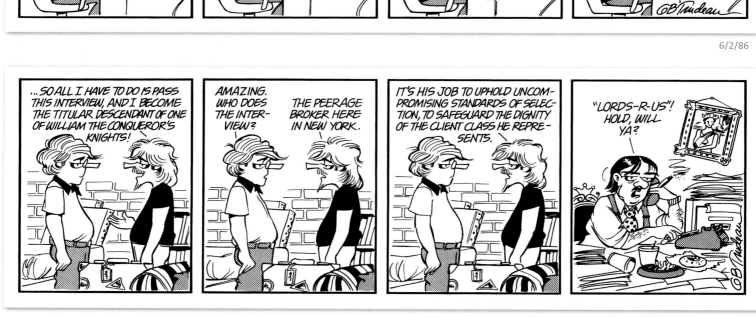

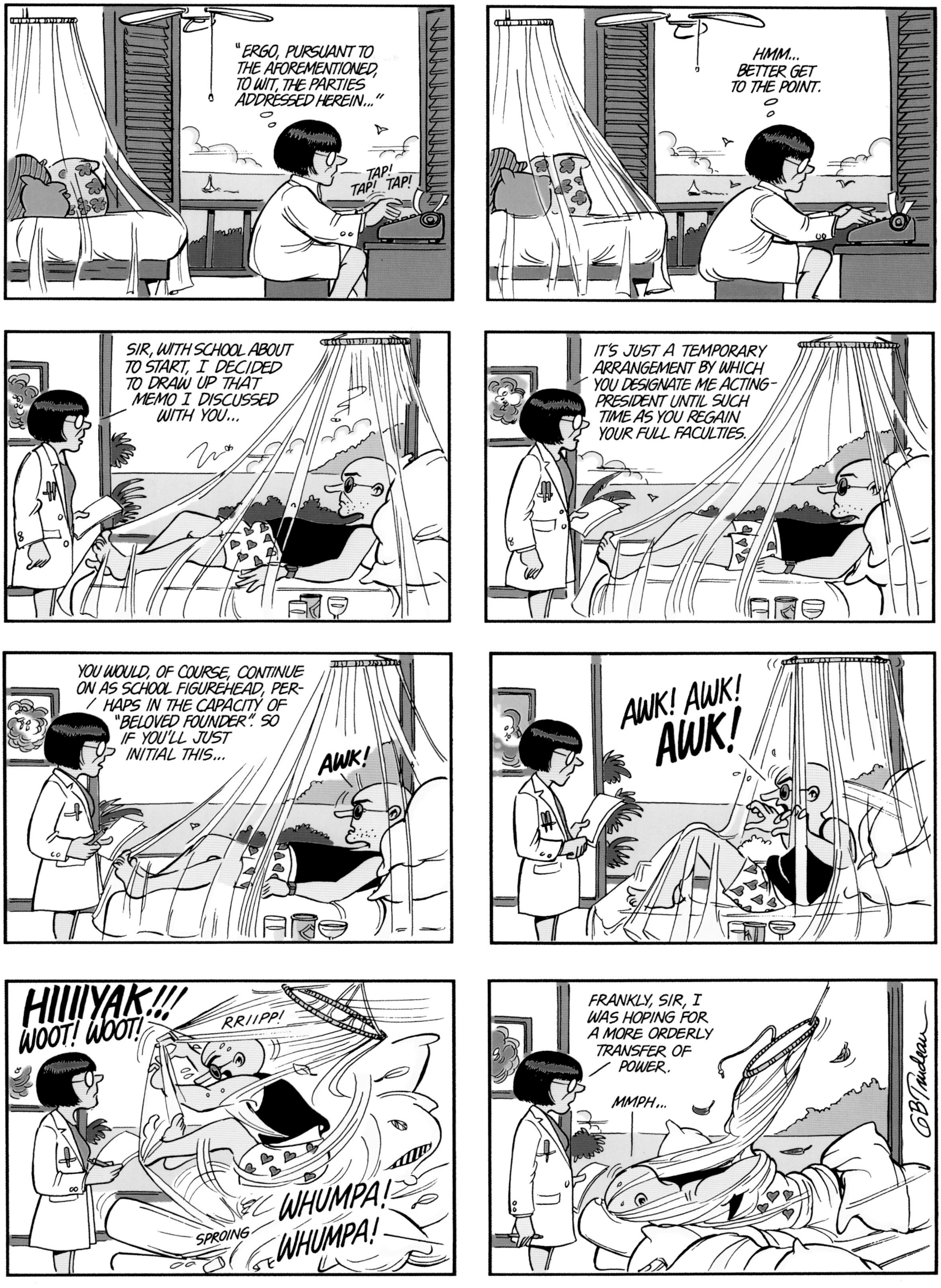
"ERGO, PURSUANT TO THE AFOREMENTIONED, TO WIT, THE PARTIES ADDRESSED HEREIN..."
TAP! TAP! TAP!
HMM... BETTER GET TO THE POINT.
SIR, WITH SCHOOL ABOUT TO START, I DECIDED TO DRAW UP THAT MEMO I DISCUSSED WITH YOU...
IT'S JUST A TEMPORARY ARRANGEMENT BY WHICH YOU DESIGNATE ME ACTING-PRESIDENT UNTIL SUCH TIME AS YOU REGAIN YOUR FULL FACULTIES.
YOU WOULD, OF COURSE, CONTINUE ON AS SCHOOL FIGUREHEAD, PERHAPS IN THE CAPACITY OF "BELOVED FOUNDER". SO IF YOU'LL JUST INITIAL THIS...
AWK!
AWK! AWK! AWK!
HIIIIYAK!!! WOOT! WOOT!
RRIIPP!
WHUMPA! WHUMPA!
SPROING
FRANKLY, SIR, I WAS HOPING FOR A MORE ORDERLY TRANSFER OF POWER.
MMPH...
GBTrudeau

9/14/86

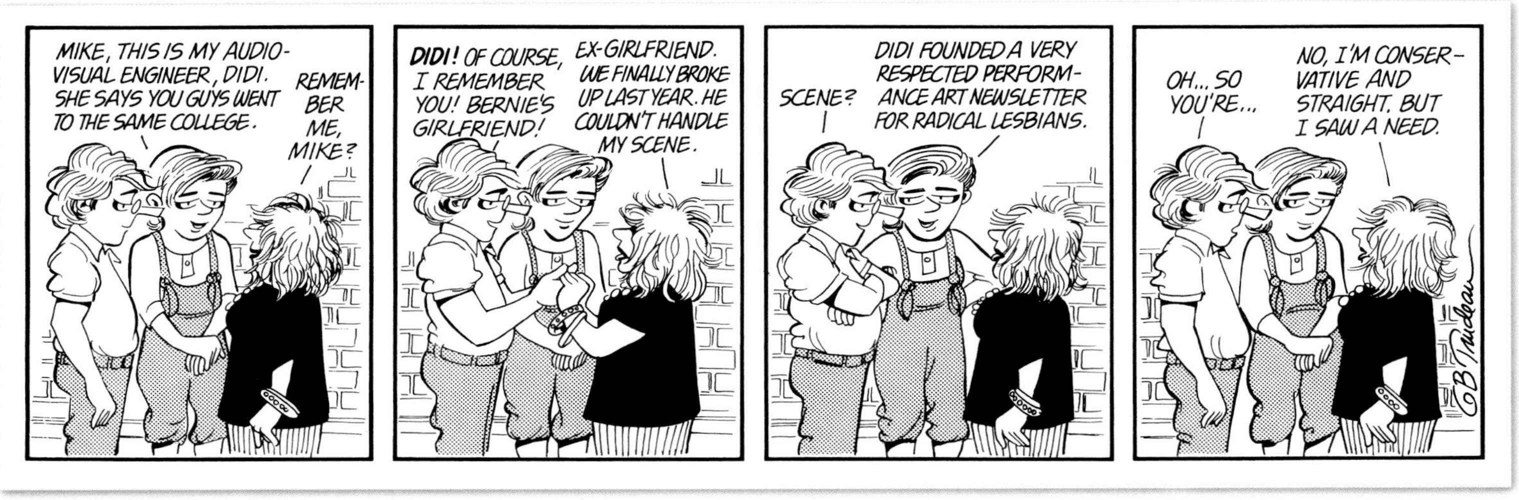
MIKE, THIS IS MY AUDIO-VISUAL ENGINEER, DIDI. SHE SAYS YOU GUYS WENT TO THE SAME COLLEGE.
REMEMBER ME, MIKE?
DIDI! OF COURSE, I REMEMBER YOU! BERNIE'S GIRLFRIEND!
EX-GIRLFRIEND. WE FINALLY BROKE UP LAST YEAR. HE COULDN'T HANDLE MY SCENE.
SCENE?
DIDI FOUNDED A VERY RESPECTED PERFORMANCE ART NEWSLETTER FOR RADICAL LESBIANS.
OH... SO YOU'RE...
NO, I'M CONSERVATIVE AND STRAIGHT. BUT I SAW A NEED.
GB Trudeau

9/9/86

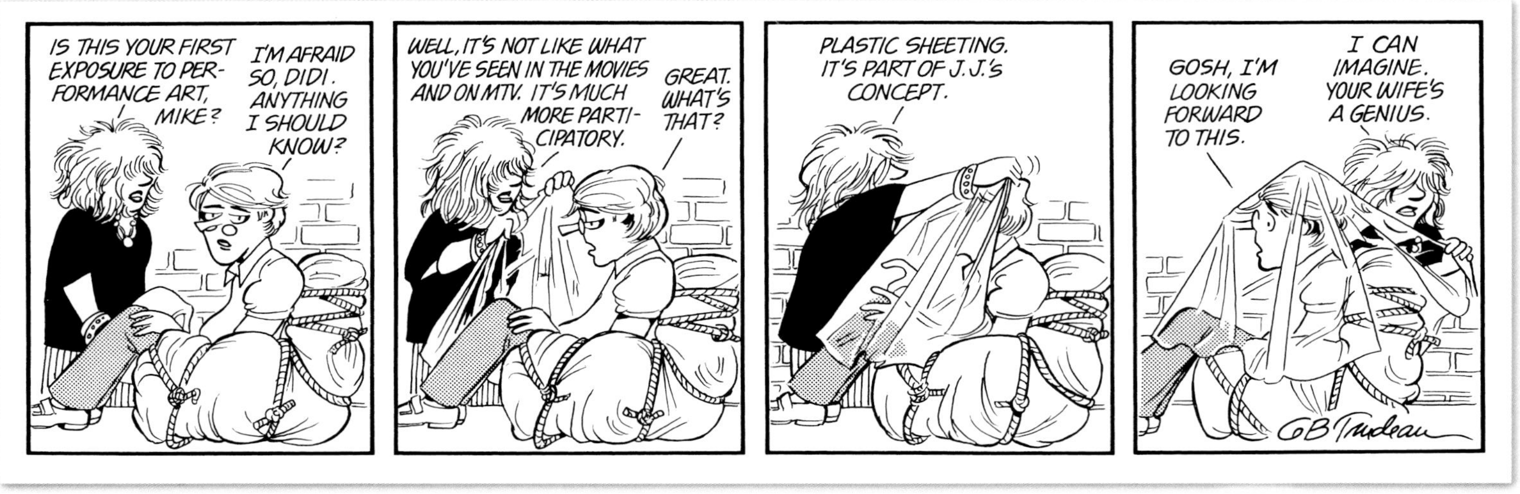
IS THIS YOUR FIRST EXPOSURE TO PERFORMANCE ART, MIKE?
I'M AFRAID SO, DIDI. ANYTHING I SHOULD KNOW?
WELL, IT'S NOT LIKE WHAT YOU'VE SEEN IN THE MOVIES AND ON MTV. IT'S MUCH MORE PARTICIPATORY.
GREAT. WHAT'S THAT?
PLASTIC SHEETING. IT'S PART OF J.J.'S CONCEPT.
GOSH, I'M LOOKING FORWARD TO THIS.
I CAN IMAGINE. YOUR WIFE'S A GENIUS.
GB Trudeau

9/10/86

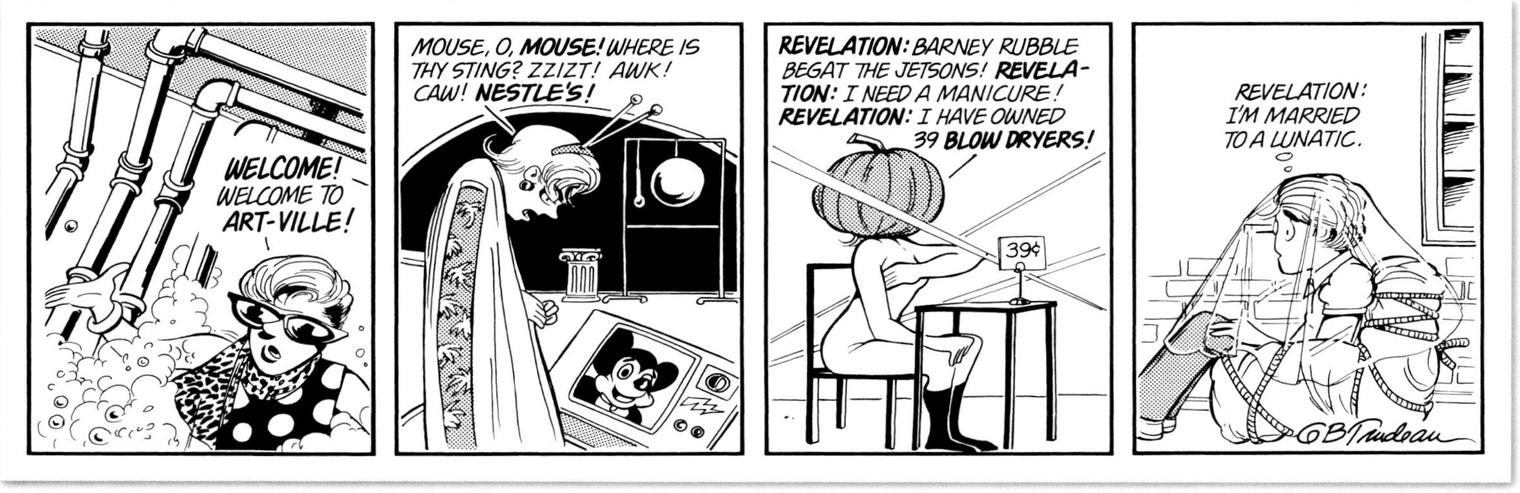
WELCOME! WELCOME TO ART-VILLE!
MOUSE, O, MOUSE! WHERE IS THY STING? ZZIZT! AWK! CAW! NESTLE'S!
REVELATION: BARNEY RUBBLE BEGAT THE JETSONS! REVELATION: I NEED A MANICURE! REVELATION: I HAVE OWNED 39 BLOW DRYERS!
39¢
REVELATION: I'M MARRIED TO A LUNATIC.
GB Trudeau

9/11/86

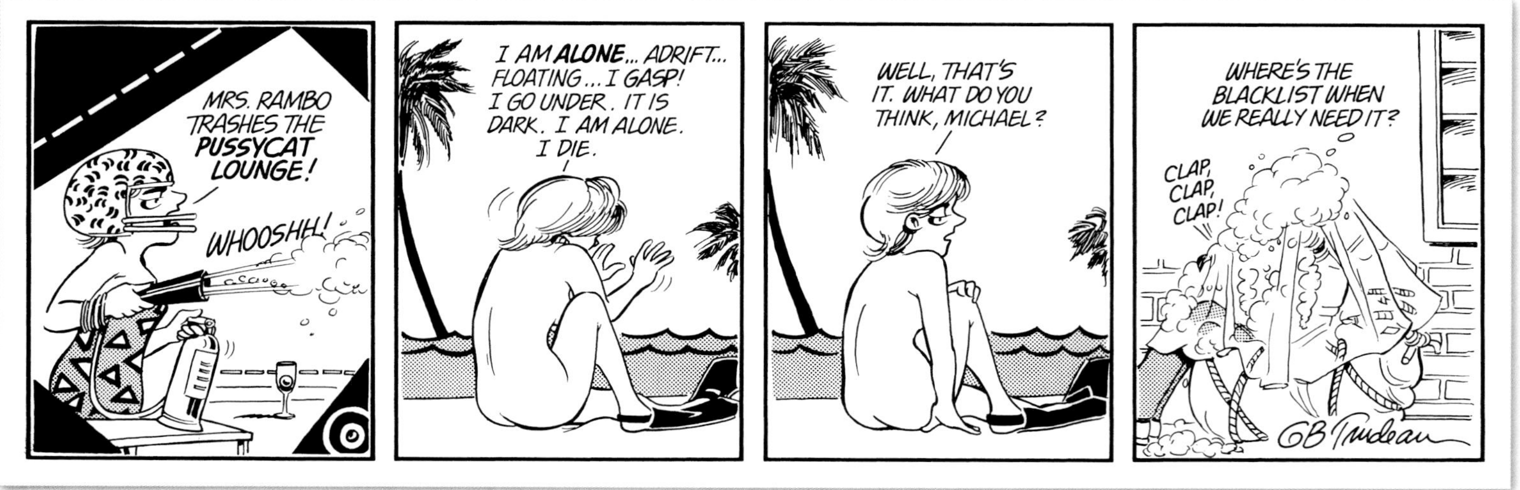
MRS. RAMBO TRASHES THE PUSSYCAT LOUNGE!
WHOOSHH!
I AM ALONE... ADRIFT... FLOATING... I GASP! I GO UNDER. IT IS DARK. I AM ALONE. I DIE.
WELL, THAT'S IT. WHAT DO YOU THINK, MICHAEL?
WHERE'S THE BLACKLIST WHEN WE REALLY NEED IT?
CLAP, CLAP, CLAP!
GB Trudeau

9/12/86

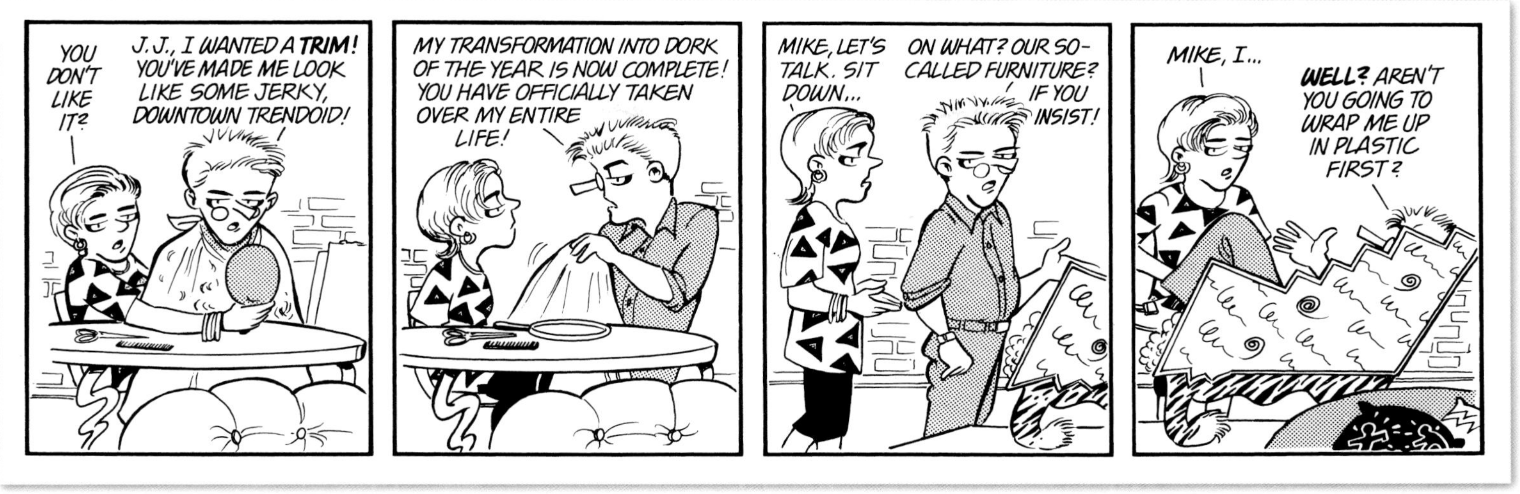
YOU DON'T LIKE IT?
J.J., I WANTED A **TRIM**! YOU'VE MADE ME LOOK LIKE SOME JERKY, DOWNTOWN TRENDOID!
MY TRANSFORMATION INTO DORK OF THE YEAR IS NOW COMPLETE! YOU HAVE OFFICIALLY TAKEN OVER MY ENTIRE LIFE!
MIKE, LET'S TALK. SIT DOWN...
ON WHAT? OUR SO-CALLED FURNITURE?
IF YOU INSIST!
MIKE, I...
WELL? AREN'T YOU GOING TO WRAP ME UP IN PLASTIC FIRST?

9/23/86

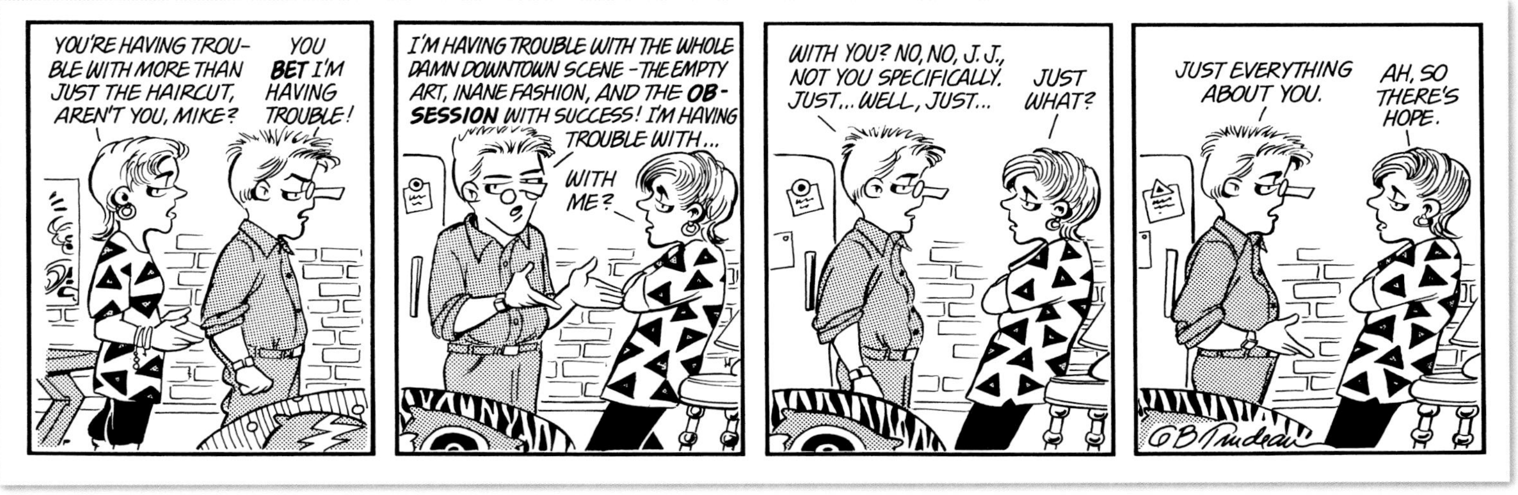
YOU'RE HAVING TROUBLE WITH MORE THAN JUST THE HAIRCUT, AREN'T YOU, MIKE?
YOU **BET** I'M HAVING TROUBLE!
I'M HAVING TROUBLE WITH THE WHOLE DAMN DOWNTOWN SCENE – THE EMPTY ART, INANE FASHION, AND THE **OBSESSION** WITH SUCCESS! I'M HAVING TROUBLE WITH...
WITH ME?
WITH YOU? NO, NO, J.J., NOT YOU SPECIFICALLY. JUST... WELL, JUST...
JUST WHAT?
JUST EVERYTHING ABOUT YOU.
AH, SO THERE'S HOPE.
GB Trudeau

9/24/86

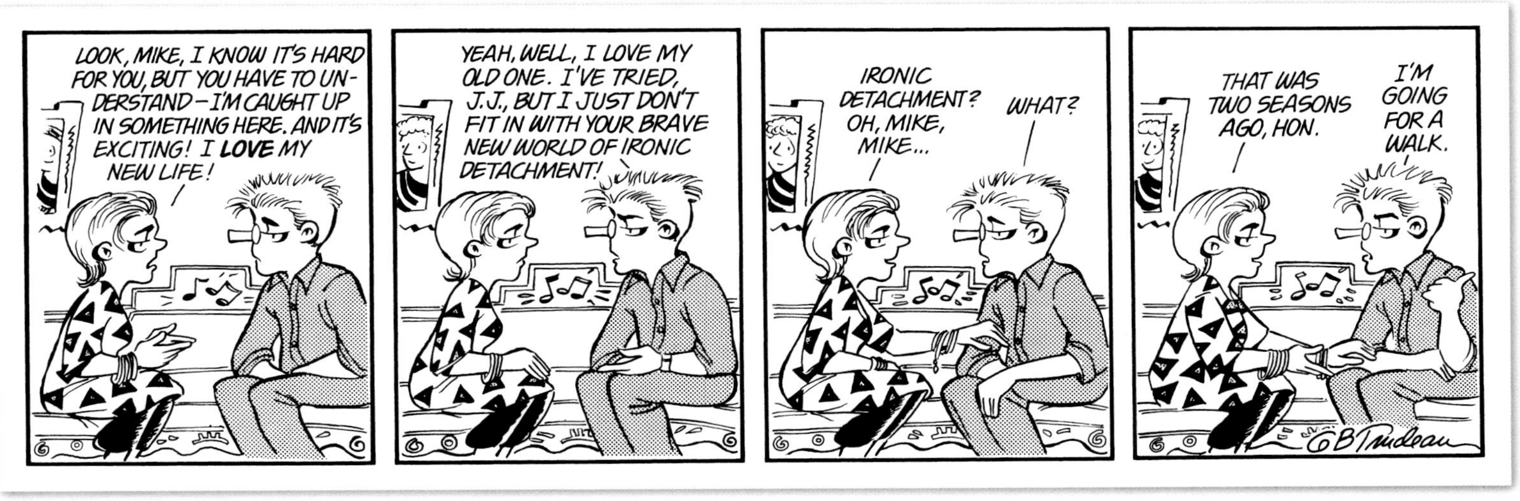
LOOK, MIKE, I KNOW IT'S HARD FOR YOU, BUT YOU HAVE TO UNDERSTAND – I'M CAUGHT UP IN SOMETHING HERE. AND IT'S EXCITING! I **LOVE** MY NEW LIFE!
YEAH, WELL, I LOVE MY OLD ONE. I'VE TRIED, J.J., BUT I JUST DON'T FIT IN WITH YOUR BRAVE NEW WORLD OF IRONIC DETACHMENT!
IRONIC DETACHMENT? OH, MIKE, MIKE...
WHAT?
THAT WAS TWO SEASONS AGO, HON.
I'M GOING FOR A WALK.
GB Trudeau

9/25/86

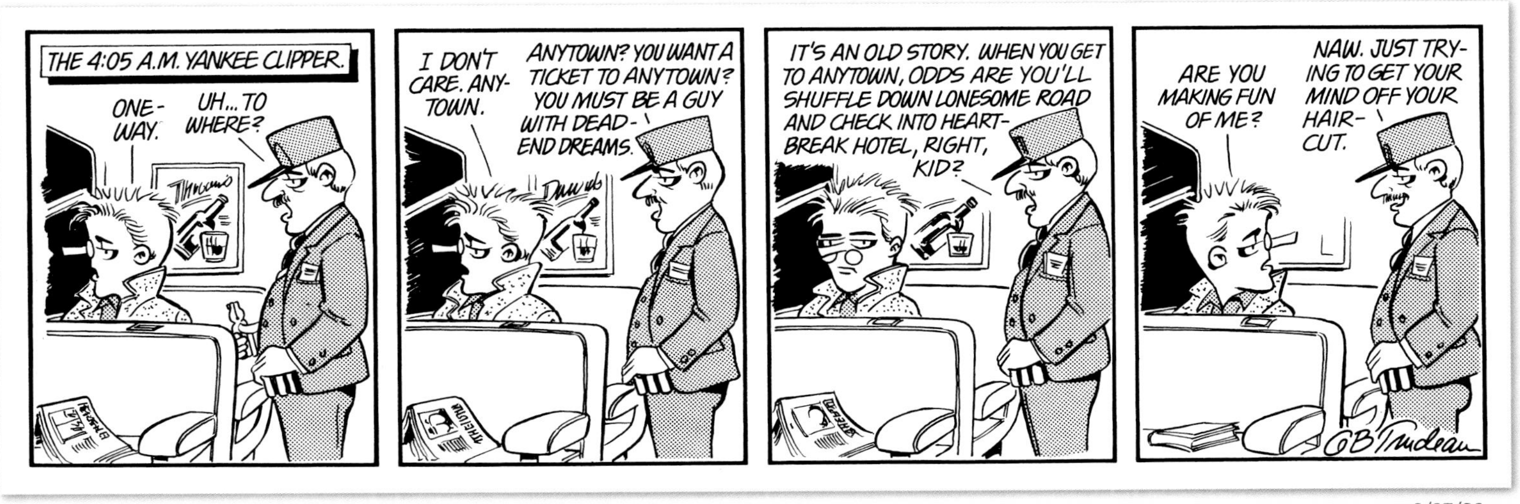
THE 4:05 A.M. YANKEE CLIPPER.
ONE-WAY.
UH... TO WHERE?
I DON'T CARE. ANYTOWN.
ANYTOWN? YOU WANT A TICKET TO ANYTOWN? YOU MUST BE A GUY WITH DEAD-END DREAMS.
IT'S AN OLD STORY. WHEN YOU GET TO ANYTOWN, ODDS ARE YOU'LL SHUFFLE DOWN LONESOME ROAD AND CHECK INTO HEARTBREAK HOTEL, RIGHT, KID?
ARE YOU MAKING FUN OF ME?
NAW. JUST TRYING TO GET YOUR MIND OFF YOUR HAIRCUT.
GB Trudeau

9/27/86

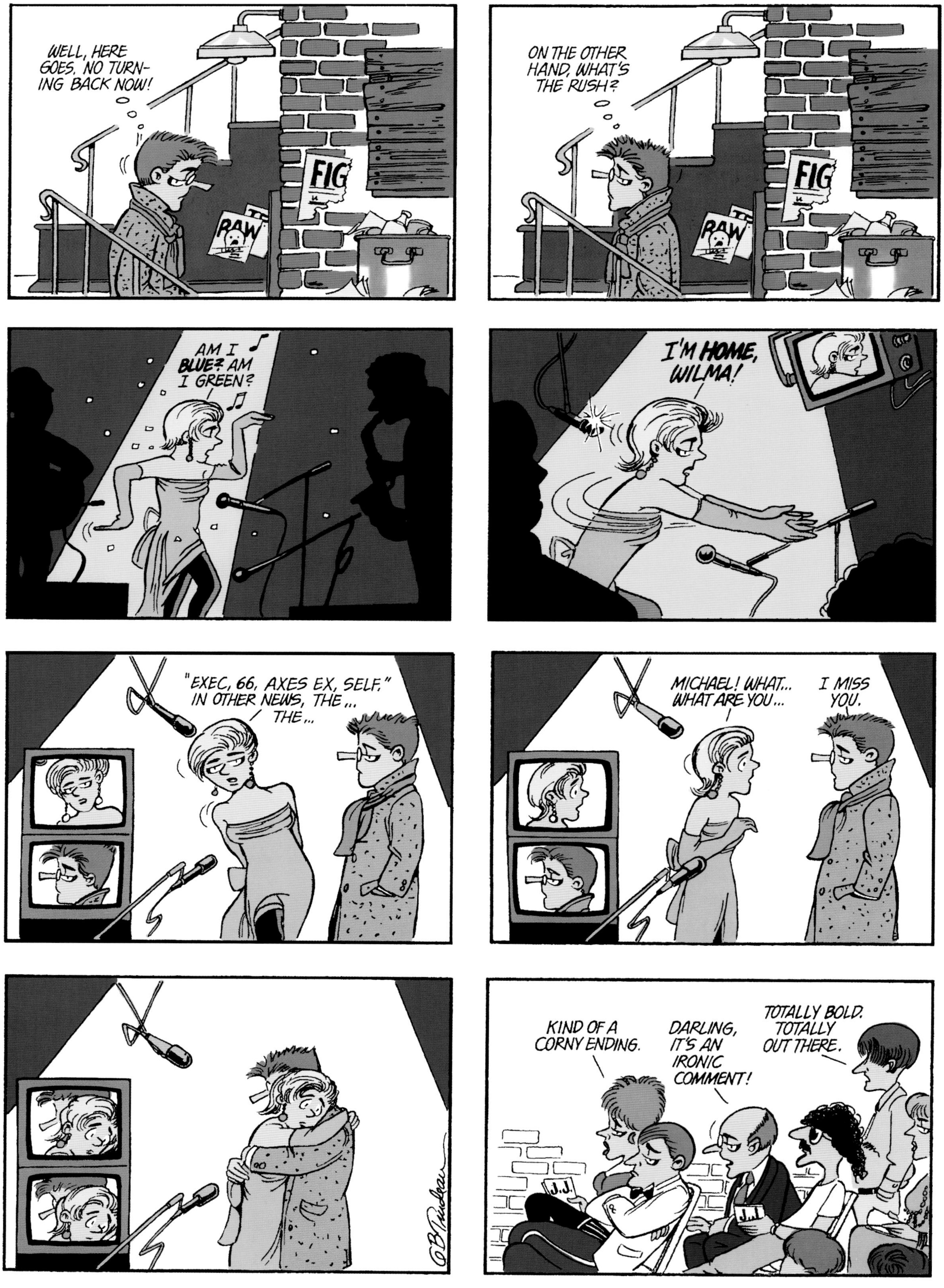
WELL, HERE GOES. NO TURNING BACK NOW!
FIG
RAW
ON THE OTHER HAND, WHAT'S THE RUSH?
FIG
RAW
AM I BLUE? AM I GREEN?
I'M HOME, WILMA!
"EXEC, 66, AXES EX, SELF." IN OTHER NEWS, THE... THE...
MICHAEL! WHAT... WHAT ARE YOU...
I MISS YOU.
KIND OF A CORNY ENDING.
DARLING, IT'S AN IRONIC COMMENT!
TOTALLY BOLD. TOTALLY OUT THERE.
J.J.
J.J.

12/14/86

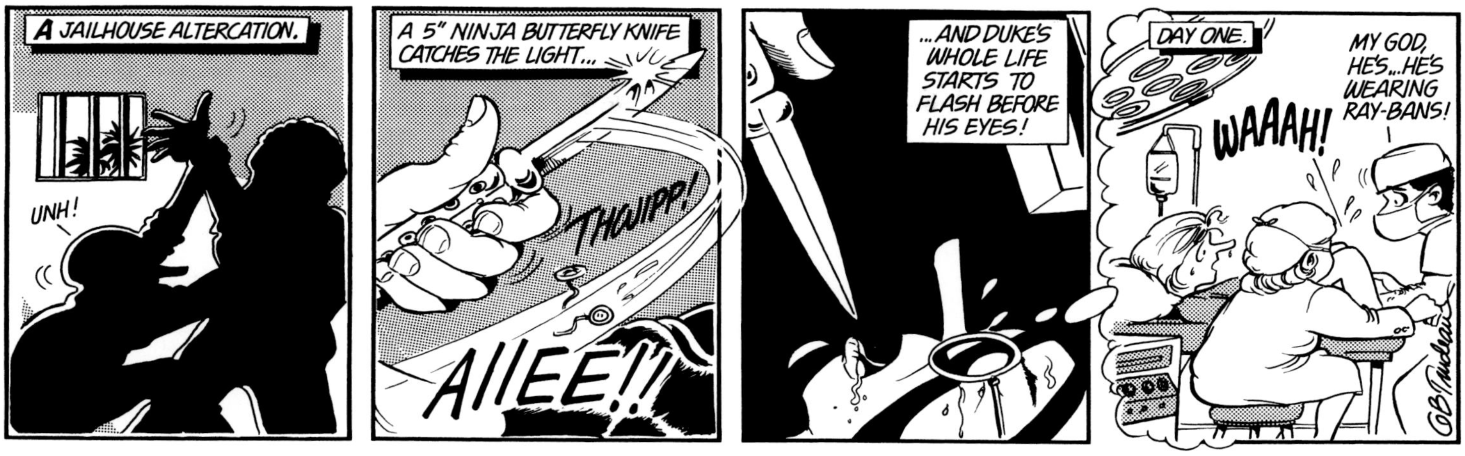
A JAILHOUSE ALTERCATION.
UNH!
A 5" NINJA BUTTERFLY KNIFE CATCHES THE LIGHT...
THWIPP!
AIIEE!!
...AND DUKE'S WHOLE LIFE STARTS TO FLASH BEFORE HIS EYES!
DAY ONE.
WAAAH!
MY GOD, HE'S... HE'S WEARING RAY-BANS!
GB Trudeau

10/20/86

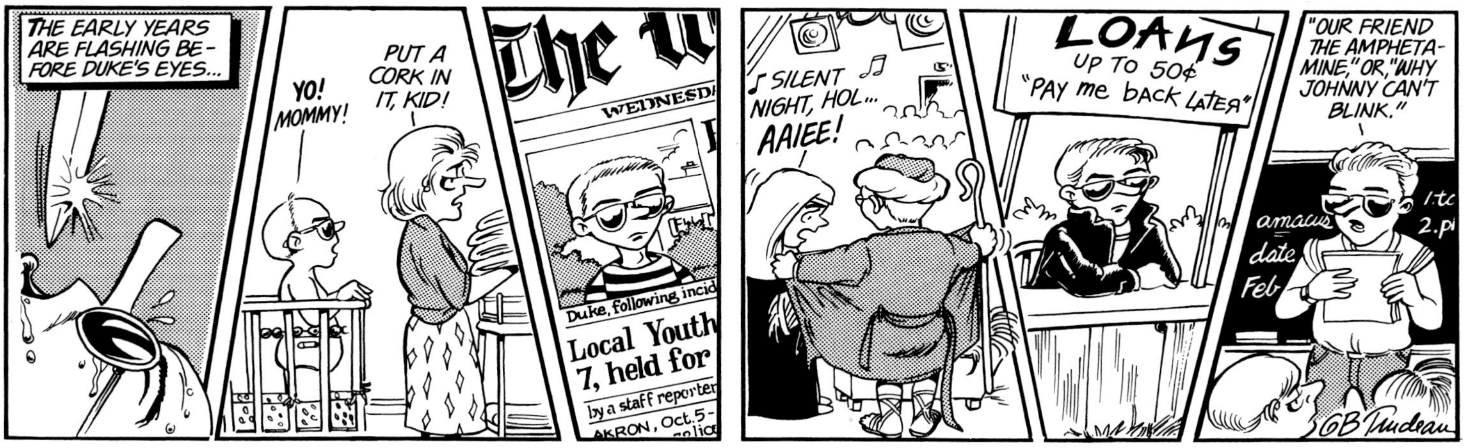
THE EARLY YEARS ARE FLASHING BEFORE DUKE'S EYES...
YO! MOMMY!
PUT A CORK IN IT, KID!
WEDNESDA
Duke, following incid
Local Youth 7, held for
by a staff reporter
AKRON, Oct.5-
SILENT NIGHT, HOL... AAIEE!
LOANS UP TO 50¢ "PAY me BACK LATER"
"OUR FRIEND THE AMPHETAMINE," OR, "WHY JOHNNY CAN'T BLINK."
GB Trudeau

10/21/86

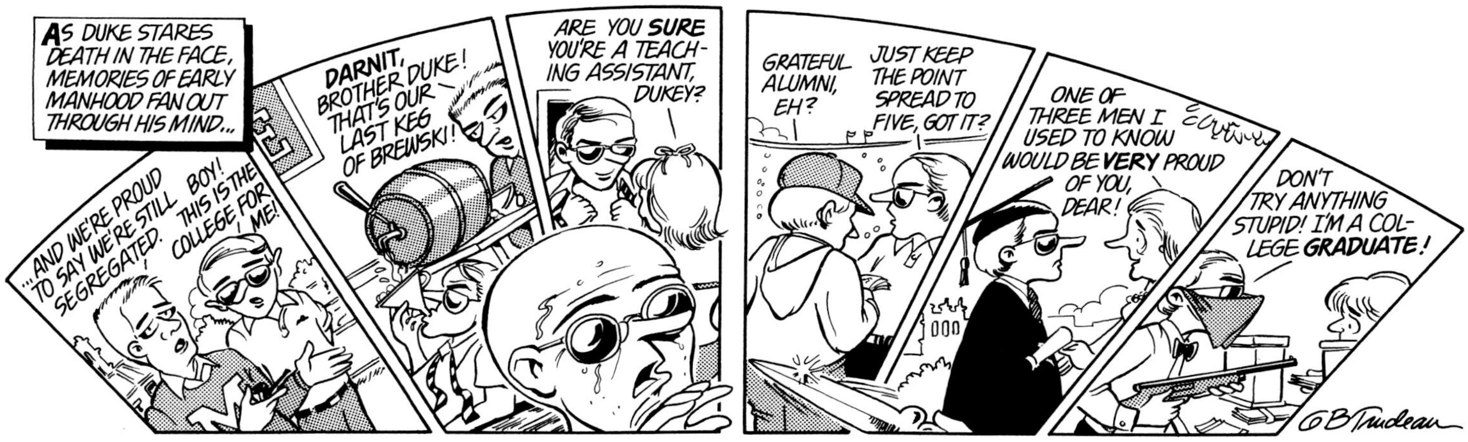
AS DUKE STARES DEATH IN THE FACE, MEMORIES OF EARLY MANHOOD FAN OUT THROUGH HIS MIND...
...AND WE'RE PROUD TO SAY WE'RE STILL SEGREGATED.
BOY! THIS IS THE COLLEGE FOR ME!
DARNIT, BROTHER DUKE! THAT'S OUR LAST KEG OF BREWSKI!
ARE YOU SURE YOU'RE A TEACHING ASSISTANT, DUKEY?
GRATEFUL ALUMNI, EH?
JUST KEEP THE POINT SPREAD TO FIVE, GOT IT?
ONE OF THREE MEN I USED TO KNOW WOULD BE VERY PROUD OF YOU, DEAR!
DON'T TRY ANYTHING STUPID! I'M A COLLEGE GRADUATE!
GB Trudeau

10/22/86

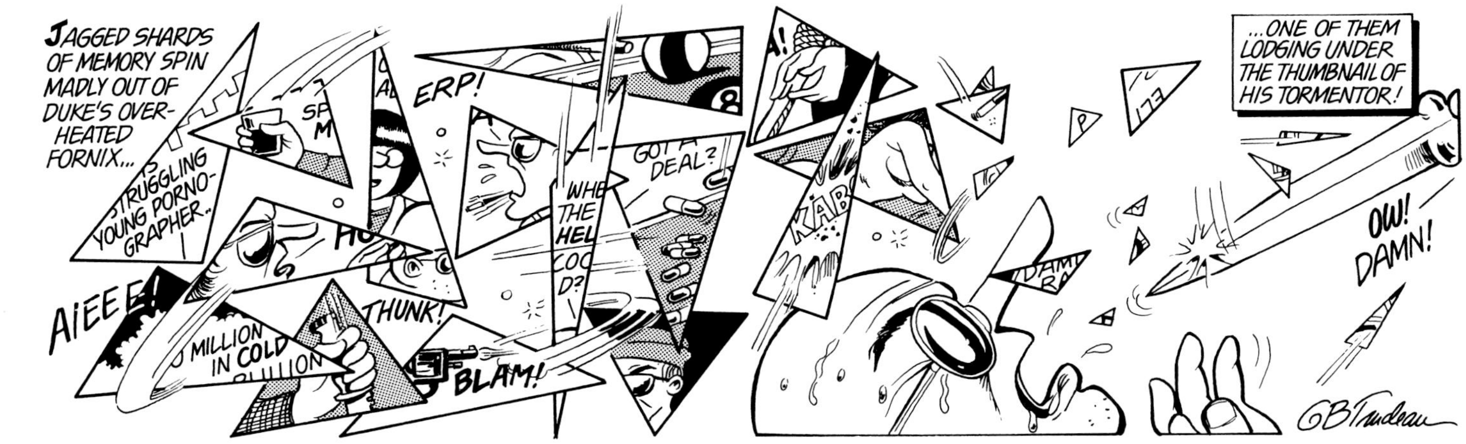
JAGGED SHARDS OF MEMORY SPIN MADLY OUT OF DUKE'S OVERHEATED FORNIX...
STRUGGLING YOUNG PORNOGRAPHER...
ERP!
GOT A DEAL?
WHE THE HEL COC D?
AIEEE!
MILLION IN COLD BULLION
THUNK!
BLAM!
...ONE OF THEM LODGING UNDER THE THUMBNAIL OF HIS TORMENTOR!
OW! DAMN!
GB Trudeau

10/24/86

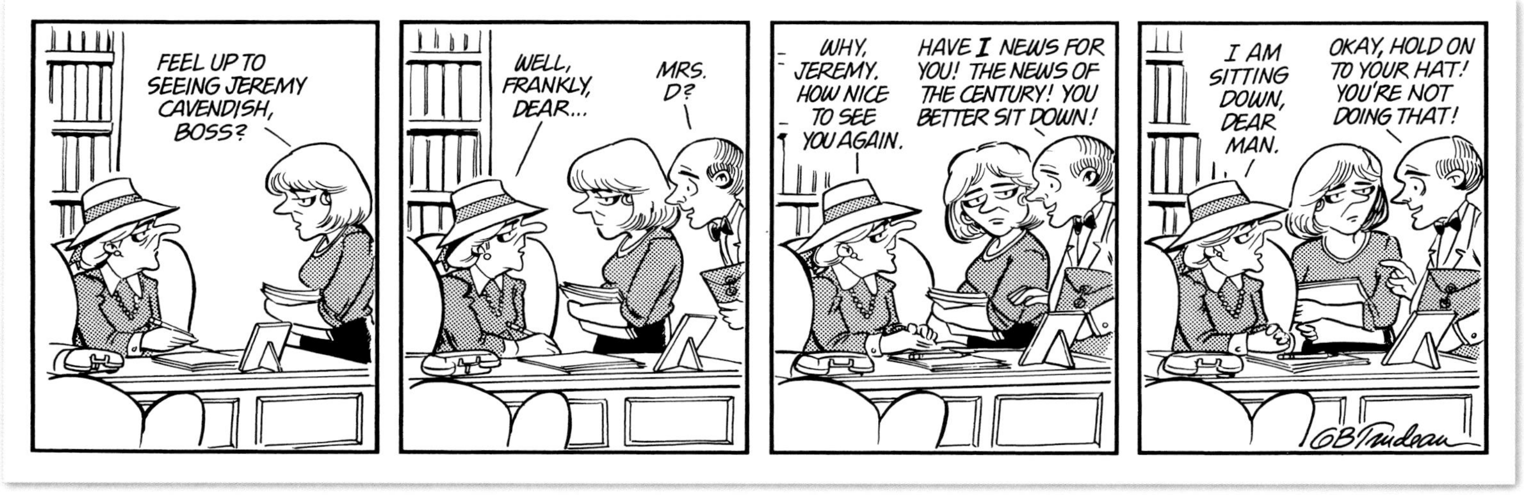
FEEL UP TO SEEING JEREMY CAVENDISH, BOSS?
WELL, FRANKLY, DEAR...
MRS. D?
WHY, JEREMY. HOW NICE TO SEE YOU AGAIN.
HAVE I NEWS FOR YOU! THE NEWS OF THE CENTURY! YOU BETTER SIT DOWN!
I AM SITTING DOWN, DEAR MAN.
OKAY, HOLD ON TO YOUR HAT! YOU'RE NOT DOING THAT!
©B Trudeau

1/6/87

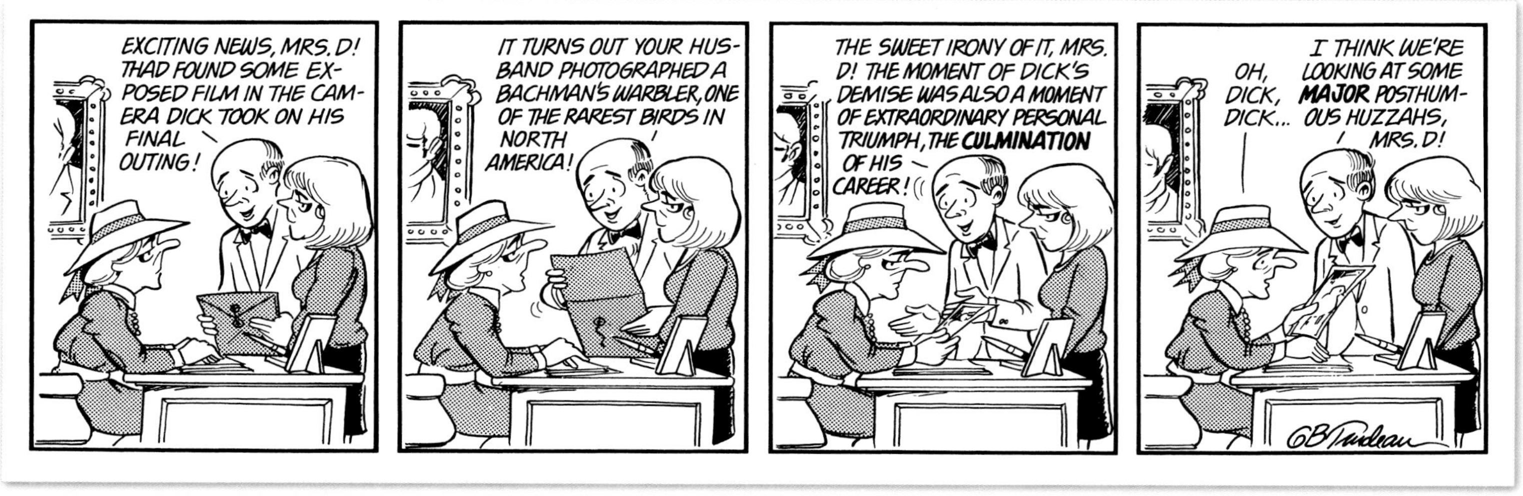
EXCITING NEWS, MRS. D! THAD FOUND SOME EXPOSED FILM IN THE CAMERA DICK TOOK ON HIS FINAL OUTING!
IT TURNS OUT YOUR HUSBAND PHOTOGRAPHED A BACHMAN'S WARBLER, ONE OF THE RAREST BIRDS IN NORTH AMERICA!
THE SWEET IRONY OF IT, MRS. D! THE MOMENT OF DICK'S DEMISE WAS ALSO A MOMENT OF EXTRAORDINARY PERSONAL TRIUMPH, THE CULMINATION OF HIS CAREER!
OH, DICK, DICK...
I THINK WE'RE LOOKING AT SOME MAJOR POSTHUMOUS HUZZAHS, MRS. D!
©B Trudeau

1/7/87

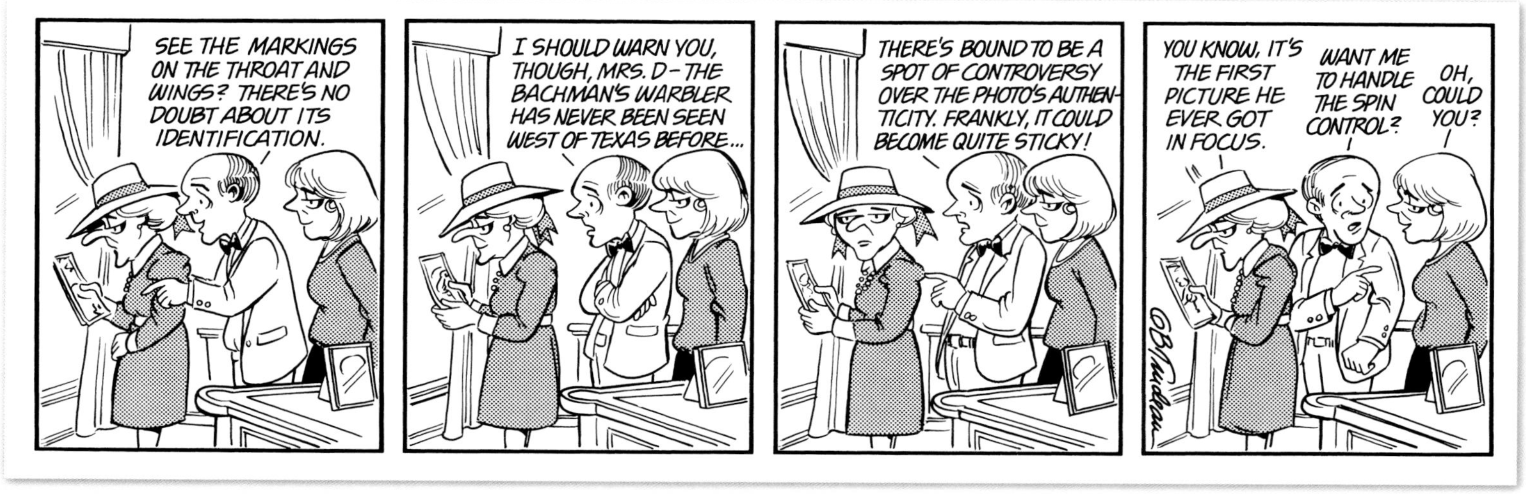
SEE THE MARKINGS ON THE THROAT AND WINGS? THERE'S NO DOUBT ABOUT ITS IDENTIFICATION.
I SHOULD WARN YOU, THOUGH, MRS. D – THE BACHMAN'S WARBLER HAS NEVER BEEN SEEN WEST OF TEXAS BEFORE...
THERE'S BOUND TO BE A SPOT OF CONTROVERSY OVER THE PHOTO'S AUTHENTICITY. FRANKLY, IT COULD BECOME QUITE STICKY!
YOU KNOW, IT'S THE FIRST PICTURE HE EVER GOT IN FOCUS.
WANT ME TO HANDLE THE SPIN CONTROL?
OH, COULD YOU?
©B Trudeau

1/8/87

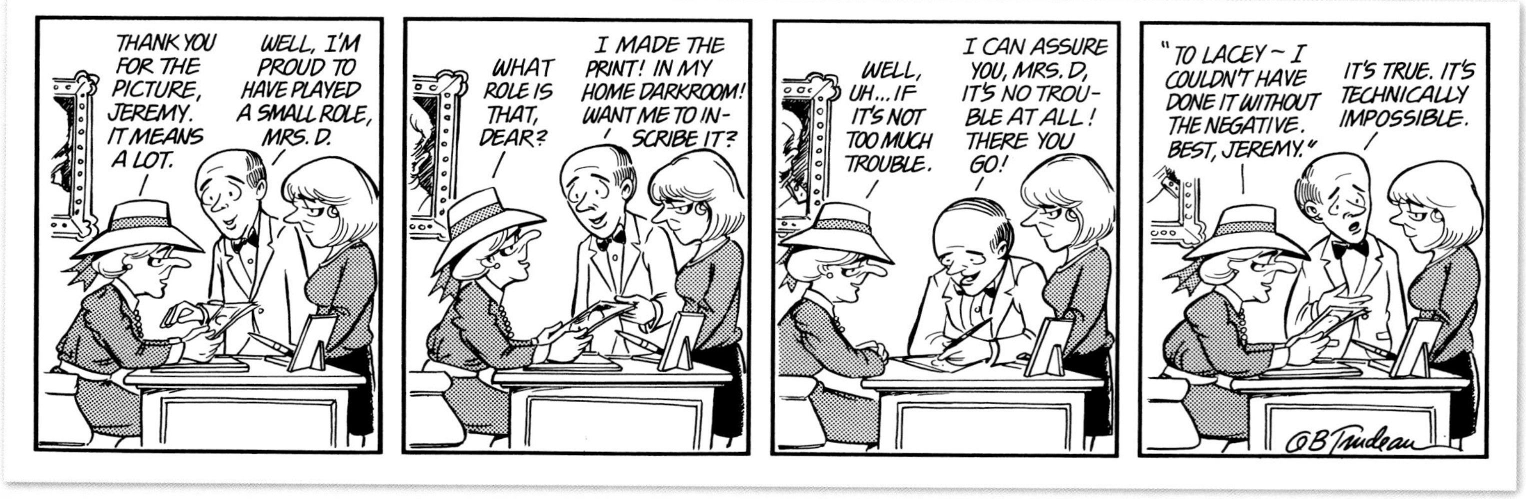
THANK YOU FOR THE PICTURE, JEREMY. IT MEANS A LOT.
WELL, I'M PROUD TO HAVE PLAYED A SMALL ROLE, MRS. D.
WHAT ROLE IS THAT, DEAR?
I MADE THE PRINT! IN MY HOME DARKROOM! WANT ME TO INSCRIBE IT?
WELL, UH... IF IT'S NOT TOO MUCH TROUBLE.
I CAN ASSURE YOU, MRS. D, IT'S NO TROUBLE AT ALL! THERE YOU GO!
"TO LACEY ~ I COULDN'T HAVE DONE IT WITHOUT THE NEGATIVE. BEST, JEREMY."
IT'S TRUE. IT'S TECHNICALLY IMPOSSIBLE.
©B Trudeau

1/10/87

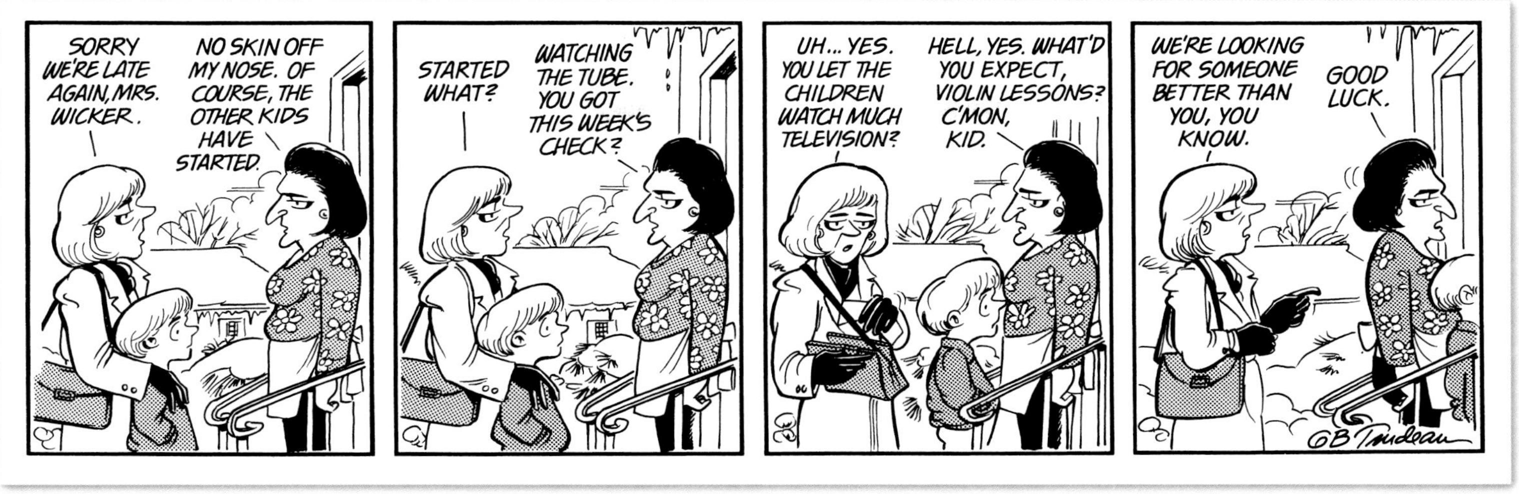
SORRY WE'RE LATE AGAIN, MRS. WICKER.
NO SKIN OFF MY NOSE. OF COURSE, THE OTHER KIDS HAVE STARTED.
STARTED WHAT?
WATCHING THE TUBE. YOU GOT THIS WEEK'S CHECK?
UH... YES. YOU LET THE CHILDREN WATCH MUCH TELEVISION?
HELL, YES. WHAT'D YOU EXPECT, VIOLIN LESSONS? C'MON, KID.
WE'RE LOOKING FOR SOMEONE BETTER THAN YOU, YOU KNOW.
GOOD LUCK.
GB Trudeau

1/20/87

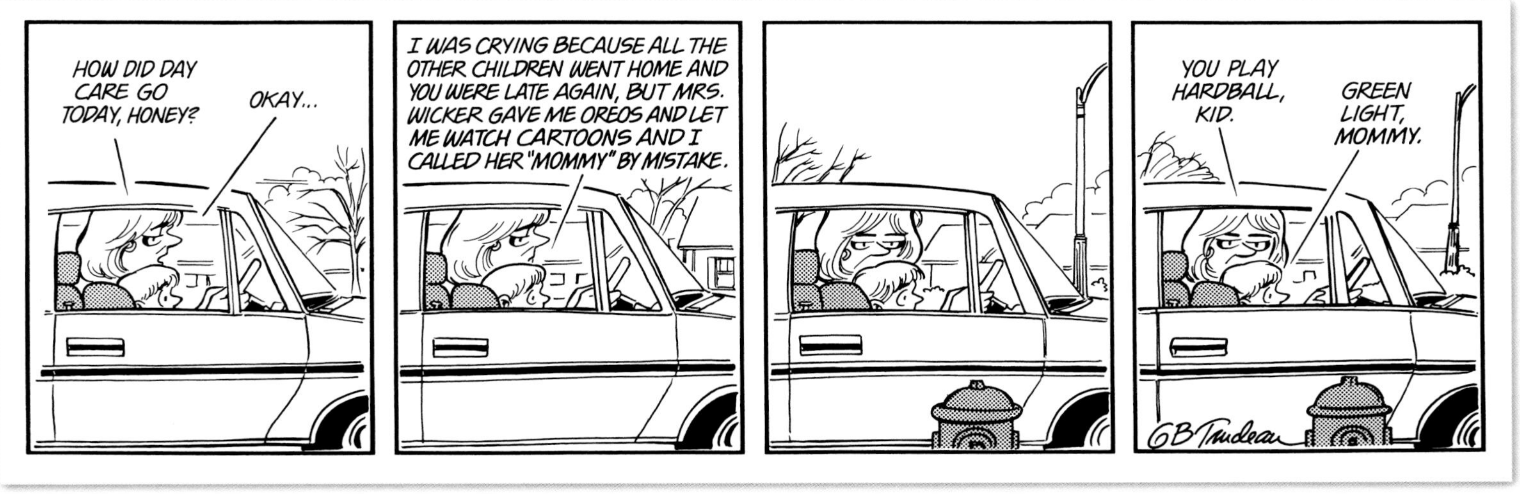
HOW DID DAY CARE GO TODAY, HONEY?
OKAY...
I WAS CRYING BECAUSE ALL THE OTHER CHILDREN WENT HOME AND YOU WERE LATE AGAIN, BUT MRS. WICKER GAVE ME OREOS AND LET ME WATCH CARTOONS AND I CALLED HER "MOMMY" BY MISTAKE.
YOU PLAY HARDBALL, KID.
GREEN LIGHT, MOMMY.
GB Trudeau

1/21/87

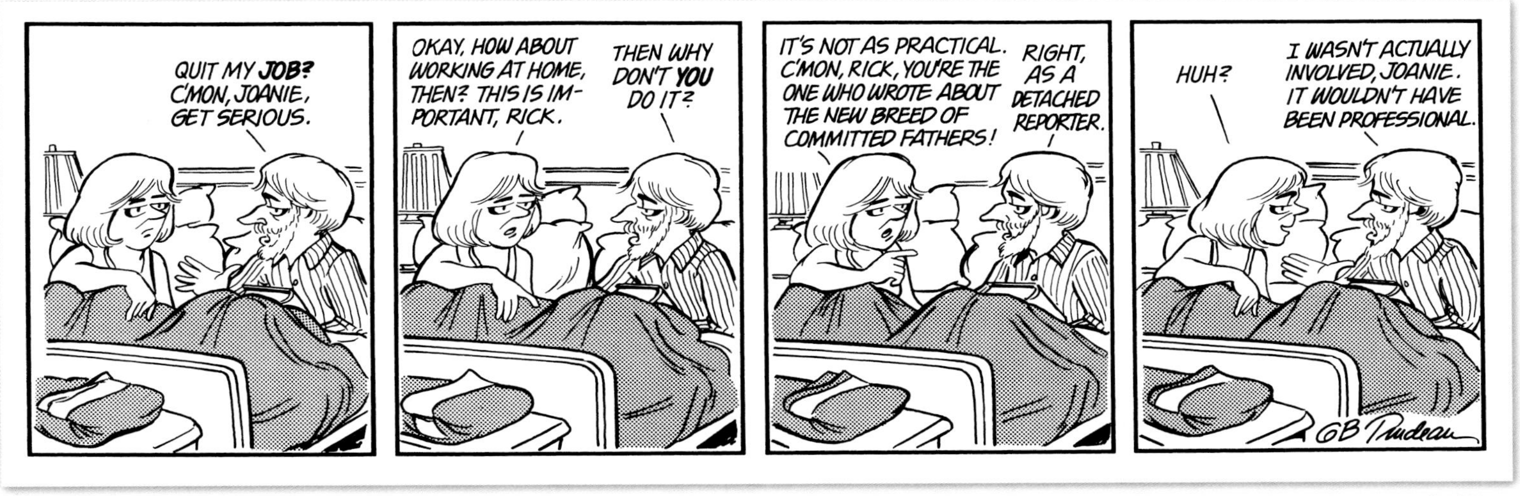
QUIT MY **JOB?** C'MON, JOANIE, GET SERIOUS.
OKAY, HOW ABOUT WORKING AT HOME, THEN? THIS IS IMPORTANT, RICK.
THEN WHY DON'T **YOU** DO IT?
IT'S NOT AS PRACTICAL. C'MON, RICK, YOU'RE THE ONE WHO WROTE ABOUT THE NEW BREED OF COMMITTED FATHERS!
RIGHT, AS A DETACHED REPORTER.
HUH?
I WASN'T ACTUALLY INVOLVED, JOANIE. IT WOULDN'T HAVE BEEN PROFESSIONAL.
GB Trudeau

1/26/87

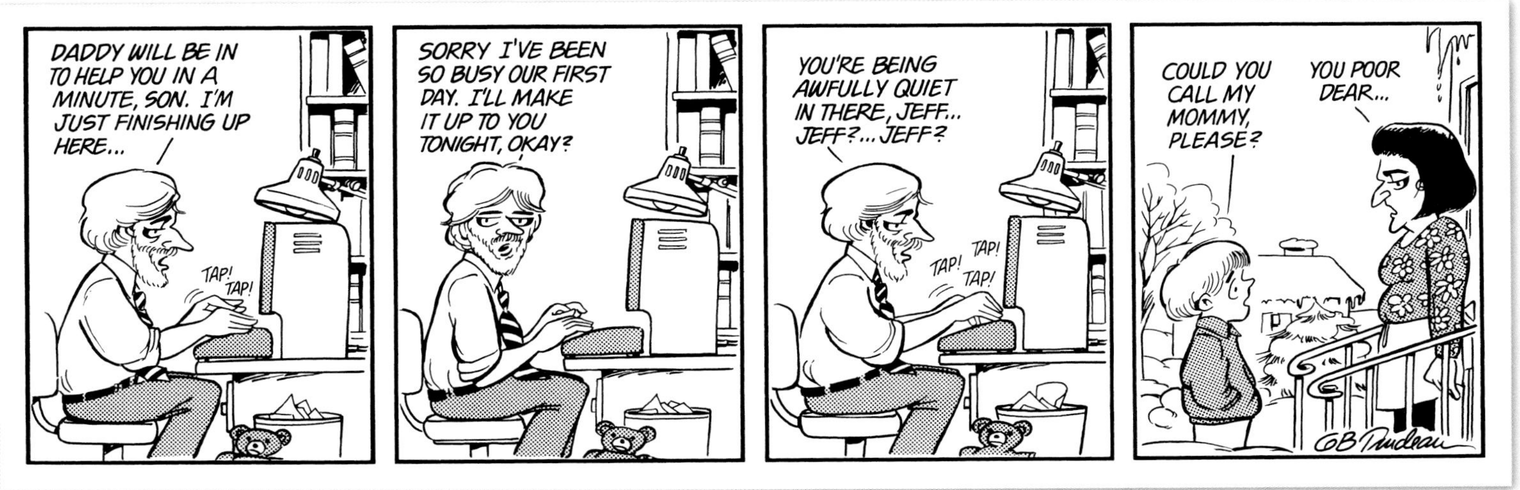
DADDY WILL BE IN TO HELP YOU IN A MINUTE, SON. I'M JUST FINISHING UP HERE...
TAP! TAP!
SORRY I'VE BEEN SO BUSY OUR FIRST DAY. I'LL MAKE IT UP TO YOU TONIGHT, OKAY?
YOU'RE BEING AWFULLY QUIET IN THERE, JEFF... JEFF?... JEFF?
TAP! TAP! TAP!
COULD YOU CALL MY MOMMY, PLEASE?
YOU POOR DEAR...
GB Trudeau

1/30/87

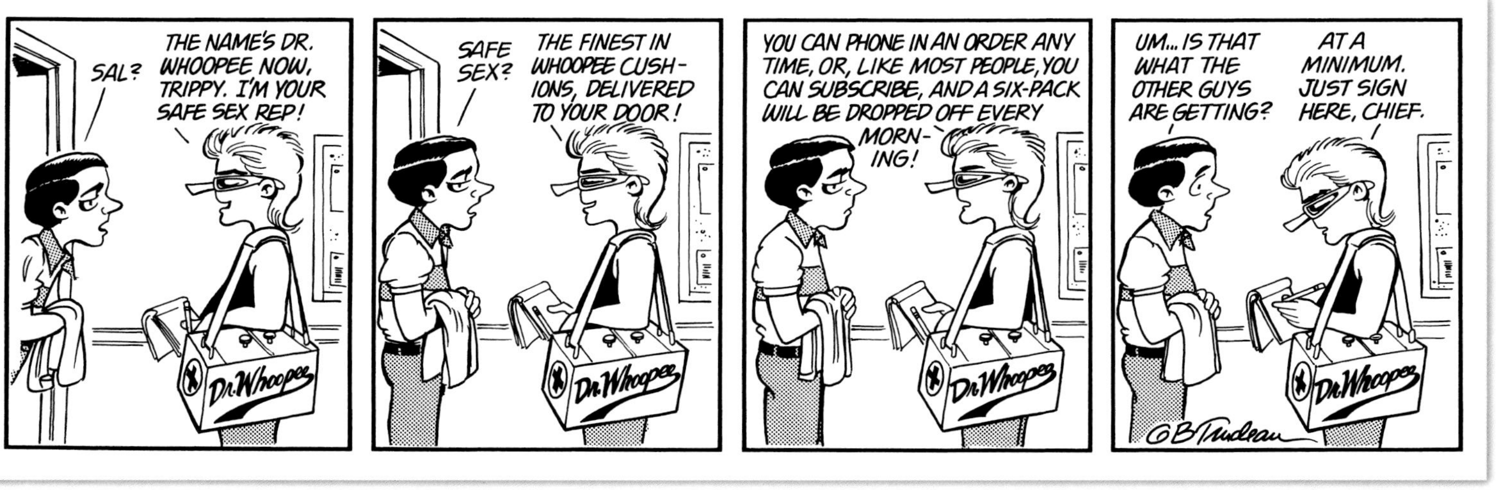
SAL?
THE NAME'S DR. WHOOPEE NOW, TRIPPY. I'M YOUR SAFE SEX REP!
SAFE SEX?
THE FINEST IN WHOOPEE CUSHIONS, DELIVERED TO YOUR DOOR!
YOU CAN PHONE IN AN ORDER ANY TIME, OR, LIKE MOST PEOPLE, YOU CAN SUBSCRIBE, AND A SIX-PACK WILL BE DROPPED OFF EVERY MORNING!
UM... IS THAT WHAT THE OTHER GUYS ARE GETTING?
AT A MINIMUM. JUST SIGN HERE, CHIEF.
Dr. Whoopee
GB Trudeau

3/10/87

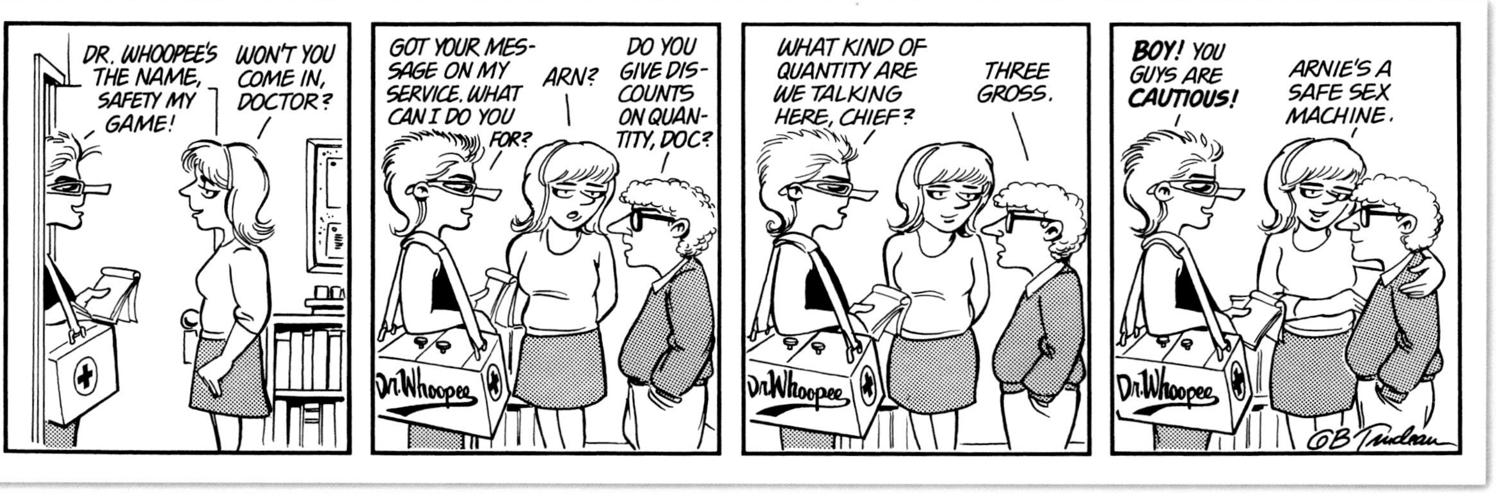
DR. WHOOPEE'S THE NAME, SAFETY MY GAME!
WON'T YOU COME IN, DOCTOR?
GOT YOUR MESSAGE ON MY SERVICE. WHAT CAN I DO YOU FOR?
ARN?
DO YOU GIVE DISCOUNTS ON QUANTITY, DOC?
WHAT KIND OF QUANTITY ARE WE TALKING HERE, CHIEF?
THREE GROSS.
BOY! YOU GUYS ARE CAUTIOUS!
ARNIE'S A SAFE SEX MACHINE.
Dr. Whoopee
GB Trudeau

3/11/87

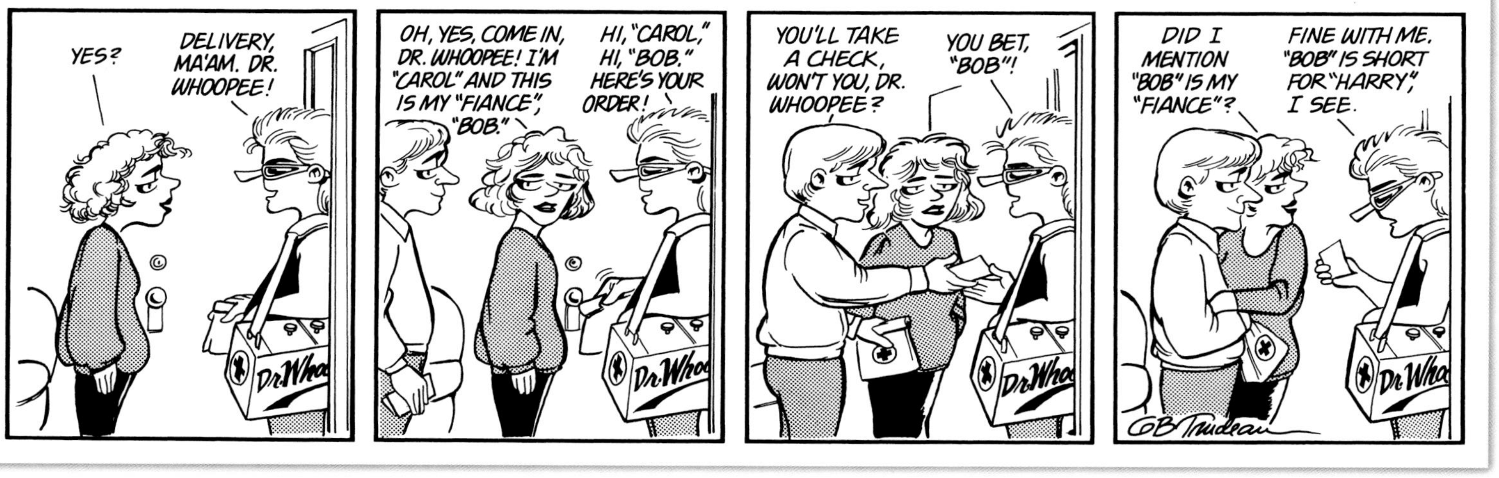
YES?
DELIVERY, MA'AM. DR. WHOOPEE!
OH, YES, COME IN, DR. WHOOPEE! I'M "CAROL" AND THIS IS MY "FIANCE", "BOB."
HI, "CAROL," HI, "BOB." HERE'S YOUR ORDER!
YOU'LL TAKE A CHECK, WON'T YOU, DR. WHOOPEE?
YOU BET, "BOB"!
DID I MENTION "BOB" IS MY "FIANCE"?
FINE WITH ME. "BOB" IS SHORT FOR "HARRY," I SEE.
GB Trudeau

3/12/87

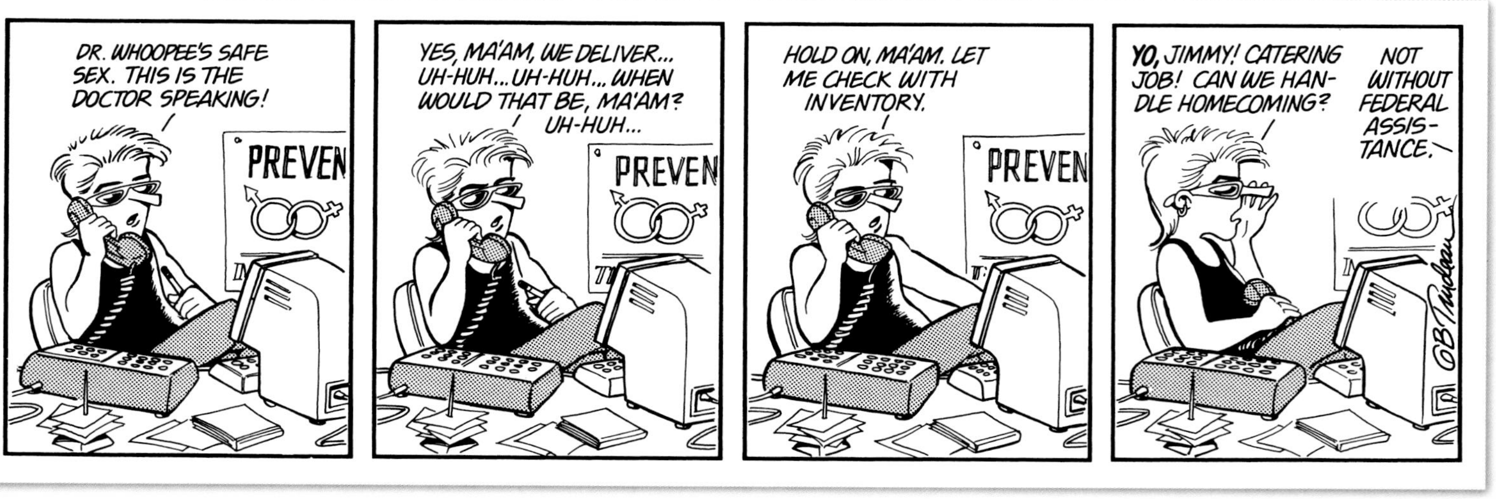
DR. WHOOPEE'S SAFE SEX. THIS IS THE DOCTOR SPEAKING!
PREVEN
YES, MA'AM, WE DELIVER... UH-HUH... UH-HUH... WHEN WOULD THAT BE, MA'AM? UH-HUH...
HOLD ON, MA'AM. LET ME CHECK WITH INVENTORY.
YO, JIMMY! CATERING JOB! CAN WE HANDLE HOMECOMING?
NOT WITHOUT FEDERAL ASSISTANCE.
GB Trudeau

3/13/87

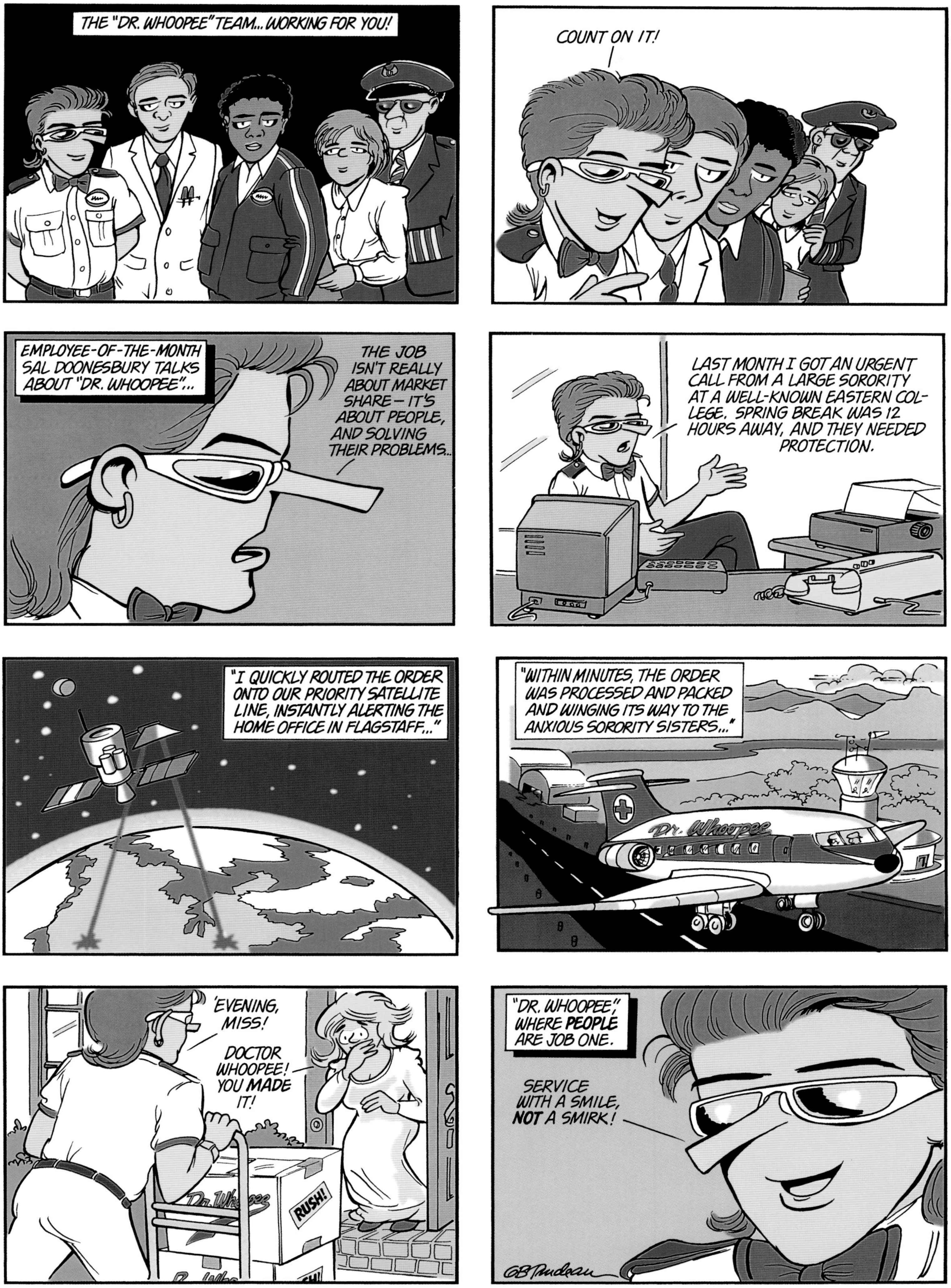
THE "DR. WHOOPEE" TEAM... WORKING FOR YOU!
COUNT ON IT!
EMPLOYEE-OF-THE-MONTH SAL DOONESBURY TALKS ABOUT "DR. WHOOPEE"...
THE JOB ISN'T REALLY ABOUT MARKET SHARE – IT'S ABOUT PEOPLE, AND SOLVING THEIR PROBLEMS...
LAST MONTH I GOT AN URGENT CALL FROM A LARGE SORORITY AT A WELL-KNOWN EASTERN COLLEGE. SPRING BREAK WAS 12 HOURS AWAY, AND THEY NEEDED PROTECTION.
"I QUICKLY ROUTED THE ORDER ONTO OUR PRIORITY SATELLITE LINE, INSTANTLY ALERTING THE HOME OFFICE IN FLAGSTAFF..."
"WITHIN MINUTES, THE ORDER WAS PROCESSED AND PACKED AND WINGING ITS WAY TO THE ANXIOUS SORORITY SISTERS..."
Dr. Whoopee
'EVENING, MISS!
DOCTOR WHOOPEE! YOU MADE IT!
Dr. Whoopee
RUSH!
"DR. WHOOPEE," WHERE PEOPLE ARE JOB ONE.
SERVICE WITH A SMILE, NOT A SMIRK!
GBTrudeau

4/5/87

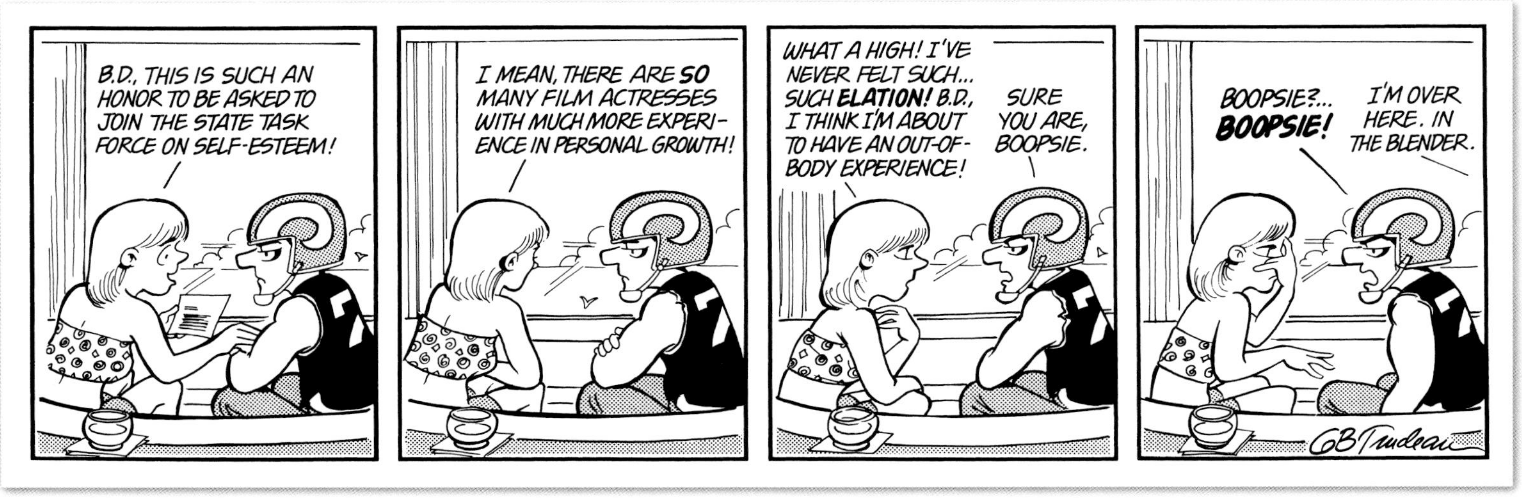
B.D., THIS IS SUCH AN HONOR TO BE ASKED TO JOIN THE STATE TASK FORCE ON SELF-ESTEEM!
I MEAN, THERE ARE **SO** MANY FILM ACTRESSES WITH MUCH MORE EXPERIENCE IN PERSONAL GROWTH!
WHAT A HIGH! I'VE NEVER FELT SUCH... SUCH **ELATION!** B.D., I THINK I'M ABOUT TO HAVE AN OUT-OF-BODY EXPERIENCE!
SURE YOU ARE, BOOPSIE.
BOOPSIE?... **BOOPSIE!**
I'M OVER HERE. IN THE BLENDER.
GBTrudeau

2/11/87

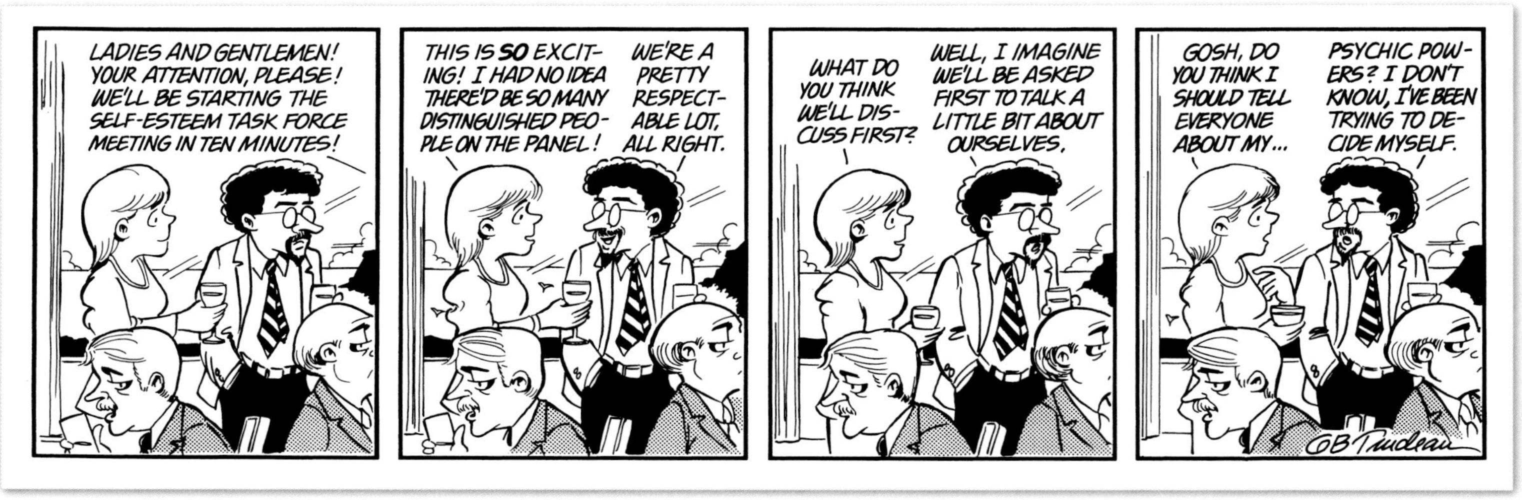
LADIES AND GENTLEMEN! YOUR ATTENTION, PLEASE! WE'LL BE STARTING THE SELF-ESTEEM TASK FORCE MEETING IN TEN MINUTES!
THIS IS **SO** EXCITING! I HAD NO IDEA THERE'D BE SO MANY DISTINGUISHED PEOPLE ON THE PANEL!
WE'RE A PRETTY RESPECTABLE LOT, ALL RIGHT.
WHAT DO YOU THINK WE'LL DISCUSS FIRST?
WELL, I IMAGINE WE'LL BE ASKED FIRST TO TALK A LITTLE BIT ABOUT OURSELVES.
GOSH, DO YOU THINK I SHOULD TELL EVERYONE ABOUT MY...
PSYCHIC POWERS? I DON'T KNOW, I'VE BEEN TRYING TO DECIDE MYSELF.
GBTrudeau

2/16/87

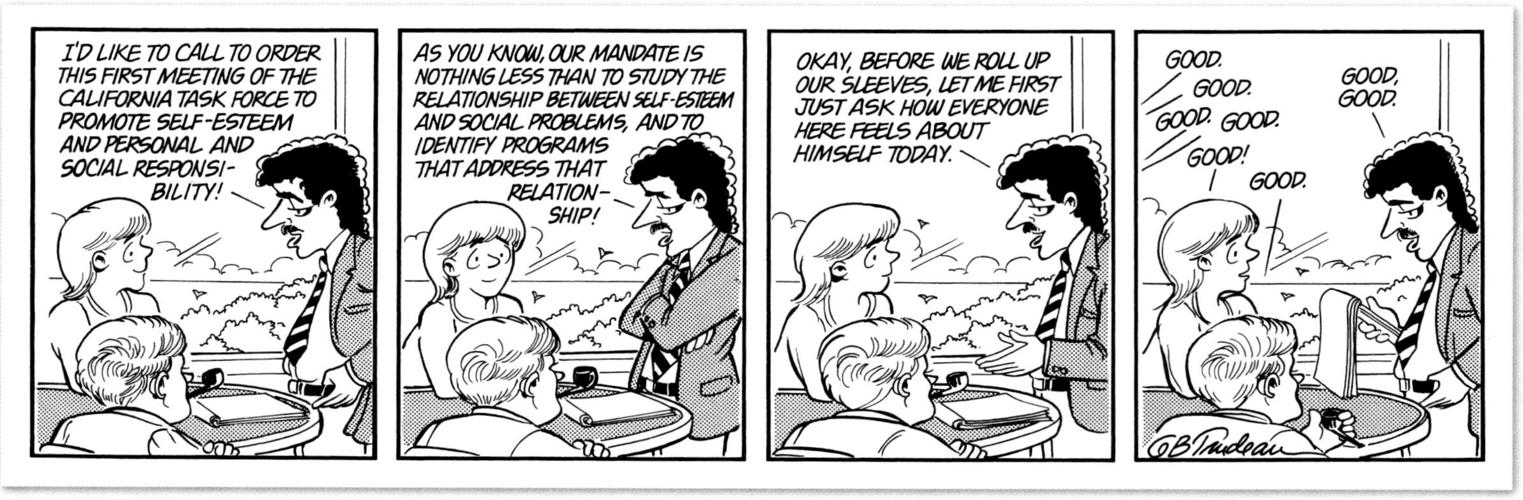
I'D LIKE TO CALL TO ORDER THIS FIRST MEETING OF THE CALIFORNIA TASK FORCE TO PROMOTE SELF-ESTEEM AND PERSONAL AND SOCIAL RESPONSIBILITY!
AS YOU KNOW, OUR MANDATE IS NOTHING LESS THAN TO STUDY THE RELATIONSHIP BETWEEN SELF-ESTEEM AND SOCIAL PROBLEMS, AND TO IDENTIFY PROGRAMS THAT ADDRESS THAT RELATIONSHIP!
OKAY, BEFORE WE ROLL UP OUR SLEEVES, LET ME FIRST JUST ASK HOW EVERYONE HERE FEELS ABOUT HIMSELF TODAY.
GOOD.
GOOD.
GOOD.
GOOD.
GOOD!
GOOD.
GOOD, GOOD.
GBTrudeau

2/17/87

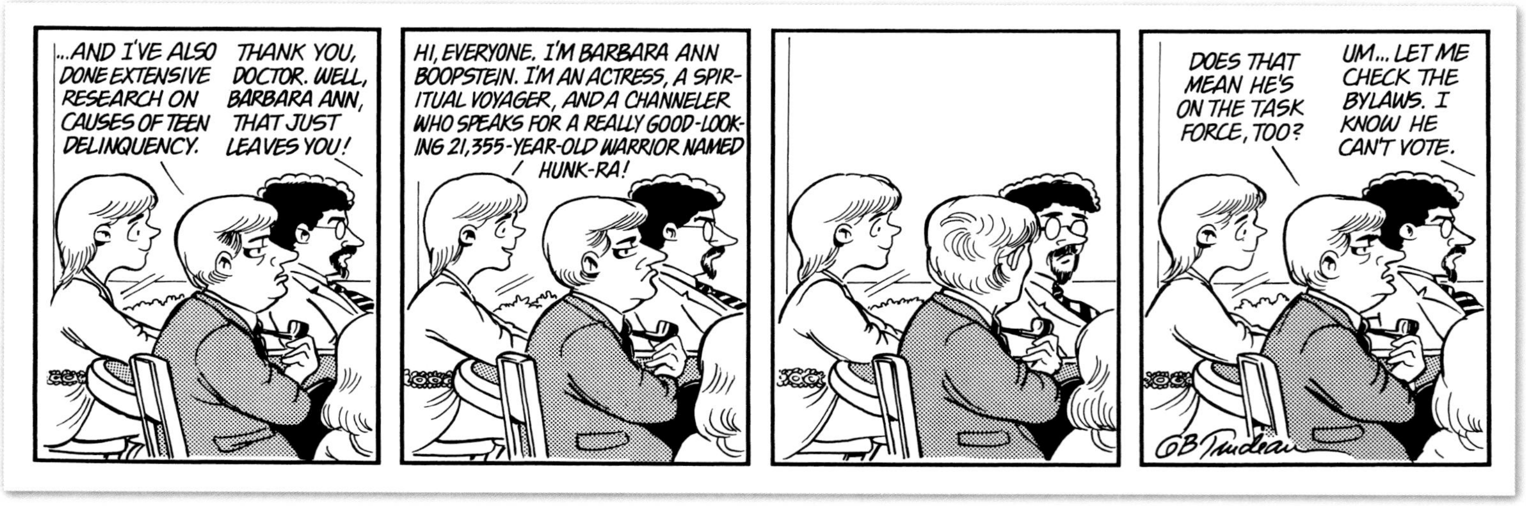
...AND I'VE ALSO DONE EXTENSIVE RESEARCH ON CAUSES OF TEEN DELINQUENCY.
THANK YOU, DOCTOR. WELL, BARBARA ANN, THAT JUST LEAVES YOU!
HI, EVERYONE. I'M BARBARA ANN BOOPSTEIN. I'M AN ACTRESS, A SPIRITUAL VOYAGER, AND A CHANNELER WHO SPEAKS FOR A REALLY GOOD-LOOKING 21,355-YEAR-OLD WARRIOR NAMED HUNK-RA!
DOES THAT MEAN HE'S ON THE TASK FORCE, TOO?
UM... LET ME CHECK THE BYLAWS. I KNOW HE CAN'T VOTE.
GBTrudeau

2/18/87

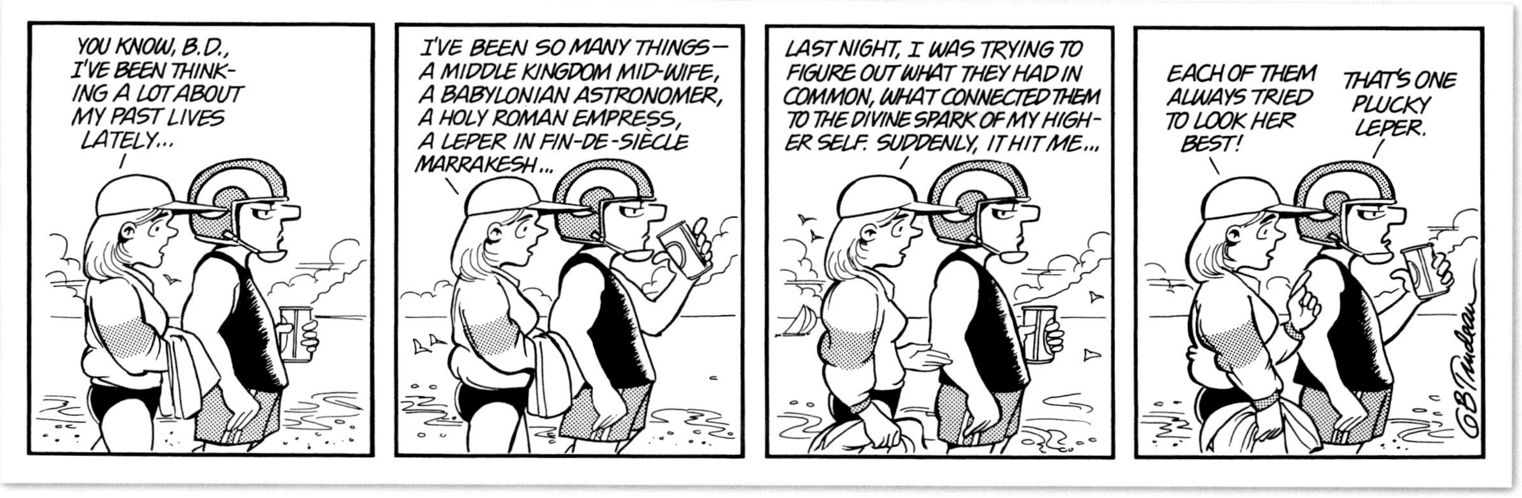
YOU KNOW, B.D., I'VE BEEN THINKING A LOT ABOUT MY PAST LIVES LATELY...
I'VE BEEN SO MANY THINGS— A MIDDLE KINGDOM MID-WIFE, A BABYLONIAN ASTRONOMER, A HOLY ROMAN EMPRESS, A LEPER IN FIN-DE-SIÈCLE MARRAKESH...
LAST NIGHT, I WAS TRYING TO FIGURE OUT WHAT THEY HAD IN COMMON, WHAT CONNECTED THEM TO THE DIVINE SPARK OF MY HIGHER SELF. SUDDENLY, IT HIT ME...
EACH OF THEM ALWAYS TRIED TO LOOK HER BEST!
THAT'S ONE PLUCKY LEPER.
©GBTrudeau

3/16/87

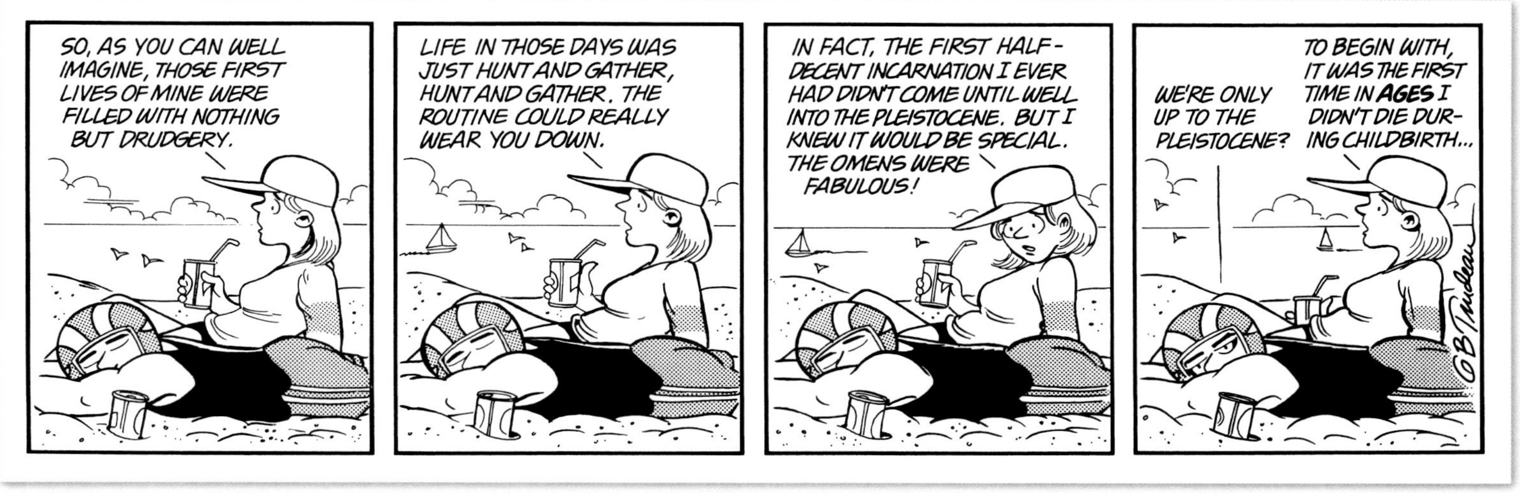
SO, AS YOU CAN WELL IMAGINE, THOSE FIRST LIVES OF MINE WERE FILLED WITH NOTHING BUT DRUDGERY.
LIFE IN THOSE DAYS WAS JUST HUNT AND GATHER, HUNT AND GATHER. THE ROUTINE COULD REALLY WEAR YOU DOWN.
IN FACT, THE FIRST HALF-DECENT INCARNATION I EVER HAD DIDN'T COME UNTIL WELL INTO THE PLEISTOCENE. BUT I KNEW IT WOULD BE SPECIAL. THE OMENS WERE FABULOUS!
WE'RE ONLY UP TO THE PLEISTOCENE?
TO BEGIN WITH, IT WAS THE FIRST TIME IN AGES I DIDN'T DIE DURING CHILDBIRTH...
©GBTrudeau

3/17/87

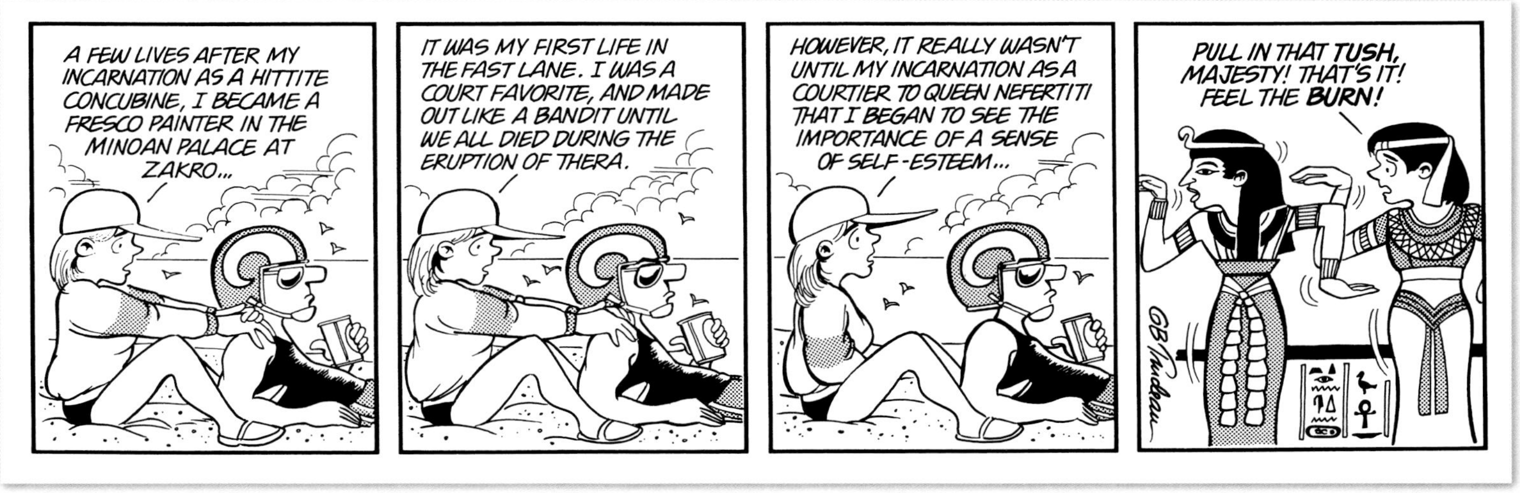
A FEW LIVES AFTER MY INCARNATION AS A HITTITE CONCUBINE, I BECAME A FRESCO PAINTER IN THE MINOAN PALACE AT ZAKRO...
IT WAS MY FIRST LIFE IN THE FAST LANE. I WAS A COURT FAVORITE, AND MADE OUT LIKE A BANDIT UNTIL WE ALL DIED DURING THE ERUPTION OF THERA.
HOWEVER, IT REALLY WASN'T UNTIL MY INCARNATION AS A COURTIER TO QUEEN NEFERTITI THAT I BEGAN TO SEE THE IMPORTANCE OF A SENSE OF SELF-ESTEEM...
PULL IN THAT TUSH, MAJESTY! THAT'S IT! FEEL THE BURN!
©GBTrudeau

3/18/87

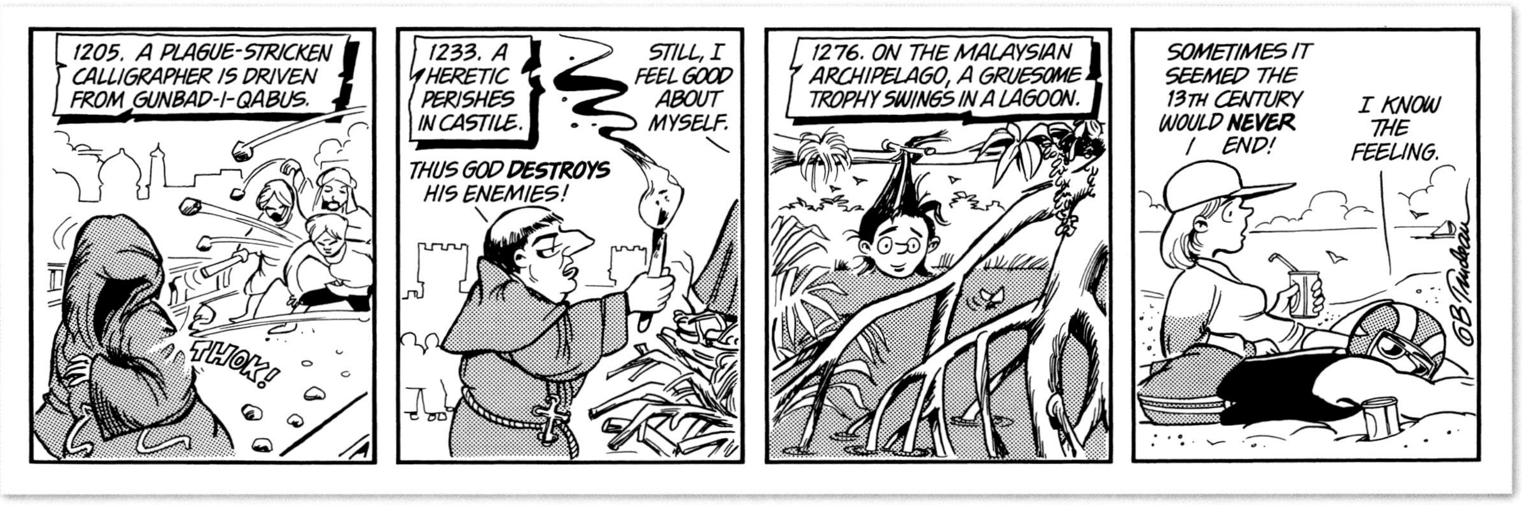
1205. A PLAGUE-STRICKEN CALLIGRAPHER IS DRIVEN FROM GUNBAD-I-QABUS.
THOK!
1233. A HERETIC PERISHES IN CASTILE.
STILL, I FEEL GOOD ABOUT MYSELF.
THUS GOD DESTROYS HIS ENEMIES!
1276. ON THE MALAYSIAN ARCHIPELAGO, A GRUESOME TROPHY SWINGS IN A LAGOON.
SOMETIMES IT SEEMED THE 13TH CENTURY WOULD NEVER END!
I KNOW THE FEELING.
©GBTrudeau

3/20/87

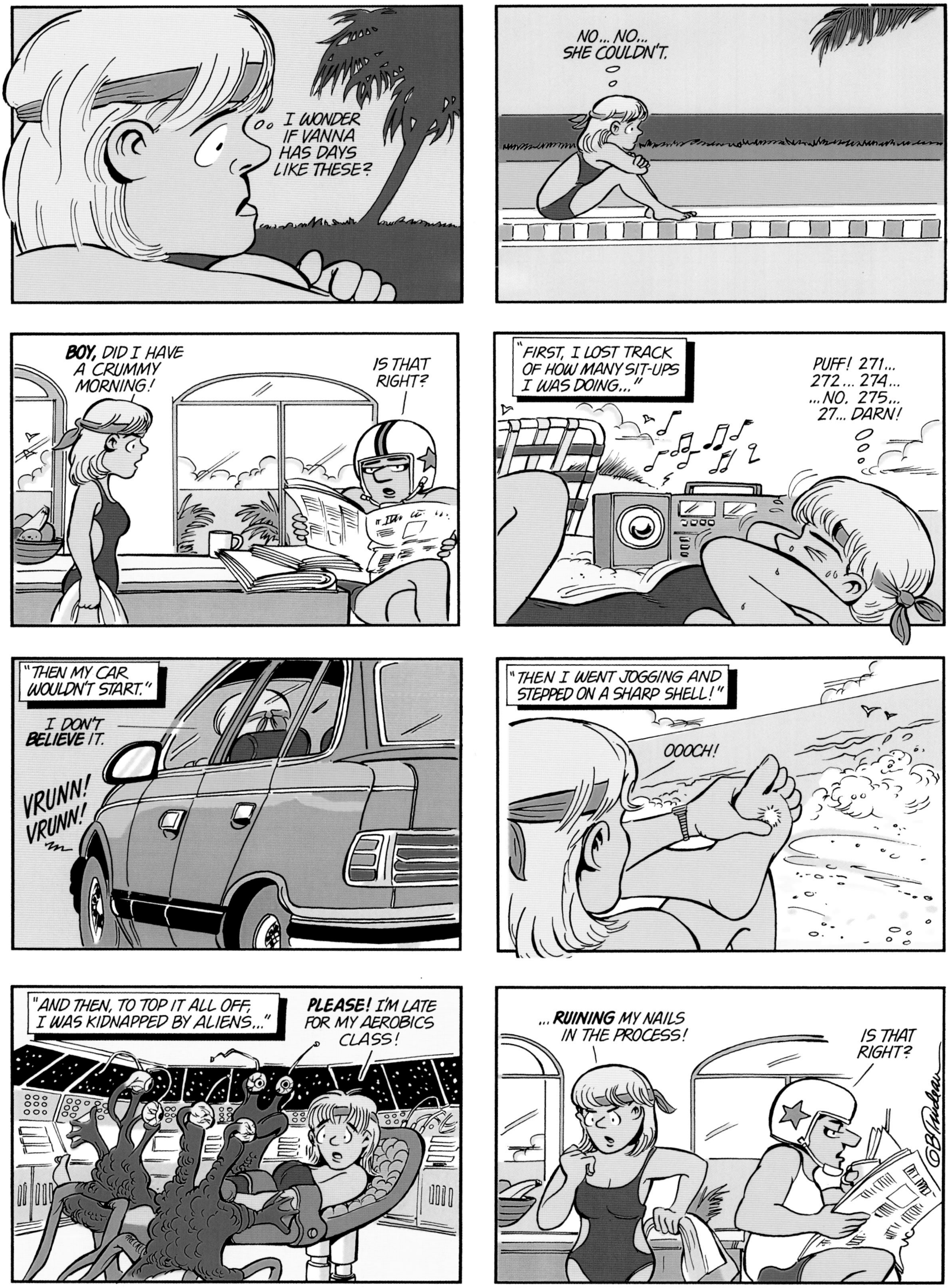

I WONDER IF VANNA HAS DAYS LIKE THESE?
NO... NO... SHE COULDN'T.
BOY, DID I HAVE A CRUMMY MORNING!
IS THAT RIGHT?
"FIRST, I LOST TRACK OF HOW MANY SIT-UPS I WAS DOING..."
PUFF! 271... 272... 274... ...NO, 275... 27... DARN!
"THEN MY CAR WOULDN'T START."
I DON'T BELIEVE IT.
VRUNN! VRUNN!
"THEN I WENT JOGGING AND STEPPED ON A SHARP SHELL!"
OOOCH!
"AND THEN, TO TOP IT ALL OFF, I WAS KIDNAPPED BY ALIENS..."
PLEASE! I'M LATE FOR MY AEROBICS CLASS!
...RUINING MY NAILS IN THE PROCESS!
IS THAT RIGHT?
©B Rudeau

8/30/87

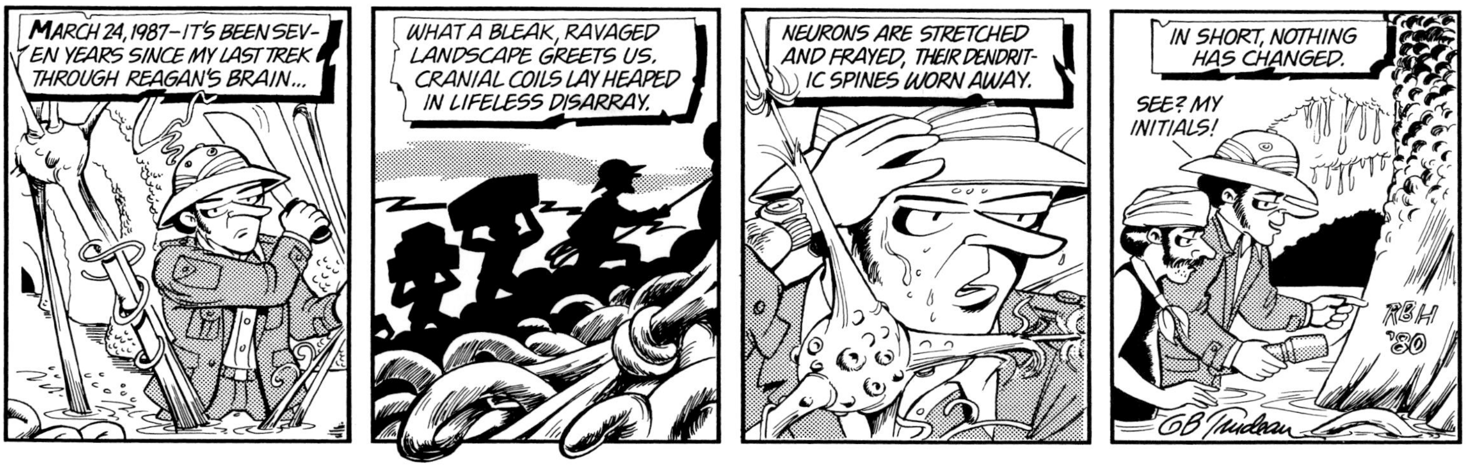
MARCH 24, 1987 – IT'S BEEN SEVEN YEARS SINCE MY LAST TREK THROUGH REAGAN'S BRAIN...
WHAT A BLEAK, RAVAGED LANDSCAPE GREETS US. CRANIAL COILS LAY HEAPED IN LIFELESS DISARRAY.
NEURONS ARE STRETCHED AND FRAYED, THEIR DENDRITIC SPINES WORN AWAY.
IN SHORT, NOTHING HAS CHANGED.
SEE? MY INITIALS!
RBH '80
GB Trudeau

3/24/87

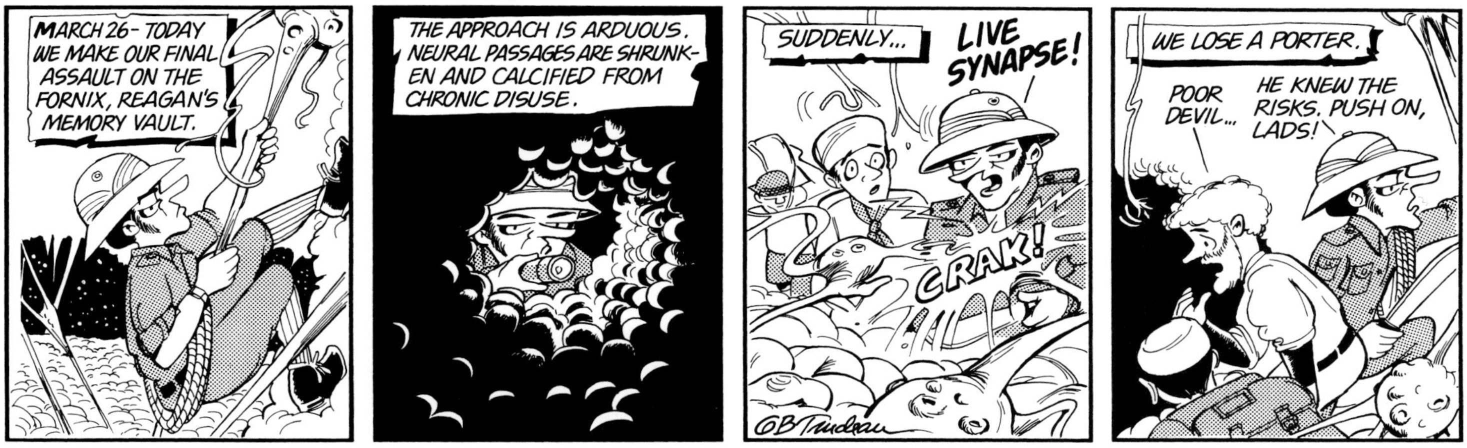
MARCH 26 – TODAY WE MAKE OUR FINAL ASSAULT ON THE FORNIX, REAGAN'S MEMORY VAULT.
THE APPROACH IS ARDUOUS. NEURAL PASSAGES ARE SHRUNKEN AND CALCIFIED FROM CHRONIC DISUSE.
SUDDENLY...
LIVE SYNAPSE!
CRAK!
WE LOSE A PORTER.
POOR DEVIL...
HE KNEW THE RISKS. PUSH ON, LADS!
GB Trudeau

3/26/87

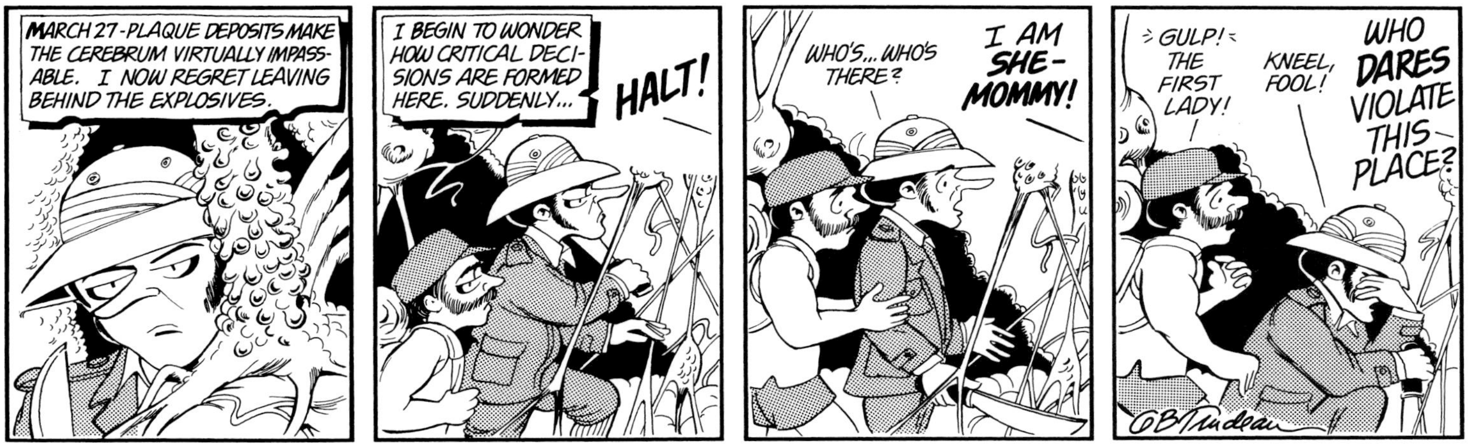
MARCH 27 – PLAQUE DEPOSITS MAKE THE CEREBRUM VIRTUALLY IMPASSABLE. I NOW REGRET LEAVING BEHIND THE EXPLOSIVES.
I BEGIN TO WONDER HOW CRITICAL DECISIONS ARE FORMED HERE. SUDDENLY...
HALT!
WHO'S... WHO'S THERE?
I AM SHE-MOMMY!
GULP! THE FIRST LADY!
KNEEL, FOOL!
WHO DARES VIOLATE THIS PLACE?
GB Trudeau

3/27/87

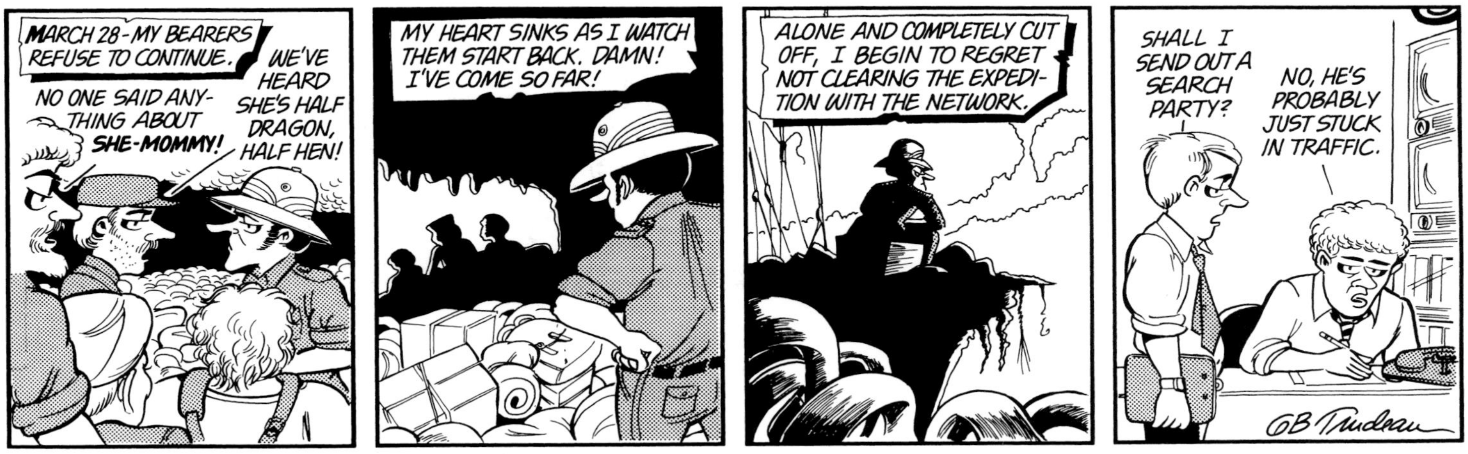
MARCH 28 – MY BEARERS REFUSE TO CONTINUE.
NO ONE SAID ANYTHING ABOUT SHE-MOMMY!
WE'VE HEARD SHE'S HALF DRAGON, HALF HEN!
MY HEART SINKS AS I WATCH THEM START BACK. DAMN! I'VE COME SO FAR!
ALONE AND COMPLETELY CUT OFF, I BEGIN TO REGRET NOT CLEARING THE EXPEDITION WITH THE NETWORK.
SHALL I SEND OUT A SEARCH PARTY?
NO, HE'S PROBABLY JUST STUCK IN TRAFFIC.
GB Trudeau

3/28/87

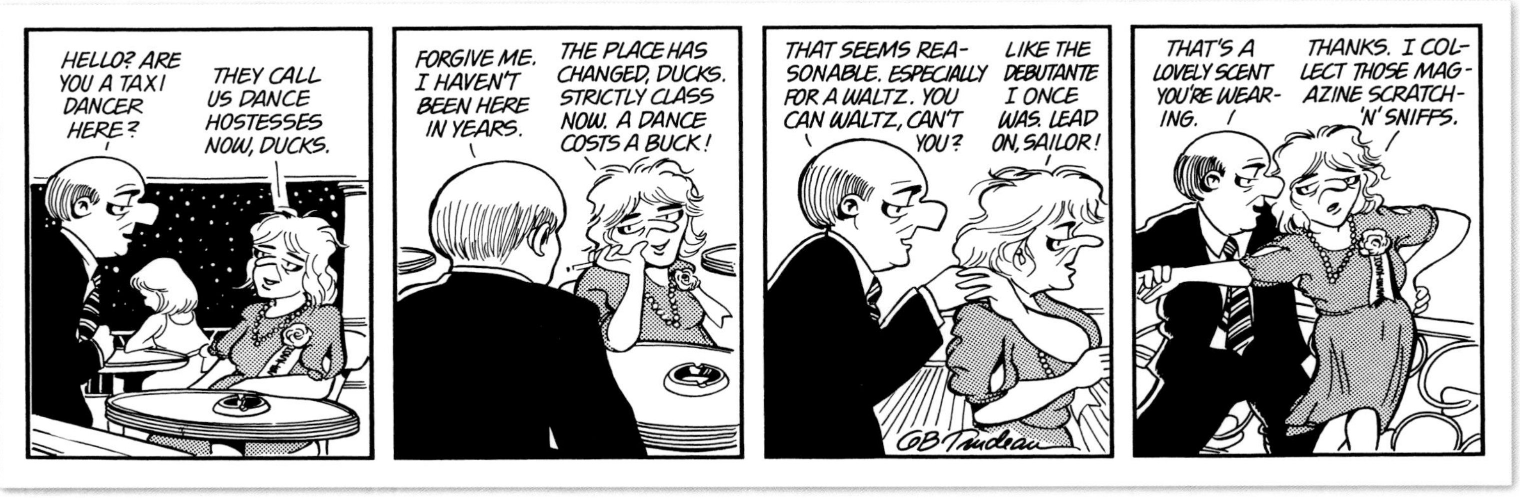
HELLO? ARE YOU A TAXI DANCER HERE?
THEY CALL US DANCE HOSTESSES NOW, DUCKS.
FORGIVE ME. I HAVEN'T BEEN HERE IN YEARS.
THE PLACE HAS CHANGED, DUCKS. STRICTLY CLASS NOW. A DANCE COSTS A BUCK!
THAT SEEMS REASONABLE. ESPECIALLY FOR A WALTZ. YOU CAN WALTZ, CAN'T YOU?
LIKE THE DEBUTANTE I ONCE WAS. LEAD ON, SAILOR!
GB Trudeau
THAT'S A LOVELY SCENT YOU'RE WEARING.
THANKS. I COLLECT THOSE MAGAZINE SCRATCH-'N'SNIFFS.

4/8/87

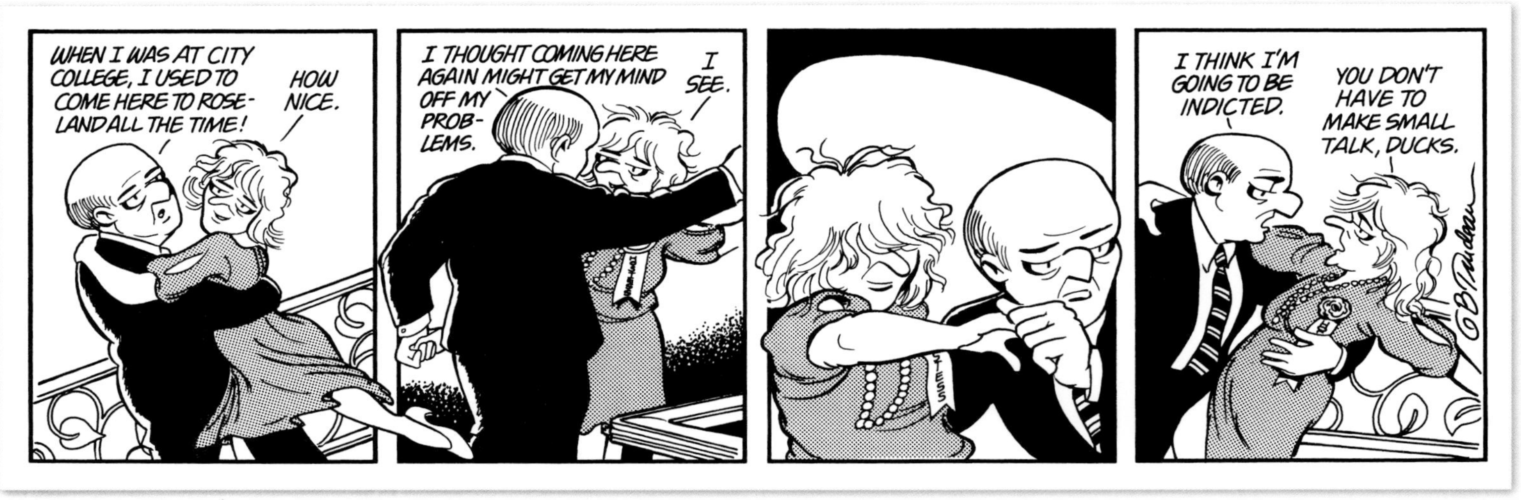
WHEN I WAS AT CITY COLLEGE, I USED TO COME HERE TO ROSELAND ALL THE TIME!
HOW NICE.
I THOUGHT COMING HERE AGAIN MIGHT GET MY MIND OFF MY PROBLEMS.
I SEE.
I THINK I'M GOING TO BE INDICTED.
YOU DON'T HAVE TO MAKE SMALL TALK, DUCKS.
GB Trudeau

4/9/87

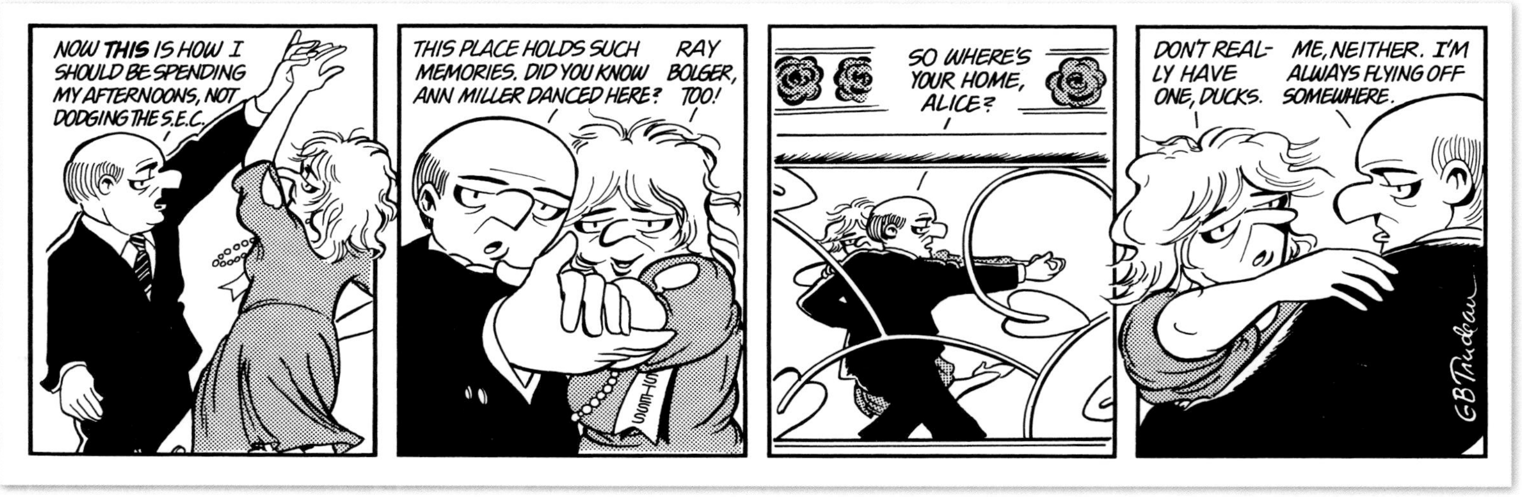
NOW **THIS** IS HOW I SHOULD BE SPENDING MY AFTERNOONS, NOT DODGING THE S.E.C.
THIS PLACE HOLDS SUCH MEMORIES. DID YOU KNOW ANN MILLER DANCED HERE?
RAY BOLGER, TOO!
SO WHERE'S YOUR HOME, ALICE?
DON'T REALLY HAVE ONE, DUCKS.
ME, NEITHER. I'M ALWAYS FLYING OFF SOMEWHERE.
GB Trudeau

4/10/87

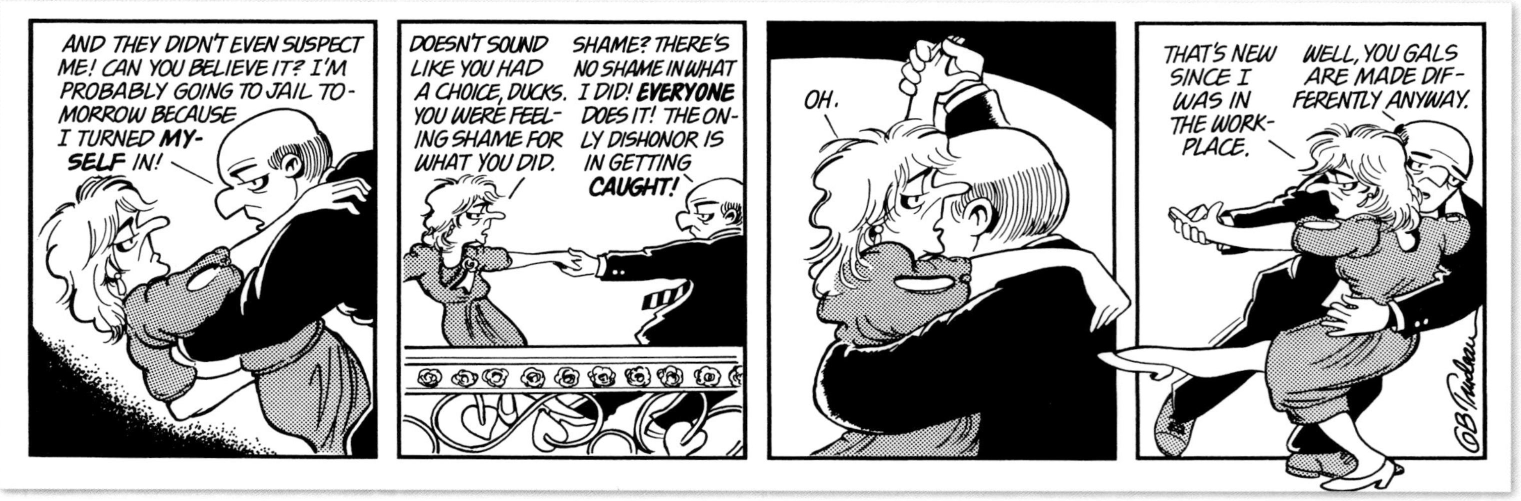
AND THEY DIDN'T EVEN SUSPECT ME! CAN YOU BELIEVE IT? I'M PROBABLY GOING TO JAIL TOMORROW BECAUSE I TURNED **MYSELF** IN!
DOESN'T SOUND LIKE YOU HAD A CHOICE, DUCKS. YOU WERE FEELING SHAME FOR WHAT YOU DID.
SHAME? THERE'S NO SHAME IN WHAT I DID! **EVERYONE** DOES IT! THE ONLY DISHONOR IS IN GETTING **CAUGHT!**
OH.
THAT'S NEW SINCE I WAS IN THE WORKPLACE.
WELL, YOU GALS ARE MADE DIFFERENTLY ANYWAY.
GB Trudeau

4/18/87

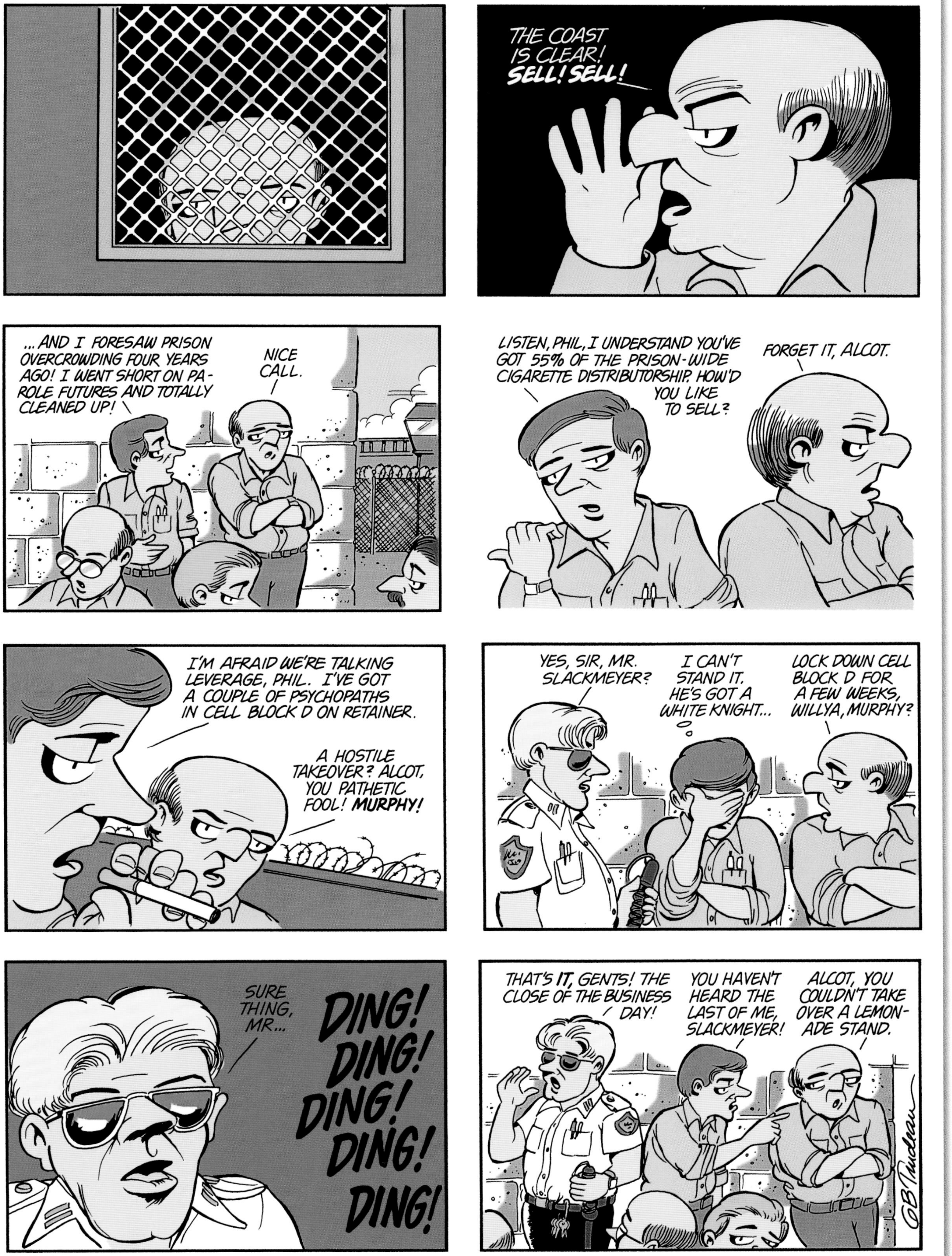
THE COAST IS CLEAR! SELL! SELL!
...AND I FORESAW PRISON OVERCROWDING FOUR YEARS AGO! I WENT SHORT ON PAROLE FUTURES AND TOTALLY CLEANED UP!
NICE CALL.
LISTEN, PHIL, I UNDERSTAND YOU'VE GOT 55% OF THE PRISON-WIDE CIGARETTE DISTRIBUTORSHIP. HOW'D YOU LIKE TO SELL?
FORGET IT, ALCOT.
I'M AFRAID WE'RE TALKING LEVERAGE, PHIL. I'VE GOT A COUPLE OF PSYCHOPATHS IN CELL BLOCK D ON RETAINER.
A HOSTILE TAKEOVER? ALCOT, YOU PATHETIC FOOL! MURPHY!
YES, SIR, MR. SLACKMEYER?
I CAN'T STAND IT. HE'S GOT A WHITE KNIGHT...
LOCK DOWN CELL BLOCK D FOR A FEW WEEKS, WILLYA, MURPHY?
SURE THING, MR...
DING! DING! DING! DING! DING!
THAT'S IT, GENTS! THE CLOSE OF THE BUSINESS DAY!
YOU HAVEN'T HEARD THE LAST OF ME, SLACKMEYER!
ALCOT, YOU COULDN'T TAKE OVER A LEMONADE STAND.
GBTrudeau

6/14/87

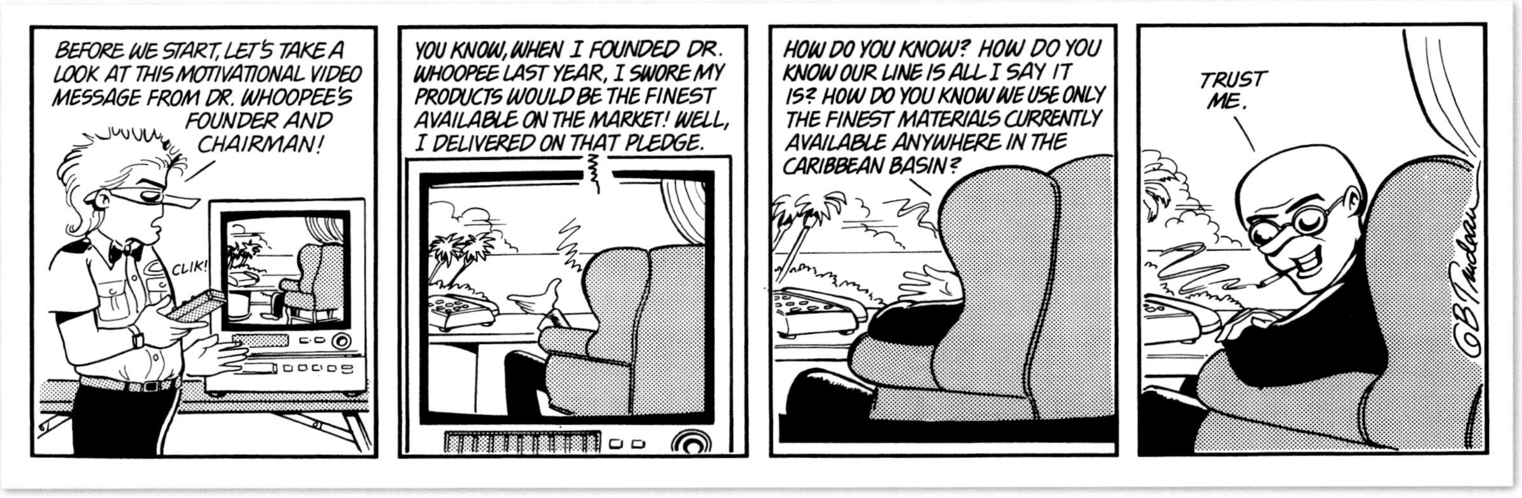
BEFORE WE START, LET'S TAKE A LOOK AT THIS MOTIVATIONAL VIDEO MESSAGE FROM DR. WHOOPEE'S FOUNDER AND CHAIRMAN!
CLIK!
YOU KNOW, WHEN I FOUNDED DR. WHOOPEE LAST YEAR, I SWORE MY PRODUCTS WOULD BE THE FINEST AVAILABLE ON THE MARKET! WELL, I DELIVERED ON THAT PLEDGE.
HOW DO YOU KNOW? HOW DO YOU KNOW OUR LINE IS ALL I SAY IT IS? HOW DO YOU KNOW WE USE ONLY THE FINEST MATERIALS CURRENTLY AVAILABLE ANYWHERE IN THE CARIBBEAN BASIN?
TRUST ME.
5/12/87

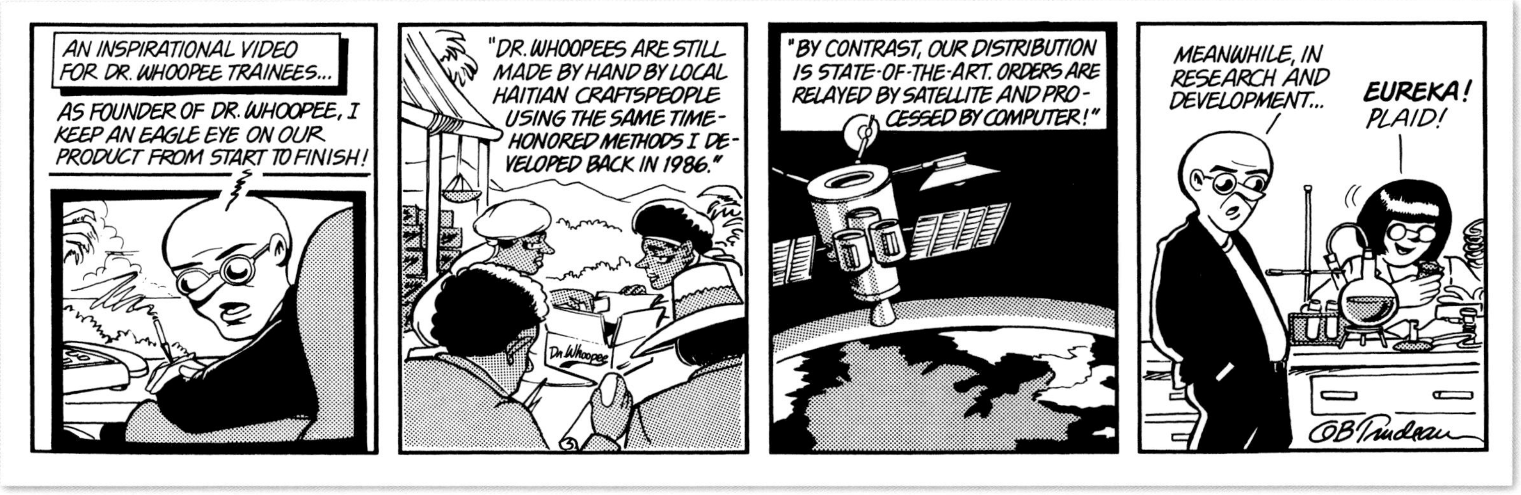
AN INSPIRATIONAL VIDEO FOR DR. WHOOPEE TRAINEES...
AS FOUNDER OF DR. WHOOPEE, I KEEP AN EAGLE EYE ON OUR PRODUCT FROM START TO FINISH!
"DR. WHOOPEES ARE STILL MADE BY HAND BY LOCAL HAITIAN CRAFTSPEOPLE USING THE SAME TIME-HONORED METHODS I DEVELOPED BACK IN 1986."
Dr. Whoopee
"BY CONTRAST, OUR DISTRIBUTION IS STATE-OF-THE-ART. ORDERS ARE RELAYED BY SATELLITE AND PROCESSED BY COMPUTER!"
MEANWHILE, IN RESEARCH AND DEVELOPMENT...
EUREKA! PLAID!
5/13/87

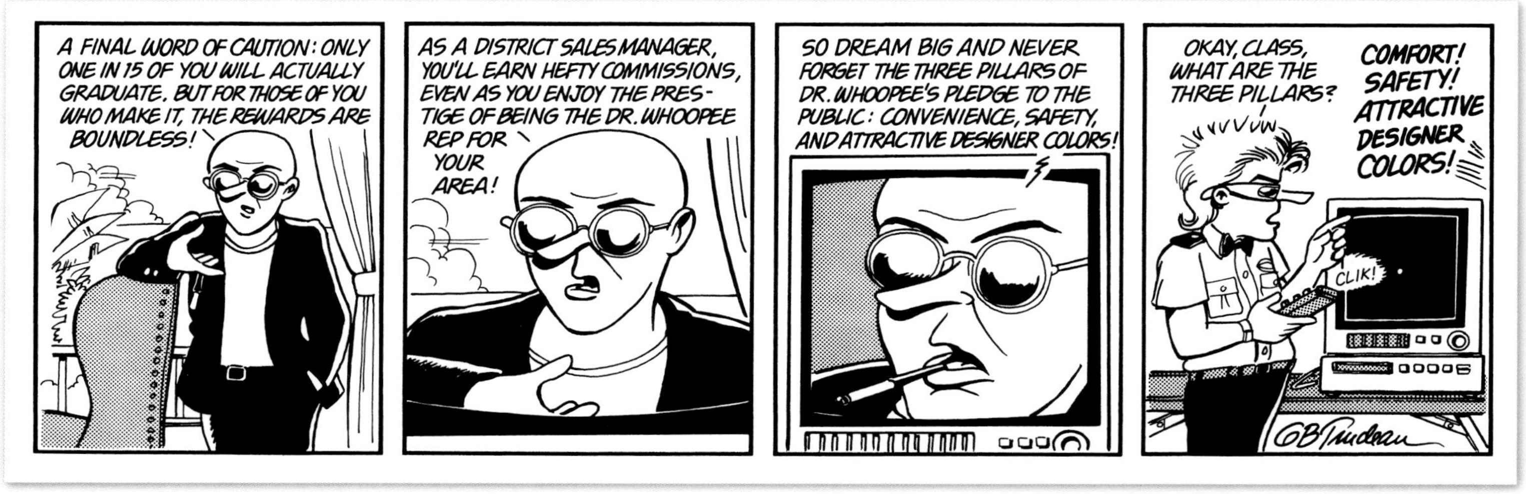
A FINAL WORD OF CAUTION: ONLY ONE IN 15 OF YOU WILL ACTUALLY GRADUATE. BUT FOR THOSE OF YOU WHO MAKE IT, THE REWARDS ARE BOUNDLESS!
AS A DISTRICT SALES MANAGER, YOU'LL EARN HEFTY COMMISSIONS, EVEN AS YOU ENJOY THE PRESTIGE OF BEING THE DR. WHOOPEE REP FOR YOUR AREA!
SO DREAM BIG AND NEVER FORGET THE THREE PILLARS OF DR. WHOOPEE'S PLEDGE TO THE PUBLIC: CONVENIENCE, SAFETY, AND ATTRACTIVE DESIGNER COLORS!
OKAY, CLASS, WHAT ARE THE THREE PILLARS?
COMFORT! SAFETY! ATTRACTIVE DESIGNER COLORS!
CLIK!
5/15/87

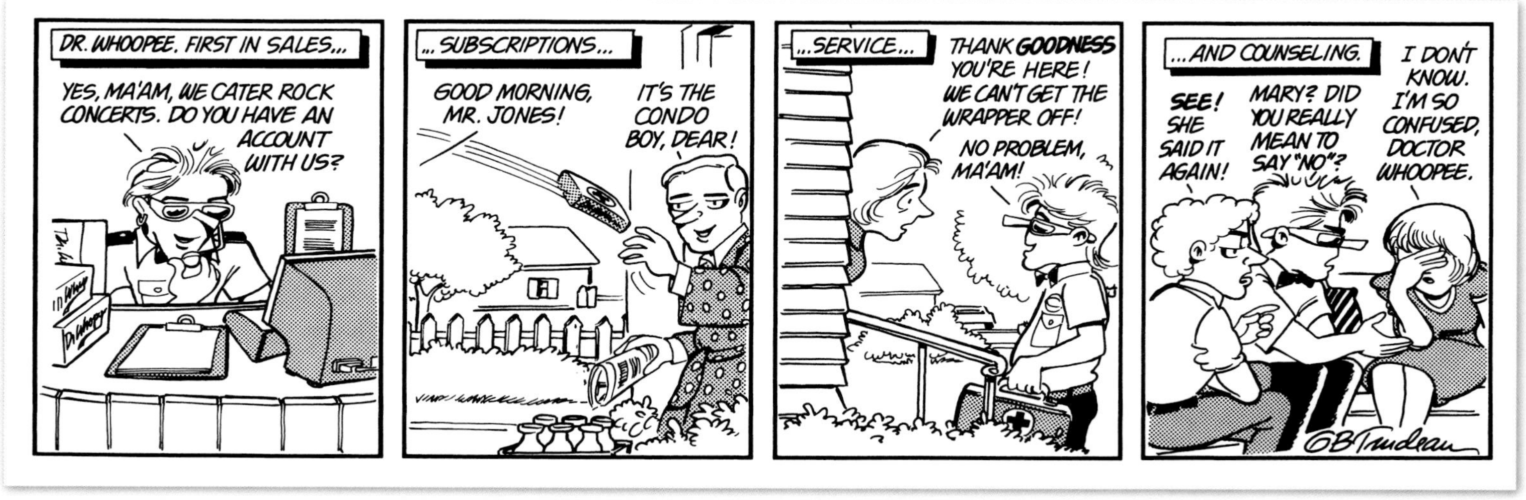
DR. WHOOPEE. FIRST IN SALES...
YES, MA'AM, WE CATER ROCK CONCERTS. DO YOU HAVE AN ACCOUNT WITH US?
...SUBSCRIPTIONS...
GOOD MORNING, MR. JONES!
IT'S THE CONDO BOY, DEAR!
...SERVICE...
THANK GOODNESS YOU'RE HERE! WE CAN'T GET THE WRAPPER OFF!
NO PROBLEM, MA'AM!
...AND COUNSELING.
SEE! SHE SAID IT AGAIN!
MARY? DID YOU REALLY MEAN TO SAY "NO"?
I DON'T KNOW. I'M SO CONFUSED, DOCTOR WHOOPEE.
5/16/87

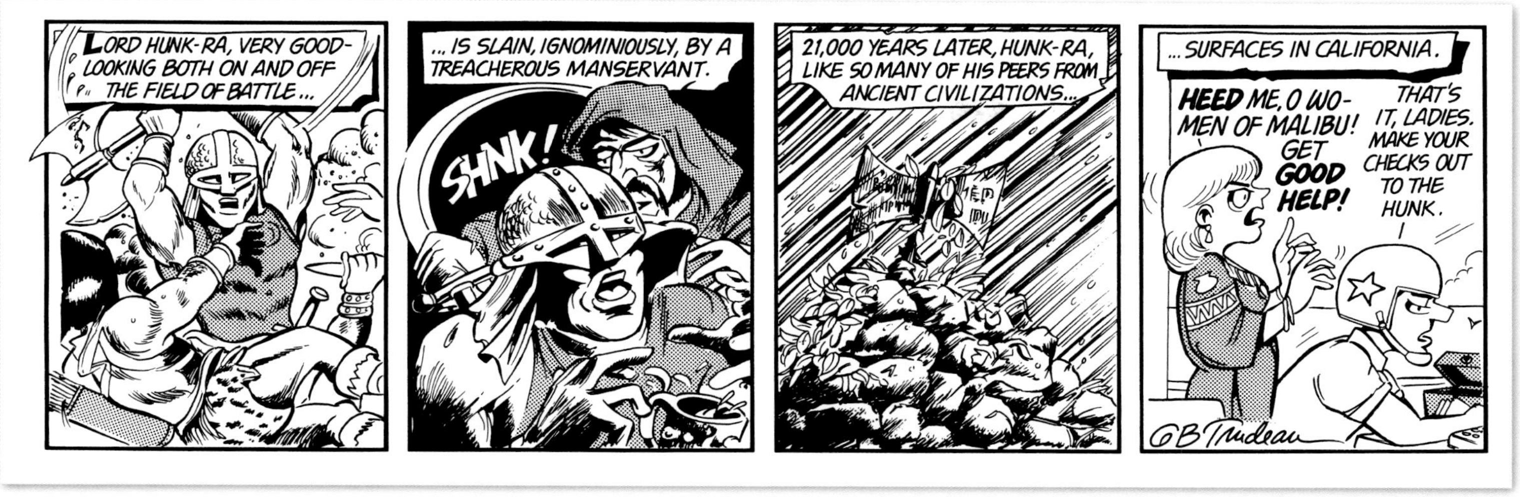
LORD HUNK-RA, VERY GOOD-LOOKING BOTH ON AND OFF THE FIELD OF BATTLE...
... IS SLAIN, IGNOMINIOUSLY, BY A TREACHEROUS MANSERVANT.
SHNK!
21,000 YEARS LATER, HUNK-RA, LIKE SO MANY OF HIS PEERS FROM ANCIENT CIVILIZATIONS...
... SURFACES IN CALIFORNIA.
HEED ME, O WOMEN OF MALIBU! GET GOOD HELP!
THAT'S IT, LADIES. MAKE YOUR CHECKS OUT TO THE HUNK.
GB Trudeau

8/3/87

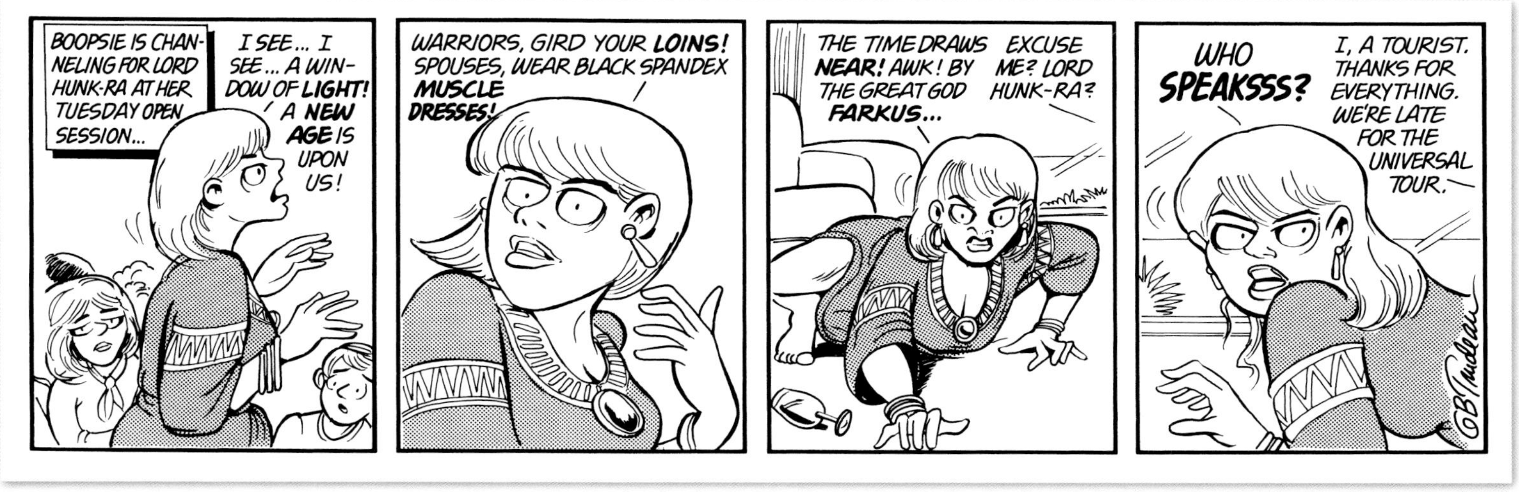
BOOPSIE IS CHANNELING FOR LORD HUNK-RA AT HER TUESDAY OPEN SESSION...
I SEE... I SEE... A WINDOW OF LIGHT! A NEW AGE IS UPON US!
WARRIORS, GIRD YOUR LOINS! SPOUSES, WEAR BLACK SPANDEX MUSCLE DRESSES!
THE TIME DRAWS NEAR! AWK! BY THE GREAT GOD FARKUS...
EXCUSE ME? LORD HUNK-RA?
WHO SPEAKSSS?
I, A TOURIST. THANKS FOR EVERYTHING. WE'RE LATE FOR THE UNIVERSAL TOUR.
GB Trudeau

8/4/87

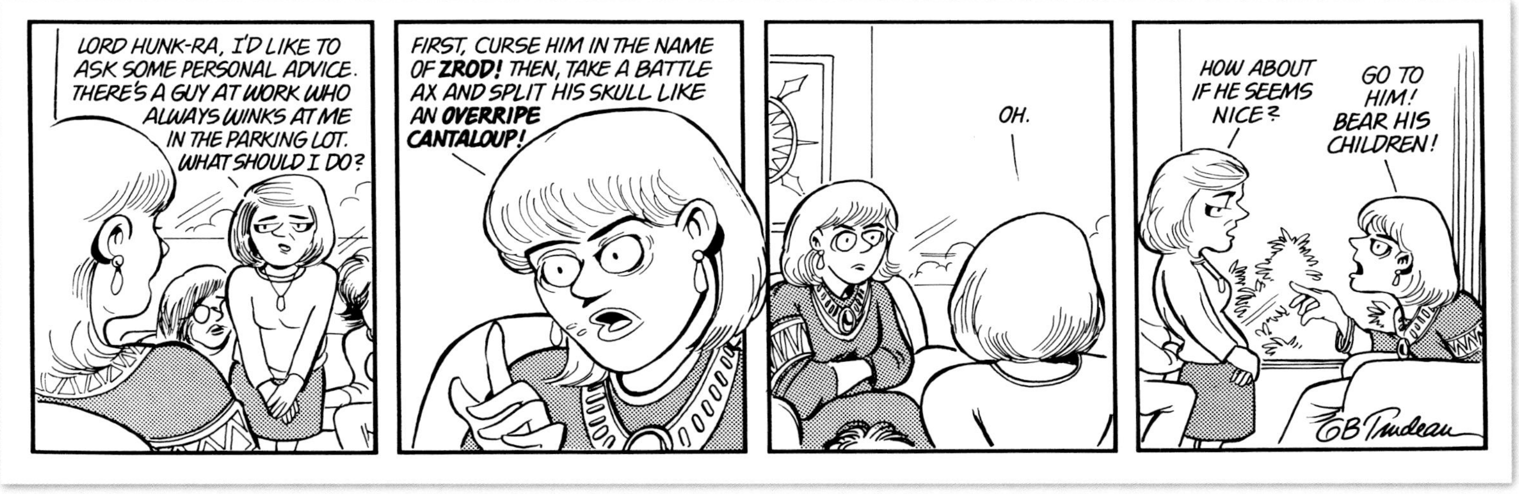
LORD HUNK-RA, I'D LIKE TO ASK SOME PERSONAL ADVICE. THERE'S A GUY AT WORK WHO ALWAYS WINKS AT ME IN THE PARKING LOT. WHAT SHOULD I DO?
FIRST, CURSE HIM IN THE NAME OF ZROD! THEN, TAKE A BATTLE AX AND SPLIT HIS SKULL LIKE AN OVERRIPE CANTALOUP!
OH.
HOW ABOUT IF HE SEEMS NICE?
GO TO HIM! BEAR HIS CHILDREN!
GB Trudeau

8/5/87

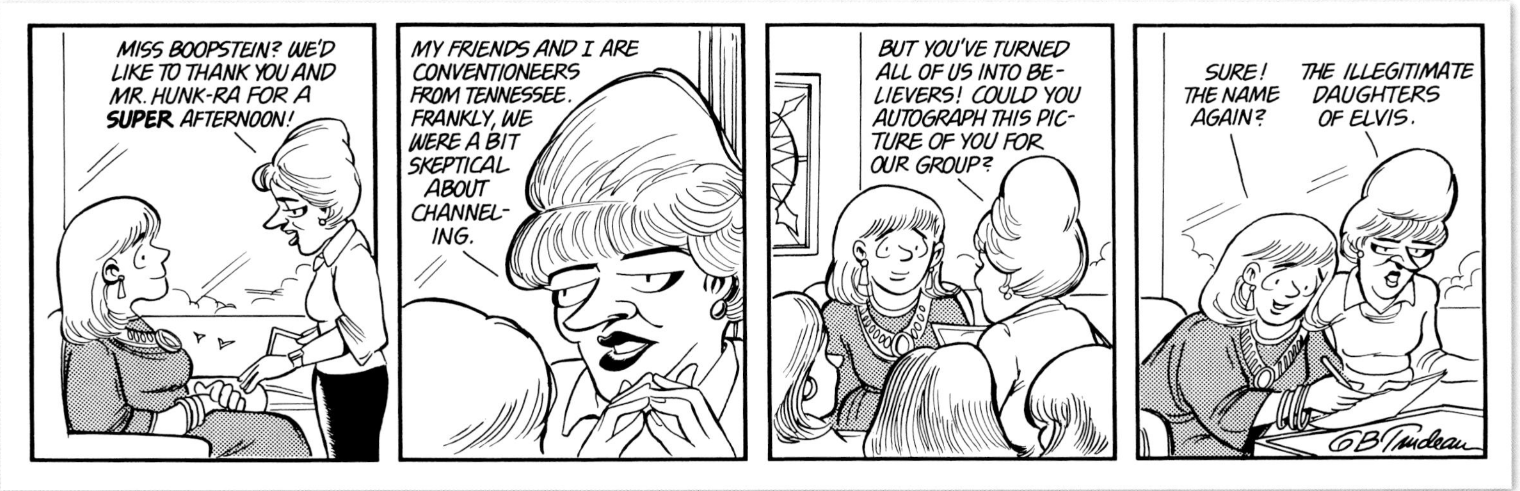
MISS BOOPSTEIN? WE'D LIKE TO THANK YOU AND MR. HUNK-RA FOR A SUPER AFTERNOON!
MY FRIENDS AND I ARE CONVENTIONEERS FROM TENNESSEE. FRANKLY, WE WERE A BIT SKEPTICAL ABOUT CHANNELING.
BUT YOU'VE TURNED ALL OF US INTO BELIEVERS! COULD YOU AUTOGRAPH THIS PICTURE OF YOU FOR OUR GROUP?
SURE! THE NAME AGAIN?
THE ILLEGITIMATE DAUGHTERS OF ELVIS.
GB Trudeau

8/6/87

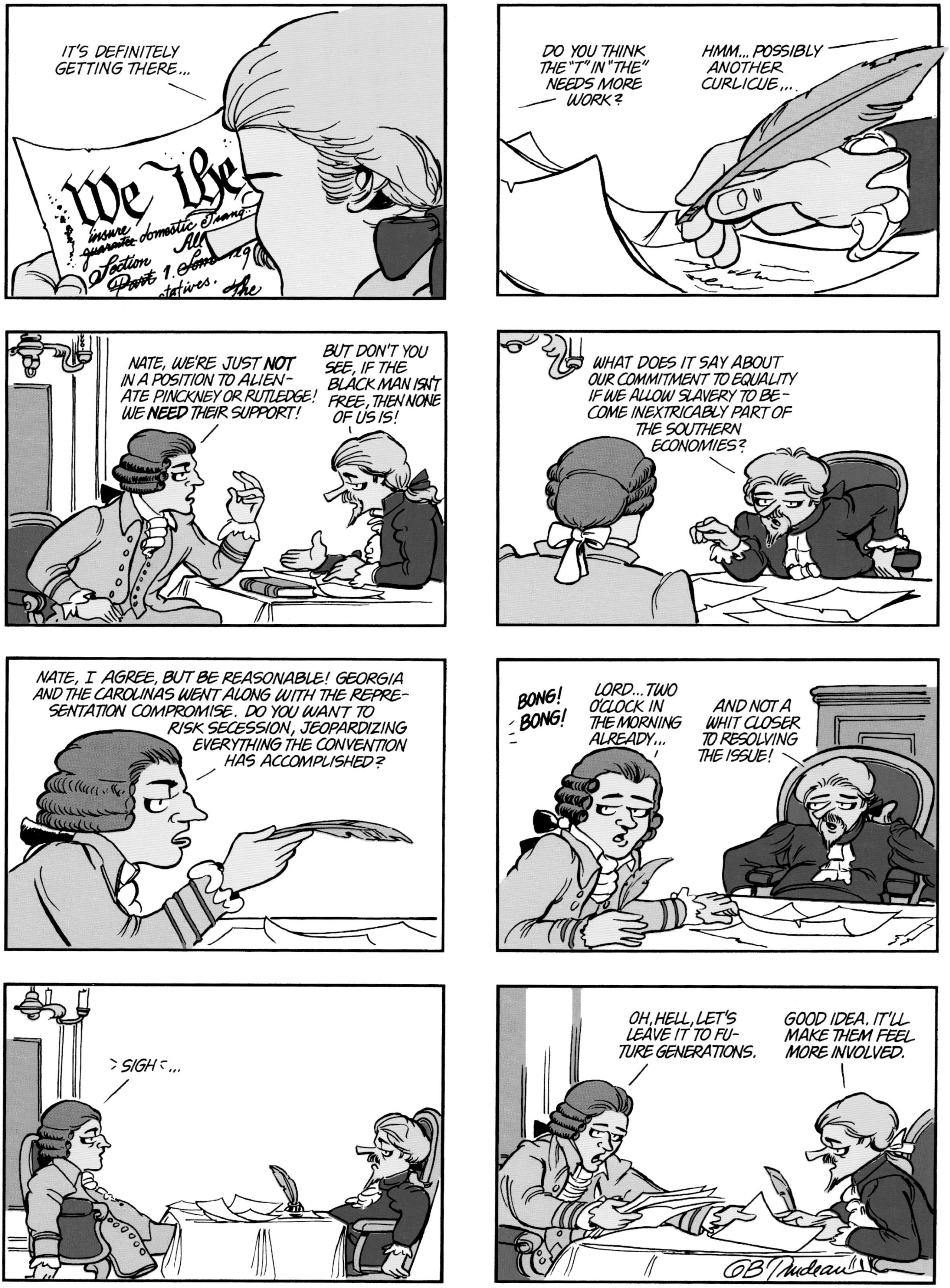
IT'S DEFINITELY GETTING THERE...
We the
insure
guarantee domestic Tranq
Section
Part 1.
statives.
DO YOU THINK THE "T" IN "THE" NEEDS MORE WORK?
HMM... POSSIBLY ANOTHER CURLICUE,...
NATE, WE'RE JUST NOT IN A POSITION TO ALIENATE PINCKNEY OR RUTLEDGE! WE NEED THEIR SUPPORT!
BUT DON'T YOU SEE, IF THE BLACK MAN ISN'T FREE, THEN NONE OF US IS!
WHAT DOES IT SAY ABOUT OUR COMMITMENT TO EQUALITY IF WE ALLOW SLAVERY TO BECOME INEXTRICABLY PART OF THE SOUTHERN ECONOMIES?
NATE, I AGREE, BUT BE REASONABLE! GEORGIA AND THE CAROLINAS WENT ALONG WITH THE REPRESENTATION COMPROMISE. DO YOU WANT TO RISK SECESSION, JEOPARDIZING EVERYTHING THE CONVENTION HAS ACCOMPLISHED?
BONG! BONG!
LORD...TWO O'CLOCK IN THE MORNING ALREADY...
AND NOT A WHIT CLOSER TO RESOLVING THE ISSUE!
>SIGH<...
OH, HELL, LET'S LEAVE IT TO FUTURE GENERATIONS.
GOOD IDEA. IT'LL MAKE THEM FEEL MORE INVOLVED.
GB Trudeau

7/19/87

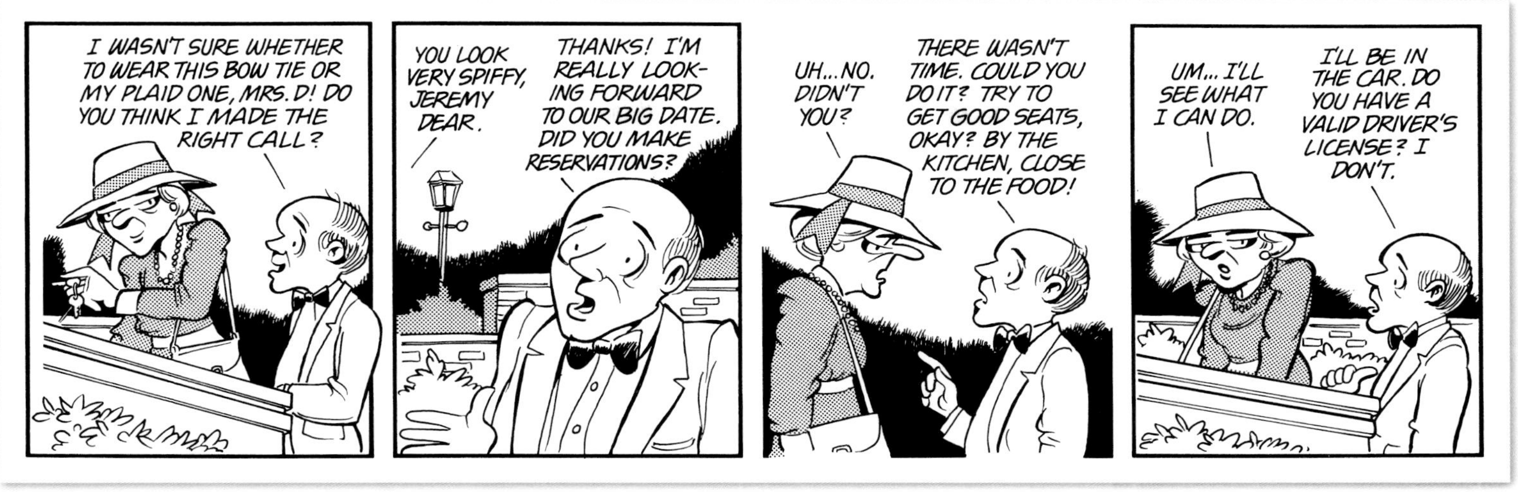
I WASN'T SURE WHETHER TO WEAR THIS BOW TIE OR MY PLAID ONE, MRS. D! DO YOU THINK I MADE THE RIGHT CALL?
YOU LOOK VERY SPIFFY, JEREMY DEAR.
THANKS! I'M REALLY LOOKING FORWARD TO OUR BIG DATE. DID YOU MAKE RESERVATIONS?
UH... NO. DIDN'T YOU?
THERE WASN'T TIME. COULD YOU DO IT? TRY TO GET GOOD SEATS, OKAY? BY THE KITCHEN, CLOSE TO THE FOOD!
UM... I'LL SEE WHAT I CAN DO.
I'LL BE IN THE CAR. DO YOU HAVE A VALID DRIVER'S LICENSE? I DON'T.

10/20/87

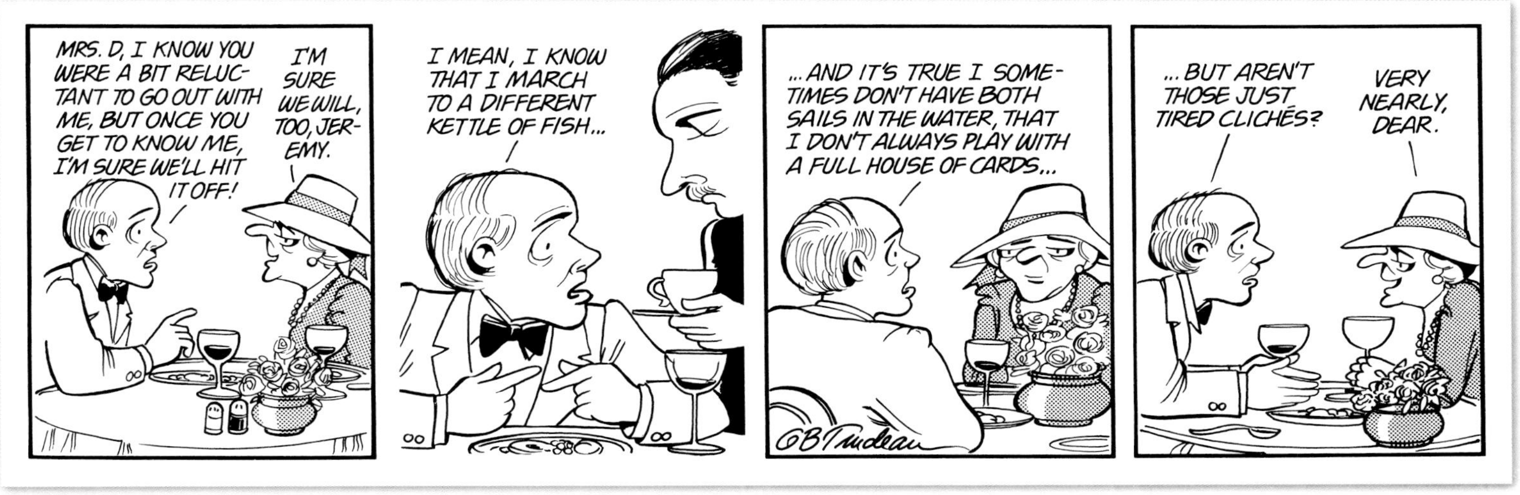
MRS. D, I KNOW YOU WERE A BIT RELUCTANT TO GO OUT WITH ME, BUT ONCE YOU GET TO KNOW ME, I'M SURE WE'LL HIT IT OFF!
I'M SURE WE WILL, TOO, JEREMY.
I MEAN, I KNOW THAT I MARCH TO A DIFFERENT KETTLE OF FISH...
...AND IT'S TRUE I SOMETIMES DON'T HAVE BOTH SAILS IN THE WATER, THAT I DON'T ALWAYS PLAY WITH A FULL HOUSE OF CARDS...
GB Trudeau
...BUT AREN'T THOSE JUST TIRED CLICHÉS?
VERY NEARLY, DEAR.

10/21/87

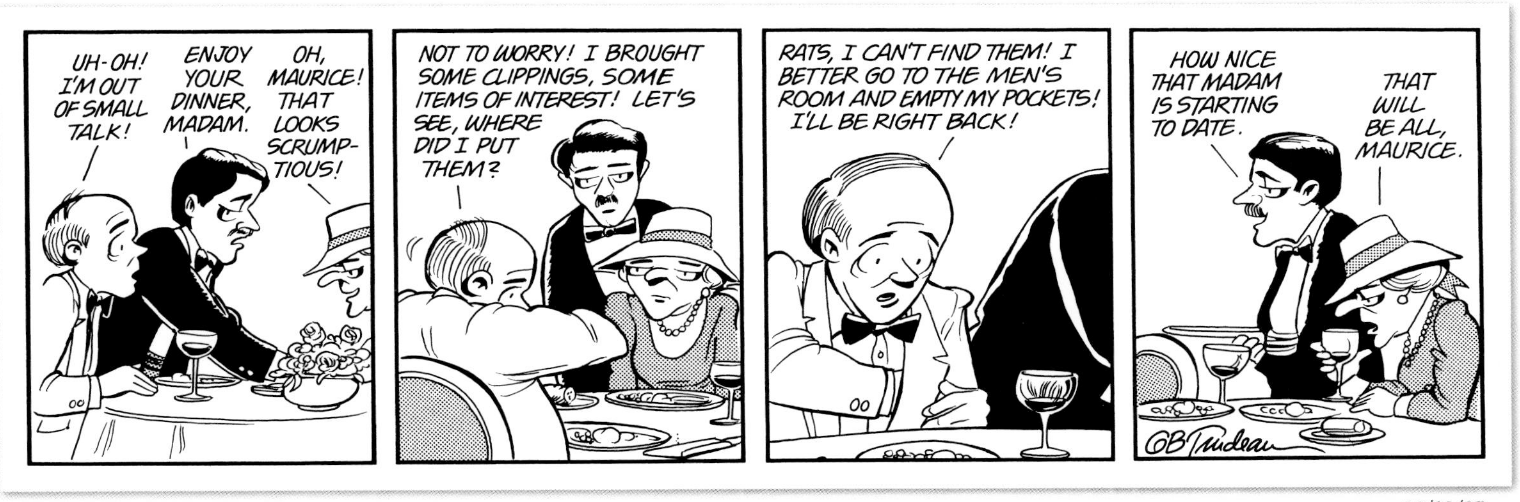
UH-OH! I'M OUT OF SMALL TALK!
ENJOY YOUR DINNER, MADAM.
OH, MAURICE! THAT LOOKS SCRUMPTIOUS!
NOT TO WORRY! I BROUGHT SOME CLIPPINGS, SOME ITEMS OF INTEREST! LET'S SEE, WHERE DID I PUT THEM?
RATS, I CAN'T FIND THEM! I BETTER GO TO THE MEN'S ROOM AND EMPTY MY POCKETS! I'LL BE RIGHT BACK!
HOW NICE THAT MADAM IS STARTING TO DATE.
THAT WILL BE ALL, MAURICE.
GB Trudeau

10/22/87

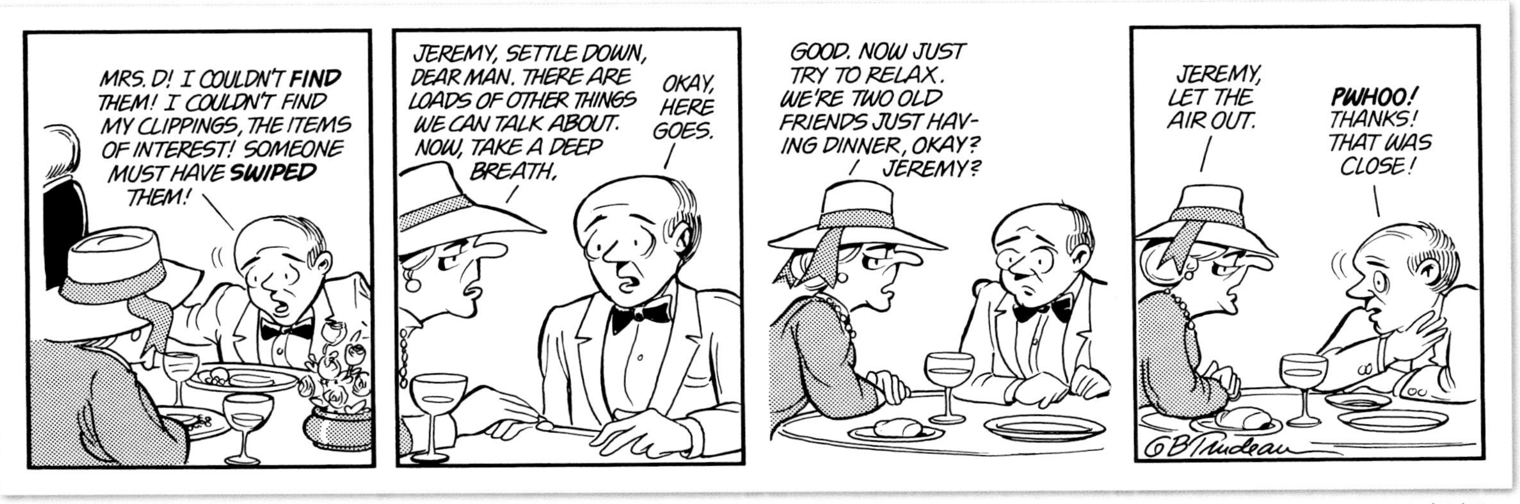
MRS. D! I COULDN'T **FIND** THEM! I COULDN'T FIND MY CLIPPINGS, THE ITEMS OF INTEREST! SOMEONE MUST HAVE **SWIPED** THEM!
JEREMY, SETTLE DOWN, DEAR MAN. THERE ARE LOADS OF OTHER THINGS WE CAN TALK ABOUT. NOW, TAKE A DEEP BREATH.
OKAY, HERE GOES.
GOOD. NOW JUST TRY TO RELAX. WE'RE TWO OLD FRIENDS JUST HAVING DINNER, OKAY? JEREMY?
JEREMY, LET THE AIR OUT.
PWHOO! THANKS! THAT WAS CLOSE!
GB Trudeau

10/23/87

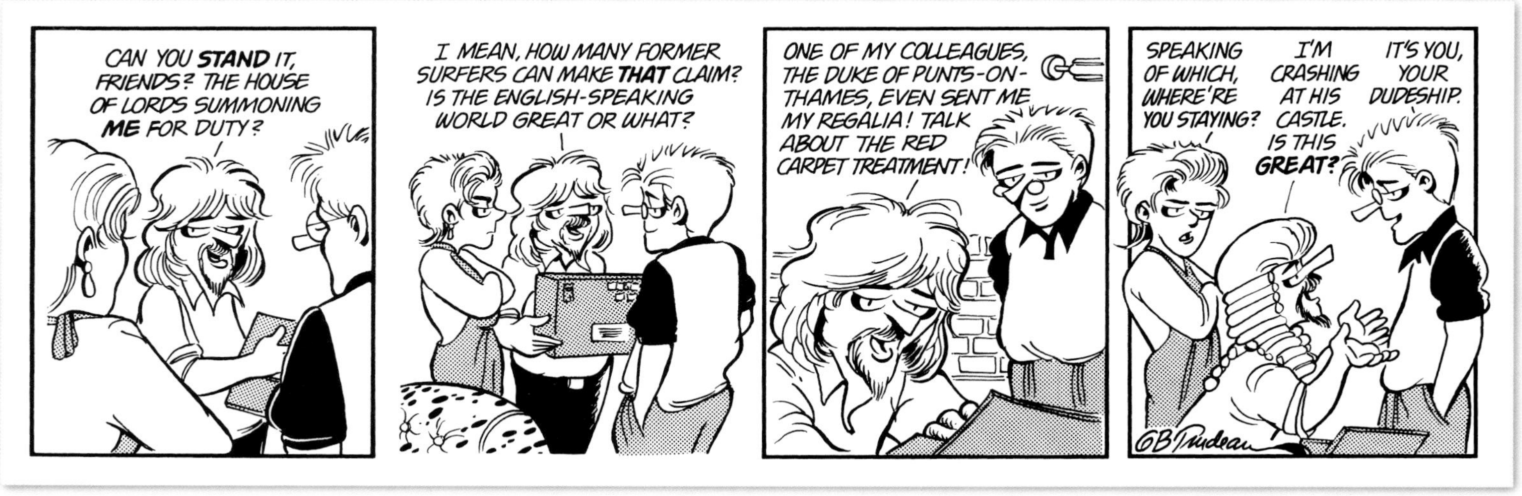
CAN YOU STAND IT, FRIENDS? THE HOUSE OF LORDS SUMMONING ME FOR DUTY?
I MEAN, HOW MANY FORMER SURFERS CAN MAKE THAT CLAIM? IS THE ENGLISH-SPEAKING WORLD GREAT OR WHAT?
ONE OF MY COLLEAGUES, THE DUKE OF PUNTS-ON-THAMES, EVEN SENT ME MY REGALIA! TALK ABOUT THE RED CARPET TREATMENT!
SPEAKING OF WHICH, WHERE'RE YOU STAYING?
I'M CRASHING AT HIS CASTLE. IS THIS GREAT?
IT'S YOU, YOUR DUDESHIP.

12/15/87

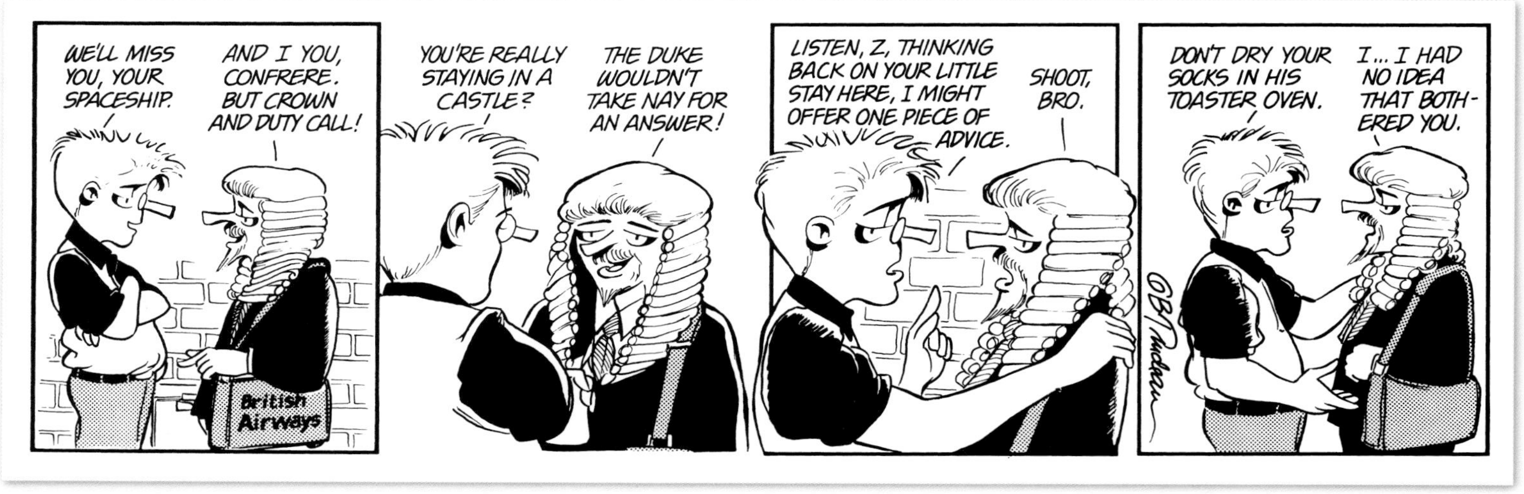
WE'LL MISS YOU, YOUR SPACESHIP.
AND I YOU, CONFRERE. BUT CROWN AND DUTY CALL!
British Airways
YOU'RE REALLY STAYING IN A CASTLE?
THE DUKE WOULDN'T TAKE NAY FOR AN ANSWER!
LISTEN, Z, THINKING BACK ON YOUR LITTLE STAY HERE, I MIGHT OFFER ONE PIECE OF ADVICE.
SHOOT, BRO.
DON'T DRY YOUR SOCKS IN HIS TOASTER OVEN.
I... I HAD NO IDEA THAT BOTHERED YOU.

12/16/87

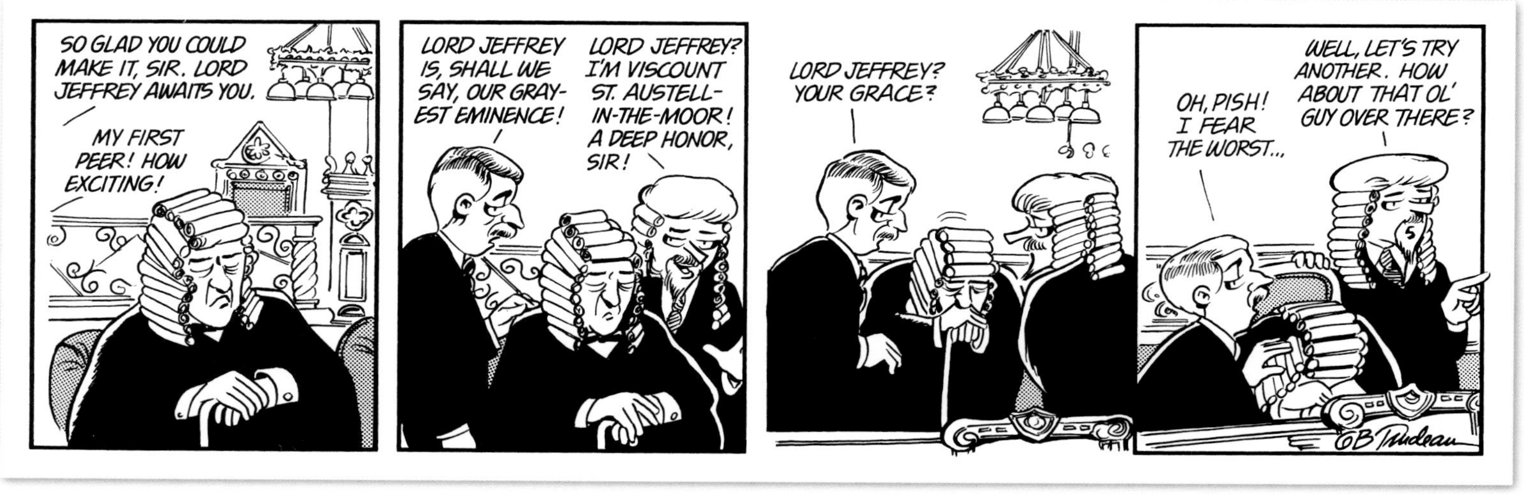
SO GLAD YOU COULD MAKE IT, SIR. LORD JEFFREY AWAITS YOU.
MY FIRST PEER! HOW EXCITING!
LORD JEFFREY IS, SHALL WE SAY, OUR GRAYEST EMINENCE!
LORD JEFFREY? I'M VISCOUNT ST. AUSTELL-IN-THE-MOOR! A DEEP HONOR, SIR!
LORD JEFFREY? YOUR GRACE?
OH, PISH! I FEAR THE WORST...
WELL, LET'S TRY ANOTHER. HOW ABOUT THAT OL' GUY OVER THERE?

12/18/87

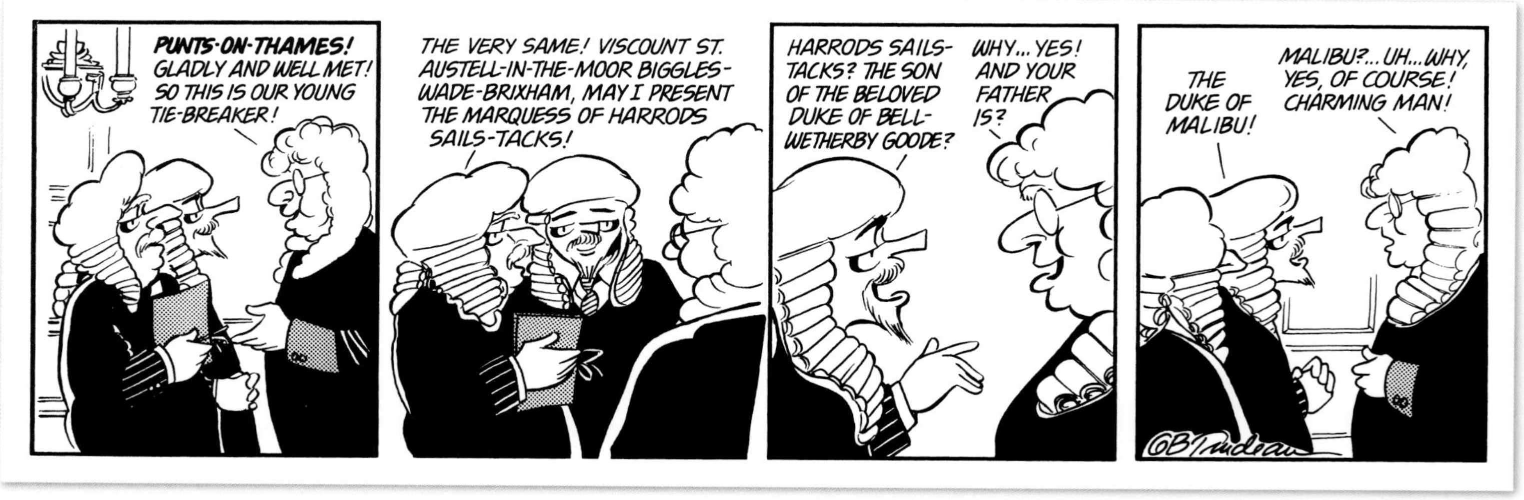
PUNTS-ON-THAMES! GLADLY AND WELL MET! SO THIS IS OUR YOUNG TIE-BREAKER!
THE VERY SAME! VISCOUNT ST. AUSTELL-IN-THE-MOOR BIGGLESWADE-BRIXHAM, MAY I PRESENT THE MARQUESS OF HARRODS SAILS-TACKS!
HARRODS SAILS-TACKS? THE SON OF THE BELOVED DUKE OF BELLWETHERBY GOODE?
WHY... YES! AND YOUR FATHER IS?
THE DUKE OF MALIBU!
MALIBU?... UH... WHY, YES, OF COURSE! CHARMING MAN!

12/22/87

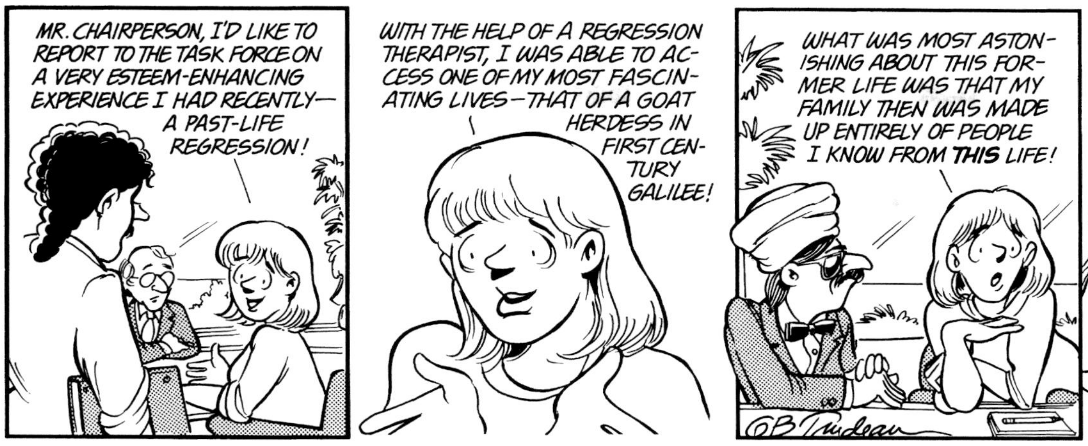
MR. CHAIRPERSON, I'D LIKE TO REPORT TO THE TASK FORCE ON A VERY ESTEEM-ENHANCING EXPERIENCE I HAD RECENTLY— A PAST-LIFE REGRESSION!
WITH THE HELP OF A REGRESSION THERAPIST, I WAS ABLE TO ACCESS ONE OF MY MOST FASCINATING LIVES—THAT OF A GOAT HERDESS IN FIRST CENTURY GALILEE!
WHAT WAS MOST ASTONISHING ABOUT THIS FORMER LIFE WAS THAT MY FAMILY THEN WAS MADE UP ENTIRELY OF PEOPLE I KNOW FROM THIS LIFE!
JOANIE! ZONKER! WHAT ARE YOU DOING HERE?
HUSH, DAUGHTER!
MOM, CAN I GO TO THE STONING OF ST. STEPHEN?
©B Trudeau

1/12/88

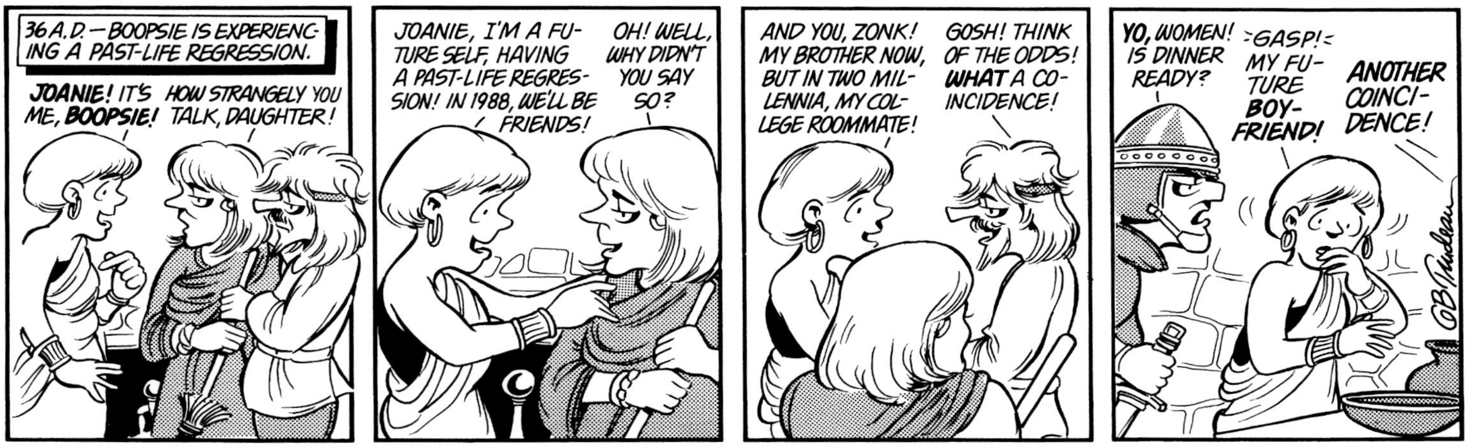
36 A.D.—BOOPSIE IS EXPERIENCING A PAST-LIFE REGRESSION.
JOANIE! IT'S ME, BOOPSIE!
HOW STRANGELY YOU TALK, DAUGHTER!
JOANIE, I'M A FUTURE SELF, HAVING A PAST-LIFE REGRESSION! IN 1988, WE'LL BE FRIENDS!
OH! WELL, WHY DIDN'T YOU SAY SO?
AND YOU, ZONK! MY BROTHER NOW, BUT IN TWO MILLENNIA, MY COLLEGE ROOMMATE!
GOSH! THINK OF THE ODDS! WHAT A COINCIDENCE!
YO, WOMEN! IS DINNER READY?
GASP! MY FUTURE BOYFRIEND!
ANOTHER COINCIDENCE!
©B Trudeau

1/13/88

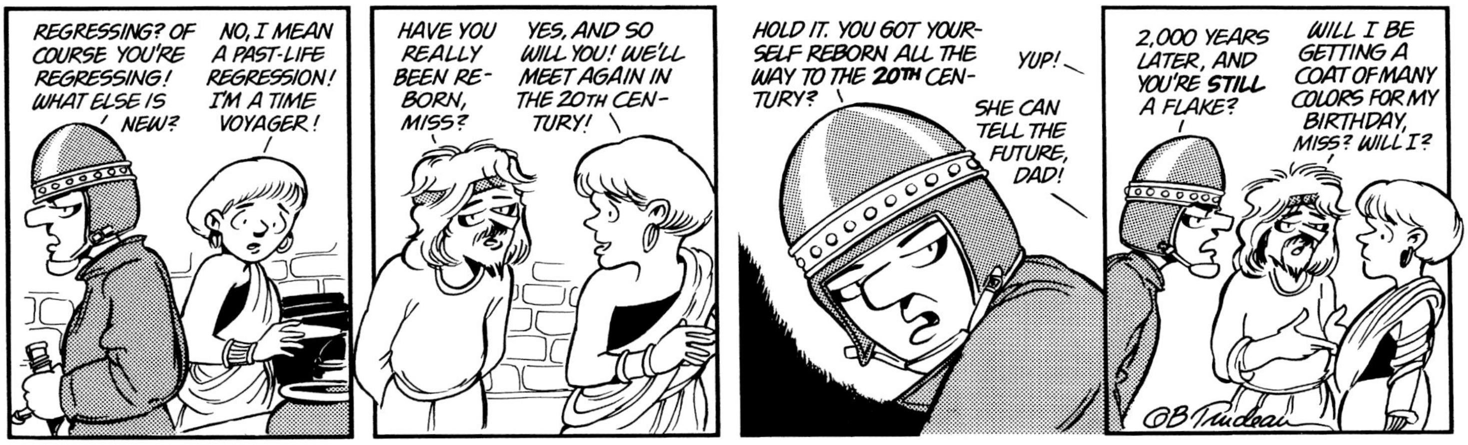
REGRESSING? OF COURSE YOU'RE REGRESSING! WHAT ELSE IS NEW?
NO, I MEAN A PAST-LIFE REGRESSION! I'M A TIME VOYAGER!
HAVE YOU REALLY BEEN REBORN, MISS?
YES, AND SO WILL YOU! WE'LL MEET AGAIN IN THE 20TH CENTURY!
HOLD IT. YOU GOT YOURSELF REBORN ALL THE WAY TO THE 20TH CENTURY?
YUP!
SHE CAN TELL THE FUTURE, DAD!
2,000 YEARS LATER, AND YOU'RE STILL A FLAKE?
WILL I BE GETTING A COAT OF MANY COLORS FOR MY BIRTHDAY, MISS? WILL I?
©B Trudeau

1/14/88

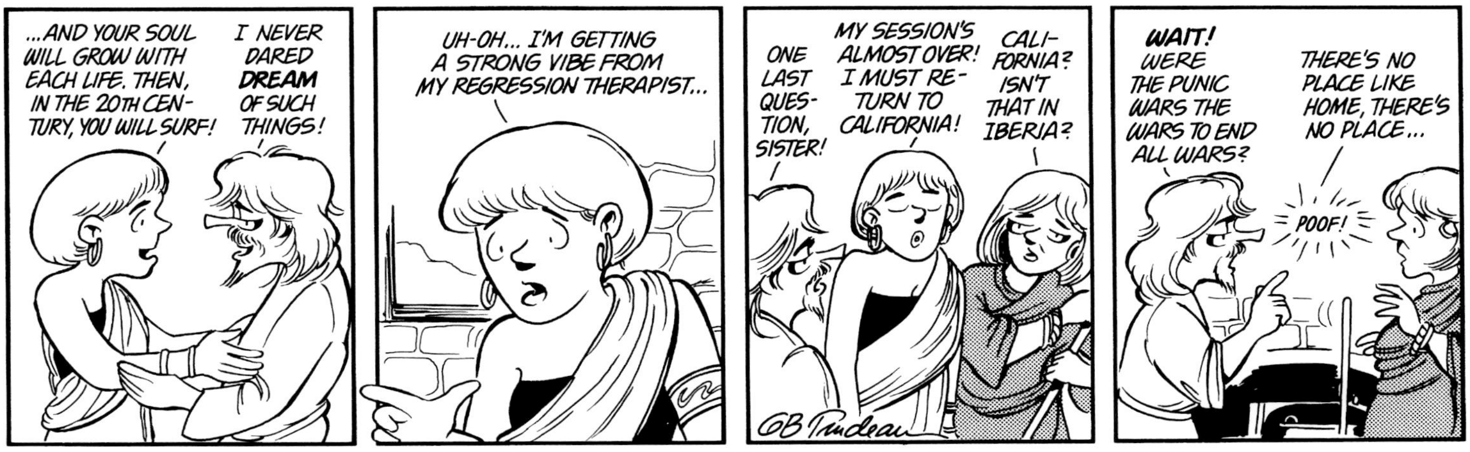
...AND YOUR SOUL WILL GROW WITH EACH LIFE. THEN, IN THE 20TH CENTURY, YOU WILL SURF!
I NEVER DARED DREAM OF SUCH THINGS!
UH-OH... I'M GETTING A STRONG VIBE FROM MY REGRESSION THERAPIST...
ONE LAST QUESTION, SISTER!
MY SESSION'S ALMOST OVER! I MUST RETURN TO CALIFORNIA!
CALIFORNIA? ISN'T THAT IN IBERIA?
WAIT! WERE THE PUNIC WARS THE WARS TO END ALL WARS?
THERE'S NO PLACE LIKE HOME, THERE'S NO PLACE...
POOF!
©B Trudeau

1/15/88

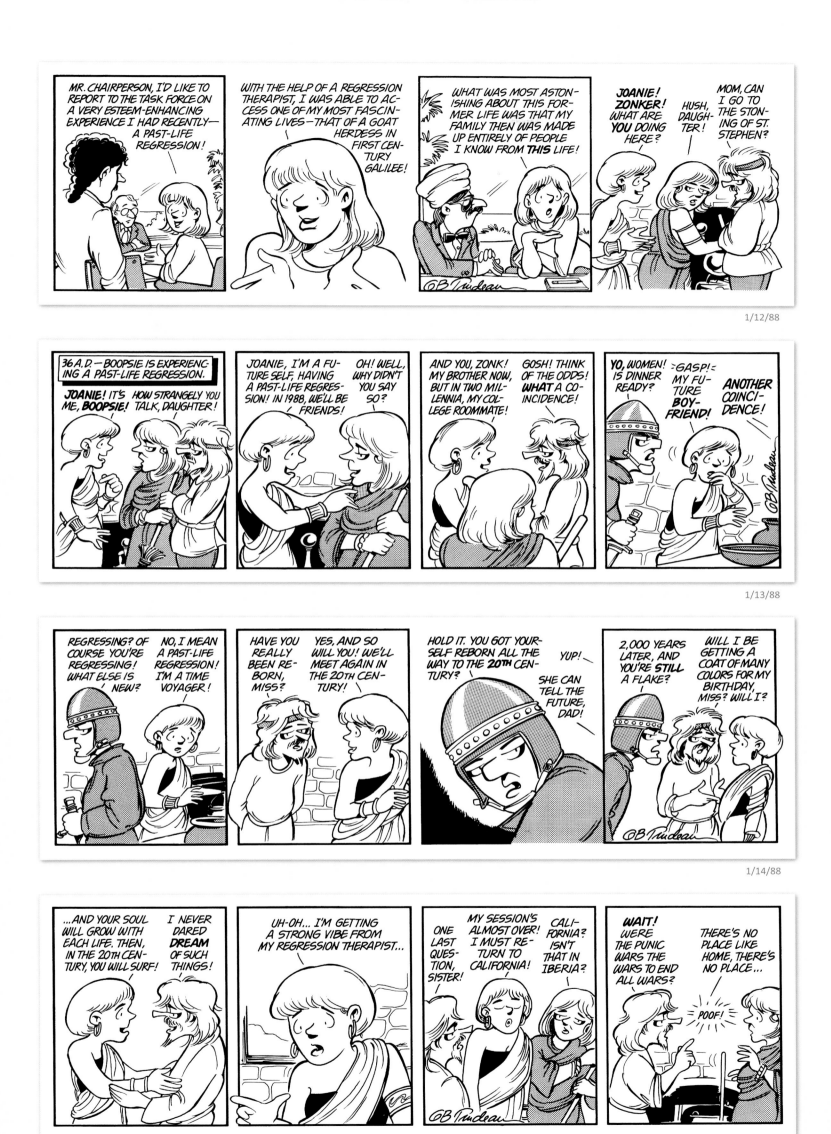

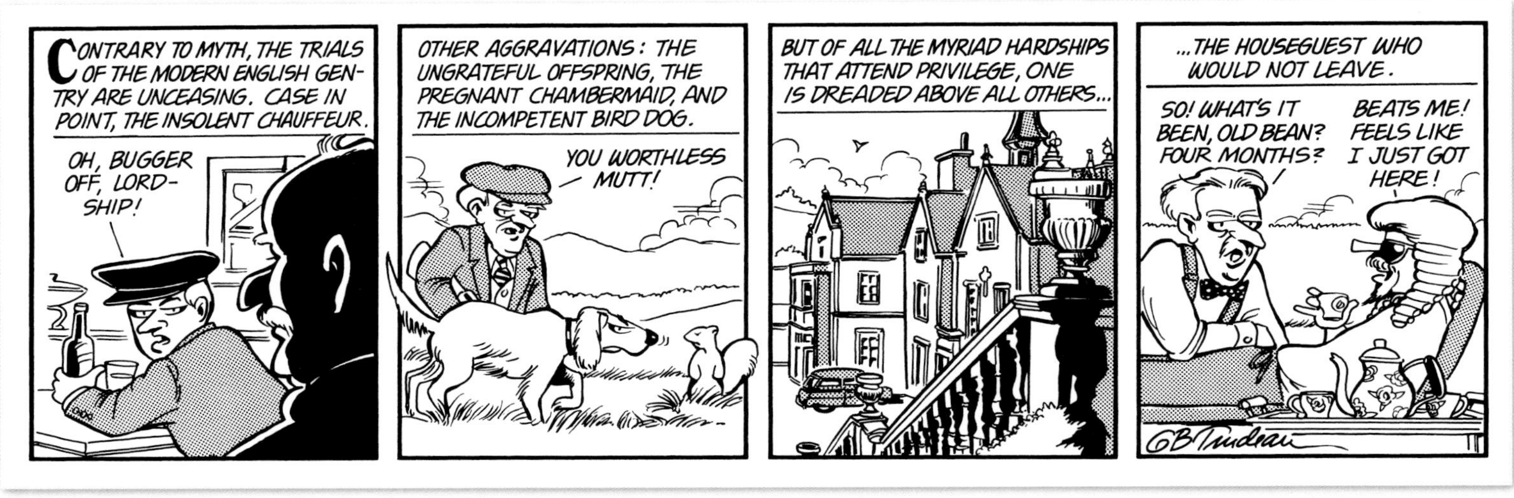
CONTRARY TO MYTH, THE TRIALS OF THE MODERN ENGLISH GENTRY ARE UNCEASING. CASE IN POINT, THE INSOLENT CHAUFFEUR.
OH, BUGGER OFF, LORDSHIP!
OTHER AGGRAVATIONS: THE UNGRATEFUL OFFSPRING, THE PREGNANT CHAMBERMAID, AND THE INCOMPETENT BIRD DOG.
YOU WORTHLESS MUTT!
BUT OF ALL THE MYRIAD HARDSHIPS THAT ATTEND PRIVILEGE, ONE IS DREADED ABOVE ALL OTHERS...
...THE HOUSEGUEST WHO WOULD NOT LEAVE.
SO! WHAT'S IT BEEN, OLD BEAN? FOUR MONTHS?
BEATS ME! FEELS LIKE I JUST GOT HERE!
GBTrudeau
3/21/88

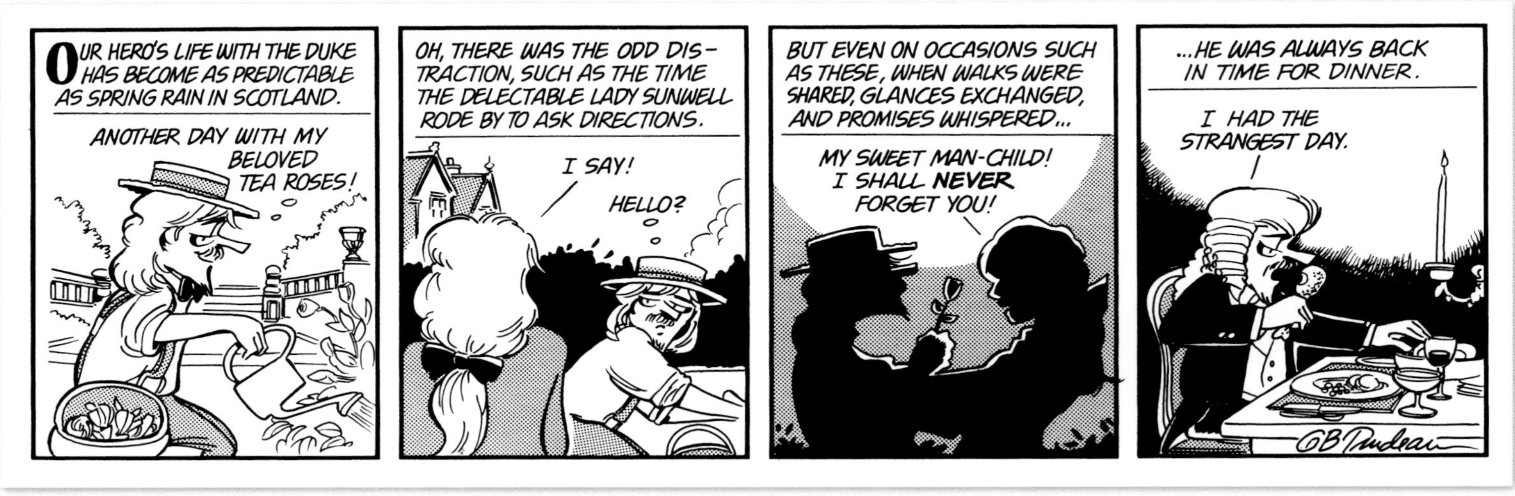
OUR HERO'S LIFE WITH THE DUKE HAS BECOME AS PREDICTABLE AS SPRING RAIN IN SCOTLAND.
ANOTHER DAY WITH MY BELOVED TEA ROSES!
OH, THERE WAS THE ODD DISTRACTION, SUCH AS THE TIME THE DELECTABLE LADY SUNWELL RODE BY TO ASK DIRECTIONS.
I SAY!
HELLO?
BUT EVEN ON OCCASIONS SUCH AS THESE, WHEN WALKS WERE SHARED, GLANCES EXCHANGED, AND PROMISES WHISPERED...
MY SWEET MAN-CHILD! I SHALL NEVER FORGET YOU!
...HE WAS ALWAYS BACK IN TIME FOR DINNER.
I HAD THE STRANGEST DAY.
GBTrudeau
3/23/88

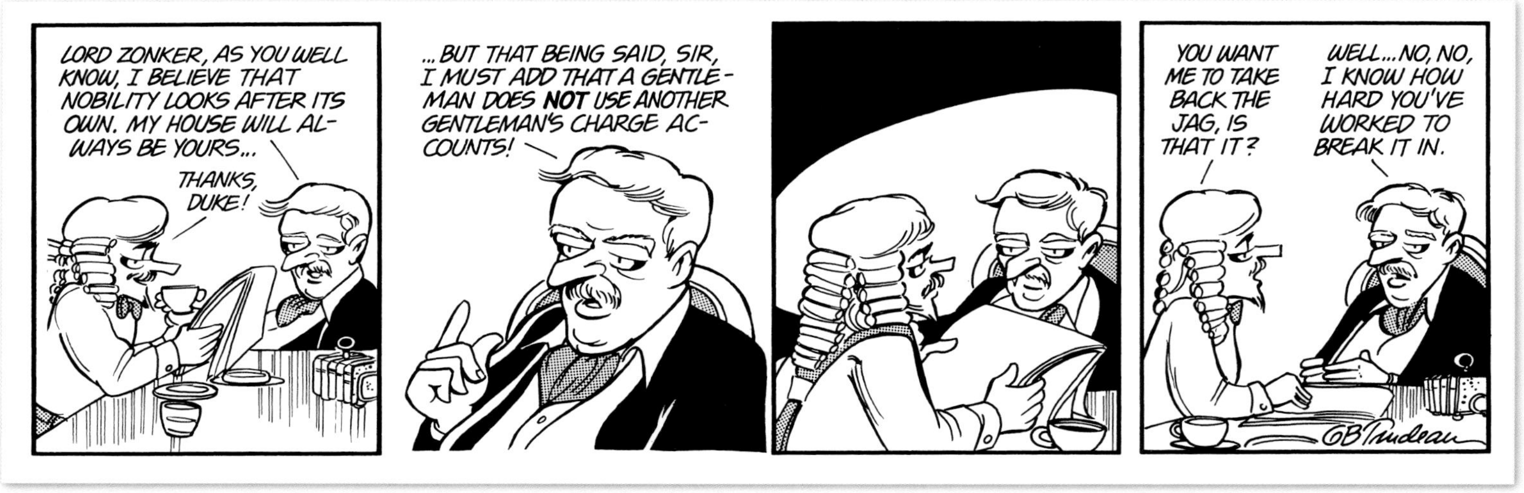
LORD ZONKER, AS YOU WELL KNOW, I BELIEVE THAT NOBILITY LOOKS AFTER ITS OWN. MY HOUSE WILL ALWAYS BE YOURS...
THANKS, DUKE!
...BUT THAT BEING SAID, SIR, I MUST ADD THAT A GENTLEMAN DOES NOT USE ANOTHER GENTLEMAN'S CHARGE ACCOUNTS!
YOU WANT ME TO TAKE BACK THE JAG, IS THAT IT?
WELL... NO, NO, I KNOW HOW HARD YOU'VE WORKED TO BREAK IT IN.
GBTrudeau
3/24/88

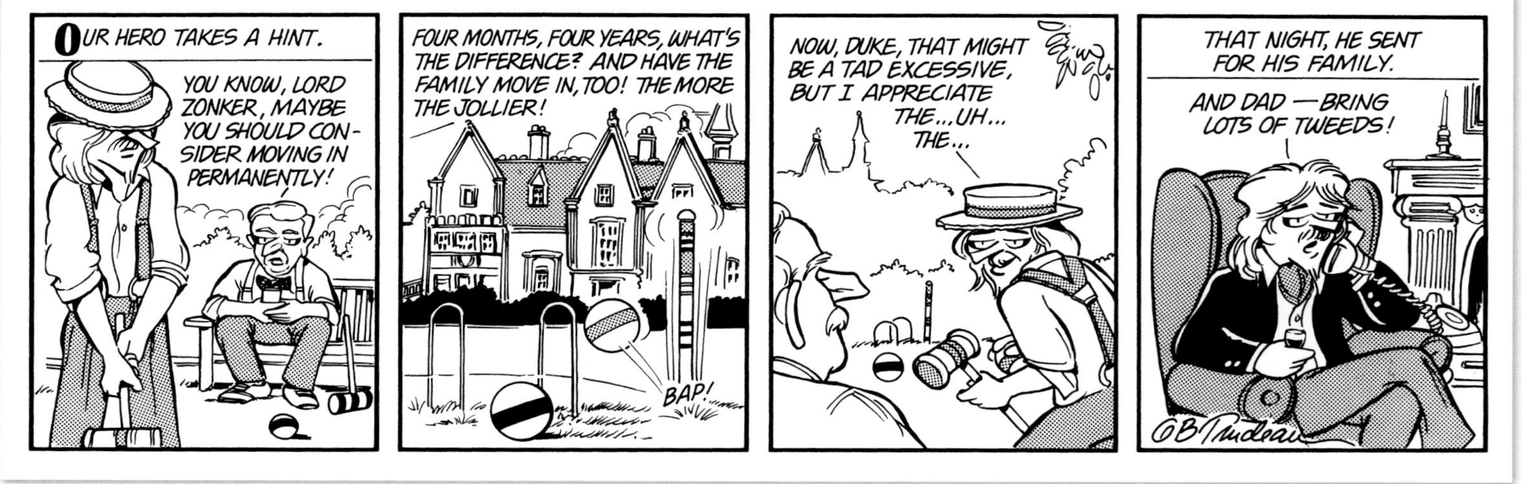
OUR HERO TAKES A HINT.
YOU KNOW, LORD ZONKER, MAYBE YOU SHOULD CONSIDER MOVING IN PERMANENTLY!
FOUR MONTHS, FOUR YEARS, WHAT'S THE DIFFERENCE? AND HAVE THE FAMILY MOVE IN, TOO! THE MORE THE JOLLIER!
BAP!
NOW, DUKE, THAT MIGHT BE A TAD EXCESSIVE, BUT I APPRECIATE THE... UH... THE...
THAT NIGHT, HE SENT FOR HIS FAMILY.
AND DAD — BRING LOTS OF TWEEDS!
GBTrudeau
3/25/88

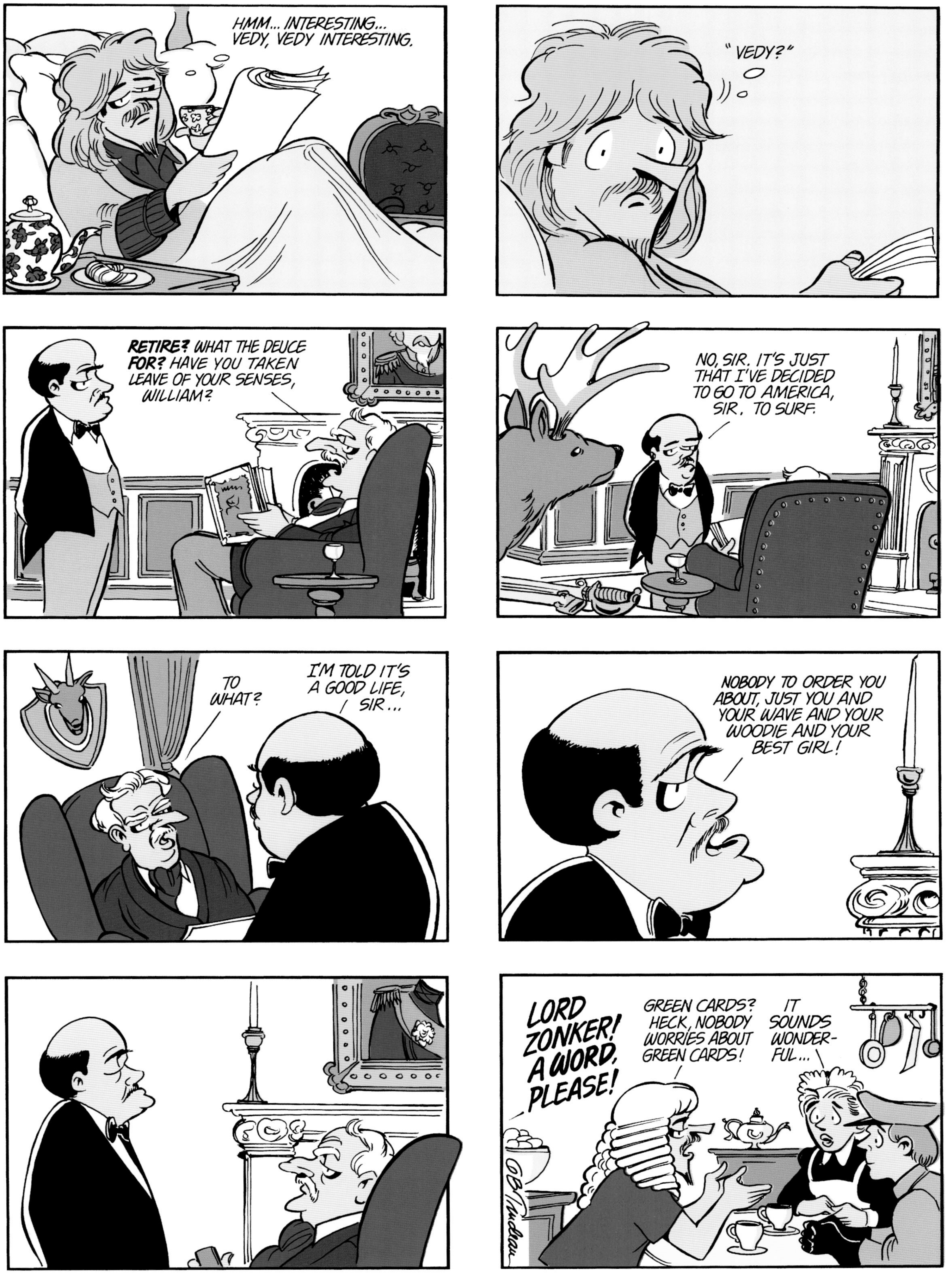

HMM... INTERESTING... VEDY, VEDY INTERESTING.
"VEDY?"
RETIRE? WHAT THE DEUCE FOR? HAVE YOU TAKEN LEAVE OF YOUR SENSES, WILLIAM?
NO, SIR. IT'S JUST THAT I'VE DECIDED TO GO TO AMERICA, SIR, TO SURF.
I'M TOLD IT'S A GOOD LIFE, SIR...
TO WHAT?
NOBODY TO ORDER YOU ABOUT, JUST YOU AND YOUR WAVE AND YOUR WOODIE AND YOUR BEST GIRL!
LORD ZONKER! A WORD, PLEASE!
GREEN CARDS? HECK, NOBODY WORRIES ABOUT GREEN CARDS!
IT SOUNDS WONDERFUL...
GBTrudeau

2/14/88

politics, that the sanctuary is too sacred a place for the grit and grime of political battle. But

8:15 Aerobic Male-bonding Night
9:30 Featured 12step Program
(TBA)

REV. SCOT SLOAN

the god of the status quo, then the church would have no prophetic role, serving the state mainly as a kind of ambulance service."
Food for thought.

Peace,

Scot

Rev. Scot Sloan
The Little Church at Walden

Saturday:
5:30-8:30 PM Potluck Organic Food Salt-free Supper

Of all the remarkable characters I encountered in college, the most unsettling was Scotty McLennan, my roommate of three years.

Scotty was a liberal arts machine. It wasn't just the sweep of his erudition that impressed; it was how effortlessly he connected it to his personal and spiritual goals, which were fixed and true. Whereas the rest of us learned in order to pass exams, Scotty put his accumulating knowledge in harness and worked one scholarly pasture after another, confident of the harvest ahead. He had come to Yale to be intellectually outfitted, and he emerged from seminar rooms grinning, his brainpan sizzling like a wok. College was exactly as anticipated, and he was acing it on schedule. So certain was he that life revealed its mysteries in predictable fashion, he once blocked out an entire semester's social calendar in advance, preassigning various women he knew to big weekends, thereby delivering to his grateful roommates a full season of hilarity.

Our scorn for his lack of spontaneity only strengthened his resolve. Gathering steam through his college years, Scott's formidable momentum carried him into both divinity school and law school (just as planned), and then out into a legal aid ministry (also as planned), followed by a college chaplaincy (yup, part of the plan). For those of us with broken compasses and low draft numbers, Scotty's direct path seemed surreal, all the more so because it was illuminated by a faith that many of us had long ago abandoned.

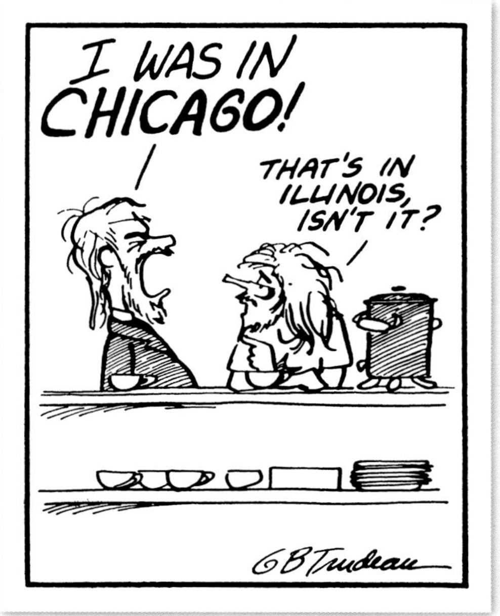
I WAS IN CHICAGO!
THAT'S IN ILLINOIS, ISN'T IT?
GBTrudeau

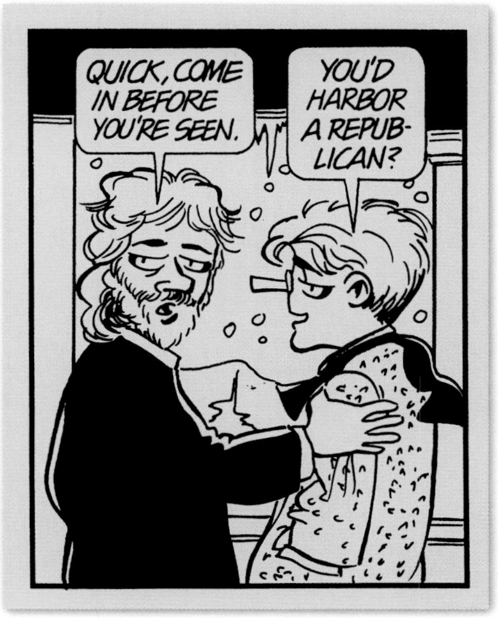
QUICK, COME IN BEFORE YOU'RE SEEN.
YOU'D HARBOR A REPUB-LICAN?

If you were twenty-three, and you were living in the just-wing-it '70s, you couldn't make up someone like this. So why would I try? I simply dragged him into the strip, ordained him on the spot (so as to fulfill one of his personal goals before he could), and set him up with the social justice ministry he had long dreamed of. I even used Scotty's likeness, although in filling out his story, I also borrowed heavily from his college mentor, the Reverend William Sloane Coffin, a campus hero and antiwar activist of near-mythic reputation.

There are, of course, significant departures from the source material. By now, you may have noticed a certain pattern emerging: real-life personalities inspiring characters who retain very few of the admirable qualities that drew me to them in the first place. My earnest cleric is no exception. Unlike the relentlessly directed real Scott, comic strip Scot is unfocused and ineffectual. And in contrast to the charismatic Coffin, whose rhetoric was passionate and robust, the cartoon version is given to listless platitudes. So the Reverend Scot Sloan, as well intentioned as he is, is hardly a salute to his origins.

Not that you'd want him to be. It's our flaws that instruct—and entertain. Whenever a writer creates a character who appears to be beyond reproach, it's almost always for the purpose of setting him up. The Bible is filled with such characters, and without their pratfalls and shortcomings, the good book wouldn't just be unteachable—it'd be unreadable. As long as Scot holds on to his core decency (a good bet), we need him to be as ungodly as the rest of us.

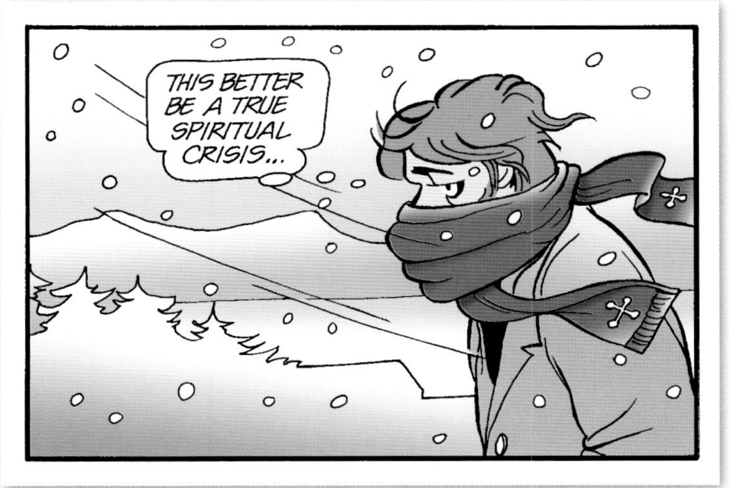
THIS BETTER BE A TRUE SPIRITUAL CRISIS...

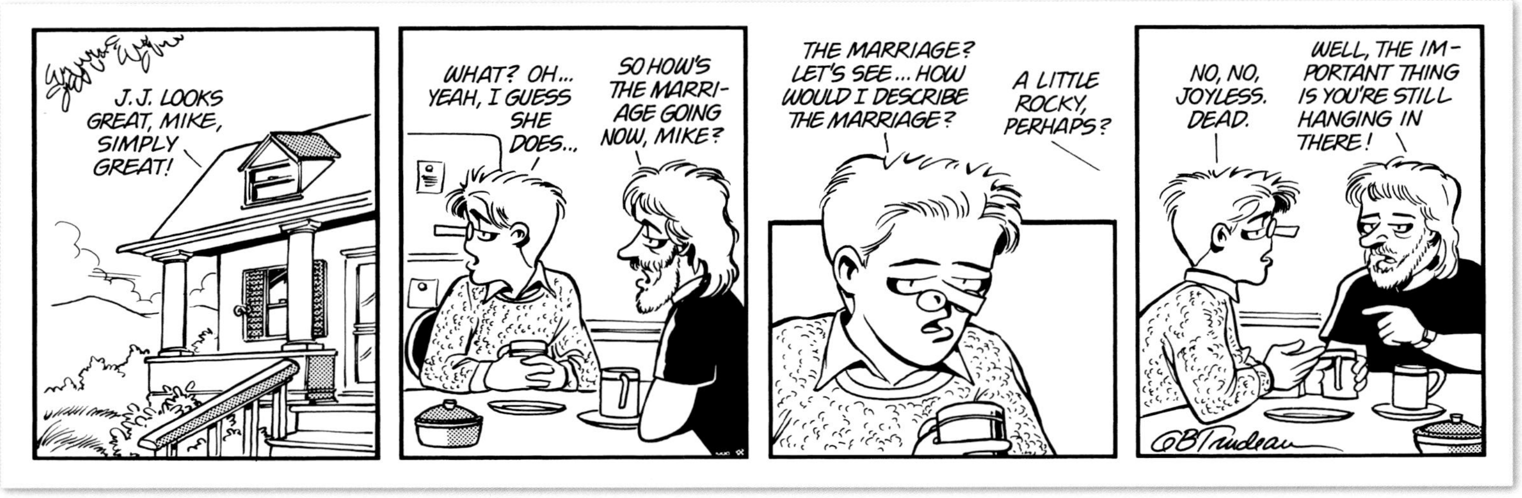
J. J. LOOKS GREAT, MIKE, SIMPLY GREAT!
WHAT? OH... YEAH, I GUESS SHE DOES...
SO HOW'S THE MARRI-AGE GOING NOW, MIKE?
THE MARRIAGE? LET'S SEE... HOW WOULD I DESCRIBE THE MARRIAGE?
A LITTLE ROCKY, PERHAPS?
NO, NO, JOYLESS. DEAD.
WELL, THE IM-PORTANT THING IS YOU'RE STILL HANGING IN THERE!
GB Trudeau

4/19/88

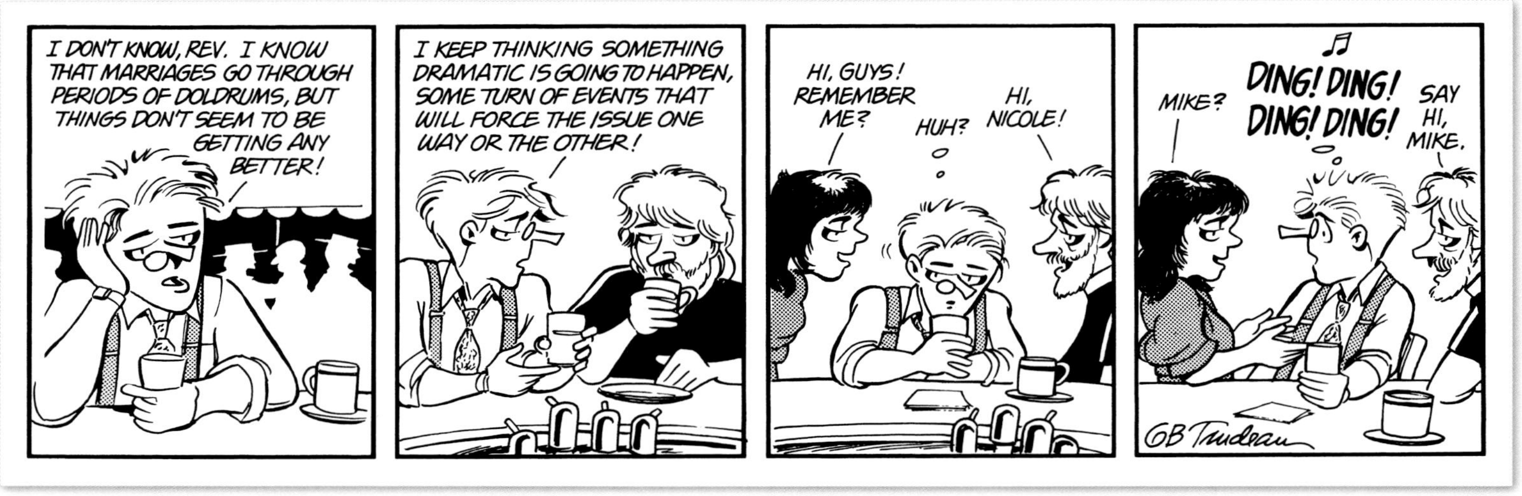
I DON'T KNOW, REV. I KNOW THAT MARRIAGES GO THROUGH PERIODS OF DOLDRUMS, BUT THINGS DON'T SEEM TO BE GETTING ANY BETTER!
I KEEP THINKING SOMETHING DRAMATIC IS GOING TO HAPPEN, SOME TURN OF EVENTS THAT WILL FORCE THE ISSUE ONE WAY OR THE OTHER!
HI, GUYS! REMEMBER ME?
HUH?
HI, NICOLE!
MIKE?
DING! DING! DING! DING!
SAY HI, MIKE.
GB Trudeau

4/25/88

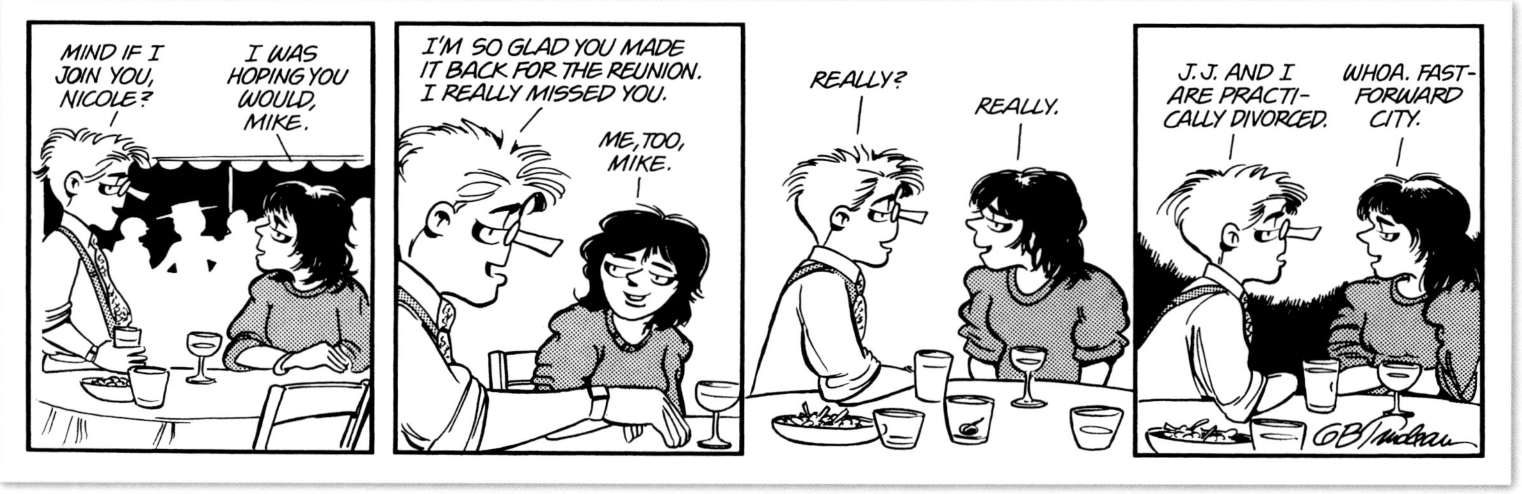
MIND IF I JOIN YOU, NICOLE?
I WAS HOPING YOU WOULD, MIKE.
I'M SO GLAD YOU MADE IT BACK FOR THE REUNION. I REALLY MISSED YOU.
ME, TOO, MIKE.
REALLY?
REALLY.
J.J. AND I ARE PRACTI-CALLY DIVORCED.
WHOA. FAST-FORWARD CITY.
GB Trudeau

4/27/88

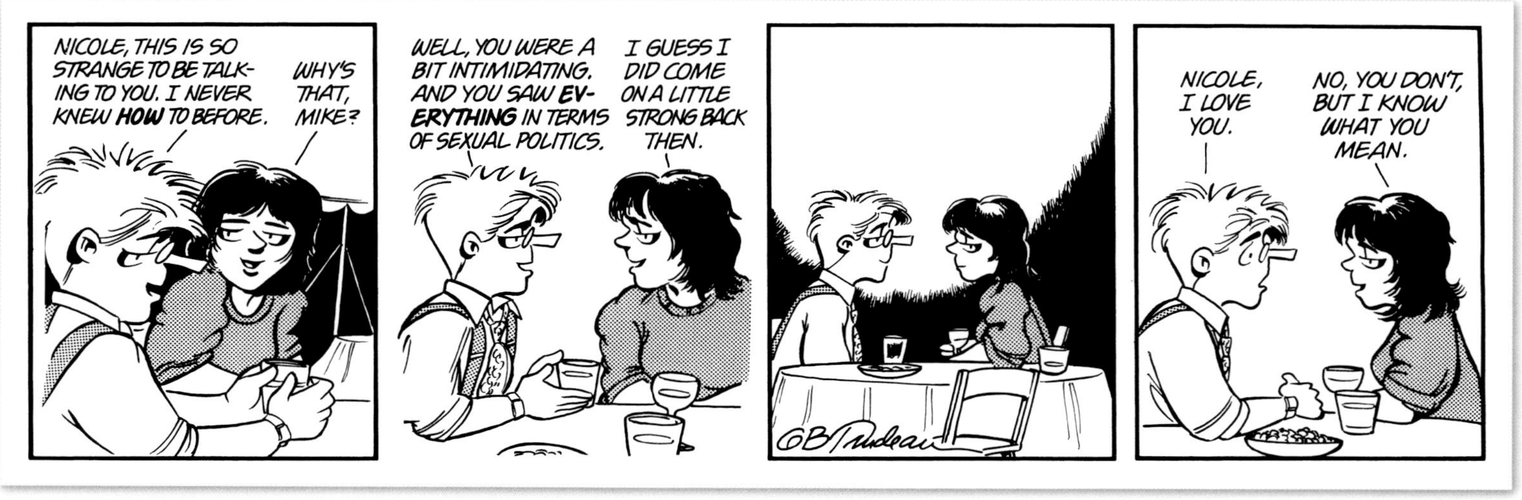
NICOLE, THIS IS SO STRANGE TO BE TALK-ING TO YOU. I NEVER KNEW **HOW** TO BEFORE.
WHY'S THAT, MIKE?
WELL, YOU WERE A BIT INTIMIDATING. AND YOU SAW **EV-ERYTHING** IN TERMS OF SEXUAL POLITICS.
I GUESS I DID COME ON A LITTLE STRONG BACK THEN.
GB Trudeau
NICOLE, I LOVE YOU.
NO, YOU DON'T, BUT I KNOW WHAT YOU MEAN.

4/28/88

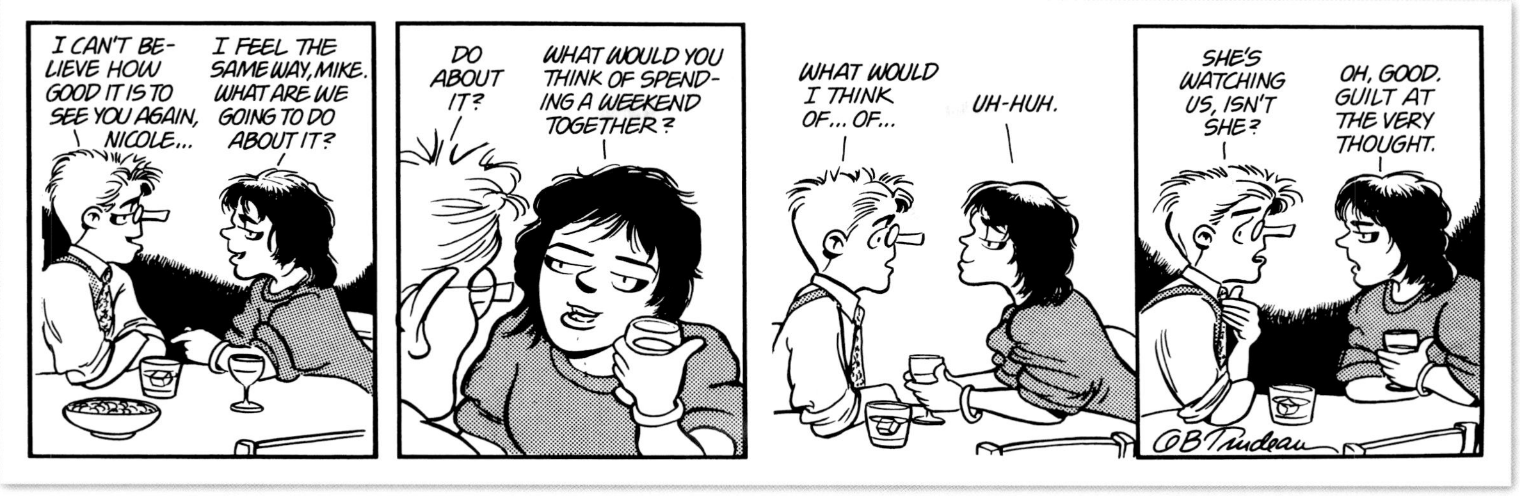
I CAN'T BELIEVE HOW GOOD IT IS TO SEE YOU AGAIN, NICOLE...
I FEEL THE SAME WAY, MIKE. WHAT ARE WE GOING TO DO ABOUT IT?
DO ABOUT IT?
WHAT WOULD YOU THINK OF SPENDING A WEEKEND TOGETHER?
WHAT WOULD I THINK OF... OF...
UH-HUH.
SHE'S WATCHING US, ISN'T SHE?
OH, GOOD. GUILT AT THE VERY THOUGHT.
©B Trudeau

4/30/88

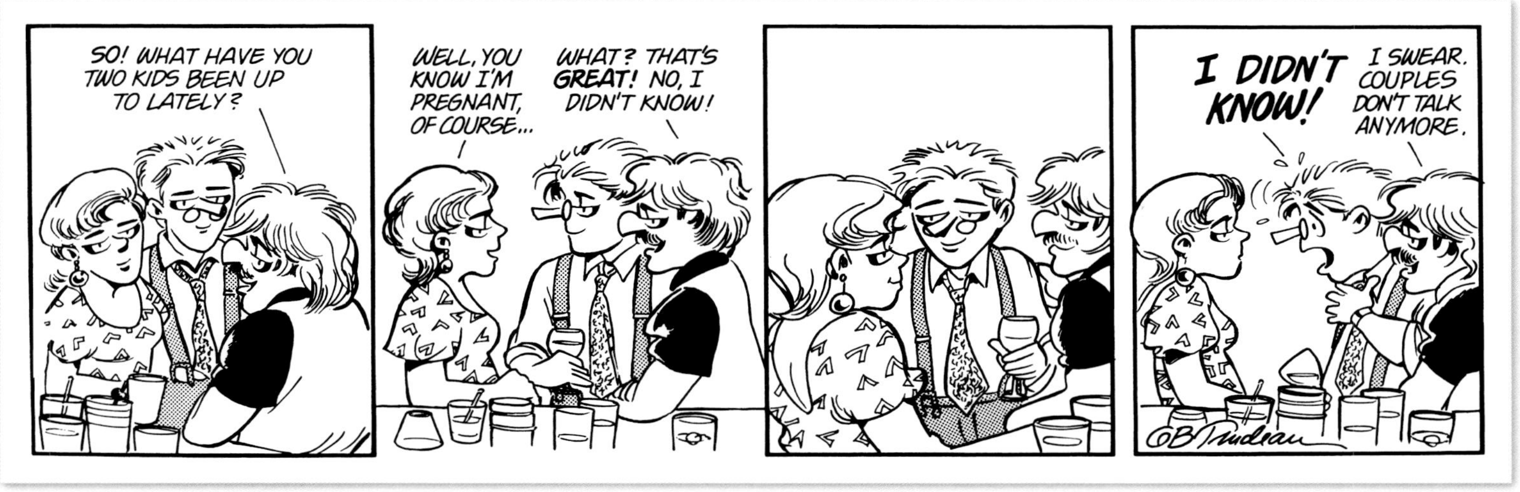
SO! WHAT HAVE YOU TWO KIDS BEEN UP TO LATELY?
WELL, YOU KNOW I'M PREGNANT, OF COURSE...
WHAT? THAT'S GREAT! NO, I DIDN'T KNOW!
I DIDN'T KNOW!
I SWEAR. COUPLES DON'T TALK ANYMORE.
©B Trudeau

5/4/88

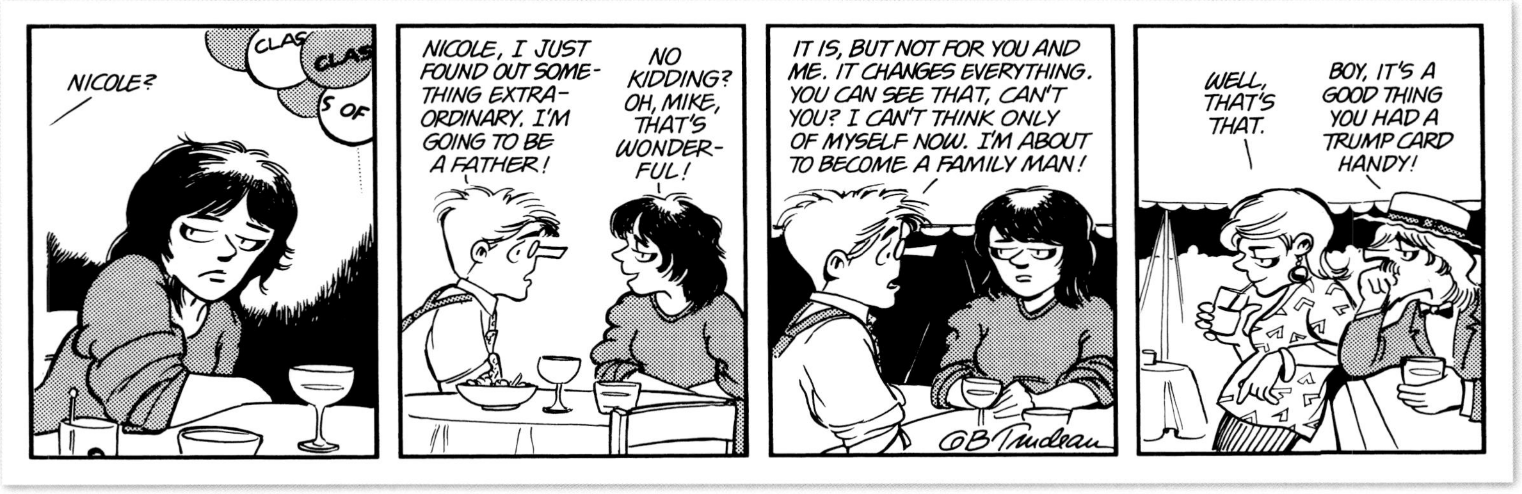
NICOLE?
NICOLE, I JUST FOUND OUT SOMETHING EXTRAORDINARY. I'M GOING TO BE A FATHER!
NO KIDDING? OH, MIKE, THAT'S WONDERFUL!
IT IS, BUT NOT FOR YOU AND ME. IT CHANGES EVERYTHING. YOU CAN SEE THAT, CAN'T YOU? I CAN'T THINK ONLY OF MYSELF NOW. I'M ABOUT TO BECOME A FAMILY MAN!
WELL, THAT'S THAT.
BOY, IT'S A GOOD THING YOU HAD A TRUMP CARD HANDY!
©B Trudeau

5/6/88

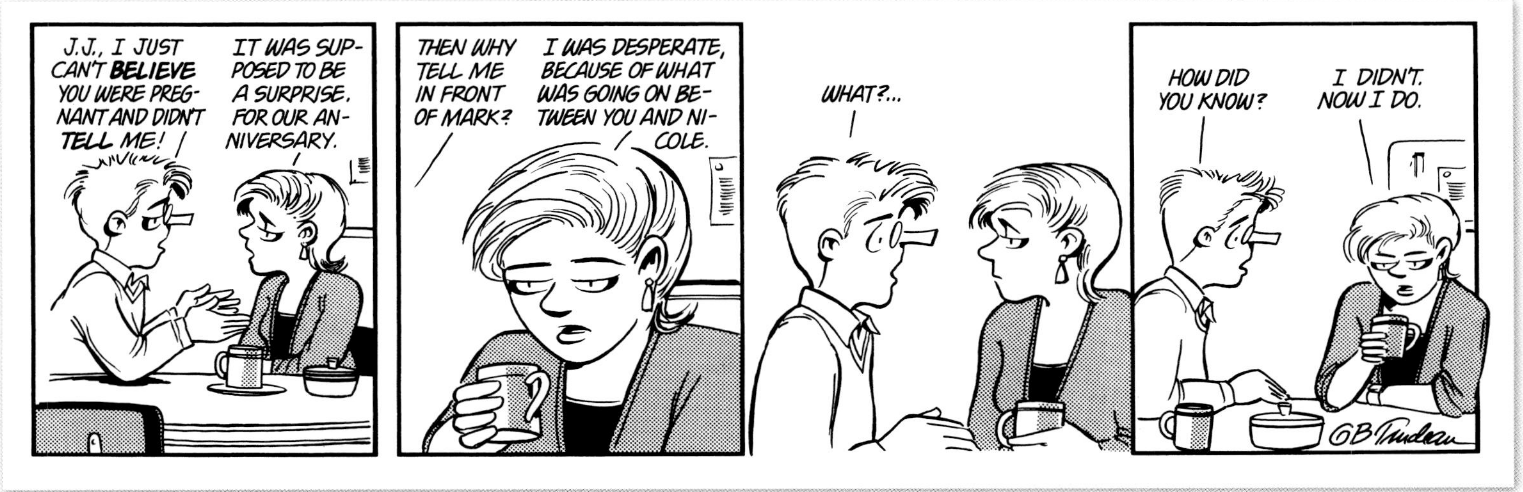
J.J., I JUST CAN'T BELIEVE YOU WERE PREGNANT AND DIDN'T TELL ME!
IT WAS SUPPOSED TO BE A SURPRISE. FOR OUR ANNIVERSARY.
THEN WHY TELL ME IN FRONT OF MARK?
I WAS DESPERATE, BECAUSE OF WHAT WAS GOING ON BETWEEN YOU AND NICOLE.
WHAT?...
HOW DID YOU KNOW?
I DIDN'T. NOW I DO.
©B Trudeau

5/10/88

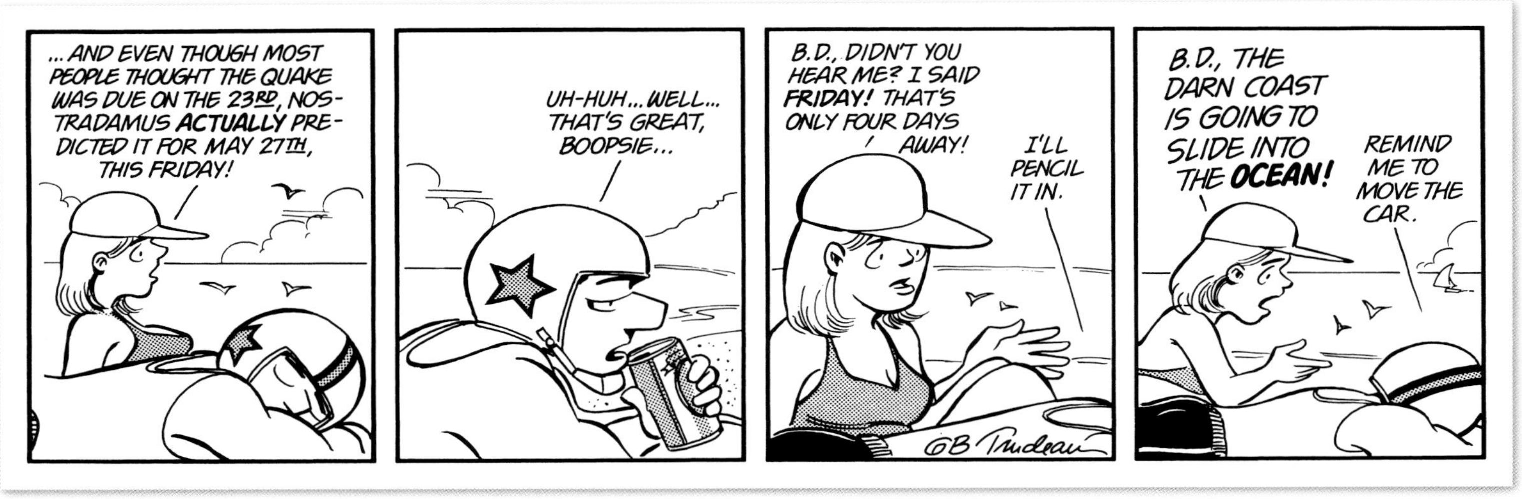
...AND EVEN THOUGH MOST PEOPLE THOUGHT THE QUAKE WAS DUE ON THE 23RD, NOSTRADAMUS ACTUALLY PREDICTED IT FOR MAY 27TH, THIS FRIDAY!
UH-HUH... WELL... THAT'S GREAT, BOOPSIE...
B.D., DIDN'T YOU HEAR ME? I SAID FRIDAY! THAT'S ONLY FOUR DAYS AWAY!
I'LL PENCIL IT IN.
B.D., THE DARN COAST IS GOING TO SLIDE INTO THE OCEAN!
REMIND ME TO MOVE THE CAR.

5/23/88

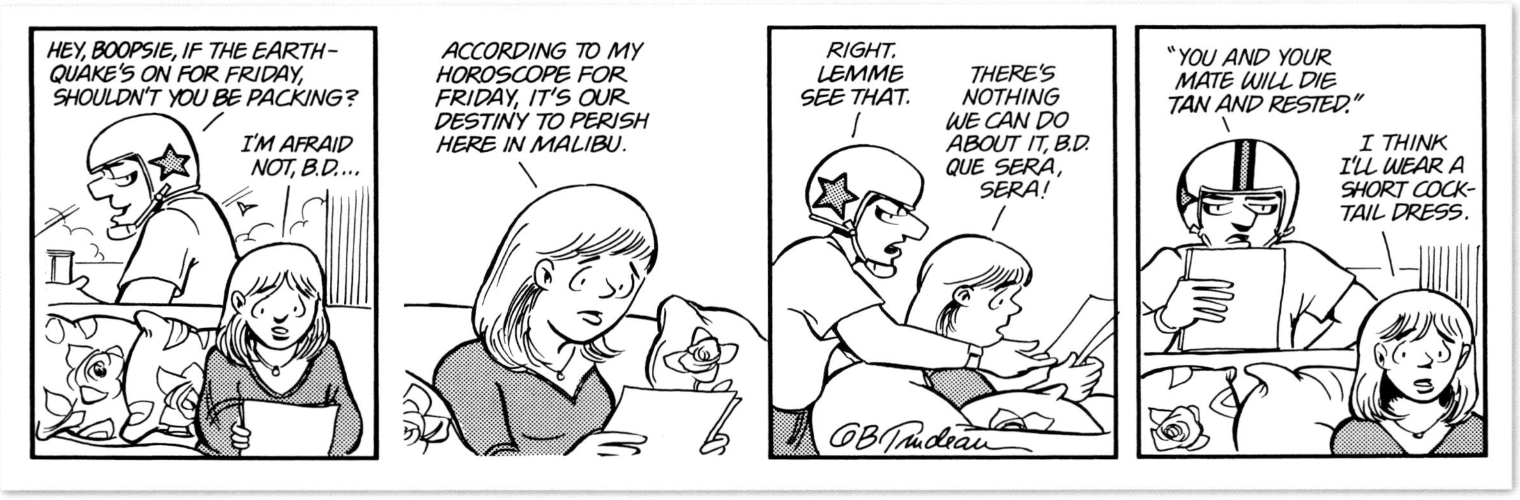
HEY, BOOPSIE, IF THE EARTHQUAKE'S ON FOR FRIDAY, SHOULDN'T YOU BE PACKING?
I'M AFRAID NOT, B.D....
ACCORDING TO MY HOROSCOPE FOR FRIDAY, IT'S OUR DESTINY TO PERISH HERE IN MALIBU.
RIGHT. LEMME SEE THAT.
THERE'S NOTHING WE CAN DO ABOUT IT, B.D. QUE SERA, SERA!
"YOU AND YOUR MATE WILL DIE TAN AND RESTED."
I THINK I'LL WEAR A SHORT COCKTAIL DRESS.

5/25/88

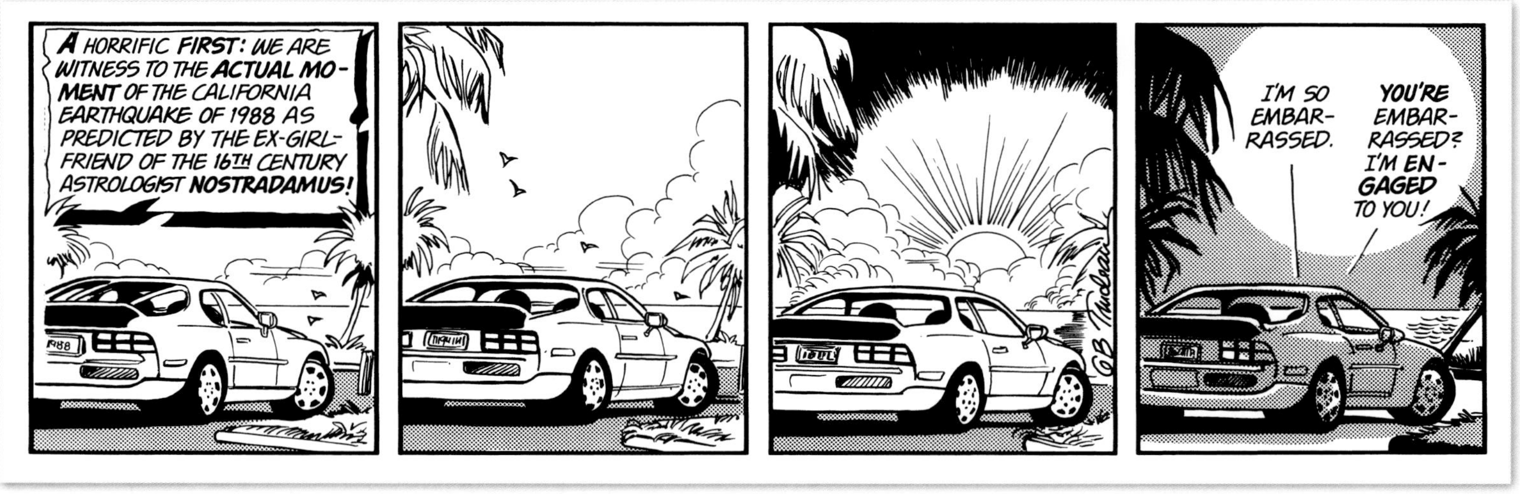
A HORRIFIC FIRST: WE ARE WITNESS TO THE ACTUAL MOMENT OF THE CALIFORNIA EARTHQUAKE OF 1988 AS PREDICTED BY THE EX-GIRLFRIEND OF THE 16TH CENTURY ASTROLOGIST NOSTRADAMUS!
I'M SO EMBARRASSED.
YOU'RE EMBARRASSED? I'M ENGAGED TO YOU!

5/27/88

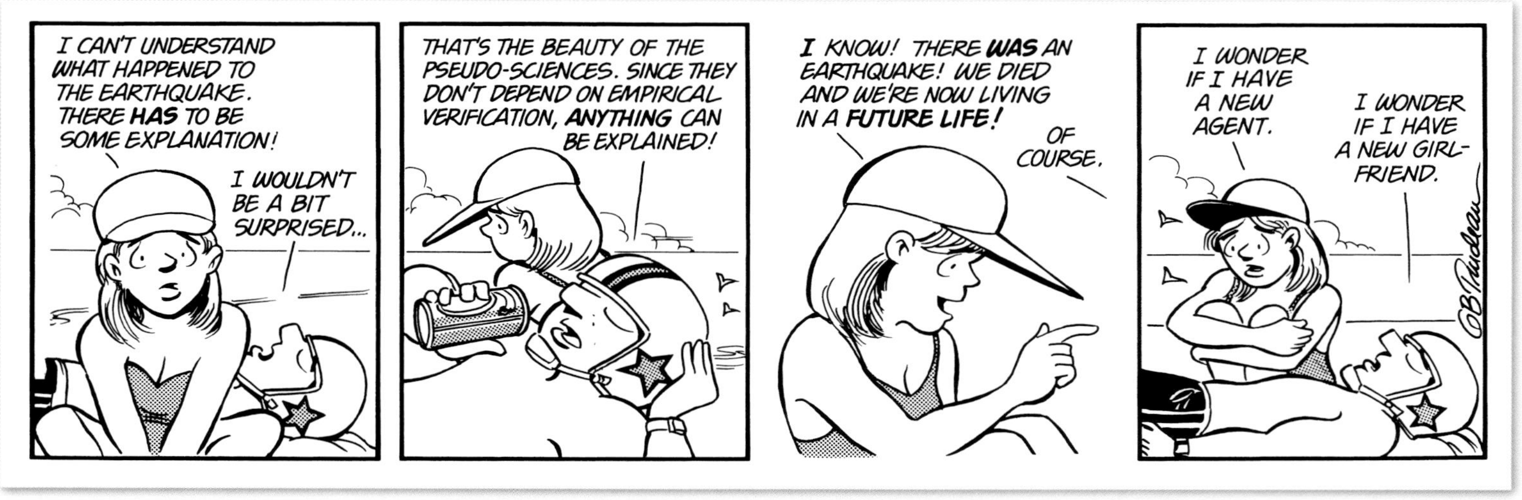
I CAN'T UNDERSTAND WHAT HAPPENED TO THE EARTHQUAKE. THERE HAS TO BE SOME EXPLANATION!
I WOULDN'T BE A BIT SURPRISED...
THAT'S THE BEAUTY OF THE PSEUDO-SCIENCES. SINCE THEY DON'T DEPEND ON EMPIRICAL VERIFICATION, ANYTHING CAN BE EXPLAINED!
I KNOW! THERE WAS AN EARTHQUAKE! WE DIED AND WE'RE NOW LIVING IN A FUTURE LIFE!
OF COURSE.
I WONDER IF I HAVE A NEW AGENT.
I WONDER IF I HAVE A NEW GIRLFRIEND.

5/28/88

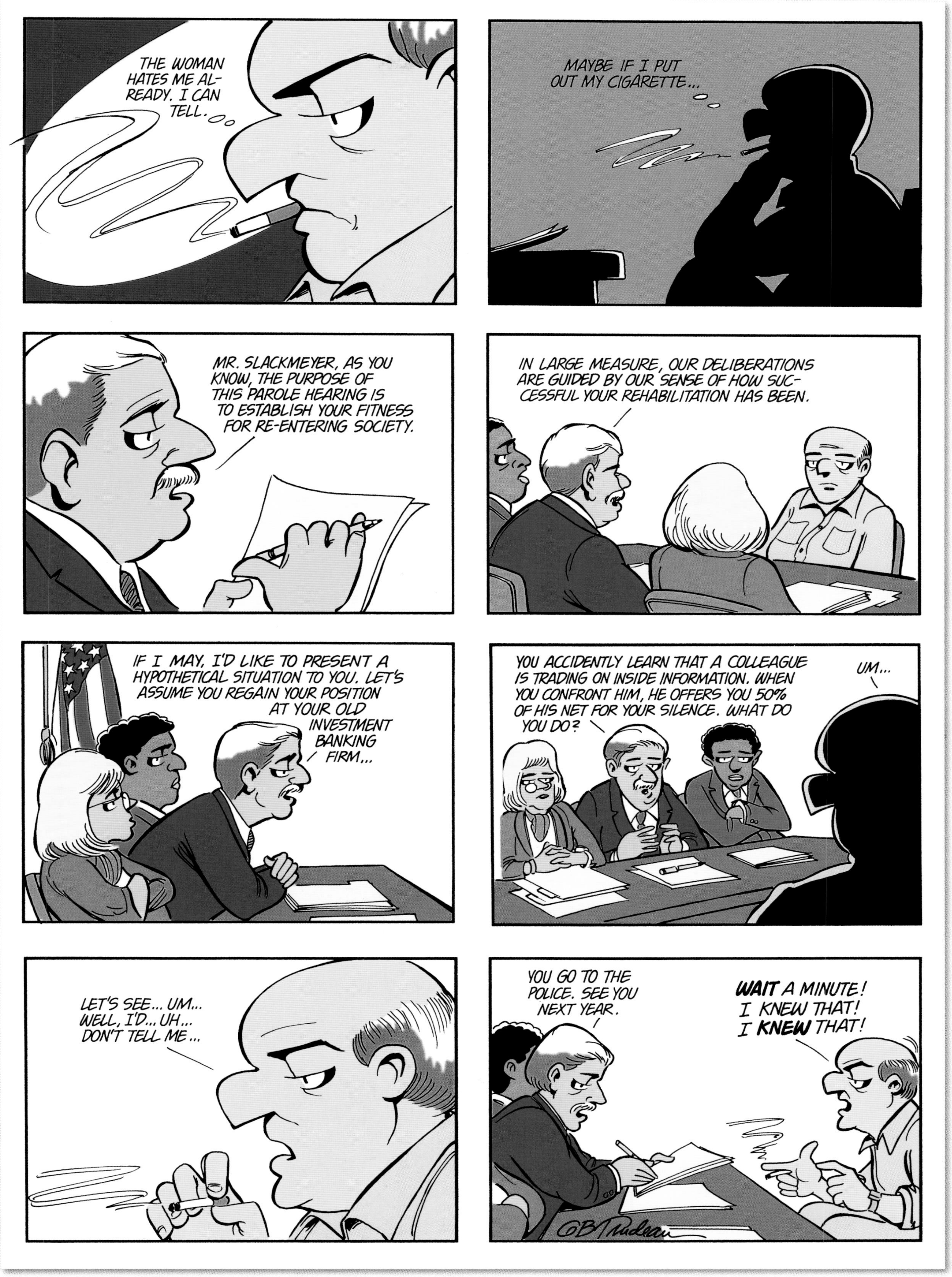
THE WOMAN HATES ME AL-READY. I CAN TELL.
MAYBE IF I PUT OUT MY CIGARETTE...
MR. SLACKMEYER, AS YOU KNOW, THE PURPOSE OF THIS PAROLE HEARING IS TO ESTABLISH YOUR FITNESS FOR RE-ENTERING SOCIETY.
IN LARGE MEASURE, OUR DELIBERATIONS ARE GUIDED BY OUR SENSE OF HOW SUC-CESSFUL YOUR REHABILITATION HAS BEEN.
IF I MAY, I'D LIKE TO PRESENT A HYPOTHETICAL SITUATION TO YOU. LET'S ASSUME YOU REGAIN YOUR POSITION AT YOUR OLD INVESTMENT BANKING FIRM...
YOU ACCIDENTLY LEARN THAT A COLLEAGUE IS TRADING ON INSIDE INFORMATION. WHEN YOU CONFRONT HIM, HE OFFERS YOU 50% OF HIS NET FOR YOUR SILENCE. WHAT DO YOU DO?
UM...
LET'S SEE... UM... WELL, I'D... UH... DON'T TELL ME...
YOU GO TO THE POLICE. SEE YOU NEXT YEAR.
WAIT A MINUTE! I KNEW THAT! I **KNEW** THAT!
©B Trudeau

4/17/88

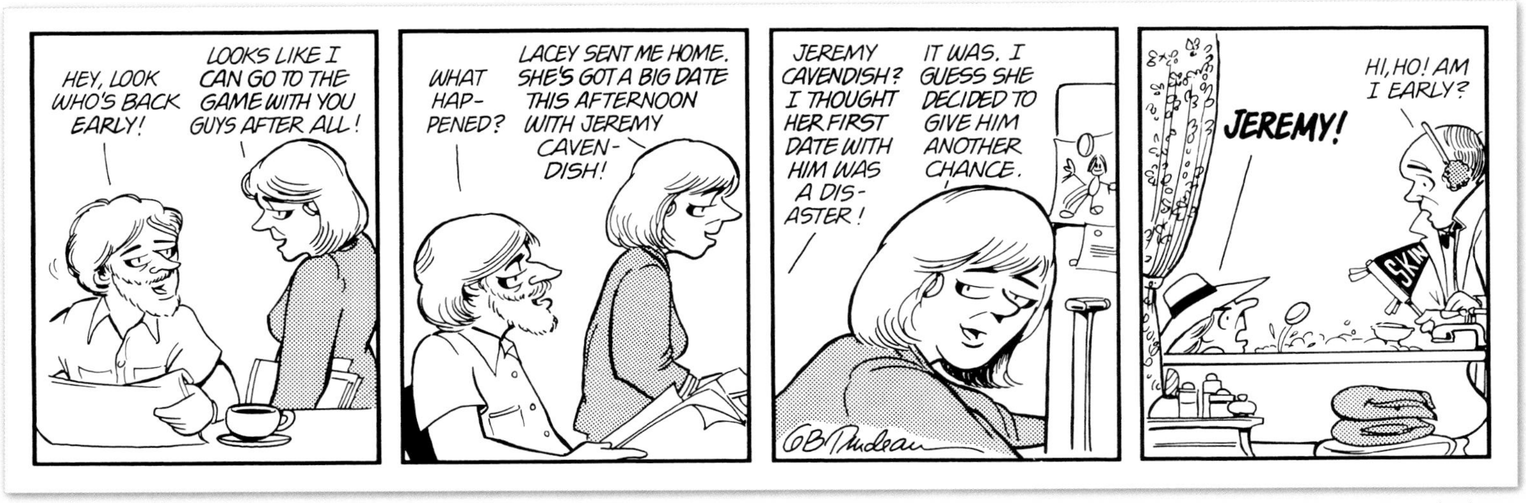
HEY, LOOK WHO'S BACK EARLY!
LOOKS LIKE I CAN GO TO THE GAME WITH YOU GUYS AFTER ALL!
WHAT HAPPENED?
LACEY SENT ME HOME. SHE'S GOT A BIG DATE THIS AFTERNOON WITH JEREMY CAVENDISH!
JEREMY CAVENDISH? I THOUGHT HER FIRST DATE WITH HIM WAS A DISASTER!
IT WAS. I GUESS SHE DECIDED TO GIVE HIM ANOTHER CHANCE.
JEREMY!
HI, HO! AM I EARLY?

12/12/88

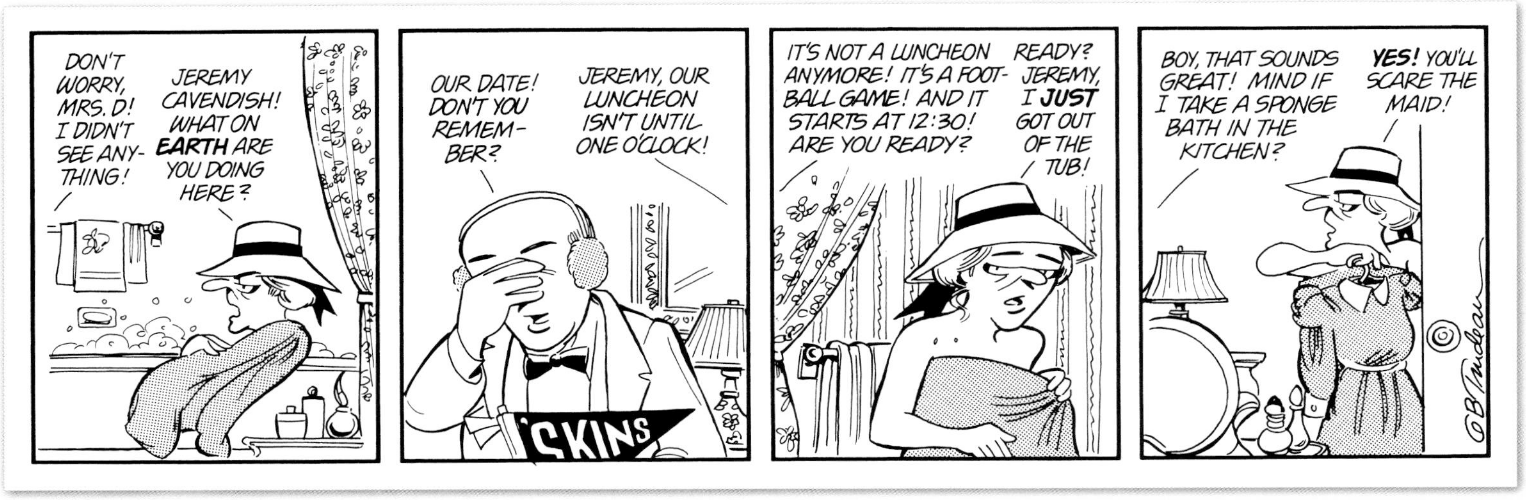
DON'T WORRY, MRS. D! I DIDN'T SEE ANYTHING!
JEREMY CAVENDISH! WHAT ON EARTH ARE YOU DOING HERE?
OUR DATE! DON'T YOU REMEMBER?
JEREMY, OUR LUNCHEON ISN'T UNTIL ONE O'CLOCK!
SKINS
IT'S NOT A LUNCHEON ANYMORE! IT'S A FOOTBALL GAME! AND IT STARTS AT 12:30! ARE YOU READY?
READY? JEREMY, I JUST GOT OUT OF THE TUB!
BOY, THAT SOUNDS GREAT! MIND IF I TAKE A SPONGE BATH IN THE KITCHEN?
YES! YOU'LL SCARE THE MAID!

12/13/88

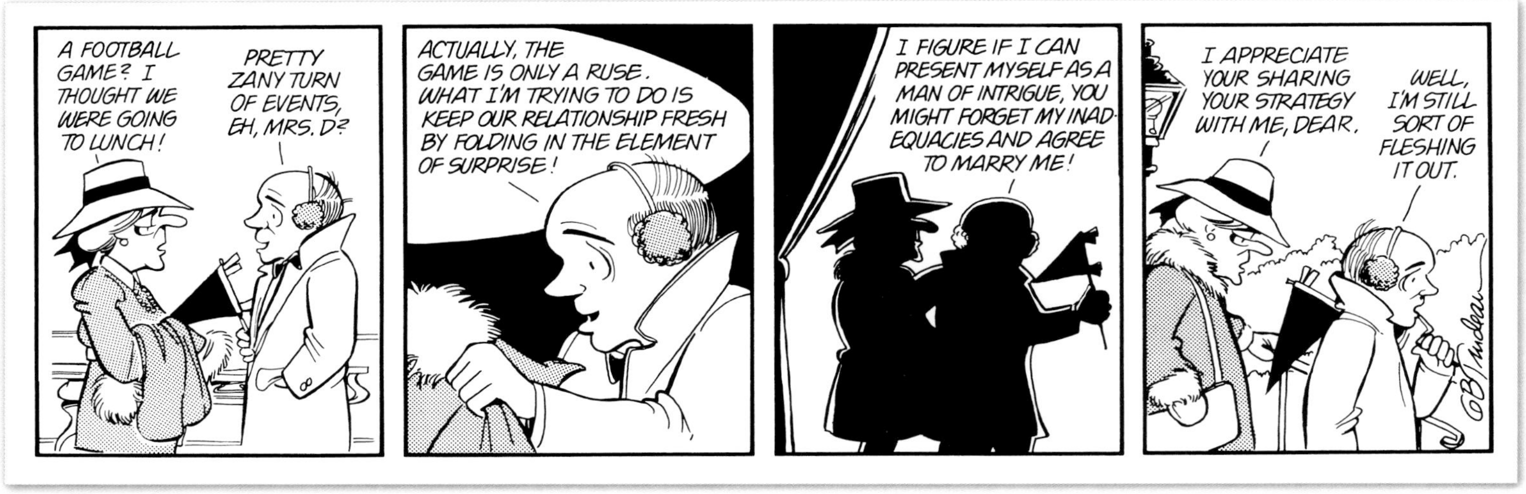
A FOOTBALL GAME? I THOUGHT WE WERE GOING TO LUNCH!
PRETTY ZANY TURN OF EVENTS, EH, MRS. D?
ACTUALLY, THE GAME IS ONLY A RUSE. WHAT I'M TRYING TO DO IS KEEP OUR RELATIONSHIP FRESH BY FOLDING IN THE ELEMENT OF SURPRISE!
I FIGURE IF I CAN PRESENT MYSELF AS A MAN OF INTRIGUE, YOU MIGHT FORGET MY INADEQUACIES AND AGREE TO MARRY ME!
I APPRECIATE YOUR SHARING YOUR STRATEGY WITH ME, DEAR.
WELL, I'M STILL SORT OF FLESHING IT OUT.

12/14/88

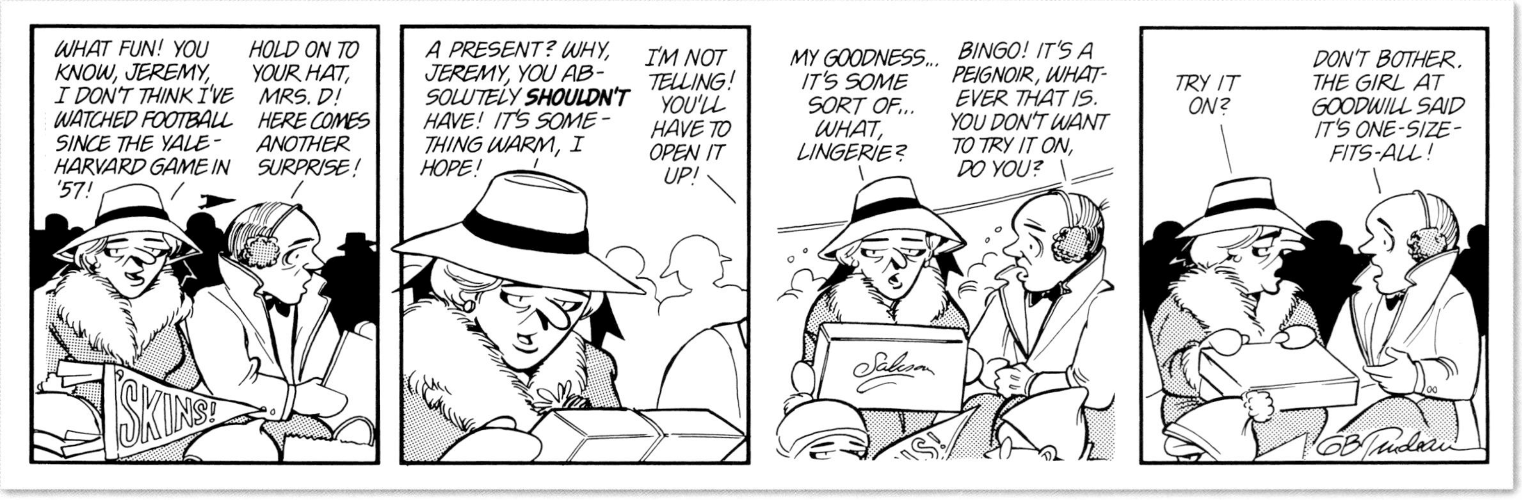
WHAT FUN! YOU KNOW, JEREMY, I DON'T THINK I'VE WATCHED FOOTBALL SINCE THE YALE-HARVARD GAME IN '57!
HOLD ON TO YOUR HAT, MRS. D! HERE COMES ANOTHER SURPRISE!
SKINS!
A PRESENT? WHY, JEREMY, YOU ABSOLUTELY SHOULDN'T HAVE! IT'S SOMETHING WARM, I HOPE!
I'M NOT TELLING! YOU'LL HAVE TO OPEN IT UP!
MY GOODNESS... IT'S SOME SORT OF... WHAT, LINGERIE?
BINGO! IT'S A PEIGNOIR, WHATEVER THAT IS. YOU DON'T WANT TO TRY IT ON, DO YOU?
TRY IT ON?
DON'T BOTHER. THE GIRL AT GOODWILL SAID IT'S ONE-SIZE-FITS-ALL!

12/16/88

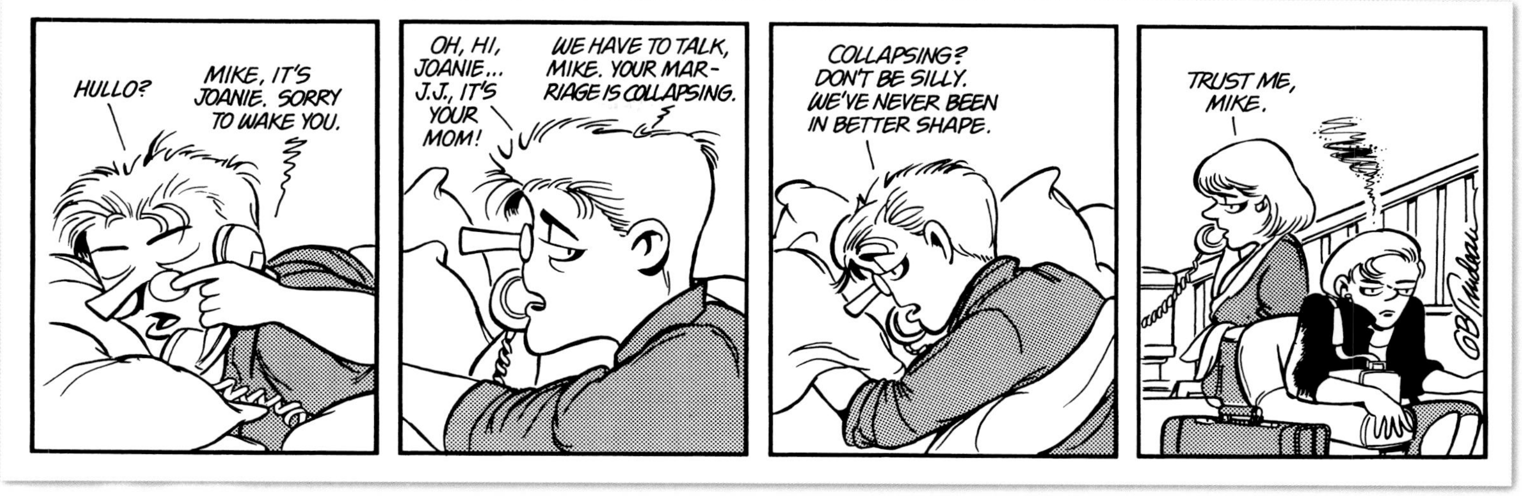
HULLO?
MIKE, IT'S JOANIE. SORRY TO WAKE YOU.
OH, HI, JOANIE... J.J., IT'S YOUR MOM!
WE HAVE TO TALK, MIKE. YOUR MARRIAGE IS COLLAPSING.
COLLAPSING? DON'T BE SILLY. WE'VE NEVER BEEN IN BETTER SHAPE.
TRUST ME, MIKE.
GBTrudeau

5/30/88

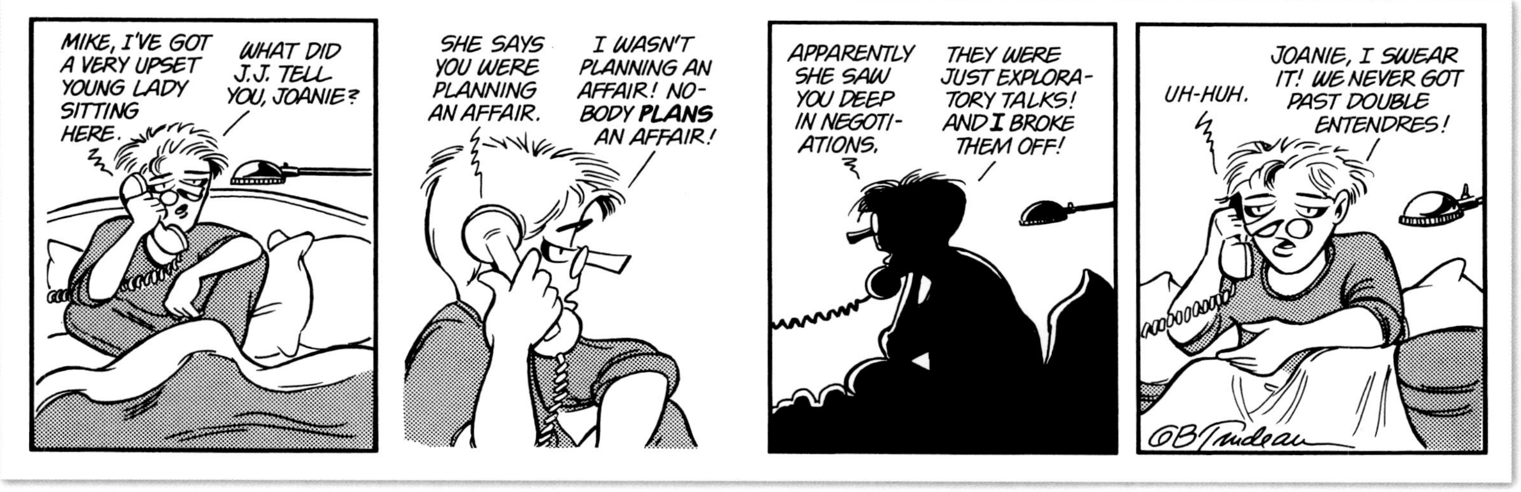
MIKE, I'VE GOT A VERY UPSET YOUNG LADY SITTING HERE.
WHAT DID J.J. TELL YOU, JOANIE?
SHE SAYS YOU WERE PLANNING AN AFFAIR.
I WASN'T PLANNING AN AFFAIR! NOBODY **PLANS** AN AFFAIR!
APPARENTLY SHE SAW YOU DEEP IN NEGOTIATIONS.
THEY WERE JUST EXPLORATORY TALKS! AND **I** BROKE THEM OFF!
UH-HUH.
JOANIE, I SWEAR IT! WE NEVER GOT PAST DOUBLE ENTENDRES!
GBTrudeau

5/31/88

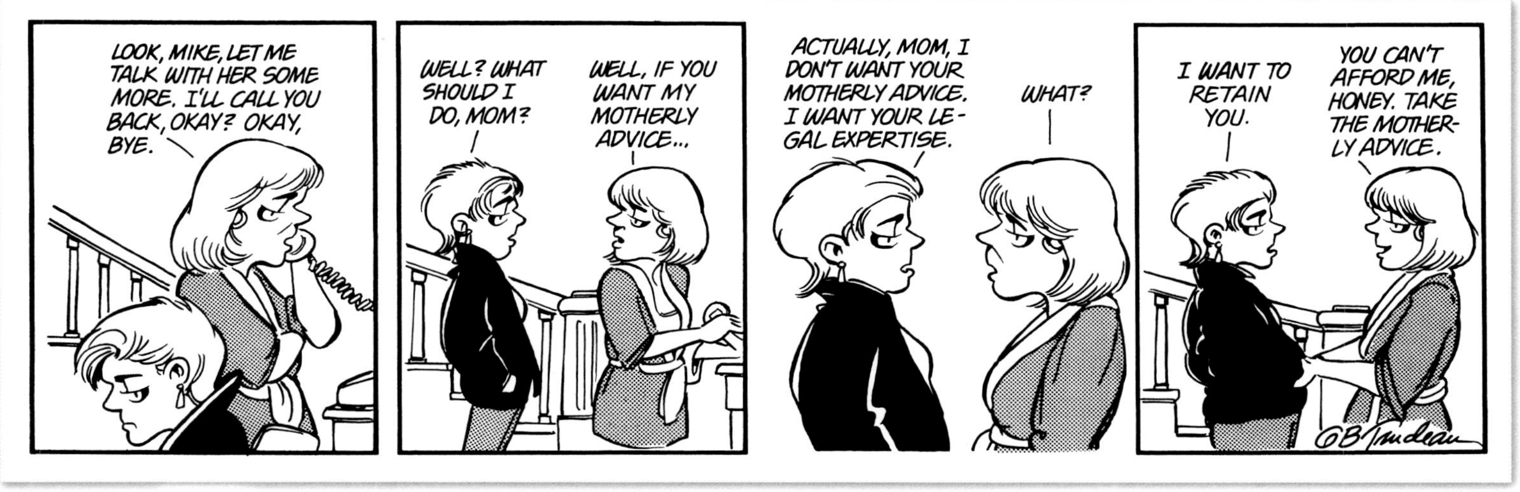
LOOK, MIKE, LET ME TALK WITH HER SOME MORE. I'LL CALL YOU BACK, OKAY? OKAY, BYE.
WELL? WHAT SHOULD I DO, MOM?
WELL, IF YOU WANT MY MOTHERLY ADVICE...
ACTUALLY, MOM, I DON'T WANT YOUR MOTHERLY ADVICE. I WANT YOUR LEGAL EXPERTISE.
WHAT?
I WANT TO RETAIN YOU.
YOU CAN'T AFFORD ME, HONEY. TAKE THE MOTHERLY ADVICE.
GBTrudeau

6/1/88

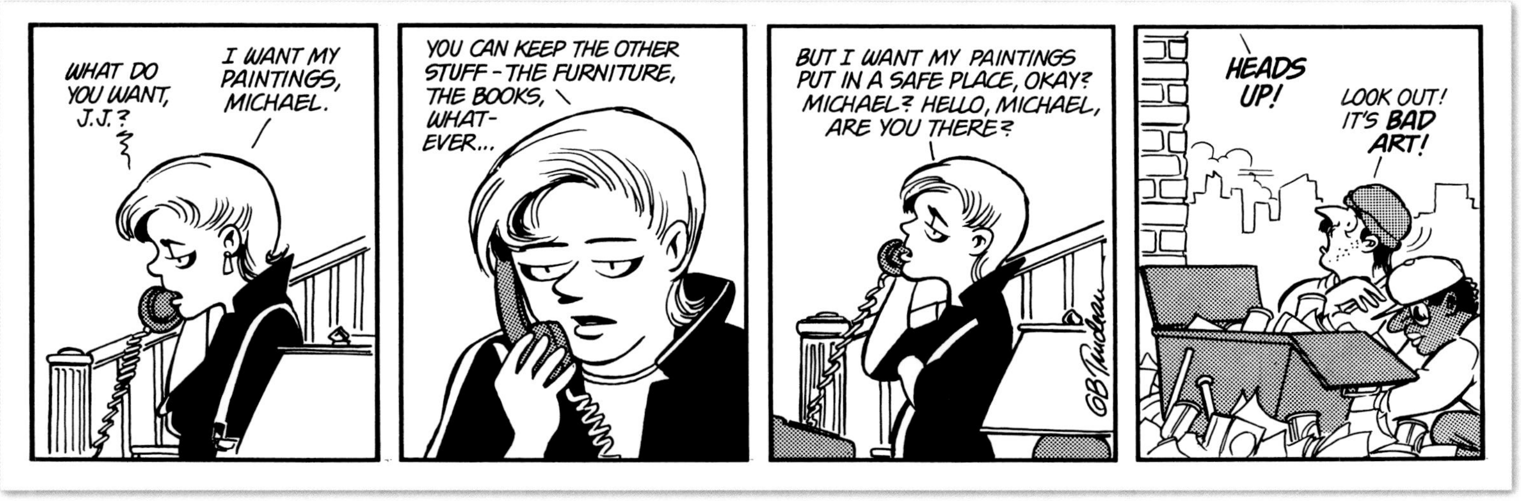
WHAT DO YOU WANT, J.J.?
I WANT MY PAINTINGS, MICHAEL.
YOU CAN KEEP THE OTHER STUFF – THE FURNITURE, THE BOOKS, WHATEVER...
BUT I WANT MY PAINTINGS PUT IN A SAFE PLACE, OKAY? MICHAEL? HELLO, MICHAEL, ARE YOU THERE?
GBTrudeau
HEADS UP!
LOOK OUT! IT'S **BAD ART!**

6/4/88

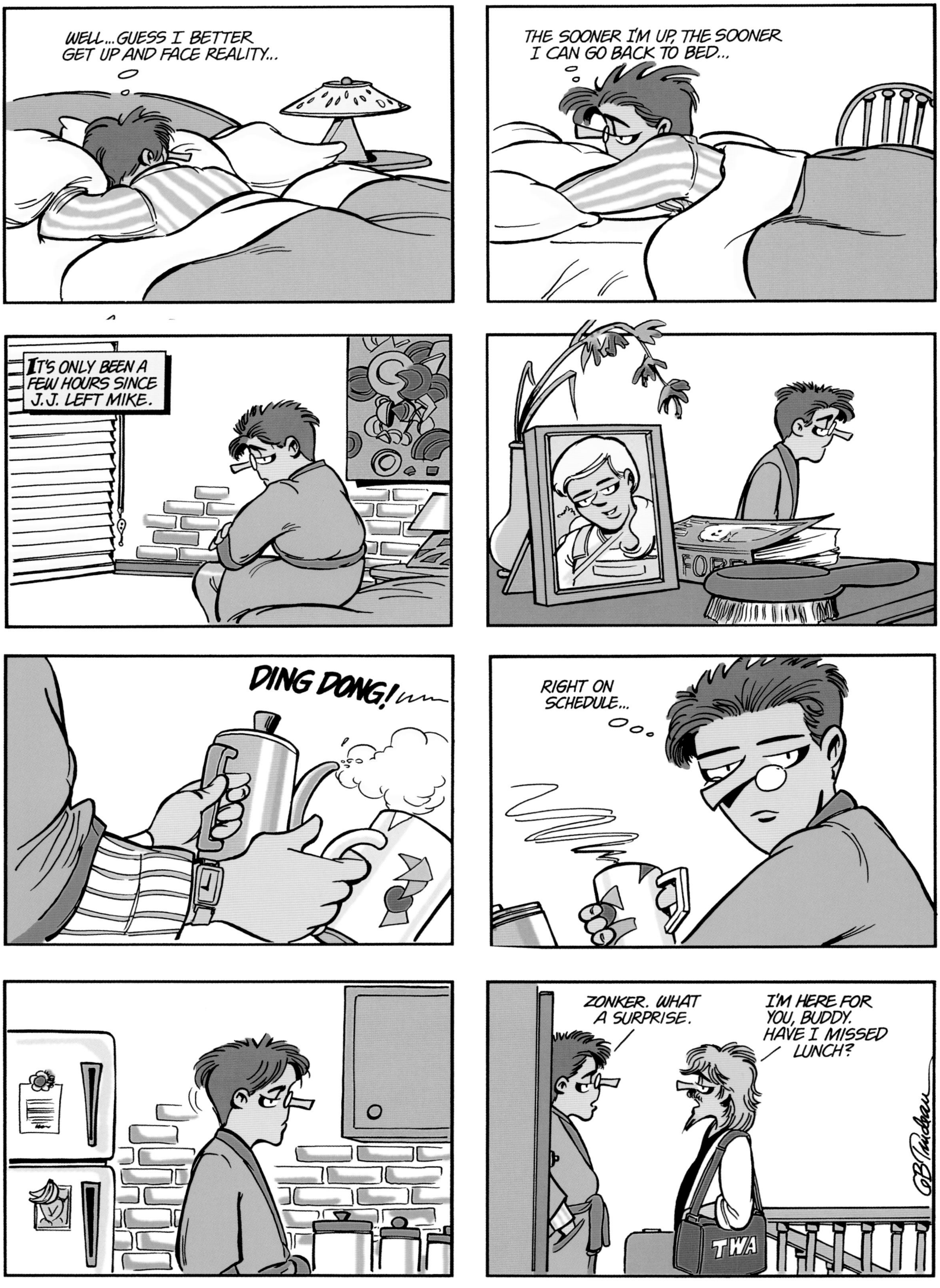
WELL...GUESS I BETTER GET UP AND FACE REALITY...
THE SOONER I'M UP, THE SOONER I CAN GO BACK TO BED...
IT'S ONLY BEEN A FEW HOURS SINCE J.J. LEFT MIKE.
DING DONG!
RIGHT ON SCHEDULE...
ZONKER. WHAT A SURPRISE.
I'M HERE FOR YOU, BUDDY. HAVE I MISSED LUNCH?
TWA

6/5/88

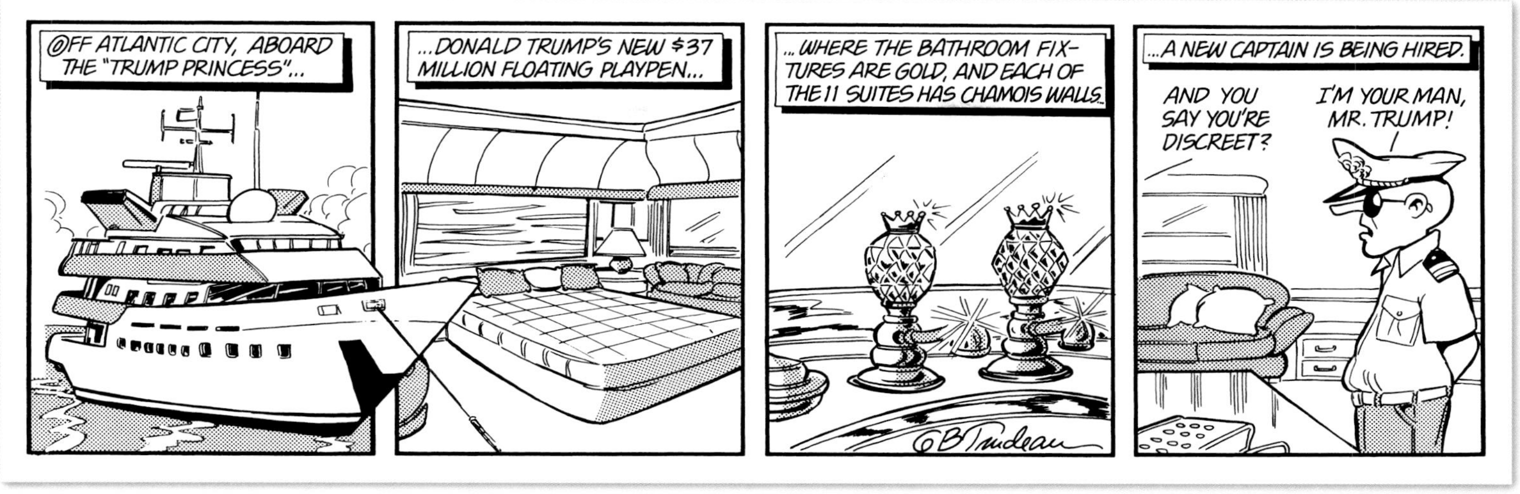
OFF ATLANTIC CITY, ABOARD THE "TRUMP PRINCESS"...
...DONALD TRUMP'S NEW $37 MILLION FLOATING PLAYPEN...
...WHERE THE BATHROOM FIXTURES ARE GOLD, AND EACH OF THE 11 SUITES HAS CHAMOIS WALLS.
...A NEW CAPTAIN IS BEING HIRED.
AND YOU SAY YOU'RE DISCREET?
I'M YOUR MAN, MR. TRUMP!

7/25/88

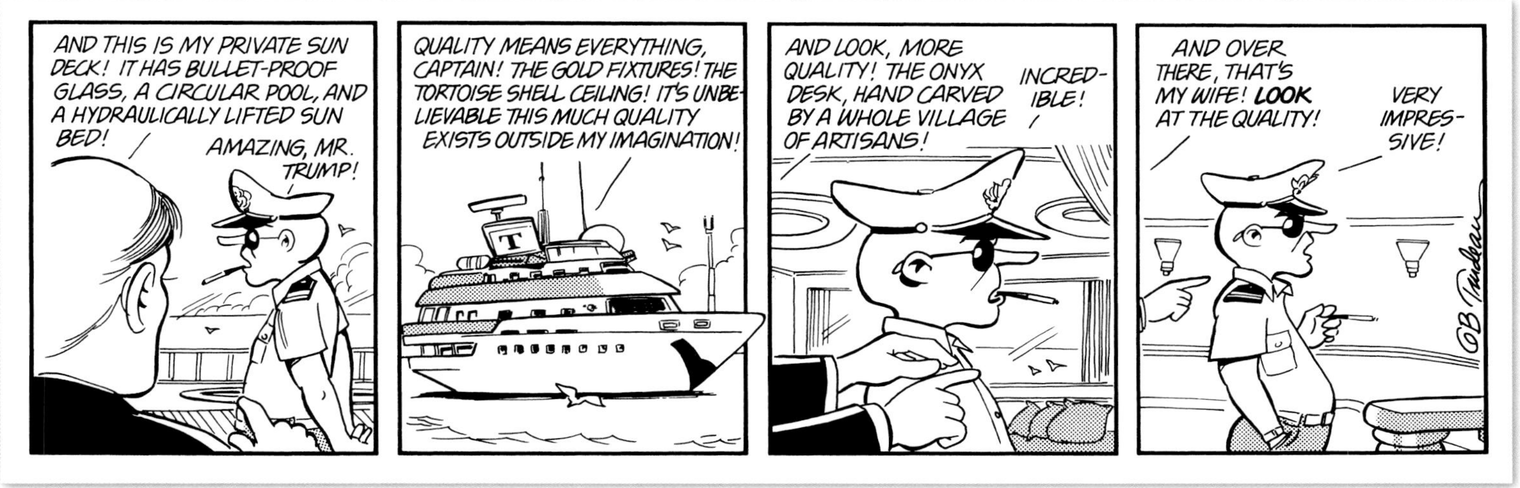
AND THIS IS MY PRIVATE SUN DECK! IT HAS BULLET-PROOF GLASS, A CIRCULAR POOL, AND A HYDRAULICALLY LIFTED SUN BED!
AMAZING, MR. TRUMP!
QUALITY MEANS EVERYTHING, CAPTAIN! THE GOLD FIXTURES! THE TORTOISE SHELL CEILING! IT'S UNBELIEVABLE THIS MUCH QUALITY EXISTS OUTSIDE MY IMAGINATION!
AND LOOK, MORE QUALITY! THE ONYX DESK, HAND CARVED BY A WHOLE VILLAGE OF ARTISANS!
INCREDIBLE!
AND OVER THERE, THAT'S MY WIFE! LOOK AT THE QUALITY!
VERY IMPRESSIVE!

7/26/88

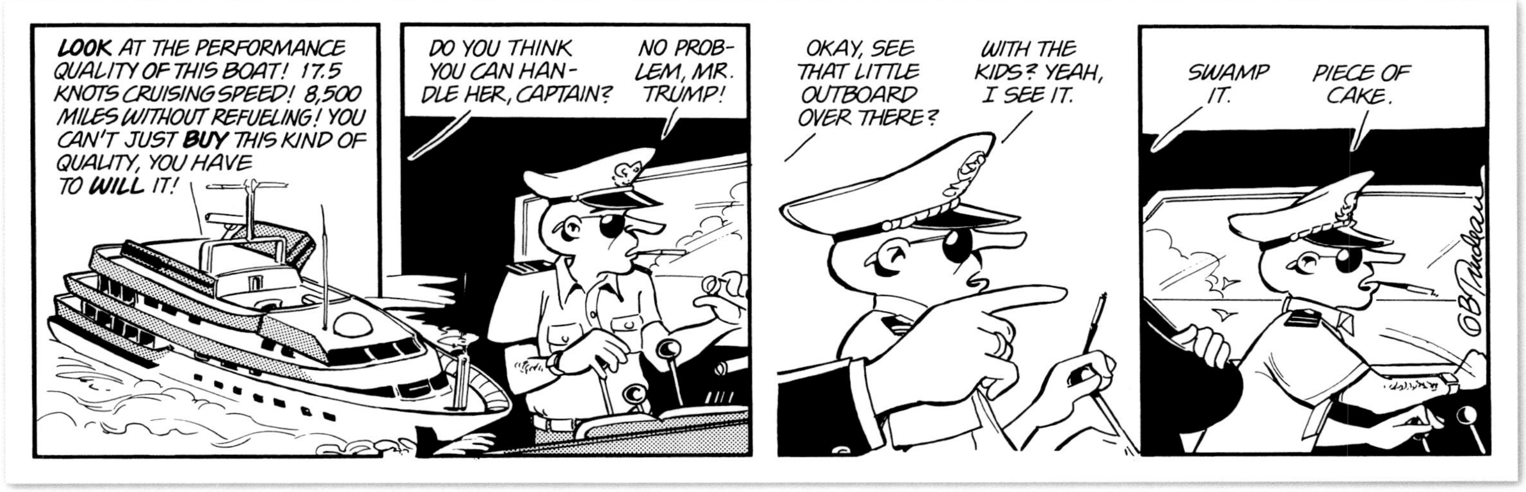
LOOK AT THE PERFORMANCE QUALITY OF THIS BOAT! 17.5 KNOTS CRUISING SPEED! 8,500 MILES WITHOUT REFUELING! YOU CAN'T JUST BUY THIS KIND OF QUALITY, YOU HAVE TO WILL IT!
DO YOU THINK YOU CAN HANDLE HER, CAPTAIN?
NO PROBLEM, MR. TRUMP!
OKAY, SEE THAT LITTLE OUTBOARD OVER THERE?
WITH THE KIDS? YEAH, I SEE IT.
SWAMP IT.
PIECE OF CAKE.

7/28/88

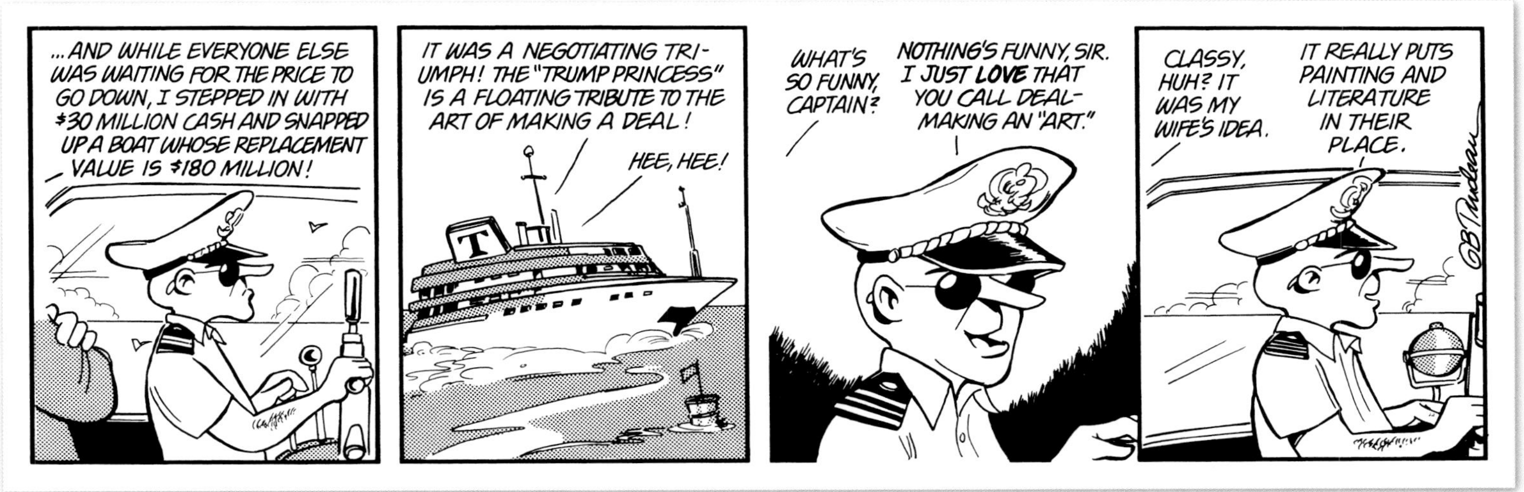
...AND WHILE EVERYONE ELSE WAS WAITING FOR THE PRICE TO GO DOWN, I STEPPED IN WITH $30 MILLION CASH AND SNAPPED UP A BOAT WHOSE REPLACEMENT VALUE IS $180 MILLION!
IT WAS A NEGOTIATING TRIUMPH! THE "TRUMP PRINCESS" IS A FLOATING TRIBUTE TO THE ART OF MAKING A DEAL!
HEE, HEE!
WHAT'S SO FUNNY, CAPTAIN?
NOTHING'S FUNNY, SIR. I JUST LOVE THAT YOU CALL DEAL-MAKING AN "ART."
CLASSY, HUH? IT WAS MY WIFE'S IDEA.
IT REALLY PUTS PAINTING AND LITERATURE IN THEIR PLACE.

8/11/88

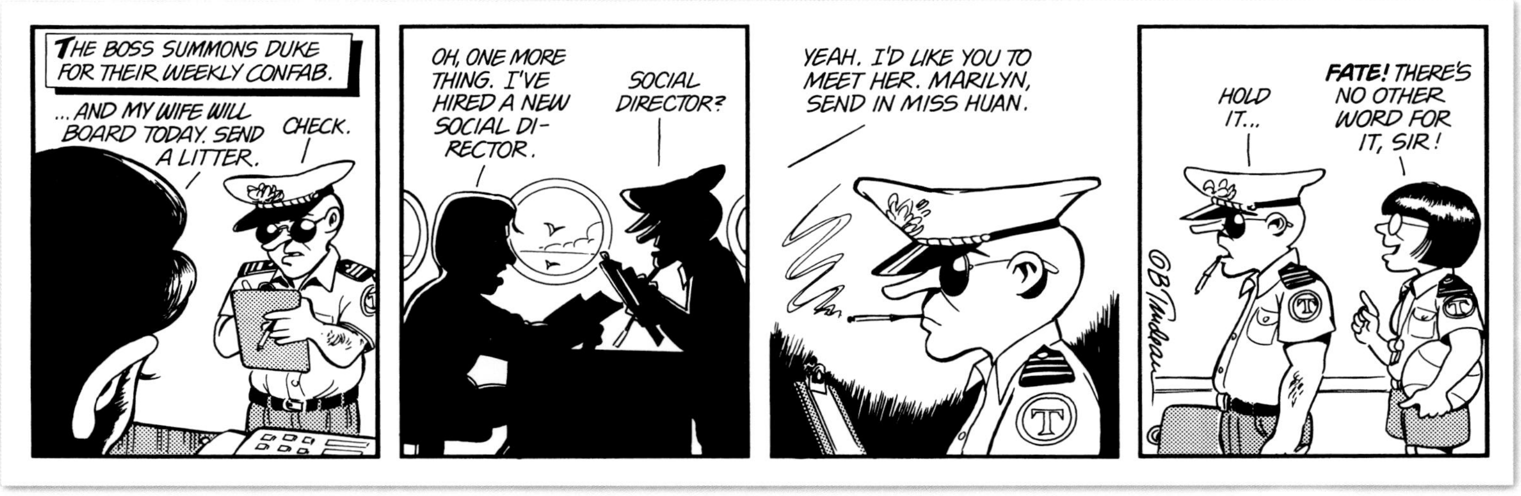
THE BOSS SUMMONS DUKE FOR THEIR WEEKLY CONFAB.
...AND MY WIFE WILL BOARD TODAY. SEND A LITTER.
CHECK.
OH, ONE MORE THING. I'VE HIRED A NEW SOCIAL DIRECTOR.
SOCIAL DIRECTOR?
YEAH. I'D LIKE YOU TO MEET HER. MARILYN, SEND IN MISS HUAN.
HOLD IT...
FATE! THERE'S NO OTHER WORD FOR IT, SIR!

10/3/88

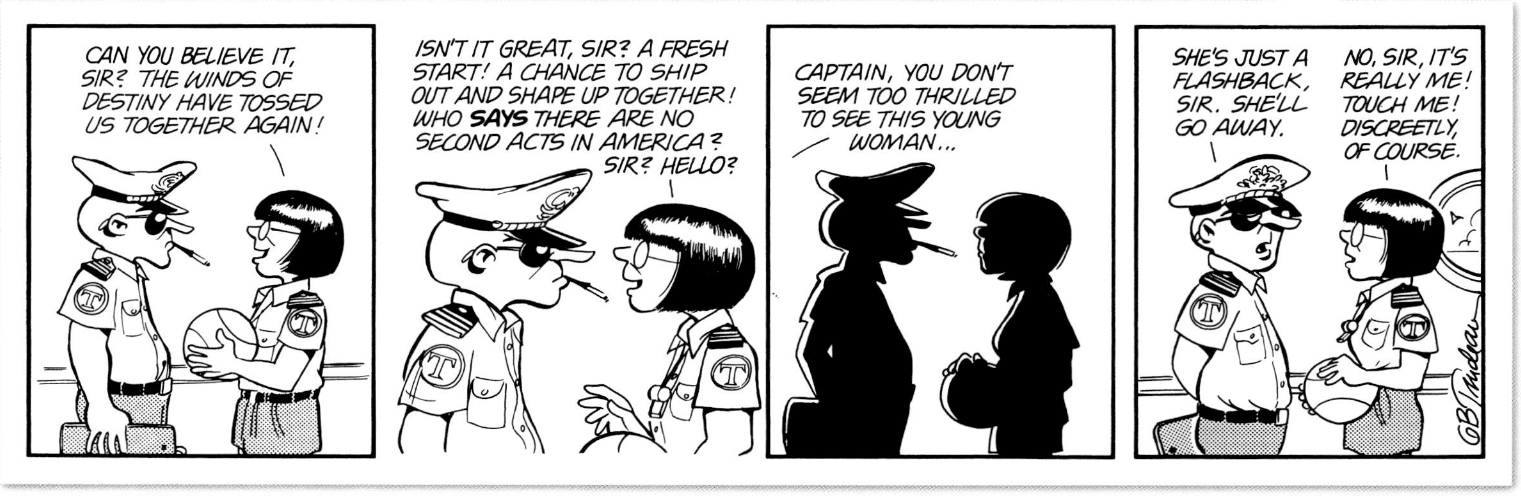
CAN YOU BELIEVE IT, SIR? THE WINDS OF DESTINY HAVE TOSSED US TOGETHER AGAIN!
ISN'T IT GREAT, SIR? A FRESH START! A CHANCE TO SHIP OUT AND SHAPE UP TOGETHER! WHO SAYS THERE ARE NO SECOND ACTS IN AMERICA? SIR? HELLO?
CAPTAIN, YOU DON'T SEEM TOO THRILLED TO SEE THIS YOUNG WOMAN...
SHE'S JUST A FLASHBACK, SIR. SHE'LL GO AWAY.
NO, SIR, IT'S REALLY ME! TOUCH ME! DISCREETLY, OF COURSE.

10/4/88

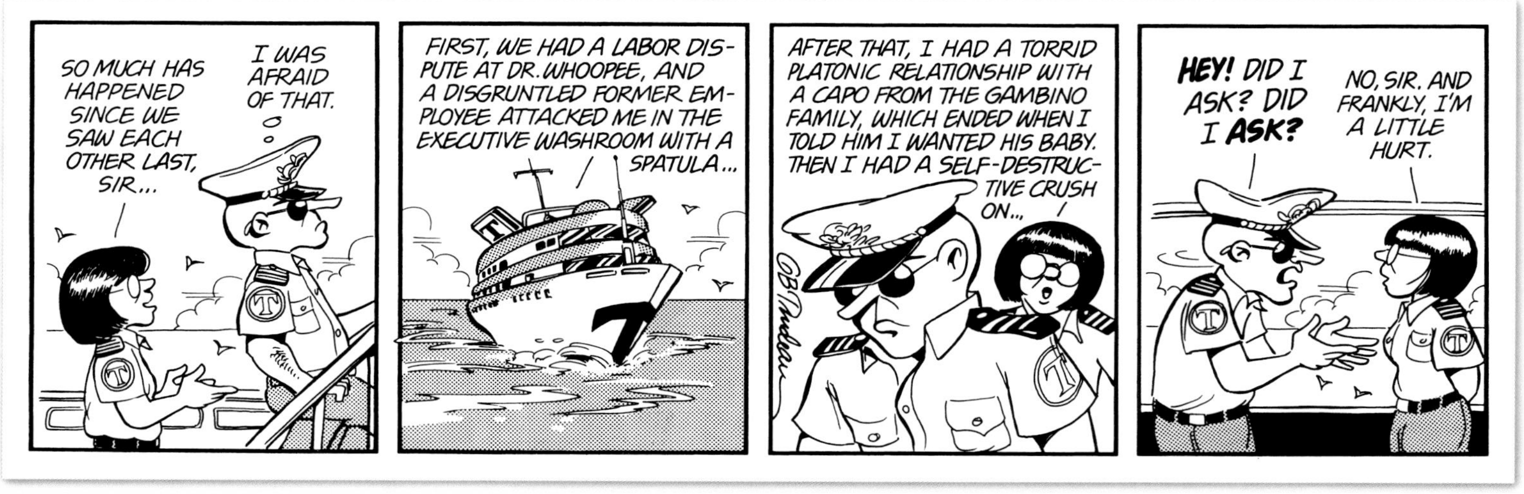
SO MUCH HAS HAPPENED SINCE WE SAW EACH OTHER LAST, SIR...
I WAS AFRAID OF THAT.
FIRST, WE HAD A LABOR DISPUTE AT DR. WHOOPEE, AND A DISGRUNTLED FORMER EMPLOYEE ATTACKED ME IN THE EXECUTIVE WASHROOM WITH A SPATULA...
AFTER THAT, I HAD A TORRID PLATONIC RELATIONSHIP WITH A CAPO FROM THE GAMBINO FAMILY, WHICH ENDED WHEN I TOLD HIM I WANTED HIS BABY. THEN I HAD A SELF-DESTRUCTIVE CRUSH ON...
HEY! DID I ASK? DID I ASK?
NO, SIR. AND FRANKLY, I'M A LITTLE HURT.

10/5/88

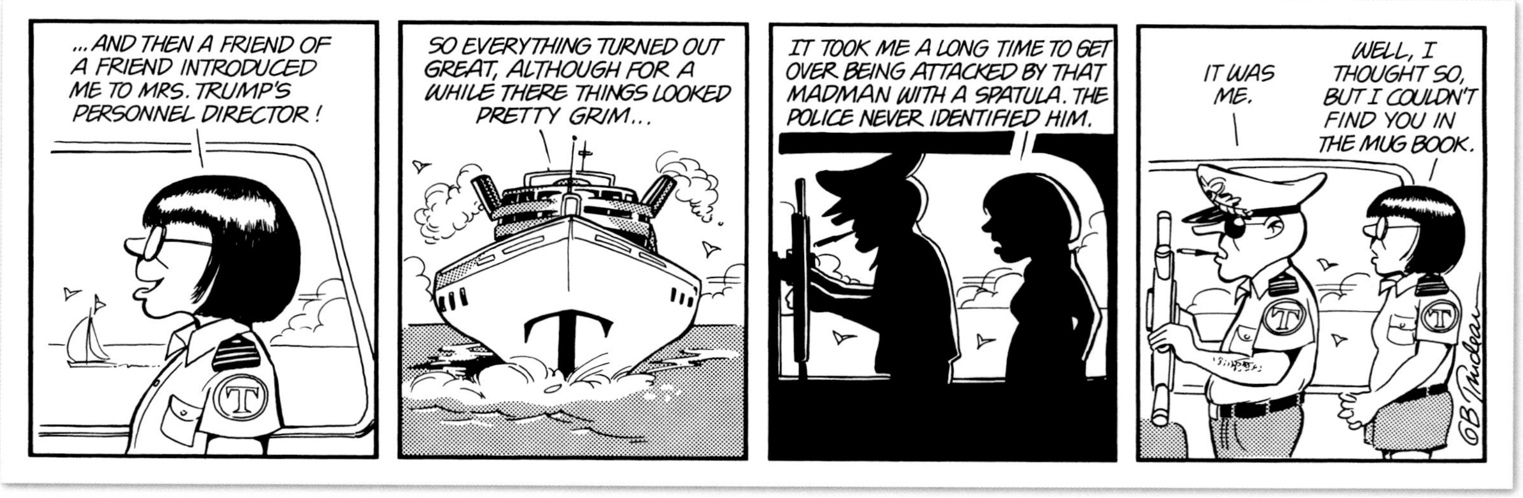
...AND THEN A FRIEND OF A FRIEND INTRODUCED ME TO MRS. TRUMP'S PERSONNEL DIRECTOR!
SO EVERYTHING TURNED OUT GREAT, ALTHOUGH FOR A WHILE THERE THINGS LOOKED PRETTY GRIM...
IT TOOK ME A LONG TIME TO GET OVER BEING ATTACKED BY THAT MADMAN WITH A SPATULA. THE POLICE NEVER IDENTIFIED HIM.
IT WAS ME.
WELL, I THOUGHT SO, BUT I COULDN'T FIND YOU IN THE MUG BOOK.

10/6/88

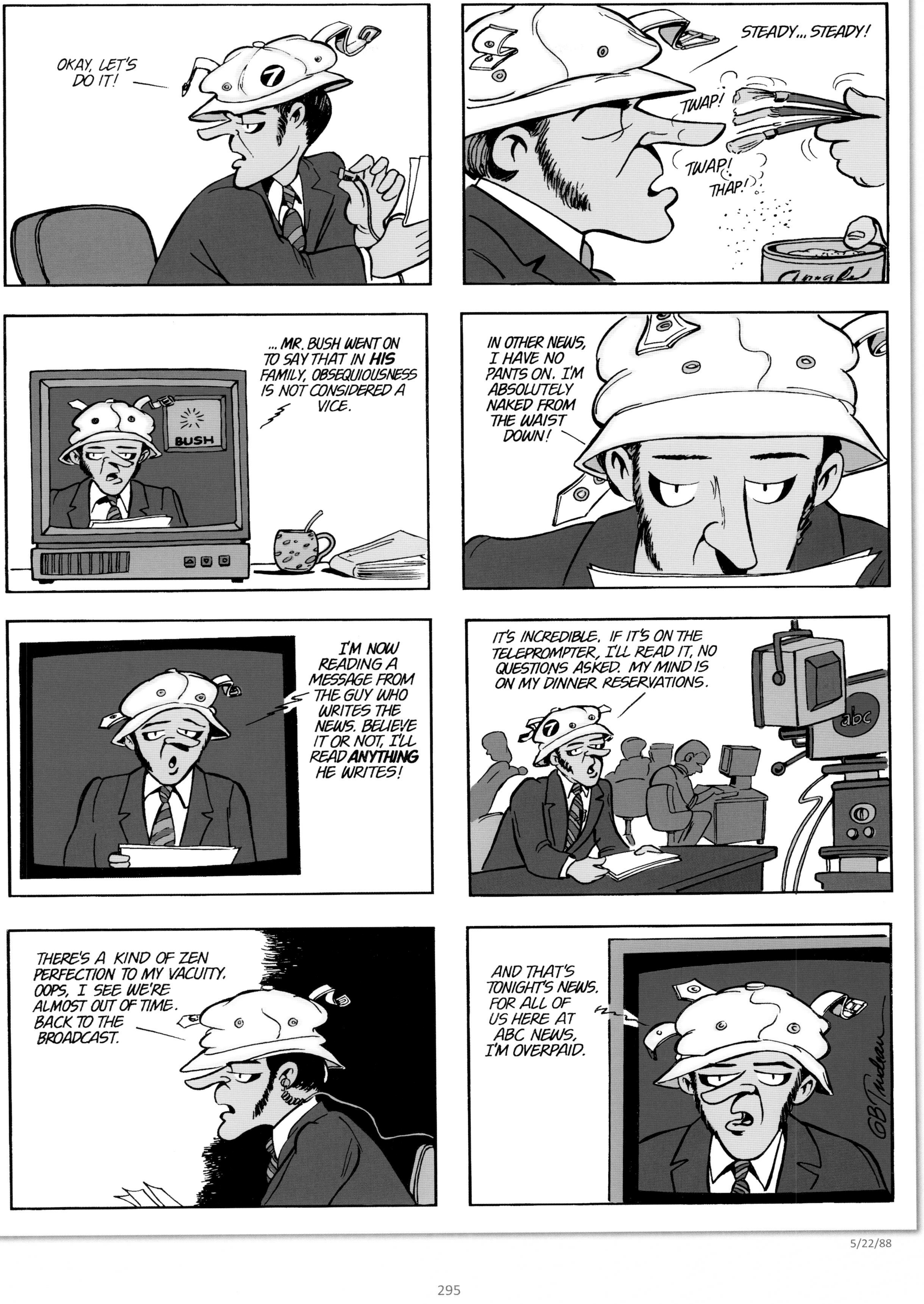
OKAY, LET'S DO IT!
STEADY... STEADY!
TWAP!
TWAP!
THAP!
... MR. BUSH WENT ON TO SAY THAT IN **HIS** FAMILY, OBSEQUIOUSNESS IS NOT CONSIDERED A VICE.
BUSH
IN OTHER NEWS, I HAVE NO PANTS ON. I'M ABSOLUTELY NAKED FROM THE WAIST DOWN!
I'M NOW READING A MESSAGE FROM THE GUY WHO WRITES THE NEWS. BELIEVE IT OR NOT, I'LL READ **ANYTHING** HE WRITES!
IT'S INCREDIBLE. IF IT'S ON THE TELEPROMPTER, I'LL READ IT, NO QUESTIONS ASKED. MY MIND IS ON MY DINNER RESERVATIONS.
abc
THERE'S A KIND OF ZEN PERFECTION TO MY VACUITY. OOPS, I SEE WE'RE ALMOST OUT OF TIME. BACK TO THE BROADCAST.
AND THAT'S TONIGHT'S NEWS. FOR ALL OF US HERE AT ABC NEWS, I'M OVERPAID.
GB Trudeau

5/22/88

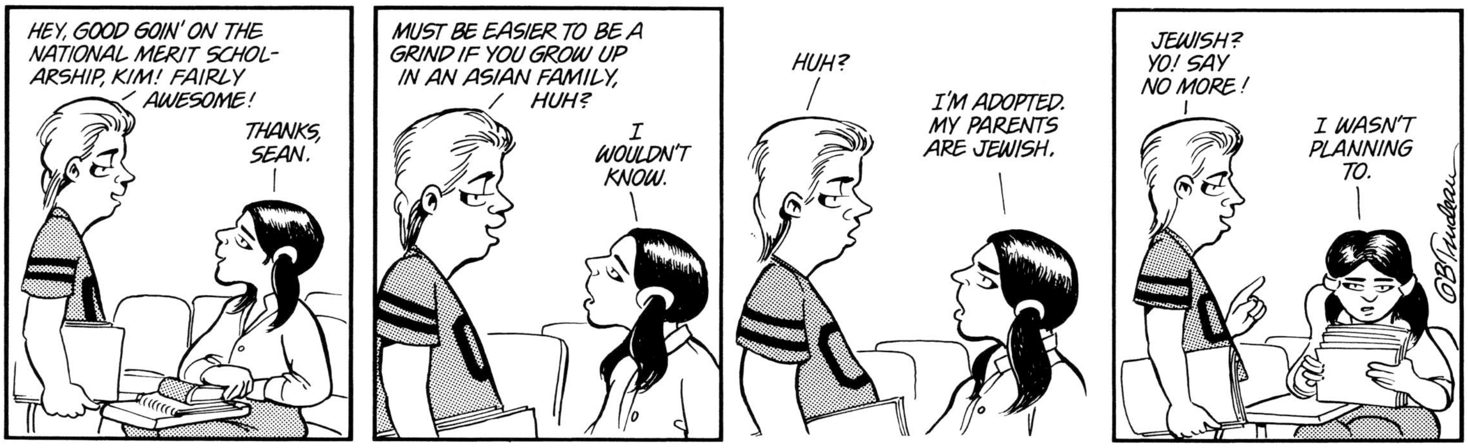
HEY, GOOD GOIN' ON THE NATIONAL MERIT SCHOLARSHIP, KIM! FAIRLY AWESOME!
THANKS, SEAN.
MUST BE EASIER TO BE A GRIND IF YOU GROW UP IN AN ASIAN FAMILY, HUH?
I WOULDN'T KNOW.
HUH?
I'M ADOPTED. MY PARENTS ARE JEWISH.
JEWISH? YO! SAY NO MORE!
I WASN'T PLANNING TO.

3/15/88

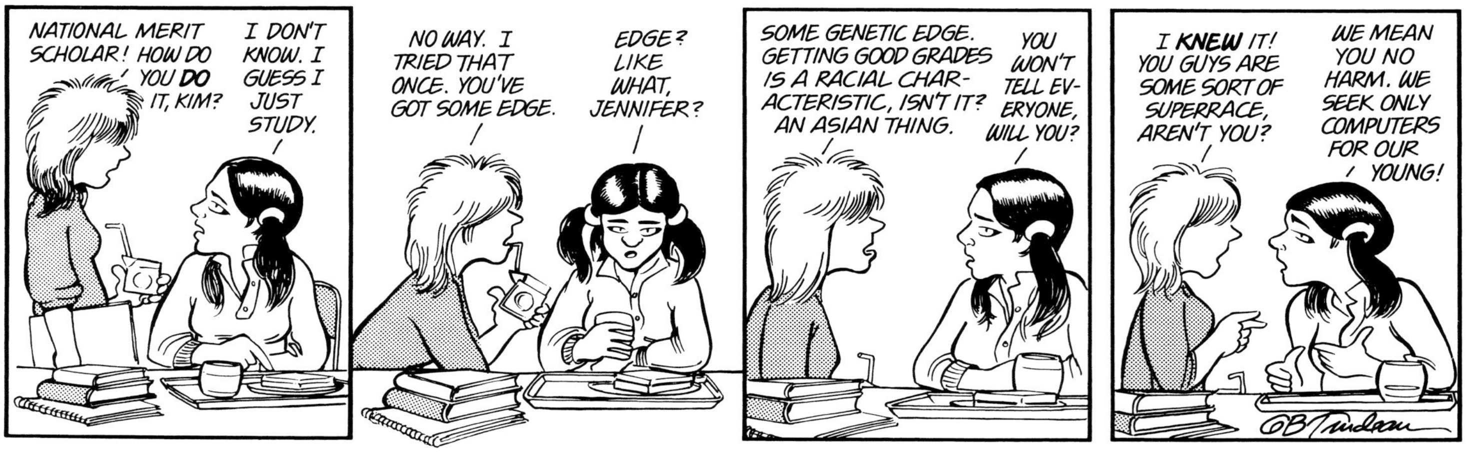
NATIONAL MERIT SCHOLAR! HOW DO YOU **DO** IT, KIM?
I DON'T KNOW. I GUESS I JUST STUDY.
NO WAY. I TRIED THAT ONCE. YOU'VE GOT SOME EDGE.
EDGE? LIKE WHAT, JENNIFER?
SOME GENETIC EDGE. GETTING GOOD GRADES IS A RACIAL CHARACTERISTIC, ISN'T IT? AN ASIAN THING.
YOU WON'T TELL EVERYONE, WILL YOU?
I **KNEW** IT! YOU GUYS ARE SOME SORT OF SUPERRACE, AREN'T YOU?
WE MEAN YOU NO HARM. WE SEEK ONLY COMPUTERS FOR OUR YOUNG!

3/16/88

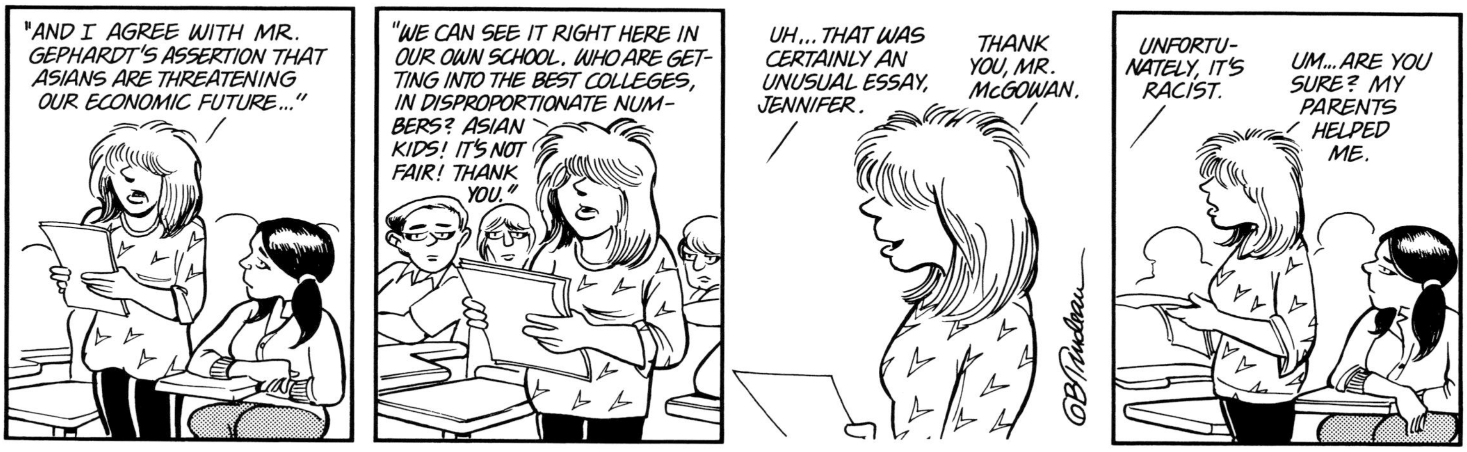
"AND I AGREE WITH MR. GEPHARDT'S ASSERTION THAT ASIANS ARE THREATENING OUR ECONOMIC FUTURE..."
"WE CAN SEE IT RIGHT HERE IN OUR OWN SCHOOL. WHO ARE GETTING INTO THE BEST COLLEGES, IN DISPROPORTIONATE NUMBERS? ASIAN KIDS! IT'S NOT FAIR! THANK YOU."
UH... THAT WAS CERTAINLY AN UNUSUAL ESSAY, JENNIFER.
THANK YOU, MR. McGOWAN.
UNFORTUNATELY, IT'S RACIST.
UM... ARE YOU SURE? MY PARENTS HELPED ME.

3/17/88

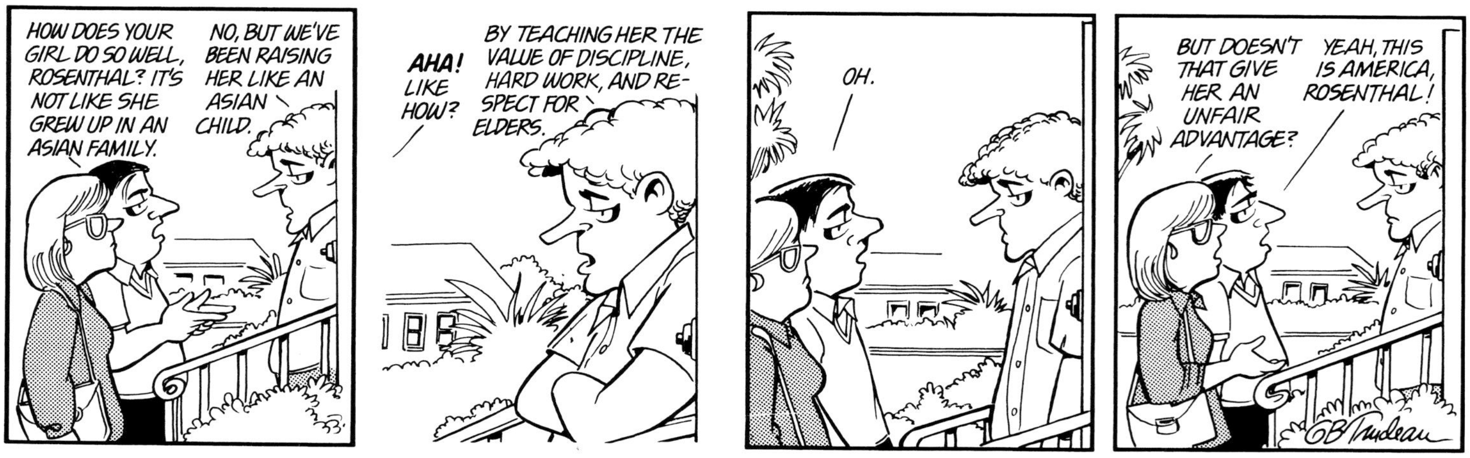
HOW DOES YOUR GIRL DO SO WELL, ROSENTHAL? IT'S NOT LIKE SHE GREW UP IN AN ASIAN FAMILY.
NO, BUT WE'VE BEEN RAISING HER LIKE AN ASIAN CHILD.
AHA! LIKE HOW?
BY TEACHING HER THE VALUE OF DISCIPLINE, HARD WORK, AND RESPECT FOR ELDERS.
OH.
BUT DOESN'T THAT GIVE HER AN UNFAIR ADVANTAGE?
YEAH, THIS IS AMERICA, ROSENTHAL!

3/19/88

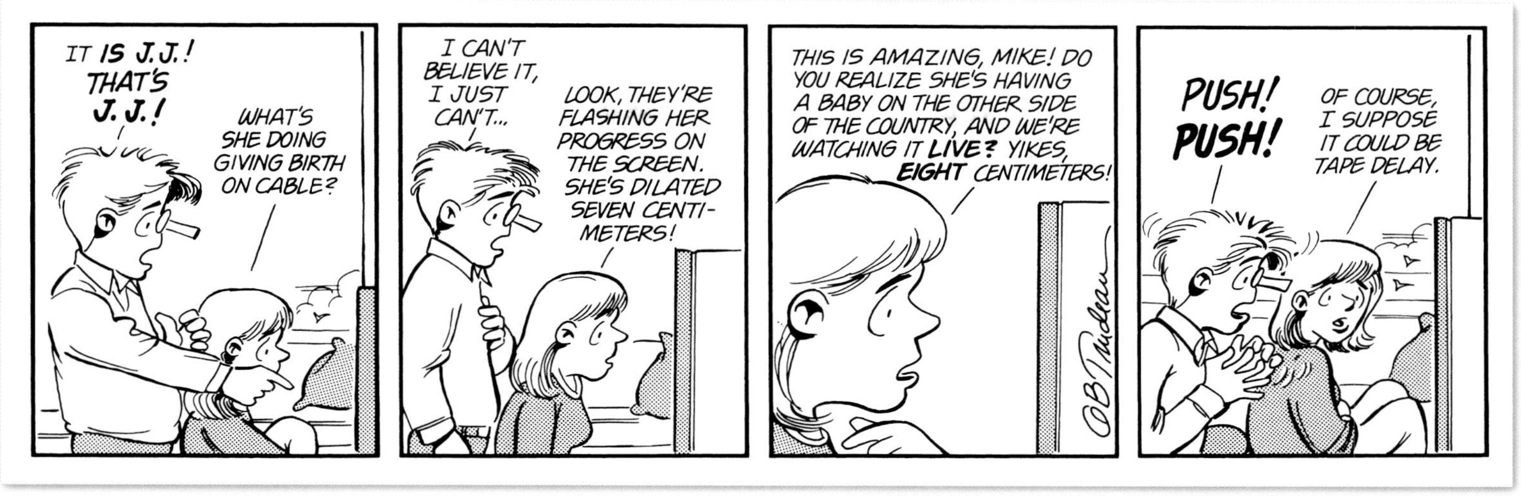
IT IS J.J.! THAT'S J.J.!
WHAT'S SHE DOING GIVING BIRTH ON CABLE?
I CAN'T BELIEVE IT, I JUST CAN'T...
LOOK, THEY'RE FLASHING HER PROGRESS ON THE SCREEN. SHE'S DILATED SEVEN CENTIMETERS!
THIS IS AMAZING, MIKE! DO YOU REALIZE SHE'S HAVING A BABY ON THE OTHER SIDE OF THE COUNTRY, AND WE'RE WATCHING IT LIVE? YIKES, EIGHT CENTIMETERS!
PUSH! PUSH!
OF COURSE, I SUPPOSE IT COULD BE TAPE DELAY.

11/29/88

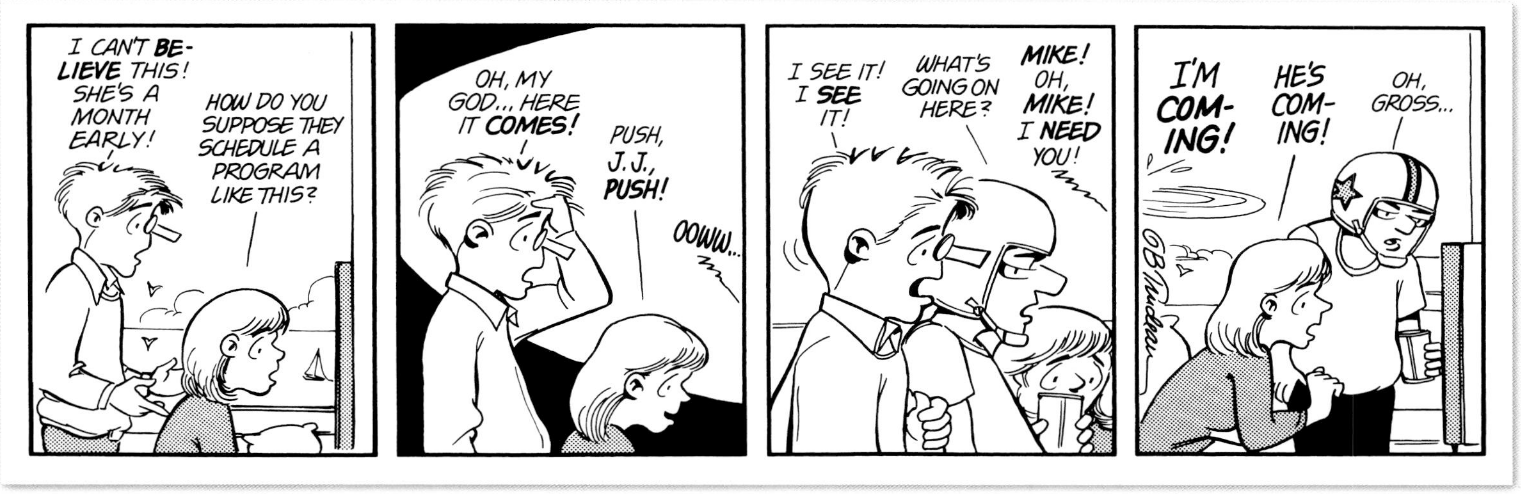
I CAN'T BELIEVE THIS! SHE'S A MONTH EARLY!
HOW DO YOU SUPPOSE THEY SCHEDULE A PROGRAM LIKE THIS?
OH, MY GOD... HERE IT COMES!
PUSH, J.J., PUSH!
OOWW...
I SEE IT! I SEE IT!
WHAT'S GOING ON HERE?
MIKE! OH, MIKE! I NEED YOU!
I'M COMING!
HE'S COMING!
OH, GROSS...

11/30/88

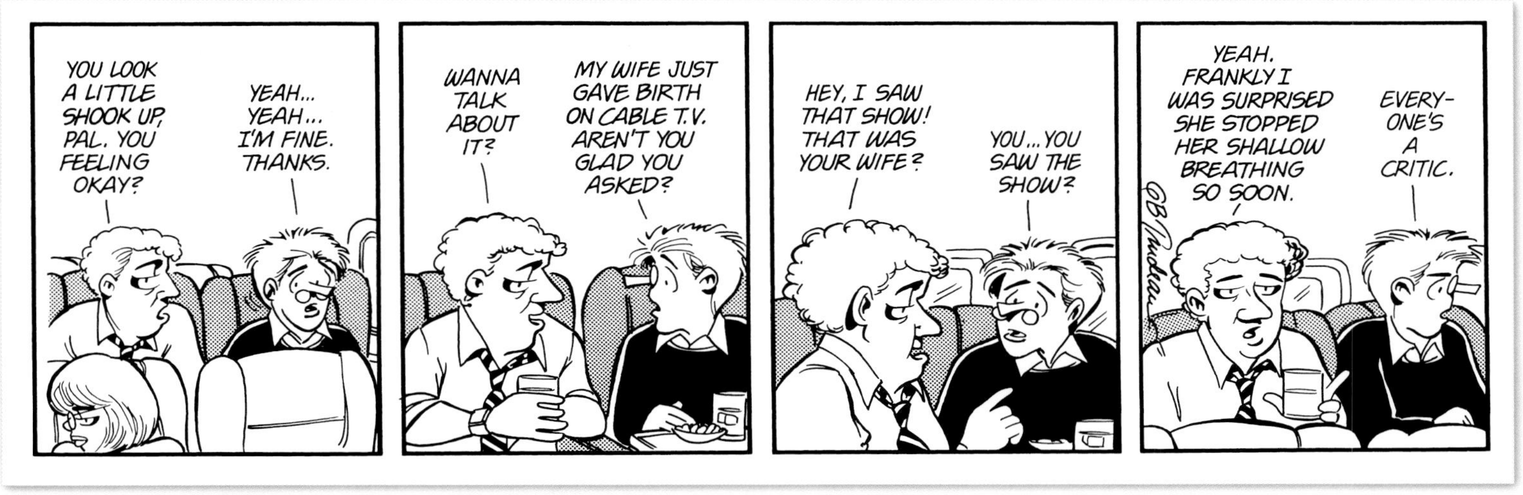
YOU LOOK A LITTLE SHOOK UP, PAL. YOU FEELING OKAY?
YEAH... YEAH... I'M FINE. THANKS.
WANNA TALK ABOUT IT?
MY WIFE JUST GAVE BIRTH ON CABLE T.V. AREN'T YOU GLAD YOU ASKED?
HEY, I SAW THAT SHOW! THAT WAS YOUR WIFE?
YOU... YOU SAW THE SHOW?
YEAH. FRANKLY I WAS SURPRISED SHE STOPPED HER SHALLOW BREATHING SO SOON.
EVERYONE'S A CRITIC.

12/1/88

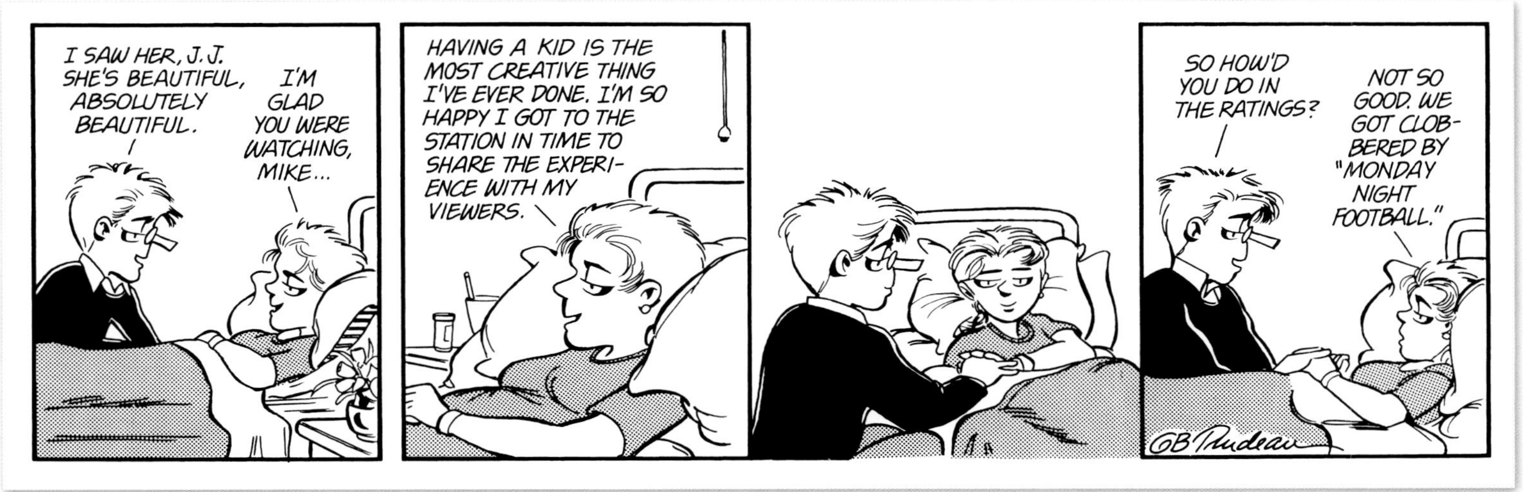
I SAW HER, J.J. SHE'S BEAUTIFUL, ABSOLUTELY BEAUTIFUL.
I'M GLAD YOU WERE WATCHING, MIKE...
HAVING A KID IS THE MOST CREATIVE THING I'VE EVER DONE. I'M SO HAPPY I GOT TO THE STATION IN TIME TO SHARE THE EXPERIENCE WITH MY VIEWERS.
SO HOW'D YOU DO IN THE RATINGS?
NOT SO GOOD. WE GOT CLOBBERED BY "MONDAY NIGHT FOOTBALL."

12/2/88

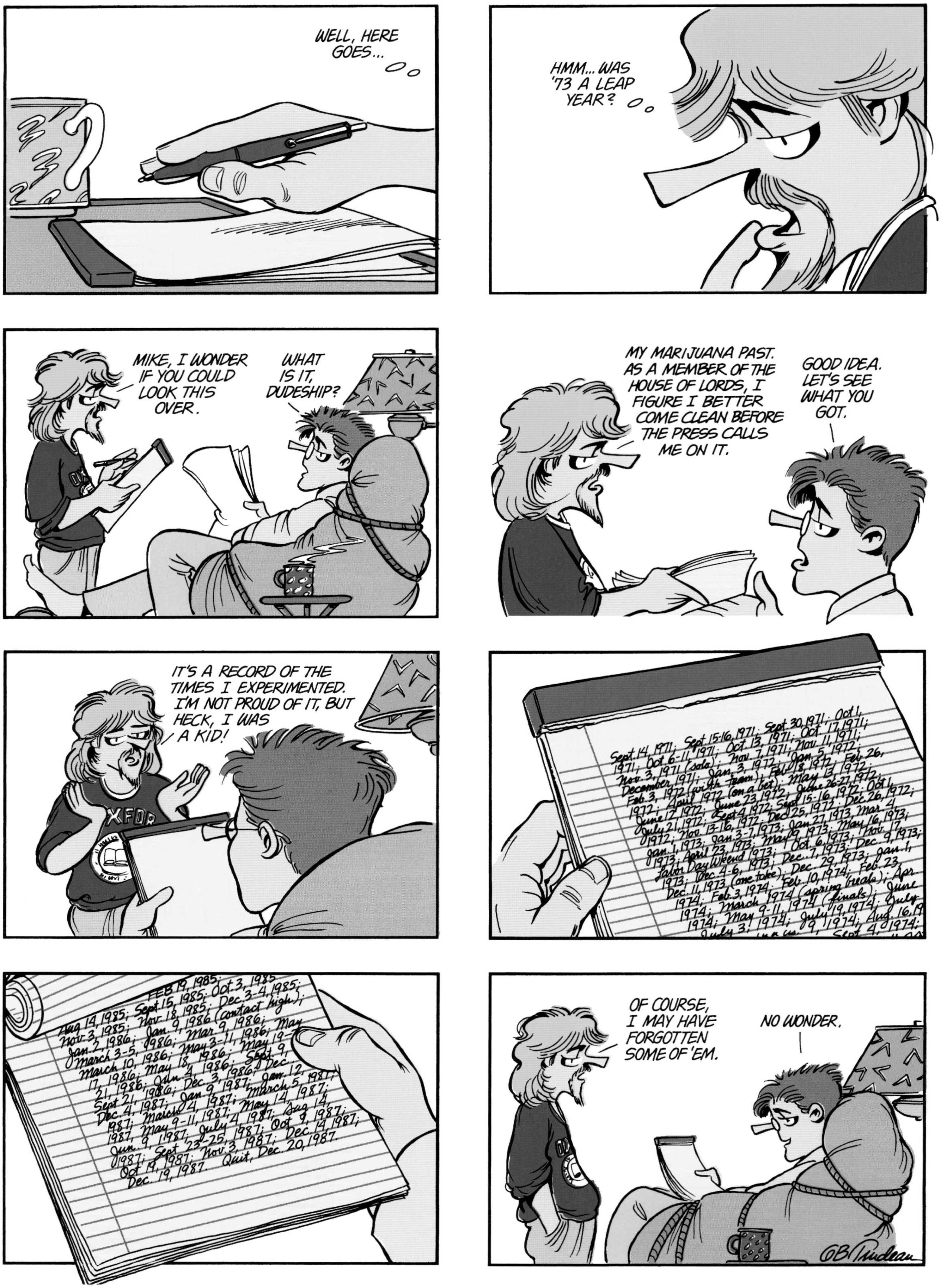
WELL, HERE GOES...
HMM... WAS '73 A LEAP YEAR?
MIKE, I WONDER IF YOU COULD LOOK THIS OVER.
WHAT IS IT, DUDESHIP?
MY MARIJUANA PAST. AS A MEMBER OF THE HOUSE OF LORDS, I FIGURE I BETTER COME CLEAN BEFORE THE PRESS CALLS ME ON IT.
GOOD IDEA. LET'S SEE WHAT YOU GOT.
IT'S A RECORD OF THE TIMES I EXPERIMENTED. I'M NOT PROUD OF IT, BUT HECK, I WAS A KID!
OF COURSE, I MAY HAVE FORGOTTEN SOME OF 'EM.
NO WONDER.
©B. Trudeau

1/10/88

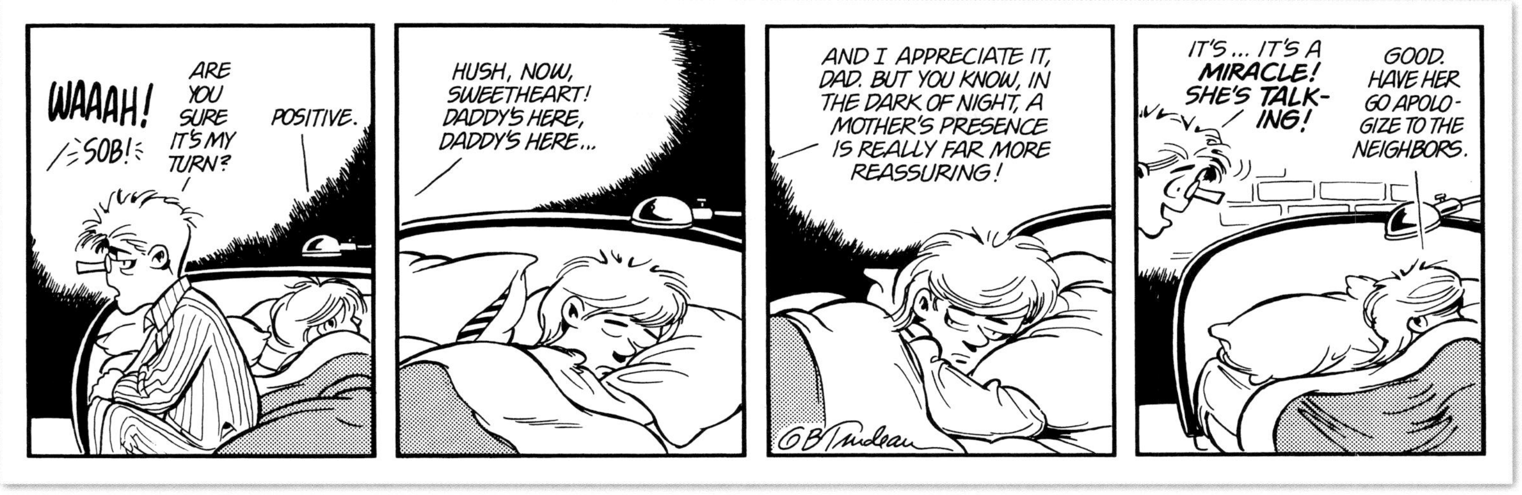
WAAAH!
SOB!
ARE YOU SURE IT'S MY TURN?
POSITIVE.
HUSH, NOW, SWEETHEART! DADDY'S HERE, DADDY'S HERE...
AND I APPRECIATE IT, DAD. BUT YOU KNOW, IN THE DARK OF NIGHT, A MOTHER'S PRESENCE IS REALLY FAR MORE REASSURING!
IT'S ... IT'S A MIRACLE! SHE'S TALKING!
GOOD. HAVE HER GO APOLOGIZE TO THE NEIGHBORS.
GB Trudeau

1/2/89

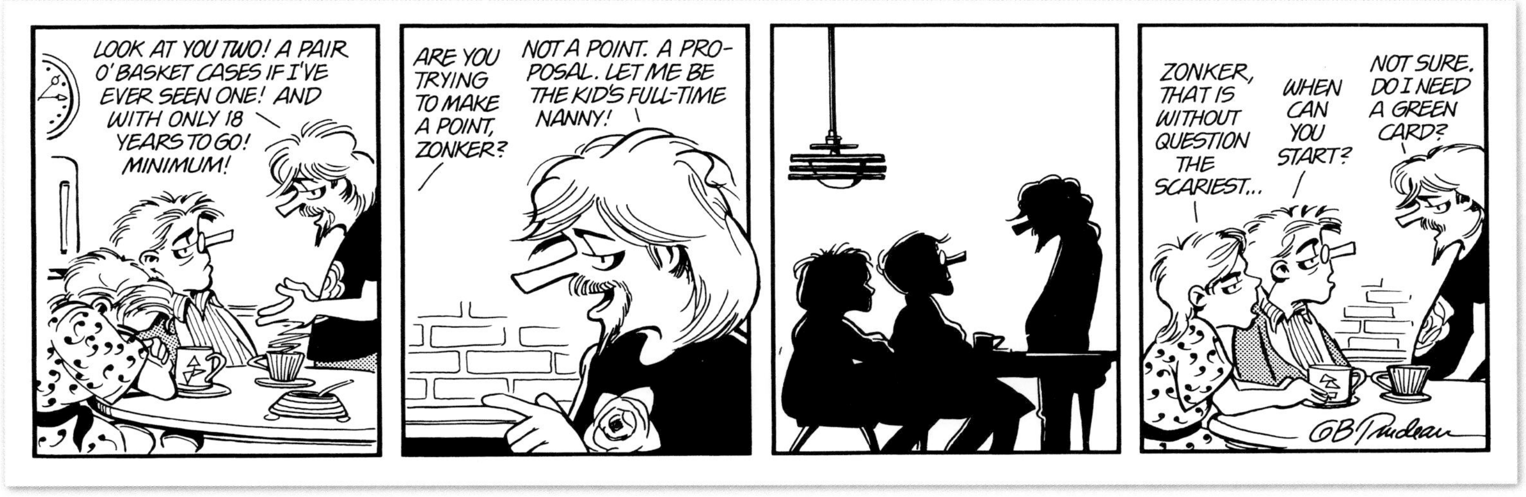
LOOK AT YOU TWO! A PAIR O' BASKET CASES IF I'VE EVER SEEN ONE! AND WITH ONLY 18 YEARS TO GO! MINIMUM!
ARE YOU TRYING TO MAKE A POINT, ZONKER?
NOT A POINT. A PROPOSAL. LET ME BE THE KID'S FULL-TIME NANNY!
ZONKER, THAT IS WITHOUT QUESTION THE SCARIEST...
WHEN CAN YOU START?
NOT SURE. DO I NEED A GREEN CARD?
GB Trudeau

1/4/89

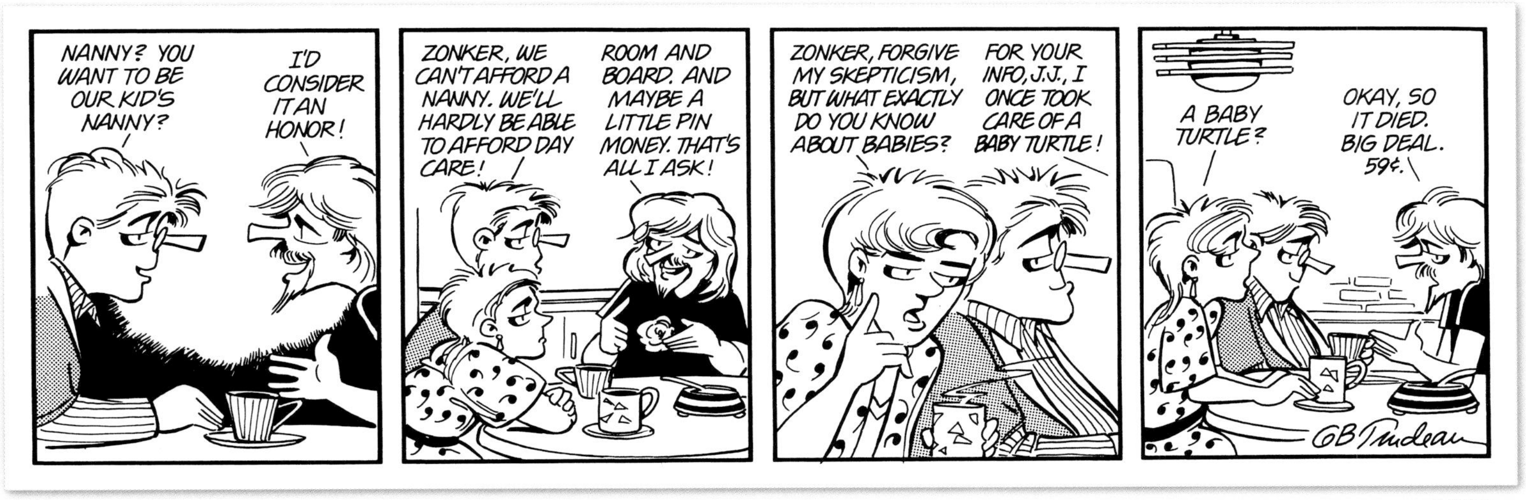
NANNY? YOU WANT TO BE OUR KID'S NANNY?
I'D CONSIDER IT AN HONOR!
ZONKER, WE CAN'T AFFORD A NANNY. WE'LL HARDLY BE ABLE TO AFFORD DAY CARE!
ROOM AND BOARD. AND MAYBE A LITTLE PIN MONEY. THAT'S ALL I ASK!
ZONKER, FORGIVE MY SKEPTICISM, BUT WHAT EXACTLY DO YOU KNOW ABOUT BABIES?
FOR YOUR INFO, J.J., I ONCE TOOK CARE OF A BABY TURTLE!
A BABY TURTLE?
OKAY, SO IT DIED. BIG DEAL. 59¢.
GB Trudeau

1/5/89

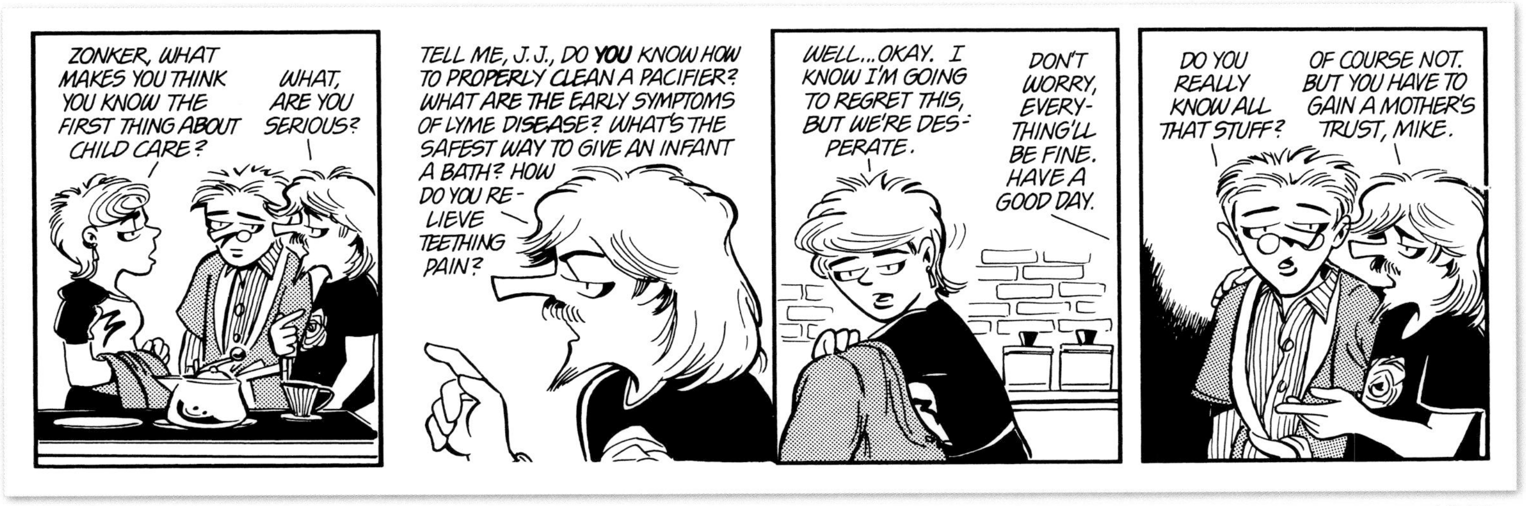
ZONKER, WHAT MAKES YOU THINK YOU KNOW THE FIRST THING ABOUT CHILD CARE?
WHAT, ARE YOU SERIOUS?
TELL ME, J.J., DO YOU KNOW HOW TO PROPERLY CLEAN A PACIFIER? WHAT ARE THE EARLY SYMPTOMS OF LYME DISEASE? WHAT'S THE SAFEST WAY TO GIVE AN INFANT A BATH? HOW DO YOU RELIEVE TEETHING PAIN?
WELL...OKAY. I KNOW I'M GOING TO REGRET THIS, BUT WE'RE DESPERATE.
DON'T WORRY, EVERYTHING'LL BE FINE. HAVE A GOOD DAY.
DO YOU REALLY KNOW ALL THAT STUFF?
OF COURSE NOT. BUT YOU HAVE TO GAIN A MOTHER'S TRUST, MIKE.

1/6/89

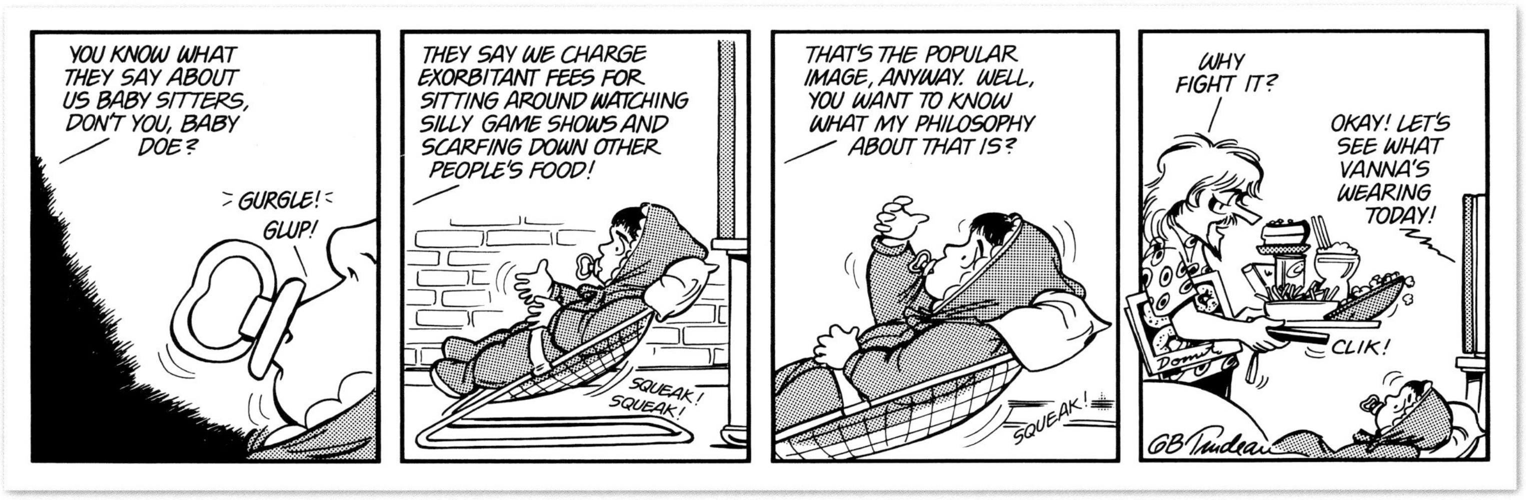
YOU KNOW WHAT THEY SAY ABOUT US BABY SITTERS, DON'T YOU, BABY DOE?
GURGLE! GLUP!
THEY SAY WE CHARGE EXORBITANT FEES FOR SITTING AROUND WATCHING SILLY GAME SHOWS AND SCARFING DOWN OTHER PEOPLE'S FOOD!
SQUEAK! SQUEAK!
THAT'S THE POPULAR IMAGE, ANYWAY. WELL, YOU WANT TO KNOW WHAT MY PHILOSOPHY ABOUT THAT IS?
SQUEAK!
WHY FIGHT IT?
OKAY! LET'S SEE WHAT VANNA'S WEARING TODAY!
CLIK!
1/10/89

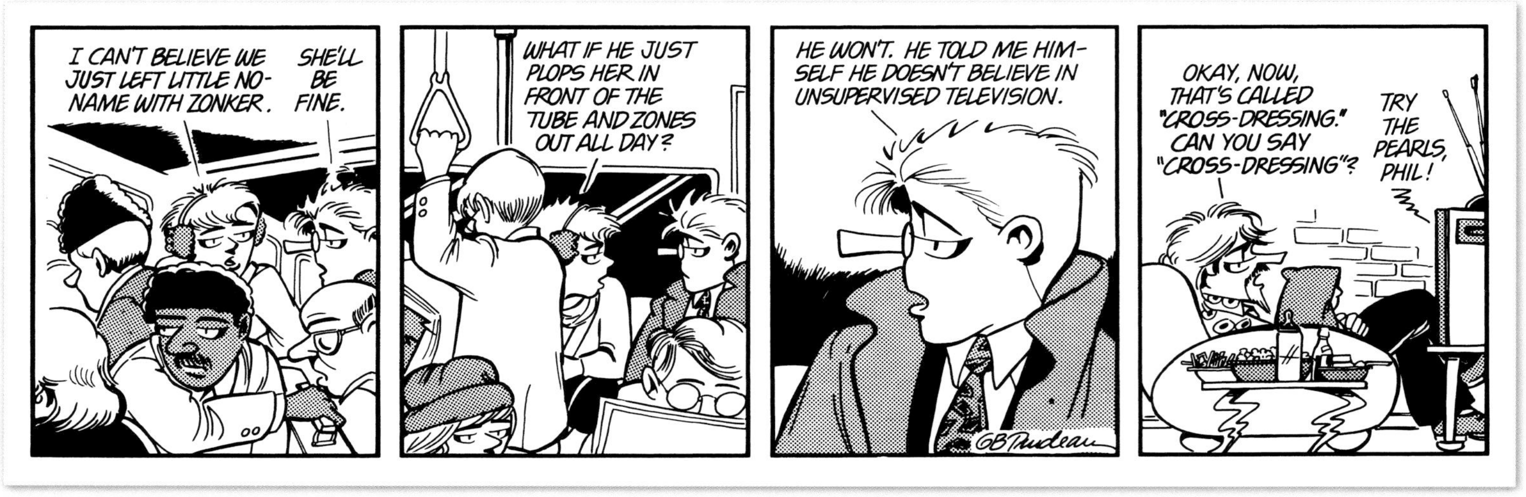
I CAN'T BELIEVE WE JUST LEFT LITTLE NO-NAME WITH ZONKER.
SHE'LL BE FINE.
WHAT IF HE JUST PLOPS HER IN FRONT OF THE TUBE AND ZONES OUT ALL DAY?
HE WON'T. HE TOLD ME HIMSELF HE DOESN'T BELIEVE IN UNSUPERVISED TELEVISION.
OKAY, NOW, THAT'S CALLED "CROSS-DRESSING." CAN YOU SAY "CROSS-DRESSING"?
TRY THE PEARLS, PHIL!
1/11/89

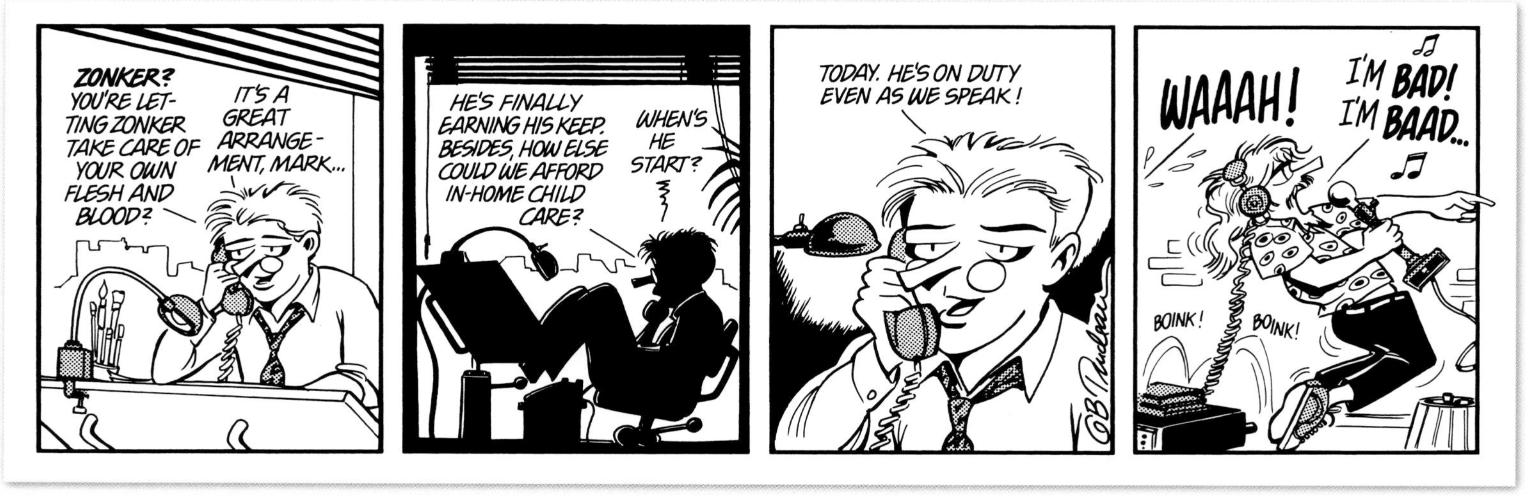
ZONKER? YOU'RE LETTING ZONKER TAKE CARE OF YOUR OWN FLESH AND BLOOD?
IT'S A GREAT ARRANGEMENT, MARK...
HE'S FINALLY EARNING HIS KEEP. BESIDES, HOW ELSE COULD WE AFFORD IN-HOME CHILD CARE?
WHEN'S HE START?
TODAY. HE'S ON DUTY EVEN AS WE SPEAK!
WAAAH!
I'M BAD! I'M BAAD...
BOINK! BOINK!
1/13/89

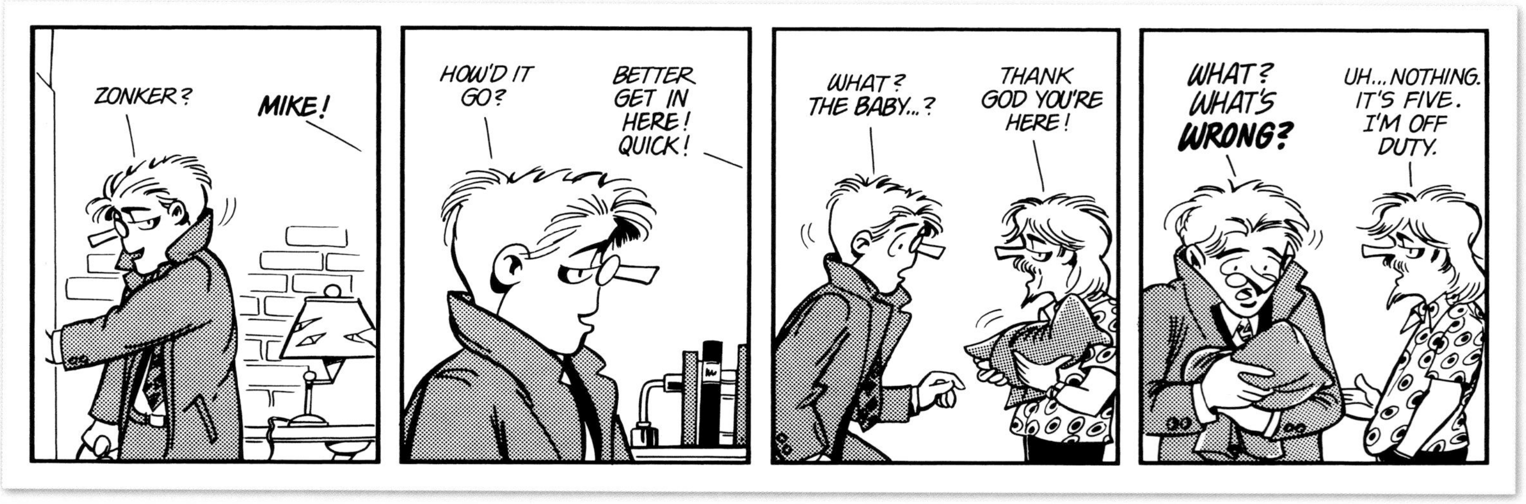
ZONKER?
MIKE!
HOW'D IT GO?
BETTER GET IN HERE! QUICK!
WHAT? THE BABY...?
THANK GOD YOU'RE HERE!
WHAT? WHAT'S WRONG?
UH... NOTHING. IT'S FIVE. I'M OFF DUTY.
1/14/89

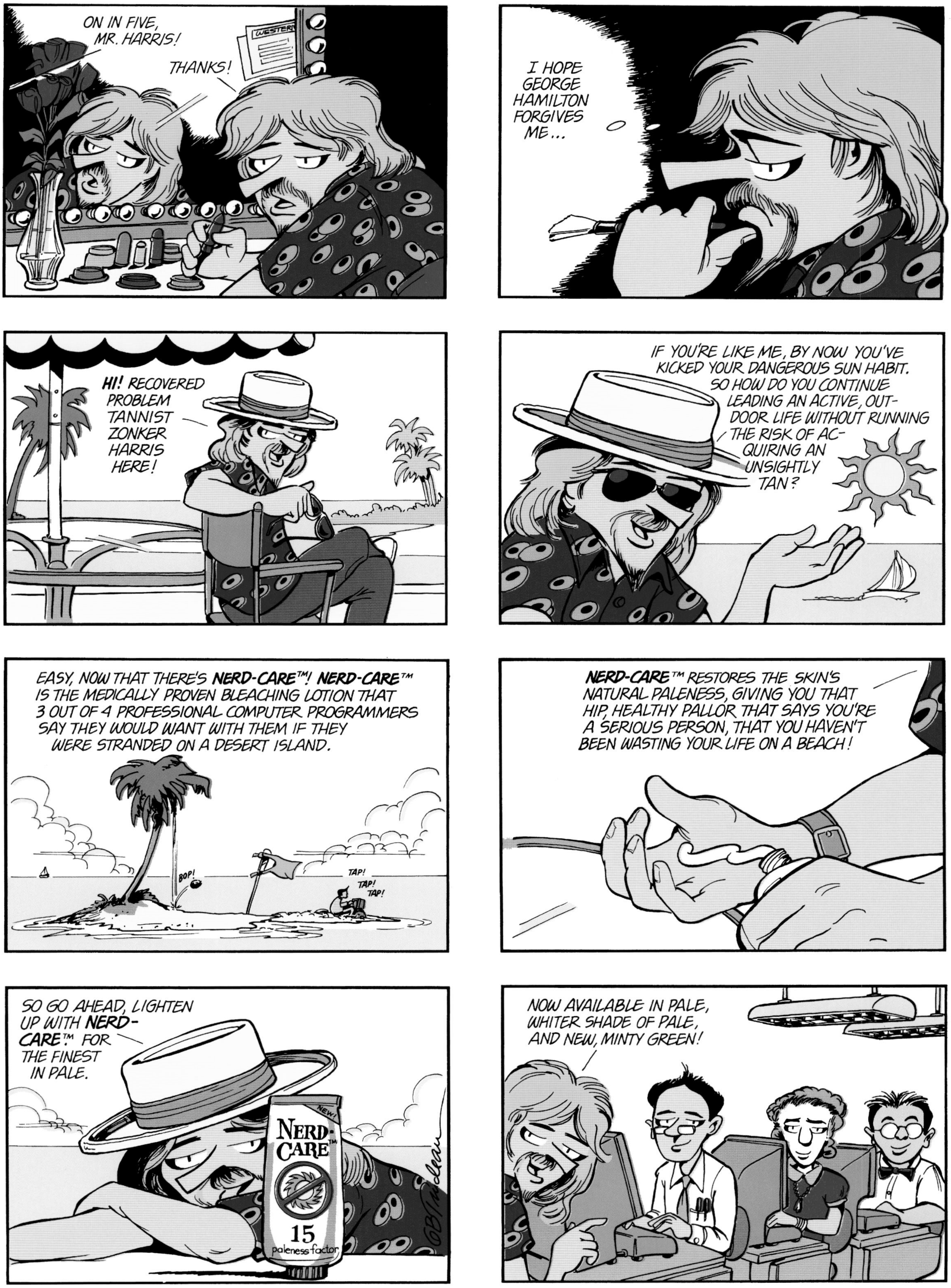

ON IN FIVE, MR. HARRIS!
THANKS!
I HOPE GEORGE HAMILTON FORGIVES ME...
HI! RECOVERED PROBLEM TANNIST ZONKER HARRIS HERE!
IF YOU'RE LIKE ME, BY NOW YOU'VE KICKED YOUR DANGEROUS SUN HABIT. SO HOW DO YOU CONTINUE LEADING AN ACTIVE, OUTDOOR LIFE WITHOUT RUNNING THE RISK OF ACQUIRING AN UNSIGHTLY TAN?
EASY, NOW THAT THERE'S NERD-CARE™! NERD-CARE™ IS THE MEDICALLY PROVEN BLEACHING LOTION THAT 3 OUT OF 4 PROFESSIONAL COMPUTER PROGRAMMERS SAY THEY WOULD WANT WITH THEM IF THEY WERE STRANDED ON A DESERT ISLAND.
BOP!
TAP! TAP! TAP!
NERD-CARE™ RESTORES THE SKIN'S NATURAL PALENESS, GIVING YOU THAT HIP, HEALTHY PALLOR THAT SAYS YOU'RE A SERIOUS PERSON, THAT YOU HAVEN'T BEEN WASTING YOUR LIFE ON A BEACH!
SO GO AHEAD, LIGHTEN UP WITH NERD-CARE™ FOR THE FINEST IN PALE.
NEW!
NERD-CARE™
15
paleness factor
NOW AVAILABLE IN PALE, WHITER SHADE OF PALE, AND NEW, MINTY GREEN!

2/19/89

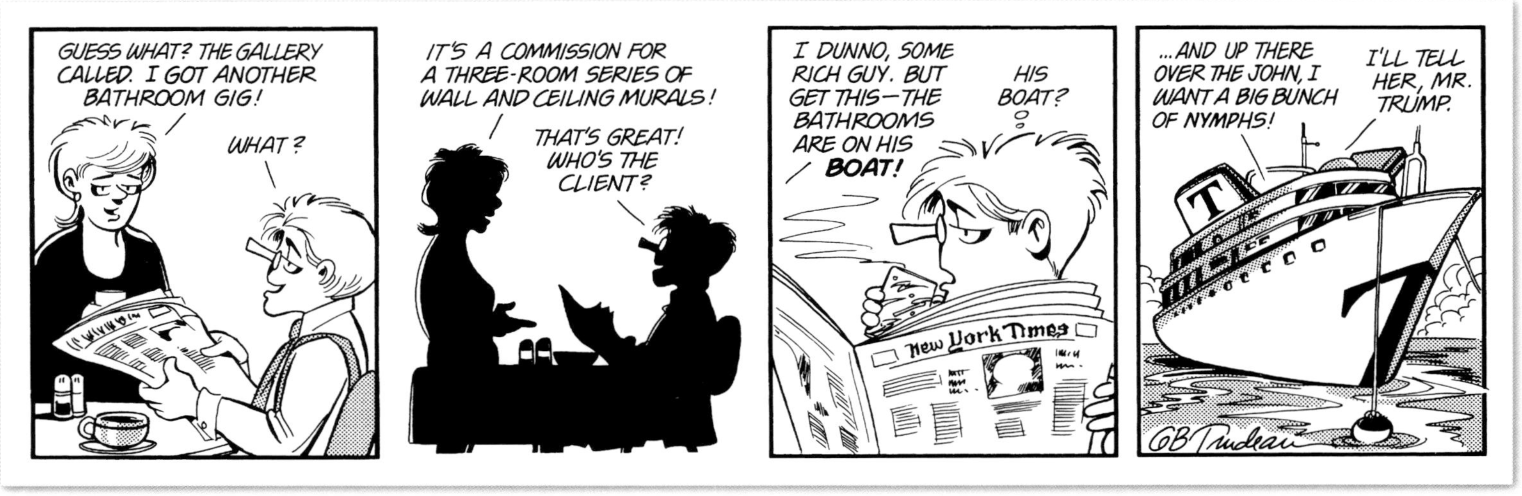
GUESS WHAT? THE GALLERY CALLED. I GOT ANOTHER BATHROOM GIG!
WHAT?
IT'S A COMMISSION FOR A THREE-ROOM SERIES OF WALL AND CEILING MURALS!
THAT'S GREAT! WHO'S THE CLIENT?
I DUNNO, SOME RICH GUY. BUT GET THIS—THE BATHROOMS ARE ON HIS **BOAT!**
HIS BOAT?
New York Times
...AND UP THERE OVER THE JOHN, I WANT A BIG BUNCH OF NYMPHS!
I'LL TELL HER, MR. TRUMP.

3/13/89

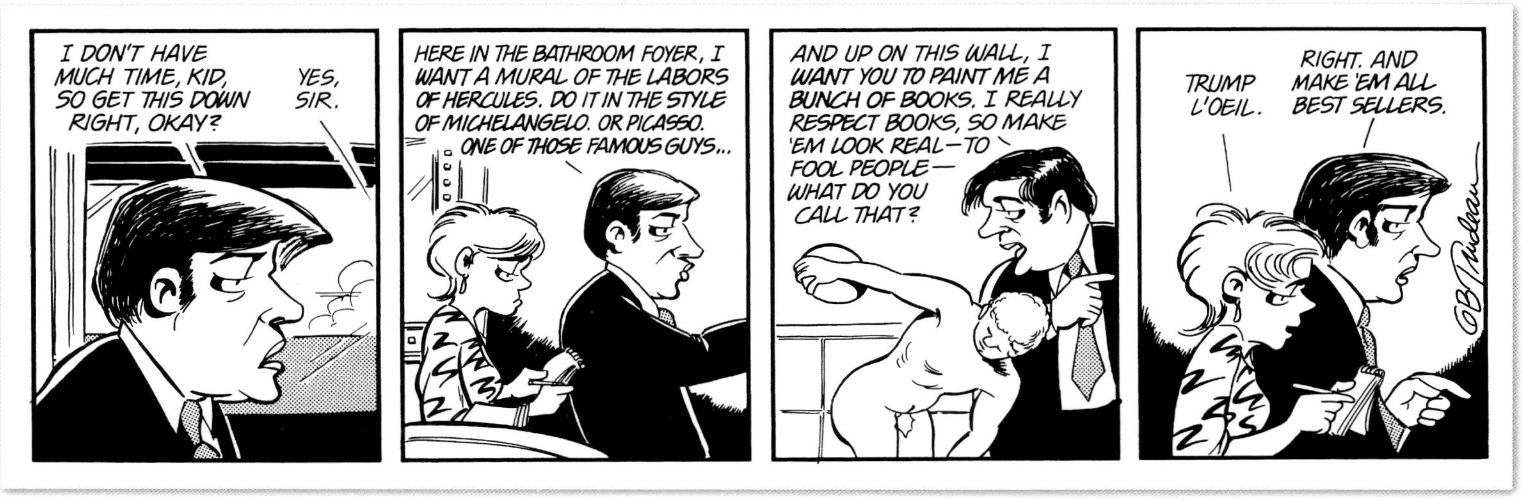
I DON'T HAVE MUCH TIME, KID, SO GET THIS DOWN RIGHT, OKAY?
YES, SIR.
HERE IN THE BATHROOM FOYER, I WANT A MURAL OF THE LABORS OF HERCULES. DO IT IN THE STYLE OF MICHELANGELO. OR PICASSO. ONE OF THOSE FAMOUS GUYS...
AND UP ON THIS WALL, I WANT YOU TO PAINT ME A BUNCH OF BOOKS. I REALLY RESPECT BOOKS, SO MAKE 'EM LOOK REAL—TO FOOL PEOPLE—WHAT DO YOU CALL THAT?
TRUMP L'OEIL.
RIGHT. AND MAKE 'EM ALL BEST SELLERS.

3/16/89

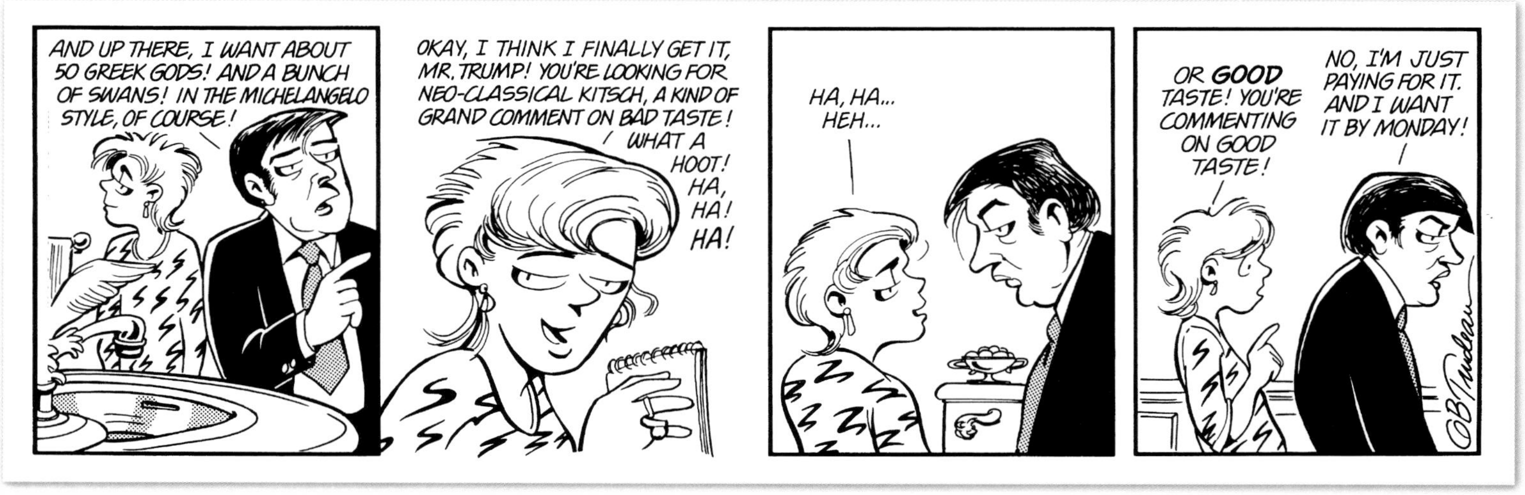
AND UP THERE, I WANT ABOUT 50 GREEK GODS! AND A BUNCH OF SWANS! IN THE MICHELANGELO STYLE, OF COURSE!
OKAY, I THINK I FINALLY GET IT, MR. TRUMP! YOU'RE LOOKING FOR NEO-CLASSICAL KITSCH, A KIND OF GRAND COMMENT ON BAD TASTE!
WHAT A HOOT! HA, HA! HA!
HA, HA... HEH...
OR **GOOD** TASTE! YOU'RE COMMENTING ON GOOD TASTE!
NO, I'M JUST PAYING FOR IT. AND I WANT IT BY MONDAY!

3/17/89

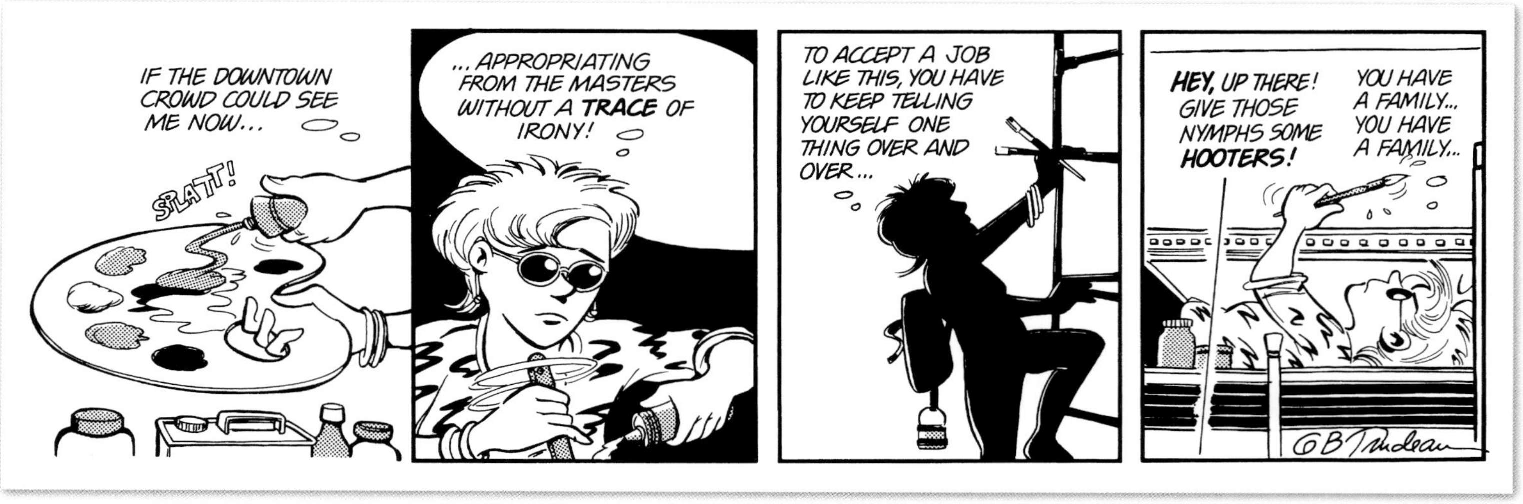
IF THE DOWNTOWN CROWD COULD SEE ME NOW...
SPLATT!
...APPROPRIATING FROM THE MASTERS WITHOUT A **TRACE** OF IRONY!
TO ACCEPT A JOB LIKE THIS, YOU HAVE TO KEEP TELLING YOURSELF ONE THING OVER AND OVER...
HEY, UP THERE! GIVE THOSE NYMPHS SOME **HOOTERS!**
YOU HAVE A FAMILY... YOU HAVE A FAMILY...

3/18/89

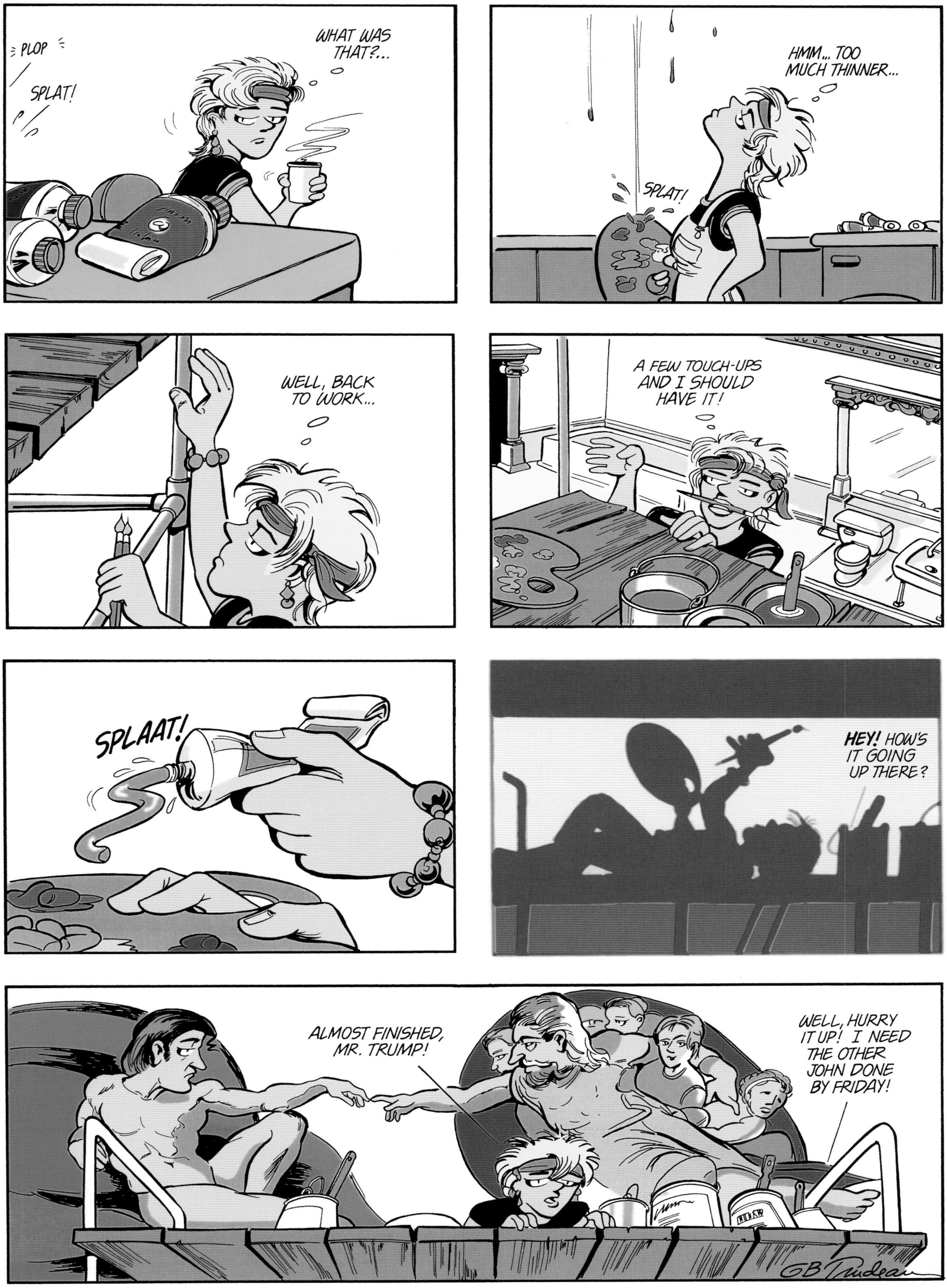
PLOP
SPLAT!
WHAT WAS THAT?...
HMM... TOO MUCH THINNER...
SPLAT!
WELL, BACK TO WORK...
A FEW TOUCH-UPS AND I SHOULD HAVE IT!
SPLAAT!
HEY! HOW'S IT GOING UP THERE?
ALMOST FINISHED, MR. TRUMP!
WELL, HURRY IT UP! I NEED THE OTHER JOHN DONE BY FRIDAY!
GB Trudeau

3/19/89

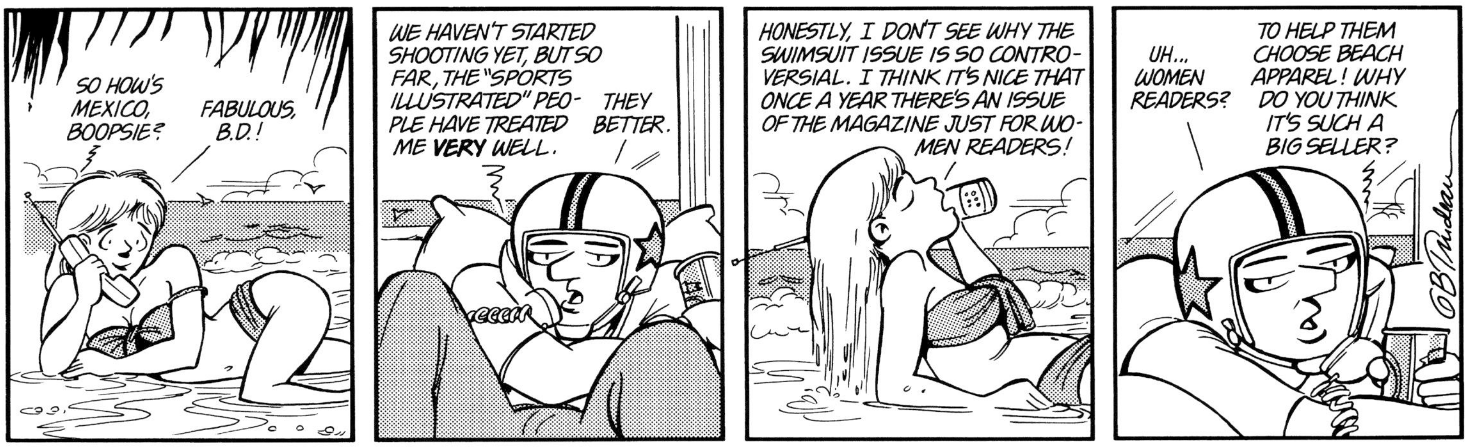
SO HOW'S MEXICO, BOOPSIE?
FABULOUS, B.D.!
WE HAVEN'T STARTED SHOOTING YET, BUT SO FAR, THE "SPORTS ILLUSTRATED" PEOPLE HAVE TREATED ME VERY WELL.
THEY BETTER.
HONESTLY, I DON'T SEE WHY THE SWIMSUIT ISSUE IS SO CONTROVERSIAL. I THINK IT'S NICE THAT ONCE A YEAR THERE'S AN ISSUE OF THE MAGAZINE JUST FOR WOMEN READERS!
UH... WOMEN READERS?
TO HELP THEM CHOOSE BEACH APPAREL! WHY DO YOU THINK IT'S SUCH A BIG SELLER?

1/23/89

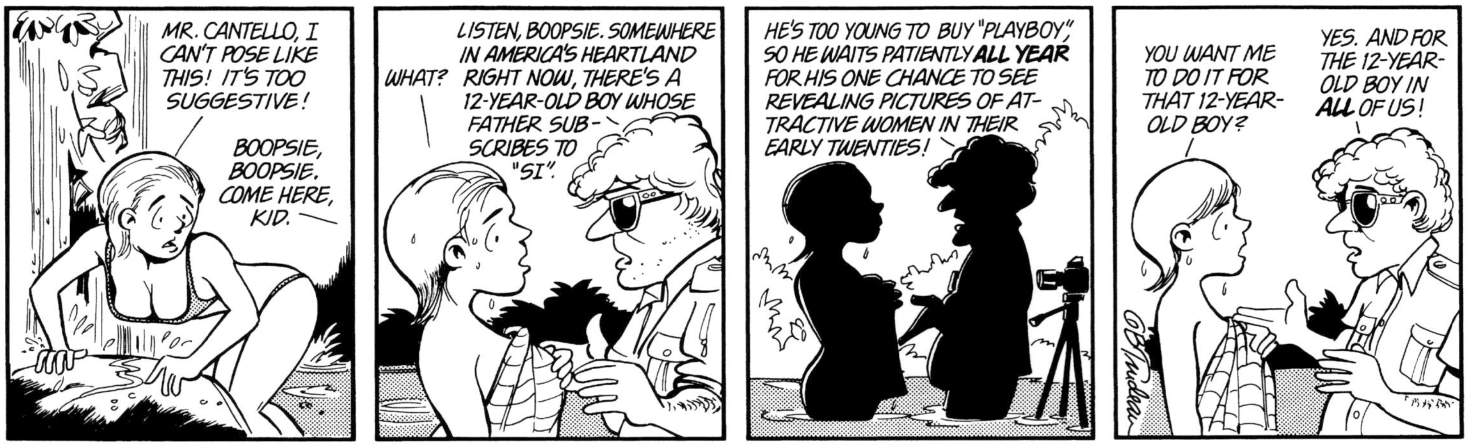
MR. CANTELLO, I CAN'T POSE LIKE THIS! IT'S TOO SUGGESTIVE!
BOOPSIE, BOOPSIE. COME HERE, KID.
WHAT?
LISTEN, BOOPSIE. SOMEWHERE IN AMERICA'S HEARTLAND RIGHT NOW, THERE'S A 12-YEAR-OLD BOY WHOSE FATHER SUBSCRIBES TO "SI".
HE'S TOO YOUNG TO BUY "PLAYBOY," SO HE WAITS PATIENTLY ALL YEAR FOR HIS ONE CHANCE TO SEE REVEALING PICTURES OF ATTRACTIVE WOMEN IN THEIR EARLY TWENTIES!
YOU WANT ME TO DO IT FOR THAT 12-YEAR-OLD BOY?
YES. AND FOR THE 12-YEAR-OLD BOY IN ALL OF US!

1/26/89

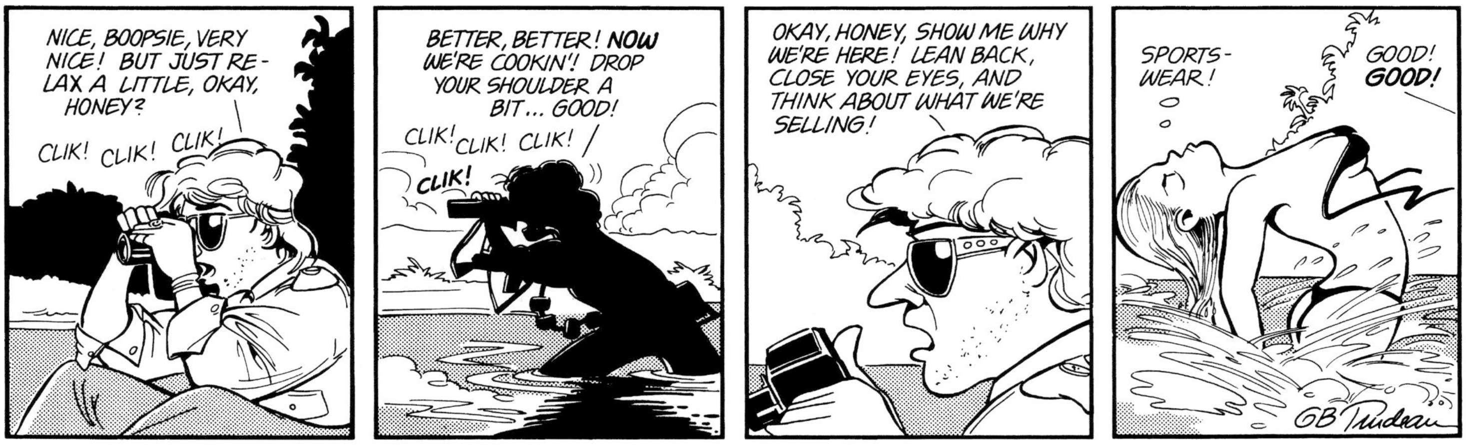
NICE, BOOPSIE, VERY NICE! BUT JUST RELAX A LITTLE, OKAY, HONEY?
CLIK! CLIK! CLIK!
BETTER, BETTER! NOW WE'RE COOKIN'! DROP YOUR SHOULDER A BIT... GOOD!
CLIK! CLIK! CLIK!
CLIK!
OKAY, HONEY, SHOW ME WHY WE'RE HERE! LEAN BACK, CLOSE YOUR EYES, AND THINK ABOUT WHAT WE'RE SELLING!
SPORTSWEAR!
GOOD! GOOD!

1/27/89

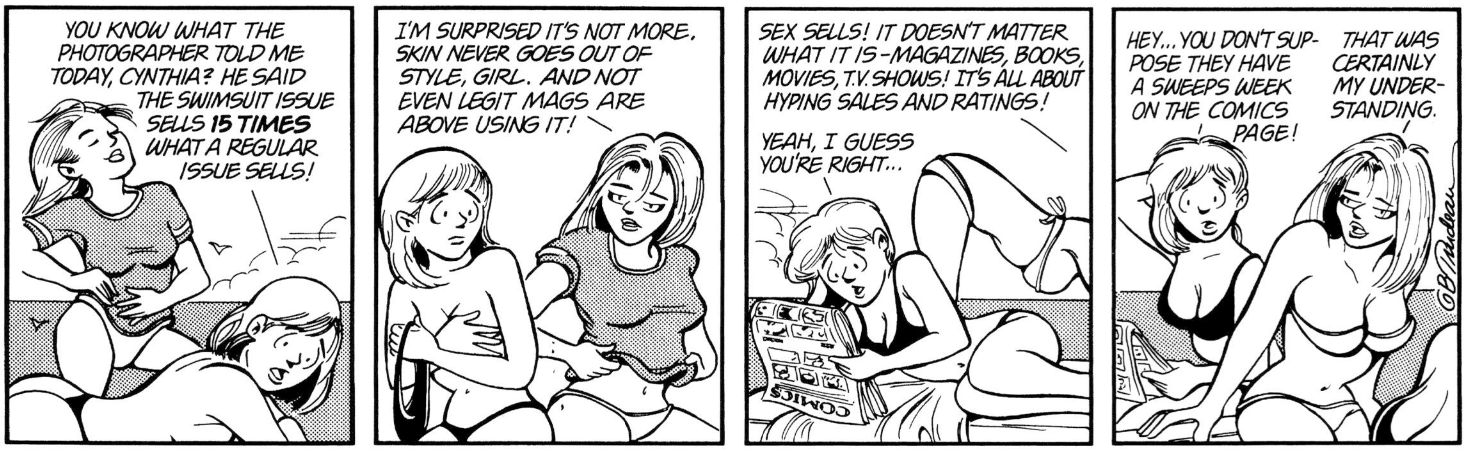
YOU KNOW WHAT THE PHOTOGRAPHER TOLD ME TODAY, CYNTHIA? HE SAID THE SWIMSUIT ISSUE SELLS 15 TIMES WHAT A REGULAR ISSUE SELLS!
I'M SURPRISED IT'S NOT MORE. SKIN NEVER GOES OUT OF STYLE, GIRL. AND NOT EVEN LEGIT MAGS ARE ABOVE USING IT!
SEX SELLS! IT DOESN'T MATTER WHAT IT IS – MAGAZINES, BOOKS, MOVIES, T.V. SHOWS! IT'S ALL ABOUT HYPING SALES AND RATINGS!
YEAH, I GUESS YOU'RE RIGHT...
COMICS
HEY... YOU DON'T SUPPOSE THEY HAVE A SWEEPS WEEK ON THE COMICS PAGE!
THAT WAS CERTAINLY MY UNDERSTANDING.

1/28/89

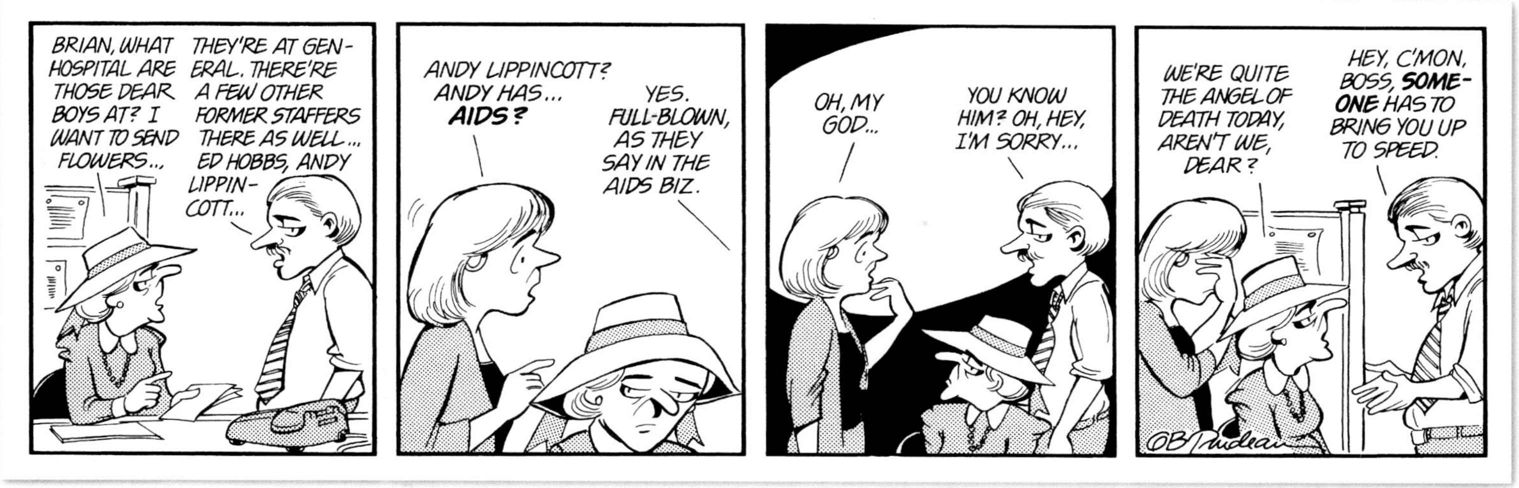
BRIAN, WHAT HOSPITAL ARE THOSE DEAR BOYS AT? I WANT TO SEND FLOWERS...
THEY'RE AT GENERAL. THERE'RE A FEW OTHER FORMER STAFFERS THERE AS WELL... ED HOBBS, ANDY LIPPINCOTT...
ANDY LIPPINCOTT? ANDY HAS... **AIDS?**
YES. FULL-BLOWN, AS THEY SAY IN THE AIDS BIZ.
OH, MY GOD...
YOU KNOW HIM? OH, HEY, I'M SORRY...
WE'RE QUITE THE ANGEL OF DEATH TODAY, AREN'T WE, DEAR?
HEY, C'MON, BOSS, **SOMEONE** HAS TO BRING YOU UP TO SPEED.

4/3/89

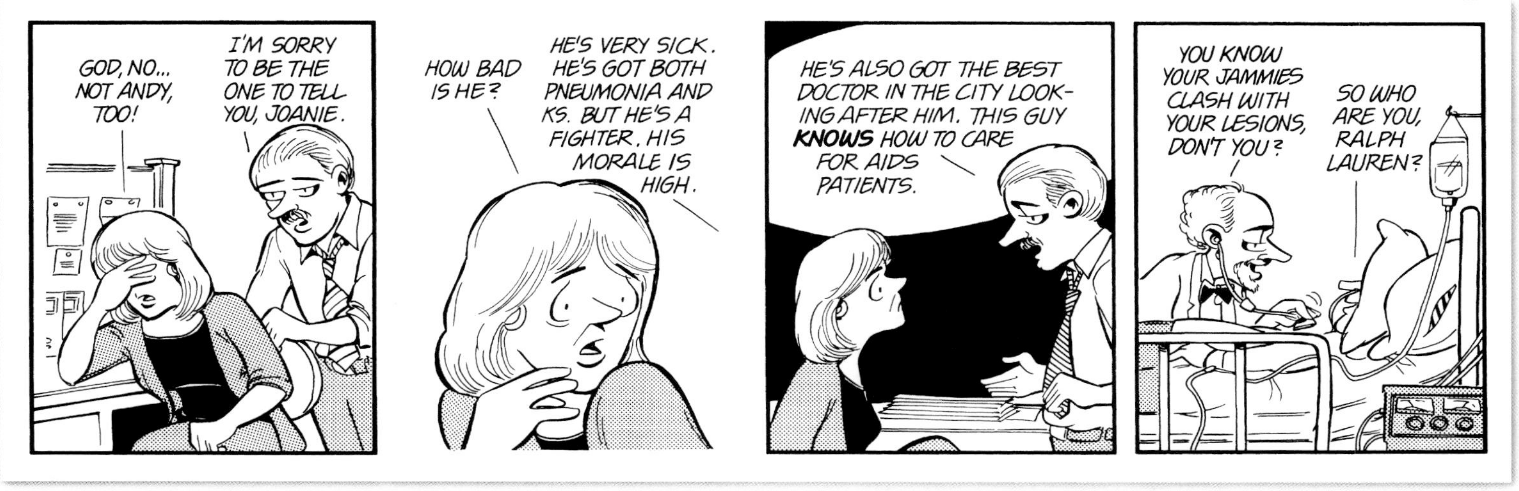
GOD, NO... NOT ANDY, TOO!
I'M SORRY TO BE THE ONE TO TELL YOU, JOANIE.
HOW BAD IS HE?
HE'S VERY SICK. HE'S GOT BOTH PNEUMONIA AND KS. BUT HE'S A FIGHTER. HIS MORALE IS HIGH.
HE'S ALSO GOT THE BEST DOCTOR IN THE CITY LOOKING AFTER HIM. THIS GUY **KNOWS** HOW TO CARE FOR AIDS PATIENTS.
YOU KNOW YOUR JAMMIES CLASH WITH YOUR LESIONS, DON'T YOU?
SO WHO ARE YOU, RALPH LAUREN?

4/4/89

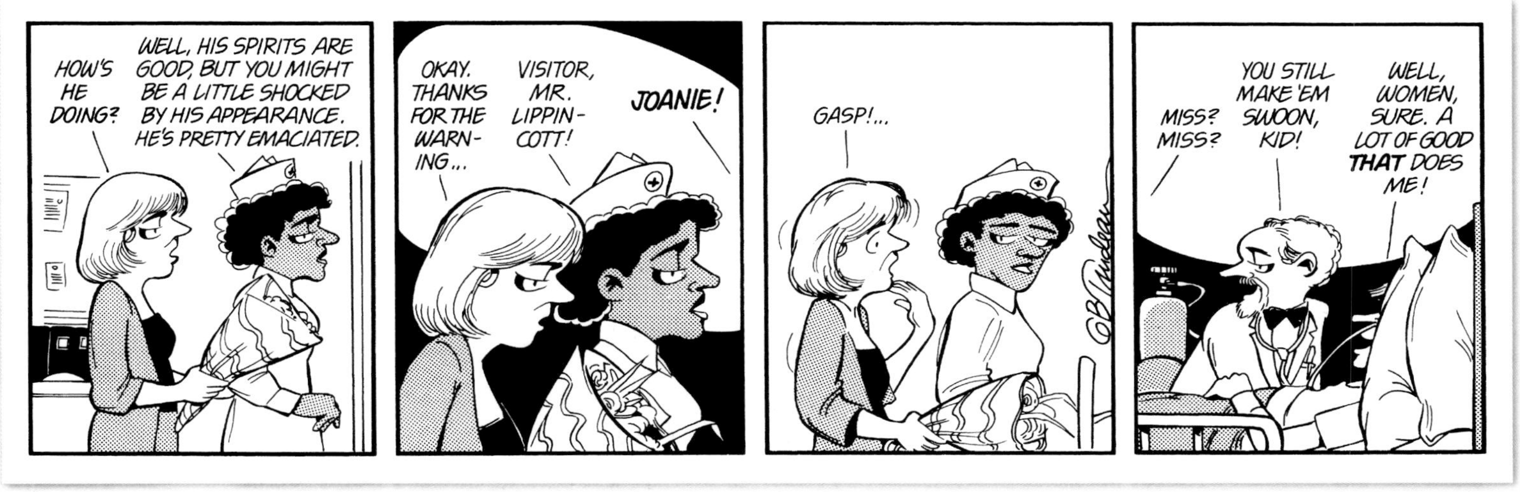
HOW'S HE DOING?
WELL, HIS SPIRITS ARE GOOD, BUT YOU MIGHT BE A LITTLE SHOCKED BY HIS APPEARANCE. HE'S PRETTY EMACIATED.
OKAY. THANKS FOR THE WARNING...
VISITOR, MR. LIPPINCOTT!
JOANIE!
GASP!...
MISS? MISS?
YOU STILL MAKE 'EM SWOON, KID!
WELL, WOMEN, SURE. A LOT OF GOOD **THAT** DOES ME!

4/5/89

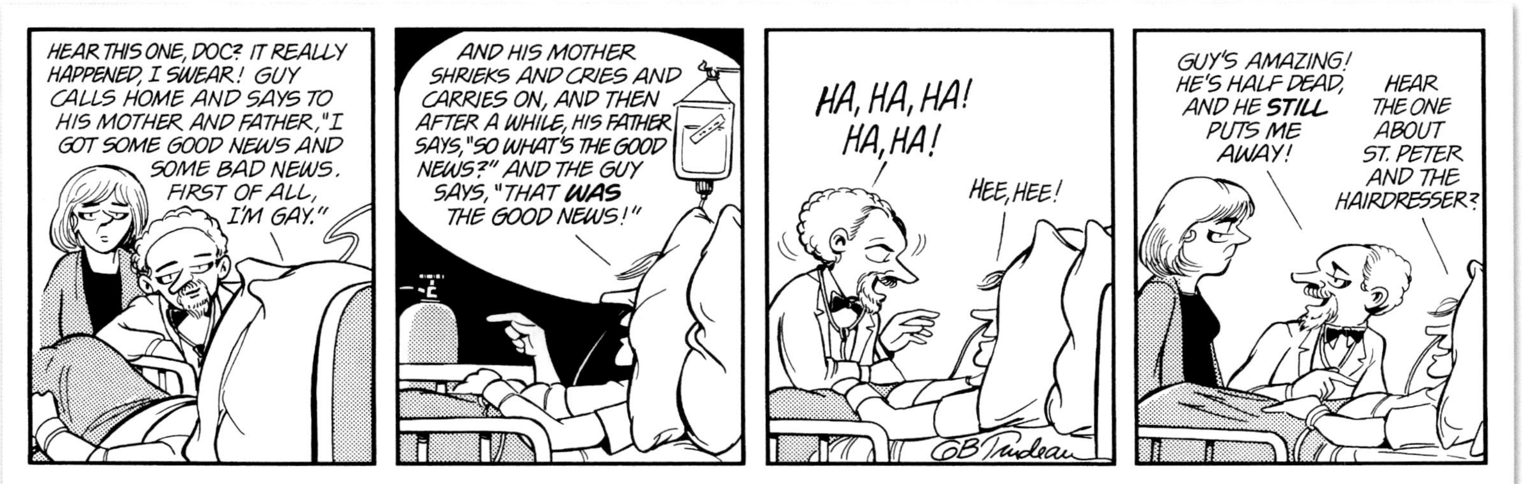
HEAR THIS ONE, DOC? IT REALLY HAPPENED, I SWEAR! GUY CALLS HOME AND SAYS TO HIS MOTHER AND FATHER, "I GOT SOME GOOD NEWS AND SOME BAD NEWS. FIRST OF ALL, I'M GAY."
AND HIS MOTHER SHRIEKS AND CRIES AND CARRIES ON, AND THEN AFTER A WHILE, HIS FATHER SAYS, "SO WHAT'S THE GOOD NEWS?" AND THE GUY SAYS, "THAT **WAS** THE GOOD NEWS!"
HA, HA, HA! HA, HA!
HEE, HEE!
GUY'S AMAZING! HE'S HALF DEAD, AND HE **STILL** PUTS ME AWAY!
HEAR THE ONE ABOUT ST. PETER AND THE HAIRDRESSER?

4/7/89

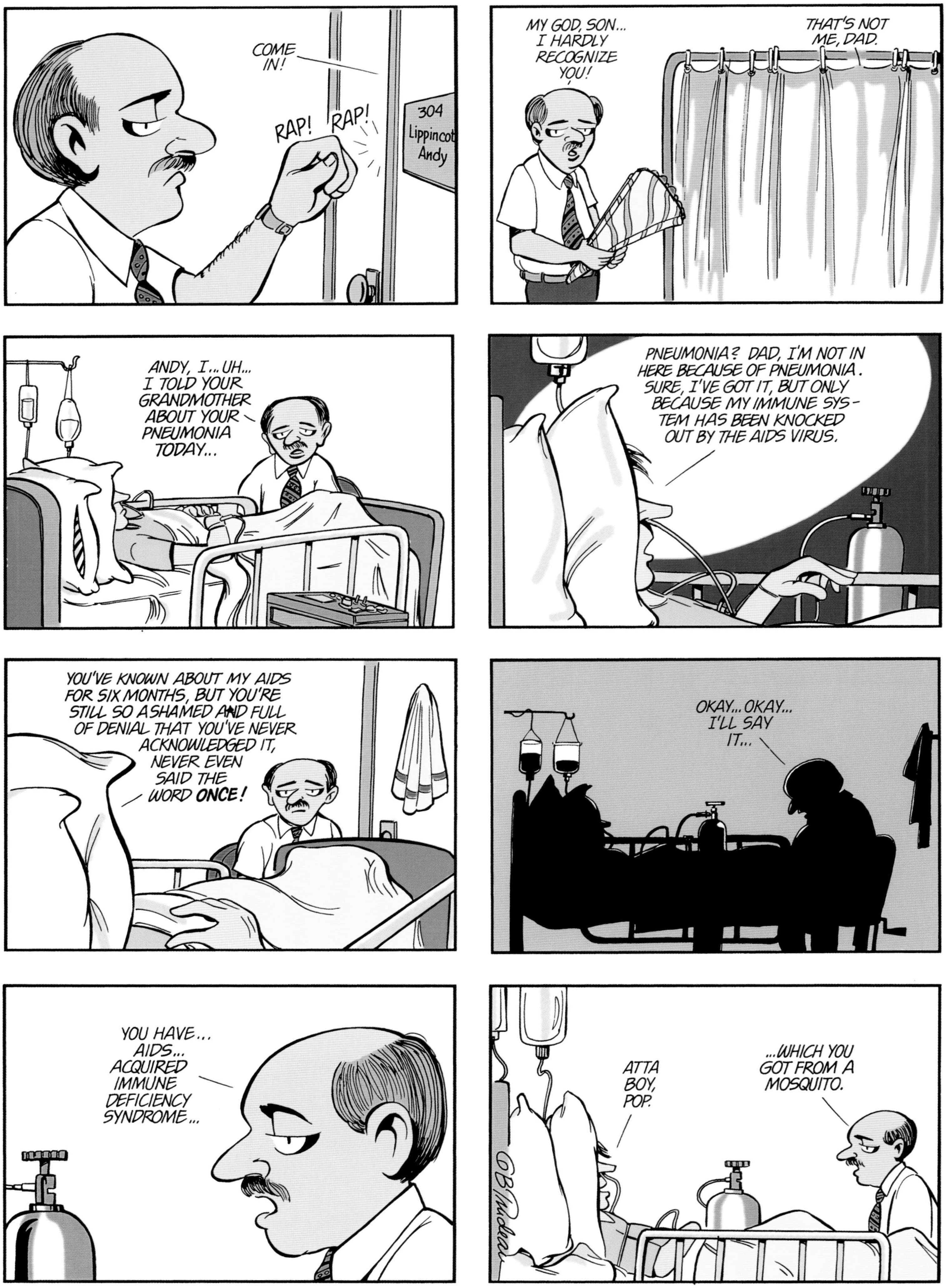
COME IN!
RAP! RAP!
304 Lippincott Andy
MY GOD, SON... I HARDLY RECOGNIZE YOU!
THAT'S NOT ME, DAD.
ANDY, I... UH... I TOLD YOUR GRANDMOTHER ABOUT YOUR PNEUMONIA TODAY...
PNEUMONIA? DAD, I'M NOT IN HERE BECAUSE OF PNEUMONIA. SURE, I'VE GOT IT, BUT ONLY BECAUSE MY IMMUNE SYS-TEM HAS BEEN KNOCKED OUT BY THE AIDS VIRUS.
YOU'VE KNOWN ABOUT MY AIDS FOR SIX MONTHS, BUT YOU'RE STILL SO ASHAMED AND FULL OF DENIAL THAT YOU'VE NEVER ACKNOWLEDGED IT, NEVER EVEN SAID THE WORD ONCE!
OKAY... OKAY... I'LL SAY IT...
YOU HAVE... AIDS... ACQUIRED IMMUNE DEFICIENCY SYNDROME...
ATTA BOY, POP.
...WHICH YOU GOT FROM A MOSQUITO.
GBTrudeau

4/30/89

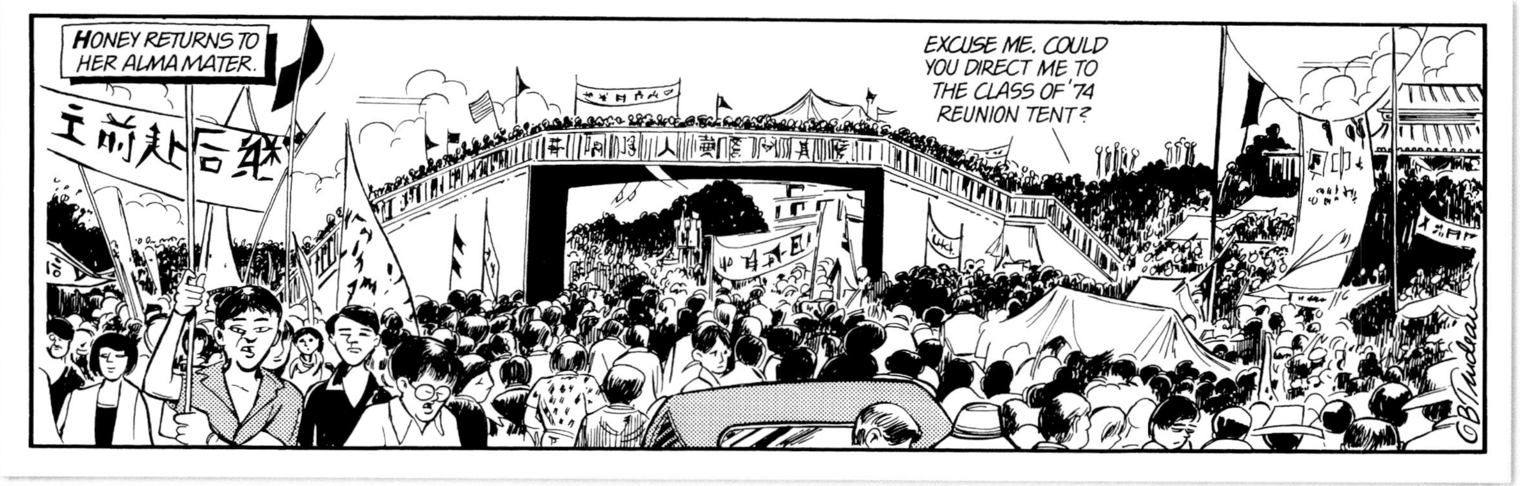
HONEY RETURNS TO HER ALMA MATER.
EXCUSE ME. COULD YOU DIRECT ME TO THE CLASS OF '74 REUNION TENT?
©B Trudeau

5/30/89

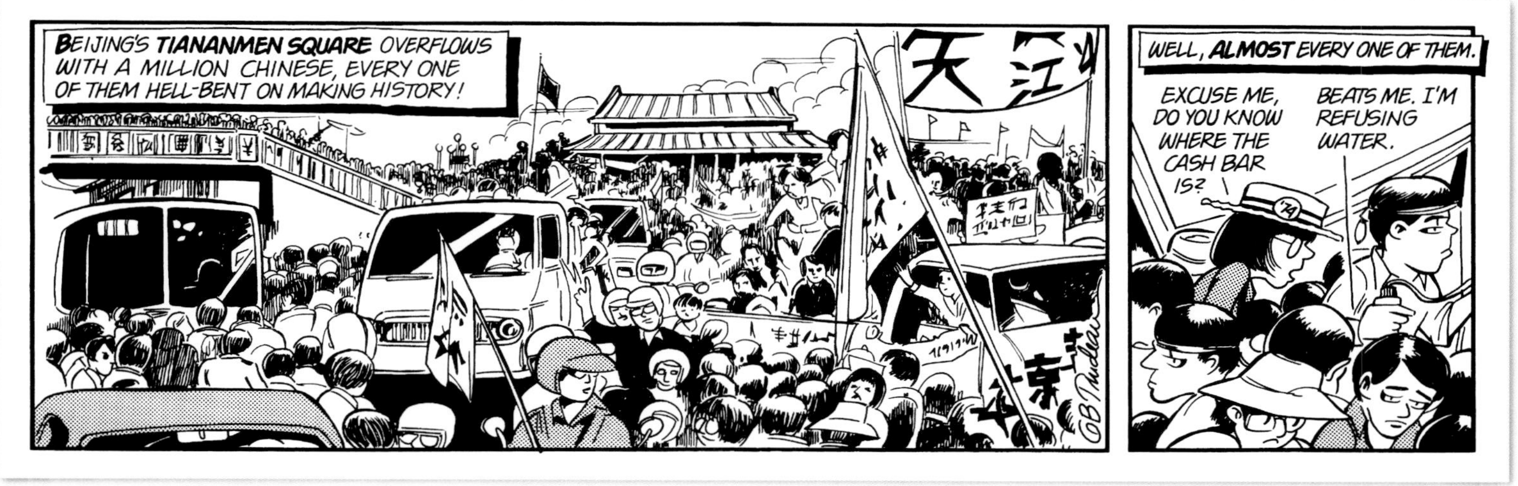
BEIJING'S TIANANMEN SQUARE OVERFLOWS WITH A MILLION CHINESE, EVERY ONE OF THEM HELL-BENT ON MAKING HISTORY!
©B Trudeau
WELL, ALMOST EVERY ONE OF THEM.
EXCUSE ME, DO YOU KNOW WHERE THE CASH BAR IS?
BEATS ME. I'M REFUSING WATER.

5/31/89

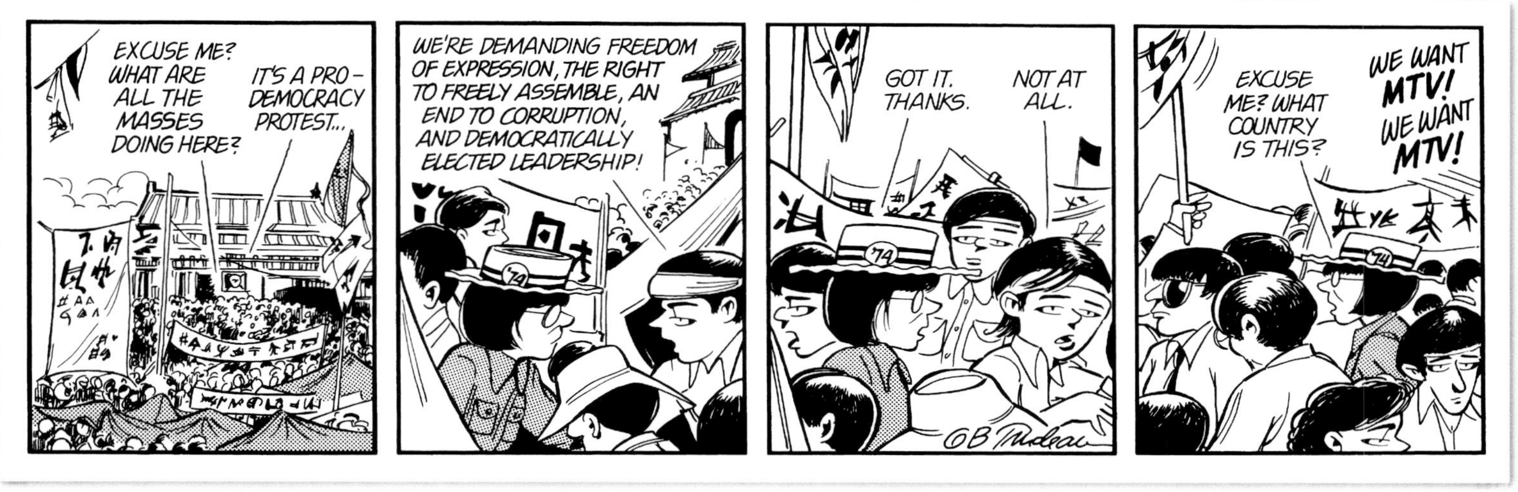
EXCUSE ME? WHAT ARE ALL THE MASSES DOING HERE?
IT'S A PRO-DEMOCRACY PROTEST...
WE'RE DEMANDING FREEDOM OF EXPRESSION, THE RIGHT TO FREELY ASSEMBLE, AN END TO CORRUPTION, AND DEMOCRATICALLY ELECTED LEADERSHIP!
GOT IT. THANKS.
NOT AT ALL.
©B Trudeau
EXCUSE ME? WHAT COUNTRY IS THIS?
WE WANT MTV! WE WANT MTV!

6/1/89

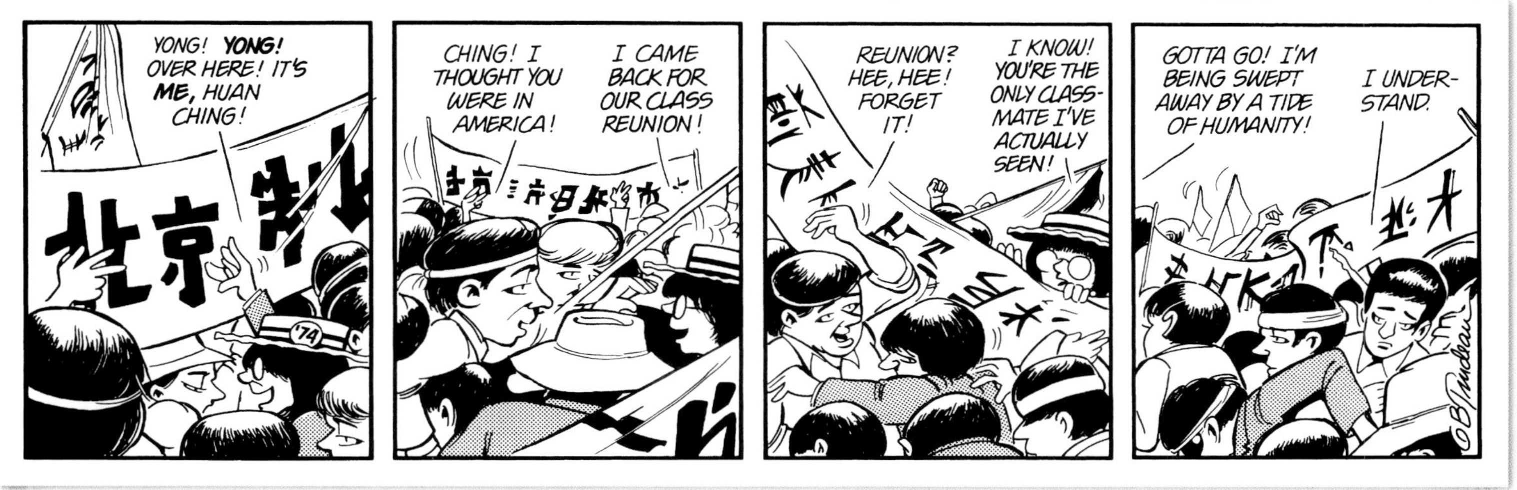
YONG! YONG! OVER HERE! IT'S ME, HUAN CHING!
CHING! I THOUGHT YOU WERE IN AMERICA!
I CAME BACK FOR OUR CLASS REUNION!
REUNION? HEE, HEE! FORGET IT!
I KNOW! YOU'RE THE ONLY CLASSMATE I'VE ACTUALLY SEEN!
GOTTA GO! I'M BEING SWEPT AWAY BY A TIDE OF HUMANITY!
I UNDERSTAND.
©B Trudeau

6/2/89

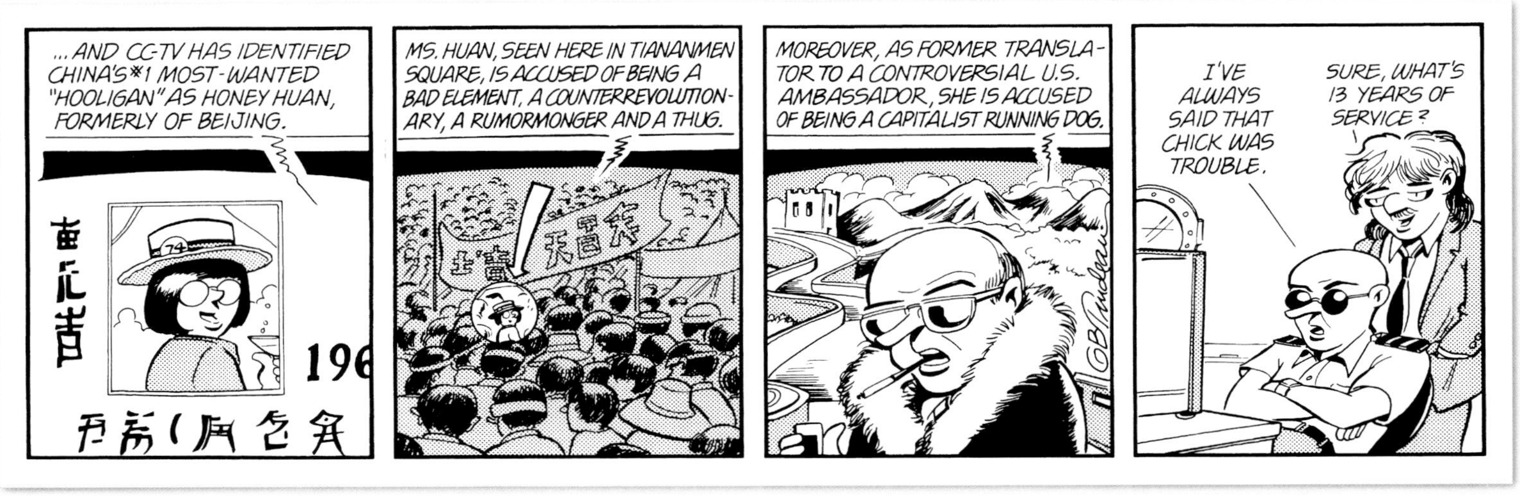
...AND CC-TV HAS IDENTIFIED CHINA'S #1 MOST-WANTED "HOOLIGAN" AS HONEY HUAN, FORMERLY OF BEIJING.
196
MS. HUAN, SEEN HERE IN TIANANMEN SQUARE, IS ACCUSED OF BEING A BAD ELEMENT, A COUNTERREVOLUTIONARY, A RUMORMONGER AND A THUG.
MOREOVER, AS FORMER TRANSLATOR TO A CONTROVERSIAL U.S. AMBASSADOR, SHE IS ACCUSED OF BEING A CAPITALIST RUNNING DOG.
I'VE ALWAYS SAID THAT CHICK WAS TROUBLE.
SURE, WHAT'S 13 YEARS OF SERVICE?

7/13/89

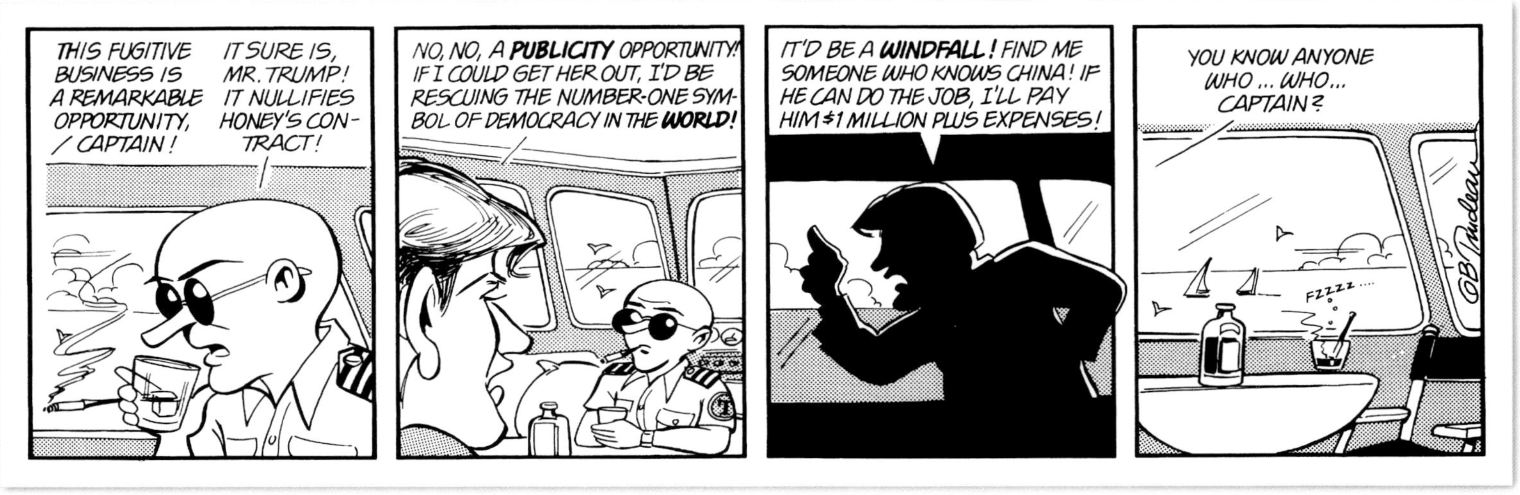
THIS FUGITIVE BUSINESS IS A REMARKABLE OPPORTUNITY, CAPTAIN!
IT SURE IS, MR. TRUMP! IT NULLIFIES HONEY'S CONTRACT!
NO, NO, A PUBLICITY OPPORTUNITY! IF I COULD GET HER OUT, I'D BE RESCUING THE NUMBER-ONE SYMBOL OF DEMOCRACY IN THE WORLD!
IT'D BE A WINDFALL! FIND ME SOMEONE WHO KNOWS CHINA! IF HE CAN DO THE JOB, I'LL PAY HIM $1 MILLION PLUS EXPENSES!
YOU KNOW ANYONE WHO ... WHO... CAPTAIN?
FZZZZ....

7/17/89

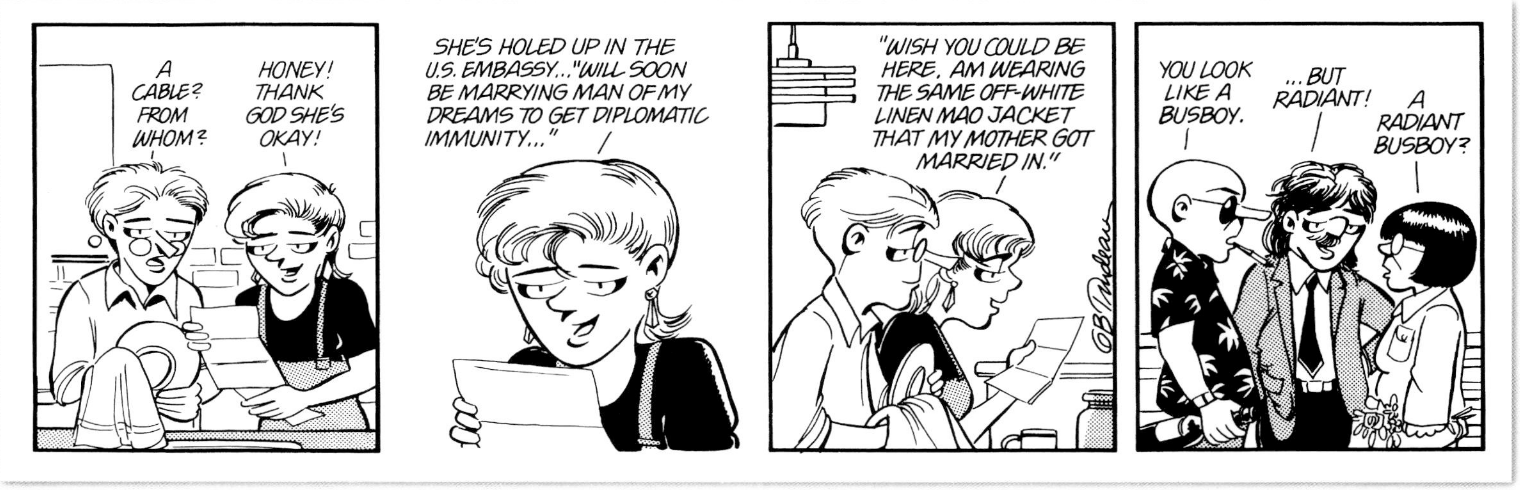
A CABLE? FROM WHOM?
HONEY! THANK GOD SHE'S OKAY!
SHE'S HOLED UP IN THE U.S. EMBASSY..."WILL SOON BE MARRYING MAN OF MY DREAMS TO GET DIPLOMATIC IMMUNITY..."
"WISH YOU COULD BE HERE. AM WEARING THE SAME OFF-WHITE LINEN MAO JACKET THAT MY MOTHER GOT MARRIED IN."
YOU LOOK LIKE A BUSBOY.
...BUT RADIANT!
A RADIANT BUSBOY?

7/24/89

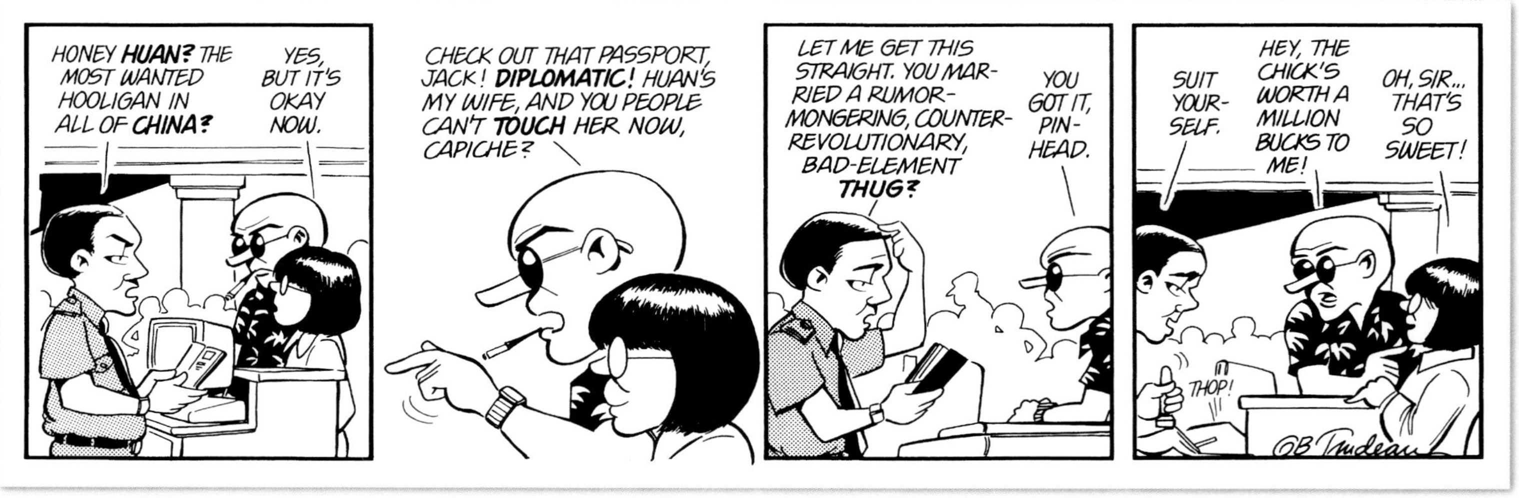
HONEY HUAN? THE MOST WANTED HOOLIGAN IN ALL OF CHINA?
YES, BUT IT'S OKAY NOW.
CHECK OUT THAT PASSPORT, JACK! DIPLOMATIC! HUAN'S MY WIFE, AND YOU PEOPLE CAN'T TOUCH HER NOW, CAPICHE?
LET ME GET THIS STRAIGHT. YOU MARRIED A RUMOR-MONGERING, COUNTER-REVOLUTIONARY, BAD-ELEMENT THUG?
YOU GOT IT, PIN-HEAD.
SUIT YOURSELF.
THOP!
HEY, THE CHICK'S WORTH A MILLION BUCKS TO ME!
OH, SIR... THAT'S SO SWEET!

7/26/89

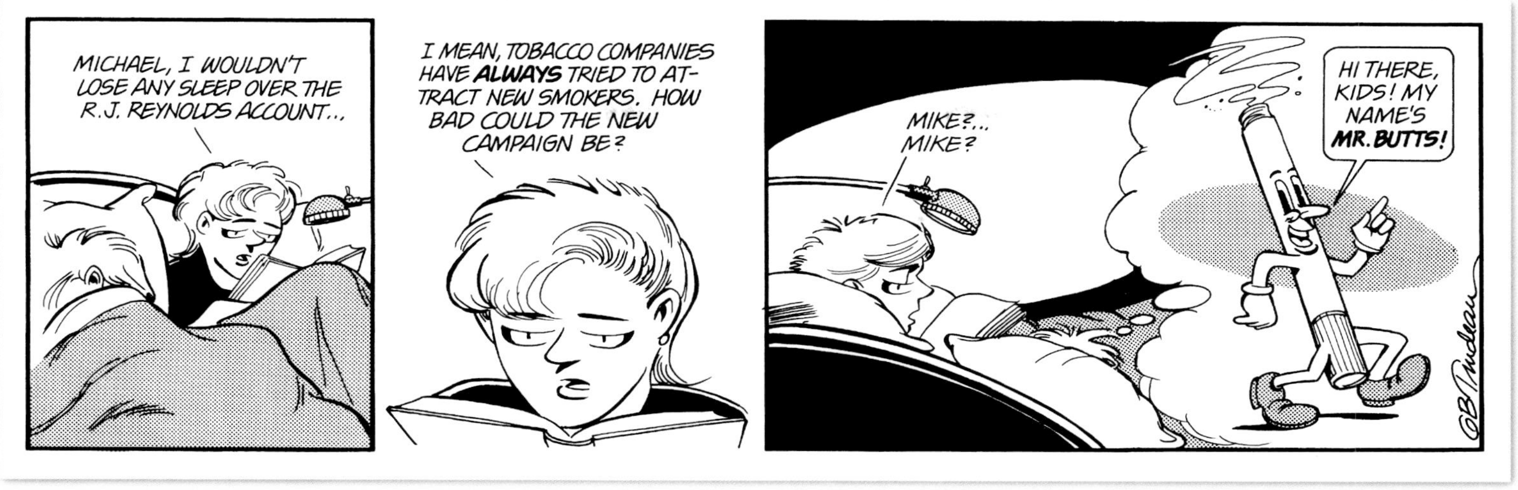

MICHAEL, I WOULDN'T LOSE ANY SLEEP OVER THE R.J. REYNOLDS ACCOUNT...
I MEAN, TOBACCO COMPANIES HAVE ALWAYS TRIED TO ATTRACT NEW SMOKERS. HOW BAD COULD THE NEW CAMPAIGN BE?
MIKE?... MIKE?
HI THERE, KIDS! MY NAME'S MR. BUTTS!

4/19/89

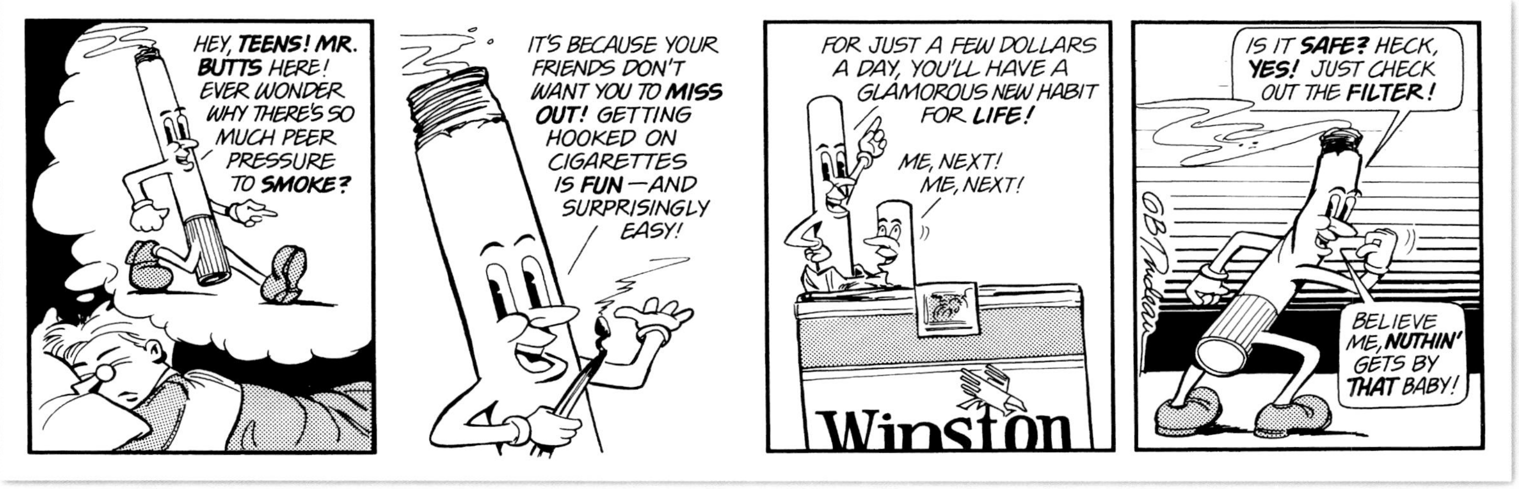

HEY, TEENS! MR. BUTTS HERE! EVER WONDER WHY THERE'S SO MUCH PEER PRESSURE TO SMOKE?
IT'S BECAUSE YOUR FRIENDS DON'T WANT YOU TO MISS OUT! GETTING HOOKED ON CIGARETTES IS FUN—AND SURPRISINGLY EASY!
FOR JUST A FEW DOLLARS A DAY, YOU'LL HAVE A GLAMOROUS NEW HABIT FOR LIFE!
ME, NEXT! ME, NEXT!
Winston
IS IT SAFE? HECK, YES! JUST CHECK OUT THE FILTER!
BELIEVE ME, NUTHIN' GETS BY THAT BABY!

4/20/89

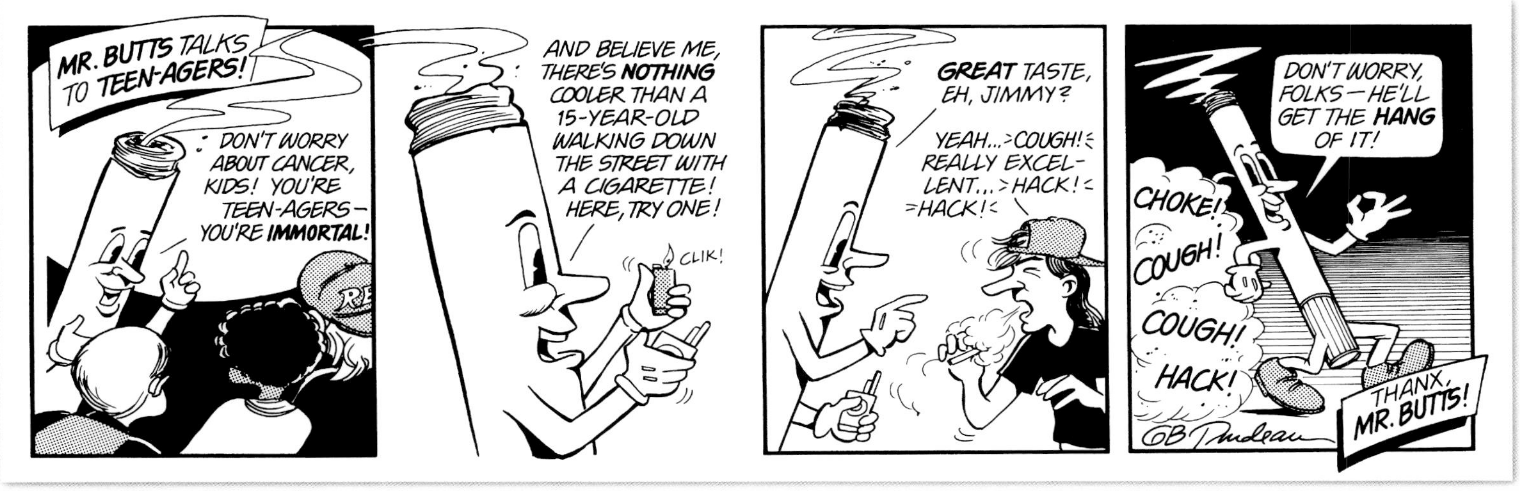

MR. BUTTS TALKS TO TEEN-AGERS!
DON'T WORRY ABOUT CANCER, KIDS! YOU'RE TEEN-AGERS—YOU'RE IMMORTAL!
AND BELIEVE ME, THERE'S NOTHING COOLER THAN A 15-YEAR-OLD WALKING DOWN THE STREET WITH A CIGARETTE! HERE, TRY ONE!
CLIK!
GREAT TASTE, EH, JIMMY?
YEAH... >COUGH!< REALLY EXCEL-LENT... >HACK!< >HACK!<
DON'T WORRY, FOLKS—HE'LL GET THE HANG OF IT!
CHOKE! COUGH! COUGH! HACK!
THANX, MR. BUTTS!

4/21/89

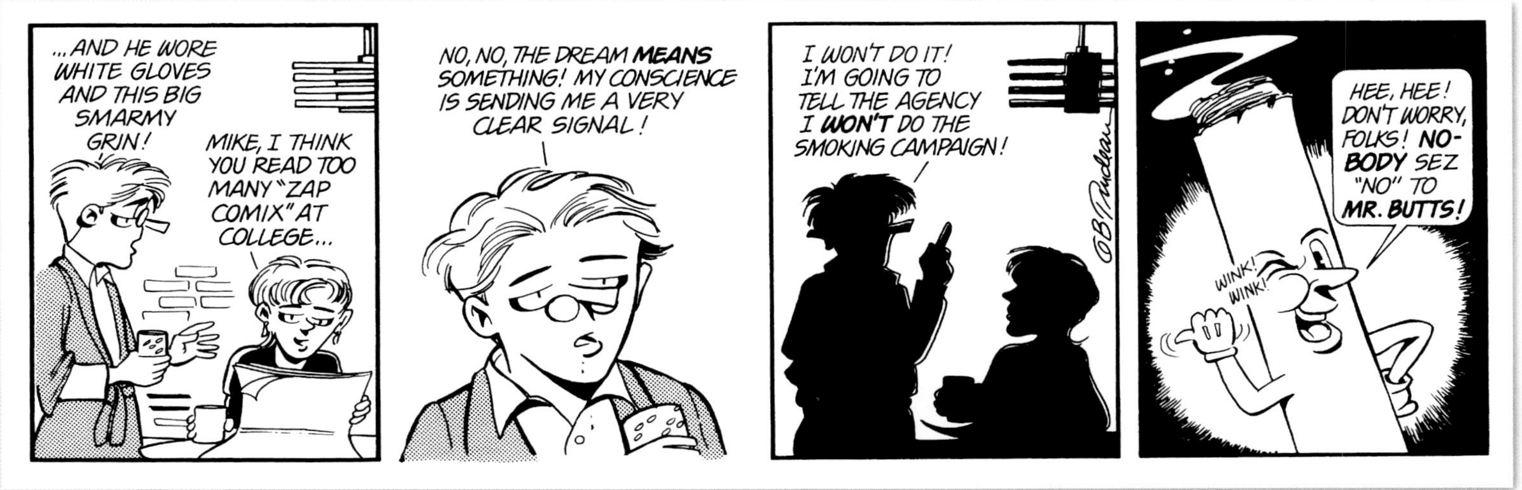

...AND HE WORE WHITE GLOVES AND THIS BIG SMARMY GRIN!
MIKE, I THINK YOU READ TOO MANY "ZAP COMIX" AT COLLEGE...
NO, NO, THE DREAM MEANS SOMETHING! MY CONSCIENCE IS SENDING ME A VERY CLEAR SIGNAL!
I WON'T DO IT! I'M GOING TO TELL THE AGENCY I WON'T DO THE SMOKING CAMPAIGN!
HEE, HEE! DON'T WORRY, FOLKS! NOBODY SEZ "NO" TO MR. BUTTS!
WINK! WINK!

4/22/89

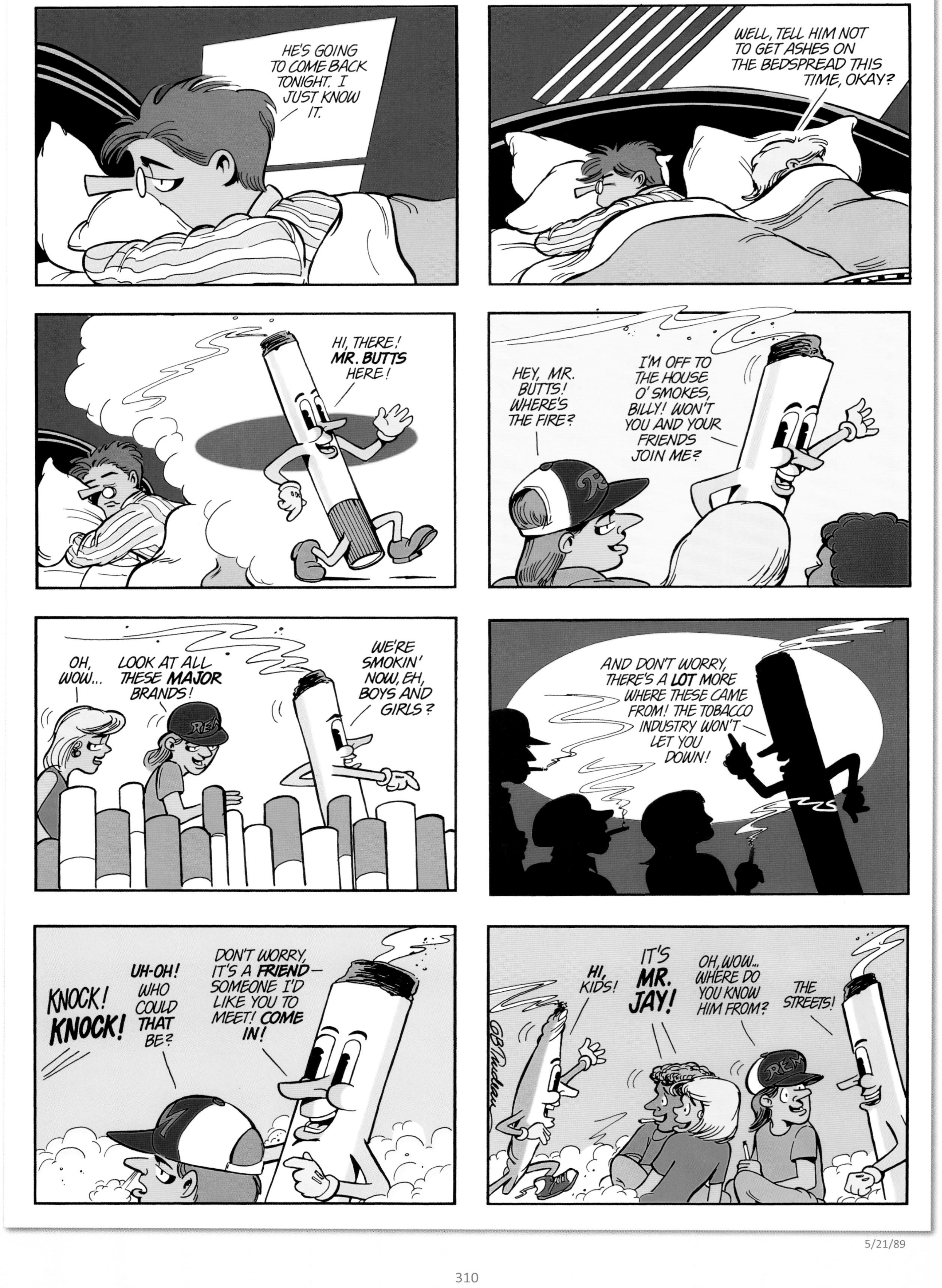
HE'S GOING TO COME BACK TONIGHT. I JUST KNOW IT.
WELL, TELL HIM NOT TO GET ASHES ON THE BEDSPREAD THIS TIME, OKAY?
HI, THERE! MR. BUTTS HERE!
HEY, MR. BUTTS! WHERE'S THE FIRE?
I'M OFF TO THE HOUSE O' SMOKES, BILLY! WON'T YOU AND YOUR FRIENDS JOIN ME?
OH, WOW...
LOOK AT ALL THESE MAJOR BRANDS!
WE'RE SMOKIN' NOW, EH, BOYS AND GIRLS?
AND DON'T WORRY, THERE'S A LOT MORE WHERE THESE CAME FROM! THE TOBACCO INDUSTRY WON'T LET YOU DOWN!
KNOCK! KNOCK!
UH-OH! WHO COULD THAT BE?
DON'T WORRY, IT'S A FRIEND— SOMEONE I'D LIKE YOU TO MEET! COME IN!
HI, KIDS!
IT'S MR. JAY!
OH, WOW... WHERE DO YOU KNOW HIM FROM?
THE STREETS!

5/21/89

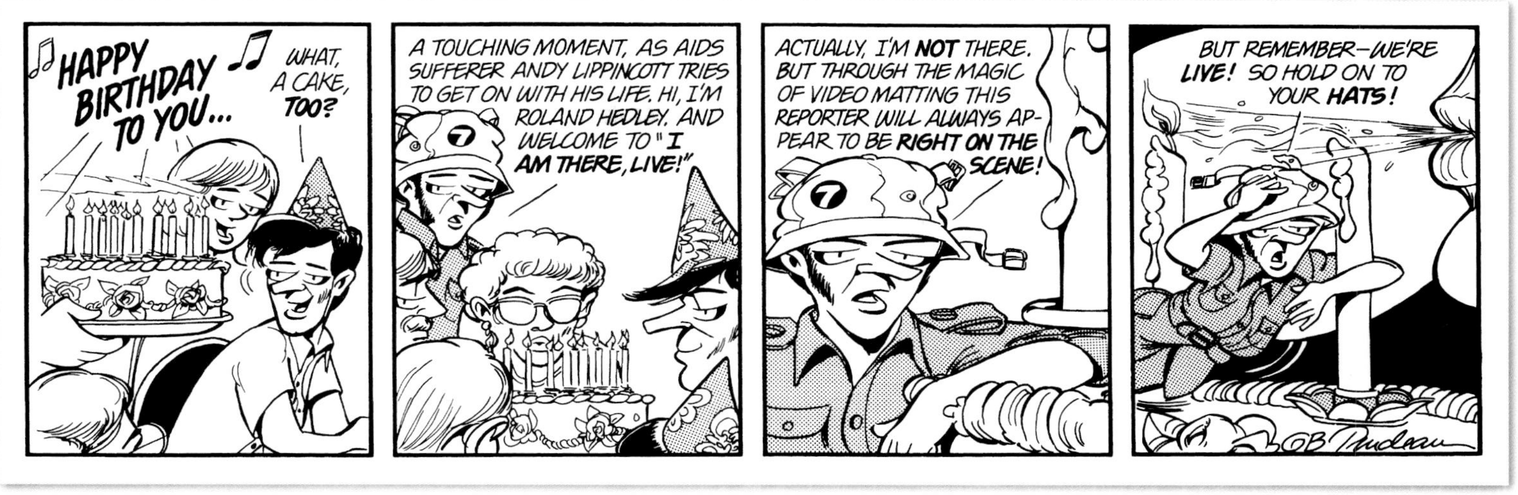
HAPPY BIRTHDAY TO YOU...
WHAT, A CAKE, TOO?
A TOUCHING MOMENT, AS AIDS SUFFERER ANDY LIPPINCOTT TRIES TO GET ON WITH HIS LIFE. HI, I'M ROLAND HEDLEY. AND WELCOME TO "I AM THERE, LIVE!"
ACTUALLY, I'M NOT THERE. BUT THROUGH THE MAGIC OF VIDEO MATTING THIS REPORTER WILL ALWAYS APPEAR TO BE RIGHT ON THE SCENE!
BUT REMEMBER—WE'RE LIVE! SO HOLD ON TO YOUR HATS!
GB Trudeau

8/14/89

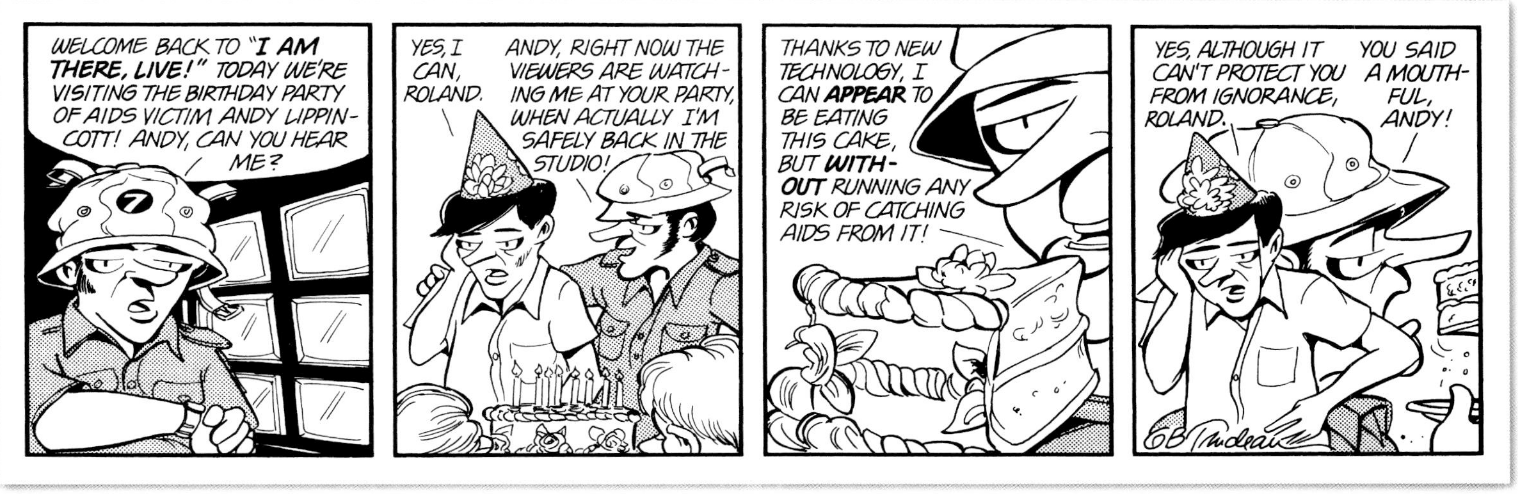
WELCOME BACK TO "I AM THERE, LIVE!" TODAY WE'RE VISITING THE BIRTHDAY PARTY OF AIDS VICTIM ANDY LIPPINCOTT! ANDY, CAN YOU HEAR ME?
YES, I CAN, ROLAND.
ANDY, RIGHT NOW THE VIEWERS ARE WATCHING ME AT YOUR PARTY, WHEN ACTUALLY I'M SAFELY BACK IN THE STUDIO!
THANKS TO NEW TECHNOLOGY, I CAN APPEAR TO BE EATING THIS CAKE, BUT WITHOUT RUNNING ANY RISK OF CATCHING AIDS FROM IT!
YES, ALTHOUGH IT CAN'T PROTECT YOU FROM IGNORANCE, ROLAND.
YOU SAID A MOUTHFUL, ANDY!
GB Trudeau

8/15/89

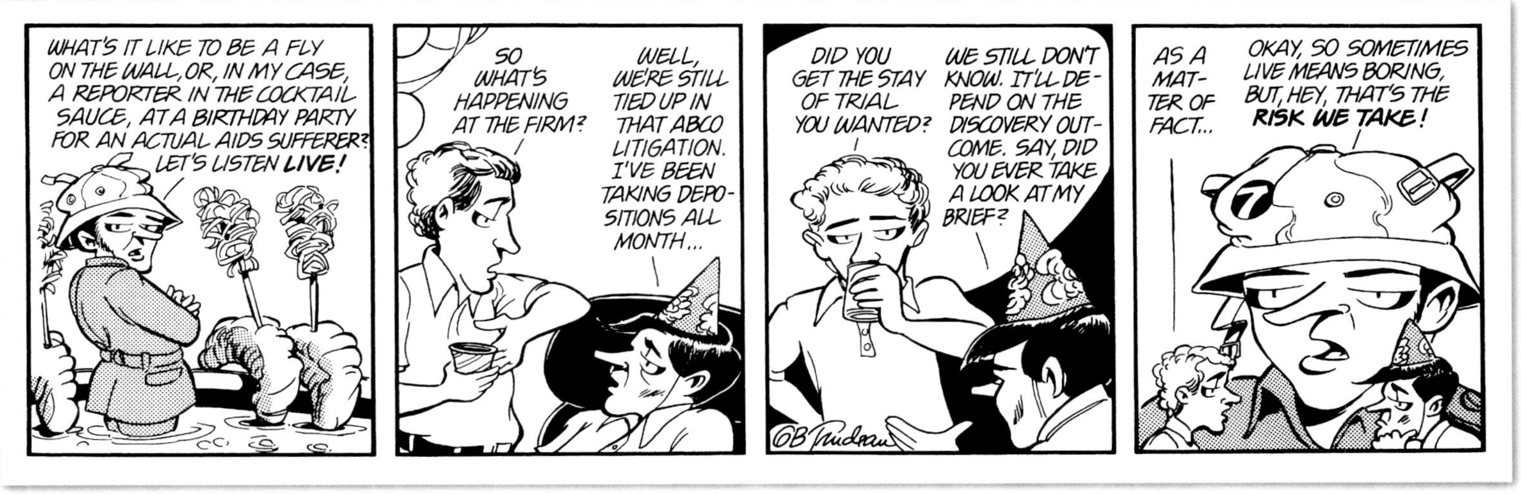
WHAT'S IT LIKE TO BE A FLY ON THE WALL, OR, IN MY CASE, A REPORTER IN THE COCKTAIL SAUCE, AT A BIRTHDAY PARTY FOR AN ACTUAL AIDS SUFFERER? LET'S LISTEN LIVE!
SO WHAT'S HAPPENING AT THE FIRM?
WELL, WE'RE STILL TIED UP IN THAT ABCO LITIGATION. I'VE BEEN TAKING DEPOSITIONS ALL MONTH...
DID YOU GET THE STAY OF TRIAL YOU WANTED?
WE STILL DON'T KNOW. IT'LL DEPEND ON THE DISCOVERY OUTCOME. SAY, DID YOU EVER TAKE A LOOK AT MY BRIEF?
GB Trudeau
AS A MATTER OF FACT...
OKAY, SO SOMETIMES LIVE MEANS BORING, BUT, HEY, THAT'S THE RISK WE TAKE!

8/16/89

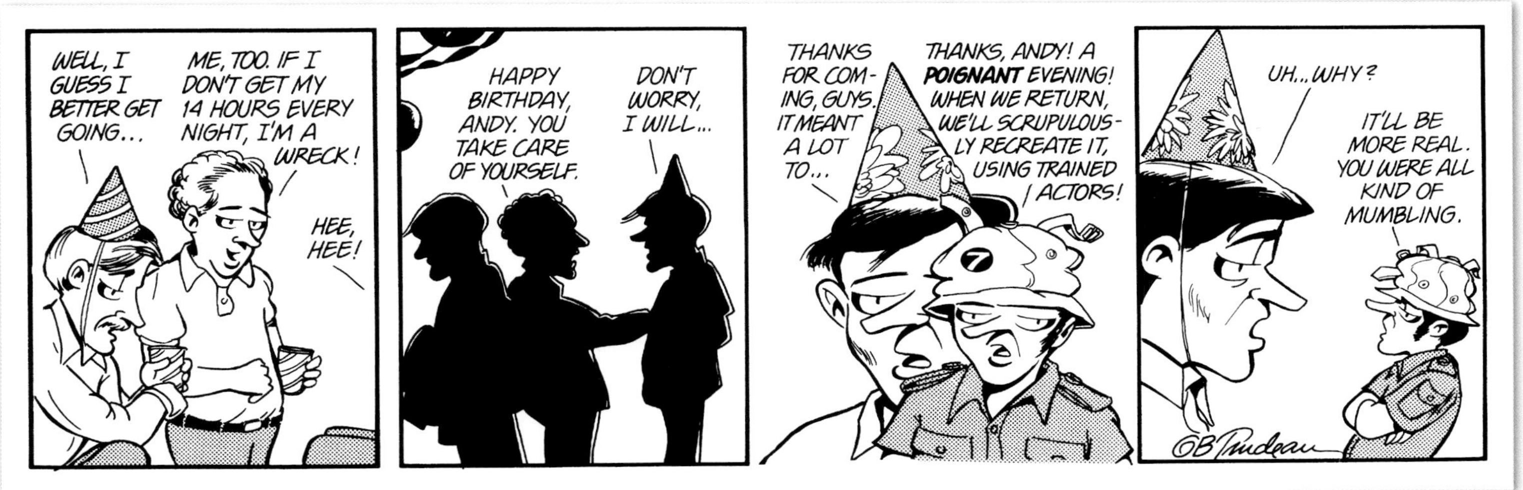
WELL, I GUESS I BETTER GET GOING...
ME, TOO. IF I DON'T GET MY 14 HOURS EVERY NIGHT, I'M A WRECK!
HEE, HEE!
HAPPY BIRTHDAY, ANDY. YOU TAKE CARE OF YOURSELF.
DON'T WORRY, I WILL...
THANKS FOR COMING, GUYS. IT MEANT A LOT TO...
THANKS, ANDY! A POIGNANT EVENING! WHEN WE RETURN, WE'LL SCRUPULOUSLY RECREATE IT, USING TRAINED ACTORS!
UH...WHY?
IT'LL BE MORE REAL. YOU WERE ALL KIND OF MUMBLING.
GB Trudeau

8/19/89

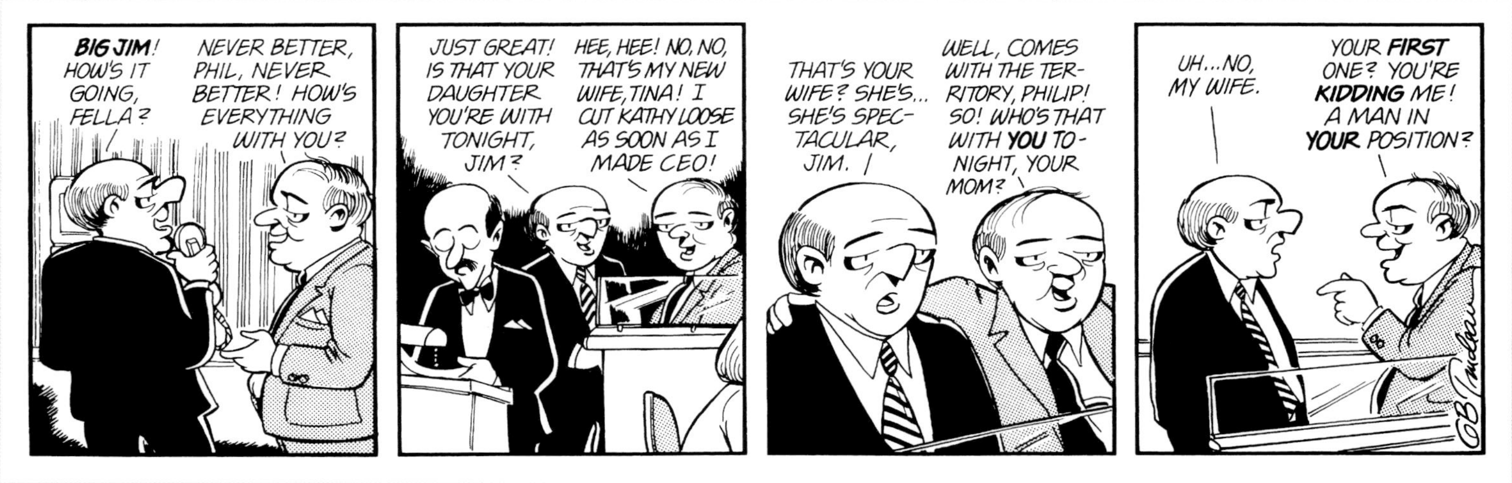
BIG JIM! HOW'S IT GOING, FELLA?
NEVER BETTER, PHIL, NEVER BETTER! HOW'S EVERYTHING WITH YOU?
JUST GREAT! IS THAT YOUR DAUGHTER YOU'RE WITH TONIGHT, JIM?
HEE, HEE! NO, NO, THAT'S MY NEW WIFE, TINA! I CUT KATHY LOOSE AS SOON AS I MADE CEO!
THAT'S YOUR WIFE? SHE'S... SHE'S SPECTACULAR, JIM.
WELL, COMES WITH THE TERRITORY, PHILIP! SO! WHO'S THAT WITH YOU TONIGHT, YOUR MOM?
UH...NO, MY WIFE.
YOUR FIRST ONE? YOU'RE KIDDING ME! A MAN IN YOUR POSITION?

8/28/89

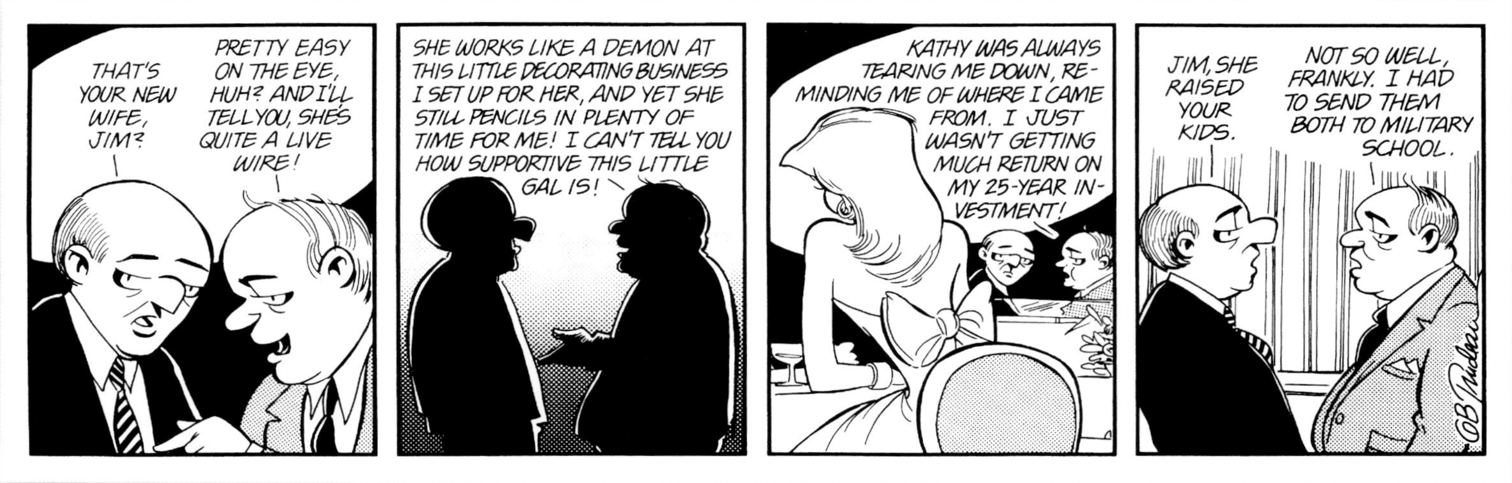
THAT'S YOUR NEW WIFE, JIM?
PRETTY EASY ON THE EYE, HUH? AND I'LL TELL YOU, SHE'S QUITE A LIVE WIRE!
SHE WORKS LIKE A DEMON AT THIS LITTLE DECORATING BUSINESS I SET UP FOR HER, AND YET SHE STILL PENCILS IN PLENTY OF TIME FOR ME! I CAN'T TELL YOU HOW SUPPORTIVE THIS LITTLE GAL IS!
KATHY WAS ALWAYS TEARING ME DOWN, REMINDING ME OF WHERE I CAME FROM. I JUST WASN'T GETTING MUCH RETURN ON MY 25-YEAR INVESTMENT!
JIM, SHE RAISED YOUR KIDS.
NOT SO WELL, FRANKLY. I HAD TO SEND THEM BOTH TO MILITARY SCHOOL.

8/29/89

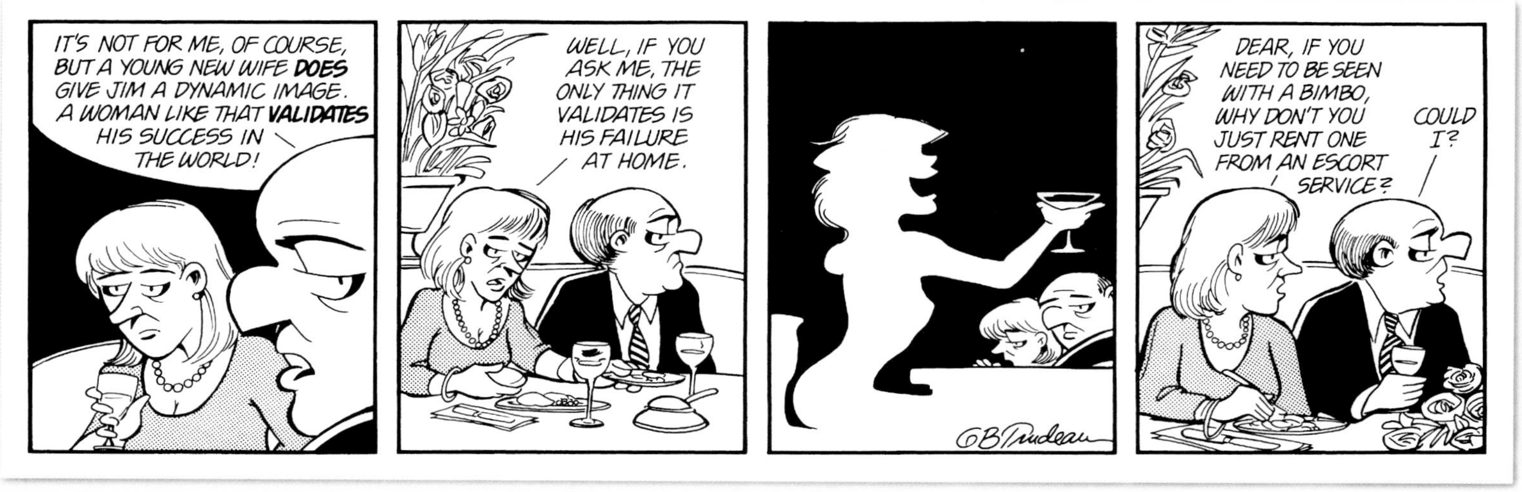
IT'S NOT FOR ME, OF COURSE, BUT A YOUNG NEW WIFE DOES GIVE JIM A DYNAMIC IMAGE. A WOMAN LIKE THAT VALIDATES HIS SUCCESS IN THE WORLD!
WELL, IF YOU ASK ME, THE ONLY THING IT VALIDATES IS HIS FAILURE AT HOME.
DEAR, IF YOU NEED TO BE SEEN WITH A BIMBO, WHY DON'T YOU JUST RENT ONE FROM AN ESCORT SERVICE?
COULD I?

8/31/89

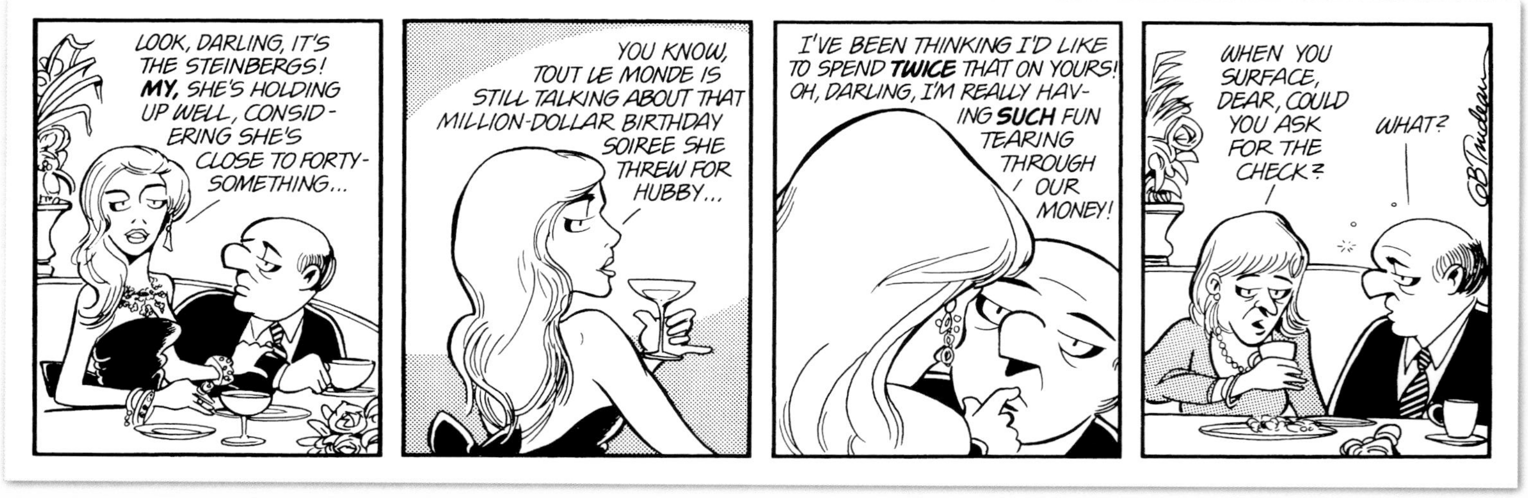
LOOK, DARLING, IT'S THE STEINBERGS! MY, SHE'S HOLDING UP WELL, CONSIDERING SHE'S CLOSE TO FORTY-SOMETHING...
YOU KNOW, TOUT LE MONDE IS STILL TALKING ABOUT THAT MILLION-DOLLAR BIRTHDAY SOIREE SHE THREW FOR HUBBY...
I'VE BEEN THINKING I'D LIKE TO SPEND TWICE THAT ON YOURS! OH, DARLING, I'M REALLY HAVING SUCH FUN TEARING THROUGH OUR MONEY!
WHEN YOU SURFACE, DEAR, COULD YOU ASK FOR THE CHECK?
WHAT?

9/1/89

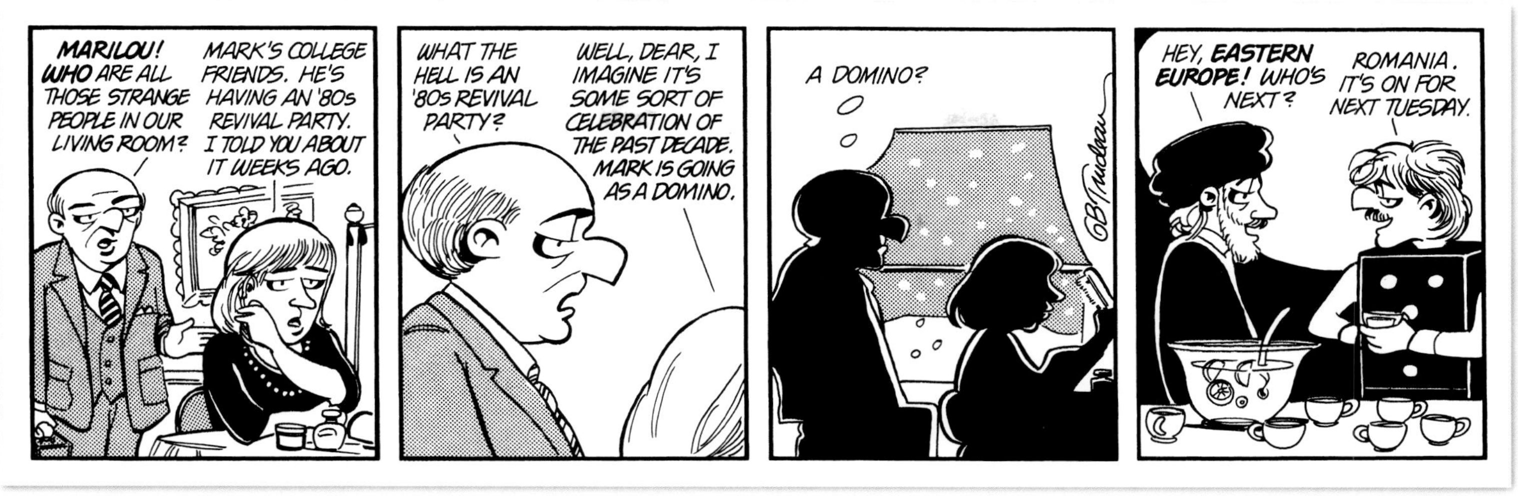
MARILOU! WHO ARE ALL THOSE STRANGE PEOPLE IN OUR LIVING ROOM?
MARK'S COLLEGE FRIENDS. HE'S HAVING AN '80s REVIVAL PARTY. I TOLD YOU ABOUT IT WEEKS AGO.
WHAT THE HELL IS AN '80s REVIVAL PARTY?
WELL, DEAR, I IMAGINE IT'S SOME SORT OF CELEBRATION OF THE PAST DECADE. MARK IS GOING AS A DOMINO.
A DOMINO?
HEY, EASTERN EUROPE! WHO'S NEXT?
ROMANIA. IT'S ON FOR NEXT TUESDAY.

12/11/89

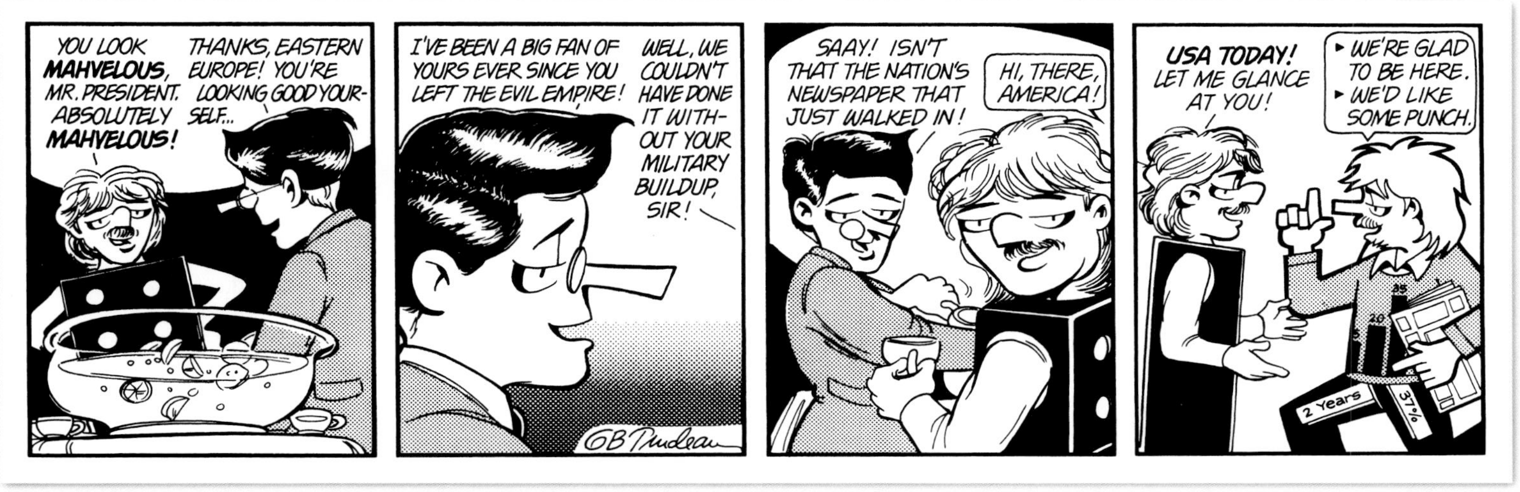
YOU LOOK MAHVELOUS, MR. PRESIDENT. ABSOLUTELY MAHVELOUS!
THANKS, EASTERN EUROPE! YOU'RE LOOKING GOOD YOURSELF...
I'VE BEEN A BIG FAN OF YOURS EVER SINCE YOU LEFT THE EVIL EMPIRE!
WELL, WE COULDN'T HAVE DONE IT WITHOUT YOUR MILITARY BUILDUP, SIR!
SAAY! ISN'T THAT THE NATION'S NEWSPAPER THAT JUST WALKED IN!
HI, THERE, AMERICA!
USA TODAY! LET ME GLANCE AT YOU!
▸ WE'RE GLAD TO BE HERE.
▸ WE'D LIKE SOME PUNCH.
2 Years
37%

12/14/89

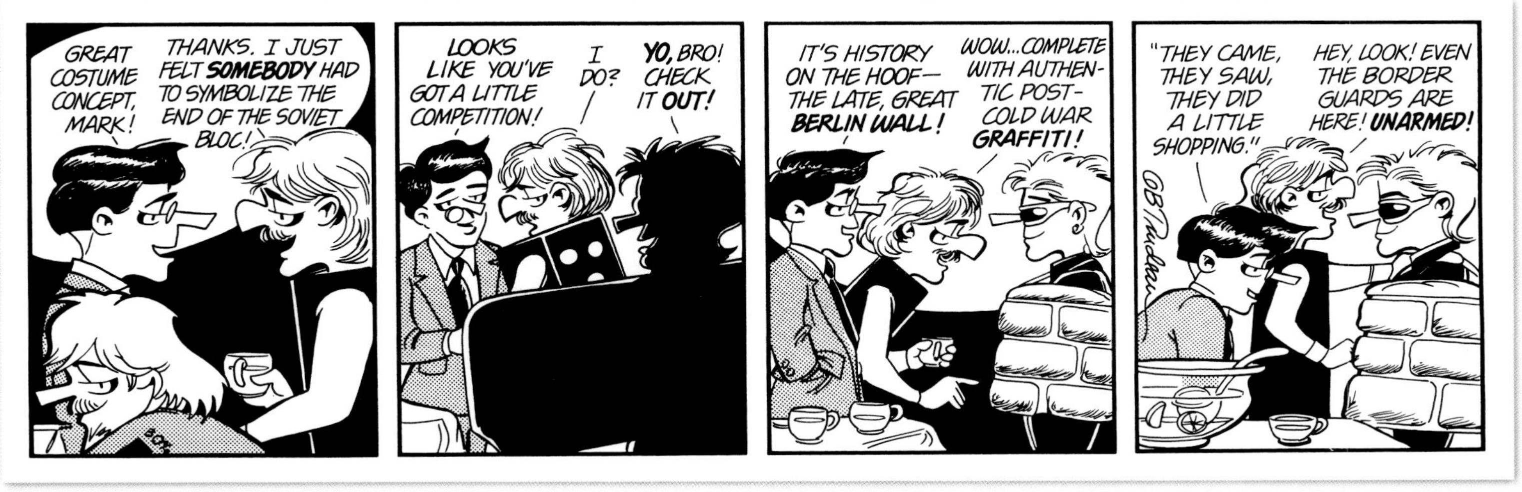
GREAT COSTUME CONCEPT, MARK!
THANKS. I JUST FELT SOMEBODY HAD TO SYMBOLIZE THE END OF THE SOVIET BLOC!
LOOKS LIKE YOU'VE GOT A LITTLE COMPETITION!
I DO?
YO, BRO! CHECK IT OUT!
IT'S HISTORY ON THE HOOF— THE LATE, GREAT BERLIN WALL!
WOW...COMPLETE WITH AUTHENTIC POST-COLD WAR GRAFFITI!
"THEY CAME, THEY SAW, THEY DID A LITTLE SHOPPING."
HEY, LOOK! EVEN THE BORDER GUARDS ARE HERE! UNARMED!

12/15/89

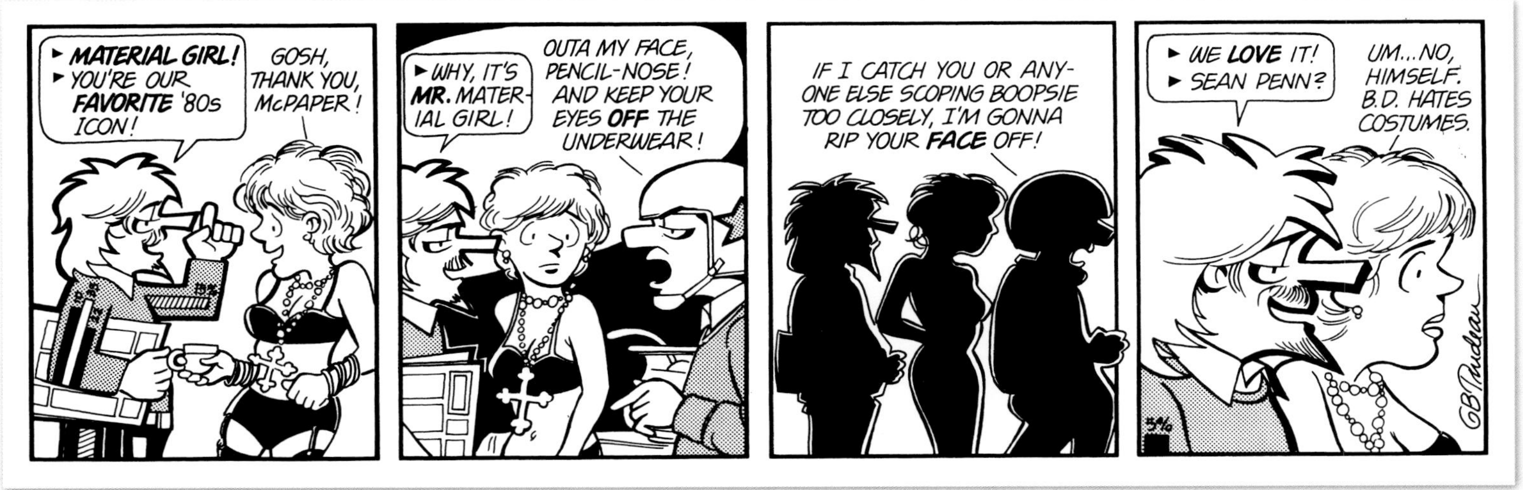
▸ MATERIAL GIRL!
▸ YOU'RE OUR FAVORITE '80s ICON!
GOSH, THANK YOU, McPAPER!
▸ WHY, IT'S MR. MATERIAL GIRL!
OUTA MY FACE, PENCIL-NOSE! AND KEEP YOUR EYES OFF THE UNDERWEAR!
IF I CATCH YOU OR ANYONE ELSE SCOPING BOOPSIE TOO CLOSELY, I'M GONNA RIP YOUR FACE OFF!
▸ WE LOVE IT!
▸ SEAN PENN?
UM...NO, HIMSELF. B.D. HATES COSTUMES.

12/16/89

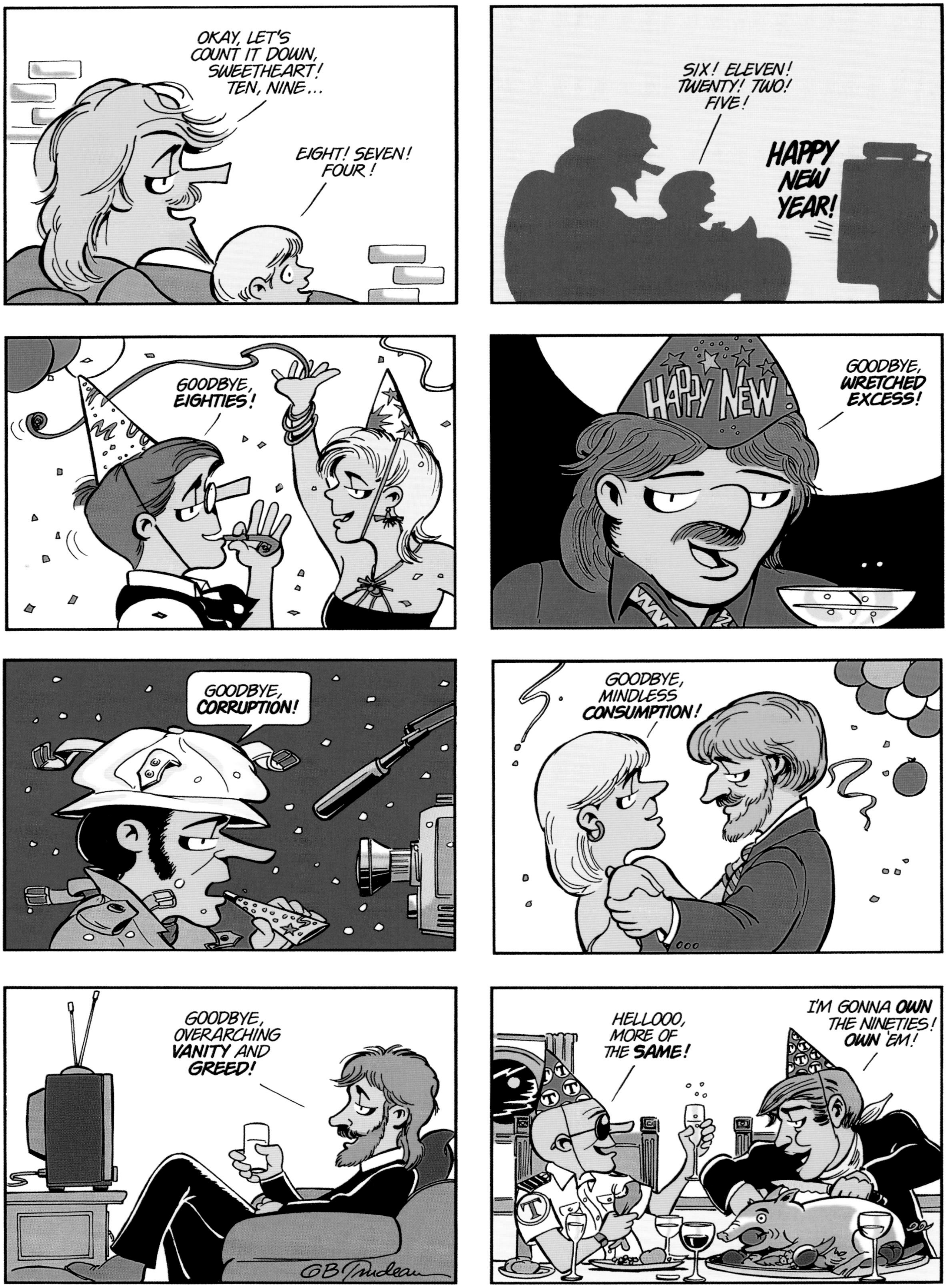
OKAY, LET'S COUNT IT DOWN, SWEETHEART! TEN, NINE...
EIGHT! SEVEN! FOUR!
SIX! ELEVEN! TWENTY! TWO! FIVE!
HAPPY NEW YEAR!
GOODBYE, **EIGHTIES!**
HAPPY NEW
GOODBYE, **WRETCHED EXCESS!**
GOODBYE, **CORRUPTION!**
GOODBYE, MINDLESS **CONSUMPTION!**
GOODBYE, OVERARCHING **VANITY** AND **GREED!**
HELLOOO, MORE OF THE **SAME!**
I'M GONNA **OWN** THE NINETIES! **OWN** 'EM!
GB Trudeau

12/31/89

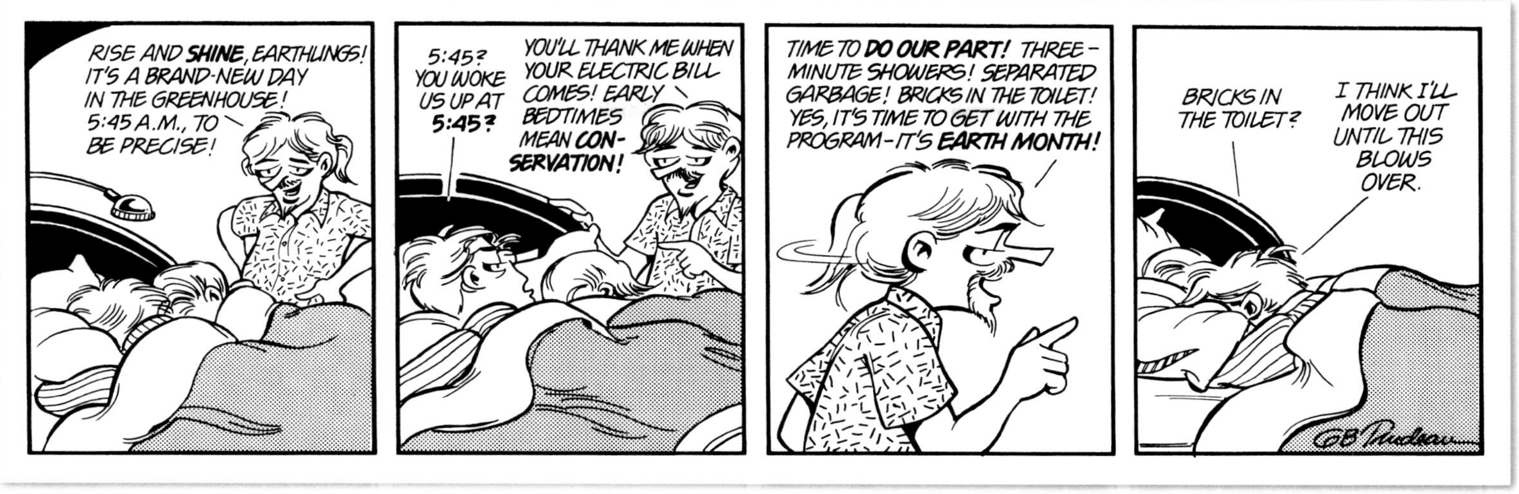
RISE AND SHINE, EARTHLINGS! IT'S A BRAND-NEW DAY IN THE GREENHOUSE! 5:45 A.M., TO BE PRECISE!
5:45? YOU WOKE US UP AT 5:45?
YOU'LL THANK ME WHEN YOUR ELECTRIC BILL COMES! EARLY BEDTIMES MEAN CONSERVATION!
TIME TO DO OUR PART! THREE-MINUTE SHOWERS! SEPARATED GARBAGE! BRICKS IN THE TOILET! YES, IT'S TIME TO GET WITH THE PROGRAM - IT'S EARTH MONTH!
BRICKS IN THE TOILET?
I THINK I'LL MOVE OUT UNTIL THIS BLOWS OVER.
GB Trudeau

4/9/90

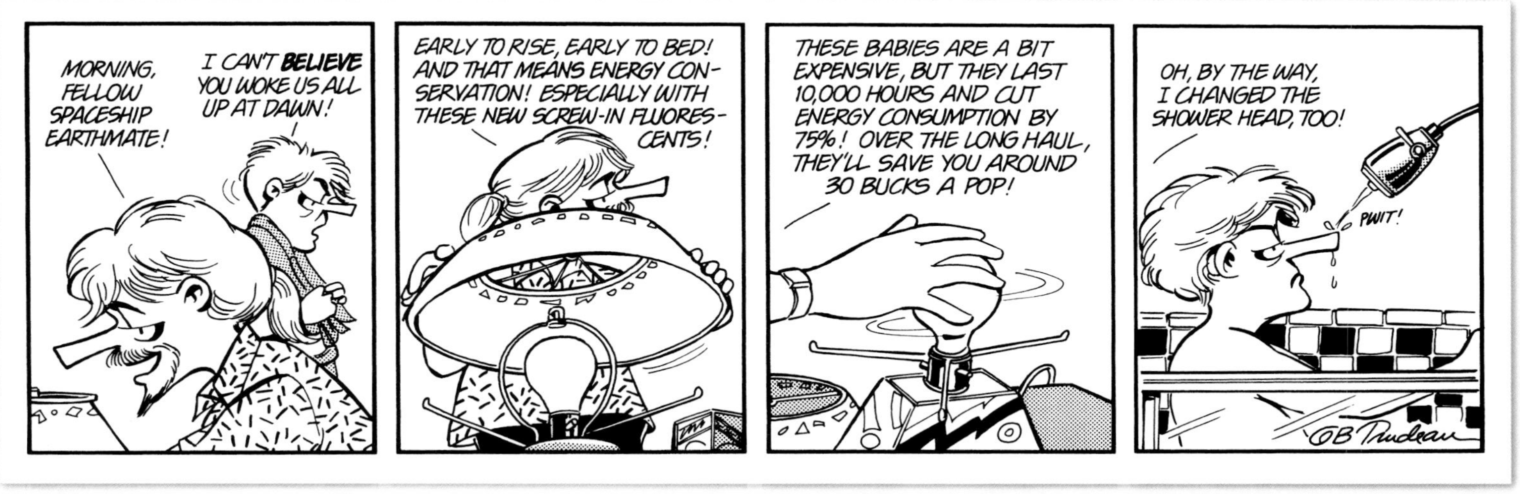
MORNING, FELLOW SPACESHIP EARTHMATE!
I CAN'T BELIEVE YOU WOKE US ALL UP AT DAWN!
EARLY TO RISE, EARLY TO BED! AND THAT MEANS ENERGY CONSERVATION! ESPECIALLY WITH THESE NEW SCREW-IN FLUORESCENTS!
THESE BABIES ARE A BIT EXPENSIVE, BUT THEY LAST 10,000 HOURS AND CUT ENERGY CONSUMPTION BY 75%! OVER THE LONG HAUL, THEY'LL SAVE YOU AROUND 30 BUCKS A POP!
OH, BY THE WAY, I CHANGED THE SHOWER HEAD, TOO!
PWIT!
GB Trudeau

4/10/90

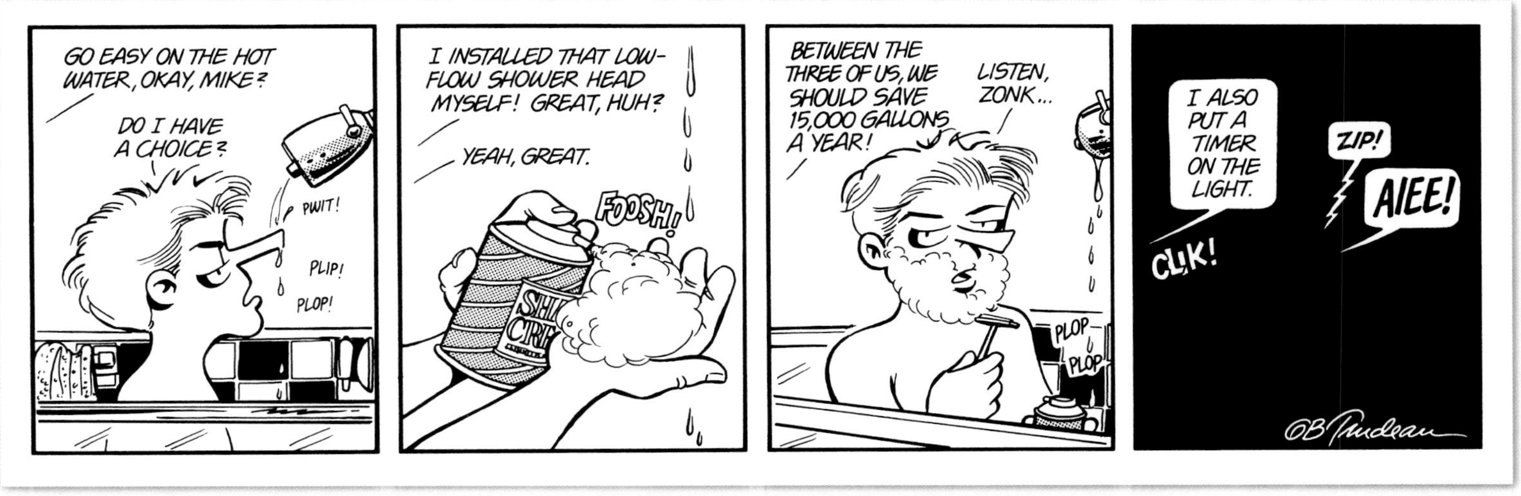
GO EASY ON THE HOT WATER, OKAY, MIKE?
DO I HAVE A CHOICE?
PWIT!
PLIP!
PLOP!
I INSTALLED THAT LOW-FLOW SHOWER HEAD MYSELF! GREAT, HUH?
YEAH, GREAT.
FOOSH!
BETWEEN THE THREE OF US, WE SHOULD SAVE 15,000 GALLONS A YEAR!
LISTEN, ZONK...
PLOP
PLOP
I ALSO PUT A TIMER ON THE LIGHT.
CLIK!
ZIP!
AIEE!
GB Trudeau

4/11/90

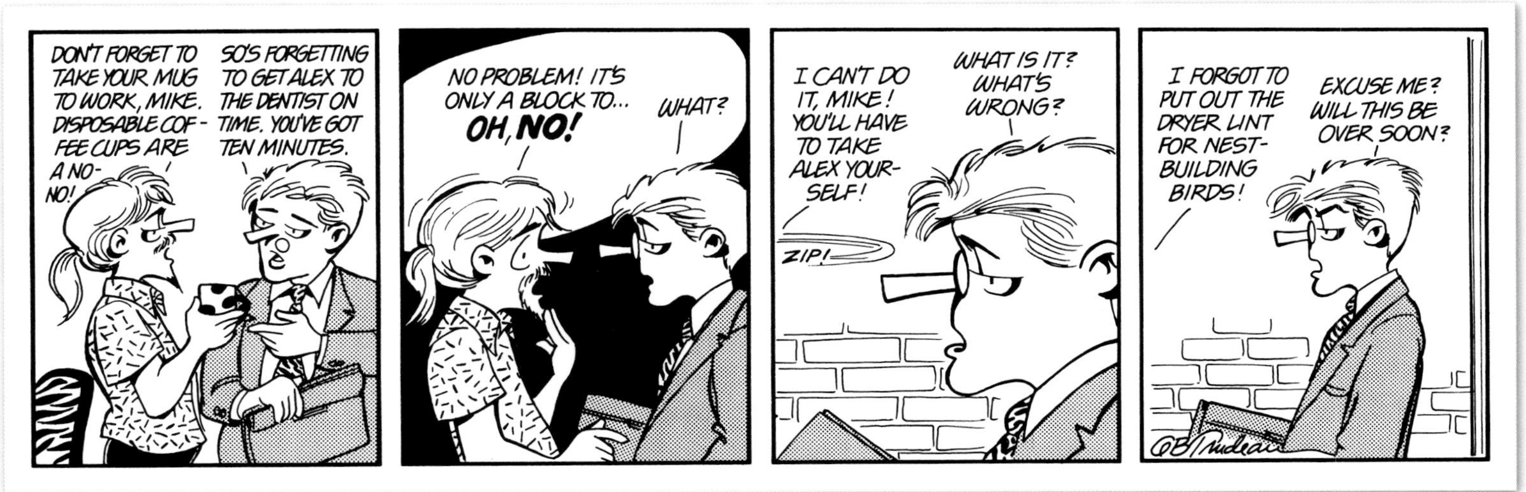
DON'T FORGET TO TAKE YOUR MUG TO WORK, MIKE. DISPOSABLE COFFEE CUPS ARE A NO-NO!
SO'S FORGETTING TO GET ALEX TO THE DENTIST ON TIME. YOU'VE GOT TEN MINUTES.
NO PROBLEM! IT'S ONLY A BLOCK TO... OH, NO!
WHAT?
I CAN'T DO IT, MIKE! YOU'LL HAVE TO TAKE ALEX YOURSELF!
WHAT IS IT? WHAT'S WRONG?
ZIP!
I FORGOT TO PUT OUT THE DRYER LINT FOR NEST-BUILDING BIRDS!
EXCUSE ME? WILL THIS BE OVER SOON?
GB Trudeau

4/13/90

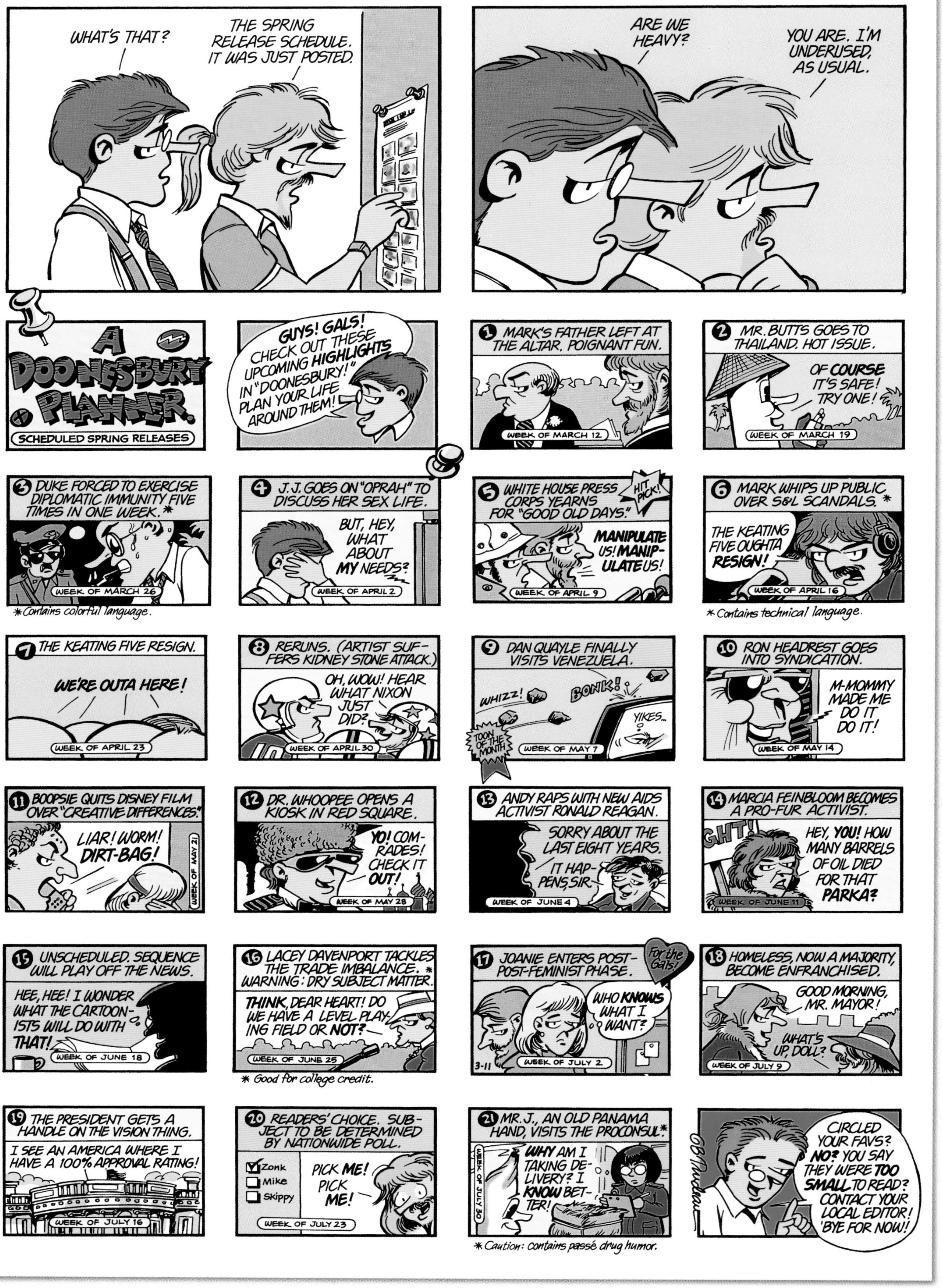
WHAT'S THAT?
THE SPRING RELEASE SCHEDULE. IT WAS JUST POSTED.
ARE WE HEAVY?
YOU ARE. I'M UNDERUSED, AS USUAL.
A DOONESBURY PLANNER.
SCHEDULED SPRING RELEASES
GUYS! GALS! CHECK OUT THESE UPCOMING HIGHLIGHTS IN "DOONESBURY!" PLAN YOUR LIFE AROUND THEM!
1 MARK'S FATHER LEFT AT THE ALTAR. POIGNANT FUN.
WEEK OF MARCH 12
2 MR. BUTTS GOES TO THAILAND. HOT ISSUE.
OF COURSE IT'S SAFE! TRY ONE!
WEEK OF MARCH 19
3 DUKE FORCED TO EXERCISE DIPLOMATIC IMMUNITY FIVE TIMES IN ONE WEEK.*
WEEK OF MARCH 26
*Contains colorful language.
4 J.J. GOES ON "OPRAH" TO DISCUSS HER SEX LIFE.
BUT, HEY, WHAT ABOUT MY NEEDS?
WEEK OF APRIL 2
5 WHITE HOUSE PRESS CORPS YEARNS FOR "GOOD OLD DAYS."
HIT PICK!
MANIPULATE US! MANIPULATE US!
WEEK OF APRIL 9
6 MARK WHIPS UP PUBLIC OVER S&L SCANDALS.*
THE KEATING FIVE OUGHTA RESIGN!
WEEK OF APRIL 16
*Contains technical language.
7 THE KEATING FIVE RESIGN.
WE'RE OUTA HERE!
WEEK OF APRIL 23
8 RERUNS. (ARTIST SUFFERS KIDNEY STONE ATTACK.)
OH, WOW! HEAR WHAT NIXON JUST DID?
WEEK OF APRIL 30
9 DAN QUAYLE FINALLY VISITS VENEZUELA.
WHIZZ!
BONK!
YIKES...
TOON OF THE MONTH
WEEK OF MAY 7
10 RON HEADREST GOES INTO SYNDICATION.
M-MOMMY MADE ME DO IT DO IT!
WEEK OF MAY 14
11 BOOPSIE QUITS DISNEY FILM OVER "CREATIVE DIFFERENCES."
LIAR! WORM! DIRT-BAG!
WEEK OF MAY 21
12 DR. WHOOPEE OPENS A KIOSK IN RED SQUARE.
YO! COMRADES! CHECK IT OUT!
WEEK OF MAY 28
13 ANDY RAPS WITH NEW AIDS ACTIVIST RONALD REAGAN.
SORRY ABOUT THE LAST EIGHT YEARS.
IT HAPPENS, SIR.
WEEK OF JUNE 4
14 MARCIA FEINBLOOM BECOMES A PRO-FUR ACTIVIST.
HEY, YOU! HOW MANY BARRELS OF OIL DIED FOR THAT PARKA?
WEEK OF JUNE 11
15 UNSCHEDULED SEQUENCE WILL PLAY OFF THE NEWS.
HEE, HEE! I WONDER WHAT THE CARTOONISTS WILL DO WITH THAT!
WEEK OF JUNE 18
16 LACEY DAVENPORT TACKLES THE TRADE IMBALANCE.* WARNING: DRY SUBJECT MATTER.
THINK, DEAR HEART! DO WE HAVE A LEVEL PLAYING FIELD OR NOT?
WEEK OF JUNE 25
*Good for college credit.
17 JOANIE ENTERS POST-POST-FEMINIST PHASE.
For the Gals!
WHO KNOWS WHAT I WANT?
WEEK OF JULY 2
18 HOMELESS, NOW A MAJORITY, BECOME ENFRANCHISED.
GOOD MORNING, MR. MAYOR!
WHAT'S UP, DOLL?
WEEK OF JULY 9
19 THE PRESIDENT GETS A HANDLE ON THE VISION THING.
I SEE AN AMERICA WHERE I HAVE A 100% APPROVAL RATING!
WEEK OF JULY 16
20 READERS' CHOICE. SUBJECT TO BE DETERMINED BY NATIONWIDE POLL.
Zonk
Mike
Skippy
PICK ME! PICK ME!
WEEK OF JULY 23
21 MR. J., AN OLD PANAMA HAND, VISITS THE PROCONSUL.*
WHY AM I TAKING DELIVERY? I KNOW BETTER!
WEEK OF JULY 30
*Caution: contains passé drug humor.
CIRCLED YOUR FAVS? NO? YOU SAY THEY WERE TOO SMALL TO READ? CONTACT YOUR LOCAL EDITOR! 'BYE FOR NOW!
G.B. Trudeau

3/11/90

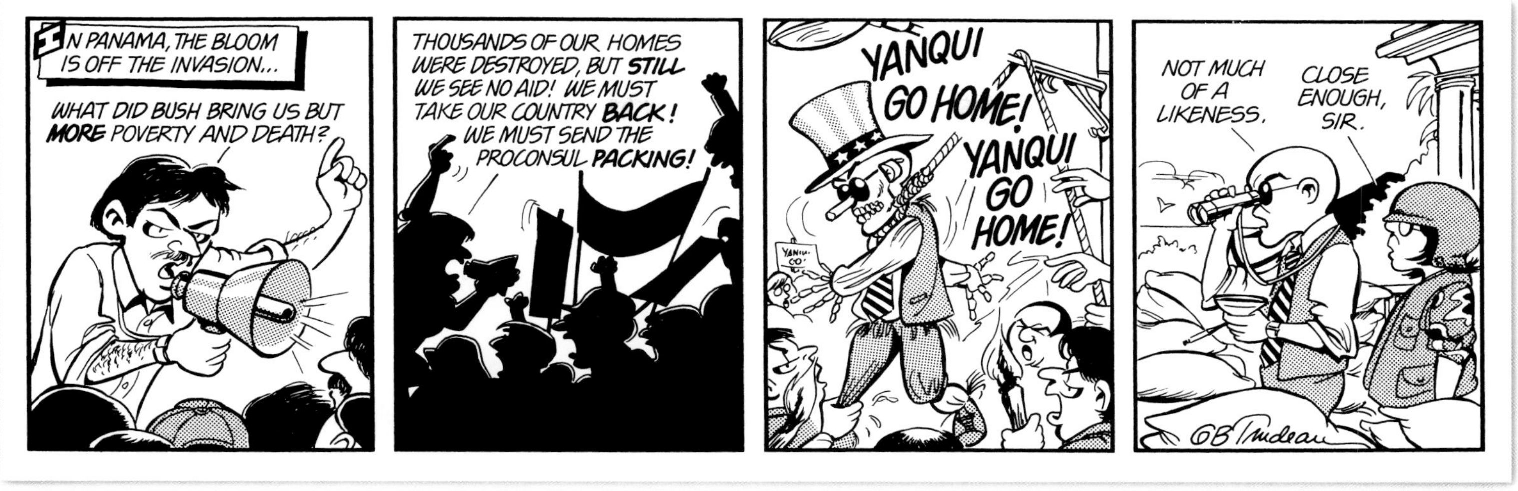
IN PANAMA, THE BLOOM IS OFF THE INVASION...
WHAT DID BUSH BRING US BUT MORE POVERTY AND DEATH?
THOUSANDS OF OUR HOMES WERE DESTROYED, BUT STILL WE SEE NO AID! WE MUST TAKE OUR COUNTRY BACK!
WE MUST SEND THE PROCONSUL PACKING!
YANQUI GO HOME!
YANQUI GO HOME!
NOT MUCH OF A LIKENESS.
CLOSE ENOUGH, SIR.

4/30/90

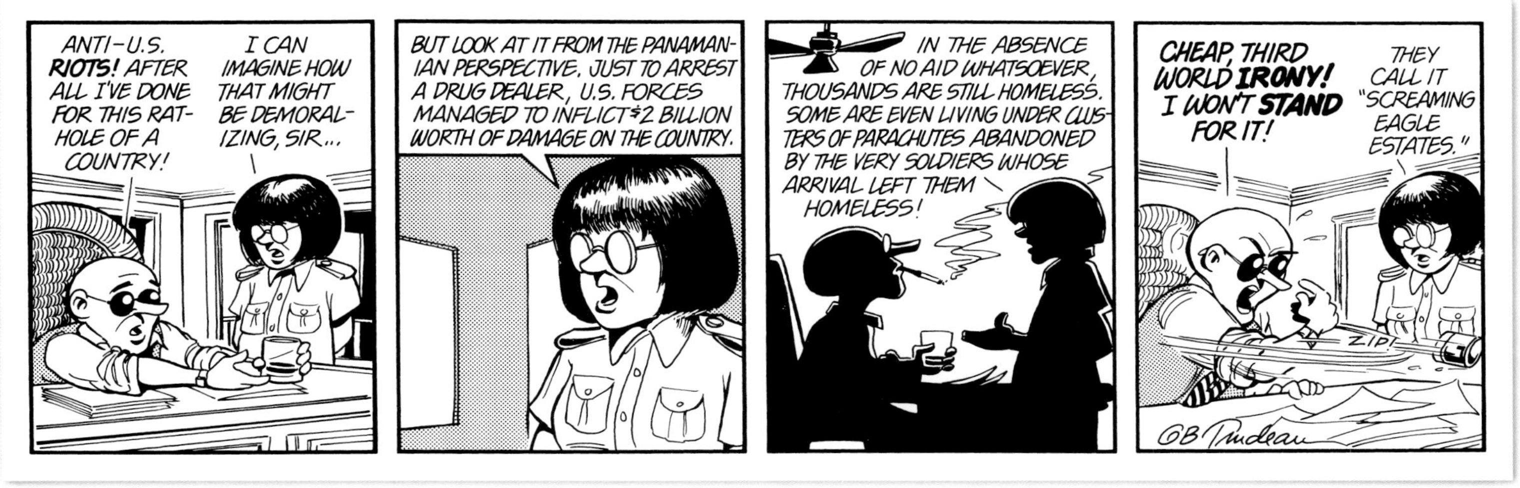
ANTI-U.S. RIOTS! AFTER ALL I'VE DONE FOR THIS RAT-HOLE OF A COUNTRY!
I CAN IMAGINE HOW THAT MIGHT BE DEMORAL-IZING, SIR...
BUT LOOK AT IT FROM THE PANAMAN-IAN PERSPECTIVE. JUST TO ARREST A DRUG DEALER, U.S. FORCES MANAGED TO INFLICT $2 BILLION WORTH OF DAMAGE ON THE COUNTRY.
IN THE ABSENCE OF NO AID WHATSOEVER, THOUSANDS ARE STILL HOMELESS. SOME ARE EVEN LIVING UNDER CLUS-TERS OF PARACHUTES ABANDONED BY THE VERY SOLDIERS WHOSE ARRIVAL LEFT THEM HOMELESS!
CHEAP, THIRD WORLD IRONY! I WON'T STAND FOR IT!
THEY CALL IT "SCREAMING EAGLE ESTATES."
ZIP!

5/1/90

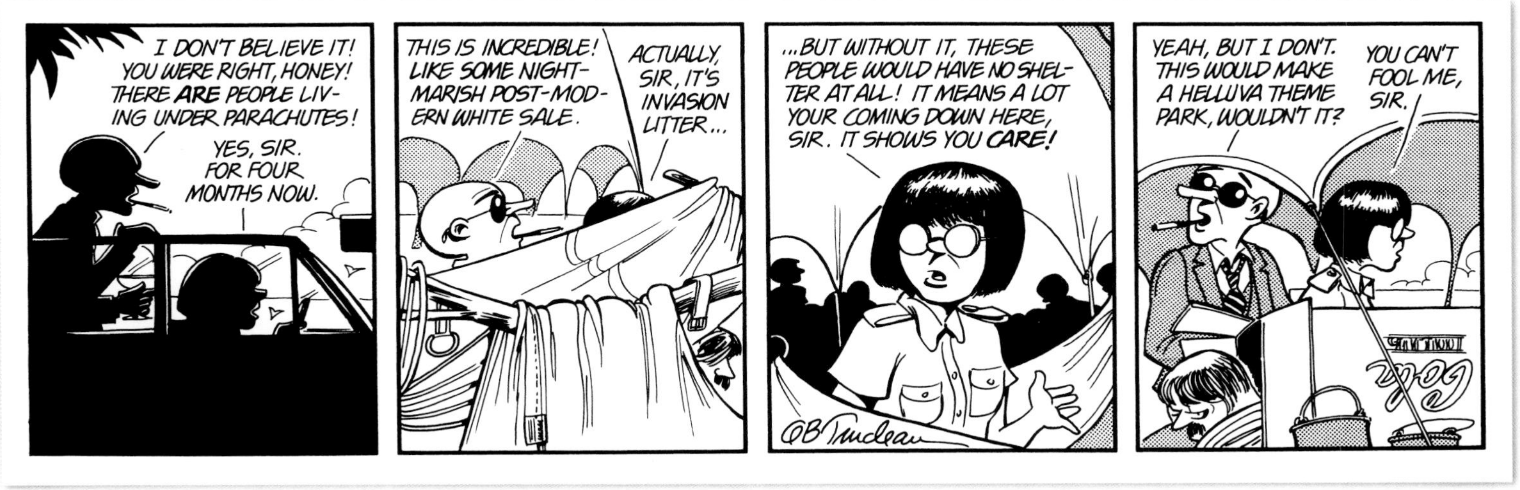
I DON'T BELIEVE IT! YOU WERE RIGHT, HONEY! THERE ARE PEOPLE LIV-ING UNDER PARACHUTES!
YES, SIR. FOR FOUR MONTHS NOW.
THIS IS INCREDIBLE! LIKE SOME NIGHT-MARISH POST-MOD-ERN WHITE SALE.
ACTUALLY, SIR, IT'S INVASION LITTER...
...BUT WITHOUT IT, THESE PEOPLE WOULD HAVE NO SHEL-TER AT ALL! IT MEANS A LOT YOUR COMING DOWN HERE, SIR. IT SHOWS YOU CARE!
YEAH, BUT I DON'T. THIS WOULD MAKE A HELLUVA THEME PARK, WOULDN'T IT?
YOU CAN'T FOOL ME, SIR.

5/2/90

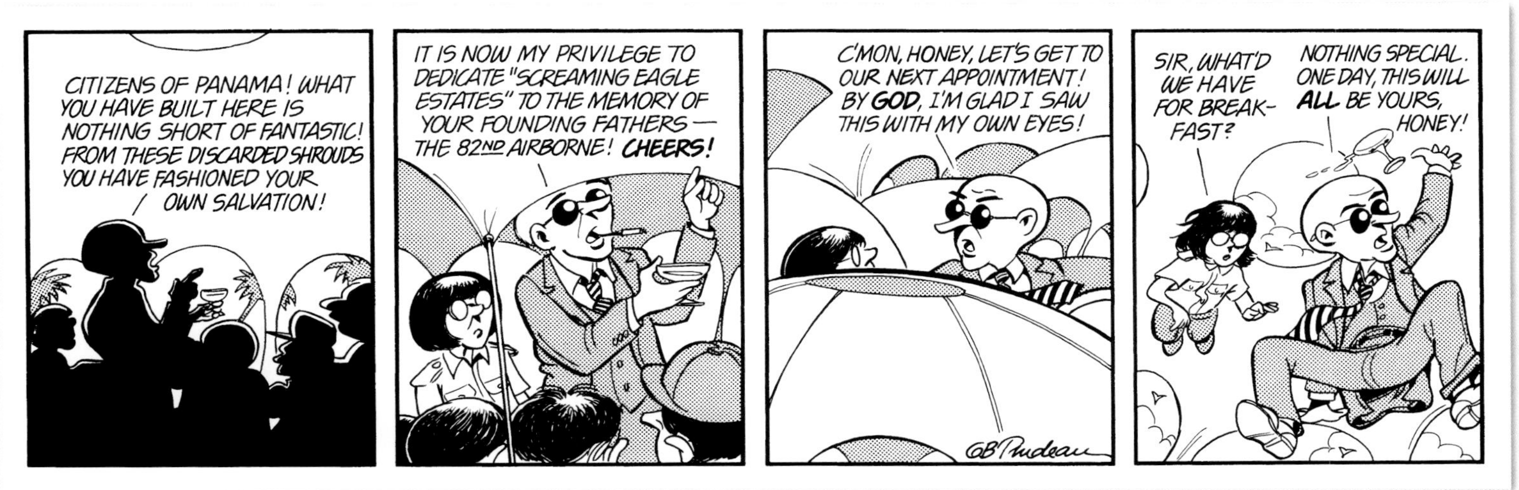
CITIZENS OF PANAMA! WHAT YOU HAVE BUILT HERE IS NOTHING SHORT OF FANTASTIC! FROM THESE DISCARDED SHROUDS YOU HAVE FASHIONED YOUR OWN SALVATION!
IT IS NOW MY PRIVILEGE TO DEDICATE "SCREAMING EAGLE ESTATES" TO THE MEMORY OF YOUR FOUNDING FATHERS — THE 82ND AIRBORNE! CHEERS!
C'MON, HONEY, LET'S GET TO OUR NEXT APPOINTMENT! BY GOD, I'M GLAD I SAW THIS WITH MY OWN EYES!
SIR, WHAT'D WE HAVE FOR BREAK-FAST?
NOTHING SPECIAL. ONE DAY, THIS WILL ALL BE YOURS, HONEY!

5/4/90

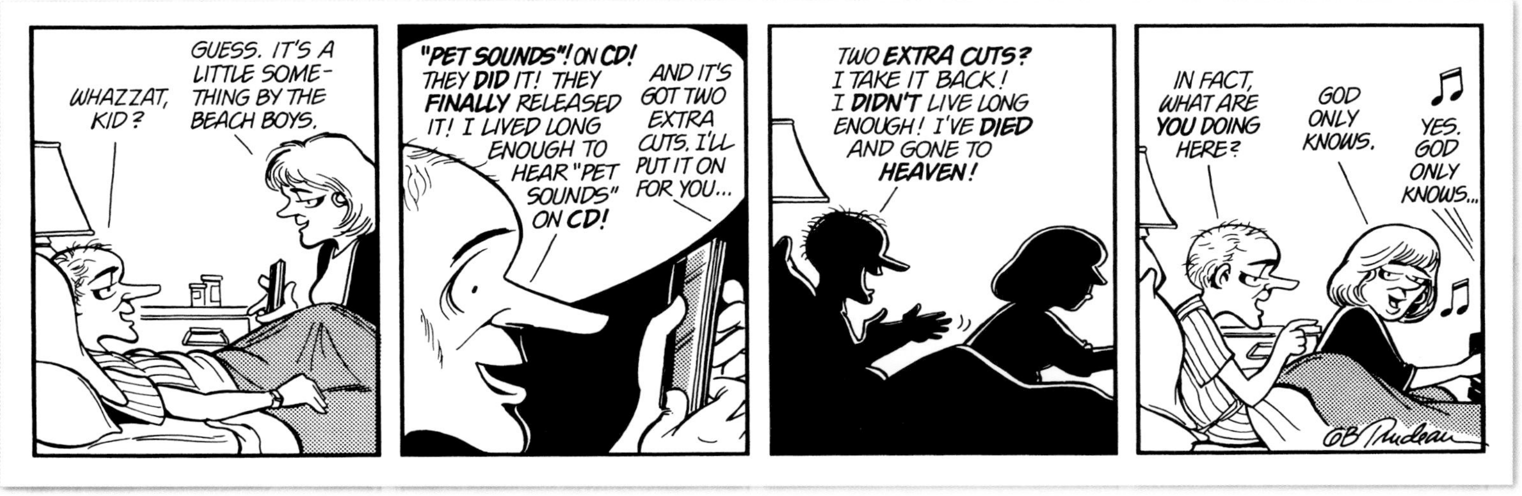
WHAZZAT, KID?
GUESS. IT'S A LITTLE SOMETHING BY THE BEACH BOYS.
"PET SOUNDS"! ON CD! THEY DID IT! THEY FINALLY RELEASED IT! I LIVED LONG ENOUGH TO HEAR "PET SOUNDS" ON CD!
AND IT'S GOT TWO EXTRA CUTS. I'LL PUT IT ON FOR YOU...
TWO EXTRA CUTS? I TAKE IT BACK! I DIDN'T LIVE LONG ENOUGH! I'VE DIED AND GONE TO HEAVEN!
IN FACT, WHAT ARE YOU DOING HERE?
GOD ONLY KNOWS.
YES. GOD ONLY KNOWS...
GB Trudeau

5/21/90

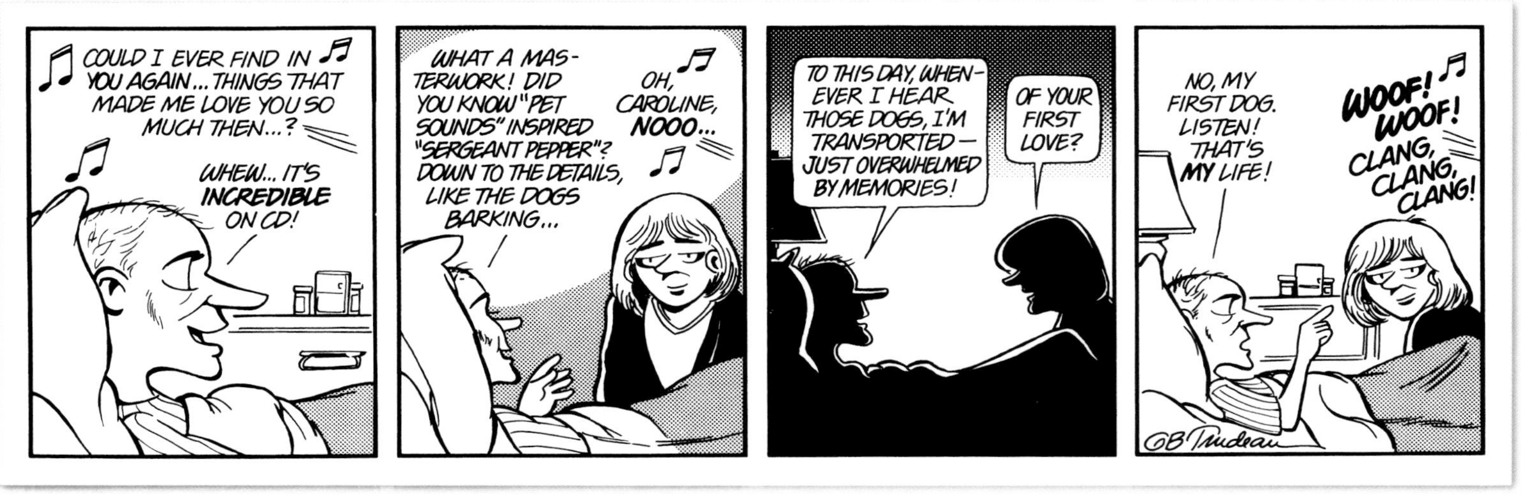
COULD I EVER FIND IN YOU AGAIN... THINGS THAT MADE ME LOVE YOU SO MUCH THEN...?
WHEW... IT'S INCREDIBLE ON CD!
WHAT A MASTERWORK! DID YOU KNOW "PET SOUNDS" INSPIRED "SERGEANT PEPPER"? DOWN TO THE DETAILS, LIKE THE DOGS BARKING...
OH, CAROLINE, NOOO...
TO THIS DAY, WHENEVER I HEAR THOSE DOGS, I'M TRANSPORTED — JUST OVERWHELMED BY MEMORIES!
OF YOUR FIRST LOVE?
NO, MY FIRST DOG. LISTEN! THAT'S MY LIFE!
WOOF! WOOF! CLANG, CLANG, CLANG!
GB Trudeau

5/22/90

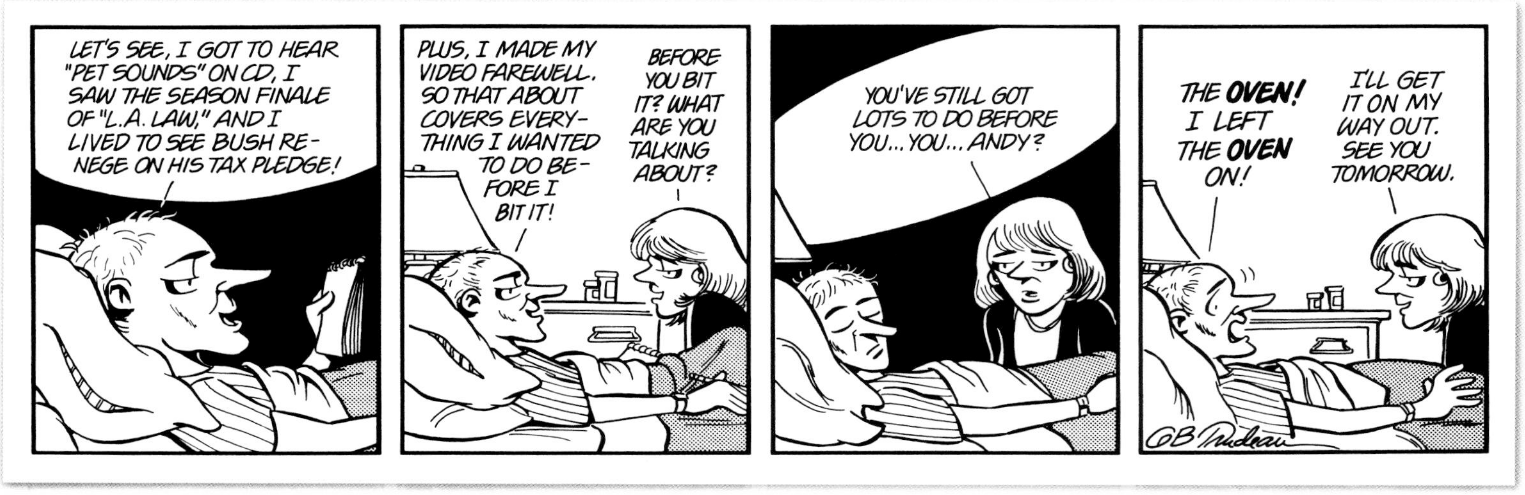
LET'S SEE, I GOT TO HEAR "PET SOUNDS" ON CD, I SAW THE SEASON FINALE OF "L.A. LAW," AND I LIVED TO SEE BUSH RENEGE ON HIS TAX PLEDGE!
PLUS, I MADE MY VIDEO FAREWELL. SO THAT ABOUT COVERS EVERYTHING I WANTED TO DO BEFORE I BIT IT!
BEFORE YOU BIT IT? WHAT ARE YOU TALKING ABOUT?
YOU'VE STILL GOT LOTS TO DO BEFORE YOU... YOU... ANDY?
THE OVEN! I LEFT THE OVEN ON!
I'LL GET IT ON MY WAY OUT. SEE YOU TOMORROW.
GB Trudeau

5/23/90

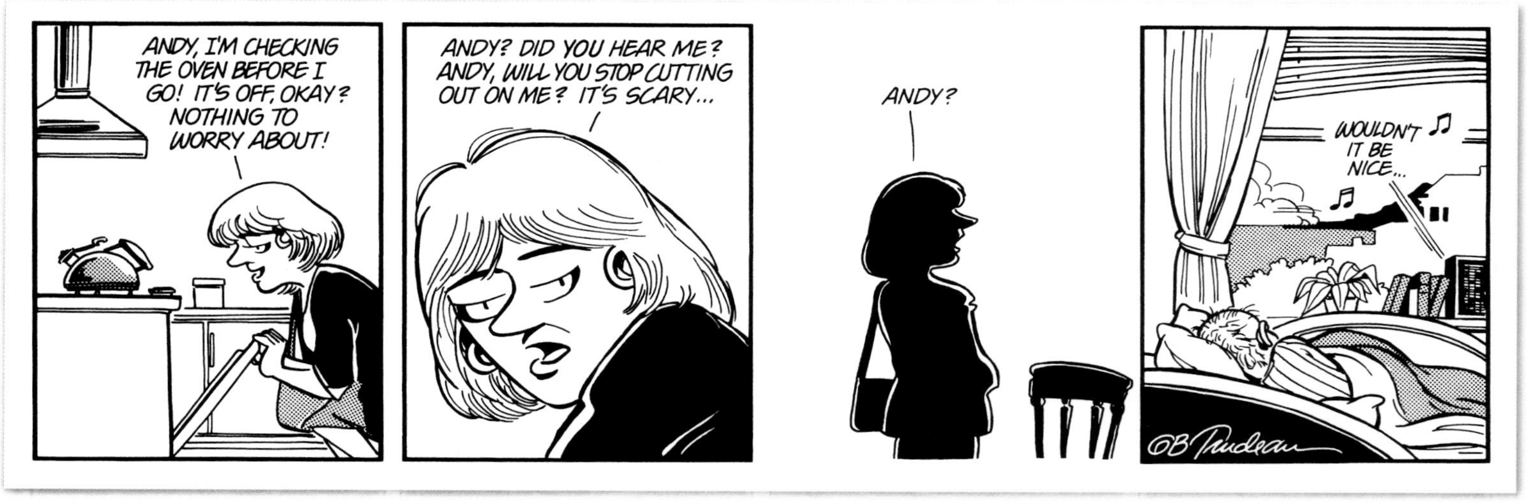
ANDY, I'M CHECKING THE OVEN BEFORE I GO! IT'S OFF, OKAY? NOTHING TO WORRY ABOUT!
ANDY? DID YOU HEAR ME? ANDY, WILL YOU STOP CUTTING OUT ON ME? IT'S SCARY...
ANDY?
WOULDN'T IT BE NICE...
GB Trudeau

5/24/90

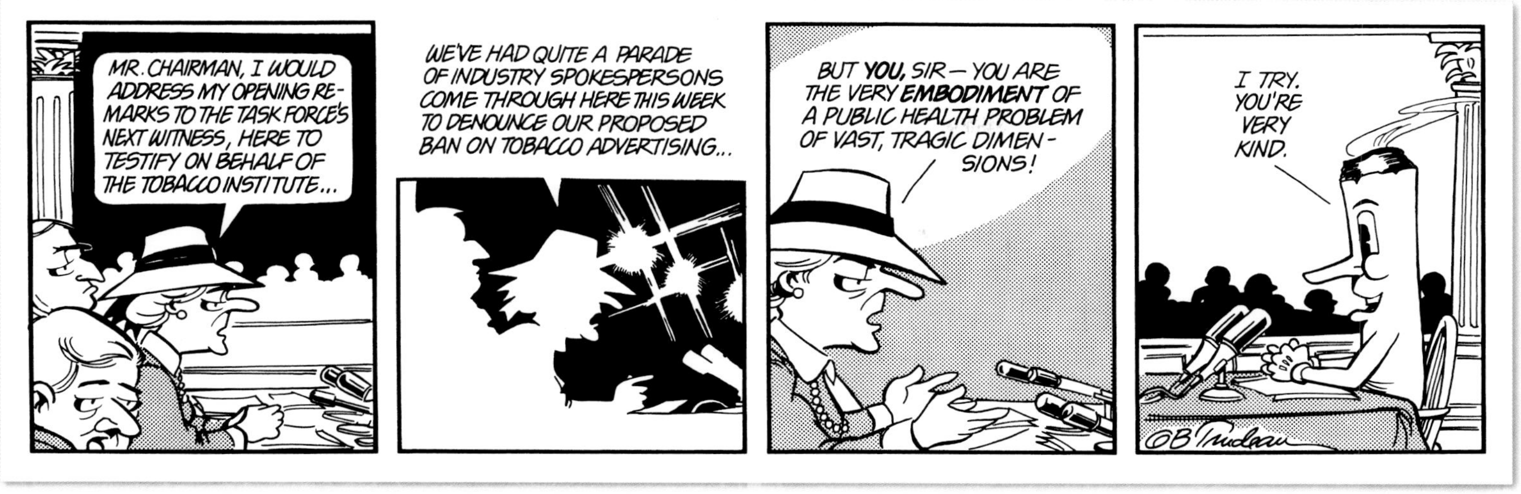

MR. CHAIRMAN, I WOULD ADDRESS MY OPENING REMARKS TO THE TASK FORCE'S NEXT WITNESS, HERE TO TESTIFY ON BEHALF OF THE TOBACCO INSTITUTE...
WE'VE HAD QUITE A PARADE OF INDUSTRY SPOKESPERSONS COME THROUGH HERE THIS WEEK TO DENOUNCE OUR PROPOSED BAN ON TOBACCO ADVERTISING...
BUT YOU, SIR — YOU ARE THE VERY EMBODIMENT OF A PUBLIC HEALTH PROBLEM OF VAST, TRAGIC DIMENSIONS!
I TRY. YOU'RE VERY KIND.

6/25/90

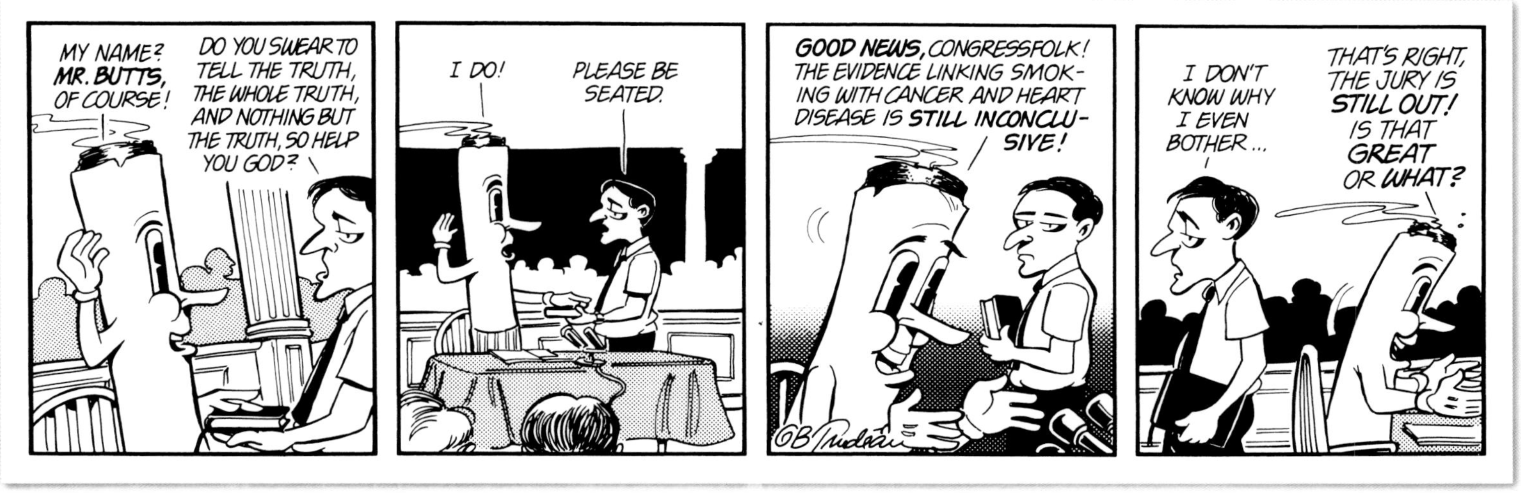

MY NAME? MR. BUTTS, OF COURSE!
DO YOU SWEAR TO TELL THE TRUTH, THE WHOLE TRUTH, AND NOTHING BUT THE TRUTH, SO HELP YOU GOD?
I DO!
PLEASE BE SEATED.
GOOD NEWS, CONGRESSFOLK! THE EVIDENCE LINKING SMOKING WITH CANCER AND HEART DISEASE IS STILL INCONCLUSIVE!
I DON'T KNOW WHY I EVEN BOTHER...
THAT'S RIGHT, THE JURY IS STILL OUT! IS THAT GREAT OR WHAT?

6/26/90

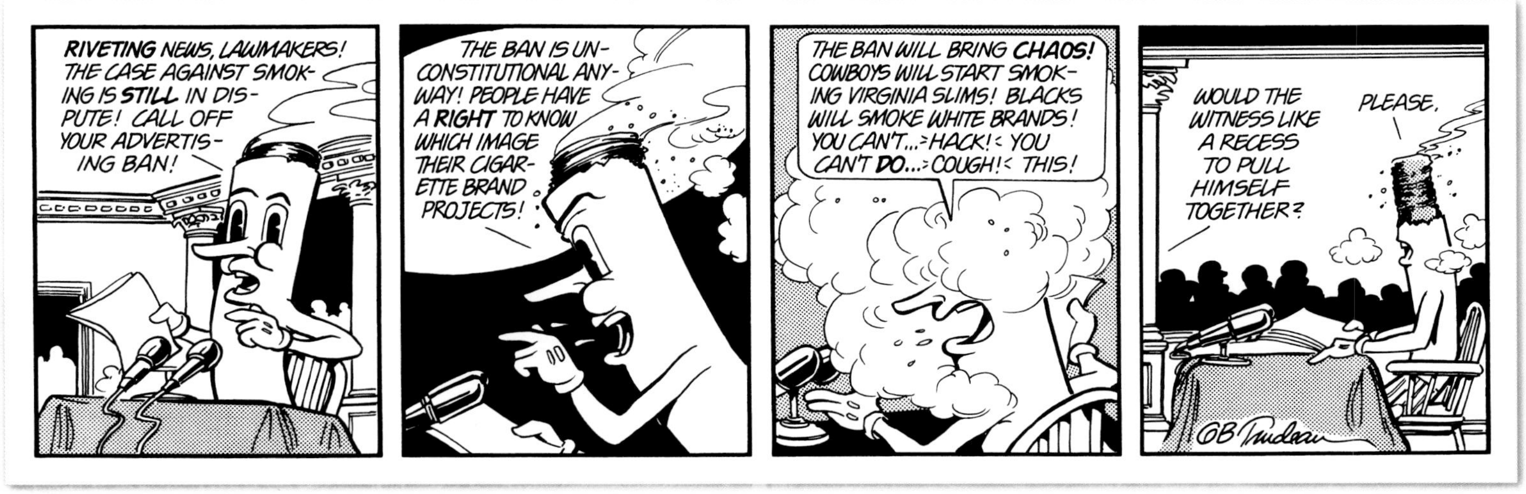

RIVETING NEWS, LAWMAKERS! THE CASE AGAINST SMOKING IS STILL IN DISPUTE! CALL OFF YOUR ADVERTISING BAN!
THE BAN IS UNCONSTITUTIONAL ANYWAY! PEOPLE HAVE A RIGHT TO KNOW WHICH IMAGE THEIR CIGARETTE BRAND PROJECTS!
THE BAN WILL BRING CHAOS! COWBOYS WILL START SMOKING VIRGINIA SLIMS! BLACKS WILL SMOKE WHITE BRANDS! YOU CAN'T... >HACK!< YOU CAN'T DO... >COUGH!< THIS!
WOULD THE WITNESS LIKE A RECESS TO PULL HIMSELF TOGETHER?
PLEASE.

6/27/90

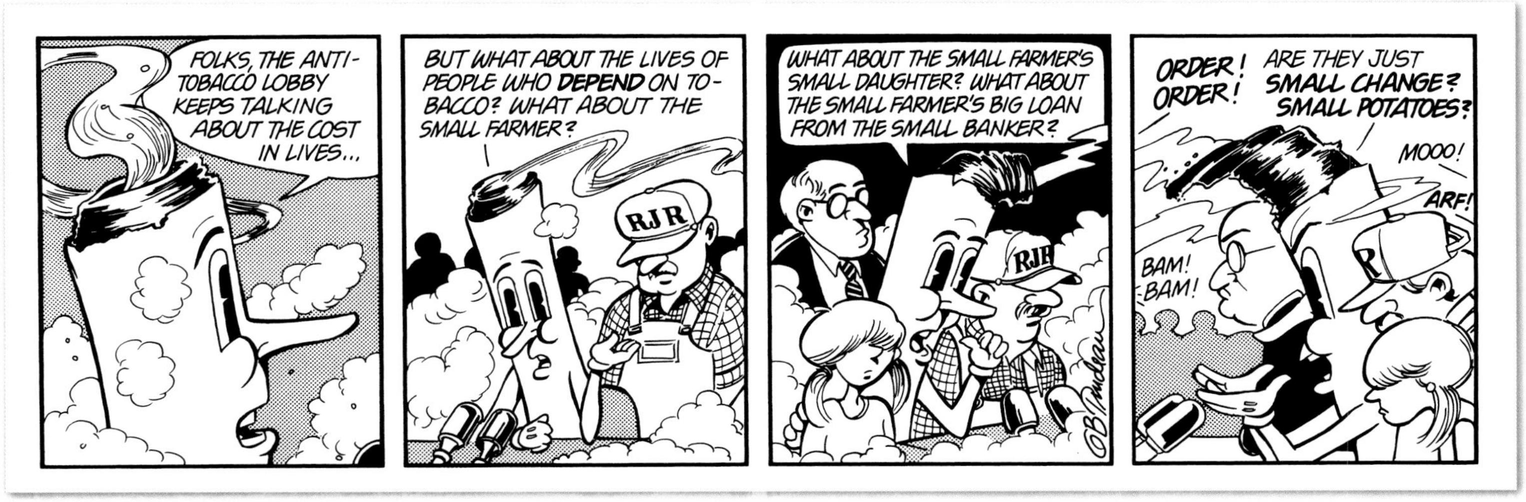

FOLKS, THE ANTI-TOBACCO LOBBY KEEPS TALKING ABOUT THE COST IN LIVES...
BUT WHAT ABOUT THE LIVES OF PEOPLE WHO DEPEND ON TOBACCO? WHAT ABOUT THE SMALL FARMER?
RJR
WHAT ABOUT THE SMALL FARMER'S SMALL DAUGHTER? WHAT ABOUT THE SMALL FARMER'S BIG LOAN FROM THE SMALL BANKER?
ORDER! ORDER!
ARE THEY JUST SMALL CHANGE? SMALL POTATOES?
MOOO!
ARF!
BAM! BAM!

6/28/90

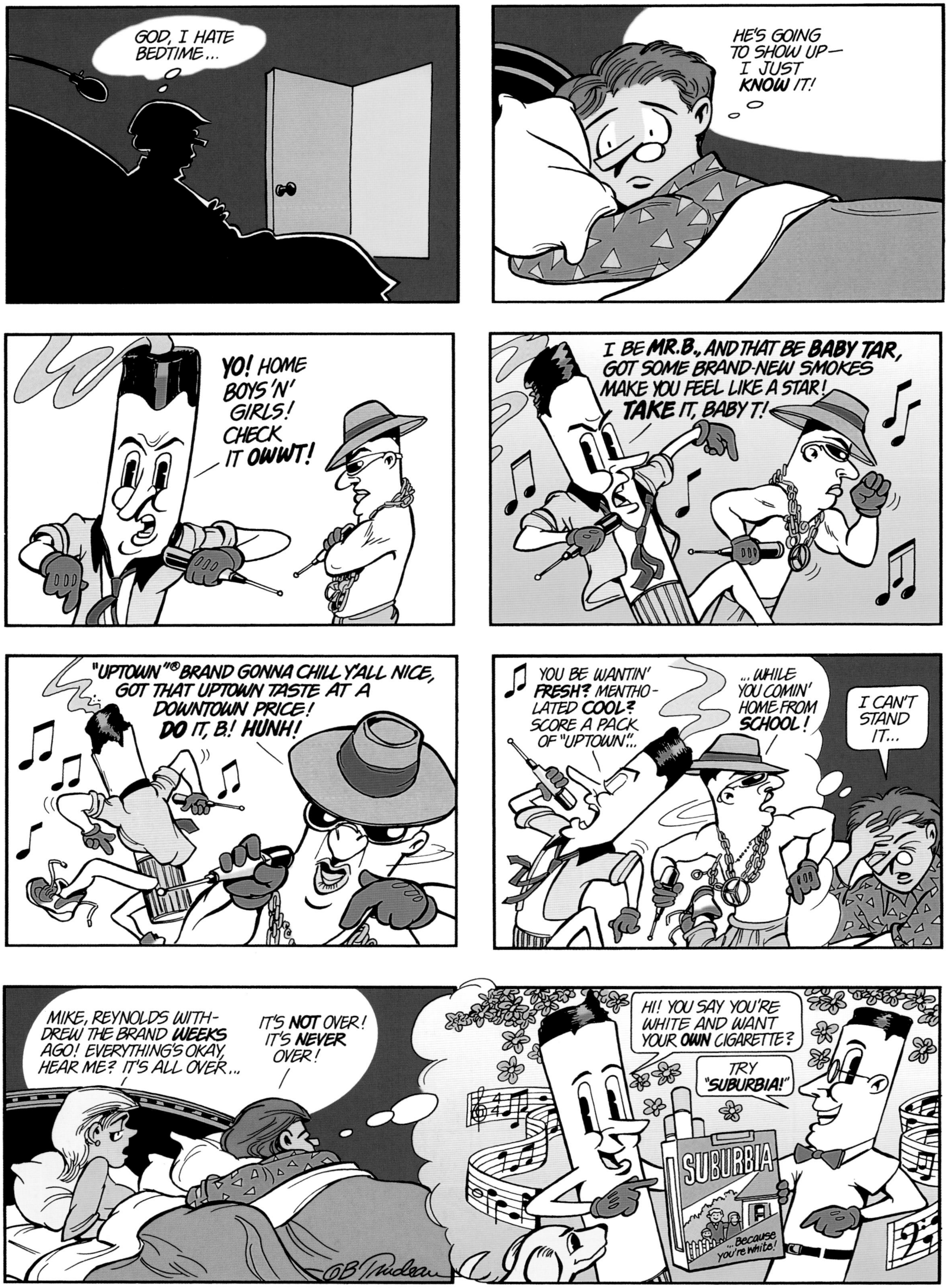
GOD, I HATE BEDTIME...
HE'S GOING TO SHOW UP— I JUST KNOW IT!
YO! HOME BOYS 'N' GIRLS! CHECK IT OWWT!
I BE MR.B., AND THAT BE BABY TAR, GOT SOME BRAND-NEW SMOKES MAKE YOU FEEL LIKE A STAR! TAKE IT, BABY T!
"UPTOWN"® BRAND GONNA CHILL Y'ALL NICE, GOT THAT UPTOWN TASTE AT A DOWNTOWN PRICE! DO IT, B! HUNH!
YOU BE WANTIN' FRESH? MENTHO-LATED COOL? SCORE A PACK OF "UPTOWN"...
...WHILE YOU COMIN' HOME FROM SCHOOL!
I CAN'T STAND IT...
MIKE, REYNOLDS WITH-DREW THE BRAND WEEKS AGO! EVERYTHING'S OKAY, HEAR ME? IT'S ALL OVER...
IT'S NOT OVER! IT'S NEVER OVER!
HI! YOU SAY YOU'RE WHITE AND WANT YOUR OWN CIGARETTE?
TRY "SUBURBIA!"
SUBURBIA
...Because you're white!
©B. Trudeau

2/25/90

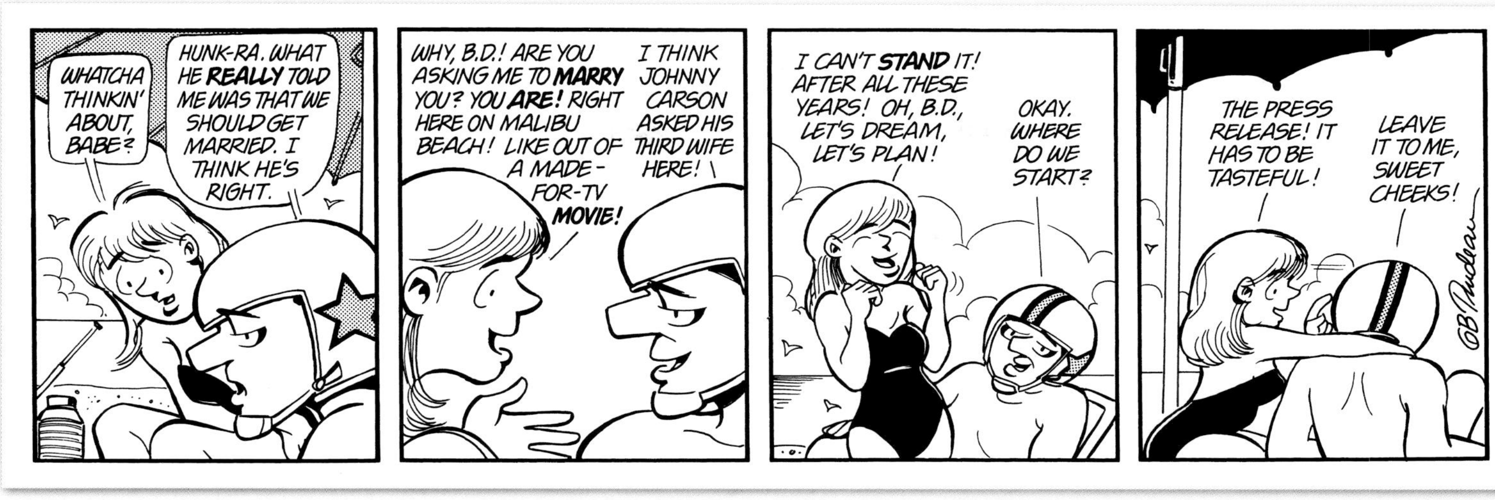
WHATCHA THINKIN' ABOUT, BABE?
HUNK-RA. WHAT HE **REALLY** TOLD ME WAS THAT WE SHOULD GET MARRIED. I THINK HE'S RIGHT.
WHY, B.D.! ARE YOU ASKING ME TO **MARRY** YOU? YOU **ARE!** RIGHT HERE ON MALIBU BEACH! LIKE OUT OF A MADE-FOR-TV **MOVIE!**
I THINK JOHNNY CARSON ASKED HIS THIRD WIFE HERE!
I CAN'T **STAND** IT! AFTER ALL THESE YEARS! OH, B.D., LET'S DREAM, LET'S PLAN!
OKAY. WHERE DO WE START?
THE PRESS RELEASE! IT HAS TO BE TASTEFUL!
LEAVE IT TO ME, SWEET CHEEKS!
GBTrudeau

7/17/90

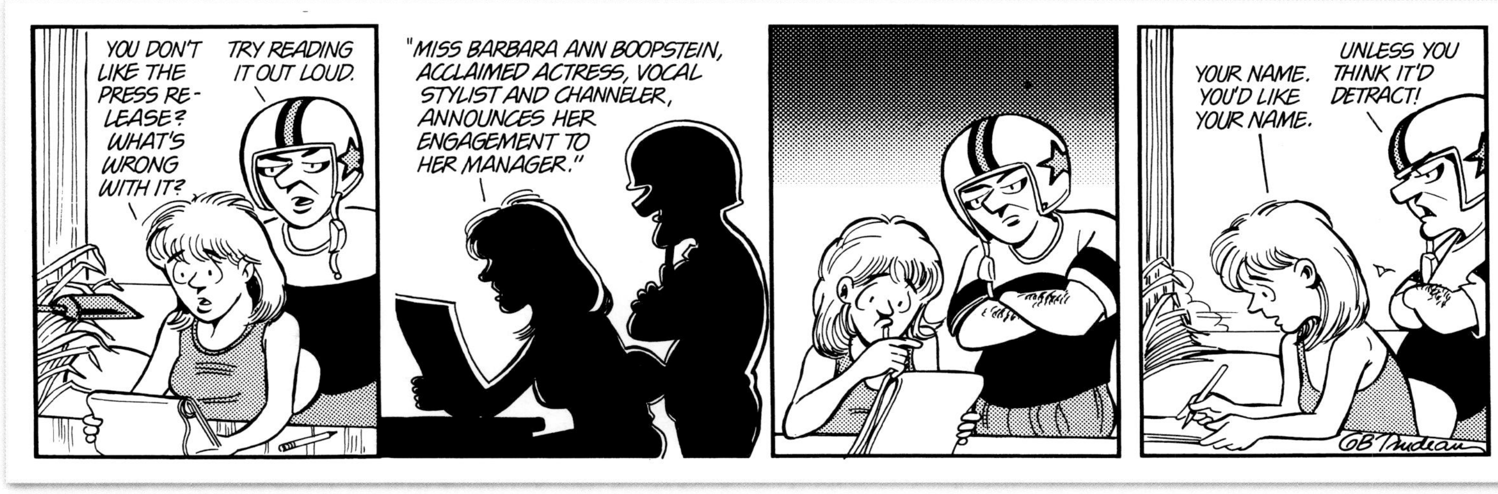
YOU DON'T LIKE THE PRESS RELEASE? WHAT'S WRONG WITH IT?
TRY READING IT OUT LOUD.
"MISS BARBARA ANN BOOPSTEIN, ACCLAIMED ACTRESS, VOCAL STYLIST AND CHANNELER, ANNOUNCES HER ENGAGEMENT TO HER MANAGER."
YOUR NAME. YOU'D LIKE YOUR NAME.
UNLESS YOU THINK IT'D DETRACT!
GBTrudeau

7/18/90

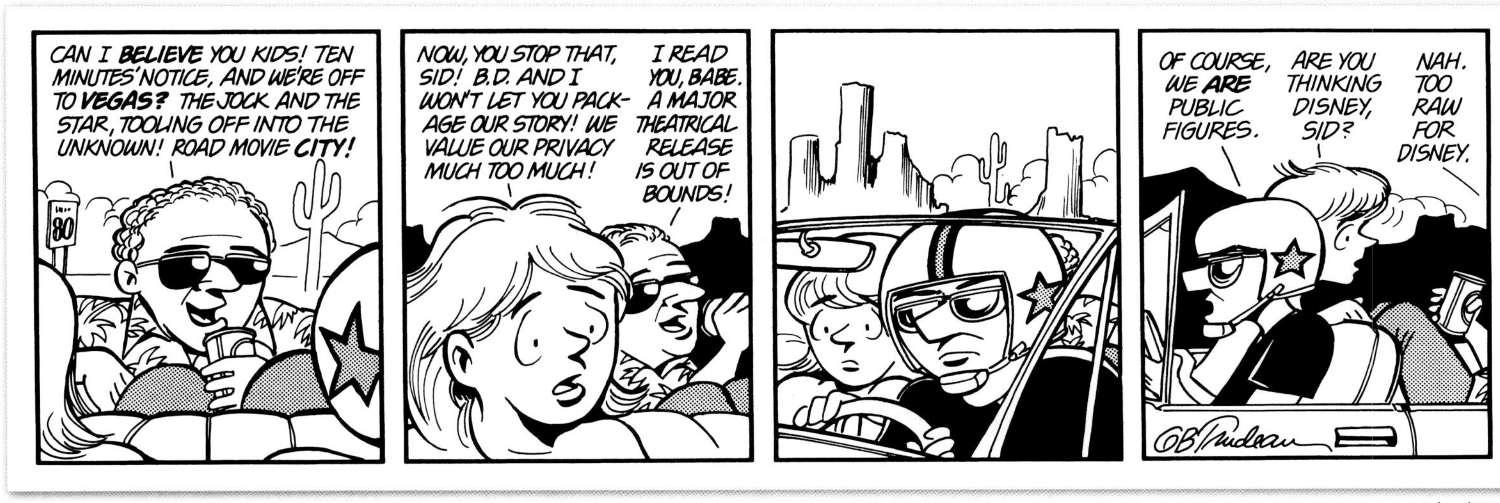
CAN I **BELIEVE** YOU KIDS! TEN MINUTES' NOTICE, AND WE'RE OFF TO **VEGAS?** THE JOCK AND THE STAR, TOOLING OFF INTO THE UNKNOWN! ROAD MOVIE **CITY!**
80
NOW, YOU STOP THAT, SID! B.D. AND I WON'T LET YOU PACKAGE OUR STORY! WE VALUE OUR PRIVACY MUCH TOO MUCH!
I READ **YOU, BABE.** A MAJOR THEATRICAL RELEASE IS OUT OF BOUNDS!
OF COURSE, WE **ARE** PUBLIC FIGURES.
ARE YOU THINKING DISNEY, SID?
NAH. TOO RAW FOR DISNEY.
GBTrudeau

7/26/90

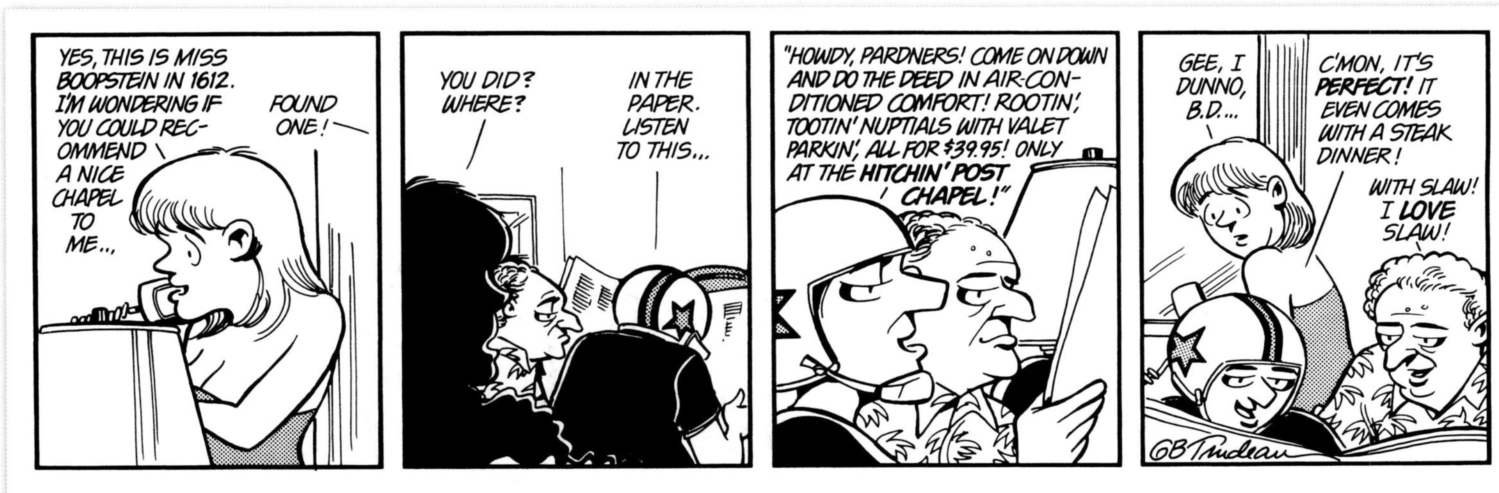
YES, THIS IS MISS BOOPSTEIN IN 1612. I'M WONDERING IF YOU COULD RECOMMEND A NICE CHAPEL TO ME...
FOUND ONE!
YOU DID? WHERE?
IN THE PAPER. LISTEN TO THIS...
"HOWDY, PARDNERS! COME ON DOWN AND DO THE DEED IN AIR-CONDITIONED COMFORT! ROOTIN', TOOTIN' NUPTIALS WITH VALET PARKIN', ALL FOR $39.95! ONLY AT THE **HITCHIN' POST CHAPEL!**"
GEE, I DUNNO, B.D...
C'MON, IT'S **PERFECT!** IT EVEN COMES WITH A STEAK DINNER!
WITH SLAW! I **LOVE** SLAW!
GBTrudeau

7/27/90

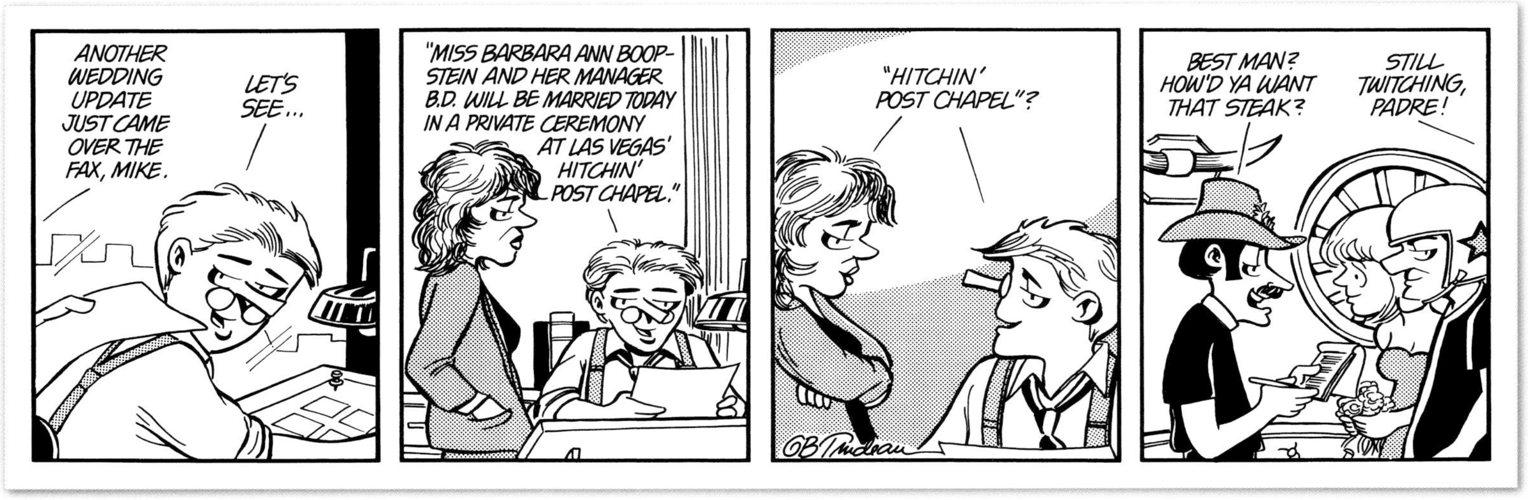
ANOTHER WEDDING UPDATE JUST CAME OVER THE FAX, MIKE.
LET'S SEE...
"MISS BARBARA ANN BOOPSTEIN AND HER MANAGER B.D. WILL BE MARRIED TODAY IN A PRIVATE CEREMONY AT LAS VEGAS' HITCHIN' POST CHAPEL."
"HITCHIN' POST CHAPEL"?
BEST MAN? HOW'D YA WANT THAT STEAK?
STILL TWITCHING, PADRE!

7/30/90

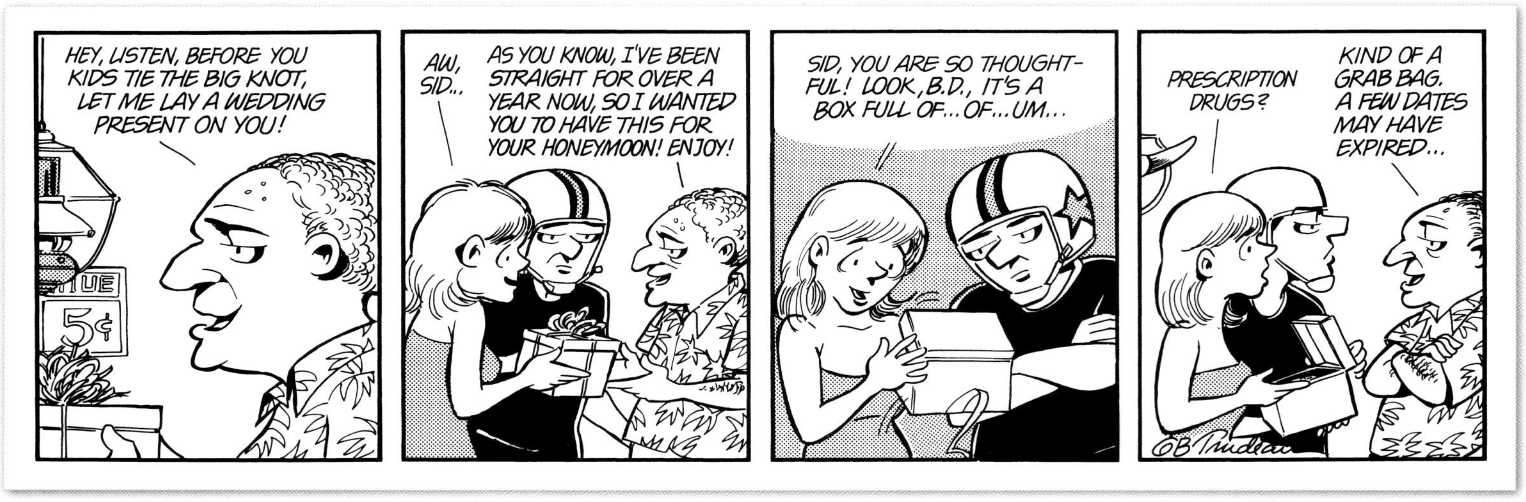
HEY, LISTEN, BEFORE YOU KIDS TIE THE BIG KNOT, LET ME LAY A WEDDING PRESENT ON YOU!
AW, SID...
AS YOU KNOW, I'VE BEEN STRAIGHT FOR OVER A YEAR NOW, SO I WANTED YOU TO HAVE THIS FOR YOUR HONEYMOON! ENJOY!
SID, YOU ARE SO THOUGHTFUL! LOOK, B.D., IT'S A BOX FULL OF... OF... UM...
PRESCRIPTION DRUGS?
KIND OF A GRAB BAG. A FEW DATES MAY HAVE EXPIRED...

7/31/90

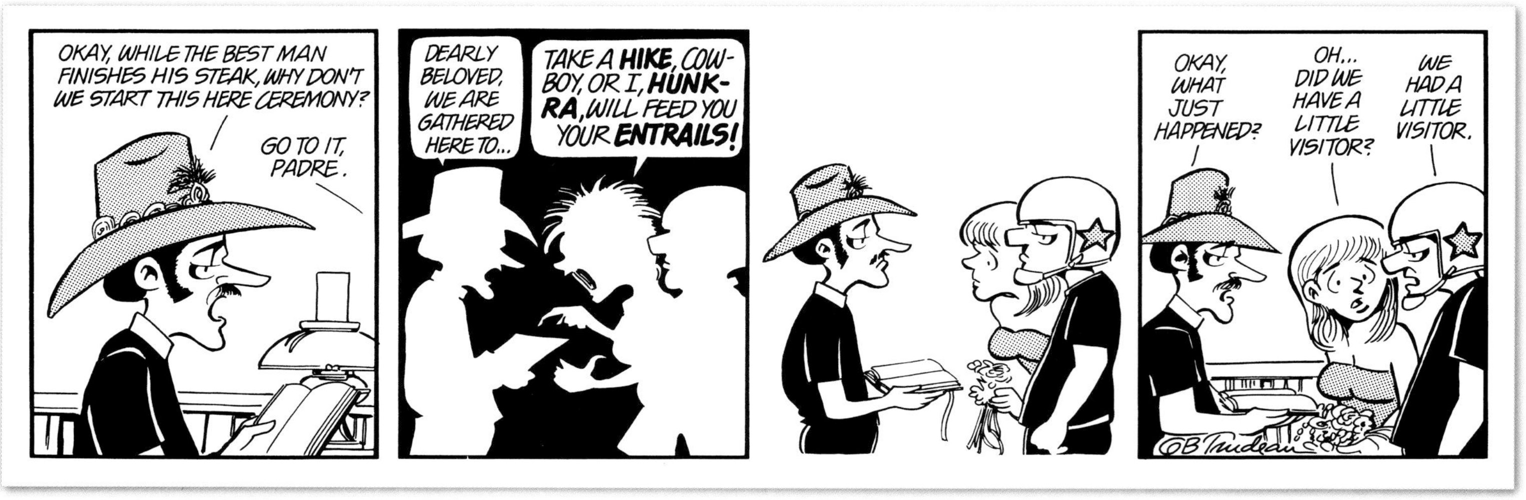
OKAY, WHILE THE BEST MAN FINISHES HIS STEAK, WHY DON'T WE START THIS HERE CEREMONY?
GO TO IT, PADRE.
DEARLY BELOVED, WE ARE GATHERED HERE TO...
TAKE A HIKE, COWBOY, OR I, HUNK-RA, WILL FEED YOU YOUR ENTRAILS!
OKAY, WHAT JUST HAPPENED?
OH... DID WE HAVE A LITTLE VISITOR?
WE HAD A LITTLE VISITOR.

8/1/90

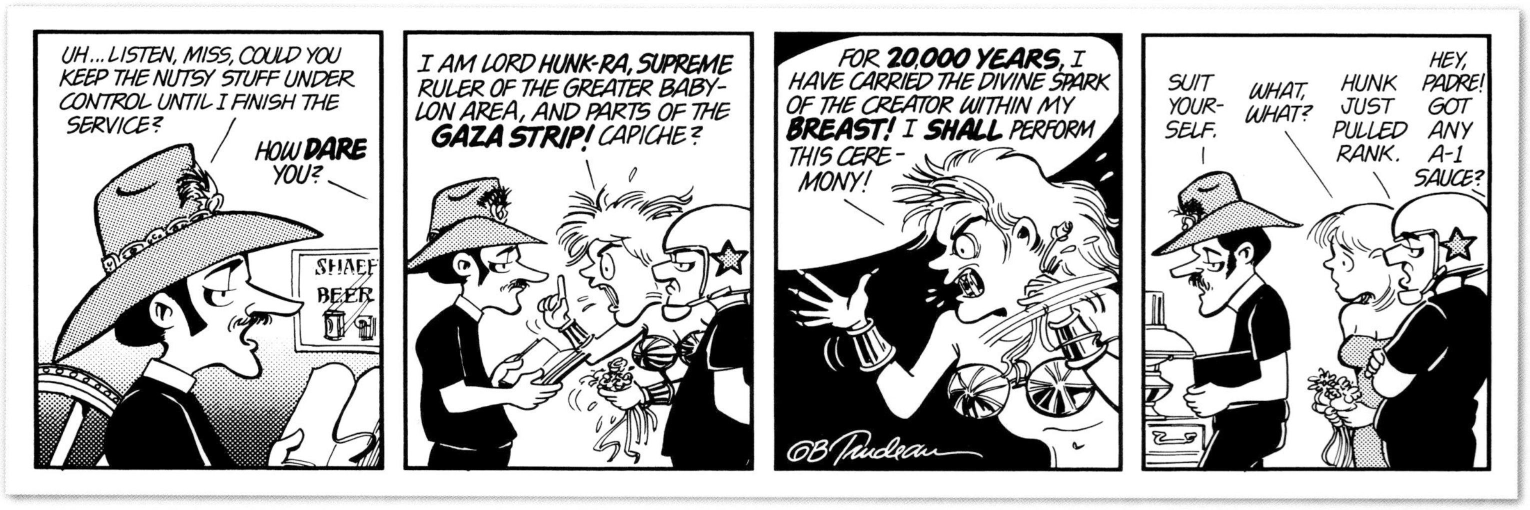
UH... LISTEN, MISS, COULD YOU KEEP THE NUTSY STUFF UNDER CONTROL UNTIL I FINISH THE SERVICE?
HOW DARE YOU?
I AM LORD HUNK-RA, SUPREME RULER OF THE GREATER BABYLON AREA, AND PARTS OF THE GAZA STRIP! CAPICHE?
FOR 20,000 YEARS, I HAVE CARRIED THE DIVINE SPARK OF THE CREATOR WITHIN MY BREAST! I SHALL PERFORM THIS CEREMONY!
SUIT YOURSELF.
WHAT, WHAT?
HUNK JUST PULLED RANK.
HEY, PADRE! GOT ANY A-1 SAUCE?

8/2/90

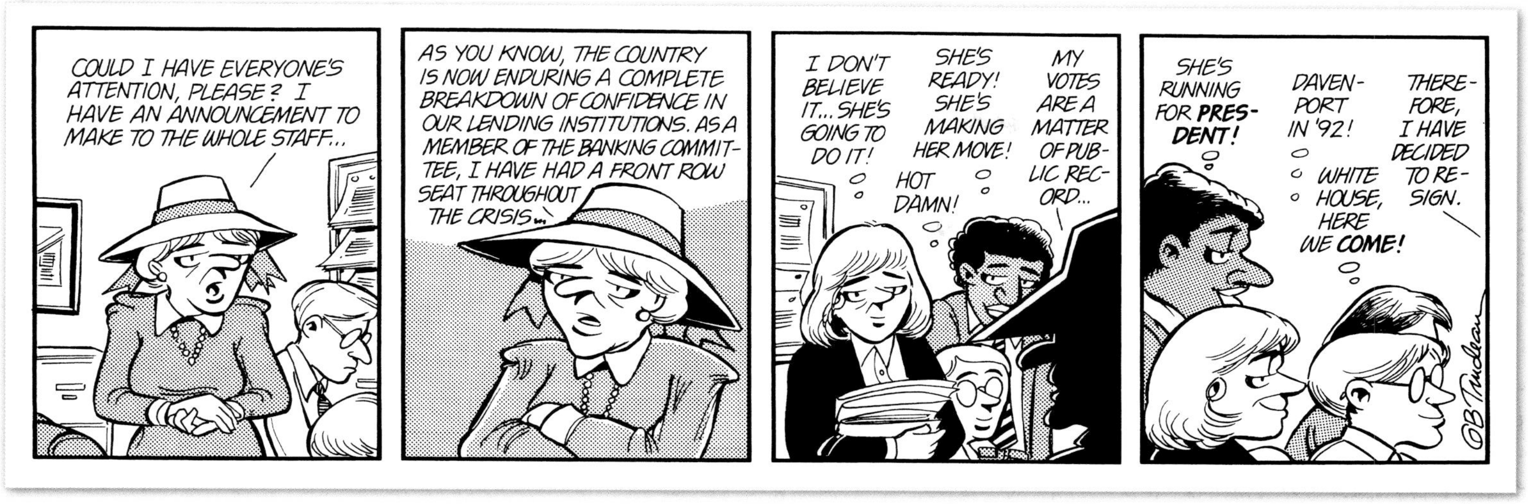
COULD I HAVE EVERYONE'S ATTENTION, PLEASE? I HAVE AN ANNOUNCEMENT TO MAKE TO THE WHOLE STAFF...
AS YOU KNOW, THE COUNTRY IS NOW ENDURING A COMPLETE BREAKDOWN OF CONFIDENCE IN OUR LENDING INSTITUTIONS. AS A MEMBER OF THE BANKING COMMITTEE, I HAVE HAD A FRONT ROW SEAT THROUGHOUT THE CRISIS...
I DON'T BELIEVE IT... SHE'S GOING TO DO IT!
SHE'S READY! SHE'S MAKING HER MOVE!
MY VOTES ARE A MATTER OF PUBLIC RECORD...
HOT DAMN!
SHE'S RUNNING FOR PRESIDENT!
DAVENPORT IN '92!
WHITE HOUSE, HERE WE COME!
THEREFORE, I HAVE DECIDED TO RESIGN.

8/13/90

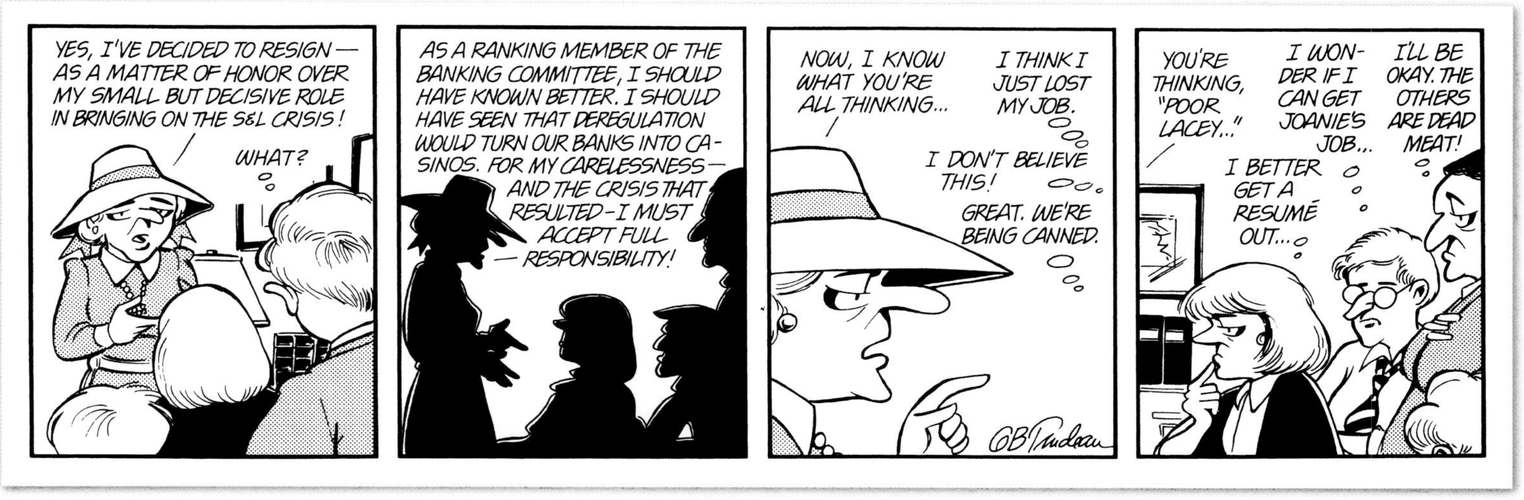
YES, I'VE DECIDED TO RESIGN — AS A MATTER OF HONOR OVER MY SMALL BUT DECISIVE ROLE IN BRINGING ON THE S&L CRISIS!
WHAT?
AS A RANKING MEMBER OF THE BANKING COMMITTEE, I SHOULD HAVE KNOWN BETTER. I SHOULD HAVE SEEN THAT DEREGULATION WOULD TURN OUR BANKS INTO CASINOS. FOR MY CARELESSNESS — AND THE CRISIS THAT RESULTED — I MUST ACCEPT FULL — RESPONSIBILITY!
NOW, I KNOW WHAT YOU'RE ALL THINKING...
I THINK I JUST LOST MY JOB.
I DON'T BELIEVE THIS!
GREAT. WE'RE BEING CANNED.
YOU'RE THINKING, "POOR LACEY..."
I WONDER IF I CAN GET JOANIE'S JOB...
I'LL BE OKAY. THE OTHERS ARE DEAD MEAT!
I BETTER GET A RESUMÉ OUT...

8/14/90

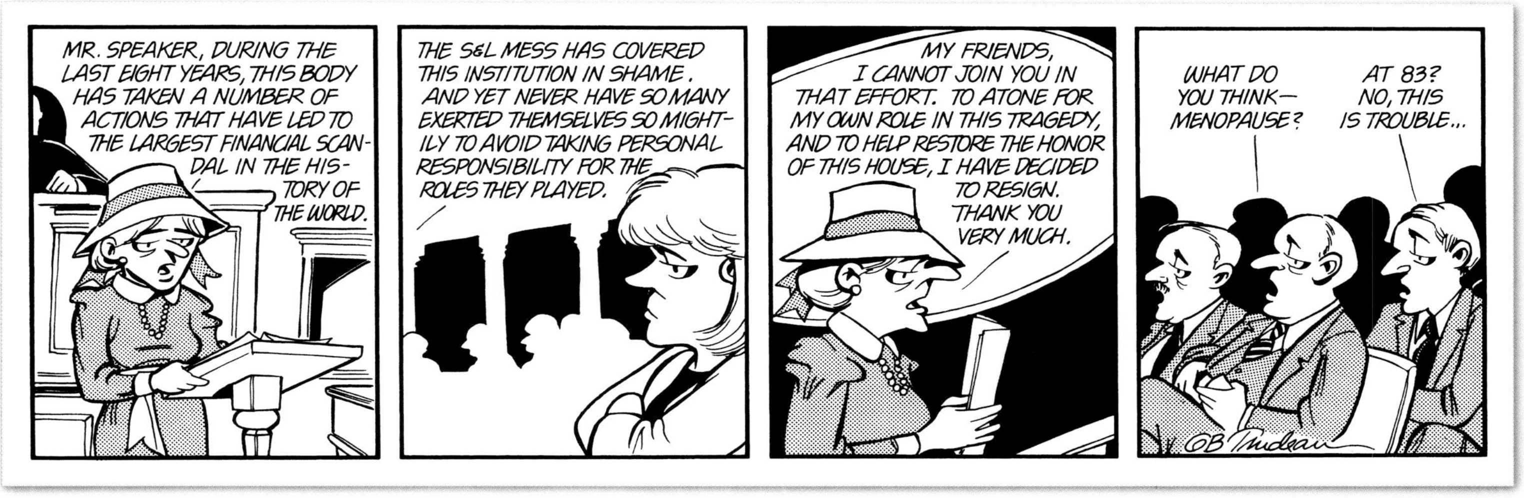
MR. SPEAKER, DURING THE LAST EIGHT YEARS, THIS BODY HAS TAKEN A NUMBER OF ACTIONS THAT HAVE LED TO THE LARGEST FINANCIAL SCANDAL IN THE HISTORY OF THE WORLD.
THE S&L MESS HAS COVERED THIS INSTITUTION IN SHAME. AND YET NEVER HAVE SO MANY EXERTED THEMSELVES SO MIGHTILY TO AVOID TAKING PERSONAL RESPONSIBILITY FOR THE ROLES THEY PLAYED.
MY FRIENDS, I CANNOT JOIN YOU IN THAT EFFORT. TO ATONE FOR MY OWN ROLE IN THIS TRAGEDY, AND TO HELP RESTORE THE HONOR OF THIS HOUSE, I HAVE DECIDED TO RESIGN. THANK YOU VERY MUCH.
WHAT DO YOU THINK — MENOPAUSE?
AT 83? NO, THIS IS TROUBLE...

8/16/90

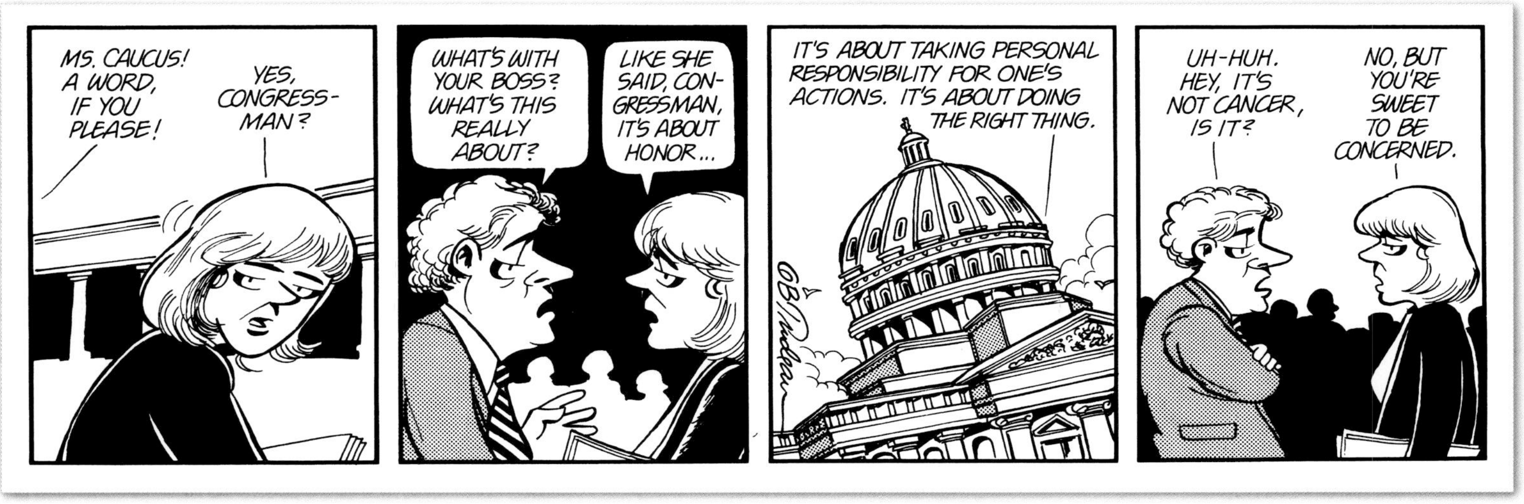
MS. CAUCUS! A WORD, IF YOU PLEASE!
YES, CONGRESSMAN?
WHAT'S WITH YOUR BOSS? WHAT'S THIS REALLY ABOUT?
LIKE SHE SAID, CONGRESSMAN, IT'S ABOUT HONOR...
IT'S ABOUT TAKING PERSONAL RESPONSIBILITY FOR ONE'S ACTIONS. IT'S ABOUT DOING THE RIGHT THING.
UH-HUH. HEY, IT'S NOT CANCER, IS IT?
NO, BUT YOU'RE SWEET TO BE CONCERNED.

8/17/90

Joanie Caucus

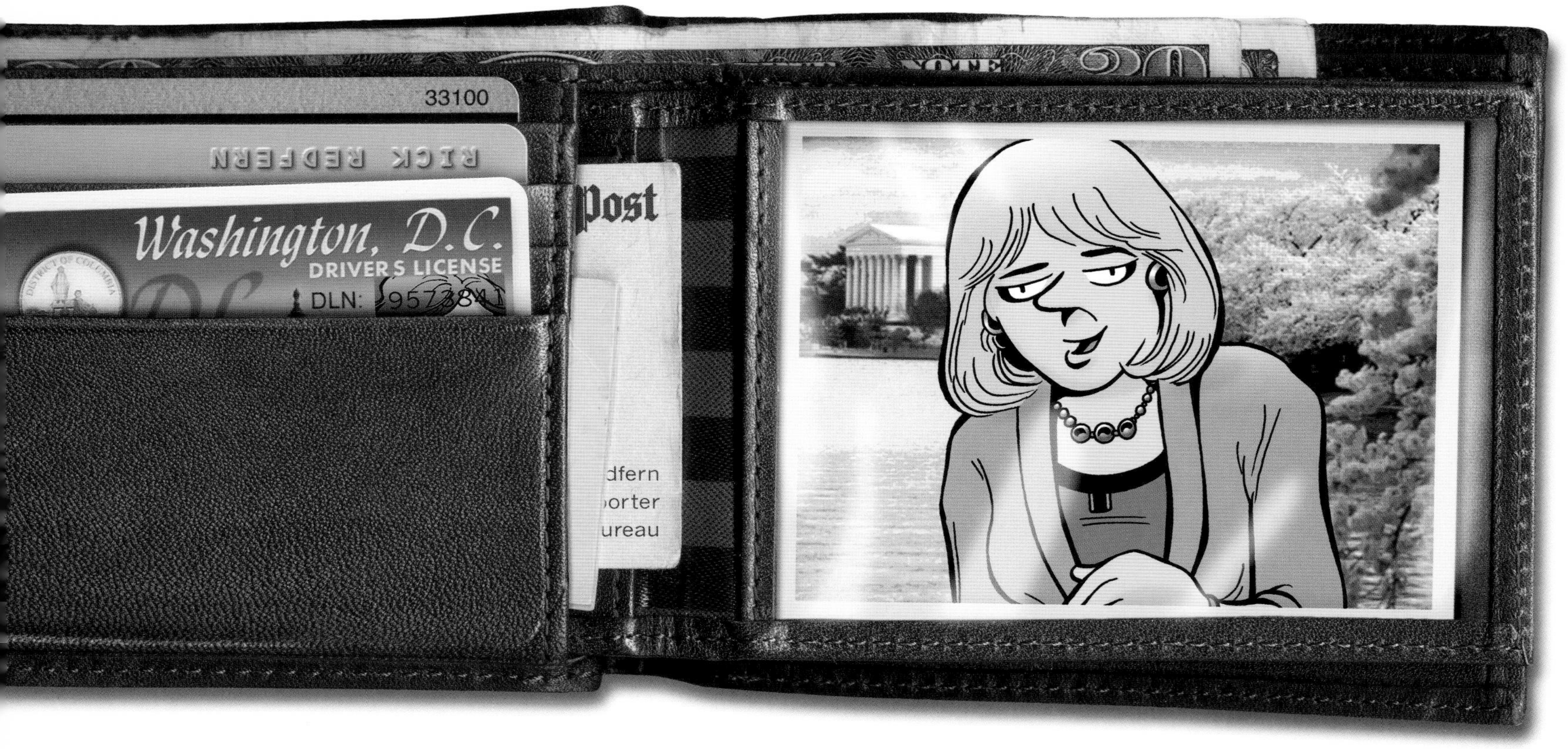
33100
Washington, D.C.
DRIVERS LICENSE
DLN:
Post
dfern
orter
ureau

This is how surreal it became: On May 27, 1977, I found myself at a podium at Boalt Hall, UC Berkeley's law school, poised to give the commencement address. I glanced down into the front row of students, and there in the center was an empty seat, upon which had been placed a program and mortarboard. This was Joanie's chair, where she would have sat in rapt anticipation had she in fact been real.

To a surprising degree, she was, if only to me and the Class of '77. There'd been the turbulent admissions drama, when I placed Joanie on the waiting lists of several real law schools. After three hundred students organized a petition demanding she be admitted, Boston University sent her an acceptance letter, as did Berkeley, the University of Virginia, and five other schools. From there, it only got stranger. Everyone played it straight. There were the innumerable forms I had to fill out on Joanie's behalf. Her student card and packet arrived, as did the university magazine. For three years, she received letters from the Berkeley community, and when she graduated, a Southern California law firm offered her a job. Soon thereafter, the Exxon Educational Foundation announced a $100,000 Joanie Caucus Exxon Fellowship Program to aid women over thirty who wanted to become lawyers.

When writers are lucky, they'll occasionally create a character in whom readers become unusually vested. The downside is a tremendous pressure to treat that character gently, to not place her in jeopardy from which she cannot escape. But in Joanie's case, I was

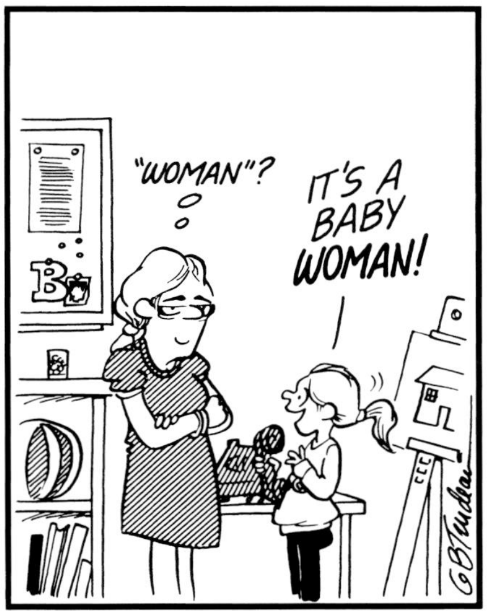
"WOMAN"?
IT'S A BABY WOMAN!

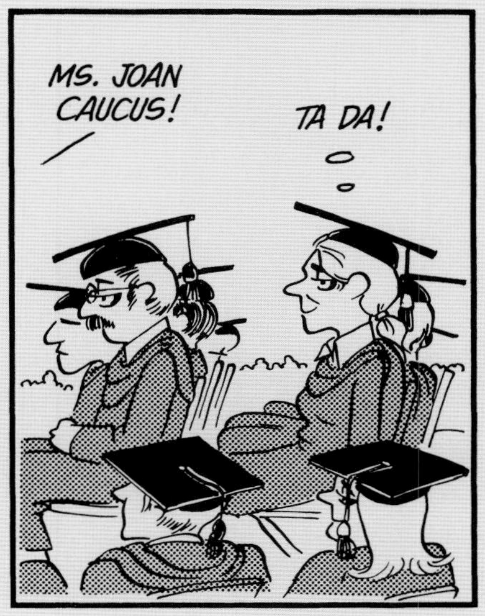
MS. JOAN CAUCUS!
TA DA!

happy to oblige, to let her survive the downdrafts and soar into a new future, becoming the kind of role model that the times seemed to demand. While it's true that role models tend not to make very interesting characters, the unfolding revolution of feminism was so inherently dramatic, I never considered giving her another path.

Especially since I was having so much fun. Joanie was joining a feminist cohort whose company I happened to enjoy; indeed, I named her after the National Women's Political Caucus. Thanks to her, I found myself at large gatherings in which I was sometimes the only man in the room. Skeptical male friends thought I had stumbled on a brilliant new dating paradigm, but mostly I had a sense that these women were on the edge of some extraordinary social shift and I didn't want to miss out.

Of course, personal transformation can sometimes inflict collateral damage, and the price Joanie paid was the enduring fury of J.J., the child she abandoned. By now, the rift is clearly beyond mending. I've painted myself into a corner with J.J.; her resentment has hardened, and there are too many people who have borne this kind of rage through their entire lives to make a tidy reconciliation fully believable. Still, Joanie's life is its own kind of triumph. She remade her life at precisely that moment when society would finally support it in a woman. That some of her choices should leave her racked with regret no longer surprises. As my wife likes to say, there are no charmed lives. Only lives.

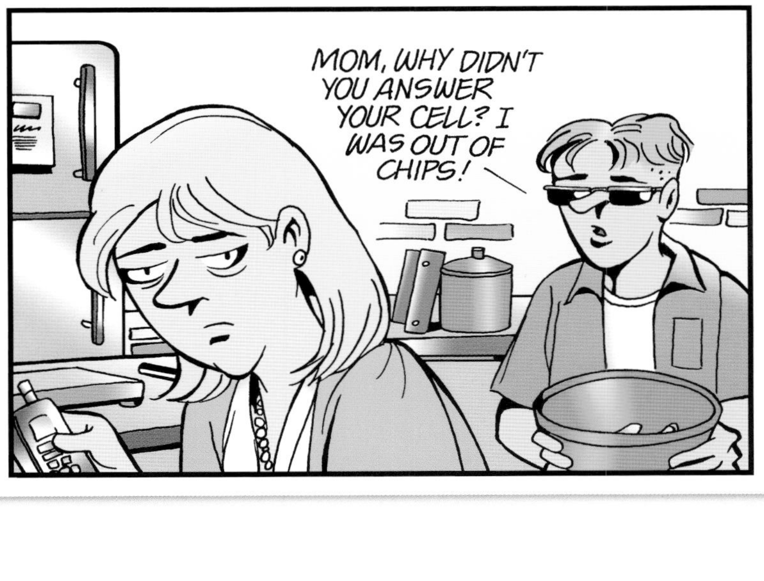
MOM, WHY DIDN'T YOU ANSWER YOUR CELL? I WAS OUT OF CHIPS!

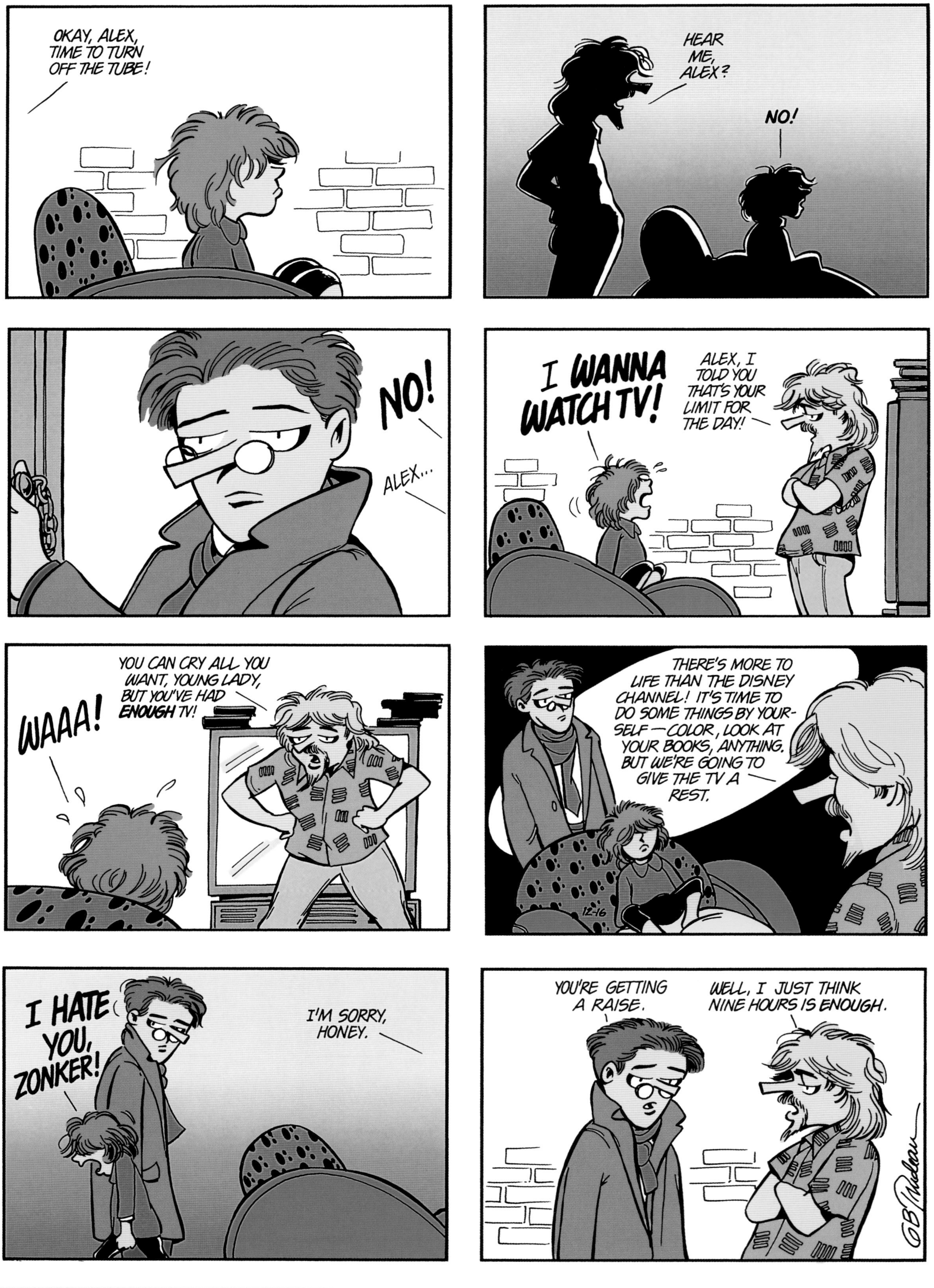
OKAY, ALEX, TIME TO TURN OFF THE TUBE!
HEAR ME, ALEX?
NO!
NO!
ALEX...
I WANNA WATCH TV!
ALEX, I TOLD YOU THAT'S YOUR LIMIT FOR THE DAY!
WAAA!
YOU CAN CRY ALL YOU WANT, YOUNG LADY, BUT YOU'VE HAD ENOUGH TV!
THERE'S MORE TO LIFE THAN THE DISNEY CHANNEL! IT'S TIME TO DO SOME THINGS BY YOURSELF—COLOR, LOOK AT YOUR BOOKS, ANYTHING. BUT WE'RE GOING TO GIVE THE TV A REST.
12-16
I HATE YOU, ZONKER!
I'M SORRY, HONEY.
YOU'RE GETTING A RAISE.
WELL, I JUST THINK NINE HOURS IS ENOUGH.
GBTrudeau

12/16/90

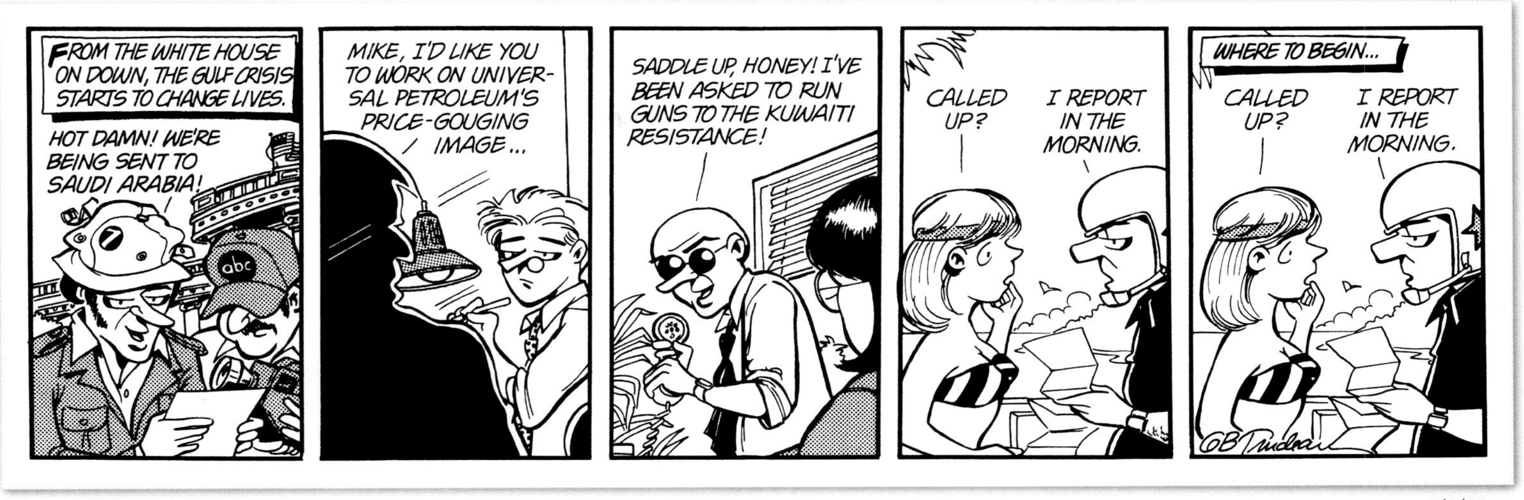
FROM THE WHITE HOUSE ON DOWN, THE GULF CRISIS STARTS TO CHANGE LIVES.
HOT DAMN! WE'RE BEING SENT TO SAUDI ARABIA!
MIKE, I'D LIKE YOU TO WORK ON UNIVERSAL PETROLEUM'S PRICE-GOUGING IMAGE...
SADDLE UP, HONEY! I'VE BEEN ASKED TO RUN GUNS TO THE KUWAITI RESISTANCE!
CALLED UP?
I REPORT IN THE MORNING.
WHERE TO BEGIN...
CALLED UP?
I REPORT IN THE MORNING.

9/5/90

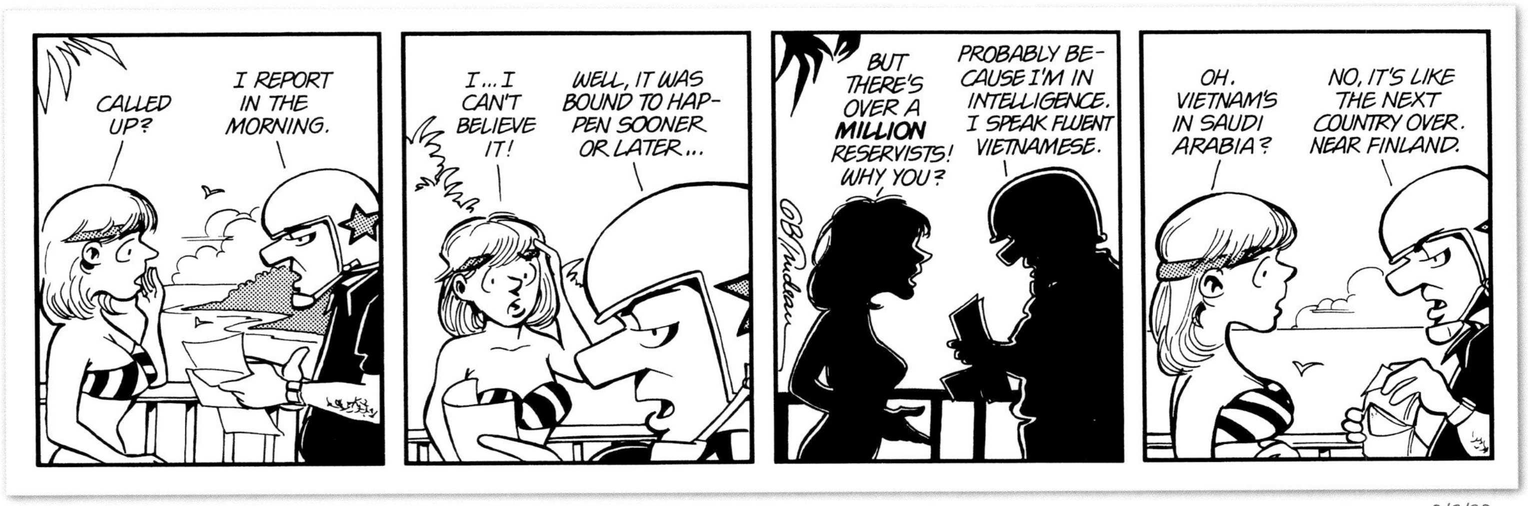
CALLED UP?
I REPORT IN THE MORNING.
I... I CAN'T BELIEVE IT!
WELL, IT WAS BOUND TO HAPPEN SOONER OR LATER...
BUT THERE'S OVER A MILLION RESERVISTS! WHY YOU?
PROBABLY BECAUSE I'M IN INTELLIGENCE. I SPEAK FLUENT VIETNAMESE.
OH. VIETNAM'S IN SAUDI ARABIA?
NO, IT'S LIKE THE NEXT COUNTRY OVER. NEAR FINLAND.

9/6/90

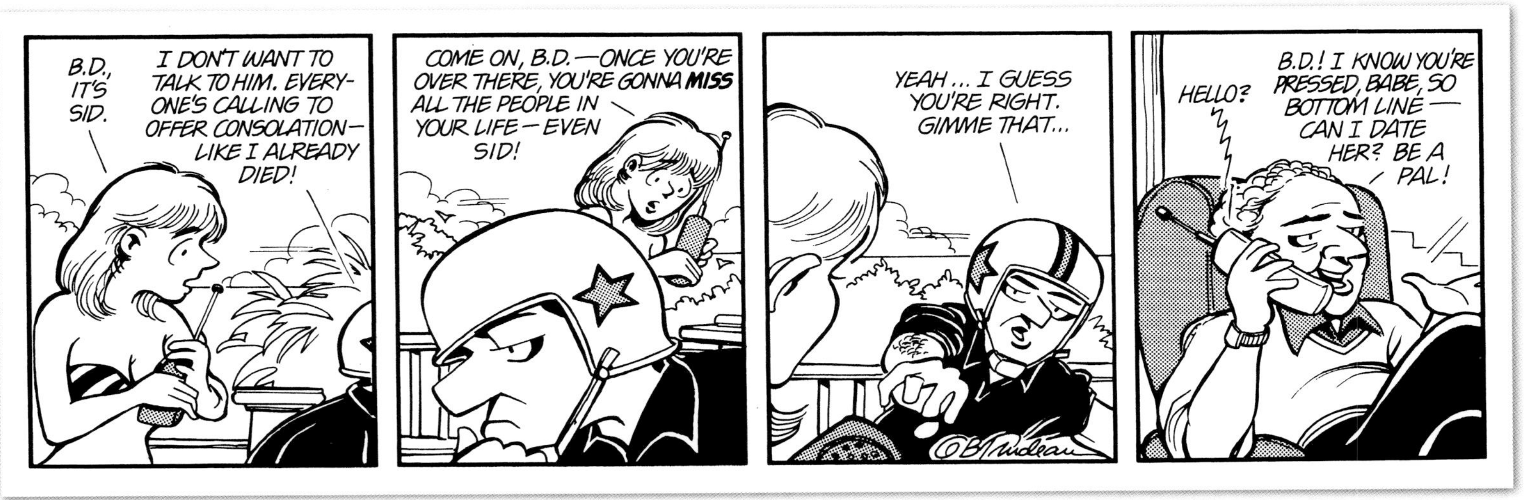
B.D., IT'S SID.
I DON'T WANT TO TALK TO HIM. EVERYONE'S CALLING TO OFFER CONSOLATION—LIKE I ALREADY DIED!
COME ON, B.D.—ONCE YOU'RE OVER THERE, YOU'RE GONNA MISS ALL THE PEOPLE IN YOUR LIFE—EVEN SID!
YEAH ... I GUESS YOU'RE RIGHT. GIMME THAT...
HELLO?
B.D.! I KNOW YOU'RE PRESSED, BABE, SO BOTTOM LINE—CAN I DATE HER? BE A PAL!

9/8/90

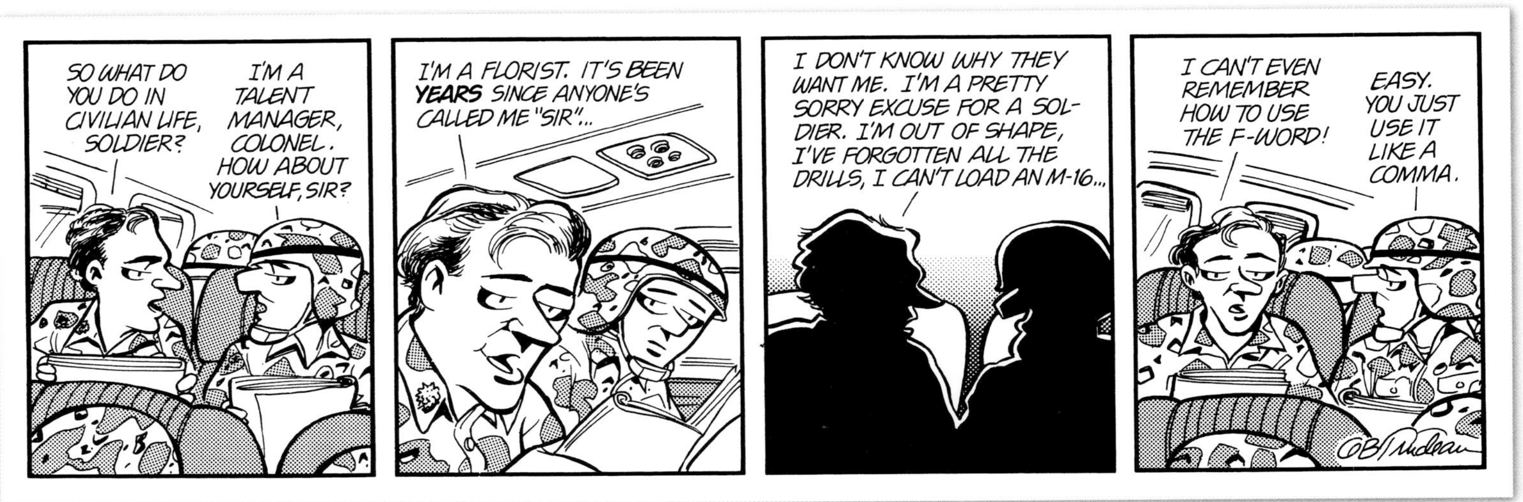
SO WHAT DO YOU DO IN CIVILIAN LIFE, SOLDIER?
I'M A TALENT MANAGER, COLONEL. HOW ABOUT YOURSELF, SIR?
I'M A FLORIST. IT'S BEEN YEARS SINCE ANYONE'S CALLED ME "SIR"...
I DON'T KNOW WHY THEY WANT ME. I'M A PRETTY SORRY EXCUSE FOR A SOLDIER. I'M OUT OF SHAPE, I'VE FORGOTTEN ALL THE DRILLS, I CAN'T LOAD AN M-16...
I CAN'T EVEN REMEMBER HOW TO USE THE F-WORD!
EASY. YOU JUST USE IT LIKE A COMMA.

9/11/90

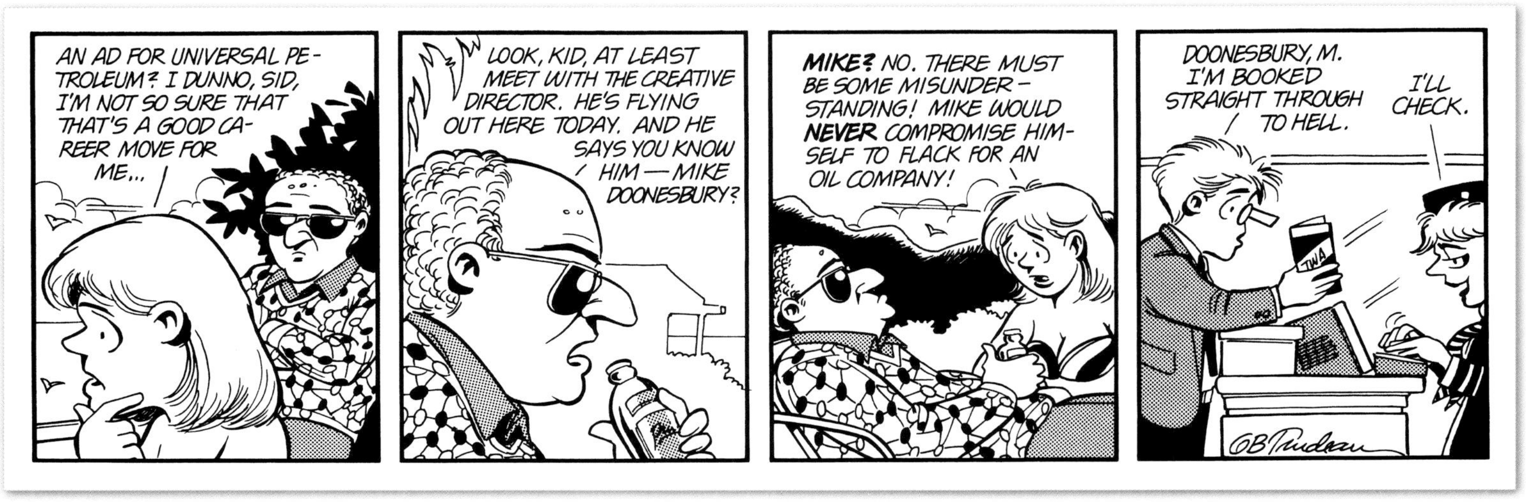
AN AD FOR UNIVERSAL PETROLEUM? I DUNNO, SID, I'M NOT SO SURE THAT THAT'S A GOOD CAREER MOVE FOR ME...
LOOK, KID, AT LEAST MEET WITH THE CREATIVE DIRECTOR. HE'S FLYING OUT HERE TODAY. AND HE SAYS YOU KNOW HIM — MIKE DOONESBURY?
MIKE? NO. THERE MUST BE SOME MISUNDERSTANDING! MIKE WOULD NEVER COMPROMISE HIMSELF TO FLACK FOR AN OIL COMPANY!
DOONESBURY, M. I'M BOOKED STRAIGHT THROUGH TO HELL.
I'LL CHECK.
TWA
GBTrudeau

10/4/90

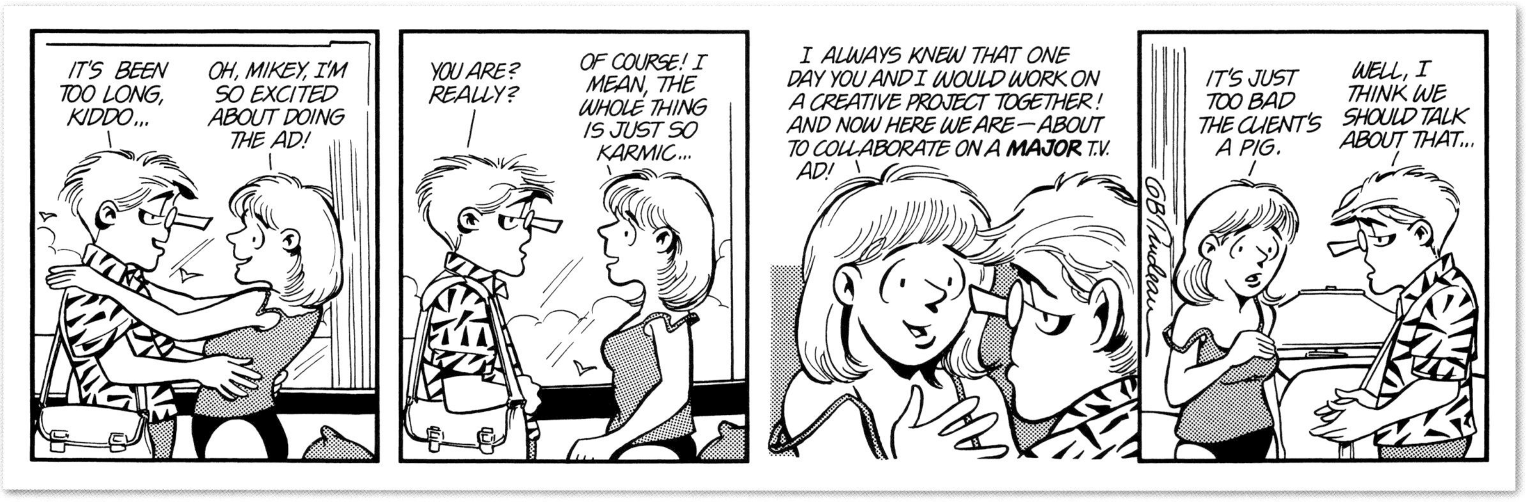
IT'S BEEN TOO LONG, KIDDO...
OH, MIKEY, I'M SO EXCITED ABOUT DOING THE AD!
YOU ARE? REALLY?
OF COURSE! I MEAN, THE WHOLE THING IS JUST SO KARMIC...
I ALWAYS KNEW THAT ONE DAY YOU AND I WOULD WORK ON A CREATIVE PROJECT TOGETHER! AND NOW HERE WE ARE — ABOUT TO COLLABORATE ON A MAJOR T.V. AD!
GBTrudeau
IT'S JUST TOO BAD THE CLIENT'S A PIG.
WELL, I THINK WE SHOULD TALK ABOUT THAT...

10/5/90

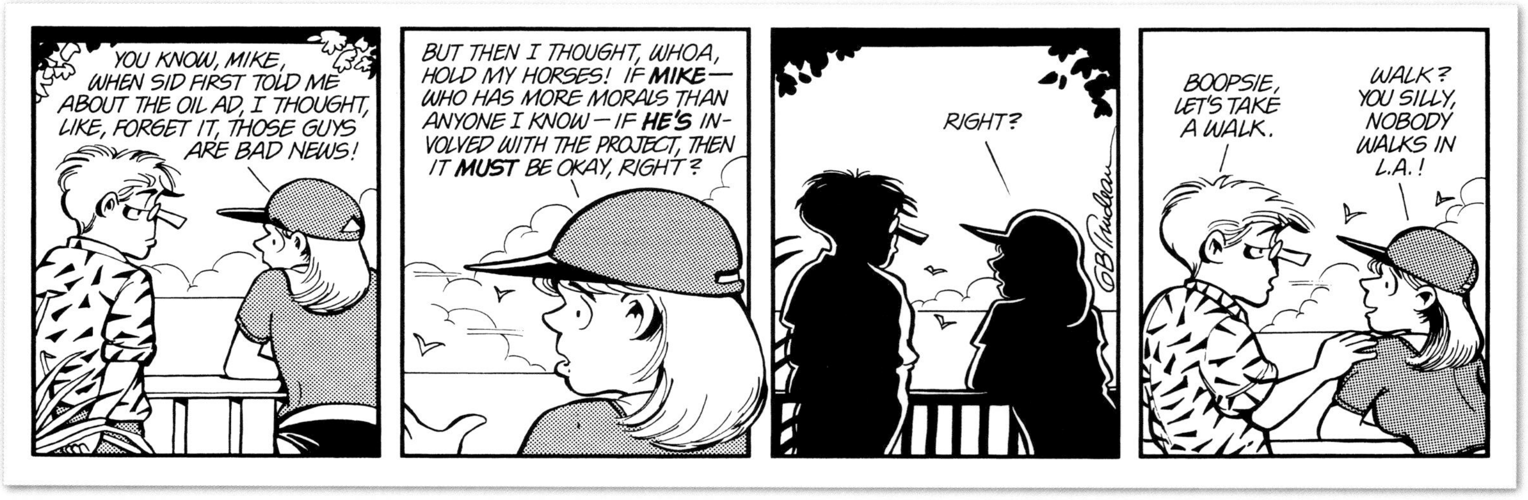
YOU KNOW, MIKE, WHEN SID FIRST TOLD ME ABOUT THE OIL AD, I THOUGHT, LIKE, FORGET IT, THOSE GUYS ARE BAD NEWS!
BUT THEN I THOUGHT, WHOA, HOLD MY HORSES! IF MIKE — WHO HAS MORE MORALS THAN ANYONE I KNOW — IF HE'S INVOLVED WITH THE PROJECT, THEN IT MUST BE OKAY, RIGHT?
RIGHT?
GBTrudeau
BOOPSIE, LET'S TAKE A WALK.
WALK? YOU SILLY, NOBODY WALKS IN L.A.!

10/6/90

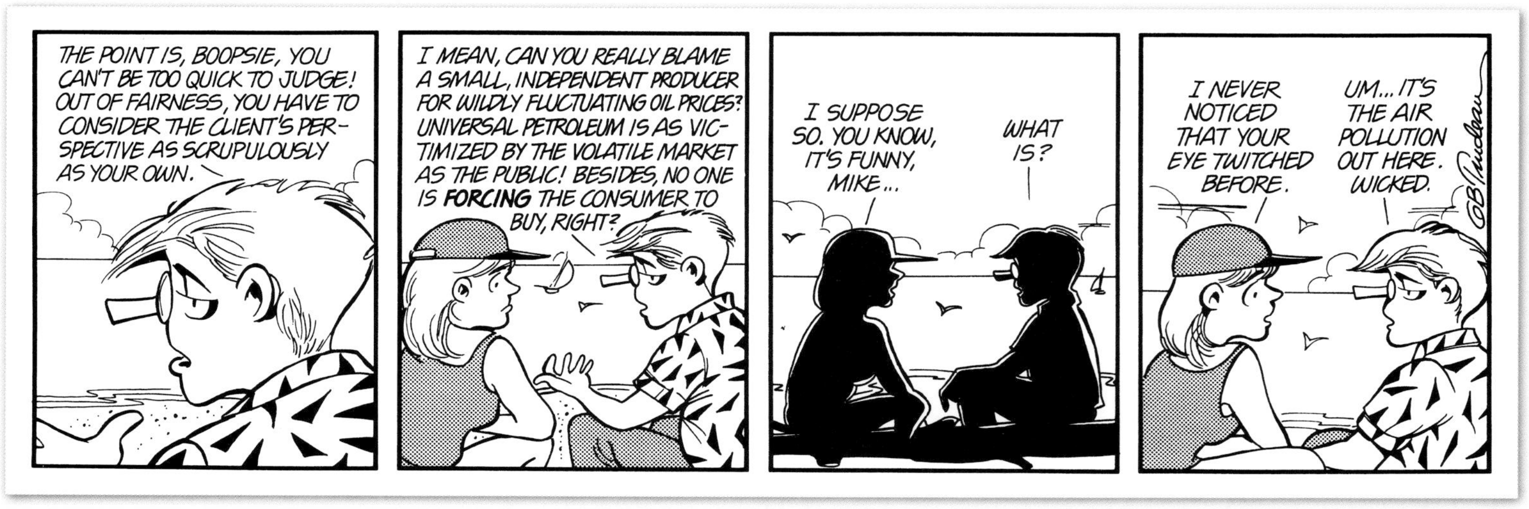
THE POINT IS, BOOPSIE, YOU CAN'T BE TOO QUICK TO JUDGE! OUT OF FAIRNESS, YOU HAVE TO CONSIDER THE CLIENT'S PERSPECTIVE AS SCRUPULOUSLY AS YOUR OWN.
I MEAN, CAN YOU REALLY BLAME A SMALL, INDEPENDENT PRODUCER FOR WILDLY FLUCTUATING OIL PRICES? UNIVERSAL PETROLEUM IS AS VICTIMIZED BY THE VOLATILE MARKET AS THE PUBLIC! BESIDES, NO ONE IS FORCING THE CONSUMER TO BUY, RIGHT?
I SUPPOSE SO. YOU KNOW, IT'S FUNNY, MIKE...
WHAT IS?
I NEVER NOTICED THAT YOUR EYE TWITCHED BEFORE.
UM... IT'S THE AIR POLLUTION OUT HERE. WICKED.
GBTrudeau

10/9/90

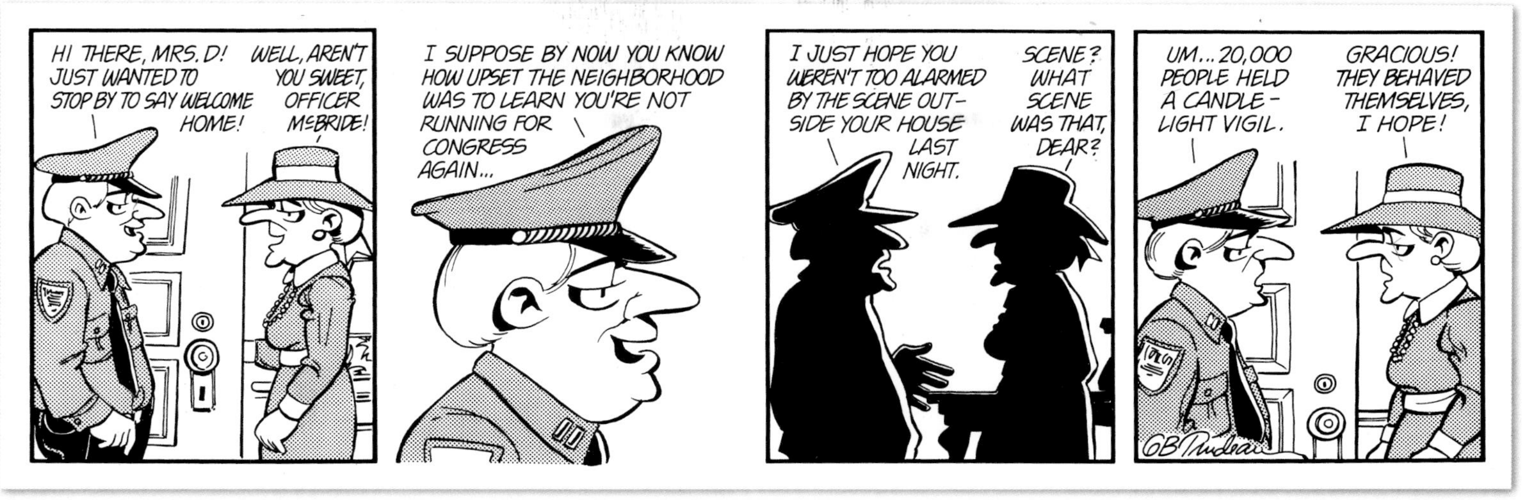
HI THERE, MRS. D! JUST WANTED TO STOP BY TO SAY WELCOME HOME!
WELL, AREN'T YOU SWEET, OFFICER McBRIDE!
I SUPPOSE BY NOW YOU KNOW HOW UPSET THE NEIGHBORHOOD WAS TO LEARN YOU'RE NOT RUNNING FOR CONGRESS AGAIN...
I JUST HOPE YOU WEREN'T TOO ALARMED BY THE SCENE OUTSIDE YOUR HOUSE LAST NIGHT.
SCENE? WHAT SCENE WAS THAT, DEAR?
UM... 20,000 PEOPLE HELD A CANDLE-LIGHT VIGIL.
GRACIOUS! THEY BEHAVED THEMSELVES, I HOPE!
GB Trudeau

10/29/90

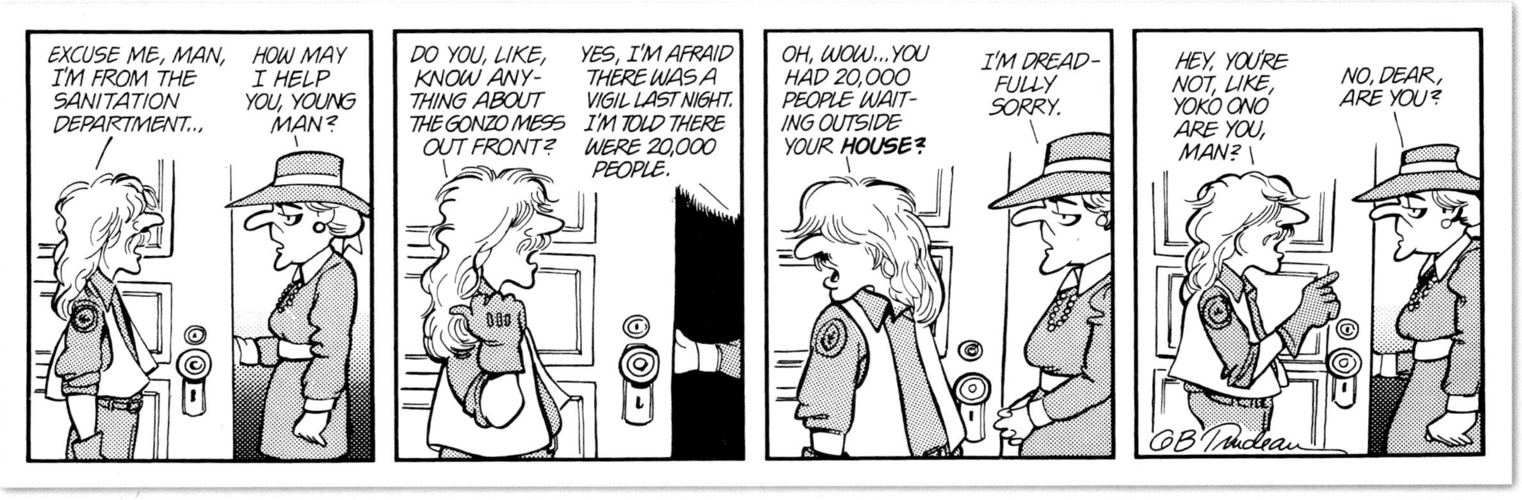
EXCUSE ME, MAN, I'M FROM THE SANITATION DEPARTMENT...,
HOW MAY I HELP YOU, YOUNG MAN?
DO YOU, LIKE, KNOW ANYTHING ABOUT THE GONZO MESS OUT FRONT?
YES, I'M AFRAID THERE WAS A VIGIL LAST NIGHT. I'M TOLD THERE WERE 20,000 PEOPLE.
OH, WOW... YOU HAD 20,000 PEOPLE WAITING OUTSIDE YOUR HOUSE?
I'M DREADFULLY SORRY.
HEY, YOU'RE NOT, LIKE, YOKO ONO ARE YOU, MAN?
NO, DEAR, ARE YOU?
GB Trudeau

10/31/90

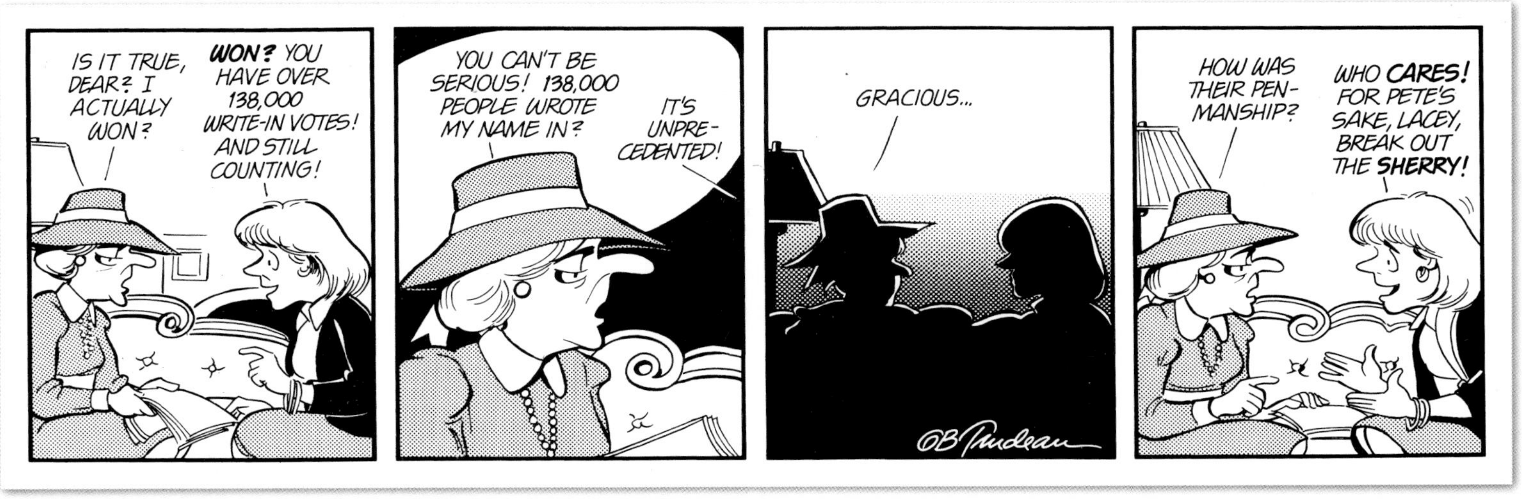
IS IT TRUE, DEAR? I ACTUALLY WON?
WON? YOU HAVE OVER 138,000 WRITE-IN VOTES! AND STILL COUNTING!
YOU CAN'T BE SERIOUS! 138,000 PEOPLE WROTE MY NAME IN?
IT'S UNPRECEDENTED!
GRACIOUS...
GB Trudeau
HOW WAS THEIR PENMANSHIP?
WHO CARES! FOR PETE'S SAKE, LACEY, BREAK OUT THE SHERRY!

11/7/90

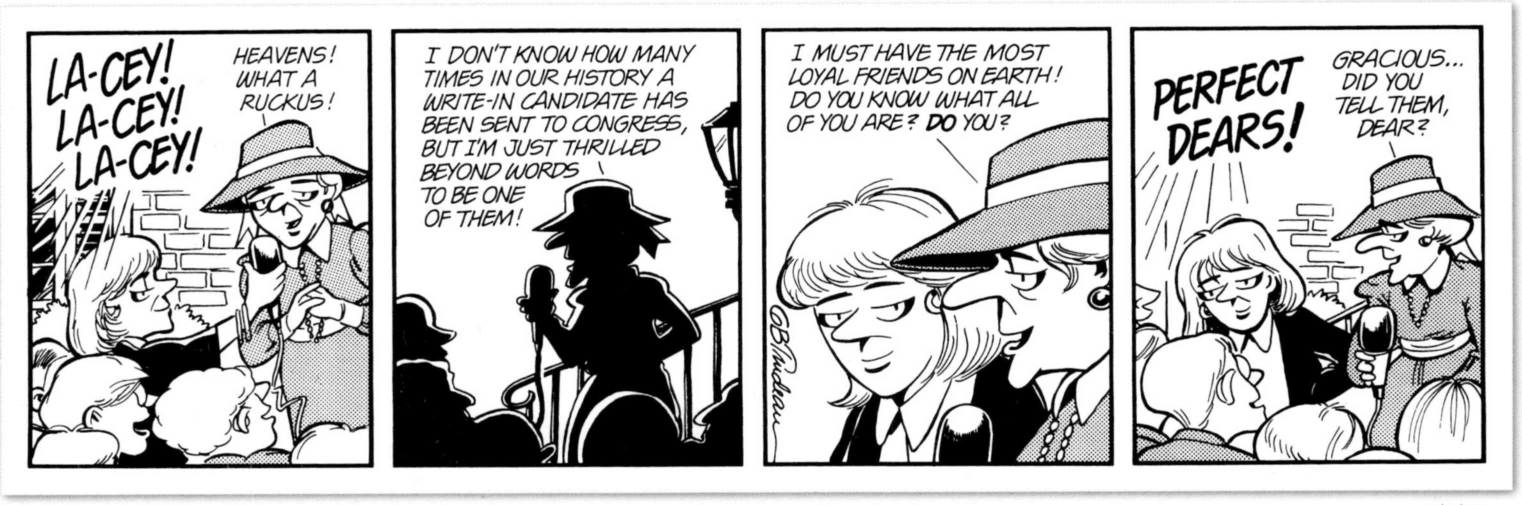
LA-CEY! LA-CEY! LA-CEY!
HEAVENS! WHAT A RUCKUS!
I DON'T KNOW HOW MANY TIMES IN OUR HISTORY A WRITE-IN CANDIDATE HAS BEEN SENT TO CONGRESS, BUT I'M JUST THRILLED BEYOND WORDS TO BE ONE OF THEM!
GB Trudeau
I MUST HAVE THE MOST LOYAL FRIENDS ON EARTH! DO YOU KNOW WHAT ALL OF YOU ARE? DO YOU?
PERFECT DEARS!
GRACIOUS... DID YOU TELL THEM, DEAR?

11/8/90

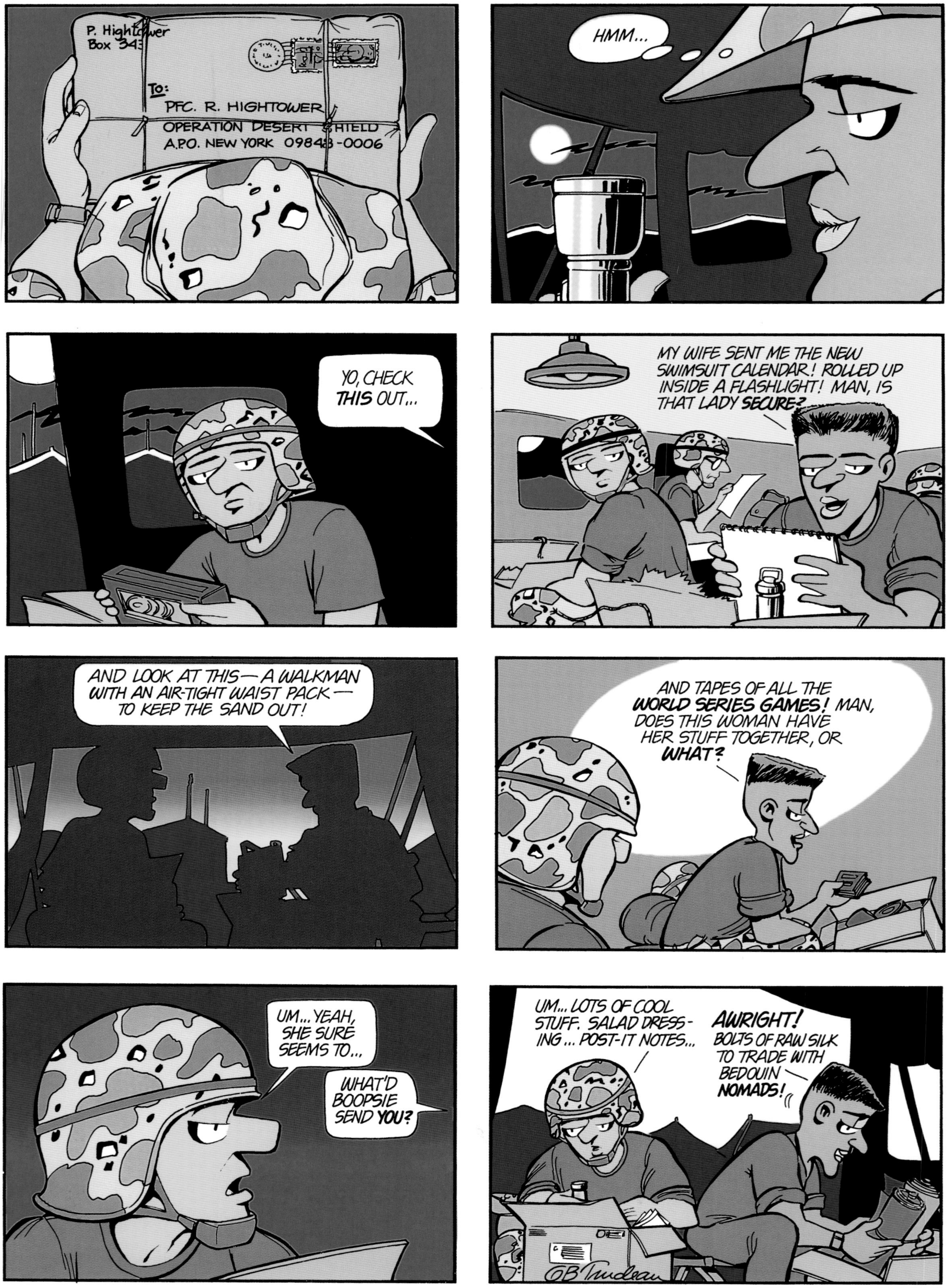
P. Hightower
Box 343
To:
PFC. R. HIGHTOWER
OPERATION DESERT SHIELD
A.P.O. NEW YORK 09848-0006
HMM...
YO, CHECK THIS OUT...
MY WIFE SENT ME THE NEW SWIMSUIT CALENDAR! ROLLED UP INSIDE A FLASHLIGHT! MAN, IS THAT LADY SECURE?
AND LOOK AT THIS— A WALKMAN WITH AN AIR-TIGHT WAIST PACK— TO KEEP THE SAND OUT!
AND TAPES OF ALL THE WORLD SERIES GAMES! MAN, DOES THIS WOMAN HAVE HER STUFF TOGETHER, OR WHAT?
UM... YEAH, SHE SURE SEEMS TO...
WHAT'D BOOPSIE SEND YOU?
UM... LOTS OF COOL STUFF. SALAD DRESSING... POST-IT NOTES...
AWRIGHT! BOLTS OF RAW SILK TO TRADE WITH BEDOUIN NOMADS!
GB Trudeau

11/4/90

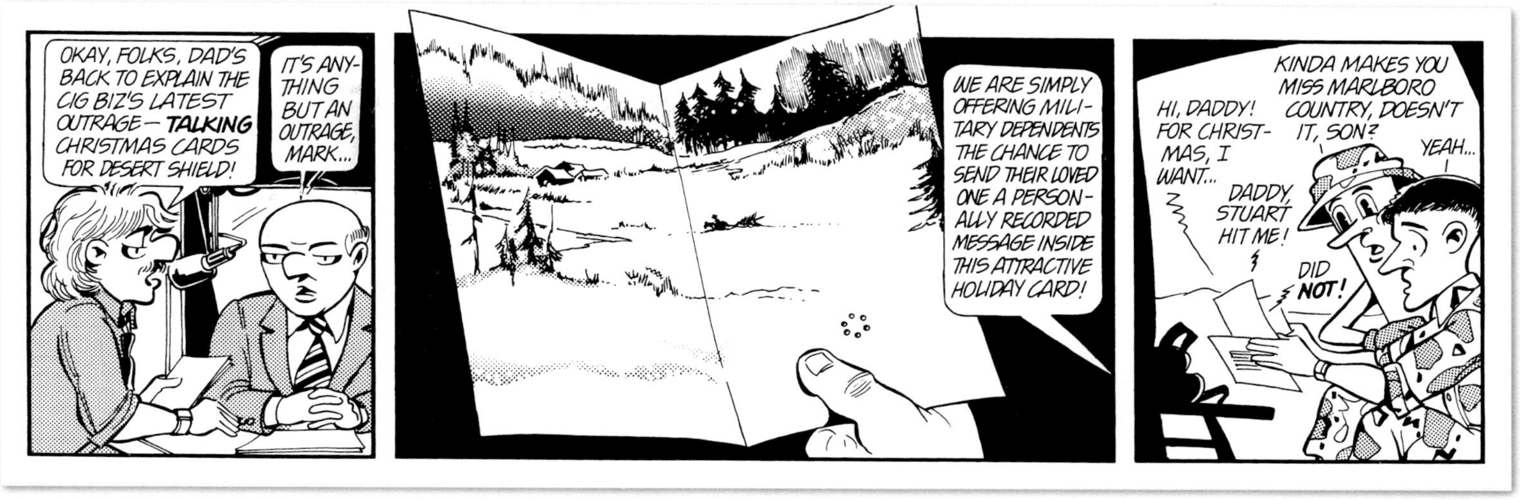
OKAY, FOLKS, DAD'S BACK TO EXPLAIN THE CIG BIZ'S LATEST OUTRAGE — TALKING CHRISTMAS CARDS FOR DESERT SHIELD!
IT'S ANYTHING BUT AN OUTRAGE, MARK...
WE ARE SIMPLY OFFERING MILITARY DEPENDENTS THE CHANCE TO SEND THEIR LOVED ONE A PERSONALLY RECORDED MESSAGE INSIDE THIS ATTRACTIVE HOLIDAY CARD!
HI, DADDY! FOR CHRISTMAS, I WANT...
DADDY, STUART HIT ME!
DID NOT!
KINDA MAKES YOU MISS MARLBORO COUNTRY, DOESN'T IT, SON?
YEAH...

12/10/90

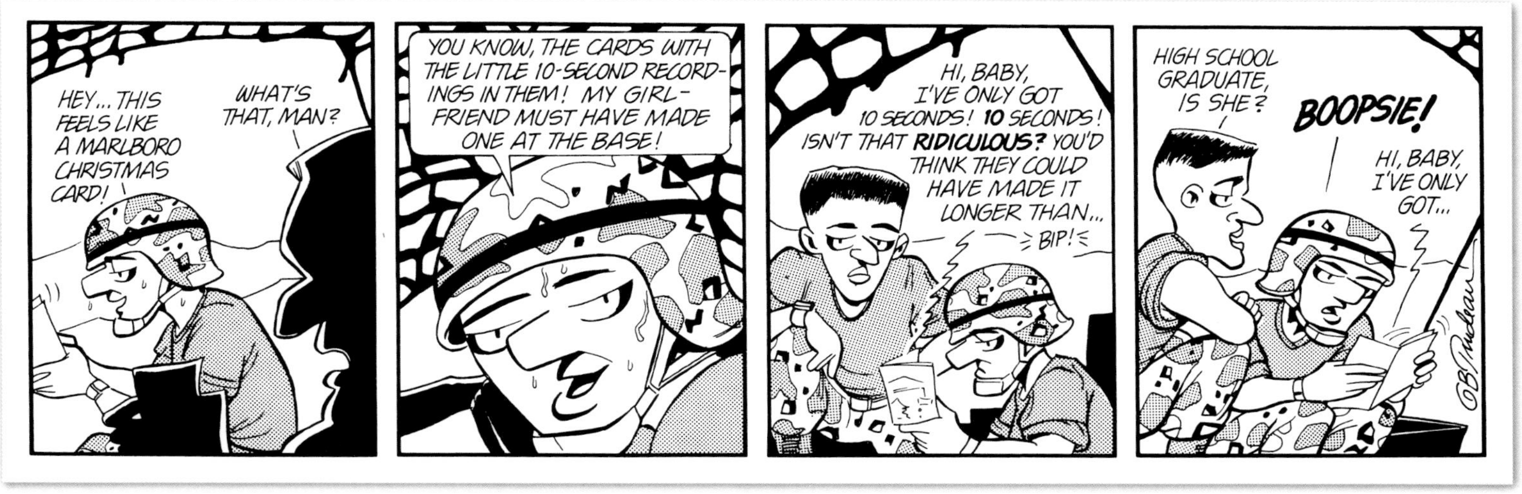
HEY... THIS FEELS LIKE A MARLBORO CHRISTMAS CARD!
WHAT'S THAT, MAN?
YOU KNOW, THE CARDS WITH THE LITTLE 10-SECOND RECORDINGS IN THEM! MY GIRLFRIEND MUST HAVE MADE ONE AT THE BASE!
HI, BABY, I'VE ONLY GOT 10 SECONDS! 10 SECONDS! ISN'T THAT RIDICULOUS? YOU'D THINK THEY COULD HAVE MADE IT LONGER THAN...
BIP!
HIGH SCHOOL GRADUATE, IS SHE?
BOOPSIE!
HI, BABY, I'VE ONLY GOT...
©B Trudeau

12/11/90

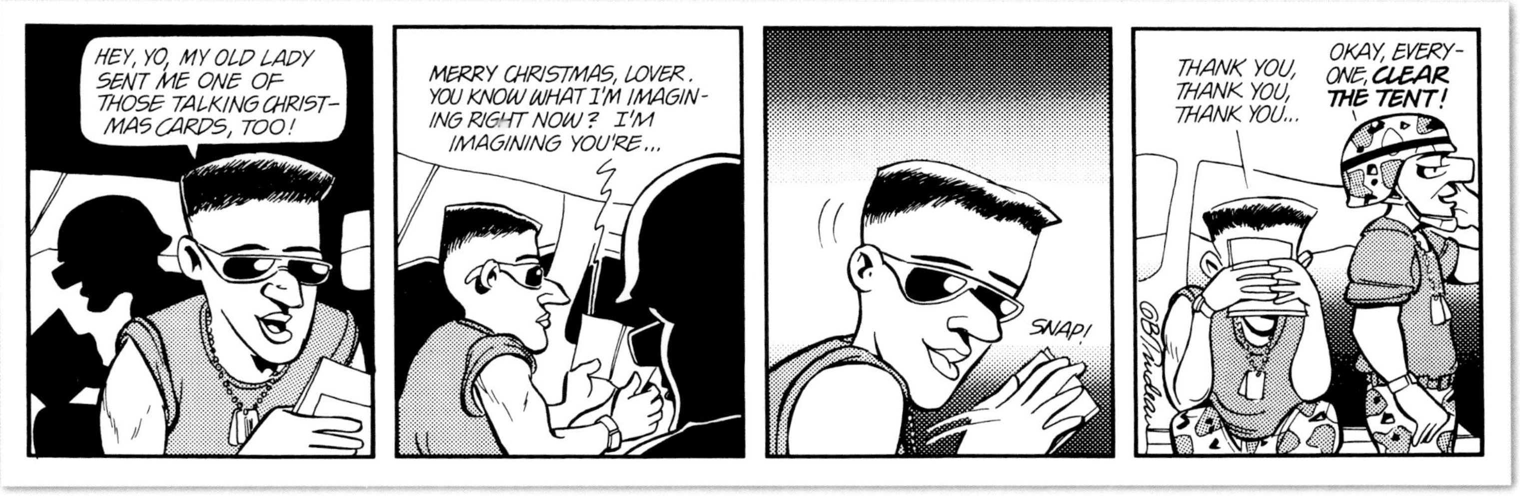
HEY, YO, MY OLD LADY SENT ME ONE OF THOSE TALKING CHRISTMAS CARDS, TOO!
MERRY CHRISTMAS, LOVER. YOU KNOW WHAT I'M IMAGINING RIGHT NOW? I'M IMAGINING YOU'RE...
SNAP!
©B Trudeau
THANK YOU, THANK YOU, THANK YOU...
OKAY, EVERYONE, CLEAR THE TENT!

12/12/90

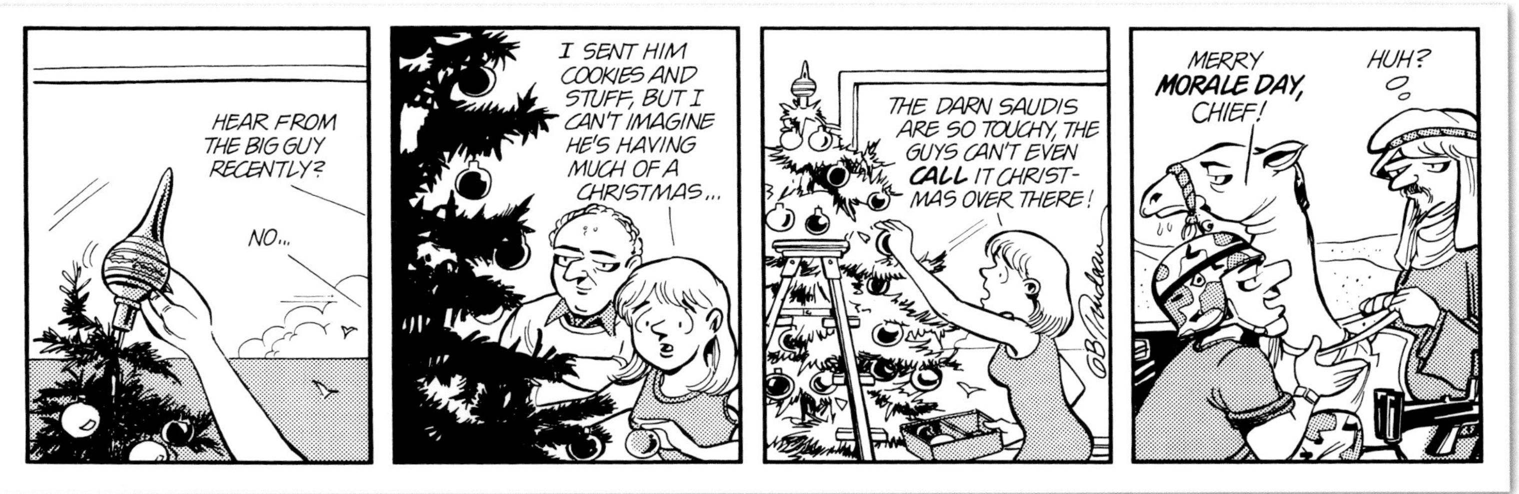
HEAR FROM THE BIG GUY RECENTLY?
NO...
I SENT HIM COOKIES AND STUFF, BUT I CAN'T IMAGINE HE'S HAVING MUCH OF A CHRISTMAS...
THE DARN SAUDIS ARE SO TOUCHY, THE GUYS CAN'T EVEN CALL IT CHRISTMAS OVER THERE!
©B Trudeau
MERRY MORALE DAY, CHIEF!
HUH?

12/25/90

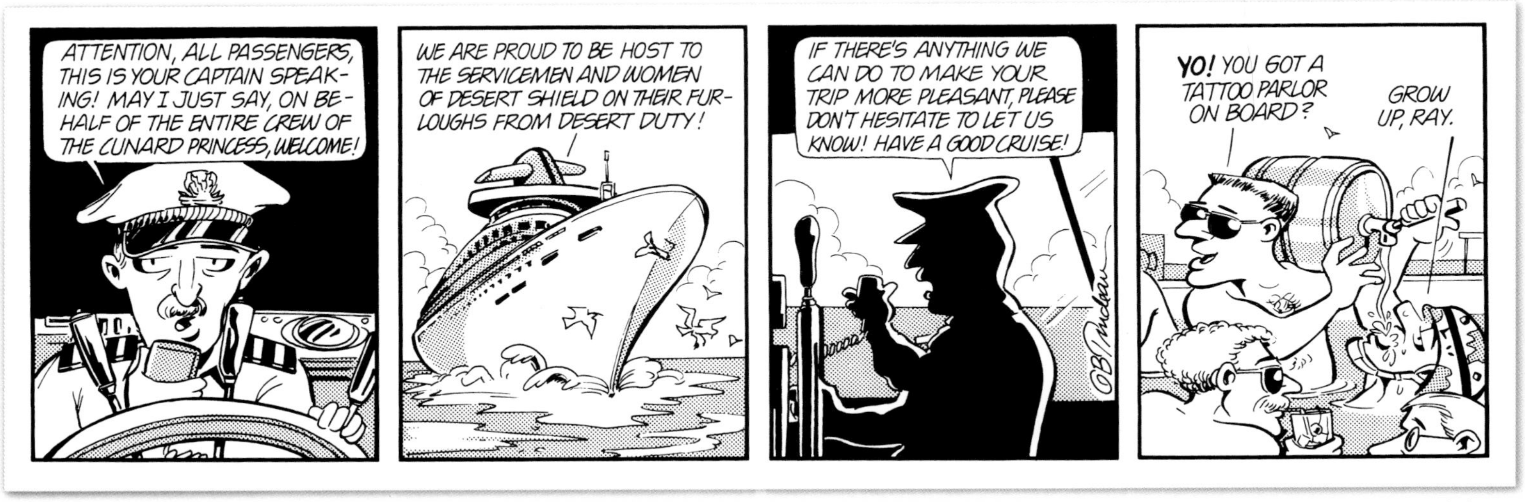
ATTENTION, ALL PASSENGERS, THIS IS YOUR CAPTAIN SPEAKING! MAY I JUST SAY, ON BEHALF OF THE ENTIRE CREW OF THE CUNARD PRINCESS, WELCOME!
WE ARE PROUD TO BE HOST TO THE SERVICEMEN AND WOMEN OF DESERT SHIELD ON THEIR FURLOUGHS FROM DESERT DUTY!
IF THERE'S ANYTHING WE CAN DO TO MAKE YOUR TRIP MORE PLEASANT, PLEASE DON'T HESITATE TO LET US KNOW! HAVE A GOOD CRUISE!
GB Trudeau
YO! YOU GOT A TATTOO PARLOR ON BOARD?
GROW UP, RAY.

1/1/91

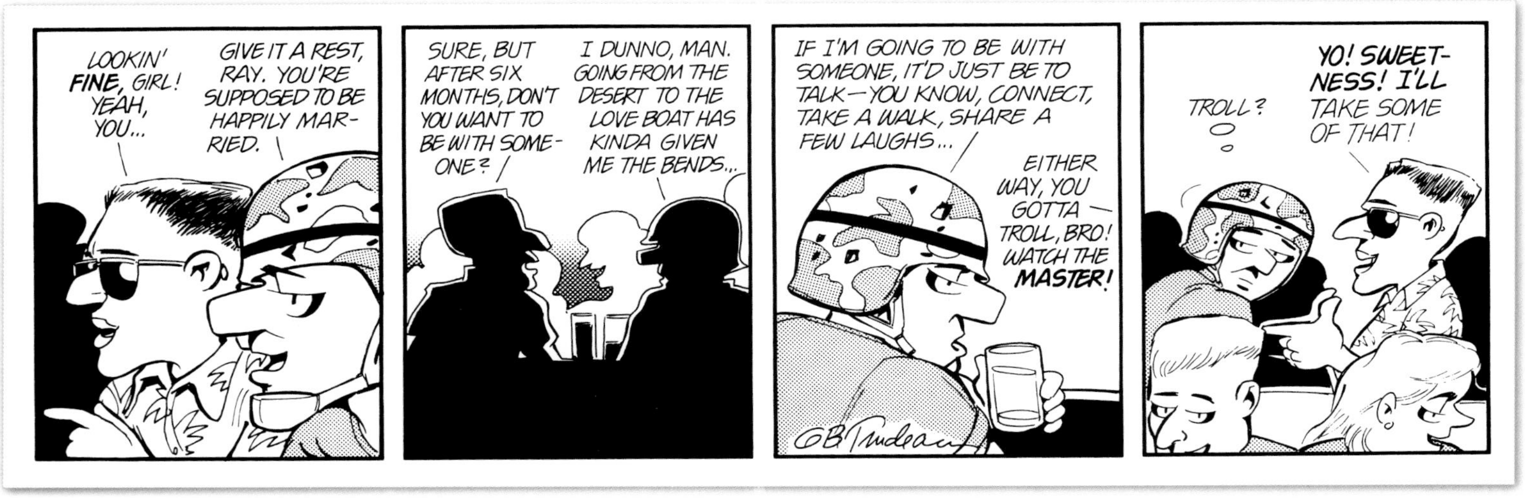
LOOKIN' FINE, GIRL! YEAH, YOU...
GIVE IT A REST, RAY. YOU'RE SUPPOSED TO BE HAPPILY MARRIED.
SURE, BUT AFTER SIX MONTHS, DON'T YOU WANT TO BE WITH SOMEONE?
I DUNNO, MAN. GOING FROM THE DESERT TO THE LOVE BOAT HAS KINDA GIVEN ME THE BENDS...
IF I'M GOING TO BE WITH SOMEONE, IT'D JUST BE TO TALK—YOU KNOW, CONNECT, TAKE A WALK, SHARE A FEW LAUGHS...
EITHER WAY, YOU GOTTA TROLL, BRO! WATCH THE MASTER!
GB Trudeau
TROLL?
YO! SWEETNESS! I'LL TAKE SOME OF THAT!

1/3/91

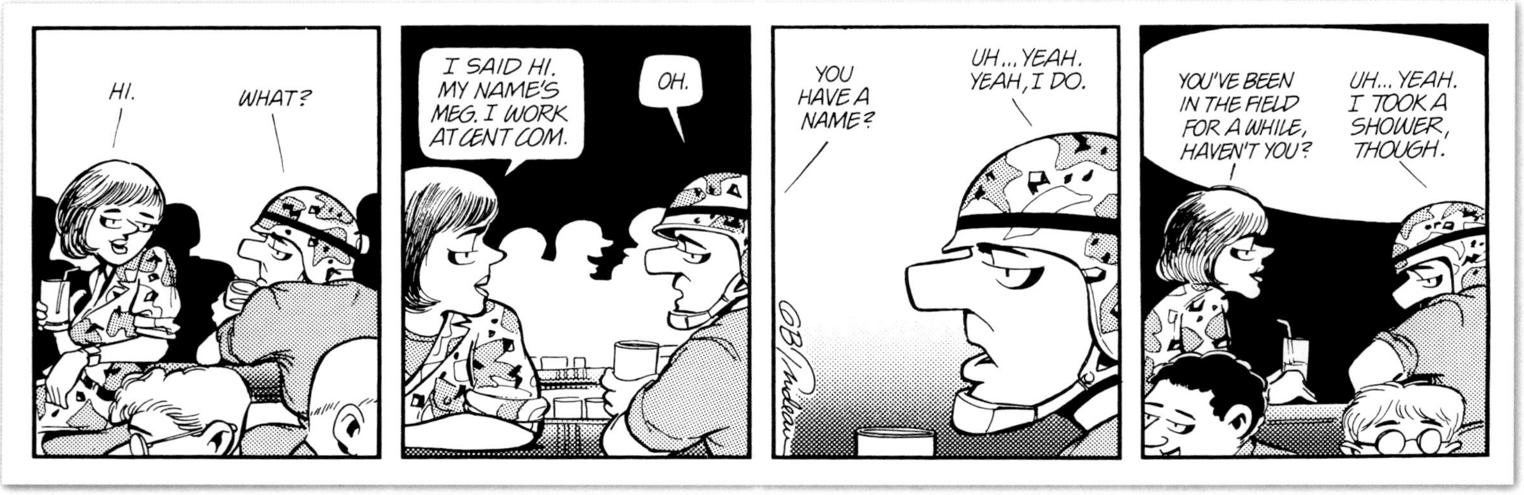
HI.
WHAT?
I SAID HI. MY NAME'S MEG. I WORK AT CENT COM.
OH.
YOU HAVE A NAME?
UH... YEAH. YEAH, I DO.
GB Trudeau
YOU'VE BEEN IN THE FIELD FOR A WHILE, HAVEN'T YOU?
UH... YEAH. I TOOK A SHOWER, THOUGH.

1/4/91

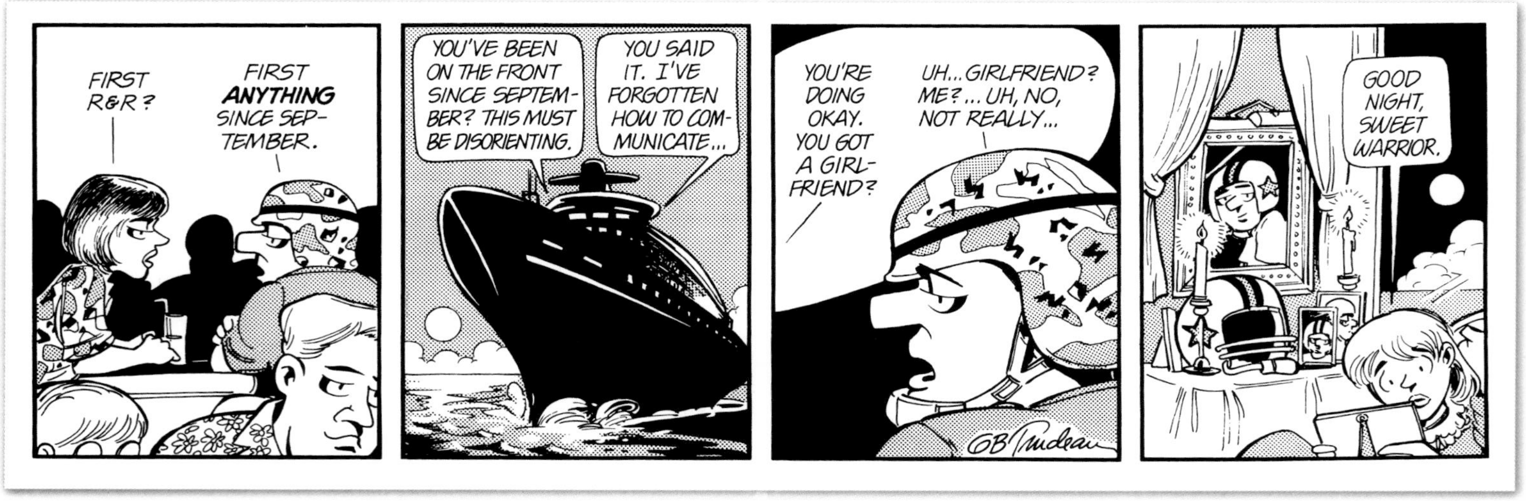
FIRST R&R?
FIRST ANYTHING SINCE SEPTEMBER.
YOU'VE BEEN ON THE FRONT SINCE SEPTEMBER? THIS MUST BE DISORIENTING.
YOU SAID IT. I'VE FORGOTTEN HOW TO COMMUNICATE...
YOU'RE DOING OKAY. YOU GOT A GIRLFRIEND?
UH... GIRLFRIEND? ME?... UH, NO, NOT REALLY...
GB Trudeau
GOOD NIGHT, SWEET WARRIOR.

1/5/91

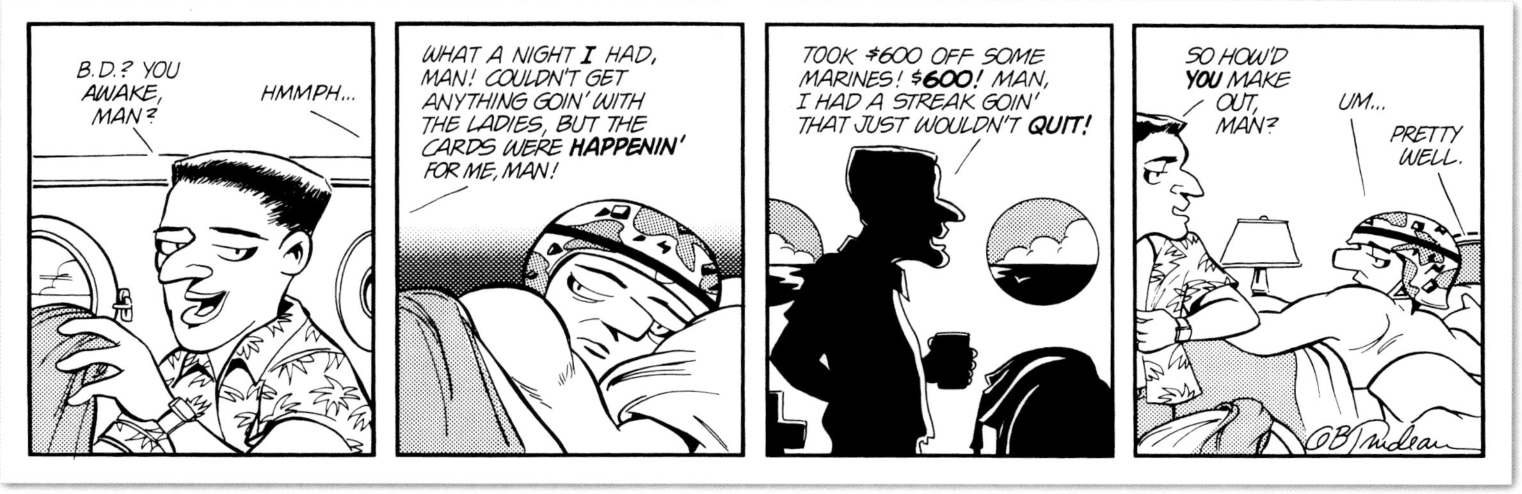
B.D.? YOU AWAKE, MAN?
HMMPH...
WHAT A NIGHT I HAD, MAN! COULDN'T GET ANYTHING GOIN' WITH THE LADIES, BUT THE CARDS WERE HAPPENIN' FOR ME, MAN!
TOOK $600 OFF SOME MARINES! $600! MAN, I HAD A STREAK GOIN' THAT JUST WOULDN'T QUIT!
SO HOW'D YOU MAKE OUT, MAN?
UM...
PRETTY WELL.

1/7/91

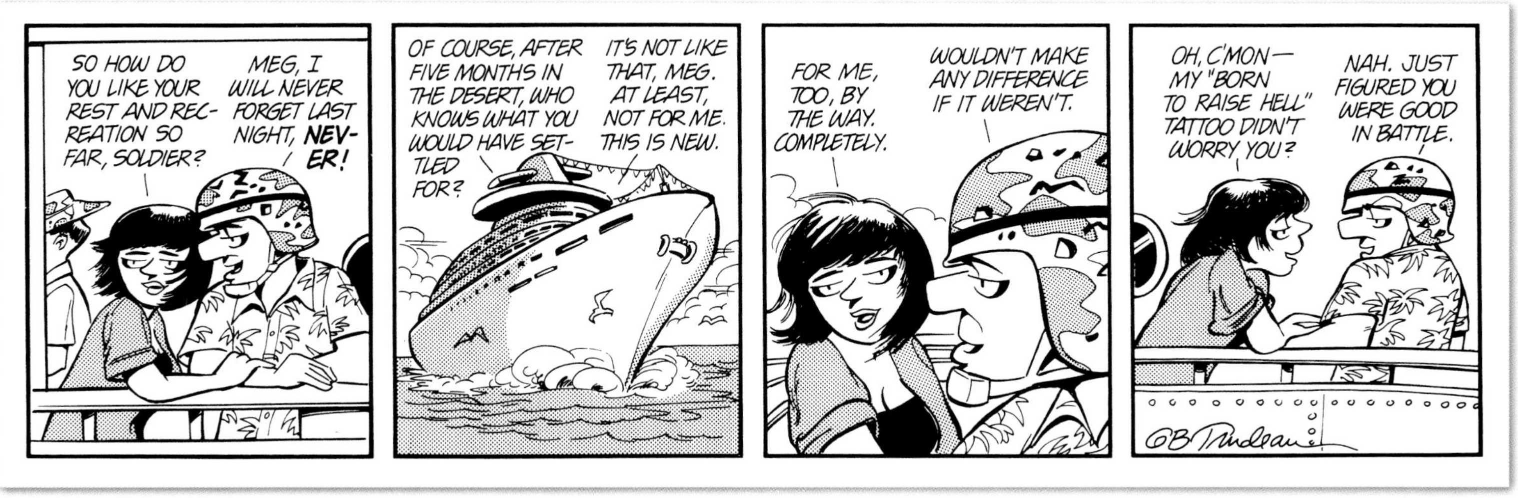
SO HOW DO YOU LIKE YOUR REST AND RECREATION SO FAR, SOLDIER?
MEG, I WILL NEVER FORGET LAST NIGHT, NEVER!
OF COURSE, AFTER FIVE MONTHS IN THE DESERT, WHO KNOWS WHAT YOU WOULD HAVE SETTLED FOR?
IT'S NOT LIKE THAT, MEG. AT LEAST, NOT FOR ME. THIS IS NEW.
FOR ME, TOO, BY THE WAY. COMPLETELY.
WOULDN'T MAKE ANY DIFFERENCE IF IT WEREN'T.
OH, C'MON— MY "BORN TO RAISE HELL" TATTOO DIDN'T WORRY YOU?
NAH. JUST FIGURED YOU WERE GOOD IN BATTLE.

1/8/91

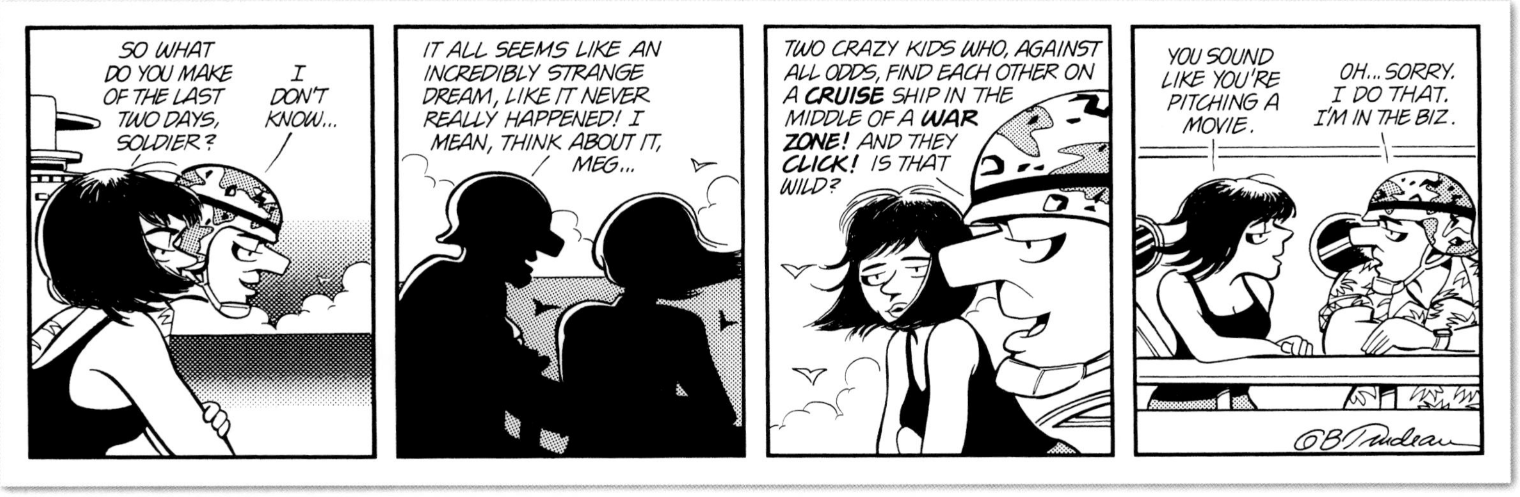
SO WHAT DO YOU MAKE OF THE LAST TWO DAYS, SOLDIER?
I DON'T KNOW...
IT ALL SEEMS LIKE AN INCREDIBLY STRANGE DREAM, LIKE IT NEVER REALLY HAPPENED! I MEAN, THINK ABOUT IT, MEG...
TWO CRAZY KIDS WHO, AGAINST ALL ODDS, FIND EACH OTHER ON A CRUISE SHIP IN THE MIDDLE OF A WAR ZONE! AND THEY CLICK! IS THAT WILD?
YOU SOUND LIKE YOU'RE PITCHING A MOVIE.
OH... SORRY. I DO THAT. I'M IN THE BIZ.

1/10/91

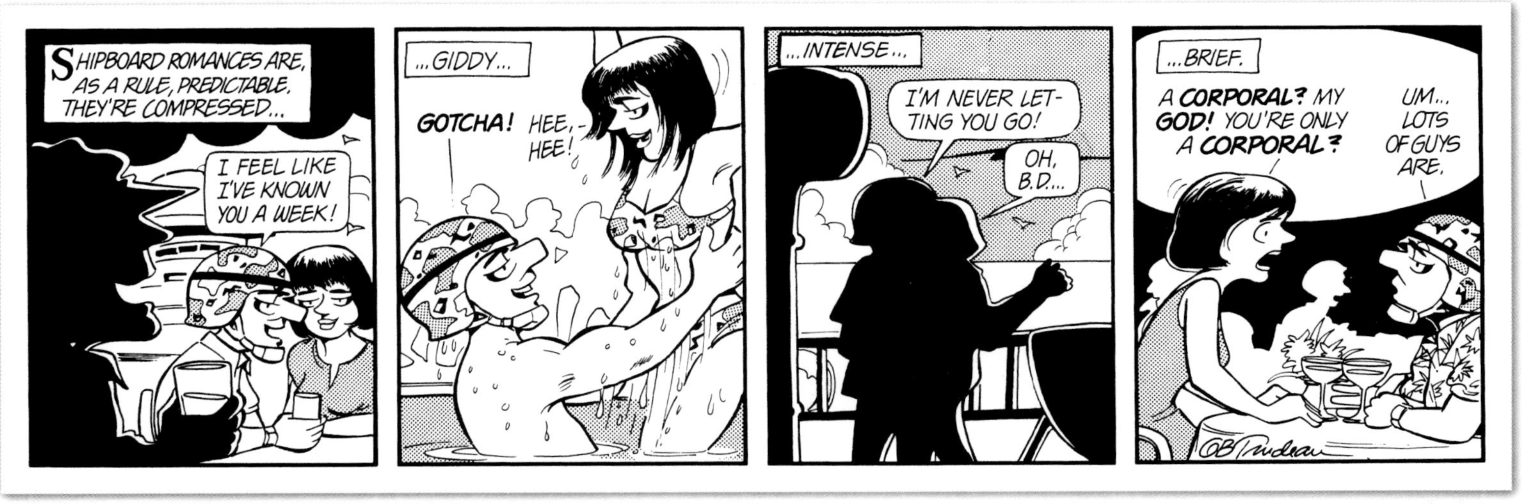
SHIPBOARD ROMANCES ARE, AS A RULE, PREDICTABLE. THEY'RE COMPRESSED...
I FEEL LIKE I'VE KNOWN YOU A WEEK!
...GIDDY...
GOTCHA!
HEE, HEE!
...INTENSE...
I'M NEVER LETTING YOU GO!
OH, B.D...
...BRIEF.
A CORPORAL? MY GOD! YOU'RE ONLY A CORPORAL?
UM... LOTS OF GUYS ARE.

1/11/91

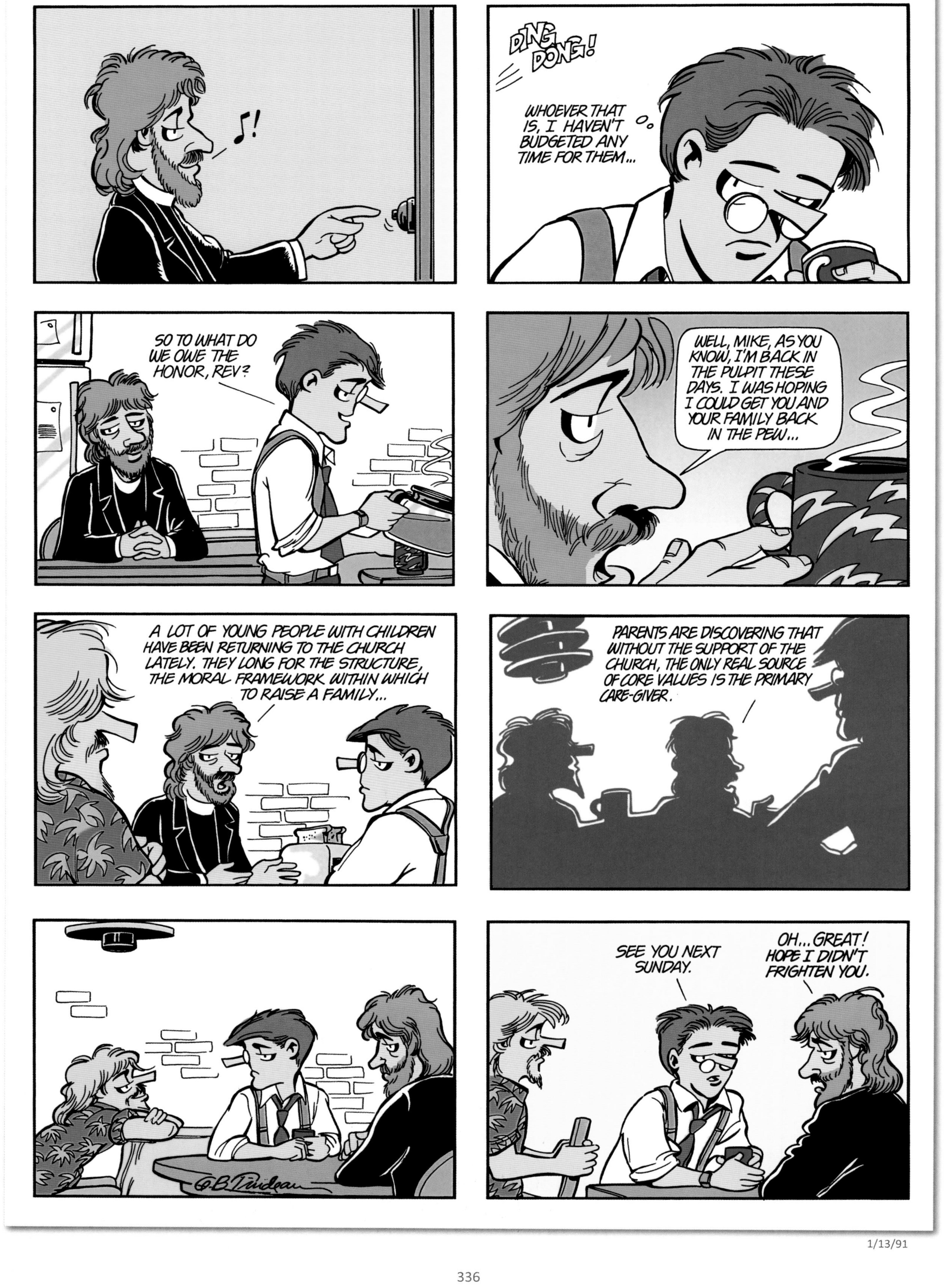
♪!
DING DONG!
WHOEVER THAT IS, I HAVEN'T BUDGETED ANY TIME FOR THEM...
SO TO WHAT DO WE OWE THE HONOR, REV?
WELL, MIKE, AS YOU KNOW, I'M BACK IN THE PULPIT THESE DAYS. I WAS HOPING I COULD GET YOU AND YOUR FAMILY BACK IN THE PEW...
A LOT OF YOUNG PEOPLE WITH CHILDREN HAVE BEEN RETURNING TO THE CHURCH LATELY. THEY LONG FOR THE STRUCTURE, THE MORAL FRAMEWORK WITHIN WHICH TO RAISE A FAMILY...
PARENTS ARE DISCOVERING THAT WITHOUT THE SUPPORT OF THE CHURCH, THE ONLY REAL SOURCE OF CORE VALUES IS THE PRIMARY CARE-GIVER.
G.B. Trudeau
SEE YOU NEXT SUNDAY.
OH... GREAT! HOPE I DIDN'T FRIGHTEN YOU.

1/13/91

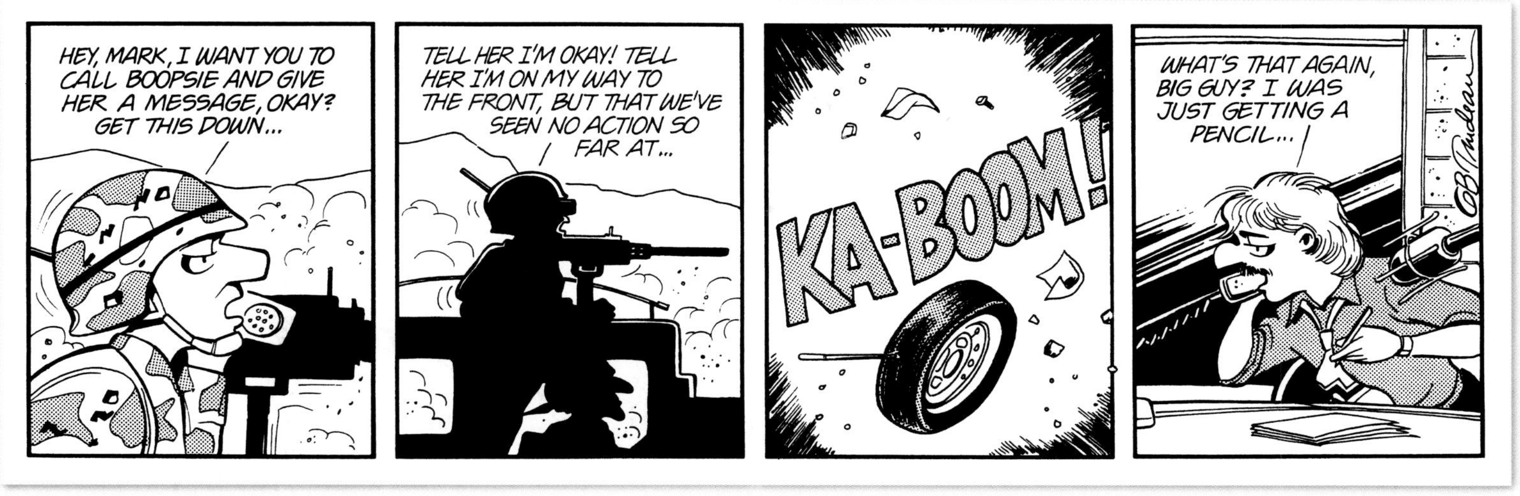
HEY, MARK, I WANT YOU TO CALL BOOPSIE AND GIVE HER A MESSAGE, OKAY? GET THIS DOWN...
TELL HER I'M OKAY! TELL HER I'M ON MY WAY TO THE FRONT, BUT THAT WE'VE SEEN NO ACTION SO FAR AT...
KA-BOOM!
WHAT'S THAT AGAIN, BIG GUY? I WAS JUST GETTING A PENCIL...

2/6/91

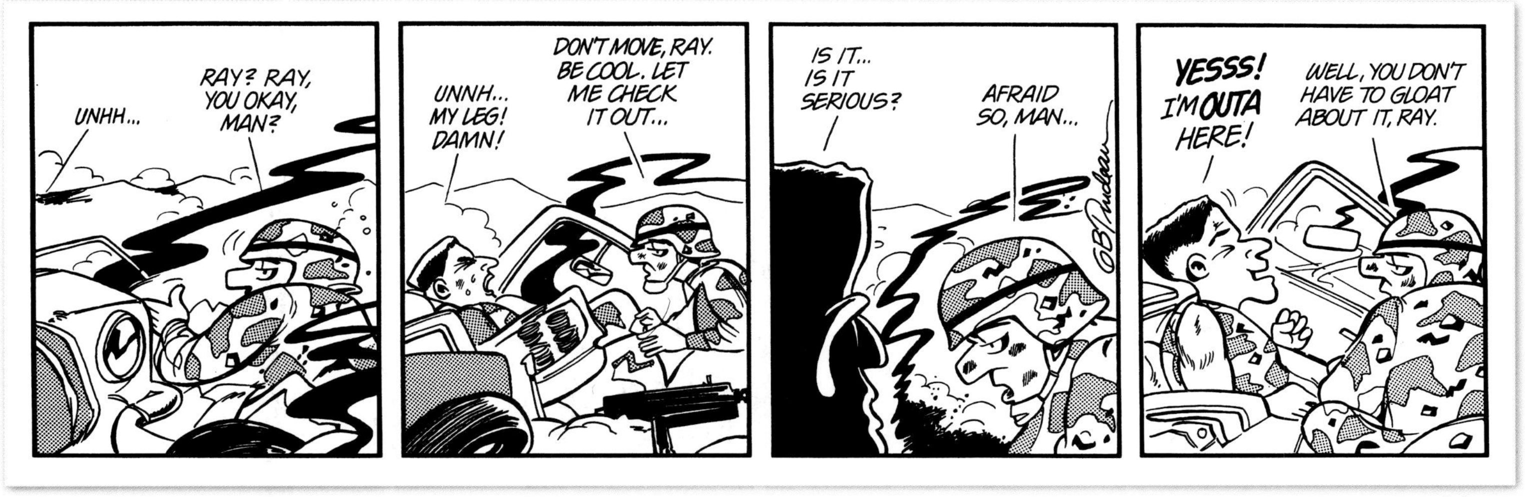
UNHH...
RAY? RAY, YOU OKAY, MAN?
UNNH... MY LEG! DAMN!
DON'T MOVE, RAY. BE COOL. LET ME CHECK IT OUT...
IS IT... IS IT SERIOUS?
AFRAID SO, MAN...
YESSS! I'M OUTA HERE!
WELL, YOU DON'T HAVE TO GLOAT ABOUT IT, RAY.

2/7/91

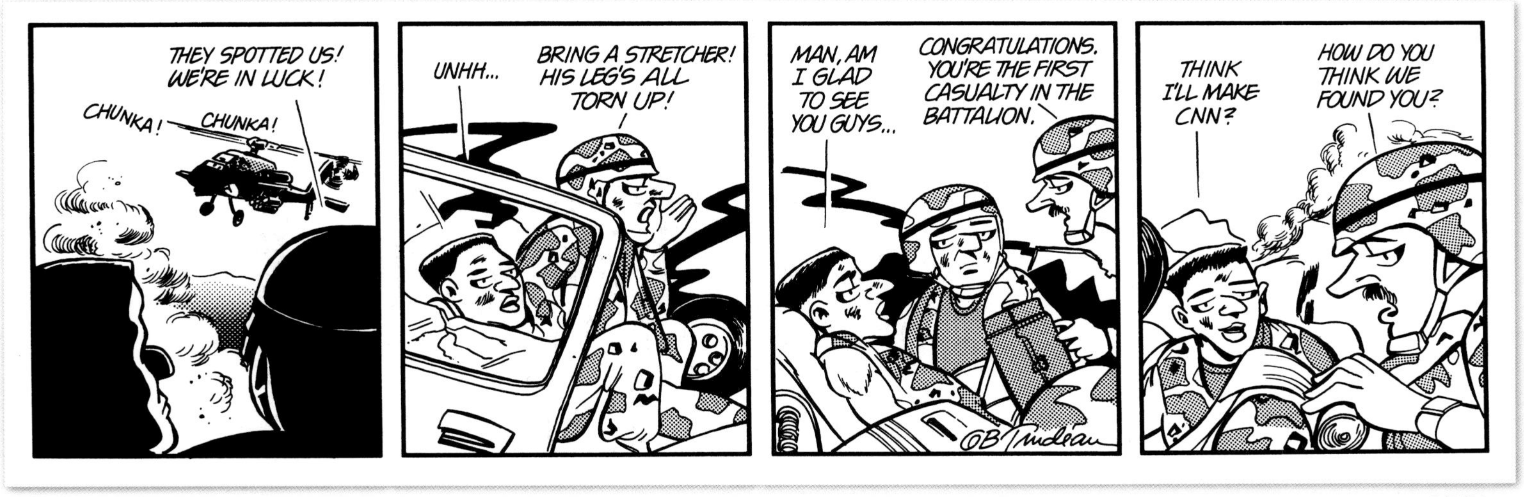
THEY SPOTTED US! WE'RE IN LUCK!
CHUNKA! CHUNKA!
UNHH...
BRING A STRETCHER! HIS LEG'S ALL TORN UP!
MAN, AM I GLAD TO SEE YOU GUYS...
CONGRATULATIONS. YOU'RE THE FIRST CASUALTY IN THE BATTALION.
THINK I'LL MAKE CNN?
HOW DO YOU THINK WE FOUND YOU?

2/8/91

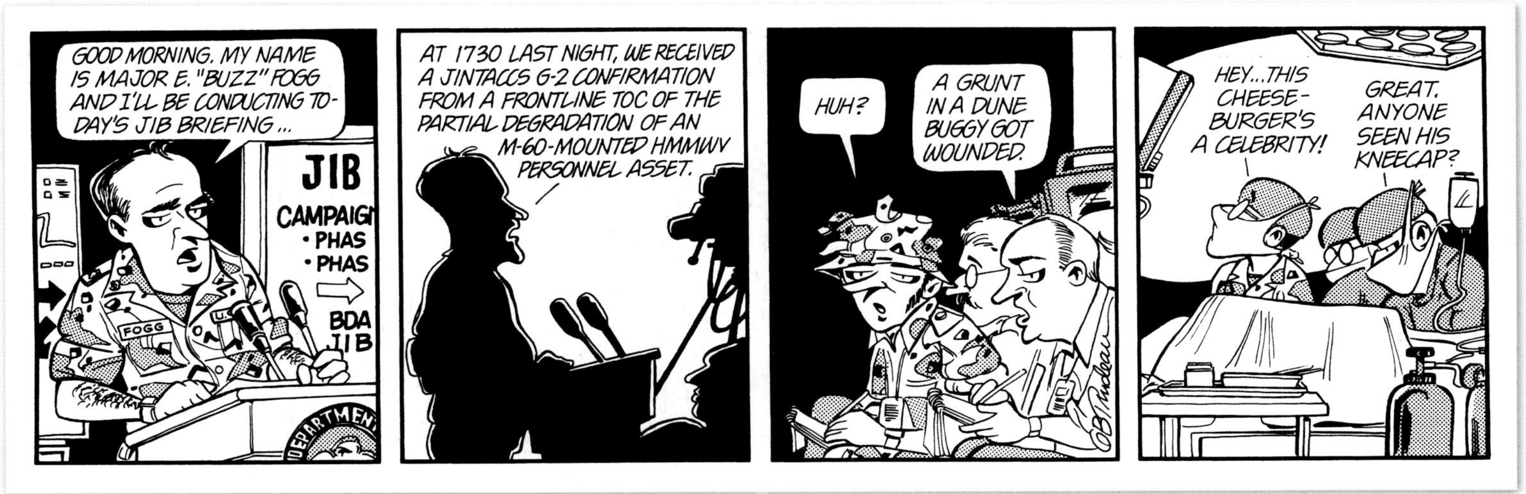
GOOD MORNING. MY NAME IS MAJOR E. "BUZZ" FOGG AND I'LL BE CONDUCTING TODAY'S JIB BRIEFING...
JIB
CAMPAIGN
• PHAS
• PHAS
BDA
JIB
FOGG
AT 1730 LAST NIGHT, WE RECEIVED A JINTACCS G-2 CONFIRMATION FROM A FRONTLINE TOC OF THE PARTIAL DEGRADATION OF AN M-60-MOUNTED HMMWV PERSONNEL ASSET.
HUH?
A GRUNT IN A DUNE BUGGY GOT WOUNDED.
HEY...THIS CHEESE-BURGER'S A CELEBRITY!
GREAT. ANYONE SEEN HIS KNEECAP?

2/11/91

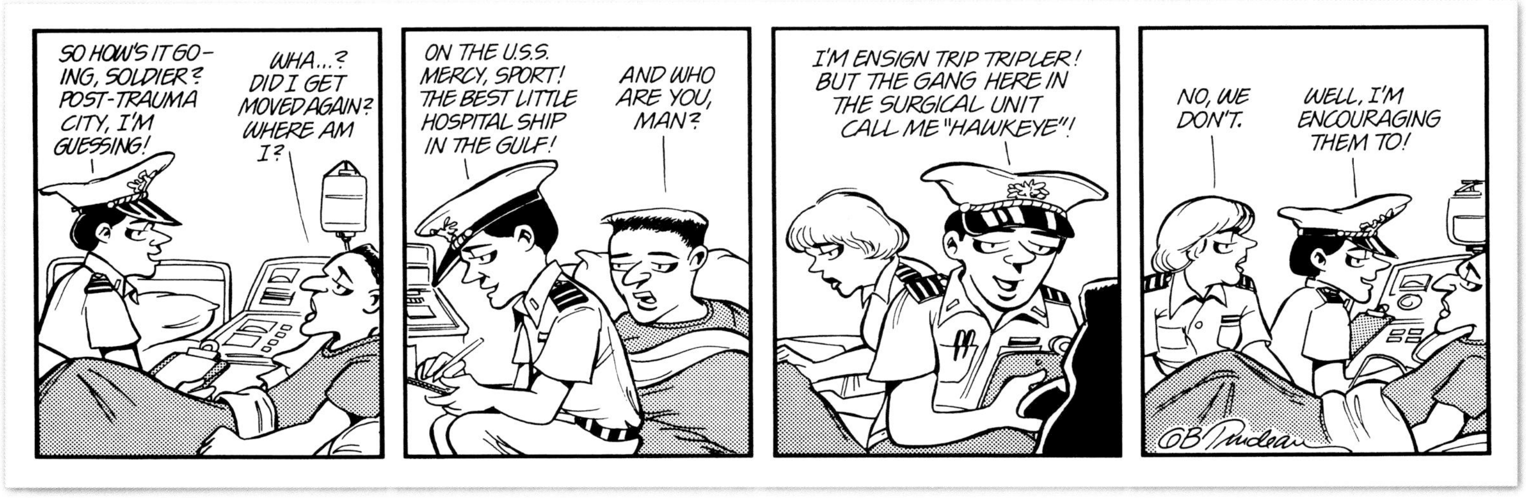
SO HOW'S IT GOING, SOLDIER? POST-TRAUMA CITY, I'M GUESSING!
WHA...? DID I GET MOVED AGAIN? WHERE AM I?
ON THE U.S.S. MERCY, SPORT! THE BEST LITTLE HOSPITAL SHIP IN THE GULF!
AND WHO ARE YOU, MAN?
I'M ENSIGN TRIP TRIPLER! BUT THE GANG HERE IN THE SURGICAL UNIT CALL ME "HAWKEYE"!
NO, WE DON'T.
WELL, I'M ENCOURAGING THEM TO!

2/15/91

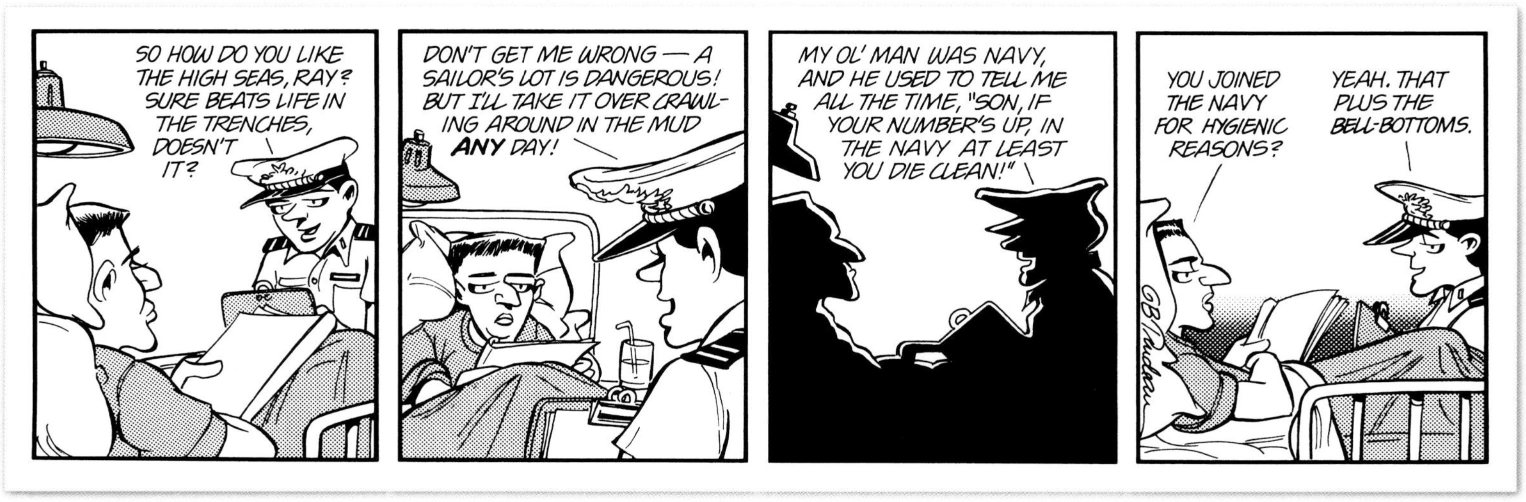
SO HOW DO YOU LIKE THE HIGH SEAS, RAY? SURE BEATS LIFE IN THE TRENCHES, DOESN'T IT?
DON'T GET ME WRONG — A SAILOR'S LOT IS DANGEROUS! BUT I'LL TAKE IT OVER CRAWLING AROUND IN THE MUD ANY DAY!
MY OL' MAN WAS NAVY, AND HE USED TO TELL ME ALL THE TIME, "SON, IF YOUR NUMBER'S UP, IN THE NAVY AT LEAST YOU DIE CLEAN!"
YOU JOINED THE NAVY FOR HYGIENIC REASONS?
YEAH. THAT PLUS THE BELL-BOTTOMS.

3/5/91

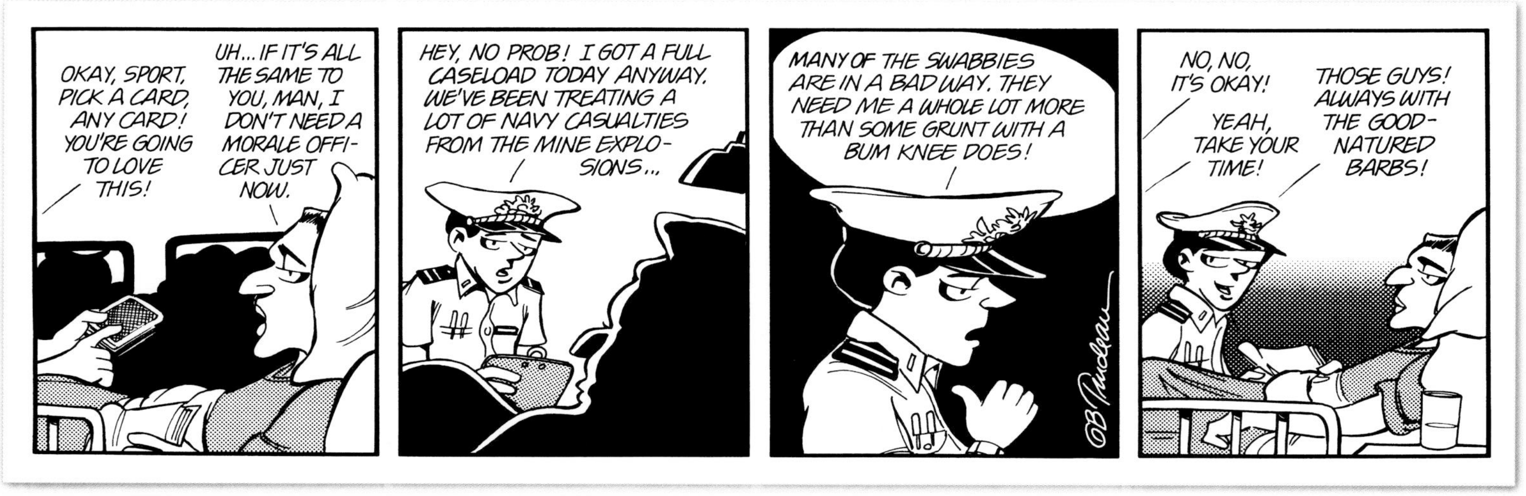
OKAY, SPORT, PICK A CARD, ANY CARD! YOU'RE GOING TO LOVE THIS!
UH... IF IT'S ALL THE SAME TO YOU, MAN, I DON'T NEED A MORALE OFFICER JUST NOW.
HEY, NO PROB! I GOT A FULL CASELOAD TODAY ANYWAY. WE'VE BEEN TREATING A LOT OF NAVY CASUALTIES FROM THE MINE EXPLOSIONS...
MANY OF THE SWABBIES ARE IN A BAD WAY. THEY NEED ME A WHOLE LOT MORE THAN SOME GRUNT WITH A BUM KNEE DOES!
NO, NO, IT'S OKAY!
YEAH, TAKE YOUR TIME!
THOSE GUYS! ALWAYS WITH THE GOOD-NATURED BARBS!

3/6/91

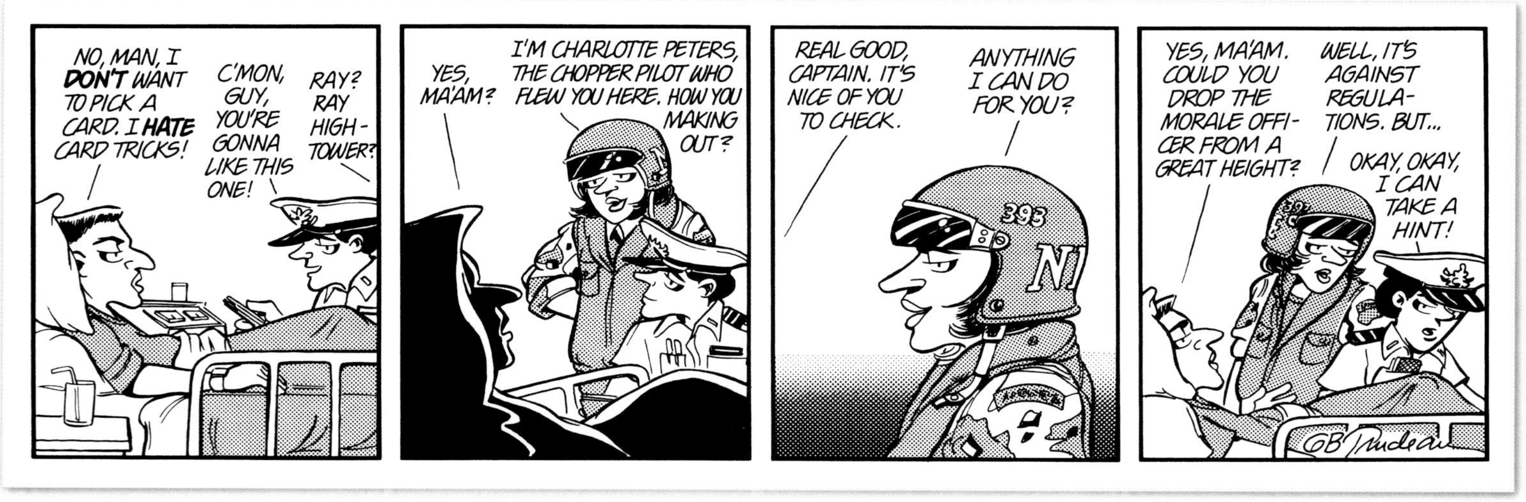
NO, MAN, I DON'T WANT TO PICK A CARD. I HATE CARD TRICKS!
C'MON, GUY, YOU'RE GONNA LIKE THIS ONE!
RAY? RAY HIGHTOWER?
YES, MA'AM?
I'M CHARLOTTE PETERS, THE CHOPPER PILOT WHO FLEW YOU HERE. HOW YOU MAKING OUT?
REAL GOOD, CAPTAIN. IT'S NICE OF YOU TO CHECK.
ANYTHING I CAN DO FOR YOU?
YES, MA'AM. COULD YOU DROP THE MORALE OFFICER FROM A GREAT HEIGHT?
WELL, IT'S AGAINST REGULATIONS. BUT...
OKAY, OKAY, I CAN TAKE A HINT!

3/7/91

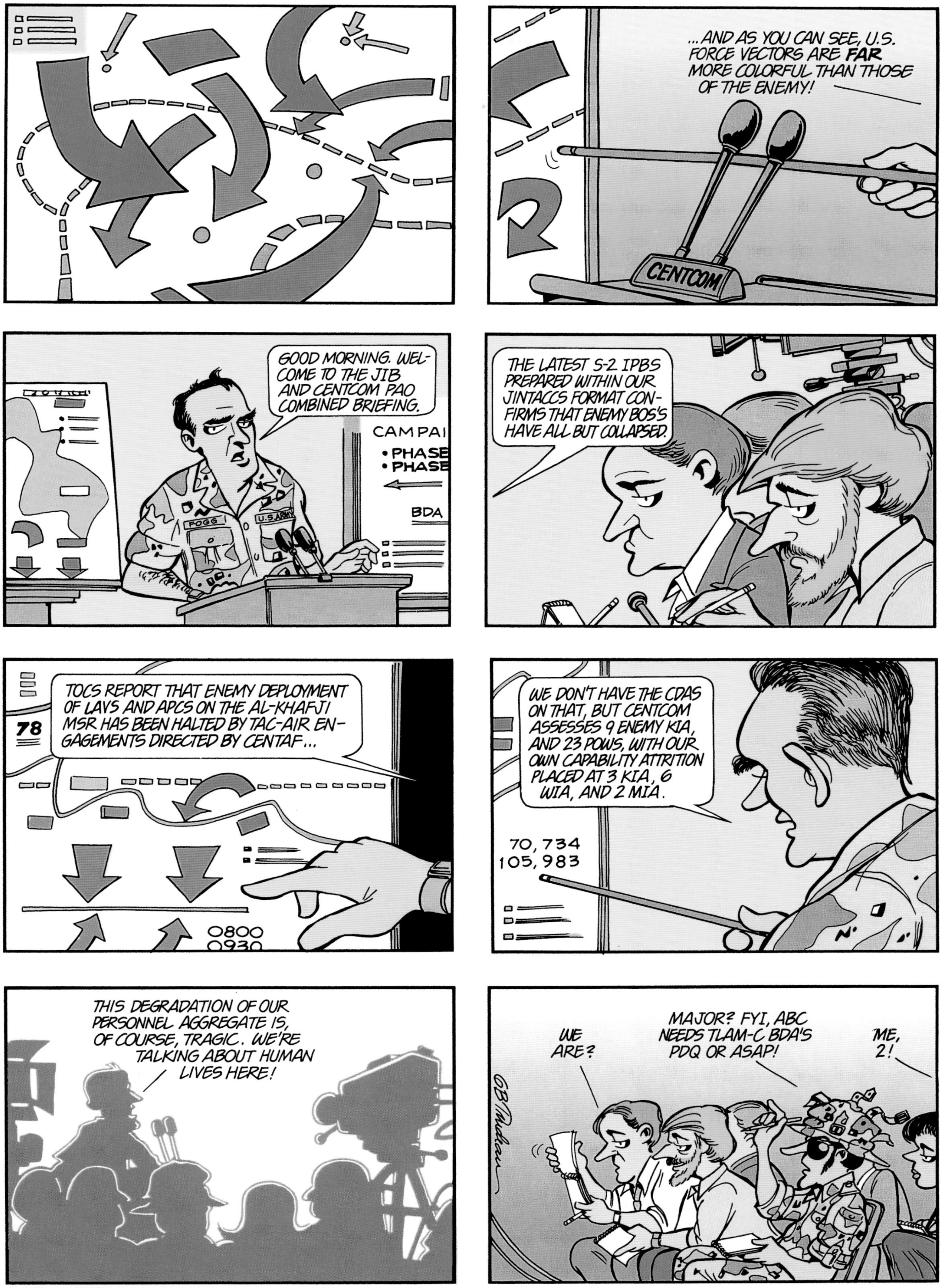
...AND AS YOU CAN SEE, U.S. FORCE VECTORS ARE FAR MORE COLORFUL THAN THOSE OF THE ENEMY!
CENTCOM
GOOD MORNING. WELCOME TO THE JIB AND CENTCOM PAO COMBINED BRIEFING.
CAMPAI
• PHASE
• PHASE
BDA
FOGG
U.S. ARMY
THE LATEST S-2 IPBS PREPARED WITHIN OUR JINTACCS FORMAT CONFIRMS THAT ENEMY BOS'S HAVE ALL BUT COLLAPSED.
TOCS REPORT THAT ENEMY DEPLOYMENT OF LAVS AND APCS ON THE AL-KHAFJI MSR HAS BEEN HALTED BY TAC-AIR ENGAGEMENTS DIRECTED BY CENTAF...
78
0800
0930
WE DON'T HAVE THE CDAS ON THAT, BUT CENTCOM ASSESSES 9 ENEMY KIA, AND 23 POWS, WITH OUR OWN CAPABILITY ATTRITION PLACED AT 3 KIA, 6 WIA, AND 2 MIA.
70,734
105,983
THIS DEGRADATION OF OUR PERSONNEL AGGREGATE IS, OF COURSE, TRAGIC. WE'RE TALKING ABOUT HUMAN LIVES HERE!
WE ARE?
MAJOR? FYI, ABC NEEDS TLAM-C BDA'S PDQ OR ASAP!
ME, 2!
GB Trudeau

3/3/91

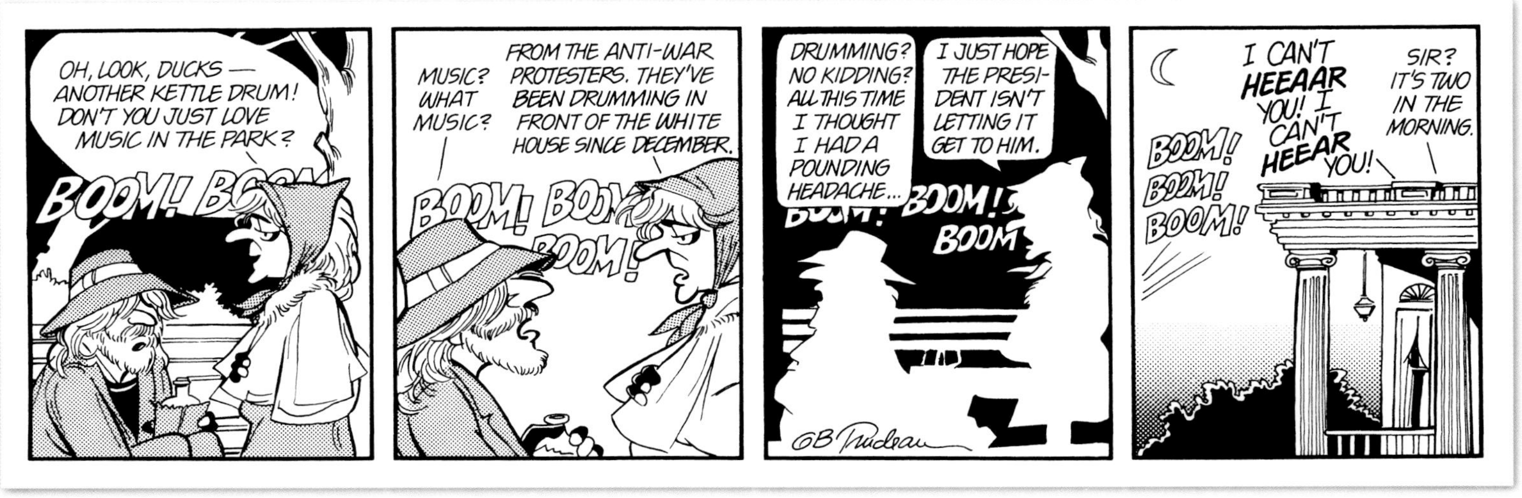
OH, LOOK, DUCKS — ANOTHER KETTLE DRUM! DON'T YOU JUST LOVE MUSIC IN THE PARK?
BOOM!
MUSIC? WHAT MUSIC?
FROM THE ANTI-WAR PROTESTERS. THEY'VE BEEN DRUMMING IN FRONT OF THE WHITE HOUSE SINCE DECEMBER.
BOOM! BOOM!
DRUMMING? NO KIDDING? ALL THIS TIME I THOUGHT I HAD A POUNDING HEADACHE...
I JUST HOPE THE PRESIDENT ISN'T LETTING IT GET TO HIM.
BOOM! BOOM
BOOM! BOOM! BOOM!
I CAN'T HEEAAR YOU! I CAN'T HEEAR YOU!
SIR? IT'S TWO IN THE MORNING.

2/18/91

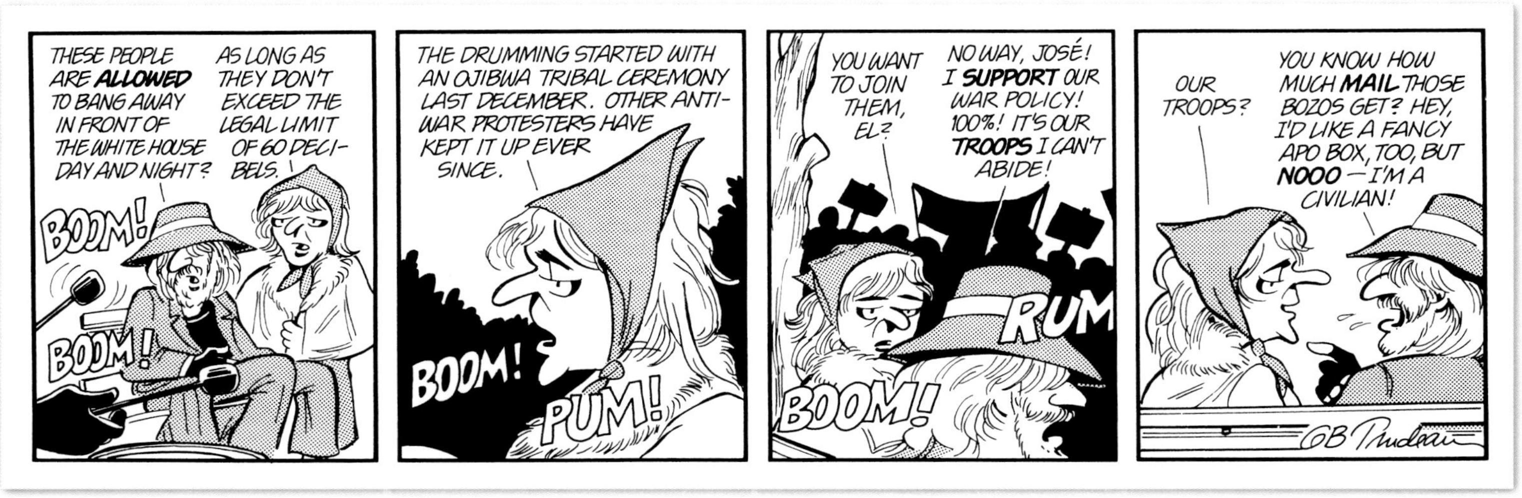
THESE PEOPLE ARE ALLOWED TO BANG AWAY IN FRONT OF THE WHITE HOUSE DAY AND NIGHT?
AS LONG AS THEY DON'T EXCEED THE LEGAL LIMIT OF 60 DECIBELS.
BOOM! BOOM!
THE DRUMMING STARTED WITH AN OJIBWA TRIBAL CEREMONY LAST DECEMBER. OTHER ANTI-WAR PROTESTERS HAVE KEPT IT UP EVER SINCE.
BOOM! PUM!
YOU WANT TO JOIN THEM, EL?
NO WAY, JOSÉ! I SUPPORT OUR WAR POLICY! 100%! IT'S OUR TROOPS I CAN'T ABIDE!
RUM BOOM!
OUR TROOPS?
YOU KNOW HOW MUCH MAIL THOSE BOZOS GET? HEY, I'D LIKE A FANCY APO BOX, TOO, BUT NOOO — I'M A CIVILIAN!

2/19/91

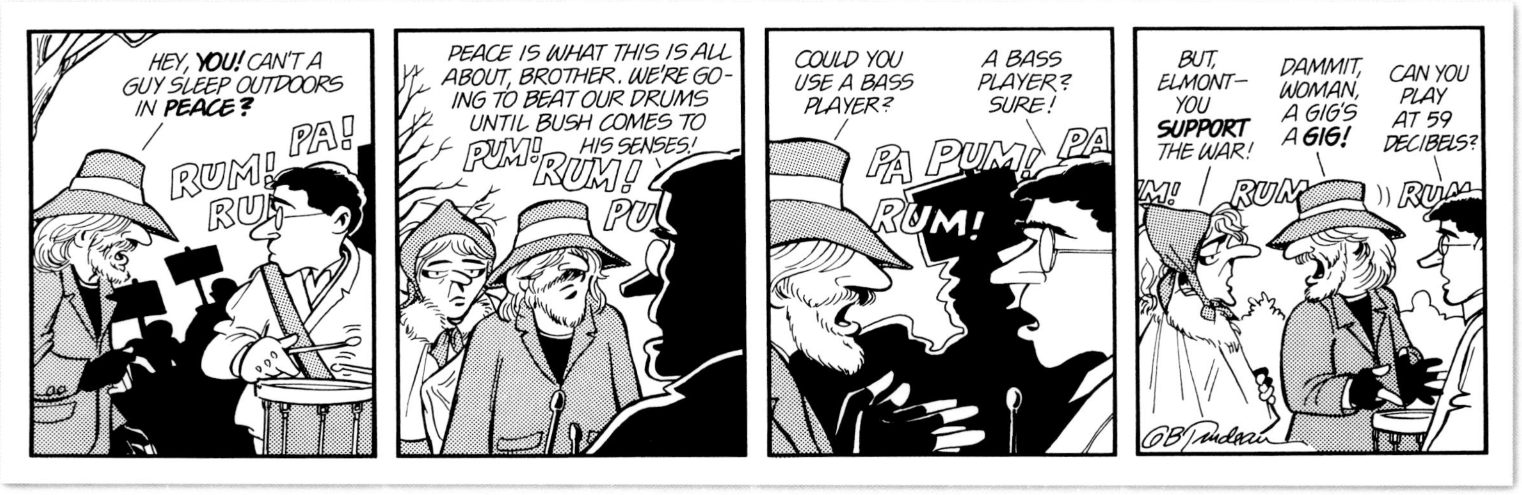
HEY, YOU! CAN'T A GUY SLEEP OUTDOORS IN PEACE?
RUM! PA!
PEACE IS WHAT THIS IS ALL ABOUT, BROTHER. WE'RE GOING TO BEAT OUR DRUMS UNTIL BUSH COMES TO HIS SENSES!
PUM! RUM!
COULD YOU USE A BASS PLAYER?
A BASS PLAYER? SURE!
PA PUM! RUM!
BUT, ELMONT — YOU SUPPORT THE WAR!
DAMMIT, WOMAN, A GIG'S A GIG!
CAN YOU PLAY AT 59 DECIBELS?

2/20/91

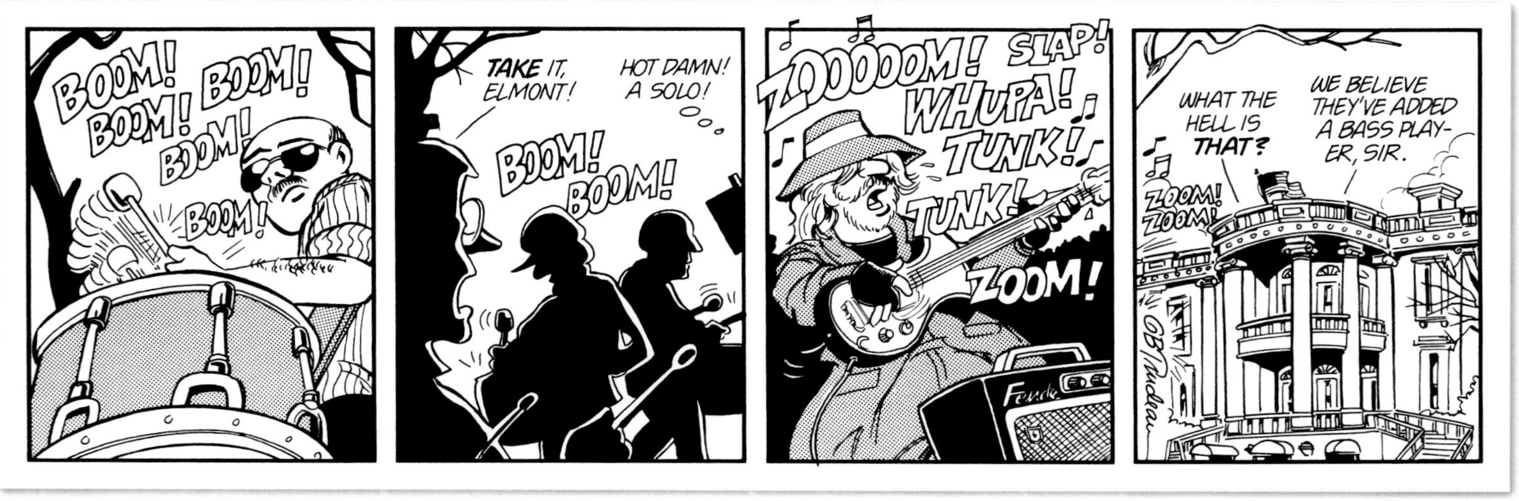
BOOM! BOOM! BOOM! BOOM! BOOM!
TAKE IT, ELMONT!
HOT DAMN! A SOLO!
BOOM! BOOM!
ZOOOOOM! SLAP! WHUPA! TUNK! TUNK! ZOOM!
WHAT THE HELL IS THAT?
WE BELIEVE THEY'VE ADDED A BASS PLAYER, SIR.
ZOOM! ZOOM!

2/21/91

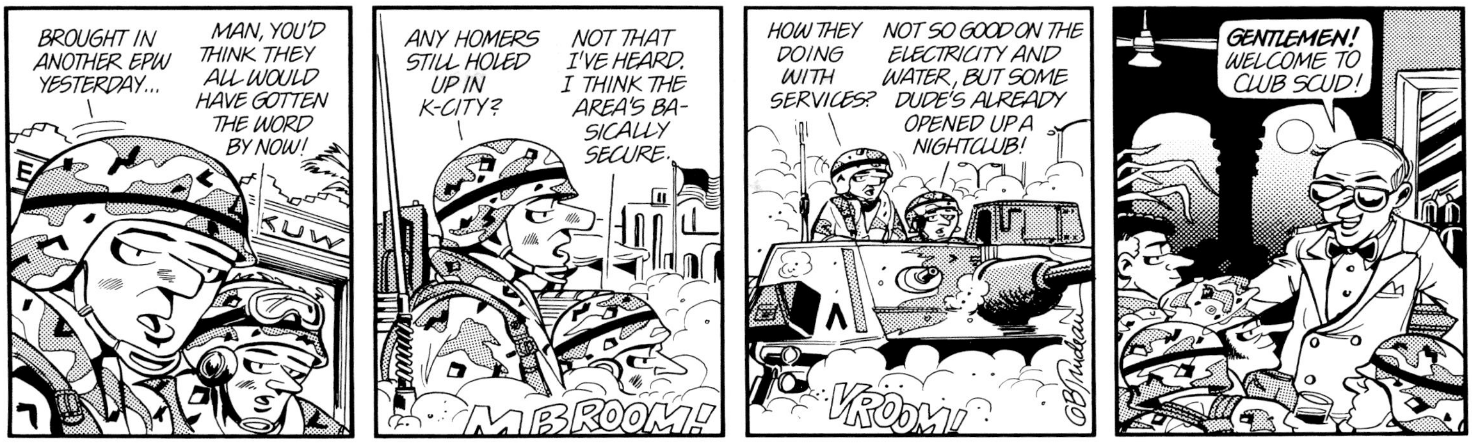
BROUGHT IN ANOTHER EPW YESTERDAY...
MAN, YOU'D THINK THEY ALL WOULD HAVE GOTTEN THE WORD BY NOW!
KUW
ANY HOMERS STILL HOLED UP IN K-CITY?
NOT THAT I'VE HEARD. I THINK THE AREA'S BASICALLY SECURE.
MBROOM!
HOW THEY DOING WITH SERVICES?
NOT SO GOOD ON THE ELECTRICITY AND WATER, BUT SOME DUDE'S ALREADY OPENED UP A NIGHTCLUB!
VROOM!
GENTLEMEN! WELCOME TO CLUB SCUD!

3/12/91

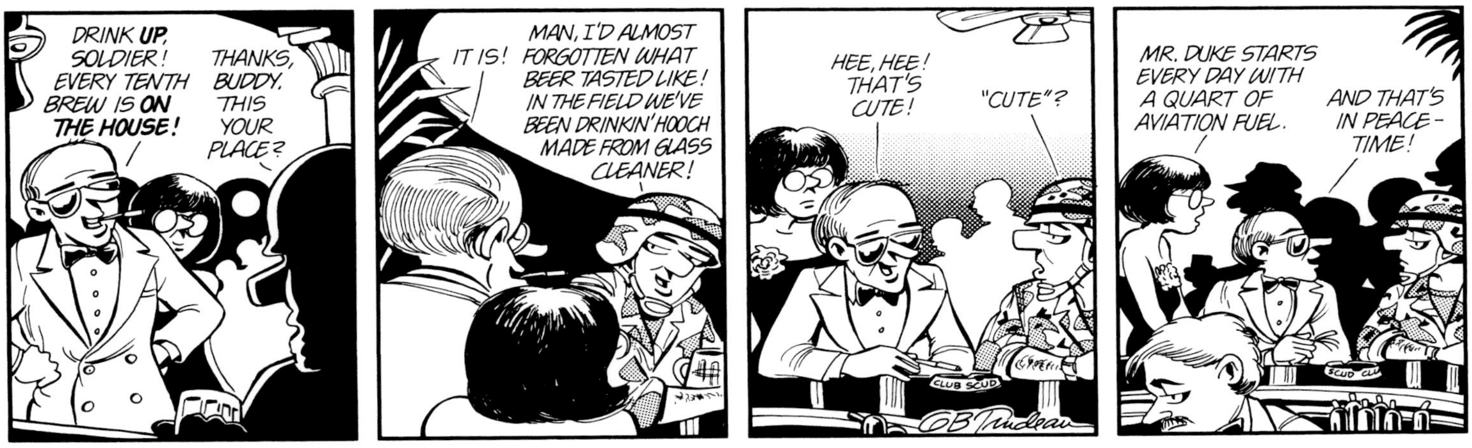
DRINK UP, SOLDIER! EVERY TENTH BREW IS ON THE HOUSE!
THANKS, BUDDY. THIS YOUR PLACE?
IT IS!
MAN, I'D ALMOST FORGOTTEN WHAT BEER TASTED LIKE! IN THE FIELD WE'VE BEEN DRINKIN' HOOCH MADE FROM GLASS CLEANER!
HEE, HEE! THAT'S CUTE!
"CUTE"?
CLUB SCUD
MR. DUKE STARTS EVERY DAY WITH A QUART OF AVIATION FUEL.
AND THAT'S IN PEACETIME!

3/14/91

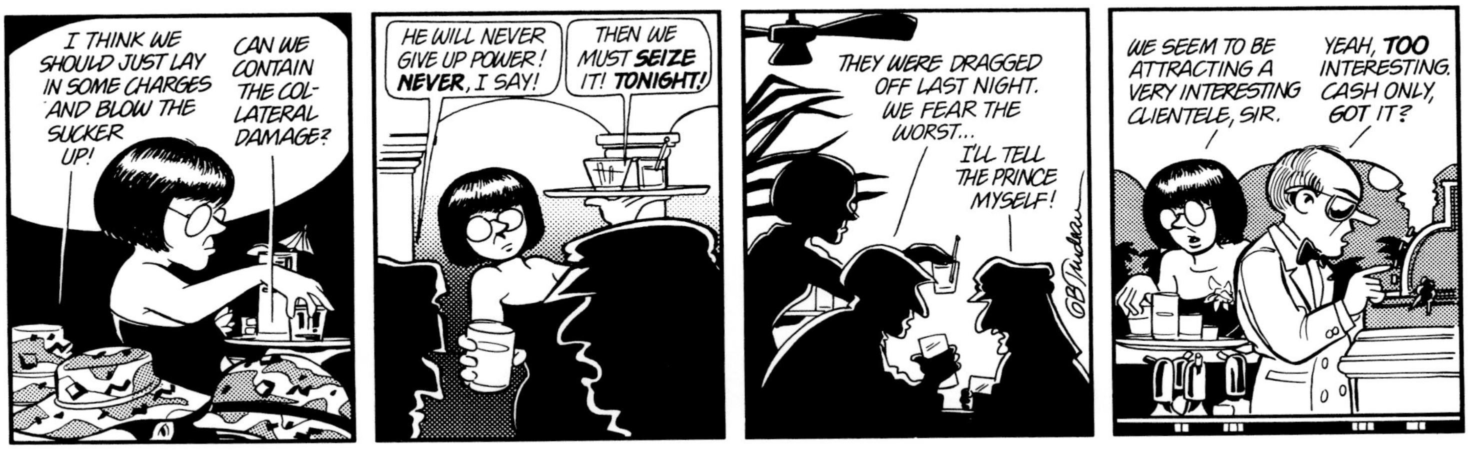
I THINK WE SHOULD JUST LAY IN SOME CHARGES AND BLOW THE SUCKER UP!
CAN WE CONTAIN THE COLLATERAL DAMAGE?
HE WILL NEVER GIVE UP POWER! NEVER, I SAY!
THEN WE MUST SEIZE IT! TONIGHT!
THEY WERE DRAGGED OFF LAST NIGHT. WE FEAR THE WORST...
I'LL TELL THE PRINCE MYSELF!
WE SEEM TO BE ATTRACTING A VERY INTERESTING CLIENTELE, SIR.
YEAH, TOO INTERESTING. CASH ONLY, GOT IT?

3/18/91

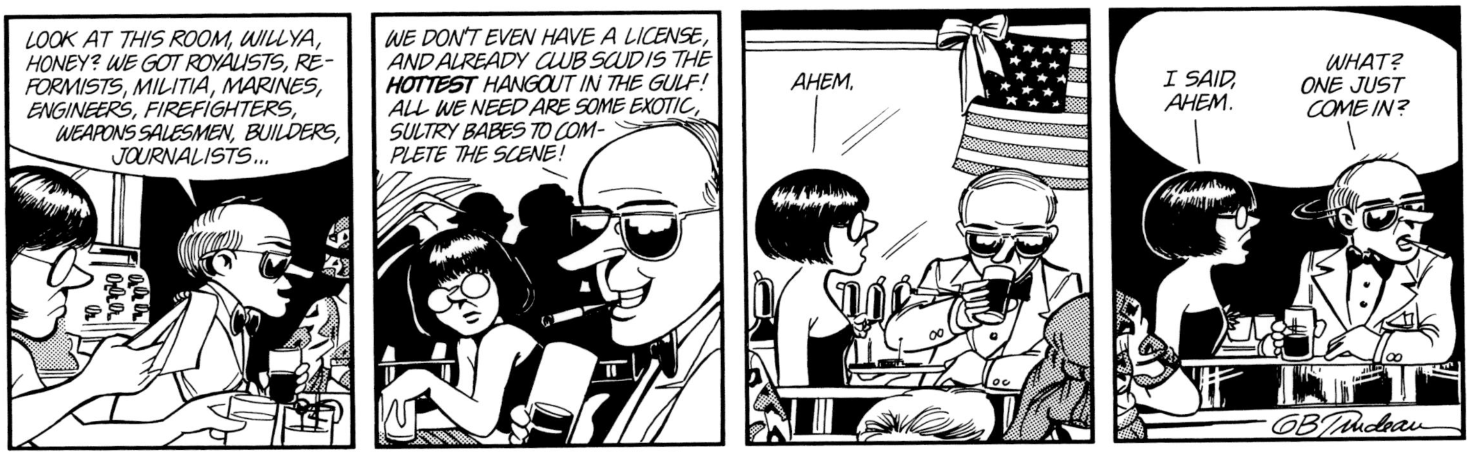
LOOK AT THIS ROOM, WILLYA, HONEY? WE GOT ROYALISTS, REFORMISTS, MILITIA, MARINES, ENGINEERS, FIREFIGHTERS, WEAPONS SALESMEN, BUILDERS, JOURNALISTS...
WE DON'T EVEN HAVE A LICENSE, AND ALREADY CLUB SCUD IS THE HOTTEST HANGOUT IN THE GULF! ALL WE NEED ARE SOME EXOTIC, SULTRY BABES TO COMPLETE THE SCENE!
AHEM.
I SAID, AHEM.
WHAT? ONE JUST COME IN?

3/19/91

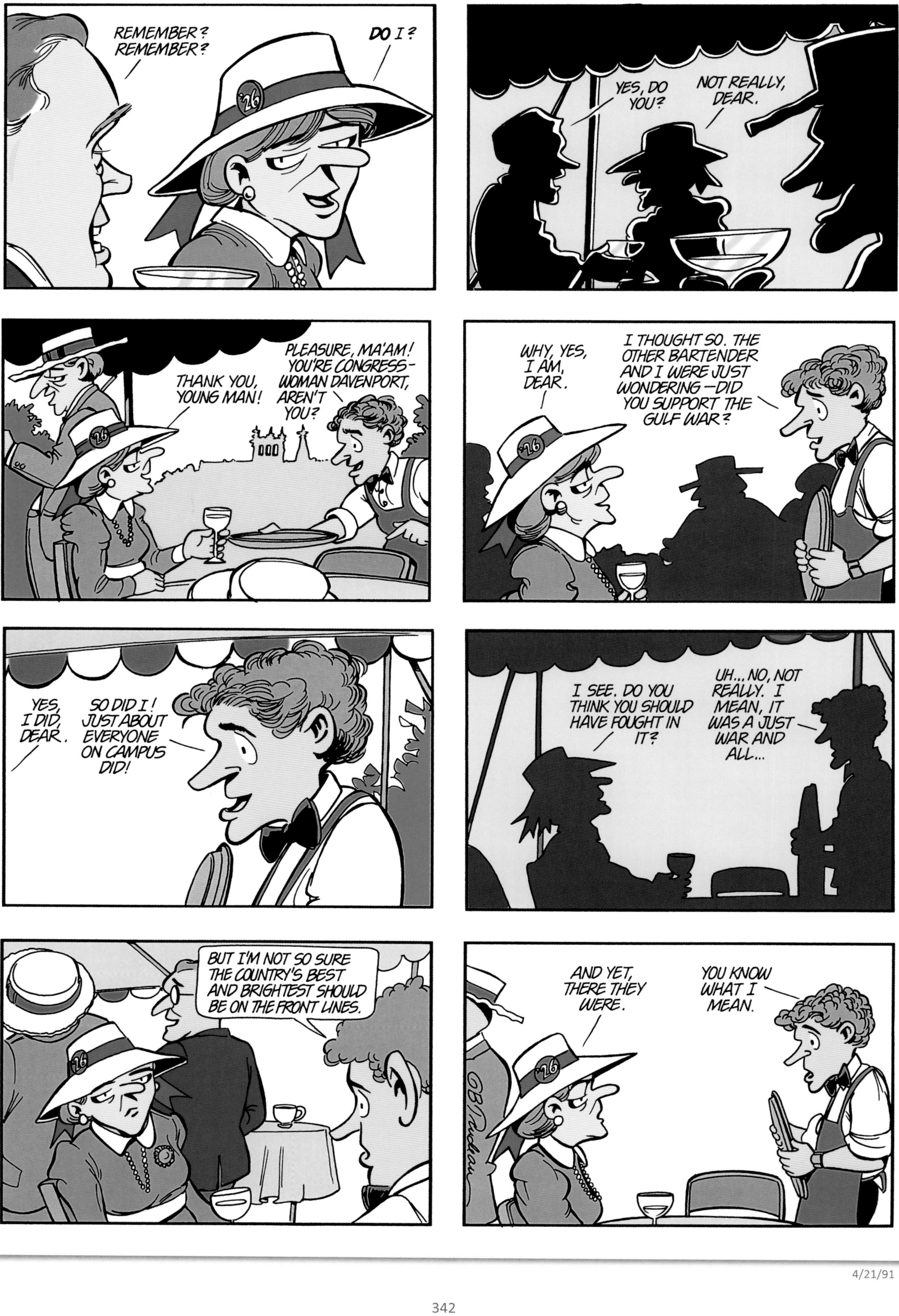
REMEMBER? REMEMBER?
DO I?
YES, DO YOU?
NOT REALLY, DEAR.
PLEASURE, MA'AM!
THANK YOU, YOUNG MAN!
YOU'RE CONGRESSWOMAN DAVENPORT, AREN'T YOU?
WHY, YES, I AM, DEAR.
I THOUGHT SO. THE OTHER BARTENDER AND I WERE JUST WONDERING—DID YOU SUPPORT THE GULF WAR?
YES, I DID, DEAR.
SO DID I! JUST ABOUT EVERYONE ON CAMPUS DID!
I SEE. DO YOU THINK YOU SHOULD HAVE FOUGHT IN IT?
UH... NO, NOT REALLY. I MEAN, IT WAS A JUST WAR AND ALL...
BUT I'M NOT SO SURE THE COUNTRY'S BEST AND BRIGHTEST SHOULD BE ON THE FRONT LINES.
AND YET, THERE THEY WERE.
YOU KNOW WHAT I MEAN.
GB Trudeau

4/21/91

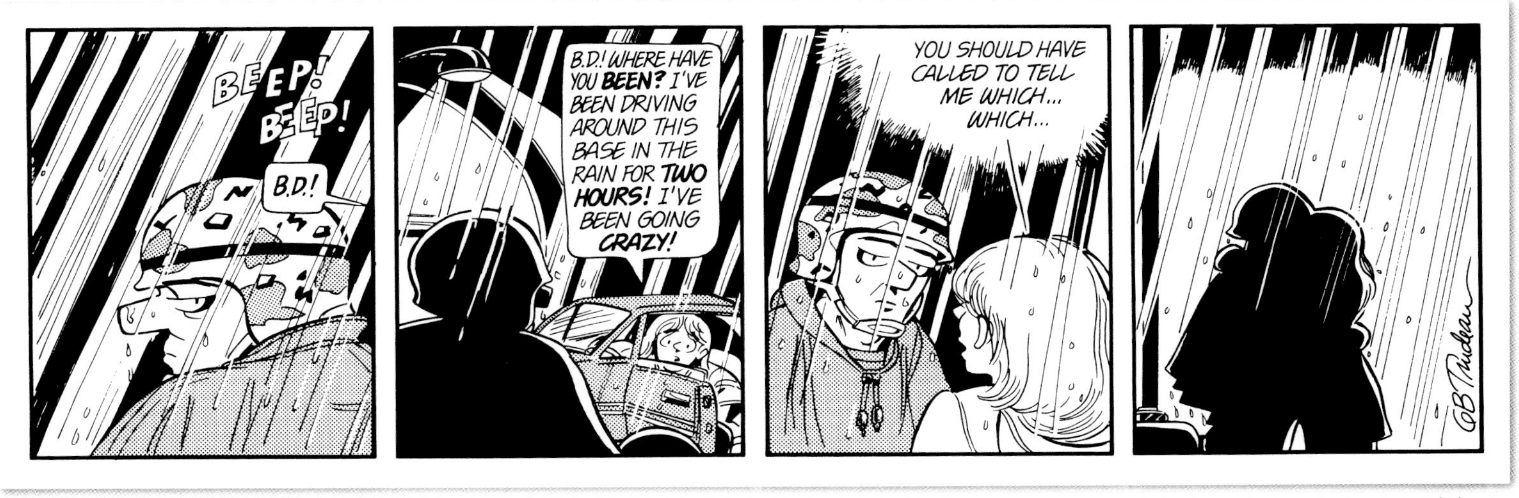
BEEP! BEEP!
B.D.!
B.D.! WHERE HAVE YOU BEEN? I'VE BEEN DRIVING AROUND THIS BASE IN THE RAIN FOR TWO HOURS! I'VE BEEN GOING CRAZY!
YOU SHOULD HAVE CALLED TO TELL ME WHICH... WHICH...

5/6/91

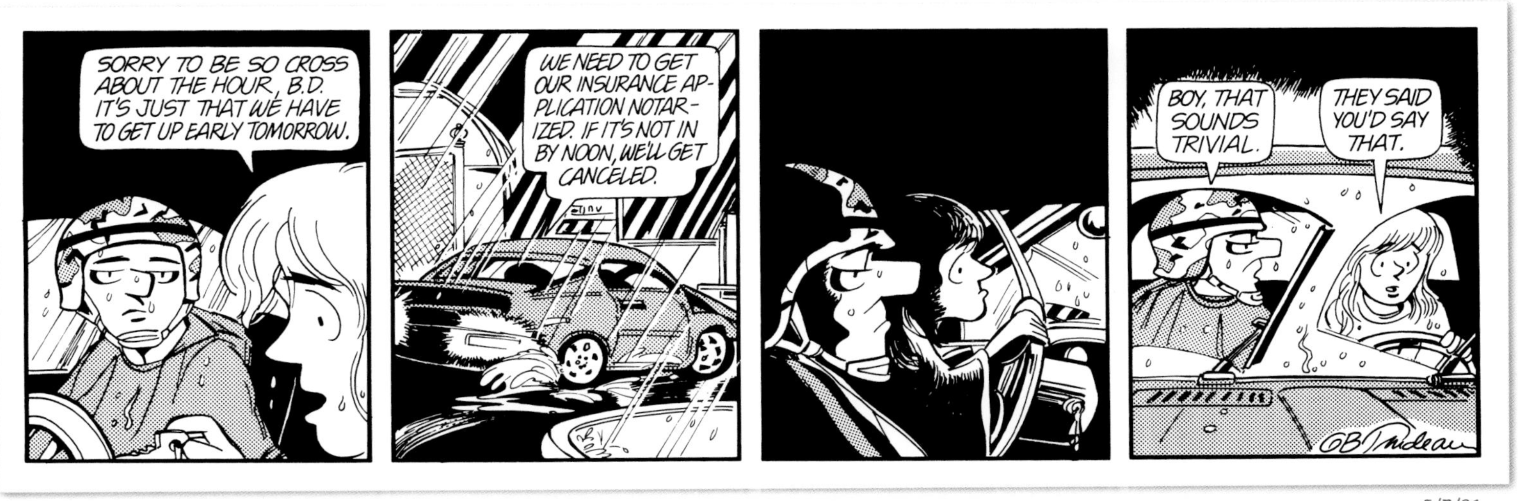
SORRY TO BE SO CROSS ABOUT THE HOUR, B.D. IT'S JUST THAT WE HAVE TO GET UP EARLY TOMORROW.
WE NEED TO GET OUR INSURANCE APPLICATION NOTARIZED. IF IT'S NOT IN BY NOON, WE'LL GET CANCELED.
BOY, THAT SOUNDS TRIVIAL.
THEY SAID YOU'D SAY THAT.

5/7/91

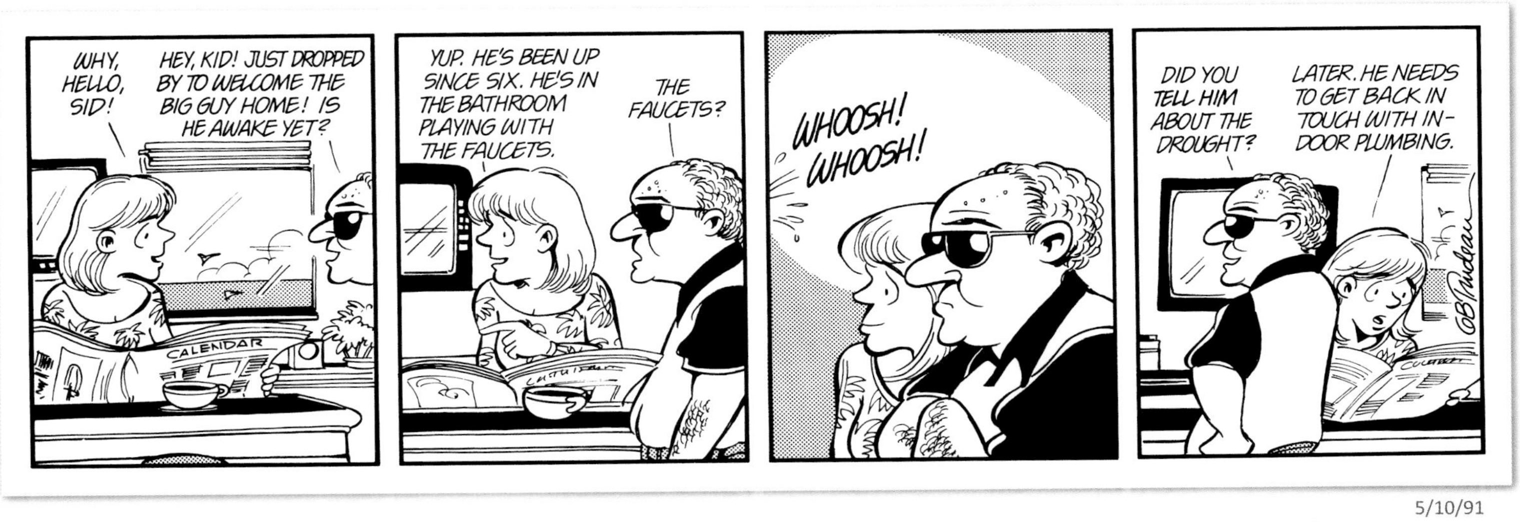
WHY, HELLO, SID!
HEY, KID! JUST DROPPED BY TO WELCOME THE BIG GUY HOME! IS HE AWAKE YET?
CALENDAR
YUP. HE'S BEEN UP SINCE SIX. HE'S IN THE BATHROOM PLAYING WITH THE FAUCETS.
THE FAUCETS?
WHOOSH! WHOOSH!
DID YOU TELL HIM ABOUT THE DROUGHT?
LATER. HE NEEDS TO GET BACK IN TOUCH WITH INDOOR PLUMBING.

5/10/91

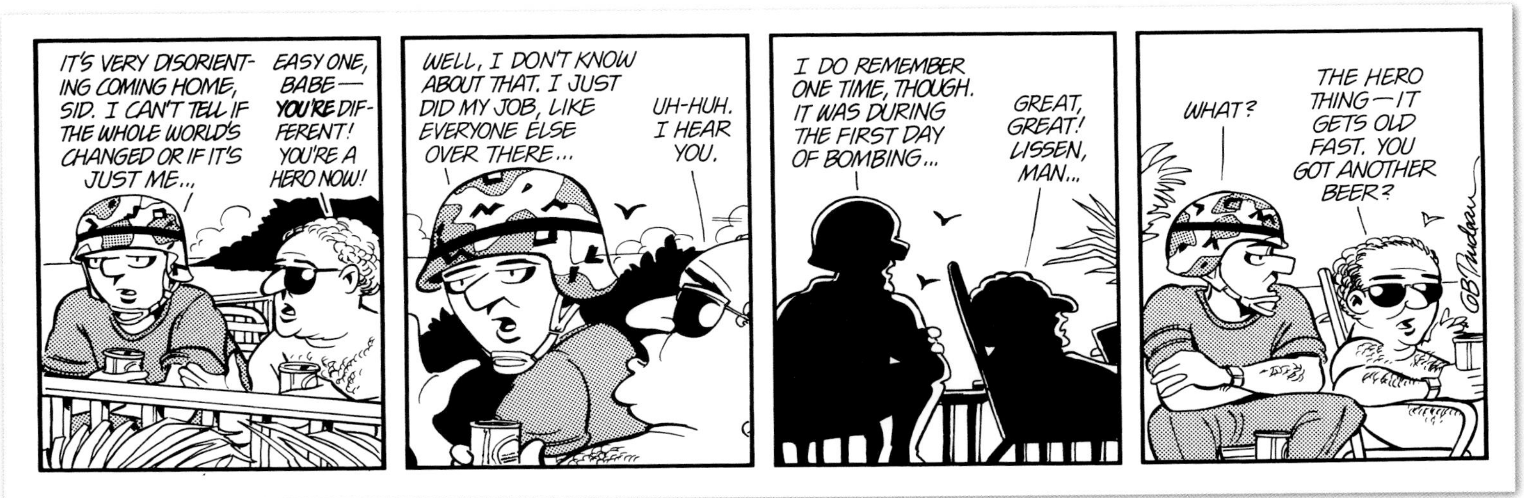
IT'S VERY DISORIENTING COMING HOME, SID. I CAN'T TELL IF THE WHOLE WORLD'S CHANGED OR IF IT'S JUST ME...
EASY ONE, BABE — YOU'RE DIFFERENT! YOU'RE A HERO NOW!
WELL, I DON'T KNOW ABOUT THAT. I JUST DID MY JOB, LIKE EVERYONE ELSE OVER THERE...
UH-HUH. I HEAR YOU.
I DO REMEMBER ONE TIME, THOUGH. IT WAS DURING THE FIRST DAY OF BOMBING...
GREAT, GREAT! LISSEN, MAN...
WHAT?
THE HERO THING — IT GETS OLD FAST. YOU GOT ANOTHER BEER?

5/11/91

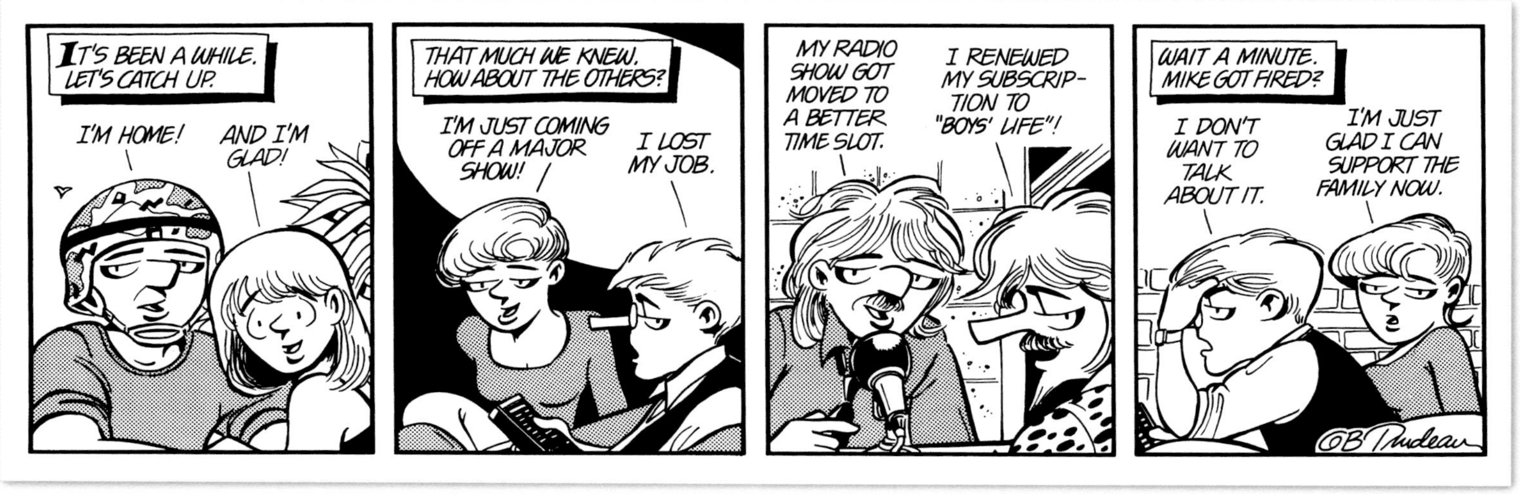
IT'S BEEN A WHILE. LET'S CATCH UP.
I'M HOME!
AND I'M GLAD!
THAT MUCH WE KNEW. HOW ABOUT THE OTHERS?
I'M JUST COMING OFF A MAJOR SHOW!
I LOST MY JOB.
MY RADIO SHOW GOT MOVED TO A BETTER TIME SLOT.
I RENEWED MY SUBSCRIPTION TO "BOYS' LIFE"!
WAIT A MINUTE. MIKE GOT FIRED?
I DON'T WANT TO TALK ABOUT IT.
I'M JUST GLAD I CAN SUPPORT THE FAMILY NOW.
©B Trudeau

6/3/91

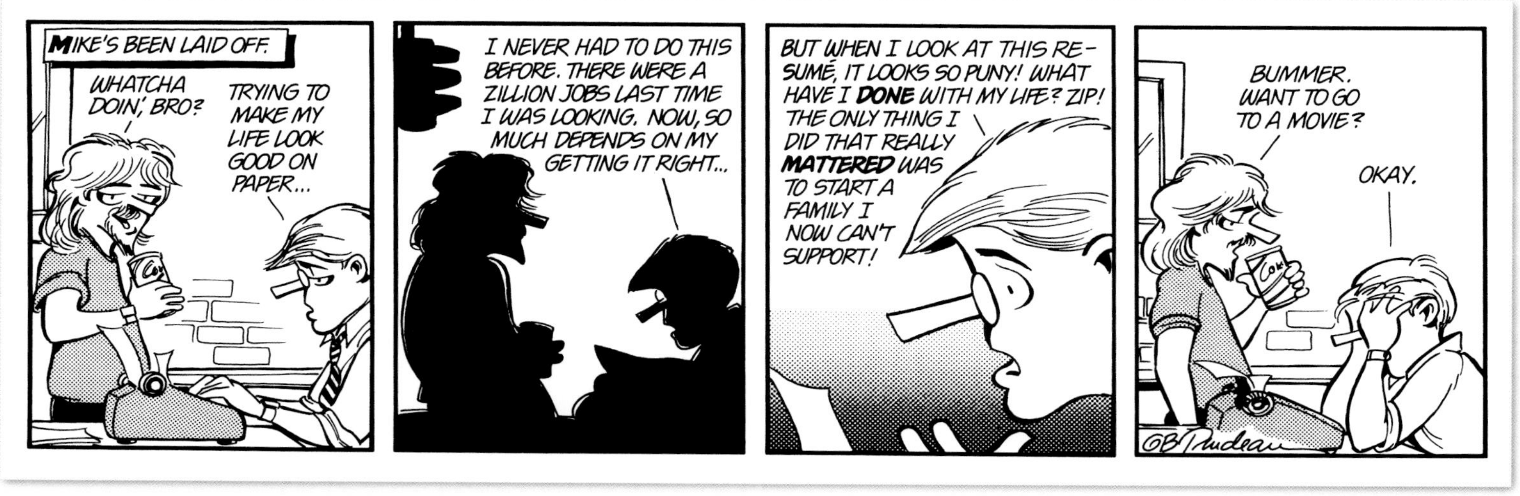
MIKE'S BEEN LAID OFF.
WHATCHA DOIN', BRO?
TRYING TO MAKE MY LIFE LOOK GOOD ON PAPER...
I NEVER HAD TO DO THIS BEFORE. THERE WERE A ZILLION JOBS LAST TIME I WAS LOOKING. NOW, SO MUCH DEPENDS ON MY GETTING IT RIGHT...
BUT WHEN I LOOK AT THIS RESUMÉ, IT LOOKS SO PUNY! WHAT HAVE I DONE WITH MY LIFE? ZIP! THE ONLY THING I DID THAT REALLY MATTERED WAS TO START A FAMILY I NOW CAN'T SUPPORT!
BUMMER. WANT TO GO TO A MOVIE?
OKAY.
©B Trudeau

6/4/91

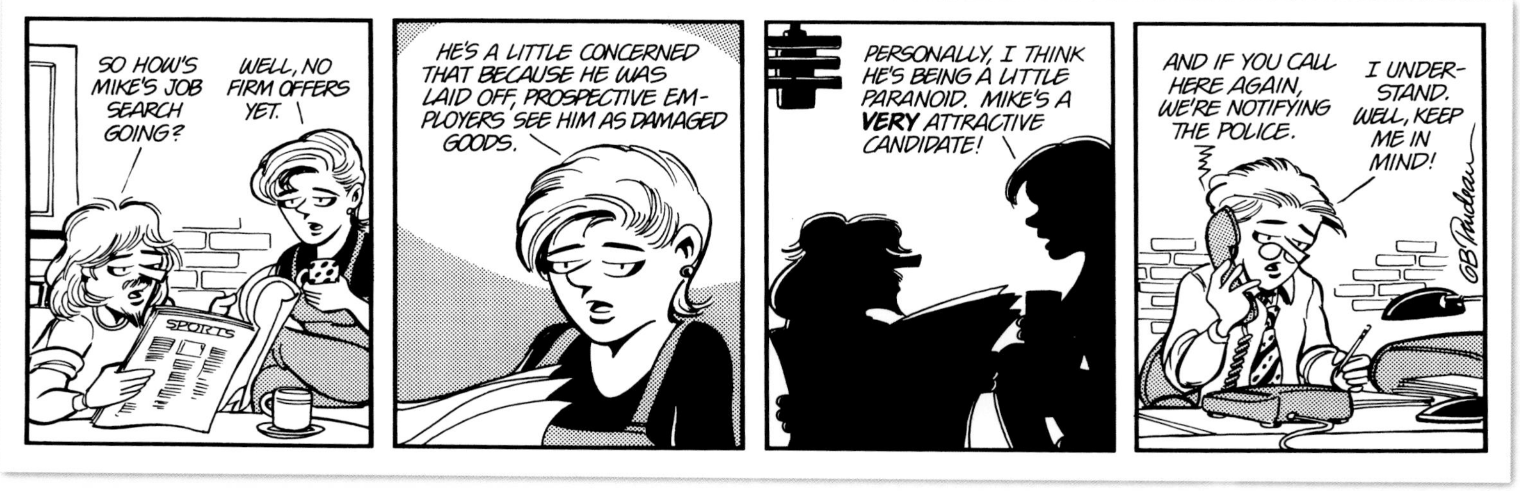
SO HOW'S MIKE'S JOB SEARCH GOING?
WELL, NO FIRM OFFERS YET.
HE'S A LITTLE CONCERNED THAT BECAUSE HE WAS LAID OFF, PROSPECTIVE EMPLOYERS SEE HIM AS DAMAGED GOODS.
PERSONALLY, I THINK HE'S BEING A LITTLE PARANOID. MIKE'S A VERY ATTRACTIVE CANDIDATE!
AND IF YOU CALL HERE AGAIN, WE'RE NOTIFYING THE POLICE.
I UNDERSTAND. WELL, KEEP ME IN MIND!
©B Trudeau

6/5/91

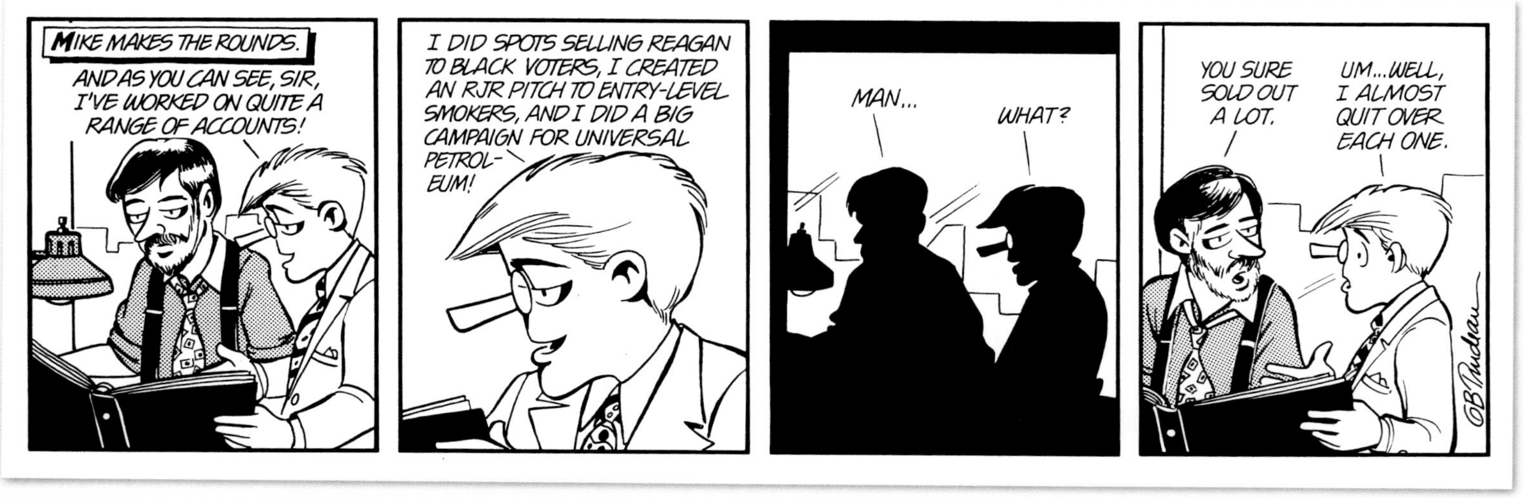
MIKE MAKES THE ROUNDS.
AND AS YOU CAN SEE, SIR, I'VE WORKED ON QUITE A RANGE OF ACCOUNTS!
I DID SPOTS SELLING REAGAN TO BLACK VOTERS, I CREATED AN RJR PITCH TO ENTRY-LEVEL SMOKERS, AND I DID A BIG CAMPAIGN FOR UNIVERSAL PETROLEUM!
MAN...
WHAT?
YOU SURE SOLD OUT A LOT.
UM...WELL, I ALMOST QUIT OVER EACH ONE.
©B Trudeau

6/7/91

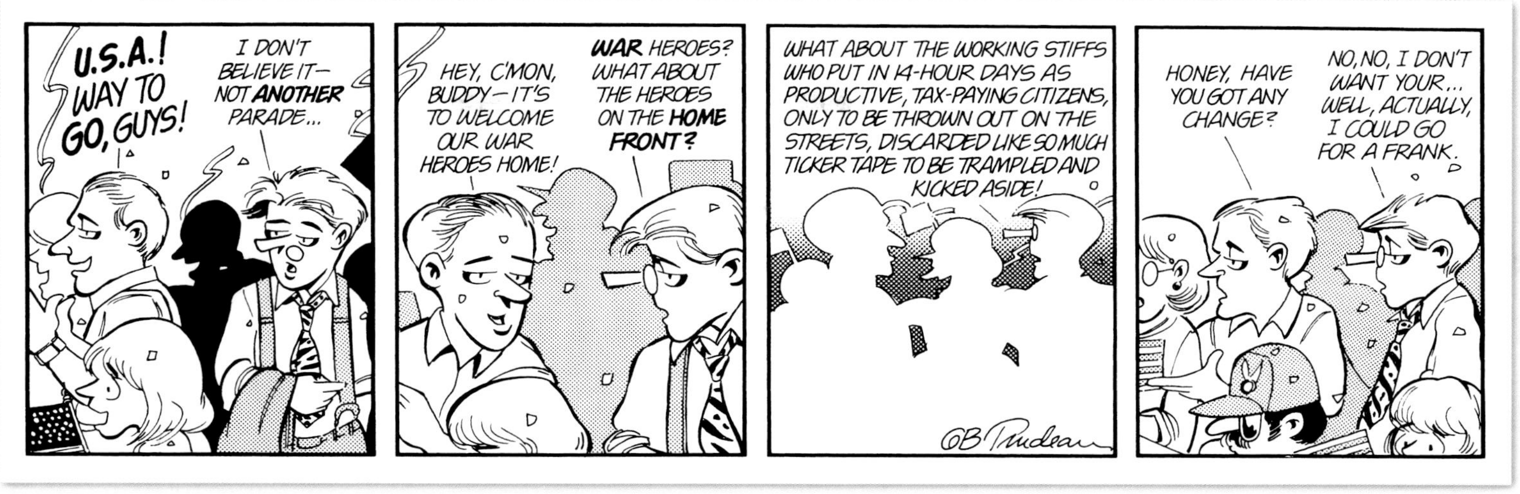
U.S.A.! WAY TO GO, GUYS!
I DON'T BELIEVE IT— NOT ANOTHER PARADE...
HEY, C'MON, BUDDY—IT'S TO WELCOME OUR WAR HEROES HOME!
WAR HEROES? WHAT ABOUT THE HEROES ON THE HOME FRONT?
WHAT ABOUT THE WORKING STIFFS WHO PUT IN 14-HOUR DAYS AS PRODUCTIVE, TAX-PAYING CITIZENS, ONLY TO BE THROWN OUT ON THE STREETS, DISCARDED LIKE SO MUCH TICKER TAPE TO BE TRAMPLED AND KICKED ASIDE!
GB Trudeau
HONEY, HAVE YOU GOT ANY CHANGE?
NO, NO, I DON'T WANT YOUR... WELL, ACTUALLY, I COULD GO FOR A FRANK.

6/10/91

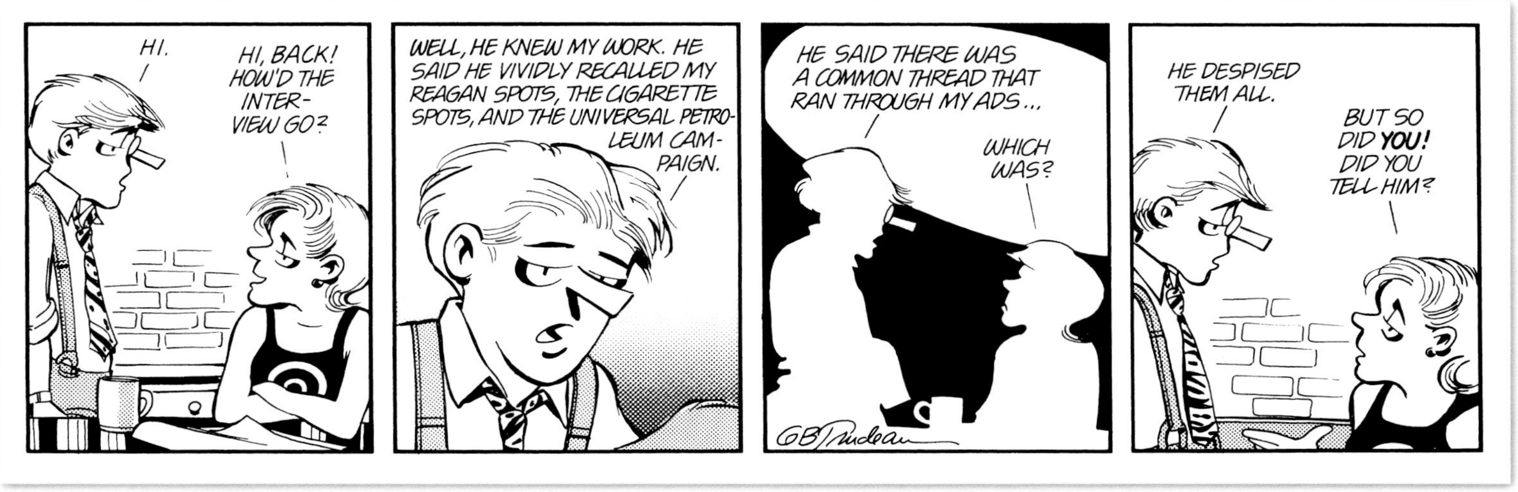
HI.
HI, BACK! HOW'D THE INTERVIEW GO?
WELL, HE KNEW MY WORK. HE SAID HE VIVIDLY RECALLED MY REAGAN SPOTS, THE CIGARETTE SPOTS, AND THE UNIVERSAL PETROLEUM CAMPAIGN.
HE SAID THERE WAS A COMMON THREAD THAT RAN THROUGH MY ADS...
WHICH WAS?
GB Trudeau
HE DESPISED THEM ALL.
BUT SO DID YOU! DID YOU TELL HIM?

6/12/91

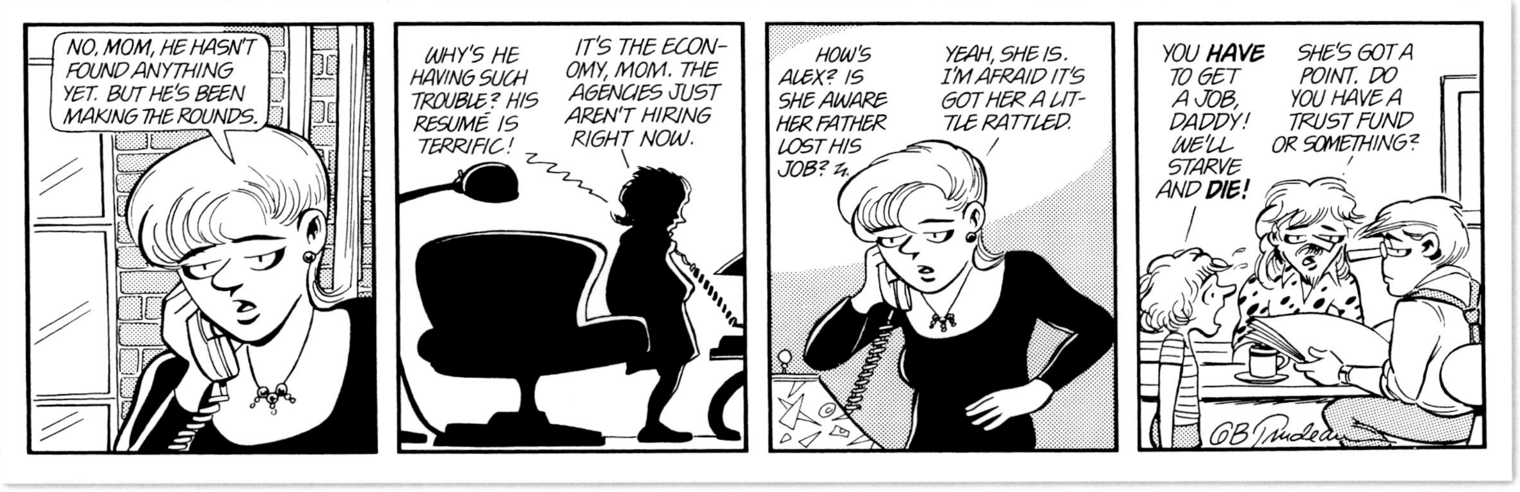
NO, MOM, HE HASN'T FOUND ANYTHING YET. BUT HE'S BEEN MAKING THE ROUNDS.
WHY'S HE HAVING SUCH TROUBLE? HIS RESUMÉ IS TERRIFIC!
IT'S THE ECONOMY, MOM. THE AGENCIES JUST AREN'T HIRING RIGHT NOW.
HOW'S ALEX? IS SHE AWARE HER FATHER LOST HIS JOB?
YEAH, SHE IS. I'M AFRAID IT'S GOT HER A LITTLE RATTLED.
YOU HAVE TO GET A JOB, DADDY! WE'LL STARVE AND DIE!
SHE'S GOT A POINT. DO YOU HAVE A TRUST FUND OR SOMETHING?
GB Trudeau

6/13/91

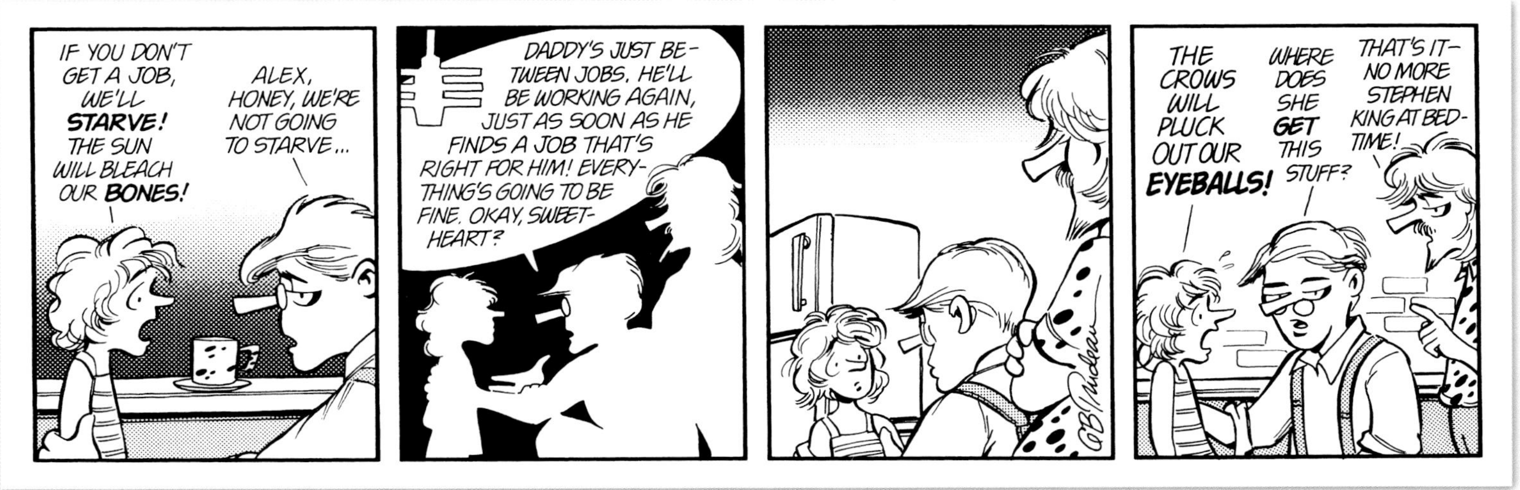
IF YOU DON'T GET A JOB, WE'LL STARVE! THE SUN WILL BLEACH OUR BONES!
ALEX, HONEY, WE'RE NOT GOING TO STARVE...
DADDY'S JUST BETWEEN JOBS. HE'LL BE WORKING AGAIN, JUST AS SOON AS HE FINDS A JOB THAT'S RIGHT FOR HIM! EVERYTHING'S GOING TO BE FINE. OKAY, SWEETHEART?
GB Trudeau
THE CROWS WILL PLUCK OUT OUR EYEBALLS!
WHERE DOES SHE GET THIS STUFF?
THAT'S IT— NO MORE STEPHEN KING AT BEDTIME!

6/14/91

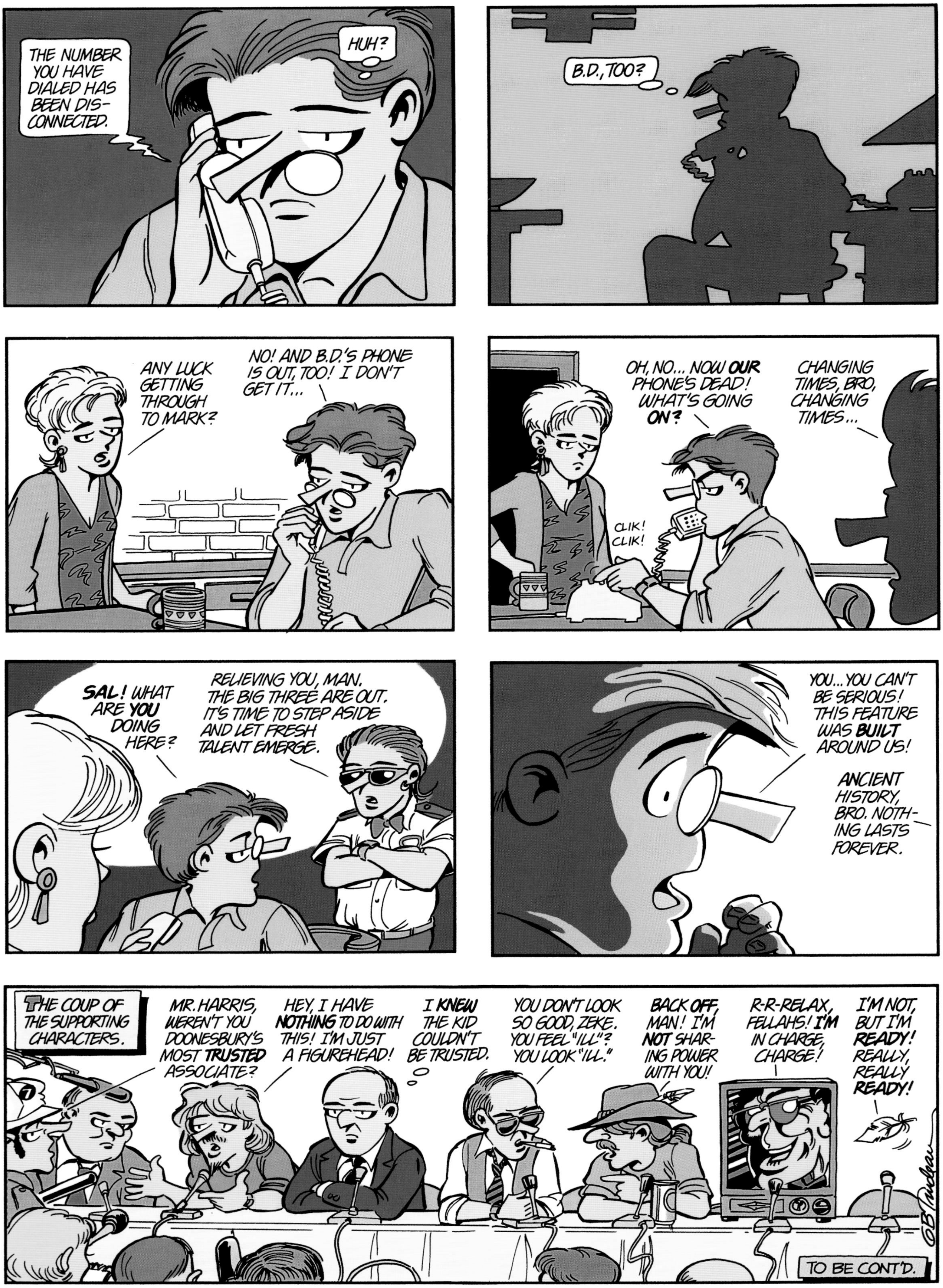
THE NUMBER YOU HAVE DIALED HAS BEEN DIS-CONNECTED.
HUH?
B.D., TOO?
ANY LUCK GETTING THROUGH TO MARK?
NO! AND B.D.'S PHONE IS OUT, TOO! I DON'T GET IT...
OH, NO... NOW OUR PHONE'S DEAD! WHAT'S GOING ON?
CLIK! CLIK!
CHANGING TIMES, BRO, CHANGING TIMES...
SAL! WHAT ARE YOU DOING HERE?
RELIEVING YOU, MAN. THE BIG THREE ARE OUT. IT'S TIME TO STEP ASIDE AND LET FRESH TALENT EMERGE.
YOU... YOU CAN'T BE SERIOUS! THIS FEATURE WAS BUILT AROUND US!
ANCIENT HISTORY, BRO. NOTHING LASTS FOREVER.
THE COUP OF THE SUPPORTING CHARACTERS.
MR. HARRIS, WEREN'T YOU DOONESBURY'S MOST TRUSTED ASSOCIATE?
HEY, I HAVE NOTHING TO DO WITH THIS! I'M JUST A FIGUREHEAD!
I KNEW THE KID COULDN'T BE TRUSTED.
YOU DON'T LOOK SO GOOD, ZEKE. YOU FEEL "ILL"? YOU LOOK "ILL."
BACK OFF, MAN! I'M NOT SHARING POWER WITH YOU!
R-R-RELAX, FELLAHS! I'M IN CHARGE, CHARGE!
I'M NOT, BUT I'M READY! REALLY, REALLY READY!
TO BE CONT'D.

9/29/91

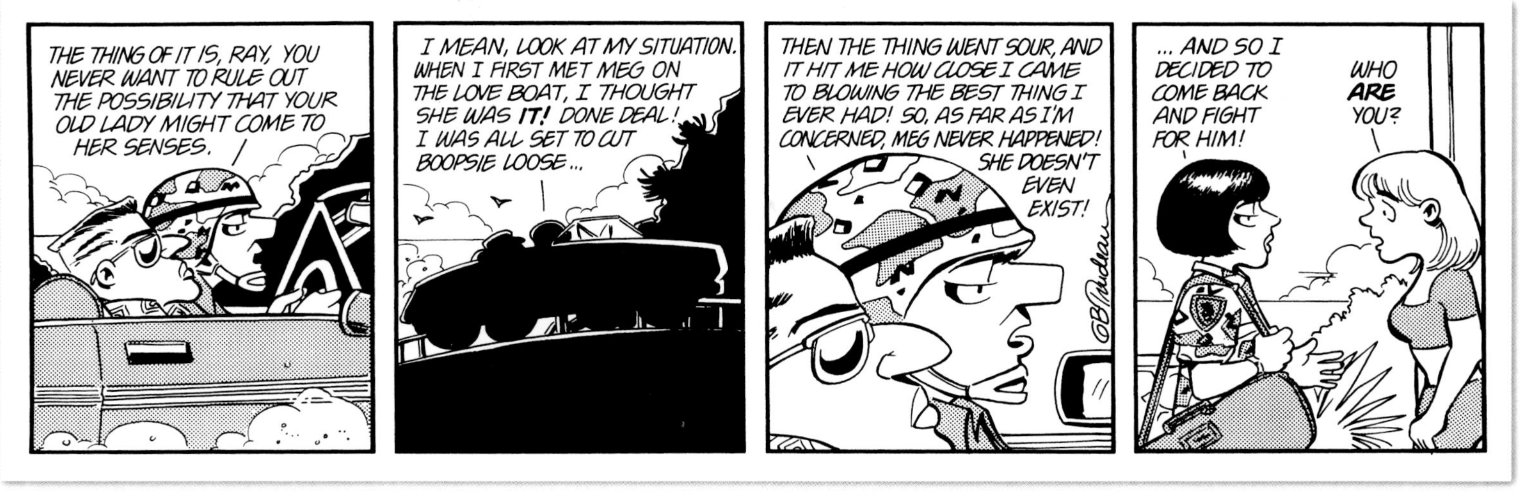
THE THING OF IT IS, RAY, YOU NEVER WANT TO RULE OUT THE POSSIBILITY THAT YOUR OLD LADY MIGHT COME TO HER SENSES.
I MEAN, LOOK AT MY SITUATION. WHEN I FIRST MET MEG ON THE LOVE BOAT, I THOUGHT SHE WAS IT! DONE DEAL! I WAS ALL SET TO CUT BOOPSIE LOOSE...
THEN THE THING WENT SOUR, AND IT HIT ME HOW CLOSE I CAME TO BLOWING THE BEST THING I EVER HAD! SO, AS FAR AS I'M CONCERNED, MEG NEVER HAPPENED!
SHE DOESN'T EVEN EXIST!
GB Trudeau
... AND SO I DECIDED TO COME BACK AND FIGHT FOR HIM!
WHO ARE YOU?

8/5/91

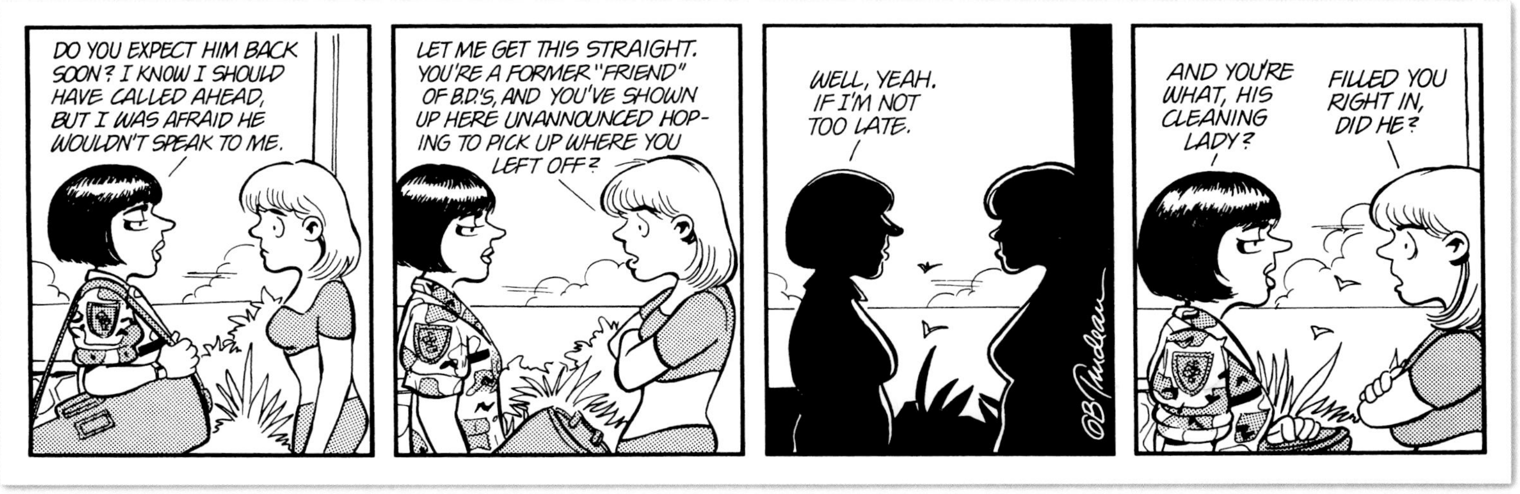
DO YOU EXPECT HIM BACK SOON? I KNOW I SHOULD HAVE CALLED AHEAD, BUT I WAS AFRAID HE WOULDN'T SPEAK TO ME.
LET ME GET THIS STRAIGHT. YOU'RE A FORMER "FRIEND" OF B.D.'S, AND YOU'VE SHOWN UP HERE UNANNOUNCED HOPING TO PICK UP WHERE YOU LEFT OFF?
WELL, YEAH. IF I'M NOT TOO LATE.
GB Trudeau
AND YOU'RE WHAT, HIS CLEANING LADY?
FILLED YOU RIGHT IN, DID HE?

8/6/91

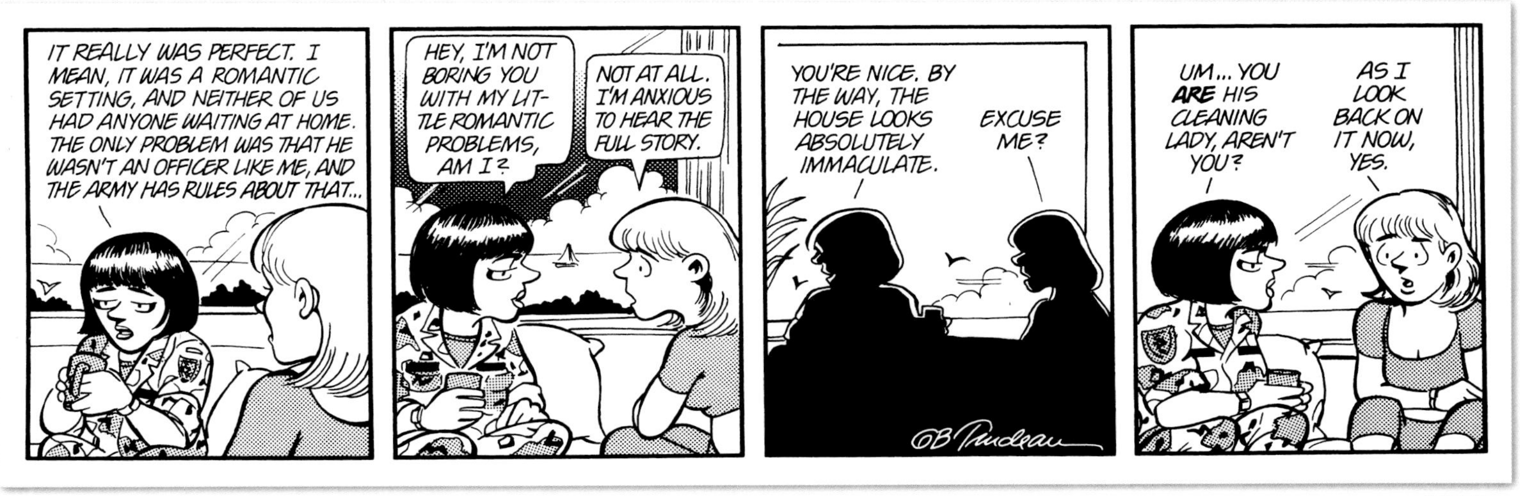
IT REALLY WAS PERFECT. I MEAN, IT WAS A ROMANTIC SETTING, AND NEITHER OF US HAD ANYONE WAITING AT HOME. THE ONLY PROBLEM WAS THAT HE WASN'T AN OFFICER LIKE ME, AND THE ARMY HAS RULES ABOUT THAT...
HEY, I'M NOT BORING YOU WITH MY LITTLE ROMANTIC PROBLEMS, AM I?
NOT AT ALL. I'M ANXIOUS TO HEAR THE FULL STORY.
YOU'RE NICE. BY THE WAY, THE HOUSE LOOKS ABSOLUTELY IMMACULATE.
EXCUSE ME?
GB Trudeau
UM... YOU ARE HIS CLEANING LADY, AREN'T YOU?
AS I LOOK BACK ON IT NOW, YES.

8/7/91

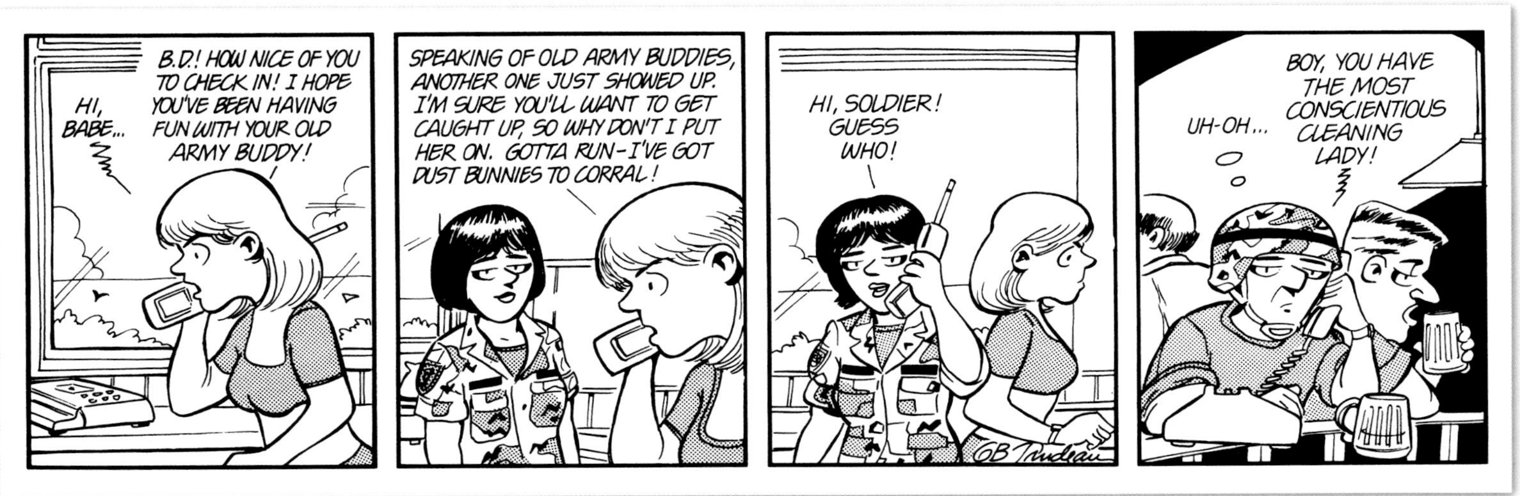
HI, BABE...
B.D.! HOW NICE OF YOU TO CHECK IN! I HOPE YOU'VE BEEN HAVING FUN WITH YOUR OLD ARMY BUDDY!
SPEAKING OF OLD ARMY BUDDIES, ANOTHER ONE JUST SHOWED UP. I'M SURE YOU'LL WANT TO GET CAUGHT UP, SO WHY DON'T I PUT HER ON. GOTTA RUN - I'VE GOT DUST BUNNIES TO CORRAL!
HI, SOLDIER! GUESS WHO!
GB Trudeau
UH-OH...
BOY, YOU HAVE THE MOST CONSCIENTIOUS CLEANING LADY!

8/10/91

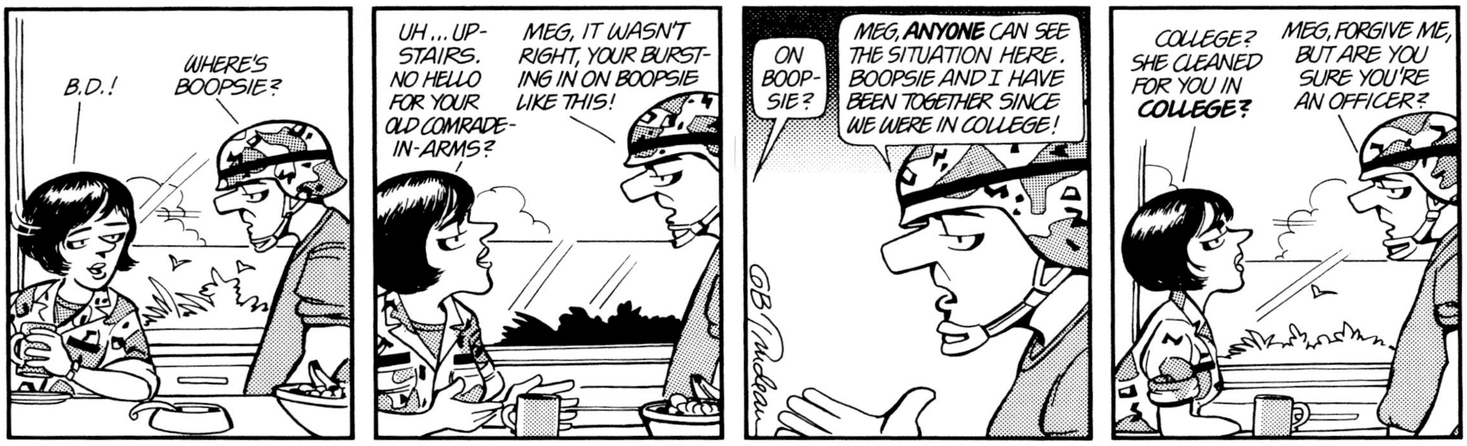
B.D.!
WHERE'S BOOPSIE?
UH... UP-STAIRS. NO HELLO FOR YOUR OLD COMRADE-IN-ARMS?
MEG, IT WASN'T RIGHT, YOUR BURSTING IN ON BOOPSIE LIKE THIS!
ON BOOP-SIE?
MEG, ANYONE CAN SEE THE SITUATION HERE. BOOPSIE AND I HAVE BEEN TOGETHER SINCE WE WERE IN COLLEGE!
COLLEGE? SHE CLEANED FOR YOU IN COLLEGE?
MEG, FORGIVE ME, BUT ARE YOU SURE YOU'RE AN OFFICER?

8/12/91

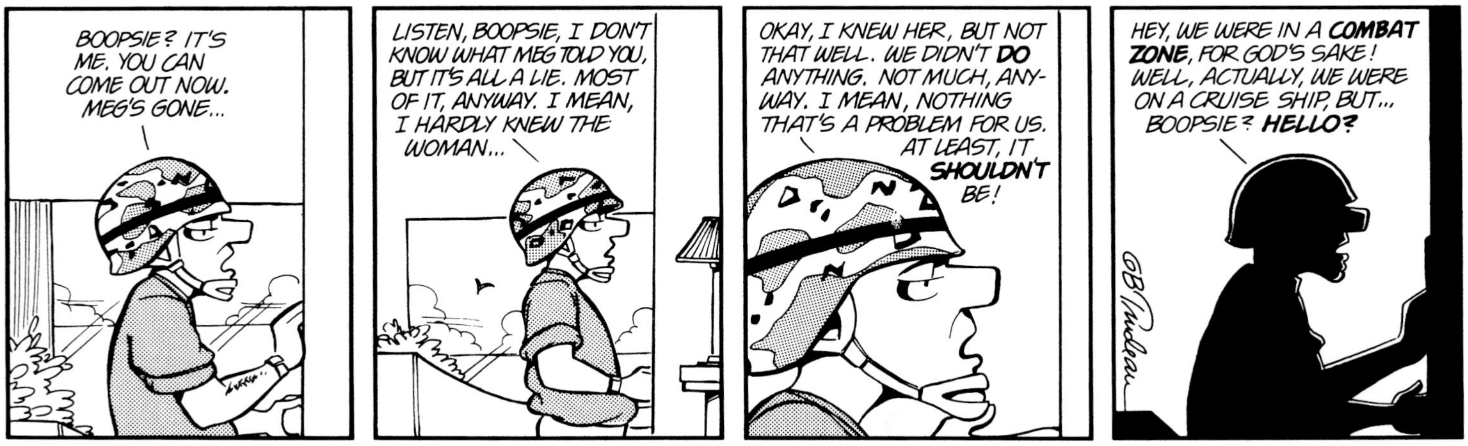
BOOPSIE? IT'S ME. YOU CAN COME OUT NOW. MEG'S GONE...
LISTEN, BOOPSIE, I DON'T KNOW WHAT MEG TOLD YOU, BUT IT'S ALL A LIE. MOST OF IT, ANYWAY. I MEAN, I HARDLY KNEW THE WOMAN...
OKAY, I KNEW HER, BUT NOT THAT WELL. WE DIDN'T DO ANYTHING. NOT MUCH, ANYWAY. I MEAN, NOTHING THAT'S A PROBLEM FOR US.
AT LEAST, IT SHOULDN'T BE!
HEY, WE WERE IN A COMBAT ZONE, FOR GOD'S SAKE! WELL, ACTUALLY, WE WERE ON A CRUISE SHIP, BUT... BOOPSIE? HELLO?

8/13/91

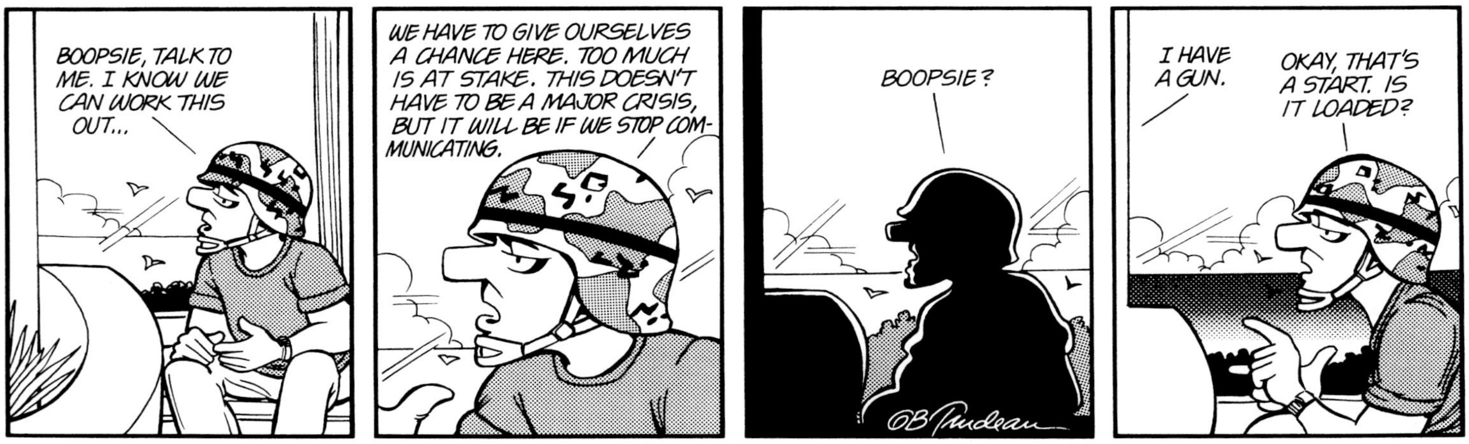
BOOPSIE, TALK TO ME. I KNOW WE CAN WORK THIS OUT...
WE HAVE TO GIVE OURSELVES A CHANCE HERE. TOO MUCH IS AT STAKE. THIS DOESN'T HAVE TO BE A MAJOR CRISIS, BUT IT WILL BE IF WE STOP COMMUNICATING.
BOOPSIE?
I HAVE A GUN.
OKAY, THAT'S A START. IS IT LOADED?

8/14/91

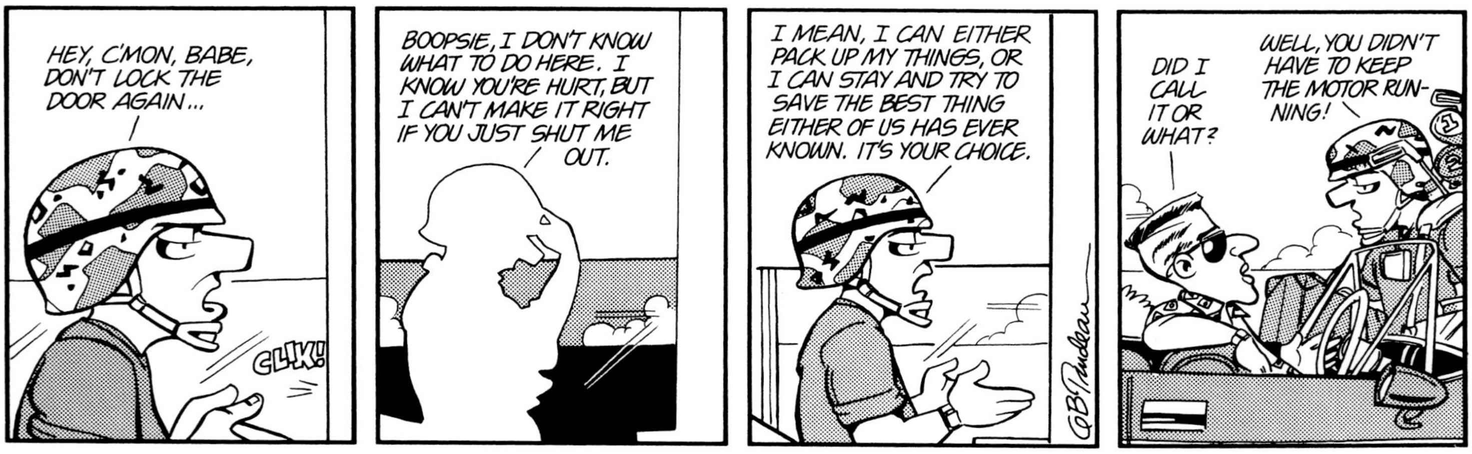
HEY, C'MON, BABE, DON'T LOCK THE DOOR AGAIN...
CLIK!
BOOPSIE, I DON'T KNOW WHAT TO DO HERE. I KNOW YOU'RE HURT, BUT I CAN'T MAKE IT RIGHT IF YOU JUST SHUT ME OUT.
I MEAN, I CAN EITHER PACK UP MY THINGS, OR I CAN STAY AND TRY TO SAVE THE BEST THING EITHER OF US HAS EVER KNOWN. IT'S YOUR CHOICE.
DID I CALL IT OR WHAT?
WELL, YOU DIDN'T HAVE TO KEEP THE MOTOR RUNNING!

8/17/91

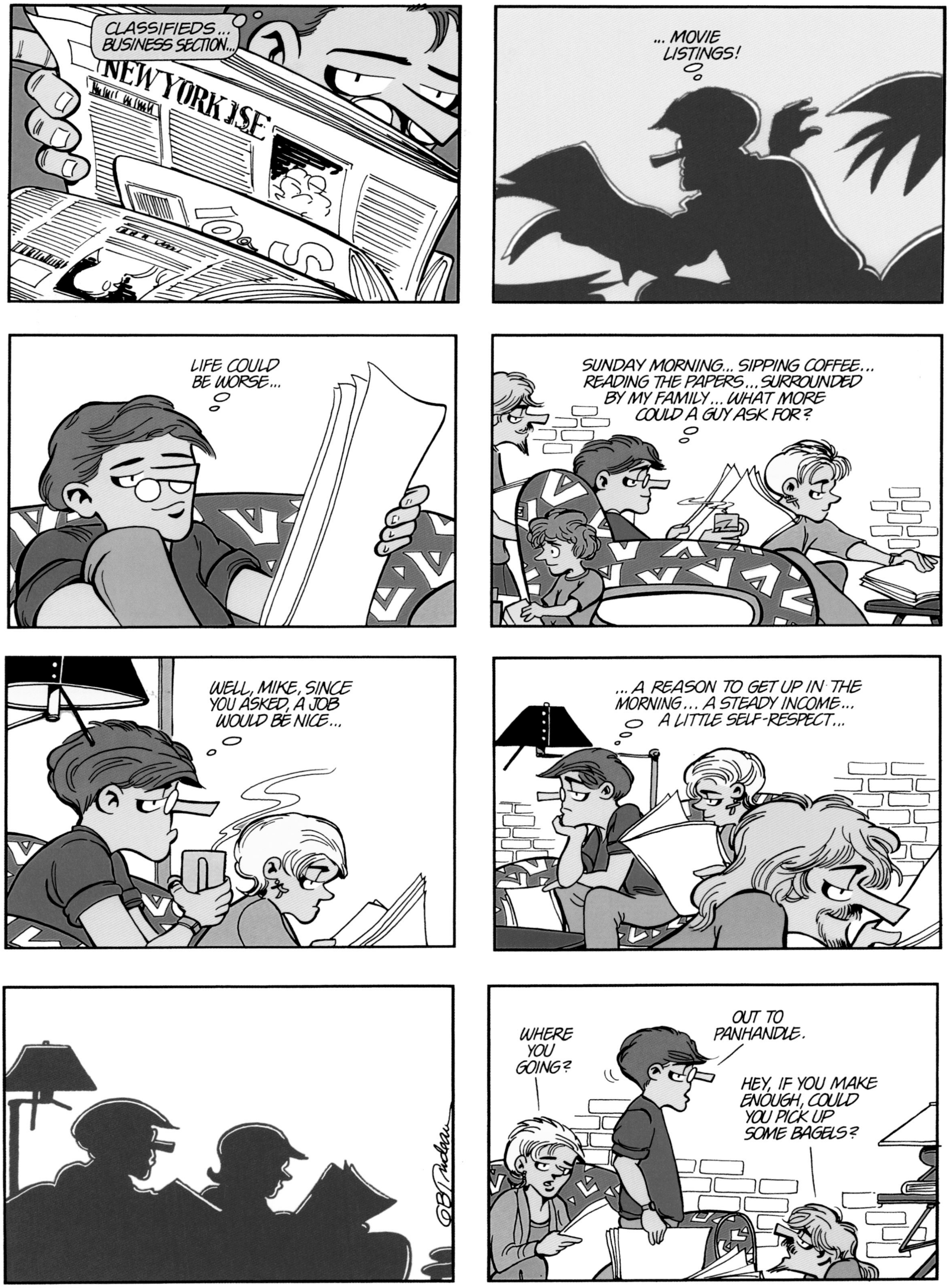
CLASSIFIEDS... BUSINESS SECTION...
NEW YORK ...SE
... MOVIE LISTINGS!
LIFE COULD BE WORSE...
SUNDAY MORNING... SIPPING COFFEE... READING THE PAPERS... SURROUNDED BY MY FAMILY... WHAT MORE COULD A GUY ASK FOR?
WELL, MIKE, SINCE YOU ASKED, A JOB WOULD BE NICE...
... A REASON TO GET UP IN THE MORNING... A STEADY INCOME... A LITTLE SELF-RESPECT...
WHERE YOU GOING?
OUT TO PANHANDLE.
HEY, IF YOU MAKE ENOUGH, COULD YOU PICK UP SOME BAGELS?

7/21/91

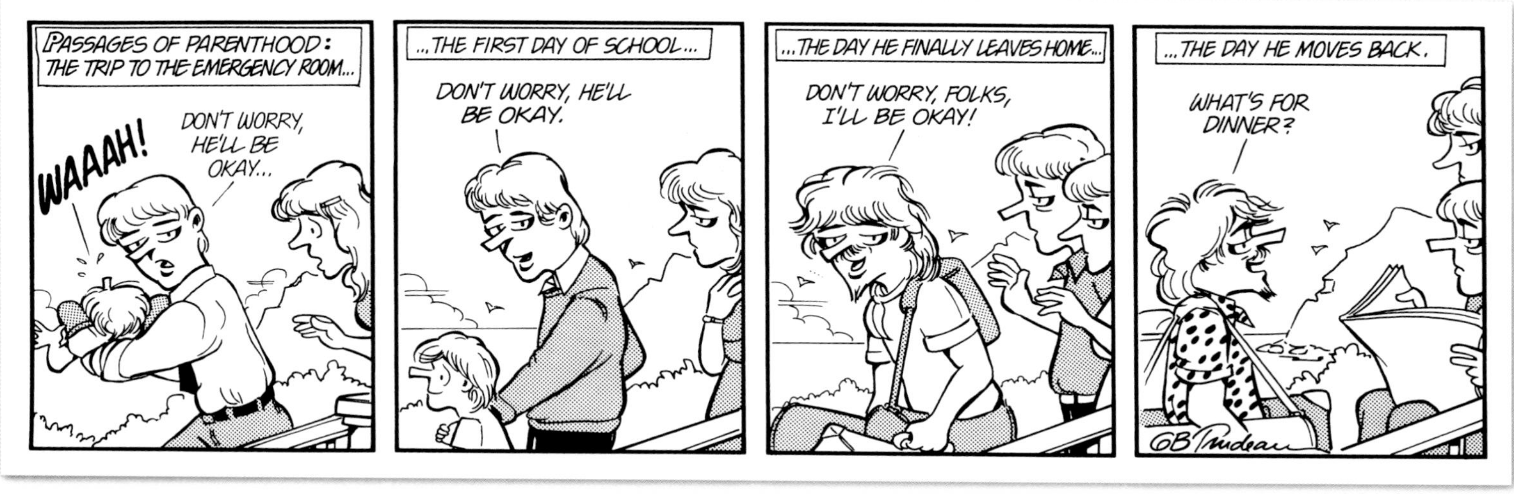
PASSAGES OF PARENTHOOD: THE TRIP TO THE EMERGENCY ROOM...
WAAAH!
DON'T WORRY, HE'LL BE OKAY...
...THE FIRST DAY OF SCHOOL...
DON'T WORRY, HE'LL BE OKAY.
...THE DAY HE FINALLY LEAVES HOME...
DON'T WORRY, FOLKS, I'LL BE OKAY!
...THE DAY HE MOVES BACK.
WHAT'S FOR DINNER?
©B Trudeau

9/2/91

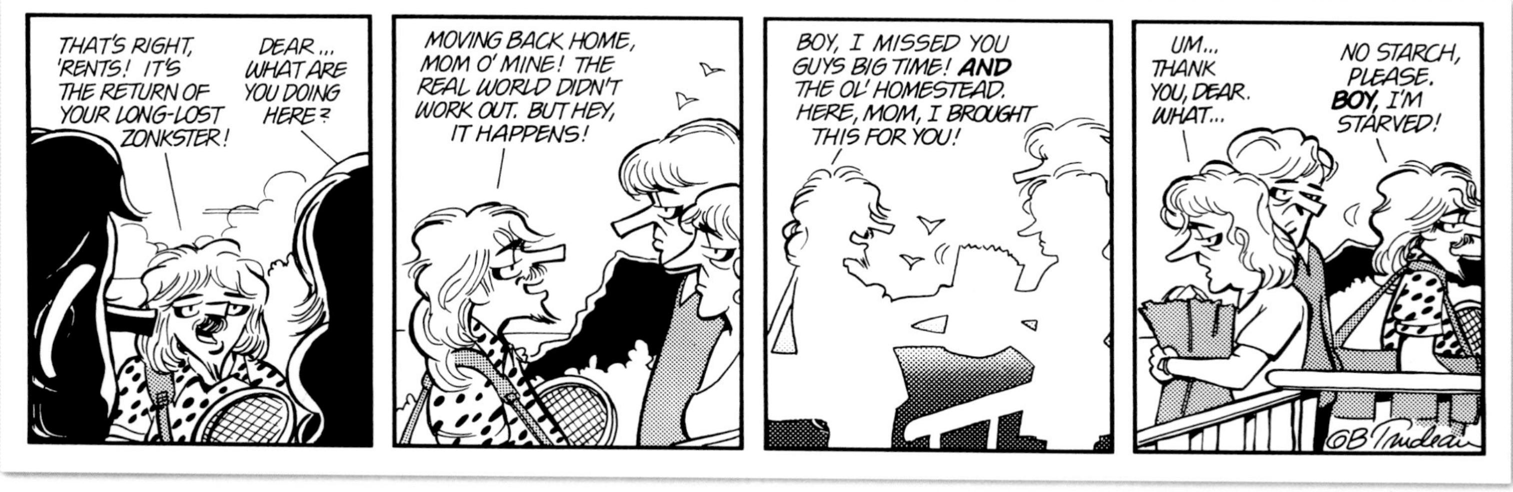
THAT'S RIGHT, 'RENTS! IT'S THE RETURN OF YOUR LONG-LOST ZONKSTER!
DEAR... WHAT ARE YOU DOING HERE?
MOVING BACK HOME, MOM O' MINE! THE REAL WORLD DIDN'T WORK OUT. BUT HEY, IT HAPPENS!
BOY, I MISSED YOU GUYS BIG TIME! AND THE OL' HOMESTEAD. HERE, MOM, I BROUGHT THIS FOR YOU!
UM... THANK YOU, DEAR. WHAT...
NO STARCH, PLEASE. BOY, I'M STARVED!
©B Trudeau

9/3/91

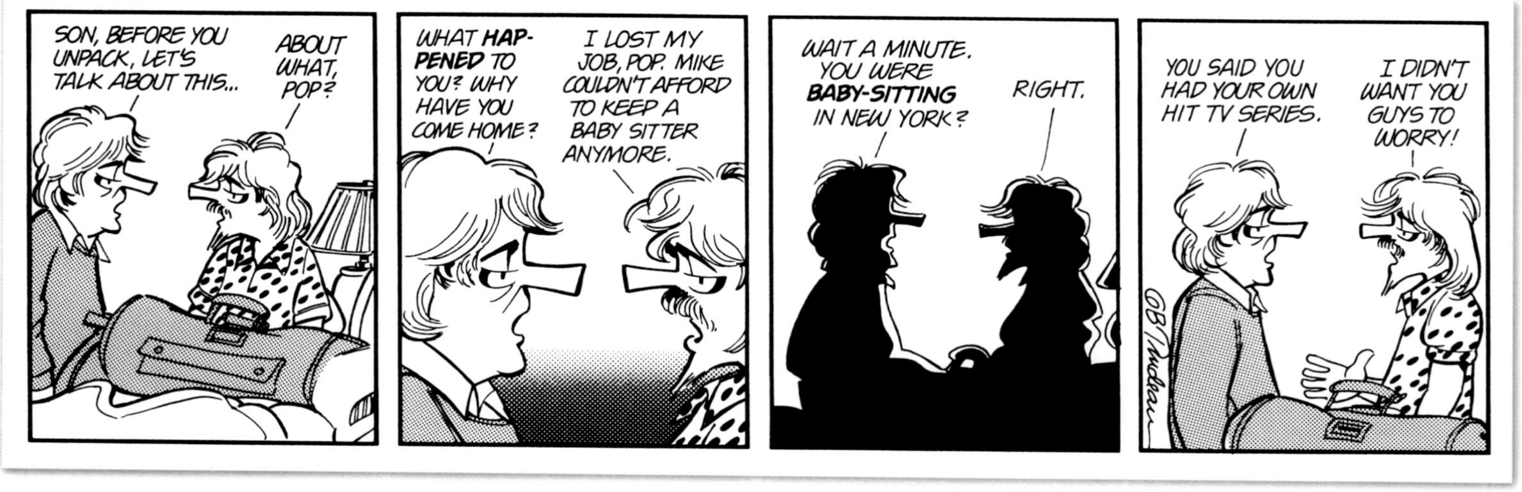
SON, BEFORE YOU UNPACK, LET'S TALK ABOUT THIS...
ABOUT WHAT, POP?
WHAT HAPPENED TO YOU? WHY HAVE YOU COME HOME?
I LOST MY JOB, POP. MIKE COULDN'T AFFORD TO KEEP A BABY SITTER ANYMORE.
WAIT A MINUTE. YOU WERE BABY-SITTING IN NEW YORK?
RIGHT.
YOU SAID YOU HAD YOUR OWN HIT TV SERIES.
I DIDN'T WANT YOU GUYS TO WORRY!
©B Trudeau

9/5/91

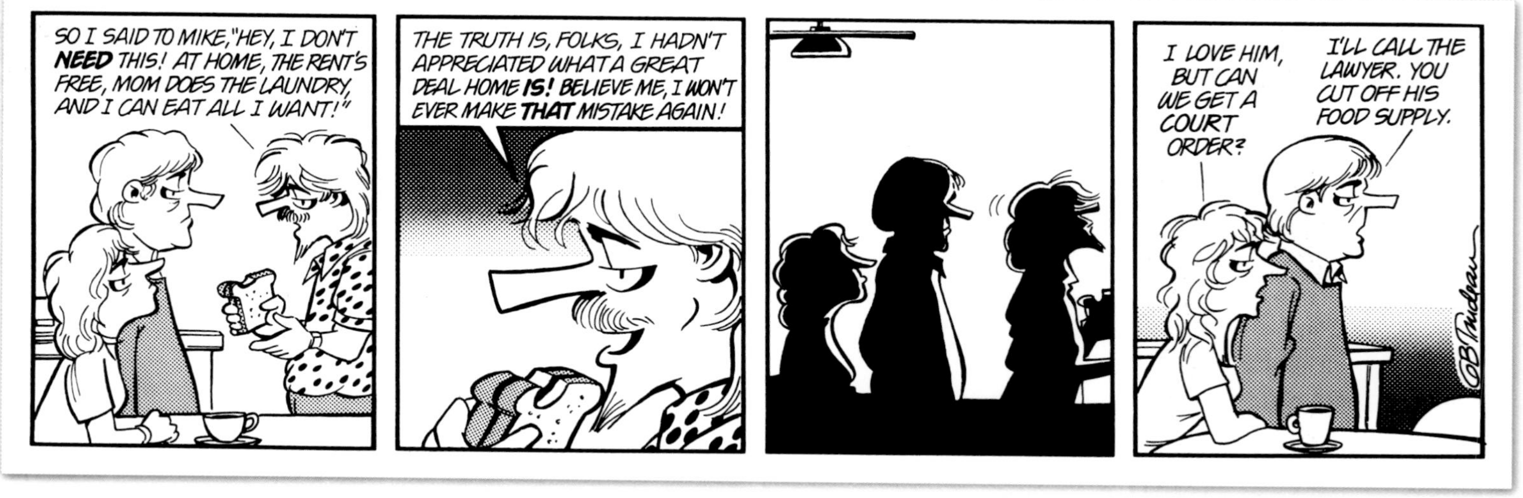
SO I SAID TO MIKE, "HEY, I DON'T NEED THIS! AT HOME, THE RENT'S FREE, MOM DOES THE LAUNDRY, AND I CAN EAT ALL I WANT!"
THE TRUTH IS, FOLKS, I HADN'T APPRECIATED WHAT A GREAT DEAL HOME IS! BELIEVE ME, I WON'T EVER MAKE THAT MISTAKE AGAIN!
I LOVE HIM, BUT CAN WE GET A COURT ORDER?
I'LL CALL THE LAWYER. YOU CUT OFF HIS FOOD SUPPLY.
©B Trudeau

9/4/91

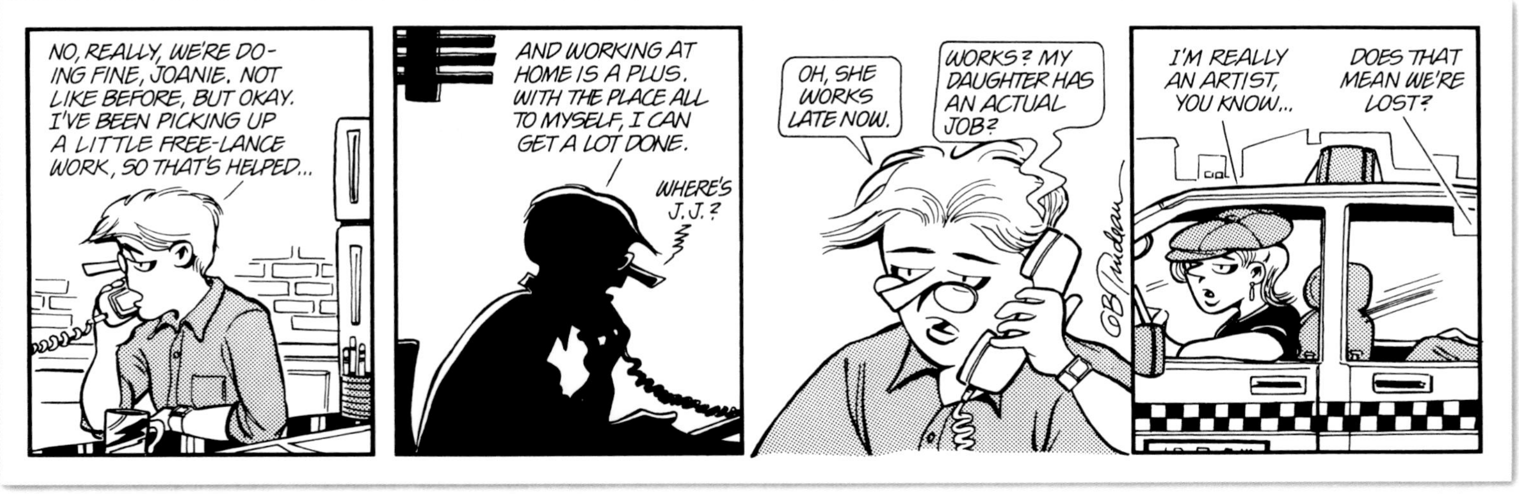
NO, REALLY, WE'RE DOING FINE, JOANIE. NOT LIKE BEFORE, BUT OKAY. I'VE BEEN PICKING UP A LITTLE FREE-LANCE WORK, SO THAT'S HELPED...
AND WORKING AT HOME IS A PLUS. WITH THE PLACE ALL TO MYSELF, I CAN GET A LOT DONE.
WHERE'S J.J.?
OH, SHE WORKS LATE NOW.
WORKS? MY DAUGHTER HAS AN ACTUAL JOB?
I'M REALLY AN ARTIST, YOU KNOW...
DOES THAT MEAN WE'RE LOST?

11/4/91

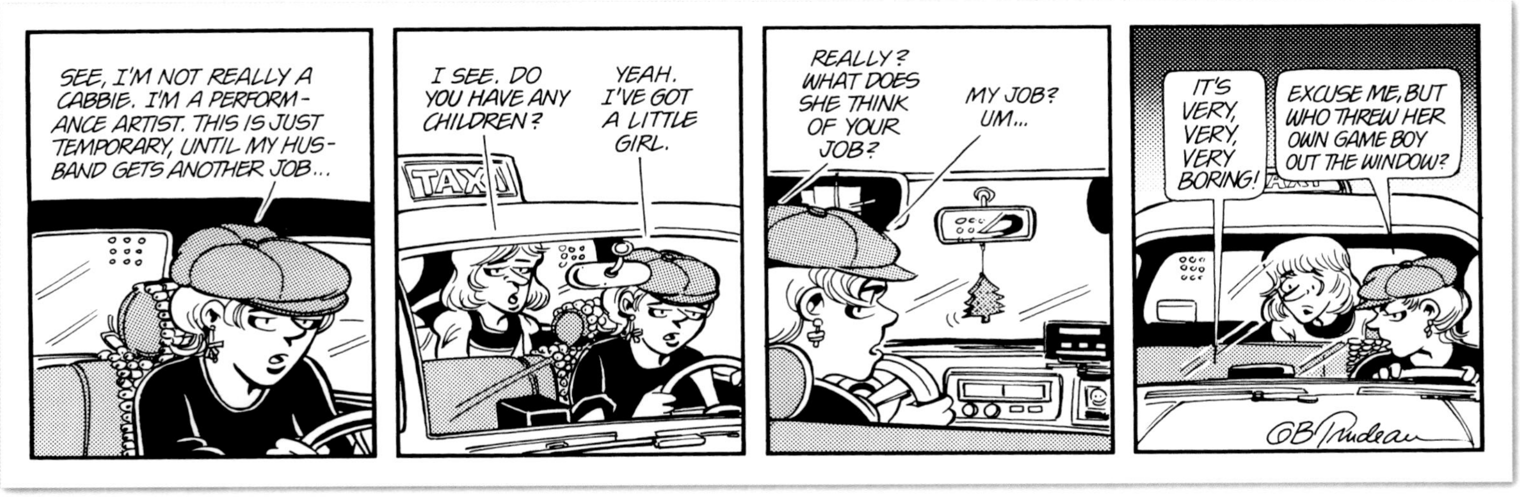
SEE, I'M NOT REALLY A CABBIE. I'M A PERFORMANCE ARTIST. THIS IS JUST TEMPORARY, UNTIL MY HUSBAND GETS ANOTHER JOB...
I SEE. DO YOU HAVE ANY CHILDREN?
YEAH. I'VE GOT A LITTLE GIRL.
TAXI
REALLY? WHAT DOES SHE THINK OF YOUR JOB?
MY JOB? UM...
IT'S VERY, VERY, VERY BORING!
EXCUSE ME, BUT WHO THREW HER OWN GAME BOY OUT THE WINDOW?

11/5/91

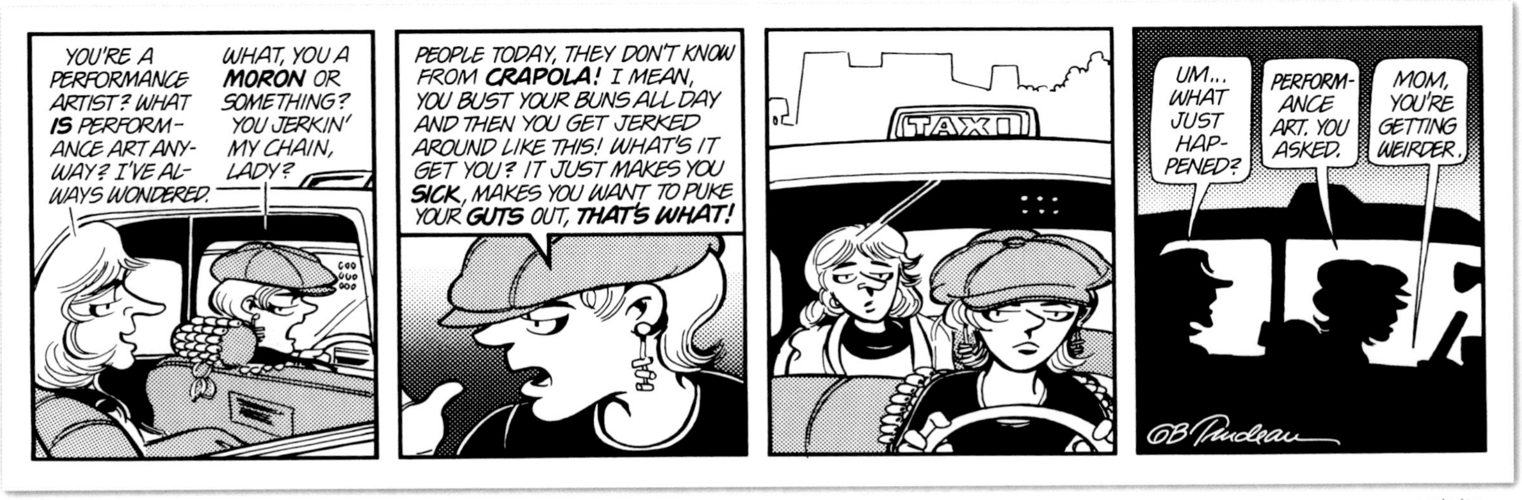
YOU'RE A PERFORMANCE ARTIST? WHAT IS PERFORMANCE ART ANYWAY? I'VE ALWAYS WONDERED.
WHAT, YOU A MORON OR SOMETHING? YOU JERKIN' MY CHAIN, LADY?
PEOPLE TODAY, THEY DON'T KNOW FROM CRAPOLA! I MEAN, YOU BUST YOUR BUNS ALL DAY AND THEN YOU GET JERKED AROUND LIKE THIS! WHAT'S IT GET YOU? IT JUST MAKES YOU SICK, MAKES YOU WANT TO PUKE YOUR GUTS OUT, THAT'S WHAT!
TAXI
UM... WHAT JUST HAPPENED?
PERFORMANCE ART. YOU ASKED.
MOM, YOU'RE GETTING WEIRDER.

11/6/91

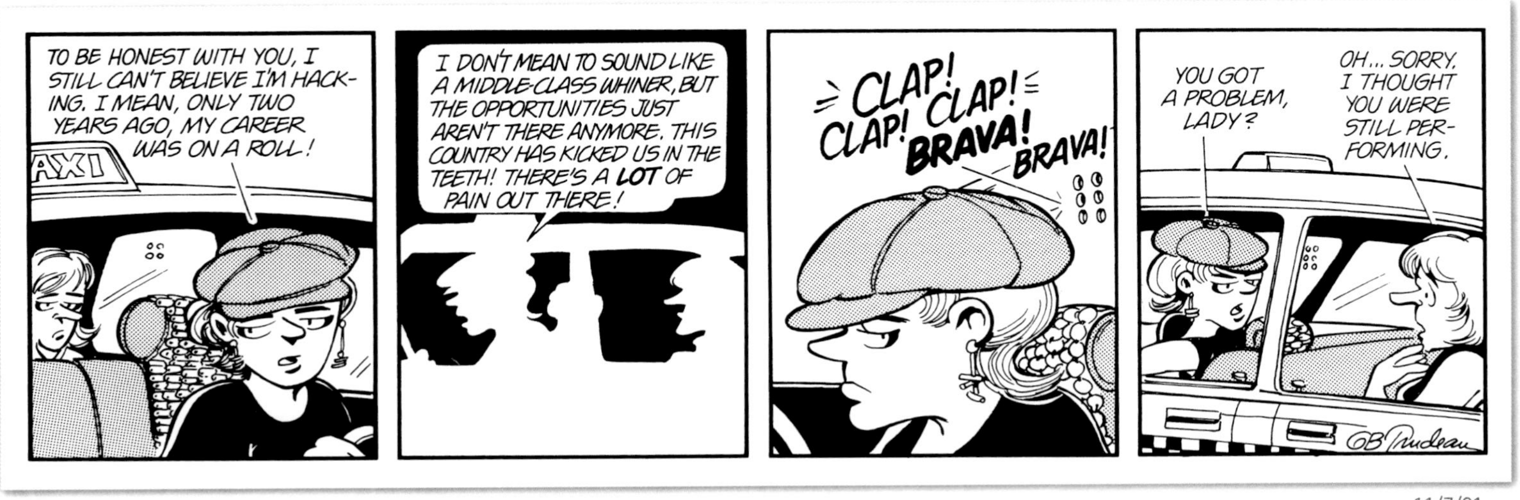
TO BE HONEST WITH YOU, I STILL CAN'T BELIEVE I'M HACKING. I MEAN, ONLY TWO YEARS AGO, MY CAREER WAS ON A ROLL!
TAXI
I DON'T MEAN TO SOUND LIKE A MIDDLE-CLASS WHINER, BUT THE OPPORTUNITIES JUST AREN'T THERE ANYMORE. THIS COUNTRY HAS KICKED US IN THE TEETH! THERE'S A LOT OF PAIN OUT THERE!
CLAP! CLAP! CLAP! BRAVA! BRAVA!
YOU GOT A PROBLEM, LADY?
OH... SORRY. I THOUGHT YOU WERE STILL PERFORMING.

11/7/91

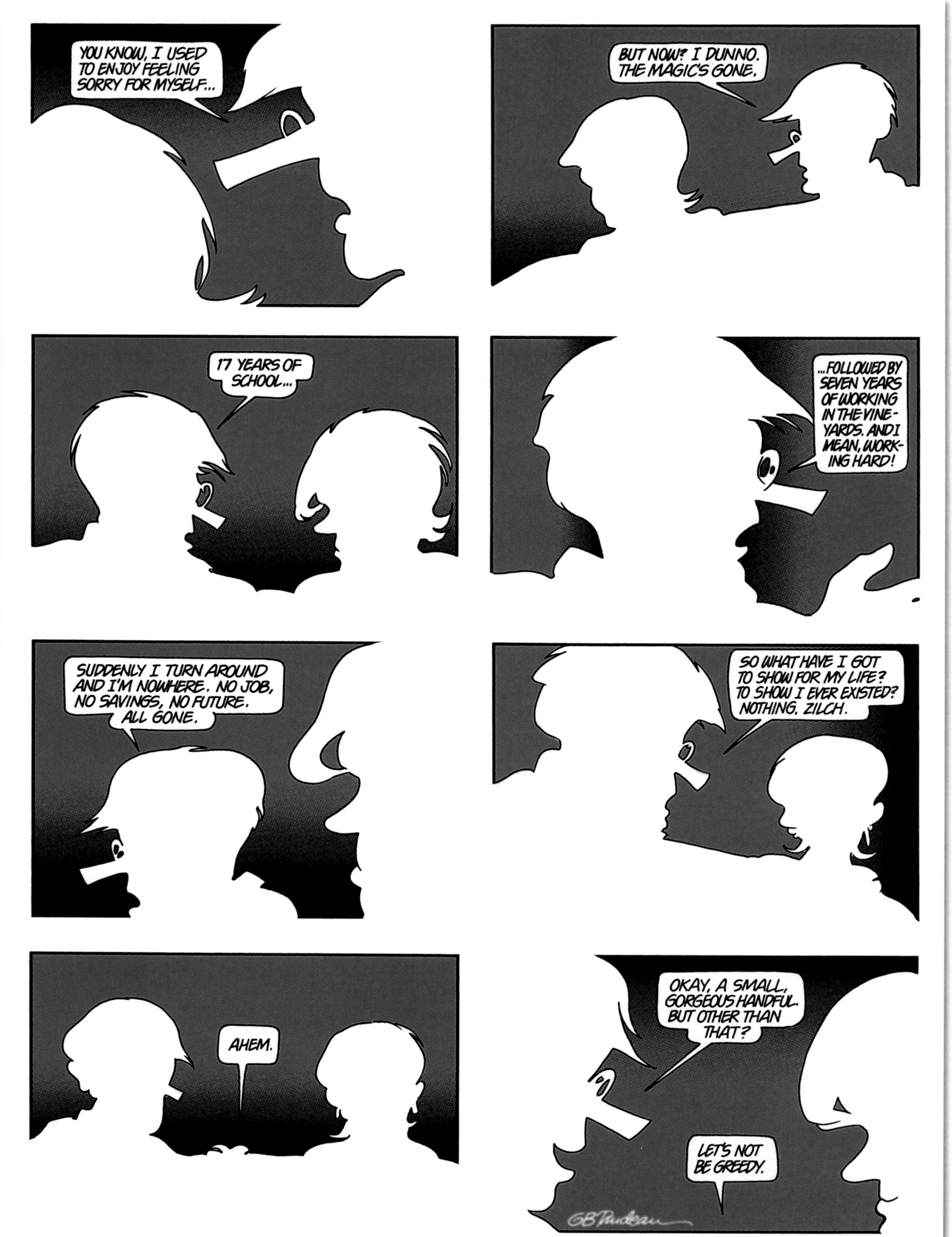
YOU KNOW, I USED TO ENJOY FEELING SORRY FOR MYSELF...
BUT NOW? I DUNNO. THE MAGIC'S GONE.
17 YEARS OF SCHOOL...
...FOLLOWED BY SEVEN YEARS OF WORKING IN THE VINE-YARDS. AND I MEAN, WORKING HARD!
SUDDENLY I TURN AROUND AND I'M NOWHERE. NO JOB, NO SAVINGS, NO FUTURE. ALL GONE.
SO WHAT HAVE I GOT TO SHOW FOR MY LIFE? TO SHOW I EVER EXISTED? NOTHING. ZILCH.
AHEM.
OKAY, A SMALL, GORGEOUS HANDFUL. BUT OTHER THAN THAT?
LET'S NOT BE GREEDY.
GB Trudeau

12/15/91

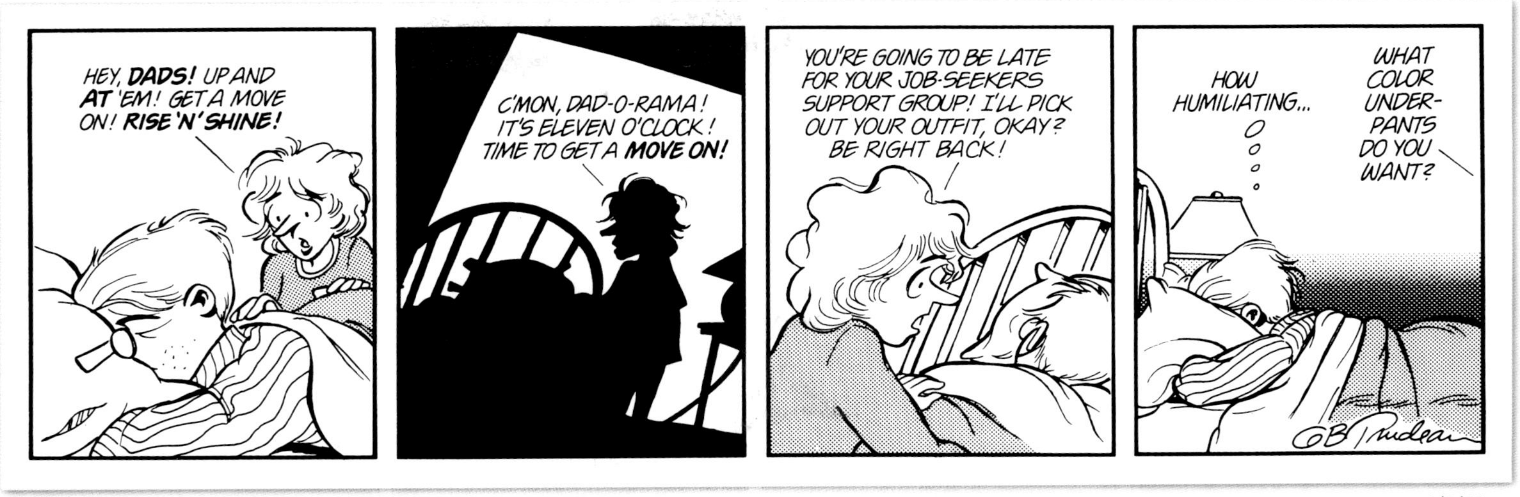
HEY, DADS! UP AND AT 'EM! GET A MOVE ON! RISE 'N' SHINE!
C'MON, DAD-O-RAMA! IT'S ELEVEN O'CLOCK! TIME TO GET A MOVE ON!
YOU'RE GOING TO BE LATE FOR YOUR JOB-SEEKERS SUPPORT GROUP! I'LL PICK OUT YOUR OUTFIT, OKAY? BE RIGHT BACK!
HOW HUMILIATING...
WHAT COLOR UNDER-PANTS DO YOU WANT?
GB Trudeau

1/6/92

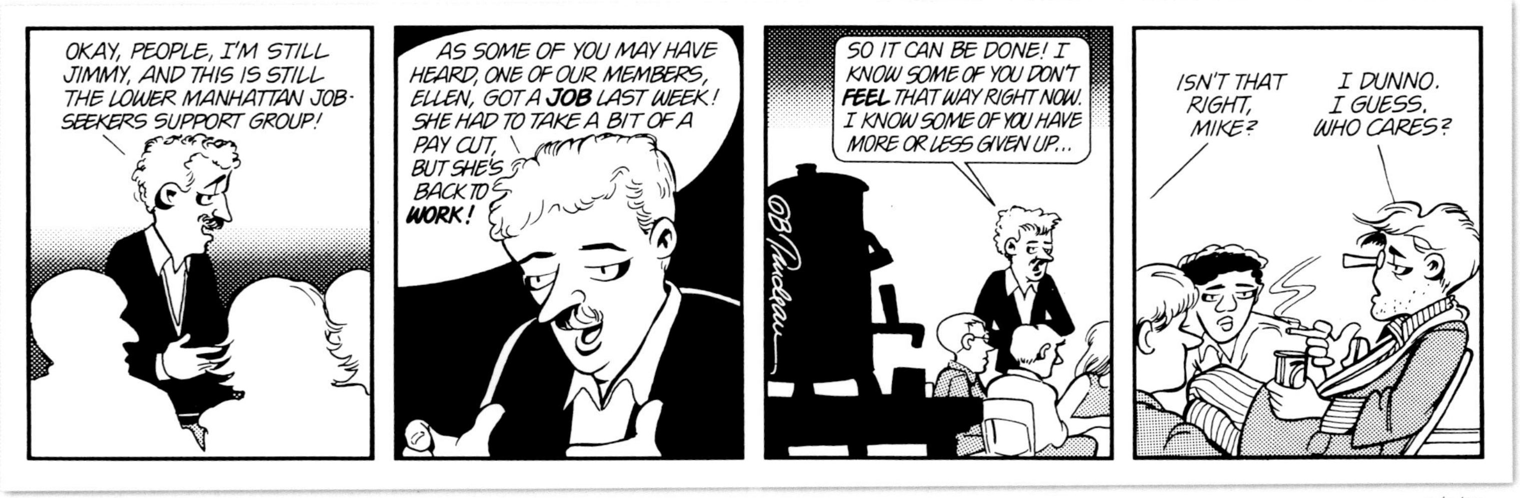
OKAY, PEOPLE, I'M STILL JIMMY, AND THIS IS STILL THE LOWER MANHATTAN JOB-SEEKERS SUPPORT GROUP!
AS SOME OF YOU MAY HAVE HEARD, ONE OF OUR MEMBERS, ELLEN, GOT A JOB LAST WEEK! SHE HAD TO TAKE A BIT OF A PAY CUT,
BUT SHE'S BACK TO WORK!
SO IT CAN BE DONE! I KNOW SOME OF YOU DON'T FEEL THAT WAY RIGHT NOW. I KNOW SOME OF YOU HAVE MORE OR LESS GIVEN UP...
GB Trudeau
ISN'T THAT RIGHT, MIKE?
I DUNNO. I GUESS. WHO CARES?

1/7/92

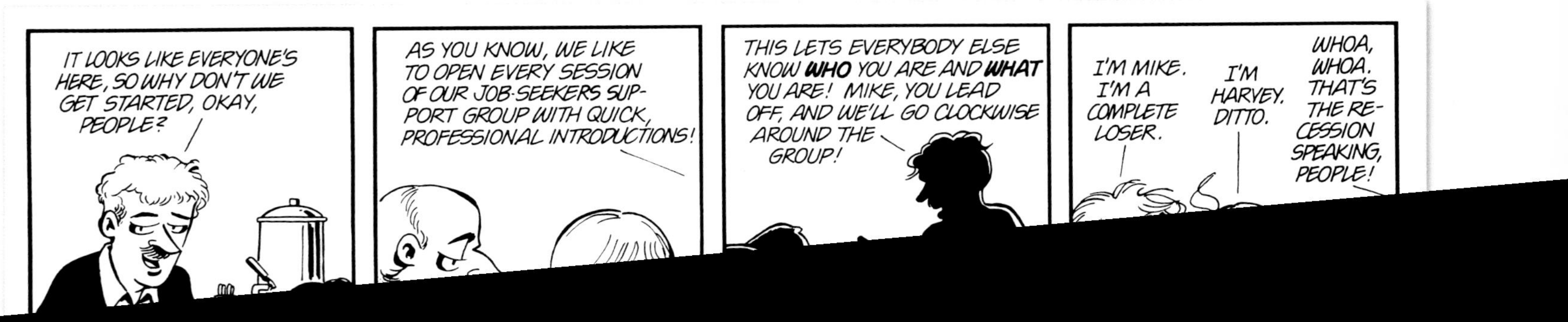
IT LOOKS LIKE EVERYONE'S HERE, SO WHY DON'T WE GET STARTED, OKAY, PEOPLE?
AS YOU KNOW, WE LIKE TO OPEN EVERY SESSION OF OUR JOB-SEEKERS SUPPORT GROUP WITH QUICK, PROFESSIONAL INTRODUCTIONS!
THIS LETS EVERYBODY ELSE KNOW WHO YOU ARE AND WHAT YOU ARE! MIKE, YOU LEAD OFF, AND WE'LL GO CLOCKWISE AROUND THE GROUP!
I'M MIKE. I'M A COMPLETE LOSER.
I'M HARVEY. DITTO.
WHOA, WHOA. THAT'S THE RECESSION SPEAKING, PEOPLE!

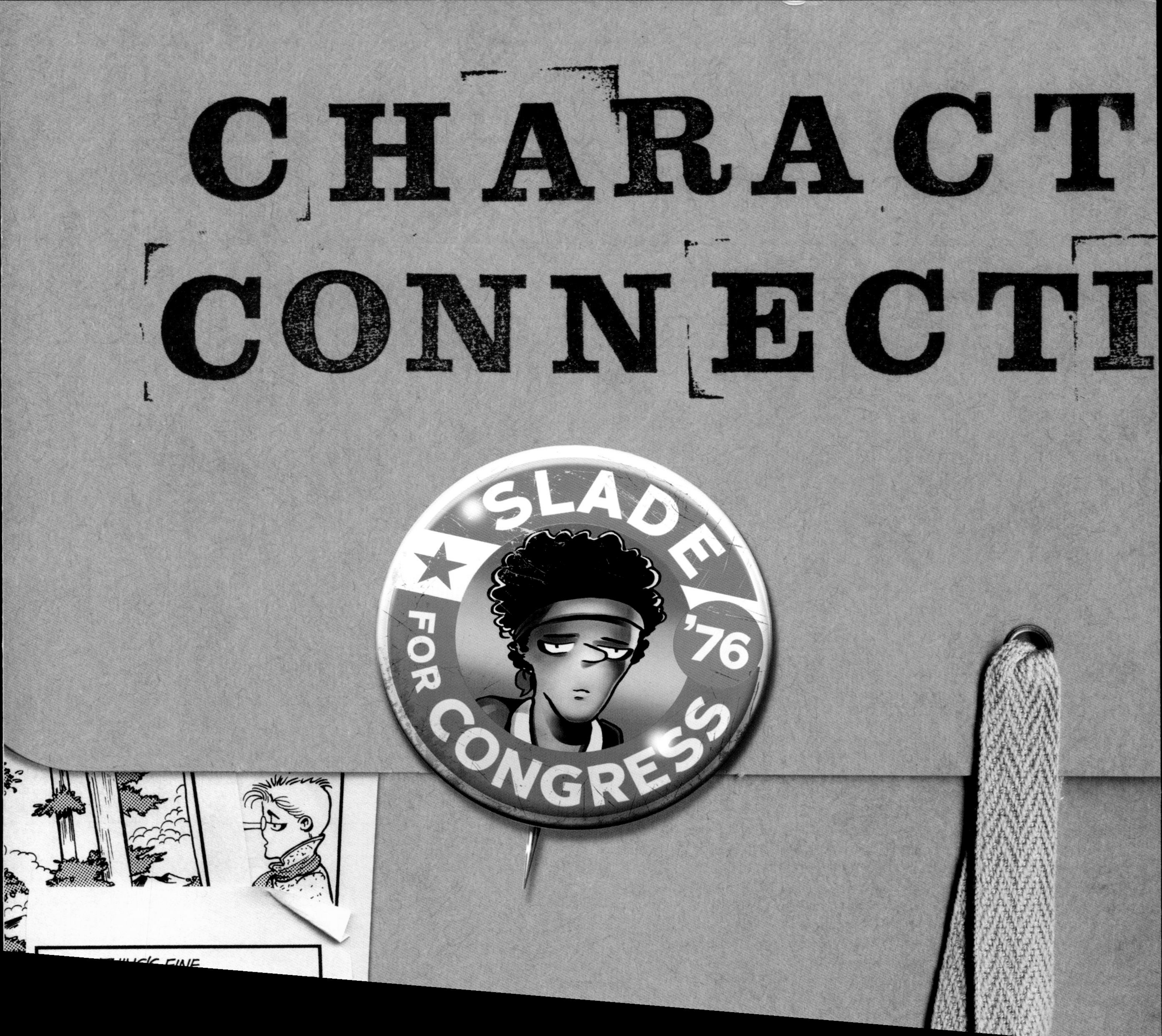
CHARACT
CONNECTI
SLADE
FOR CONGRESS
'76

ER

ONS

1970–2010

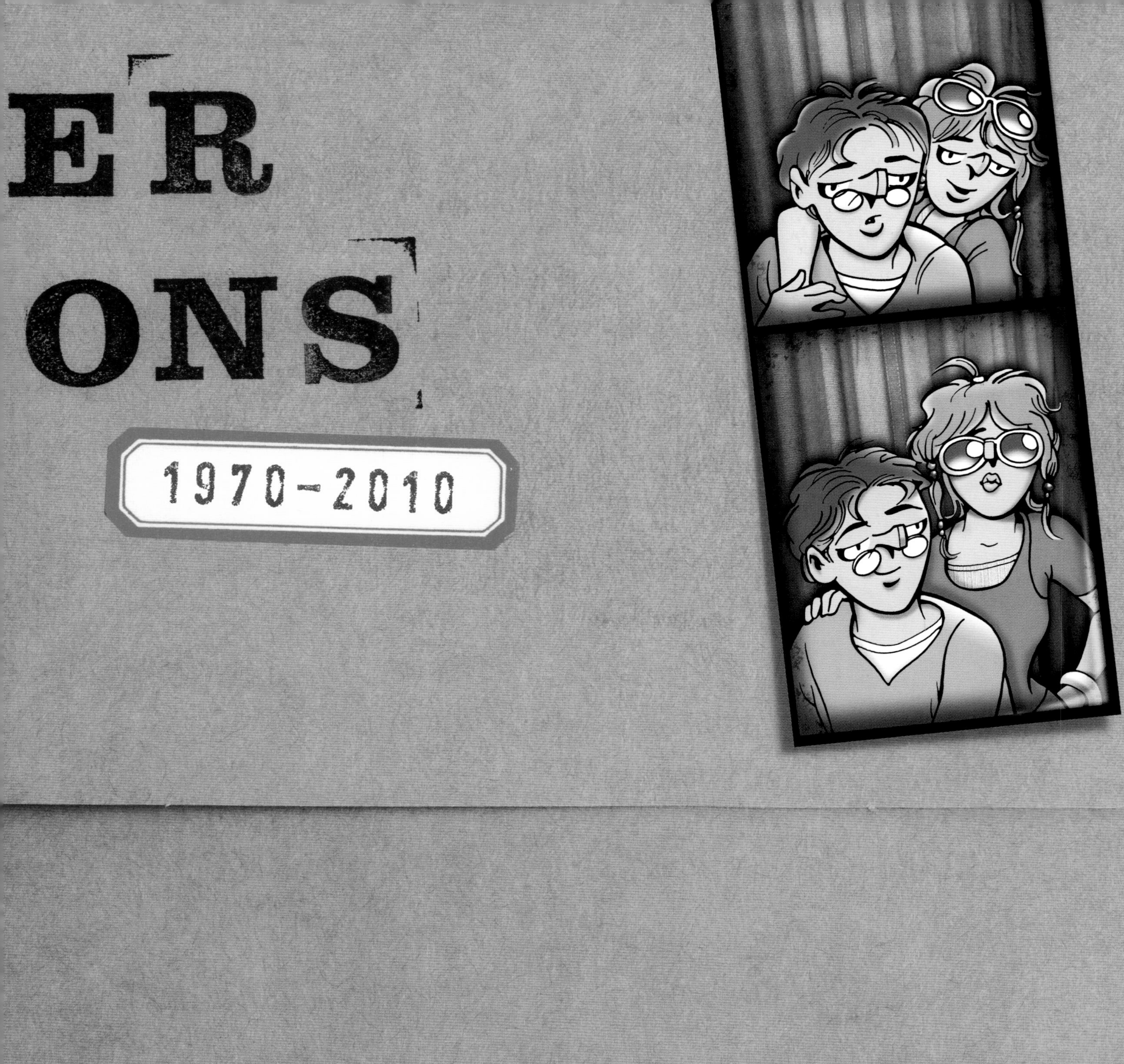

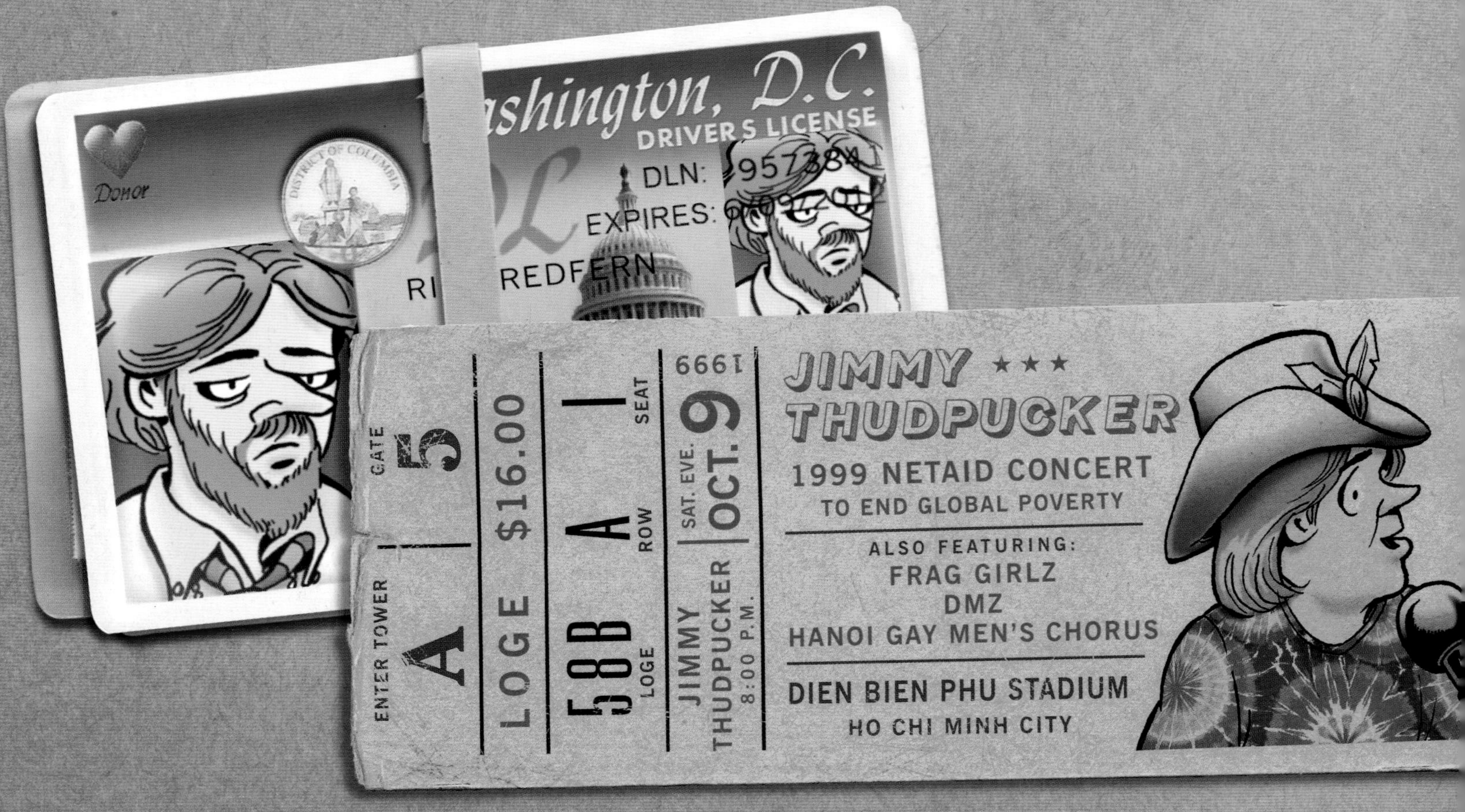

ashington, D.C.
DRIVERS LICENSE
Donor
DISTRICT OF COLUMBIA
DLN:
EXPIRES:
REDFERN
ENTER TOWER
A
GATE
5
LOGE $16.00
58B
LOGE
A
ROW
1
SEAT
JIMMY THUDPUCKER
8:00 P.M.
SAT. EVE.
OCT. 9
1999
JIMMY ★★★
THUDPUCKER
1999 NETAID CONCERT
TO END GLOBAL POVERTY
ALSO FEATURING:
FRAG GIRLZ
DMZ
HANOI GAY MEN'S CHORUS
DIEN BIEN PHU STADIUM
HO CHI MINH CITY

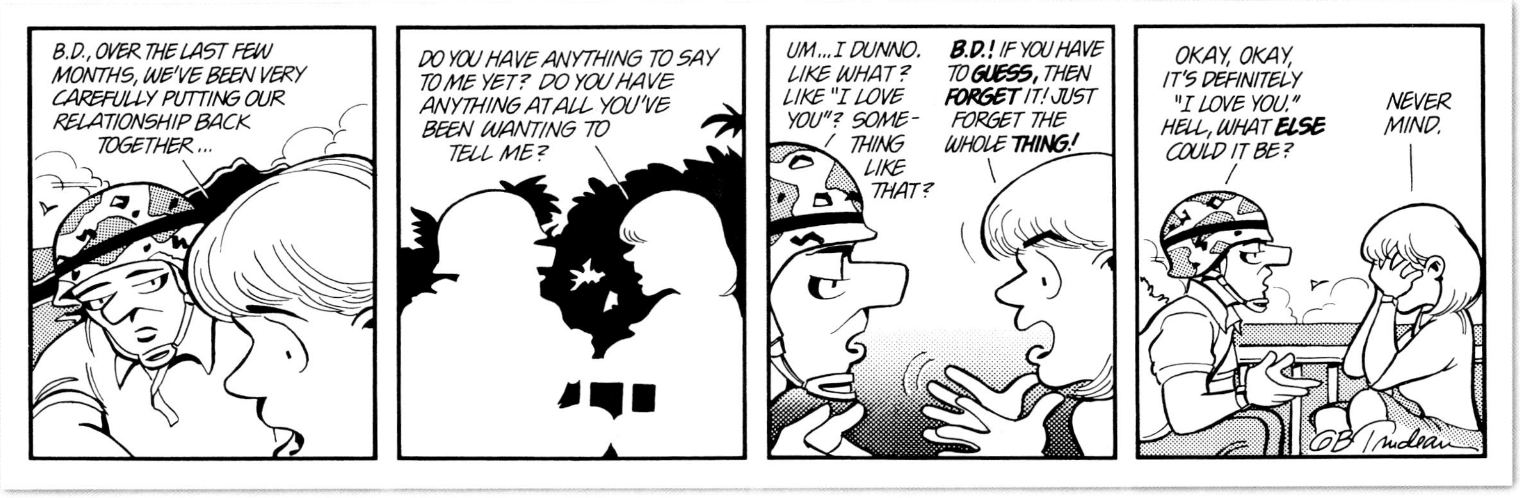
B.D., OVER THE LAST FEW MONTHS, WE'VE BEEN VERY CAREFULLY PUTTING OUR RELATIONSHIP BACK TOGETHER...
DO YOU HAVE ANYTHING TO SAY TO ME YET? DO YOU HAVE ANYTHING AT ALL YOU'VE BEEN WANTING TO TELL ME?
UM...I DUNNO. LIKE WHAT? LIKE "I LOVE YOU"? SOMETHING LIKE THAT?
B.D.! IF YOU HAVE TO GUESS, THEN FORGET IT! JUST FORGET THE WHOLE THING!
OKAY, OKAY, IT'S DEFINITELY "I LOVE YOU." HELL, WHAT ELSE COULD IT BE?
NEVER MIND.

1/14/92

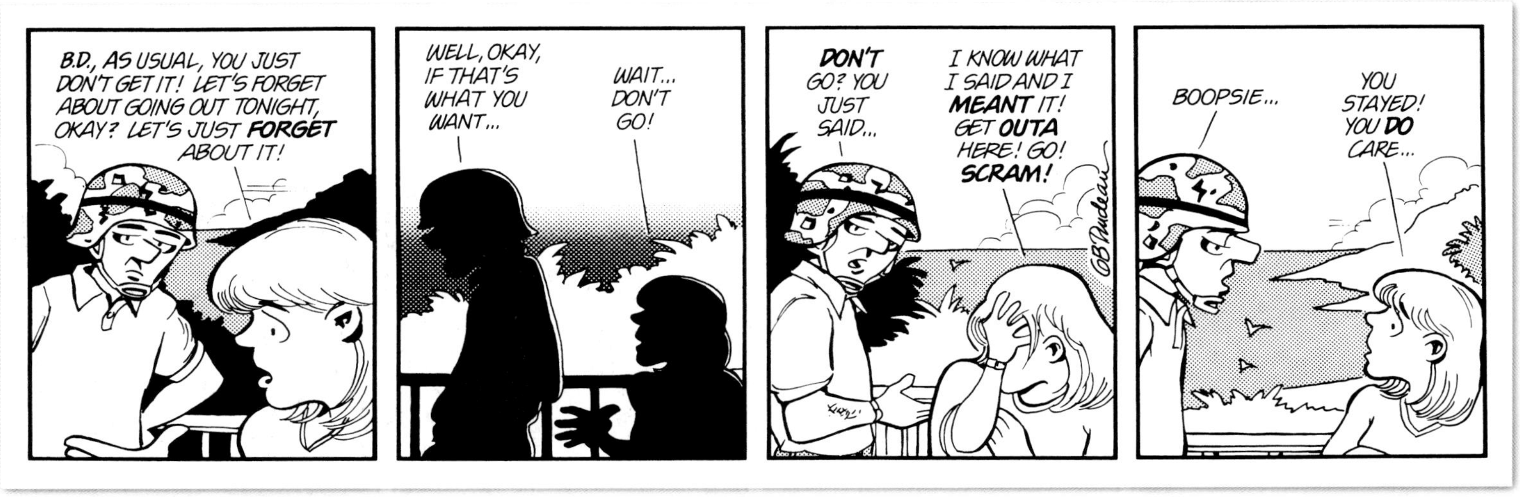
B.D., AS USUAL, YOU JUST DON'T GET IT! LET'S FORGET ABOUT GOING OUT TONIGHT, OKAY? LET'S JUST FORGET ABOUT IT!
WELL, OKAY, IF THAT'S WHAT YOU WANT...
WAIT... DON'T GO!
DON'T GO? YOU JUST SAID...
I KNOW WHAT I SAID AND I MEANT IT! GET OUTA HERE! GO! SCRAM!
BOOPSIE...
YOU STAYED! YOU DO CARE...

1/15/92

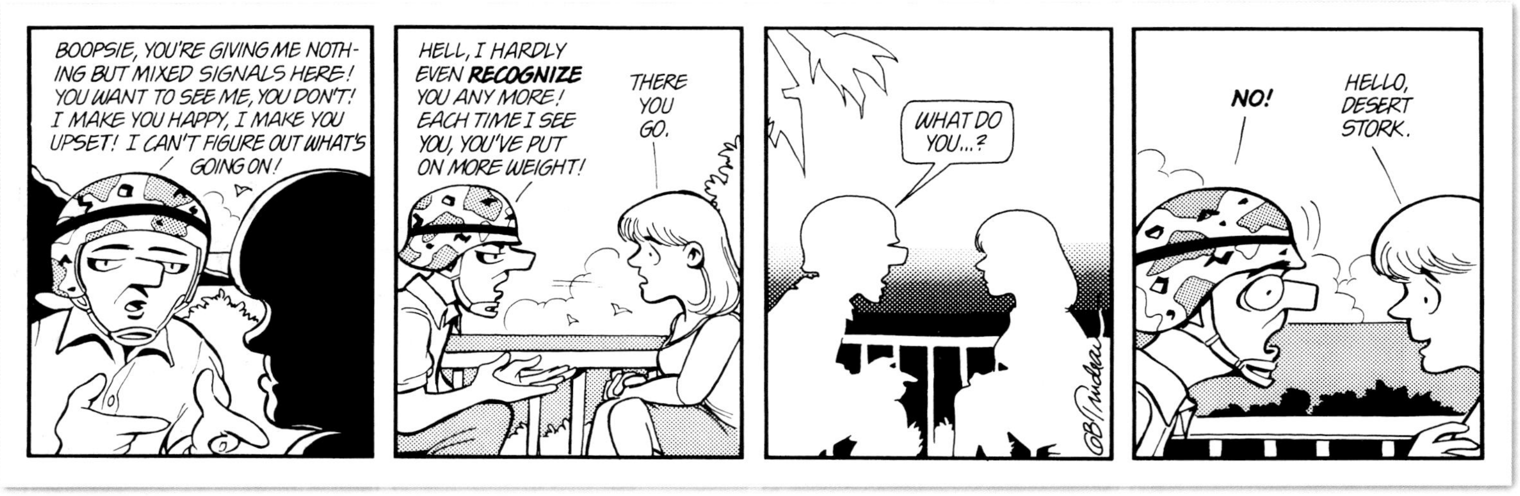
BOOPSIE, YOU'RE GIVING ME NOTHING BUT MIXED SIGNALS HERE! YOU WANT TO SEE ME, YOU DON'T! I MAKE YOU HAPPY, I MAKE YOU UPSET! I CAN'T FIGURE OUT WHAT'S GOING ON!
HELL, I HARDLY EVEN RECOGNIZE YOU ANY MORE! EACH TIME I SEE YOU, YOU'VE PUT ON MORE WEIGHT!
THERE YOU GO.
WHAT DO YOU...?
NO!
HELLO, DESERT STORK.

1/16/92

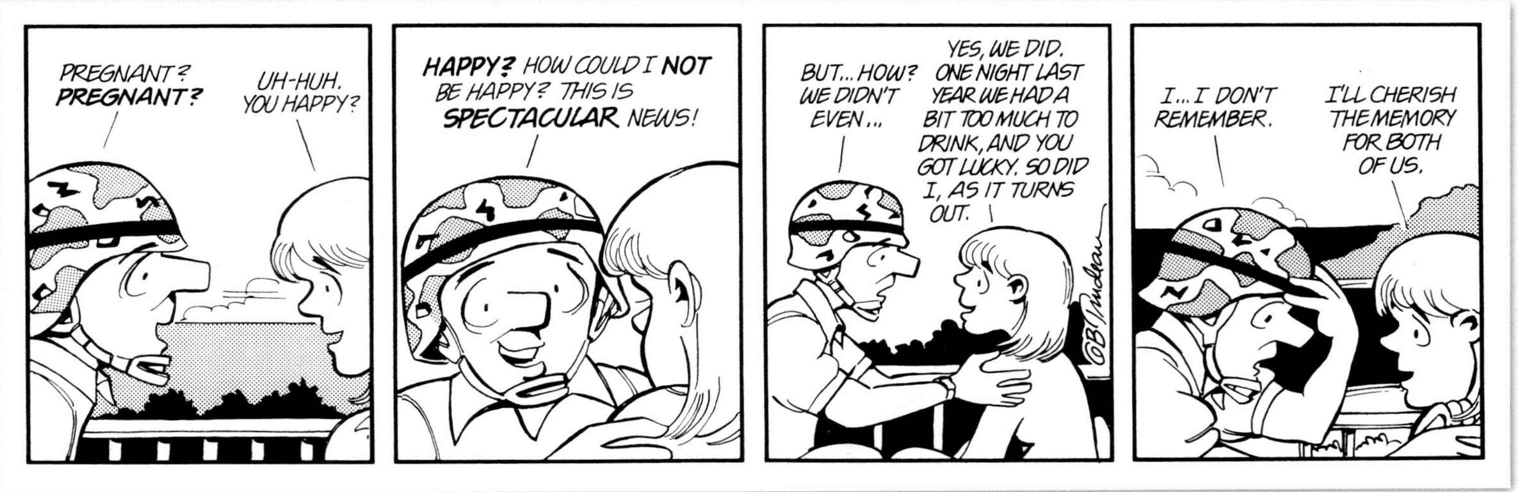
PREGNANT? PREGNANT?
UH-HUH. YOU HAPPY?
HAPPY? HOW COULD I NOT BE HAPPY? THIS IS SPECTACULAR NEWS!
BUT...HOW? WE DIDN'T EVEN...
YES, WE DID. ONE NIGHT LAST YEAR WE HAD A BIT TOO MUCH TO DRINK, AND YOU GOT LUCKY. SO DID I, AS IT TURNS OUT.
I...I DON'T REMEMBER.
I'LL CHERISH THE MEMORY FOR BOTH OF US.

1/17/92

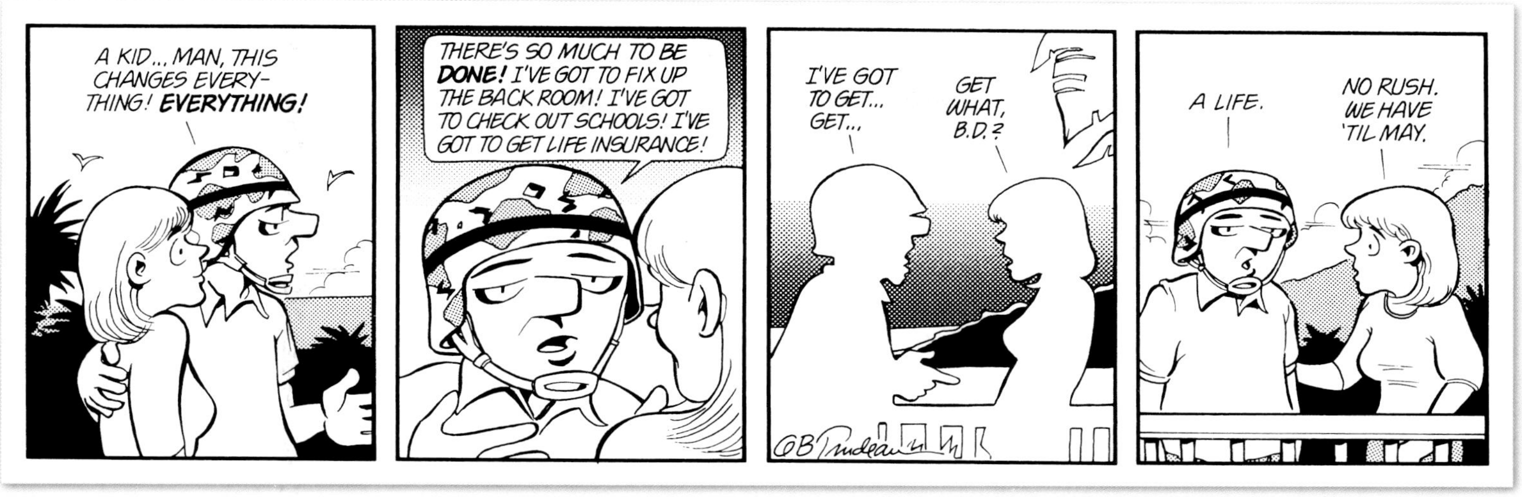
A KID... MAN, THIS CHANGES EVERYTHING! **EVERYTHING!**
THERE'S SO MUCH TO BE **DONE!** I'VE GOT TO FIX UP THE BACK ROOM! I'VE GOT TO CHECK OUT SCHOOLS! I'VE GOT TO GET LIFE INSURANCE!
I'VE GOT TO GET... GET...
GET WHAT, B.D.?
A LIFE.
NO RUSH. WE HAVE 'TIL MAY.
©B Trudeau

1/20/92

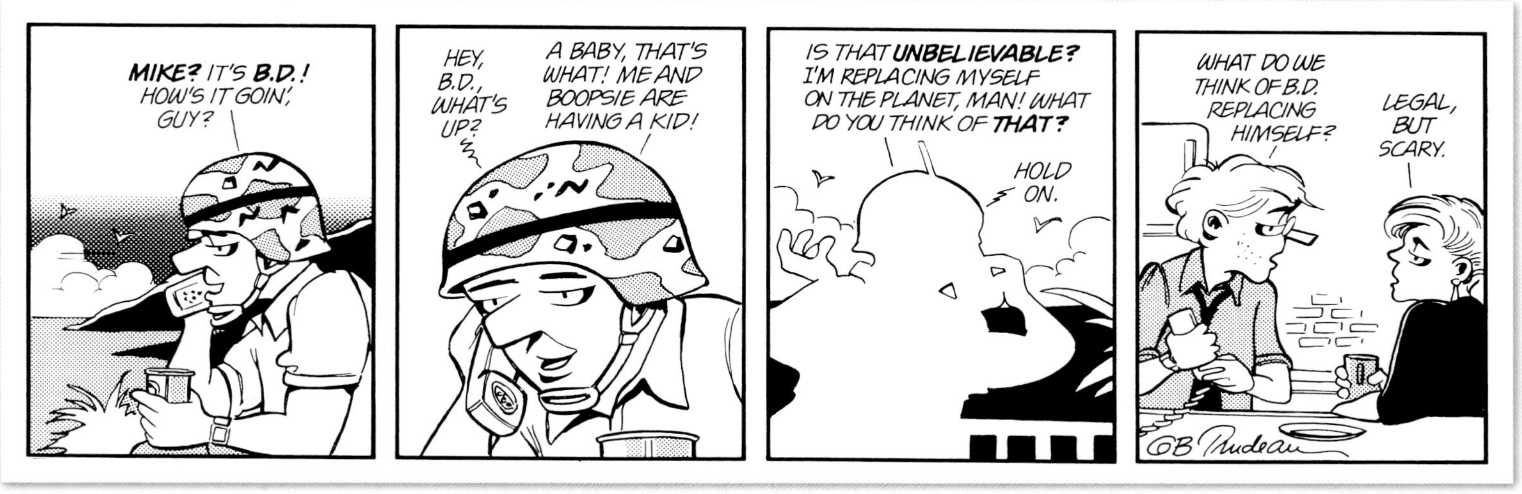
MIKE? IT'S **B.D.!** HOW'S IT GOIN', GUY?
HEY, B.D., WHAT'S UP?
A BABY, THAT'S WHAT! ME AND BOOPSIE ARE HAVING A KID!
IS THAT **UNBELIEVABLE?** I'M REPLACING MYSELF ON THE PLANET, MAN! WHAT DO YOU THINK OF **THAT?**
HOLD ON.
WHAT DO WE THINK OF B.D. REPLACING HIMSELF?
LEGAL, BUT SCARY.
©B Trudeau

1/21/92

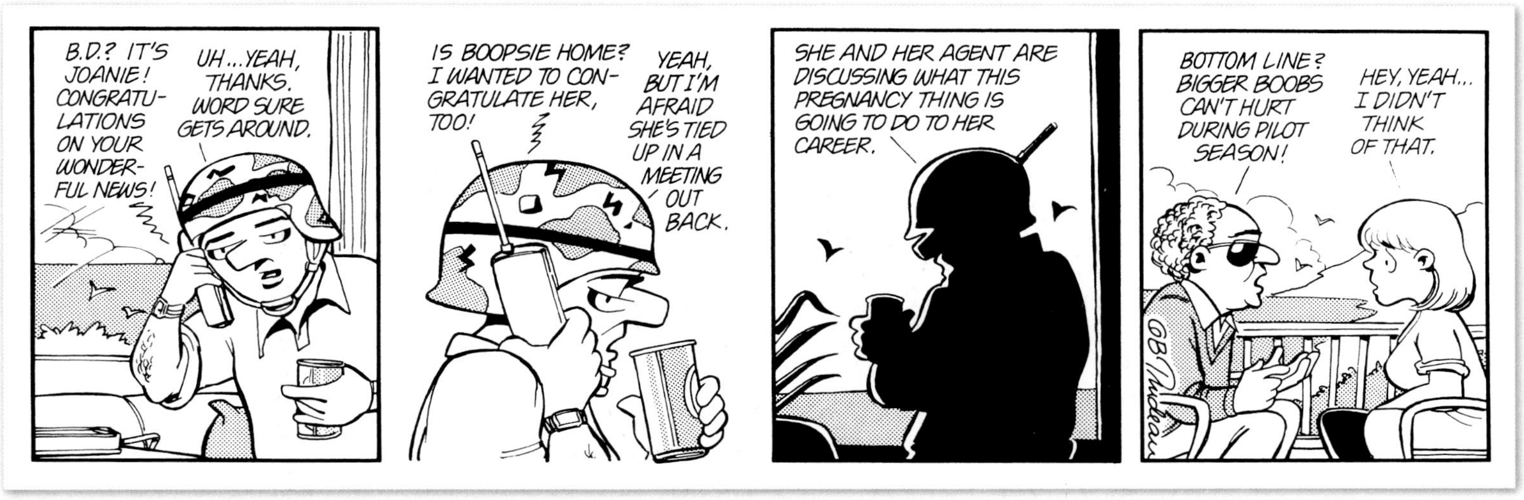
B.D.? IT'S JOANIE! CONGRATULATIONS ON YOUR WONDERFUL NEWS!
UH... YEAH, THANKS. WORD SURE GETS AROUND.
IS BOOPSIE HOME? I WANTED TO CONGRATULATE HER, TOO!
YEAH, BUT I'M AFRAID SHE'S TIED UP IN A MEETING OUT BACK.
SHE AND HER AGENT ARE DISCUSSING WHAT THIS PREGNANCY THING IS GOING TO DO TO HER CAREER.
BOTTOM LINE? BIGGER BOOBS CAN'T HURT DURING PILOT SEASON!
HEY, YEAH... I DIDN'T THINK OF THAT.
©B Trudeau

1/23/92

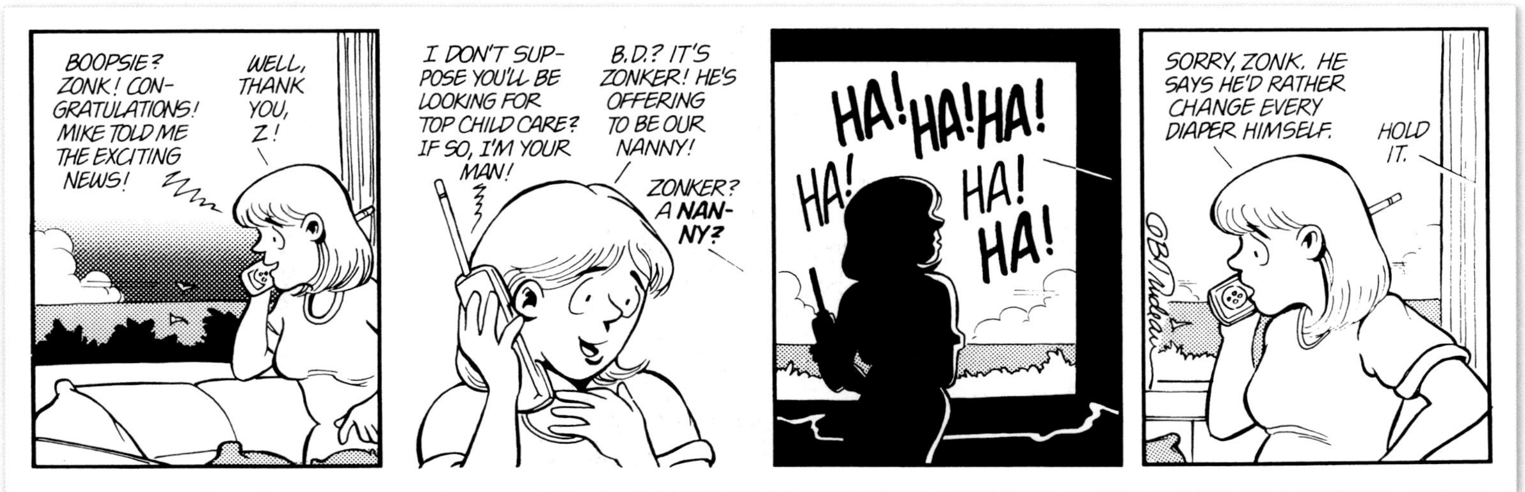
BOOPSIE? ZONK! CONGRATULATIONS! MIKE TOLD ME THE EXCITING NEWS!
WELL, THANK YOU, Z!
I DON'T SUPPOSE YOU'LL BE LOOKING FOR TOP CHILD CARE? IF SO, I'M YOUR MAN!
B.D.? IT'S ZONKER! HE'S OFFERING TO BE OUR NANNY!
ZONKER? A **NANNY?**
HA! HA! HA! HA! HA! HA!
SORRY, ZONK. HE SAYS HE'D RATHER CHANGE EVERY DIAPER HIMSELF.
HOLD IT.
©B Trudeau

1/25/92

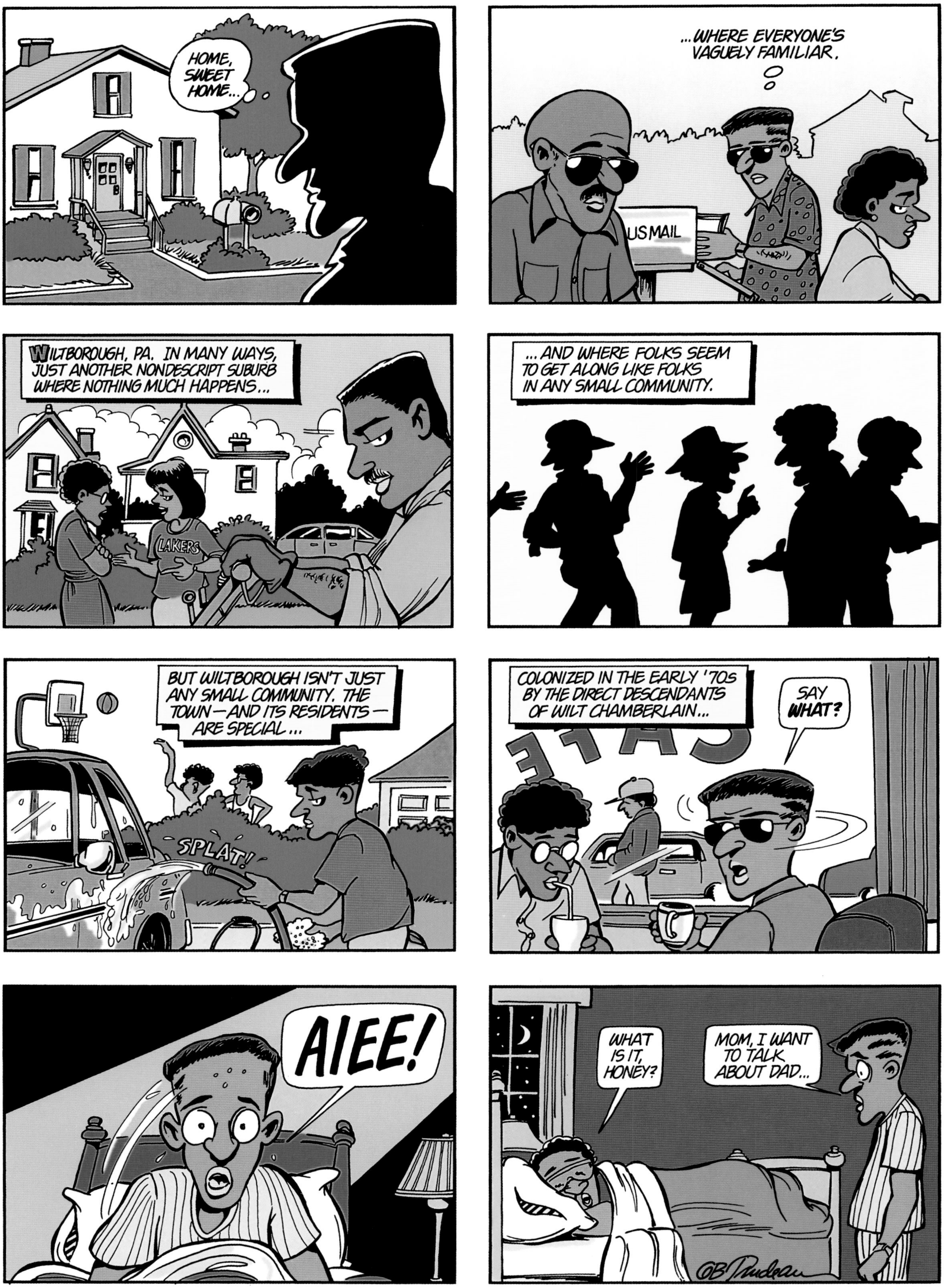
HOME, SWEET HOME...
...WHERE EVERYONE'S VAGUELY FAMILIAR.
US MAIL
WILTBOROUGH, PA. IN MANY WAYS, JUST ANOTHER NONDESCRIPT SUBURB WHERE NOTHING MUCH HAPPENS...
LAKERS
...AND WHERE FOLKS SEEM TO GET ALONG LIKE FOLKS IN ANY SMALL COMMUNITY.
BUT WILTBOROUGH ISN'T JUST ANY SMALL COMMUNITY. THE TOWN—AND ITS RESIDENTS—ARE SPECIAL...
SPLAT!
COLONIZED IN THE EARLY '70s BY THE DIRECT DESCENDANTS OF WILT CHAMBERLAIN...
SAY WHAT?
CAFE
AIEE!
WHAT IS IT, HONEY?
MOM, I WANT TO TALK ABOUT DAD...
©B Trudeau

1/19/92

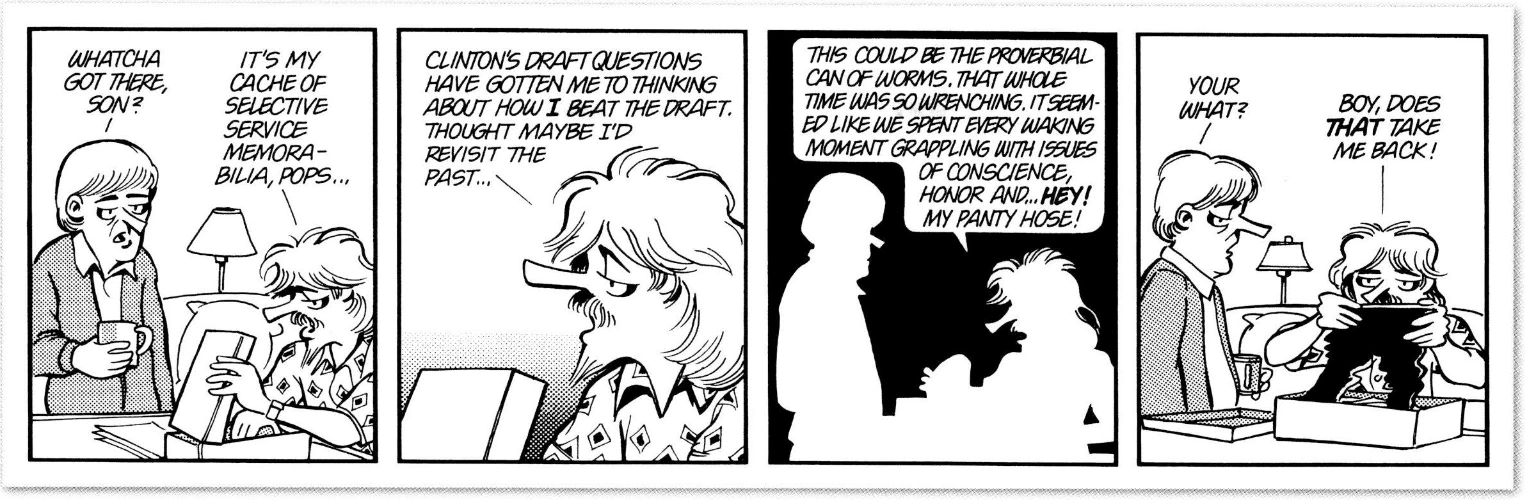
WHATCHA GOT THERE, SON?
IT'S MY CACHE OF SELECTIVE SERVICE MEMORABILIA, POPS...
CLINTON'S DRAFT QUESTIONS HAVE GOTTEN ME TO THINKING ABOUT HOW I BEAT THE DRAFT. THOUGHT MAYBE I'D REVISIT THE PAST...
THIS COULD BE THE PROVERBIAL CAN OF WORMS. THAT WHOLE TIME WAS SO WRENCHING. IT SEEMED LIKE WE SPENT EVERY WAKING MOMENT GRAPPLING WITH ISSUES OF CONSCIENCE, HONOR AND... HEY! MY PANTY HOSE!
YOUR WHAT?
BOY, DOES THAT TAKE ME BACK!

2/24/92

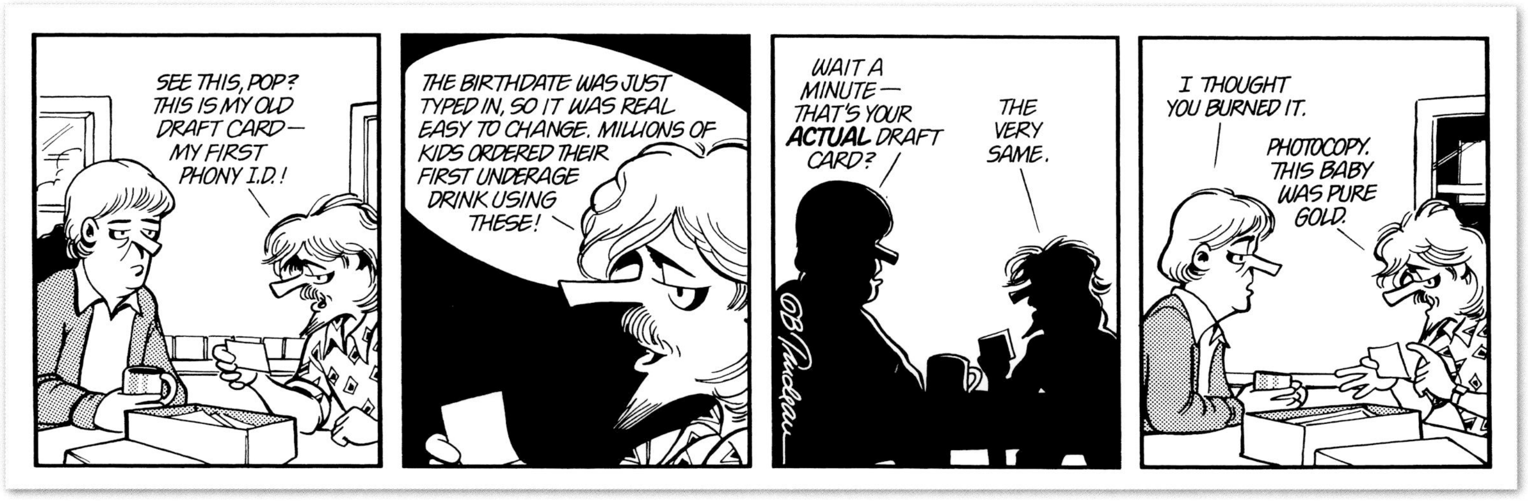
SEE THIS, POP? THIS IS MY OLD DRAFT CARD— MY FIRST PHONY I.D.!
THE BIRTHDATE WAS JUST TYPED IN, SO IT WAS REAL EASY TO CHANGE. MILLIONS OF KIDS ORDERED THEIR FIRST UNDERAGE DRINK USING THESE!
WAIT A MINUTE— THAT'S YOUR ACTUAL DRAFT CARD?
THE VERY SAME.
I THOUGHT YOU BURNED IT.
PHOTOCOPY. THIS BABY WAS PURE GOLD.

2/25/92

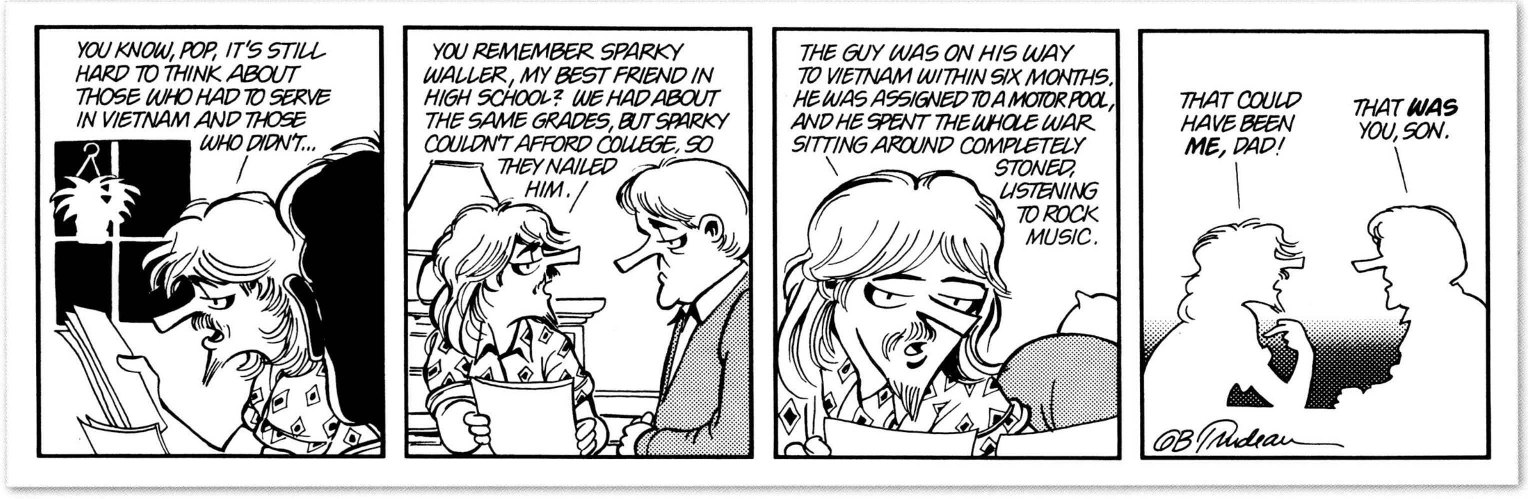
YOU KNOW, POP, IT'S STILL HARD TO THINK ABOUT THOSE WHO HAD TO SERVE IN VIETNAM AND THOSE WHO DIDN'T...
YOU REMEMBER SPARKY WALLER, MY BEST FRIEND IN HIGH SCHOOL? WE HAD ABOUT THE SAME GRADES, BUT SPARKY COULDN'T AFFORD COLLEGE, SO THEY NAILED HIM.
THE GUY WAS ON HIS WAY TO VIETNAM WITHIN SIX MONTHS. HE WAS ASSIGNED TO A MOTOR POOL, AND HE SPENT THE WHOLE WAR SITTING AROUND COMPLETELY STONED, LISTENING TO ROCK MUSIC.
THAT COULD HAVE BEEN ME, DAD!
THAT WAS YOU, SON.

2/27/92

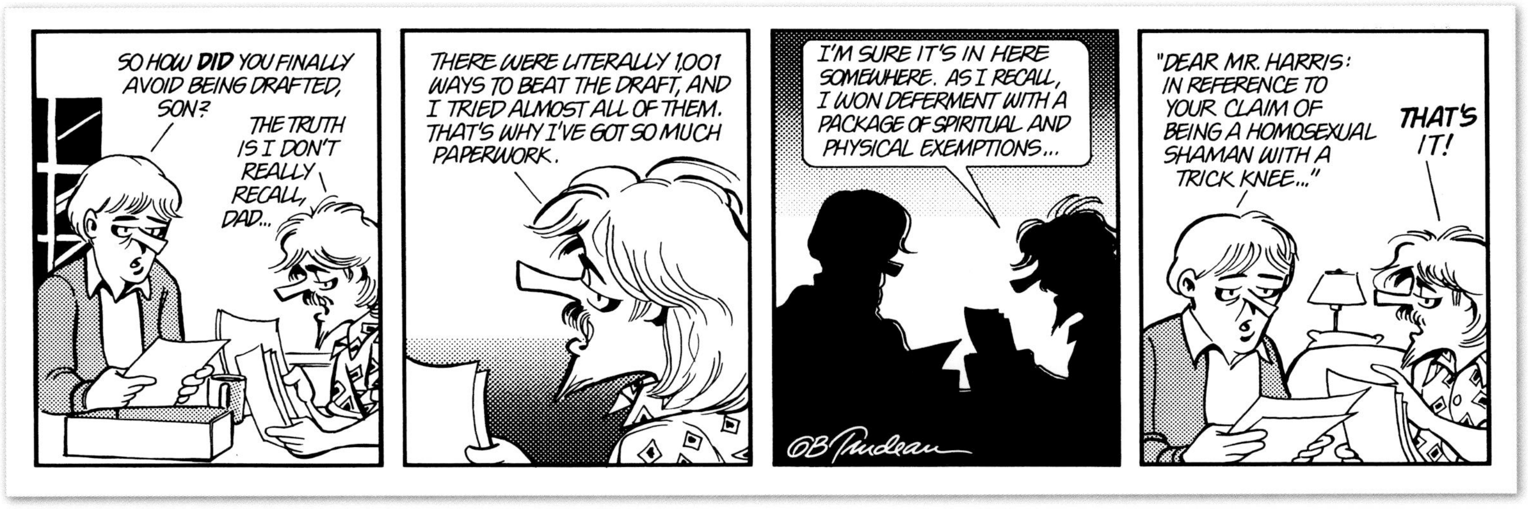
SO HOW DID YOU FINALLY AVOID BEING DRAFTED, SON?
THE TRUTH IS I DON'T REALLY RECALL, DAD...
THERE WERE LITERALLY 1,001 WAYS TO BEAT THE DRAFT, AND I TRIED ALMOST ALL OF THEM. THAT'S WHY I'VE GOT SO MUCH PAPERWORK.
I'M SURE IT'S IN HERE SOMEWHERE. AS I RECALL, I WON DEFERMENT WITH A PACKAGE OF SPIRITUAL AND PHYSICAL EXEMPTIONS...
"DEAR MR. HARRIS: IN REFERENCE TO YOUR CLAIM OF BEING A HOMOSEXUAL SHAMAN WITH A TRICK KNEE..."
THAT'S IT!

2/28/92

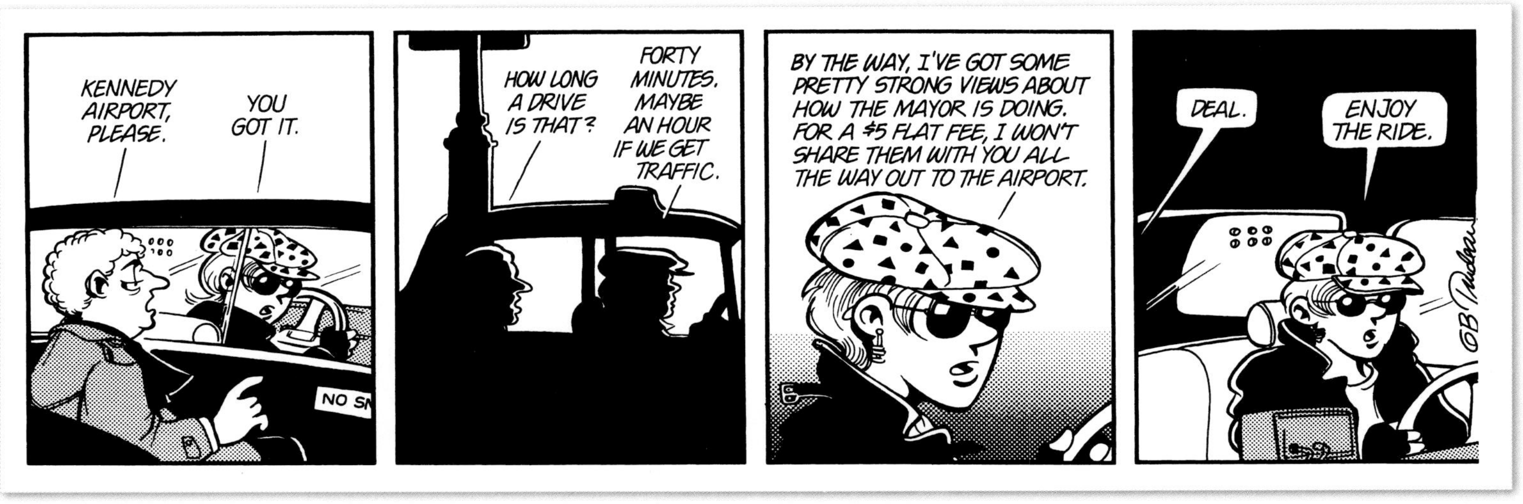
KENNEDY AIRPORT, PLEASE.
YOU GOT IT.
HOW LONG A DRIVE IS THAT?
FORTY MINUTES. MAYBE AN HOUR IF WE GET TRAFFIC.
BY THE WAY, I'VE GOT SOME PRETTY STRONG VIEWS ABOUT HOW THE MAYOR IS DOING. FOR A $5 FLAT FEE, I WON'T SHARE THEM WITH YOU ALL THE WAY OUT TO THE AIRPORT.
DEAL.
ENJOY THE RIDE.
GB Trudeau

3/2/92

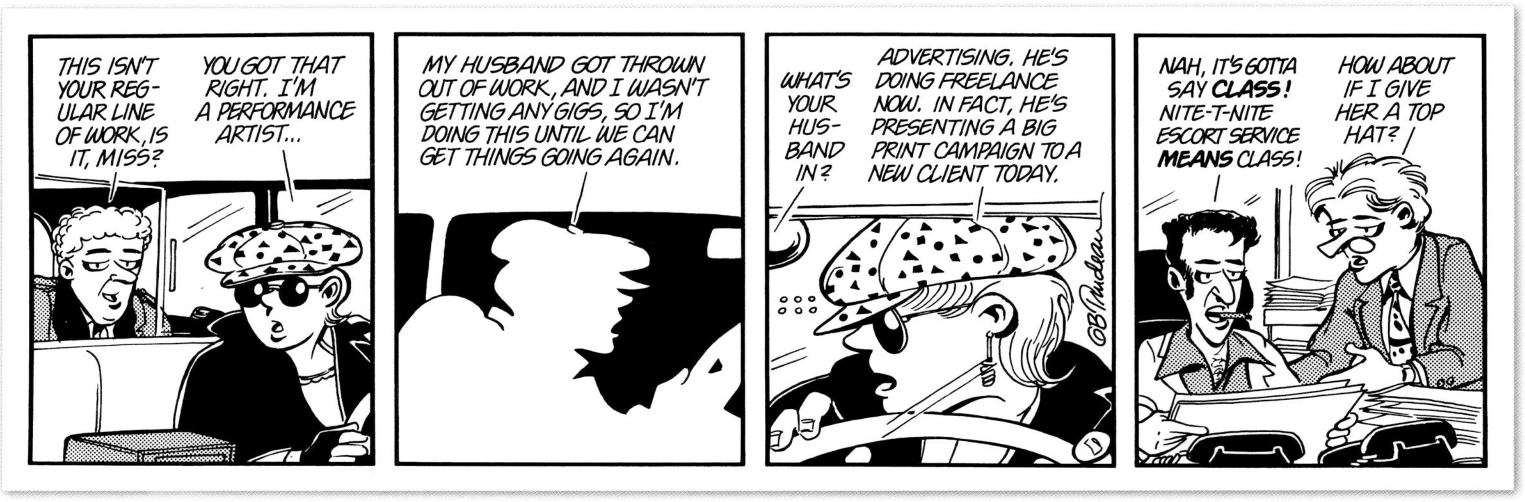
THIS ISN'T YOUR REGULAR LINE OF WORK, IS IT, MISS?
YOU GOT THAT RIGHT. I'M A PERFORMANCE ARTIST...
MY HUSBAND GOT THROWN OUT OF WORK, AND I WASN'T GETTING ANY GIGS, SO I'M DOING THIS UNTIL WE CAN GET THINGS GOING AGAIN.
WHAT'S YOUR HUSBAND IN?
ADVERTISING. HE'S DOING FREELANCE NOW. IN FACT, HE'S PRESENTING A BIG PRINT CAMPAIGN TO A NEW CLIENT TODAY.
GB Trudeau
NAH, IT'S GOTTA SAY CLASS! NITE-T-NITE ESCORT SERVICE MEANS CLASS!
HOW ABOUT IF I GIVE HER A TOP HAT?

3/4/92

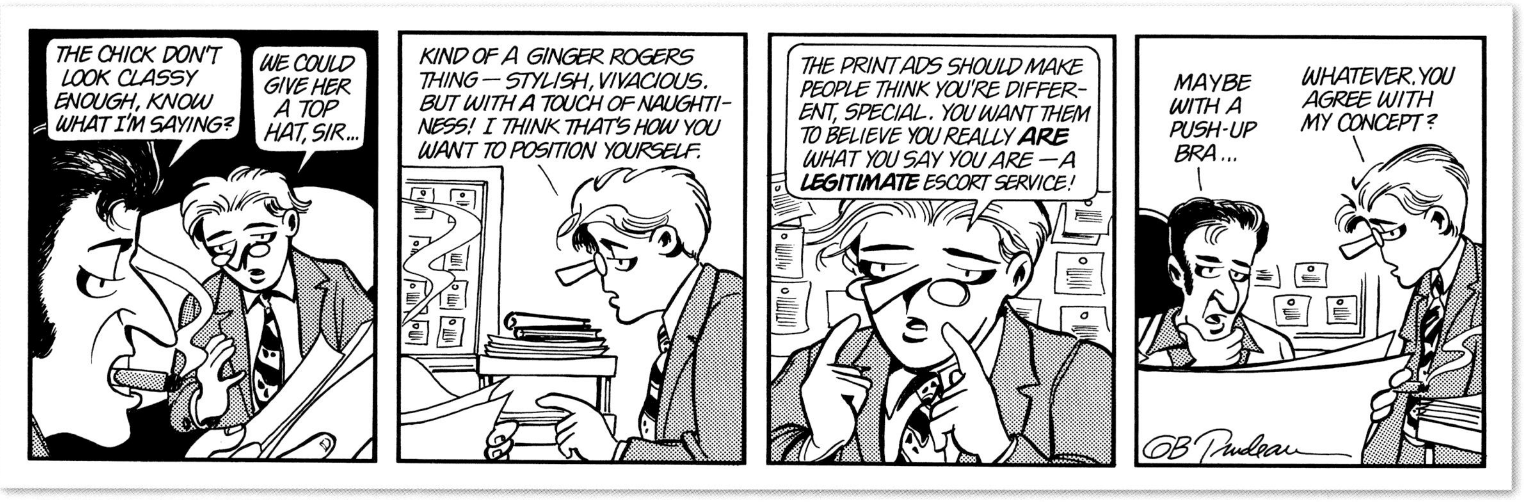
THE CHICK DON'T LOOK CLASSY ENOUGH, KNOW WHAT I'M SAYING?
WE COULD GIVE HER A TOP HAT, SIR...
KIND OF A GINGER ROGERS THING — STYLISH, VIVACIOUS. BUT WITH A TOUCH OF NAUGHTINESS! I THINK THAT'S HOW YOU WANT TO POSITION YOURSELF.
THE PRINT ADS SHOULD MAKE PEOPLE THINK YOU'RE DIFFERENT, SPECIAL. YOU WANT THEM TO BELIEVE YOU REALLY ARE WHAT YOU SAY YOU ARE — A LEGITIMATE ESCORT SERVICE!
MAYBE WITH A PUSH-UP BRA...
WHATEVER. YOU AGREE WITH MY CONCEPT?
GB Trudeau

3/5/92

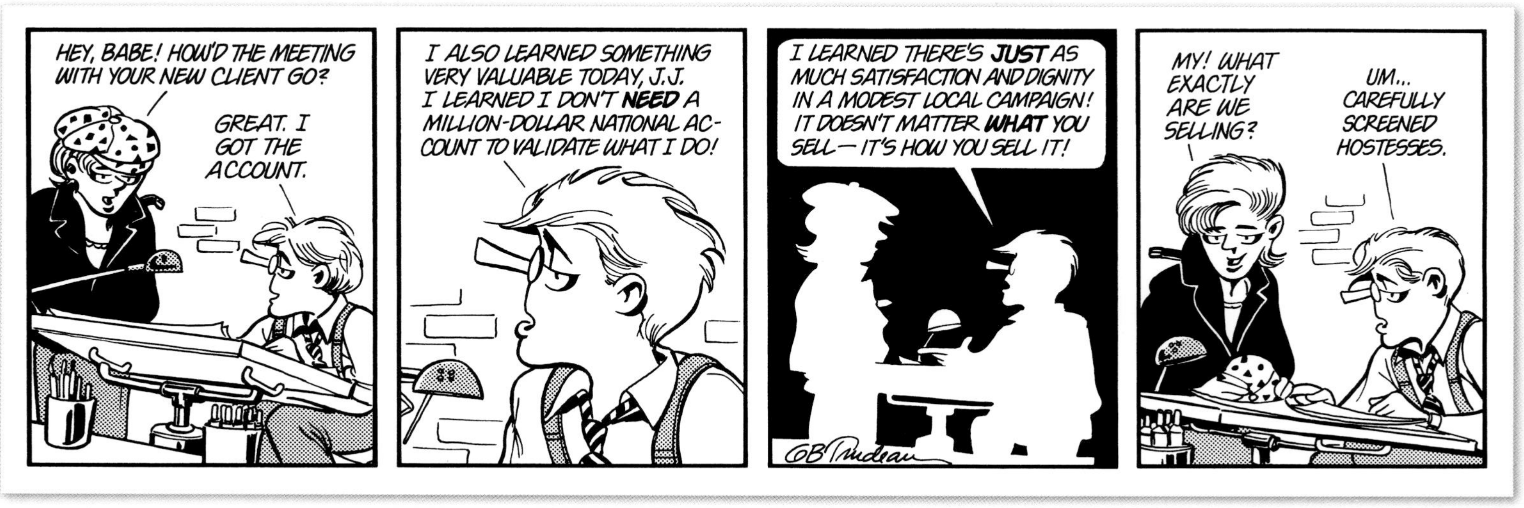
HEY, BABE! HOW'D THE MEETING WITH YOUR NEW CLIENT GO?
GREAT. I GOT THE ACCOUNT.
I ALSO LEARNED SOMETHING VERY VALUABLE TODAY, J.J. I LEARNED I DON'T NEED A MILLION-DOLLAR NATIONAL ACCOUNT TO VALIDATE WHAT I DO!
I LEARNED THERE'S JUST AS MUCH SATISFACTION AND DIGNITY IN A MODEST LOCAL CAMPAIGN! IT DOESN'T MATTER WHAT YOU SELL — IT'S HOW YOU SELL IT!
GB Trudeau
MY! WHAT EXACTLY ARE WE SELLING?
UM... CAREFULLY SCREENED HOSTESSES.

3/6/92

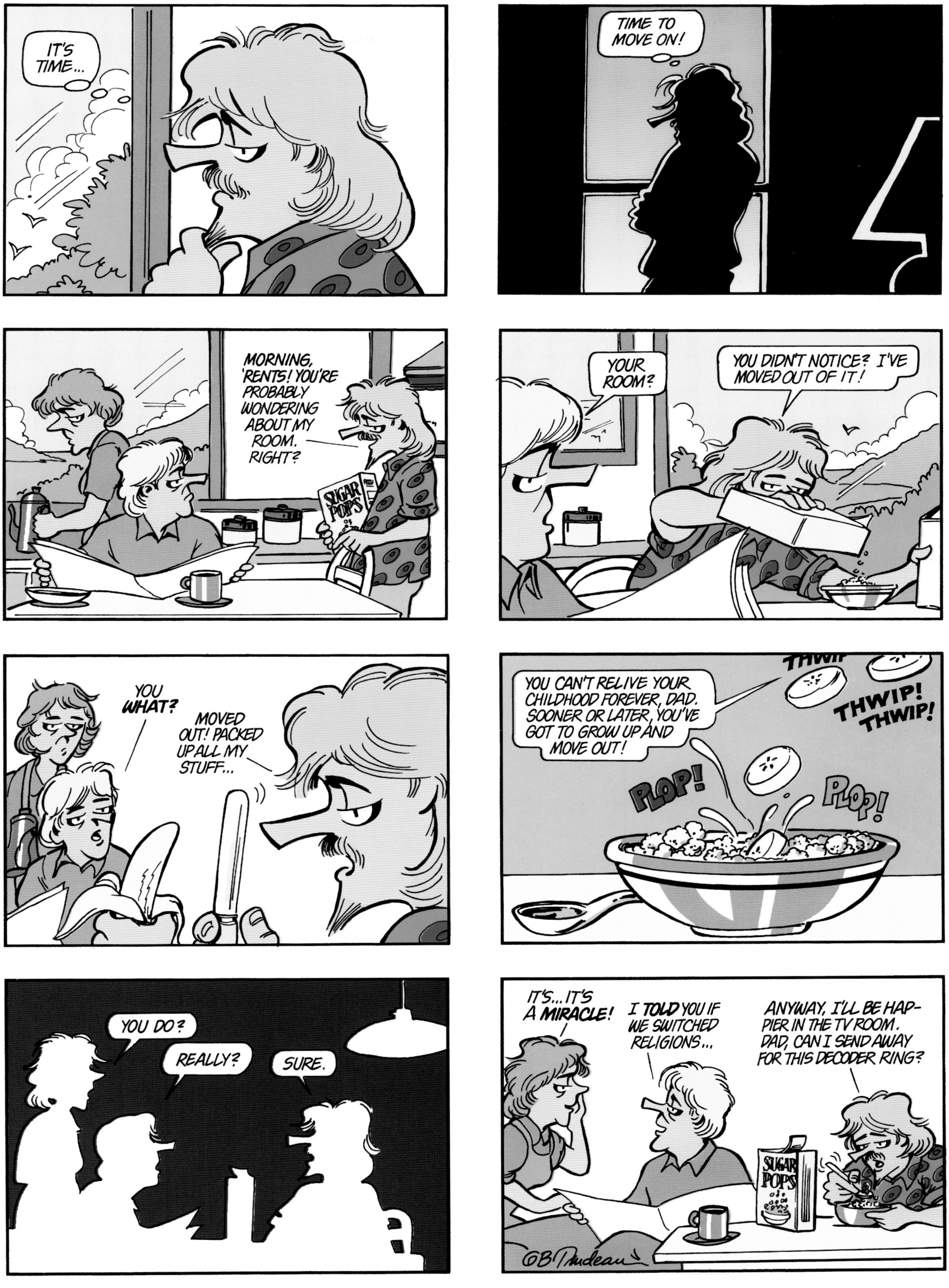
IT'S TIME...
TIME TO MOVE ON!
MORNING, 'RENTS! YOU'RE PROBABLY WONDERING ABOUT MY ROOM. RIGHT?
SUGAR POPS
YOUR ROOM?
YOU DIDN'T NOTICE? I'VE MOVED OUT OF IT!
YOU WHAT?
MOVED OUT! PACKED UP ALL MY STUFF...
YOU CAN'T RELIVE YOUR CHILDHOOD FOREVER, DAD. SOONER OR LATER, YOU'VE GOT TO GROW UP AND MOVE OUT!
THWIP! THWIP!
PLOP! PLOP!
YOU DO?
REALLY?
SURE.
IT'S... IT'S A MIRACLE!
I TOLD YOU IF WE SWITCHED RELIGIONS...
ANYWAY, I'LL BE HAPPIER IN THE TV ROOM. DAD, CAN I SEND AWAY FOR THIS DECODER RING?
SUGAR POPS
GB Trudeau

9/13/92

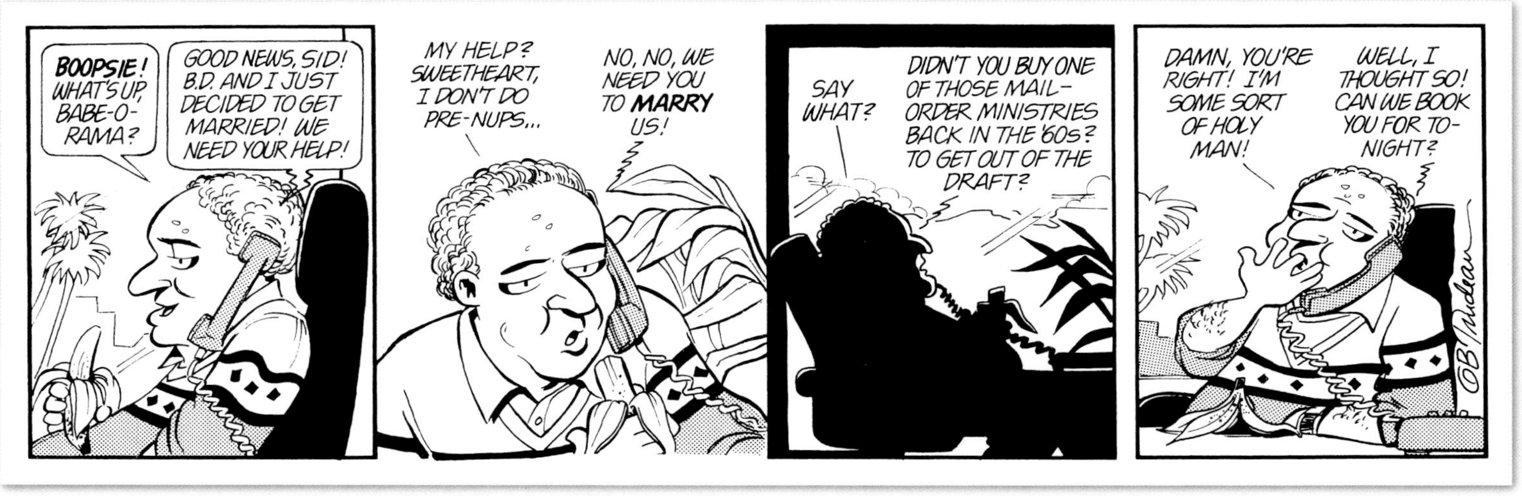
BOOPSIE! WHAT'S UP, BABE-O-RAMA?
GOOD NEWS, SID! B.D. AND I JUST DECIDED TO GET MARRIED! WE NEED YOUR HELP!
MY HELP? SWEETHEART, I DON'T DO PRE-NUPS...
NO, NO, WE NEED YOU TO MARRY US!
SAY WHAT?
DIDN'T YOU BUY ONE OF THOSE MAIL-ORDER MINISTRIES BACK IN THE '60s? TO GET OUT OF THE DRAFT?
DAMN, YOU'RE RIGHT! I'M SOME SORT OF HOLY MAN!
WELL, I THOUGHT SO! CAN WE BOOK YOU FOR TONIGHT?
GB Trudeau

4/13/92

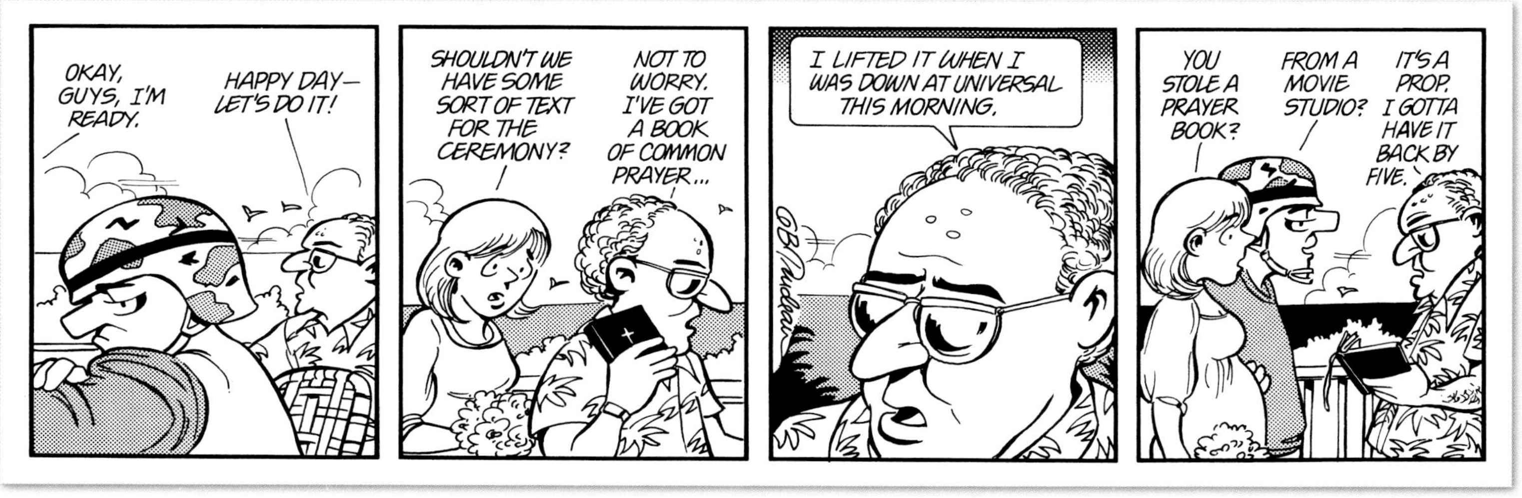
OKAY, GUYS, I'M READY.
HAPPY DAY— LET'S DO IT!
SHOULDN'T WE HAVE SOME SORT OF TEXT FOR THE CEREMONY?
NOT TO WORRY. I'VE GOT A BOOK OF COMMON PRAYER...
GB Trudeau
I LIFTED IT WHEN I WAS DOWN AT UNIVERSAL THIS MORNING.
YOU STOLE A PRAYER BOOK?
FROM A MOVIE STUDIO?
IT'S A PROP. I GOTTA HAVE IT BACK BY FIVE.

4/16/92

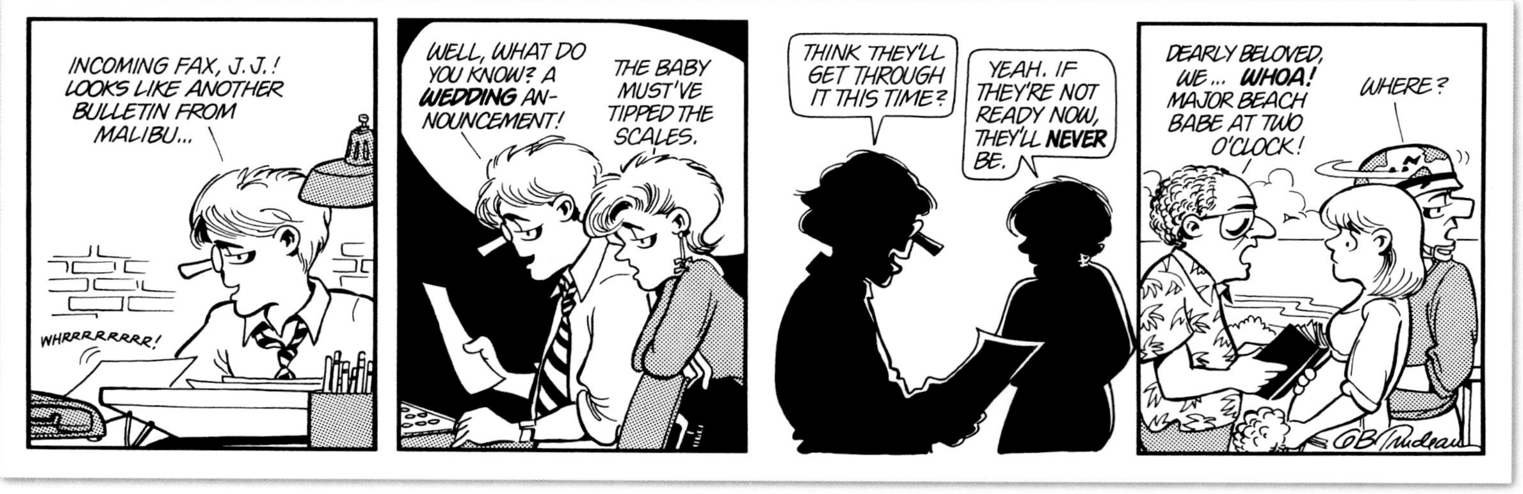
INCOMING FAX, J.J.! LOOKS LIKE ANOTHER BULLETIN FROM MALIBU...
WHRRRRRRRR!
WELL, WHAT DO YOU KNOW? A WEDDING ANNOUNCEMENT!
THE BABY MUST'VE TIPPED THE SCALES.
THINK THEY'LL GET THROUGH IT THIS TIME?
YEAH. IF THEY'RE NOT READY NOW, THEY'LL NEVER BE.
DEARLY BELOVED, WE... WHOA! MAJOR BEACH BABE AT TWO O'CLOCK!
WHERE?
GB Trudeau

4/17/92

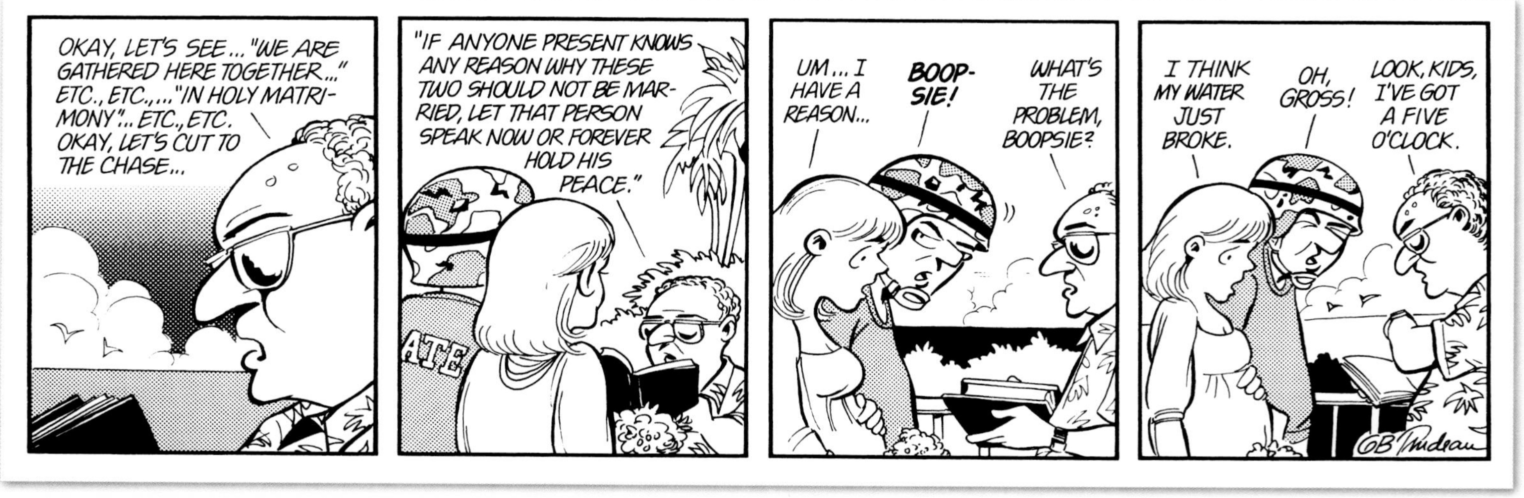
OKAY, LET'S SEE... "WE ARE GATHERED HERE TOGETHER..." ETC., ETC.,..."IN HOLY MATRIMONY"... ETC., ETC. OKAY, LET'S CUT TO THE CHASE...
"IF ANYONE PRESENT KNOWS ANY REASON WHY THESE TWO SHOULD NOT BE MARRIED, LET THAT PERSON SPEAK NOW OR FOREVER HOLD HIS PEACE."
UM... I HAVE A REASON...
BOOPSIE!
WHAT'S THE PROBLEM, BOOPSIE?
I THINK MY WATER JUST BROKE.
OH, GROSS!
LOOK, KIDS, I'VE GOT A FIVE O'CLOCK.
GB Trudeau

4/18/92

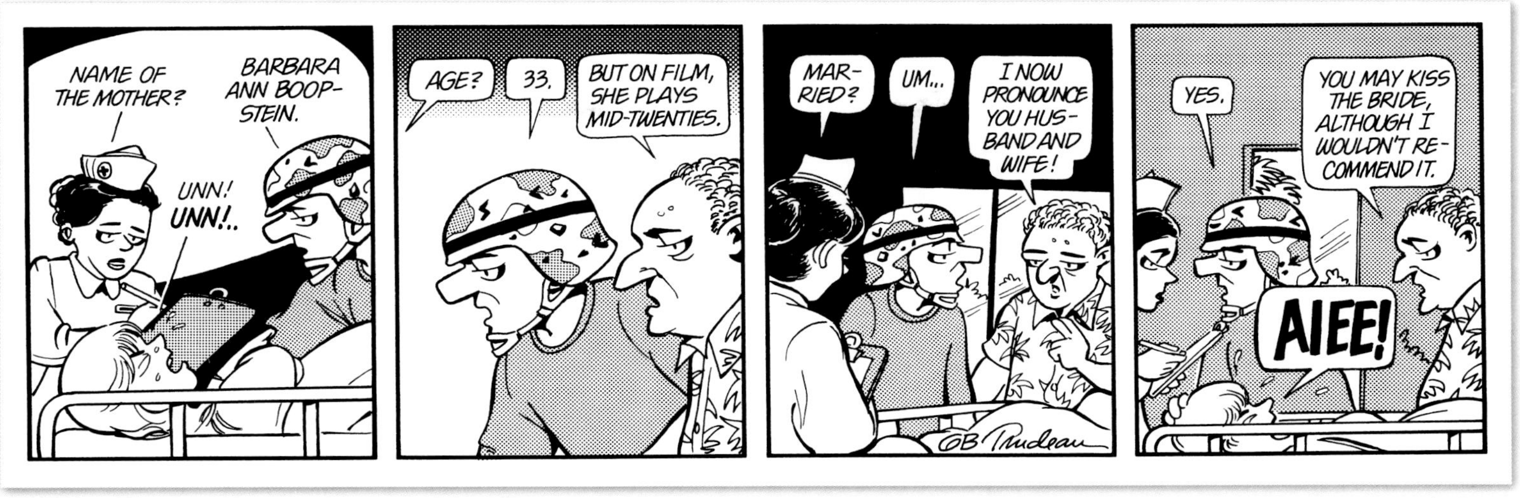
NAME OF THE MOTHER?
BARBARA ANN BOOPSTEIN.
UNN! UNN!..
AGE?
33.
BUT ON FILM, SHE PLAYS MID-TWENTIES.
MARRIED?
UM...
I NOW PRONOUNCE YOU HUSBAND AND WIFE!
YES.
YOU MAY KISS THE BRIDE, ALTHOUGH I WOULDN'T RECOMMEND IT.
AIEE!
©B Trudeau

4/20/92

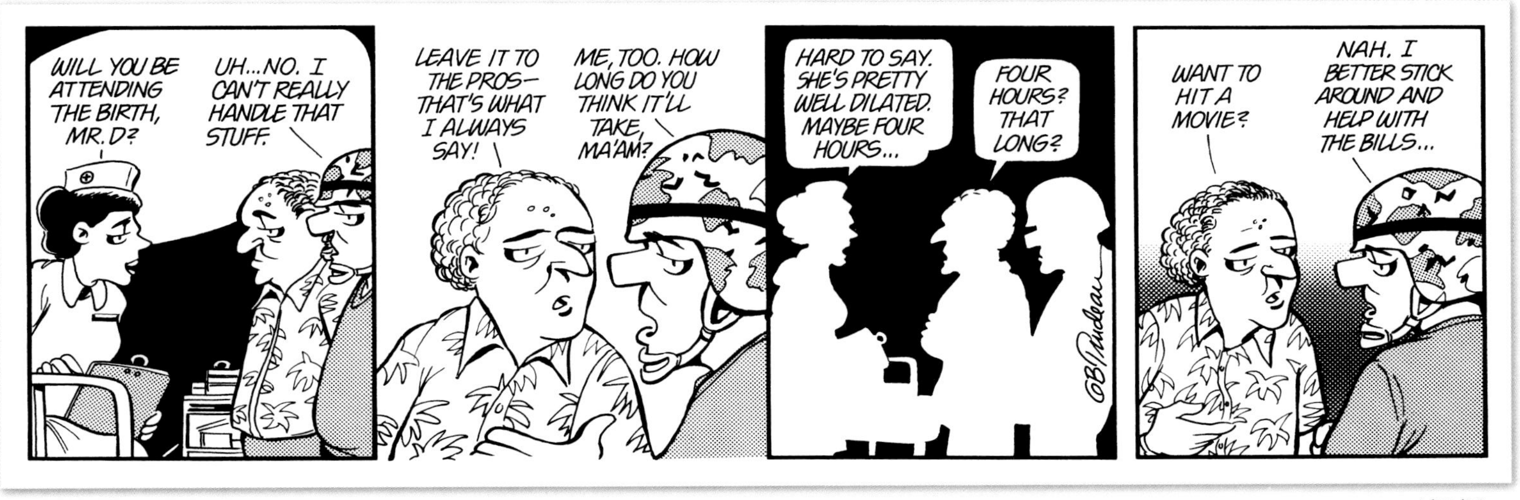
WILL YOU BE ATTENDING THE BIRTH, MR. D?
UH...NO. I CAN'T REALLY HANDLE THAT STUFF.
LEAVE IT TO THE PROS—THAT'S WHAT I ALWAYS SAY!
ME, TOO. HOW LONG DO YOU THINK IT'LL TAKE, MA'AM?
HARD TO SAY. SHE'S PRETTY WELL DILATED. MAYBE FOUR HOURS...
FOUR HOURS? THAT LONG?
WANT TO HIT A MOVIE?
NAH. I BETTER STICK AROUND AND HELP WITH THE BILLS...
©B Trudeau

4/21/92

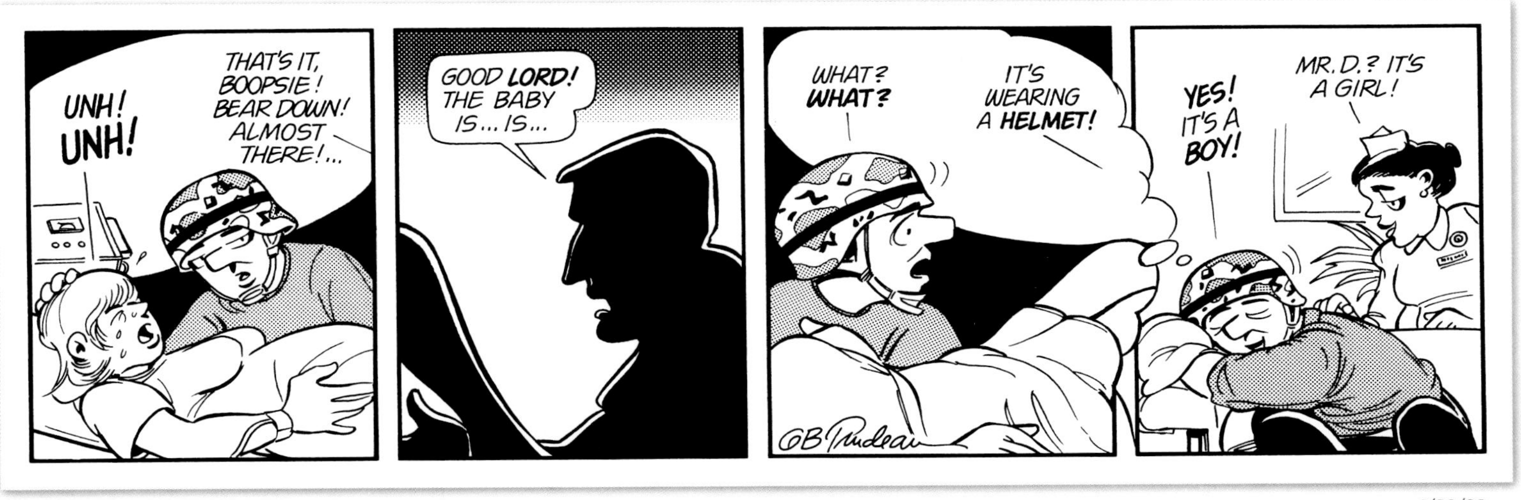
UNH! UNH!
THAT'S IT, BOOPSIE! BEAR DOWN! ALMOST THERE!...
GOOD LORD! THE BABY IS... IS...
WHAT? WHAT?
IT'S WEARING A HELMET!
YES! IT'S A BOY!
MR. D.? IT'S A GIRL!
©B Trudeau

4/23/92

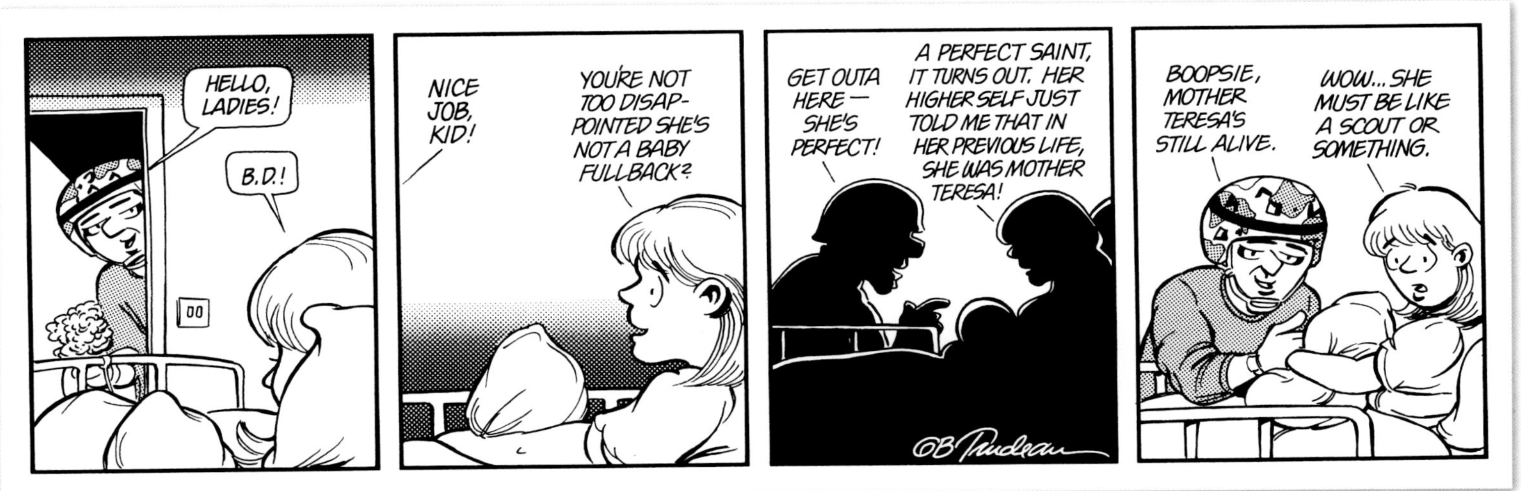
HELLO, LADIES!
B.D.!
NICE JOB, KID!
YOU'RE NOT TOO DISAPPOINTED SHE'S NOT A BABY FULLBACK?
GET OUTA HERE—SHE'S PERFECT!
A PERFECT SAINT, IT TURNS OUT. HER HIGHER SELF JUST TOLD ME THAT IN HER PREVIOUS LIFE, SHE WAS MOTHER TERESA!
BOOPSIE, MOTHER TERESA'S STILL ALIVE.
WOW... SHE MUST BE LIKE A SCOUT OR SOMETHING.
©B Trudeau

4/24/92

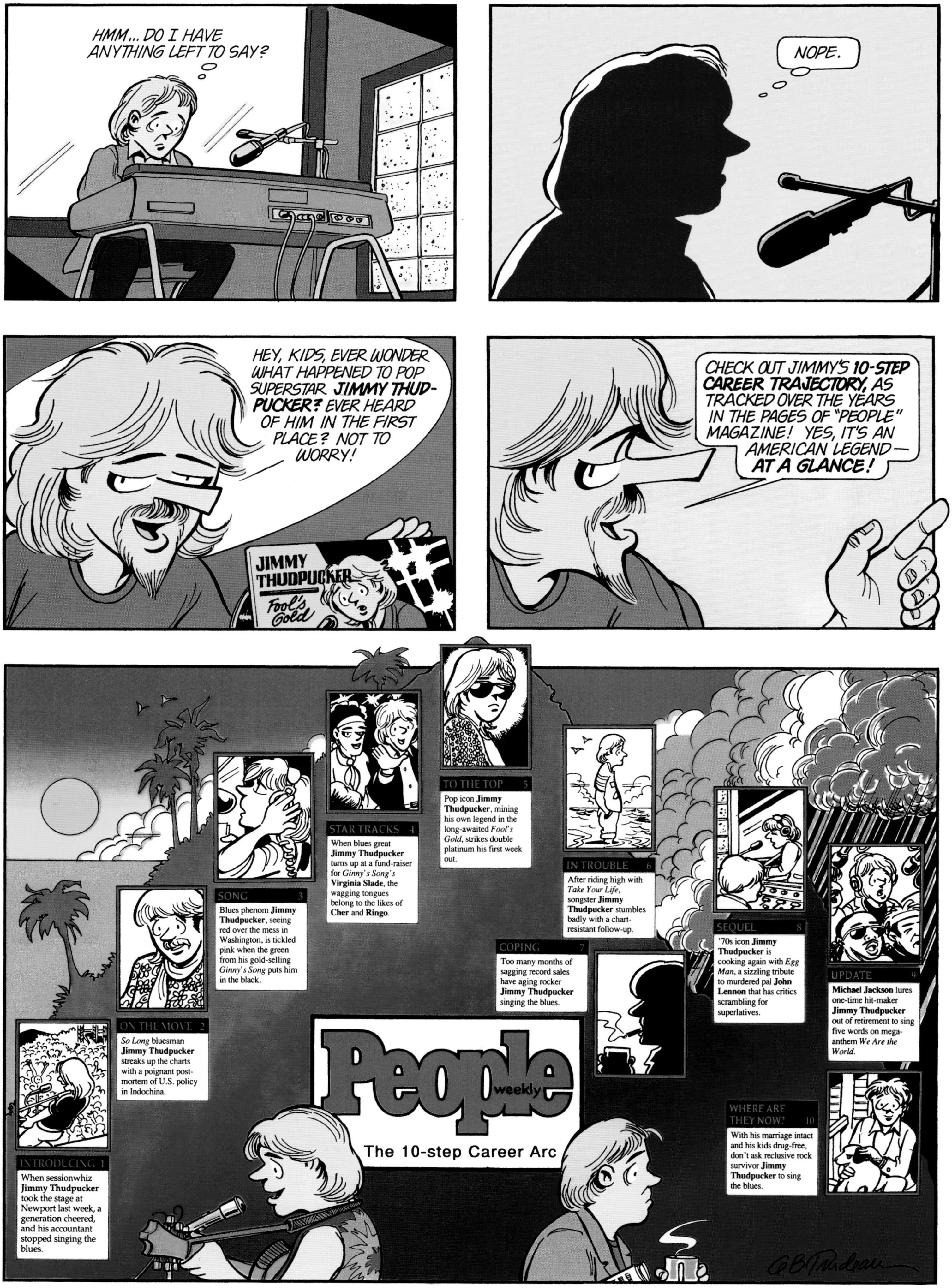
HMM... DO I HAVE ANYTHING LEFT TO SAY?
NOPE.
HEY, KIDS, EVER WONDER WHAT HAPPENED TO POP SUPERSTAR JIMMY THUDPUCKER? EVER HEARD OF HIM IN THE FIRST PLACE? NOT TO WORRY!
JIMMY THUDPUCKER
Fool's Gold
CHECK OUT JIMMY'S 10-STEP CAREER TRAJECTORY, AS TRACKED OVER THE YEARS IN THE PAGES OF "PEOPLE" MAGAZINE! YES, IT'S AN AMERICAN LEGEND— AT A GLANCE!
People weekly
The 10-step Career Arc
INTRODUCING 1
When sessionwhiz Jimmy Thudpucker took the stage at Newport last week, a generation cheered, and his accountant stopped singing the blues.
ON THE MOVE 2
So Long bluesman Jimmy Thudpucker streaks up the charts with a poignant post-mortem of U.S. policy in Indochina.
SONG 3
Blues phenom Jimmy Thudpucker, seeing red over the mess in Washington, is tickled pink when the green from his gold-selling Ginny's Song puts him in the black.
STAR TRACKS 4
When blues great Jimmy Thudpucker turns up at a fund-raiser for Ginny's Song's Virginia Slade, the wagging tongues belong to the likes of Cher and Ringo.
TO THE TOP 5
Pop icon Jimmy Thudpucker, mining his own legend in the long-awaited Fool's Gold, strikes double platinum his first week out.
IN TROUBLE 6
After riding high with Take Your Life, songster Jimmy Thudpucker stumbles badly with a chart-resistant follow-up.
COPING 7
Too many months of sagging record sales have aging rocker Jimmy Thudpucker singing the blues.
SEQUEL 8
'70s icon Jimmy Thudpucker is cooking again with Egg Man, a sizzling tribute to murdered pal John Lennon that has critics scrambling for superlatives.
UPDATE 9
Michael Jackson lures one-time hit-maker Jimmy Thudpucker out of retirement to sing five words on mega-anthem We Are the World.
WHERE ARE THEY NOW? 10
With his marriage intact and his kids drug-free, don't ask reclusive rock survivor Jimmy Thudpucker to sing the blues.
G.B. Trudeau

5/31/92

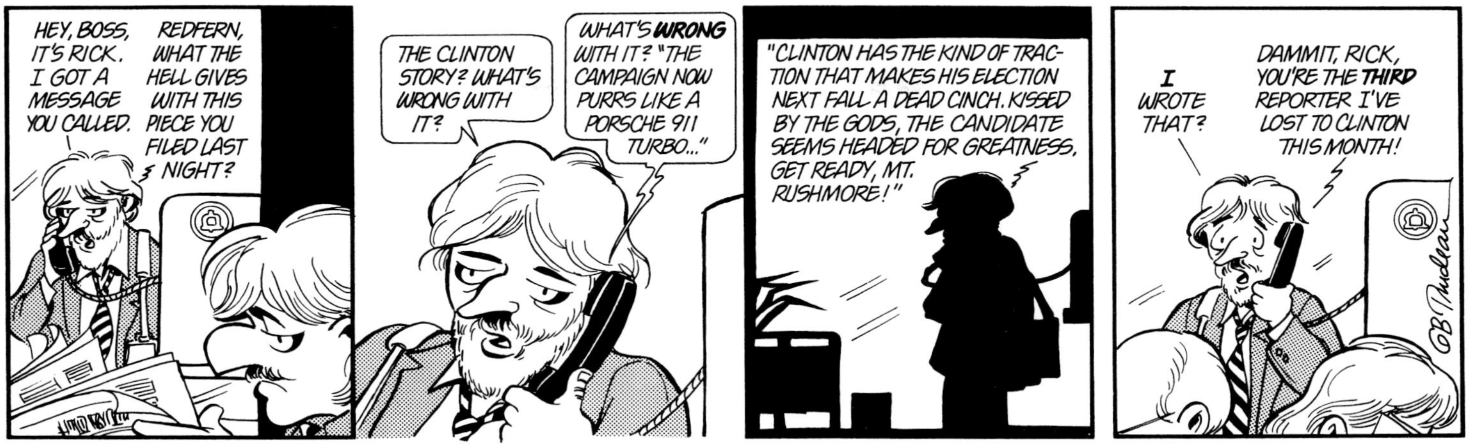
HEY, BOSS, IT'S RICK. I GOT A MESSAGE YOU CALLED.
REDFERN, WHAT THE HELL GIVES WITH THIS PIECE YOU FILED LAST NIGHT?
THE CLINTON STORY? WHAT'S WRONG WITH IT?
WHAT'S WRONG WITH IT? "THE CAMPAIGN NOW PURRS LIKE A PORSCHE 911 TURBO..."
"CLINTON HAS THE KIND OF TRACTION THAT MAKES HIS ELECTION NEXT FALL A DEAD CINCH. KISSED BY THE GODS, THE CANDIDATE SEEMS HEADED FOR GREATNESS. GET READY, MT. RUSHMORE!"
I WROTE THAT?
DAMMIT, RICK, YOU'RE THE THIRD REPORTER I'VE LOST TO CLINTON THIS MONTH!

3/23/92

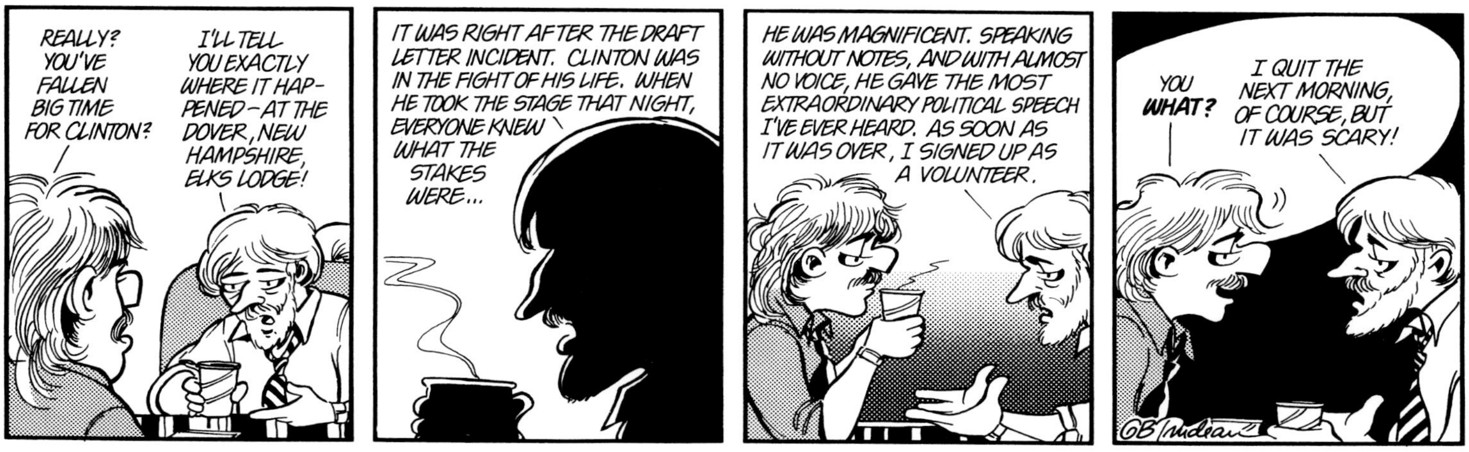
REALLY? YOU'VE FALLEN BIG TIME FOR CLINTON?
I'LL TELL YOU EXACTLY WHERE IT HAPPENED—AT THE DOVER, NEW HAMPSHIRE, ELKS LODGE!
IT WAS RIGHT AFTER THE DRAFT LETTER INCIDENT. CLINTON WAS IN THE FIGHT OF HIS LIFE. WHEN HE TOOK THE STAGE THAT NIGHT, EVERYONE KNEW WHAT THE STAKES WERE...
HE WAS MAGNIFICENT. SPEAKING WITHOUT NOTES, AND WITH ALMOST NO VOICE, HE GAVE THE MOST EXTRAORDINARY POLITICAL SPEECH I'VE EVER HEARD. AS SOON AS IT WAS OVER, I SIGNED UP AS A VOLUNTEER.
YOU WHAT?
I QUIT THE NEXT MORNING, OF COURSE, BUT IT WAS SCARY!

3/25/92

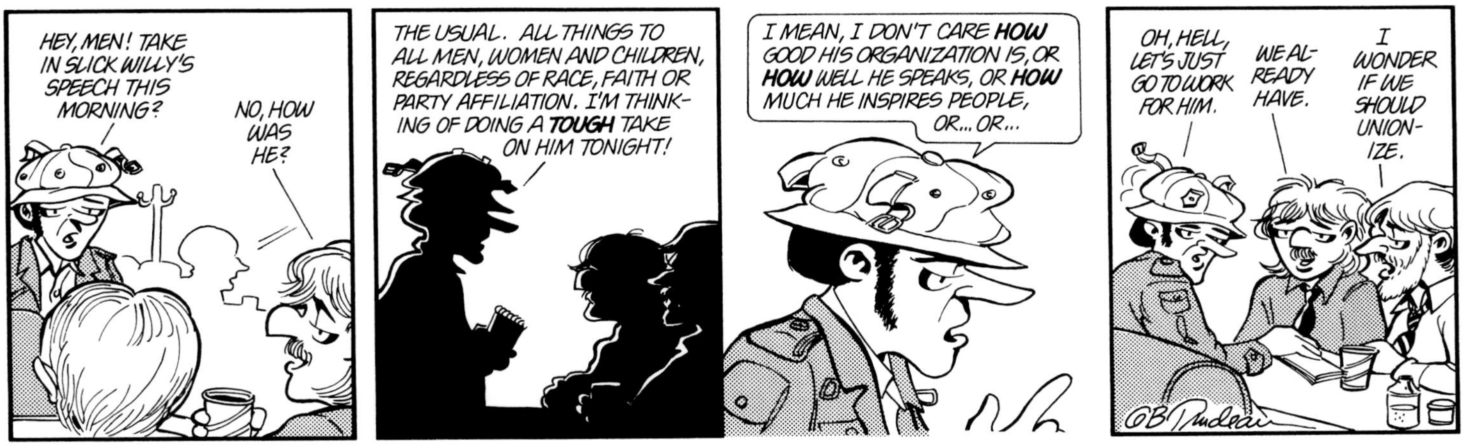
HEY, MEN! TAKE IN SLICK WILLY'S SPEECH THIS MORNING?
NO, HOW WAS HE?
THE USUAL. ALL THINGS TO ALL MEN, WOMEN AND CHILDREN, REGARDLESS OF RACE, FAITH OR PARTY AFFILIATION. I'M THINKING OF DOING A TOUGH TAKE ON HIM TONIGHT!
I MEAN, I DON'T CARE HOW GOOD HIS ORGANIZATION IS, OR HOW WELL HE SPEAKS, OR HOW MUCH HE INSPIRES PEOPLE, OR... OR...
OH, HELL, LET'S JUST GO TO WORK FOR HIM.
WE ALREADY HAVE.
I WONDER IF WE SHOULD UNIONIZE.

3/26/92

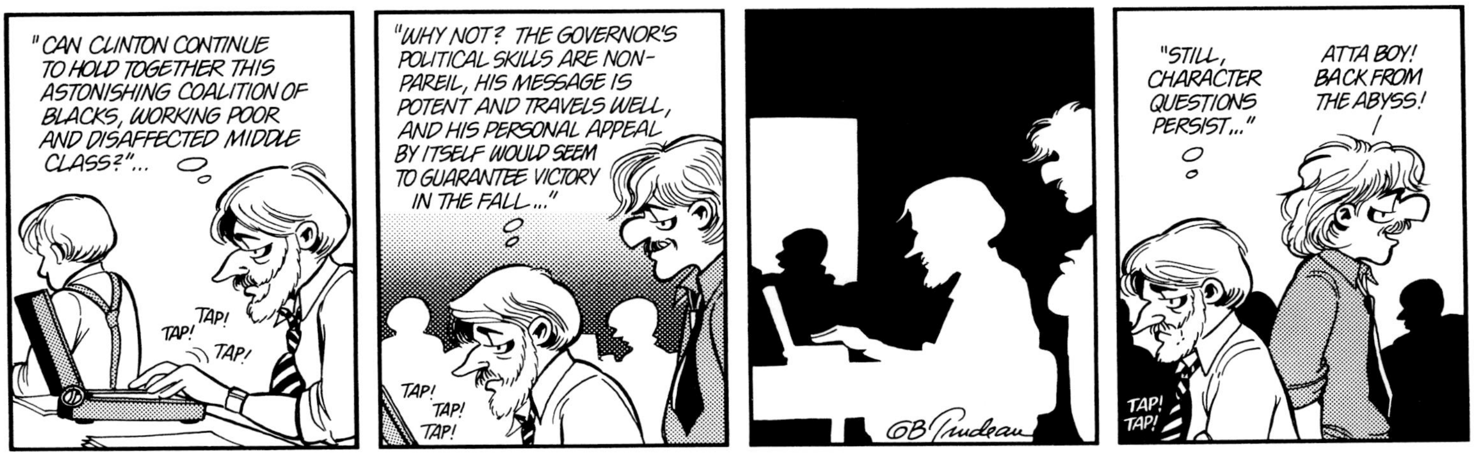
"CAN CLINTON CONTINUE TO HOLD TOGETHER THIS ASTONISHING COALITION OF BLACKS, WORKING POOR AND DISAFFECTED MIDDLE CLASS?"...
TAP! TAP! TAP!
"WHY NOT? THE GOVERNOR'S POLITICAL SKILLS ARE NONPAREIL, HIS MESSAGE IS POTENT AND TRAVELS WELL, AND HIS PERSONAL APPEAL BY ITSELF WOULD SEEM TO GUARANTEE VICTORY IN THE FALL..."
TAP! TAP! TAP!
"STILL, CHARACTER QUESTIONS PERSIST..."
ATTA BOY! BACK FROM THE ABYSS!
TAP! TAP!

3/27/92

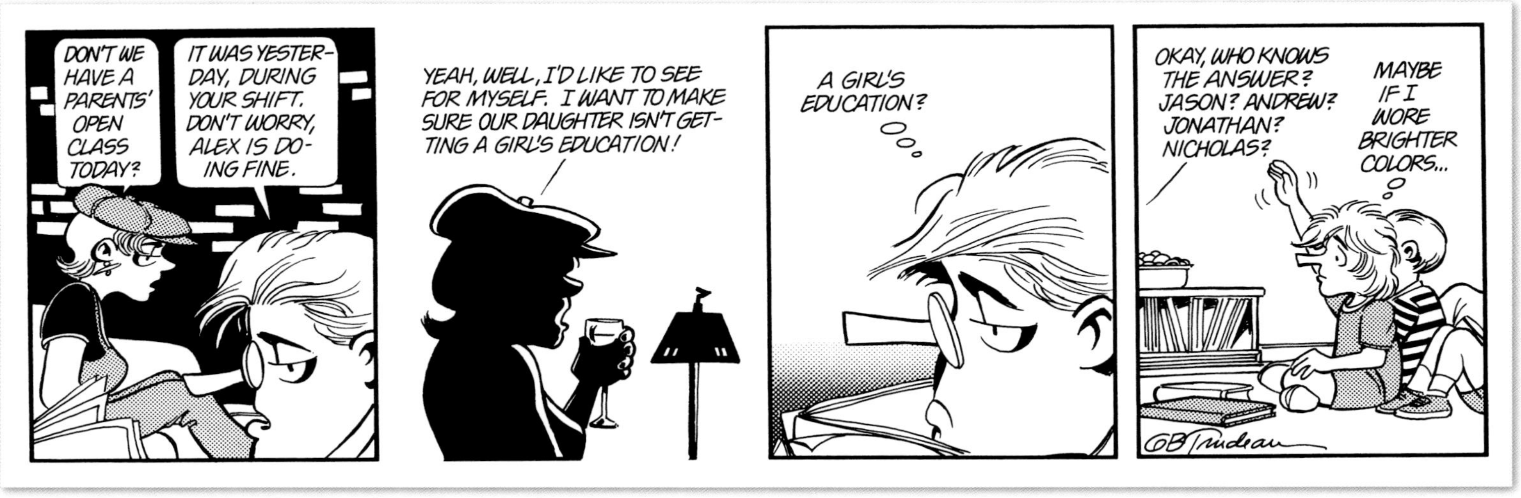
DON'T WE HAVE A PARENTS' OPEN CLASS TODAY?
IT WAS YESTERDAY, DURING YOUR SHIFT. DON'T WORRY, ALEX IS DOING FINE.
YEAH, WELL, I'D LIKE TO SEE FOR MYSELF. I WANT TO MAKE SURE OUR DAUGHTER ISN'T GETTING A GIRL'S EDUCATION!
A GIRL'S EDUCATION?
OKAY, WHO KNOWS THE ANSWER? JASON? ANDREW? JONATHAN? NICHOLAS?
MAYBE IF I WORE BRIGHTER COLORS...

4/27/92

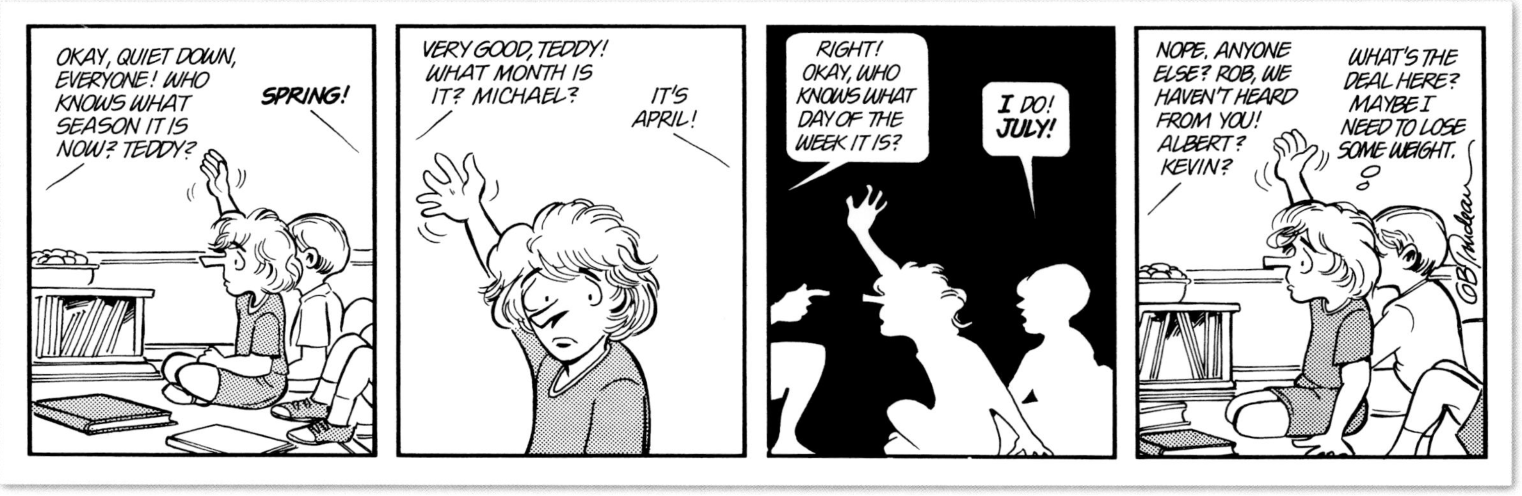
OKAY, QUIET DOWN, EVERYONE! WHO KNOWS WHAT SEASON IT IS NOW? TEDDY?
SPRING!
VERY GOOD, TEDDY! WHAT MONTH IS IT? MICHAEL?
IT'S APRIL!
RIGHT! OKAY, WHO KNOWS WHAT DAY OF THE WEEK IT IS?
I DO! JULY!
NOPE, ANYONE ELSE? ROB, WE HAVEN'T HEARD FROM YOU! ALBERT? KEVIN?
WHAT'S THE DEAL HERE? MAYBE I NEED TO LOSE SOME WEIGHT.

4/28/92

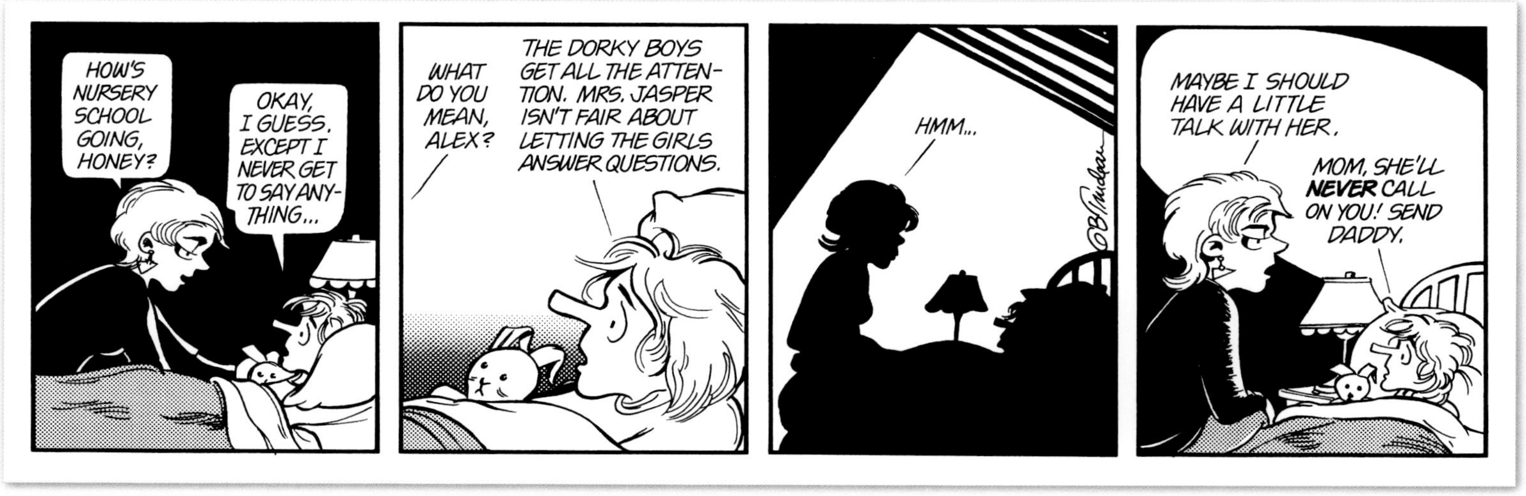
HOW'S NURSERY SCHOOL GOING, HONEY?
OKAY, I GUESS. EXCEPT I NEVER GET TO SAY ANYTHING...
WHAT DO YOU MEAN, ALEX?
THE DORKY BOYS GET ALL THE ATTENTION. MRS. JASPER ISN'T FAIR ABOUT LETTING THE GIRLS ANSWER QUESTIONS.
HMM...
MAYBE I SHOULD HAVE A LITTLE TALK WITH HER.
MOM, SHE'LL NEVER CALL ON YOU! SEND DADDY.

4/29/92

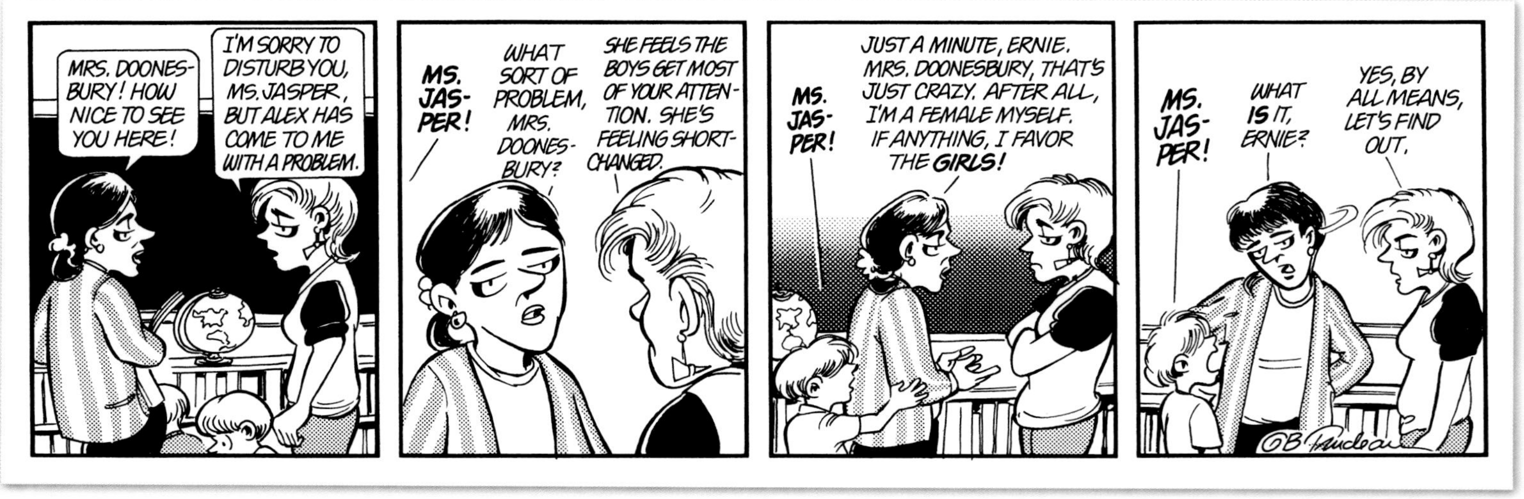
MRS. DOONESBURY! HOW NICE TO SEE YOU HERE!
I'M SORRY TO DISTURB YOU, MS. JASPER, BUT ALEX HAS COME TO ME WITH A PROBLEM.
MS. JASPER!
WHAT SORT OF PROBLEM, MRS. DOONESBURY?
SHE FEELS THE BOYS GET MOST OF YOUR ATTENTION. SHE'S FEELING SHORT-CHANGED.
MS. JASPER!
JUST A MINUTE, ERNIE. MRS. DOONESBURY, THAT'S JUST CRAZY. AFTER ALL, I'M A FEMALE MYSELF. IF ANYTHING, I FAVOR THE GIRLS!
MS. JASPER!
WHAT IS IT, ERNIE?
YES, BY ALL MEANS, LET'S FIND OUT.

4/30/92

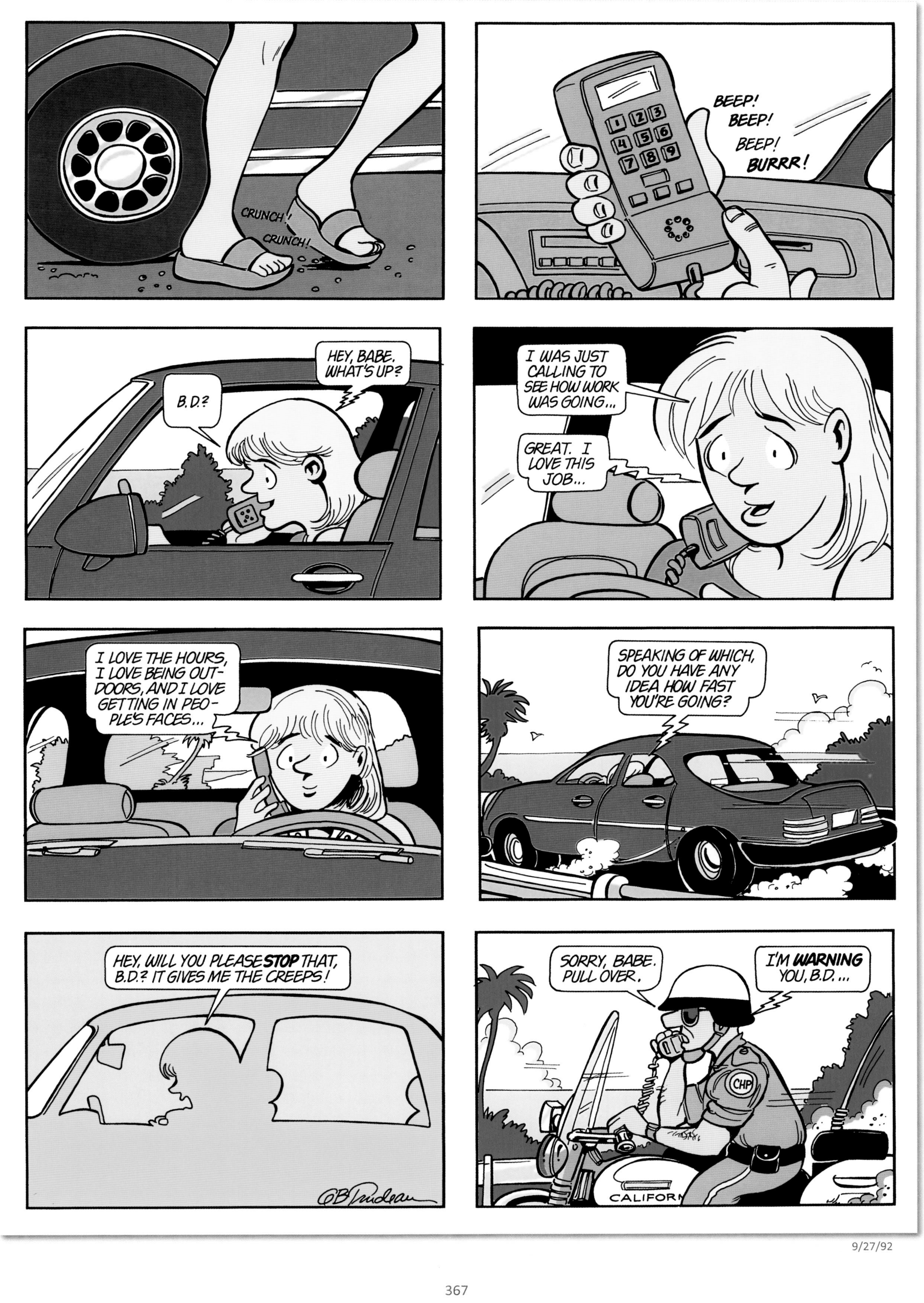
CRUNCH!
CRUNCH!
BEEP!
BEEP!
BEEP!
BURRR!
B.D.?
HEY, BABE. WHAT'S UP?
I WAS JUST CALLING TO SEE HOW WORK WAS GOING...
GREAT. I LOVE THIS JOB...
I LOVE THE HOURS, I LOVE BEING OUT-DOORS, AND I LOVE GETTING IN PEO-PLE'S FACES...
SPEAKING OF WHICH, DO YOU HAVE ANY IDEA HOW FAST YOU'RE GOING?
HEY, WILL YOU PLEASE **STOP** THAT, B.D.? IT GIVES ME THE CREEPS!
SORRY, BABE. PULL OVER.
I'M **WARNING** YOU, B.D. ...
CHP
CALIFORN

9/27/92

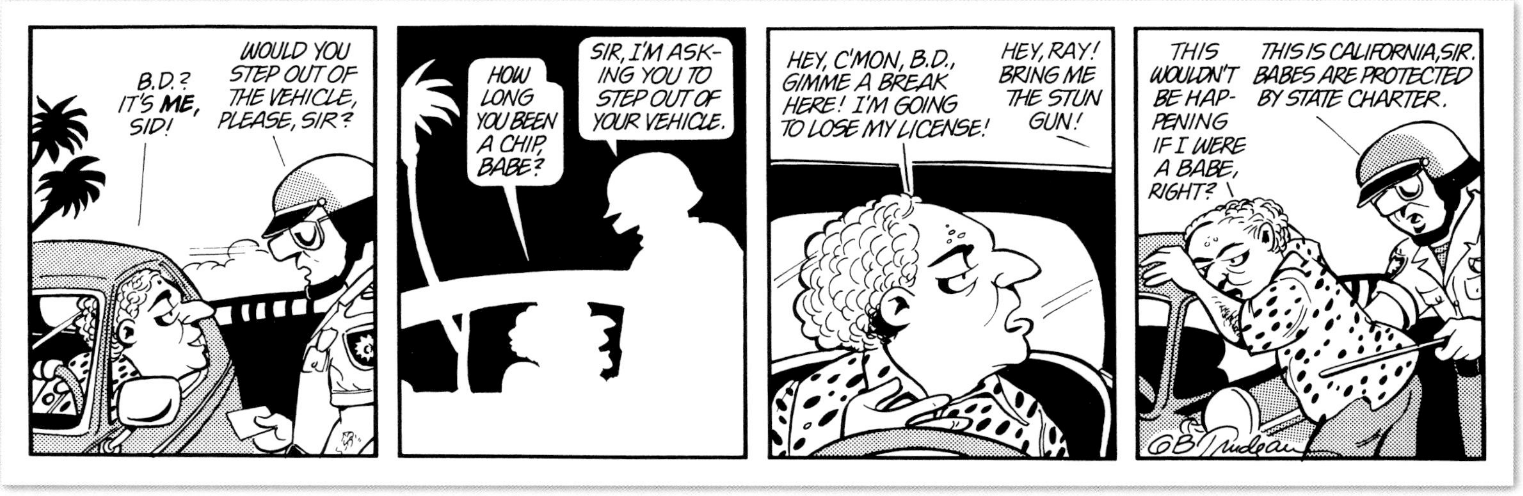
B.D.? IT'S **ME**, SID!
WOULD YOU STEP OUT OF THE VEHICLE, PLEASE, SIR?
HOW LONG YOU BEEN A CHIP, BABE?
SIR, I'M ASKING YOU TO STEP OUT OF YOUR VEHICLE.
HEY, C'MON, B.D., GIMME A BREAK HERE! I'M GOING TO LOSE MY LICENSE!
HEY, RAY! BRING ME THE STUN GUN!
THIS WOULDN'T BE HAPPENING IF I WERE A BABE, RIGHT?
THIS IS CALIFORNIA, SIR. BABES ARE PROTECTED BY STATE CHARTER.
GB Trudeau

9/29/92

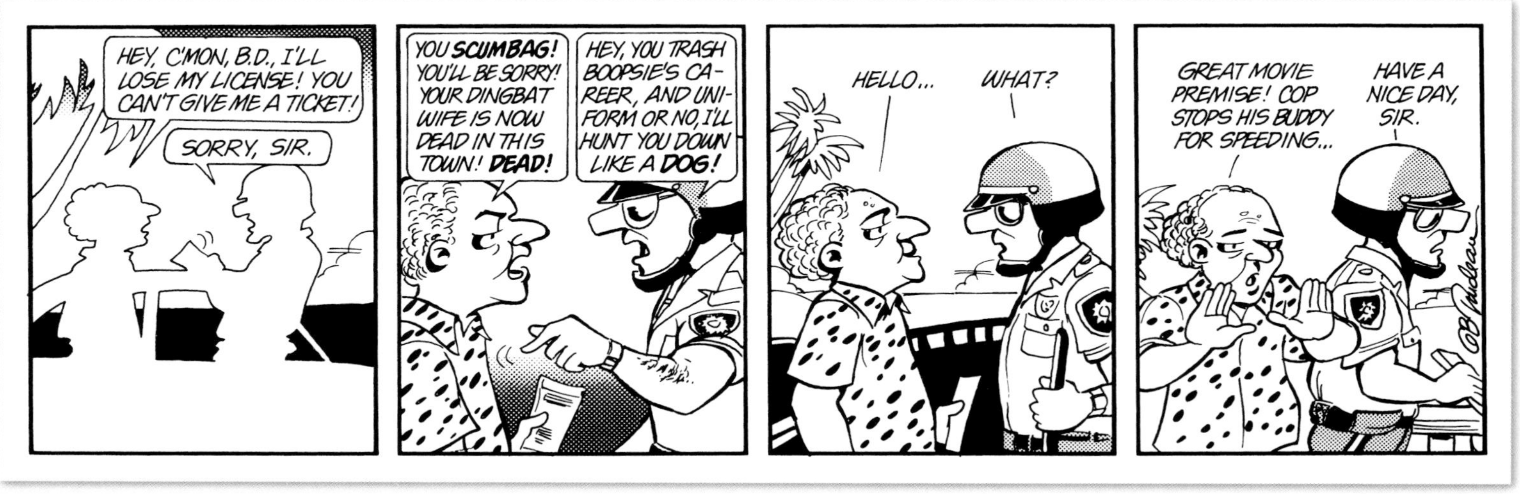
HEY, C'MON, B.D., I'LL LOSE MY LICENSE! YOU CAN'T GIVE ME A TICKET!
SORRY, SIR.
YOU **SCUMBAG!** YOU'LL BE SORRY! YOUR DINGBAT WIFE IS NOW DEAD IN THIS TOWN! **DEAD!**
HEY, YOU TRASH BOOPSIE'S CAREER, AND UNIFORM OR NO, I'LL HUNT YOU DOWN LIKE A **DOG!**
HELLO...
WHAT?
GREAT MOVIE PREMISE! COP STOPS HIS BUDDY FOR SPEEDING...
HAVE A NICE DAY, SIR.
GB Trudeau

9/30/92

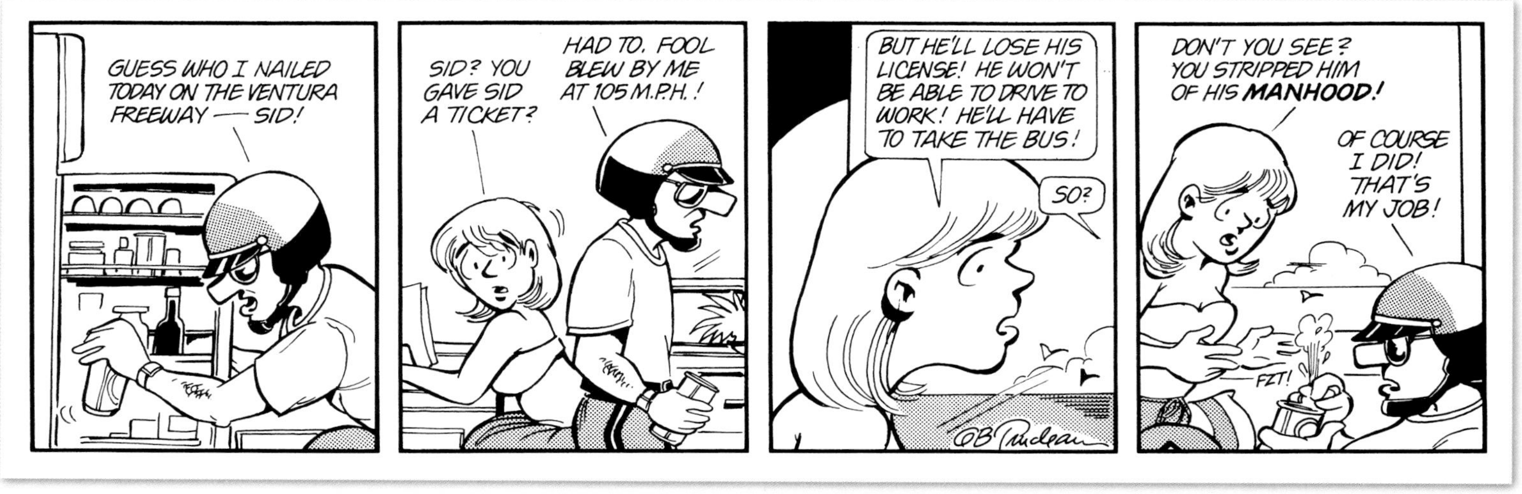
GUESS WHO I NAILED TODAY ON THE VENTURA FREEWAY — SID!
SID? YOU GAVE SID A TICKET?
HAD TO. FOOL BLEW BY ME AT 105 M.P.H.!
BUT HE'LL LOSE HIS LICENSE! HE WON'T BE ABLE TO DRIVE TO WORK! HE'LL HAVE TO TAKE THE BUS!
SO?
DON'T YOU SEE? YOU STRIPPED HIM OF HIS **MANHOOD!**
OF COURSE I DID! THAT'S MY JOB!
FZT!
GB Trudeau

10/1/92

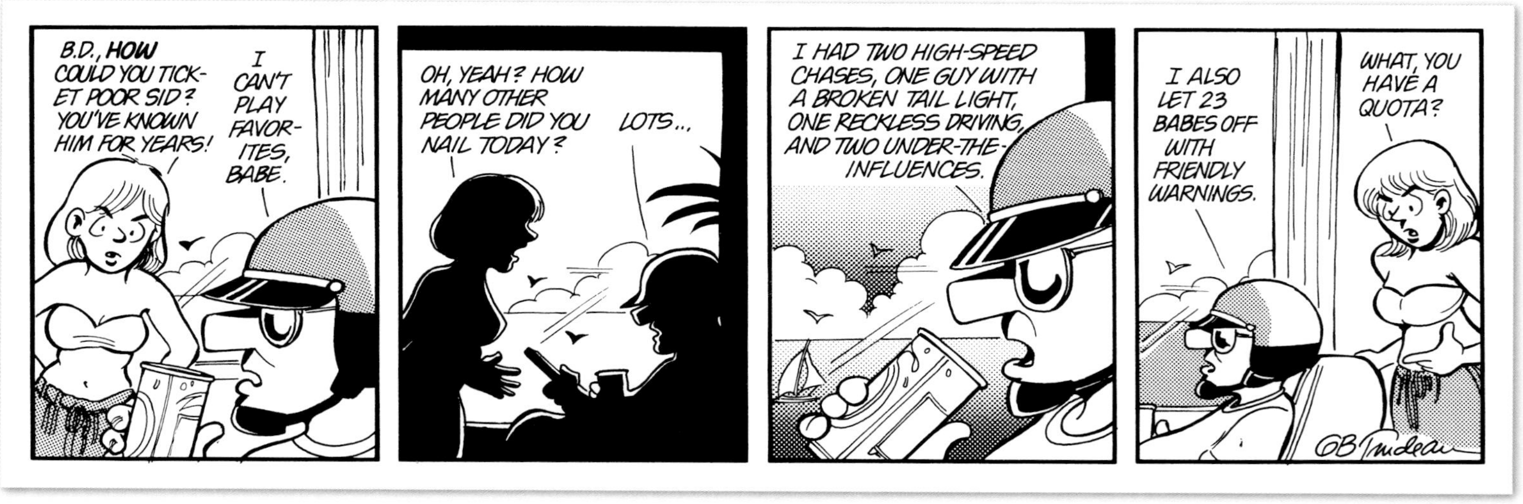
B.D., **HOW** COULD YOU TICKET POOR SID? YOU'VE KNOWN HIM FOR YEARS!
I CAN'T PLAY FAVORITES, BABE.
OH, YEAH? HOW MANY OTHER PEOPLE DID YOU NAIL TODAY?
LOTS...
I HAD TWO HIGH-SPEED CHASES, ONE GUY WITH A BROKEN TAIL LIGHT, ONE RECKLESS DRIVING, AND TWO UNDER-THE-INFLUENCES.
I ALSO LET 23 BABES OFF WITH FRIENDLY WARNINGS.
WHAT, YOU HAVE A QUOTA?
GB Trudeau

10/2/92

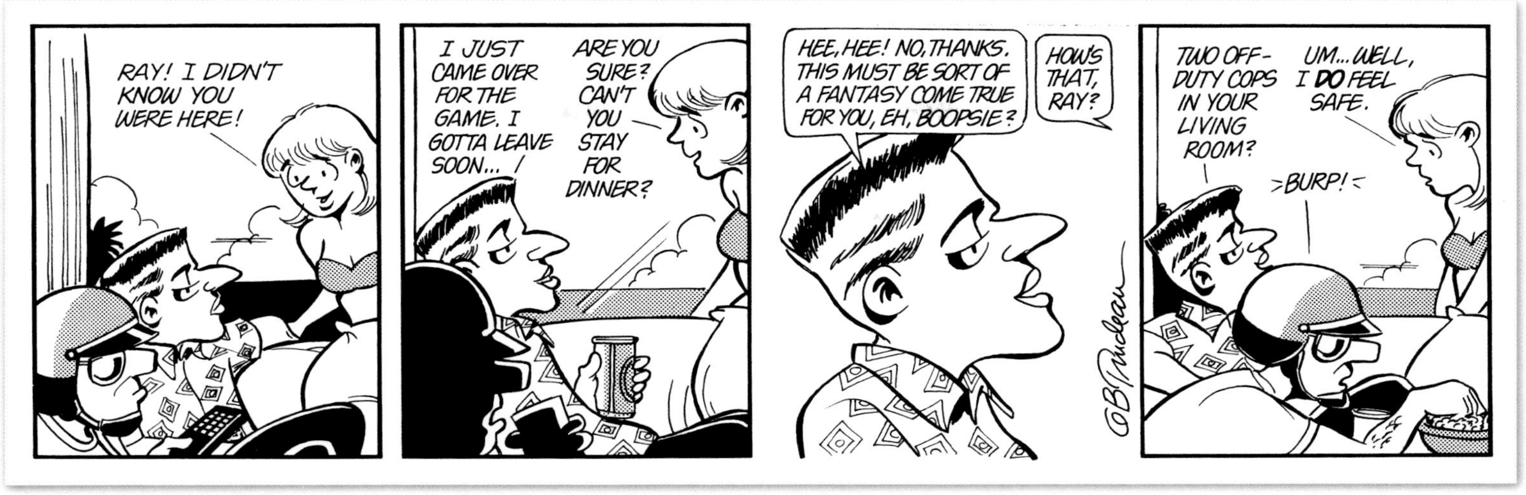
RAY! I DIDN'T KNOW YOU WERE HERE!
I JUST CAME OVER FOR THE GAME. I GOTTA LEAVE SOON...
ARE YOU SURE? CAN'T YOU STAY FOR DINNER?
HEE, HEE! NO, THANKS. THIS MUST BE SORT OF A FANTASY COME TRUE FOR YOU, EH, BOOPSIE?
HOW'S THAT, RAY?
TWO OFF-DUTY COPS IN YOUR LIVING ROOM?
UM... WELL, I DO FEEL SAFE.
BURP!

10/5/92

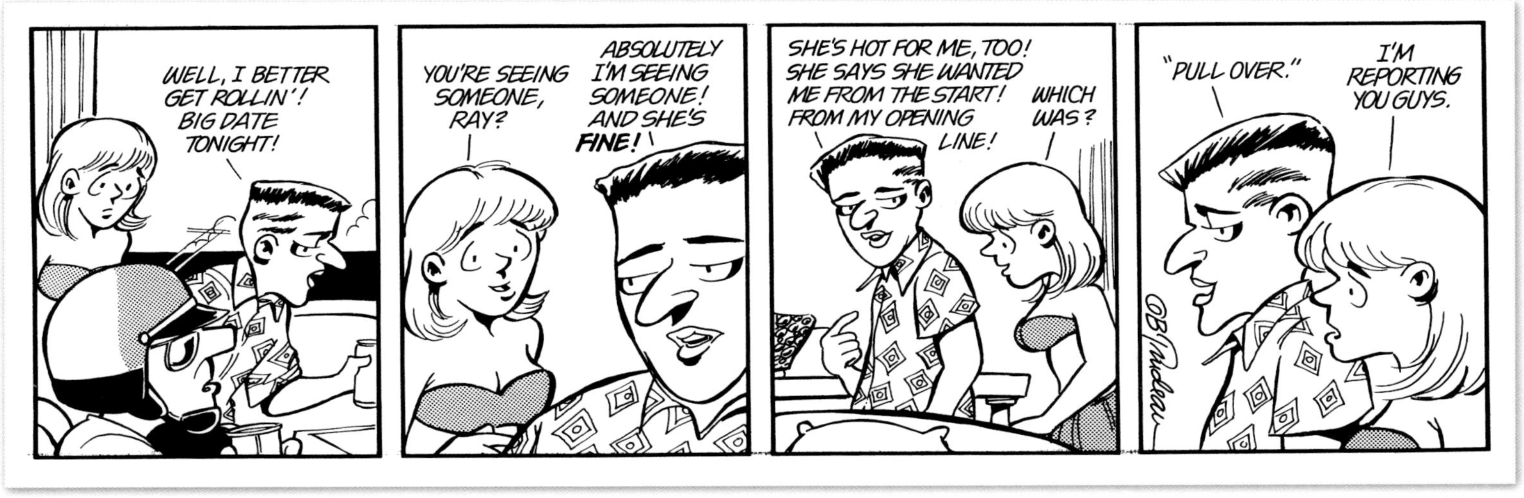
WELL, I BETTER GET ROLLIN'! BIG DATE TONIGHT!
YOU'RE SEEING SOMEONE, RAY?
ABSOLUTELY I'M SEEING SOMEONE! AND SHE'S FINE!
SHE'S HOT FOR ME, TOO! SHE SAYS SHE WANTED ME FROM THE START! FROM MY OPENING LINE!
WHICH WAS?
"PULL OVER."
I'M REPORTING YOU GUYS.

10/7/92

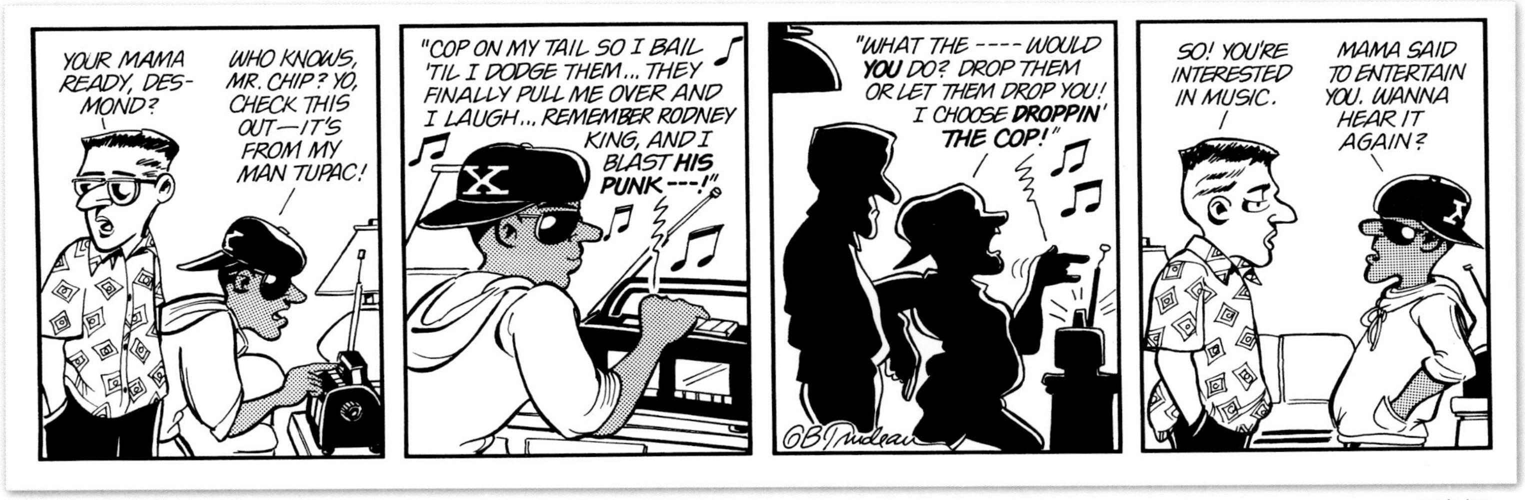
YOUR MAMA READY, DESMOND?
WHO KNOWS, MR. CHIP? YO, CHECK THIS OUT—IT'S FROM MY MAN TUPAC!
"COP ON MY TAIL SO I BAIL 'TIL I DODGE THEM... THEY FINALLY PULL ME OVER AND I LAUGH... REMEMBER RODNEY KING, AND I BLAST HIS PUNK---!"
"WHAT THE ---- WOULD YOU DO? DROP THEM OR LET THEM DROP YOU! I CHOOSE DROPPIN' THE COP!"
SO! YOU'RE INTERESTED IN MUSIC.
MAMA SAID TO ENTERTAIN YOU. WANNA HEAR IT AGAIN?

10/9/92

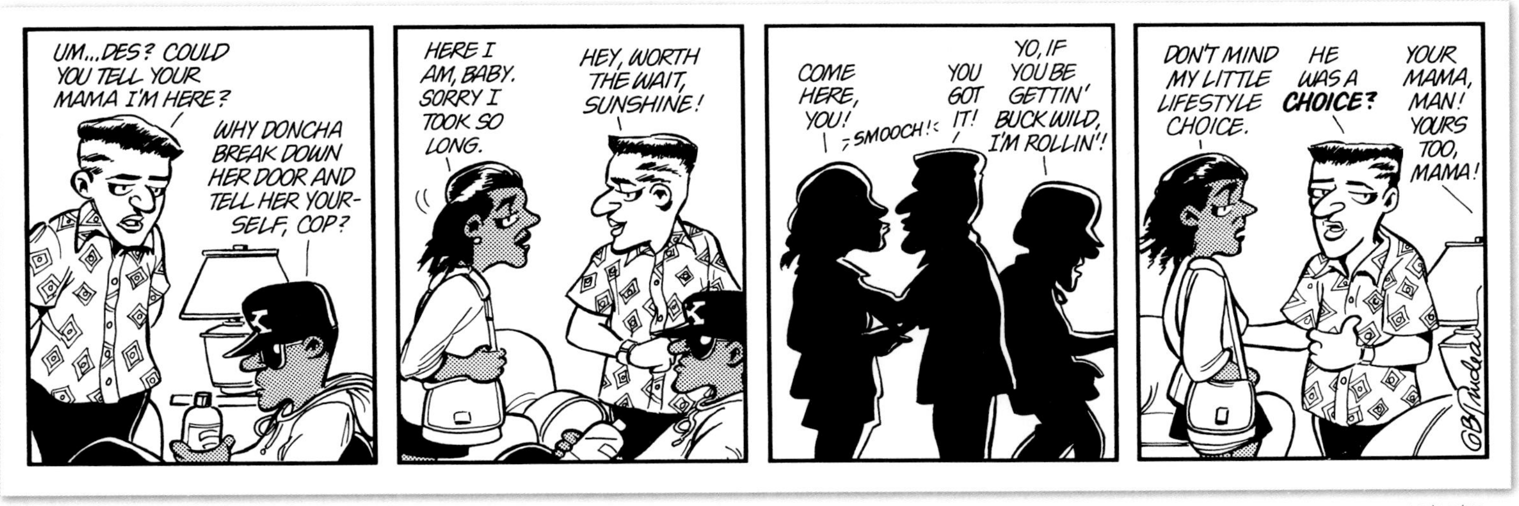
UM...DES? COULD YOU TELL YOUR MAMA I'M HERE?
WHY DONCHA BREAK DOWN HER DOOR AND TELL HER YOURSELF, COP?
HERE I AM, BABY. SORRY I TOOK SO LONG.
HEY, WORTH THE WAIT, SUNSHINE!
COME HERE, YOU!
SMOOCH!
YOU GOT IT!
YO, IF YOU BE GETTIN' BUCK WILD, I'M ROLLIN'!
DON'T MIND MY LITTLE LIFESTYLE CHOICE.
HE WAS A CHOICE?
YOUR MAMA, MAN! YOURS TOO, MAMA!

10/10/92

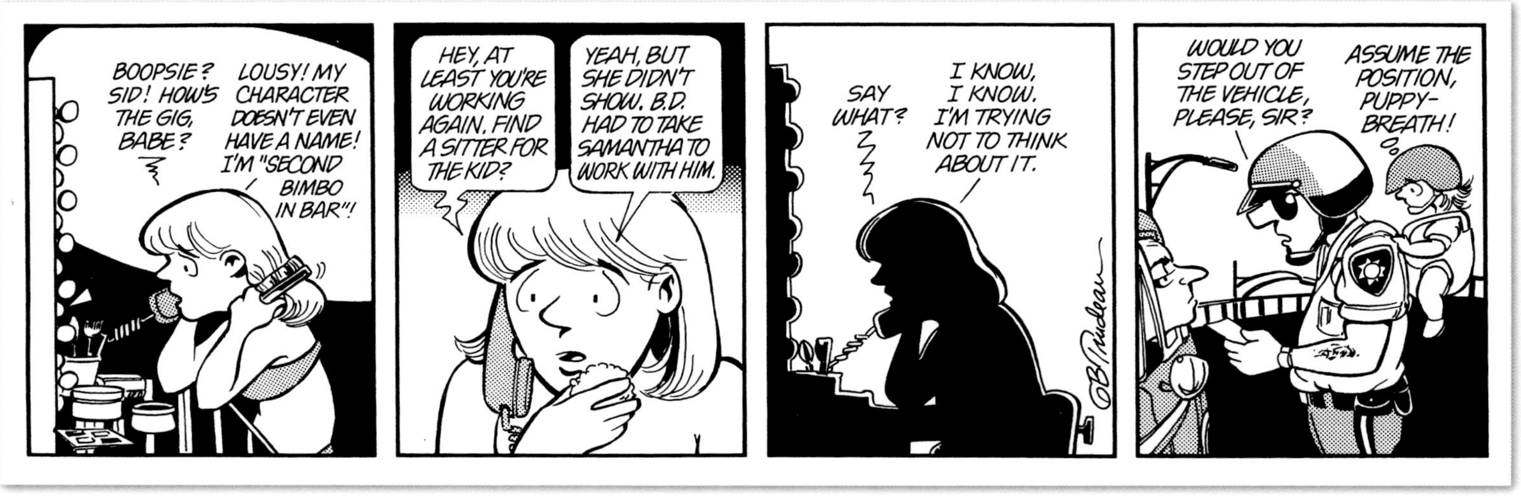
BOOPSIE? SID! HOW'S THE GIG, BABE?
LOUSY! MY CHARACTER DOESN'T EVEN HAVE A NAME! I'M "SECOND BIMBO IN BAR"!
HEY, AT LEAST YOU'RE WORKING AGAIN. FIND A SITTER FOR THE KID?
YEAH, BUT SHE DIDN'T SHOW. B.D. HAD TO TAKE SAMANTHA TO WORK WITH HIM.
SAY WHAT?
I KNOW, I KNOW. I'M TRYING NOT TO THINK ABOUT IT.
WOULD YOU STEP OUT OF THE VEHICLE, PLEASE, SIR?
ASSUME THE POSITION, PUPPY-BREATH!

11/9/92

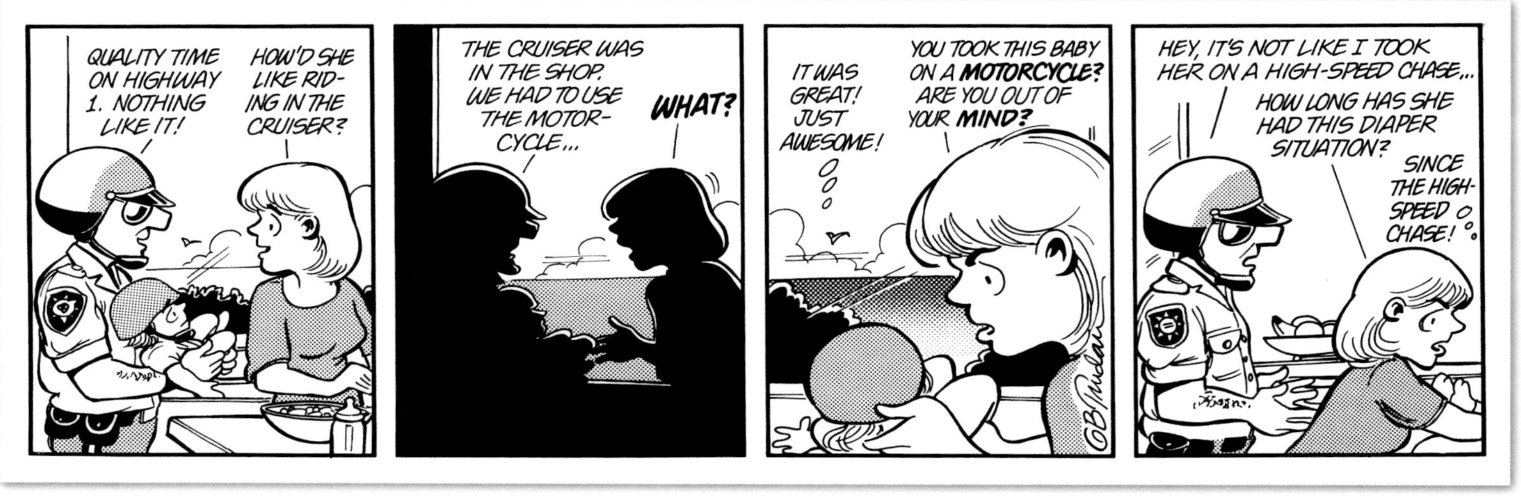
QUALITY TIME ON HIGHWAY 1. NOTHING LIKE IT!
HOW'D SHE LIKE RIDING IN THE CRUISER?
THE CRUISER WAS IN THE SHOP. WE HAD TO USE THE MOTORCYCLE...
WHAT?
IT WAS GREAT! JUST AWESOME!
YOU TOOK THIS BABY ON A MOTORCYCLE? ARE YOU OUT OF YOUR MIND?
HEY, IT'S NOT LIKE I TOOK HER ON A HIGH-SPEED CHASE...
HOW LONG HAS SHE HAD THIS DIAPER SITUATION?
SINCE THE HIGH-SPEED CHASE!

11/11/92

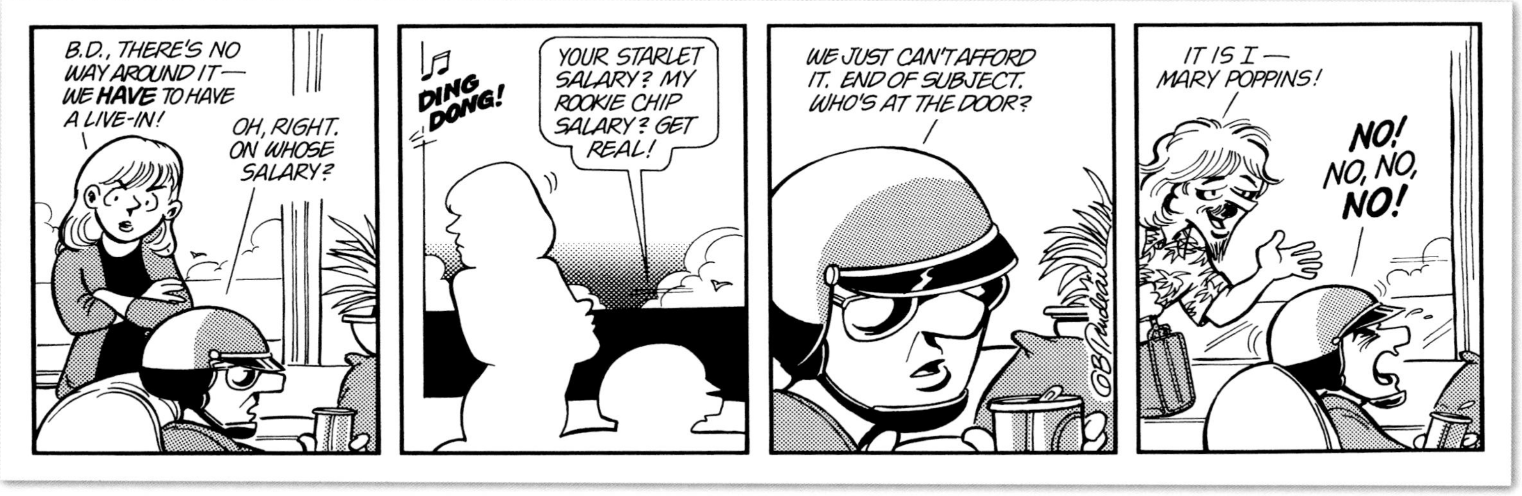
B.D., THERE'S NO WAY AROUND IT — WE HAVE TO HAVE A LIVE-IN!
OH, RIGHT. ON WHOSE SALARY?
DING DONG!
YOUR STARLET SALARY? MY ROOKIE CHIP SALARY? GET REAL!
WE JUST CAN'T AFFORD IT. END OF SUBJECT. WHO'S AT THE DOOR?
IT IS I — MARY POPPINS!
NO! NO, NO, NO!

11/14/92

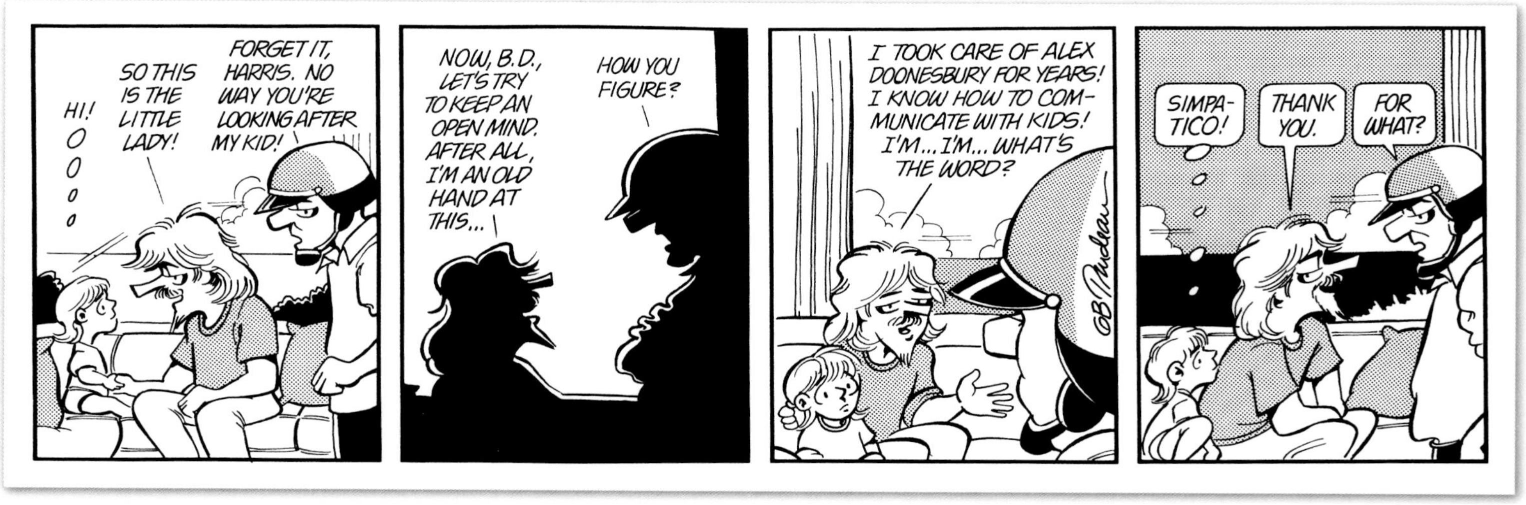
HI!
SO THIS IS THE LITTLE LADY!
FORGET IT, HARRIS. NO WAY YOU'RE LOOKING AFTER MY KID!
NOW, B.D., LET'S TRY TO KEEP AN OPEN MIND. AFTER ALL, I'M AN OLD HAND AT THIS...
HOW YOU FIGURE?
I TOOK CARE OF ALEX DOONESBURY FOR YEARS! I KNOW HOW TO COMMUNICATE WITH KIDS! I'M... I'M... WHAT'S THE WORD?
SIMPATICO!
THANK YOU.
FOR WHAT?

11/16/92

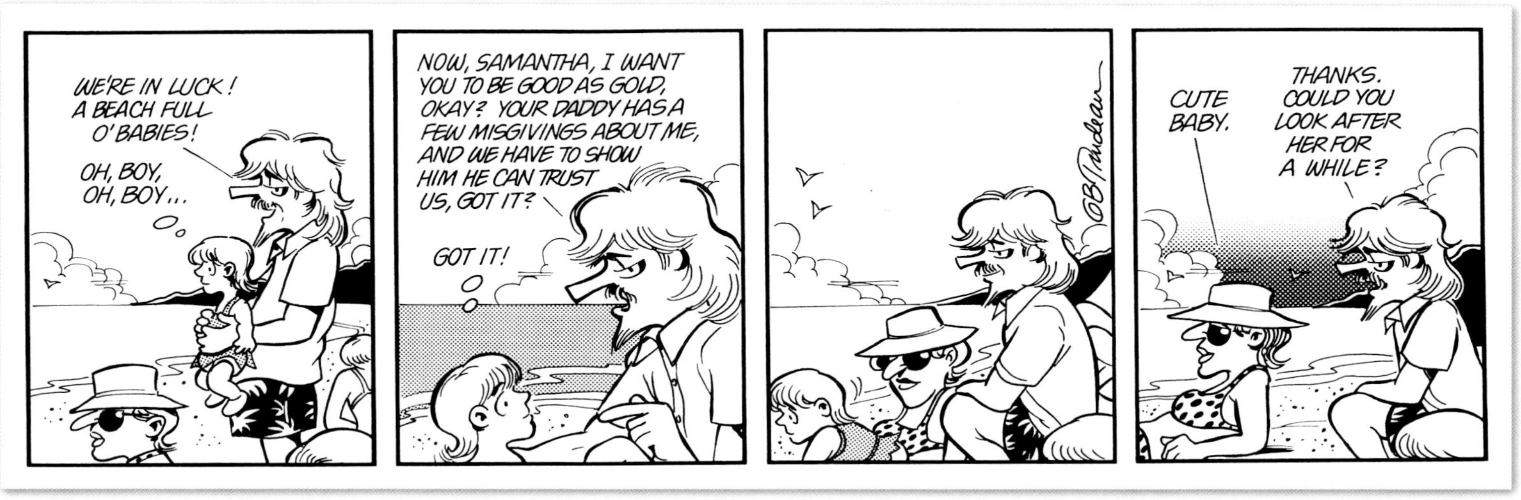
WE'RE IN LUCK! A BEACH FULL O' BABIES!
OH, BOY, OH, BOY...
NOW, SAMANTHA, I WANT YOU TO BE GOOD AS GOLD, OKAY? YOUR DADDY HAS A FEW MISGIVINGS ABOUT ME, AND WE HAVE TO SHOW HIM HE CAN TRUST US, GOT IT?
GOT IT!
CUTE BABY.
THANKS. COULD YOU LOOK AFTER HER FOR A WHILE?

11/17/92

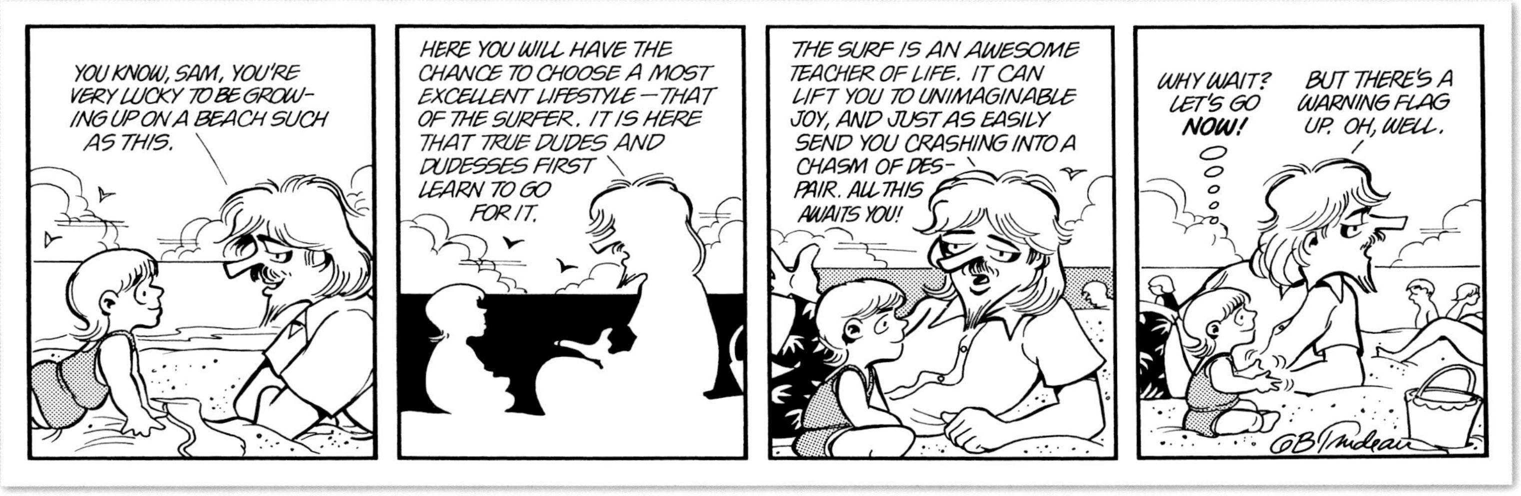
YOU KNOW, SAM, YOU'RE VERY LUCKY TO BE GROWING UP ON A BEACH SUCH AS THIS.
HERE YOU WILL HAVE THE CHANCE TO CHOOSE A MOST EXCELLENT LIFESTYLE—THAT OF THE SURFER. IT IS HERE THAT TRUE DUDES AND DUDESSES FIRST LEARN TO GO FOR IT.
THE SURF IS AN AWESOME TEACHER OF LIFE. IT CAN LIFT YOU TO UNIMAGINABLE JOY, AND JUST AS EASILY SEND YOU CRASHING INTO A CHASM OF DESPAIR. ALL THIS AWAITS YOU!
WHY WAIT? LET'S GO NOW!
BUT THERE'S A WARNING FLAG UP. OH, WELL.

11/19/92

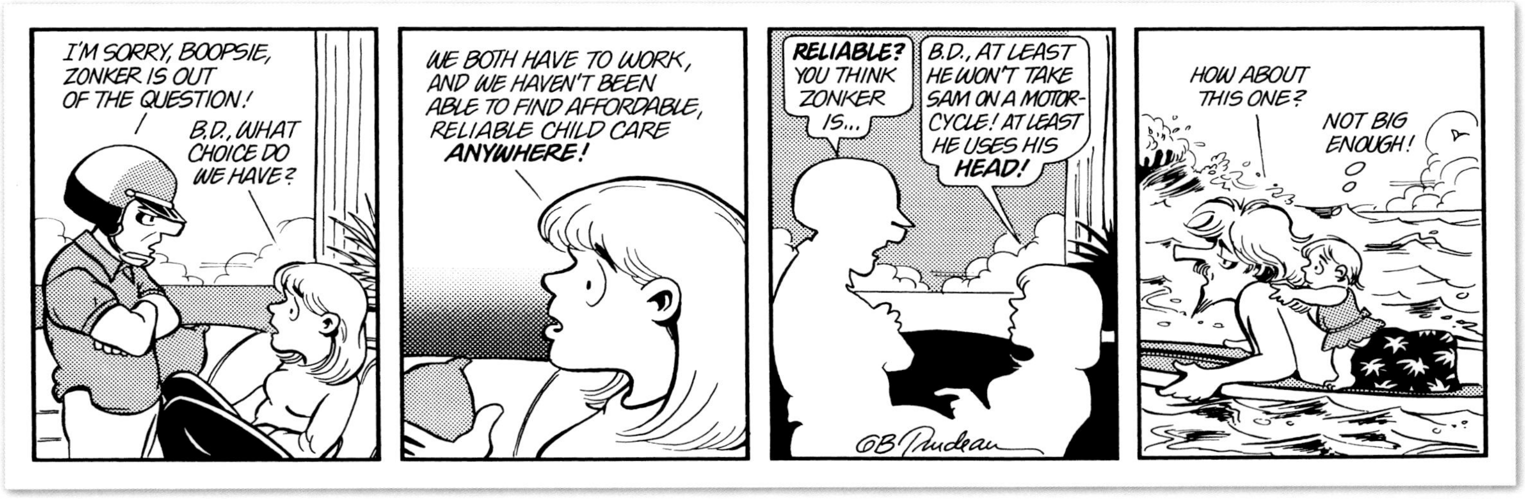
I'M SORRY, BOOPSIE, ZONKER IS OUT OF THE QUESTION!
B.D., WHAT CHOICE DO WE HAVE?
WE BOTH HAVE TO WORK, AND WE HAVEN'T BEEN ABLE TO FIND AFFORDABLE, RELIABLE CHILD CARE ANYWHERE!
RELIABLE? YOU THINK ZONKER IS...
B.D., AT LEAST HE WON'T TAKE SAM ON A MOTORCYCLE! AT LEAST HE USES HIS HEAD!
HOW ABOUT THIS ONE?
NOT BIG ENOUGH!

11/20/92

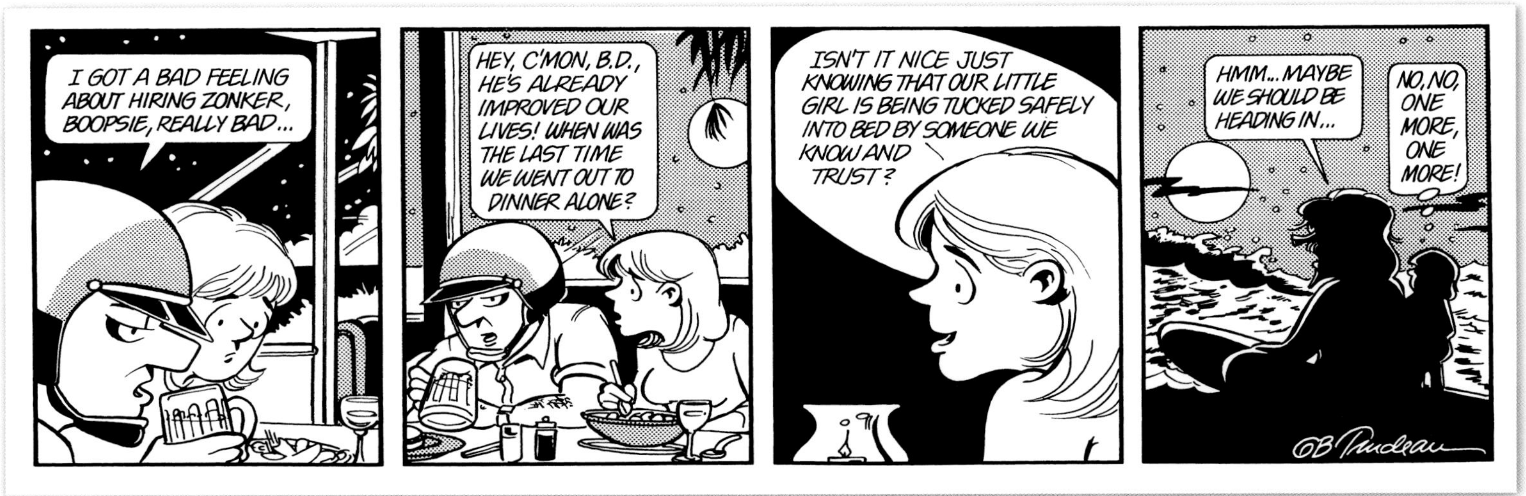
I GOT A BAD FEELING ABOUT HIRING ZONKER, BOOPSIE, REALLY BAD...
HEY, C'MON, B.D., HE'S ALREADY IMPROVED OUR LIVES! WHEN WAS THE LAST TIME WE WENT OUT TO DINNER ALONE?
ISN'T IT NICE JUST KNOWING THAT OUR LITTLE GIRL IS BEING TUCKED SAFELY INTO BED BY SOMEONE WE KNOW AND TRUST?
HMM... MAYBE WE SHOULD BE HEADING IN...
NO, NO, ONE MORE, ONE MORE!

11/21/92

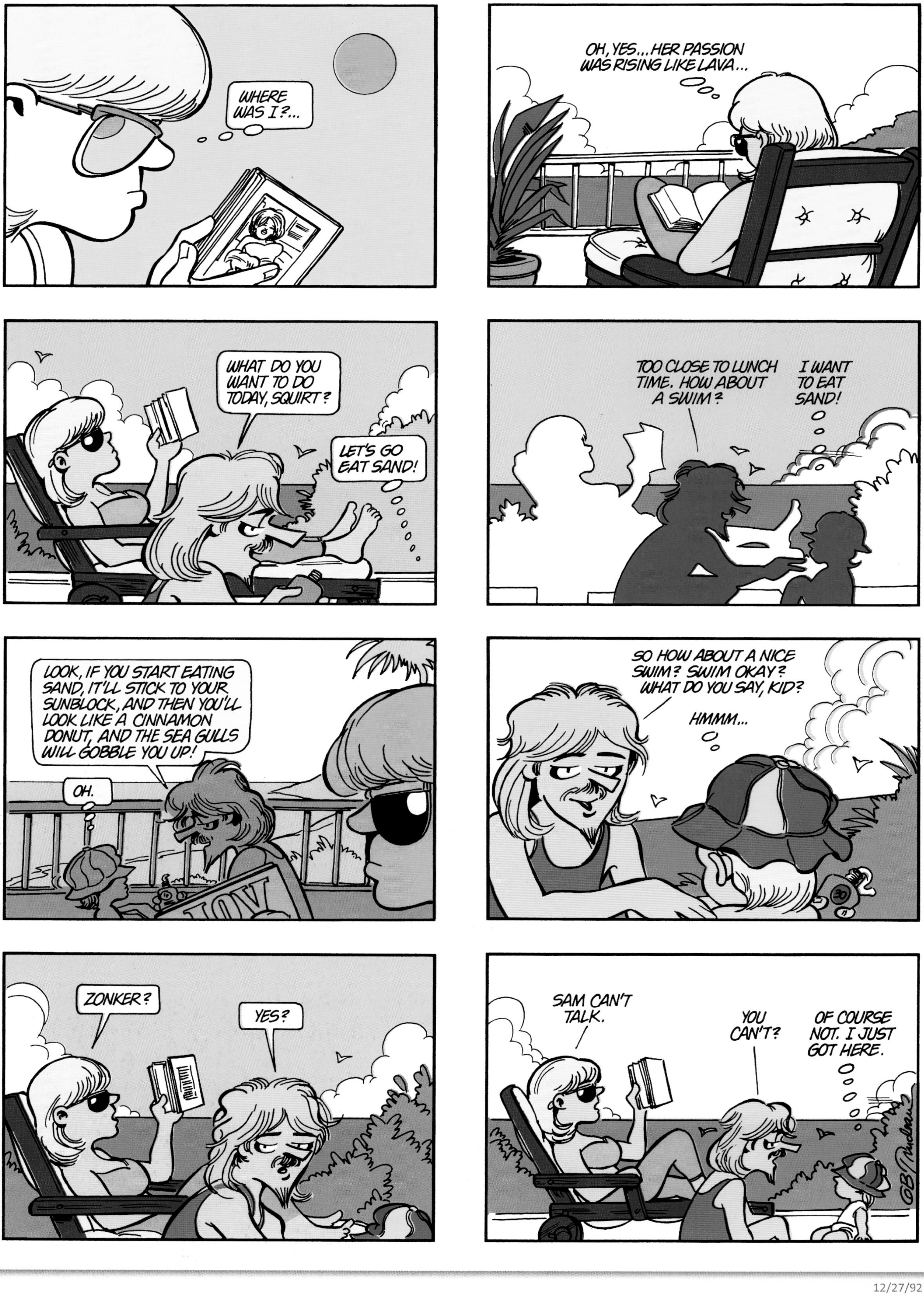
WHERE WAS I?...
OH, YES... HER PASSION WAS RISING LIKE LAVA...
WHAT DO YOU WANT TO DO TODAY, SQUIRT?
LET'S GO EAT SAND!
TOO CLOSE TO LUNCH TIME. HOW ABOUT A SWIM?
I WANT TO EAT SAND!
LOOK, IF YOU START EATING SAND, IT'LL STICK TO YOUR SUNBLOCK, AND THEN YOU'LL LOOK LIKE A CINNAMON DONUT, AND THE SEA GULLS WILL GOBBLE YOU UP!
OH.
SO HOW ABOUT A NICE SWIM? SWIM OKAY? WHAT DO YOU SAY, KID?
HMMM...
ZONKER?
YES?
SAM CAN'T TALK.
YOU CAN'T?
OF COURSE NOT. I JUST GOT HERE.

12/27/92

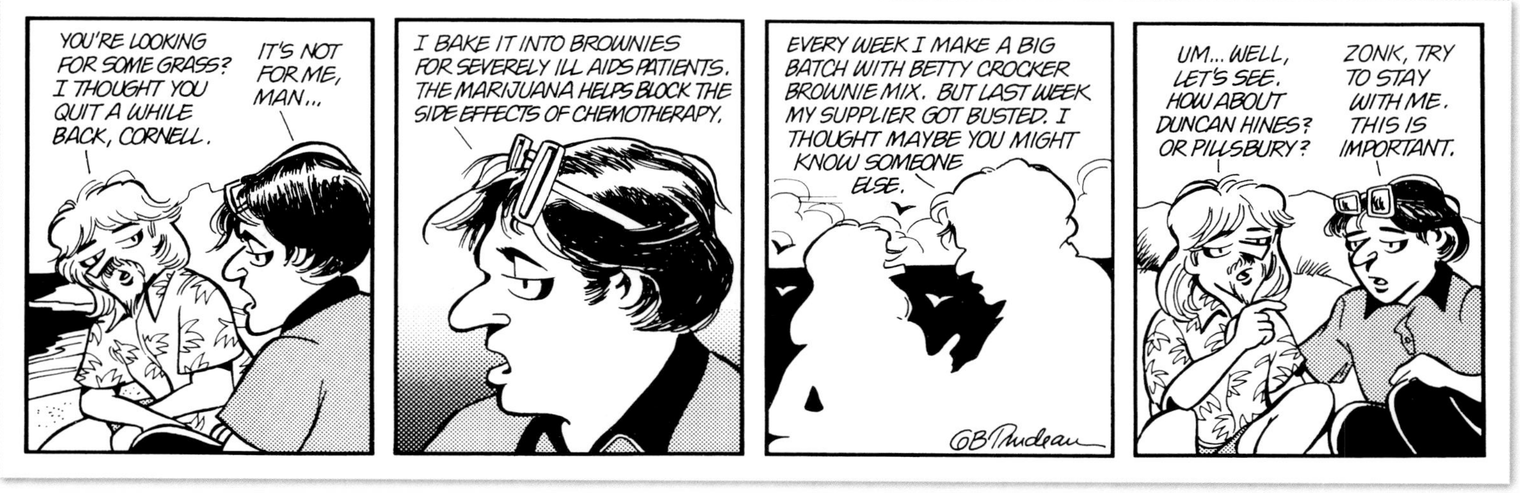
YOU'RE LOOKING FOR SOME GRASS? I THOUGHT YOU QUIT A WHILE BACK, CORNELL.
IT'S NOT FOR ME, MAN...
I BAKE IT INTO BROWNIES FOR SEVERELY ILL AIDS PATIENTS. THE MARIJUANA HELPS BLOCK THE SIDE EFFECTS OF CHEMOTHERAPY.
EVERY WEEK I MAKE A BIG BATCH WITH BETTY CROCKER BROWNIE MIX. BUT LAST WEEK MY SUPPLIER GOT BUSTED. I THOUGHT MAYBE YOU MIGHT KNOW SOMEONE ELSE.
UM... WELL, LET'S SEE. HOW ABOUT DUNCAN HINES? OR PILLSBURY?
ZONK, TRY TO STAY WITH ME. THIS IS IMPORTANT.

2/10/93

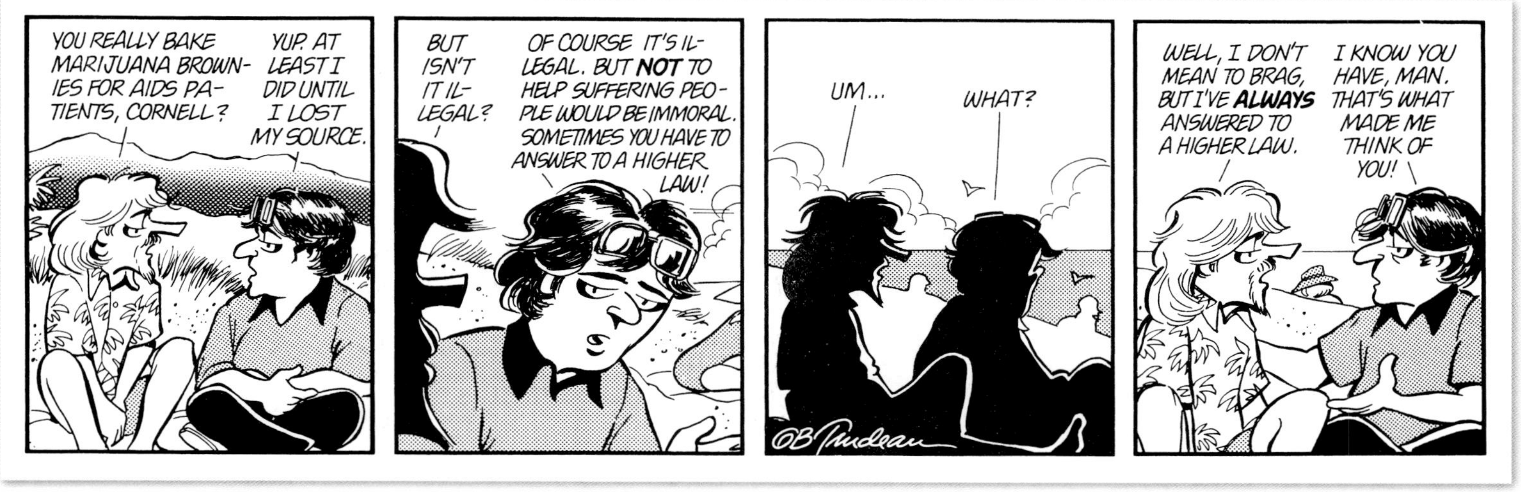
YOU REALLY BAKE MARIJUANA BROWNIES FOR AIDS PATIENTS, CORNELL?
YUP. AT LEAST I DID UNTIL I LOST MY SOURCE.
BUT ISN'T IT ILLEGAL?
OF COURSE IT'S ILLEGAL. BUT **NOT** TO HELP SUFFERING PEOPLE WOULD BE IMMORAL. SOMETIMES YOU HAVE TO ANSWER TO A HIGHER LAW!
UM...
WHAT?
WELL, I DON'T MEAN TO BRAG, BUT I'VE **ALWAYS** ANSWERED TO A HIGHER LAW.
I KNOW YOU HAVE, MAN. THAT'S WHAT MADE ME THINK OF YOU!

2/11/93

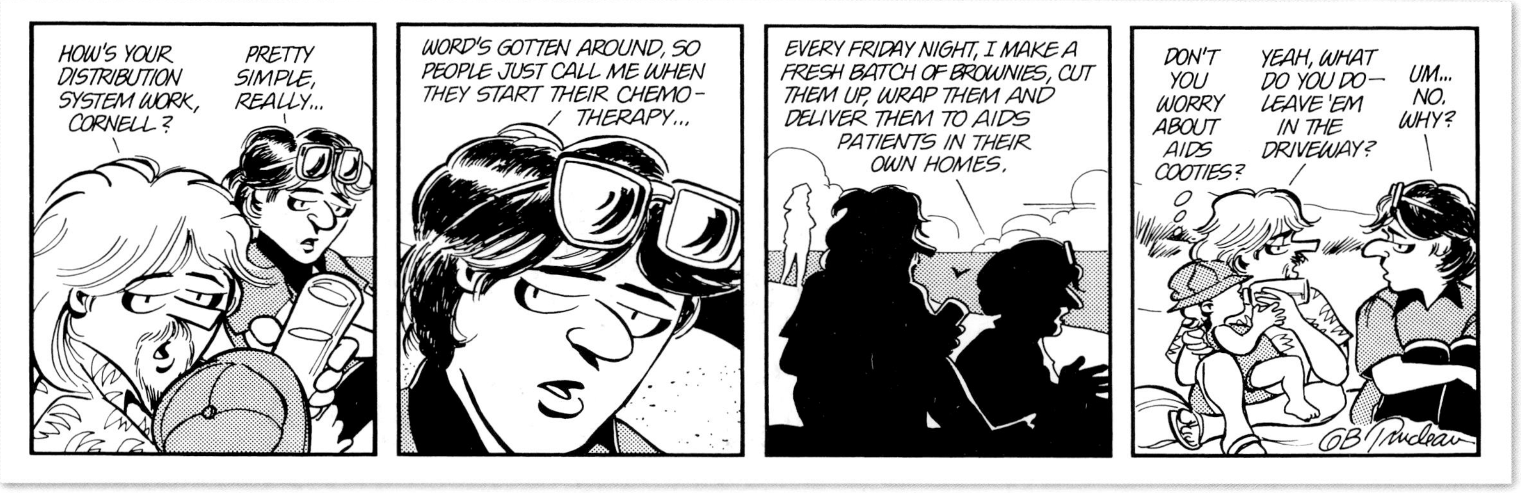
HOW'S YOUR DISTRIBUTION SYSTEM WORK, CORNELL?
PRETTY SIMPLE, REALLY...
WORD'S GOTTEN AROUND, SO PEOPLE JUST CALL ME WHEN THEY START THEIR CHEMOTHERAPY...
EVERY FRIDAY NIGHT, I MAKE A FRESH BATCH OF BROWNIES, CUT THEM UP, WRAP THEM AND DELIVER THEM TO AIDS PATIENTS IN THEIR OWN HOMES.
DON'T YOU WORRY ABOUT AIDS COOTIES?
YEAH, WHAT DO YOU DO— LEAVE 'EM IN THE DRIVEWAY?
UM... NO. WHY?

2/12/93

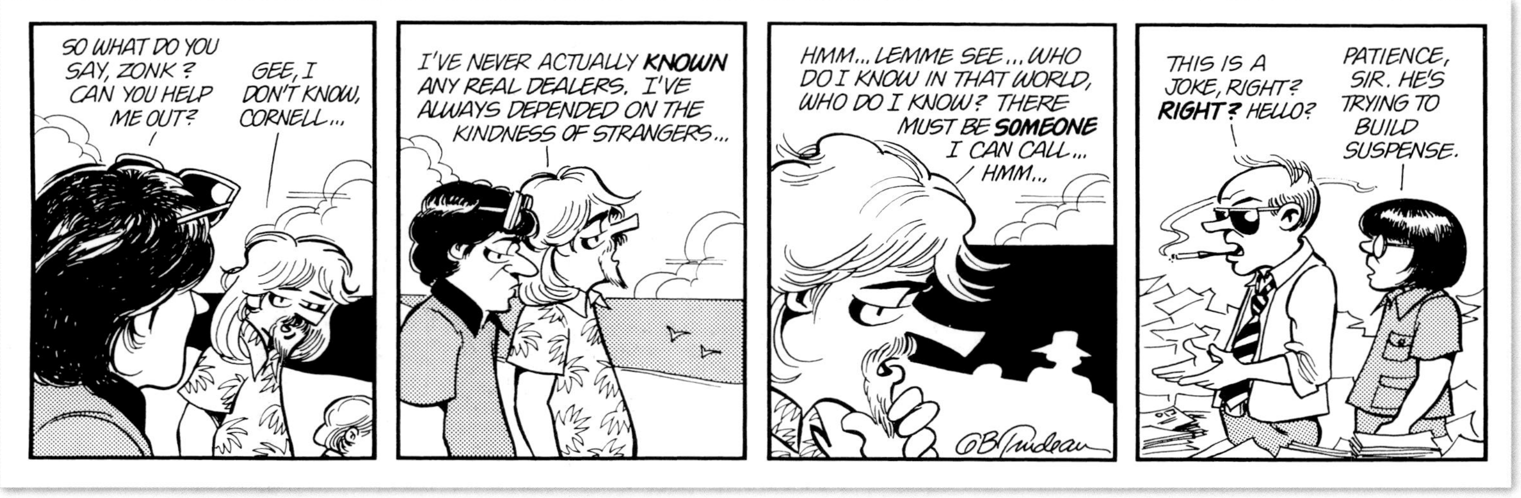
SO WHAT DO YOU SAY, ZONK? CAN YOU HELP ME OUT?
GEE, I DON'T KNOW, CORNELL...
I'VE NEVER ACTUALLY **KNOWN** ANY REAL DEALERS. I'VE ALWAYS DEPENDED ON THE KINDNESS OF STRANGERS...
HMM... LEMME SEE... WHO DO I KNOW IN THAT WORLD, WHO DO I KNOW? THERE MUST BE **SOMEONE** I CAN CALL... HMM...
THIS IS A JOKE, RIGHT? **RIGHT?** HELLO?
PATIENCE, SIR. HE'S TRYING TO BUILD SUSPENSE.

2/15/93

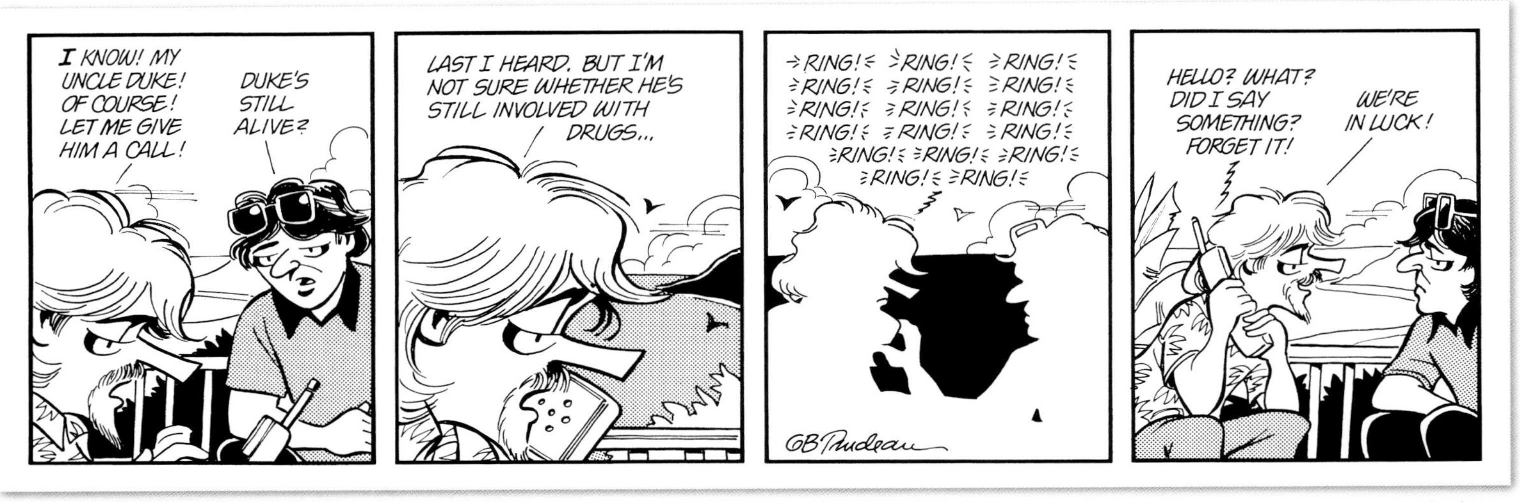
I KNOW! MY UNCLE DUKE! OF COURSE! LET ME GIVE HIM A CALL!
DUKE'S STILL ALIVE?
LAST I HEARD. BUT I'M NOT SURE WHETHER HE'S STILL INVOLVED WITH DRUGS...
RING! RING! RING! RING! RING! RING! RING! RING! RING! RING! RING! RING! RING! RING! RING! RING! RING!
HELLO? WHAT? DID I SAY SOMETHING? FORGET IT!
WE'RE IN LUCK!
GB Trudeau

2/16/93

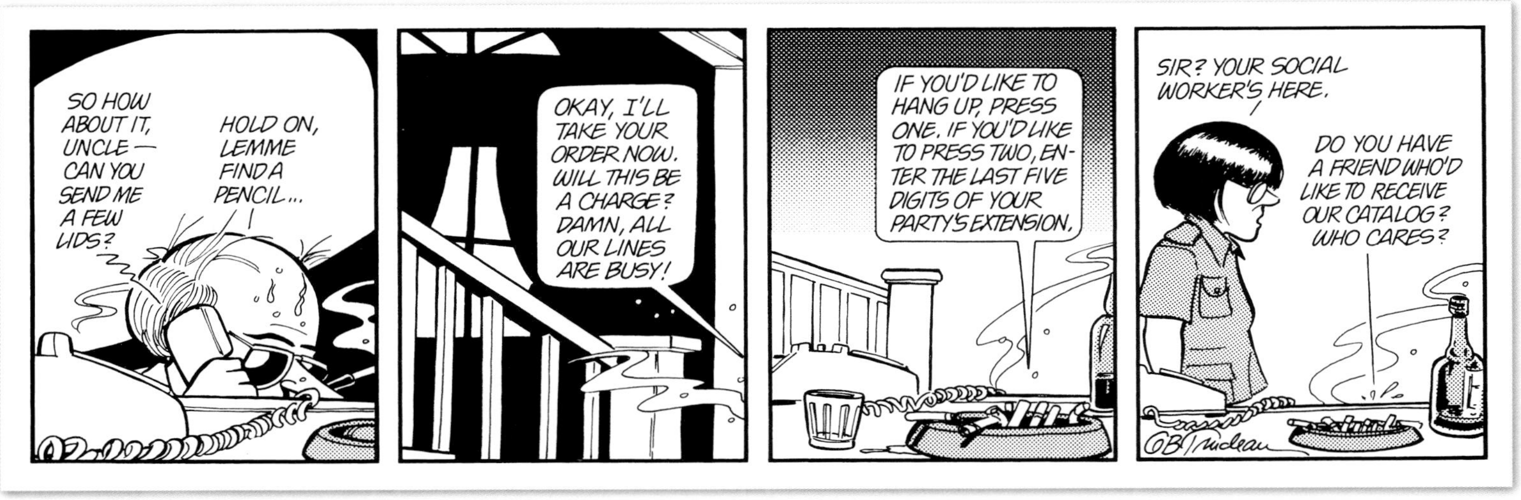
SO HOW ABOUT IT, UNCLE— CAN YOU SEND ME A FEW LIDS?
HOLD ON, LEMME FIND A PENCIL...
OKAY, I'LL TAKE YOUR ORDER NOW. WILL THIS BE A CHARGE? DAMN, ALL OUR LINES ARE BUSY!
IF YOU'D LIKE TO HANG UP, PRESS ONE. IF YOU'D LIKE TO PRESS TWO, ENTER THE LAST FIVE DIGITS OF YOUR PARTY'S EXTENSION.
SIR? YOUR SOCIAL WORKER'S HERE.
DO YOU HAVE A FRIEND WHO'D LIKE TO RECEIVE OUR CATALOG? WHO CARES?
GB Trudeau

2/18/93

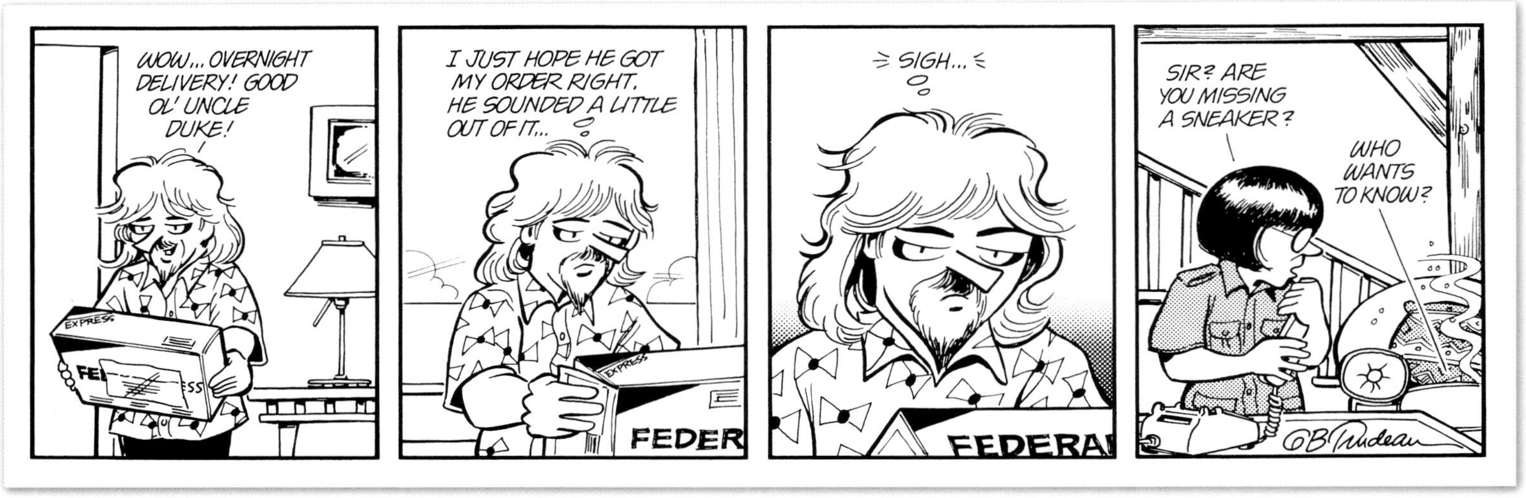
WOW... OVERNIGHT DELIVERY! GOOD OL' UNCLE DUKE!
I JUST HOPE HE GOT MY ORDER RIGHT. HE SOUNDED A LITTLE OUT OF IT...
SIGH...
SIR? ARE YOU MISSING A SNEAKER?
WHO WANTS TO KNOW?
GB Trudeau

2/19/93

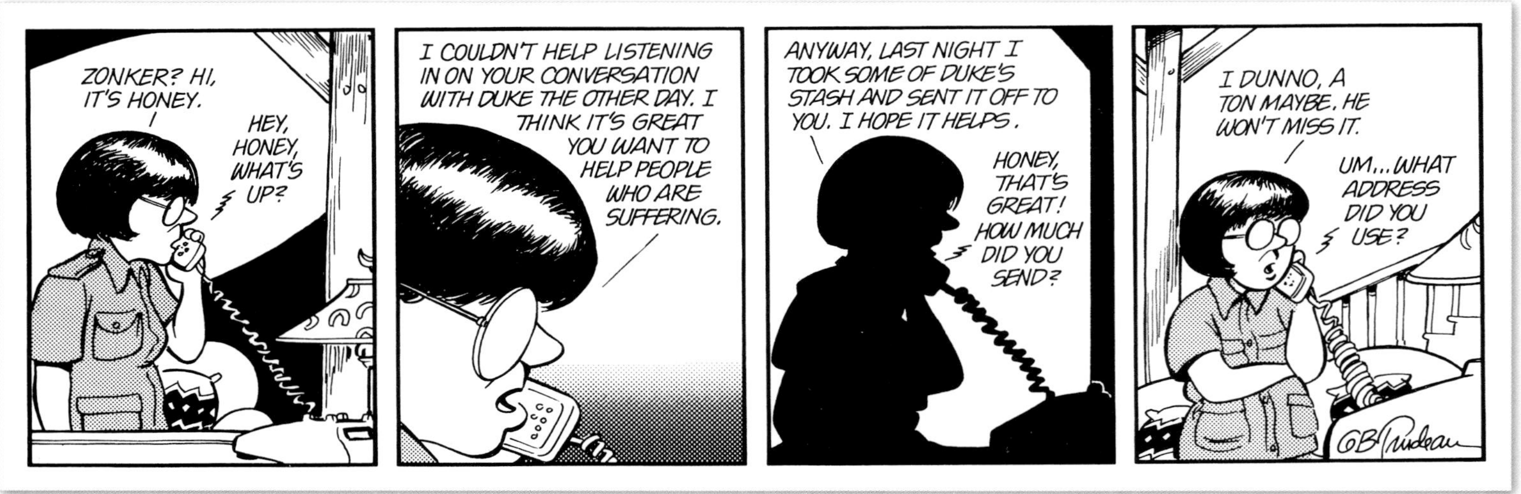
ZONKER? HI, IT'S HONEY.
HEY, HONEY, WHAT'S UP?
I COULDN'T HELP LISTENING IN ON YOUR CONVERSATION WITH DUKE THE OTHER DAY. I THINK IT'S GREAT YOU WANT TO HELP PEOPLE WHO ARE SUFFERING.
ANYWAY, LAST NIGHT I TOOK SOME OF DUKE'S STASH AND SENT IT OFF TO YOU. I HOPE IT HELPS.
HONEY, THAT'S GREAT! HOW MUCH DID YOU SEND?
I DUNNO, A TON MAYBE. HE WON'T MISS IT.
UM... WHAT ADDRESS DID YOU USE?
GB Trudeau

2/20/93

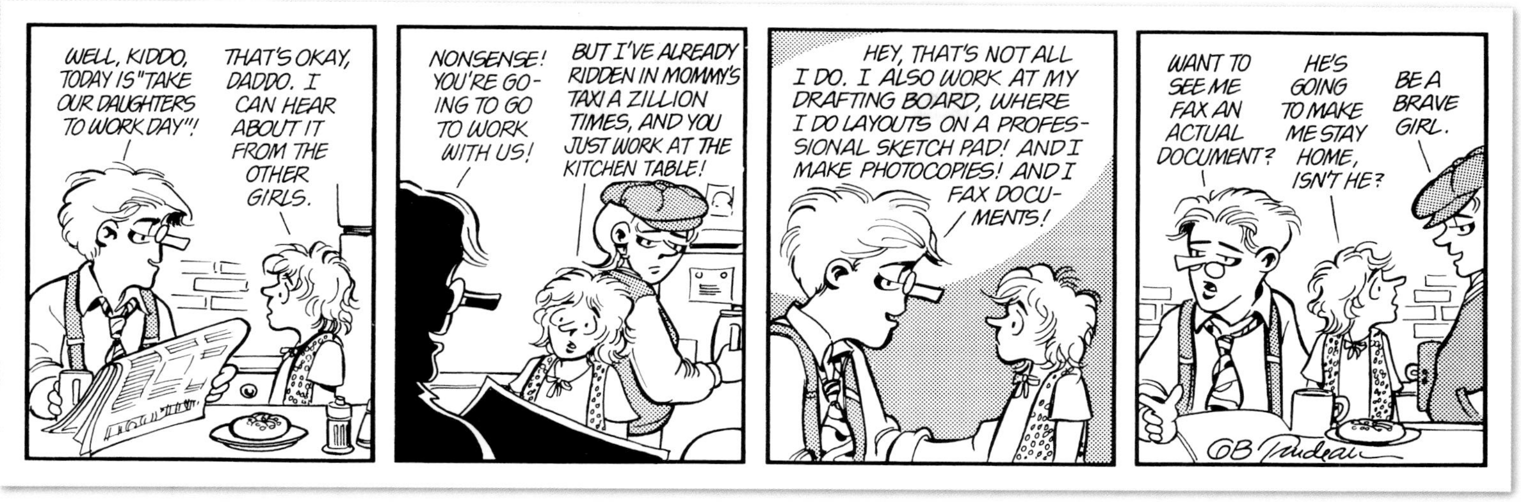
WELL, KIDDO, TODAY IS "TAKE OUR DAUGHTERS TO WORK DAY"!
THAT'S OKAY, DADDO. I CAN HEAR ABOUT IT FROM THE OTHER GIRLS.
NONSENSE! YOU'RE GOING TO GO TO WORK WITH US!
BUT I'VE ALREADY RIDDEN IN MOMMY'S TAXI A ZILLION TIMES, AND YOU JUST WORK AT THE KITCHEN TABLE!
HEY, THAT'S NOT ALL I DO. I ALSO WORK AT MY DRAFTING BOARD, WHERE I DO LAYOUTS ON A PROFESSIONAL SKETCH PAD! AND I MAKE PHOTOCOPIES! AND I FAX DOCUMENTS!
WANT TO SEE ME FAX AN ACTUAL DOCUMENT?
HE'S GOING TO MAKE ME STAY HOME, ISN'T HE?
BE A BRAVE GIRL.
GB Trudeau

4/27/93

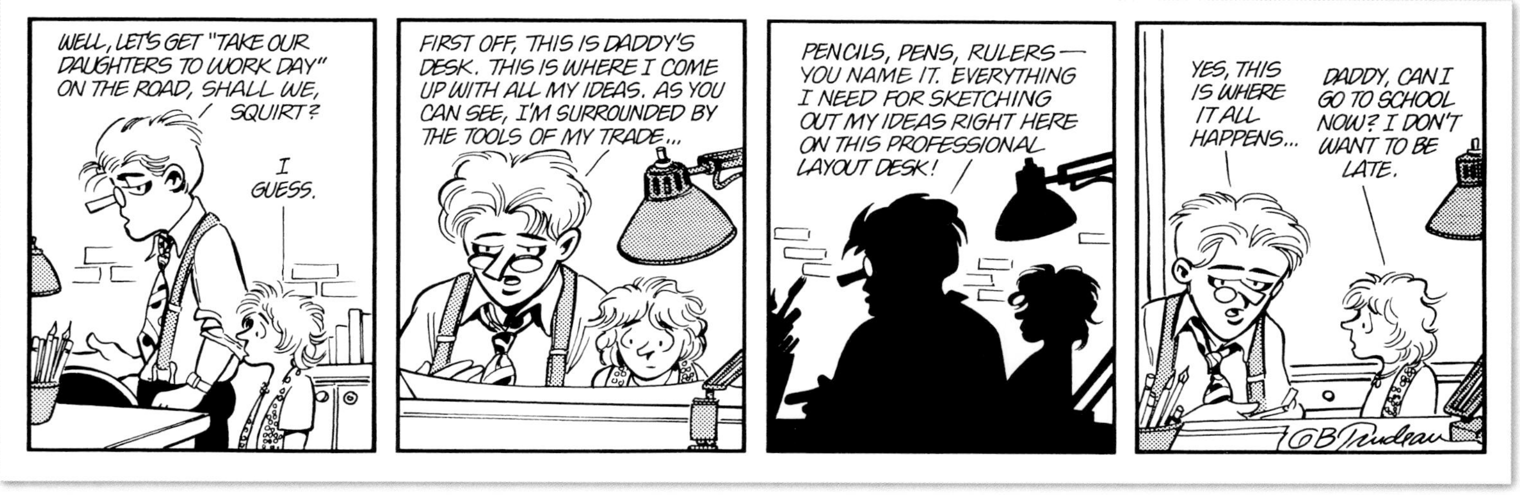
WELL, LET'S GET "TAKE OUR DAUGHTERS TO WORK DAY" ON THE ROAD, SHALL WE, SQUIRT?
I GUESS.
FIRST OFF, THIS IS DADDY'S DESK. THIS IS WHERE I COME UP WITH ALL MY IDEAS. AS YOU CAN SEE, I'M SURROUNDED BY THE TOOLS OF MY TRADE...
PENCILS, PENS, RULERS — YOU NAME IT. EVERYTHING I NEED FOR SKETCHING OUT MY IDEAS RIGHT HERE ON THIS PROFESSIONAL LAYOUT DESK!
YES, THIS IS WHERE IT ALL HAPPENS...
DADDY, CAN I GO TO SCHOOL NOW? I DON'T WANT TO BE LATE.
GB Trudeau

4/28/93

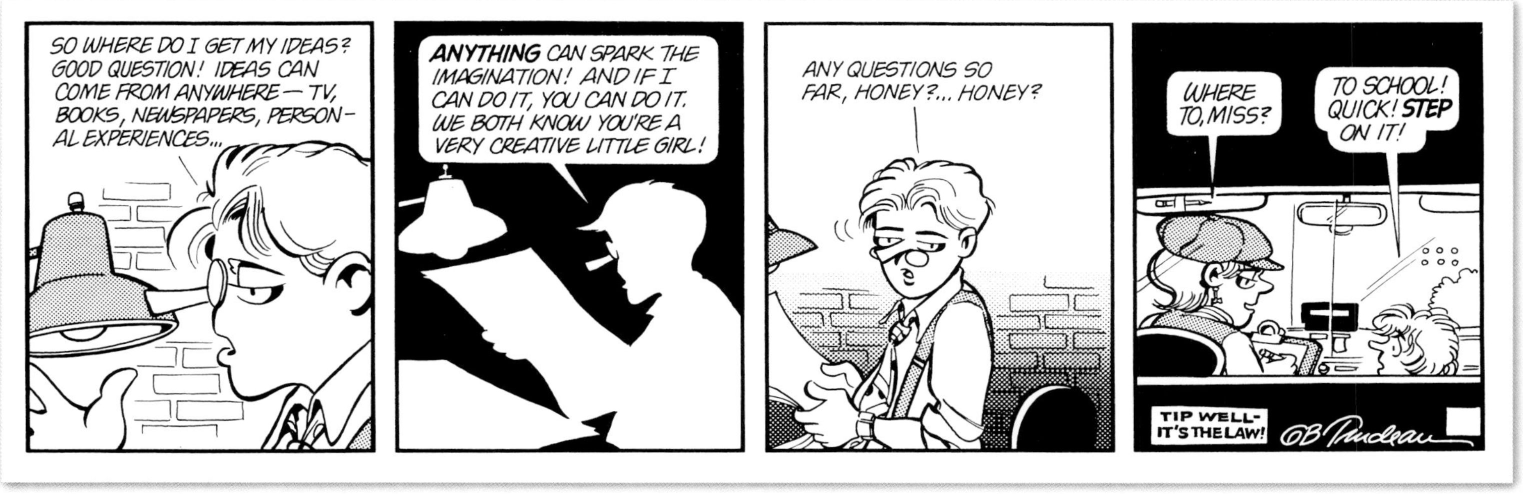
SO WHERE DO I GET MY IDEAS? GOOD QUESTION! IDEAS CAN COME FROM ANYWHERE — TV, BOOKS, NEWSPAPERS, PERSONAL EXPERIENCES...
ANYTHING CAN SPARK THE IMAGINATION! AND IF I CAN DO IT, YOU CAN DO IT. WE BOTH KNOW YOU'RE A VERY CREATIVE LITTLE GIRL!
ANY QUESTIONS SO FAR, HONEY?... HONEY?
WHERE TO, MISS?
TO SCHOOL! QUICK! STEP ON IT!
TIP WELL- IT'S THE LAW!
GB Trudeau

4/29/93

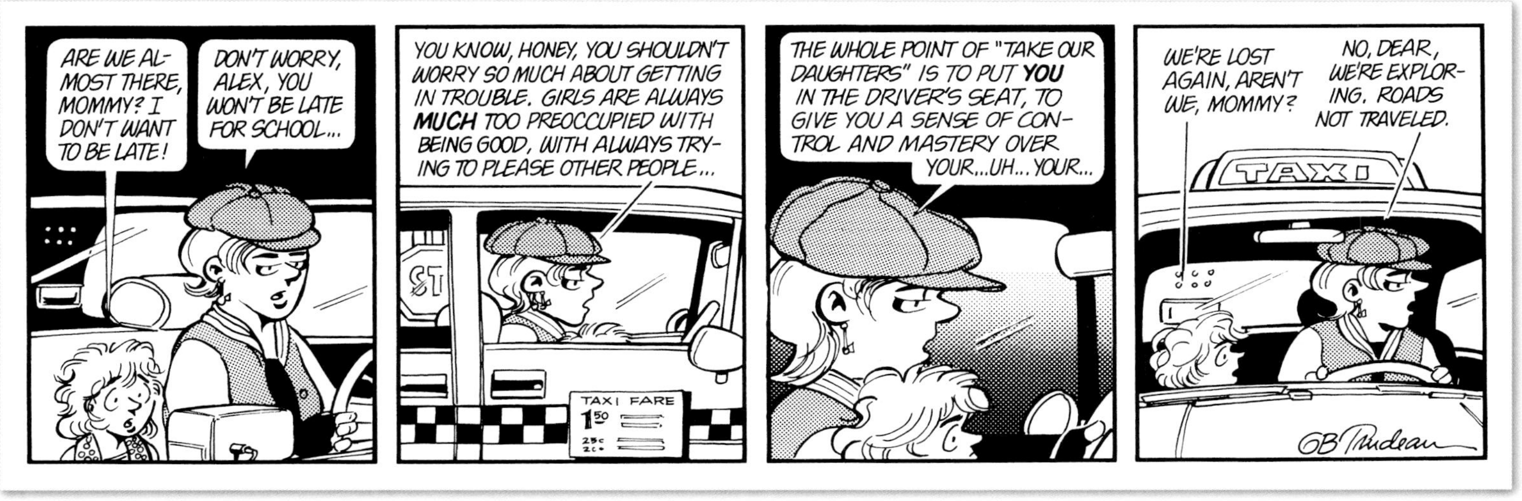
ARE WE ALMOST THERE, MOMMY? I DON'T WANT TO BE LATE!
DON'T WORRY, ALEX, YOU WON'T BE LATE FOR SCHOOL...
YOU KNOW, HONEY, YOU SHOULDN'T WORRY SO MUCH ABOUT GETTING IN TROUBLE. GIRLS ARE ALWAYS MUCH TOO PREOCCUPIED WITH BEING GOOD, WITH ALWAYS TRYING TO PLEASE OTHER PEOPLE...
TAXI FARE
THE WHOLE POINT OF "TAKE OUR DAUGHTERS" IS TO PUT YOU IN THE DRIVER'S SEAT, TO GIVE YOU A SENSE OF CONTROL AND MASTERY OVER YOUR...UH... YOUR...
WE'RE LOST AGAIN, AREN'T WE, MOMMY?
NO, DEAR, WE'RE EXPLORING. ROADS NOT TRAVELED.
TAXI
GB Trudeau

5/1/93

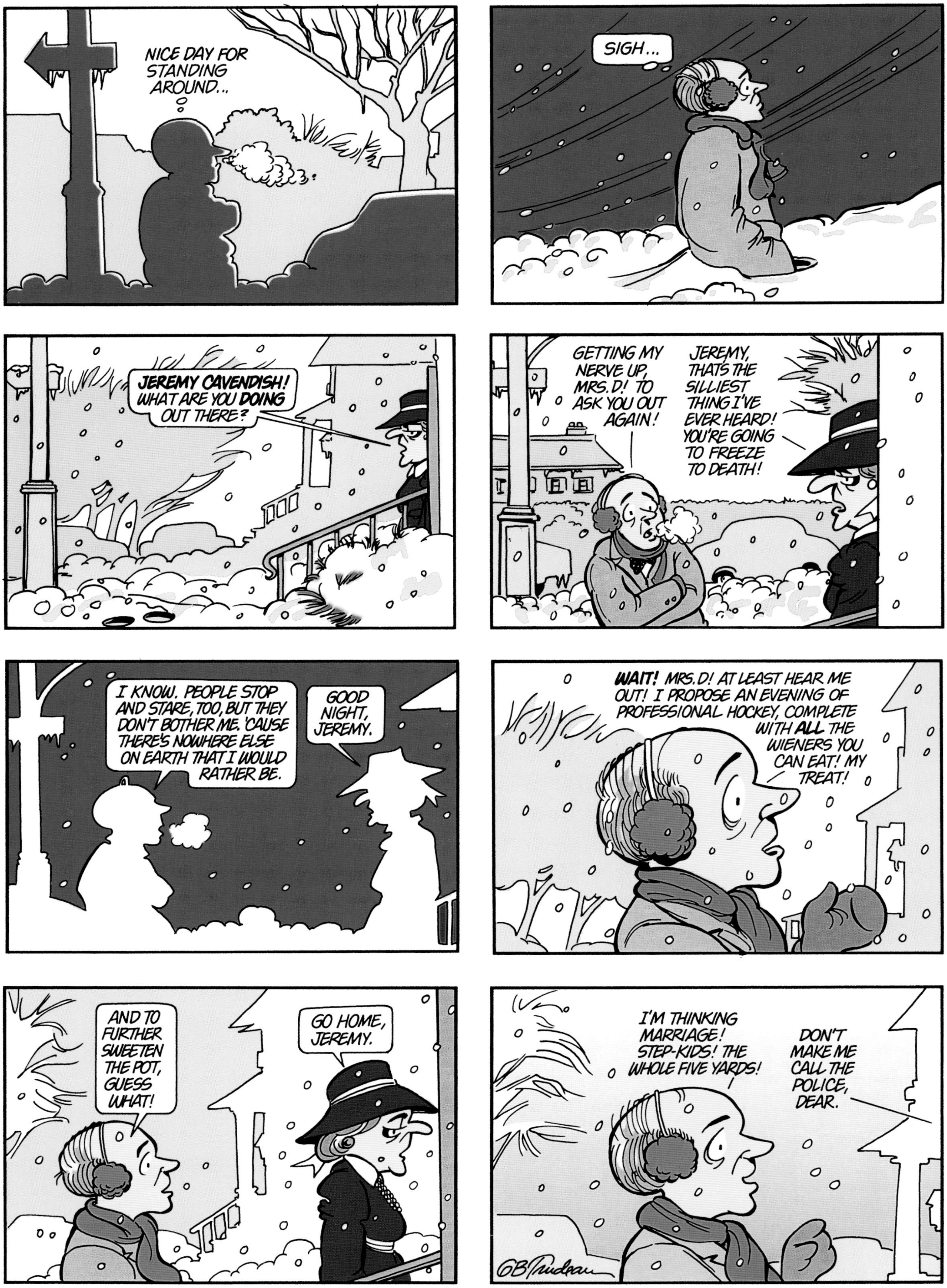
NICE DAY FOR STANDING AROUND...
SIGH...
JEREMY CAVENDISH! WHAT ARE YOU DOING OUT THERE?
GETTING MY NERVE UP, MRS. D! TO ASK YOU OUT AGAIN!
JEREMY, THAT'S THE SILLIEST THING I'VE EVER HEARD! YOU'RE GOING TO FREEZE TO DEATH!
I KNOW. PEOPLE STOP AND STARE, TOO, BUT THEY DON'T BOTHER ME. 'CAUSE THERE'S NOWHERE ELSE ON EARTH THAT I WOULD RATHER BE.
GOOD NIGHT, JEREMY.
WAIT! MRS. D! AT LEAST HEAR ME OUT! I PROPOSE AN EVENING OF PROFESSIONAL HOCKEY, COMPLETE WITH ALL THE WIENERS YOU CAN EAT! MY TREAT!
AND TO FURTHER SWEETEN THE POT, GUESS WHAT!
GO HOME, JEREMY.
I'M THINKING MARRIAGE! STEP-KIDS! THE WHOLE FIVE YARDS!
DON'T MAKE ME CALL THE POLICE, DEAR.
GB Trudeau

1/31/93

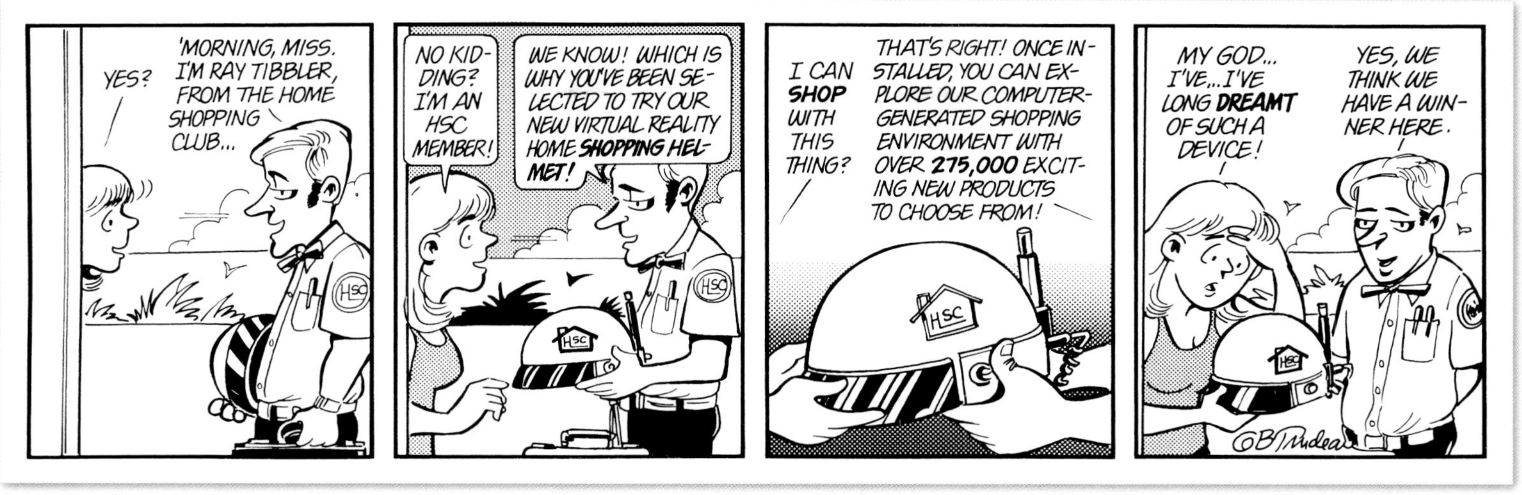
YES?
'MORNING, MISS. I'M RAY TIBBLER, FROM THE HOME SHOPPING CLUB...
NO KIDDING? I'M AN HSC MEMBER!
WE KNOW! WHICH IS WHY YOU'VE BEEN SELECTED TO TRY OUR NEW VIRTUAL REALITY HOME **SHOPPING HELMET!**
I CAN **SHOP** WITH THIS THING?
THAT'S RIGHT! ONCE INSTALLED, YOU CAN EXPLORE OUR COMPUTER-GENERATED SHOPPING ENVIRONMENT WITH OVER **275,000** EXCITING NEW PRODUCTS TO CHOOSE FROM!
MY GOD... I'VE... I'VE LONG **DREAMT** OF SUCH A DEVICE!
YES, WE THINK WE HAVE A WINNER HERE.
©B Trudeau

5/3/93

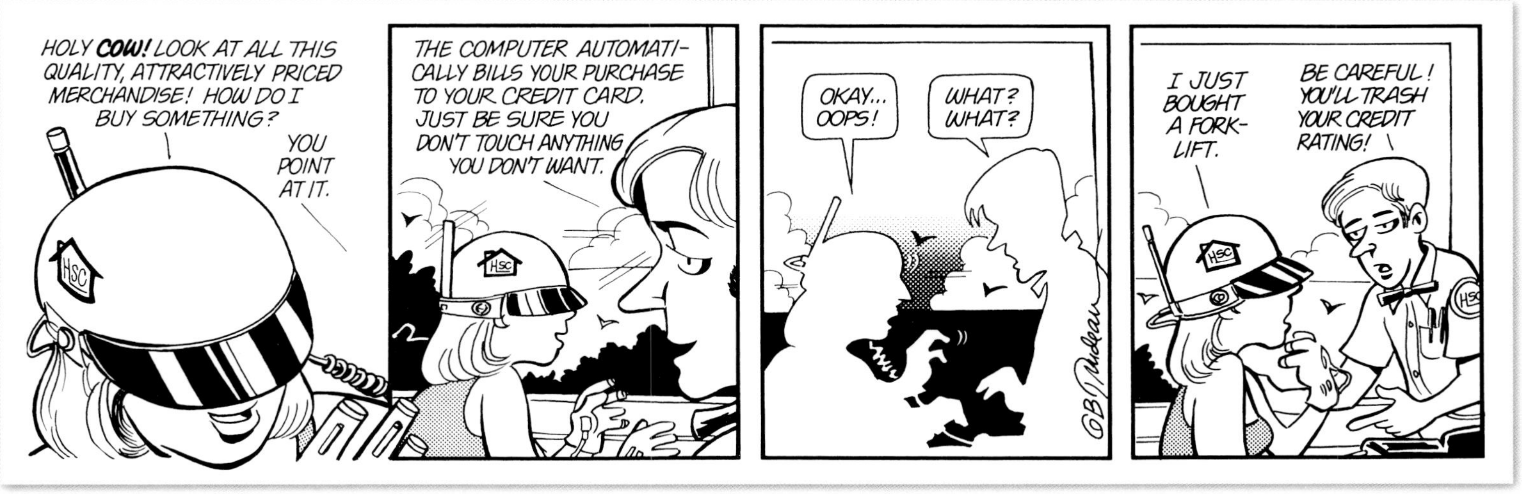
HOLY **COW!** LOOK AT ALL THIS QUALITY, ATTRACTIVELY PRICED MERCHANDISE! HOW DO I BUY SOMETHING?
YOU POINT AT IT.
THE COMPUTER AUTOMATICALLY BILLS YOUR PURCHASE TO YOUR CREDIT CARD. JUST BE SURE YOU DON'T TOUCH ANYTHING YOU DON'T WANT.
OKAY... OOPS!
WHAT? WHAT?
©B Trudeau
I JUST BOUGHT A FORK-LIFT.
BE CAREFUL! YOU'LL TRASH YOUR CREDIT RATING!

5/5/93

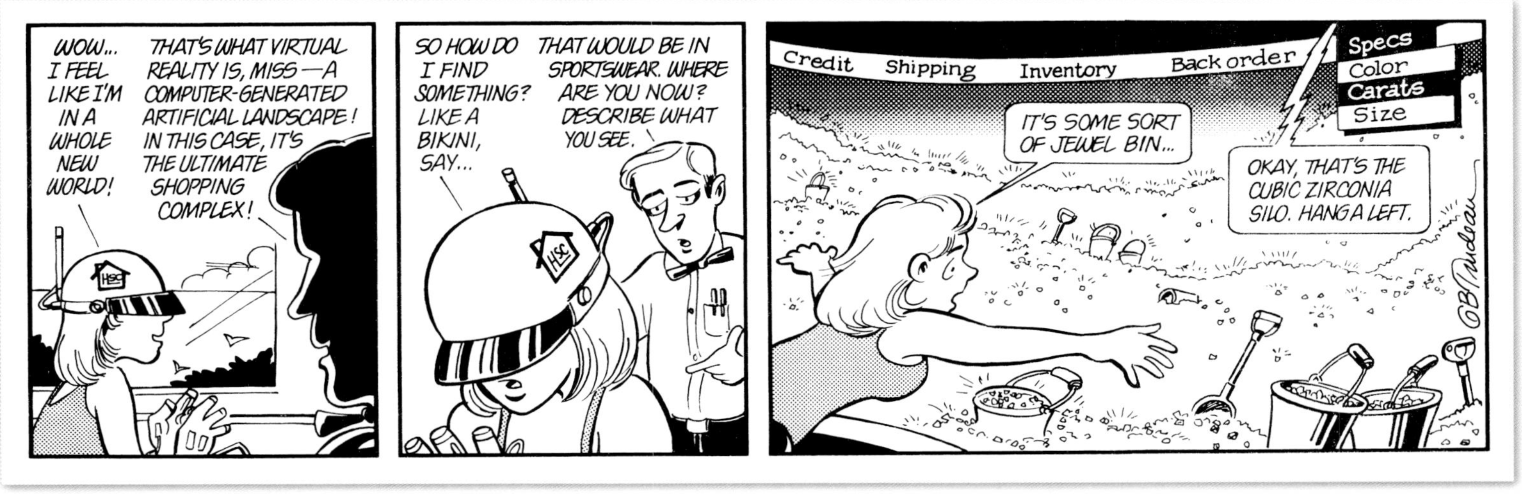
WOW... I FEEL LIKE I'M IN A WHOLE NEW WORLD!
THAT'S WHAT VIRTUAL REALITY IS, MISS — A COMPUTER-GENERATED ARTIFICIAL LANDSCAPE! IN THIS CASE, IT'S THE ULTIMATE SHOPPING COMPLEX!
SO HOW DO I FIND SOMETHING? LIKE A BIKINI, SAY...
THAT WOULD BE IN SPORTSWEAR. WHERE ARE YOU NOW? DESCRIBE WHAT YOU SEE.
Credit
Shipping
Inventory
Back order
Specs
Color
Carats
Size
IT'S SOME SORT OF JEWEL BIN...
OKAY, THAT'S THE CUBIC ZIRCONIA SILO. HANG A LEFT.
©B Trudeau

5/6/93

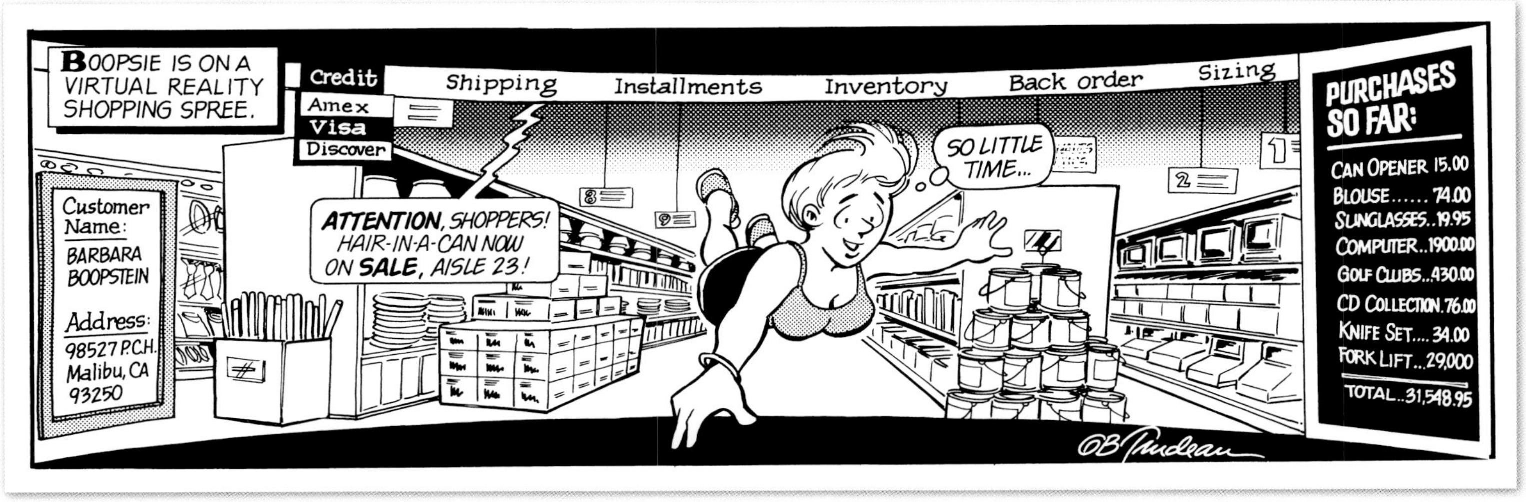
BOOPSIE IS ON A VIRTUAL REALITY SHOPPING SPREE.
Credit
Amex
Visa
Discover
Shipping
Installments
Inventory
Back order
Sizing
Customer Name:
BARBARA BOOPSTEIN
Address:
98527 P.C.H.
Malibu, CA
93250
ATTENTION, SHOPPERS! HAIR-IN-A-CAN NOW ON **SALE**, AISLE 23!
SO LITTLE TIME...
PURCHASES SO FAR:
CAN OPENER 15.00
BLOUSE...... 74.00
SUNGLASSES..19.95
COMPUTER..1900.00
GOLF CLUBS..430.00
CD COLLECTION.76.00
KNIFE SET.... 34.00
FORK LIFT...29,000
TOTAL..31,548.95
©B Trudeau

5/7/93

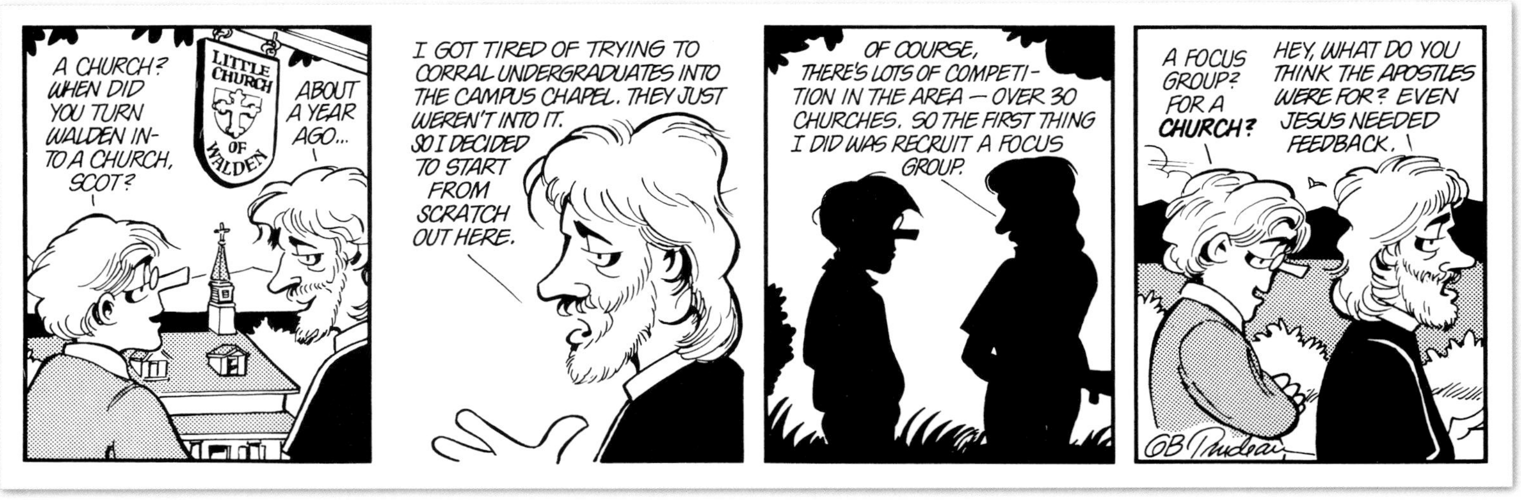
A CHURCH? WHEN DID YOU TURN WALDEN INTO A CHURCH, SCOT?
LITTLE CHURCH OF WALDEN
ABOUT A YEAR AGO...
I GOT TIRED OF TRYING TO CORRAL UNDERGRADUATES INTO THE CAMPUS CHAPEL. THEY JUST WEREN'T INTO IT. SO I DECIDED TO START FROM SCRATCH OUT HERE.
OF COURSE, THERE'S LOTS OF COMPETITION IN THE AREA — OVER 30 CHURCHES. SO THE FIRST THING I DID WAS RECRUIT A FOCUS GROUP.
A FOCUS GROUP? FOR A CHURCH?
HEY, WHAT DO YOU THINK THE APOSTLES WERE FOR? EVEN JESUS NEEDED FEEDBACK.
GB Trudeau

5/18/93

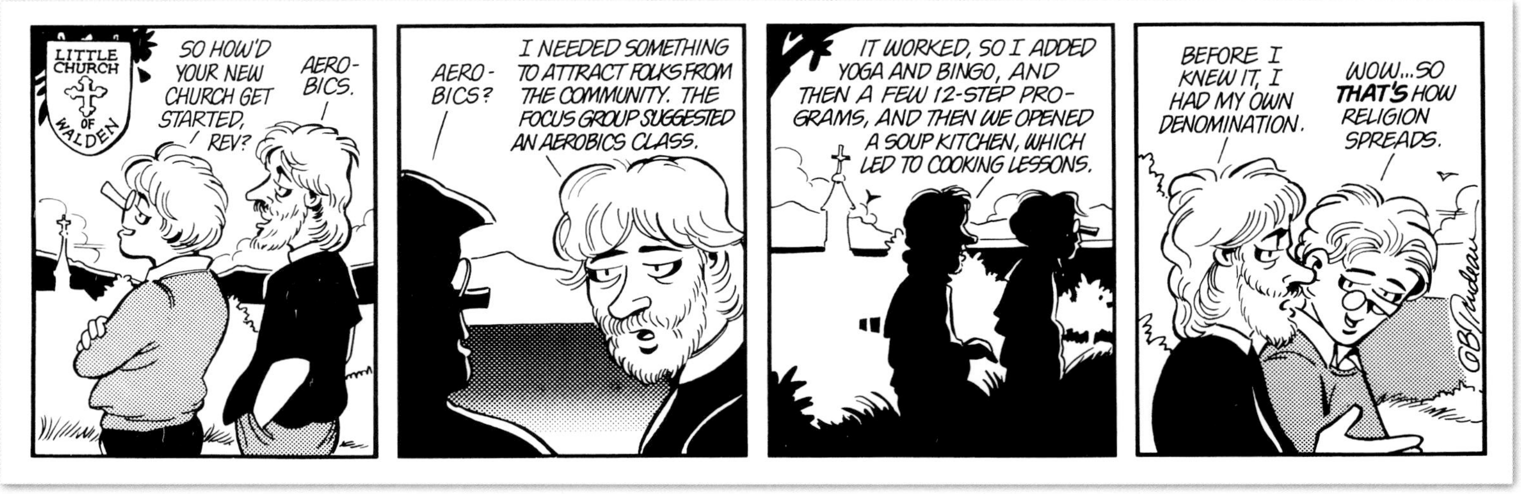
LITTLE CHURCH OF WALDEN
SO HOW'D YOUR NEW CHURCH GET STARTED, REV?
AEROBICS.
AEROBICS?
I NEEDED SOMETHING TO ATTRACT FOLKS FROM THE COMMUNITY. THE FOCUS GROUP SUGGESTED AN AEROBICS CLASS.
IT WORKED, SO I ADDED YOGA AND BINGO, AND THEN A FEW 12-STEP PROGRAMS, AND THEN WE OPENED A SOUP KITCHEN, WHICH LED TO COOKING LESSONS.
BEFORE I KNEW IT, I HAD MY OWN DENOMINATION.
WOW...SO THAT'S HOW RELIGION SPREADS.
GB Trudeau

5/19/93

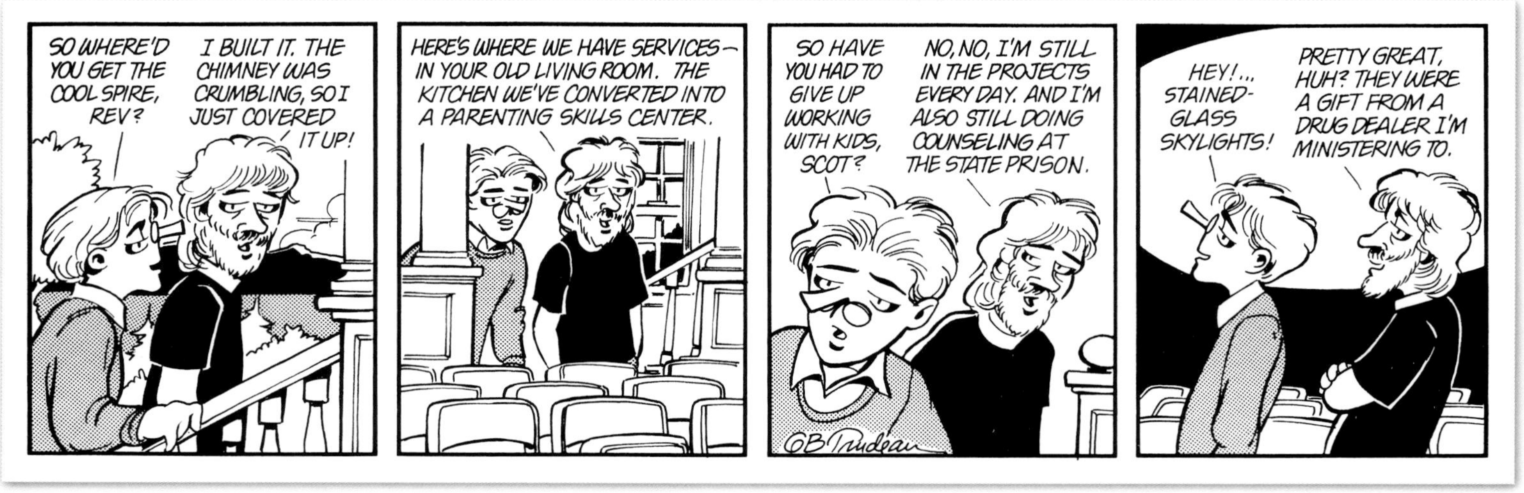
SO WHERE'D YOU GET THE COOL SPIRE, REV?
I BUILT IT. THE CHIMNEY WAS CRUMBLING, SO I JUST COVERED IT UP!
HERE'S WHERE WE HAVE SERVICES — IN YOUR OLD LIVING ROOM. THE KITCHEN WE'VE CONVERTED INTO A PARENTING SKILLS CENTER.
SO HAVE YOU HAD TO GIVE UP WORKING WITH KIDS, SCOT?
NO, NO, I'M STILL IN THE PROJECTS EVERY DAY. AND I'M ALSO STILL DOING COUNSELING AT THE STATE PRISON.
GB Trudeau
HEY!... STAINED-GLASS SKYLIGHTS!
PRETTY GREAT, HUH? THEY WERE A GIFT FROM A DRUG DEALER I'M MINISTERING TO.

5/20/93

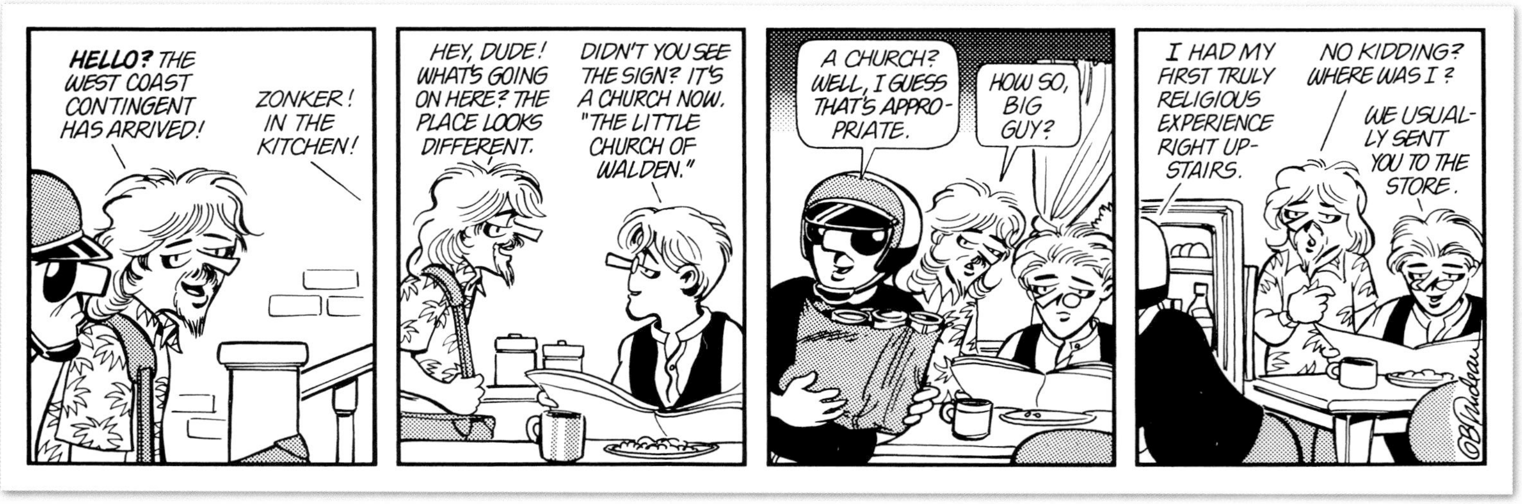
HELLO? THE WEST COAST CONTINGENT HAS ARRIVED!
ZONKER! IN THE KITCHEN!
HEY, DUDE! WHAT'S GOING ON HERE? THE PLACE LOOKS DIFFERENT.
DIDN'T YOU SEE THE SIGN? IT'S A CHURCH NOW. "THE LITTLE CHURCH OF WALDEN."
A CHURCH? WELL, I GUESS THAT'S APPROPRIATE.
HOW SO, BIG GUY?
I HAD MY FIRST TRULY RELIGIOUS EXPERIENCE RIGHT UPSTAIRS.
NO KIDDING? WHERE WAS I?
WE USUALLY SENT YOU TO THE STORE.
GB Trudeau

5/22/93

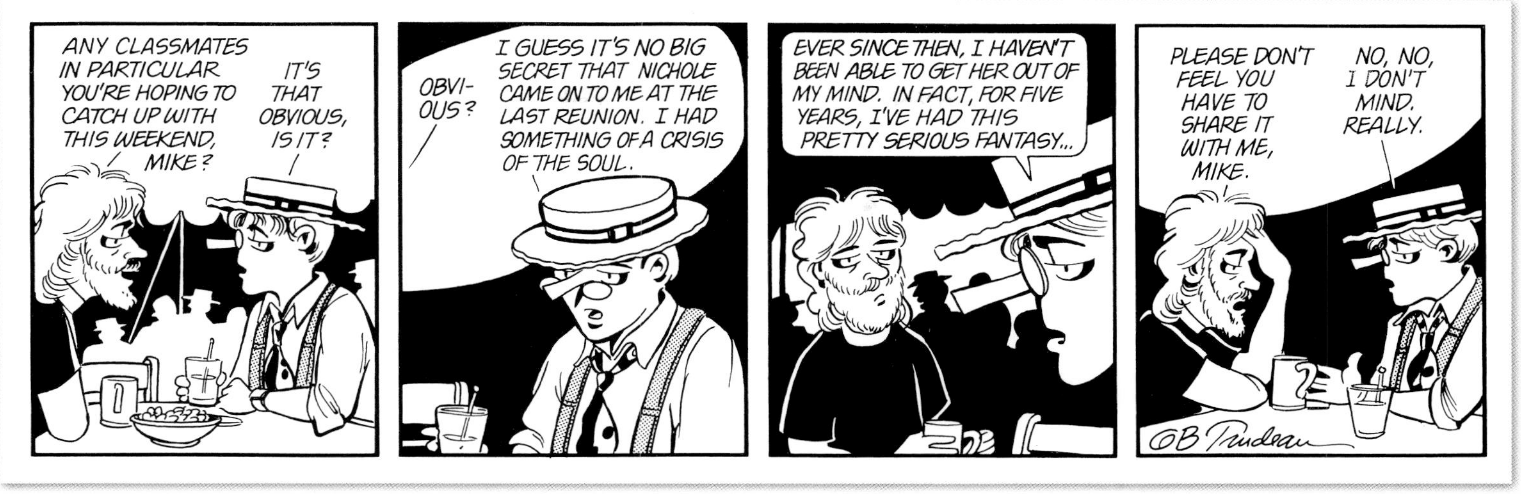
ANY CLASSMATES IN PARTICULAR YOU'RE HOPING TO CATCH UP WITH THIS WEEKEND, MIKE?
IT'S THAT OBVIOUS, IS IT?
OBVIOUS?
I GUESS IT'S NO BIG SECRET THAT NICHOLE CAME ON TO ME AT THE LAST REUNION. I HAD SOMETHING OF A CRISIS OF THE SOUL.
EVER SINCE THEN, I HAVEN'T BEEN ABLE TO GET HER OUT OF MY MIND. IN FACT, FOR FIVE YEARS, I'VE HAD THIS PRETTY SERIOUS FANTASY...
PLEASE DON'T FEEL YOU HAVE TO SHARE IT WITH ME, MIKE.
NO, NO, I DON'T MIND. REALLY.

5/24/93

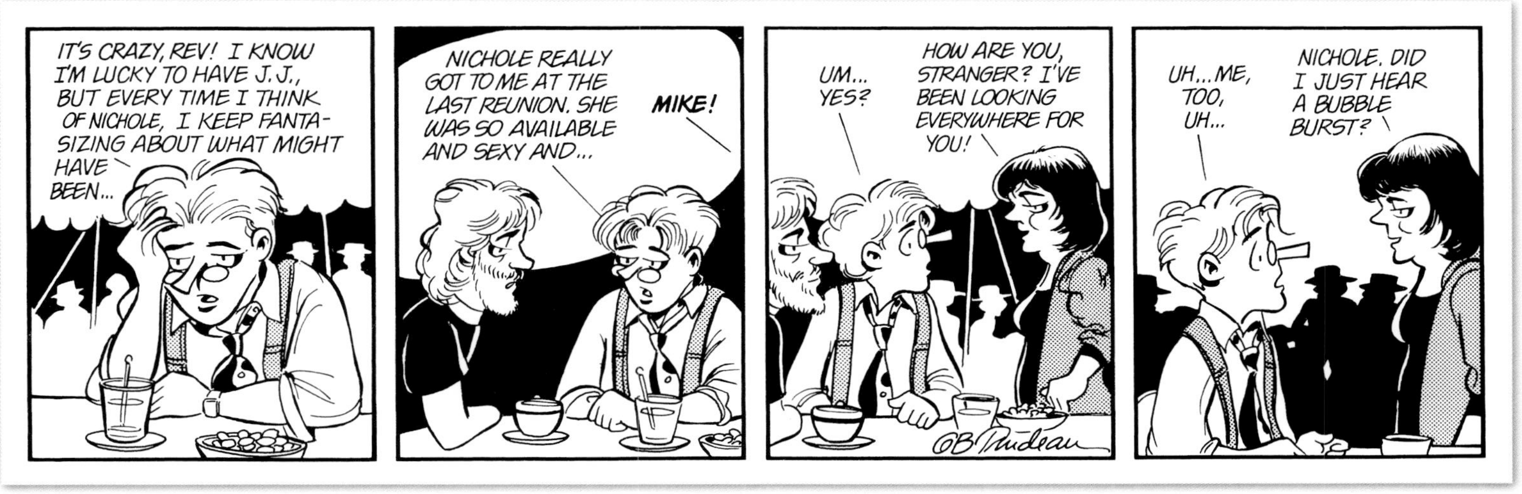
IT'S CRAZY, REV! I KNOW I'M LUCKY TO HAVE J.J., BUT EVERY TIME I THINK OF NICHOLE, I KEEP FANTASIZING ABOUT WHAT MIGHT HAVE BEEN...
NICHOLE REALLY GOT TO ME AT THE LAST REUNION. SHE WAS SO AVAILABLE AND SEXY AND...
MIKE!
UM... YES?
HOW ARE YOU, STRANGER? I'VE BEEN LOOKING EVERYWHERE FOR YOU!
UH... ME, TOO, UH...
NICHOLE. DID I JUST HEAR A BUBBLE BURST?

5/25/93

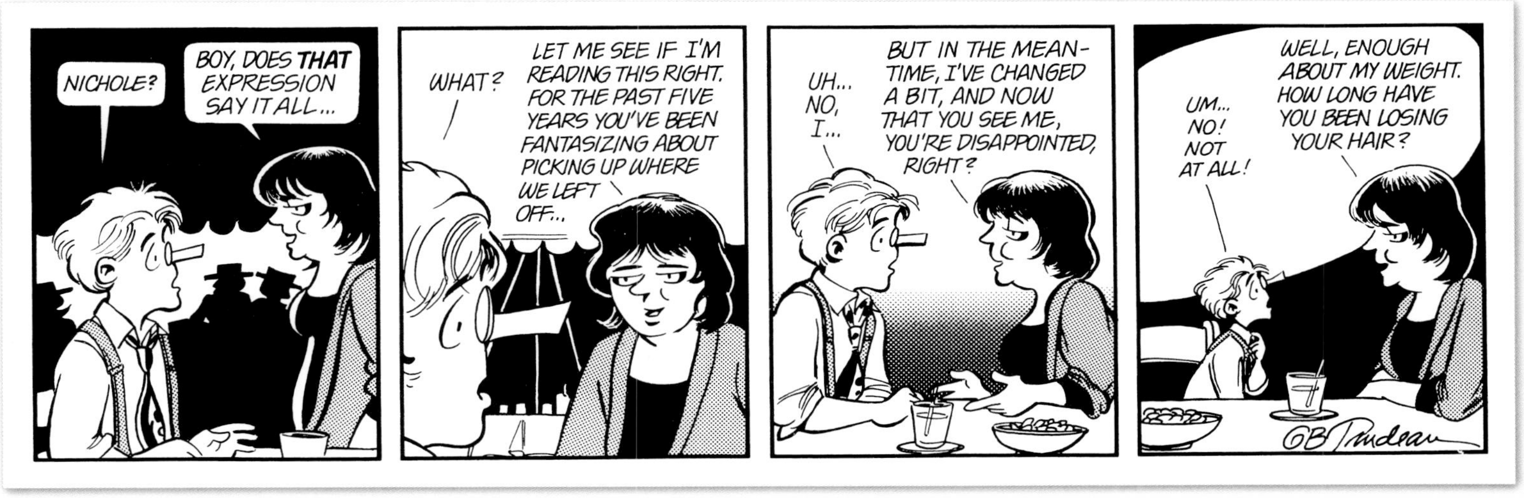
NICHOLE?
BOY, DOES THAT EXPRESSION SAY IT ALL...
WHAT?
LET ME SEE IF I'M READING THIS RIGHT. FOR THE PAST FIVE YEARS YOU'VE BEEN FANTASIZING ABOUT PICKING UP WHERE WE LEFT OFF...
UH... NO, I...
BUT IN THE MEANTIME, I'VE CHANGED A BIT, AND NOW THAT YOU SEE ME, YOU'RE DISAPPOINTED, RIGHT?
UM... NO! NOT AT ALL!
WELL, ENOUGH ABOUT MY WEIGHT. HOW LONG HAVE YOU BEEN LOSING YOUR HAIR?

5/26/93

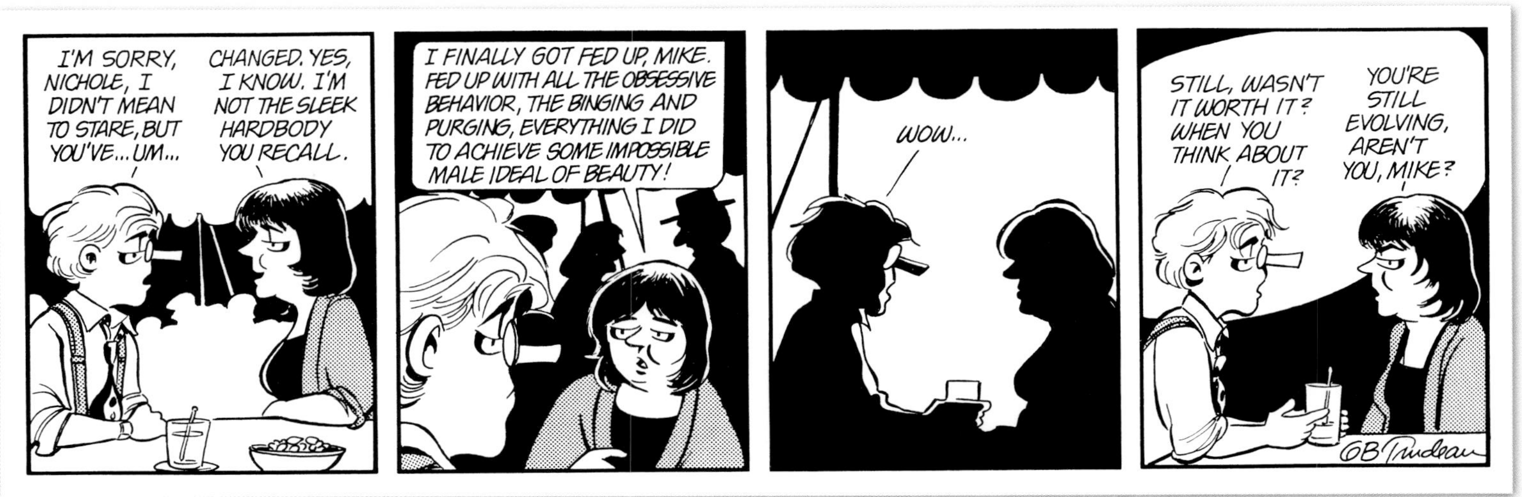
I'M SORRY, NICHOLE, I DIDN'T MEAN TO STARE, BUT YOU'VE... UM...
CHANGED. YES, I KNOW. I'M NOT THE SLEEK HARDBODY YOU RECALL.
I FINALLY GOT FED UP, MIKE. FED UP WITH ALL THE OBSESSIVE BEHAVIOR, THE BINGING AND PURGING, EVERYTHING I DID TO ACHIEVE SOME IMPOSSIBLE MALE IDEAL OF BEAUTY!
WOW...
STILL, WASN'T IT WORTH IT? WHEN YOU THINK ABOUT IT?
YOU'RE STILL EVOLVING, AREN'T YOU, MIKE?

5/27/93

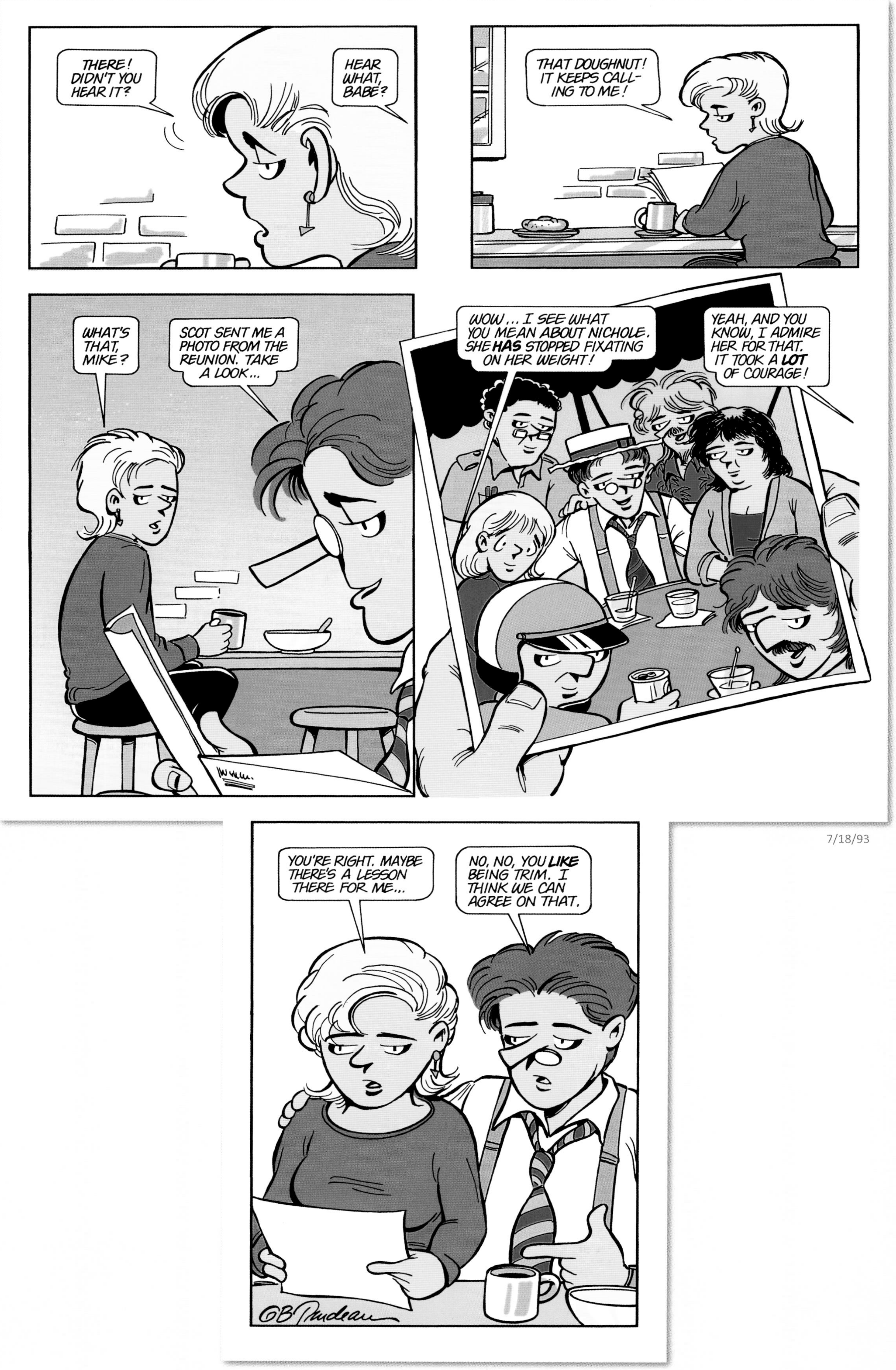
THERE! DIDN'T YOU HEAR IT?
HEAR WHAT, BABE?
THAT DOUGHNUT! IT KEEPS CALLING TO ME!
WHAT'S THAT, MIKE?
SCOT SENT ME A PHOTO FROM THE REUNION. TAKE A LOOK...
WOW... I SEE WHAT YOU MEAN ABOUT NICHOLE. SHE HAS STOPPED FIXATING ON HER WEIGHT!
YEAH, AND YOU KNOW, I ADMIRE HER FOR THAT. IT TOOK A LOT OF COURAGE!
YOU'RE RIGHT. MAYBE THERE'S A LESSON THERE FOR ME...
NO, NO, YOU LIKE BEING TRIM. I THINK WE CAN AGREE ON THAT.
©B. Trudeau

7/18/93

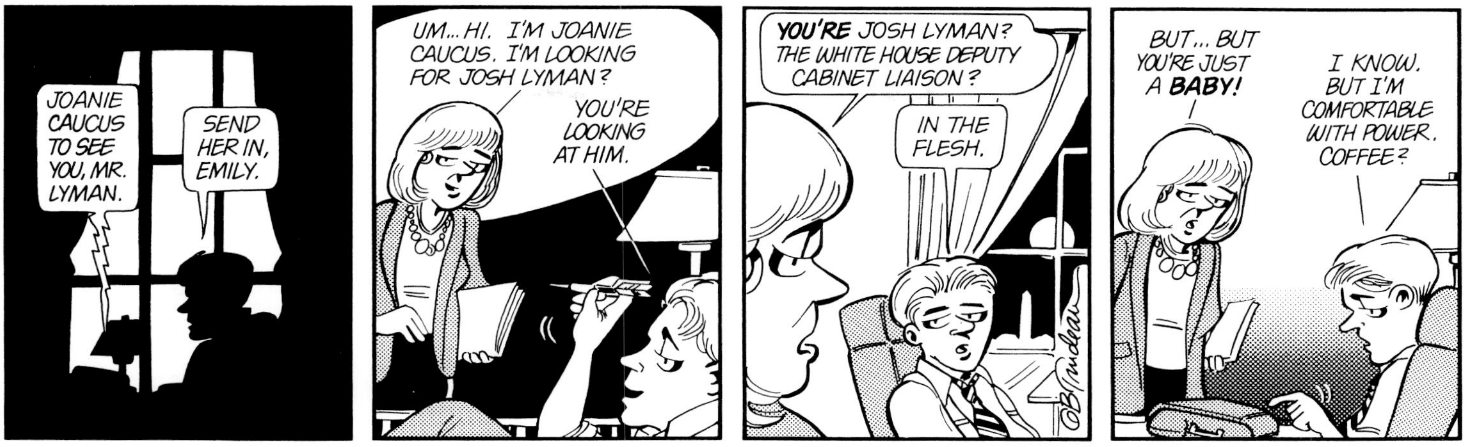
JOANIE CAUCUS TO SEE YOU, MR. LYMAN.
SEND HER IN, EMILY.
UM... HI. I'M JOANIE CAUCUS. I'M LOOKING FOR JOSH LYMAN?
YOU'RE LOOKING AT HIM.
YOU'RE JOSH LYMAN? THE WHITE HOUSE DEPUTY CABINET LIAISON?
IN THE FLESH.
BUT... BUT YOU'RE JUST A BABY!
I KNOW. BUT I'M COMFORTABLE WITH POWER. COFFEE?

5/11/93

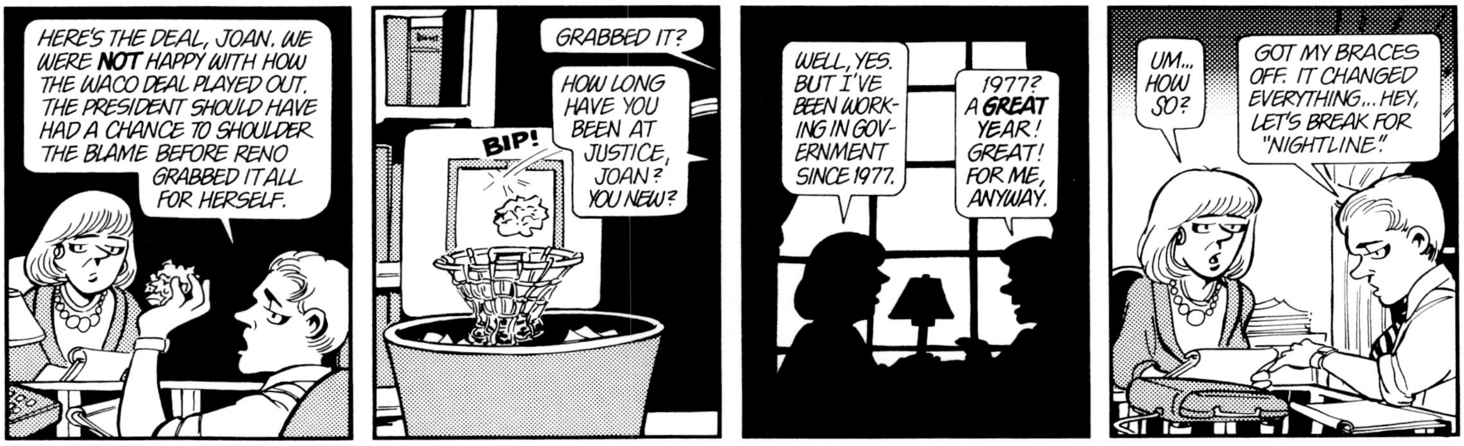
HERE'S THE DEAL, JOAN. WE WERE NOT HAPPY WITH HOW THE WACO DEAL PLAYED OUT. THE PRESIDENT SHOULD HAVE HAD A CHANCE TO SHOULDER THE BLAME BEFORE RENO GRABBED IT ALL FOR HERSELF.
GRABBED IT?
HOW LONG HAVE YOU BEEN AT JUSTICE, JOAN? YOU NEW?
BIP!
WELL, YES. BUT I'VE BEEN WORKING IN GOVERNMENT SINCE 1977.
1977? A GREAT YEAR! GREAT! FOR ME, ANYWAY.
UM... HOW SO?
GOT MY BRACES OFF. IT CHANGED EVERYTHING... HEY, LET'S BREAK FOR "NIGHTLINE."

5/12/93

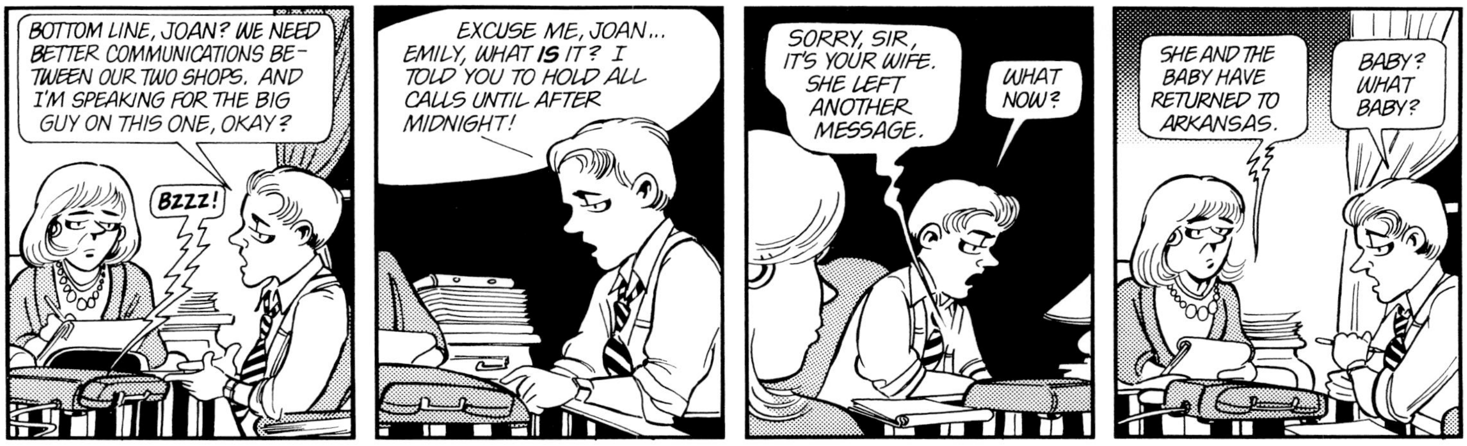
BOTTOM LINE, JOAN? WE NEED BETTER COMMUNICATIONS BETWEEN OUR TWO SHOPS. AND I'M SPEAKING FOR THE BIG GUY ON THIS ONE, OKAY?
BZZZ!
EXCUSE ME, JOAN... EMILY, WHAT IS IT? I TOLD YOU TO HOLD ALL CALLS UNTIL AFTER MIDNIGHT!
SORRY, SIR, IT'S YOUR WIFE. SHE LEFT ANOTHER MESSAGE.
WHAT NOW?
SHE AND THE BABY HAVE RETURNED TO ARKANSAS.
BABY? WHAT BABY?

5/13/93

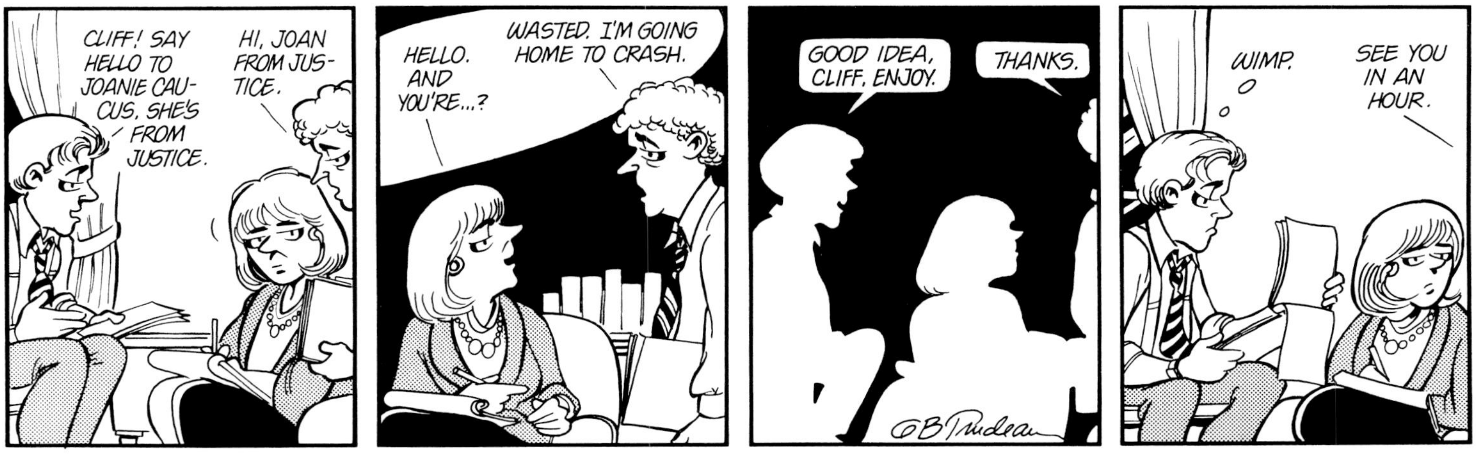
CLIFF! SAY HELLO TO JOANIE CAUCUS. SHE'S FROM JUSTICE.
HI, JOAN FROM JUSTICE.
HELLO. AND YOU'RE...?
WASTED. I'M GOING HOME TO CRASH.
GOOD IDEA, CLIFF. ENJOY.
THANKS.
WIMP.
SEE YOU IN AN HOUR.

5/14/93

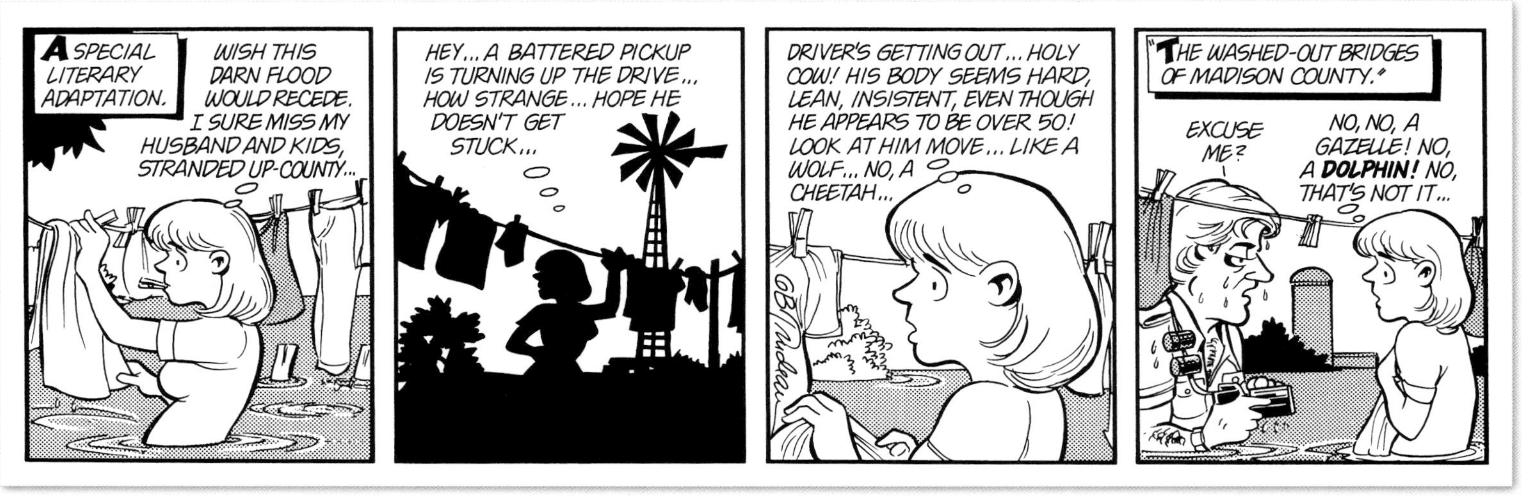
A SPECIAL LITERARY ADAPTATION.
WISH THIS DARN FLOOD WOULD RECEDE. I SURE MISS MY HUSBAND AND KIDS, STRANDED UP-COUNTY...
HEY... A BATTERED PICKUP IS TURNING UP THE DRIVE... HOW STRANGE... HOPE HE DOESN'T GET STUCK...
DRIVER'S GETTING OUT... HOLY COW! HIS BODY SEEMS HARD, LEAN, INSISTENT, EVEN THOUGH HE APPEARS TO BE OVER 50! LOOK AT HIM MOVE... LIKE A WOLF... NO, A CHEETAH...
"THE WASHED-OUT BRIDGES OF MADISON COUNTY."
EXCUSE ME?
NO, NO, A GAZELLE! NO, A **DOLPHIN!** NO, THAT'S NOT IT...

8/16/93

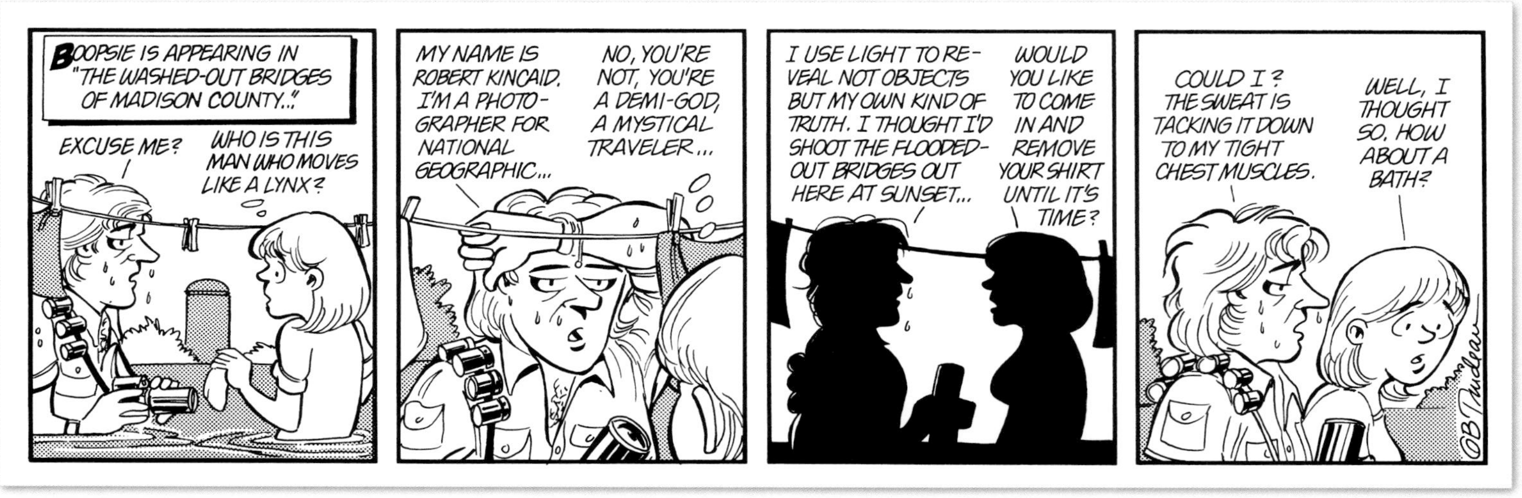
BOOPSIE IS APPEARING IN "THE WASHED-OUT BRIDGES OF MADISON COUNTY."
EXCUSE ME?
WHO IS THIS MAN WHO MOVES LIKE A LYNX?
MY NAME IS ROBERT KINCAID. I'M A PHOTO-GRAPHER FOR NATIONAL GEOGRAPHIC...
NO, YOU'RE NOT, YOU'RE A DEMI-GOD, A MYSTICAL TRAVELER...
I USE LIGHT TO RE-VEAL NOT OBJECTS BUT MY OWN KIND OF TRUTH. I THOUGHT I'D SHOOT THE FLOODED-OUT BRIDGES OUT HERE AT SUNSET...
WOULD YOU LIKE TO COME IN AND REMOVE YOUR SHIRT UNTIL IT'S TIME?
COULD I? THE SWEAT IS TACKING IT DOWN TO MY TIGHT CHEST MUSCLES.
WELL, I THOUGHT SO. HOW ABOUT A BATH?

8/17/93

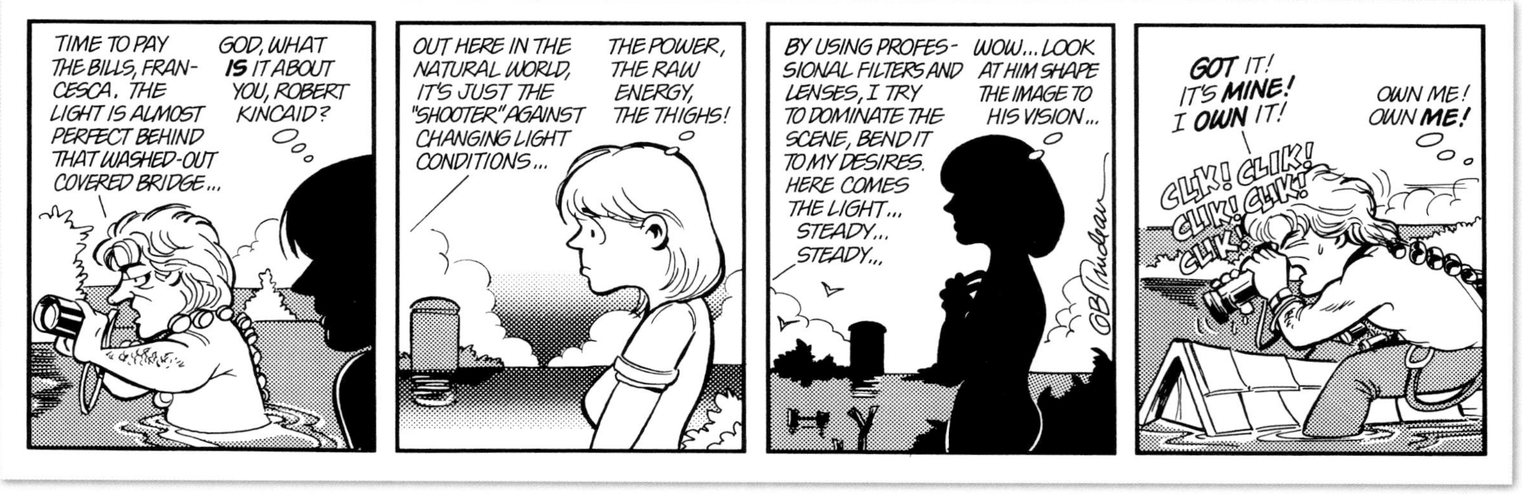
TIME TO PAY THE BILLS, FRAN-CESCA. THE LIGHT IS ALMOST PERFECT BEHIND THAT WASHED-OUT COVERED BRIDGE...
GOD, WHAT **IS** IT ABOUT YOU, ROBERT KINCAID?
OUT HERE IN THE NATURAL WORLD, IT'S JUST THE "SHOOTER" AGAINST CHANGING LIGHT CONDITIONS...
THE POWER, THE RAW ENERGY, THE THIGHS!
BY USING PROFES-SIONAL FILTERS AND LENSES, I TRY TO DOMINATE THE SCENE, BEND IT TO MY DESIRES. HERE COMES THE LIGHT... STEADY... STEADY...
WOW... LOOK AT HIM SHAPE THE IMAGE TO HIS VISION...
GOT IT! IT'S **MINE!** I **OWN** IT!
CLIK! CLIK! CLIK! CLIK! CLIK!
OWN ME! OWN **ME!**

8/18/93

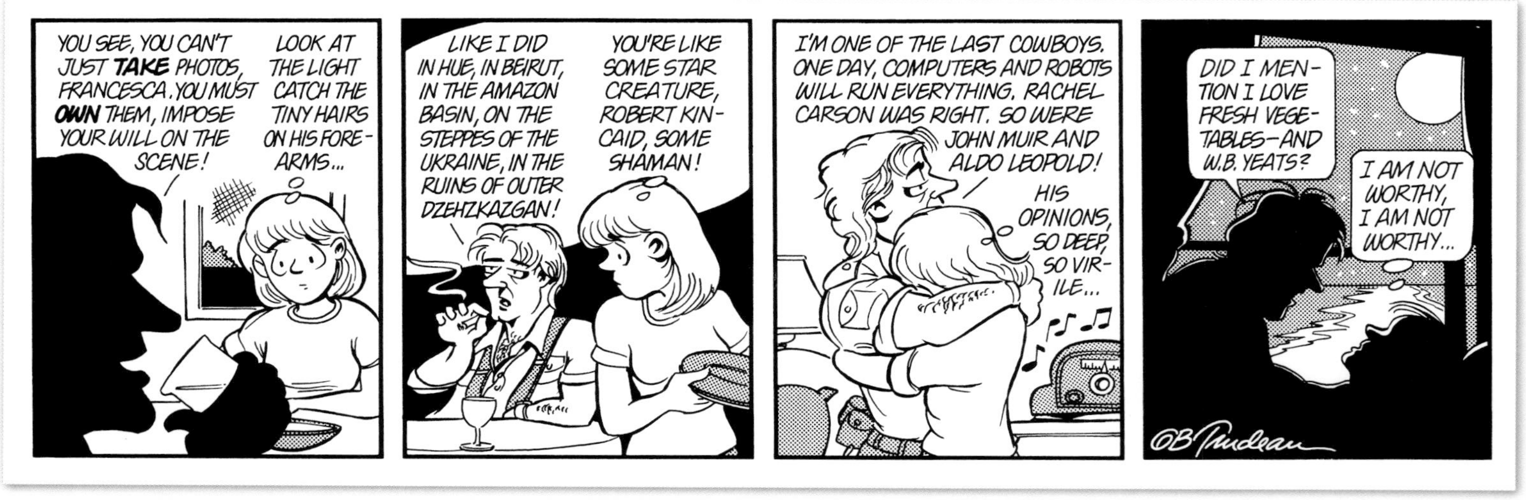
YOU SEE, YOU CAN'T JUST **TAKE** PHOTOS, FRANCESCA. YOU MUST **OWN** THEM, IMPOSE YOUR WILL ON THE SCENE!
LOOK AT THE LIGHT CATCH THE TINY HAIRS ON HIS FORE-ARMS...
LIKE I DID IN HUE, IN BEIRUT, IN THE AMAZON BASIN, ON THE STEPPES OF THE UKRAINE, IN THE RUINS OF OUTER DZEHZKAZGAN!
YOU'RE LIKE SOME STAR CREATURE, ROBERT KIN-CAID, SOME SHAMAN!
I'M ONE OF THE LAST COWBOYS. ONE DAY, COMPUTERS AND ROBOTS WILL RUN EVERYTHING. RACHEL CARSON WAS RIGHT. SO WERE JOHN MUIR AND ALDO LEOPOLD!
HIS OPINIONS, SO DEEP, SO VIR-ILE...
DID I MEN-TION I LOVE FRESH VEGE-TABLES—AND W.B. YEATS?
I AM NOT WORTHY, I AM NOT WORTHY...

8/19/93

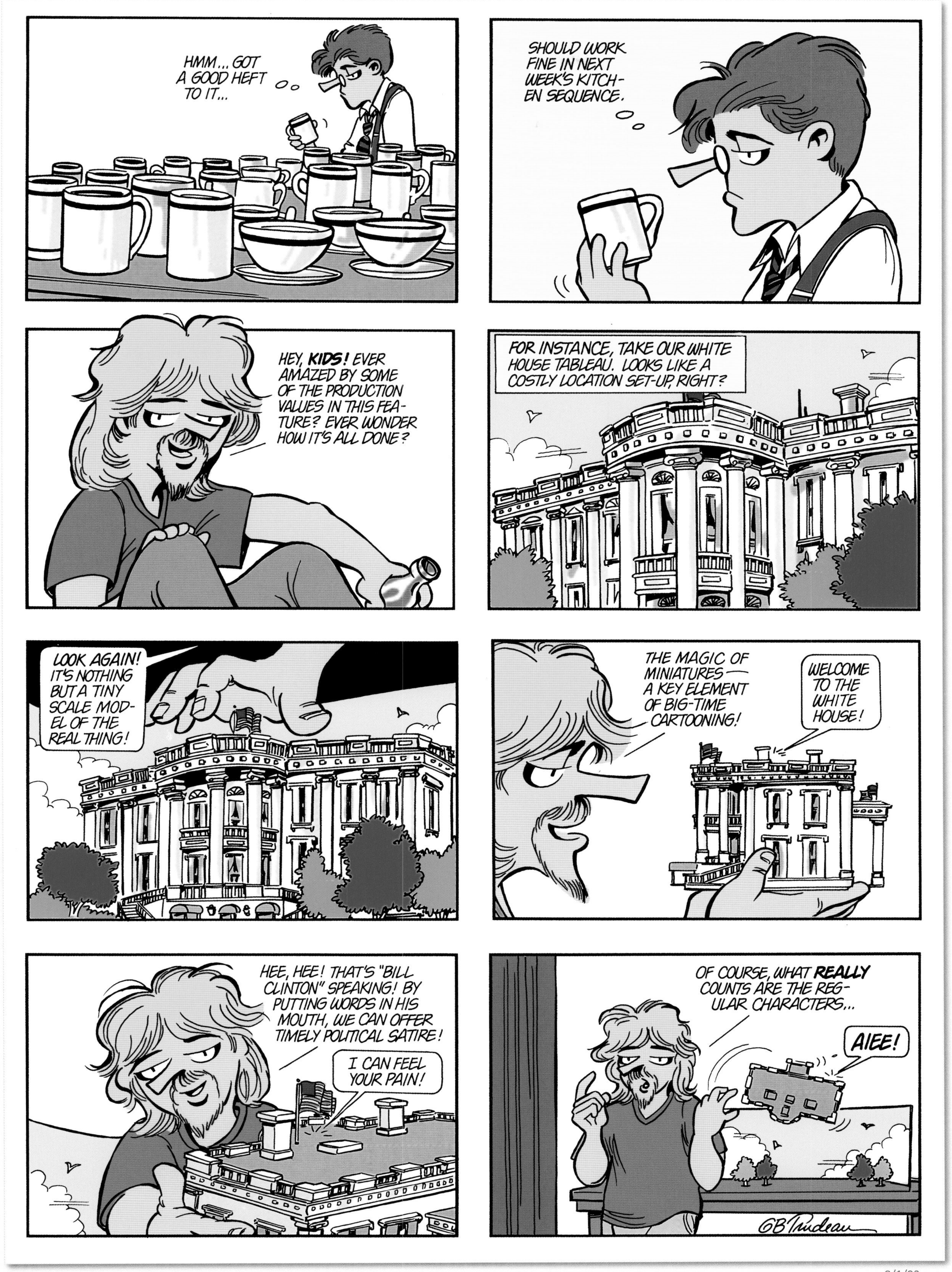
HMM... GOT A GOOD HEFT TO IT...
SHOULD WORK FINE IN NEXT WEEK'S KITCH-EN SEQUENCE.
HEY, KIDS! EVER AMAZED BY SOME OF THE PRODUCTION VALUES IN THIS FEA-TURE? EVER WONDER HOW IT'S ALL DONE?
FOR INSTANCE, TAKE OUR WHITE HOUSE TABLEAU. LOOKS LIKE A COSTLY LOCATION SET-UP, RIGHT?
LOOK AGAIN! IT'S NOTHING BUT A TINY SCALE MOD-EL OF THE REAL THING!
THE MAGIC OF MINIATURES — A KEY ELEMENT OF BIG-TIME CARTOONING!
WELCOME TO THE WHITE HOUSE!
HEE, HEE! THAT'S "BILL CLINTON" SPEAKING! BY PUTTING WORDS IN HIS MOUTH, WE CAN OFFER TIMELY POLITICAL SATIRE!
I CAN FEEL YOUR PAIN!
OF COURSE, WHAT REALLY COUNTS ARE THE REG-ULAR CHARACTERS...
AIEE!
GBTrudeau

8/1/93

ROLAND HEDLEY

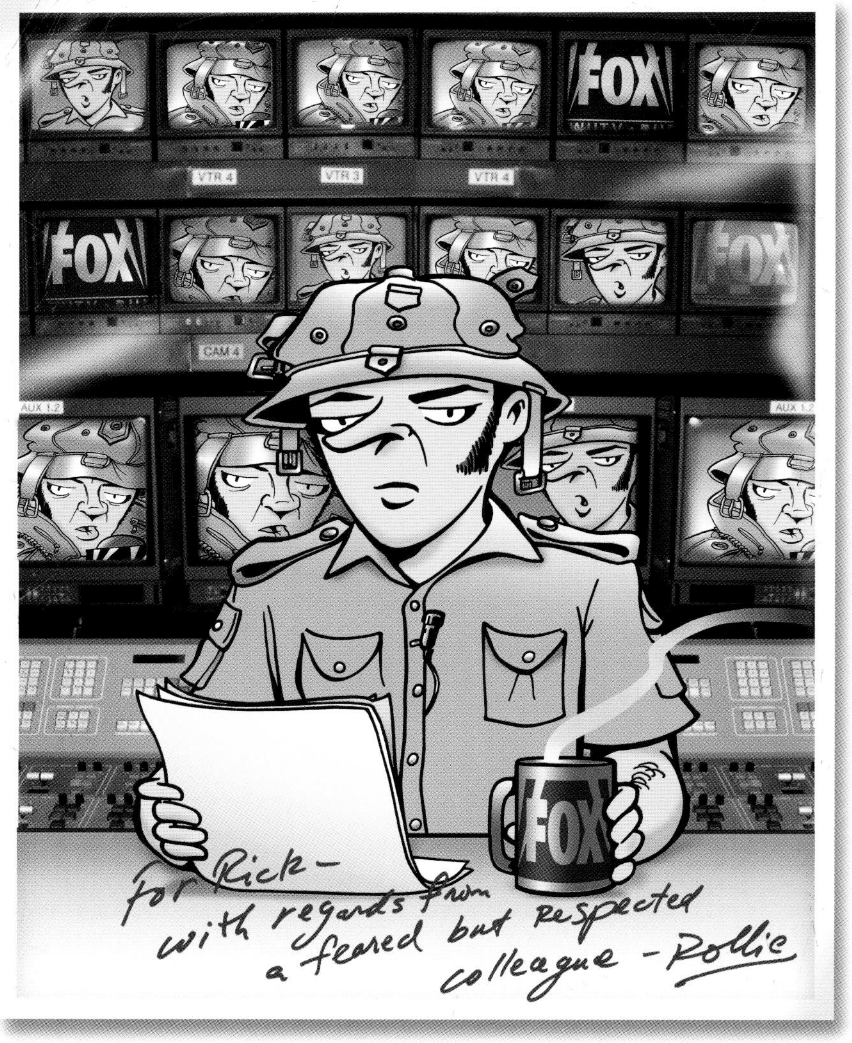
FOX
VTR 4
VTR 3
VTR 4
FOX
FOX
CAM 4
AUX 1.2
AUX 1.2
FOX
for Rick –
with regards from
a feared but respected
colleague – Rollie

From time to time, I have tagged along with the White House traveling press corps on overseas trips. Many news organizations can no longer afford to send people abroad, but in flusher days, there were enough reporters and support personnel to fill two charter planes.

The first was reserved for stars like Roland and Rick, alpha dogs from the networks and major papers, but the second aircraft, dubbed the Zoo Plane, carried those further down the pecking order—reporters from less exalted publications, field producers, cameramen, White House staffers, and assorted riffraff like me.

Of the two planes, the Zoo was by far the more fun. With an open bar, suspended safety rules, and unusually solicitous stewardesses, the cabin had the look and feel of a frat house during pledge week. Reporters rolled fruit down the aisles and taped jangling, purloined hotel keys to the overhead bins. On one long trip across the Pacific, several dozen inebriated passengers suddenly stood up and started gyrating wildly in the aisles—in complete silence. All of them were wearing headsets tuned to the same disco channel on the aircraft sound

"Wonder what I used 2 do with 2 hrs/day I now spend on Twitter. Probably just wasted them."

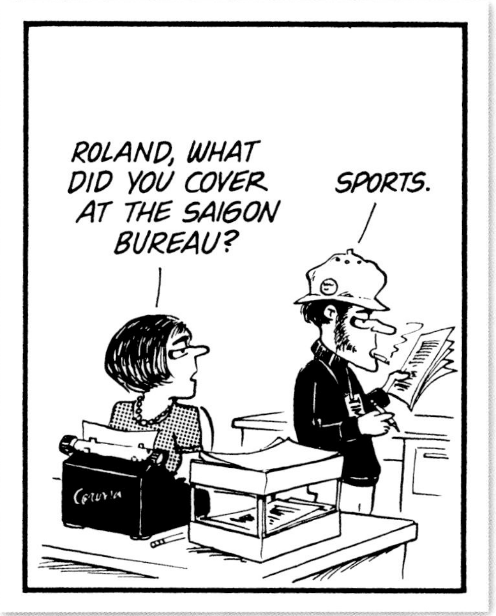
ROLAND, WHAT DID YOU COVER AT THE SAIGON BUREAU?
SPORTS.

system. Aside from the occasional whoop or laugh, there was nothing to disturb the concentration of those few reporters still tapping away on their keyboards. The scene was beyond bizarre.

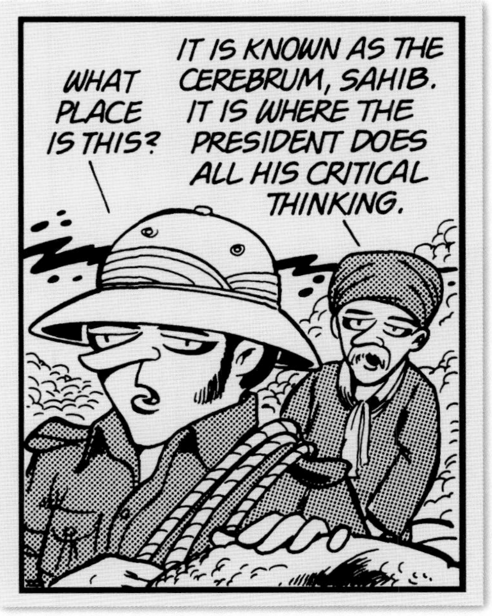
WHAT PLACE IS THIS?
IT IS KNOWN AS THE CEREBRUM, SAHIB. IT IS WHERE THE PRESIDENT DOES ALL HIS CRITICAL THINKING.

I took copious notes about my fellow travelers, frequently working them into the strip. Although Roland began life as a print journalist, the real animating force behind him was a television reporter, ABC's Sam Donaldson. Dubbed the Human Bullhorn, Sam possessed the most formidable voice in all of journalism. Such was its stopping power that only the septuagenarian Reagan could convincingly pretend not to hear Donaldson boom out a question, and only then when it was covered by helicopter prop wash.

But Sam wasn't just bombast and epaulets; he was also hapless. One night at a Warsaw club, several bottles of champagne were sent over to his table from "two gentlemen from ABC News." He basked in this affirmation of his star status. Only after we had finished the champagne did Sam finally notice there was no one from ABC News in the room. He paid up.

Fortunately, Sam has a robust sense of humor, especially about himself, and in this critical respect he differs wildly from the character he inspired. Roland's vanity and lack of self-awareness is so complete that his peers can direct the cruelest comments in his direction without any fear of giving offense. I've always believed that cluelessness evolved as an adaption to allow the truly appalling to live with themselves. Imagine, for instance, looking in the mirror one day and seeing Geraldo Rivera staring back at you; only Geraldo Rivera could survive such a shock.

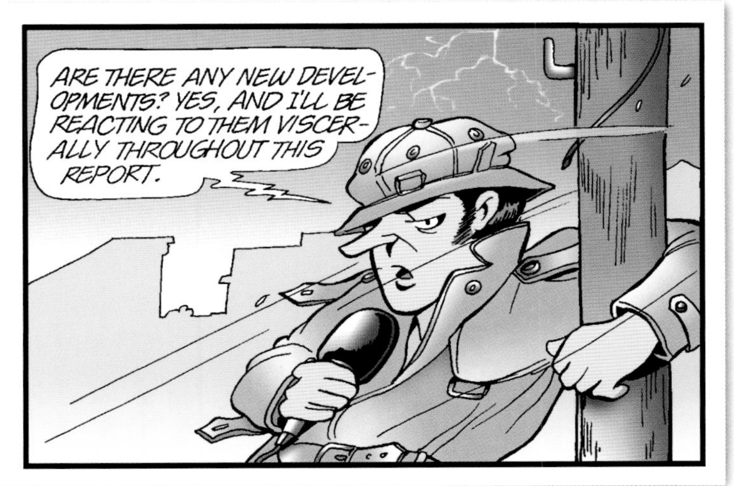
ARE THERE ANY NEW DEVELOPMENTS? YES, AND I'LL BE REACTING TO THEM VISCERALLY THROUGHOUT THIS REPORT.

Or Roland.

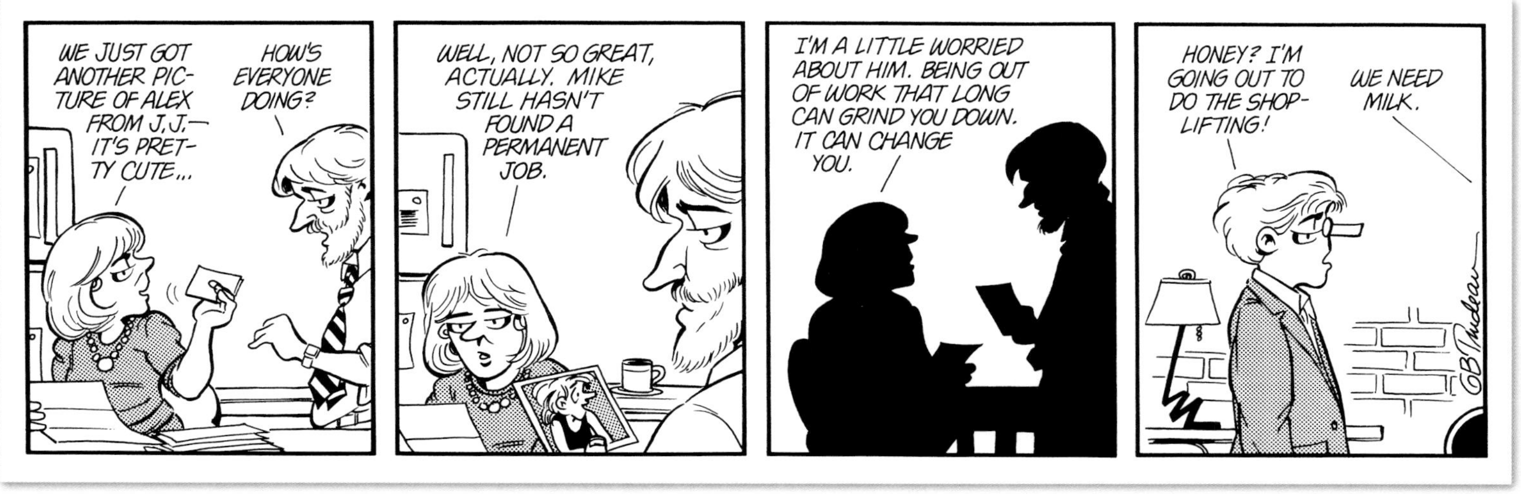
WE JUST GOT ANOTHER PICTURE OF ALEX FROM J.J.— IT'S PRETTY CUTE...
HOW'S EVERYONE DOING?
WELL, NOT SO GREAT, ACTUALLY. MIKE STILL HASN'T FOUND A PERMANENT JOB.
I'M A LITTLE WORRIED ABOUT HIM. BEING OUT OF WORK THAT LONG CAN GRIND YOU DOWN. IT CAN CHANGE YOU.
HONEY? I'M GOING OUT TO DO THE SHOPLIFTING!
WE NEED MILK.
GB Trudeau

7/5/93

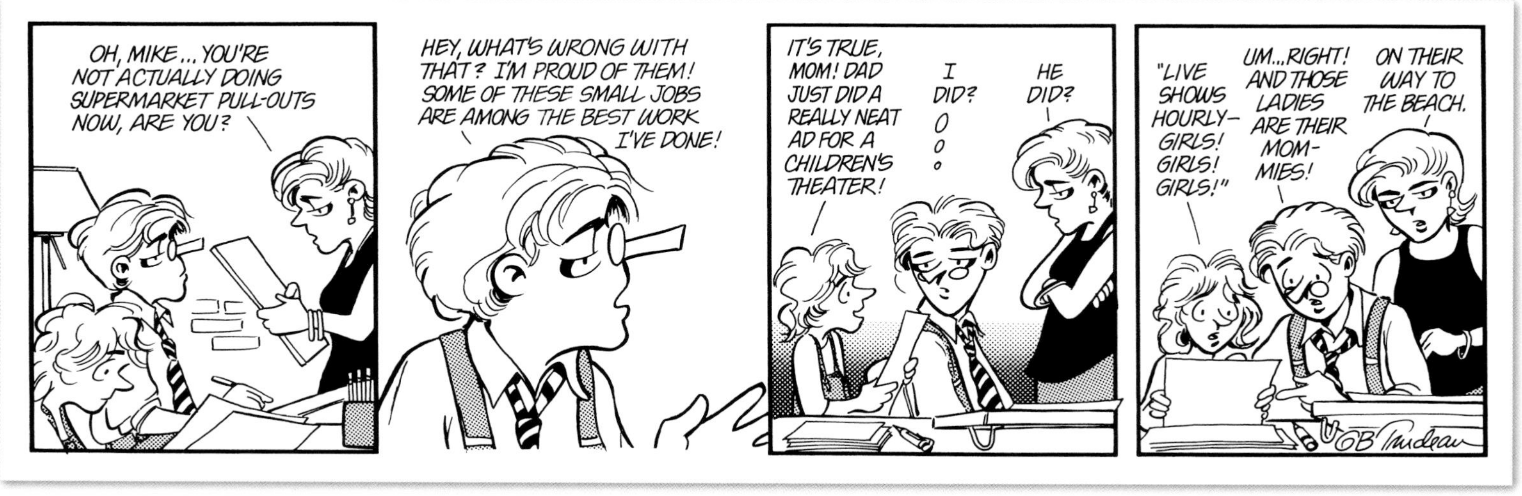
OH, MIKE... YOU'RE NOT ACTUALLY DOING SUPERMARKET PULL-OUTS NOW, ARE YOU?
HEY, WHAT'S WRONG WITH THAT? I'M PROUD OF THEM! SOME OF THESE SMALL JOBS ARE AMONG THE BEST WORK I'VE DONE!
IT'S TRUE, MOM! DAD JUST DID A REALLY NEAT AD FOR A CHILDREN'S THEATER!
I DID?
HE DID?
"LIVE SHOWS HOURLY—GIRLS! GIRLS! GIRLS!"
UM...RIGHT! AND THOSE LADIES ARE THEIR MOMMIES!
ON THEIR WAY TO THE BEACH.
GB Trudeau

7/7/93

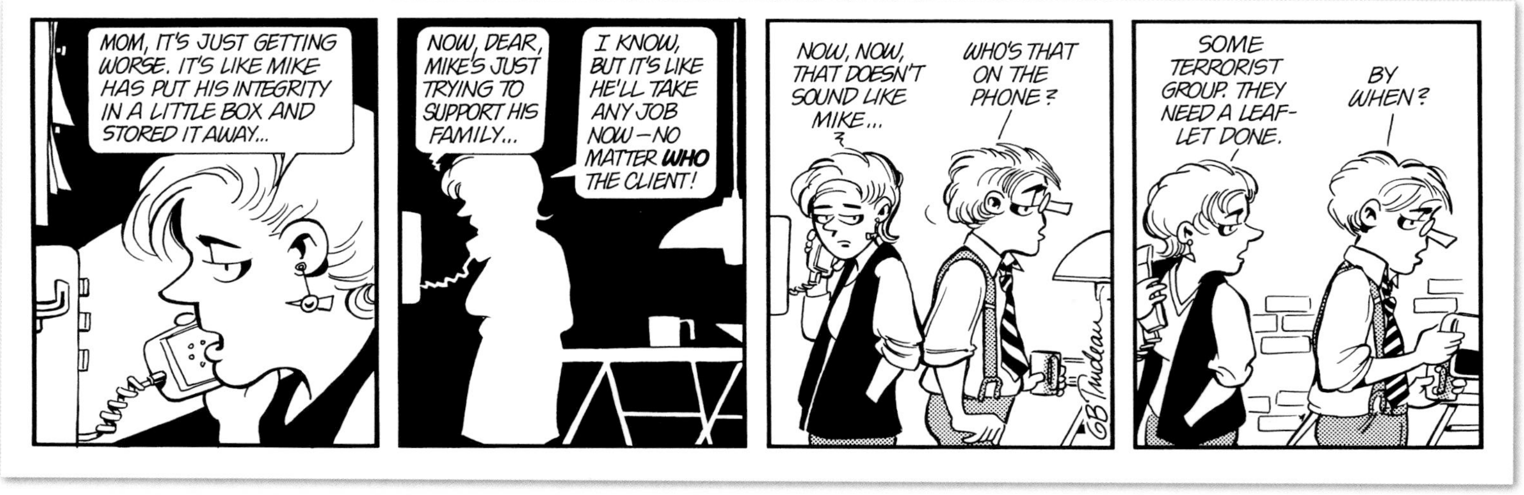
MOM, IT'S JUST GETTING WORSE. IT'S LIKE MIKE HAS PUT HIS INTEGRITY IN A LITTLE BOX AND STORED IT AWAY...
NOW, DEAR, MIKE'S JUST TRYING TO SUPPORT HIS FAMILY...
I KNOW, BUT IT'S LIKE HE'LL TAKE ANY JOB NOW—NO MATTER WHO THE CLIENT!
NOW, NOW, THAT DOESN'T SOUND LIKE MIKE...
WHO'S THAT ON THE PHONE?
SOME TERRORIST GROUP. THEY NEED A LEAFLET DONE.
BY WHEN?
GB Trudeau

7/8/93

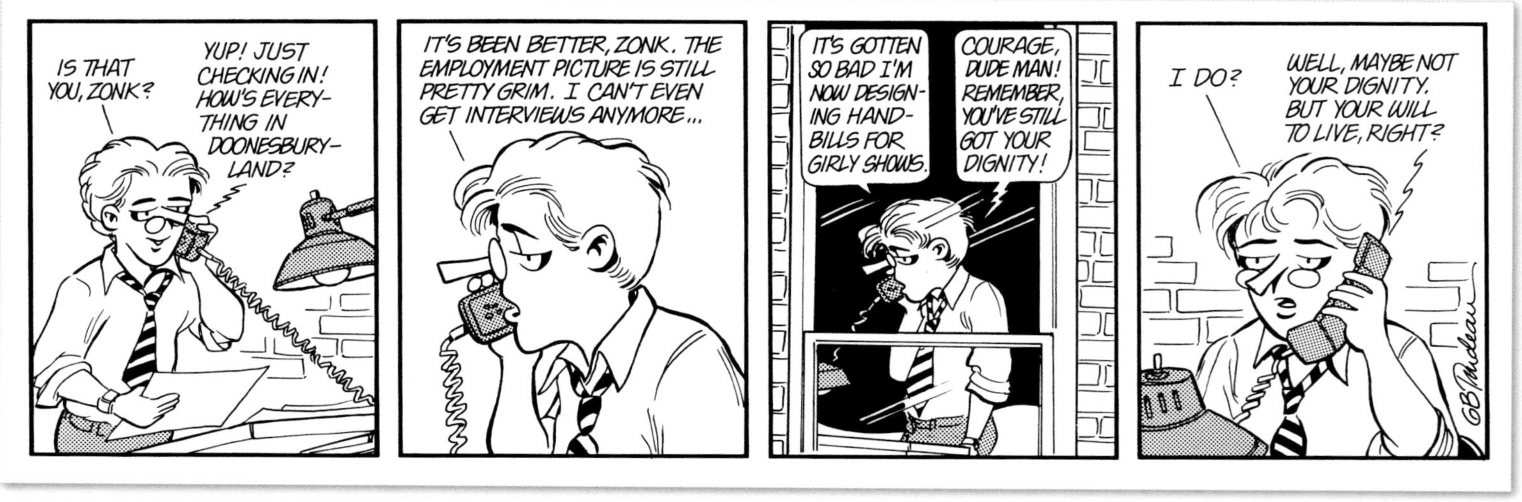
IS THAT YOU, ZONK?
YUP! JUST CHECKING IN! HOW'S EVERYTHING IN DOONESBURYLAND?
IT'S BEEN BETTER, ZONK. THE EMPLOYMENT PICTURE IS STILL PRETTY GRIM. I CAN'T EVEN GET INTERVIEWS ANYMORE...
IT'S GOTTEN SO BAD I'M NOW DESIGNING HANDBILLS FOR GIRLY SHOWS.
COURAGE, DUDE MAN! REMEMBER, YOU'VE STILL GOT YOUR DIGNITY!
I DO?
WELL, MAYBE NOT YOUR DIGNITY. BUT YOUR WILL TO LIVE, RIGHT?
GB Trudeau

7/9/93

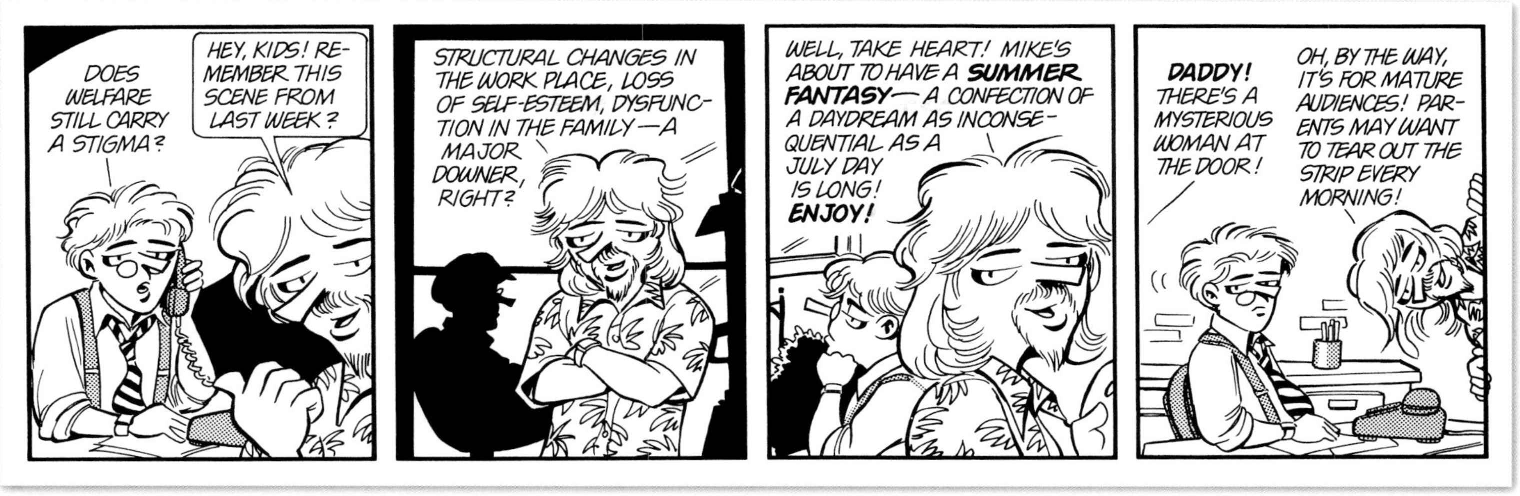
DOES WELFARE STILL CARRY A STIGMA?
HEY, KIDS! REMEMBER THIS SCENE FROM LAST WEEK?
STRUCTURAL CHANGES IN THE WORK PLACE, LOSS OF SELF-ESTEEM, DYSFUNCTION IN THE FAMILY—A MAJOR DOWNER, RIGHT?
WELL, TAKE HEART! MIKE'S ABOUT TO HAVE A **SUMMER FANTASY**—A CONFECTION OF A DAYDREAM AS INCONSEQUENTIAL AS A JULY DAY IS LONG! **ENJOY!**
DADDY! THERE'S A MYSTERIOUS WOMAN AT THE DOOR!
OH, BY THE WAY, IT'S FOR MATURE AUDIENCES! PARENTS MAY WANT TO TEAR OUT THE STRIP EVERY MORNING!

7/12/93

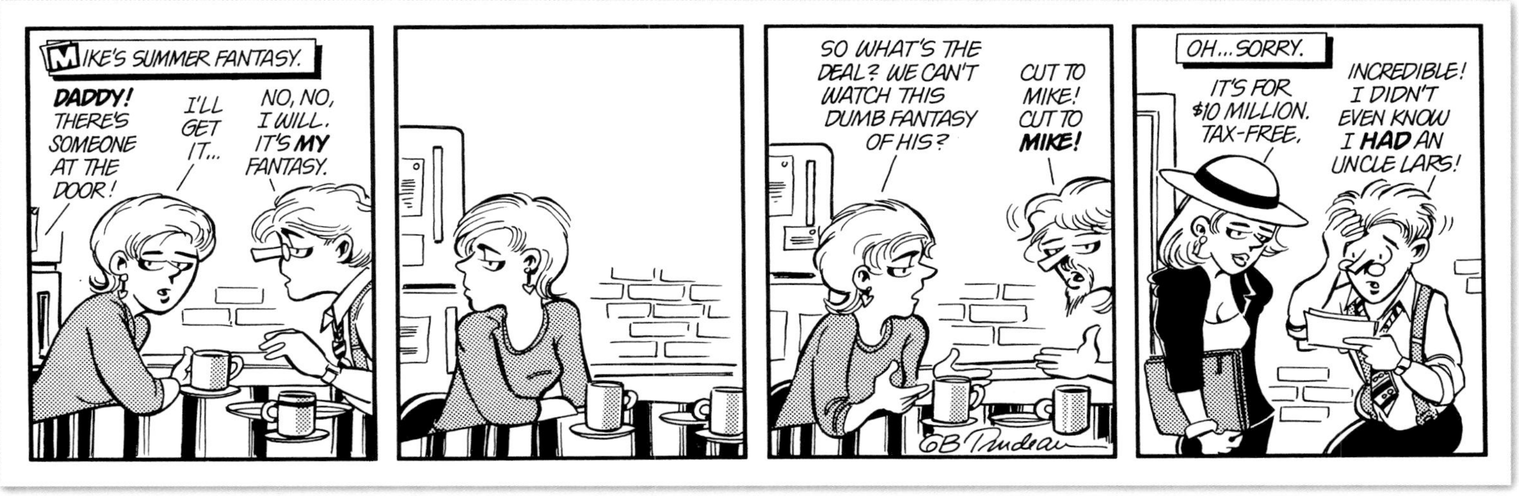
MIKE'S SUMMER FANTASY.
DADDY! THERE'S SOMEONE AT THE DOOR!
I'LL GET IT...
NO, NO, I WILL. IT'S **MY** FANTASY.
SO WHAT'S THE DEAL? WE CAN'T WATCH THIS DUMB FANTASY OF HIS?
CUT TO MIKE! CUT TO **MIKE!**
OH... SORRY.
IT'S FOR $10 MILLION. TAX-FREE.
INCREDIBLE! I DIDN'T EVEN KNOW I **HAD** AN UNCLE LARS!

7/13/93

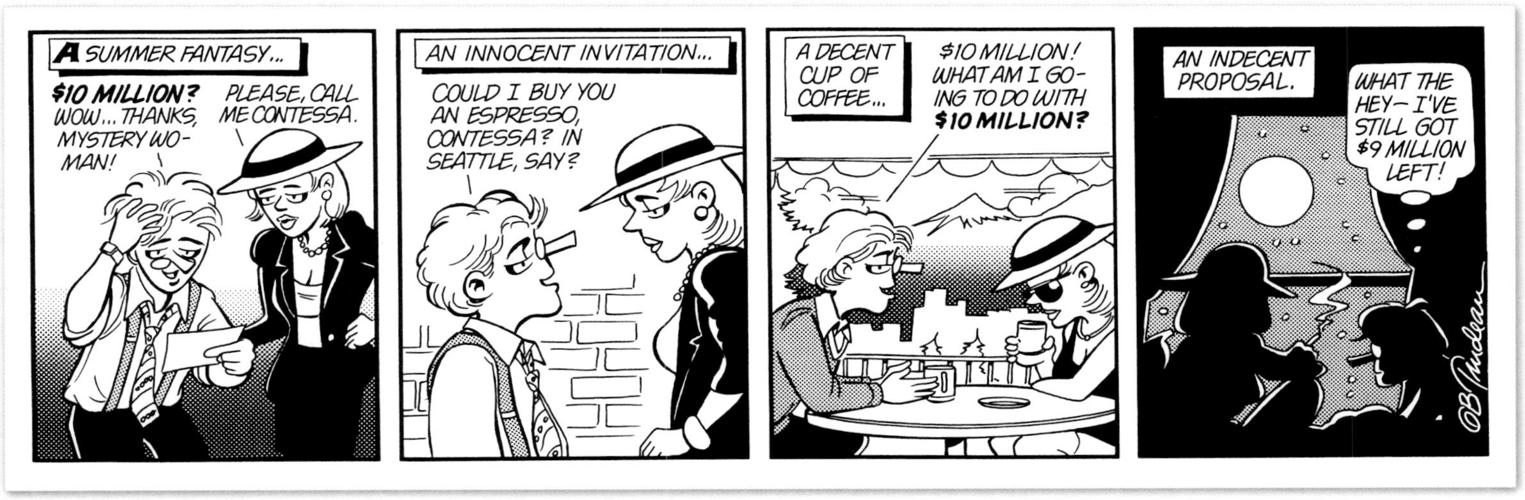
A SUMMER FANTASY...
$10 MILLION? WOW... THANKS, MYSTERY WOMAN!
PLEASE, CALL ME CONTESSA.
AN INNOCENT INVITATION...
COULD I BUY YOU AN ESPRESSO, CONTESSA? IN SEATTLE, SAY?
A DECENT CUP OF COFFEE...
$10 MILLION! WHAT AM I GOING TO DO WITH **$10 MILLION?**
AN INDECENT PROPOSAL.
WHAT THE HEY— I'VE STILL GOT $9 MILLION LEFT!

7/14/93

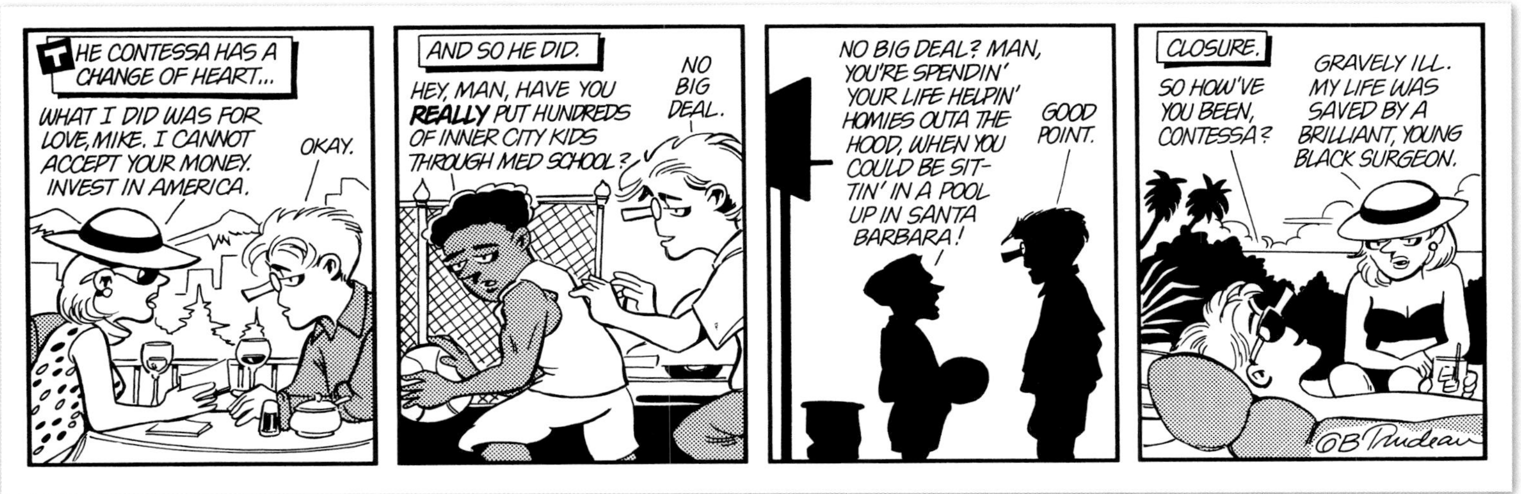
THE CONTESSA HAS A CHANGE OF HEART...
WHAT I DID WAS FOR LOVE, MIKE. I CANNOT ACCEPT YOUR MONEY. INVEST IN AMERICA.
OKAY.
AND SO HE DID.
HEY, MAN, HAVE YOU **REALLY** PUT HUNDREDS OF INNER CITY KIDS THROUGH MED SCHOOL?
NO BIG DEAL.
NO BIG DEAL? MAN, YOU'RE SPENDIN' YOUR LIFE HELPIN' HOMIES OUTA THE HOOD, WHEN YOU COULD BE SITTIN' IN A POOL UP IN SANTA BARBARA!
GOOD POINT.
CLOSURE.
SO HOW'VE YOU BEEN, CONTESSA?
GRAVELY ILL. MY LIFE WAS SAVED BY A BRILLIANT, YOUNG BLACK SURGEON.

7/15/93

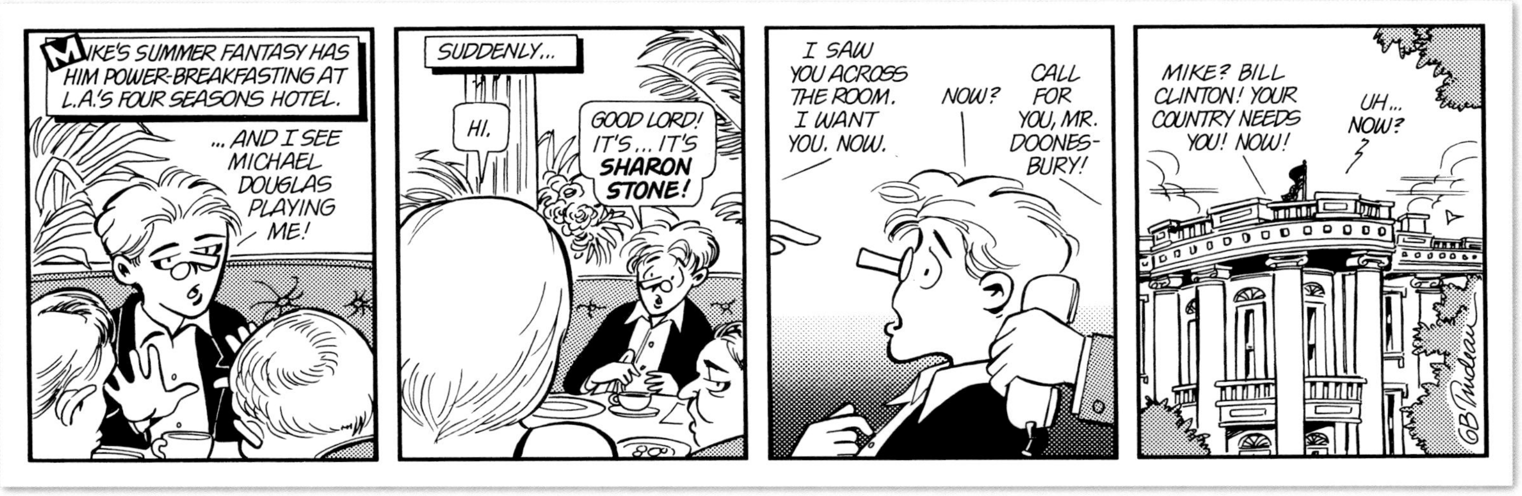
MIKE'S SUMMER FANTASY HAS HIM POWER-BREAKFASTING AT L.A.'S FOUR SEASONS HOTEL.
... AND I SEE MICHAEL DOUGLAS PLAYING ME!
SUDDENLY...
HI.
GOOD LORD! IT'S ... IT'S SHARON STONE!
I SAW YOU ACROSS THE ROOM. I WANT YOU. NOW.
NOW?
CALL FOR YOU, MR. DOONESBURY!
MIKE? BILL CLINTON! YOUR COUNTRY NEEDS YOU! NOW!
UH... NOW?

7/16/93

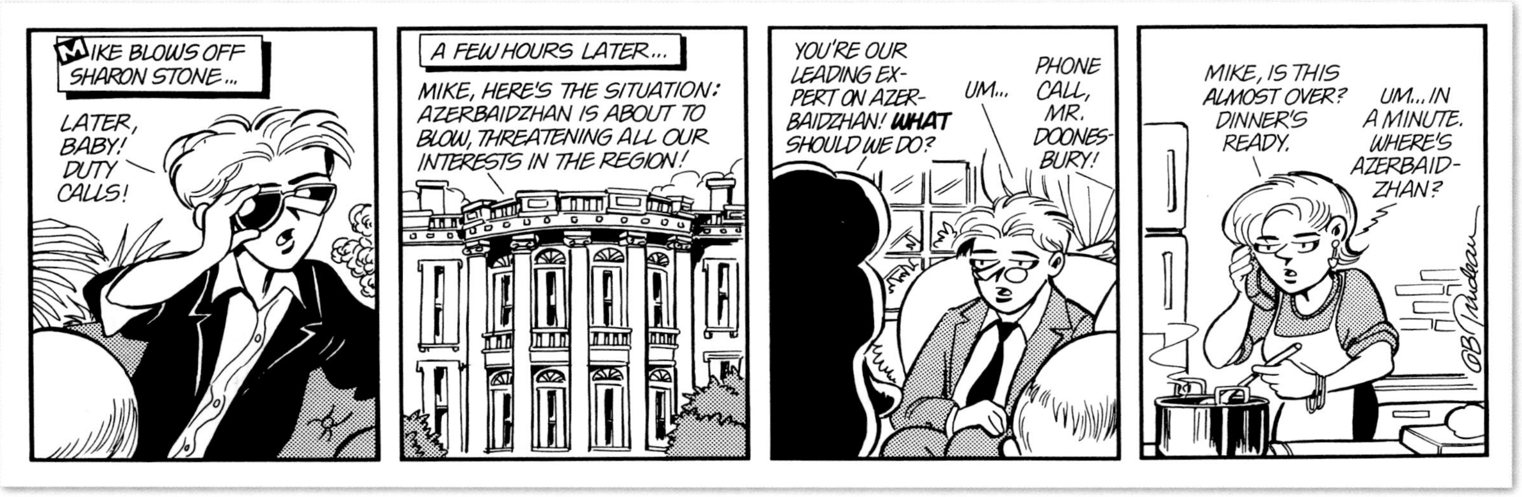
MIKE BLOWS OFF SHARON STONE...
LATER, BABY! DUTY CALLS!
A FEW HOURS LATER...
MIKE, HERE'S THE SITUATION: AZERBAIDZHAN IS ABOUT TO BLOW, THREATENING ALL OUR INTERESTS IN THE REGION!
YOU'RE OUR LEADING EXPERT ON AZERBAIDZHAN! WHAT SHOULD WE DO?
UM...
PHONE CALL, MR. DOONESBURY!
MIKE, IS THIS ALMOST OVER? DINNER'S READY.
UM... IN A MINUTE. WHERE'S AZERBAIDZHAN?

7/17/93

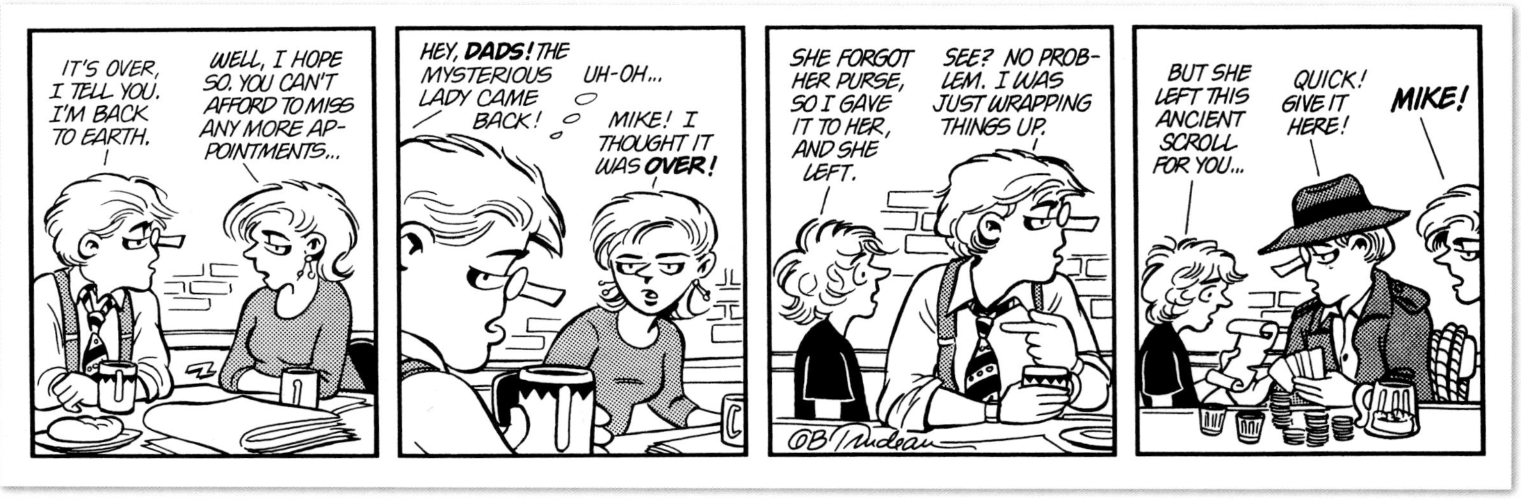
IT'S OVER, I TELL YOU. I'M BACK TO EARTH.
WELL, I HOPE SO. YOU CAN'T AFFORD TO MISS ANY MORE APPOINTMENTS...
HEY, DADS! THE MYSTERIOUS LADY CAME BACK!
UH-OH...
MIKE! I THOUGHT IT WAS OVER!
SHE FORGOT HER PURSE, SO I GAVE IT TO HER, AND SHE LEFT.
SEE? NO PROBLEM. I WAS JUST WRAPPING THINGS UP.
BUT SHE LEFT THIS ANCIENT SCROLL FOR YOU...
QUICK! GIVE IT HERE!
MIKE!

7/19/93

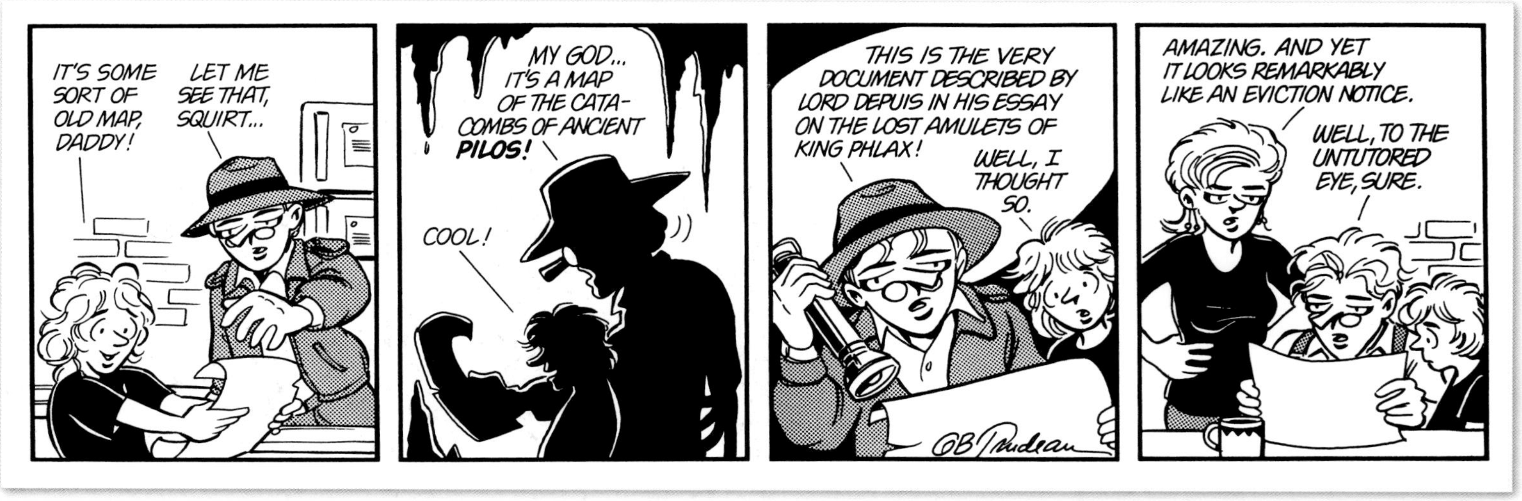
IT'S SOME SORT OF OLD MAP, DADDY!
LET ME SEE THAT, SQUIRT...
MY GOD... IT'S A MAP OF THE CATACOMBS OF ANCIENT PILOS!
COOL!
THIS IS THE VERY DOCUMENT DESCRIBED BY LORD DEPUIS IN HIS ESSAY ON THE LOST AMULETS OF KING PHLAX!
WELL, I THOUGHT SO.
AMAZING. AND YET IT LOOKS REMARKABLY LIKE AN EVICTION NOTICE.
WELL, TO THE UNTUTORED EYE, SURE.

7/20/93

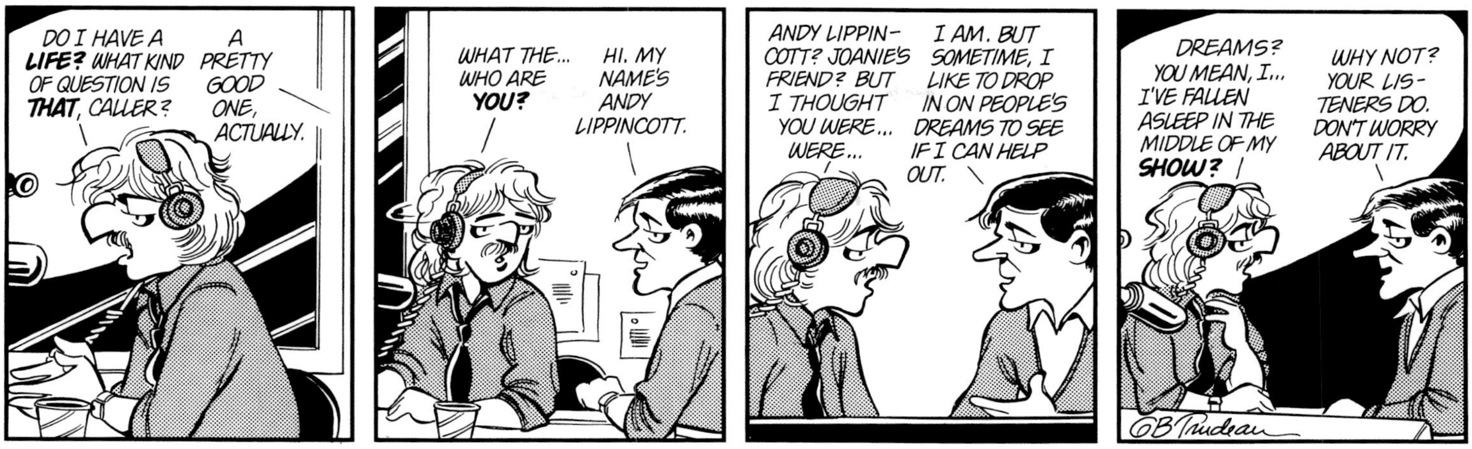
DO I HAVE A LIFE? WHAT KIND OF QUESTION IS THAT, CALLER?
A PRETTY GOOD ONE, ACTUALLY.
WHAT THE... WHO ARE YOU?
HI. MY NAME'S ANDY LIPPINCOTT.
ANDY LIPPINCOTT? JOANIE'S FRIEND? BUT I THOUGHT YOU WERE... WERE...
I AM. BUT SOMETIME, I LIKE TO DROP IN ON PEOPLE'S DREAMS TO SEE IF I CAN HELP OUT.
DREAMS? YOU MEAN, I... I'VE FALLEN ASLEEP IN THE MIDDLE OF MY SHOW?
WHY NOT? YOUR LISTENERS DO. DON'T WORRY ABOUT IT.
GB Trudeau

8/31/93

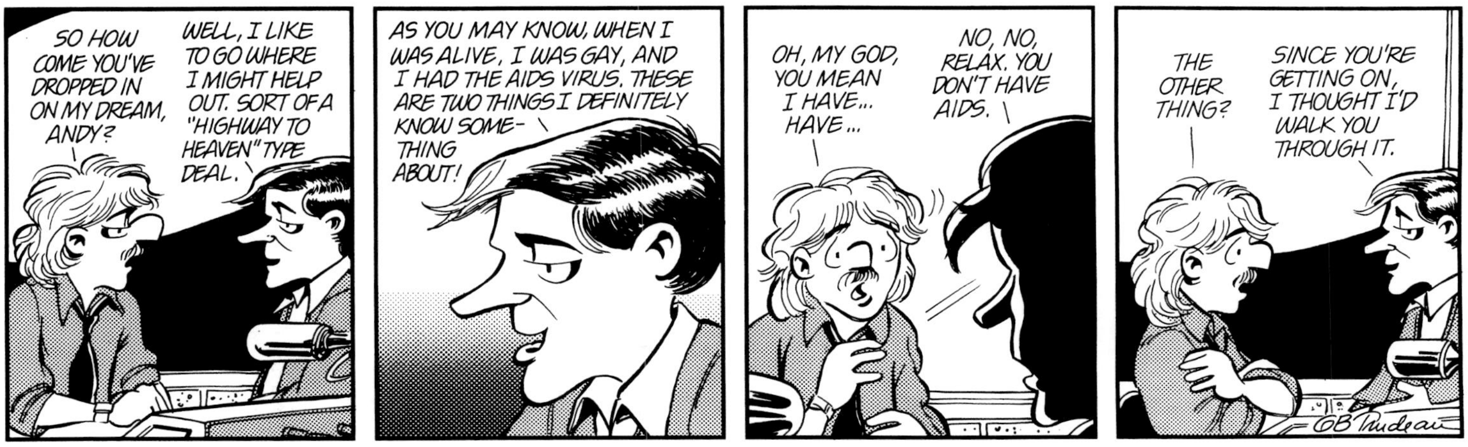
SO HOW COME YOU'VE DROPPED IN ON MY DREAM, ANDY?
WELL, I LIKE TO GO WHERE I MIGHT HELP OUT. SORT OF A "HIGHWAY TO HEAVEN" TYPE DEAL.
AS YOU MAY KNOW, WHEN I WAS ALIVE, I WAS GAY, AND I HAD THE AIDS VIRUS. THESE ARE TWO THINGS I DEFINITELY KNOW SOMETHING ABOUT!
OH, MY GOD, YOU MEAN I HAVE... HAVE...
NO, NO, RELAX. YOU DON'T HAVE AIDS.
THE OTHER THING?
SINCE YOU'RE GETTING ON, I THOUGHT I'D WALK YOU THROUGH IT.
GB Trudeau

9/1/93

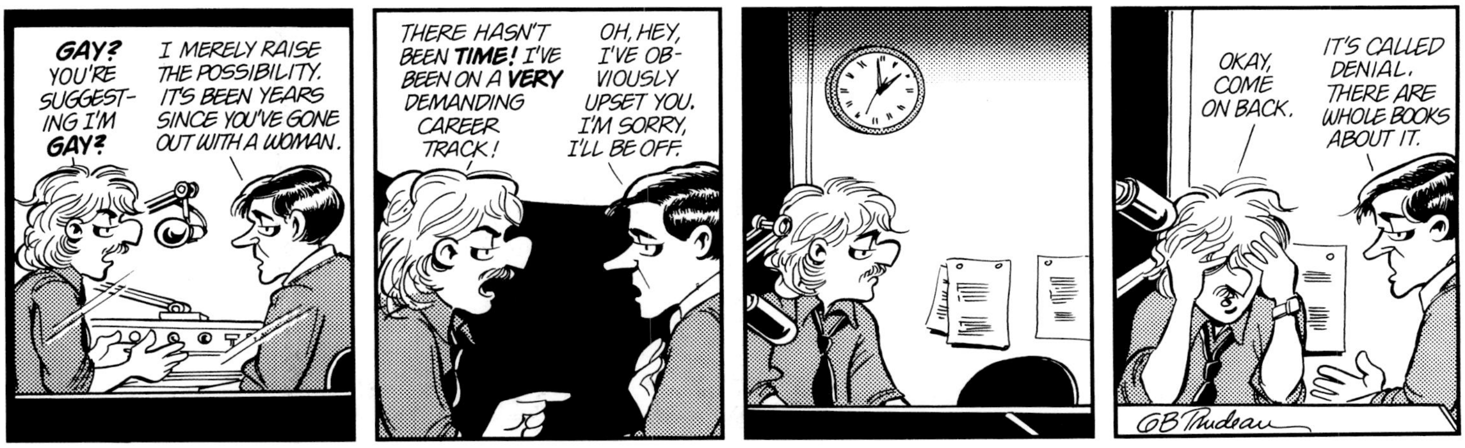
GAY? YOU'RE SUGGESTING I'M GAY?
I MERELY RAISE THE POSSIBILITY. IT'S BEEN YEARS SINCE YOU'VE GONE OUT WITH A WOMAN.
THERE HASN'T BEEN TIME! I'VE BEEN ON A VERY DEMANDING CAREER TRACK!
OH, HEY, I'VE OBVIOUSLY UPSET YOU. I'M SORRY, I'LL BE OFF.
OKAY, COME ON BACK.
IT'S CALLED DENIAL. THERE ARE WHOLE BOOKS ABOUT IT.
GB Trudeau

9/2/93

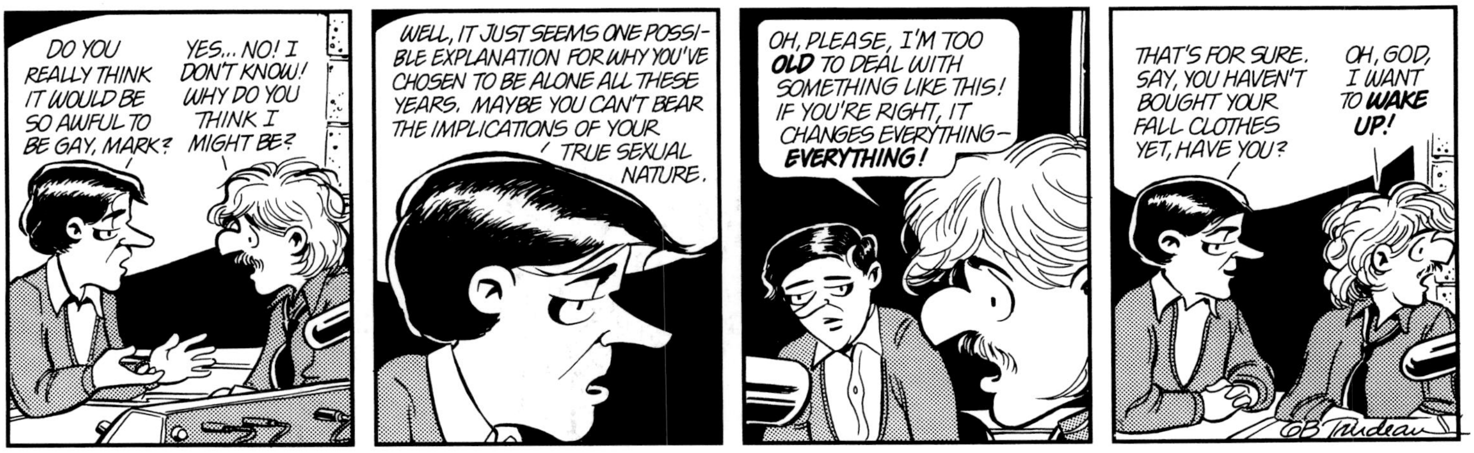
DO YOU REALLY THINK IT WOULD BE SO AWFUL TO BE GAY, MARK?
YES... NO! I DON'T KNOW! WHY DO YOU THINK I MIGHT BE?
WELL, IT JUST SEEMS ONE POSSIBLE EXPLANATION FOR WHY YOU'VE CHOSEN TO BE ALONE ALL THESE YEARS. MAYBE YOU CAN'T BEAR THE IMPLICATIONS OF YOUR TRUE SEXUAL NATURE.
OH, PLEASE, I'M TOO OLD TO DEAL WITH SOMETHING LIKE THIS! IF YOU'RE RIGHT, IT CHANGES EVERYTHING— EVERYTHING!
THAT'S FOR SURE. SAY, YOU HAVEN'T BOUGHT YOUR FALL CLOTHES YET, HAVE YOU?
OH, GOD, I WANT TO WAKE UP!
GB Trudeau

9/3/93

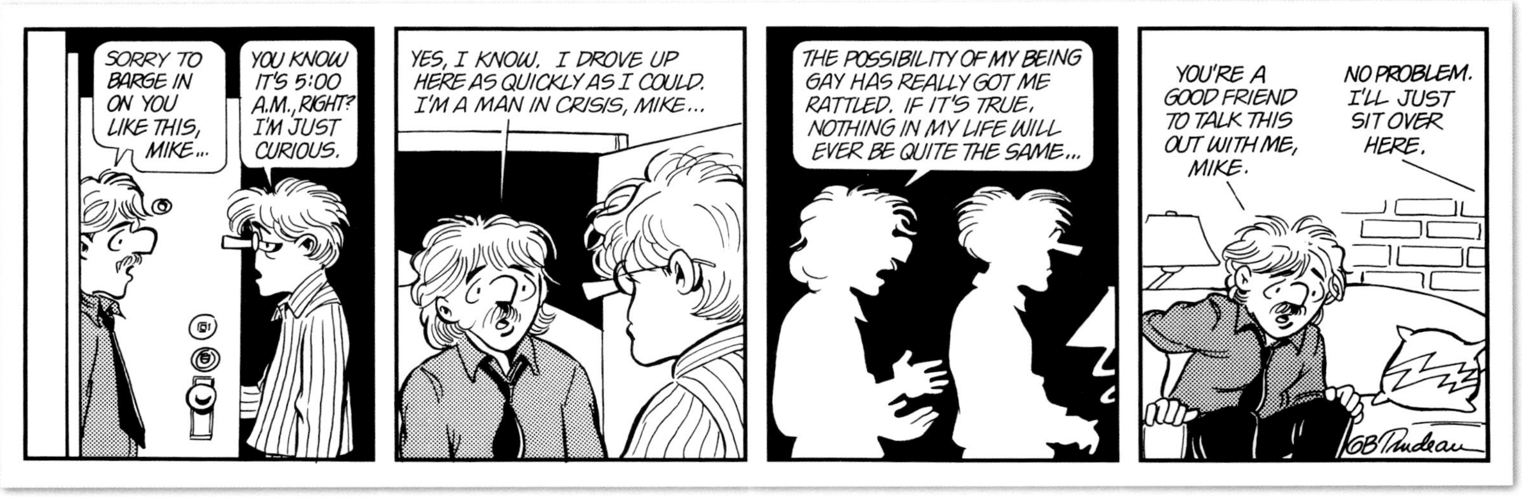
SORRY TO BARGE IN ON YOU LIKE THIS, MIKE...
YOU KNOW IT'S 5:00 A.M., RIGHT? I'M JUST CURIOUS.
YES, I KNOW. I DROVE UP HERE AS QUICKLY AS I COULD. I'M A MAN IN CRISIS, MIKE...
THE POSSIBILITY OF MY BEING GAY HAS REALLY GOT ME RATTLED. IF IT'S TRUE, NOTHING IN MY LIFE WILL EVER BE QUITE THE SAME...
YOU'RE A GOOD FRIEND TO TALK THIS OUT WITH ME, MIKE.
NO PROBLEM. I'LL JUST SIT OVER HERE.
GB Trudeau

9/6/93

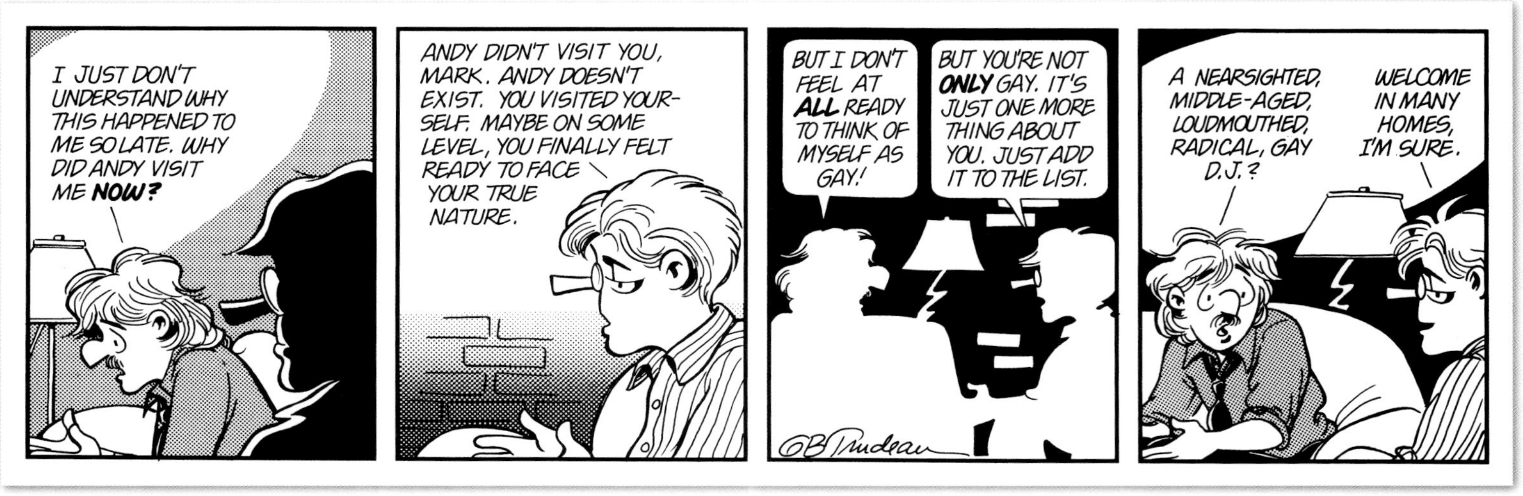
I JUST DON'T UNDERSTAND WHY THIS HAPPENED TO ME SO LATE. WHY DID ANDY VISIT ME **NOW?**
ANDY DIDN'T VISIT YOU, MARK. ANDY DOESN'T EXIST. YOU VISITED YOURSELF. MAYBE ON SOME LEVEL, YOU FINALLY FELT READY TO FACE YOUR TRUE NATURE.
BUT I DON'T FEEL AT **ALL** READY TO THINK OF MYSELF AS GAY!
BUT YOU'RE NOT **ONLY** GAY. IT'S JUST ONE MORE THING ABOUT YOU. JUST ADD IT TO THE LIST.
A NEARSIGHTED, MIDDLE-AGED, LOUDMOUTHED, RADICAL, GAY D.J.?
WELCOME IN MANY HOMES, I'M SURE.
GB Trudeau

9/7/93

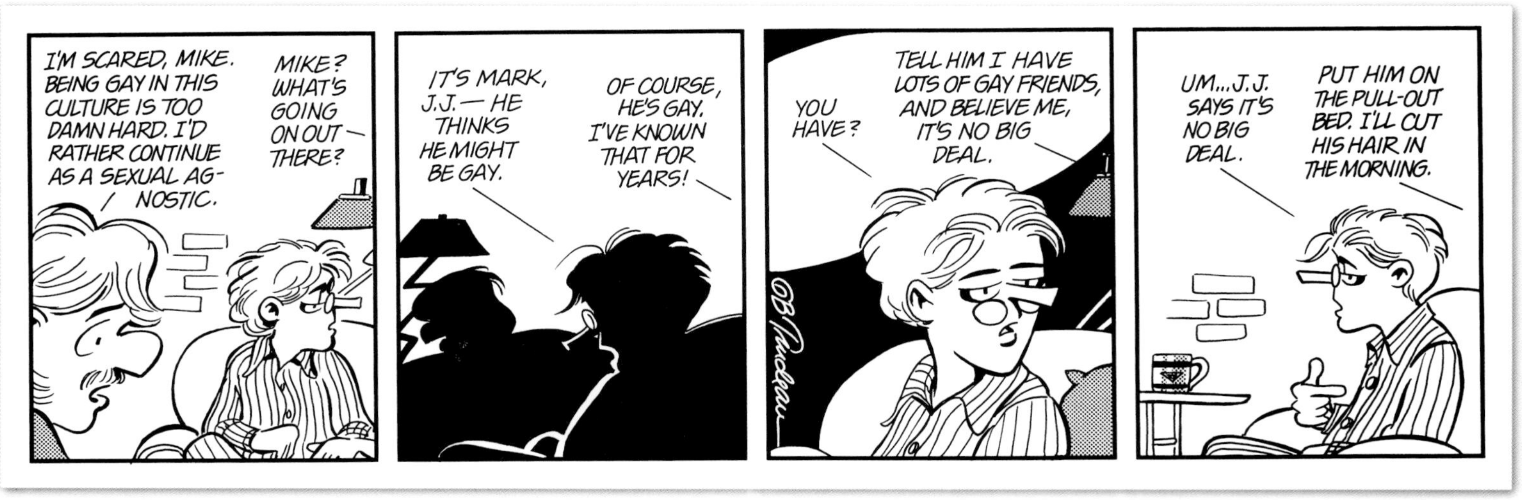
I'M SCARED, MIKE. BEING GAY IN THIS CULTURE IS TOO DAMN HARD. I'D RATHER CONTINUE AS A SEXUAL AGNOSTIC.
MIKE? WHAT'S GOING ON OUT THERE?
IT'S MARK, J.J. — HE THINKS HE MIGHT BE GAY.
OF COURSE, HE'S GAY. I'VE KNOWN THAT FOR YEARS!
YOU HAVE?
TELL HIM I HAVE LOTS OF GAY FRIENDS, AND BELIEVE ME, IT'S NO BIG DEAL.
GB Trudeau
UM... J.J. SAYS IT'S NO BIG DEAL.
PUT HIM ON THE PULL-OUT BED. I'LL CUT HIS HAIR IN THE MORNING.

9/8/93

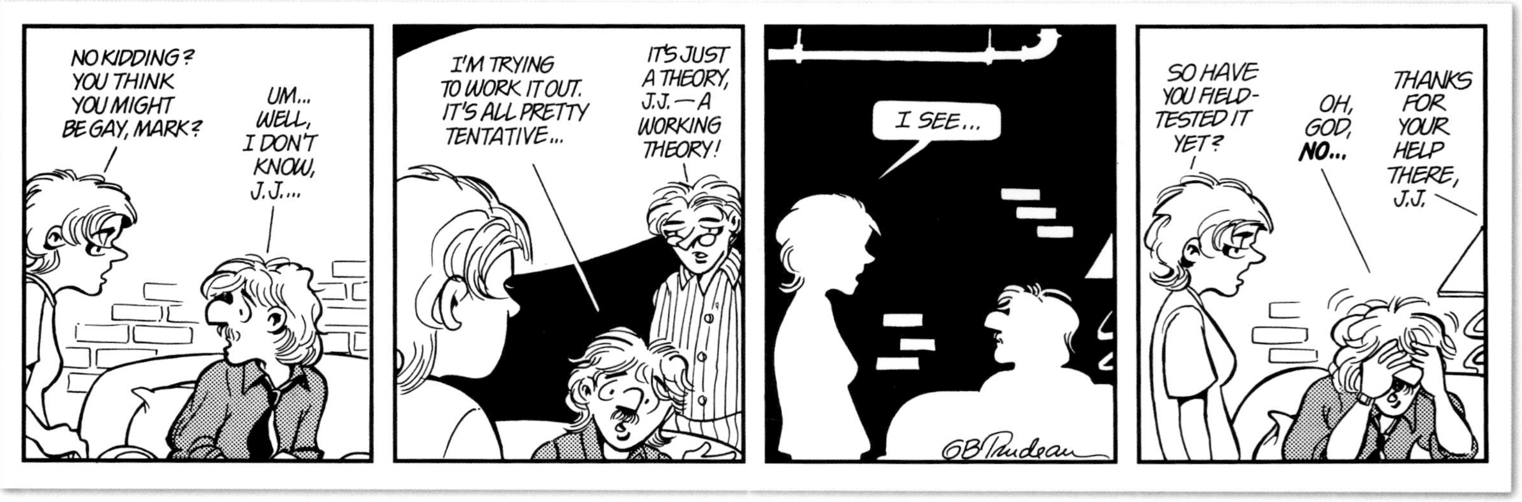
NO KIDDING? YOU THINK YOU MIGHT BE GAY, MARK?
UM... WELL, I DON'T KNOW, J.J...
I'M TRYING TO WORK IT OUT. IT'S ALL PRETTY TENTATIVE...
IT'S JUST A THEORY, J.J. — A WORKING THEORY!
I SEE...
GB Trudeau
SO HAVE YOU FIELD-TESTED IT YET?
OH, GOD, **NO...**
THANKS FOR YOUR HELP THERE, J.J.

9/9/93

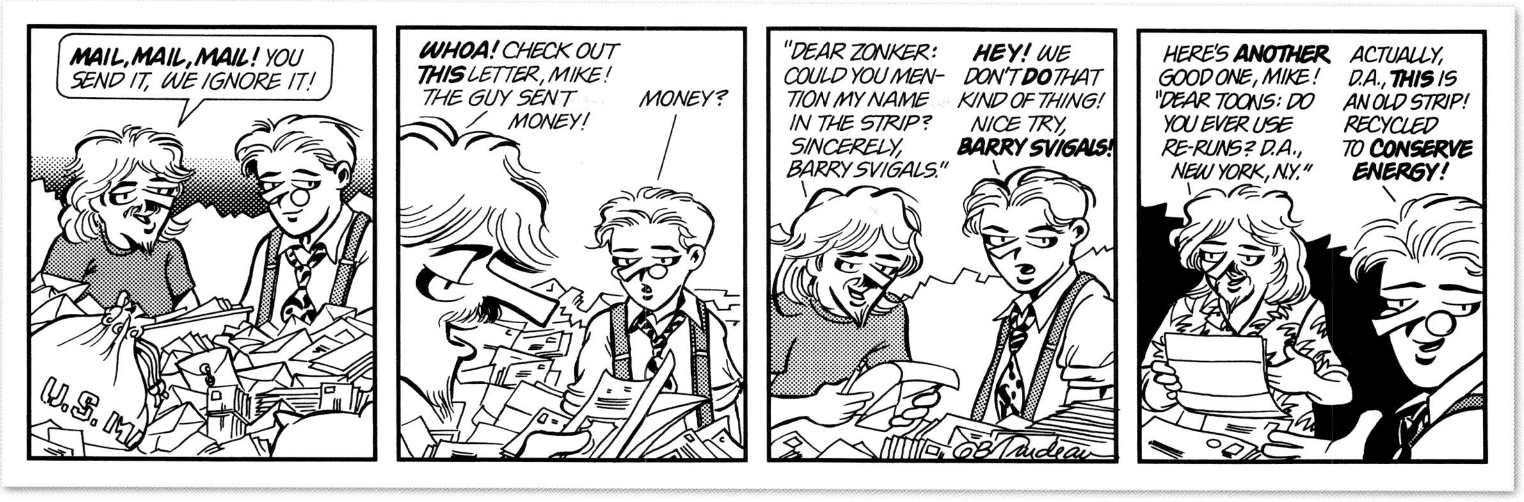
MAIL, MAIL, MAIL! YOU SEND IT, WE IGNORE IT!
U.S.M
WHOA! CHECK OUT THIS LETTER, MIKE! THE GUY SENT MONEY!
MONEY?
"DEAR ZONKER: COULD YOU MENTION MY NAME IN THE STRIP? SINCERELY, BARRY SVIGALS."
HEY! WE DON'T DO THAT KIND OF THING! NICE TRY, BARRY SVIGALS!
HERE'S ANOTHER GOOD ONE, MIKE! "DEAR TOONS: DO YOU EVER USE RE-RUNS? D.A., NEW YORK, N.Y."
ACTUALLY, D.A., THIS IS AN OLD STRIP! RECYCLED TO CONSERVE ENERGY!

1/11/94

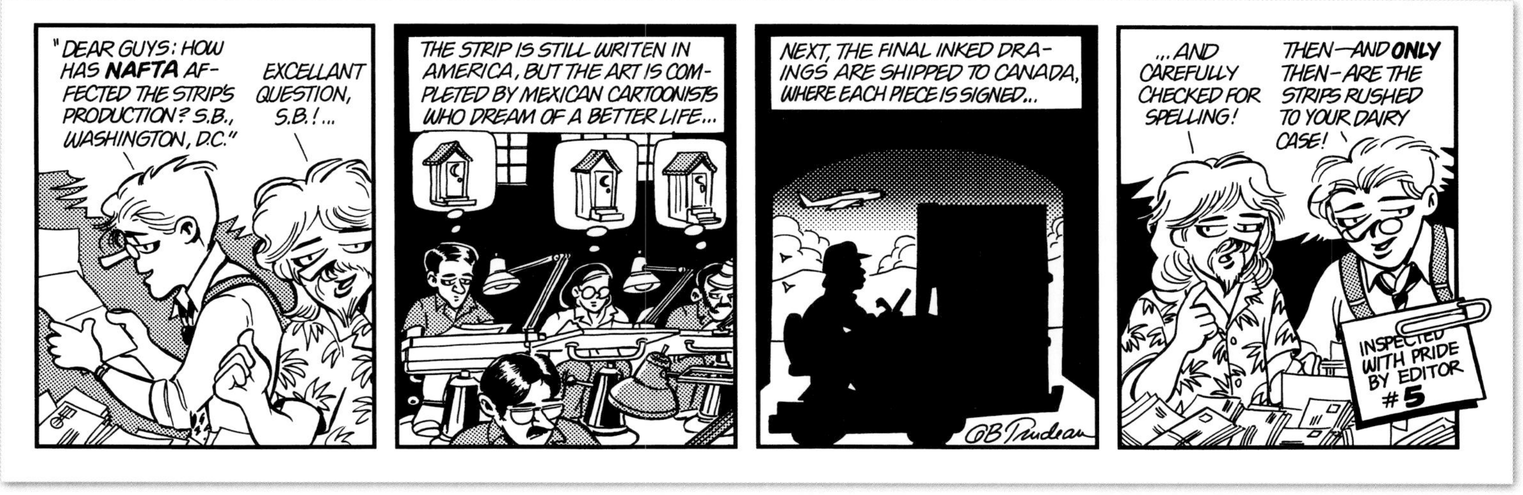
"DEAR GUYS: HOW HAS NAFTA AFFECTED THE STRIP'S PRODUCTION? S.B., WASHINGTON, D.C."
EXCELLANT QUESTION, S.B.! ...
THE STRIP IS STILL WRITEN IN AMERICA, BUT THE ART IS COMPLETED BY MEXICAN CARTOONISTS WHO DREAM OF A BETTER LIFE...
NEXT, THE FINAL INKED DRAINGS ARE SHIPPED TO CANADA, WHERE EACH PIECE IS SIGNED...
...AND CAREFULLY CHECKED FOR SPELLING!
THEN—AND ONLY THEN—ARE THE STRIPS RUSHED TO YOUR DAIRY CASE!
INSPECTED WITH PRIDE BY EDITOR #5

1/12/94

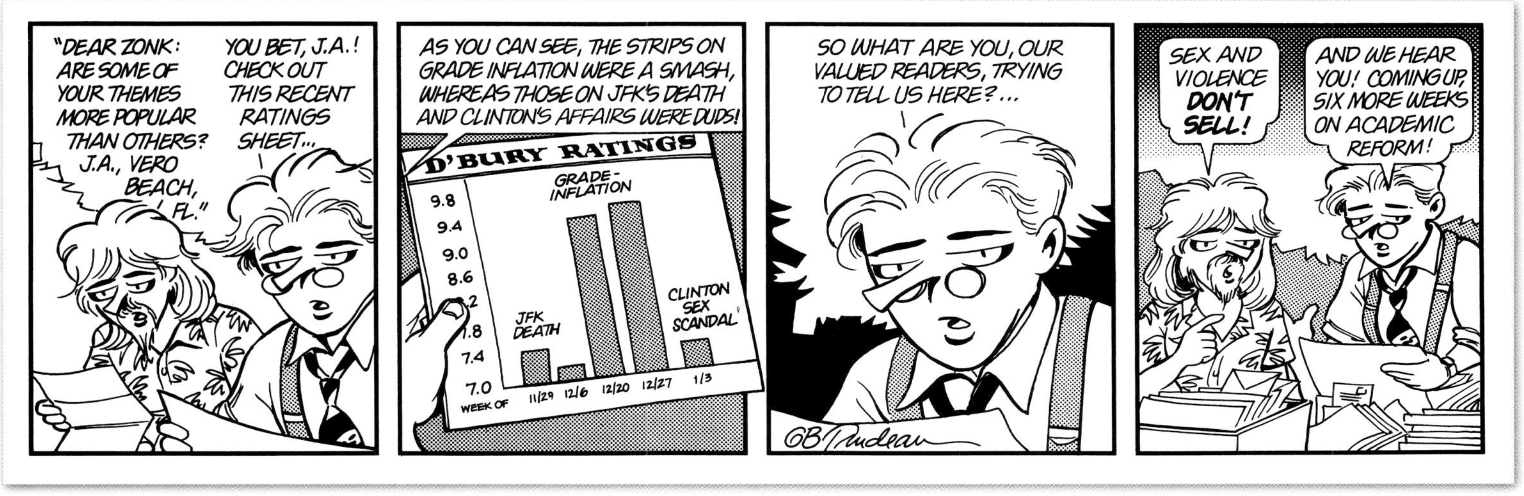
"DEAR ZONK: ARE SOME OF YOUR THEMES MORE POPULAR THAN OTHERS? J.A., VERO BEACH, FL."
YOU BET, J.A.! CHECK OUT THIS RECENT RATINGS SHEET...
AS YOU CAN SEE, THE STRIPS ON GRADE INFLATION WERE A SMASH, WHEREAS THOSE ON JFK'S DEATH AND CLINTON'S AFFAIRS WERE DUDS!
D'BURY RATINGS
GRADE-INFLATION
JFK DEATH
CLINTON SEX SCANDAL
9.8
9.4
9.0
8.6
7.4
7.0
WEEK OF 11/29 12/6 12/20 12/27 1/3
SO WHAT ARE YOU, OUR VALUED READERS, TRYING TO TELL US HERE?...
SEX AND VIOLENCE DON'T SELL!
AND WE HEAR YOU! COMING UP, SIX MORE WEEKS ON ACADEMIC REFORM!

1/13/94

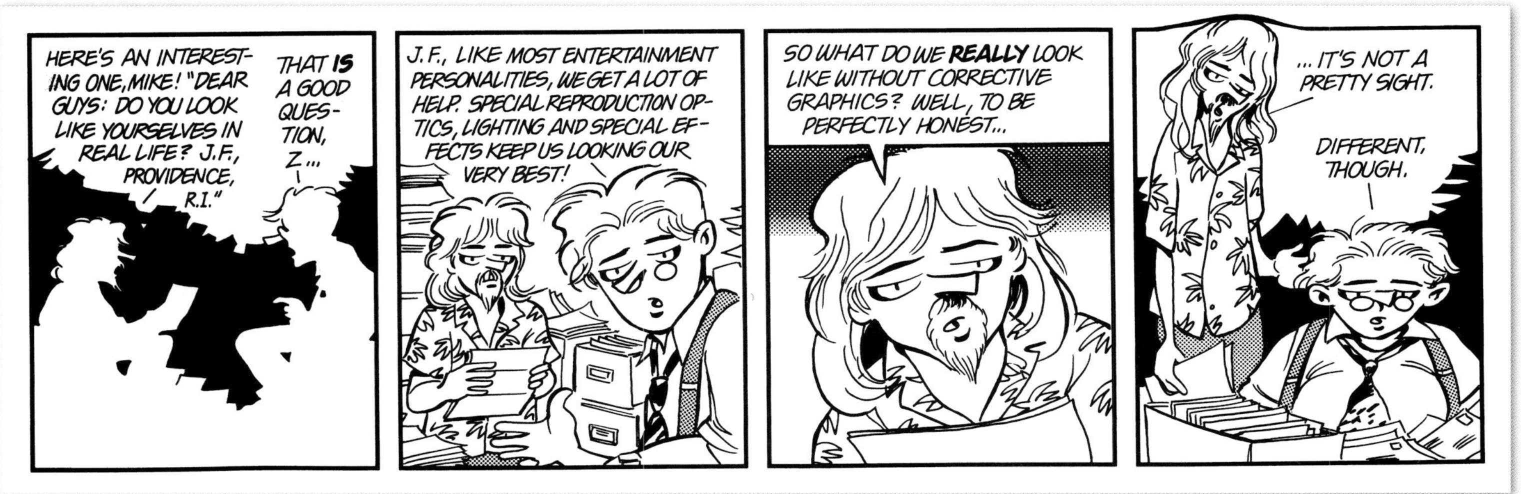
HERE'S AN INTERESTING ONE, MIKE! "DEAR GUYS: DO YOU LOOK LIKE YOURSELVES IN REAL LIFE? J.F., PROVIDENCE, R.I."
THAT IS A GOOD QUESTION, Z...
J.F., LIKE MOST ENTERTAINMENT PERSONALITIES, WE GET A LOT OF HELP. SPECIAL REPRODUCTION OPTICS, LIGHTING AND SPECIAL EFFECTS KEEP US LOOKING OUR VERY BEST!
SO WHAT DO WE REALLY LOOK LIKE WITHOUT CORRECTIVE GRAPHICS? WELL, TO BE PERFECTLY HONEST...
... IT'S NOT A PRETTY SIGHT.
DIFFERENT, THOUGH.

1/14/94

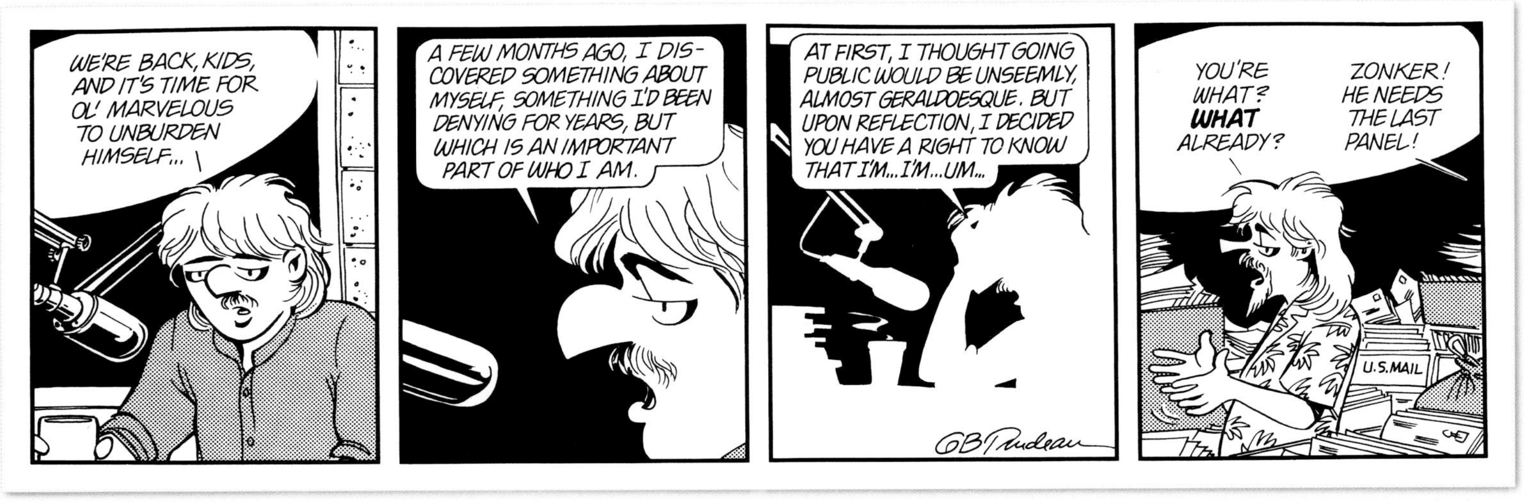
WE'RE BACK, KIDS, AND IT'S TIME FOR OL' MARVELOUS TO UNBURDEN HIMSELF...
A FEW MONTHS AGO, I DISCOVERED SOMETHING ABOUT MYSELF, SOMETHING I'D BEEN DENYING FOR YEARS, BUT WHICH IS AN IMPORTANT PART OF WHO I AM.
AT FIRST, I THOUGHT GOING PUBLIC WOULD BE UNSEEMLY, ALMOST GERALDOESQUE. BUT UPON REFLECTION, I DECIDED YOU HAVE A RIGHT TO KNOW THAT I'M...I'M...UM...
YOU'RE WHAT? **WHAT** ALREADY?
ZONKER! HE NEEDS THE LAST PANEL!
U.S. MAIL
GBTrudeau

1/17/94

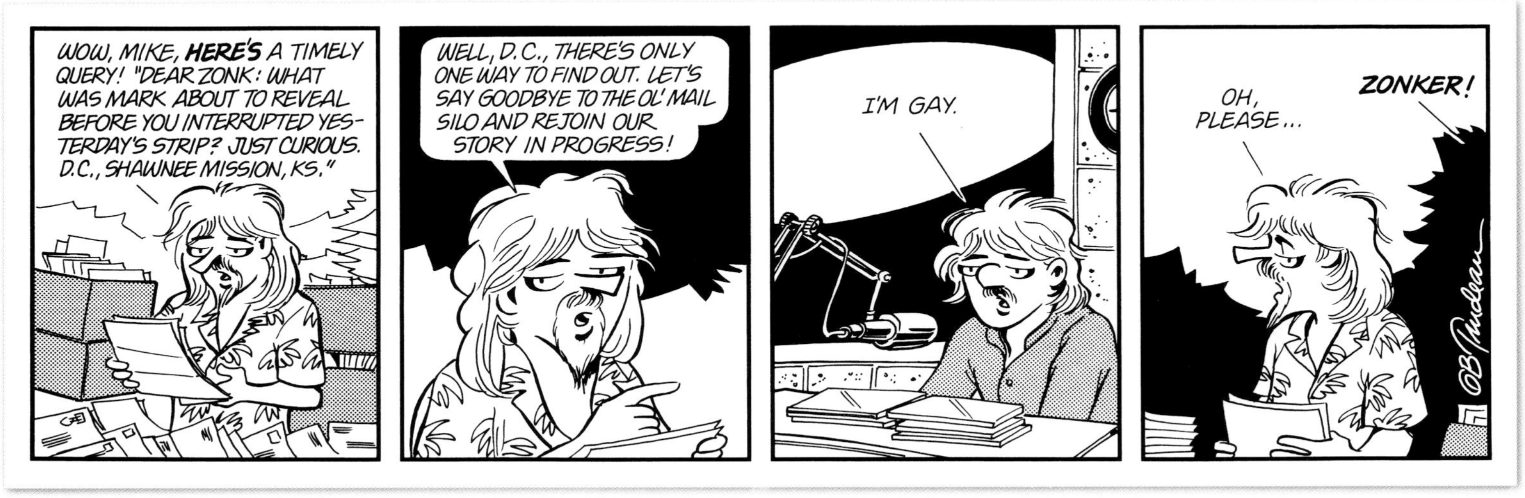
WOW, MIKE, **HERE'S** A TIMELY QUERY! "DEAR ZONK: WHAT WAS MARK ABOUT TO REVEAL BEFORE YOU INTERRUPTED YESTERDAY'S STRIP? JUST CURIOUS. D.C., SHAWNEE MISSION, KS."
WELL, D.C., THERE'S ONLY ONE WAY TO FIND OUT. LET'S SAY GOODBYE TO THE OL' MAIL SILO AND REJOIN OUR STORY IN PROGRESS!
I'M GAY.
OH, PLEASE...
ZONKER!
GBTrudeau

1/18/94

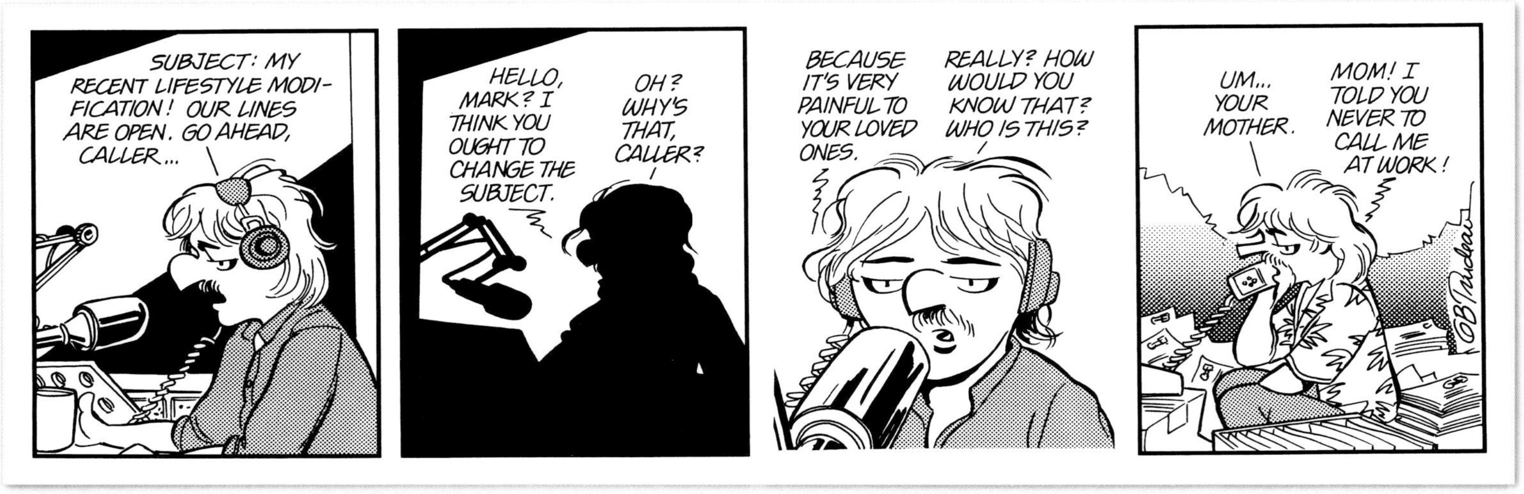
SUBJECT: MY RECENT LIFESTYLE MODIFICATION! OUR LINES ARE OPEN. GO AHEAD, CALLER...
HELLO, MARK? I THINK YOU OUGHT TO CHANGE THE SUBJECT.
OH? WHY'S THAT, CALLER?
BECAUSE IT'S VERY PAINFUL TO YOUR LOVED ONES.
REALLY? HOW WOULD YOU KNOW THAT? WHO IS THIS?
UM... YOUR MOTHER.
MOM! I TOLD YOU NEVER TO CALL ME AT WORK!
GBTrudeau

1/19/94

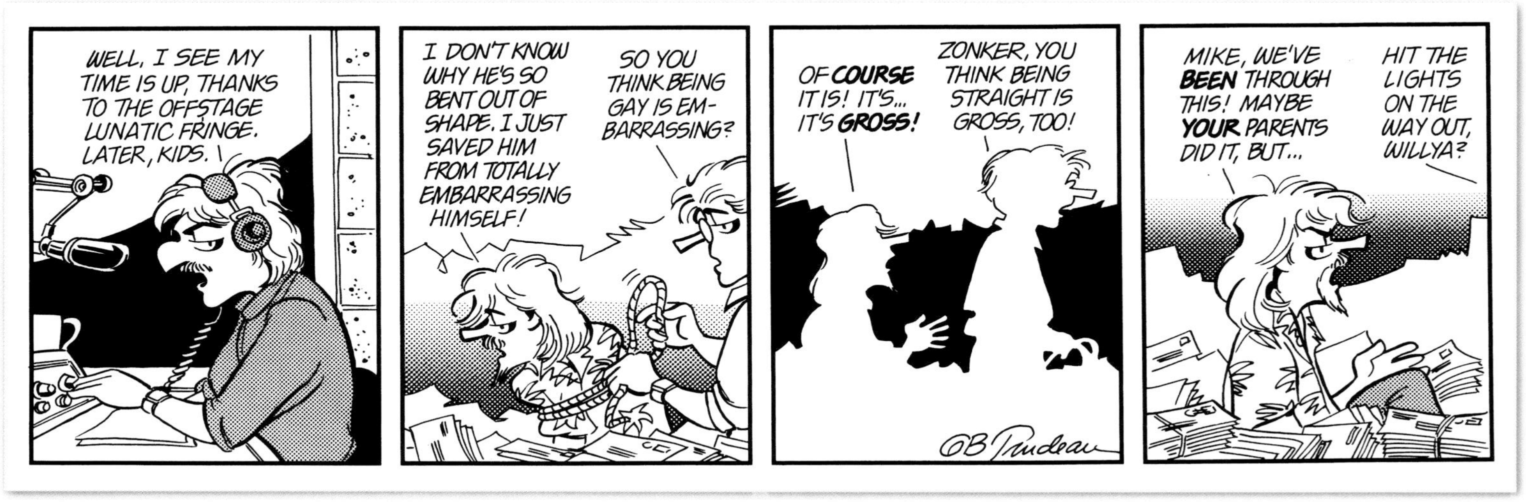
WELL, I SEE MY TIME IS UP, THANKS TO THE OFFSTAGE LUNATIC FRINGE. LATER, KIDS.
I DON'T KNOW WHY HE'S SO BENT OUT OF SHAPE. I JUST SAVED HIM FROM TOTALLY EMBARRASSING HIMSELF!
SO YOU THINK BEING GAY IS EMBARRASSING?
OF **COURSE** IT IS! IT'S... IT'S **GROSS!**
ZONKER, YOU THINK BEING STRAIGHT IS GROSS, TOO!
MIKE, WE'VE **BEEN** THROUGH THIS! MAYBE **YOUR** PARENTS DID IT, BUT...
HIT THE LIGHTS ON THE WAY OUT, WILLYA?
GBTrudeau

1/22/94

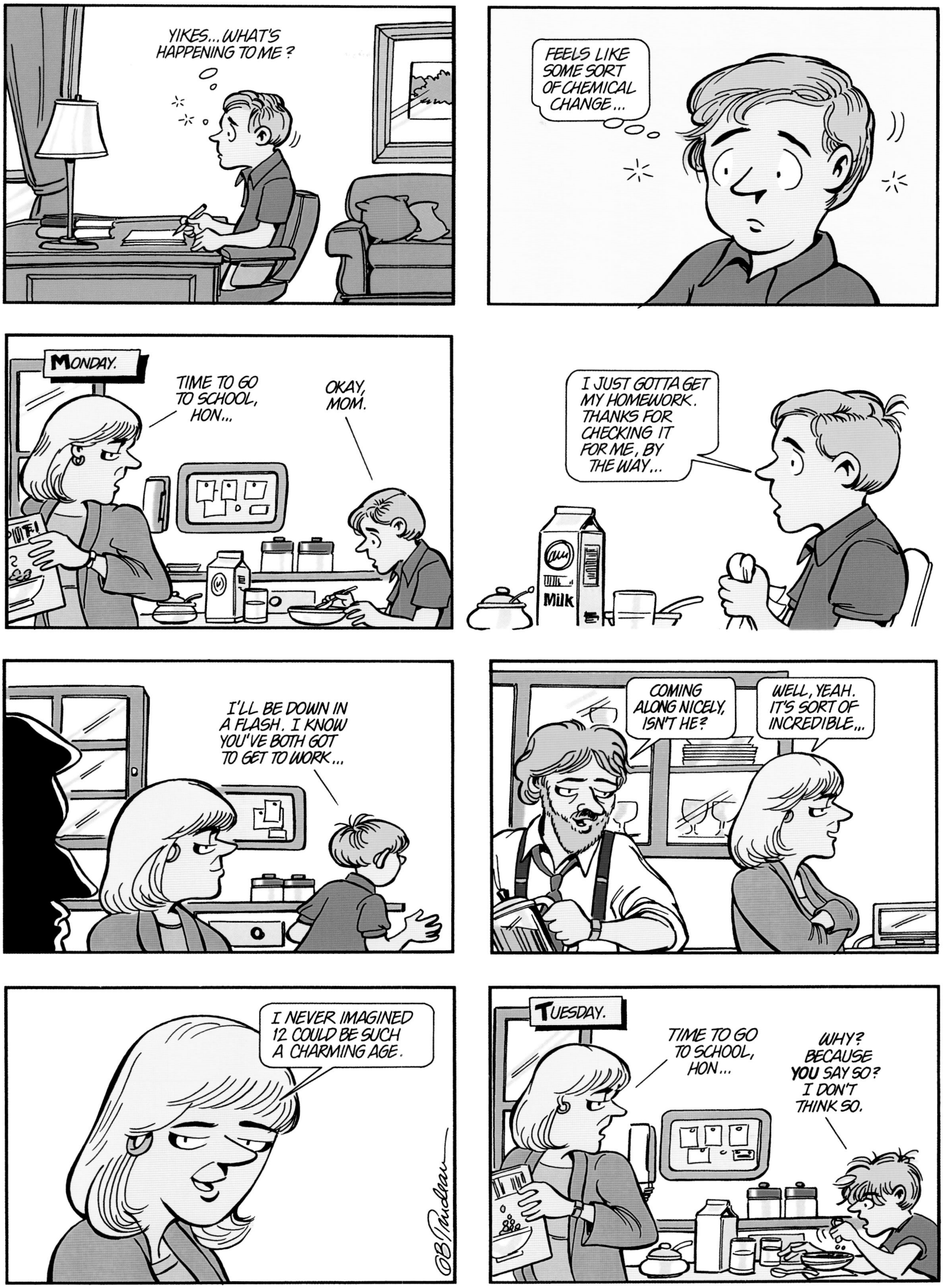

YIKES... WHAT'S HAPPENING TO ME?
FEELS LIKE SOME SORT OF CHEMICAL CHANGE...
MONDAY.
TIME TO GO TO SCHOOL, HON...
OKAY, MOM.
I JUST GOTTA GET MY HOMEWORK. THANKS FOR CHECKING IT FOR ME, BY THE WAY...
MILK
I'LL BE DOWN IN A FLASH. I KNOW YOU'VE BOTH GOT TO GET TO WORK...
COMING ALONG NICELY, ISN'T HE?
WELL, YEAH. IT'S SORT OF INCREDIBLE...
I NEVER IMAGINED 12 COULD BE SUCH A CHARMING AGE.
TUESDAY.
TIME TO GO TO SCHOOL, HON...
WHY? BECAUSE YOU SAY SO? I DON'T THINK SO.

7/3/94

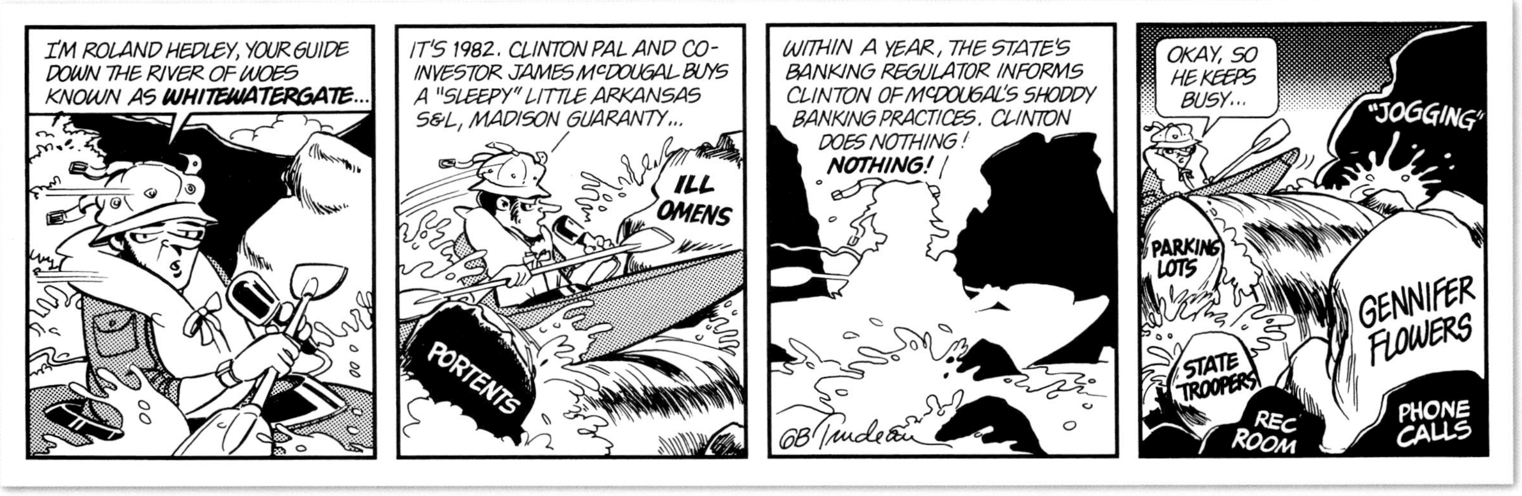
I'M ROLAND HEDLEY, YOUR GUIDE DOWN THE RIVER OF WOES KNOWN AS **WHITEWATERGATE**...
IT'S 1982. CLINTON PAL AND CO-INVESTOR JAMES McDOUGAL BUYS A "SLEEPY" LITTLE ARKANSAS S&L, MADISON GUARANTY...
ILL OMENS
PORTENTS
WITHIN A YEAR, THE STATE'S BANKING REGULATOR INFORMS CLINTON OF McDOUGAL'S SHODDY BANKING PRACTICES. CLINTON DOES NOTHING! **NOTHING!**
OKAY, SO HE KEEPS BUSY...
"JOGGING"
PARKING LOTS
GENNIFER FLOWERS
STATE TROOPERS
REC ROOM
PHONE CALLS

1/25/94

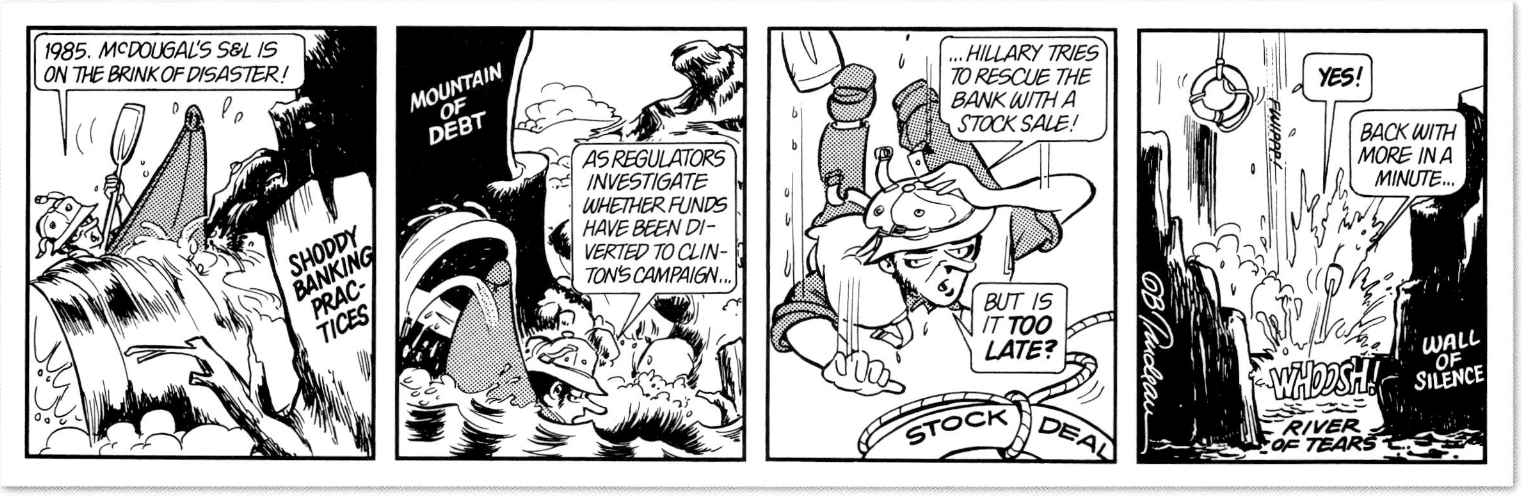
1985. McDOUGAL'S S&L IS ON THE BRINK OF DISASTER!
SHODDY BANKING PRAC-TICES
MOUNTAIN OF DEBT
AS REGULATORS INVESTIGATE WHETHER FUNDS HAVE BEEN DI-VERTED TO CLIN-TON'S CAMPAIGN...
...HILLARY TRIES TO RESCUE THE BANK WITH A STOCK SALE!
BUT IS IT **TOO LATE?**
STOCK DEAL
YES!
BACK WITH MORE IN A MINUTE...
FWUPP!
WHOOSH!
WALL OF SILENCE
RIVER OF TEARS

1/26/94

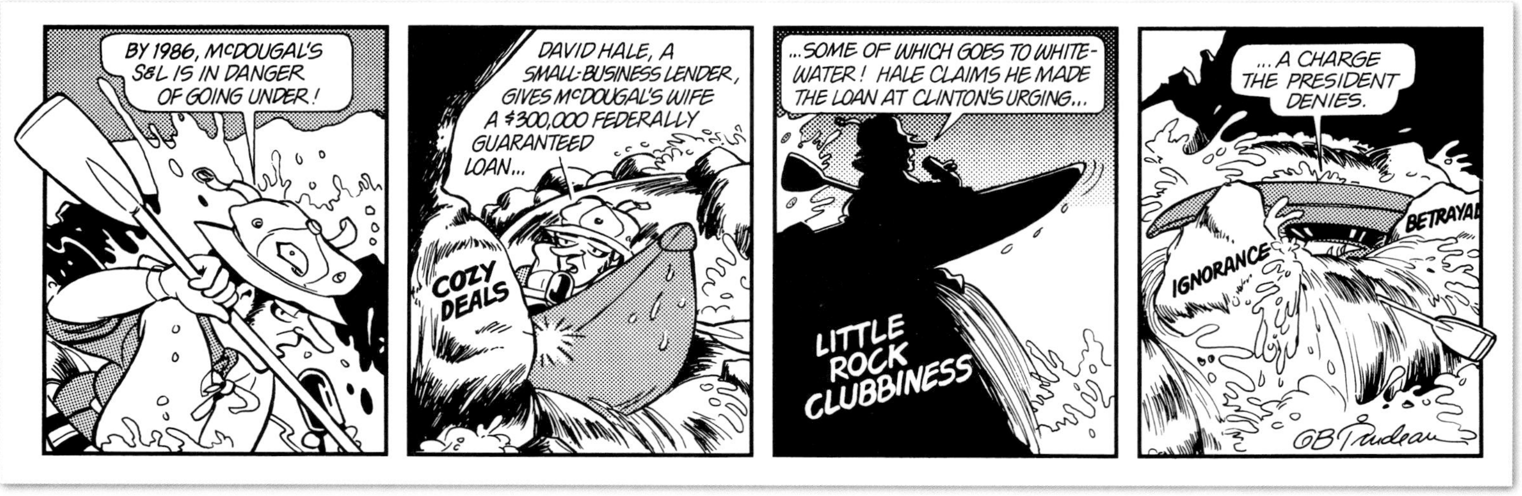
BY 1986, McDOUGAL'S S&L IS IN DANGER OF GOING UNDER!
DAVID HALE, A SMALL-BUSINESS LENDER, GIVES McDOUGAL'S WIFE A $300,000 FEDERALLY GUARANTEED LOAN...
COZY DEALS
...SOME OF WHICH GOES TO WHITE-WATER! HALE CLAIMS HE MADE THE LOAN AT CLINTON'S URGING...
LITTLE ROCK CLUBBINESS
...A CHARGE THE PRESIDENT DENIES.
IGNORANCE
BETRAYAL

1/27/94

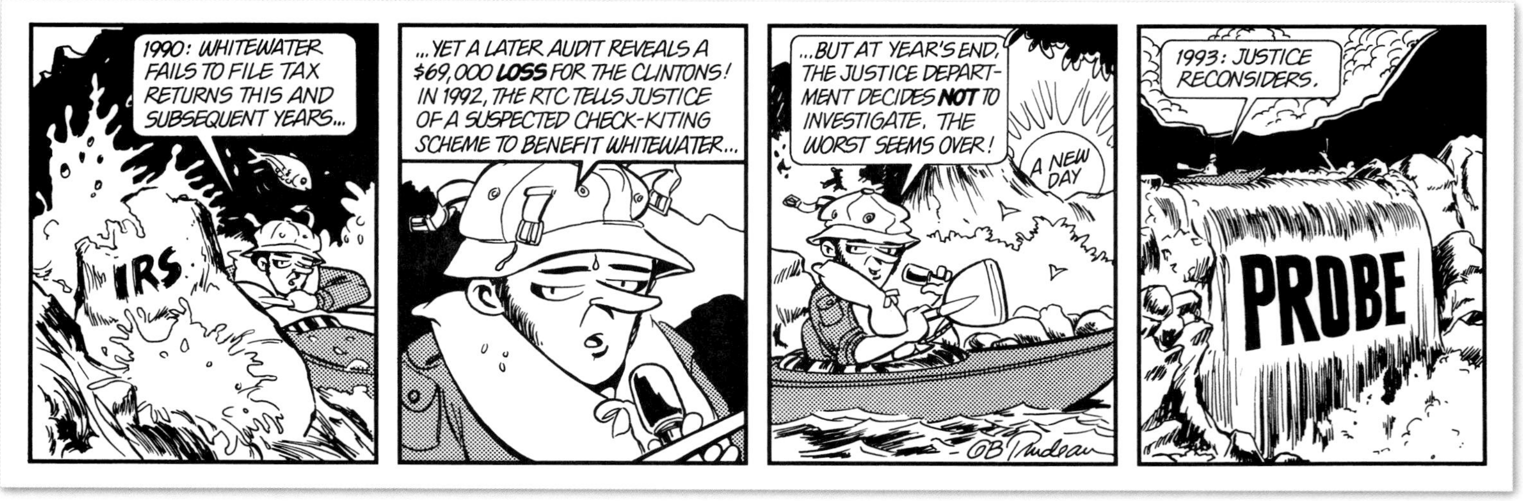
1990: WHITEWATER FAILS TO FILE TAX RETURNS THIS AND SUBSEQUENT YEARS...
IRS
...YET A LATER AUDIT REVEALS A $69,000 **LOSS** FOR THE CLINTONS! IN 1992, THE RTC TELLS JUSTICE OF A SUSPECTED CHECK-KITING SCHEME TO BENEFIT WHITEWATER...
...BUT AT YEAR'S END, THE JUSTICE DEPART-MENT DECIDES **NOT** TO INVESTIGATE. THE WORST SEEMS OVER!
A NEW DAY
1993: JUSTICE RECONSIDERS.
PROBE

1/28/94

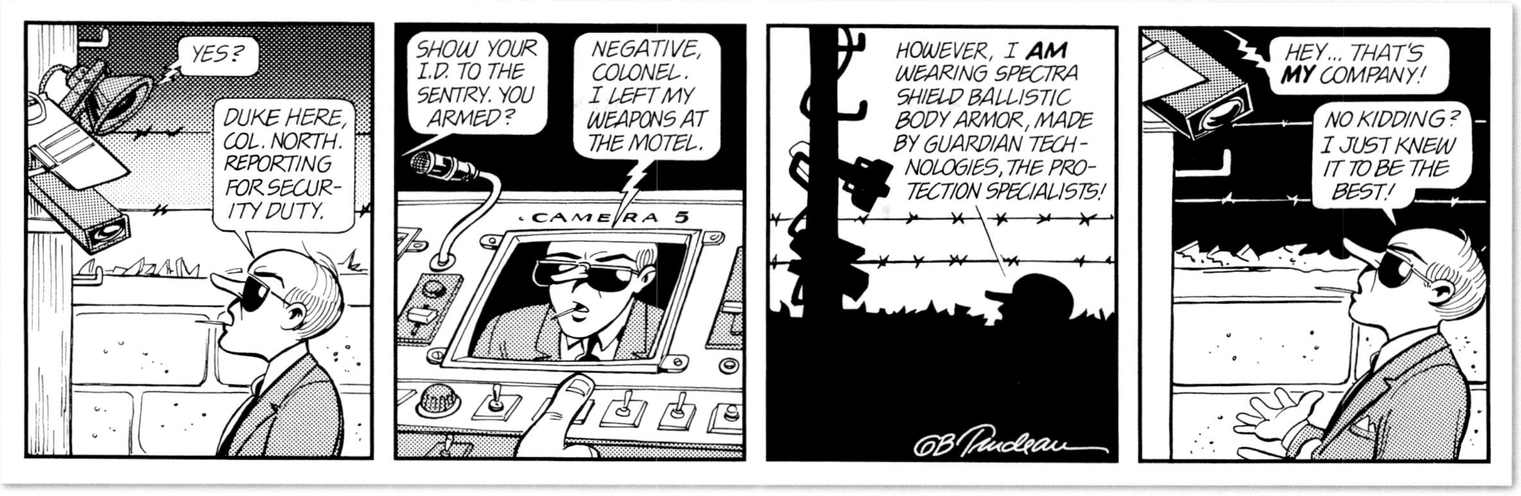
YES?
DUKE HERE, COL. NORTH. REPORTING FOR SECURITY DUTY.
SHOW YOUR I.D. TO THE SENTRY. YOU ARMED?
NEGATIVE, COLONEL. I LEFT MY WEAPONS AT THE MOTEL.
CAMERA 5
HOWEVER, I **AM** WEARING SPECTRA SHIELD BALLISTIC BODY ARMOR, MADE BY GUARDIAN TECHNOLOGIES, THE PROTECTION SPECIALISTS!
HEY... THAT'S **MY** COMPANY!
NO KIDDING? I JUST KNEW IT TO BE THE BEST!

2/14/94

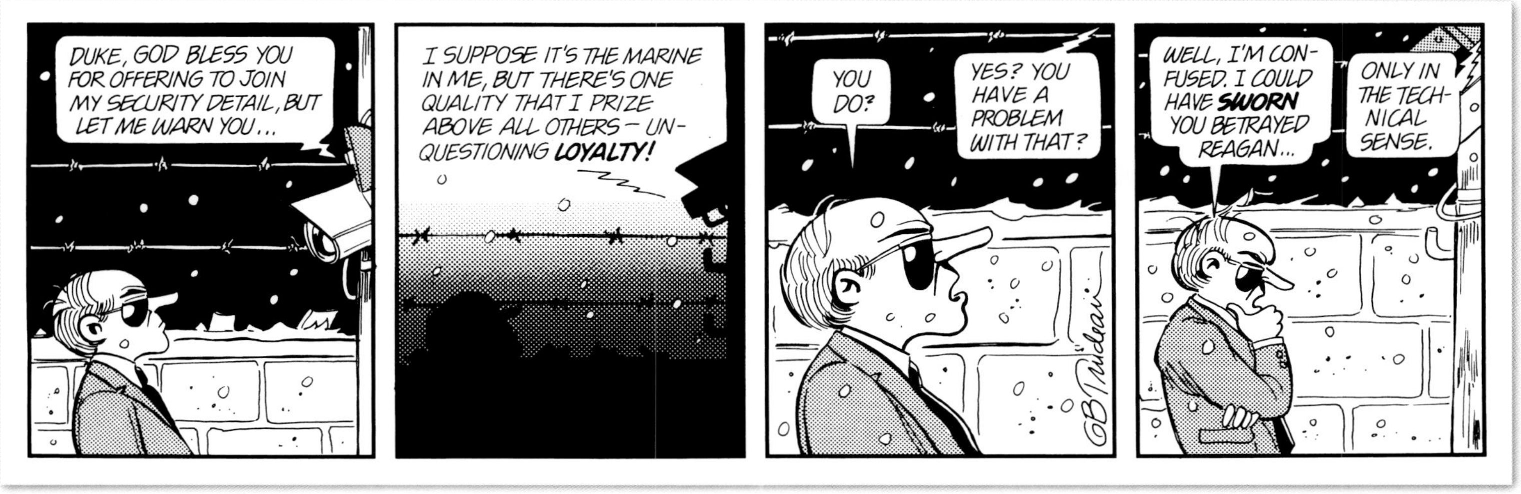
DUKE, GOD BLESS YOU FOR OFFERING TO JOIN MY SECURITY DETAIL, BUT LET ME WARN YOU...
I SUPPOSE IT'S THE MARINE IN ME, BUT THERE'S ONE QUALITY THAT I PRIZE ABOVE ALL OTHERS — UNQUESTIONING **LOYALTY!**
YOU DO?
YES? YOU HAVE A PROBLEM WITH THAT?
WELL, I'M CONFUSED. I COULD HAVE **SWORN** YOU BETRAYED REAGAN...
ONLY IN THE TECHNICAL SENSE.

2/15/94

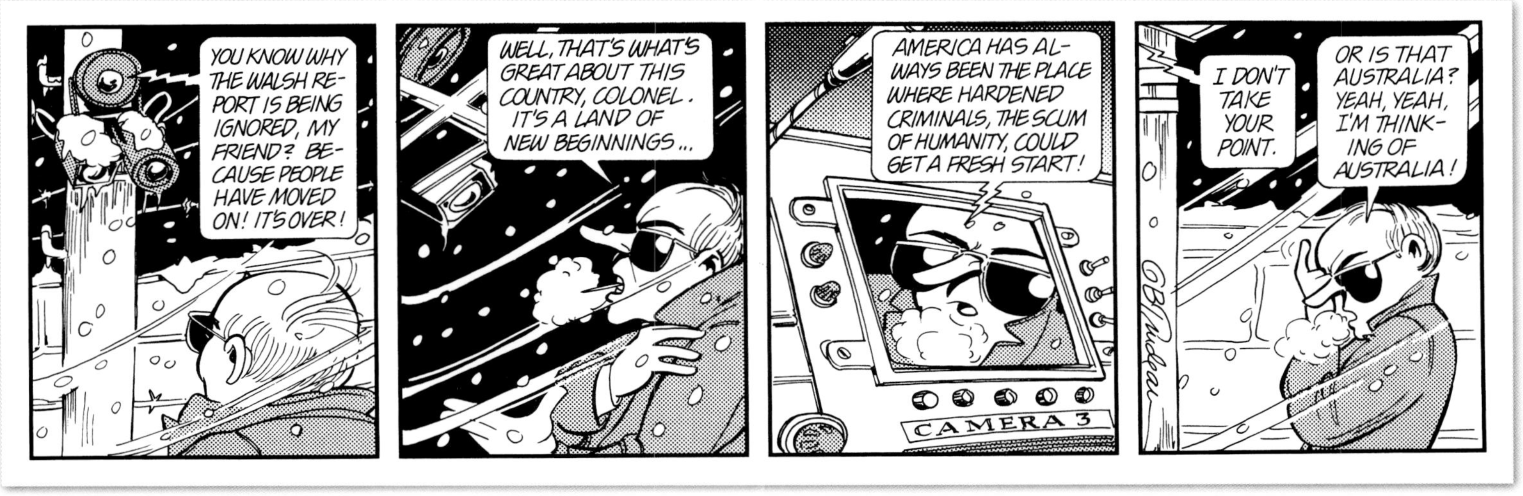
YOU KNOW WHY THE WALSH REPORT IS BEING IGNORED, MY FRIEND? BECAUSE PEOPLE HAVE MOVED ON! IT'S OVER!
WELL, THAT'S WHAT'S GREAT ABOUT THIS COUNTRY, COLONEL. IT'S A LAND OF NEW BEGINNINGS...
AMERICA HAS ALWAYS BEEN THE PLACE WHERE HARDENED CRIMINALS, THE SCUM OF HUMANITY, COULD GET A FRESH START!
CAMERA 3
I DON'T TAKE YOUR POINT.
OR IS THAT AUSTRALIA? YEAH, YEAH, I'M THINKING OF AUSTRALIA!

2/17/94

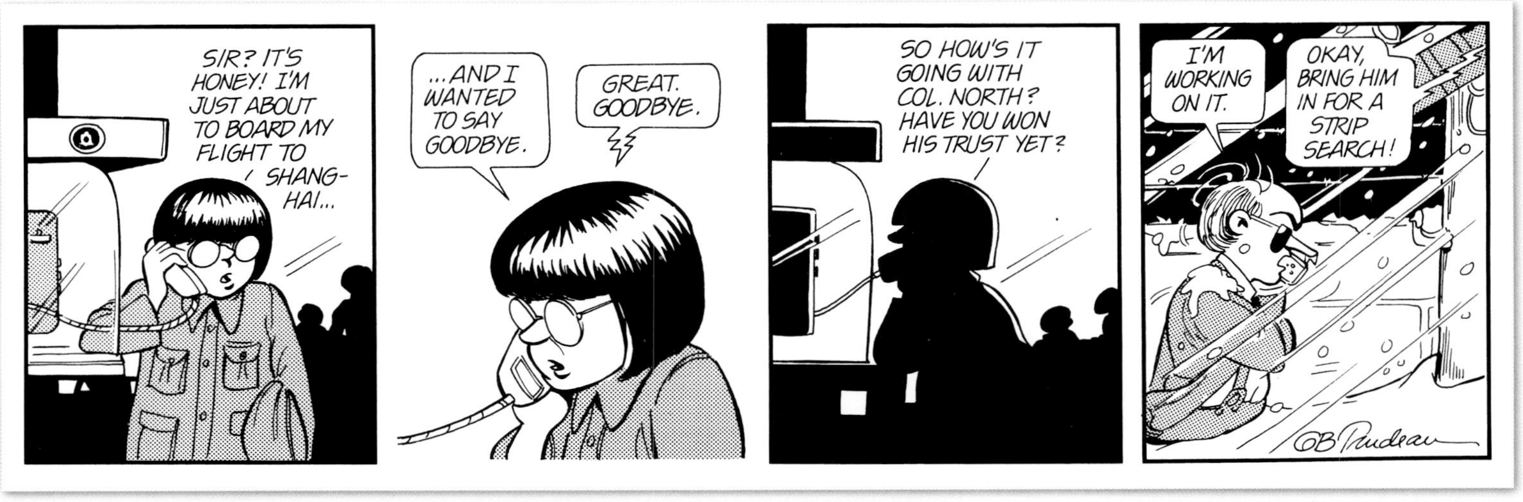
SIR? IT'S HONEY! I'M JUST ABOUT TO BOARD MY FLIGHT TO SHANGHAI...
...AND I WANTED TO SAY GOODBYE.
GREAT. GOODBYE.
SO HOW'S IT GOING WITH COL. NORTH? HAVE YOU WON HIS TRUST YET?
I'M WORKING ON IT.
OKAY, BRING HIM IN FOR A STRIP SEARCH!

2/19/94

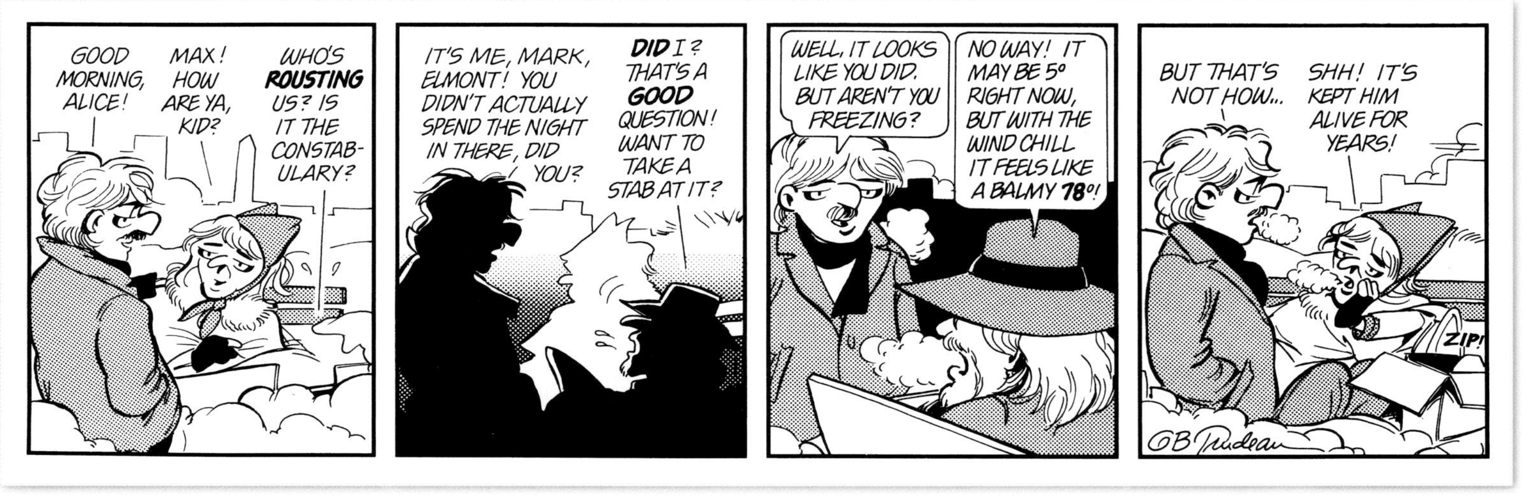
GOOD MORNING, ALICE!
MAX! HOW ARE YA, KID?
WHO'S **ROUSTING** US? IS IT THE CONSTABULARY?
IT'S ME, MARK, ELMONT! YOU DIDN'T ACTUALLY SPEND THE NIGHT IN THERE, DID YOU?
DID I? THAT'S A **GOOD** QUESTION! WANT TO TAKE A STAB AT IT?
WELL, IT LOOKS LIKE YOU DID. BUT AREN'T YOU FREEZING?
NO WAY! IT MAY BE 5° RIGHT NOW, BUT WITH THE WIND CHILL IT FEELS LIKE A BALMY **78°**!
BUT THAT'S NOT HOW...
SHH! IT'S KEPT HIM ALIVE FOR YEARS!
ZIP!
GBTrudeau

2/2/94

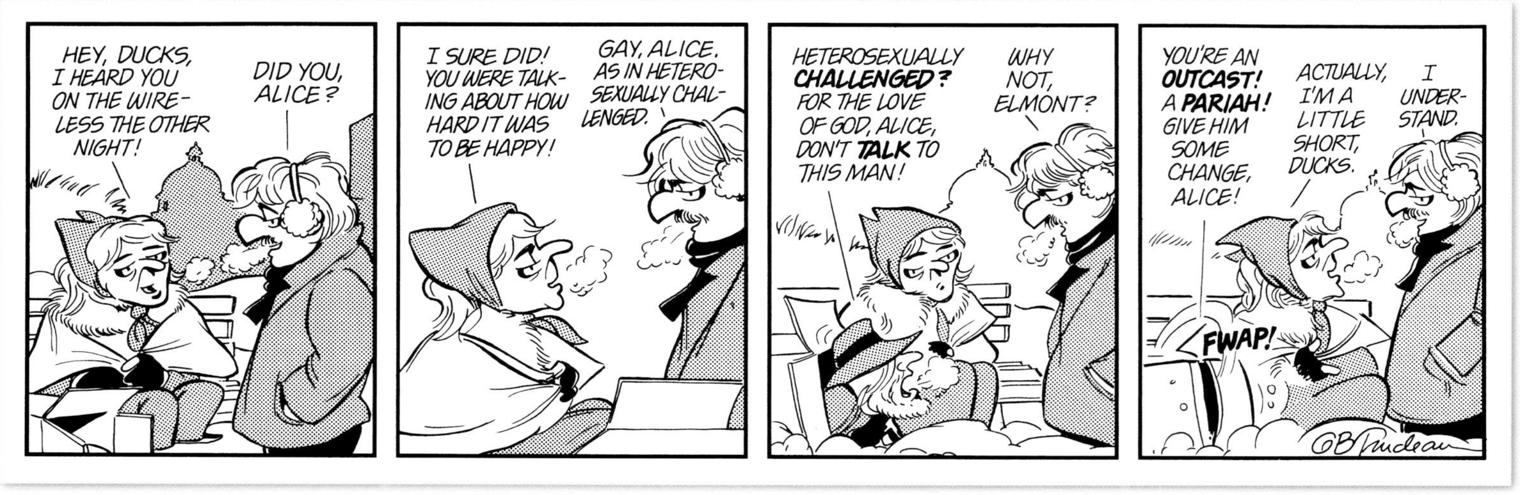
HEY, DUCKS, I HEARD YOU ON THE WIRELESS THE OTHER NIGHT!
DID YOU, ALICE?
I SURE DID! YOU WERE TALKING ABOUT HOW HARD IT WAS TO BE HAPPY!
GAY, ALICE. AS IN HETEROSEXUALLY CHALLENGED.
HETEROSEXUALLY **CHALLENGED?** FOR THE LOVE OF GOD, ALICE, DON'T **TALK** TO THIS MAN!
WHY NOT, ELMONT?
YOU'RE AN **OUTCAST!** A **PARIAH!** GIVE HIM SOME CHANGE, ALICE!
ACTUALLY, I'M A LITTLE SHORT, DUCKS.
I UNDERSTAND.
FWAP!
GBTrudeau

2/3/94

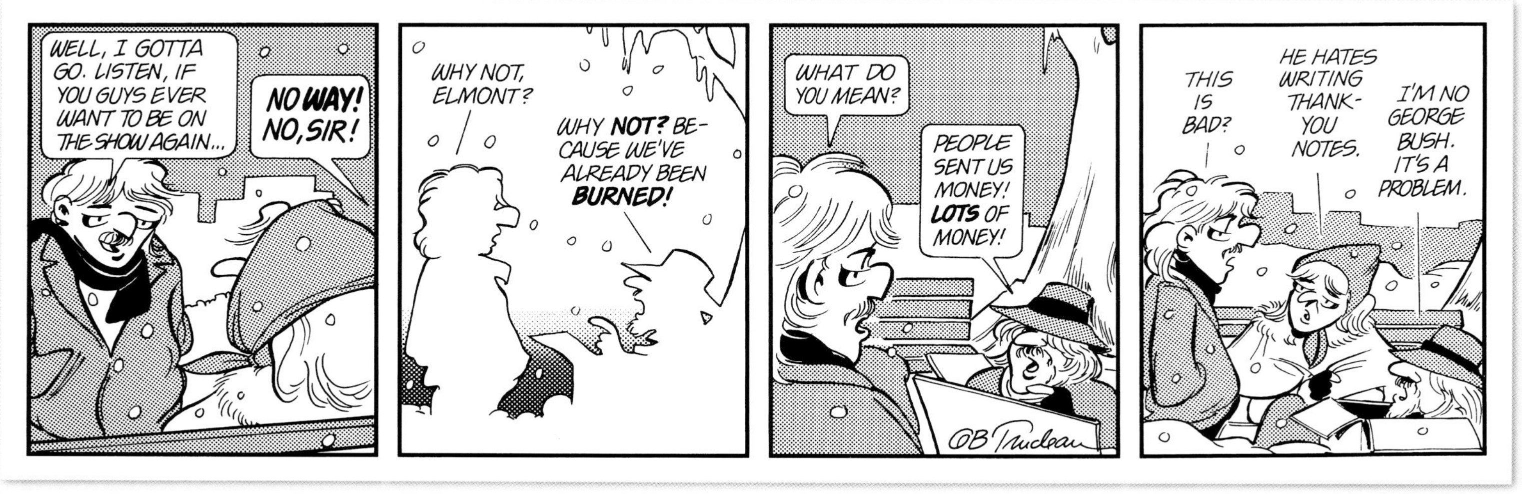
WELL, I GOTTA GO. LISTEN, IF YOU GUYS EVER WANT TO BE ON THE SHOW AGAIN...
NO WAY! NO, SIR!
WHY NOT, ELMONT?
WHY **NOT?** BECAUSE WE'VE ALREADY BEEN **BURNED!**
WHAT DO YOU MEAN?
PEOPLE SENT US MONEY! **LOTS** OF MONEY!
GBTrudeau
THIS IS BAD?
HE HATES WRITING THANK-YOU NOTES.
I'M NO GEORGE BUSH. IT'S A PROBLEM.

2/4/94

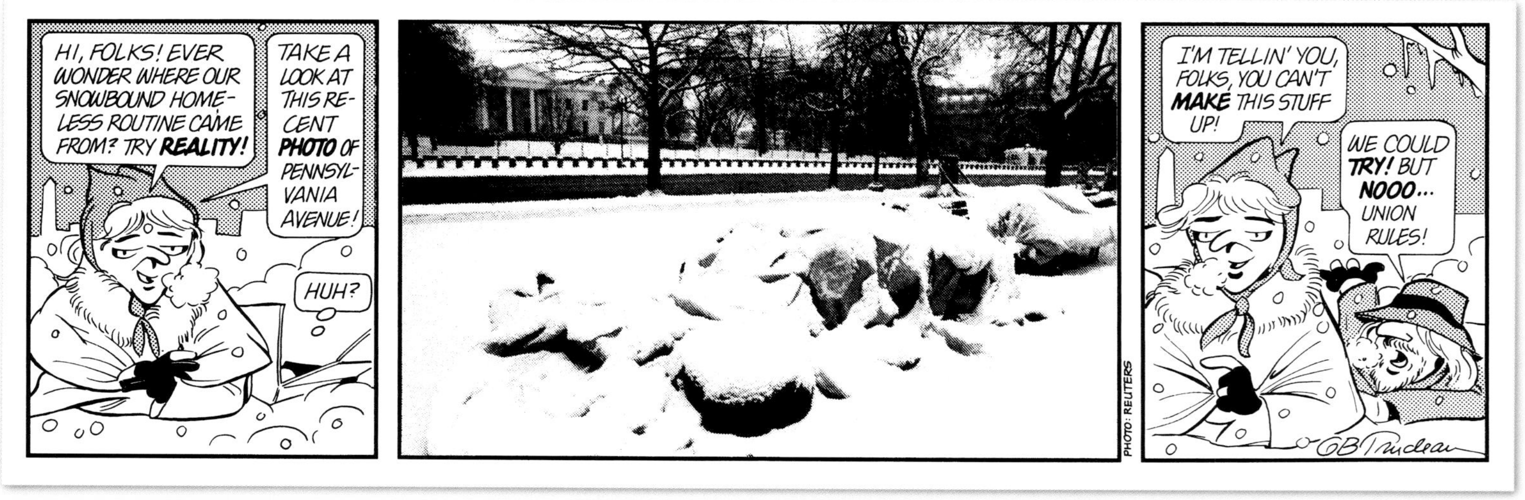
HI, FOLKS! EVER WONDER WHERE OUR SNOWBOUND HOMELESS ROUTINE CAME FROM? TRY **REALITY!**
TAKE A LOOK AT THIS RECENT **PHOTO** OF PENNSYLVANIA AVENUE!
HUH?
PHOTO: REUTERS
I'M TELLIN' YOU, FOLKS, YOU CAN'T **MAKE** THIS STUFF UP!
WE COULD **TRY!** BUT **NOOO**... UNION RULES!
GBTrudeau

2/5/94

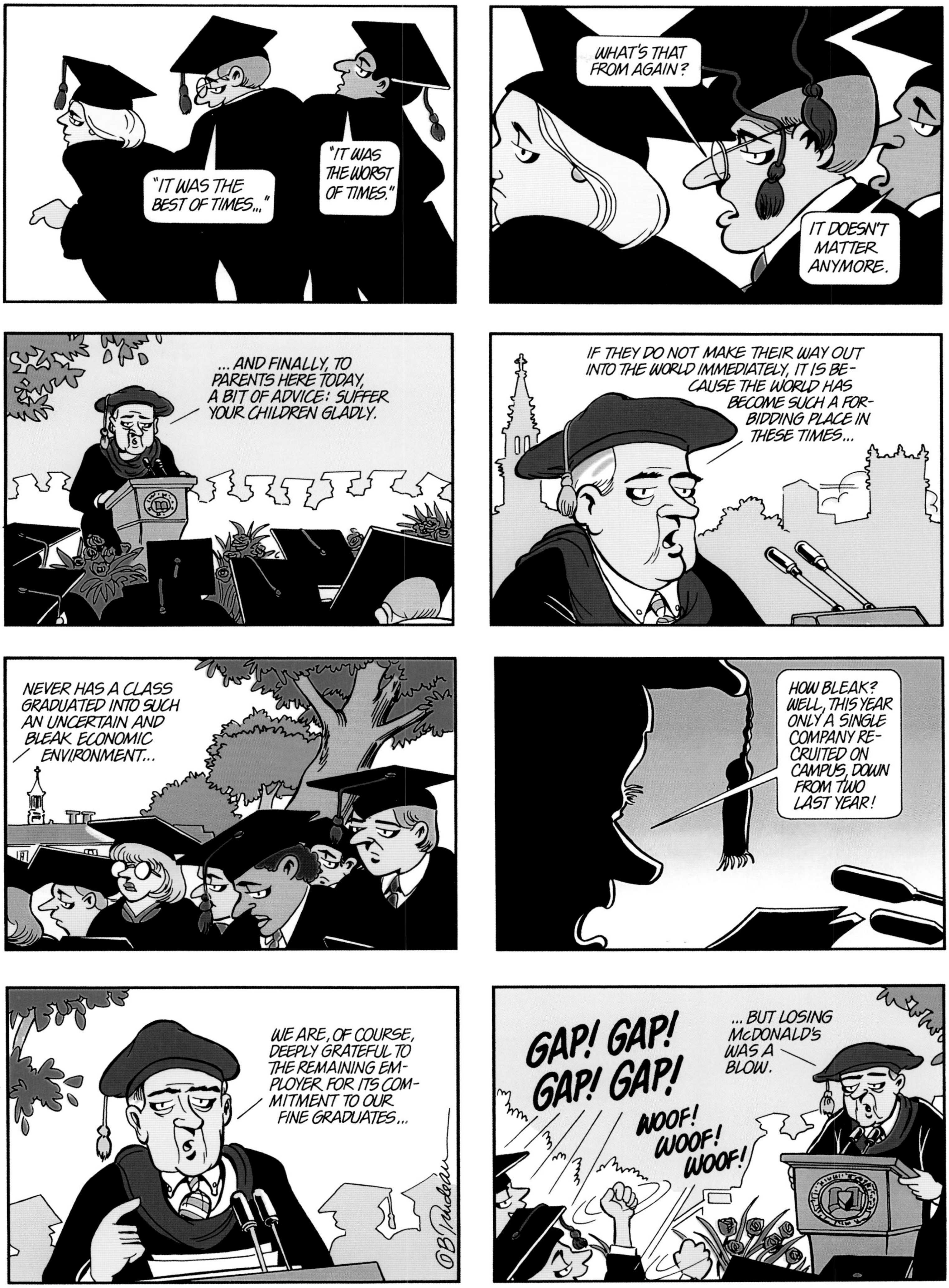
"IT WAS THE BEST OF TIMES..."
"IT WAS THE WORST OF TIMES."
WHAT'S THAT FROM AGAIN?
IT DOESN'T MATTER ANYMORE.
... AND FINALLY, TO PARENTS HERE TODAY, A BIT OF ADVICE: SUFFER YOUR CHILDREN GLADLY.
IF THEY DO NOT MAKE THEIR WAY OUT INTO THE WORLD IMMEDIATELY, IT IS BECAUSE THE WORLD HAS BECOME SUCH A FORBIDDING PLACE IN THESE TIMES...
NEVER HAS A CLASS GRADUATED INTO SUCH AN UNCERTAIN AND BLEAK ECONOMIC ENVIRONMENT...
HOW BLEAK? WELL, THIS YEAR ONLY A SINGLE COMPANY RECRUITED ON CAMPUS, DOWN FROM TWO LAST YEAR!
WE ARE, OF COURSE, DEEPLY GRATEFUL TO THE REMAINING EMPLOYER FOR ITS COMMITMENT TO OUR FINE GRADUATES...
©BTrudeau
GAP! GAP! GAP! GAP!
WOOF! WOOF! WOOF!
... BUT LOSING McDONALD'S WAS A BLOW.

5/15/94

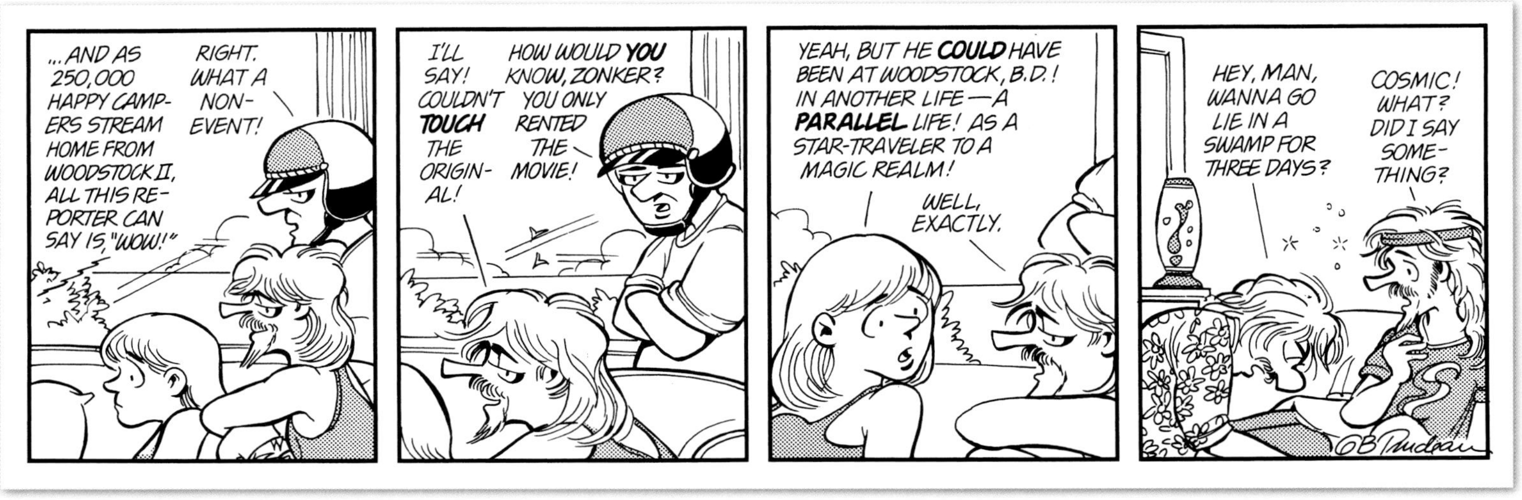
...AND AS 250,000 HAPPY CAMPERS STREAM HOME FROM WOODSTOCK II, ALL THIS REPORTER CAN SAY IS, "WOW!"
RIGHT. WHAT A NON-EVENT!
I'LL SAY! COULDN'T TOUCH THE ORIGINAL!
HOW WOULD YOU KNOW, ZONKER? YOU ONLY RENTED THE MOVIE!
YEAH, BUT HE COULD HAVE BEEN AT WOODSTOCK, B.D.! IN ANOTHER LIFE — A PARALLEL LIFE! AS A STAR-TRAVELER TO A MAGIC REALM!
WELL, EXACTLY.
HEY, MAN, WANNA GO LIE IN A SWAMP FOR THREE DAYS?
COSMIC! WHAT? DID I SAY SOMETHING?

8/15/94

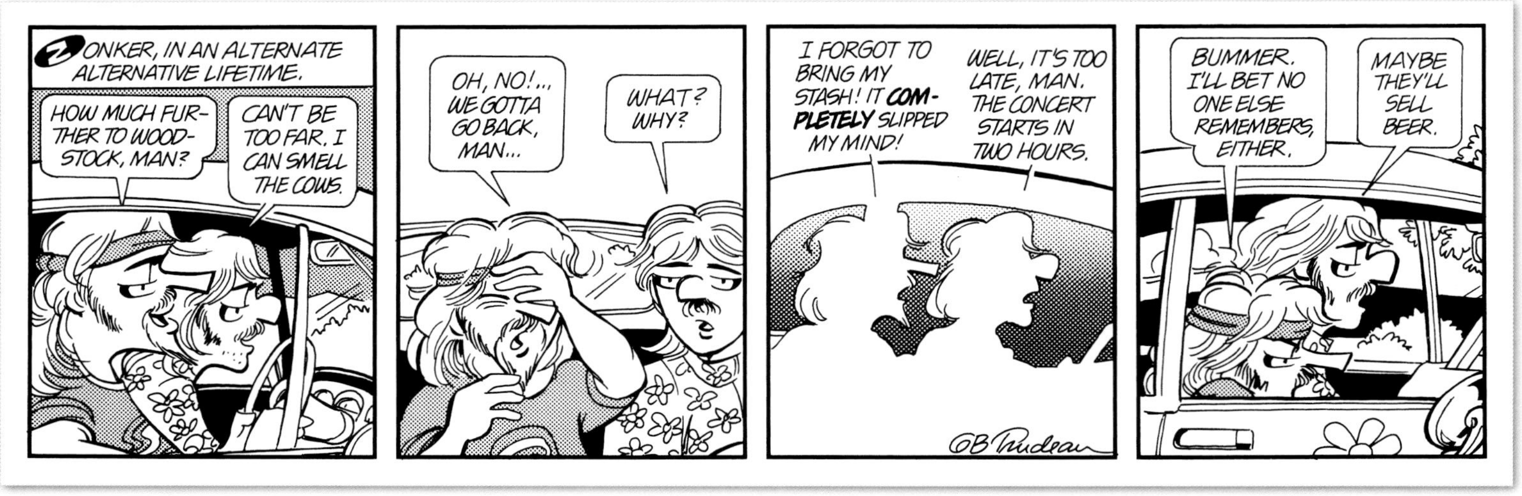
ZONKER, IN AN ALTERNATE ALTERNATIVE LIFETIME.
HOW MUCH FURTHER TO WOODSTOCK, MAN?
CAN'T BE TOO FAR. I CAN SMELL THE COWS.
OH, NO!.. WE GOTTA GO BACK, MAN...
WHAT? WHY?
I FORGOT TO BRING MY STASH! IT COMPLETELY SLIPPED MY MIND!
WELL, IT'S TOO LATE, MAN. THE CONCERT STARTS IN TWO HOURS.
BUMMER. I'LL BET NO ONE ELSE REMEMBERS, EITHER.
MAYBE THEY'LL SELL BEER.

8/16/94

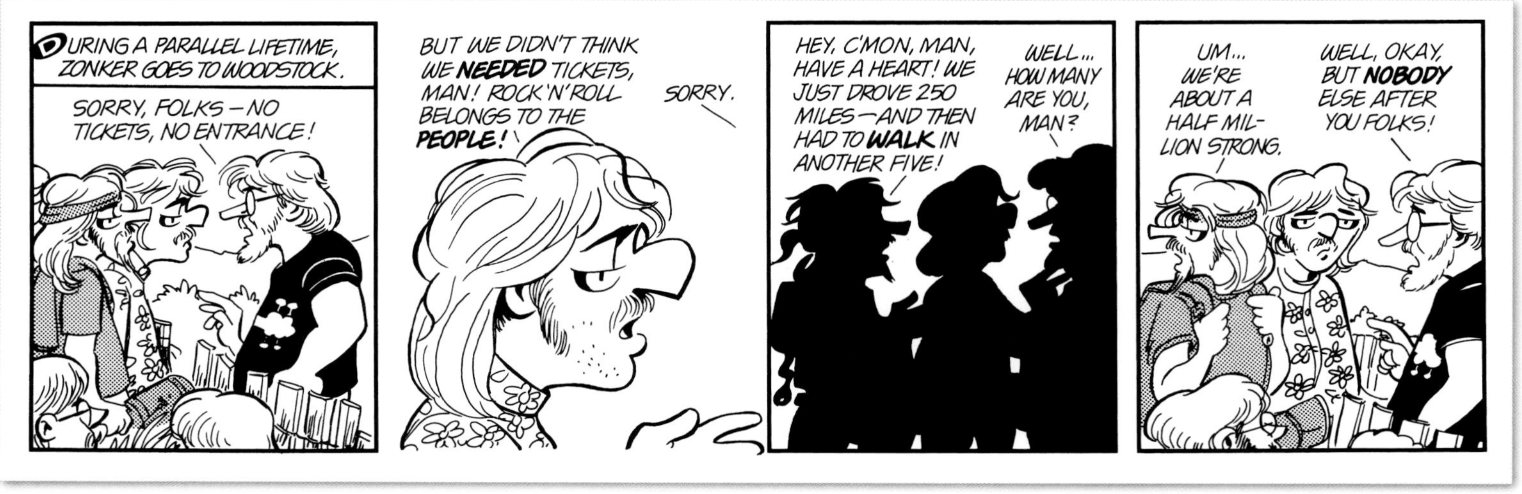
DURING A PARALLEL LIFETIME, ZONKER GOES TO WOODSTOCK.
SORRY, FOLKS — NO TICKETS, NO ENTRANCE!
BUT WE DIDN'T THINK WE NEEDED TICKETS, MAN! ROCK 'N' ROLL BELONGS TO THE PEOPLE!
SORRY.
HEY, C'MON, MAN, HAVE A HEART! WE JUST DROVE 250 MILES — AND THEN HAD TO WALK IN ANOTHER FIVE!
WELL... HOW MANY ARE YOU, MAN?
UM... WE'RE ABOUT A HALF MILLION STRONG.
WELL, OKAY, BUT NOBODY ELSE AFTER YOU FOLKS!

8/17/94

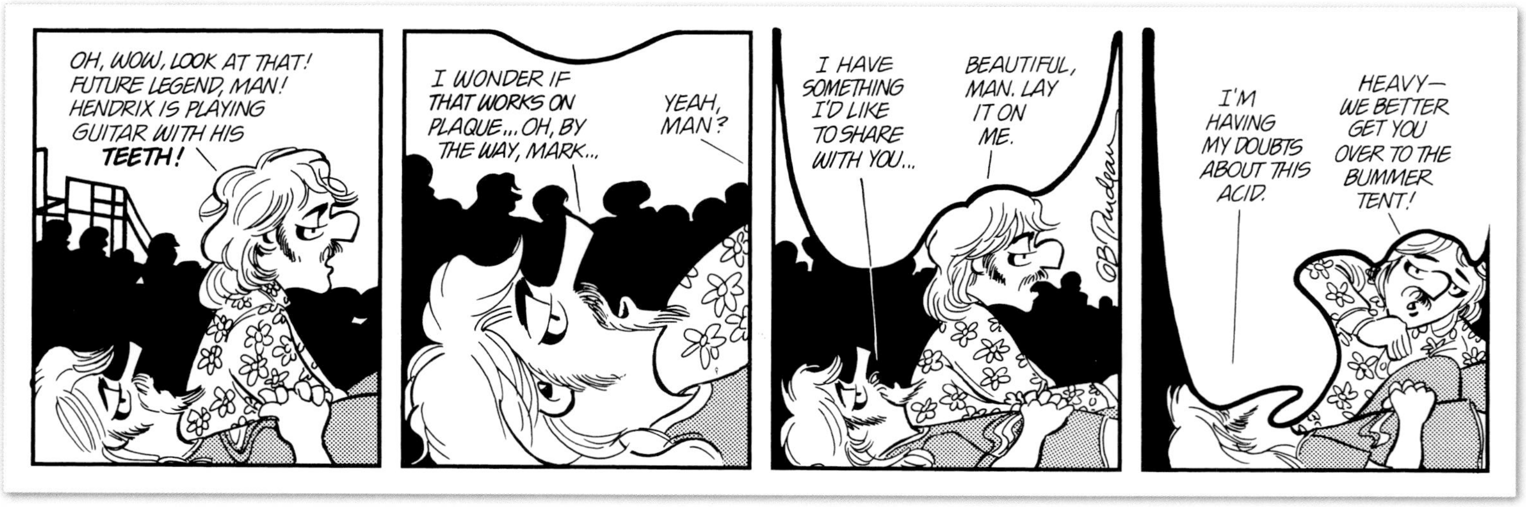
OH, WOW, LOOK AT THAT! FUTURE LEGEND, MAN! HENDRIX IS PLAYING GUITAR WITH HIS TEETH!
I WONDER IF THAT WORKS ON PLAQUE... OH, BY THE WAY, MARK...
YEAH, MAN?
I HAVE SOMETHING I'D LIKE TO SHARE WITH YOU...
BEAUTIFUL, MAN. LAY IT ON ME.
I'M HAVING MY DOUBTS ABOUT THIS ACID.
HEAVY — WE BETTER GET YOU OVER TO THE BUMMER TENT!

8/18/94

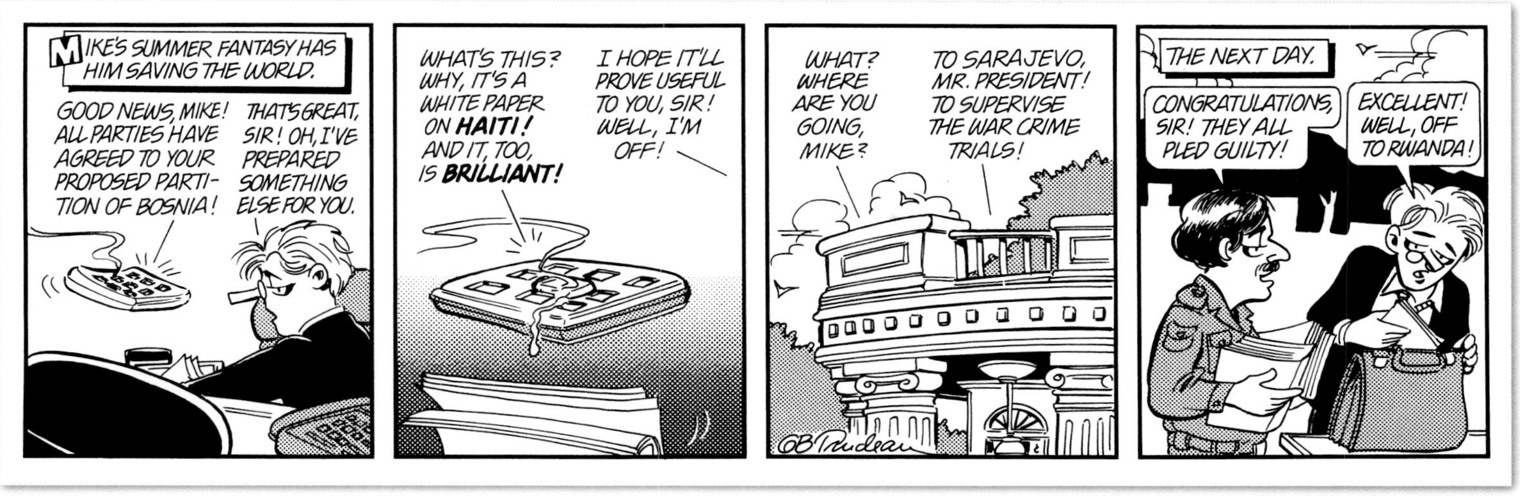
MIKE'S SUMMER FANTASY HAS HIM SAVING THE WORLD.
GOOD NEWS, MIKE! ALL PARTIES HAVE AGREED TO YOUR PROPOSED PARTITION OF BOSNIA!
THAT'S GREAT, SIR! OH, I'VE PREPARED SOMETHING ELSE FOR YOU.
WHAT'S THIS? WHY, IT'S A WHITE PAPER ON HAITI! AND IT, TOO, IS BRILLIANT!
I HOPE IT'LL PROVE USEFUL TO YOU, SIR! WELL, I'M OFF!
WHAT? WHERE ARE YOU GOING, MIKE?
TO SARAJEVO, MR. PRESIDENT! TO SUPERVISE THE WAR CRIME TRIALS!
THE NEXT DAY.
CONGRATULATIONS, SIR! THEY ALL PLED GUILTY!
EXCELLENT! WELL, OFF TO RWANDA!

8/30/94

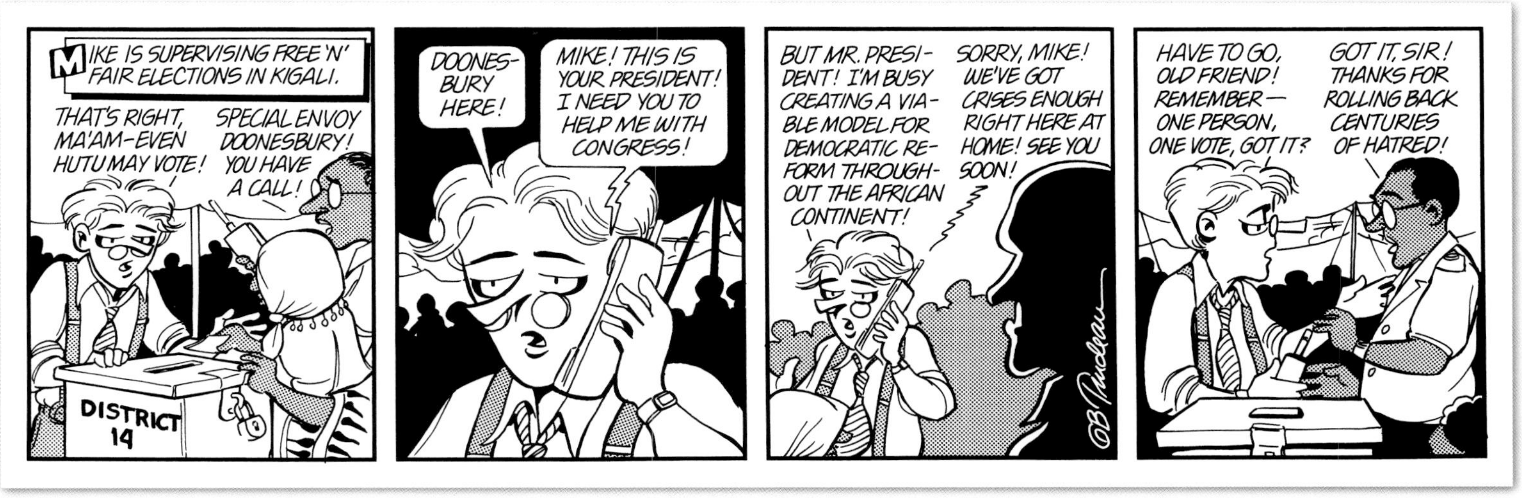
MIKE IS SUPERVISING FREE 'N' FAIR ELECTIONS IN KIGALI.
THAT'S RIGHT, MA'AM—EVEN HUTU MAY VOTE!
SPECIAL ENVOY DOONESBURY! YOU HAVE A CALL!
DISTRICT 14
DOONESBURY HERE!
MIKE! THIS IS YOUR PRESIDENT! I NEED YOU TO HELP ME WITH CONGRESS!
BUT MR. PRESIDENT! I'M BUSY CREATING A VIABLE MODEL FOR DEMOCRATIC REFORM THROUGHOUT THE AFRICAN CONTINENT!
SORRY, MIKE! WE'VE GOT CRISES ENOUGH RIGHT HERE AT HOME! SEE YOU SOON!
HAVE TO GO, OLD FRIEND! REMEMBER—ONE PERSON, ONE VOTE, GOT IT?
GOT IT, SIR! THANKS FOR ROLLING BACK CENTURIES OF HATRED!

8/31/94

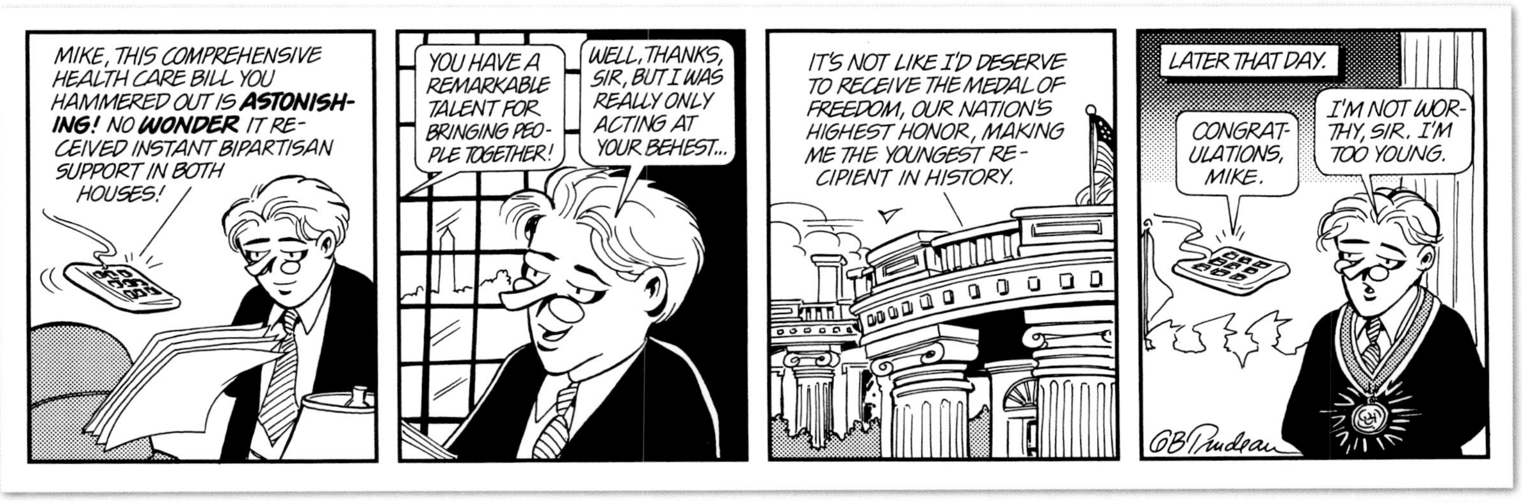
MIKE, THIS COMPREHENSIVE HEALTH CARE BILL YOU HAMMERED OUT IS ASTONISHING! NO WONDER IT RECEIVED INSTANT BIPARTISAN SUPPORT IN BOTH HOUSES!
YOU HAVE A REMARKABLE TALENT FOR BRINGING PEOPLE TOGETHER!
WELL, THANKS, SIR, BUT I WAS REALLY ONLY ACTING AT YOUR BEHEST...
IT'S NOT LIKE I'D DESERVE TO RECEIVE THE MEDAL OF FREEDOM, OUR NATION'S HIGHEST HONOR, MAKING ME THE YOUNGEST RECIPIENT IN HISTORY.
LATER THAT DAY.
CONGRATULATIONS, MIKE.
I'M NOT WORTHY, SIR. I'M TOO YOUNG.

9/2/94

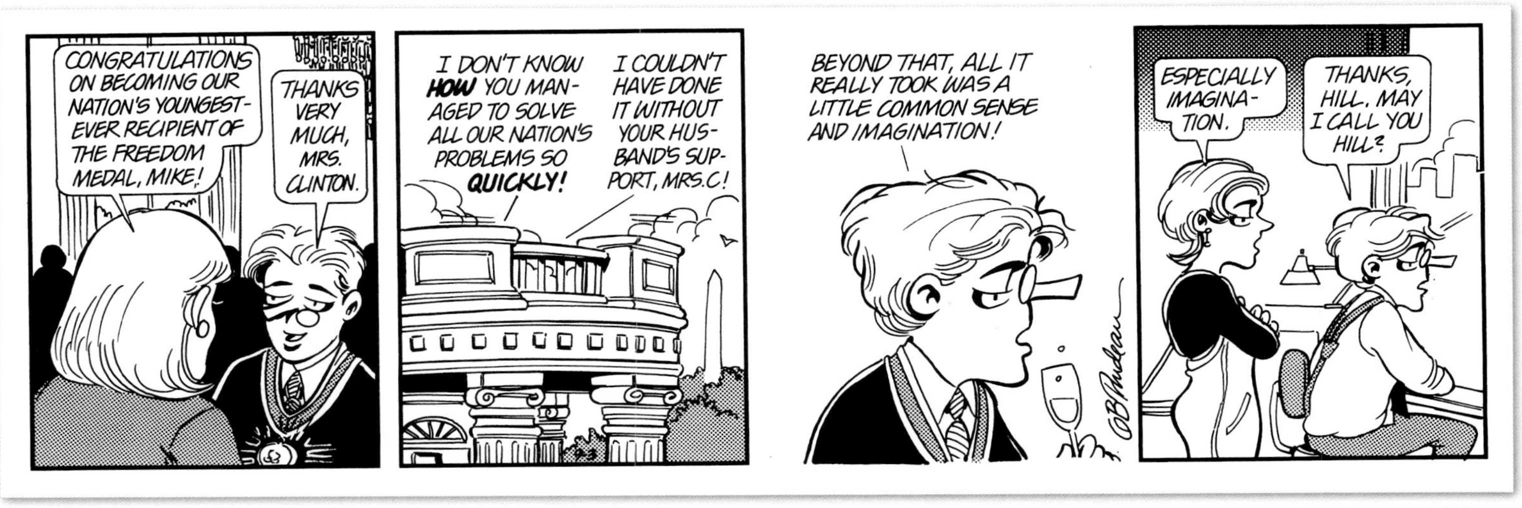
CONGRATULATIONS ON BECOMING OUR NATION'S YOUNGEST-EVER RECIPIENT OF THE FREEDOM MEDAL, MIKE!
THANKS VERY MUCH, MRS. CLINTON.
I DON'T KNOW HOW YOU MANAGED TO SOLVE ALL OUR NATION'S PROBLEMS SO QUICKLY!
I COULDN'T HAVE DONE IT WITHOUT YOUR HUSBAND'S SUPPORT, MRS. C!
BEYOND THAT, ALL IT REALLY TOOK WAS A LITTLE COMMON SENSE AND IMAGINATION!
ESPECIALLY IMAGINATION.
THANKS, HILL. MAY I CALL YOU HILL?

9/3/94

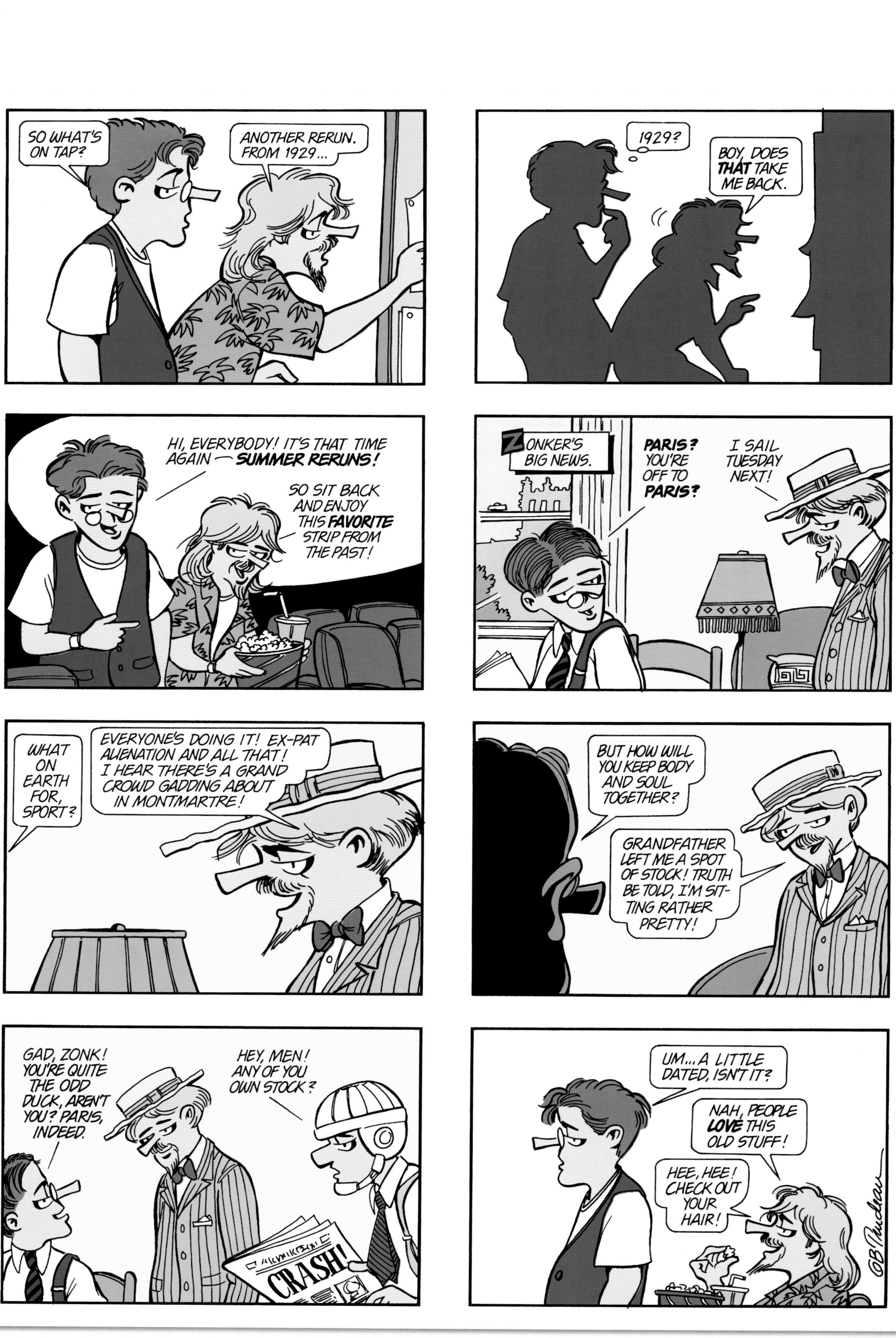
SO WHAT'S ON TAP?
ANOTHER RERUN. FROM 1929...
1929?
BOY, DOES **THAT** TAKE ME BACK.
HI, EVERYBODY! IT'S THAT TIME AGAIN — **SUMMER RERUNS!**
SO SIT BACK AND ENJOY THIS **FAVORITE** STRIP FROM THE PAST!
ZONKER'S BIG NEWS.
PARIS? YOU'RE OFF TO **PARIS?**
I SAIL TUESDAY NEXT!
WHAT ON EARTH FOR, SPORT?
EVERYONE'S DOING IT! EX-PAT ALIENATION AND ALL THAT! I HEAR THERE'S A GRAND CROWD GADDING ABOUT IN MONTMARTRE!
BUT HOW WILL YOU KEEP BODY AND SOUL TOGETHER?
GRANDFATHER LEFT ME A SPOT OF STOCK! TRUTH BE TOLD, I'M SITTING RATHER PRETTY!
GAD, ZONK! YOU'RE QUITE THE ODD DUCK, AREN'T YOU? PARIS, INDEED.
HEY, MEN! ANY OF YOU OWN STOCK?
CRASH!
UM... A LITTLE DATED, ISN'T IT?
NAH, PEOPLE **LOVE** THIS OLD STUFF!
HEE, HEE! CHECK OUT YOUR HAIR!

7/24/94

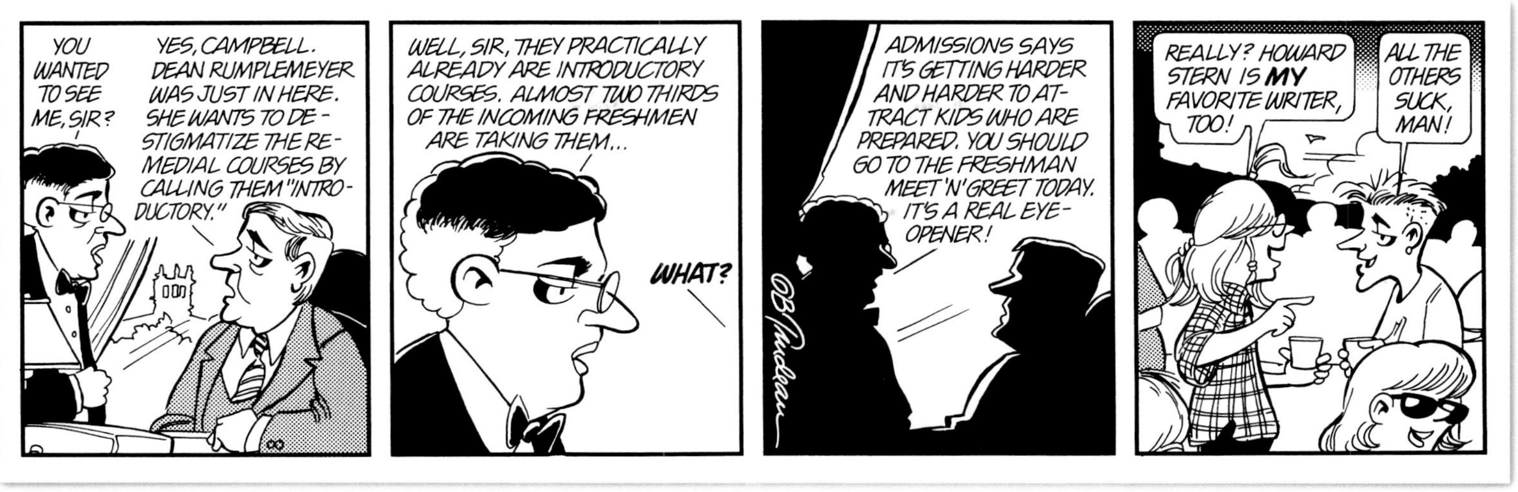
YOU WANTED TO SEE ME, SIR?
YES, CAMPBELL. DEAN RUMPLEMEYER WAS JUST IN HERE. SHE WANTS TO DE-STIGMATIZE THE REMEDIAL COURSES BY CALLING THEM "INTRODUCTORY."
WELL, SIR, THEY PRACTICALLY ALREADY ARE INTRODUCTORY COURSES. ALMOST TWO THIRDS OF THE INCOMING FRESHMEN ARE TAKING THEM...
WHAT?
ADMISSIONS SAYS IT'S GETTING HARDER AND HARDER TO ATTRACT KIDS WHO ARE PREPARED. YOU SHOULD GO TO THE FRESHMAN MEET 'N' GREET TODAY. IT'S A REAL EYE-OPENER!
REALLY? HOWARD STERN IS **MY** FAVORITE WRITER, TOO!
ALL THE OTHERS SUCK, MAN!

9/6/94

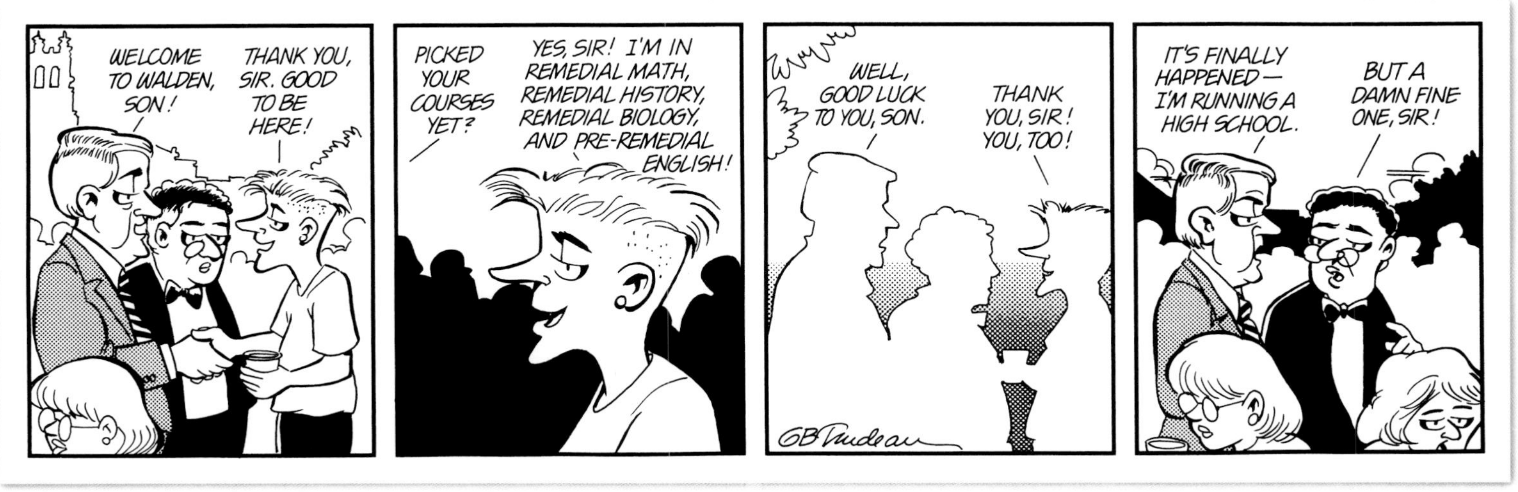
WELCOME TO WALDEN, SON!
THANK YOU, SIR. GOOD TO BE HERE!
PICKED YOUR COURSES YET?
YES, SIR! I'M IN REMEDIAL MATH, REMEDIAL HISTORY, REMEDIAL BIOLOGY, AND PRE-REMEDIAL ENGLISH!
WELL, GOOD LUCK TO YOU, SON.
THANK YOU, SIR! YOU, TOO!
IT'S FINALLY HAPPENED— I'M RUNNING A HIGH SCHOOL.
BUT A DAMN FINE ONE, SIR!

9/7/94

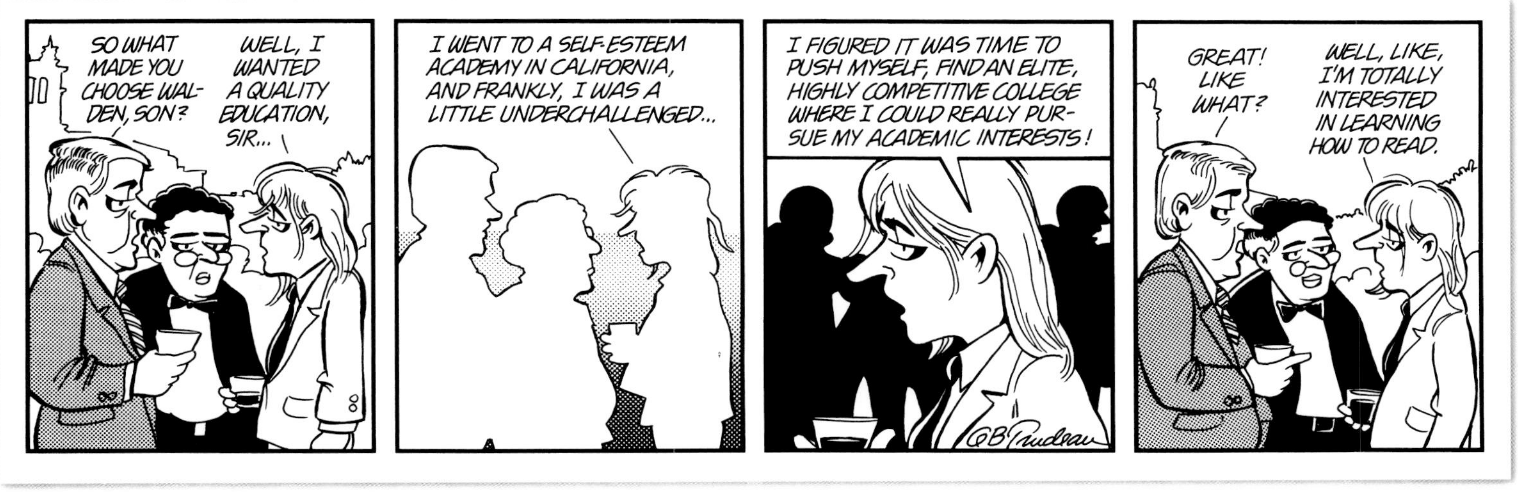
SO WHAT MADE YOU CHOOSE WALDEN, SON?
WELL, I WANTED A QUALITY EDUCATION, SIR...
I WENT TO A SELF-ESTEEM ACADEMY IN CALIFORNIA, AND FRANKLY, I WAS A LITTLE UNDERCHALLENGED...
I FIGURED IT WAS TIME TO PUSH MYSELF, FIND AN ELITE, HIGHLY COMPETITIVE COLLEGE WHERE I COULD REALLY PURSUE MY ACADEMIC INTERESTS!
GREAT! LIKE WHAT?
WELL, LIKE, I'M TOTALLY INTERESTED IN LEARNING HOW TO READ.

9/8/94

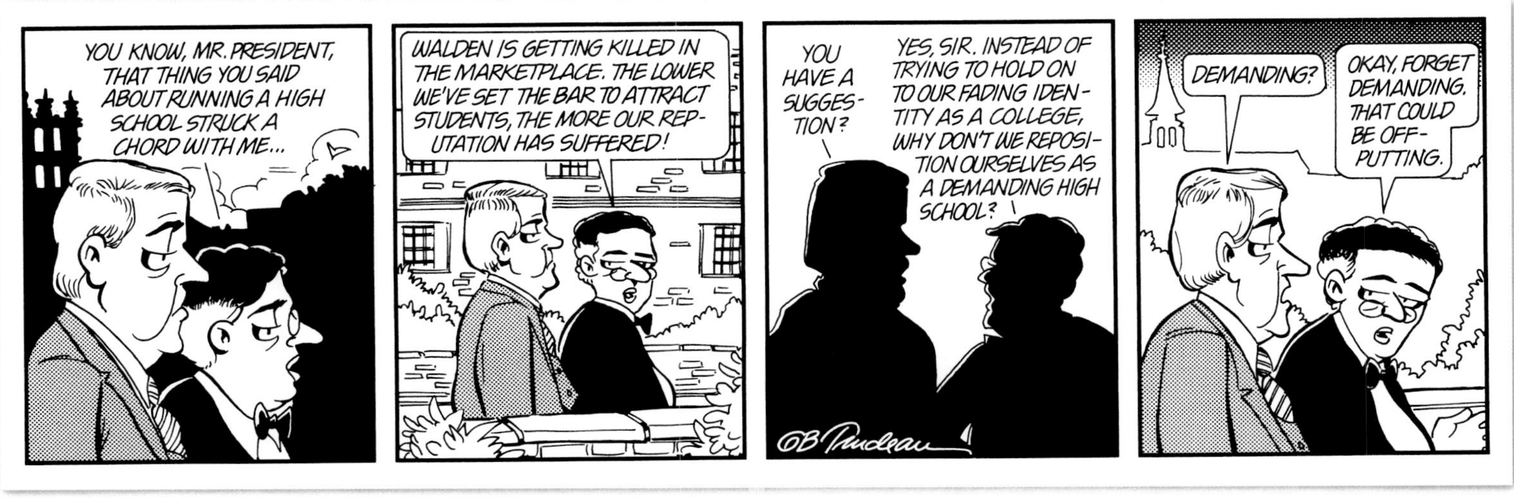
YOU KNOW, MR. PRESIDENT, THAT THING YOU SAID ABOUT RUNNING A HIGH SCHOOL STRUCK A CHORD WITH ME...
WALDEN IS GETTING KILLED IN THE MARKETPLACE. THE LOWER WE'VE SET THE BAR TO ATTRACT STUDENTS, THE MORE OUR REPUTATION HAS SUFFERED!
YOU HAVE A SUGGESTION?
YES, SIR. INSTEAD OF TRYING TO HOLD ON TO OUR FADING IDENTITY AS A COLLEGE, WHY DON'T WE REPOSITION OURSELVES AS A DEMANDING HIGH SCHOOL?
DEMANDING?
OKAY, FORGET DEMANDING. THAT COULD BE OFF-PUTTING.

9/9/94

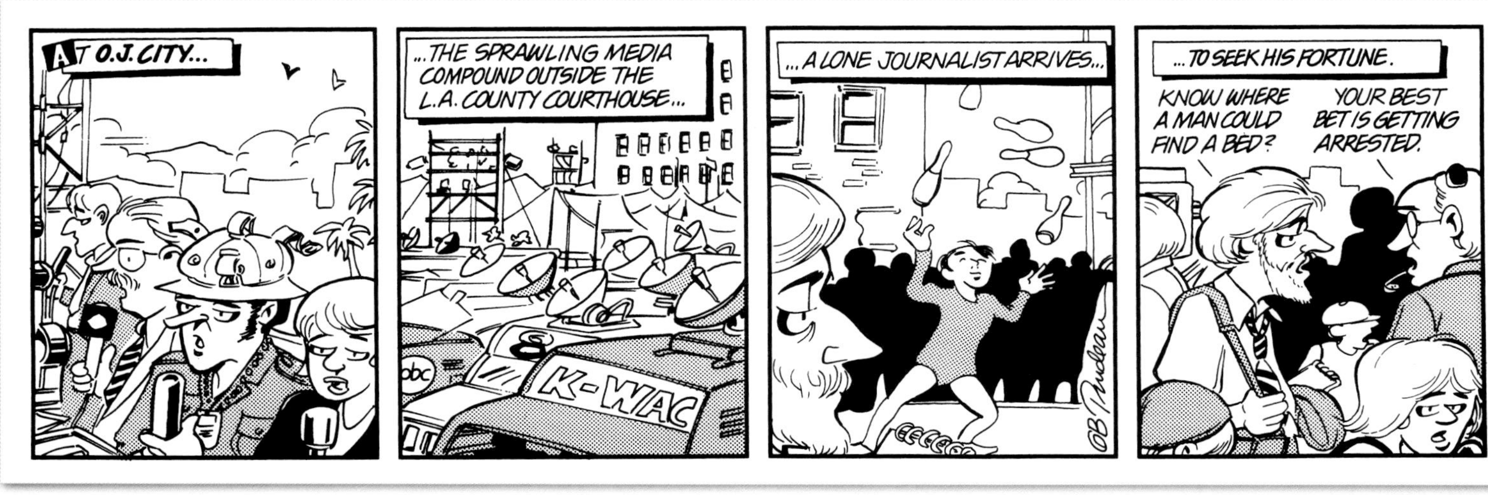
AT O.J. CITY...
...THE SPRAWLING MEDIA COMPOUND OUTSIDE THE L.A. COUNTY COURTHOUSE...
abc
K-WAC
...A LONE JOURNALIST ARRIVES...
...TO SEEK HIS FORTUNE.
KNOW WHERE A MAN COULD FIND A BED?
YOUR BEST BET IS GETTING ARRESTED.

11/21/94

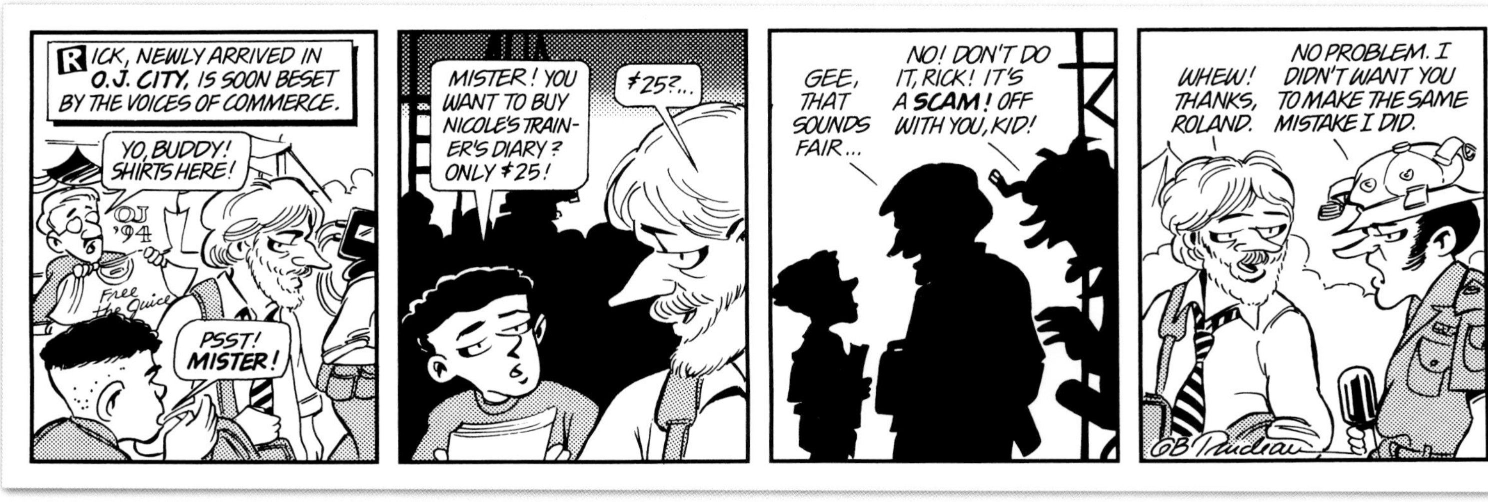
RICK, NEWLY ARRIVED IN O.J. CITY, IS SOON BESET BY THE VOICES OF COMMERCE.
YO, BUDDY! SHIRTS HERE!
OJ '94
Free the Juice
PSST! MISTER!
MISTER! YOU WANT TO BUY NICOLE'S TRAINER'S DIARY? ONLY $25!
$25?...
GEE, THAT SOUNDS FAIR...
NO! DON'T DO IT, RICK! IT'S A SCAM! OFF WITH YOU, KID!
WHEW! THANKS, ROLAND.
NO PROBLEM. I DIDN'T WANT YOU TO MAKE THE SAME MISTAKE I DID.

11/22/94

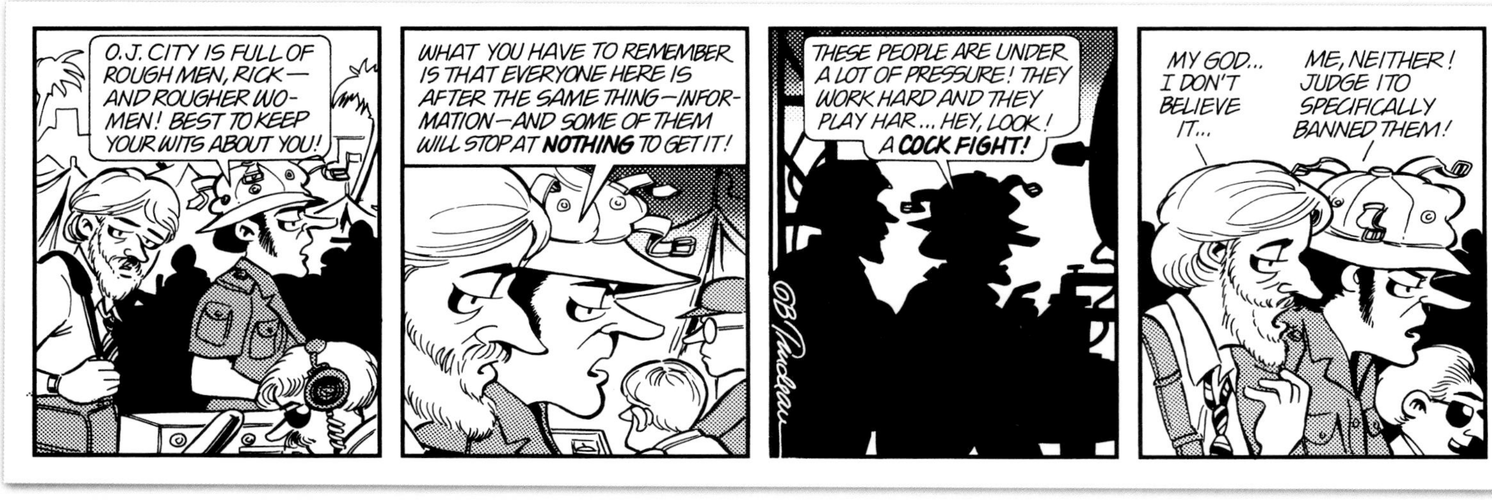
O.J. CITY IS FULL OF ROUGH MEN, RICK—AND ROUGHER WOMEN! BEST TO KEEP YOUR WITS ABOUT YOU!
WHAT YOU HAVE TO REMEMBER IS THAT EVERYONE HERE IS AFTER THE SAME THING—INFORMATION—AND SOME OF THEM WILL STOP AT NOTHING TO GET IT!
THESE PEOPLE ARE UNDER A LOT OF PRESSURE! THEY WORK HARD AND THEY PLAY HAR... HEY, LOOK! A COCK FIGHT!
MY GOD... I DON'T BELIEVE IT...
ME, NEITHER! JUDGE ITO SPECIFICALLY BANNED THEM!

11/25/94

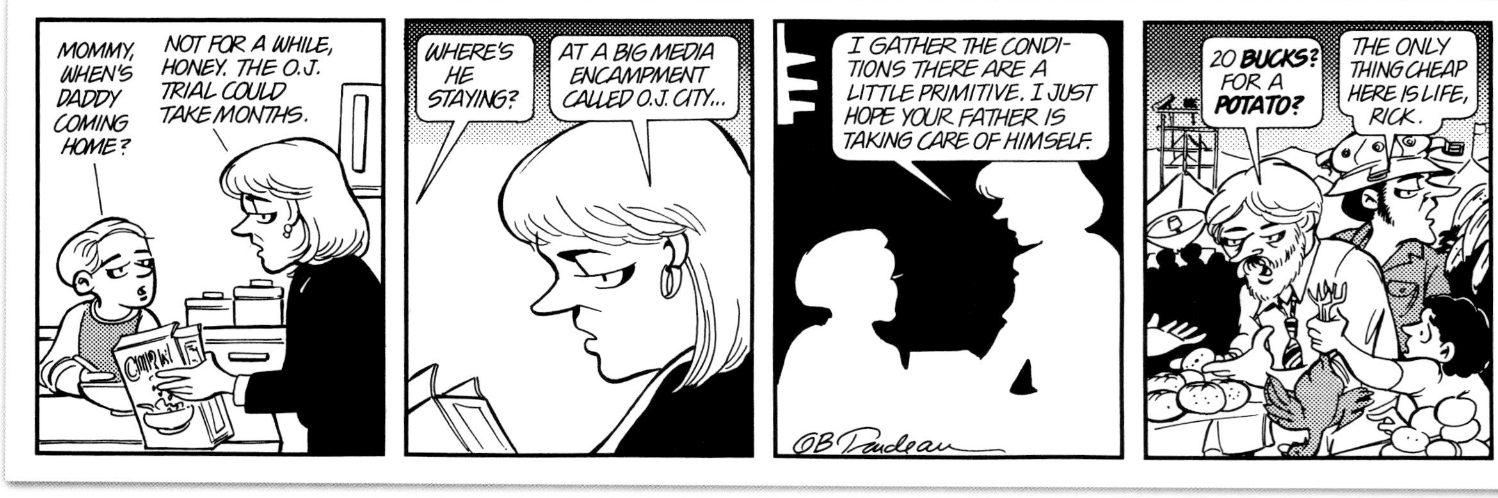
MOMMY, WHEN'S DADDY COMING HOME?
NOT FOR A WHILE, HONEY. THE O.J. TRIAL COULD TAKE MONTHS.
WHERE'S HE STAYING?
AT A BIG MEDIA ENCAMPMENT CALLED O.J. CITY...
I GATHER THE CONDITIONS THERE ARE A LITTLE PRIMITIVE. I JUST HOPE YOUR FATHER IS TAKING CARE OF HIMSELF.
20 BUCKS? FOR A POTATO?
THE ONLY THING CHEAP HERE IS LIFE, RICK.

11/26/94

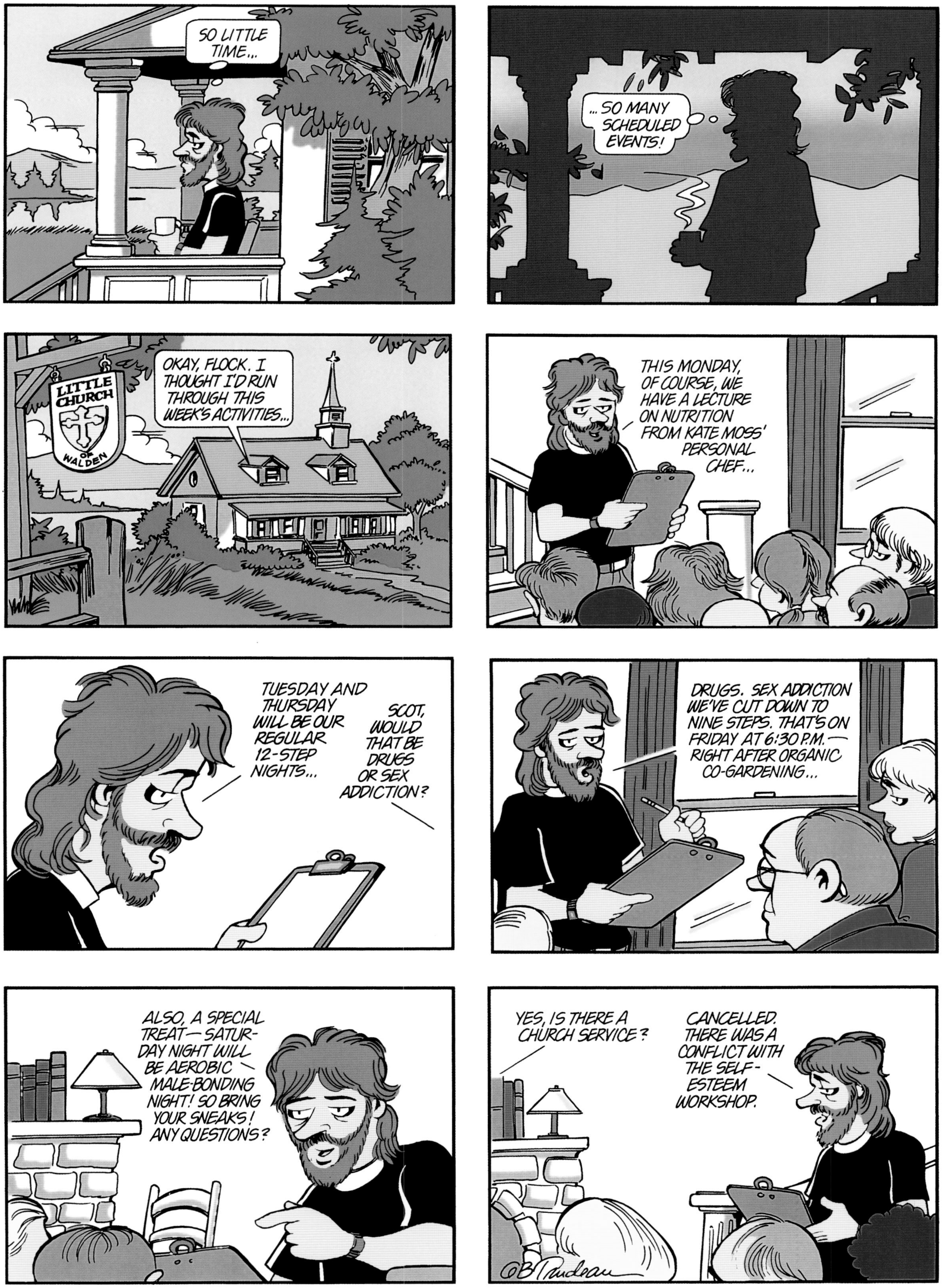
SO LITTLE TIME...
...SO MANY SCHEDULED EVENTS!
LITTLE CHURCH OF WALDEN
OKAY, FLOCK. I THOUGHT I'D RUN THROUGH THIS WEEK'S ACTIVITIES...
THIS MONDAY, OF COURSE, WE HAVE A LECTURE ON NUTRITION FROM KATE MOSS' PERSONAL CHEF...
TUESDAY AND THURSDAY WILL BE OUR REGULAR 12-STEP NIGHTS...
SCOT, WOULD THAT BE DRUGS OR SEX ADDICTION?
DRUGS. SEX ADDICTION WE'VE CUT DOWN TO NINE STEPS. THAT'S ON FRIDAY AT 6:30 P.M.— RIGHT AFTER ORGANIC CO-GARDENING...
ALSO, A SPECIAL TREAT— SATURDAY NIGHT WILL BE AEROBIC MALE-BONDING NIGHT! SO BRING YOUR SNEAKS! ANY QUESTIONS?
YES, IS THERE A CHURCH SERVICE?
CANCELLED. THERE WAS A CONFLICT WITH THE SELF-ESTEEM WORKSHOP.
©B Trudeau

6/19/94

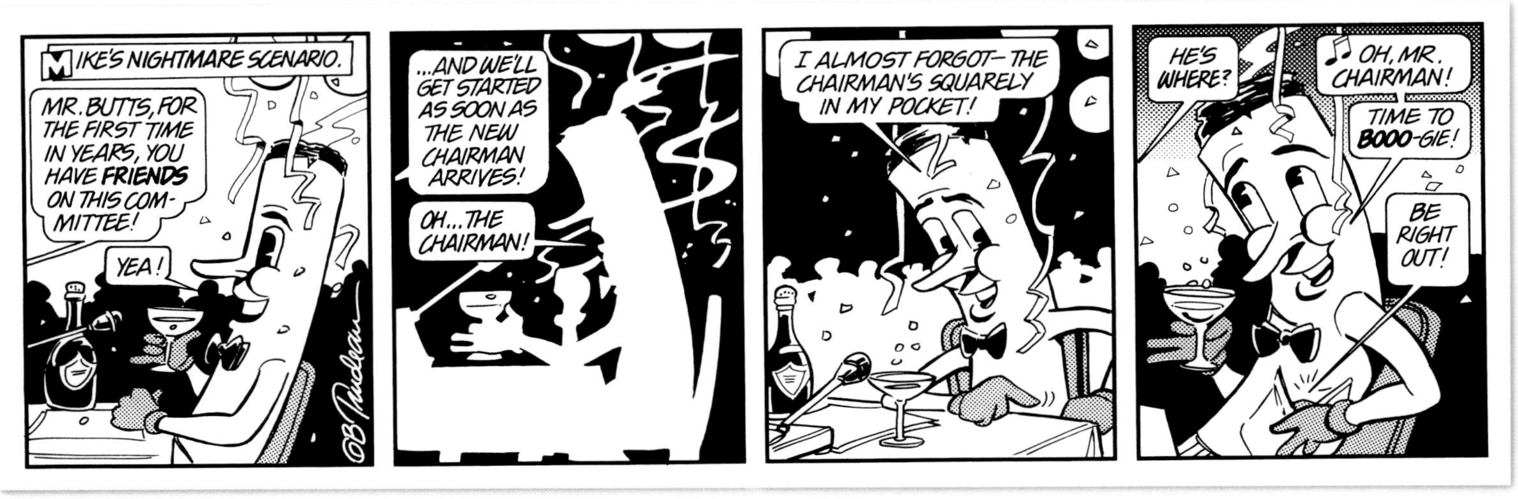
MIKE'S NIGHTMARE SCENARIO.
MR. BUTTS, FOR THE FIRST TIME IN YEARS, YOU HAVE **FRIENDS** ON THIS COMMITTEE!
YEA!
...AND WE'LL GET STARTED AS SOON AS THE NEW CHAIRMAN ARRIVES!
OH... THE CHAIRMAN!
I ALMOST FORGOT— THE CHAIRMAN'S SQUARELY IN MY POCKET!
HE'S WHERE?
♪ OH, MR. CHAIRMAN!
TIME TO **BOOO**-GIE!
BE RIGHT OUT!

12/6/94

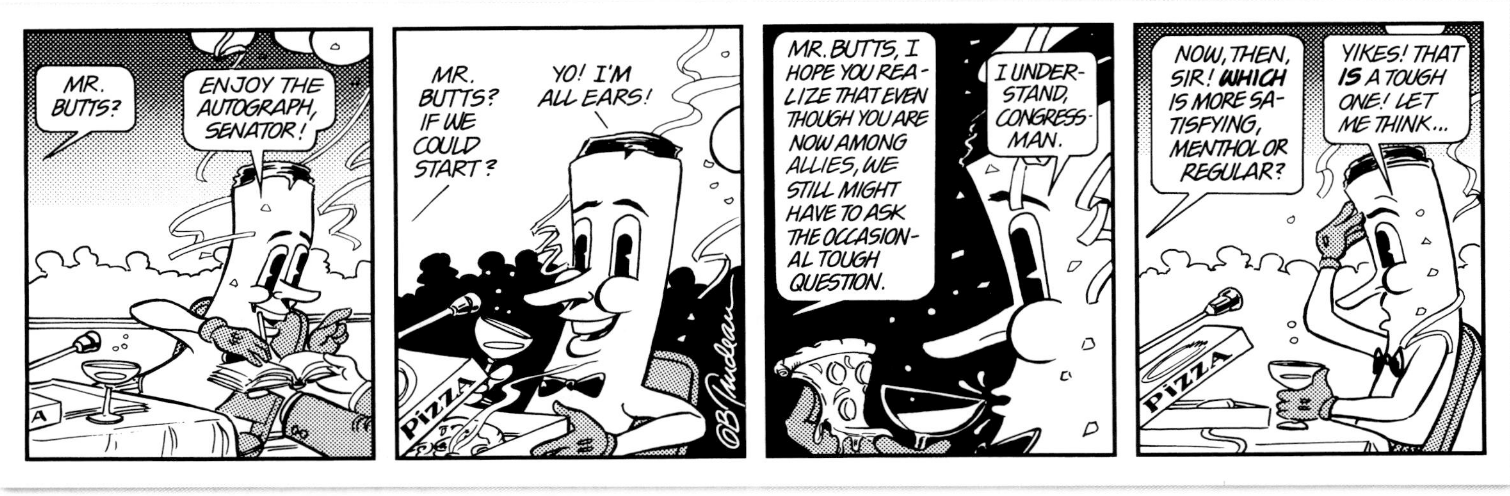
MR. BUTTS?
ENJOY THE AUTOGRAPH, SENATOR!
MR. BUTTS? IF WE COULD START?
YO! I'M ALL EARS!
MR. BUTTS, I HOPE YOU REALIZE THAT EVEN THOUGH YOU ARE NOW AMONG ALLIES, WE STILL MIGHT HAVE TO ASK THE OCCASIONAL TOUGH QUESTION.
I UNDERSTAND, CONGRESSMAN.
NOW, THEN, SIR! **WHICH** IS MORE SATISFYING, MENTHOL OR REGULAR?
YIKES! THAT **IS** A TOUGH ONE! LET ME THINK...

12/7/94

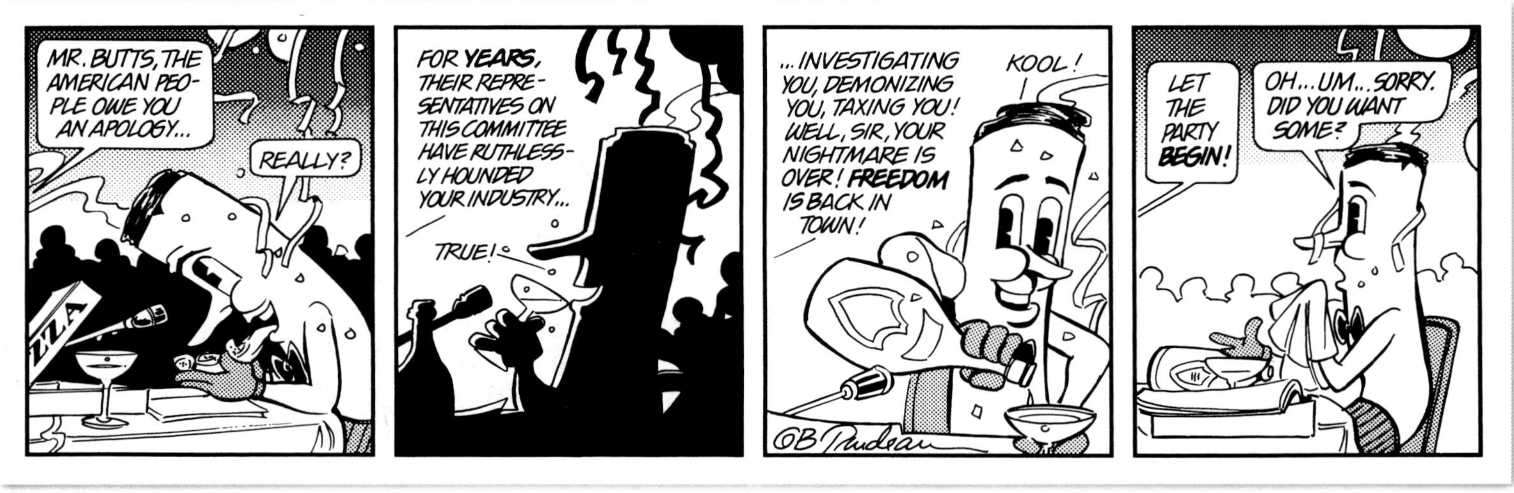
MR. BUTTS, THE AMERICAN PEOPLE OWE YOU AN APOLOGY...
REALLY?
FOR **YEARS**, THEIR REPRESENTATIVES ON THIS COMMITTEE HAVE RUTHLESSLY HOUNDED YOUR INDUSTRY...
TRUE!
...INVESTIGATING YOU, DEMONIZING YOU, TAXING YOU! WELL, SIR, YOUR NIGHTMARE IS OVER! **FREEDOM** IS BACK IN TOWN!
KOOL!
LET THE PARTY **BEGIN**!
OH... UM... SORRY. DID YOU WANT SOME?

12/8/94

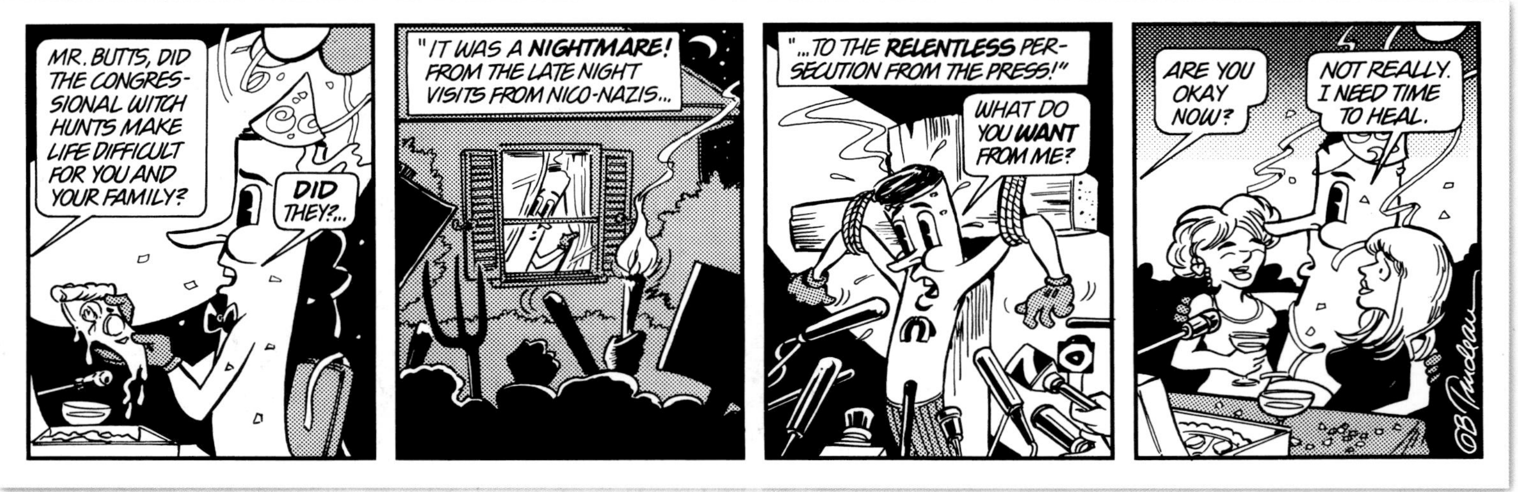
MR. BUTTS, DID THE CONGRESSIONAL WITCH HUNTS MAKE LIFE DIFFICULT FOR YOU AND YOUR FAMILY?
DID THEY?...
"IT WAS A **NIGHTMARE**! FROM THE LATE NIGHT VISITS FROM NICO-NAZIS...
"...TO THE **RELENTLESS** PERSECUTION FROM THE PRESS!"
WHAT DO YOU **WANT** FROM ME?
ARE YOU OKAY NOW?
NOT REALLY. I NEED TIME TO HEAL.

12/9/94

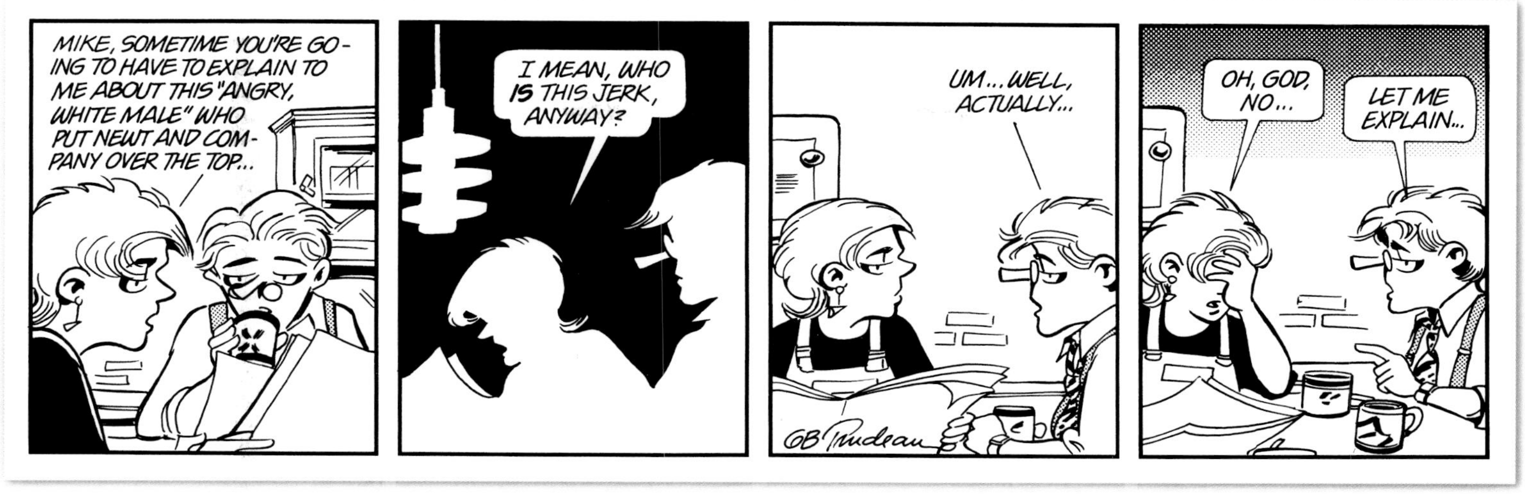
MIKE, SOMETIME YOU'RE GOING TO HAVE TO EXPLAIN TO ME ABOUT THIS "ANGRY, WHITE MALE" WHO PUT NEWT AND COMPANY OVER THE TOP...
I MEAN, WHO **IS** THIS JERK, ANYWAY?
UM... WELL, ACTUALLY...
GB Trudeau
OH, GOD, NO...
LET ME EXPLAIN...

12/12/94

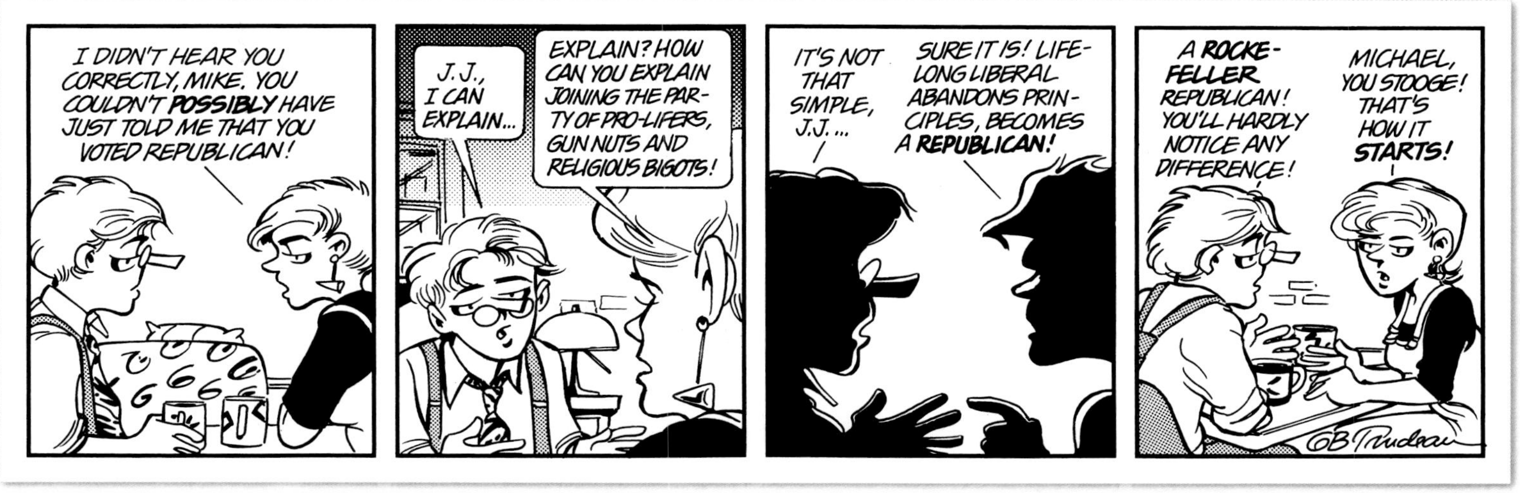
I DIDN'T HEAR YOU CORRECTLY, MIKE. YOU COULDN'T **POSSIBLY** HAVE JUST TOLD ME THAT YOU VOTED REPUBLICAN!
J.J., I CAN EXPLAIN...
EXPLAIN? HOW CAN YOU EXPLAIN JOINING THE PARTY OF PRO-LIFERS, GUN NUTS AND RELIGIOUS BIGOTS!
IT'S NOT THAT SIMPLE, J.J. ...
SURE IT IS! LIFELONG LIBERAL ABANDONS PRINCIPLES, BECOMES A **REPUBLICAN!**
A **ROCKEFELLER** REPUBLICAN! YOU'LL HARDLY NOTICE ANY DIFFERENCE!
MICHAEL, YOU STOOGE! THAT'S HOW IT **STARTS!**
GB Trudeau

12/13/94

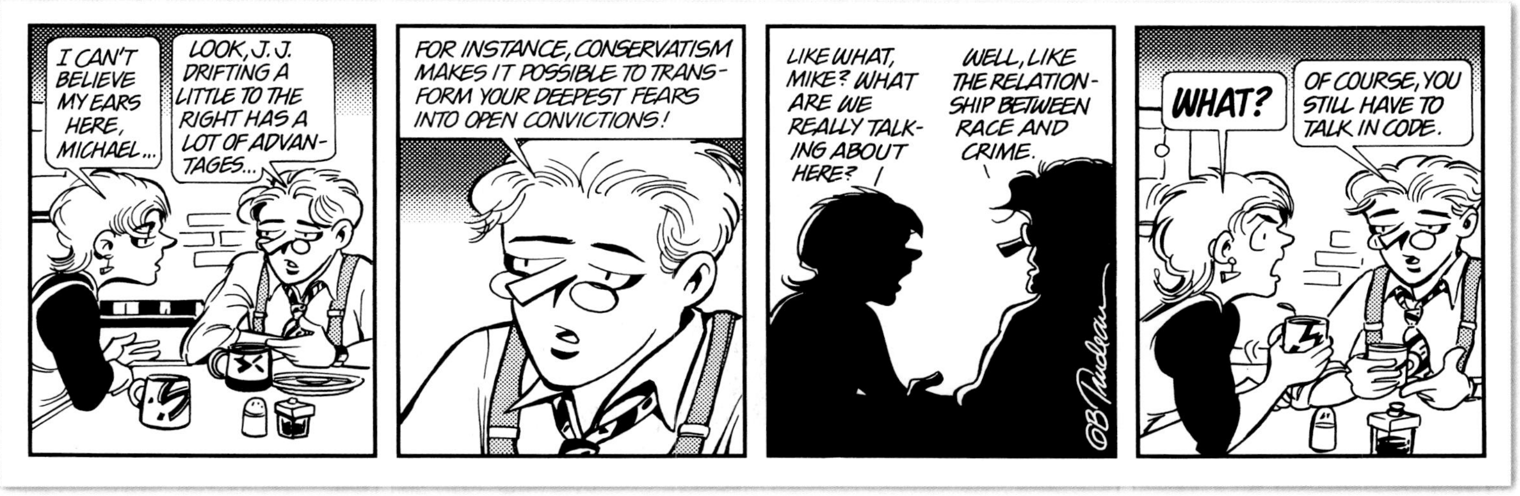
I CAN'T BELIEVE MY EARS HERE, MICHAEL...
LOOK, J.J. DRIFTING A LITTLE TO THE RIGHT HAS A LOT OF ADVANTAGES...
FOR INSTANCE, CONSERVATISM MAKES IT POSSIBLE TO TRANSFORM YOUR DEEPEST FEARS INTO OPEN CONVICTIONS!
LIKE WHAT, MIKE? WHAT ARE WE REALLY TALKING ABOUT HERE?
WELL, LIKE THE RELATIONSHIP BETWEEN RACE AND CRIME.
GB Trudeau
WHAT?
OF COURSE, YOU STILL HAVE TO TALK IN CODE.

12/14/94

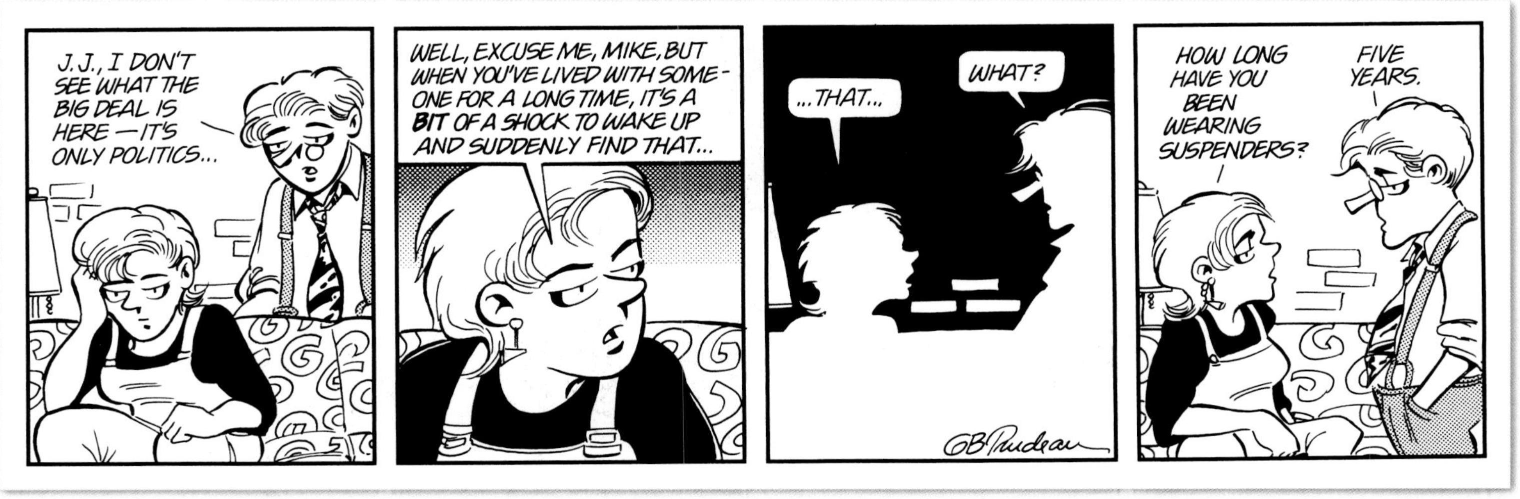
J.J., I DON'T SEE WHAT THE BIG DEAL IS HERE — IT'S ONLY POLITICS...
WELL, EXCUSE ME, MIKE, BUT WHEN YOU'VE LIVED WITH SOMEONE FOR A LONG TIME, IT'S A **BIT** OF A SHOCK TO WAKE UP AND SUDDENLY FIND THAT...
...THAT...
WHAT?
GB Trudeau
HOW LONG HAVE YOU BEEN WEARING SUSPENDERS?
FIVE YEARS.

12/16/94

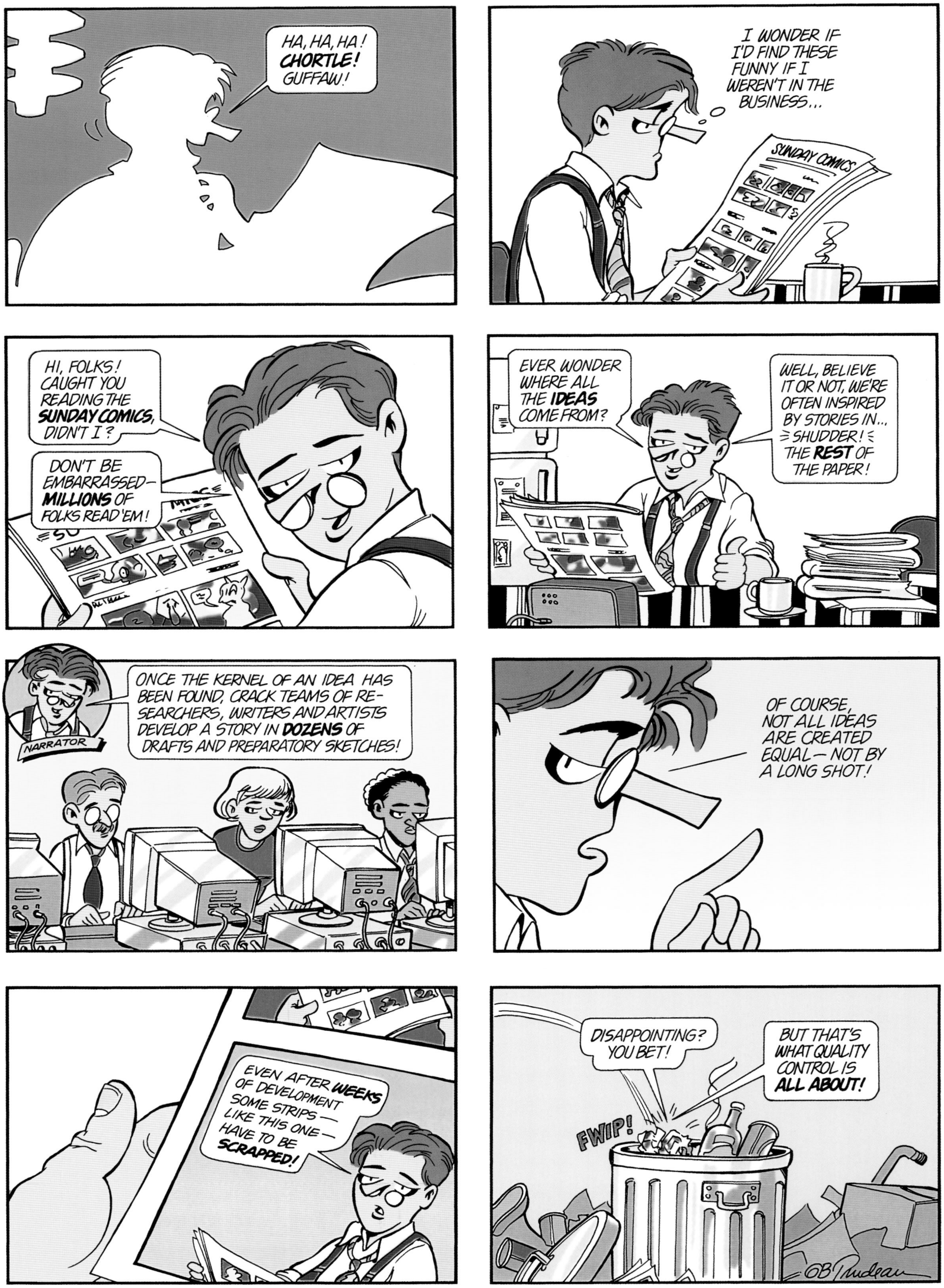
HA, HA, HA! CHORTLE! GUFFAW!
I WONDER IF I'D FIND THESE FUNNY IF I WEREN'T IN THE BUSINESS...
SUNDAY COMICS
HI, FOLKS! CAUGHT YOU READING THE SUNDAY COMICS, DIDN'T I?
DON'T BE EMBARRASSED– MILLIONS OF FOLKS READ 'EM!
EVER WONDER WHERE ALL THE IDEAS COME FROM?
WELL, BELIEVE IT OR NOT, WE'RE OFTEN INSPIRED BY STORIES IN... SHUDDER! THE REST OF THE PAPER!
NARRATOR
ONCE THE KERNEL OF AN IDEA HAS BEEN FOUND, CRACK TEAMS OF RE-SEARCHERS, WRITERS AND ARTISTS DEVELOP A STORY IN DOZENS OF DRAFTS AND PREPARATORY SKETCHES!
OF COURSE, NOT ALL IDEAS ARE CREATED EQUAL— NOT BY A LONG SHOT!
EVEN AFTER WEEKS OF DEVELOPMENT SOME STRIPS— LIKE THIS ONE— HAVE TO BE SCRAPPED!
DISAPPOINTING? YOU BET!
BUT THAT'S WHAT QUALITY CONTROL IS ALL ABOUT!
FWIP!
GB Trudeau

9/4/94

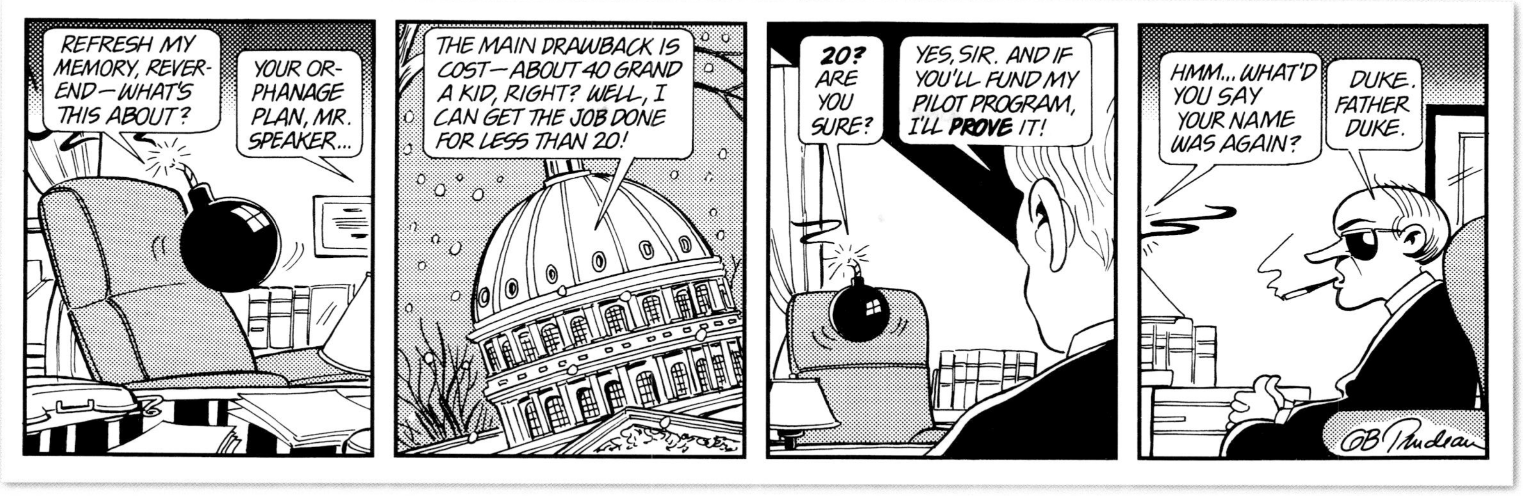
REFRESH MY MEMORY, REVEREND — WHAT'S THIS ABOUT?
YOUR ORPHANAGE PLAN, MR. SPEAKER...
THE MAIN DRAWBACK IS COST — ABOUT 40 GRAND A KID, RIGHT? WELL, I CAN GET THE JOB DONE FOR LESS THAN 20!
20? ARE YOU SURE?
YES, SIR. AND IF YOU'LL FUND MY PILOT PROGRAM, I'LL **PROVE** IT!
HMM... WHAT'D YOU SAY YOUR NAME WAS AGAIN?
DUKE. FATHER DUKE.
©B Trudeau

1/9/95

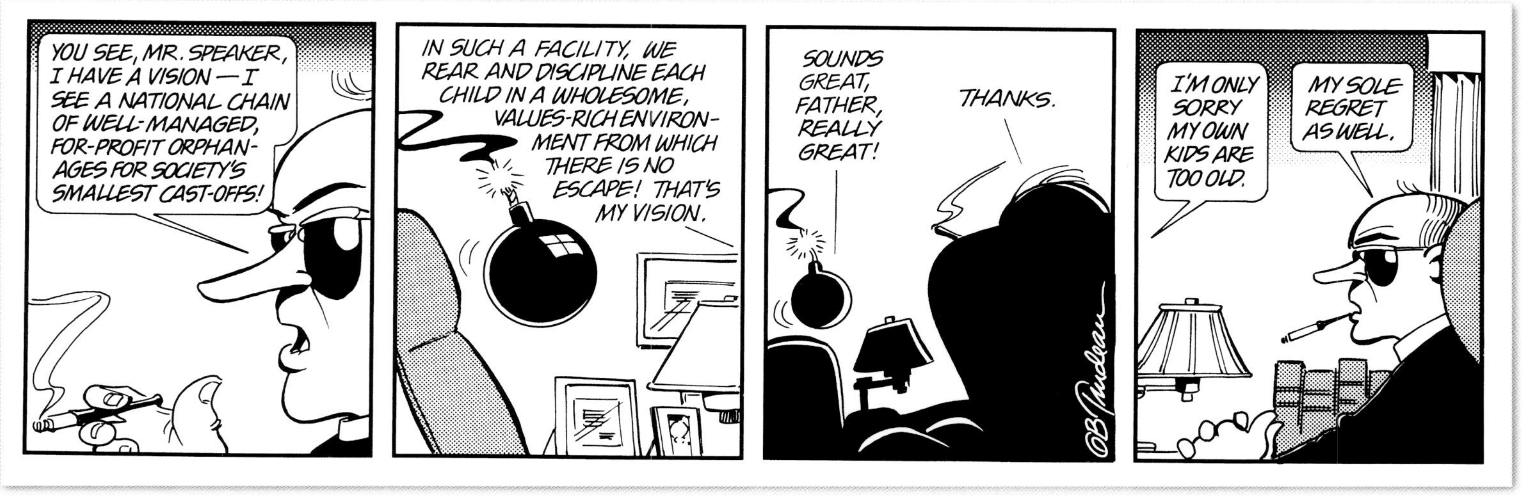
YOU SEE, MR. SPEAKER, I HAVE A VISION — I SEE A NATIONAL CHAIN OF WELL-MANAGED, FOR-PROFIT ORPHANAGES FOR SOCIETY'S SMALLEST CAST-OFFS!
IN SUCH A FACILITY, WE REAR AND DISCIPLINE EACH CHILD IN A WHOLESOME, VALUES-RICH ENVIRONMENT FROM WHICH THERE IS NO ESCAPE! THAT'S MY VISION.
SOUNDS GREAT, FATHER, REALLY GREAT!
THANKS.
I'M ONLY SORRY MY OWN KIDS ARE TOO OLD.
MY SOLE REGRET AS WELL.
©B Trudeau

1/11/95

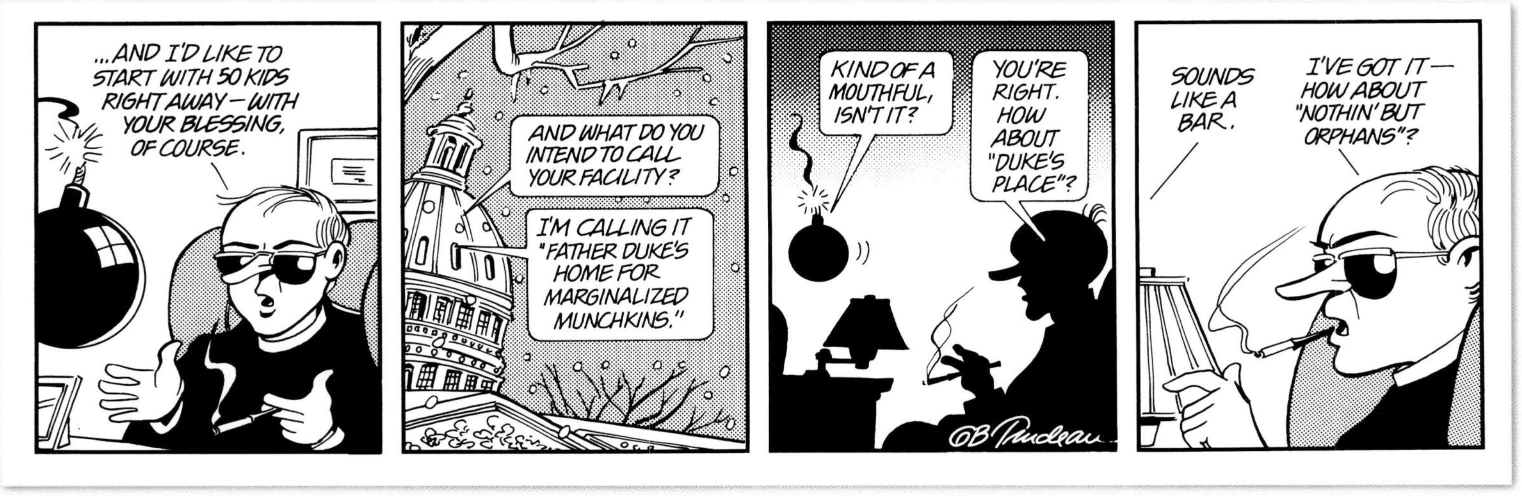
...AND I'D LIKE TO START WITH 50 KIDS RIGHT AWAY — WITH YOUR BLESSING, OF COURSE.
AND WHAT DO YOU INTEND TO CALL YOUR FACILITY?
I'M CALLING IT "FATHER DUKE'S HOME FOR MARGINALIZED MUNCHKINS."
KIND OF A MOUTHFUL, ISN'T IT?
YOU'RE RIGHT. HOW ABOUT "DUKE'S PLACE"?
SOUNDS LIKE A BAR.
I'VE GOT IT — HOW ABOUT "NOTHIN' BUT ORPHANS"?
©B Trudeau

1/13/95

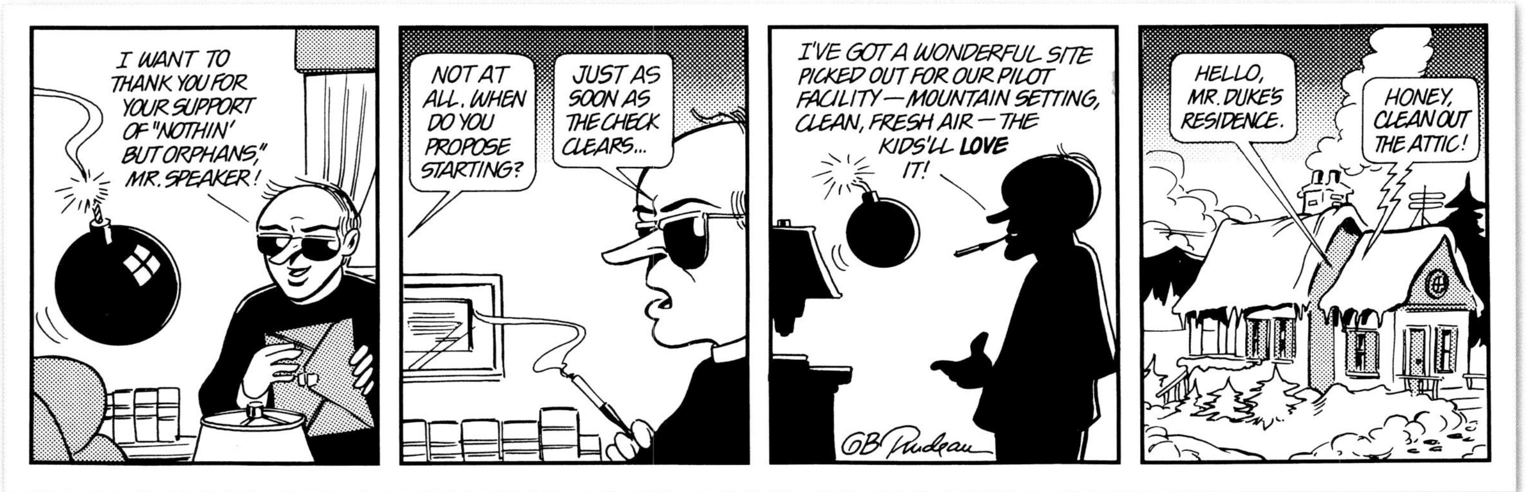
I WANT TO THANK YOU FOR YOUR SUPPORT OF "NOTHIN' BUT ORPHANS," MR. SPEAKER!
NOT AT ALL. WHEN DO YOU PROPOSE STARTING?
JUST AS SOON AS THE CHECK CLEARS...
I'VE GOT A WONDERFUL SITE PICKED OUT FOR OUR PILOT FACILITY — MOUNTAIN SETTING, CLEAN, FRESH AIR — THE KIDS'LL **LOVE** IT!
HELLO, MR. DUKE'S RESIDENCE.
HONEY, CLEAN OUT THE ATTIC!
©B Trudeau

1/14/95

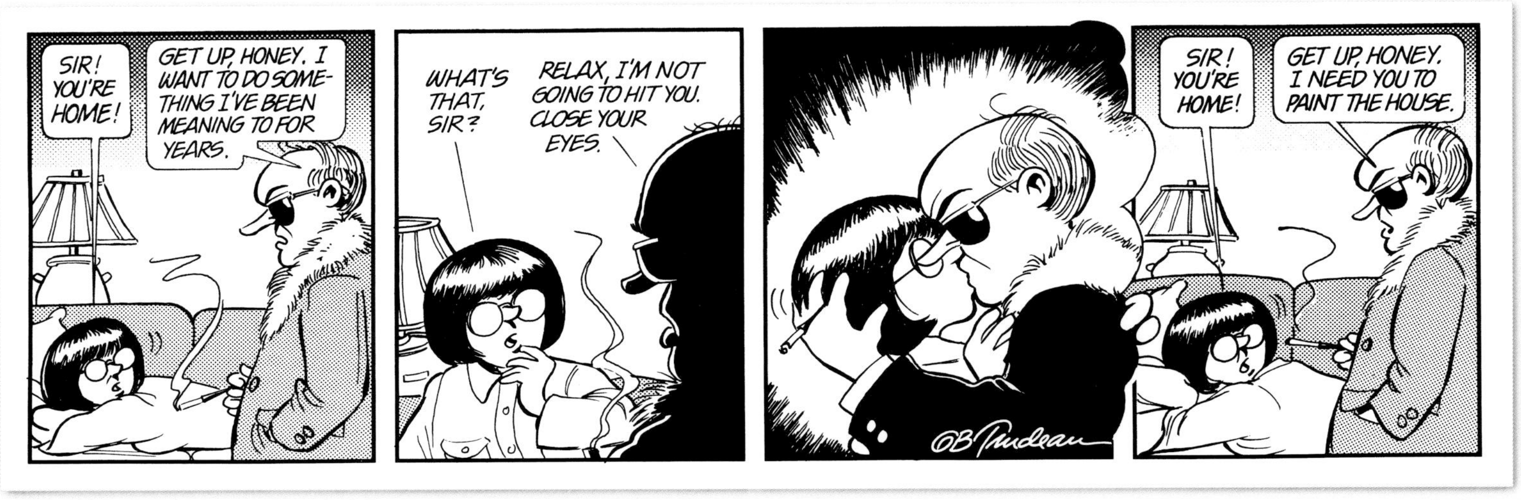
SIR! YOU'RE HOME!
GET UP, HONEY. I WANT TO DO SOMETHING I'VE BEEN MEANING TO FOR YEARS.
WHAT'S THAT, SIR?
RELAX, I'M NOT GOING TO HIT YOU. CLOSE YOUR EYES.
SIR! YOU'RE HOME!
GET UP, HONEY. I NEED YOU TO PAINT THE HOUSE.

1/16/95

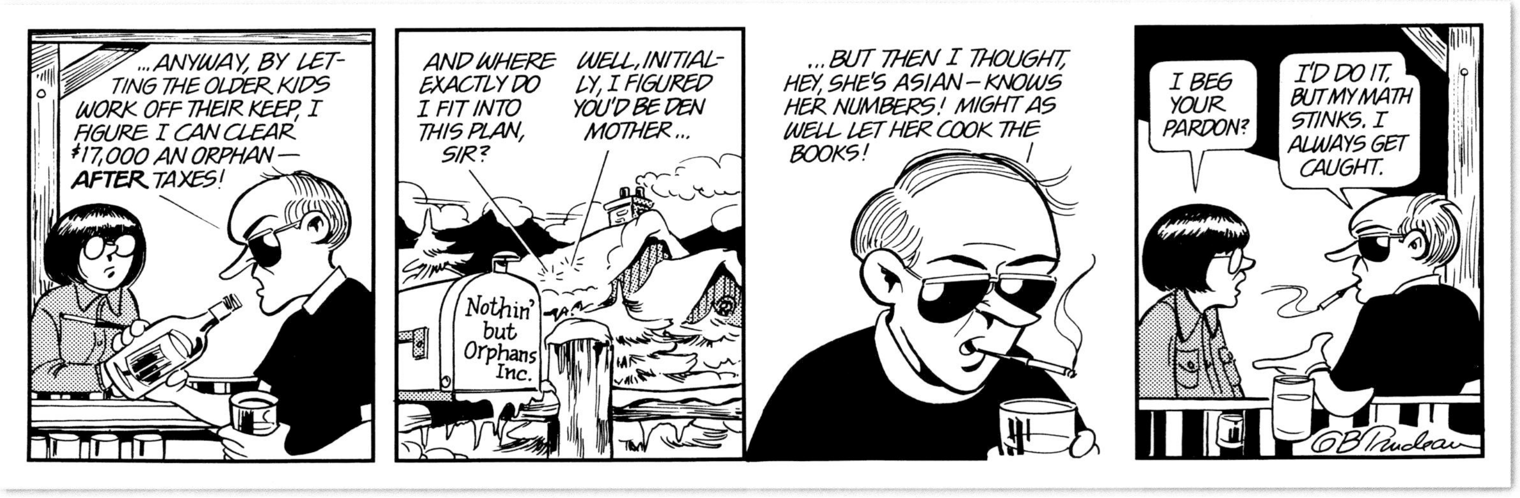
...ANYWAY, BY LETTING THE OLDER KIDS WORK OFF THEIR KEEP, I FIGURE I CAN CLEAR $17,000 AN ORPHAN— AFTER TAXES!
AND WHERE EXACTLY DO I FIT INTO THIS PLAN, SIR?
WELL, INITIALLY, I FIGURED YOU'D BE DEN MOTHER...
Nothin' but Orphans Inc.
...BUT THEN I THOUGHT, HEY, SHE'S ASIAN—KNOWS HER NUMBERS! MIGHT AS WELL LET HER COOK THE BOOKS!
I BEG YOUR PARDON?
I'D DO IT, BUT MY MATH STINKS. I ALWAYS GET CAUGHT.

1/18/95

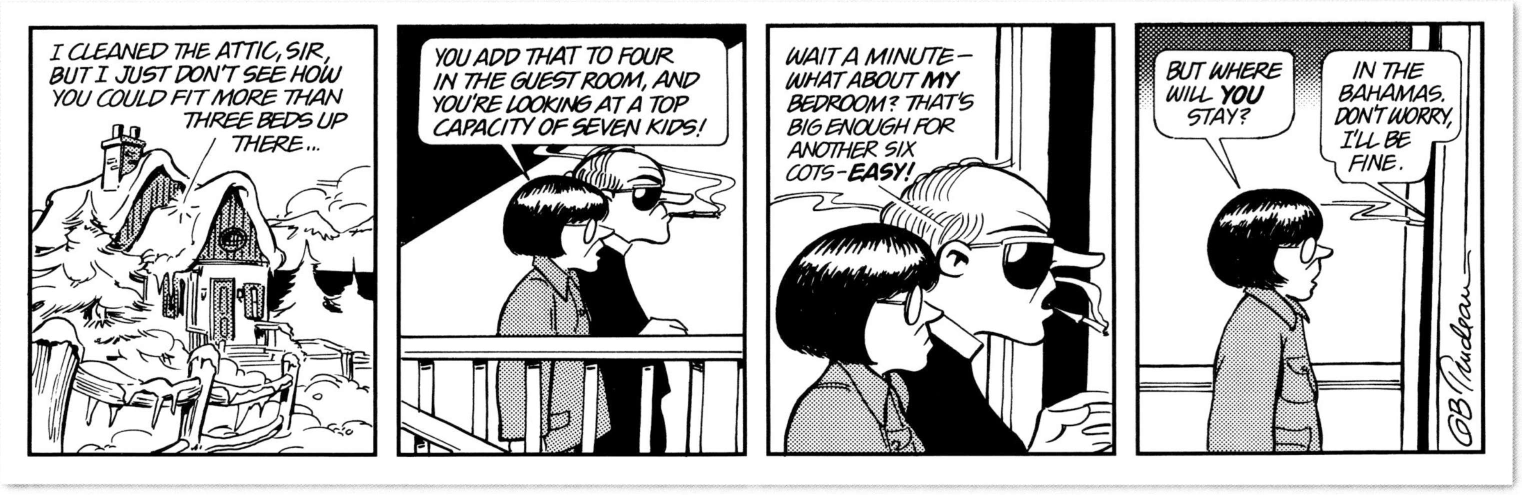
I CLEANED THE ATTIC, SIR, BUT I JUST DON'T SEE HOW YOU COULD FIT MORE THAN THREE BEDS UP THERE...
YOU ADD THAT TO FOUR IN THE GUEST ROOM, AND YOU'RE LOOKING AT A TOP CAPACITY OF SEVEN KIDS!
WAIT A MINUTE— WHAT ABOUT MY BEDROOM? THAT'S BIG ENOUGH FOR ANOTHER SIX COTS—EASY!
BUT WHERE WILL YOU STAY?
IN THE BAHAMAS. DON'T WORRY, I'LL BE FINE.

1/19/95

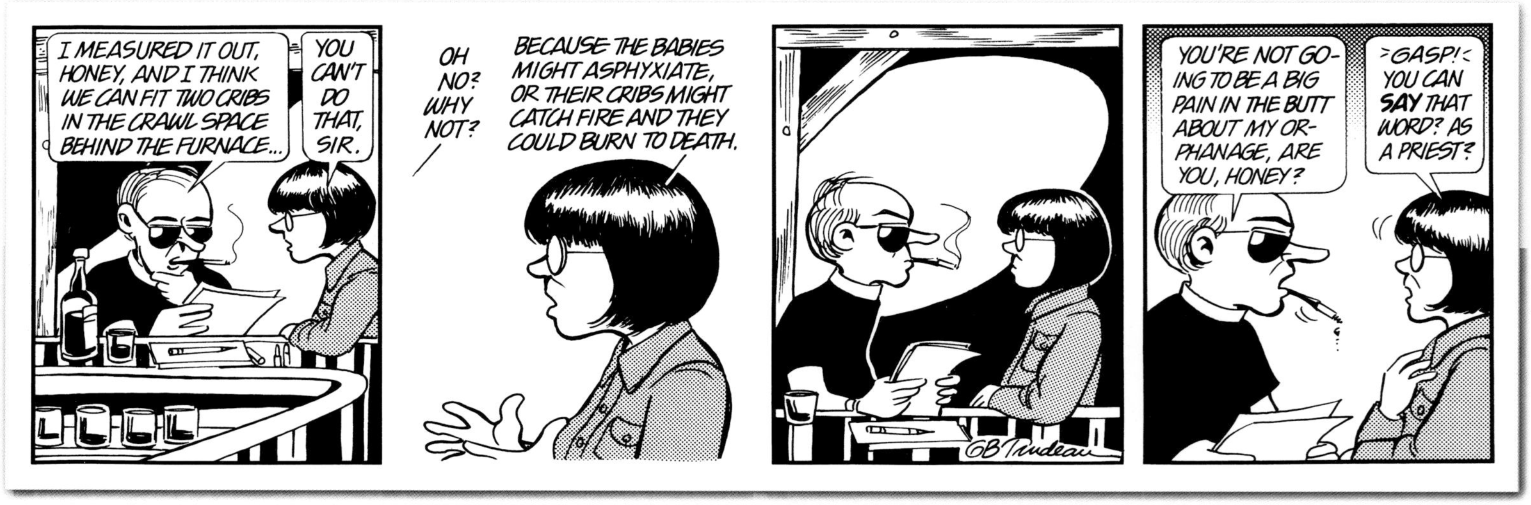
I MEASURED IT OUT, HONEY, AND I THINK WE CAN FIT TWO CRIBS IN THE CRAWL SPACE BEHIND THE FURNACE...
YOU CAN'T DO THAT, SIR.
OH NO? WHY NOT?
BECAUSE THE BABIES MIGHT ASPHYXIATE, OR THEIR CRIBS MIGHT CATCH FIRE AND THEY COULD BURN TO DEATH.
YOU'RE NOT GOING TO BE A BIG PAIN IN THE BUTT ABOUT MY ORPHANAGE, ARE YOU, HONEY?
>GASP!< YOU CAN SAY THAT WORD? AS A PRIEST?

1/21/95

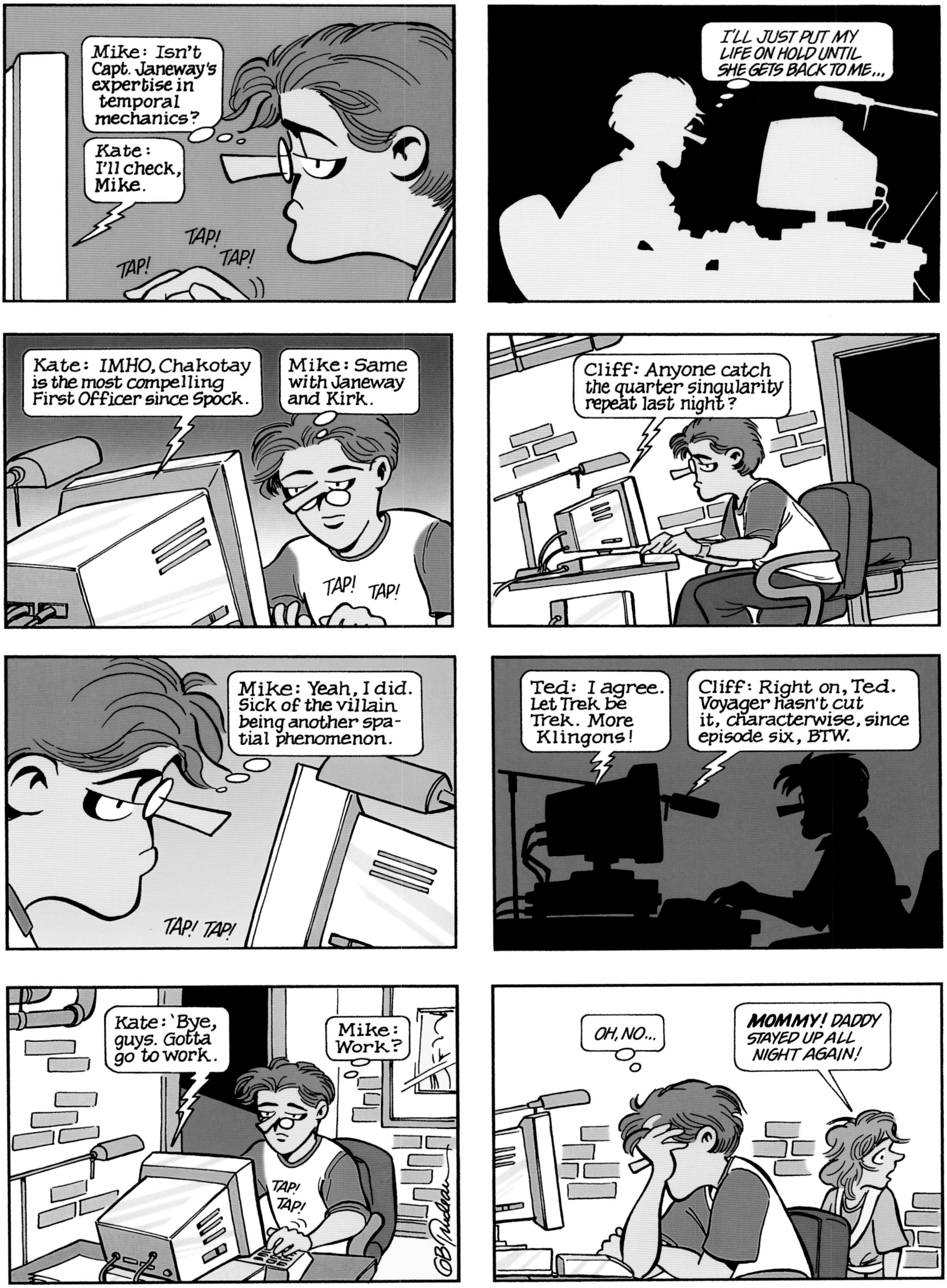

Mike: Isn't Capt. Janeway's expertise in temporal mechanics?
Kate: I'll check, Mike.
TAP! TAP! TAP!
I'LL JUST PUT MY LIFE ON HOLD UNTIL SHE GETS BACK TO ME...
Kate: IMHO, Chakotay is the most compelling First Officer since Spock.
Mike: Same with Janeway and Kirk.
TAP! TAP!
Cliff: Anyone catch the quarter singularity repeat last night?
Mike: Yeah, I did. Sick of the villain being another spatial phenomenon.
TAP! TAP!
Ted: I agree. Let Trek be Trek. More Klingons!
Cliff: Right on, Ted. Voyager hasn't cut it, characterwise, since episode six, BTW.
Kate: 'Bye, guys. Gotta go to work.
Mike: Work?
TAP! TAP!
OH, NO...
MOMMY! DADDY STAYED UP ALL NIGHT AGAIN!

2/26/95

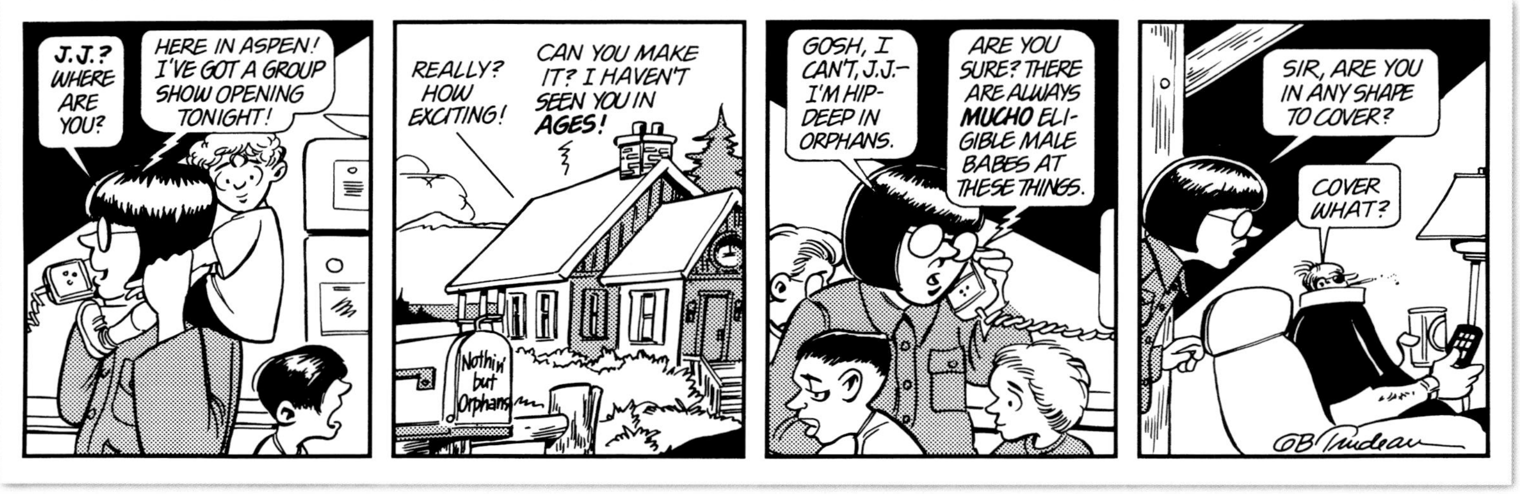
J.J.? WHERE ARE YOU?
HERE IN ASPEN! I'VE GOT A GROUP SHOW OPENING TONIGHT!
REALLY? HOW EXCITING!
CAN YOU MAKE IT? I HAVEN'T SEEN YOU IN AGES!
Nothin' but Orphans
GOSH, I CAN'T, J.J.— I'M HIP-DEEP IN ORPHANS.
ARE YOU SURE? THERE ARE ALWAYS MUCHO ELIGIBLE MALE BABES AT THESE THINGS.
SIR, ARE YOU IN ANY SHAPE TO COVER?
COVER WHAT?
GB Trudeau

6/5/95

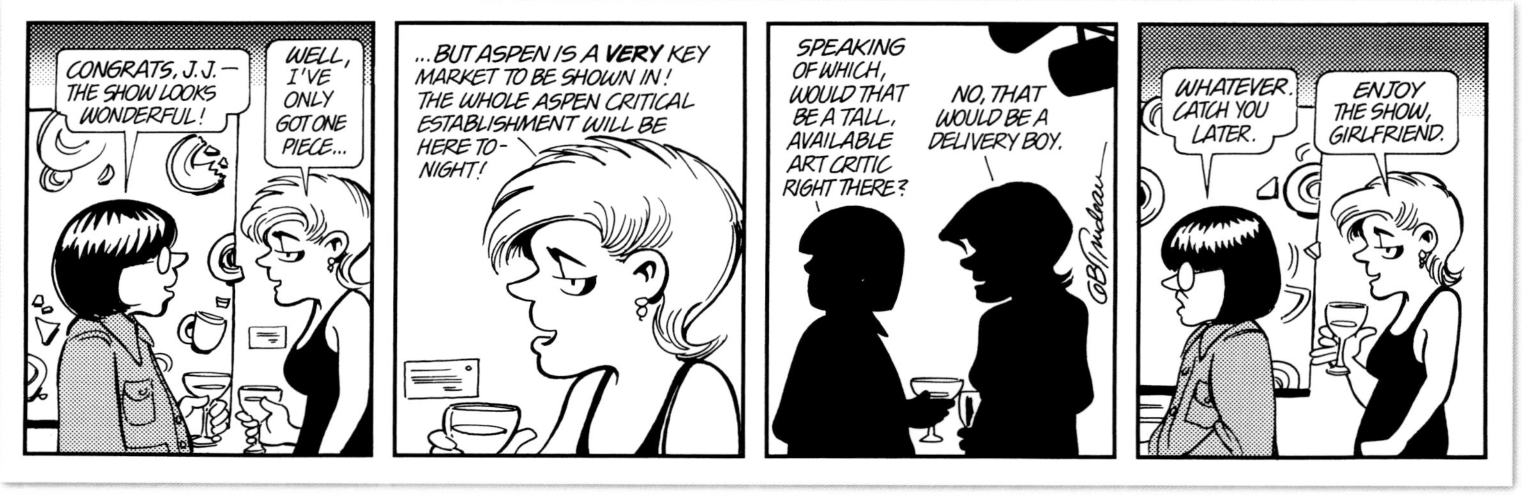
CONGRATS, J.J.— THE SHOW LOOKS WONDERFUL!
WELL, I'VE ONLY GOT ONE PIECE...
...BUT ASPEN IS A VERY KEY MARKET TO BE SHOWN IN! THE WHOLE ASPEN CRITICAL ESTABLISHMENT WILL BE HERE TONIGHT!
SPEAKING OF WHICH, WOULD THAT BE A TALL, AVAILABLE ART CRITIC RIGHT THERE?
NO, THAT WOULD BE A DELIVERY BOY.
GB Trudeau
WHATEVER. CATCH YOU LATER.
ENJOY THE SHOW, GIRLFRIEND.

6/6/95

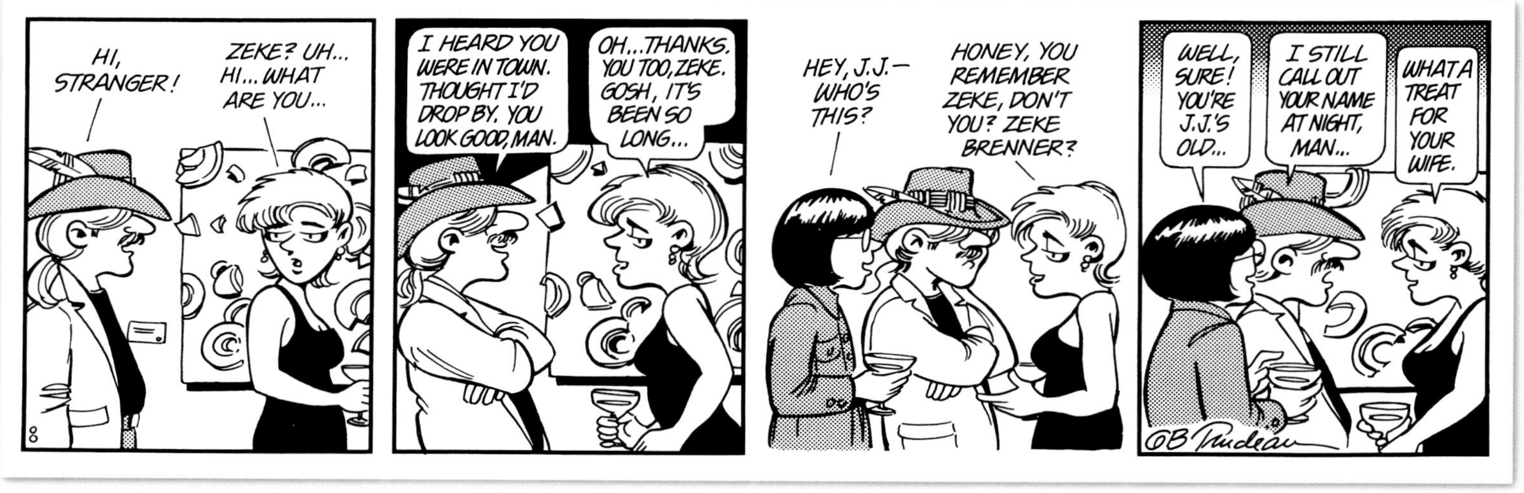
HI, STRANGER!
ZEKE? UH... HI... WHAT ARE YOU...
I HEARD YOU WERE IN TOWN. THOUGHT I'D DROP BY. YOU LOOK GOOD, MAN.
OH... THANKS. YOU TOO, ZEKE. GOSH, IT'S BEEN SO LONG...
HEY, J.J.— WHO'S THIS?
HONEY, YOU REMEMBER ZEKE, DON'T YOU? ZEKE BRENNER?
WELL, SURE! YOU'RE J.J.'S OLD...
I STILL CALL OUT YOUR NAME AT NIGHT, MAN...
WHAT A TREAT FOR YOUR WIFE.
GB Trudeau

6/7/95

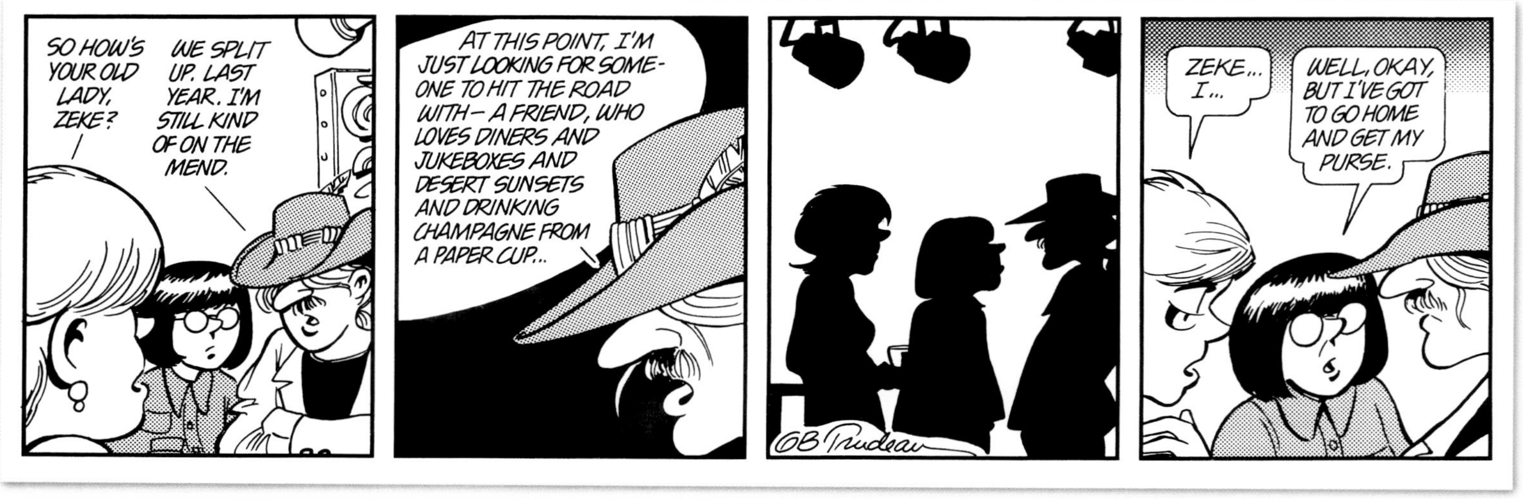
SO HOW'S YOUR OLD LADY, ZEKE?
WE SPLIT UP. LAST YEAR. I'M STILL KIND OF ON THE MEND.
AT THIS POINT, I'M JUST LOOKING FOR SOMEONE TO HIT THE ROAD WITH— A FRIEND, WHO LOVES DINERS AND JUKEBOXES AND DESERT SUNSETS AND DRINKING CHAMPAGNE FROM A PAPER CUP...
GB Trudeau
ZEKE... I...
WELL, OKAY, BUT I'VE GOT TO GO HOME AND GET MY PURSE.

6/8/95

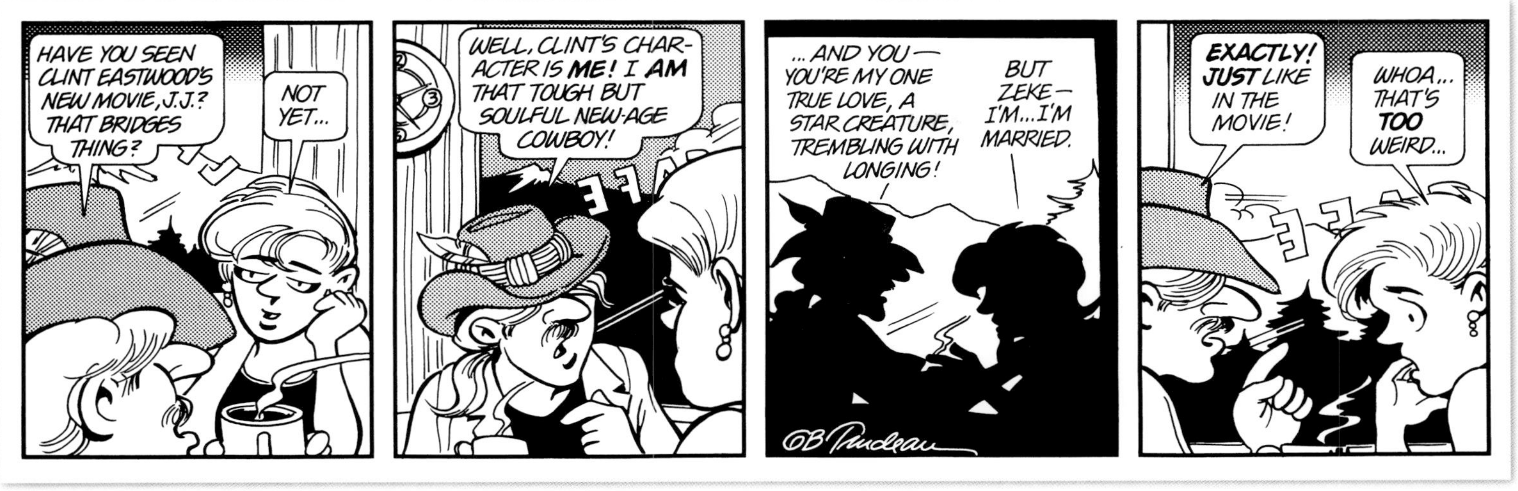
HAVE YOU SEEN CLINT EASTWOOD'S NEW MOVIE, J.J.? THAT BRIDGES THING?
NOT YET...
WELL, CLINT'S CHARACTER IS ME! I AM THAT TOUGH BUT SOULFUL NEW-AGE COWBOY!
...AND YOU— YOU'RE MY ONE TRUE LOVE, A STAR CREATURE, TREMBLING WITH LONGING!
BUT ZEKE— I'M...I'M MARRIED.
EXACTLY! JUST LIKE IN THE MOVIE!
WHOA... THAT'S TOO WEIRD...

6/10/95

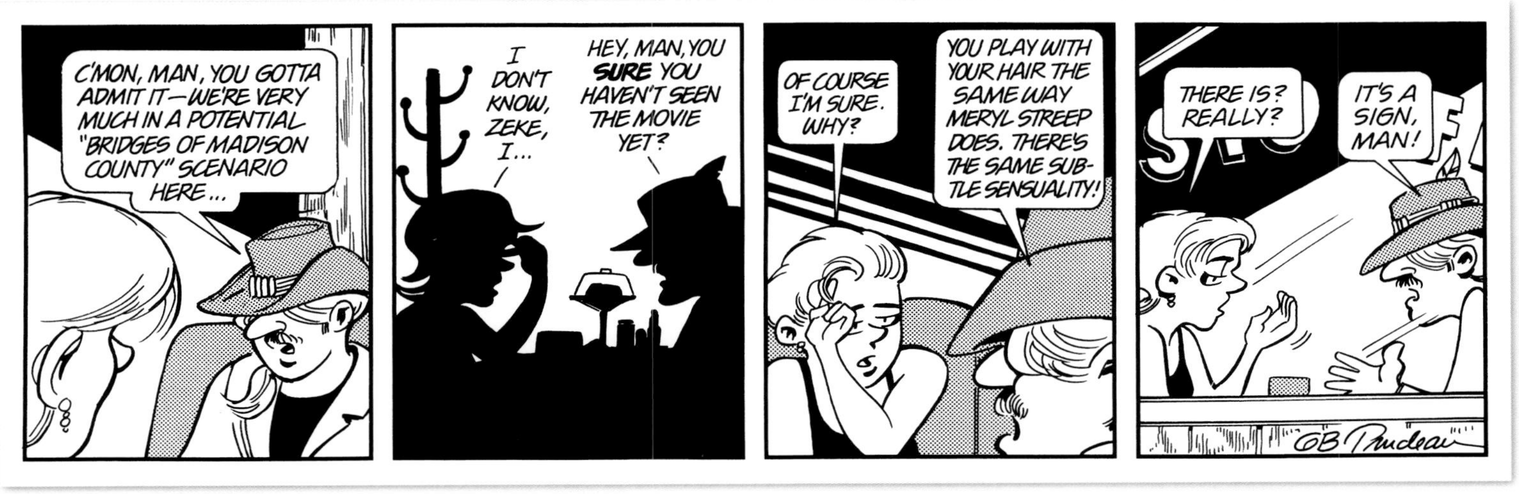
C'MON, MAN, YOU GOTTA ADMIT IT—WE'RE VERY MUCH IN A POTENTIAL "BRIDGES OF MADISON COUNTY" SCENARIO HERE...
I DON'T KNOW, ZEKE, I...
HEY, MAN, YOU SURE YOU HAVEN'T SEEN THE MOVIE YET?
OF COURSE I'M SURE. WHY?
YOU PLAY WITH YOUR HAIR THE SAME WAY MERYL STREEP DOES. THERE'S THE SAME SUBTLE SENSUALITY!
THERE IS? REALLY?
IT'S A SIGN, MAN!

6/12/95

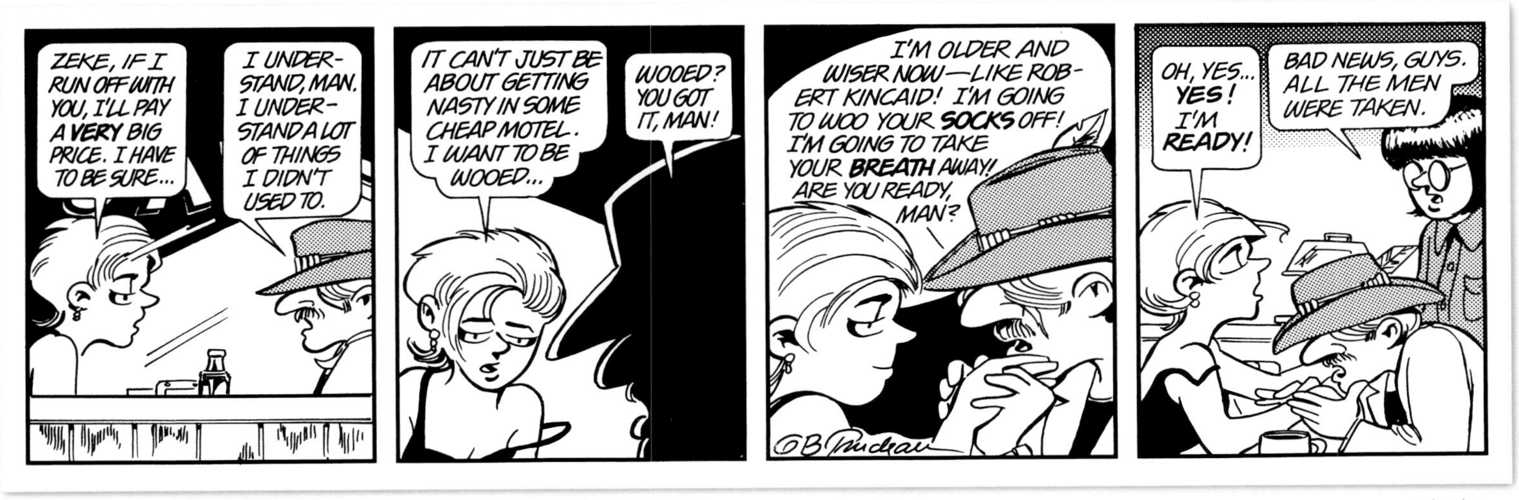
ZEKE, IF I RUN OFF WITH YOU, I'LL PAY A VERY BIG PRICE. I HAVE TO BE SURE...
I UNDERSTAND, MAN. I UNDERSTAND A LOT OF THINGS I DIDN'T USED TO.
IT CAN'T JUST BE ABOUT GETTING NASTY IN SOME CHEAP MOTEL. I WANT TO BE WOOED...
WOOED? YOU GOT IT, MAN!
I'M OLDER AND WISER NOW—LIKE ROBERT KINCAID! I'M GOING TO WOO YOUR SOCKS OFF! I'M GOING TO TAKE YOUR BREATH AWAY! ARE YOU READY, MAN?
OH, YES... YES! I'M READY!
BAD NEWS, GUYS. ALL THE MEN WERE TAKEN.

6/15/95

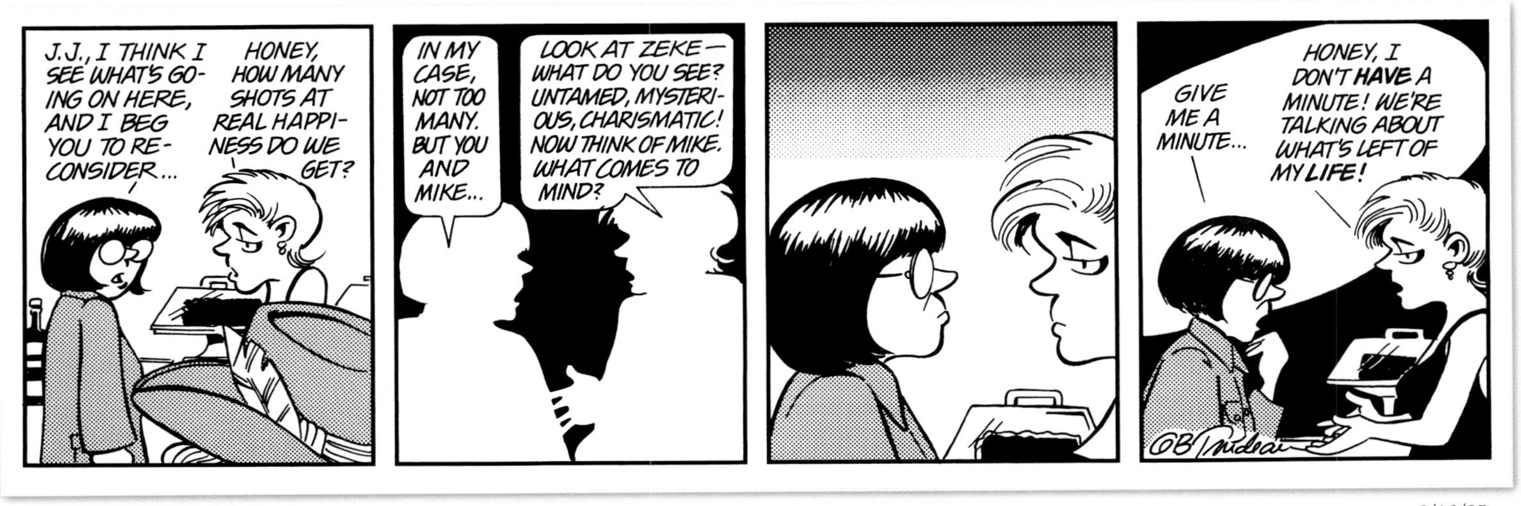
J.J., I THINK I SEE WHAT'S GOING ON HERE, AND I BEG YOU TO RECONSIDER...
HONEY, HOW MANY SHOTS AT REAL HAPPINESS DO WE GET?
IN MY CASE, NOT TOO MANY. BUT YOU AND MIKE...
LOOK AT ZEKE— WHAT DO YOU SEE? UNTAMED, MYSTERIOUS, CHARISMATIC! NOW THINK OF MIKE. WHAT COMES TO MIND?
GIVE ME A MINUTE...
HONEY, I DON'T HAVE A MINUTE! WE'RE TALKING ABOUT WHAT'S LEFT OF MY LIFE!

6/16/95

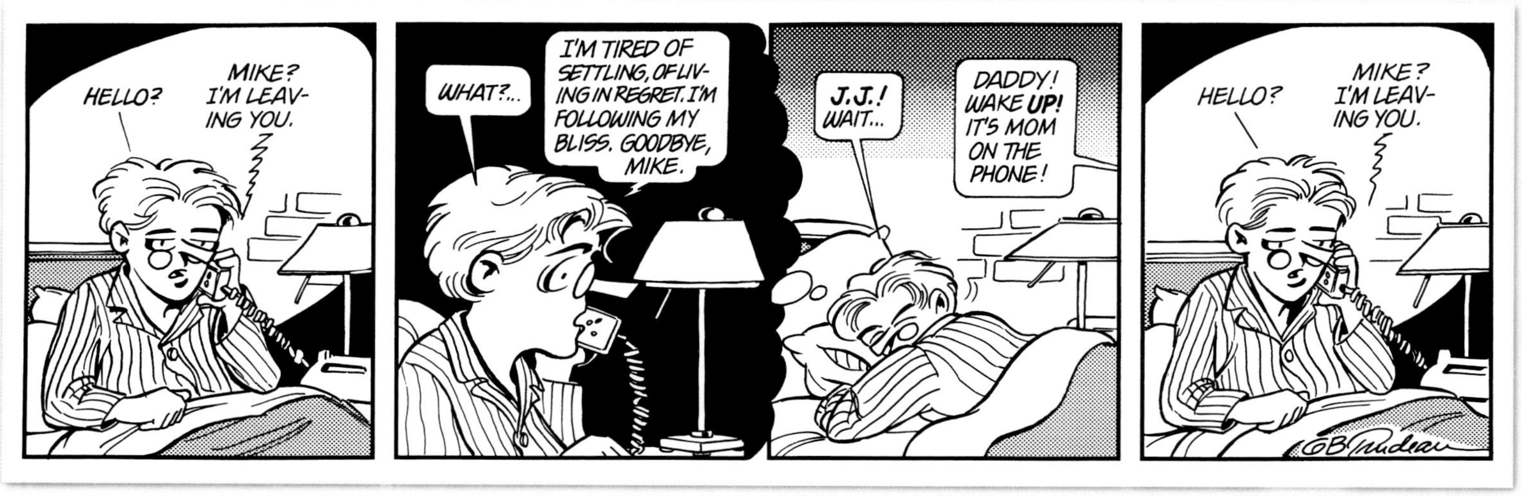
HELLO?
MIKE? I'M LEAVING YOU.
WHAT?...
I'M TIRED OF SETTLING, OF LIVING IN REGRET. I'M FOLLOWING MY BLISS. GOODBYE, MIKE.
J.J.! WAIT...
DADDY! WAKE UP! IT'S MOM ON THE PHONE!
HELLO?
MIKE? I'M LEAVING YOU.

6/19/95

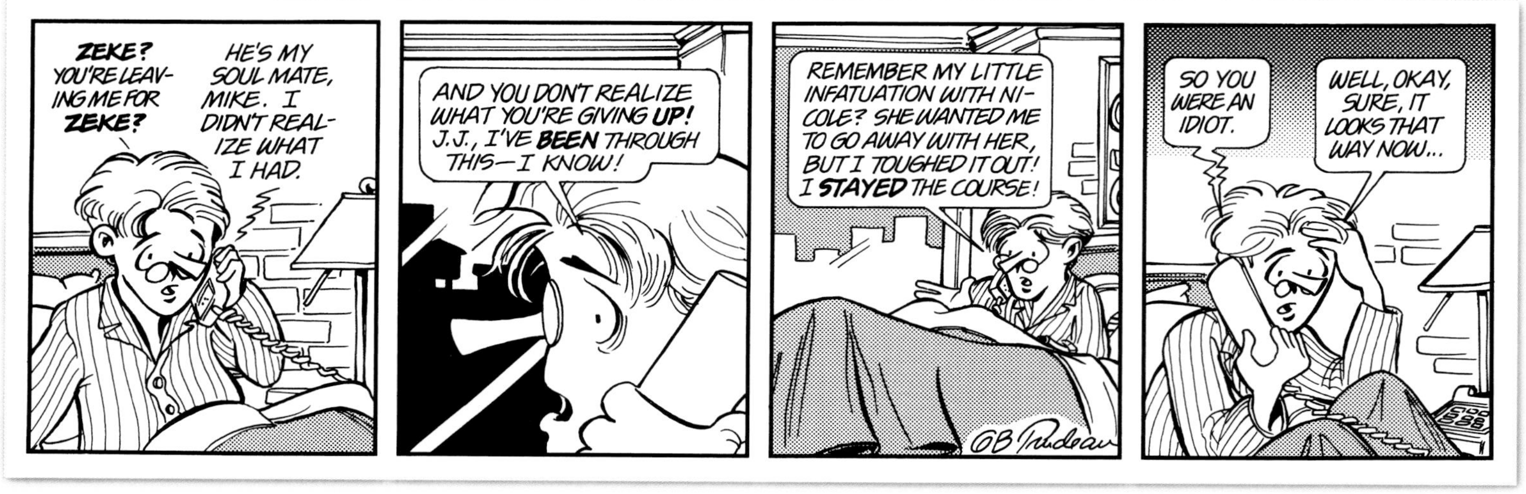
ZEKE? YOU'RE LEAVING ME FOR ZEKE?
HE'S MY SOUL MATE, MIKE. I DIDN'T REALIZE WHAT I HAD.
AND YOU DON'T REALIZE WHAT YOU'RE GIVING UP! J.J., I'VE BEEN THROUGH THIS—I KNOW!
REMEMBER MY LITTLE INFATUATION WITH NICOLE? SHE WANTED ME TO GO AWAY WITH HER, BUT I TOUGHED IT OUT! I STAYED THE COURSE!
SO YOU WERE AN IDIOT.
WELL, OKAY, SURE, IT LOOKS THAT WAY NOW...

6/20/95

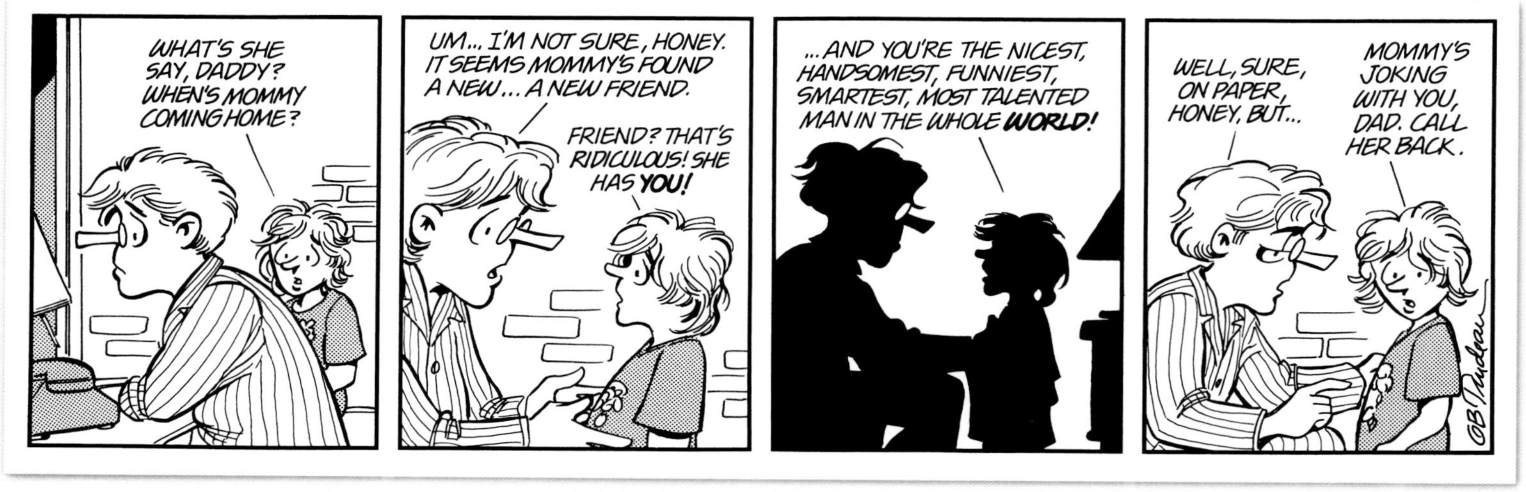
WHAT'S SHE SAY, DADDY? WHEN'S MOMMY COMING HOME?
UM... I'M NOT SURE, HONEY. IT SEEMS MOMMY'S FOUND A NEW... A NEW FRIEND.
FRIEND? THAT'S RIDICULOUS! SHE HAS YOU!
...AND YOU'RE THE NICEST, HANDSOMEST, FUNNIEST, SMARTEST, MOST TALENTED MAN IN THE WHOLE WORLD!
WELL, SURE, ON PAPER, HONEY, BUT...
MOMMY'S JOKING WITH YOU, DAD. CALL HER BACK.

6/21/95

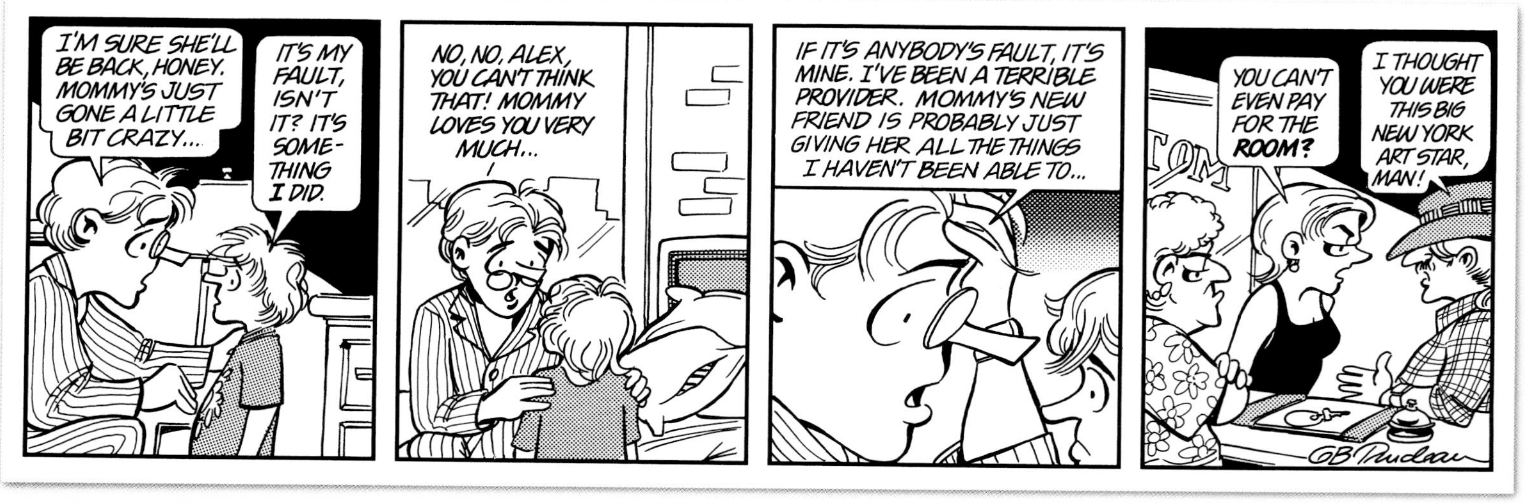
I'M SURE SHE'LL BE BACK, HONEY. MOMMY'S JUST GONE A LITTLE BIT CRAZY...
IT'S MY FAULT, ISN'T IT? IT'S SOMETHING I DID.
NO, NO, ALEX, YOU CAN'T THINK THAT! MOMMY LOVES YOU VERY MUCH...
IF IT'S ANYBODY'S FAULT, IT'S MINE. I'VE BEEN A TERRIBLE PROVIDER. MOMMY'S NEW FRIEND IS PROBABLY JUST GIVING HER ALL THE THINGS I HAVEN'T BEEN ABLE TO...
YOU CAN'T EVEN PAY FOR THE ROOM?
I THOUGHT YOU WERE THIS BIG NEW YORK ART STAR, MAN!

6/22/95

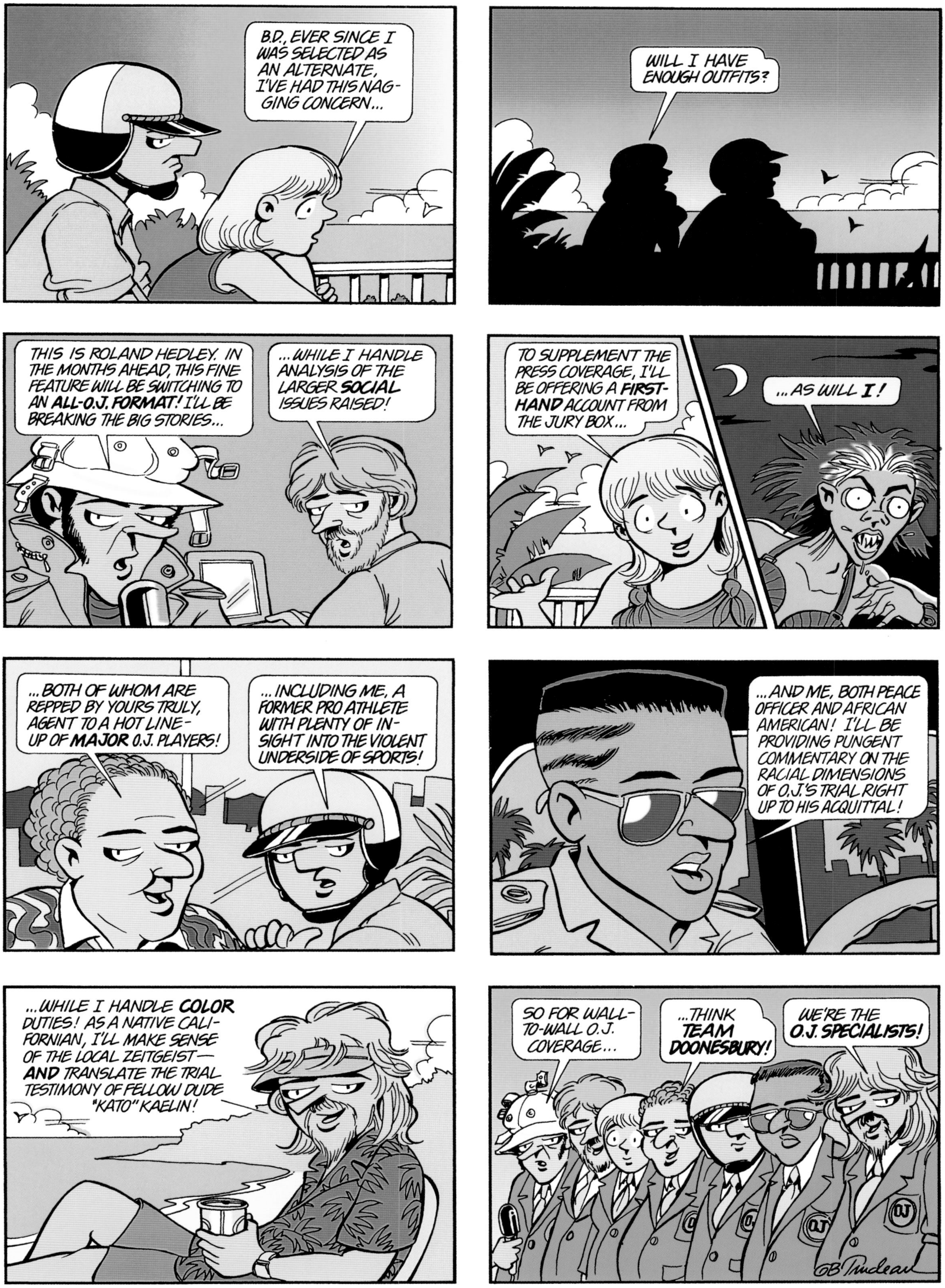
B.D., EVER SINCE I WAS SELECTED AS AN ALTERNATE, I'VE HAD THIS NAG-GING CONCERN...
WILL I HAVE ENOUGH OUTFITS?
THIS IS ROLAND HEDLEY. IN THE MONTHS AHEAD, THIS FINE FEATURE WILL BE SWITCHING TO AN ALL-O.J. FORMAT! I'LL BE BREAKING THE BIG STORIES...
...WHILE I HANDLE ANALYSIS OF THE LARGER SOCIAL ISSUES RAISED!
TO SUPPLEMENT THE PRESS COVERAGE, I'LL BE OFFERING A FIRST-HAND ACCOUNT FROM THE JURY BOX...
...AS WILL I!
...BOTH OF WHOM ARE REPPED BY YOURS TRULY, AGENT TO A HOT LINE-UP OF MAJOR O.J. PLAYERS!
...INCLUDING ME, A FORMER PRO ATHLETE WITH PLENTY OF IN-SIGHT INTO THE VIOLENT UNDERSIDE OF SPORTS!
...AND ME, BOTH PEACE OFFICER AND AFRICAN AMERICAN! I'LL BE PROVIDING PUNGENT COMMENTARY ON THE RACIAL DIMENSIONS OF O.J.'S TRIAL RIGHT UP TO HIS ACQUITTAL!
...WHILE I HANDLE COLOR DUTIES! AS A NATIVE CALI-FORNIAN, I'LL MAKE SENSE OF THE LOCAL ZEITGEIST—AND TRANSLATE THE TRIAL TESTIMONY OF FELLOW DUDE "KATO" KAELIN!
SO FOR WALL-TO-WALL O.J. COVERAGE...
...THINK TEAM DOONESBURY!
WE'RE THE O.J. SPECIALISTS!
GB Trudeau

1/22/95

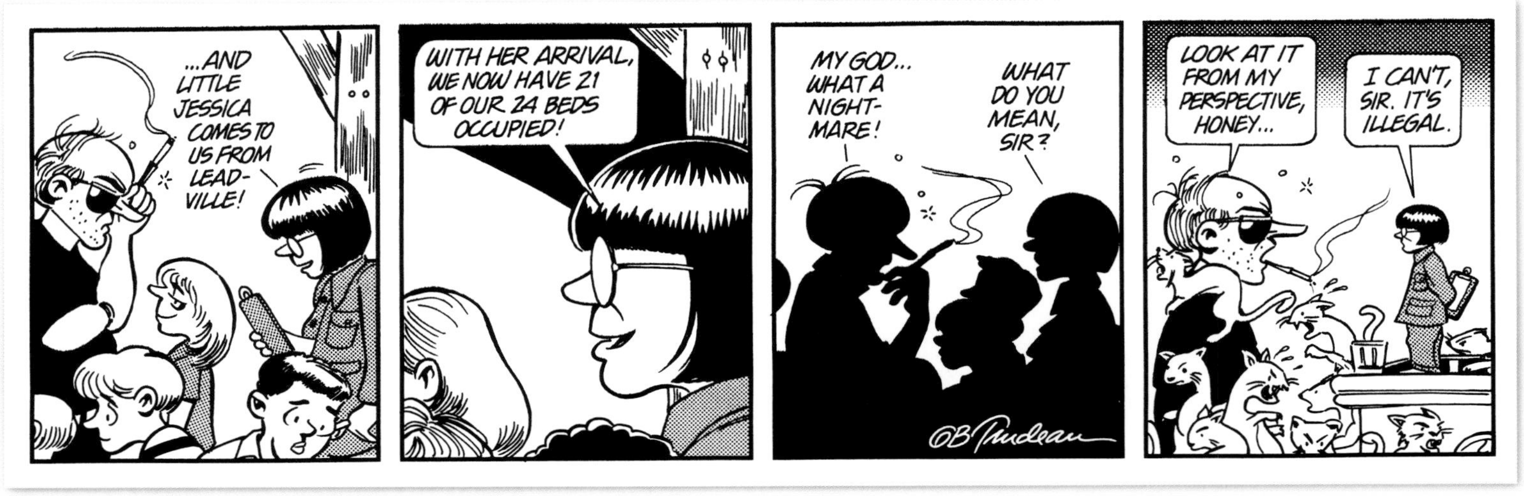

...AND LITTLE JESSICA COMES TO US FROM LEAD-VILLE!
WITH HER ARRIVAL, WE NOW HAVE 21 OF OUR 24 BEDS OCCUPIED!
MY GOD... WHAT A NIGHT-MARE!
WHAT DO YOU MEAN, SIR?
LOOK AT IT FROM MY PERSPECTIVE, HONEY...
I CAN'T, SIR. IT'S ILLEGAL.

4/10/95

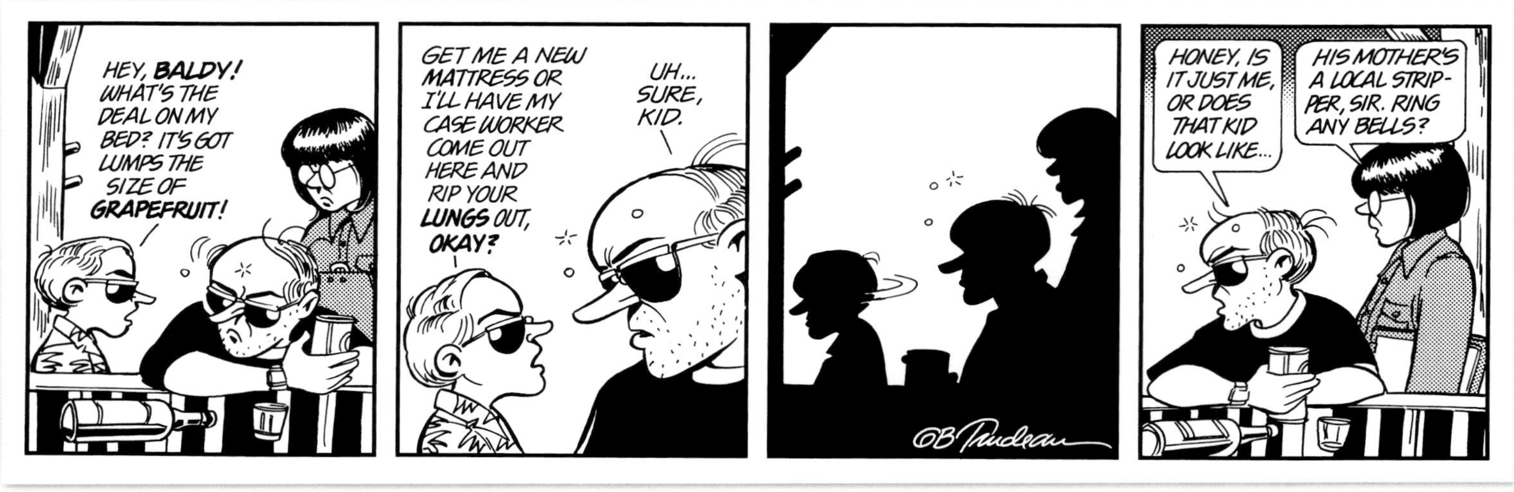

HEY, **BALDY!** WHAT'S THE DEAL ON MY BED? IT'S GOT LUMPS THE SIZE OF **GRAPEFRUIT!**
GET ME A NEW MATTRESS OR I'LL HAVE MY CASE WORKER COME OUT HERE AND RIP YOUR **LUNGS** OUT, **OKAY?**
UH... SURE, KID.
HONEY, IS IT JUST ME, OR DOES THAT KID LOOK LIKE...
HIS MOTHER'S A LOCAL STRIP-PER, SIR. RING ANY BELLS?

4/12/95

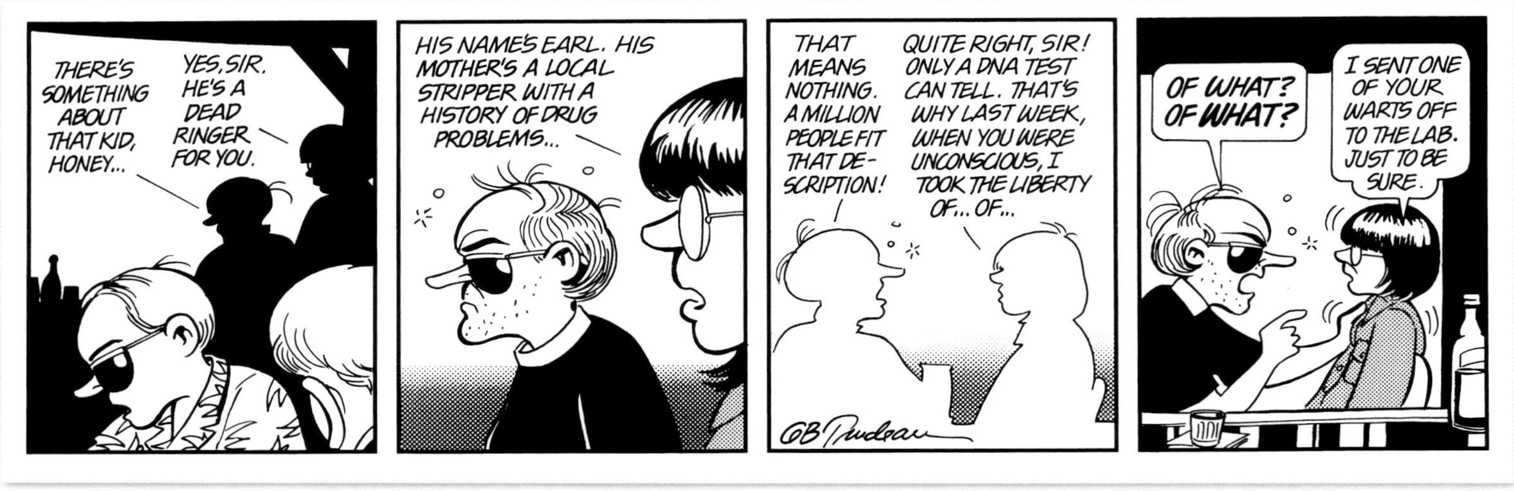

THERE'S SOMETHING ABOUT THAT KID, HONEY...
YES, SIR. HE'S A DEAD RINGER FOR YOU.
HIS NAME'S EARL. HIS MOTHER'S A LOCAL STRIPPER WITH A HISTORY OF DRUG PROBLEMS...
THAT MEANS NOTHING. A MILLION PEOPLE FIT THAT DE-SCRIPTION!
QUITE RIGHT, SIR! ONLY A DNA TEST CAN TELL. THAT'S WHY LAST WEEK, WHEN YOU WERE UNCONSCIOUS, I TOOK THE LIBERTY OF... OF...
OF WHAT? OF **WHAT?**
I SENT ONE OF YOUR WARTS OFF TO THE LAB. JUST TO BE SURE.

4/13/95

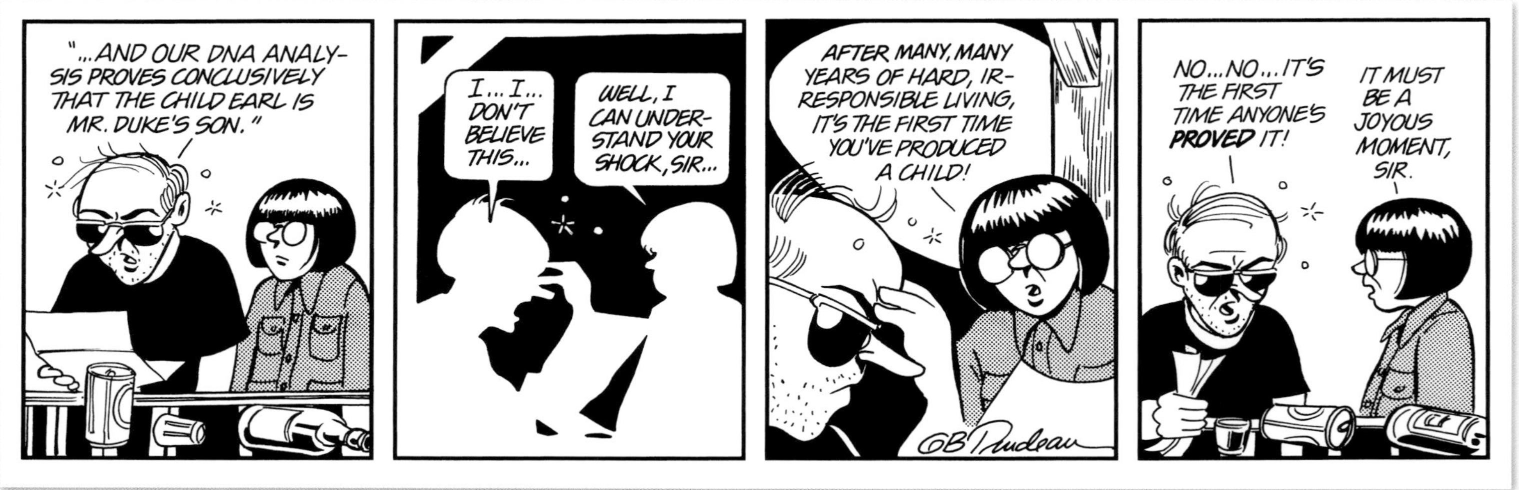

"...AND OUR DNA ANALY-SIS PROVES CONCLUSIVELY THAT THE CHILD EARL IS MR. DUKE'S SON."
I... I... DON'T BELIEVE THIS...
WELL, I CAN UNDER-STAND YOUR SHOCK, SIR...
AFTER MANY, MANY YEARS OF HARD, IR-RESPONSIBLE LIVING, IT'S THE FIRST TIME YOU'VE PRODUCED A CHILD!
NO... NO... IT'S THE FIRST TIME ANYONE'S **PROVED** IT!
IT MUST BE A JOYOUS MOMENT, SIR.

4/15/95

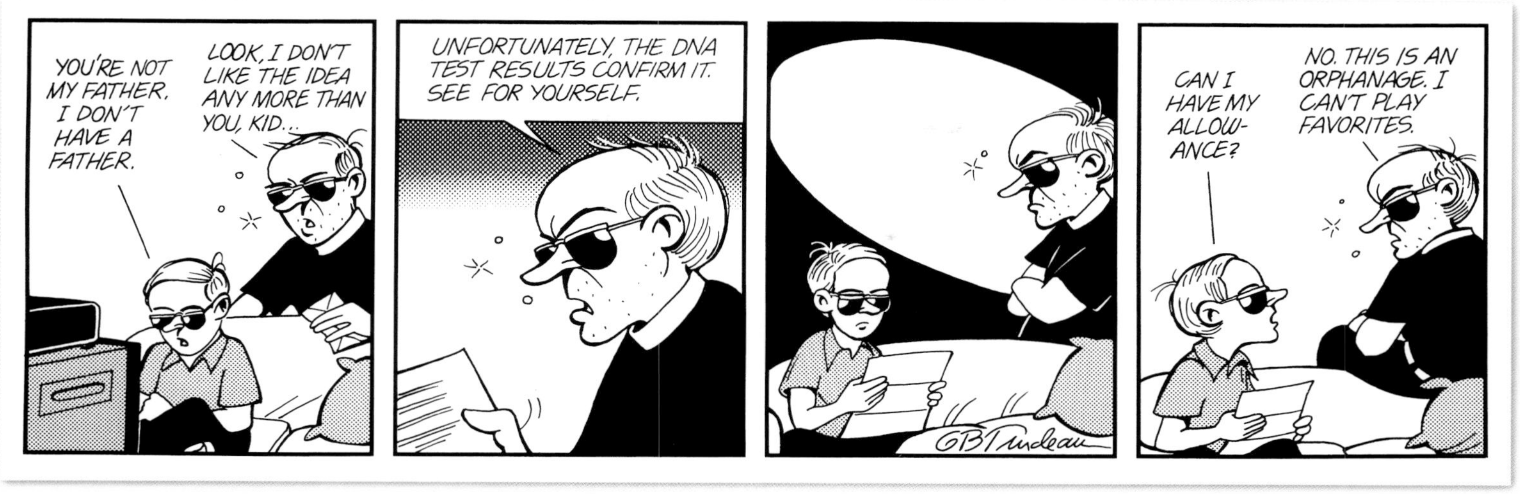
YOU'RE NOT MY FATHER. I DON'T HAVE A FATHER.
LOOK, I DON'T LIKE THE IDEA ANY MORE THAN YOU, KID...
UNFORTUNATELY, THE DNA TEST RESULTS CONFIRM IT. SEE FOR YOURSELF.
CAN I HAVE MY ALLOW-ANCE?
NO. THIS IS AN ORPHANAGE. I CAN'T PLAY FAVORITES.
GBTrudeau

4/18/95

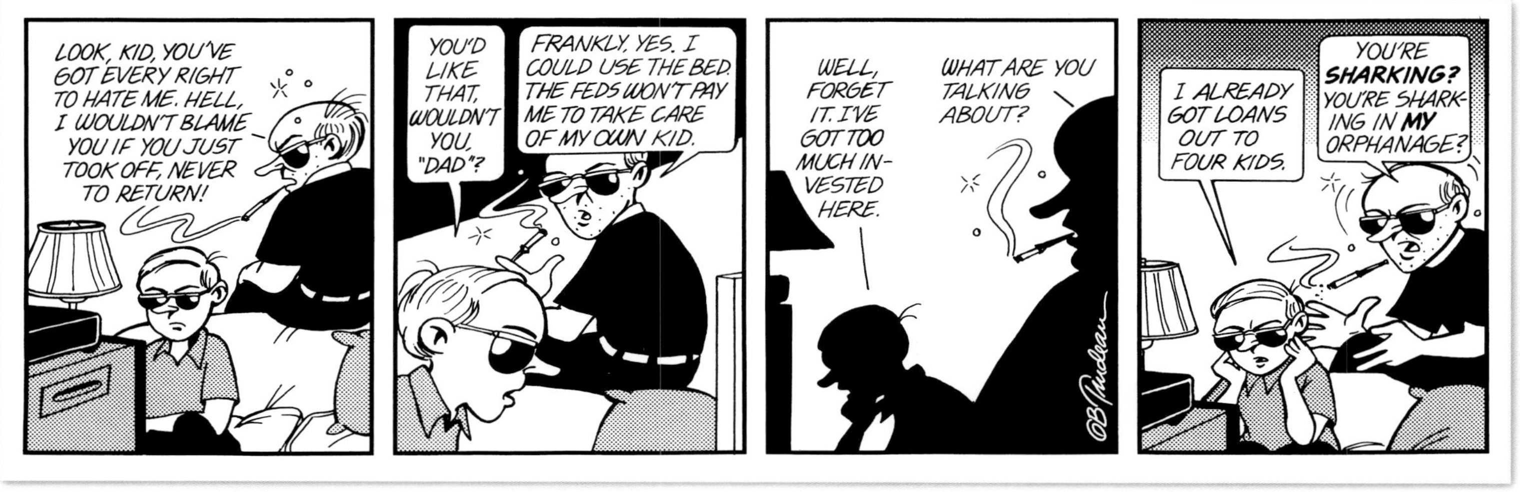
LOOK, KID, YOU'VE GOT EVERY RIGHT TO HATE ME. HELL, I WOULDN'T BLAME YOU IF YOU JUST TOOK OFF, NEVER TO RETURN!
YOU'D LIKE THAT, WOULDN'T YOU, "DAD"?
FRANKLY, YES. I COULD USE THE BED. THE FEDS WON'T PAY ME TO TAKE CARE OF MY OWN KID.
WELL, FORGET IT. I'VE GOT TOO MUCH IN-VESTED HERE.
WHAT ARE YOU TALKING ABOUT?
I ALREADY GOT LOANS OUT TO FOUR KIDS.
YOU'RE SHARKING? YOU'RE SHARK-ING IN MY ORPHANAGE?
GBTrudeau

4/19/95

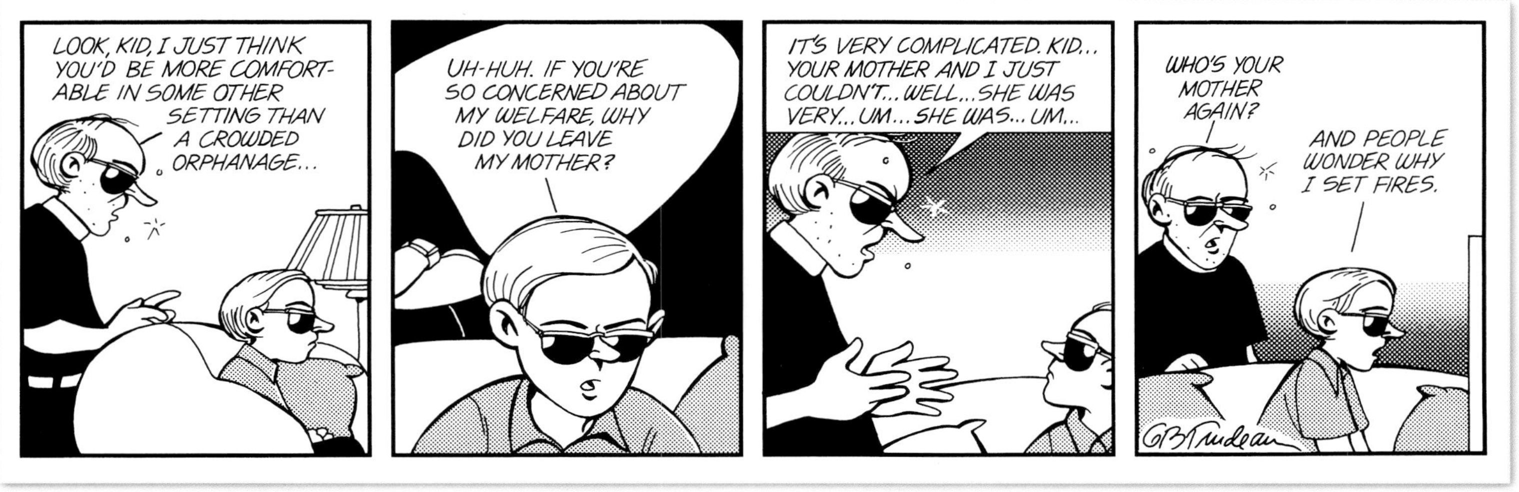
LOOK, KID, I JUST THINK YOU'D BE MORE COMFORT-ABLE IN SOME OTHER SETTING THAN A CROWDED ORPHANAGE...
UH-HUH. IF YOU'RE SO CONCERNED ABOUT MY WELFARE, WHY DID YOU LEAVE MY MOTHER?
IT'S VERY COMPLICATED, KID... YOUR MOTHER AND I JUST COULDN'T... WELL... SHE WAS VERY... UM... SHE WAS... UM...
WHO'S YOUR MOTHER AGAIN?
AND PEOPLE WONDER WHY I SET FIRES.
GBTrudeau

4/20/95

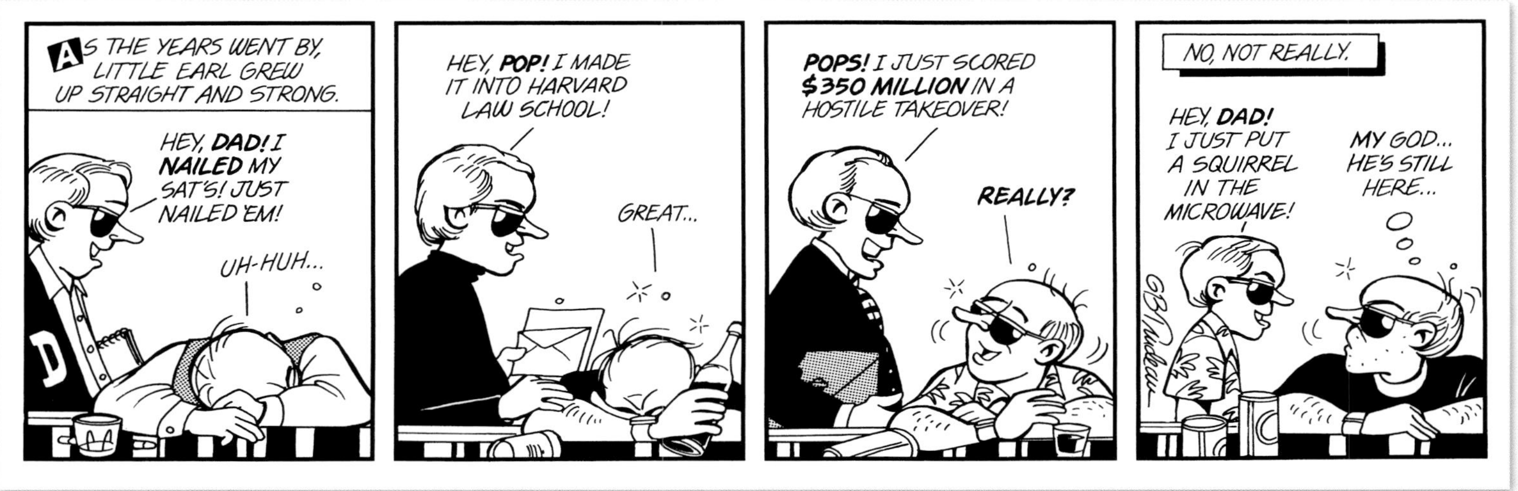
AS THE YEARS WENT BY, LITTLE EARL GREW UP STRAIGHT AND STRONG.
HEY, DAD! I NAILED MY SAT'S! JUST NAILED 'EM!
UH-HUH...
HEY, POP! I MADE IT INTO HARVARD LAW SCHOOL!
GREAT...
POPS! I JUST SCORED $350 MILLION IN A HOSTILE TAKEOVER!
REALLY?
NO, NOT REALLY.
HEY, DAD! I JUST PUT A SQUIRREL IN THE MICROWAVE!
MY GOD... HE'S STILL HERE...
GBTrudeau

4/22/95

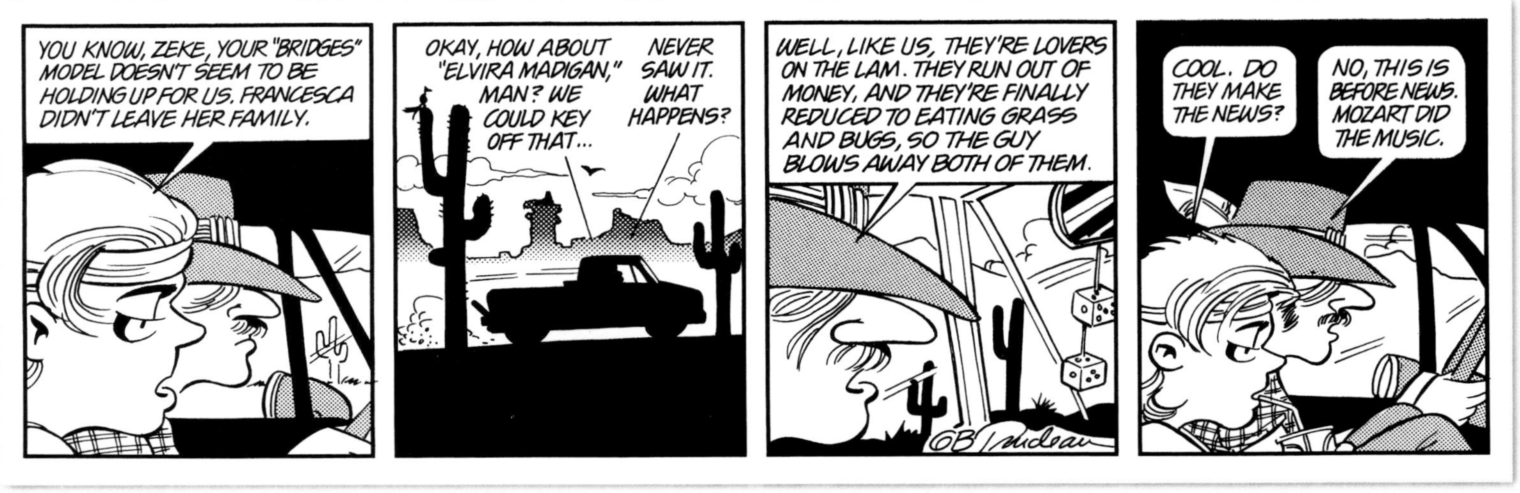
YOU KNOW, ZEKE, YOUR "BRIDGES" MODEL DOESN'T SEEM TO BE HOLDING UP FOR US. FRANCESCA DIDN'T LEAVE HER FAMILY.
OKAY, HOW ABOUT "ELVIRA MADIGAN," MAN? WE COULD KEY OFF THAT...
NEVER SAW IT. WHAT HAPPENS?
WELL, LIKE US, THEY'RE LOVERS ON THE LAM. THEY RUN OUT OF MONEY, AND THEY'RE FINALLY REDUCED TO EATING GRASS AND BUGS, SO THE GUY BLOWS AWAY BOTH OF THEM.
COOL. DO THEY MAKE THE NEWS?
NO, THIS IS BEFORE NEWS. MOZART DID THE MUSIC.
GB Trudeau

7/10/95

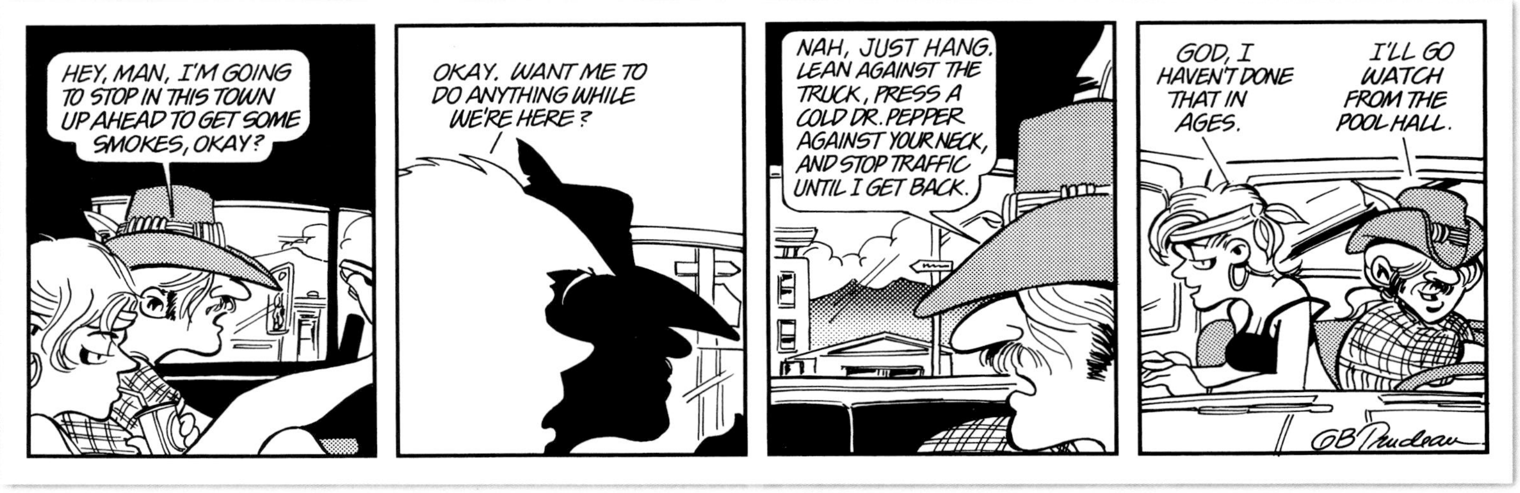
HEY, MAN, I'M GOING TO STOP IN THIS TOWN UP AHEAD TO GET SOME SMOKES, OKAY?
OKAY. WANT ME TO DO ANYTHING WHILE WE'RE HERE?
NAH, JUST HANG. LEAN AGAINST THE TRUCK, PRESS A COLD DR. PEPPER AGAINST YOUR NECK, AND STOP TRAFFIC UNTIL I GET BACK.
GOD, I HAVEN'T DONE THAT IN AGES.
I'LL GO WATCH FROM THE POOL HALL.
GB Trudeau

7/11/95

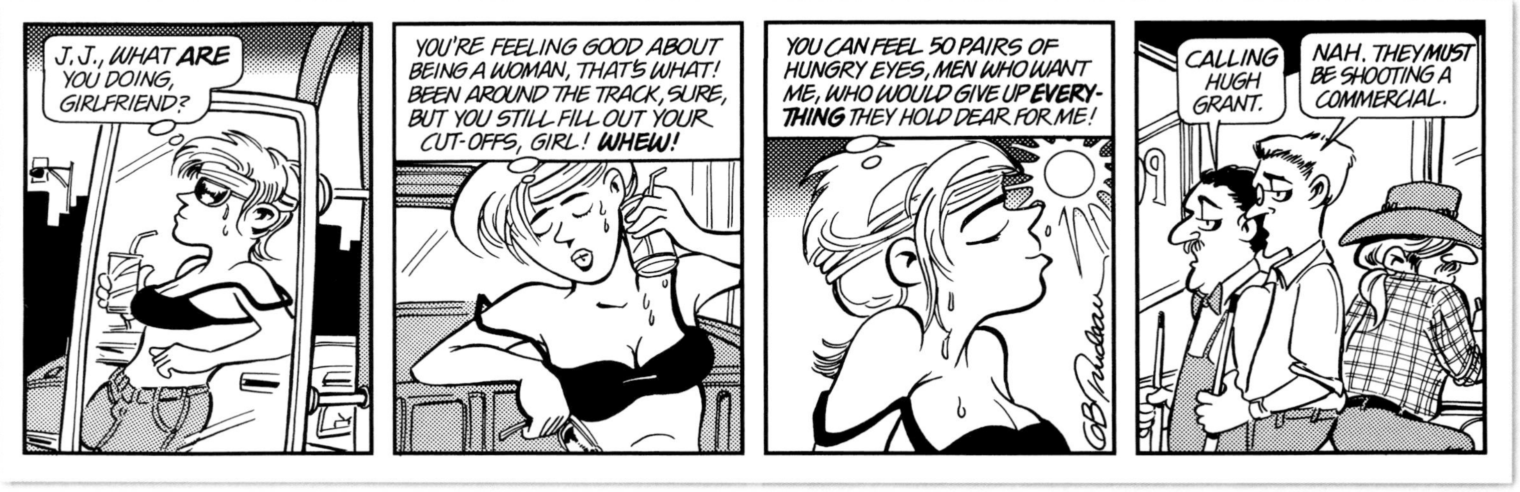
J.J., WHAT ARE YOU DOING, GIRLFRIEND?
YOU'RE FEELING GOOD ABOUT BEING A WOMAN, THAT'S WHAT! BEEN AROUND THE TRACK, SURE, BUT YOU STILL FILL OUT YOUR CUT-OFFS, GIRL! WHEW!
YOU CAN FEEL 50 PAIRS OF HUNGRY EYES, MEN WHO WANT ME, WHO WOULD GIVE UP EVERYTHING THEY HOLD DEAR FOR ME!
GB Trudeau
CALLING HUGH GRANT.
NAH. THEY MUST BE SHOOTING A COMMERCIAL.

7/12/95

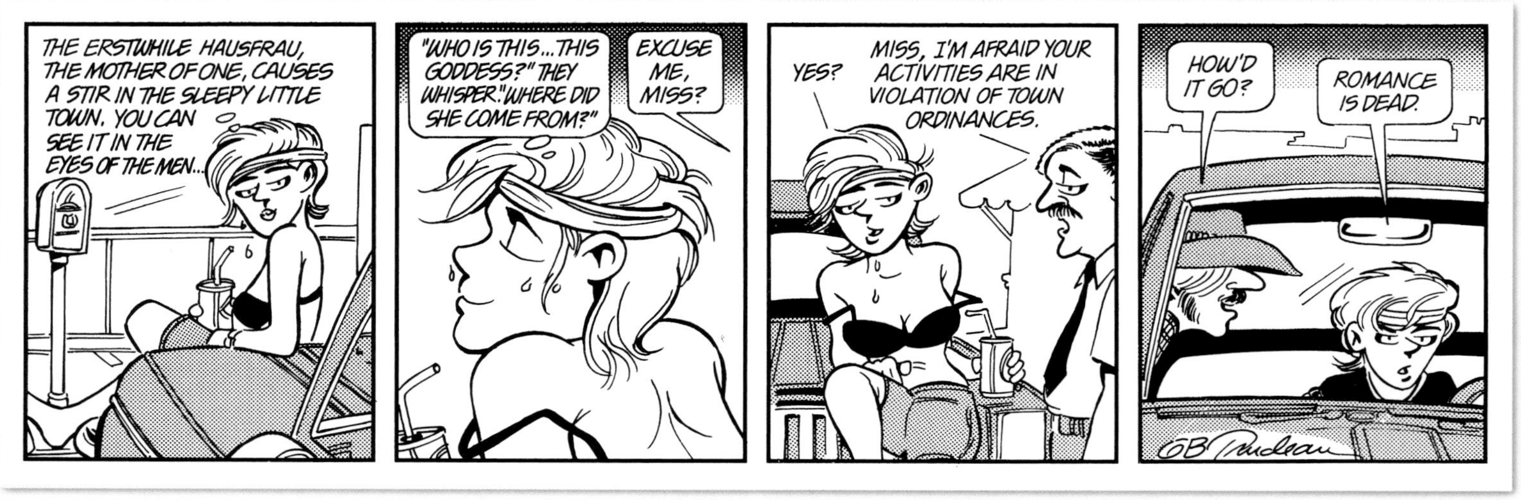
THE ERSTWHILE HAUSFRAU, THE MOTHER OF ONE, CAUSES A STIR IN THE SLEEPY LITTLE TOWN. YOU CAN SEE IT IN THE EYES OF THE MEN...
"WHO IS THIS... THIS GODDESS?" THEY WHISPER. "WHERE DID SHE COME FROM?"
EXCUSE ME, MISS?
YES?
MISS, I'M AFRAID YOUR ACTIVITIES ARE IN VIOLATION OF TOWN ORDINANCES.
HOW'D IT GO?
ROMANCE IS DEAD.
GB Trudeau

7/13/95

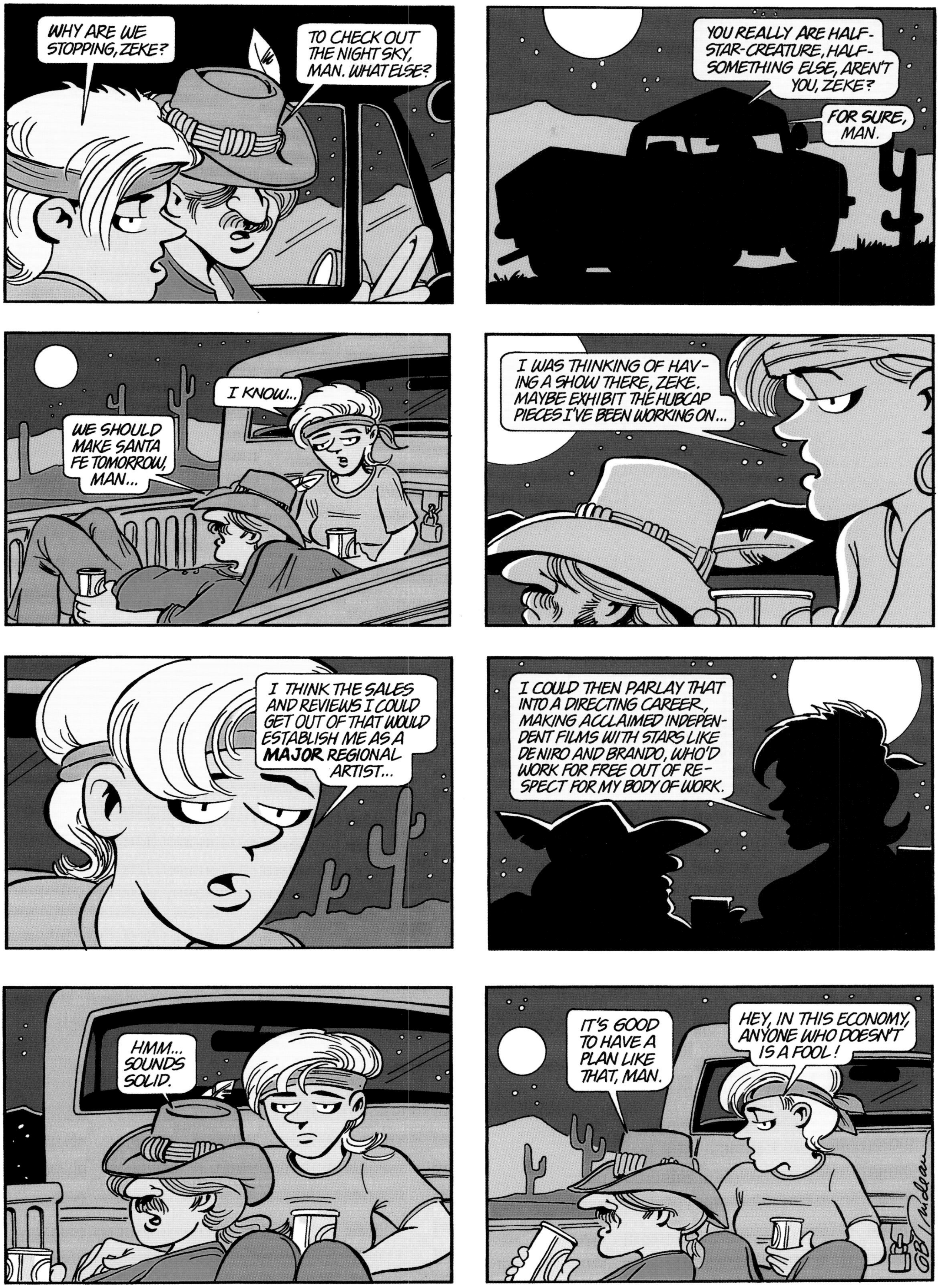
WHY ARE WE STOPPING, ZEKE?
TO CHECK OUT THE NIGHT SKY, MAN. WHAT ELSE?
YOU REALLY ARE HALF-STAR-CREATURE, HALF-SOMETHING ELSE, AREN'T YOU, ZEKE?
FOR SURE, MAN.
WE SHOULD MAKE SANTA FE TOMORROW, MAN...
I KNOW...
I WAS THINKING OF HAVING A SHOW THERE, ZEKE. MAYBE EXHIBIT THE HUBCAP PIECES I'VE BEEN WORKING ON...
I THINK THE SALES AND REVIEWS I COULD GET OUT OF THAT WOULD ESTABLISH ME AS A MAJOR REGIONAL ARTIST...
I COULD THEN PARLAY THAT INTO A DIRECTING CAREER, MAKING ACCLAIMED INDEPENDENT FILMS WITH STARS LIKE DE NIRO AND BRANDO, WHO'D WORK FOR FREE OUT OF RESPECT FOR MY BODY OF WORK.
HMM... SOUNDS SOLID.
IT'S GOOD TO HAVE A PLAN LIKE THAT, MAN.
HEY, IN THIS ECONOMY, ANYONE WHO DOESN'T IS A FOOL!

7/30/95

Duke

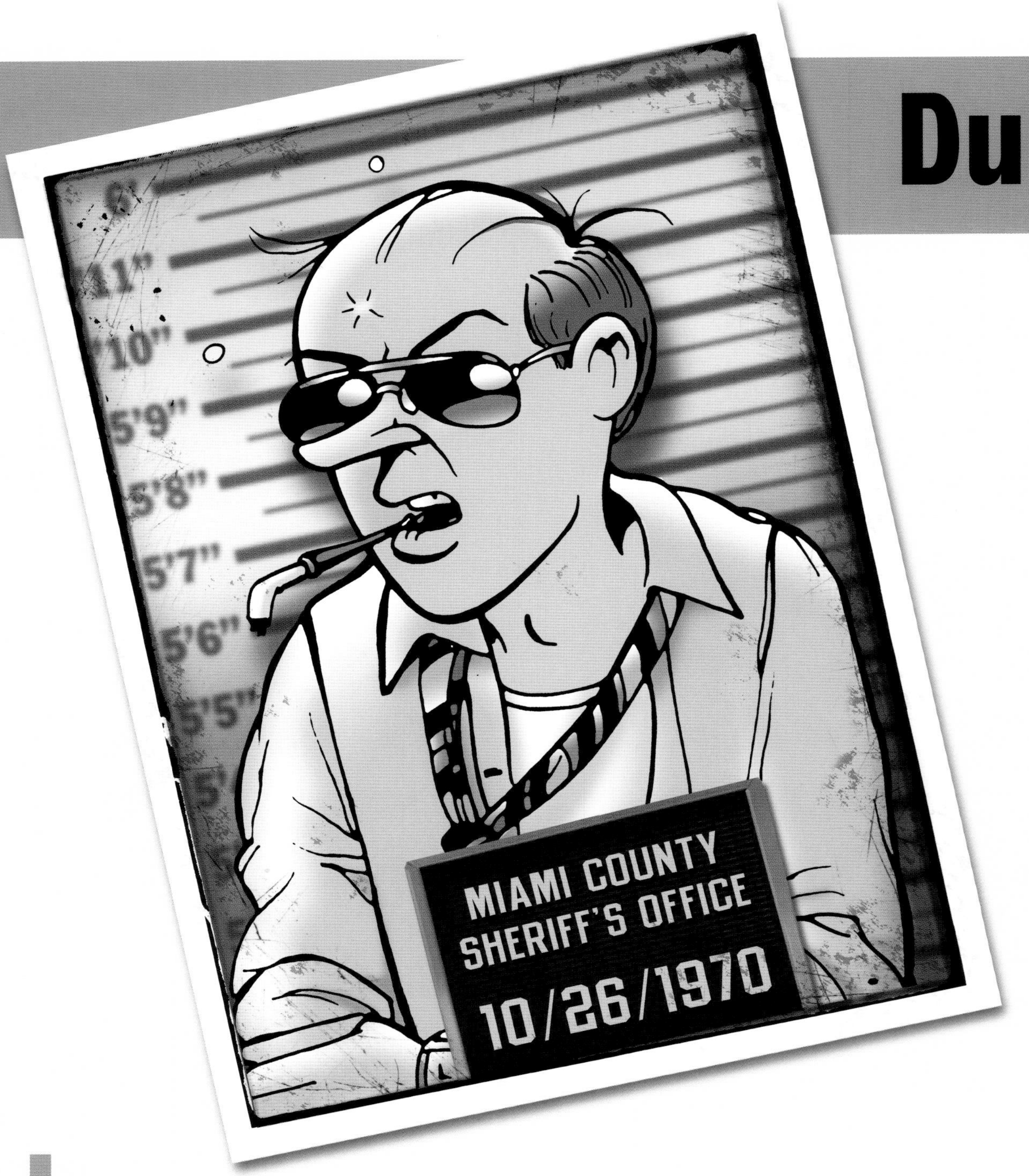
11"
10"
5'9"
5'8"
5'7"
5'6"
5'5"
MIAMI COUNTY
SHERIFF'S OFFICE
10/26/1970

Like most people, I never met Hunter S. Thompson. It's just as well.

Duke, alone among the main characters, arrived in the strip as straight-ahead parody. Duke wasn't inspired by Thompson, he was Thompson—right down to the name, taken from "Raoul Duke," Thompson's pseudonym. Many public figures are parodied, but Thompson, who viewed writing as serious business, apparently found it unnerving to have such an unserious version of himself on the loose. He'd worked hard to become the star of his own work, and consequently viewed the HST brand as proprietary.

Of course, in turning himself into a celebrity, Thompson, like all public figures, had made himself available to caricature. But to him, the creation of Duke was nothing less than intellectual property theft. In this view, I had appropriated his greatest asset—his wild-man image—and simultaneously devalued it through ridicule (even though Duke had inarguably contributed to his fame). The loss of control seemed to unhinge him. Mutual friends conveyed word of his outrage. An attorney was dispatched to demand royalties for using

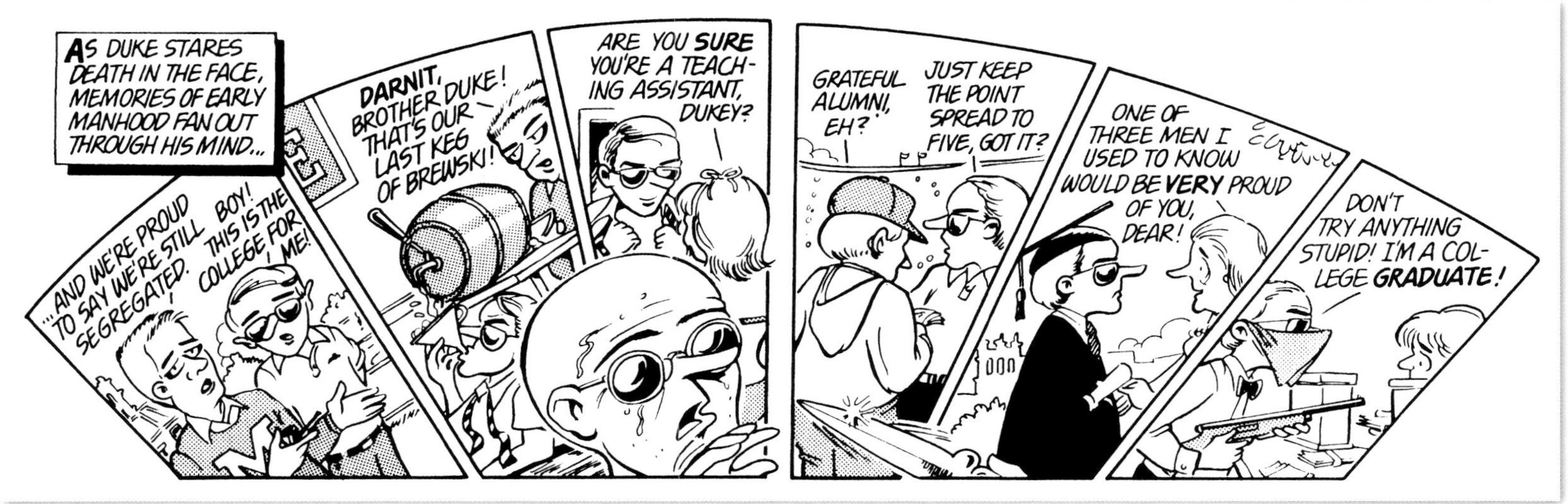
AS DUKE STARES DEATH IN THE FACE, MEMORIES OF EARLY MANHOOD FAN OUT THROUGH HIS MIND...
...AND WE'RE PROUD TO SAY WE'RE STILL SEGREGATED.
BOY! THIS IS THE COLLEGE FOR ME!
DARNIT, BROTHER DUKE! THAT'S OUR LAST KEG OF BREWSKI!
ARE YOU SURE YOU'RE A TEACHING ASSISTANT, DUKEY?
GRATEFUL ALUMNI, EH?
JUST KEEP THE POINT SPREAD TO FIVE, GOT IT?
ONE OF THREE MEN I USED TO KNOW WOULD BE VERY PROUD OF YOU, DEAR!
DON'T TRY ANYTHING STUPID! I'M A COLLEGE GRADUATE!

his "likeness" in a Duke action figure. In rambling college speeches, Thompson hurled invective at me, threatening to rip out my lungs or force me to sweep peacock dung from his porch. These declarations were comical, but only up to a point; it was never clear how seriously I should be taking his threats, especially after he mailed me an envelope stuffed with used toilet paper.

Unlike Thompson's Gonzo act, my parody of it ran its course in short order. Duke soon shed the *Rolling Stone* connection and shipped out to the world's trouble spots, contriving a never-ending series of debauched schemes that had little or nothing to do with Thompson or his career. But Duke's origins as a parody had an oddly limiting effect on his evolution as a character. He was frozen in a permanent state of opportunism, binary in his reaction to any given situation. To act, he need only ask himself, "Is this in my self-interest or not?" In my early determination to make him as "outrageous" as the source, I'd left no room for ambivalence. In Dukeworld, the only lessons learned affect his tradecraft, not his behavior. In that sense, he's the least relatable character in the strip, and why I have filled his life with such unrelenting chaos. Duke at rest is not just implausible—he's no fun.

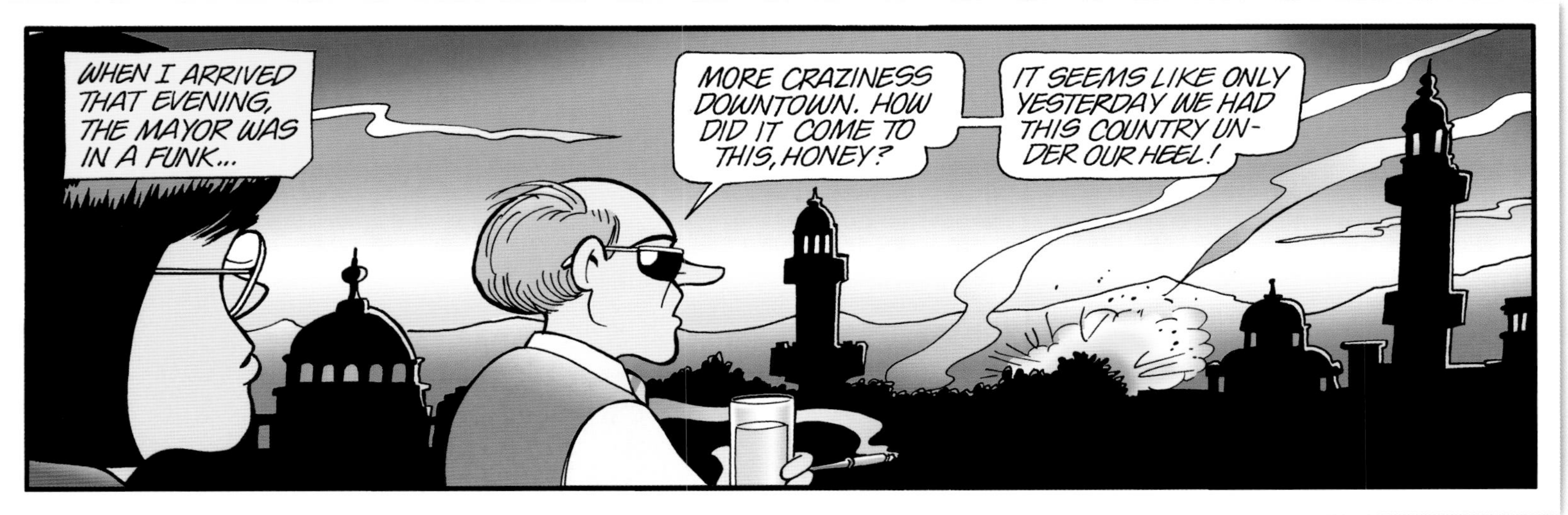
WHEN I ARRIVED THAT EVENING, THE MAYOR WAS IN A FUNK...
MORE CRAZINESS DOWNTOWN. HOW DID IT COME TO THIS, HONEY?
IT SEEMS LIKE ONLY YESTERDAY WE HAD THIS COUNTRY UNDER OUR HEEL!

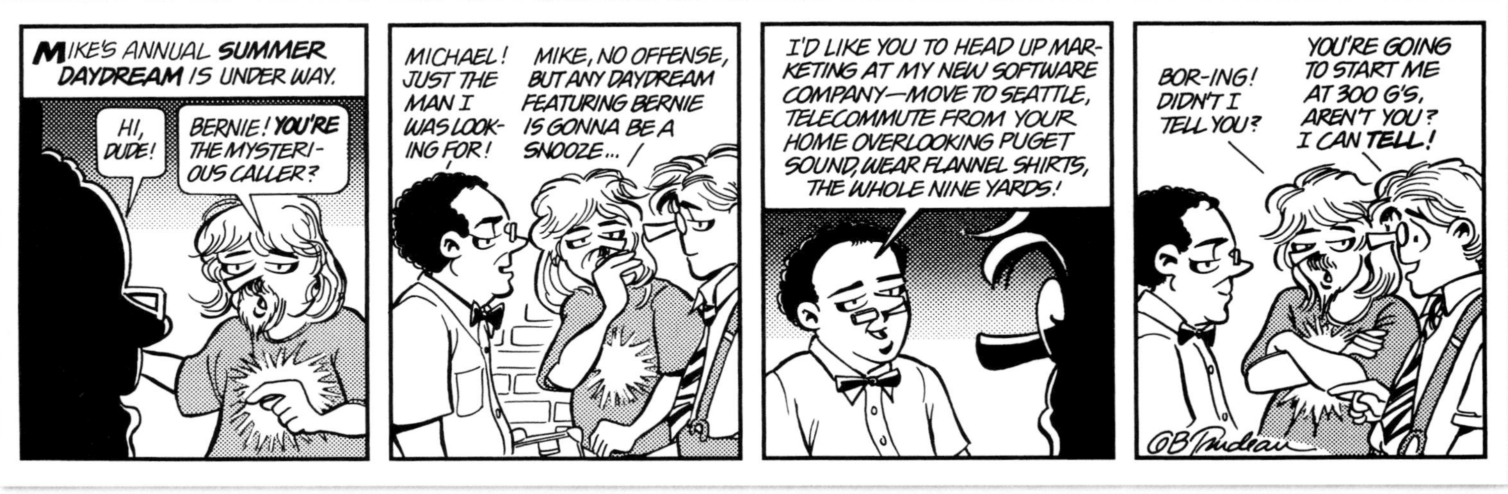
MIKE'S ANNUAL SUMMER DAYDREAM IS UNDER WAY.
HI, DUDE!
BERNIE! YOU'RE THE MYSTERIOUS CALLER?
MICHAEL! JUST THE MAN I WAS LOOKING FOR!
MIKE, NO OFFENSE, BUT ANY DAYDREAM FEATURING BERNIE IS GONNA BE A SNOOZE...
I'D LIKE YOU TO HEAD UP MARKETING AT MY NEW SOFTWARE COMPANY—MOVE TO SEATTLE, TELECOMMUTE FROM YOUR HOME OVERLOOKING PUGET SOUND, WEAR FLANNEL SHIRTS, THE WHOLE NINE YARDS!
BOR-ING! DIDN'T I TELL YOU?
YOU'RE GOING TO START ME AT 300 G'S, AREN'T YOU? I CAN TELL!
©B Trudeau

7/25/95

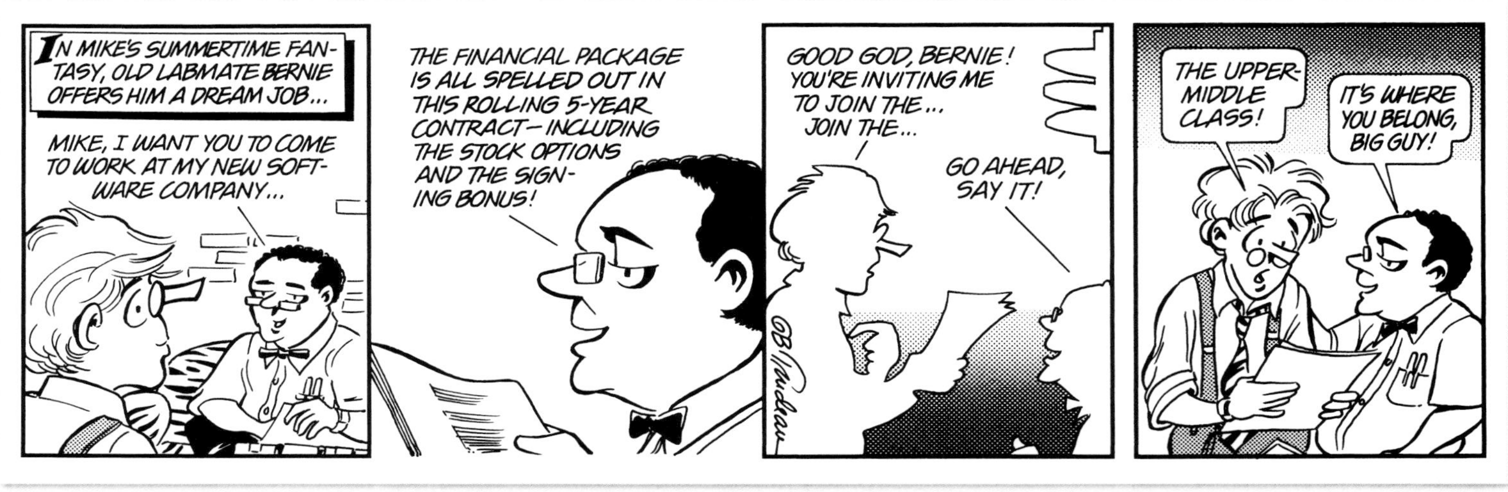
IN MIKE'S SUMMERTIME FANTASY, OLD LABMATE BERNIE OFFERS HIM A DREAM JOB...
MIKE, I WANT YOU TO COME TO WORK AT MY NEW SOFTWARE COMPANY...
THE FINANCIAL PACKAGE IS ALL SPELLED OUT IN THIS ROLLING 5-YEAR CONTRACT—INCLUDING THE STOCK OPTIONS AND THE SIGNING BONUS!
GOOD GOD, BERNIE! YOU'RE INVITING ME TO JOIN THE... JOIN THE...
GO AHEAD, SAY IT!
THE UPPER-MIDDLE CLASS!
IT'S WHERE YOU BELONG, BIG GUY!
©B Trudeau

7/26/95

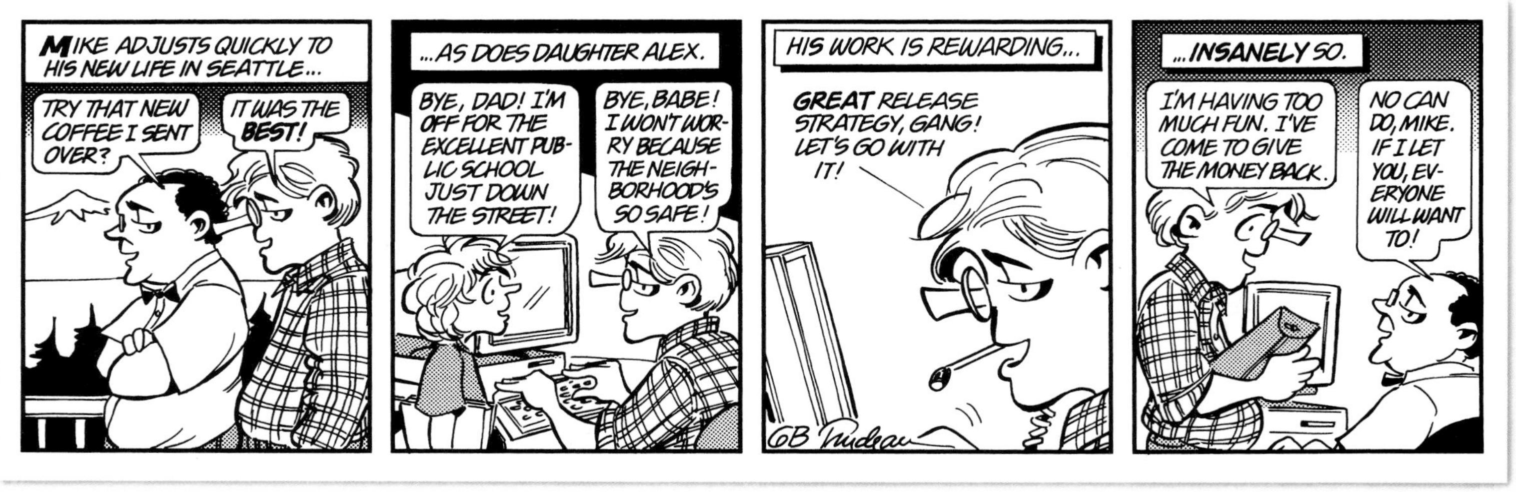
MIKE ADJUSTS QUICKLY TO HIS NEW LIFE IN SEATTLE...
TRY THAT NEW COFFEE I SENT OVER?
IT WAS THE BEST!
...AS DOES DAUGHTER ALEX.
BYE, DAD! I'M OFF FOR THE EXCELLENT PUBLIC SCHOOL JUST DOWN THE STREET!
BYE, BABE! I WON'T WORRY BECAUSE THE NEIGHBORHOOD'S SO SAFE!
HIS WORK IS REWARDING...
GREAT RELEASE STRATEGY, GANG! LET'S GO WITH IT!
...INSANELY SO.
I'M HAVING TOO MUCH FUN. I'VE COME TO GIVE THE MONEY BACK.
NO CAN DO, MIKE. IF I LET YOU, EVERYONE WILL WANT TO!
©B Trudeau

7/28/95

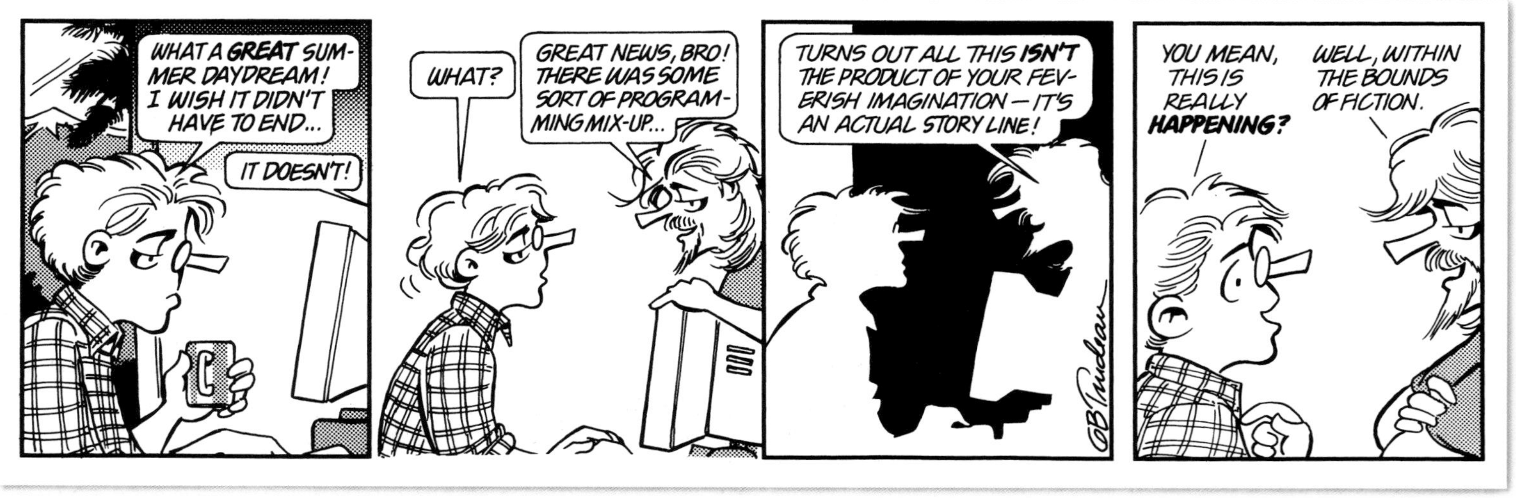
WHAT A GREAT SUMMER DAYDREAM! I WISH IT DIDN'T HAVE TO END...
IT DOESN'T!
WHAT?
GREAT NEWS, BRO! THERE WAS SOME SORT OF PROGRAMMING MIX-UP...
TURNS OUT ALL THIS ISN'T THE PRODUCT OF YOUR FEVERISH IMAGINATION—IT'S AN ACTUAL STORY LINE!
YOU MEAN, THIS IS REALLY HAPPENING?
WELL, WITHIN THE BOUNDS OF FICTION.
©B Trudeau

7/29/95

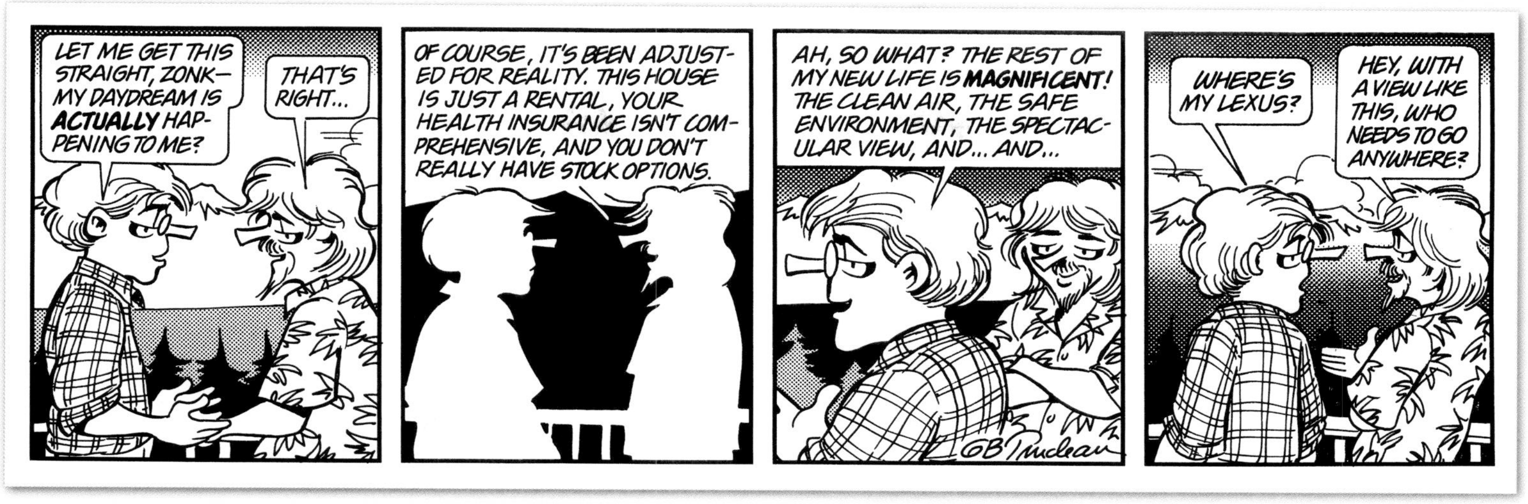
LET ME GET THIS STRAIGHT, ZONK— MY DAYDREAM IS ACTUALLY HAPPENING TO ME?
THAT'S RIGHT...
OF COURSE, IT'S BEEN ADJUSTED FOR REALITY. THIS HOUSE IS JUST A RENTAL, YOUR HEALTH INSURANCE ISN'T COMPREHENSIVE, AND YOU DON'T REALLY HAVE STOCK OPTIONS.
AH, SO WHAT? THE REST OF MY NEW LIFE IS MAGNIFICENT! THE CLEAN AIR, THE SAFE ENVIRONMENT, THE SPECTACULAR VIEW, AND... AND...
WHERE'S MY LEXUS?
HEY, WITH A VIEW LIKE THIS, WHO NEEDS TO GO ANYWHERE?
GB Trudeau

8/7/95

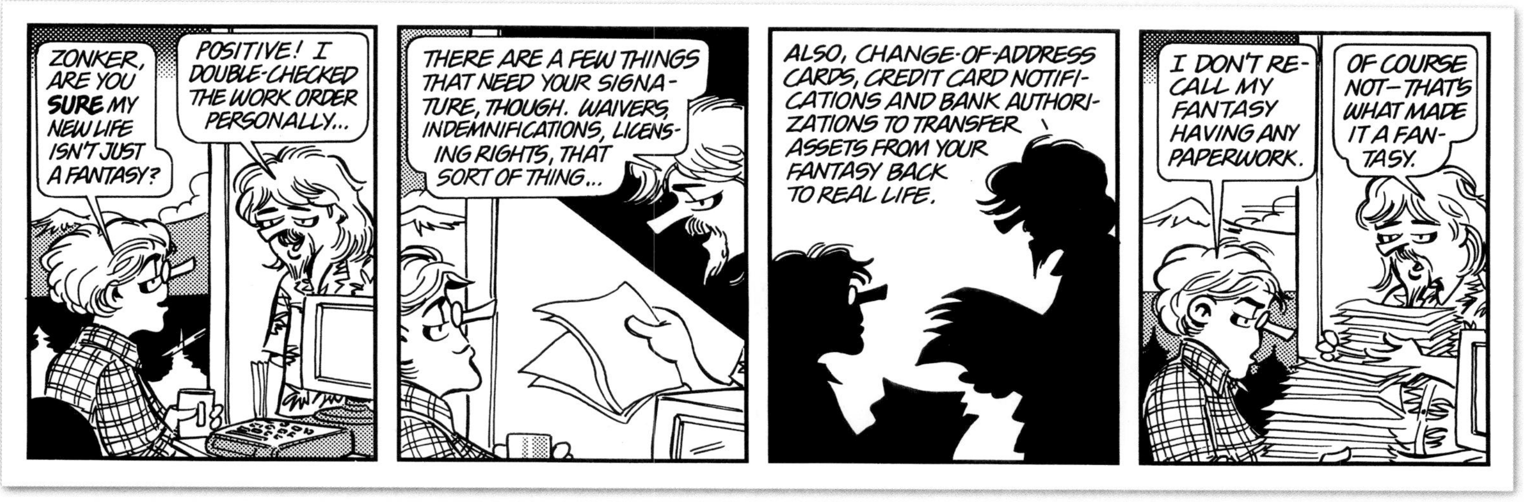
ZONKER, ARE YOU SURE MY NEW LIFE ISN'T JUST A FANTASY?
POSITIVE! I DOUBLE-CHECKED THE WORK ORDER PERSONALLY...
THERE ARE A FEW THINGS THAT NEED YOUR SIGNATURE, THOUGH. WAIVERS, INDEMNIFICATIONS, LICENSING RIGHTS, THAT SORT OF THING...
ALSO, CHANGE-OF-ADDRESS CARDS, CREDIT CARD NOTIFICATIONS AND BANK AUTHORIZATIONS TO TRANSFER ASSETS FROM YOUR FANTASY BACK TO REAL LIFE.
I DON'T RECALL MY FANTASY HAVING ANY PAPERWORK.
OF COURSE NOT—THAT'S WHAT MADE IT A FANTASY.

8/8/95

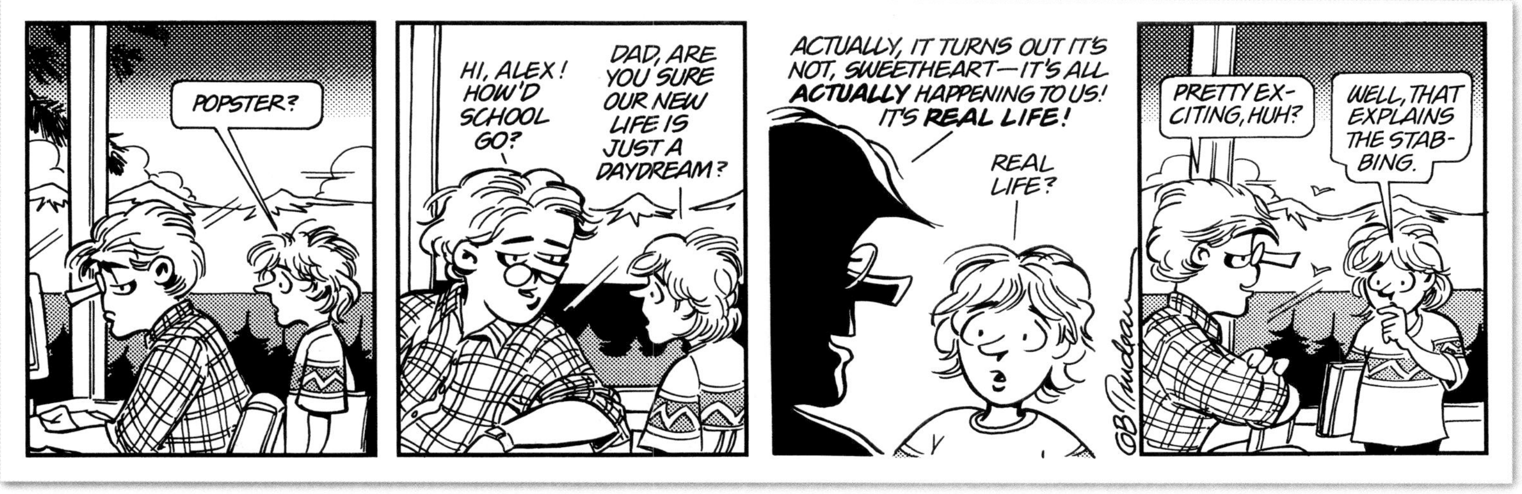
POPSTER?
HI, ALEX! HOW'D SCHOOL GO?
DAD, ARE YOU SURE OUR NEW LIFE IS JUST A DAYDREAM?
ACTUALLY, IT TURNS OUT IT'S NOT, SWEETHEART—IT'S ALL ACTUALLY HAPPENING TO US! IT'S REAL LIFE!
REAL LIFE?
PRETTY EXCITING, HUH?
WELL, THAT EXPLAINS THE STABBING.
GB Trudeau

8/11/95

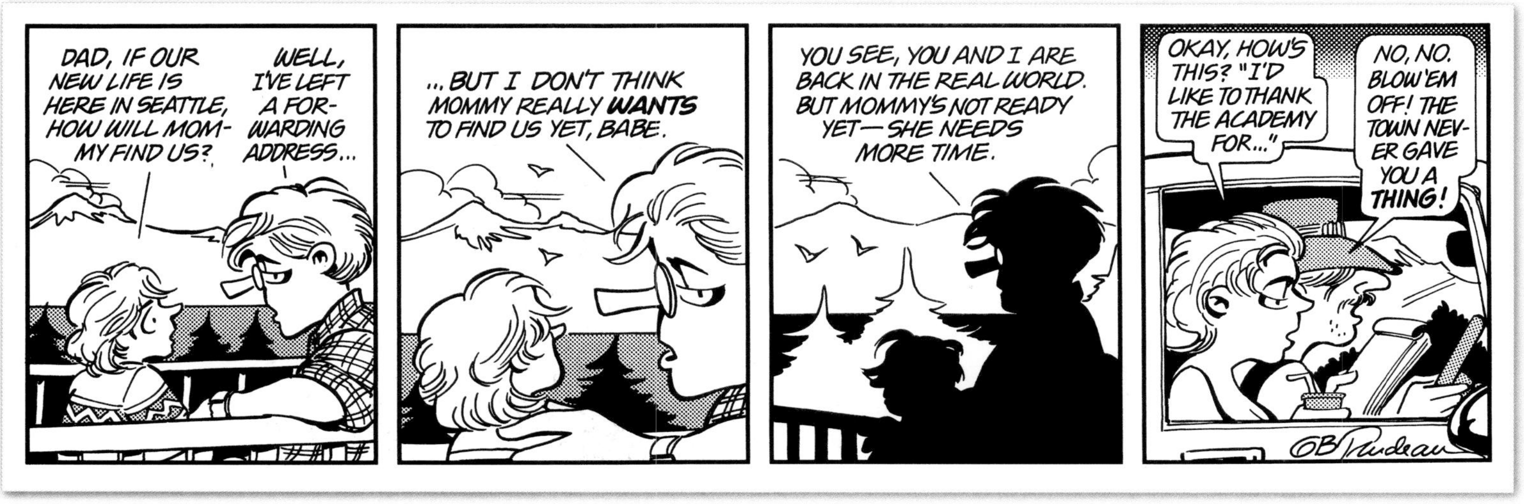
DAD, IF OUR NEW LIFE IS HERE IN SEATTLE, HOW WILL MOMMY FIND US?
WELL, I'VE LEFT A FORWARDING ADDRESS...
...BUT I DON'T THINK MOMMY REALLY WANTS TO FIND US YET, BABE.
YOU SEE, YOU AND I ARE BACK IN THE REAL WORLD. BUT MOMMY'S NOT READY YET—SHE NEEDS MORE TIME.
OKAY, HOW'S THIS? "I'D LIKE TO THANK THE ACADEMY FOR..."
NO, NO. BLOW 'EM OFF! THE TOWN NEVER GAVE YOU A THING!
GB Trudeau

8/12/95

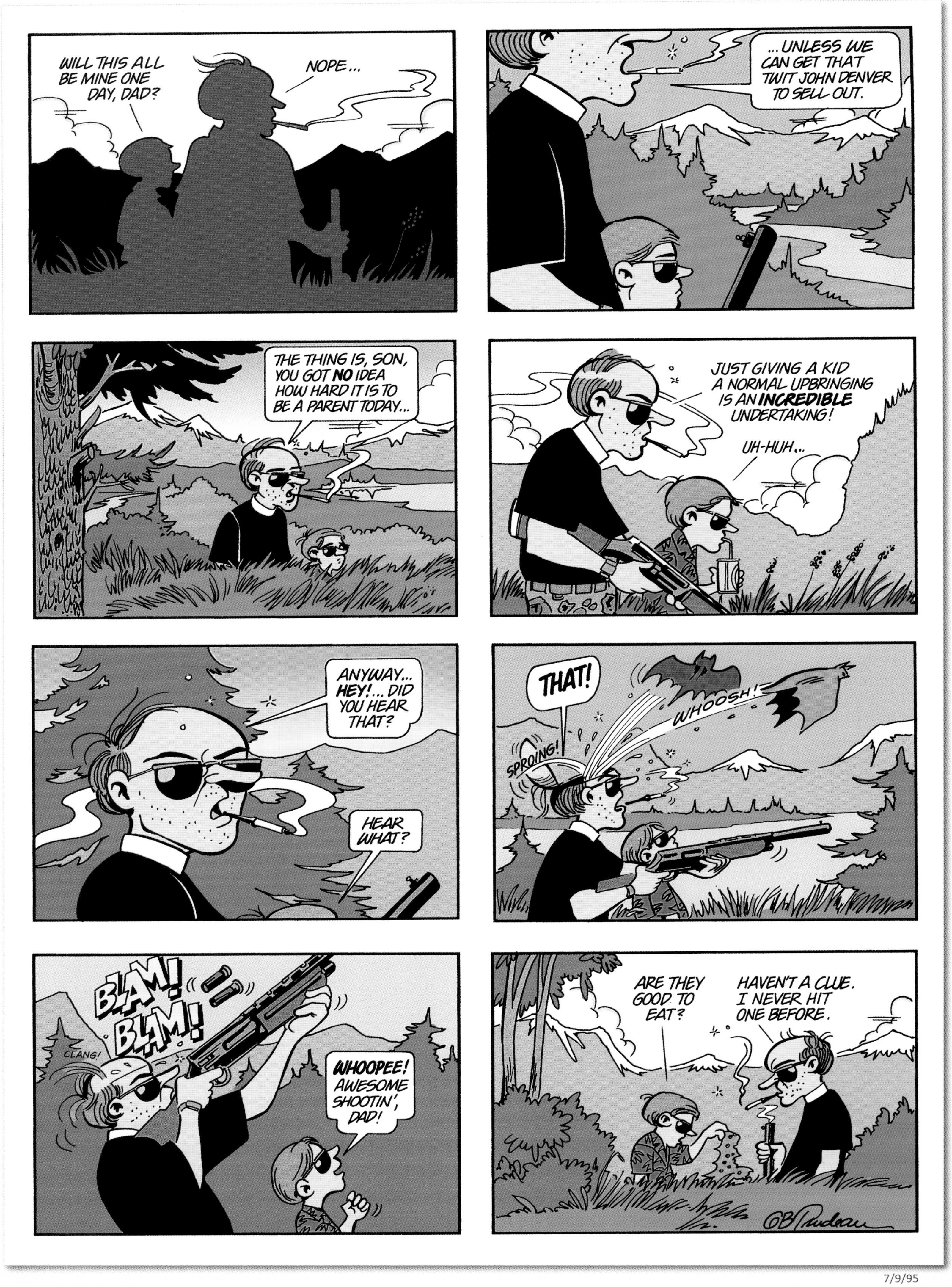

WILL THIS ALL BE MINE ONE DAY, DAD?
NOPE...
...UNLESS WE CAN GET THAT TWIT JOHN DENVER TO SELL OUT.
THE THING IS, SON, YOU GOT NO IDEA HOW HARD IT IS TO BE A PARENT TODAY...
JUST GIVING A KID A NORMAL UPBRINGING IS AN INCREDIBLE UNDERTAKING!
UH-HUH...
ANYWAY... HEY!... DID YOU HEAR THAT?
HEAR WHAT?
THAT!
SPROING!
WHOOSH!
BLAM! BLAM!
CLANG!
WHOOPEE! AWESOME SHOOTIN', DAD!
ARE THEY GOOD TO EAT?
HAVEN'T A CLUE. I NEVER HIT ONE BEFORE.
©B Trudeau

7/9/95

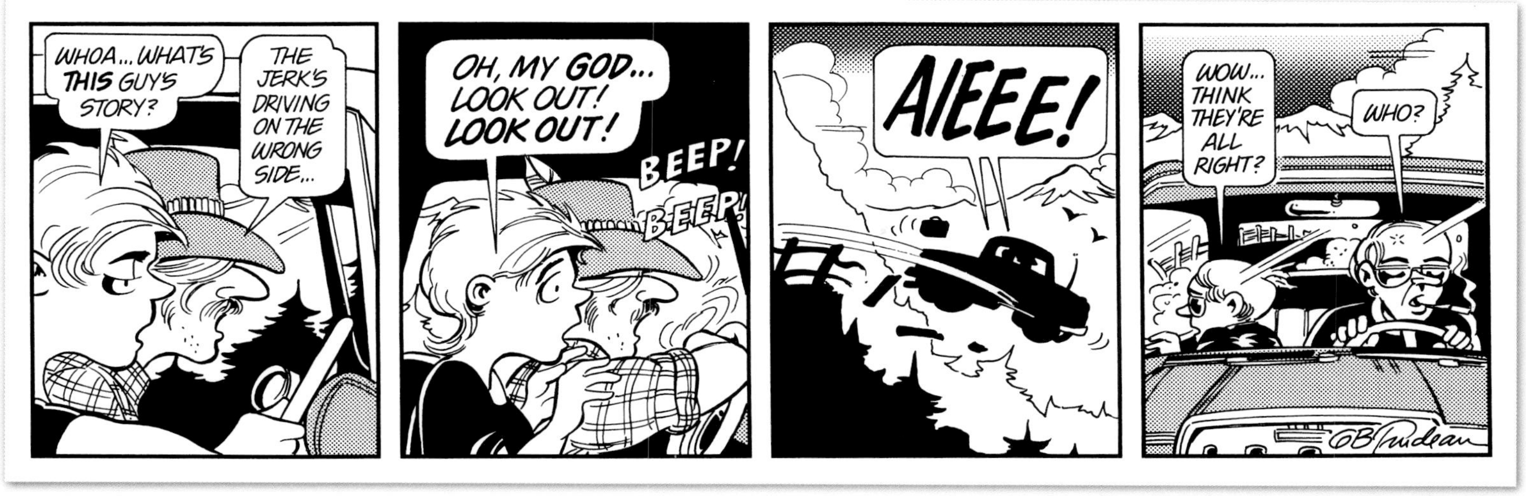
WHOA... WHAT'S **THIS** GUY'S STORY?
THE JERK'S DRIVING ON THE WRONG SIDE...
OH, MY **GOD**... LOOK OUT! **LOOK OUT!**
BEEP! B-EEP!
AIEEE!
WOW... THINK THEY'RE ALL RIGHT?
WHO?

10/3/95

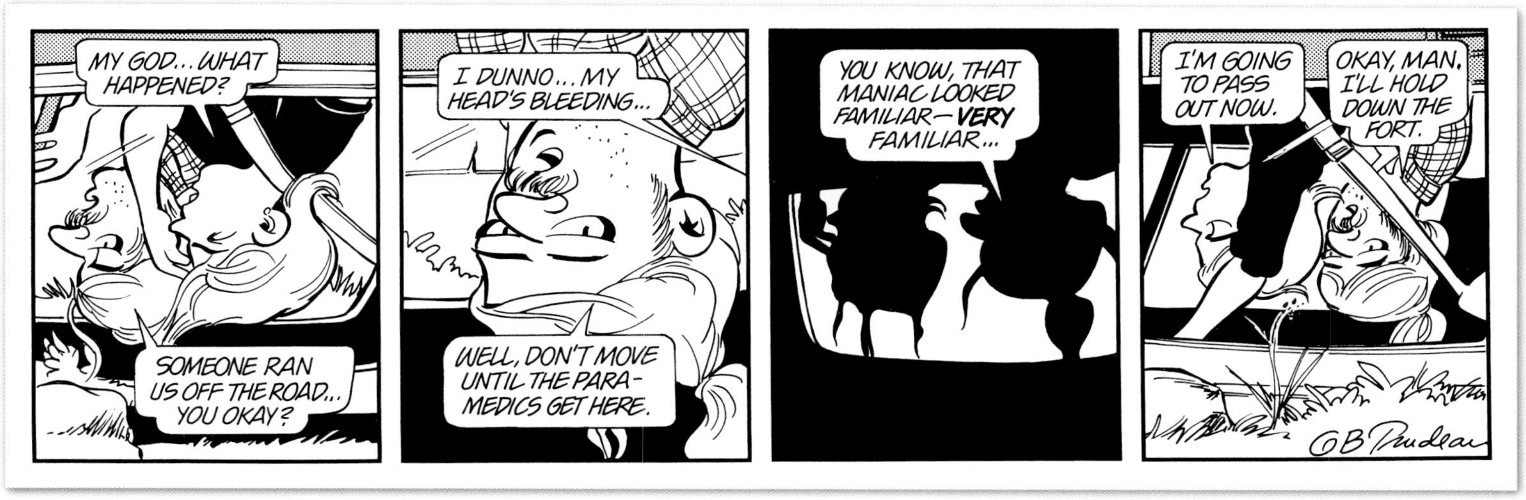
MY GOD... WHAT HAPPENED?
SOMEONE RAN US OFF THE ROAD... YOU OKAY?
I DUNNO... MY HEAD'S BLEEDING...
WELL, DON'T MOVE UNTIL THE PARA-MEDICS GET HERE.
YOU KNOW, THAT MANIAC LOOKED FAMILIAR—**VERY** FAMILIAR...
I'M GOING TO PASS OUT NOW.
OKAY, MAN. I'LL HOLD DOWN THE FORT.

10/4/95

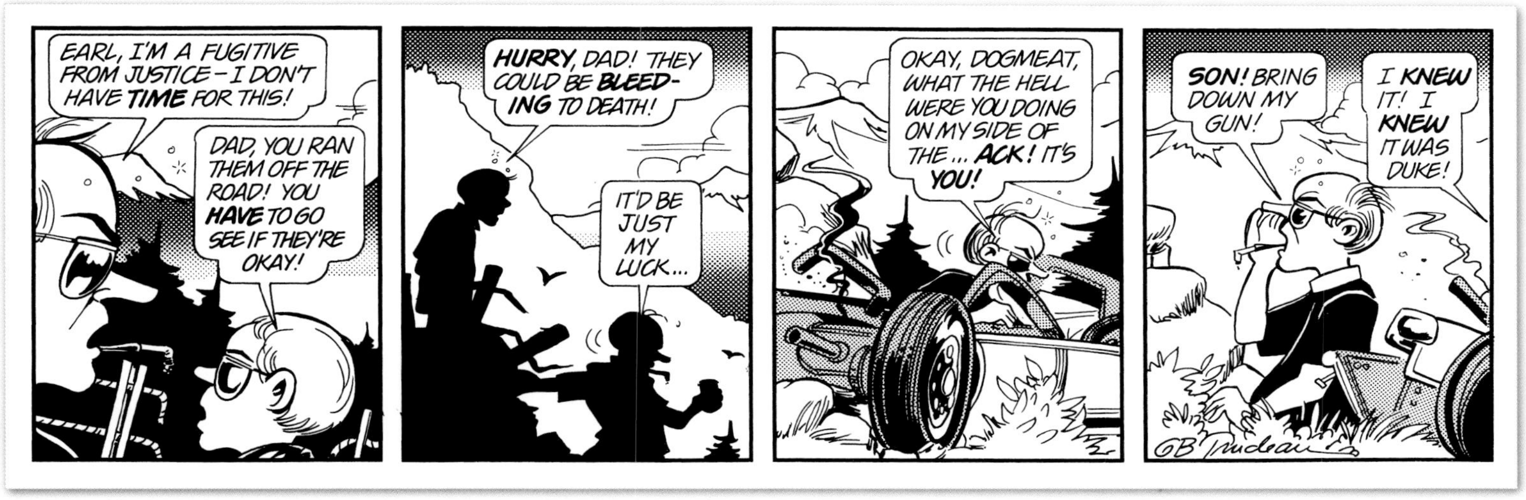
EARL, I'M A FUGITIVE FROM JUSTICE - I DON'T HAVE **TIME** FOR THIS!
DAD, YOU RAN THEM OFF THE ROAD! YOU **HAVE** TO GO SEE IF THEY'RE OKAY!
HURRY, DAD! THEY COULD BE **BLEED-ING** TO DEATH!
IT'D BE JUST MY LUCK...
OKAY, DOGMEAT, WHAT THE HELL WERE YOU DOING ON MY SIDE OF THE... **ACK!** IT'S **YOU!**
SON! BRING DOWN MY GUN!
I **KNEW** IT! I **KNEW** IT WAS DUKE!

10/5/95

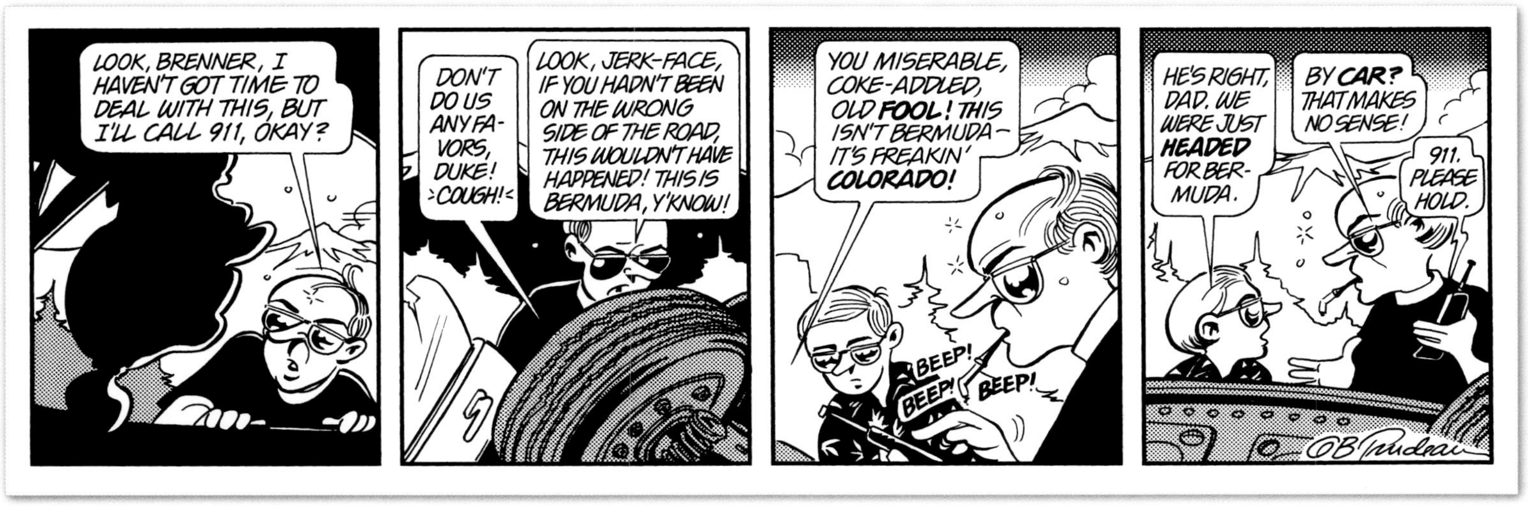
LOOK, BRENNER, I HAVEN'T GOT TIME TO DEAL WITH THIS, BUT I'LL CALL 911, OKAY?
DON'T DO US ANY FA-VORS, DUKE! >COUGH!<
LOOK, JERK-FACE, IF YOU HADN'T BEEN ON THE WRONG SIDE OF THE ROAD, THIS WOULDN'T HAVE HAPPENED! THIS IS BERMUDA, Y'KNOW!
YOU MISERABLE, COKE-ADDLED, OLD **FOOL!** THIS ISN'T BERMUDA - IT'S FREAKIN' **COLORADO!**
BEEP! BEEP! BEEP!
HE'S RIGHT, DAD. WE WERE JUST **HEADED** FOR BER-MUDA.
BY **CAR?** THAT MAKES NO SENSE!
911. PLEASE HOLD.

10/6/95

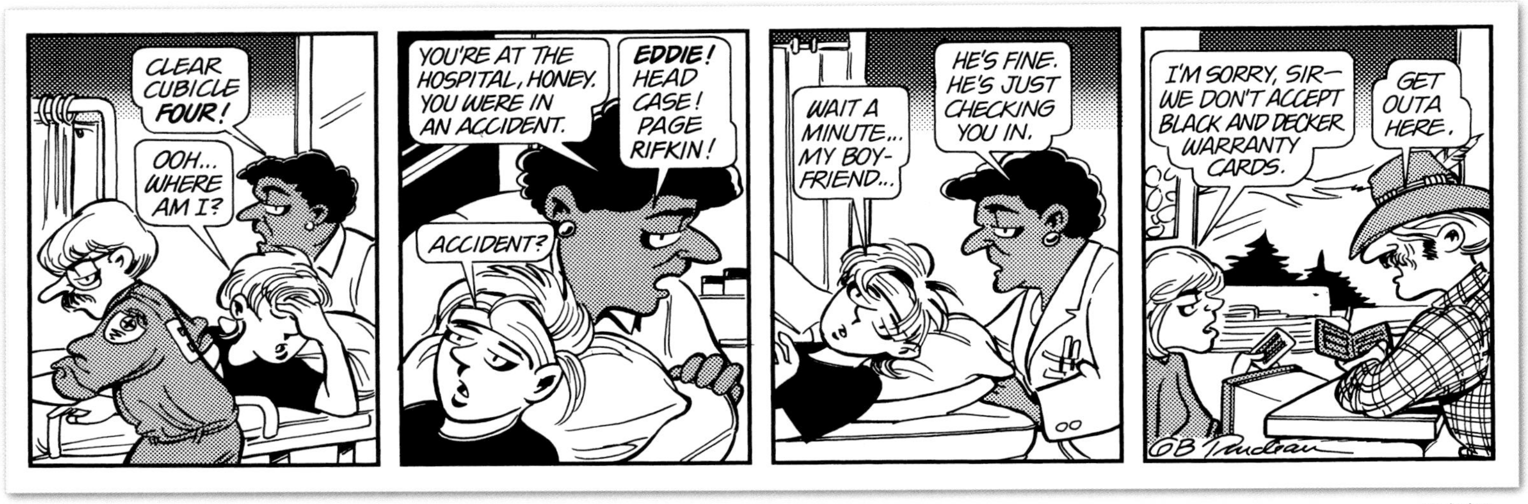
CLEAR CUBICLE FOUR!
OOH... WHERE AM I?
YOU'RE AT THE HOSPITAL, HONEY. YOU WERE IN AN ACCIDENT.
EDDIE! HEAD CASE! PAGE RIFKIN!
ACCIDENT?
WAIT A MINUTE... MY BOY-FRIEND...
HE'S FINE. HE'S JUST CHECKING YOU IN.
I'M SORRY, SIR— WE DON'T ACCEPT BLACK AND DECKER WARRANTY CARDS.
GET OUTA HERE.

10/9/95

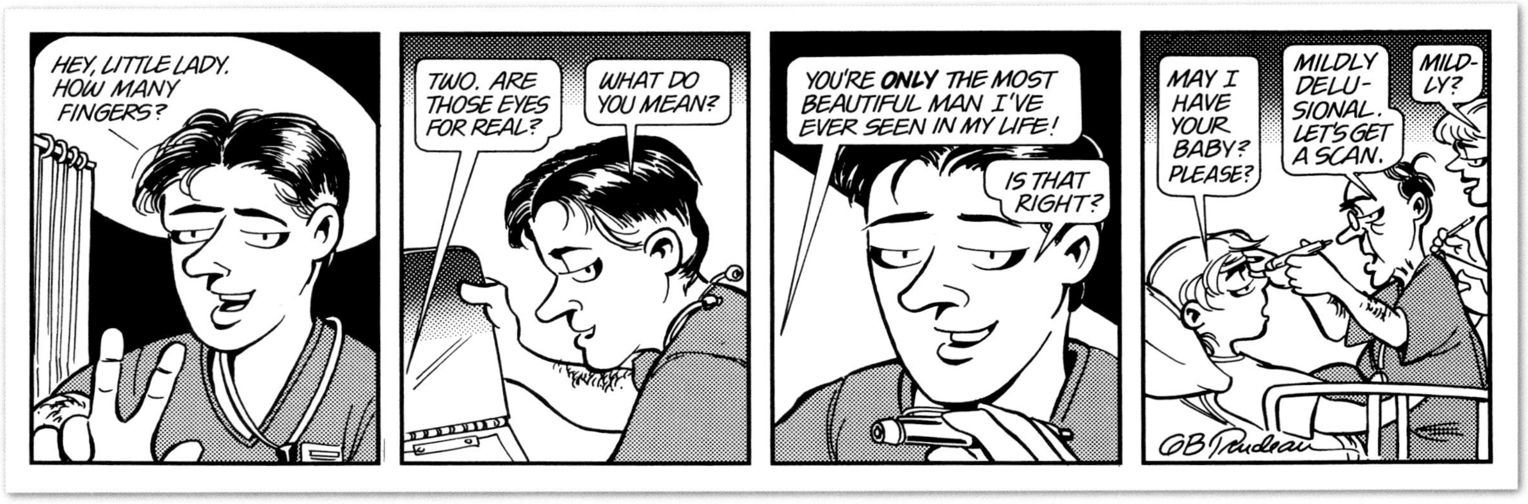
HEY, LITTLE LADY. HOW MANY FINGERS?
TWO. ARE THOSE EYES FOR REAL?
WHAT DO YOU MEAN?
YOU'RE ONLY THE MOST BEAUTIFUL MAN I'VE EVER SEEN IN MY LIFE!
IS THAT RIGHT?
MAY I HAVE YOUR BABY? PLEASE?
MILDLY DELU-SIONAL. LET'S GET A SCAN.
MILD-LY?

10/10/95

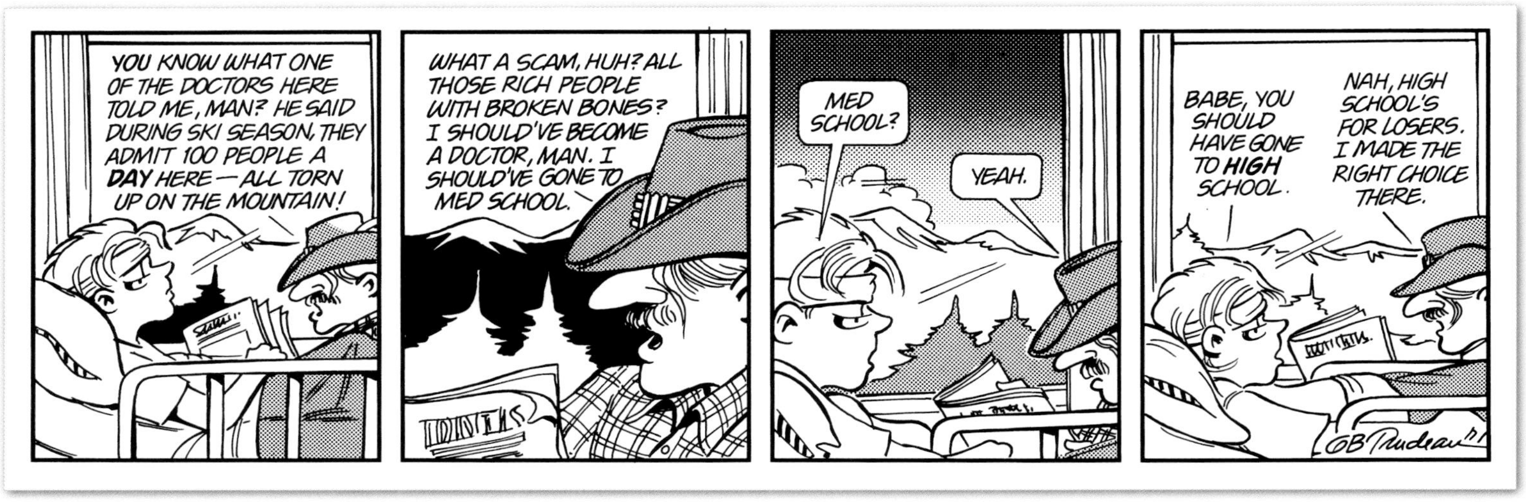
YOU KNOW WHAT ONE OF THE DOCTORS HERE TOLD ME, MAN? HE SAID DURING SKI SEASON, THEY ADMIT 100 PEOPLE A DAY HERE — ALL TORN UP ON THE MOUNTAIN!
WHAT A SCAM, HUH? ALL THOSE RICH PEOPLE WITH BROKEN BONES? I SHOULD'VE BECOME A DOCTOR, MAN. I SHOULD'VE GONE TO MED SCHOOL.
MED SCHOOL?
YEAH.
BABE, YOU SHOULD HAVE GONE TO HIGH SCHOOL.
NAH, HIGH SCHOOL'S FOR LOSERS. I MADE THE RIGHT CHOICE THERE.

10/14/95

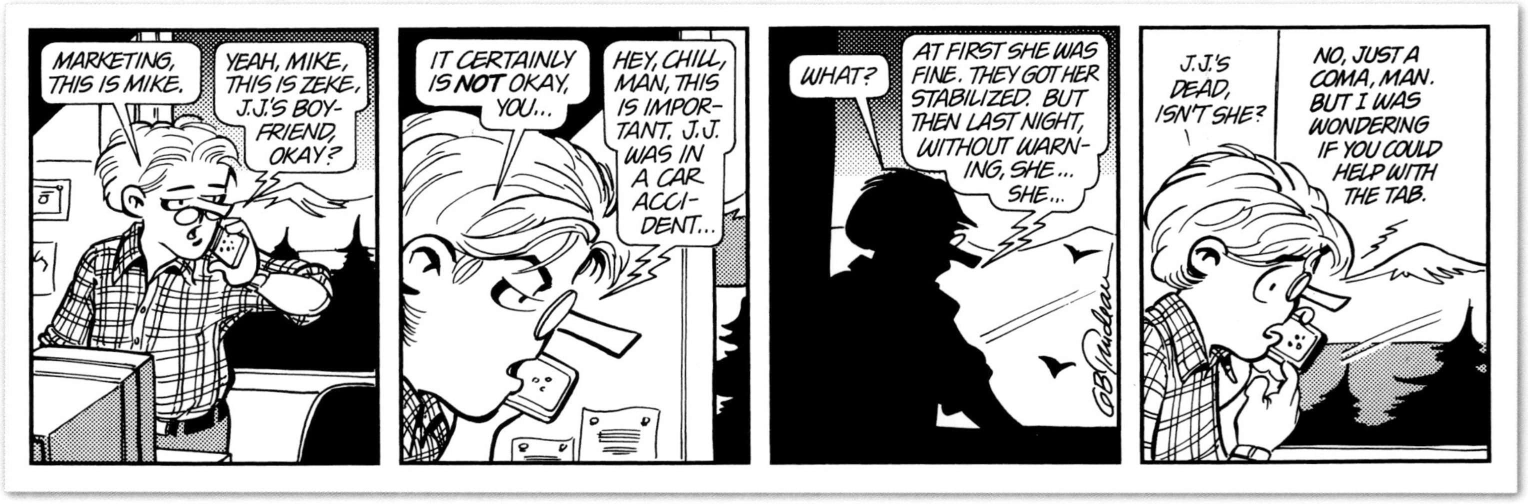
MARKETING, THIS IS MIKE.
YEAH, MIKE, THIS IS ZEKE, J.J.'S BOY-FRIEND, OKAY?
IT CERTAINLY IS NOT OKAY, YOU...
HEY, CHILL, MAN, THIS IS IMPOR-TANT. J.J. WAS IN A CAR ACCI-DENT...
WHAT?
AT FIRST SHE WAS FINE. THEY GOT HER STABILIZED. BUT THEN LAST NIGHT, WITHOUT WARN-ING, SHE... SHE...
J.J.'S DEAD, ISN'T SHE?
NO, JUST A COMA, MAN. BUT I WAS WONDERING IF YOU COULD HELP WITH THE TAB.

10/23/95

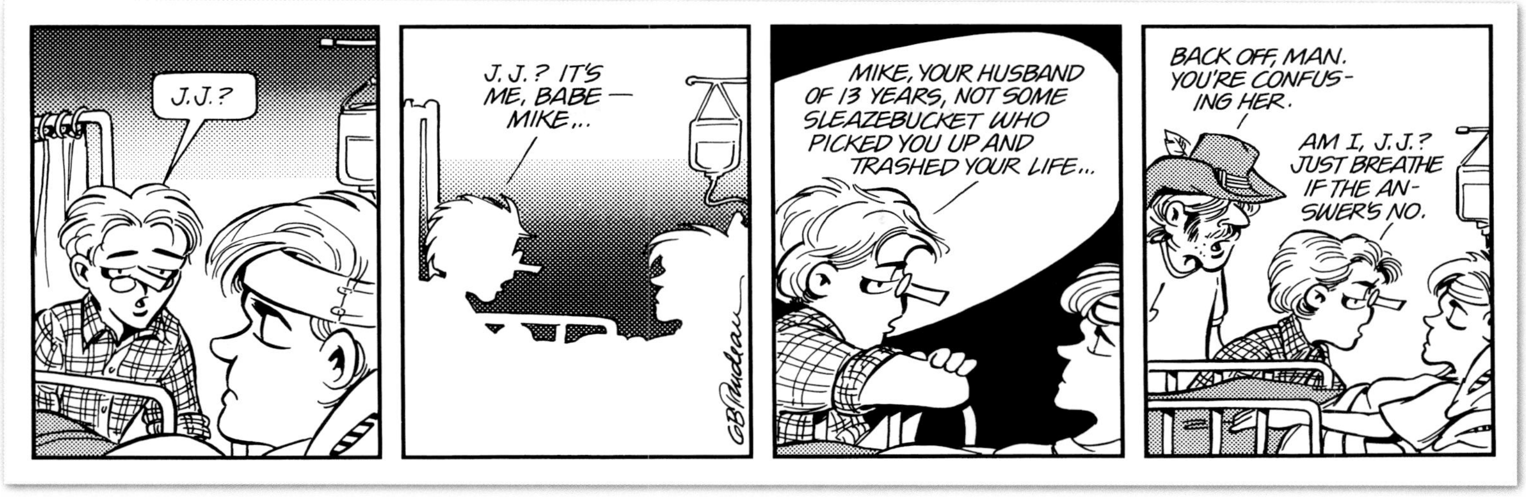
J.J.?
J.J.? IT'S ME, BABE — MIKE...
MIKE, YOUR HUSBAND OF 13 YEARS, NOT SOME SLEAZEBUCKET WHO PICKED YOU UP AND TRASHED YOUR LIFE...
BACK OFF, MAN. YOU'RE CONFUSING HER.
AM I, J.J.? JUST BREATHE IF THE ANSWER'S NO.

10/25/95

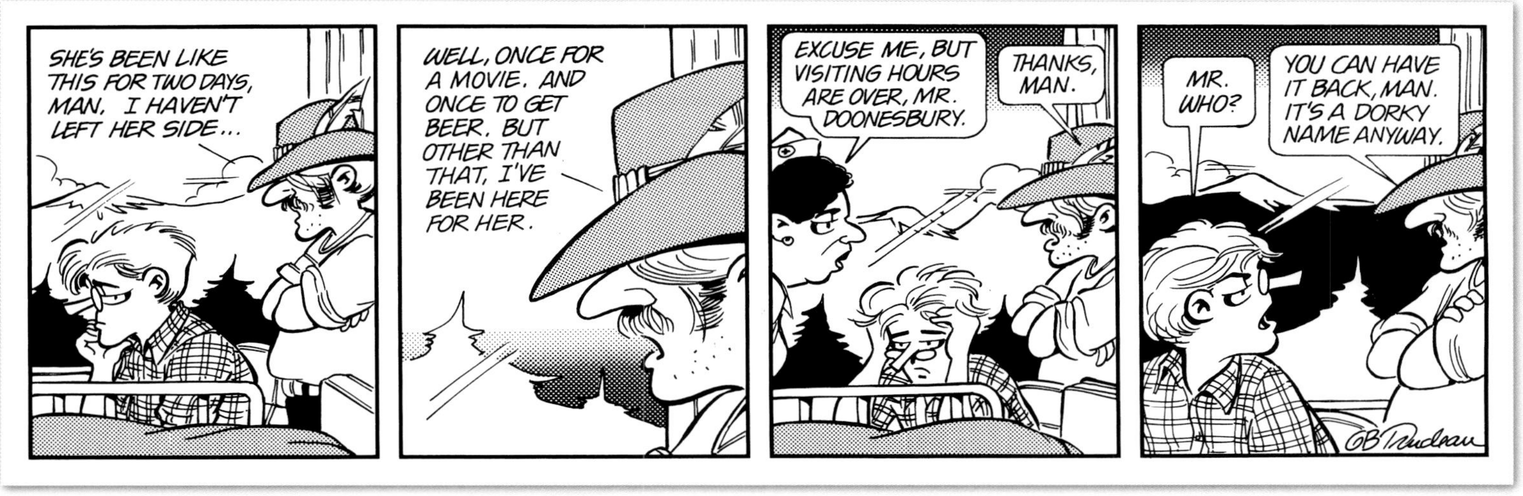
SHE'S BEEN LIKE THIS FOR TWO DAYS, MAN. I HAVEN'T LEFT HER SIDE...
WELL, ONCE FOR A MOVIE. AND ONCE TO GET BEER. BUT OTHER THAN THAT, I'VE BEEN HERE FOR HER.
EXCUSE ME, BUT VISITING HOURS ARE OVER, MR. DOONESBURY.
THANKS, MAN.
MR. WHO?
YOU CAN HAVE IT BACK, MAN. IT'S A DORKY NAME ANYWAY.

10/26/95

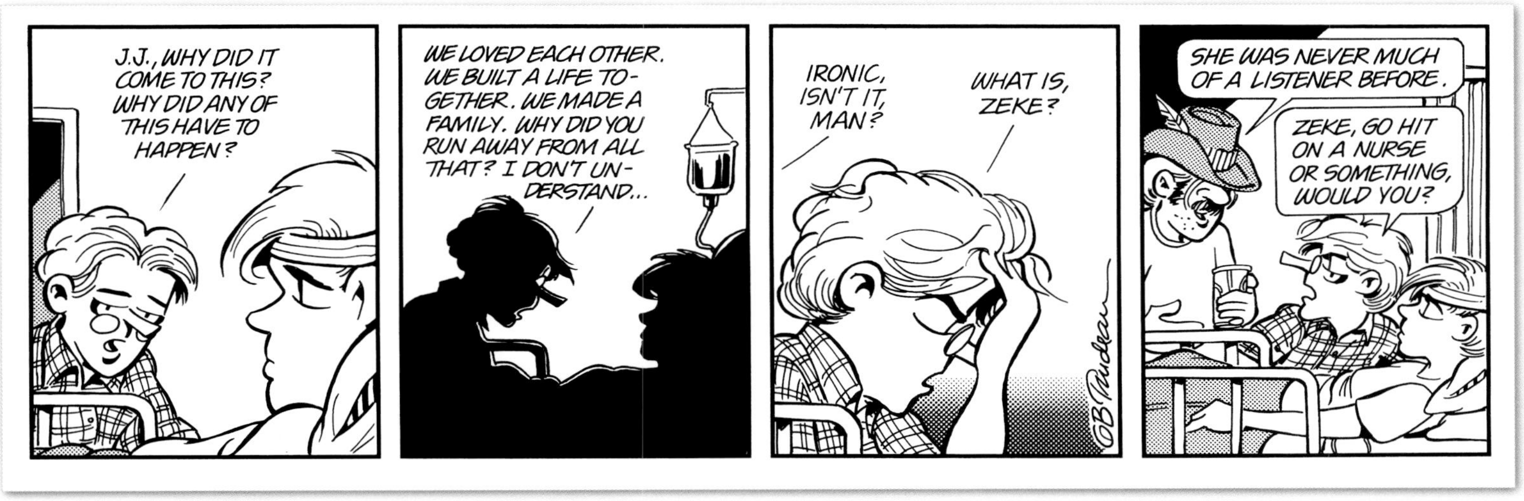
J.J., WHY DID IT COME TO THIS? WHY DID ANY OF THIS HAVE TO HAPPEN?
WE LOVED EACH OTHER. WE BUILT A LIFE TOGETHER. WE MADE A FAMILY. WHY DID YOU RUN AWAY FROM ALL THAT? I DON'T UNDERSTAND...
IRONIC, ISN'T IT, MAN?
WHAT IS, ZEKE?
SHE WAS NEVER MUCH OF A LISTENER BEFORE.
ZEKE, GO HIT ON A NURSE OR SOMETHING, WOULD YOU?

10/27/95

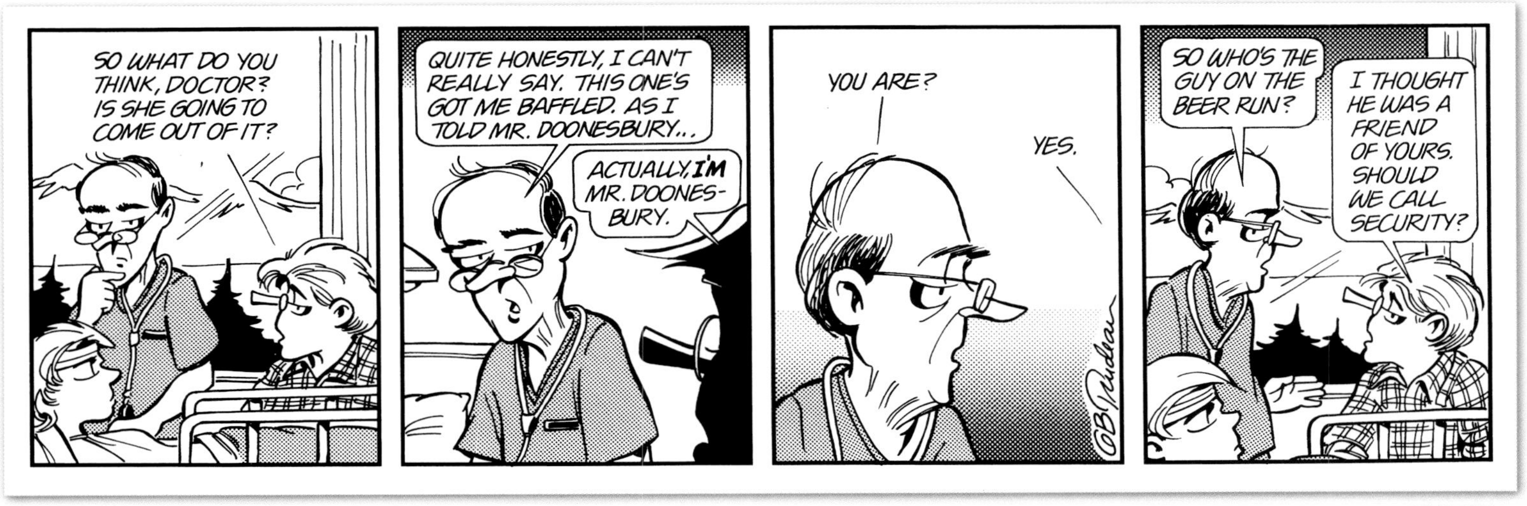
SO WHAT DO YOU THINK, DOCTOR? IS SHE GOING TO COME OUT OF IT?
QUITE HONESTLY, I CAN'T REALLY SAY. THIS ONE'S GOT ME BAFFLED. AS I TOLD MR. DOONESBURY...
ACTUALLY, I'M MR. DOONESBURY.
YOU ARE?
YES.
SO WHO'S THE GUY ON THE BEER RUN?
I THOUGHT HE WAS A FRIEND OF YOURS. SHOULD WE CALL SECURITY?

10/28/95

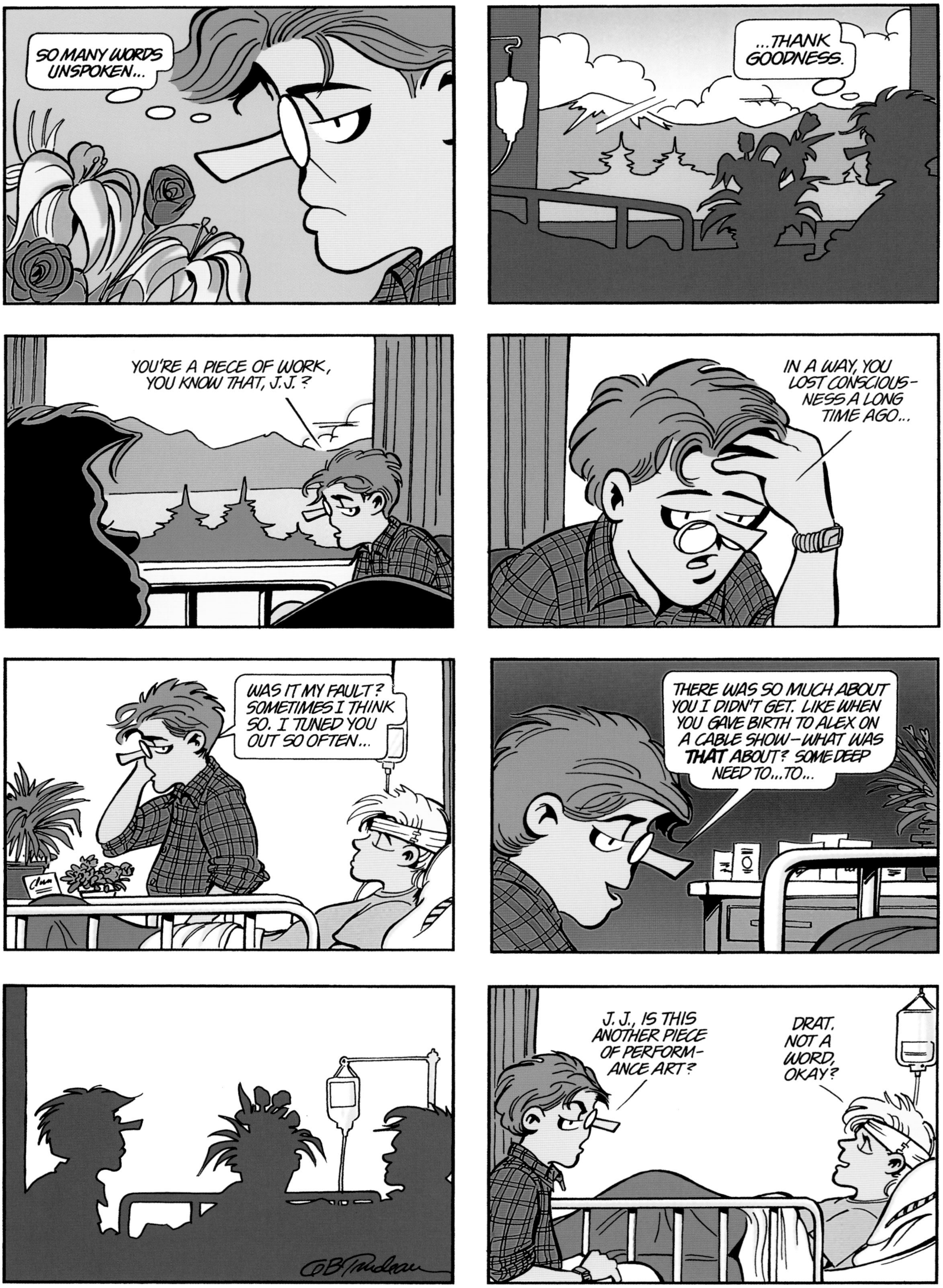
SO MANY WORDS UNSPOKEN...
...THANK GOODNESS.
YOU'RE A PIECE OF WORK, YOU KNOW THAT, J.J.?
IN A WAY, YOU LOST CONSCIOUS-NESS A LONG TIME AGO...
WAS IT MY FAULT? SOMETIMES I THINK SO. I TUNED YOU OUT SO OFTEN...
THERE WAS SO MUCH ABOUT YOU I DIDN'T GET. LIKE WHEN YOU GAVE BIRTH TO ALEX ON A CABLE SHOW—WHAT WAS **THAT** ABOUT? SOME DEEP NEED TO...TO...
J.J., IS THIS ANOTHER PIECE OF PERFORM-ANCE ART?
DRAT. NOT A WORD, OKAY?

10/29/95

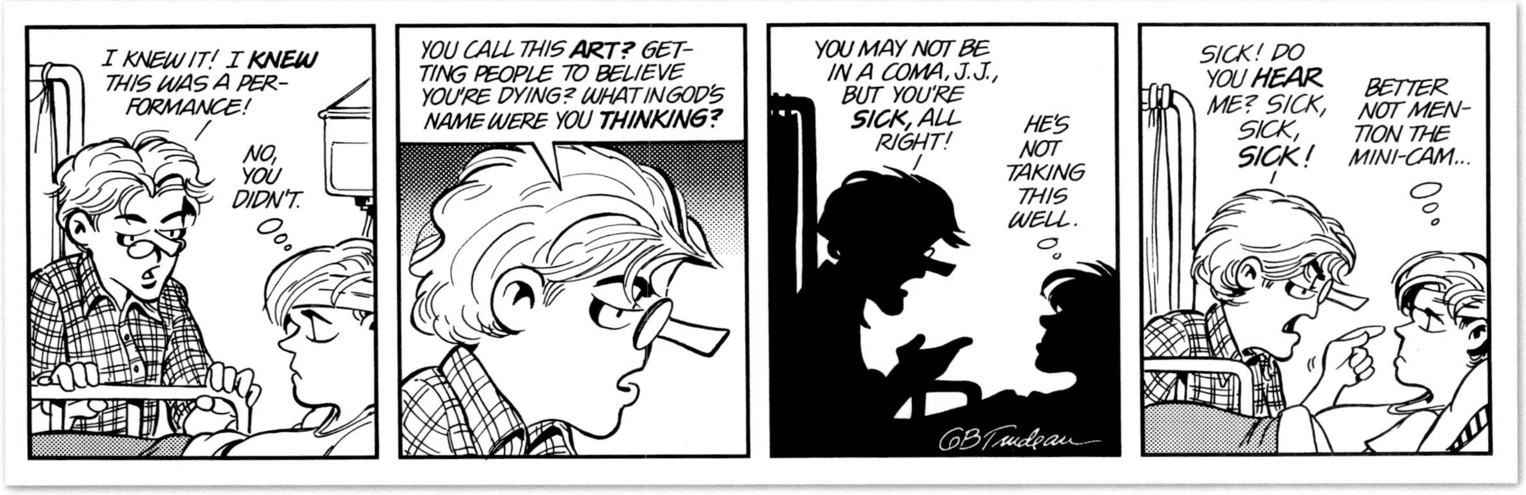
I KNEW IT! I KNEW THIS WAS A PERFORMANCE!
NO, YOU DIDN'T.
YOU CALL THIS ART? GETTING PEOPLE TO BELIEVE YOU'RE DYING? WHAT IN GOD'S NAME WERE YOU THINKING?
YOU MAY NOT BE IN A COMA, J.J., BUT YOU'RE SICK, ALL RIGHT!
HE'S NOT TAKING THIS WELL.
SICK! DO YOU HEAR ME? SICK, SICK, SICK!
BETTER NOT MENTION THE MINI-CAM...
GBTrudeau

10/30/95

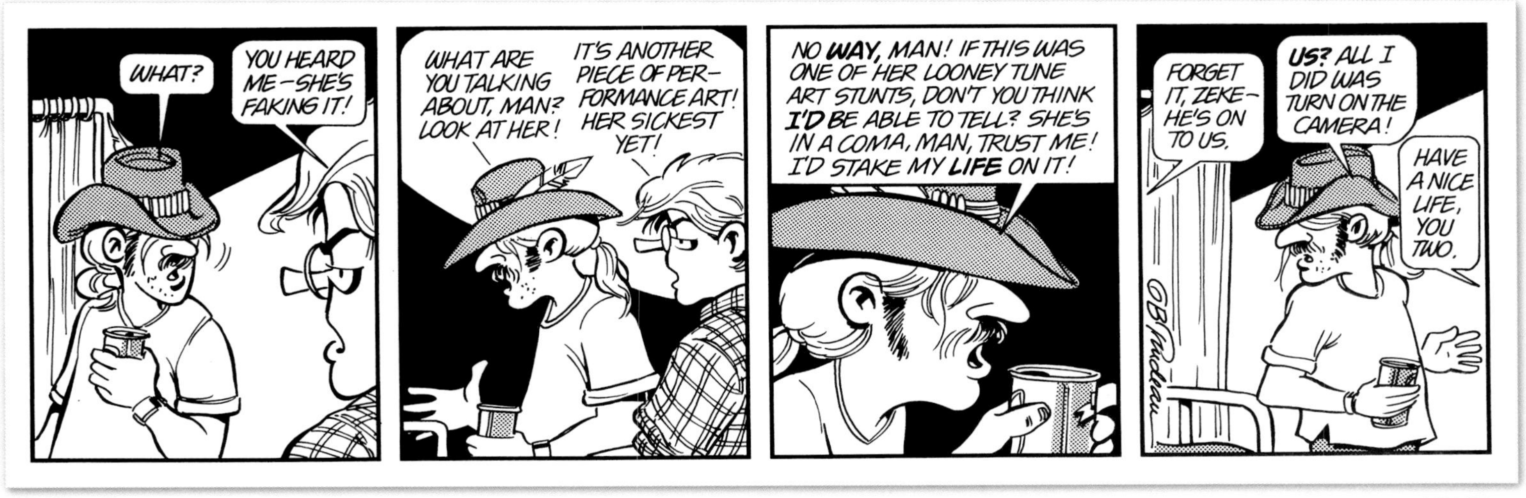
WHAT?
YOU HEARD ME–SHE'S FAKING IT!
WHAT ARE YOU TALKING ABOUT, MAN? LOOK AT HER!
IT'S ANOTHER PIECE OF PERFORMANCE ART! HER SICKEST YET!
NO WAY, MAN! IF THIS WAS ONE OF HER LOONEY TUNE ART STUNTS, DON'T YOU THINK I'D BE ABLE TO TELL? SHE'S IN A COMA, MAN, TRUST ME! I'D STAKE MY LIFE ON IT!
FORGET IT, ZEKE–HE'S ON TO US.
US? ALL I DID WAS TURN ON THE CAMERA!
HAVE A NICE LIFE, YOU TWO.
GBTrudeau

10/31/95

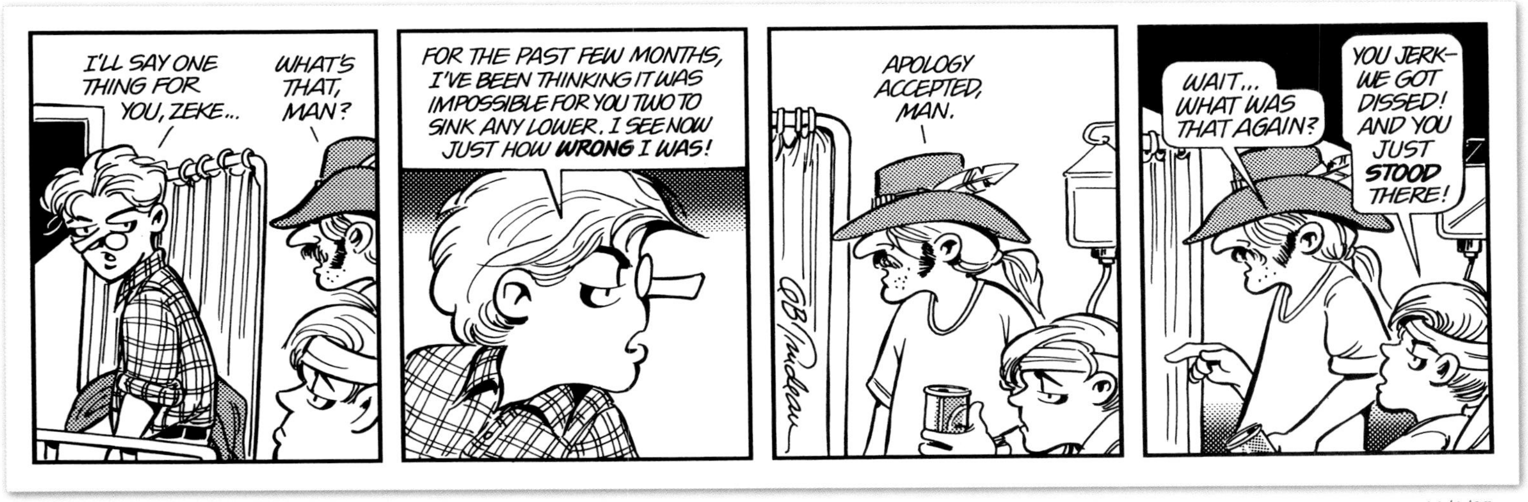
I'LL SAY ONE THING FOR YOU, ZEKE...
WHAT'S THAT, MAN?
FOR THE PAST FEW MONTHS, I'VE BEEN THINKING IT WAS IMPOSSIBLE FOR YOU TWO TO SINK ANY LOWER. I SEE NOW JUST HOW WRONG I WAS!
APOLOGY ACCEPTED, MAN.
WAIT... WHAT WAS THAT AGAIN?
YOU JERK–WE GOT DISSED! AND YOU JUST STOOD THERE!
GBTrudeau

11/1/95

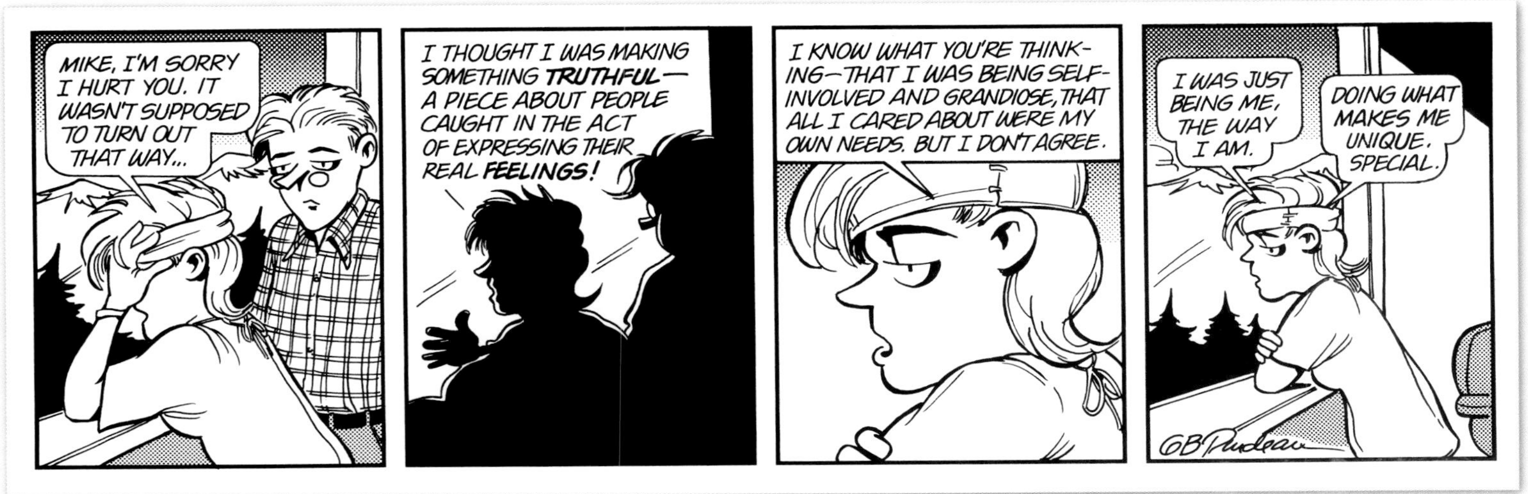
MIKE, I'M SORRY I HURT YOU. IT WASN'T SUPPOSED TO TURN OUT THAT WAY...
I THOUGHT I WAS MAKING SOMETHING TRUTHFUL–A PIECE ABOUT PEOPLE CAUGHT IN THE ACT OF EXPRESSING THEIR REAL FEELINGS!
I KNOW WHAT YOU'RE THINKING–THAT I WAS BEING SELF-INVOLVED AND GRANDIOSE, THAT ALL I CARED ABOUT WERE MY OWN NEEDS. BUT I DON'T AGREE.
I WAS JUST BEING ME, THE WAY I AM.
DOING WHAT MAKES ME UNIQUE. SPECIAL.
GBTrudeau

11/3/95

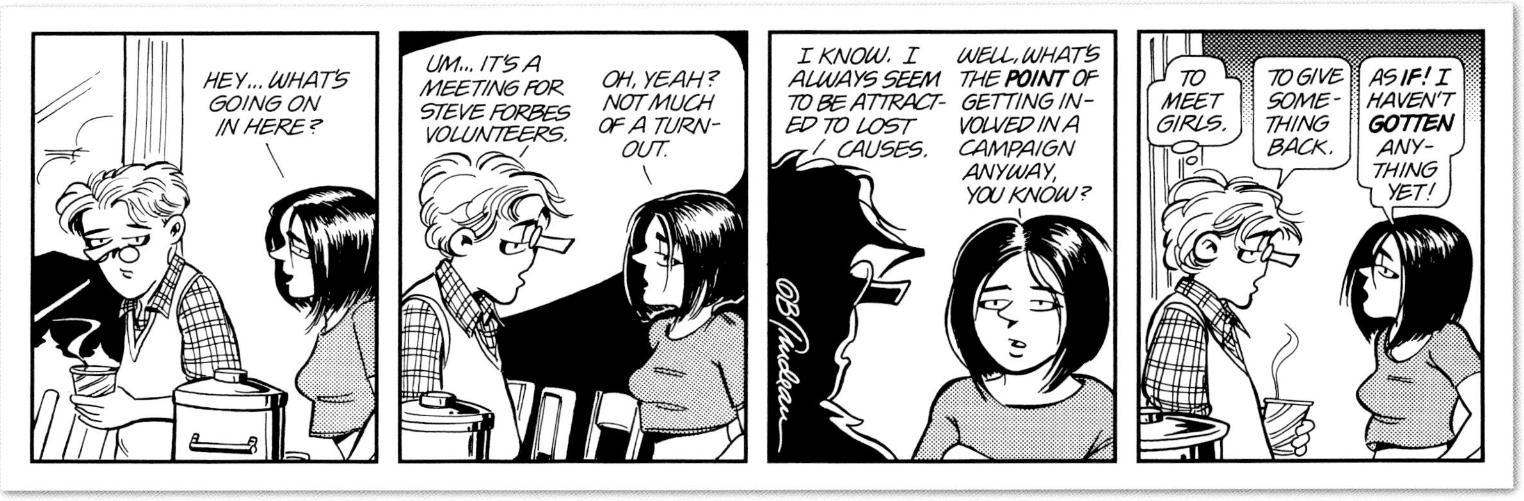
HEY... WHAT'S GOING ON IN HERE?
UM... IT'S A MEETING FOR STEVE FORBES VOLUNTEERS.
OH, YEAH? NOT MUCH OF A TURN-OUT.
I KNOW. I ALWAYS SEEM TO BE ATTRACTED TO LOST CAUSES.
WELL, WHAT'S THE **POINT** OF GETTING INVOLVED IN A CAMPAIGN ANYWAY, YOU KNOW?
TO MEET GIRLS.
TO GIVE SOMETHING BACK.
AS **IF**! I HAVEN'T **GOTTEN** ANYTHING YET!

2/7/96

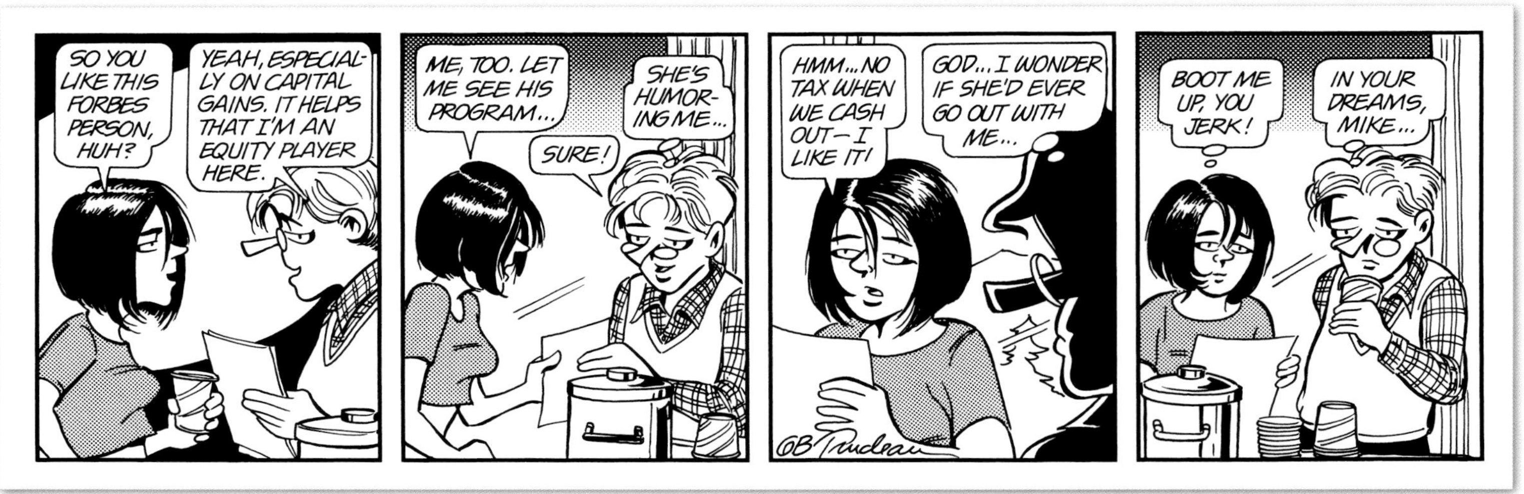
SO YOU LIKE THIS FORBES PERSON, HUH?
YEAH, ESPECIALLY ON CAPITAL GAINS. IT HELPS THAT I'M AN EQUITY PLAYER HERE.
ME, TOO. LET ME SEE HIS PROGRAM...
SHE'S HUMORING ME...
SURE!
HMM... NO TAX WHEN WE CASH OUT— I LIKE IT!
GOD... I WONDER IF SHE'D EVER GO OUT WITH ME...
BOOT ME UP, YOU JERK!
IN YOUR DREAMS, MIKE...

2/9/96

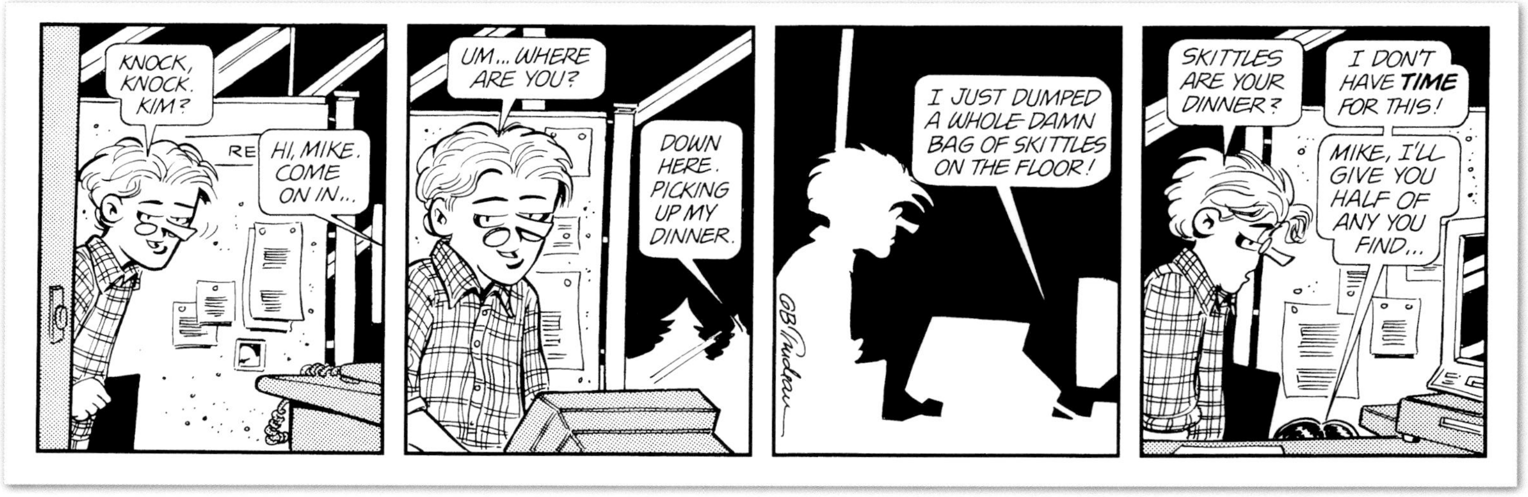
KNOCK, KNOCK. KIM?
HI, MIKE. COME ON IN...
UM... WHERE ARE YOU?
DOWN HERE. PICKING UP MY DINNER.
I JUST DUMPED A WHOLE-DAMN BAG OF SKITTLES ON THE FLOOR!
SKITTLES ARE YOUR DINNER?
I DON'T HAVE **TIME** FOR THIS!
MIKE, I'LL GIVE YOU HALF OF ANY YOU FIND...

2/19/96

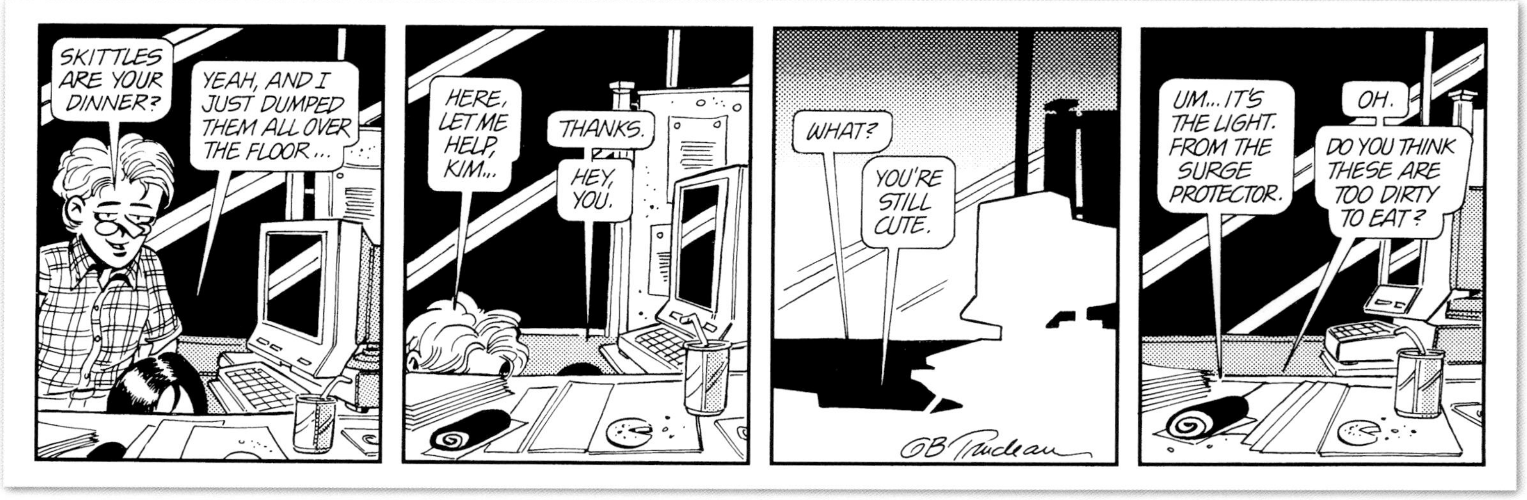
SKITTLES ARE YOUR DINNER?
YEAH, AND I JUST DUMPED THEM ALL OVER THE FLOOR...
HERE, LET ME HELP, KIM...
THANKS.
HEY, YOU.
WHAT?
YOU'RE STILL CUTE.
UM... IT'S THE LIGHT. FROM THE SURGE PROTECTOR.
OH.
DO YOU THINK THESE ARE TOO DIRTY TO EAT?

2/20/96

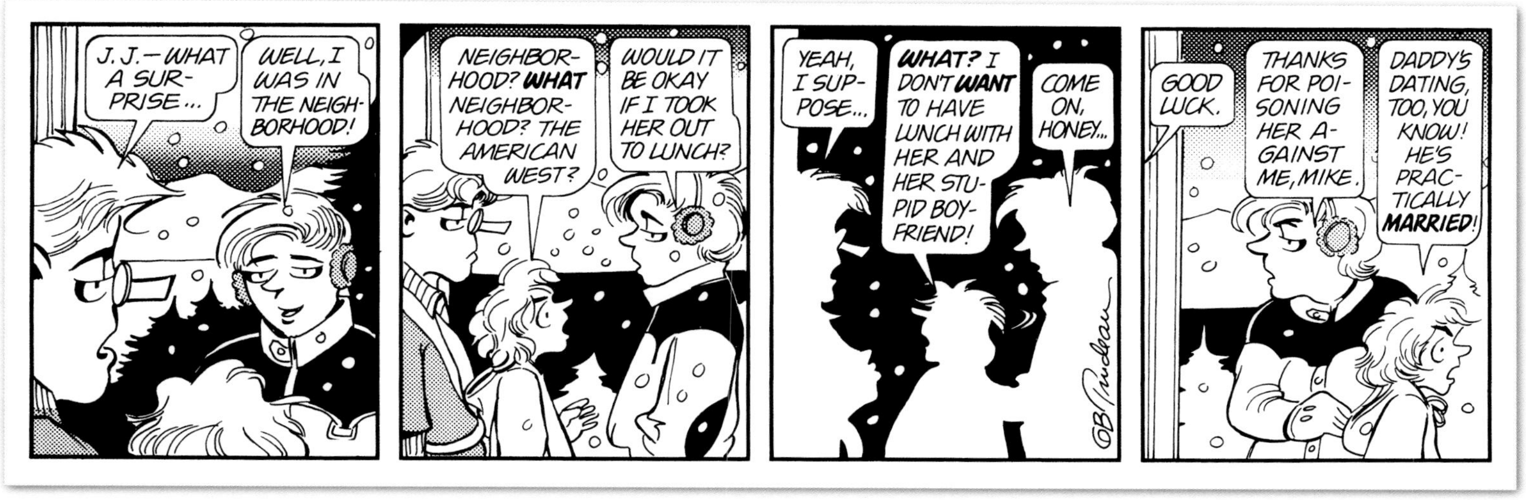
J. J.—WHAT A SURPRISE...
WELL, I WAS IN THE NEIGHBORHOOD!
NEIGHBORHOOD? WHAT NEIGHBORHOOD? THE AMERICAN WEST?
WOULD IT BE OKAY IF I TOOK HER OUT TO LUNCH?
YEAH, I SUPPOSE...
WHAT? I DON'T WANT TO HAVE LUNCH WITH HER AND HER STUPID BOYFRIEND!
COME ON, HONEY...
GOOD LUCK.
THANKS FOR POISONING HER AGAINST ME, MIKE.
DADDY'S DATING, TOO, YOU KNOW! HE'S PRACTICALLY MARRIED!
GB Trudeau

12/29/95

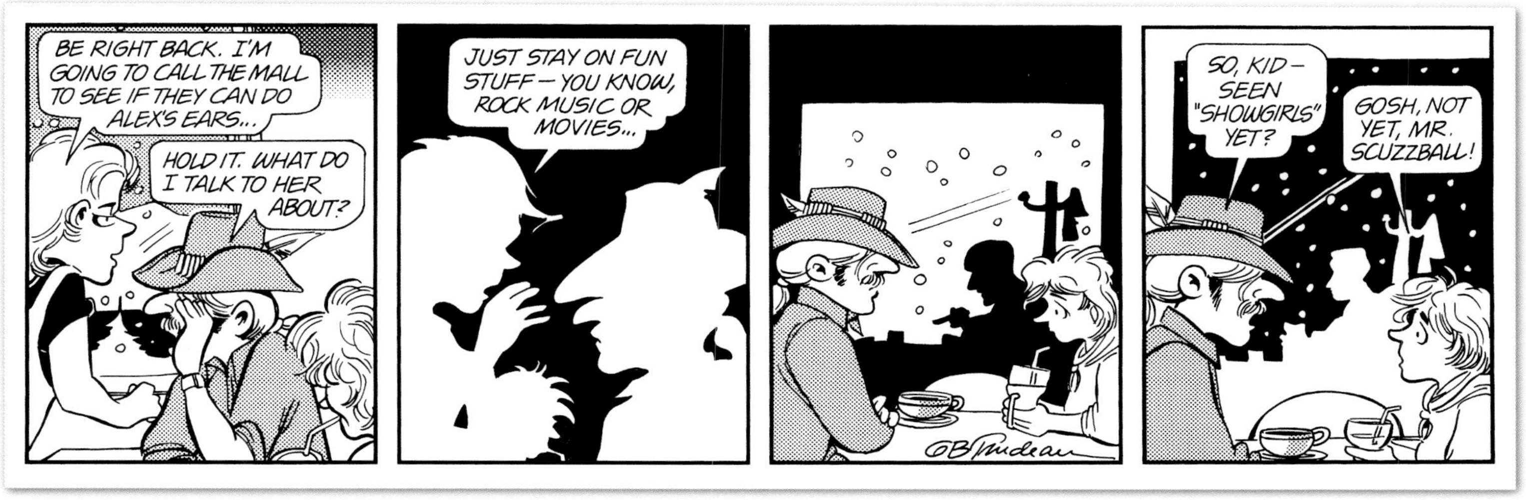
BE RIGHT BACK. I'M GOING TO CALL THE MALL TO SEE IF THEY CAN DO ALEX'S EARS...
HOLD IT. WHAT DO I TALK TO HER ABOUT?
JUST STAY ON FUN STUFF—YOU KNOW, ROCK MUSIC OR MOVIES...
GB Trudeau
SO, KID—SEEN "SHOWGIRLS" YET?
GOSH, NOT YET, MR. SCUZZBALL!

1/2/96

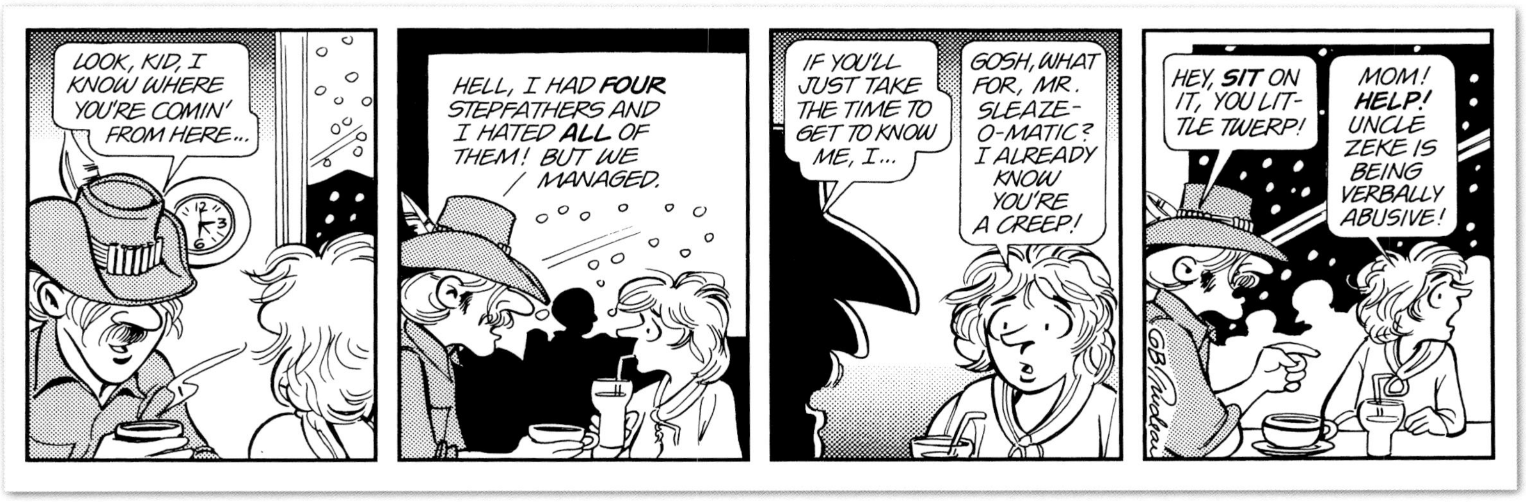
LOOK, KID, I KNOW WHERE YOU'RE COMIN' FROM HERE...
HELL, I HAD FOUR STEPFATHERS AND I HATED ALL OF THEM! BUT WE MANAGED.
IF YOU'LL JUST TAKE THE TIME TO GET TO KNOW ME, I...
GOSH, WHAT FOR, MR. SLEAZE-O-MATIC? I ALREADY KNOW YOU'RE A CREEP!
HEY, SIT ON IT, YOU LITTLE TWERP!
MOM! HELP! UNCLE ZEKE IS BEING VERBALLY ABUSIVE!
GB Trudeau

1/3/96

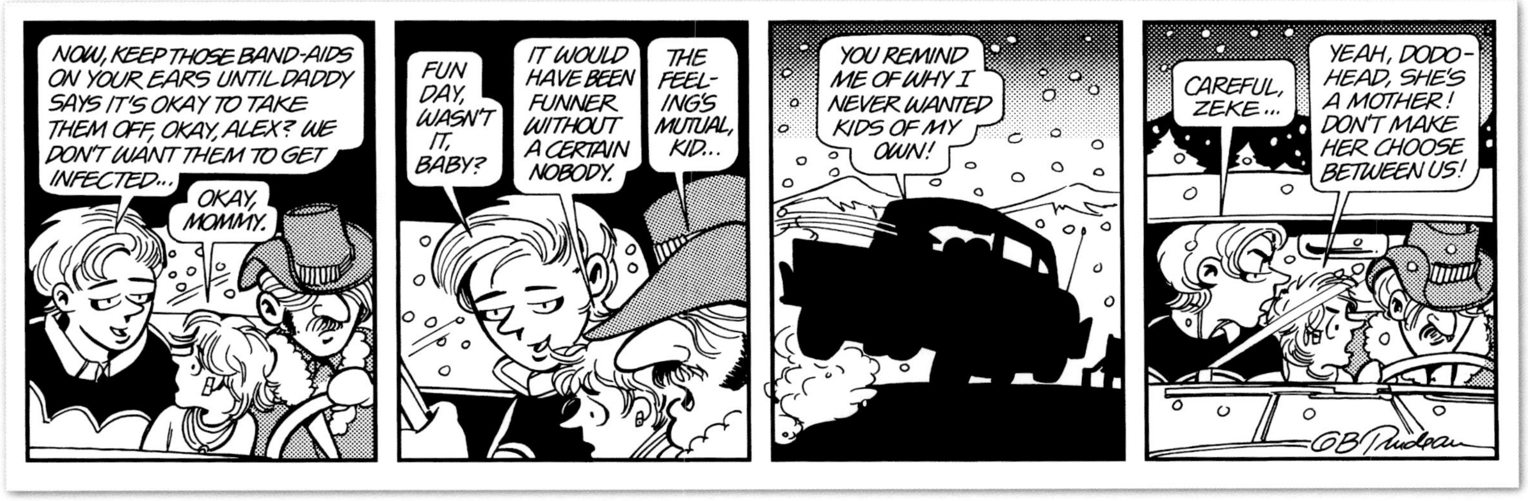
NOW, KEEP THOSE BAND-AIDS ON YOUR EARS UNTIL DADDY SAYS IT'S OKAY TO TAKE THEM OFF, OKAY, ALEX? WE DON'T WANT THEM TO GET INFECTED...
OKAY, MOMMY.
FUN DAY, WASN'T IT, BABY?
IT WOULD HAVE BEEN FUNNER WITHOUT A CERTAIN NOBODY.
THE FEELING'S MUTUAL, KID...
YOU REMIND ME OF WHY I NEVER WANTED KIDS OF MY OWN!
CAREFUL, ZEKE...
YEAH, DODOHEAD, SHE'S A MOTHER! DON'T MAKE HER CHOOSE BETWEEN US!
GB Trudeau

1/4/96

2/7/96

2/9/96

2/19/96

2/20/96

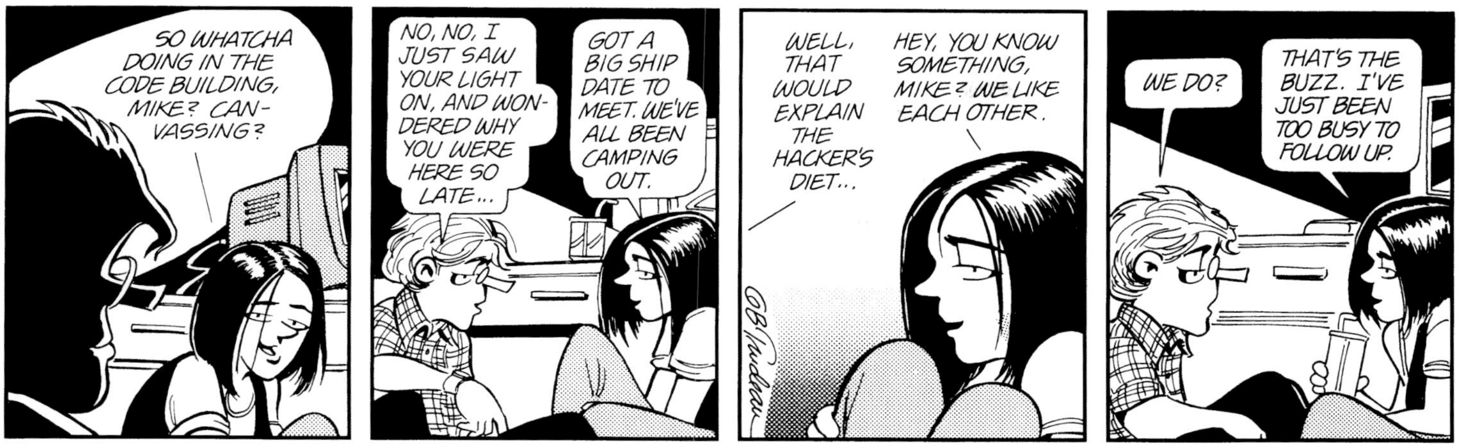
SO WHATCHA DOING IN THE CODE BUILDING, MIKE? CAN-VASSING?
NO, NO, I JUST SAW YOUR LIGHT ON, AND WON-DERED WHY YOU WERE HERE SO LATE...
GOT A BIG SHIP DATE TO MEET. WE'VE ALL BEEN CAMPING OUT.
WELL, THAT WOULD EXPLAIN THE HACKER'S DIET...
HEY, YOU KNOW SOMETHING, MIKE? WE LIKE EACH OTHER.
WE DO?
THAT'S THE BUZZ. I'VE JUST BEEN TOO BUSY TO FOLLOW UP.
GB Trudeau

2/22/96

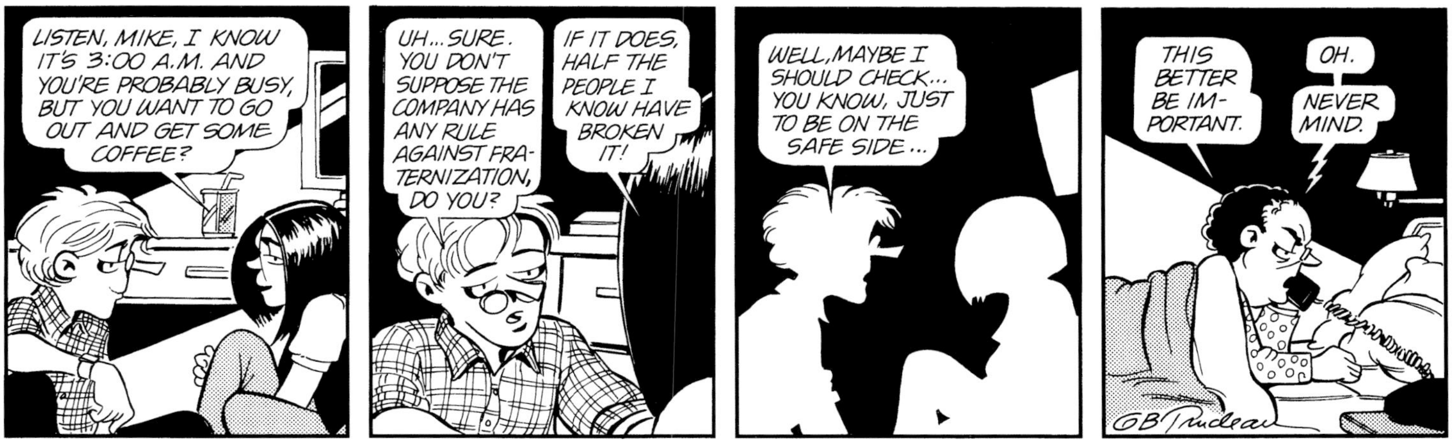
LISTEN, MIKE, I KNOW IT'S 3:00 A.M. AND YOU'RE PROBABLY BUSY, BUT YOU WANT TO GO OUT AND GET SOME COFFEE?
UH... SURE. YOU DON'T SUPPOSE THE COMPANY HAS ANY RULE AGAINST FRA-TERNIZATION, DO YOU?
IF IT DOES, HALF THE PEOPLE I KNOW HAVE BROKEN IT!
WELL, MAYBE I SHOULD CHECK... YOU KNOW, JUST TO BE ON THE SAFE SIDE...
THIS BETTER BE IM-PORTANT.
OH.
NEVER MIND.
GB Trudeau

2/23/96

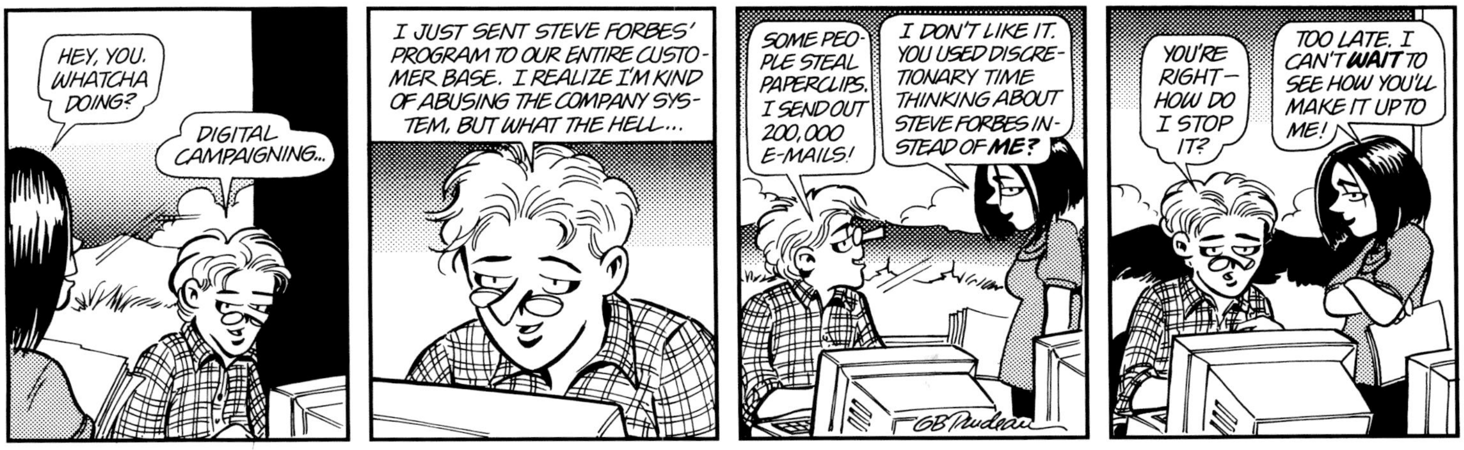
HEY, YOU. WHATCHA DOING?
DIGITAL CAMPAIGNING...
I JUST SENT STEVE FORBES' PROGRAM TO OUR ENTIRE CUSTO-MER BASE. I REALIZE I'M KIND OF ABUSING THE COMPANY SYS-TEM, BUT WHAT THE HELL...
SOME PEO-PLE STEAL PAPERCLIPS. I SEND OUT 200,000 E-MAILS!
I DON'T LIKE IT. YOU USED DISCRE-TIONARY TIME THINKING ABOUT STEVE FORBES IN-STEAD OF ME?
YOU'RE RIGHT— HOW DO I STOP IT?
TOO LATE. I CAN'T WAIT TO SEE HOW YOU'LL MAKE IT UP TO ME!
GB Trudeau

3/11/96

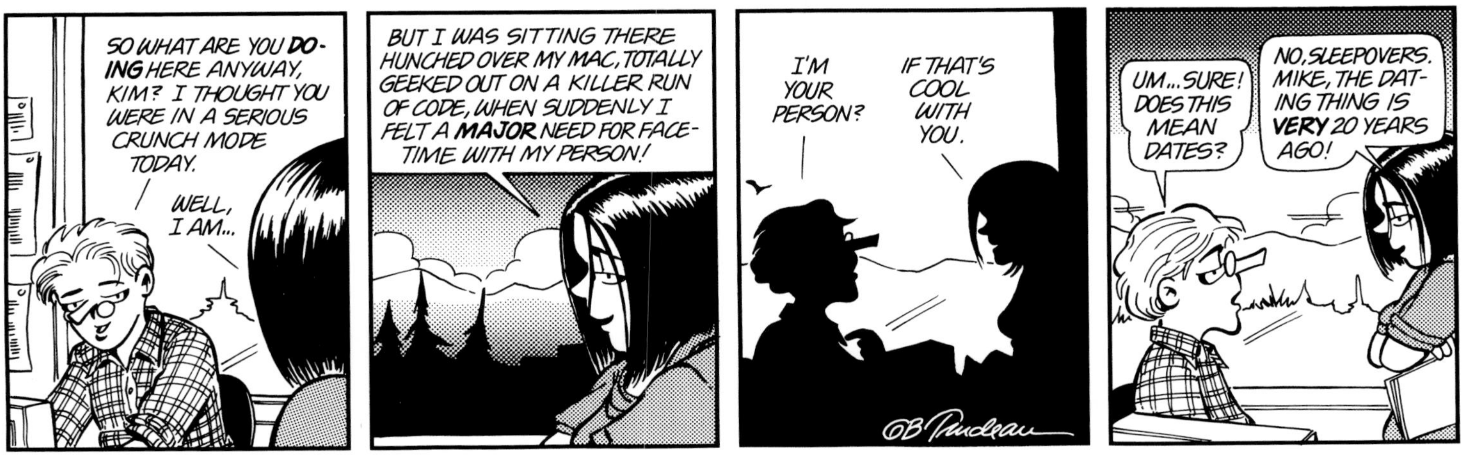
SO WHAT ARE YOU DO-ING HERE ANYWAY, KIM? I THOUGHT YOU WERE IN A SERIOUS CRUNCH MODE TODAY.
WELL, I AM...
BUT I WAS SITTING THERE HUNCHED OVER MY MAC, TOTALLY GEEKED OUT ON A KILLER RUN OF CODE, WHEN SUDDENLY I FELT A MAJOR NEED FOR FACE-TIME WITH MY PERSON!
I'M YOUR PERSON?
IF THAT'S COOL WITH YOU.
UM... SURE! DOES THIS MEAN DATES?
NO, SLEEPOVERS. MIKE, THE DAT-ING THING IS VERY 20 YEARS AGO!
GB Trudeau

3/13/96

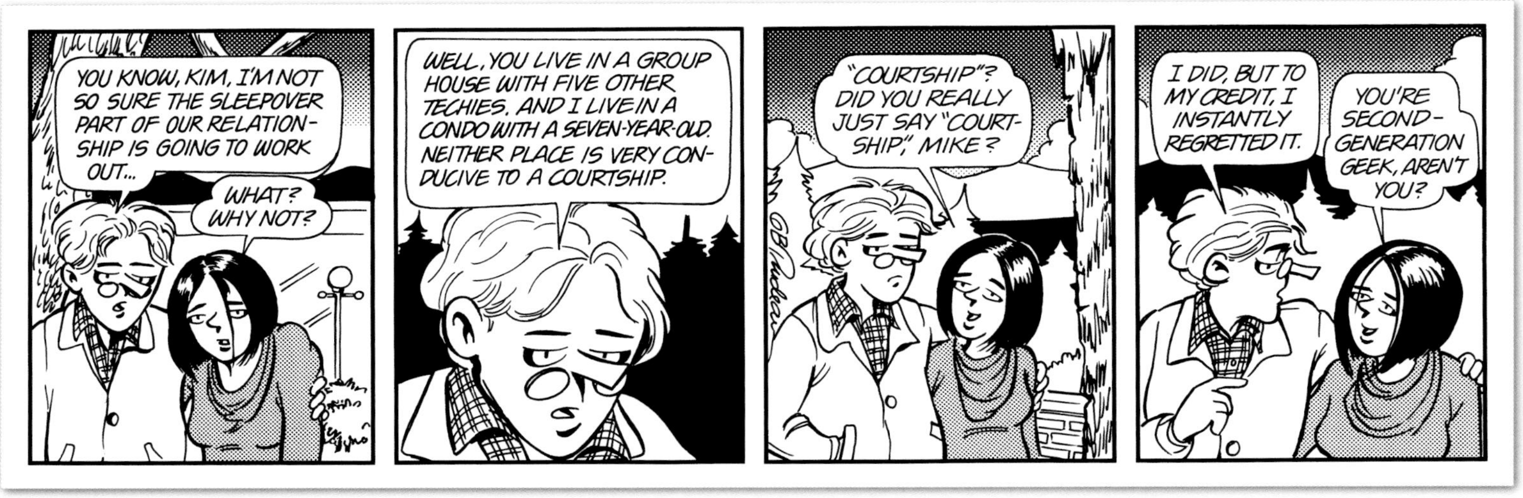
YOU KNOW, KIM, I'M NOT SO SURE THE SLEEPOVER PART OF OUR RELATIONSHIP IS GOING TO WORK OUT...
WHAT? WHY NOT?
WELL, YOU LIVE IN A GROUP HOUSE WITH FIVE OTHER TECHIES. AND I LIVE IN A CONDO WITH A SEVEN-YEAR-OLD. NEITHER PLACE IS VERY CONDUCIVE TO A COURTSHIP.
"COURTSHIP"? DID YOU REALLY JUST SAY "COURTSHIP," MIKE?
I DID, BUT TO MY CREDIT, I INSTANTLY REGRETTED IT.
YOU'RE SECOND-GENERATION GEEK, AREN'T YOU?

3/16/96

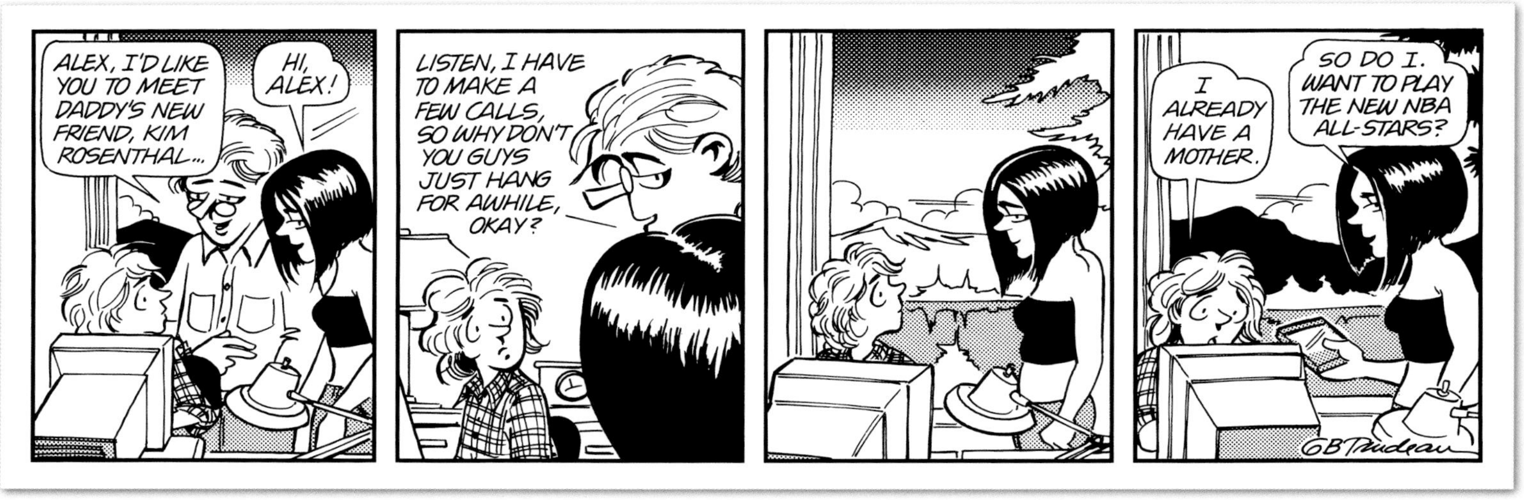
ALEX, I'D LIKE YOU TO MEET DADDY'S NEW FRIEND, KIM ROSENTHAL...
HI, ALEX!
LISTEN, I HAVE TO MAKE A FEW CALLS, SO WHY DON'T YOU GUYS JUST HANG FOR AWHILE, OKAY?
I ALREADY HAVE A MOTHER.
SO DO I. WANT TO PLAY THE NEW NBA ALL-STARS?

3/18/96

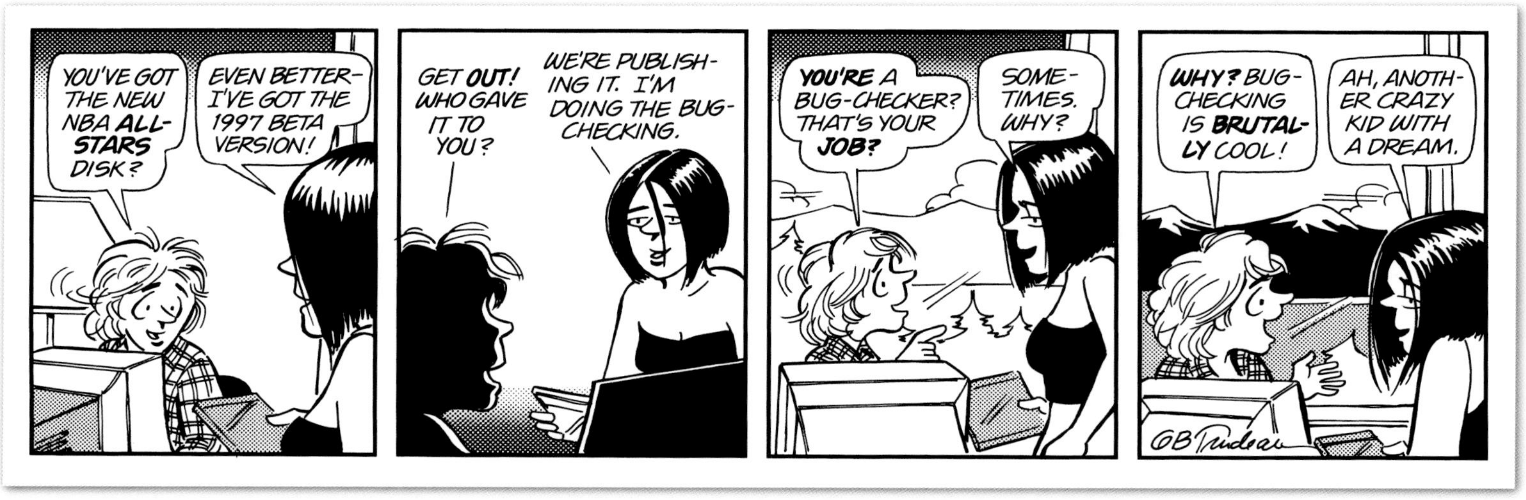
YOU'VE GOT THE NEW NBA ALL-STARS DISK?
EVEN BETTER—I'VE GOT THE 1997 BETA VERSION!
GET OUT! WHO GAVE IT TO YOU?
WE'RE PUBLISHING IT. I'M DOING THE BUG-CHECKING.
YOU'RE A BUG-CHECKER? THAT'S YOUR JOB?
SOMETIMES. WHY?
WHY? BUG-CHECKING IS BRUTALLY COOL!
AH, ANOTHER CRAZY KID WITH A DREAM.

3/19/96

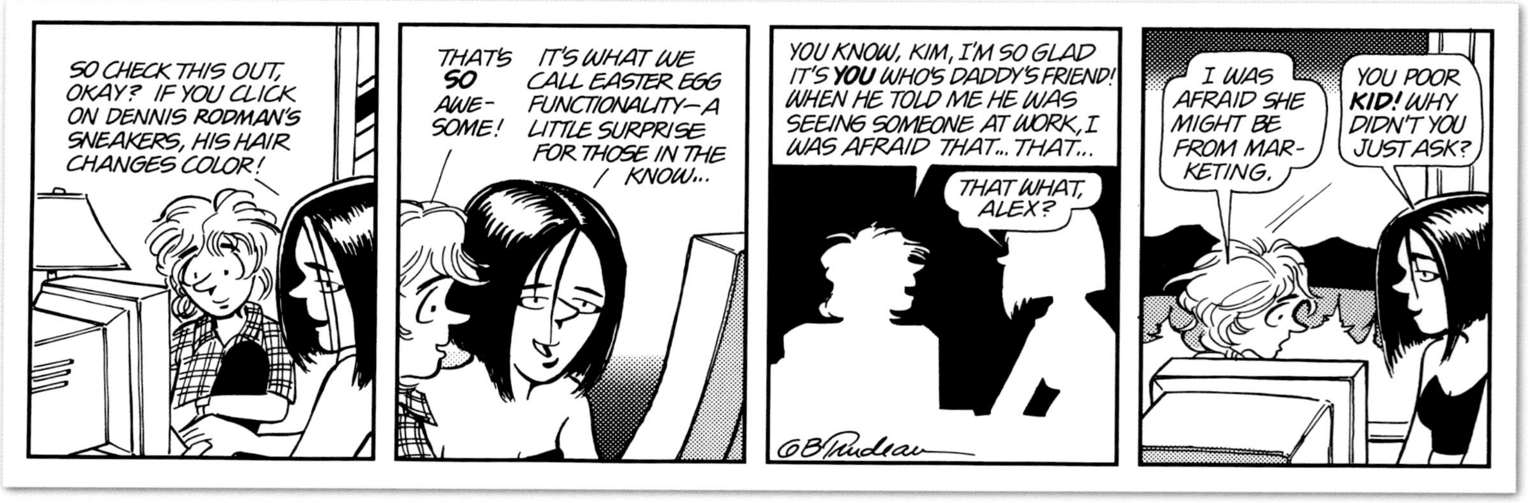
SO CHECK THIS OUT, OKAY? IF YOU CLICK ON DENNIS RODMAN'S SNEAKERS, HIS HAIR CHANGES COLOR!
THAT'S SO AWESOME!
IT'S WHAT WE CALL EASTER EGG FUNCTIONALITY—A LITTLE SURPRISE FOR THOSE IN THE KNOW...
YOU KNOW, KIM, I'M SO GLAD IT'S YOU WHO'S DADDY'S FRIEND! WHEN HE TOLD ME HE WAS SEEING SOMEONE AT WORK, I WAS AFRAID THAT... THAT...
THAT WHAT, ALEX?
I WAS AFRAID SHE MIGHT BE FROM MARKETING.
YOU POOR KID! WHY DIDN'T YOU JUST ASK?

3/20/96

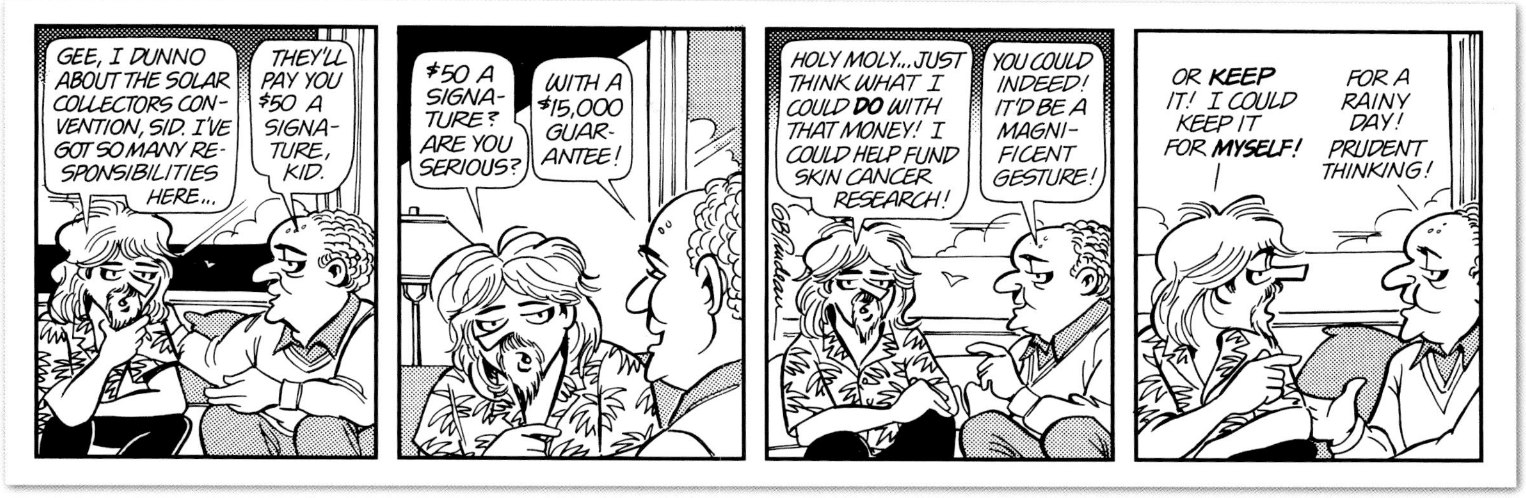
GEE, I DUNNO ABOUT THE SOLAR COLLECTORS CONVENTION, SID. I'VE GOT SO MANY RESPONSIBILITIES HERE...
THEY'LL PAY YOU $50 A SIGNATURE, KID.
$50 A SIGNATURE? ARE YOU SERIOUS?
WITH A $15,000 GUARANTEE!
HOLY MOLY... JUST THINK WHAT I COULD **DO** WITH THAT MONEY! I COULD HELP FUND SKIN CANCER RESEARCH!
YOU COULD INDEED! IT'D BE A MAGNIFICENT GESTURE!
OR **KEEP** IT! I COULD KEEP IT FOR **MYSELF**!
FOR A RAINY DAY! PRUDENT THINKING!

4/16/96

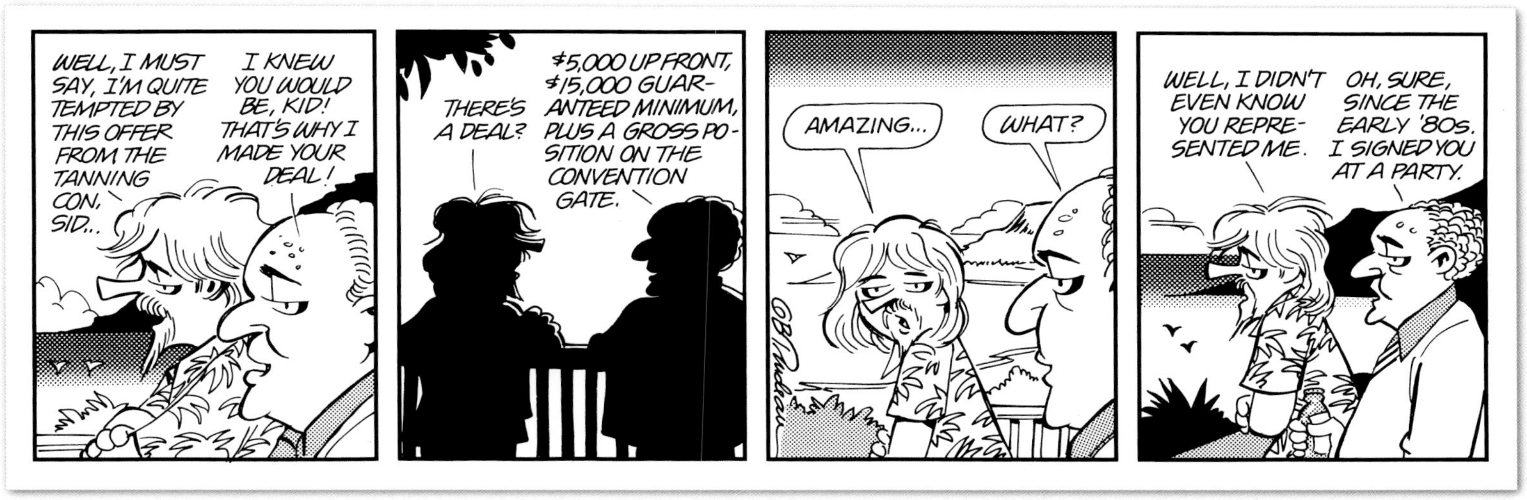
WELL, I MUST SAY, I'M QUITE TEMPTED BY THIS OFFER FROM THE TANNING CON, SID...
I KNEW YOU WOULD BE, KID! THAT'S WHY I MADE YOUR DEAL!
THERE'S A DEAL?
$5,000 UP FRONT, $15,000 GUARANTEED MINIMUM, PLUS A GROSS POSITION ON THE CONVENTION GATE.
AMAZING...
WHAT?
WELL, I DIDN'T EVEN KNOW YOU REPRESENTED ME.
OH, SURE, SINCE THE EARLY '80S. I SIGNED YOU AT A PARTY.

4/17/96

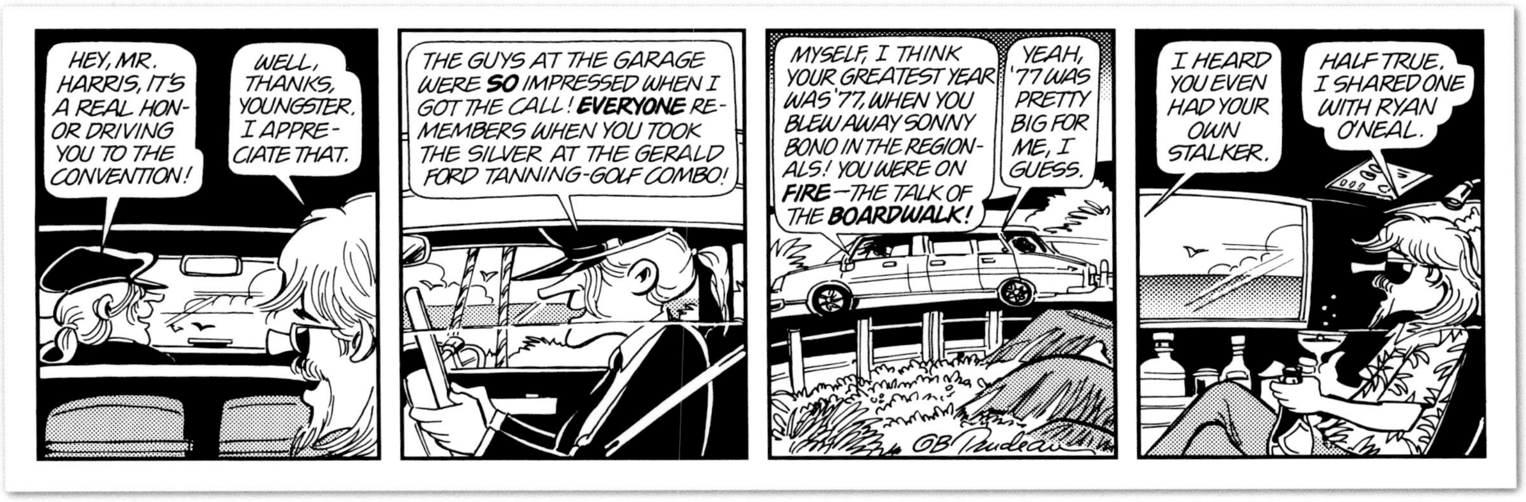
HEY, MR. HARRIS, IT'S A REAL HONOR DRIVING YOU TO THE CONVENTION!
WELL, THANKS, YOUNGSTER. I APPRECIATE THAT.
THE GUYS AT THE GARAGE WERE **SO** IMPRESSED WHEN I GOT THE CALL! **EVERYONE** REMEMBERS WHEN YOU TOOK THE SILVER AT THE GERALD FORD TANNING-GOLF COMBO!
MYSELF, I THINK YOUR GREATEST YEAR WAS '77, WHEN YOU BLEW AWAY SONNY BONO IN THE REGIONALS! YOU WERE ON **FIRE**—THE TALK OF THE **BOARDWALK**!
YEAH, '77 WAS PRETTY BIG FOR ME, I GUESS.
I HEARD YOU EVEN HAD YOUR OWN STALKER.
HALF TRUE. I SHARED ONE WITH RYAN O'NEAL.

4/19/96

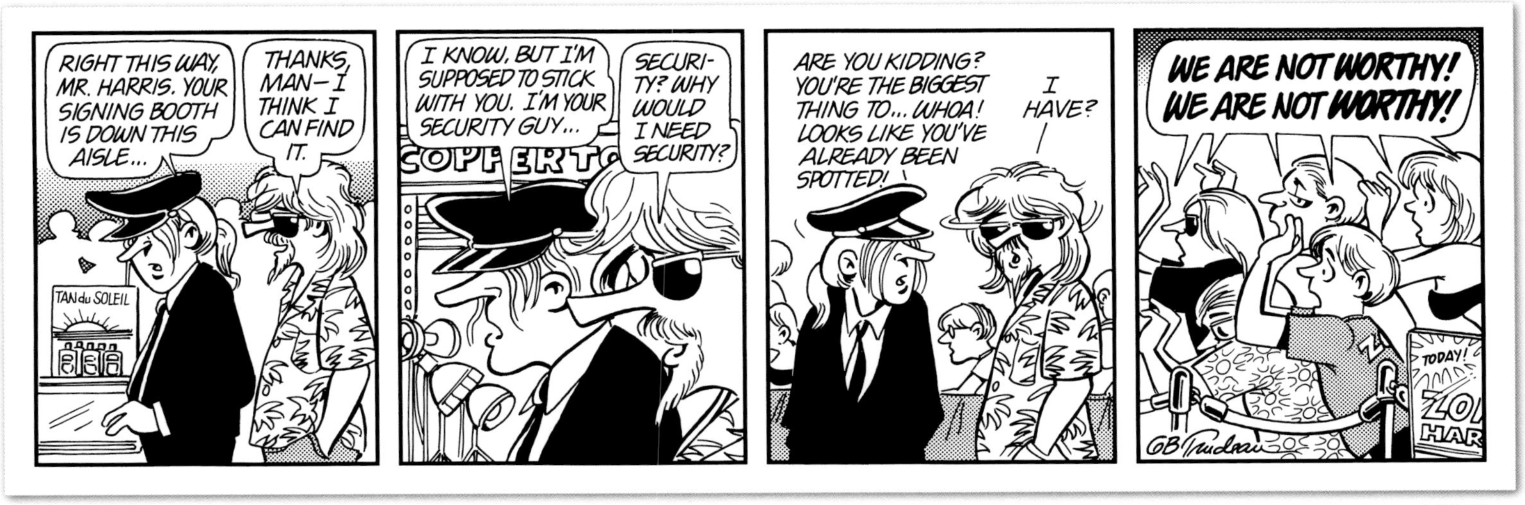
RIGHT THIS WAY, MR. HARRIS. YOUR SIGNING BOOTH IS DOWN THIS AISLE...
THANKS, MAN—I THINK I CAN FIND IT.
TAN du SOLEIL
I KNOW, BUT I'M SUPPOSED TO STICK WITH YOU. I'M YOUR SECURITY GUY...
SECURITY? WHY WOULD I NEED SECURITY?
ARE YOU KIDDING? YOU'RE THE BIGGEST THING TO... WHOA! LOOKS LIKE YOU'VE ALREADY BEEN SPOTTED!
I HAVE?
WE ARE NOT WORTHY! WE ARE NOT WORTHY!
TODAY!

4/22/96

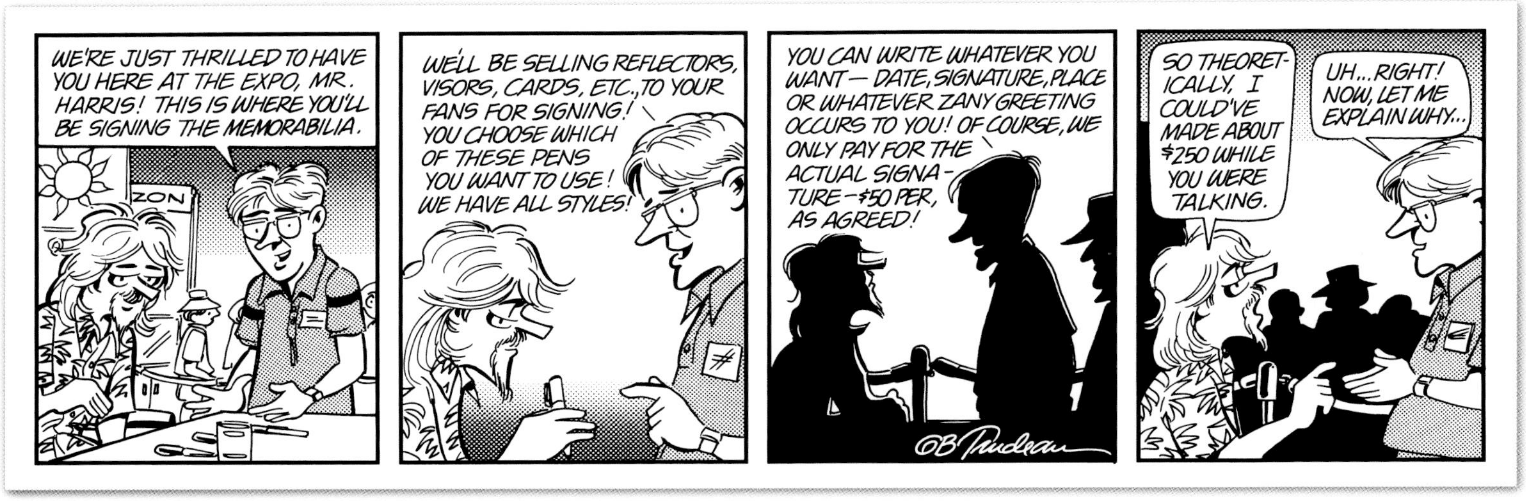
WE'RE JUST THRILLED TO HAVE YOU HERE AT THE EXPO, MR. HARRIS! THIS IS WHERE YOU'LL BE SIGNING THE MEMORABILIA.
WE'LL BE SELLING REFLECTORS, VISORS, CARDS, ETC., TO YOUR FANS FOR SIGNING! YOU CHOOSE WHICH OF THESE PENS YOU WANT TO USE! WE HAVE ALL STYLES!
YOU CAN WRITE WHATEVER YOU WANT — DATE, SIGNATURE, PLACE OR WHATEVER ZANY GREETING OCCURS TO YOU! OF COURSE, WE ONLY PAY FOR THE ACTUAL SIGNATURE — $50 PER, AS AGREED!
SO THEORETICALLY, I COULD'VE MADE ABOUT $250 WHILE YOU WERE TALKING.
UH... RIGHT! NOW, LET ME EXPLAIN WHY...

4/23/96

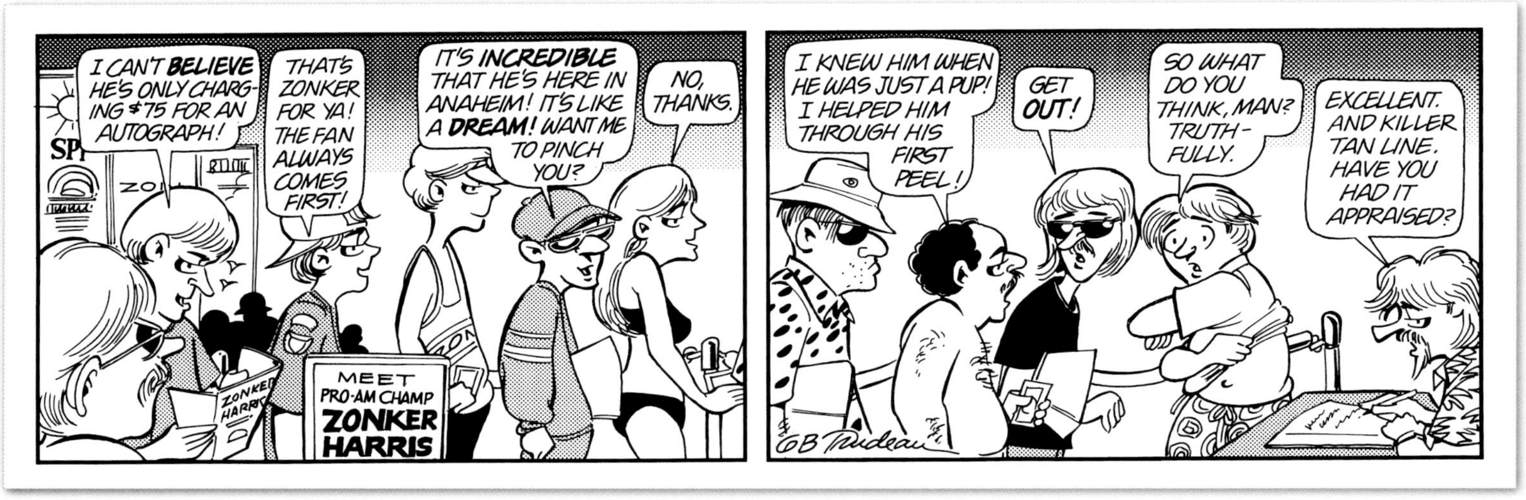
I CAN'T BELIEVE HE'S ONLY CHARGING $75 FOR AN AUTOGRAPH!
THAT'S ZONKER FOR YA! THE FAN ALWAYS COMES FIRST!
IT'S INCREDIBLE THAT HE'S HERE IN ANAHEIM! IT'S LIKE A DREAM! WANT ME TO PINCH YOU?
NO, THANKS.
MEET PRO-AM CHAMP ZONKER HARRIS
I KNEW HIM WHEN HE WAS JUST A PUP! I HELPED HIM THROUGH HIS FIRST PEEL!
GET OUT!
SO WHAT DO YOU THINK, MAN? TRUTHFULLY.
EXCELLENT. AND KILLER TAN LINE. HAVE YOU HAD IT APPRAISED?

4/24/96

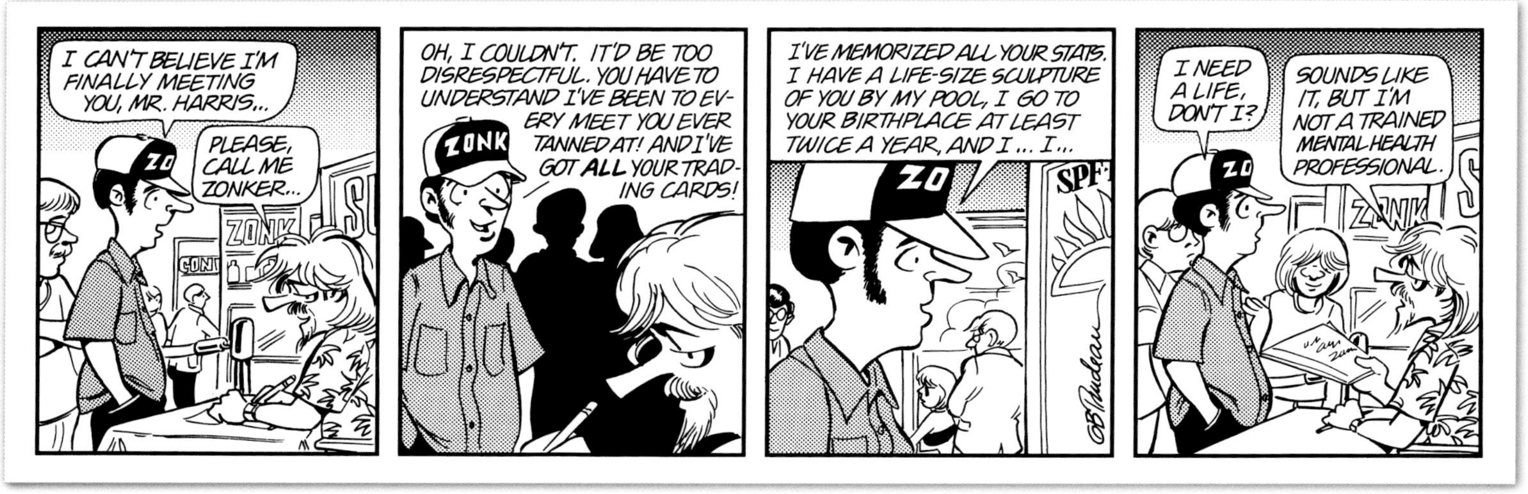
I CAN'T BELIEVE I'M FINALLY MEETING YOU, MR. HARRIS...
PLEASE, CALL ME ZONKER...
OH, I COULDN'T. IT'D BE TOO DISRESPECTFUL. YOU HAVE TO UNDERSTAND I'VE BEEN TO EVERY MEET YOU EVER TANNED AT! AND I'VE GOT ALL YOUR TRADING CARDS!
I'VE MEMORIZED ALL YOUR STATS. I HAVE A LIFE-SIZE SCULPTURE OF YOU BY MY POOL, I GO TO YOUR BIRTHPLACE AT LEAST TWICE A YEAR, AND I... I...
I NEED A LIFE, DON'T I?
SOUNDS LIKE IT, BUT I'M NOT A TRAINED MENTAL-HEALTH PROFESSIONAL.

4/25/96

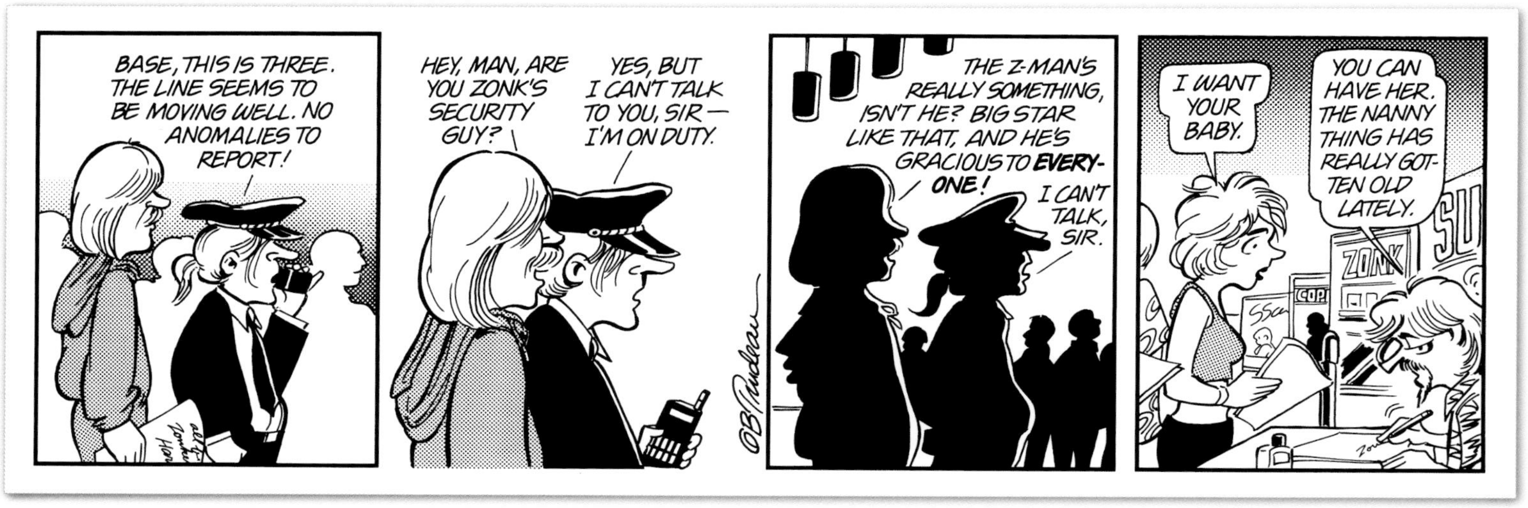
BASE, THIS IS THREE. THE LINE SEEMS TO BE MOVING WELL. NO ANOMALIES TO REPORT!
HEY, MAN, ARE YOU ZONK'S SECURITY GUY?
YES, BUT I CAN'T TALK TO YOU, SIR — I'M ON DUTY.
THE Z-MAN'S REALLY SOMETHING, ISN'T HE? BIG STAR LIKE THAT, AND HE'S GRACIOUS TO EVERYONE!
I CAN'T TALK, SIR.
I WANT YOUR BABY.
YOU CAN HAVE HER. THE NANNY THING HAS REALLY GOTTEN OLD LATELY.

4/27/96

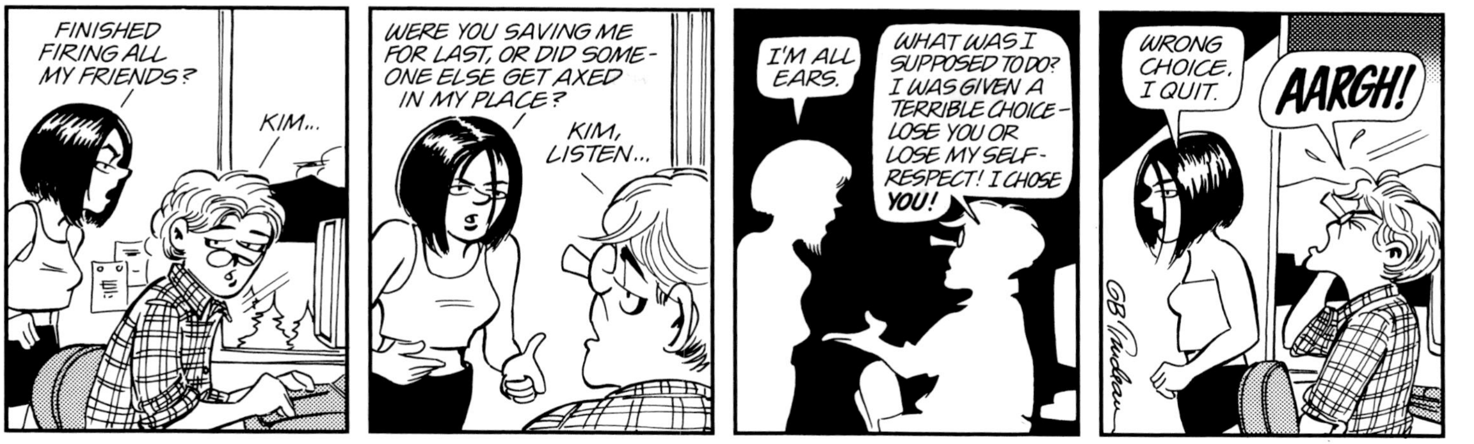
FINISHED FIRING ALL MY FRIENDS?
KIM...
WERE YOU SAVING ME FOR LAST, OR DID SOME-ONE ELSE GET AXED IN MY PLACE?
KIM, LISTEN...
I'M ALL EARS.
WHAT WAS I SUPPOSED TO DO? I WAS GIVEN A TERRIBLE CHOICE - LOSE YOU OR LOSE MY SELF-RESPECT! I CHOSE **YOU**!
WRONG CHOICE. I QUIT.
AARGH!

5/4/96

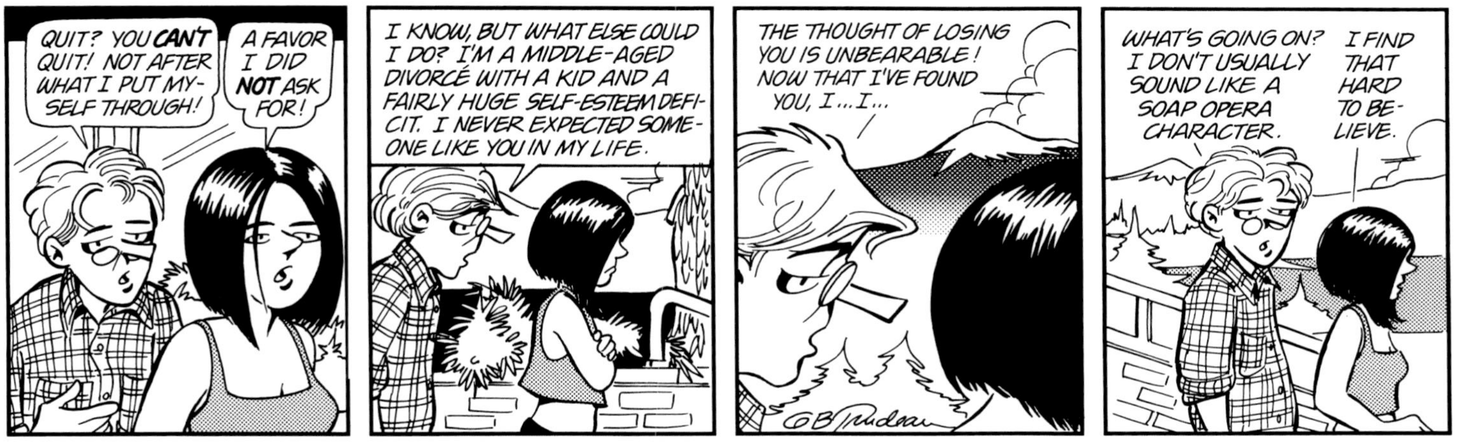
QUIT? YOU **CAN'T** QUIT! NOT AFTER WHAT I PUT MY-SELF THROUGH!
A FAVOR I DID **NOT** ASK FOR!
I KNOW, BUT WHAT ELSE COULD I DO? I'M A MIDDLE-AGED DIVORCÉ WITH A KID AND A FAIRLY HUGE SELF-ESTEEM DEFI-CIT. I NEVER EXPECTED SOME-ONE LIKE YOU IN MY LIFE.
THE THOUGHT OF LOSING YOU IS UNBEARABLE! NOW THAT I'VE FOUND YOU, I... I...
WHAT'S GOING ON? I DON'T USUALLY SOUND LIKE A SOAP OPERA CHARACTER.
I FIND THAT HARD TO BE-LIEVE.

5/6/96

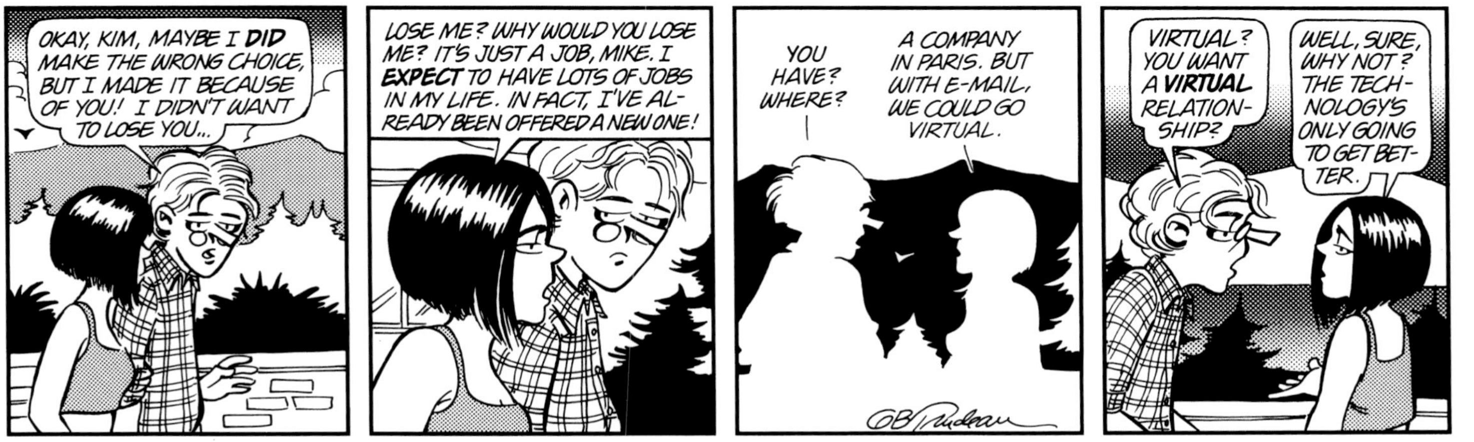
OKAY, KIM, MAYBE I **DID** MAKE THE WRONG CHOICE, BUT I MADE IT BECAUSE OF YOU! I DIDN'T WANT TO LOSE YOU...
LOSE ME? WHY WOULD YOU LOSE ME? IT'S JUST A JOB, MIKE. I **EXPECT** TO HAVE LOTS OF JOBS IN MY LIFE. IN FACT, I'VE AL-READY BEEN OFFERED A NEW ONE!
YOU HAVE? WHERE?
A COMPANY IN PARIS. BUT WITH E-MAIL, WE COULD GO VIRTUAL.
VIRTUAL? YOU WANT A **VIRTUAL** RELATION-SHIP?
WELL, SURE, WHY NOT? THE TECH-NOLOGY'S ONLY GOING TO GET BET-TER.

5/7/96

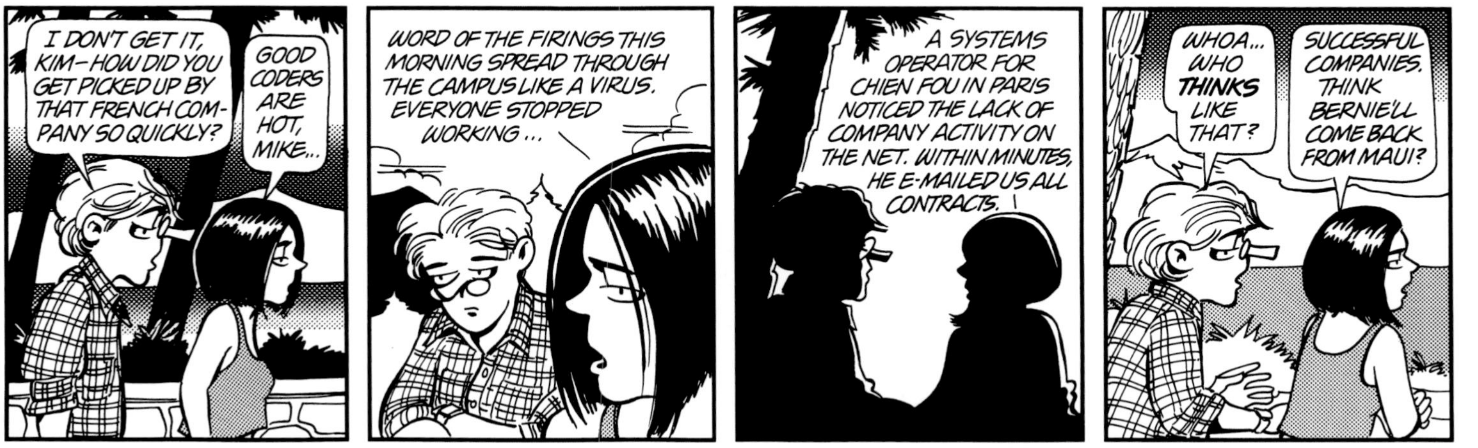
I DON'T GET IT, KIM—HOW DID YOU GET PICKED UP BY THAT FRENCH COM-PANY SO QUICKLY?
GOOD CODERS ARE HOT, MIKE...
WORD OF THE FIRINGS THIS MORNING SPREAD THROUGH THE CAMPUS LIKE A VIRUS. EVERYONE STOPPED WORKING...
A SYSTEMS OPERATOR FOR CHIEN FOU IN PARIS NOTICED THE LACK OF COMPANY ACTIVITY ON THE NET. WITHIN MINUTES, HE E-MAILED US ALL CONTRACTS.
WHOA... WHO **THINKS** LIKE THAT?
SUCCESSFUL COMPANIES. THINK BERNIE'LL COME BACK FROM MAUI?

5/8/96

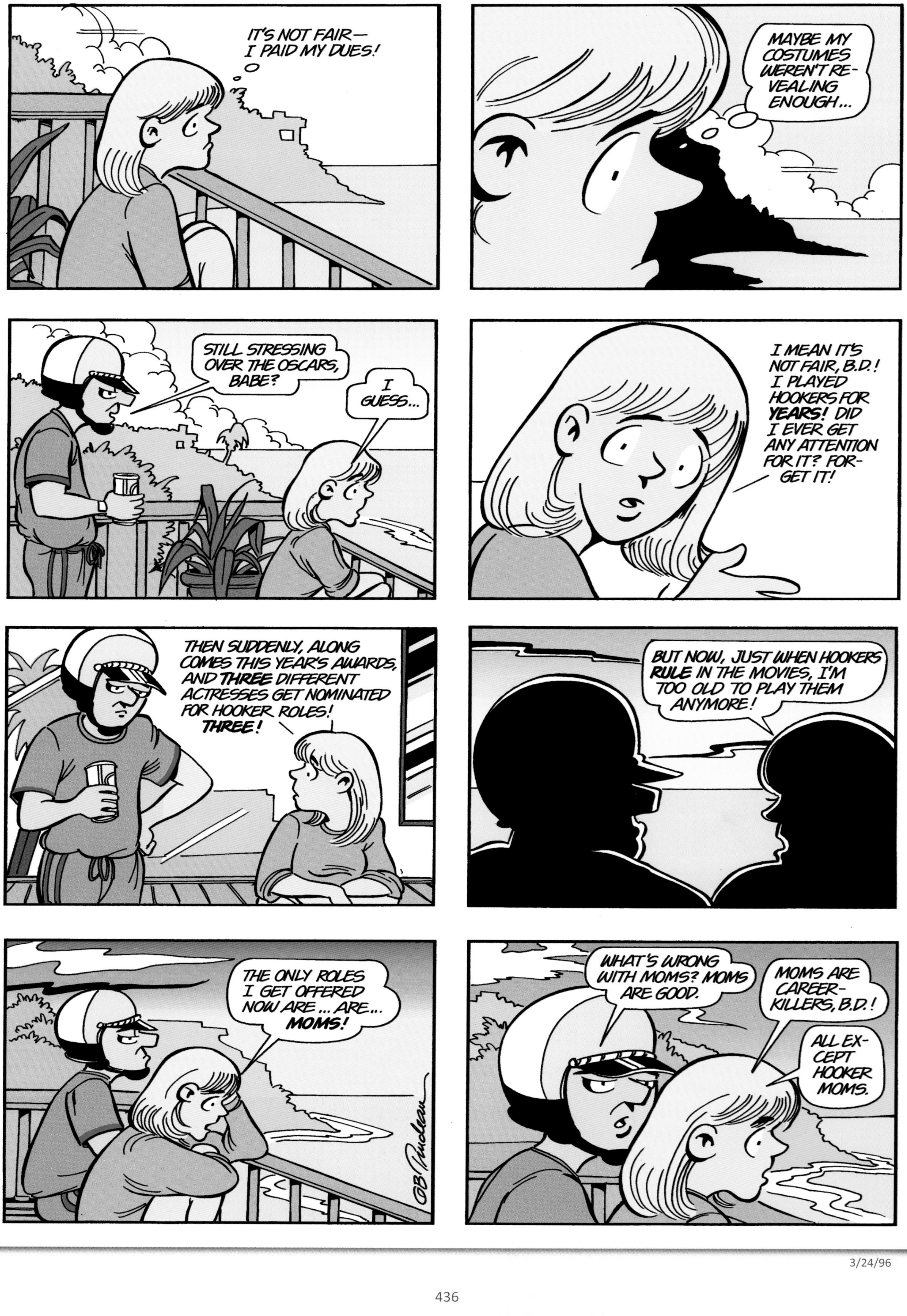
IT'S NOT FAIR—
I PAID MY DUES!
MAYBE MY COSTUMES WEREN'T RE-VEALING ENOUGH...
STILL STRESSING OVER THE OSCARS, BABE?
I GUESS...
I MEAN IT'S NOT FAIR, B.D.! I PLAYED HOOKERS FOR **YEARS!** DID I EVER GET ANY ATTENTION FOR IT? FOR-GET IT!
THEN SUDDENLY, ALONG COMES THIS YEAR'S AWARDS, AND **THREE** DIFFERENT ACTRESSES GET NOMINATED FOR HOOKER ROLES! **THREE!**
BUT NOW, JUST WHEN HOOKERS **RULE** IN THE MOVIES, I'M TOO OLD TO PLAY THEM ANYMORE!
THE ONLY ROLES I GET OFFERED NOW ARE ... ARE... **MOMS!**
WHAT'S WRONG WITH MOMS? MOMS ARE GOOD.
MOMS ARE CAREER-KILLERS, B.D.!
ALL EX-CEPT HOOKER MOMS.

3/24/96

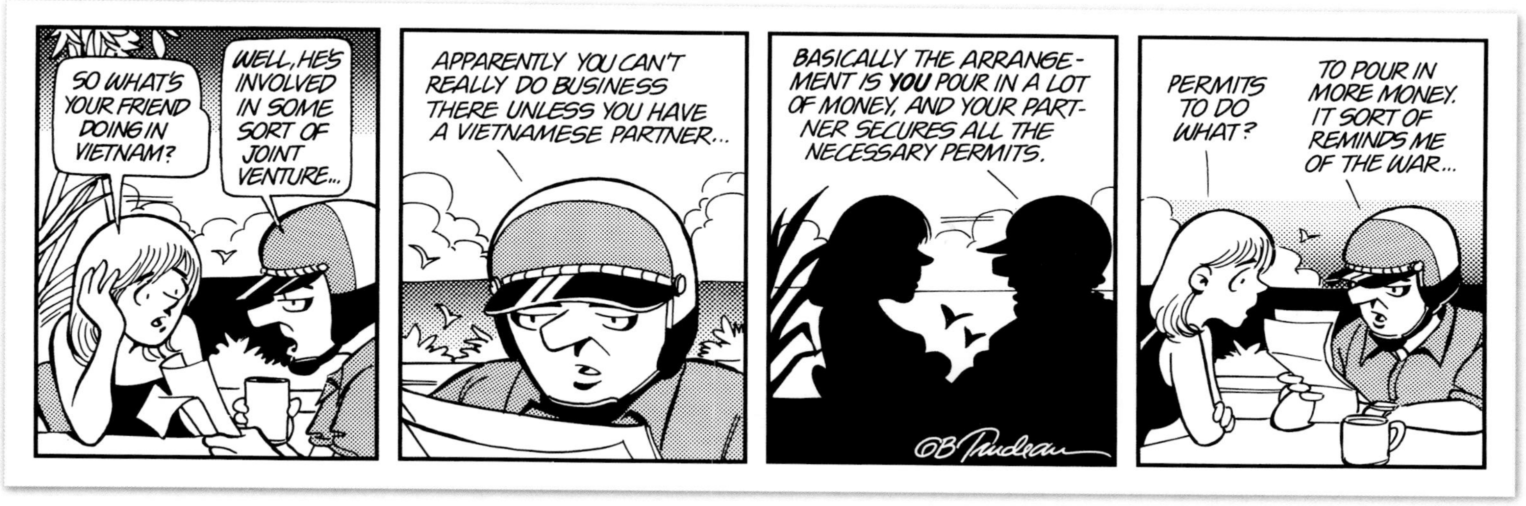
SO WHAT'S YOUR FRIEND DOING IN VIETNAM?
WELL, HE'S INVOLVED IN SOME SORT OF JOINT VENTURE...
APPARENTLY YOU CAN'T REALLY DO BUSINESS THERE UNLESS YOU HAVE A VIETNAMESE PARTNER...
BASICALLY THE ARRANGEMENT IS **YOU** POUR IN A LOT OF MONEY, AND YOUR PARTNER SECURES ALL THE NECESSARY PERMITS.
PERMITS TO DO WHAT?
TO POUR IN MORE MONEY. IT SORT OF REMINDS ME OF THE WAR...

5/29/96

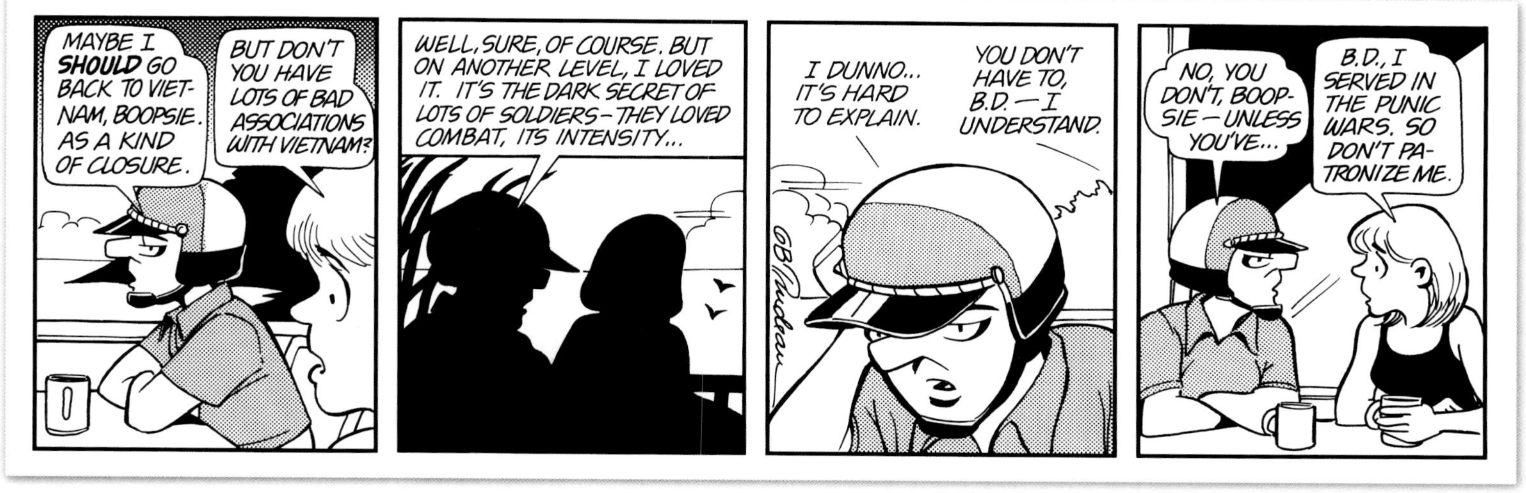
MAYBE I **SHOULD** GO BACK TO VIETNAM, BOOPSIE. AS A KIND OF CLOSURE.
BUT DON'T YOU HAVE LOTS OF BAD ASSOCIATIONS WITH VIETNAM?
WELL, SURE, OF COURSE. BUT ON ANOTHER LEVEL, I LOVED IT. IT'S THE DARK SECRET OF LOTS OF SOLDIERS–THEY LOVED COMBAT, ITS INTENSITY...
I DUNNO... IT'S HARD TO EXPLAIN.
YOU DON'T HAVE TO, B.D.—I UNDERSTAND.
NO, YOU DON'T, BOOPSIE—UNLESS YOU'VE...
B.D., I SERVED IN THE PUNIC WARS. SO DON'T PATRONIZE ME.

6/1/96

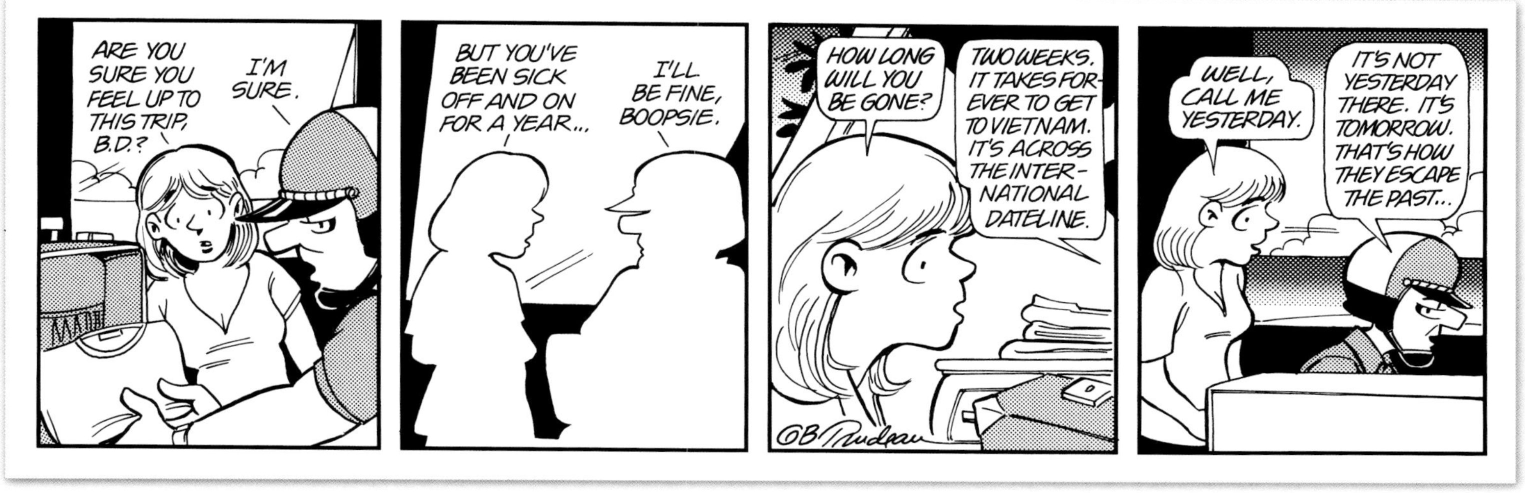
ARE YOU SURE YOU FEEL UP TO THIS TRIP, B.D.?
I'M SURE.
BUT YOU'VE BEEN SICK OFF AND ON FOR A YEAR...
I'LL BE FINE, BOOPSIE.
HOW LONG WILL YOU BE GONE?
TWO WEEKS. IT TAKES FOREVER TO GET TO VIETNAM. IT'S ACROSS THE INTERNATIONAL DATELINE.
WELL, CALL ME YESTERDAY.
IT'S NOT YESTERDAY THERE. IT'S TOMORROW. THAT'S HOW THEY ESCAPE THE PAST...

6/3/96

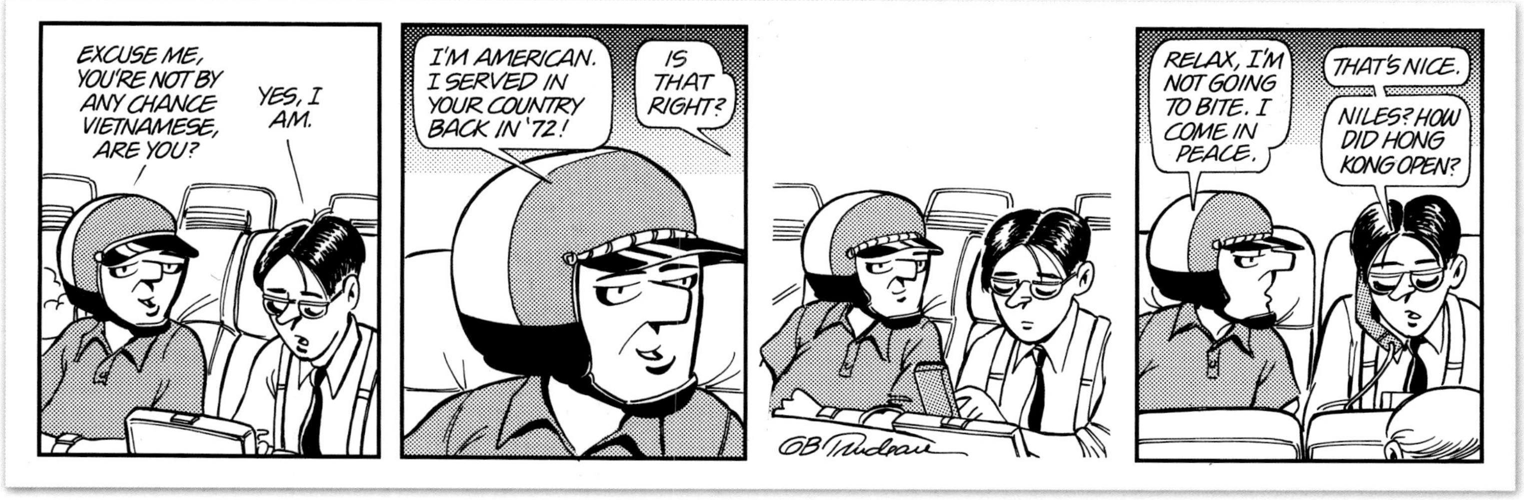
EXCUSE ME, YOU'RE NOT BY ANY CHANCE VIETNAMESE, ARE YOU?
YES, I AM.
I'M AMERICAN. I SERVED IN YOUR COUNTRY BACK IN '72!
IS THAT RIGHT?
RELAX, I'M NOT GOING TO BITE. I COME IN PEACE.
THAT'S NICE.
NILES? HOW DID HONG KONG OPEN?

6/4/96

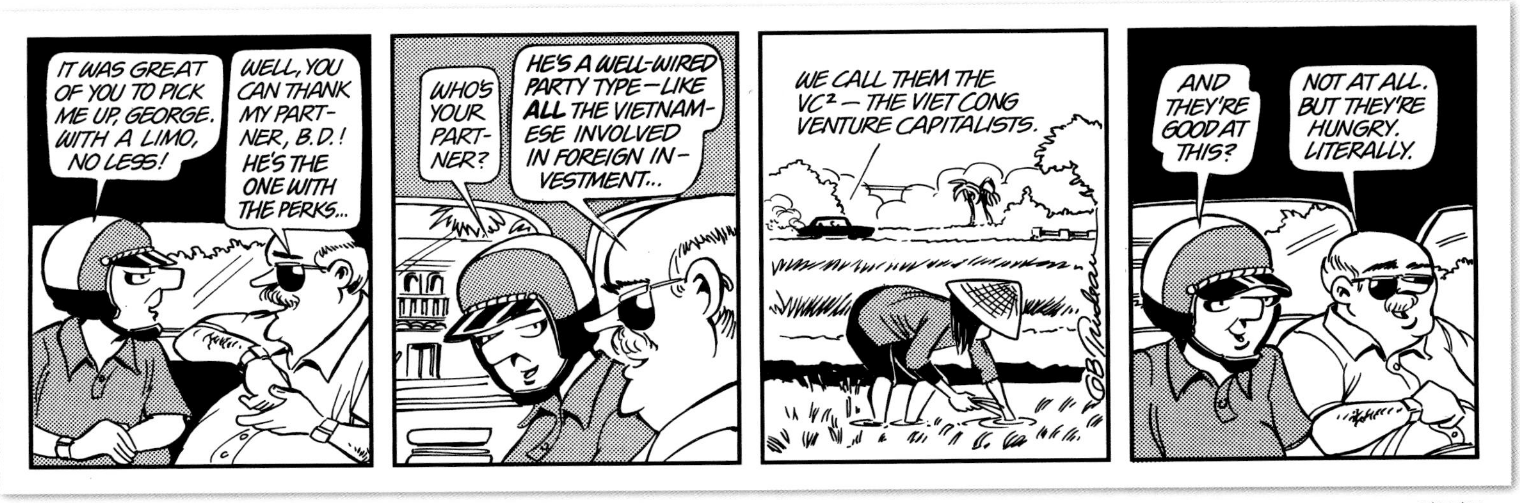
IT WAS GREAT OF YOU TO PICK ME UP, GEORGE. WITH A LIMO, NO LESS!
WELL, YOU CAN THANK MY PART-NER, B.D.! HE'S THE ONE WITH THE PERKS...
WHO'S YOUR PART-NER?
HE'S A WELL-WIRED PARTY TYPE—LIKE ALL THE VIETNAM-ESE INVOLVED IN FOREIGN IN-VESTMENT...
WE CALL THEM THE VC^2—THE VIET CONG VENTURE CAPITALISTS.
AND THEY'RE GOOD AT THIS?
NOT AT ALL. BUT THEY'RE HUNGRY. LITERALLY.
6/10/96

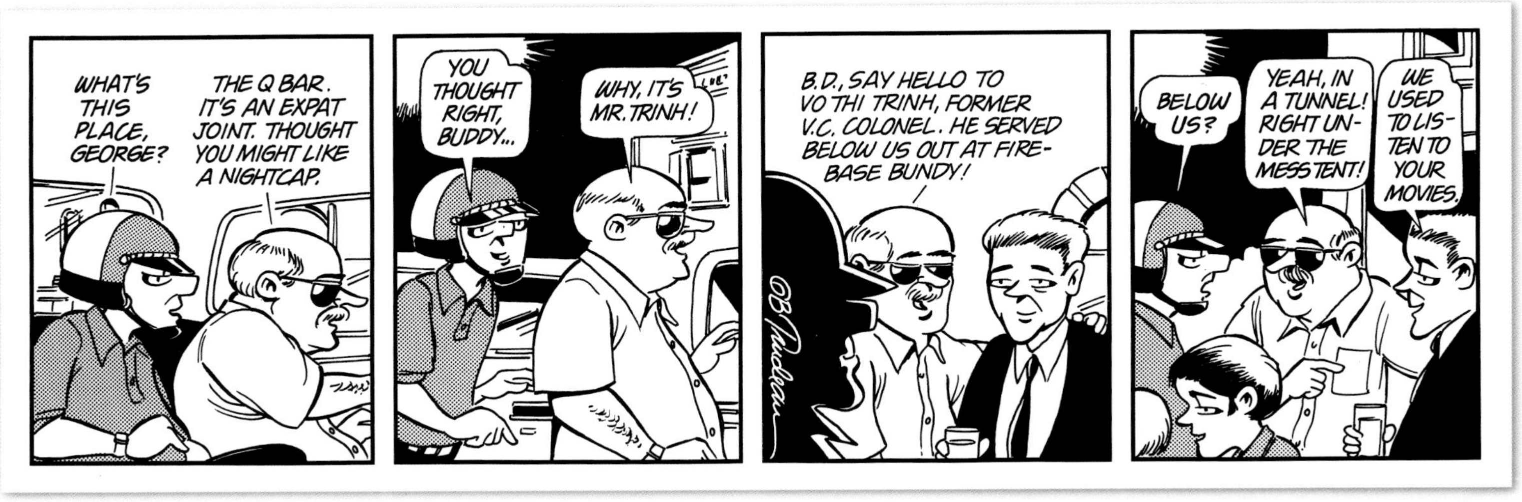
WHAT'S THIS PLACE, GEORGE?
THE Q BAR. IT'S AN EXPAT JOINT. THOUGHT YOU MIGHT LIKE A NIGHTCAP.
YOU THOUGHT RIGHT, BUDDY...
WHY, IT'S MR. TRINH!
B.D., SAY HELLO TO VO THI TRINH, FORMER V.C. COLONEL. HE SERVED BELOW US OUT AT FIRE-BASE BUNDY!
BELOW US?
YEAH, IN A TUNNEL! RIGHT UN-DER THE MESS TENT!
WE USED TO LIS-TEN TO YOUR MOVIES.
6/12/96

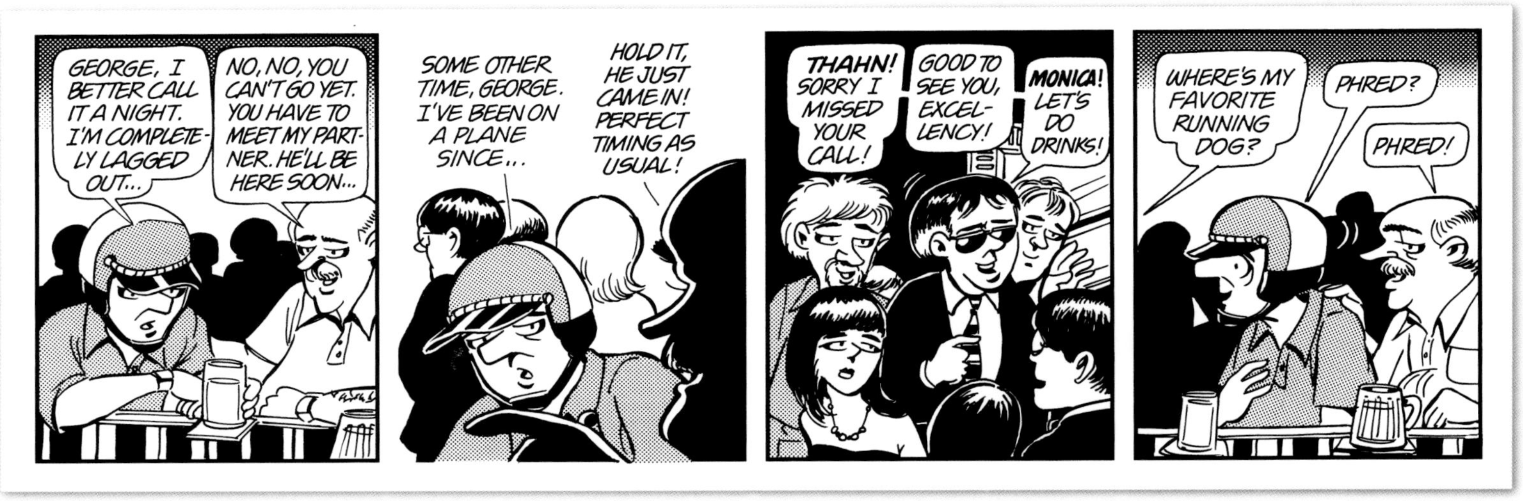
GEORGE, I BETTER CALL IT A NIGHT. I'M COMPLETE-LY LAGGED OUT...
NO, NO, YOU CAN'T GO YET. YOU HAVE TO MEET MY PART-NER. HE'LL BE HERE SOON...
SOME OTHER TIME, GEORGE. I'VE BEEN ON A PLANE SINCE...
HOLD IT, HE JUST CAME IN! PERFECT TIMING AS USUAL!
THAHN! SORRY I MISSED YOUR CALL!
GOOD TO SEE YOU, EXCEL-LENCY!
MONICA! LET'S DO DRINKS!
WHERE'S MY FAVORITE RUNNING DOG?
PHRED?
PHRED!
6/20/96

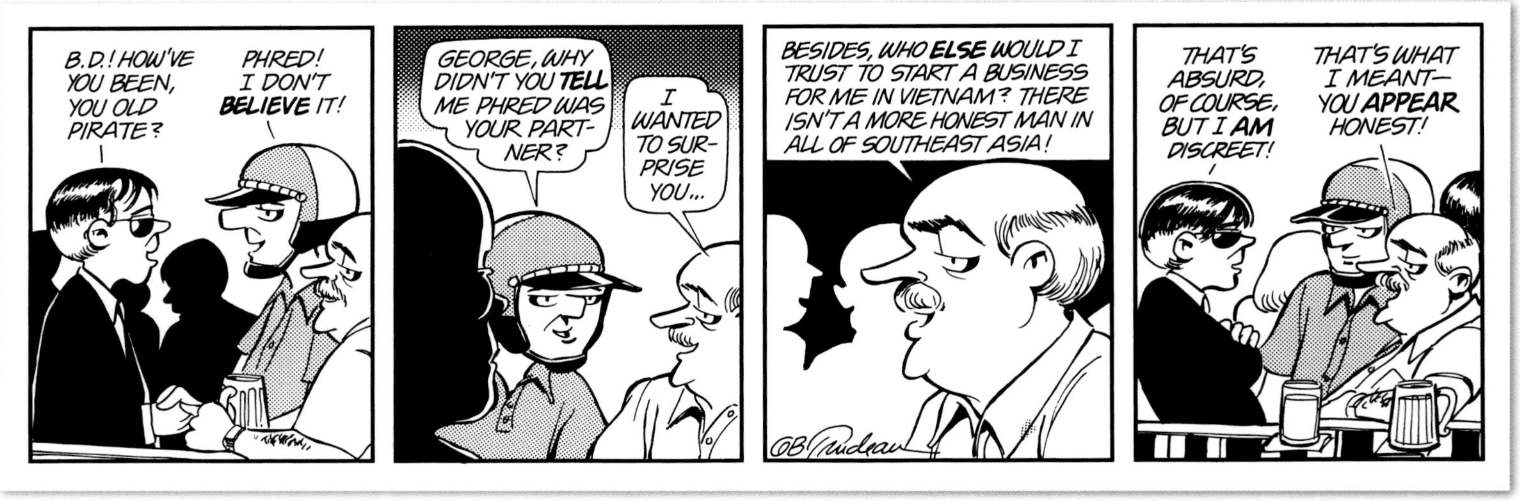
B.D.! HOW'VE YOU BEEN, YOU OLD PIRATE?
PHRED! I DON'T BELIEVE IT!
GEORGE, WHY DIDN'T YOU TELL ME PHRED WAS YOUR PART-NER?
I WANTED TO SUR-PRISE YOU...
BESIDES, WHO ELSE WOULD I TRUST TO START A BUSINESS FOR ME IN VIETNAM? THERE ISN'T A MORE HONEST MAN IN ALL OF SOUTHEAST ASIA!
THAT'S ABSURD, OF COURSE, BUT I AM DISCREET!
THAT'S WHAT I MEANT—YOU APPEAR HONEST!
6/21/96

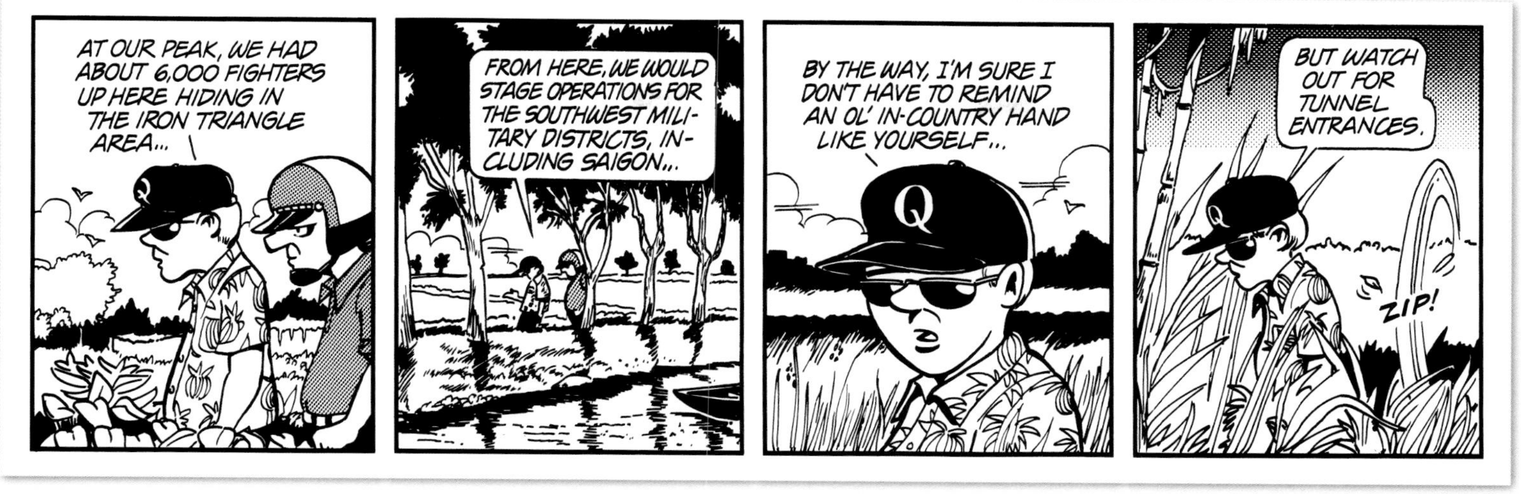
AT OUR PEAK, WE HAD ABOUT 6,000 FIGHTERS UP HERE HIDING IN THE IRON TRIANGLE AREA...
FROM HERE, WE WOULD STAGE OPERATIONS FOR THE SOUTHWEST MILITARY DISTRICTS, INCLUDING SAIGON...
BY THE WAY, I'M SURE I DON'T HAVE TO REMIND AN OL' IN-COUNTRY HAND LIKE YOURSELF...
BUT WATCH OUT FOR TUNNEL ENTRANCES.
ZIP!

6/29/96

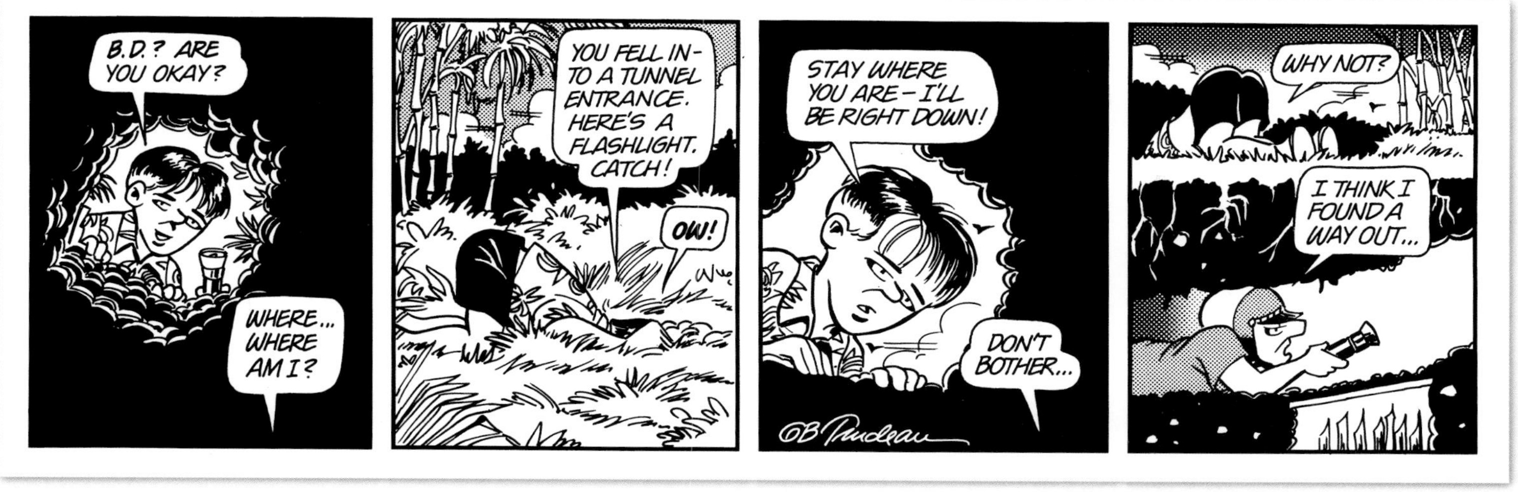
B.D.? ARE YOU OKAY?
WHERE... WHERE AM I?
YOU FELL INTO A TUNNEL ENTRANCE. HERE'S A FLASHLIGHT. CATCH!
OW!
STAY WHERE YOU ARE – I'LL BE RIGHT DOWN!
DON'T BOTHER...
WHY NOT?
I THINK I FOUND A WAY OUT...

7/8/96

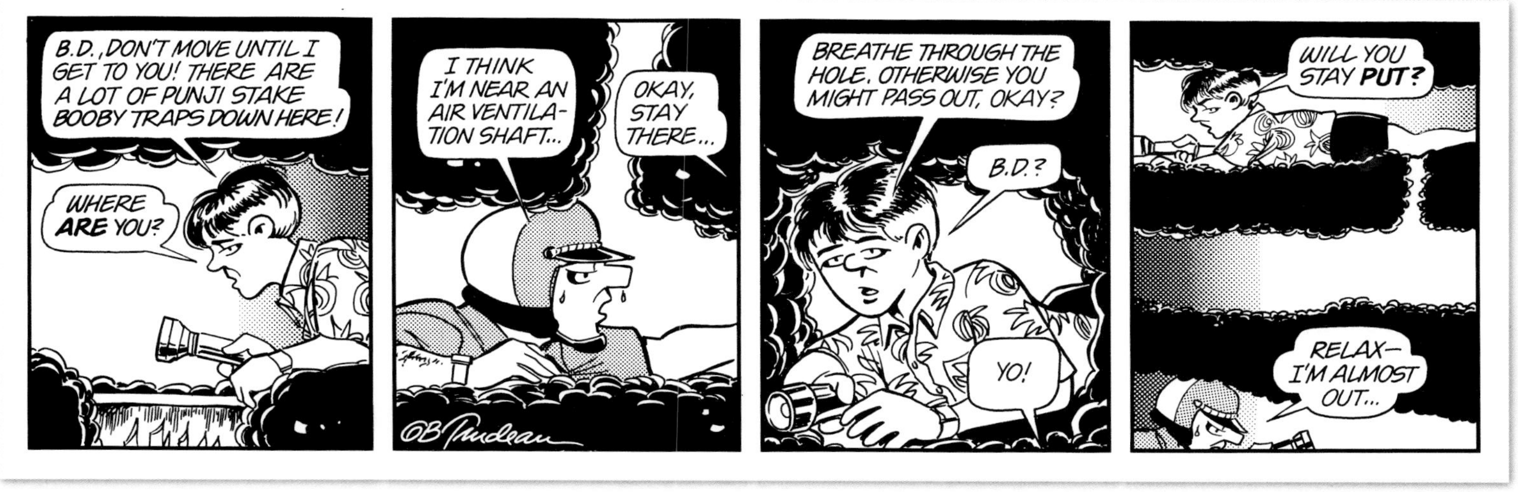
B.D., DON'T MOVE UNTIL I GET TO YOU! THERE ARE A LOT OF PUNJI STAKE BOOBY TRAPS DOWN HERE!
WHERE ARE YOU?
I THINK I'M NEAR AN AIR VENTILATION SHAFT...
OKAY, STAY THERE...
BREATHE THROUGH THE HOLE. OTHERWISE YOU MIGHT PASS OUT, OKAY?
B.D.?
YO!
WILL YOU STAY PUT?
RELAX– I'M ALMOST OUT...

7/9/96

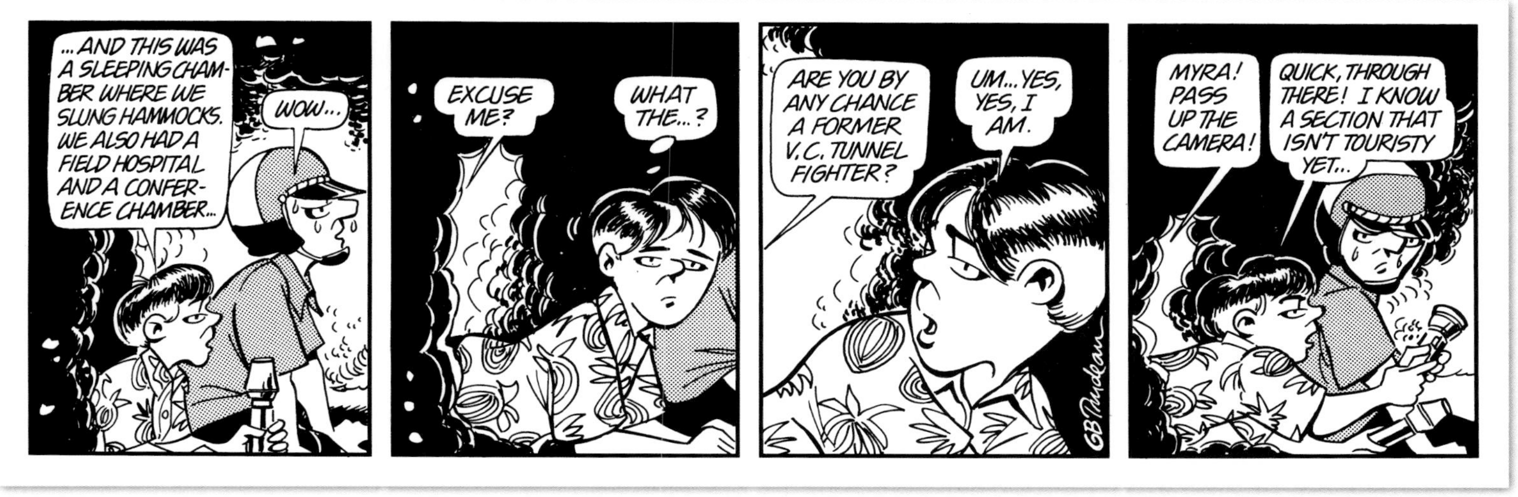
...AND THIS WAS A SLEEPING CHAMBER WHERE WE SLUNG HAMMOCKS. WE ALSO HAD A FIELD HOSPITAL AND A CONFERENCE CHAMBER...
WOW...
EXCUSE ME?
WHAT THE...?
ARE YOU BY ANY CHANCE A FORMER V.C. TUNNEL FIGHTER?
UM... YES, YES, I AM.
MYRA! PASS UP THE CAMERA!
QUICK, THROUGH THERE! I KNOW A SECTION THAT ISN'T TOURISTY YET...

7/12/96

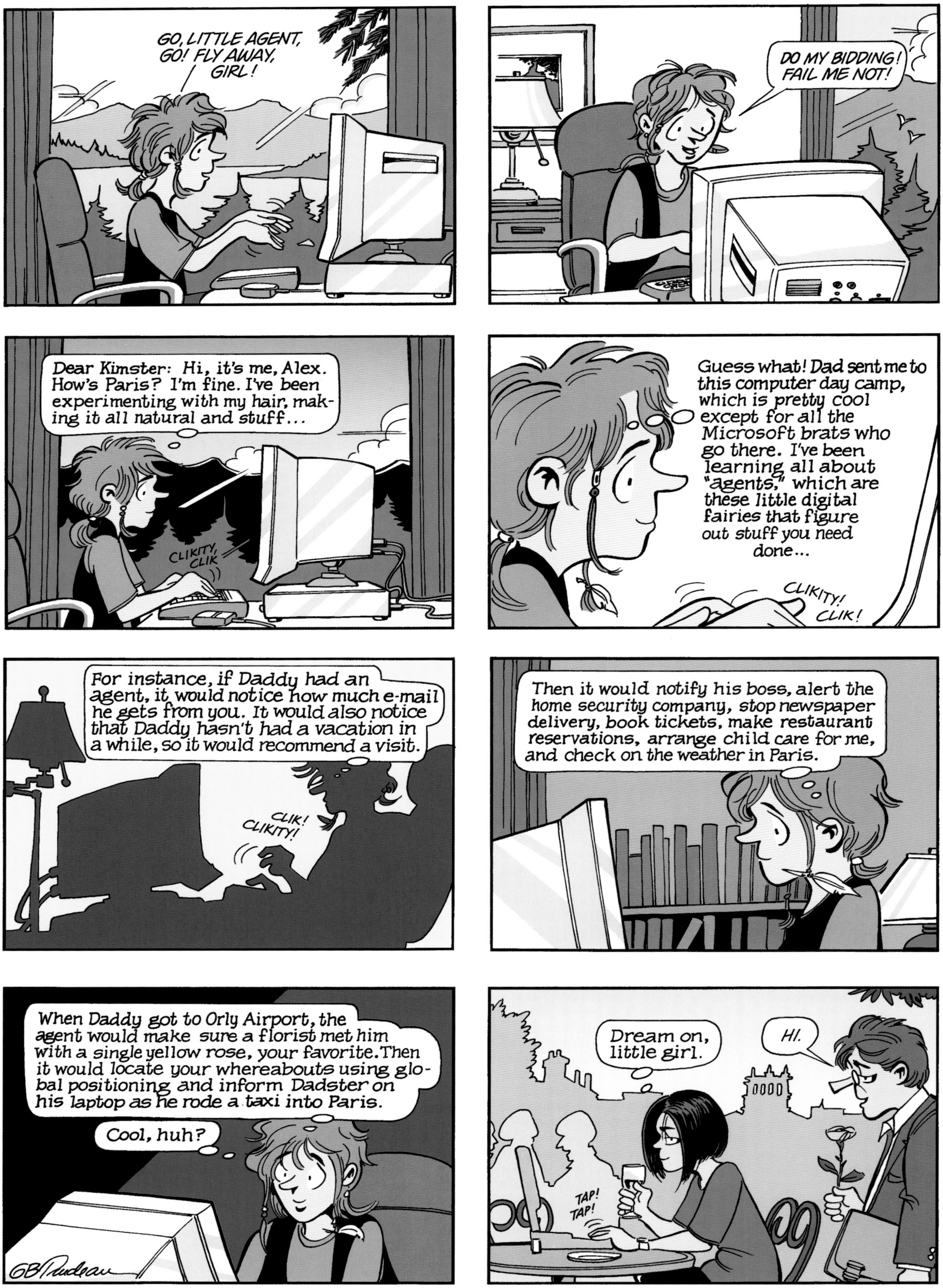
GO, LITTLE AGENT, GO! FLY AWAY, GIRL!
DO MY BIDDING! FAIL ME NOT!
Dear Kimster: Hi, it's me, Alex. How's Paris? I'm fine. I've been experimenting with my hair, making it all natural and stuff...
CLIKITY, CLIK
Guess what! Dad sent me to this computer day camp, which is pretty cool except for all the Microsoft brats who go there. I've been learning all about "agents," which are these little digital fairies that figure out stuff you need done...
CLIKITY! CLIK!
For instance, if Daddy had an agent, it would notice how much e-mail he gets from you. It would also notice that Daddy hasn't had a vacation in a while, so it would recommend a visit.
CLIK! CLIKITY!
Then it would notify his boss, alert the home security company, stop newspaper delivery, book tickets, make restaurant reservations, arrange child care for me, and check on the weather in Paris.
When Daddy got to Orly Airport, the agent would make sure a florist met him with a single yellow rose, your favorite. Then it would locate your whereabouts using global positioning and inform Dadster on his laptop as he rode a taxi into Paris.
Cool, huh?
GBTrudeau
Dream on, little girl.
HI.
TAP! TAP!

8/4/96

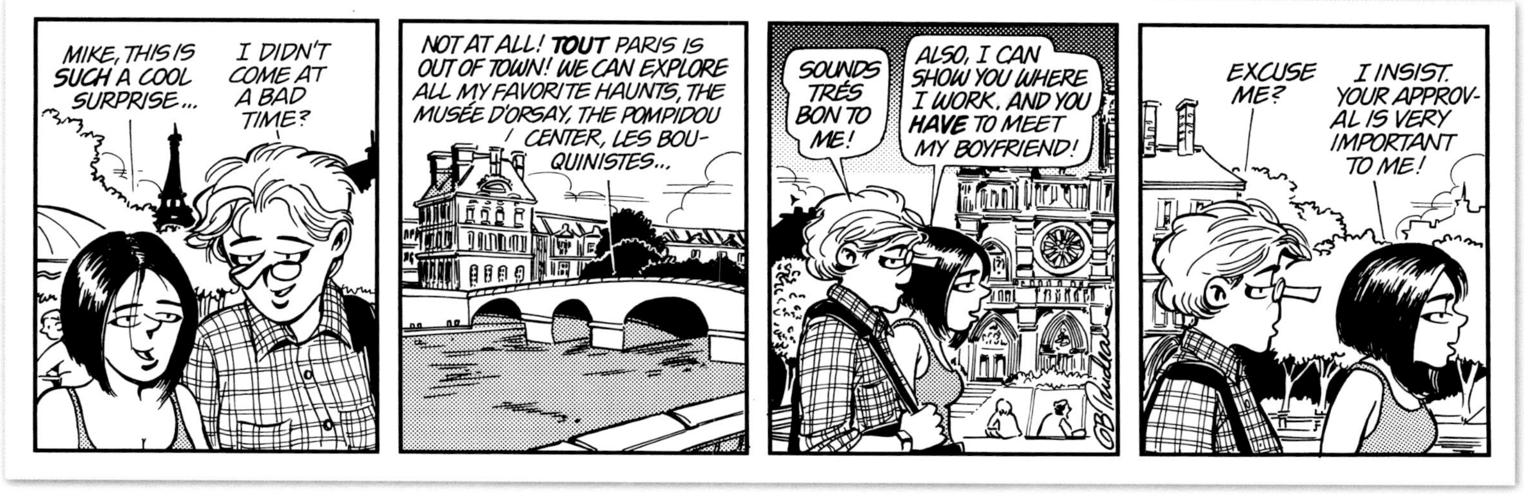
MIKE, THIS IS SUCH A COOL SURPRISE...
I DIDN'T COME AT A BAD TIME?
NOT AT ALL! TOUT PARIS IS OUT OF TOWN! WE CAN EXPLORE ALL MY FAVORITE HAUNTS, THE MUSÉE D'ORSAY, THE POMPIDOU CENTER, LES BOUQUINISTES...
SOUNDS TRÉS BON TO ME!
ALSO, I CAN SHOW YOU WHERE I WORK. AND YOU HAVE TO MEET MY BOYFRIEND!
EXCUSE ME?
I INSIST. YOUR APPROVAL IS VERY IMPORTANT TO ME!

8/7/96

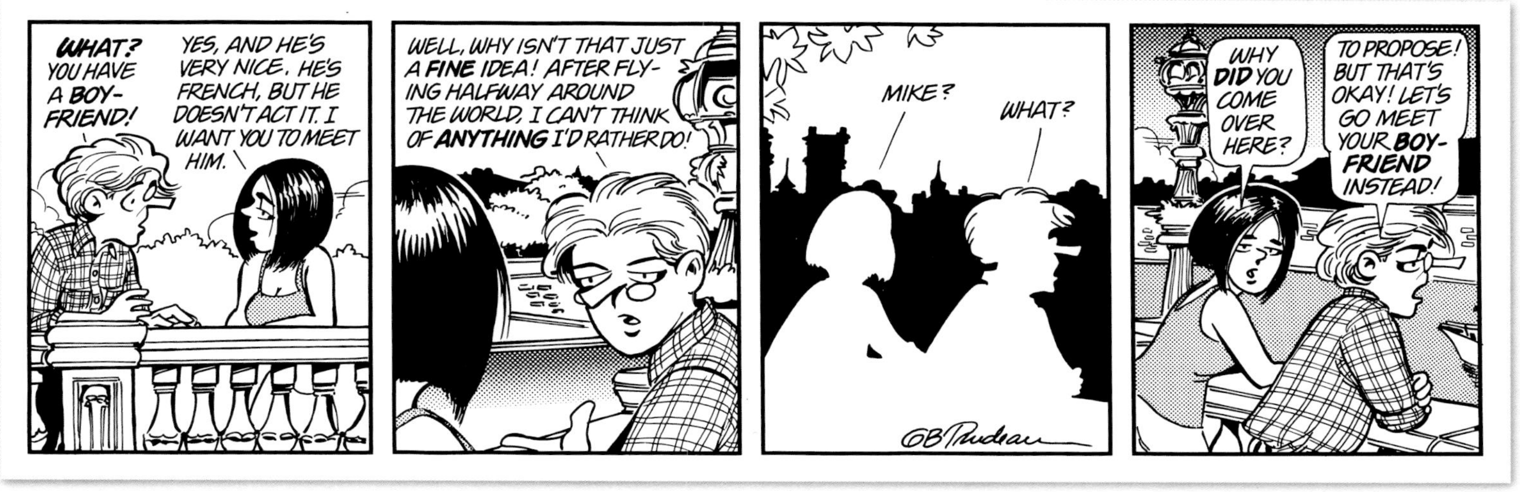
WHAT? YOU HAVE A BOYFRIEND!
YES, AND HE'S VERY NICE. HE'S FRENCH, BUT HE DOESN'T ACT IT. I WANT YOU TO MEET HIM.
WELL, WHY ISN'T THAT JUST A FINE IDEA! AFTER FLYING HALFWAY AROUND THE WORLD, I CAN'T THINK OF ANYTHING I'D RATHER DO!
MIKE?
WHAT?
WHY DID YOU COME OVER HERE?
TO PROPOSE! BUT THAT'S OKAY! LET'S GO MEET YOUR BOYFRIEND INSTEAD!

8/8/96

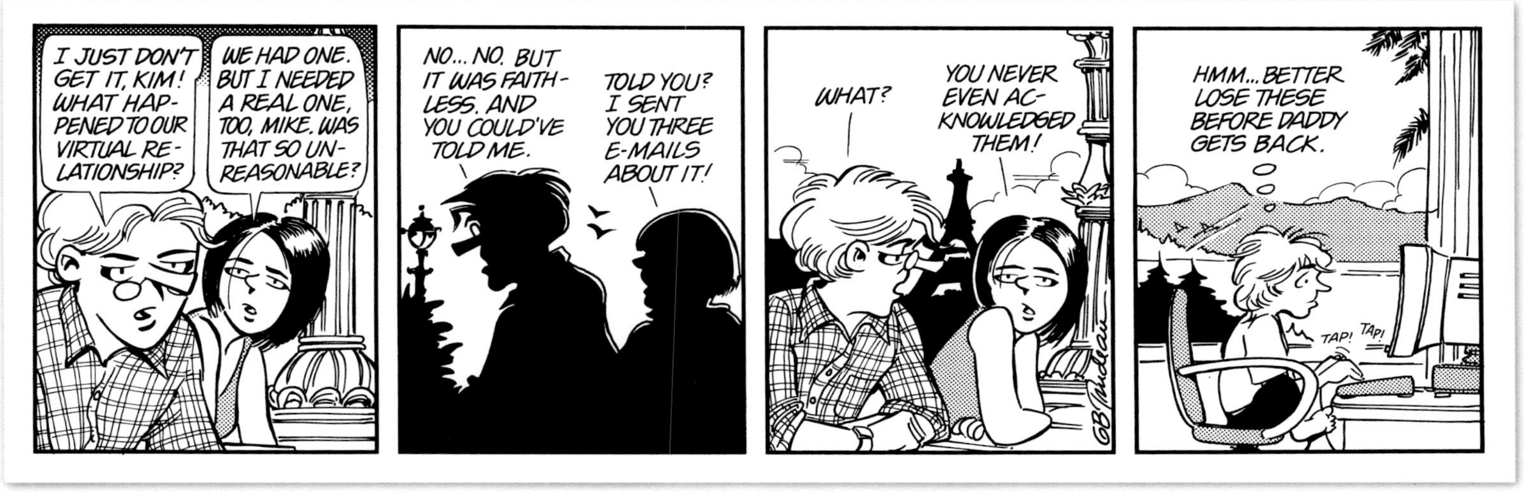
I JUST DON'T GET IT, KIM! WHAT HAPPENED TO OUR VIRTUAL RELATIONSHIP?
WE HAD ONE. BUT I NEEDED A REAL ONE, TOO, MIKE. WAS THAT SO UNREASONABLE?
NO... NO. BUT IT WAS FAITHLESS. AND YOU COULD'VE TOLD ME.
TOLD YOU? I SENT YOU THREE E-MAILS ABOUT IT!
WHAT?
YOU NEVER EVEN ACKNOWLEDGED THEM!
HMM... BETTER LOSE THESE BEFORE DADDY GETS BACK.
TAP! TAP!

8/9/96

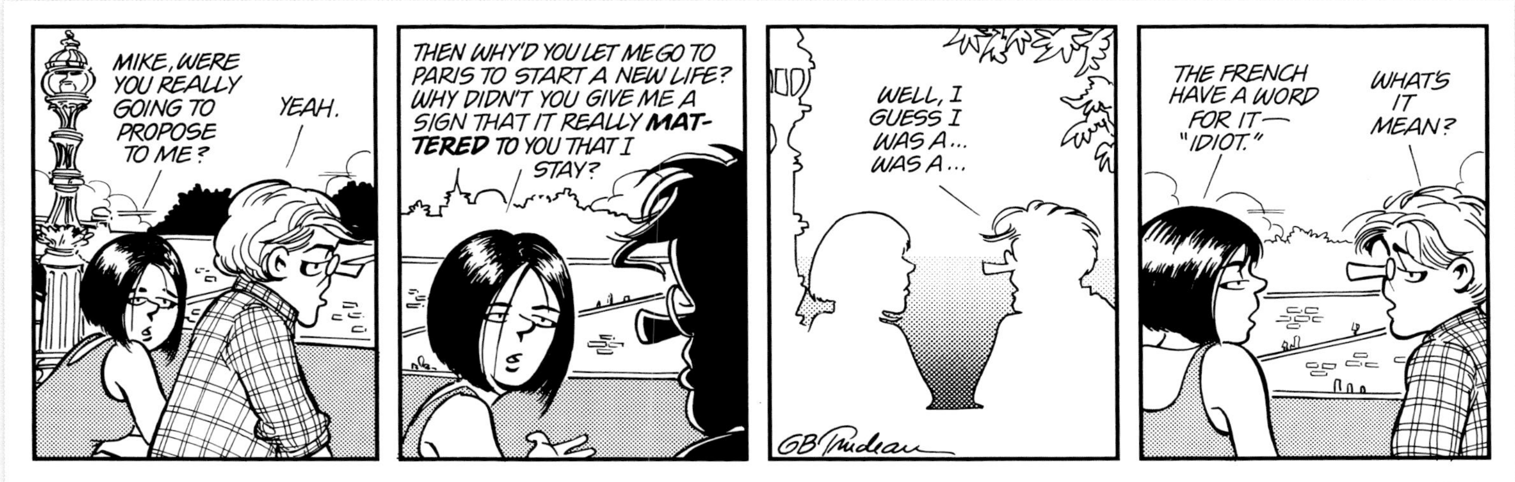
MIKE, WERE YOU REALLY GOING TO PROPOSE TO ME?
YEAH.
THEN WHY'D YOU LET ME GO TO PARIS TO START A NEW LIFE? WHY DIDN'T YOU GIVE ME A SIGN THAT IT REALLY MATTERED TO YOU THAT I STAY?
WELL, I GUESS I WAS A... WAS A...
THE FRENCH HAVE A WORD FOR IT— "IDIOT."
WHAT'S IT MEAN?

8/10/96

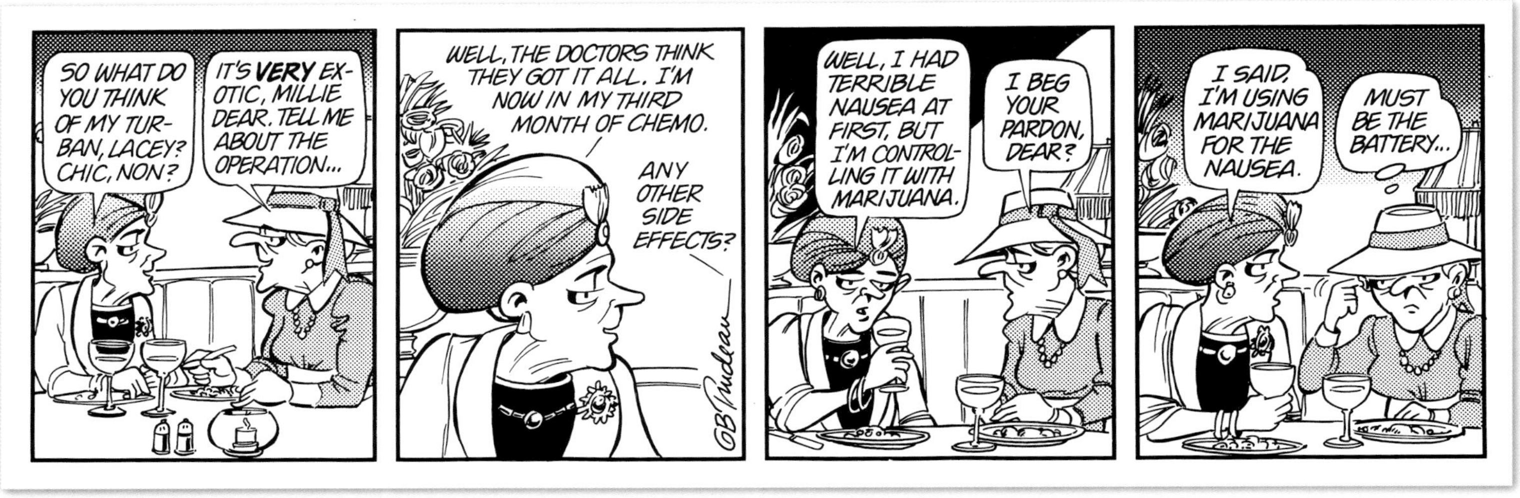
SO WHAT DO YOU THINK OF MY TURBAN, LACEY? CHIC, NON?
IT'S **VERY** EXOTIC, MILLIE DEAR. TELL ME ABOUT THE OPERATION...
WELL, THE DOCTORS THINK THEY GOT IT ALL. I'M NOW IN MY THIRD MONTH OF CHEMO.
ANY OTHER SIDE EFFECTS?
GB Trudeau
WELL, I HAD TERRIBLE NAUSEA AT FIRST, BUT I'M CONTROLLING IT WITH MARIJUANA.
I BEG YOUR PARDON, DEAR?
I SAID, I'M USING MARIJUANA FOR THE NAUSEA.
MUST BE THE BATTERY...

10/21/96

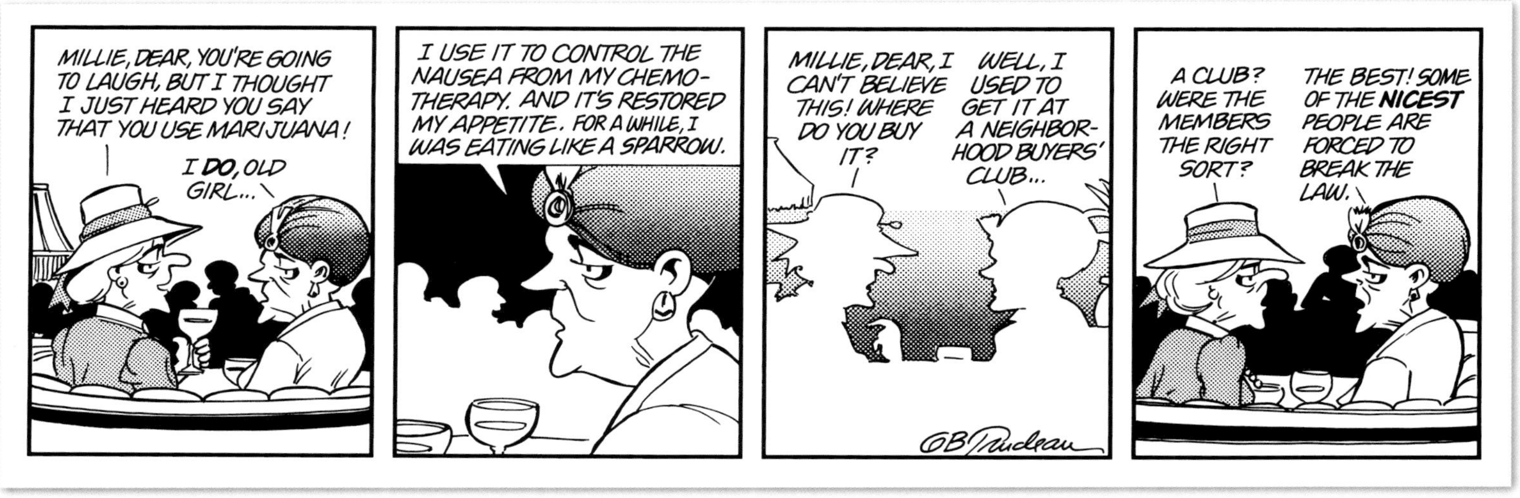
MILLIE, DEAR, YOU'RE GOING TO LAUGH, BUT I THOUGHT I JUST HEARD YOU SAY THAT YOU USE MARIJUANA!
I **DO**, OLD GIRL...
I USE IT TO CONTROL THE NAUSEA FROM MY CHEMOTHERAPY. AND IT'S RESTORED MY APPETITE. FOR A WHILE, I WAS EATING LIKE A SPARROW.
MILLIE, DEAR, I CAN'T BELIEVE THIS! WHERE DO YOU BUY IT?
WELL, I USED TO GET IT AT A NEIGHBORHOOD BUYERS' CLUB...
GB Trudeau
A CLUB? WERE THE MEMBERS THE RIGHT SORT?
THE BEST! SOME OF THE **NICEST** PEOPLE ARE FORCED TO BREAK THE LAW.

10/22/96

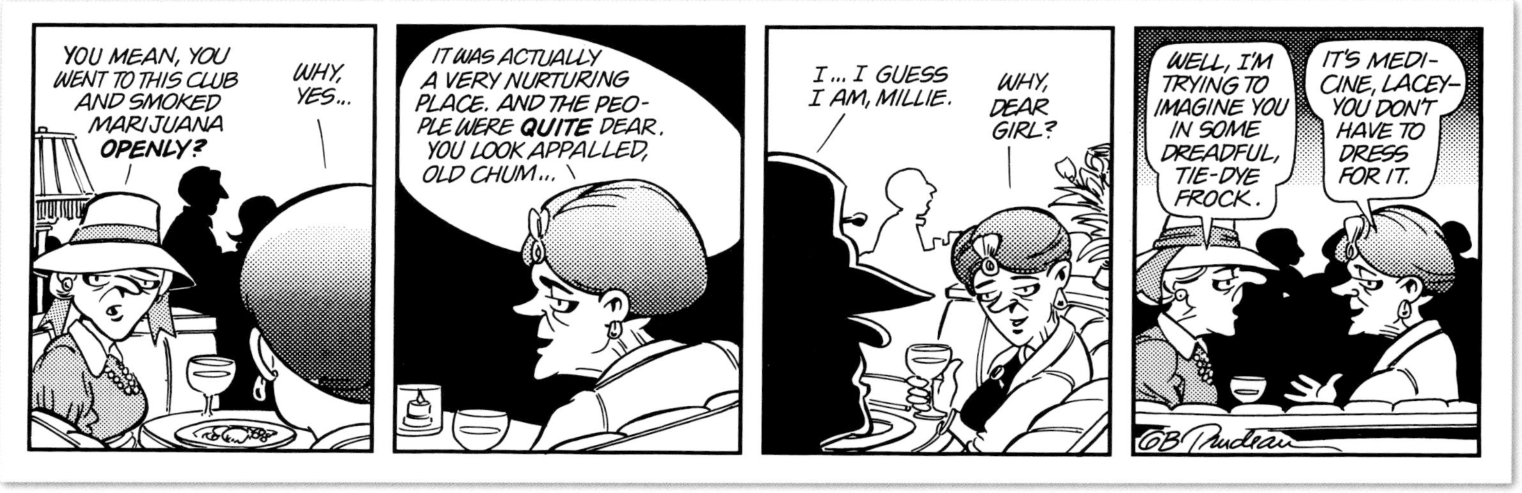
YOU MEAN, YOU WENT TO THIS CLUB AND SMOKED MARIJUANA **OPENLY?**
WHY, YES...
IT WAS ACTUALLY A VERY NURTURING PLACE. AND THE PEOPLE WERE **QUITE** DEAR. YOU LOOK APPALLED, OLD CHUM...
I... I GUESS I AM, MILLIE.
WHY, DEAR GIRL?
WELL, I'M TRYING TO IMAGINE YOU IN SOME DREADFUL, TIE-DYE FROCK.
IT'S MEDICINE, LACEY—YOU DON'T HAVE TO DRESS FOR IT.
GB Trudeau

10/23/96

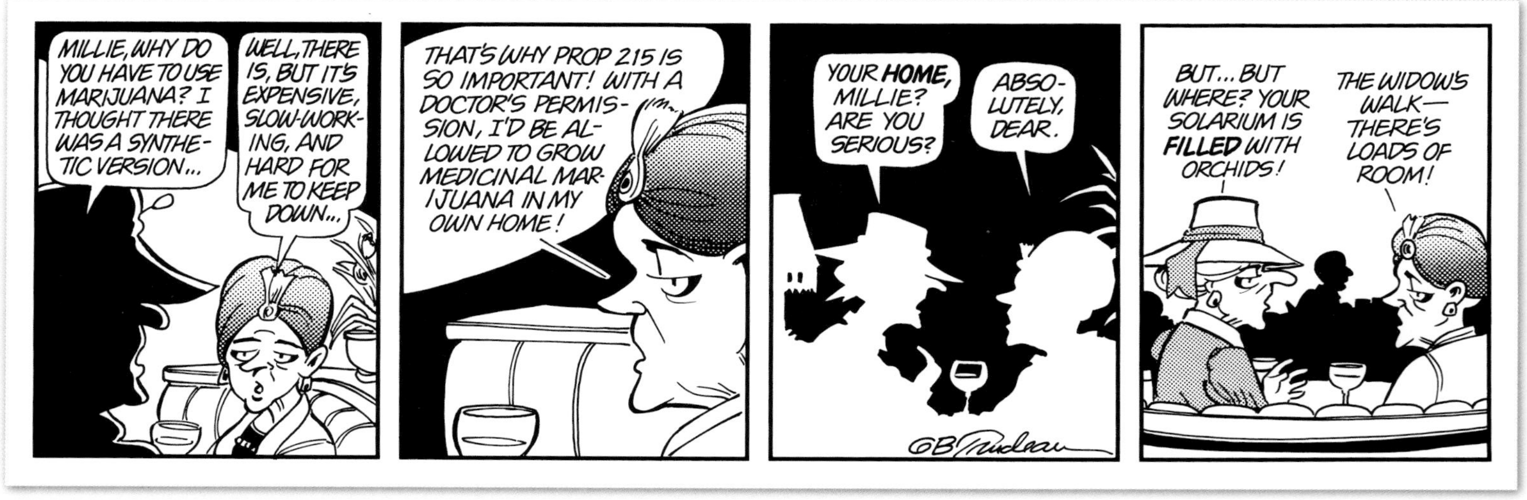
MILLIE, WHY DO YOU HAVE TO USE MARIJUANA? I THOUGHT THERE WAS A SYNTHETIC VERSION...
WELL, THERE IS, BUT IT'S EXPENSIVE, SLOW-WORKING, AND HARD FOR ME TO KEEP DOWN...
THAT'S WHY PROP 215 IS SO IMPORTANT! WITH A DOCTOR'S PERMISSION, I'D BE ALLOWED TO GROW MEDICINAL MARIJUANA IN MY OWN HOME!
YOUR **HOME**, MILLIE? ARE YOU SERIOUS?
ABSOLUTELY, DEAR.
GB Trudeau
BUT... BUT WHERE? YOUR SOLARIUM IS **FILLED** WITH ORCHIDS!
THE WIDOW'S WALK—THERE'S LOADS OF ROOM!

10/25/96

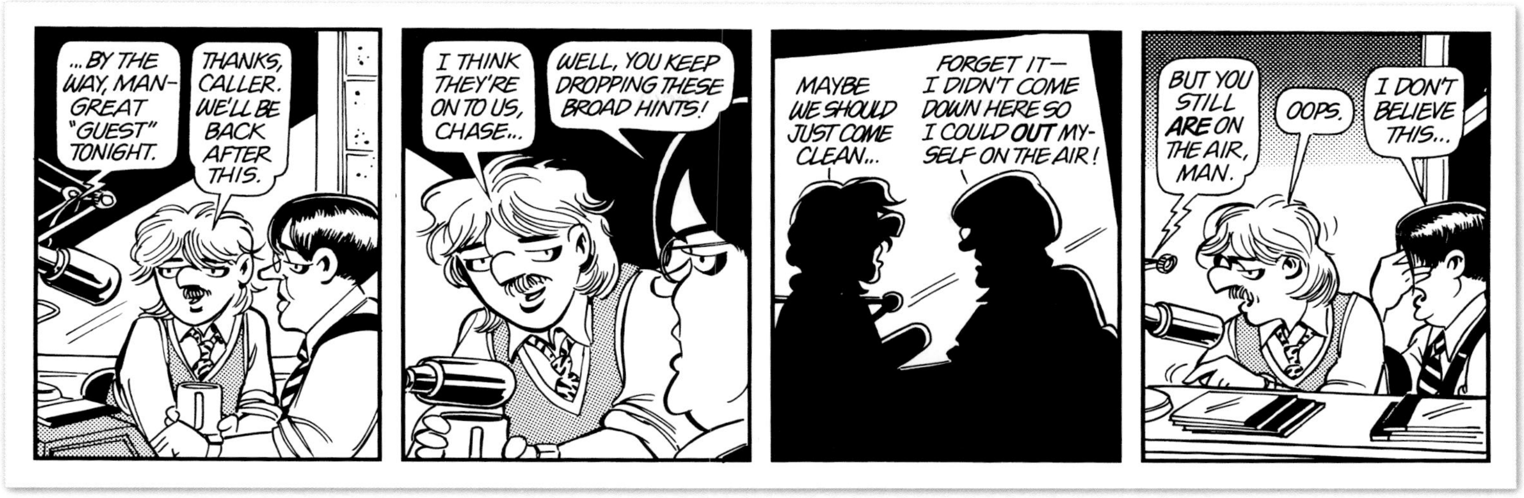

...BY THE WAY, MAN-GREAT "GUEST" TONIGHT.
THANKS, CALLER. WE'LL BE BACK AFTER THIS.
I THINK THEY'RE ON TO US, CHASE...
WELL, YOU KEEP DROPPING THESE BROAD HINTS!
MAYBE WE SHOULD JUST COME CLEAN...
FORGET IT— I DIDN'T COME DOWN HERE SO I COULD **OUT** MY-SELF ON THE AIR!
BUT YOU STILL **ARE** ON THE AIR, MAN.
OOPS.
I DON'T BELIEVE THIS...

11/4/96

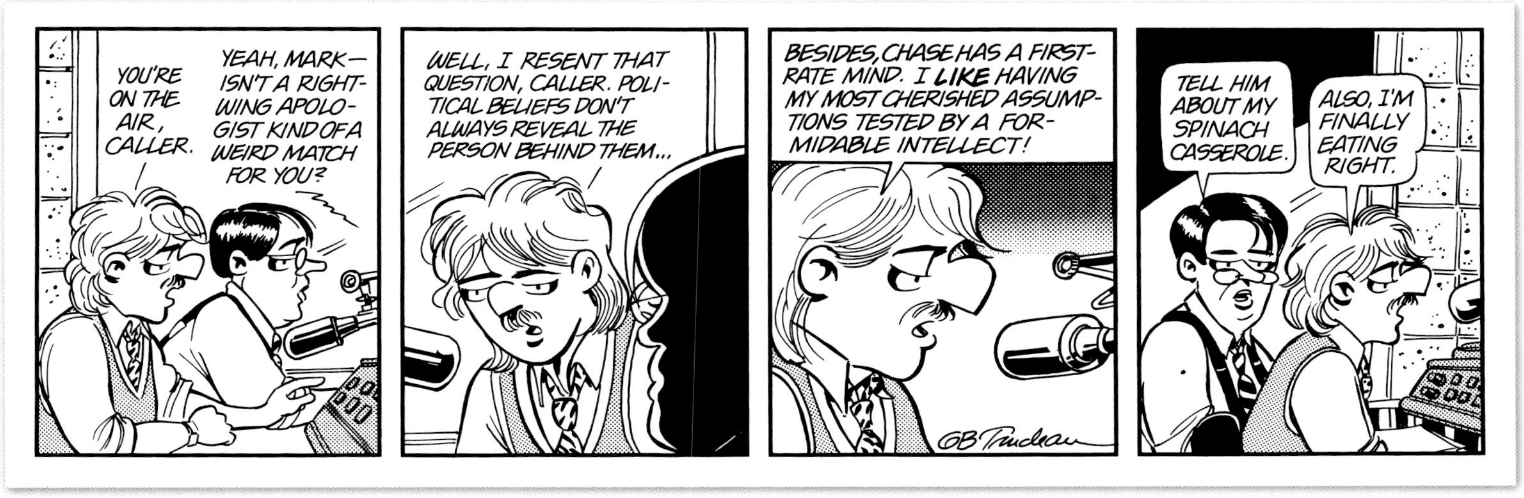

YOU'RE ON THE AIR, CALLER.
YEAH, MARK— ISN'T A RIGHT-WING APOLO-GIST KIND OF A WEIRD MATCH FOR YOU?
WELL, I RESENT THAT QUESTION, CALLER. POLI-TICAL BELIEFS DON'T ALWAYS REVEAL THE PERSON BEHIND THEM...
BESIDES, CHASE HAS A FIRST-RATE MIND. I **LIKE** HAVING MY MOST CHERISHED ASSUMP-TIONS TESTED BY A FOR-MIDABLE INTELLECT!
TELL HIM ABOUT MY SPINACH CASSEROLE.
ALSO, I'M FINALLY EATING RIGHT.

11/6/96

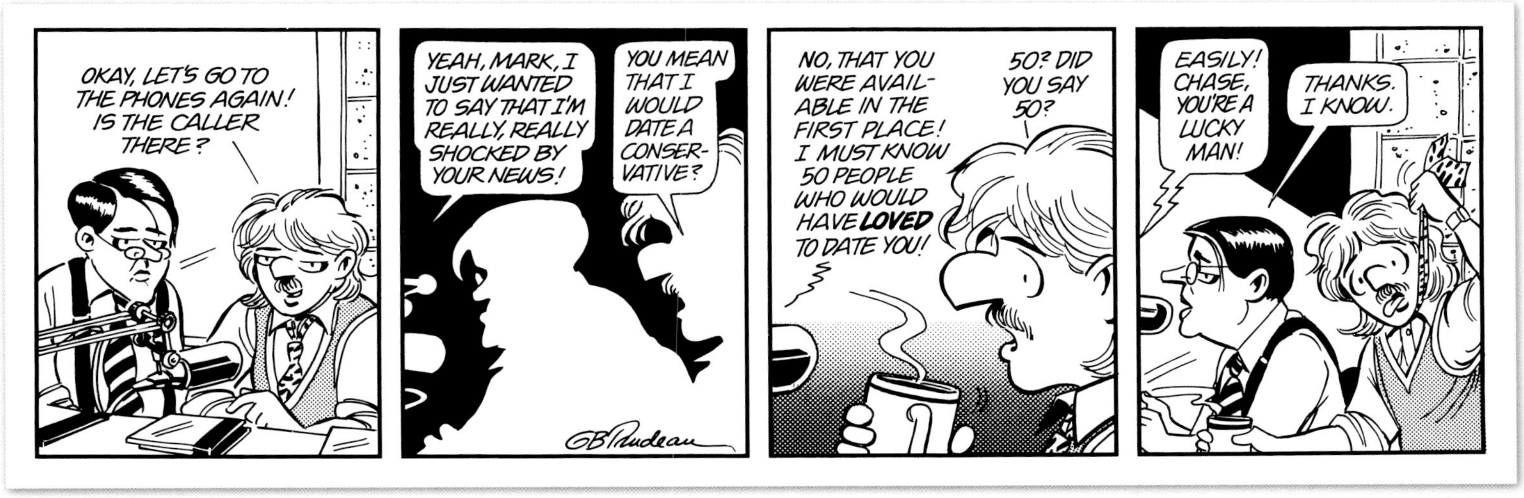

OKAY, LET'S GO TO THE PHONES AGAIN! IS THE CALLER THERE?
YEAH, MARK, I JUST WANTED TO SAY THAT I'M REALLY, REALLY SHOCKED BY YOUR NEWS!
YOU MEAN THAT I WOULD DATE A CONSER-VATIVE?
NO, THAT YOU WERE AVAIL-ABLE IN THE FIRST PLACE! I MUST KNOW 50 PEOPLE WHO WOULD HAVE **LOVED** TO DATE YOU!
50? DID YOU SAY 50?
EASILY! CHASE, YOU'RE A LUCKY MAN!
THANKS. I KNOW.

11/7/96

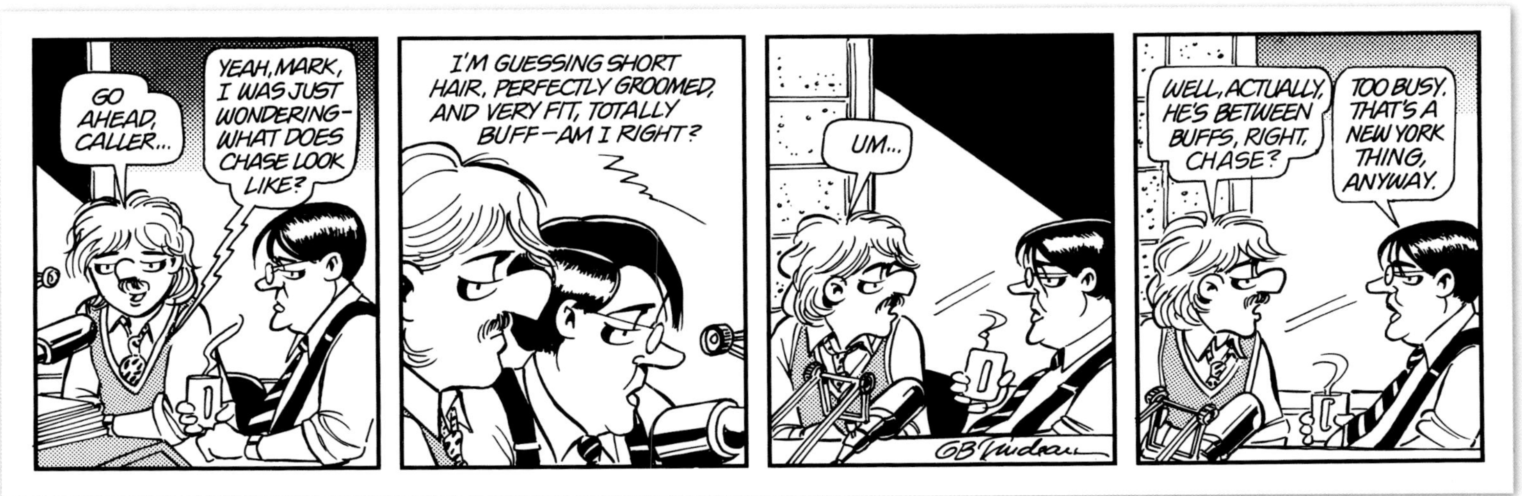

GO AHEAD, CALLER...
YEAH, MARK, I WAS JUST WONDERING-WHAT DOES CHASE LOOK LIKE?
I'M GUESSING SHORT HAIR, PERFECTLY GROOMED, AND VERY FIT, TOTALLY BUFF—AM I RIGHT?
UM...
WELL, ACTUALLY, HE'S BETWEEN BUFFS, RIGHT, CHASE?
TOO BUSY. THAT'S A NEW YORK THING, ANYWAY.

11/8/96

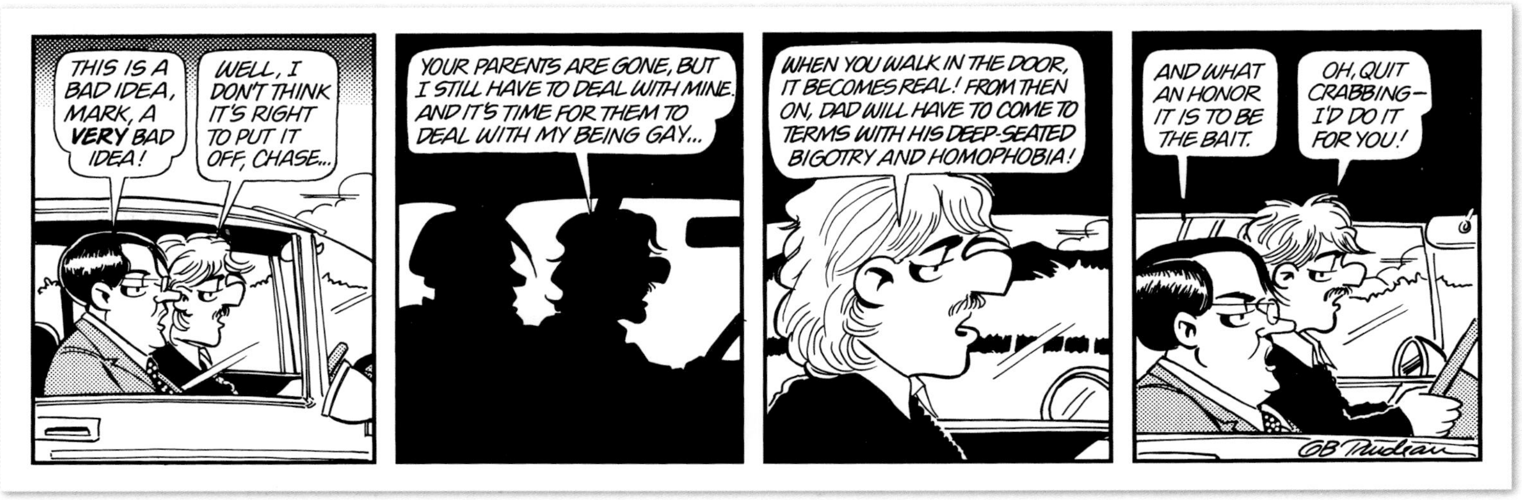
THIS IS A BAD IDEA, MARK, A **VERY** BAD IDEA!
WELL, I DON'T THINK IT'S RIGHT TO PUT IT OFF, CHASE...
YOUR PARENTS ARE GONE, BUT I STILL HAVE TO DEAL WITH MINE. AND IT'S TIME FOR THEM TO DEAL WITH MY BEING GAY...
WHEN YOU WALK IN THE DOOR, IT BECOMES REAL! FROM THEN ON, DAD WILL HAVE TO COME TO TERMS WITH HIS DEEP-SEATED BIGOTRY AND HOMOPHOBIA!
AND WHAT AN HONOR IT IS TO BE THE BAIT.
OH, QUIT CRABBING— I'D DO IT FOR YOU!
GB Trudeau

12/16/96

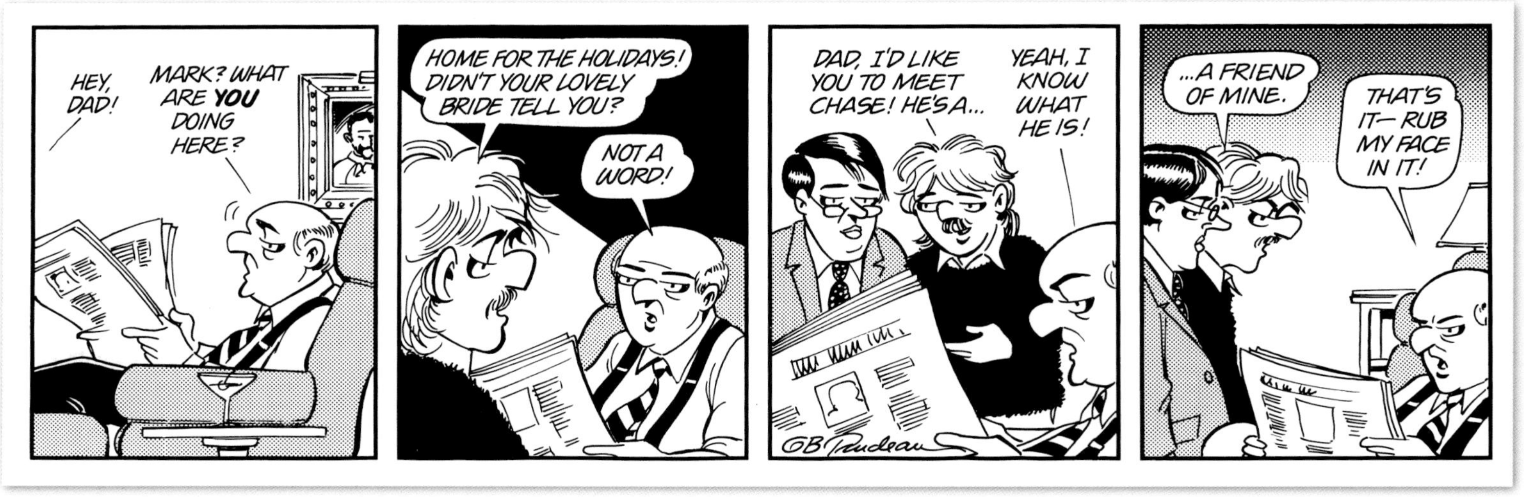
HEY, DAD!
MARK? WHAT ARE **YOU** DOING HERE?
HOME FOR THE HOLIDAYS! DIDN'T YOUR LOVELY BRIDE TELL YOU?
NOT A WORD!
DAD, I'D LIKE YOU TO MEET CHASE! HE'S A...
YEAH, I KNOW WHAT HE IS!
GB Trudeau
...A FRIEND OF MINE.
THAT'S IT— RUB MY FACE IN IT!

12/17/96

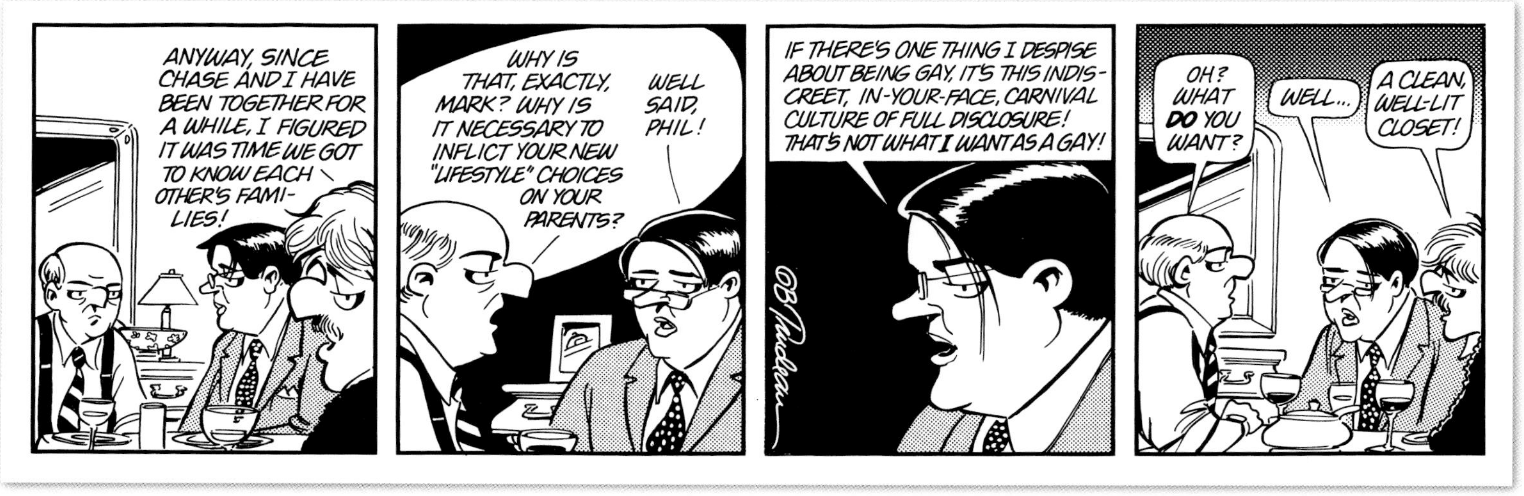
ANYWAY, SINCE CHASE AND I HAVE BEEN TOGETHER FOR A WHILE, I FIGURED IT WAS TIME WE GOT TO KNOW EACH OTHER'S FAMILIES!
WHY IS THAT, EXACTLY, MARK? WHY IS IT NECESSARY TO INFLICT YOUR NEW "LIFESTYLE" CHOICES ON YOUR PARENTS?
WELL SAID, PHIL!
GB Trudeau
IF THERE'S ONE THING I DESPISE ABOUT BEING GAY, IT'S THIS INDISCREET, IN-YOUR-FACE, CARNIVAL CULTURE OF FULL DISCLOSURE! THAT'S NOT WHAT **I** WANT AS A GAY!
OH? WHAT **DO** YOU WANT?
WELL...
A CLEAN, WELL-LIT CLOSET!

12/18/96

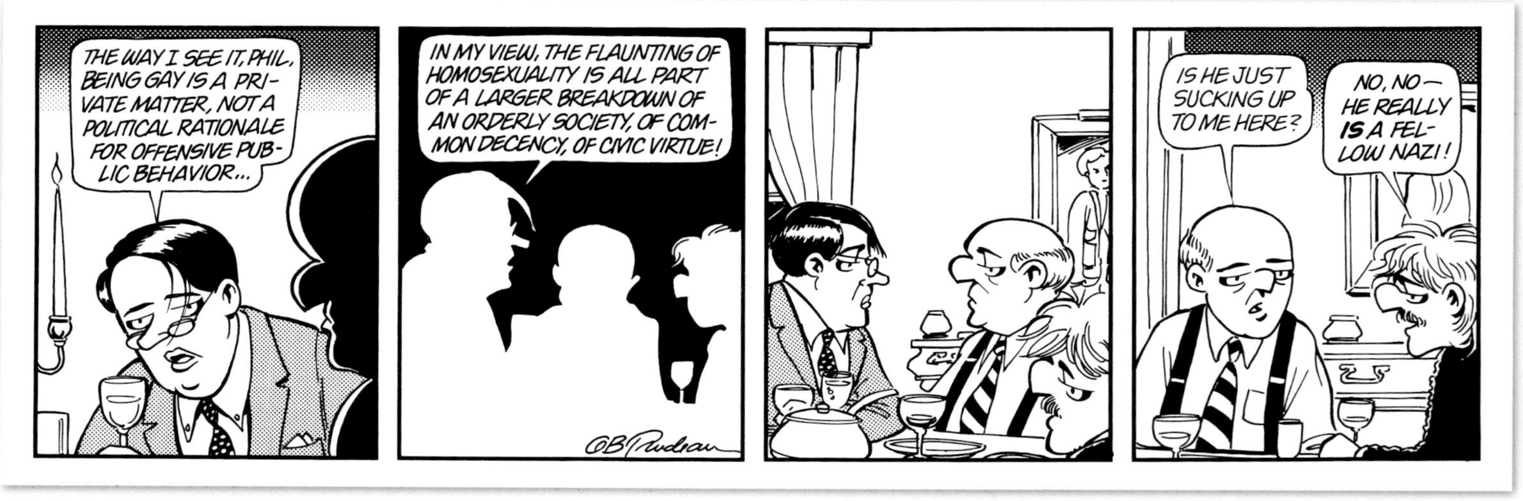
THE WAY I SEE IT, PHIL, BEING GAY IS A PRIVATE MATTER, NOT A POLITICAL RATIONALE FOR OFFENSIVE PUBLIC BEHAVIOR...
IN MY VIEW, THE FLAUNTING OF HOMOSEXUALITY IS ALL PART OF A LARGER BREAKDOWN OF AN ORDERLY SOCIETY, OF COMMON DECENCY, OF CIVIC VIRTUE!
GB Trudeau
IS HE JUST SUCKING UP TO ME HERE?
NO, NO— HE REALLY **IS** A FELLOW NAZI!

12/19/96

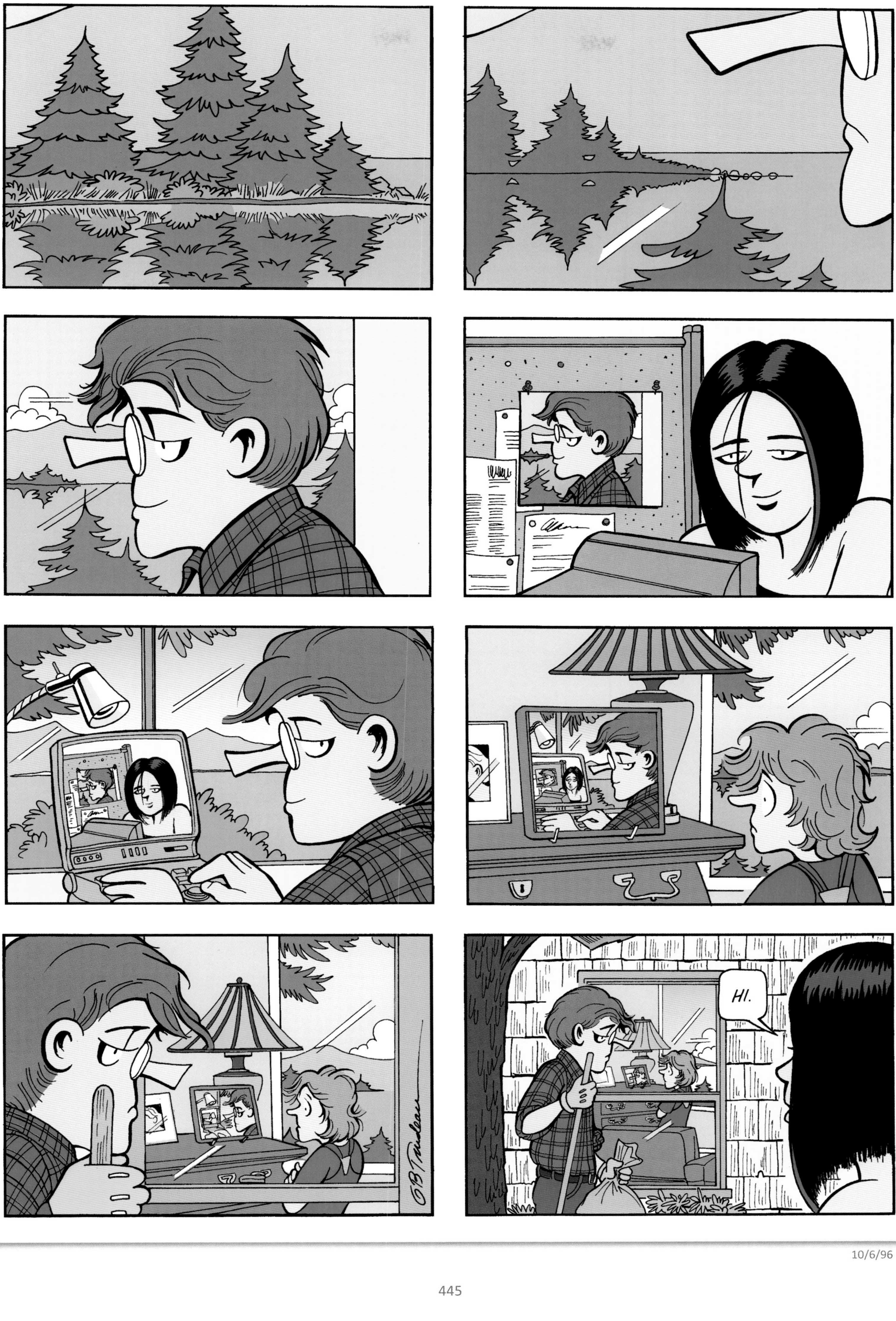
HI.

10/6/96

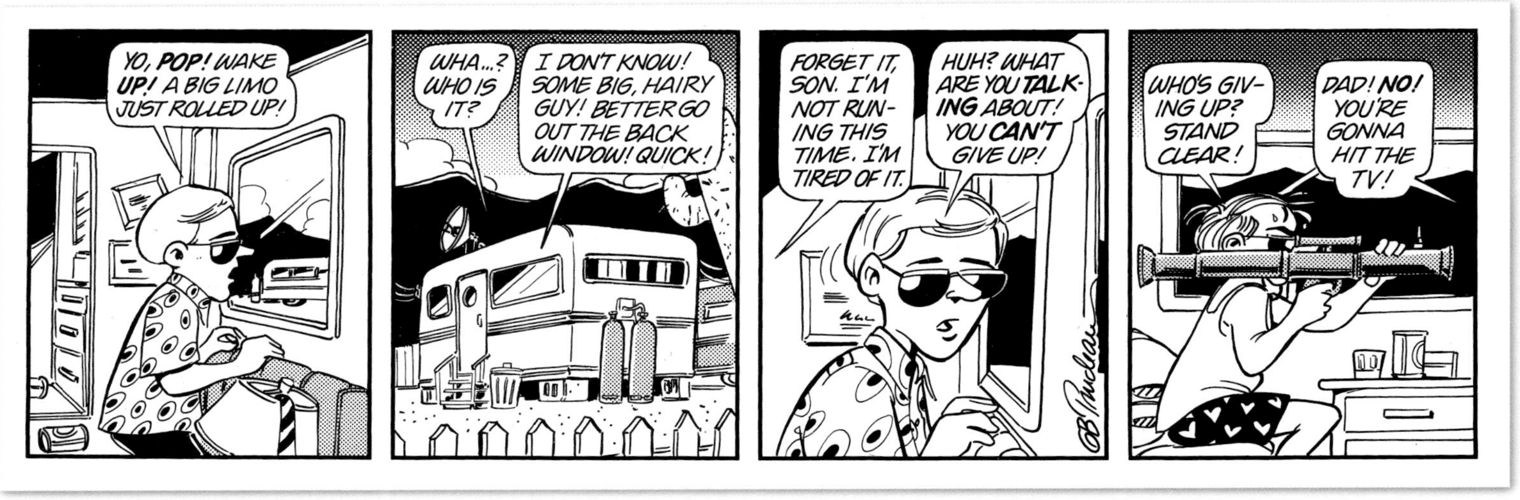
YO, POP! WAKE UP! A BIG LIMO JUST ROLLED UP!
WHA...? WHO IS IT?
I DON'T KNOW! SOME BIG, HAIRY GUY! BETTER GO OUT THE BACK WINDOW! QUICK!
FORGET IT, SON. I'M NOT RUNNING THIS TIME. I'M TIRED OF IT.
HUH? WHAT ARE YOU TALKING ABOUT! YOU CAN'T GIVE UP!
WHO'S GIVING UP? STAND CLEAR!
DAD! NO! YOU'RE GONNA HIT THE TV!

2/24/97

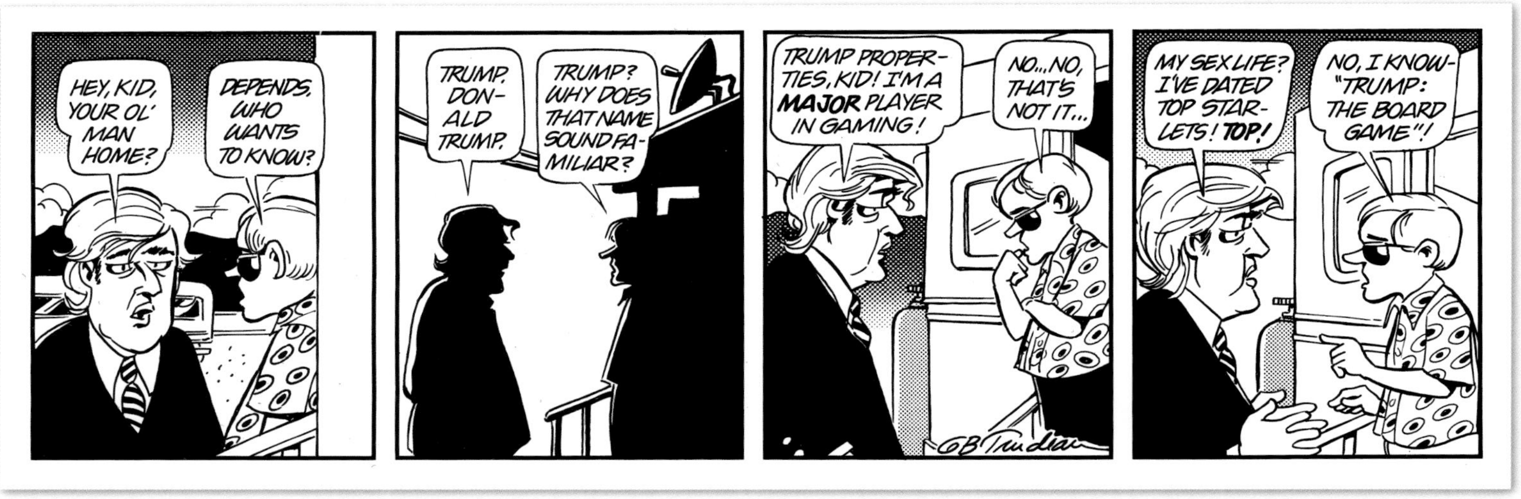
HEY, KID, YOUR OL' MAN HOME?
DEPENDS. WHO WANTS TO KNOW?
TRUMP. DONALD TRUMP.
TRUMP? WHY DOES THAT NAME SOUND FAMILIAR?
TRUMP PROPERTIES, KID! I'M A MAJOR PLAYER IN GAMING!
NO... NO, THAT'S NOT IT...
MY SEX LIFE? I'VE DATED TOP STARLETS! TOP!
NO, I KNOW— "TRUMP: THE BOARD GAME"!

2/25/97

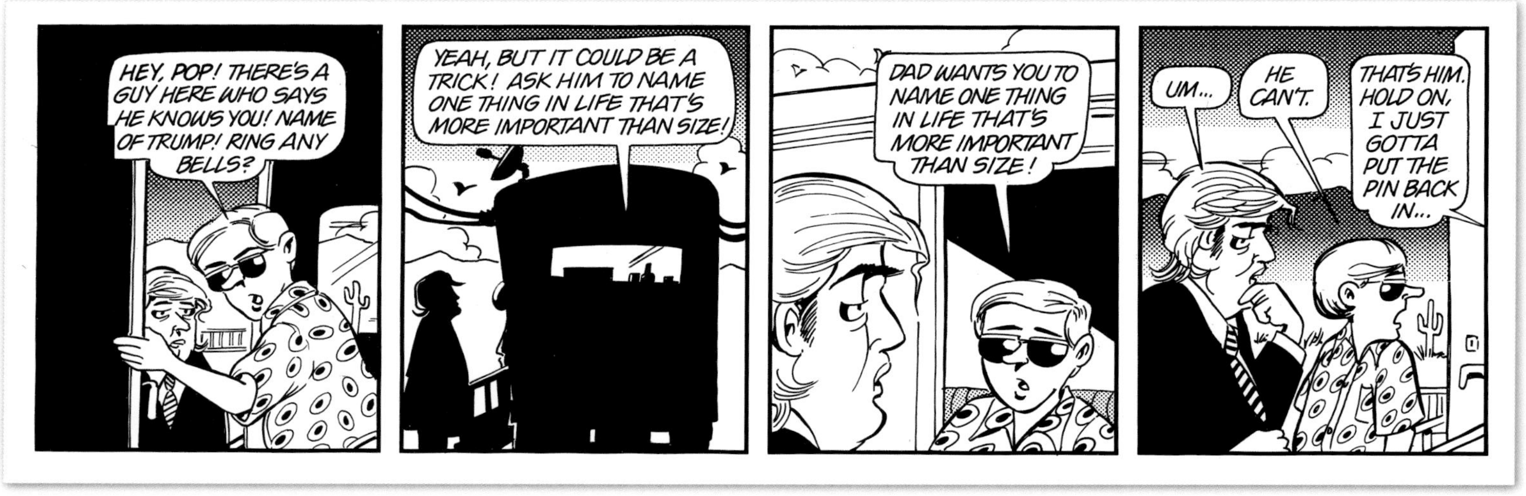
HEY, POP! THERE'S A GUY HERE WHO SAYS HE KNOWS YOU! NAME OF TRUMP! RING ANY BELLS?
YEAH, BUT IT COULD BE A TRICK! ASK HIM TO NAME ONE THING IN LIFE THAT'S MORE IMPORTANT THAN SIZE!
DAD WANTS YOU TO NAME ONE THING IN LIFE THAT'S MORE IMPORTANT THAN SIZE!
UM...
HE CAN'T.
THAT'S HIM. HOLD ON, I JUST GOTTA PUT THE PIN BACK IN...

2/26/97

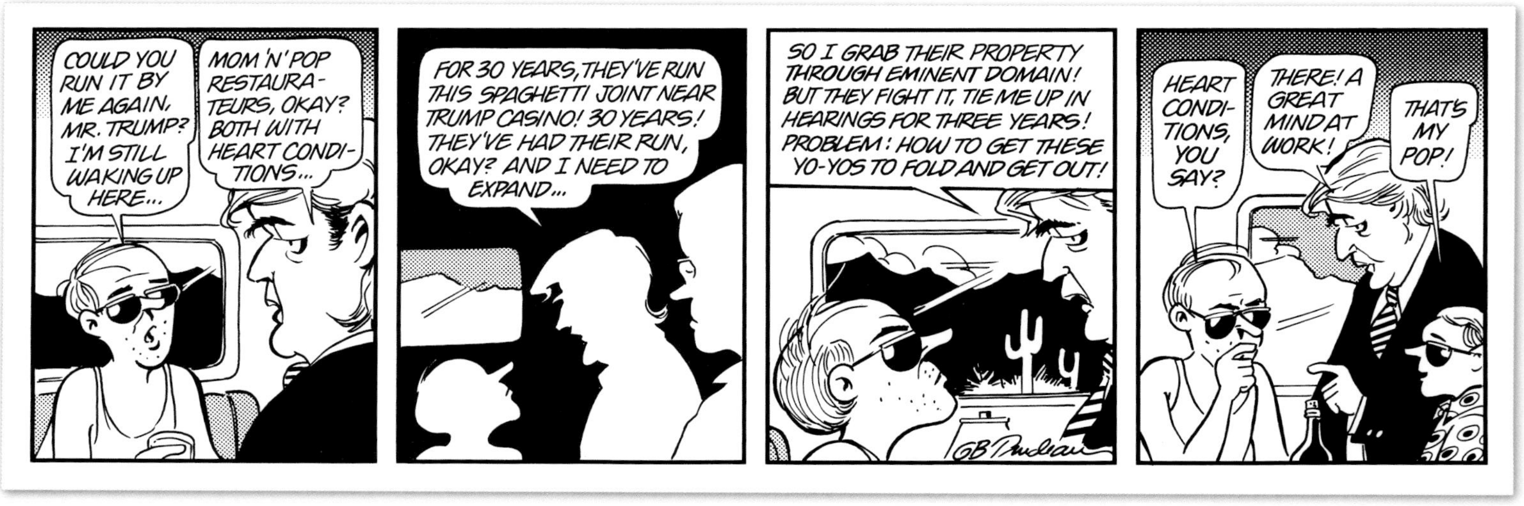
COULD YOU RUN IT BY ME AGAIN, MR. TRUMP? I'M STILL WAKING UP HERE...
MOM 'N' POP RESTAURATEURS, OKAY? BOTH WITH HEART CONDITIONS...
FOR 30 YEARS, THEY'VE RUN THIS SPAGHETTI JOINT NEAR TRUMP CASINO! 30 YEARS! THEY'VE HAD THEIR RUN, OKAY? AND I NEED TO EXPAND...
SO I GRAB THEIR PROPERTY THROUGH EMINENT DOMAIN! BUT THEY FIGHT IT, TIE ME UP IN HEARINGS FOR THREE YEARS! PROBLEM: HOW TO GET THESE YO-YOS TO FOLD AND GET OUT!
HEART CONDITIONS, YOU SAY?
THERE! A GREAT MIND AT WORK!
THAT'S MY POP!

2/28/97

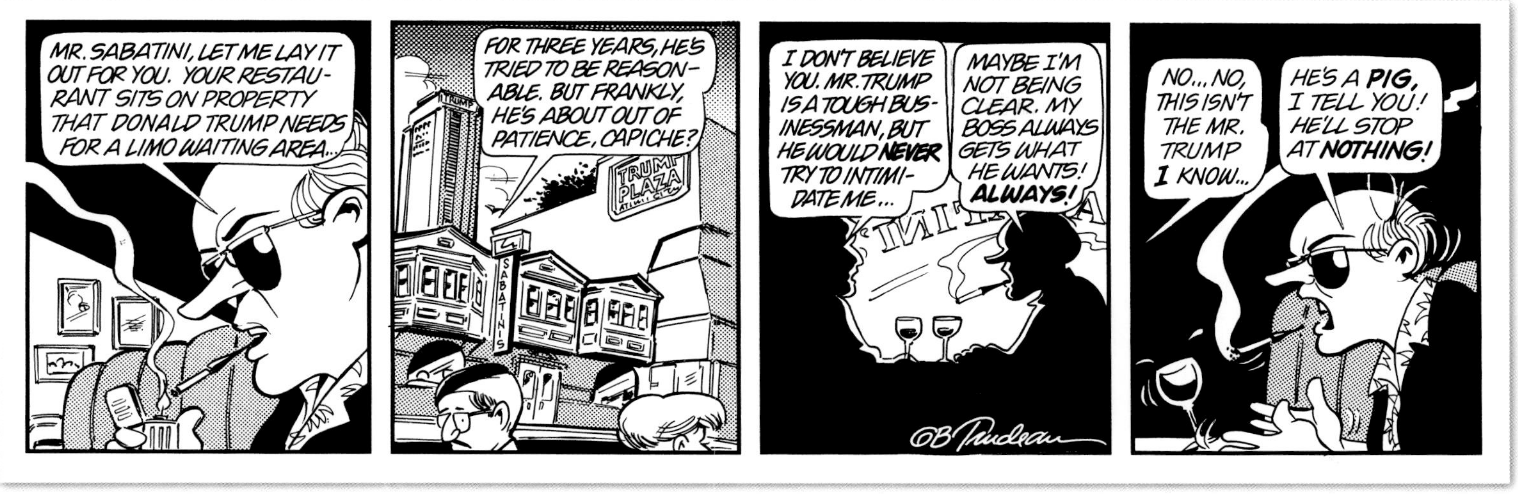
MR. SABATINI, LET ME LAY IT OUT FOR YOU. YOUR RESTAURANT SITS ON PROPERTY THAT DONALD TRUMP NEEDS FOR A LIMO WAITING AREA...
FOR THREE YEARS, HE'S TRIED TO BE REASONABLE. BUT FRANKLY, HE'S ABOUT OUT OF PATIENCE, CAPICHE?
TRUMP PLAZA
SABATINI'S
I DON'T BELIEVE YOU. MR. TRUMP IS A TOUGH BUSINESSMAN, BUT HE WOULD NEVER TRY TO INTIMIDATE ME...
MAYBE I'M NOT BEING CLEAR. MY BOSS ALWAYS GETS WHAT HE WANTS! ALWAYS!
NO... NO, THIS ISN'T THE MR. TRUMP I KNOW...
HE'S A PIG, I TELL YOU! HE'LL STOP AT NOTHING!

3/10/97

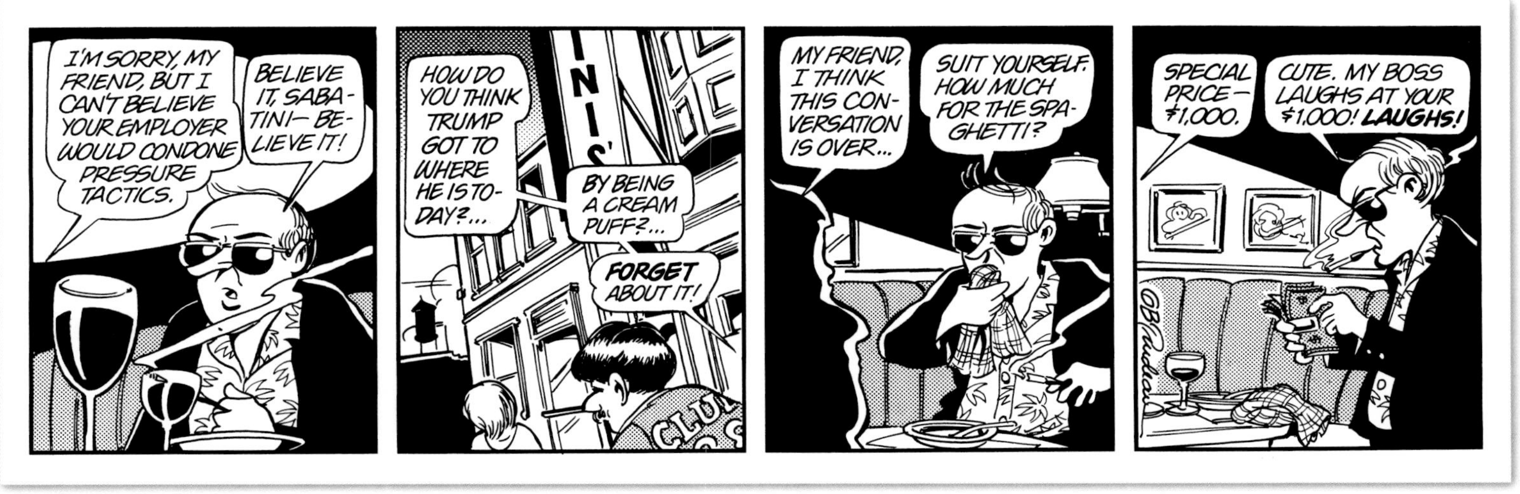
I'M SORRY, MY FRIEND, BUT I CAN'T BELIEVE YOUR EMPLOYER WOULD CONDONE PRESSURE TACTICS.
BELIEVE IT, SABATINI— BELIEVE IT!
HOW DO YOU THINK TRUMP GOT TO WHERE HE IS TODAY?...
BY BEING A CREAM PUFF?...
FORGET ABOUT IT!
MY FRIEND, I THINK THIS CONVERSATION IS OVER...
SUIT YOURSELF. HOW MUCH FOR THE SPAGHETTI?
SPECIAL PRICE— $1,000.
CUTE. MY BOSS LAUGHS AT YOUR $1,000! LAUGHS!

3/11/97

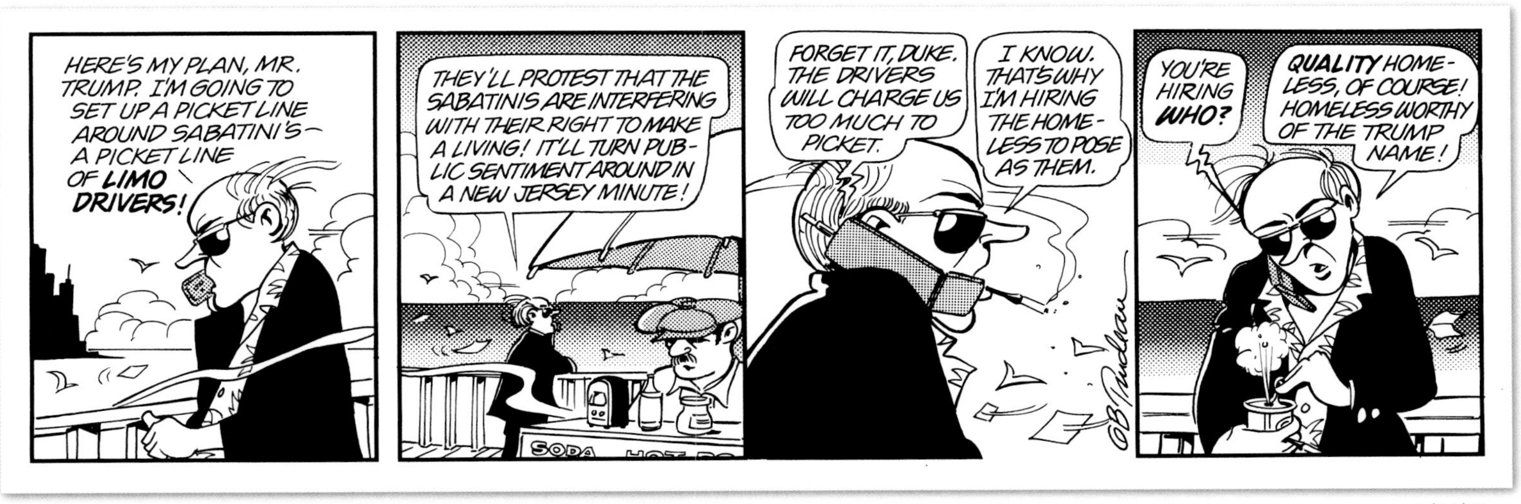
HERE'S MY PLAN, MR. TRUMP. I'M GOING TO SET UP A PICKET LINE AROUND SABATINI'S— A PICKET LINE OF LIMO DRIVERS!
THEY'LL PROTEST THAT THE SABATINIS ARE INTERFERING WITH THEIR RIGHT TO MAKE A LIVING! IT'LL TURN PUBLIC SENTIMENT AROUND IN A NEW JERSEY MINUTE!
FORGET IT, DUKE. THE DRIVERS WILL CHARGE US TOO MUCH TO PICKET.
I KNOW. THAT'S WHY I'M HIRING THE HOMELESS TO POSE AS THEM.
YOU'RE HIRING WHO?
QUALITY HOMELESS, OF COURSE! HOMELESS WORTHY OF THE TRUMP NAME!

3/14/97

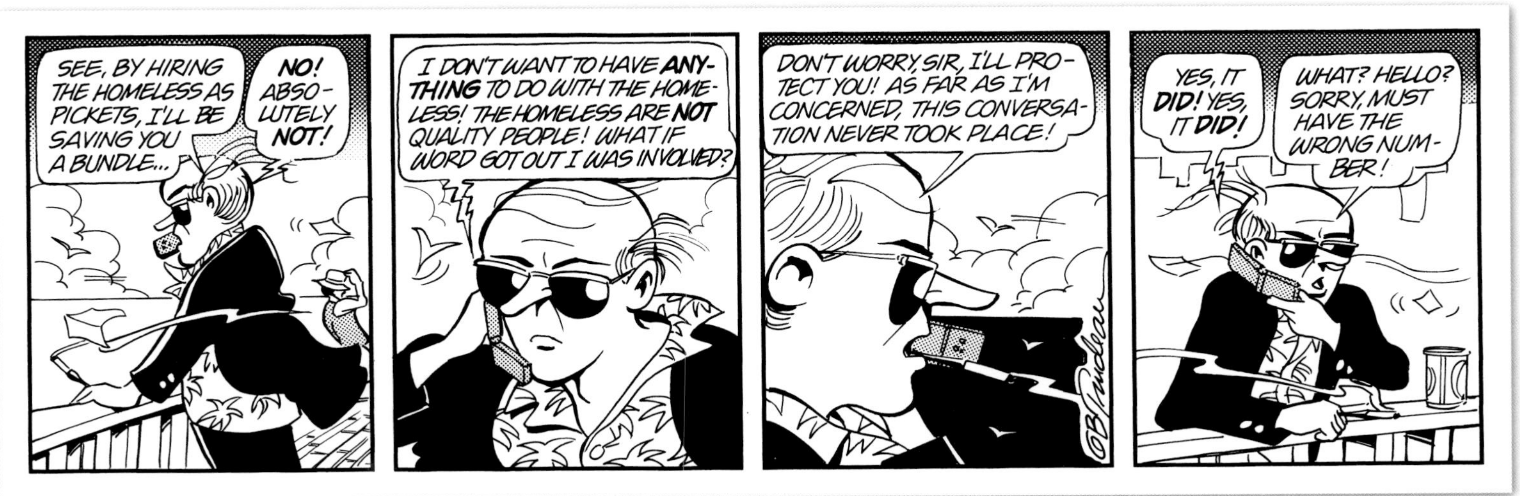
SEE, BY HIRING THE HOMELESS AS PICKETS, I'LL BE SAVING YOU A BUNDLE...
NO! ABSOLUTELY NOT!
I DON'T WANT TO HAVE ANYTHING TO DO WITH THE HOMELESS! THE HOMELESS ARE NOT QUALITY PEOPLE! WHAT IF WORD GOT OUT I WAS INVOLVED?
DON'T WORRY, SIR, I'LL PROTECT YOU! AS FAR AS I'M CONCERNED, THIS CONVERSATION NEVER TOOK PLACE!
YES, IT DID! YES, IT DID!
WHAT? HELLO? SORRY, MUST HAVE THE WRONG NUMBER!

3/15/97

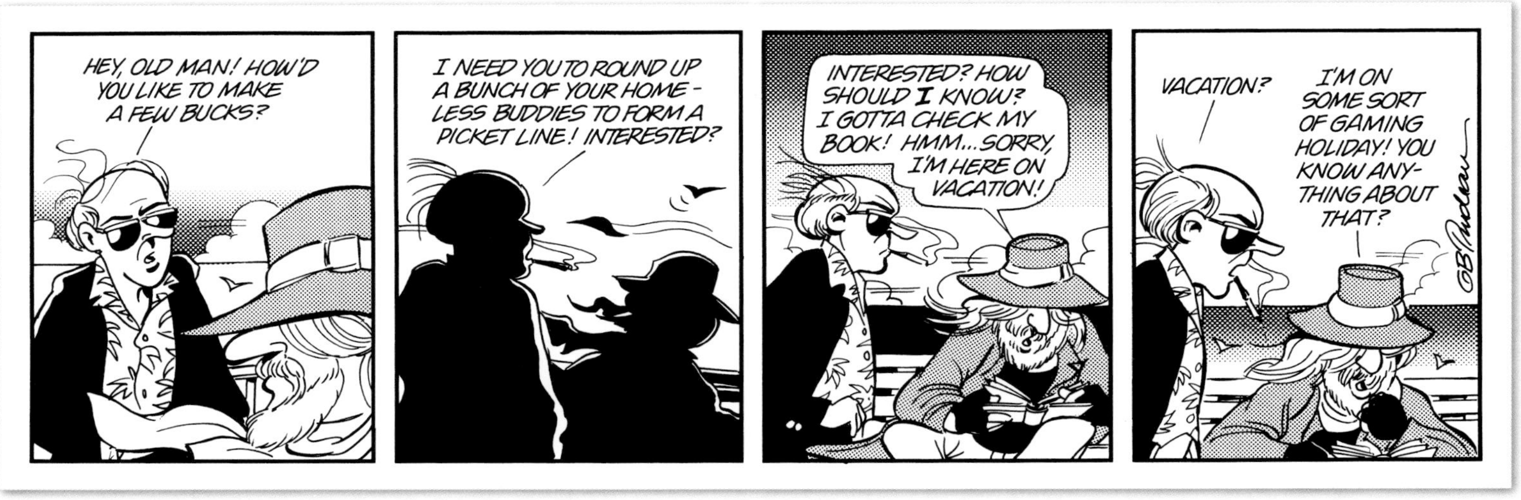
HEY, OLD MAN! HOW'D YOU LIKE TO MAKE A FEW BUCKS?
I NEED YOU TO ROUND UP A BUNCH OF YOUR HOME-LESS BUDDIES TO FORM A PICKET LINE! INTERESTED?
INTERESTED? HOW SHOULD **I** KNOW? I GOTTA CHECK MY BOOK! HMM... SORRY, I'M HERE ON VACATION!
VACATION?
I'M ON SOME SORT OF GAMING HOLIDAY! YOU KNOW ANY-THING ABOUT THAT?

3/17/97

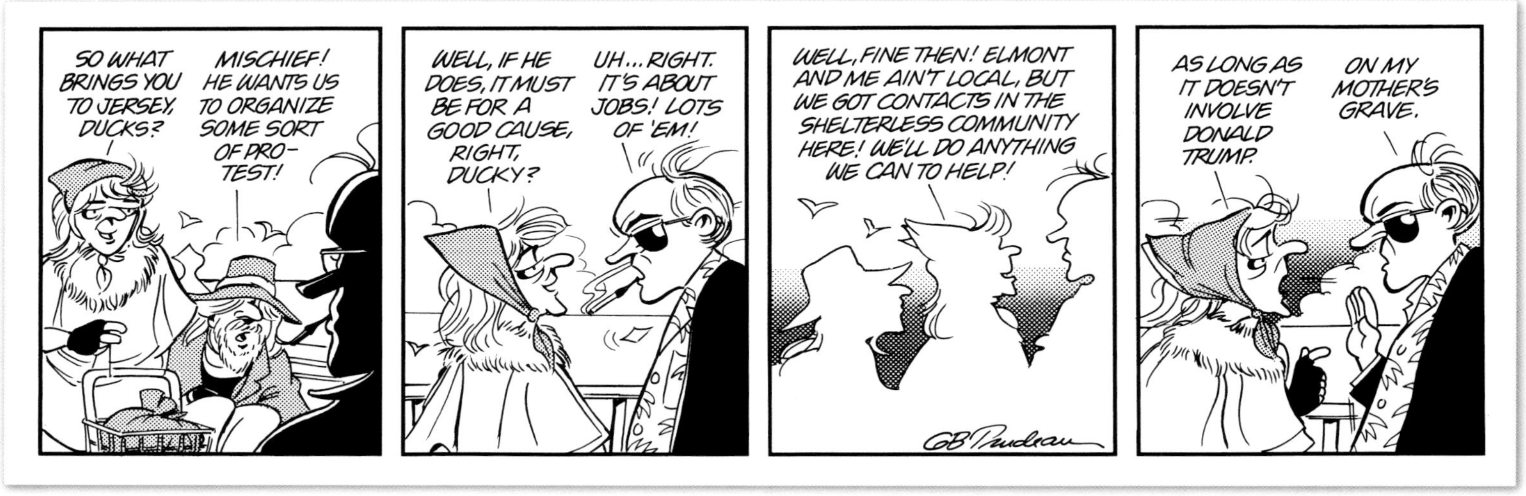
SO WHAT BRINGS YOU TO JERSEY, DUCKS?
MISCHIEF! HE WANTS US TO ORGANIZE SOME SORT OF PRO-TEST!
WELL, IF HE DOES, IT MUST BE FOR A GOOD CAUSE, RIGHT, DUCKY?
UH... RIGHT. IT'S ABOUT JOBS! LOTS OF 'EM!
WELL, FINE THEN! ELMONT AND ME AIN'T LOCAL, BUT WE GOT CONTACTS IN THE SHELTERLESS COMMUNITY HERE! WE'LL DO ANYTHING WE CAN TO HELP!
AS LONG AS IT DOESN'T INVOLVE DONALD TRUMP.
ON MY MOTHER'S GRAVE.

3/19/97

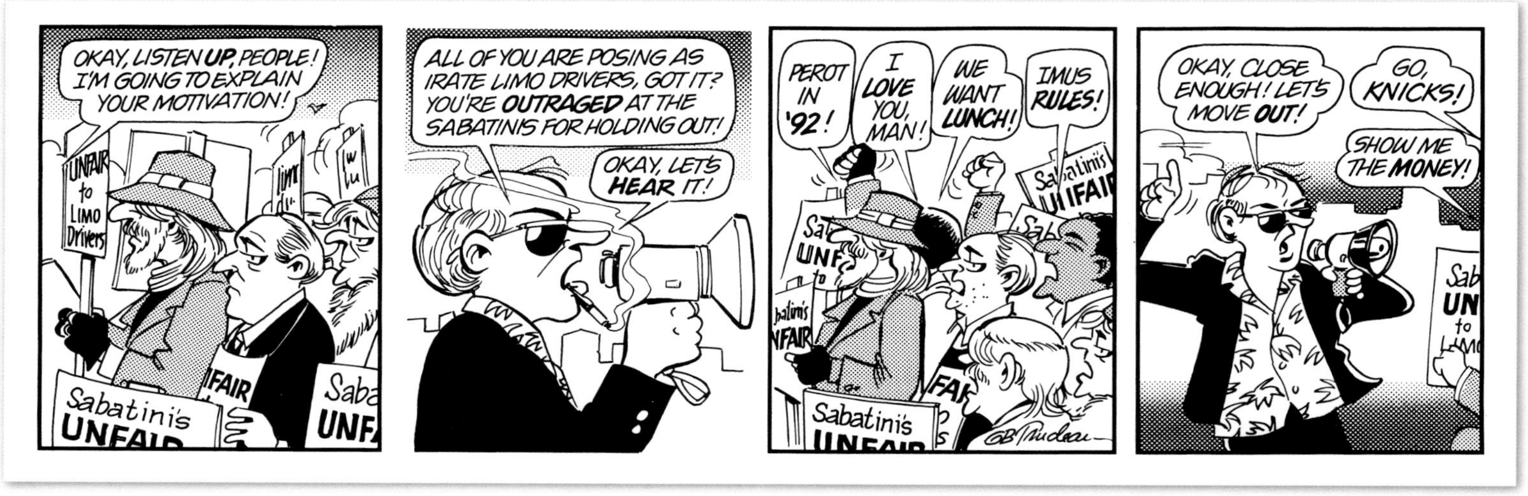
OKAY, LISTEN **UP**, PEOPLE! I'M GOING TO EXPLAIN YOUR MOTIVATION!
UNFAIR to LIMO Drivers
ALL OF YOU ARE POSING AS IRATE LIMO DRIVERS, GOT IT? YOU'RE **OUTRAGED** AT THE SABATINIS FOR HOLDING OUT!
OKAY, LET'S **HEAR** IT!
PEROT IN **'92**!
I **LOVE** YOU, MAN!
WE WANT **LUNCH**!
IMUS **RULES**!
OKAY, CLOSE ENOUGH! LET'S MOVE **OUT**!
GO, **KNICKS**!
SHOW ME THE **MONEY**!

3/20/97

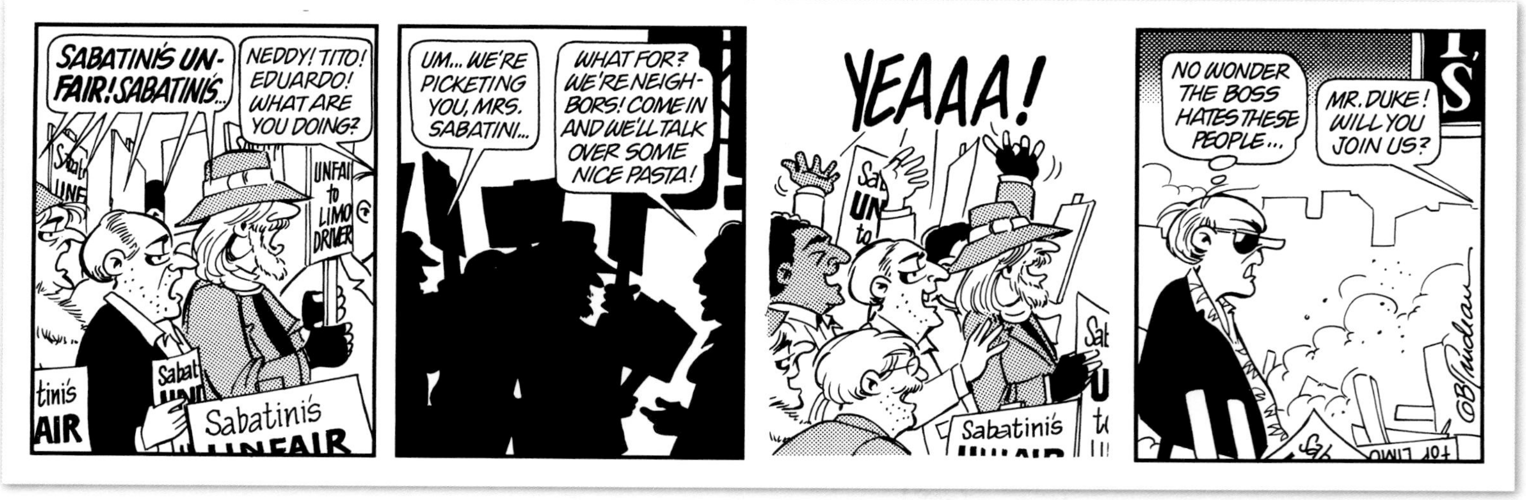
SABATINI'S UN-FAIR! SABATINI'S...
NEDDY! TITO! EDUARDO! WHAT ARE YOU DOING?
UM... WE'RE PICKETING YOU, MRS. SABATINI...
WHAT FOR? WE'RE NEIGH-BORS! COME IN AND WE'LL TALK OVER SOME NICE PASTA!
YEAAA!
NO WONDER THE BOSS HATES THESE PEOPLE...
MR. DUKE! WILL YOU JOIN US?

3/21/97

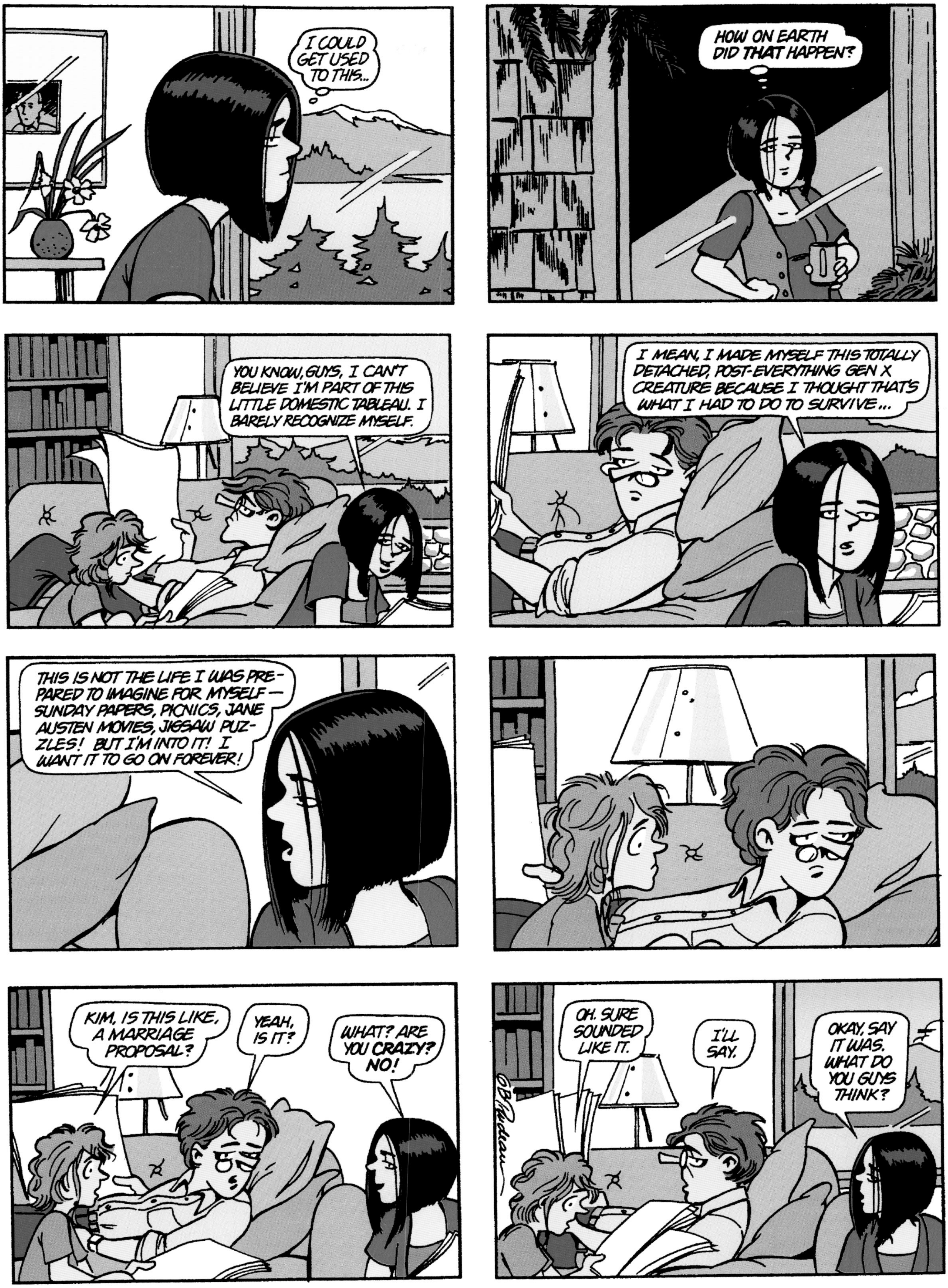
I COULD GET USED TO THIS...
HOW ON EARTH DID THAT HAPPEN?
YOU KNOW, GUYS, I CAN'T BELIEVE I'M PART OF THIS LITTLE DOMESTIC TABLEAU. I BARELY RECOGNIZE MYSELF.
I MEAN, I MADE MYSELF THIS TOTALLY DETACHED, POST-EVERYTHING GEN X CREATURE BECAUSE I THOUGHT THAT'S WHAT I HAD TO DO TO SURVIVE...
THIS IS NOT THE LIFE I WAS PREPARED TO IMAGINE FOR MYSELF— SUNDAY PAPERS, PICNICS, JANE AUSTEN MOVIES, JIGSAW PUZZLES! BUT I'M INTO IT! I WANT IT TO GO ON FOREVER!
KIM, IS THIS LIKE, A MARRIAGE PROPOSAL?
YEAH, IS IT?
WHAT? ARE YOU CRAZY? NO!
OH. SURE SOUNDED LIKE IT.
I'LL SAY.
OKAY, SAY IT WAS. WHAT DO YOU GUYS THINK?

1/5/97

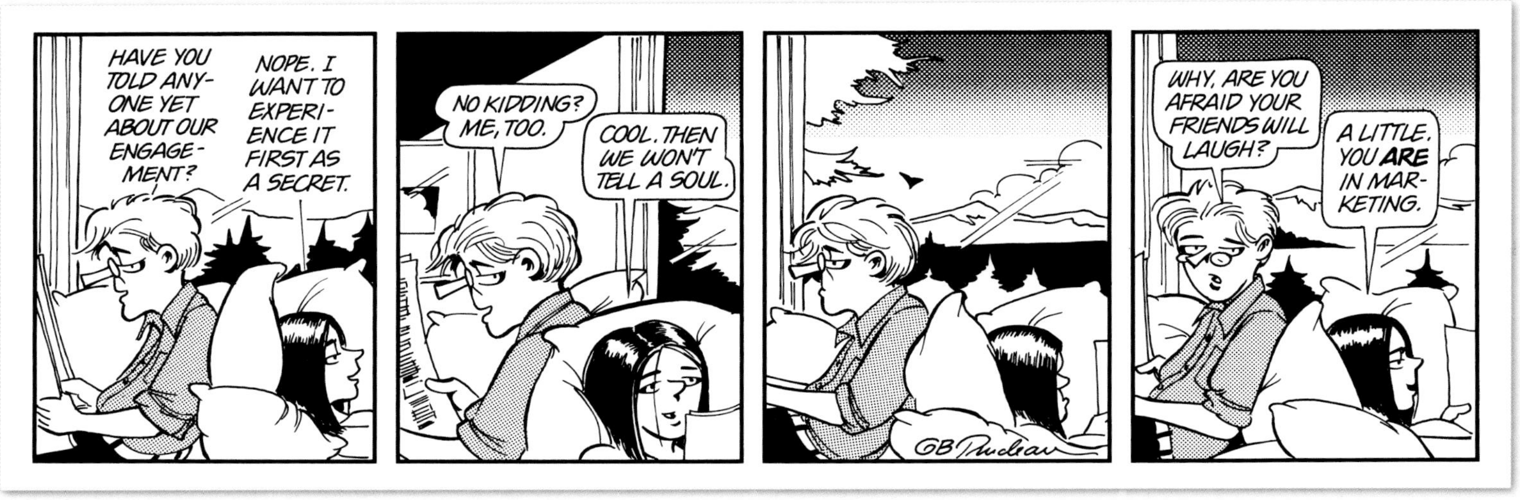
HAVE YOU TOLD ANYONE YET ABOUT OUR ENGAGEMENT?
NOPE. I WANT TO EXPERIENCE IT FIRST AS A SECRET.
NO KIDDING? ME, TOO.
COOL. THEN WE WON'T TELL A SOUL.
WHY, ARE YOU AFRAID YOUR FRIENDS WILL LAUGH?
A LITTLE. YOU ARE IN MARKETING.

1/21/97

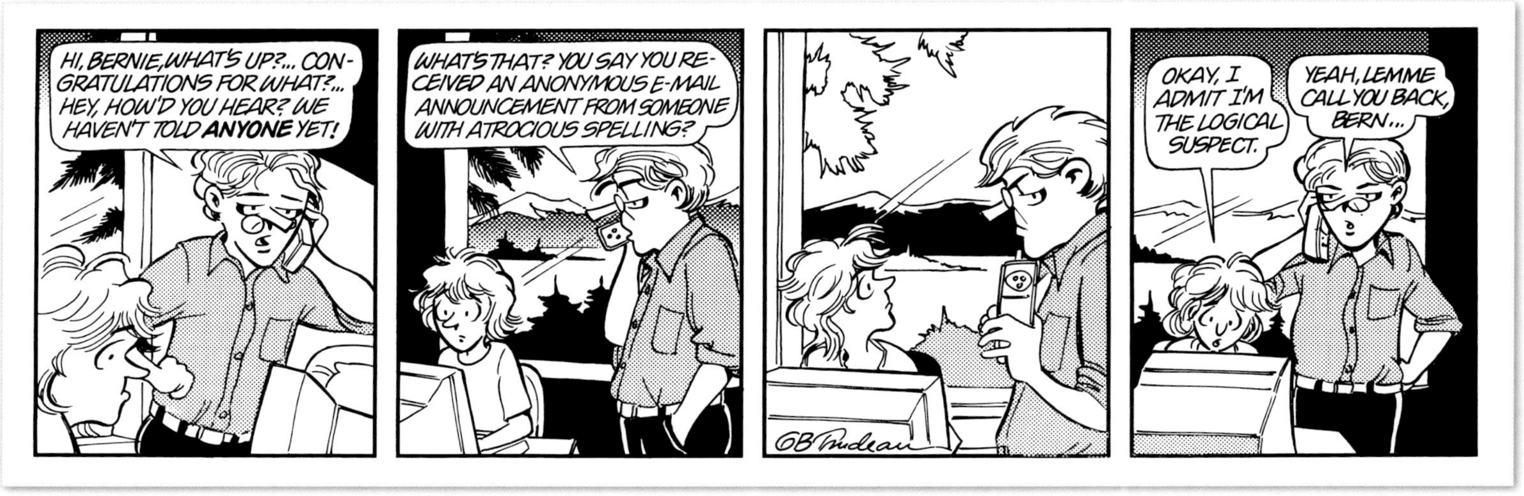
HI, BERNIE, WHAT'S UP?... CONGRATULATIONS FOR WHAT?... HEY, HOW'D YOU HEAR? WE HAVEN'T TOLD ANYONE YET!
WHAT'S THAT? YOU SAY YOU RECEIVED AN ANONYMOUS E-MAIL ANNOUNCEMENT FROM SOMEONE WITH ATROCIOUS SPELLING?
OKAY, I ADMIT I'M THE LOGICAL SUSPECT.
YEAH, LEMME CALL YOU BACK, BERN...

1/22/97

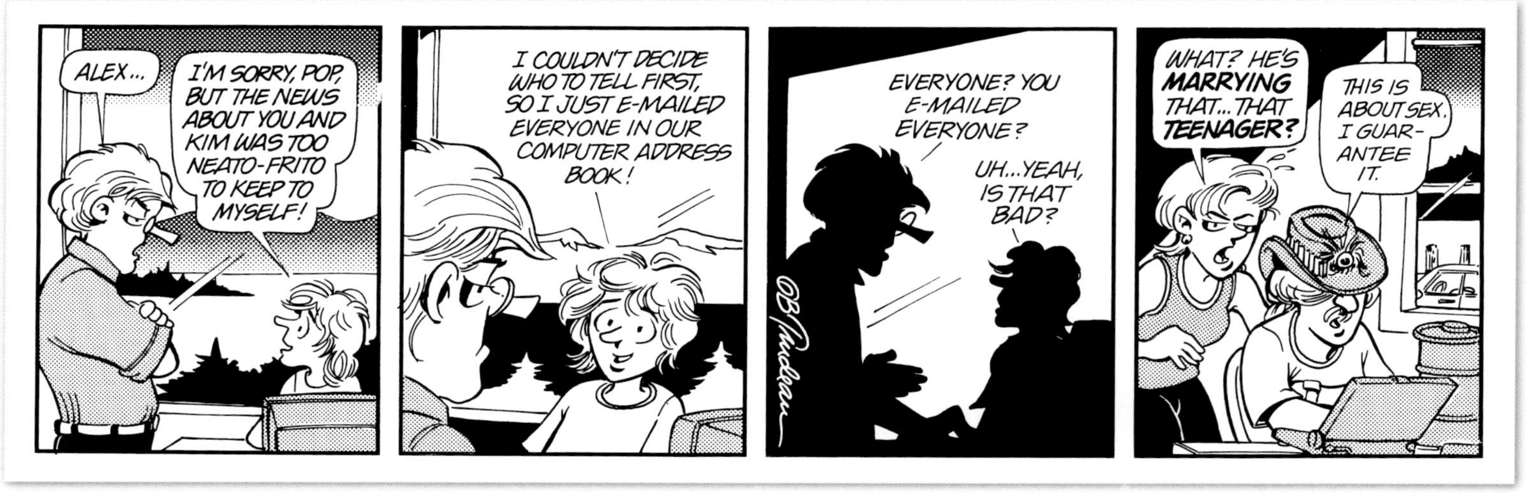
ALEX...
I'M SORRY, POP, BUT THE NEWS ABOUT YOU AND KIM WAS TOO NEATO-FRITO TO KEEP TO MYSELF!
I COULDN'T DECIDE WHO TO TELL FIRST, SO I JUST E-MAILED EVERYONE IN OUR COMPUTER ADDRESS BOOK!
EVERYONE? YOU E-MAILED EVERYONE?
UH...YEAH, IS THAT BAD?
WHAT? HE'S MARRYING THAT...THAT TEENAGER?
THIS IS ABOUT SEX. I GUARANTEE IT.

1/23/97

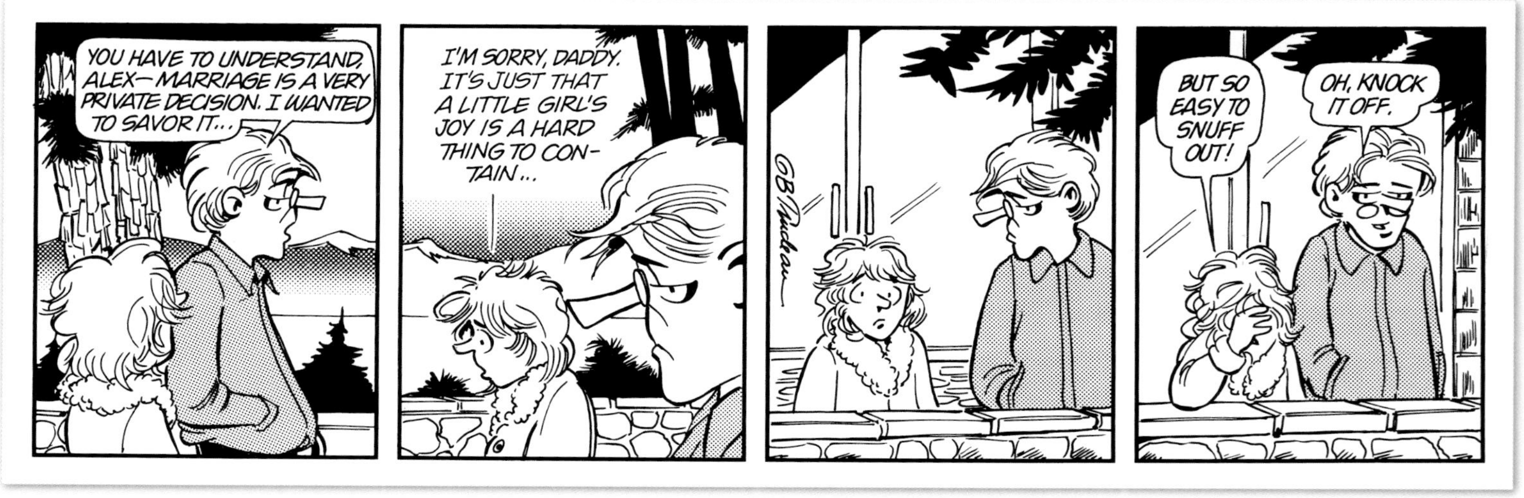
YOU HAVE TO UNDERSTAND, ALEX—MARRIAGE IS A VERY PRIVATE DECISION. I WANTED TO SAVOR IT...
I'M SORRY, DADDY. IT'S JUST THAT A LITTLE GIRL'S JOY IS A HARD THING TO CONTAIN...
BUT SO EASY TO SNUFF OUT!
OH, KNOCK IT OFF.

1/24/97

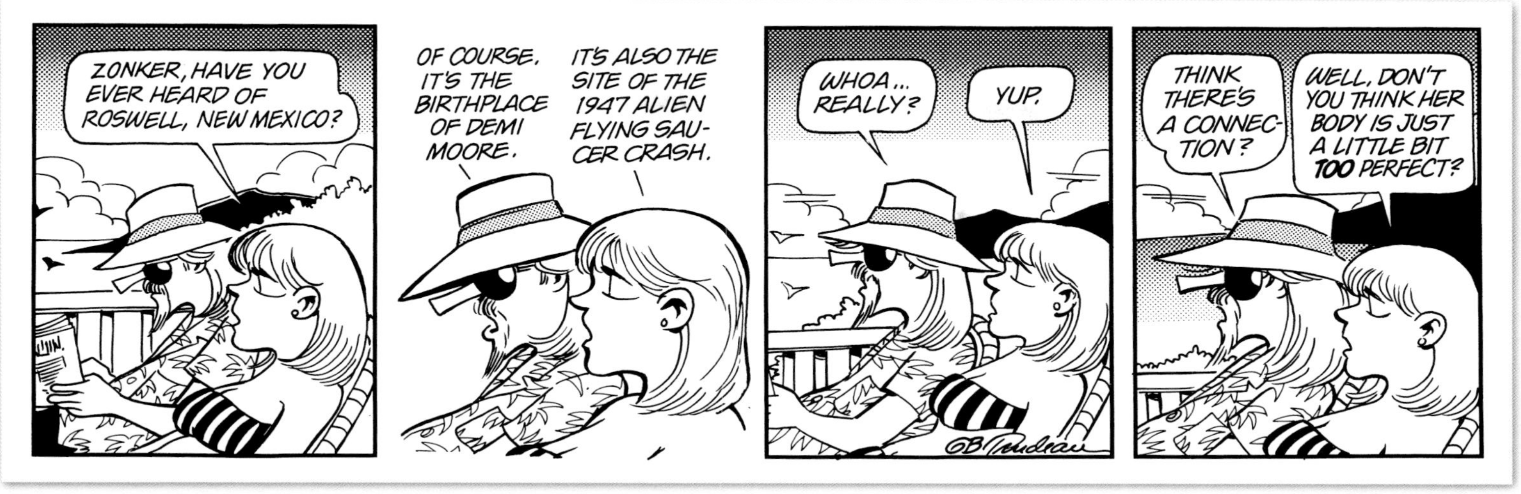
ZONKER, HAVE YOU EVER HEARD OF ROSWELL, NEW MEXICO?
OF COURSE. IT'S THE BIRTHPLACE OF DEMI MOORE.
IT'S ALSO THE SITE OF THE 1947 ALIEN FLYING SAUCER CRASH.
WHOA... REALLY?
YUP.
THINK THERE'S A CONNECTION?
WELL, DON'T YOU THINK HER BODY IS JUST A LITTLE BIT **TOO** PERFECT?
©B Trudeau

7/7/97

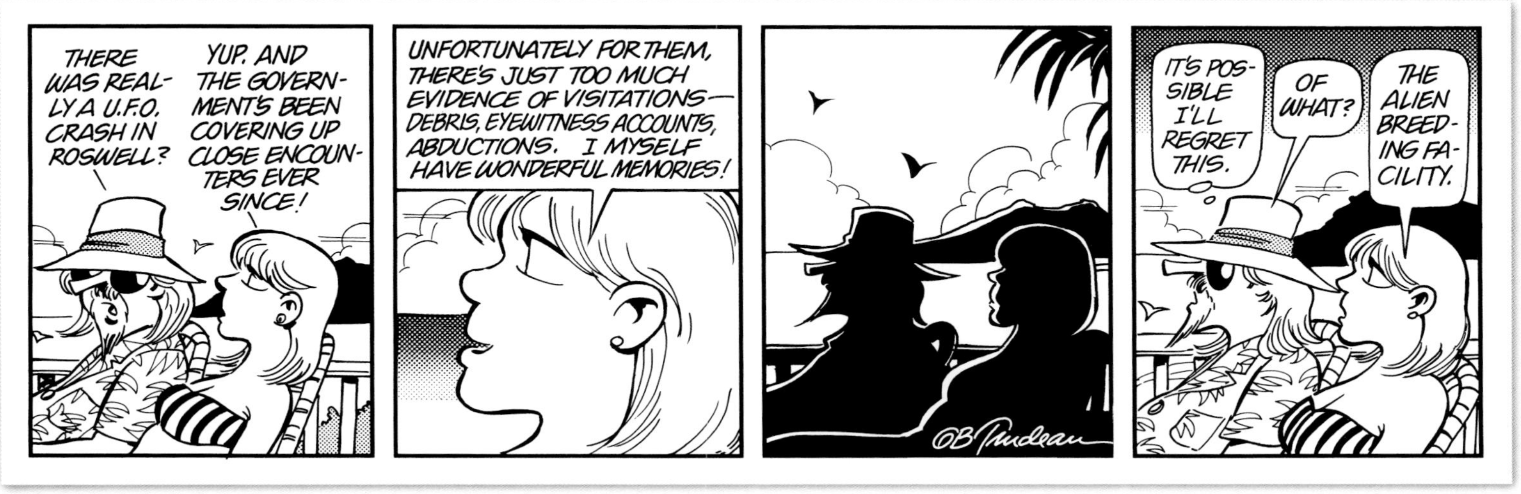
THERE WAS REALLY A U.F.O. CRASH IN ROSWELL?
YUP. AND THE GOVERNMENT'S BEEN COVERING UP CLOSE ENCOUNTERS EVER SINCE!
UNFORTUNATELY FOR THEM, THERE'S JUST TOO MUCH EVIDENCE OF VISITATIONS— DEBRIS, EYEWITNESS ACCOUNTS, ABDUCTIONS. I MYSELF HAVE WONDERFUL MEMORIES!
©B Trudeau
IT'S POSSIBLE I'LL REGRET THIS.
OF WHAT?
THE ALIEN BREEDING FACILITY.

7/8/97

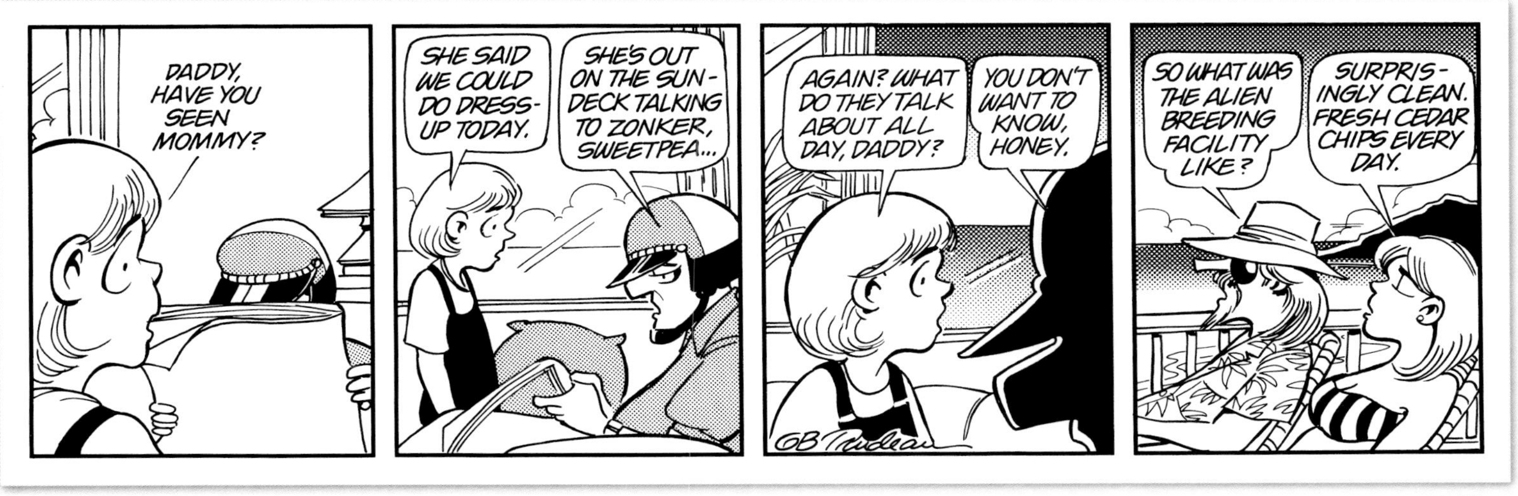
DADDY, HAVE YOU SEEN MOMMY?
SHE SAID WE COULD DO DRESS-UP TODAY.
SHE'S OUT ON THE SUNDECK TALKING TO ZONKER, SWEETPEA...
AGAIN? WHAT DO THEY TALK ABOUT ALL DAY, DADDY?
YOU DON'T WANT TO KNOW, HONEY.
©B Trudeau
SO WHAT WAS THE ALIEN BREEDING FACILITY LIKE?
SURPRISINGLY CLEAN. FRESH CEDAR CHIPS EVERY DAY.

7/9/97

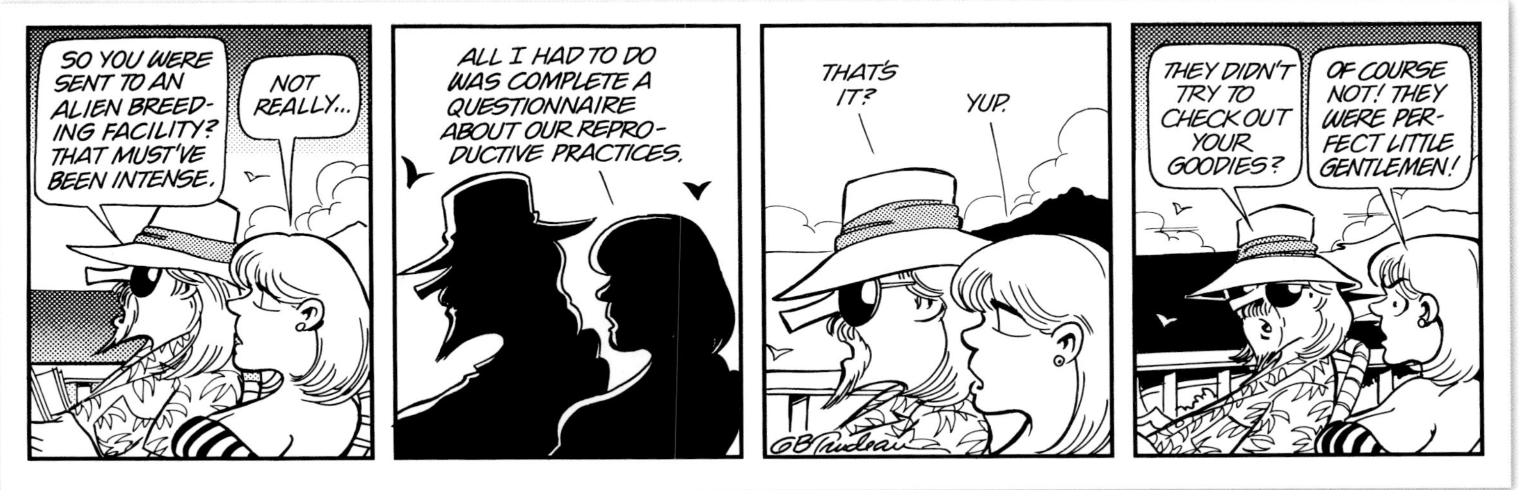
SO YOU WERE SENT TO AN ALIEN BREEDING FACILITY? THAT MUST'VE BEEN INTENSE.
NOT REALLY...
ALL I HAD TO DO WAS COMPLETE A QUESTIONNAIRE ABOUT OUR REPRODUCTIVE PRACTICES.
THAT'S IT?
YUP.
©B Trudeau
THEY DIDN'T TRY TO CHECK OUT YOUR GOODIES?
OF COURSE NOT! THEY WERE PERFECT LITTLE GENTLEMEN!

7/10/97

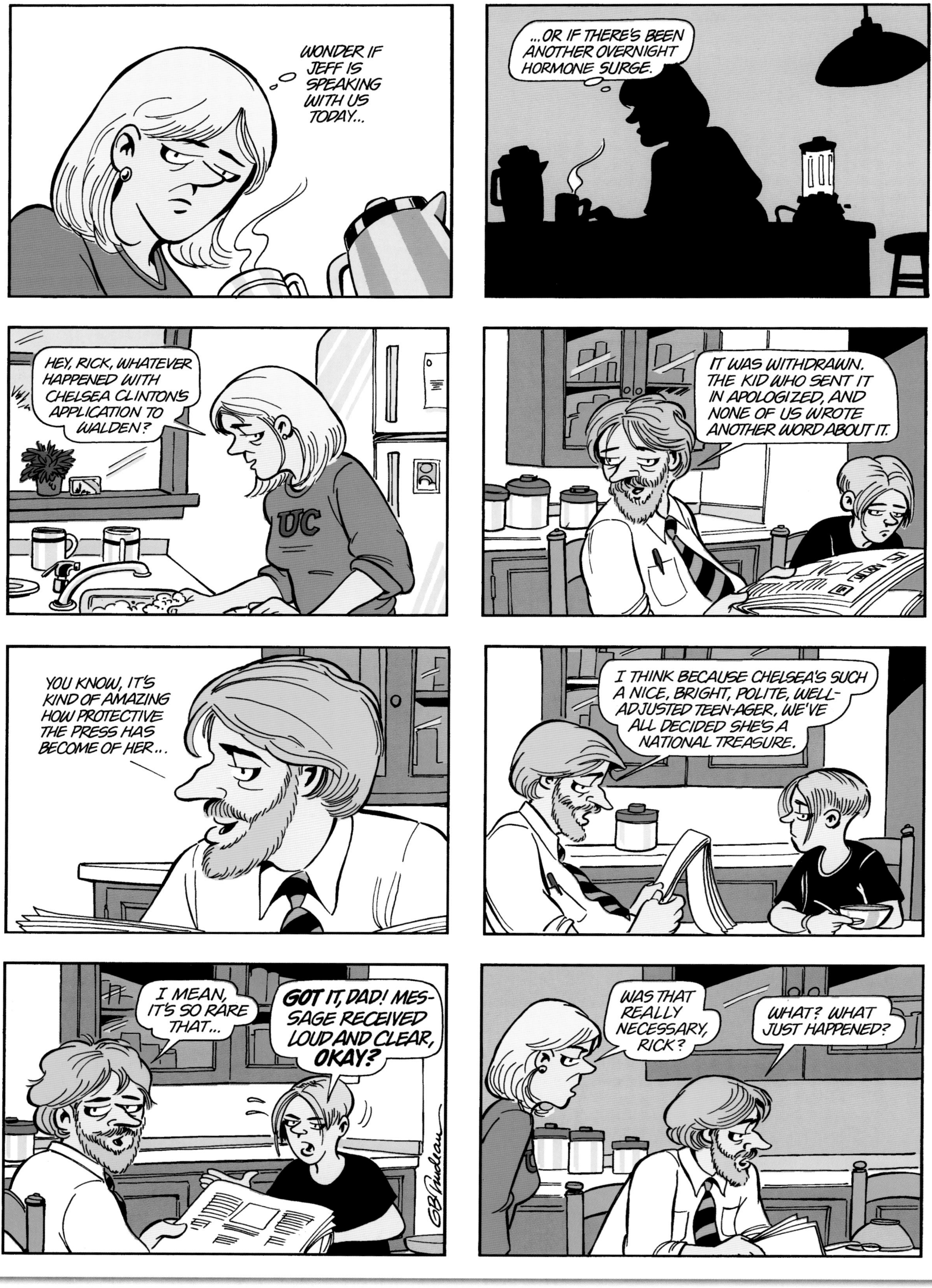
WONDER IF JEFF IS SPEAKING WITH US TODAY...
...OR IF THERE'S BEEN ANOTHER OVERNIGHT HORMONE SURGE.
HEY, RICK, WHATEVER HAPPENED WITH CHELSEA CLINTON'S APPLICATION TO WALDEN?
IT WAS WITHDRAWN. THE KID WHO SENT IT IN APOLOGIZED, AND NONE OF US WROTE ANOTHER WORD ABOUT IT.
YOU KNOW, IT'S KIND OF AMAZING HOW PROTECTIVE THE PRESS HAS BECOME OF HER...
I THINK BECAUSE CHELSEA'S SUCH A NICE, BRIGHT, POLITE, WELL-ADJUSTED TEEN-AGER, WE'VE ALL DECIDED SHE'S A NATIONAL TREASURE.
I MEAN, IT'S SO RARE THAT...
GOT IT, DAD! MESSAGE RECEIVED LOUD AND CLEAR, OKAY?
WAS THAT REALLY NECESSARY, RICK?
WHAT? WHAT JUST HAPPENED?

2/23/97

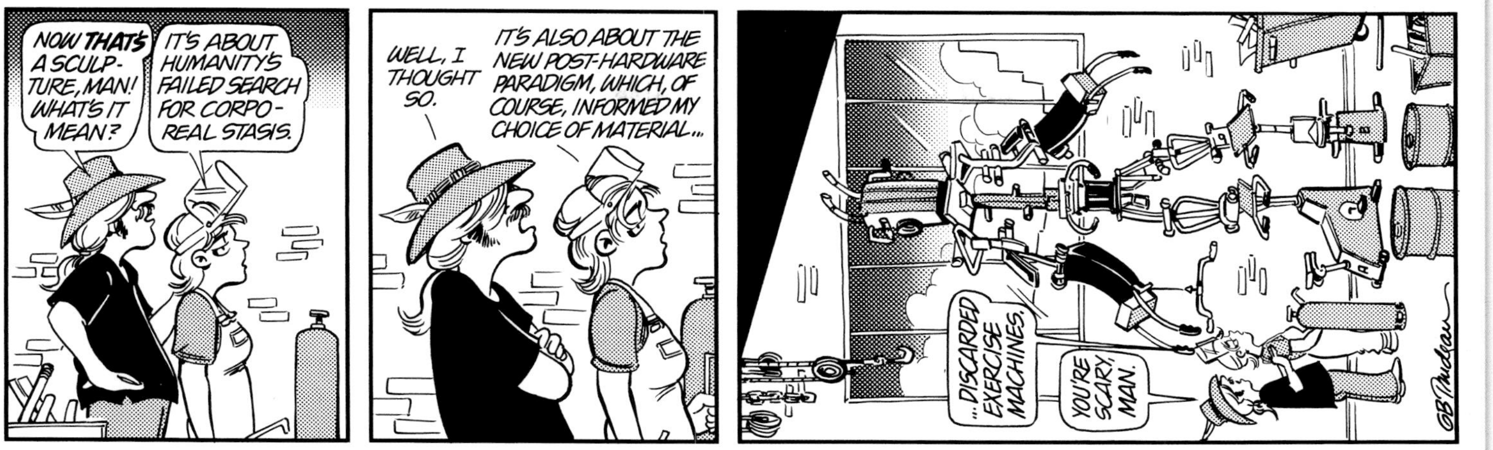
NOW THAT'S A SCULPTURE, MAN! WHAT'S IT MEAN?
IT'S ABOUT HUMANITY'S FAILED SEARCH FOR CORPOREAL STASIS.
WELL, I THOUGHT SO.
IT'S ALSO ABOUT THE NEW POST-HARDWARE PARADIGM, WHICH, OF COURSE, INFORMED MY CHOICE OF MATERIAL...
...DISCARDED EXERCISE MACHINES.
YOU'RE SCARY, MAN.

4/14/97

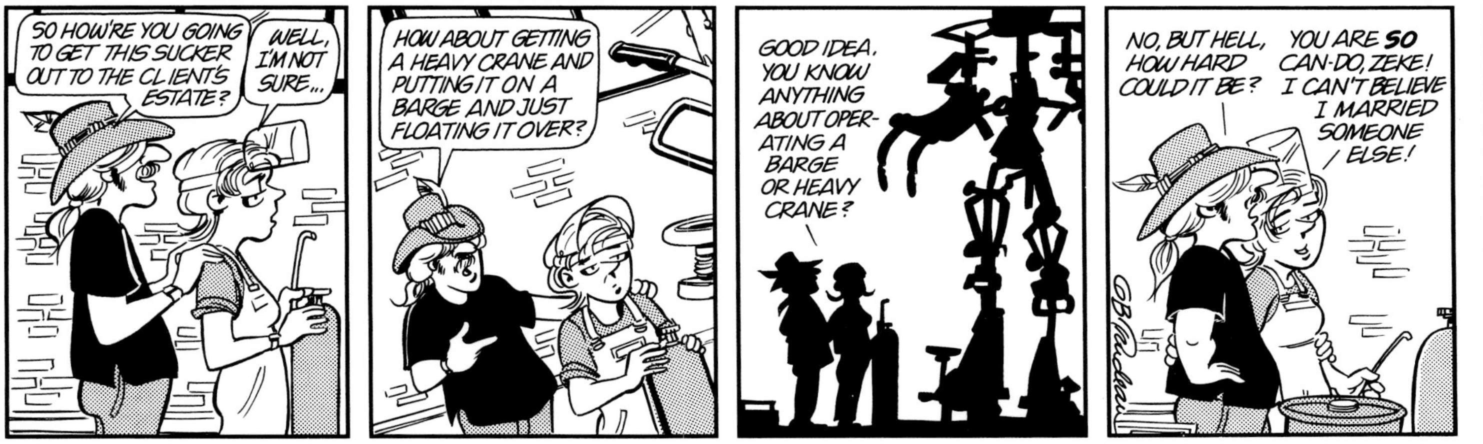
SO HOW'RE YOU GOING TO GET THIS SUCKER OUT TO THE CLIENT'S ESTATE?
WELL, I'M NOT SURE...
HOW ABOUT GETTING A HEAVY CRANE AND PUTTING IT ON A BARGE AND JUST FLOATING IT OVER?
GOOD IDEA. YOU KNOW ANYTHING ABOUT OPERATING A BARGE OR HEAVY CRANE?
NO, BUT HELL, HOW HARD COULD IT BE?
YOU ARE SO CAN-DO, ZEKE! I CAN'T BELIEVE I MARRIED SOMEONE ELSE!

4/15/97

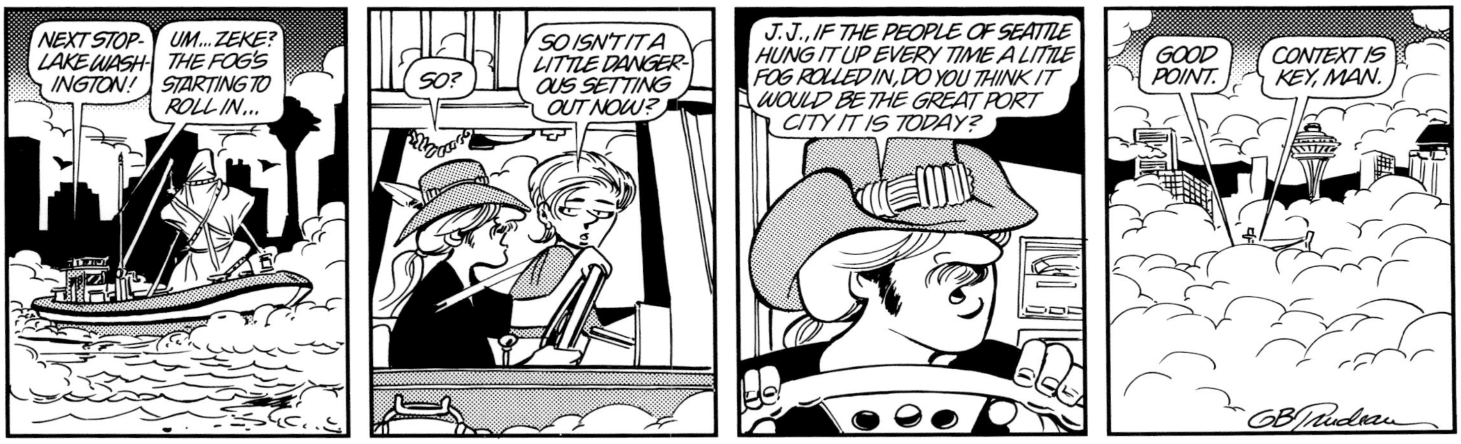
NEXT STOP-LAKE WASHINGTON!
UM...ZEKE? THE FOG'S STARTING TO ROLL IN...
SO?
SO ISN'T IT A LITTLE DANGEROUS SETTING OUT NOW?
J.J., IF THE PEOPLE OF SEATTLE HUNG IT UP EVERY TIME A LITTLE FOG ROLLED IN, DO YOU THINK IT WOULD BE THE GREAT PORT CITY IT IS TODAY?
GOOD POINT.
CONTEXT IS KEY, MAN.

4/17/97

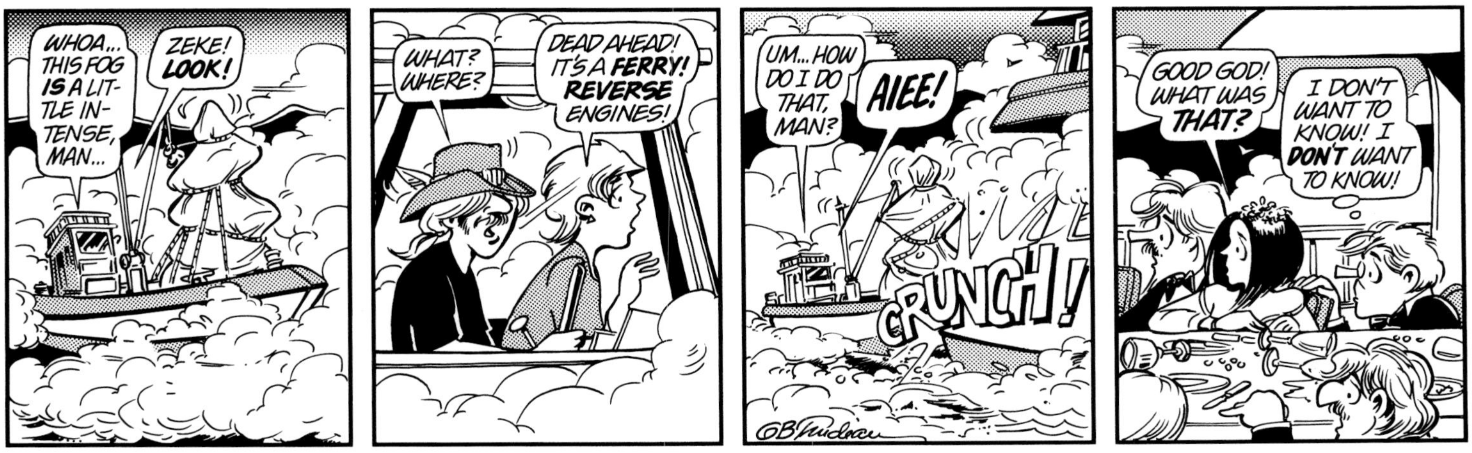
WHOA... THIS FOG IS A LITTLE INTENSE, MAN...
ZEKE! LOOK!
WHAT? WHERE?
DEAD AHEAD! IT'S A FERRY! REVERSE ENGINES!
UM... HOW DO I DO THAT, MAN?
AIEE!
CRUNCH!
GOOD GOD! WHAT WAS THAT?
I DON'T WANT TO KNOW! I DON'T WANT TO KNOW!

4/18/97

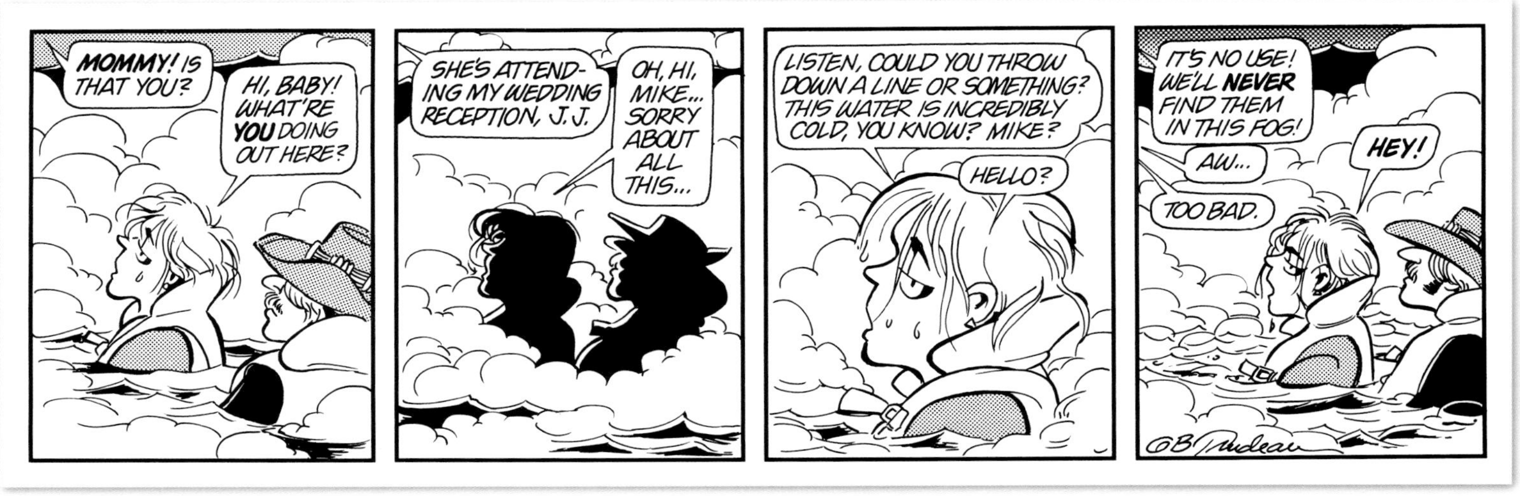
MOMMY! IS THAT YOU?
HI, BABY! WHAT'RE YOU DOING OUT HERE?
SHE'S ATTENDING MY WEDDING RECEPTION, J.J.
OH, HI, MIKE... SORRY ABOUT ALL THIS...
LISTEN, COULD YOU THROW DOWN A LINE OR SOMETHING? THIS WATER IS INCREDIBLY COLD, YOU KNOW? MIKE?
HELLO?
IT'S NO USE! WE'LL NEVER FIND THEM IN THIS FOG!
AW...
TOO BAD.
HEY!
©B. Trudeau

4/21/97

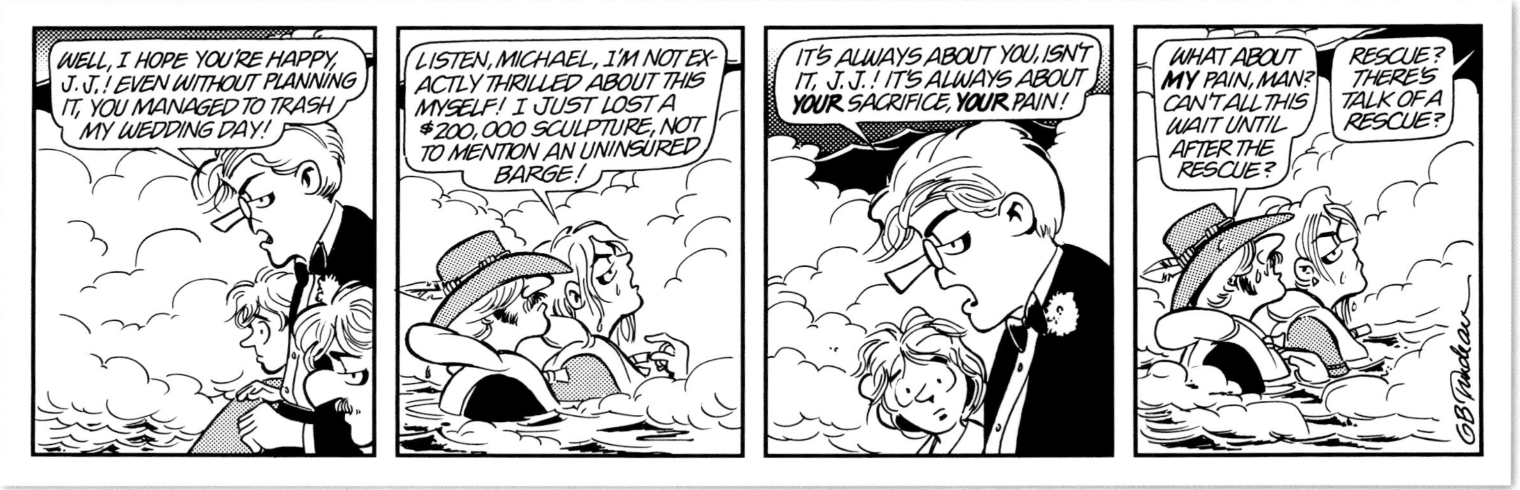
WELL, I HOPE YOU'RE HAPPY, J.J.! EVEN WITHOUT PLANNING IT, YOU MANAGED TO TRASH MY WEDDING DAY!
LISTEN, MICHAEL, I'M NOT EXACTLY THRILLED ABOUT THIS MYSELF! I JUST LOST A $200,000 SCULPTURE, NOT TO MENTION AN UNINSURED BARGE!
IT'S ALWAYS ABOUT YOU, ISN'T IT, J.J.! IT'S ALWAYS ABOUT YOUR SACRIFICE, YOUR PAIN!
WHAT ABOUT MY PAIN, MAN? CAN'T ALL THIS WAIT UNTIL AFTER THE RESCUE?
RESCUE? THERE'S TALK OF A RESCUE?
©B. Trudeau

4/22/97

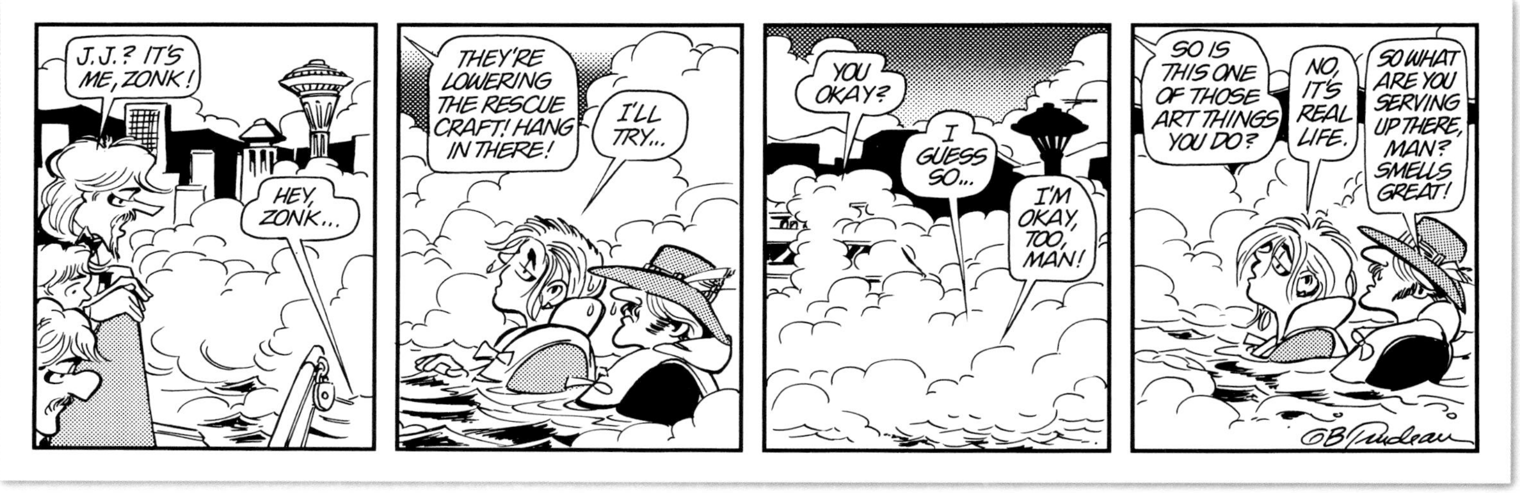
J.J.? IT'S ME, ZONK!
HEY, ZONK...
THEY'RE LOWERING THE RESCUE CRAFT! HANG IN THERE!
I'LL TRY...
YOU OKAY?
I GUESS SO...
I'M OKAY, TOO, MAN!
SO IS THIS ONE OF THOSE ART THINGS YOU DO?
NO, IT'S REAL LIFE.
SO WHAT ARE YOU SERVING UP THERE, MAN? SMELLS GREAT!
©B. Trudeau

4/23/97

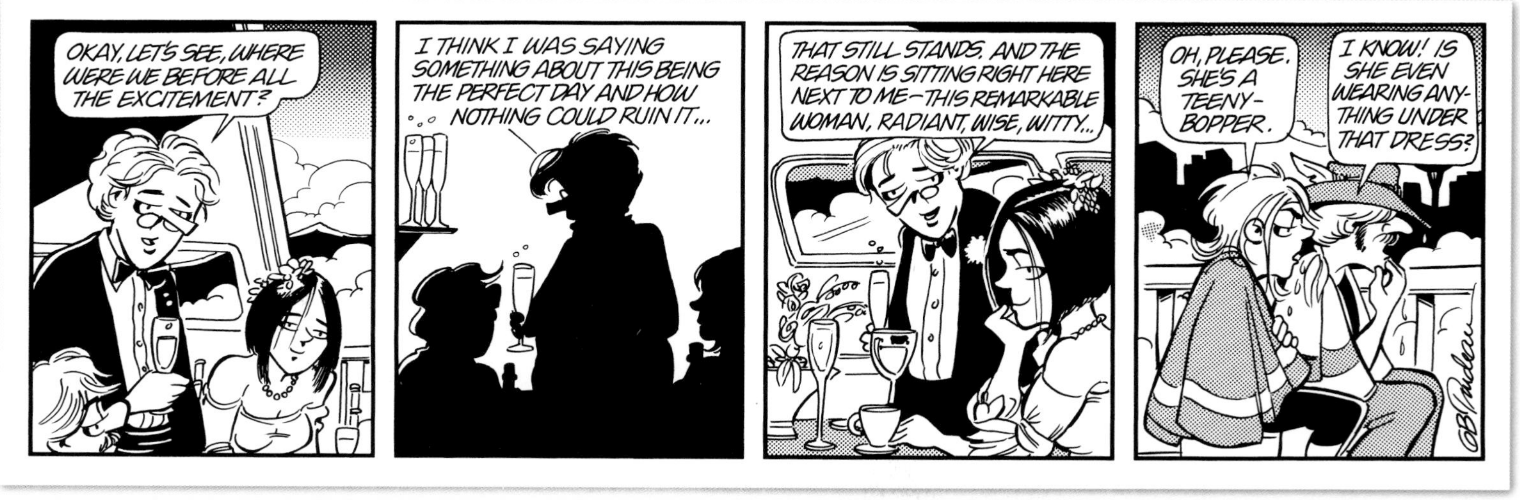
OKAY, LET'S SEE, WHERE WERE WE BEFORE ALL THE EXCITEMENT?
I THINK I WAS SAYING SOMETHING ABOUT THIS BEING THE PERFECT DAY AND HOW NOTHING COULD RUIN IT...
THAT STILL STANDS, AND THE REASON IS SITTING RIGHT HERE NEXT TO ME—THIS REMARKABLE WOMAN, RADIANT, WISE, WITTY...
OH, PLEASE. SHE'S A TEENY-BOPPER.
I KNOW! IS SHE EVEN WEARING ANYTHING UNDER THAT DRESS?
©B. Trudeau

4/25/97

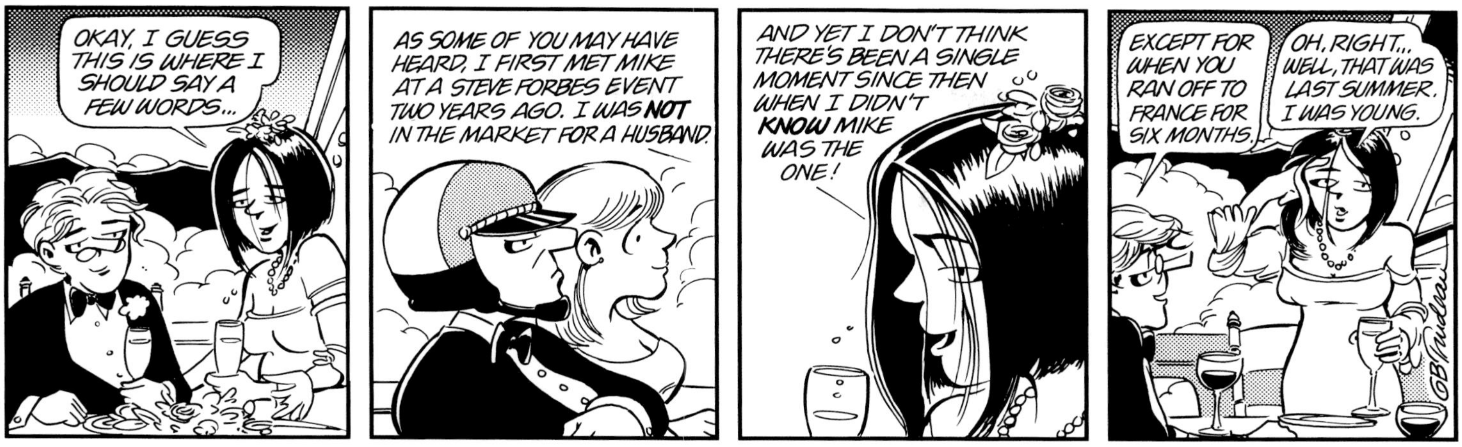
OKAY, I GUESS THIS IS WHERE I SHOULD SAY A FEW WORDS...
AS SOME OF YOU MAY HAVE HEARD, I FIRST MET MIKE AT A STEVE FORBES EVENT TWO YEARS AGO. I WAS NOT IN THE MARKET FOR A HUSBAND.
AND YET I DON'T THINK THERE'S BEEN A SINGLE MOMENT SINCE THEN WHEN I DIDN'T KNOW MIKE WAS THE ONE!
EXCEPT FOR WHEN YOU RAN OFF TO FRANCE FOR SIX MONTHS.
OH, RIGHT... WELL, THAT WAS LAST SUMMER. I WAS YOUNG.

4/28/97

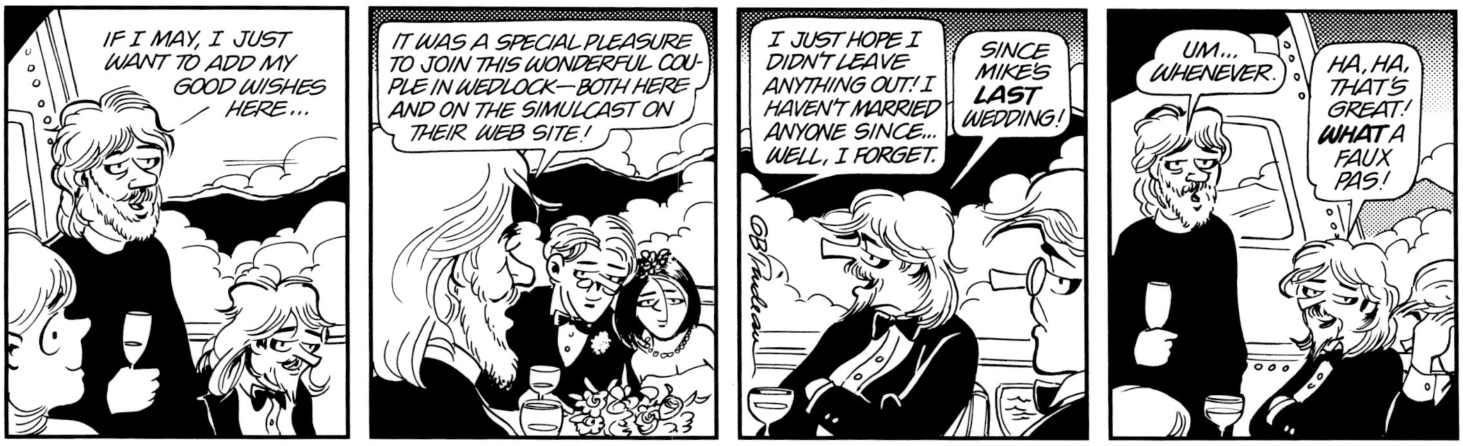
IF I MAY, I JUST WANT TO ADD MY GOOD WISHES HERE...
IT WAS A SPECIAL PLEASURE TO JOIN THIS WONDERFUL COUPLE IN WEDLOCK—BOTH HERE AND ON THE SIMULCAST ON THEIR WEB SITE!
I JUST HOPE I DIDN'T LEAVE ANYTHING OUT! I HAVEN'T MARRIED ANYONE SINCE... WELL, I FORGET.
SINCE MIKE'S LAST WEDDING!
UM... WHENEVER.
HA, HA, THAT'S GREAT! WHAT A FAUX PAS!

4/29/97

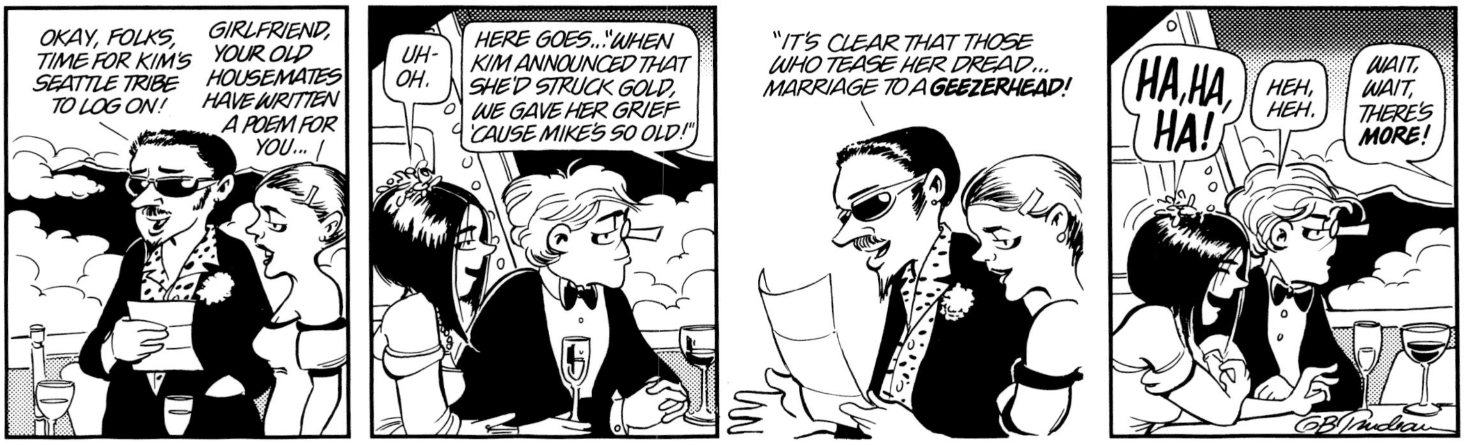
OKAY, FOLKS, TIME FOR KIM'S SEATTLE TRIBE TO LOG ON!
GIRLFRIEND, YOUR OLD HOUSEMATES HAVE WRITTEN A POEM FOR YOU...
UH-OH.
HERE GOES... "WHEN KIM ANNOUNCED THAT SHE'D STRUCK GOLD, WE GAVE HER GRIEF 'CAUSE MIKE'S SO OLD!"
"IT'S CLEAR THAT THOSE WHO TEASE HER DREAD... MARRIAGE TO A GEEZERHEAD!
HA, HA, HA!
HEH, HEH.
WAIT, WAIT, THERE'S MORE!

4/30/97

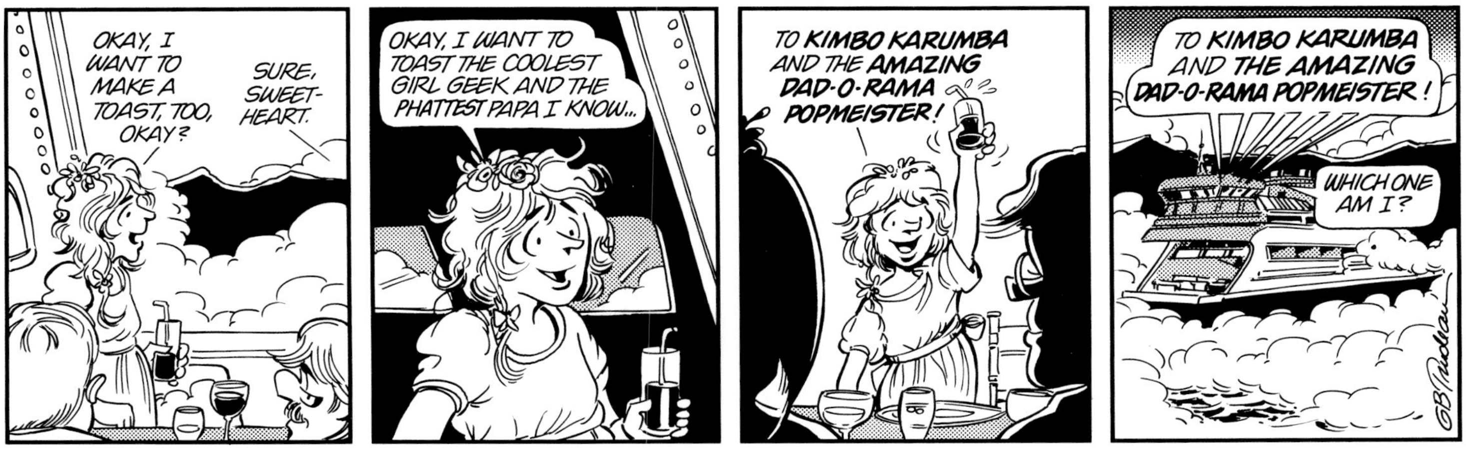
OKAY, I WANT TO MAKE A TOAST, TOO, OKAY?
SURE, SWEETHEART.
OKAY, I WANT TO TOAST THE COOLEST GIRL GEEK AND THE PHATTEST PAPA I KNOW...
TO KIMBO KARUMBA AND THE AMAZING DAD-O-RAMA POPMEISTER!
TO KIMBO KARUMBA AND THE AMAZING DAD-O-RAMA POPMEISTER!
WHICH ONE AM I?

5/1/97

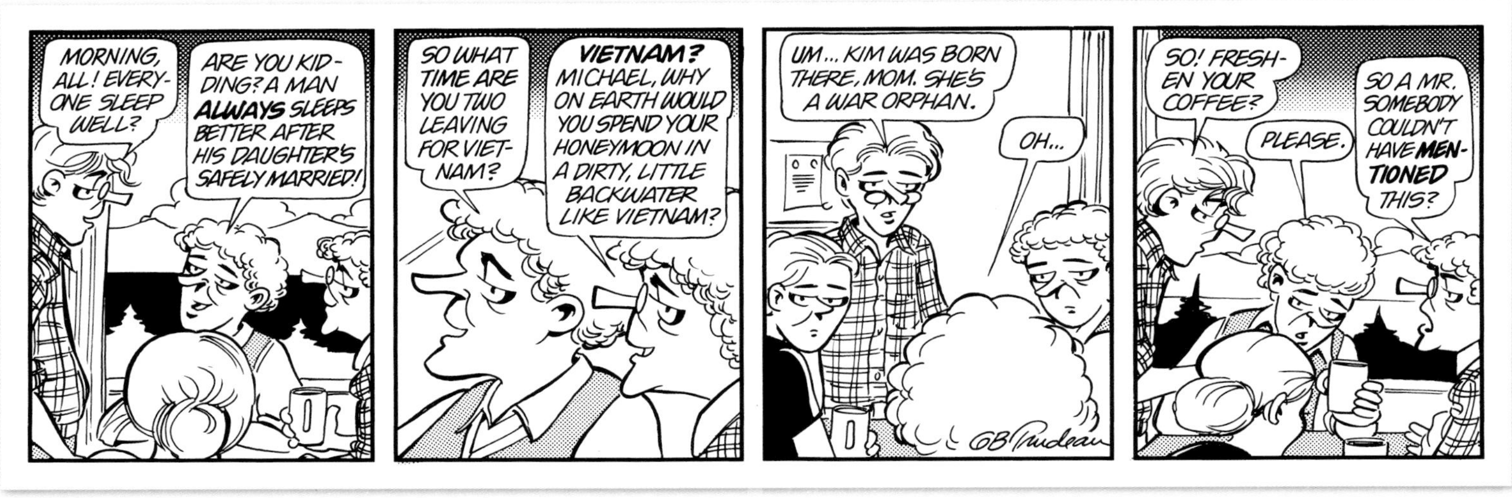
MORNING, ALL! EVERYONE SLEEP WELL?
ARE YOU KIDDING? A MAN ALWAYS SLEEPS BETTER AFTER HIS DAUGHTER'S SAFELY MARRIED!
SO WHAT TIME ARE YOU TWO LEAVING FOR VIETNAM?
VIETNAM? MICHAEL, WHY ON EARTH WOULD YOU SPEND YOUR HONEYMOON IN A DIRTY, LITTLE BACKWATER LIKE VIETNAM?
UM... KIM WAS BORN THERE, MOM. SHE'S A WAR ORPHAN.
OH...
SO! FRESHEN YOUR COFFEE?
PLEASE.
SO A MR. SOMEBODY COULDN'T HAVE MENTIONED THIS?

5/5/97

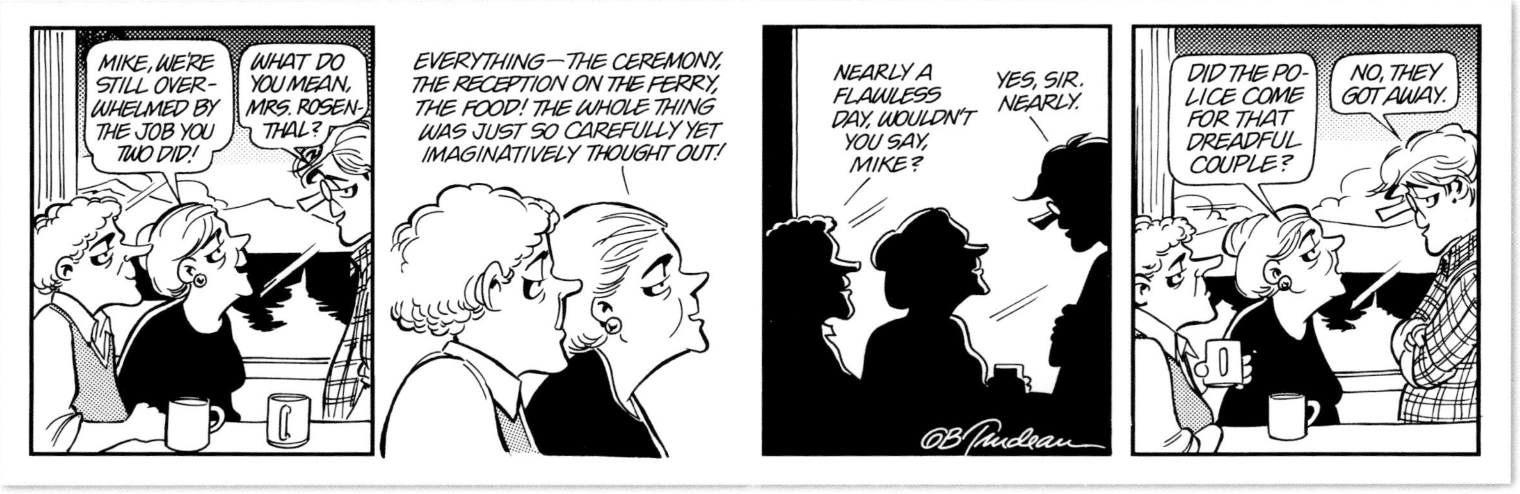
MIKE, WE'RE STILL OVERWHELMED BY THE JOB YOU TWO DID!
WHAT DO YOU MEAN, MRS. ROSENTHAL?
EVERYTHING—THE CEREMONY, THE RECEPTION ON THE FERRY, THE FOOD! THE WHOLE THING WAS JUST SO CAREFULLY YET IMAGINATIVELY THOUGHT OUT!
NEARLY A FLAWLESS DAY, WOULDN'T YOU SAY, MIKE?
YES, SIR. NEARLY.
DID THE POLICE COME FOR THAT DREADFUL COUPLE?
NO, THEY GOT AWAY.

5/6/97

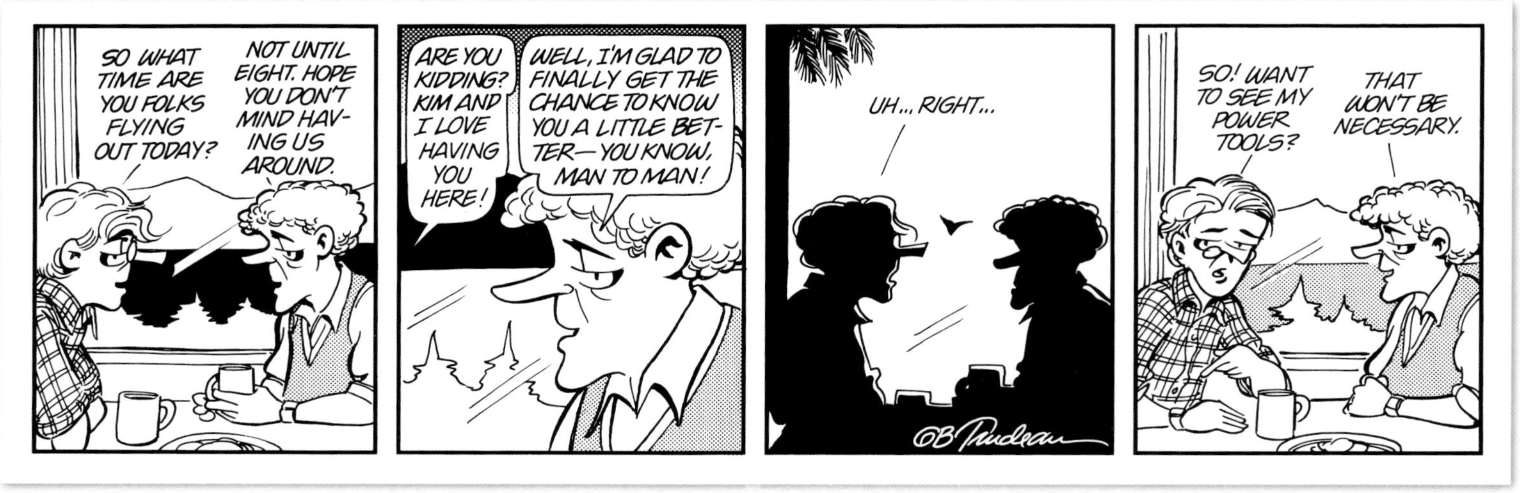
SO WHAT TIME ARE YOU FOLKS FLYING OUT TODAY?
NOT UNTIL EIGHT. HOPE YOU DON'T MIND HAVING US AROUND.
ARE YOU KIDDING? KIM AND I LOVE HAVING YOU HERE!
WELL, I'M GLAD TO FINALLY GET THE CHANCE TO KNOW YOU A LITTLE BETTER—YOU KNOW, MAN TO MAN!
UH... RIGHT...
SO! WANT TO SEE MY POWER TOOLS?
THAT WON'T BE NECESSARY.

5/8/97

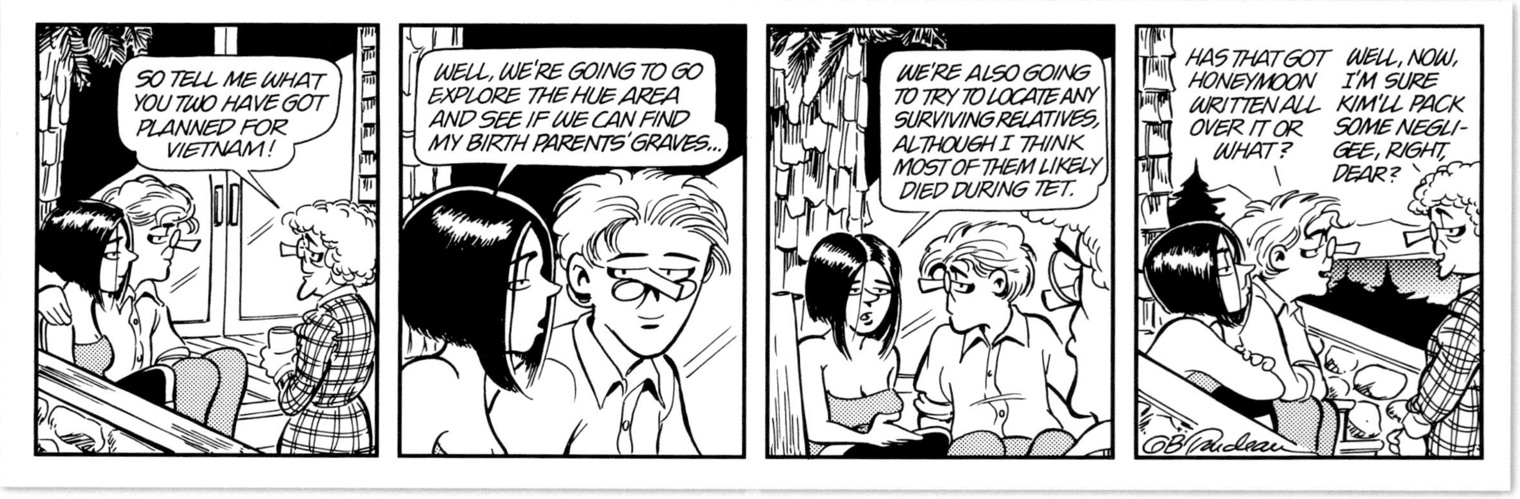
SO TELL ME WHAT YOU TWO HAVE GOT PLANNED FOR VIETNAM!
WELL, WE'RE GOING TO GO EXPLORE THE HUE AREA AND SEE IF WE CAN FIND MY BIRTH PARENTS' GRAVES...
WE'RE ALSO GOING TO TRY TO LOCATE ANY SURVIVING RELATIVES, ALTHOUGH I THINK MOST OF THEM LIKELY DIED DURING TET.
HAS THAT GOT HONEYMOON WRITTEN ALL OVER IT OR WHAT?
WELL, NOW, I'M SURE KIM'LL PACK SOME NEGLIGEE, RIGHT, DEAR?

5/9/97

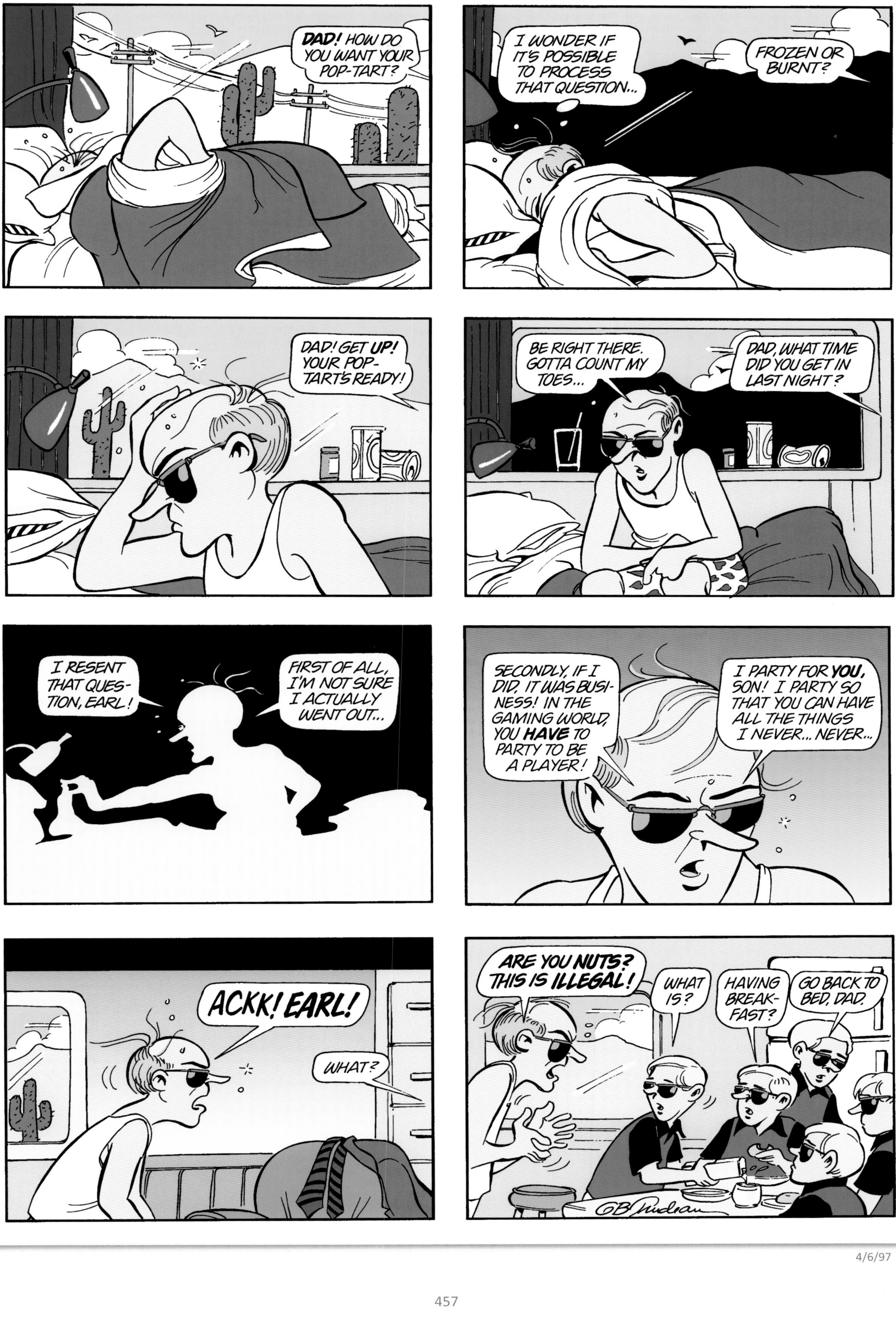
DAD! HOW DO YOU WANT YOUR POP-TART?
I WONDER IF IT'S POSSIBLE TO PROCESS THAT QUESTION...
FROZEN OR BURNT?
DAD! GET UP! YOUR POP-TART'S READY!
BE RIGHT THERE. GOTTA COUNT MY TOES...
DAD, WHAT TIME DID YOU GET IN LAST NIGHT?
I RESENT THAT QUESTION, EARL!
FIRST OF ALL, I'M NOT SURE I ACTUALLY WENT OUT...
SECONDLY, IF I DID, IT WAS BUSINESS! IN THE GAMING WORLD, YOU HAVE TO PARTY TO BE A PLAYER!
I PARTY FOR YOU, SON! I PARTY SO THAT YOU CAN HAVE ALL THE THINGS I NEVER... NEVER...
ACKK! EARL!
WHAT?
ARE YOU NUTS? THIS IS ILLEGAL!
WHAT IS?
HAVING BREAKFAST?
GO BACK TO BED, DAD.
GB Trudeau

4/6/97

JIMMY THUDPUCKER

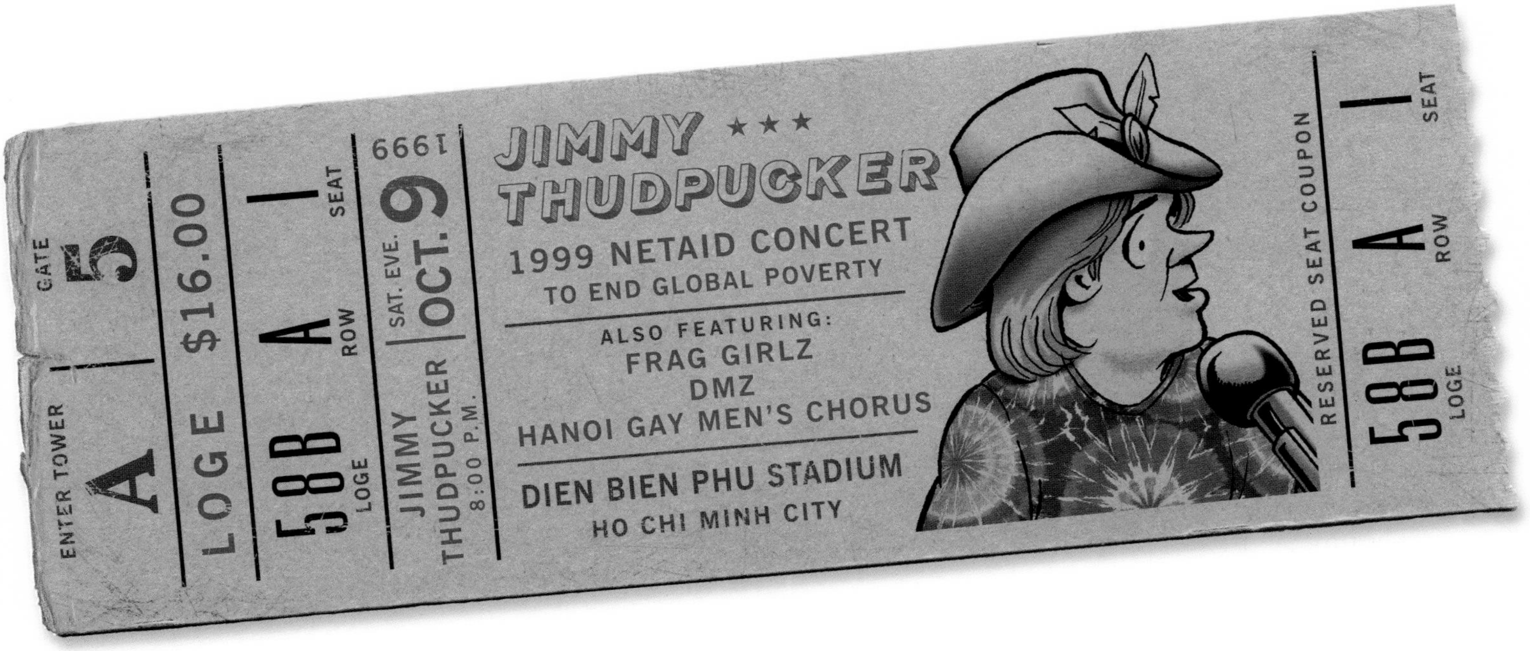

ENTER TOWER
A
GATE
5
LOGE $16.00
58B
LOGE
A
ROW
SEAT
SAT. EVE.
OCT. 9
1999
JIMMY THUDPUCKER
8:00 P.M.
JIMMY ★★★
THUDPUCKER
1999 NETAID CONCERT
TO END GLOBAL POVERTY
ALSO FEATURING:
FRAG GIRLZ
DMZ
HANOI GAY MEN'S CHORUS
DIEN BIEN PHU STADIUM
HO CHI MINH CITY
RESERVED SEAT COUPON
58B
LOGE
A
ROW
SEAT

Here's what I owe Jimmy Thudpucker—and what he owes me. In the early hours of January 29, 1985, I was standing in the back of a room at A&M Studios in Hollywood, watching forty-five of the most famous recording artists in the world mingle during a break. They were recording what would become the massively successful anthem "We Are the World," and a photographer from *Life* and I were the only outsiders present.

With no entourages permitted, the musicians were on their own, and they proved surprisingly shy. Bob Dylan and Bruce Springsteen circled each other nervously. Paul Simon looked dazed. Cyndi Lauper talked much too fast. Everyone seemed awed by someone else in the room.

At one point, Ray Charles sat down behind a grand piano and started to noodle. Off to his left stood Billy Joel, mouth agape, transfixed by Ray's tossed-off virtuosity. Periodically, Joel would smile and shake his head in helpless wonder. (Later that year, Joel would name his newborn daughter Alexa Ray after his hero, which led to their collaboration on "Baby Grand.")

So why was I there? As Jimmy Thudpucker's proxy. Ken Kragen, one of USA for Africa's founders, called to invite Jimmy to "participate" in the project, figuring that a two-week

"Stop / in the middle of your life for askin' / when, where, why, who and what became of you."

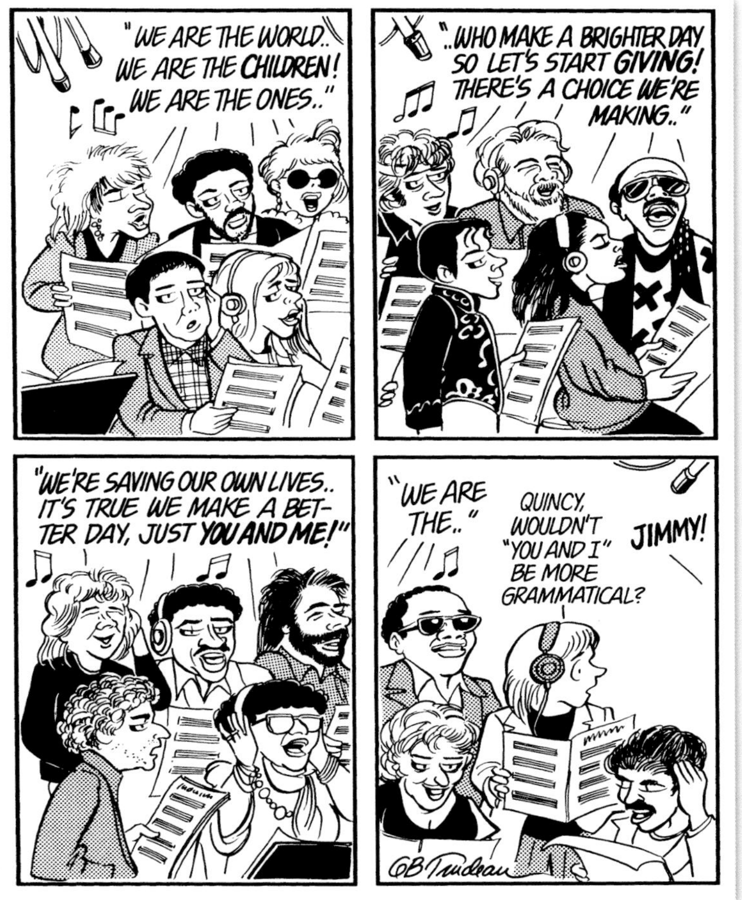
"WE ARE THE WORLD.. WE ARE THE CHILDREN! WE ARE THE ONES.."
"..WHO MAKE A BRIGHTER DAY SO LET'S START GIVING! THERE'S A CHOICE WE'RE MAKING.."
"WE'RE SAVING OUR OWN LIVES.. IT'S TRUE WE MAKE A BETTER DAY, JUST YOU AND ME!"
"WE ARE THE.."
QUINCY, WOULDN'T "YOU AND I" BE MORE GRAMMATICAL?
JIMMY!
GB Trudeau

rollout in the comics couldn't hurt the record's launch. The globally-hyped project hardly needed any help from me, but I was happy to pitch in, and two weeks of strips featuring Jimmy at the session followed.

It was not the first time Thudpucker had put me in a studio. I had earlier written a story line about Jimmy creating a song for Virginia Slade's congressional campaign. On a whim, we hired an L.A. session singer, recorded the tune, and released it under Jimmy's name. The single led to the cover of *Rolling Stone*, two more songs for an NBC animated special, and then a full album of Jimmy's "greatest hits," produced and performed by, among others, Steve Cropper and his band mates from Booker T & the MGs (later to back up another faux act, the Blues Brothers). This, in turn, led to Jimmy's second appearance on the cover of *Rolling Stone*, the only imaginary pop star ever to be so honored.

That Jimmy's output was strictly novelty music didn't seem to dim his prospects. Power pop took care of that. The era of the sensitive singer/songwriter over, Jimmy's career went into a controlled dive. Over the years, he's tried everything to pull out of it, from standards to soft rock covers to downloads to ringtones, but nothing has quite seemed to work. Even as a legacy act, Jimmy's pretty much over.

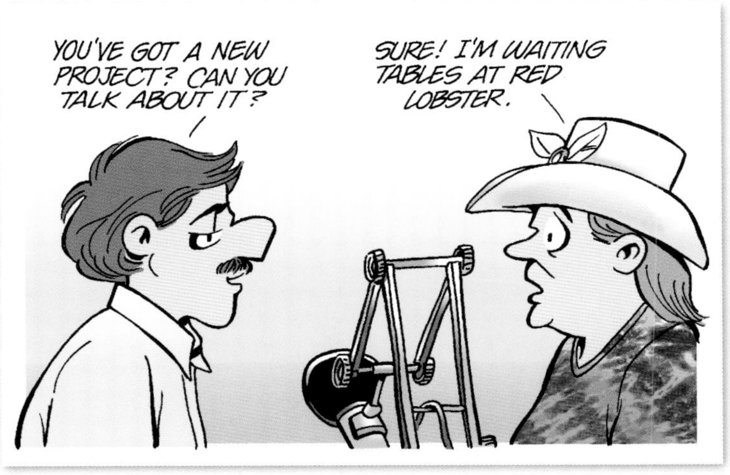
YOU'VE GOT A NEW PROJECT? CAN YOU TALK ABOUT IT?
SURE! I'M WAITING TABLES AT RED LOBSTER.

Not that he's noticed. Jimmy moves ahead doggedly, and to his credit, he's never once recalled that night at A&M studios as the high-water mark it so clearly was.

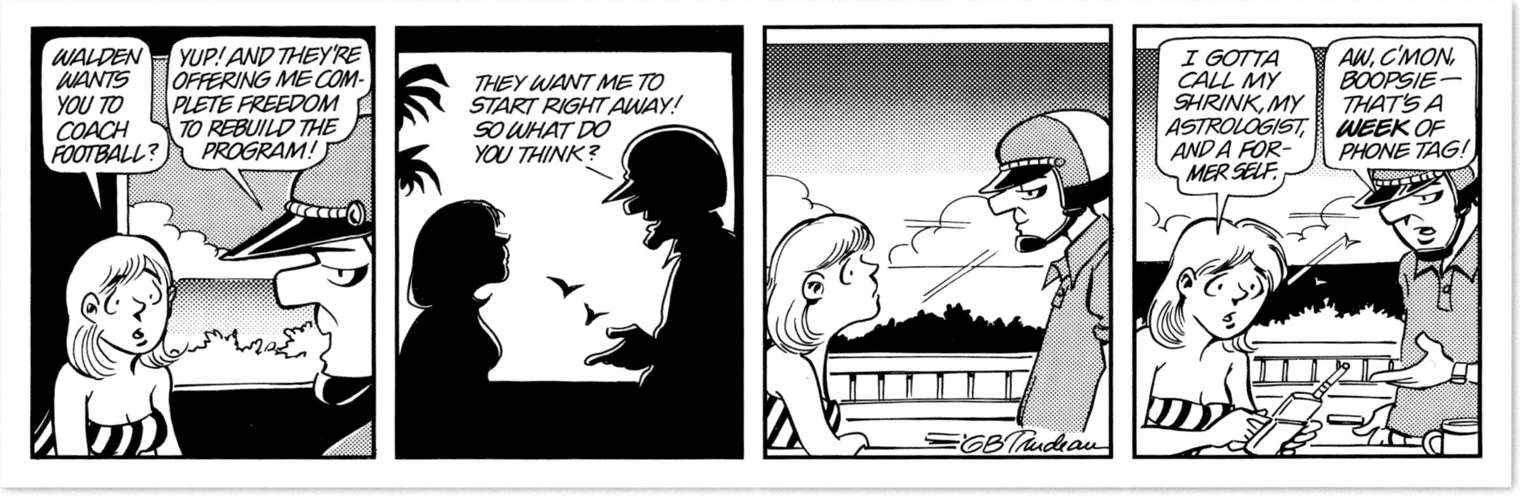

WALDEN WANTS YOU TO COACH FOOTBALL?
YUP! AND THEY'RE OFFERING ME COMPLETE FREEDOM TO REBUILD THE PROGRAM!
THEY WANT ME TO START RIGHT AWAY! SO WHAT DO YOU THINK?
I GOTTA CALL MY SHRINK, MY ASTROLOGIST, AND A FORMER SELF.
AW, C'MON, BOOPSIE— THAT'S A **WEEK** OF PHONE TAG!

9/11/97

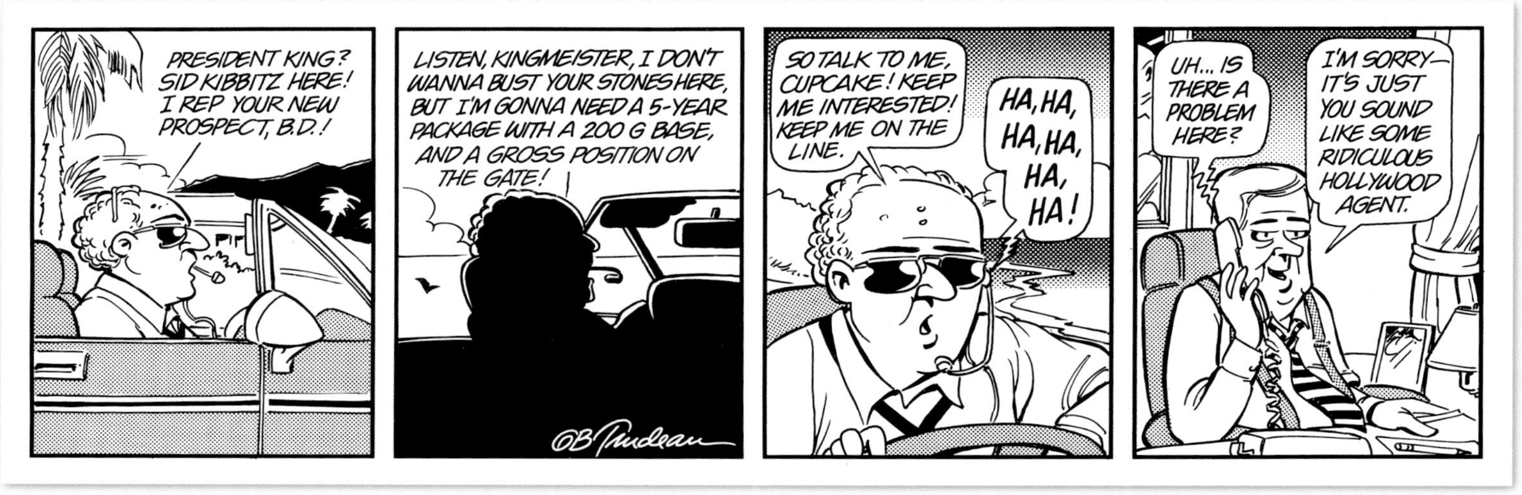

PRESIDENT KING? SID KIBBITZ HERE! I REP YOUR NEW PROSPECT, B.D.!
LISTEN, KINGMEISTER, I DON'T WANNA BUST YOUR STONES HERE, BUT I'M GONNA NEED A 5-YEAR PACKAGE WITH A 200 G BASE, AND A GROSS POSITION ON THE GATE!
SO TALK TO ME, CUPCAKE! KEEP ME INTERESTED! KEEP ME ON THE LINE.
HA, HA, HA, HA, HA, HA!
UH... IS THERE A PROBLEM HERE?
I'M SORRY— IT'S JUST YOU SOUND LIKE SOME RIDICULOUS HOLLYWOOD AGENT.

9/15/97

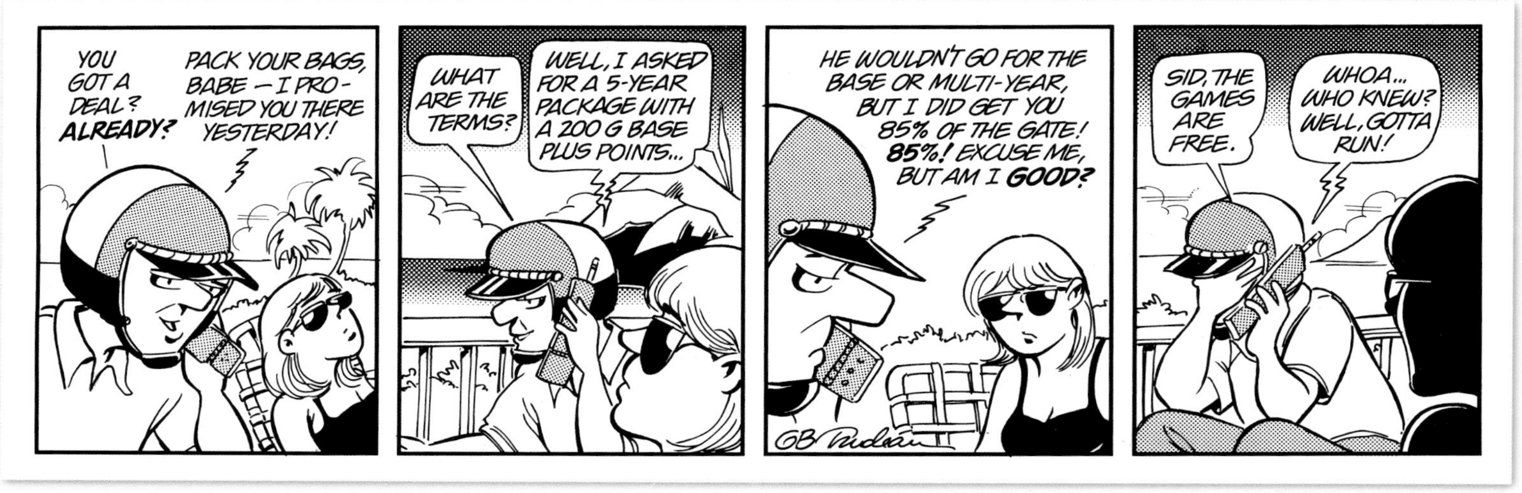

YOU GOT A DEAL? **ALREADY?**
PACK YOUR BAGS, BABE — I PROMISED YOU THERE YESTERDAY!
WHAT ARE THE TERMS?
WELL, I ASKED FOR A 5-YEAR PACKAGE WITH A 200 G BASE PLUS POINTS...
HE WOULDN'T GO FOR THE BASE OR MULTI-YEAR, BUT I DID GET YOU 85% OF THE GATE! **85%!** EXCUSE ME, BUT AM I **GOOD?**
SID, THE GAMES ARE FREE.
WHOA... WHO KNEW? WELL, GOTTA RUN!

9/16/97

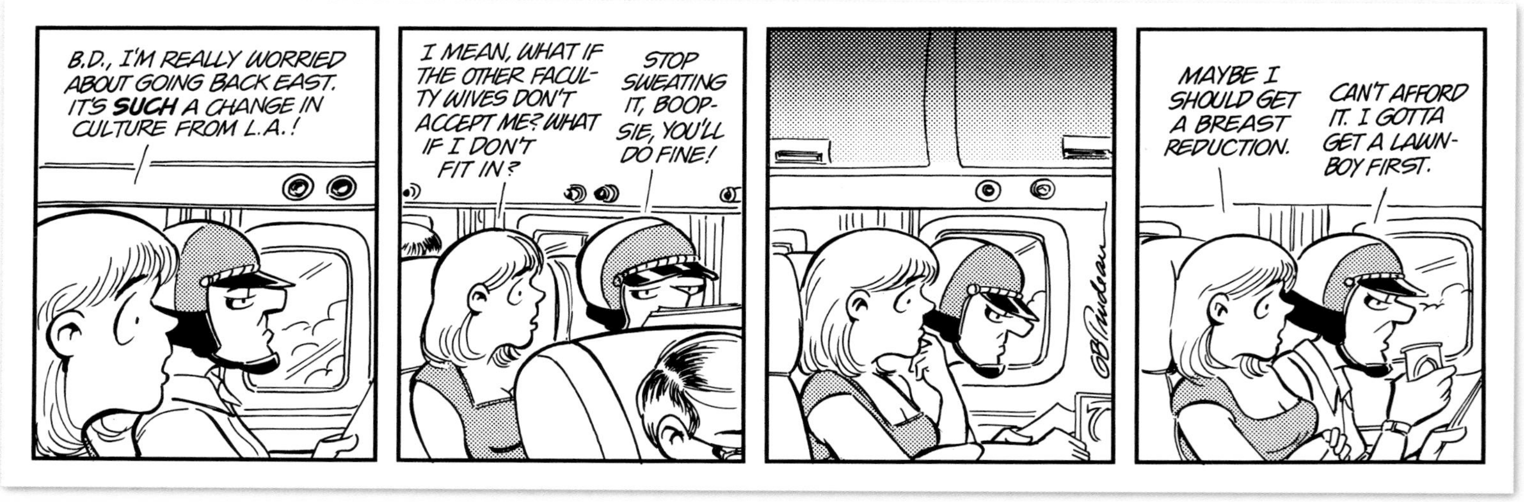

B.D., I'M REALLY WORRIED ABOUT GOING BACK EAST. IT'S **SUCH** A CHANGE IN CULTURE FROM L.A.!
I MEAN, WHAT IF THE OTHER FACULTY WIVES DON'T ACCEPT ME? WHAT IF I DON'T FIT IN?
STOP SWEATING IT, BOOPSIE, YOU'LL DO FINE!
MAYBE I SHOULD GET A BREAST REDUCTION.
CAN'T AFFORD IT. I GOTTA GET A LAWNBOY FIRST.

9/19/97

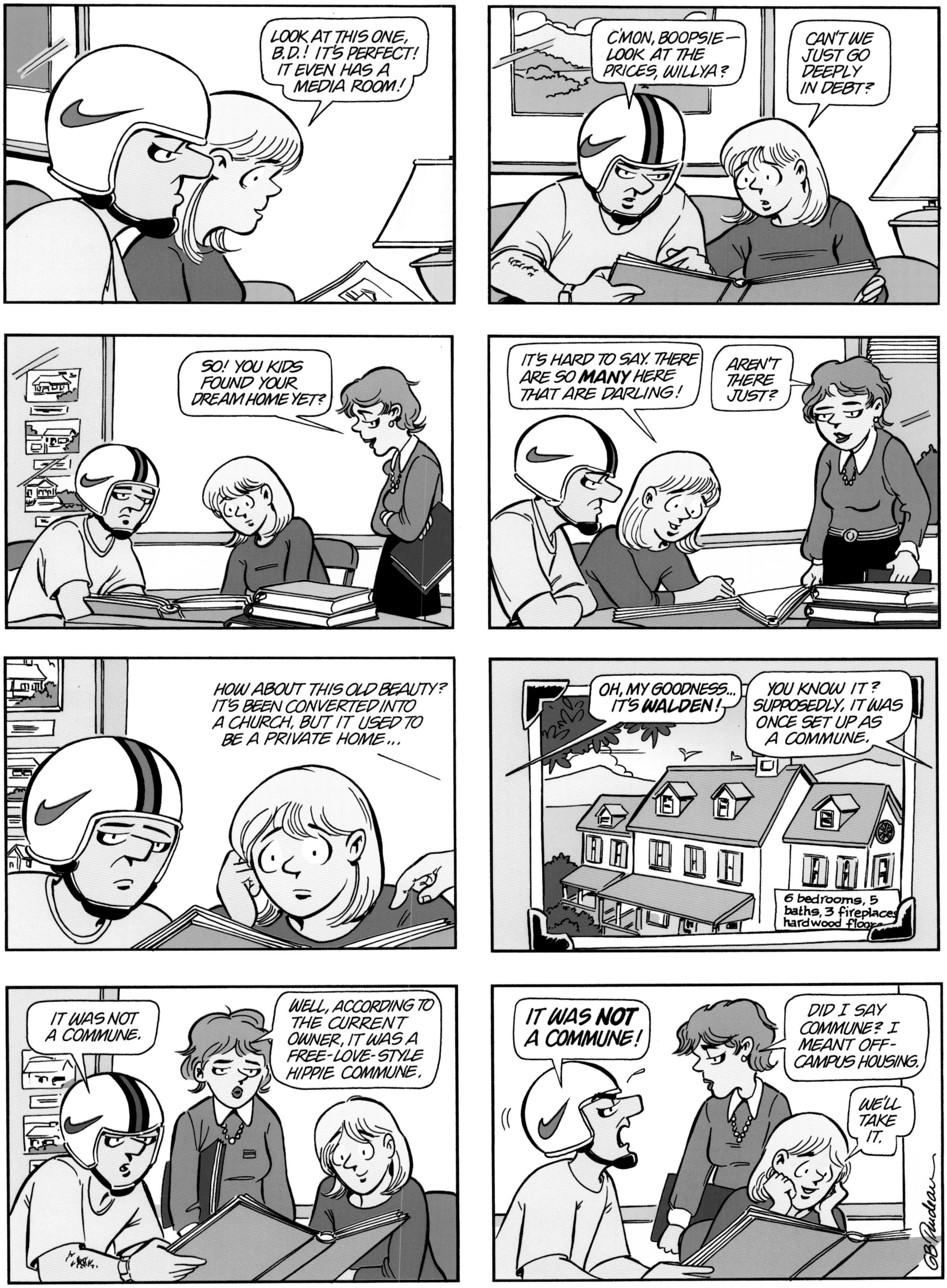
LOOK AT THIS ONE, B.D.! IT'S PERFECT! IT EVEN HAS A MEDIA ROOM!
C'MON, BOOPSIE— LOOK AT THE PRICES, WILLYA?
CAN'T WE JUST GO DEEPLY IN DEBT?
SO! YOU KIDS FOUND YOUR DREAM HOME YET?
IT'S HARD TO SAY. THERE ARE SO MANY HERE THAT ARE DARLING!
AREN'T THERE JUST?
HOW ABOUT THIS OLD BEAUTY? IT'S BEEN CONVERTED INTO A CHURCH, BUT IT USED TO BE A PRIVATE HOME...
OH, MY GOODNESS... IT'S WALDEN!
YOU KNOW IT? SUPPOSEDLY, IT WAS ONCE SET UP AS A COMMUNE.
6 bedrooms, 5 baths, 3 fireplaces hardwood floo
IT WAS NOT A COMMUNE.
WELL, ACCORDING TO THE CURRENT OWNER, IT WAS A FREE-LOVE-STYLE HIPPIE COMMUNE.
IT WAS NOT A COMMUNE!
DID I SAY COMMUNE? I MEANT OFF-CAMPUS HOUSING.
WE'LL TAKE IT.
GBTrudeau

11/23/97

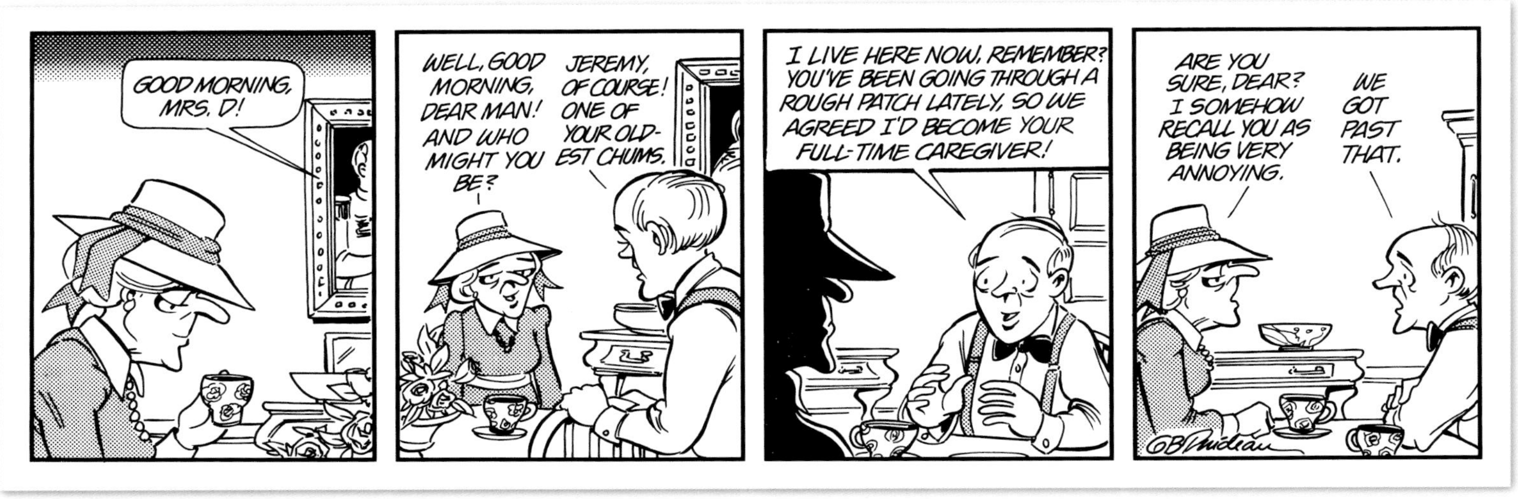
GOOD MORNING, MRS. D!
WELL, GOOD MORNING, DEAR MAN! AND WHO MIGHT YOU BE?
JEREMY, OF COURSE! ONE OF YOUR OLDEST CHUMS.
I LIVE HERE NOW, REMEMBER? YOU'VE BEEN GOING THROUGH A ROUGH PATCH LATELY, SO WE AGREED I'D BECOME YOUR FULL-TIME CAREGIVER!
ARE YOU SURE, DEAR? I SOMEHOW RECALL YOU AS BEING VERY ANNOYING.
WE GOT PAST THAT.

11/3/97

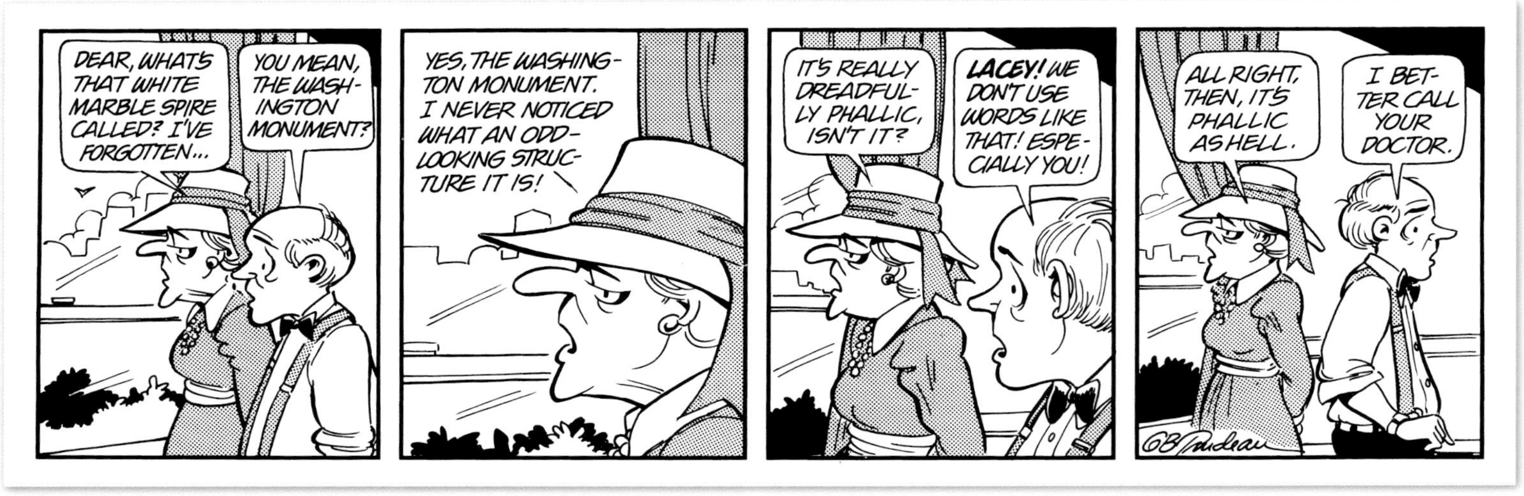
DEAR, WHAT'S THAT WHITE MARBLE SPIRE CALLED? I'VE FORGOTTEN...
YOU MEAN, THE WASHINGTON MONUMENT?
YES, THE WASHINGTON MONUMENT. I NEVER NOTICED WHAT AN ODD-LOOKING STRUCTURE IT IS!
IT'S REALLY DREADFULLY PHALLIC, ISN'T IT?
LACEY! WE DON'T USE WORDS LIKE THAT! ESPECIALLY YOU!
ALL RIGHT, THEN, IT'S PHALLIC AS HELL.
I BETTER CALL YOUR DOCTOR.

11/6/97

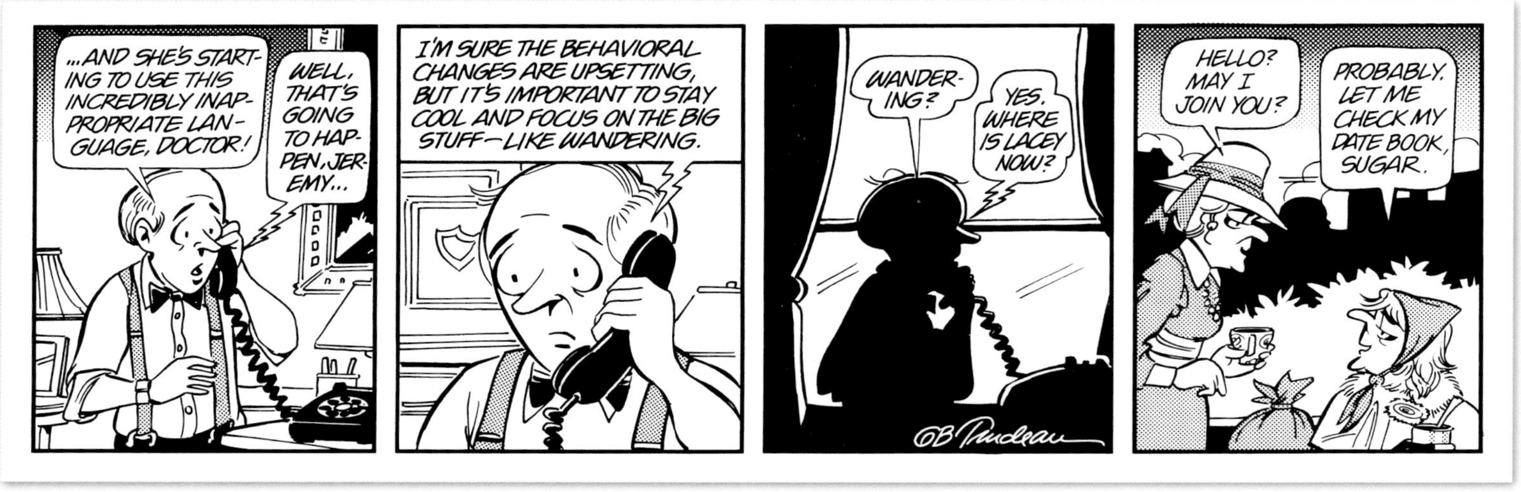
...AND SHE'S STARTING TO USE THIS INCREDIBLY INAPPROPRIATE LANGUAGE, DOCTOR!
WELL, THAT'S GOING TO HAPPEN, JEREMY...
I'M SURE THE BEHAVIORAL CHANGES ARE UPSETTING, BUT IT'S IMPORTANT TO STAY COOL AND FOCUS ON THE BIG STUFF—LIKE WANDERING.
WANDERING?
YES. WHERE IS LACEY NOW?
HELLO? MAY I JOIN YOU?
PROBABLY. LET ME CHECK MY DATE BOOK, SUGAR.

11/7/97

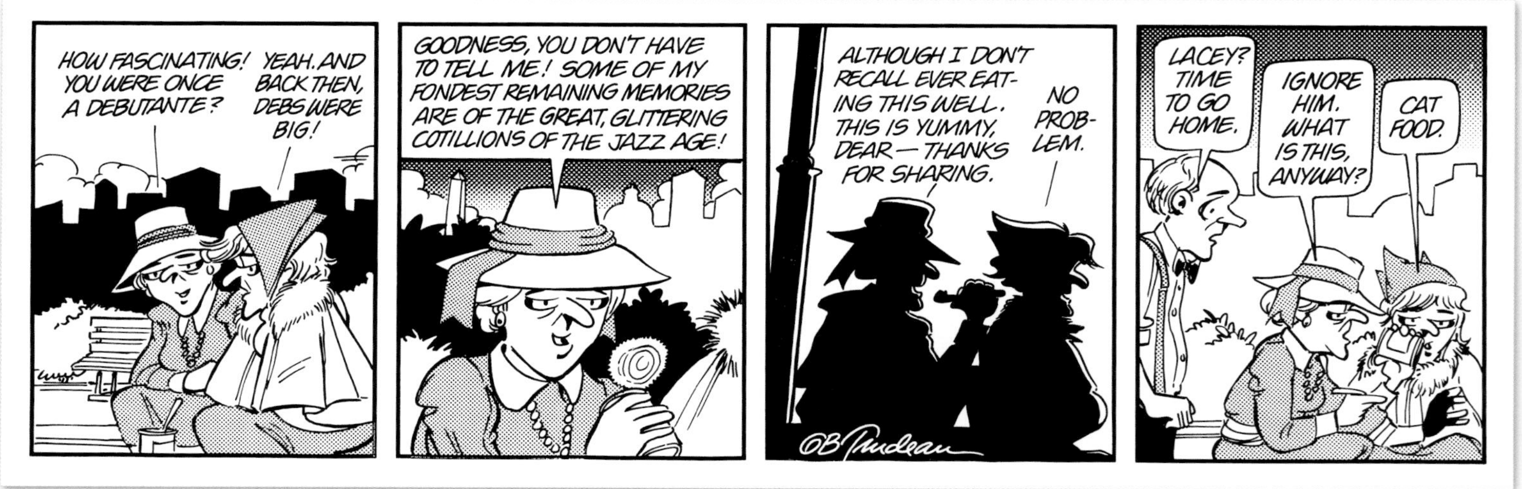
HOW FASCINATING! YOU WERE ONCE A DEBUTANTE?
YEAH. AND BACK THEN, DEBS WERE BIG!
GOODNESS, YOU DON'T HAVE TO TELL ME! SOME OF MY FONDEST REMAINING MEMORIES ARE OF THE GREAT, GLITTERING COTILLIONS OF THE JAZZ AGE!
ALTHOUGH I DON'T RECALL EVER EATING THIS WELL. THIS IS YUMMY, DEAR—THANKS FOR SHARING.
NO PROBLEM.
LACEY? TIME TO GO HOME.
IGNORE HIM. WHAT IS THIS, ANYWAY?
CAT FOOD.

11/8/97

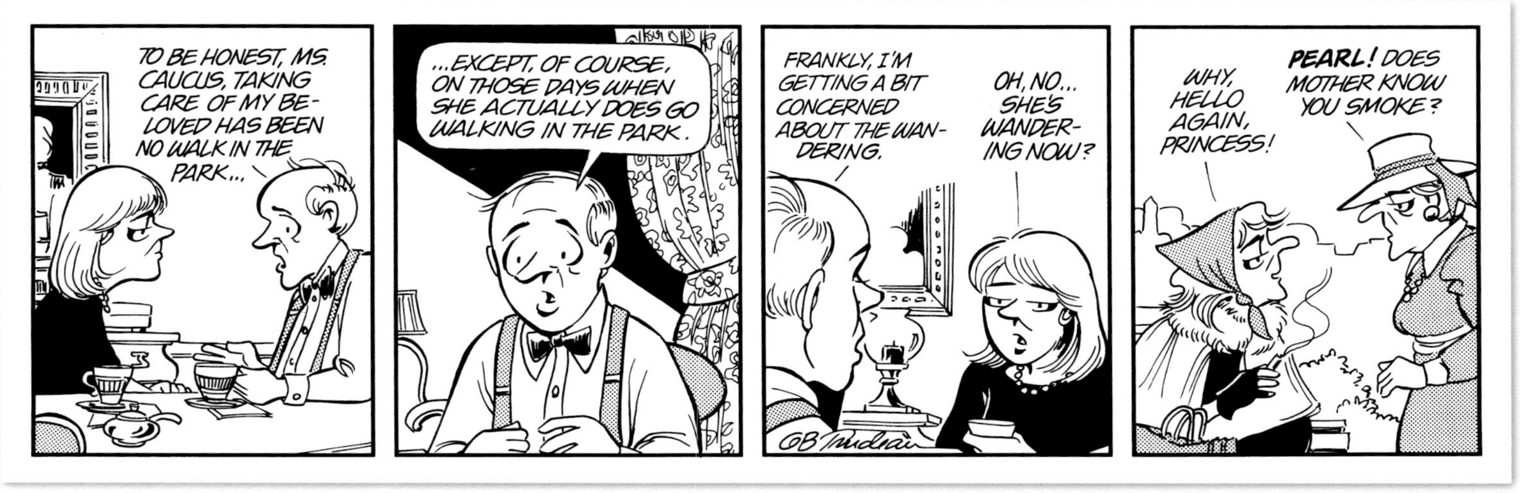
TO BE HONEST, MS. CAUCUS, TAKING CARE OF MY BELOVED HAS BEEN NO WALK IN THE PARK...
...EXCEPT, OF COURSE, ON THOSE DAYS WHEN SHE ACTUALLY DOES GO WALKING IN THE PARK.
FRANKLY, I'M GETTING A BIT CONCERNED ABOUT THE WANDERING.
OH, NO... SHE'S WANDERING NOW?
WHY, HELLO AGAIN, PRINCESS!
PEARL! DOES MOTHER KNOW YOU SMOKE?

11/10/97

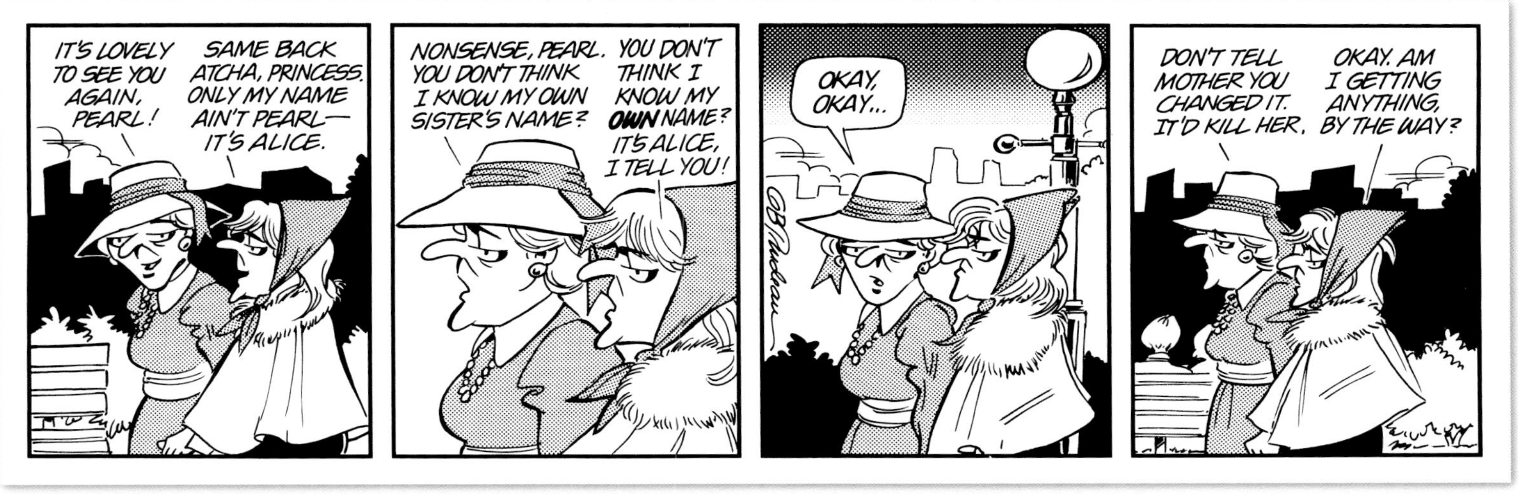
IT'S LOVELY TO SEE YOU AGAIN, PEARL!
SAME BACK ATCHA, PRINCESS. ONLY MY NAME AIN'T PEARL— IT'S ALICE.
NONSENSE, PEARL. YOU DON'T THINK I KNOW MY OWN SISTER'S NAME?
YOU DON'T THINK I KNOW MY OWN NAME? IT'S ALICE, I TELL YOU!
OKAY, OKAY...
DON'T TELL MOTHER YOU CHANGED IT. IT'D KILL HER.
OKAY. AM I GETTING ANYTHING, BY THE WAY?

11/11/97

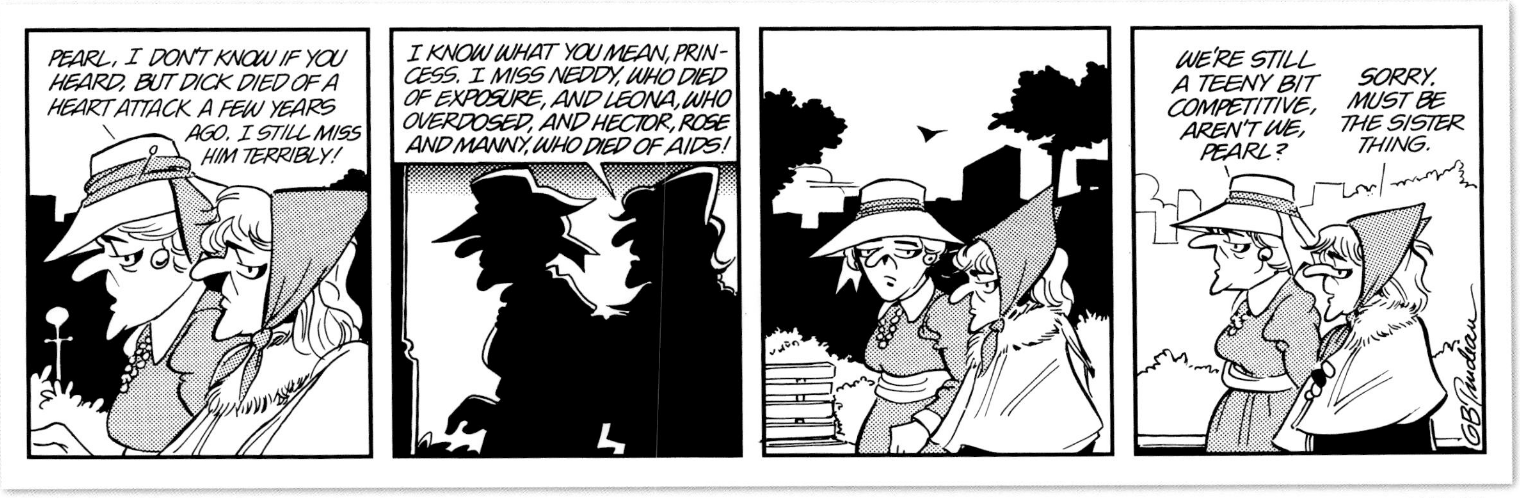
PEARL, I DON'T KNOW IF YOU HEARD, BUT DICK DIED OF A HEART ATTACK A FEW YEARS AGO. I STILL MISS HIM TERRIBLY!
I KNOW WHAT YOU MEAN, PRINCESS. I MISS NEDDY, WHO DIED OF EXPOSURE, AND LEONA, WHO OVERDOSED, AND HECTOR, ROSE AND MANNY, WHO DIED OF AIDS!
WE'RE STILL A TEENY BIT COMPETITIVE, AREN'T WE, PEARL?
SORRY. MUST BE THE SISTER THING.

11/12/97

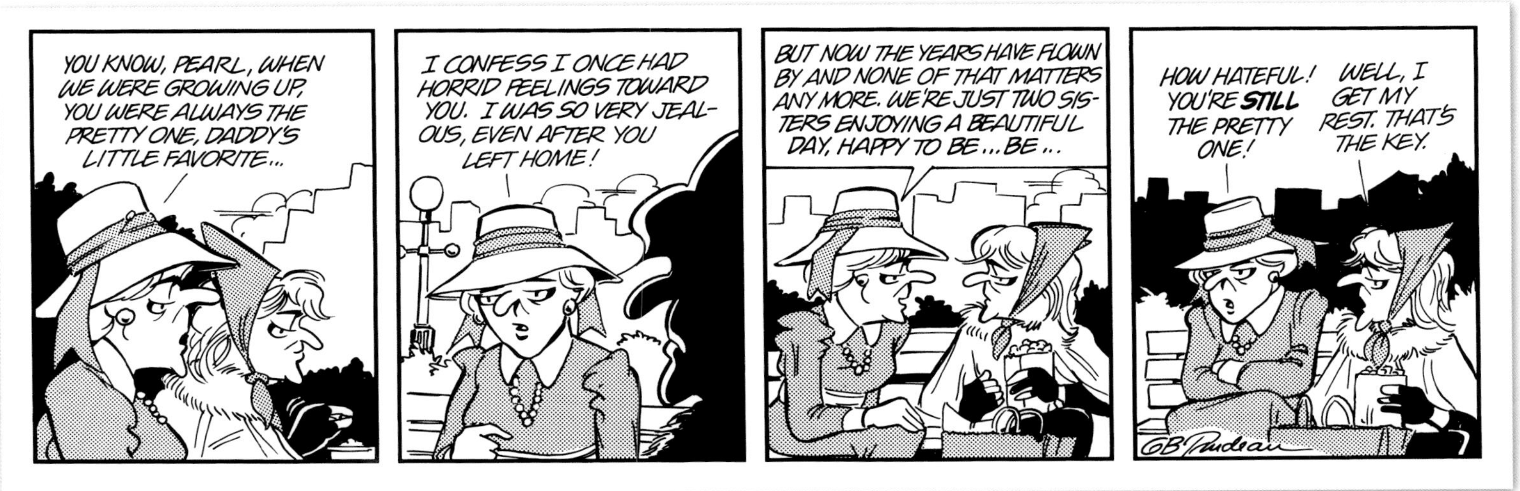
YOU KNOW, PEARL, WHEN WE WERE GROWING UP, YOU WERE ALWAYS THE PRETTY ONE, DADDY'S LITTLE FAVORITE...
I CONFESS I ONCE HAD HORRID FEELINGS TOWARD YOU. I WAS SO VERY JEALOUS, EVEN AFTER YOU LEFT HOME!
BUT NOW THE YEARS HAVE FLOWN BY AND NONE OF THAT MATTERS ANY MORE. WE'RE JUST TWO SISTERS ENJOYING A BEAUTIFUL DAY, HAPPY TO BE ... BE ...
HOW HATEFUL! YOU'RE STILL THE PRETTY ONE!
WELL, I GET MY REST. THAT'S THE KEY.

11/13/97

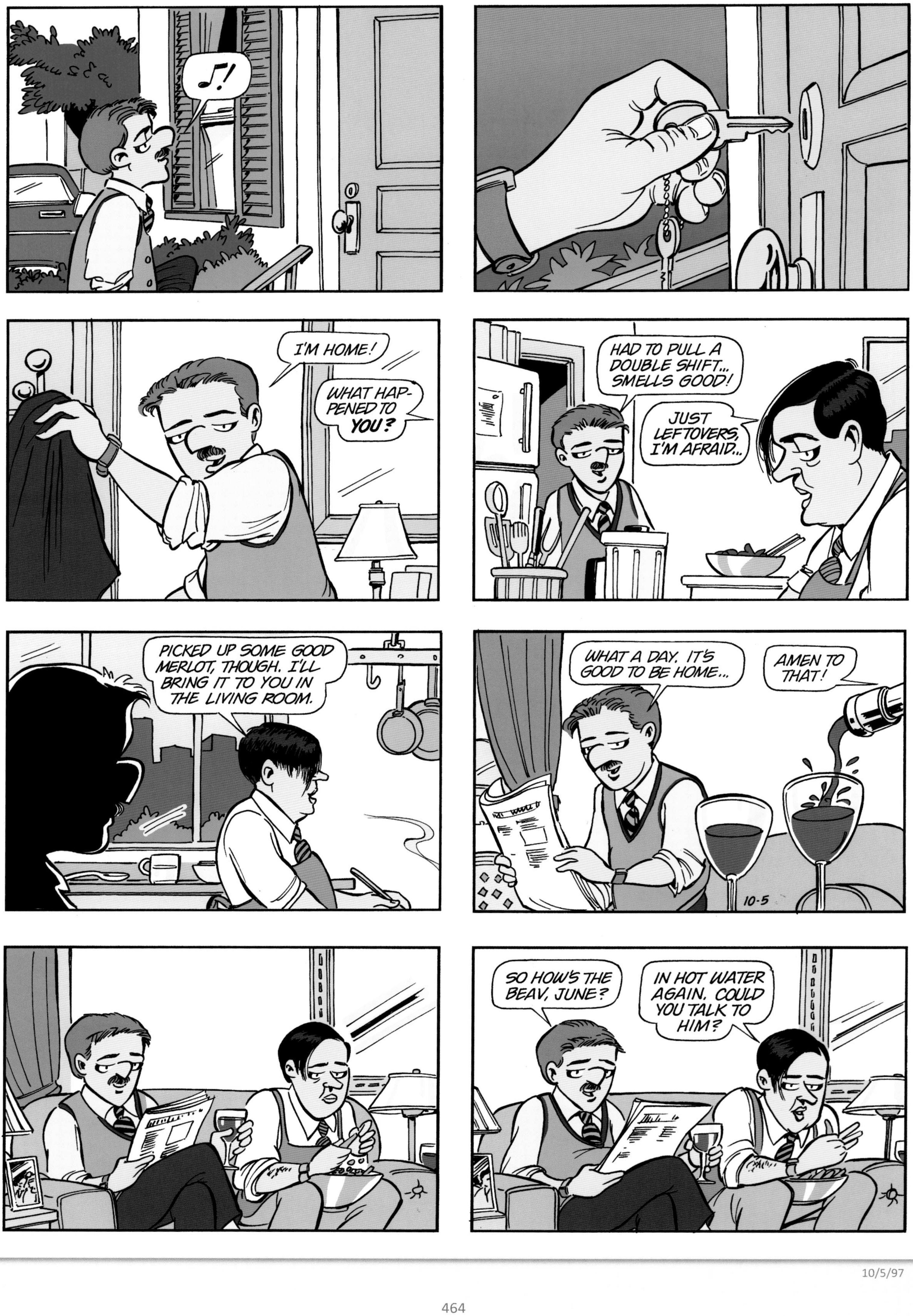
♪!
I'M HOME!
WHAT HAP-PENED TO YOU?
HAD TO PULL A DOUBLE SHIFT... SMELLS GOOD!
JUST LEFTOVERS, I'M AFRAID...
PICKED UP SOME GOOD MERLOT, THOUGH. I'LL BRING IT TO YOU IN THE LIVING ROOM.
WHAT A DAY. IT'S GOOD TO BE HOME...
AMEN TO THAT!
10-5
SO HOW'S THE BEAV, JUNE?
IN HOT WATER AGAIN. COULD YOU TALK TO HIM?

10/5/97

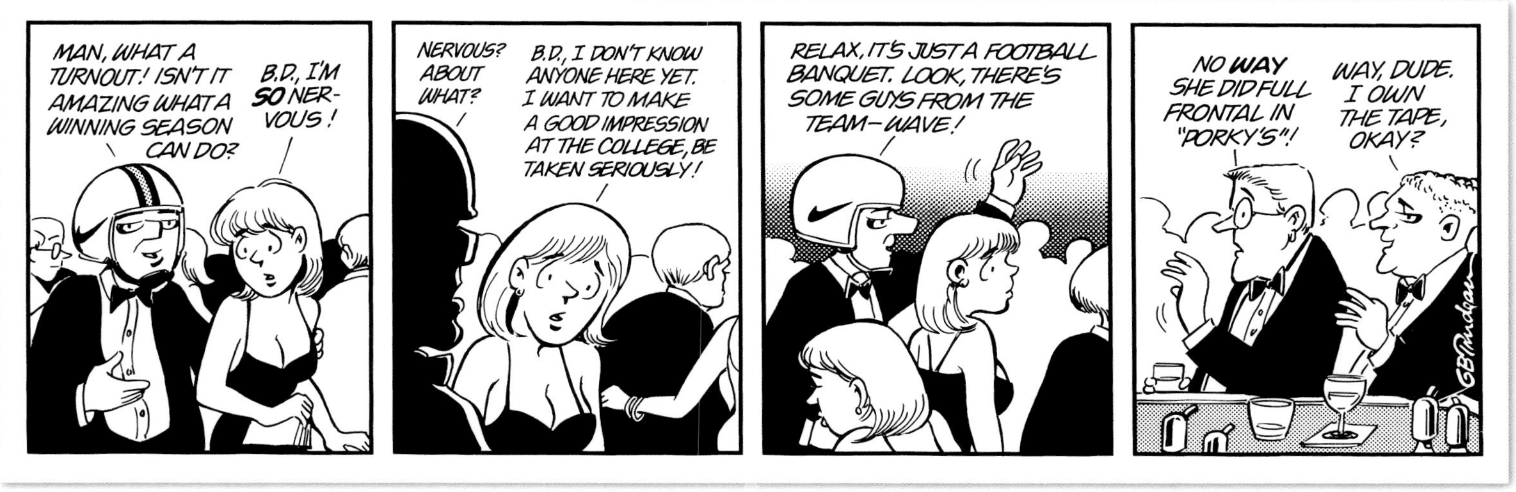
MAN, WHAT A TURNOUT! ISN'T IT AMAZING WHAT A WINNING SEASON CAN DO?
B.D., I'M **SO** NERVOUS!
NERVOUS? ABOUT WHAT?
B.D., I DON'T KNOW ANYONE HERE YET. I WANT TO MAKE A GOOD IMPRESSION AT THE COLLEGE, BE TAKEN SERIOUSLY!
RELAX, IT'S JUST A FOOTBALL BANQUET. LOOK, THERE'S SOME GUYS FROM THE TEAM—WAVE!
NO **WAY** SHE DID FULL FRONTAL IN "PORKY'S"!
WAY, DUDE. I OWN THE TAPE, OKAY?

12/8/97

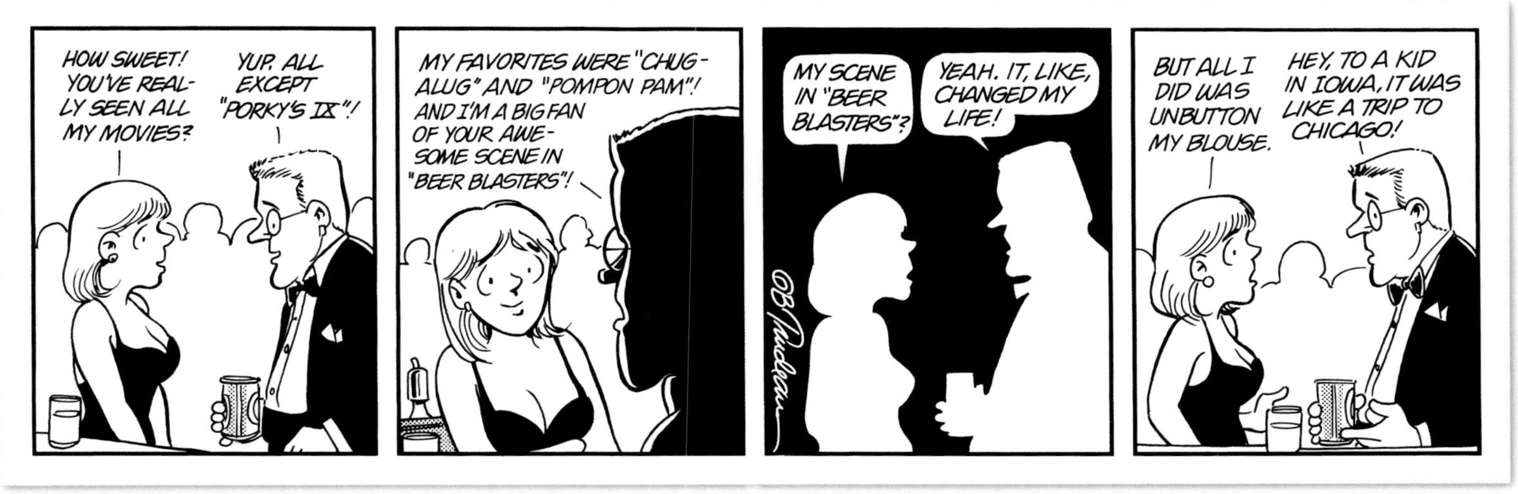
HOW SWEET! YOU'VE REALLY SEEN ALL MY MOVIES?
YUP. ALL EXCEPT "PORKY'S IX"!
MY FAVORITES WERE "CHUG-A-LUG" AND "POMPON PAM"! AND I'M A BIG FAN OF YOUR AWESOME SCENE IN "BEER BLASTERS"!
MY SCENE IN "BEER BLASTERS"?
YEAH. IT, LIKE, CHANGED MY LIFE!
BUT ALL I DID WAS UNBUTTON MY BLOUSE.
HEY, TO A KID IN IOWA, IT WAS LIKE A TRIP TO CHICAGO!

12/10/97

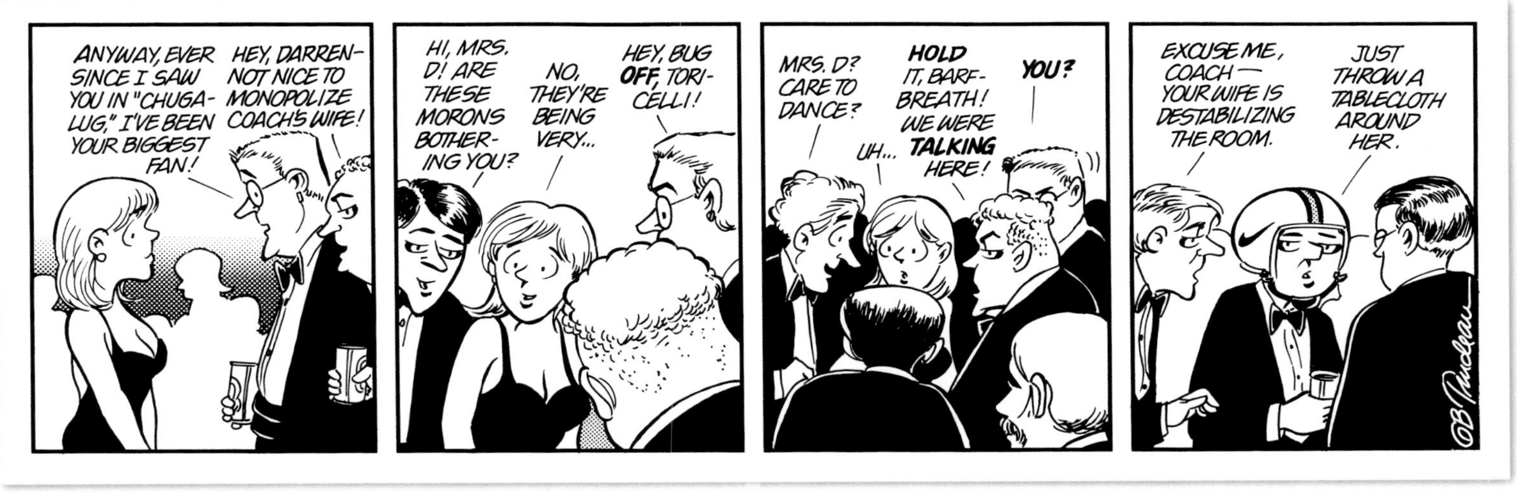
ANYWAY, EVER SINCE I SAW YOU IN "CHUGALUG," I'VE BEEN YOUR BIGGEST FAN!
HEY, DARREN—NOT NICE TO MONOPOLIZE COACH'S WIFE!
HI, MRS. D! ARE THESE MORONS BOTHERING YOU?
NO, THEY'RE BEING VERY...
HEY, BUG **OFF**, TORICELLI!
MRS. D? CARE TO DANCE?
UH...
HOLD IT, BARF-BREATH! WE WERE **TALKING** HERE!
YOU?
EXCUSE ME, COACH—YOUR WIFE IS DESTABILIZING THE ROOM.
JUST THROW A TABLECLOTH AROUND HER.

12/11/97

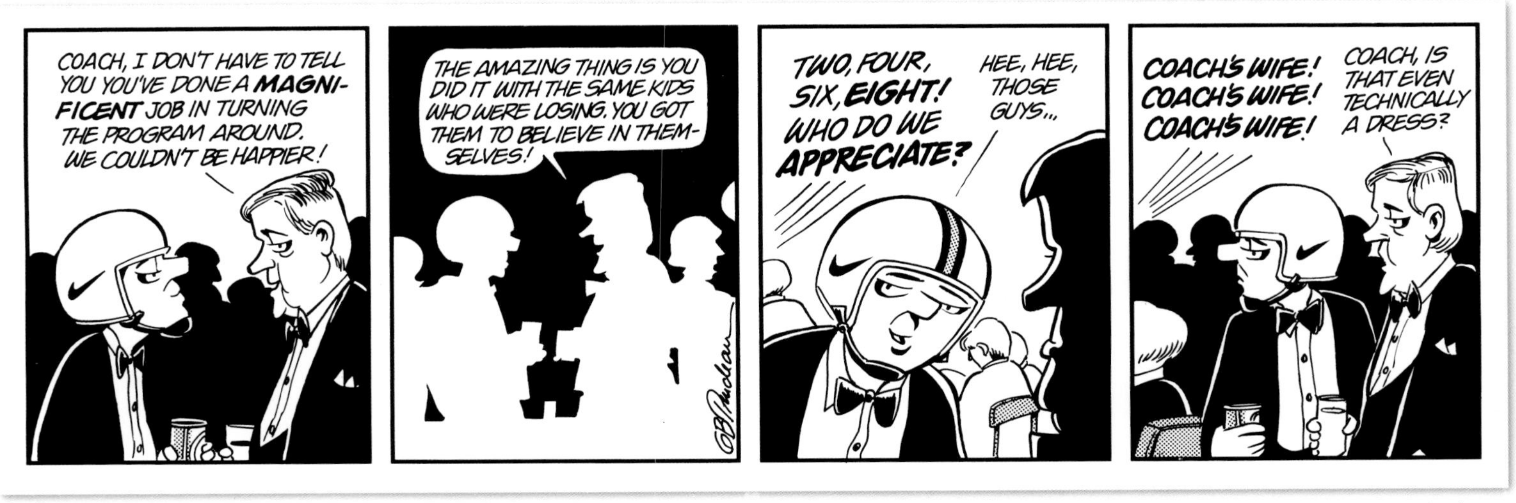
COACH, I DON'T HAVE TO TELL YOU YOU'VE DONE A **MAGNIFICENT** JOB IN TURNING THE PROGRAM AROUND. WE COULDN'T BE HAPPIER!
THE AMAZING THING IS YOU DID IT WITH THE SAME KIDS WHO WERE LOSING. YOU GOT THEM TO BELIEVE IN THEMSELVES!
TWO, FOUR, SIX, EIGHT! WHO DO WE APPRECIATE?
HEE, HEE, THOSE GUYS...
COACH'S WIFE! COACH'S WIFE! COACH'S WIFE!
COACH, IS THAT EVEN TECHNICALLY A DRESS?

12/12/97

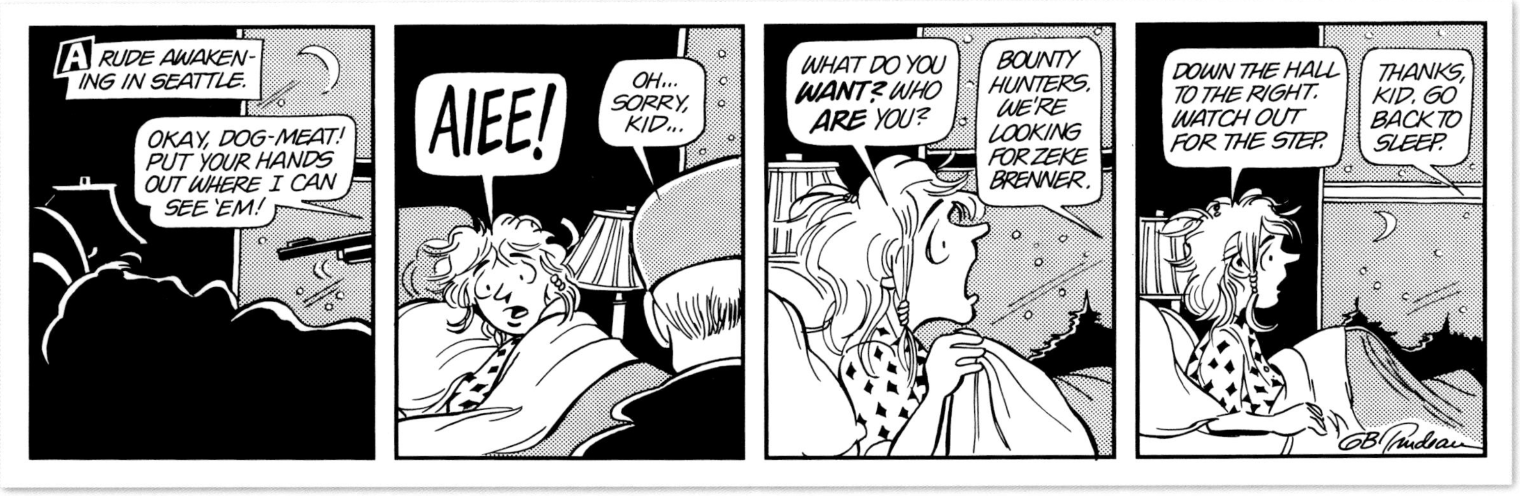
A RUDE AWAKENING IN SEATTLE.
OKAY, DOG-MEAT! PUT YOUR HANDS OUT WHERE I CAN SEE 'EM!
AIEE!
OH... SORRY, KID...
WHAT DO YOU WANT? WHO ARE YOU?
BOUNTY HUNTERS. WE'RE LOOKING FOR ZEKE BRENNER.
DOWN THE HALL TO THE RIGHT. WATCH OUT FOR THE STEP.
THANKS, KID. GO BACK TO SLEEP.
GB Trudeau

1/26/98

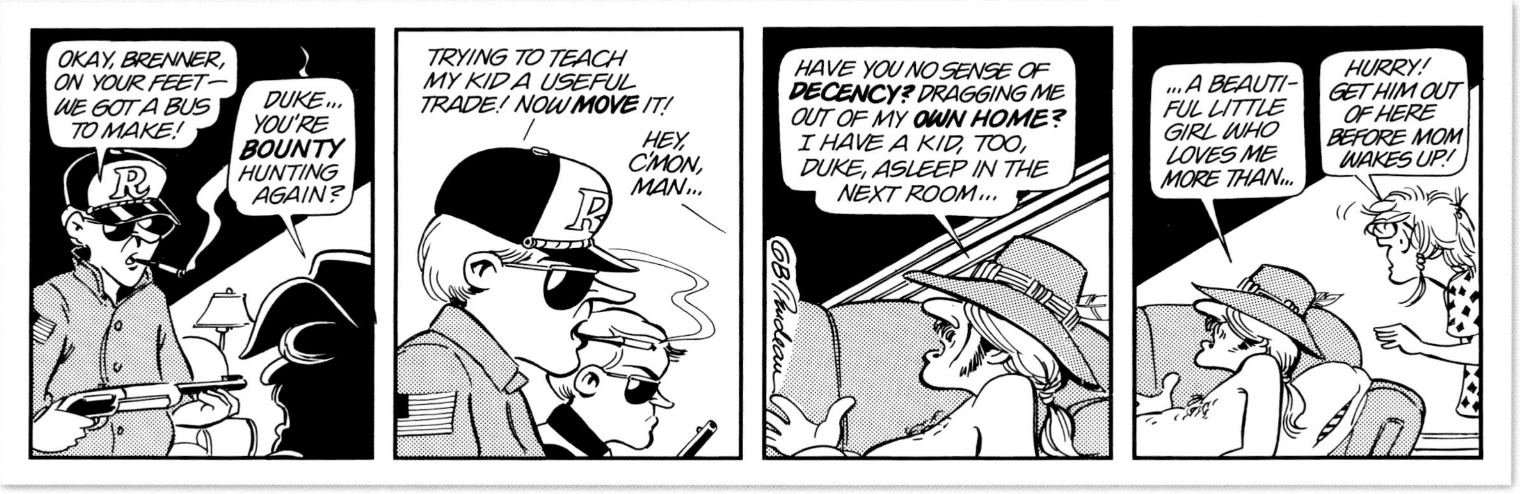
OKAY, BRENNER, ON YOUR FEET—WE GOT A BUS TO MAKE!
DUKE... YOU'RE BOUNTY HUNTING AGAIN?
TRYING TO TEACH MY KID A USEFUL TRADE! NOW MOVE IT!
HEY, C'MON, MAN...
HAVE YOU NO SENSE OF DECENCY? DRAGGING ME OUT OF MY OWN HOME? I HAVE A KID, TOO, DUKE, ASLEEP IN THE NEXT ROOM...
...A BEAUTIFUL LITTLE GIRL WHO LOVES ME MORE THAN...
HURRY! GET HIM OUT OF HERE BEFORE MOM WAKES UP!
GB Trudeau

1/28/98

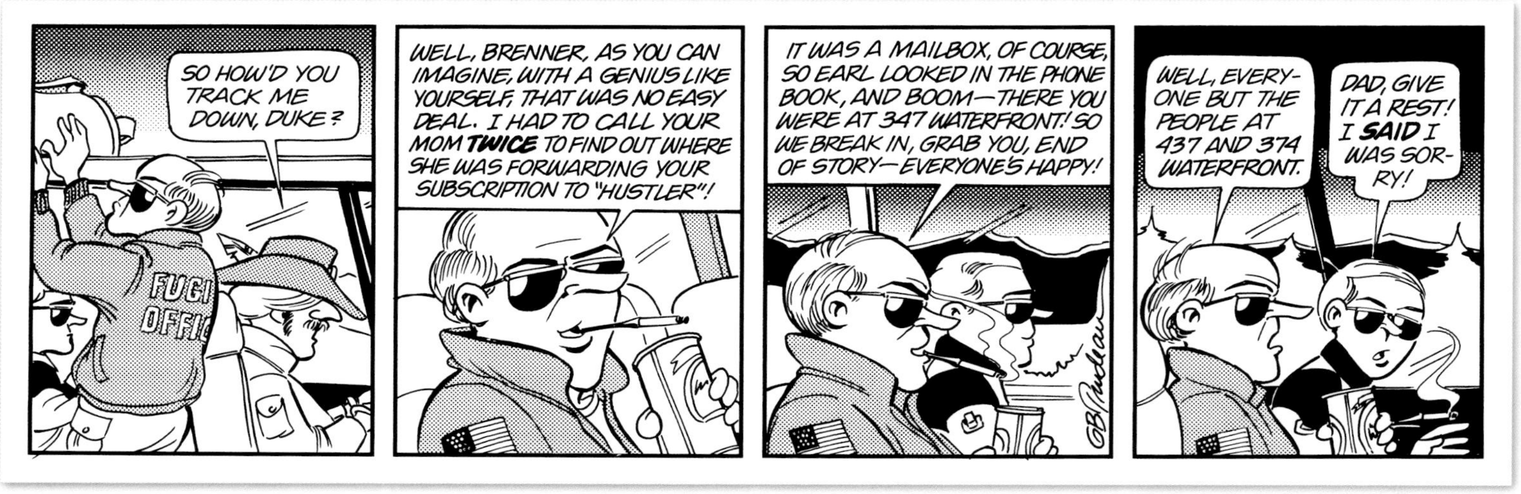
SO HOW'D YOU TRACK ME DOWN, DUKE?
WELL, BRENNER, AS YOU CAN IMAGINE, WITH A GENIUS LIKE YOURSELF, THAT WAS NO EASY DEAL. I HAD TO CALL YOUR MOM TWICE TO FIND OUT WHERE SHE WAS FORWARDING YOUR SUBSCRIPTION TO "HUSTLER"!
IT WAS A MAILBOX, OF COURSE, SO EARL LOOKED IN THE PHONE BOOK, AND BOOM—THERE YOU WERE AT 347 WATERFRONT! SO WE BREAK IN, GRAB YOU, END OF STORY—EVERYONE'S HAPPY!
WELL, EVERYONE BUT THE PEOPLE AT 437 AND 374 WATERFRONT.
DAD, GIVE IT A REST! I SAID I WAS SORRY!
GB Trudeau

1/30/98

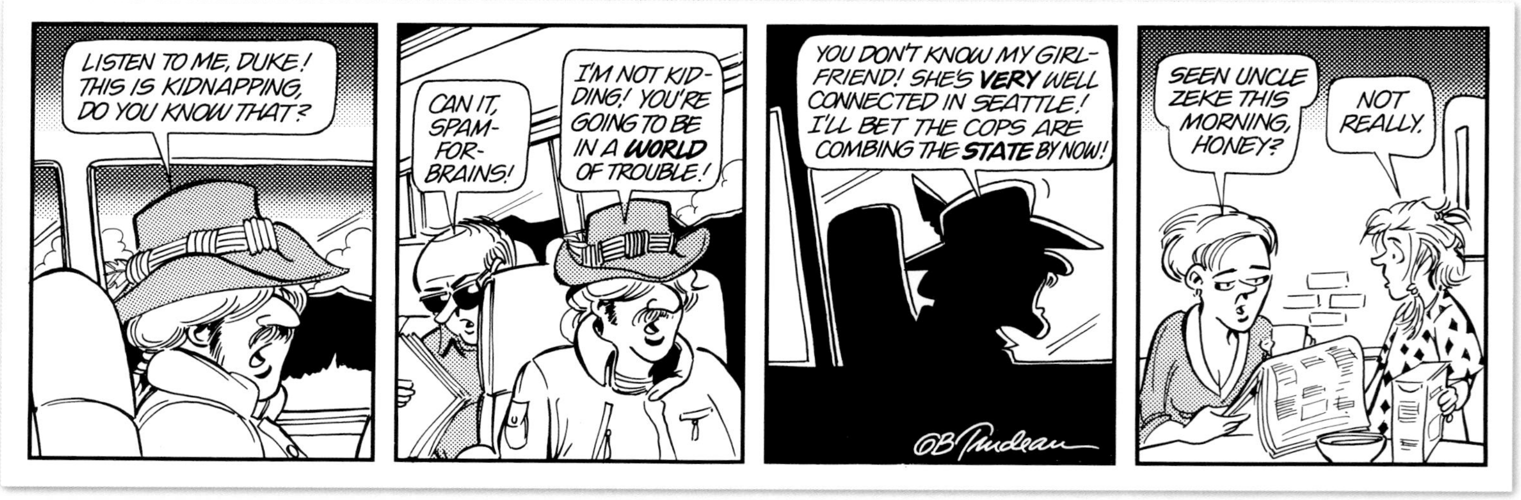
LISTEN TO ME, DUKE! THIS IS KIDNAPPING, DO YOU KNOW THAT?
CAN IT, SPAM-FOR-BRAINS!
I'M NOT KIDDING! YOU'RE GOING TO BE IN A WORLD OF TROUBLE!
YOU DON'T KNOW MY GIRLFRIEND! SHE'S VERY WELL CONNECTED IN SEATTLE! I'LL BET THE COPS ARE COMBING THE STATE BY NOW!
SEEN UNCLE ZEKE THIS MORNING, HONEY?
NOT REALLY.
GB Trudeau

1/31/98

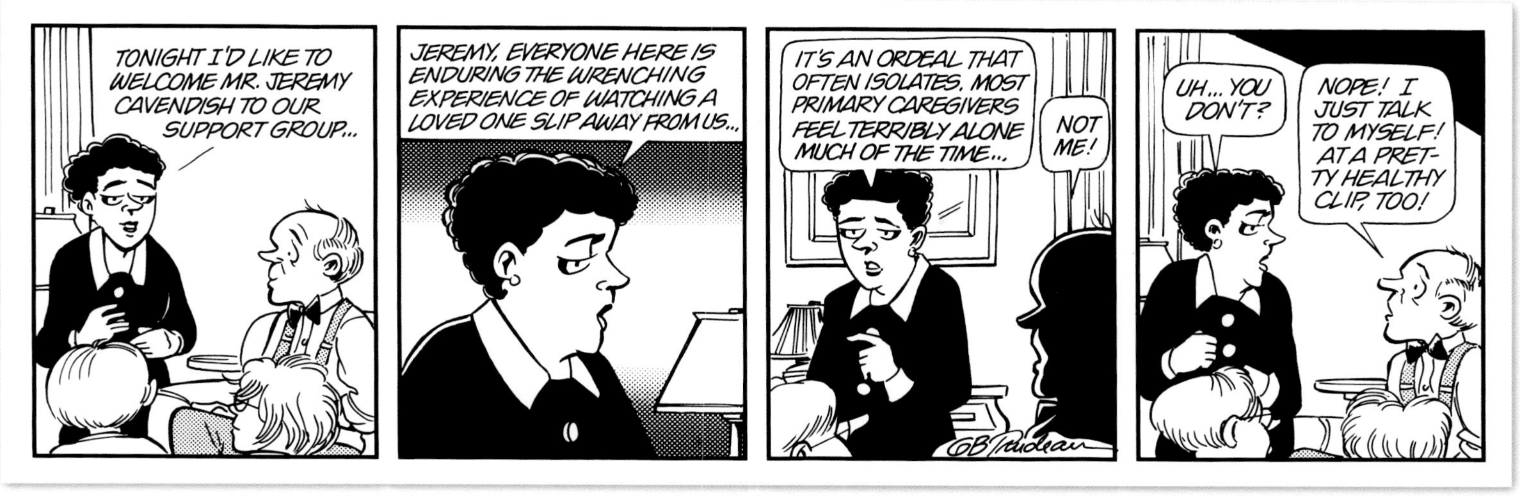
TONIGHT I'D LIKE TO WELCOME MR. JEREMY CAVENDISH TO OUR SUPPORT GROUP...
JEREMY, EVERYONE HERE IS ENDURING THE WRENCHING EXPERIENCE OF WATCHING A LOVED ONE SLIP AWAY FROM US...
IT'S AN ORDEAL THAT OFTEN ISOLATES. MOST PRIMARY CAREGIVERS FEEL TERRIBLY ALONE MUCH OF THE TIME...
NOT ME!
UH... YOU DON'T?
NOPE! I JUST TALK TO MYSELF! AT A PRETTY HEALTHY CLIP, TOO!

2/25/98

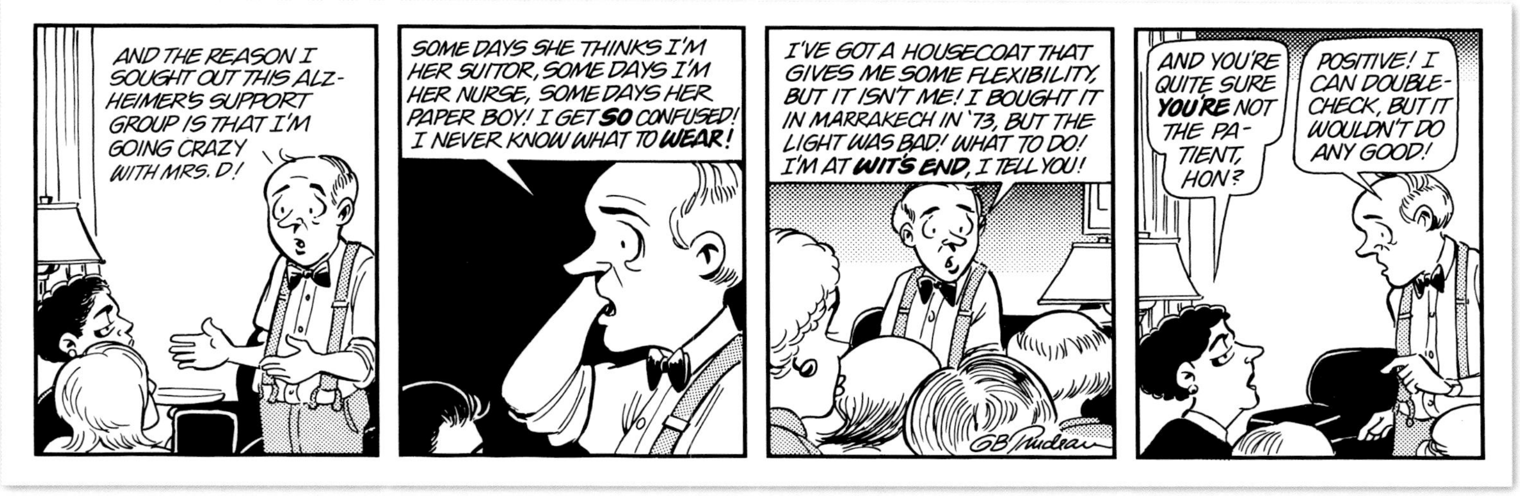
AND THE REASON I SOUGHT OUT THIS ALZHEIMER'S SUPPORT GROUP IS THAT I'M GOING CRAZY WITH MRS. D!
SOME DAYS SHE THINKS I'M HER SUITOR, SOME DAYS I'M HER NURSE, SOME DAYS HER PAPER BOY! I GET SO CONFUSED! I NEVER KNOW WHAT TO WEAR!
I'VE GOT A HOUSECOAT THAT GIVES ME SOME FLEXIBILITY, BUT IT ISN'T ME! I BOUGHT IT IN MARRAKECH IN '73, BUT THE LIGHT WAS BAD! WHAT TO DO! I'M AT WIT'S END, I TELL YOU!
AND YOU'RE QUITE SURE YOU'RE NOT THE PATIENT, HON?
POSITIVE! I CAN DOUBLE-CHECK, BUT IT WOULDN'T DO ANY GOOD!

2/26/98

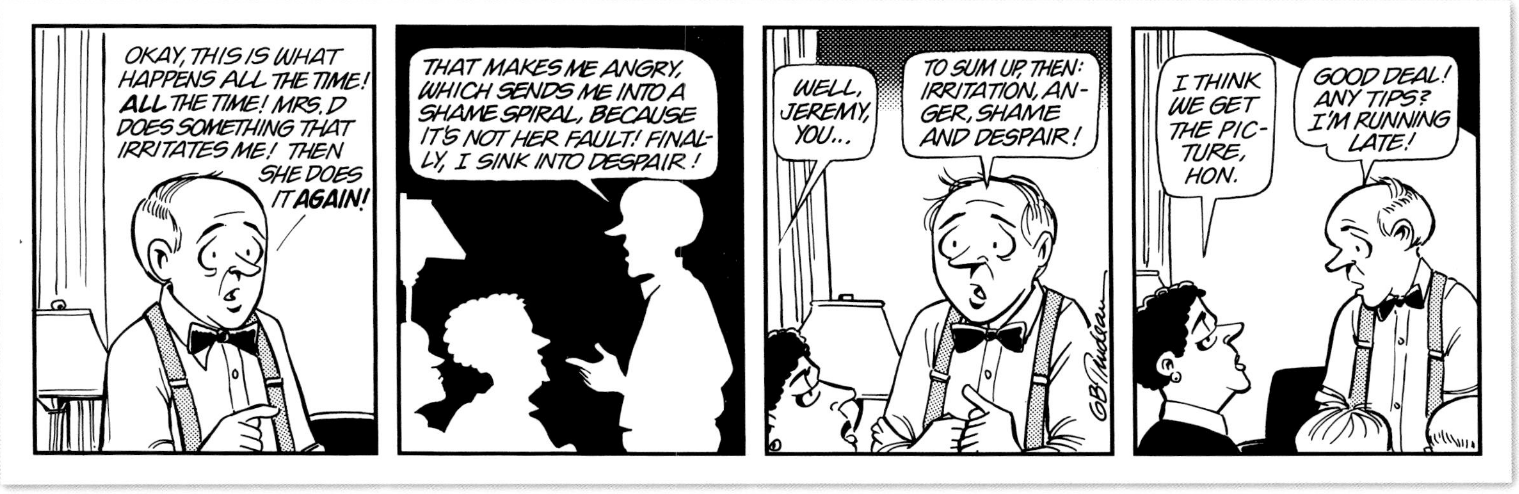
OKAY, THIS IS WHAT HAPPENS ALL THE TIME! ALL THE TIME! MRS. D DOES SOMETHING THAT IRRITATES ME! THEN SHE DOES IT AGAIN!
THAT MAKES ME ANGRY, WHICH SENDS ME INTO A SHAME SPIRAL, BECAUSE IT'S NOT HER FAULT! FINALLY, I SINK INTO DESPAIR!
WELL, JEREMY, YOU...
TO SUM UP, THEN: IRRITATION, ANGER, SHAME AND DESPAIR!
I THINK WE GET THE PICTURE, HON.
GOOD DEAL! ANY TIPS? I'M RUNNING LATE!

2/27/98

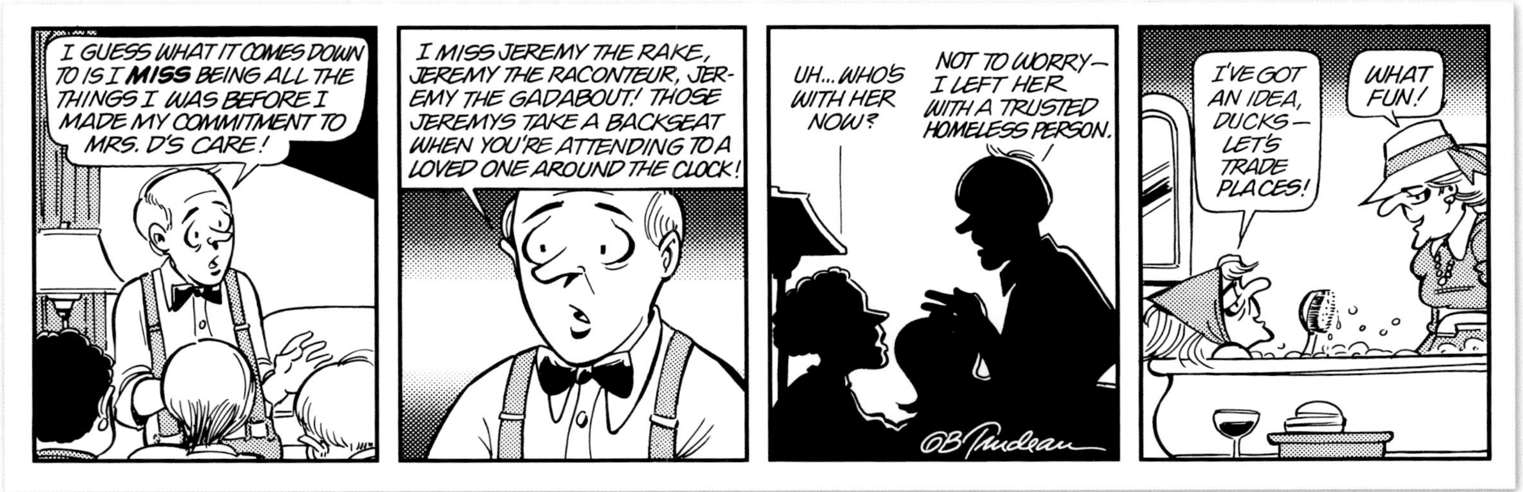
I GUESS WHAT IT COMES DOWN TO IS I MISS BEING ALL THE THINGS I WAS BEFORE I MADE MY COMMITMENT TO MRS. D'S CARE!
I MISS JEREMY THE RAKE, JEREMY THE RACONTEUR, JEREMY THE GADABOUT! THOSE JEREMYS TAKE A BACKSEAT WHEN YOU'RE ATTENDING TO A LOVED ONE AROUND THE CLOCK!
UH... WHO'S WITH HER NOW?
NOT TO WORRY— I LEFT HER WITH A TRUSTED HOMELESS PERSON.
I'VE GOT AN IDEA, DUCKS— LET'S TRADE PLACES!
WHAT FUN!

2/28/98

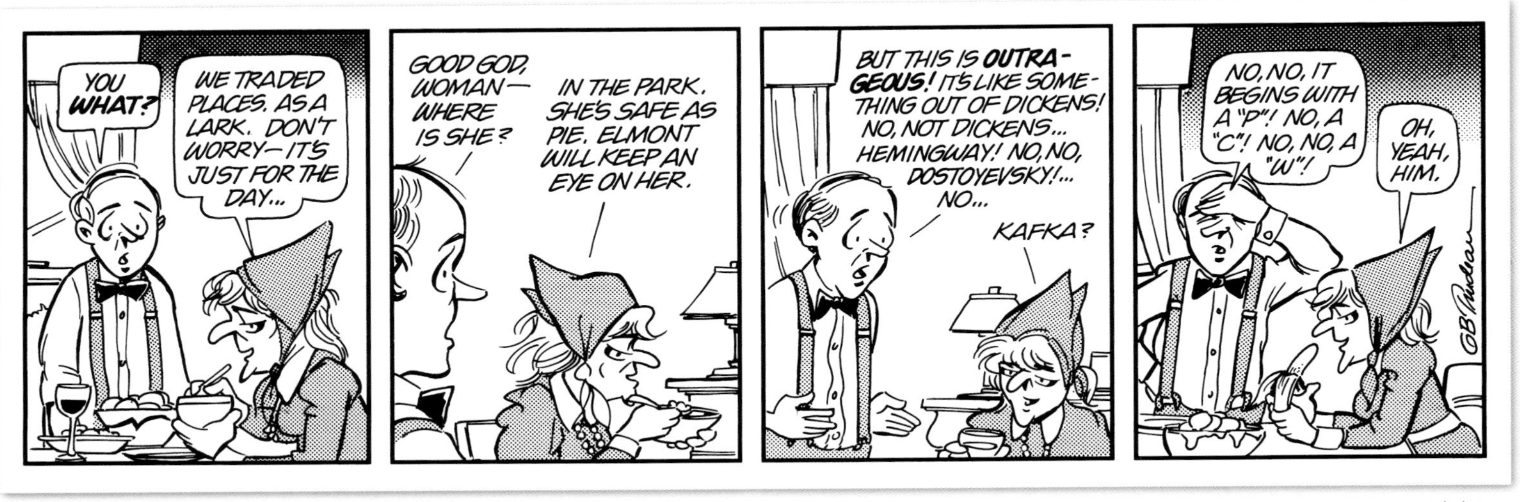
YOU **WHAT?**
WE TRADED PLACES. AS A LARK. DON'T WORRY—IT'S JUST FOR THE DAY...
GOOD GOD, WOMAN—WHERE IS SHE?
IN THE PARK. SHE'S SAFE AS PIE. ELMONT WILL KEEP AN EYE ON HER.
BUT THIS IS **OUTRAGEOUS!** IT'S LIKE SOMETHING OUT OF DICKENS! NO, NOT DICKENS... HEMINGWAY! NO, NO, DOSTOYEVSKY!... NO...
KAFKA?
NO, NO, IT BEGINS WITH A "P"! NO, A "C"! NO, NO, A "W"!
OH, YEAH, HIM.

3/3/98

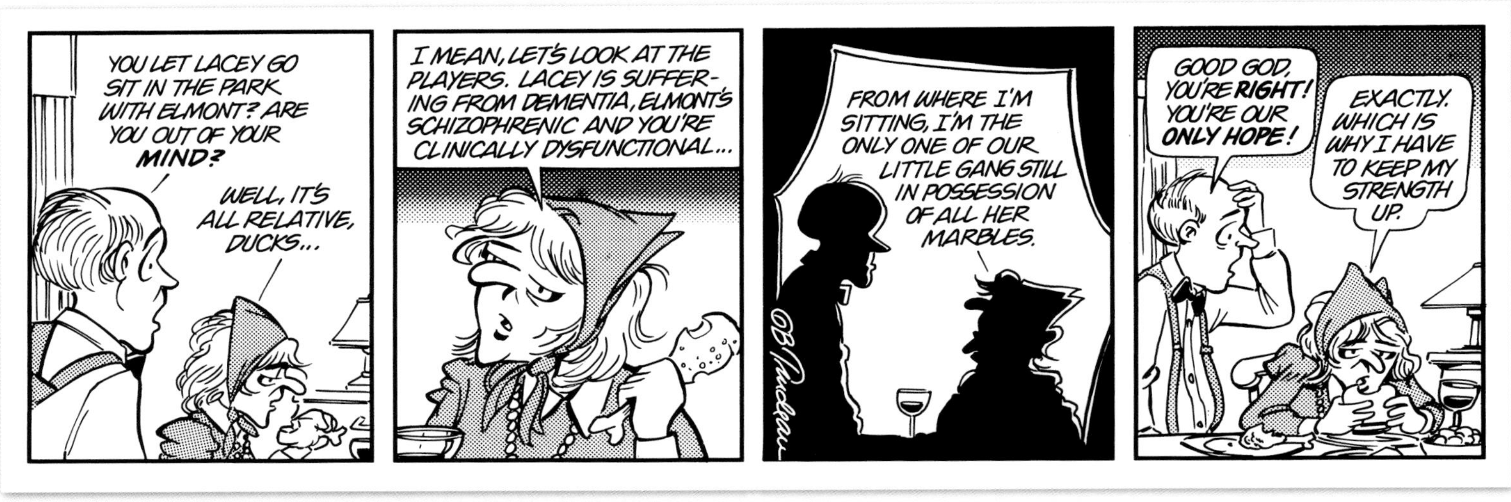
YOU LET LACEY GO SIT IN THE PARK WITH ELMONT? ARE YOU OUT OF YOUR **MIND?**
WELL, IT'S ALL RELATIVE, DUCKS...
I MEAN, LET'S LOOK AT THE PLAYERS. LACEY IS SUFFERING FROM DEMENTIA, ELMONT'S SCHIZOPHRENIC AND YOU'RE CLINICALLY DYSFUNCTIONAL...
FROM WHERE I'M SITTING, I'M THE ONLY ONE OF OUR LITTLE GANG STILL IN POSSESSION OF ALL HER MARBLES.
GOOD GOD, YOU'RE **RIGHT!** YOU'RE OUR **ONLY HOPE!**
EXACTLY. WHICH IS WHY I HAVE TO KEEP MY STRENGTH UP.

3/4/98

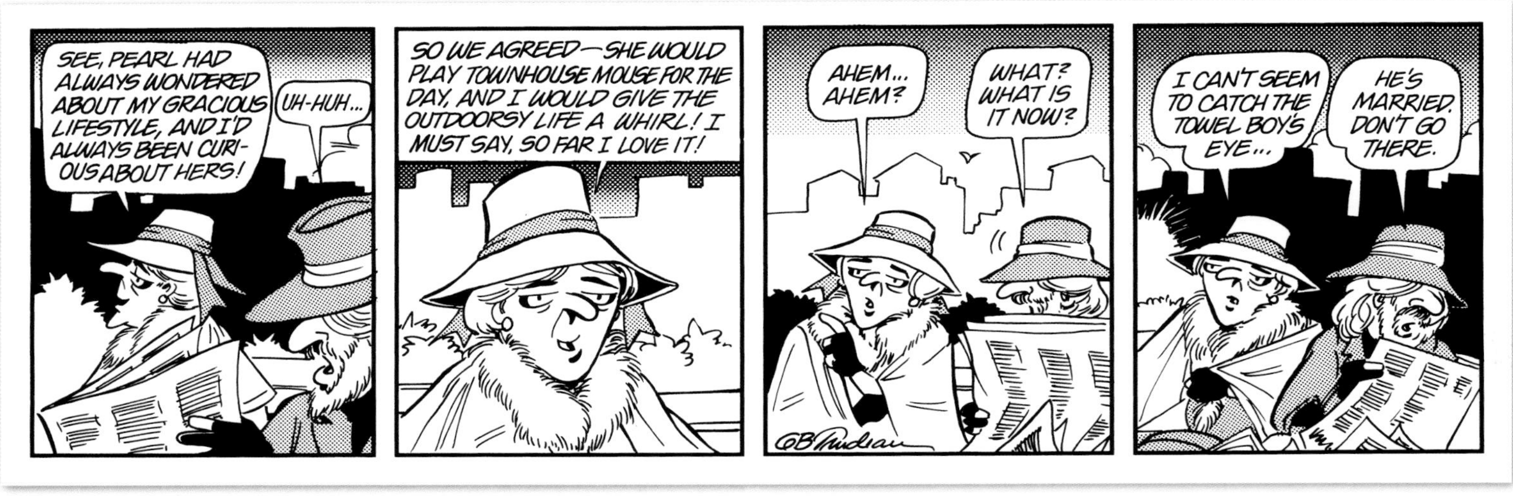
SEE, PEARL HAD ALWAYS WONDERED ABOUT MY GRACIOUS LIFESTYLE, AND I'D ALWAYS BEEN CURIOUS ABOUT HERS!
UH-HUH...
SO WE AGREED—SHE WOULD PLAY TOWNHOUSE MOUSE FOR THE DAY, AND I WOULD GIVE THE OUTDOORSY LIFE A WHIRL! I MUST SAY, SO FAR I LOVE IT!
AHEM... AHEM?
WHAT? WHAT IS IT NOW?
I CAN'T SEEM TO CATCH THE TOWEL BOY'S EYE...
HE'S MARRIED. DON'T GO THERE.

3/5/98

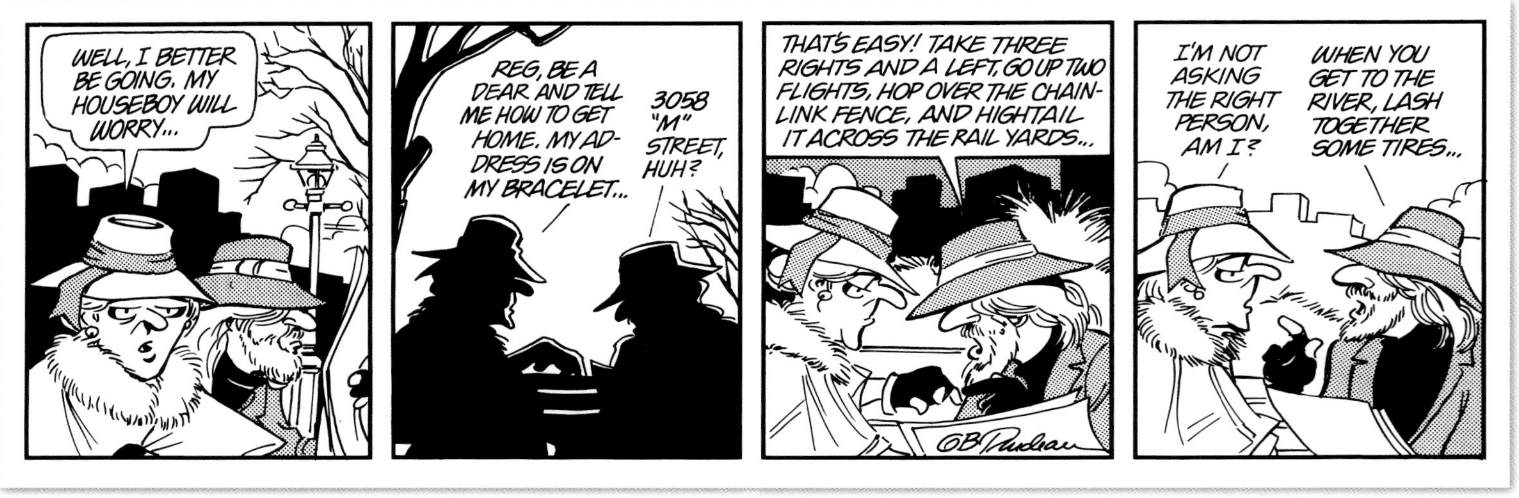
WELL, I BETTER BE GOING. MY HOUSEBOY WILL WORRY...
REG, BE A DEAR AND TELL ME HOW TO GET HOME. MY ADDRESS IS ON MY BRACELET...
3058 "M" STREET, HUH?
THAT'S EASY! TAKE THREE RIGHTS AND A LEFT, GO UP TWO FLIGHTS, HOP OVER THE CHAIN-LINK FENCE, AND HIGHTAIL IT ACROSS THE RAIL YARDS...
I'M NOT ASKING THE RIGHT PERSON, AM I?
WHEN YOU GET TO THE RIVER, LASH TOGETHER SOME TIRES...

3/7/98

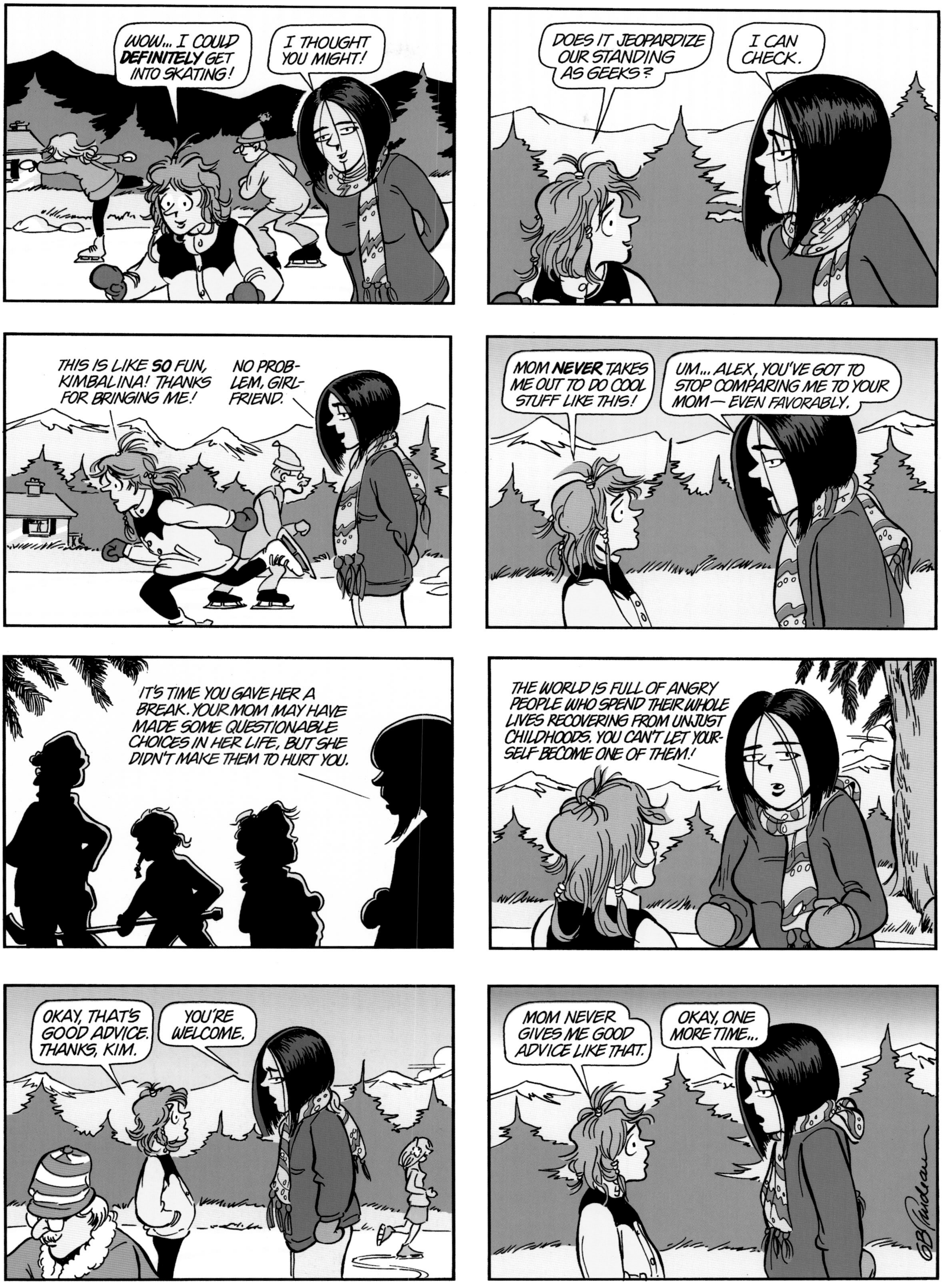
WOW... I COULD DEFINITELY GET INTO SKATING!
I THOUGHT YOU MIGHT!
DOES IT JEOPARDIZE OUR STANDING AS GEEKS?
I CAN CHECK.
THIS IS LIKE SO FUN, KIMBALINA! THANKS FOR BRINGING ME!
NO PROBLEM, GIRLFRIEND.
MOM NEVER TAKES ME OUT TO DO COOL STUFF LIKE THIS!
UM... ALEX, YOU'VE GOT TO STOP COMPARING ME TO YOUR MOM — EVEN FAVORABLY.
IT'S TIME YOU GAVE HER A BREAK. YOUR MOM MAY HAVE MADE SOME QUESTIONABLE CHOICES IN HER LIFE, BUT SHE DIDN'T MAKE THEM TO HURT YOU.
THE WORLD IS FULL OF ANGRY PEOPLE WHO SPEND THEIR WHOLE LIVES RECOVERING FROM UNJUST CHILDHOODS. YOU CAN'T LET YOURSELF BECOME ONE OF THEM!
OKAY, THAT'S GOOD ADVICE. THANKS, KIM.
YOU'RE WELCOME.
MOM NEVER GIVES ME GOOD ADVICE LIKE THAT.
OKAY, ONE MORE TIME...
GB Trudeau

1/18/98

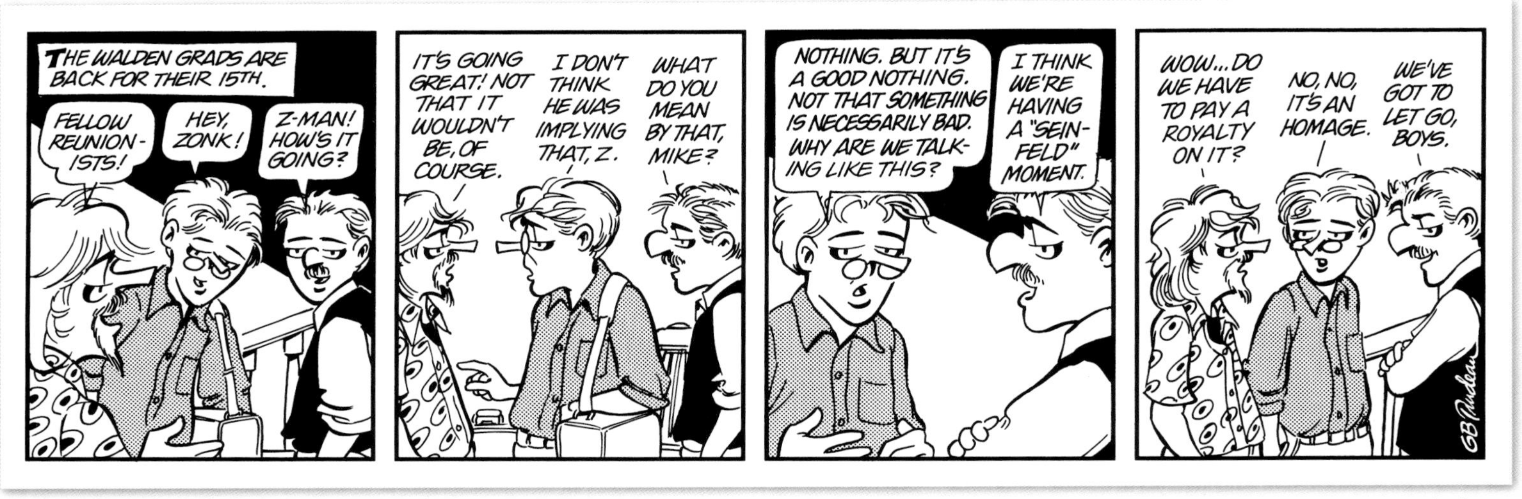
THE WALDEN GRADS ARE BACK FOR THEIR 15TH.
FELLOW REUNIONISTS!
HEY, ZONK!
Z-MAN! HOW'S IT GOING?
IT'S GOING GREAT! NOT THAT IT WOULDN'T BE, OF COURSE.
I DON'T THINK HE WAS IMPLYING THAT, Z.
WHAT DO YOU MEAN BY THAT, MIKE?
NOTHING. BUT IT'S A GOOD NOTHING. NOT THAT SOMETHING IS NECESSARILY BAD. WHY ARE WE TALKING LIKE THIS?
I THINK WE'RE HAVING A "SEINFELD" MOMENT.
WOW... DO WE HAVE TO PAY A ROYALTY ON IT?
NO, NO, IT'S AN HOMAGE.
WE'VE GOT TO LET GO, BOYS.

4/27/98

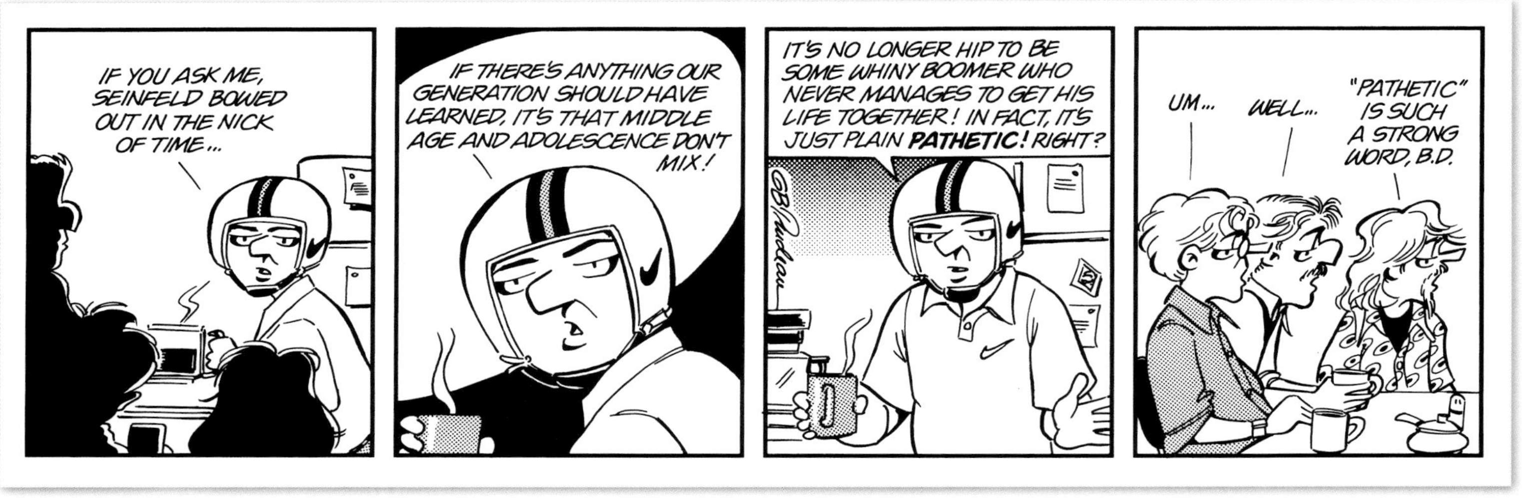
IF YOU ASK ME, SEINFELD BOWED OUT IN THE NICK OF TIME...
IF THERE'S ANYTHING OUR GENERATION SHOULD HAVE LEARNED, IT'S THAT MIDDLE AGE AND ADOLESCENCE DON'T MIX!
IT'S NO LONGER HIP TO BE SOME WHINY BOOMER WHO NEVER MANAGES TO GET HIS LIFE TOGETHER! IN FACT, IT'S JUST PLAIN PATHETIC! RIGHT?
UM...
WELL...
"PATHETIC" IS SUCH A STRONG WORD, B.D.

4/30/98

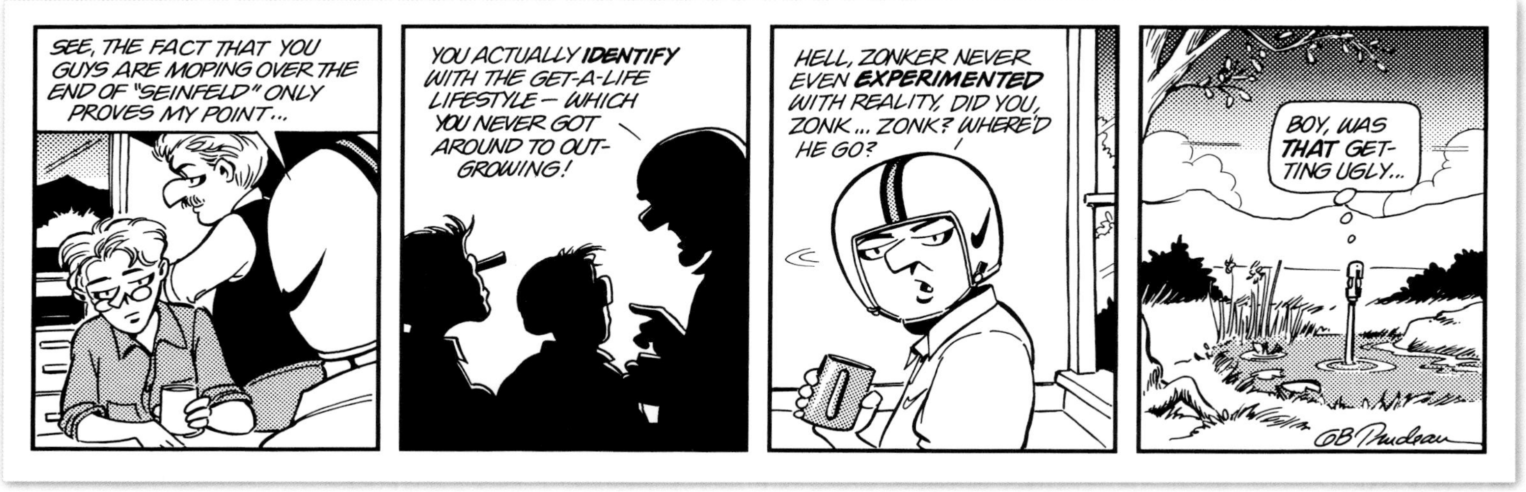
SEE, THE FACT THAT YOU GUYS ARE MOPING OVER THE END OF "SEINFELD" ONLY PROVES MY POINT...
YOU ACTUALLY IDENTIFY WITH THE GET-A-LIFE LIFESTYLE — WHICH YOU NEVER GOT AROUND TO OUTGROWING!
HELL, ZONKER NEVER EVEN EXPERIMENTED WITH REALITY, DID YOU, ZONK... ZONK? WHERE'D HE GO?
BOY, WAS THAT GETTING UGLY...

5/1/98

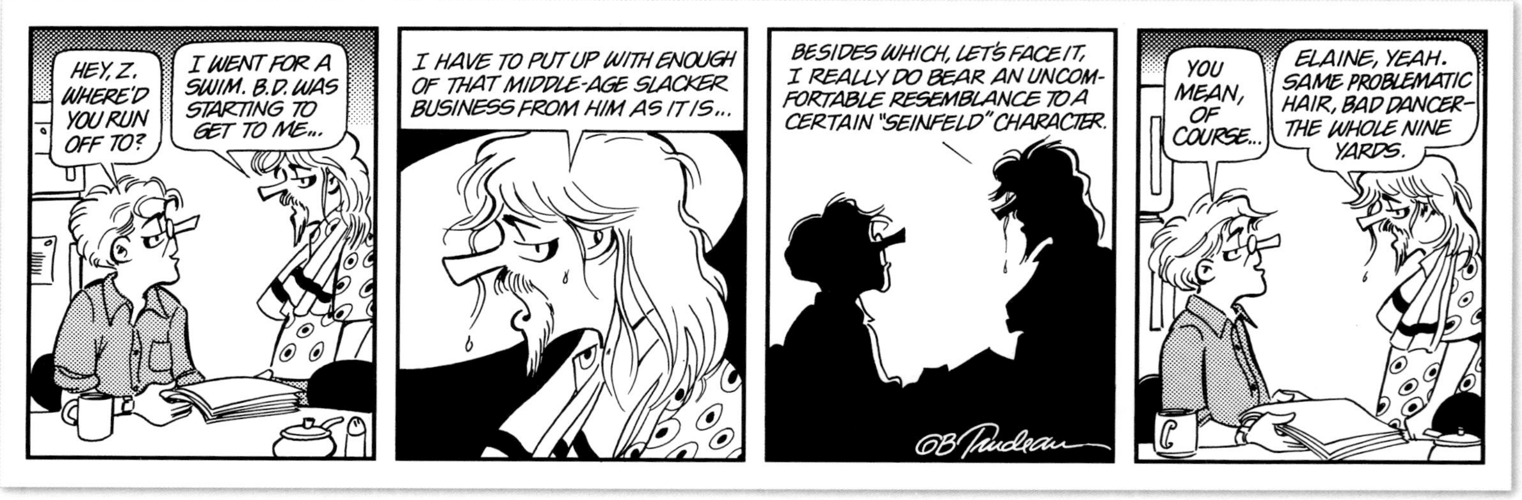
HEY, Z. WHERE'D YOU RUN OFF TO?
I WENT FOR A SWIM. B.D. WAS STARTING TO GET TO ME...
I HAVE TO PUT UP WITH ENOUGH OF THAT MIDDLE-AGE SLACKER BUSINESS FROM HIM AS IT IS...
BESIDES WHICH, LET'S FACE IT, I REALLY DO BEAR AN UNCOMFORTABLE RESEMBLANCE TO A CERTAIN "SEINFELD" CHARACTER.
YOU MEAN, OF COURSE...
ELAINE, YEAH. SAME PROBLEMATIC HAIR, BAD DANCER — THE WHOLE NINE YARDS.

5/2/98

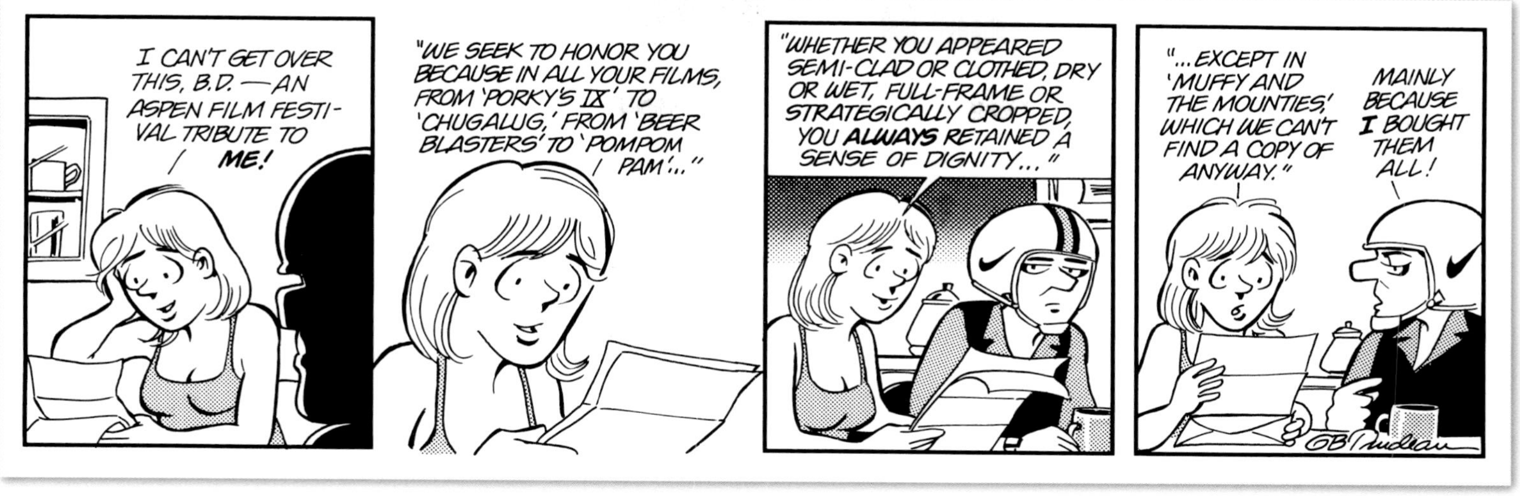
I CAN'T GET OVER THIS, B.D. — AN ASPEN FILM FESTIVAL TRIBUTE TO **ME!**
"WE SEEK TO HONOR YOU BECAUSE IN ALL YOUR FILMS, FROM 'PORKY'S IX' TO 'CHUGALUG,' FROM 'BEER BLASTERS' TO 'POMPOM PAM'..."
"WHETHER YOU APPEARED SEMI-CLAD OR CLOTHED, DRY OR WET, FULL-FRAME OR STRATEGICALLY CROPPED, YOU **ALWAYS** RETAINED A SENSE OF DIGNITY..."
"...EXCEPT IN 'MUFFY AND THE MOUNTIES,' WHICH WE CAN'T FIND A COPY OF ANYWAY."
MAINLY BECAUSE **I** BOUGHT THEM ALL!
G.B. Trudeau

6/9/98

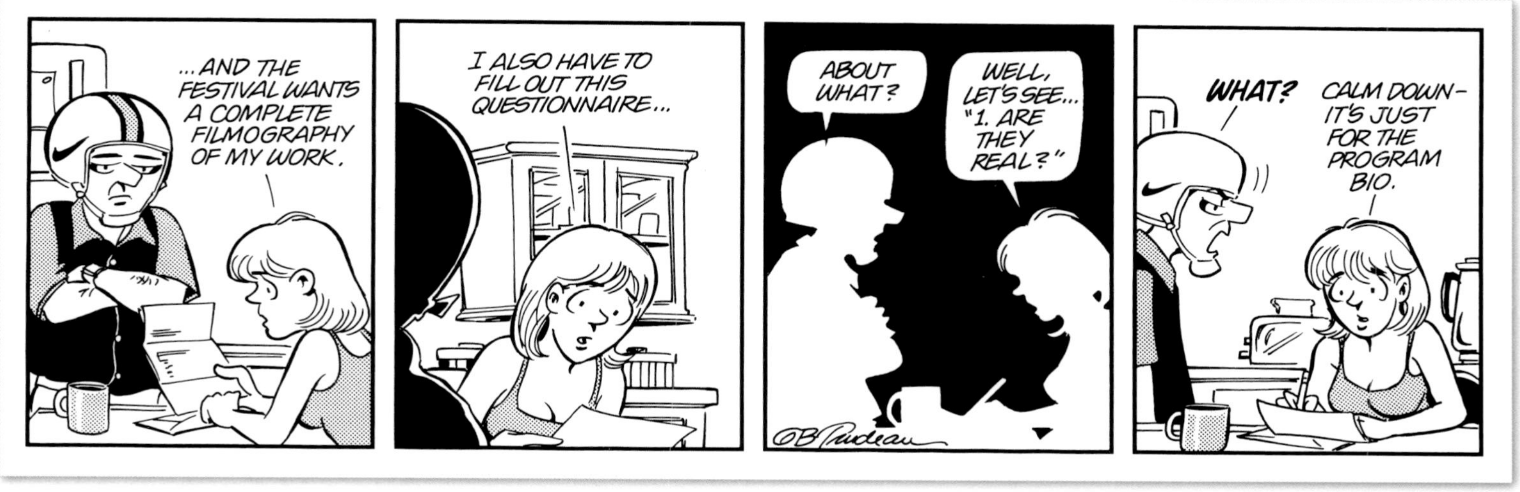
...AND THE FESTIVAL WANTS A COMPLETE FILMOGRAPHY OF MY WORK.
I ALSO HAVE TO FILL OUT THIS QUESTIONNAIRE...
ABOUT WHAT?
WELL, LET'S SEE... "1. ARE THEY REAL?"
G.B. Trudeau
WHAT?
CALM DOWN — IT'S JUST FOR THE PROGRAM BIO.

6/10/98

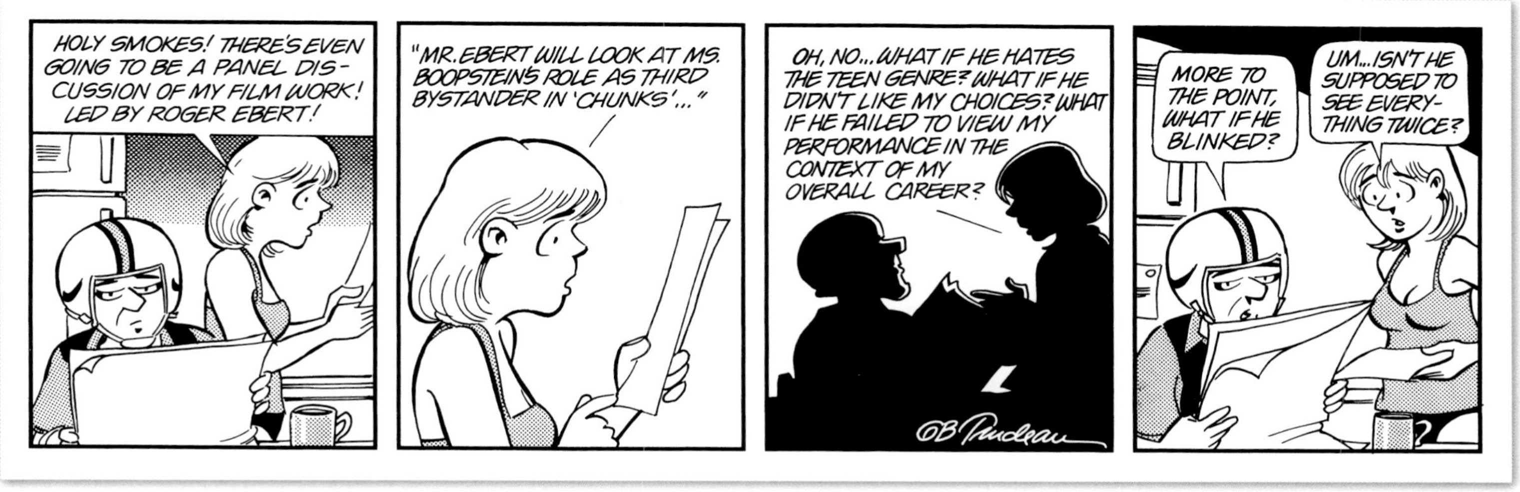
HOLY SMOKES! THERE'S EVEN GOING TO BE A PANEL DISCUSSION OF MY FILM WORK! LED BY ROGER EBERT!
"MR. EBERT WILL LOOK AT MS. BOOPSTEIN'S ROLE AS THIRD BYSTANDER IN 'CHUNKS'..."
OH, NO... WHAT IF HE HATES THE TEEN GENRE? WHAT IF HE DIDN'T LIKE MY CHOICES? WHAT IF HE FAILED TO VIEW MY PERFORMANCE IN THE CONTEXT OF MY OVERALL CAREER?
G.B. Trudeau
MORE TO THE POINT, WHAT IF HE BLINKED?
UM... ISN'T HE SUPPOSED TO SEE EVERYTHING TWICE?

6/11/98

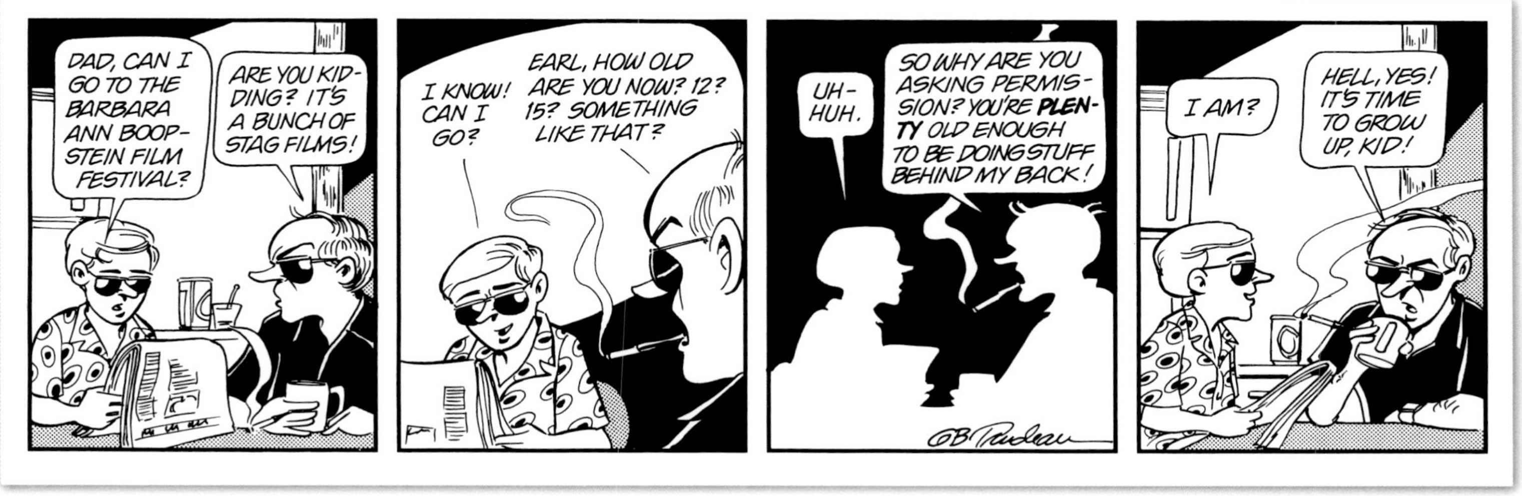
DAD, CAN I GO TO THE BARBARA ANN BOOPSTEIN FILM FESTIVAL?
ARE YOU KIDDING? IT'S A BUNCH OF STAG FILMS!
I KNOW! CAN I GO?
EARL, HOW OLD ARE YOU NOW? 12? 15? SOMETHING LIKE THAT?
UH-HUH.
SO WHY ARE YOU ASKING PERMISSION? YOU'RE **PLENTY** OLD ENOUGH TO BE DOING STUFF BEHIND MY BACK!
G.B. Trudeau
I AM?
HELL, YES! IT'S TIME TO GROW UP, KID!

6/15/98

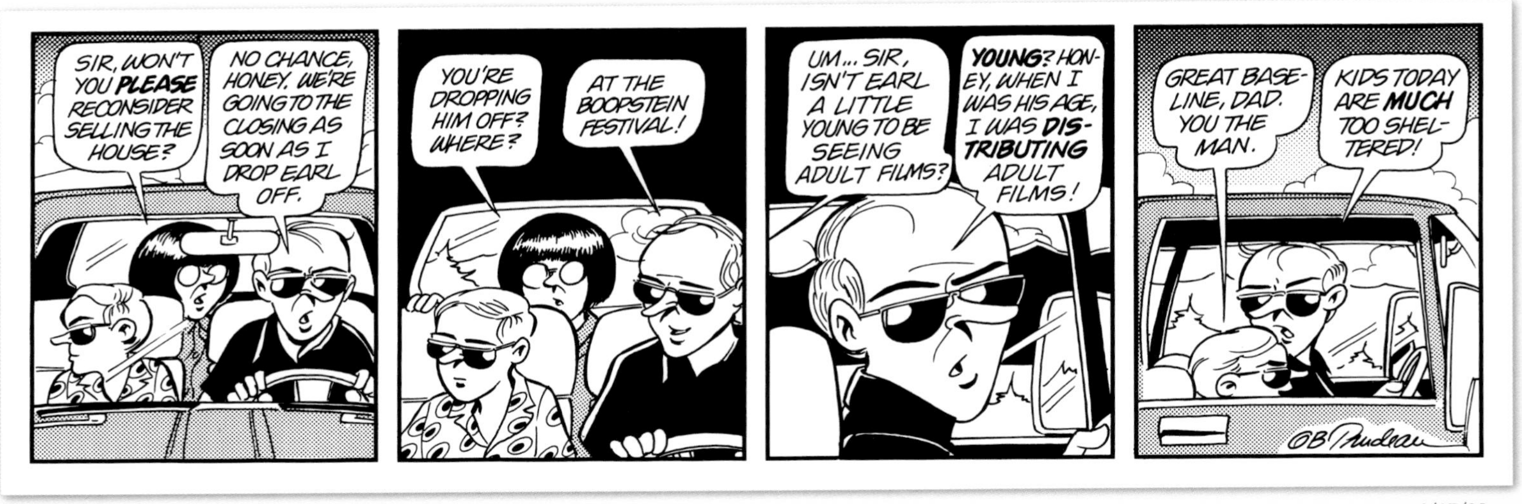
SIR, WON'T YOU **PLEASE** RECONSIDER SELLING THE HOUSE?
NO CHANCE, HONEY. WE'RE GOING TO THE CLOSING AS SOON AS I DROP EARL OFF.
YOU'RE DROPPING HIM OFF? WHERE?
AT THE BOOPSTEIN FESTIVAL!
UM... SIR, ISN'T EARL A LITTLE YOUNG TO BE SEEING ADULT FILMS?
YOUNG? HONEY, WHEN I WAS HIS AGE, I WAS **DISTRIBUTING** ADULT FILMS!
GREAT BASELINE, DAD. YOU THE MAN.
KIDS TODAY ARE **MUCH** TOO SHELTERED!
GB Trudeau

6/17/98

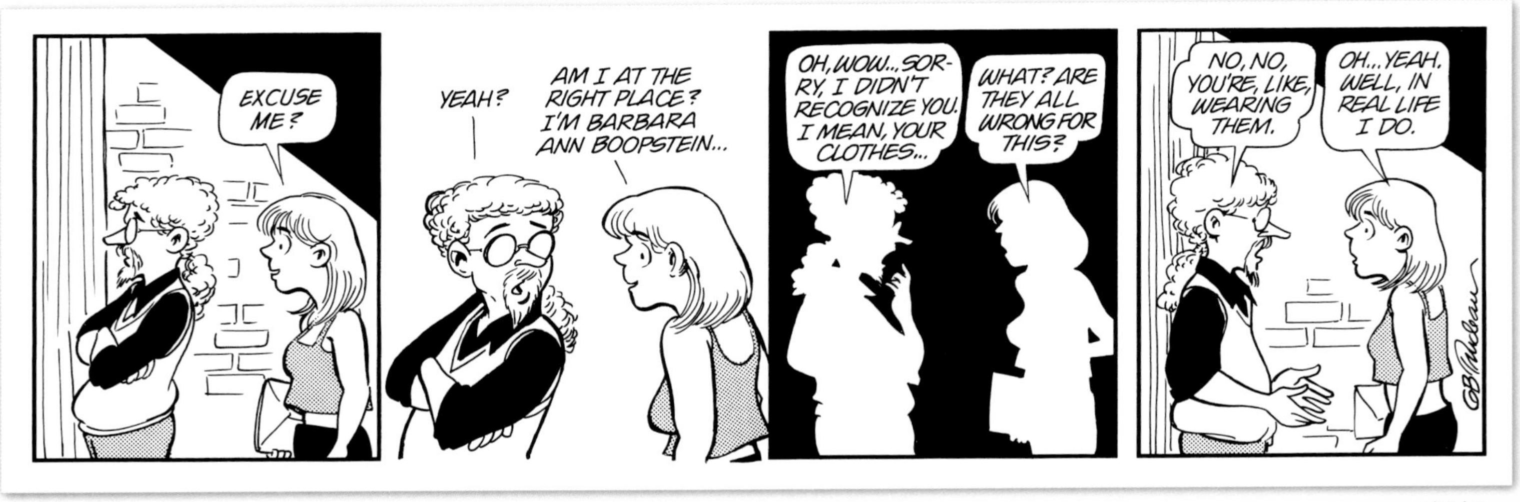
EXCUSE ME?
YEAH?
AM I AT THE RIGHT PLACE? I'M BARBARA ANN BOOPSTEIN...
OH, WOW... SORRY, I DIDN'T RECOGNIZE YOU. I MEAN, YOUR CLOTHES...
WHAT? ARE THEY ALL WRONG FOR THIS?
NO, NO, YOU'RE, LIKE, WEARING THEM.
OH... YEAH. WELL, IN REAL LIFE I DO.
GB Trudeau

6/22/98

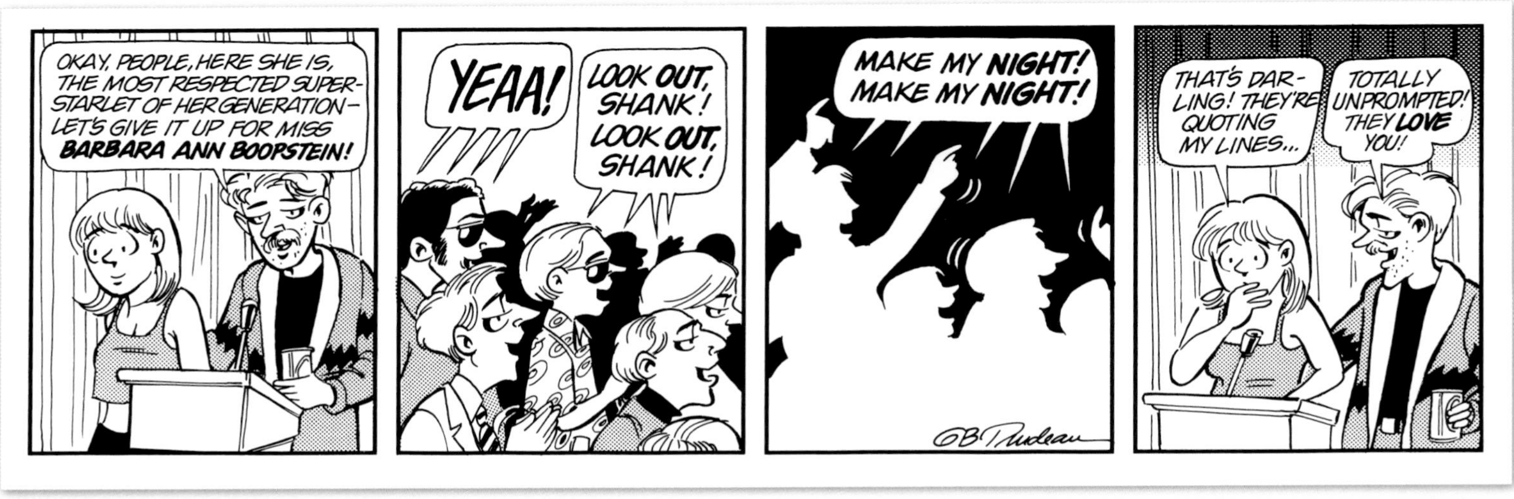
OKAY, PEOPLE, HERE SHE IS, THE MOST RESPECTED SUPERSTARLET OF HER GENERATION— LET'S GIVE IT UP FOR MISS **BARBARA ANN BOOPSTEIN!**
YEAA!
LOOK **OUT**, SHANK! LOOK **OUT**, SHANK!
MAKE MY **NIGHT!** MAKE MY **NIGHT!**
THAT'S DARLING! THEY'RE QUOTING MY LINES...
TOTALLY UNPROMPTED! THEY **LOVE** YOU!
GB Trudeau

6/24/98

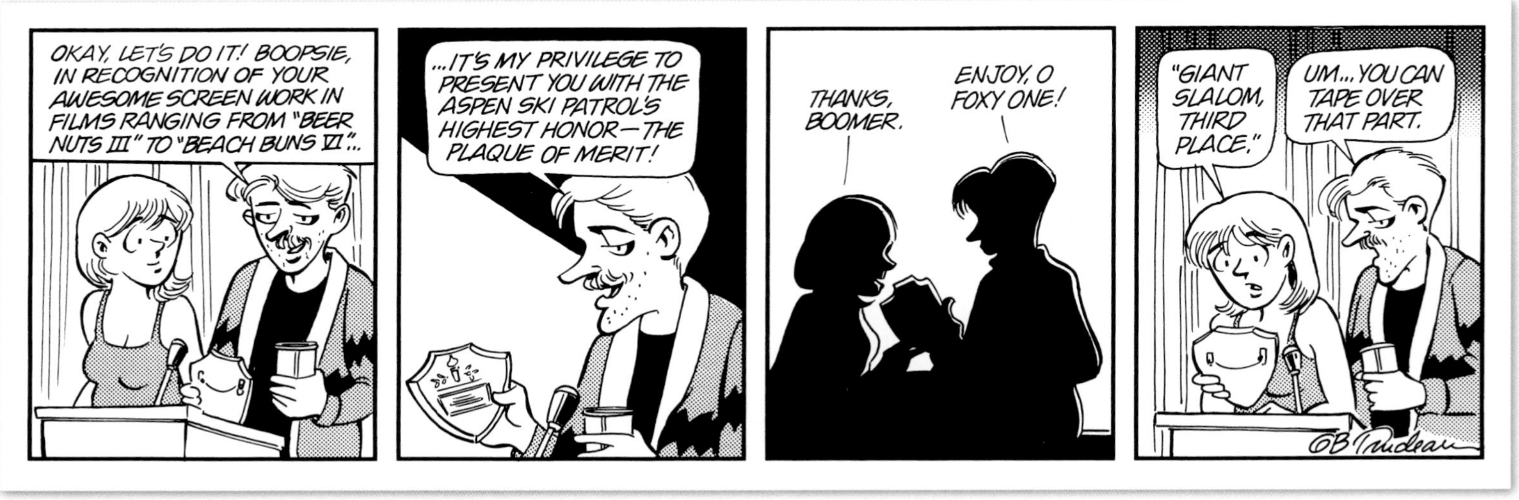
OKAY, LET'S DO IT! BOOPSIE, IN RECOGNITION OF YOUR AWESOME SCREEN WORK IN FILMS RANGING FROM "BEER NUTS III" TO "BEACH BUNS VI"...
...IT'S MY PRIVILEGE TO PRESENT YOU WITH THE ASPEN SKI PATROL'S HIGHEST HONOR—THE PLAQUE OF MERIT!
THANKS, BOOMER.
ENJOY, O FOXY ONE!
"GIANT SLALOM, THIRD PLACE."
UM... YOU CAN TAPE OVER THAT PART.
GB Trudeau

6/25/98

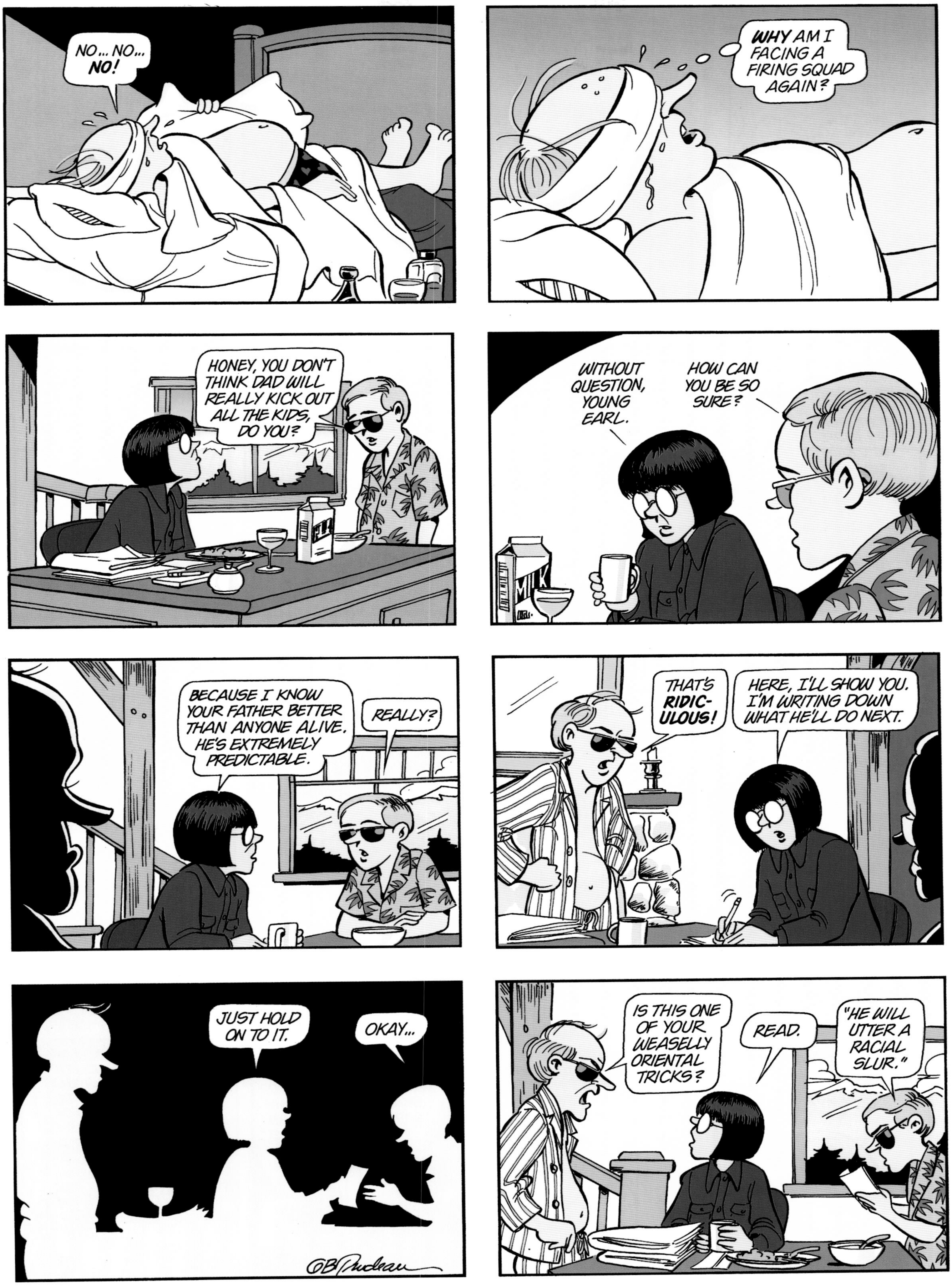

NO... NO... NO!
WHY AM I FACING A FIRING SQUAD AGAIN?
HONEY, YOU DON'T THINK DAD WILL REALLY KICK OUT ALL THE KIDS, DO YOU?
WITHOUT QUESTION, YOUNG EARL.
HOW CAN YOU BE SO SURE?
BECAUSE I KNOW YOUR FATHER BETTER THAN ANYONE ALIVE. HE'S EXTREMELY PREDICTABLE.
REALLY?
THAT'S RIDICULOUS!
HERE, I'LL SHOW YOU. I'M WRITING DOWN WHAT HE'LL DO NEXT.
JUST HOLD ON TO IT.
OKAY...
IS THIS ONE OF YOUR WEASELLY ORIENTAL TRICKS?
READ.
"HE WILL UTTER A RACIAL SLUR."

6/14/98

8/15/98

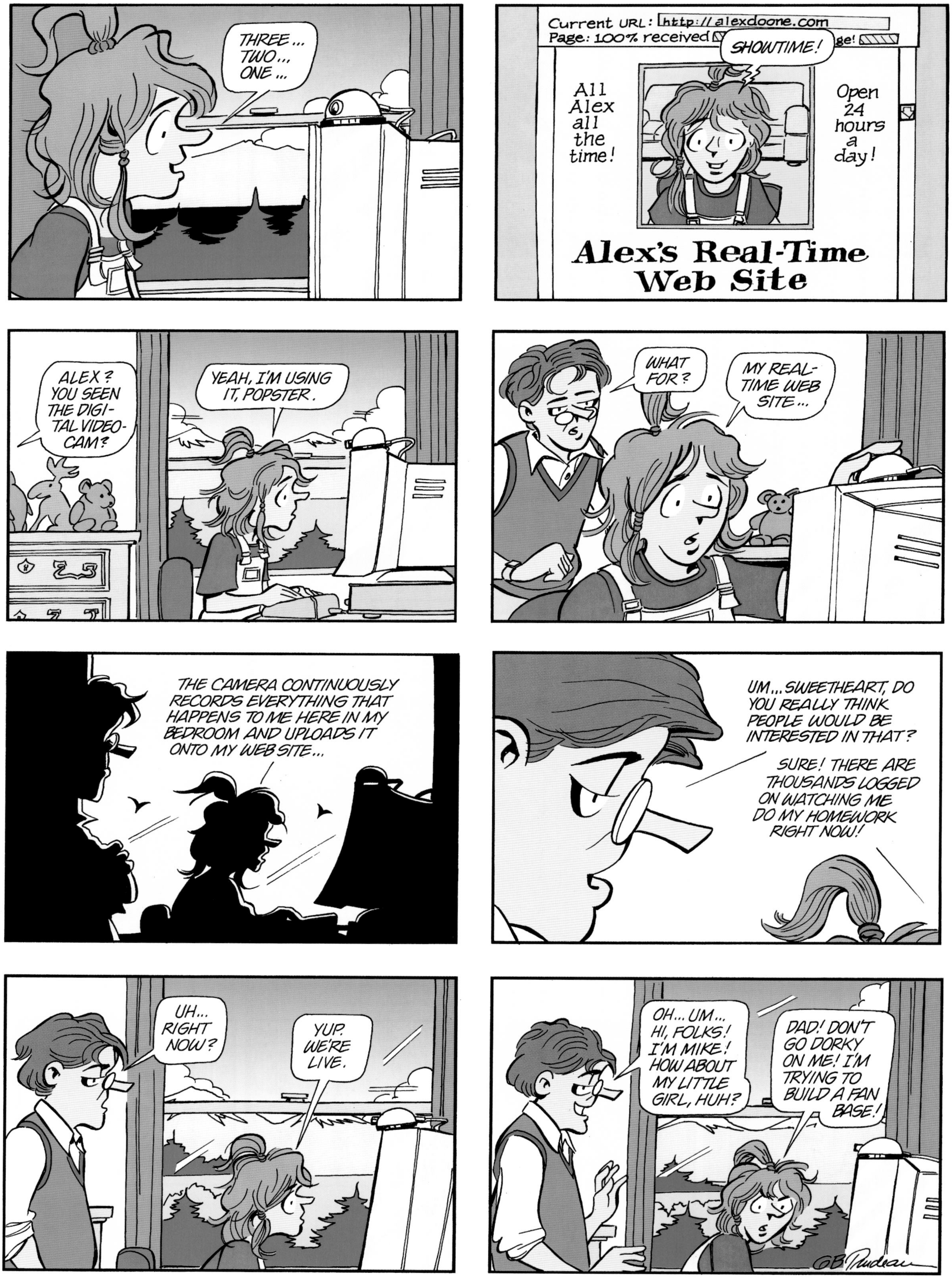

THREE... TWO... ONE...
Current URL: http://alexdoone.com
Page: 100% received
SHOWTIME!
All Alex all the time!
Open 24 hours a day!
Alex's Real-Time Web Site
ALEX? YOU SEEN THE DIGITAL VIDEO-CAM?
YEAH, I'M USING IT, POPSTER.
WHAT FOR?
MY REAL-TIME WEB SITE...
THE CAMERA CONTINUOUSLY RECORDS EVERYTHING THAT HAPPENS TO ME HERE IN MY BEDROOM AND UPLOADS IT ONTO MY WEB SITE...
UM... SWEETHEART, DO YOU REALLY THINK PEOPLE WOULD BE INTERESTED IN THAT?
SURE! THERE ARE THOUSANDS LOGGED ON WATCHING ME DO MY HOMEWORK RIGHT NOW!
UH... RIGHT NOW?
YUP. WE'RE LIVE.
OH... UM... HI, FOLKS! I'M MIKE! HOW ABOUT MY LITTLE GIRL, HUH?
DAD! DON'T GO DORKY ON ME! I'M TRYING TO BUILD A FAN BASE!
GB Trudeau

12/20/98

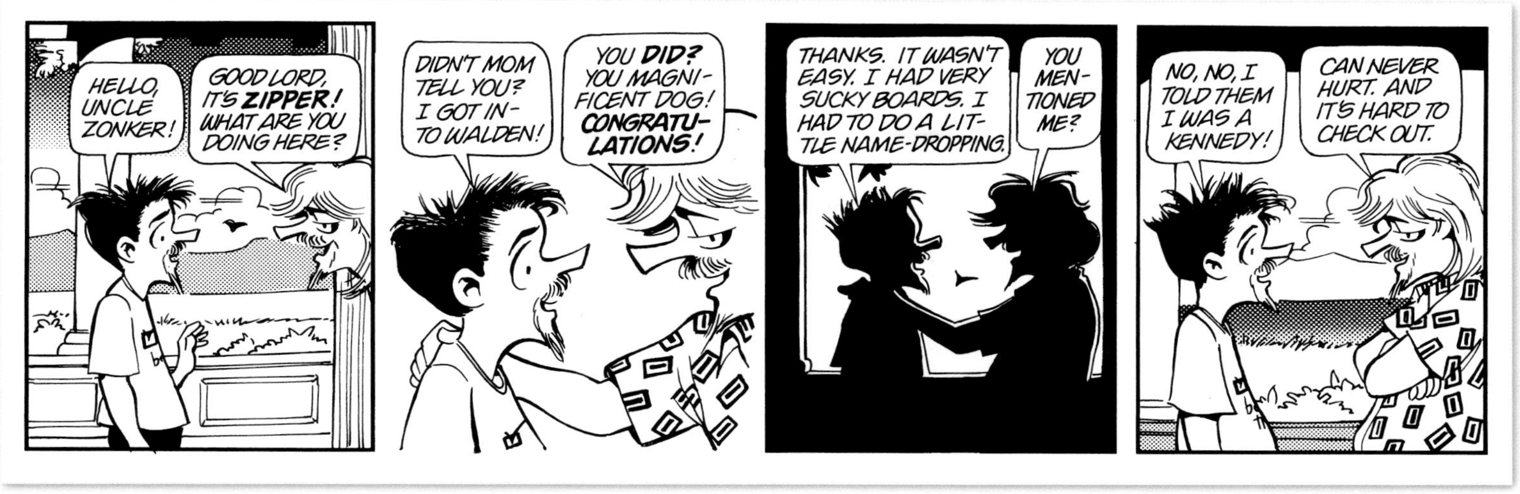
HELLO, UNCLE ZONKER!
GOOD LORD, IT'S **ZIPPER**! WHAT ARE YOU DOING HERE?
DIDN'T MOM TELL YOU? I GOT INTO WALDEN!
YOU **DID?** YOU MAGNIFICENT DOG! **CONGRATULATIONS!**
THANKS. IT WASN'T EASY. I HAD VERY SUCKY BOARDS. I HAD TO DO A LITTLE NAME-DROPPING.
YOU MENTIONED ME?
NO, NO, I TOLD THEM I WAS A KENNEDY!
CAN NEVER HURT. AND IT'S HARD TO CHECK OUT.

9/7/98

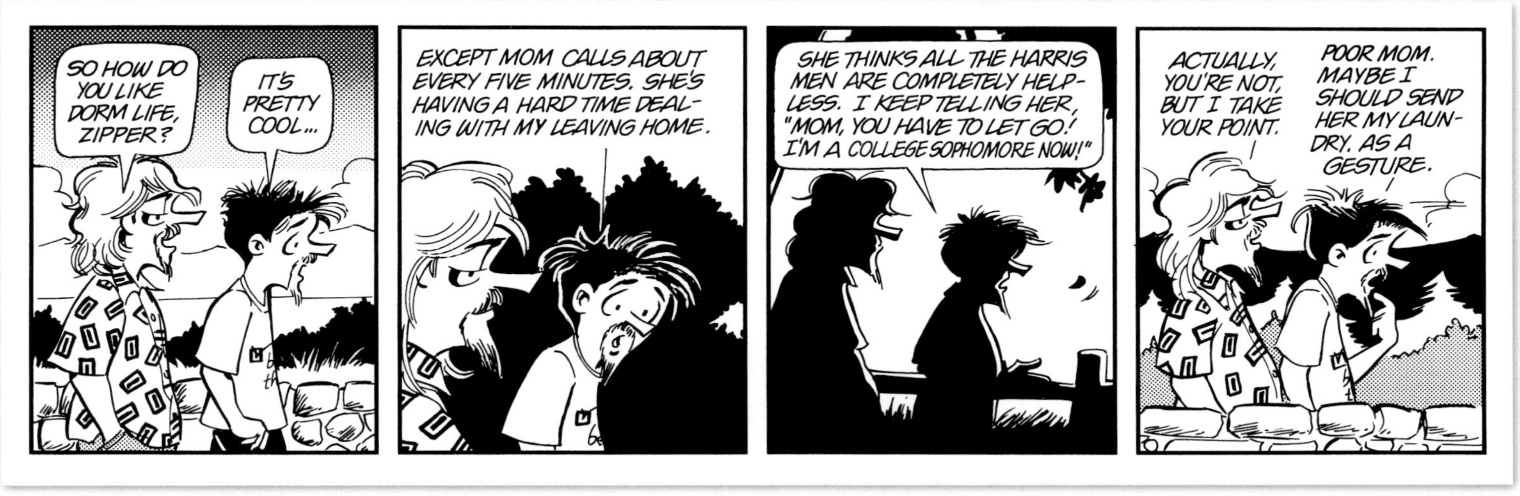
SO HOW DO YOU LIKE DORM LIFE, ZIPPER?
IT'S PRETTY COOL...
EXCEPT MOM CALLS ABOUT EVERY FIVE MINUTES. SHE'S HAVING A HARD TIME DEALING WITH MY LEAVING HOME.
SHE THINKS ALL THE HARRIS MEN ARE COMPLETELY HELPLESS. I KEEP TELLING HER, "MOM, YOU HAVE TO LET GO! I'M A COLLEGE SOPHOMORE NOW!"
ACTUALLY, YOU'RE NOT, BUT I TAKE YOUR POINT.
POOR MOM. MAYBE I SHOULD SEND HER MY LAUNDRY, AS A GESTURE.

9/8/98

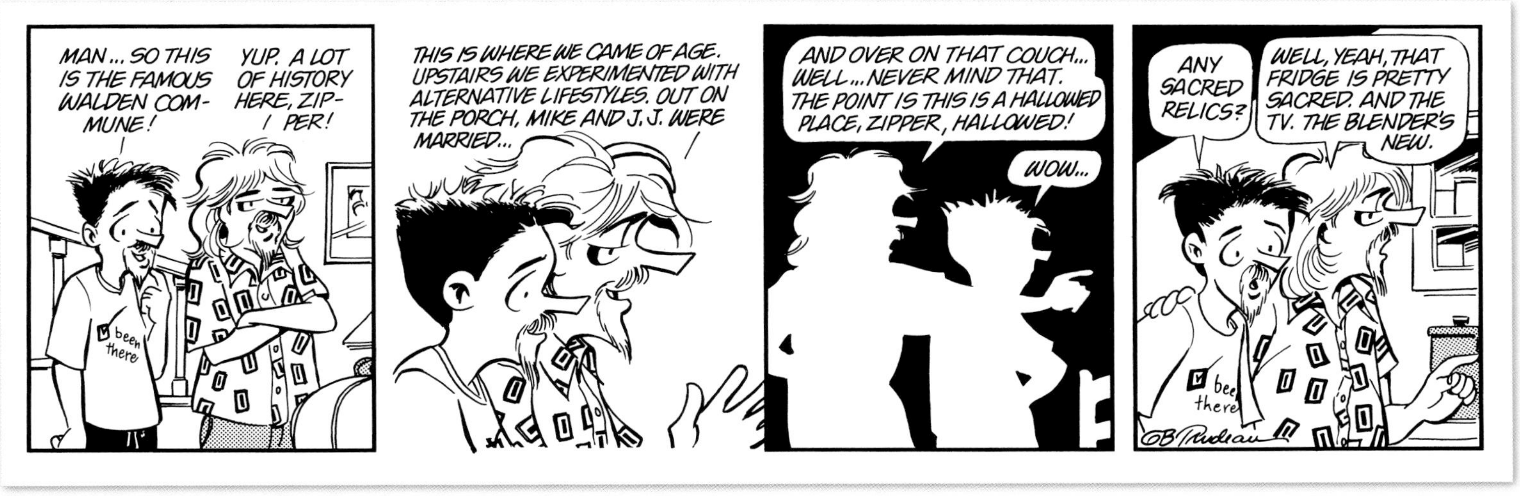
MAN... SO THIS IS THE FAMOUS WALDEN COMMUNE!
YUP. A LOT OF HISTORY HERE, ZIPPER!
THIS IS WHERE WE CAME OF AGE. UPSTAIRS WE EXPERIMENTED WITH ALTERNATIVE LIFESTYLES. OUT ON THE PORCH, MIKE AND J.J. WERE MARRIED...
AND OVER ON THAT COUCH... WELL... NEVER MIND THAT. THE POINT IS THIS IS A HALLOWED PLACE, ZIPPER, HALLOWED!
WOW...
ANY SACRED RELICS?
WELL, YEAH, THAT FRIDGE IS PRETTY SACRED. AND THE TV. THE BLENDER'S NEW.

9/9/98

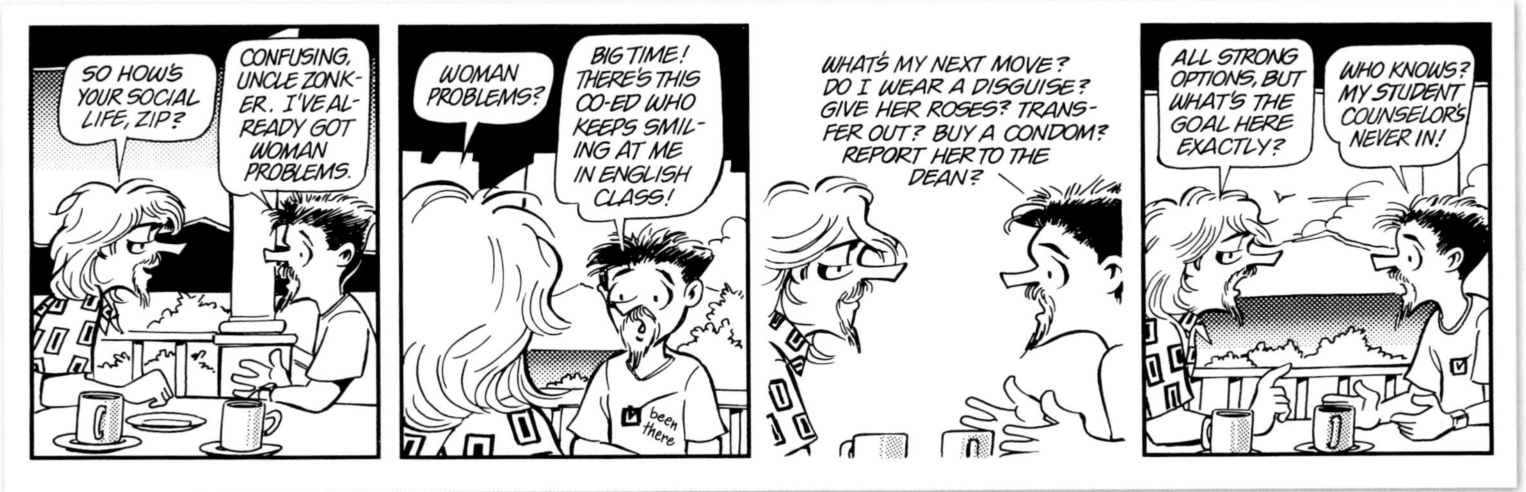
SO HOW'S YOUR SOCIAL LIFE, ZIP?
CONFUSING, UNCLE ZONKER. I'VE ALREADY GOT WOMAN PROBLEMS.
WOMAN PROBLEMS?
BIG TIME! THERE'S THIS CO-ED WHO KEEPS SMILING AT ME IN ENGLISH CLASS!
WHAT'S MY NEXT MOVE? DO I WEAR A DISGUISE? GIVE HER ROSES? TRANSFER OUT? BUY A CONDOM? REPORT HER TO THE DEAN?
ALL STRONG OPTIONS, BUT WHAT'S THE GOAL HERE EXACTLY?
WHO KNOWS? MY STUDENT COUNSELOR'S NEVER IN!

9/10/98

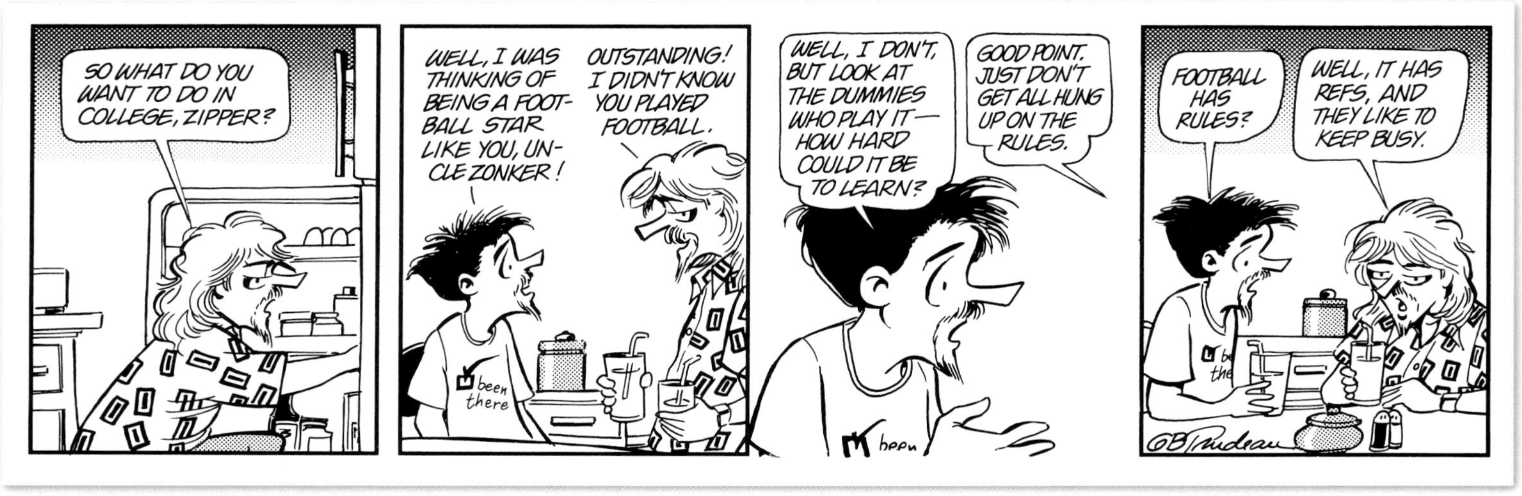
SO WHAT DO YOU WANT TO DO IN COLLEGE, ZIPPER?
WELL, I WAS THINKING OF BEING A FOOTBALL STAR LIKE YOU, UNCLE ZONKER!
OUTSTANDING! I DIDN'T KNOW YOU PLAYED FOOTBALL.
WELL, I DON'T, BUT LOOK AT THE DUMMIES WHO PLAY IT— HOW HARD COULD IT BE TO LEARN?
GOOD POINT. JUST DON'T GET ALL HUNG UP ON THE RULES.
FOOTBALL HAS RULES?
WELL, IT HAS REFS, AND THEY LIKE TO KEEP BUSY.

9/11/98

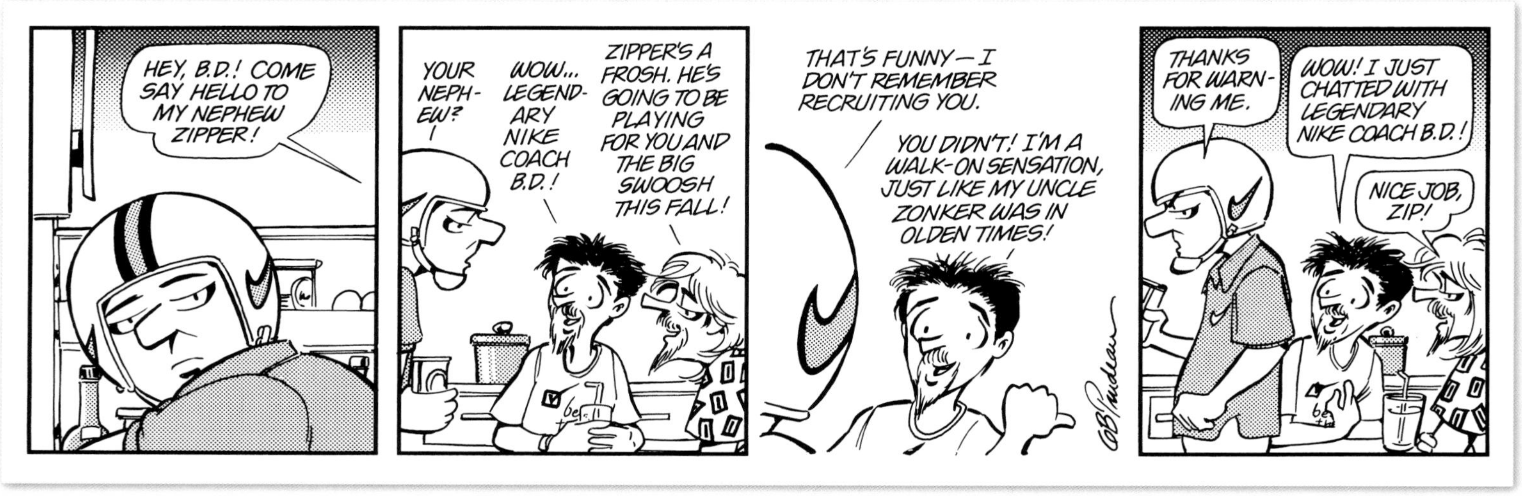
HEY, B.D.! COME SAY HELLO TO MY NEPHEW ZIPPER!
YOUR NEPHEW?
WOW... LEGENDARY NIKE COACH B.D.!
ZIPPER'S A FROSH. HE'S GOING TO BE PLAYING FOR YOU AND THE BIG SWOOSH THIS FALL!
THAT'S FUNNY— I DON'T REMEMBER RECRUITING YOU.
YOU DIDN'T! I'M A WALK-ON SENSATION, JUST LIKE MY UNCLE ZONKER WAS IN OLDEN TIMES!
THANKS FOR WARNING ME.
WOW! I JUST CHATTED WITH LEGENDARY NIKE COACH B.D.!
NICE JOB, ZIP!

9/12/98

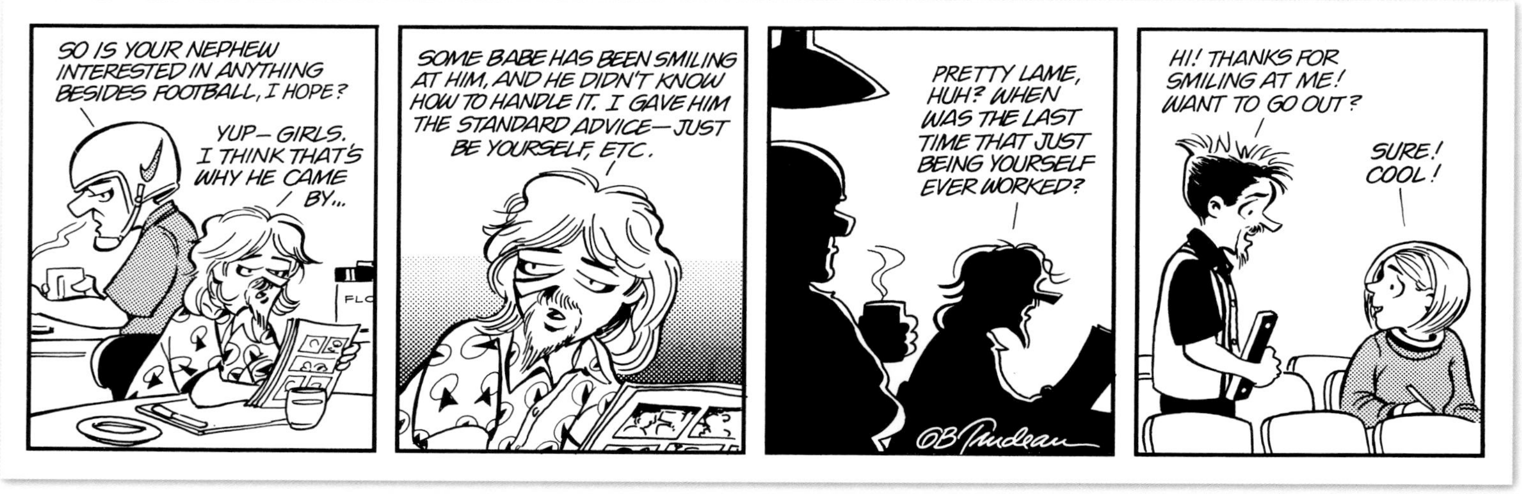
SO IS YOUR NEPHEW INTERESTED IN ANYTHING BESIDES FOOTBALL, I HOPE?
YUP— GIRLS. I THINK THAT'S WHY HE CAME BY...
SOME BABE HAS BEEN SMILING AT HIM, AND HE DIDN'T KNOW HOW TO HANDLE IT. I GAVE HIM THE STANDARD ADVICE— JUST BE YOURSELF, ETC.
PRETTY LAME, HUH? WHEN WAS THE LAST TIME THAT JUST BEING YOURSELF EVER WORKED?
HI! THANKS FOR SMILING AT ME! WANT TO GO OUT?
SURE! COOL!

9/14/98

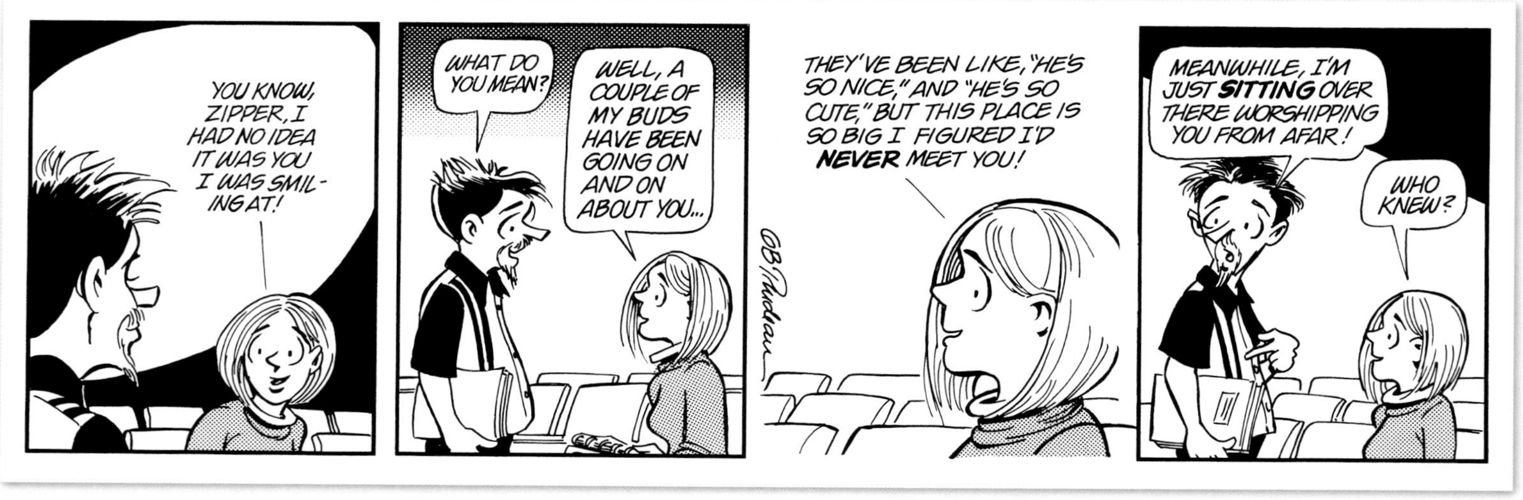
YOU KNOW, ZIPPER, I HAD NO IDEA IT WAS YOU I WAS SMILING AT!
WHAT DO YOU MEAN?
WELL, A COUPLE OF MY BUDS HAVE BEEN GOING ON AND ON ABOUT YOU...
THEY'VE BEEN LIKE, "HE'S SO NICE," AND "HE'S SO CUTE," BUT THIS PLACE IS SO BIG I FIGURED I'D NEVER MEET YOU!
MEANWHILE, I'M JUST SITTING OVER THERE WORSHIPPING YOU FROM AFAR!
WHO KNEW?

9/16/98

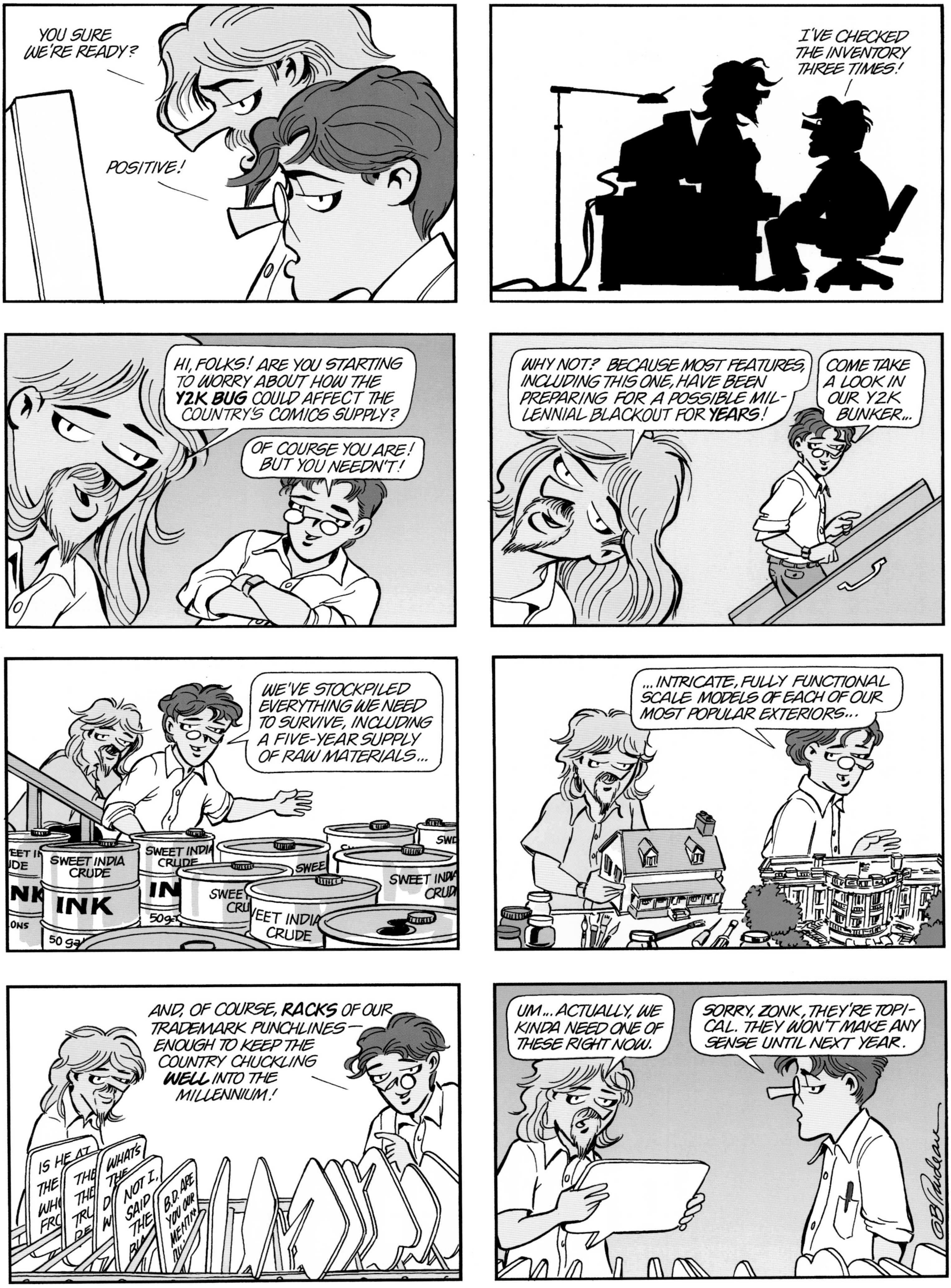
YOU SURE WE'RE READY?
POSITIVE!
I'VE CHECKED THE INVENTORY THREE TIMES!
HI, FOLKS! ARE YOU STARTING TO WORRY ABOUT HOW THE **Y2K BUG** COULD AFFECT THE COUNTRY'S COMICS SUPPLY?
OF COURSE YOU ARE! BUT YOU NEEDN'T!
WHY NOT? BECAUSE MOST FEATURES, INCLUDING THIS ONE, HAVE BEEN PREPARING FOR A POSSIBLE MILLENNIAL BLACKOUT FOR **YEARS**!
COME TAKE A LOOK IN OUR Y2K BUNKER...
WE'VE STOCKPILED EVERYTHING WE NEED TO SURVIVE, INCLUDING A FIVE-YEAR SUPPLY OF RAW MATERIALS...
SWEET INDIA CRUDE
INK
...INTRICATE, FULLY FUNCTIONAL SCALE MODELS OF EACH OF OUR MOST POPULAR EXTERIORS...
AND, OF COURSE, **RACKS** OF OUR TRADEMARK PUNCHLINES — ENOUGH TO KEEP THE COUNTRY CHUCKLING **WELL** INTO THE MILLENNIUM!
UM... ACTUALLY, WE KINDA NEED ONE OF THESE RIGHT NOW.
SORRY, ZONK, THEY'RE TOPICAL. THEY WON'T MAKE ANY SENSE UNTIL NEXT YEAR.

12/27/98

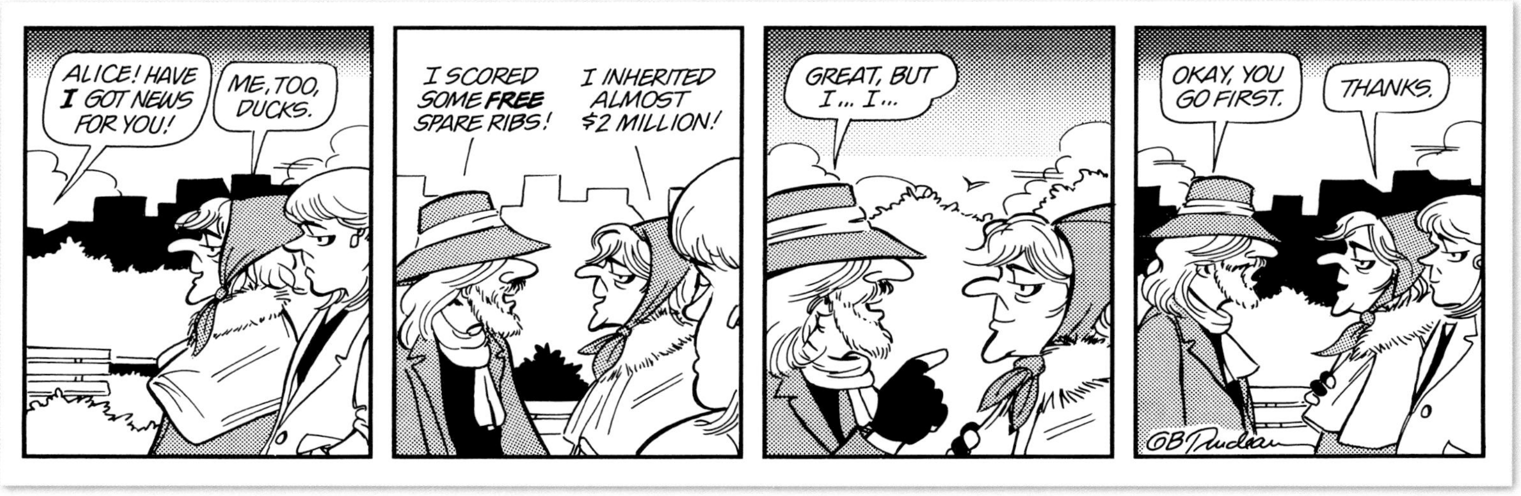
ALICE! HAVE I GOT NEWS FOR YOU!
ME, TOO, DUCKS.
I SCORED SOME FREE SPARE RIBS!
I INHERITED ALMOST $2 MILLION!
GREAT, BUT I... I...
OKAY, YOU GO FIRST.
THANKS.
GB Trudeau

11/2/98

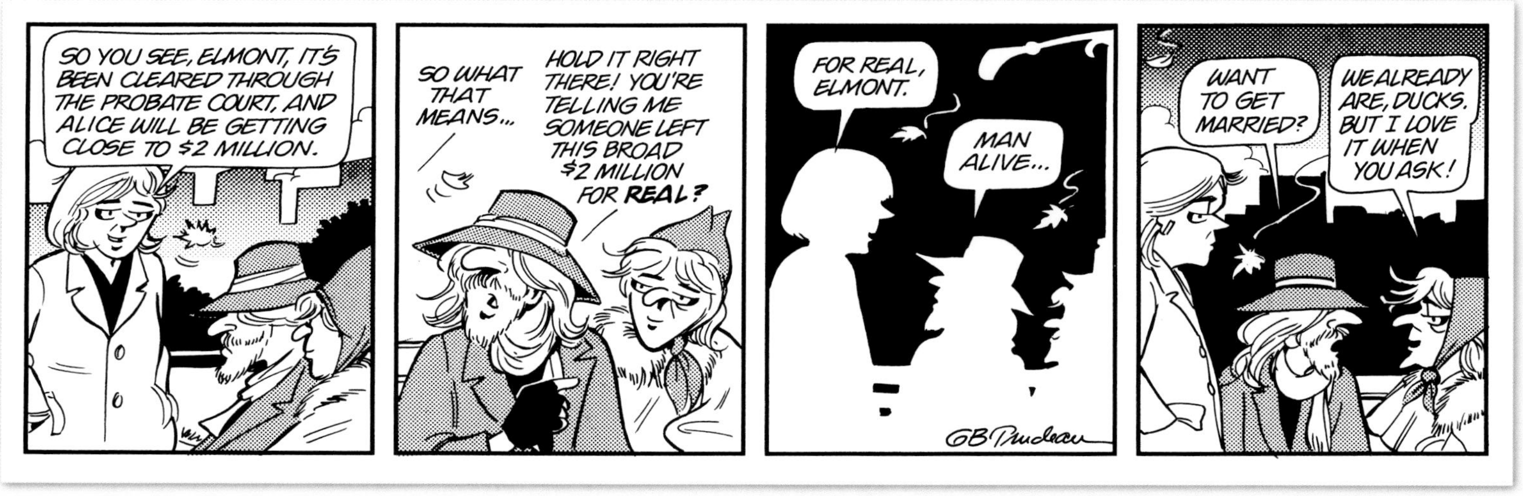
SO YOU SEE, ELMONT, IT'S BEEN CLEARED THROUGH THE PROBATE COURT, AND ALICE WILL BE GETTING CLOSE TO $2 MILLION.
SO WHAT THAT MEANS...
HOLD IT RIGHT THERE! YOU'RE TELLING ME SOMEONE LEFT THIS BROAD $2 MILLION FOR REAL?
FOR REAL, ELMONT.
MAN ALIVE...
WANT TO GET MARRIED?
WE ALREADY ARE, DUCKS. BUT I LOVE IT WHEN YOU ASK!
GB Trudeau

11/3/98

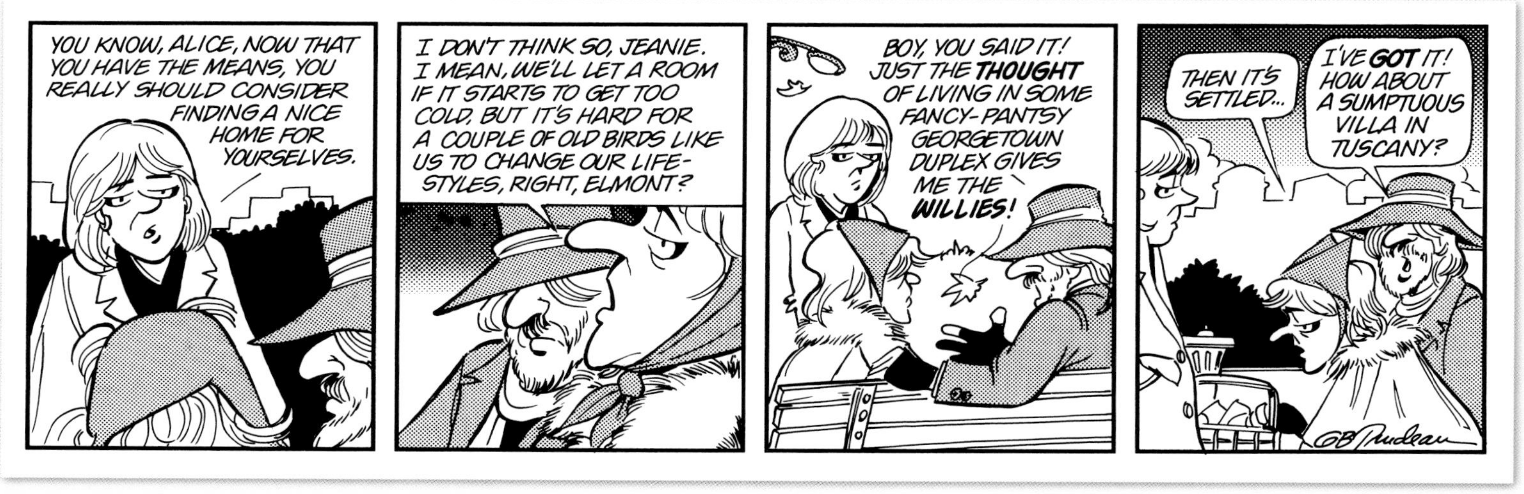
YOU KNOW, ALICE, NOW THAT YOU HAVE THE MEANS, YOU REALLY SHOULD CONSIDER FINDING A NICE HOME FOR YOURSELVES.
I DON'T THINK SO, JEANIE. I MEAN, WE'LL LET A ROOM IF IT STARTS TO GET TOO COLD, BUT IT'S HARD FOR A COUPLE OF OLD BIRDS LIKE US TO CHANGE OUR LIFESTYLES, RIGHT, ELMONT?
BOY, YOU SAID IT! JUST THE THOUGHT OF LIVING IN SOME FANCY-PANTSY GEORGETOWN DUPLEX GIVES ME THE WILLIES!
THEN IT'S SETTLED...
I'VE GOT IT! HOW ABOUT A SUMPTUOUS VILLA IN TUSCANY?
GB Trudeau

11/6/98

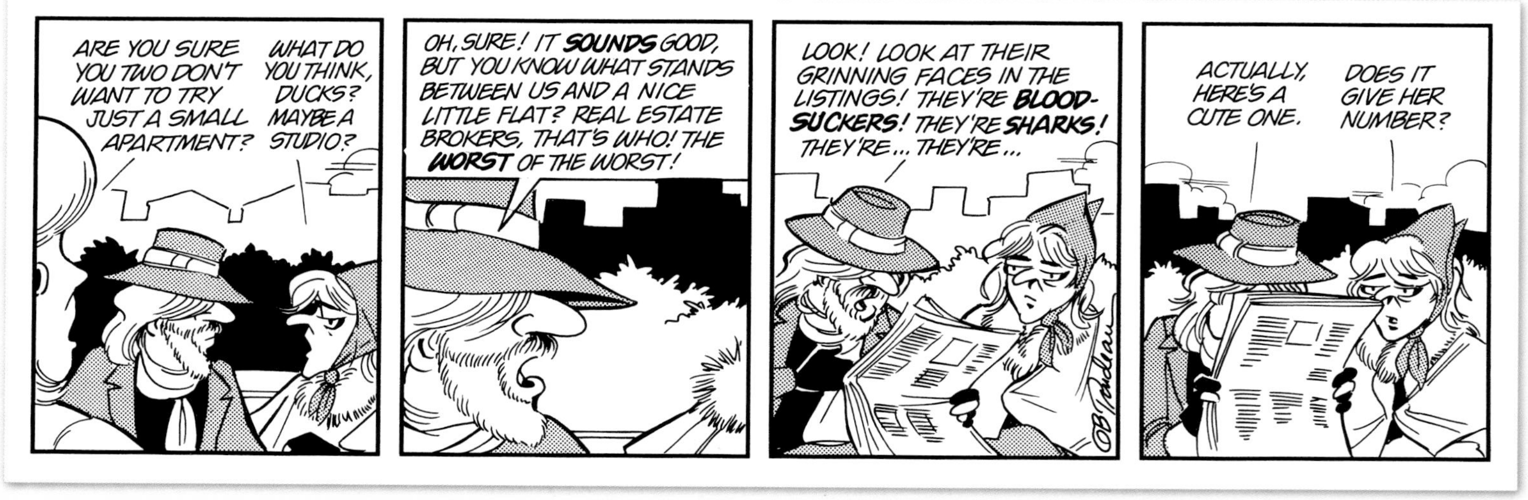
ARE YOU SURE YOU TWO DON'T WANT TO TRY JUST A SMALL APARTMENT?
WHAT DO YOU THINK, DUCKS? MAYBE A STUDIO?
OH, SURE! IT SOUNDS GOOD, BUT YOU KNOW WHAT STANDS BETWEEN US AND A NICE LITTLE FLAT? REAL ESTATE BROKERS, THAT'S WHO! THE WORST OF THE WORST!
LOOK! LOOK AT THEIR GRINNING FACES IN THE LISTINGS! THEY'RE BLOODSUCKERS! THEY'RE SHARKS! THEY'RE... THEY'RE...
ACTUALLY, HERE'S A CUTE ONE.
DOES IT GIVE HER NUMBER?
GB Trudeau

11/7/98

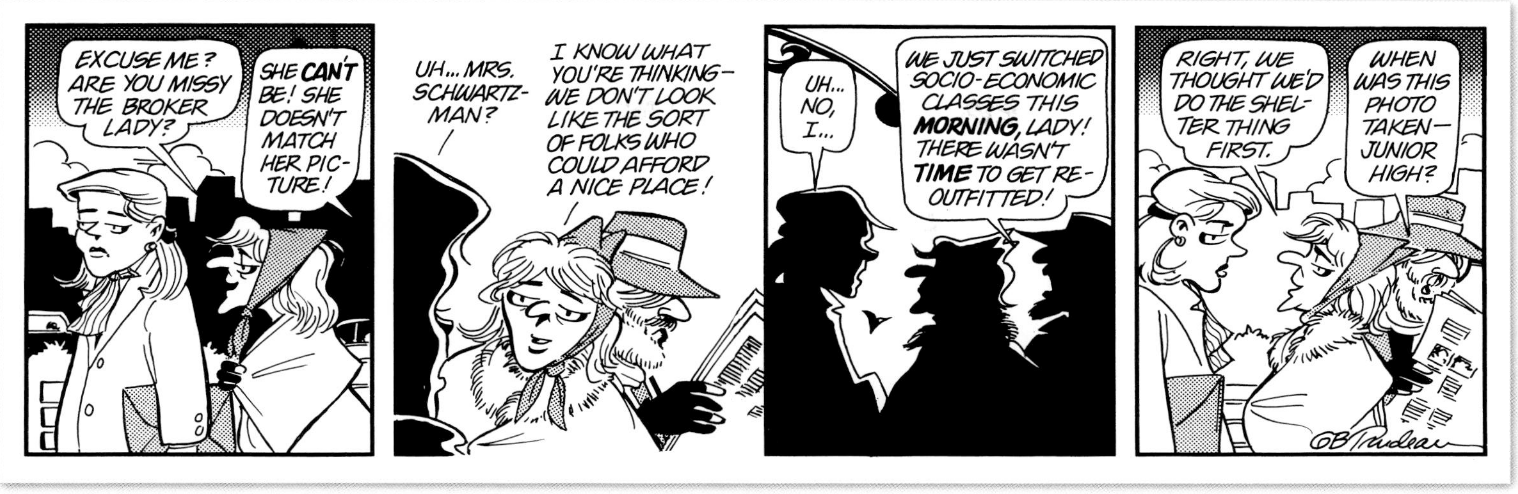
EXCUSE ME? ARE YOU MISSY THE BROKER LADY?
SHE **CAN'T** BE! SHE DOESN'T MATCH HER PICTURE!
UH... MRS. SCHWARTZMAN?
I KNOW WHAT YOU'RE THINKING— WE DON'T LOOK LIKE THE SORT OF FOLKS WHO COULD AFFORD A NICE PLACE!
UH... NO, I...
WE JUST SWITCHED SOCIO-ECONOMIC CLASSES THIS **MORNING**, LADY! THERE WASN'T **TIME** TO GET RE-OUTFITTED!
RIGHT, WE THOUGHT WE'D DO THE SHELTER THING FIRST.
WHEN WAS THIS PHOTO TAKEN— JUNIOR HIGH?
©B Trudeau

11/11/98

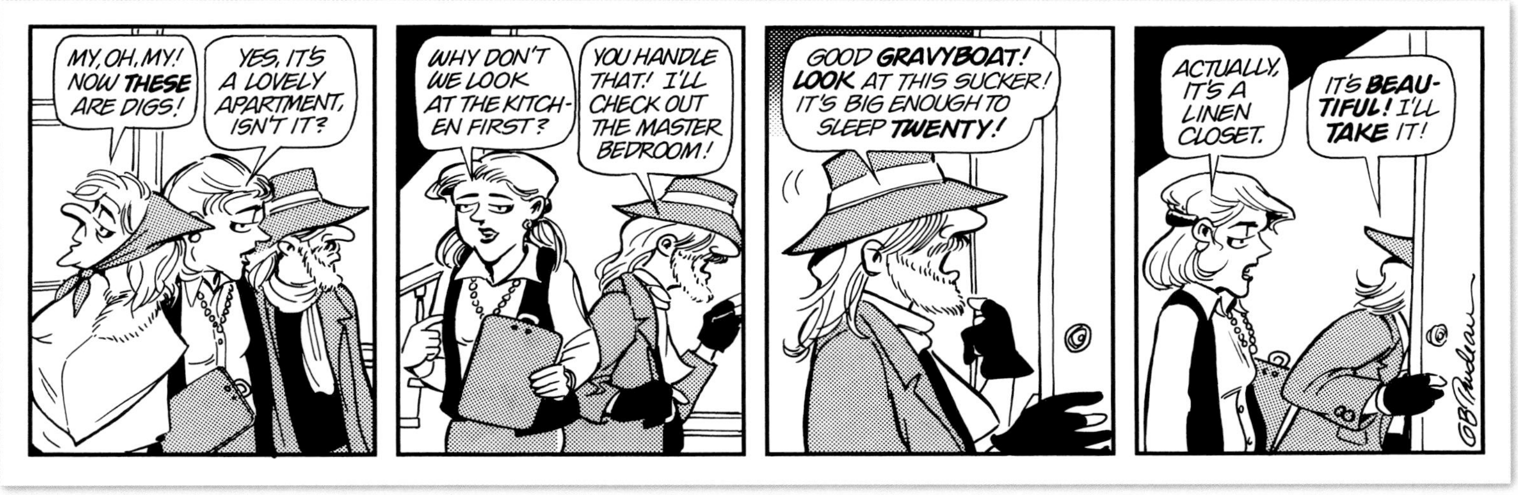
MY, OH, MY! NOW **THESE** ARE DIGS!
YES, IT'S A LOVELY APARTMENT, ISN'T IT?
WHY DON'T WE LOOK AT THE KITCHEN FIRST?
YOU HANDLE THAT! I'LL CHECK OUT THE MASTER BEDROOM!
GOOD **GRAVYBOAT**! **LOOK** AT THIS SUCKER! IT'S BIG ENOUGH TO SLEEP **TWENTY**!
ACTUALLY, IT'S A LINEN CLOSET.
IT'S **BEAUTIFUL**! I'LL **TAKE** IT!
©B Trudeau

11/12/98

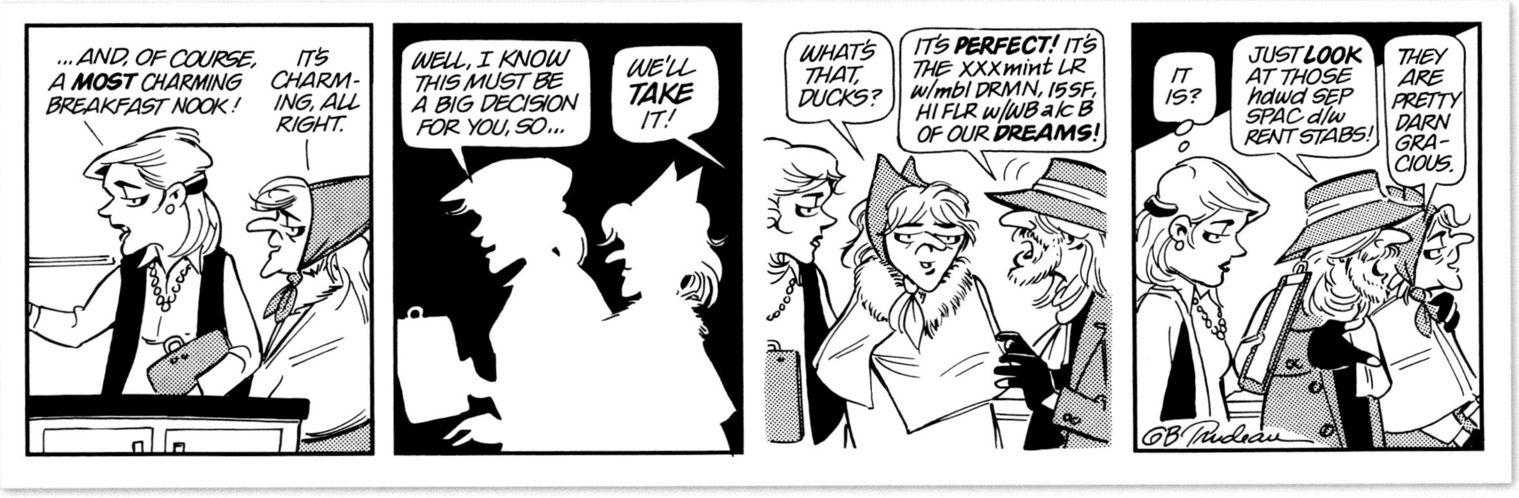
...AND, OF COURSE, A **MOST** CHARMING BREAKFAST NOOK!
IT'S CHARMING, ALL RIGHT.
WELL, I KNOW THIS MUST BE A BIG DECISION FOR YOU, SO...
WE'LL **TAKE** IT!
WHAT'S THAT, DUCKS?
IT'S **PERFECT**! IT'S THE XXXmint LR w/mbl DRMN, 15SF, HI FLR w/WB a/c B OF OUR **DREAMS**!
IT IS?
JUST **LOOK** AT THOSE hdwd SEP SPAC d/w RENT STABS!
THEY ARE PRETTY DARN GRACIOUS.
©B Trudeau

11/13/98

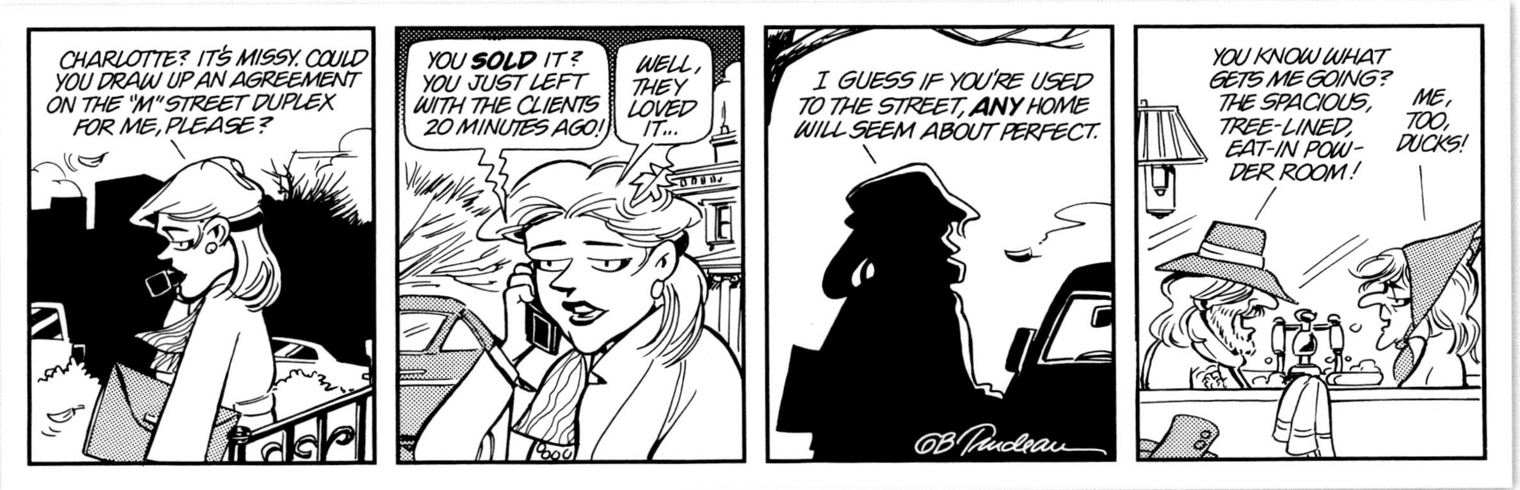
CHARLOTTE? IT'S MISSY. COULD YOU DRAW UP AN AGREEMENT ON THE "M" STREET DUPLEX FOR ME, PLEASE?
YOU **SOLD** IT? YOU JUST LEFT WITH THE CLIENTS 20 MINUTES AGO!
WELL, THEY LOVED IT...
I GUESS IF YOU'RE USED TO THE STREET, **ANY** HOME WILL SEEM ABOUT PERFECT.
YOU KNOW WHAT GETS ME GOING? THE SPACIOUS, TREE-LINED, EAT-IN POWDER ROOM!
ME, TOO, DUCKS!
©B Trudeau

11/14/98

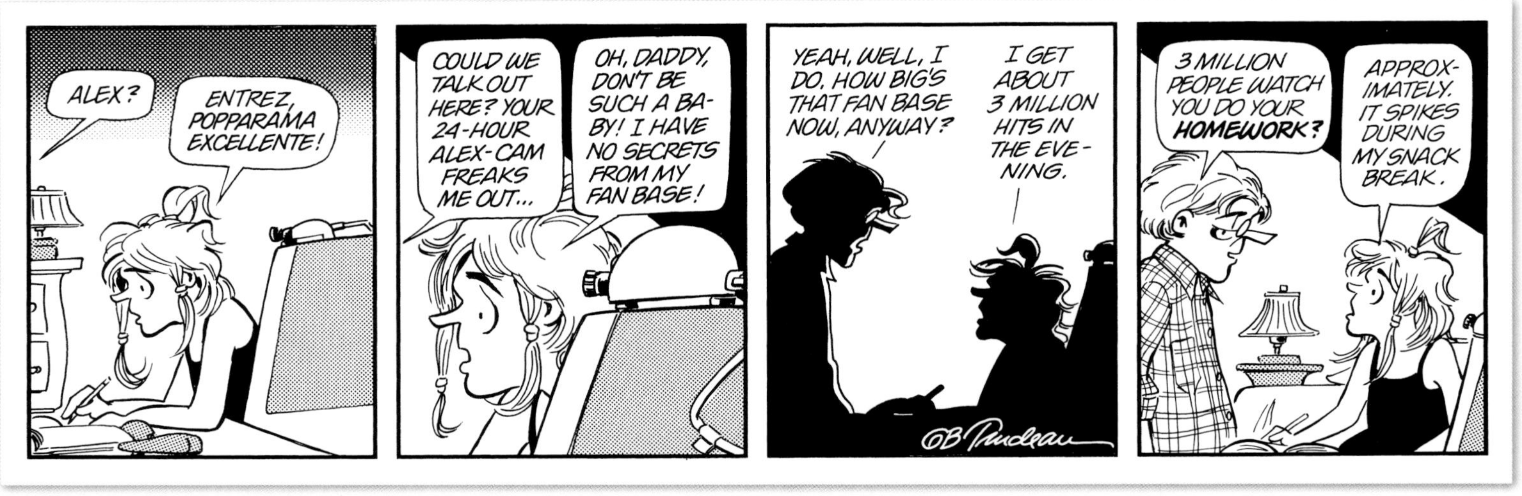
ALEX?
ENTREZ, POPPARAMA EXCELLENTE!
COULD WE TALK OUT HERE? YOUR 24-HOUR ALEX-CAM FREAKS ME OUT...
OH, DADDY, DON'T BE SUCH A BABY! I HAVE NO SECRETS FROM MY FAN BASE!
YEAH, WELL, I DO. HOW BIG'S THAT FAN BASE NOW, ANYWAY?
I GET ABOUT 3 MILLION HITS IN THE EVENING.
3 MILLION PEOPLE WATCH YOU DO YOUR HOMEWORK?
APPROXIMATELY. IT SPIKES DURING MY SNACK BREAK.

4/5/99

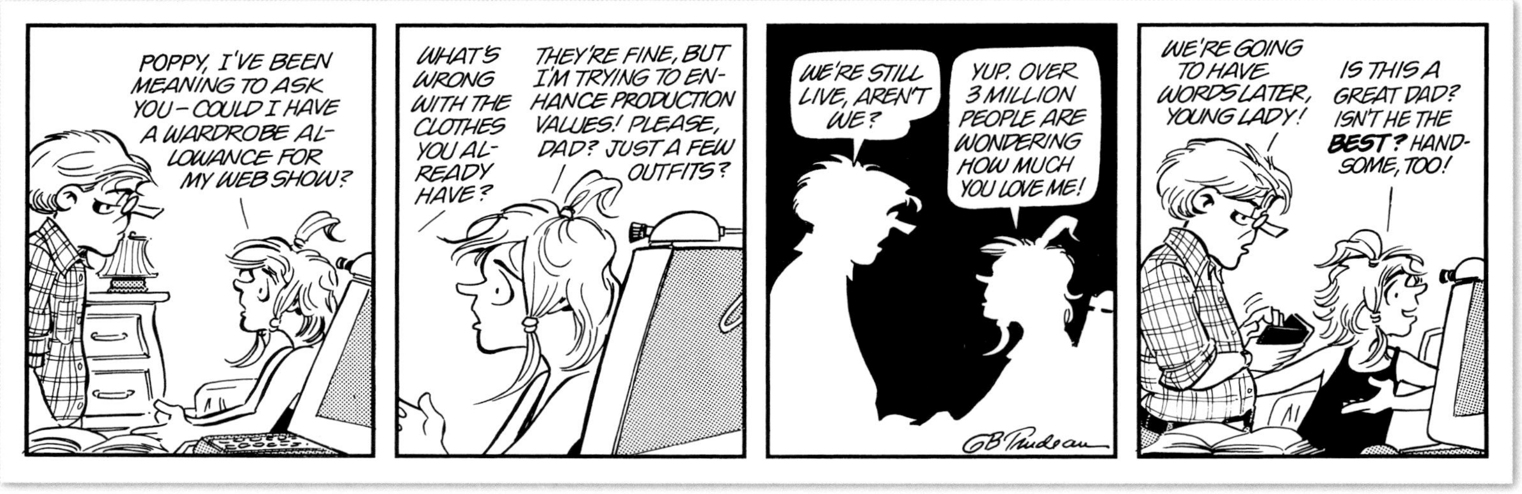
POPPY, I'VE BEEN MEANING TO ASK YOU – COULD I HAVE A WARDROBE ALLOWANCE FOR MY WEB SHOW?
WHAT'S WRONG WITH THE CLOTHES YOU ALREADY HAVE?
THEY'RE FINE, BUT I'M TRYING TO ENHANCE PRODUCTION VALUES! PLEASE, DAD? JUST A FEW OUTFITS?
WE'RE STILL LIVE, AREN'T WE?
YUP. OVER 3 MILLION PEOPLE ARE WONDERING HOW MUCH YOU LOVE ME!
WE'RE GOING TO HAVE WORDS LATER, YOUNG LADY!
IS THIS A GREAT DAD? ISN'T HE THE BEST? HANDSOME, TOO!

4/6/99

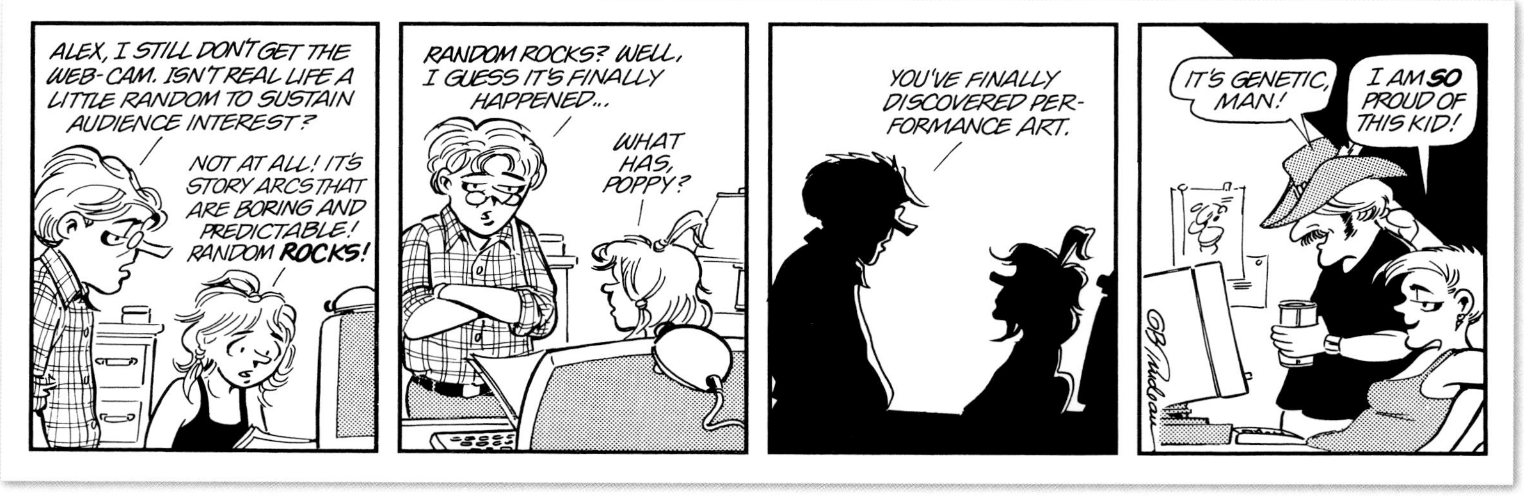
ALEX, I STILL DON'T GET THE WEB-CAM. ISN'T REAL LIFE A LITTLE RANDOM TO SUSTAIN AUDIENCE INTEREST?
NOT AT ALL! IT'S STORY ARCS THAT ARE BORING AND PREDICTABLE! RANDOM ROCKS!
RANDOM ROCKS? WELL, I GUESS IT'S FINALLY HAPPENED...
WHAT HAS, POPPY?
YOU'VE FINALLY DISCOVERED PERFORMANCE ART.
IT'S GENETIC, MAN!
I AM SO PROUD OF THIS KID!

4/7/99

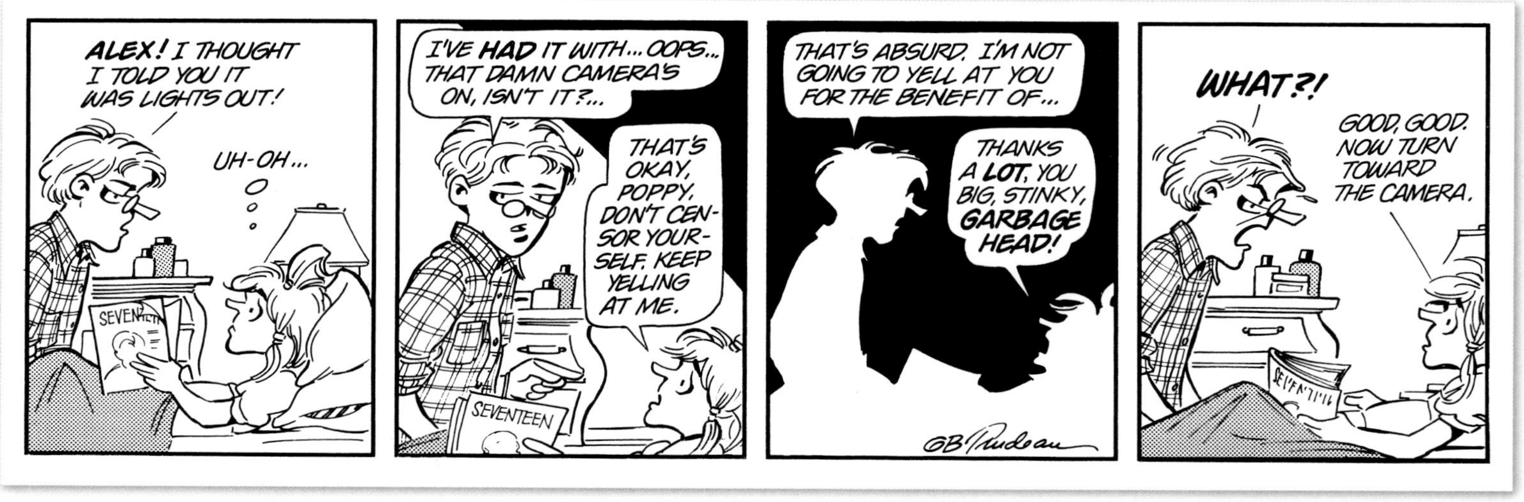
ALEX! I THOUGHT I TOLD YOU IT WAS LIGHTS OUT!
UH-OH...
I'VE HAD IT WITH... OOPS... THAT DAMN CAMERA'S ON, ISN'T IT?...
THAT'S OKAY, POPPY, DON'T CENSOR YOURSELF. KEEP YELLING AT ME.
SEVENTEEN
THAT'S ABSURD. I'M NOT GOING TO YELL AT YOU FOR THE BENEFIT OF...
THANKS A LOT, YOU BIG, STINKY, GARBAGE HEAD!
WHAT?!
GOOD, GOOD. NOW TURN TOWARD THE CAMERA.

4/10/99

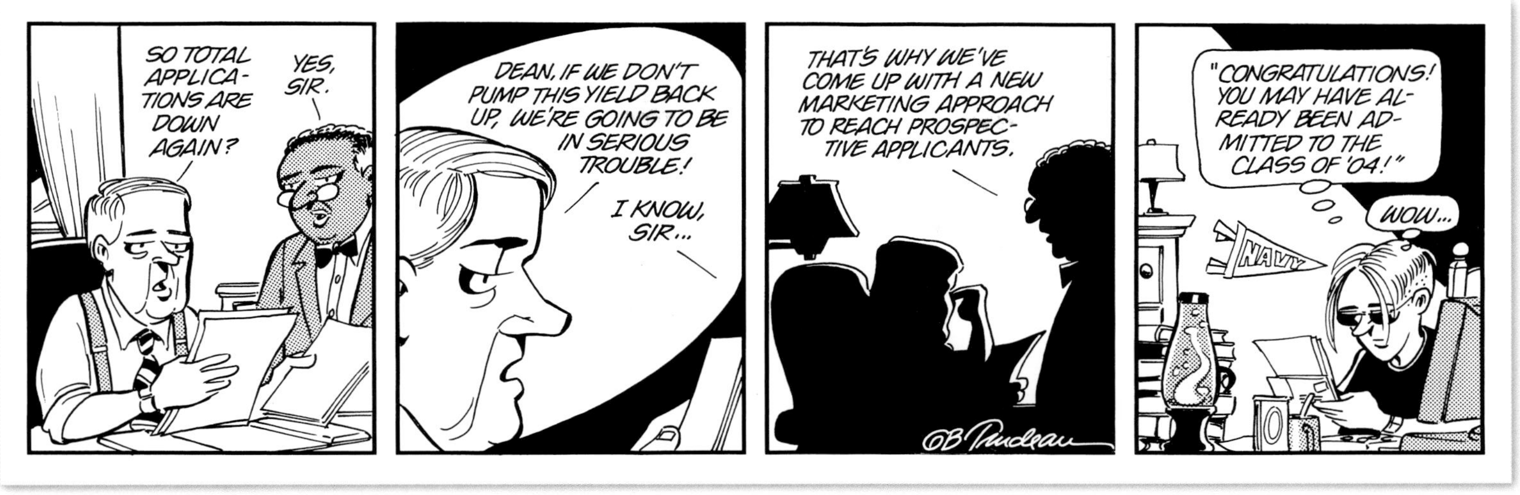
SO TOTAL APPLICATIONS ARE DOWN AGAIN?
YES, SIR.
DEAN, IF WE DON'T PUMP THIS YIELD BACK UP, WE'RE GOING TO BE IN SERIOUS TROUBLE!
I KNOW, SIR...
THAT'S WHY WE'VE COME UP WITH A NEW MARKETING APPROACH TO REACH PROSPECTIVE APPLICANTS.
©B Trudeau
"CONGRATULATIONS! YOU MAY HAVE ALREADY BEEN ADMITTED TO THE CLASS OF '04!"
WOW...
NAVY

4/12/99

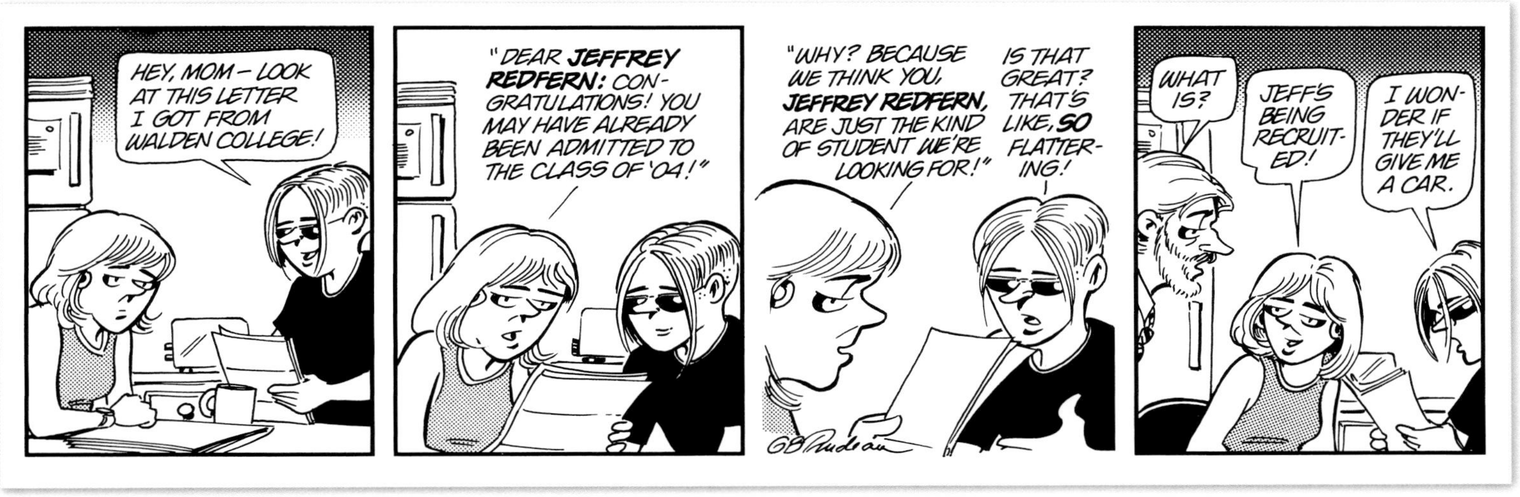
HEY, MOM – LOOK AT THIS LETTER I GOT FROM WALDEN COLLEGE!
"DEAR **JEFFREY REDFERN:** CONGRATULATIONS! YOU MAY HAVE ALREADY BEEN ADMITTED TO THE CLASS OF '04!"
"WHY? BECAUSE WE THINK YOU, **JEFFREY REDFERN,** ARE JUST THE KIND OF STUDENT WE'RE LOOKING FOR!"
IS THAT GREAT? THAT'S LIKE, **SO** FLATTERING!
©B Trudeau
WHAT IS?
JEFF'S BEING RECRUITED!
I WONDER IF THEY'LL GIVE ME A CAR.

4/13/99

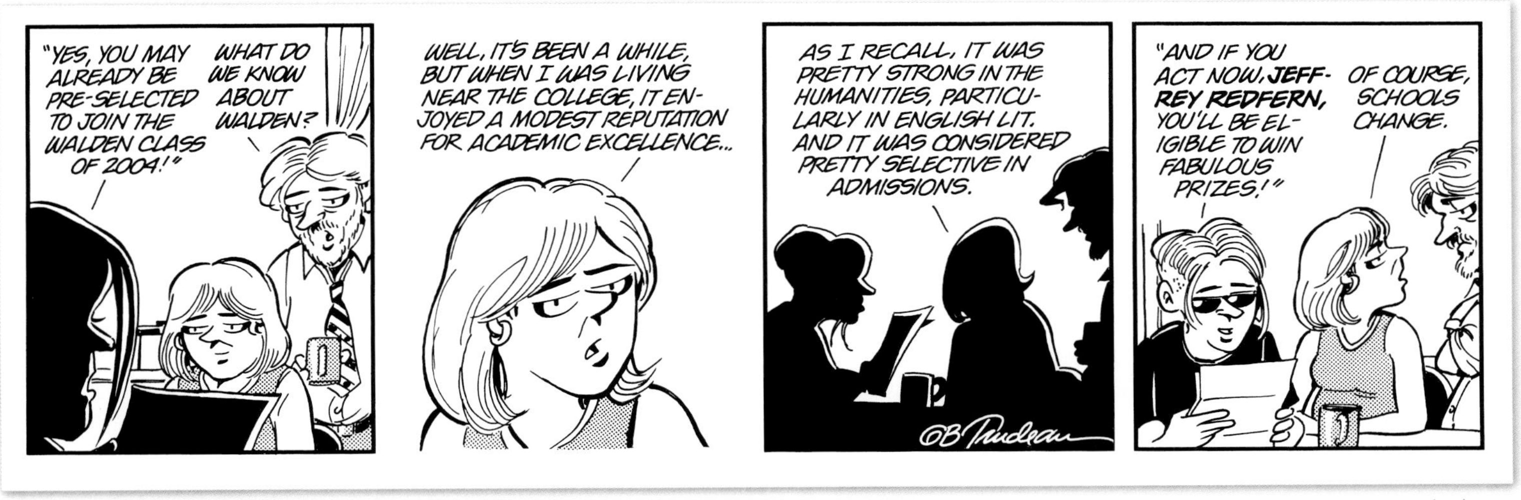
"YES, YOU MAY ALREADY BE PRE-SELECTED TO JOIN THE WALDEN CLASS OF 2004!"
WHAT DO WE KNOW ABOUT WALDEN?
WELL, IT'S BEEN A WHILE, BUT WHEN I WAS LIVING NEAR THE COLLEGE, IT ENJOYED A MODEST REPUTATION FOR ACADEMIC EXCELLENCE...
AS I RECALL, IT WAS PRETTY STRONG IN THE HUMANITIES, PARTICULARLY IN ENGLISH LIT. AND IT WAS CONSIDERED PRETTY SELECTIVE IN ADMISSIONS.
©B Trudeau
"AND IF YOU ACT NOW, **JEFFREY REDFERN,** YOU'LL BE ELIGIBLE TO WIN FABULOUS PRIZES!"
OF COURSE, SCHOOLS CHANGE.

4/14/99

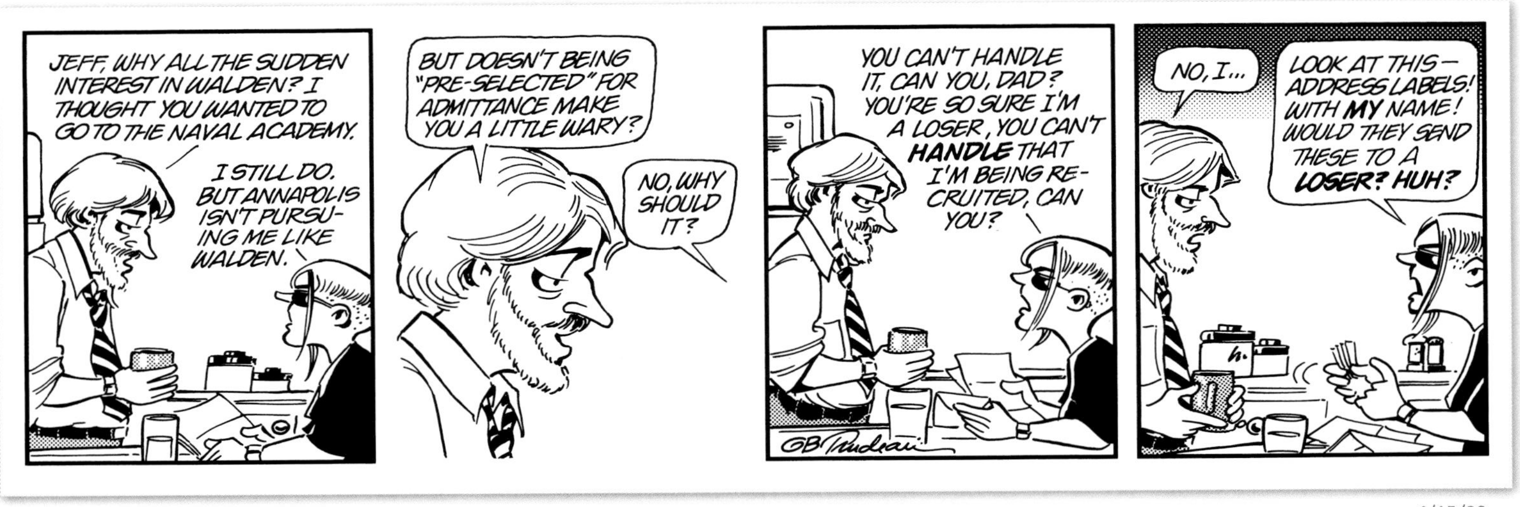
JEFF, WHY ALL THE SUDDEN INTEREST IN WALDEN? I THOUGHT YOU WANTED TO GO TO THE NAVAL ACADEMY.
I STILL DO. BUT ANNAPOLIS ISN'T PURSUING ME LIKE WALDEN.
BUT DOESN'T BEING "PRE-SELECTED" FOR ADMITTANCE MAKE YOU A LITTLE WARY?
NO, WHY SHOULD IT?
YOU CAN'T HANDLE IT, CAN YOU, DAD? YOU'RE SO SURE I'M A LOSER, YOU CAN'T **HANDLE** THAT I'M BEING RECRUITED, CAN YOU?
©B Trudeau
NO, I...
LOOK AT THIS – ADDRESS LABELS! WITH **MY** NAME! WOULD THEY SEND THESE TO A **LOSER? HUH?**

4/15/99

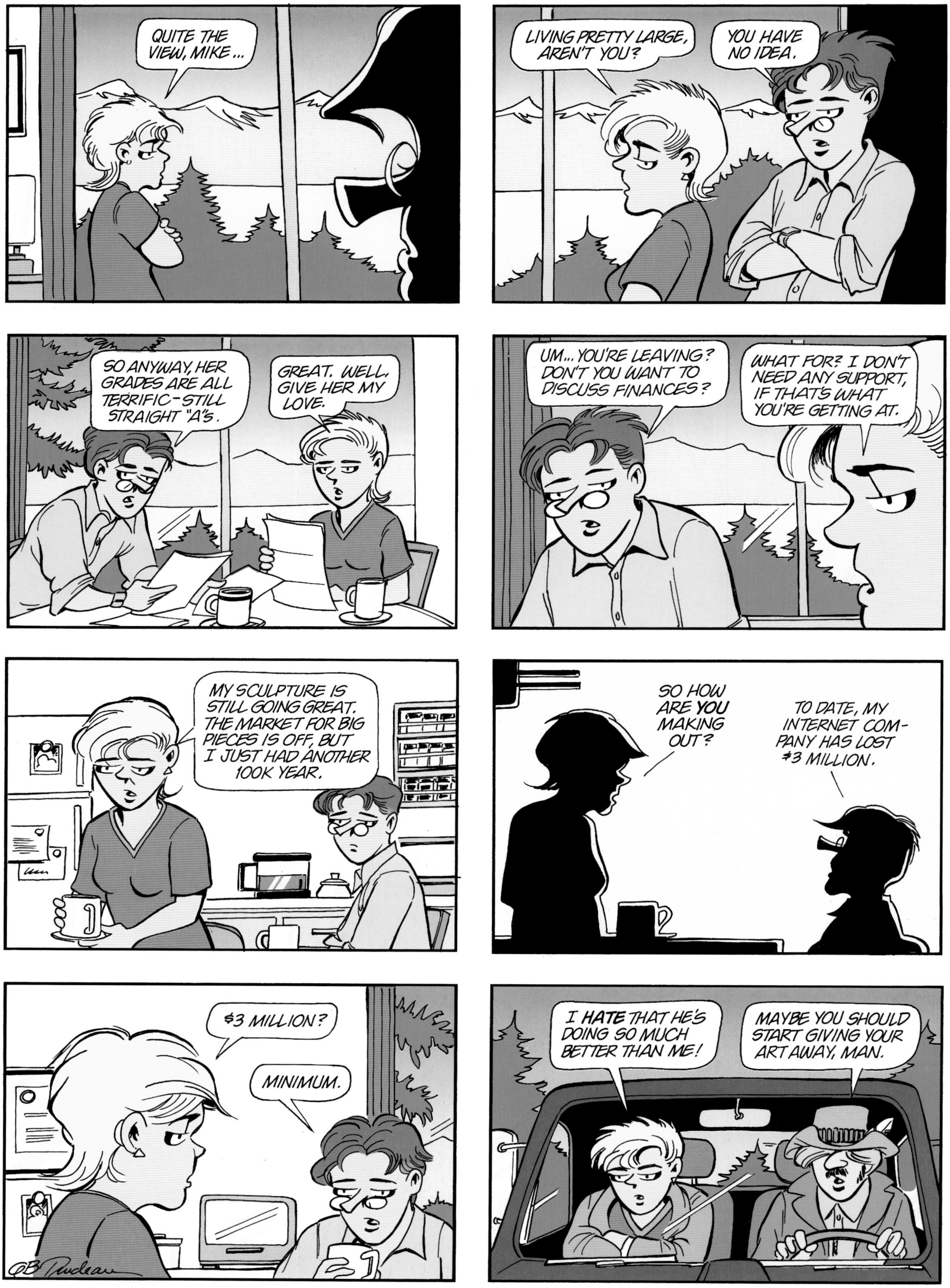
QUITE THE VIEW, MIKE...
LIVING PRETTY LARGE, AREN'T YOU?
YOU HAVE NO IDEA.
SO ANYWAY, HER GRADES ARE ALL TERRIFIC–STILL STRAIGHT "A"S.
GREAT. WELL, GIVE HER MY LOVE.
UM... YOU'RE LEAVING? DON'T YOU WANT TO DISCUSS FINANCES?
WHAT FOR? I DON'T NEED ANY SUPPORT, IF THAT'S WHAT YOU'RE GETTING AT.
MY SCULPTURE IS STILL GOING GREAT. THE MARKET FOR BIG PIECES IS OFF, BUT I JUST HAD ANOTHER 100K YEAR.
SO HOW ARE YOU MAKING OUT?
TO DATE, MY INTERNET COMPANY HAS LOST $3 MILLION.
$3 MILLION?
MINIMUM.
I HATE THAT HE'S DOING SO MUCH BETTER THAN ME!
MAYBE YOU SHOULD START GIVING YOUR ART AWAY, MAN.
GB Trudeau

1/3/99

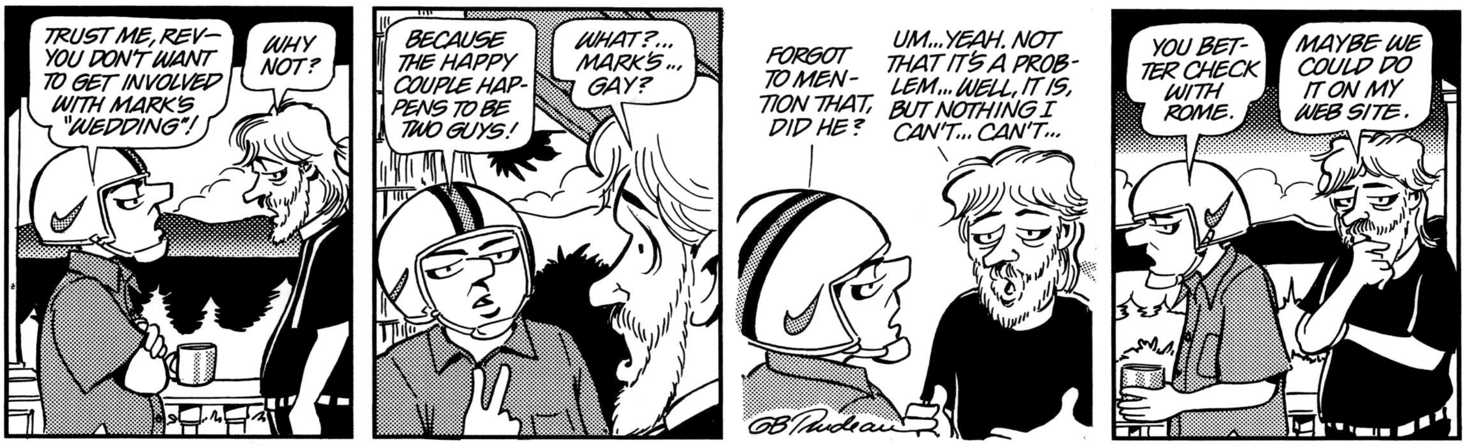
TRUST ME, REV— YOU DON'T WANT TO GET INVOLVED WITH MARK'S "WEDDING"!
WHY NOT?
BECAUSE THE HAPPY COUPLE HAPPENS TO BE TWO GUYS!
WHAT?... MARK'S... GAY?
FORGOT TO MENTION THAT, DID HE?
UM...YEAH. NOT THAT IT'S A PROBLEM... WELL, IT IS, BUT NOTHING I CAN'T... CAN'T...
YOU BETTER CHECK WITH ROME.
MAYBE WE COULD DO IT ON MY WEB SITE.
GB Trudeau

6/15/99

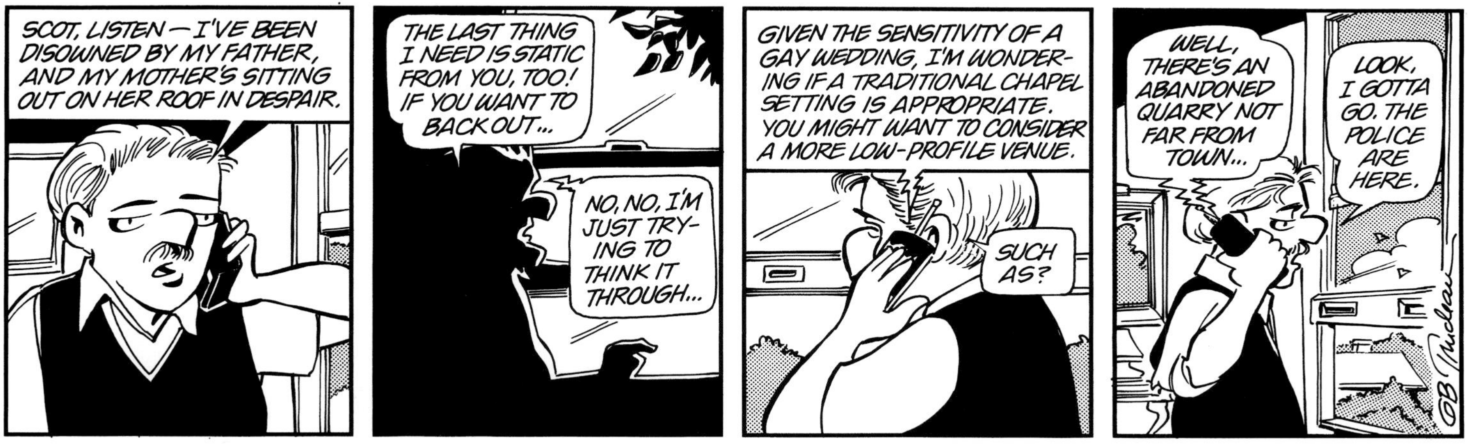
SCOT, LISTEN — I'VE BEEN DISOWNED BY MY FATHER, AND MY MOTHER'S SITTING OUT ON HER ROOF IN DESPAIR.
THE LAST THING I NEED IS STATIC FROM YOU, TOO! IF YOU WANT TO BACK OUT...
NO, NO, I'M JUST TRYING TO THINK IT THROUGH...
GIVEN THE SENSITIVITY OF A GAY WEDDING, I'M WONDERING IF A TRADITIONAL CHAPEL SETTING IS APPROPRIATE. YOU MIGHT WANT TO CONSIDER A MORE LOW-PROFILE VENUE.
SUCH AS?
WELL, THERE'S AN ABANDONED QUARRY NOT FAR FROM TOWN...
LOOK, I GOTTA GO. THE POLICE ARE HERE.
GB Trudeau

6/19/99

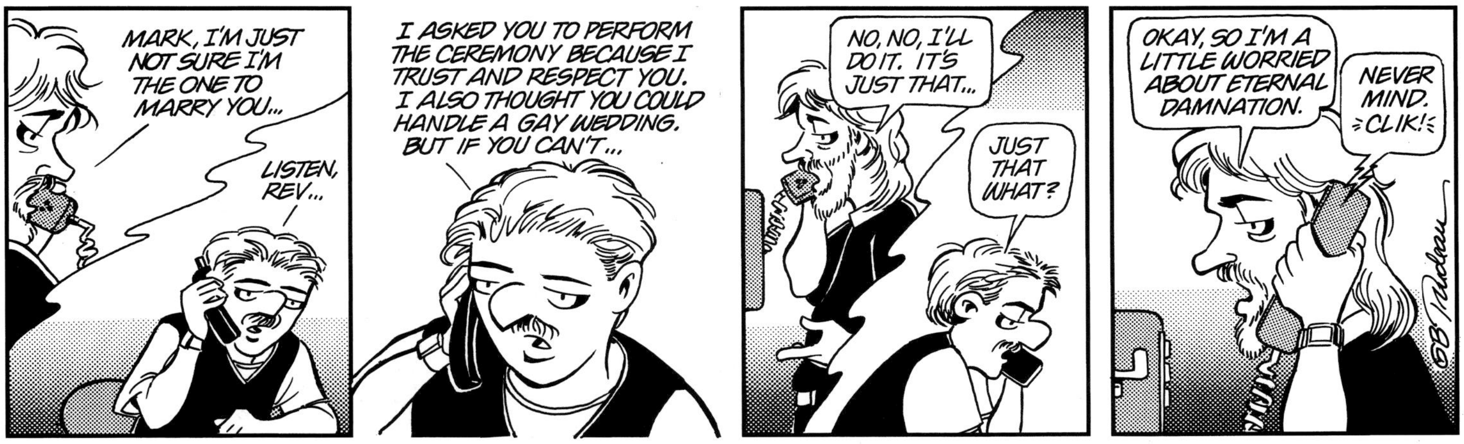
MARK, I'M JUST NOT SURE I'M THE ONE TO MARRY YOU...
LISTEN, REV...
I ASKED YOU TO PERFORM THE CEREMONY BECAUSE I TRUST AND RESPECT YOU. I ALSO THOUGHT YOU COULD HANDLE A GAY WEDDING. BUT IF YOU CAN'T...
NO, NO, I'LL DO IT. IT'S JUST THAT...
JUST THAT WHAT?
OKAY, SO I'M A LITTLE WORRIED ABOUT ETERNAL DAMNATION.
NEVER MIND. CLIK!
GB Trudeau

6/23/99

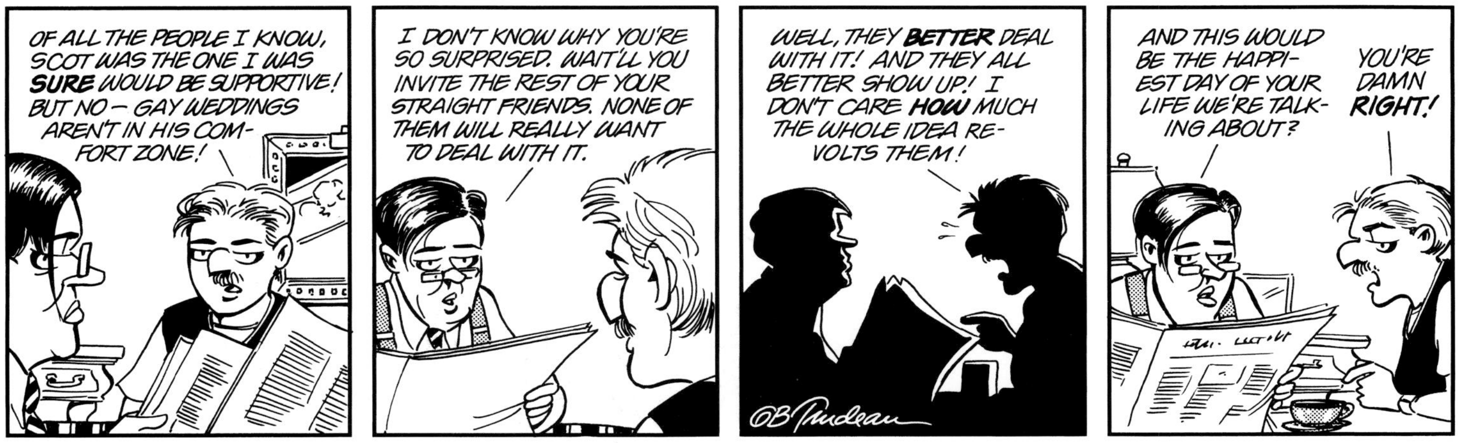
OF ALL THE PEOPLE I KNOW, SCOT WAS THE ONE I WAS SURE WOULD BE SUPPORTIVE! BUT NO — GAY WEDDINGS AREN'T IN HIS COMFORT ZONE!
I DON'T KNOW WHY YOU'RE SO SURPRISED. WAIT'LL YOU INVITE THE REST OF YOUR STRAIGHT FRIENDS. NONE OF THEM WILL REALLY WANT TO DEAL WITH IT.
WELL, THEY BETTER DEAL WITH IT! AND THEY ALL BETTER SHOW UP! I DON'T CARE HOW MUCH THE WHOLE IDEA REVOLTS THEM!
AND THIS WOULD BE THE HAPPIEST DAY OF YOUR LIFE WE'RE TALKING ABOUT?
YOU'RE DAMN RIGHT!
GB Trudeau

6/24/99

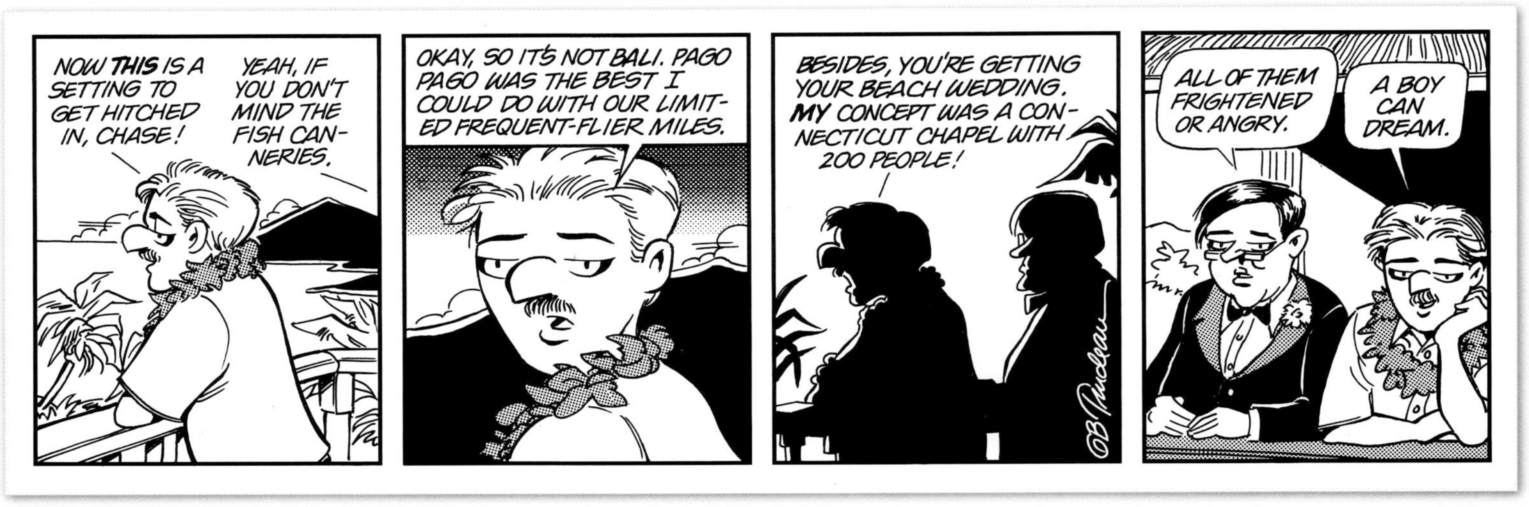
NOW THIS IS A SETTING TO GET HITCHED IN, CHASE!
YEAH, IF YOU DON'T MIND THE FISH CANNERIES.
OKAY, SO IT'S NOT BALI. PAGO PAGO WAS THE BEST I COULD DO WITH OUR LIMITED FREQUENT-FLIER MILES.
BESIDES, YOU'RE GETTING YOUR BEACH WEDDING. MY CONCEPT WAS A CONNECTICUT CHAPEL WITH 200 PEOPLE!
ALL OF THEM FRIGHTENED OR ANGRY.
A BOY CAN DREAM.

7/20/99

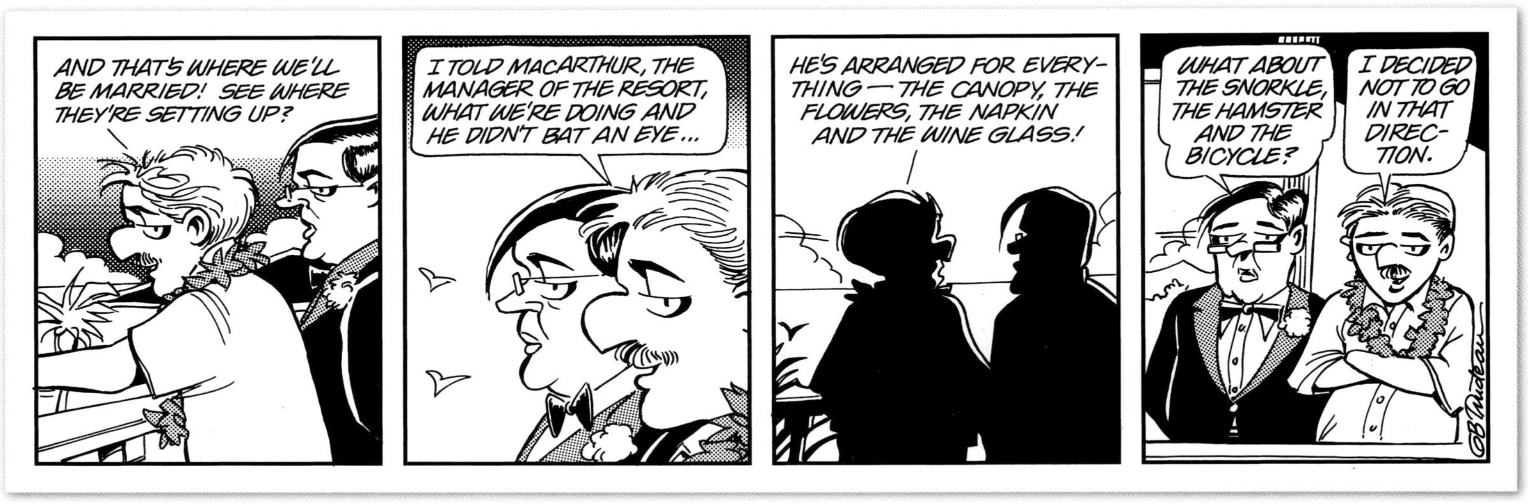
AND THAT'S WHERE WE'LL BE MARRIED! SEE WHERE THEY'RE SETTING UP?
I TOLD MACARTHUR, THE MANAGER OF THE RESORT, WHAT WE'RE DOING AND HE DIDN'T BAT AN EYE...
HE'S ARRANGED FOR EVERYTHING — THE CANOPY, THE FLOWERS, THE NAPKIN AND THE WINE GLASS!
WHAT ABOUT THE SNORKLE, THE HAMSTER AND THE BICYCLE?
I DECIDED NOT TO GO IN THAT DIRECTION.

7/21/99

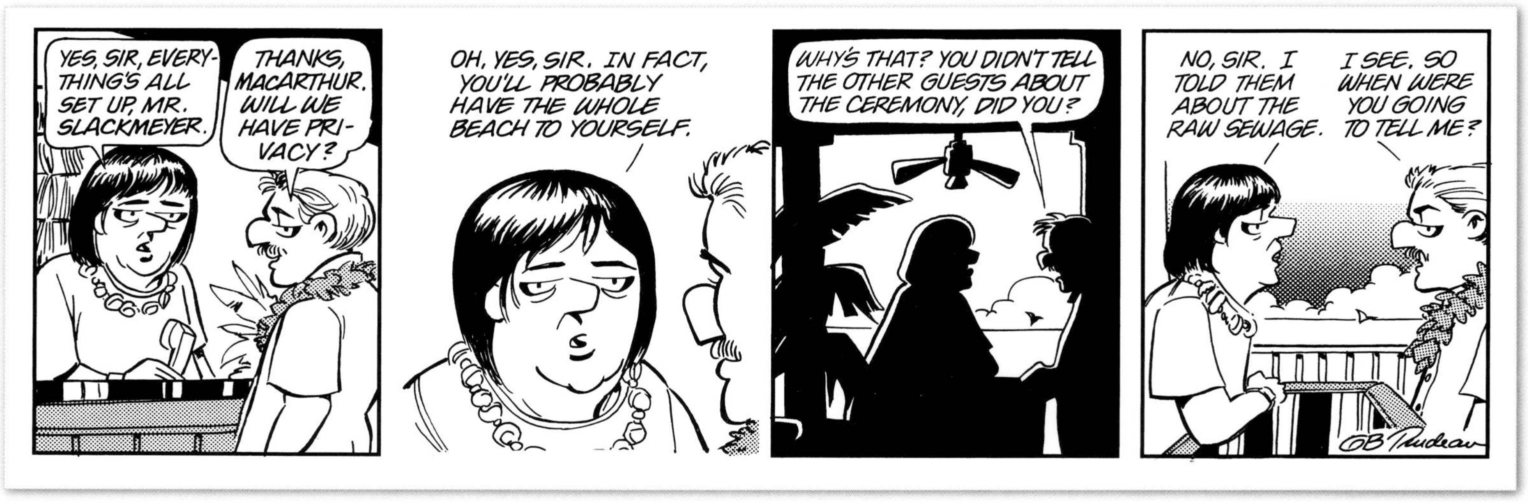
YES, SIR, EVERYTHING'S ALL SET UP, MR. SLACKMEYER.
THANKS, MACARTHUR. WILL WE HAVE PRIVACY?
OH, YES, SIR. IN FACT, YOU'LL PROBABLY HAVE THE WHOLE BEACH TO YOURSELF.
WHY'S THAT? YOU DIDN'T TELL THE OTHER GUESTS ABOUT THE CEREMONY, DID YOU?
NO, SIR. I TOLD THEM ABOUT THE RAW SEWAGE.
I SEE. SO WHEN WERE YOU GOING TO TELL ME?

7/22/99

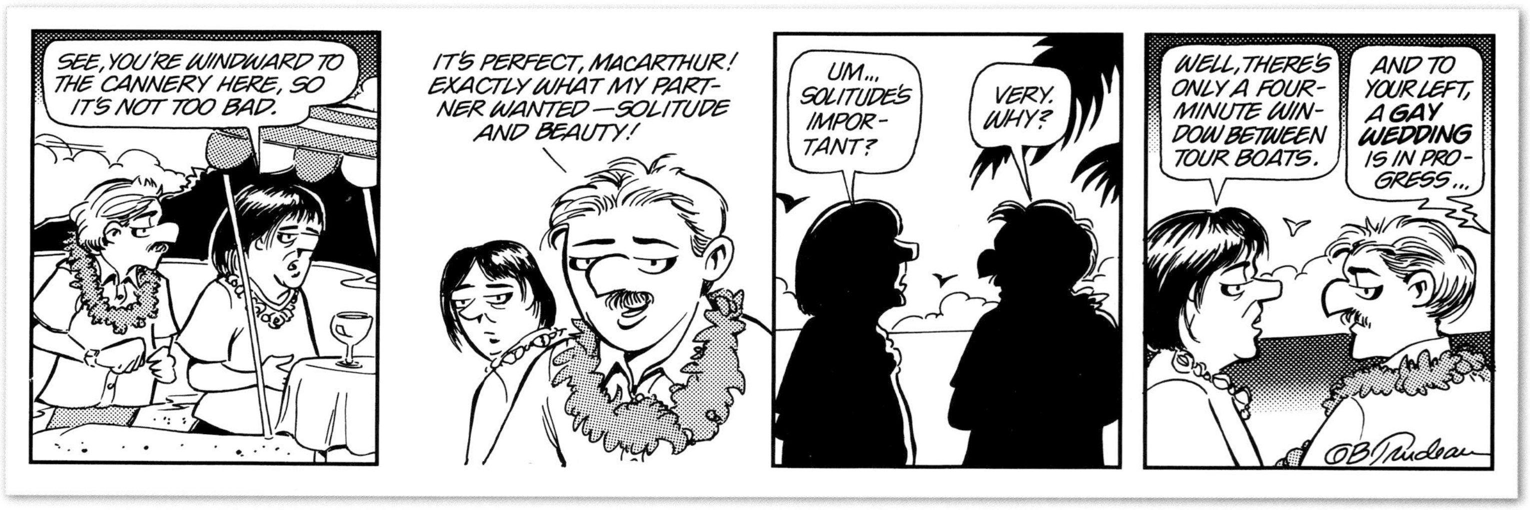
SEE, YOU'RE WINDWARD TO THE CANNERY HERE, SO IT'S NOT TOO BAD.
IT'S PERFECT, MACARTHUR! EXACTLY WHAT MY PARTNER WANTED — SOLITUDE AND BEAUTY!
UM... SOLITUDE'S IMPORTANT?
VERY. WHY?
WELL, THERE'S ONLY A FOUR-MINUTE WINDOW BETWEEN TOUR BOATS.
AND TO YOUR LEFT, A GAY WEDDING IS IN PROGRESS...

7/24/99

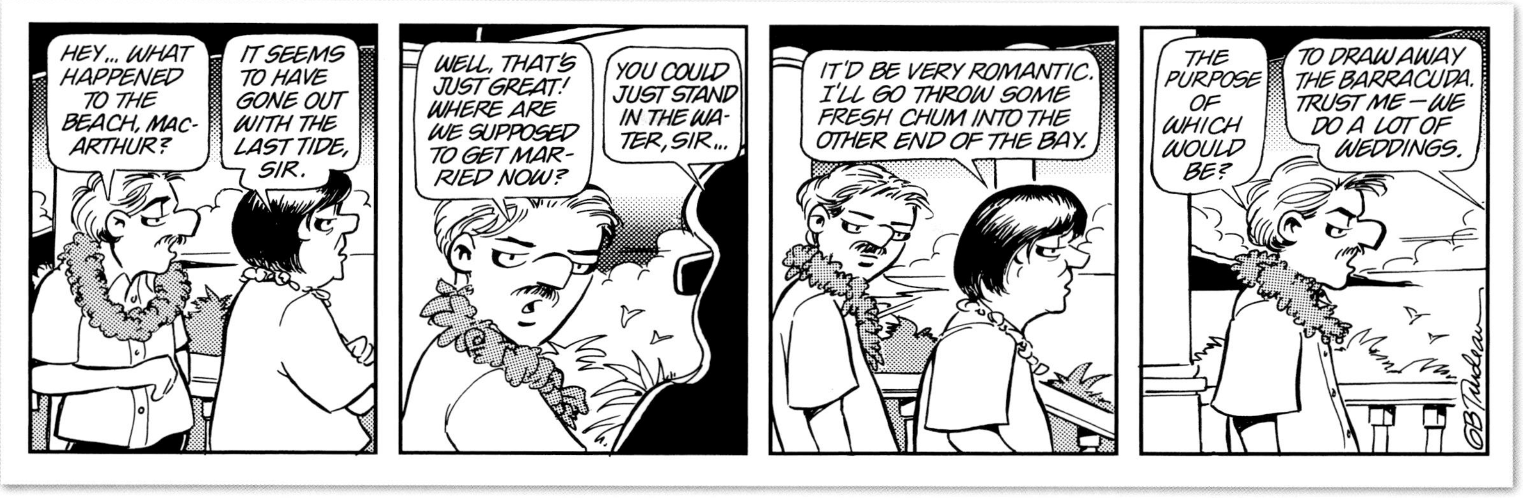
HEY... WHAT HAPPENED TO THE BEACH, MACARTHUR?
IT SEEMS TO HAVE GONE OUT WITH THE LAST TIDE, SIR.
WELL, THAT'S JUST GREAT! WHERE ARE WE SUPPOSED TO GET MARRIED NOW?
YOU COULD JUST STAND IN THE WATER, SIR...
IT'D BE VERY ROMANTIC. I'LL GO THROW SOME FRESH CHUM INTO THE OTHER END OF THE BAY.
THE PURPOSE OF WHICH WOULD BE?
TO DRAW AWAY THE BARRACUDA. TRUST ME — WE DO A LOT OF WEDDINGS.
GB Trudeau

7/26/99

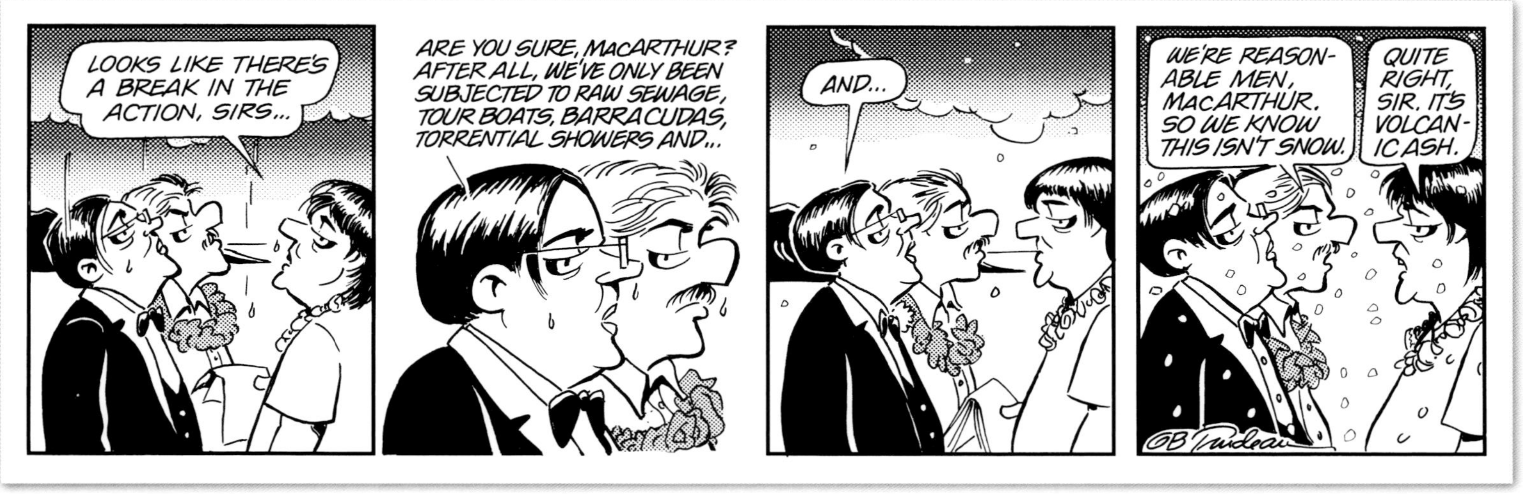
LOOKS LIKE THERE'S A BREAK IN THE ACTION, SIRS...
ARE YOU SURE, MACARTHUR? AFTER ALL, WE'VE ONLY BEEN SUBJECTED TO RAW SEWAGE, TOUR BOATS, BARRACUDAS, TORRENTIAL SHOWERS AND...
AND...
WE'RE REASONABLE MEN, MacARTHUR. SO WE KNOW THIS ISN'T SNOW.
QUITE RIGHT, SIR. IT'S VOLCANIC ASH.
GB Trudeau

7/28/99

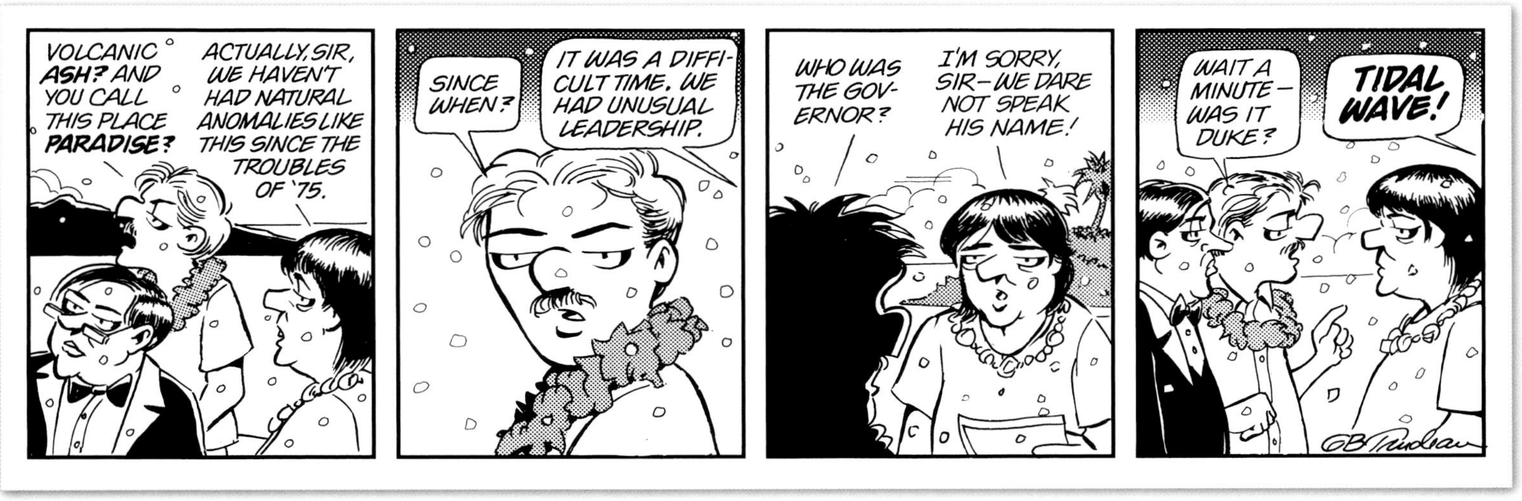
VOLCANIC ASH? AND YOU CALL THIS PLACE PARADISE?
ACTUALLY, SIR, WE HAVEN'T HAD NATURAL ANOMALIES LIKE THIS SINCE THE TROUBLES OF '75.
SINCE WHEN?
IT WAS A DIFFICULT TIME. WE HAD UNUSUAL LEADERSHIP.
WHO WAS THE GOVERNOR?
I'M SORRY, SIR — WE DARE NOT SPEAK HIS NAME!
WAIT A MINUTE — WAS IT DUKE?
TIDAL WAVE!
GB Trudeau

7/29/99

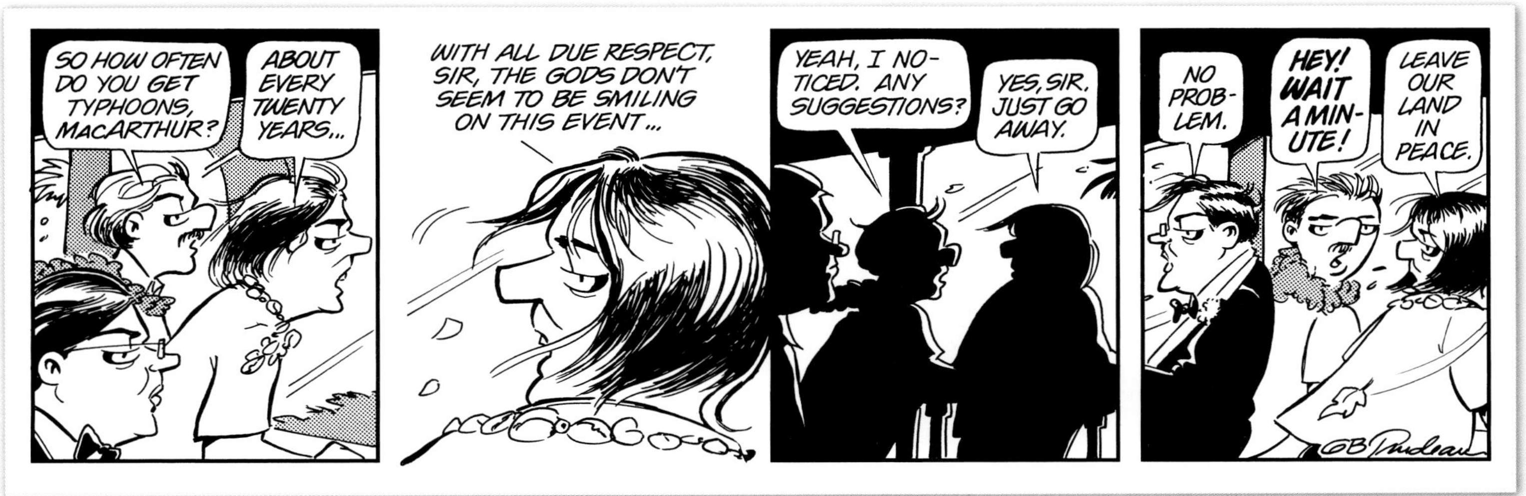
SO HOW OFTEN DO YOU GET TYPHOONS, MACARTHUR?
ABOUT EVERY TWENTY YEARS...
WITH ALL DUE RESPECT, SIR, THE GODS DON'T SEEM TO BE SMILING ON THIS EVENT...
YEAH, I NOTICED. ANY SUGGESTIONS?
YES, SIR. JUST GO AWAY.
NO PROBLEM.
HEY! WAIT A MINUTE!
LEAVE OUR LAND IN PEACE.
GB Trudeau

7/30/99

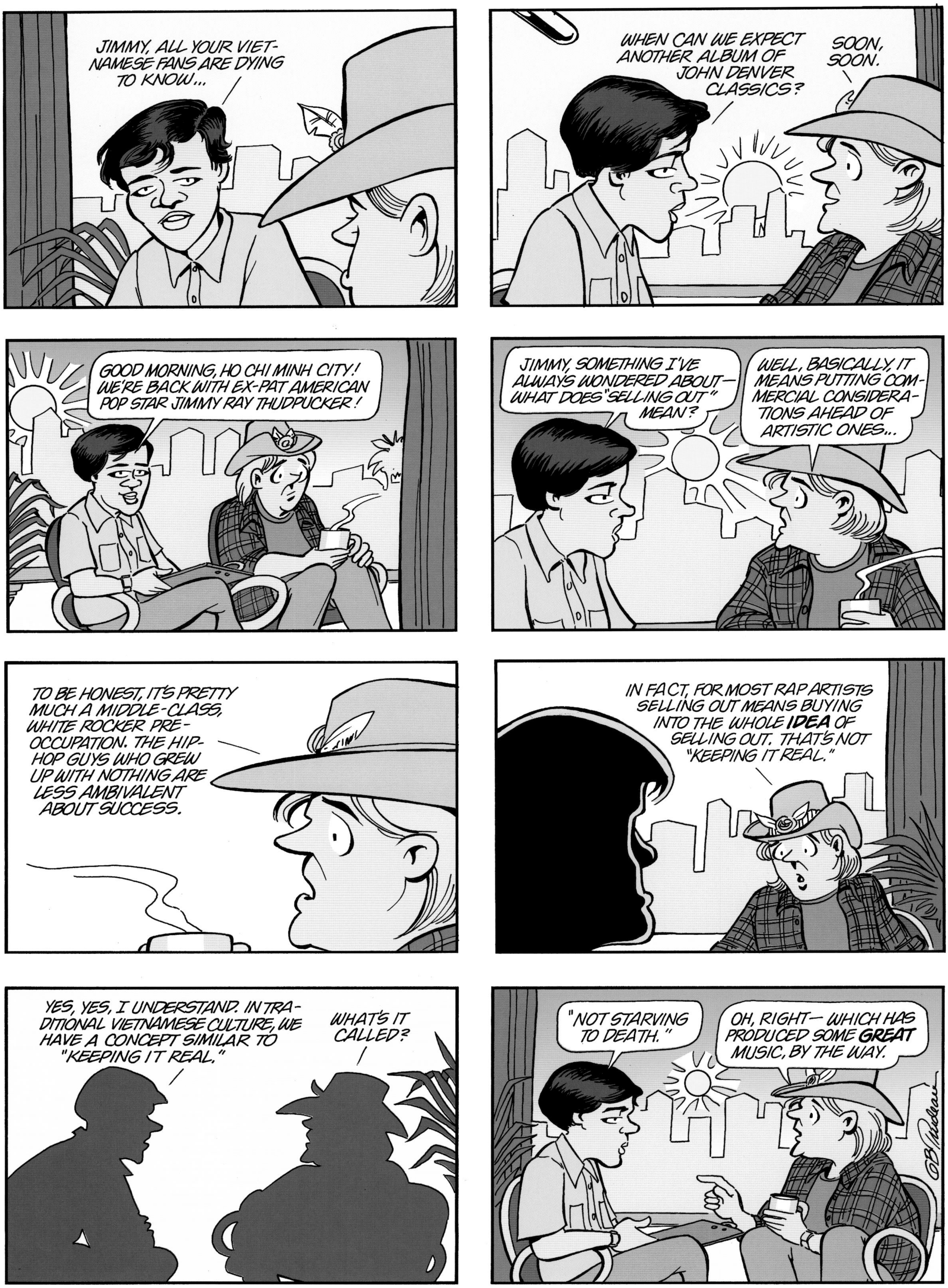

JIMMY, ALL YOUR VIET-NAMESE FANS ARE DYING TO KNOW...
WHEN CAN WE EXPECT ANOTHER ALBUM OF JOHN DENVER CLASSICS?
SOON, SOON.
GOOD MORNING, HO CHI MINH CITY! WE'RE BACK WITH EX-PAT AMERICAN POP STAR JIMMY RAY THUDPUCKER!
JIMMY, SOMETHING I'VE ALWAYS WONDERED ABOUT— WHAT DOES "SELLING OUT" MEAN?
WELL, BASICALLY, IT MEANS PUTTING COM-MERCIAL CONSIDERA-TIONS AHEAD OF ARTISTIC ONES...
TO BE HONEST, IT'S PRETTY MUCH A MIDDLE-CLASS, WHITE ROCKER PRE-OCCUPATION. THE HIP-HOP GUYS WHO GREW UP WITH NOTHING ARE LESS AMBIVALENT ABOUT SUCCESS.
IN FACT, FOR MOST RAP ARTISTS SELLING OUT MEANS BUYING INTO THE WHOLE **IDEA** OF SELLING OUT. THAT'S NOT "KEEPING IT REAL."
YES, YES, I UNDERSTAND. IN TRA-DITIONAL VIETNAMESE CULTURE, WE HAVE A CONCEPT SIMILAR TO "KEEPING IT REAL."
WHAT'S IT CALLED?
"NOT STARVING TO DEATH."
OH, RIGHT— WHICH HAS PRODUCED SOME **GREAT** MUSIC, BY THE WAY.
©B. Trudeau

3/14/99

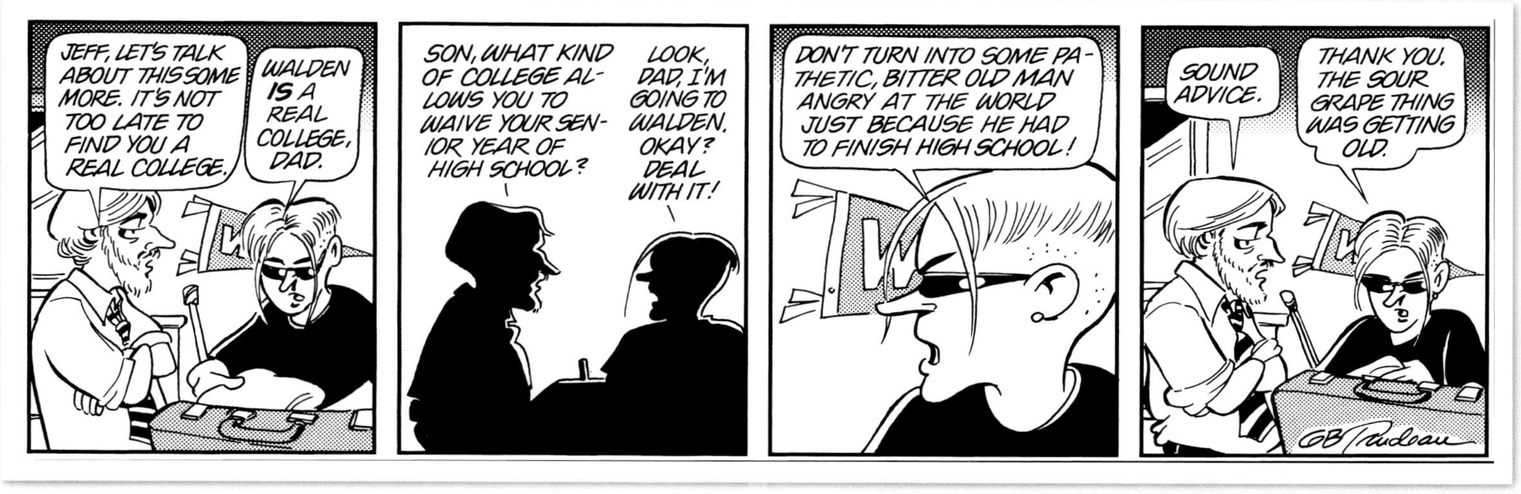
JEFF, LET'S TALK ABOUT THIS SOME MORE. IT'S NOT TOO LATE TO FIND YOU A REAL COLLEGE.
WALDEN IS A REAL COLLEGE, DAD.
SON, WHAT KIND OF COLLEGE ALLOWS YOU TO WAIVE YOUR SENIOR YEAR OF HIGH SCHOOL?
LOOK, DAD, I'M GOING TO WALDEN. OKAY? DEAL WITH IT!
DON'T TURN INTO SOME PATHETIC, BITTER OLD MAN ANGRY AT THE WORLD JUST BECAUSE HE HAD TO FINISH HIGH SCHOOL!
SOUND ADVICE.
THANK YOU. THE SOUR GRAPE THING WAS GETTING OLD.

8/23/99

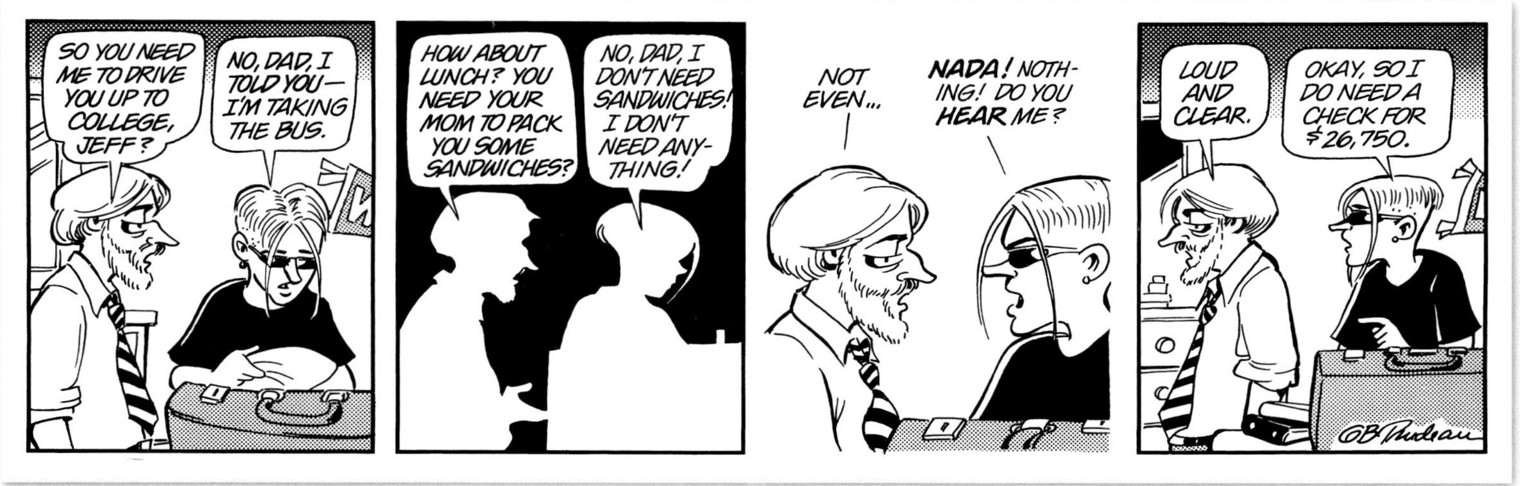
SO YOU NEED ME TO DRIVE YOU UP TO COLLEGE, JEFF?
NO, DAD, I TOLD YOU— I'M TAKING THE BUS.
HOW ABOUT LUNCH? YOU NEED YOUR MOM TO PACK YOU SOME SANDWICHES?
NO, DAD, I DON'T NEED SANDWICHES! I DON'T NEED ANYTHING!
NOT EVEN...
NADA! NOTHING! DO YOU HEAR ME?
LOUD AND CLEAR.
OKAY, SO I DO NEED A CHECK FOR $26,750.

8/24/99

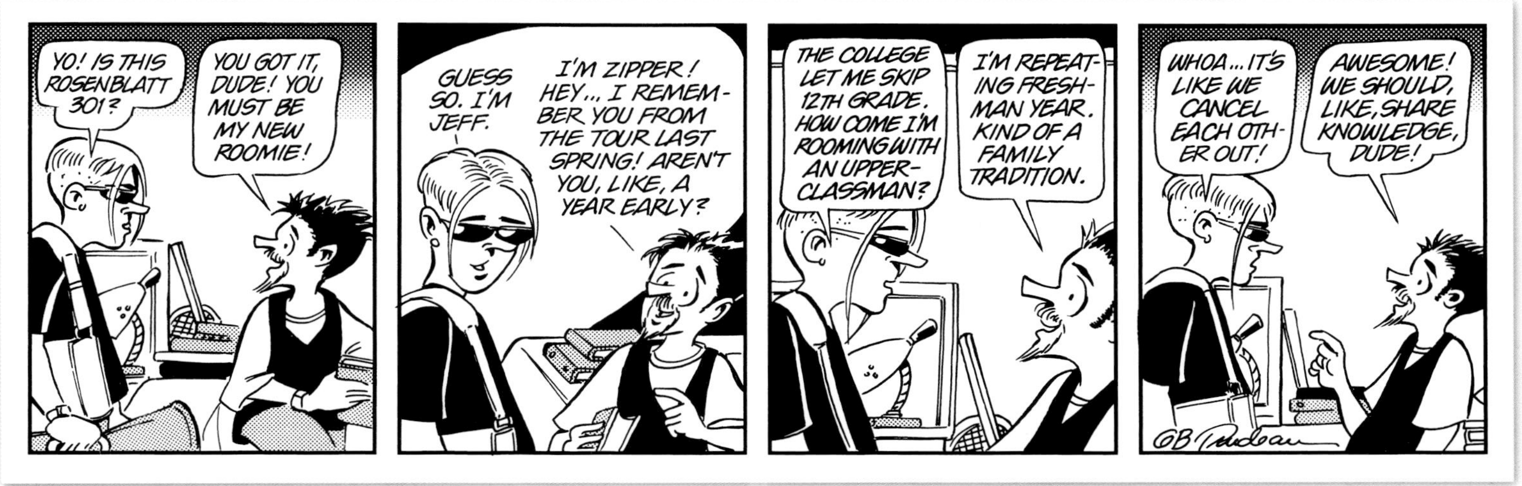
YO! IS THIS ROSENBLATT 301?
YOU GOT IT, DUDE! YOU MUST BE MY NEW ROOMIE!
GUESS SO. I'M JEFF.
I'M ZIPPER! HEY... I REMEMBER YOU FROM THE TOUR LAST SPRING! AREN'T YOU, LIKE, A YEAR EARLY?
THE COLLEGE LET ME SKIP 12TH GRADE. HOW COME I'M ROOMING WITH AN UPPERCLASSMAN?
I'M REPEATING FRESHMAN YEAR. KIND OF A FAMILY TRADITION.
WHOA... IT'S LIKE WE CANCEL EACH OTHER OUT!
AWESOME! WE SHOULD, LIKE, SHARE KNOWLEDGE, DUDE!

8/25/99

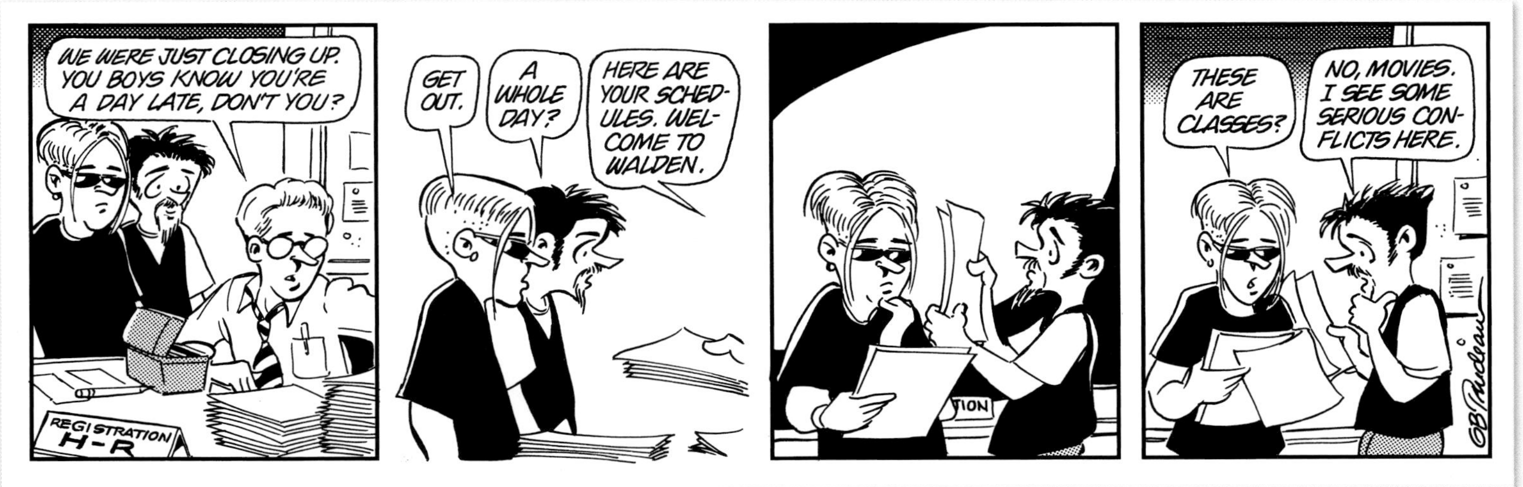
WE WERE JUST CLOSING UP. YOU BOYS KNOW YOU'RE A DAY LATE, DON'T YOU?
REGISTRATION H-R
GET OUT.
A WHOLE DAY?
HERE ARE YOUR SCHEDULES. WELCOME TO WALDEN.
THESE ARE CLASSES?
NO, MOVIES. I SEE SOME SERIOUS CONFLICTS HERE.

8/28/99

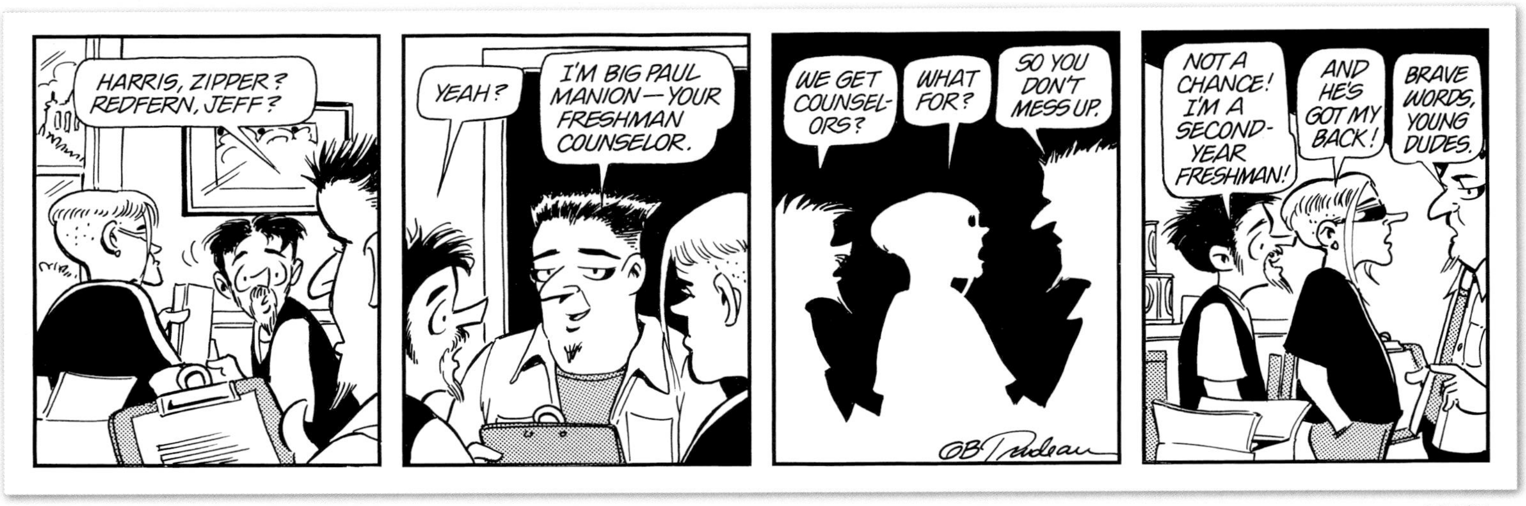
HARRIS, ZIPPER? REDFERN, JEFF?
YEAH?
I'M BIG PAUL MANION — YOUR FRESHMAN COUNSELOR.
WE GET COUNSEL-ORS?
WHAT FOR?
SO YOU DON'T MESS UP.
NOT A CHANCE! I'M A SECOND-YEAR FRESHMAN!
AND HE'S GOT MY BACK!
BRAVE WORDS, YOUNG DUDES.

8/30/99

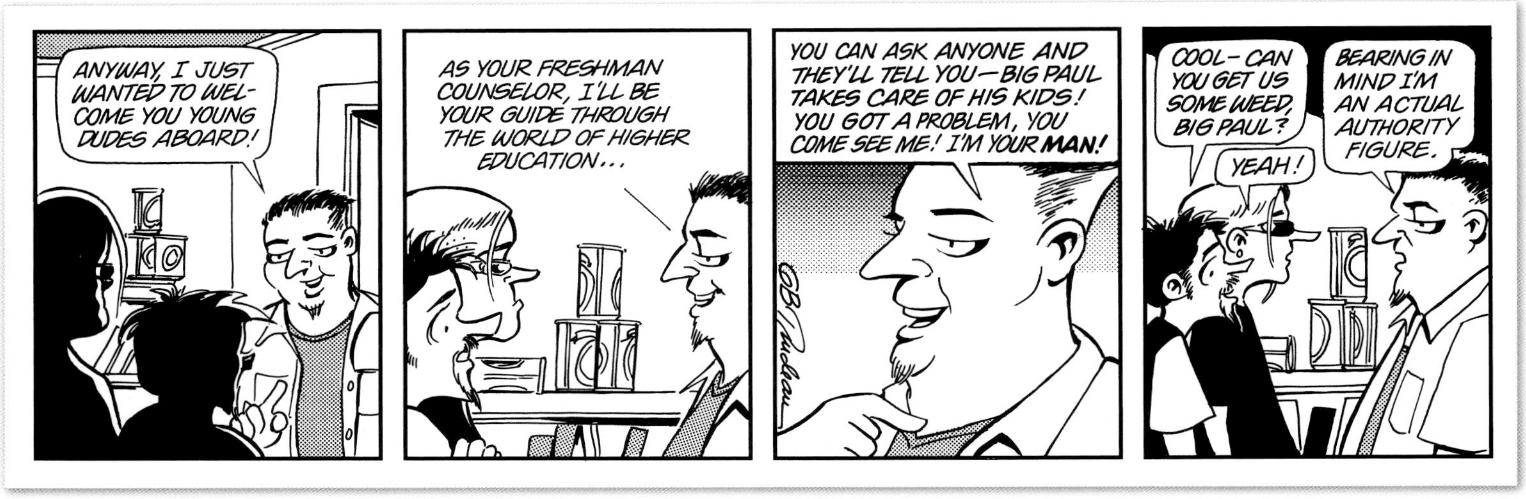
ANYWAY, I JUST WANTED TO WEL-COME YOU YOUNG DUDES ABOARD!
AS YOUR FRESHMAN COUNSELOR, I'LL BE YOUR GUIDE THROUGH THE WORLD OF HIGHER EDUCATION...
YOU CAN ASK ANYONE AND THEY'LL TELL YOU — BIG PAUL TAKES CARE OF HIS KIDS! YOU GOT A PROBLEM, YOU COME SEE ME! I'M YOUR MAN!
COOL — CAN YOU GET US SOME WEED, BIG PAUL?
YEAH!
BEARING IN MIND I'M AN ACTUAL AUTHORITY FIGURE.

8/31/99

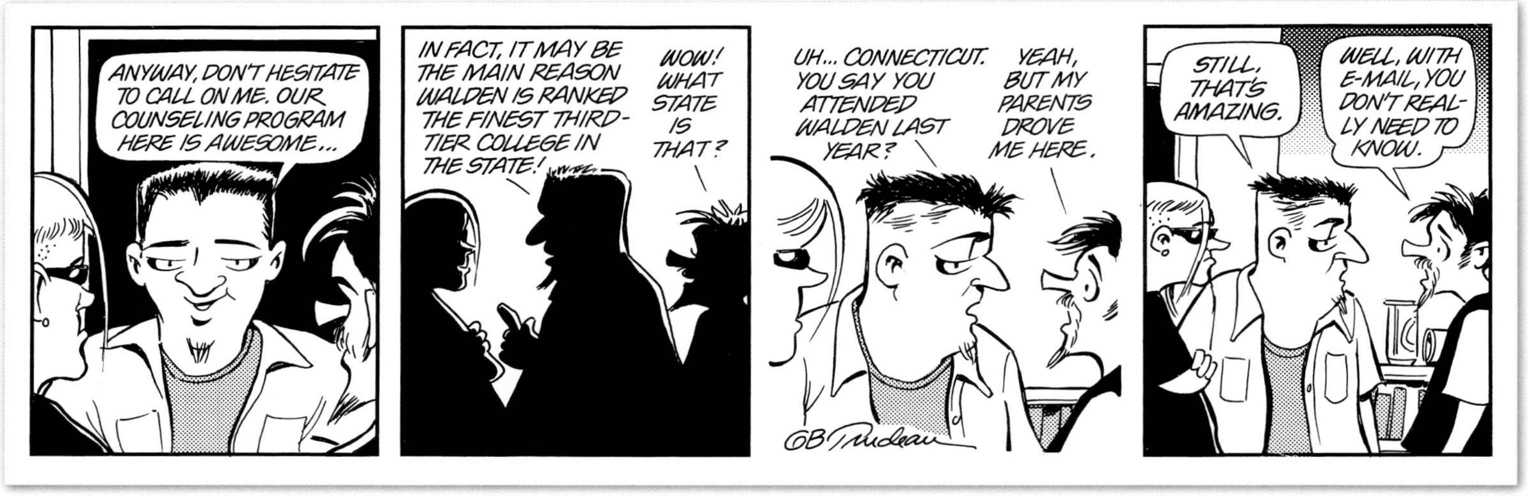
ANYWAY, DON'T HESITATE TO CALL ON ME. OUR COUNSELING PROGRAM HERE IS AWESOME...
IN FACT, IT MAY BE THE MAIN REASON WALDEN IS RANKED THE FINEST THIRD-TIER COLLEGE IN THE STATE!
WOW! WHAT STATE IS THAT?
UH... CONNECTICUT. YOU SAY YOU ATTENDED WALDEN LAST YEAR?
YEAH, BUT MY PARENTS DROVE ME HERE.
STILL, THAT'S AMAZING.
WELL, WITH E-MAIL, YOU DON'T REAL-LY NEED TO KNOW.

9/1/99

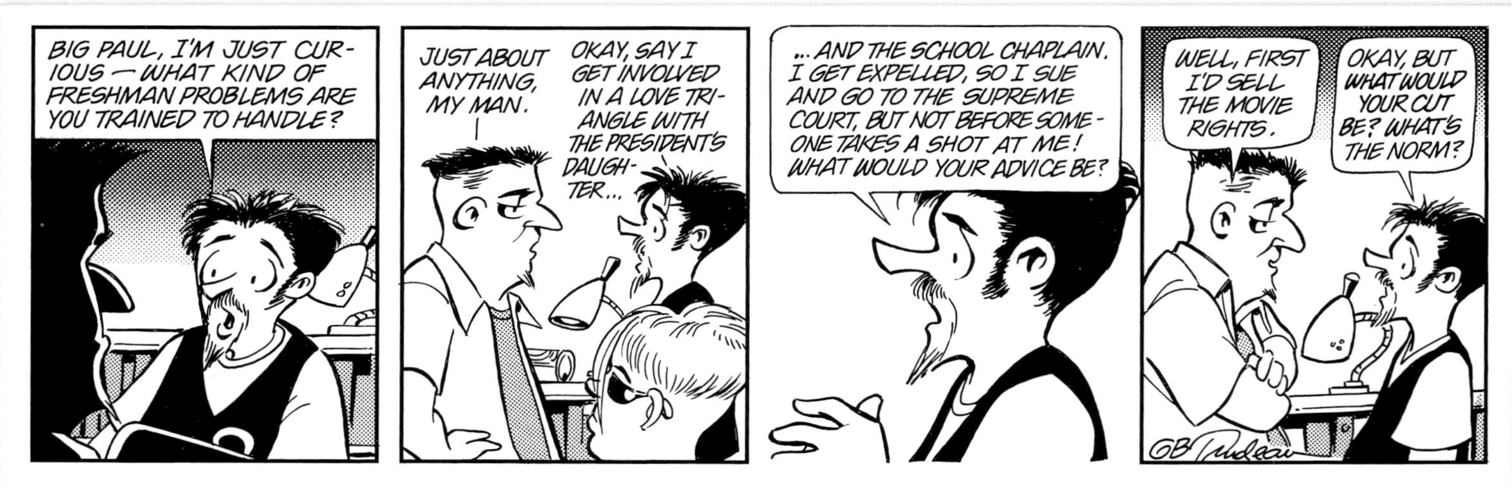
BIG PAUL, I'M JUST CUR-IOUS — WHAT KIND OF FRESHMAN PROBLEMS ARE YOU TRAINED TO HANDLE?
JUST ABOUT ANYTHING, MY MAN.
OKAY, SAY I GET INVOLVED IN A LOVE TRI-ANGLE WITH THE PRESIDENT'S DAUGH-TER...
...AND THE SCHOOL CHAPLAIN. I GET EXPELLED, SO I SUE AND GO TO THE SUPREME COURT, BUT NOT BEFORE SOME-ONE TAKES A SHOT AT ME! WHAT WOULD YOUR ADVICE BE?
WELL, FIRST I'D SELL THE MOVIE RIGHTS.
OKAY, BUT WHAT WOULD YOUR CUT BE? WHAT'S THE NORM?

9/2/99

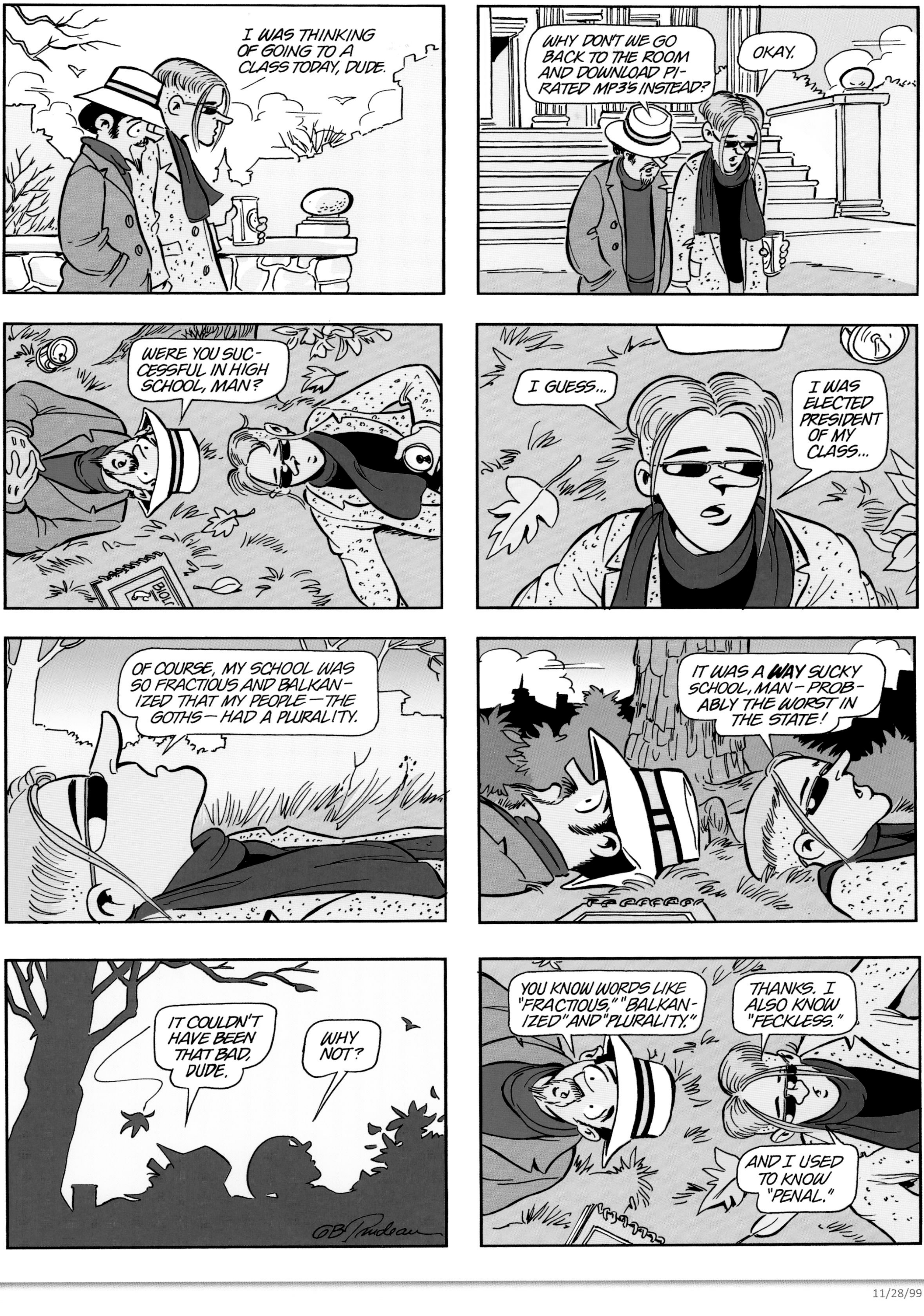
I WAS THINKING OF GOING TO A CLASS TODAY, DUDE.
WHY DON'T WE GO BACK TO THE ROOM AND DOWNLOAD PI-RATED MP3'S INSTEAD?
OKAY.
WERE YOU SUC-CESSFUL IN HIGH SCHOOL, MAN?
I GUESS...
I WAS ELECTED PRESIDENT OF MY CLASS...
OF COURSE, MY SCHOOL WAS SO FRACTIOUS AND BALKAN-IZED THAT MY PEOPLE—THE GOTHS—HAD A PLURALITY.
IT WAS A WAY SUCKY SCHOOL, MAN—PROB-ABLY THE WORST IN THE STATE!
IT COULDN'T HAVE BEEN THAT BAD, DUDE.
WHY NOT?
YOU KNOW WORDS LIKE "FRACTIOUS," "BALKAN-IZED" AND "PLURALITY."
THANKS. I ALSO KNOW "FECKLESS."
AND I USED TO KNOW "PENAL."
GB Trudeau

11/28/99

Lacey Davenport

On June 16, 1978, I received a telegram from House Speaker Tip O'Neill requesting the withdrawal of some upcoming strips that featured Lacey Davenport discussing the so-called Koreagate scandal. O'Neill's efforts to block the strips backfired, of course, drawing even more attention to the Speaker's role in the matter. All of which was just fine with Republican representative Millicent Fenwick, who commented at the time, "Quite delightful. I'm in favor of all kinds of irreverence in that way."

Fenwick had been asked for her views because, of course, it was widely assumed that she was the model for Lacey. In fact, Lacey made her first appearance, along with longtime companion Dick Davenport, under a Walden College reunion tent in May of 1974—eight months before Fenwick arrived in Washington. But by the time Lacey followed her to Congress in 1976, Fenwick had already made an impression, and observers speculated that surely art must be imitating life.

Actually, the parallels between the two progressive Republicans were striking: same age, same elegant bearing, same patrician inflections, and same blazing integrity. Even Lacey's

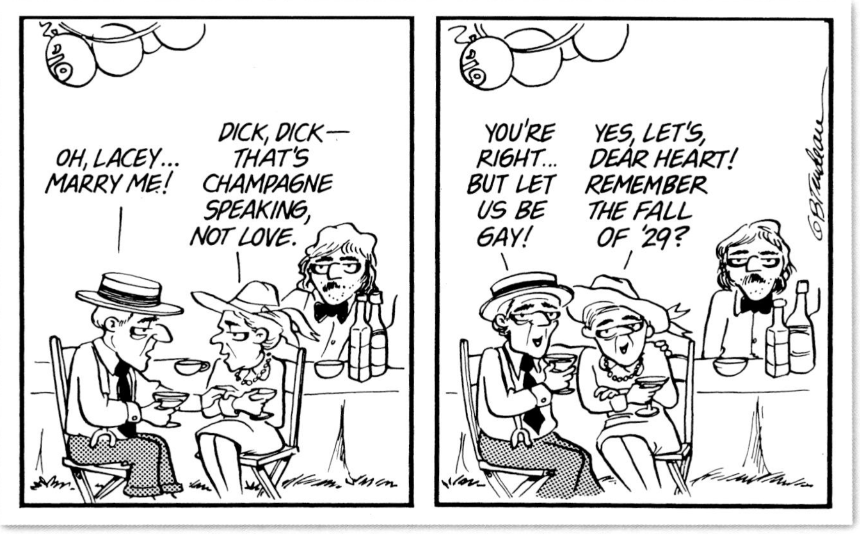
OH, LACEY... MARRY ME!
DICK, DICK— THAT'S CHAMPAGNE SPEAKING, NOT LOVE.
YOU'RE RIGHT... BUT LET US BE GAY!
YES, LET'S, DEAR HEART! REMEMBER THE FALL OF '29?

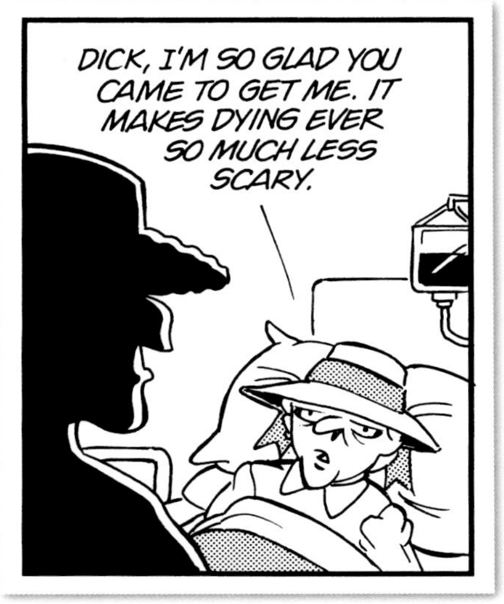
DICK, I'M SO GLAD YOU CAME TO GET ME. IT MAKES DYING EVER SO MUCH LESS SCARY.

floppy hat and heirloom brooches suggested an homage. It quickly became obvious to me that there was no advantage to clearing up the confusion. Not only was it an honor to be associated with the wholly admirable Fenwick, it seemed almost ungallant to challenge the association. For her part, the congresswoman seemed to regard her supposed avatar with some affection, and her family later sent me what had become a symbol of her unique style—a tiny, exceedingly ladylike pipe.

As the years passed, there was also serendipity in the causes Lacey championed. Unbeknownst to me, Fenwick had served for sixteen years on the U.S. Commission on Civil Rights, so when Lacey kicked up a storm over a little-known law in Palm Beach that required servants to carry identity cards, she was again perfectly aligned with the Fenwick legacy. When the Florida state legislature subsequently passed a "Doonesbury Bill" banning such ordinances, I was sent the governor's signing pen to put next to my pipe.

Lacey, like Fenwick, was also a pariah in her own party. Neither of them received the memo about a Reagan Revolution, and each held true to the sensible moderation that had once been welcome within the GOP. When Lacey finally retired in the shadow of Alzheimer's, I tried to capture a sense of the shifting political landscape that had proved so vexing to her real-life counterpart.

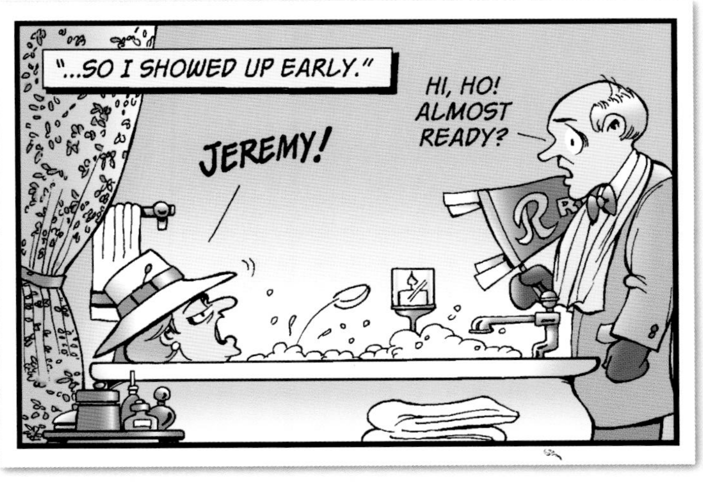
"...SO I SHOWED UP EARLY."
JEREMY!
HI, HO! ALMOST READY?

I finally met Fenwick, over lunch, after she had retired from Congress. I was not disappointed; the class act was real. What I didn't say to her, but should have, is this: If Lacey Davenport wasn't Millicent Fenwick, she was a tribute to women like her. But since no one else was like Millicent Fenwick, the tribute was hers alone.

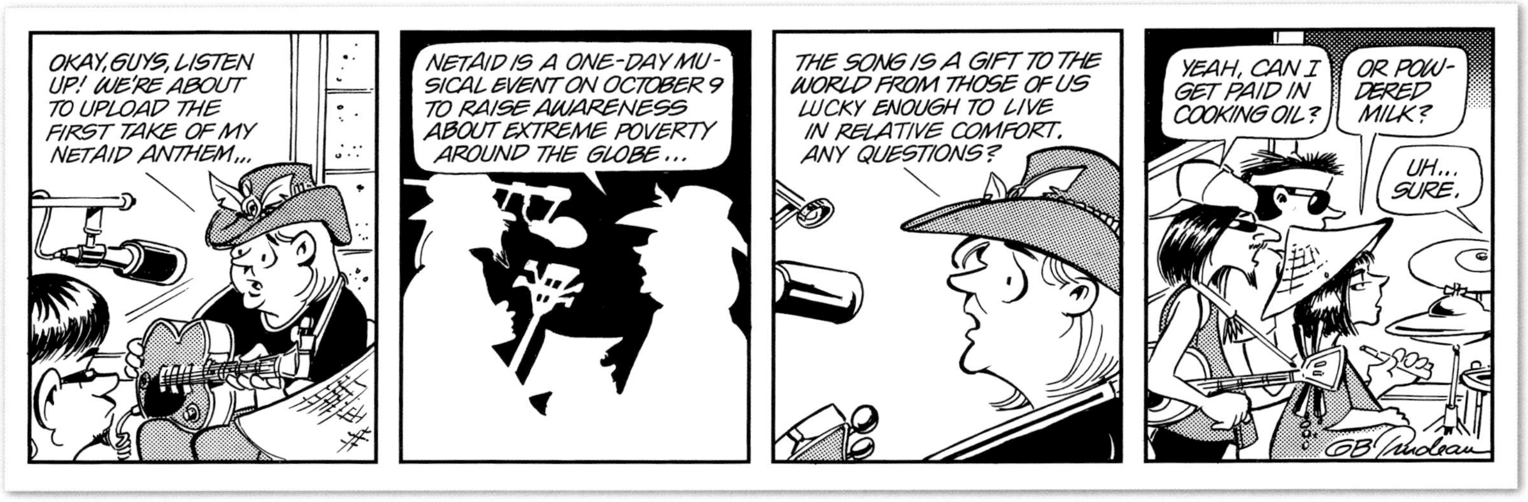
OKAY, GUYS, LISTEN UP! WE'RE ABOUT TO UPLOAD THE FIRST TAKE OF MY NETAID ANTHEM...
NETAID IS A ONE-DAY MUSICAL EVENT ON OCTOBER 9 TO RAISE AWARENESS ABOUT EXTREME POVERTY AROUND THE GLOBE...
THE SONG IS A GIFT TO THE WORLD FROM THOSE OF US LUCKY ENOUGH TO LIVE IN RELATIVE COMFORT. ANY QUESTIONS?
YEAH, CAN I GET PAID IN COOKING OIL?
OR POWDERED MILK?
UH... SURE.

9/7/99

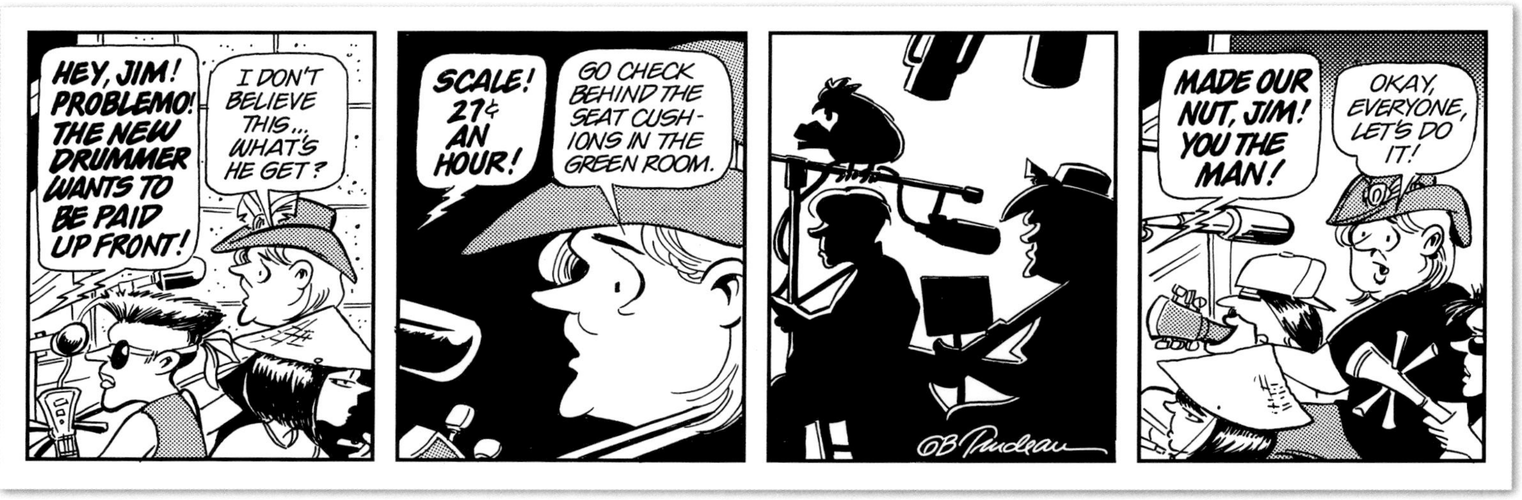
HEY, JIM! PROBLEMO! THE NEW DRUMMER WANTS TO BE PAID UP FRONT!
I DON'T BELIEVE THIS... WHAT'S HE GET?
SCALE! 27¢ AN HOUR!
GO CHECK BEHIND THE SEAT CUSHIONS IN THE GREEN ROOM.
MADE OUR NUT, JIM! YOU THE MAN!
OKAY, EVERYONE, LET'S DO IT!

9/8/99

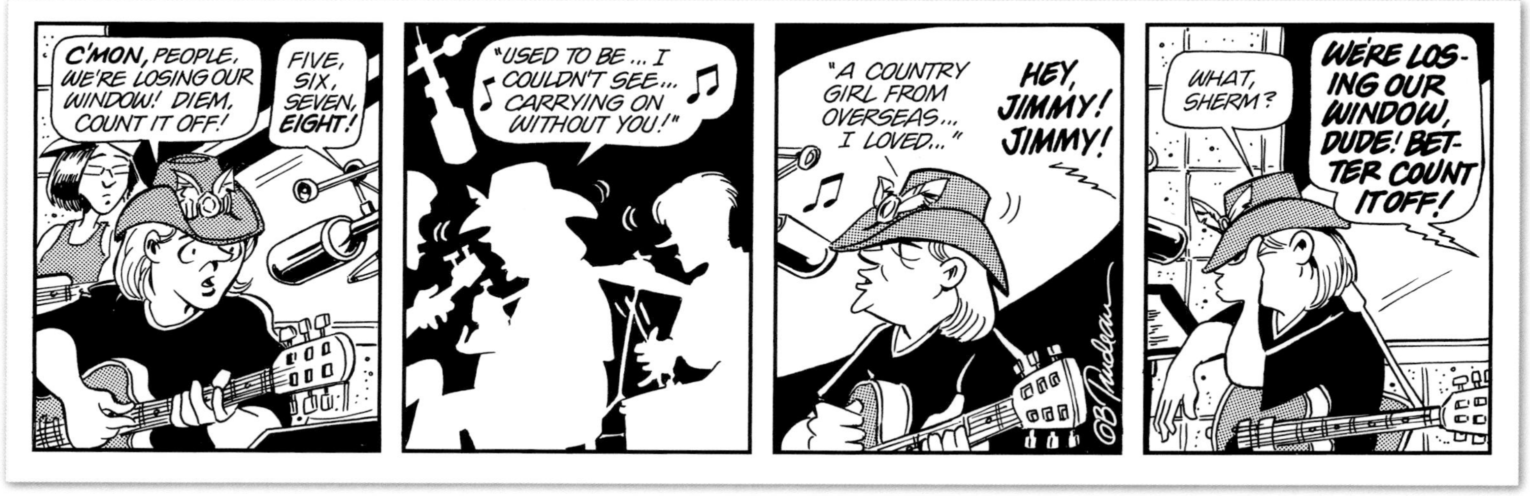
C'MON, PEOPLE, WE'RE LOSING OUR WINDOW! DIEM, COUNT IT OFF!
FIVE, SIX, SEVEN, EIGHT!
"USED TO BE... I COULDN'T SEE... CARRYING ON WITHOUT YOU!"
"A COUNTRY GIRL FROM OVERSEAS... I LOVED..."
HEY, JIMMY! JIMMY!
WHAT, SHERM?
WE'RE LOSING OUR WINDOW, DUDE! BETTER COUNT IT OFF!

9/10/99

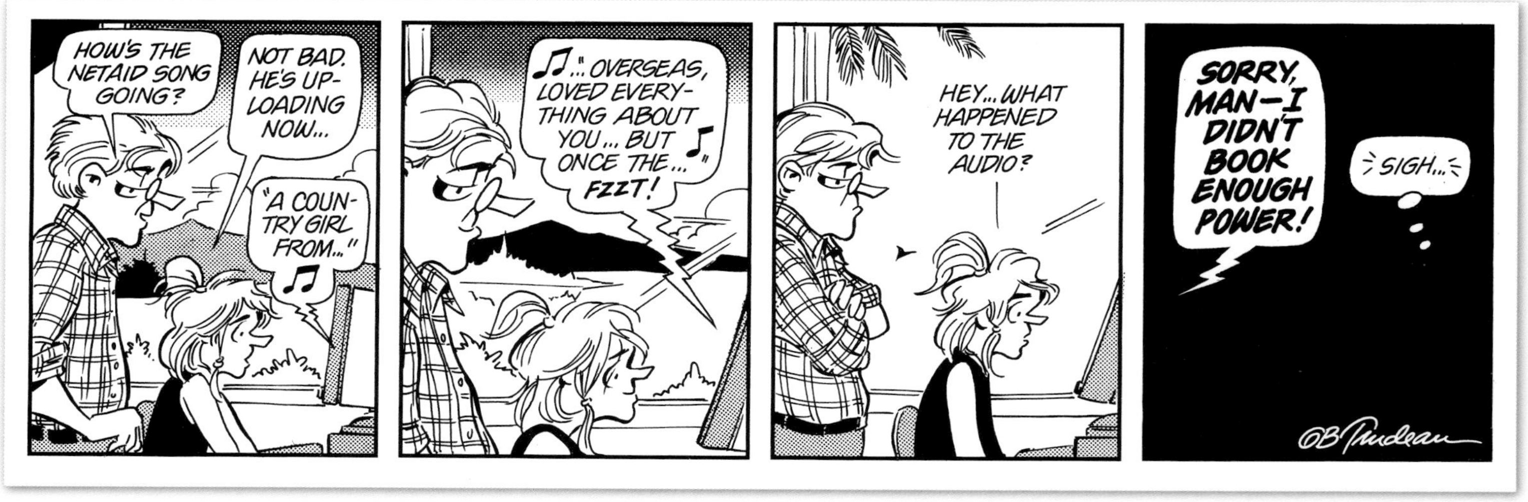
HOW'S THE NETAID SONG GOING?
NOT BAD. HE'S UPLOADING NOW...
"A COUNTRY GIRL FROM..."
"...OVERSEAS, LOVED EVERYTHING ABOUT YOU... BUT ONCE THE..."
FZZT!
HEY... WHAT HAPPENED TO THE AUDIO?
SORRY, MAN—I DIDN'T BOOK ENOUGH POWER!
SIGH...

9/11/99

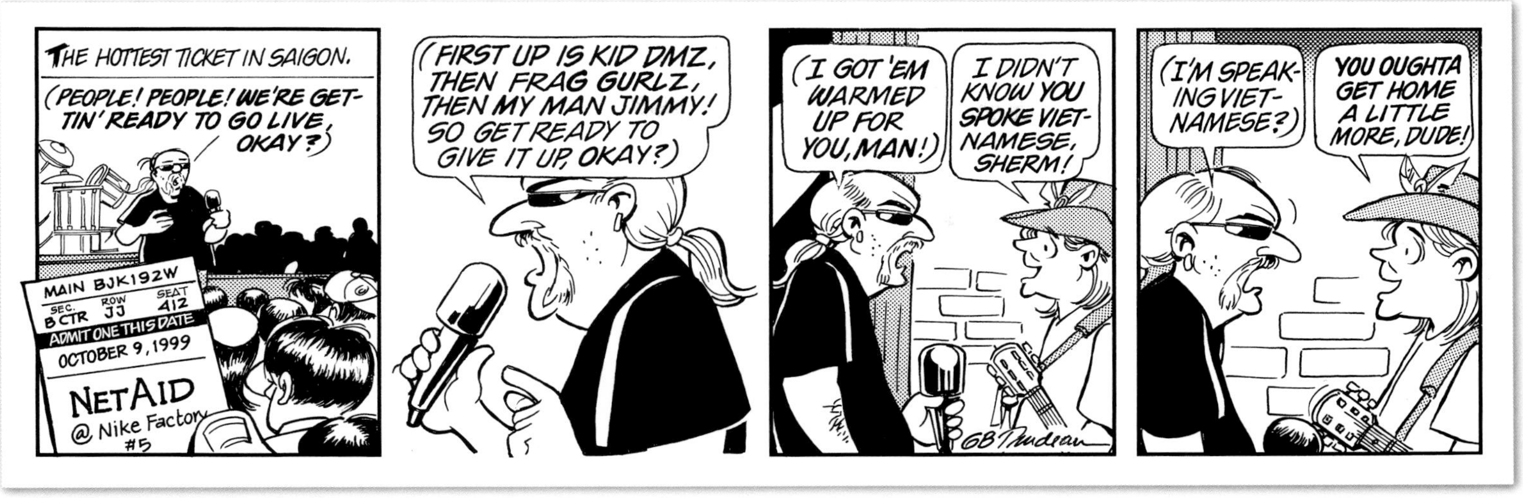
THE HOTTEST TICKET IN SAIGON.
(PEOPLE! PEOPLE! WE'RE GETTIN' READY TO GO LIVE, OKAY?)
MAIN BJK192W
SEC. BCTR ROW JJ SEAT 412
ADMIT ONE THIS DATE
OCTOBER 9, 1999
NETAID @ Nike Factory #5
(FIRST UP IS KID DMZ, THEN FRAG GURLZ, THEN MY MAN JIMMY! SO GET READY TO GIVE IT UP, OKAY?)
(I GOT 'EM WARMED UP FOR YOU, MAN!)
I DIDN'T KNOW YOU SPOKE VIETNAMESE, SHERM!
(I'M SPEAKING VIETNAMESE?)
YOU OUGHTA GET HOME A LITTLE MORE, DUDE!

10/4/99

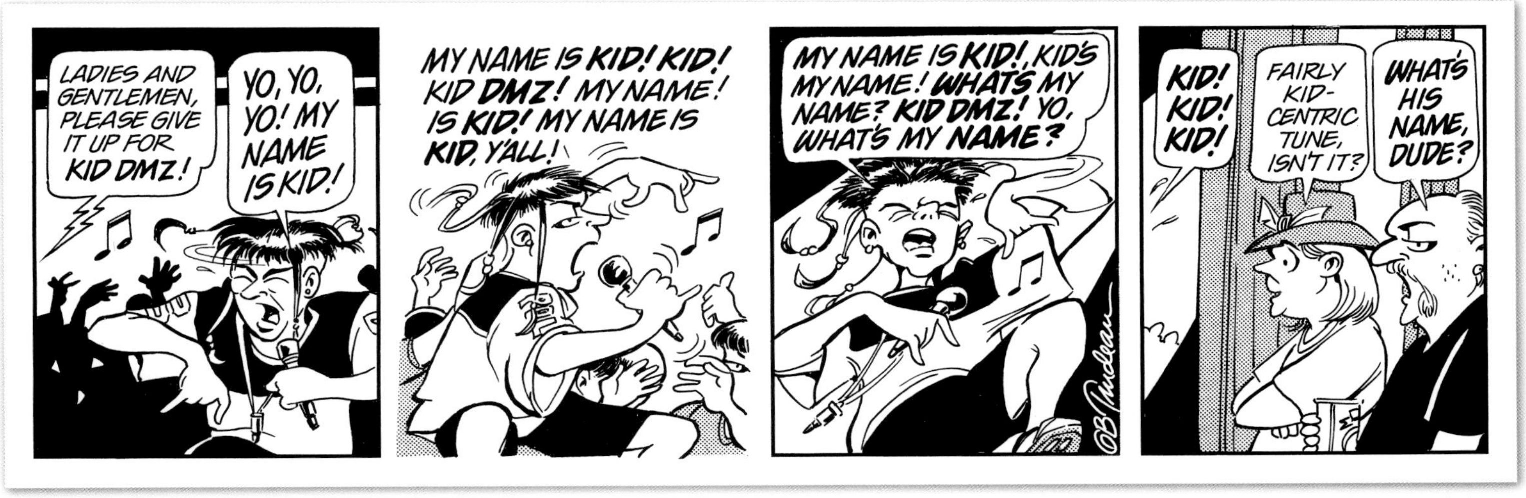
LADIES AND GENTLEMEN, PLEASE GIVE IT UP FOR KID DMZ!
YO, YO, YO! MY NAME IS KID!
MY NAME IS KID! KID! KID DMZ! MY NAME! IS KID! MY NAME IS KID, Y'ALL!
MY NAME IS KID!, KID'S MY NAME! WHAT'S MY NAME? KID DMZ! YO, WHAT'S MY NAME?
KID! KID! KID!
FAIRLY KID-CENTRIC TUNE, ISN'T IT?
WHAT'S HIS NAME, DUDE?

10/5/99

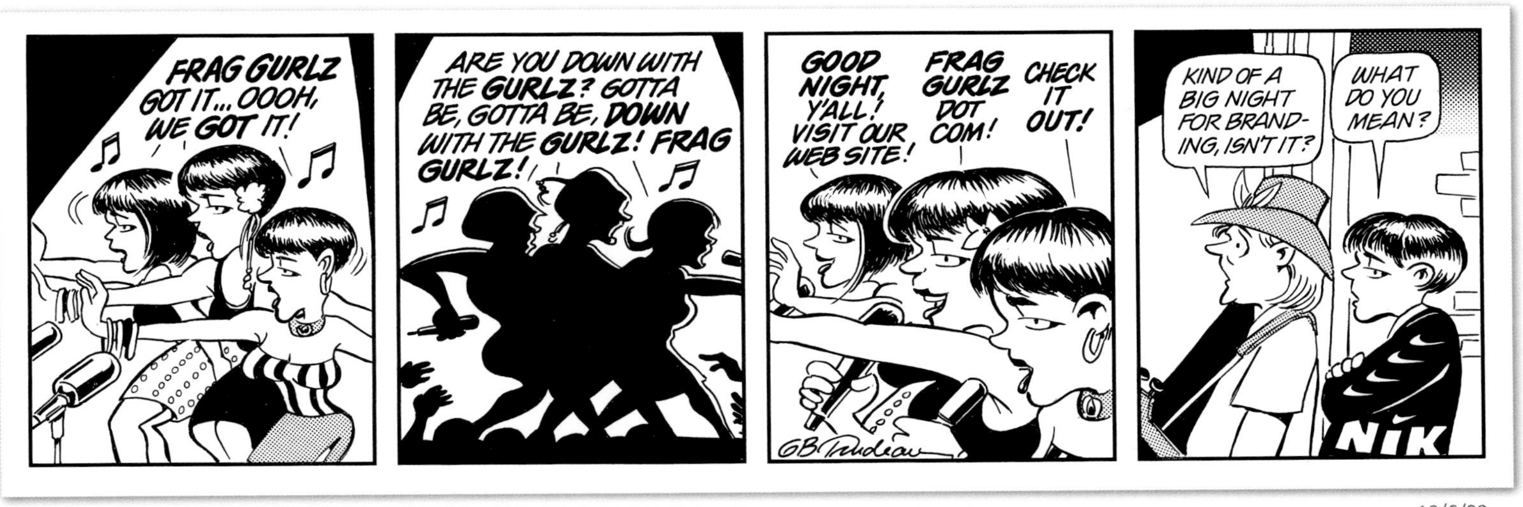
FRAG GURLZ GOT IT... OOOH, WE GOT IT!
ARE YOU DOWN WITH THE GURLZ? GOTTA BE, GOTTA BE, DOWN WITH THE GURLZ! FRAG GURLZ!
GOOD NIGHT, Y'ALL! VISIT OUR WEB SITE!
FRAG GURLZ DOT COM!
CHECK IT OUT!
KIND OF A BIG NIGHT FOR BRANDING, ISN'T IT?
WHAT DO YOU MEAN?
NIK

10/6/99

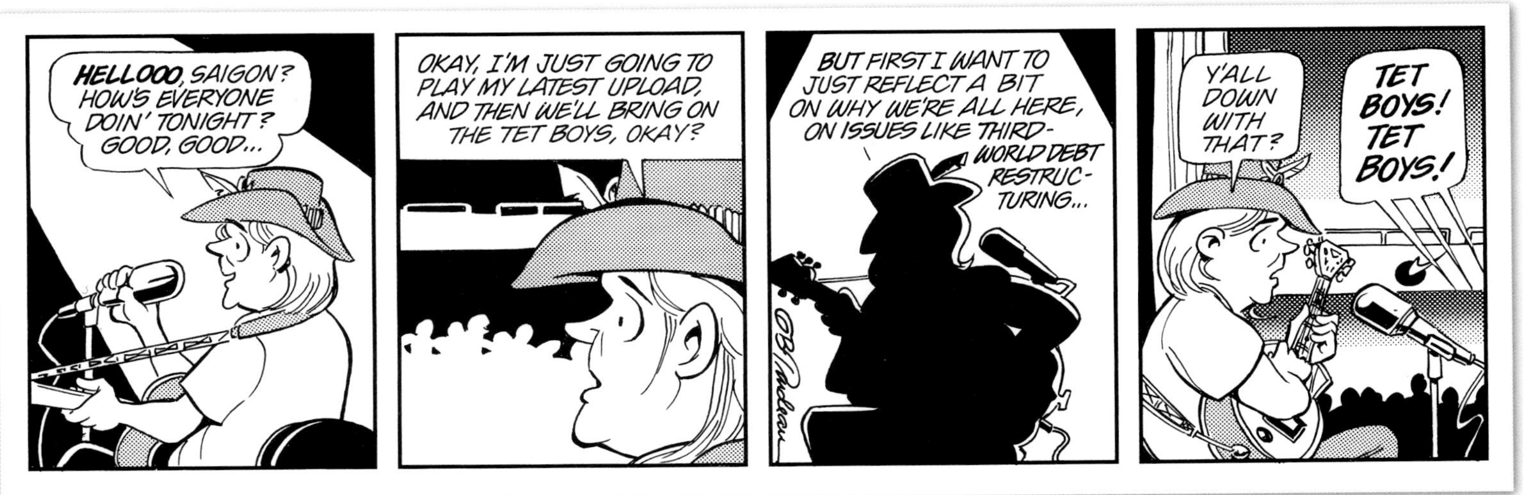
HELLOOO, SAIGON? HOW'S EVERYONE DOIN' TONIGHT? GOOD, GOOD...
OKAY, I'M JUST GOING TO PLAY MY LATEST UPLOAD, AND THEN WE'LL BRING ON THE TET BOYS, OKAY?
BUT FIRST I WANT TO JUST REFLECT A BIT ON WHY WE'RE ALL HERE, ON ISSUES LIKE THIRD-WORLD DEBT RESTRUCTURING...
Y'ALL DOWN WITH THAT?
TET BOYS! TET BOYS!

10/8/99

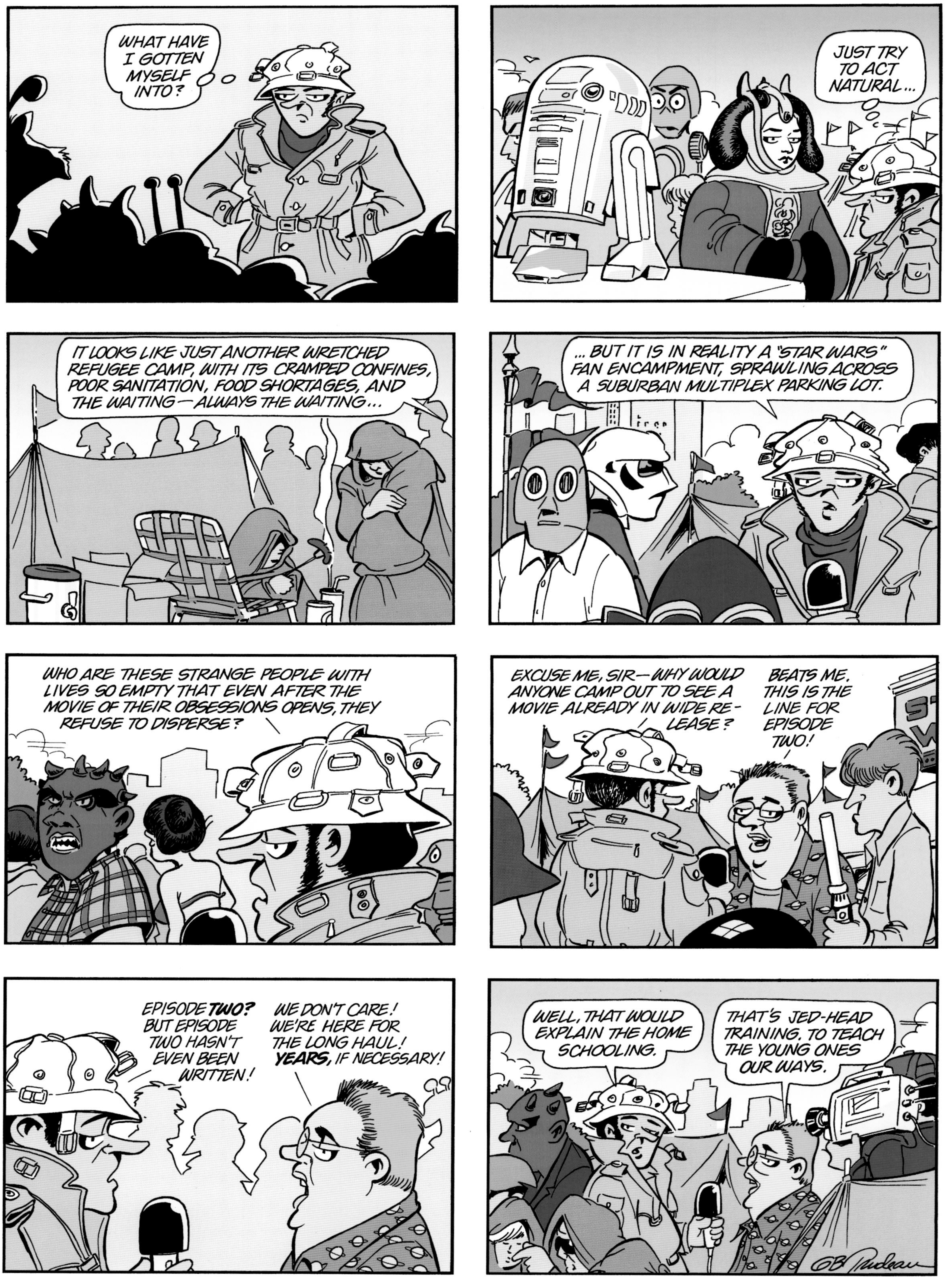
WHAT HAVE I GOTTEN MYSELF INTO?
JUST TRY TO ACT NATURAL...
IT LOOKS LIKE JUST ANOTHER WRETCHED REFUGEE CAMP, WITH ITS CRAMPED CONFINES, POOR SANITATION, FOOD SHORTAGES, AND THE WAITING—ALWAYS THE WAITING...
...BUT IT IS IN REALITY A "STAR WARS" FAN ENCAMPMENT, SPRAWLING ACROSS A SUBURBAN MULTIPLEX PARKING LOT.
WHO ARE THESE STRANGE PEOPLE WITH LIVES SO EMPTY THAT EVEN AFTER THE MOVIE OF THEIR OBSESSIONS OPENS, THEY REFUSE TO DISPERSE?
EXCUSE ME, SIR—WHY WOULD ANYONE CAMP OUT TO SEE A MOVIE ALREADY IN WIDE RELEASE?
BEATS ME. THIS IS THE LINE FOR EPISODE TWO!
EPISODE **TWO?** BUT EPISODE TWO HASN'T EVEN BEEN WRITTEN!
WE DON'T CARE! WE'RE HERE FOR THE LONG HAUL! **YEARS**, IF NECESSARY!
WELL, THAT WOULD EXPLAIN THE HOME SCHOOLING.
THAT'S JED-HEAD TRAINING, TO TEACH THE YOUNG ONES OUR WAYS.
GB Trudeau

6/13/99

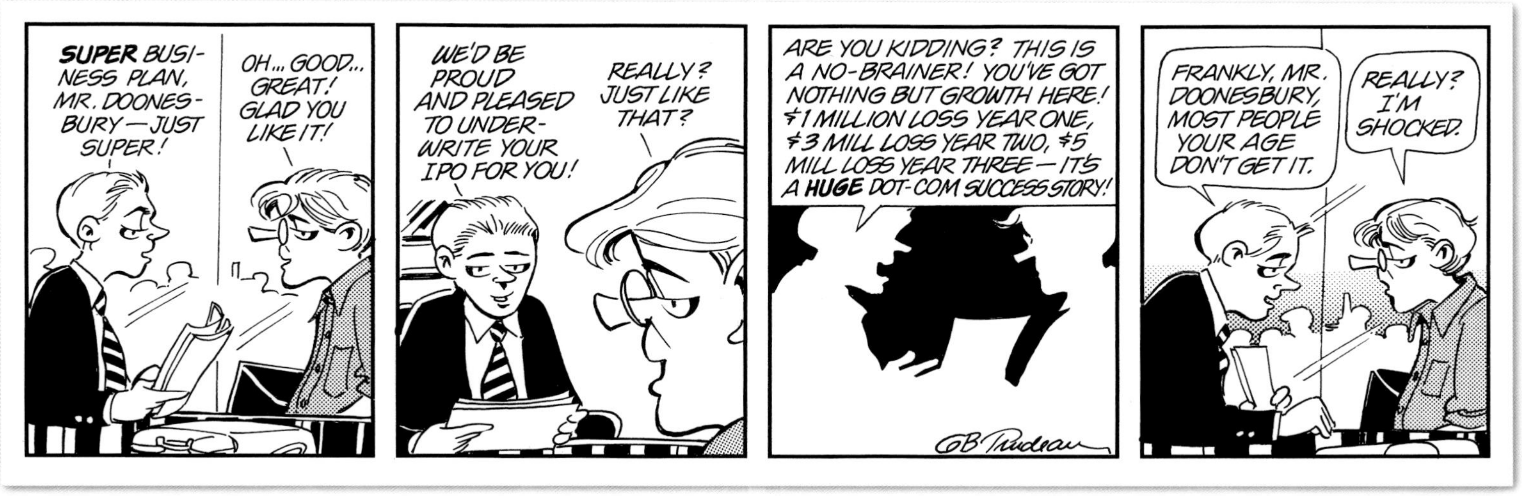
SUPER BUSINESS PLAN, MR. DOONESBURY—JUST SUPER!
OH... GOOD... GREAT! GLAD YOU LIKE IT!
WE'D BE PROUD AND PLEASED TO UNDERWRITE YOUR IPO FOR YOU!
REALLY? JUST LIKE THAT?
ARE YOU KIDDING? THIS IS A NO-BRAINER! YOU'VE GOT NOTHING BUT GROWTH HERE! $1 MILLION LOSS YEAR ONE, $3 MILL LOSS YEAR TWO, $5 MILL LOSS YEAR THREE—IT'S A HUGE DOT-COM SUCCESS STORY!
FRANKLY, MR. DOONESBURY, MOST PEOPLE YOUR AGE DON'T GET IT.
REALLY? I'M SHOCKED.

10/11/99

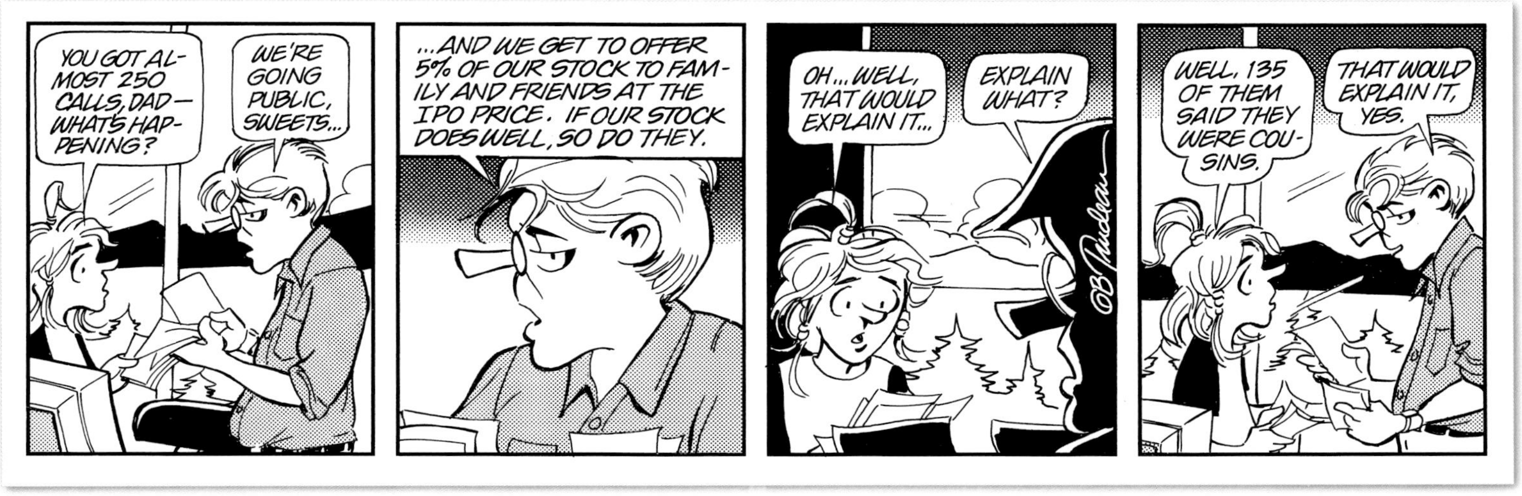
YOU GOT ALMOST 250 CALLS, DAD—WHAT'S HAPPENING?
WE'RE GOING PUBLIC, SWEETS...
...AND WE GET TO OFFER 5% OF OUR STOCK TO FAMILY AND FRIENDS AT THE IPO PRICE. IF OUR STOCK DOES WELL, SO DO THEY.
OH... WELL, THAT WOULD EXPLAIN IT...
EXPLAIN WHAT?
WELL, 135 OF THEM SAID THEY WERE COUSINS.
THAT WOULD EXPLAIN IT, YES.

10/13/99

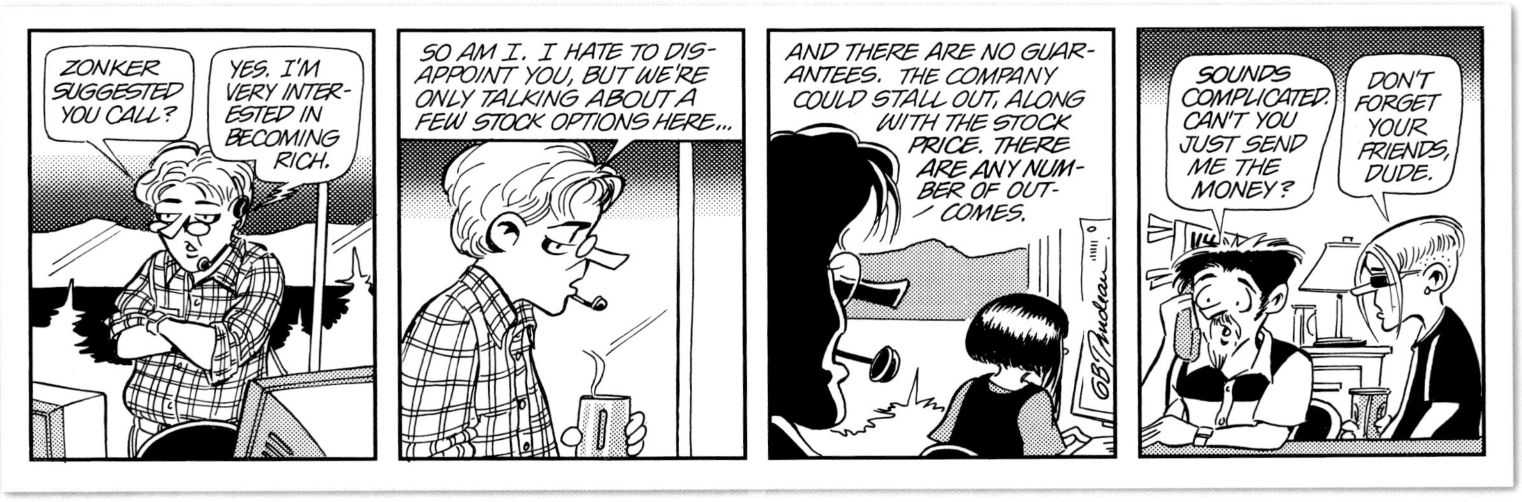
ZONKER SUGGESTED YOU CALL?
YES. I'M VERY INTERESTED IN BECOMING RICH.
SO AM I. I HATE TO DISAPPOINT YOU, BUT WE'RE ONLY TALKING ABOUT A FEW STOCK OPTIONS HERE...
AND THERE ARE NO GUARANTEES. THE COMPANY COULD STALL OUT, ALONG WITH THE STOCK PRICE. THERE ARE ANY NUMBER OF OUTCOMES.
SOUNDS COMPLICATED. CAN'T YOU JUST SEND ME THE MONEY?
DON'T FORGET YOUR FRIENDS, DUDE.

10/18/99

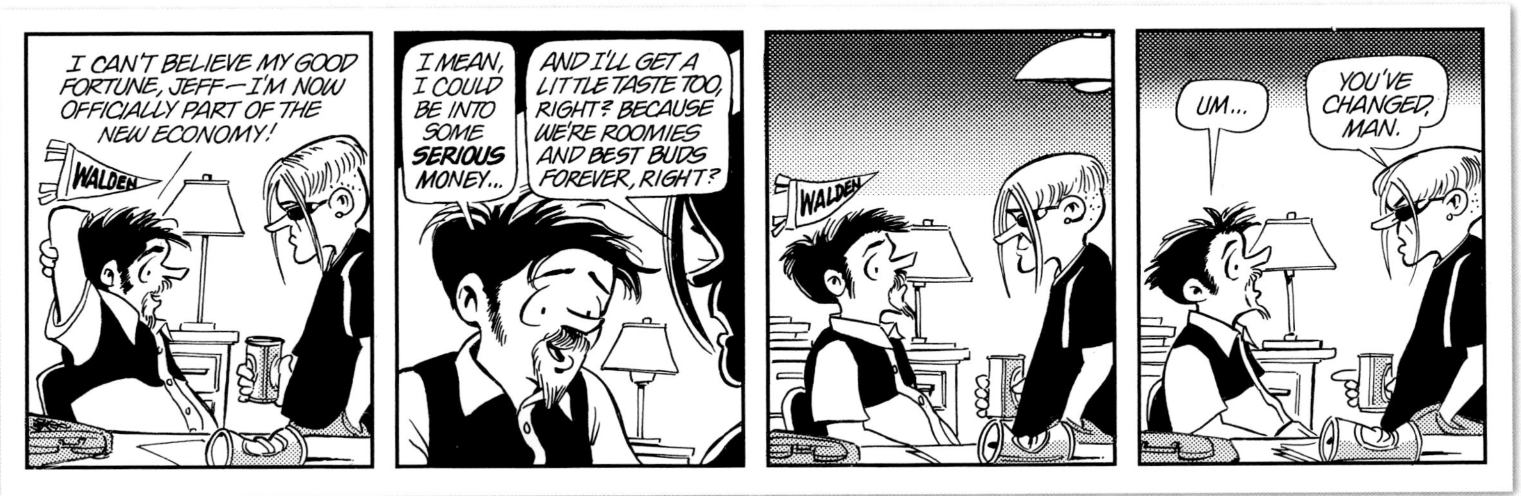
I CAN'T BELIEVE MY GOOD FORTUNE, JEFF—I'M NOW OFFICIALLY PART OF THE NEW ECONOMY!
WALDEN
I MEAN, I COULD BE INTO SOME SERIOUS MONEY...
AND I'LL GET A LITTLE TASTE TOO, RIGHT? BECAUSE WE'RE ROOMIES AND BEST BUDS FOREVER, RIGHT?
WALDEN
UM...
YOU'VE CHANGED, MAN.

10/20/99

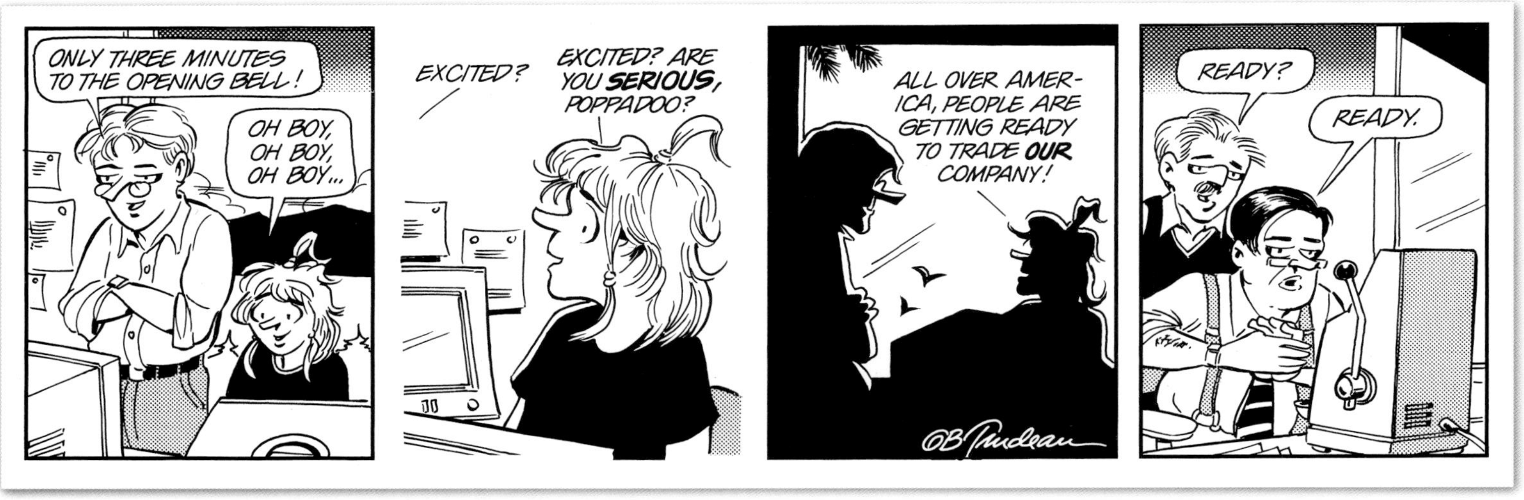
ONLY THREE MINUTES TO THE OPENING BELL!
OH BOY, OH BOY, OH BOY...
EXCITED?
EXCITED? ARE YOU **SERIOUS,** POPPADOO?
ALL OVER AMERICA, PEOPLE ARE GETTING READY TO TRADE **OUR** COMPANY!
READY?
READY.

11/1/99

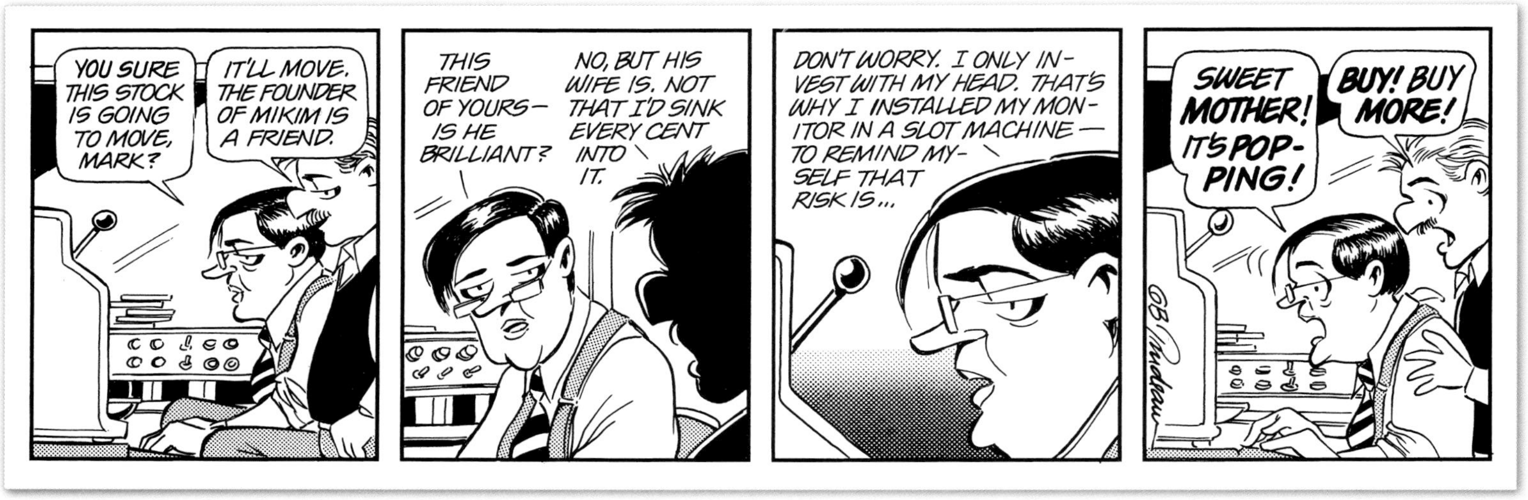
YOU SURE THIS STOCK IS GOING TO MOVE, MARK?
IT'LL MOVE. THE FOUNDER OF MIKIM IS A FRIEND.
THIS FRIEND OF YOURS— IS HE BRILLIANT?
NO, BUT HIS WIFE IS. NOT THAT I'D SINK EVERY CENT INTO IT.
DON'T WORRY. I ONLY INVEST WITH MY HEAD. THAT'S WHY I INSTALLED MY MONITOR IN A SLOT MACHINE— TO REMIND MYSELF THAT RISK IS...
SWEET MOTHER! IT'S POPPING!
BUY! BUY MORE!

11/2/99

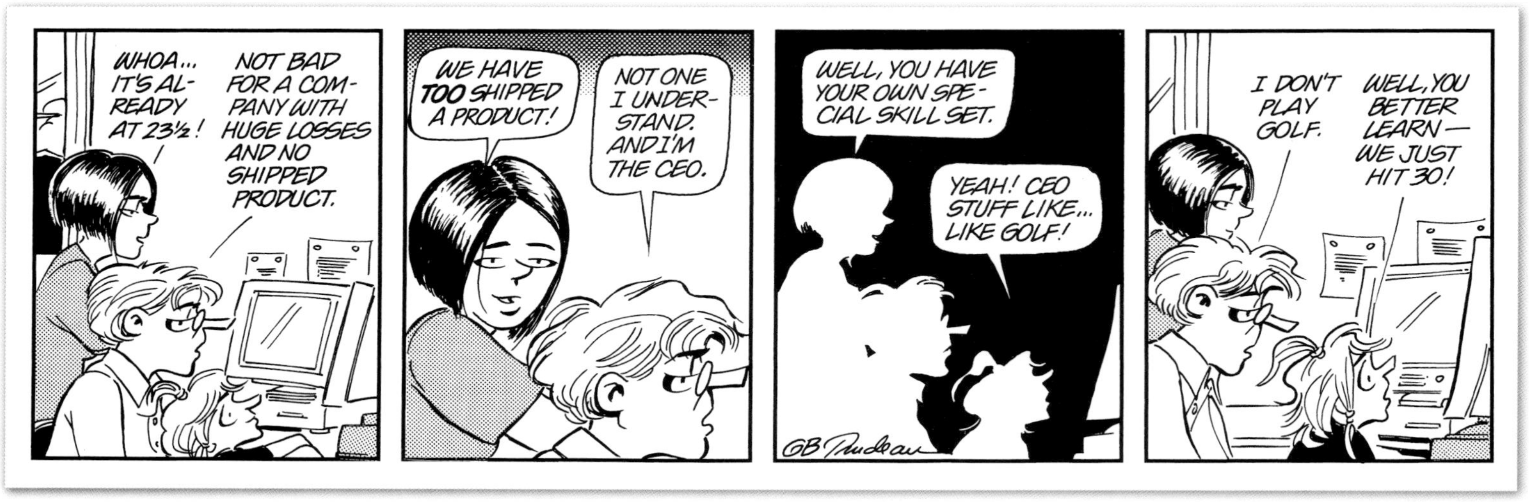
WHOA... IT'S ALREADY AT 23½!
NOT BAD FOR A COMPANY WITH HUGE LOSSES AND NO SHIPPED PRODUCT.
WE HAVE **TOO** SHIPPED A PRODUCT!
NOT ONE I UNDERSTAND. AND I'M THE CEO.
WELL, YOU HAVE YOUR OWN SPECIAL SKILL SET.
YEAH! CEO STUFF LIKE... LIKE GOLF!
I DON'T PLAY GOLF.
WELL, YOU BETTER LEARN— WE JUST HIT 30!

11/3/99

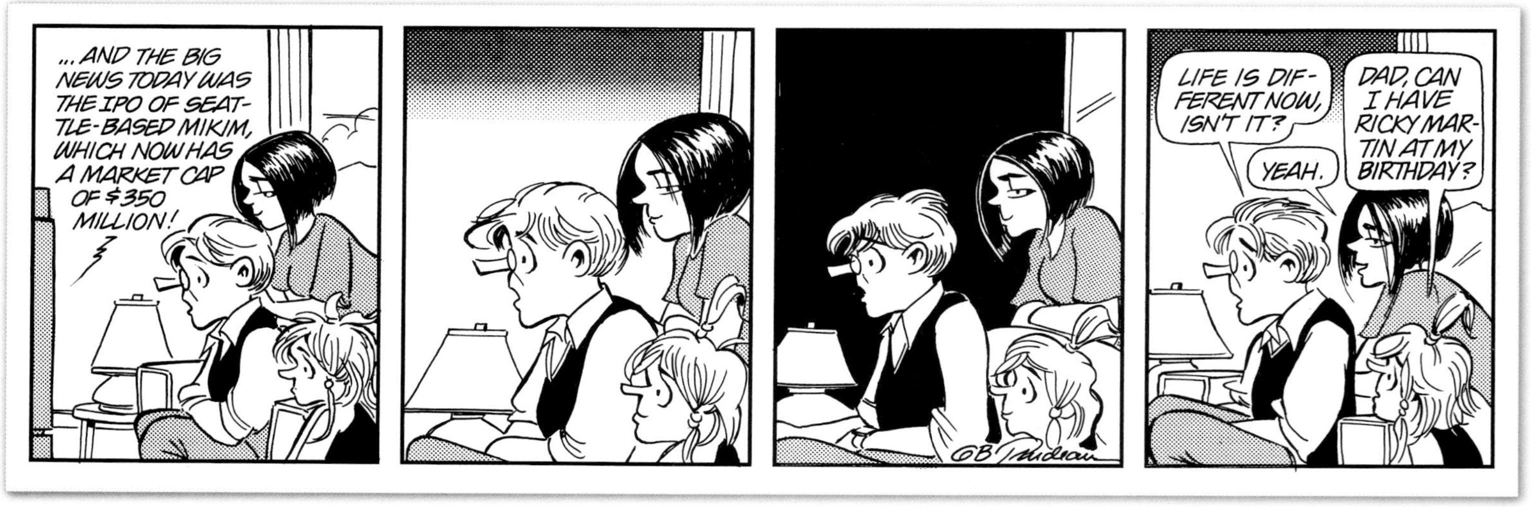
...AND THE BIG NEWS TODAY WAS THE IPO OF SEATTLE-BASED MIKIM, WHICH NOW HAS A MARKET CAP OF $350 MILLION!
LIFE IS DIFFERENT NOW, ISN'T IT?
YEAH.
DAD, CAN I HAVE RICKY MARTIN AT MY BIRTHDAY?

11/5/99

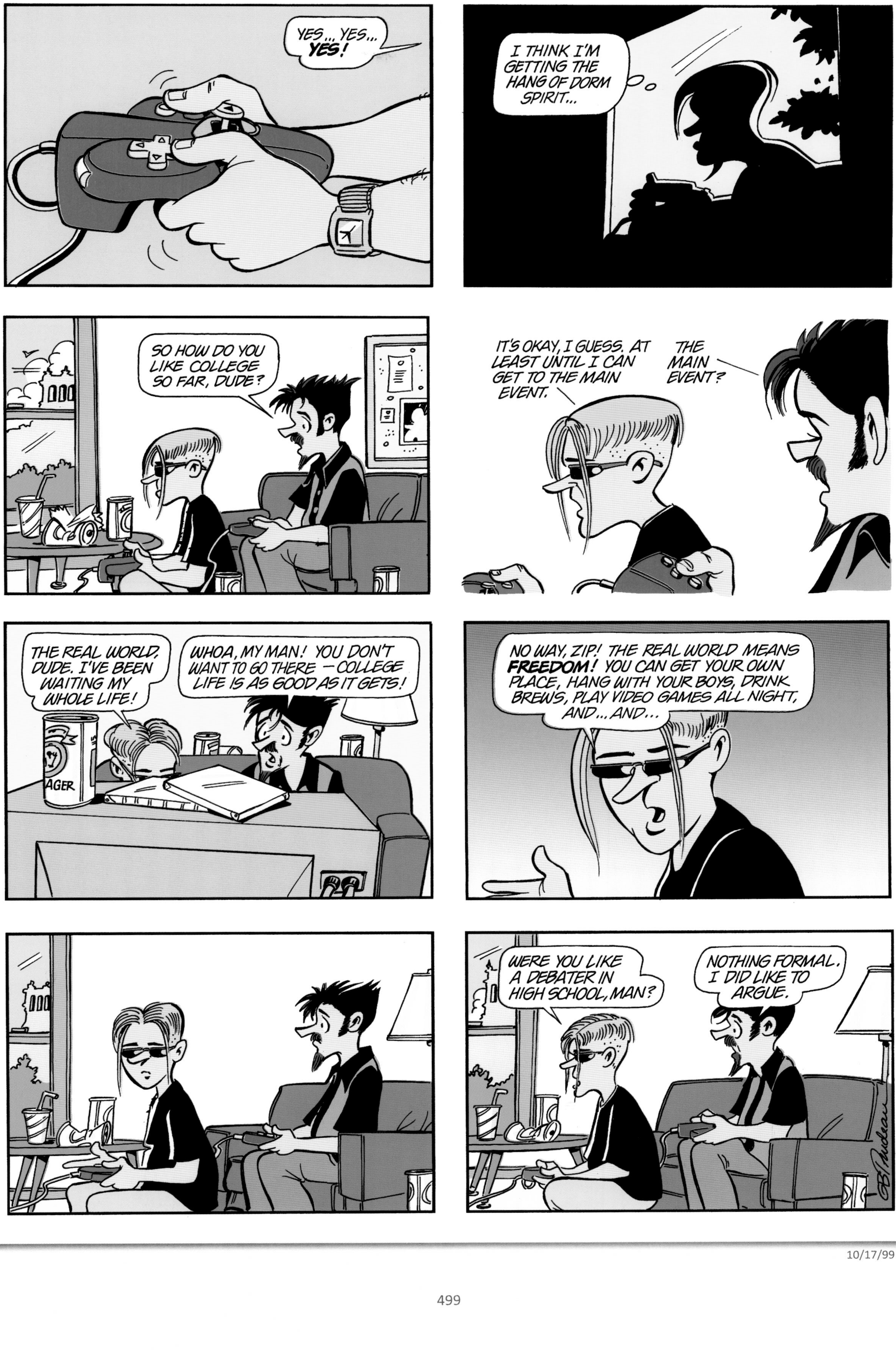
YES... YES... **YES!**
I THINK I'M GETTING THE HANG OF DORM SPIRIT...
SO HOW DO YOU LIKE COLLEGE SO FAR, DUDE?
IT'S OKAY, I GUESS. AT LEAST UNTIL I CAN GET TO THE MAIN EVENT.
THE MAIN EVENT?
THE REAL WORLD, DUDE. I'VE BEEN WAITING MY WHOLE LIFE!
WHOA, MY MAN! YOU DON'T WANT TO GO THERE — COLLEGE LIFE IS AS GOOD AS IT GETS!
AGER
NO WAY, ZIP! THE REAL WORLD MEANS **FREEDOM!** YOU CAN GET YOUR OWN PLACE, HANG WITH YOUR BOYS, DRINK BREWS, PLAY VIDEO GAMES ALL NIGHT, AND... AND...
WERE YOU LIKE A DEBATER IN HIGH SCHOOL, MAN?
NOTHING FORMAL. I DID LIKE TO ARGUE.

10/17/99

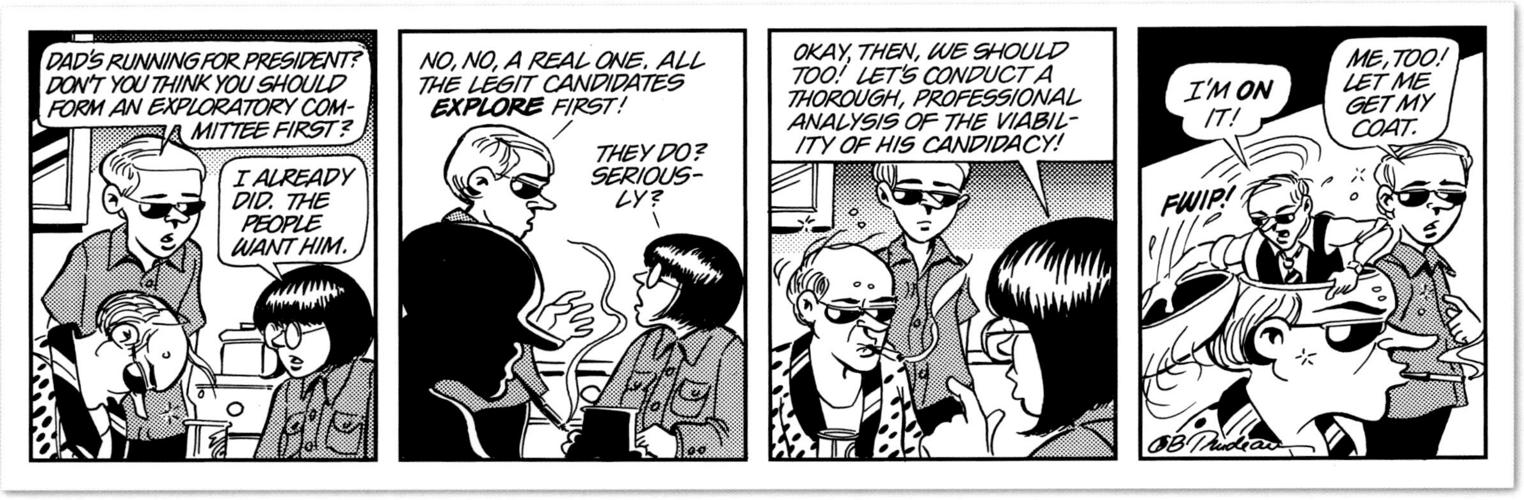
DAD'S RUNNING FOR PRESIDENT? DON'T YOU THINK YOU SHOULD FORM AN EXPLORATORY COMMITTEE FIRST?
I ALREADY DID. THE PEOPLE WANT HIM.
NO, NO, A REAL ONE. ALL THE LEGIT CANDIDATES EXPLORE FIRST!
THEY DO? SERIOUSLY?
OKAY, THEN, WE SHOULD TOO! LET'S CONDUCT A THOROUGH, PROFESSIONAL ANALYSIS OF THE VIABILITY OF HIS CANDIDACY!
I'M ON IT!
FWIP!
ME, TOO! LET ME GET MY COAT.
GB Trudeau

11/29/99

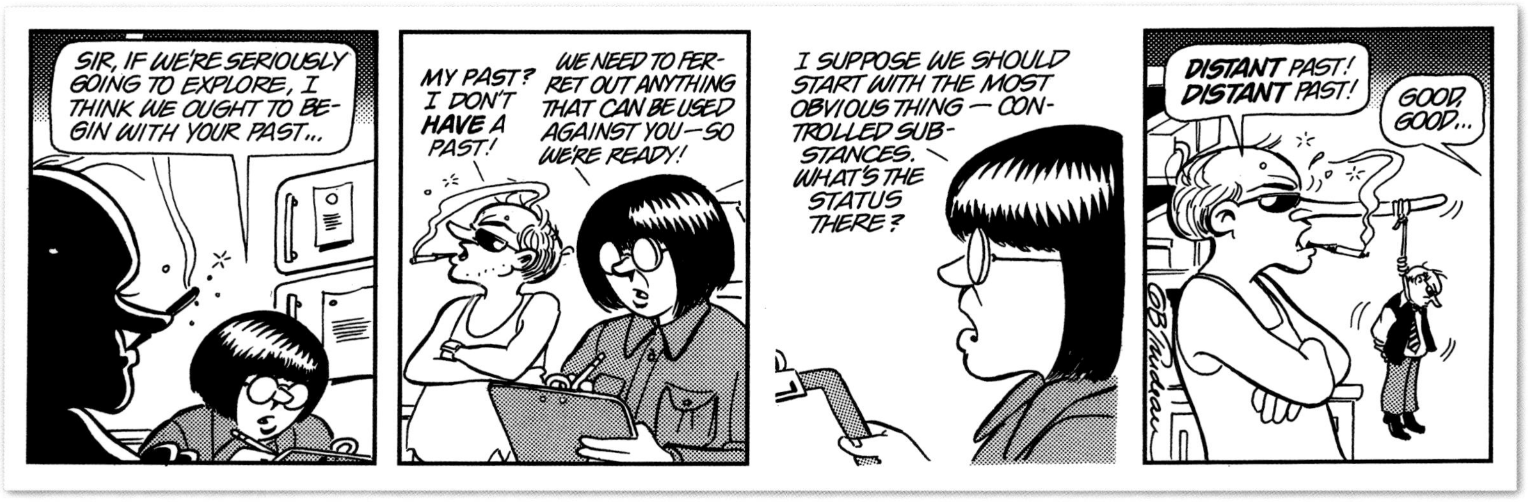
SIR, IF WE'RE SERIOUSLY GOING TO EXPLORE, I THINK WE OUGHT TO BEGIN WITH YOUR PAST...
MY PAST? I DON'T HAVE A PAST!
WE NEED TO FERRET OUT ANYTHING THAT CAN BE USED AGAINST YOU—SO WE'RE READY!
I SUPPOSE WE SHOULD START WITH THE MOST OBVIOUS THING — CONTROLLED SUBSTANCES. WHAT'S THE STATUS THERE?
DISTANT PAST! DISTANT PAST!
GOOD, GOOD...
GB Trudeau

11/30/99

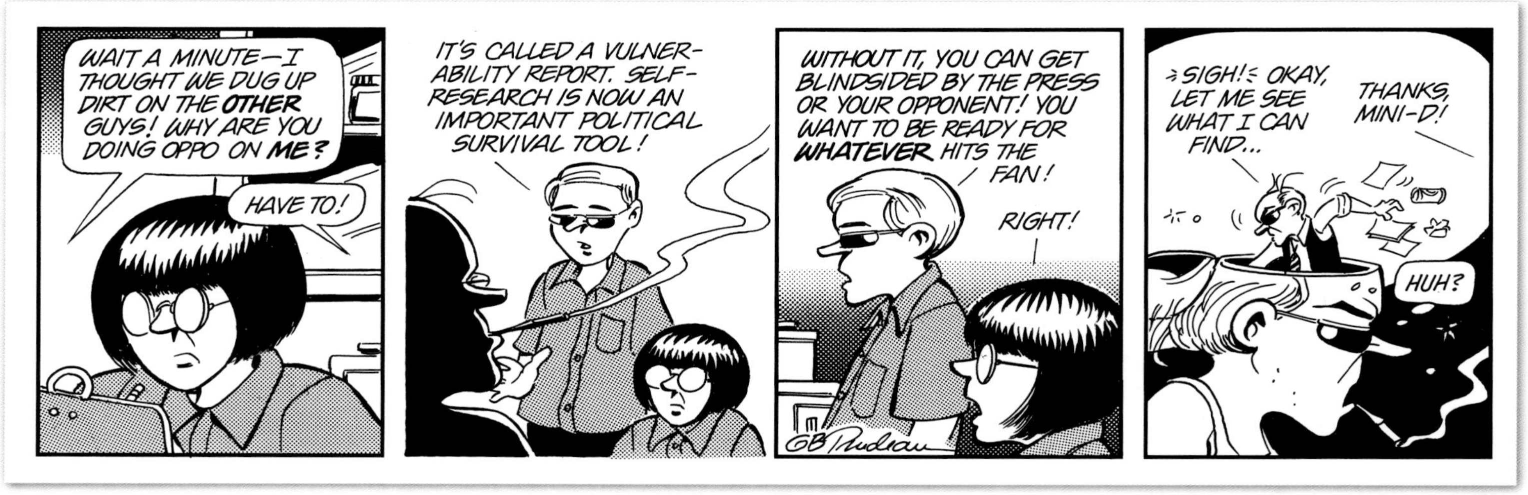
WAIT A MINUTE—I THOUGHT WE DUG UP DIRT ON THE OTHER GUYS! WHY ARE YOU DOING OPPO ON ME?
HAVE TO!
IT'S CALLED A VULNERABILITY REPORT. SELF-RESEARCH IS NOW AN IMPORTANT POLITICAL SURVIVAL TOOL!
WITHOUT IT, YOU CAN GET BLINDSIDED BY THE PRESS OR YOUR OPPONENT! YOU WANT TO BE READY FOR WHATEVER HITS THE FAN!
RIGHT!
GB Trudeau
SIGH! OKAY, LET ME SEE WHAT I CAN FIND...
THANKS, MINI-D!
HUH?

12/1/99

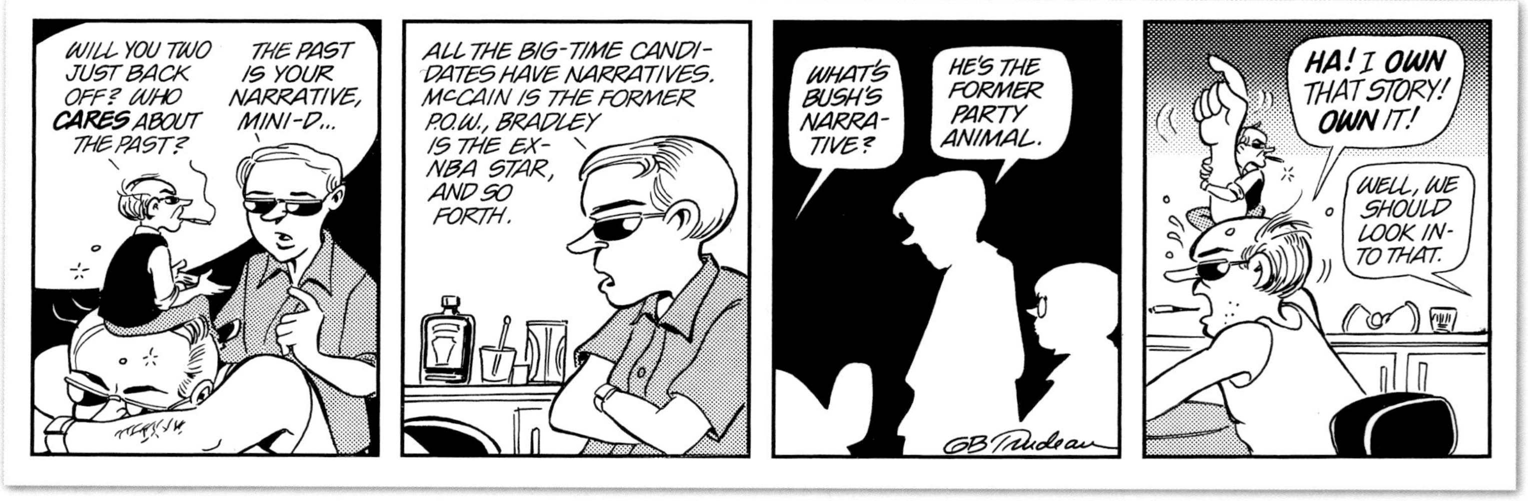
WILL YOU TWO JUST BACK OFF? WHO CARES ABOUT THE PAST?
THE PAST IS YOUR NARRATIVE, MINI-D...
ALL THE BIG-TIME CANDIDATES HAVE NARRATIVES. McCAIN IS THE FORMER P.O.W., BRADLEY IS THE EX-NBA STAR, AND SO FORTH.
WHAT'S BUSH'S NARRATIVE?
HE'S THE FORMER PARTY ANIMAL.
GB Trudeau
HA! I OWN THAT STORY! OWN IT!
WELL, WE SHOULD LOOK INTO THAT.

12/4/99

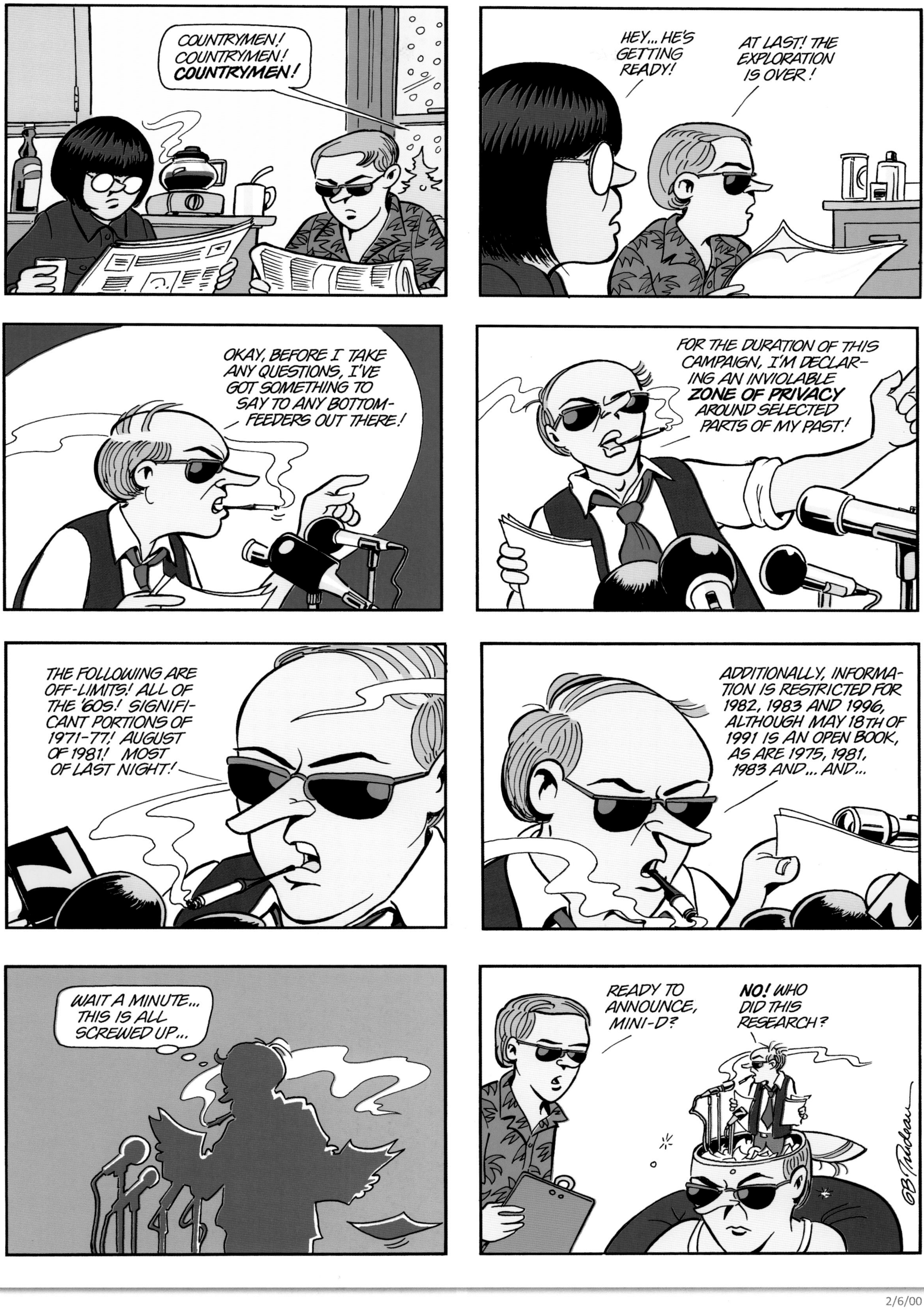
COUNTRYMEN! COUNTRYMEN! COUNTRYMEN!
HEY... HE'S GETTING READY!
AT LAST! THE EXPLORATION IS OVER!
OKAY, BEFORE I TAKE ANY QUESTIONS, I'VE GOT SOMETHING TO SAY TO ANY BOTTOM-FEEDERS OUT THERE!
FOR THE DURATION OF THIS CAMPAIGN, I'M DECLARING AN INVIOLABLE ZONE OF PRIVACY AROUND SELECTED PARTS OF MY PAST!
THE FOLLOWING ARE OFF-LIMITS! ALL OF THE '60S! SIGNIFICANT PORTIONS OF 1971-77! AUGUST OF 1981! MOST OF LAST NIGHT!
ADDITIONALLY, INFORMATION IS RESTRICTED FOR 1982, 1983 AND 1996, ALTHOUGH MAY 18TH OF 1991 IS AN OPEN BOOK, AS ARE 1975, 1981, 1983 AND... AND...
WAIT A MINUTE... THIS IS ALL SCREWED UP...
READY TO ANNOUNCE, MINI-D?
NO! WHO DID THIS RESEARCH?
GB Trudeau

2/6/00

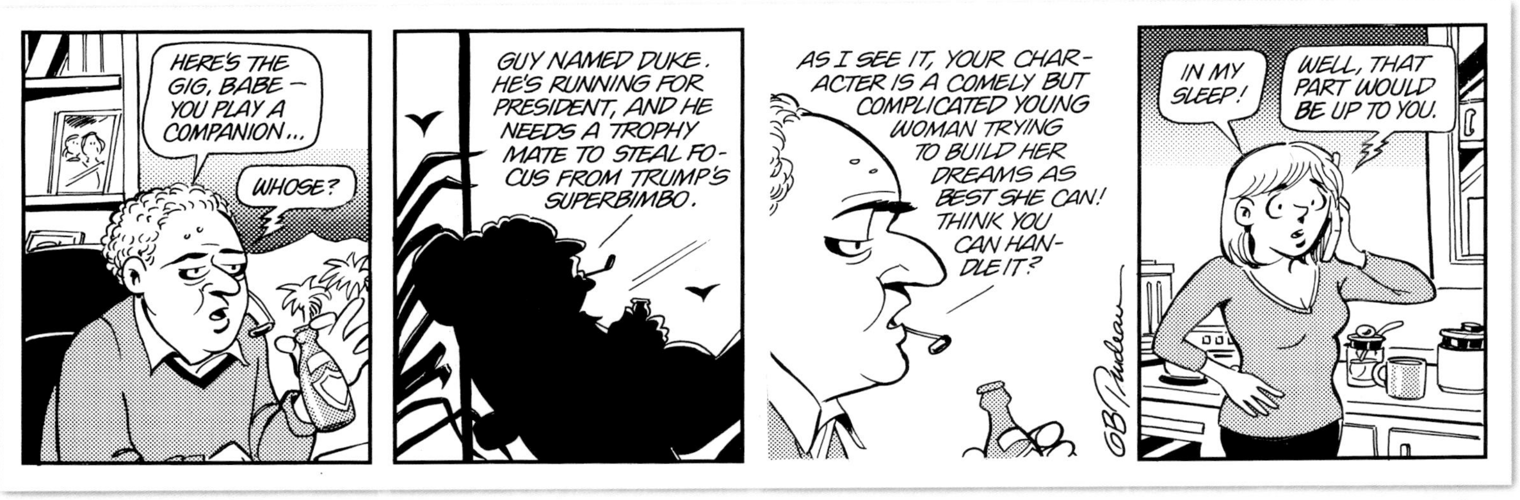
HERE'S THE GIG, BABE — YOU PLAY A COMPANION...
WHOSE?
GUY NAMED DUKE. HE'S RUNNING FOR PRESIDENT, AND HE NEEDS A TROPHY MATE TO STEAL FOCUS FROM TRUMP'S SUPERBIMBO.
AS I SEE IT, YOUR CHARACTER IS A COMELY BUT COMPLICATED YOUNG WOMAN TRYING TO BUILD HER DREAMS AS BEST SHE CAN! THINK YOU CAN HANDLE IT?
IN MY SLEEP!
WELL, THAT PART WOULD BE UP TO YOU.

1/10/00

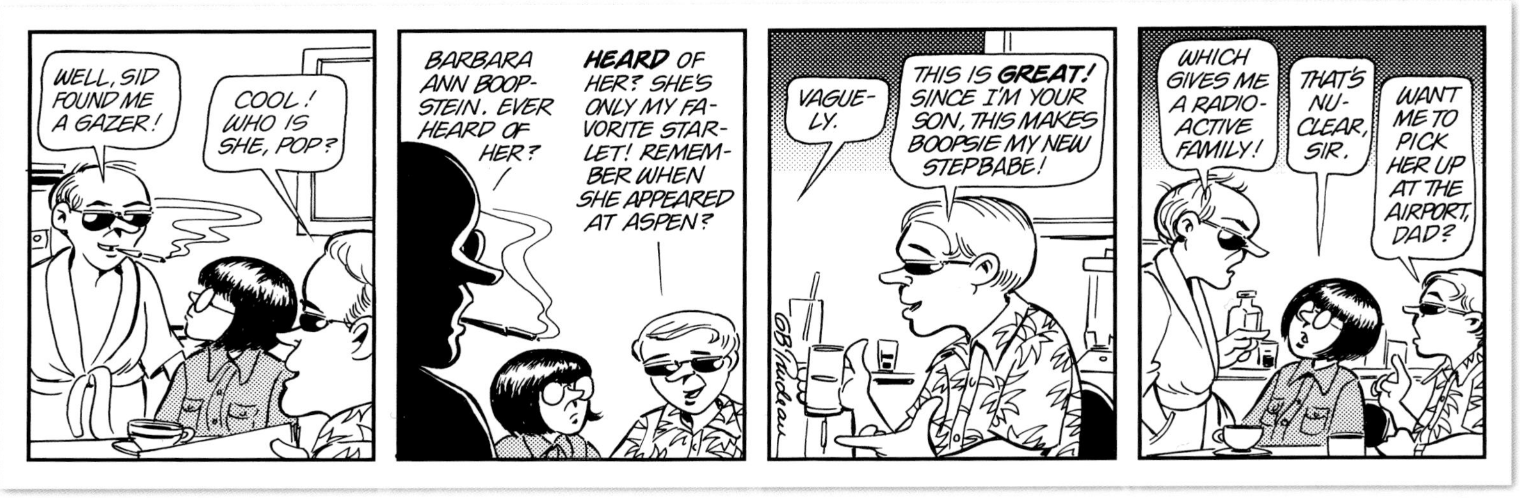
WELL, SID FOUND ME A GAZER!
COOL! WHO IS SHE, POP?
BARBARA ANN BOOPSTEIN. EVER HEARD OF HER?
HEARD OF HER? SHE'S ONLY MY FAVORITE STARLET! REMEMBER WHEN SHE APPEARED AT ASPEN?
VAGUELY.
THIS IS GREAT! SINCE I'M YOUR SON, THIS MAKES BOOPSIE MY NEW STEPBABE!
WHICH GIVES ME A RADIOACTIVE FAMILY!
THAT'S NUCLEAR, SIR.
WANT ME TO PICK HER UP AT THE AIRPORT, DAD?

1/12/00

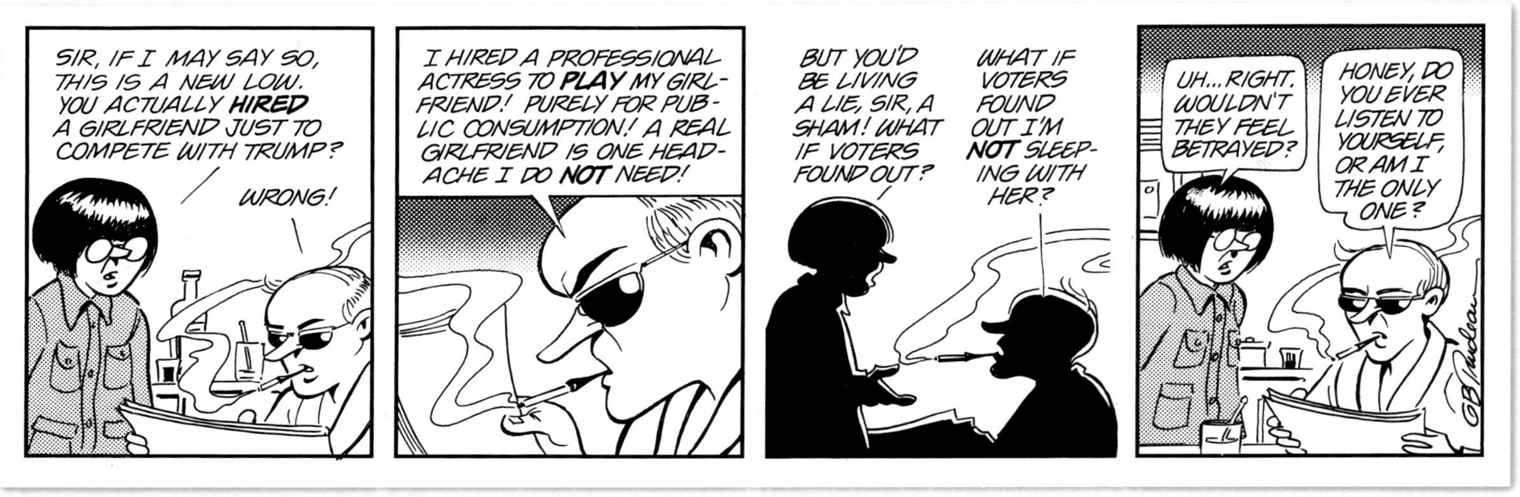
SIR, IF I MAY SAY SO, THIS IS A NEW LOW. YOU ACTUALLY HIRED A GIRLFRIEND JUST TO COMPETE WITH TRUMP?
WRONG!
I HIRED A PROFESSIONAL ACTRESS TO PLAY MY GIRLFRIEND! PURELY FOR PUBLIC CONSUMPTION! A REAL GIRLFRIEND IS ONE HEADACHE I DO NOT NEED!
BUT YOU'D BE LIVING A LIE, SIR, A SHAM! WHAT IF VOTERS FOUND OUT?
WHAT IF VOTERS FOUND OUT I'M NOT SLEEPING WITH HER?
UH...RIGHT. WOULDN'T THEY FEEL BETRAYED?
HONEY, DO YOU EVER LISTEN TO YOURSELF, OR AM I THE ONLY ONE?

1/13/00

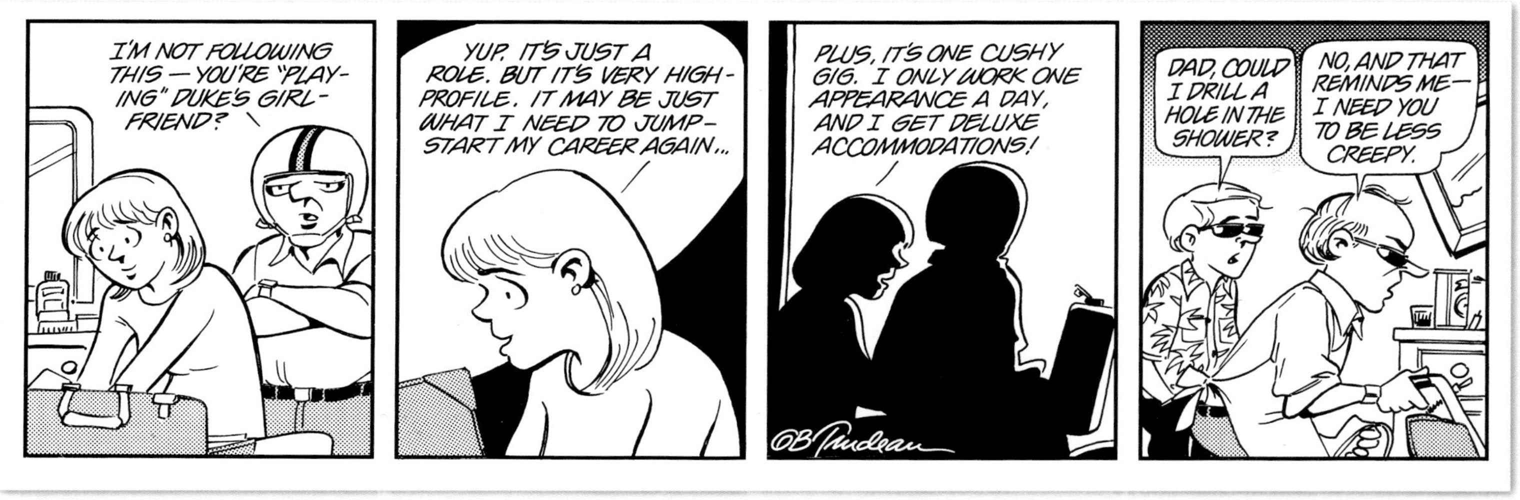
I'M NOT FOLLOWING THIS — YOU'RE "PLAYING" DUKE'S GIRLFRIEND?
YUP. IT'S JUST A ROLE. BUT IT'S VERY HIGH-PROFILE. IT MAY BE JUST WHAT I NEED TO JUMP-START MY CAREER AGAIN...
PLUS, IT'S ONE CUSHY GIG. I ONLY WORK ONE APPEARANCE A DAY, AND I GET DELUXE ACCOMMODATIONS!
DAD, COULD I DRILL A HOLE IN THE SHOWER?
NO, AND THAT REMINDS ME — I NEED YOU TO BE LESS CREEPY.

1/15/00

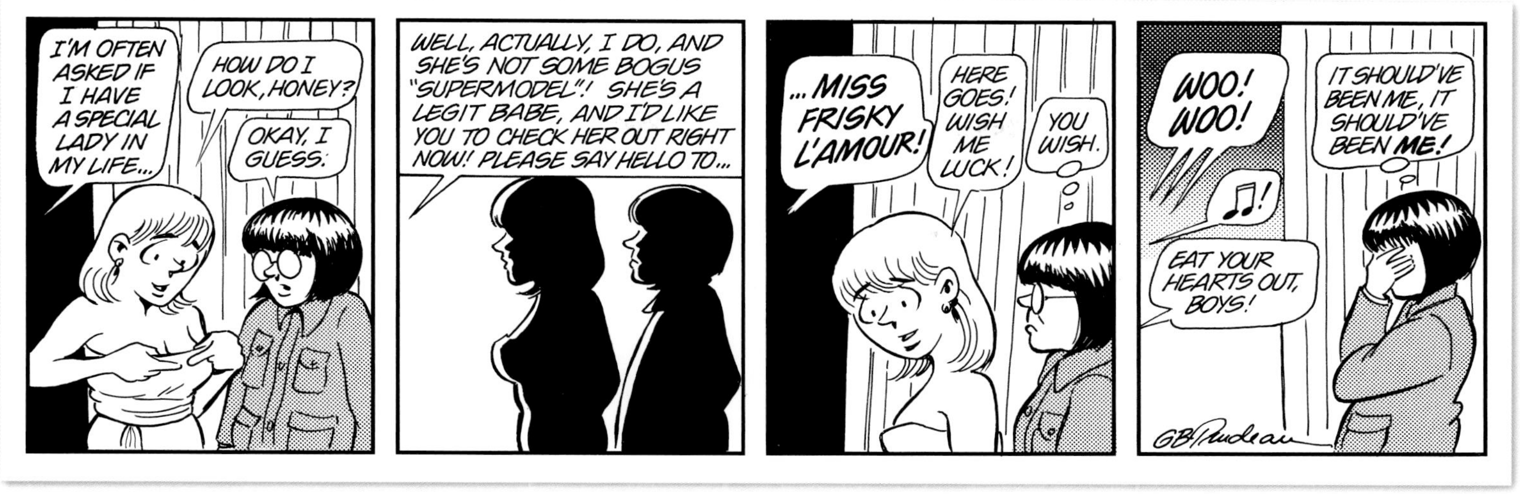
I'M OFTEN ASKED IF I HAVE A SPECIAL LADY IN MY LIFE...
HOW DO I LOOK, HONEY?
OKAY, I GUESS.
WELL, ACTUALLY, I DO, AND SHE'S NOT SOME BOGUS "SUPERMODEL"! SHE'S A LEGIT BABE, AND I'D LIKE YOU TO CHECK HER OUT RIGHT NOW! PLEASE SAY HELLO TO...
...MISS FRISKY L'AMOUR!
HERE GOES! WISH ME LUCK!
YOU WISH.
WOO! WOO!
♫!
EAT YOUR HEARTS OUT, BOYS!
IT SHOULD'VE BEEN ME, IT SHOULD'VE BEEN ME!
GBTrudeau

2/21/00

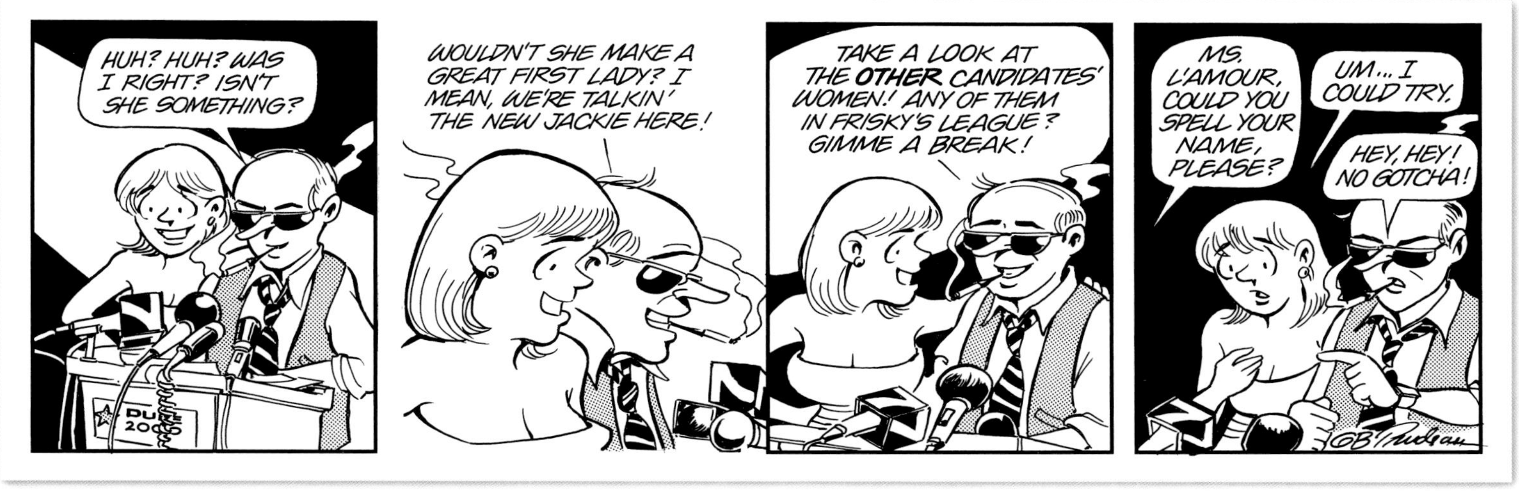
HUH? HUH? WAS I RIGHT? ISN'T SHE SOMETHING?
DUKE 2000
WOULDN'T SHE MAKE A GREAT FIRST LADY? I MEAN, WE'RE TALKIN' THE NEW JACKIE HERE!
TAKE A LOOK AT THE OTHER CANDIDATES' WOMEN! ANY OF THEM IN FRISKY'S LEAGUE? GIMME A BREAK!
MS. L'AMOUR, COULD YOU SPELL YOUR NAME, PLEASE?
UM... I COULD TRY.
HEY, HEY! NO GOTCHA!
GBTrudeau

2/22/00

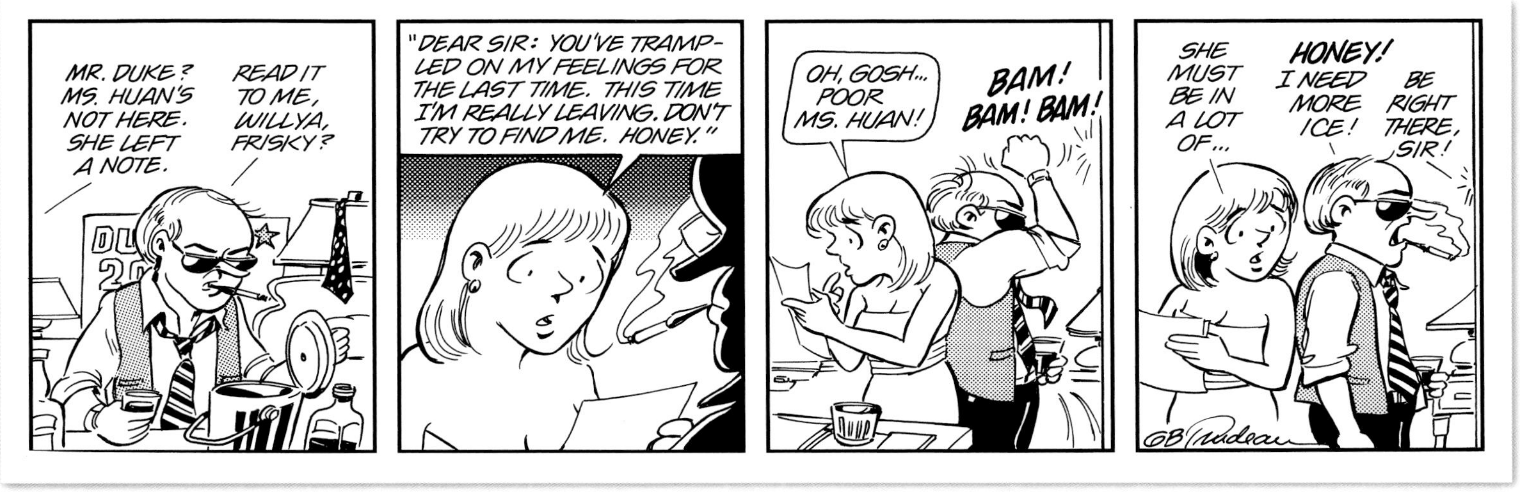
MR. DUKE? MS. HUAN'S NOT HERE. SHE LEFT A NOTE.
READ IT TO ME, WILLYA, FRISKY?
"DEAR SIR: YOU'VE TRAMPLED ON MY FEELINGS FOR THE LAST TIME. THIS TIME I'M REALLY LEAVING. DON'T TRY TO FIND ME. HONEY."
OH, GOSH... POOR MS. HUAN!
BAM! BAM! BAM!
SHE MUST BE IN A LOT OF...
HONEY! I NEED MORE ICE!
BE RIGHT THERE, SIR!
GBTrudeau

2/24/00

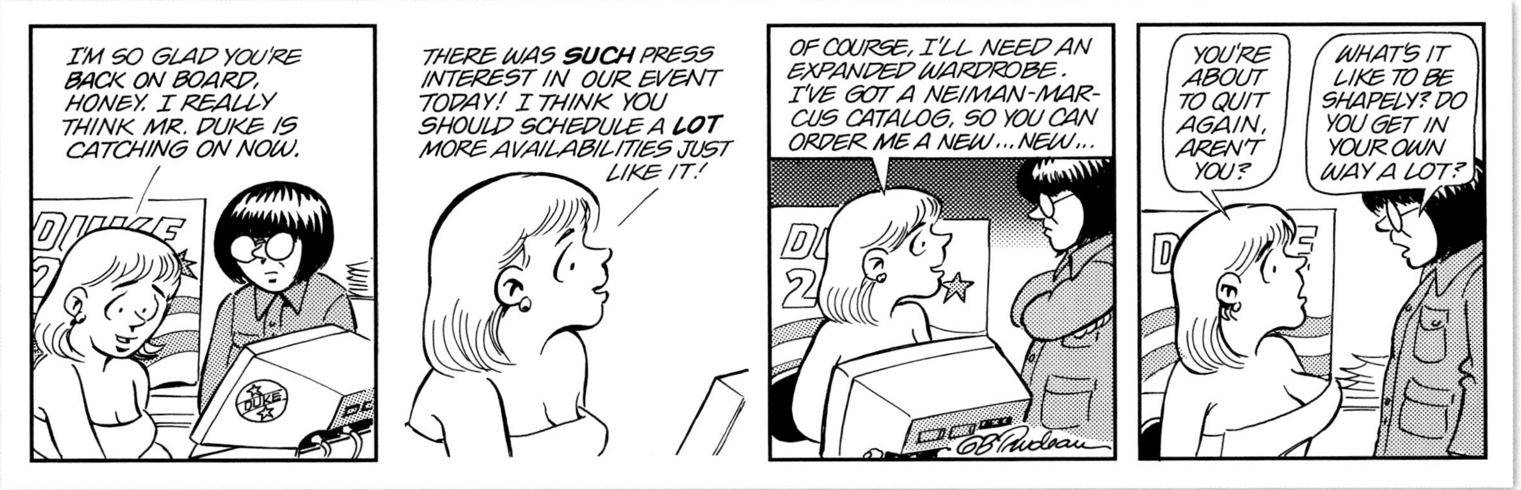
I'M SO GLAD YOU'RE BACK ON BOARD, HONEY. I REALLY THINK MR. DUKE IS CATCHING ON NOW.
THERE WAS SUCH PRESS INTEREST IN OUR EVENT TODAY! I THINK YOU SHOULD SCHEDULE A LOT MORE AVAILABILITIES JUST LIKE IT!
OF COURSE, I'LL NEED AN EXPANDED WARDROBE. I'VE GOT A NEIMAN-MARCUS CATALOG, SO YOU CAN ORDER ME A NEW... NEW...
YOU'RE ABOUT TO QUIT AGAIN, AREN'T YOU?
WHAT'S IT LIKE TO BE SHAPELY? DO YOU GET IN YOUR OWN WAY A LOT?
GBTrudeau

2/25/00

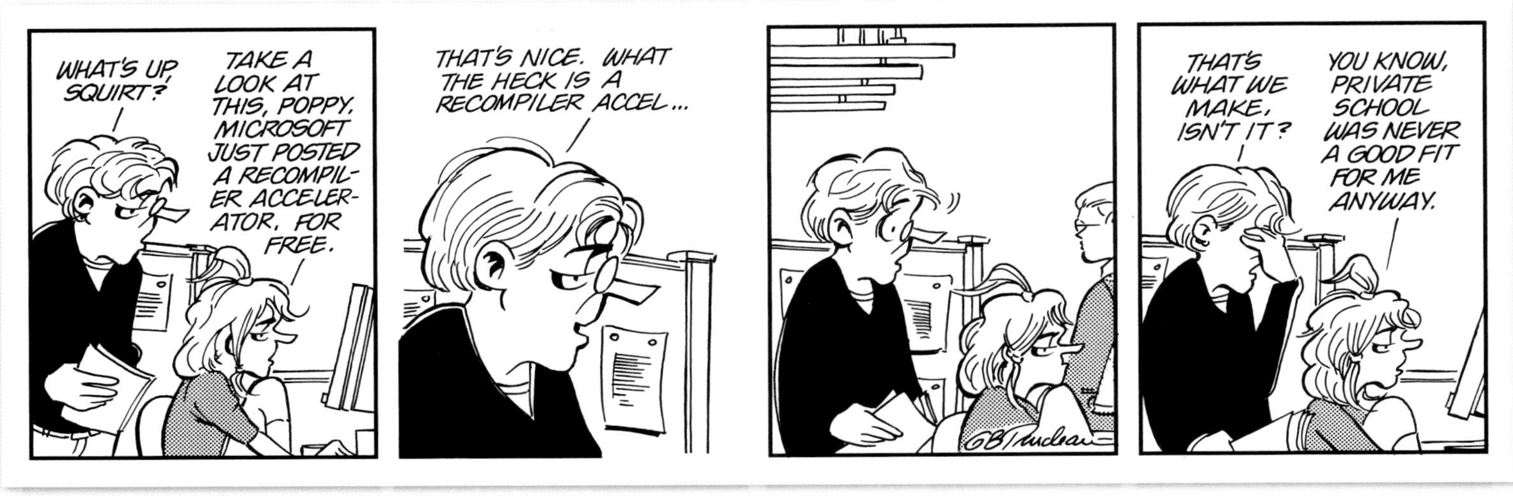
WHAT'S UP, SQUIRT?
TAKE A LOOK AT THIS, POPPY. MICROSOFT JUST POSTED A RECOMPILER ACCELERATOR. FOR FREE.
THAT'S NICE. WHAT THE HECK IS A RECOMPILER ACCEL...
THAT'S WHAT WE MAKE, ISN'T IT?
YOU KNOW, PRIVATE SCHOOL WAS NEVER A GOOD FIT FOR ME ANYWAY.
©B Trudeau

1/24/00

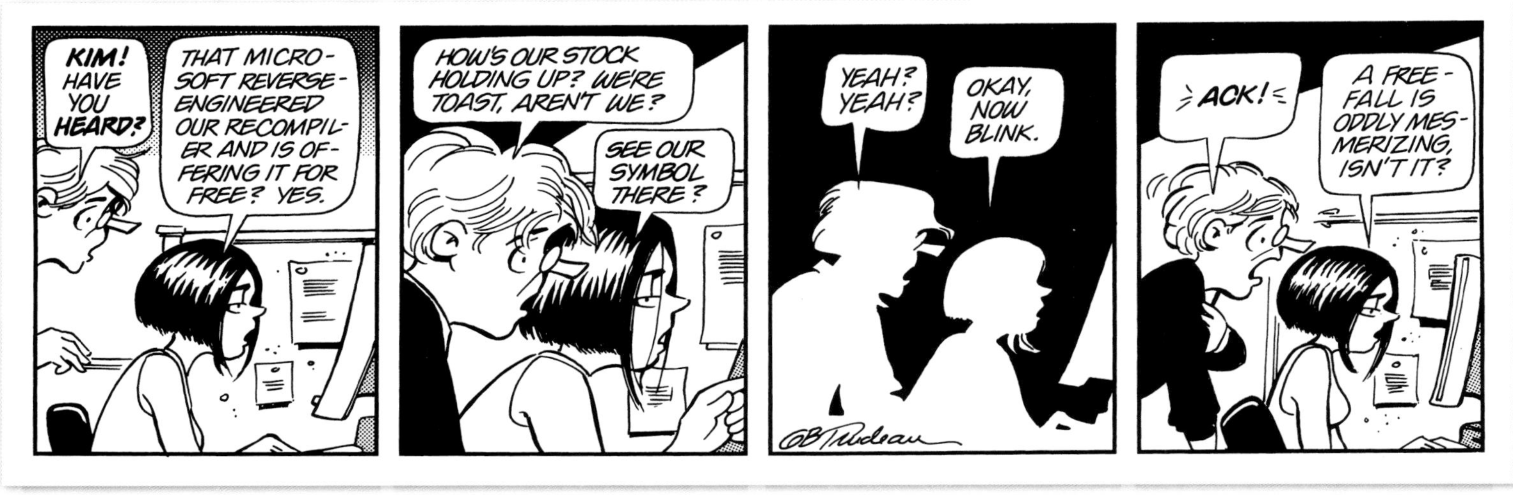
KIM! HAVE YOU HEARD?
THAT MICROSOFT REVERSE-ENGINEERED OUR RECOMPILER AND IS OFFERING IT FOR FREE? YES.
HOW'S OUR STOCK HOLDING UP? WE'RE TOAST, AREN'T WE?
SEE OUR SYMBOL THERE?
YEAH? YEAH?
OKAY, NOW BLINK.
©B Trudeau
>ACK!<
A FREE-FALL IS ODDLY MESMERIZING, ISN'T IT?

1/25/00

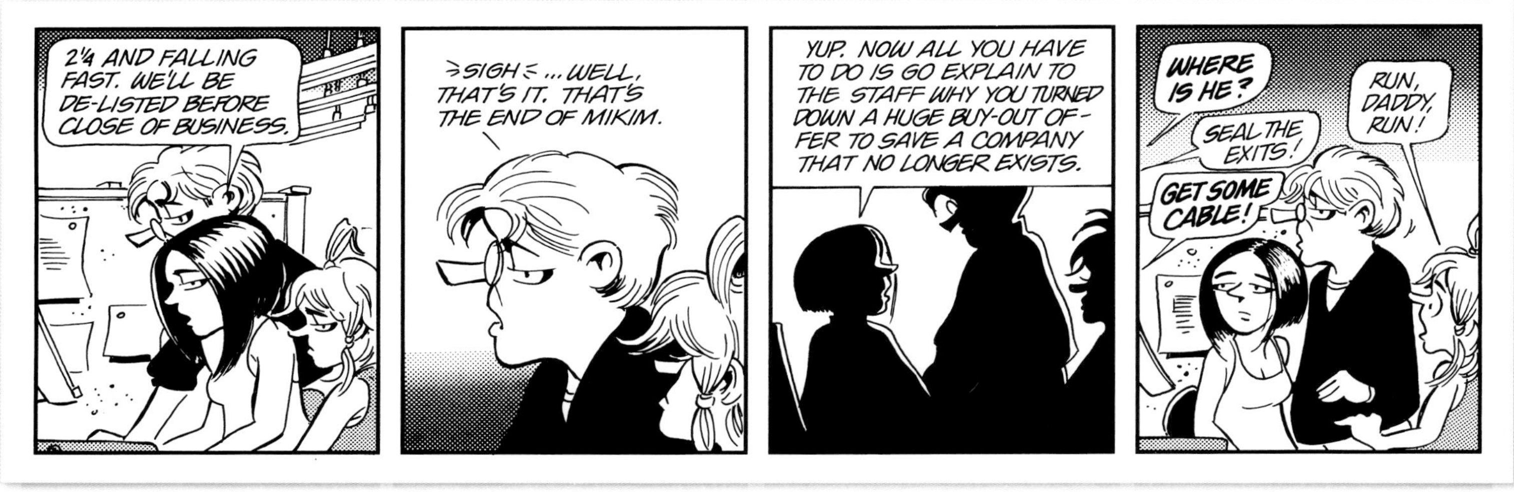
2¼ AND FALLING FAST. WE'LL BE DE-LISTED BEFORE CLOSE OF BUSINESS.
>SIGH< ...WELL, THAT'S IT. THAT'S THE END OF MIKIM.
YUP. NOW ALL YOU HAVE TO DO IS GO EXPLAIN TO THE STAFF WHY YOU TURNED DOWN A HUGE BUY-OUT OFFER TO SAVE A COMPANY THAT NO LONGER EXISTS.
WHERE IS HE?
SEAL THE EXITS!
GET SOME CABLE!
RUN, DADDY, RUN!

1/27/00

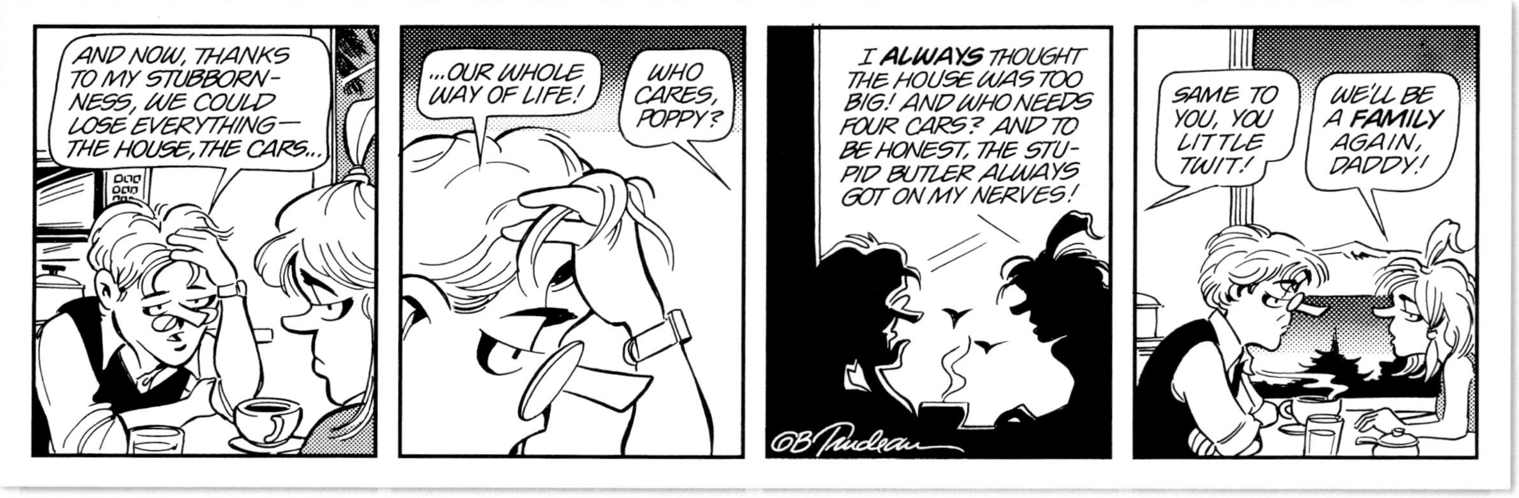
AND NOW, THANKS TO MY STUBBORNNESS, WE COULD LOSE EVERYTHING—THE HOUSE, THE CARS...
...OUR WHOLE WAY OF LIFE!
WHO CARES, POPPY?
I ALWAYS THOUGHT THE HOUSE WAS TOO BIG! AND WHO NEEDS FOUR CARS? AND TO BE HONEST, THE STUPID BUTLER ALWAYS GOT ON MY NERVES!
©B Trudeau
SAME TO YOU, YOU LITTLE TWIT!
WE'LL BE A FAMILY AGAIN, DADDY!

1/29/00

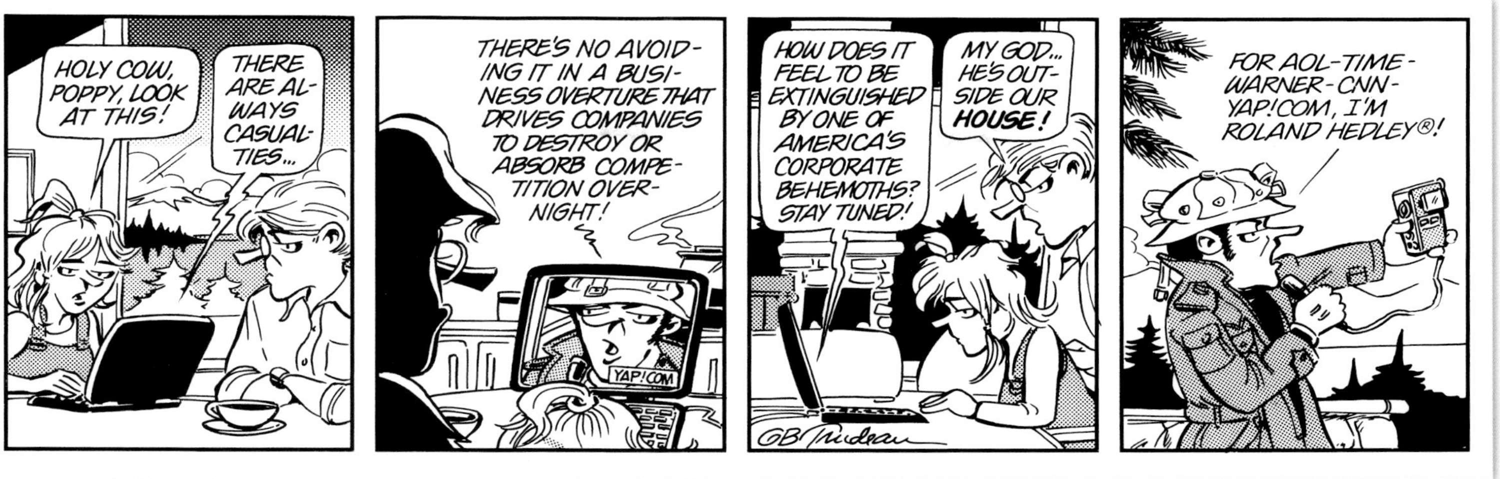
HOLY COW, POPPY, LOOK AT THIS!
THERE ARE ALWAYS CASUALTIES...
THERE'S NO AVOIDING IT IN A BUSINESS OVERTURE THAT DRIVES COMPANIES TO DESTROY OR ABSORB COMPETITION OVERNIGHT!
YAP!COM
HOW DOES IT FEEL TO BE EXTINGUISHED BY ONE OF AMERICA'S CORPORATE BEHEMOTHS? STAY TUNED!
MY GOD... HE'S OUTSIDE OUR HOUSE!
FOR AOL-TIME-WARNER-CNN-YAP!COM, I'M ROLAND HEDLEY®!
GB Trudeau

1/31/00

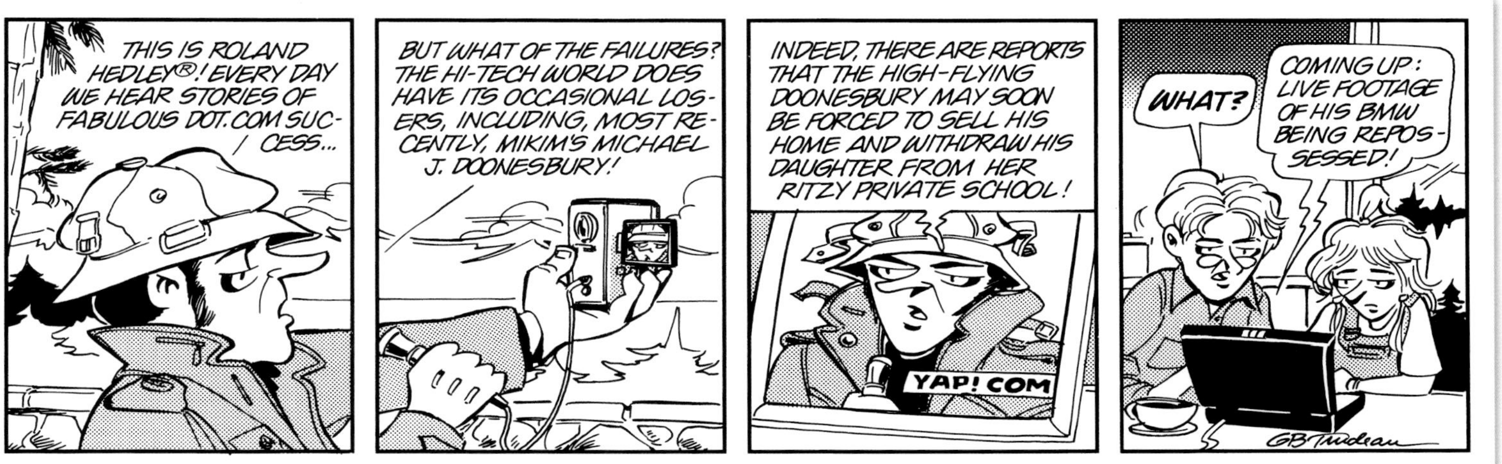
THIS IS ROLAND HEDLEY®! EVERY DAY WE HEAR STORIES OF FABULOUS DOT.COM SUCCESS...
BUT WHAT OF THE FAILURES? THE HI-TECH WORLD DOES HAVE ITS OCCASIONAL LOSERS, INCLUDING, MOST RECENTLY, MIKIM'S MICHAEL J. DOONESBURY!
INDEED, THERE ARE REPORTS THAT THE HIGH-FLYING DOONESBURY MAY SOON BE FORCED TO SELL HIS HOME AND WITHDRAW HIS DAUGHTER FROM HER RITZY PRIVATE SCHOOL!
YAP!COM
WHAT?
COMING UP: LIVE FOOTAGE OF HIS BMW BEING REPOSSESSED!
GB Trudeau

2/1/00

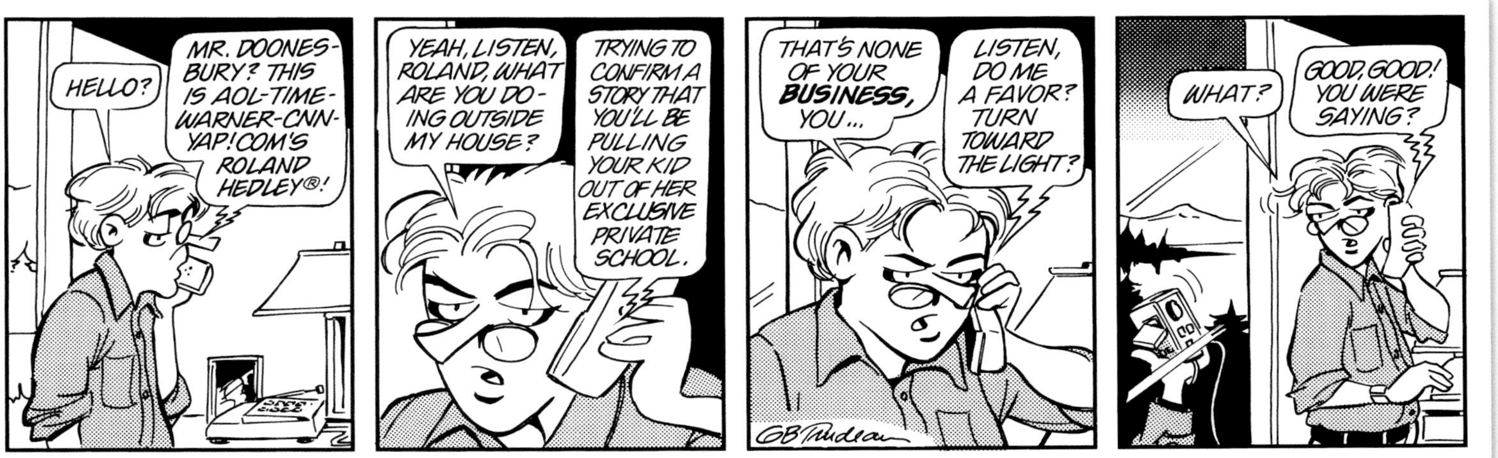
HELLO?
MR. DOONESBURY? THIS IS AOL-TIME-WARNER-CNN-YAP!COM'S ROLAND HEDLEY®!
YEAH, LISTEN, ROLAND, WHAT ARE YOU DOING OUTSIDE MY HOUSE?
TRYING TO CONFIRM A STORY THAT YOU'LL BE PULLING YOUR KID OUT OF HER EXCLUSIVE PRIVATE SCHOOL.
THAT'S NONE OF YOUR BUSINESS, YOU...
LISTEN, DO ME A FAVOR? TURN TOWARD THE LIGHT?
WHAT?
GOOD, GOOD! YOU WERE SAYING?
GB Trudeau

2/2/00

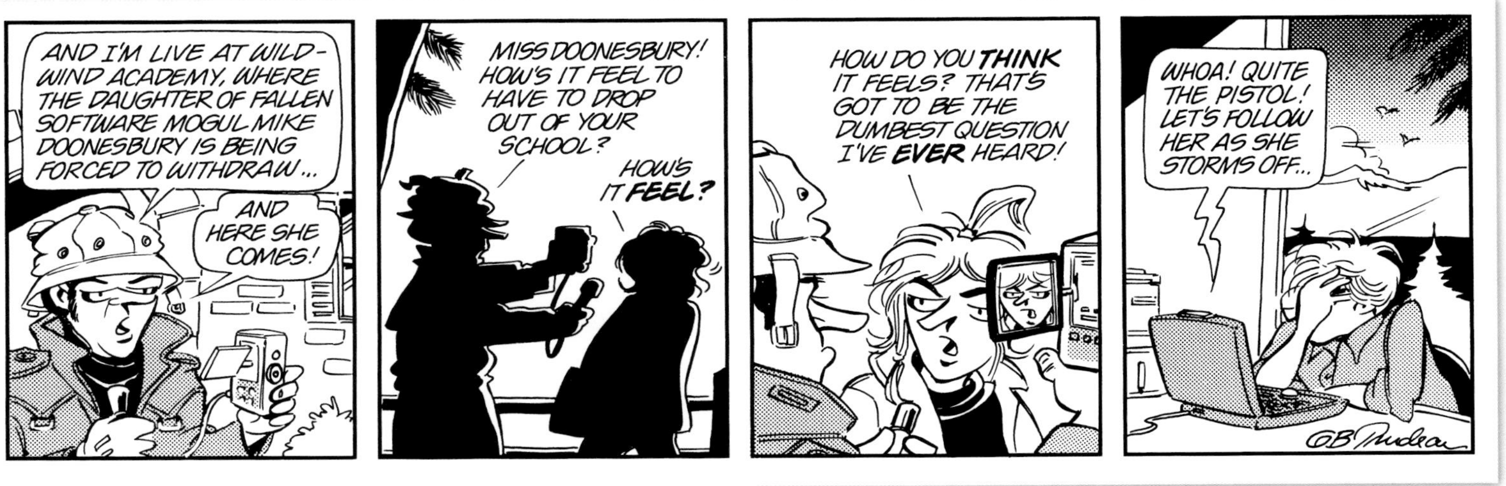
AND I'M LIVE AT WILDWIND ACADEMY, WHERE THE DAUGHTER OF FALLEN SOFTWARE MOGUL MIKE DOONESBURY IS BEING FORCED TO WITHDRAW...
AND HERE SHE COMES!
MISS DOONESBURY! HOW'S IT FEEL TO HAVE TO DROP OUT OF YOUR SCHOOL?
HOW'S IT FEEL?
HOW DO YOU THINK IT FEELS? THAT'S GOT TO BE THE DUMBEST QUESTION I'VE EVER HEARD!
WHOA! QUITE THE PISTOL! LET'S FOLLOW HER AS SHE STORMS OFF...
GB Trudeau

2/3/00

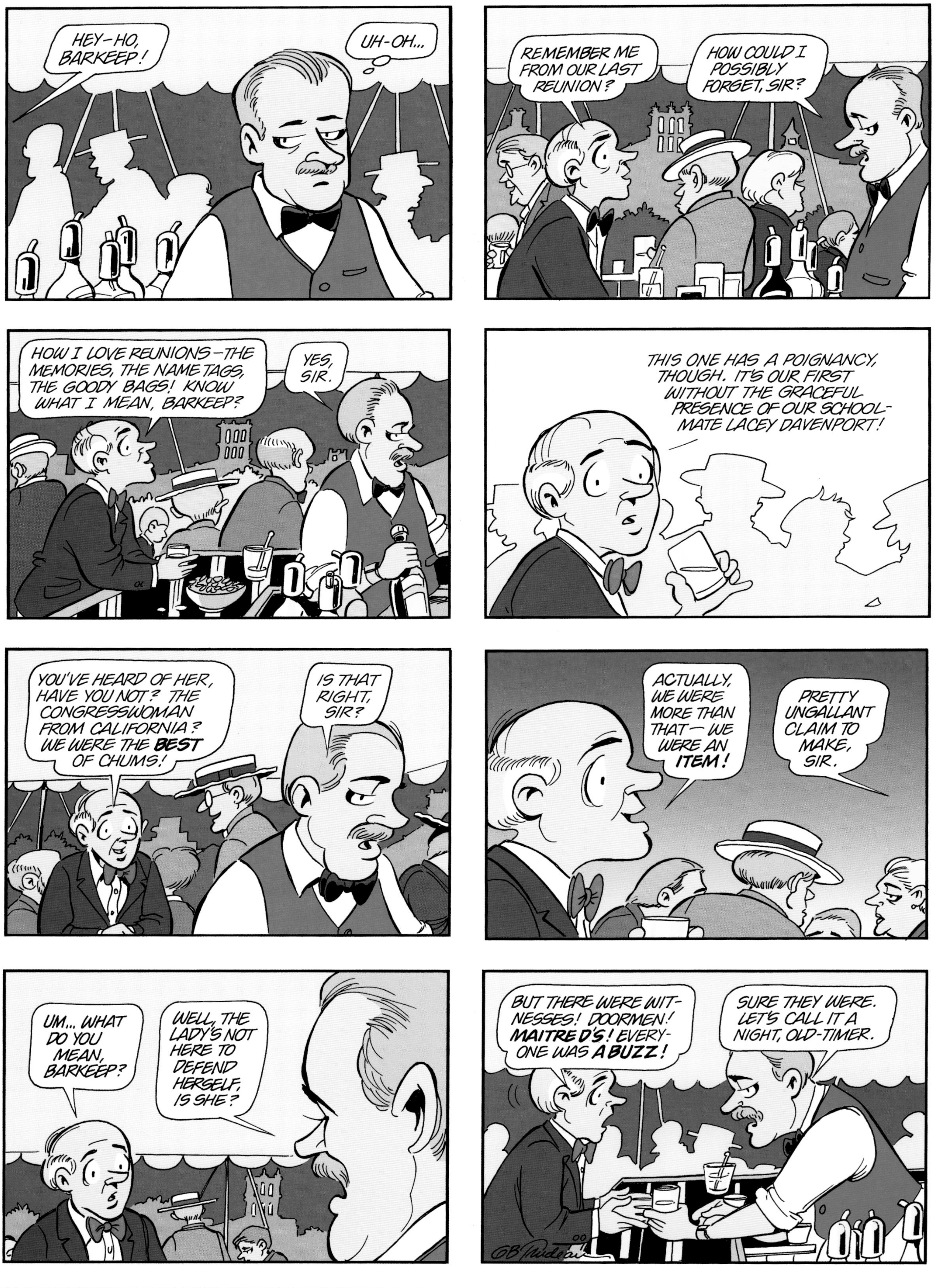
HEY-HO, BARKEEP!
UH-OH...
REMEMBER ME FROM OUR LAST REUNION?
HOW COULD I POSSIBLY FORGET, SIR?
HOW I LOVE REUNIONS—THE MEMORIES, THE NAME TAGS, THE GOODY BAGS! KNOW WHAT I MEAN, BARKEEP?
YES, SIR.
THIS ONE HAS A POIGNANCY, THOUGH. IT'S OUR FIRST WITHOUT THE GRACEFUL PRESENCE OF OUR SCHOOL-MATE LACEY DAVENPORT!
YOU'VE HEARD OF HER, HAVE YOU NOT? THE CONGRESSWOMAN FROM CALIFORNIA? WE WERE THE BEST OF CHUMS!
IS THAT RIGHT, SIR?
ACTUALLY, WE WERE MORE THAN THAT—WE WERE AN ITEM!
PRETTY UNGALLANT CLAIM TO MAKE, SIR.
UM... WHAT DO YOU MEAN, BARKEEP?
WELL, THE LADY'S NOT HERE TO DEFEND HERSELF, IS SHE?
BUT THERE WERE WITNESSES! DOORMEN! MAITRE D'S! EVERYONE WAS A BUZZ!
SURE THEY WERE. LET'S CALL IT A NIGHT, OLD-TIMER.
GB Trudeau

5/14/00

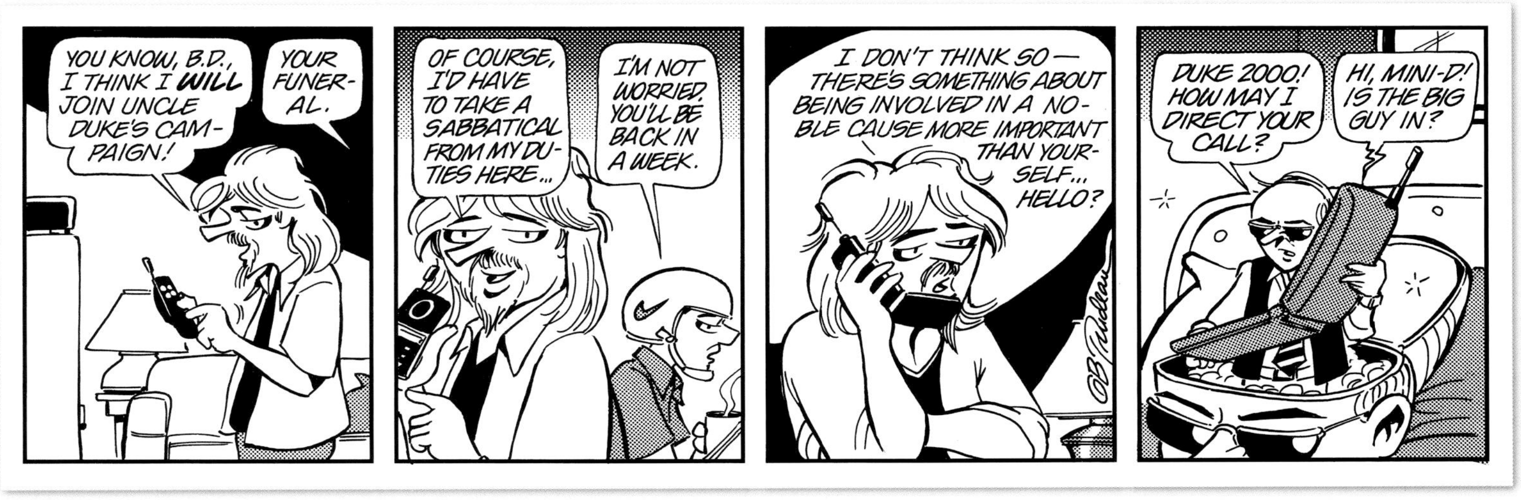
YOU KNOW, B.D., I THINK I WILL JOIN UNCLE DUKE'S CAMPAIGN!
YOUR FUNERAL.
OF COURSE, I'D HAVE TO TAKE A SABBATICAL FROM MY DUTIES HERE...
I'M NOT WORRIED. YOU'LL BE BACK IN A WEEK.
I DON'T THINK SO — THERE'S SOMETHING ABOUT BEING INVOLVED IN A NOBLE CAUSE MORE IMPORTANT THAN YOURSELF... HELLO?
DUKE 2000! HOW MAY I DIRECT YOUR CALL?
HI, MINI-D! IS THE BIG GUY IN?

4/20/00

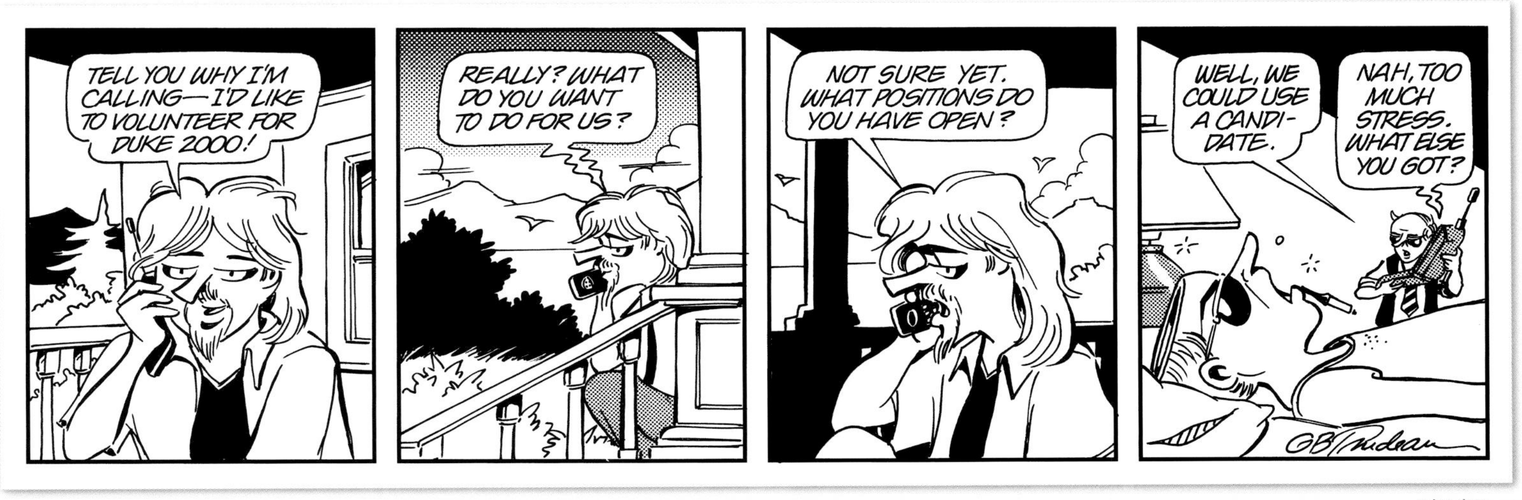
TELL YOU WHY I'M CALLING—I'D LIKE TO VOLUNTEER FOR DUKE 2000!
REALLY? WHAT DO YOU WANT TO DO FOR US?
NOT SURE YET. WHAT POSITIONS DO YOU HAVE OPEN?
WELL, WE COULD USE A CANDIDATE.
NAH, TOO MUCH STRESS. WHAT ELSE YOU GOT?

4/21/00

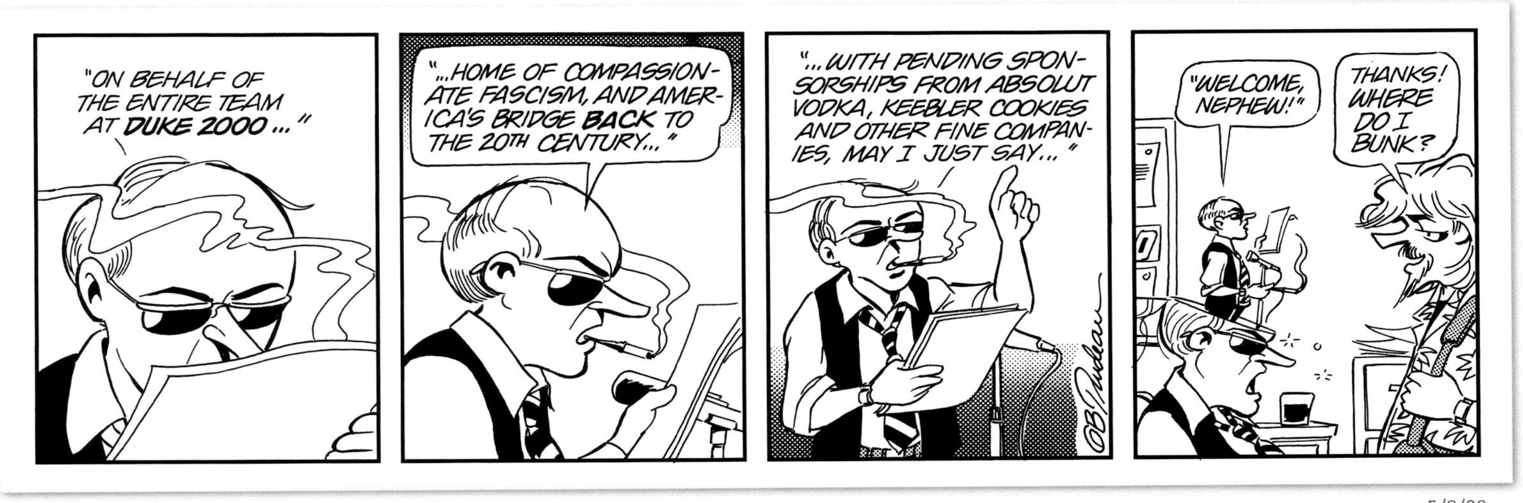
"ON BEHALF OF THE ENTIRE TEAM AT DUKE 2000..."
"...HOME OF COMPASSIONATE FASCISM, AND AMERICA'S BRIDGE BACK TO THE 20TH CENTURY..."
"...WITH PENDING SPONSORSHIPS FROM ABSOLUT VODKA, KEEBLER COOKIES AND OTHER FINE COMPANIES, MAY I JUST SAY..."
"WELCOME, NEPHEW!"
THANKS! WHERE DO I BUNK?

5/8/00

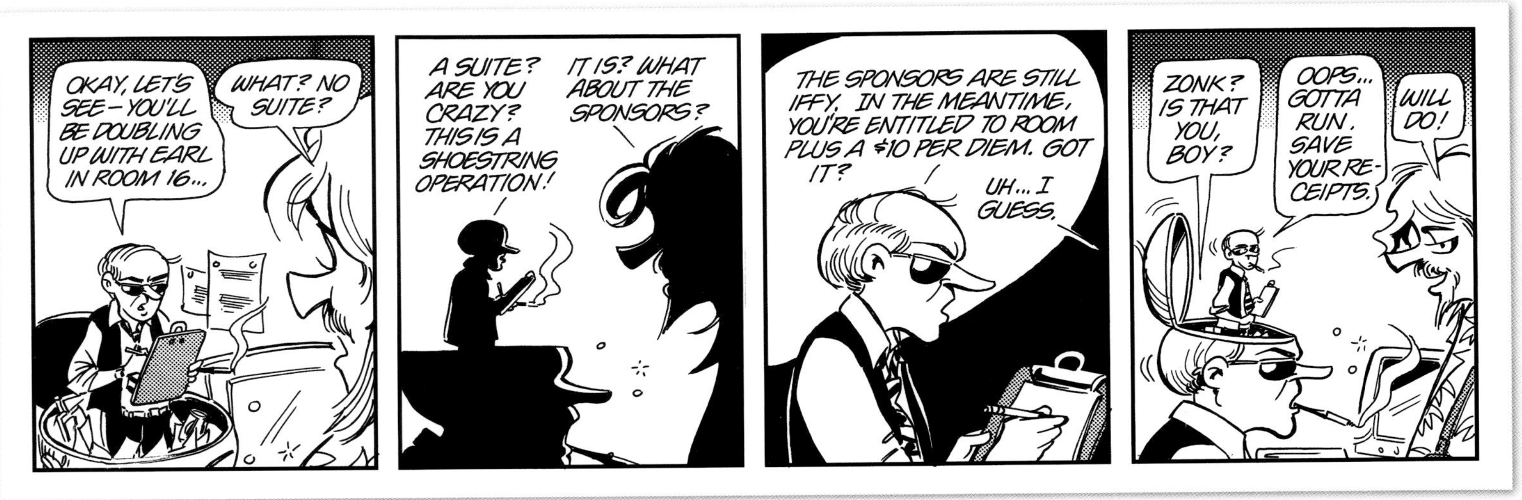
OKAY, LET'S SEE—YOU'LL BE DOUBLING UP WITH EARL IN ROOM 16...
WHAT? NO SUITE?
A SUITE? ARE YOU CRAZY? THIS IS A SHOESTRING OPERATION!
IT IS? WHAT ABOUT THE SPONSORS?
THE SPONSORS ARE STILL IFFY. IN THE MEANTIME, YOU'RE ENTITLED TO ROOM PLUS A $10 PER DIEM. GOT IT?
UH... I GUESS.
ZONK? IS THAT YOU, BOY?
OOPS... GOTTA RUN. SAVE YOUR RECEIPTS.
WILL DO!

5/9/00

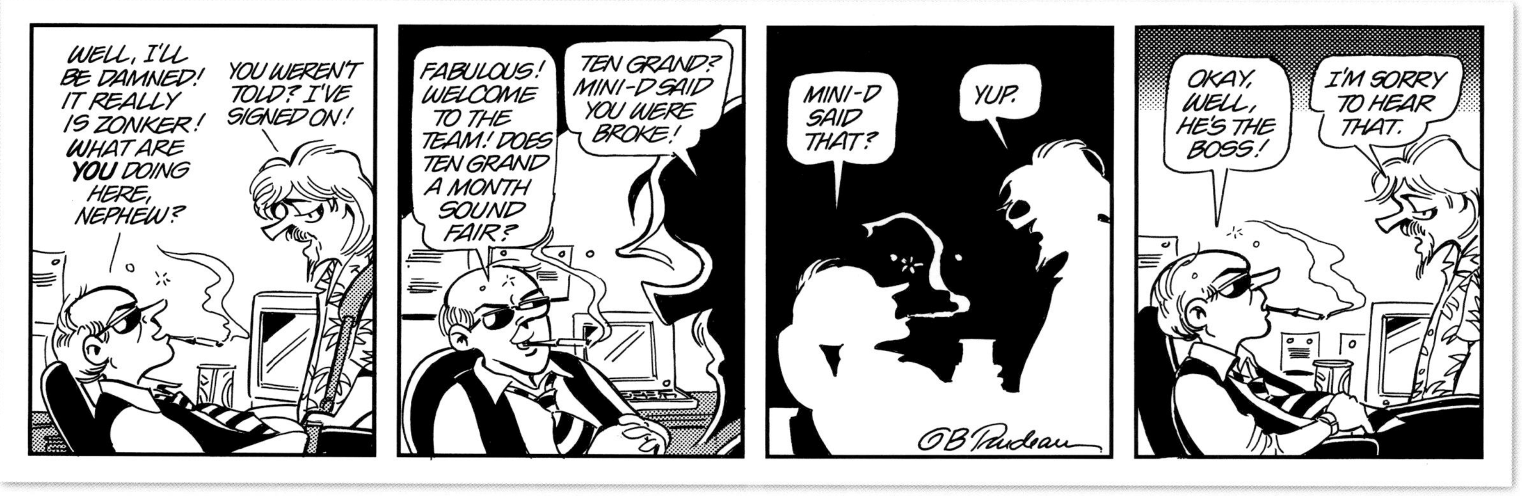
WELL, I'LL BE DAMNED! IT REALLY IS ZONKER! WHAT ARE YOU DOING HERE, NEPHEW?
YOU WEREN'T TOLD? I'VE SIGNED ON!
FABULOUS! WELCOME TO THE TEAM! DOES TEN GRAND A MONTH SOUND FAIR?
TEN GRAND? MINI-D SAID YOU WERE BROKE!
MINI-D SAID THAT?
YUP.
OKAY. WELL, HE'S THE BOSS!
I'M SORRY TO HEAR THAT.

5/10/00

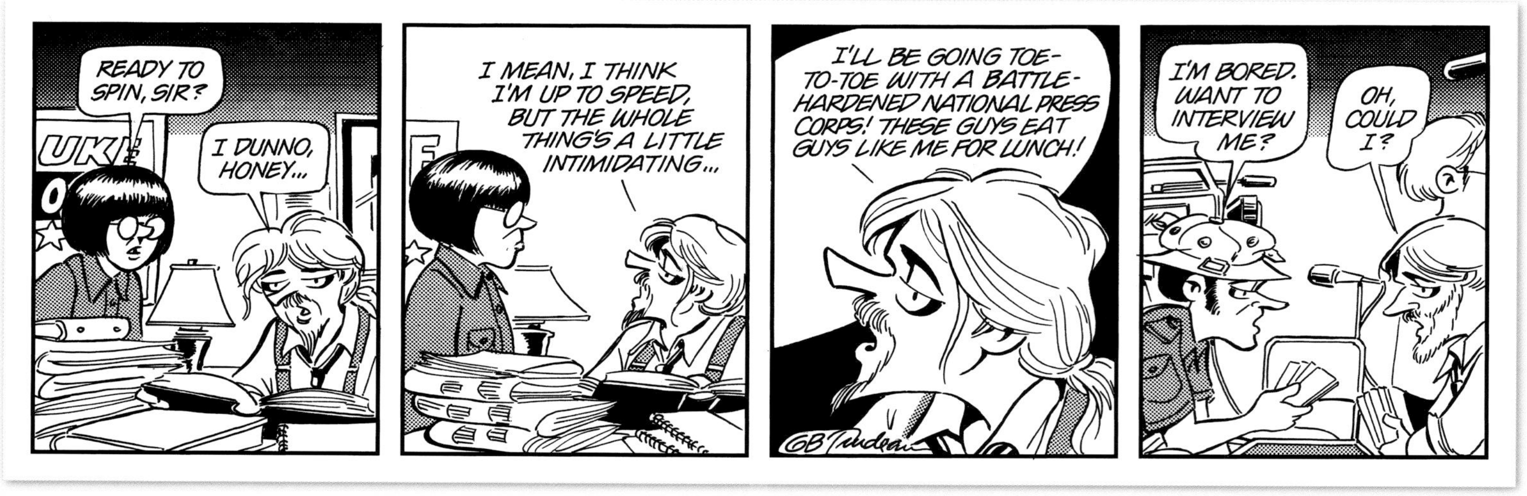
READY TO SPIN, SIR?
I DUNNO, HONEY...
I MEAN, I THINK I'M UP TO SPEED, BUT THE WHOLE THING'S A LITTLE INTIMIDATING...
I'LL BE GOING TOE-TO-TOE WITH A BATTLE-HARDENED NATIONAL PRESS CORPS! THESE GUYS EAT GUYS LIKE ME FOR LUNCH!
I'M BORED. WANT TO INTERVIEW ME?
OH, COULD I?

6/20/00

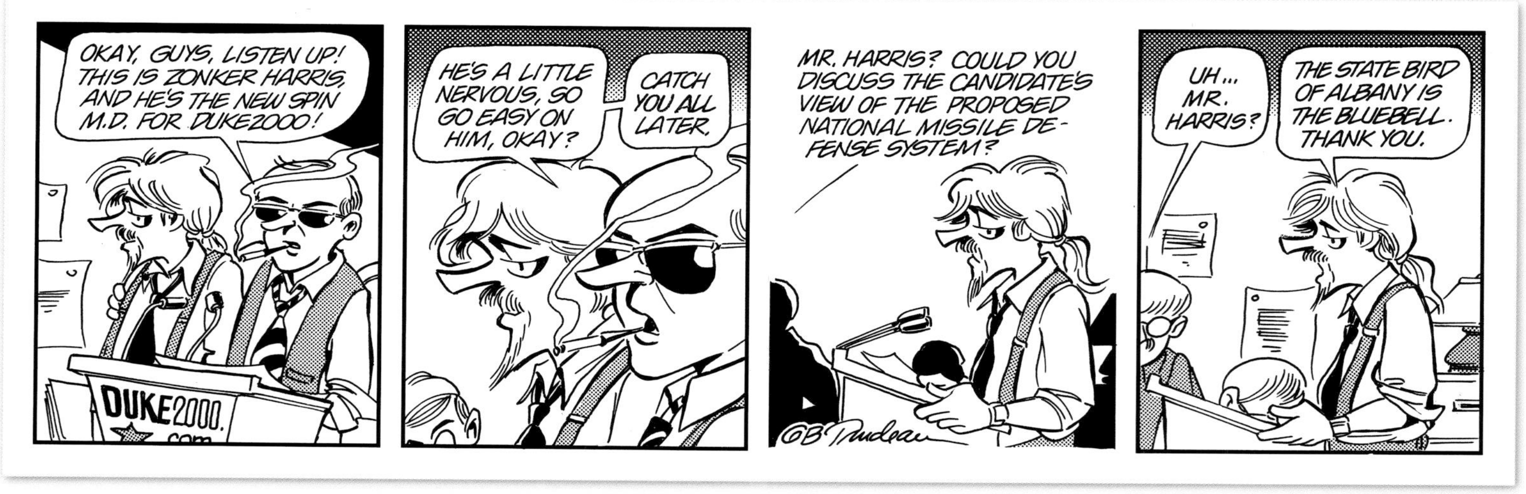
OKAY, GUYS, LISTEN UP! THIS IS ZONKER HARRIS, AND HE'S THE NEW SPIN M.D. FOR DUKE2000!
DUKE2000.com
HE'S A LITTLE NERVOUS, SO GO EASY ON HIM, OKAY?
CATCH YOU ALL LATER.
MR. HARRIS? COULD YOU DISCUSS THE CANDIDATE'S VIEW OF THE PROPOSED NATIONAL MISSILE DEFENSE SYSTEM?
UH... MR. HARRIS?
THE STATE BIRD OF ALBANY IS THE BLUEBELL. THANK YOU.

6/21/00

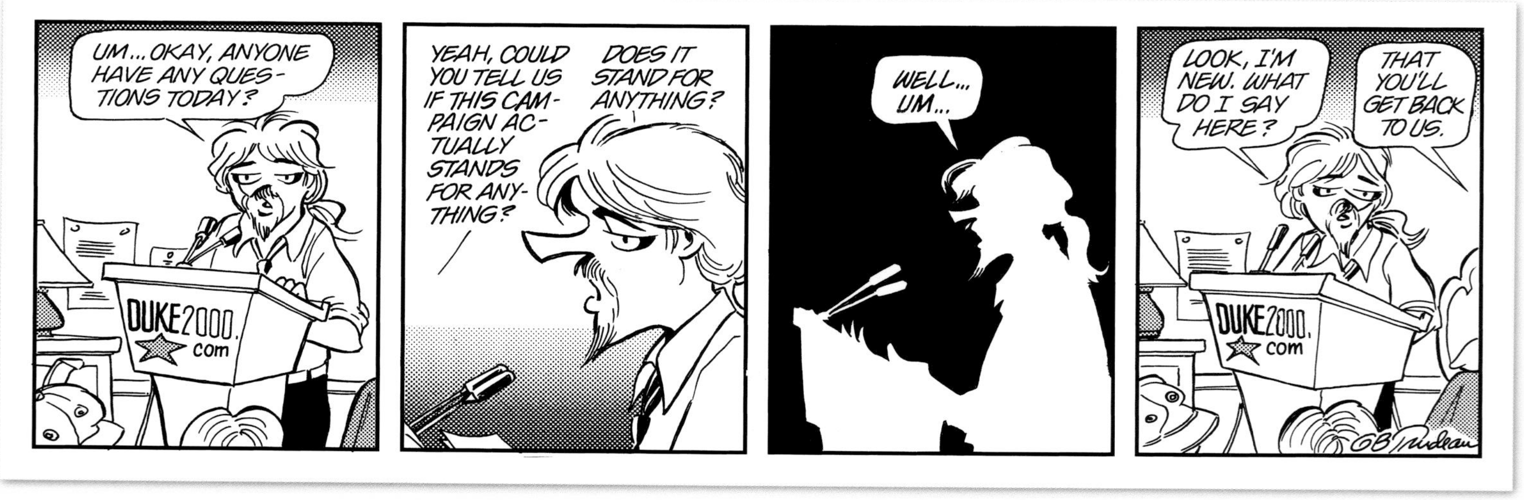
UM... OKAY, ANYONE HAVE ANY QUESTIONS TODAY?
DUKE2000.com
YEAH, COULD YOU TELL US IF THIS CAMPAIGN ACTUALLY STANDS FOR ANYTHING?
DOES IT STAND FOR ANYTHING?
WELL... UM...
LOOK, I'M NEW. WHAT DO I SAY HERE?
THAT YOU'LL GET BACK TO US.
DUKE2000.com

6/23/00

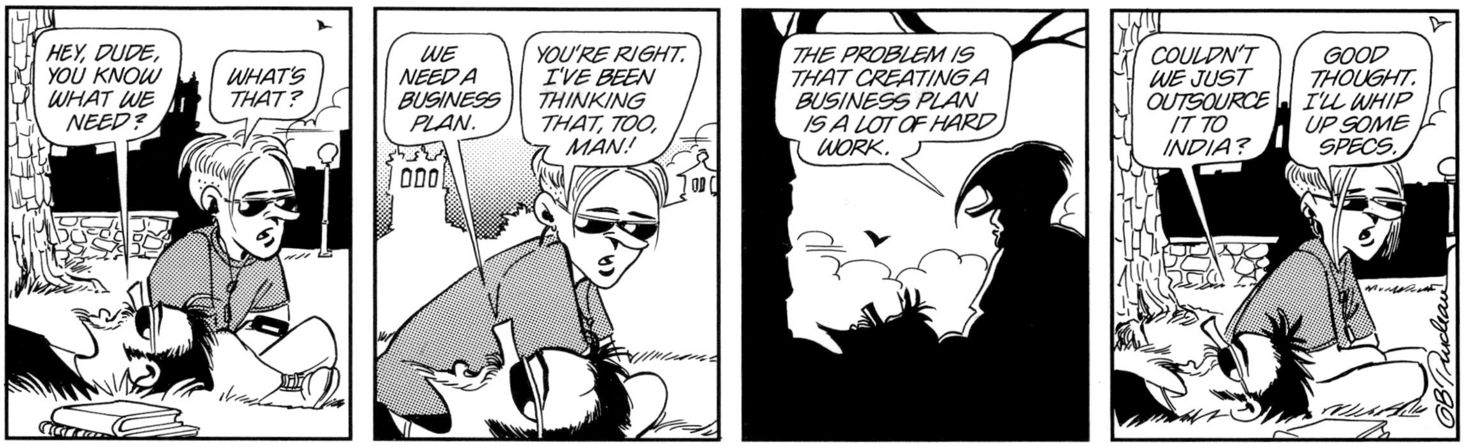
HEY, DUDE, YOU KNOW WHAT WE NEED?
WHAT'S THAT?
WE NEED A BUSINESS PLAN.
YOU'RE RIGHT. I'VE BEEN THINKING THAT, TOO, MAN!
THE PROBLEM IS THAT CREATING A BUSINESS PLAN IS A LOT OF HARD WORK.
COULDN'T WE JUST OUTSOURCE IT TO INDIA?
GOOD THOUGHT. I'LL WHIP UP SOME SPECS.

4/24/00

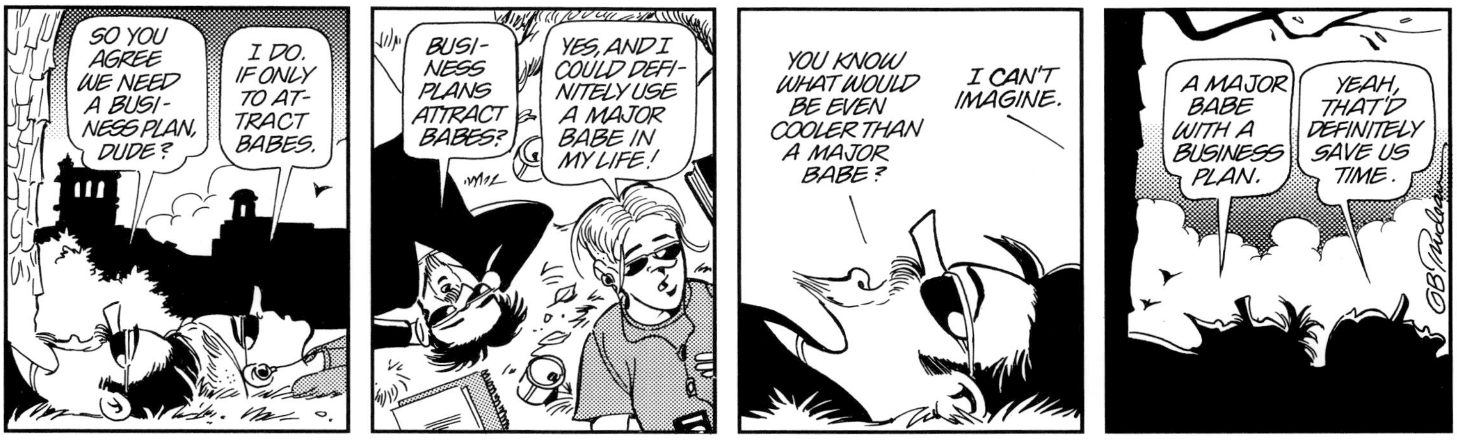
SO YOU AGREE WE NEED A BUSINESS PLAN, DUDE?
I DO. IF ONLY TO ATTRACT BABES.
BUSINESS PLANS ATTRACT BABES?
YES, AND I COULD DEFINITELY USE A MAJOR BABE IN MY LIFE!
YOU KNOW WHAT WOULD BE EVEN COOLER THAN A MAJOR BABE?
I CAN'T IMAGINE.
A MAJOR BABE WITH A BUSINESS PLAN.
YEAH, THAT'D DEFINITELY SAVE US TIME.

4/25/00

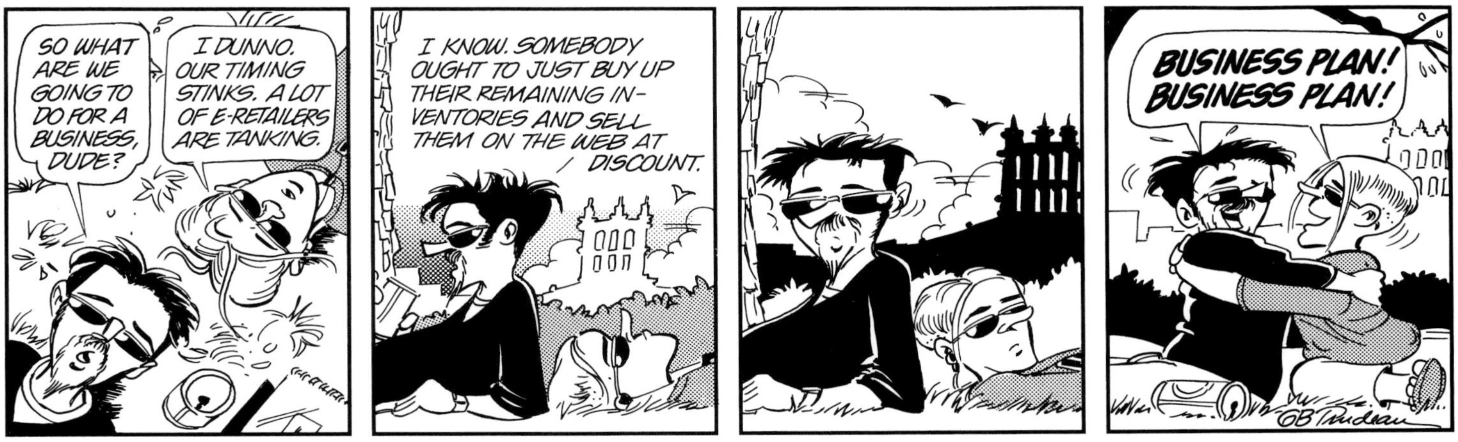
SO WHAT ARE WE GOING TO DO FOR A BUSINESS, DUDE?
I DUNNO. OUR TIMING STINKS. A LOT OF E-RETAILERS ARE TANKING.
I KNOW. SOMEBODY OUGHT TO JUST BUY UP THEIR REMAINING INVENTORIES AND SELL THEM ON THE WEB AT DISCOUNT.
BUSINESS PLAN! BUSINESS PLAN!

4/26/00

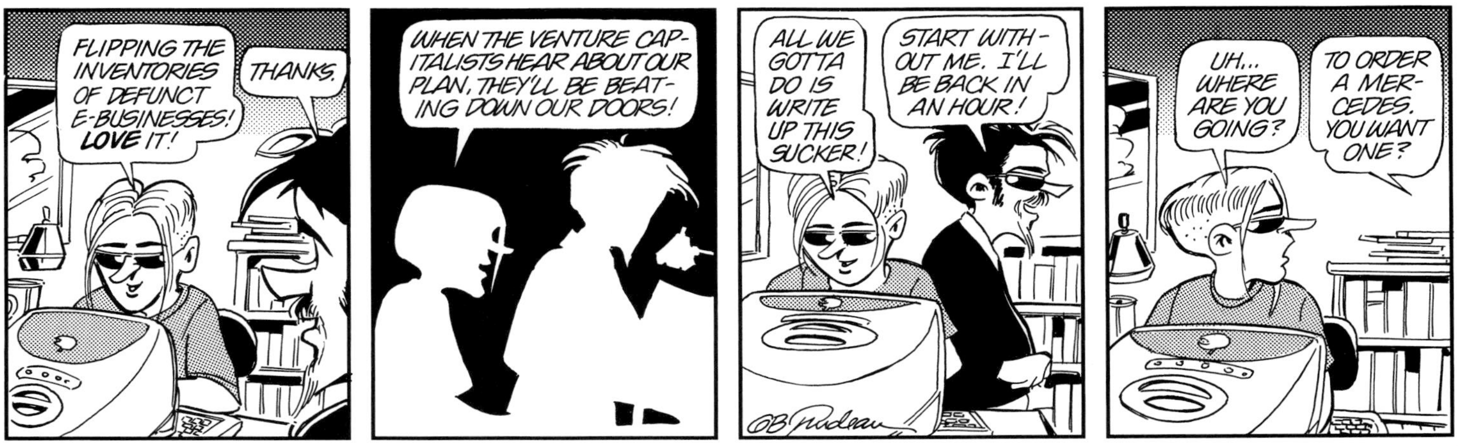
FLIPPING THE INVENTORIES OF DEFUNCT E-BUSINESSES! LOVE IT!
THANKS.
WHEN THE VENTURE CAPITALISTS HEAR ABOUT OUR PLAN, THEY'LL BE BEATING DOWN OUR DOORS!
ALL WE GOTTA DO IS WRITE UP THIS SUCKER!
START WITHOUT ME. I'LL BE BACK IN AN HOUR!
UH... WHERE ARE YOU GOING?
TO ORDER A MERCEDES. YOU WANT ONE?

4/28/00

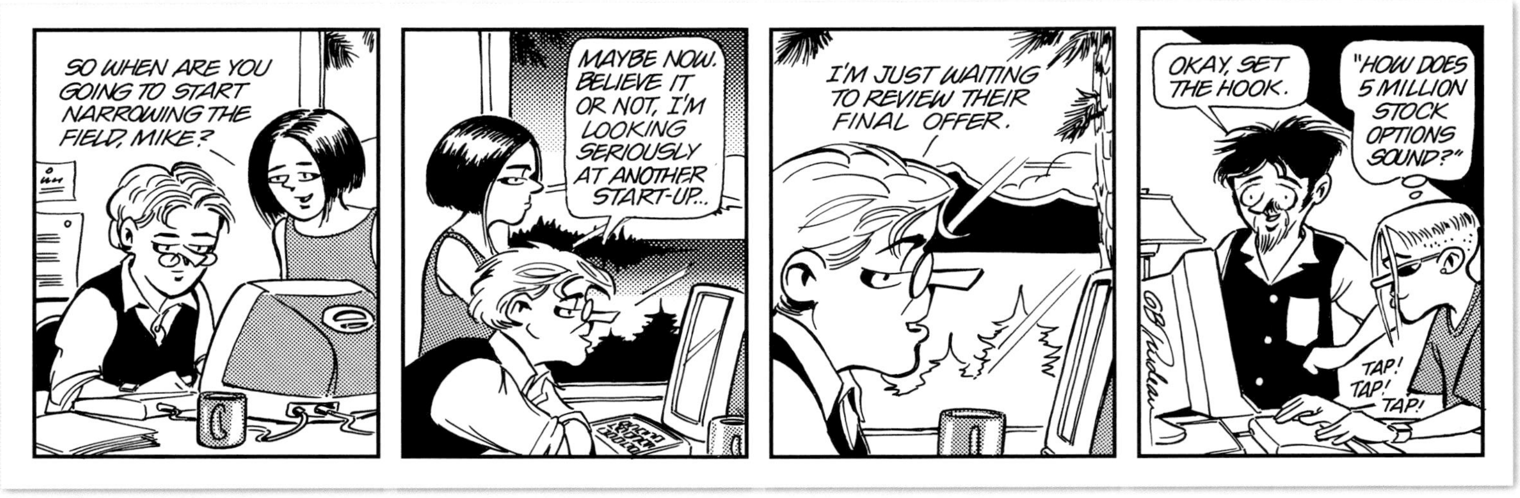
SO WHEN ARE YOU GOING TO START NARROWING THE FIELD, MIKE?
MAYBE NOW. BELIEVE IT OR NOT, I'M LOOKING SERIOUSLY AT ANOTHER START-UP...
I'M JUST WAITING TO REVIEW THEIR FINAL OFFER.
OKAY, SET THE HOOK.
"HOW DOES 5 MILLION STOCK OPTIONS SOUND?"
TAP! TAP! TAP!

5/22/00

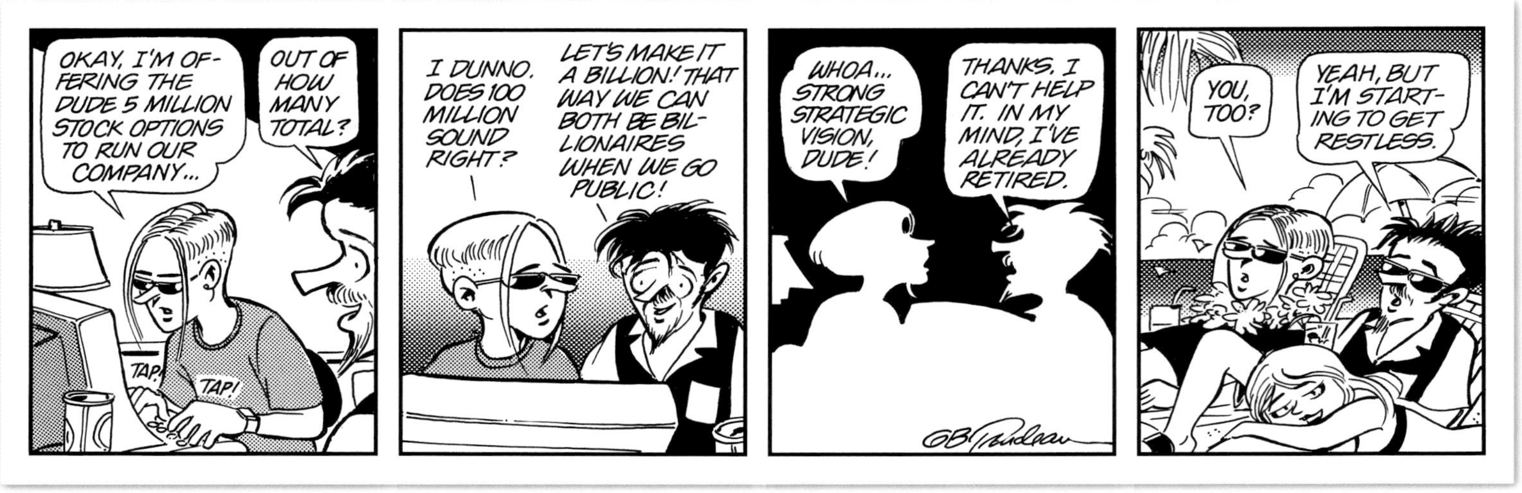
OKAY, I'M OFFERING THE DUDE 5 MILLION STOCK OPTIONS TO RUN OUR COMPANY...
OUT OF HOW MANY TOTAL?
TAP! TAP!
I DUNNO. DOES 100 MILLION SOUND RIGHT?
LET'S MAKE IT A BILLION! THAT WAY WE CAN BOTH BE BILLIONAIRES WHEN WE GO PUBLIC!
WHOA... STRONG STRATEGIC VISION, DUDE!
THANKS, I CAN'T HELP IT. IN MY MIND, I'VE ALREADY RETIRED.
YOU, TOO?
YEAH, BUT I'M STARTING TO GET RESTLESS.

5/23/00

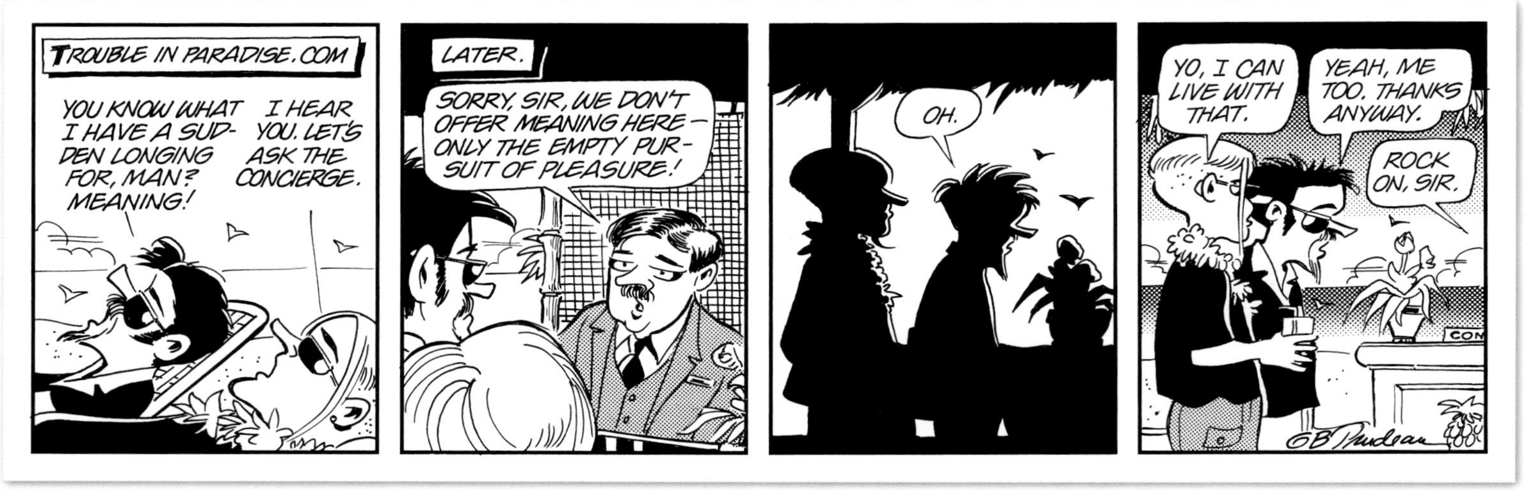
TROUBLE IN PARADISE.COM
YOU KNOW WHAT I HAVE A SUDDEN LONGING FOR, MAN? MEANING!
I HEAR YOU. LET'S ASK THE CONCIERGE.
LATER.
SORRY, SIR, WE DON'T OFFER MEANING HERE — ONLY THE EMPTY PURSUIT OF PLEASURE!
OH.
YO, I CAN LIVE WITH THAT.
YEAH, ME TOO. THANKS ANYWAY.
ROCK ON, SIR.

5/25/00

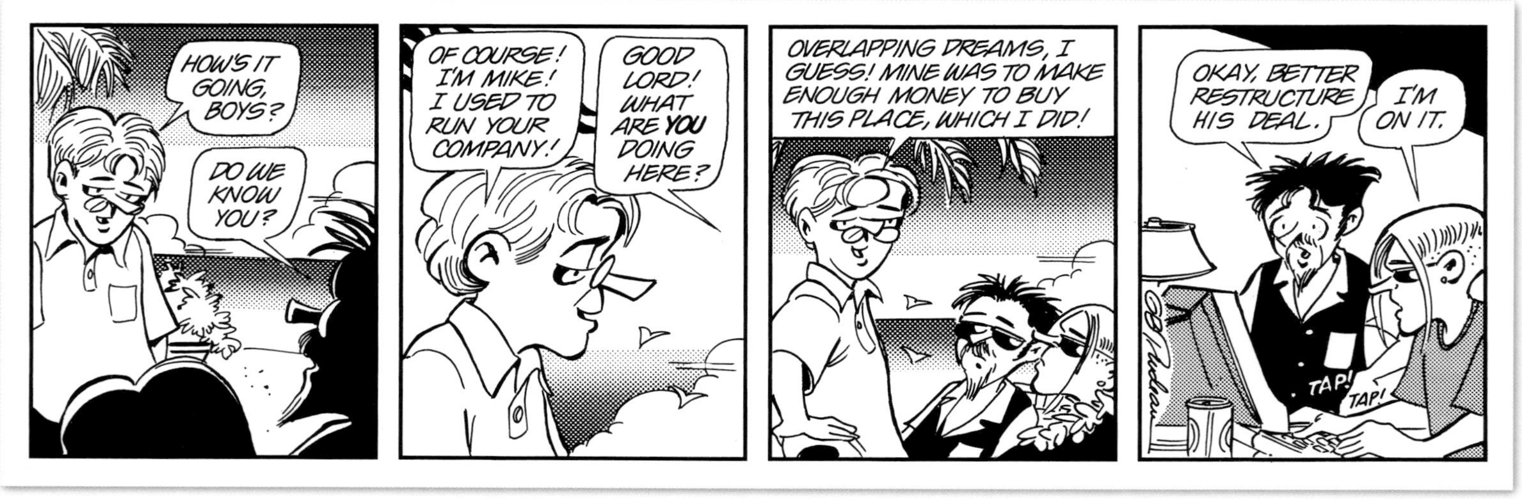
HOW'S IT GOING, BOYS?
DO WE KNOW YOU?
OF COURSE! I'M MIKE! I USED TO RUN YOUR COMPANY!
GOOD LORD! WHAT ARE YOU DOING HERE?
OVERLAPPING DREAMS, I GUESS! MINE WAS TO MAKE ENOUGH MONEY TO BUY THIS PLACE, WHICH I DID!
OKAY, BETTER RESTRUCTURE HIS DEAL.
I'M ON IT.
TAP! TAP!

5/27/00

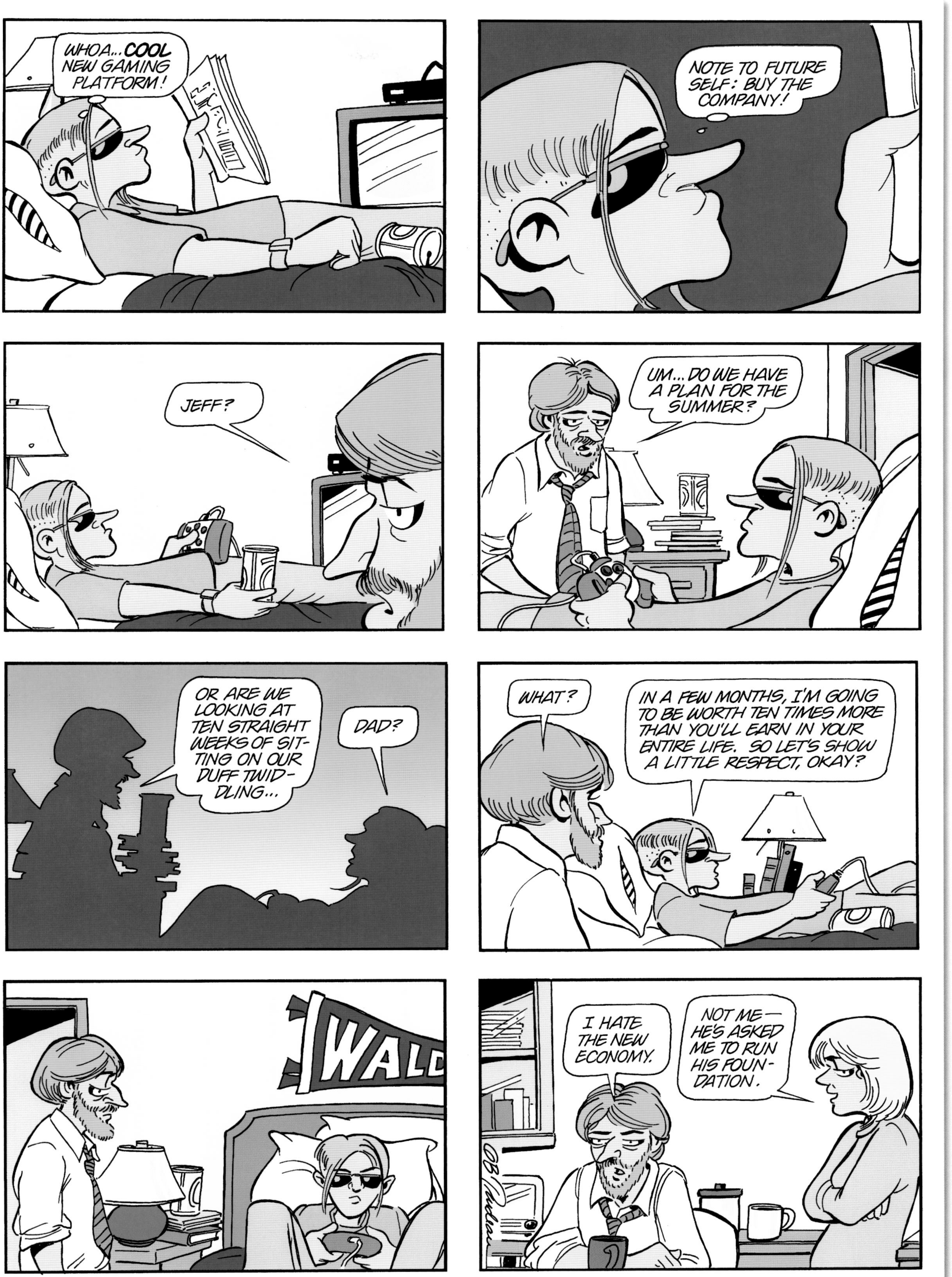
WHOA...**COOL** NEW GAMING PLATFORM!
NOTE TO FUTURE SELF: BUY THE COMPANY!
JEFF?
UM...DO WE HAVE A PLAN FOR THE SUMMER?
OR ARE WE LOOKING AT TEN STRAIGHT WEEKS OF SIT-TING ON OUR DUFF TWID-DLING...
DAD?
WHAT?
IN A FEW MONTHS, I'M GOING TO BE WORTH TEN TIMES MORE THAN YOU'LL EARN IN YOUR ENTIRE LIFE. SO LET'S SHOW A LITTLE RESPECT, OKAY?
WALD
I HATE THE NEW ECONOMY.
NOT ME—HE'S ASKED ME TO RUN HIS FOUN-DATION.

6/4/00

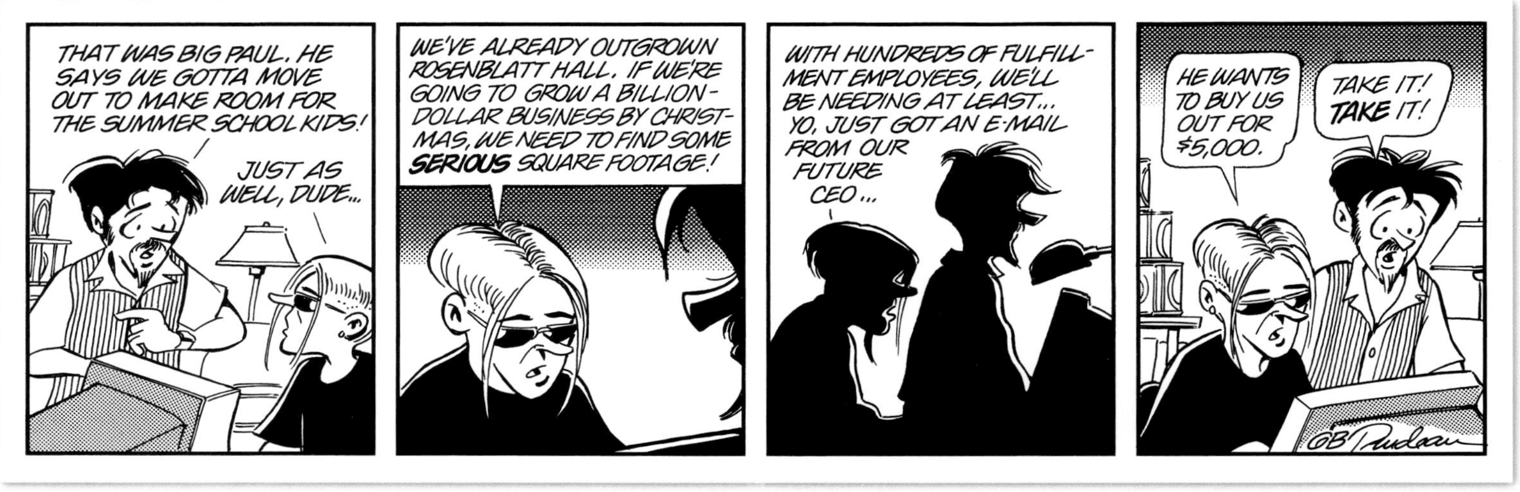
THAT WAS BIG PAUL. HE SAYS WE GOTTA MOVE OUT TO MAKE ROOM FOR THE SUMMER SCHOOL KIDS!
JUST AS WELL, DUDE...
WE'VE ALREADY OUTGROWN ROSENBLATT HALL. IF WE'RE GOING TO GROW A BILLION-DOLLAR BUSINESS BY CHRISTMAS, WE NEED TO FIND SOME SERIOUS SQUARE FOOTAGE!
WITH HUNDREDS OF FULFILLMENT EMPLOYEES, WE'LL BE NEEDING AT LEAST... YO, JUST GOT AN E-MAIL FROM OUR FUTURE CEO...
HE WANTS TO BUY US OUT FOR $5,000.
TAKE IT! TAKE IT!

6/3/00

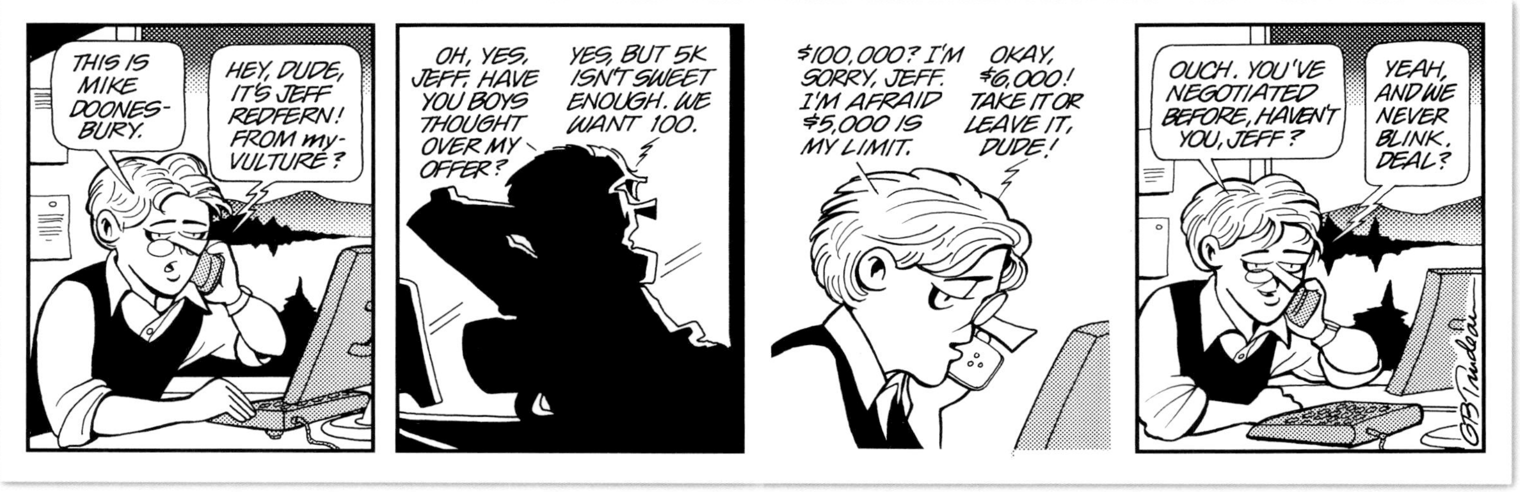
THIS IS MIKE DOONESBURY.
HEY, DUDE, IT'S JEFF REDFERN! FROM myVULTURE?
OH, YES, JEFF. HAVE YOU BOYS THOUGHT OVER MY OFFER?
YES, BUT 5K ISN'T SWEET ENOUGH. WE WANT 100.
$100,000? I'M SORRY, JEFF. I'M AFRAID $5,000 IS MY LIMIT.
OKAY, $6,000! TAKE IT OR LEAVE IT, DUDE!
OUCH. YOU'VE NEGOTIATED BEFORE, HAVEN'T YOU, JEFF?
YEAH, AND WE NEVER BLINK. DEAL?

7/5/00

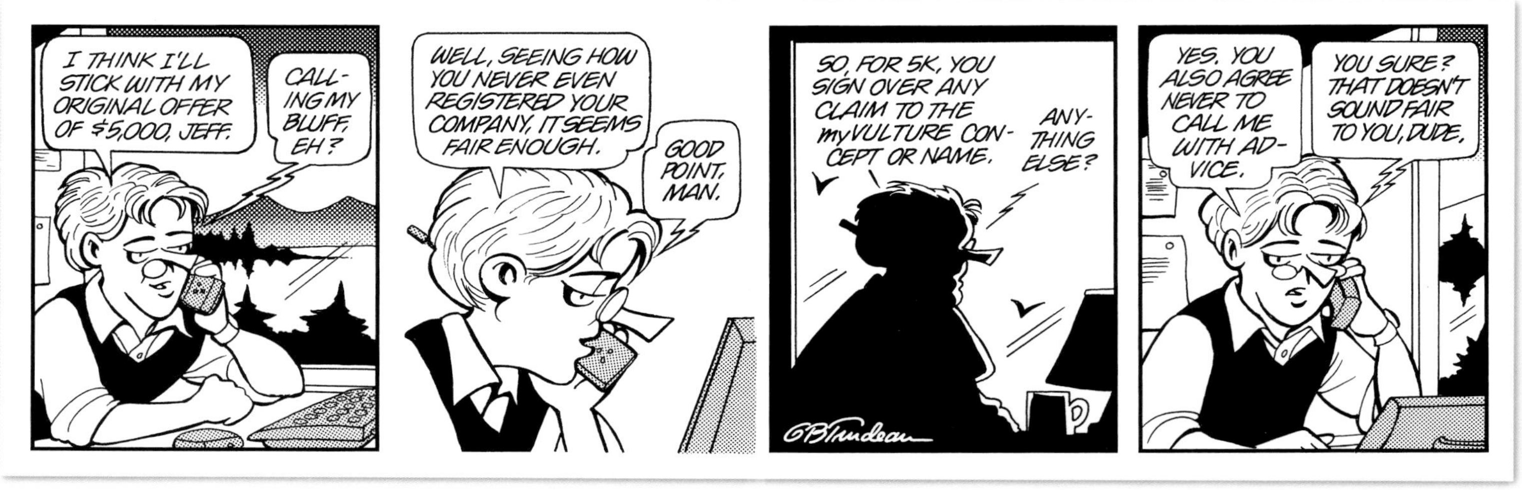
I THINK I'LL STICK WITH MY ORIGINAL OFFER OF $5,000, JEFF.
CALLING MY BLUFF, EH?
WELL, SEEING HOW YOU NEVER EVEN REGISTERED YOUR COMPANY, IT SEEMS FAIR ENOUGH.
GOOD POINT, MAN.
SO, FOR 5K, YOU SIGN OVER ANY CLAIM TO THE myVULTURE CONCEPT OR NAME.
ANYTHING ELSE?
YES. YOU ALSO AGREE NEVER TO CALL ME WITH ADVICE.
YOU SURE? THAT DOESN'T SOUND FAIR TO YOU, DUDE.

7/6/00

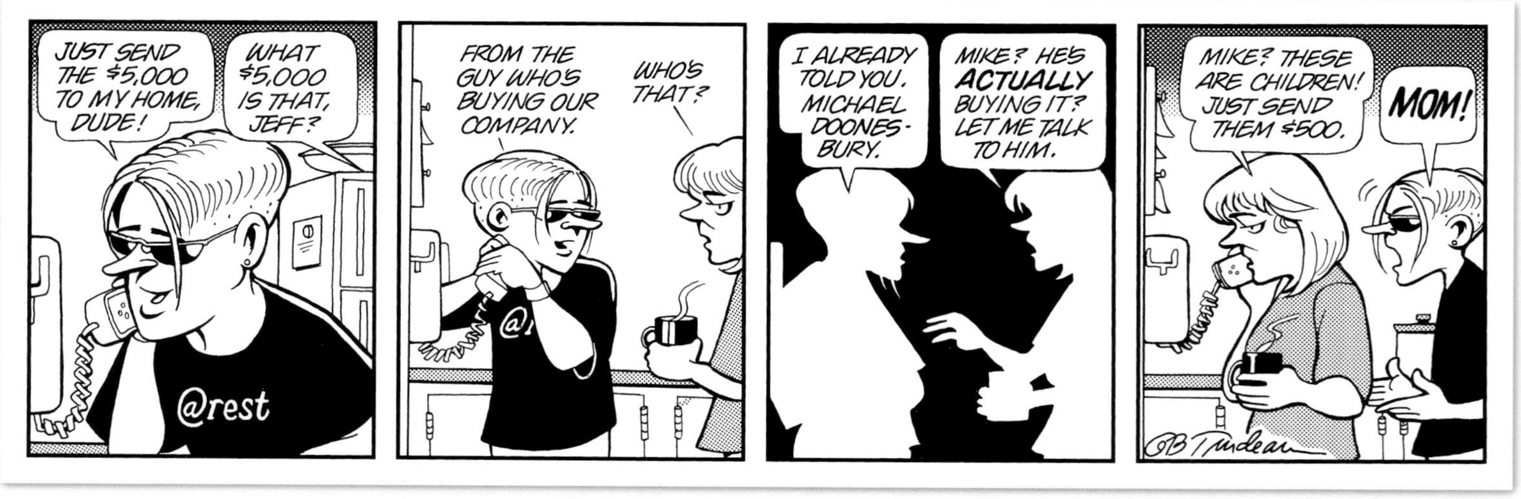
JUST SEND THE $5,000 TO MY HOME, DUDE!
WHAT $5,000 IS THAT, JEFF?
@rest
FROM THE GUY WHO'S BUYING OUR COMPANY.
WHO'S THAT?
I ALREADY TOLD YOU. MICHAEL DOONESBURY.
MIKE? HE'S ACTUALLY BUYING IT? LET ME TALK TO HIM.
MIKE? THESE ARE CHILDREN! JUST SEND THEM $500.
MOM!

7/7/00

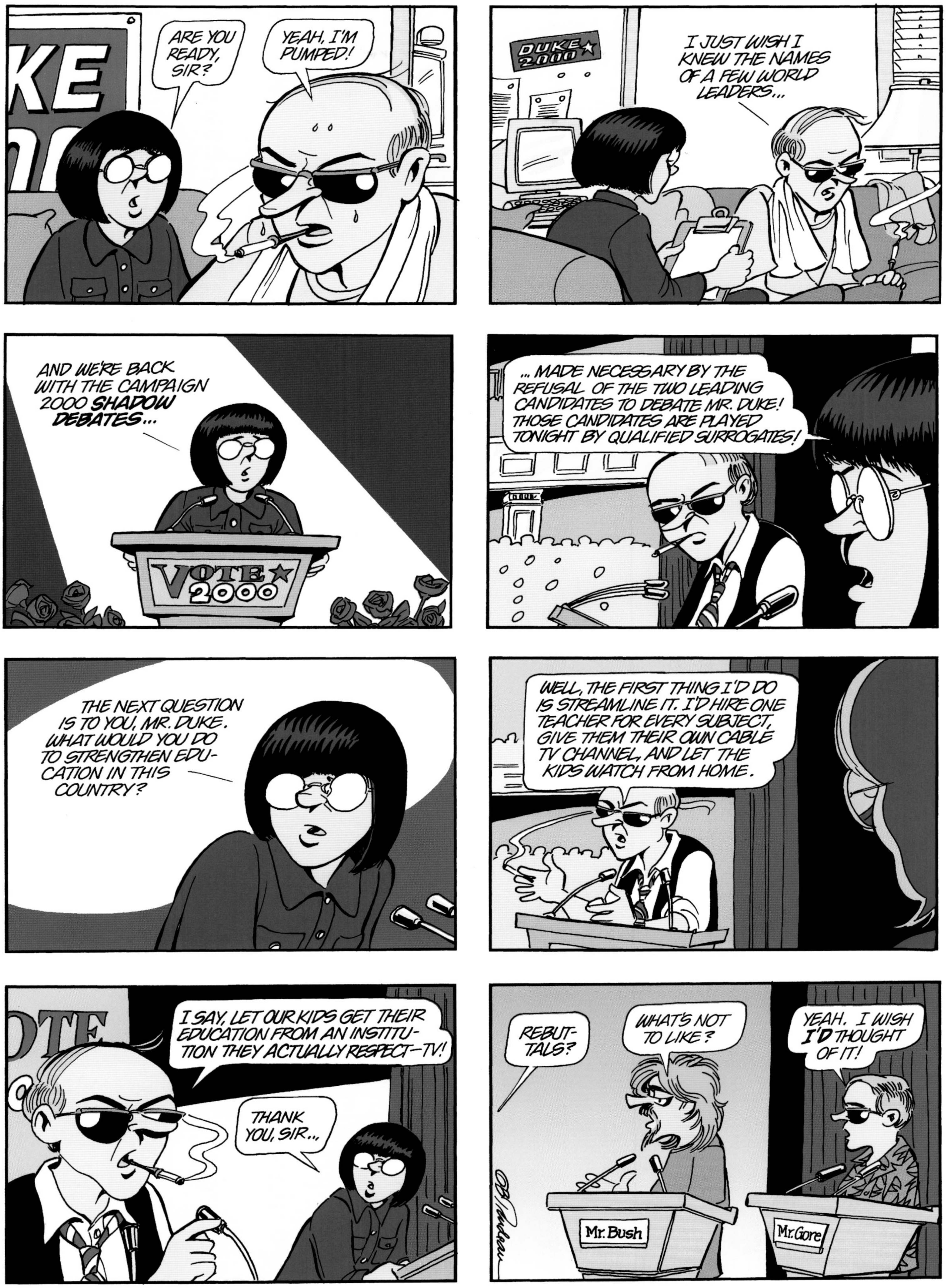
DUKE 2000
ARE YOU READY, SIR?
YEAH, I'M PUMPED!
I JUST WISH I KNEW THE NAMES OF A FEW WORLD LEADERS...
AND WE'RE BACK WITH THE CAMPAIGN 2000 SHADOW DEBATES...
VOTE 2000
... MADE NECESSARY BY THE REFUSAL OF THE TWO LEADING CANDIDATES TO DEBATE MR. DUKE! THOSE CANDIDATES ARE PLAYED TONIGHT BY QUALIFIED SURROGATES!
THE NEXT QUESTION IS TO YOU, MR. DUKE. WHAT WOULD YOU DO TO STRENGTHEN EDUCATION IN THIS COUNTRY?
WELL, THE FIRST THING I'D DO IS STREAMLINE IT. I'D HIRE ONE TEACHER FOR EVERY SUBJECT, GIVE THEM THEIR OWN CABLE TV CHANNEL, AND LET THE KIDS WATCH FROM HOME.
I SAY, LET OUR KIDS GET THEIR EDUCATION FROM AN INSTITUTION THEY ACTUALLY RESPECT—TV!
THANK YOU, SIR...
REBUTTALS?
WHAT'S NOT TO LIKE?
YEAH. I WISH I'D THOUGHT OF IT!
Mr. Bush
Mr. Gore

10/1/00

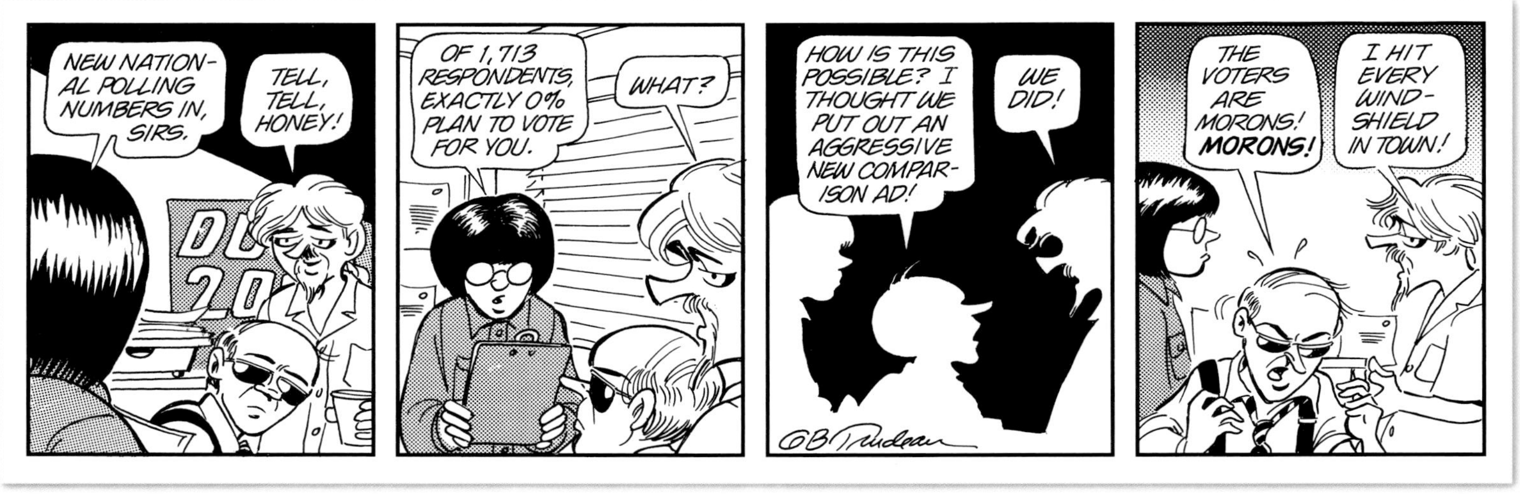
NEW NATIONAL POLLING NUMBERS IN, SIRS.
TELL, TELL, HONEY!
OF 1,713 RESPONDENTS, EXACTLY 0% PLAN TO VOTE FOR YOU.
WHAT?
HOW IS THIS POSSIBLE? I THOUGHT WE PUT OUT AN AGGRESSIVE NEW COMPARISON AD!
WE DID!
THE VOTERS ARE MORONS! **MORONS!**
I HIT EVERY WINDSHIELD IN TOWN!

10/30/00

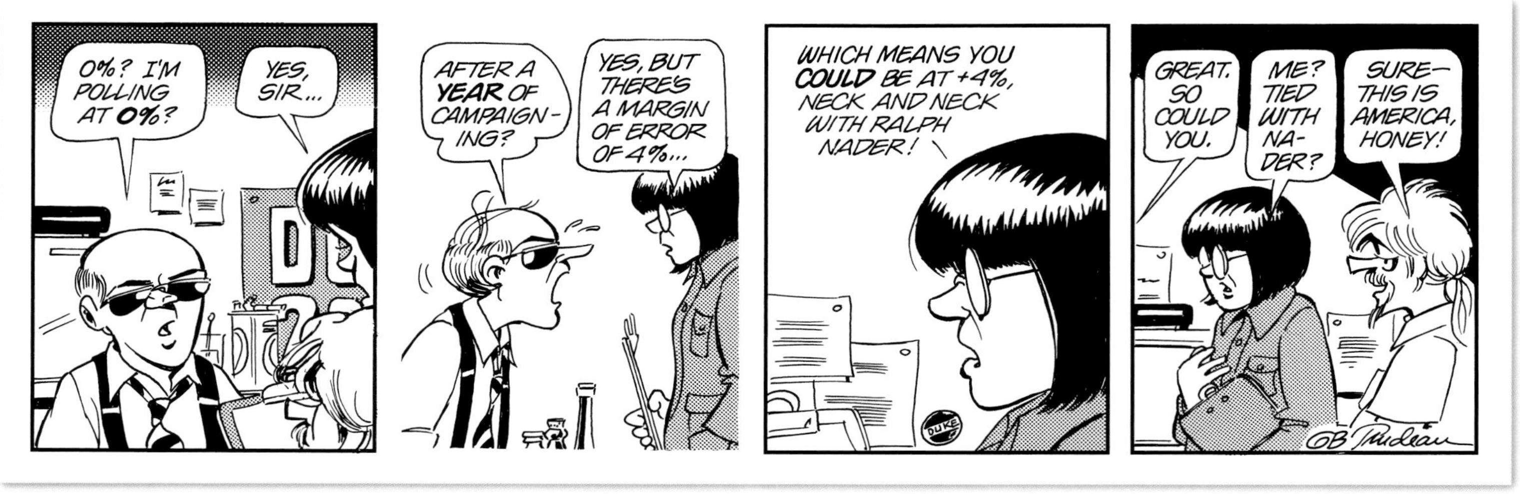
0%? I'M POLLING AT **0%**?
YES, SIR...
AFTER A **YEAR** OF CAMPAIGNING?
YES, BUT THERE'S A MARGIN OF ERROR OF 4%...
WHICH MEANS YOU **COULD** BE AT +4%, NECK AND NECK WITH RALPH NADER!
GREAT. SO COULD YOU.
ME? TIED WITH NADER?
SURE—THIS IS AMERICA, HONEY!

10/31/00

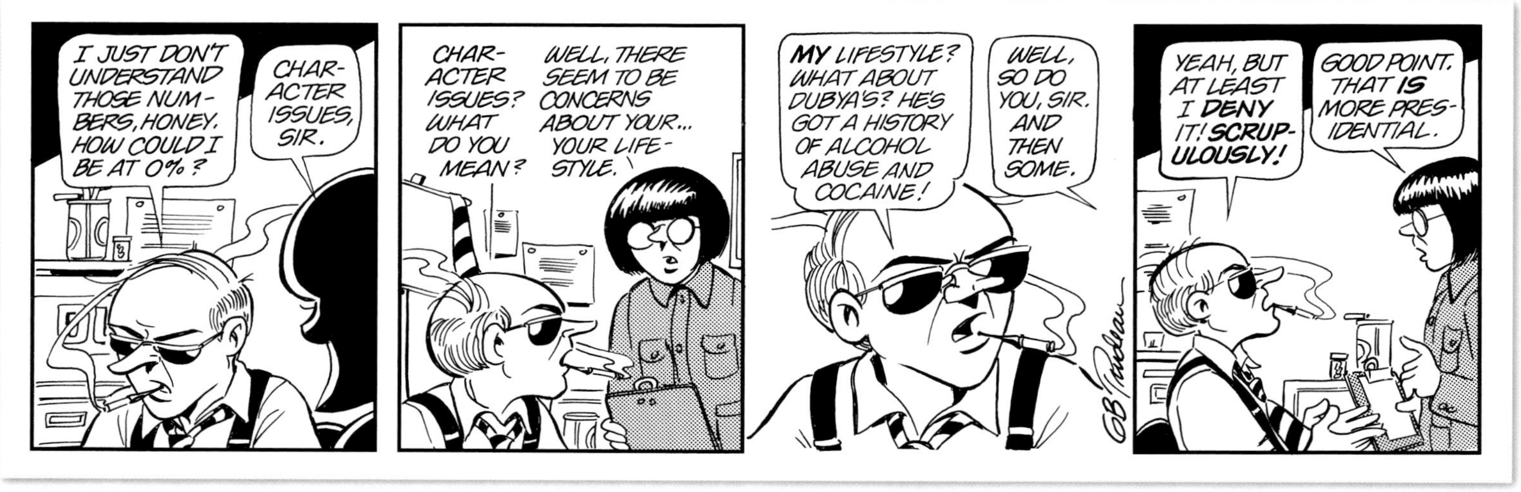
I JUST DON'T UNDERSTAND THOSE NUMBERS, HONEY. HOW COULD I BE AT 0%?
CHARACTER ISSUES, SIR.
CHARACTER ISSUES? WHAT DO YOU MEAN?
WELL, THERE SEEM TO BE CONCERNS ABOUT YOUR... YOUR LIFESTYLE.
MY LIFESTYLE? WHAT ABOUT DUBYA'S? HE'S GOT A HISTORY OF ALCOHOL ABUSE AND COCAINE!
WELL, SO DO YOU, SIR. AND THEN SOME.
YEAH, BUT AT LEAST I **DENY** IT! **SCRUPULOUSLY!**
GOOD POINT. THAT **IS** MORE PRESIDENTIAL.

11/1/00

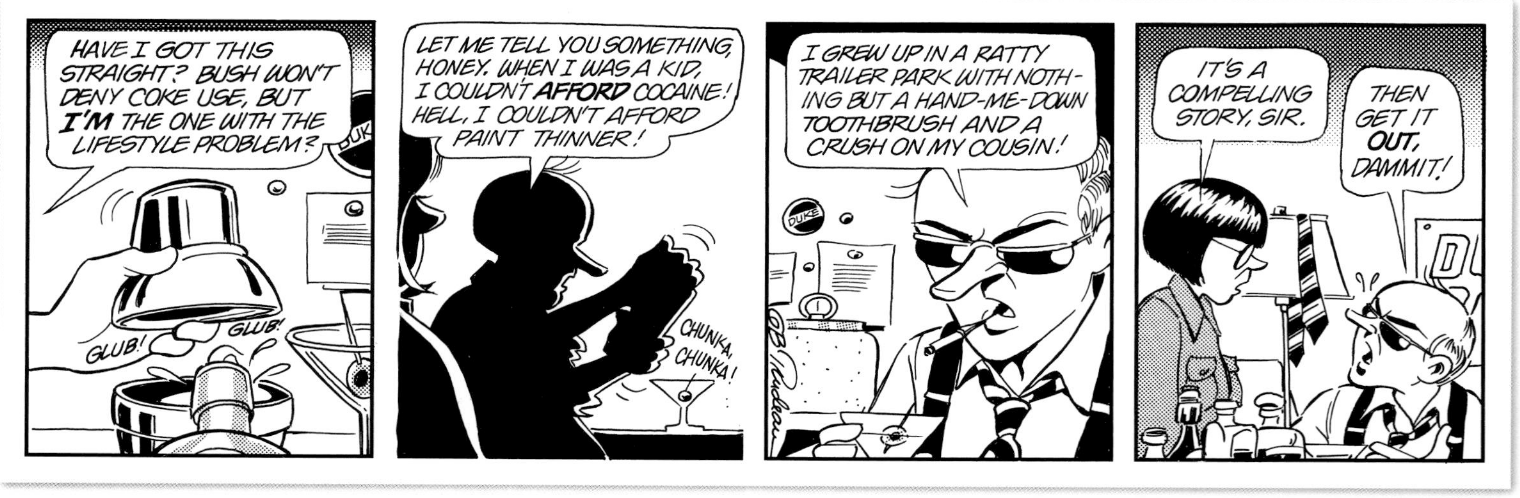
HAVE I GOT THIS STRAIGHT? BUSH WON'T DENY COKE USE, BUT **I'M** THE ONE WITH THE LIFESTYLE PROBLEM?
GLUB! GLUB!
LET ME TELL YOU SOMETHING, HONEY. WHEN I WAS A KID, I COULDN'T **AFFORD** COCAINE! HELL, I COULDN'T AFFORD PAINT THINNER!
CHUNKA, CHUNKA!
I GREW UP IN A RATTY TRAILER PARK WITH NOTHING BUT A HAND-ME-DOWN TOOTHBRUSH AND A CRUSH ON MY COUSIN!
IT'S A COMPELLING STORY, SIR.
THEN GET IT **OUT**, DAMMIT!

11/2/00

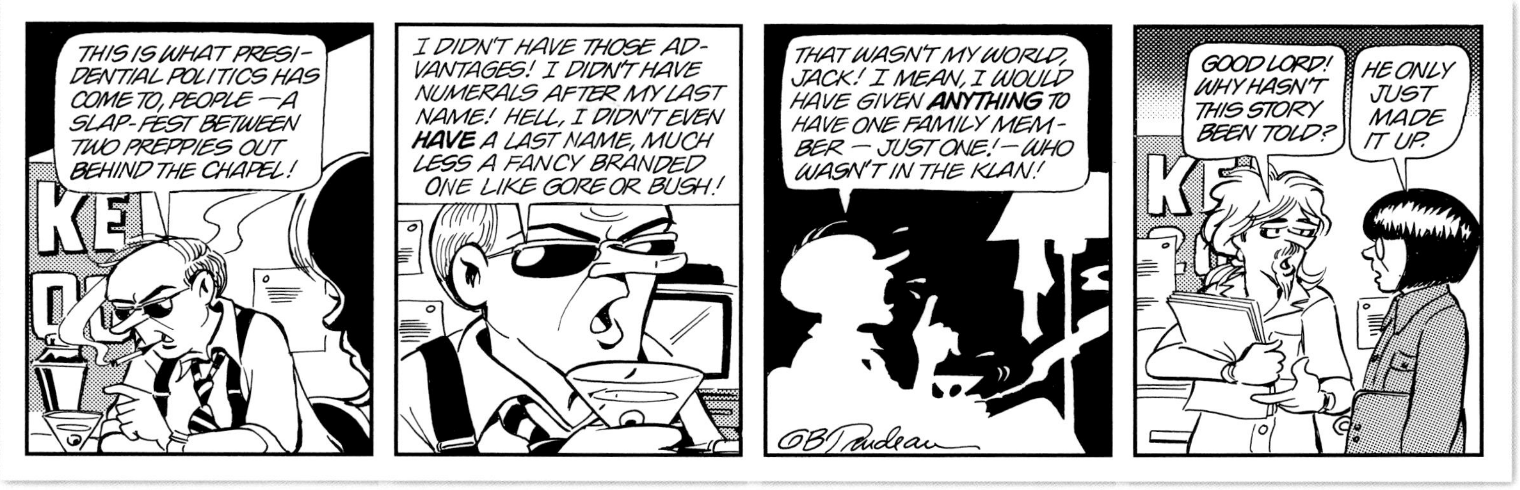
THIS IS WHAT PRESIDENTIAL POLITICS HAS COME TO, PEOPLE — A SLAP-FEST BETWEEN TWO PREPPIES OUT BEHIND THE CHAPEL!
I DIDN'T HAVE THOSE ADVANTAGES! I DIDN'T HAVE NUMERALS AFTER MY LAST NAME! HELL, I DIDN'T EVEN HAVE A LAST NAME, MUCH LESS A FANCY BRANDED ONE LIKE GORE OR BUSH!
THAT WASN'T MY WORLD, JACK! I MEAN, I WOULD HAVE GIVEN ANYTHING TO HAVE ONE FAMILY MEMBER — JUST ONE! — WHO WASN'T IN THE KLAN!
GOOD LORD! WHY HASN'T THIS STORY BEEN TOLD?
HE ONLY JUST MADE IT UP.

11/3/00

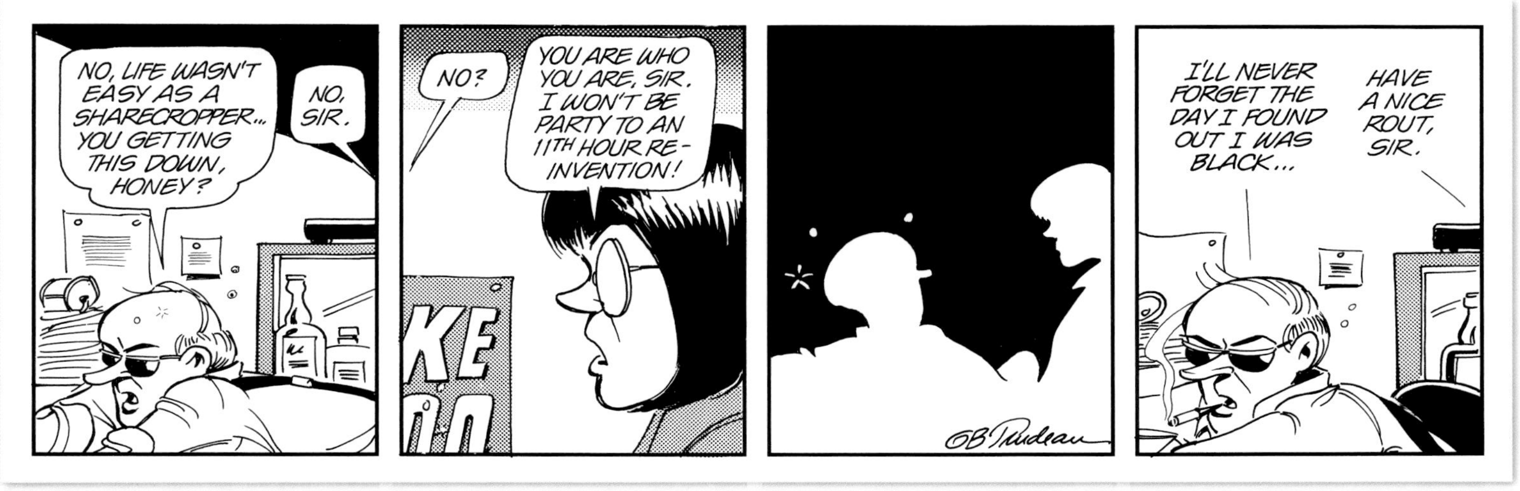
NO, LIFE WASN'T EASY AS A SHARECROPPER... YOU GETTING THIS DOWN, HONEY?
NO, SIR.
NO?
YOU ARE WHO YOU ARE, SIR. I WON'T BE PARTY TO AN 11TH HOUR REINVENTION!
I'LL NEVER FORGET THE DAY I FOUND OUT I WAS BLACK...
HAVE A NICE ROUT, SIR.

11/4/00

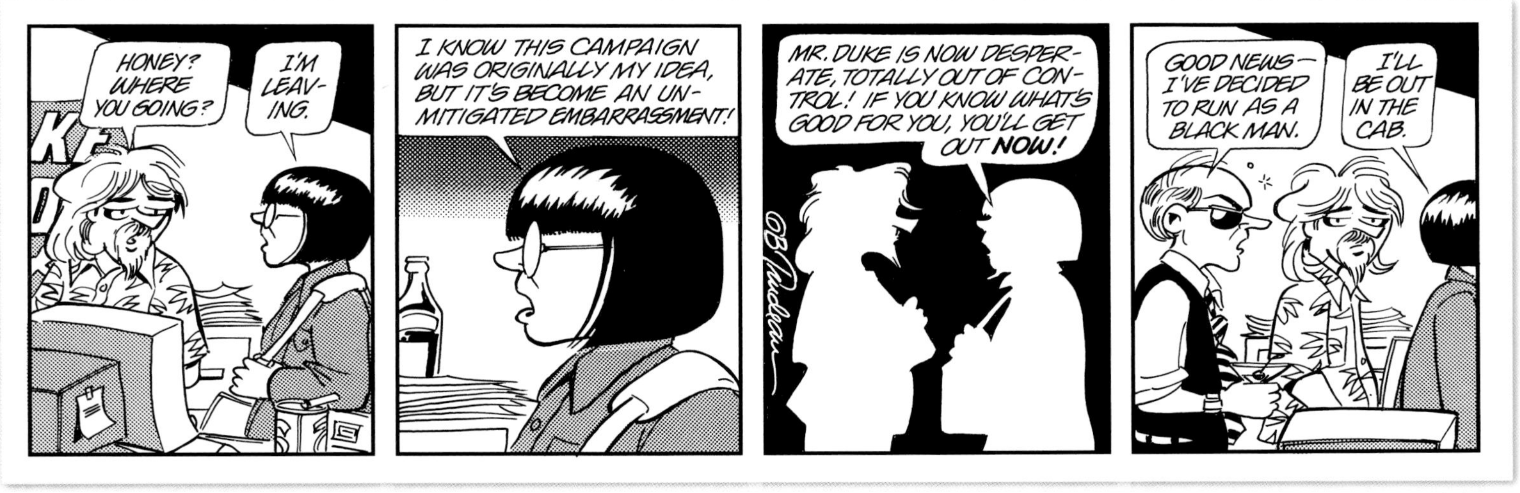
HONEY? WHERE YOU GOING?
I'M LEAVING.
I KNOW THIS CAMPAIGN WAS ORIGINALLY MY IDEA, BUT IT'S BECOME AN UNMITIGATED EMBARRASSMENT!
MR. DUKE IS NOW DESPERATE, TOTALLY OUT OF CONTROL! IF YOU KNOW WHAT'S GOOD FOR YOU, YOU'LL GET OUT NOW!
GOOD NEWS — I'VE DECIDED TO RUN AS A BLACK MAN.
I'LL BE OUT IN THE CAB.

11/6/00

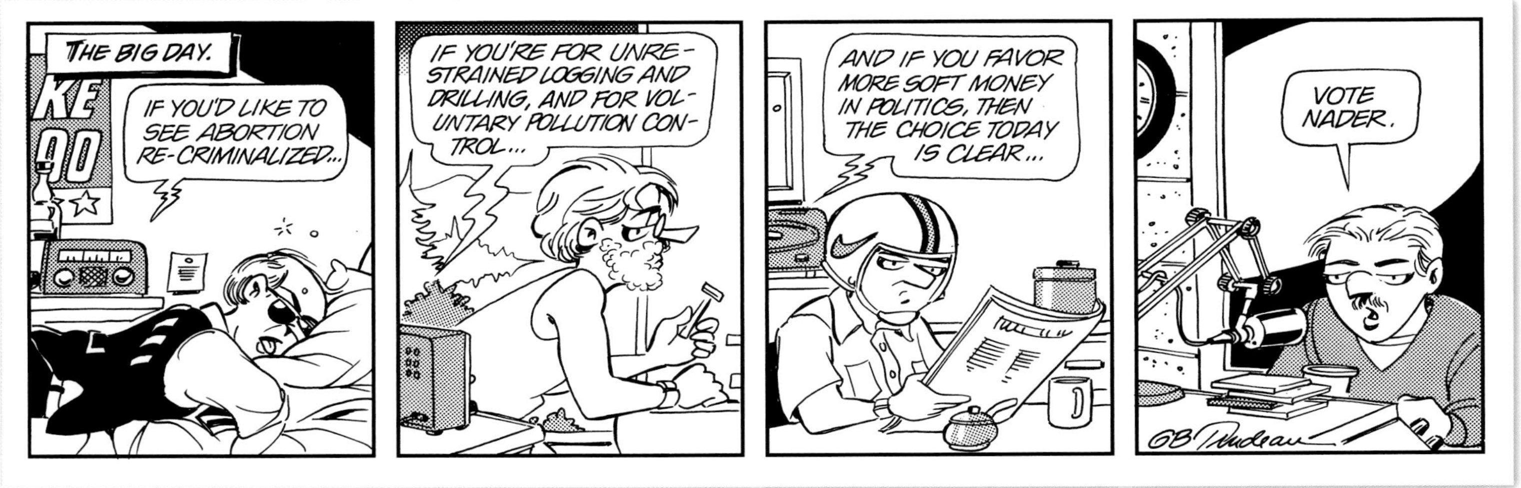
THE BIG DAY.
IF YOU'D LIKE TO SEE ABORTION RE-CRIMINALIZED...
IF YOU'RE FOR UNRESTRAINED LOGGING AND DRILLING, AND FOR VOLUNTARY POLLUTION CONTROL...
AND IF YOU FAVOR MORE SOFT MONEY IN POLITICS, THEN THE CHOICE TODAY IS CLEAR...
VOTE NADER.

11/7/00

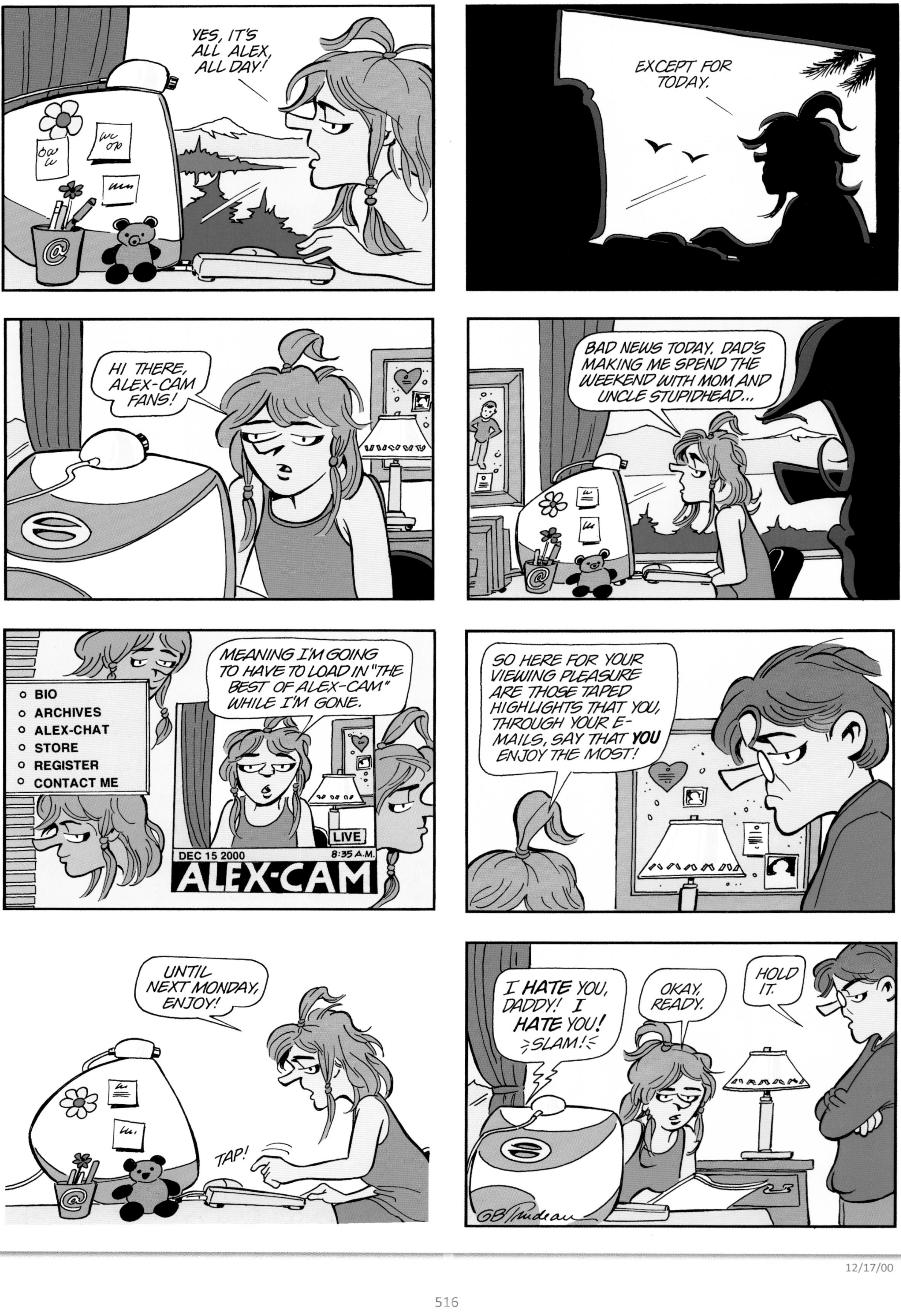
YES, IT'S ALL ALEX, ALL DAY!
EXCEPT FOR TODAY.
HI THERE, ALEX-CAM FANS!
BAD NEWS TODAY. DAD'S MAKING ME SPEND THE WEEKEND WITH MOM AND UNCLE STUPIDHEAD...
BIO
ARCHIVES
ALEX-CHAT
STORE
REGISTER
CONTACT ME
MEANING I'M GOING TO HAVE TO LOAD IN "THE BEST OF ALEX-CAM" WHILE I'M GONE.
LIVE
DEC 15 2000
8:35 A.M.
ALEX-CAM
SO HERE FOR YOUR VIEWING PLEASURE ARE THOSE TAPED HIGHLIGHTS THAT YOU, THROUGH YOUR E-MAILS, SAY THAT YOU ENJOY THE MOST!
UNTIL NEXT MONDAY, ENJOY!
TAP!
I HATE YOU, DADDY! I HATE YOU! SLAM!
OKAY, READY.
HOLD IT.
GBTrudeau

12/17/00

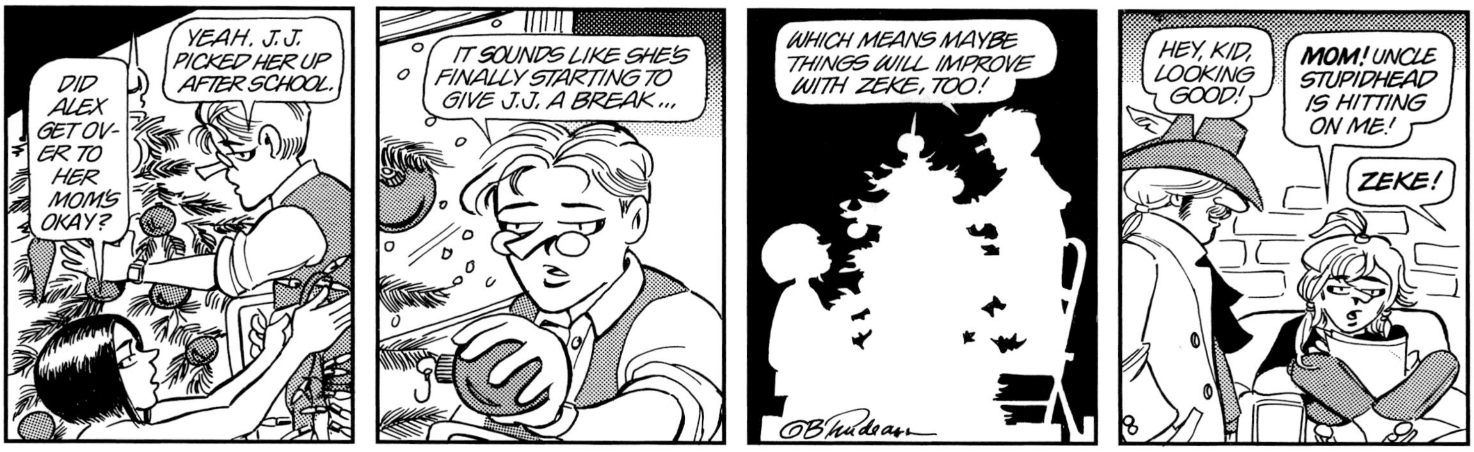
DID ALEX GET OVER TO HER MOM'S OKAY?
YEAH. J.J. PICKED HER UP AFTER SCHOOL.
IT SOUNDS LIKE SHE'S FINALLY STARTING TO GIVE J.J. A BREAK...
WHICH MEANS MAYBE THINGS WILL IMPROVE WITH ZEKE, TOO!
HEY, KID, LOOKING GOOD!
MOM! UNCLE STUPIDHEAD IS HITTING ON ME!
ZEKE!

12/18/00

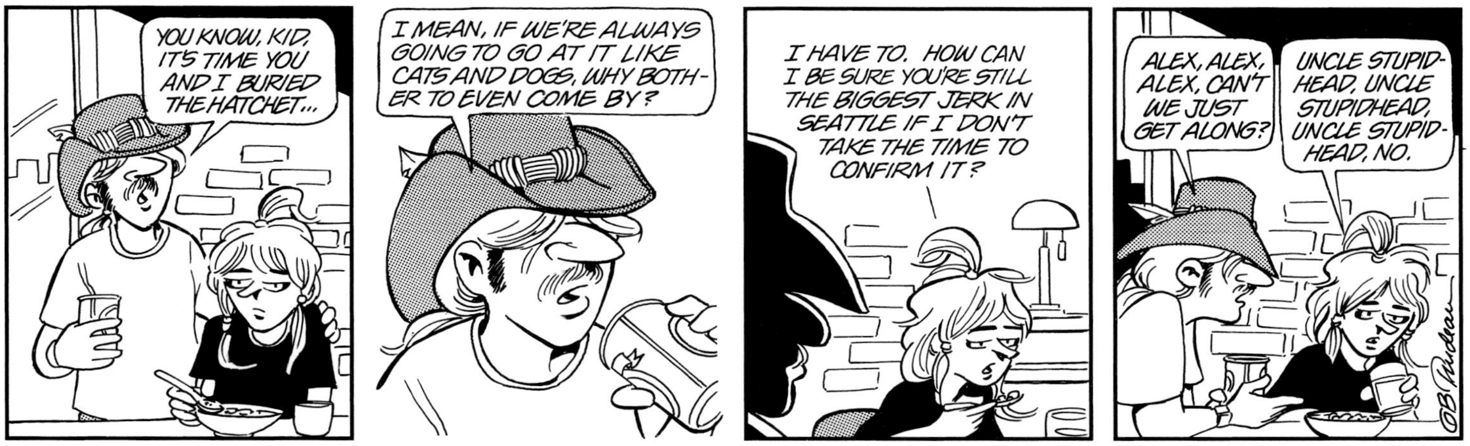
YOU KNOW, KID, IT'S TIME YOU AND I BURIED THE HATCHET...
I MEAN, IF WE'RE ALWAYS GOING TO GO AT IT LIKE CATS AND DOGS, WHY BOTHER TO EVEN COME BY?
I HAVE TO. HOW CAN I BE SURE YOU'RE STILL THE BIGGEST JERK IN SEATTLE IF I DON'T TAKE THE TIME TO CONFIRM IT?
ALEX, ALEX, ALEX, CAN'T WE JUST GET ALONG?
UNCLE STUPIDHEAD, UNCLE STUPIDHEAD, UNCLE STUPIDHEAD, NO.

12/19/00

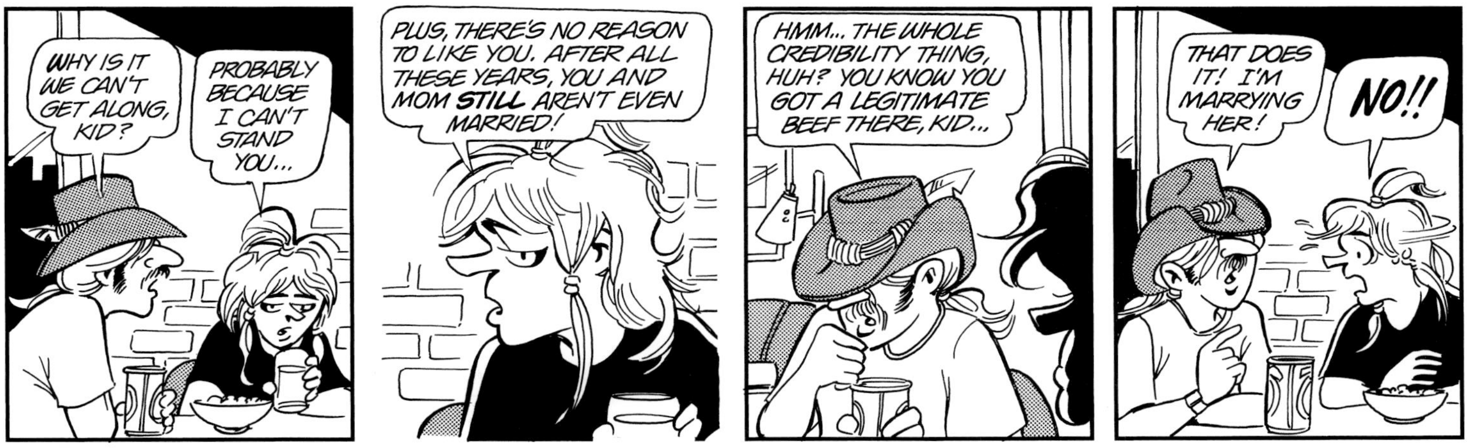
WHY IS IT WE CAN'T GET ALONG, KID?
PROBABLY BECAUSE I CAN'T STAND YOU...
PLUS, THERE'S NO REASON TO LIKE YOU. AFTER ALL THESE YEARS, YOU AND MOM STILL AREN'T EVEN MARRIED!
HMM... THE WHOLE CREDIBILITY THING, HUH? YOU KNOW YOU GOT A LEGITIMATE BEEF THERE, KID...
THAT DOES IT! I'M MARRYING HER!
NO!!

12/20/00

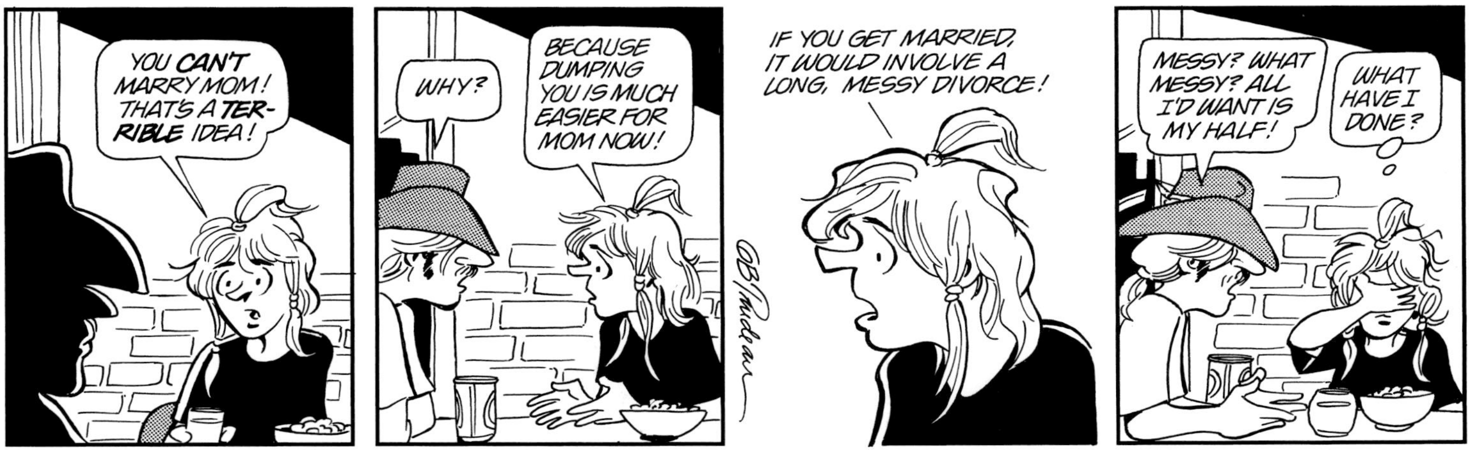
YOU CAN'T MARRY MOM! THAT'S A TERRIBLE IDEA!
WHY?
BECAUSE DUMPING YOU IS MUCH EASIER FOR MOM NOW!
IF YOU GET MARRIED, IT WOULD INVOLVE A LONG, MESSY DIVORCE!
MESSY? WHAT MESSY? ALL I'D WANT IS MY HALF!
WHAT HAVE I DONE?

12/21/00

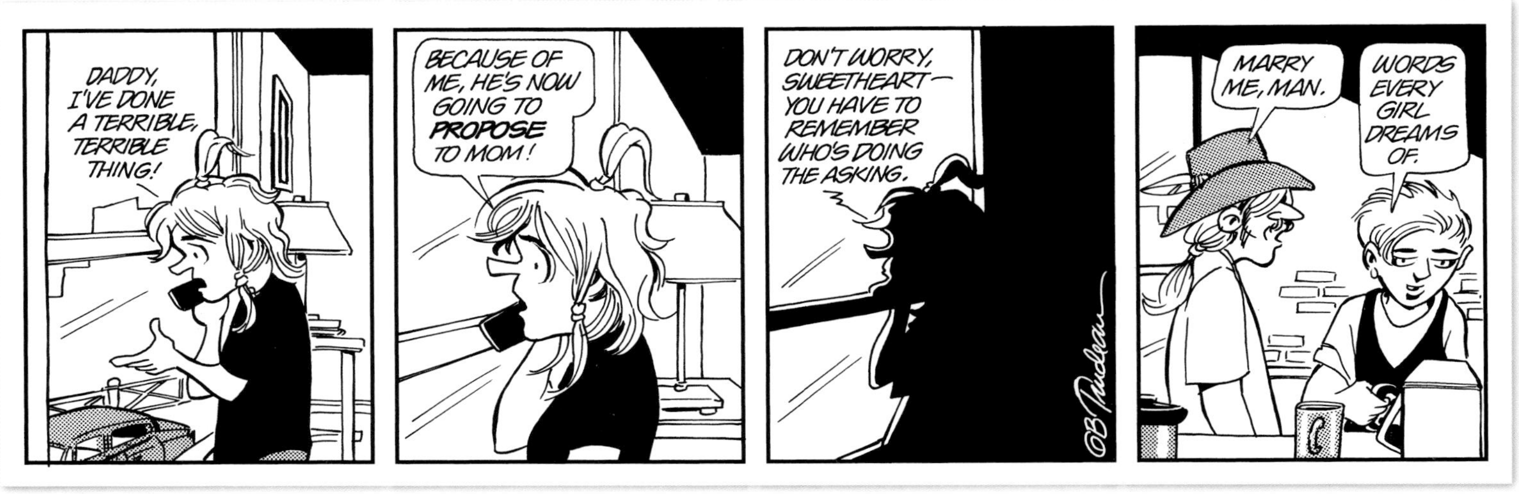
DADDY, I'VE DONE A TERRIBLE, TERRIBLE THING!
BECAUSE OF ME, HE'S NOW GOING TO **PROPOSE** TO MOM!
DON'T WORRY, SWEETHEART— YOU HAVE TO REMEMBER WHO'S DOING THE ASKING.
MARRY ME, MAN.
WORDS EVERY GIRL DREAMS OF.

12/22/00

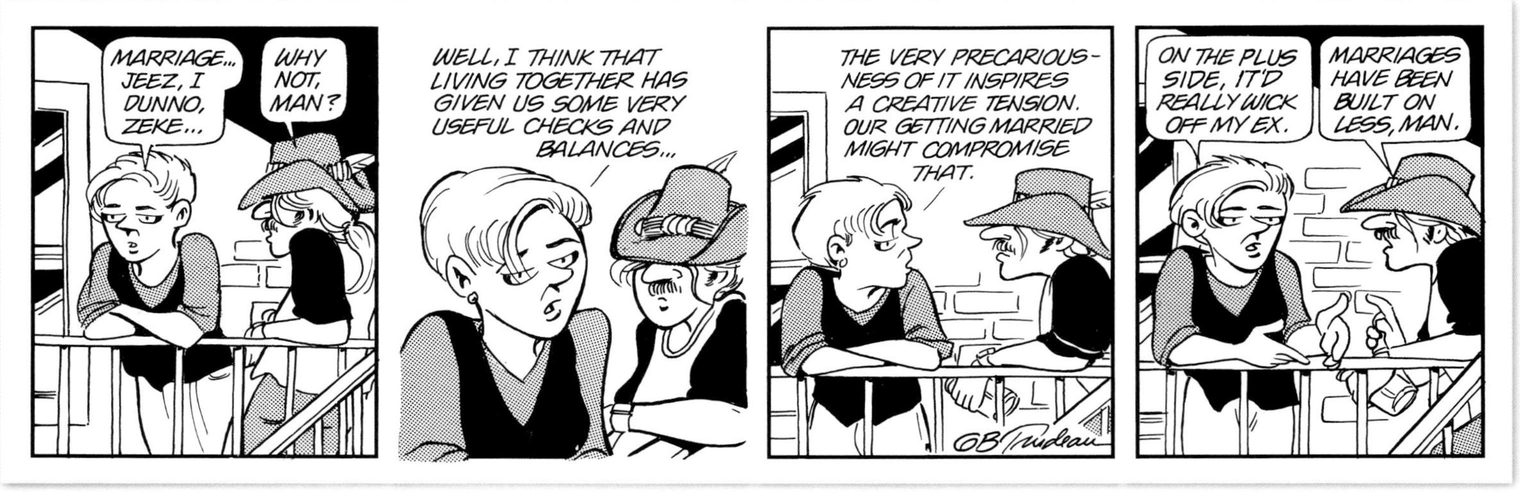
MARRIAGE... JEEZ, I DUNNO, ZEKE...
WHY NOT, MAN?
WELL, I THINK THAT LIVING TOGETHER HAS GIVEN US SOME VERY USEFUL CHECKS AND BALANCES...
THE VERY PRECARIOUSNESS OF IT INSPIRES A CREATIVE TENSION. OUR GETTING MARRIED MIGHT COMPROMISE THAT.
ON THE PLUS SIDE, IT'D REALLY WICK OFF MY EX.
MARRIAGES HAVE BEEN BUILT ON LESS, MAN.

12/25/00

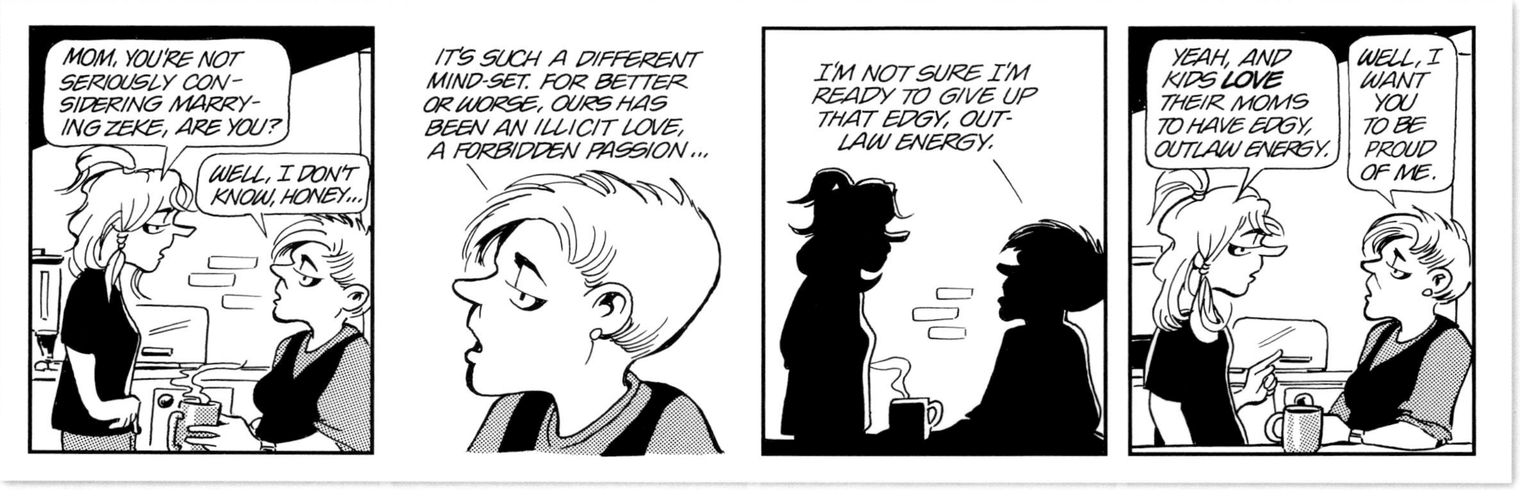
MOM, YOU'RE NOT SERIOUSLY CONSIDERING MARRYING ZEKE, ARE YOU?
WELL, I DON'T KNOW, HONEY...
IT'S SUCH A DIFFERENT MIND-SET. FOR BETTER OR WORSE, OURS HAS BEEN AN ILLICIT LOVE, A FORBIDDEN PASSION...
I'M NOT SURE I'M READY TO GIVE UP THAT EDGY, OUTLAW ENERGY.
YEAH, AND KIDS **LOVE** THEIR MOMS TO HAVE EDGY, OUTLAW ENERGY.
WELL, I WANT YOU TO BE PROUD OF ME.

12/27/00

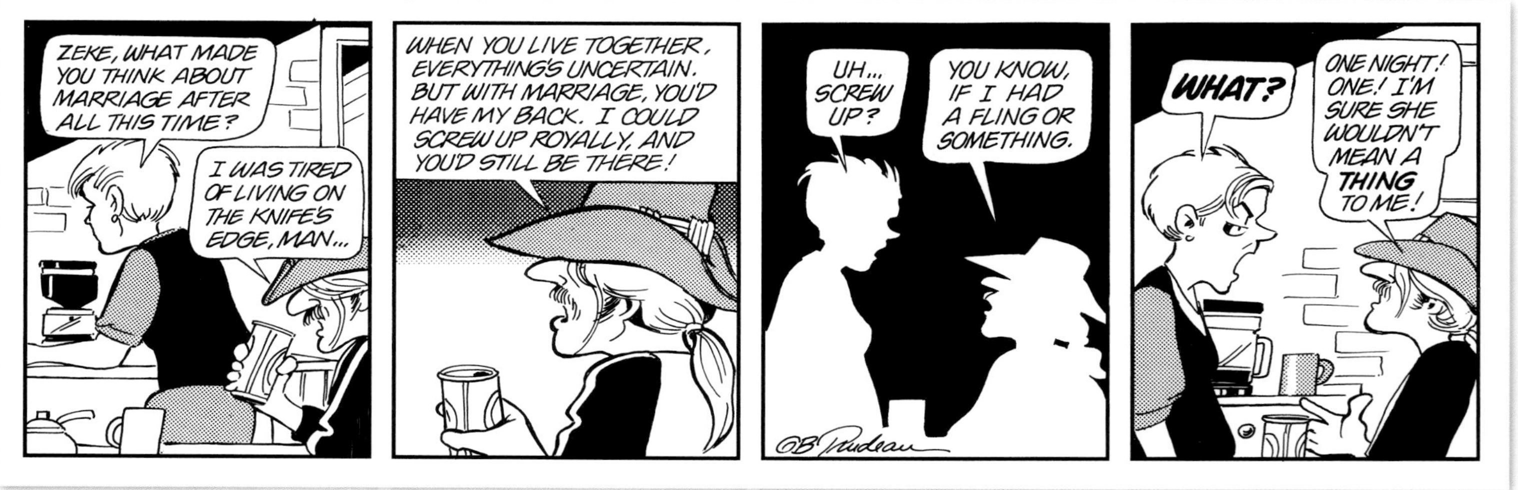
ZEKE, WHAT MADE YOU THINK ABOUT MARRIAGE AFTER ALL THIS TIME?
I WAS TIRED OF LIVING ON THE KNIFE'S EDGE, MAN...
WHEN YOU LIVE TOGETHER, EVERYTHING'S UNCERTAIN. BUT WITH MARRIAGE, YOU'D HAVE MY BACK. I COULD SCREW UP ROYALLY, AND YOU'D STILL BE THERE!
UH... SCREW UP?
YOU KNOW, IF I HAD A FLING OR SOMETHING.
WHAT?
ONE NIGHT! ONE! I'M SURE SHE WOULDN'T MEAN A **THING** TO ME!

12/29/00

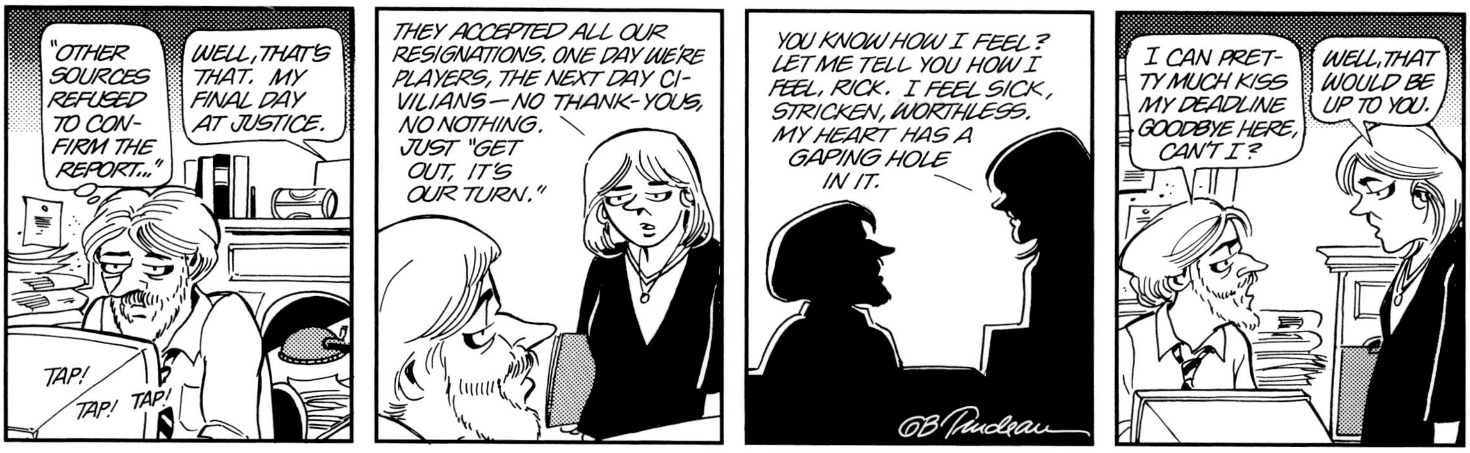
"OTHER SOURCES REFUSED TO CONFIRM THE REPORT..."
WELL, THAT'S THAT. MY FINAL DAY AT JUSTICE.
TAP! TAP! TAP!
THEY ACCEPTED ALL OUR RESIGNATIONS. ONE DAY WE'RE PLAYERS, THE NEXT DAY CIVILIANS—NO THANK-YOUS, NO NOTHING. JUST "GET OUT, IT'S OUR TURN."
YOU KNOW HOW I FEEL? LET ME TELL YOU HOW I FEEL, RICK. I FEEL SICK, STRICKEN, WORTHLESS. MY HEART HAS A GAPING HOLE IN IT.
I CAN PRETTY MUCH KISS MY DEADLINE GOODBYE HERE, CAN'T I?
WELL, THAT WOULD BE UP TO YOU.

1/29/01

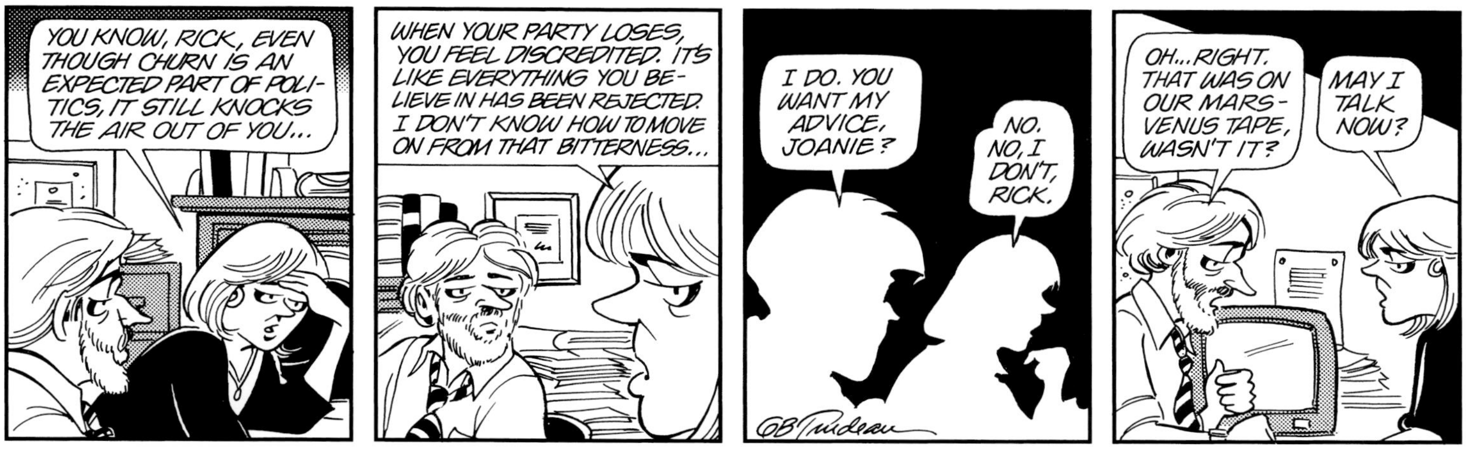
YOU KNOW, RICK, EVEN THOUGH CHURN IS AN EXPECTED PART OF POLITICS, IT STILL KNOCKS THE AIR OUT OF YOU...
WHEN YOUR PARTY LOSES, YOU FEEL DISCREDITED. IT'S LIKE EVERYTHING YOU BELIEVE IN HAS BEEN REJECTED. I DON'T KNOW HOW TO MOVE ON FROM THAT BITTERNESS...
I DO. YOU WANT MY ADVICE, JOANIE?
NO. NO, I DON'T, RICK.
OH... RIGHT. THAT WAS ON OUR MARS-VENUS TAPE, WASN'T IT?
MAY I TALK NOW?

1/30/01

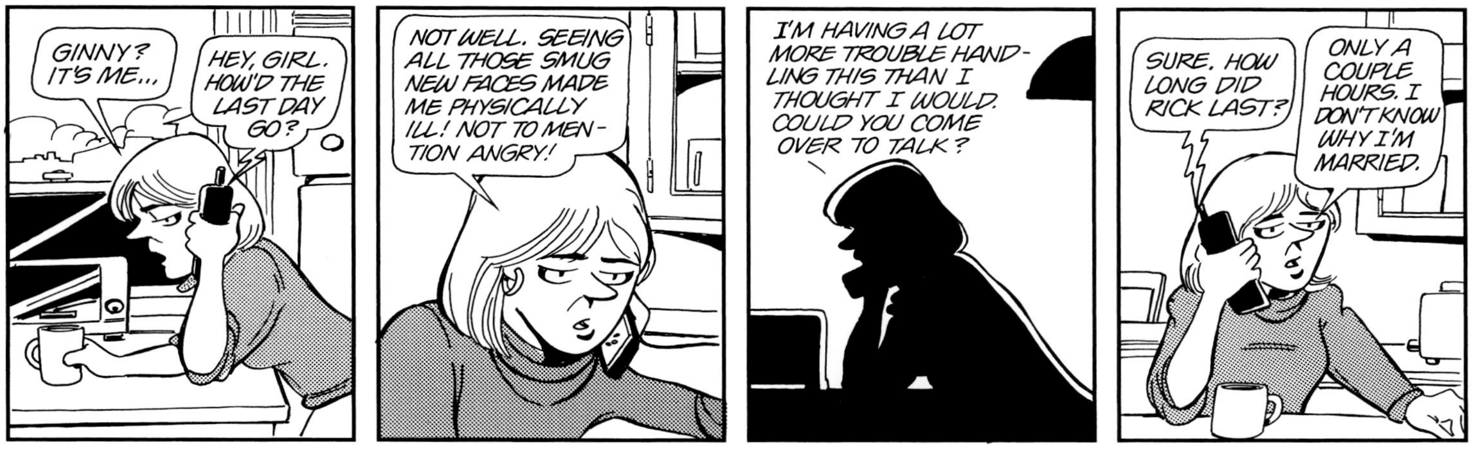
GINNY? IT'S ME...
HEY, GIRL. HOW'D THE LAST DAY GO?
NOT WELL. SEEING ALL THOSE SMUG NEW FACES MADE ME PHYSICALLY ILL! NOT TO MENTION ANGRY!
I'M HAVING A LOT MORE TROUBLE HANDLING THIS THAN I THOUGHT I WOULD. COULD YOU COME OVER TO TALK?
SURE. HOW LONG DID RICK LAST?
ONLY A COUPLE HOURS. I DON'T KNOW WHY I'M MARRIED.

2/1/01

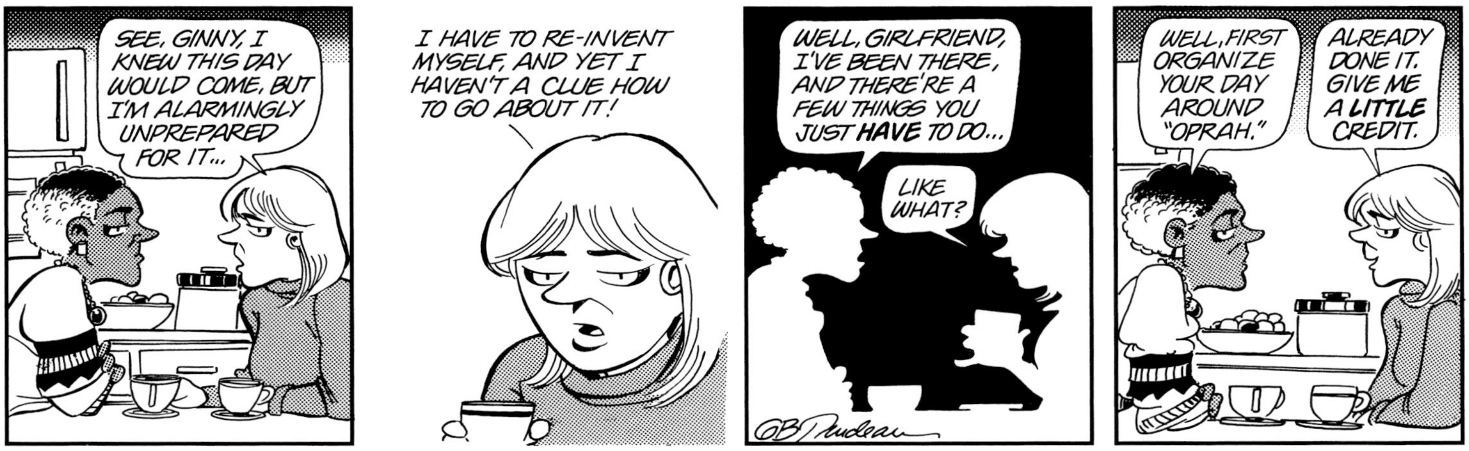
SEE, GINNY, I KNEW THIS DAY WOULD COME, BUT I'M ALARMINGLY UNPREPARED FOR IT...
I HAVE TO RE-INVENT MYSELF, AND YET I HAVEN'T A CLUE HOW TO GO ABOUT IT!
WELL, GIRLFRIEND, I'VE BEEN THERE, AND THERE'RE A FEW THINGS YOU JUST HAVE TO DO...
LIKE WHAT?
WELL, FIRST ORGANIZE YOUR DAY AROUND "OPRAH."
ALREADY DONE IT. GIVE ME A LITTLE CREDIT.

2/2/01

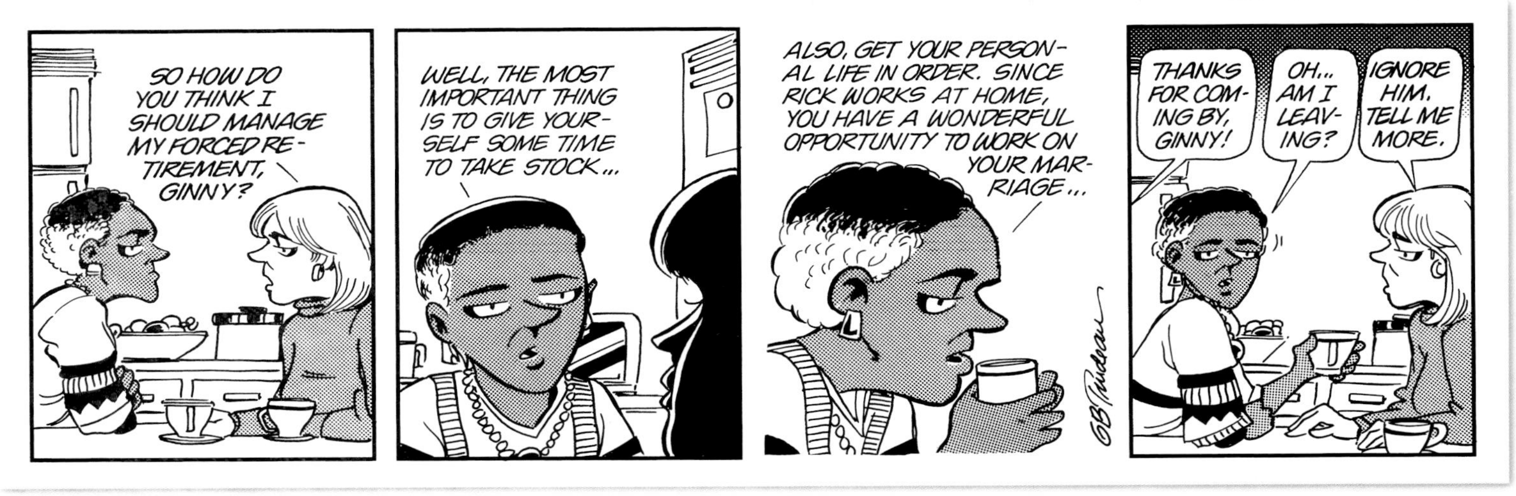
SO HOW DO YOU THINK I SHOULD MANAGE MY FORCED RETIREMENT, GINNY?
WELL, THE MOST IMPORTANT THING IS TO GIVE YOURSELF SOME TIME TO TAKE STOCK...
ALSO, GET YOUR PERSONAL LIFE IN ORDER. SINCE RICK WORKS AT HOME, YOU HAVE A WONDERFUL OPPORTUNITY TO WORK ON YOUR MARRIAGE...
THANKS FOR COMING BY, GINNY!
OH... AM I LEAVING?
IGNORE HIM. TELL ME MORE.

2/3/01

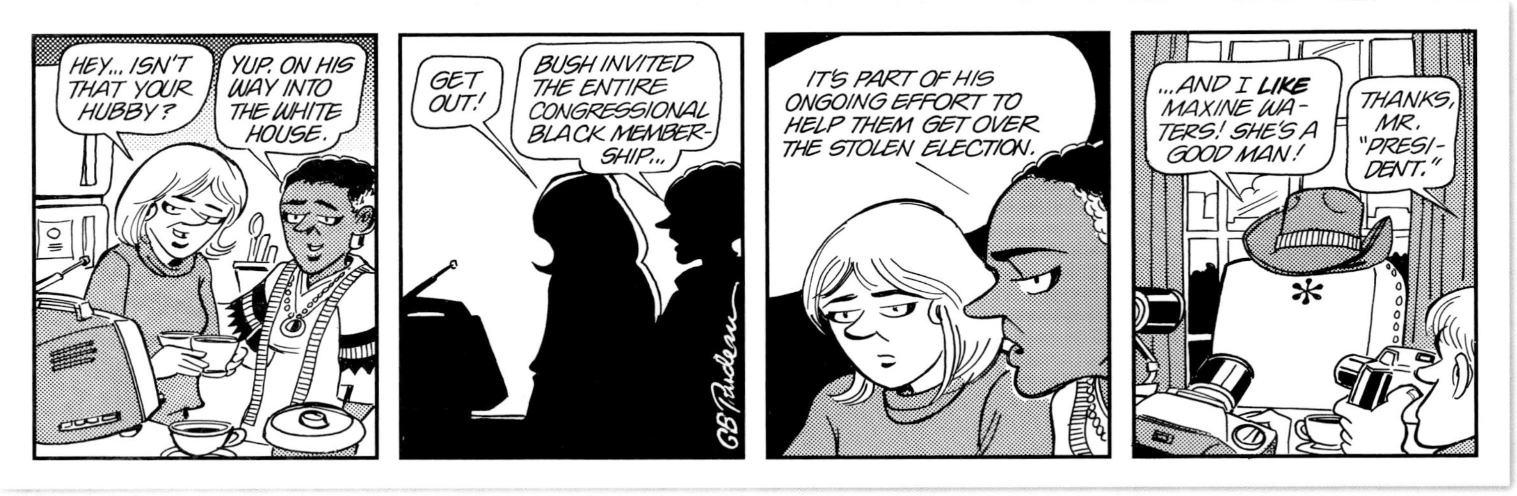
HEY... ISN'T THAT YOUR HUBBY?
YUP, ON HIS WAY INTO THE WHITE HOUSE.
GET OUT!
BUSH INVITED THE ENTIRE CONGRESSIONAL BLACK MEMBERSHIP...
IT'S PART OF HIS ONGOING EFFORT TO HELP THEM GET OVER THE STOLEN ELECTION.
...AND I **LIKE** MAXINE WATERS! SHE'S A GOOD MAN!
THANKS, MR. "PRESIDENT."

2/5/01

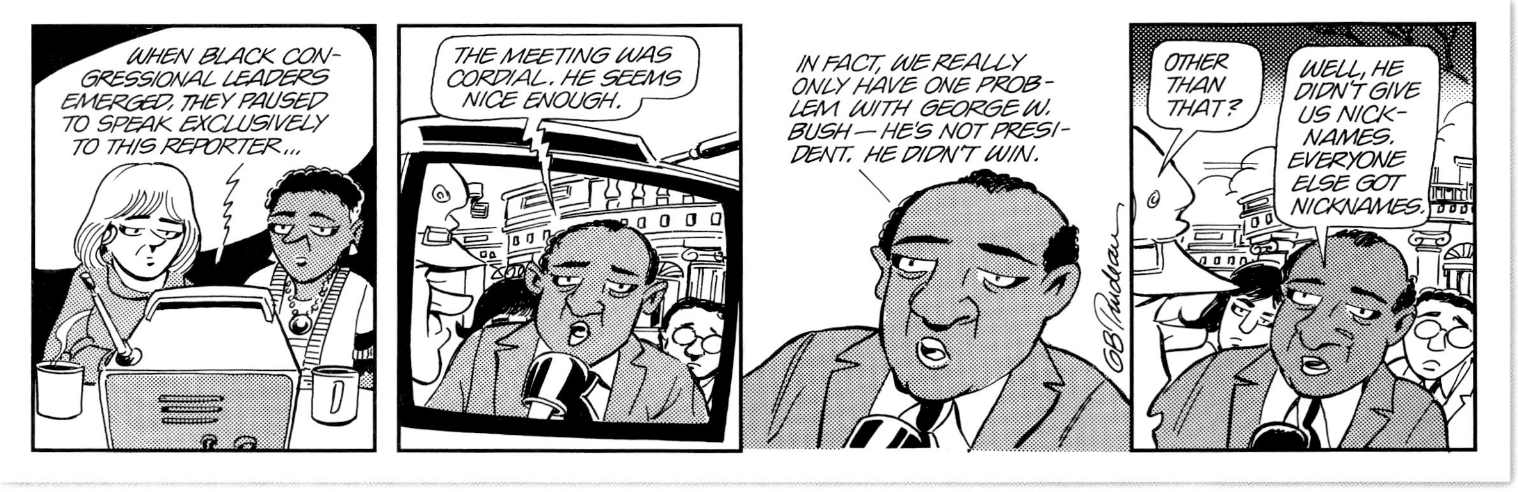
WHEN BLACK CONGRESSIONAL LEADERS EMERGED, THEY PAUSED TO SPEAK EXCLUSIVELY TO THIS REPORTER...
THE MEETING WAS CORDIAL. HE SEEMS NICE ENOUGH.
IN FACT, WE REALLY ONLY HAVE ONE PROBLEM WITH GEORGE W. BUSH — HE'S NOT PRESIDENT. HE DIDN'T WIN.
OTHER THAN THAT?
WELL, HE DIDN'T GIVE US NICKNAMES. EVERYONE ELSE GOT NICKNAMES.

2/8/01

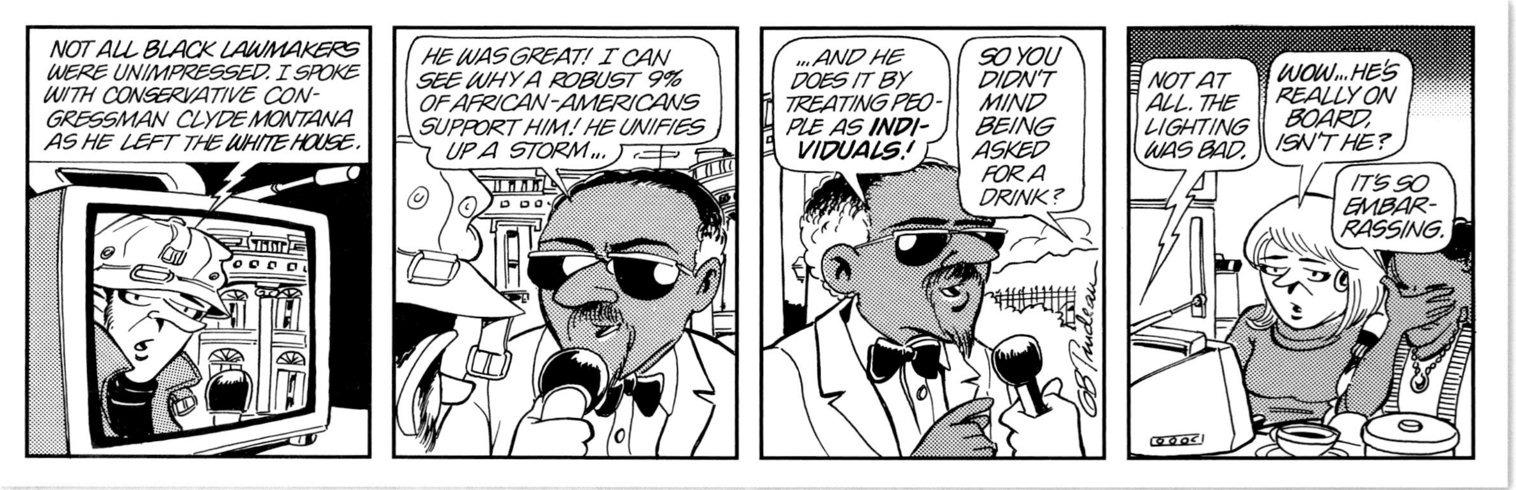
NOT ALL BLACK LAWMAKERS WERE UNIMPRESSED. I SPOKE WITH CONSERVATIVE CONGRESSMAN CLYDE MONTANA AS HE LEFT THE WHITE HOUSE.
HE WAS GREAT! I CAN SEE WHY A ROBUST 9% OF AFRICAN-AMERICANS SUPPORT HIM! HE UNIFIES UP A STORM...
...AND HE DOES IT BY TREATING PEOPLE AS **INDIVIDUALS**!
SO YOU DIDN'T MIND BEING ASKED FOR A DRINK?
NOT AT ALL. THE LIGHTING WAS BAD.
WOW... HE'S REALLY ON BOARD, ISN'T HE?
IT'S SO EMBARRASSING.

2/9/01

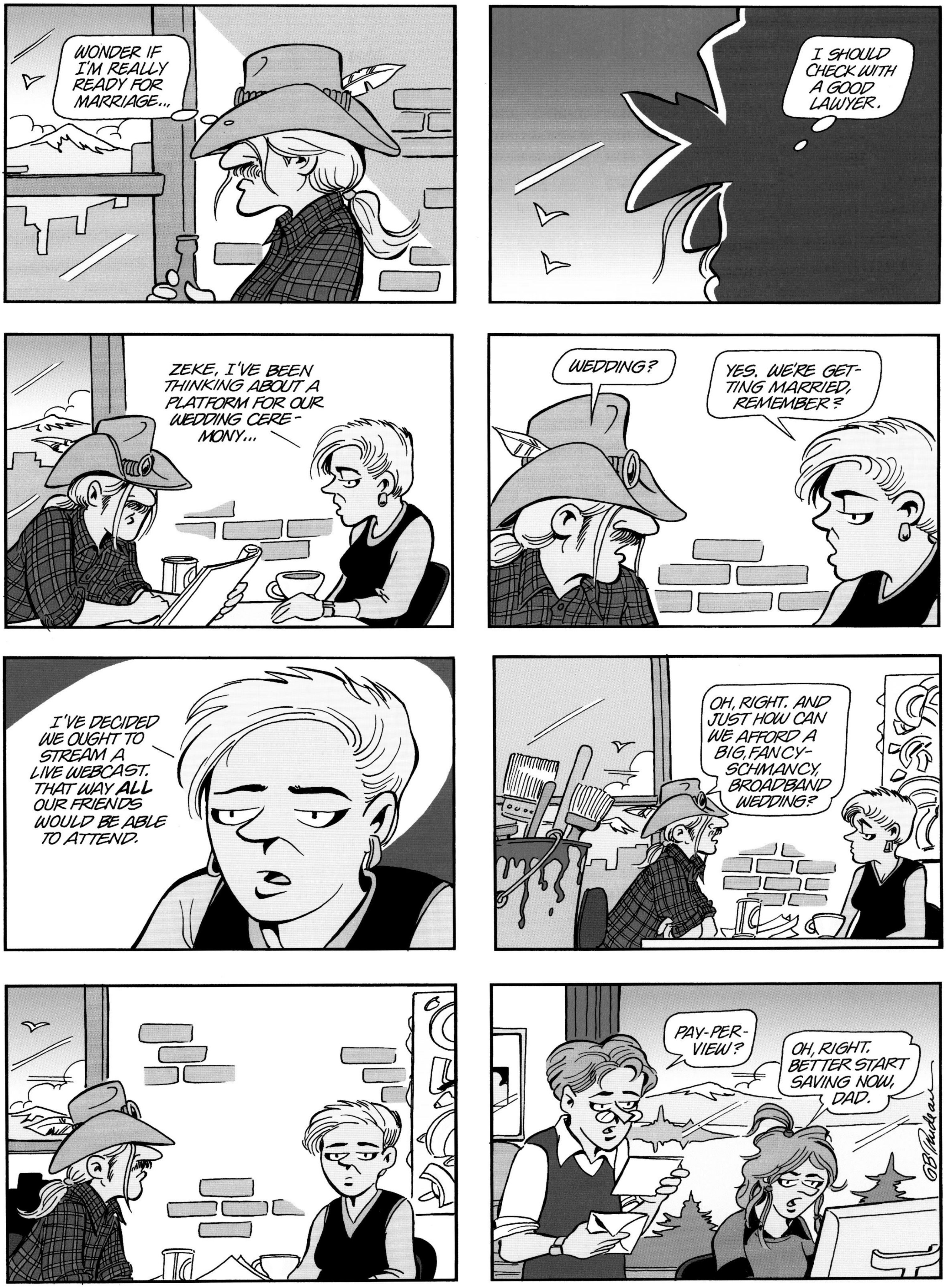

WONDER IF I'M REALLY READY FOR MARRIAGE...
I SHOULD CHECK WITH A GOOD LAWYER.
ZEKE, I'VE BEEN THINKING ABOUT A PLATFORM FOR OUR WEDDING CEREMONY...
WEDDING?
YES. WE'RE GETTING MARRIED, REMEMBER?
I'VE DECIDED WE OUGHT TO STREAM A LIVE WEBCAST. THAT WAY **ALL** OUR FRIENDS WOULD BE ABLE TO ATTEND.
OH, RIGHT. AND JUST HOW CAN WE AFFORD A BIG, FANCY-SCHMANCY, BROADBAND WEDDING?
PAY-PER-VIEW?
OH, RIGHT. BETTER START SAVING NOW, DAD.
GBTrudeau

3/4/01

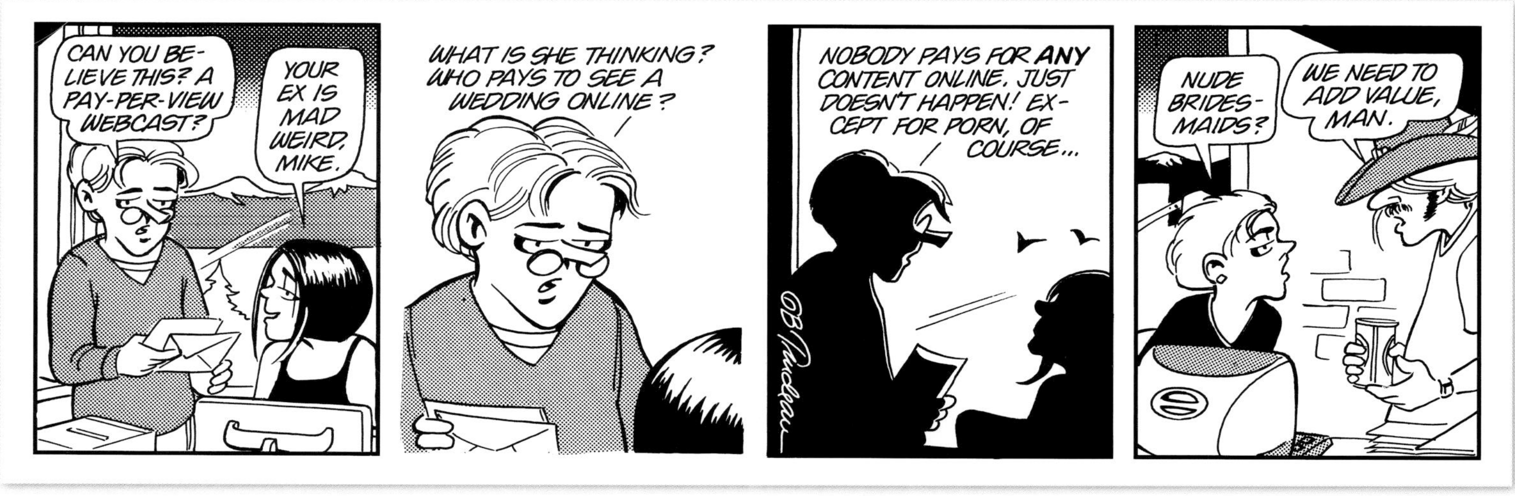
CAN YOU BE-LIEVE THIS? A PAY-PER-VIEW WEBCAST?
YOUR EX IS MAD WEIRD, MIKE.
WHAT IS SHE THINKING? WHO PAYS TO SEE A WEDDING ONLINE?
NOBODY PAYS FOR ANY CONTENT ONLINE. JUST DOESN'T HAPPEN! EX-CEPT FOR PORN, OF COURSE...
NUDE BRIDES-MAIDS?
WE NEED TO ADD VALUE, MAN.

3/14/01

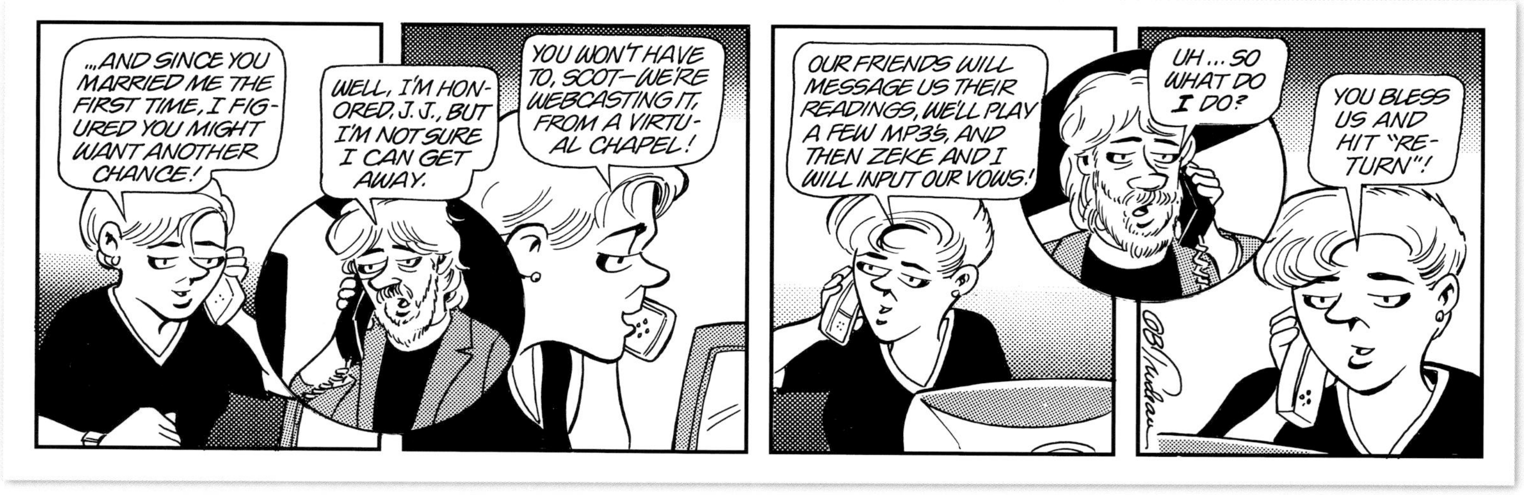
...AND SINCE YOU MARRIED ME THE FIRST TIME, I FIG-URED YOU MIGHT WANT ANOTHER CHANCE!
WELL, I'M HON-ORED, J.J., BUT I'M NOT SURE I CAN GET AWAY.
YOU WON'T HAVE TO, SCOT—WE'RE WEBCASTING IT, FROM A VIRTU-AL CHAPEL!
OUR FRIENDS WILL MESSAGE US THEIR READINGS, WE'LL PLAY A FEW MP3'S, AND THEN ZEKE AND I WILL INPUT OUR VOWS!
UH... SO WHAT DO I DO?
YOU BLESS US AND HIT "RE-TURN"!

3/17/01

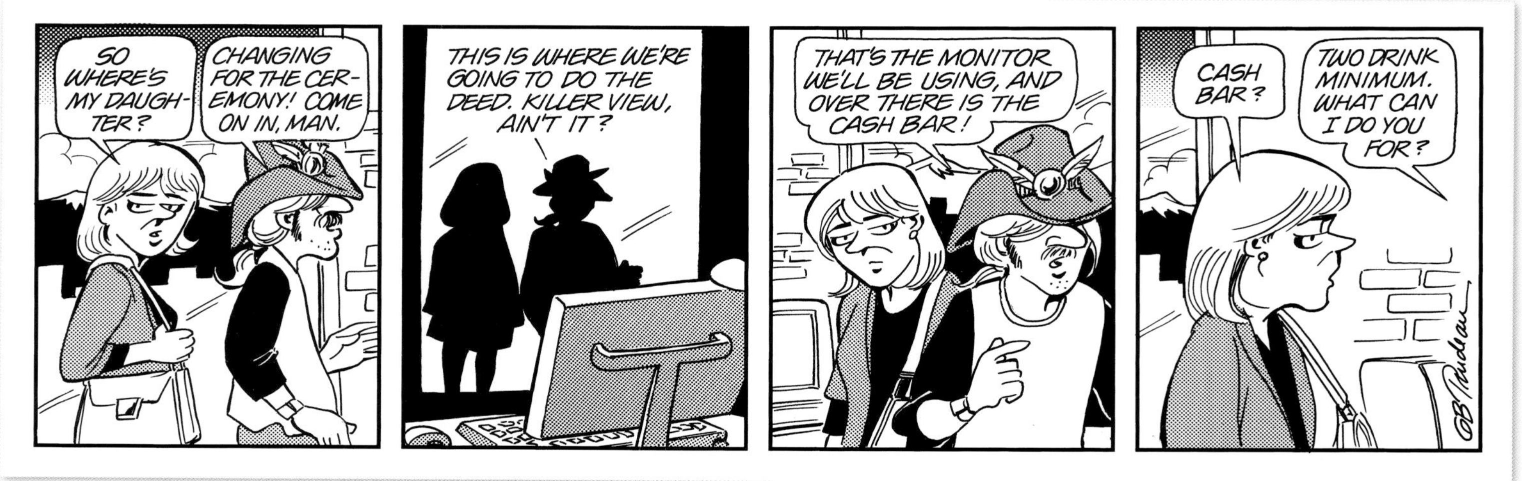
SO WHERE'S MY DAUGH-TER?
CHANGING FOR THE CER-EMONY! COME ON IN, MAN.
THIS IS WHERE WE'RE GOING TO DO THE DEED. KILLER VIEW, AIN'T IT?
THAT'S THE MONITOR WE'LL BE USING, AND OVER THERE IS THE CASH BAR!
CASH BAR?
TWO DRINK MINIMUM. WHAT CAN I DO YOU FOR?

3/19/01

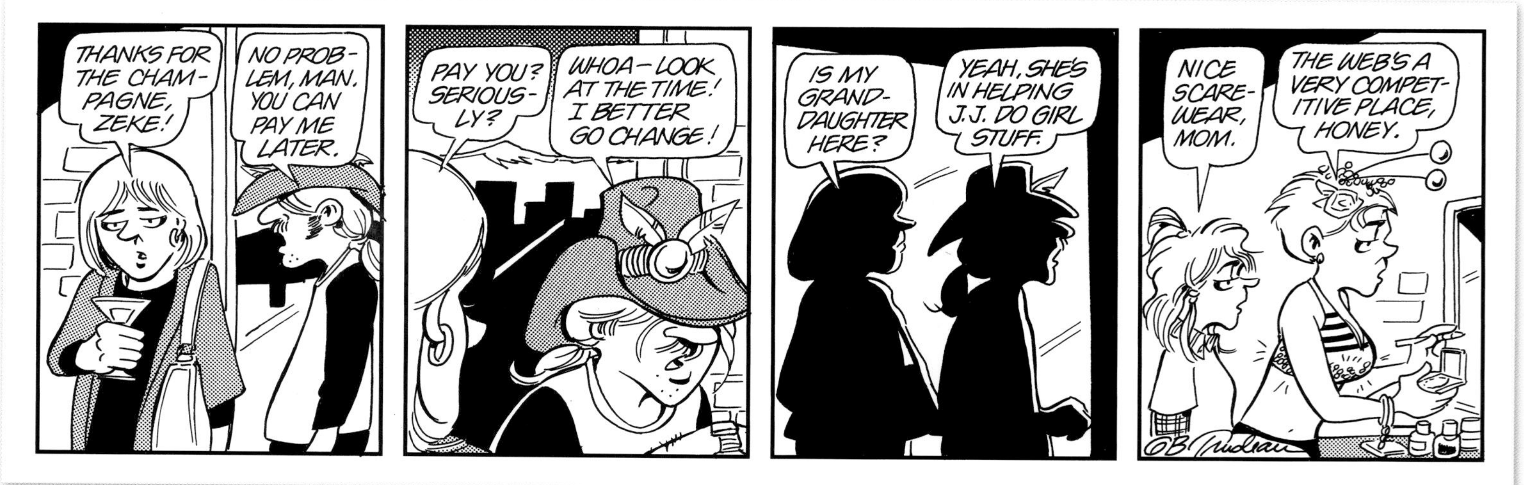
THANKS FOR THE CHAM-PAGNE, ZEKE!
NO PROB-LEM, MAN. YOU CAN PAY ME LATER.
PAY YOU? SERIOUS-LY?
WHOA—LOOK AT THE TIME! I BETTER GO CHANGE!
IS MY GRAND-DAUGHTER HERE?
YEAH, SHE'S IN HELPING J.J. DO GIRL STUFF.
NICE SCARE-WEAR, MOM.
THE WEB'S A VERY COMPET-ITIVE PLACE, HONEY.

3/20/01

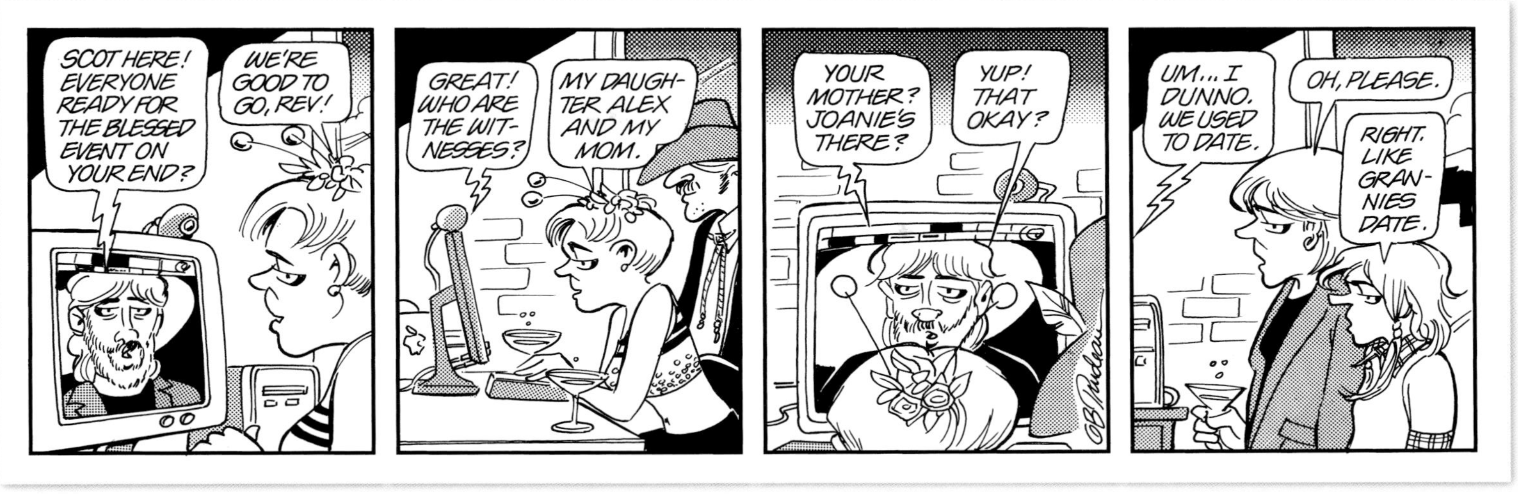
SCOT HERE! EVERYONE READY FOR THE BLESSED EVENT ON YOUR END?
WE'RE GOOD TO GO, REV!
GREAT! WHO ARE THE WITNESSES?
MY DAUGHTER ALEX AND MY MOM.
YOUR MOTHER? JOANIE'S THERE?
YUP! THAT OKAY?
UM... I DUNNO. WE USED TO DATE.
OH, PLEASE.
RIGHT. LIKE GRANNIES DATE.

3/21/01

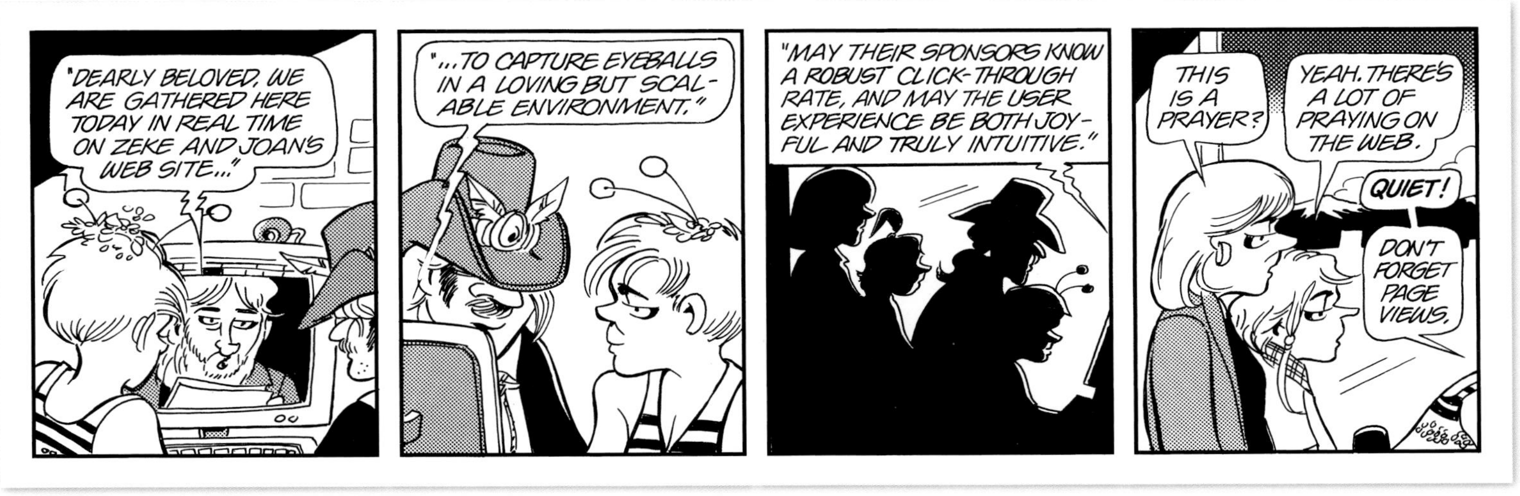
"DEARLY BELOVED, WE ARE GATHERED HERE TODAY IN REAL TIME ON ZEKE AND JOAN'S WEB SITE..."
"...TO CAPTURE EYEBALLS IN A LOVING BUT SCALABLE ENVIRONMENT."
"MAY THEIR SPONSORS KNOW A ROBUST CLICK-THROUGH RATE, AND MAY THE USER EXPERIENCE BE BOTH JOYFUL AND TRULY INTUITIVE."
THIS IS A PRAYER?
YEAH. THERE'S A LOT OF PRAYING ON THE WEB.
QUIET!
DON'T FORGET PAGE VIEWS.

3/22/01

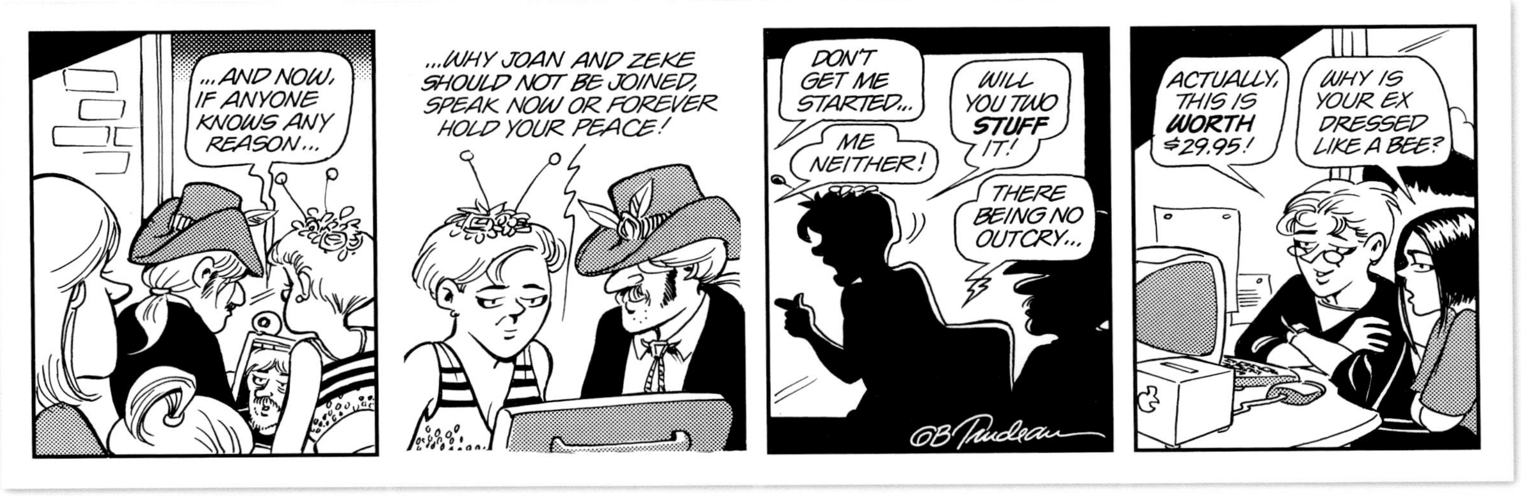
...AND NOW, IF ANYONE KNOWS ANY REASON...
...WHY JOAN AND ZEKE SHOULD NOT BE JOINED, SPEAK NOW OR FOREVER HOLD YOUR PEACE!
DON'T GET ME STARTED...
ME NEITHER!
WILL YOU TWO STUFF IT!
THERE BEING NO OUTCRY...
ACTUALLY, THIS IS WORTH $29.95!
WHY IS YOUR EX DRESSED LIKE A BEE?

3/23/01

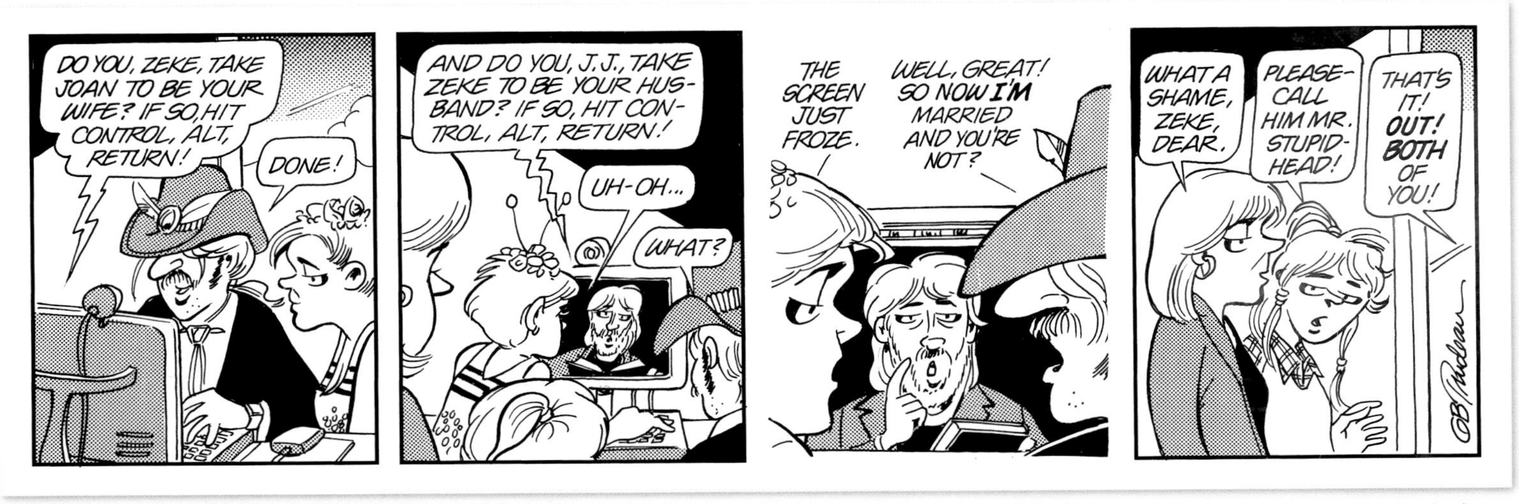
DO YOU, ZEKE, TAKE JOAN TO BE YOUR WIFE? IF SO, HIT CONTROL, ALT, RETURN!
DONE!
AND DO YOU, J.J., TAKE ZEKE TO BE YOUR HUSBAND? IF SO, HIT CONTROL, ALT, RETURN!
UH-OH...
WHAT?
THE SCREEN JUST FROZE.
WELL, GREAT! SO NOW I'M MARRIED AND YOU'RE NOT?
WHAT A SHAME, ZEKE, DEAR.
PLEASE-CALL HIM MR. STUPIDHEAD!
THAT'S IT! OUT! BOTH OF YOU!

3/24/01

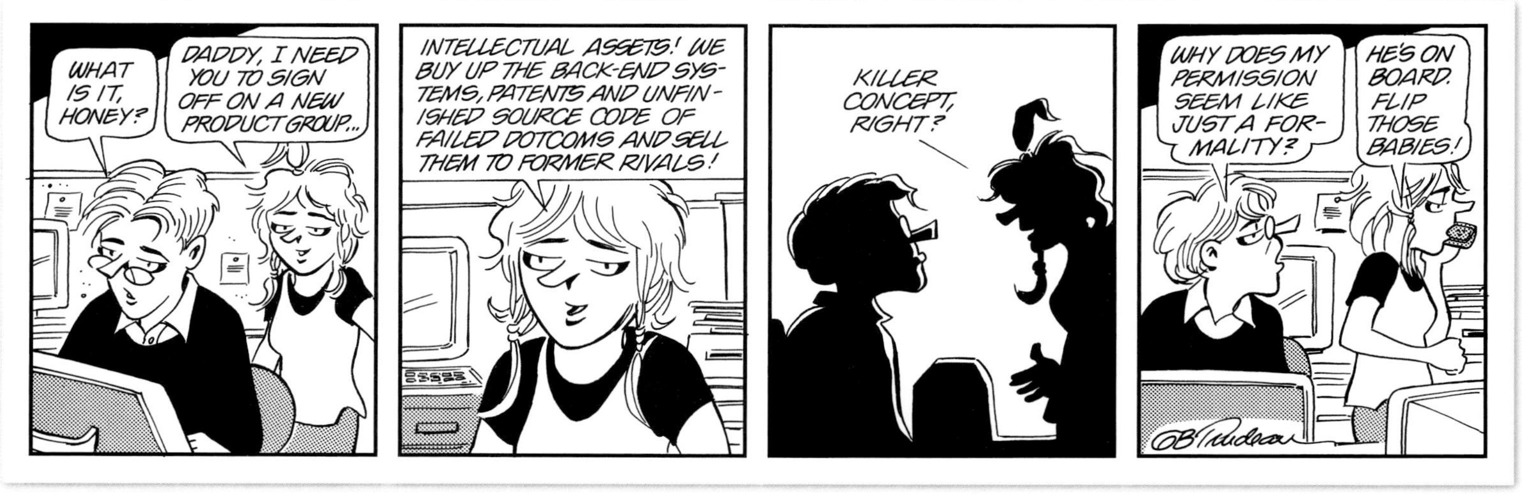
WHAT IS IT, HONEY?
DADDY, I NEED YOU TO SIGN OFF ON A NEW PRODUCT GROUP...
INTELLECTUAL ASSETS! WE BUY UP THE BACK-END SYSTEMS, PATENTS AND UNFINISHED SOURCE CODE OF FAILED DOTCOMS AND SELL THEM TO FORMER RIVALS!
KILLER CONCEPT, RIGHT?
WHY DOES MY PERMISSION SEEM LIKE JUST A FORMALITY?
HE'S ON BOARD. FLIP THOSE BABIES!
GBTrudeau

7/2/01

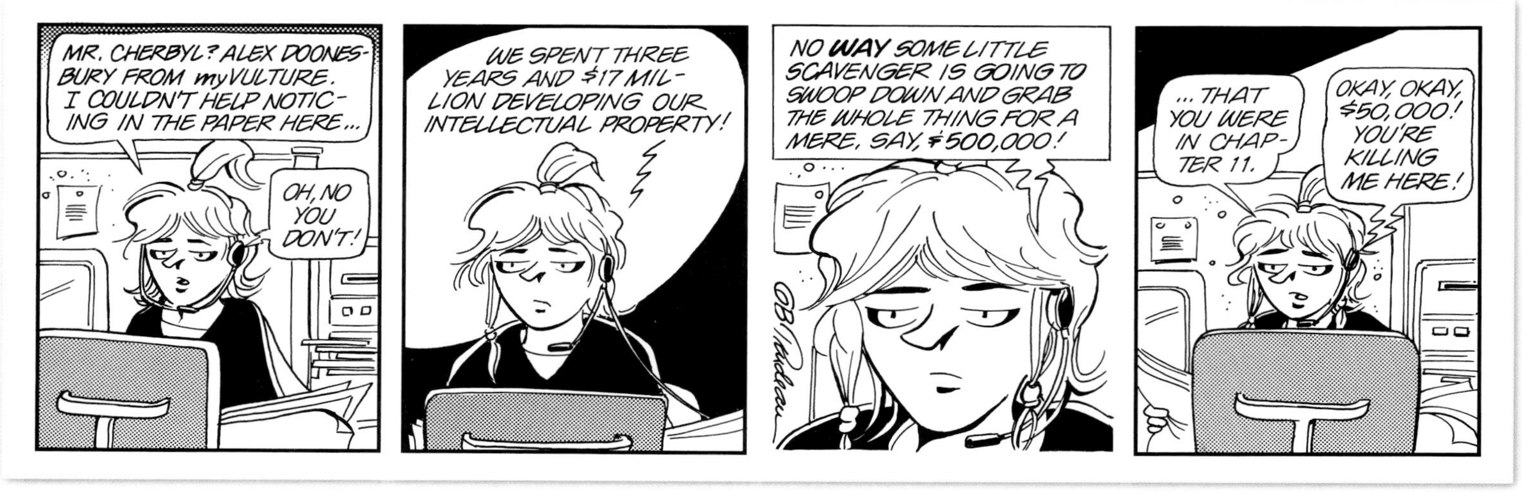
MR. CHERBYL? ALEX DOONESBURY FROM myVULTURE. I COULDN'T HELP NOTICING IN THE PAPER HERE...
OH, NO YOU DON'T!
WE SPENT THREE YEARS AND $17 MILLION DEVELOPING OUR INTELLECTUAL PROPERTY!
NO WAY SOME LITTLE SCAVENGER IS GOING TO SWOOP DOWN AND GRAB THE WHOLE THING FOR A MERE, SAY, $500,000!
...THAT YOU WERE IN CHAPTER 11.
OKAY, OKAY, $50,000! YOU'RE KILLING ME HERE!
GBTrudeau

7/3/01

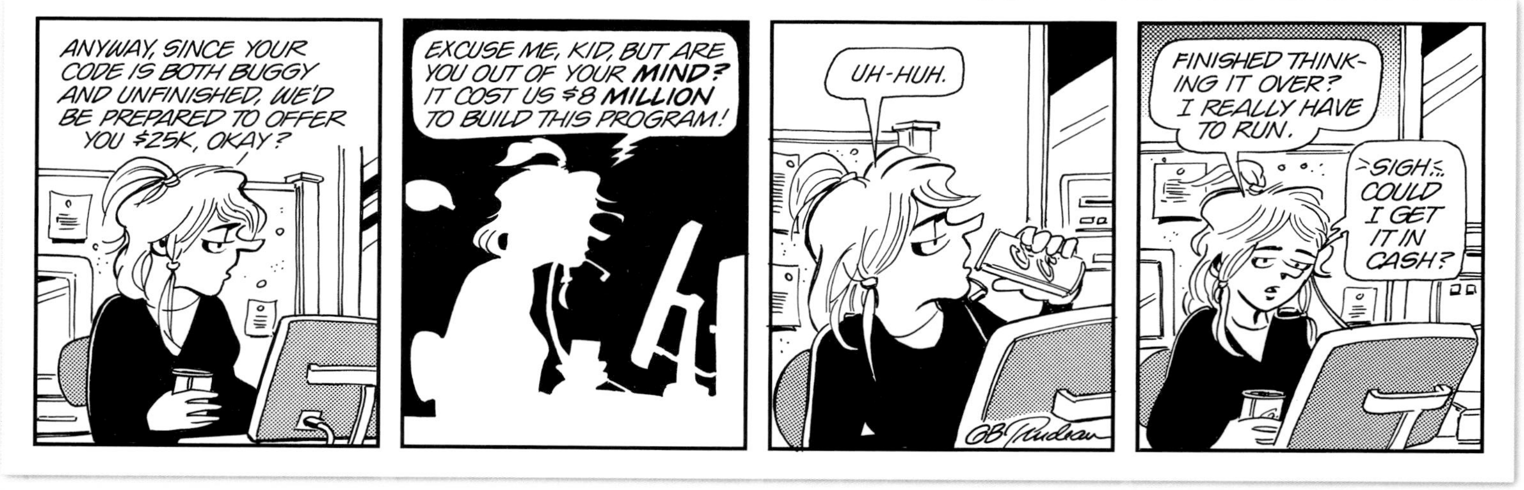
ANYWAY, SINCE YOUR CODE IS BOTH BUGGY AND UNFINISHED, WE'D BE PREPARED TO OFFER YOU $25K, OKAY?
EXCUSE ME, KID, BUT ARE YOU OUT OF YOUR MIND? IT COST US $8 MILLION TO BUILD THIS PROGRAM!
UH-HUH.
FINISHED THINKING IT OVER? I REALLY HAVE TO RUN.
>SIGH<... COULD I GET IT IN CASH?
GBTrudeau

7/4/01

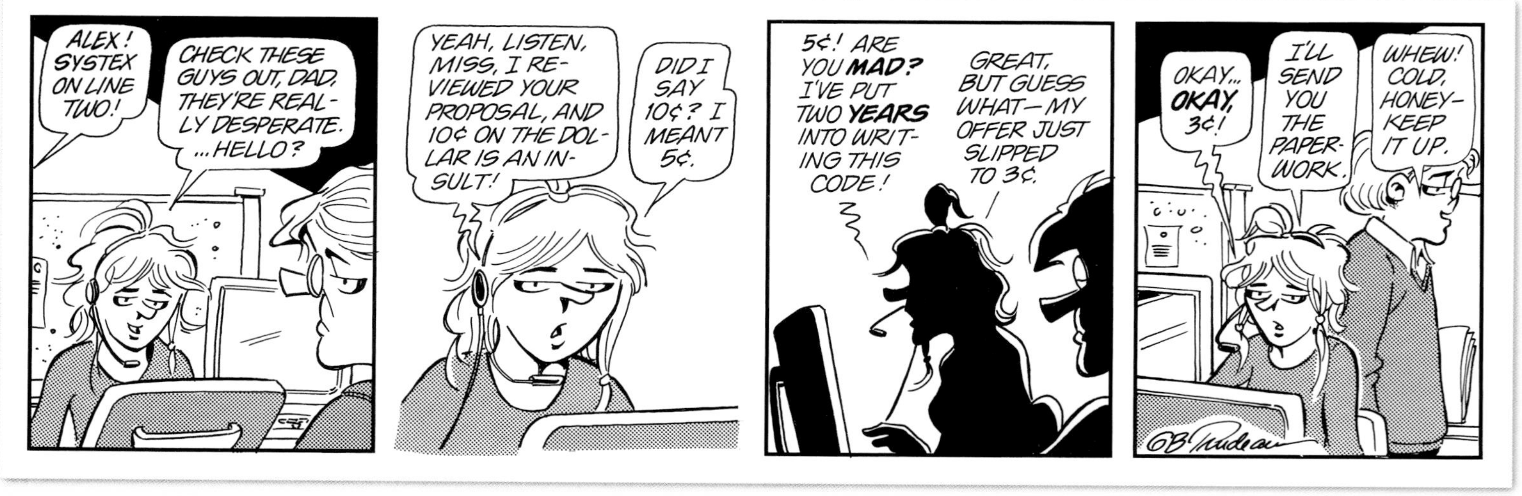
ALEX! SYSTEX ON LINE TWO!
CHECK THESE GUYS OUT, DAD, THEY'RE REALLY DESPERATE. ...HELLO?
YEAH, LISTEN, MISS, I REVIEWED YOUR PROPOSAL, AND 10¢ ON THE DOLLAR IS AN INSULT!
DID I SAY 10¢? I MEANT 5¢.
5¢! ARE YOU MAD? I'VE PUT TWO YEARS INTO WRITING THIS CODE!
GREAT, BUT GUESS WHAT—MY OFFER JUST SLIPPED TO 3¢.
OKAY... OKAY, 3¢!
I'LL SEND YOU THE PAPERWORK.
WHEW! COLD, HONEY—KEEP IT UP.
GBTrudeau

7/6/01

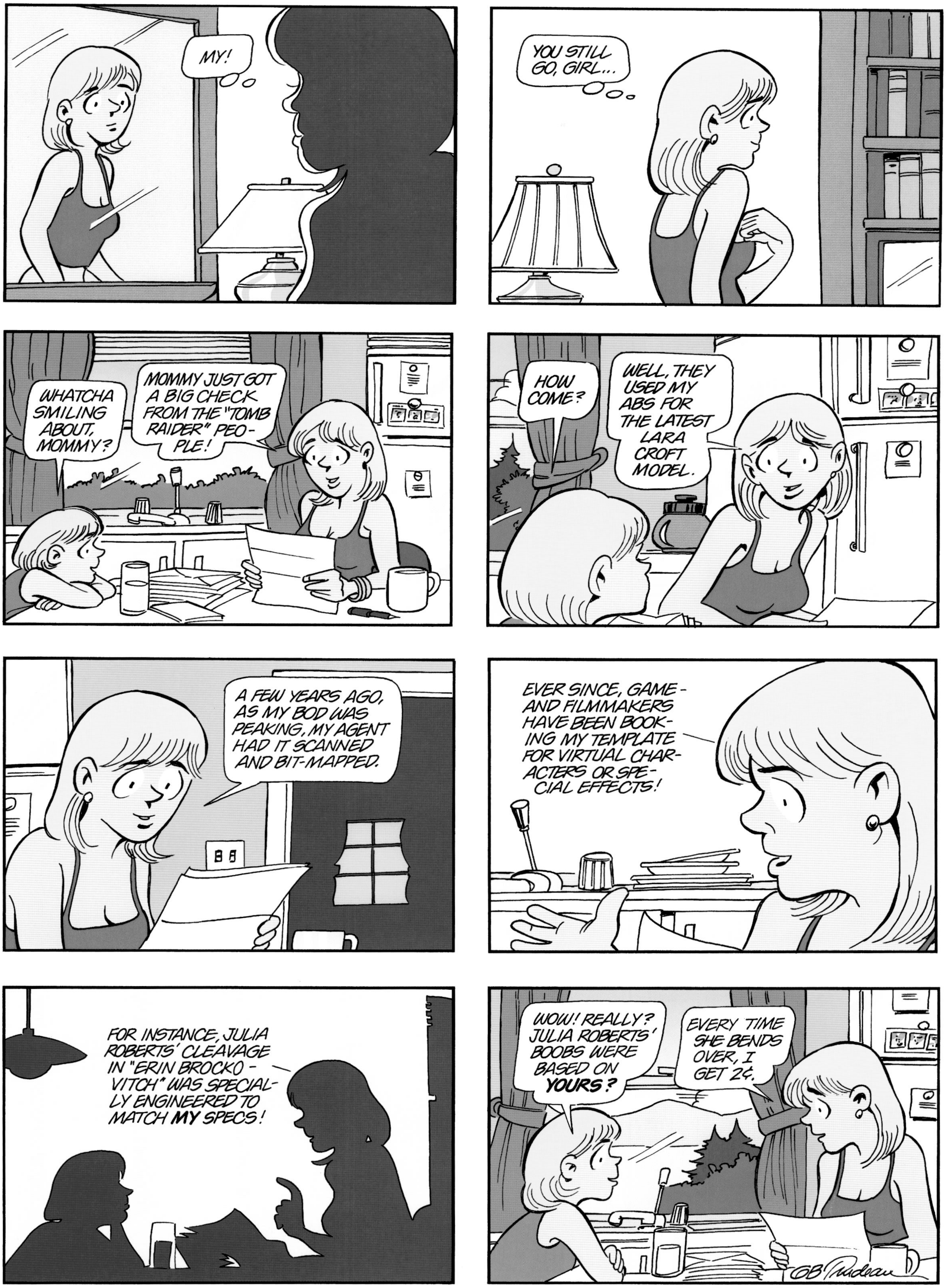
MY!
YOU STILL GO, GIRL...
WHATCHA SMILING ABOUT, MOMMY?
MOMMY JUST GOT A BIG CHECK FROM THE "TOMB RAIDER" PEO-PLE!
HOW COME?
WELL, THEY USED MY ABS FOR THE LATEST LARA CROFT MODEL.
A FEW YEARS AGO, AS MY BOD WAS PEAKING, MY AGENT HAD IT SCANNED AND BIT-MAPPED.
EVER SINCE, GAME- AND FILMMAKERS HAVE BEEN BOOK-ING MY TEMPLATE FOR VIRTUAL CHAR-ACTERS OR SPE-CIAL EFFECTS!
FOR INSTANCE, JULIA ROBERTS' CLEAVAGE IN "ERIN BROCKO-VITCH" WAS SPECIAL-LY ENGINEERED TO MATCH **MY** SPECS!
WOW! REALLY? JULIA ROBERTS' BOOBS WERE BASED ON **YOURS**?
EVERY TIME SHE BENDS OVER, I GET 2¢.
GB Trudeau

8/26/01

Alice Schwartzman

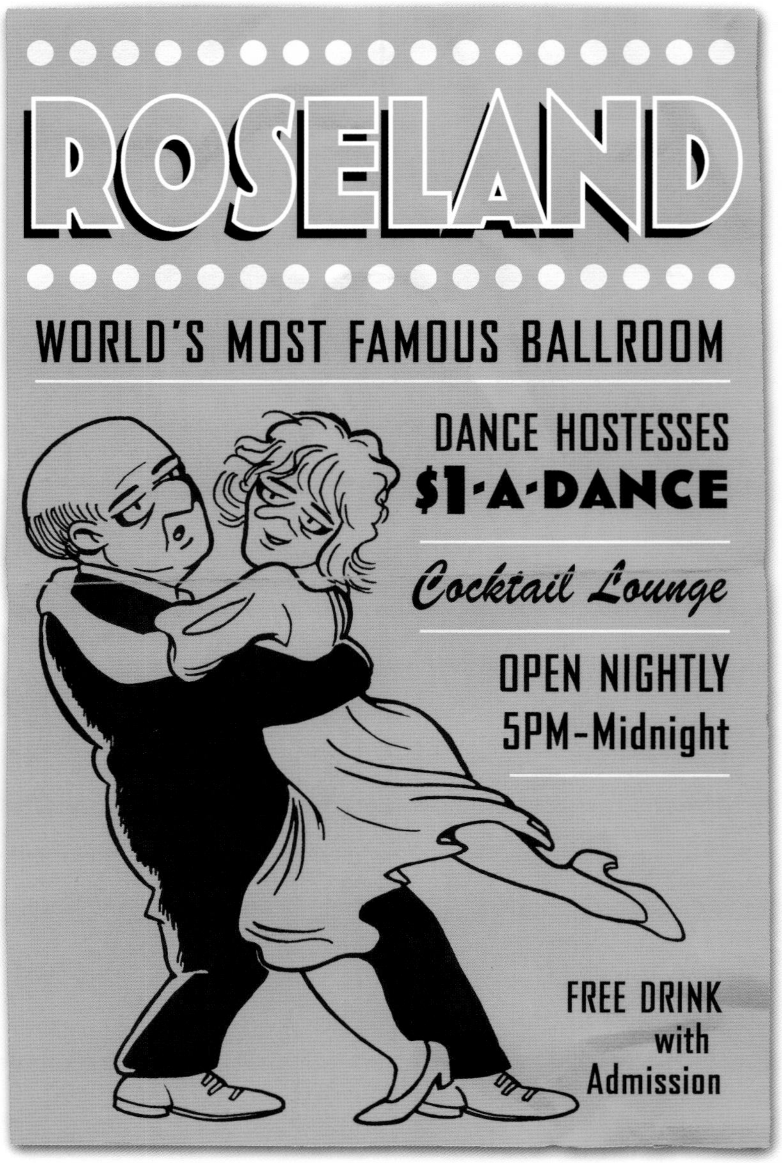
ROSELAND
WORLD'S MOST FAMOUS BALLROOM
DANCE HOSTESSES
$1-A-DANCE
Cocktail Lounge
OPEN NIGHTLY
5PM-Midnight
FREE DRINK
with
Admission

By 1987, New York's legendary Roseland Ballroom was a dingy, forlorn place. Its glory days as the city's premier swing band showcase long behind it, all that remained of its glamorous legacy was the afternoon taxi dancing. Eight bucks got you in the door, and once there, a spin around the floor with a "dance hostess" set you back a dollar.

One warm spring day, I paid a visit to Roseland, thinking it might provide the perfect setting for Alice, my ruined debutante, to reconnect with happier times. My idea was to have her migrate up to the city every spring, and with a borrowed chiffon gown, join the ballroom's band of hired hoofers. Accustomed to the melancholy of lost souls, Alice would be in her element, free to summon the gaiety of her younger self—the one who stopped hearts with her dips and swirls at schoolgirl cotillions. (It helped that I'd met such a person at a local shelter—an elderly bag lady who talked ceaselessly and, it turned out, truthfully, about her days in the Ziegfeld Follies.)

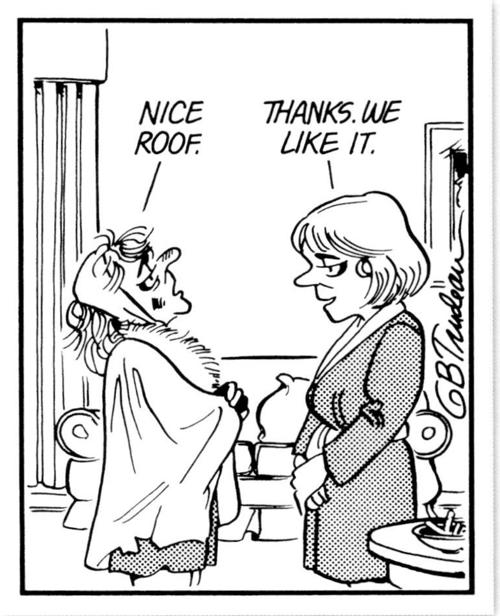
NICE ROOF.
THANKS. WE LIKE IT.

The place seemed ideal, and set in motion a simple tale of convergence: Alice is seated behind the taxi table when out of the afternoon sunlight wanders troubled financier Phil Slackmeyer. A refugee from a different story line, Phil encounters Alice at the nadir of his fortunes. Like Alice, Phil is there to recall a more innocent time, when as a City College student, he used to watch Ann Miller flash her gams in the hottest club in town.

Phil hands over his ticket, and as the unlikely couple floats around the empty ballroom, the cares of both are momentarily lifted. The scene might have seemed irredeemably sentimental had I not arranged for Phil to be arrested for insider trading the next morning. This was to be his last tango before the trip upriver. But Alice never learns this; her time with Phil is just a pleasant, metered interlude among many. Soon enough, she's back on the streets of Washington, sharing a steam grate with Elmont, her beloved head case of a husband. And life rolls on.

The temptation with homeless characters is to make them content with their circumstances—happy hobos who've somehow reconciled themselves to life's harshness. And some of the indigent I've met do in fact project a kind of irrepressible dignity. My friend Roger knew a homeless man who had set up a living room on the sidewalk outside his apartment building. One day, Roger sat down in one of the tattered armchairs and engaged the squatter in small talk. After a few moments of polite chitchat, the man looked at his watch and said, "Roger, I'm sorry to cut this short, but I'm expecting company."

Delusion can seem charming at such moments, but from there, it's straight to heartbreak. It's a challenge to keep the stories of the homeless bearable, and sometimes I don't even try. The *Washington Post* once ran a photograph of a homeless couple buried in a snowdrift in front of the White House. A decade earlier, I'd drawn Alice buried in snow in that precise spot, but this time, I just clipped the photo and pasted it into the strip.

Here, folks, I was saying, this is real, this is happening. Try smiling at this.

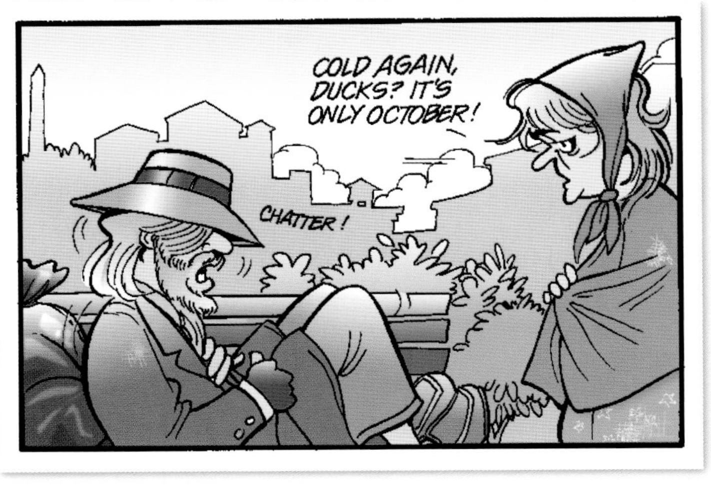
COLD AGAIN, DUCKS? IT'S ONLY OCTOBER!
CHATTER!

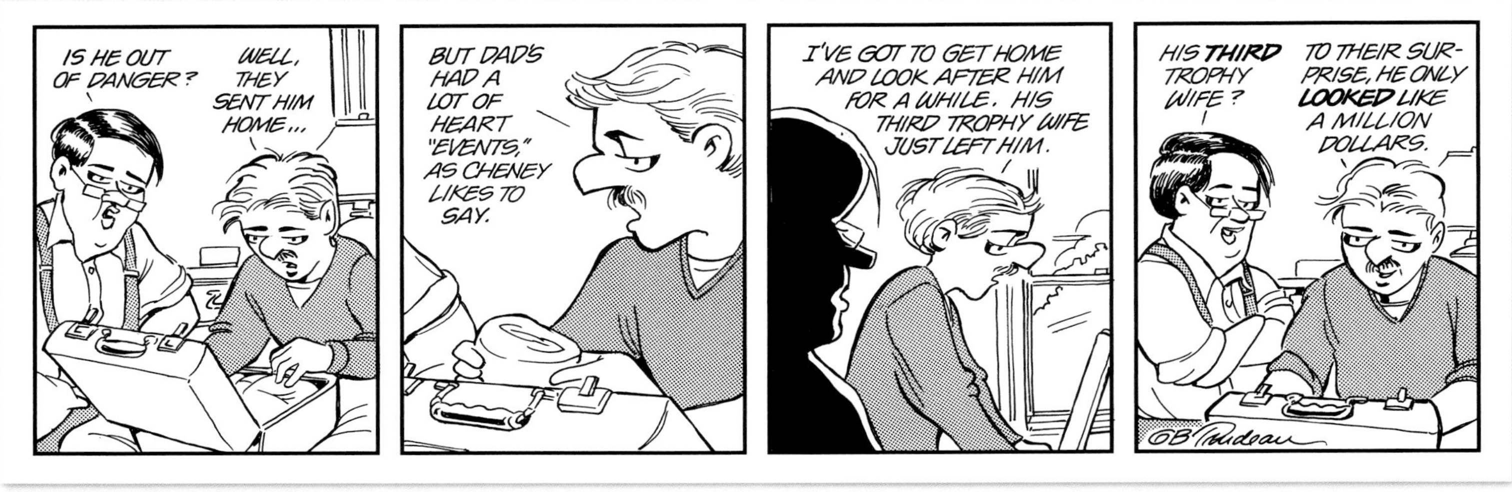
IS HE OUT OF DANGER?
WELL, THEY SENT HIM HOME...
BUT DAD'S HAD A LOT OF HEART "EVENTS," AS CHENEY LIKES TO SAY.
I'VE GOT TO GET HOME AND LOOK AFTER HIM FOR A WHILE. HIS THIRD TROPHY WIFE JUST LEFT HIM.
HIS **THIRD** TROPHY WIFE?
TO THEIR SURPRISE, HE ONLY **LOOKED** LIKE A MILLION DOLLARS.
GBTrudeau

9/3/01

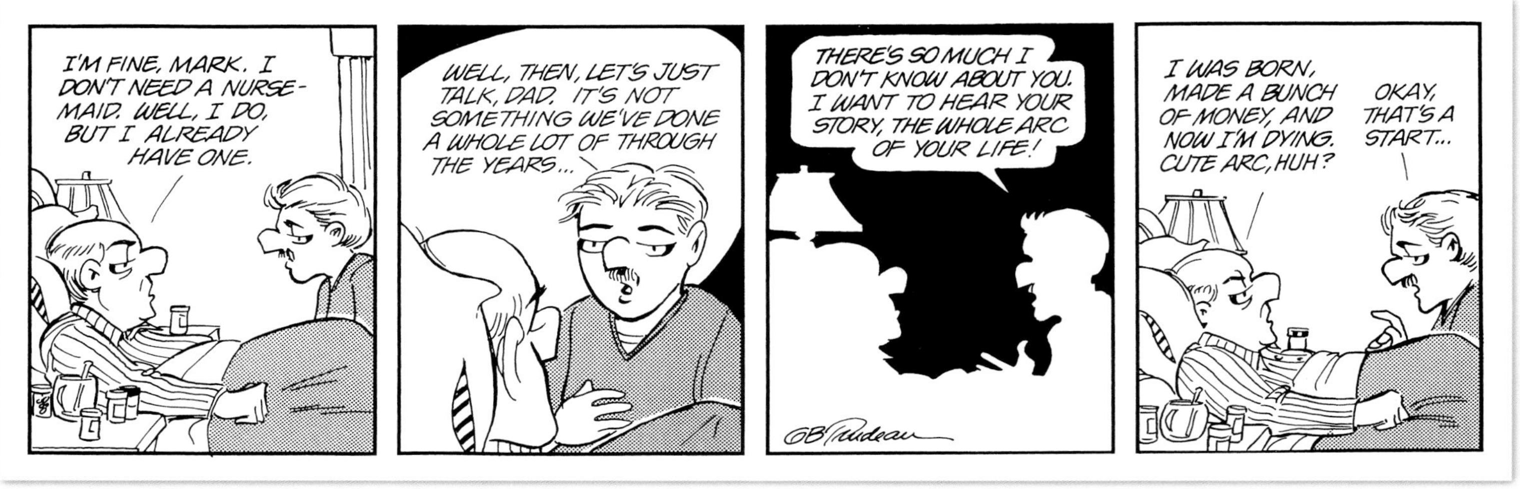
I'M FINE, MARK. I DON'T NEED A NURSEMAID. WELL, I DO, BUT I ALREADY HAVE ONE.
WELL, THEN, LET'S JUST TALK, DAD. IT'S NOT SOMETHING WE'VE DONE A WHOLE LOT OF THROUGH THE YEARS...
THERE'S SO MUCH I DON'T KNOW ABOUT YOU. I WANT TO HEAR YOUR STORY, THE WHOLE ARC OF YOUR LIFE!
GBTrudeau
I WAS BORN, MADE A BUNCH OF MONEY, AND NOW I'M DYING. CUTE ARC, HUH?
OKAY, THAT'S A START...

9/4/01

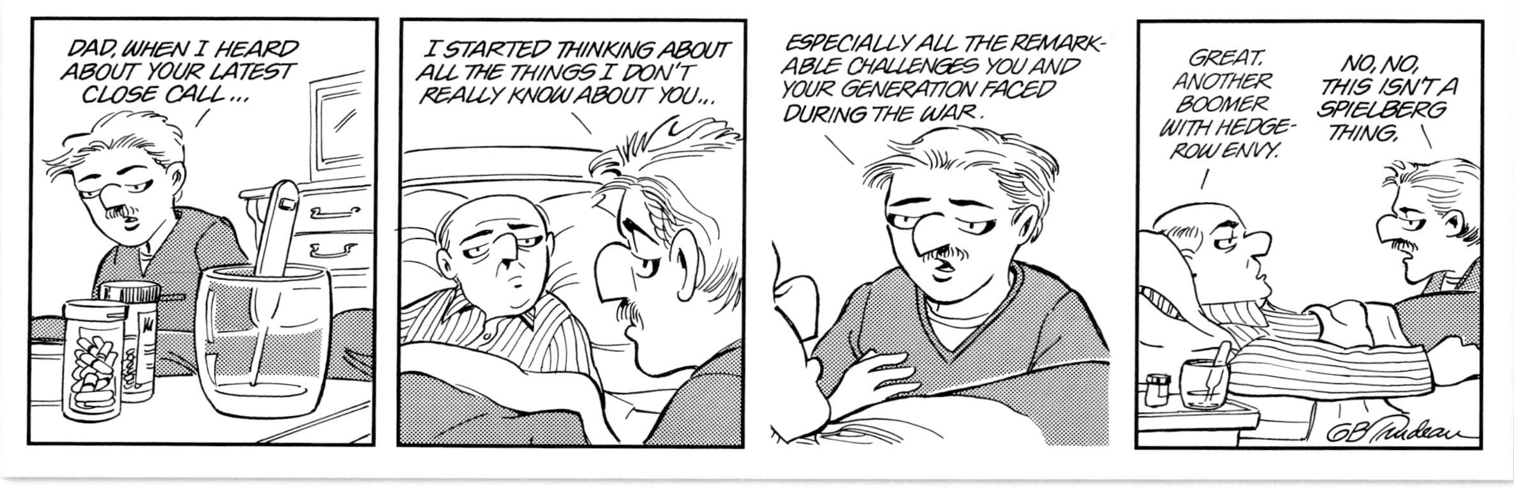
DAD, WHEN I HEARD ABOUT YOUR LATEST CLOSE CALL...
I STARTED THINKING ABOUT ALL THE THINGS I DON'T REALLY KNOW ABOUT YOU...
ESPECIALLY ALL THE REMARKABLE CHALLENGES YOU AND YOUR GENERATION FACED DURING THE WAR.
GREAT. ANOTHER BOOMER WITH HEDGEROW ENVY.
NO, NO, THIS ISN'T A SPIELBERG THING.
GBTrudeau

9/5/01

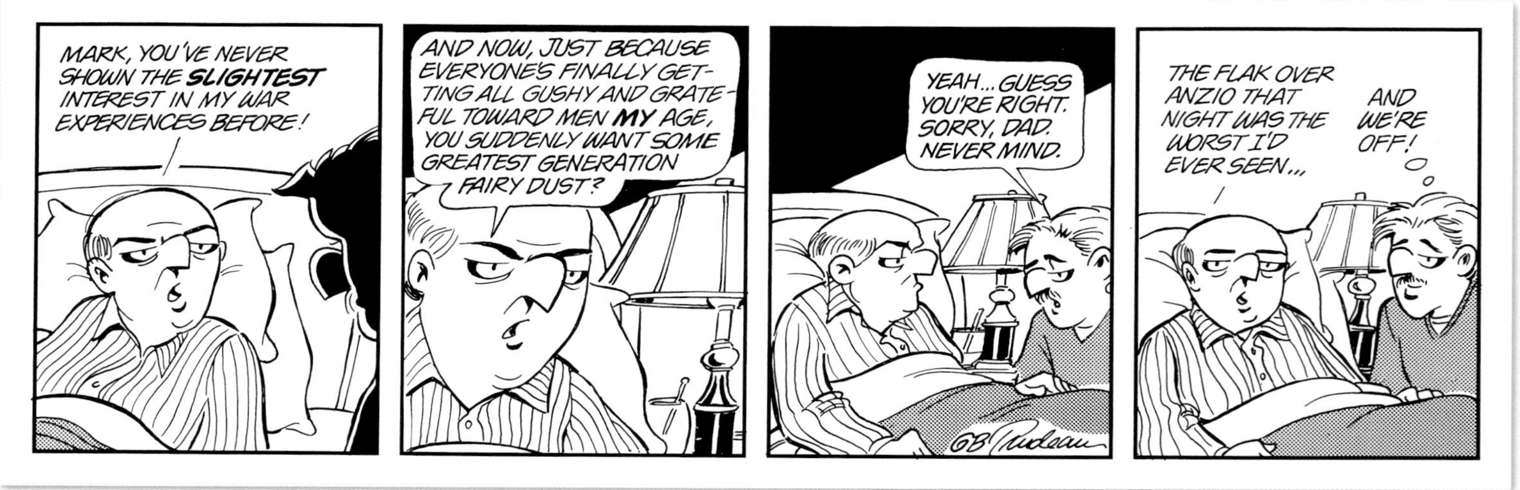
MARK, YOU'VE NEVER SHOWN THE **SLIGHTEST** INTEREST IN MY WAR EXPERIENCES BEFORE!
AND NOW, JUST BECAUSE EVERYONE'S FINALLY GETTING ALL GUSHY AND GRATEFUL TOWARD MEN **MY** AGE, YOU SUDDENLY WANT SOME GREATEST GENERATION FAIRY DUST?
YEAH... GUESS YOU'RE RIGHT. SORRY, DAD. NEVER MIND.
GBTrudeau
THE FLAK OVER ANZIO THAT NIGHT WAS THE WORST I'D EVER SEEN...
AND WE'RE OFF!

9/8/01

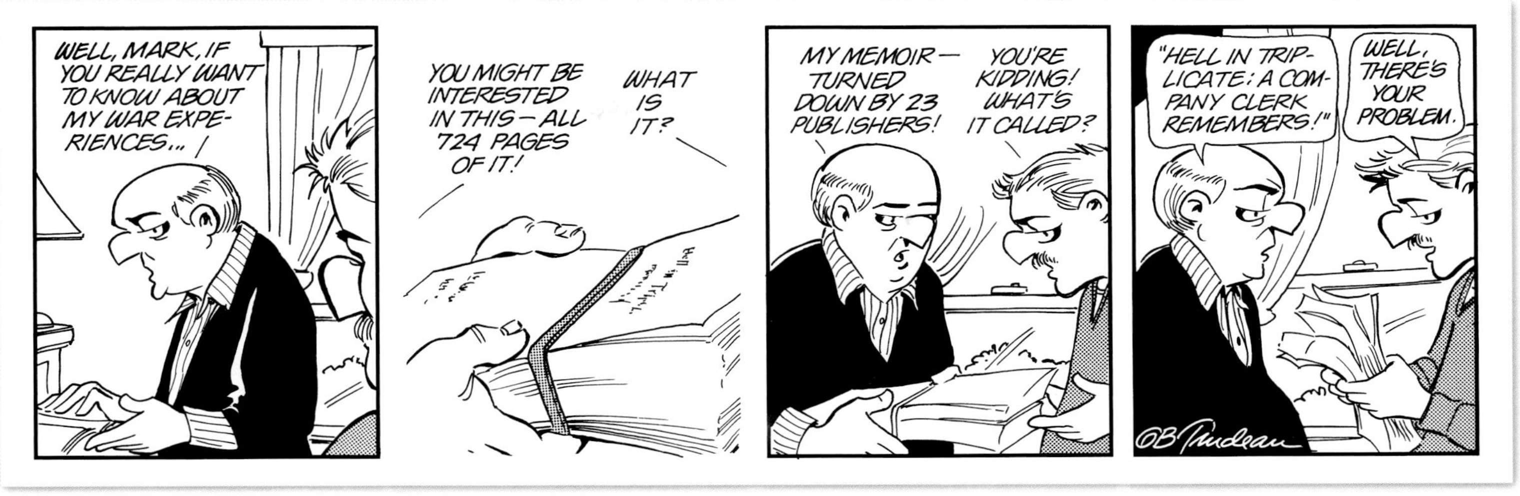
WELL, MARK, IF YOU REALLY WANT TO KNOW ABOUT MY WAR EXPERIENCES... !
YOU MIGHT BE INTERESTED IN THIS — ALL 724 PAGES OF IT!
WHAT IS IT?
MY MEMOIR — TURNED DOWN BY 23 PUBLISHERS!
YOU'RE KIDDING! WHAT'S IT CALLED?
"HELL IN TRIPLICATE: A COMPANY CLERK REMEMBERS!"
WELL, THERE'S YOUR PROBLEM.

9/10/01

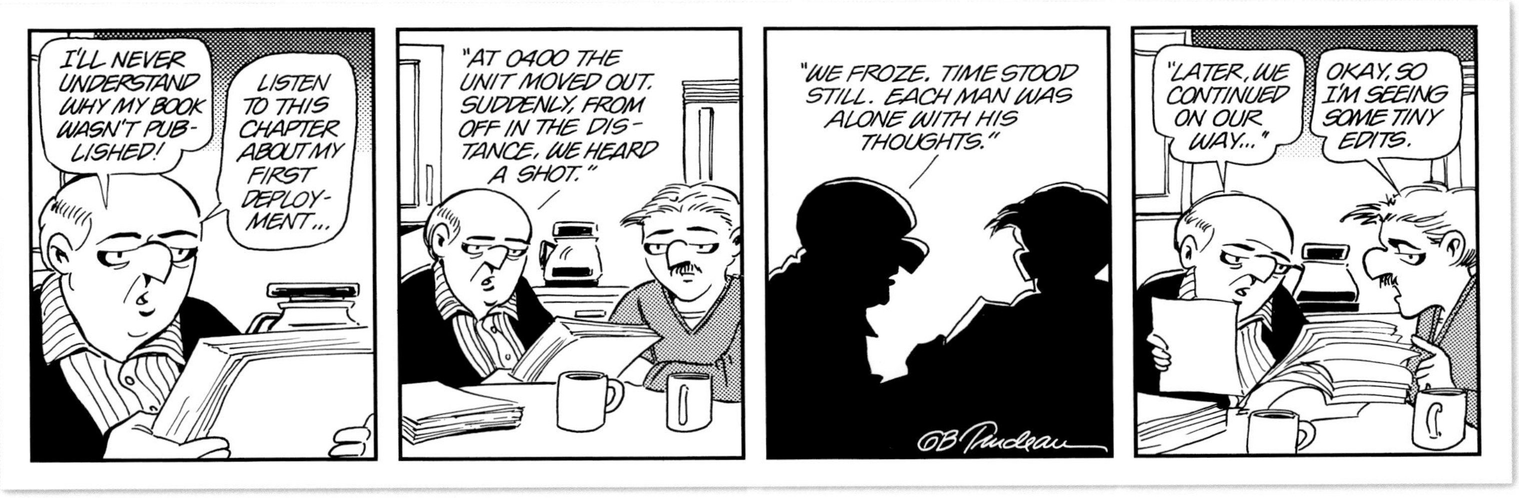
I'LL NEVER UNDERSTAND WHY MY BOOK WASN'T PUBLISHED!
LISTEN TO THIS CHAPTER ABOUT MY FIRST DEPLOYMENT...
"AT 0400 THE UNIT MOVED OUT. SUDDENLY, FROM OFF IN THE DISTANCE, WE HEARD A SHOT."
"WE FROZE. TIME STOOD STILL. EACH MAN WAS ALONE WITH HIS THOUGHTS."
"LATER, WE CONTINUED ON OUR WAY..."
OKAY, SO I'M SEEING SOME TINY EDITS.

9/11/01

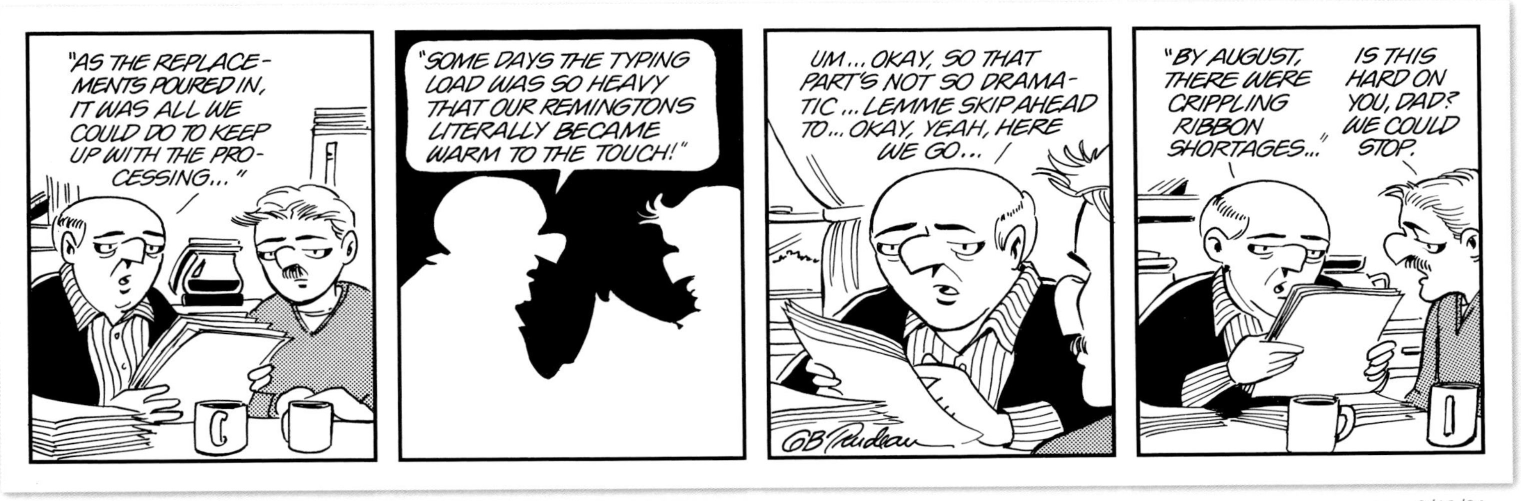
"AS THE REPLACEMENTS POURED IN, IT WAS ALL WE COULD DO TO KEEP UP WITH THE PROCESSING..."
"SOME DAYS THE TYPING LOAD WAS SO HEAVY THAT OUR REMINGTONS LITERALLY BECAME WARM TO THE TOUCH!"
UM... OKAY, SO THAT PART'S NOT SO DRAMATIC... LEMME SKIP AHEAD TO... OKAY, YEAH, HERE WE GO... !
"BY AUGUST, THERE WERE CRIPPLING RIBBON SHORTAGES..."
IS THIS HARD ON YOU, DAD? WE COULD STOP.

9/12/01

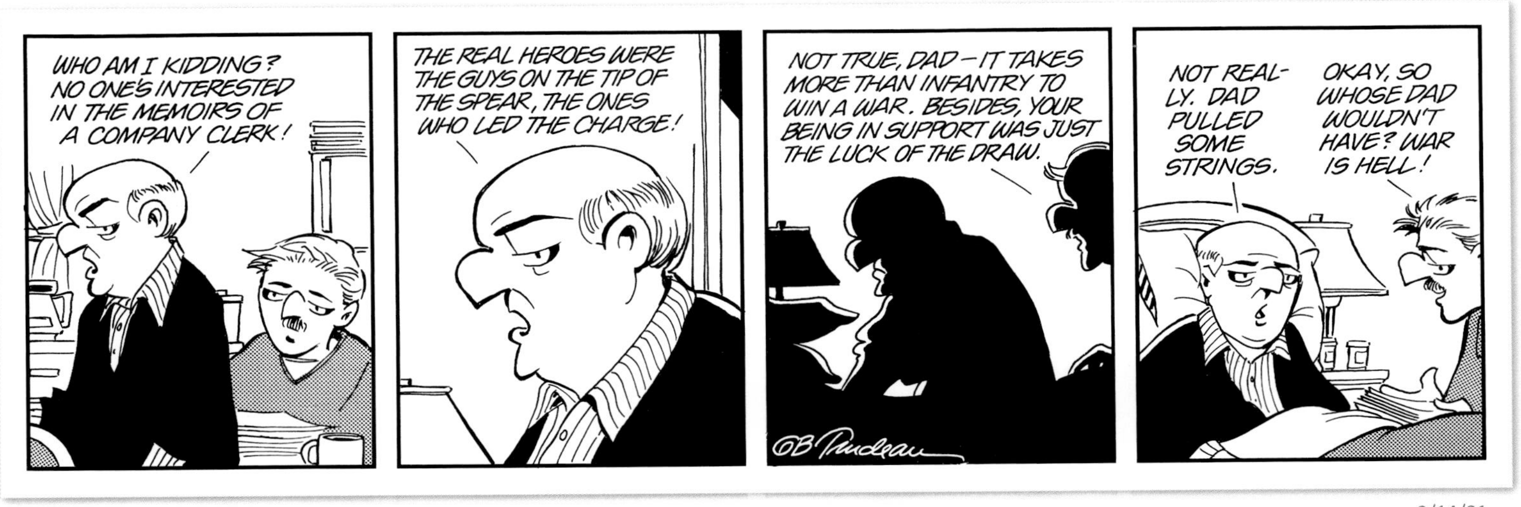
WHO AM I KIDDING? NO ONE'S INTERESTED IN THE MEMOIRS OF A COMPANY CLERK!
THE REAL HEROES WERE THE GUYS ON THE TIP OF THE SPEAR, THE ONES WHO LED THE CHARGE!
NOT TRUE, DAD — IT TAKES MORE THAN INFANTRY TO WIN A WAR. BESIDES, YOUR BEING IN SUPPORT WAS JUST THE LUCK OF THE DRAW.
NOT REALLY. DAD PULLED SOME STRINGS.
OKAY, SO WHOSE DAD WOULDN'T HAVE? WAR IS HELL!

9/14/01

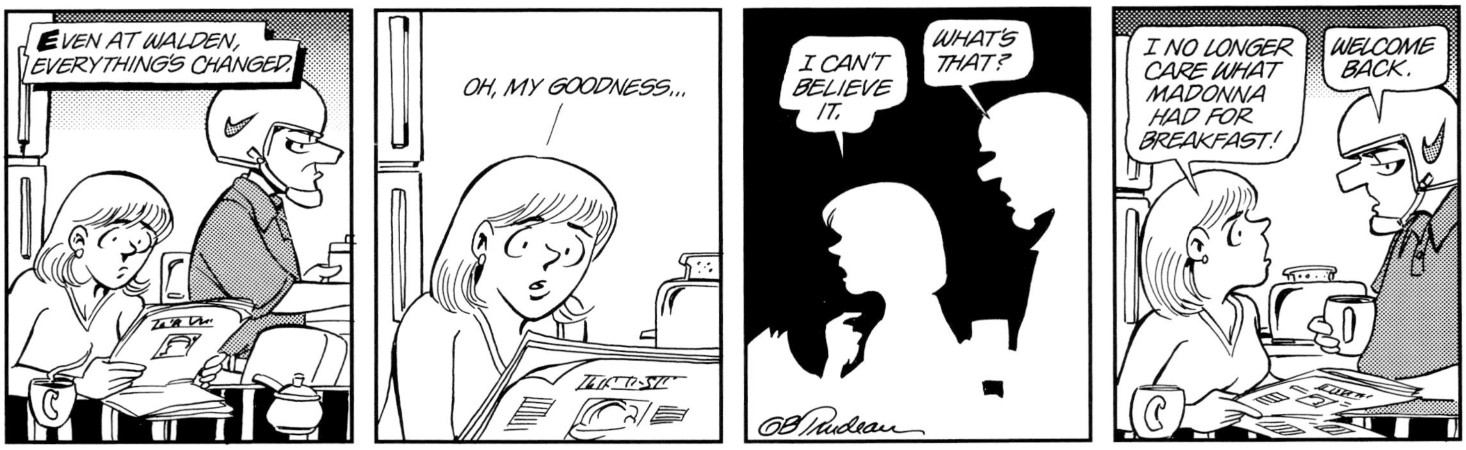
EVEN AT WALDEN, EVERYTHING'S CHANGED.
OH, MY GOODNESS...
I CAN'T BELIEVE IT.
WHAT'S THAT?
I NO LONGER CARE WHAT MADONNA HAD FOR BREAKFAST!
WELCOME BACK.

10/1/01

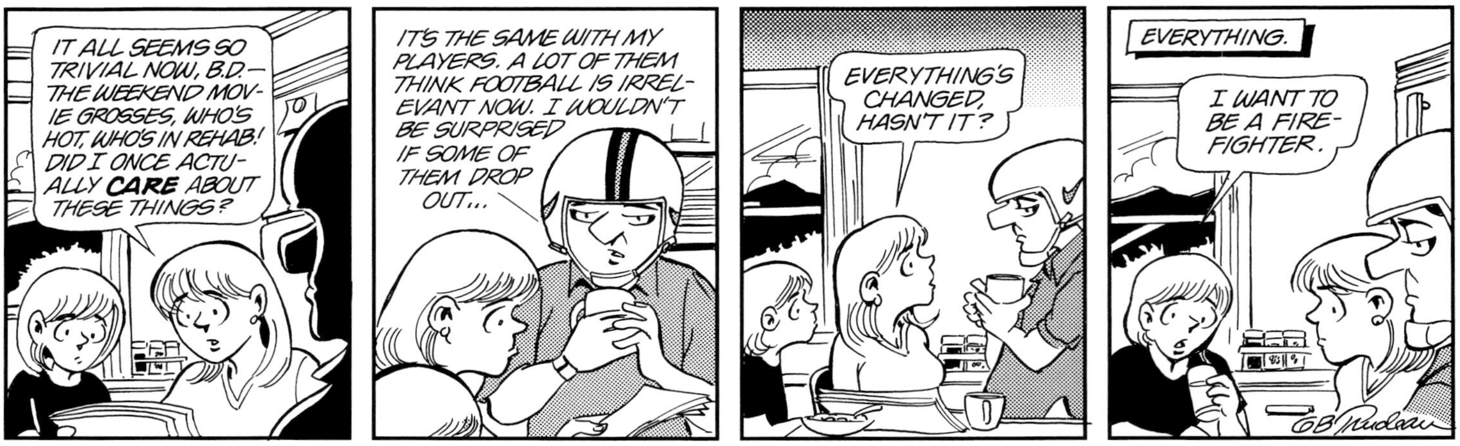
IT ALL SEEMS SO TRIVIAL NOW, B.D.— THE WEEKEND MOVIE GROSSES, WHO'S HOT, WHO'S IN REHAB! DID I ONCE ACTUALLY CARE ABOUT THESE THINGS?
IT'S THE SAME WITH MY PLAYERS. A LOT OF THEM THINK FOOTBALL IS IRRELEVANT NOW. I WOULDN'T BE SURPRISED IF SOME OF THEM DROP OUT...
EVERYTHING'S CHANGED, HASN'T IT?
EVERYTHING.
I WANT TO BE A FIRE-FIGHTER.

10/2/01

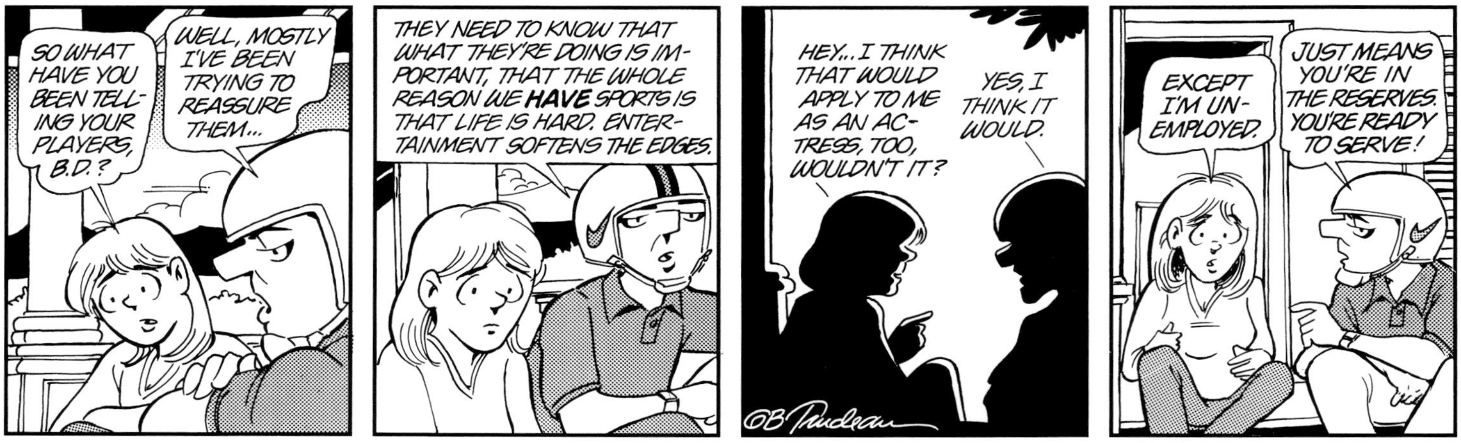
SO WHAT HAVE YOU BEEN TELLING YOUR PLAYERS, B.D.?
WELL, MOSTLY I'VE BEEN TRYING TO REASSURE THEM...
THEY NEED TO KNOW THAT WHAT THEY'RE DOING IS IMPORTANT, THAT THE WHOLE REASON WE HAVE SPORTS IS THAT LIFE IS HARD. ENTERTAINMENT SOFTENS THE EDGES.
HEY... I THINK THAT WOULD APPLY TO ME AS AN ACTRESS, TOO, WOULDN'T IT?
YES, I THINK IT WOULD.
EXCEPT I'M UNEMPLOYED.
JUST MEANS YOU'RE IN THE RESERVES. YOU'RE READY TO SERVE!

10/3/01

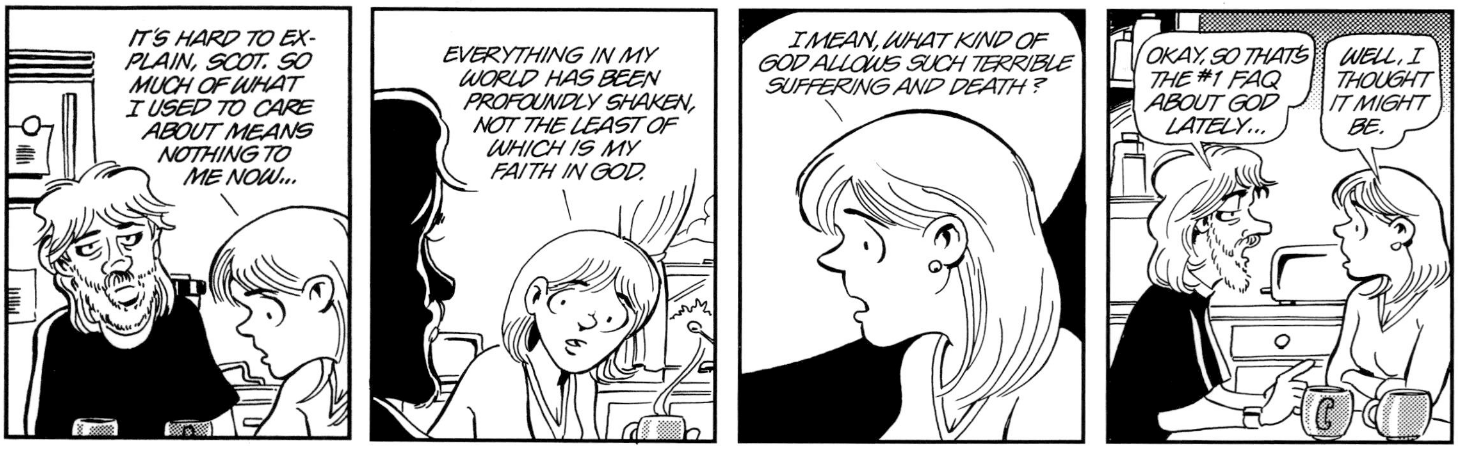
IT'S HARD TO EXPLAIN, SCOT. SO MUCH OF WHAT I USED TO CARE ABOUT MEANS NOTHING TO ME NOW...
EVERYTHING IN MY WORLD HAS BEEN PROFOUNDLY SHAKEN, NOT THE LEAST OF WHICH IS MY FAITH IN GOD.
I MEAN, WHAT KIND OF GOD ALLOWS SUCH TERRIBLE SUFFERING AND DEATH?
OKAY, SO THAT'S THE #1 FAQ ABOUT GOD LATELY...
WELL, I THOUGHT IT MIGHT BE.

10/5/01

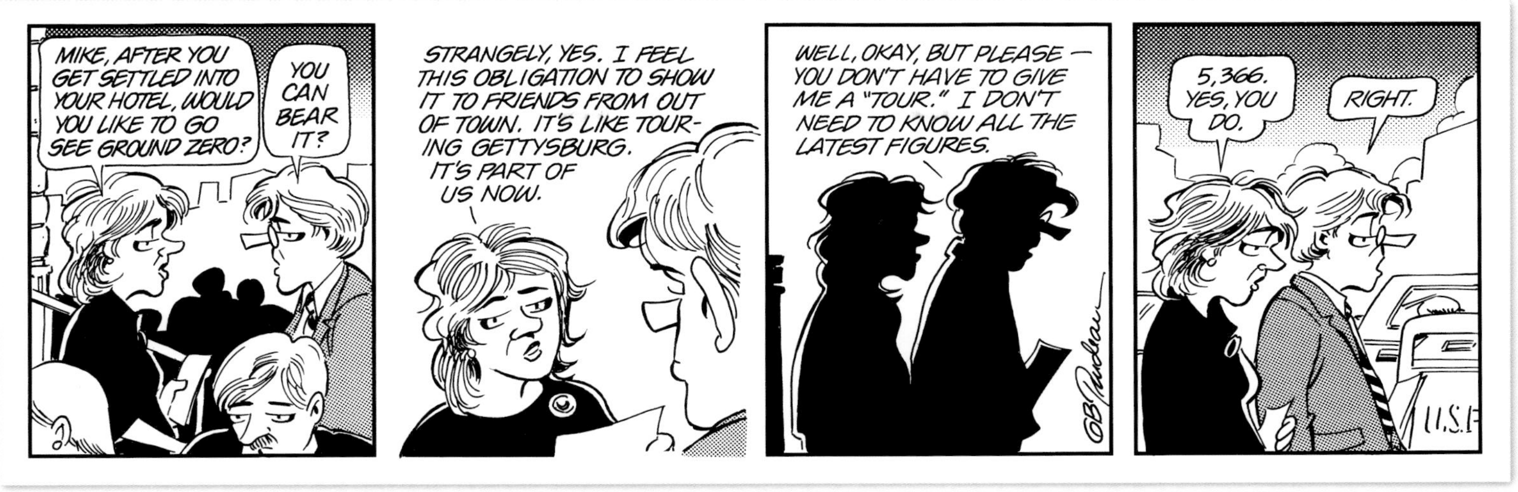
MIKE, AFTER YOU GET SETTLED INTO YOUR HOTEL, WOULD YOU LIKE TO GO SEE GROUND ZERO?
YOU CAN BEAR IT?
STRANGELY, YES. I FEEL THIS OBLIGATION TO SHOW IT TO FRIENDS FROM OUT OF TOWN. IT'S LIKE TOURING GETTYSBURG. IT'S PART OF US NOW.
WELL, OKAY, BUT PLEASE — YOU DON'T HAVE TO GIVE ME A "TOUR." I DON'T NEED TO KNOW ALL THE LATEST FIGURES.
5,366. YES, YOU DO.
RIGHT.
U.S.P.

10/19/01

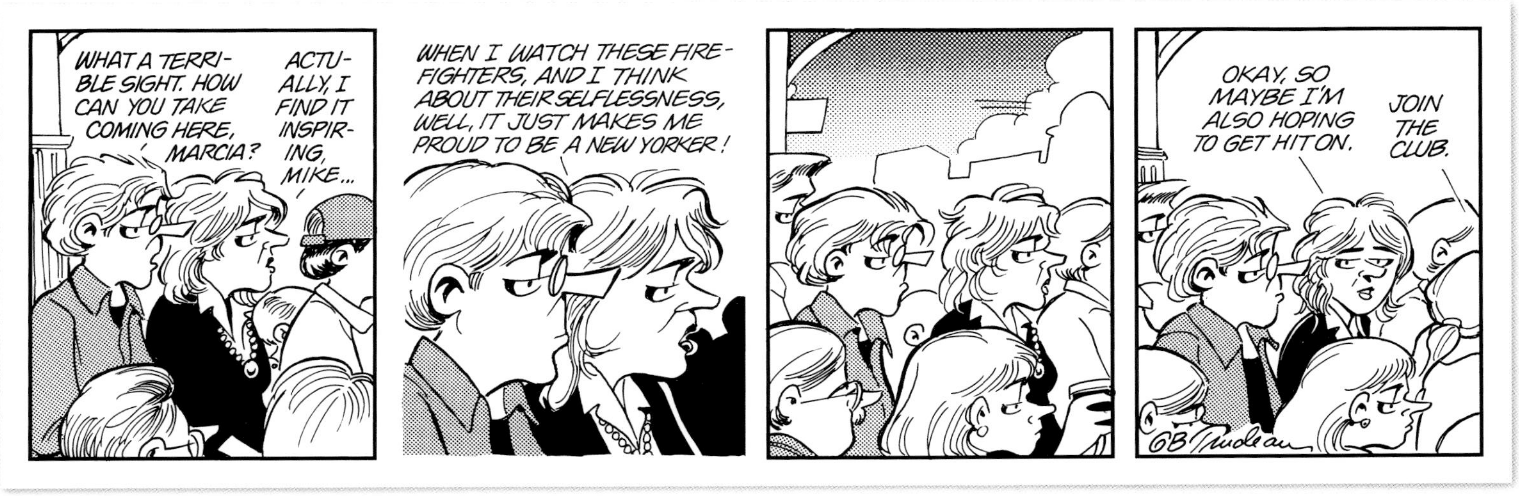
WHAT A TERRIBLE SIGHT. HOW CAN YOU TAKE COMING HERE, MARCIA?
ACTUALLY, I FIND IT INSPIRING, MIKE...
WHEN I WATCH THESE FIREFIGHTERS, AND I THINK ABOUT THEIR SELFLESSNESS, WELL, IT JUST MAKES ME PROUD TO BE A NEW YORKER!
OKAY, SO MAYBE I'M ALSO HOPING TO GET HIT ON.
JOIN THE CLUB.

10/22/01

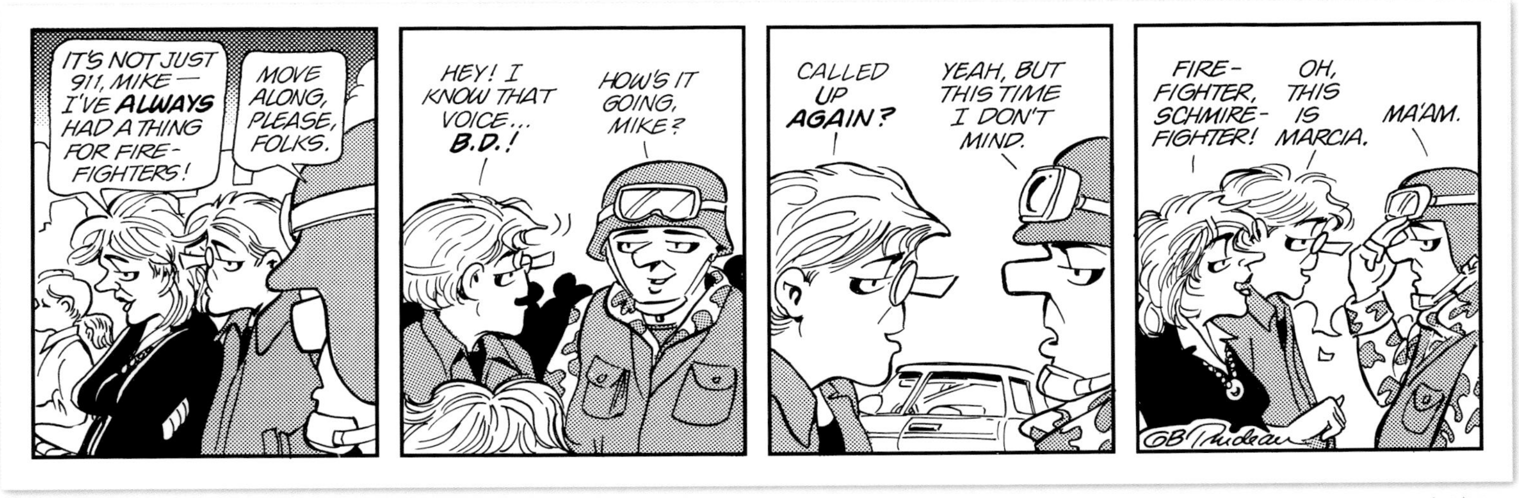
IT'S NOT JUST 9/11, MIKE — I'VE ALWAYS HAD A THING FOR FIREFIGHTERS!
MOVE ALONG, PLEASE, FOLKS.
HEY! I KNOW THAT VOICE... B.D.!
HOW'S IT GOING, MIKE?
CALLED UP AGAIN?
YEAH, BUT THIS TIME I DON'T MIND.
FIREFIGHTER, SCHMIREFIGHTER!
OH, THIS IS MARCIA.
MA'AM.

10/23/01

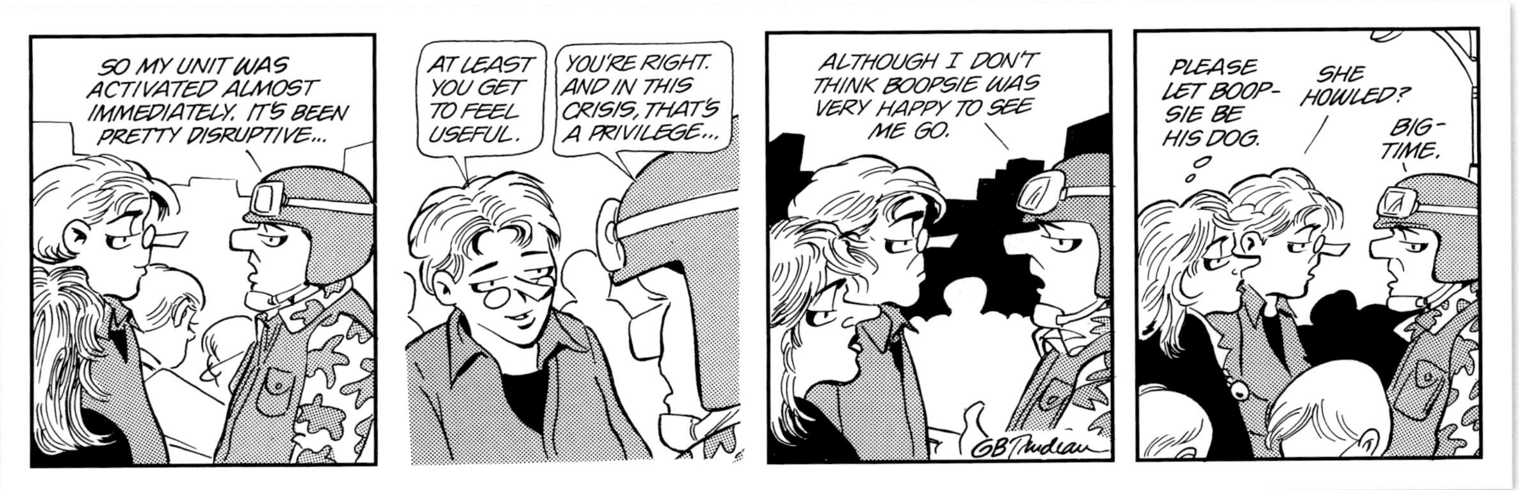
SO MY UNIT WAS ACTIVATED ALMOST IMMEDIATELY. IT'S BEEN PRETTY DISRUPTIVE...
AT LEAST YOU GET TO FEEL USEFUL.
YOU'RE RIGHT. AND IN THIS CRISIS, THAT'S A PRIVILEGE...
ALTHOUGH I DON'T THINK BOOPSIE WAS VERY HAPPY TO SEE ME GO.
PLEASE LET BOOPSIE BE HIS DOG.
SHE HOWLED?
BIG-TIME.

10/24/01

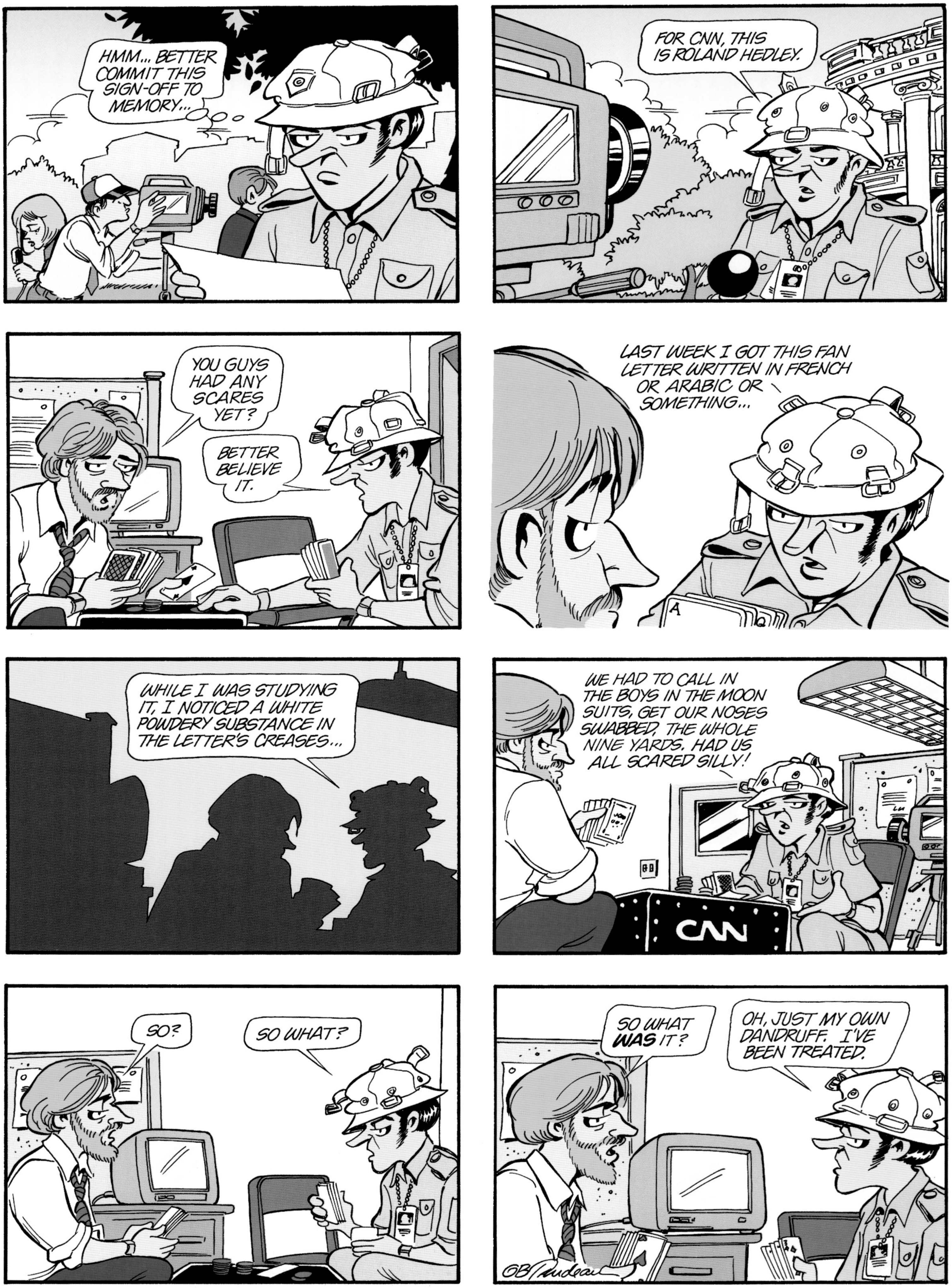
HMM... BETTER COMMIT THIS SIGN-OFF TO MEMORY...
FOR CNN, THIS IS ROLAND HEDLEY.
YOU GUYS HAD ANY SCARES YET?
BETTER BELIEVE IT.
LAST WEEK I GOT THIS FAN LETTER WRITTEN IN FRENCH OR ARABIC OR SOMETHING...
WHILE I WAS STUDYING IT, I NOTICED A WHITE POWDERY SUBSTANCE IN THE LETTER'S CREASES...
WE HAD TO CALL IN THE BOYS IN THE MOON SUITS, GET OUR NOSES SWABBED, THE WHOLE NINE YARDS. HAD US ALL SCARED SILLY!
CNN
SO?
SO WHAT?
SO WHAT **WAS** IT?
OH, JUST MY OWN DANDRUFF. I'VE BEEN TREATED.
©BTrudeau

12/2/01

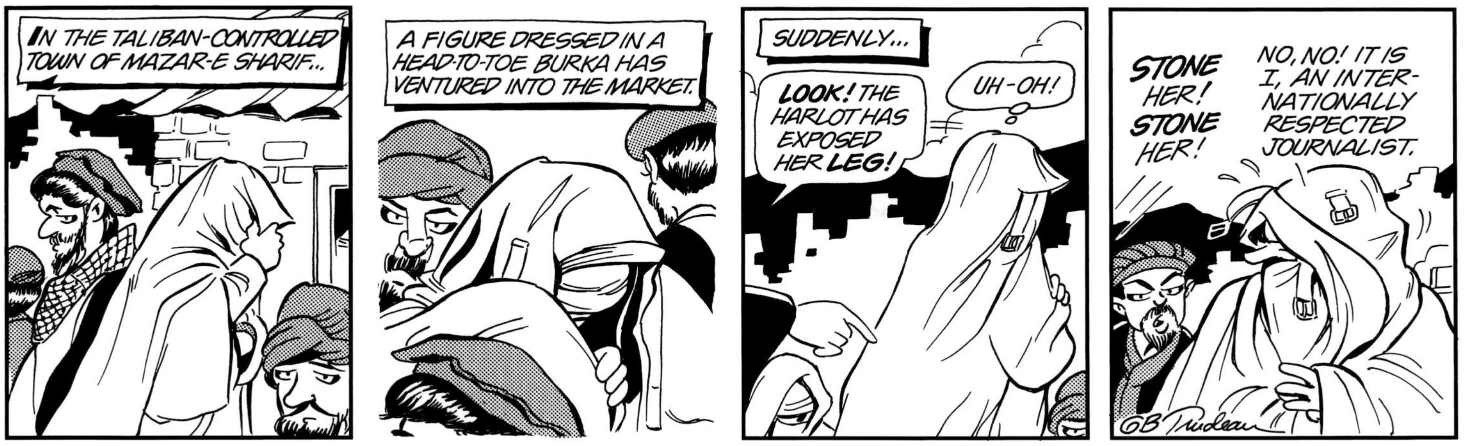
IN THE TALIBAN-CONTROLLED TOWN OF MAZAR-E SHARIF...
A FIGURE DRESSED IN A HEAD-TO-TOE BURKA HAS VENTURED INTO THE MARKET.
SUDDENLY...
LOOK! THE HARLOT HAS EXPOSED HER LEG!
UH-OH!
STONE HER! STONE HER!
NO, NO! IT IS I, AN INTERNATIONALLY RESPECTED JOURNALIST.
GB Trudeau

10/29/01

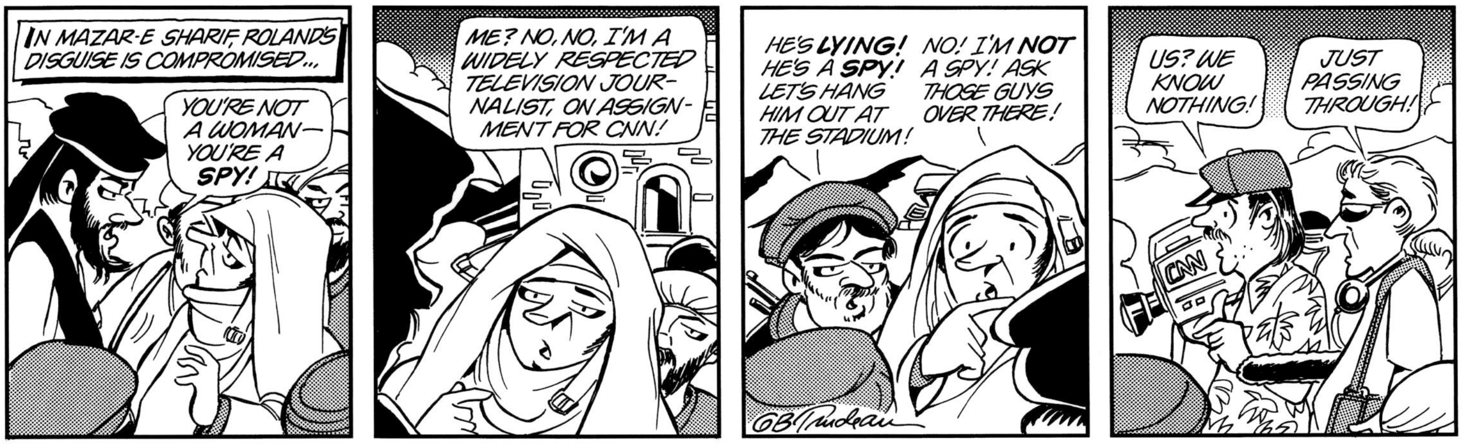
IN MAZAR-E SHARIF, ROLAND'S DISGUISE IS COMPROMISED...
YOU'RE NOT A WOMAN— YOU'RE A SPY!
ME? NO, NO, I'M A WIDELY RESPECTED TELEVISION JOURNALIST, ON ASSIGNMENT FOR CNN!
HE'S LYING! HE'S A SPY! LET'S HANG HIM OUT AT THE STADIUM!
NO! I'M NOT A SPY! ASK THOSE GUYS OVER THERE!
US? WE KNOW NOTHING!
JUST PASSING THROUGH!
CNN
GB Trudeau

10/30/01

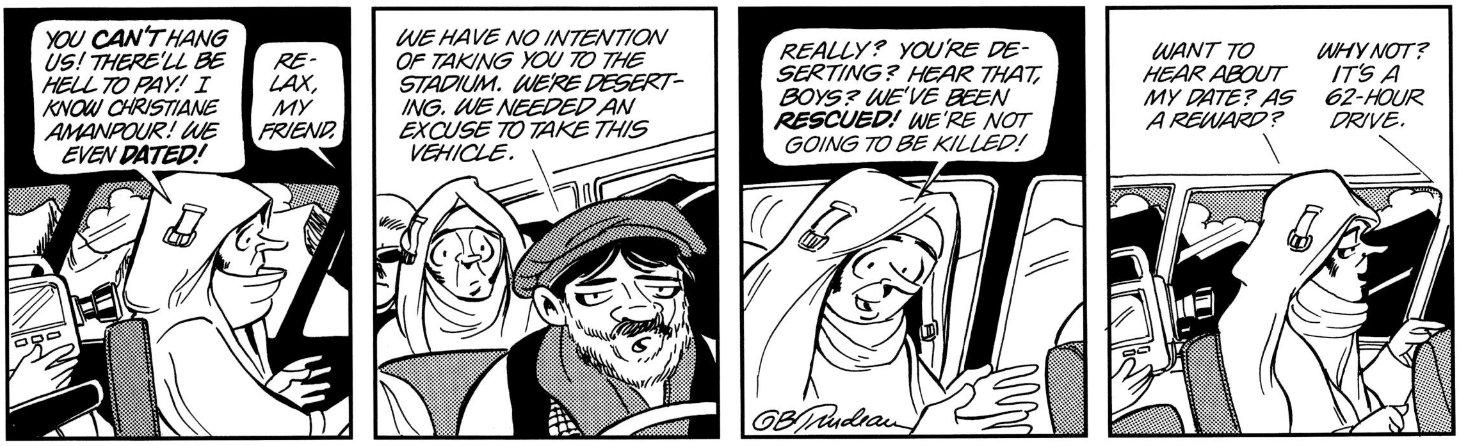
YOU CAN'T HANG US! THERE'LL BE HELL TO PAY! I KNOW CHRISTIANE AMANPOUR! WE EVEN DATED!
RELAX, MY FRIEND.
WE HAVE NO INTENTION OF TAKING YOU TO THE STADIUM. WE'RE DESERTING. WE NEEDED AN EXCUSE TO TAKE THIS VEHICLE.
REALLY? YOU'RE DESERTING? HEAR THAT, BOYS? WE'VE BEEN RESCUED! WE'RE NOT GOING TO BE KILLED!
WANT TO HEAR ABOUT MY DATE? AS A REWARD?
WHY NOT? IT'S A 62-HOUR DRIVE.
GB Trudeau

10/31/01

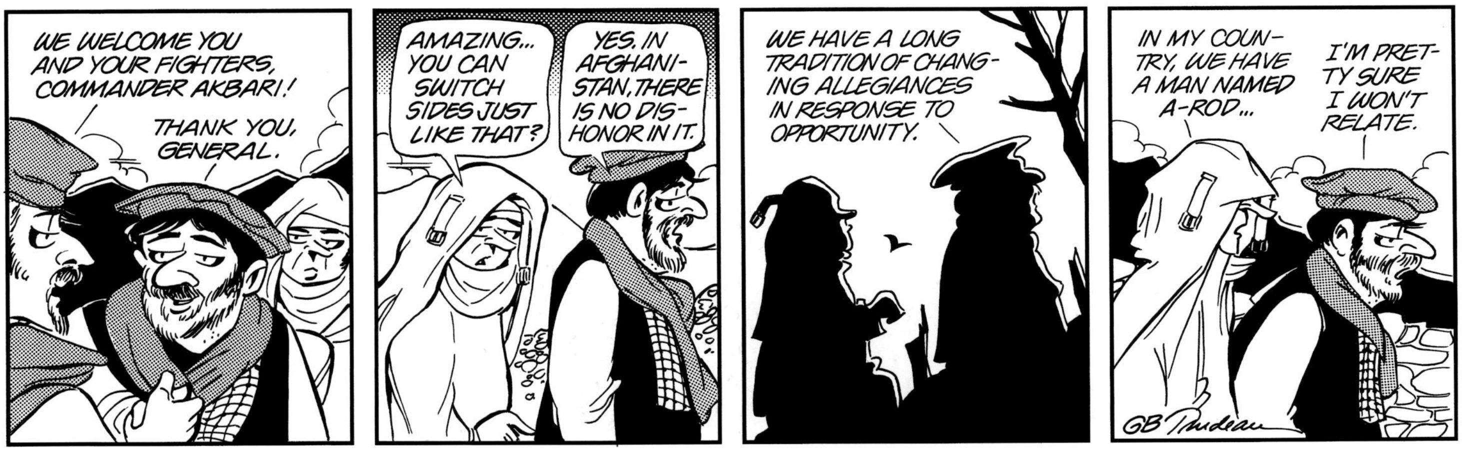
WE WELCOME YOU AND YOUR FIGHTERS, COMMANDER AKBARI!
THANK YOU, GENERAL.
AMAZING... YOU CAN SWITCH SIDES JUST LIKE THAT?
YES. IN AFGHANISTAN, THERE IS NO DISHONOR IN IT.
WE HAVE A LONG TRADITION OF CHANGING ALLEGIANCES IN RESPONSE TO OPPORTUNITY.
IN MY COUNTRY, WE HAVE A MAN NAMED A-ROD...
I'M PRETTY SURE I WON'T RELATE.
GB Trudeau

11/1/01

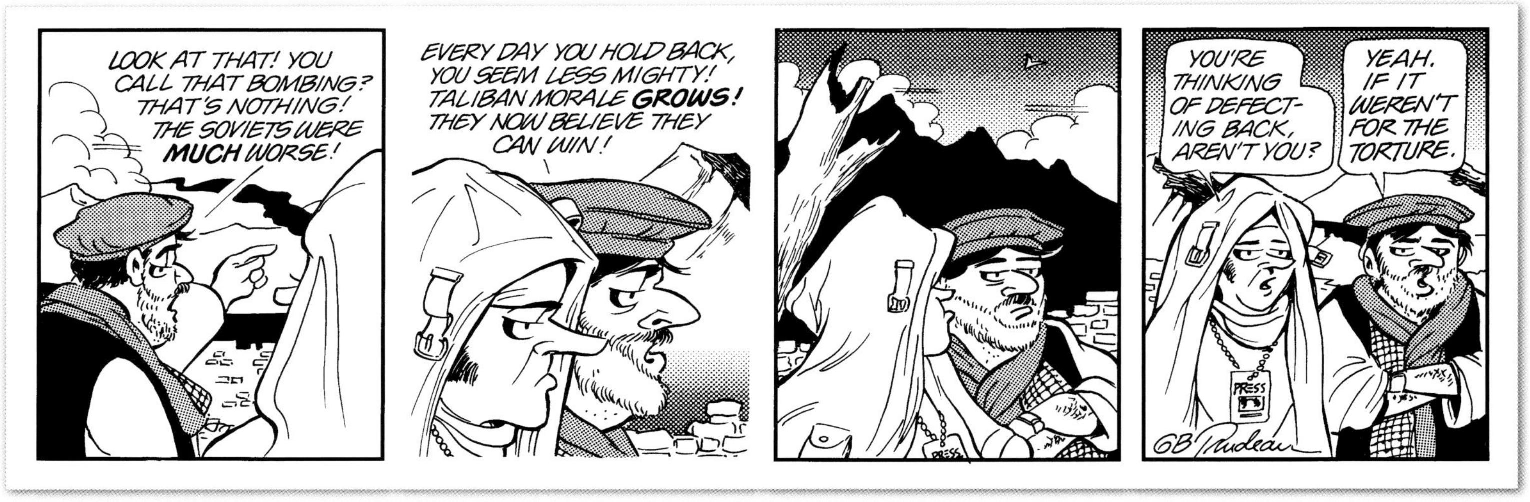
LOOK AT THAT! YOU CALL THAT BOMBING? THAT'S NOTHING! THE SOVIETS WERE **MUCH** WORSE!
EVERY DAY YOU HOLD BACK, YOU SEEM LESS MIGHTY! TALIBAN MORALE **GROWS!** THEY NOW BELIEVE THEY CAN WIN!
YOU'RE THINKING OF DEFECTING BACK, AREN'T YOU?
YEAH. IF IT WEREN'T FOR THE TORTURE.
PRESS
GB Trudeau

11/5/01

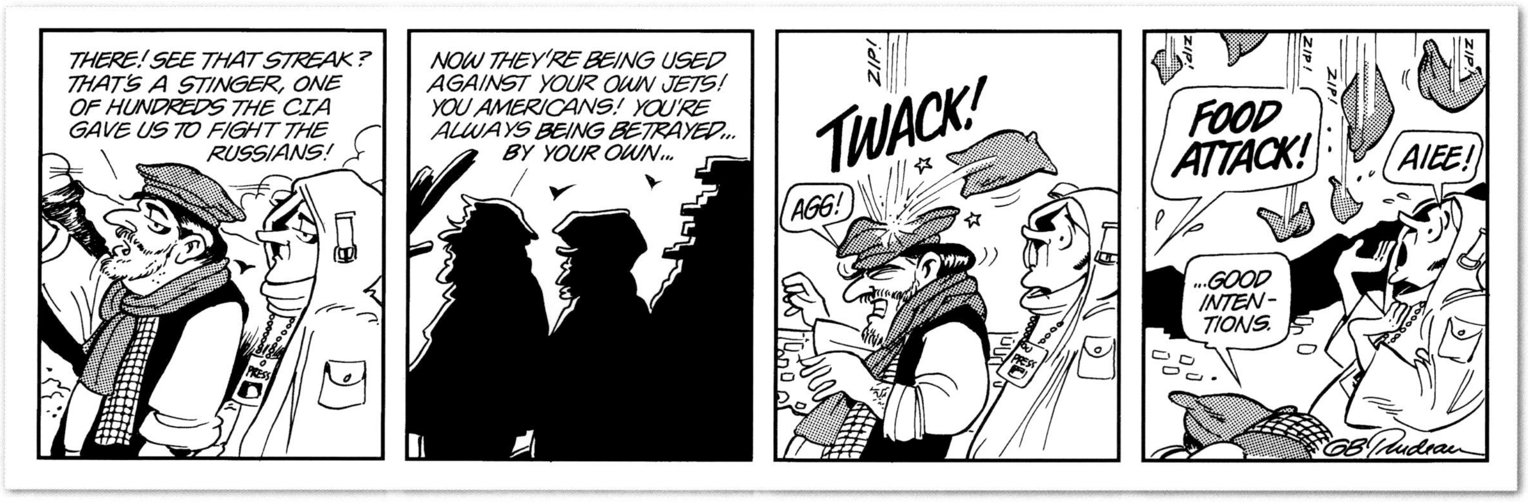
THERE! SEE THAT STREAK? THAT'S A STINGER, ONE OF HUNDREDS THE CIA GAVE US TO FIGHT THE RUSSIANS!
PRESS
NOW THEY'RE BEING USED AGAINST YOUR OWN JETS! YOU AMERICANS! YOU'RE ALWAYS BEING BETRAYED... BY YOUR OWN...
ZIP!
TWACK!
AGG!
FOOD ATTACK!
AIEE!
...GOOD INTENTIONS.
ZIP!
GB Trudeau

11/6/01

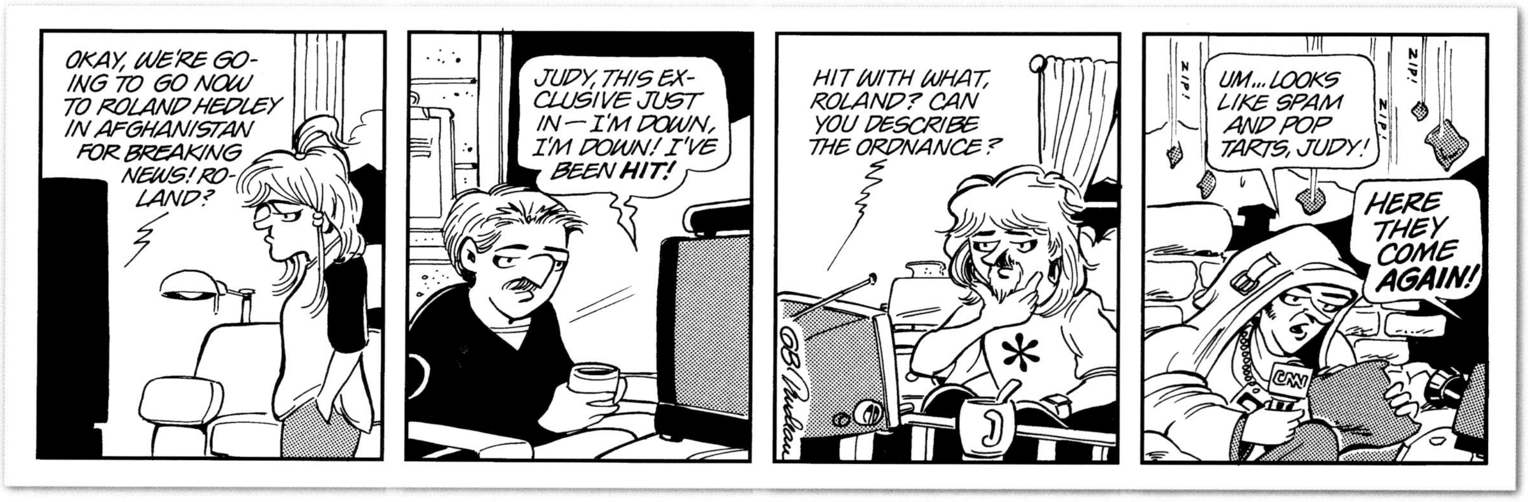
OKAY, WE'RE GOING TO GO NOW TO ROLAND HEDLEY IN AFGHANISTAN FOR BREAKING NEWS! ROLAND?
JUDY, THIS EXCLUSIVE JUST IN — I'M DOWN, I'M DOWN! I'VE BEEN **HIT!**
HIT WITH WHAT, ROLAND? CAN YOU DESCRIBE THE ORDNANCE?
GB Trudeau
ZIP!
UM... LOOKS LIKE SPAM AND POP TARTS, JUDY!
HERE THEY COME AGAIN!
CNN

11/7/01

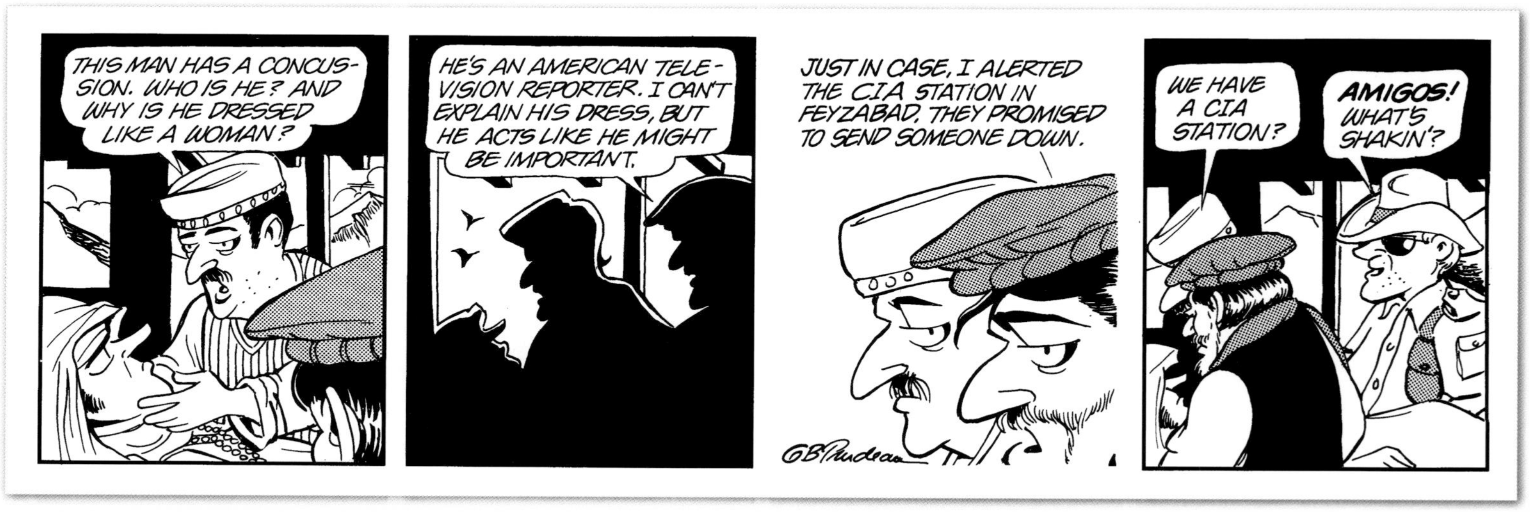
THIS MAN HAS A CONCUSSION. WHO IS HE? AND WHY IS HE DRESSED LIKE A WOMAN?
HE'S AN AMERICAN TELEVISION REPORTER. I CAN'T EXPLAIN HIS DRESS, BUT HE ACTS LIKE HE MIGHT BE IMPORTANT.
JUST IN CASE, I ALERTED THE C.I.A. STATION IN FEYZABAD. THEY PROMISED TO SEND SOMEONE DOWN.
GB Trudeau
WE HAVE A CIA STATION?
AMIGOS! WHAT'S SHAKIN'?

11/9/01

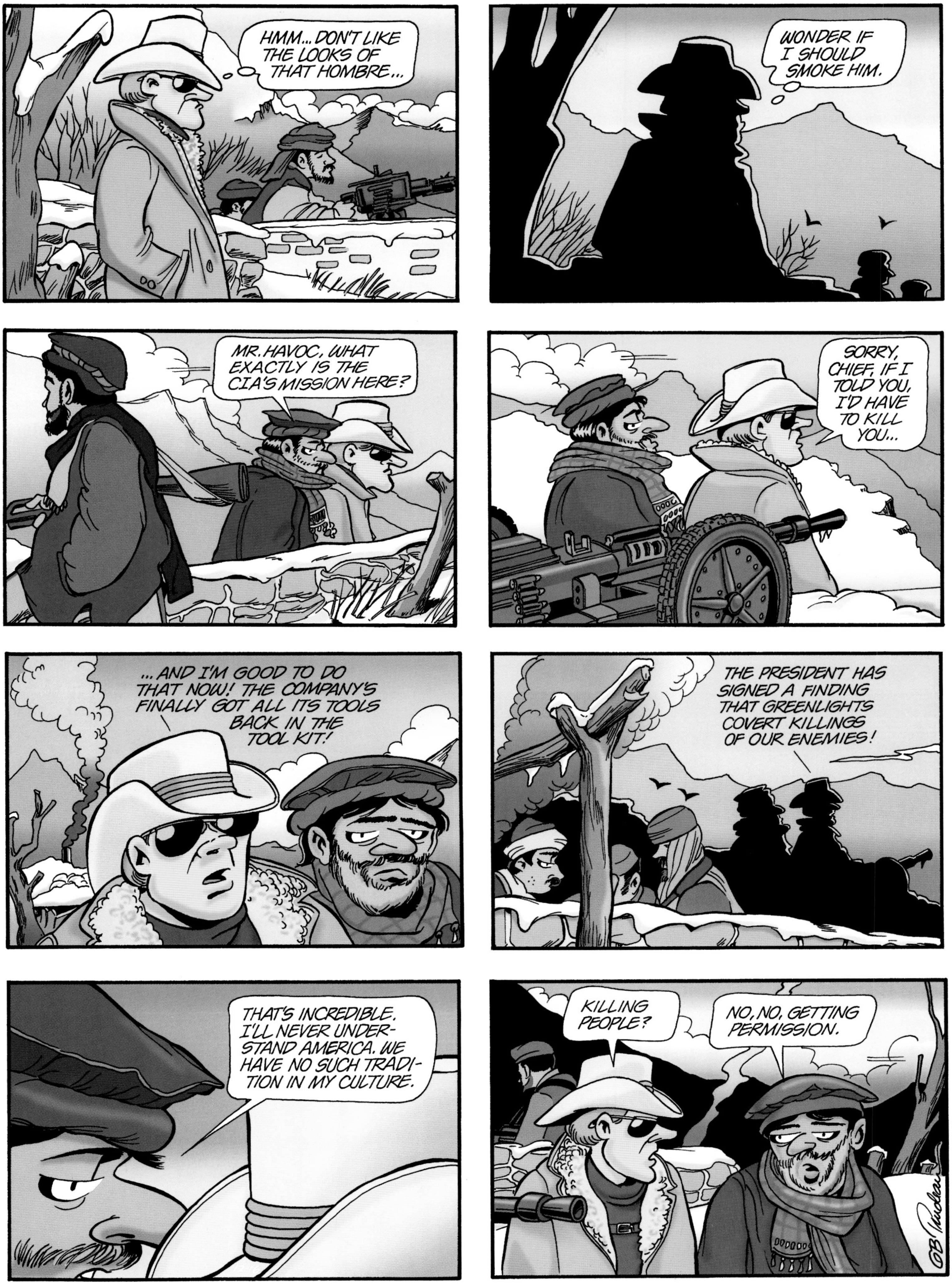
HMM... DON'T LIKE THE LOOKS OF THAT HOMBRE...
WONDER IF I SHOULD SMOKE HIM.
MR. HAVOC, WHAT EXACTLY IS THE CIA'S MISSION HERE?
SORRY, CHIEF, IF I TOLD YOU, I'D HAVE TO KILL YOU...
...AND I'M GOOD TO DO THAT NOW! THE COMPANY'S FINALLY GOT ALL ITS TOOLS BACK IN THE TOOL KIT!
THE PRESIDENT HAS SIGNED A FINDING THAT GREENLIGHTS COVERT KILLINGS OF OUR ENEMIES!
THAT'S INCREDIBLE. I'LL NEVER UNDERSTAND AMERICA. WE HAVE NO SUCH TRADITION IN MY CULTURE.
KILLING PEOPLE?
NO, NO, GETTING PERMISSION.
GBTrudeau

12/16/01

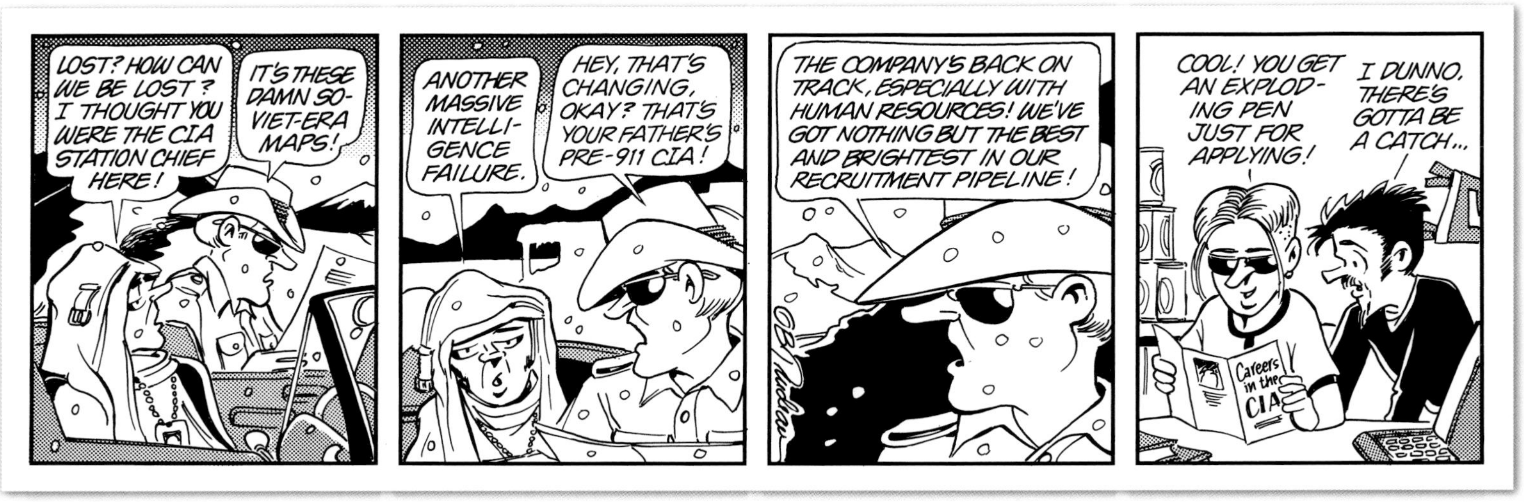

LOST? HOW CAN WE BE LOST? I THOUGHT YOU WERE THE CIA STATION CHIEF HERE!
IT'S THESE DAMN SOVIET-ERA MAPS!
ANOTHER MASSIVE INTELLIGENCE FAILURE.
HEY, THAT'S CHANGING, OKAY? THAT'S YOUR FATHER'S PRE-911 CIA!
THE COMPANY'S BACK ON TRACK, ESPECIALLY WITH HUMAN RESOURCES! WE'VE GOT NOTHING BUT THE BEST AND BRIGHTEST IN OUR RECRUITMENT PIPELINE!
COOL! YOU GET AN EXPLODING PEN JUST FOR APPLYING!
I DUNNO. THERE'S GOTTA BE A CATCH...
Careers in the CIA

11/12/01

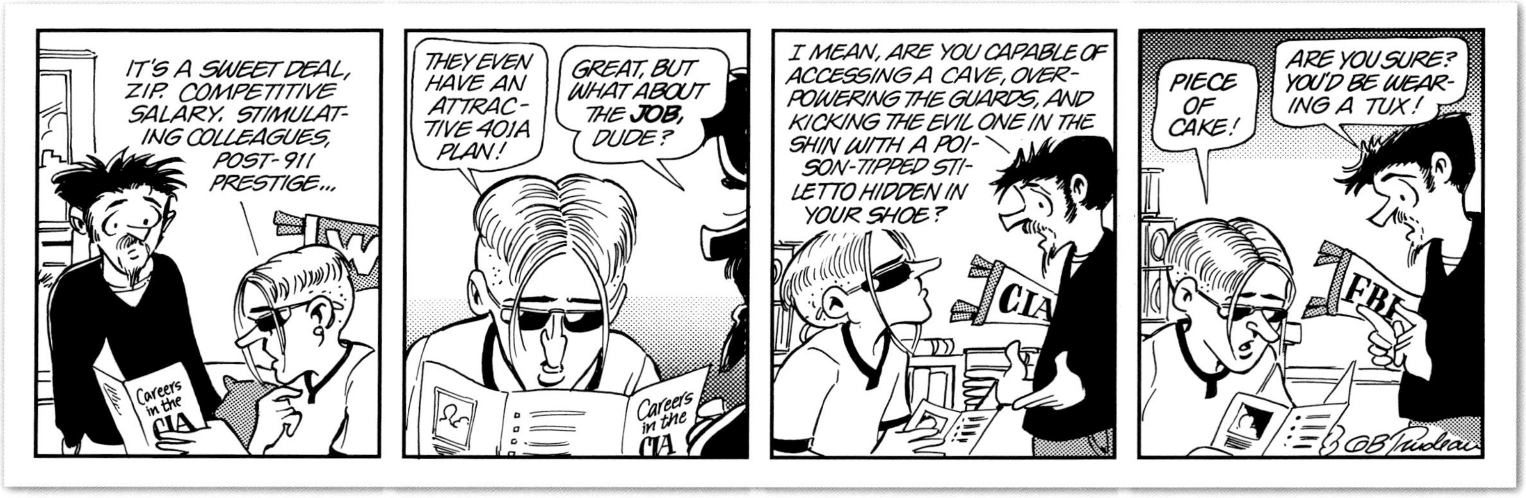

IT'S A SWEET DEAL, ZIP. COMPETITIVE SALARY. STIMULATING COLLEAGUES, POST-911 PRESTIGE...
Careers in the CIA
THEY EVEN HAVE AN ATTRACTIVE 401A PLAN!
GREAT, BUT WHAT ABOUT THE JOB, DUDE?
I MEAN, ARE YOU CAPABLE OF ACCESSING A CAVE, OVERPOWERING THE GUARDS, AND KICKING THE EVIL ONE IN THE SHIN WITH A POISON-TIPPED STILETTO HIDDEN IN YOUR SHOE?
CIA
PIECE OF CAKE!
ARE YOU SURE? YOU'D BE WEARING A TUX!
FBI

11/14/01

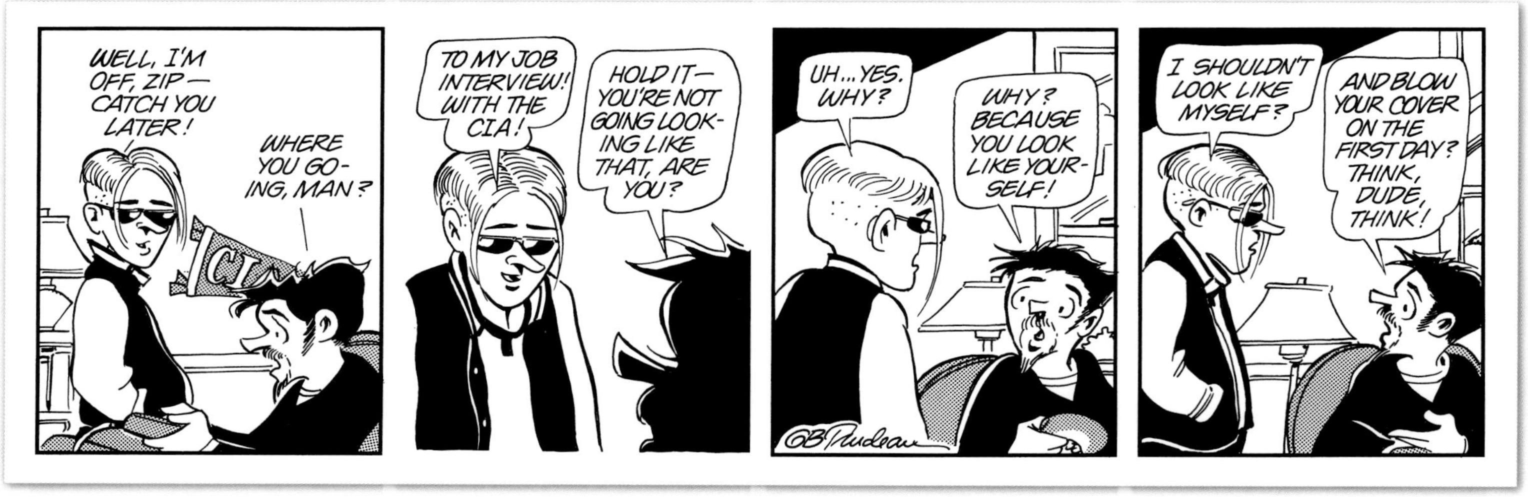

WELL, I'M OFF, ZIP— CATCH YOU LATER!
WHERE YOU GOING, MAN?
CIA
TO MY JOB INTERVIEW! WITH THE CIA!
HOLD IT— YOU'RE NOT GOING LOOKING LIKE THAT, ARE YOU?
UH... YES. WHY?
WHY? BECAUSE YOU LOOK LIKE YOURSELF!
I SHOULDN'T LOOK LIKE MYSELF?
AND BLOW YOUR COVER ON THE FIRST DAY? THINK, DUDE, THINK!

11/15/01

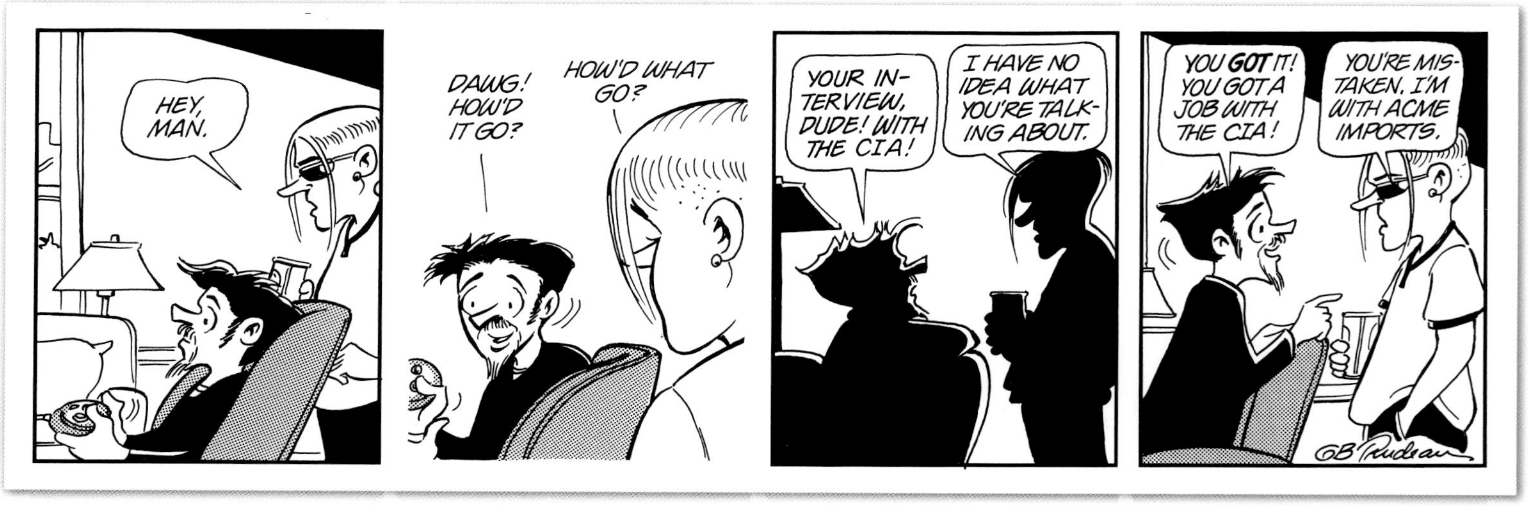

HEY, MAN.
DAWG! HOW'D IT GO?
HOW'D WHAT GO?
YOUR INTERVIEW, DUDE! WITH THE CIA!
I HAVE NO IDEA WHAT YOU'RE TALKING ABOUT.
YOU GOT IT! YOU GOT A JOB WITH THE CIA!
YOU'RE MISTAKEN. I'M WITH ACME IMPORTS.

11/16/01

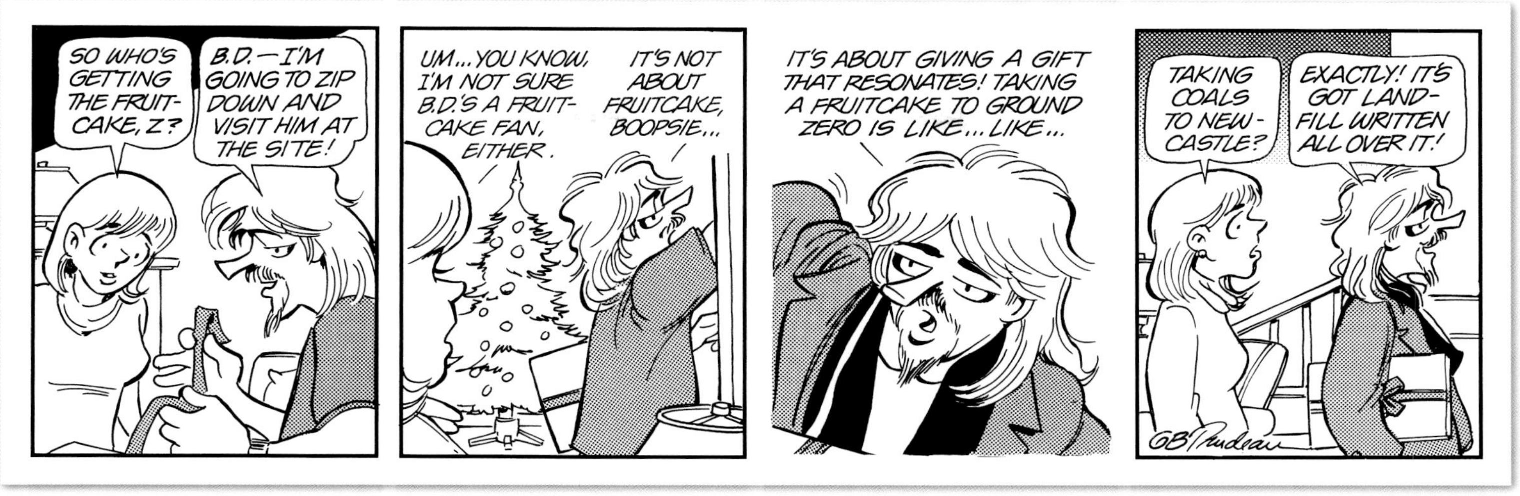
SO WHO'S GETTING THE FRUIT-CAKE, Z?
B.D.—I'M GOING TO ZIP DOWN AND VISIT HIM AT THE SITE!
UM... YOU KNOW, I'M NOT SURE B.D.'S A FRUIT-CAKE FAN, EITHER.
IT'S NOT ABOUT FRUITCAKE, BOOPSIE...
IT'S ABOUT GIVING A GIFT THAT RESONATES! TAKING A FRUITCAKE TO GROUND ZERO IS LIKE... LIKE...
TAKING COALS TO NEW-CASTLE?
EXACTLY! IT'S GOT LAND-FILL WRITTEN ALL OVER IT!
GB Trudeau

12/18/01

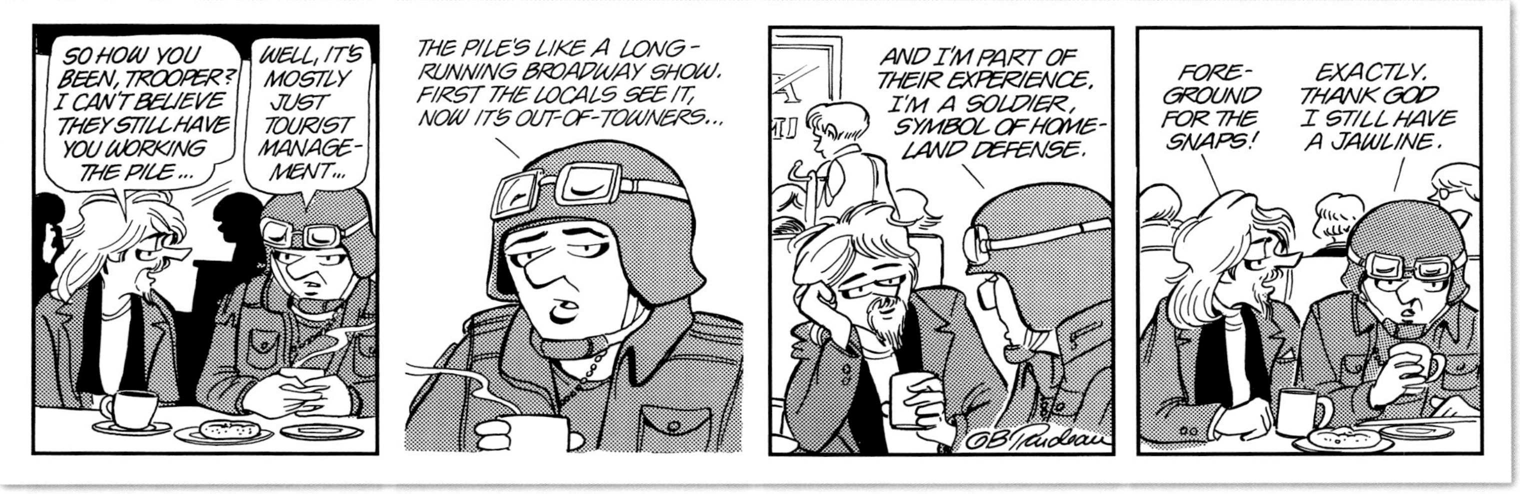
SO HOW YOU BEEN, TROOPER? I CAN'T BELIEVE THEY STILL HAVE YOU WORKING THE PILE...
WELL, IT'S MOSTLY JUST TOURIST MANAGE-MENT...
THE PILE'S LIKE A LONG-RUNNING BROADWAY SHOW. FIRST THE LOCALS SEE IT, NOW IT'S OUT-OF-TOWNERS...
AND I'M PART OF THEIR EXPERIENCE. I'M A SOLDIER, SYMBOL OF HOME-LAND DEFENSE.
FORE-GROUND FOR THE SNAPS!
EXACTLY. THANK GOD I STILL HAVE A JAWLINE.
GB Trudeau

12/19/01

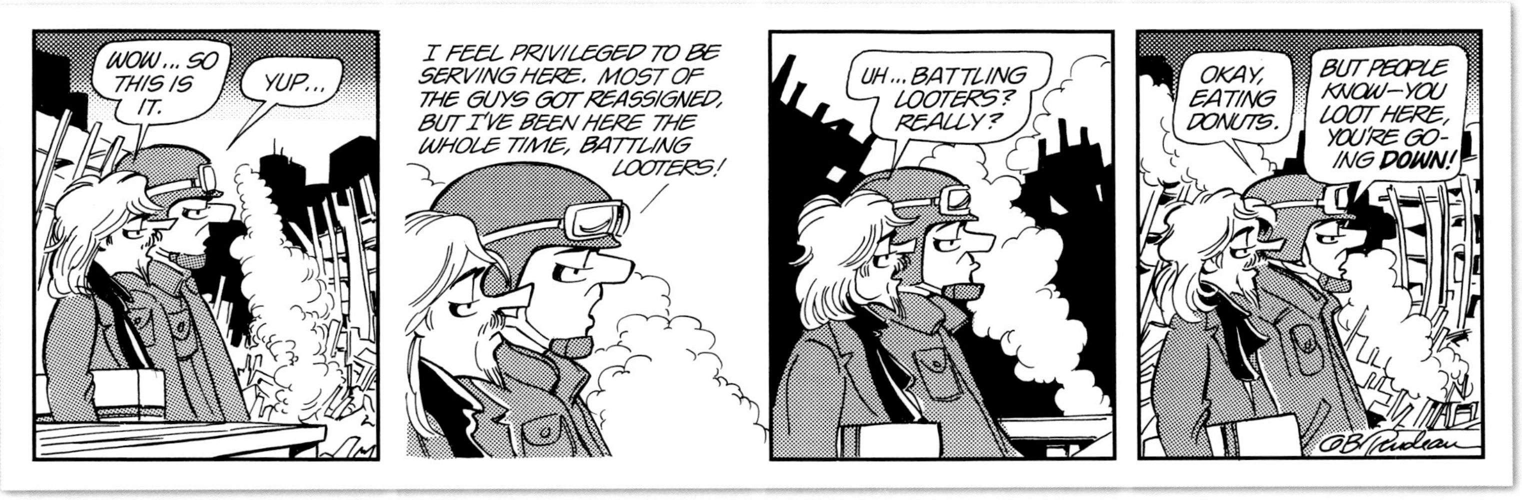
WOW... SO THIS IS IT.
YUP...
I FEEL PRIVILEGED TO BE SERVING HERE. MOST OF THE GUYS GOT REASSIGNED, BUT I'VE BEEN HERE THE WHOLE TIME, BATTLING LOOTERS!
UH... BATTLING LOOTERS? REALLY?
OKAY, EATING DONUTS.
BUT PEOPLE KNOW—YOU LOOT HERE, YOU'RE GO-ING DOWN!
GB Trudeau

12/20/01

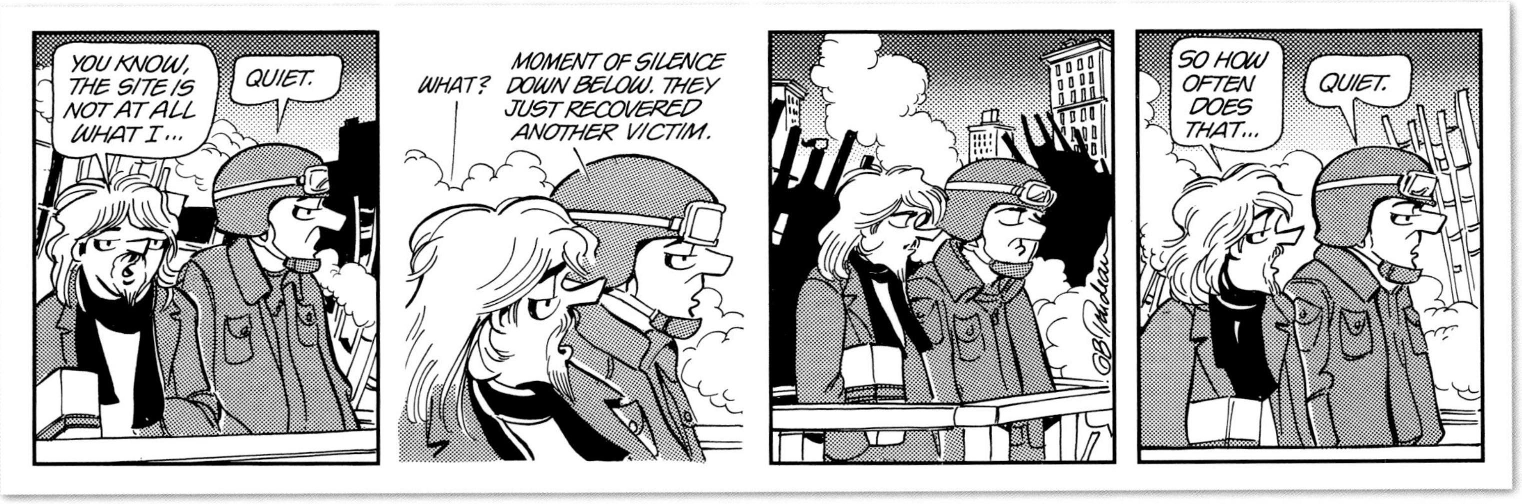
YOU KNOW, THE SITE IS NOT AT ALL WHAT I...
QUIET.
WHAT?
MOMENT OF SILENCE DOWN BELOW. THEY JUST RECOVERED ANOTHER VICTIM.
GB Trudeau
SO HOW OFTEN DOES THAT...
QUIET.

12/21/01

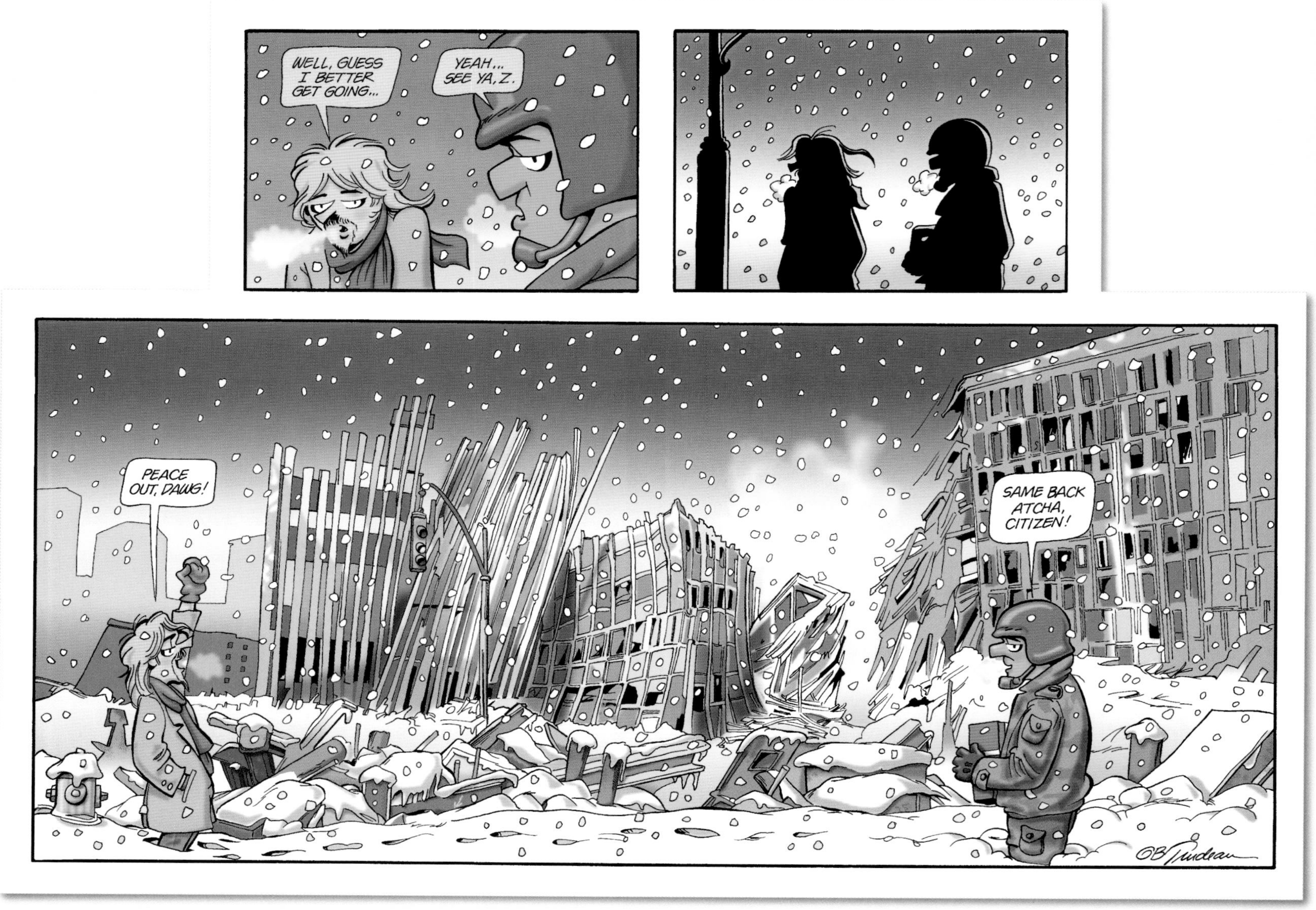
WELL, GUESS I BETTER GET GOING...
YEAH... SEE YA, Z.
PEACE OUT, DAWG!
SAME BACK ATCHA, CITIZEN!
©B Trudeau

12/23/01

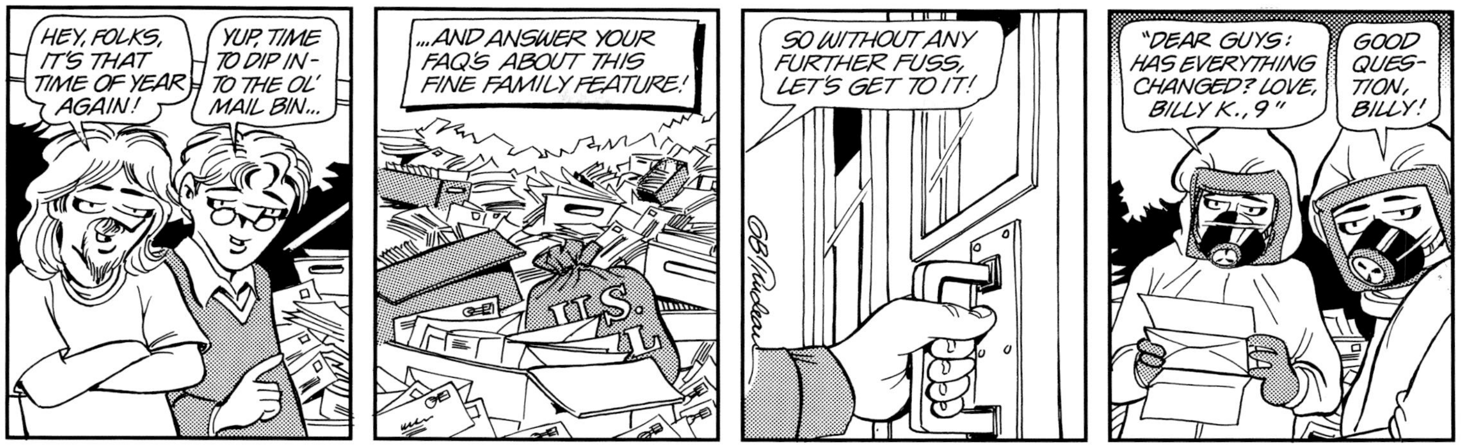
HEY, FOLKS, IT'S THAT TIME OF YEAR AGAIN!
YUP, TIME TO DIP INTO THE OL' MAIL BIN...
...AND ANSWER YOUR FAQ'S ABOUT THIS FINE FAMILY FEATURE!
U.S.
SO WITHOUT ANY FURTHER FUSS, LET'S GET TO IT!
GB Trudeau
"DEAR GUYS: HAS EVERYTHING CHANGED? LOVE, BILLY K., 9"
GOOD QUESTION, BILLY!

1/14/02

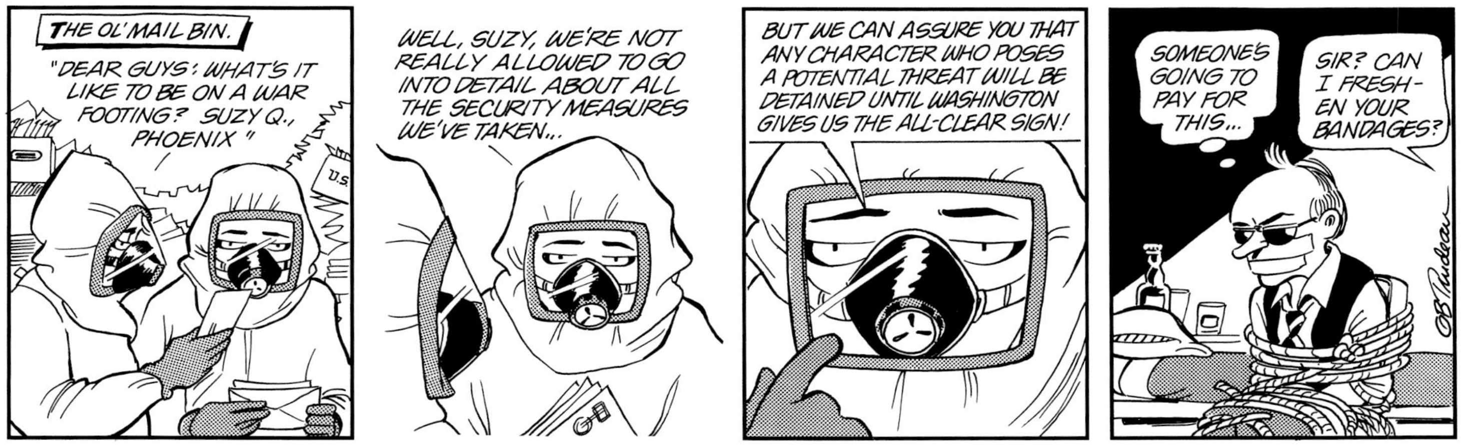
THE OL' MAIL BIN.
"DEAR GUYS: WHAT'S IT LIKE TO BE ON A WAR FOOTING? SUZY Q., PHOENIX"
WELL, SUZY, WE'RE NOT REALLY ALLOWED TO GO INTO DETAIL ABOUT ALL THE SECURITY MEASURES WE'VE TAKEN...
BUT WE CAN ASSURE YOU THAT ANY CHARACTER WHO POSES A POTENTIAL THREAT WILL BE DETAINED UNTIL WASHINGTON GIVES US THE ALL-CLEAR SIGN!
SOMEONE'S GOING TO PAY FOR THIS...
SIR? CAN I FRESHEN YOUR BANDAGES?
GB Trudeau

1/15/02

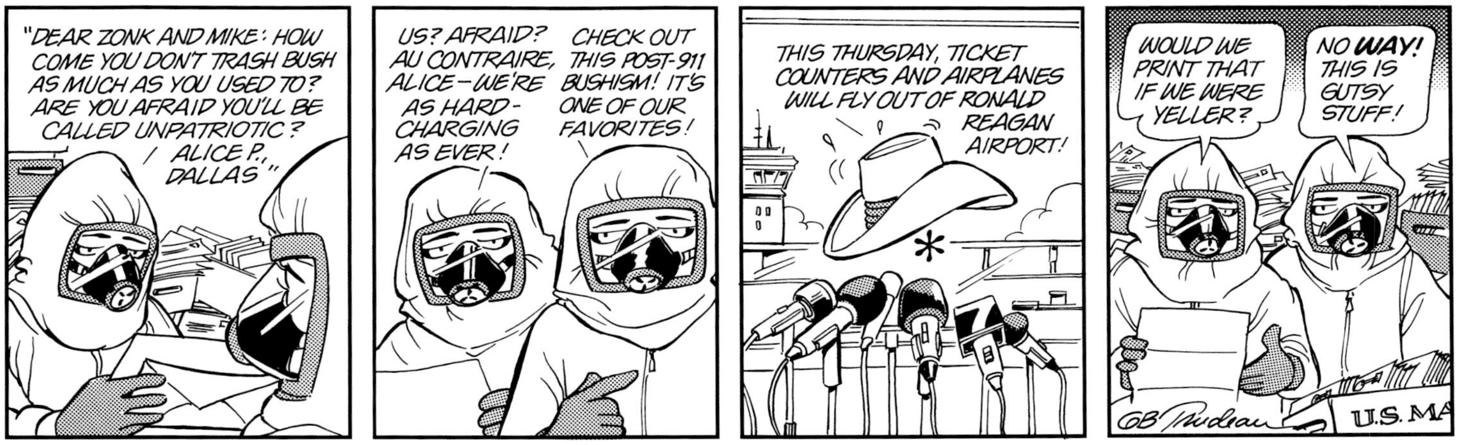
"DEAR ZONK AND MIKE: HOW COME YOU DON'T TRASH BUSH AS MUCH AS YOU USED TO? ARE YOU AFRAID YOU'LL BE CALLED UNPATRIOTIC? ALICE P., DALLAS"
US? AFRAID? AU CONTRAIRE, ALICE—WE'RE AS HARD-CHARGING AS EVER!
CHECK OUT THIS POST-911 BUSHISM! IT'S ONE OF OUR FAVORITES!
THIS THURSDAY, TICKET COUNTERS AND AIRPLANES WILL FLY OUT OF RONALD REAGAN AIRPORT!
WOULD WE PRINT THAT IF WE WERE YELLER?
NO WAY! THIS IS GUTSY STUFF!
GB Trudeau
U.S. MA

1/16/02

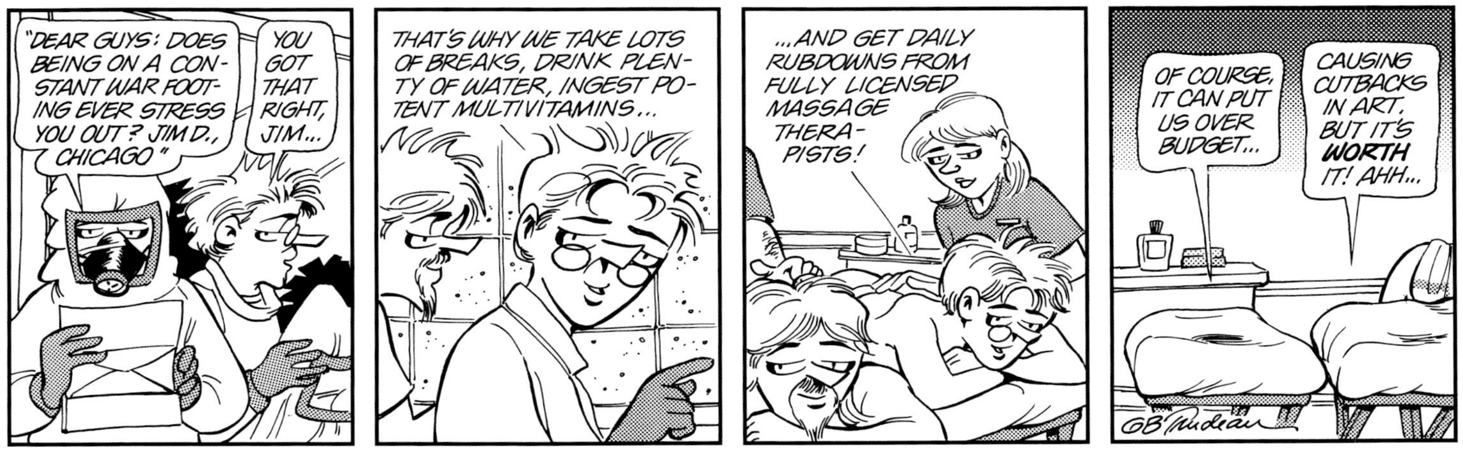
"DEAR GUYS: DOES BEING ON A CONSTANT WAR FOOTING EVER STRESS YOU OUT? JIM D., CHICAGO"
YOU GOT THAT RIGHT, JIM...
THAT'S WHY WE TAKE LOTS OF BREAKS, DRINK PLENTY OF WATER, INGEST POTENT MULTIVITAMINS...
...AND GET DAILY RUBDOWNS FROM FULLY LICENSED MASSAGE THERAPISTS!
OF COURSE, IT CAN PUT US OVER BUDGET...
CAUSING CUTBACKS IN ART. BUT IT'S WORTH IT! AHH...
GB Trudeau

1/19/02

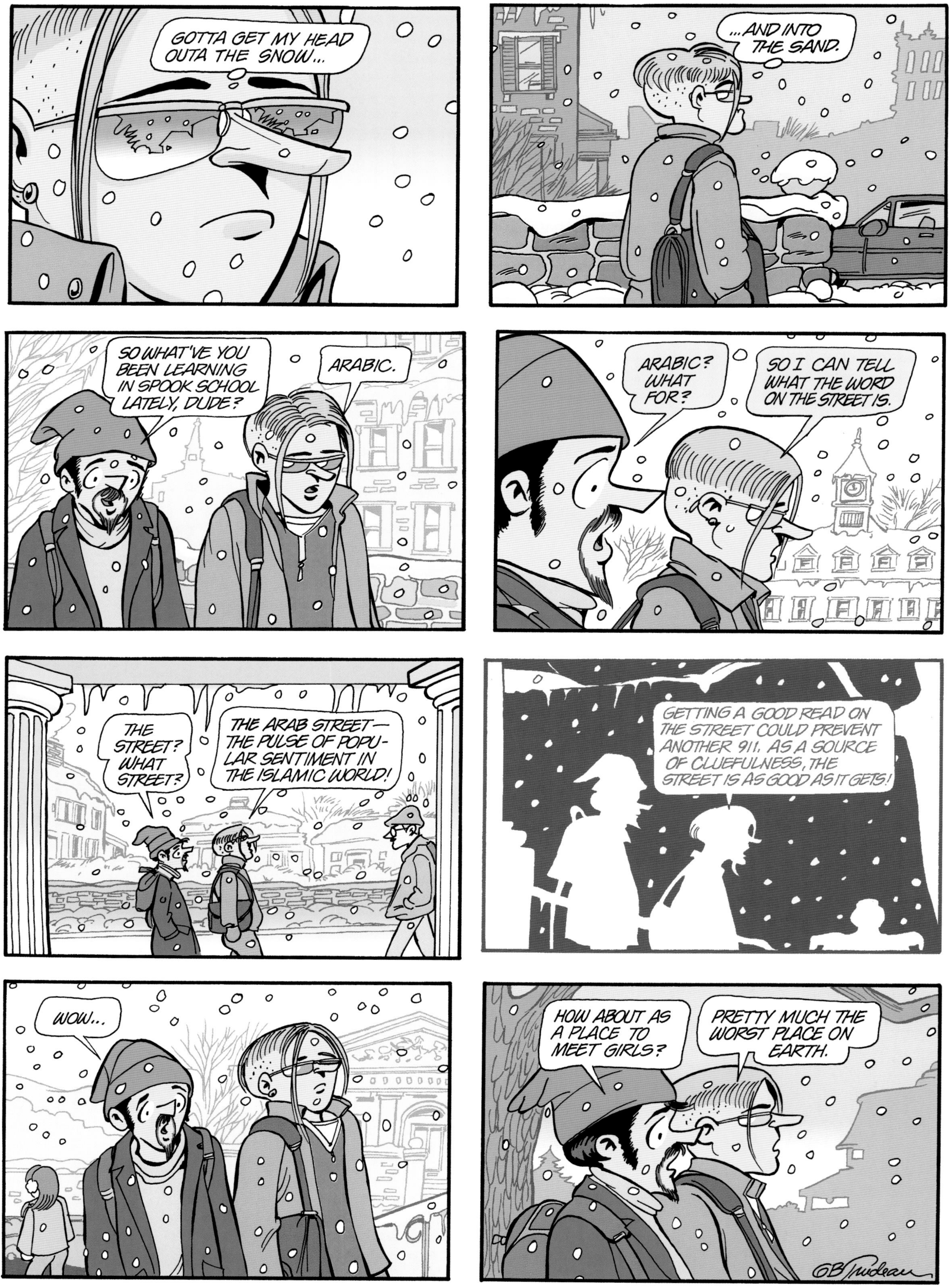
GOTTA GET MY HEAD OUTA THE SNOW...
...AND INTO THE SAND.
SO WHAT'VE YOU BEEN LEARNING IN SPOOK SCHOOL LATELY, DUDE?
ARABIC.
ARABIC? WHAT FOR?
SO I CAN TELL WHAT THE WORD ON THE STREET IS.
THE STREET? WHAT STREET?
THE ARAB STREET— THE PULSE OF POPULAR SENTIMENT IN THE ISLAMIC WORLD!
GETTING A GOOD READ ON THE STREET COULD PREVENT ANOTHER 911. AS A SOURCE OF CLUEFULNESS, THE STREET IS AS GOOD AS IT GETS!
WOW...
HOW ABOUT AS A PLACE TO MEET GIRLS?
PRETTY MUCH THE WORST PLACE ON EARTH.
GB Trudeau

2/17/02

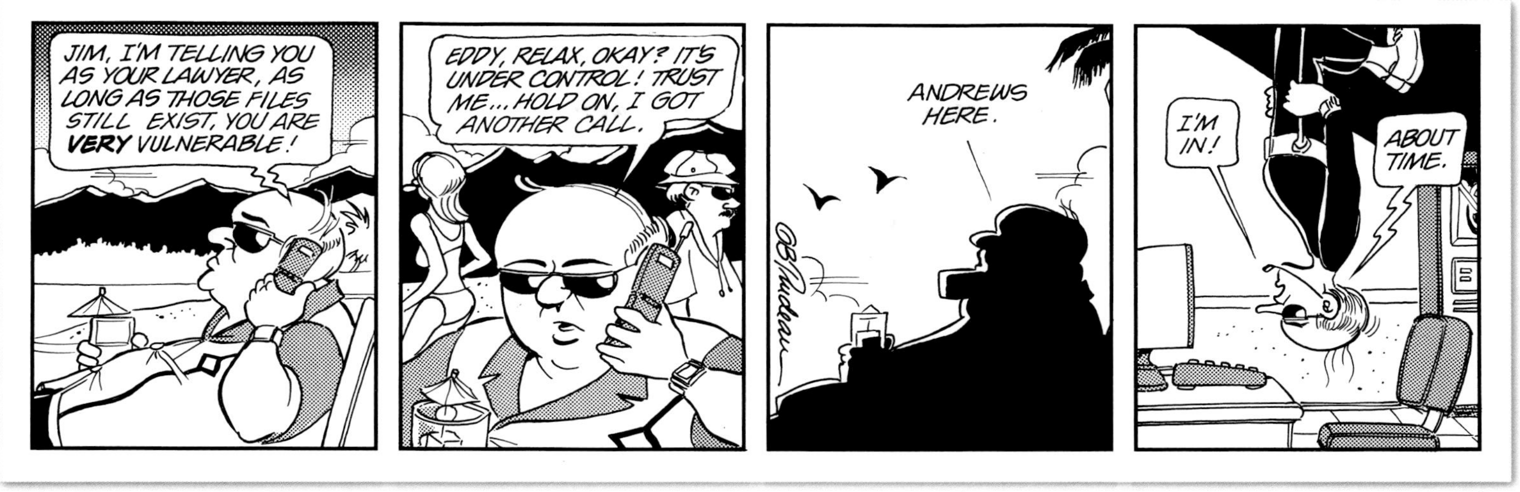
JIM, I'M TELLING YOU AS YOUR LAWYER, AS LONG AS THOSE FILES STILL EXIST, YOU ARE **VERY** VULNERABLE!
EDDY, RELAX, OKAY? IT'S UNDER CONTROL! TRUST ME... HOLD ON, I GOT ANOTHER CALL.
ANDREWS HERE.
I'M IN!
ABOUT TIME.

3/4/02

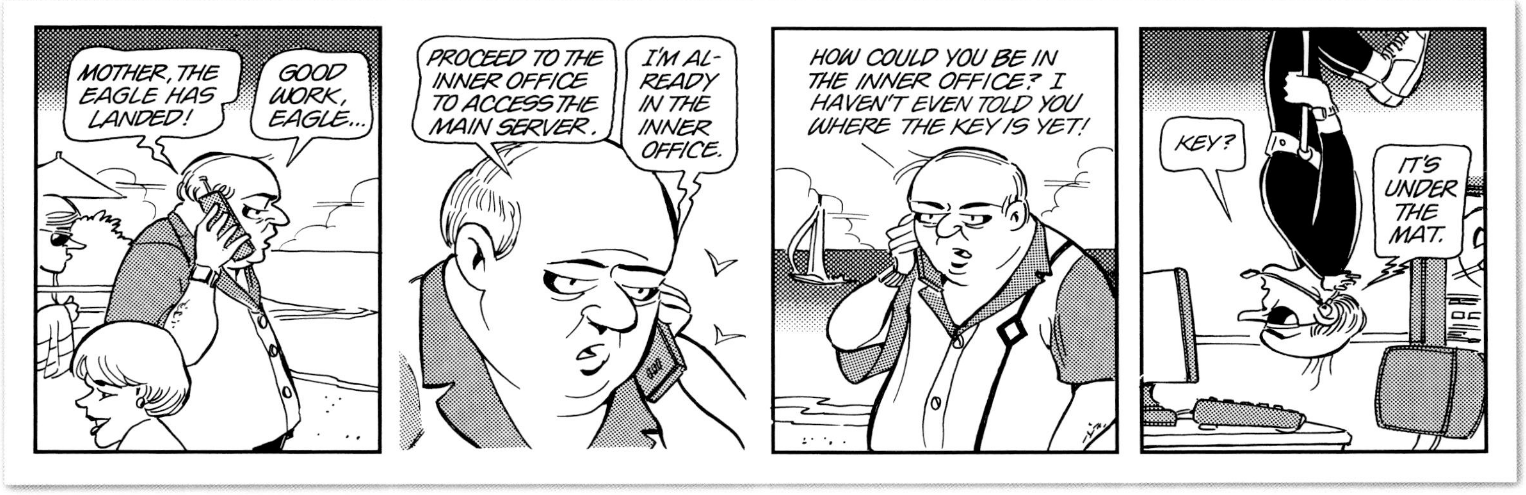
MOTHER, THE EAGLE HAS LANDED!
GOOD WORK, EAGLE...
PROCEED TO THE INNER OFFICE TO ACCESS THE MAIN SERVER.
I'M ALREADY IN THE INNER OFFICE.
HOW COULD YOU BE IN THE INNER OFFICE? I HAVEN'T EVEN TOLD YOU WHERE THE KEY IS YET!
KEY?
IT'S UNDER THE MAT.

3/5/02

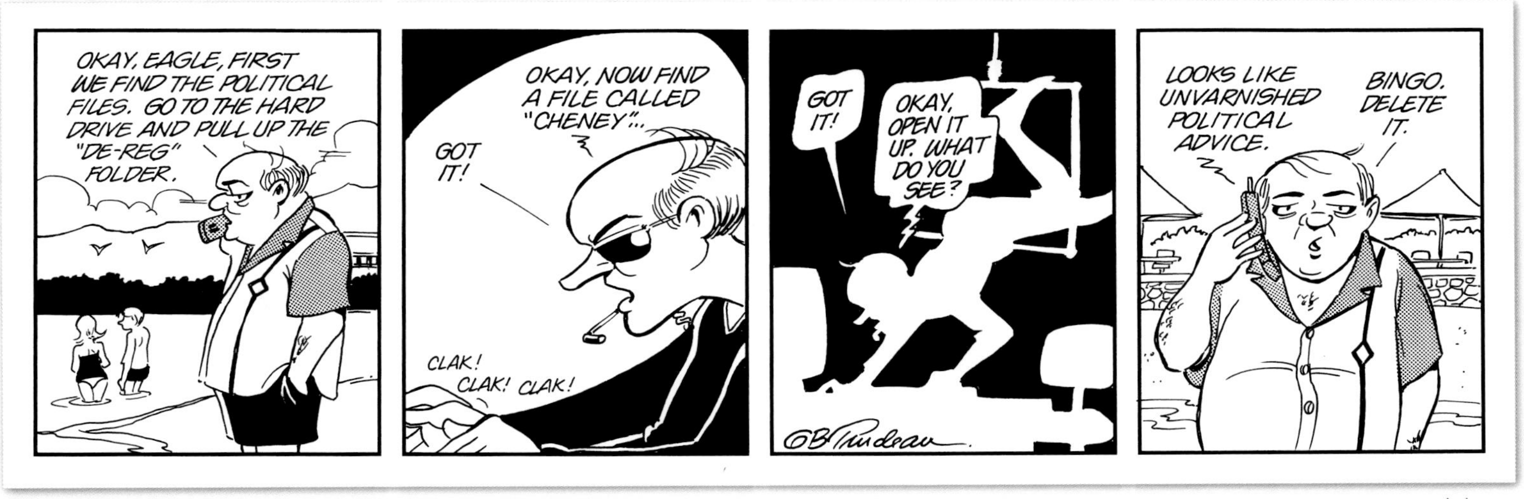
OKAY, EAGLE, FIRST WE FIND THE POLITICAL FILES. GO TO THE HARD DRIVE AND PULL UP THE "DE-REG" FOLDER.
OKAY, NOW FIND A FILE CALLED "CHENEY"...
GOT IT!
CLAK! CLAK! CLAK!
GOT IT!
OKAY, OPEN IT UP. WHAT DO YOU SEE?
LOOKS LIKE UNVARNISHED POLITICAL ADVICE.
BINGO. DELETE IT.

3/6/02

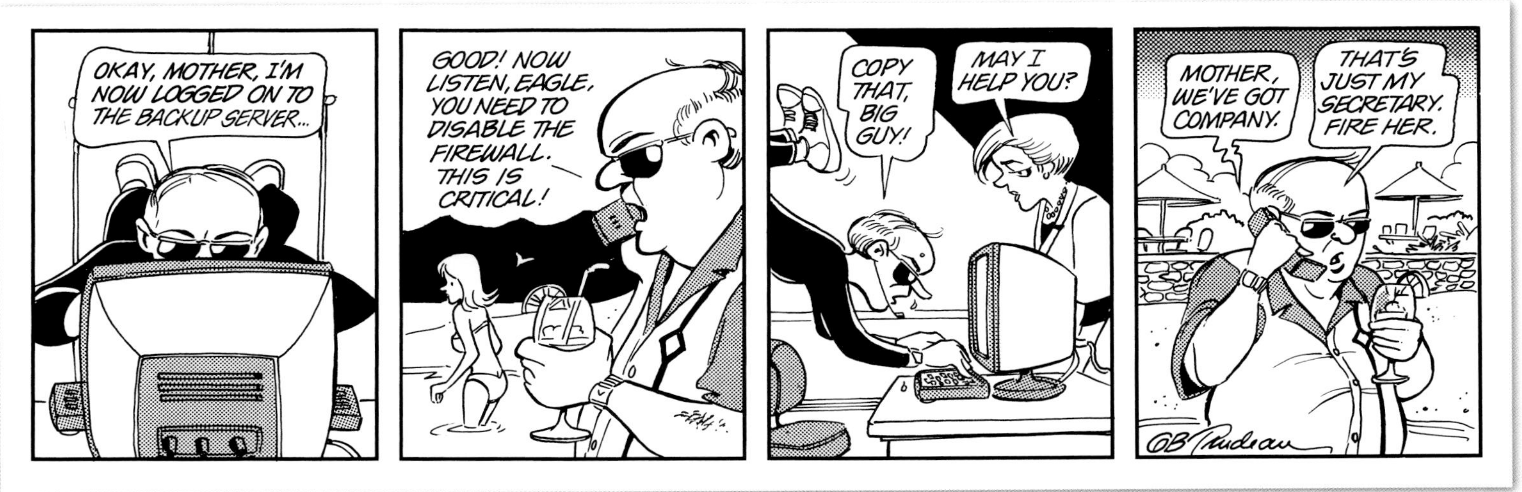
OKAY, MOTHER, I'M NOW LOGGED ON TO THE BACKUP SERVER...
GOOD! NOW LISTEN, EAGLE, YOU NEED TO DISABLE THE FIREWALL. THIS IS CRITICAL!
COPY THAT, BIG GUY!
MAY I HELP YOU?
MOTHER, WE'VE GOT COMPANY.
THAT'S JUST MY SECRETARY. FIRE HER.

3/7/02

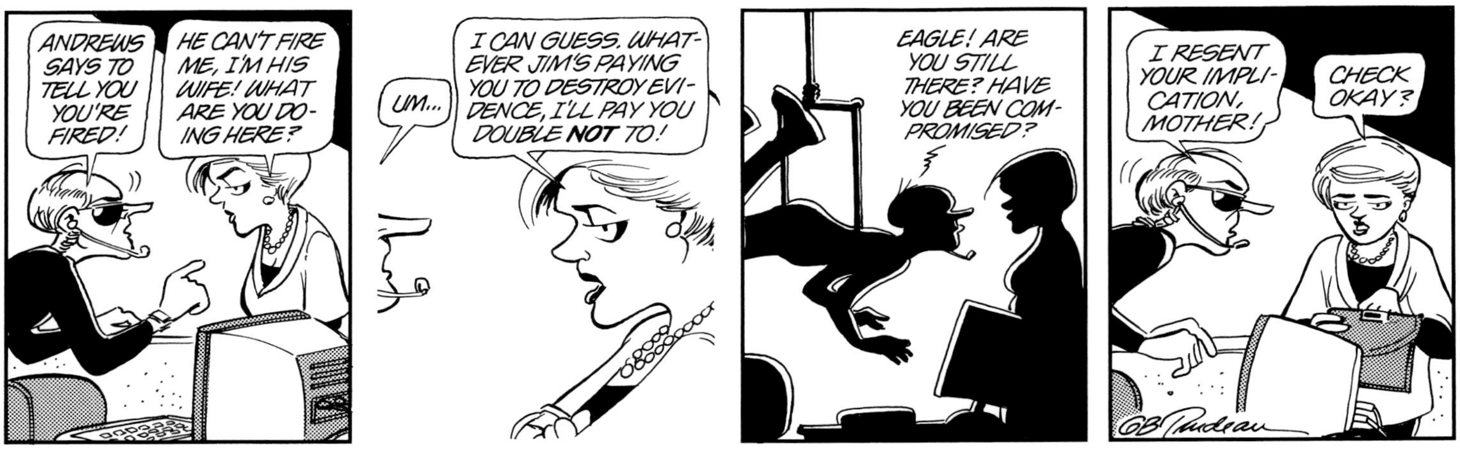
ANDREWS SAYS TO TELL YOU YOU'RE FIRED!
HE CAN'T FIRE ME, I'M HIS WIFE! WHAT ARE YOU DOING HERE?
UM...
I CAN GUESS. WHATEVER JIM'S PAYING YOU TO DESTROY EVIDENCE, I'LL PAY YOU DOUBLE **NOT** TO!
EAGLE! ARE YOU STILL THERE? HAVE YOU BEEN COMPROMISED?
I RESENT YOUR IMPLICATION, MOTHER!
CHECK OKAY?
GBTrudeau

3/8/02

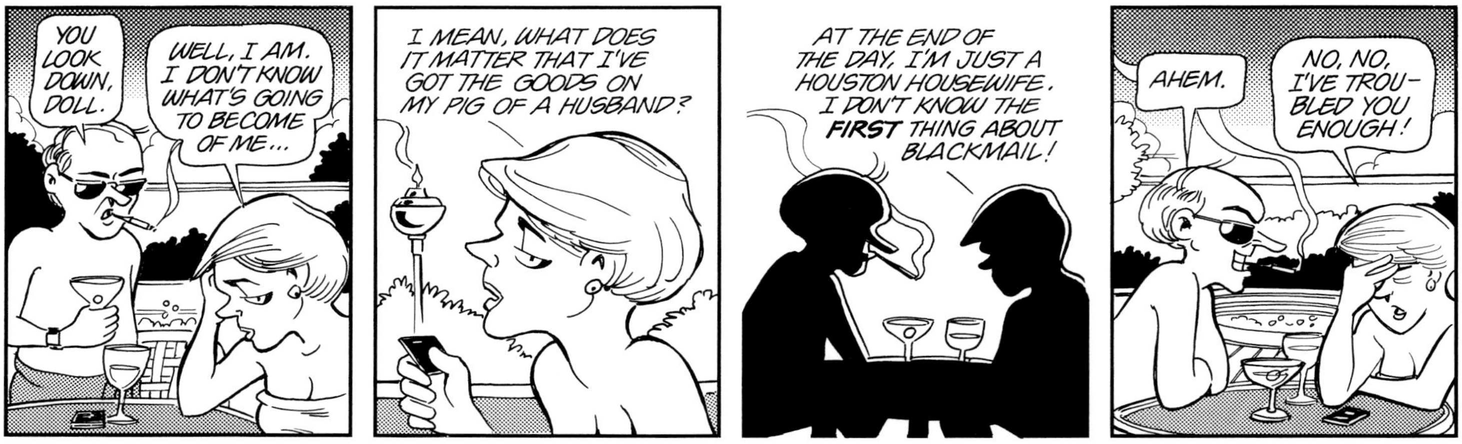
YOU LOOK DOWN, DOLL.
WELL, I AM. I DON'T KNOW WHAT'S GOING TO BECOME OF ME...
I MEAN, WHAT DOES IT MATTER THAT I'VE GOT THE GOODS ON MY PIG OF A HUSBAND?
AT THE END OF THE DAY, I'M JUST A HOUSTON HOUSEWIFE. I DON'T KNOW THE **FIRST** THING ABOUT BLACKMAIL!
AHEM.
NO, NO, I'VE TROUBLED YOU ENOUGH!

3/12/02

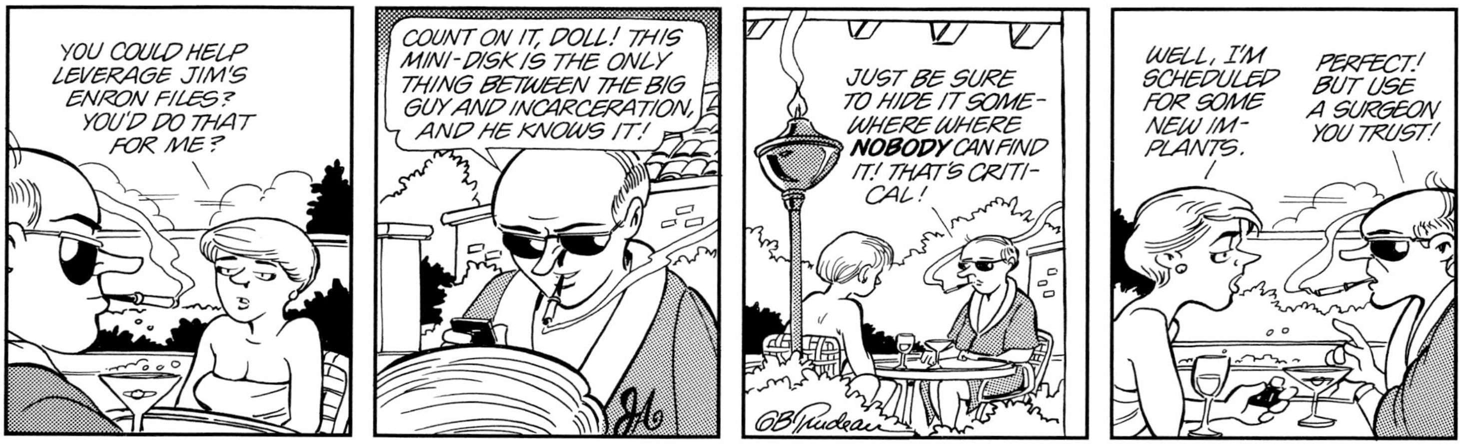
YOU COULD HELP LEVERAGE JIM'S ENRON FILES? YOU'D DO THAT FOR ME?
COUNT ON IT, DOLL! THIS MINI-DISK IS THE ONLY THING BETWEEN THE BIG GUY AND INCARCERATION, AND HE KNOWS IT!
JUST BE SURE TO HIDE IT SOMEWHERE WHERE **NOBODY** CAN FIND IT! THAT'S CRITICAL!
WELL, I'M SCHEDULED FOR SOME NEW IMPLANTS.
PERFECT! BUT USE A SURGEON YOU TRUST!
GBTrudeau

3/13/02

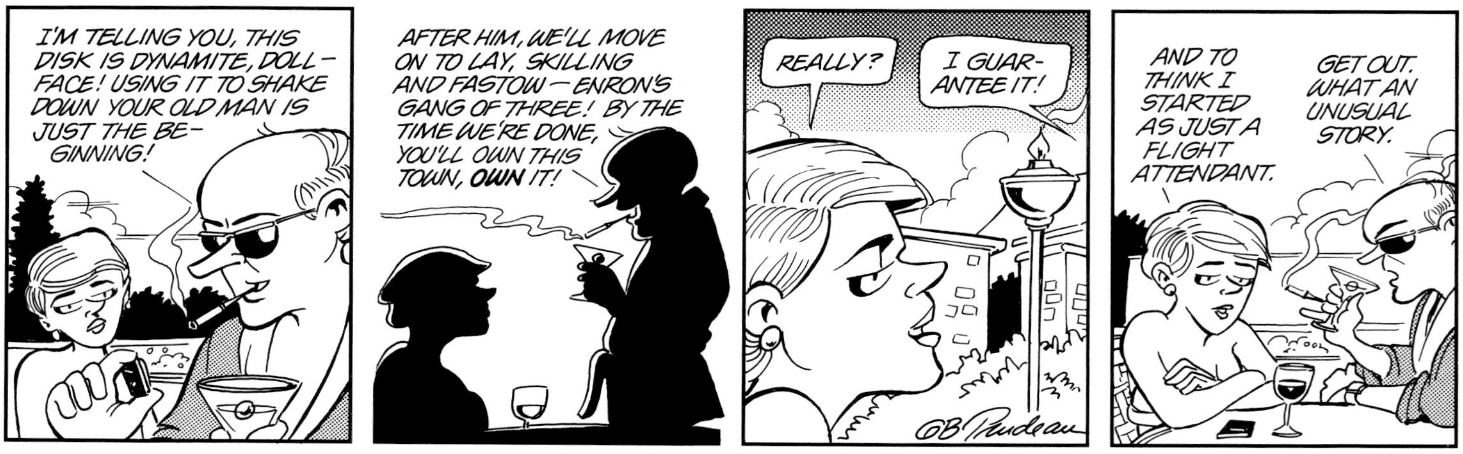
I'M TELLING YOU, THIS DISK IS DYNAMITE, DOLLFACE! USING IT TO SHAKE DOWN YOUR OLD MAN IS JUST THE BEGINNING!
AFTER HIM, WE'LL MOVE ON TO LAY, SKILLING AND FASTOW — ENRON'S GANG OF THREE! BY THE TIME WE'RE DONE, YOU'LL OWN THIS TOWN, **OWN** IT!
REALLY?
I GUARANTEE IT!
AND TO THINK I STARTED AS JUST A FLIGHT ATTENDANT.
GET OUT. WHAT AN UNUSUAL STORY.
GBTrudeau

3/14/02

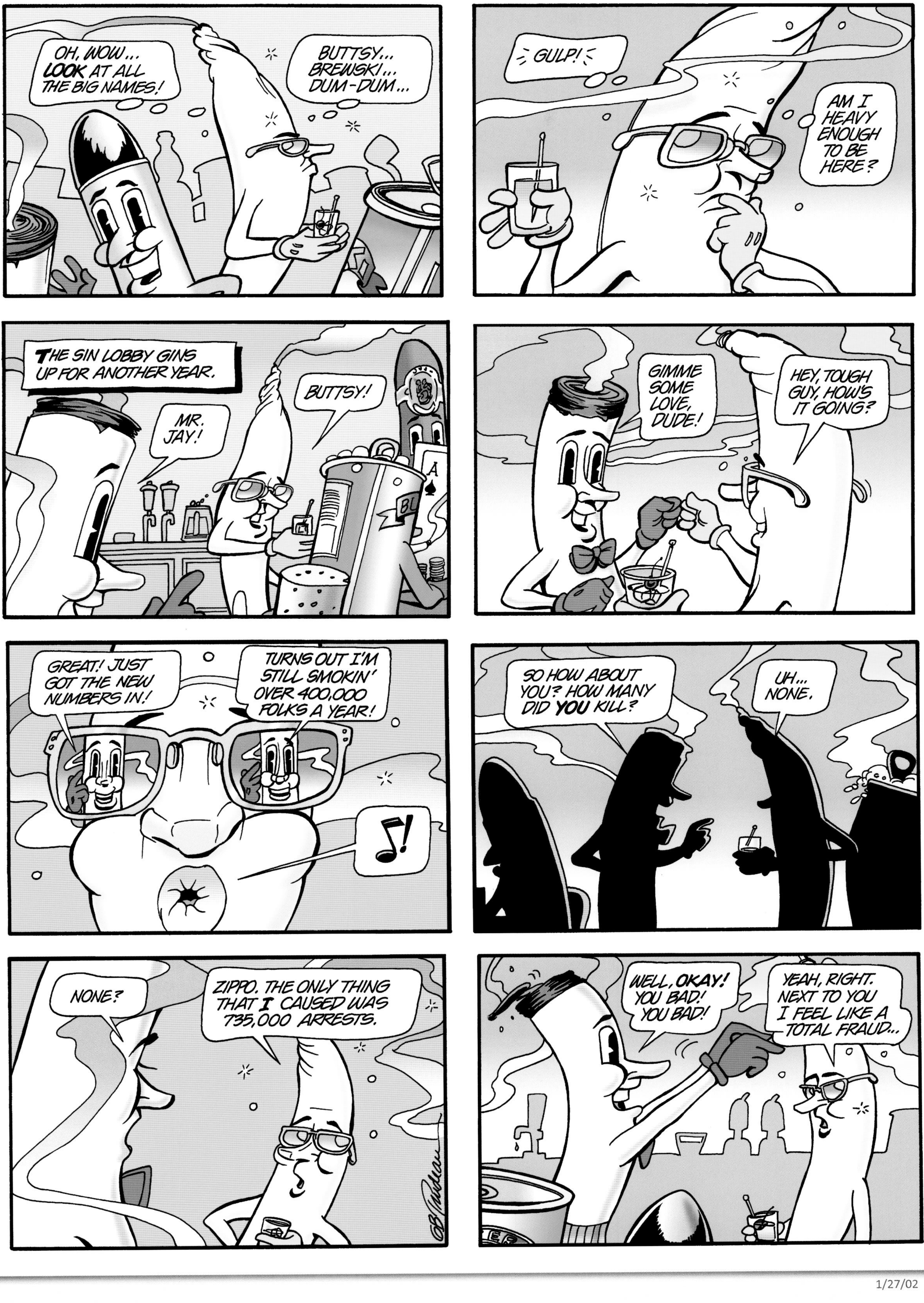
OH, WOW... LOOK AT ALL THE BIG NAMES!
BUTTSY... BREWSKI... DUM-DUM...
GULP!
AM I HEAVY ENOUGH TO BE HERE?
THE SIN LOBBY GINS UP FOR ANOTHER YEAR.
MR. JAY!
BUTTSY!
GIMME SOME LOVE, DUDE!
HEY, TOUGH GUY, HOW'S IT GOING?
GREAT! JUST GOT THE NEW NUMBERS IN!
TURNS OUT I'M STILL SMOKIN' OVER 400,000 FOLKS A YEAR!
♪!
SO HOW ABOUT YOU? HOW MANY DID YOU KILL?
UH... NONE.
NONE?
ZIPPO. THE ONLY THING THAT I CAUSED WAS 735,000 ARRESTS.
WELL, OKAY! YOU BAD! YOU BAD!
YEAH, RIGHT. NEXT TO YOU I FEEL LIKE A TOTAL FRAUD...

1/27/02

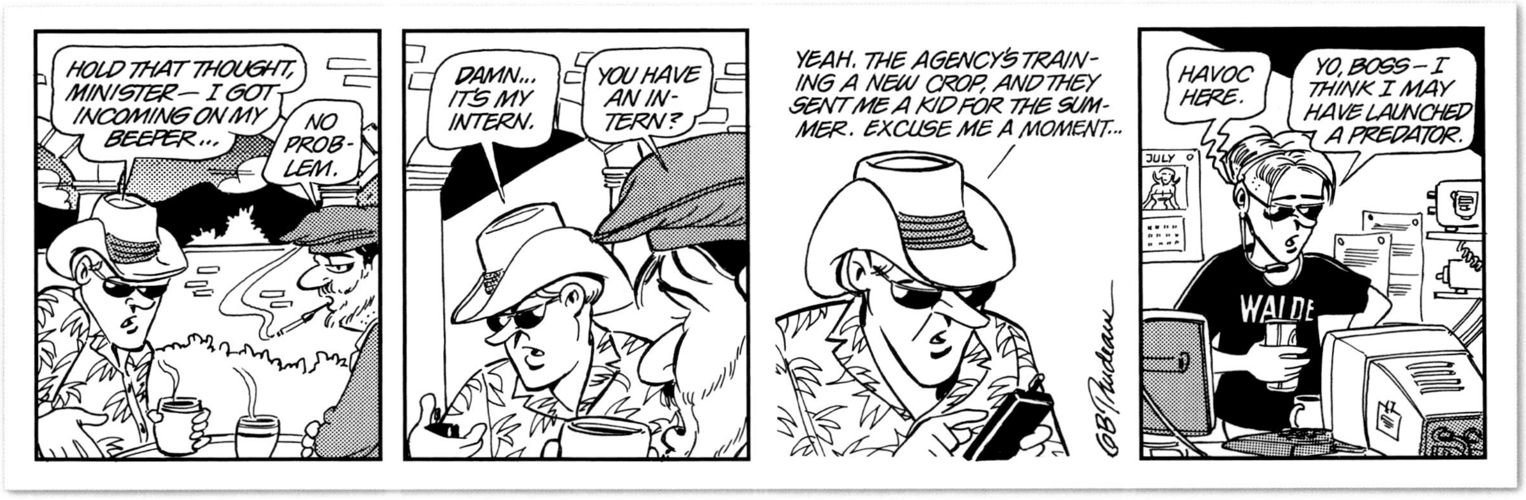
HOLD THAT THOUGHT, MINISTER— I GOT INCOMING ON MY BEEPER...
NO PROBLEM.
DAMN... IT'S MY INTERN.
YOU HAVE AN INTERN?
YEAH. THE AGENCY'S TRAINING A NEW CROP, AND THEY SENT ME A KID FOR THE SUMMER. EXCUSE ME A MOMENT...
HAVOC HERE.
YO, BOSS— I THINK I MAY HAVE LAUNCHED A PREDATOR.
WALDE

7/5/02

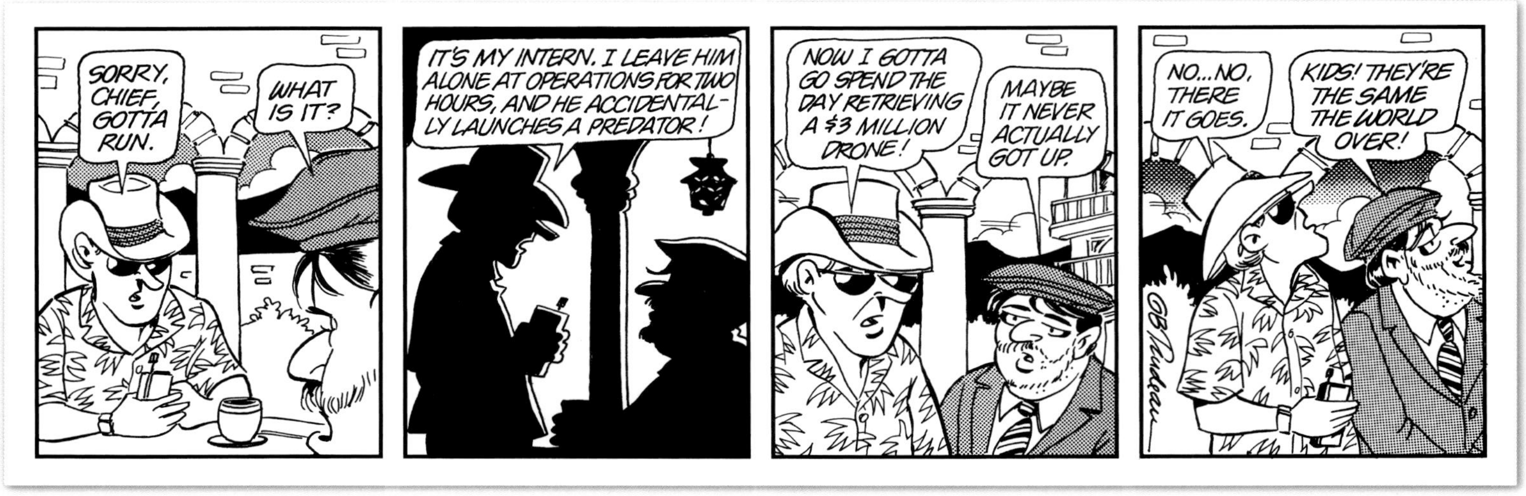
SORRY, CHIEF, GOTTA RUN.
WHAT IS IT?
IT'S MY INTERN. I LEAVE HIM ALONE AT OPERATIONS FOR TWO HOURS, AND HE ACCIDENTALLY LAUNCHES A PREDATOR!
NOW I GOTTA GO SPEND THE DAY RETRIEVING A $3 MILLION DRONE!
MAYBE IT NEVER ACTUALLY GOT UP.
NO...NO, THERE IT GOES.
KIDS! THEY'RE THE SAME THE WORLD OVER!

7/6/02

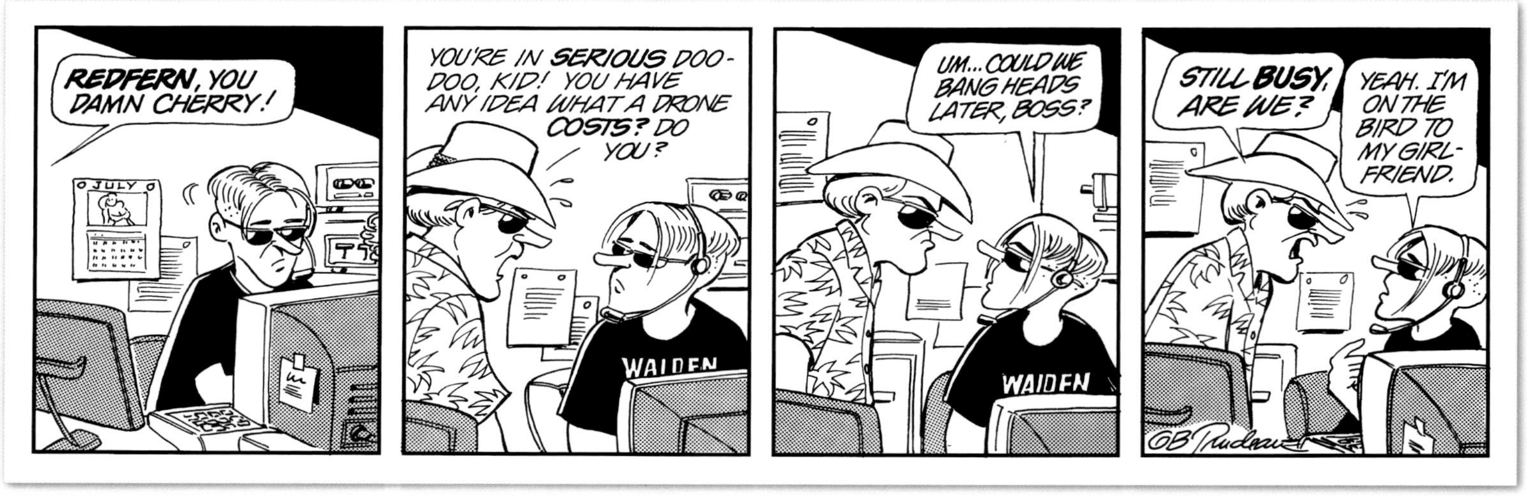
REDFERN, YOU DAMN CHERRY!
JULY
YOU'RE IN SERIOUS DOO-DOO, KID! YOU HAVE ANY IDEA WHAT A DRONE COSTS? DO YOU?
WALDEN
UM...COULD WE BANG HEADS LATER, BOSS?
WALDEN
STILL BUSY, ARE WE?
YEAH. I'M ON THE BIRD TO MY GIRLFRIEND.

7/8/02

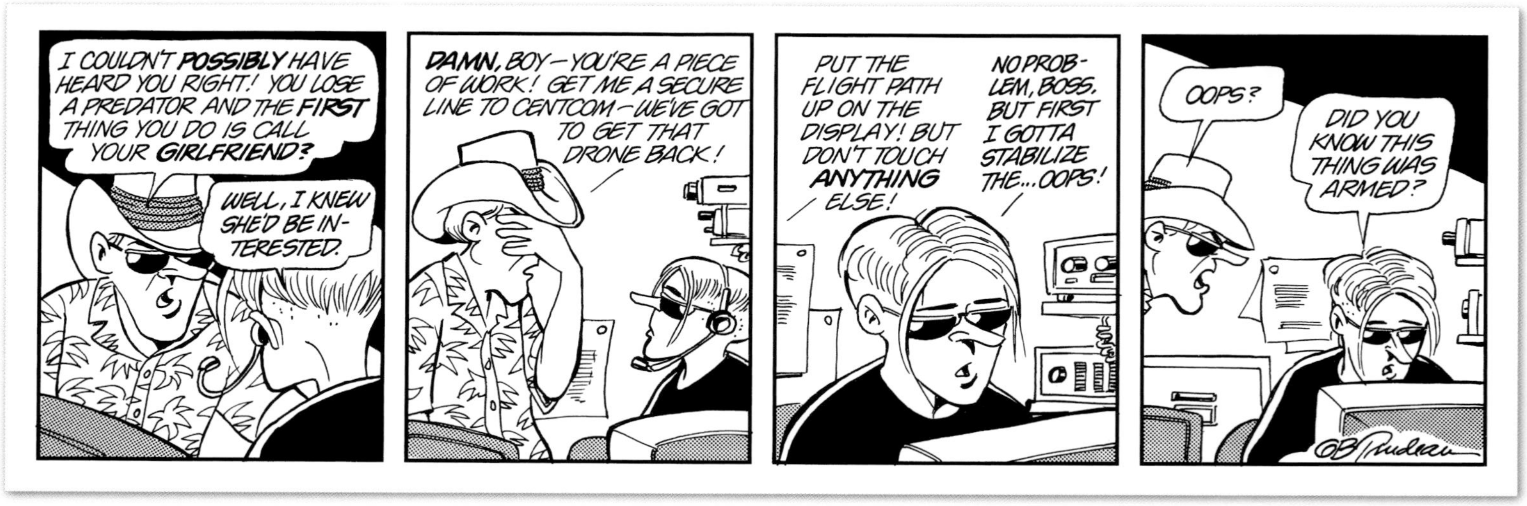
I COULDN'T POSSIBLY HAVE HEARD YOU RIGHT! YOU LOSE A PREDATOR AND THE FIRST THING YOU DO IS CALL YOUR GIRLFRIEND?
WELL, I KNEW SHE'D BE INTERESTED.
DAMN, BOY— YOU'RE A PIECE OF WORK! GET ME A SECURE LINE TO CENTCOM— WE'VE GOT TO GET THAT DRONE BACK!
PUT THE FLIGHT PATH UP ON THE DISPLAY! BUT DON'T TOUCH ANYTHING ELSE!
NO PROBLEM, BOSS. BUT FIRST I GOTTA STABILIZE THE...OOPS!
OOPS?
DID YOU KNOW THIS THING WAS ARMED?

7/9/02

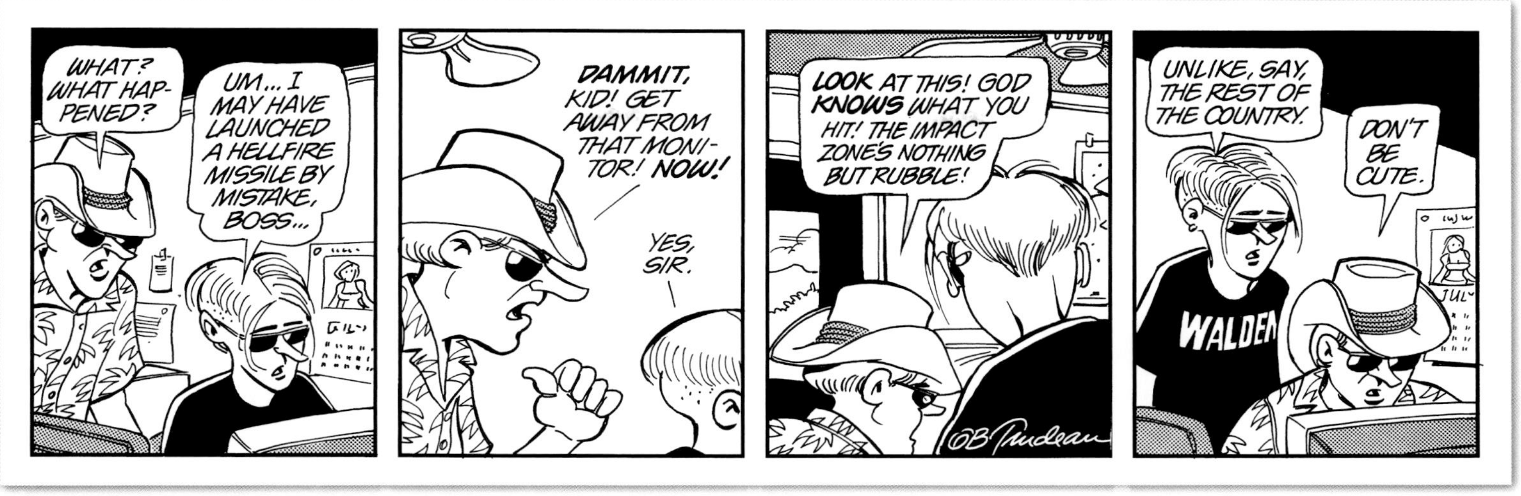
WHAT? WHAT HAPPENED?
UM... I MAY HAVE LAUNCHED A HELLFIRE MISSILE BY MISTAKE, BOSS...
DAMMIT, KID! GET AWAY FROM THAT MONITOR! NOW!
YES, SIR.
LOOK AT THIS! GOD KNOWS WHAT YOU HIT! THE IMPACT ZONE'S NOTHING BUT RUBBLE!
UNLIKE, SAY, THE REST OF THE COUNTRY.
DON'T BE CUTE.
WALDEN

7/10/02

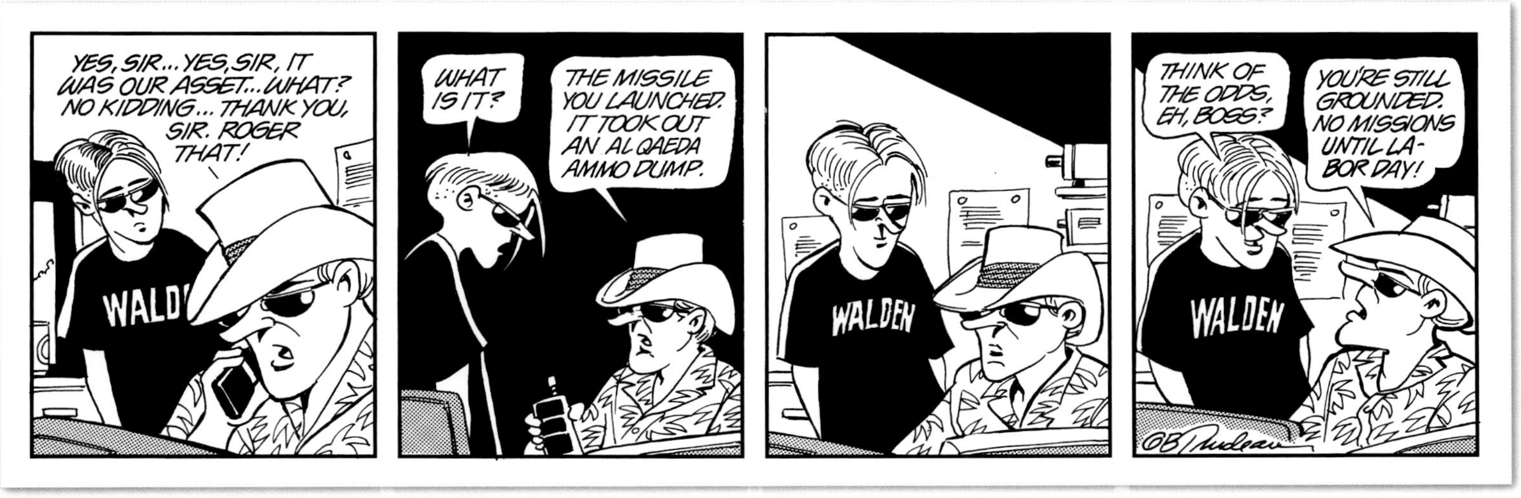
YES, SIR... YES, SIR, IT WAS OUR ASSET... WHAT? NO KIDDING... THANK YOU, SIR. ROGER THAT!
WHAT IS IT?
THE MISSILE YOU LAUNCHED. IT TOOK OUT AN AL QAEDA AMMO DUMP.
THINK OF THE ODDS, EH, BOSS?
YOU'RE STILL GROUNDED. NO MISSIONS UNTIL LABOR DAY!
WALDEN

7/11/02

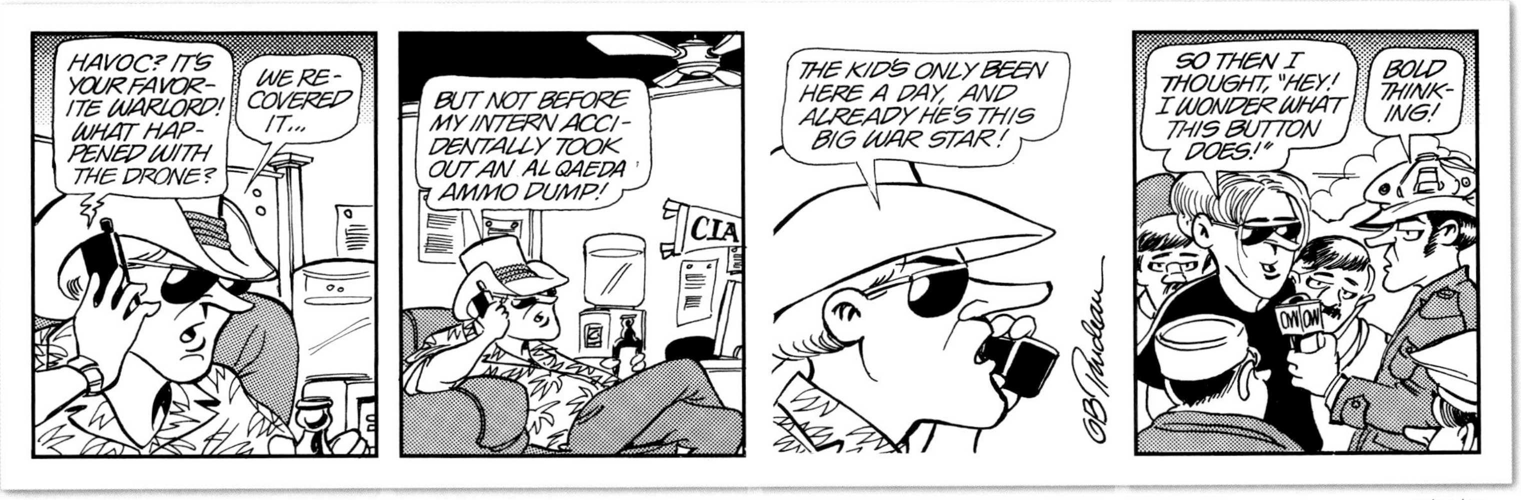
HAVOC? IT'S YOUR FAVORITE WARLORD! WHAT HAPPENED WITH THE DRONE?
WE RECOVERED IT...
BUT NOT BEFORE MY INTERN ACCIDENTALLY TOOK OUT AN AL QAEDA AMMO DUMP!
CIA
THE KID'S ONLY BEEN HERE A DAY, AND ALREADY HE'S THIS BIG WAR STAR!
SO THEN I THOUGHT, "HEY! I WONDER WHAT THIS BUTTON DOES!"
BOLD THINKING!

7/13/02

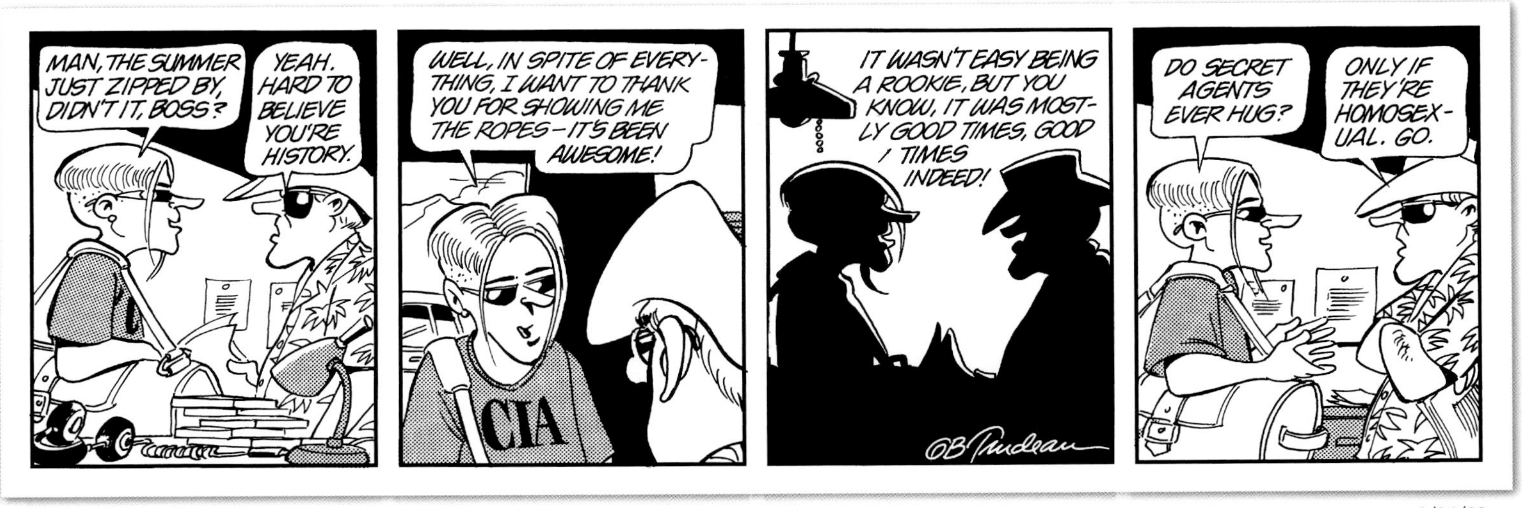
MAN, THE SUMMER JUST ZIPPED BY, DIDN'T IT, BOSS?
YEAH. HARD TO BELIEVE YOU'RE HISTORY.
WELL, IN SPITE OF EVERYTHING, I WANT TO THANK YOU FOR SHOWING ME THE ROPES—IT'S BEEN AWESOME!
CIA
IT WASN'T EASY BEING A ROOKIE, BUT YOU KNOW, IT WAS MOSTLY GOOD TIMES, GOOD TIMES INDEED!
DO SECRET AGENTS EVER HUG?
ONLY IF THEY'RE HOMOSEXUAL. GO.

8/24/02

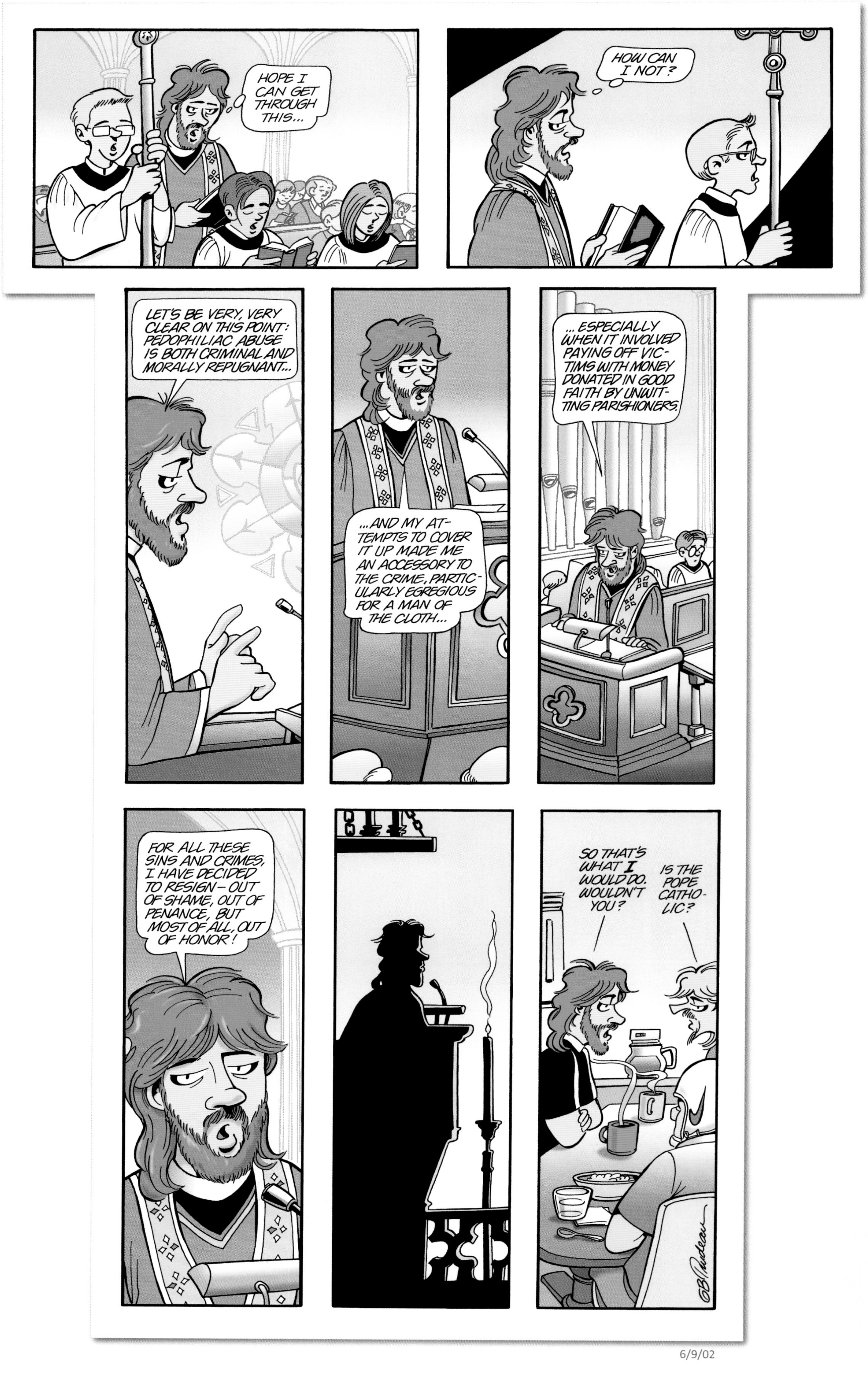
HOPE I CAN GET THROUGH THIS...
HOW CAN I NOT?
LET'S BE VERY, VERY CLEAR ON THIS POINT: PEDOPHILIAC ABUSE IS BOTH CRIMINAL AND MORALLY REPUGNANT...
...AND MY ATTEMPTS TO COVER IT UP MADE ME AN ACCESSORY TO THE CRIME, PARTICULARLY EGREGIOUS FOR A MAN OF THE CLOTH...
...ESPECIALLY WHEN IT INVOLVED PAYING OFF VICTIMS WITH MONEY DONATED IN GOOD FAITH BY UNWITTING PARISHIONERS.
FOR ALL THESE SINS AND CRIMES, I HAVE DECIDED TO RESIGN – OUT OF SHAME, OUT OF PENANCE, BUT MOST OF ALL, OUT OF HONOR!
SO THAT'S WHAT I WOULD DO. WOULDN'T YOU?
IS THE POPE CATHOLIC?
GBTrudeau

6/9/02

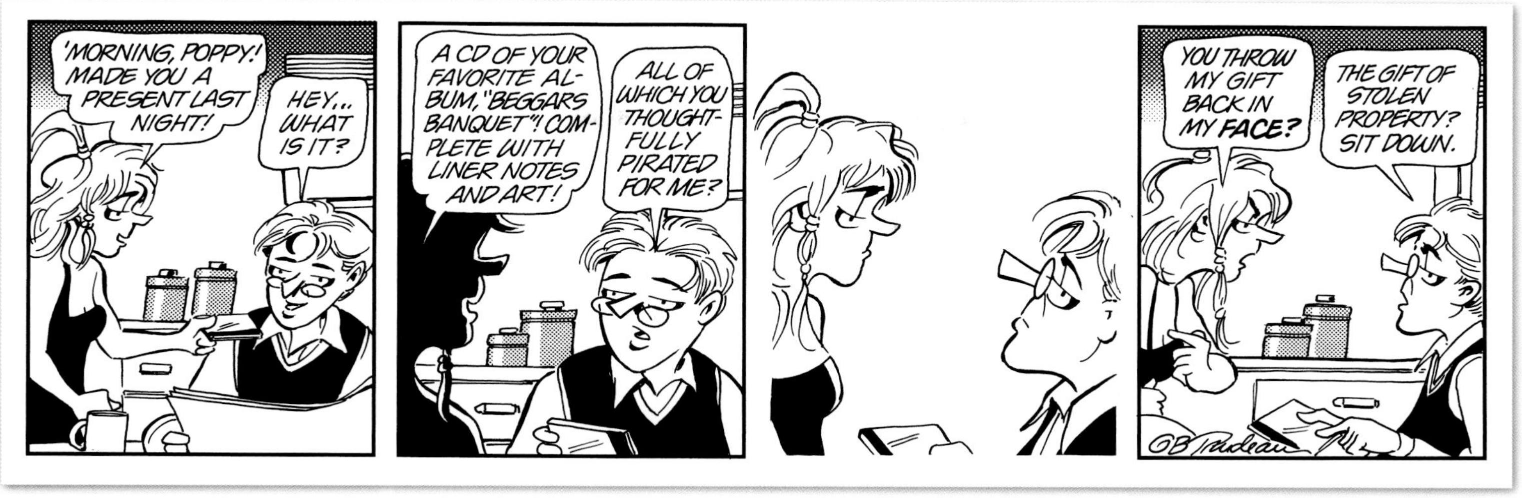
'MORNING, POPPY! MADE YOU A PRESENT LAST NIGHT!
HEY... WHAT IS IT?
A CD OF YOUR FAVORITE ALBUM, "BEGGARS BANQUET"! COMPLETE WITH LINER NOTES AND ART!
ALL OF WHICH YOU THOUGHTFULLY PIRATED FOR ME?
YOU THROW MY GIFT BACK IN MY **FACE?**
THE GIFT OF STOLEN PROPERTY? SIT DOWN.

3/25/02

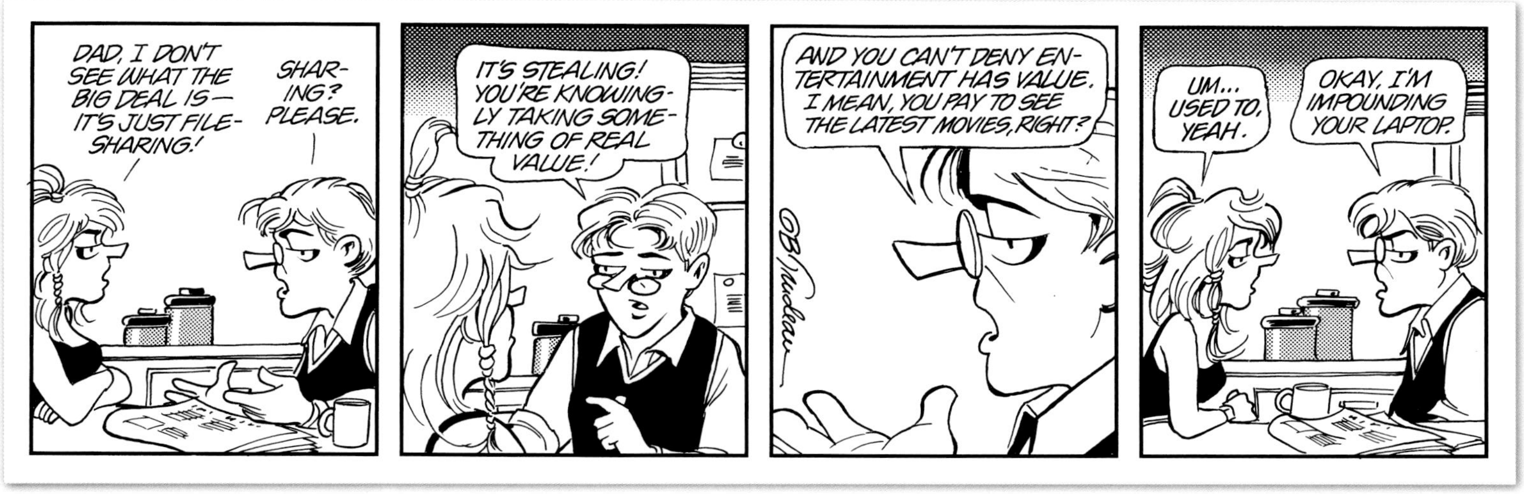
DAD, I DON'T SEE WHAT THE BIG DEAL IS — IT'S JUST FILE-SHARING!
SHARING? PLEASE.
IT'S STEALING! YOU'RE KNOWINGLY TAKING SOMETHING OF REAL VALUE!
AND YOU CAN'T DENY ENTERTAINMENT HAS VALUE. I MEAN, YOU PAY TO SEE THE LATEST MOVIES, RIGHT?
UM... USED TO, YEAH.
OKAY, I'M IMPOUNDING YOUR LAPTOP.

3/27/02

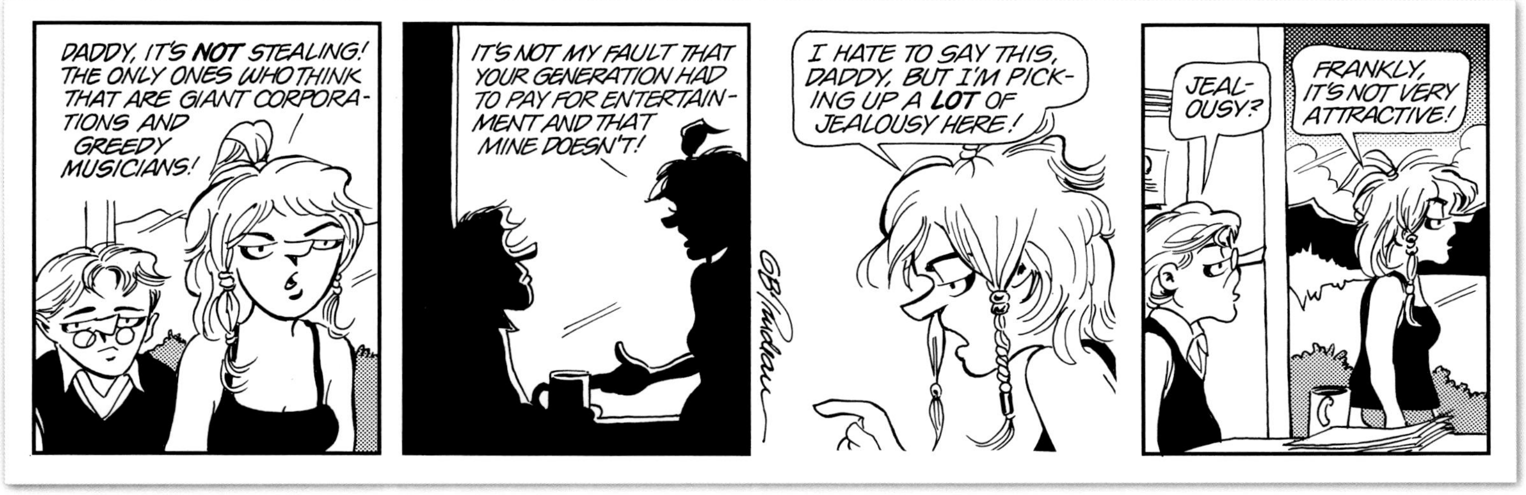
DADDY, IT'S **NOT** STEALING! THE ONLY ONES WHO THINK THAT ARE GIANT CORPORATIONS AND GREEDY MUSICIANS!
IT'S NOT MY FAULT THAT YOUR GENERATION HAD TO PAY FOR ENTERTAINMENT AND THAT MINE DOESN'T!
I HATE TO SAY THIS, DADDY, BUT I'M PICKING UP A **LOT** OF JEALOUSY HERE!
JEALOUSY?
FRANKLY, IT'S NOT VERY ATTRACTIVE!

3/28/02

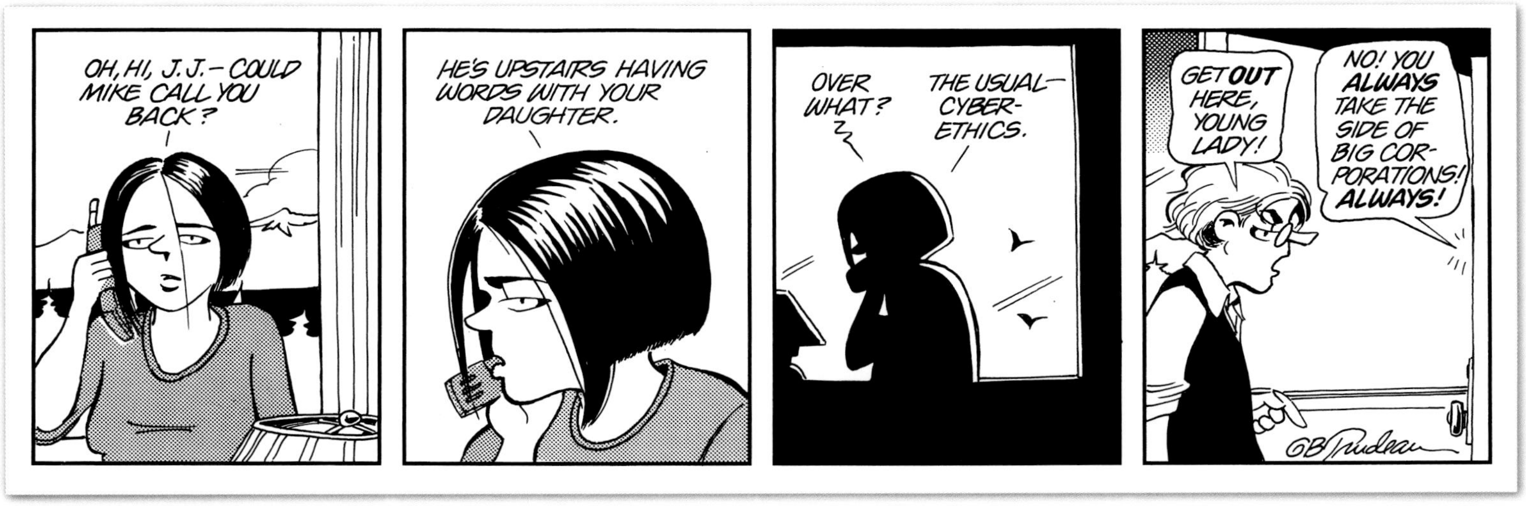
OH, HI, J.J. — COULD MIKE CALL YOU BACK?
HE'S UPSTAIRS HAVING WORDS WITH YOUR DAUGHTER.
OVER WHAT?
THE USUAL — CYBER-ETHICS.
GET **OUT** HERE, YOUNG LADY!
NO! YOU **ALWAYS** TAKE THE SIDE OF BIG CORPORATIONS! **ALWAYS!**

3/29/02

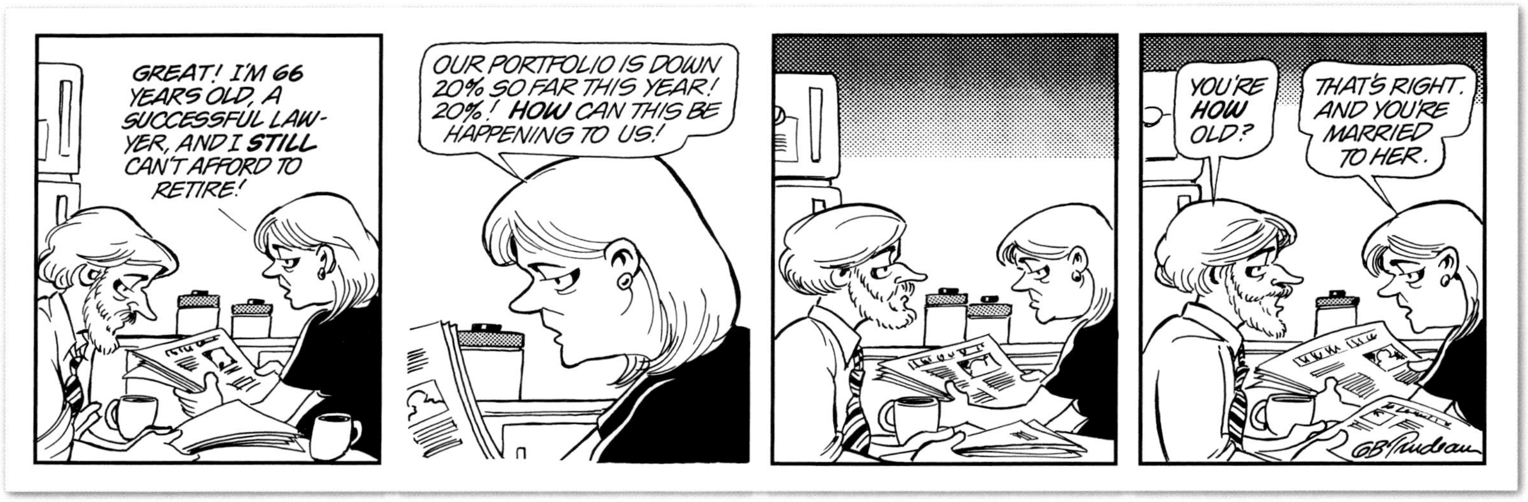
GREAT! I'M 66 YEARS OLD, A SUCCESSFUL LAWYER, AND I STILL CAN'T AFFORD TO RETIRE!
OUR PORTFOLIO IS DOWN 20% SO FAR THIS YEAR! 20%! HOW CAN THIS BE HAPPENING TO US!
YOU'RE HOW OLD?
THAT'S RIGHT. AND YOU'RE MARRIED TO HER.
©B Trudeau

7/29/02

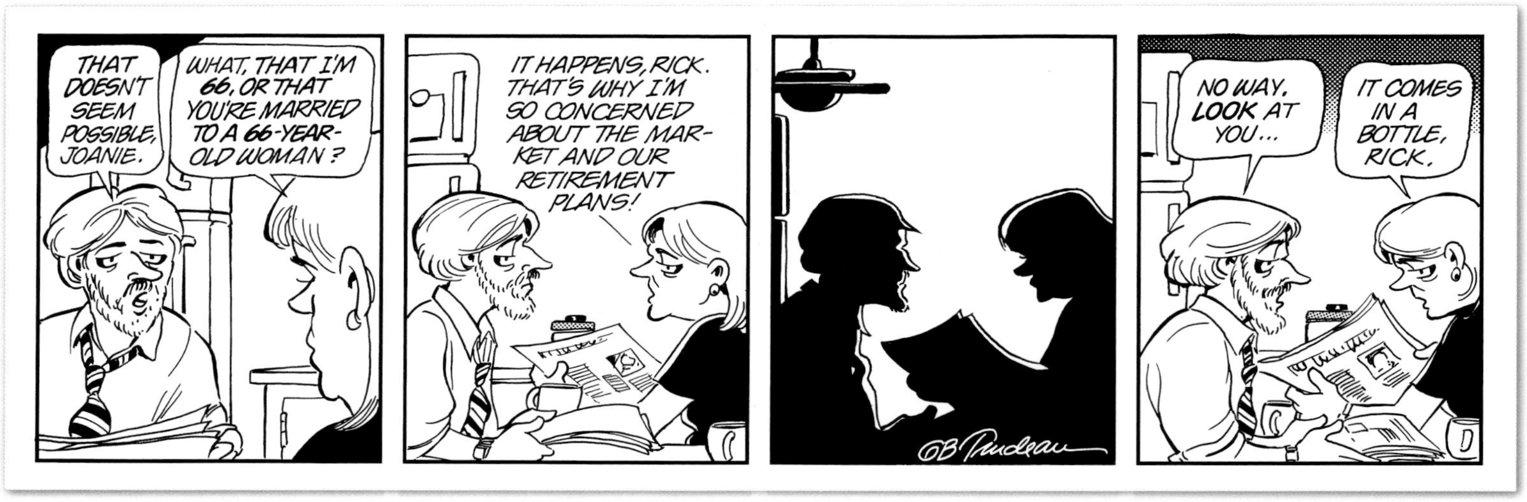
THAT DOESN'T SEEM POSSIBLE, JOANIE.
WHAT, THAT I'M 66, OR THAT YOU'RE MARRIED TO A 66-YEAR-OLD WOMAN?
IT HAPPENS, RICK. THAT'S WHY I'M SO CONCERNED ABOUT THE MARKET AND OUR RETIREMENT PLANS!
©B Trudeau
NO WAY. LOOK AT YOU...
IT COMES IN A BOTTLE, RICK.

7/30/02

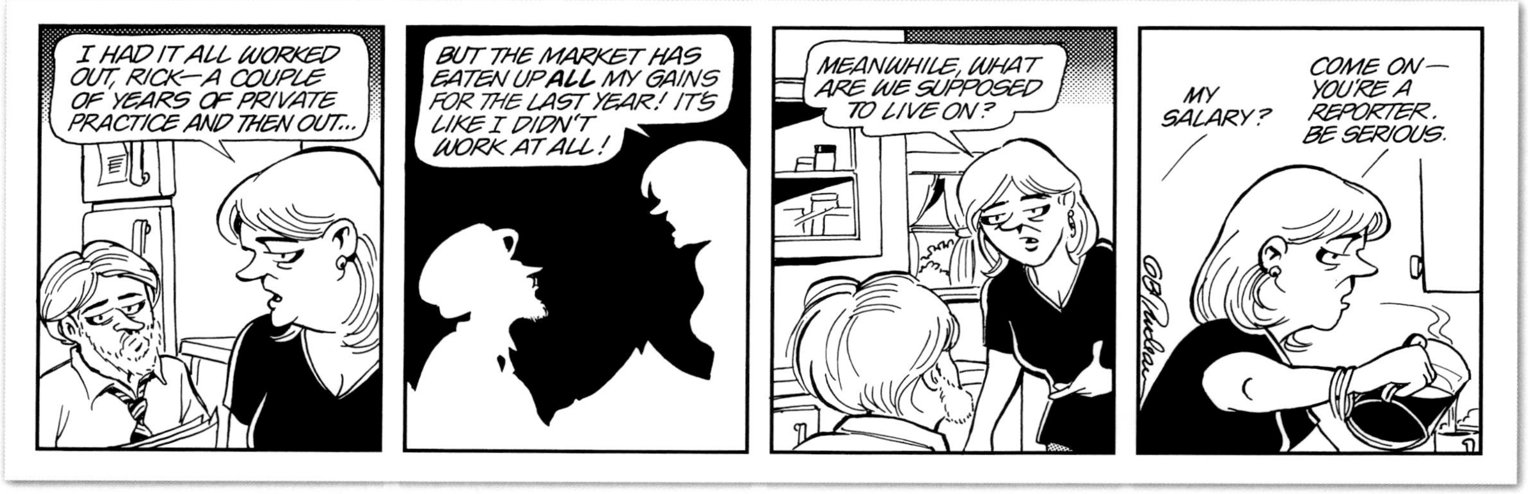
I HAD IT ALL WORKED OUT, RICK—A COUPLE OF YEARS OF PRIVATE PRACTICE AND THEN OUT...
BUT THE MARKET HAS EATEN UP ALL MY GAINS FOR THE LAST YEAR! IT'S LIKE I DIDN'T WORK AT ALL!
MEANWHILE, WHAT ARE WE SUPPOSED TO LIVE ON?
MY SALARY?
COME ON— YOU'RE A REPORTER. BE SERIOUS.

8/1/02

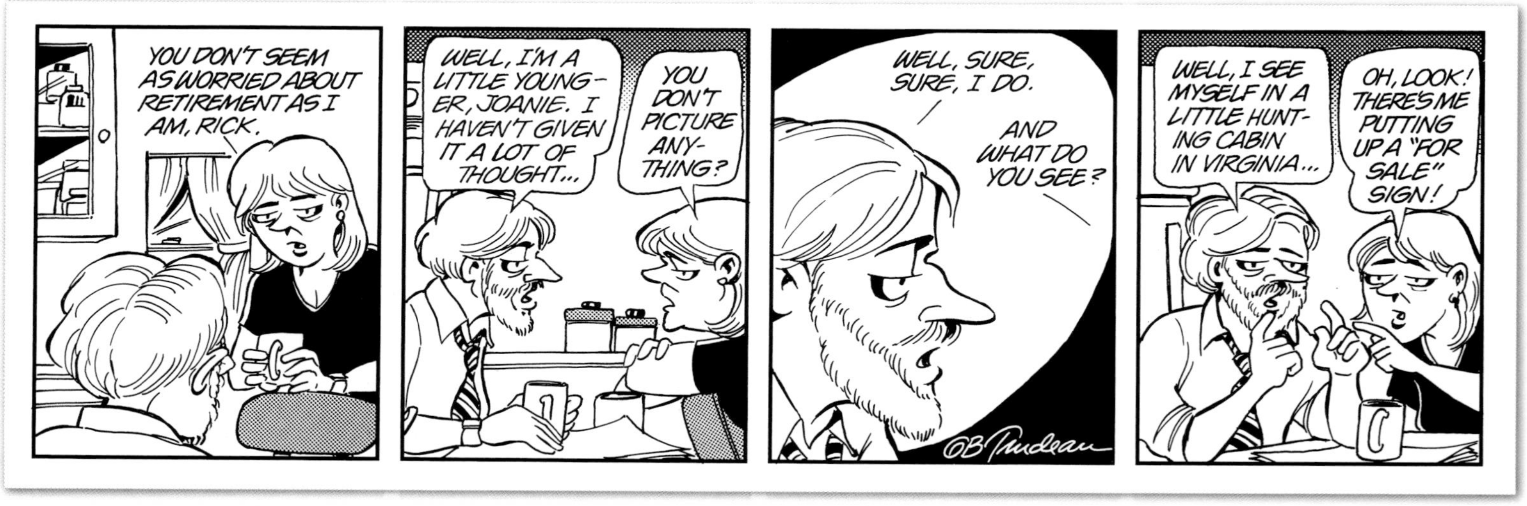
YOU DON'T SEEM AS WORRIED ABOUT RETIREMENT AS I AM, RICK.
WELL, I'M A LITTLE YOUNGER, JOANIE. I HAVEN'T GIVEN IT A LOT OF THOUGHT...
YOU DON'T PICTURE ANYTHING?
WELL, SURE, SURE, I DO.
AND WHAT DO YOU SEE?
©B Trudeau
WELL, I SEE MYSELF IN A LITTLE HUNTING CABIN IN VIRGINIA...
OH, LOOK! THERE'S ME PUTTING UP A "FOR SALE" SIGN!

8/2/02

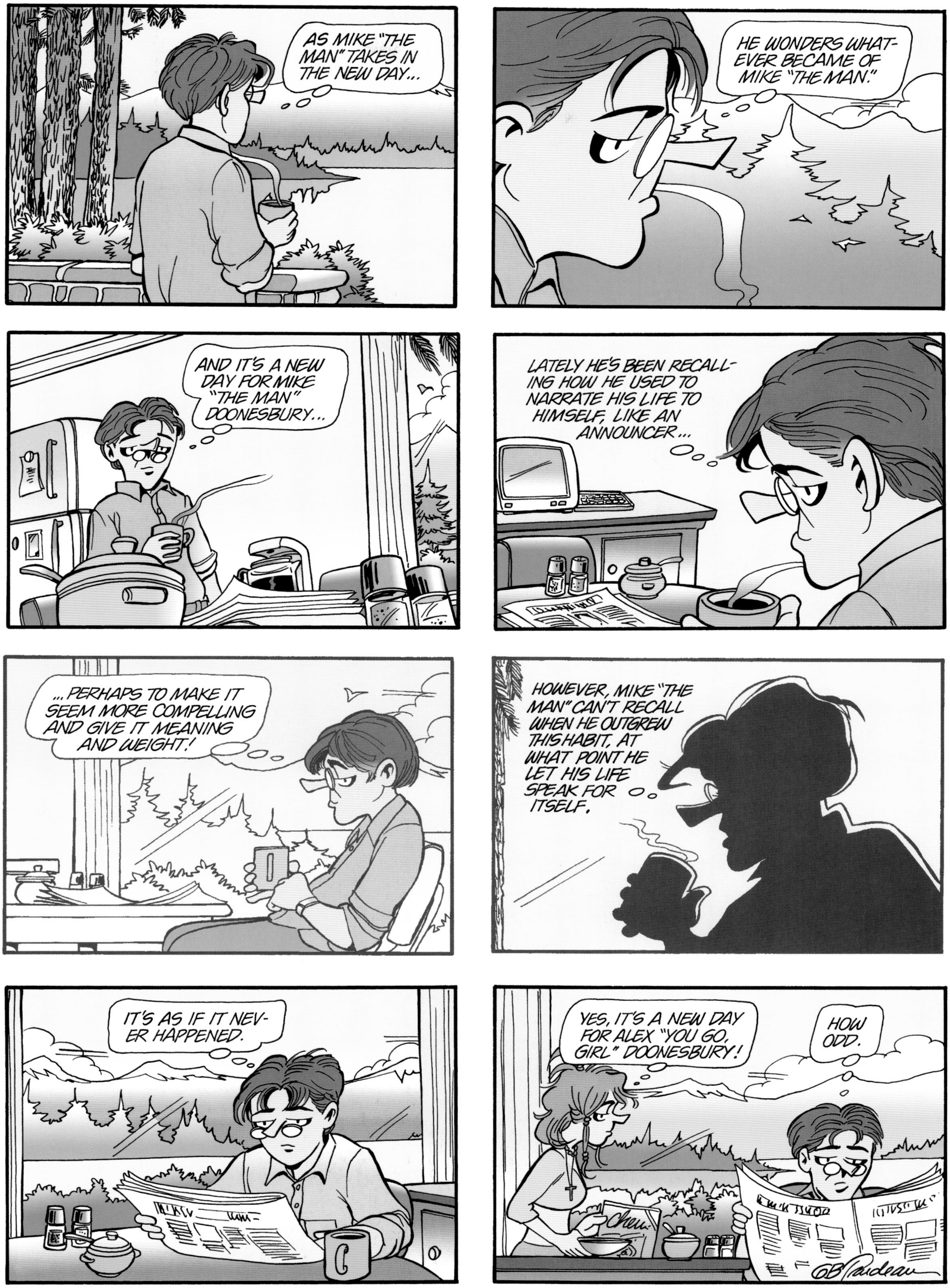
AS MIKE "THE MAN" TAKES IN THE NEW DAY...
HE WONDERS WHATEVER BECAME OF MIKE "THE MAN."
AND IT'S A NEW DAY FOR MIKE "THE MAN" DOONESBURY...
LATELY HE'S BEEN RECALLING HOW HE USED TO NARRATE HIS LIFE TO HIMSELF, LIKE AN ANNOUNCER...
...PERHAPS TO MAKE IT SEEM MORE COMPELLING AND GIVE IT MEANING AND WEIGHT!
HOWEVER, MIKE "THE MAN" CAN'T RECALL WHEN HE OUTGREW THIS HABIT, AT WHAT POINT HE LET HIS LIFE SPEAK FOR ITSELF.
IT'S AS IF IT NEVER HAPPENED.
YES, IT'S A NEW DAY FOR ALEX "YOU GO, GIRL" DOONESBURY!
HOW ODD.
GBTrudeau

7/14/02

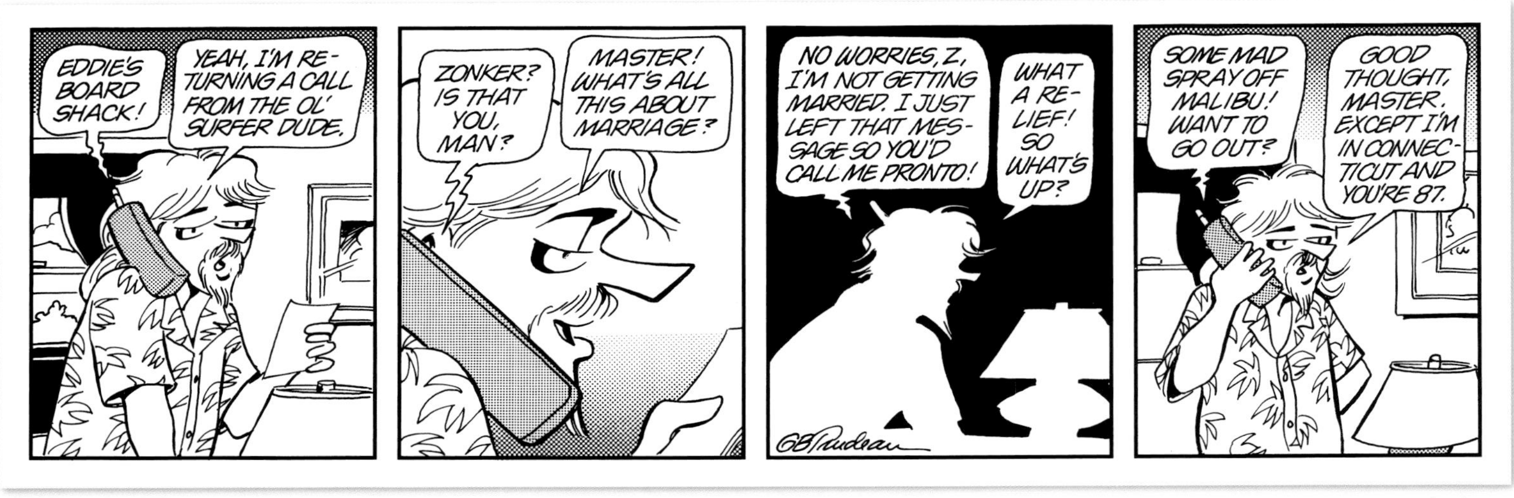
EDDIE'S BOARD SHACK!
YEAH, I'M RETURNING A CALL FROM THE OL' SURFER DUDE.
ZONKER? IS THAT YOU, MAN?
MASTER! WHAT'S ALL THIS ABOUT MARRIAGE?
NO WORRIES, Z, I'M NOT GETTING MARRIED. I JUST LEFT THAT MESSAGE SO YOU'D CALL ME PRONTO!
WHAT A RELIEF! SO WHAT'S UP?
SOME MAD SPRAY OFF MALIBU! WANT TO GO OUT?
GOOD THOUGHT, MASTER. EXCEPT I'M IN CONNECTICUT AND YOU'RE 87.

9/10/02

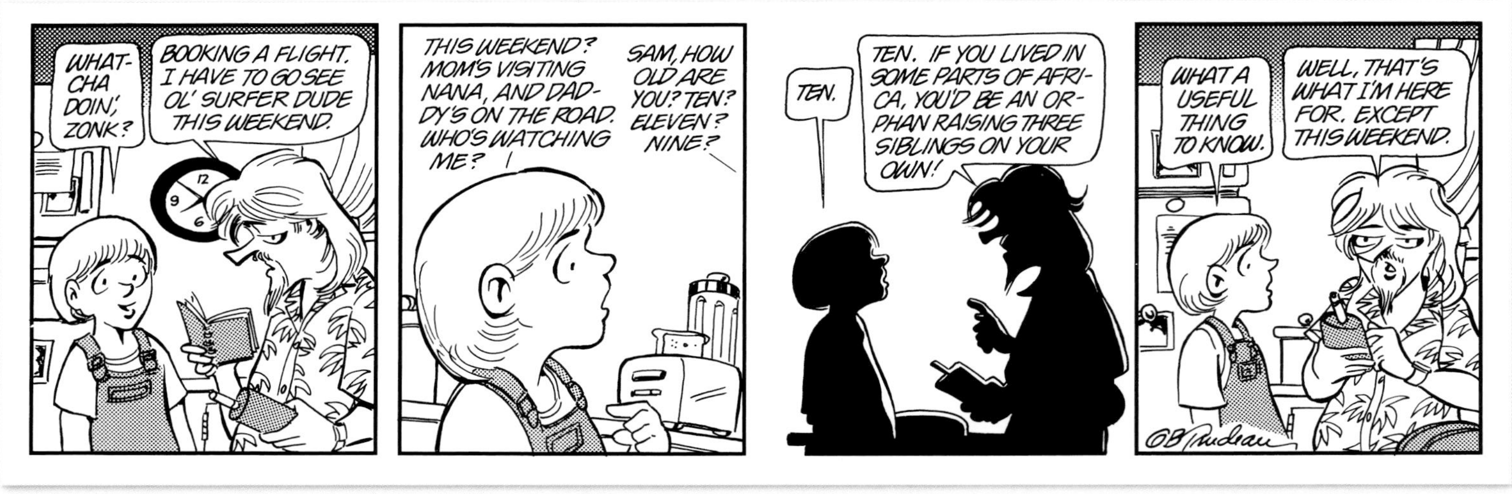
WHATCHA DOIN', ZONK?
BOOKING A FLIGHT. I HAVE TO GO SEE OL' SURFER DUDE THIS WEEKEND.
THIS WEEKEND? MOM'S VISITING NANA, AND DADDY'S ON THE ROAD. WHO'S WATCHING ME?
SAM, HOW OLD ARE YOU? TEN? ELEVEN? NINE?
TEN.
TEN. IF YOU LIVED IN SOME PARTS OF AFRICA, YOU'D BE AN ORPHAN RAISING THREE SIBLINGS ON YOUR OWN!
WHAT A USEFUL THING TO KNOW.
WELL, THAT'S WHAT I'M HERE FOR. EXCEPT THIS WEEKEND.

9/12/02

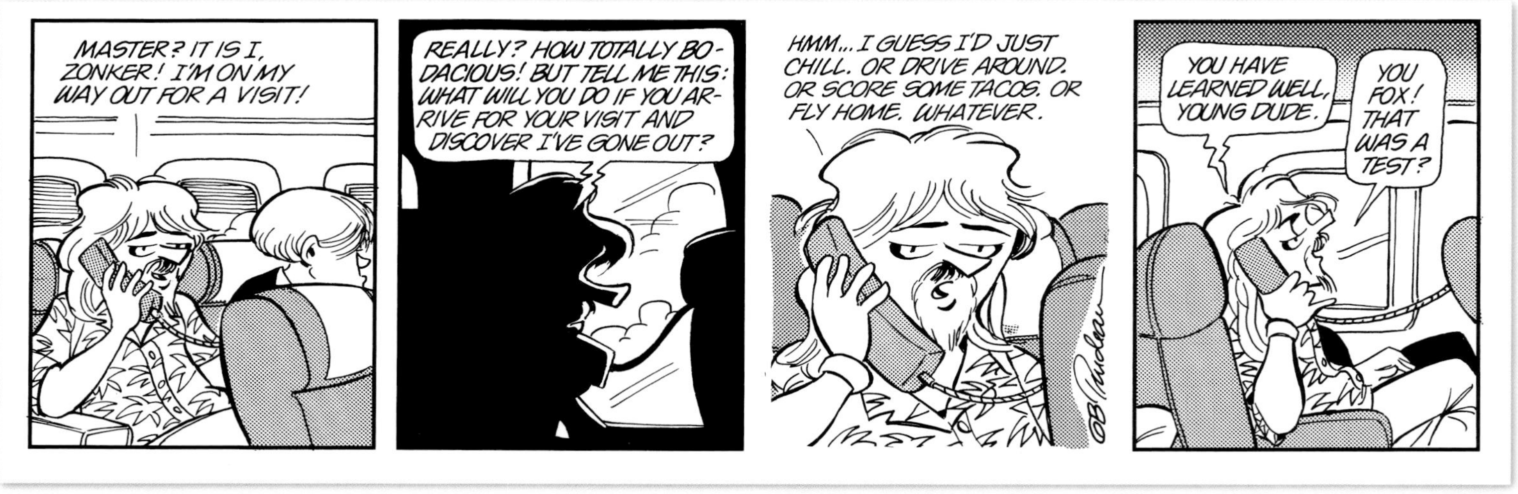
MASTER? IT IS I, ZONKER! I'M ON MY WAY OUT FOR A VISIT!
REALLY? HOW TOTALLY BODACIOUS! BUT TELL ME THIS: WHAT WILL YOU DO IF YOU ARRIVE FOR YOUR VISIT AND DISCOVER I'VE GONE OUT?
HMM... I GUESS I'D JUST CHILL. OR DRIVE AROUND. OR SCORE SOME TACOS. OR FLY HOME. WHATEVER.
YOU HAVE LEARNED WELL, YOUNG DUDE.
YOU FOX! THAT WAS A TEST?

9/14/02

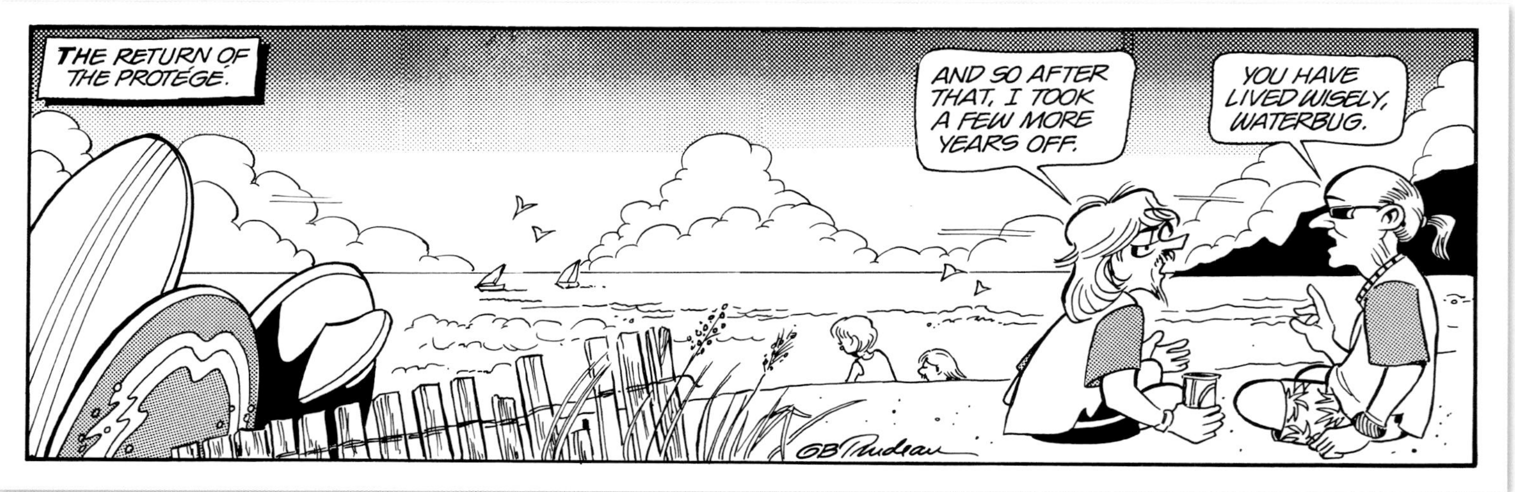
THE RETURN OF THE PROTÉGÉ.
AND SO AFTER THAT, I TOOK A FEW MORE YEARS OFF.
YOU HAVE LIVED WISELY, WATERBUG.

9/16/02

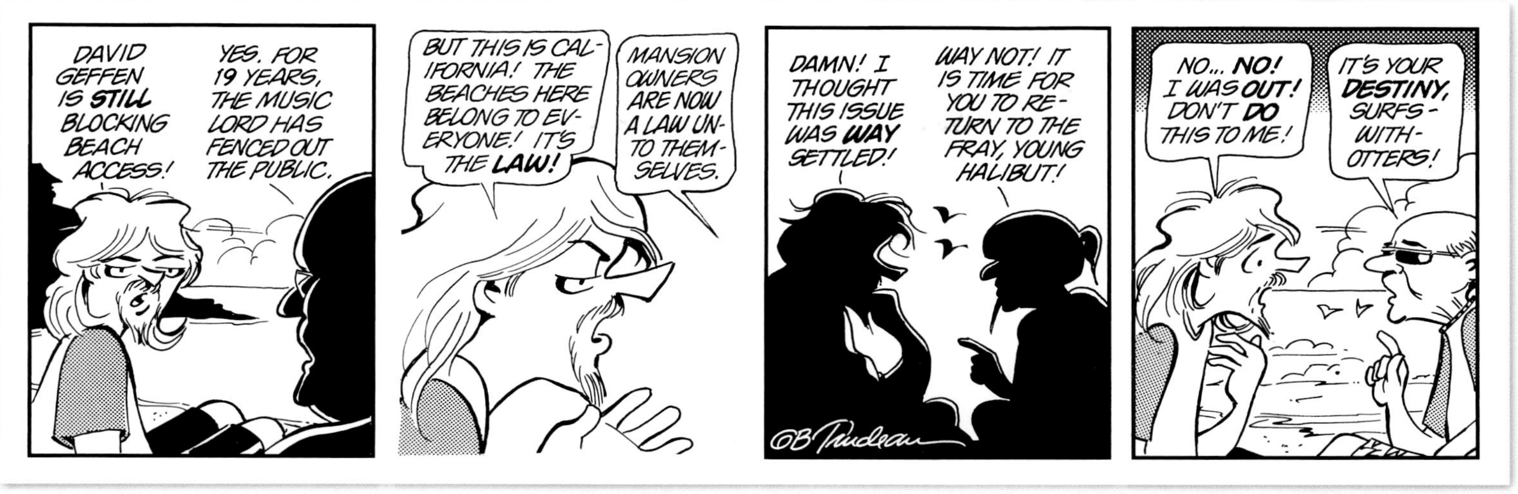

DAVID GEFFEN IS **STILL** BLOCKING BEACH ACCESS!
YES. FOR 19 YEARS, THE MUSIC LORD HAS FENCED OUT THE PUBLIC.
BUT THIS IS CALIFORNIA! THE BEACHES HERE BELONG TO EVERYONE! IT'S THE **LAW!**
MANSION OWNERS ARE NOW A LAW UNTO THEMSELVES.
DAMN! I THOUGHT THIS ISSUE WAS **WAY** SETTLED!
WAY NOT! IT IS TIME FOR YOU TO RETURN TO THE FRAY, YOUNG HALIBUT!
©B Trudeau
NO... **NO!** I WAS **OUT!** DON'T **DO** THIS TO ME!
IT'S YOUR **DESTINY,** SURFS-WITH-OTTERS!

9/18/02

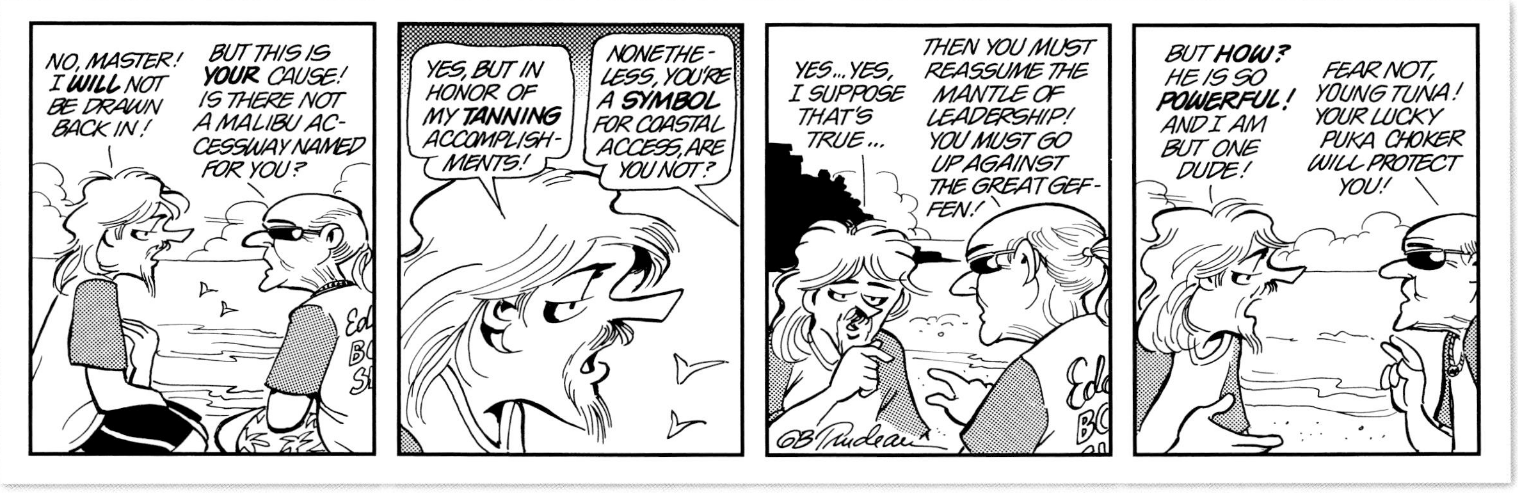

NO, MASTER! I **WILL** NOT BE DRAWN BACK IN!
BUT THIS IS **YOUR** CAUSE! IS THERE NOT A MALIBU ACCESSWAY NAMED FOR YOU?
YES, BUT IN HONOR OF MY **TANNING** ACCOMPLISHMENTS!
NONETHELESS, YOU'RE A **SYMBOL** FOR COASTAL ACCESS, ARE YOU NOT?
YES... YES, I SUPPOSE THAT'S TRUE...
THEN YOU MUST REASSUME THE MANTLE OF LEADERSHIP! YOU MUST GO UP AGAINST THE GREAT GEFFEN!
©B Trudeau
BUT **HOW?** HE IS SO **POWERFUL!** AND I AM BUT ONE DUDE!
FEAR NOT, YOUNG TUNA! YOUR LUCKY PUKA CHOKER WILL PROTECT YOU!

9/19/02

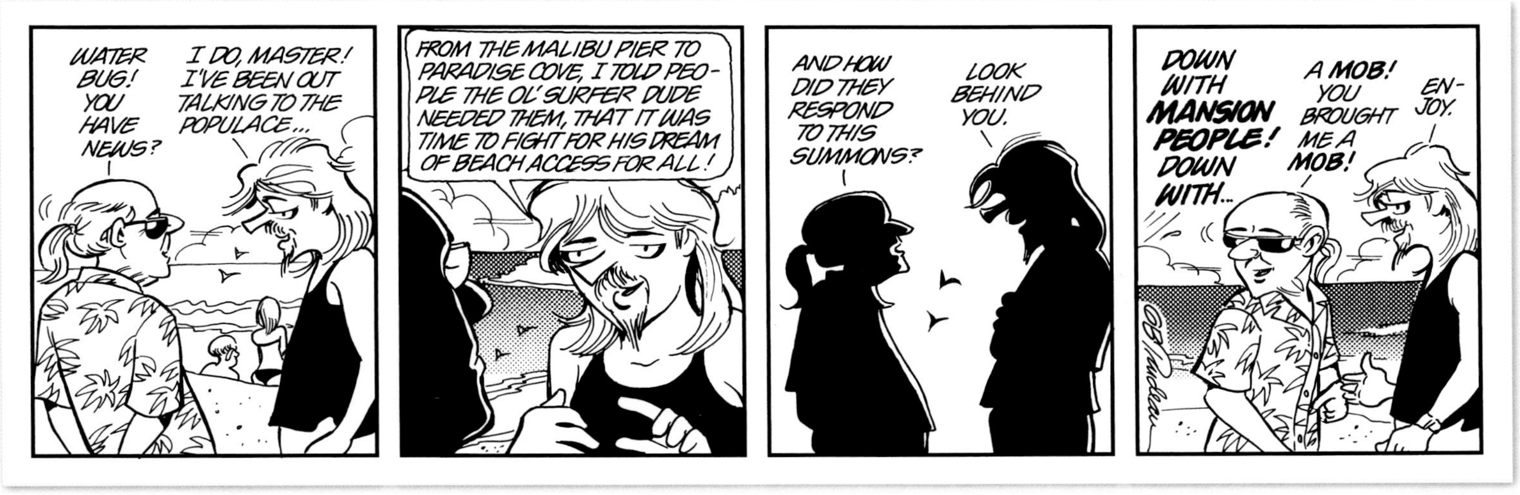

WATER BUG! YOU HAVE NEWS?
I DO, MASTER! I'VE BEEN OUT TALKING TO THE POPULACE...
FROM THE MALIBU PIER TO PARADISE COVE, I TOLD PEOPLE THE OL' SURFER DUDE NEEDED THEM, THAT IT WAS TIME TO FIGHT FOR HIS DREAM OF BEACH ACCESS FOR ALL!
AND HOW DID THEY RESPOND TO THIS SUMMONS?
LOOK BEHIND YOU.
DOWN WITH MANSION PEOPLE! DOWN WITH...
A **MOB!** YOU BROUGHT ME A **MOB!**
ENJOY.
©B Trudeau

9/23/02

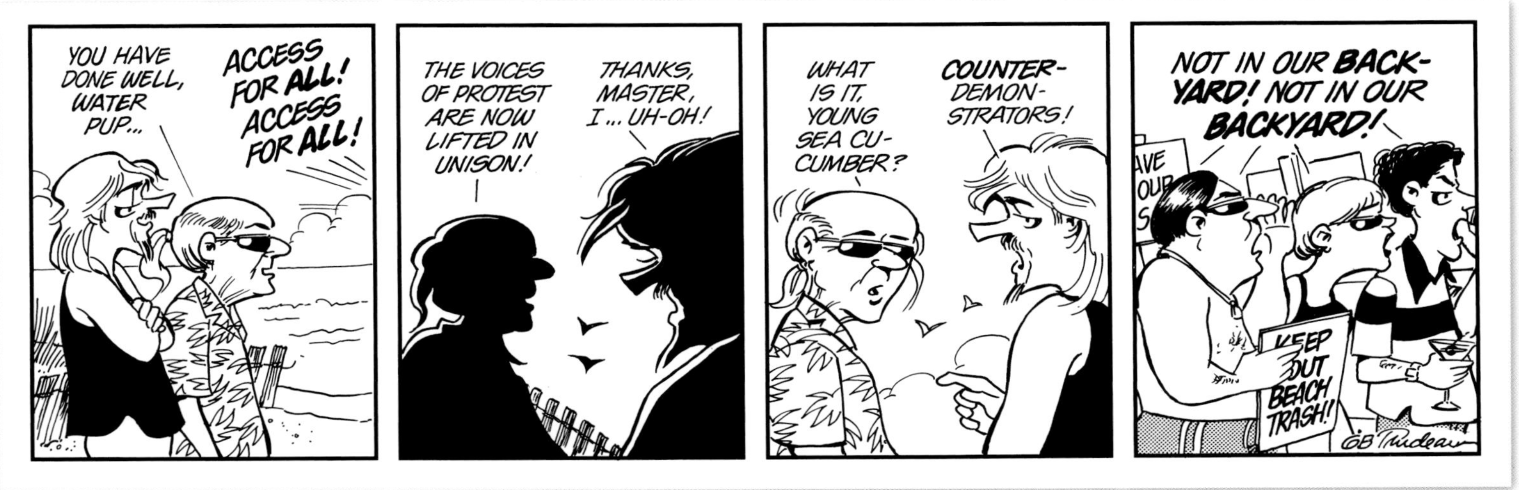

YOU HAVE DONE WELL, WATER PUP...
ACCESS FOR ALL! ACCESS FOR ALL!
THE VOICES OF PROTEST ARE NOW LIFTED IN UNISON!
THANKS, MASTER, I... UH-OH!
WHAT IS IT, YOUNG SEA CUCUMBER?
COUNTER-DEMONSTRATORS!
NOT IN OUR BACKYARD! NOT IN OUR BACKYARD!
KEEP OUT BEACH TRASH!
©B Trudeau

9/25/02

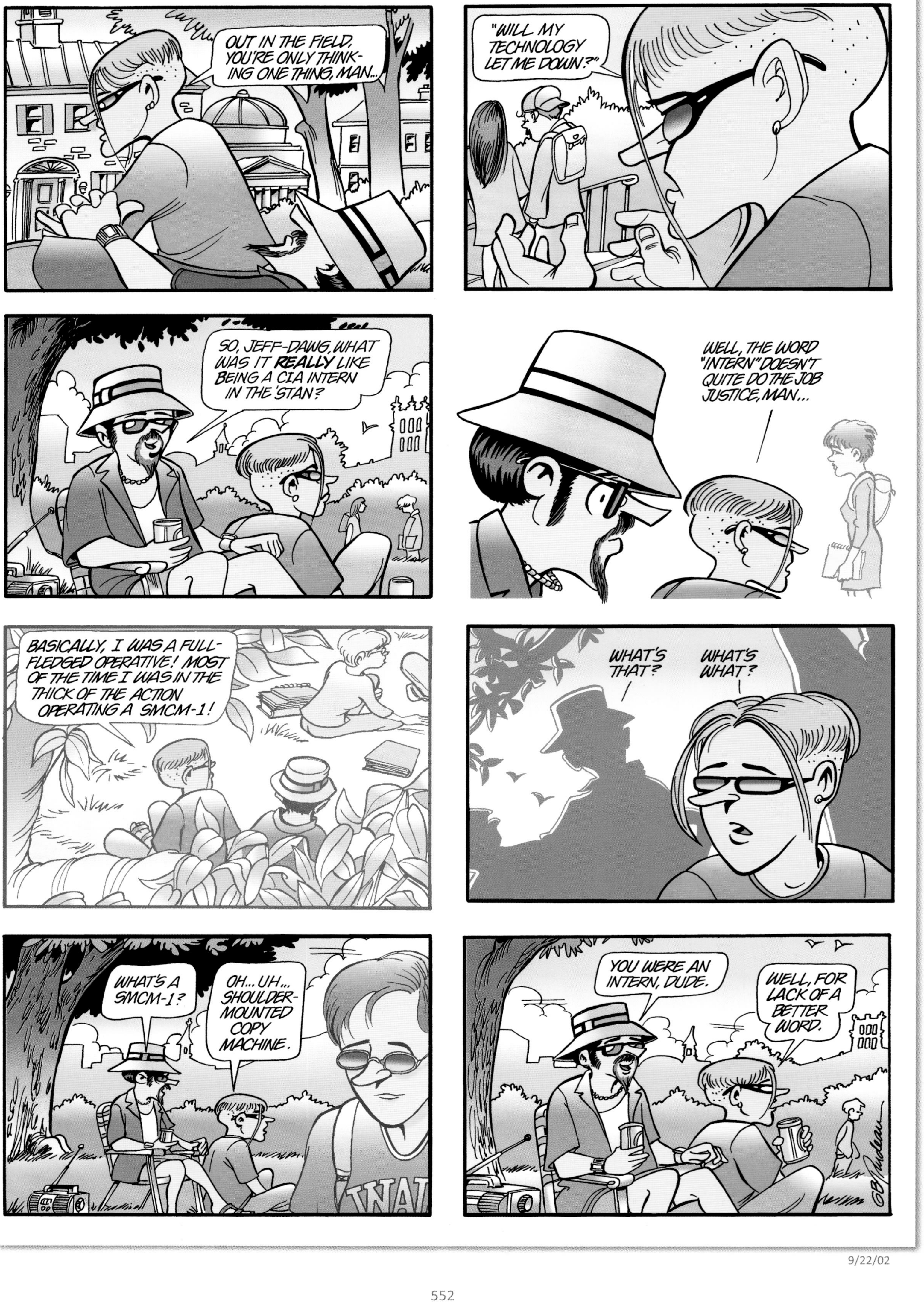
OUT IN THE FIELD, YOU'RE ONLY THINKING ONE THING, MAN...
"WILL MY TECHNOLOGY LET ME DOWN?"
SO, JEFF-DAWG, WHAT WAS IT REALLY LIKE BEING A CIA INTERN IN THE 'STAN?
WELL, THE WORD "INTERN" DOESN'T QUITE DO THE JOB JUSTICE, MAN...
BASICALLY, I WAS A FULL-FLEDGED OPERATIVE! MOST OF THE TIME I WAS IN THE THICK OF THE ACTION OPERATING A SMCM-1!
WHAT'S THAT?
WHAT'S WHAT?
WHAT'S A SMCM-1?
OH... UH... SHOULDER-MOUNTED COPY MACHINE.
YOU WERE AN INTERN, DUDE.
WELL, FOR LACK OF A BETTER WORD.

9/22/02

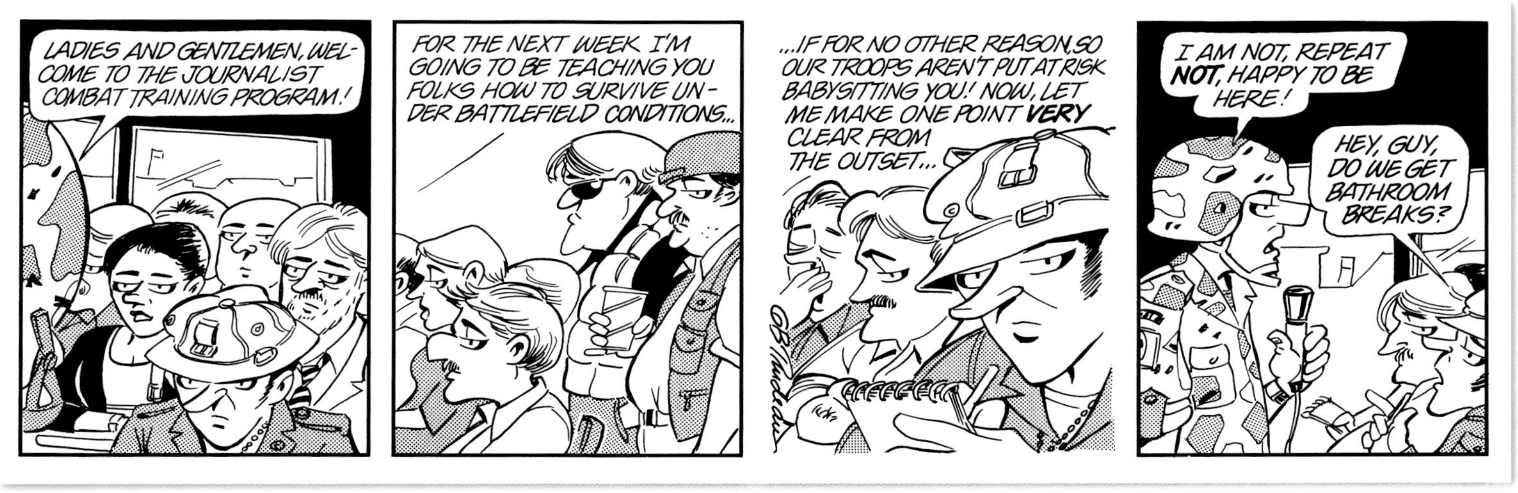
LADIES AND GENTLEMEN, WELCOME TO THE JOURNALIST COMBAT TRAINING PROGRAM!
FOR THE NEXT WEEK I'M GOING TO BE TEACHING YOU FOLKS HOW TO SURVIVE UNDER BATTLEFIELD CONDITIONS...
...IF FOR NO OTHER REASON, SO OUR TROOPS AREN'T PUT AT RISK BABYSITTING YOU! NOW, LET ME MAKE ONE POINT VERY CLEAR FROM THE OUTSET...
I AM NOT, REPEAT NOT, HAPPY TO BE HERE!
HEY, GUY, DO WE GET BATHROOM BREAKS?

11/26/02

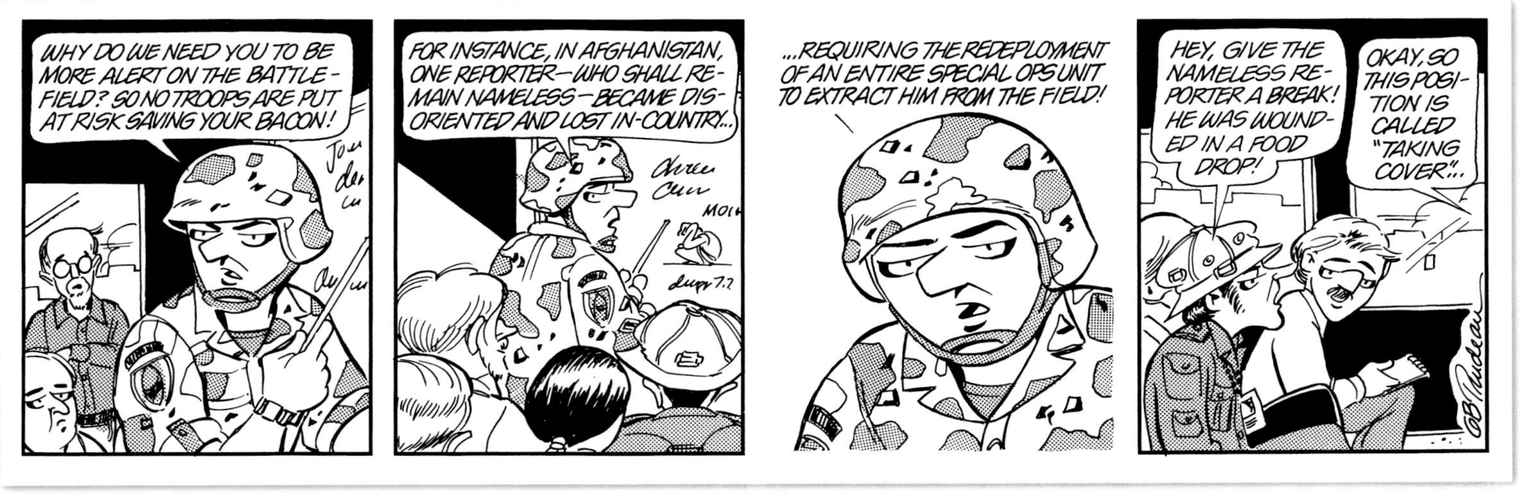
WHY DO WE NEED YOU TO BE MORE ALERT ON THE BATTLEFIELD? SO NO TROOPS ARE PUT AT RISK SAVING YOUR BACON!
FOR INSTANCE, IN AFGHANISTAN, ONE REPORTER—WHO SHALL REMAIN NAMELESS—BECAME DISORIENTED AND LOST IN-COUNTRY...
...REQUIRING THE REDEPLOYMENT OF AN ENTIRE SPECIAL OPS UNIT TO EXTRACT HIM FROM THE FIELD!
HEY, GIVE THE NAMELESS REPORTER A BREAK! HE WAS WOUNDED IN A FOOD DROP!
OKAY, SO THIS POSITION IS CALLED "TAKING COVER"...

11/28/02

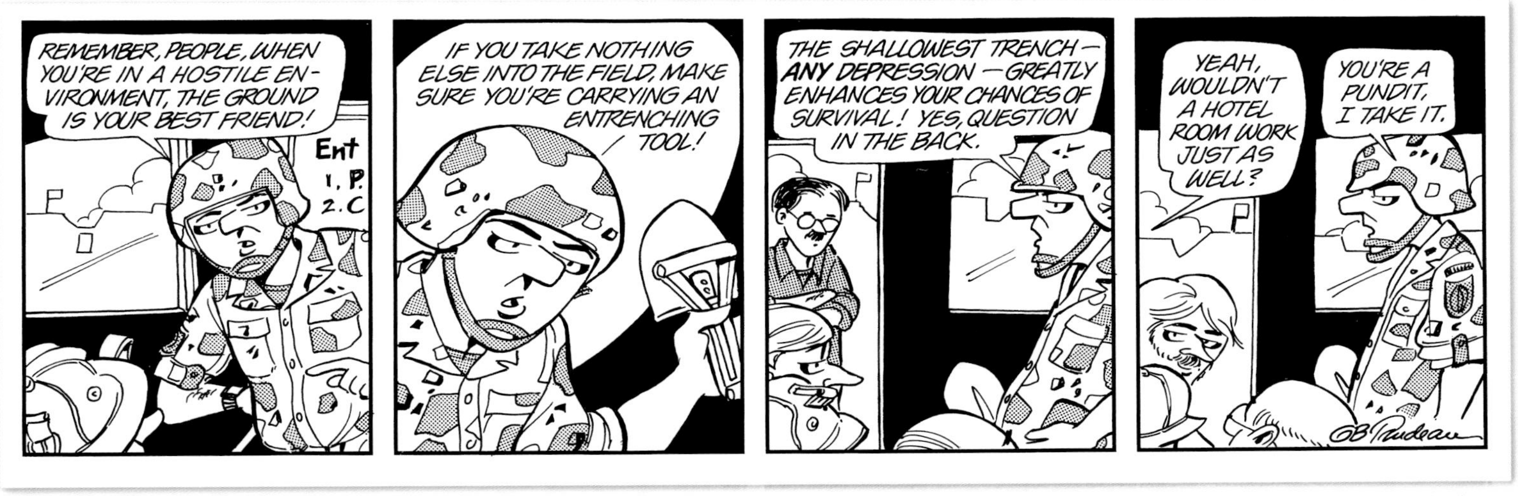
REMEMBER, PEOPLE, WHEN YOU'RE IN A HOSTILE ENVIRONMENT, THE GROUND IS YOUR BEST FRIEND!
Ent
IF YOU TAKE NOTHING ELSE INTO THE FIELD, MAKE SURE YOU'RE CARRYING AN ENTRENCHING TOOL!
THE SHALLOWEST TRENCH—ANY DEPRESSION—GREATLY ENHANCES YOUR CHANCES OF SURVIVAL! YES, QUESTION IN THE BACK.
YEAH, WOULDN'T A HOTEL ROOM WORK JUST AS WELL?
YOU'RE A PUNDIT, I TAKE IT.

11/29/02

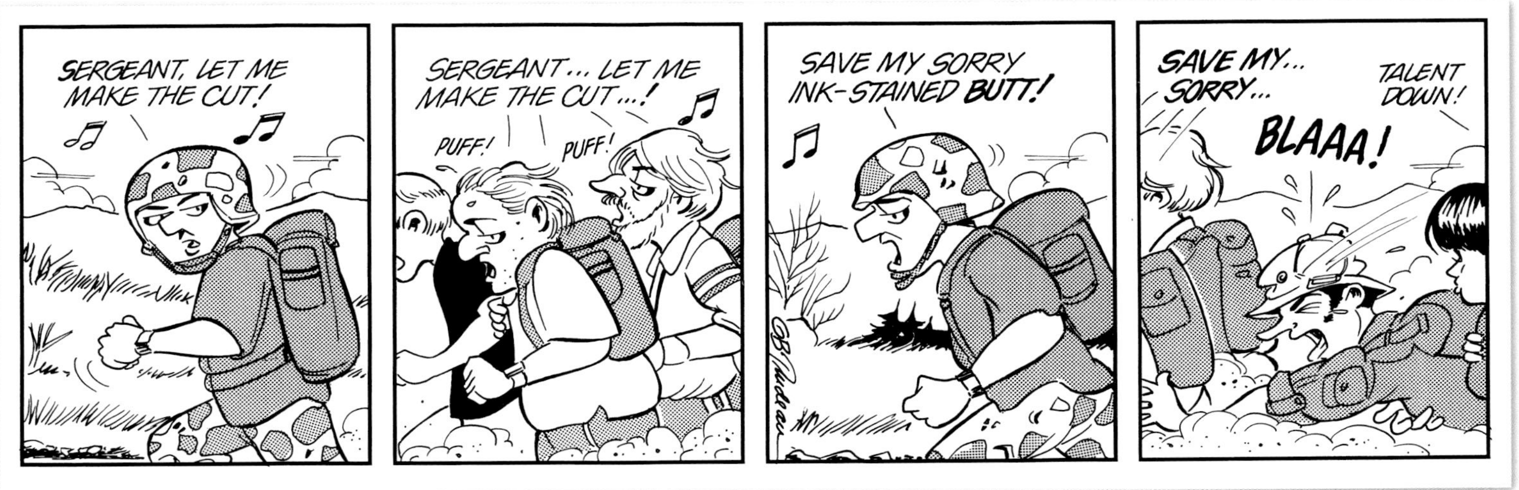
SERGEANT, LET ME MAKE THE CUT!
SERGEANT... LET ME MAKE THE CUT...!
PUFF!
PUFF!
SAVE MY SORRY INK-STAINED BUTT!
SAVE MY... SORRY...
TALENT DOWN!
BLAAA!

11/30/02

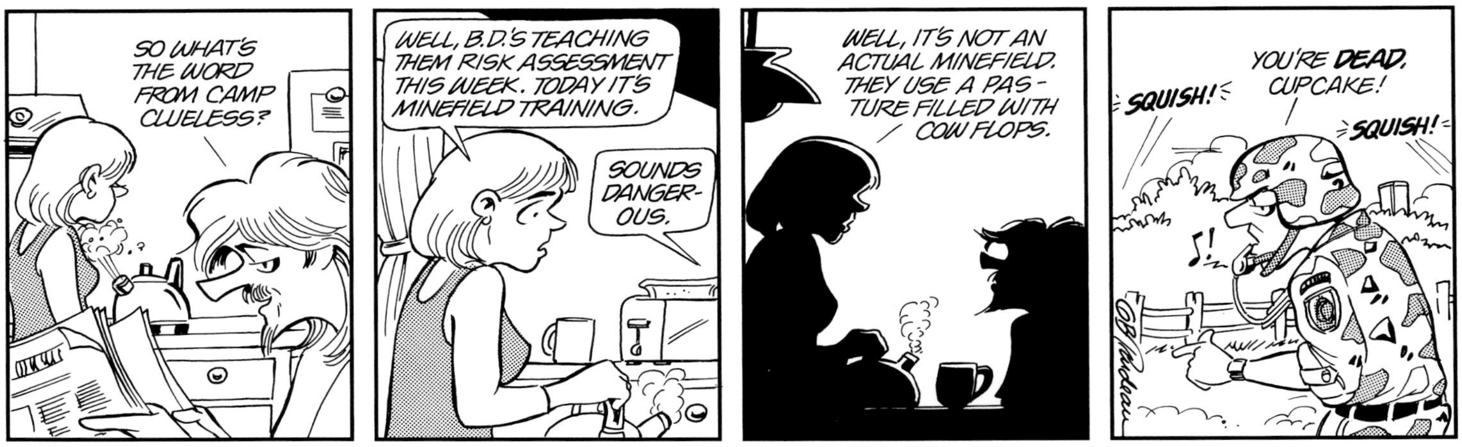
SO WHAT'S THE WORD FROM CAMP CLUELESS?
WELL, B.D.'S TEACHING THEM RISK ASSESSMENT THIS WEEK. TODAY IT'S MINEFIELD TRAINING.
SOUNDS DANGEROUS.
WELL, IT'S NOT AN ACTUAL MINEFIELD. THEY USE A PASTURE FILLED WITH COW FLOPS.
SQUISH!
YOU'RE **DEAD,** CUPCAKE!
SQUISH!

12/2/02

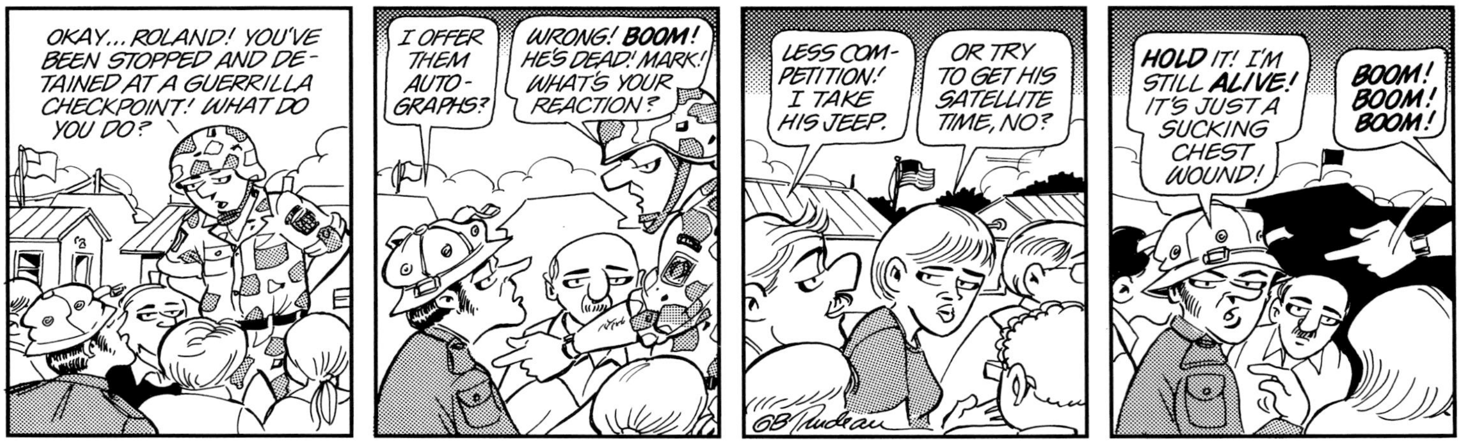
OKAY... ROLAND! YOU'VE BEEN STOPPED AND DETAINED AT A GUERRILLA CHECKPOINT! WHAT DO YOU DO?
I OFFER THEM AUTOGRAPHS?
WRONG! **BOOM!** HE'S DEAD! MARK! WHAT'S YOUR REACTION?
LESS COMPETITION! I TAKE HIS JEEP.
OR TRY TO GET HIS SATELLITE TIME, NO?
HOLD IT! I'M STILL **ALIVE!** IT'S JUST A SUCKING CHEST WOUND!
BOOM! BOOM! BOOM!

12/3/02

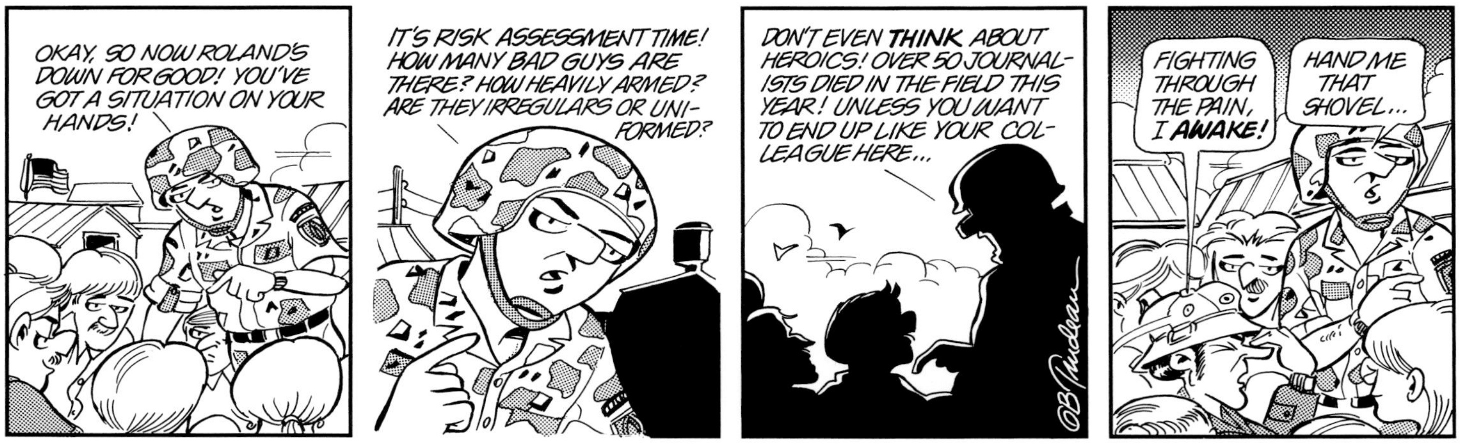
OKAY, SO NOW ROLAND'S DOWN FOR GOOD! YOU'VE GOT A SITUATION ON YOUR HANDS!
IT'S RISK ASSESSMENT TIME! HOW MANY BAD GUYS ARE THERE? HOW HEAVILY ARMED? ARE THEY IRREGULARS OR UNIFORMED?
DON'T EVEN **THINK** ABOUT HEROICS! OVER 50 JOURNALISTS DIED IN THE FIELD THIS YEAR! UNLESS YOU WANT TO END UP LIKE YOUR COLLEAGUE HERE...
FIGHTING THROUGH THE PAIN, I **AWAKE!**
HAND ME THAT SHOVEL...

12/4/02

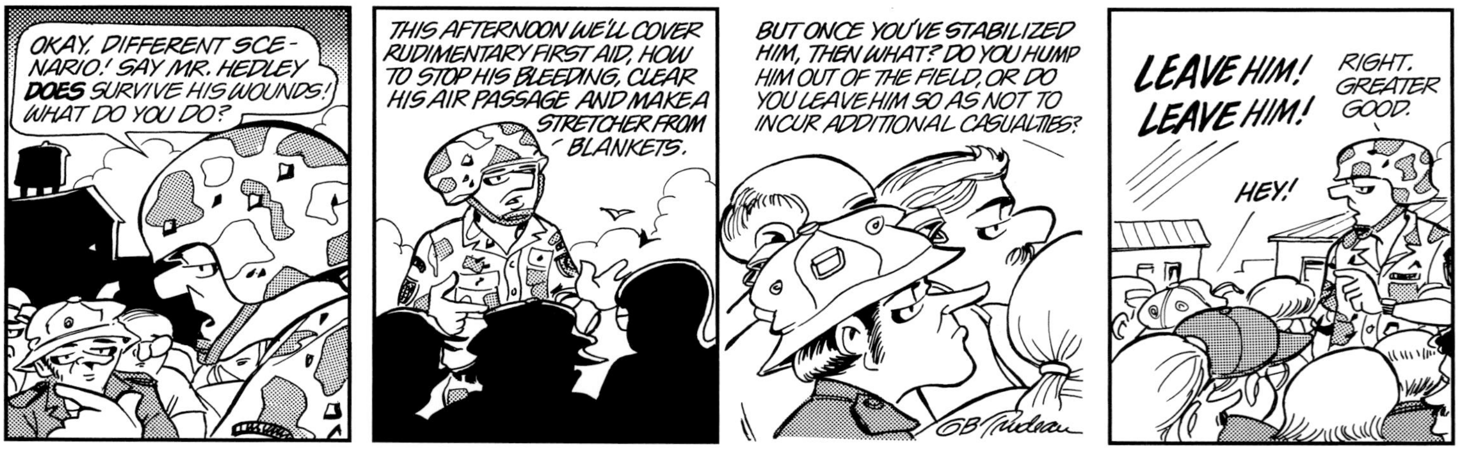
OKAY, DIFFERENT SCENARIO! SAY MR. HEDLEY **DOES** SURVIVE HIS WOUNDS! WHAT DO YOU DO?
THIS AFTERNOON WE'LL COVER RUDIMENTARY FIRST AID, HOW TO STOP HIS BLEEDING, CLEAR HIS AIR PASSAGE AND MAKE A STRETCHER FROM BLANKETS.
BUT ONCE YOU'VE STABILIZED HIM, THEN WHAT? DO YOU HUMP HIM OUT OF THE FIELD, OR DO YOU LEAVE HIM SO AS NOT TO INCUR ADDITIONAL CASUALTIES?
LEAVE HIM! LEAVE HIM!
RIGHT. GREATER GOOD.
HEY!

12/5/02

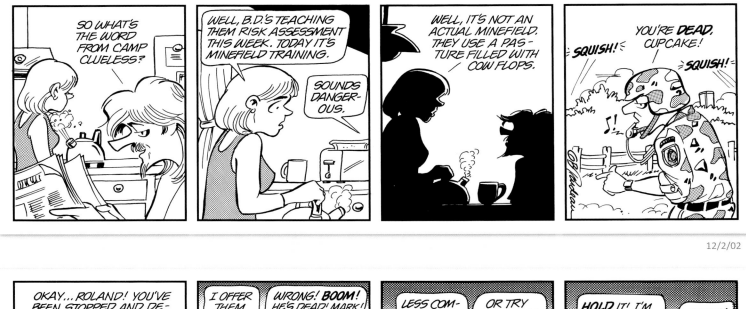

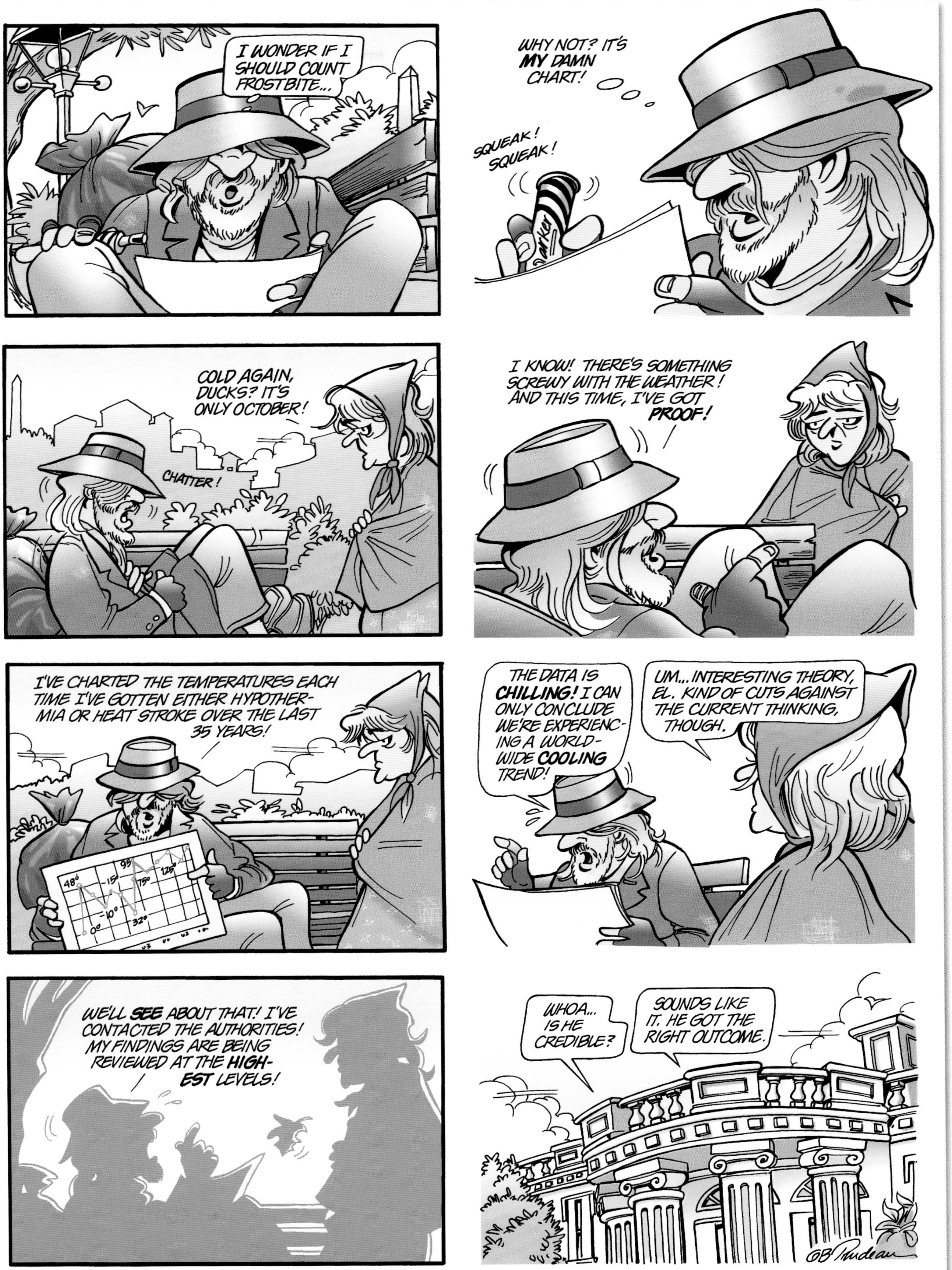
I WONDER IF I SHOULD COUNT FROSTBITE...
WHY NOT? IT'S MY DAMN CHART!
SQUEAK! SQUEAK!
COLD AGAIN, DUCKS? IT'S ONLY OCTOBER!
CHATTER!
I KNOW! THERE'S SOMETHING SCREWY WITH THE WEATHER! AND THIS TIME, I'VE GOT PROOF!
I'VE CHARTED THE TEMPERATURES EACH TIME I'VE GOTTEN EITHER HYPOTHERMIA OR HEAT STROKE OVER THE LAST 35 YEARS!
48°
-15°
95°
75°
125°
-10°
32°
0°
THE DATA IS CHILLING! I CAN ONLY CONCLUDE WE'RE EXPERIENCING A WORLD-WIDE COOLING TREND!
UM... INTERESTING THEORY, EL. KIND OF CUTS AGAINST THE CURRENT THINKING, THOUGH.
WE'LL SEE ABOUT THAT! I'VE CONTACTED THE AUTHORITIES! MY FINDINGS ARE BEING REVIEWED AT THE HIGHEST LEVELS!
WHOA... IS HE CREDIBLE?
SOUNDS LIKE IT. HE GOT THE RIGHT OUTCOME.
GB Trudeau

10/20/02

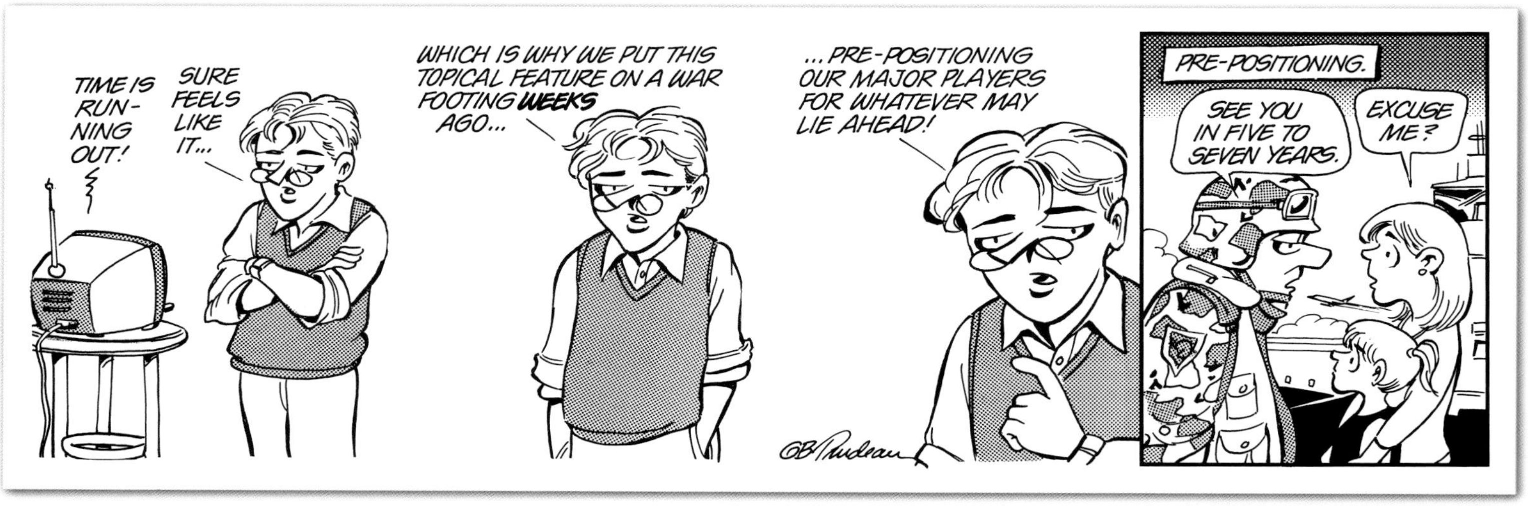
TIME IS RUN-NING OUT!
SURE FEELS LIKE IT...
WHICH IS WHY WE PUT THIS TOPICAL FEATURE ON A WAR FOOTING WEEKS AGO...
...PRE-POSITIONING OUR MAJOR PLAYERS FOR WHATEVER MAY LIE AHEAD!
PRE-POSITIONING.
SEE YOU IN FIVE TO SEVEN YEARS.
EXCUSE ME?

2/10/03

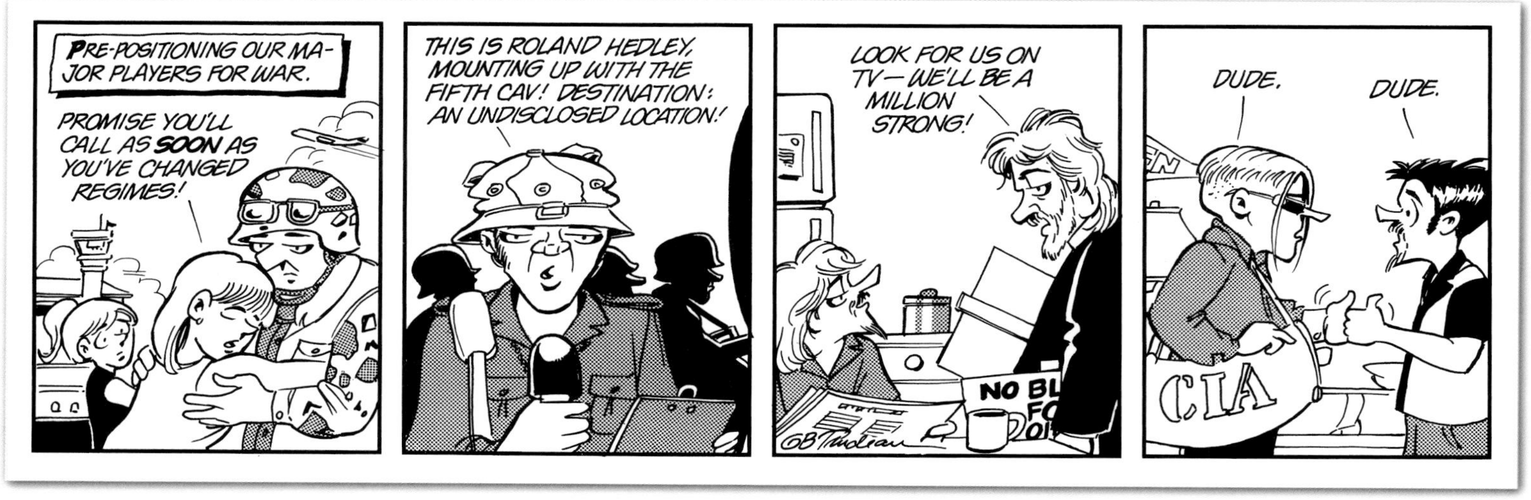
PRE-POSITIONING OUR MA-JOR PLAYERS FOR WAR.
PROMISE YOU'LL CALL AS SOON AS YOU'VE CHANGED REGIMES!
THIS IS ROLAND HEDLEY, MOUNTING UP WITH THE FIFTH CAV! DESTINATION: AN UNDISCLOSED LOCATION!
LOOK FOR US ON TV—WE'LL BE A MILLION STRONG!
DUDE.
DUDE.
CIA

2/11/03

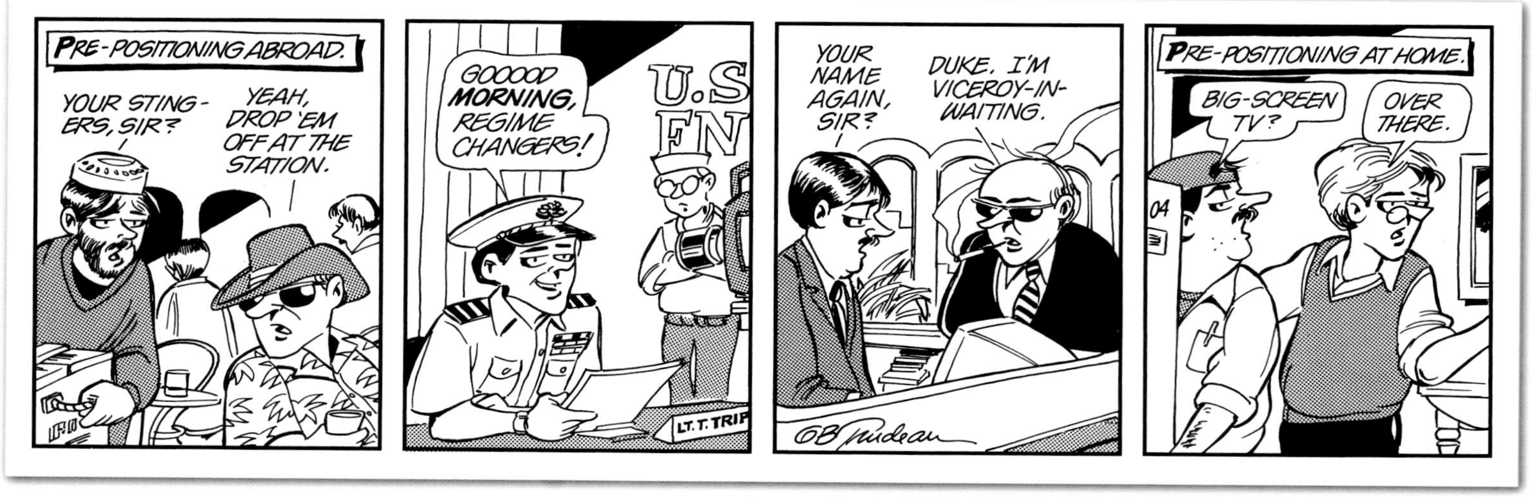
PRE-POSITIONING ABROAD.
YOUR STING-ERS, SIR?
YEAH, DROP 'EM OFF AT THE STATION.
GOOOOD MORNING, REGIME CHANGERS!
LT. T. TRIP
YOUR NAME AGAIN, SIR?
DUKE. I'M VICEROY-IN-WAITING.
PRE-POSITIONING AT HOME.
BIG-SCREEN TV?
OVER THERE.

2/12/03

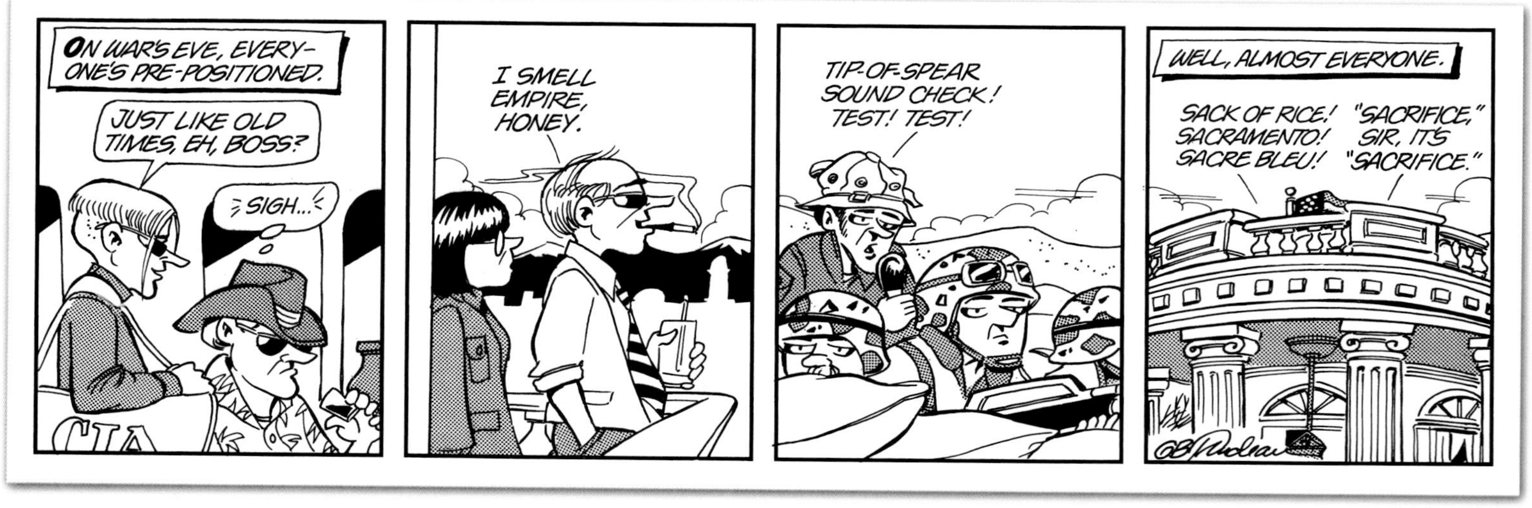
ON WAR'S EVE, EVERY-ONE'S PRE-POSITIONED.
JUST LIKE OLD TIMES, EH, BOSS?
SIGH...
CIA
I SMELL EMPIRE, HONEY.
TIP-OF-SPEAR SOUND CHECK! TEST! TEST!
WELL, ALMOST EVERYONE.
SACK OF RICE! SACRAMENTO! SACRE BLEU!
"SACRIFICE," SIR, IT'S "SACRIFICE."

2/15/03

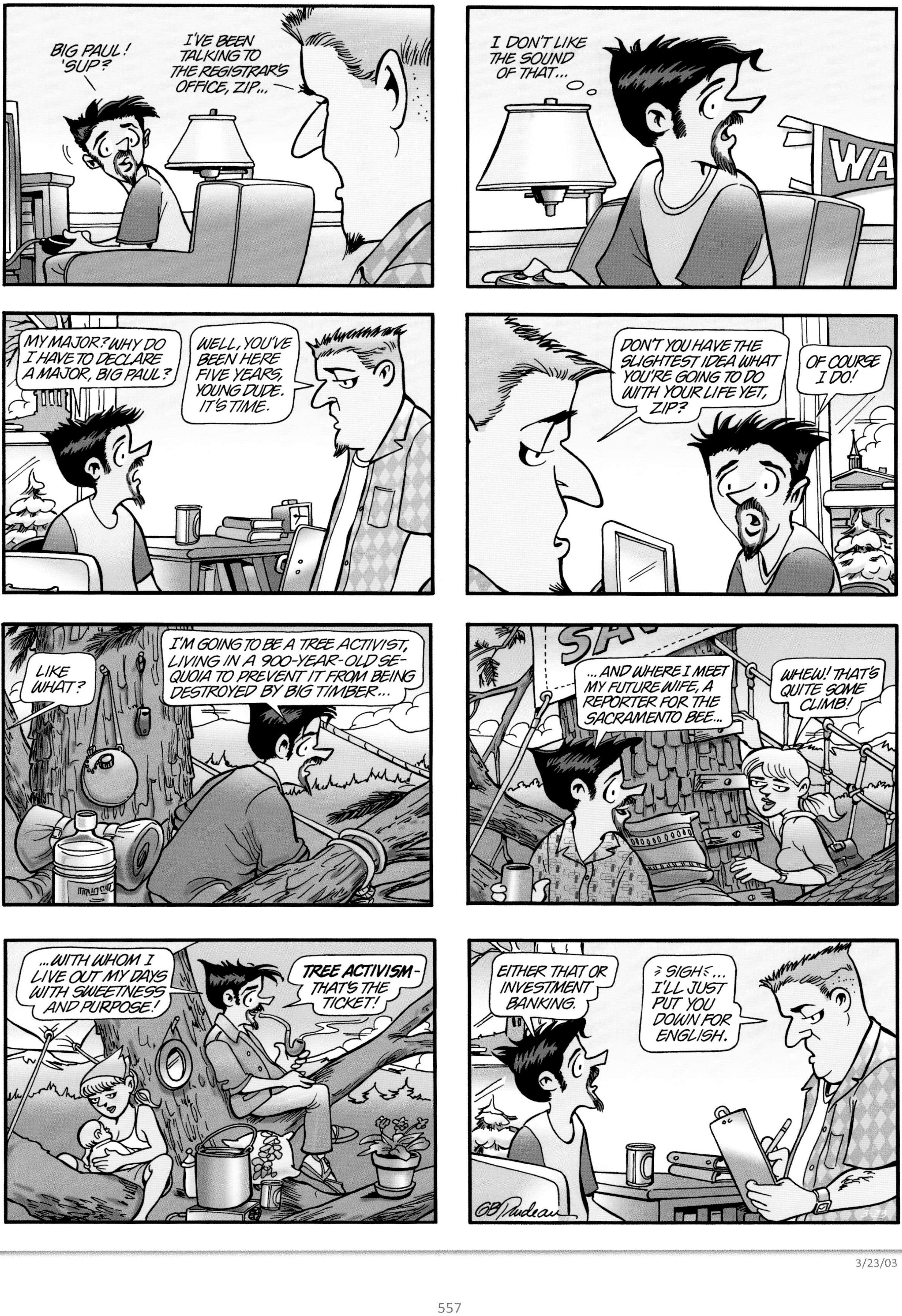
BIG PAUL! 'SUP?
I'VE BEEN TALKING TO THE REGISTRAR'S OFFICE, ZIP...
I DON'T LIKE THE SOUND OF THAT...
MY MAJOR? WHY DO I HAVE TO DECLARE A MAJOR, BIG PAUL?
WELL, YOU'VE BEEN HERE FIVE YEARS, YOUNG DUDE. IT'S TIME.
DON'T YOU HAVE THE SLIGHTEST IDEA WHAT YOU'RE GOING TO DO WITH YOUR LIFE YET, ZIP?
OF COURSE I DO!
LIKE WHAT?
I'M GOING TO BE A TREE ACTIVIST, LIVING IN A 900-YEAR-OLD SEQUOIA TO PREVENT IT FROM BEING DESTROYED BY BIG TIMBER...
...AND WHERE I MEET MY FUTURE WIFE, A REPORTER FOR THE SACRAMENTO BEE...
WHEW! THAT'S QUITE SOME CLIMB!
...WITH WHOM I LIVE OUT MY DAYS WITH SWEETNESS AND PURPOSE!
TREE ACTIVISM - THAT'S THE TICKET!
EITHER THAT OR INVESTMENT BANKING.
SIGH... I'LL JUST PUT YOU DOWN FOR ENGLISH.
GB Trudeau

3/23/03

J.J. CAUCUS

In the final two decades of the 20th century, something wholly unexpected happened to the culture: It ran out of ideas, or at least the kind of big, widely influential ideas that coalesce into movements. The previous era's creative giants—artists such as Warhol and Mailer and Lennon-McCartney—had no obvious successors. After the endgames of minimalism and subjective nonfiction and spoken song (a.k.a. rap), the arts seemed exhausted. We'd heard and seen it all.

With no establishment to scandalize, no conventions to overturn, and no icons to smash, artists looked inward and backward for inspiration—appropriating, recycling, sampling, all of it made infinitely easier by cheap digital tools that lowered the bar for entry. Talent still abounded, but with Photoshop, anyone could airbrush; Final Cut created instant auteurs; pitchy vocalists were Auto-Tuned into stars; blogging allowed 100 million of us to become published writers. In such a broadly democratic and competitive environment, the indispensable skill was no longer craft but marketing.

"The viewer won't know it's our wedding china. To him, it's the shards of the American dream."

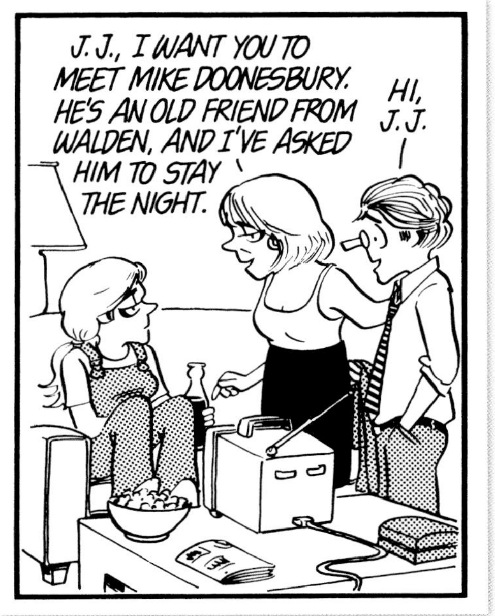
J.J., I WANT YOU TO MEET MIKE DOONESBURY. HE'S AN OLD FRIEND FROM WALDEN, AND I'VE ASKED HIM TO STAY THE NIGHT.
HI, J.J.

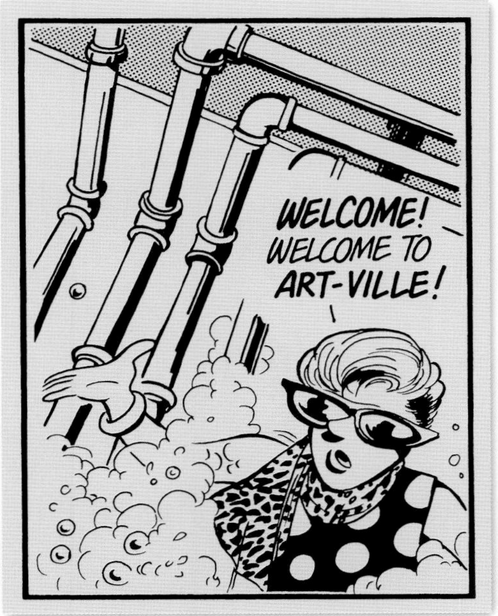
WELCOME! WELCOME TO ART-VILLE!

Enter J.J., princess of self-promotion. From the beginning, she was an outrider, a harbinger of the cut-and-paste career. Dragging Mike to the East Village just as speculators were scouring it for the Next Big Thing, J.J. lurched from crockery painting to urinal installations to performance art, always one step behind anyone caring. When she finally caught up with the Zeitgeist, it was in Seattle, where she fashioned trophy sculptures for cyberbarons out of discarded exercise machines—one fad building on the detritus of another. Her success fed her grandiosity, and before long she was spending whole evenings curating her entry on Wikipedia.

I never intended J.J. to be eaten alive by narcissism—it just happened. Mike certainly deserved better, but better seemed unlikely in the presence of such overweening ambition. Besides, I'd long been fascinated by improbable success, having survived my own. Plucked from a college newspaper at an early age, I had unexpectedly found myself in big-time cartooning without the benefit of a relevant skill set. It was harrowing, on-the-job training, with my learning curve in full public view. The only thing I had going for me was my youth, which allowed the syndicate to frame my amateurish drawing as authentic, as urgent scribblings from the front lines of generational change.

At least that was the rap. Unlike J.J., I waited anxiously for the jig to be up. Paul Simon's voice floated through my thoughts: "I know I'm fakin' it / I'm not really makin' it." It's a truism that at some point in their lives, most people are plagued by feelings of fraudulence or unworthiness. My gift to J.J. was their utter absence.

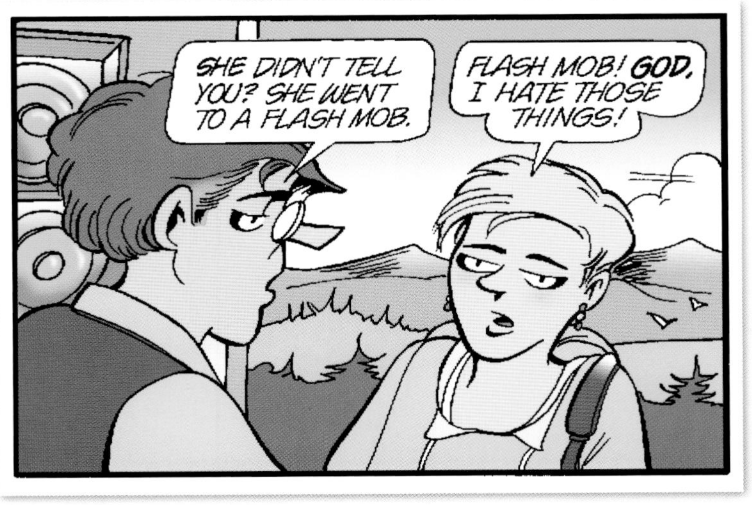
SHE DIDN'T TELL YOU? SHE WENT TO A FLASH MOB.
FLASH MOB! GOD, I HATE THOSE THINGS!

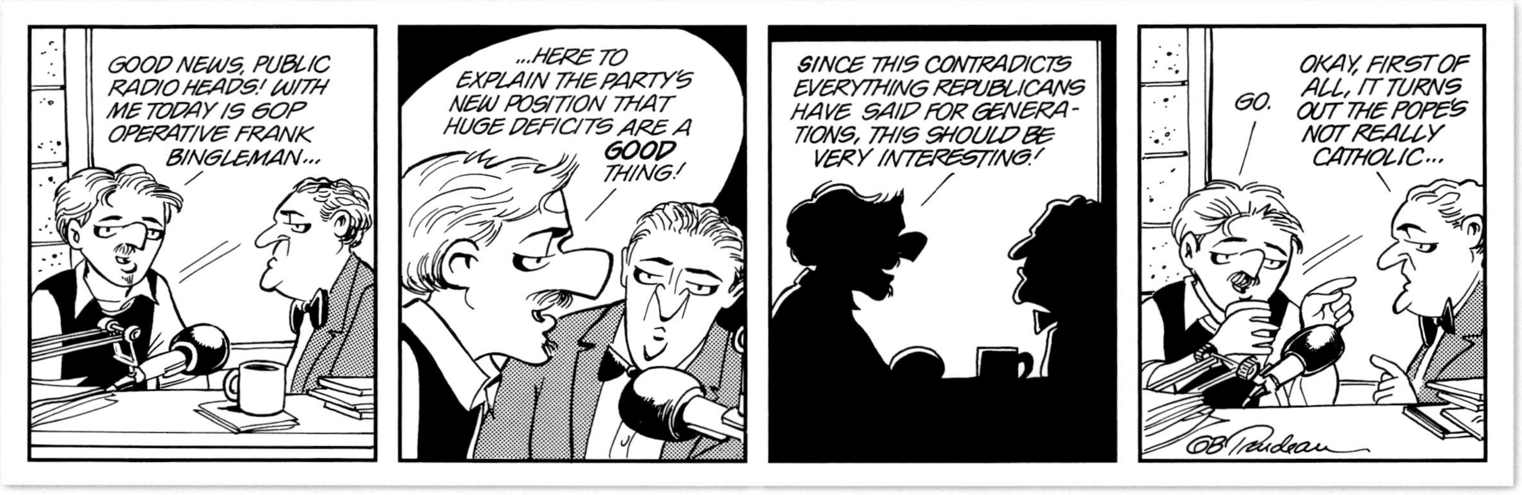
GOOD NEWS, PUBLIC RADIO HEADS! WITH ME TODAY IS GOP OPERATIVE FRANK BINGLEMAN...
...HERE TO EXPLAIN THE PARTY'S NEW POSITION THAT HUGE DEFICITS ARE A GOOD THING!
SINCE THIS CONTRADICTS EVERYTHING REPUBLICANS HAVE SAID FOR GENERATIONS, THIS SHOULD BE VERY INTERESTING!
GO.
OKAY, FIRST OF ALL, IT TURNS OUT THE POPE'S NOT REALLY CATHOLIC...
GBTrudeau

3/10/03

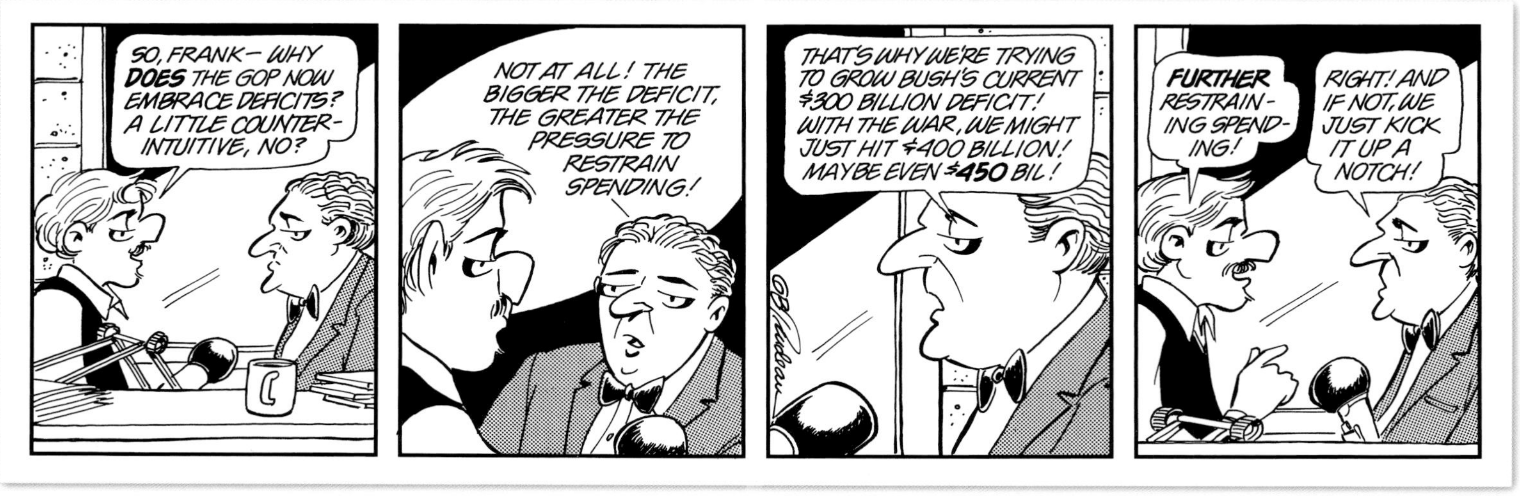
SO, FRANK– WHY DOES THE GOP NOW EMBRACE DEFICITS? A LITTLE COUNTER-INTUITIVE, NO?
NOT AT ALL! THE BIGGER THE DEFICIT, THE GREATER THE PRESSURE TO RESTRAIN SPENDING!
THAT'S WHY WE'RE TRYING TO GROW BUSH'S CURRENT $300 BILLION DEFICIT! WITH THE WAR, WE MIGHT JUST HIT $400 BILLION! MAYBE EVEN $450 BIL!
GBTrudeau
FURTHER RESTRAINING SPENDING!
RIGHT! AND IF NOT, WE JUST KICK IT UP A NOTCH!

3/11/03

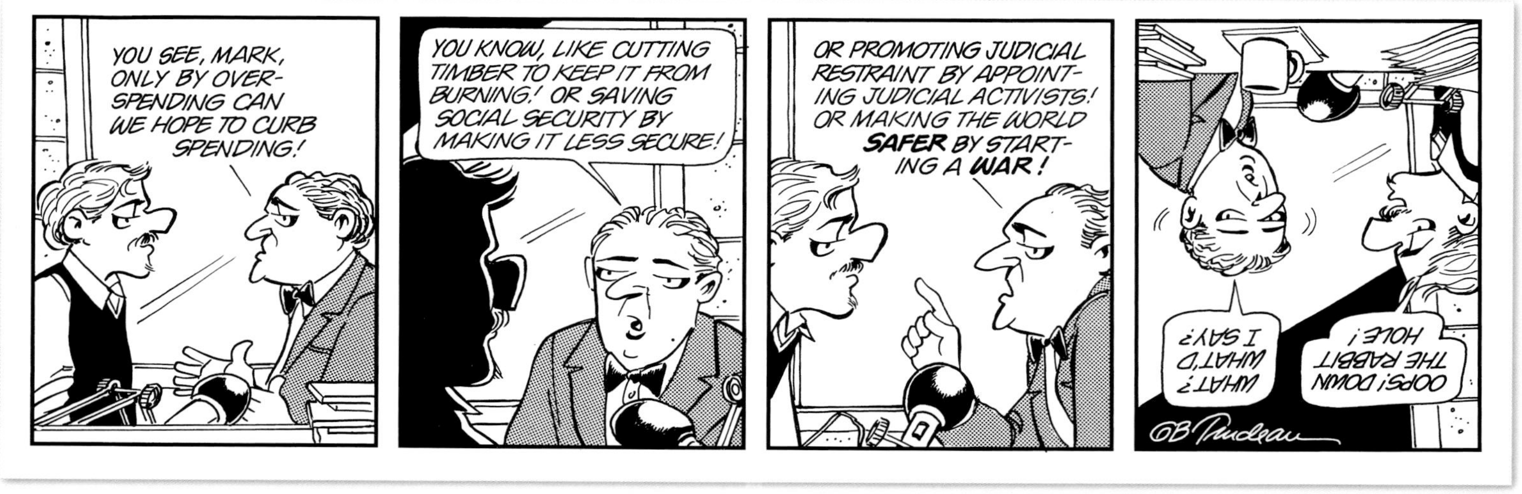
YOU SEE, MARK, ONLY BY OVER-SPENDING CAN WE HOPE TO CURB SPENDING!
YOU KNOW, LIKE CUTTING TIMBER TO KEEP IT FROM BURNING! OR SAVING SOCIAL SECURITY BY MAKING IT LESS SECURE!
OR PROMOTING JUDICIAL RESTRAINT BY APPOINTING JUDICIAL ACTIVISTS! OR MAKING THE WORLD SAFER BY STARTING A WAR!
OOPS! DOWN THE RABBIT HOLE!
WHAT? WHAT'D I SAY?
GBTrudeau

3/13/03

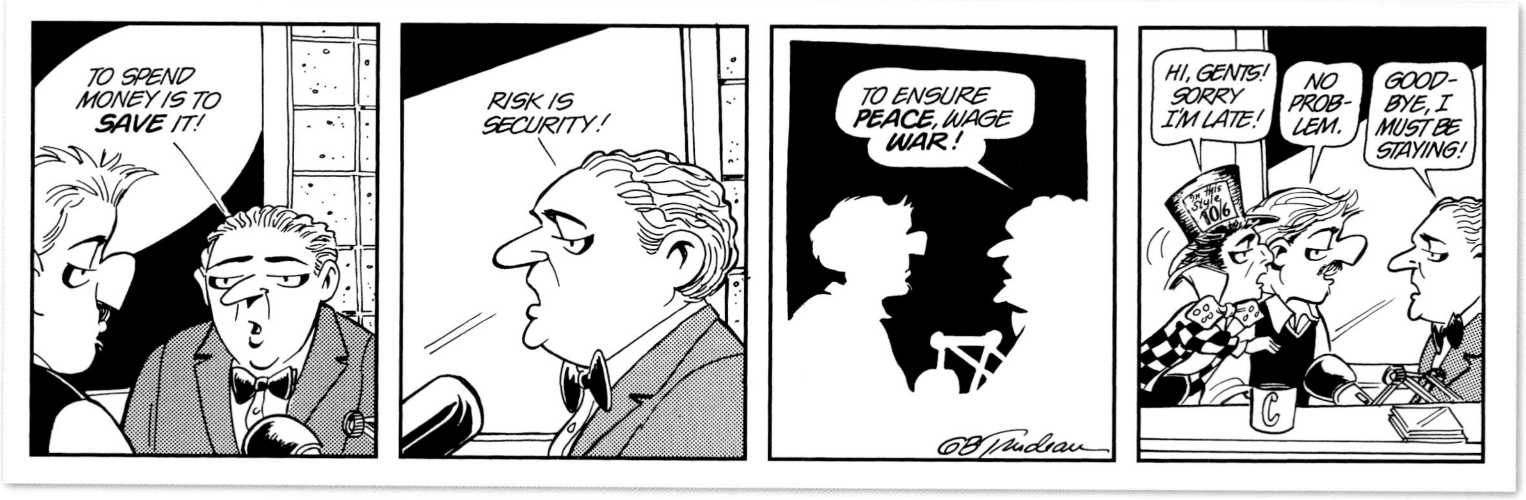
TO SPEND MONEY IS TO SAVE IT!
RISK IS SECURITY!
TO ENSURE PEACE, WAGE WAR!
GBTrudeau
HI, GENTS! SORRY I'M LATE!
NO PROBLEM.
GOOD-BYE, I MUST BE STAYING!

3/15/03

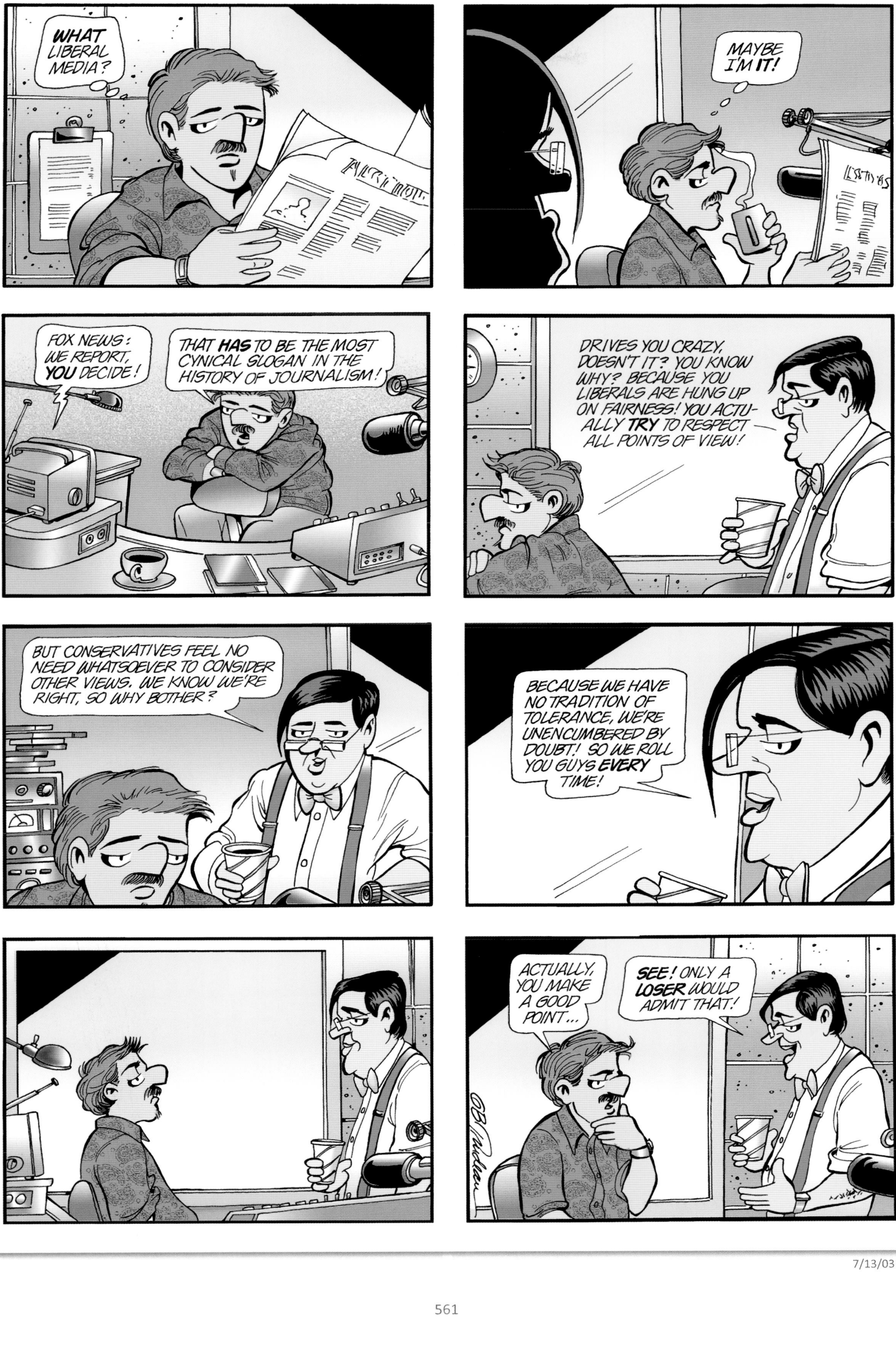
WHAT LIBERAL MEDIA?
MAYBE I'M IT!
FOX NEWS: WE REPORT, YOU DECIDE!
THAT HAS TO BE THE MOST CYNICAL SLOGAN IN THE HISTORY OF JOURNALISM!
DRIVES YOU CRAZY, DOESN'T IT? YOU KNOW WHY? BECAUSE YOU LIBERALS ARE HUNG UP ON FAIRNESS! YOU ACTUALLY TRY TO RESPECT ALL POINTS OF VIEW!
BUT CONSERVATIVES FEEL NO NEED WHATSOEVER TO CONSIDER OTHER VIEWS. WE KNOW WE'RE RIGHT, SO WHY BOTHER?
BECAUSE WE HAVE NO TRADITION OF TOLERANCE, WE'RE UNENCUMBERED BY DOUBT! SO WE ROLL YOU GUYS EVERY TIME!
ACTUALLY, YOU MAKE A GOOD POINT...
SEE! ONLY A LOSER WOULD ADMIT THAT!

7/13/03

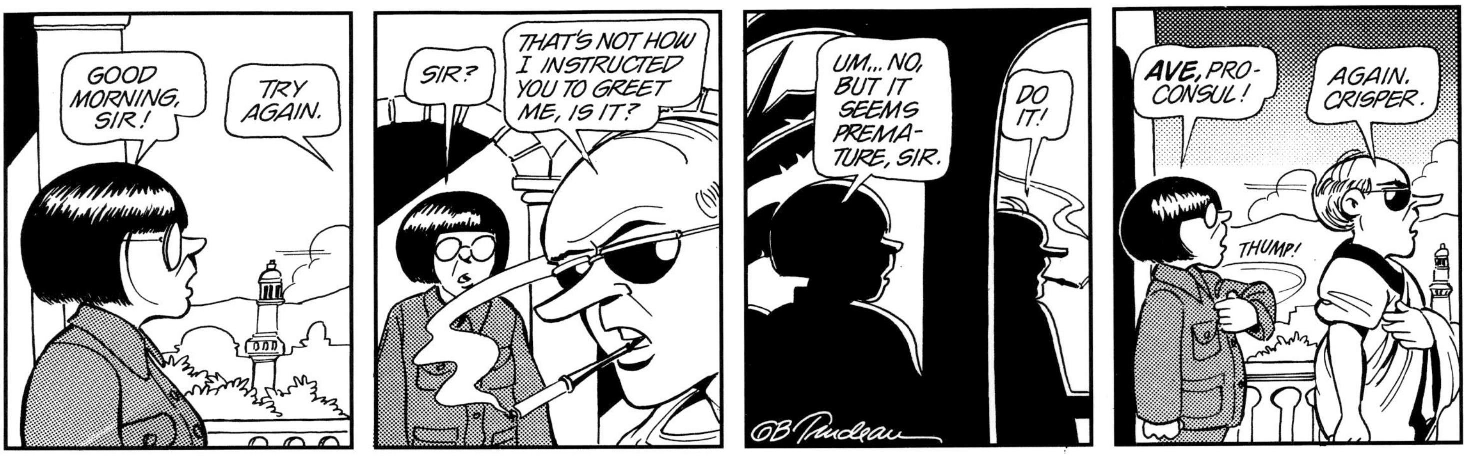
GOOD MORNING, SIR!
TRY AGAIN.
SIR?
THAT'S NOT HOW I INSTRUCTED YOU TO GREET ME, IS IT?
UM... NO, BUT IT SEEMS PREMATURE, SIR.
DO IT!
AVE, PROCONSUL!
AGAIN. CRISPER.
THUMP!

3/17/03

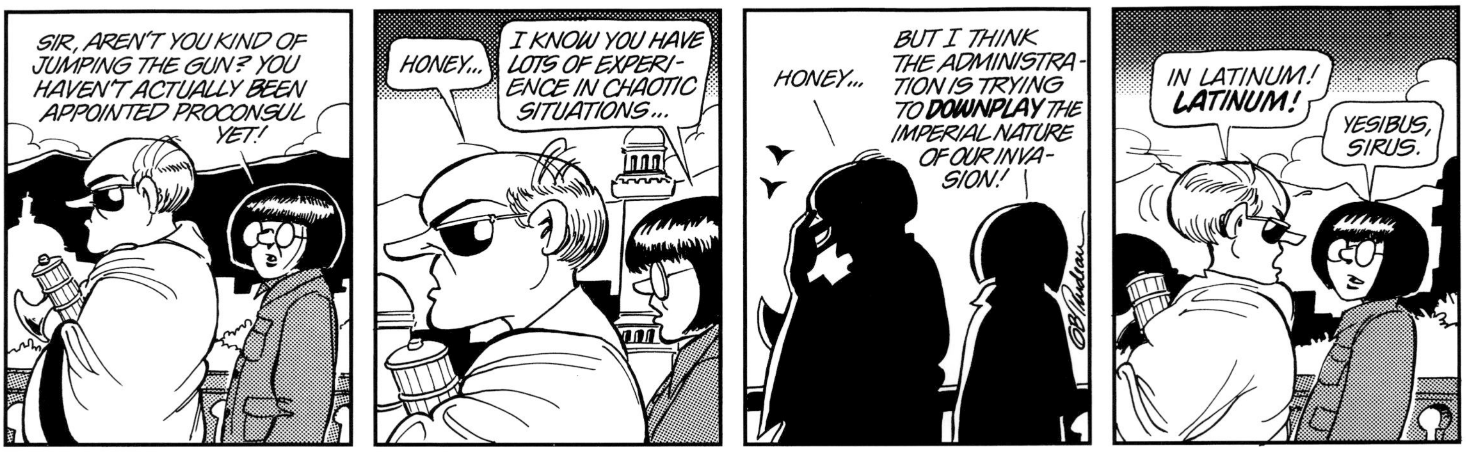
SIR, AREN'T YOU KIND OF JUMPING THE GUN? YOU HAVEN'T ACTUALLY BEEN APPOINTED PROCONSUL YET!
HONEY...
I KNOW YOU HAVE LOTS OF EXPERIENCE IN CHAOTIC SITUATIONS...
HONEY...
BUT I THINK THE ADMINISTRATION IS TRYING TO DOWNPLAY THE IMPERIAL NATURE OF OUR INVASION!
IN LATINUM! LATINUM!
YESIBUS, SIRUS.

3/18/03

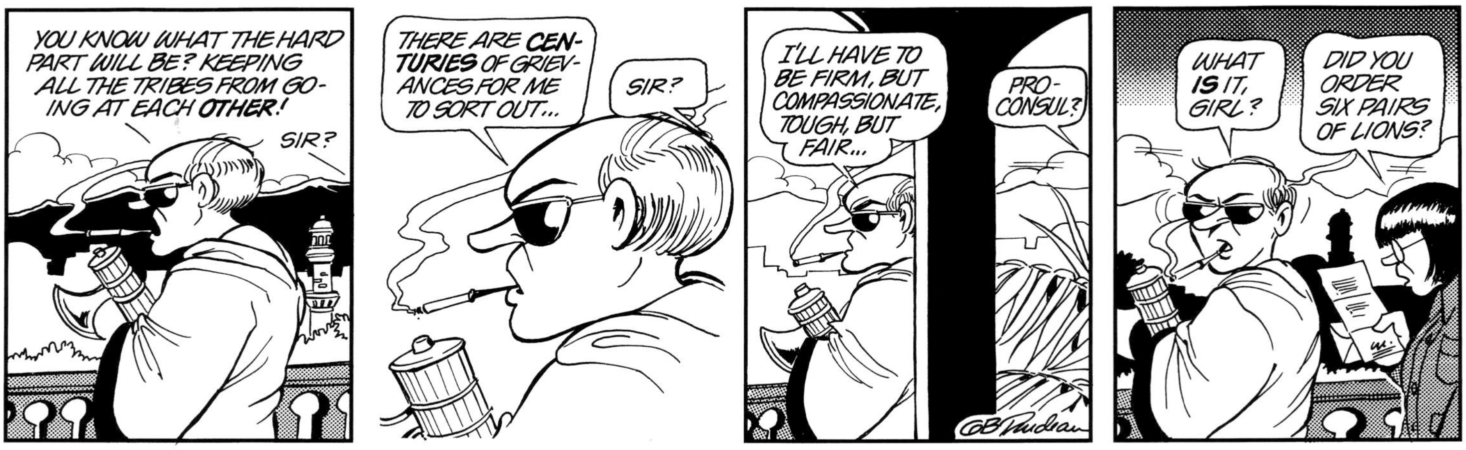
YOU KNOW WHAT THE HARD PART WILL BE? KEEPING ALL THE TRIBES FROM GOING AT EACH OTHER!
SIR?
THERE ARE CENTURIES OF GRIEVANCES FOR ME TO SORT OUT...
SIR?
I'LL HAVE TO BE FIRM, BUT COMPASSIONATE, TOUGH, BUT FAIR...
PROCONSUL?
WHAT IS IT, GIRL?
DID YOU ORDER SIX PAIRS OF LIONS?

3/20/03

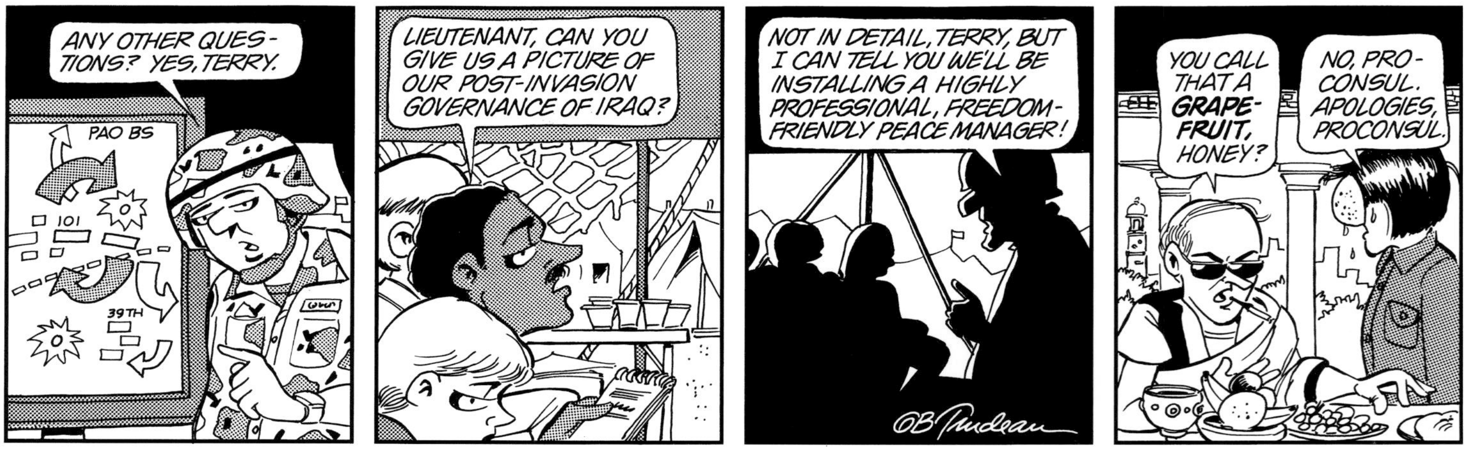
ANY OTHER QUESTIONS? YES, TERRY.
PAO BS
101
39TH
LIEUTENANT, CAN YOU GIVE US A PICTURE OF OUR POST-INVASION GOVERNANCE OF IRAQ?
NOT IN DETAIL, TERRY, BUT I CAN TELL YOU WE'LL BE INSTALLING A HIGHLY PROFESSIONAL, FREEDOM-FRIENDLY PEACE MANAGER!
YOU CALL THAT A GRAPEFRUIT, HONEY?
NO, PROCONSUL. APOLOGIES, PROCONSUL.

3/22/03

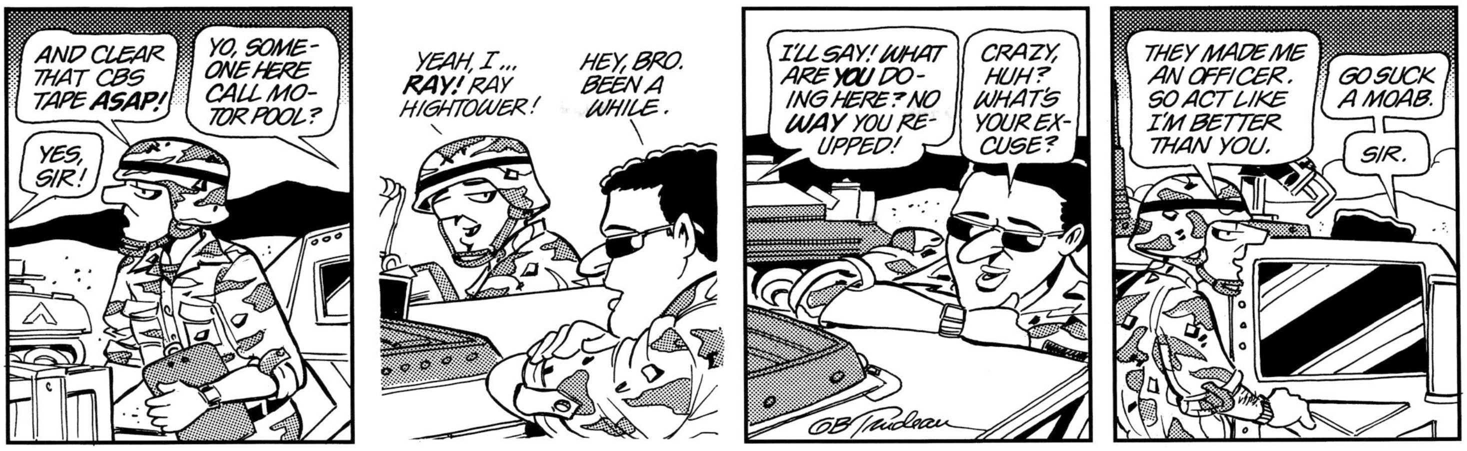
AND CLEAR THAT CBS TAPE ASAP!
YES, SIR!
YO, SOME-ONE HERE CALL MO-TOR POOL?
YEAH, I... RAY! RAY HIGHTOWER!
HEY, BRO. BEEN A WHILE.
I'LL SAY! WHAT ARE YOU DO-ING HERE? NO WAY YOU RE-UPPED!
CRAZY, HUH? WHAT'S YOUR EX-CUSE?
THEY MADE ME AN OFFICER. SO ACT LIKE I'M BETTER THAN YOU.
GO SUCK A MOAB.
SIR.

3/24/03

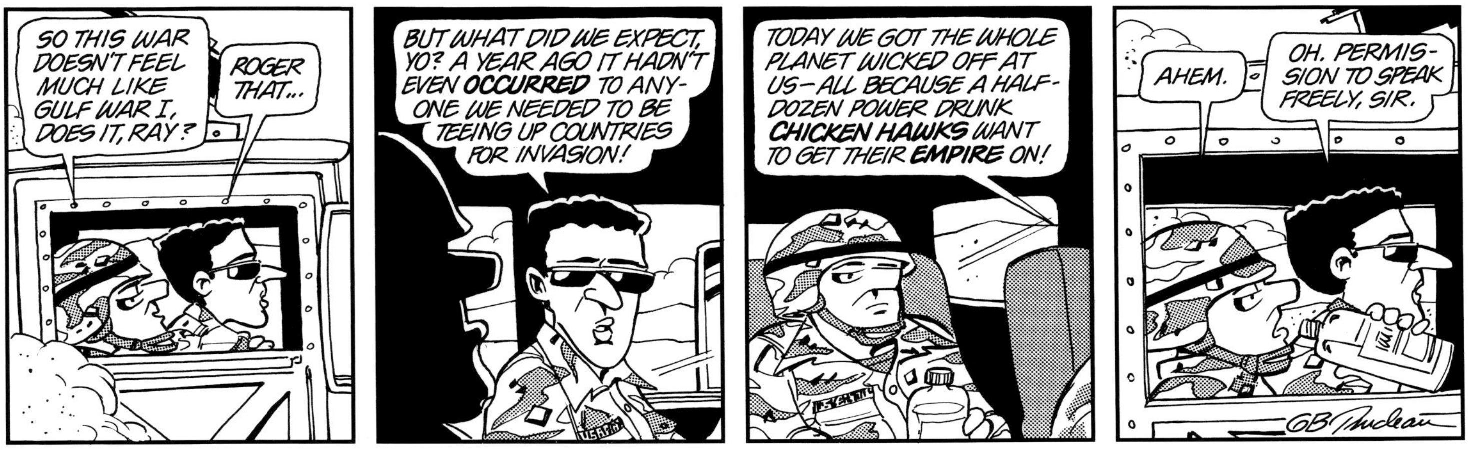
SO THIS WAR DOESN'T FEEL MUCH LIKE GULF WAR I, DOES IT, RAY?
ROGER THAT...
BUT WHAT DID WE EXPECT, YO? A YEAR AGO IT HADN'T EVEN OCCURRED TO ANY-ONE WE NEEDED TO BE TEEING UP COUNTRIES FOR INVASION!
TODAY WE GOT THE WHOLE PLANET WICKED OFF AT US—ALL BECAUSE A HALF-DOZEN POWER DRUNK CHICKEN HAWKS WANT TO GET THEIR EMPIRE ON!
AHEM.
OH. PERMIS-SION TO SPEAK FREELY, SIR.

3/25/03

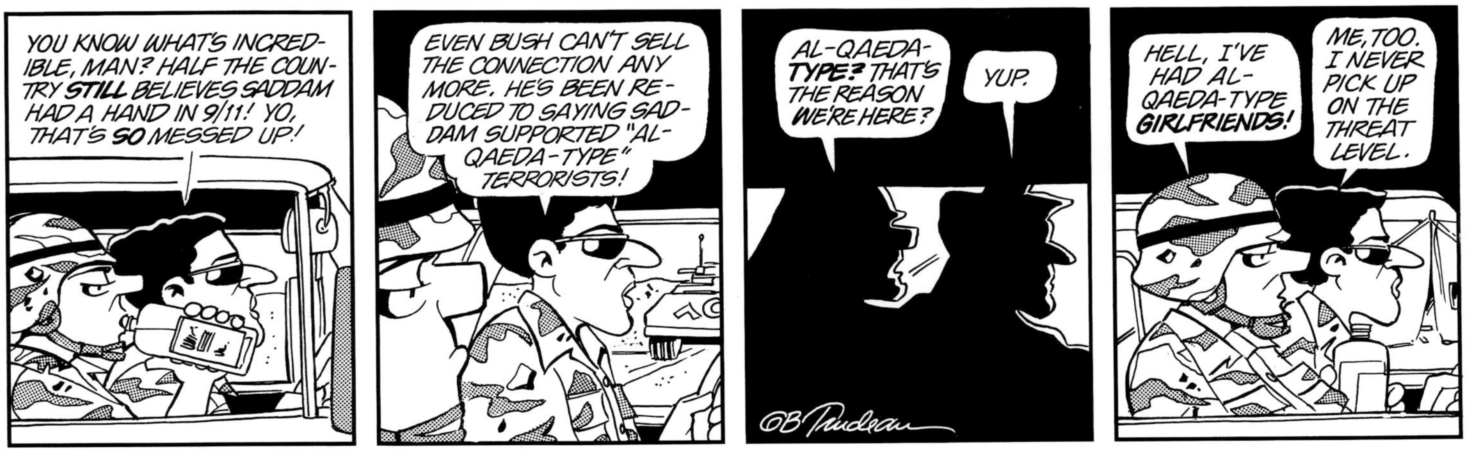
YOU KNOW WHAT'S INCRED-IBLE, MAN? HALF THE COUN-TRY STILL BELIEVES SADDAM HAD A HAND IN 9/11! YO, THAT'S SO MESSED UP!
EVEN BUSH CAN'T SELL THE CONNECTION ANY MORE. HE'S BEEN RE-DUCED TO SAYING SAD-DAM SUPPORTED "AL-QAEDA-TYPE" TERRORISTS!
AL-QAEDA-TYPE? THAT'S THE REASON WE'RE HERE?
YUP.
HELL, I'VE HAD AL-QAEDA-TYPE GIRLFRIENDS!
ME, TOO. I NEVER PICK UP ON THE THREAT LEVEL.

3/26/03

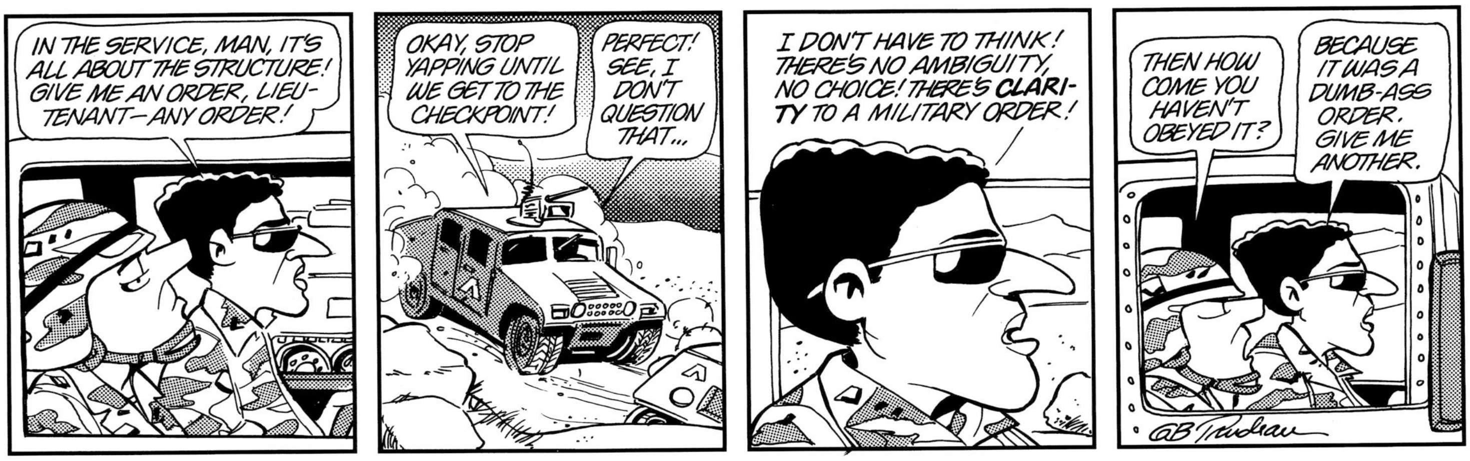
IN THE SERVICE, MAN, IT'S ALL ABOUT THE STRUCTURE! GIVE ME AN ORDER, LIEU-TENANT—ANY ORDER!
OKAY, STOP YAPPING UNTIL WE GET TO THE CHECKPOINT!
PERFECT! SEE, I DON'T QUESTION THAT...
I DON'T HAVE TO THINK! THERE'S NO AMBIGUITY, NO CHOICE! THERE'S CLARI-TY TO A MILITARY ORDER!
THEN HOW COME YOU HAVEN'T OBEYED IT?
BECAUSE IT WAS A DUMB-ASS ORDER. GIVE ME ANOTHER.

3/28/03

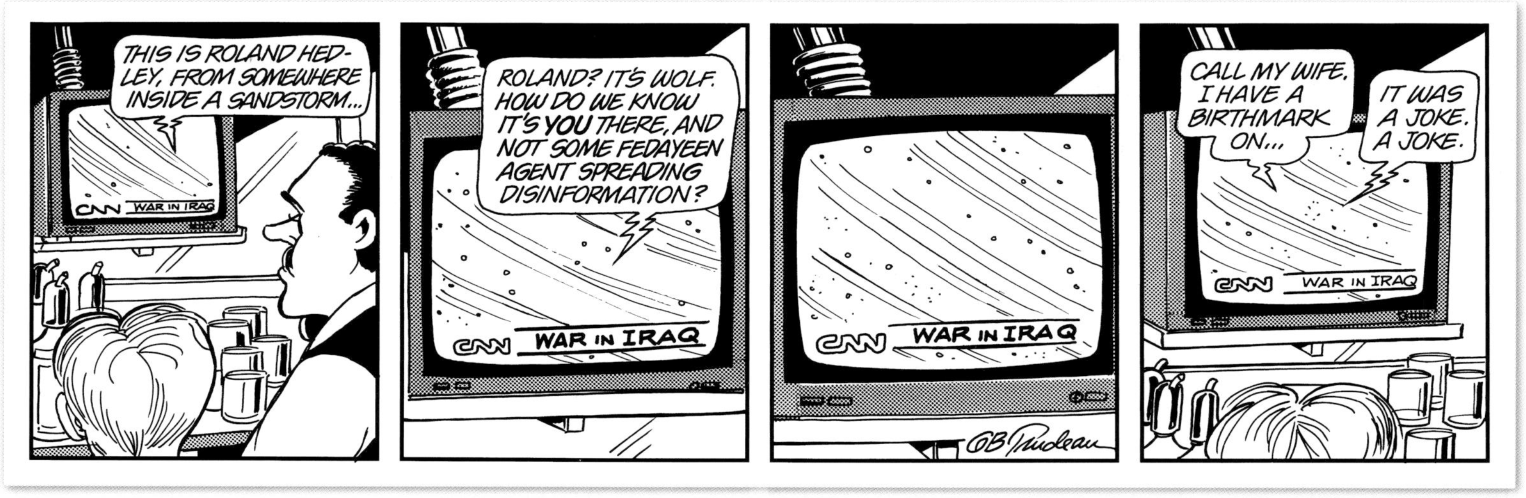
THIS IS ROLAND HEDLEY, FROM SOMEWHERE INSIDE A SANDSTORM...
CNN WAR IN IRAQ
ROLAND? IT'S WOLF. HOW DO WE KNOW IT'S YOU THERE, AND NOT SOME FEDAYEEN AGENT SPREADING DISINFORMATION?
CNN WAR IN IRAQ
CNN WAR IN IRAQ
GB Trudeau
CALL MY WIFE. I HAVE A BIRTHMARK ON...
IT WAS A JOKE. A JOKE.
CNN WAR IN IRAQ

4/9/03

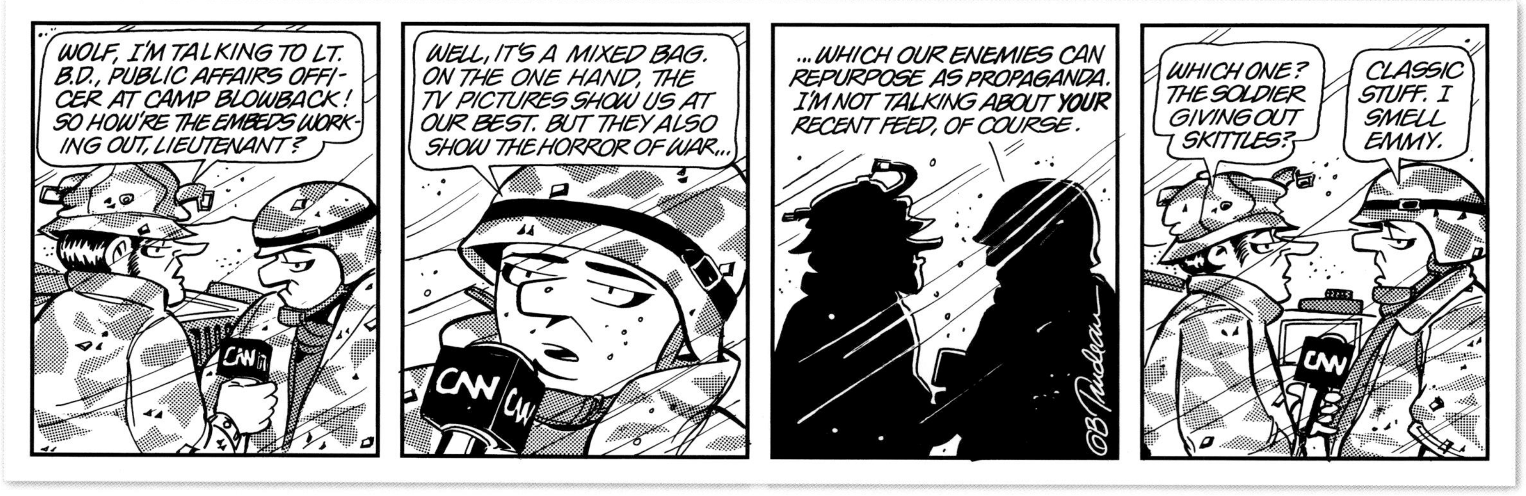
WOLF, I'M TALKING TO LT. B.D., PUBLIC AFFAIRS OFFICER AT CAMP BLOWBACK! SO HOW'RE THE EMBEDS WORKING OUT, LIEUTENANT?
WELL, IT'S A MIXED BAG. ON THE ONE HAND, THE TV PICTURES SHOW US AT OUR BEST. BUT THEY ALSO SHOW THE HORROR OF WAR...
...WHICH OUR ENEMIES CAN REPURPOSE AS PROPAGANDA. I'M NOT TALKING ABOUT YOUR RECENT FEED, OF COURSE.
GB Trudeau
WHICH ONE? THE SOLDIER GIVING OUT SKITTLES?
CLASSIC STUFF. I SMELL EMMY.

4/10/03

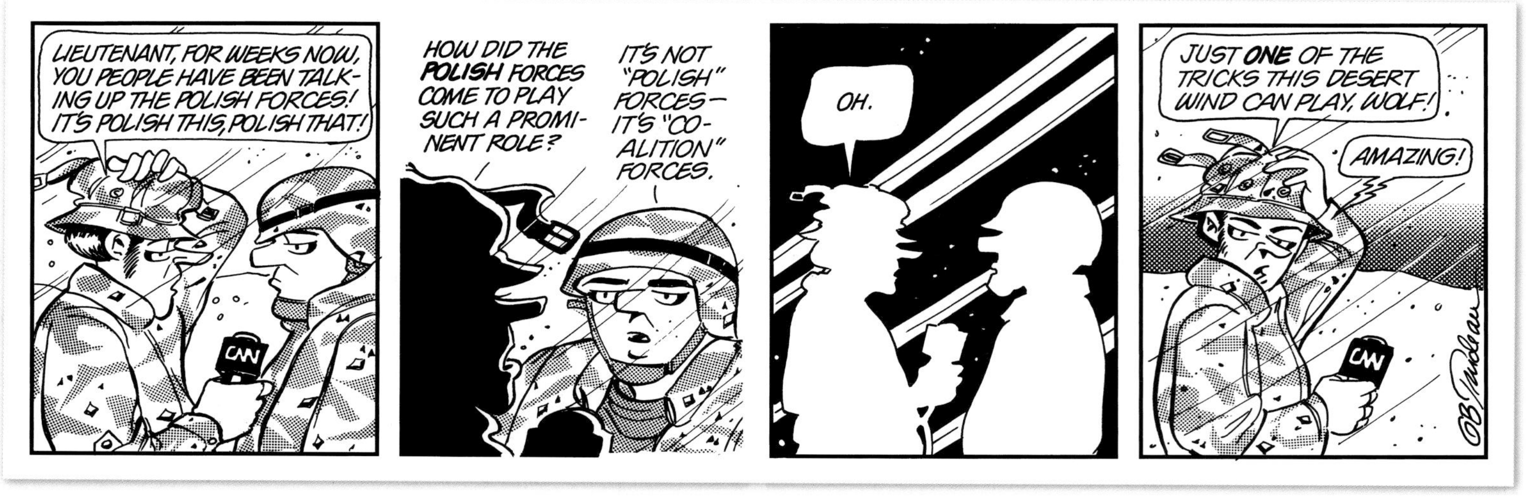
LIEUTENANT, FOR WEEKS NOW, YOU PEOPLE HAVE BEEN TALKING UP THE POLISH FORCES! IT'S POLISH THIS, POLISH THAT!
HOW DID THE POLISH FORCES COME TO PLAY SUCH A PROMINENT ROLE?
IT'S NOT "POLISH" FORCES— IT'S "COALITION" FORCES.
OH.
JUST ONE OF THE TRICKS THIS DESERT WIND CAN PLAY, WOLF!
AMAZING!
GB Trudeau

4/11/03

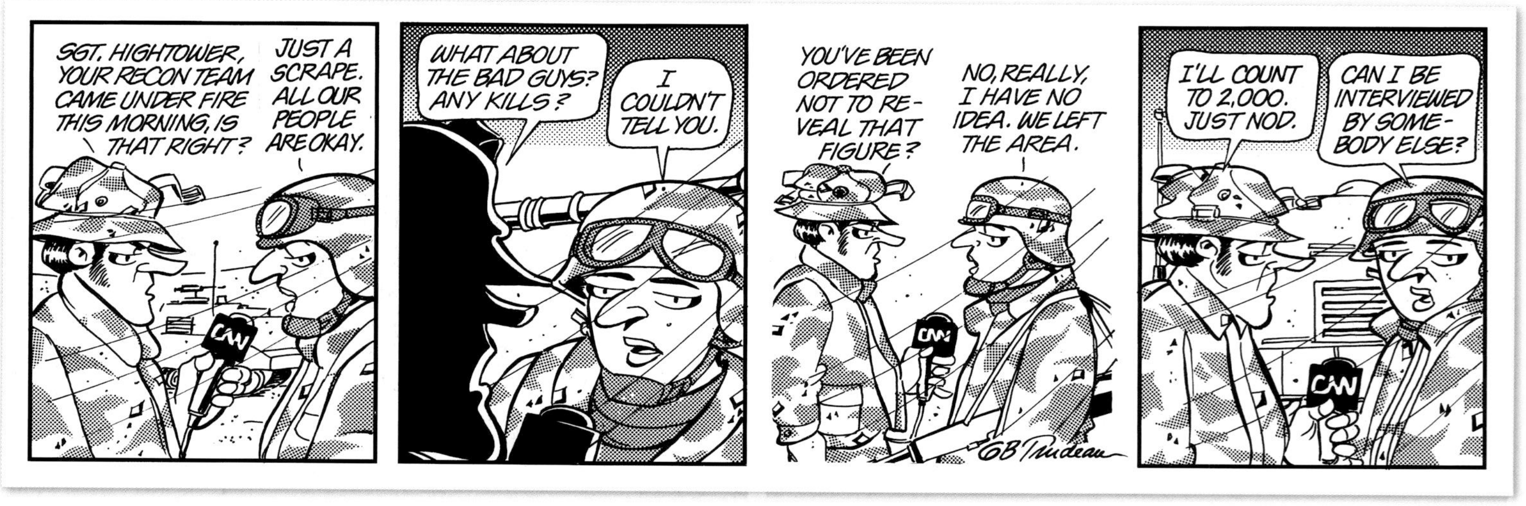
SGT. HIGHTOWER, YOUR RECON TEAM CAME UNDER FIRE THIS MORNING, IS THAT RIGHT?
JUST A SCRAPE. ALL OUR PEOPLE ARE OKAY.
WHAT ABOUT THE BAD GUYS? ANY KILLS?
I COULDN'T TELL YOU.
YOU'VE BEEN ORDERED NOT TO REVEAL THAT FIGURE?
NO, REALLY, I HAVE NO IDEA. WE LEFT THE AREA.
GB Trudeau
I'LL COUNT TO 2,000. JUST NOD.
CAN I BE INTERVIEWED BY SOMEBODY ELSE?

4/12/03

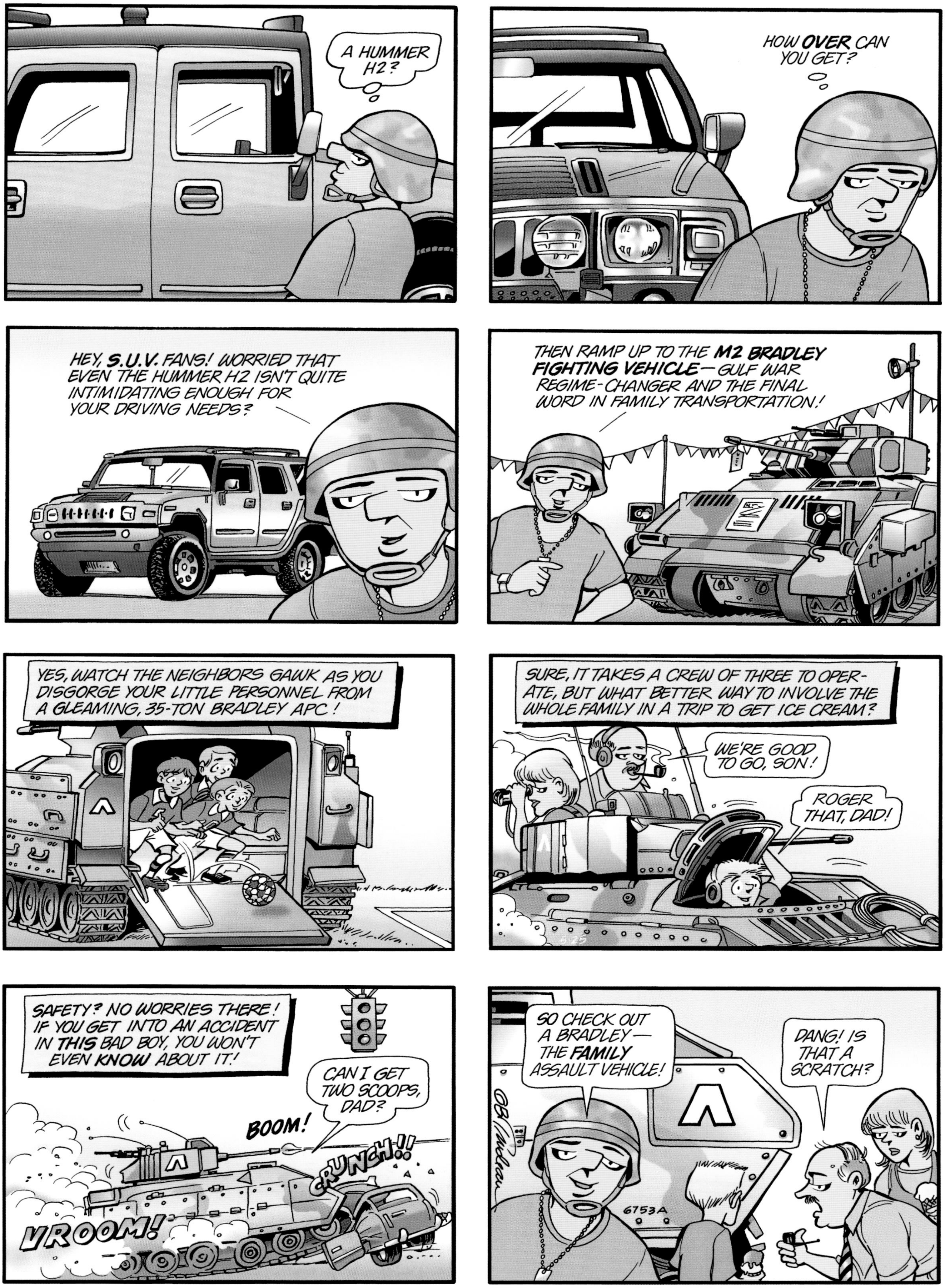
A HUMMER H2?
HOW OVER CAN YOU GET?
HEY, S.U.V. FANS! WORRIED THAT EVEN THE HUMMER H2 ISN'T QUITE INTIMIDATING ENOUGH FOR YOUR DRIVING NEEDS?
THEN RAMP UP TO THE M2 BRADLEY FIGHTING VEHICLE — GULF WAR REGIME-CHANGER AND THE FINAL WORD IN FAMILY TRANSPORTATION!
YES, WATCH THE NEIGHBORS GAWK AS YOU DISGORGE YOUR LITTLE PERSONNEL FROM A GLEAMING, 35-TON BRADLEY APC!
SURE, IT TAKES A CREW OF THREE TO OPERATE, BUT WHAT BETTER WAY TO INVOLVE THE WHOLE FAMILY IN A TRIP TO GET ICE CREAM?
WE'RE GOOD TO GO, SON!
ROGER THAT, DAD!
SAFETY? NO WORRIES THERE! IF YOU GET INTO AN ACCIDENT IN THIS BAD BOY, YOU WON'T EVEN KNOW ABOUT IT!
CAN I GET TWO SCOOPS, DAD?
BOOM!
CRUNCH!!
VROOM!
SO CHECK OUT A BRADLEY — THE FAMILY ASSAULT VEHICLE!
DANG! IS THAT A SCRATCH?
6753A

5/25/03

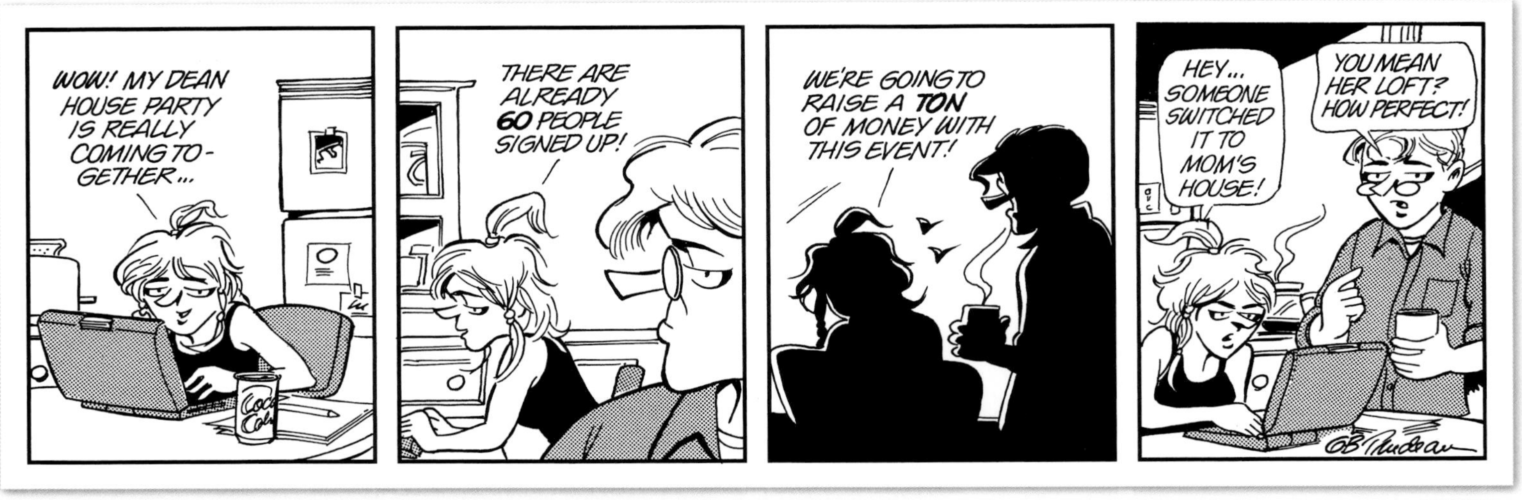
WOW! MY DEAN HOUSE PARTY IS REALLY COMING TO-GETHER...
THERE ARE ALREADY 60 PEOPLE SIGNED UP!
WE'RE GOING TO RAISE A TON OF MONEY WITH THIS EVENT!
HEY... SOMEONE SWITCHED IT TO MOM'S HOUSE!
YOU MEAN HER LOFT? HOW PERFECT!

7/7/03

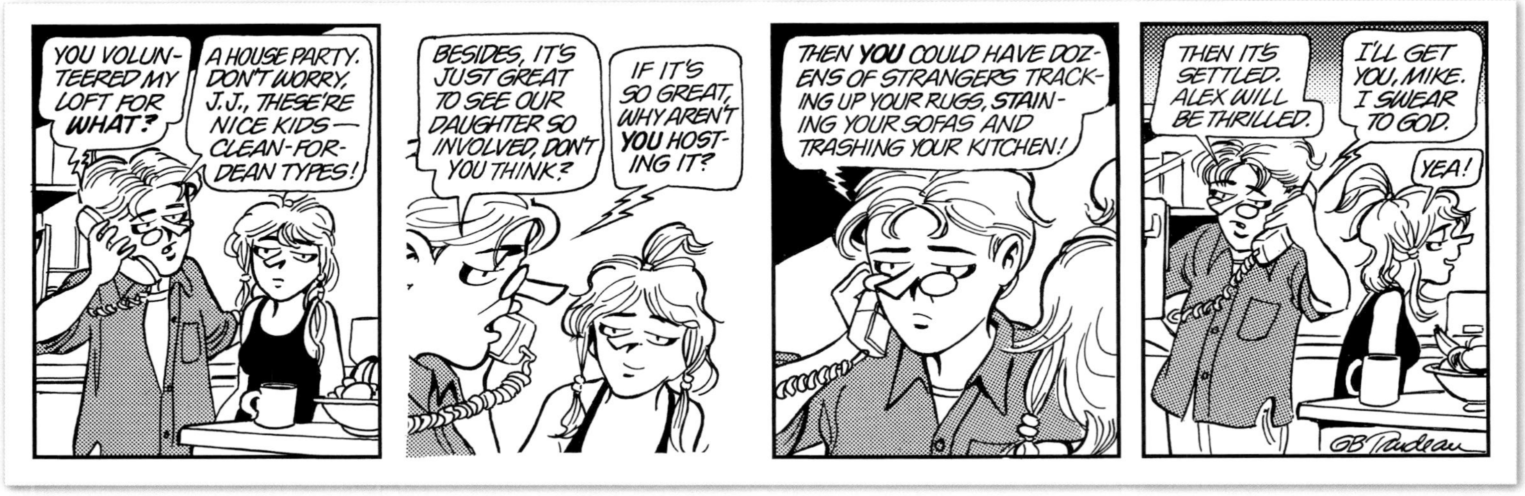
YOU VOLUN-TEERED MY LOFT FOR WHAT?
A HOUSE PARTY. DON'T WORRY, J.J., THESE'RE NICE KIDS— CLEAN-FOR-DEAN TYPES!
BESIDES, IT'S JUST GREAT TO SEE OUR DAUGHTER SO INVOLVED, DON'T YOU THINK?
IF IT'S SO GREAT, WHY AREN'T YOU HOST-ING IT?
THEN YOU COULD HAVE DOZ-ENS OF STRANGERS TRACK-ING UP YOUR RUGS, STAIN-ING YOUR SOFAS AND TRASHING YOUR KITCHEN!
THEN IT'S SETTLED. ALEX WILL BE THRILLED.
I'LL GET YOU, MIKE. I SWEAR TO GOD.
YEA!

7/9/03

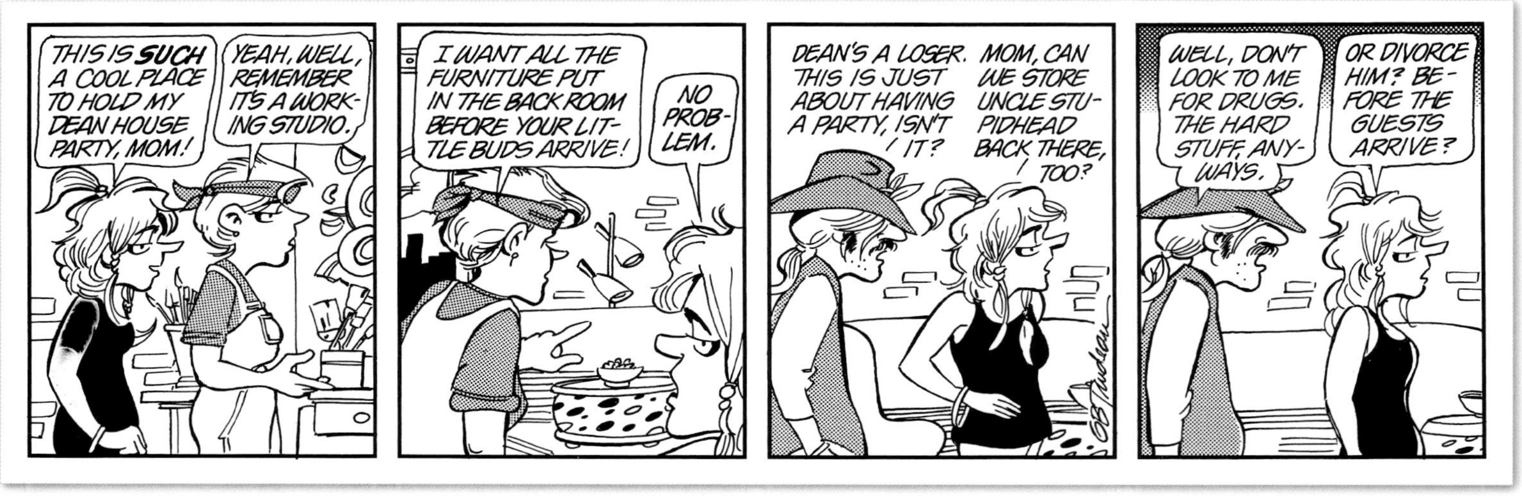
THIS IS SUCH A COOL PLACE TO HOLD MY DEAN HOUSE PARTY, MOM!
YEAH, WELL, REMEMBER IT'S A WORK-ING STUDIO.
I WANT ALL THE FURNITURE PUT IN THE BACK ROOM BEFORE YOUR LIT-TLE BUDS ARRIVE!
NO PROB-LEM.
DEAN'S A LOSER. THIS IS JUST ABOUT HAVING A PARTY, ISN'T IT?
MOM, CAN WE STORE UNCLE STU-PIDHEAD BACK THERE, TOO?
WELL, DON'T LOOK TO ME FOR DRUGS. THE HARD STUFF, ANY-WAYS.
OR DIVORCE HIM? BE-FORE THE GUESTS ARRIVE?

7/10/03

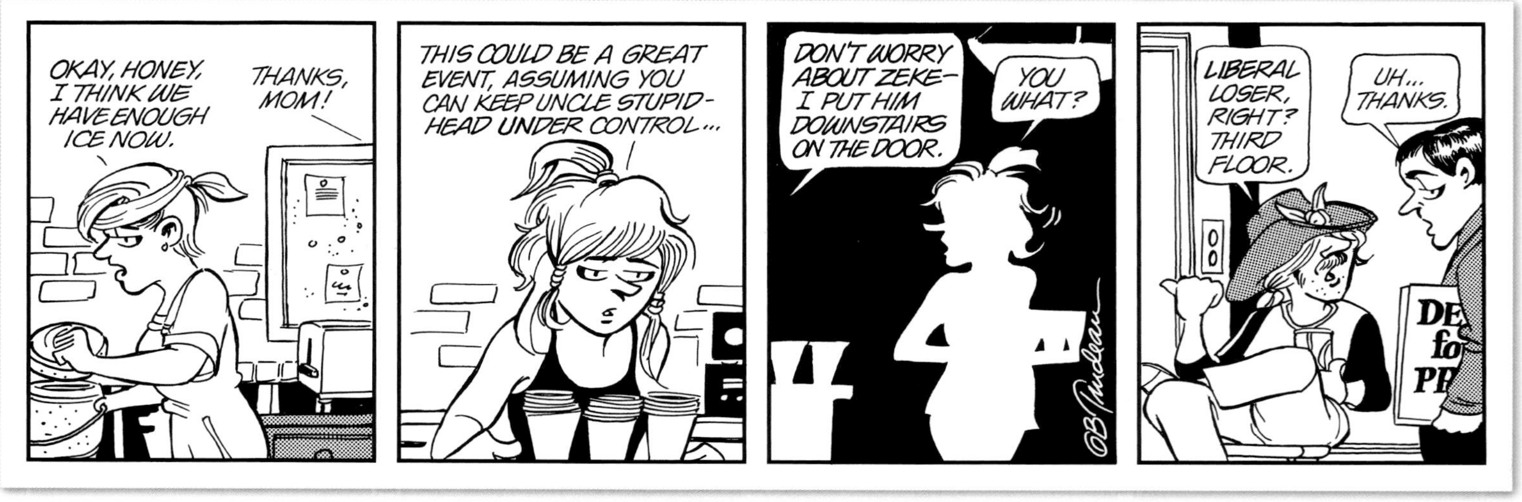
OKAY, HONEY, I THINK WE HAVE ENOUGH ICE NOW.
THANKS, MOM!
THIS COULD BE A GREAT EVENT, ASSUMING YOU CAN KEEP UNCLE STUPID-HEAD UNDER CONTROL...
DON'T WORRY ABOUT ZEKE— I PUT HIM DOWNSTAIRS ON THE DOOR.
YOU WHAT?
LIBERAL LOSER, RIGHT? THIRD FLOOR.
UH... THANKS.

7/12/03

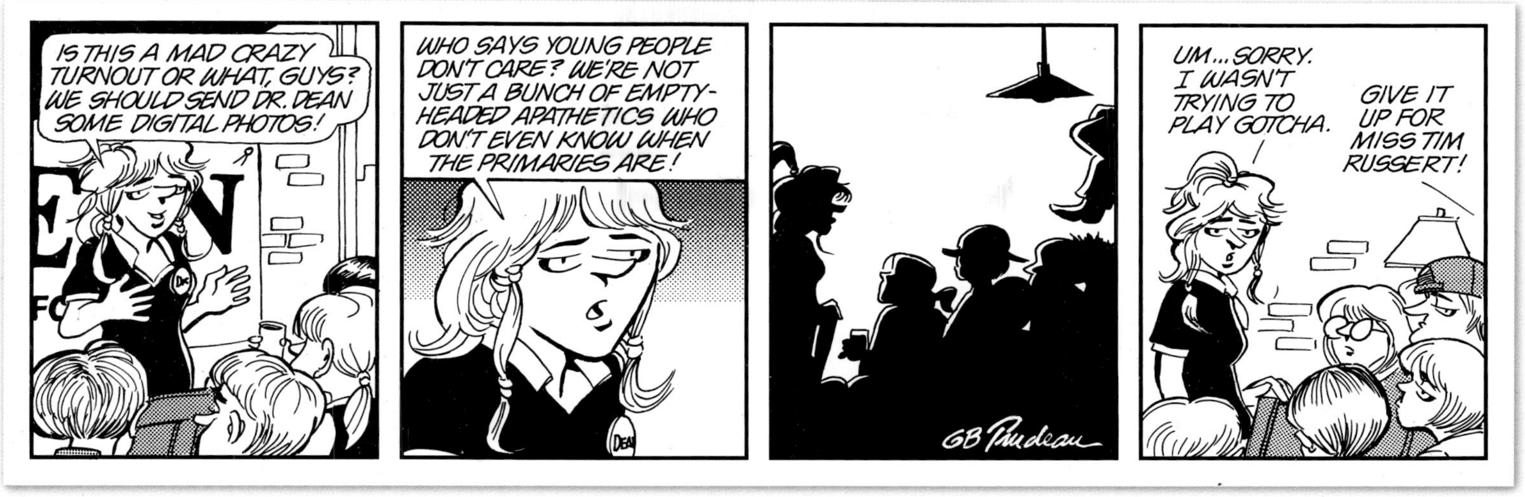
IS THIS A MAD CRAZY TURNOUT OR WHAT, GUYS? WE SHOULD SEND DR. DEAN SOME DIGITAL PHOTOS!
WHO SAYS YOUNG PEOPLE DON'T CARE? WE'RE NOT JUST A BUNCH OF EMPTY-HEADED APATHETICS WHO DON'T EVEN KNOW WHEN THE PRIMARIES ARE!
UM... SORRY. I WASN'T TRYING TO PLAY GOTCHA.
GIVE IT UP FOR MISS TIM RUSSERT!

7/15/03

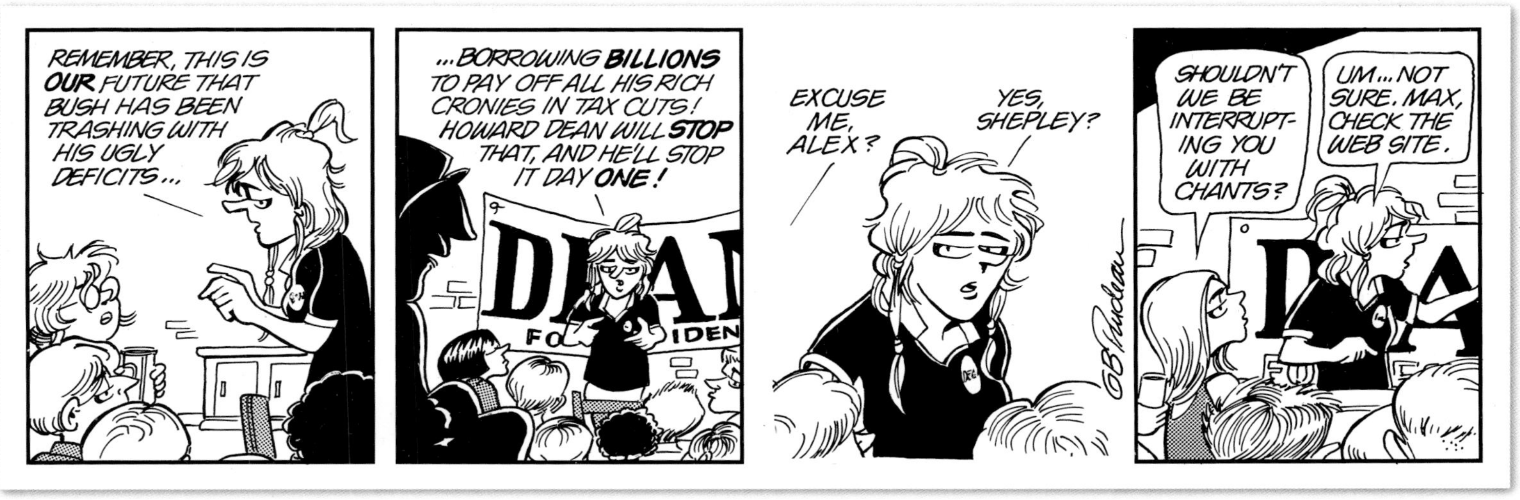
REMEMBER, THIS IS OUR FUTURE THAT BUSH HAS BEEN TRASHING WITH HIS UGLY DEFICITS...
...BORROWING BILLIONS TO PAY OFF ALL HIS RICH CRONIES IN TAX CUTS! HOWARD DEAN WILL STOP THAT, AND HE'LL STOP IT DAY ONE!
EXCUSE ME, ALEX?
YES, SHEPLEY?
SHOULDN'T WE BE INTERRUPTING YOU WITH CHANTS?
UM... NOT SURE. MAX, CHECK THE WEB SITE.

7/16/03

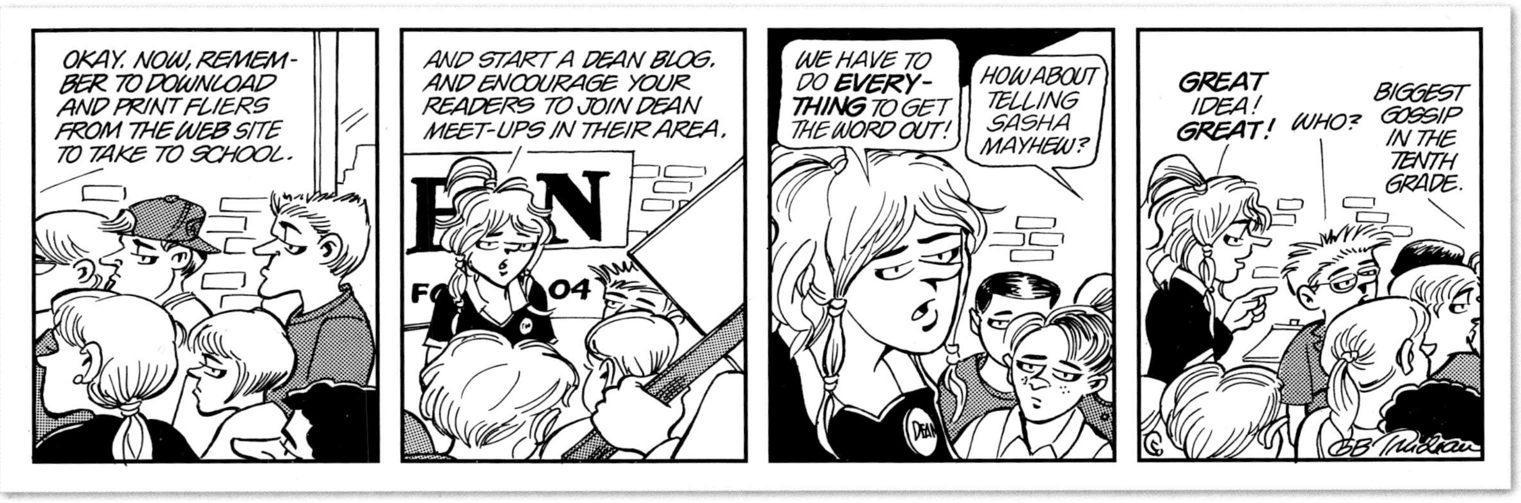
OKAY. NOW, REMEMBER TO DOWNLOAD AND PRINT FLIERS FROM THE WEB SITE TO TAKE TO SCHOOL.
AND START A DEAN BLOG. AND ENCOURAGE YOUR READERS TO JOIN DEAN MEET-UPS IN THEIR AREA.
WE HAVE TO DO EVERYTHING TO GET THE WORD OUT!
HOW ABOUT TELLING SASHA MAYHEW?
GREAT IDEA! GREAT!
WHO?
BIGGEST GOSSIP IN THE TENTH GRADE.

7/18/03

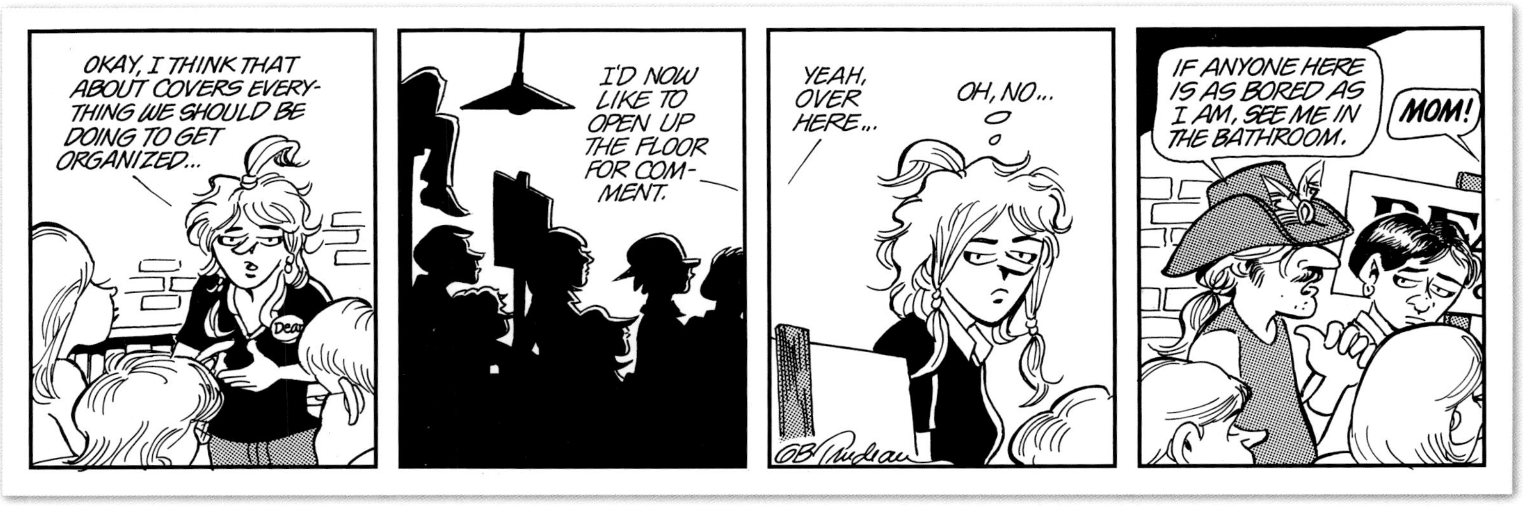
OKAY, I THINK THAT ABOUT COVERS EVERYTHING WE SHOULD BE DOING TO GET ORGANIZED...
I'D NOW LIKE TO OPEN UP THE FLOOR FOR COMMENT.
YEAH, OVER HERE...
OH, NO...
IF ANYONE HERE IS AS BORED AS I AM, SEE ME IN THE BATHROOM.
MOM!

7/19/03

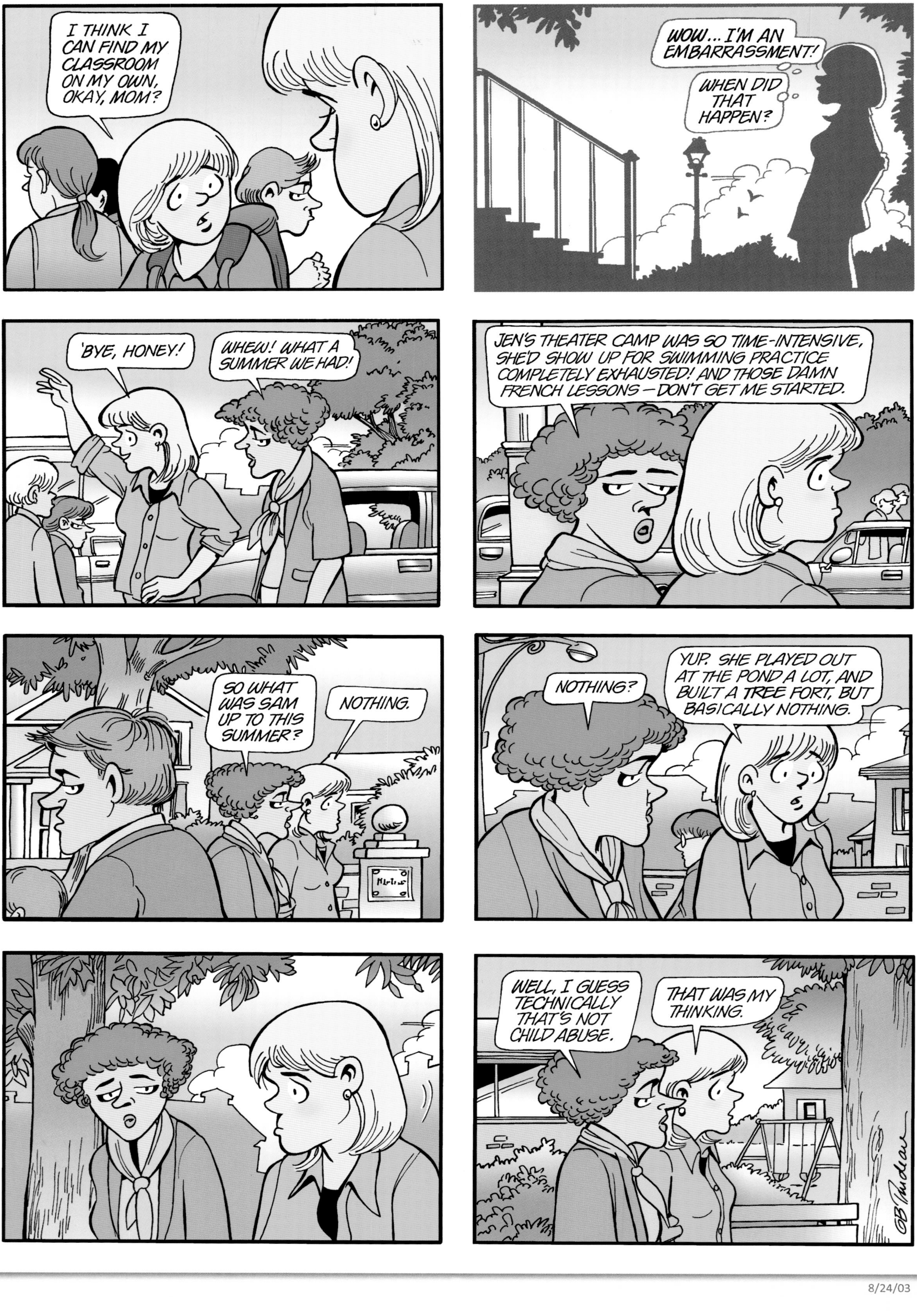
I THINK I CAN FIND MY CLASSROOM ON MY OWN, OKAY, MOM?
WOW... I'M AN EMBARRASSMENT!
WHEN DID THAT HAPPEN?
'BYE, HONEY!
WHEW! WHAT A SUMMER WE HAD!
JEN'S THEATER CAMP WAS SO TIME-INTENSIVE, SHE'D SHOW UP FOR SWIMMING PRACTICE COMPLETELY EXHAUSTED! AND THOSE DAMN FRENCH LESSONS – DON'T GET ME STARTED.
SO WHAT WAS SAM UP TO THIS SUMMER?
NOTHING.
NOTHING?
YUP. SHE PLAYED OUT AT THE POND A LOT, AND BUILT A TREE FORT, BUT BASICALLY NOTHING.
WELL, I GUESS TECHNICALLY THAT'S NOT CHILD ABUSE.
THAT WAS MY THINKING.
GB Trudeau

8/24/03

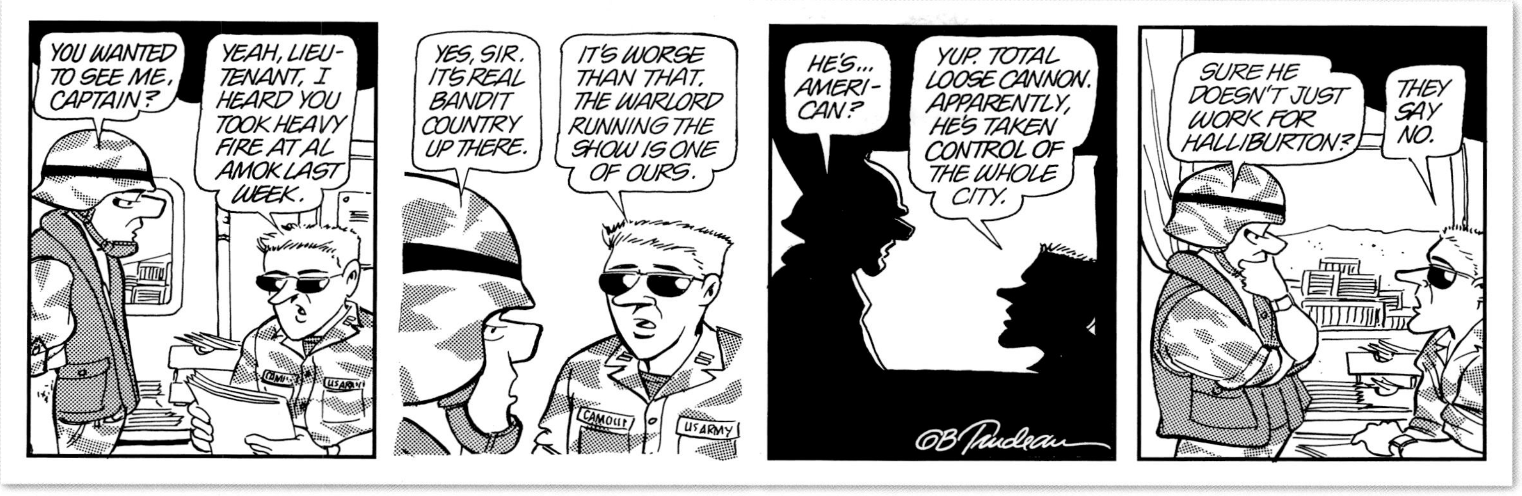
YOU WANTED TO SEE ME, CAPTAIN?
YEAH, LIEUTENANT, I HEARD YOU TOOK HEAVY FIRE AT AL AMOK LAST WEEK.
YES, SIR. IT'S REAL BANDIT COUNTRY UP THERE.
IT'S WORSE THAN THAT. THE WARLORD RUNNING THE SHOW IS ONE OF OURS.
HE'S... AMERICAN?
YUP. TOTAL LOOSE CANNON. APPARENTLY, HE'S TAKEN CONTROL OF THE WHOLE CITY.
SURE HE DOESN'T JUST WORK FOR HALLIBURTON?
THEY SAY NO.

8/18/03

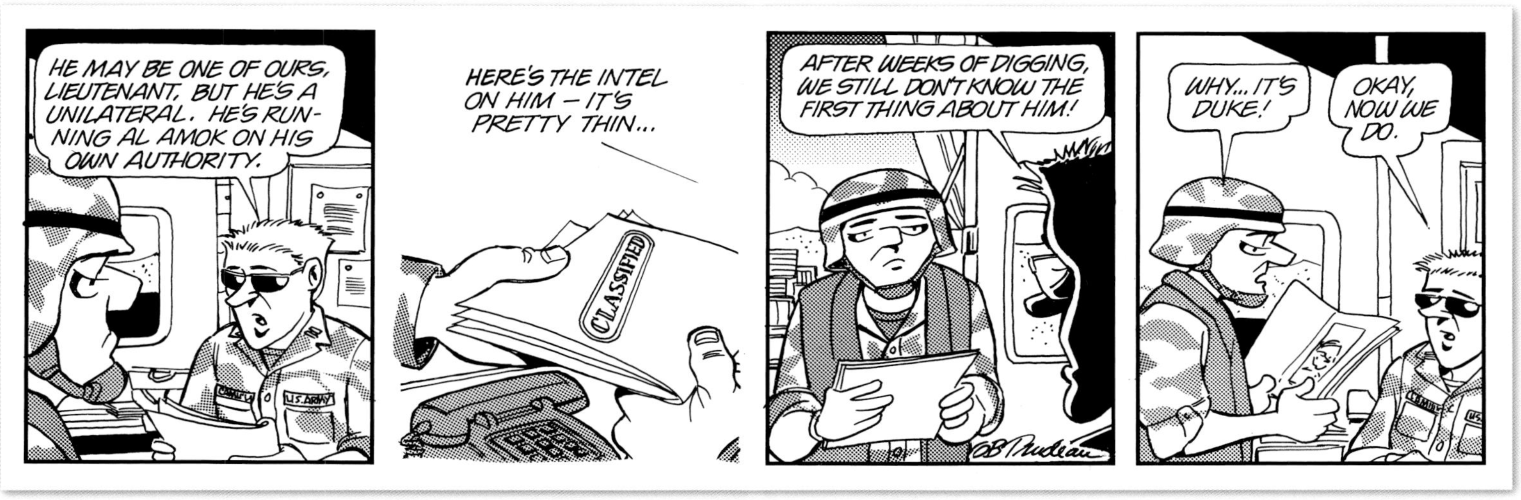
HE MAY BE ONE OF OURS, LIEUTENANT, BUT HE'S A UNILATERAL. HE'S RUNNING AL AMOK ON HIS OWN AUTHORITY.
HERE'S THE INTEL ON HIM — IT'S PRETTY THIN...
CLASSIFIED
AFTER WEEKS OF DIGGING, WE STILL DON'T KNOW THE FIRST THING ABOUT HIM!
WHY... IT'S DUKE!
OKAY, NOW WE DO.

8/19/03

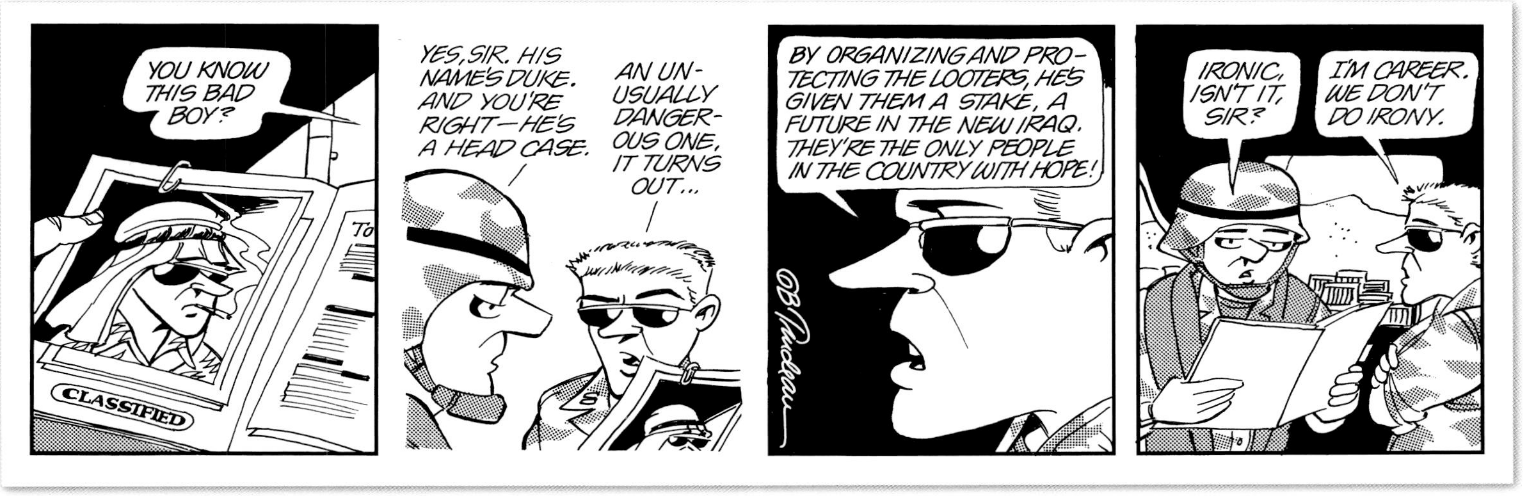
YOU KNOW THIS BAD BOY?
CLASSIFIED
YES, SIR. HIS NAME'S DUKE. AND YOU'RE RIGHT—HE'S A HEAD CASE.
AN UNUSUALLY DANGEROUS ONE, IT TURNS OUT...
BY ORGANIZING AND PROTECTING THE LOOTERS, HE'S GIVEN THEM A STAKE, A FUTURE IN THE NEW IRAQ. THEY'RE THE ONLY PEOPLE IN THE COUNTRY WITH HOPE!
IRONIC, ISN'T IT, SIR?
I'M CAREER. WE DON'T DO IRONY.

8/20/03

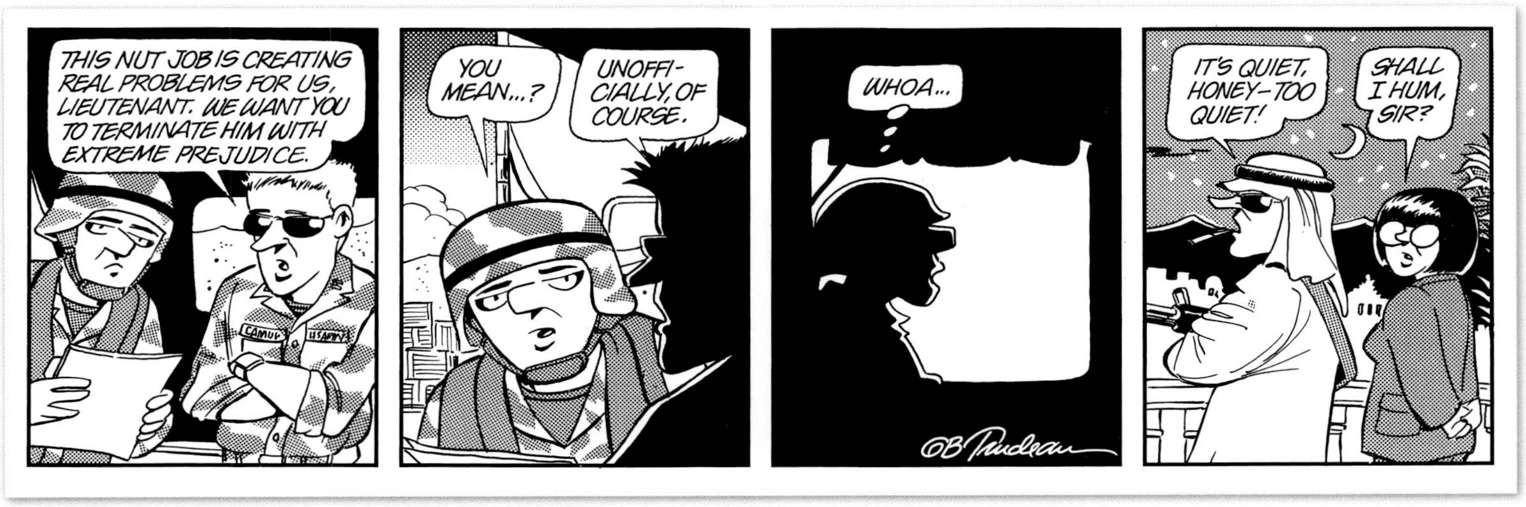
THIS NUT JOB IS CREATING REAL PROBLEMS FOR US, LIEUTENANT. WE WANT YOU TO TERMINATE HIM WITH EXTREME PREJUDICE.
YOU MEAN...?
UNOFFICIALLY, OF COURSE.
WHOA...
IT'S QUIET, HONEY—TOO QUIET!
SHALL I HUM, SIR?

8/21/03

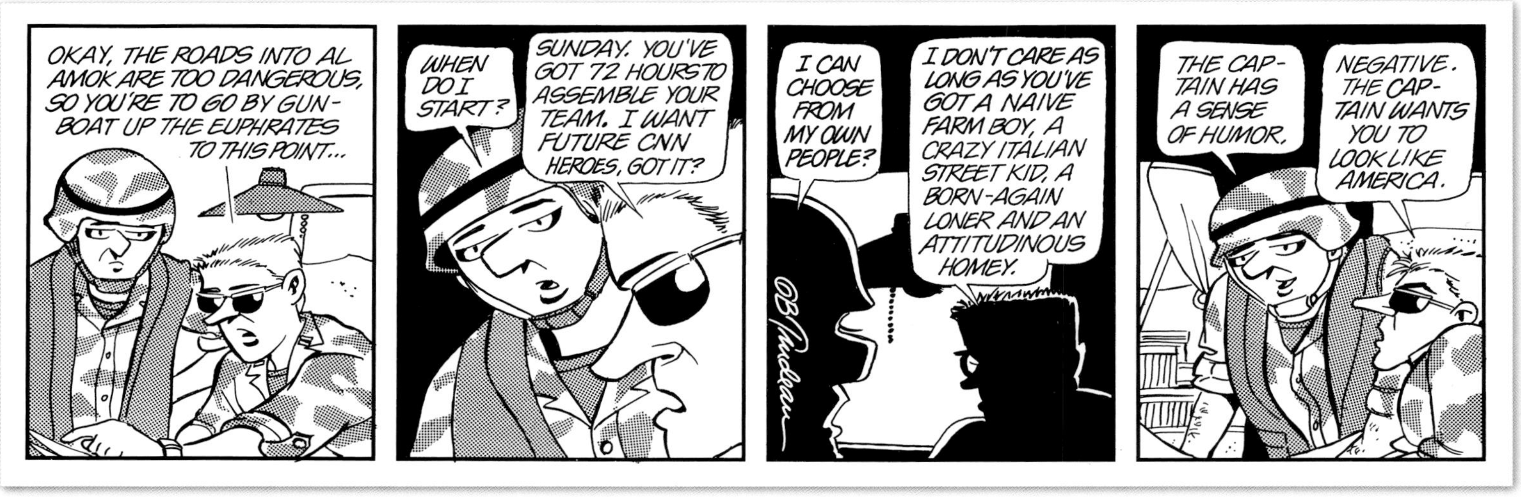
OKAY, THE ROADS INTO AL AMOK ARE TOO DANGEROUS, SO YOU'RE TO GO BY GUNBOAT UP THE EUPHRATES TO THIS POINT...
WHEN DO I START?
SUNDAY. YOU'VE GOT 72 HOURS TO ASSEMBLE YOUR TEAM. I WANT FUTURE CNN HEROES, GOT IT?
I CAN CHOOSE FROM MY OWN PEOPLE?
I DON'T CARE AS LONG AS YOU'VE GOT A NAIVE FARM BOY, A CRAZY ITALIAN STREET KID, A BORN-AGAIN LONER AND AN ATTITUDINOUS HOMEY.
THE CAPTAIN HAS A SENSE OF HUMOR.
NEGATIVE. THE CAPTAIN WANTS YOU TO LOOK LIKE AMERICA.
8/22/03

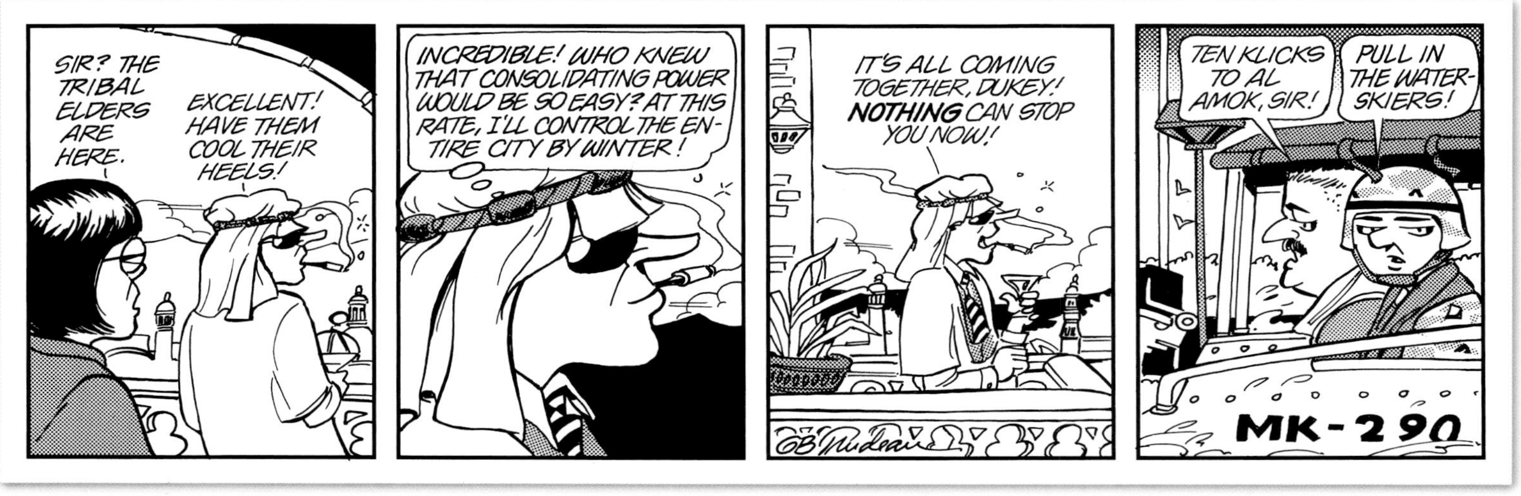
SIR? THE TRIBAL ELDERS ARE HERE.
EXCELLENT! HAVE THEM COOL THEIR HEELS!
INCREDIBLE! WHO KNEW THAT CONSOLIDATING POWER WOULD BE SO EASY? AT THIS RATE, I'LL CONTROL THE ENTIRE CITY BY WINTER!
IT'S ALL COMING TOGETHER, DUKEY! NOTHING CAN STOP YOU NOW!
TEN KLICKS TO AL AMOK, SIR!
PULL IN THE WATER-SKIERS!
MK-290
10/6/03

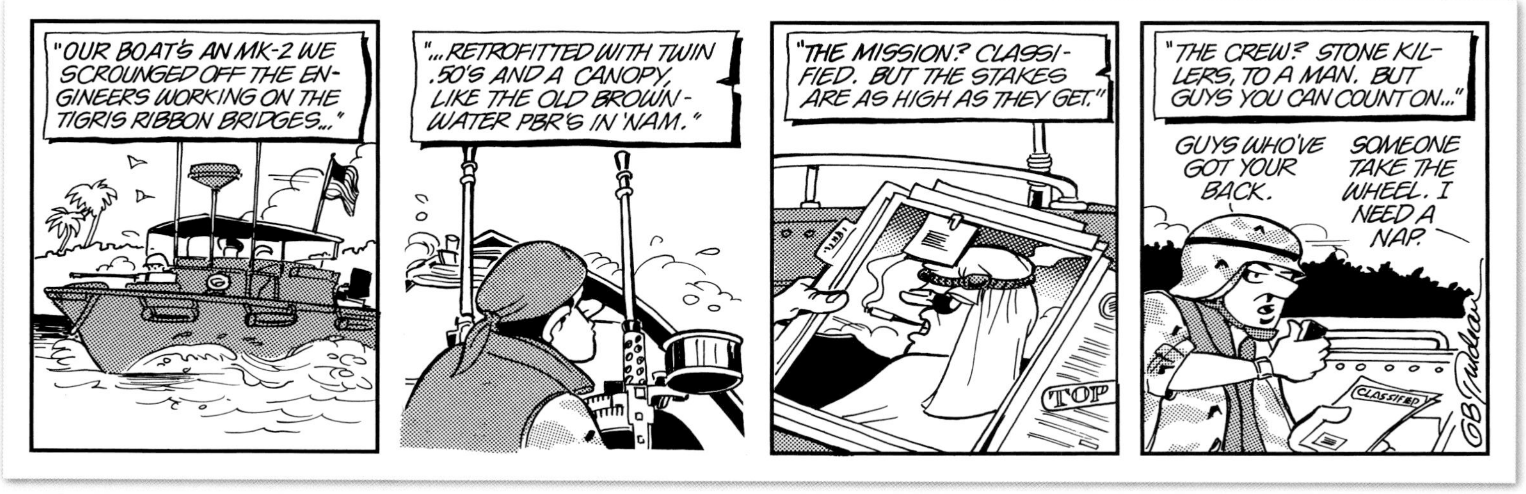
"OUR BOAT'S AN MK-2 WE SCROUNGED OFF THE ENGINEERS WORKING ON THE TIGRIS RIBBON BRIDGES..."
"...RETROFITTED WITH TWIN .50'S AND A CANOPY, LIKE THE OLD BROWN-WATER PBR'S IN 'NAM."
"THE MISSION? CLASSIFIED. BUT THE STAKES ARE AS HIGH AS THEY GET."
TOP
"THE CREW? STONE KILLERS, TO A MAN. BUT GUYS YOU CAN COUNT ON..."
GUYS WHO'VE GOT YOUR BACK.
SOMEONE TAKE THE WHEEL. I NEED A NAP.
CLASSIFIED
10/7/03

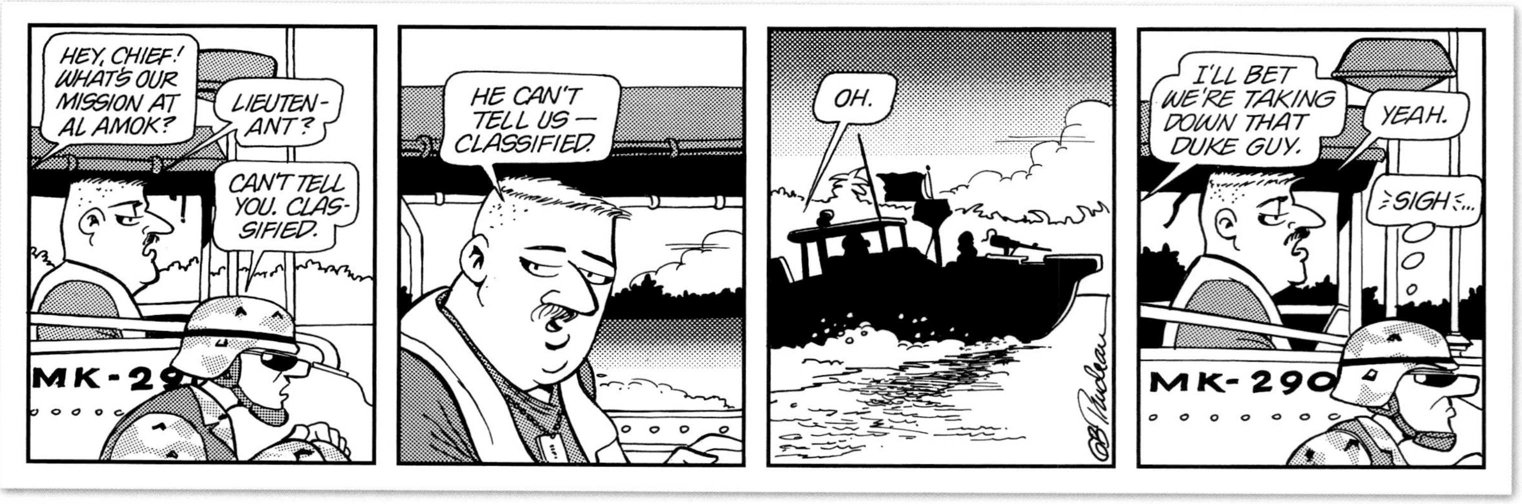
HEY, CHIEF! WHAT'S OUR MISSION AT AL AMOK?
LIEUTENANT?
CAN'T TELL YOU. CLASSIFIED.
MK-29
HE CAN'T TELL US — CLASSIFIED.
OH.
I'LL BET WE'RE TAKING DOWN THAT DUKE GUY.
YEAH.
SIGH...
MK-290
10/10/03

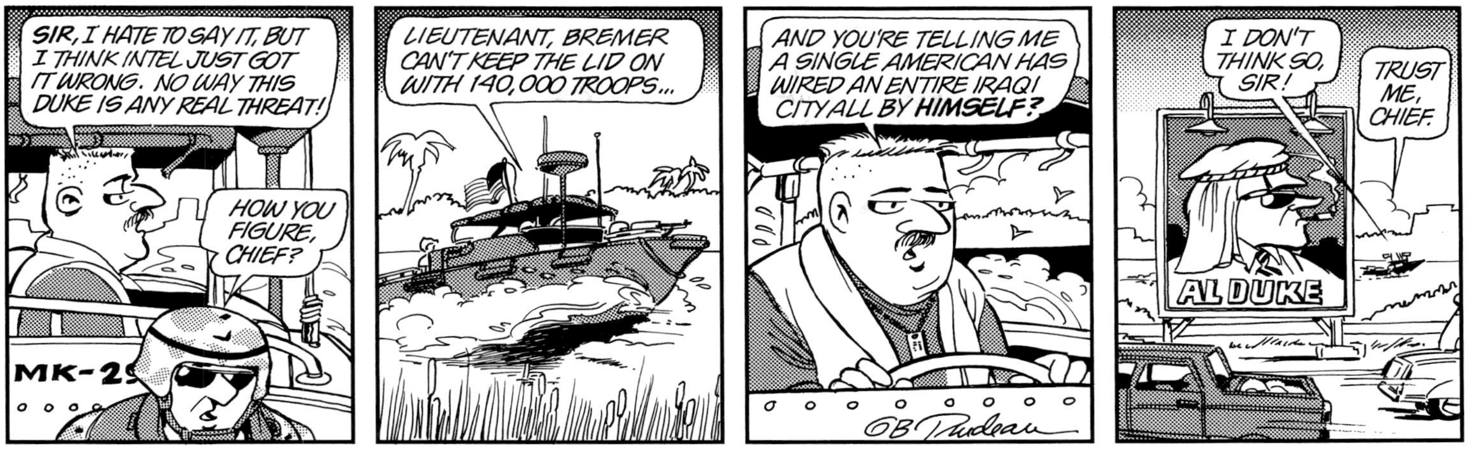
SIR, I HATE TO SAY IT, BUT I THINK INTEL JUST GOT IT WRONG. NO WAY THIS DUKE IS ANY REAL THREAT!
HOW YOU FIGURE, CHIEF?
LIEUTENANT, BREMER CAN'T KEEP THE LID ON WITH 140,000 TROOPS...
AND YOU'RE TELLING ME A SINGLE AMERICAN HAS WIRED AN ENTIRE IRAQI CITY ALL BY HIMSELF?
I DON'T THINK SO, SIR!
TRUST ME, CHIEF.
AL DUKE

10/11/03

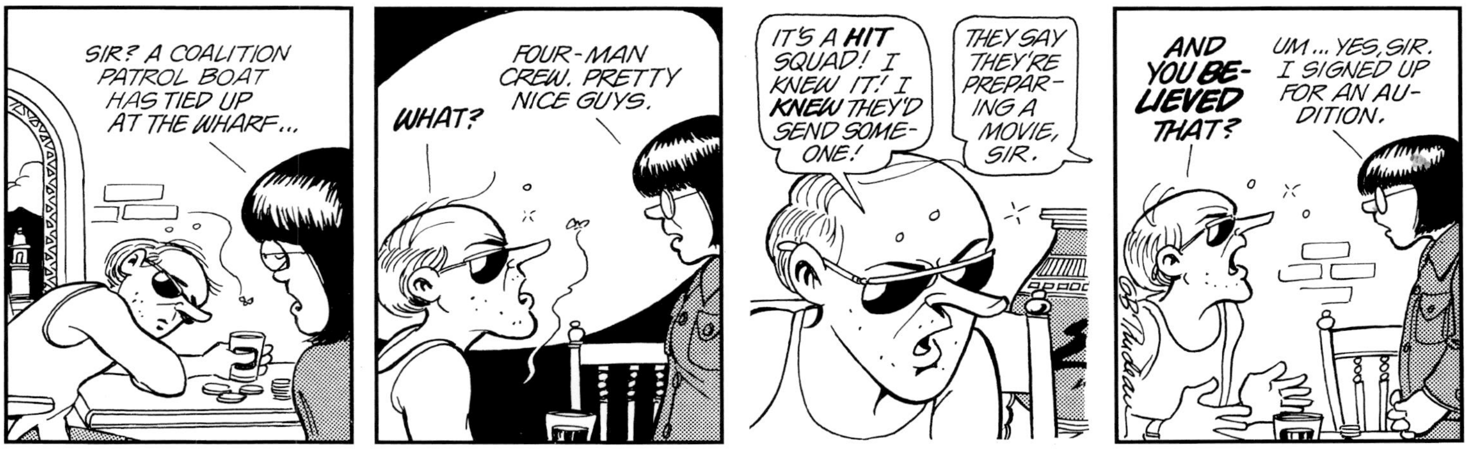
SIR? A COALITION PATROL BOAT HAS TIED UP AT THE WHARF...
WHAT?
FOUR-MAN CREW. PRETTY NICE GUYS.
IT'S A HIT SQUAD! I KNEW IT! I KNEW THEY'D SEND SOMEONE!
THEY SAY THEY'RE PREPARING A MOVIE, SIR.
AND YOU BELIEVED THAT?
UM... YES, SIR. I SIGNED UP FOR AN AUDITION.

10/13/03

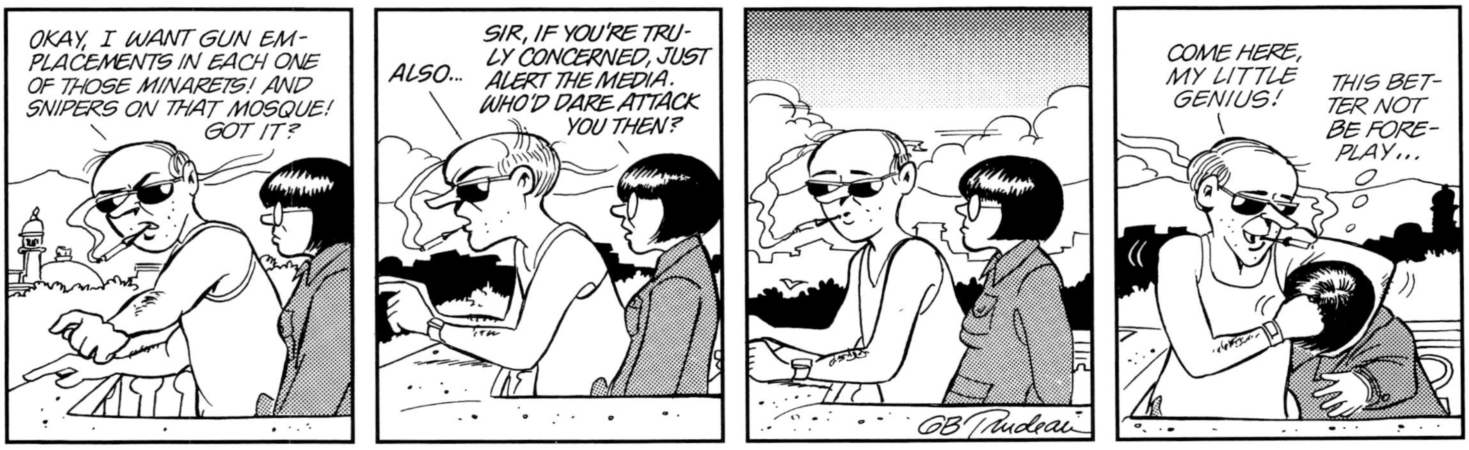
OKAY, I WANT GUN EMPLACEMENTS IN EACH ONE OF THOSE MINARETS! AND SNIPERS ON THAT MOSQUE! GOT IT?
ALSO...
SIR, IF YOU'RE TRULY CONCERNED, JUST ALERT THE MEDIA. WHO'D DARE ATTACK YOU THEN?
COME HERE, MY LITTLE GENIUS!
THIS BETTER NOT BE FOREPLAY...

10/15/03

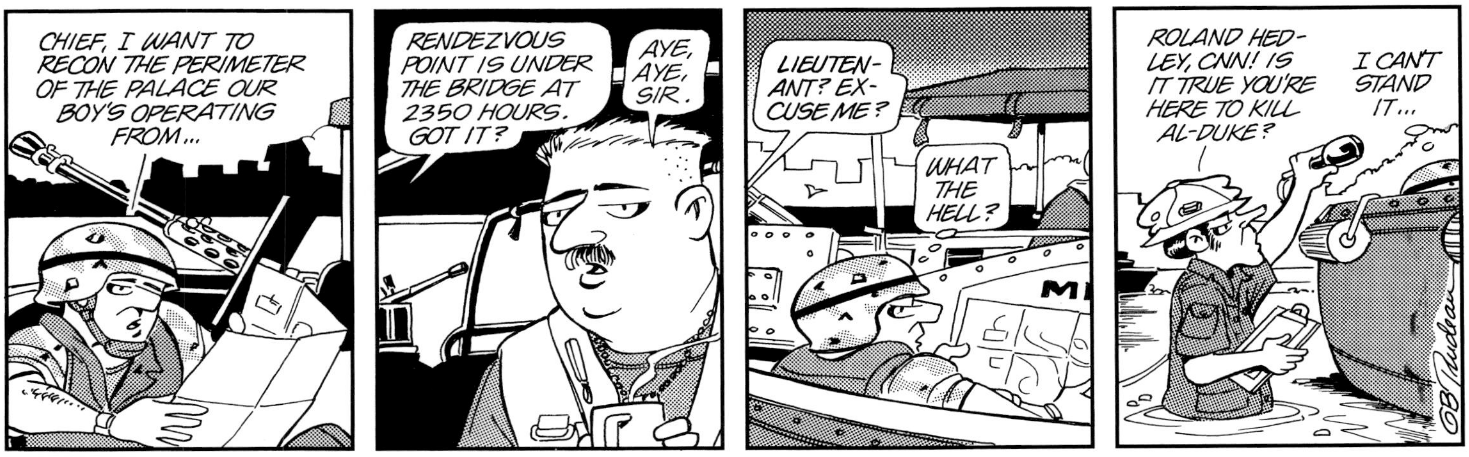
CHIEF, I WANT TO RECON THE PERIMETER OF THE PALACE OUR BOY'S OPERATING FROM...
RENDEZVOUS POINT IS UNDER THE BRIDGE AT 2350 HOURS. GOT IT?
AYE, AYE, SIR.
LIEUTENANT? EXCUSE ME?
WHAT THE HELL?
ROLAND HEDLEY, CNN! IS IT TRUE YOU'RE HERE TO KILL AL-DUKE?
I CAN'T STAND IT...

10/16/03

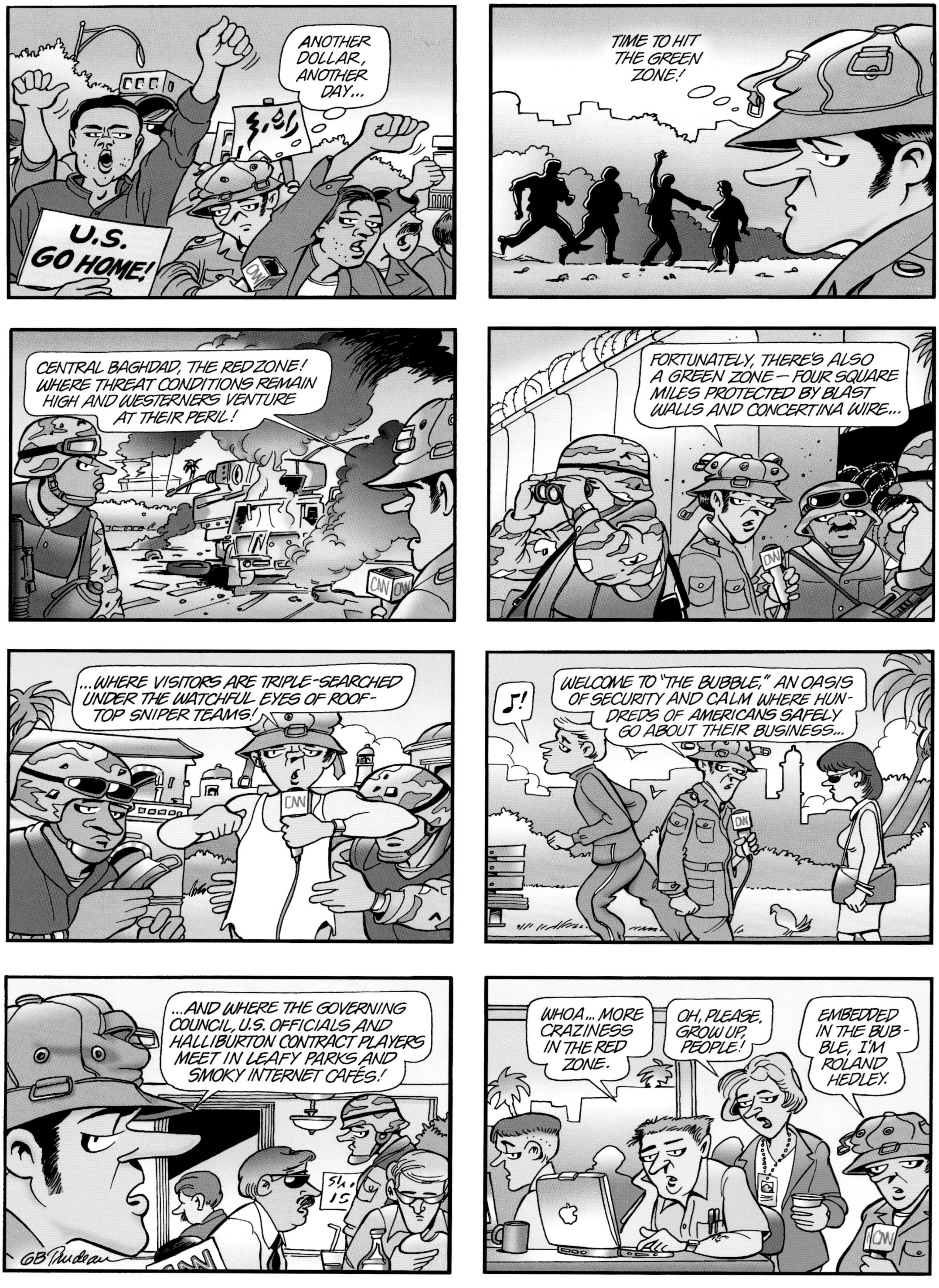
ANOTHER DOLLAR, ANOTHER DAY...
U.S. GO HOME!
TIME TO HIT THE GREEN ZONE!
CENTRAL BAGHDAD, THE RED ZONE! WHERE THREAT CONDITIONS REMAIN HIGH AND WESTERNERS VENTURE AT THEIR PERIL!
FORTUNATELY, THERE'S ALSO A GREEN ZONE — FOUR SQUARE MILES PROTECTED BY BLAST WALLS AND CONCERTINA WIRE...
...WHERE VISITORS ARE TRIPLE-SEARCHED UNDER THE WATCHFUL EYES OF ROOF-TOP SNIPER TEAMS!
♪!
WELCOME TO "THE BUBBLE," AN OASIS OF SECURITY AND CALM WHERE HUN-DREDS OF AMERICANS SAFELY GO ABOUT THEIR BUSINESS...
...AND WHERE THE GOVERNING COUNCIL, U.S. OFFICIALS AND HALLIBURTON CONTRACT PLAYERS MEET IN LEAFY PARKS AND SMOKY INTERNET CAFÉS!
WHOA... MORE CRAZINESS IN THE RED ZONE.
OH, PLEASE, GROW UP, PEOPLE!
EMBEDDED IN THE BUB-BLE, I'M ROLAND HEDLEY.
GB Trudeau

12/7/03

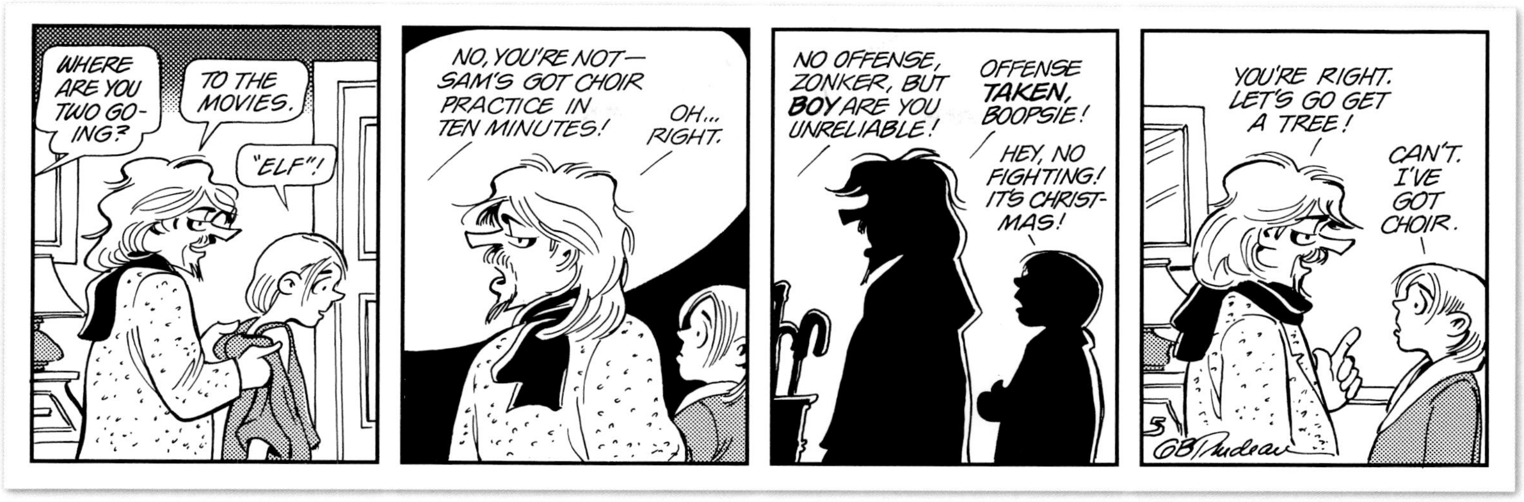
WHERE ARE YOU TWO GOING?
TO THE MOVIES.
"ELF"!
NO, YOU'RE NOT— SAM'S GOT CHOIR PRACTICE IN TEN MINUTES!
OH... RIGHT.
NO OFFENSE, ZONKER, BUT BOY ARE YOU UNRELIABLE!
OFFENSE TAKEN, BOOPSIE!
HEY, NO FIGHTING! IT'S CHRISTMAS!
YOU'RE RIGHT. LET'S GO GET A TREE!
CAN'T. I'VE GOT CHOIR.

12/17/03

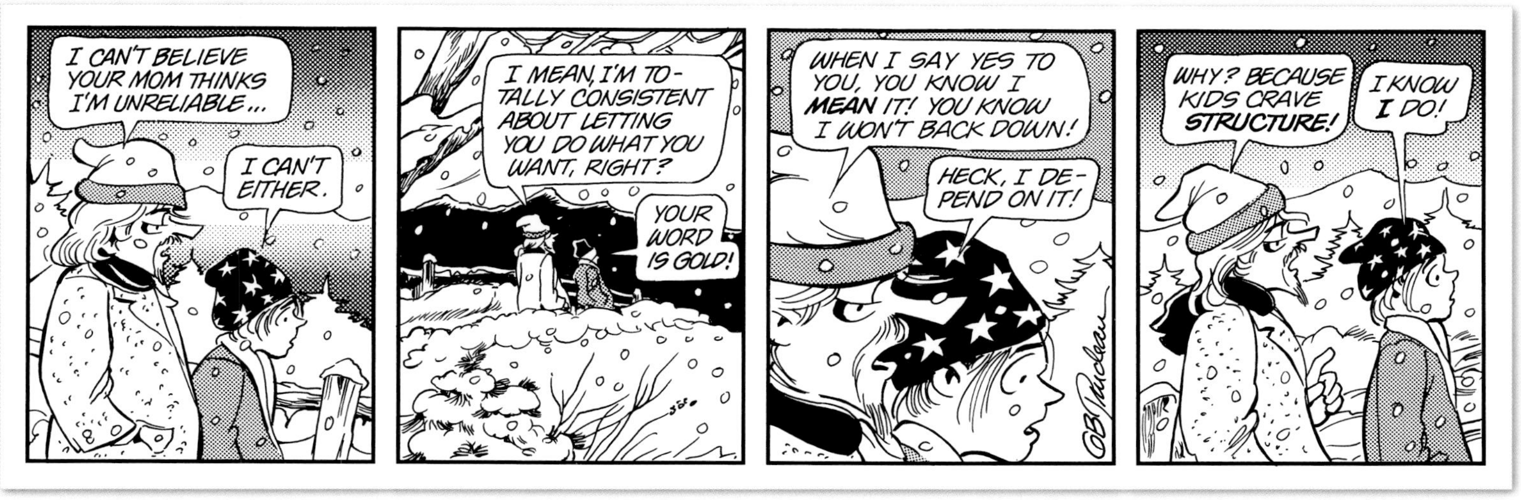
I CAN'T BELIEVE YOUR MOM THINKS I'M UNRELIABLE...
I CAN'T EITHER.
I MEAN, I'M TOTALLY CONSISTENT ABOUT LETTING YOU DO WHAT YOU WANT, RIGHT?
YOUR WORD IS GOLD!
WHEN I SAY YES TO YOU, YOU KNOW I MEAN IT! YOU KNOW I WON'T BACK DOWN!
HECK, I DEPEND ON IT!
WHY? BECAUSE KIDS CRAVE STRUCTURE!
I KNOW I DO!

12/18/03

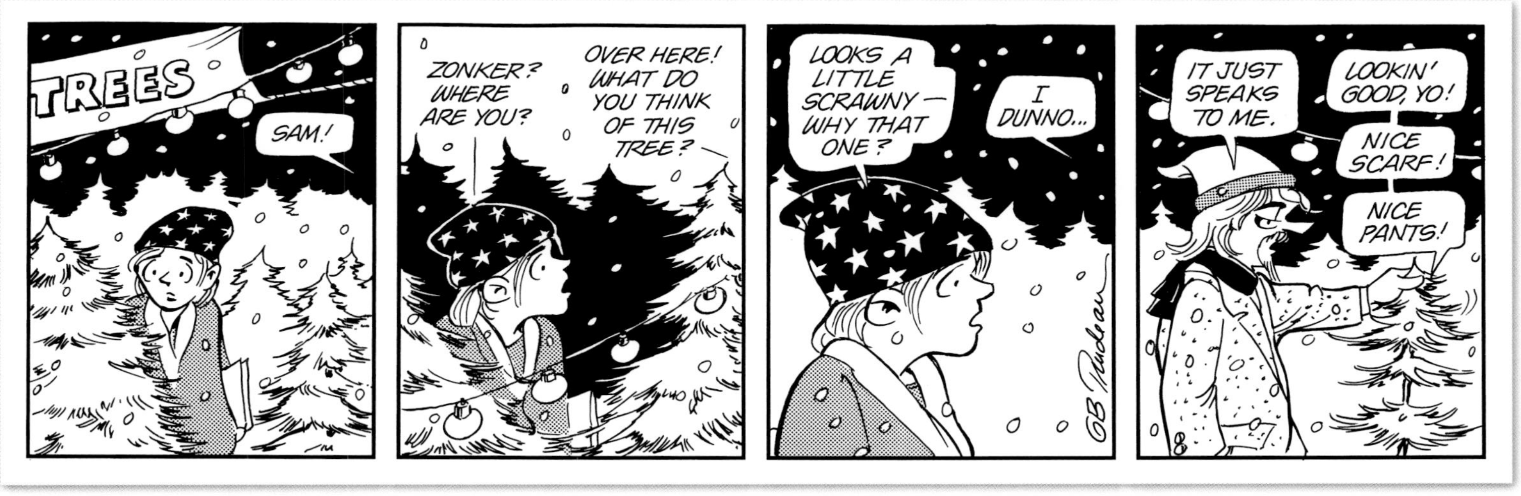
TREES
SAM!
ZONKER? WHERE ARE YOU?
OVER HERE! WHAT DO YOU THINK OF THIS TREE?
LOOKS A LITTLE SCRAWNY— WHY THAT ONE?
I DUNNO...
IT JUST SPEAKS TO ME.
LOOKIN' GOOD, YO!
NICE SCARF!
NICE PANTS!

12/20/03

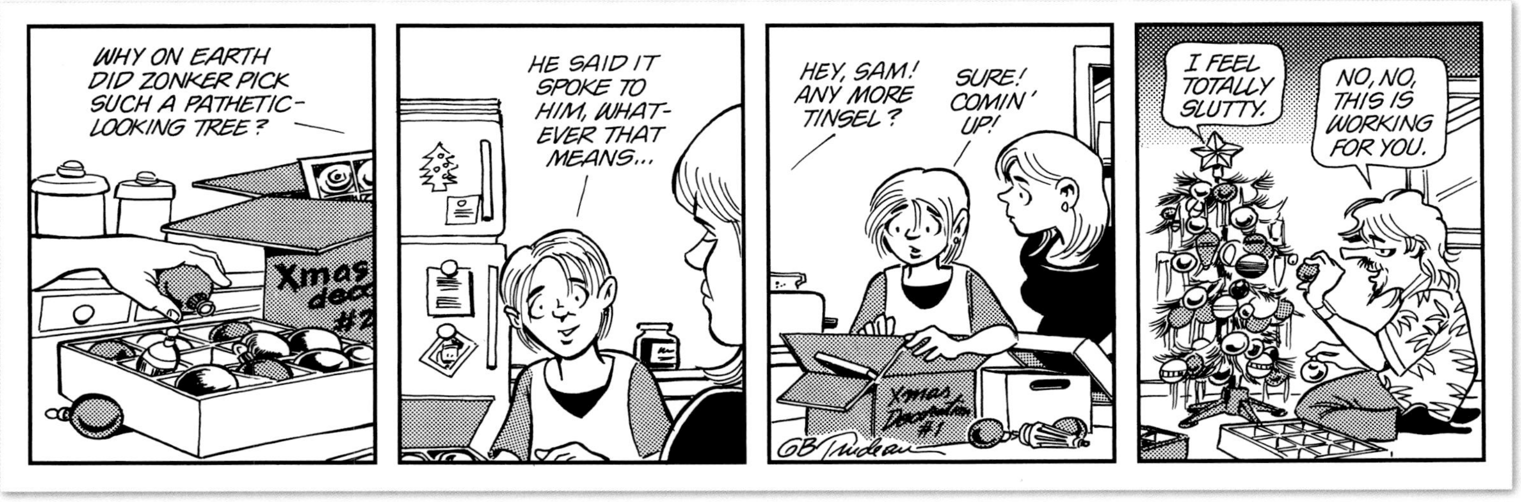
WHY ON EARTH DID ZONKER PICK SUCH A PATHETIC-LOOKING TREE?
HE SAID IT SPOKE TO HIM, WHATEVER THAT MEANS...
HEY, SAM! ANY MORE TINSEL?
SURE! COMIN' UP!
I FEEL TOTALLY SLUTTY.
NO, NO, THIS IS WORKING FOR YOU.

12/22/03

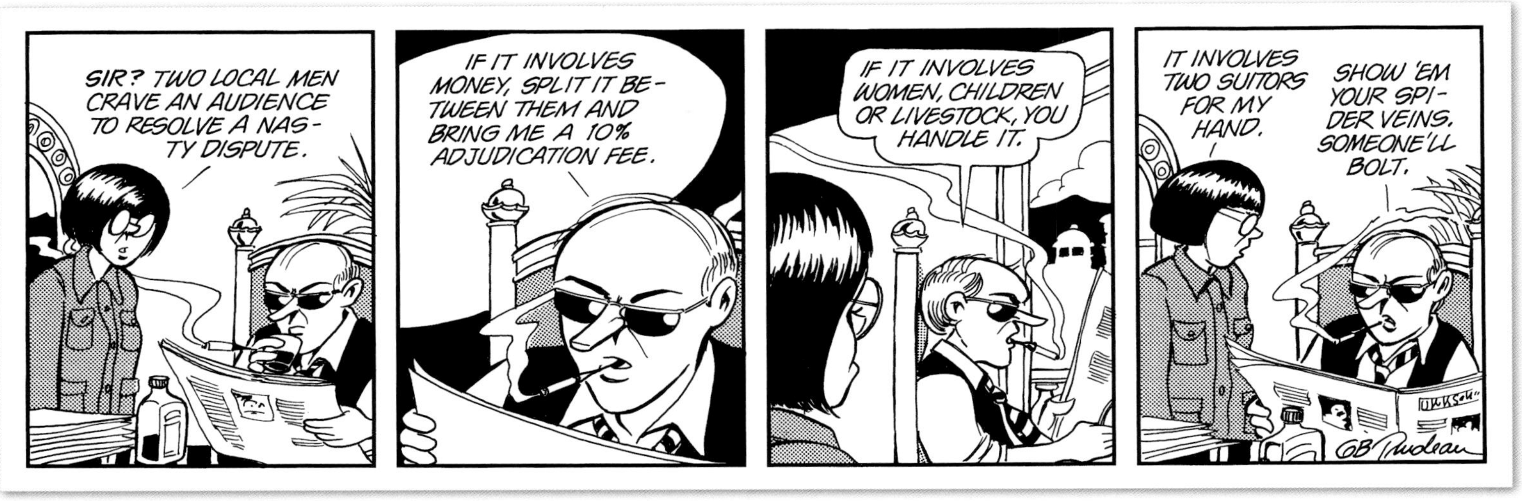
SIR? TWO LOCAL MEN CRAVE AN AUDIENCE TO RESOLVE A NASTY DISPUTE.
IF IT INVOLVES MONEY, SPLIT IT BETWEEN THEM AND BRING ME A 10% ADJUDICATION FEE.
IF IT INVOLVES WOMEN, CHILDREN OR LIVESTOCK, YOU HANDLE IT.
IT INVOLVES TWO SUITORS FOR MY HAND.
SHOW 'EM YOUR SPIDER VEINS. SOMEONE'LL BOLT.

1/19/04

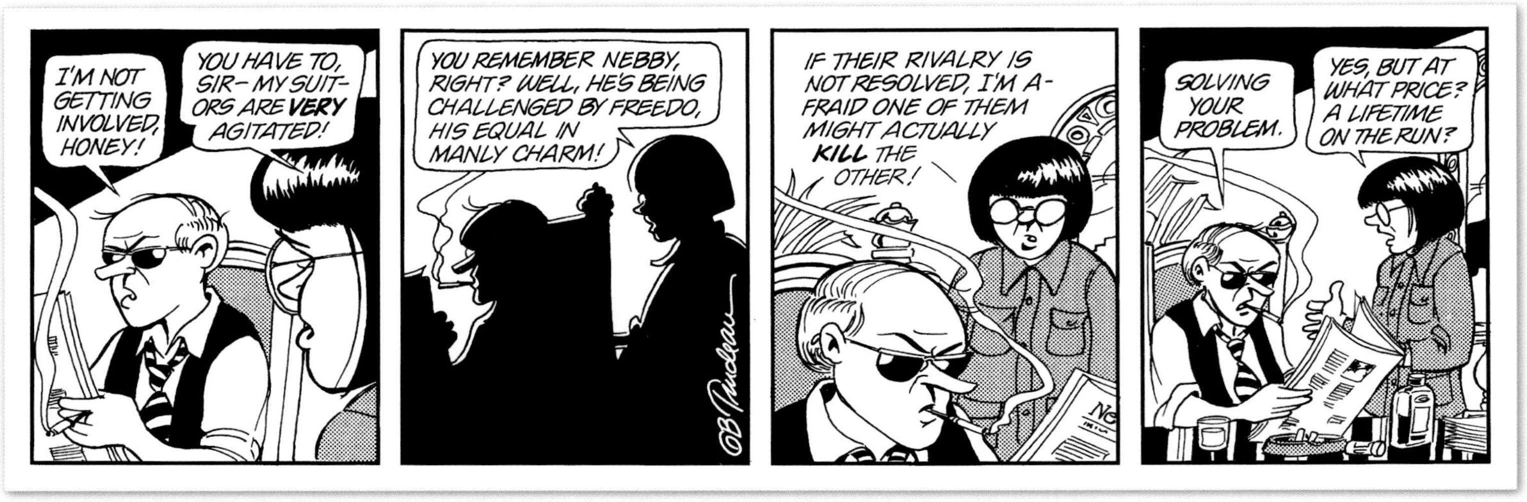
I'M NOT GETTING INVOLVED, HONEY!
YOU HAVE TO, SIR– MY SUITORS ARE **VERY** AGITATED!
YOU REMEMBER NEBBY, RIGHT? WELL, HE'S BEING CHALLENGED BY FREEDO, HIS EQUAL IN MANLY CHARM!
IF THEIR RIVALRY IS NOT RESOLVED, I'M AFRAID ONE OF THEM MIGHT ACTUALLY **KILL** THE OTHER!
SOLVING YOUR PROBLEM.
YES, BUT AT WHAT PRICE? A LIFETIME ON THE RUN?

1/20/04

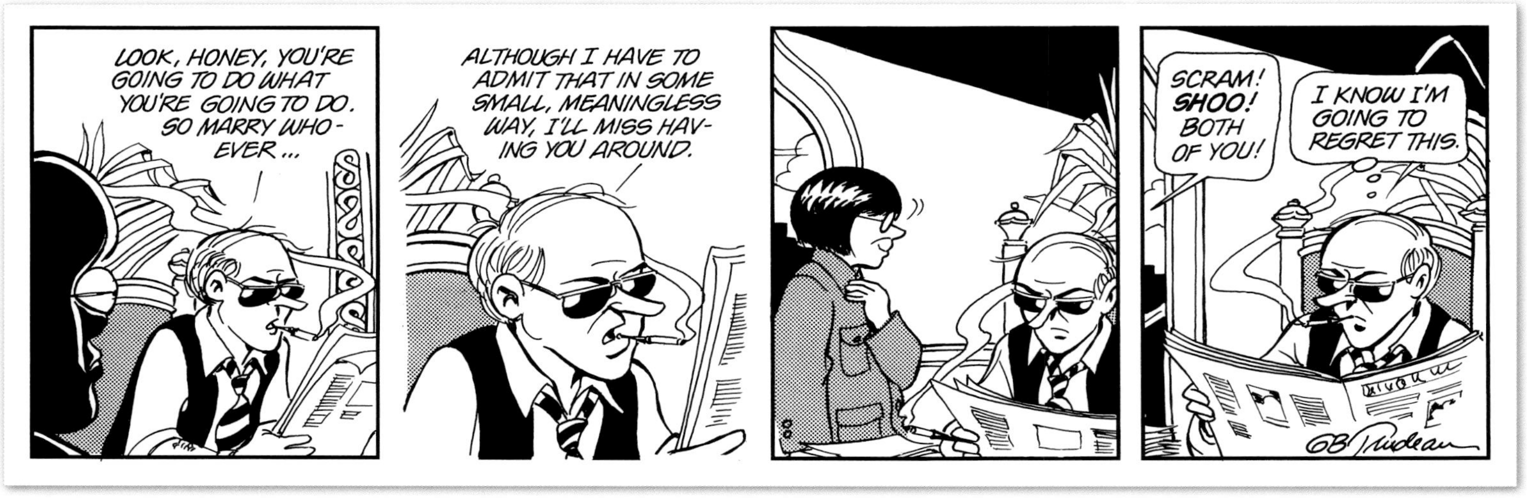
LOOK, HONEY, YOU'RE GOING TO DO WHAT YOU'RE GOING TO DO. SO MARRY WHOEVER...
ALTHOUGH I HAVE TO ADMIT THAT IN SOME SMALL, MEANINGLESS WAY, I'LL MISS HAVING YOU AROUND.
SCRAM! **SHOO!** BOTH OF YOU!
I KNOW I'M GOING TO REGRET THIS.

1/22/04

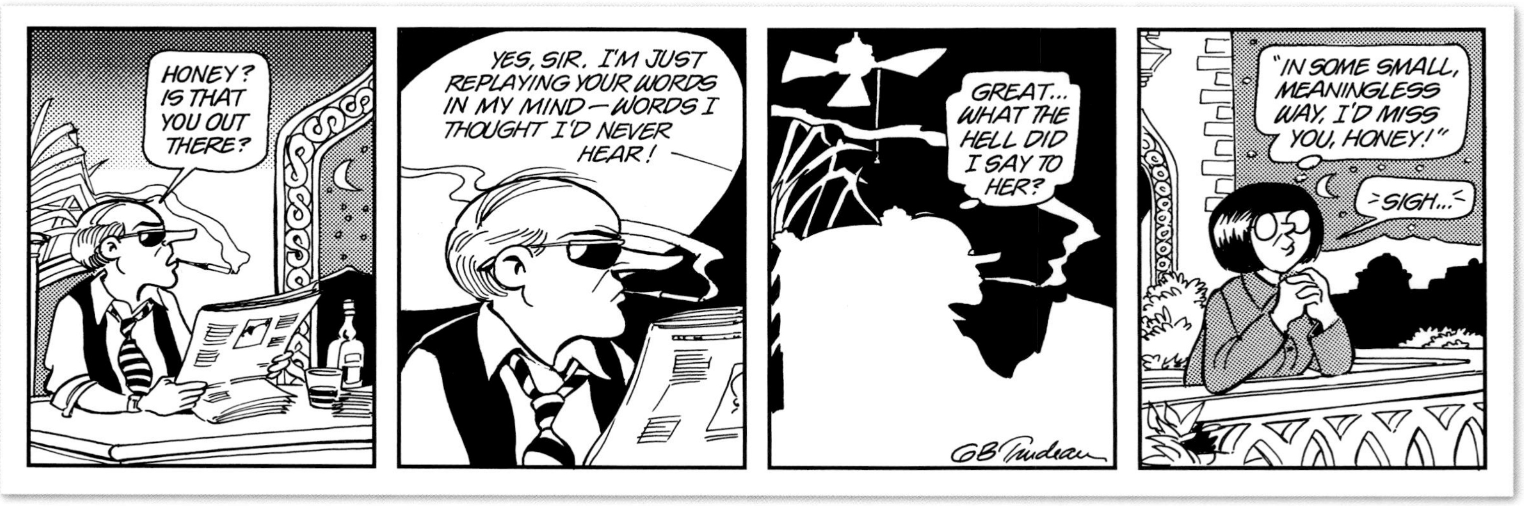
HONEY? IS THAT YOU OUT THERE?
YES, SIR. I'M JUST REPLAYING YOUR WORDS IN MY MIND—WORDS I THOUGHT I'D NEVER HEAR!
GREAT... WHAT THE HELL DID I SAY TO HER?
"IN SOME SMALL, MEANINGLESS WAY, I'D MISS YOU, HONEY!"
SIGH...

1/23/04

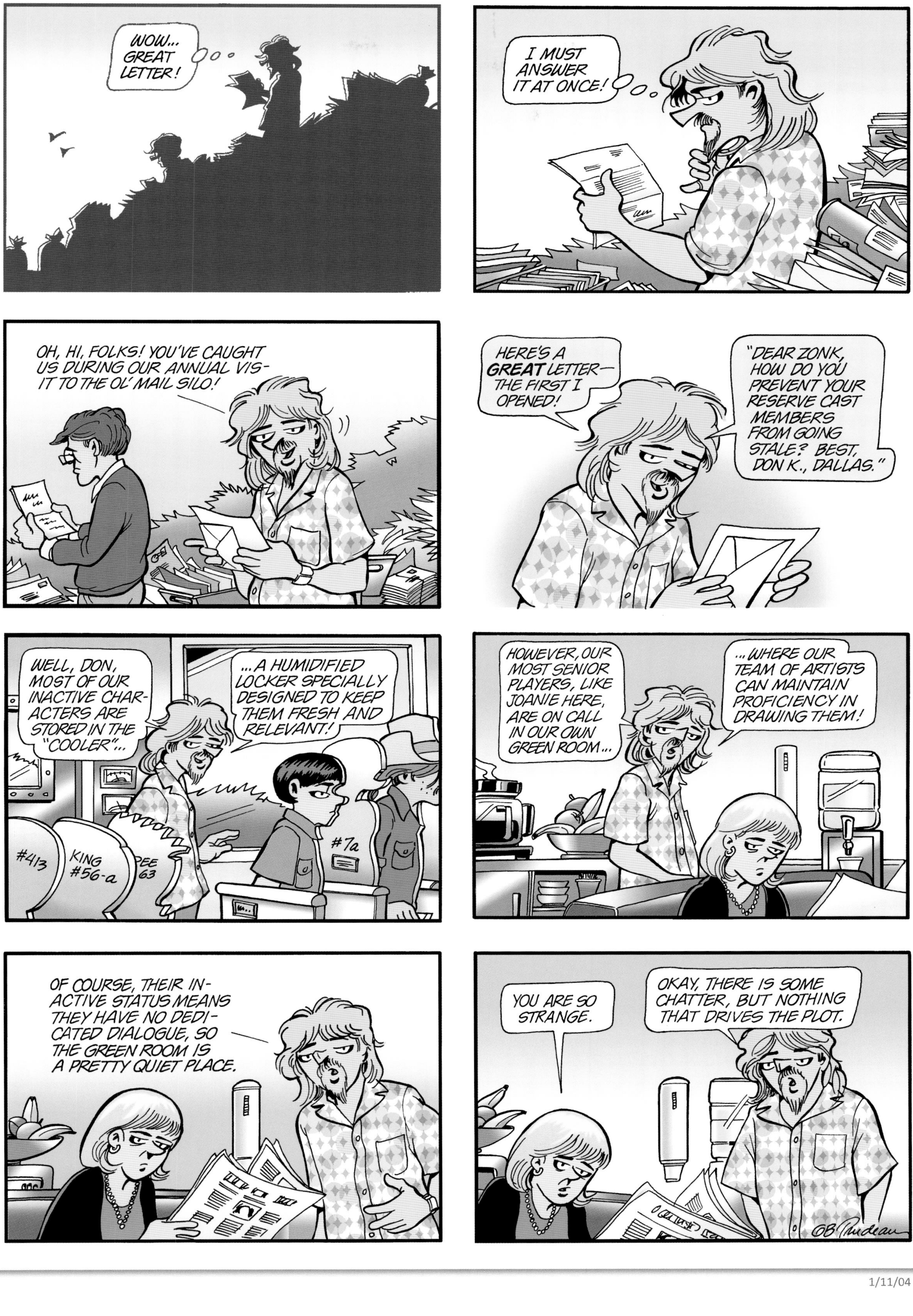
WOW... GREAT LETTER!
I MUST ANSWER IT AT ONCE!
OH, HI, FOLKS! YOU'VE CAUGHT US DURING OUR ANNUAL VISIT TO THE OL' MAIL SILO!
HERE'S A GREAT LETTER— THE FIRST I OPENED!
"DEAR ZONK, HOW DO YOU PREVENT YOUR RESERVE CAST MEMBERS FROM GOING STALE? BEST, DON K., DALLAS."
WELL, DON, MOST OF OUR INACTIVE CHARACTERS ARE STORED IN THE "COOLER"...
...A HUMIDIFIED LOCKER SPECIALLY DESIGNED TO KEEP THEM FRESH AND RELEVANT!
#413
KING #56-a
#7a
HOWEVER, OUR MOST SENIOR PLAYERS, LIKE JOANIE HERE, ARE ON CALL IN OUR OWN GREEN ROOM...
...WHERE OUR TEAM OF ARTISTS CAN MAINTAIN PROFICIENCY IN DRAWING THEM!
OF COURSE, THEIR INACTIVE STATUS MEANS THEY HAVE NO DEDICATED DIALOGUE, SO THE GREEN ROOM IS A PRETTY QUIET PLACE.
YOU ARE SO STRANGE.
OKAY, THERE IS SOME CHATTER, BUT NOTHING THAT DRIVES THE PLOT.
GB Trudeau

1/11/04

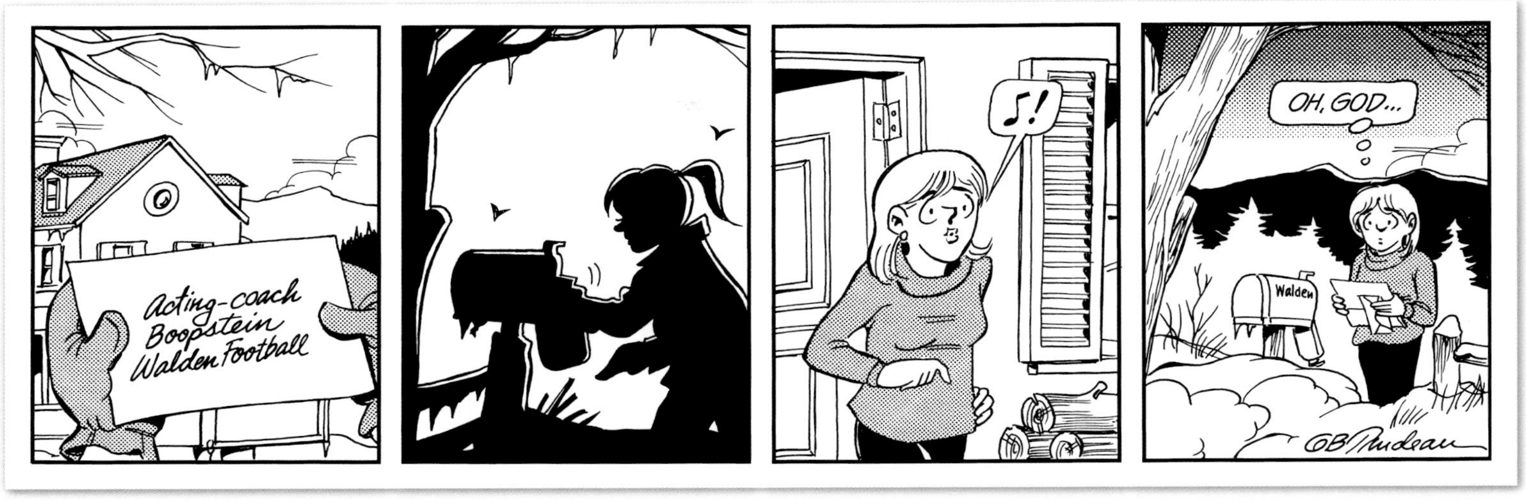

Acting-coach Boopstein Walden Football
♪!
OH, GOD...
Walden

3/1/04

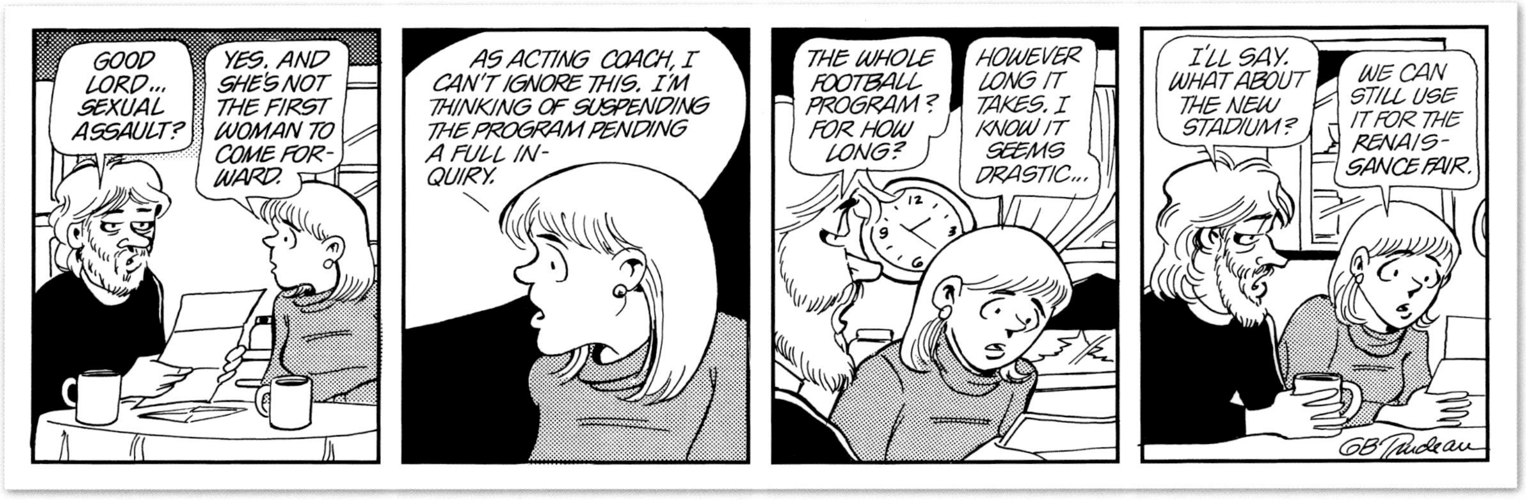

GOOD LORD... SEXUAL ASSAULT?
YES. AND SHE'S NOT THE FIRST WOMAN TO COME FORWARD.
AS ACTING COACH, I CAN'T IGNORE THIS. I'M THINKING OF SUSPENDING THE PROGRAM PENDING A FULL INQUIRY.
THE WHOLE FOOTBALL PROGRAM? FOR HOW LONG?
HOWEVER LONG IT TAKES. I KNOW IT SEEMS DRASTIC...
I'LL SAY. WHAT ABOUT THE NEW STADIUM?
WE CAN STILL USE IT FOR THE RENAISSANCE FAIR.

3/2/04

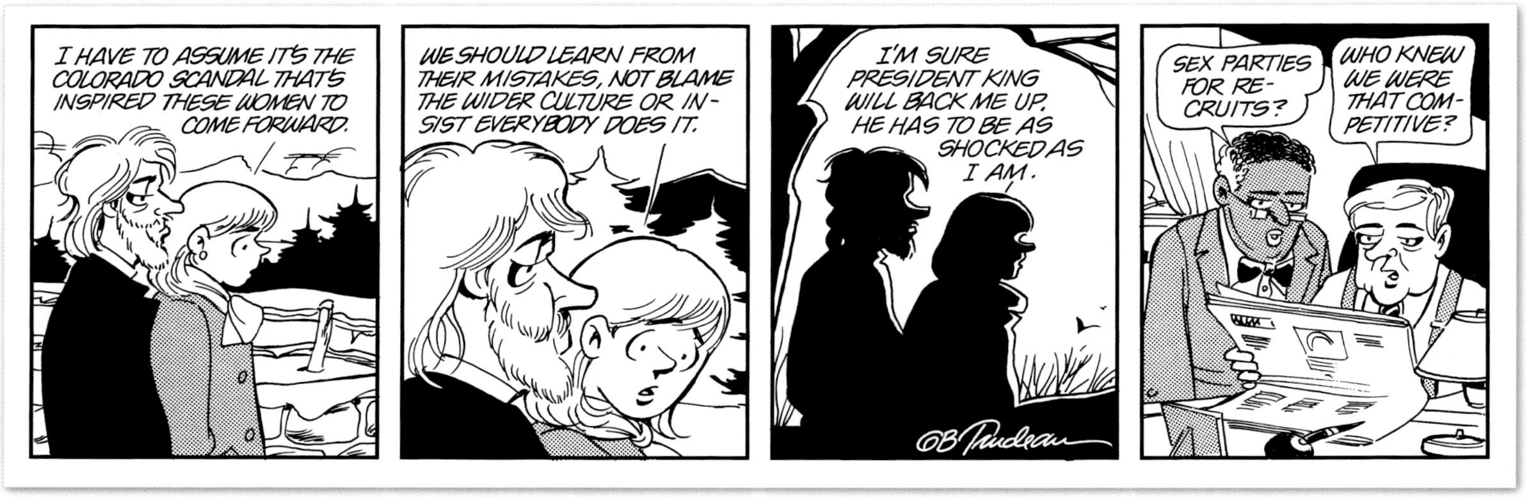

I HAVE TO ASSUME IT'S THE COLORADO SCANDAL THAT'S INSPIRED THESE WOMEN TO COME FORWARD.
WE SHOULD LEARN FROM THEIR MISTAKES, NOT BLAME THE WIDER CULTURE OR INSIST EVERYBODY DOES IT.
I'M SURE PRESIDENT KING WILL BACK ME UP. HE HAS TO BE AS SHOCKED AS I AM.
SEX PARTIES FOR RECRUITS?
WHO KNEW WE WERE THAT COMPETITIVE?

3/6/04

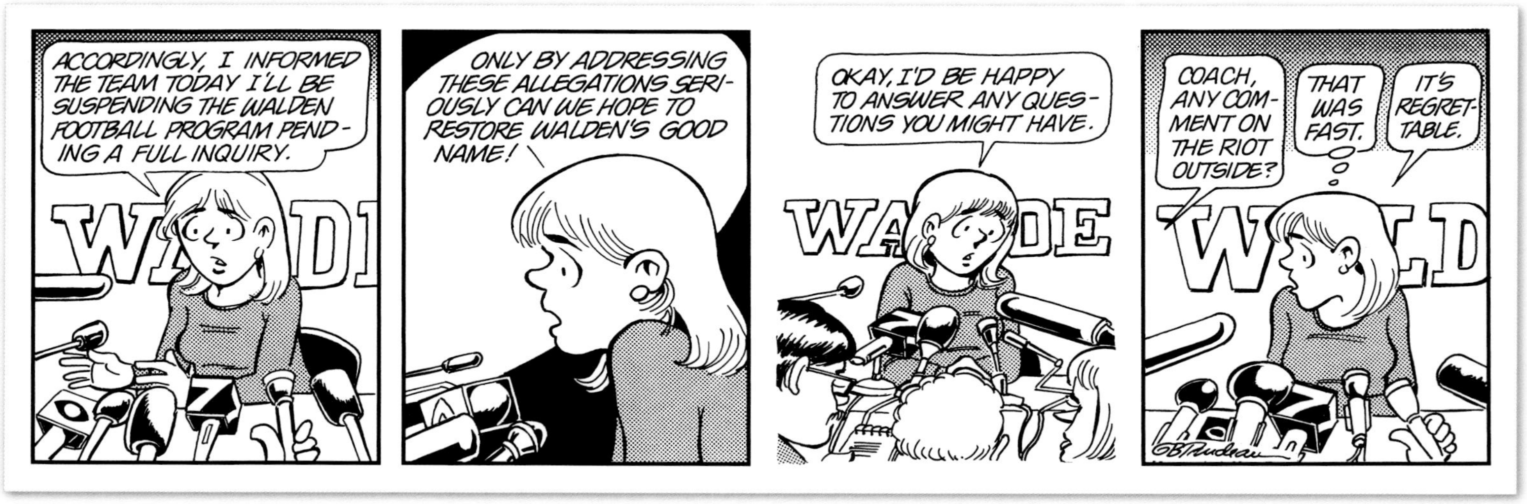

ACCORDINGLY, I INFORMED THE TEAM TODAY I'LL BE SUSPENDING THE WALDEN FOOTBALL PROGRAM PENDING A FULL INQUIRY.
ONLY BY ADDRESSING THESE ALLEGATIONS SERIOUSLY CAN WE HOPE TO RESTORE WALDEN'S GOOD NAME!
OKAY, I'D BE HAPPY TO ANSWER ANY QUESTIONS YOU MIGHT HAVE.
COACH, ANY COMMENT ON THE RIOT OUTSIDE?
THAT WAS FAST.
IT'S REGRETTABLE.

3/8/04

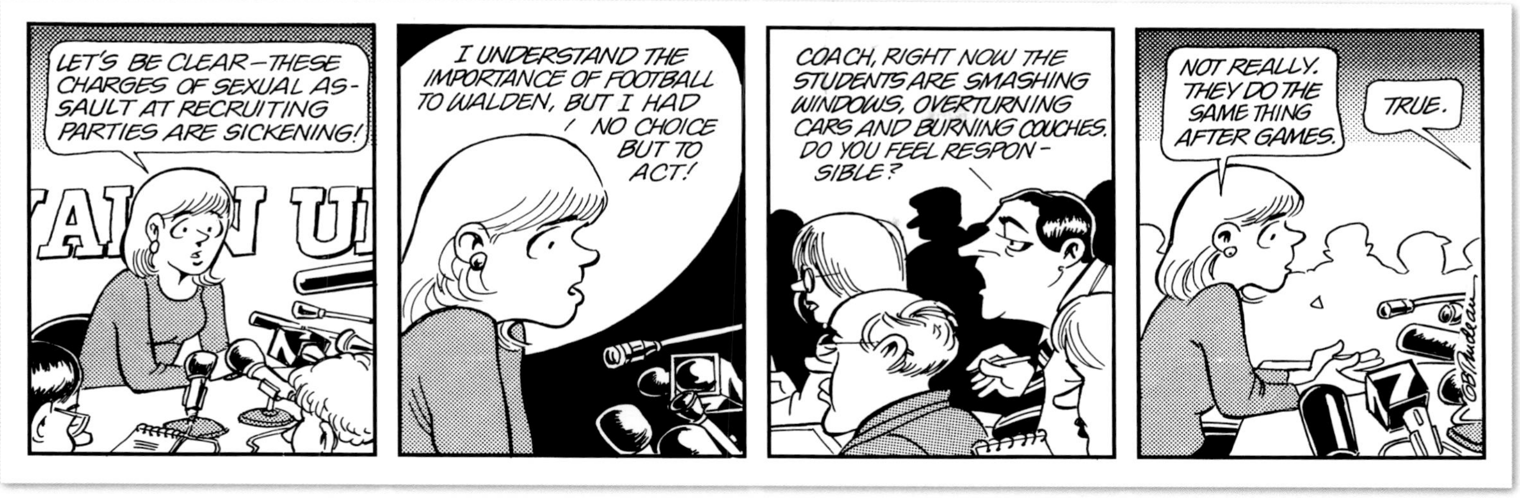
LET'S BE CLEAR—THESE CHARGES OF SEXUAL ASSAULT AT RECRUITING PARTIES ARE SICKENING!
I UNDERSTAND THE IMPORTANCE OF FOOTBALL TO WALDEN, BUT I HAD NO CHOICE BUT TO ACT!
COACH, RIGHT NOW THE STUDENTS ARE SMASHING WINDOWS, OVERTURNING CARS AND BURNING COUCHES. DO YOU FEEL RESPONSIBLE?
NOT REALLY. THEY DO THE SAME THING AFTER GAMES.
TRUE.

3/9/04

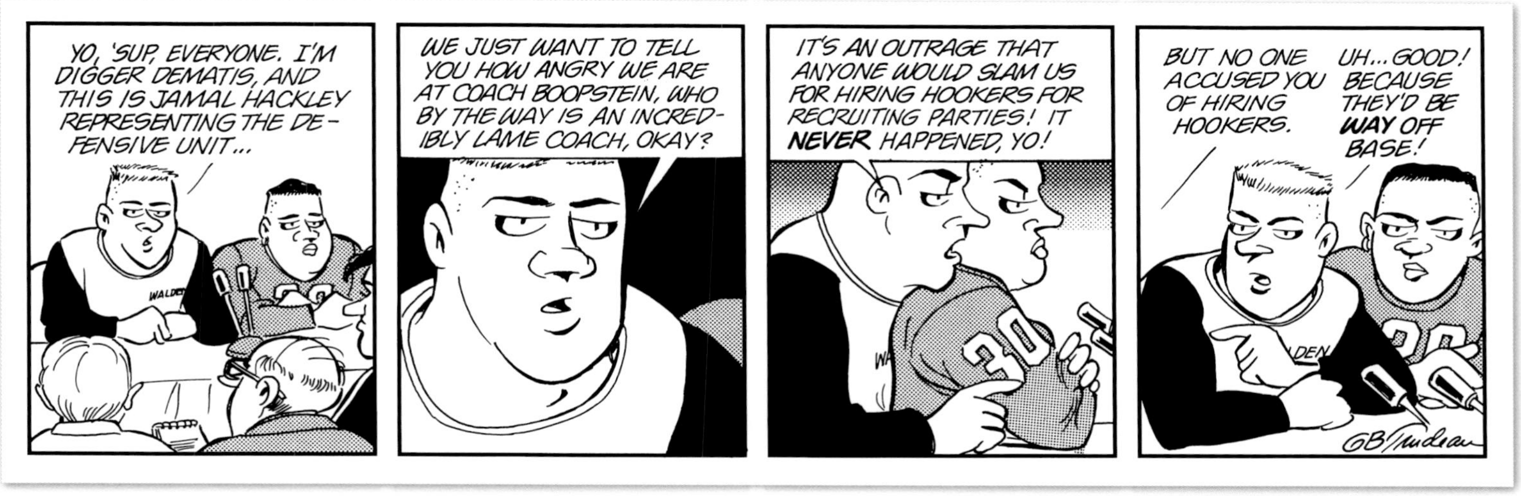
YO, 'SUP, EVERYONE. I'M DIGGER DEMATIS, AND THIS IS JAMAL HACKLEY REPRESENTING THE DEFENSIVE UNIT...
WE JUST WANT TO TELL YOU HOW ANGRY WE ARE AT COACH BOOPSTEIN, WHO BY THE WAY IS AN INCREDIBLY LAME COACH, OKAY?
IT'S AN OUTRAGE THAT ANYONE WOULD SLAM US FOR HIRING HOOKERS FOR RECRUITING PARTIES! IT NEVER HAPPENED, YO!
BUT NO ONE ACCUSED YOU OF HIRING HOOKERS.
UH... GOOD! BECAUSE THEY'D BE WAY OFF BASE!

3/11/04

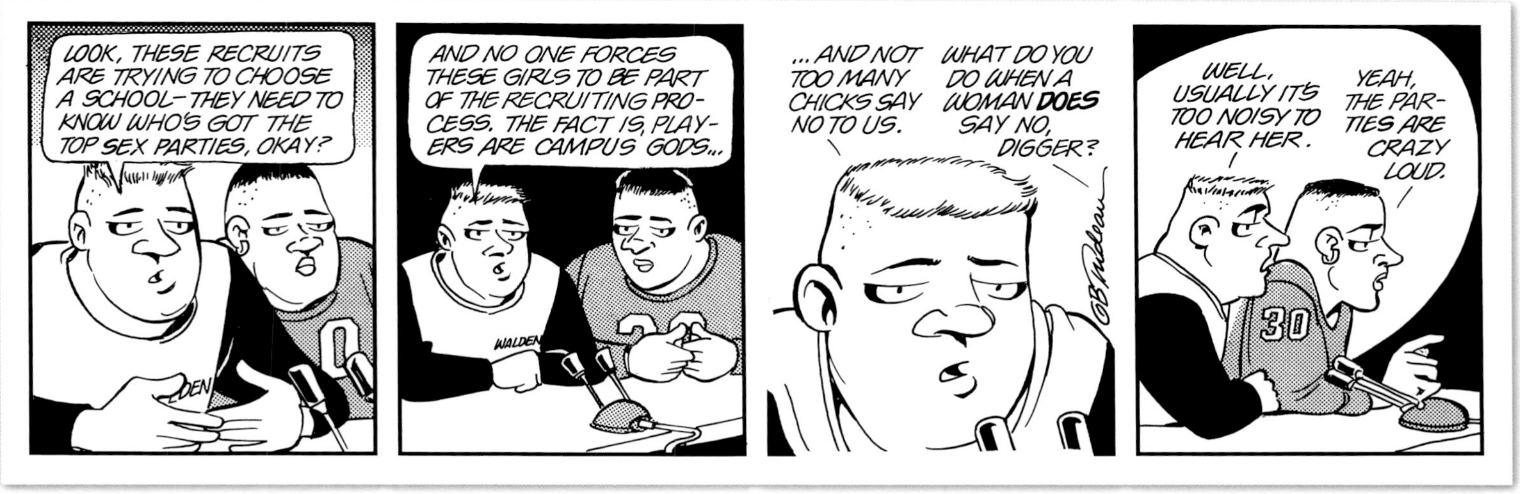
LOOK, THESE RECRUITS ARE TRYING TO CHOOSE A SCHOOL—THEY NEED TO KNOW WHO'S GOT THE TOP SEX PARTIES, OKAY?
AND NO ONE FORCES THESE GIRLS TO BE PART OF THE RECRUITING PROCESS. THE FACT IS, PLAYERS ARE CAMPUS GODS...
...AND NOT TOO MANY CHICKS SAY NO TO US.
WHAT DO YOU DO WHEN A WOMAN DOES SAY NO, DIGGER?
WELL, USUALLY IT'S TOO NOISY TO HEAR HER.
YEAH, THE PARTIES ARE CRAZY LOUD.

3/12/04

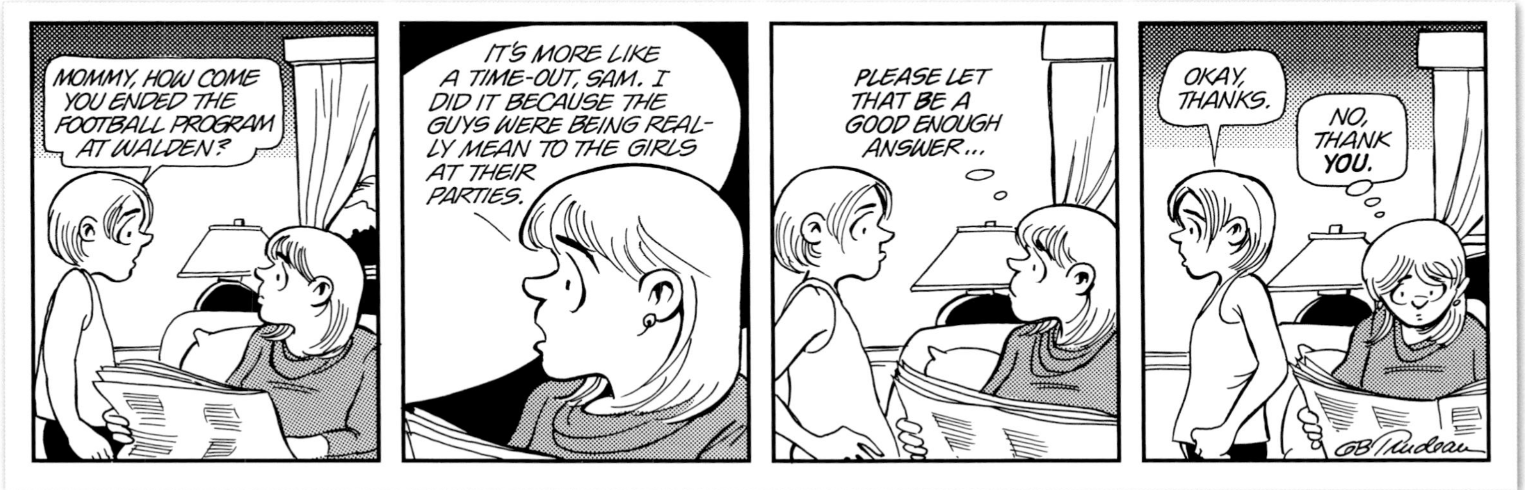
MOMMY, HOW COME YOU ENDED THE FOOTBALL PROGRAM AT WALDEN?
IT'S MORE LIKE A TIME-OUT, SAM. I DID IT BECAUSE THE GUYS WERE BEING REALLY MEAN TO THE GIRLS AT THEIR PARTIES.
PLEASE LET THAT BE A GOOD ENOUGH ANSWER...
OKAY, THANKS.
NO, THANK YOU.

3/23/04

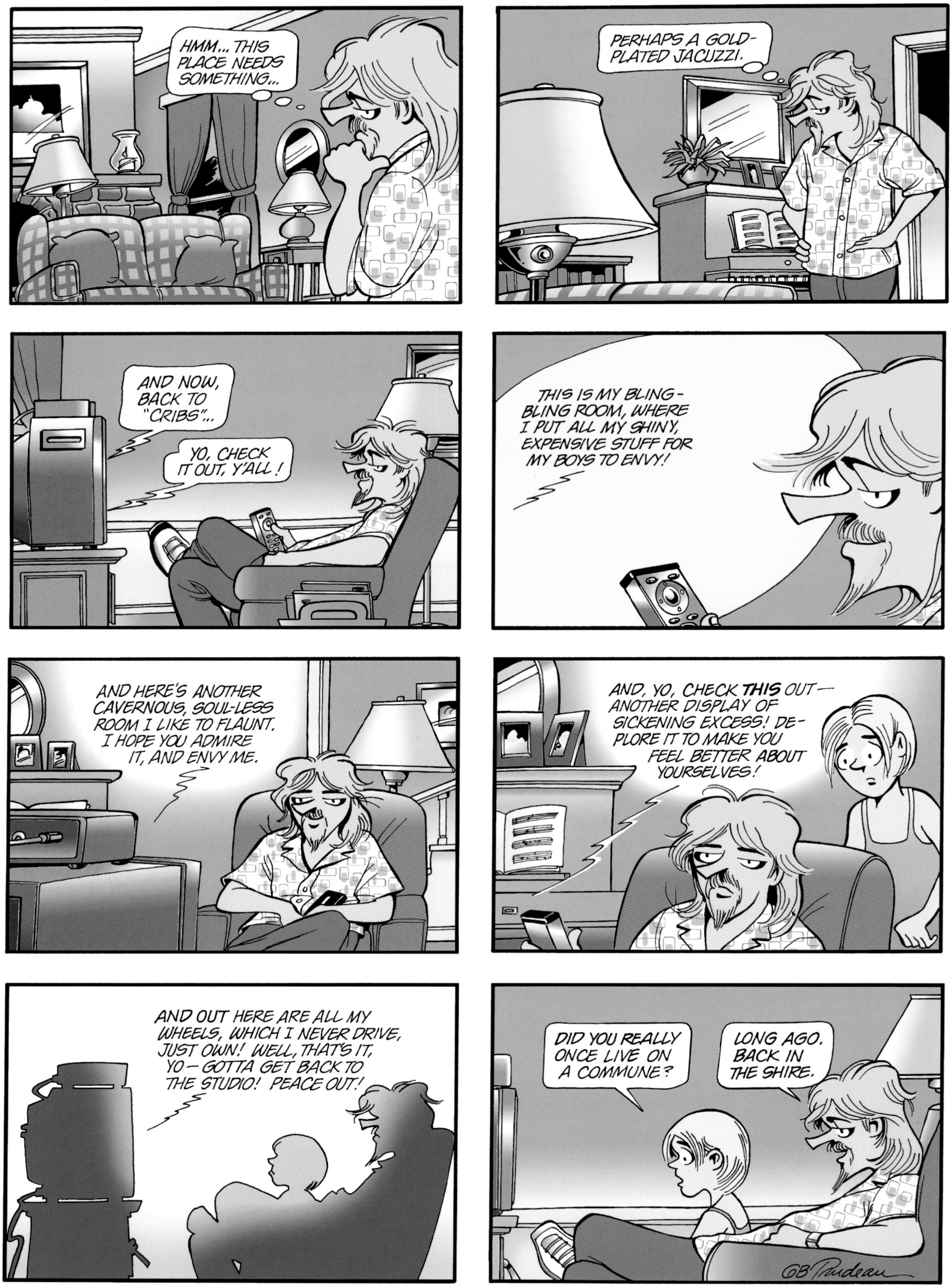
HMM... THIS PLACE NEEDS SOMETHING...
PERHAPS A GOLD-PLATED JACUZZI.
AND NOW, BACK TO "CRIBS"...
YO, CHECK IT OUT, Y'ALL!
THIS IS MY BLING-BLING ROOM, WHERE I PUT ALL MY SHINY, EXPENSIVE STUFF FOR MY BOYS TO ENVY!
AND HERE'S ANOTHER CAVERNOUS, SOUL-LESS ROOM I LIKE TO FLAUNT. I HOPE YOU ADMIRE IT, AND ENVY ME.
AND, YO, CHECK THIS OUT— ANOTHER DISPLAY OF SICKENING EXCESS! DEPLORE IT TO MAKE YOU FEEL BETTER ABOUT YOURSELVES!
AND OUT HERE ARE ALL MY WHEELS, WHICH I NEVER DRIVE, JUST OWN! WELL, THAT'S IT, YO— GOTTA GET BACK TO THE STUDIO! PEACE OUT!
DID YOU REALLY ONCE LIVE ON A COMMUNE?
LONG AGO. BACK IN THE SHIRE.
GB Trudeau

2/15/04

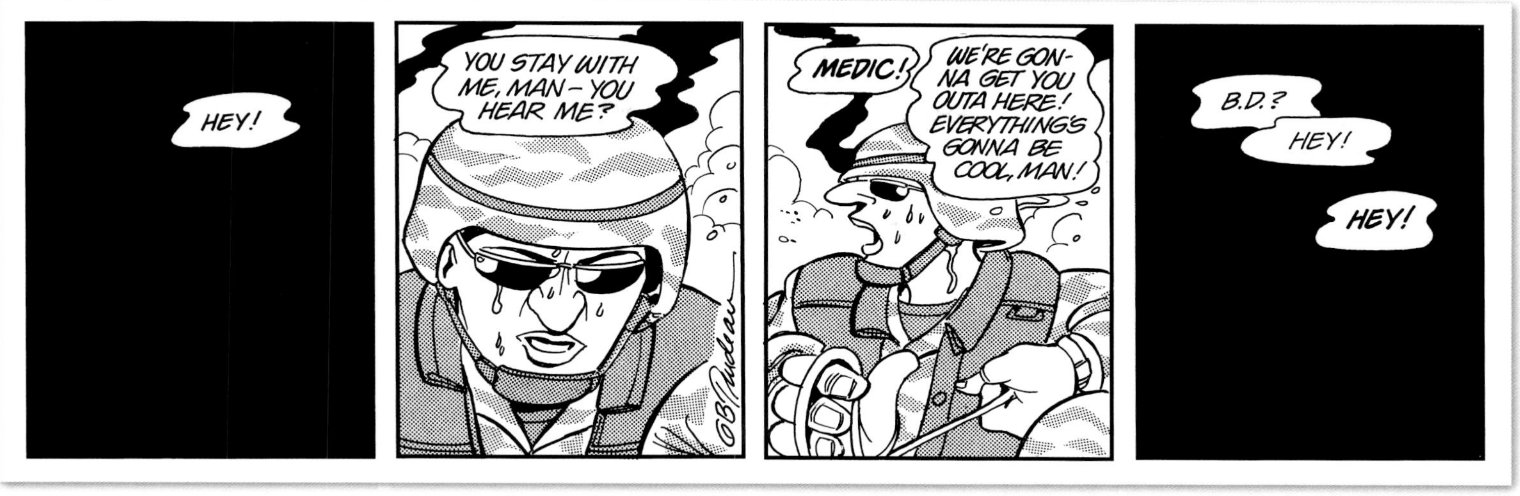
HEY!
YOU STAY WITH ME, MAN – YOU HEAR ME?
MEDIC!
WE'RE GONNA GET YOU OUTA HERE! EVERYTHING'S GONNA BE COOL, MAN!
B.D.?
HEY!
HEY!

4/19/04

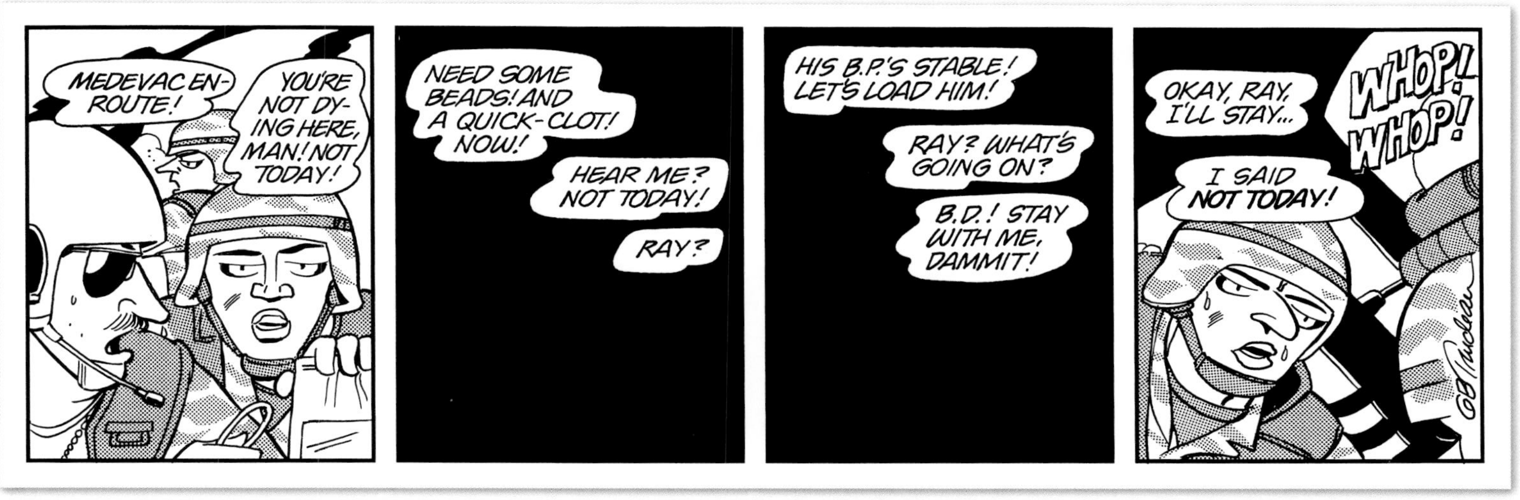
MEDEVAC EN-ROUTE!
YOU'RE NOT DYING HERE, MAN! NOT TODAY!
NEED SOME BEADS! AND A QUICK-CLOT! NOW!
HEAR ME? NOT TODAY!
RAY?
HIS B.P.'S STABLE! LET'S LOAD HIM!
RAY? WHAT'S GOING ON?
B.D.! STAY WITH ME, DAMMIT!
OKAY, RAY. I'LL STAY...
WHOP! WHOP!
I SAID NOT TODAY!

4/20/04

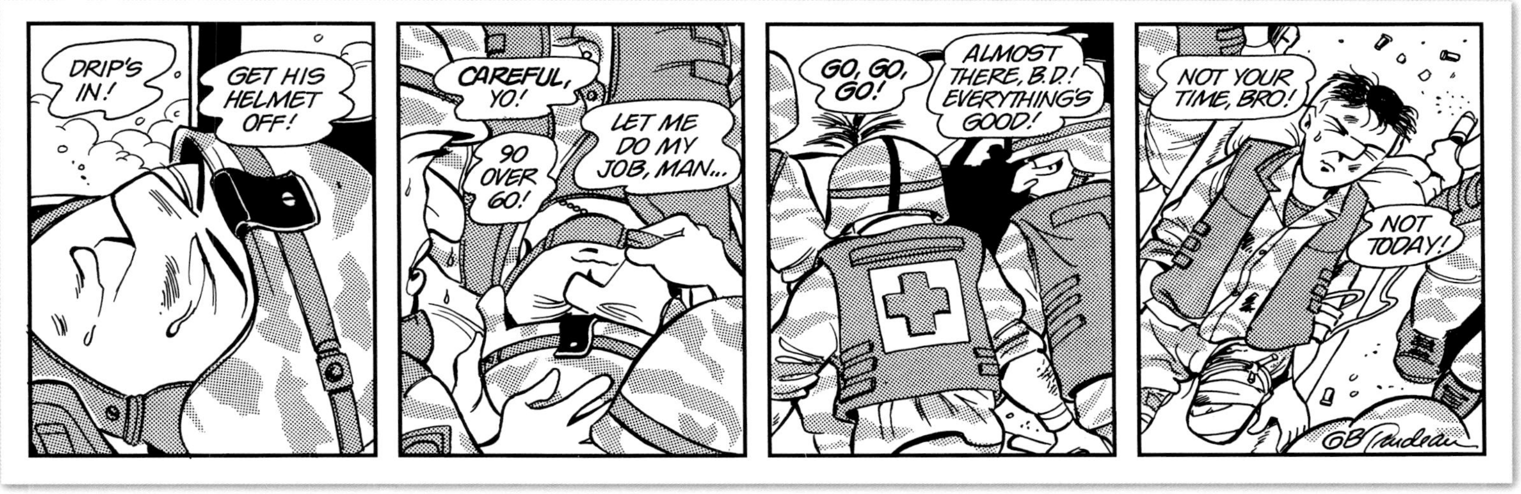
DRIP'S IN!
GET HIS HELMET OFF!
CAREFUL, YO!
LET ME DO MY JOB, MAN...
90 OVER 60!
GO, GO, GO!
ALMOST THERE, B.D.! EVERYTHING'S GOOD!
NOT YOUR TIME, BRO!
NOT TODAY!

4/21/04

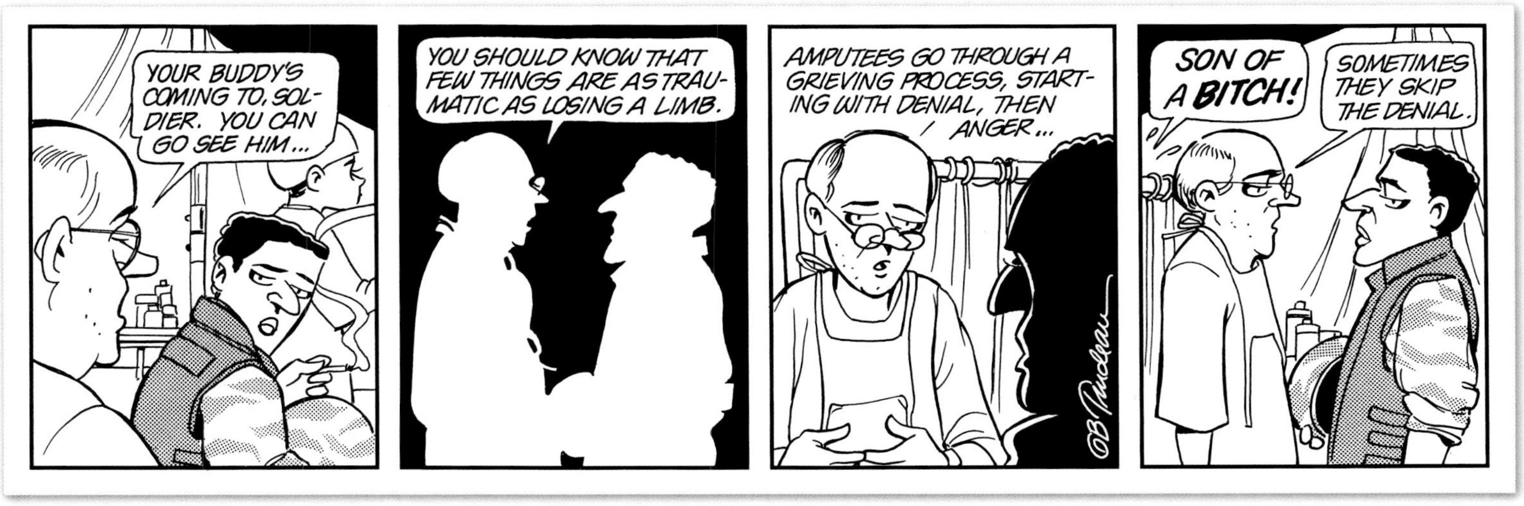
YOUR BUDDY'S COMING TO, SOLDIER. YOU CAN GO SEE HIM...
YOU SHOULD KNOW THAT FEW THINGS ARE AS TRAUMATIC AS LOSING A LIMB.
AMPUTEES GO THROUGH A GRIEVING PROCESS, STARTING WITH DENIAL, THEN ANGER...
SON OF A BITCH!
SOMETIMES THEY SKIP THE DENIAL.

4/23/04

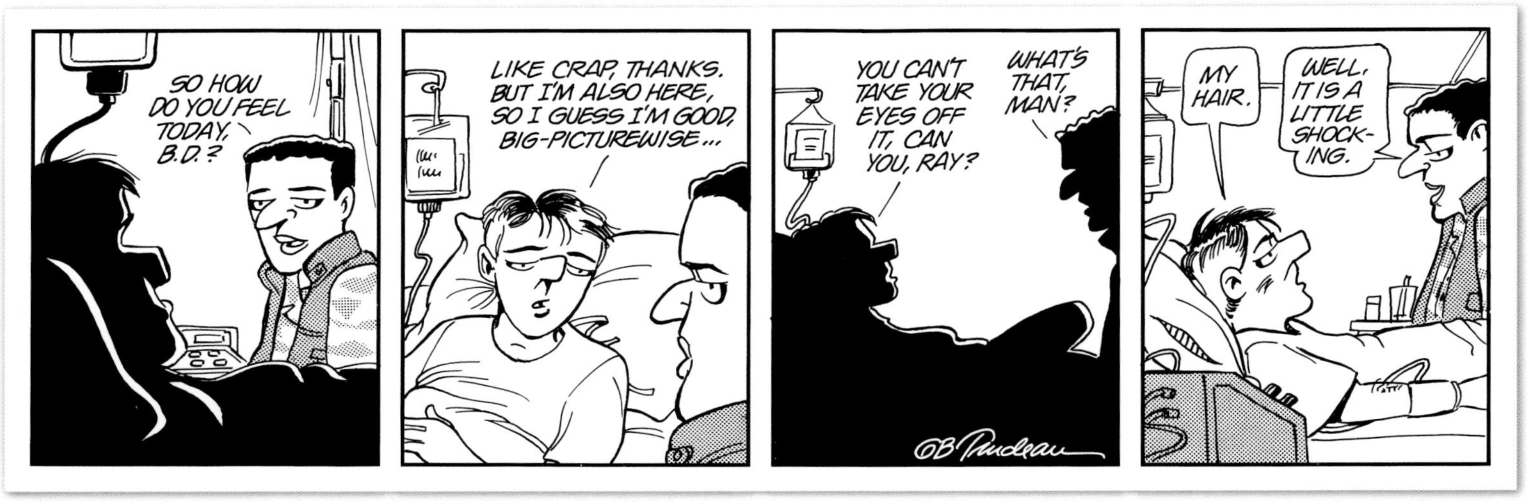
SO HOW DO YOU FEEL TODAY, B.D.?
LIKE CRAP, THANKS. BUT I'M ALSO HERE, SO I GUESS I'M GOOD, BIG-PICTUREWISE...
YOU CAN'T TAKE YOUR EYES OFF IT, CAN YOU, RAY?
WHAT'S THAT, MAN?
MY HAIR.
WELL, IT IS A LITTLE SHOCKING.
©B Trudeau

4/26/04

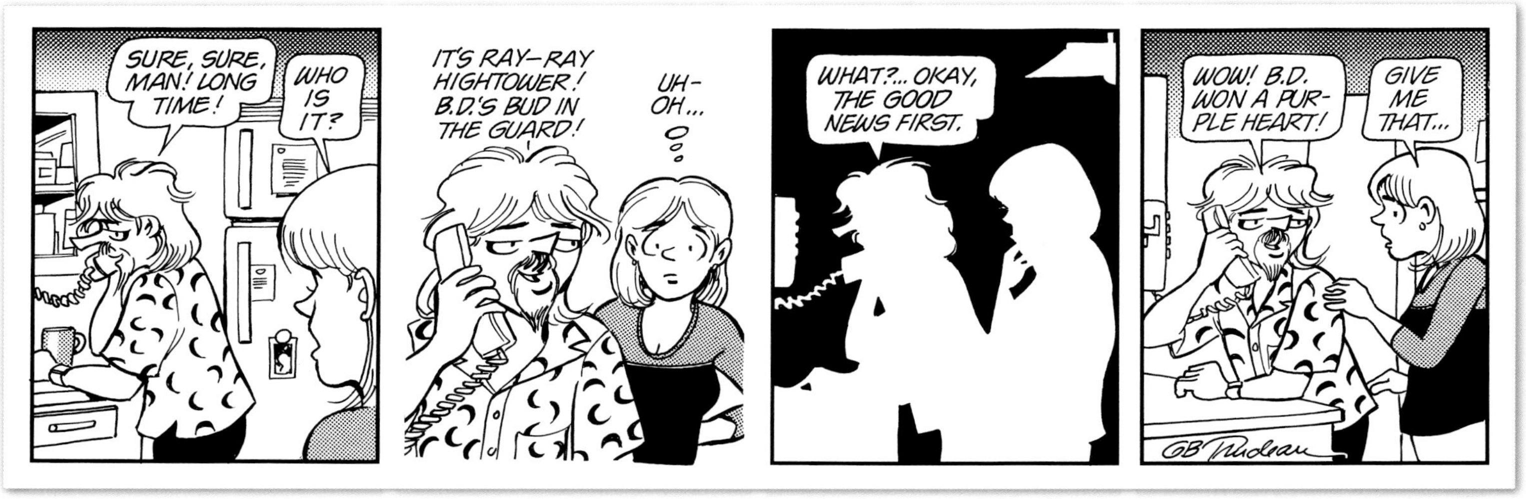
SURE, SURE, MAN! LONG TIME!
WHO IS IT?
IT'S RAY—RAY HIGHTOWER! B.D.'S BUD IN THE GUARD!
UH-OH...
WHAT?... OKAY, THE GOOD NEWS FIRST.
WOW! B.D. WON A PURPLE HEART!
GIVE ME THAT...
©B Trudeau

4/28/04

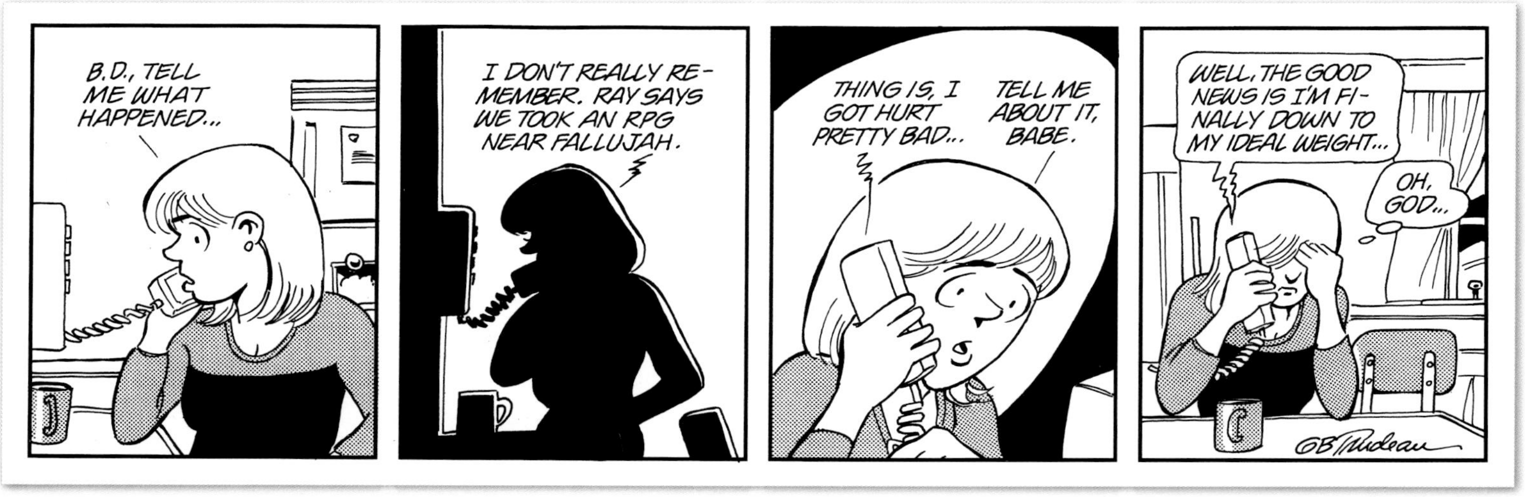
B.D., TELL ME WHAT HAPPENED...
I DON'T REALLY REMEMBER. RAY SAYS WE TOOK AN RPG NEAR FALLUJAH.
THING IS, I GOT HURT PRETTY BAD...
TELL ME ABOUT IT, BABE.
WELL, THE GOOD NEWS IS I'M FINALLY DOWN TO MY IDEAL WEIGHT...
OH, GOD...
©B Trudeau

4/29/04

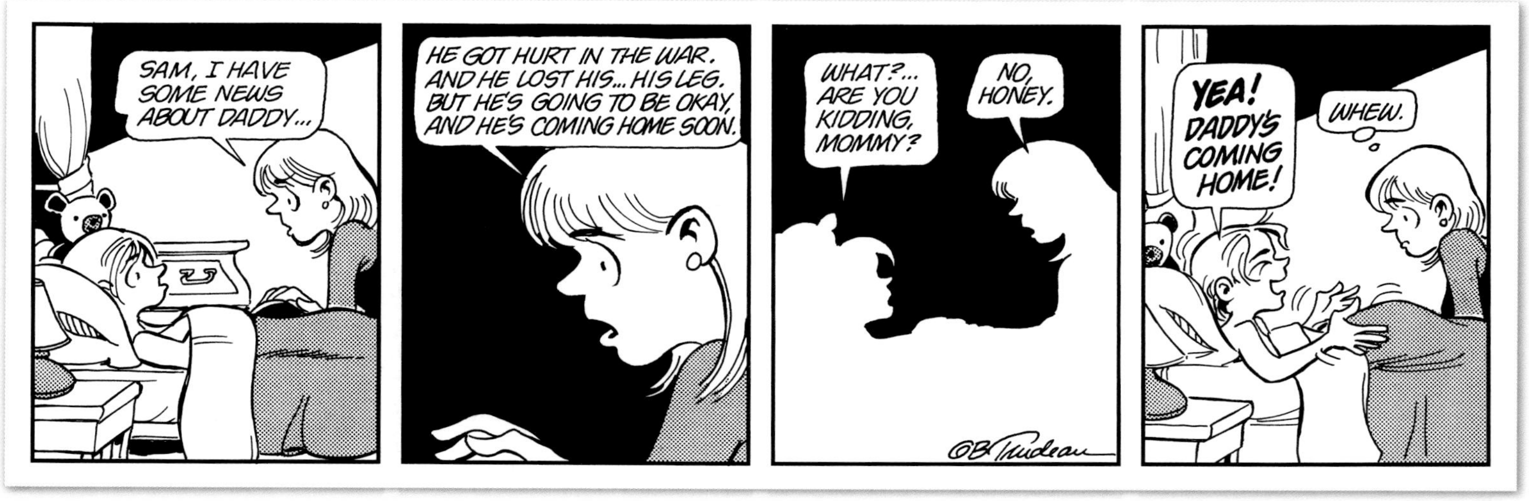
SAM, I HAVE SOME NEWS ABOUT DADDY...
HE GOT HURT IN THE WAR. AND HE LOST HIS... HIS LEG. BUT HE'S GOING TO BE OKAY, AND HE'S COMING HOME SOON.
WHAT?... ARE YOU KIDDING, MOMMY?
NO, HONEY.
YEA! DADDY'S COMING HOME!
WHEW.
©B Trudeau

5/1/04

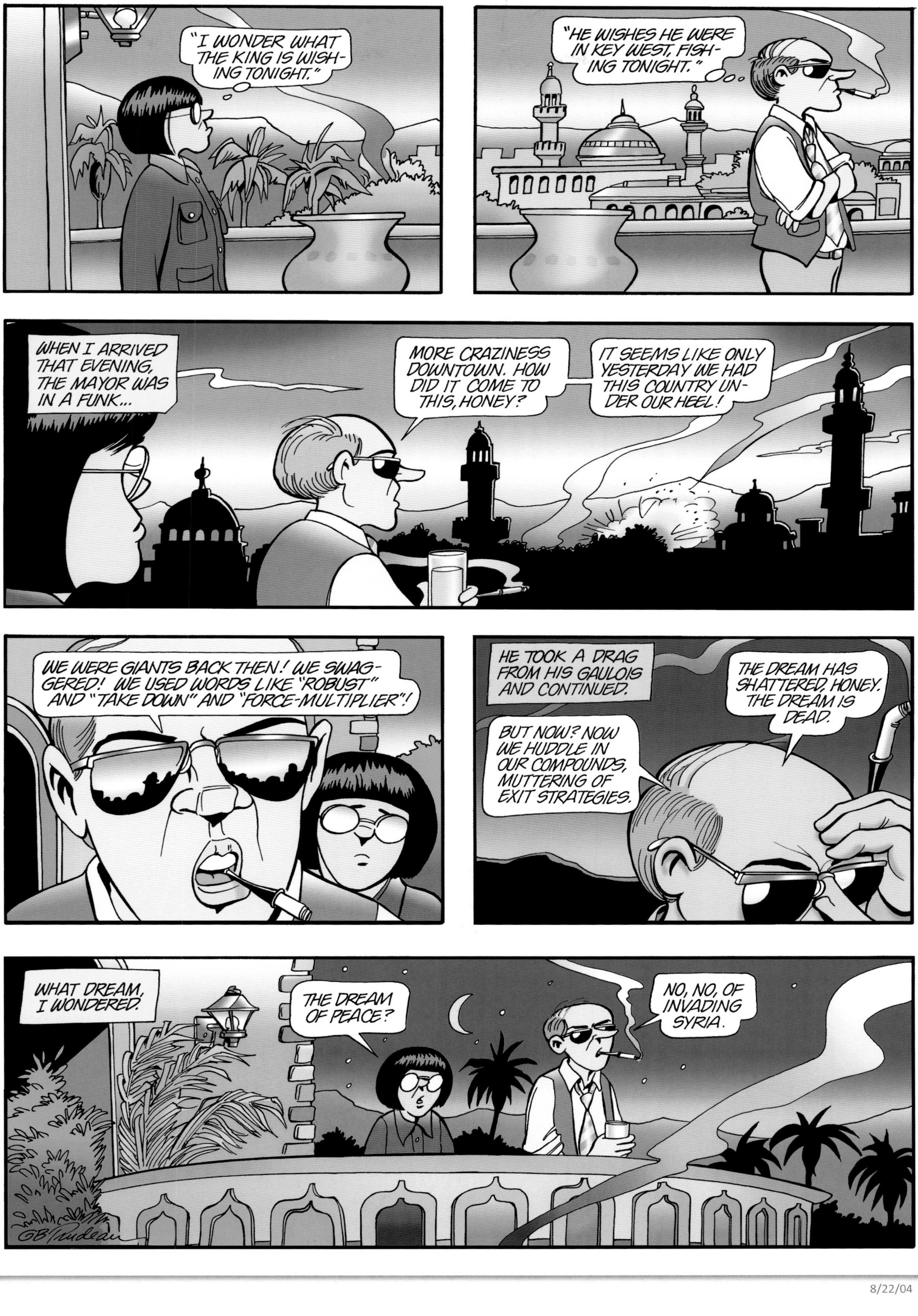
"I WONDER WHAT THE KING IS WISHING TONIGHT."
"HE WISHES HE WERE IN KEY WEST, FISHING TONIGHT."
WHEN I ARRIVED THAT EVENING, THE MAYOR WAS IN A FUNK...
MORE CRAZINESS DOWNTOWN. HOW DID IT COME TO THIS, HONEY?
IT SEEMS LIKE ONLY YESTERDAY WE HAD THIS COUNTRY UNDER OUR HEEL!
WE WERE GIANTS BACK THEN! WE SWAGGERED! WE USED WORDS LIKE "ROBUST" AND "TAKE DOWN" AND "FORCE-MULTIPLIER"!
HE TOOK A DRAG FROM HIS GAULOIS AND CONTINUED.
BUT NOW? NOW WE HUDDLE IN OUR COMPOUNDS, MUTTERING OF EXIT STRATEGIES.
THE DREAM HAS SHATTERED, HONEY. THE DREAM IS DEAD.
WHAT DREAM, I WONDERED.
THE DREAM OF PEACE?
NO, NO, OF INVADING SYRIA.
GBTrudeau

8/22/04

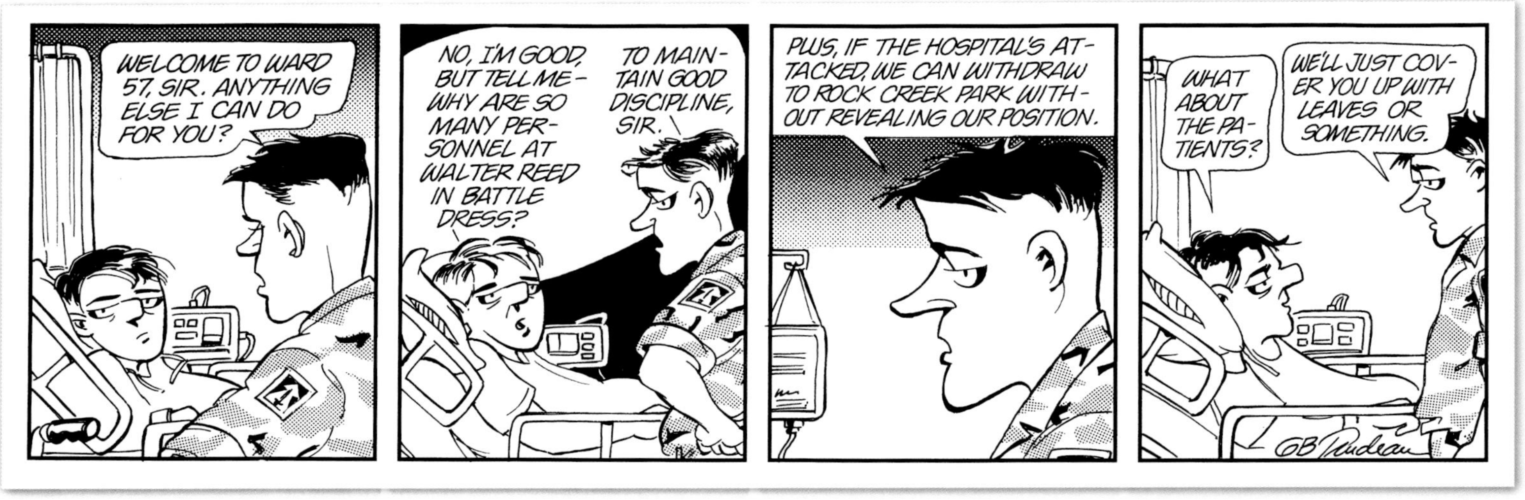
WELCOME TO WARD 57, SIR. ANYTHING ELSE I CAN DO FOR YOU?
NO, I'M GOOD, BUT TELL ME– WHY ARE SO MANY PERSONNEL AT WALTER REED IN BATTLE DRESS?
TO MAINTAIN GOOD DISCIPLINE, SIR.
PLUS, IF THE HOSPITAL'S ATTACKED, WE CAN WITHDRAW TO ROCK CREEK PARK WITHOUT REVEALING OUR POSITION.
WHAT ABOUT THE PATIENTS?
WE'LL JUST COVER YOU UP WITH LEAVES OR SOMETHING.
GB Trudeau

6/21/04

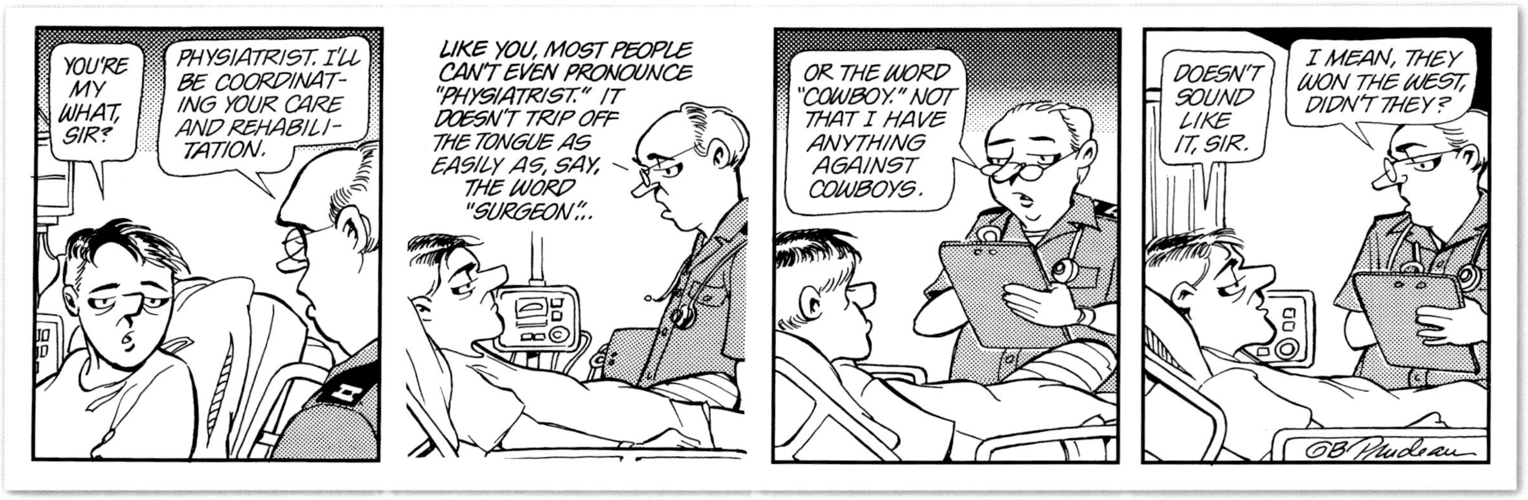
YOU'RE MY WHAT, SIR?
PHYSIATRIST. I'LL BE COORDINATING YOUR CARE AND REHABILITATION.
LIKE YOU, MOST PEOPLE CAN'T EVEN PRONOUNCE "PHYSIATRIST." IT DOESN'T TRIP OFF THE TONGUE AS EASILY AS, SAY, THE WORD "SURGEON"...
OR THE WORD "COWBOY." NOT THAT I HAVE ANYTHING AGAINST COWBOYS.
DOESN'T SOUND LIKE IT, SIR.
I MEAN, THEY WON THE WEST, DIDN'T THEY?
GB Trudeau

6/22/04

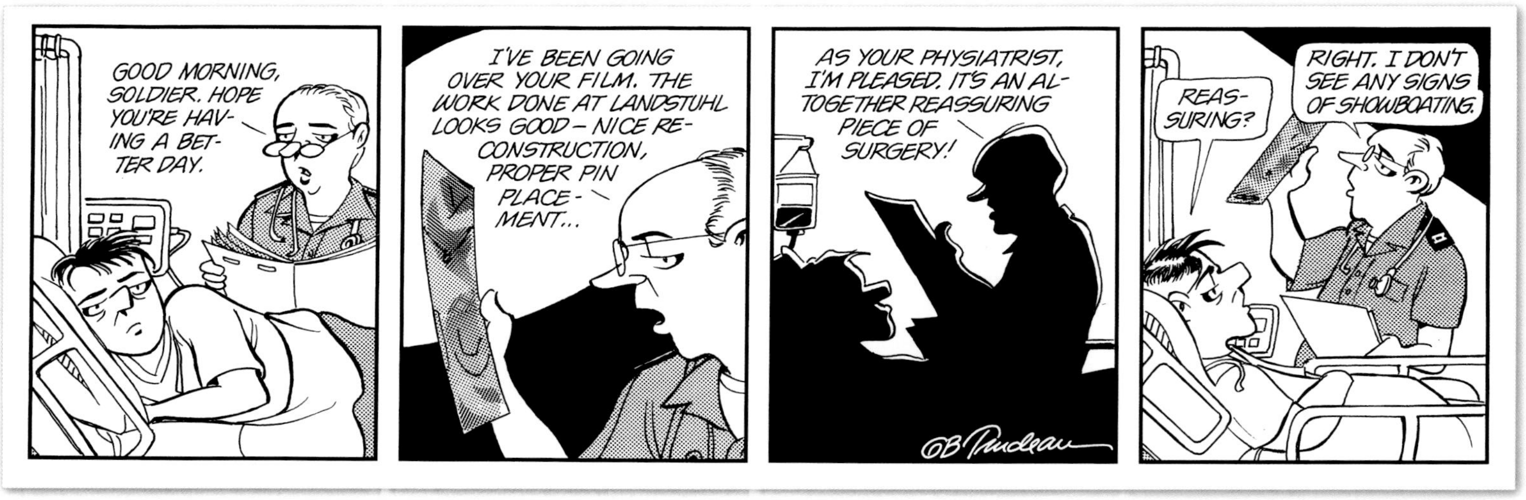
GOOD MORNING, SOLDIER. HOPE YOU'RE HAVING A BETTER DAY.
I'VE BEEN GOING OVER YOUR FILM. THE WORK DONE AT LANDSTUHL LOOKS GOOD – NICE RECONSTRUCTION, PROPER PIN PLACEMENT...
AS YOUR PHYSIATRIST, I'M PLEASED. IT'S AN ALTOGETHER REASSURING PIECE OF SURGERY!
GB Trudeau
REASSURING?
RIGHT. I DON'T SEE ANY SIGNS OF SHOWBOATING.

6/24/04

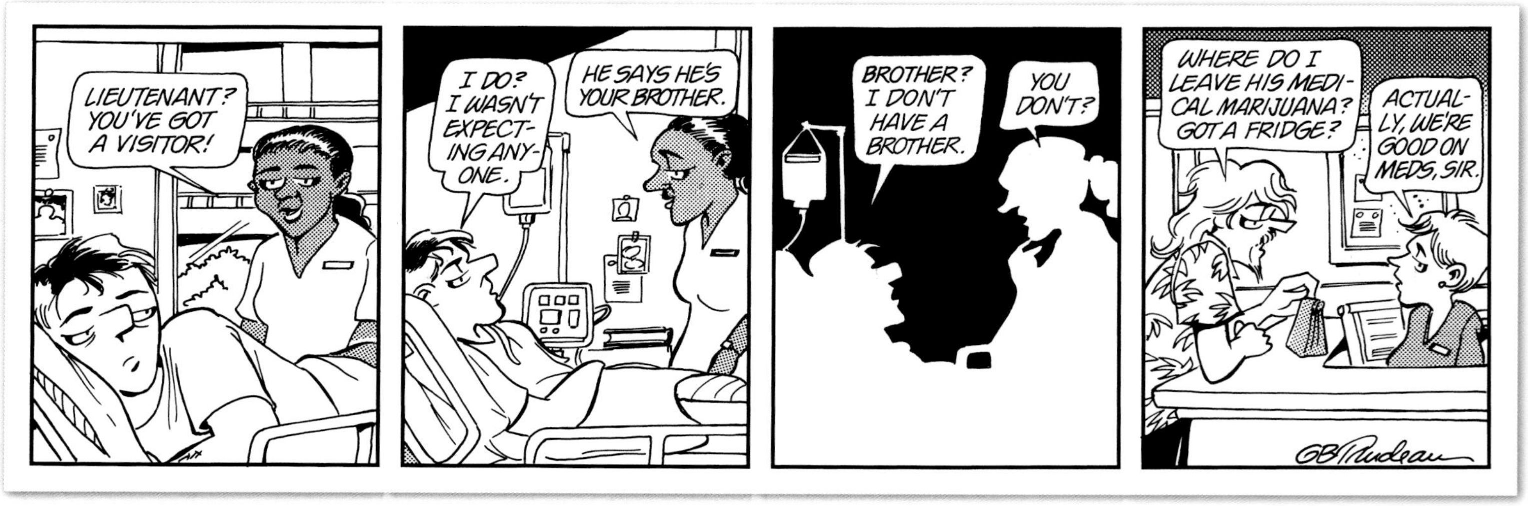
LIEUTENANT? YOU'VE GOT A VISITOR!
I DO? I WASN'T EXPECTING ANYONE.
HE SAYS HE'S YOUR BROTHER.
BROTHER? I DON'T HAVE A BROTHER.
YOU DON'T?
WHERE DO I LEAVE HIS MEDICAL MARIJUANA? GOT A FRIDGE?
ACTUALLY, WE'RE GOOD ON MEDS, SIR.
GB Trudeau

6/26/04

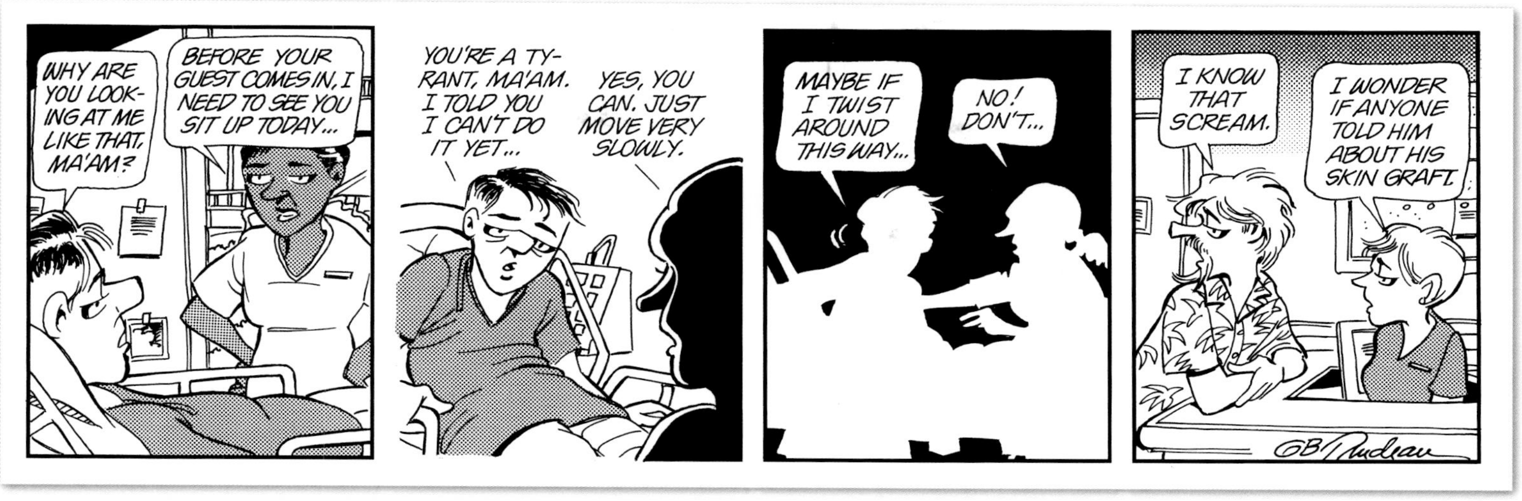
WHY ARE YOU LOOKING AT ME LIKE THAT, MA'AM?
BEFORE YOUR GUEST COMES IN, I NEED TO SEE YOU SIT UP TODAY...
YOU'RE A TYRANT, MA'AM. I TOLD YOU I CAN'T DO IT YET...
YES, YOU CAN. JUST MOVE VERY SLOWLY.
MAYBE IF I TWIST AROUND THIS WAY...
NO! DON'T...
I KNOW THAT SCREAM.
I WONDER IF ANYONE TOLD HIM ABOUT HIS SKIN GRAFT.

6/28/04

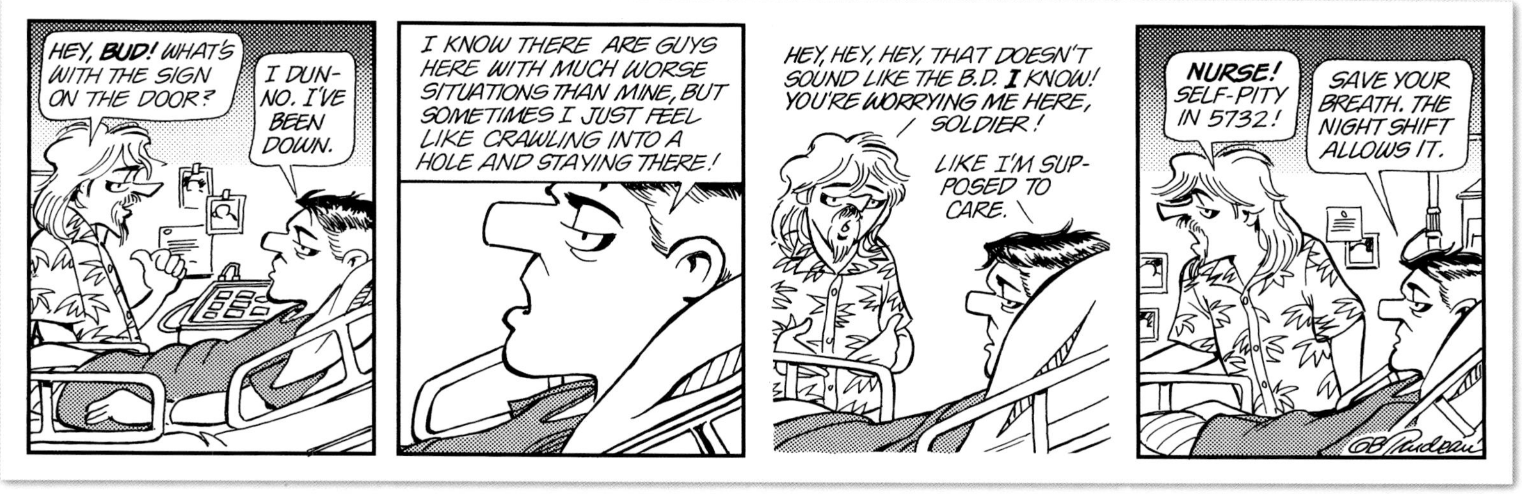
HEY, BUD! WHAT'S WITH THE SIGN ON THE DOOR?
I DUNNO. I'VE BEEN DOWN.
I KNOW THERE ARE GUYS HERE WITH MUCH WORSE SITUATIONS THAN MINE, BUT SOMETIMES I JUST FEEL LIKE CRAWLING INTO A HOLE AND STAYING THERE!
HEY, HEY, HEY, THAT DOESN'T SOUND LIKE THE B.D. I KNOW! YOU'RE WORRYING ME HERE, SOLDIER!
LIKE I'M SUPPOSED TO CARE.
NURSE! SELF-PITY IN 5732!
SAVE YOUR BREATH. THE NIGHT SHIFT ALLOWS IT.

6/29/04

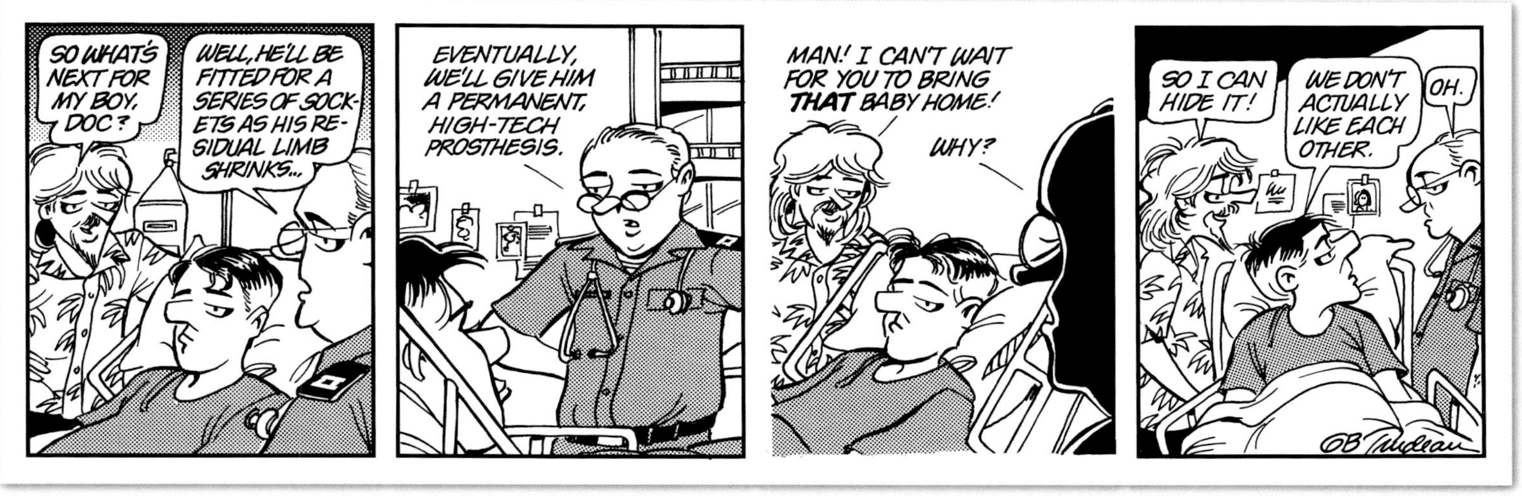
SO WHAT'S NEXT FOR MY BOY, DOC?
WELL, HE'LL BE FITTED FOR A SERIES OF SOCKETS AS HIS RESIDUAL LIMB SHRINKS...
EVENTUALLY, WE'LL GIVE HIM A PERMANENT, HIGH-TECH PROSTHESIS.
MAN! I CAN'T WAIT FOR YOU TO BRING THAT BABY HOME!
WHY?
SO I CAN HIDE IT!
WE DON'T ACTUALLY LIKE EACH OTHER.
OH.

7/1/04

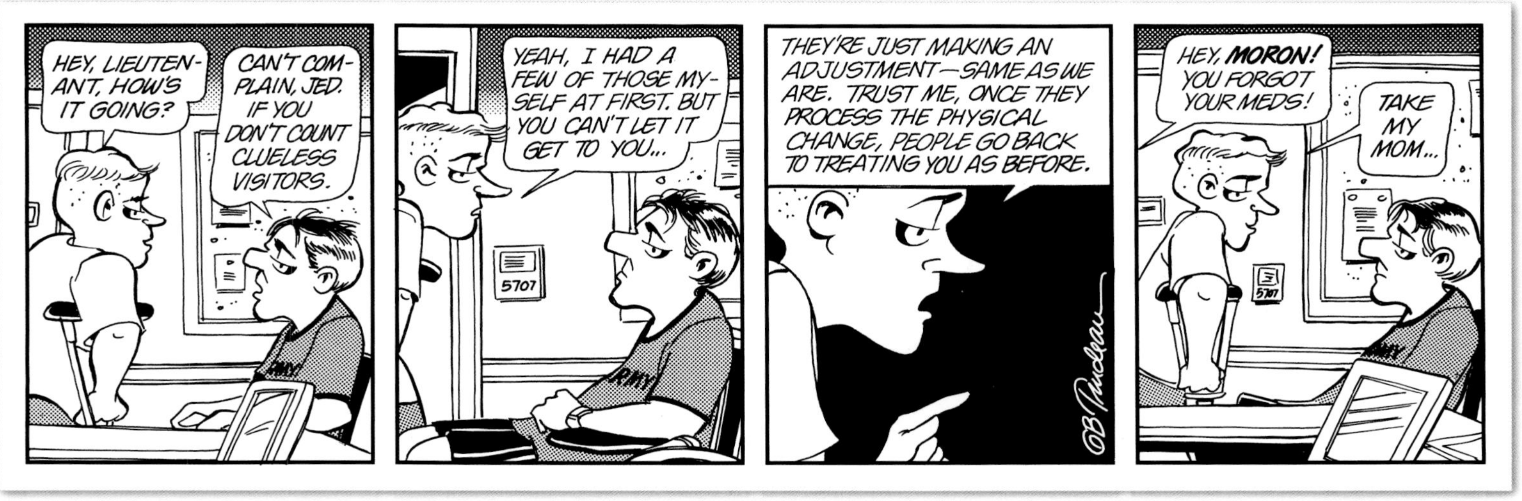
HEY, LIEUTENANT, HOW'S IT GOING?
CAN'T COMPLAIN, JED. IF YOU DON'T COUNT CLUELESS VISITORS.
YEAH, I HAD A FEW OF THOSE MYSELF AT FIRST. BUT YOU CAN'T LET IT GET TO YOU...
THEY'RE JUST MAKING AN ADJUSTMENT—SAME AS WE ARE. TRUST ME, ONCE THEY PROCESS THE PHYSICAL CHANGE, PEOPLE GO BACK TO TREATING YOU AS BEFORE.
HEY, MORON! YOU FORGOT YOUR MEDS!
TAKE MY MOM...

8/27/04

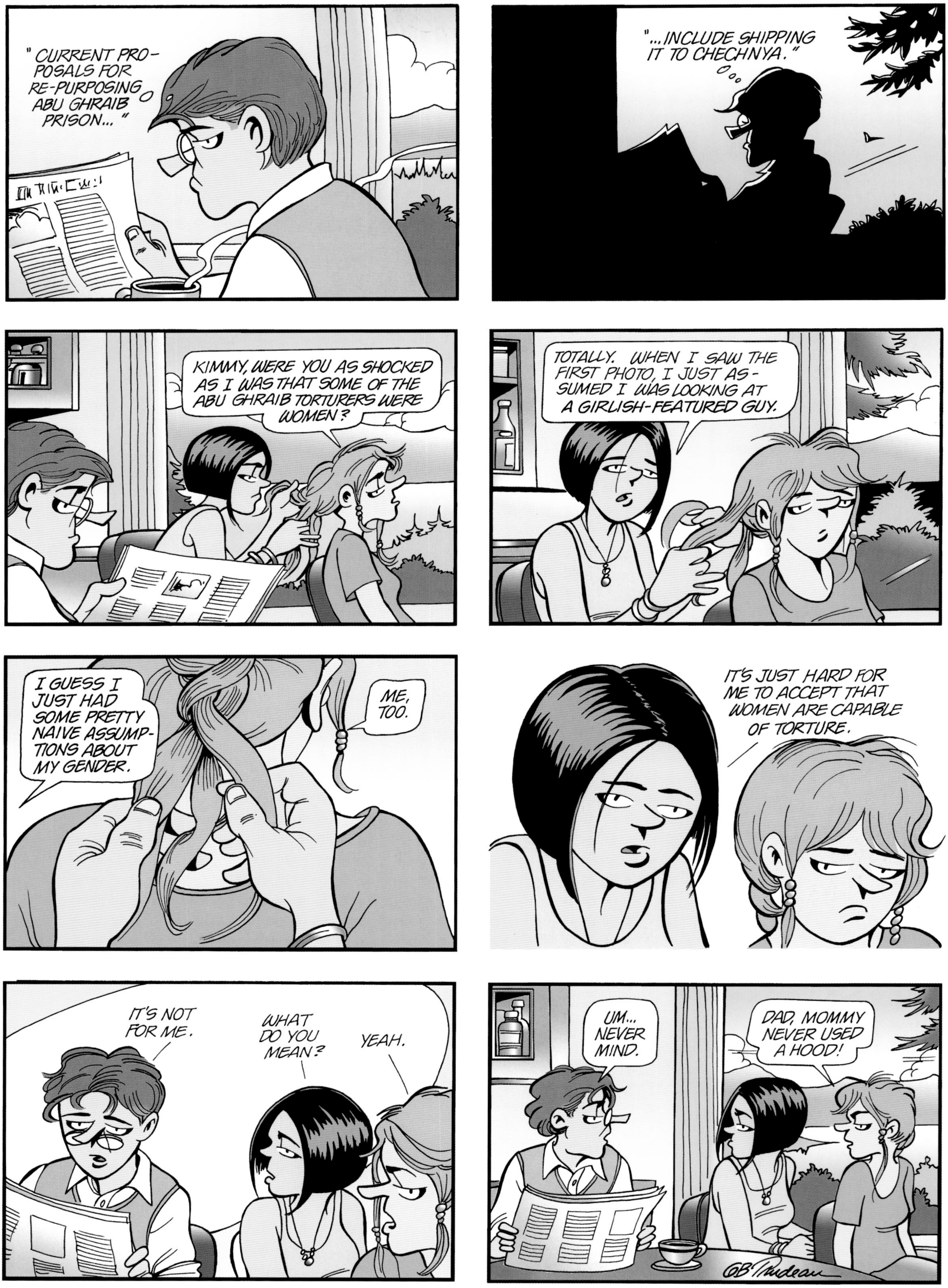
"CURRENT PRO-POSALS FOR RE-PURPOSING ABU GHRAIB PRISON..."
"...INCLUDE SHIPPING IT TO CHECHNYA."
KIMMY, WERE YOU AS SHOCKED AS I WAS THAT SOME OF THE ABU GHRAIB TORTURERS WERE WOMEN?
TOTALLY. WHEN I SAW THE FIRST PHOTO, I JUST AS-SUMED I WAS LOOKING AT A GIRLISH-FEATURED GUY.
I GUESS I JUST HAD SOME PRETTY NAIVE ASSUMP-TIONS ABOUT MY GENDER.
ME, TOO.
IT'S JUST HARD FOR ME TO ACCEPT THAT WOMEN ARE CAPABLE OF TORTURE.
IT'S NOT FOR ME.
WHAT DO YOU MEAN?
YEAH.
UM... NEVER MIND.
DAD, MOMMY NEVER USED A HOOD!
GBTrudeau

7/4/04

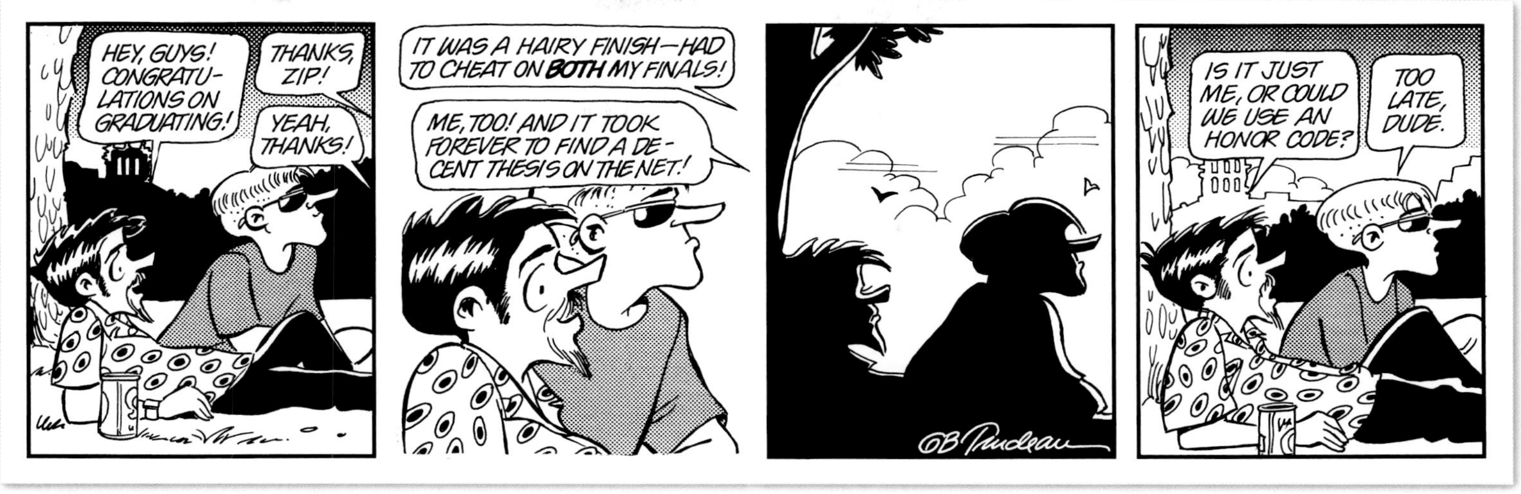
HEY, GUYS! CONGRATULATIONS ON GRADUATING!
THANKS, ZIP!
YEAH, THANKS!
IT WAS A HAIRY FINISH—HAD TO CHEAT ON **BOTH** MY FINALS!
ME, TOO! AND IT TOOK FOREVER TO FIND A DECENT THESIS ON THE NET!
IS IT JUST ME, OR COULD WE USE AN HONOR CODE?
TOO LATE, DUDE.

5/10/04

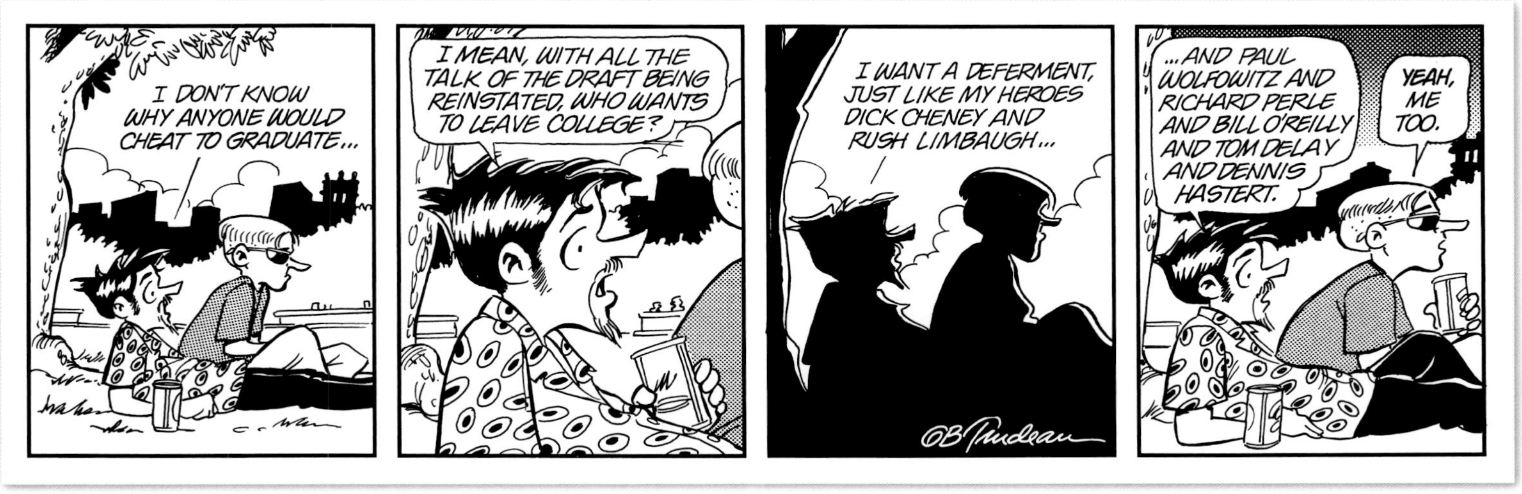
I DON'T KNOW WHY ANYONE WOULD CHEAT TO GRADUATE...
I MEAN, WITH ALL THE TALK OF THE DRAFT BEING REINSTATED, WHO WANTS TO LEAVE COLLEGE?
I WANT A DEFERMENT, JUST LIKE MY HEROES DICK CHENEY AND RUSH LIMBAUGH...
...AND PAUL WOLFOWITZ AND RICHARD PERLE AND BILL O'REILLY AND TOM DELAY AND DENNIS HASTERT.
YEAH, ME TOO.

5/12/04

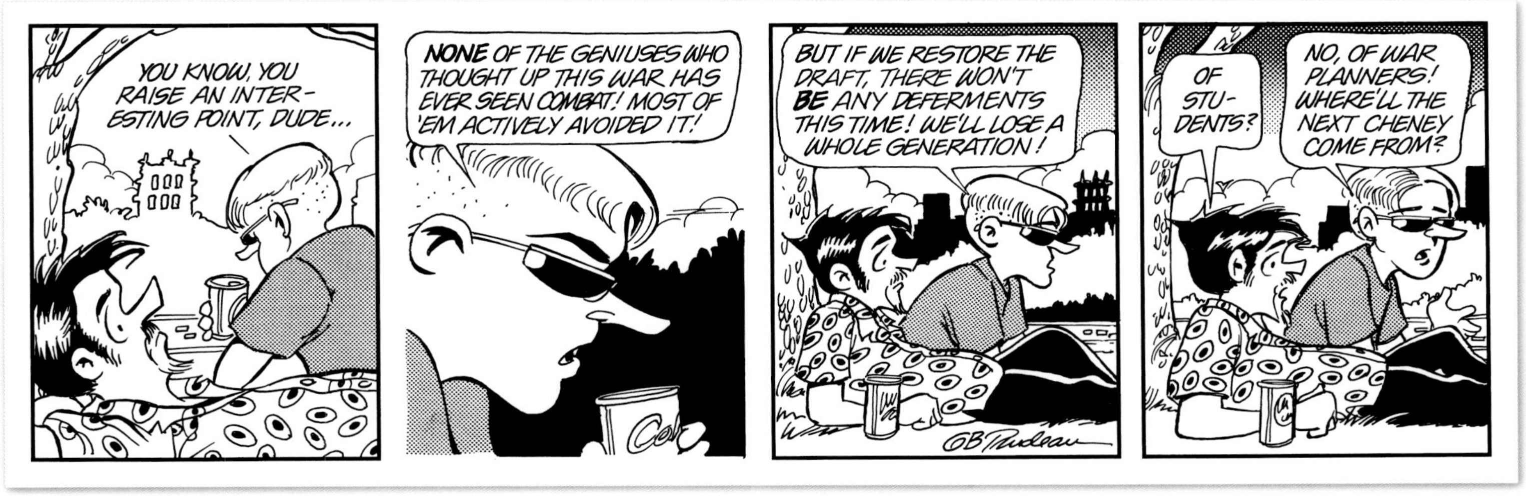
YOU KNOW, YOU RAISE AN INTERESTING POINT, DUDE...
NONE OF THE GENIUSES WHO THOUGHT UP THIS WAR HAS EVER SEEN COMBAT! MOST OF 'EM ACTIVELY AVOIDED IT!
BUT IF WE RESTORE THE DRAFT, THERE WON'T **BE** ANY DEFERMENTS THIS TIME! WE'LL LOSE A WHOLE GENERATION!
OF STUDENTS?
NO, OF WAR PLANNERS! WHERE'LL THE NEXT CHENEY COME FROM?

5/13/04

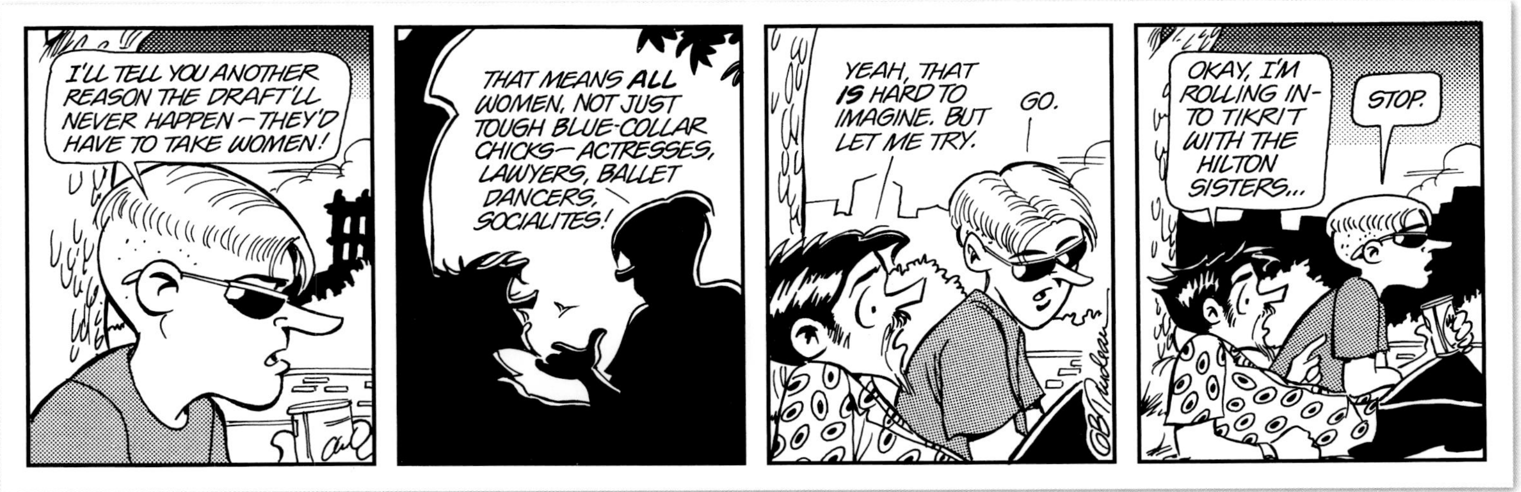
I'LL TELL YOU ANOTHER REASON THE DRAFT'LL NEVER HAPPEN—THEY'D HAVE TO TAKE WOMEN!
THAT MEANS **ALL** WOMEN, NOT JUST TOUGH BLUE-COLLAR CHICKS—ACTRESSES, LAWYERS, BALLET DANCERS, SOCIALITES!
YEAH, THAT **IS** HARD TO IMAGINE. BUT LET ME TRY.
GO.
OKAY, I'M ROLLING INTO TIKRIT WITH THE HILTON SISTERS...
STOP.

5/15/04

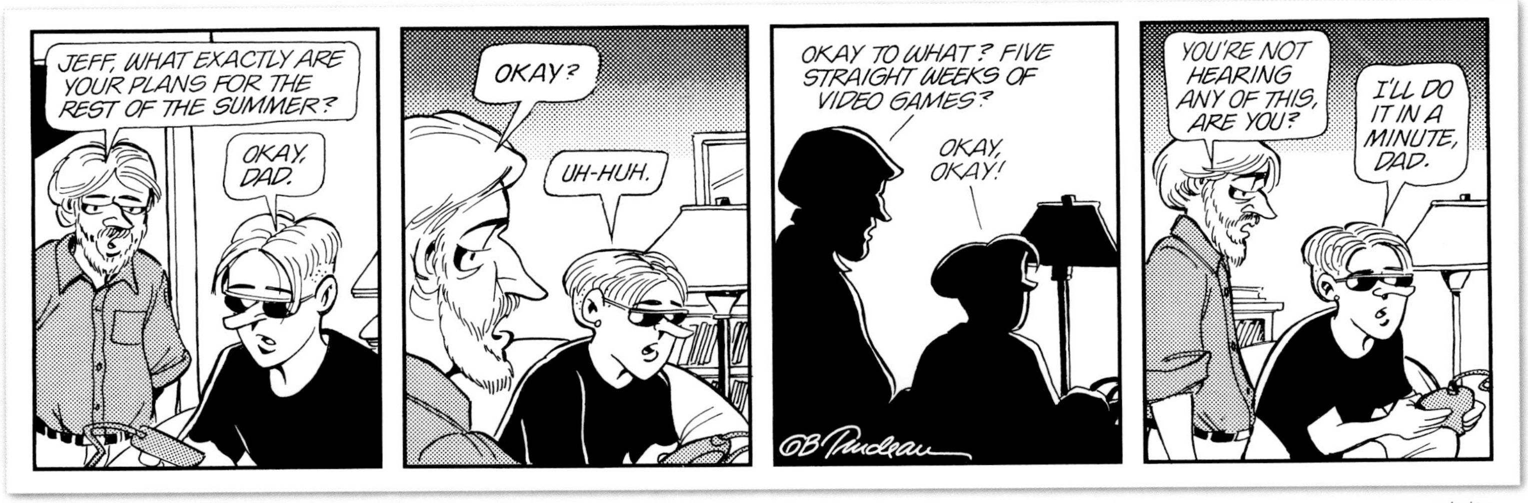
JEFF, WHAT EXACTLY ARE YOUR PLANS FOR THE REST OF THE SUMMER?
OKAY, DAD.
OKAY?
UH-HUH.
OKAY TO WHAT? FIVE STRAIGHT WEEKS OF VIDEO GAMES?
OKAY, OKAY!
YOU'RE NOT HEARING ANY OF THIS, ARE YOU?
I'LL DO IT IN A MINUTE, DAD.

8/2/04

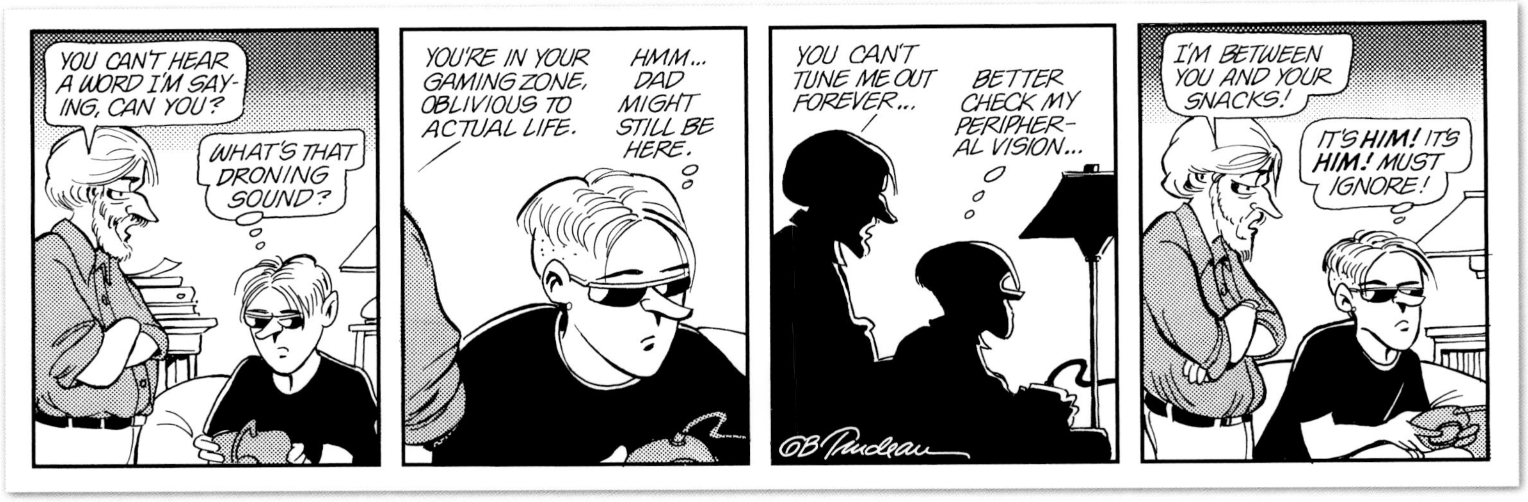
YOU CAN'T HEAR A WORD I'M SAYING, CAN YOU?
WHAT'S THAT DRONING SOUND?
YOU'RE IN YOUR GAMING ZONE, OBLIVIOUS TO ACTUAL LIFE.
HMM... DAD MIGHT STILL BE HERE.
YOU CAN'T TUNE ME OUT FOREVER...
BETTER CHECK MY PERIPHERAL VISION...
I'M BETWEEN YOU AND YOUR SNACKS!
IT'S HIM! IT'S HIM! MUST IGNORE!

8/3/04

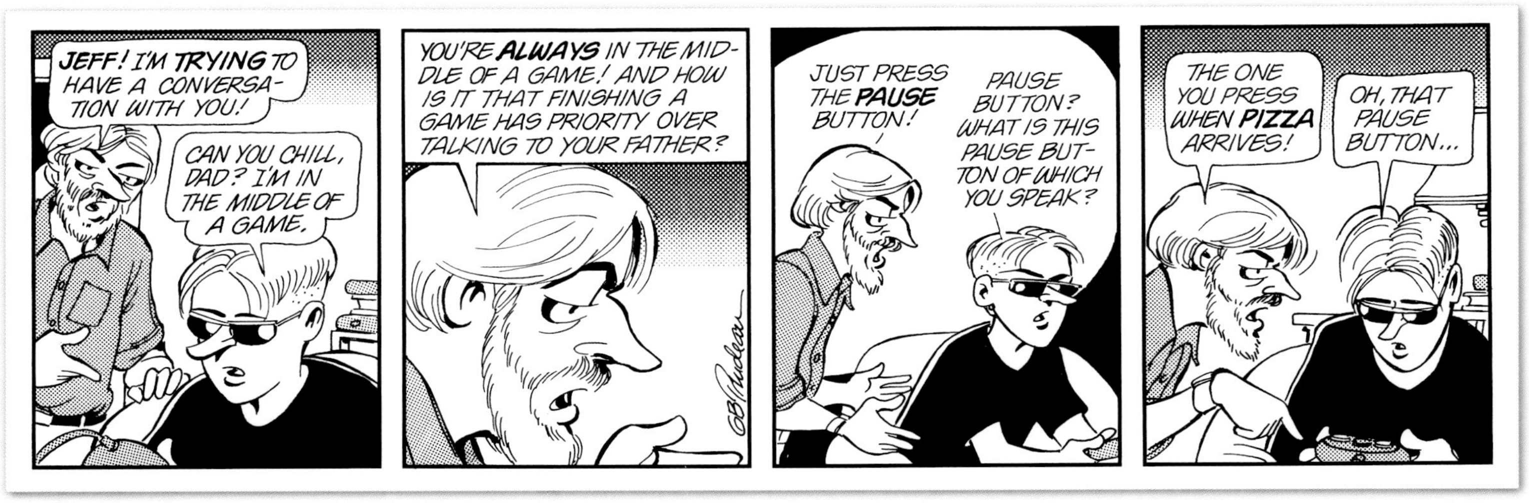
JEFF! I'M TRYING TO HAVE A CONVERSATION WITH YOU!
CAN YOU CHILL, DAD? I'M IN THE MIDDLE OF A GAME.
YOU'RE ALWAYS IN THE MIDDLE OF A GAME! AND HOW IS IT THAT FINISHING A GAME HAS PRIORITY OVER TALKING TO YOUR FATHER?
JUST PRESS THE PAUSE BUTTON!
PAUSE BUTTON? WHAT IS THIS PAUSE BUTTON OF WHICH YOU SPEAK?
THE ONE YOU PRESS WHEN PIZZA ARRIVES!
OH, THAT PAUSE BUTTON...

8/4/04

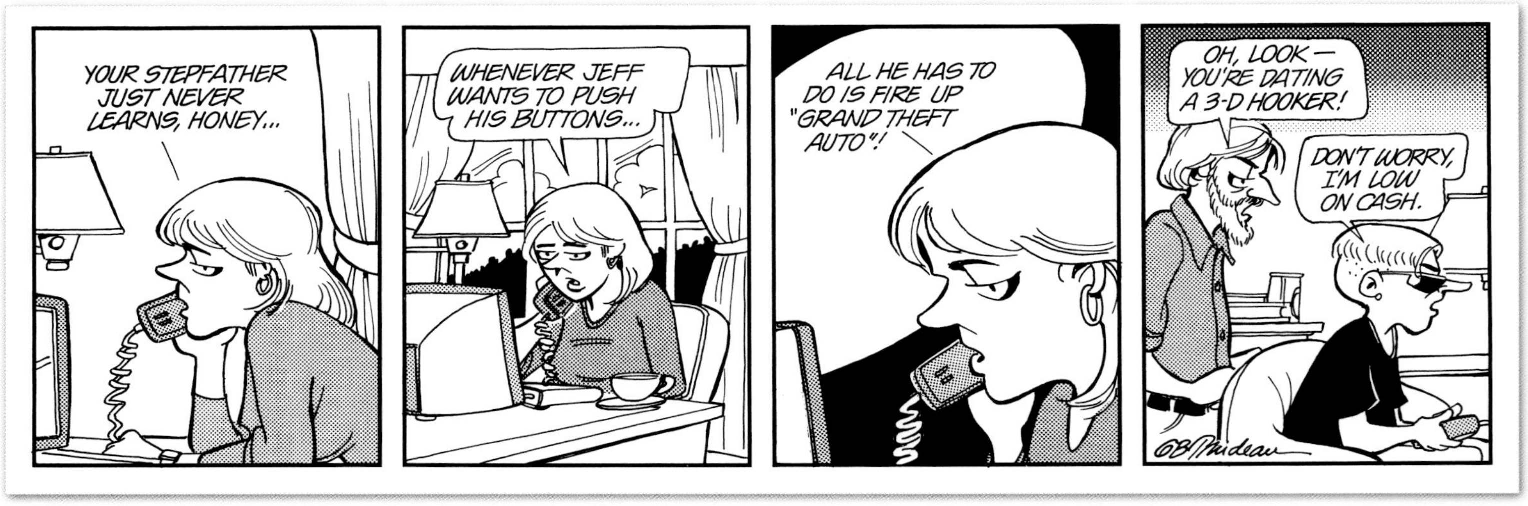
YOUR STEPFATHER JUST NEVER LEARNS, HONEY...
WHENEVER JEFF WANTS TO PUSH HIS BUTTONS...
ALL HE HAS TO DO IS FIRE UP "GRAND THEFT AUTO"!
OH, LOOK — YOU'RE DATING A 3-D HOOKER!
DON'T WORRY, I'M LOW ON CASH.

8/6/04

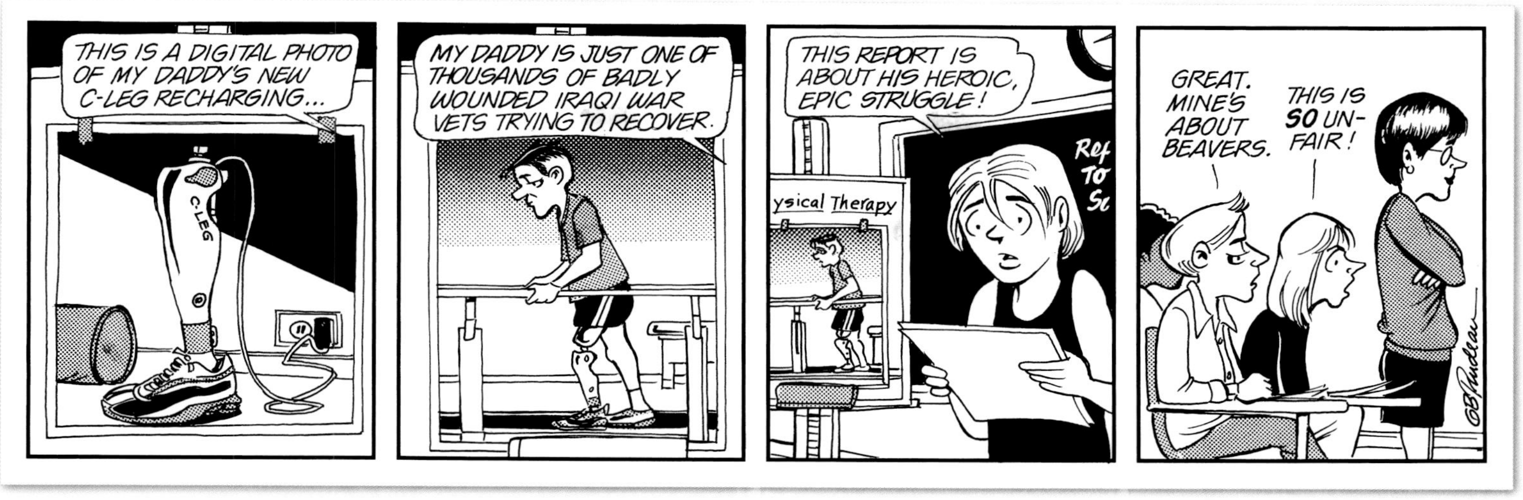
THIS IS A DIGITAL PHOTO OF MY DADDY'S NEW C-LEG RECHARGING...
C-LEG
MY DADDY IS JUST ONE OF THOUSANDS OF BADLY WOUNDED IRAQI WAR VETS TRYING TO RECOVER.
THIS REPORT IS ABOUT HIS HEROIC, EPIC STRUGGLE!
GREAT. MINE'S ABOUT BEAVERS.
THIS IS **SO** UNFAIR!

9/20/04

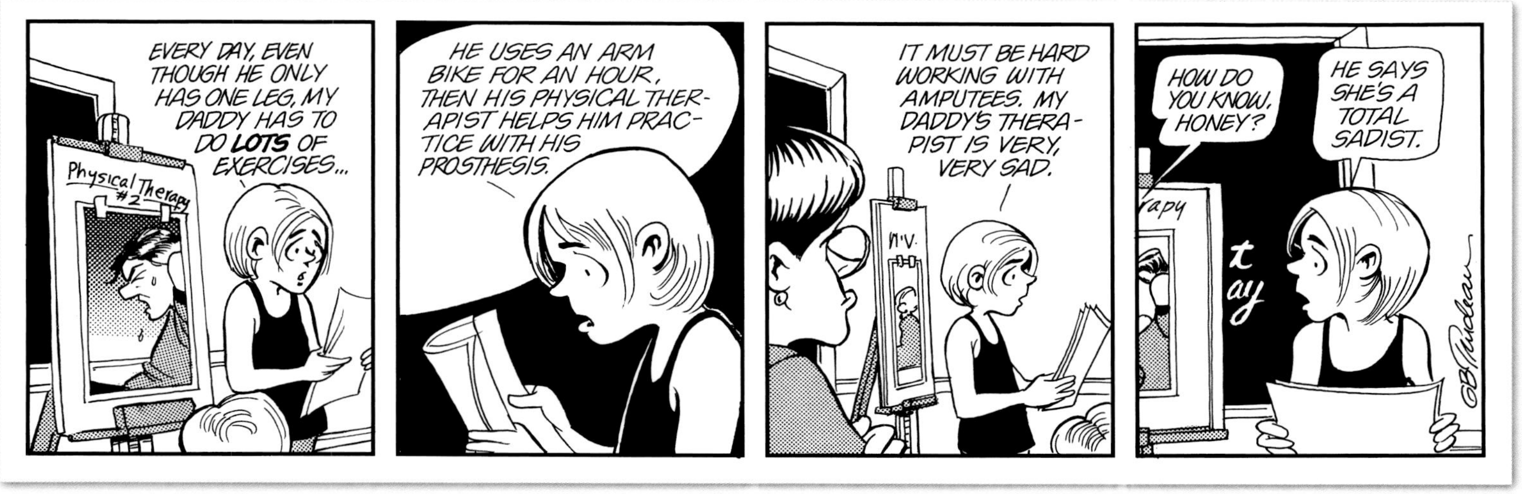
EVERY DAY, EVEN THOUGH HE ONLY HAS ONE LEG, MY DADDY HAS TO DO **LOTS** OF EXERCISES...
Physical Therapy #2
HE USES AN ARM BIKE FOR AN HOUR, THEN HIS PHYSICAL THERAPIST HELPS HIM PRACTICE WITH HIS PROSTHESIS.
IT MUST BE HARD WORKING WITH AMPUTEES. MY DADDY'S THERAPIST IS VERY, VERY SAD.
HOW DO YOU KNOW, HONEY?
HE SAYS SHE'S A TOTAL SADIST.

9/21/04

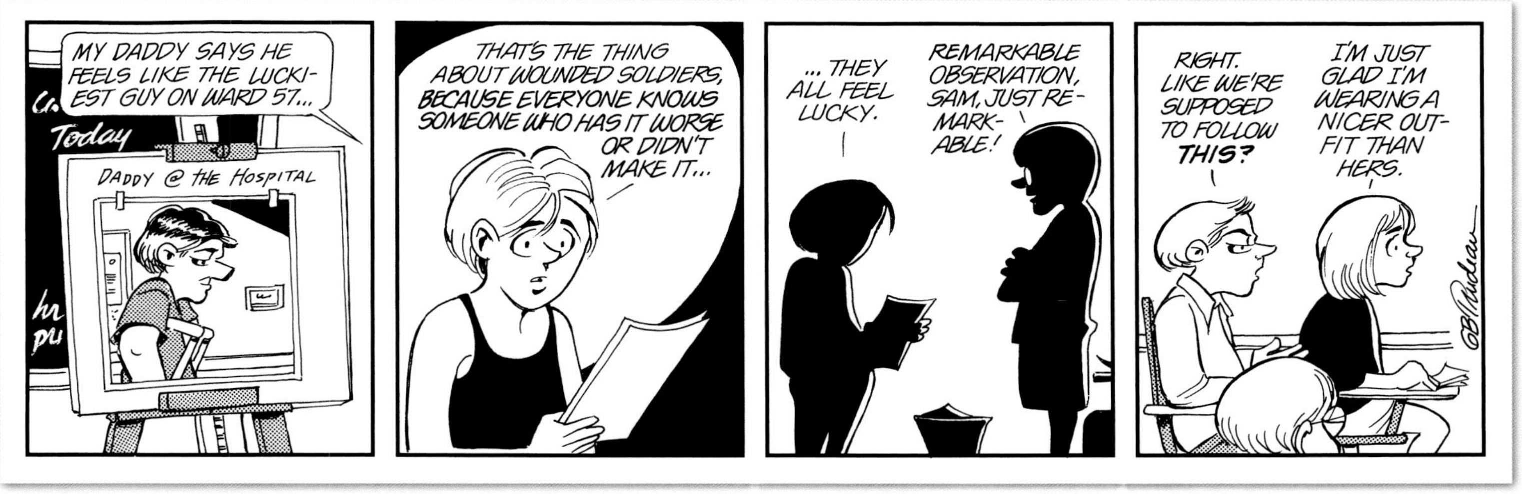
MY DADDY SAYS HE FEELS LIKE THE LUCKIEST GUY ON WARD 57...
Today
DADDY @ THE HOSPITAL
THAT'S THE THING ABOUT WOUNDED SOLDIERS, **BECAUSE EVERYONE KNOWS** SOMEONE WHO HAS IT WORSE OR DIDN'T MAKE IT...
... THEY ALL FEEL LUCKY.
REMARKABLE OBSERVATION, SAM, JUST REMARKABLE!
RIGHT. LIKE WE'RE SUPPOSED TO FOLLOW **THIS?**
I'M JUST GLAD I'M WEARING A NICER OUTFIT THAN HERS.

9/22/04

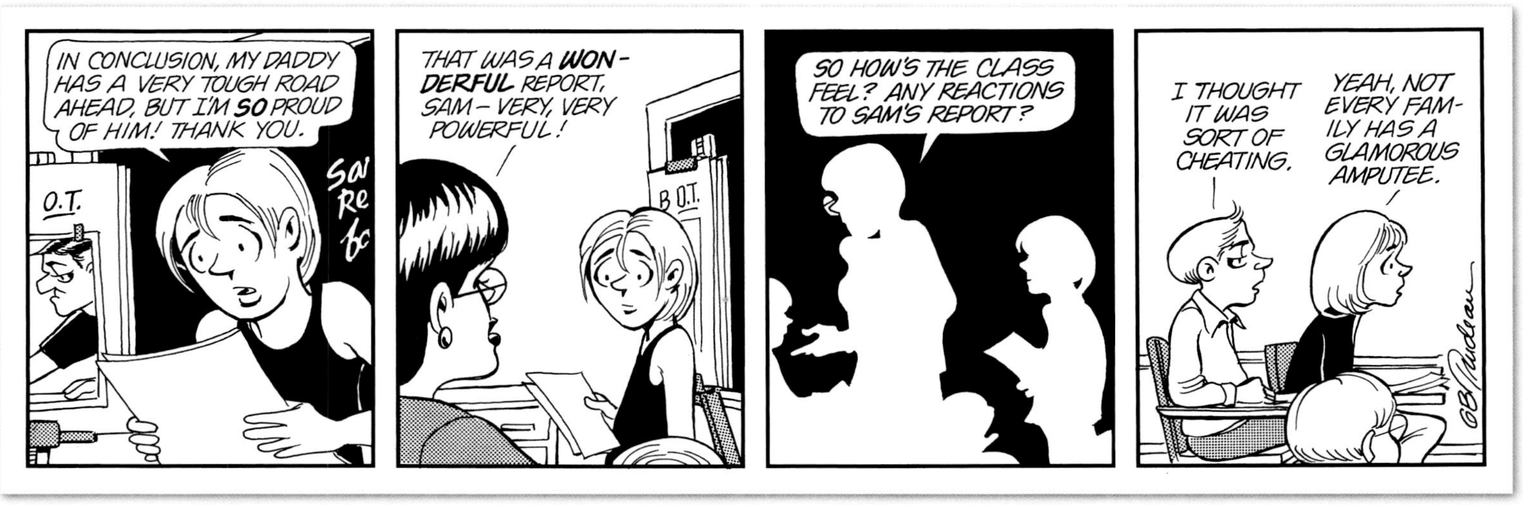
IN CONCLUSION, MY DADDY HAS A VERY TOUGH ROAD AHEAD, BUT I'M **SO** PROUD OF HIM! THANK YOU.
O.T.
THAT WAS A **WONDERFUL** REPORT, SAM – VERY, VERY POWERFUL!
SO HOW'S THE CLASS FEEL? ANY REACTIONS TO SAM'S REPORT?
I THOUGHT IT WAS SORT OF CHEATING.
YEAH, NOT EVERY FAMILY HAS A GLAMOROUS AMPUTEE.

9/24/04

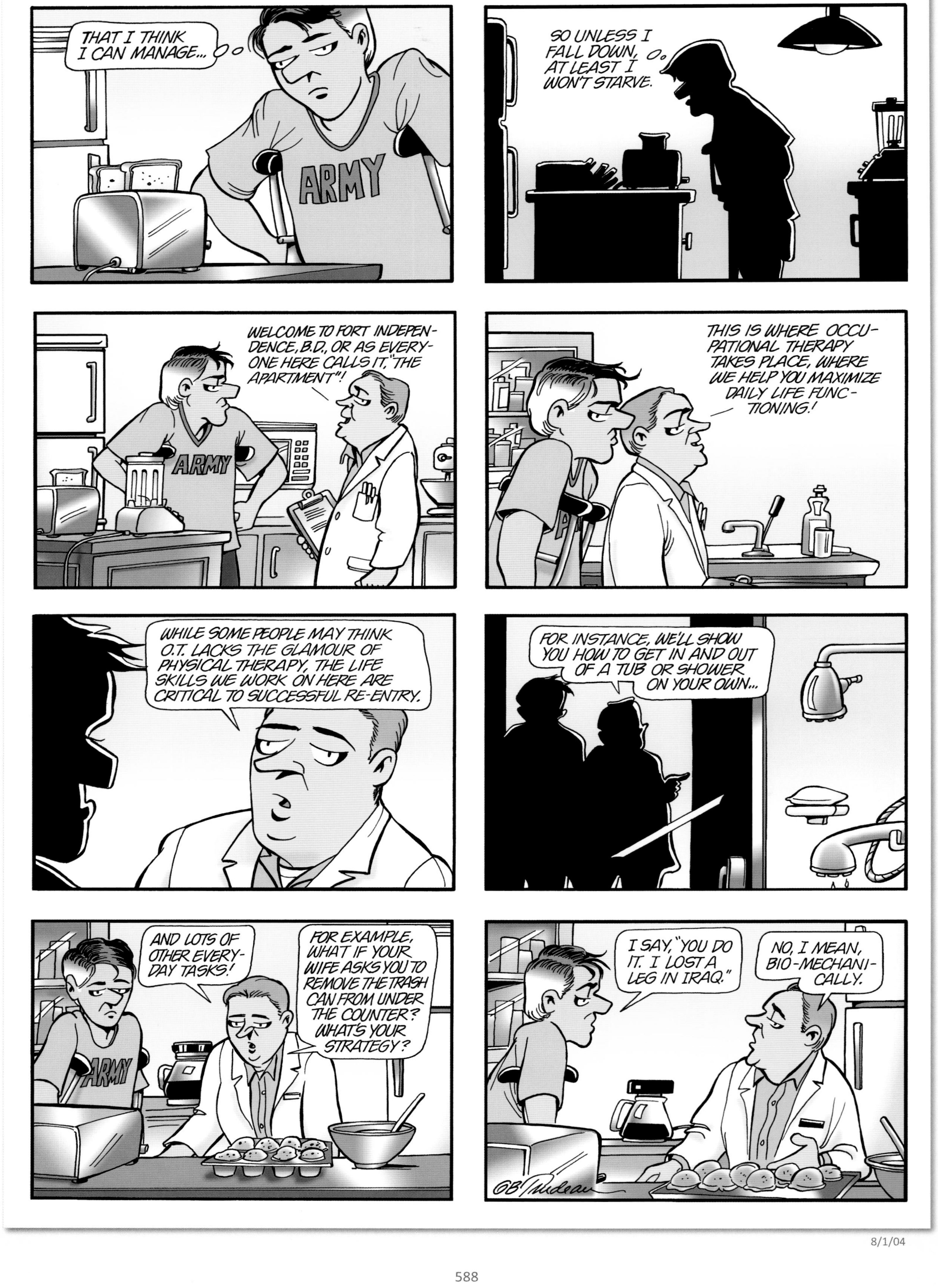
THAT I THINK I CAN MANAGE...
ARMY
SO UNLESS I FALL DOWN, AT LEAST I WON'T STARVE.
WELCOME TO FORT INDEPENDENCE, B.D., OR AS EVERYONE HERE CALLS IT, "THE APARTMENT"!
ARMY
THIS IS WHERE OCCUPATIONAL THERAPY TAKES PLACE, WHERE WE HELP YOU MAXIMIZE DAILY LIFE FUNCTIONING!
WHILE SOME PEOPLE MAY THINK O.T. LACKS THE GLAMOUR OF PHYSICAL THERAPY, THE LIFE SKILLS WE WORK ON HERE ARE CRITICAL TO SUCCESSFUL RE-ENTRY.
FOR INSTANCE, WE'LL SHOW YOU HOW TO GET IN AND OUT OF A TUB OR SHOWER ON YOUR OWN...
AND LOTS OF OTHER EVERYDAY TASKS!
FOR EXAMPLE, WHAT IF YOUR WIFE ASKS YOU TO REMOVE THE TRASH CAN FROM UNDER THE COUNTER? WHAT'S YOUR STRATEGY?
ARMY
I SAY, "YOU DO IT. I LOST A LEG IN IRAQ."
NO, I MEAN, BIO-MECHANICALLY.
GB Trudeau

8/1/04

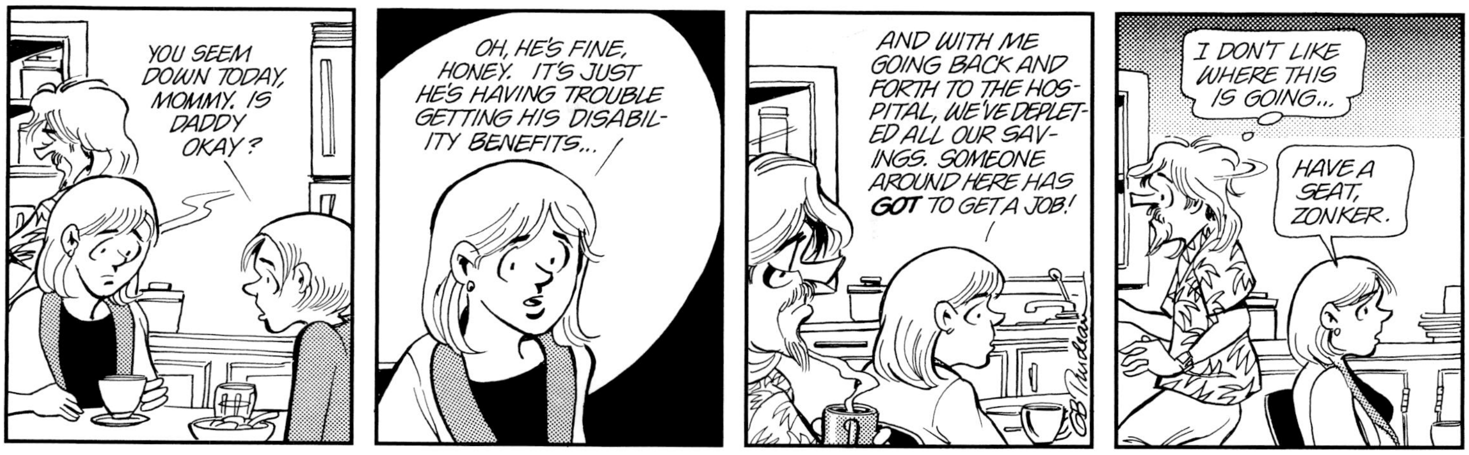
YOU SEEM DOWN TODAY, MOMMY. IS DADDY OKAY?
OH, HE'S FINE, HONEY. IT'S JUST HE'S HAVING TROUBLE GETTING HIS DISABILITY BENEFITS...
AND WITH ME GOING BACK AND FORTH TO THE HOSPITAL, WE'VE DEPLETED ALL OUR SAVINGS. SOMEONE AROUND HERE HAS **GOT** TO GET A JOB!
I DON'T LIKE WHERE THIS IS GOING...
HAVE A SEAT, ZONKER.

11/8/04

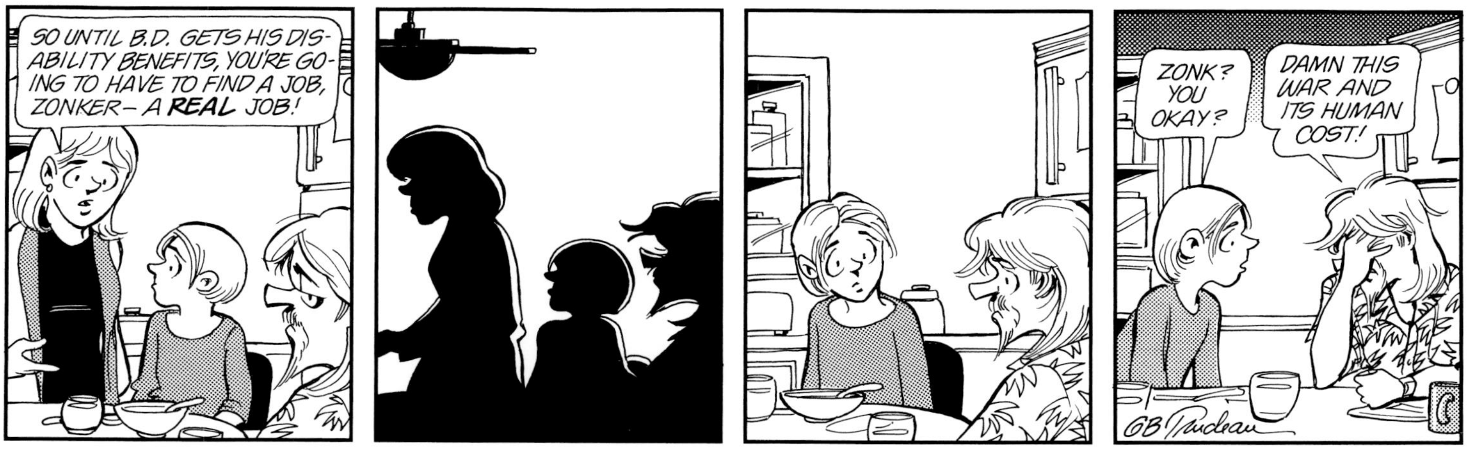
SO UNTIL B.D. GETS HIS DISABILITY BENEFITS, YOU'RE GOING TO HAVE TO FIND A JOB, ZONKER– A **REAL** JOB!
ZONK? YOU OKAY?
DAMN THIS WAR AND ITS HUMAN COST!

11/9/04

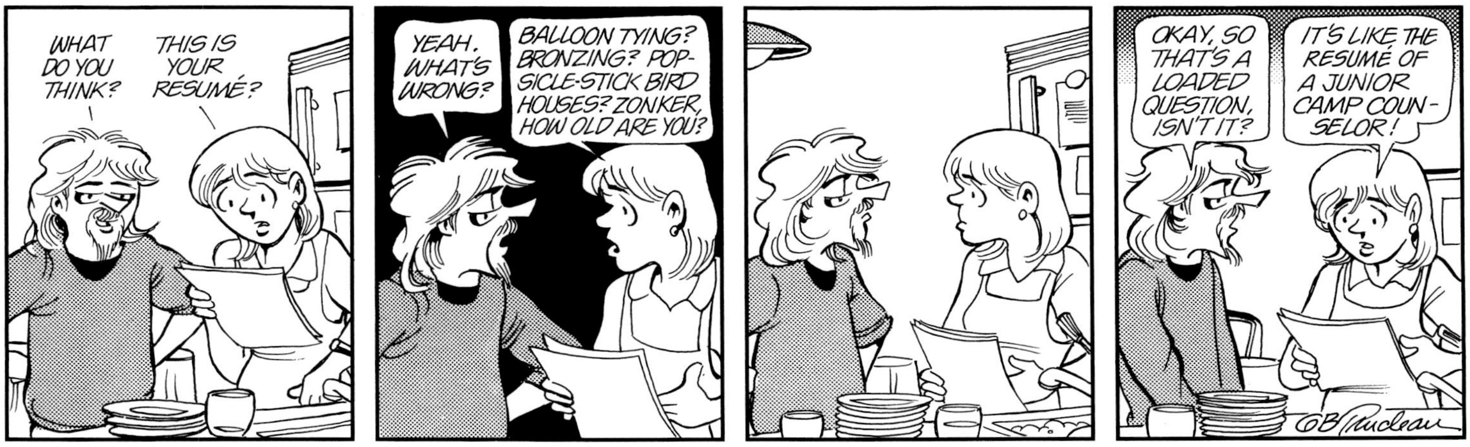
WHAT DO YOU THINK?
THIS IS YOUR RESUMÉ?
YEAH. WHAT'S WRONG?
BALLOON TYING? BRONZING? POPSICLE-STICK BIRD HOUSES? ZONKER, HOW OLD ARE YOU?
OKAY, SO THAT'S A LOADED QUESTION, ISN'T IT?
IT'S LIKE THE RESUMÉ OF A JUNIOR CAMP COUNSELOR!

11/15/04

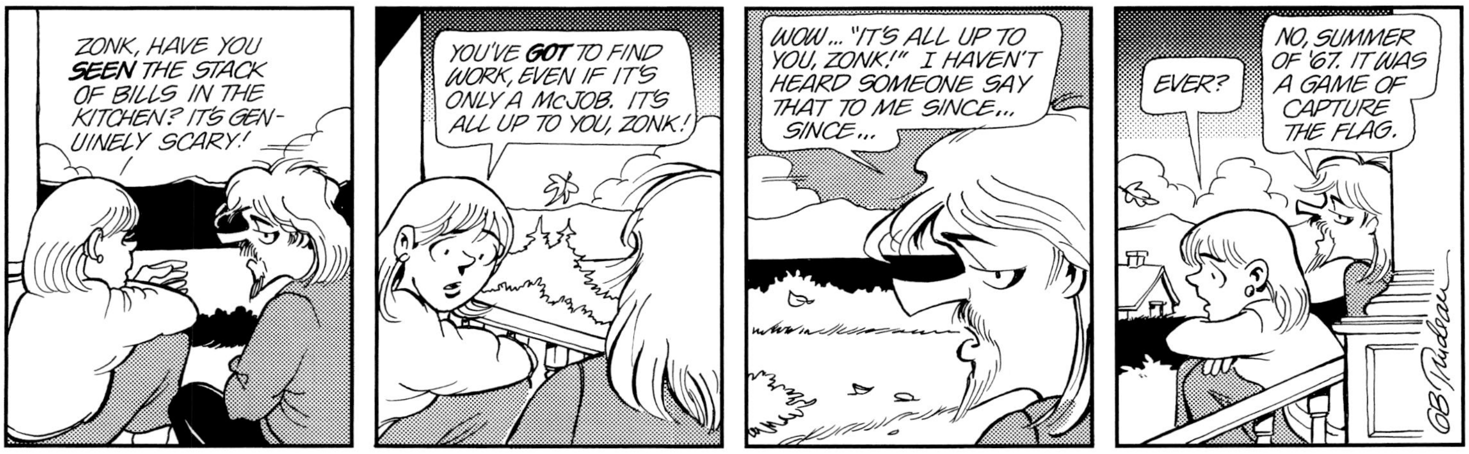
ZONK, HAVE YOU **SEEN** THE STACK OF BILLS IN THE KITCHEN? IT'S GENUINELY SCARY!
YOU'VE **GOT** TO FIND WORK, EVEN IF IT'S ONLY A McJOB. IT'S ALL UP TO YOU, ZONK!
WOW... "IT'S ALL UP TO YOU, ZONK!" I HAVEN'T HEARD SOMEONE SAY THAT TO ME SINCE... SINCE...
EVER?
NO, SUMMER OF '67. IT WAS A GAME OF CAPTURE THE FLAG.

11/18/04

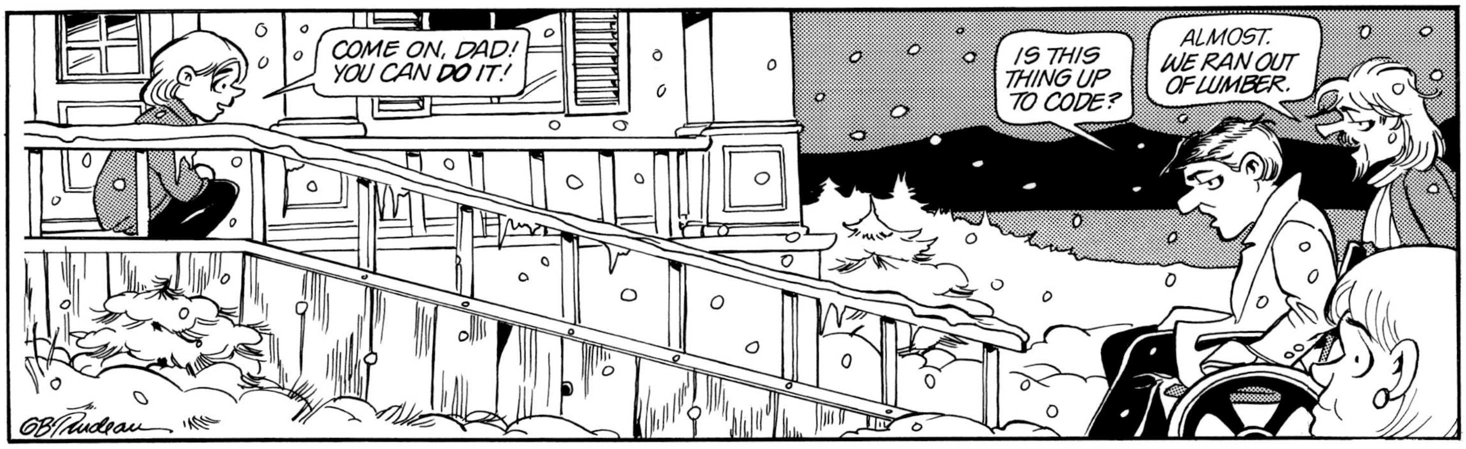
COME ON, DAD! YOU CAN DO IT!
IS THIS THING UP TO CODE?
ALMOST. WE RAN OUT OF LUMBER.

12/20/04

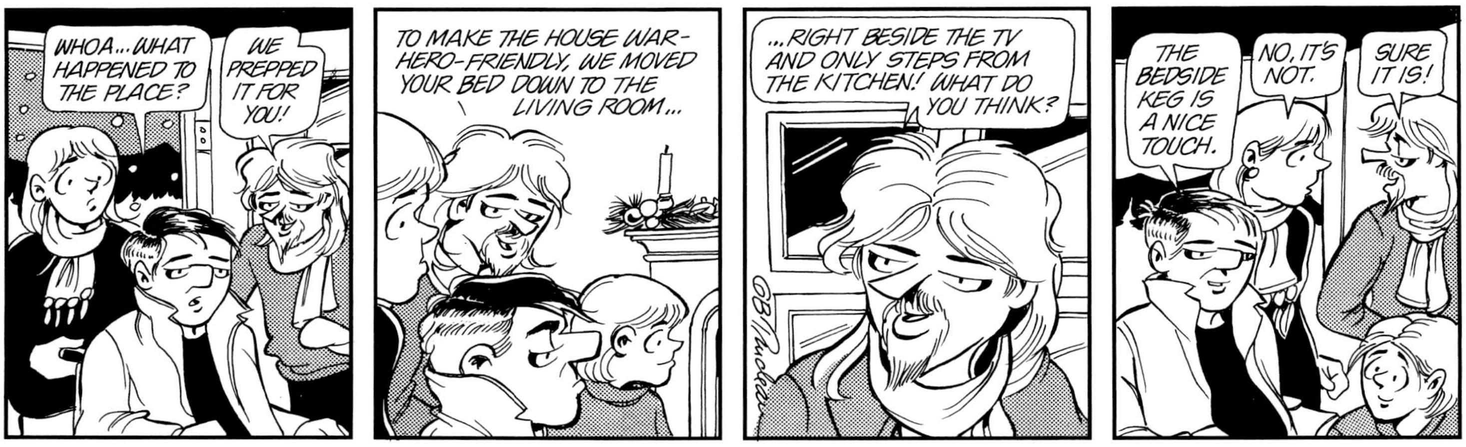
WHOA... WHAT HAPPENED TO THE PLACE?
WE PREPPED IT FOR YOU!
TO MAKE THE HOUSE WAR-HERO-FRIENDLY, WE MOVED YOUR BED DOWN TO THE LIVING ROOM...
...RIGHT BESIDE THE TV AND ONLY STEPS FROM THE KITCHEN! WHAT DO YOU THINK?
THE BEDSIDE KEG IS A NICE TOUCH.
NO, IT'S NOT.
SURE IT IS!

12/21/04

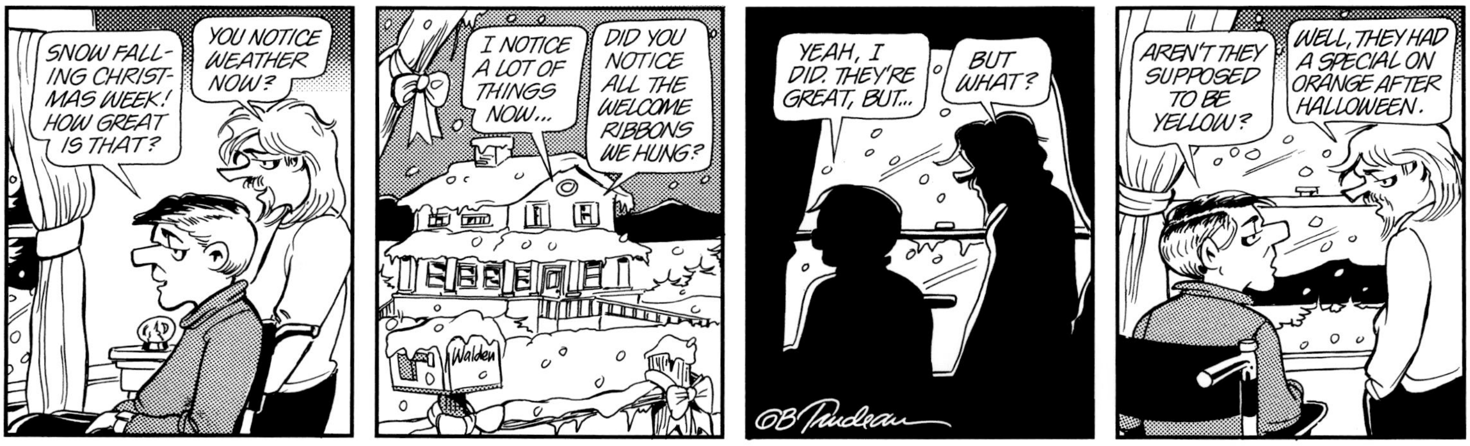
SNOW FALLING CHRISTMAS WEEK! HOW GREAT IS THAT?
YOU NOTICE WEATHER NOW?
I NOTICE A LOT OF THINGS NOW...
DID YOU NOTICE ALL THE WELCOME RIBBONS WE HUNG?
Walden
YEAH, I DID. THEY'RE GREAT, BUT...
BUT WHAT?
AREN'T THEY SUPPOSED TO BE YELLOW?
WELL, THEY HAD A SPECIAL ON ORANGE AFTER HALLOWEEN.

12/22/04

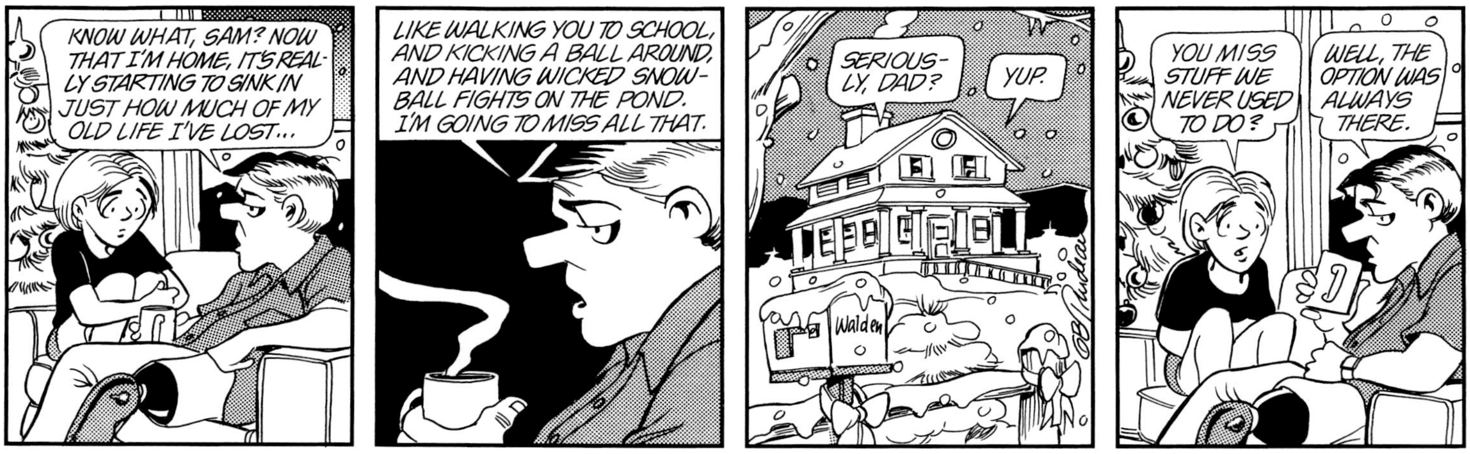
KNOW WHAT, SAM? NOW THAT I'M HOME, IT'S REALLY STARTING TO SINK IN JUST HOW MUCH OF MY OLD LIFE I'VE LOST...
LIKE WALKING YOU TO SCHOOL, AND KICKING A BALL AROUND, AND HAVING WICKED SNOWBALL FIGHTS ON THE POND. I'M GOING TO MISS ALL THAT.
SERIOUSLY, DAD?
YUP.
Walden
YOU MISS STUFF WE NEVER USED TO DO?
WELL, THE OPTION WAS ALWAYS THERE.

12/24/04

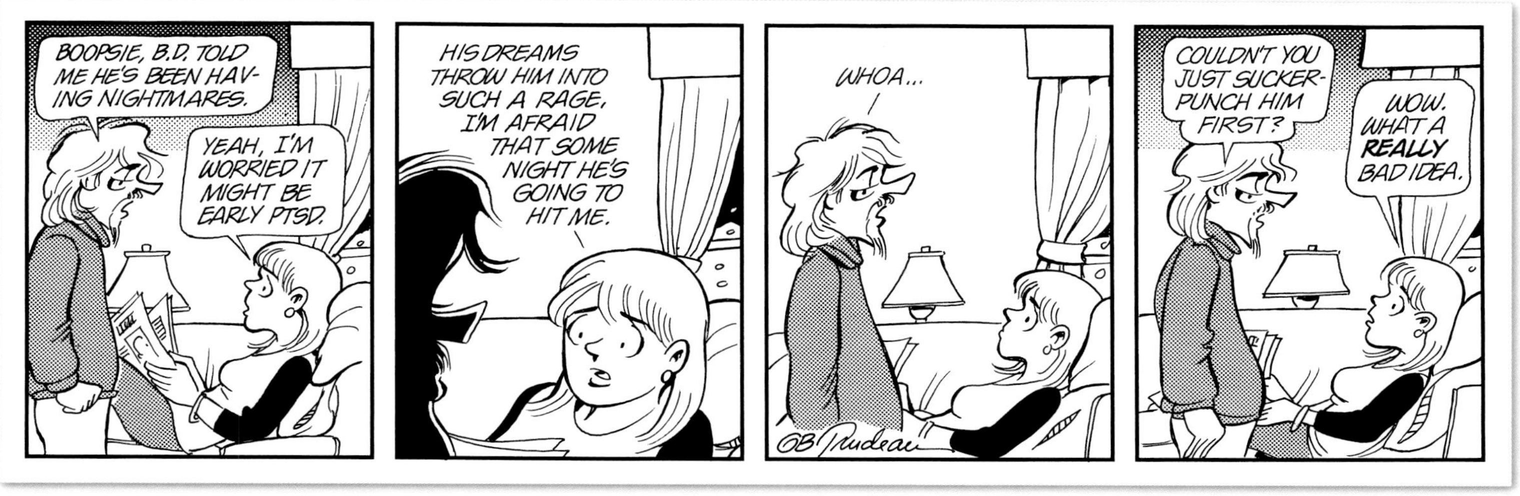
BOOPSIE, B.D. TOLD ME HE'S BEEN HAVING NIGHTMARES.
YEAH, I'M WORRIED IT MIGHT BE EARLY PTSD.
HIS DREAMS THROW HIM INTO SUCH A RAGE, I'M AFRAID THAT SOME NIGHT HE'S GOING TO HIT ME.
WHOA...
G.B. Trudeau
COULDN'T YOU JUST SUCKER-PUNCH HIM FIRST?
WOW. WHAT A **REALLY** BAD IDEA.

1/12/05

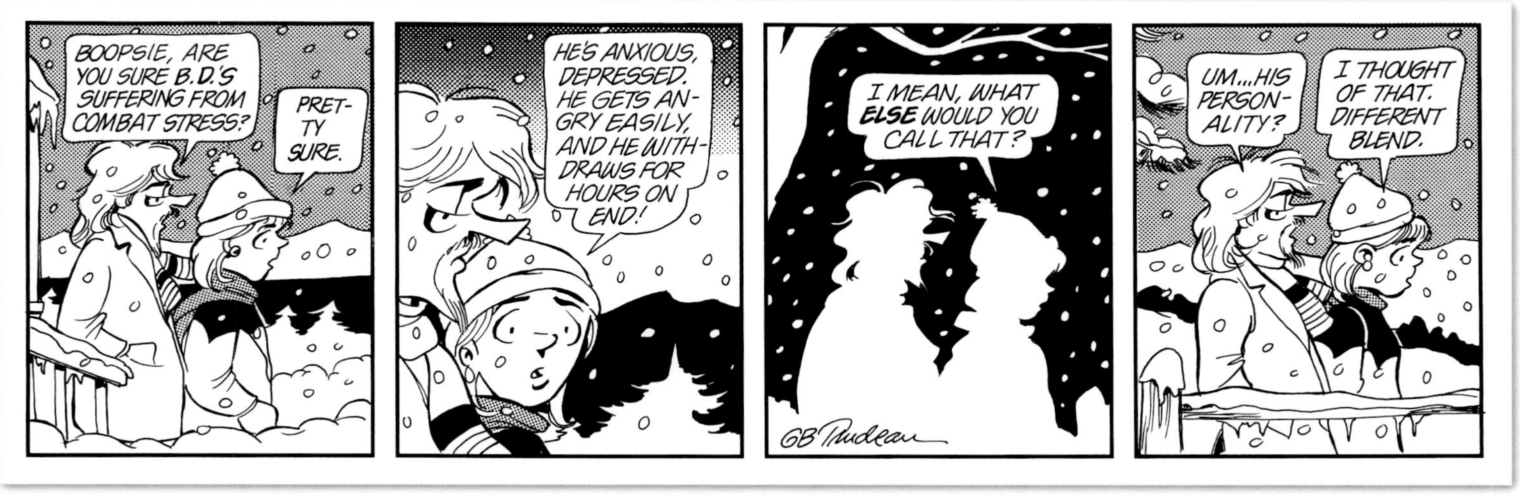
BOOPSIE, ARE YOU SURE B.D.'S SUFFERING FROM COMBAT STRESS?
PRETTY SURE.
HE'S ANXIOUS, DEPRESSED. HE GETS ANGRY EASILY, AND HE WITHDRAWS FOR HOURS ON END!
I MEAN, WHAT **ELSE** WOULD YOU CALL THAT?
G.B. Trudeau
UM...HIS PERSONALITY?
I THOUGHT OF THAT. DIFFERENT BLEND.

1/13/05

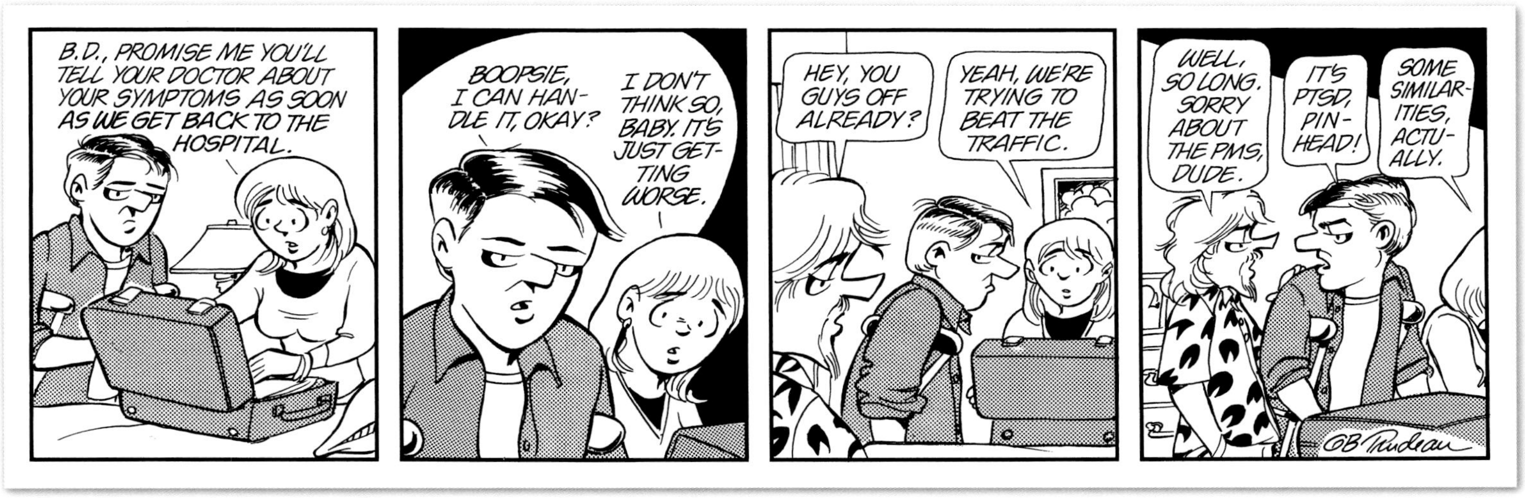
B.D., PROMISE ME YOU'LL TELL YOUR DOCTOR ABOUT YOUR SYMPTOMS AS SOON AS WE GET BACK TO THE HOSPITAL.
BOOPSIE, I CAN HANDLE IT, OKAY?
I DON'T THINK SO, BABY. IT'S JUST GETTING WORSE.
HEY, YOU GUYS OFF ALREADY?
YEAH, WE'RE TRYING TO BEAT THE TRAFFIC.
WELL, SO LONG. SORRY ABOUT THE PMS, DUDE.
IT'S PTSD, PINHEAD!
SOME SIMILARITIES, ACTUALLY.
G.B. Trudeau

1/14/05

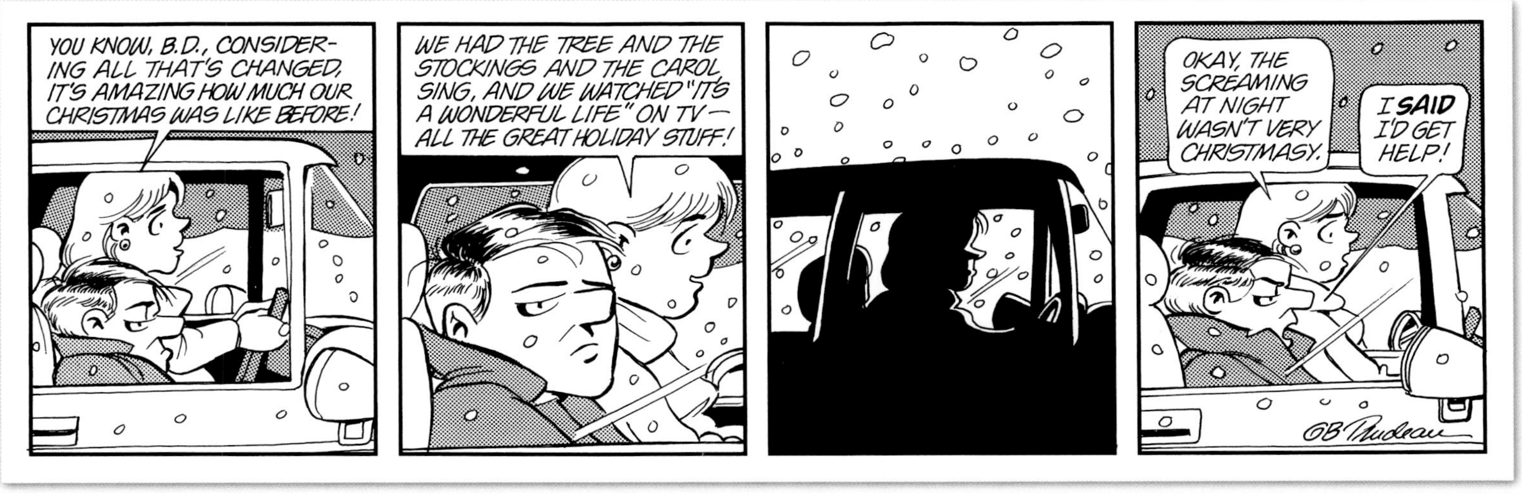
YOU KNOW, B.D., CONSIDERING ALL THAT'S CHANGED, IT'S AMAZING HOW MUCH OUR CHRISTMAS WAS LIKE BEFORE!
WE HAD THE TREE AND THE STOCKINGS AND THE CAROL SING, AND WE WATCHED "IT'S A WONDERFUL LIFE" ON TV — ALL THE GREAT HOLIDAY STUFF!
OKAY, THE SCREAMING AT NIGHT WASN'T VERY CHRISTMASY.
I **SAID** I'D GET HELP!
G.B. Trudeau

1/15/05

Alex Doonesbury

For the most part, I've drawn a bright line between my family members and the strip's characters, but occasionally it's been blurred. For instance, my daughter, Rickie, and Mike's daughter, Alex, have one big thing in common: They were both born on TV.

Rickie went first; viewers of *The Today Show* watched my wife grow rounder for months, although fortunately, the blessed event itself took place off camera. Rickie and her twin brother, Ross, made their debut in a hospital. Alex was not so fortunate. Thanks to her mother's passion for oversharing, she was born on air, live, making her the first public access cable baby—and an unwitting pioneer of reality TV. As her appalled father watched on Channel Z in Malibu, Boopsie narrated Alex's progress via the screen crawl ("Eight centimeters!"), and fretted over whether there might be a tape delay.

Not many artistes would take performance art to such an extreme, but J.J.'s need for attention was profound and her faith in the material unshakable. Some of this grandiosity has made its way downstream; there's clearly a lot of the mother in the daughter. Dreams pour off of Alex, far outpacing the reality of her life. But unlike J.J., Alex *knows* she can be grating—and actually aspires not to be. She's starting to edit, although usually after it's too late to matter.

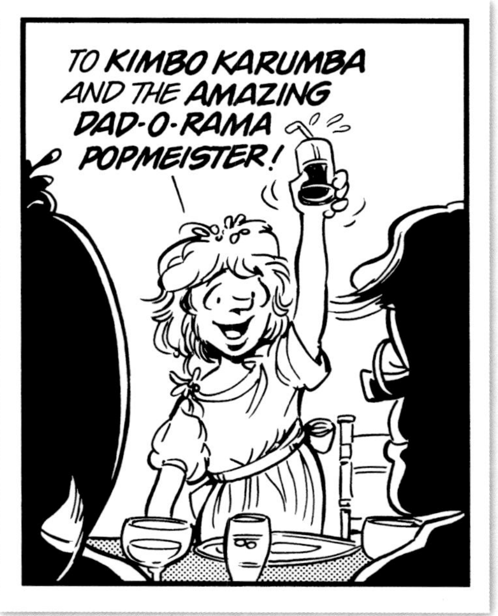
TO KIMBO KARUMBA AND THE AMAZING DAD-O-RAMA POPMEISTER!

In any event, it's a bit surprising that Alex has come to dominate the franchise. As her father drifts along, his importance to the main action receding, the life and times of Alex Doonesbury have taken center stage. While a few readers find her irritating, most seem to root for her, especially now that her world has expanded to accommodate another soul. Toggle, with his humility and good heart, is a godsend. He calms Alex down, quietly modeling restraint. Such is his equanimity that Alex self-regulates in his presence, digging herself out of holes he pretends she was never in.

Alex knows she has a good deal in Toggle. She calls him Leo, his given name, out of respect; she doesn't feel entitled to use the name bestowed on him by his comrades-in-arms. Besides, it's not uncommon for girlfriends to avoid the nicknames young men accumulate; it's a measure of their seriousness that they prefer the baggage-free original.

The opposite is true when girls address their fathers. Alex has extravagant nicknames for Mike, most of which have been furnished by Rickie. "Poppadoodle," "Popsicle," "Daddykins"—I answer to them all, and can discern my daughter's mood by which name is in play. "Popsicle" means it's all good; a simple "Dad" means it could be better. "You evil earwig" means what it sounds like.

To be honest, it's quite a helpful system.

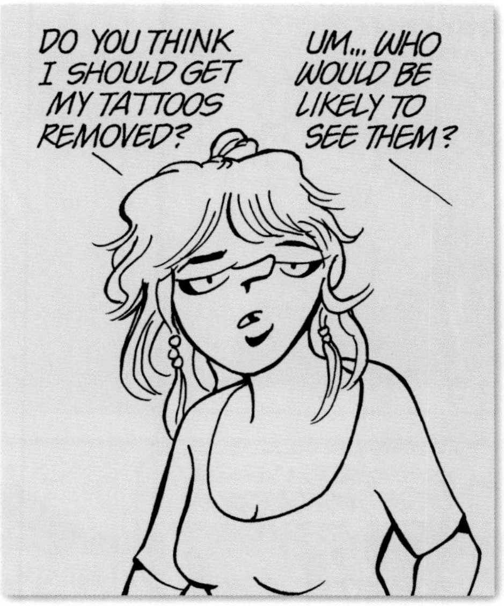
DO YOU THINK I SHOULD GET MY TATTOOS REMOVED?
UM... WHO WOULD BE LIKELY TO SEE THEM?

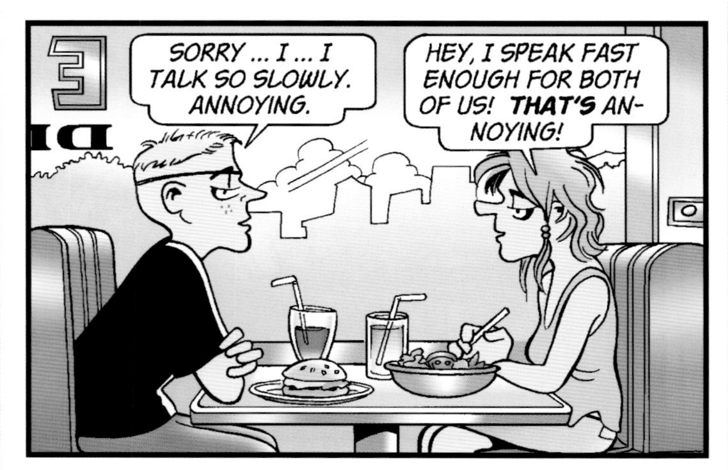
SORRY ... I ... I TALK SO SLOWLY. ANNOYING.
HEY, I SPEAK FAST ENOUGH FOR BOTH OF US! THAT'S AN-NOYING!

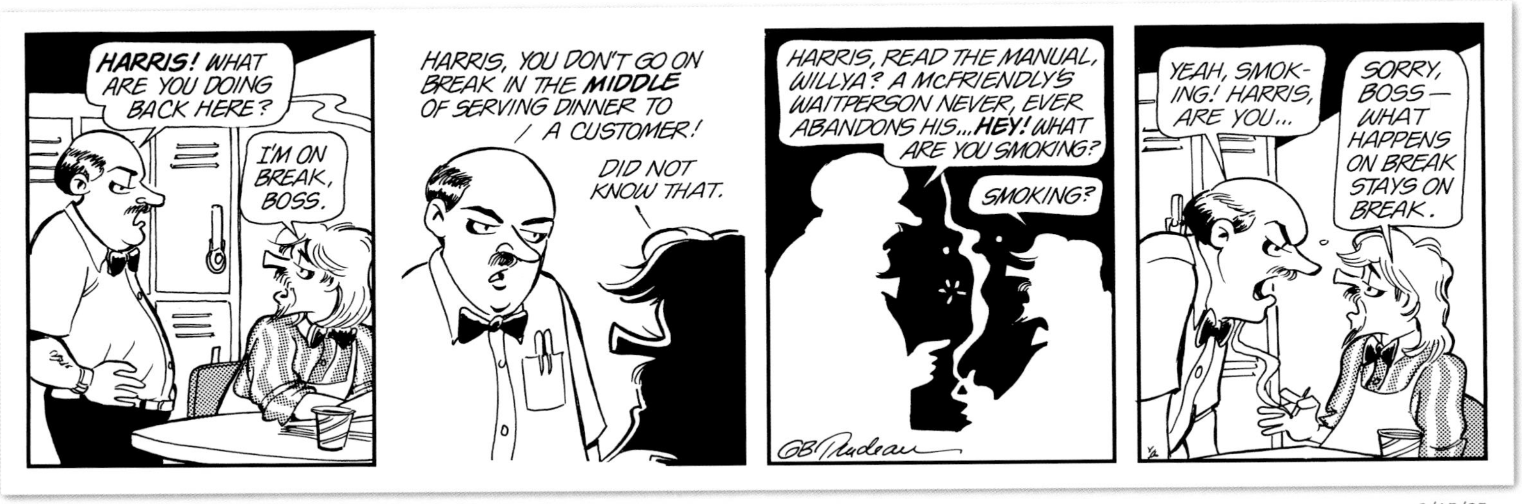
HARRIS! WHAT ARE YOU DOING BACK HERE?
I'M ON BREAK, BOSS.
HARRIS, YOU DON'T GO ON BREAK IN THE MIDDLE OF SERVING DINNER TO A CUSTOMER!
DID NOT KNOW THAT.
HARRIS, READ THE MANUAL, WILLYA? A McFRIENDLY'S WAITPERSON NEVER, EVER ABANDONS HIS... HEY! WHAT ARE YOU SMOKING?
SMOKING?
YEAH, SMOKING! HARRIS, ARE YOU...
SORRY, BOSS— WHAT HAPPENS ON BREAK STAYS ON BREAK.
GB Trudeau

2/15/05

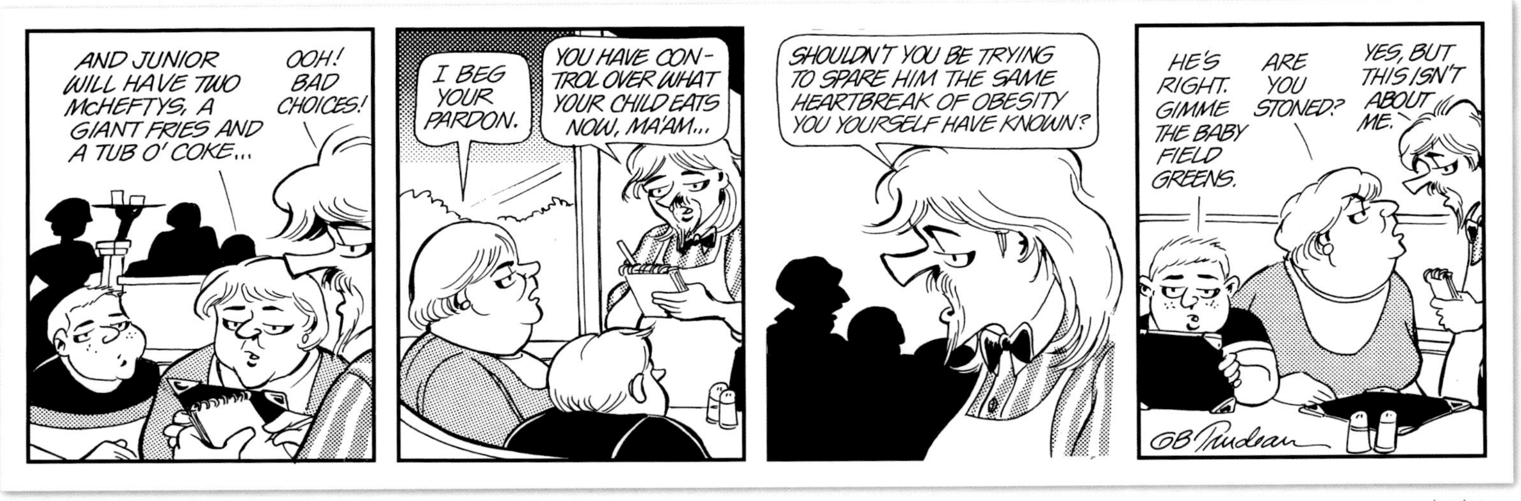
AND JUNIOR WILL HAVE TWO McHEFTYS, A GIANT FRIES AND A TUB O' COKE...
OOH! BAD CHOICES!
I BEG YOUR PARDON.
YOU HAVE CONTROL OVER WHAT YOUR CHILD EATS NOW, MA'AM...
SHOULDN'T YOU BE TRYING TO SPARE HIM THE SAME HEARTBREAK OF OBESITY YOU YOURSELF HAVE KNOWN?
HE'S RIGHT. GIMME THE BABY FIELD GREENS.
ARE YOU STONED?
YES, BUT THIS ISN'T ABOUT ME.
GB Trudeau

2/16/05

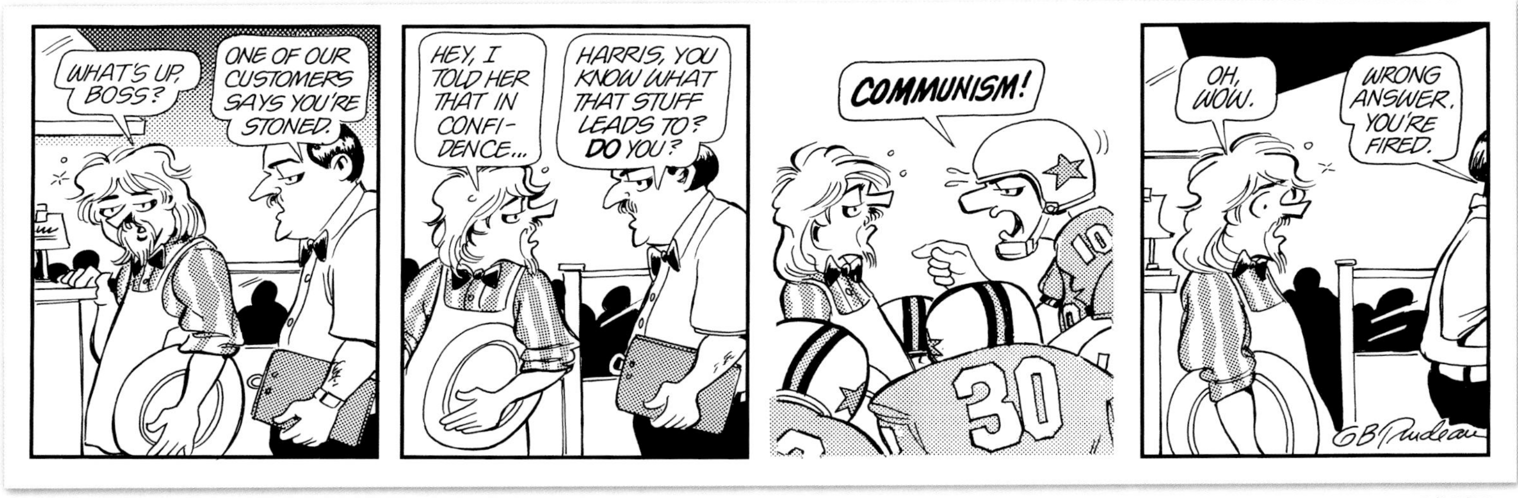
WHAT'S UP, BOSS?
ONE OF OUR CUSTOMERS SAYS YOU'RE STONED.
HEY, I TOLD HER THAT IN CONFIDENCE...
HARRIS, YOU KNOW WHAT THAT STUFF LEADS TO? DO YOU?
COMMUNISM!
OH, WOW.
WRONG ANSWER. YOU'RE FIRED.
GB Trudeau

2/17/05

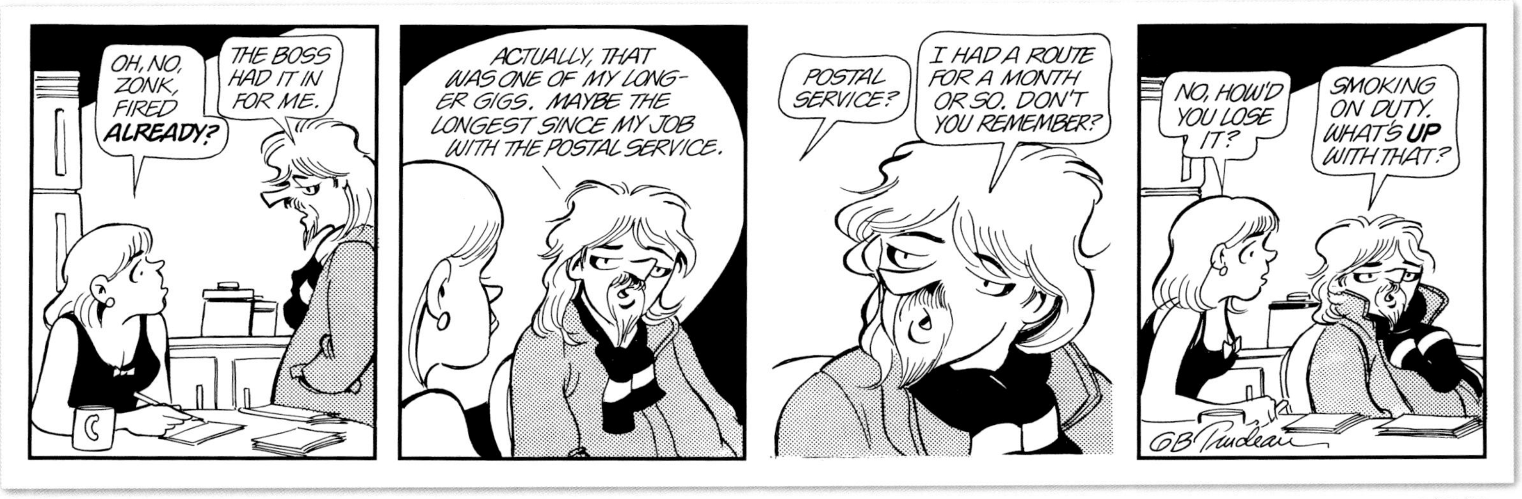
OH, NO, ZONK, FIRED ALREADY?
THE BOSS HAD IT IN FOR ME.
ACTUALLY, THAT WAS ONE OF MY LONGER GIGS. MAYBE THE LONGEST SINCE MY JOB WITH THE POSTAL SERVICE.
POSTAL SERVICE?
I HAD A ROUTE FOR A MONTH OR SO. DON'T YOU REMEMBER?
NO, HOW'D YOU LOSE IT?
SMOKING ON DUTY. WHAT'S UP WITH THAT?
GB Trudeau

2/18/05

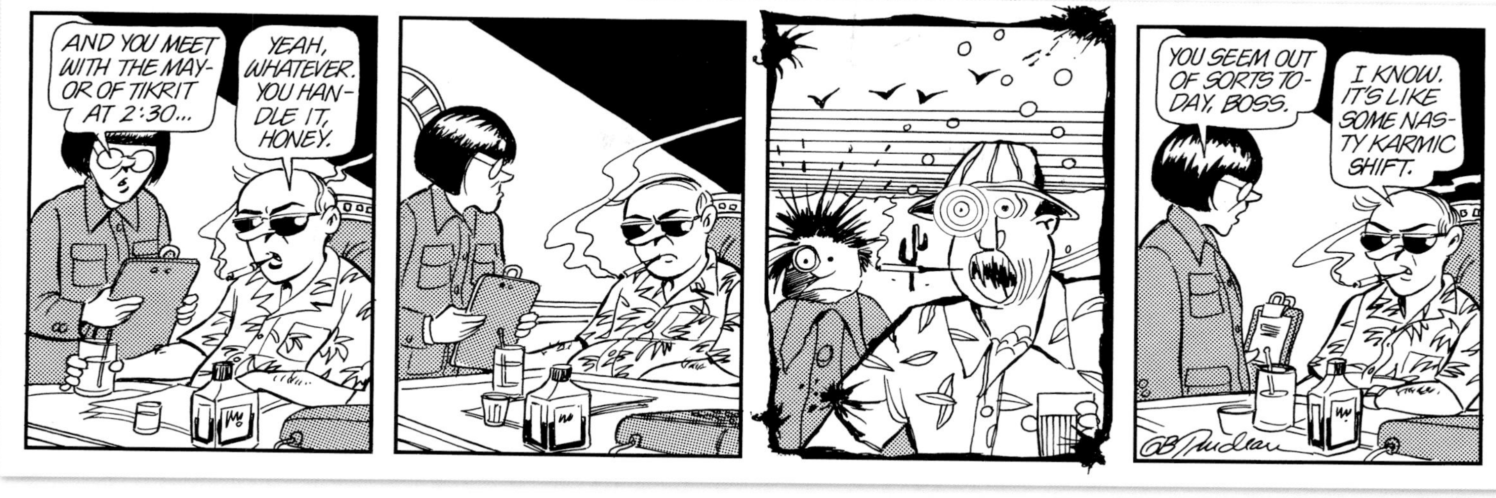
AND YOU MEET WITH THE MAYOR OF TIKRIT AT 2:30...
YEAH, WHATEVER. YOU HANDLE IT, HONEY.
YOU SEEM OUT OF SORTS TODAY, BOSS.
I KNOW. IT'S LIKE SOME NASTY KARMIC SHIFT.

3/7/05

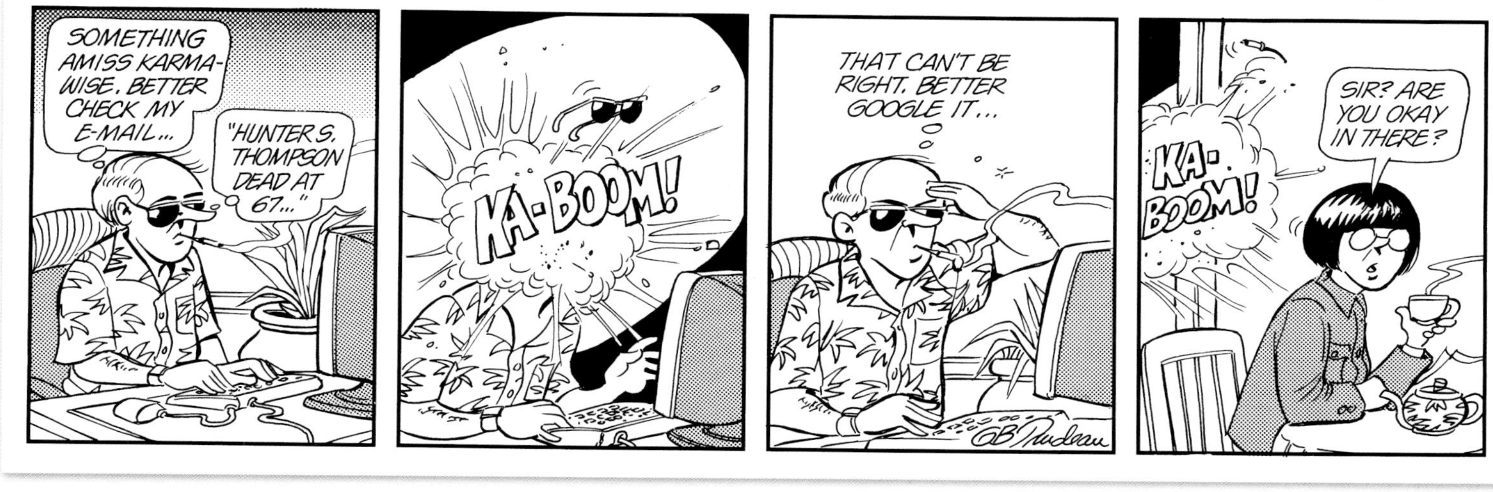
SOMETHING AMISS KARMAWISE. BETTER CHECK MY E-MAIL...
"HUNTER S. THOMPSON DEAD AT 67..."
KA-BOOM!
THAT CAN'T BE RIGHT. BETTER GOOGLE IT...
KA-BOOM!
SIR? ARE YOU OKAY IN THERE?

3/8/05

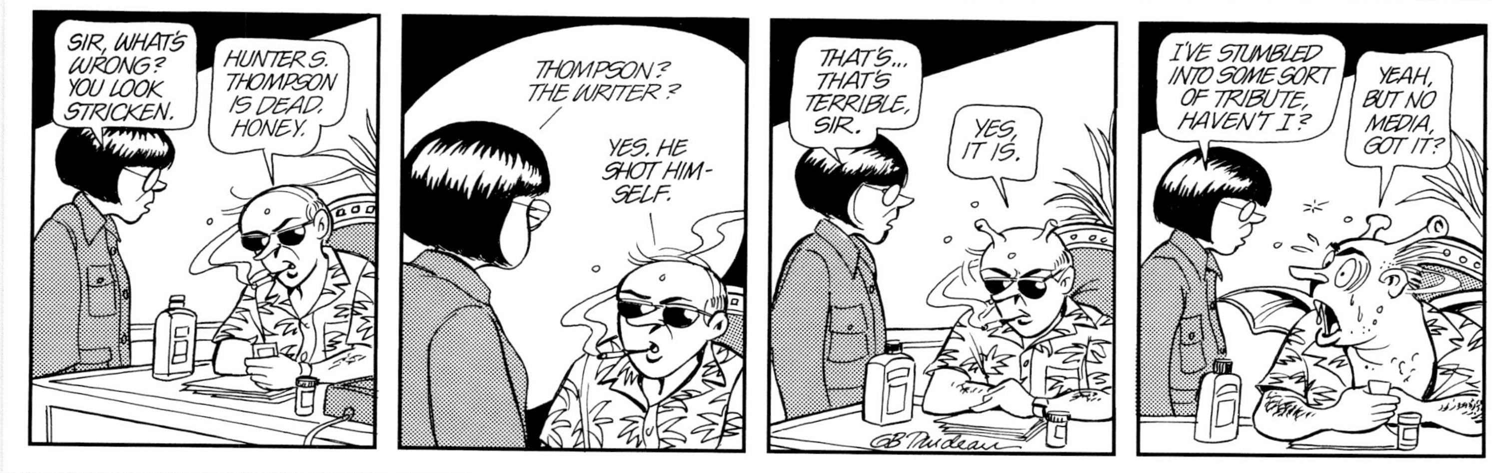
SIR, WHAT'S WRONG? YOU LOOK STRICKEN.
HUNTER S. THOMPSON IS DEAD, HONEY.
THOMPSON? THE WRITER?
YES. HE SHOT HIMSELF.
THAT'S... THAT'S TERRIBLE, SIR.
YES, IT IS.
I'VE STUMBLED INTO SOME SORT OF TRIBUTE, HAVEN'T I?
YEAH, BUT NO MEDIA, GOT IT?

3/9/05

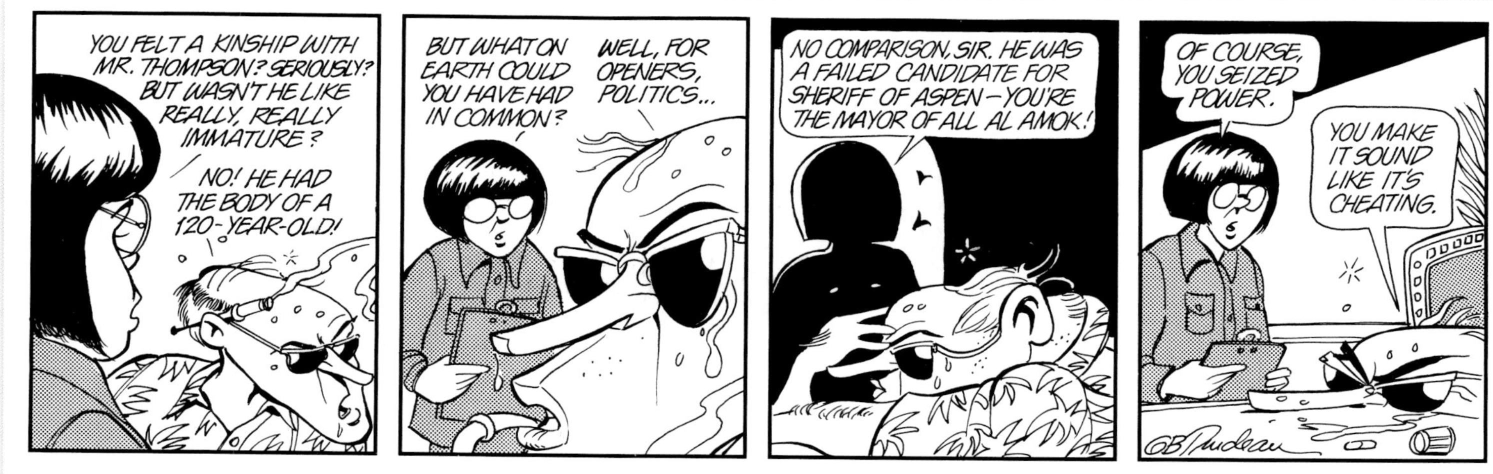
YOU FELT A KINSHIP WITH MR. THOMPSON? SERIOUSLY? BUT WASN'T HE LIKE REALLY, REALLY IMMATURE?
NO! HE HAD THE BODY OF A 120-YEAR-OLD!
BUT WHAT ON EARTH COULD YOU HAVE HAD IN COMMON?
WELL, FOR OPENERS, POLITICS...
NO COMPARISON, SIR. HE WAS A FAILED CANDIDATE FOR SHERIFF OF ASPEN – YOU'RE THE MAYOR OF ALL AL AMOK!
OF COURSE, YOU SEIZED POWER.
YOU MAKE IT SOUND LIKE IT'S CHEATING.

3/10/05

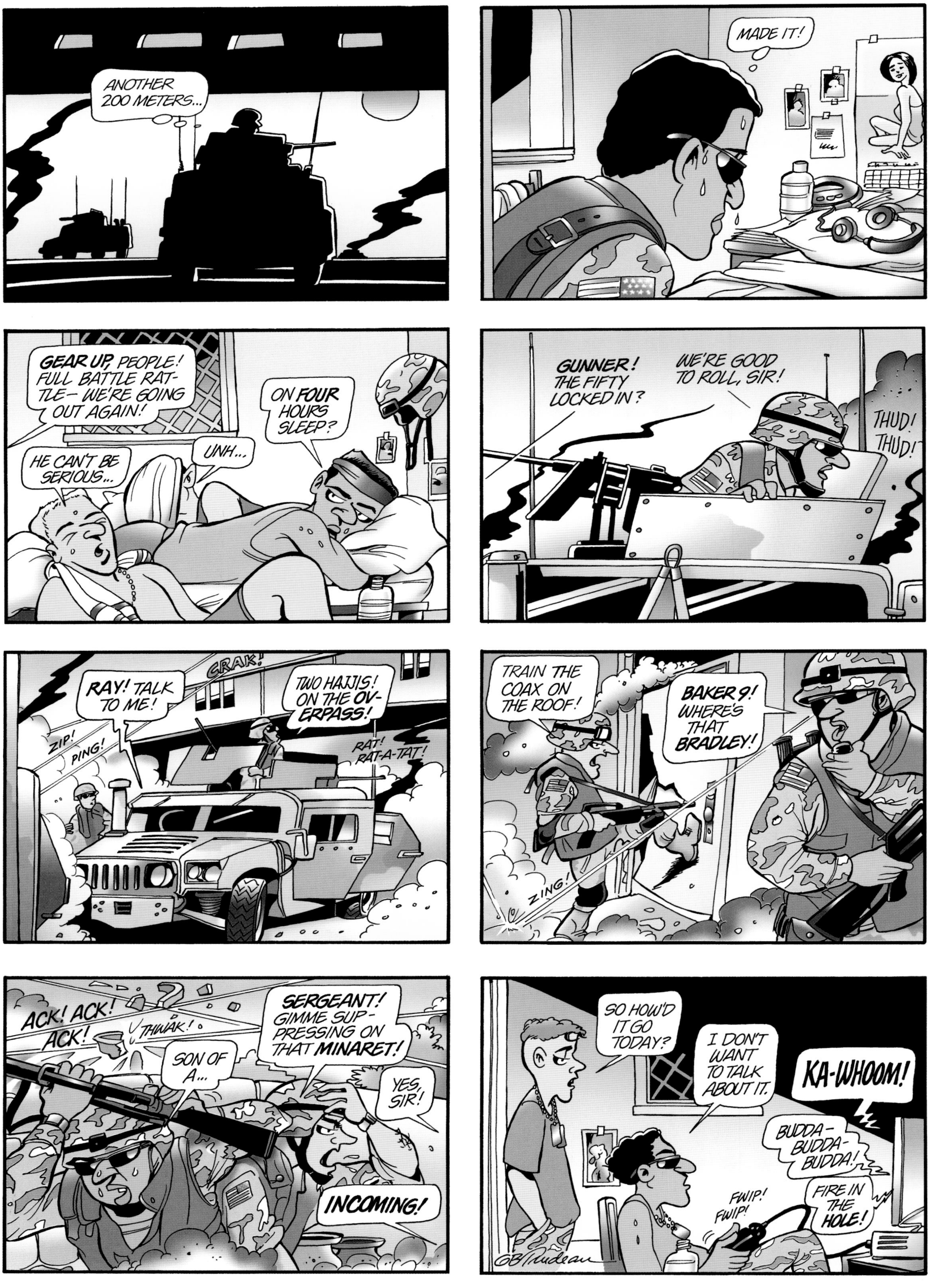
ANOTHER 200 METERS...
MADE IT!
GEAR UP, PEOPLE! FULL BATTLE RATTLE— WE'RE GOING OUT AGAIN!
ON FOUR HOURS SLEEP?
HE CAN'T BE SERIOUS...
UNH...
GUNNER! THE FIFTY LOCKED IN?
WE'RE GOOD TO ROLL, SIR!
THUD! THUD!
CRAK!
RAY! TALK TO ME!
TWO HAJJIS! ON THE OVERPASS!
ZIP!
PING!
RAT! RAT-A-TAT!
TRAIN THE COAX ON THE ROOF!
BAKER 9! WHERE'S THAT BRADLEY!
ZING!
ACK! ACK! ACK!
THWAK!
SERGEANT! GIMME SUPPRESSING ON THAT MINARET!
SON OF A...
YES, SIR!
INCOMING!
SO HOW'D IT GO TODAY?
I DON'T WANT TO TALK ABOUT IT.
KA-WHOOM!
BUDDA-BUDDA-BUDDA!
FWIP! FWIP!
FIRE IN THE HOLE!
GB Trudeau

9/11/05

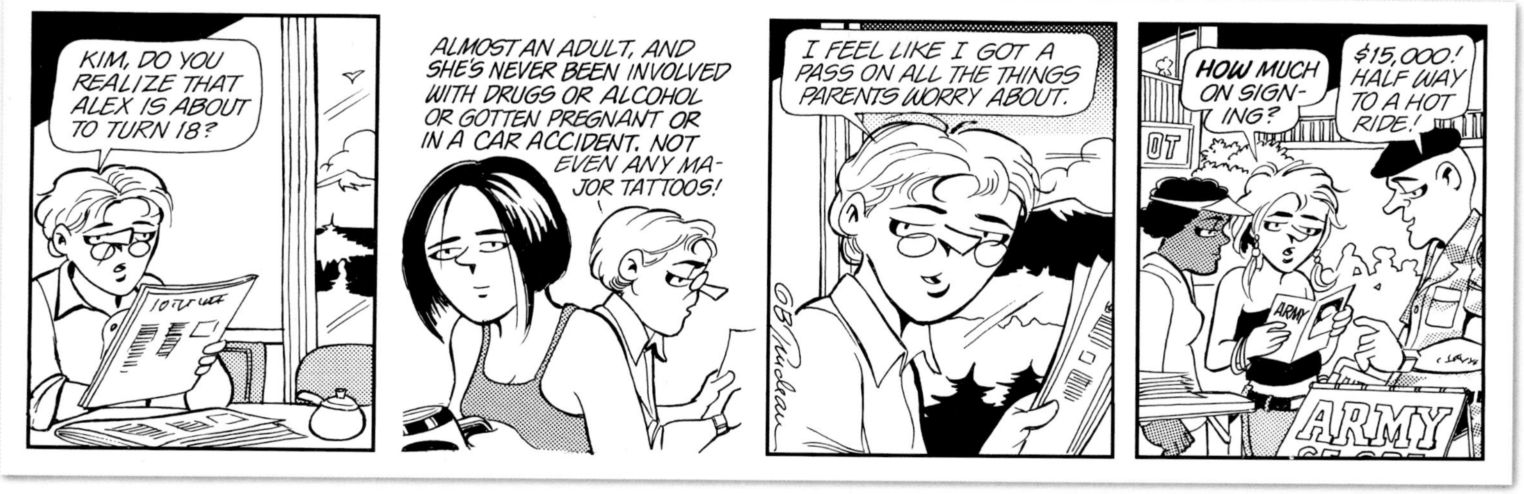
KIM, DO YOU REALIZE THAT ALEX IS ABOUT TO TURN 18?
ALMOST AN ADULT, AND SHE'S NEVER BEEN INVOLVED WITH DRUGS OR ALCOHOL OR GOTTEN PREGNANT OR IN A CAR ACCIDENT. NOT EVEN ANY MAJOR TATTOOS!
I FEEL LIKE I GOT A PASS ON ALL THE THINGS PARENTS WORRY ABOUT.
HOW MUCH ON SIGNING?
$15,000! HALF WAY TO A HOT RIDE!
ARMY

4/4/05

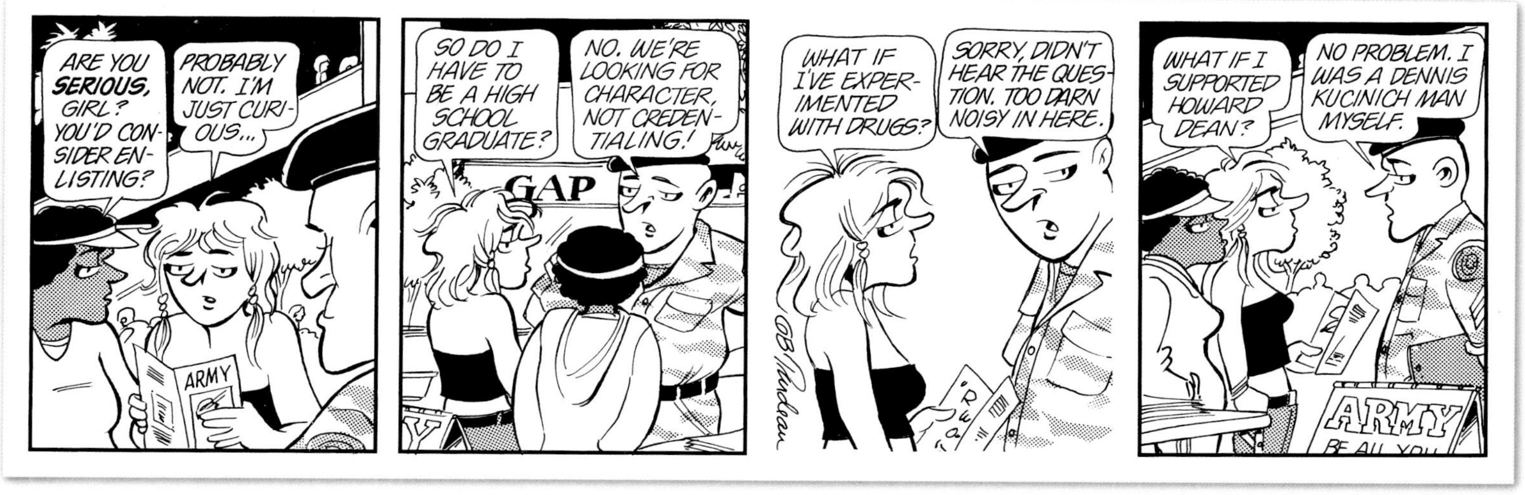
ARE YOU SERIOUS, GIRL? YOU'D CONSIDER ENLISTING?
PROBABLY NOT. I'M JUST CURIOUS...
ARMY
SO DO I HAVE TO BE A HIGH SCHOOL GRADUATE?
NO. WE'RE LOOKING FOR CHARACTER, NOT CREDENTIALING!
GAP
WHAT IF I'VE EXPERIMENTED WITH DRUGS?
SORRY, DIDN'T HEAR THE QUESTION. TOO DARN NOISY IN HERE.
WHAT IF I SUPPORTED HOWARD DEAN?
NO PROBLEM. I WAS A DENNIS KUCINICH MAN MYSELF.
ARMY

4/5/05

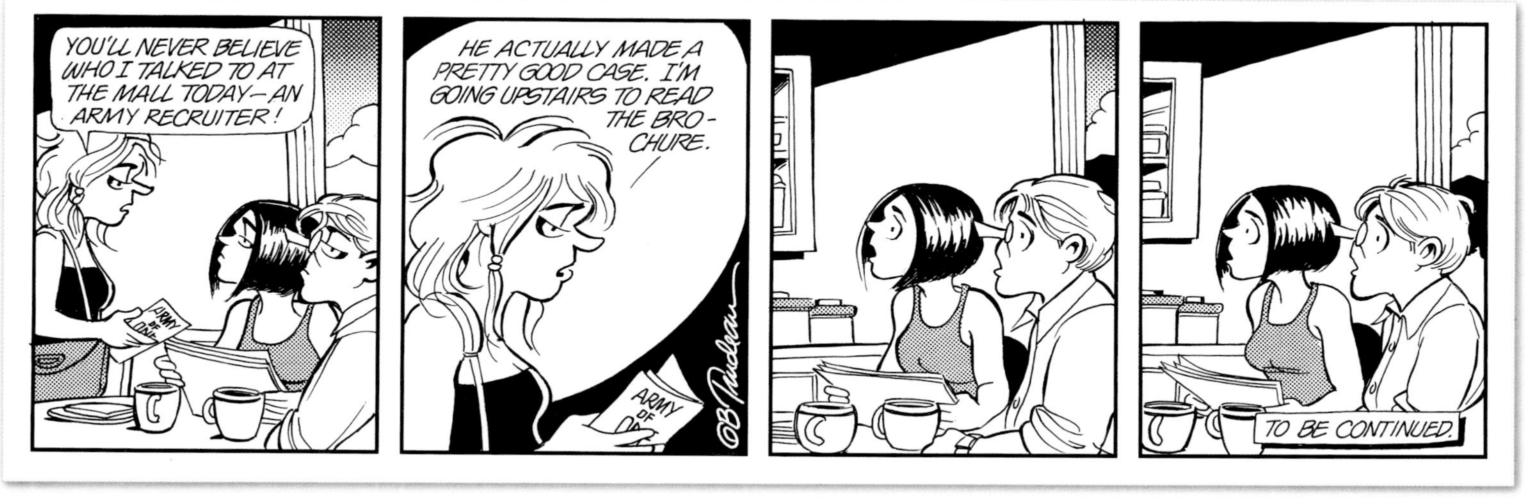
YOU'LL NEVER BELIEVE WHO I TALKED TO AT THE MALL TODAY—AN ARMY RECRUITER!
HE ACTUALLY MADE A PRETTY GOOD CASE. I'M GOING UPSTAIRS TO READ THE BROCHURE.
TO BE CONTINUED.

4/8/05

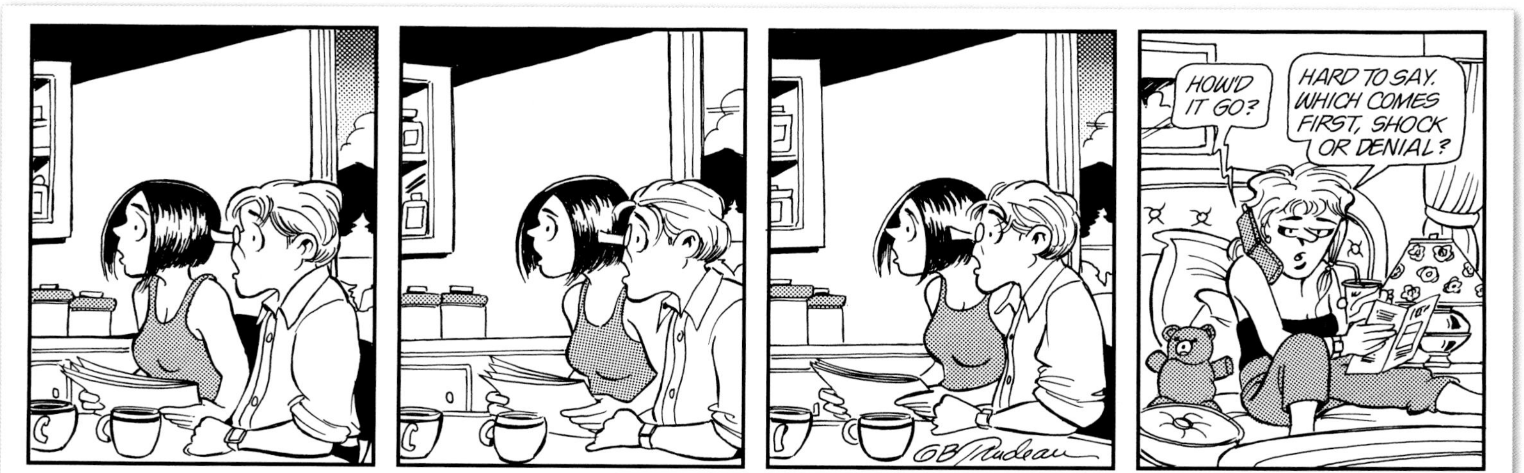
HOW'D IT GO?
HARD TO SAY. WHICH COMES FIRST, SHOCK OR DENIAL?

4/9/05

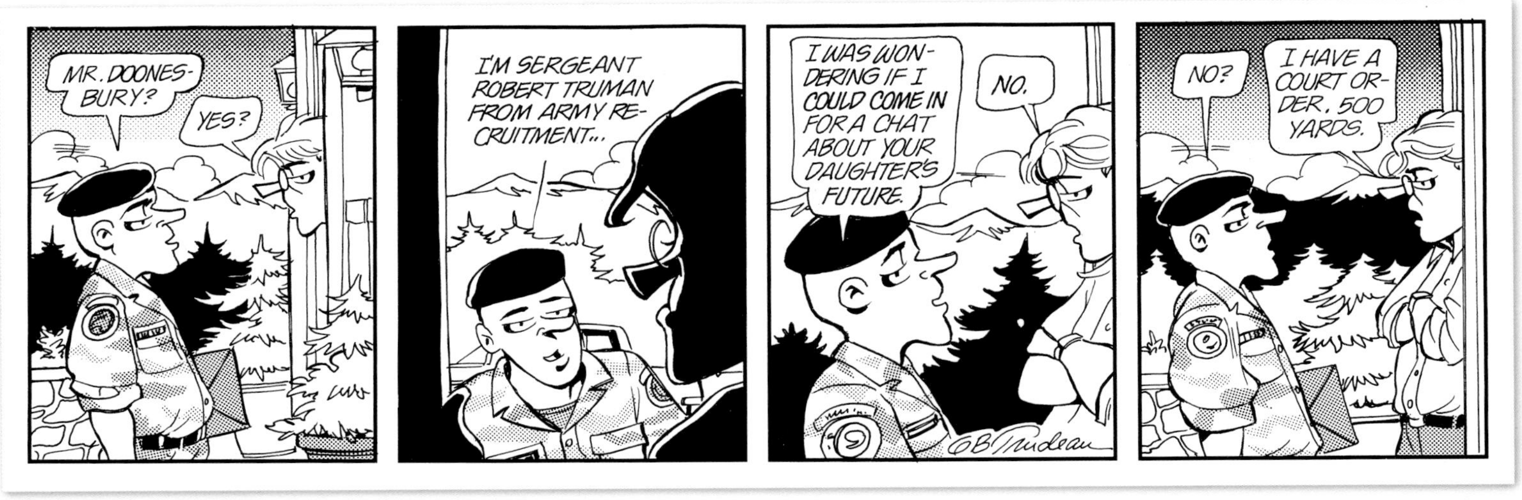
MR. DOONESBURY?
YES?
I'M SERGEANT ROBERT TRUMAN FROM ARMY RECRUITMENT...
I WAS WONDERING IF I COULD COME IN FOR A CHAT ABOUT YOUR DAUGHTER'S FUTURE.
NO.
NO?
I HAVE A COURT ORDER. 500 YARDS.

4/11/05

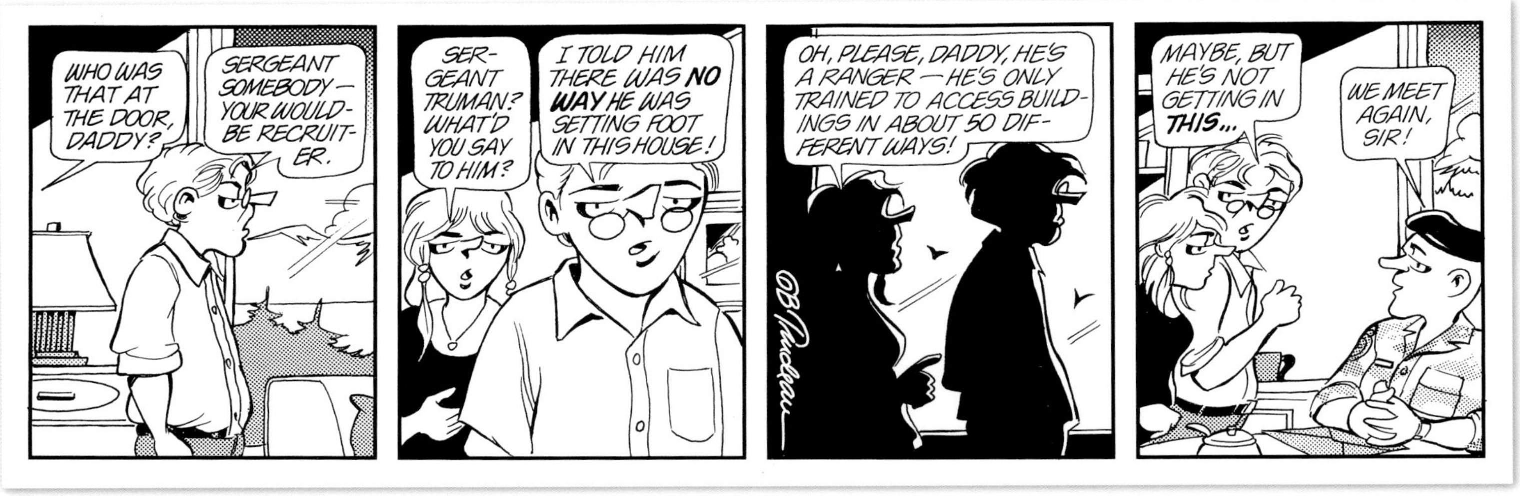
WHO WAS THAT AT THE DOOR, DADDY?
SERGEANT SOMEBODY — YOUR WOULD-BE RECRUITER.
SERGEANT TRUMAN? WHAT'D YOU SAY TO HIM?
I TOLD HIM THERE WAS NO WAY HE WAS SETTING FOOT IN THIS HOUSE!
OH, PLEASE, DADDY, HE'S A RANGER — HE'S ONLY TRAINED TO ACCESS BUILDINGS IN ABOUT 50 DIFFERENT WAYS!
MAYBE, BUT HE'S NOT GETTING IN THIS...
WE MEET AGAIN, SIR!

4/12/05

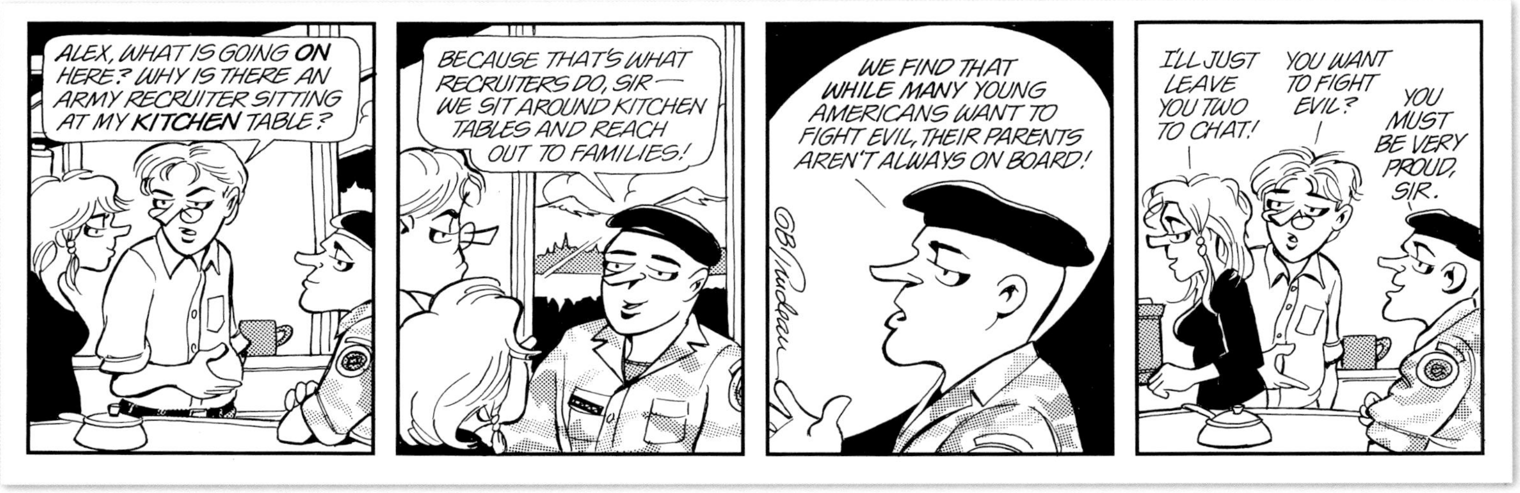
ALEX, WHAT IS GOING ON HERE? WHY IS THERE AN ARMY RECRUITER SITTING AT MY KITCHEN TABLE?
BECAUSE THAT'S WHAT RECRUITERS DO, SIR — WE SIT AROUND KITCHEN TABLES AND REACH OUT TO FAMILIES!
WE FIND THAT WHILE MANY YOUNG AMERICANS WANT TO FIGHT EVIL, THEIR PARENTS AREN'T ALWAYS ON BOARD!
I'LL JUST LEAVE YOU TWO TO CHAT!
YOU WANT TO FIGHT EVIL?
YOU MUST BE VERY PROUD, SIR.

4/13/05

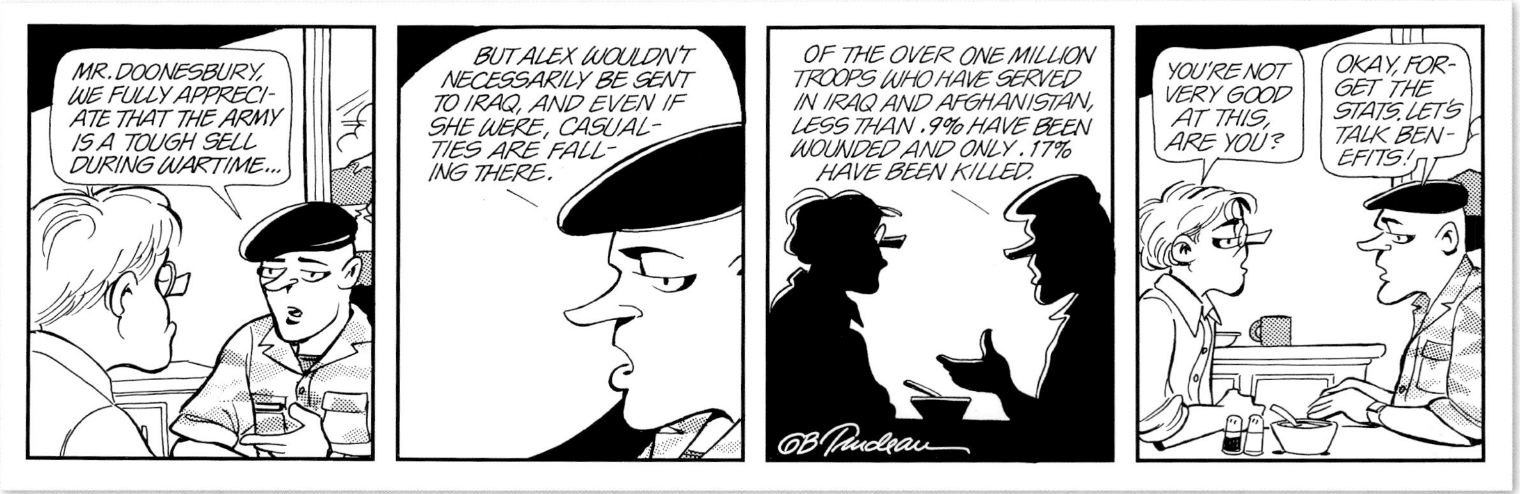
MR. DOONESBURY, WE FULLY APPRECIATE THAT THE ARMY IS A TOUGH SELL DURING WARTIME...
BUT ALEX WOULDN'T NECESSARILY BE SENT TO IRAQ, AND EVEN IF SHE WERE, CASUALTIES ARE FALLING THERE.
OF THE OVER ONE MILLION TROOPS WHO HAVE SERVED IN IRAQ AND AFGHANISTAN, LESS THAN .9% HAVE BEEN WOUNDED AND ONLY .17% HAVE BEEN KILLED.
YOU'RE NOT VERY GOOD AT THIS, ARE YOU?
OKAY, FORGET THE STATS. LET'S TALK BENEFITS!

4/14/05

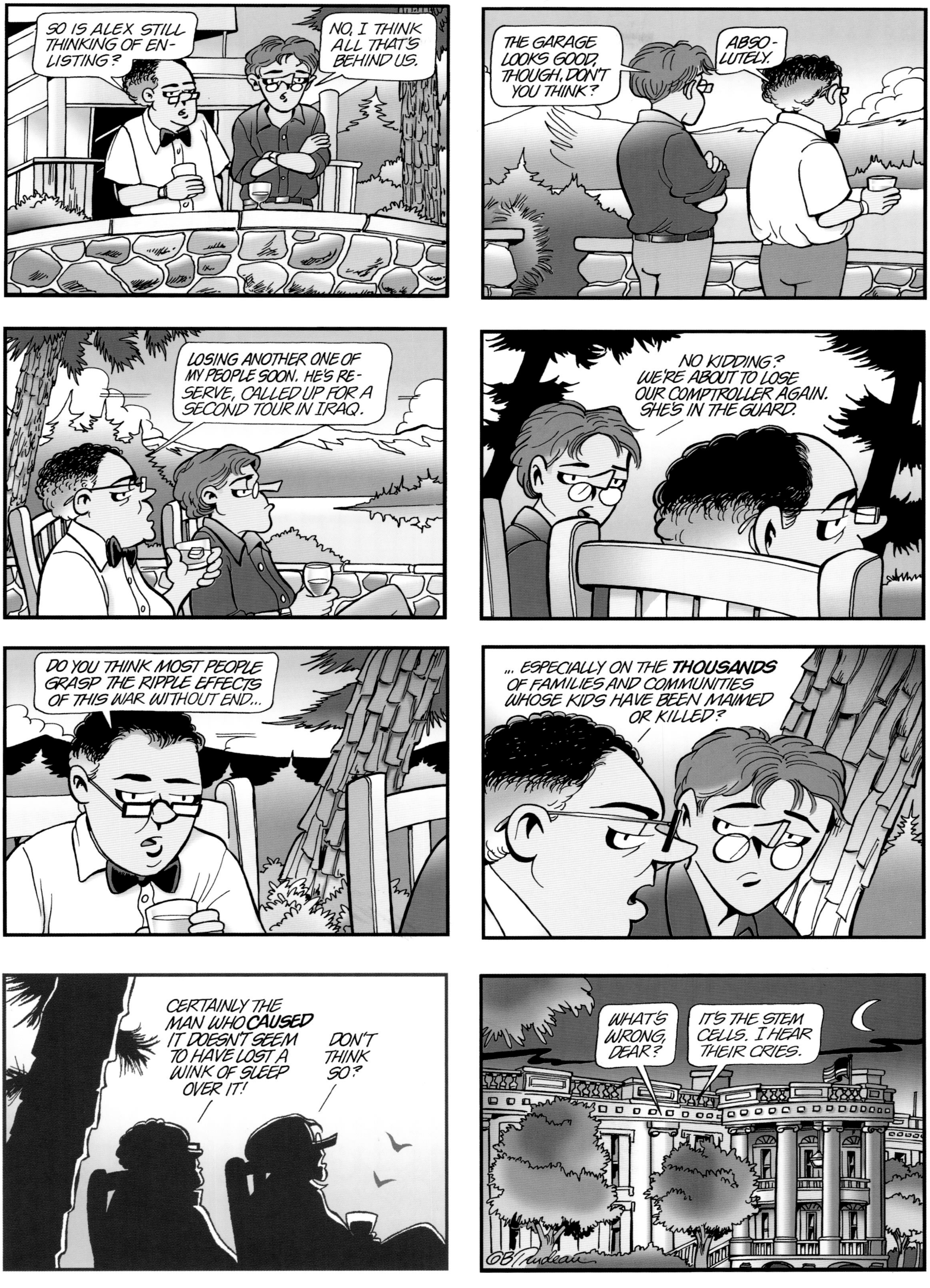
SO IS ALEX STILL THINKING OF EN-LISTING?
NO, I THINK ALL THAT'S BEHIND US.
THE GARAGE LOOKS GOOD, THOUGH, DON'T YOU THINK?
ABSO-LUTELY.
LOSING ANOTHER ONE OF MY PEOPLE SOON. HE'S RE-SERVE, CALLED UP FOR A SECOND TOUR IN IRAQ.
NO KIDDING? WE'RE ABOUT TO LOSE OUR COMPTROLLER AGAIN. SHE'S IN THE GUARD.
DO YOU THINK MOST PEOPLE GRASP THE RIPPLE EFFECTS OF THIS WAR WITHOUT END...
... ESPECIALLY ON THE **THOUSANDS** OF FAMILIES AND COMMUNITIES WHOSE KIDS HAVE BEEN MAIMED OR KILLED?
CERTAINLY THE MAN WHO **CAUSED** IT DOESN'T SEEM TO HAVE LOST A WINK OF SLEEP OVER IT!
DON'T THINK SO?
WHAT'S WRONG, DEAR?
IT'S THE STEM CELLS. I HEAR THEIR CRIES.
©B. Trudeau

7/10/05

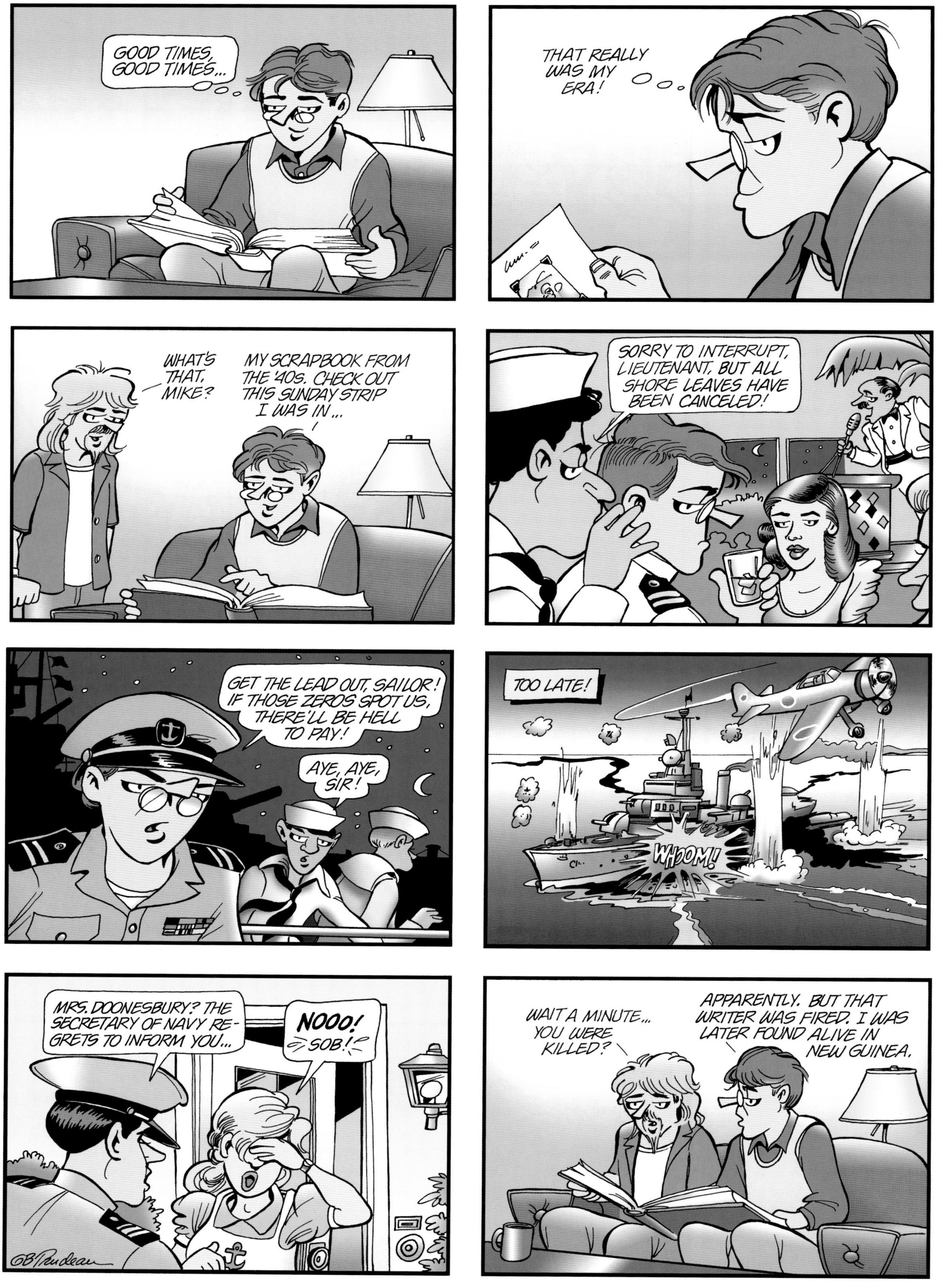

GOOD TIMES, GOOD TIMES...
THAT REALLY WAS MY ERA!
WHAT'S THAT, MIKE?
MY SCRAPBOOK FROM THE '40S. CHECK OUT THIS SUNDAY STRIP I WAS IN...
SORRY TO INTERRUPT, LIEUTENANT, BUT ALL SHORE LEAVES HAVE BEEN CANCELED!
GET THE LEAD OUT, SAILOR! IF THOSE ZEROS SPOT US, THERE'LL BE HELL TO PAY!
AYE, AYE, SIR!
TOO LATE!
WHOOM!
MRS. DOONESBURY? THE SECRETARY OF NAVY REGRETS TO INFORM YOU...
NOOO!
SOB!
WAIT A MINUTE... YOU WERE KILLED?
APPARENTLY. BUT THAT WRITER WAS FIRED. I WAS LATER FOUND ALIVE IN NEW GUINEA.
GB Trudeau

8/14/05

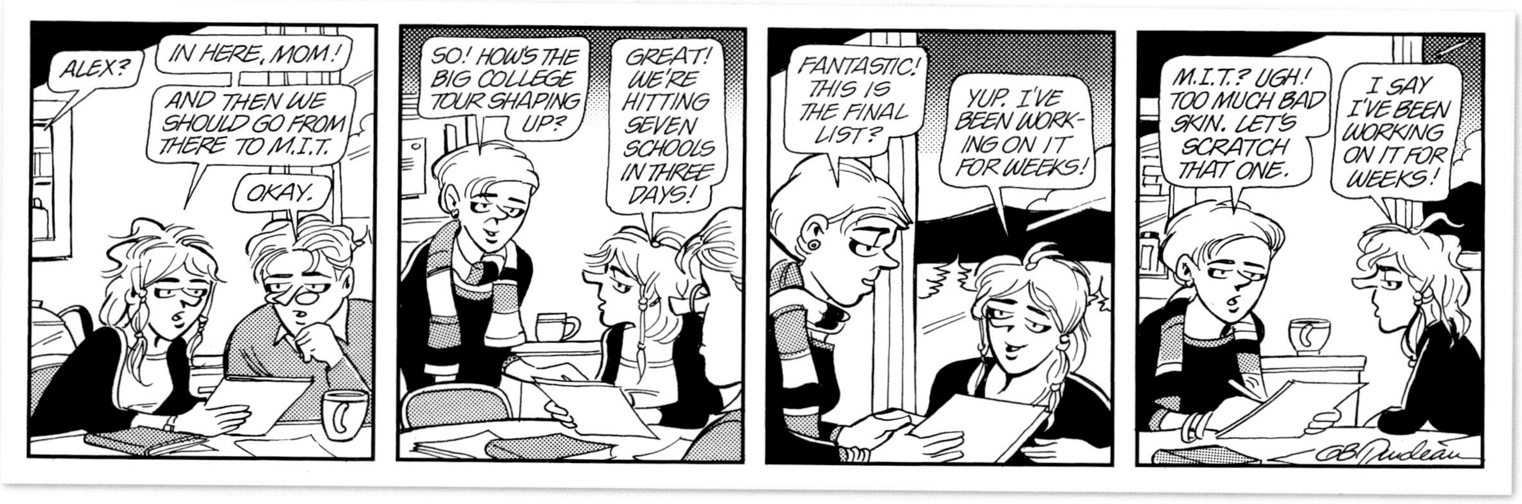
ALEX?
IN HERE, MOM!
AND THEN WE SHOULD GO FROM THERE TO M.I.T.
OKAY.
SO! HOW'S THE BIG COLLEGE TOUR SHAPING UP?
GREAT! WE'RE HITTING SEVEN SCHOOLS IN THREE DAYS!
FANTASTIC! THIS IS THE FINAL LIST?
YUP. I'VE BEEN WORKING ON IT FOR WEEKS!
M.I.T.? UGH! TOO MUCH BAD SKIN. LET'S SCRATCH THAT ONE.
I SAY I'VE BEEN WORKING ON IT FOR WEEKS!
GB Trudeau

10/24/05

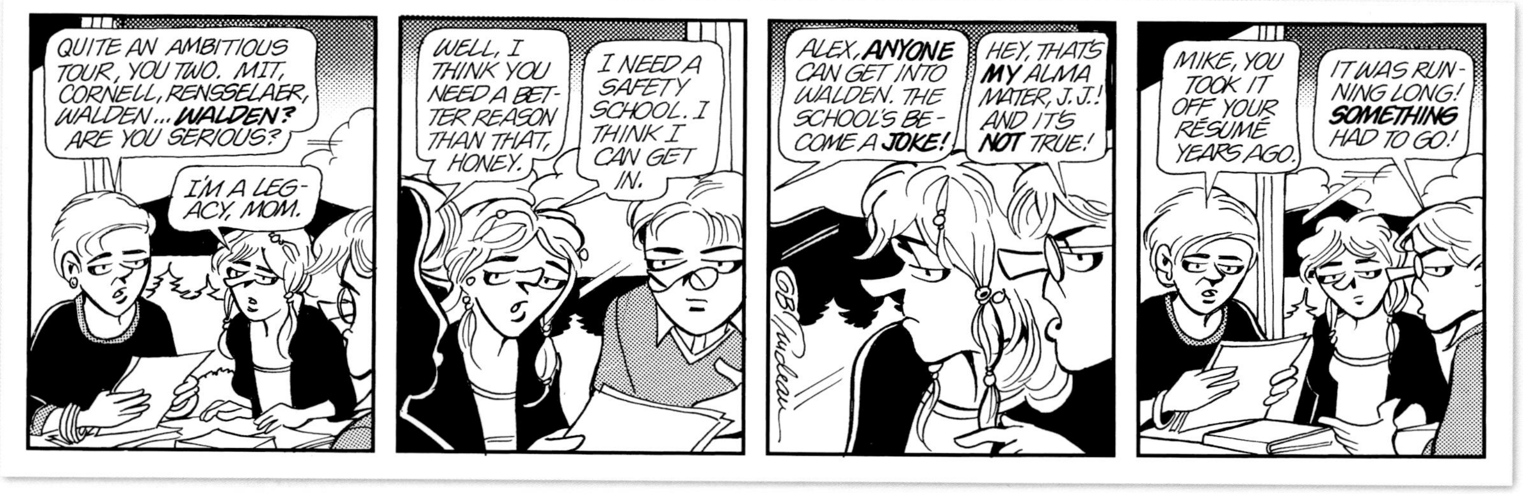
QUITE AN AMBITIOUS TOUR, YOU TWO. MIT, CORNELL, RENSSELAER, WALDEN... WALDEN? ARE YOU SERIOUS?
I'M A LEGACY, MOM.
WELL, I THINK YOU NEED A BETTER REASON THAN THAT, HONEY.
I NEED A SAFETY SCHOOL. I THINK I CAN GET IN.
ALEX, ANYONE CAN GET INTO WALDEN. THE SCHOOL'S BECOME A JOKE!
HEY, THAT'S MY ALMA MATER, J.J.! AND IT'S NOT TRUE!
MIKE, YOU TOOK IT OFF YOUR RÉSUMÉ YEARS AGO.
IT WAS RUNNING LONG! SOMETHING HAD TO GO!
GB Trudeau

10/25/05

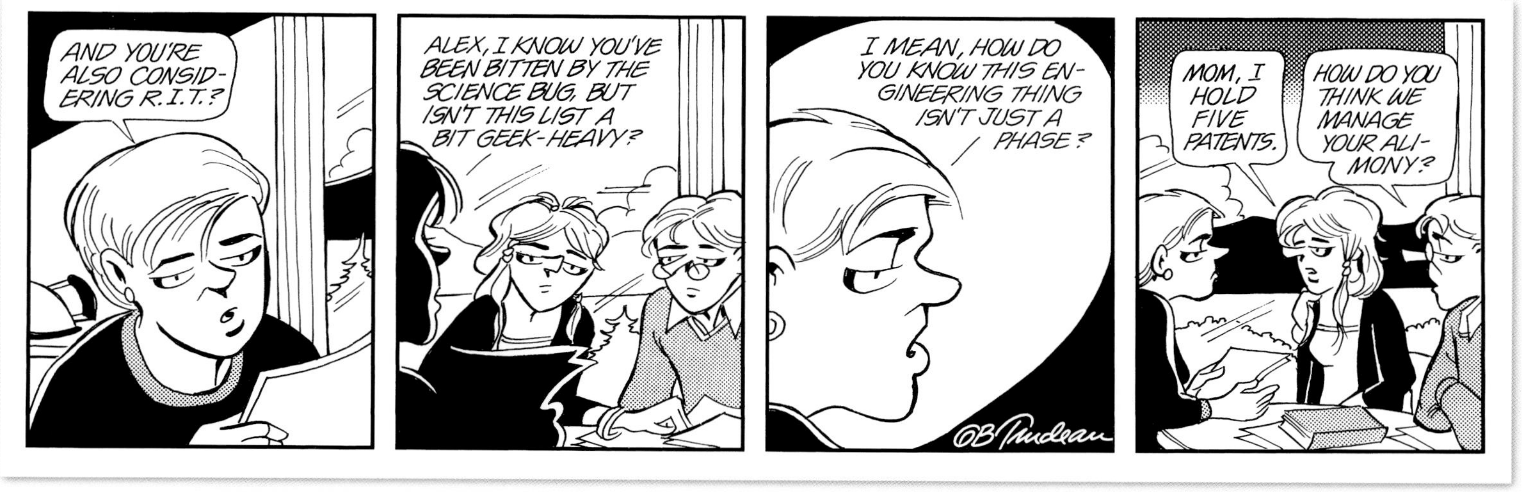
AND YOU'RE ALSO CONSIDERING R.I.T.?
ALEX, I KNOW YOU'VE BEEN BITTEN BY THE SCIENCE BUG, BUT ISN'T THIS LIST A BIT GEEK-HEAVY?
I MEAN, HOW DO YOU KNOW THIS ENGINEERING THING ISN'T JUST A PHASE?
MOM, I HOLD FIVE PATENTS.
HOW DO YOU THINK WE MANAGE YOUR ALIMONY?
GB Trudeau

10/26/05

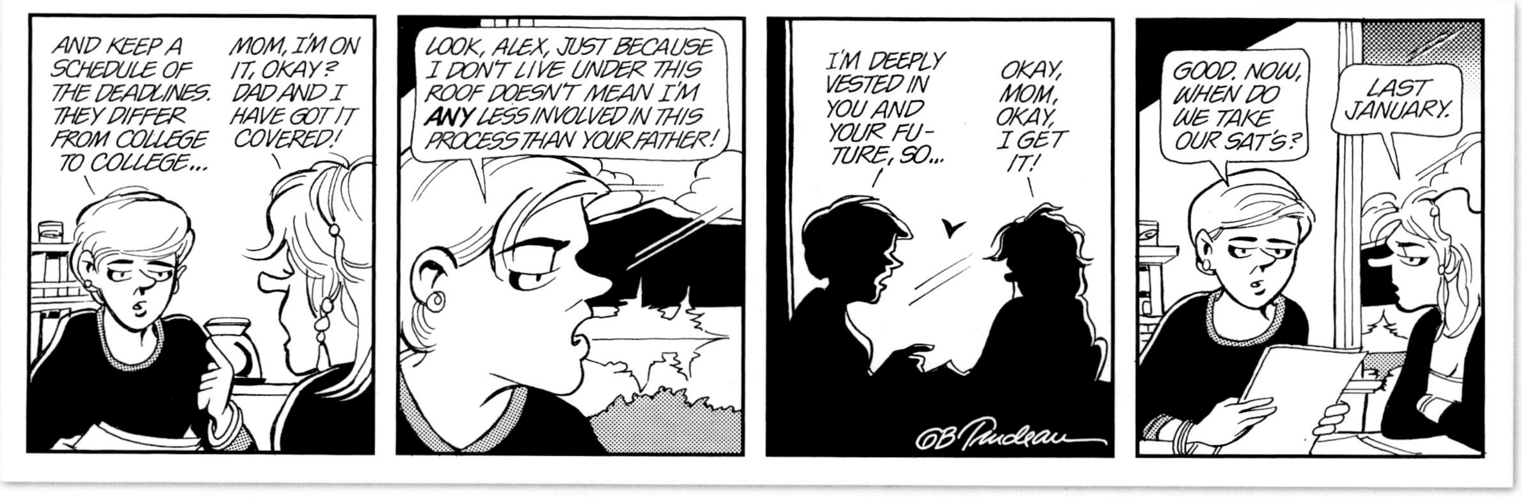
AND KEEP A SCHEDULE OF THE DEADLINES. THEY DIFFER FROM COLLEGE TO COLLEGE...
MOM, I'M ON IT, OKAY? DAD AND I HAVE GOT IT COVERED!
LOOK, ALEX, JUST BECAUSE I DON'T LIVE UNDER THIS ROOF DOESN'T MEAN I'M ANY LESS INVOLVED IN THIS PROCESS THAN YOUR FATHER!
I'M DEEPLY VESTED IN YOU AND YOUR FUTURE, SO...
OKAY, MOM, OKAY, I GET IT!
GOOD. NOW, WHEN DO WE TAKE OUR SAT'S?
LAST JANUARY.
GB Trudeau

10/27/05

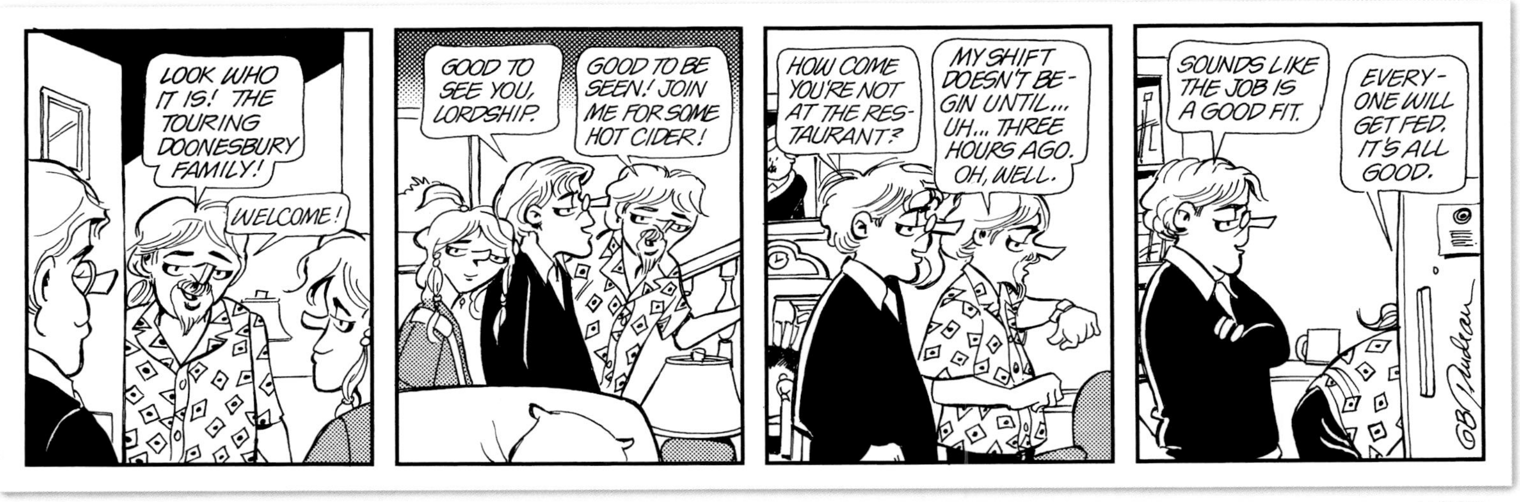
LOOK WHO IT IS! THE TOURING DOONESBURY FAMILY!
WELCOME!
GOOD TO SEE YOU, LORDSHIP.
GOOD TO BE SEEN! JOIN ME FOR SOME HOT CIDER!
HOW COME YOU'RE NOT AT THE RESTAURANT?
MY SHIFT DOESN'T BEGIN UNTIL... UH... THREE HOURS AGO. OH, WELL.
SOUNDS LIKE THE JOB IS A GOOD FIT.
EVERYONE WILL GET FED. IT'S ALL GOOD.
GB Trudeau

11/7/05

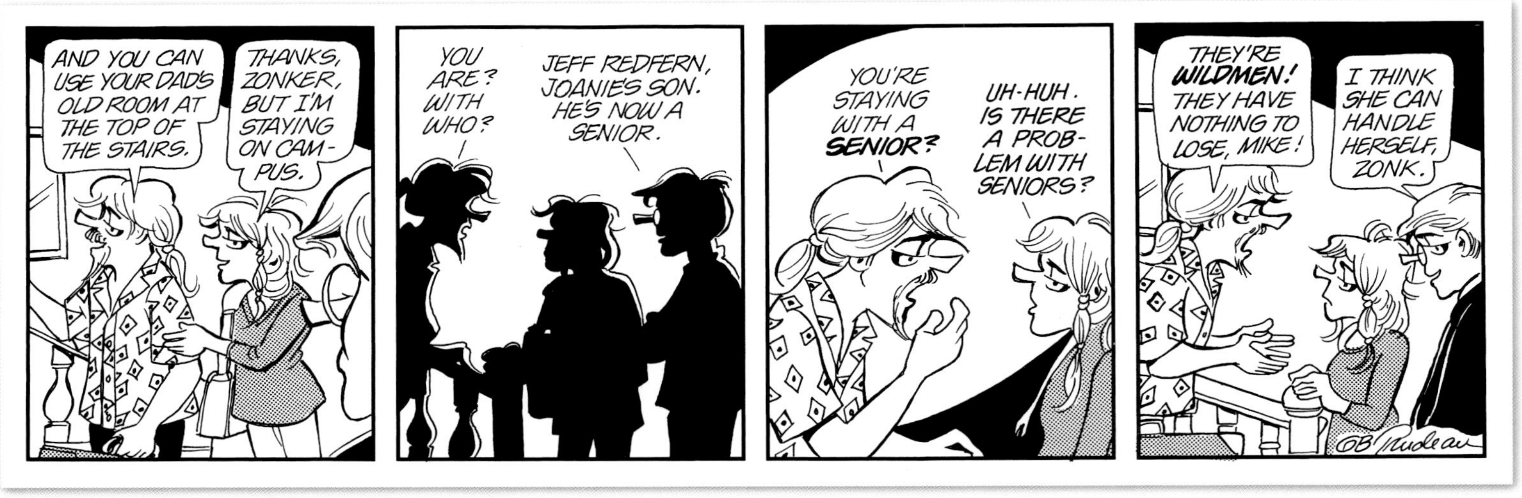
AND YOU CAN USE YOUR DAD'S OLD ROOM AT THE TOP OF THE STAIRS.
THANKS, ZONKER, BUT I'M STAYING ON CAMPUS.
YOU ARE? WITH WHO?
JEFF REDFERN, JOANIE'S SON. HE'S NOW A SENIOR.
YOU'RE STAYING WITH A SENIOR?
UH-HUH. IS THERE A PROBLEM WITH SENIORS?
THEY'RE WILDMEN! THEY HAVE NOTHING TO LOSE, MIKE!
I THINK SHE CAN HANDLE HERSELF, ZONK.
GB Trudeau

11/8/05

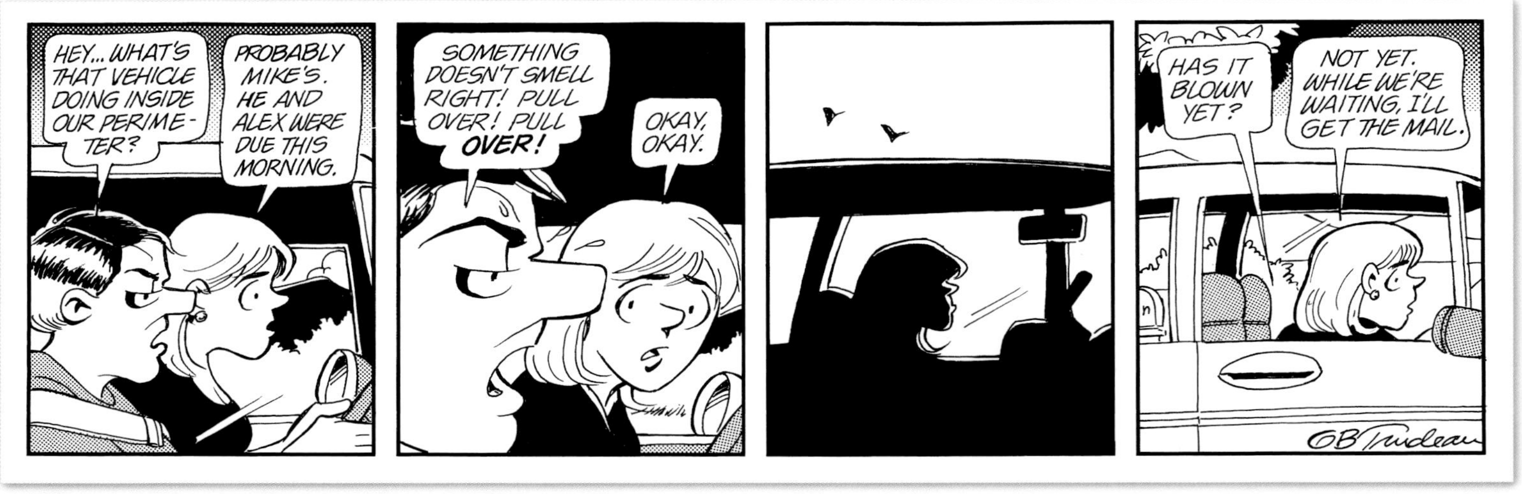
HEY... WHAT'S THAT VEHICLE DOING INSIDE OUR PERIMETER?
PROBABLY MIKE'S. HE AND ALEX WERE DUE THIS MORNING.
SOMETHING DOESN'T SMELL RIGHT! PULL OVER! PULL OVER!
OKAY, OKAY.
HAS IT BLOWN YET?
NOT YET. WHILE WE'RE WAITING, I'LL GET THE MAIL.
GB Trudeau

11/21/05

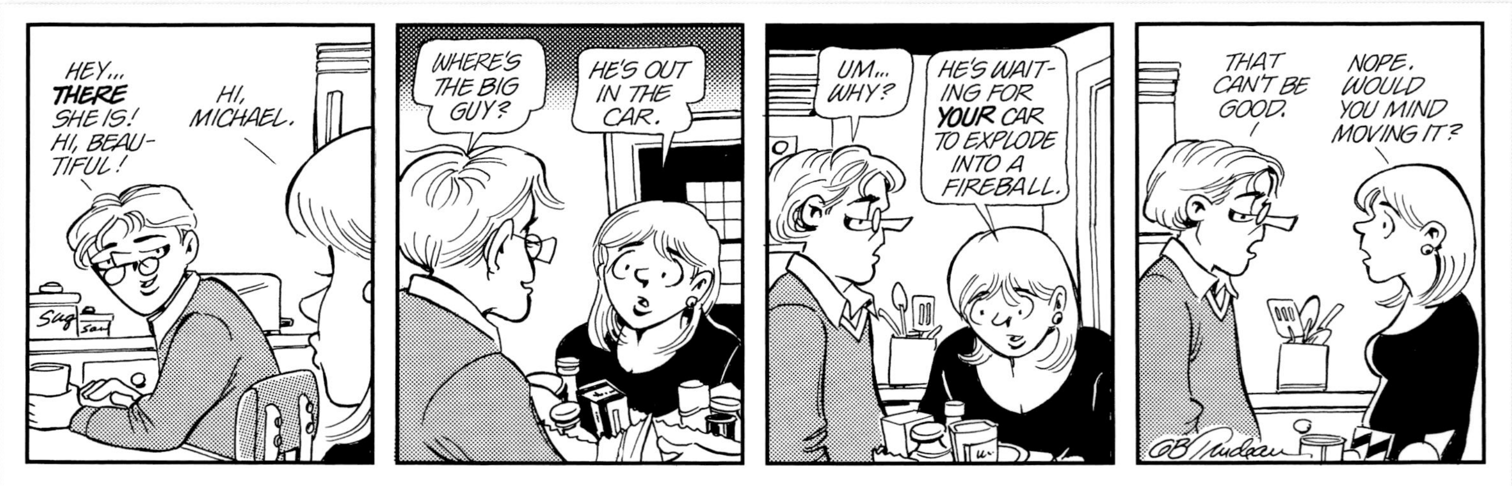
HEY... THERE SHE IS! HI, BEAUTIFUL!
HI, MICHAEL.
WHERE'S THE BIG GUY?
HE'S OUT IN THE CAR.
UM... WHY?
HE'S WAITING FOR YOUR CAR TO EXPLODE INTO A FIREBALL.
THAT CAN'T BE GOOD.
NOPE. WOULD YOU MIND MOVING IT?
GB Trudeau

11/22/05

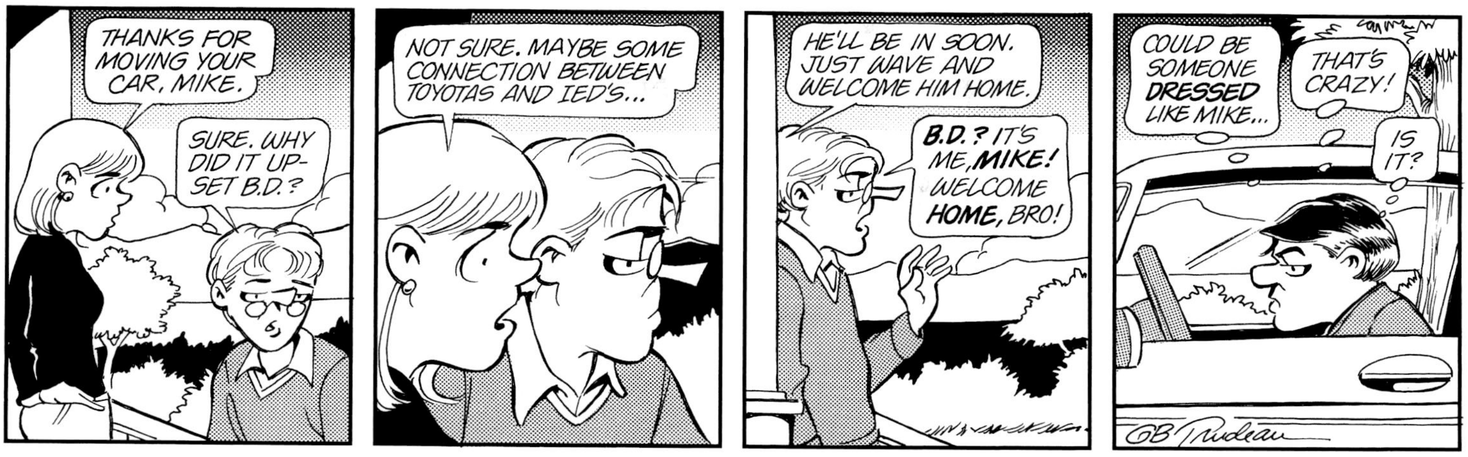
THANKS FOR MOVING YOUR CAR, MIKE.
SURE. WHY DID IT UPSET B.D.?
NOT SURE. MAYBE SOME CONNECTION BETWEEN TOYOTAS AND IED'S...
HE'LL BE IN SOON. JUST WAVE AND WELCOME HIM HOME.
B.D.? IT'S ME, MIKE! WELCOME HOME, BRO!
COULD BE SOMEONE DRESSED LIKE MIKE...
THAT'S CRAZY!
IS IT?

11/23/05

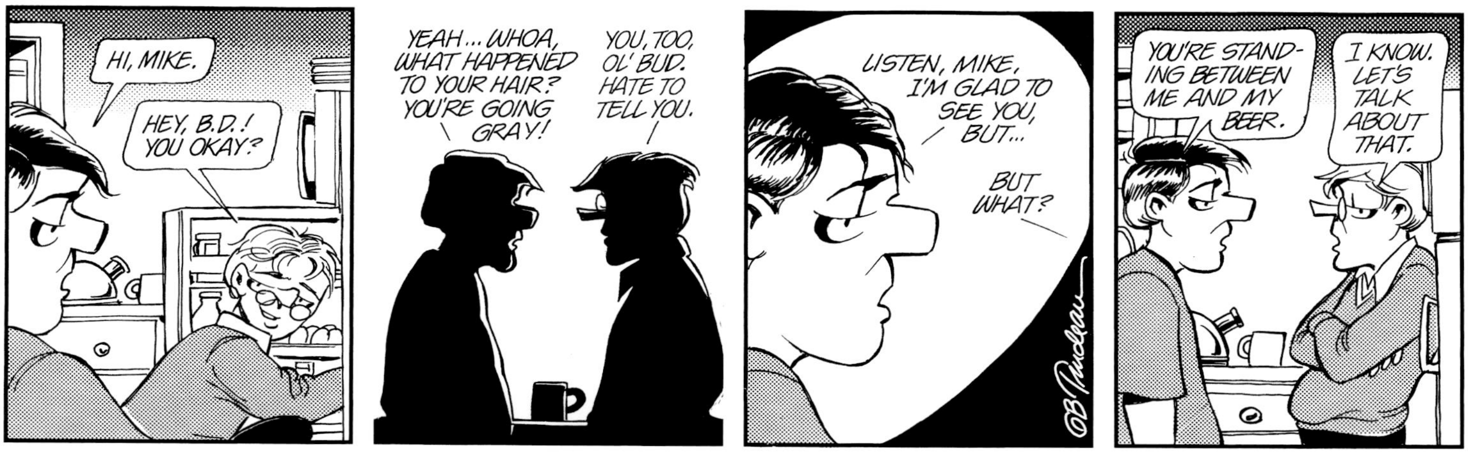
HI, MIKE.
HEY, B.D.! YOU OKAY?
YEAH... WHOA, WHAT HAPPENED TO YOUR HAIR? YOU'RE GOING GRAY!
YOU, TOO, OL' BUD. HATE TO TELL YOU.
LISTEN, MIKE, I'M GLAD TO SEE YOU, BUT...
BUT WHAT?
YOU'RE STANDING BETWEEN ME AND MY BEER.
I KNOW. LET'S TALK ABOUT THAT.

11/26/05

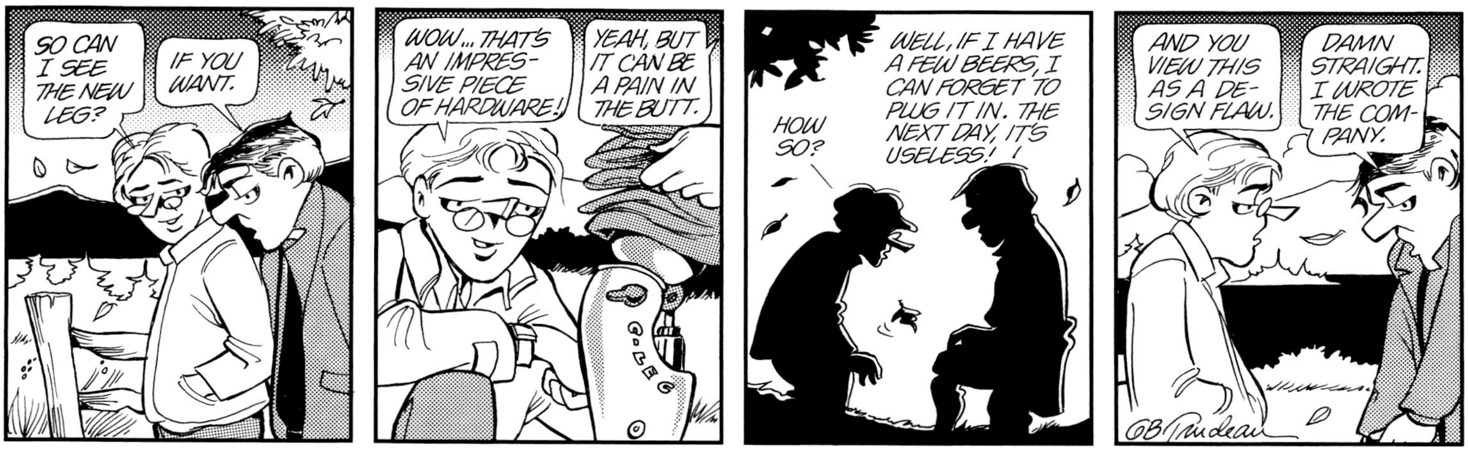
SO CAN I SEE THE NEW LEG?
IF YOU WANT.
WOW... THAT'S AN IMPRESSIVE PIECE OF HARDWARE!
YEAH, BUT IT CAN BE A PAIN IN THE BUTT.
HOW SO?
WELL, IF I HAVE A FEW BEERS, I CAN FORGET TO PLUG IT IN. THE NEXT DAY, IT'S USELESS!
AND YOU VIEW THIS AS A DESIGN FLAW.
DAMN STRAIGHT. I WROTE THE COMPANY.

11/28/05

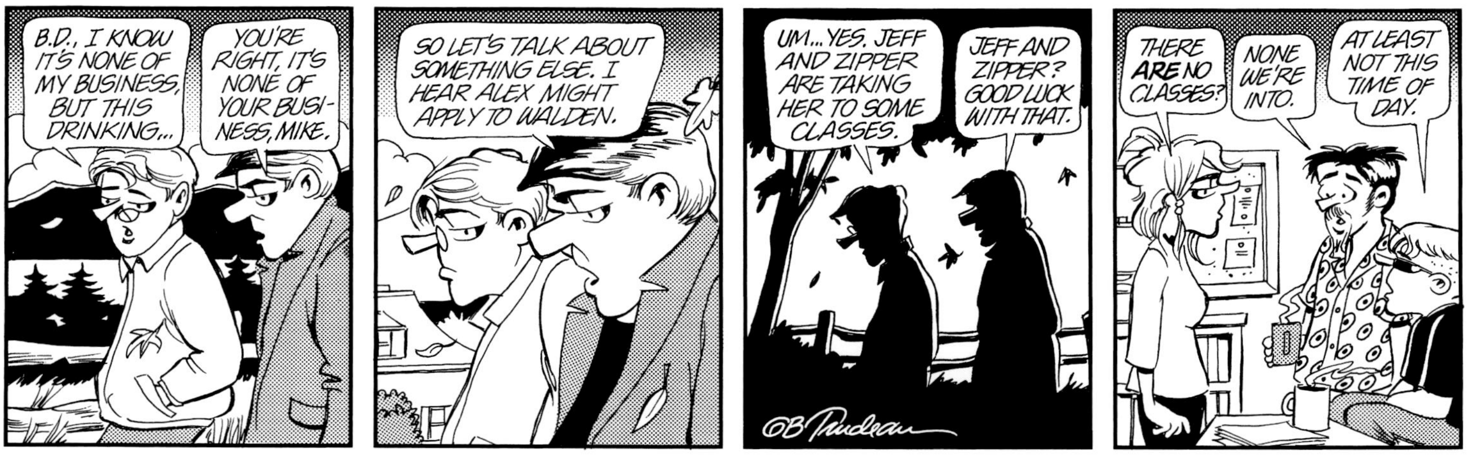
B.D., I KNOW IT'S NONE OF MY BUSINESS, BUT THIS DRINKING...
YOU'RE RIGHT, IT'S NONE OF YOUR BUSINESS, MIKE.
SO LET'S TALK ABOUT SOMETHING ELSE. I HEAR ALEX MIGHT APPLY TO WALDEN.
UM... YES. JEFF AND ZIPPER ARE TAKING HER TO SOME CLASSES.
JEFF AND ZIPPER? GOOD LUCK WITH THAT.
THERE ARE NO CLASSES?
NONE WE'RE INTO.
AT LEAST NOT THIS TIME OF DAY.

11/29/05

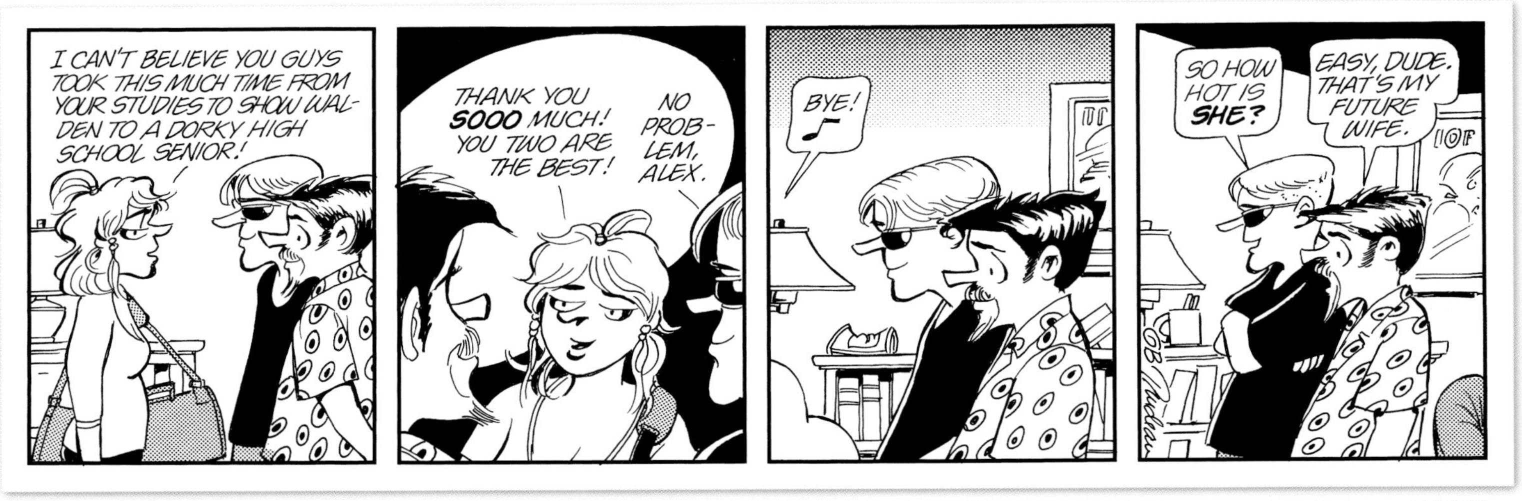
I CAN'T BELIEVE YOU GUYS TOOK THIS MUCH TIME FROM YOUR STUDIES TO SHOW WALDEN TO A DORKY HIGH SCHOOL SENIOR!
THANK YOU SOOO MUCH! YOU TWO ARE THE BEST!
NO PROBLEM, ALEX.
BYE!
SO HOW HOT IS SHE?
EASY, DUDE. THAT'S MY FUTURE WIFE.

11/30/05

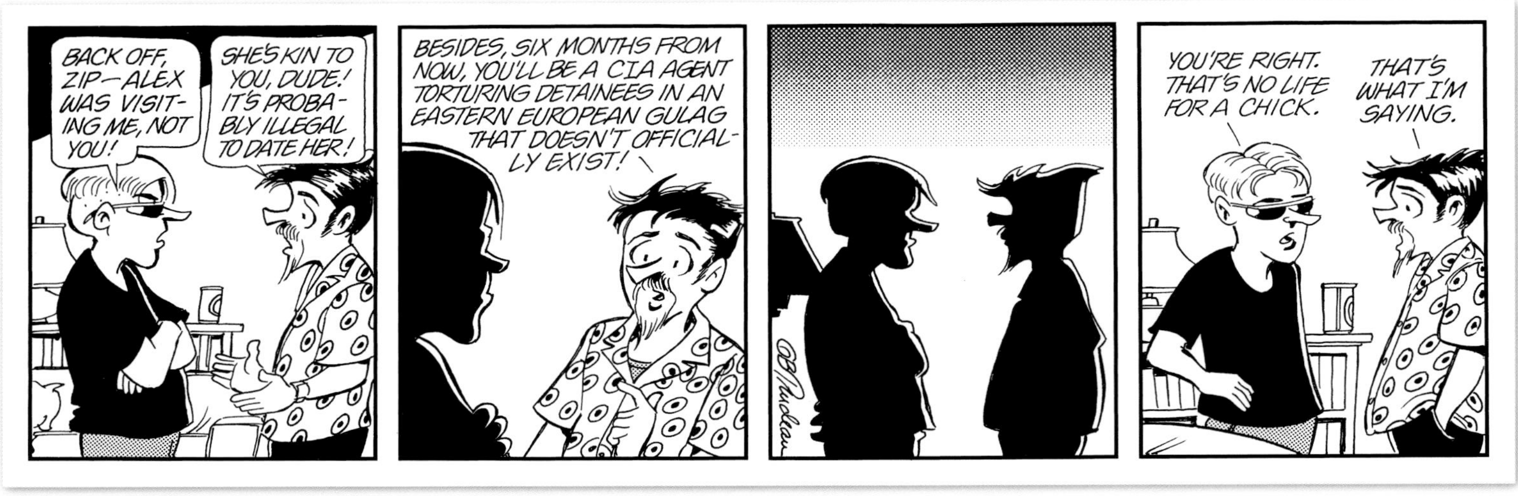
BACK OFF, ZIP—ALEX WAS VISITING ME, NOT YOU!
SHE'S KIN TO YOU, DUDE! IT'S PROBABLY ILLEGAL TO DATE HER!
BESIDES, SIX MONTHS FROM NOW, YOU'LL BE A CIA AGENT TORTURING DETAINEES IN AN EASTERN EUROPEAN GULAG THAT DOESN'T OFFICIALLY EXIST!
YOU'RE RIGHT. THAT'S NO LIFE FOR A CHICK.
THAT'S WHAT I'M SAYING.

12/1/05

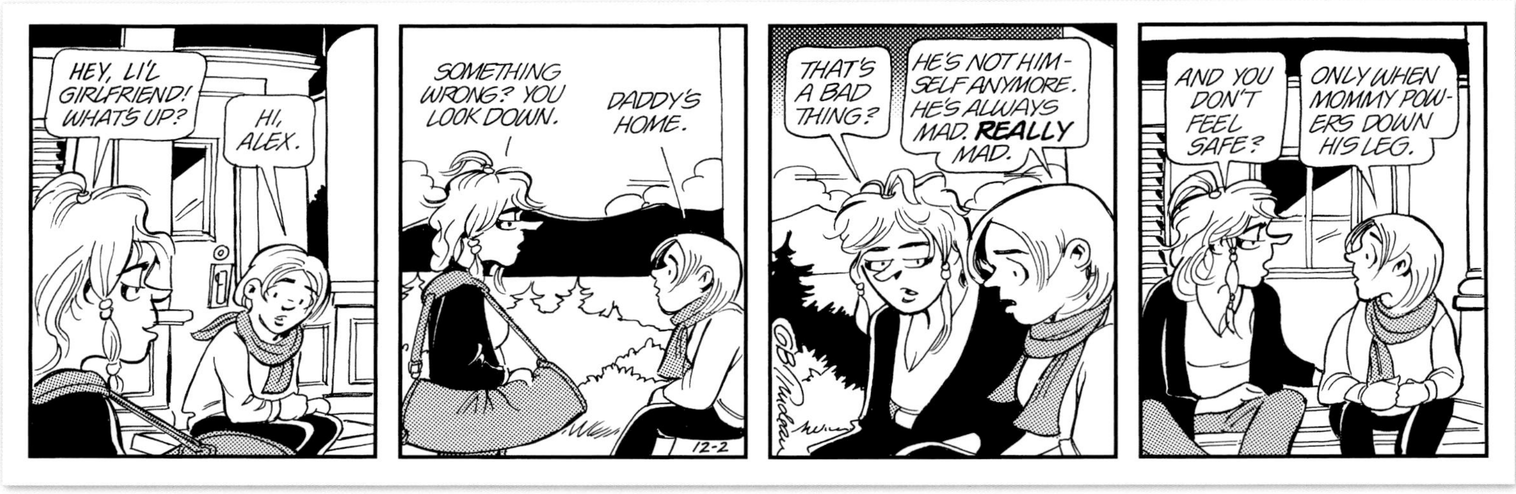
HEY, LI'L GIRLFRIEND! WHAT'S UP?
HI, ALEX.
SOMETHING WRONG? YOU LOOK DOWN.
DADDY'S HOME.
THAT'S A BAD THING?
HE'S NOT HIMSELF ANYMORE. HE'S ALWAYS MAD. REALLY MAD.
AND YOU DON'T FEEL SAFE?
ONLY WHEN MOMMY POWERS DOWN HIS LEG.

12/2/05

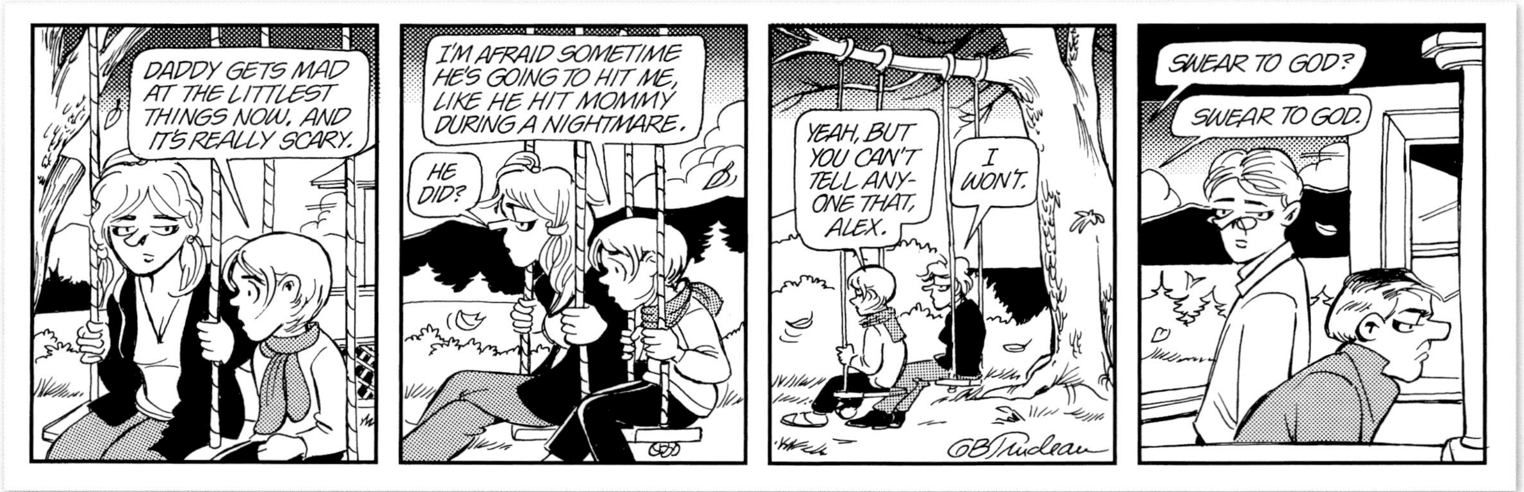
DADDY GETS MAD AT THE LITTLEST THINGS NOW, AND IT'S REALLY SCARY.
I'M AFRAID SOMETIME HE'S GOING TO HIT ME, LIKE HE HIT MOMMY DURING A NIGHTMARE.
HE DID?
YEAH, BUT YOU CAN'T TELL ANYONE THAT, ALEX.
I WON'T.
SWEAR TO GOD?
SWEAR TO GOD.

12/3/05

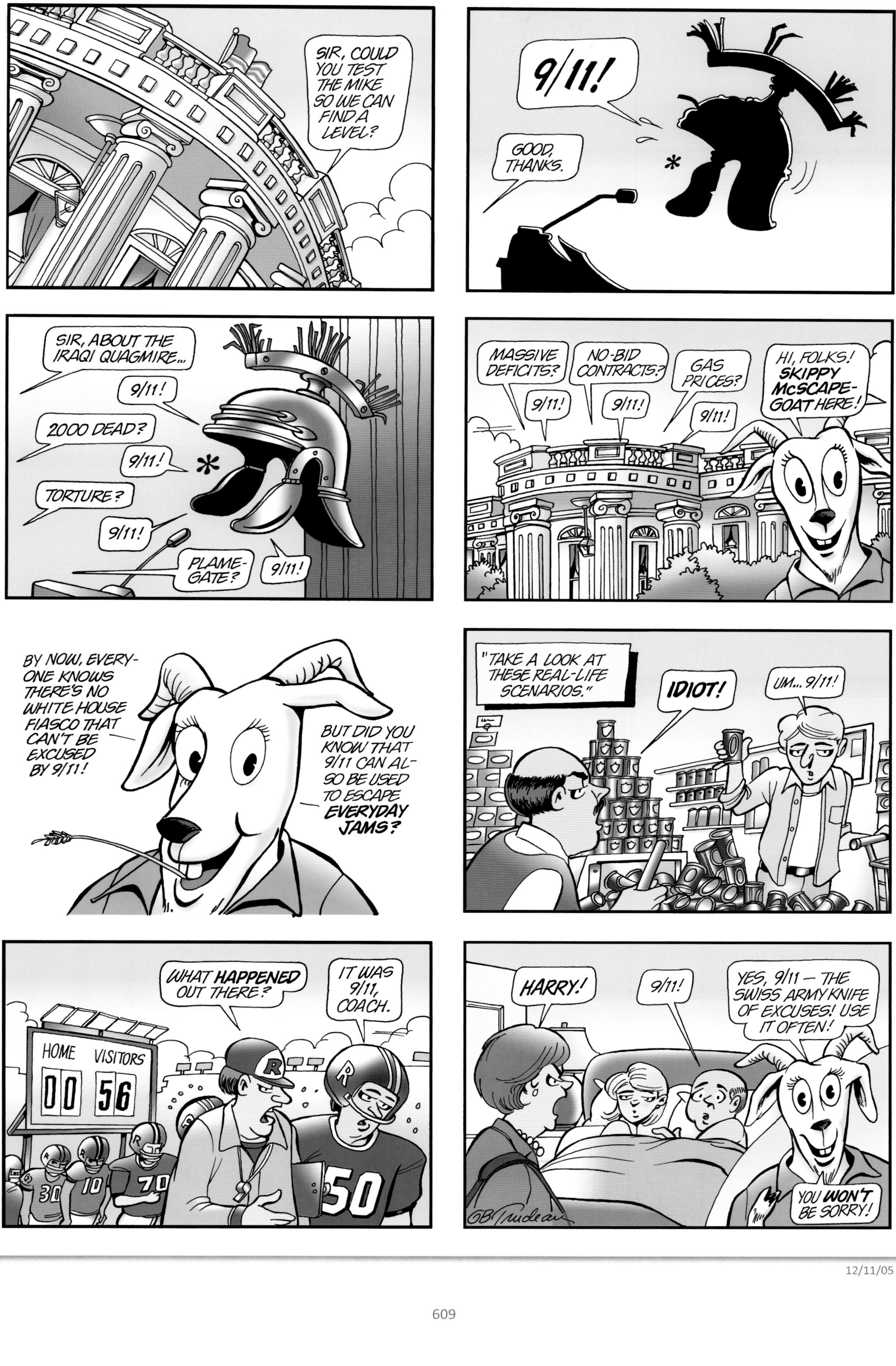
SIR, COULD YOU TEST THE MIKE SO WE CAN FIND A LEVEL?
9/11!
GOOD, THANKS.
*
SIR, ABOUT THE IRAQI QUAGMIRE...
9/11!
2000 DEAD?
9/11!
*
TORTURE?
9/11!
PLAME-GATE?
9/11!
MASSIVE DEFICITS?
9/11!
NO-BID CONTRACTS?
9/11!
GAS PRICES?
9/11!
HI, FOLKS! SKIPPY McSCAPE-GOAT HERE!
BY NOW, EVERY-ONE KNOWS THERE'S NO WHITE HOUSE FIASCO THAT CAN'T BE EXCUSED BY 9/11!
BUT DID YOU KNOW THAT 9/11 CAN AL-SO BE USED TO ESCAPE EVERYDAY JAMS?
"TAKE A LOOK AT THESE REAL-LIFE SCENARIOS."
IDIOT!
UM... 9/11!
WHAT HAPPENED OUT THERE?
IT WAS 9/11, COACH.
HOME VISITORS
00 56
HARRY!
9/11!
YES, 9/11 – THE SWISS ARMY KNIFE OF EXCUSES! USE IT OFTEN!
YOU WON'T BE SORRY!

12/11/05

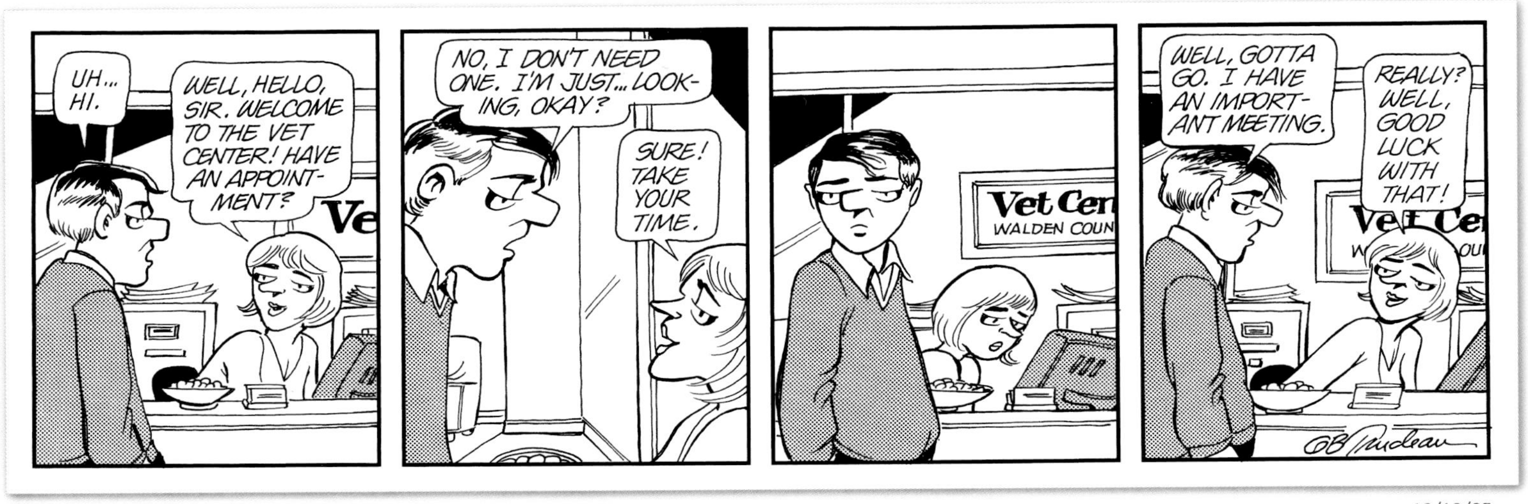
UH... HI.
WELL, HELLO, SIR. WELCOME TO THE VET CENTER! HAVE AN APPOINT-MENT?
NO, I DON'T NEED ONE. I'M JUST... LOOK-ING, OKAY?
SURE! TAKE YOUR TIME.
Vet Cen
WALDEN COUN
WELL, GOTTA GO. I HAVE AN IMPORT-ANT MEETING.
REALLY? WELL, GOOD LUCK WITH THAT!

12/12/05

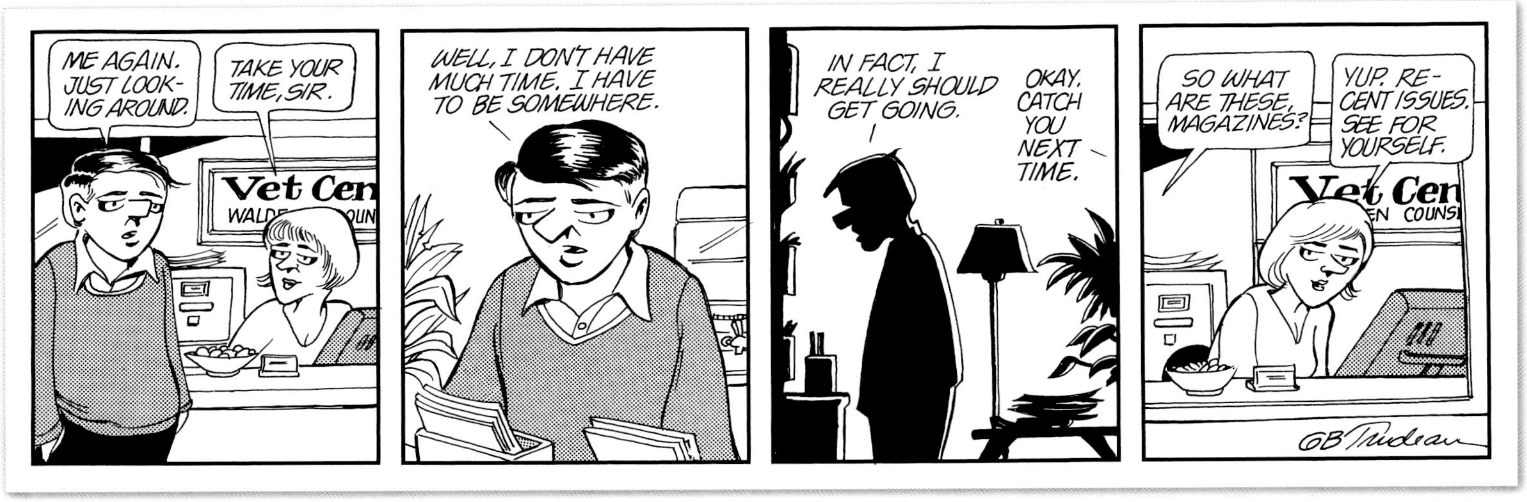
ME AGAIN. JUST LOOK-ING AROUND.
TAKE YOUR TIME, SIR.
WELL, I DON'T HAVE MUCH TIME. I HAVE TO BE SOMEWHERE.
IN FACT, I REALLY SHOULD GET GOING.
OKAY. CATCH YOU NEXT TIME.
SO WHAT ARE THESE, MAGAZINES?
YUP. RE-CENT ISSUES. SEE FOR YOURSELF.

12/13/05

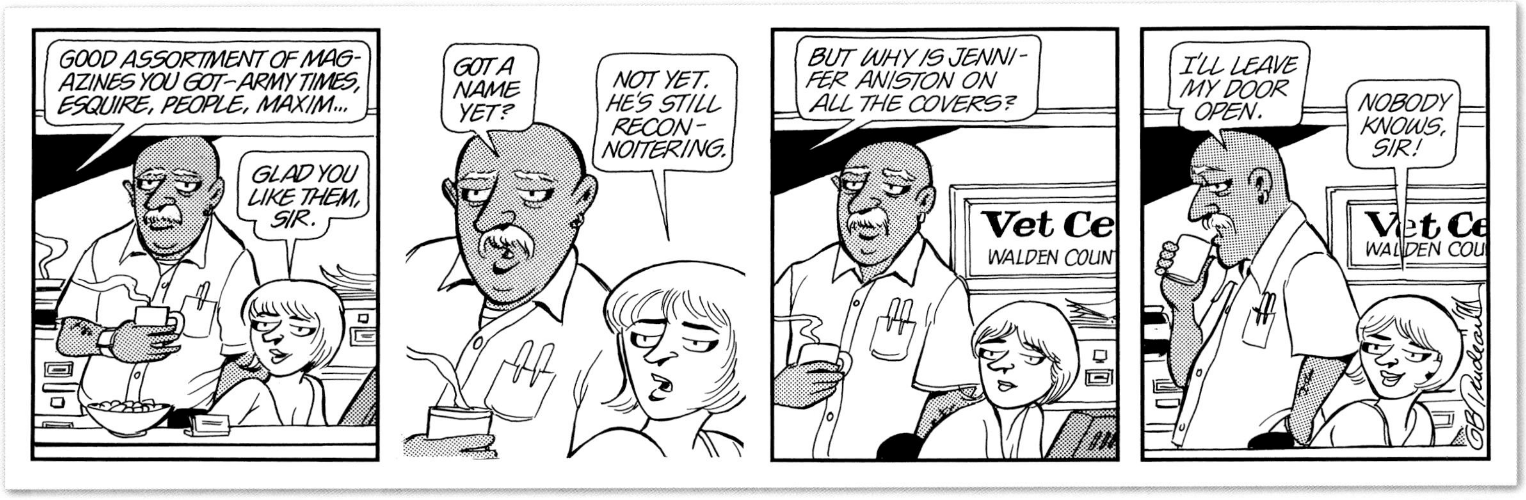
GOOD ASSORTMENT OF MAG-AZINES YOU GOT - ARMY TIMES, ESQUIRE, PEOPLE, MAXIM...
GLAD YOU LIKE THEM, SIR.
GOT A NAME YET?
NOT YET. HE'S STILL RECON-NOITERING.
BUT WHY IS JENNI-FER ANISTON ON ALL THE COVERS?
Vet Ce
WALDEN COUN
I'LL LEAVE MY DOOR OPEN.
NOBODY KNOWS, SIR!

12/14/05

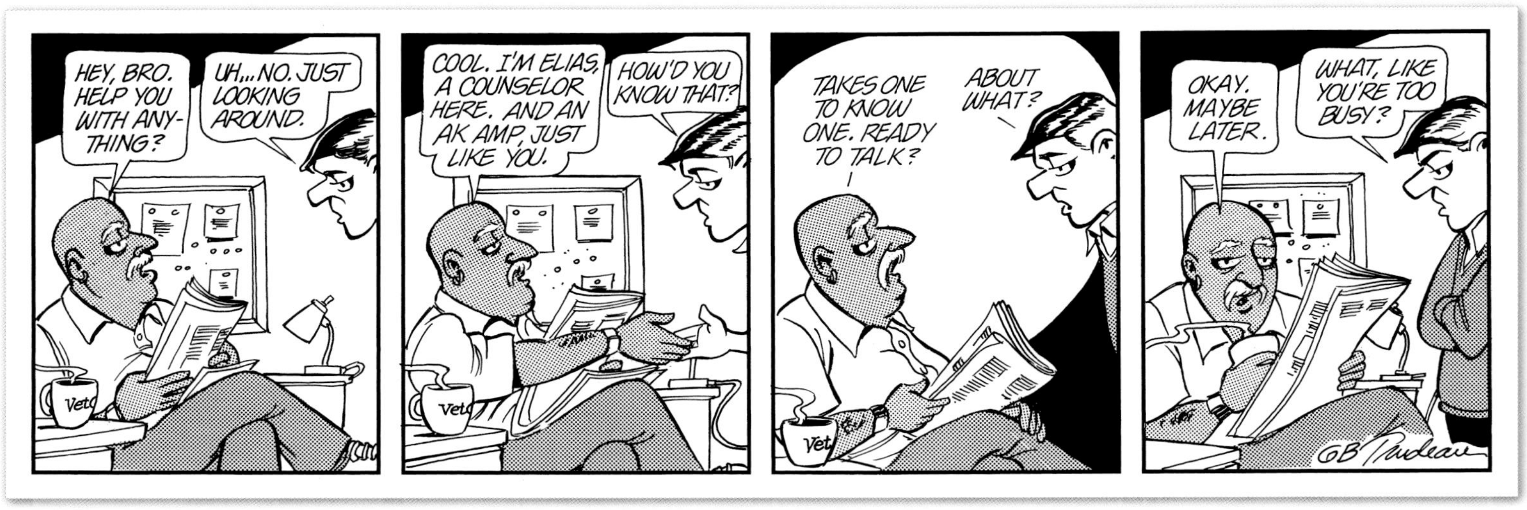
HEY, BRO. HELP YOU WITH ANY-THING?
UH... NO. JUST LOOKING AROUND.
COOL. I'M ELIAS, A COUNSELOR HERE. AND AN AK AMP, JUST LIKE YOU.
HOW'D YOU KNOW THAT?
TAKES ONE TO KNOW ONE. READY TO TALK?
ABOUT WHAT?
OKAY. MAYBE LATER.
WHAT, LIKE YOU'RE TOO BUSY?

12/15/05

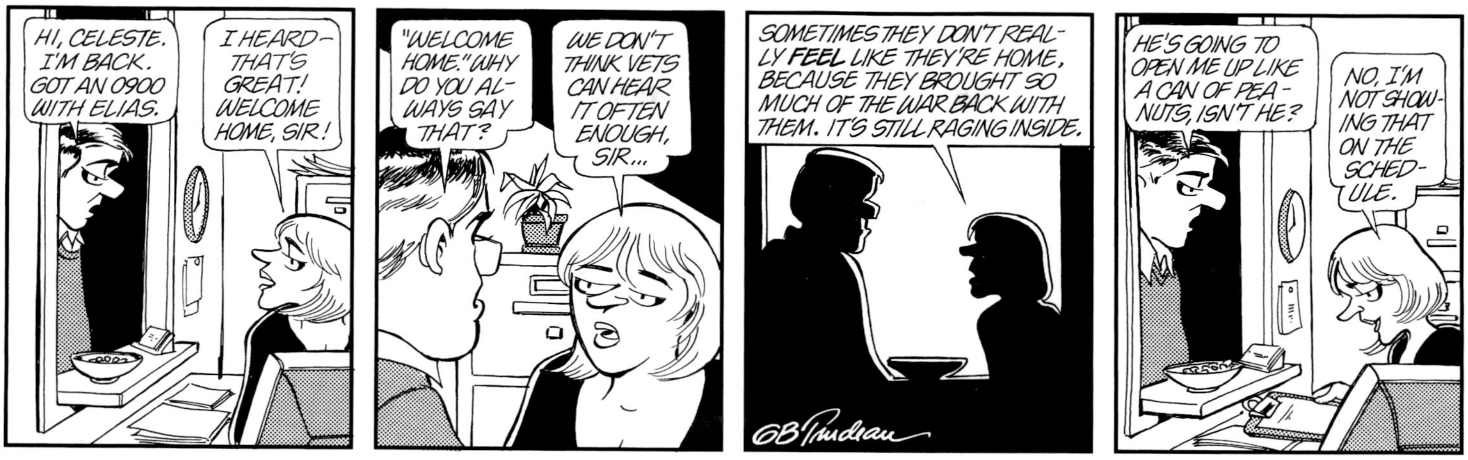
HI, CELESTE. I'M BACK. GOT AN 0900 WITH ELIAS.
I HEARD— THAT'S GREAT! WELCOME HOME, SIR!
"WELCOME HOME." WHY DO YOU ALWAYS SAY THAT?
WE DON'T THINK VETS CAN HEAR IT OFTEN ENOUGH, SIR...
SOMETIMES THEY DON'T REALLY FEEL LIKE THEY'RE HOME, BECAUSE THEY BROUGHT SO MUCH OF THE WAR BACK WITH THEM. IT'S STILL RAGING INSIDE.
GB Trudeau
HE'S GOING TO OPEN ME UP LIKE A CAN OF PEANUTS, ISN'T HE?
NO, I'M NOT SHOWING THAT ON THE SCHEDULE.

1/23/06

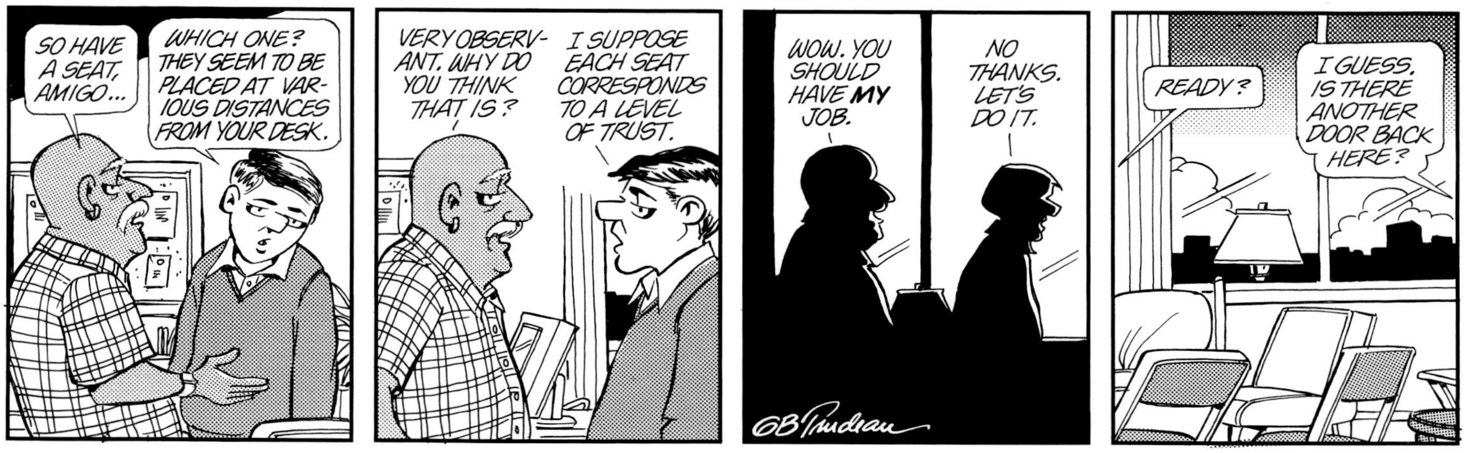
SO HAVE A SEAT, AMIGO...
WHICH ONE? THEY SEEM TO BE PLACED AT VARIOUS DISTANCES FROM YOUR DESK.
VERY OBSERVANT. WHY DO YOU THINK THAT IS?
I SUPPOSE EACH SEAT CORRESPONDS TO A LEVEL OF TRUST.
WOW. YOU SHOULD HAVE MY JOB.
NO THANKS. LET'S DO IT.
GB Trudeau
READY?
I GUESS. IS THERE ANOTHER DOOR BACK HERE?

1/24/06

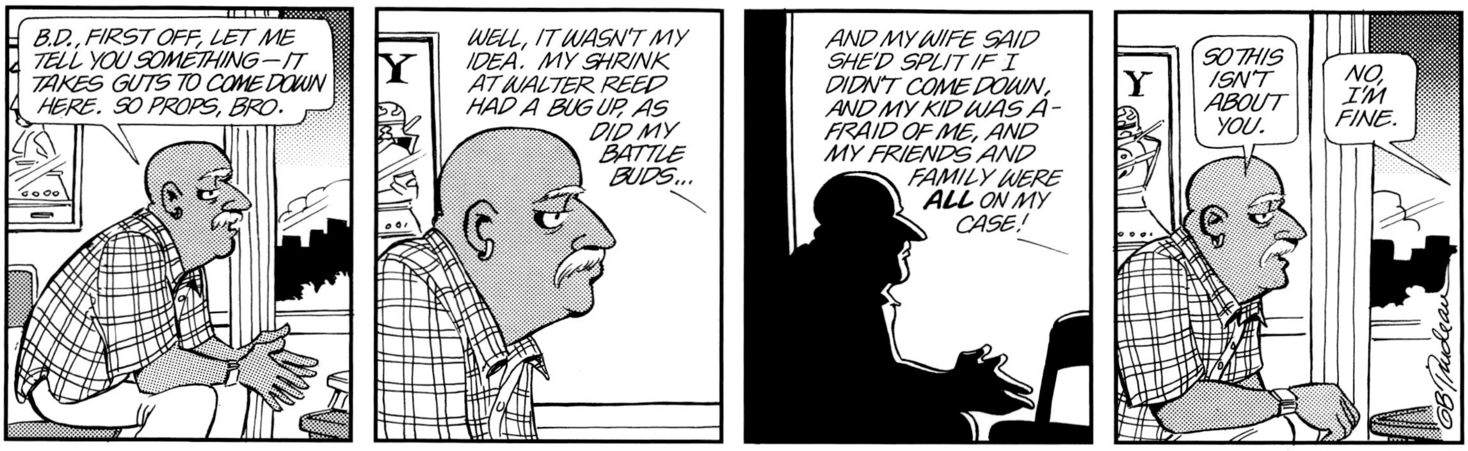
B.D., FIRST OFF, LET ME TELL YOU SOMETHING—IT TAKES GUTS TO COME DOWN HERE. SO PROPS, BRO.
WELL, IT WASN'T MY IDEA. MY SHRINK AT WALTER REED HAD A BUG UP, AS DID MY BATTLE BUDS...
AND MY WIFE SAID SHE'D SPLIT IF I DIDN'T COME DOWN, AND MY KID WAS AFRAID OF ME, AND MY FRIENDS AND FAMILY WERE ALL ON MY CASE!
SO THIS ISN'T ABOUT YOU.
NO, I'M FINE.
GB Trudeau

1/25/06

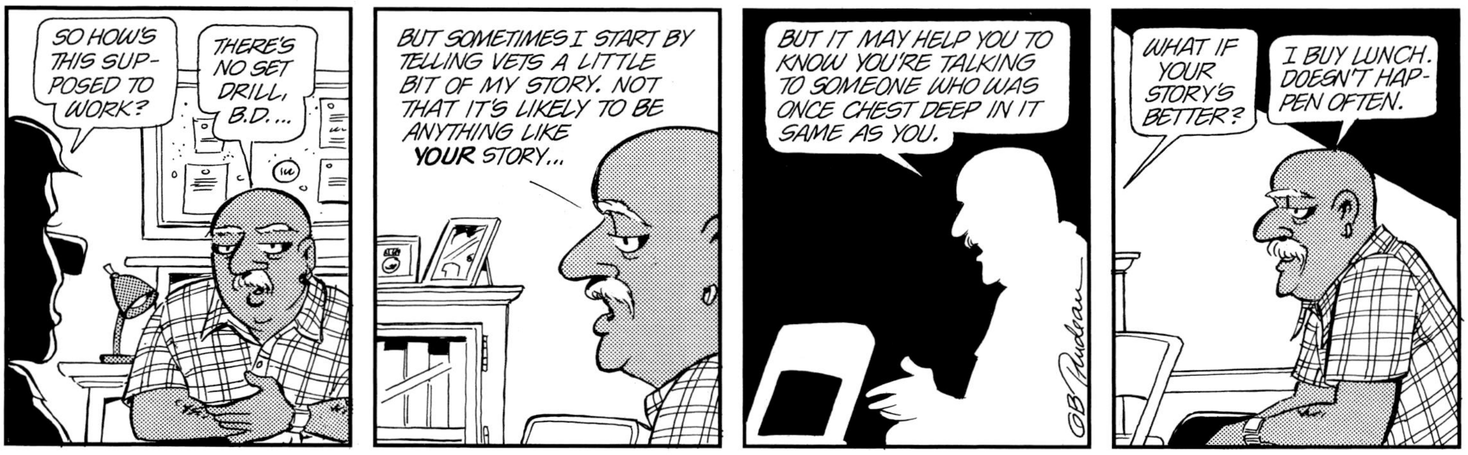
SO HOW'S THIS SUPPOSED TO WORK?
THERE'S NO SET DRILL, B.D....
BUT SOMETIMES I START BY TELLING VETS A LITTLE BIT OF MY STORY. NOT THAT IT'S LIKELY TO BE ANYTHING LIKE YOUR STORY...
BUT IT MAY HELP YOU TO KNOW YOU'RE TALKING TO SOMEONE WHO WAS ONCE CHEST DEEP IN IT SAME AS YOU.
GB Trudeau
WHAT IF YOUR STORY'S BETTER?
I BUY LUNCH. DOESN'T HAPPEN OFTEN.

1/26/06

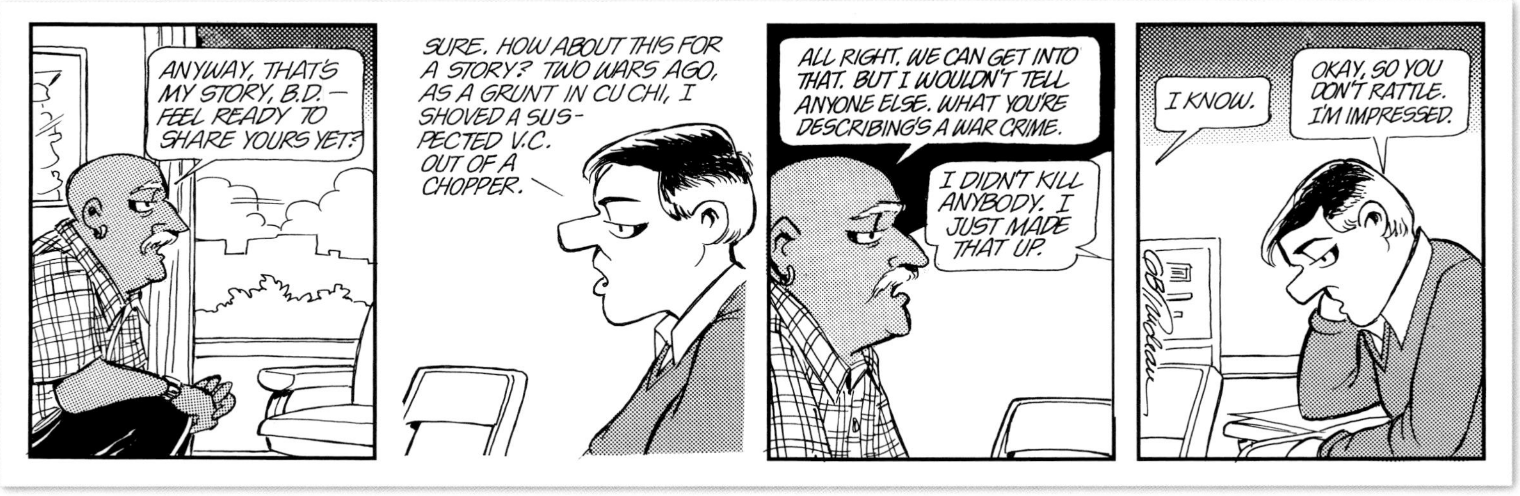
ANYWAY, THAT'S MY STORY, B.D.— FEEL READY TO SHARE YOURS YET?
SURE. HOW ABOUT THIS FOR A STORY? TWO WARS AGO, AS A GRUNT IN CU CHI, I SHOVED A SUSPECTED V.C. OUT OF A CHOPPER.
ALL RIGHT, WE CAN GET INTO THAT. BUT I WOULDN'T TELL ANYONE ELSE. WHAT YOU'RE DESCRIBING'S A WAR CRIME.
I DIDN'T KILL ANYBODY. I JUST MADE THAT UP.
I KNOW.
OKAY, SO YOU DON'T RATTLE. I'M IMPRESSED.

1/28/06

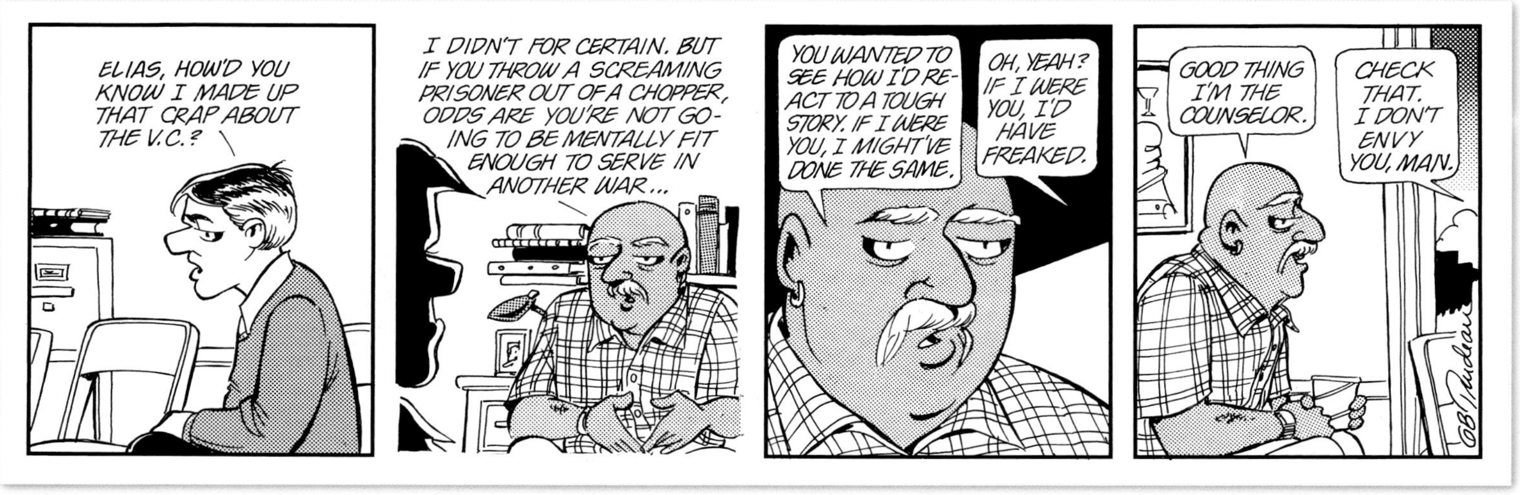
ELIAS, HOW'D YOU KNOW I MADE UP THAT CRAP ABOUT THE V.C.?
I DIDN'T FOR CERTAIN. BUT IF YOU THROW A SCREAMING PRISONER OUT OF A CHOPPER, ODDS ARE YOU'RE NOT GOING TO BE MENTALLY FIT ENOUGH TO SERVE IN ANOTHER WAR...
YOU WANTED TO SEE HOW I'D REACT TO A TOUGH STORY. IF I WERE YOU, I MIGHT'VE DONE THE SAME.
OH, YEAH? IF I WERE YOU, I'D HAVE FREAKED.
GOOD THING I'M THE COUNSELOR.
CHECK THAT. I DON'T ENVY YOU, MAN.

1/30/06

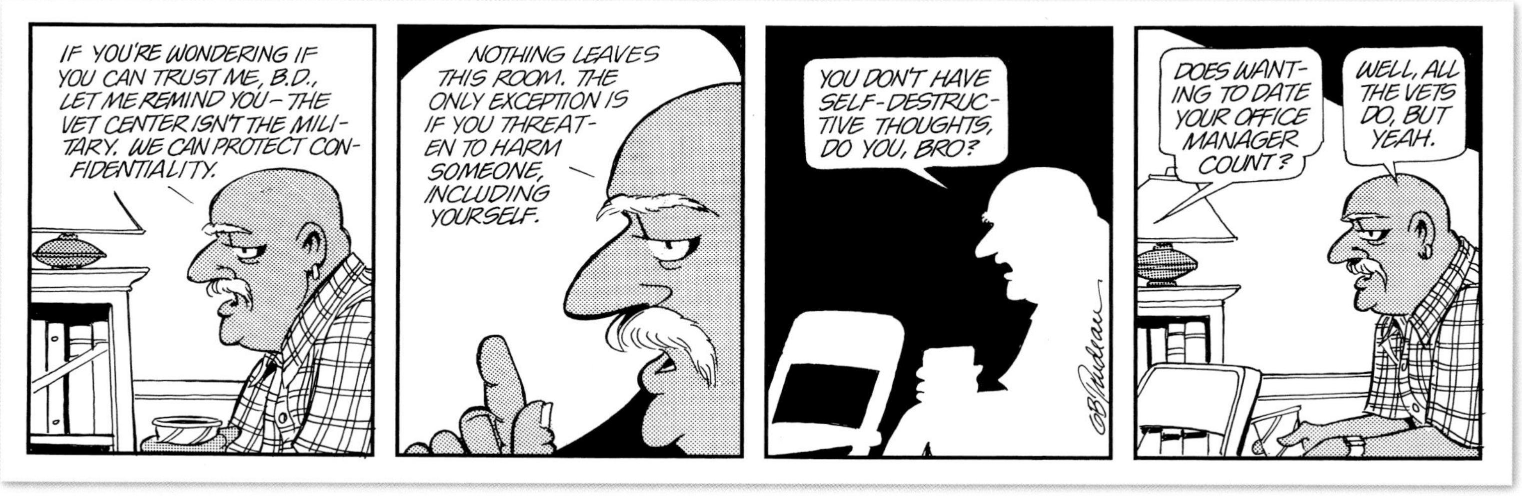
IF YOU'RE WONDERING IF YOU CAN TRUST ME, B.D., LET ME REMIND YOU— THE VET CENTER ISN'T THE MILITARY. WE CAN PROTECT CONFIDENTIALITY.
NOTHING LEAVES THIS ROOM. THE ONLY EXCEPTION IS IF YOU THREATEN TO HARM SOMEONE, INCLUDING YOURSELF.
YOU DON'T HAVE SELF-DESTRUCTIVE THOUGHTS, DO YOU, BRO?
DOES WANTING TO DATE YOUR OFFICE MANAGER COUNT?
WELL, ALL THE VETS DO, BUT YEAH.

1/31/06

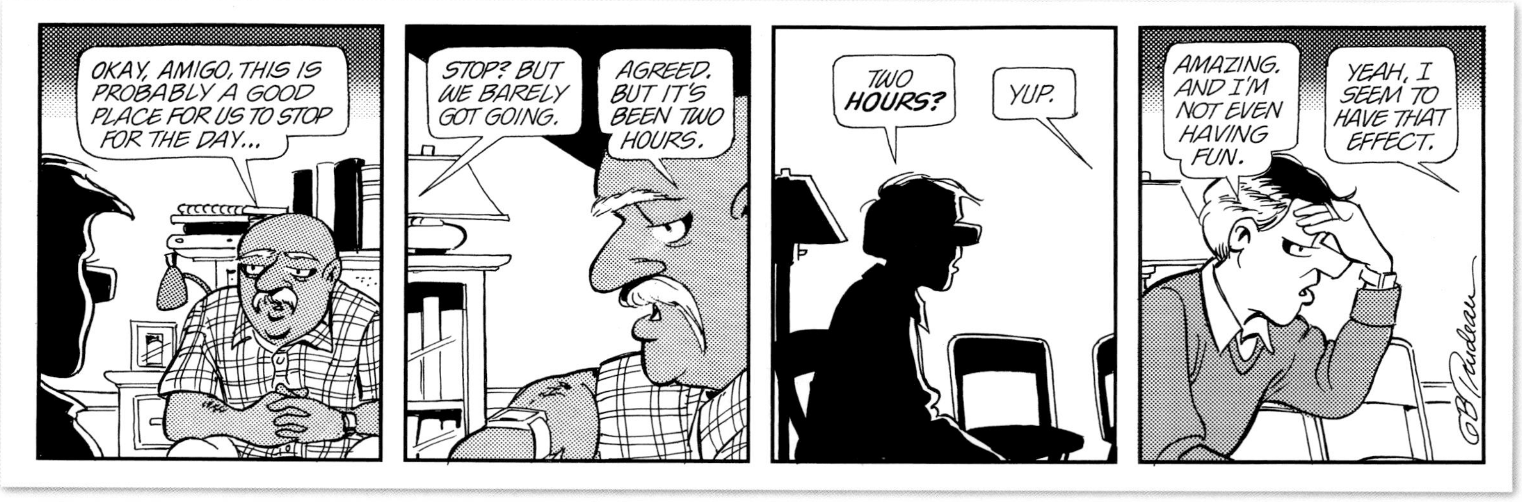
OKAY, AMIGO, THIS IS PROBABLY A GOOD PLACE FOR US TO STOP FOR THE DAY...
STOP? BUT WE BARELY GOT GOING.
AGREED. BUT IT'S BEEN TWO HOURS.
TWO HOURS?
YUP.
AMAZING. AND I'M NOT EVEN HAVING FUN.
YEAH, I SEEM TO HAVE THAT EFFECT.

2/1/06

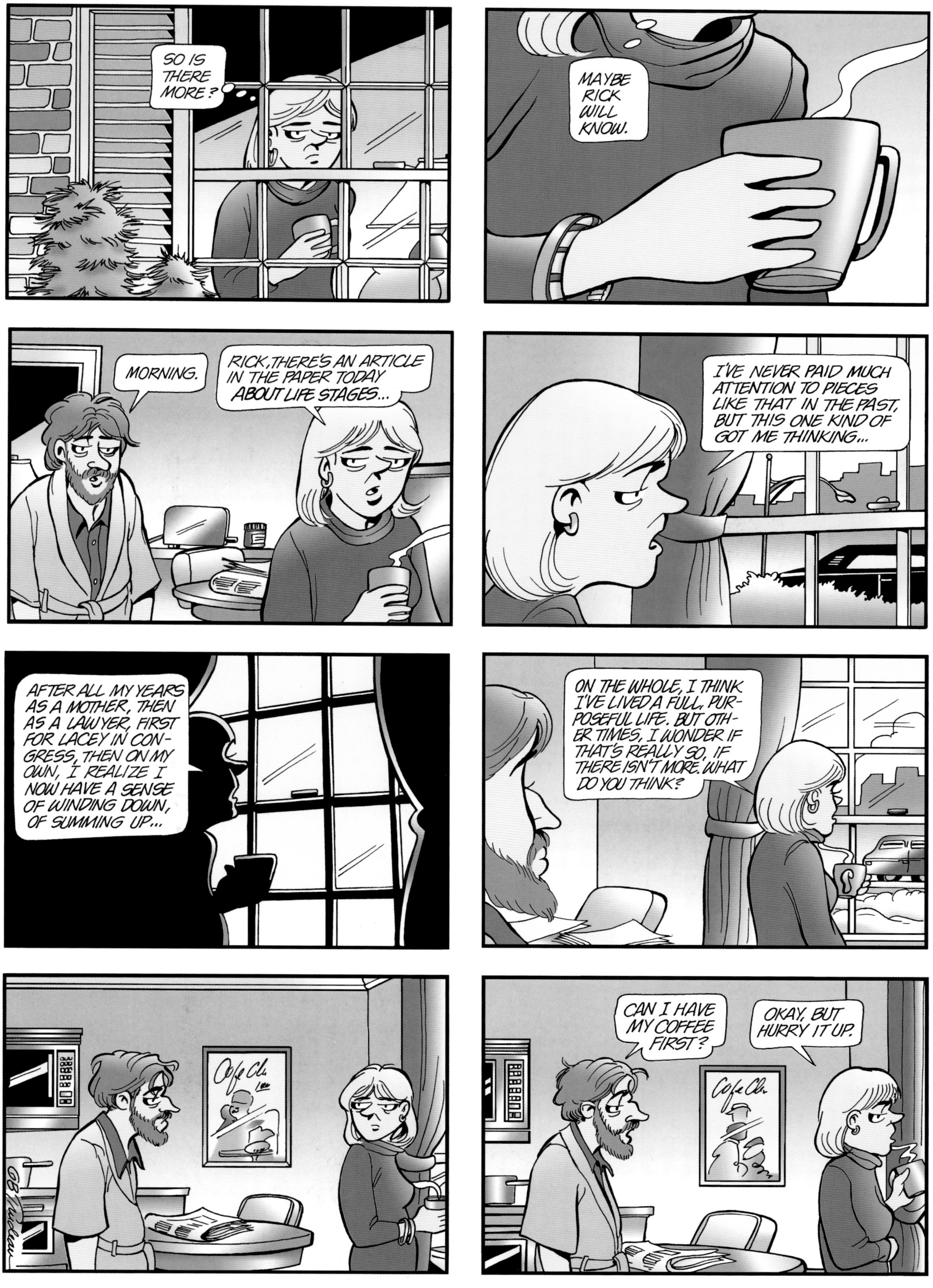
SO IS THERE MORE?
MAYBE RICK WILL KNOW.
MORNING.
RICK, THERE'S AN ARTICLE IN THE PAPER TODAY ABOUT LIFE STAGES...
I'VE NEVER PAID MUCH ATTENTION TO PIECES LIKE THAT IN THE PAST, BUT THIS ONE KIND OF GOT ME THINKING...
AFTER ALL MY YEARS AS A MOTHER, THEN AS A LAWYER, FIRST FOR LACEY IN CONGRESS, THEN ON MY OWN, I REALIZE I NOW HAVE A SENSE OF WINDING DOWN, OF SUMMING UP...
ON THE WHOLE, I THINK I'VE LIVED A FULL, PURPOSEFUL LIFE. BUT OTHER TIMES, I WONDER IF THAT'S REALLY SO, IF THERE ISN'T MORE. WHAT DO YOU THINK?
CAN I HAVE MY COFFEE FIRST?
OKAY, BUT HURRY IT UP.

2/5/06

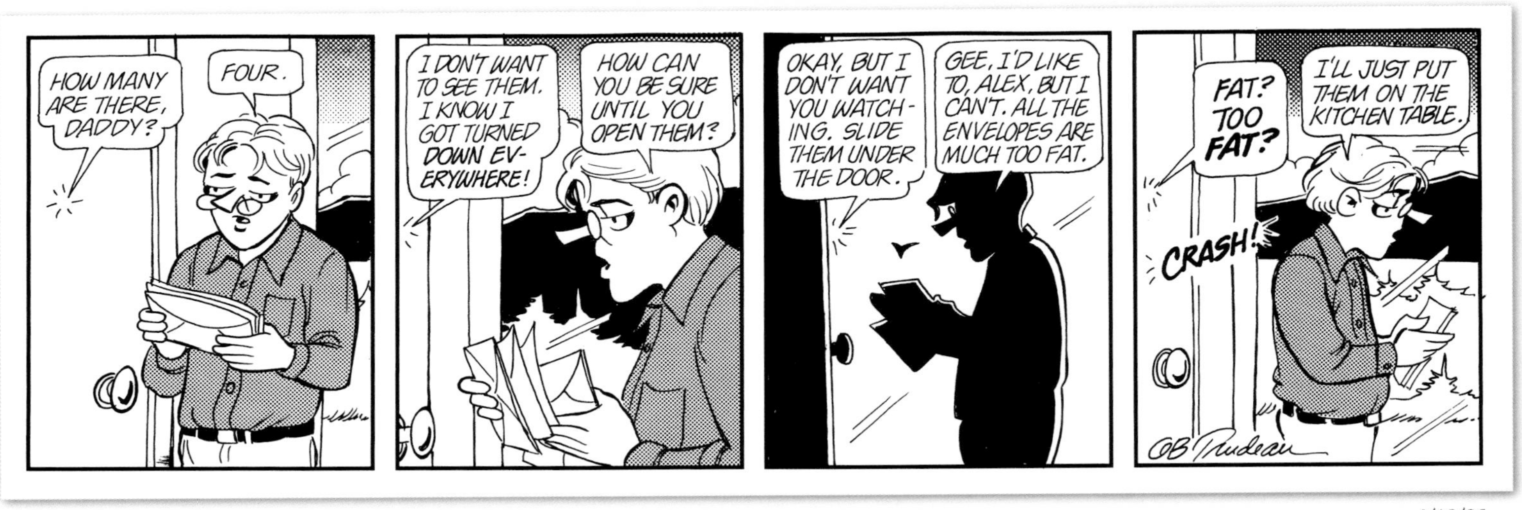

HOW MANY ARE THERE, DADDY?
FOUR.
I DON'T WANT TO SEE THEM. I KNOW I GOT TURNED **DOWN** EVERYWHERE!
HOW CAN YOU BE SURE UNTIL YOU OPEN THEM?
OKAY, BUT I DON'T WANT YOU WATCHING. SLIDE THEM UNDER THE DOOR.
GEE, I'D LIKE TO, ALEX, BUT I CAN'T. ALL THE ENVELOPES ARE MUCH TOO FAT.
FAT? TOO FAT?
CRASH!
I'LL JUST PUT THEM ON THE KITCHEN TABLE.
GB Trudeau

4/10/06

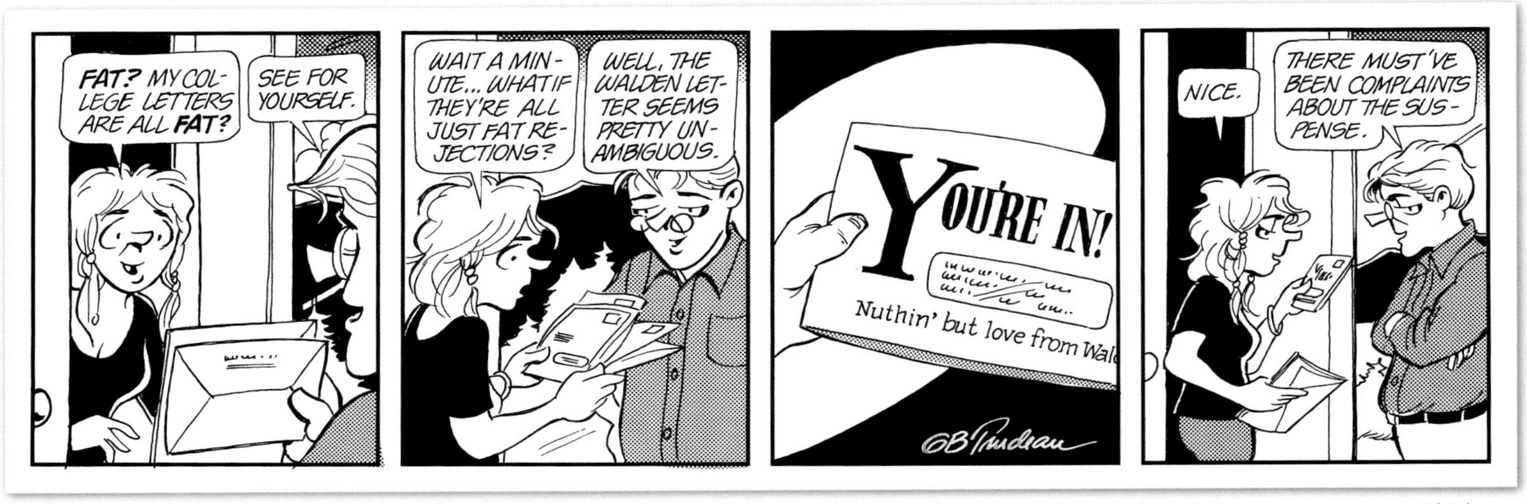

FAT? MY COLLEGE LETTERS ARE ALL **FAT**?
SEE FOR YOURSELF.
WAIT A MINUTE... WHAT IF THEY'RE ALL JUST FAT REJECTIONS?
WELL, THE WALDEN LETTER SEEMS PRETTY UNAMBIGUOUS.
YOU'RE IN!
Nuthin' but love from Wal
GB Trudeau
NICE.
THERE MUST'VE BEEN COMPLAINTS ABOUT THE SUSPENSE.

4/11/06

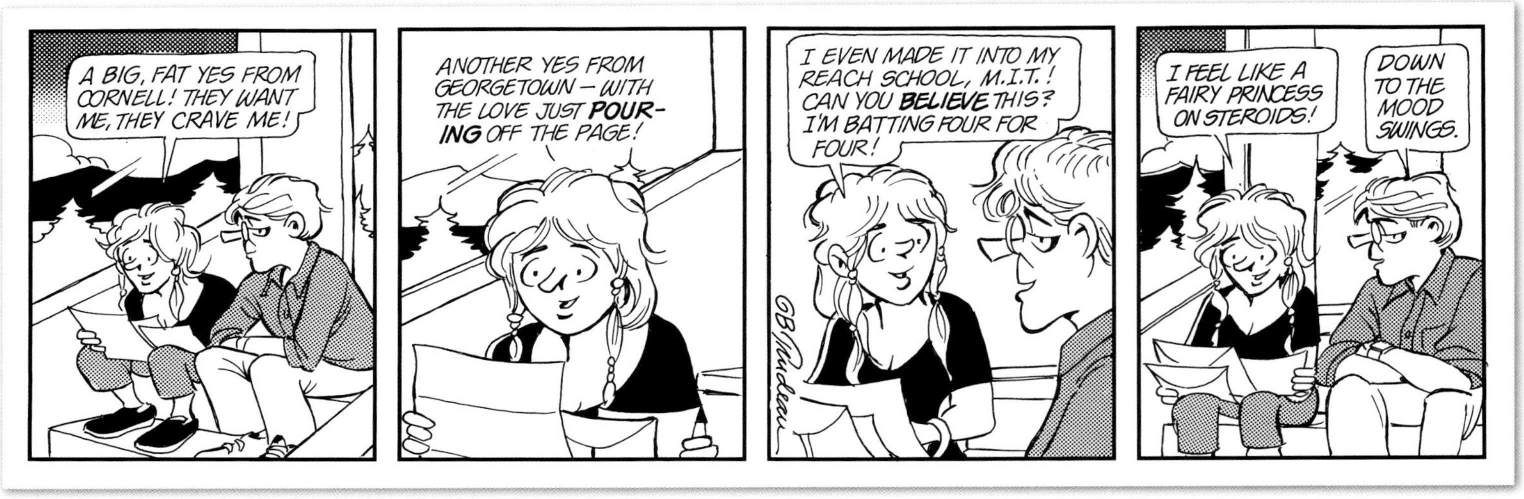

A BIG, FAT YES FROM CORNELL! THEY WANT ME, THEY CRAVE ME!
ANOTHER YES FROM GEORGETOWN — WITH THE LOVE JUST **POURING** OFF THE PAGE!
I EVEN MADE IT INTO MY REACH SCHOOL, M.I.T.! CAN YOU **BELIEVE** THIS? I'M BATTING FOUR FOR FOUR!
GB Trudeau
I FEEL LIKE A FAIRY PRINCESS ON STEROIDS!
DOWN TO THE MOOD SWINGS.

4/12/06

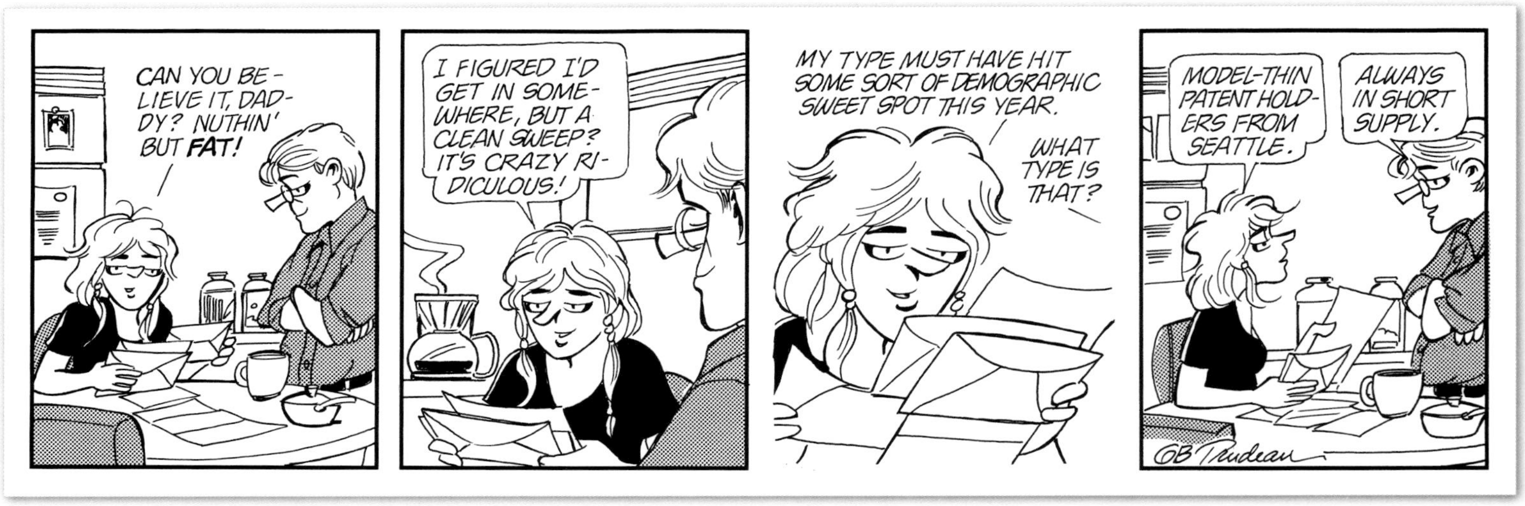

CAN YOU BELIEVE IT, DADDY? NUTHIN' BUT **FAT!**
I FIGURED I'D GET IN SOMEWHERE, BUT A CLEAN SWEEP? IT'S CRAZY RIDICULOUS!
MY TYPE MUST HAVE HIT SOME SORT OF DEMOGRAPHIC SWEET SPOT THIS YEAR.
WHAT TYPE IS THAT?
MODEL-THIN PATENT HOLDERS FROM SEATTLE.
ALWAYS IN SHORT SUPPLY.
GB Trudeau

4/14/06

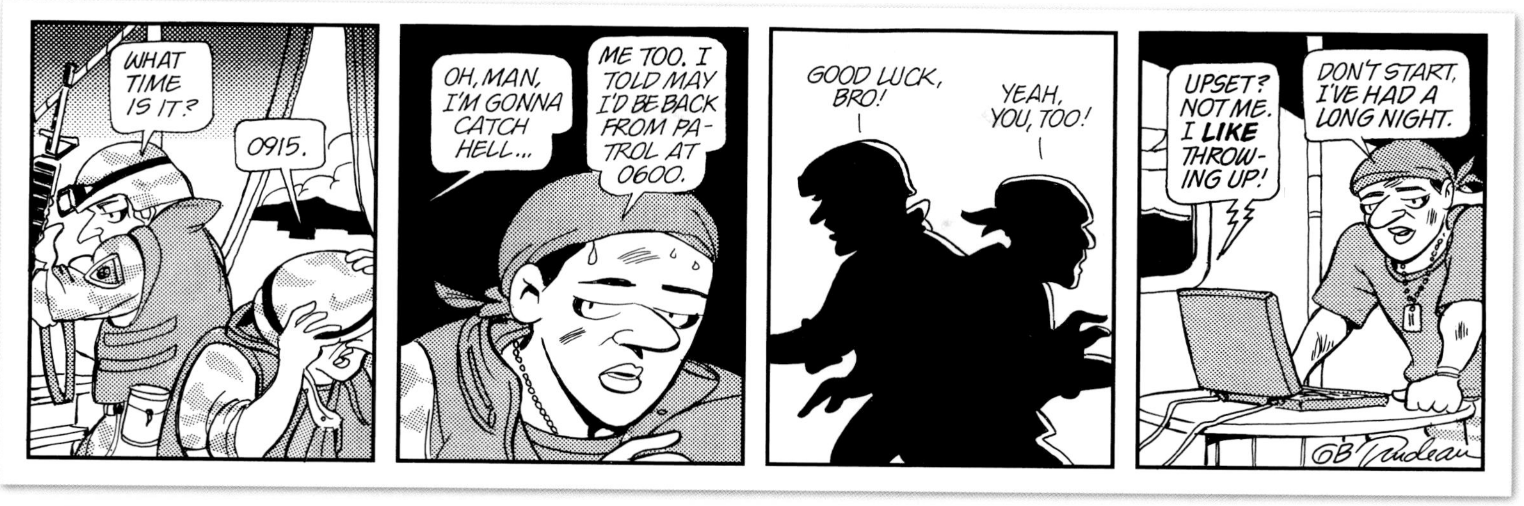
WHAT TIME IS IT?
0915.
OH, MAN, I'M GONNA CATCH HELL...
ME TOO. I TOLD MAY I'D BE BACK FROM PATROL AT 0600.
GOOD LUCK, BRO!
YEAH, YOU, TOO!
UPSET? NOT ME. I **LIKE** THROWING UP!
DON'T START, I'VE HAD A LONG NIGHT.
©B Trudeau

9/4/06

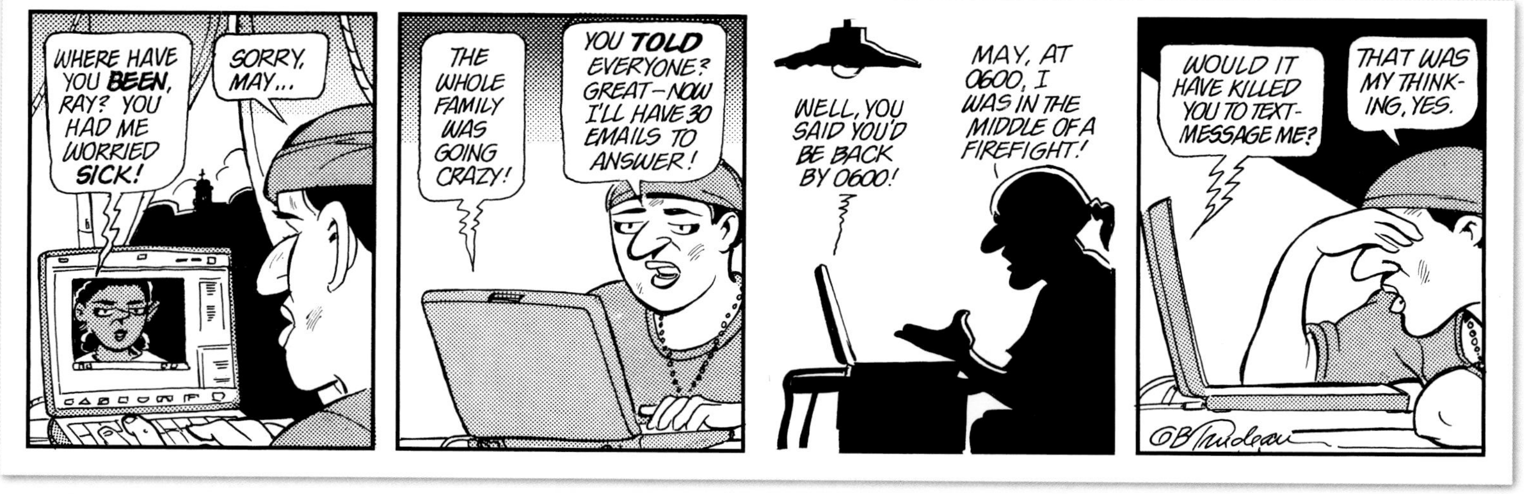
WHERE HAVE YOU **BEEN**, RAY? YOU HAD ME WORRIED **SICK**!
SORRY, MAY...
THE WHOLE FAMILY WAS GOING CRAZY!
YOU **TOLD** EVERYONE? GREAT—NOW I'LL HAVE 30 EMAILS TO ANSWER!
WELL, YOU SAID YOU'D BE BACK BY 0600!
MAY, AT 0600, I WAS IN THE MIDDLE OF A FIREFIGHT!
WOULD IT HAVE KILLED YOU TO TEXT-MESSAGE ME?
THAT WAS MY THINKING, YES.
©B Trudeau

9/5/06

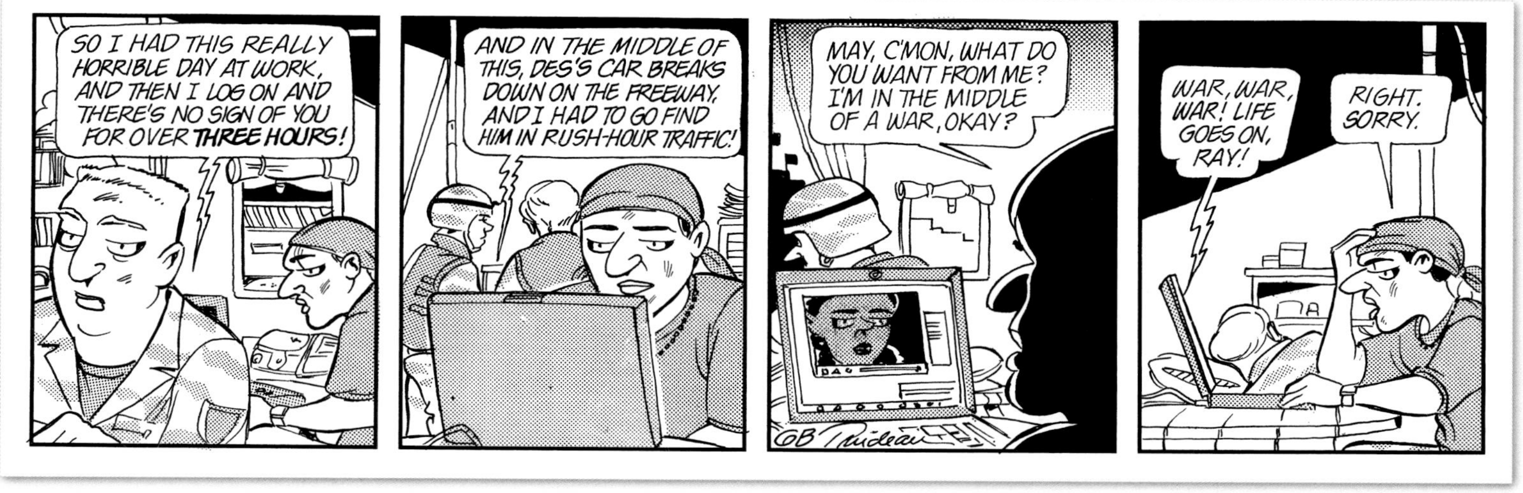
SO I HAD THIS REALLY HORRIBLE DAY AT WORK, AND THEN I LOG ON AND THERE'S NO SIGN OF YOU FOR OVER **THREE HOURS**!
AND IN THE MIDDLE OF THIS, DES'S CAR BREAKS DOWN ON THE FREEWAY, AND I HAD TO GO FIND HIM IN RUSH-HOUR TRAFFIC!
MAY, C'MON, WHAT DO YOU WANT FROM ME? I'M IN THE MIDDLE OF A WAR, OKAY?
WAR, WAR, WAR! LIFE GOES ON, RAY!
RIGHT. SORRY.
©B Trudeau

9/6/06

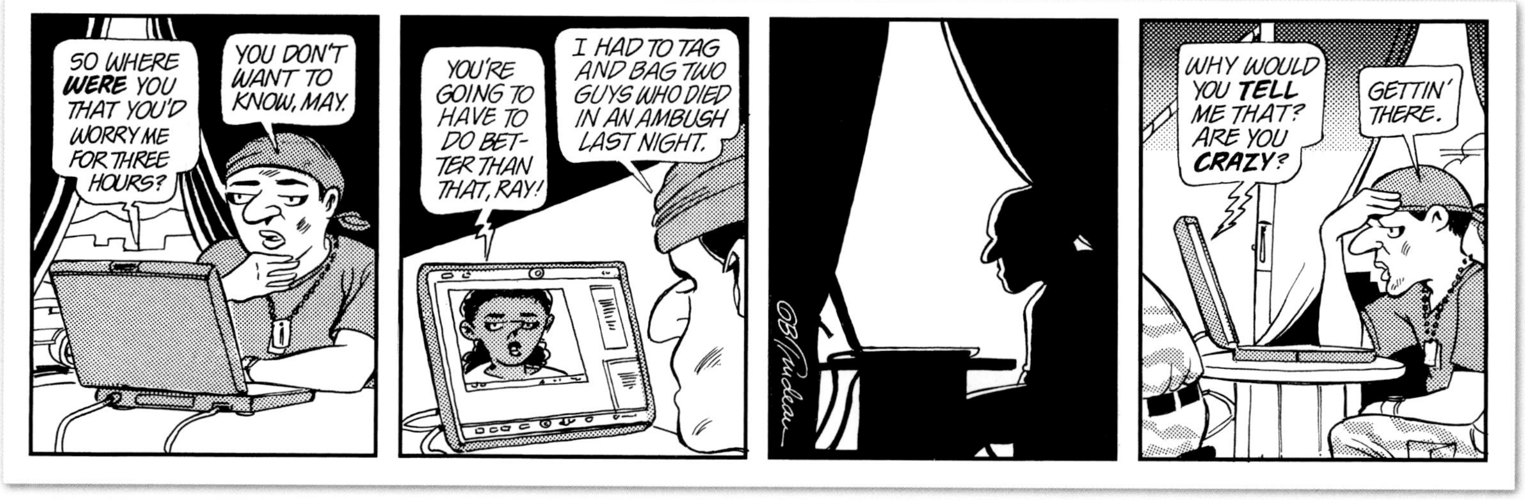
SO WHERE **WERE** YOU THAT YOU'D WORRY ME FOR THREE HOURS?
YOU DON'T WANT TO KNOW, MAY.
YOU'RE GOING TO HAVE TO DO BETTER THAN THAT, RAY!
I HAD TO TAG AND BAG TWO GUYS WHO DIED IN AN AMBUSH LAST NIGHT.
©B Trudeau
WHY WOULD YOU **TELL** ME THAT? ARE YOU **CRAZY**?
GETTIN' THERE.

9/7/06

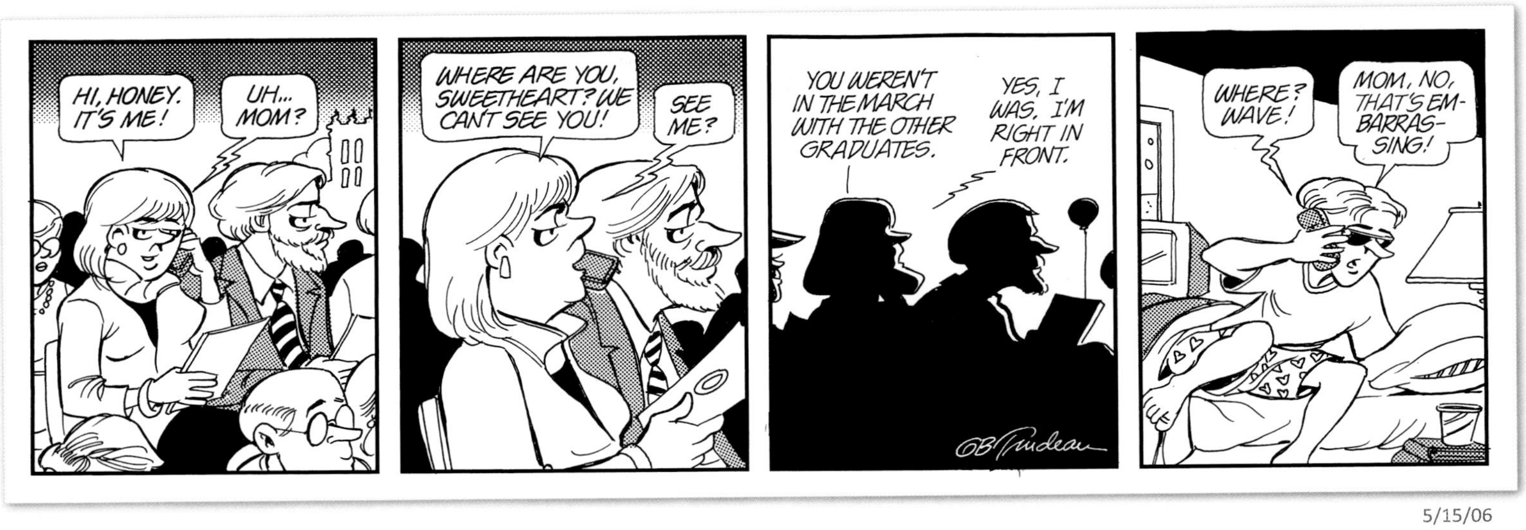

HI, HONEY. IT'S ME!
UH... MOM?
WHERE ARE YOU, SWEETHEART? WE CAN'T SEE YOU!
SEE ME?
YOU WEREN'T IN THE MARCH WITH THE OTHER GRADUATES.
YES, I WAS, I'M RIGHT IN FRONT.
WHERE? WAVE!
MOM, NO, THAT'S EMBARRASSING!
GB Trudeau

5/15/06

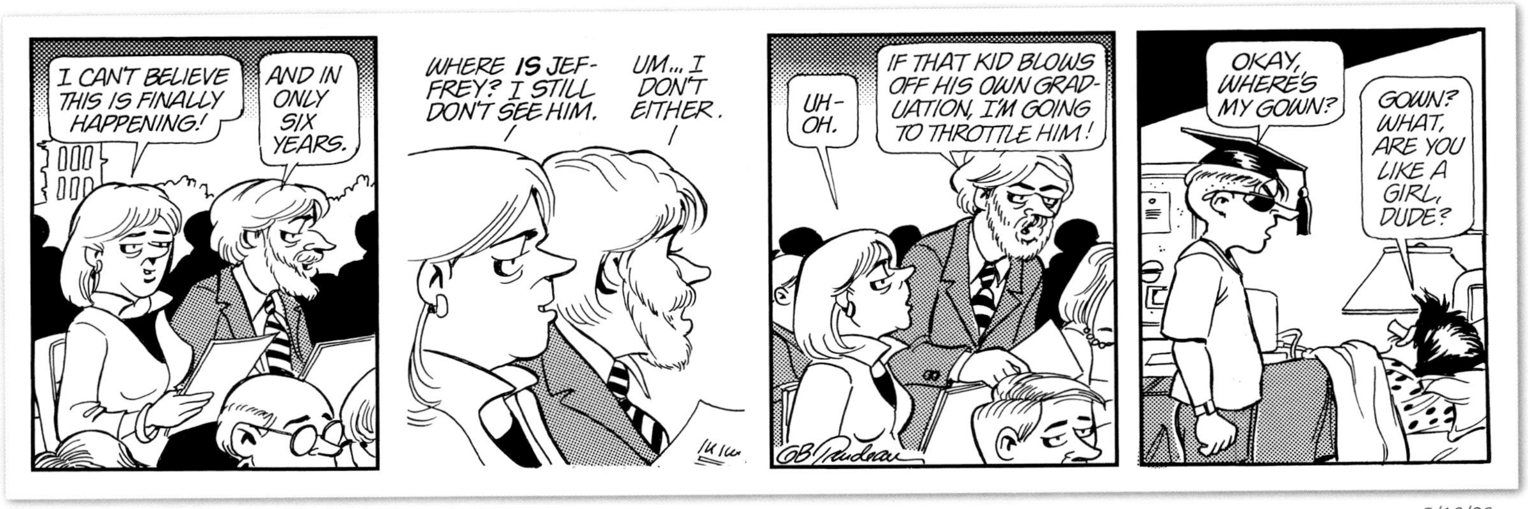

I CAN'T BELIEVE THIS IS FINALLY HAPPENING!
AND IN ONLY SIX YEARS.
WHERE IS JEFFREY? I STILL DON'T SEE HIM.
UM... I DON'T EITHER.
UH-OH.
IF THAT KID BLOWS OFF HIS OWN GRADUATION, I'M GOING TO THROTTLE HIM!
GB Trudeau
OKAY, WHERE'S MY GOWN?
GOWN? WHAT, ARE YOU LIKE A GIRL, DUDE?

5/16/06

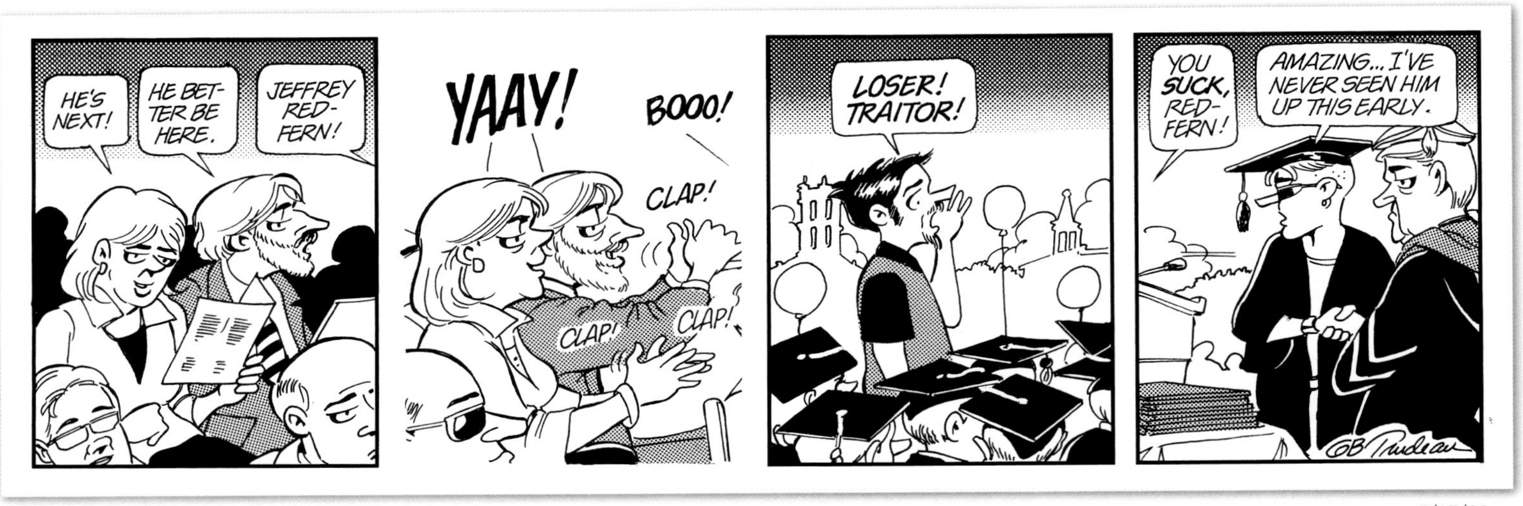

HE'S NEXT!
HE BETTER BE HERE.
JEFFREY REDFERN!
YAAY!
BOOO!
CLAP!
CLAP!
CLAP!
LOSER! TRAITOR!
YOU SUCK, REDFERN!
AMAZING... I'VE NEVER SEEN HIM UP THIS EARLY.
GB Trudeau

5/17/06

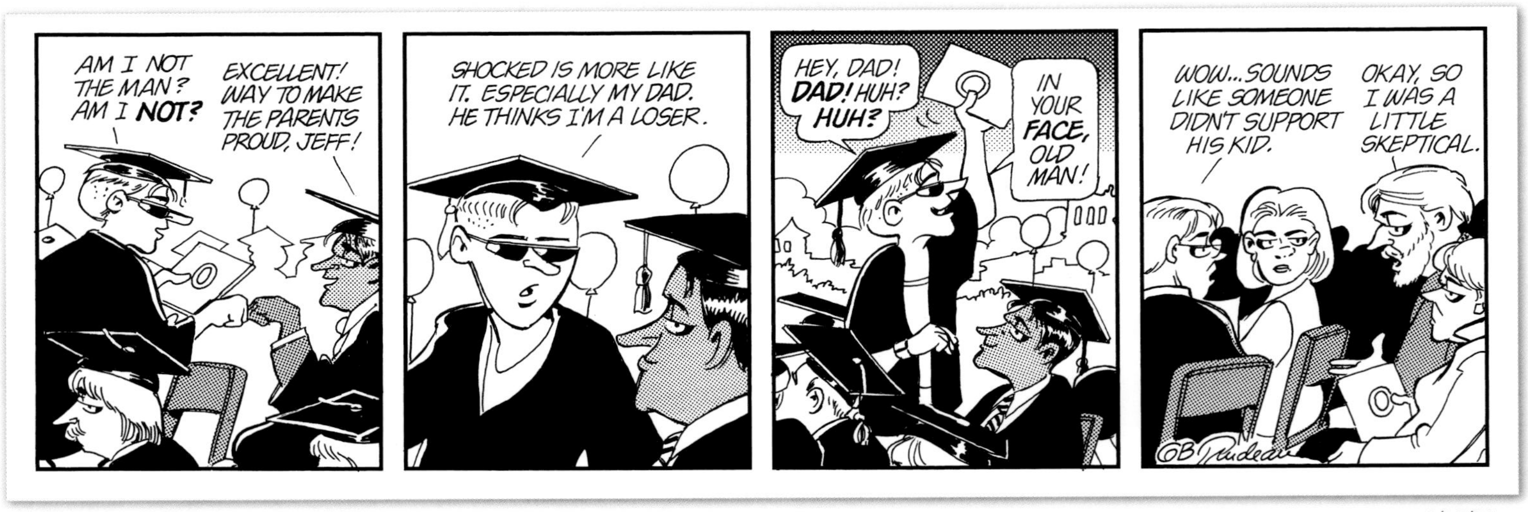

AM I NOT THE MAN? AM I NOT?
EXCELLENT! WAY TO MAKE THE PARENTS PROUD, JEFF!
SHOCKED IS MORE LIKE IT. ESPECIALLY MY DAD. HE THINKS I'M A LOSER.
HEY, DAD! DAD! HUH? HUH?
IN YOUR FACE, OLD MAN!
WOW... SOUNDS LIKE SOMEONE DIDN'T SUPPORT HIS KID.
OKAY, SO I WAS A LITTLE SKEPTICAL.
GB Trudeau

5/18/06

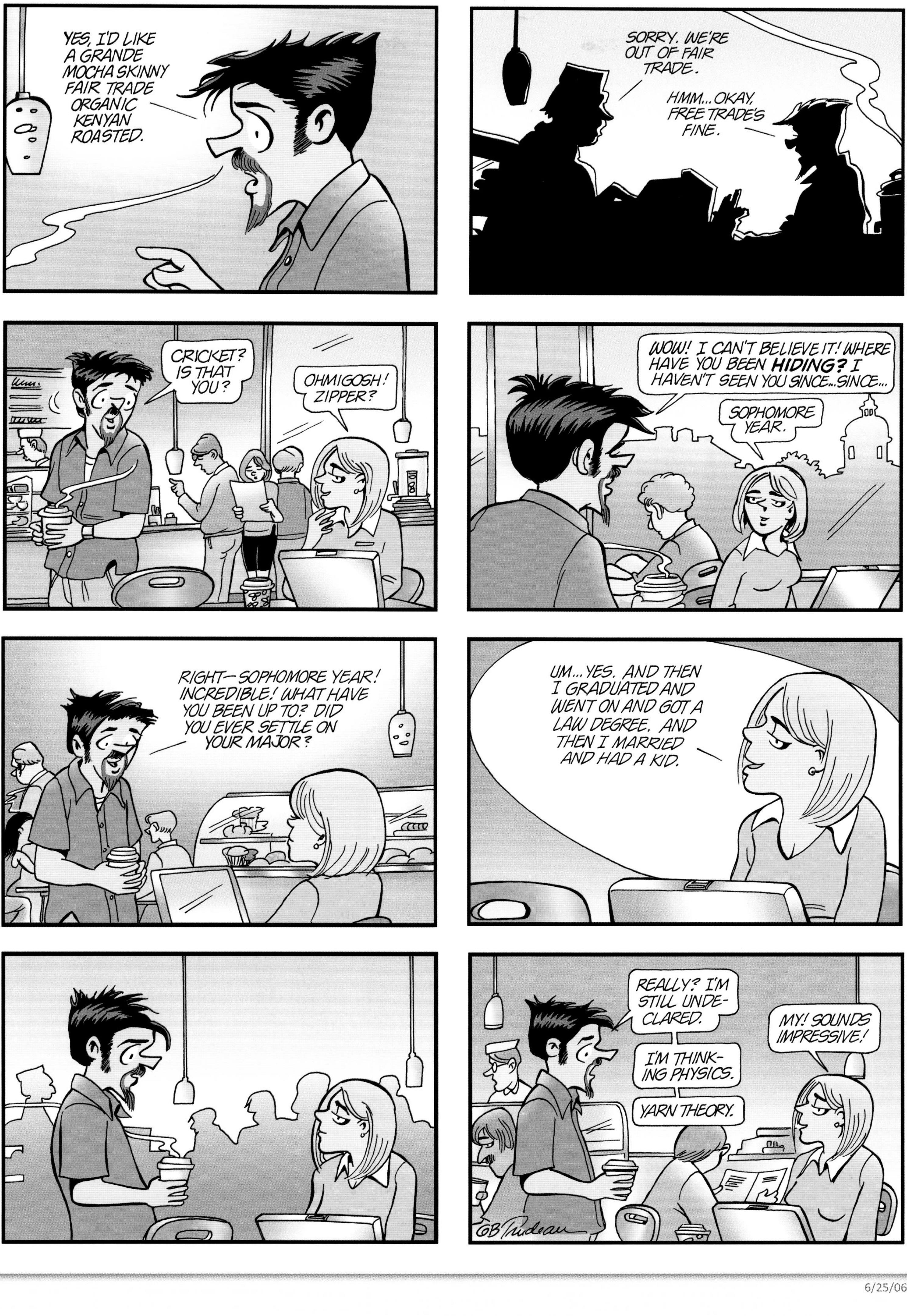
YES, I'D LIKE A GRANDE MOCHA SKINNY FAIR TRADE ORGANIC KENYAN ROASTED.
SORRY. WE'RE OUT OF FAIR TRADE.
HMM... OKAY, FREE TRADE'S FINE.
CRICKET? IS THAT YOU?
OHMIGOSH! ZIPPER?
WOW! I CAN'T BELIEVE IT! WHERE HAVE YOU BEEN HIDING? I HAVEN'T SEEN YOU SINCE... SINCE...
SOPHOMORE YEAR.
RIGHT—SOPHOMORE YEAR! INCREDIBLE! WHAT HAVE YOU BEEN UP TO? DID YOU EVER SETTLE ON YOUR MAJOR?
UM... YES. AND THEN I GRADUATED AND WENT ON AND GOT A LAW DEGREE. AND THEN I MARRIED AND HAD A KID.
REALLY? I'M STILL UNDE-CLARED.
I'M THINKING PHYSICS.
YARN THEORY.
MY! SOUNDS IMPRESSIVE!
GB Trudeau

6/25/06

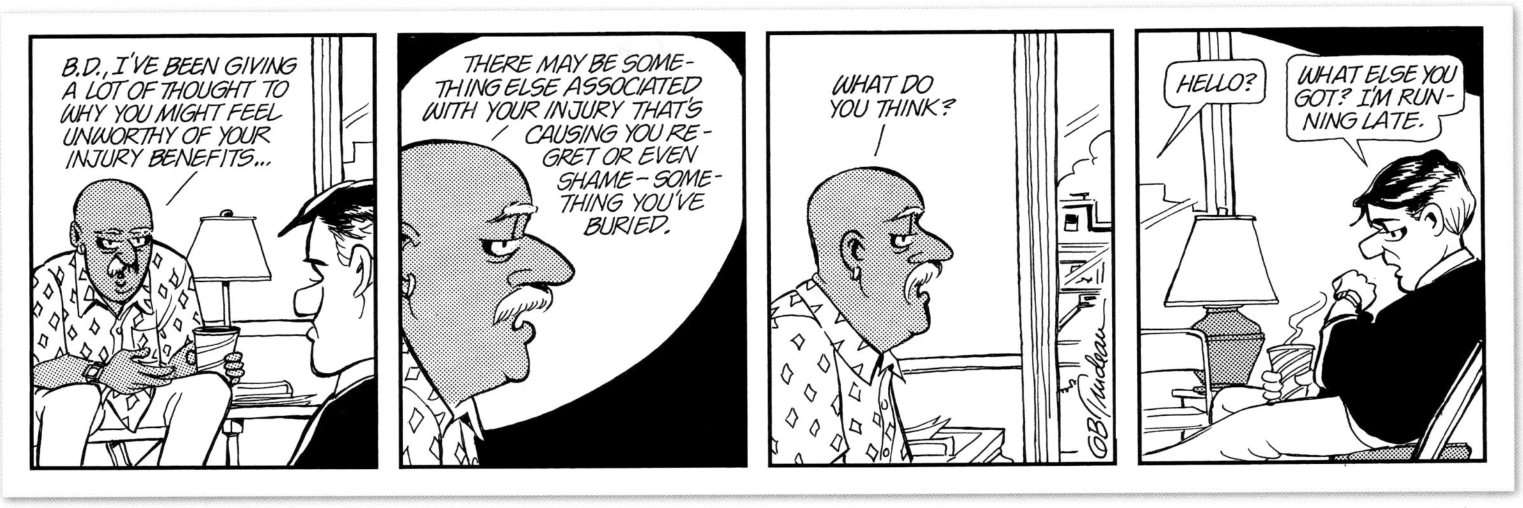
B.D., I'VE BEEN GIVING A LOT OF THOUGHT TO WHY YOU MIGHT FEEL UNWORTHY OF YOUR INJURY BENEFITS...
THERE MAY BE SOMETHING ELSE ASSOCIATED WITH YOUR INJURY THAT'S CAUSING YOU REGRET OR EVEN SHAME – SOMETHING YOU'VE BURIED.
WHAT DO YOU THINK?
HELLO?
WHAT ELSE YOU GOT? I'M RUNNING LATE.

4/19/06

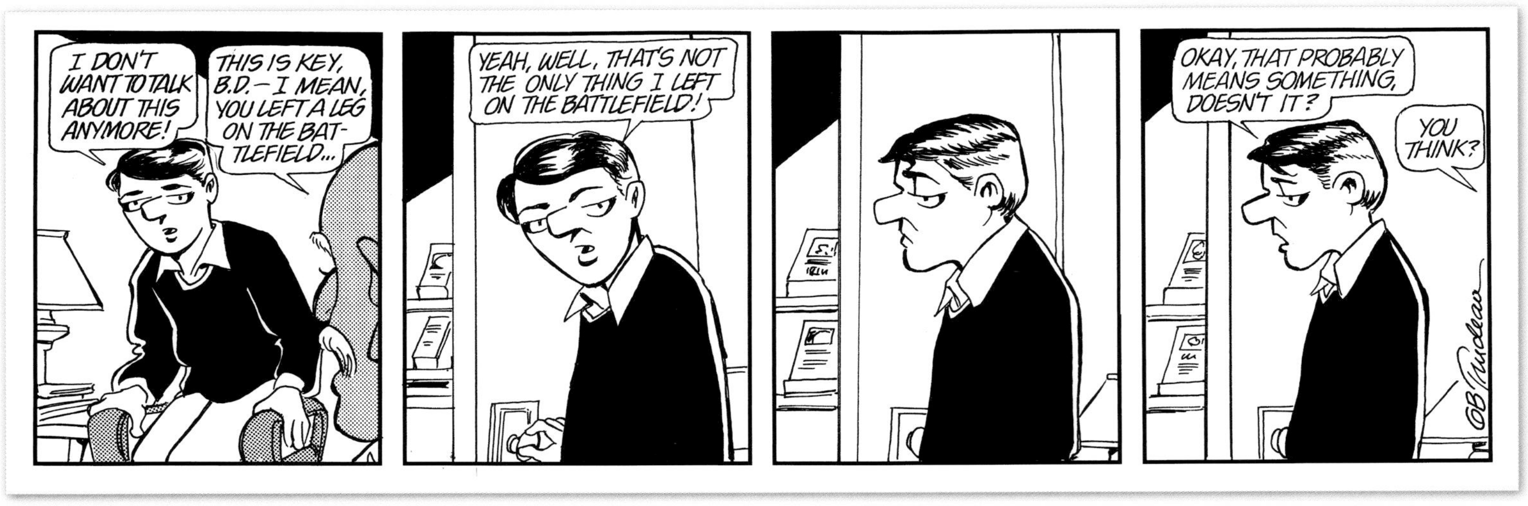
I DON'T WANT TO TALK ABOUT THIS ANYMORE!
THIS IS KEY, B.D. – I MEAN, YOU LEFT A LEG ON THE BATTLEFIELD...
YEAH, WELL, THAT'S NOT THE ONLY THING I LEFT ON THE BATTLEFIELD!
OKAY, THAT PROBABLY MEANS SOMETHING, DOESN'T IT?
YOU THINK?

4/21/06

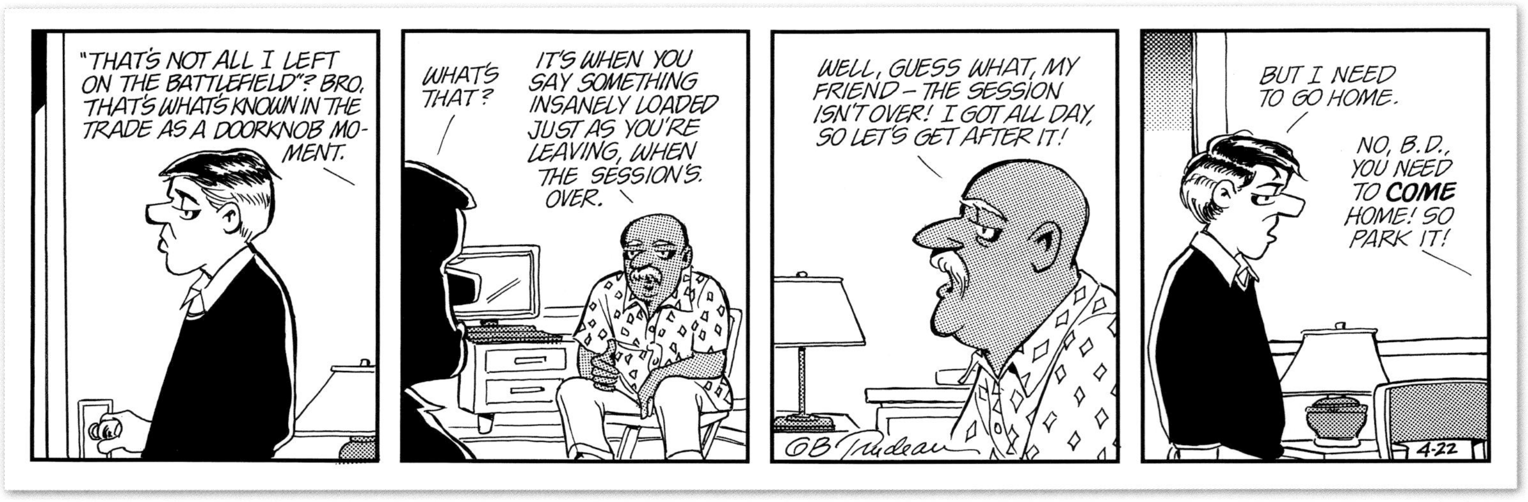
"THAT'S NOT ALL I LEFT ON THE BATTLEFIELD"? BRO, THAT'S WHAT'S KNOWN IN THE TRADE AS A DOORKNOB MOMENT.
WHAT'S THAT?
IT'S WHEN YOU SAY SOMETHING INSANELY LOADED JUST AS YOU'RE LEAVING, WHEN THE SESSION'S OVER.
WELL, GUESS WHAT, MY FRIEND – THE SESSION ISN'T OVER! I GOT ALL DAY, SO LET'S GET AFTER IT!
BUT I NEED TO GO HOME.
NO, B.D., YOU NEED TO **COME** HOME! SO PARK IT!
4-22

4/22/06

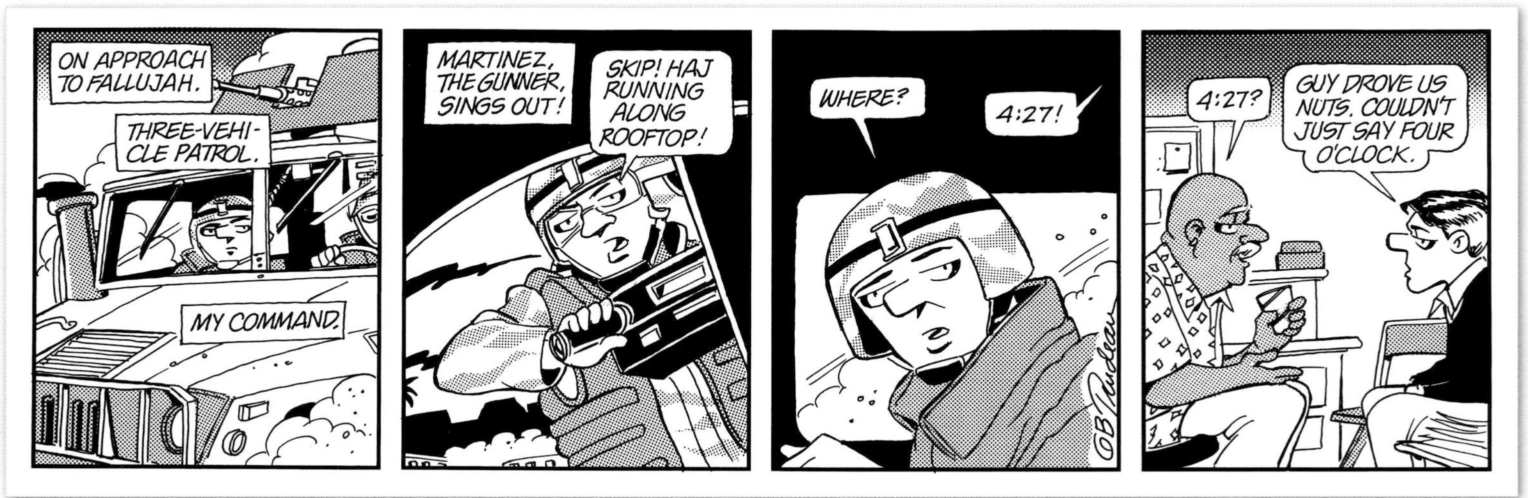
ON APPROACH TO FALLUJAH.
THREE-VEHICLE PATROL.
MY COMMAND.
MARTINEZ, THE GUNNER, SINGS OUT!
SKIP! HAJ RUNNING ALONG ROOFTOP!
WHERE?
4:27!
4:27?
GUY DROVE US NUTS. COULDN'T JUST SAY FOUR O'CLOCK.

4/24/06

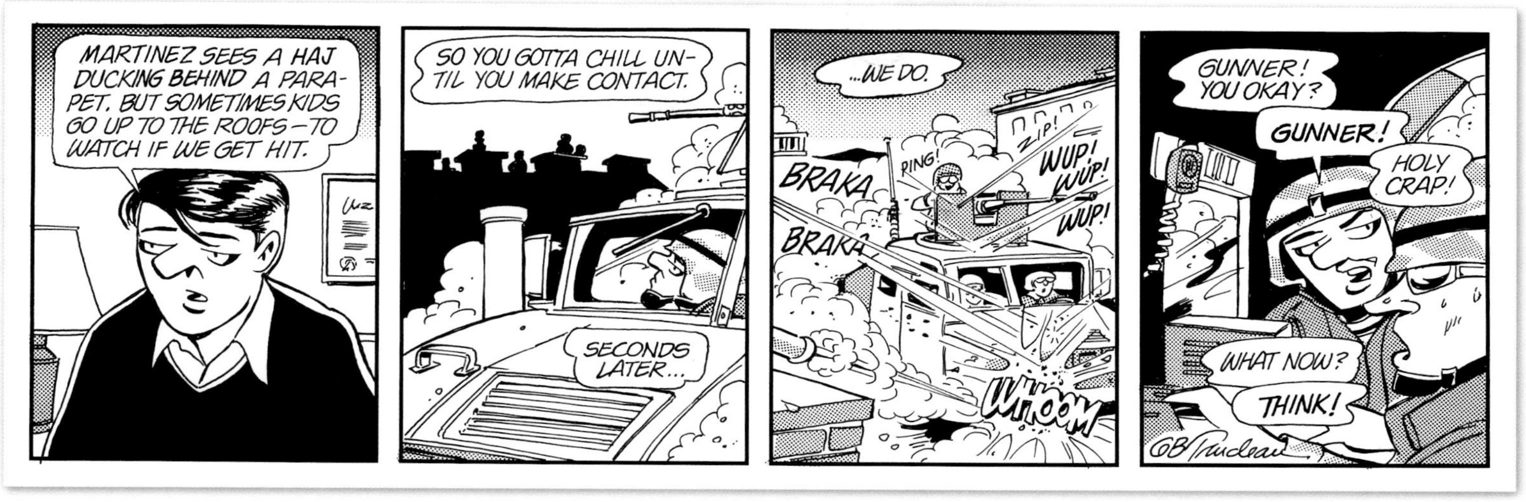
MARTINEZ SEES A HAJ DUCKING BEHIND A PARAPET. BUT SOMETIMES KIDS GO UP TO THE ROOFS—TO WATCH IF WE GET HIT.
SO YOU GOTTA CHILL UNTIL YOU MAKE CONTACT.
SECONDS LATER...
...WE DO.
BRAKA
BRAKA
PING!
ZIP!
WUP!
WUP!
WUP!
WHOOM
GUNNER! YOU OKAY?
GUNNER!
HOLY CRAP!
WHAT NOW?
THINK!
GB Trudeau

4/25/06

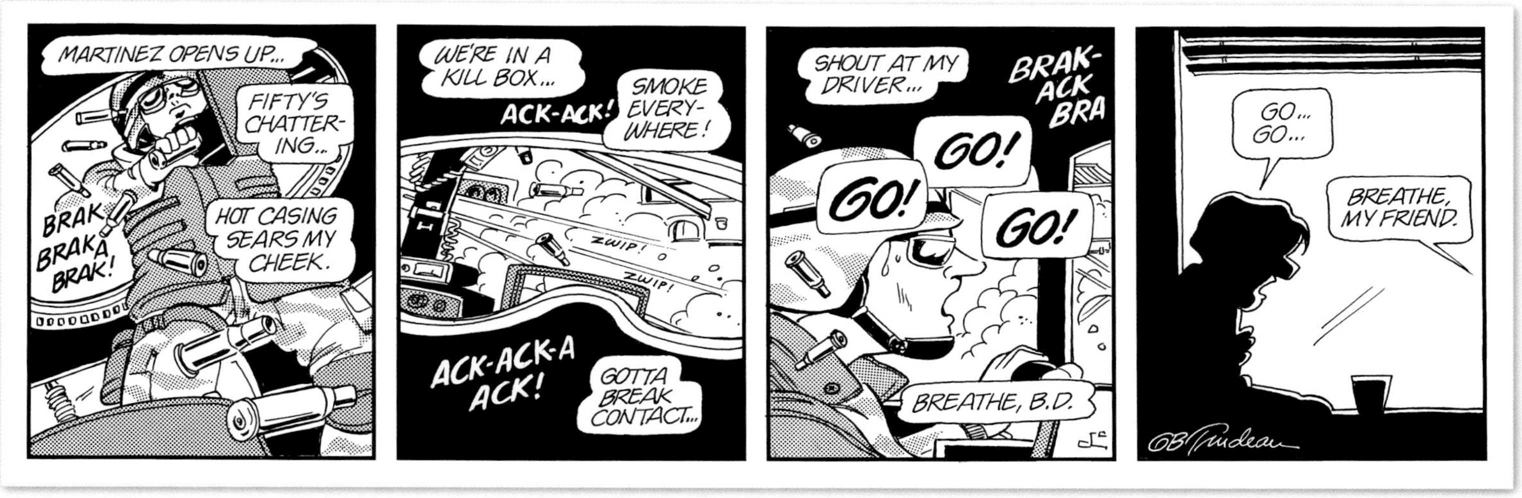
MARTINEZ OPENS UP...
FIFTY'S CHATTERING...
BRAK BRAK A BRAK!
HOT CASING SEARS MY CHEEK.
WE'RE IN A KILL BOX...
SMOKE EVERYWHERE!
ACK-ACK!
ZWIP!
ZWIP!
ACK-ACK-A ACK!
GOTTA BREAK CONTACT...
SHOUT AT MY DRIVER...
BRAK-ACK BRA
GO!
GO!
GO!
BREATHE, B.D.
GO... GO...
BREATHE, MY FRIEND.
GB Trudeau

4/26/06

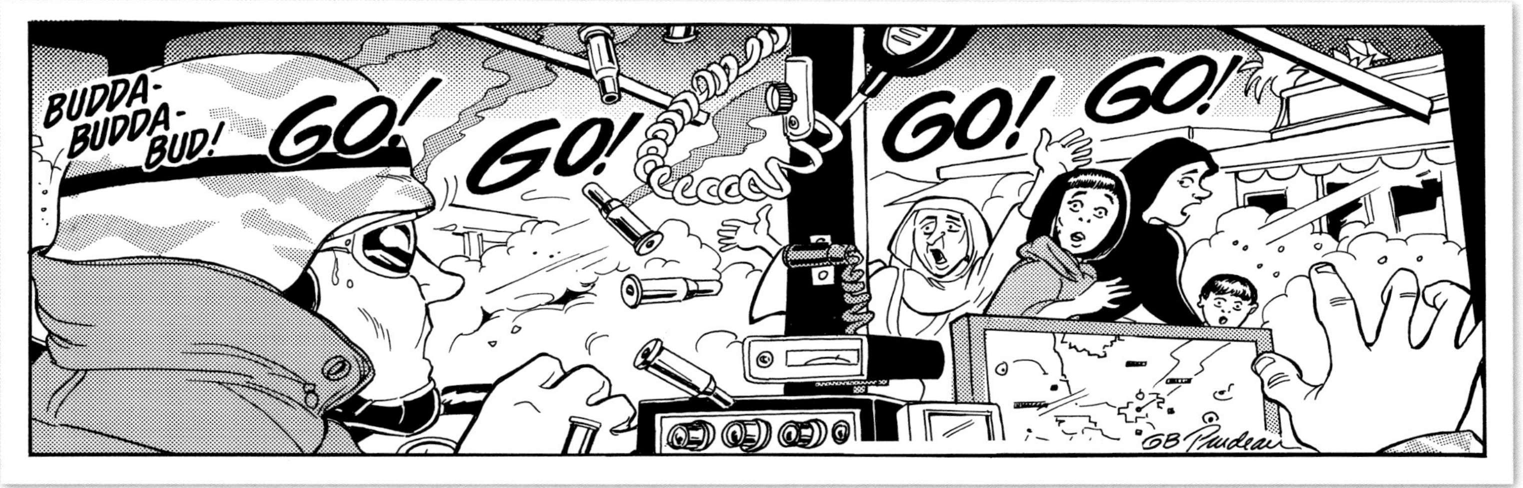
BUDDA-BUDDA-BUD!
GO!
GO!
GO!
GO!
GB Trudeau

4/27/06

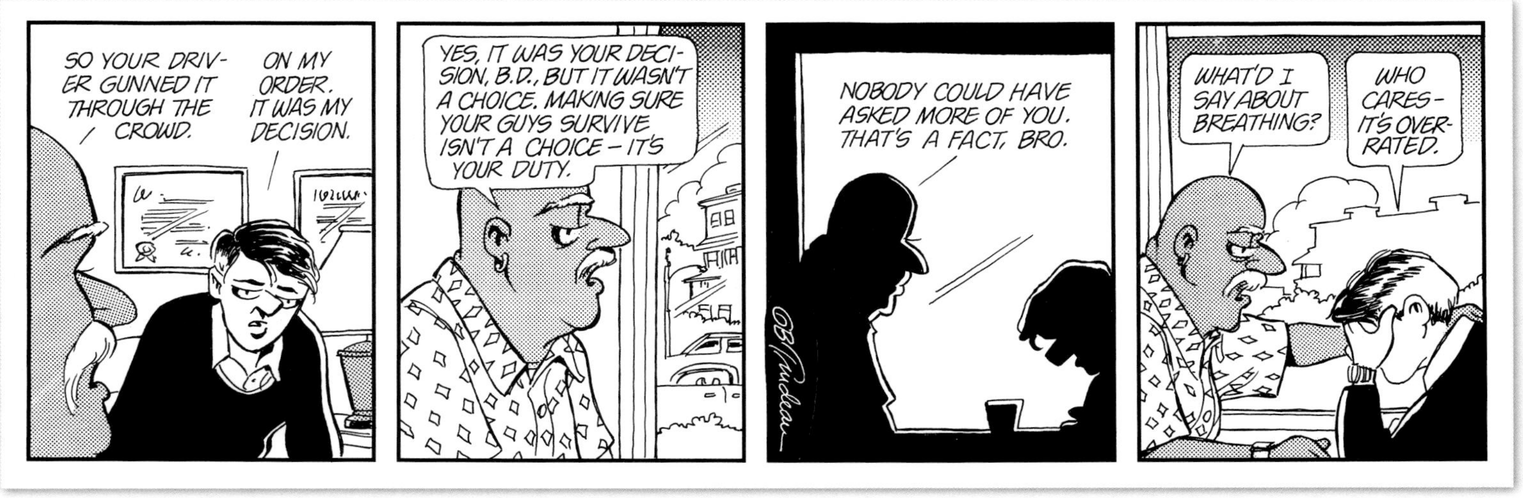
SO YOUR DRIVER GUNNED IT THROUGH THE CROWD.
ON MY ORDER. IT WAS MY DECISION.
YES, IT WAS YOUR DECISION, B.D., BUT IT WASN'T A CHOICE. MAKING SURE YOUR GUYS SURVIVE ISN'T A CHOICE—IT'S YOUR DUTY.
NOBODY COULD HAVE ASKED MORE OF YOU. THAT'S A FACT, BRO.
GB Trudeau
WHAT'D I SAY ABOUT BREATHING?
WHO CARES—IT'S OVERRATED.

4/28/06

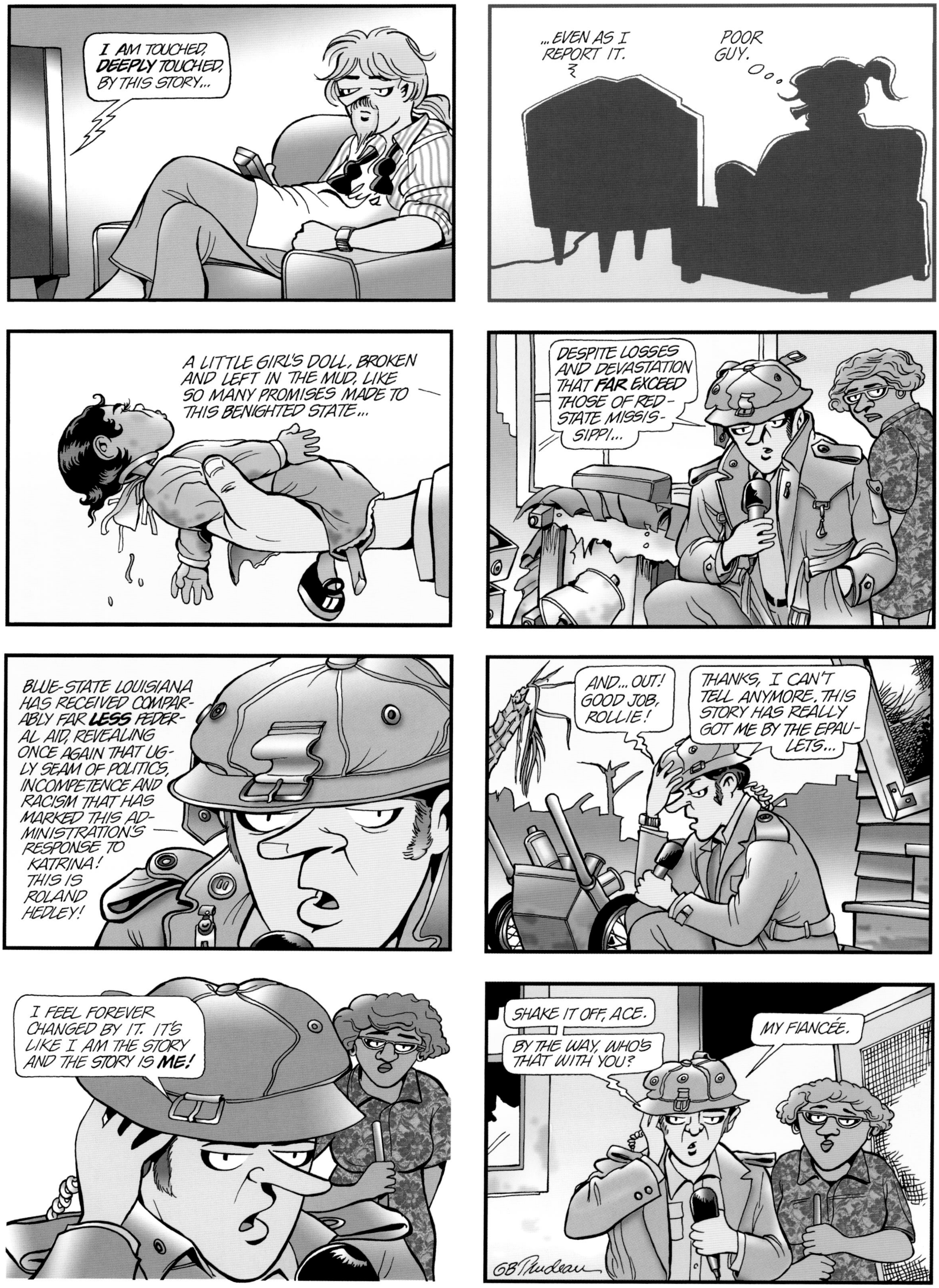
I AM TOUCHED, DEEPLY TOUCHED, BY THIS STORY...
...EVEN AS I REPORT IT.
POOR GUY.
A LITTLE GIRL'S DOLL, BROKEN AND LEFT IN THE MUD, LIKE SO MANY PROMISES MADE TO THIS BENIGHTED STATE...
DESPITE LOSSES AND DEVASTATION THAT FAR EXCEED THOSE OF RED-STATE MISSISSIPPI...
BLUE-STATE LOUISIANA HAS RECEIVED COMPARABLY FAR LESS FEDERAL AID, REVEALING ONCE AGAIN THAT UGLY SEAM OF POLITICS, INCOMPETENCE AND RACISM THAT HAS MARKED THIS ADMINISTRATION'S RESPONSE TO KATRINA! THIS IS ROLAND HEDLEY!
AND... OUT! GOOD JOB, ROLLIE!
THANKS, I CAN'T TELL ANYMORE. THIS STORY HAS REALLY GOT ME BY THE EPAULETS...
I FEEL FOREVER CHANGED BY IT. IT'S LIKE I AM THE STORY AND THE STORY IS ME!
SHAKE IT OFF, ACE.
BY THE WAY, WHO'S THAT WITH YOU?
MY FIANCÉE.
GB Trudeau

3/12/06

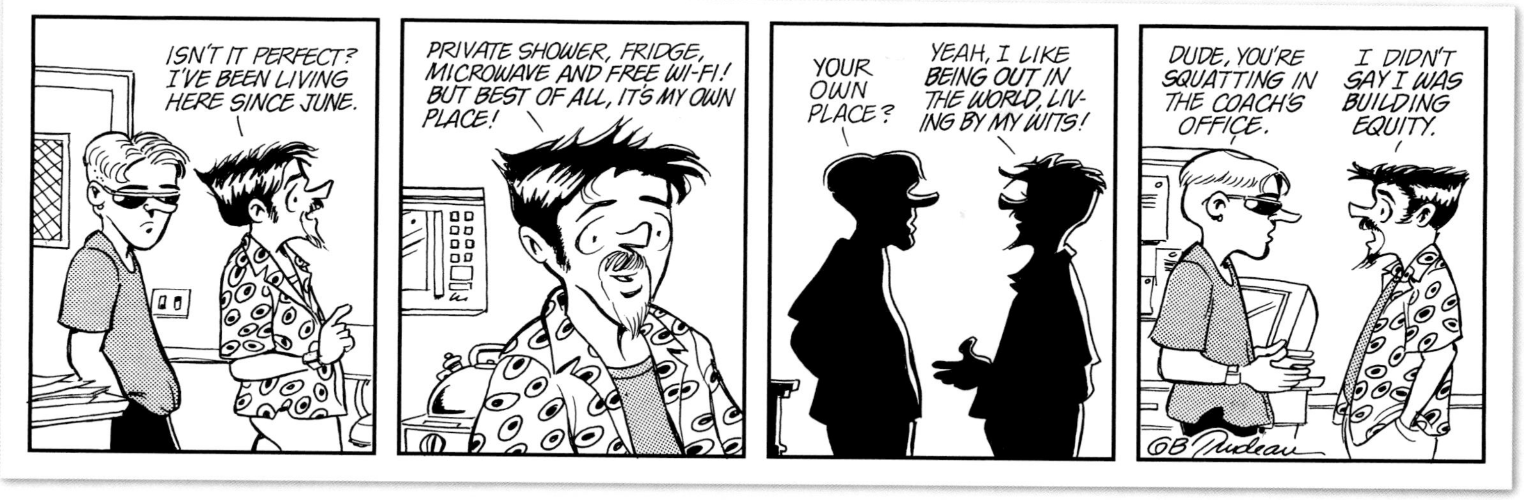
ISN'T IT PERFECT? I'VE BEEN LIVING HERE SINCE JUNE.
PRIVATE SHOWER, FRIDGE, MICROWAVE AND FREE WI-FI! BUT BEST OF ALL, IT'S MY OWN PLACE!
YOUR OWN PLACE?
YEAH, I LIKE BEING OUT IN THE WORLD, LIVING BY MY WITS!
DUDE, YOU'RE SQUATTING IN THE COACH'S OFFICE.
I DIDN'T SAY I WAS BUILDING EQUITY.
©B Trudeau

8/14/06

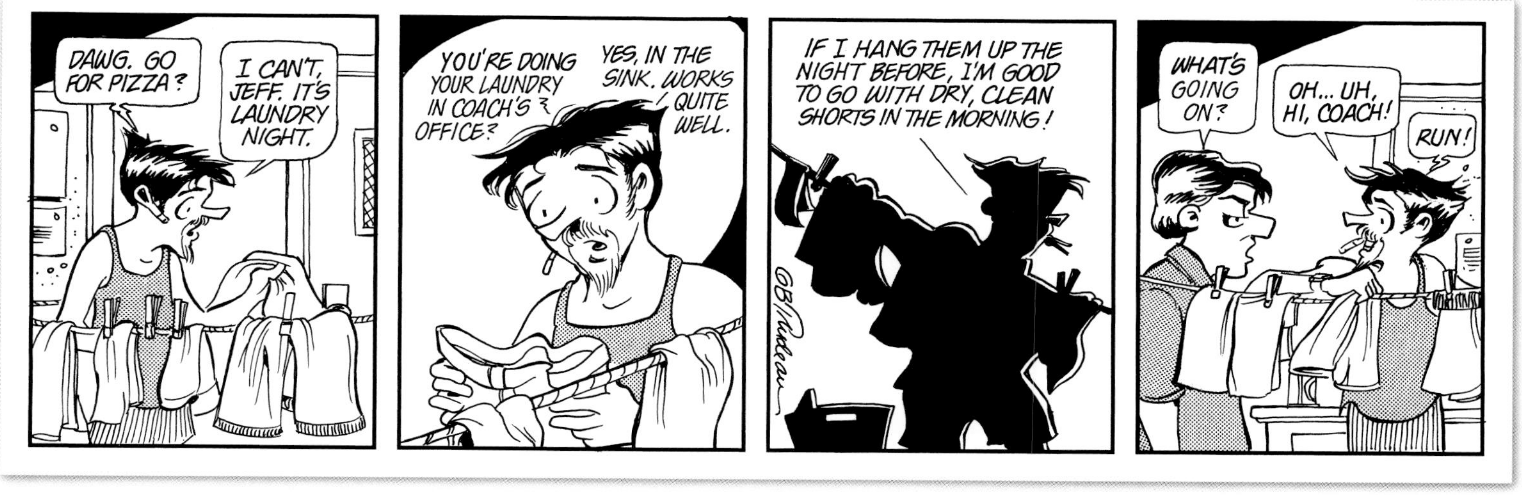
DAWG. GO FOR PIZZA?
I CAN'T, JEFF. IT'S LAUNDRY NIGHT.
YOU'RE DOING YOUR LAUNDRY IN COACH'S OFFICE?
YES, IN THE SINK. WORKS QUITE WELL.
IF I HANG THEM UP THE NIGHT BEFORE, I'M GOOD TO GO WITH DRY, CLEAN SHORTS IN THE MORNING!
WHAT'S GOING ON?
OH... UH, HI, COACH!
RUN!

8/15/06

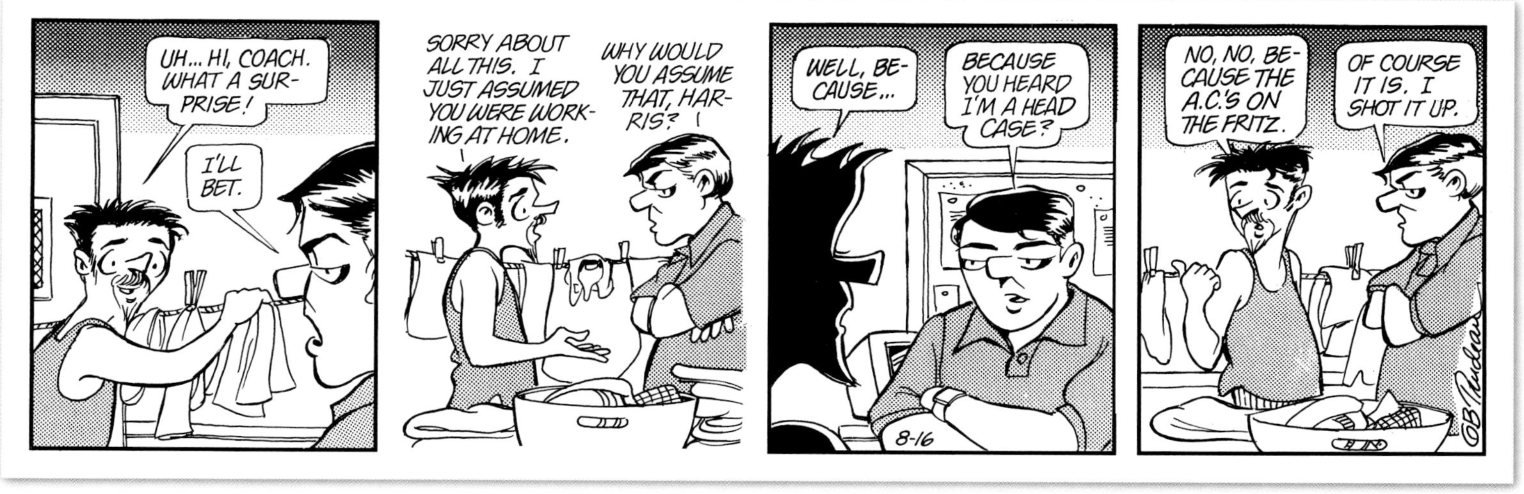
UH... HI, COACH. WHAT A SURPRISE!
I'LL BET.
SORRY ABOUT ALL THIS. I JUST ASSUMED YOU WERE WORKING AT HOME.
WHY WOULD YOU ASSUME THAT, HARRIS?
WELL, BECAUSE...
BECAUSE YOU HEARD I'M A HEAD CASE?
NO, NO, BECAUSE THE A.C.'S ON THE FRITZ.
OF COURSE IT IS. I SHOT IT UP.

8/16/06

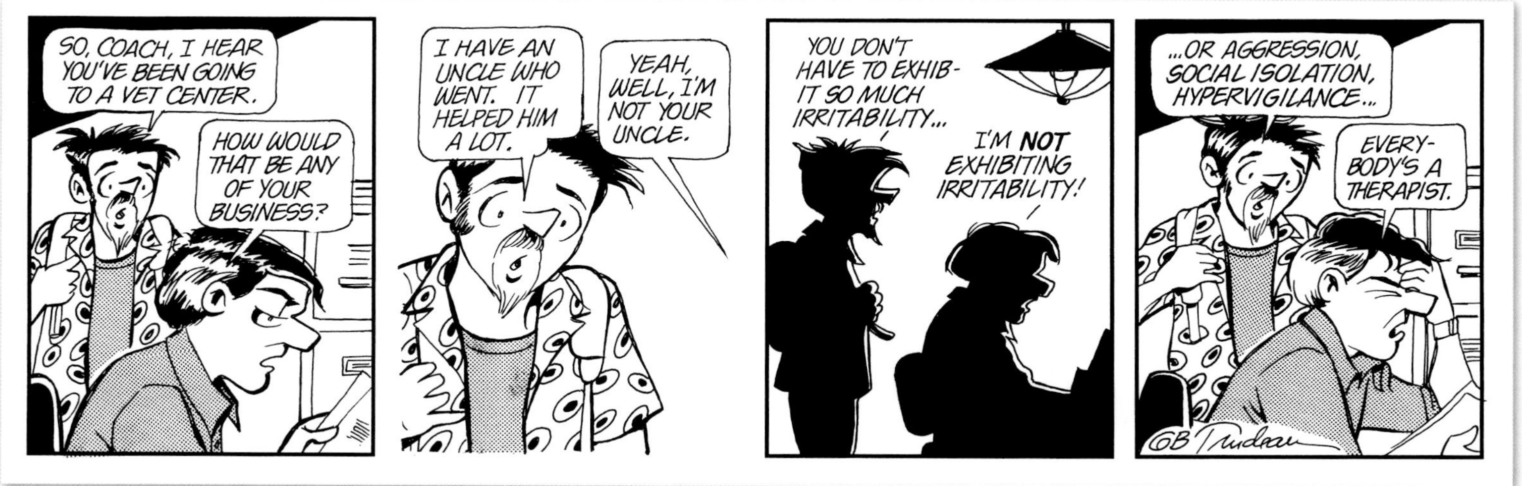
SO, COACH, I HEAR YOU'VE BEEN GOING TO A VET CENTER.
HOW WOULD THAT BE ANY OF YOUR BUSINESS?
I HAVE AN UNCLE WHO WENT. IT HELPED HIM A LOT.
YEAH, WELL, I'M NOT YOUR UNCLE.
YOU DON'T HAVE TO EXHIBIT SO MUCH IRRITABILITY...
I'M NOT EXHIBITING IRRITABILITY!
...OR AGGRESSION, SOCIAL ISOLATION, HYPERVIGILANCE...
EVERYBODY'S A THERAPIST.

8/18/06

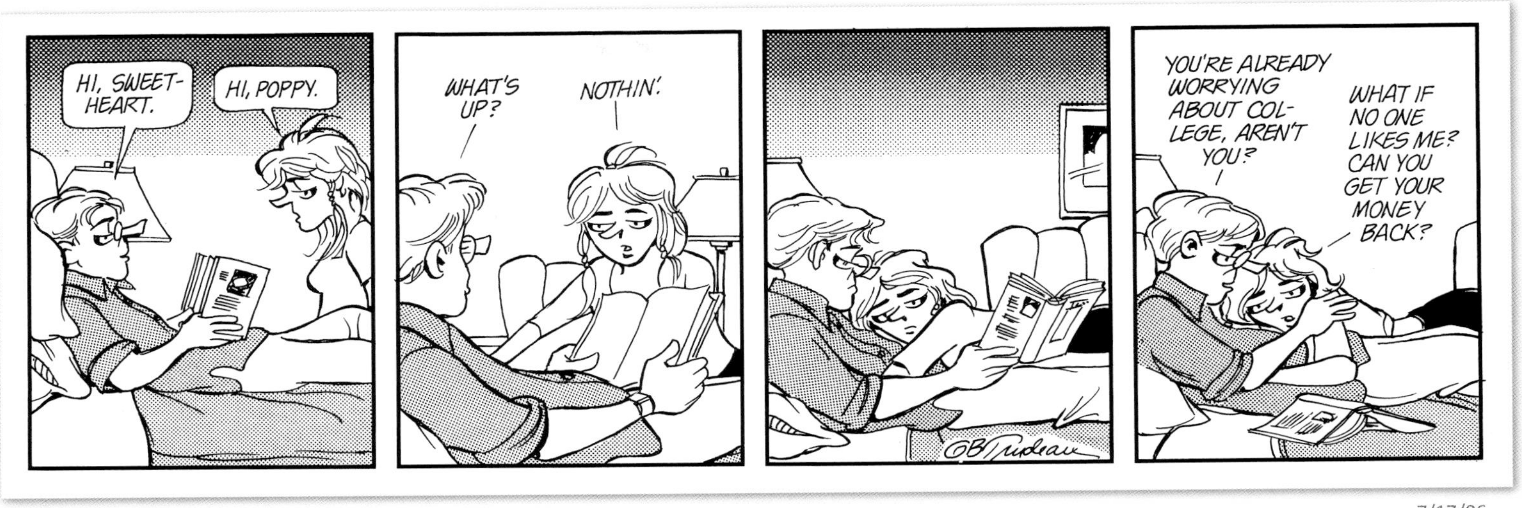
HI, SWEET-HEART.
HI, POPPY.
WHAT'S UP?
NOTHIN'.
YOU'RE ALREADY WORRYING ABOUT COL-LEGE, AREN'T YOU?
WHAT IF NO ONE LIKES ME? CAN YOU GET YOUR MONEY BACK?

7/17/06

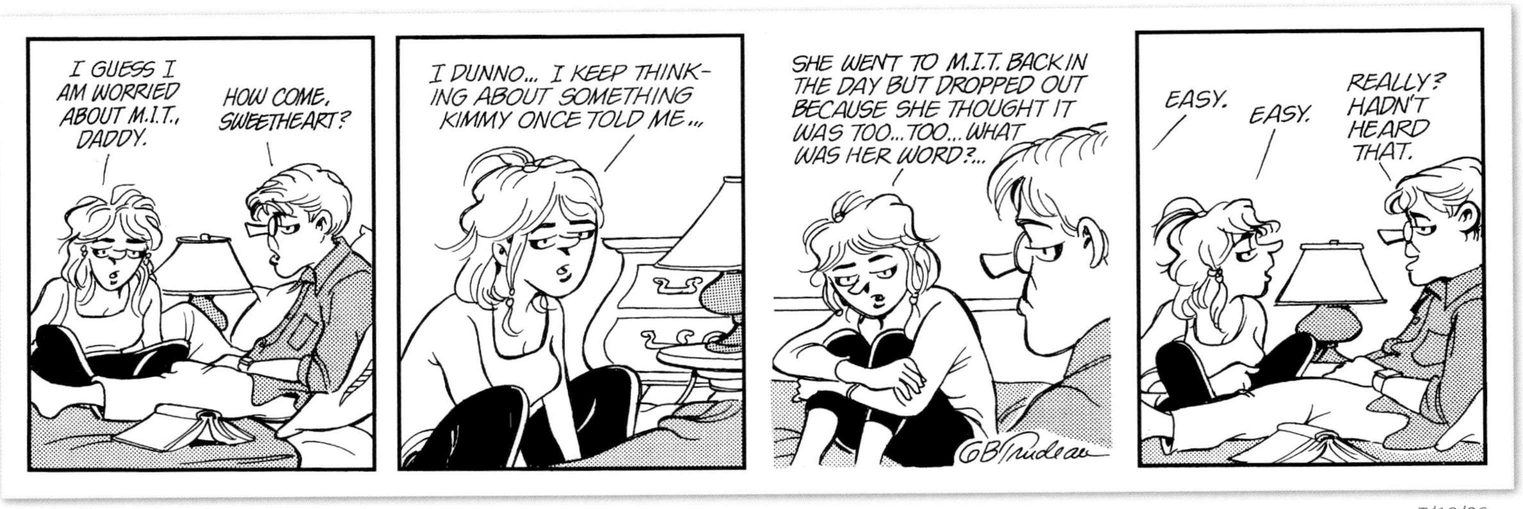
I GUESS I AM WORRIED ABOUT M.I.T., DADDY.
HOW COME, SWEETHEART?
I DUNNO... I KEEP THINK-ING ABOUT SOMETHING KIMMY ONCE TOLD ME...
SHE WENT TO M.I.T. BACK IN THE DAY BUT DROPPED OUT BECAUSE SHE THOUGHT IT WAS TOO...TOO...WHAT WAS HER WORD?...
EASY.
EASY.
REALLY? HADN'T HEARD THAT.

7/18/06

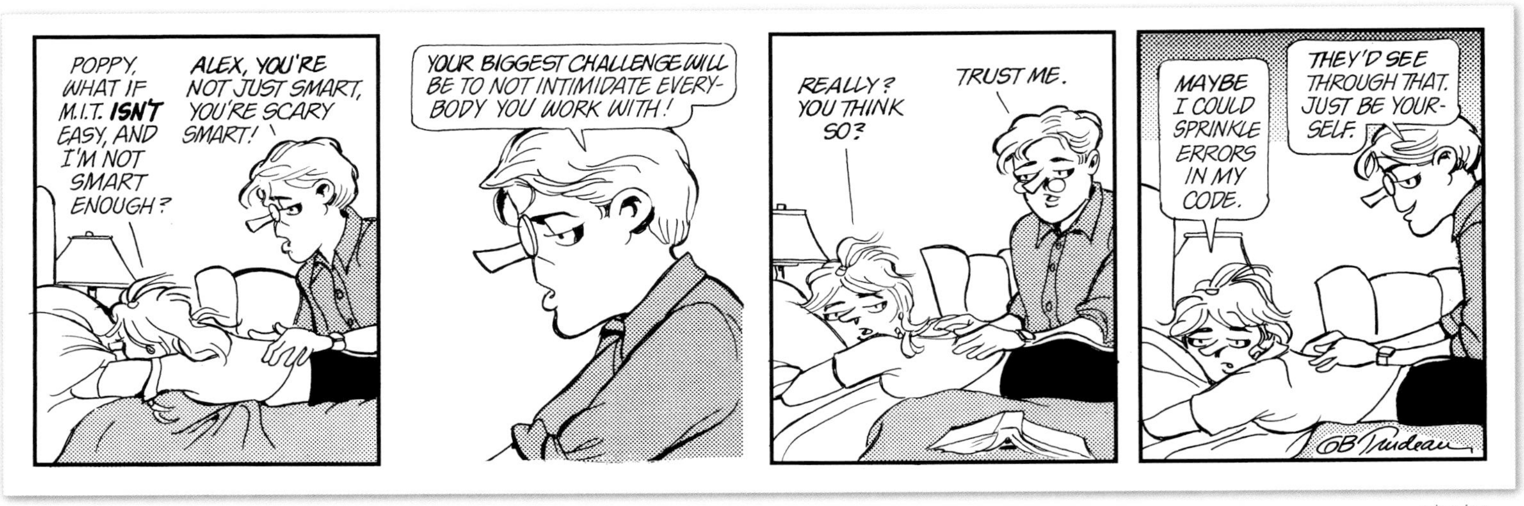
POPPY, WHAT IF M.I.T. **ISN'T** EASY, AND I'M NOT SMART ENOUGH?
ALEX, YOU'RE NOT JUST SMART, YOU'RE SCARY SMART!
YOUR BIGGEST CHALLENGE WILL BE TO NOT INTIMIDATE EVERY-BODY YOU WORK WITH!
REALLY? YOU THINK SO?
TRUST ME.
MAYBE I COULD SPRINKLE ERRORS IN MY CODE.
THEY'D SEE THROUGH THAT. JUST BE YOUR-SELF.

7/19/06

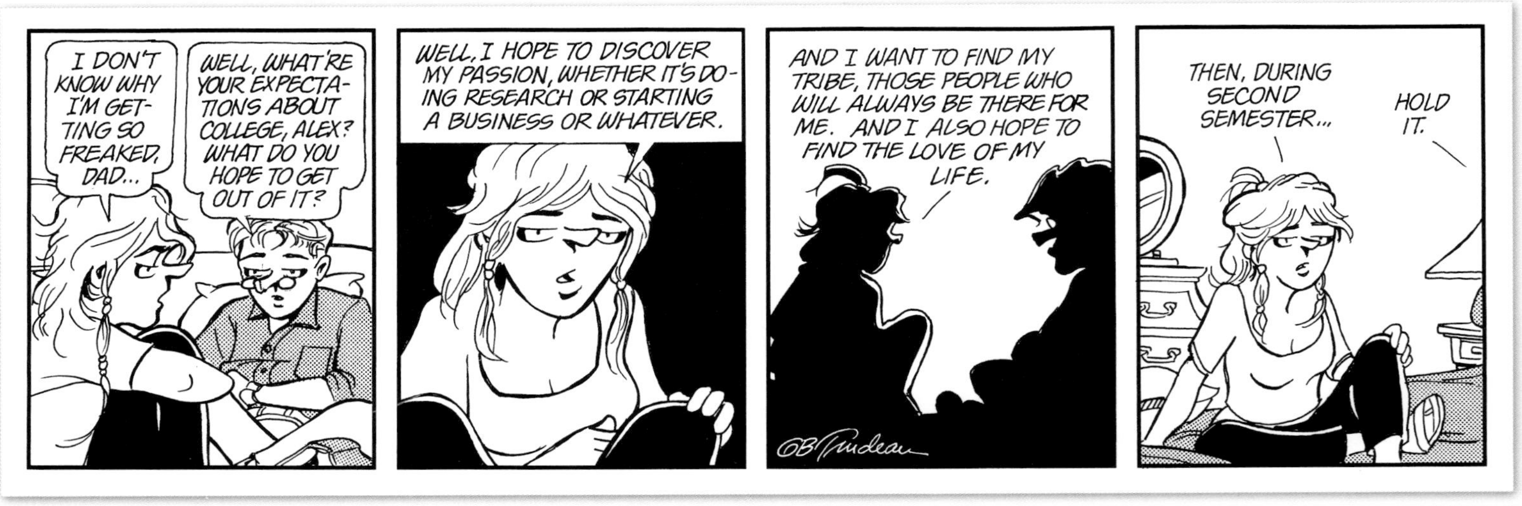
I DON'T KNOW WHY I'M GET-TING SO FREAKED, DAD...
WELL, WHAT'RE YOUR EXPECTA-TIONS ABOUT COLLEGE, ALEX? WHAT DO YOU HOPE TO GET OUT OF IT?
WELL, I HOPE TO DISCOVER MY PASSION, WHETHER IT'S DO-ING RESEARCH OR STARTING A BUSINESS OR WHATEVER.
AND I WANT TO FIND MY TRIBE, THOSE PEOPLE WHO WILL ALWAYS BE THERE FOR ME. AND I ALSO HOPE TO FIND THE LOVE OF MY LIFE.
THEN, DURING SECOND SEMESTER...
HOLD IT.

7/20/06

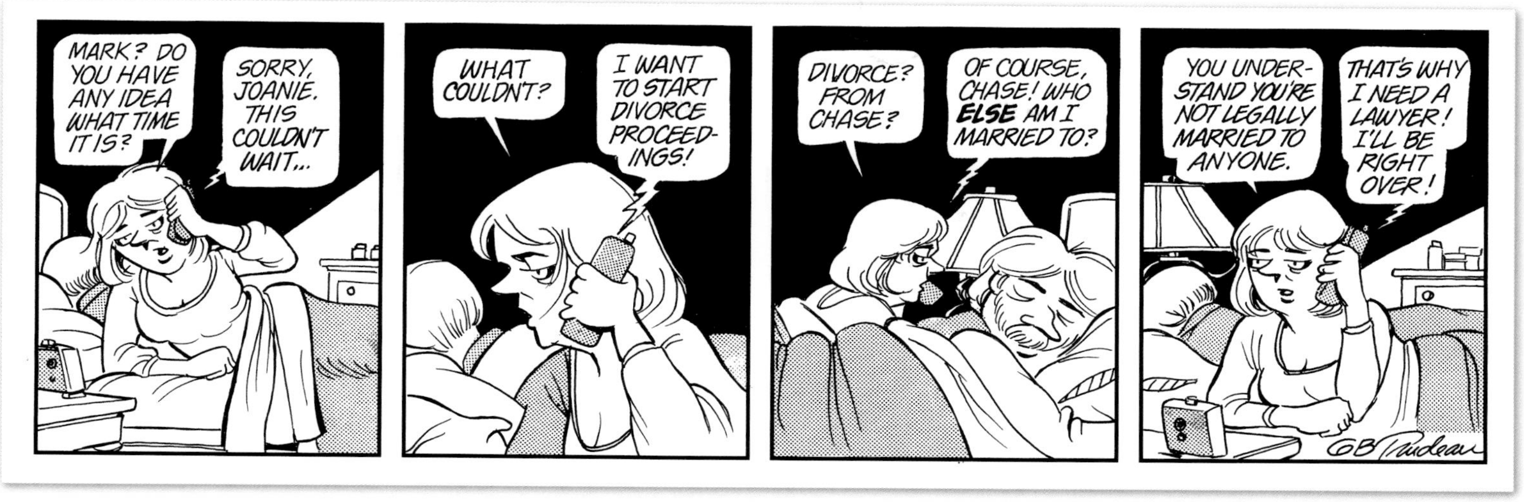
MARK? DO YOU HAVE ANY IDEA WHAT TIME IT IS?
SORRY, JOANIE. THIS COULDN'T WAIT...
WHAT COULDN'T?
I WANT TO START DIVORCE PROCEEDINGS!
DIVORCE? FROM CHASE?
OF COURSE, CHASE! WHO ELSE AM I MARRIED TO?
YOU UNDERSTAND YOU'RE NOT LEGALLY MARRIED TO ANYONE.
THAT'S WHY I NEED A LAWYER! I'LL BE RIGHT OVER!
GB Trudeau

10/23/06

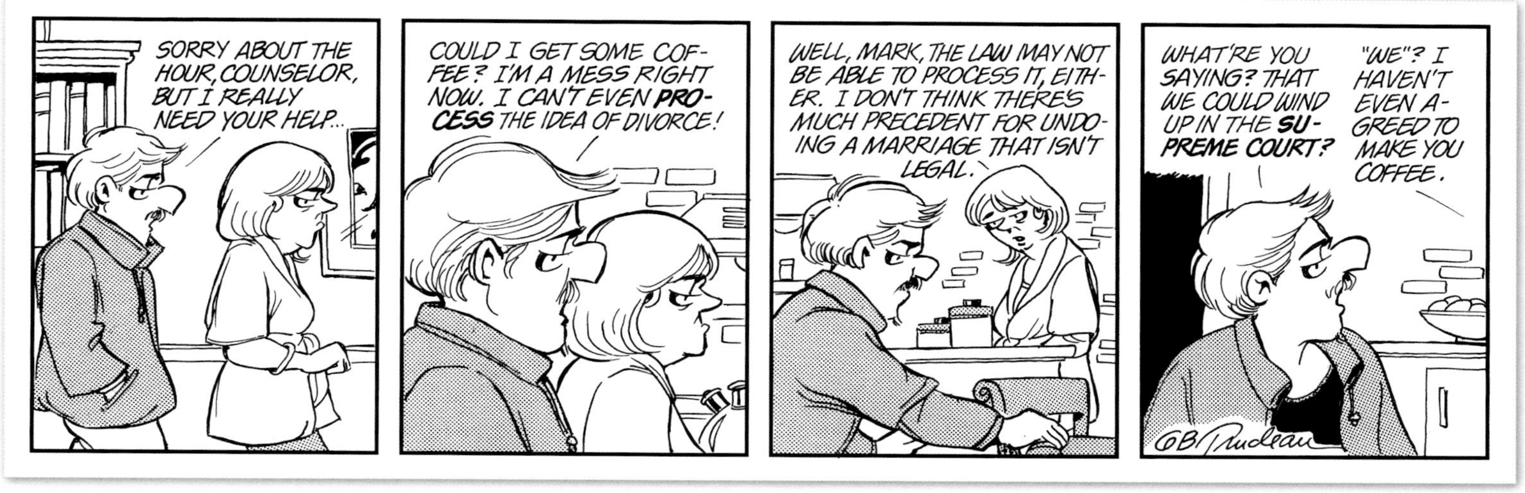
SORRY ABOUT THE HOUR, COUNSELOR, BUT I REALLY NEED YOUR HELP...
COULD I GET SOME COFFEE? I'M A MESS RIGHT NOW. I CAN'T EVEN PROCESS THE IDEA OF DIVORCE!
WELL, MARK, THE LAW MAY NOT BE ABLE TO PROCESS IT, EITHER. I DON'T THINK THERE'S MUCH PRECEDENT FOR UNDOING A MARRIAGE THAT ISN'T LEGAL.
WHAT'RE YOU SAYING? THAT WE COULD WIND UP IN THE SUPREME COURT?
"WE"? I HAVEN'T EVEN AGREED TO MAKE YOU COFFEE.
GB Trudeau

10/24/06

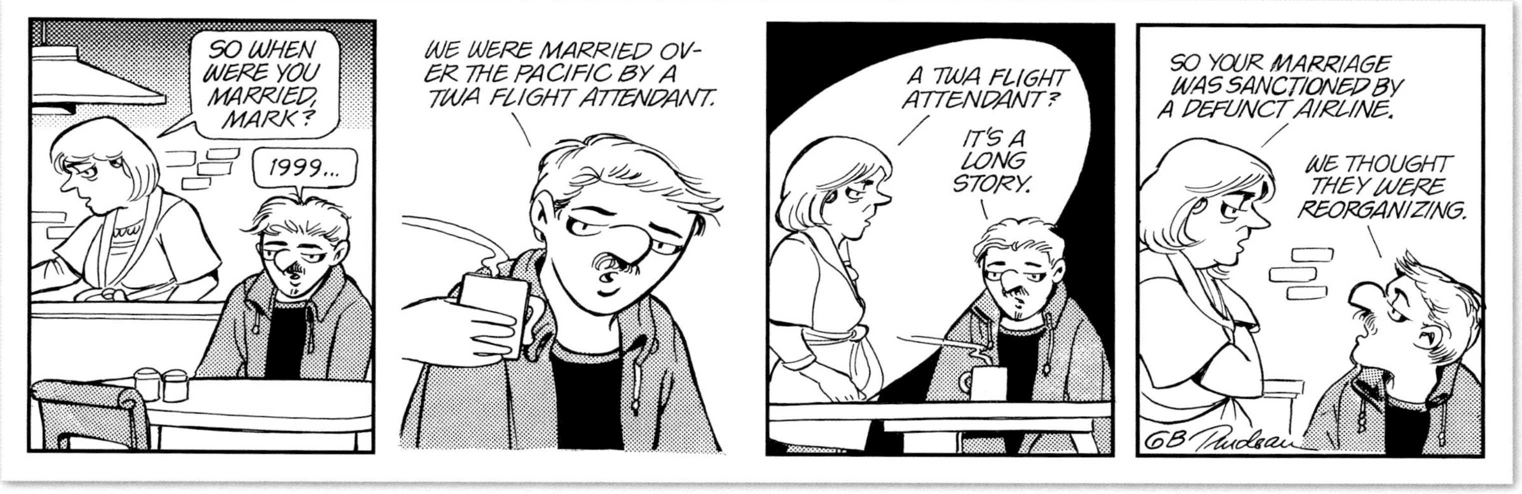
SO WHEN WERE YOU MARRIED, MARK?
1999...
WE WERE MARRIED OVER THE PACIFIC BY A TWA FLIGHT ATTENDANT.
A TWA FLIGHT ATTENDANT?
IT'S A LONG STORY.
SO YOUR MARRIAGE WAS SANCTIONED BY A DEFUNCT AIRLINE.
WE THOUGHT THEY WERE REORGANIZING.
GB Trudeau

10/25/06

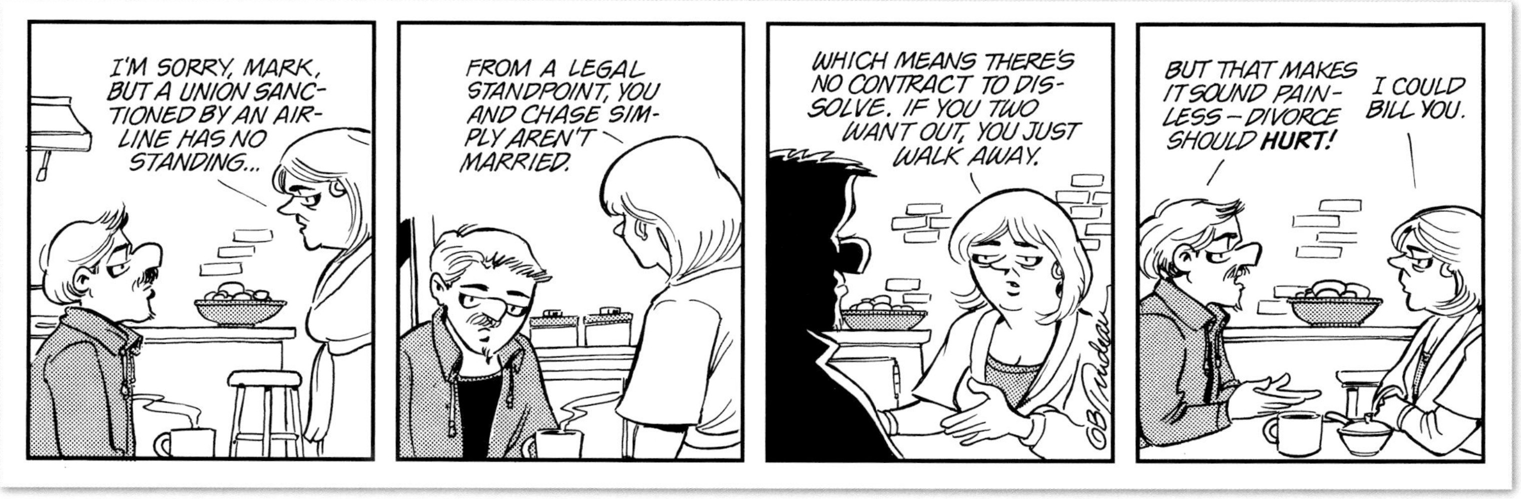
I'M SORRY, MARK, BUT A UNION SANCTIONED BY AN AIRLINE HAS NO STANDING...
FROM A LEGAL STANDPOINT, YOU AND CHASE SIMPLY AREN'T MARRIED.
WHICH MEANS THERE'S NO CONTRACT TO DISSOLVE. IF YOU TWO WANT OUT, YOU JUST WALK AWAY.
GB Trudeau
BUT THAT MAKES IT SOUND PAINLESS—DIVORCE SHOULD HURT!
I COULD BILL YOU.

10/26/06

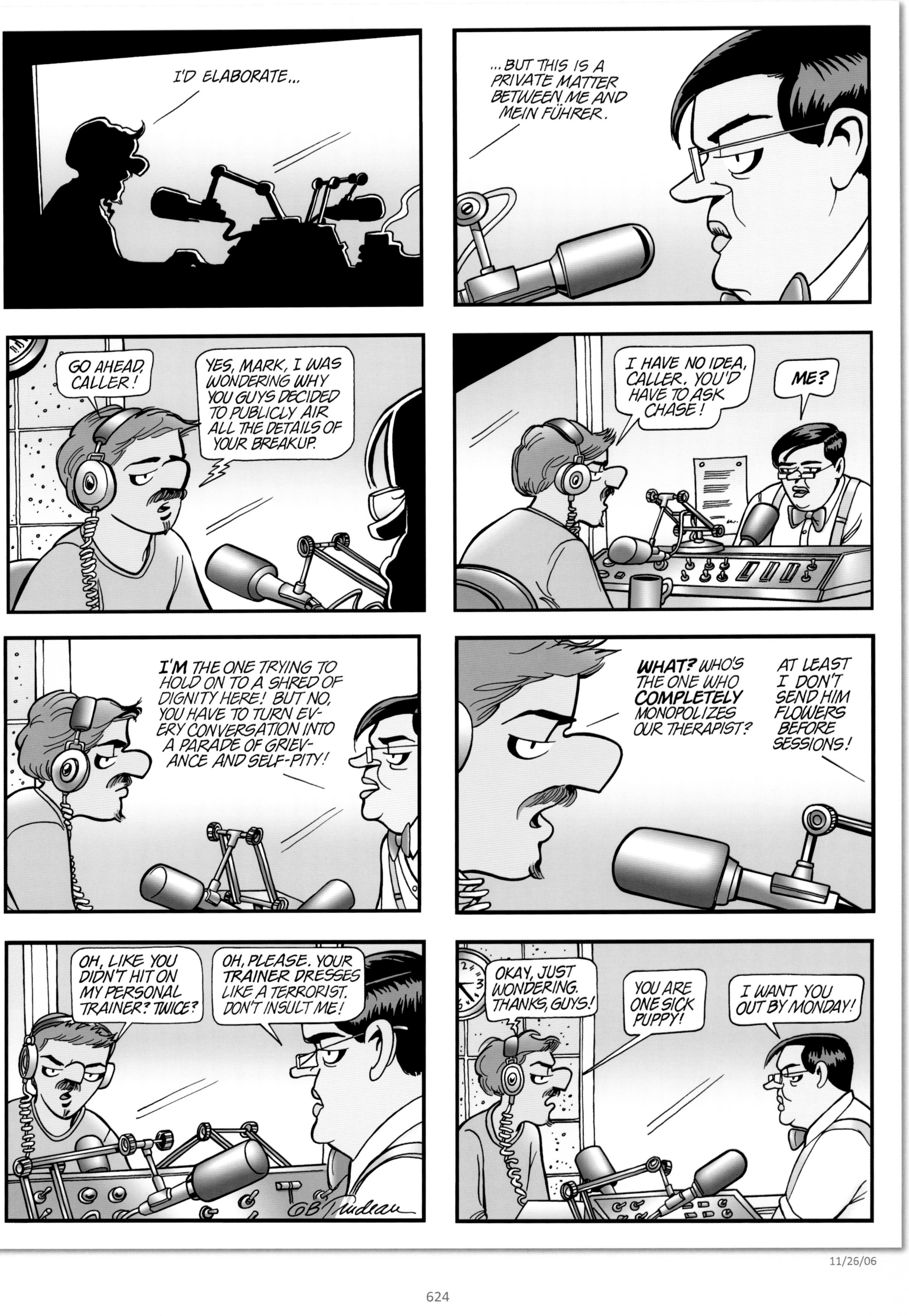
I'D ELABORATE...
...BUT THIS IS A PRIVATE MATTER BETWEEN ME AND MEIN FÜHRER.
GO AHEAD, CALLER!
YES, MARK, I WAS WONDERING WHY YOU GUYS DECIDED TO PUBLICLY AIR ALL THE DETAILS OF YOUR BREAKUP.
I HAVE NO IDEA, CALLER. YOU'D HAVE TO ASK CHASE!
ME?
I'M THE ONE TRYING TO HOLD ON TO A SHRED OF DIGNITY HERE! BUT NO, YOU HAVE TO TURN EVERY CONVERSATION INTO A PARADE OF GRIEVANCE AND SELF-PITY!
WHAT? WHO'S THE ONE WHO COMPLETELY MONOPOLIZES OUR THERAPIST?
AT LEAST I DON'T SEND HIM FLOWERS BEFORE SESSIONS!
OH, LIKE YOU DIDN'T HIT ON MY PERSONAL TRAINER? TWICE?
OH, PLEASE. YOUR TRAINER DRESSES LIKE A TERRORIST. DON'T INSULT ME!
GB Trudeau
OKAY, JUST WONDERING. THANKS, GUYS!
YOU ARE ONE SICK PUPPY!
I WANT YOU OUT BY MONDAY!

11/26/06

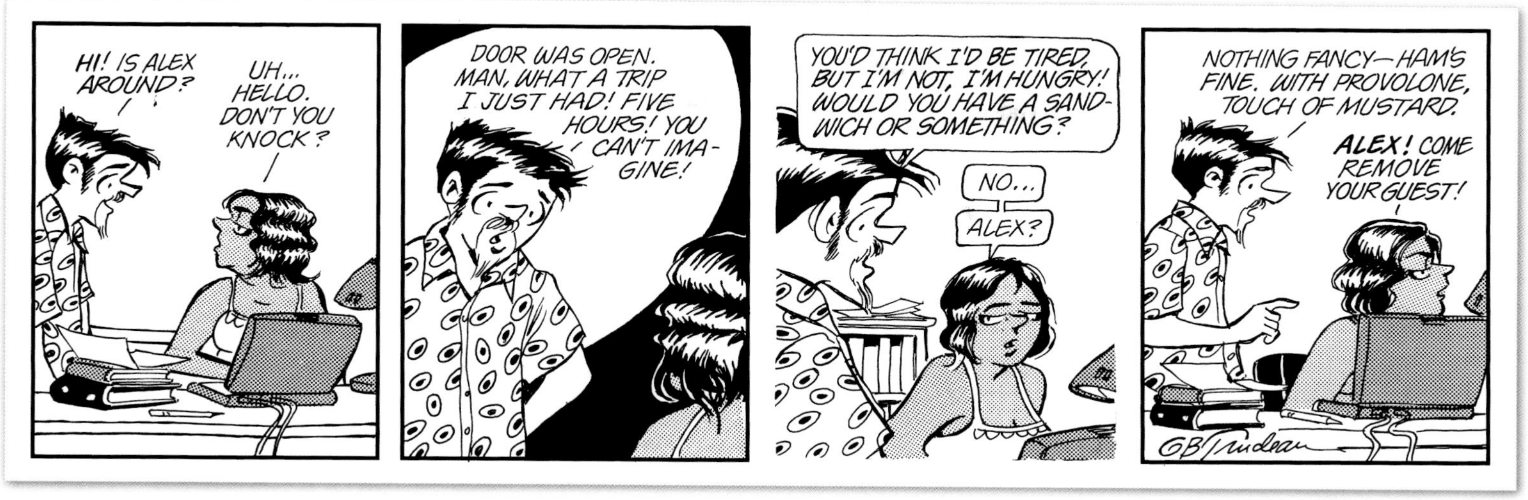

HI! IS ALEX AROUND?
UH... HELLO. DON'T YOU KNOCK?
DOOR WAS OPEN. MAN, WHAT A TRIP I JUST HAD! FIVE HOURS! YOU CAN'T IMAGINE!
YOU'D THINK I'D BE TIRED, BUT I'M NOT, I'M HUNGRY! WOULD YOU HAVE A SANDWICH OR SOMETHING?
NO...
ALEX?
NOTHING FANCY—HAM'S FINE. WITH PROVOLONE, TOUCH OF MUSTARD.
ALEX! COME REMOVE YOUR GUEST!
GB Trudeau

9/27/06

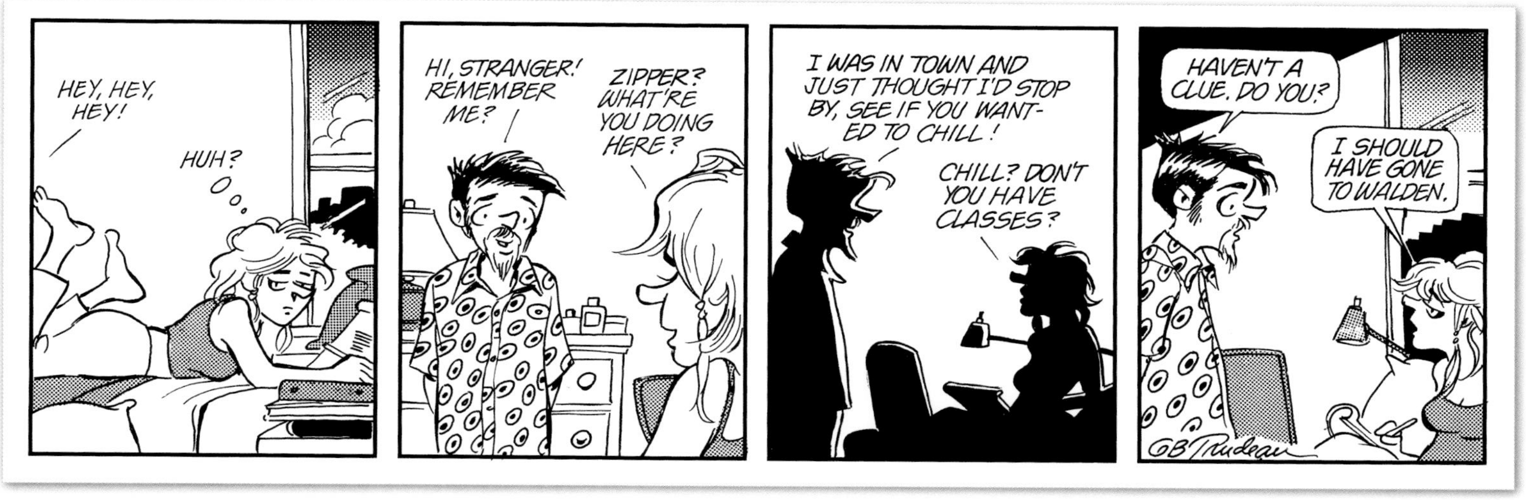

HEY, HEY, HEY!
HUH?
HI, STRANGER! REMEMBER ME?
ZIPPER? WHAT'RE YOU DOING HERE?
I WAS IN TOWN AND JUST THOUGHT I'D STOP BY, SEE IF YOU WANTED TO CHILL!
CHILL? DON'T YOU HAVE CLASSES?
HAVEN'T A CLUE. DO YOU?
I SHOULD HAVE GONE TO WALDEN.
GB Trudeau

9/28/06

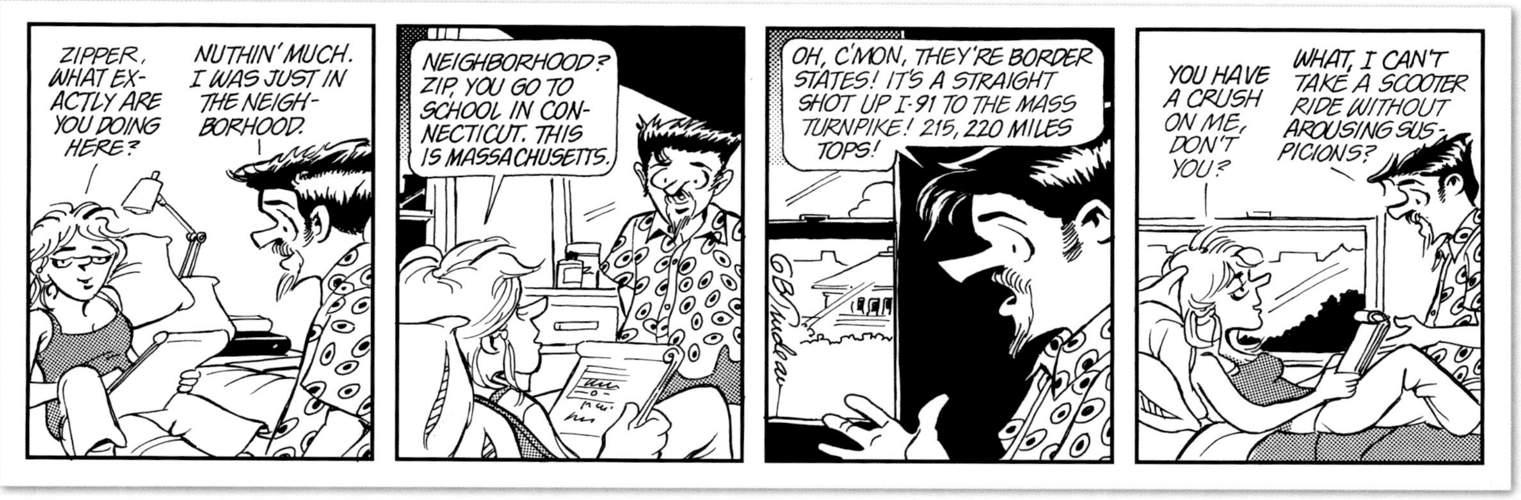

ZIPPER, WHAT EXACTLY ARE YOU DOING HERE?
NUTHIN' MUCH. I WAS JUST IN THE NEIGHBORHOOD.
NEIGHBORHOOD? ZIP, YOU GO TO SCHOOL IN CONNECTICUT. THIS IS MASSACHUSETTS.
OH, C'MON, THEY'RE BORDER STATES! IT'S A STRAIGHT SHOT UP I-91 TO THE MASS TURNPIKE! 215, 220 MILES TOPS!
GB Trudeau
YOU HAVE A CRUSH ON ME, DON'T YOU?
WHAT, I CAN'T TAKE A SCOOTER RIDE WITHOUT AROUSING SUSPICIONS?

9/29/06

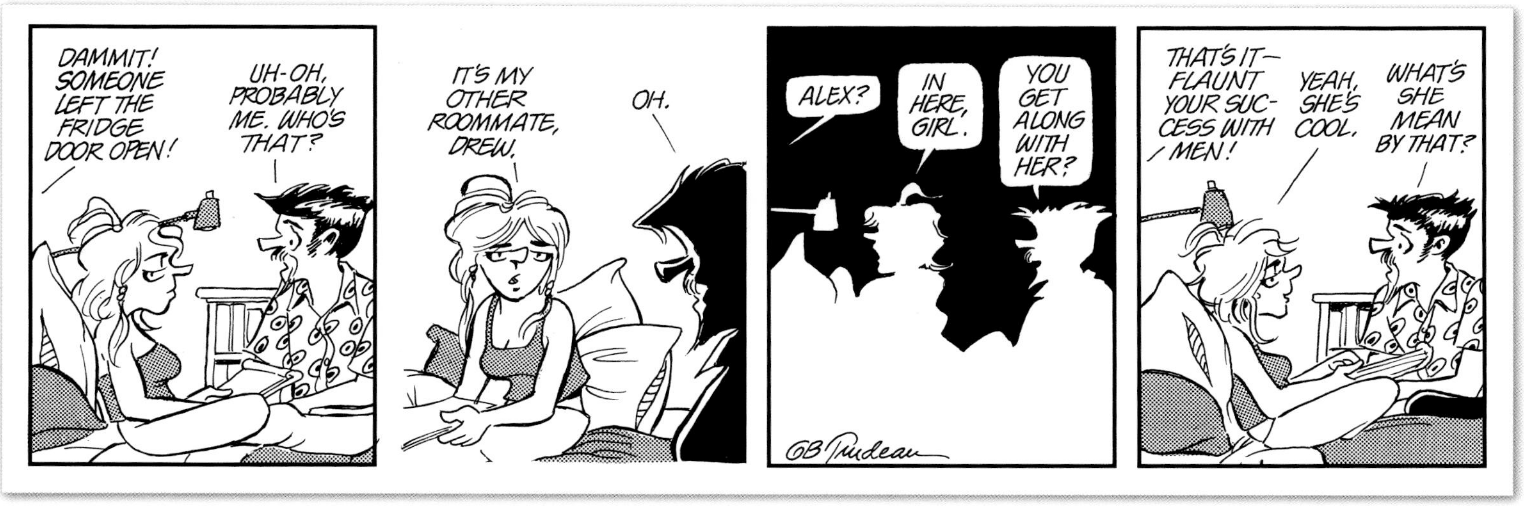

DAMMIT! SOMEONE LEFT THE FRIDGE DOOR OPEN!
UH-OH, PROBABLY ME. WHO'S THAT?
IT'S MY OTHER ROOMMATE, DREW.
OH.
ALEX?
IN HERE, GIRL.
YOU GET ALONG WITH HER?
GB Trudeau
THAT'S IT—FLAUNT YOUR SUCCESS WITH MEN!
YEAH, SHE'S COOL.
WHAT'S SHE MEAN BY THAT?

9/30/06

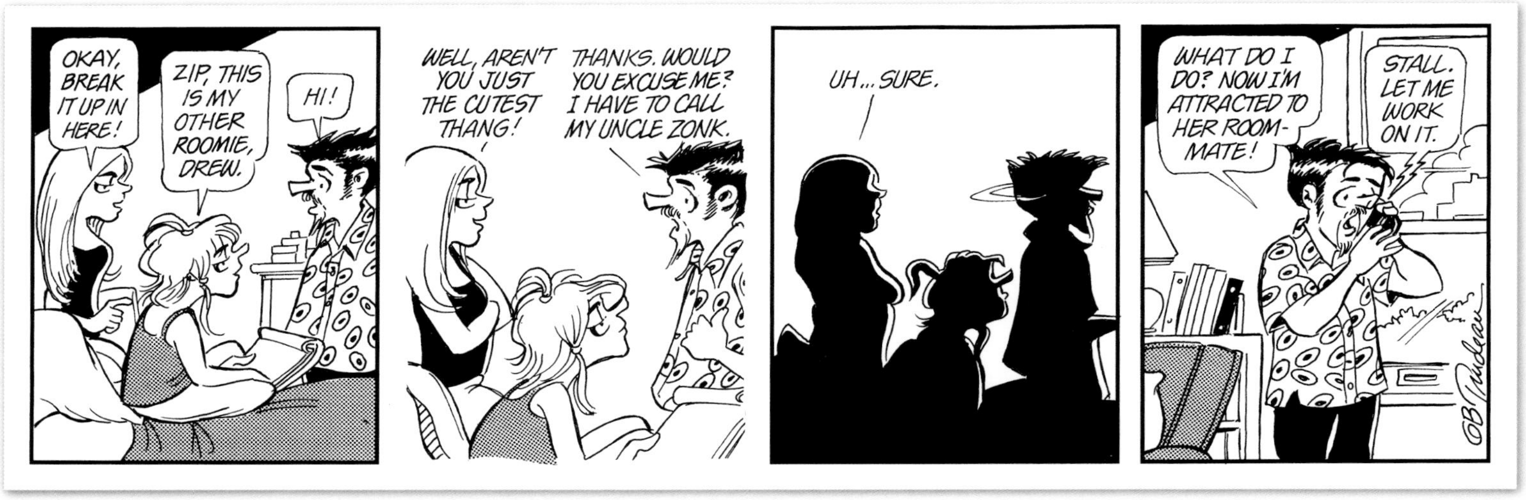
OKAY, BREAK IT UP IN HERE!
ZIP, THIS IS MY OTHER ROOMIE, DREW.
HI!
WELL, AREN'T YOU JUST THE CUTEST THANG!
THANKS. WOULD YOU EXCUSE ME? I HAVE TO CALL MY UNCLE ZONK.
UH... SURE.
WHAT DO I DO? NOW I'M ATTRACTED TO HER ROOM-MATE!
STALL. LET ME WORK ON IT.
GB Trudeau

10/2/06

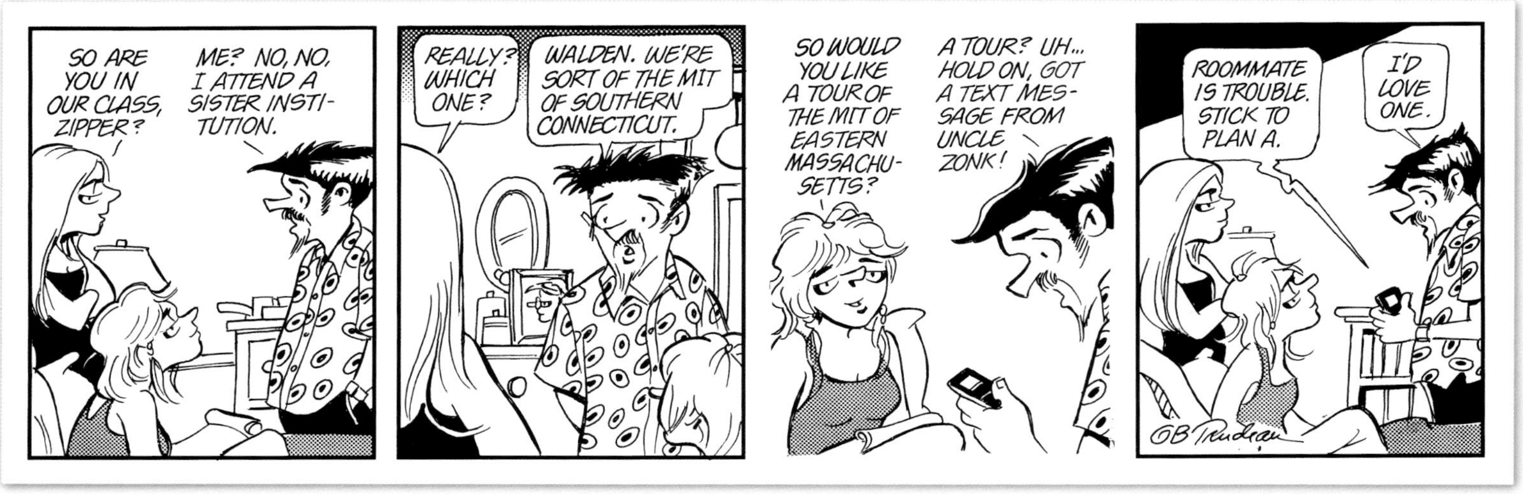
SO ARE YOU IN OUR CLASS, ZIPPER?
ME? NO, NO, I ATTEND A SISTER INSTI-TUTION.
REALLY? WHICH ONE?
WALDEN. WE'RE SORT OF THE MIT OF SOUTHERN CONNECTICUT.
SO WOULD YOU LIKE A TOUR OF THE MIT OF EASTERN MASSACHU-SETTS?
A TOUR? UH... HOLD ON, GOT A TEXT MES-SAGE FROM UNCLE ZONK!
ROOMMATE IS TROUBLE. STICK TO PLAN A.
I'D LOVE ONE.
GB Trudeau

10/3/06

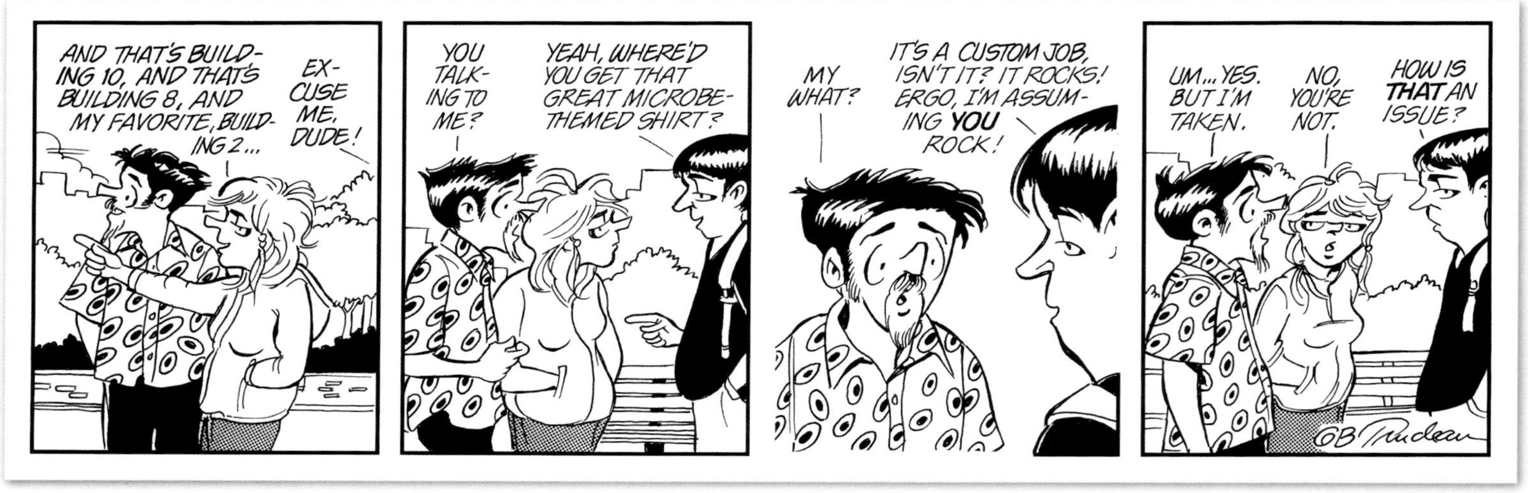
AND THAT'S BUILD-ING 10, AND THAT'S BUILDING 8, AND MY FAVORITE, BUILD-ING 2...
EX-CUSE ME, DUDE!
YOU TALK-ING TO ME?
YEAH, WHERE'D YOU GET THAT GREAT MICROBE-THEMED SHIRT?
MY WHAT?
IT'S A CUSTOM JOB, ISN'T IT? IT ROCKS! ERGO, I'M ASSUM-ING YOU ROCK!
UM... YES. BUT I'M TAKEN.
NO, YOU'RE NOT.
HOW IS THAT AN ISSUE?
GB Trudeau

10/6/06

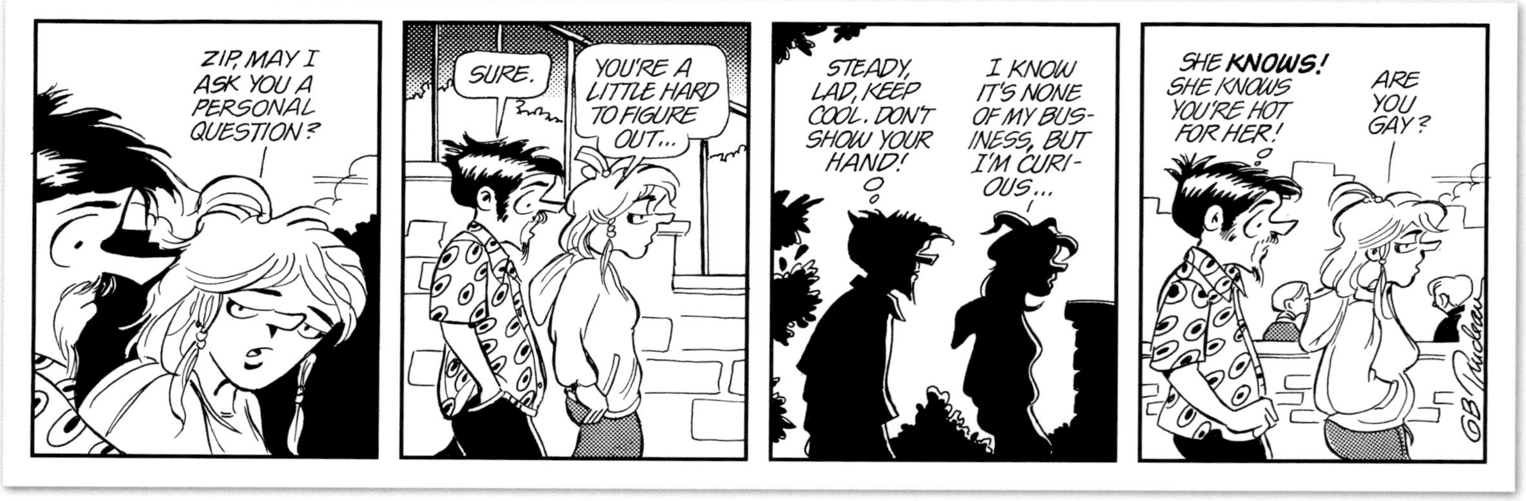
ZIP, MAY I ASK YOU A PERSONAL QUESTION?
SURE.
YOU'RE A LITTLE HARD TO FIGURE OUT...
STEADY, LAD, KEEP COOL. DON'T SHOW YOUR HAND!
I KNOW IT'S NONE OF MY BUS-INESS, BUT I'M CURI-OUS...
SHE KNOWS! SHE KNOWS YOU'RE HOT FOR HER!
ARE YOU GAY?
GB Trudeau

10/7/06

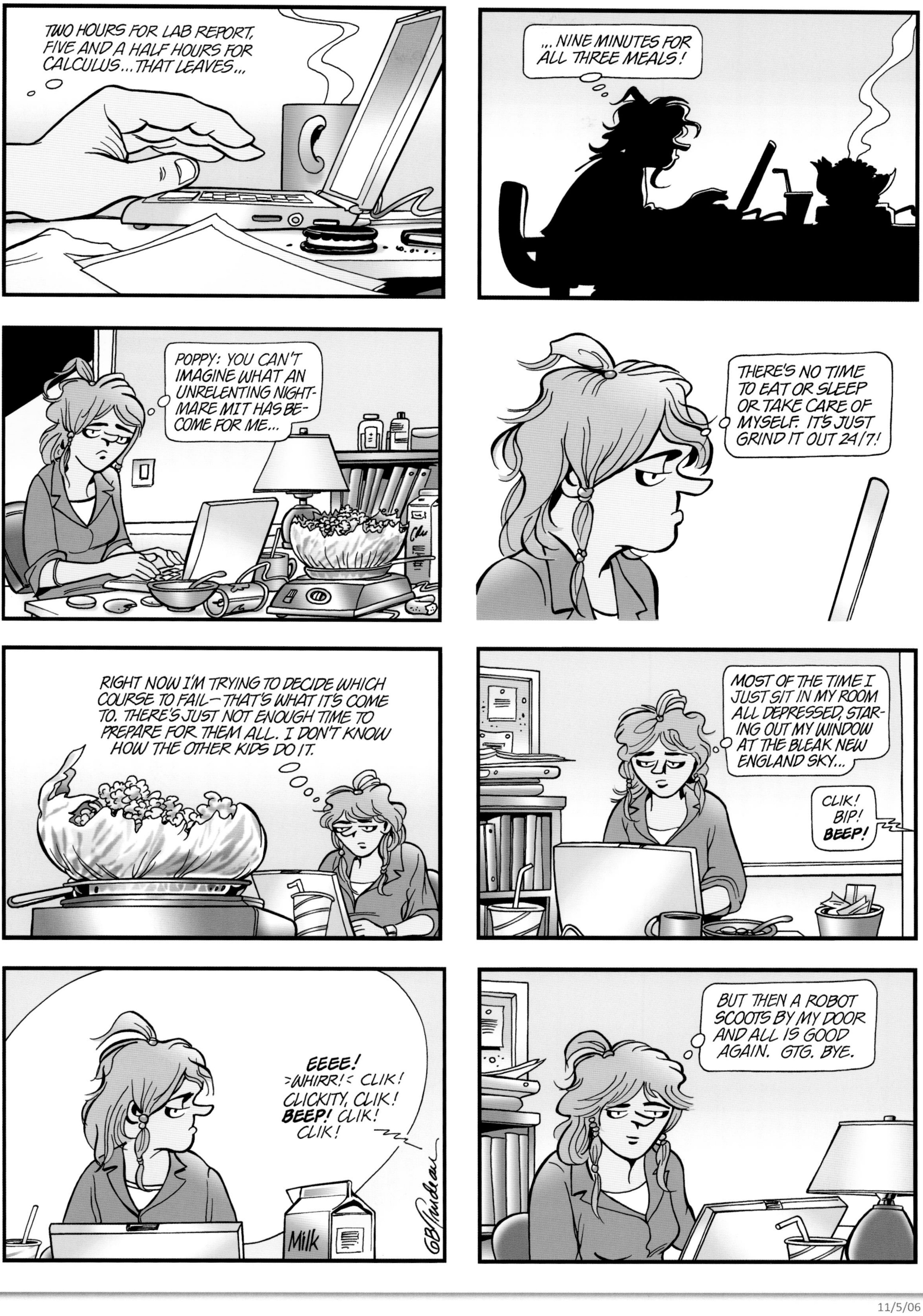

TWO HOURS FOR LAB REPORT, FIVE AND A HALF HOURS FOR CALCULUS... THAT LEAVES...
... NINE MINUTES FOR ALL THREE MEALS!
POPPY: YOU CAN'T IMAGINE WHAT AN UNRELENTING NIGHT-MARE MIT HAS BE-COME FOR ME...
THERE'S NO TIME TO EAT OR SLEEP OR TAKE CARE OF MYSELF. IT'S JUST GRIND IT OUT 24/7!
RIGHT NOW I'M TRYING TO DECIDE WHICH COURSE TO FAIL—THAT'S WHAT IT'S COME TO. THERE'S JUST NOT ENOUGH TIME TO PREPARE FOR THEM ALL. I DON'T KNOW HOW THE OTHER KIDS DO IT.
MOST OF THE TIME I JUST SIT IN MY ROOM ALL DEPRESSED, STAR-ING OUT MY WINDOW AT THE BLEAK NEW ENGLAND SKY...
CLIK! BIP! BEEP!
EEEE! >WHIRR!< CLIK! CLICKITY, CLIK! BEEP! CLIK! CLIK!
GBTrudeau
MILK
BUT THEN A ROBOT SCOOTS BY MY DOOR AND ALL IS GOOD AGAIN. GTG. BYE.

11/5/06

Zipper & Jeff

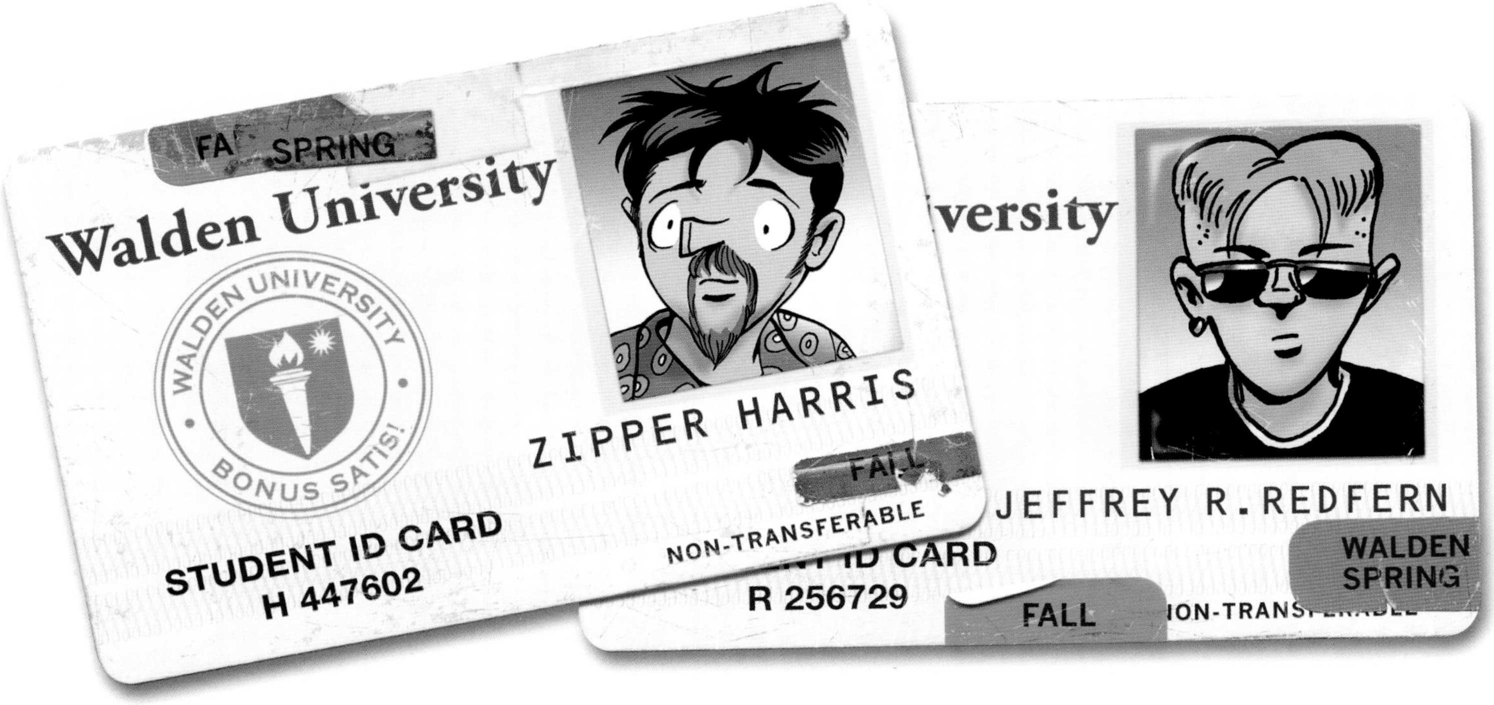
FA SPRING
Walden University
WALDEN UNIVERSITY
BONUS SATIS!
ZIPPER HARRIS
FALL
NON-TRANSFERABLE
STUDENT ID CARD
H 447602
versity
JEFFREY R. REDFERN
R 256729
FALL
WALDEN
SPRING

A few years ago, my wife Jane heard from a former professor of hers at Indiana University. He reported that he was still teaching the history course she had taken from him years ago, but that it had changed considerably. Whereas there were once nine challenging books on the required reading list, the professor now taught the class with five, all of them short. And while his course had once been one of the most popular on campus, in recent years it was one of the least. Reason: too much reading.

Zipper and Jeff didn't make this world of declining expectations, but they sure don't mind living in it. And nowhere is academic free fall more celebrated than at their beloved Walden, a college so unfettered by standards that high school juniors are considered fully prepared for admission. At Walden, grade inflation isn't just the norm, it's enforced, as is graduating with distinction. (Any resistance from the faculty crumbled after a successful suit brought by a fraternity member claiming grade bias against "the Greco-American community.")

While it's tempting to think of Zip and Jeff as dawg 'n' dude, Los Dos Amigos, there are significant differences in their narratives. First, Jeff has actual ambitions, albeit way beyond his capabilities. Second, his attention span exceeds that of a hummingbird, a boast Zipper is not in a position to make. And last, Jeff actually graduates, much to

"Mom, do you have a couch we could burn?"

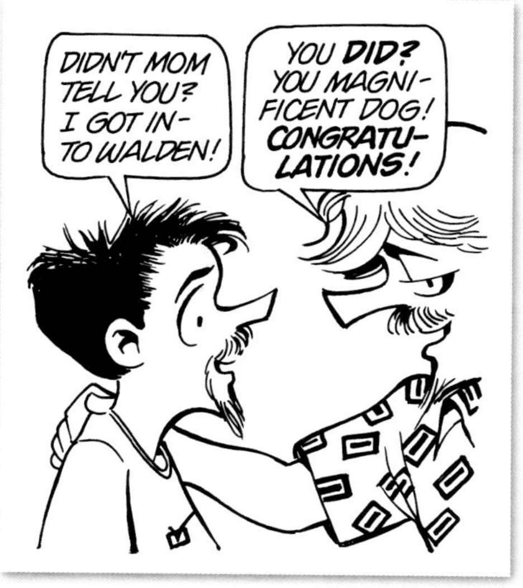
DIDN'T MOM TELL YOU? I GOT IN-TO WALDEN!
YOU DID? YOU MAGNI-FICENT DOG! CONGRATU-LATIONS!

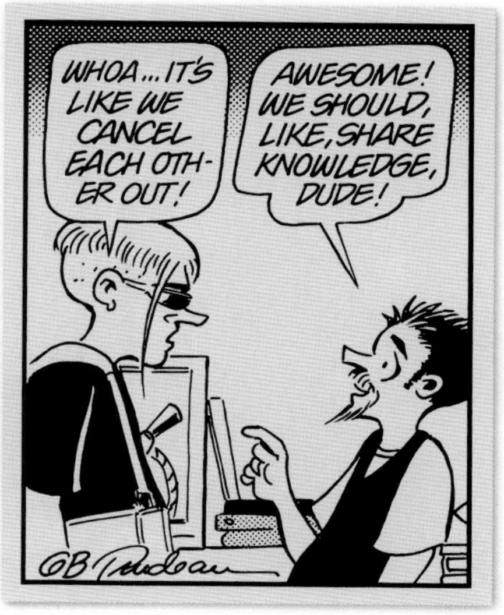
WHOA... IT'S LIKE WE CANCEL EACH OTH-ER OUT!
AWESOME! WE SHOULD, LIKE, SHARE KNOWLEDGE, DUDE!

the despair of his roomie, who had seen the warning signs (Jeff occasionally went to classes) but failed to act in time.

Fortunately, Zipper does not resent Jeff's diploma, worthless in any event (Walden is not accredited), and they remain tight as ticks. Zipper continues to squat at college, satisfied that his compadre's erratic career as a spook is enthralling enough for the both of them, especially with the addition of Jeff's imaginary adventures as the Red Rascal of Afghanistan. Together, they make stagnation look viable, if not exactly desirable. As the two lads age, they are in no obvious danger of maturing—a point of contention with some readers of their generation. Zip and Jeff, the beef goes, are the creations of a baby boomer disdainful of a successor cohort, the millennials.

It's a variation of a familiar complaint. Whenever I create a character who's less than admirable, I always run the danger of someone assuming I mean him to be categoric, a stand-in for the whole of whatever group he's part of. But by that metric, I'm in contempt of all generations, races, tribes, faiths, and affiliation groups. To which sterling baby boomer do Zip and Jeff stand in contrast, exactly? Zonker? Mark? Mike? Which powerhouse of personal togetherness is the baseline here? While some of the earliest characters may indeed have begun their runs as stereotypes, it's the accumulated peculiarities and contradictions that give them breath—and longevity. Without any mitigating nuance, characters can quickly turn into forgettable mouthpieces for whatever point of view they've been assigned. I know this because I've created a few, and they are forgotten, and they deserve to be.

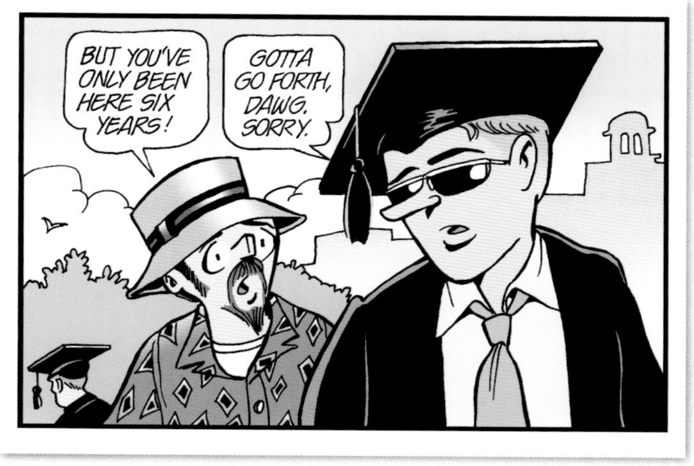
BUT YOU'VE ONLY BEEN HERE SIX YEARS!
GOTTA GO FORTH, DAWG. SORRY.

Zipper and Jeff do not. Dudes are as dudes do, but this duo's a little different.

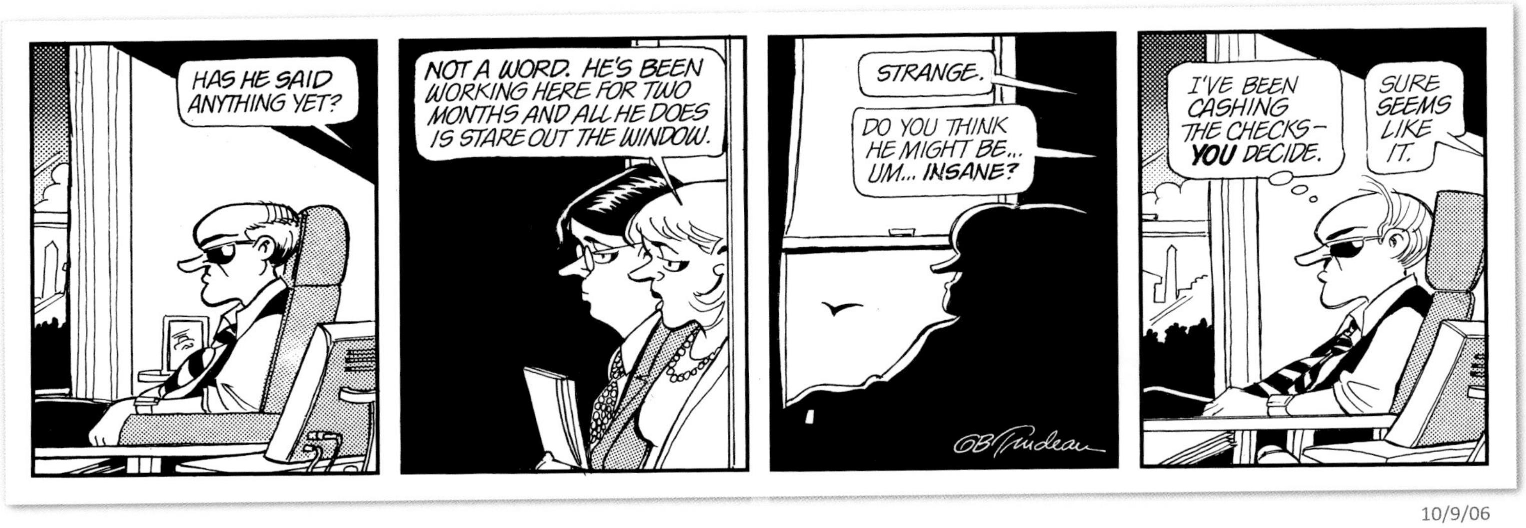
HAS HE SAID ANYTHING YET?
NOT A WORD. HE'S BEEN WORKING HERE FOR TWO MONTHS AND ALL HE DOES IS STARE OUT THE WINDOW.
STRANGE.
DO YOU THINK HE MIGHT BE... UM... **INSANE?**
I'VE BEEN CASHING THE CHECKS— **YOU** DECIDE.
SURE SEEMS LIKE IT.

10/9/06

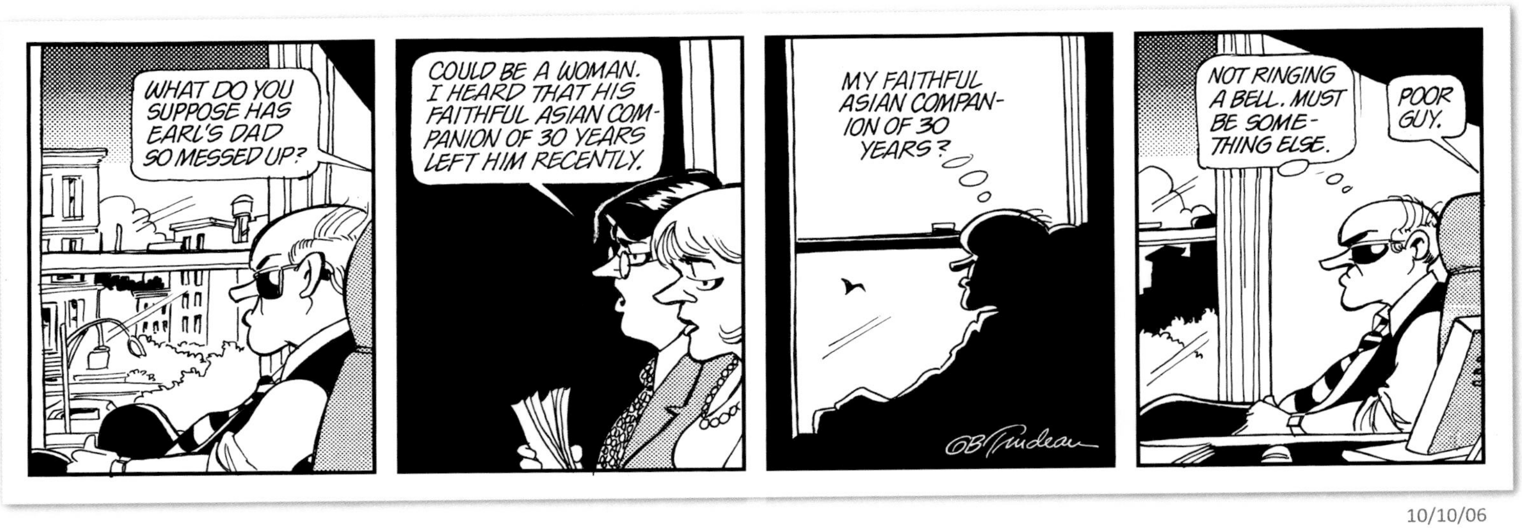
WHAT DO YOU SUPPOSE HAS EARL'S DAD SO MESSED UP?
COULD BE A WOMAN. I HEARD THAT HIS FAITHFUL ASIAN COMPANION OF 30 YEARS LEFT HIM RECENTLY.
MY FAITHFUL ASIAN COMPANION OF 30 YEARS?
NOT RINGING A BELL.. MUST BE SOMETHING ELSE.
POOR GUY.

10/10/06

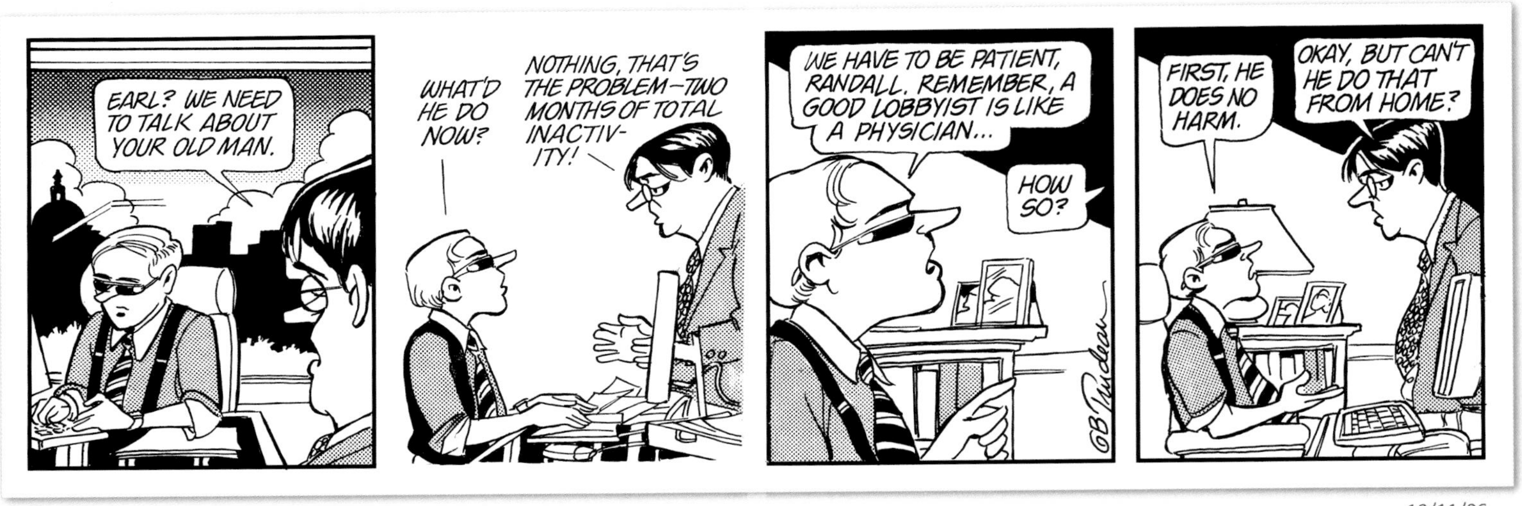
EARL? WE NEED TO TALK ABOUT YOUR OLD MAN.
WHAT'D HE DO NOW?
NOTHING, THAT'S THE PROBLEM—TWO MONTHS OF TOTAL INACTIVITY!
WE HAVE TO BE PATIENT, RANDALL. REMEMBER, A GOOD LOBBYIST IS LIKE A PHYSICIAN...
HOW SO?
FIRST, HE DOES NO HARM.
OKAY, BUT CAN'T HE DO THAT FROM HOME?

10/11/06

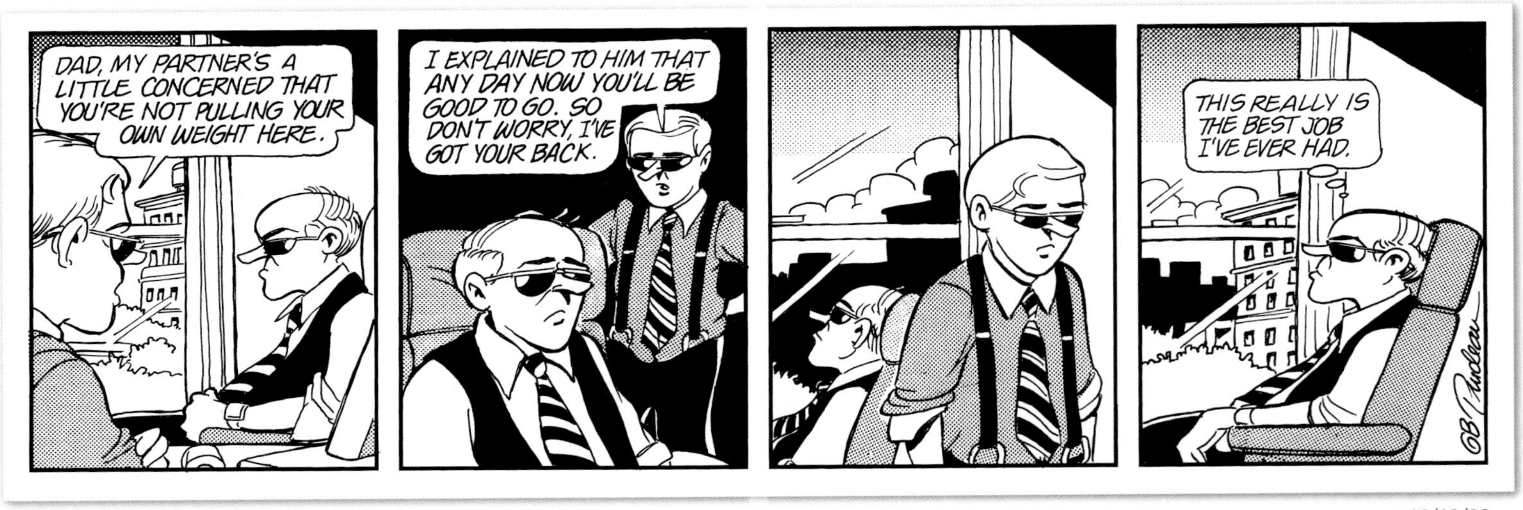
DAD, MY PARTNER'S A LITTLE CONCERNED THAT YOU'RE NOT PULLING YOUR OWN WEIGHT HERE.
I EXPLAINED TO HIM THAT ANY DAY NOW YOU'LL BE GOOD TO GO. SO DON'T WORRY, I'VE GOT YOUR BACK.
THIS REALLY IS THE BEST JOB I'VE EVER HAD.

10/13/06

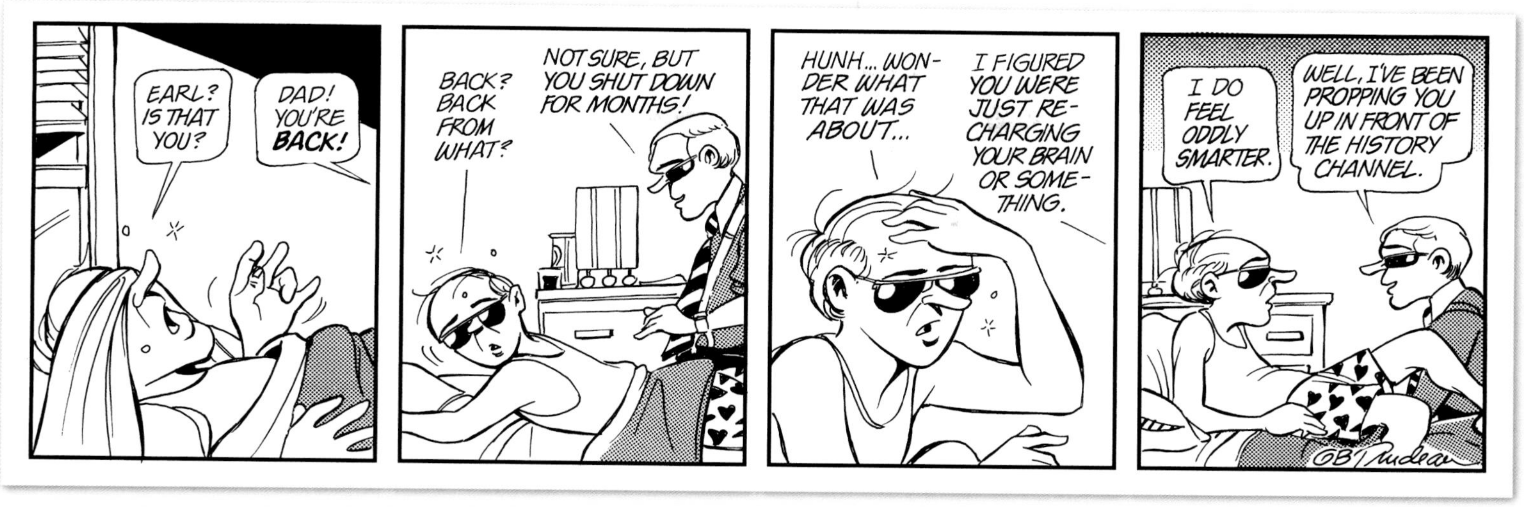
EARL? IS THAT YOU?
DAD! YOU'RE BACK!
BACK? BACK FROM WHAT?
NOT SURE, BUT YOU SHUT DOWN FOR MONTHS!
HUNH... WONDER WHAT THAT WAS ABOUT...
I FIGURED YOU WERE JUST RECHARGING YOUR BRAIN OR SOMETHING.
I DO FEEL ODDLY SMARTER.
WELL, I'VE BEEN PROPPING YOU UP IN FRONT OF THE HISTORY CHANNEL.
©B Trudeau

11/13/06

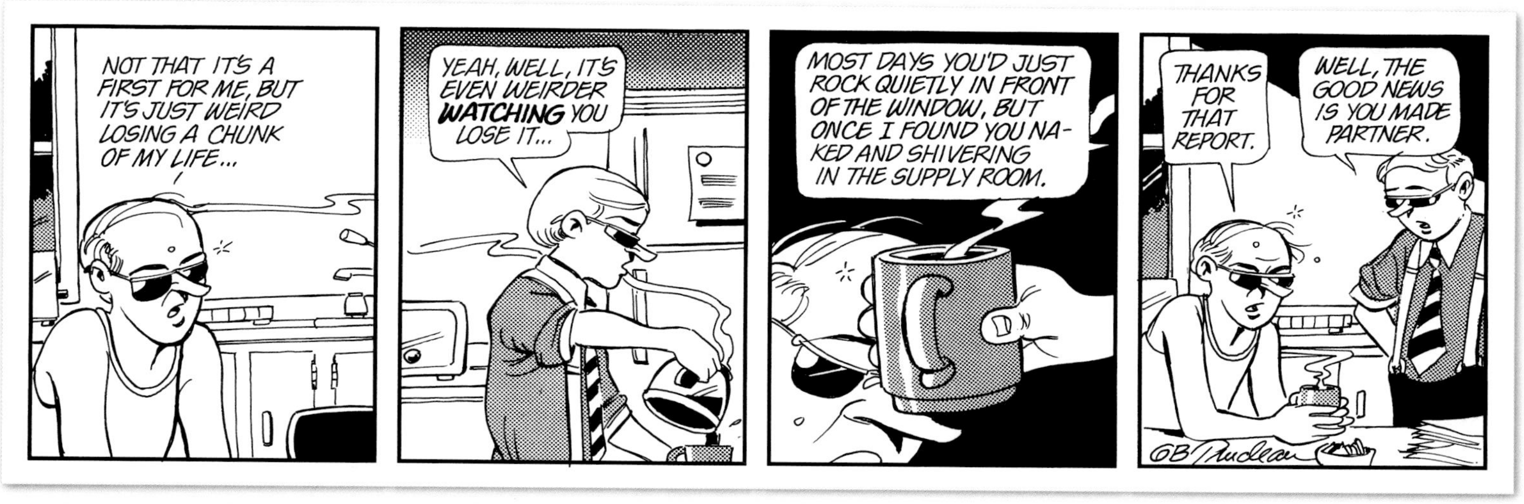
NOT THAT IT'S A FIRST FOR ME, BUT IT'S JUST WEIRD LOSING A CHUNK OF MY LIFE...
YEAH, WELL, IT'S EVEN WEIRDER WATCHING YOU LOSE IT...
MOST DAYS YOU'D JUST ROCK QUIETLY IN FRONT OF THE WINDOW, BUT ONCE I FOUND YOU NAKED AND SHIVERING IN THE SUPPLY ROOM.
THANKS FOR THAT REPORT.
WELL, THE GOOD NEWS IS YOU MADE PARTNER.
©B Trudeau

11/16/06

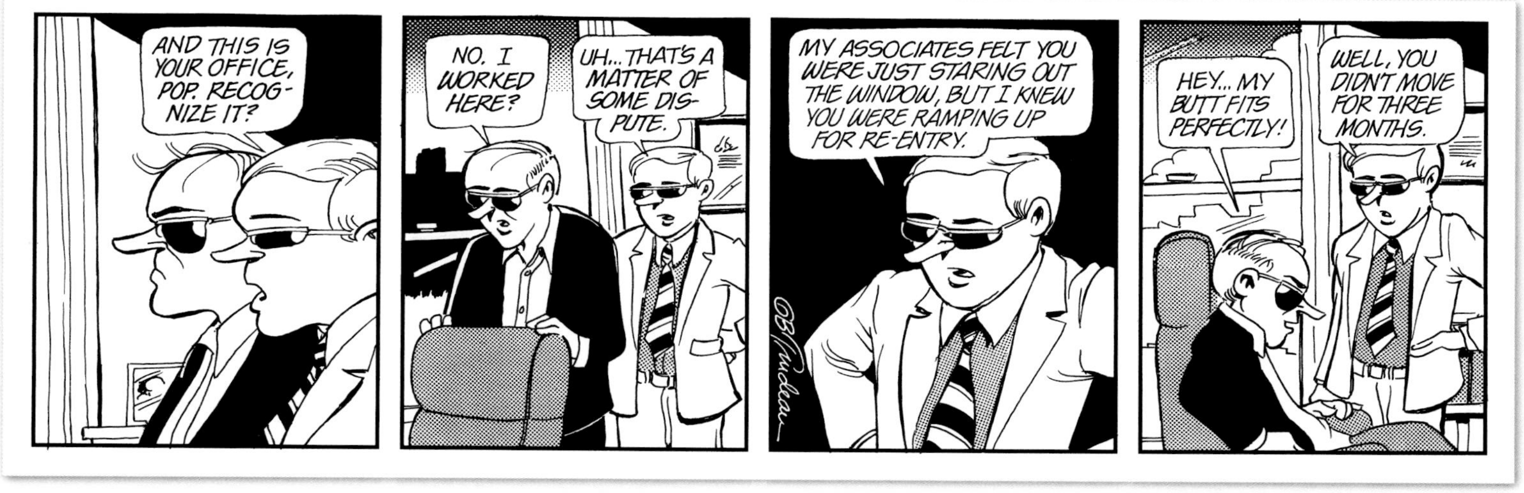
AND THIS IS YOUR OFFICE, POP. RECOGNIZE IT?
NO. I WORKED HERE?
UH... THAT'S A MATTER OF SOME DISPUTE.
MY ASSOCIATES FELT YOU WERE JUST STARING OUT THE WINDOW, BUT I KNEW YOU WERE RAMPING UP FOR RE-ENTRY.
HEY... MY BUTT FITS PERFECTLY!
WELL, YOU DIDN'T MOVE FOR THREE MONTHS.
©B Trudeau

12/4/06

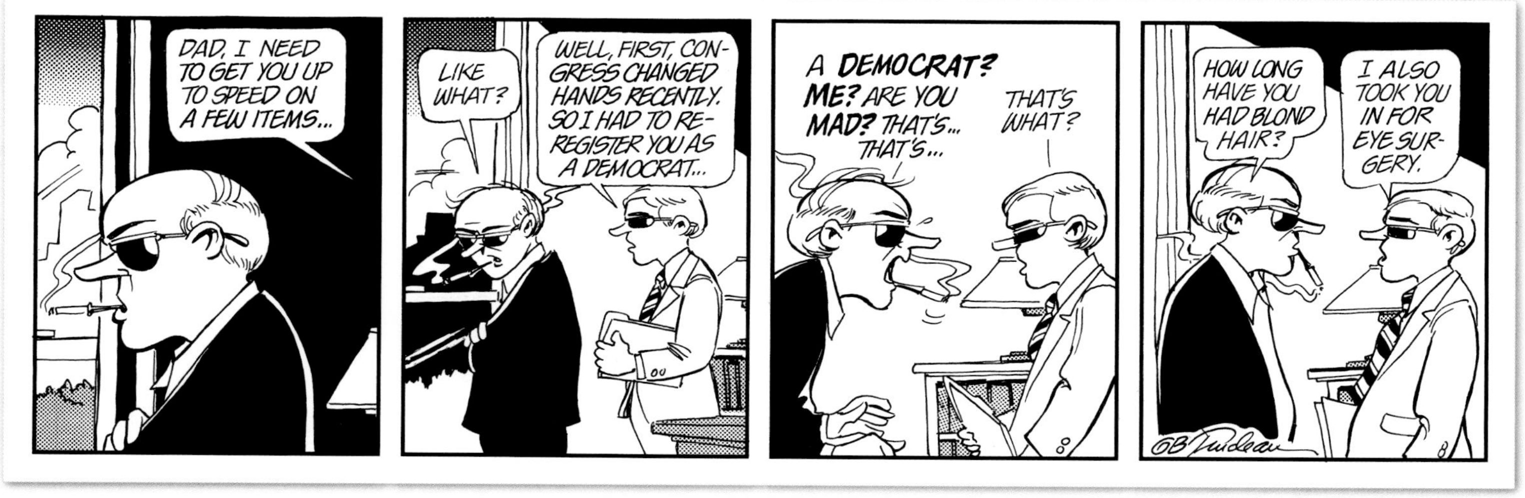
DAD, I NEED TO GET YOU UP TO SPEED ON A FEW ITEMS...
LIKE WHAT?
WELL, FIRST, CONGRESS CHANGED HANDS RECENTLY. SO I HAD TO RE-REGISTER YOU AS A DEMOCRAT...
A DEMOCRAT? ME? ARE YOU MAD? THAT'S... THAT'S...
THAT'S WHAT?
HOW LONG HAVE YOU HAD BLOND HAIR?
I ALSO TOOK YOU IN FOR EYE SURGERY.
©B Trudeau

12/6/06

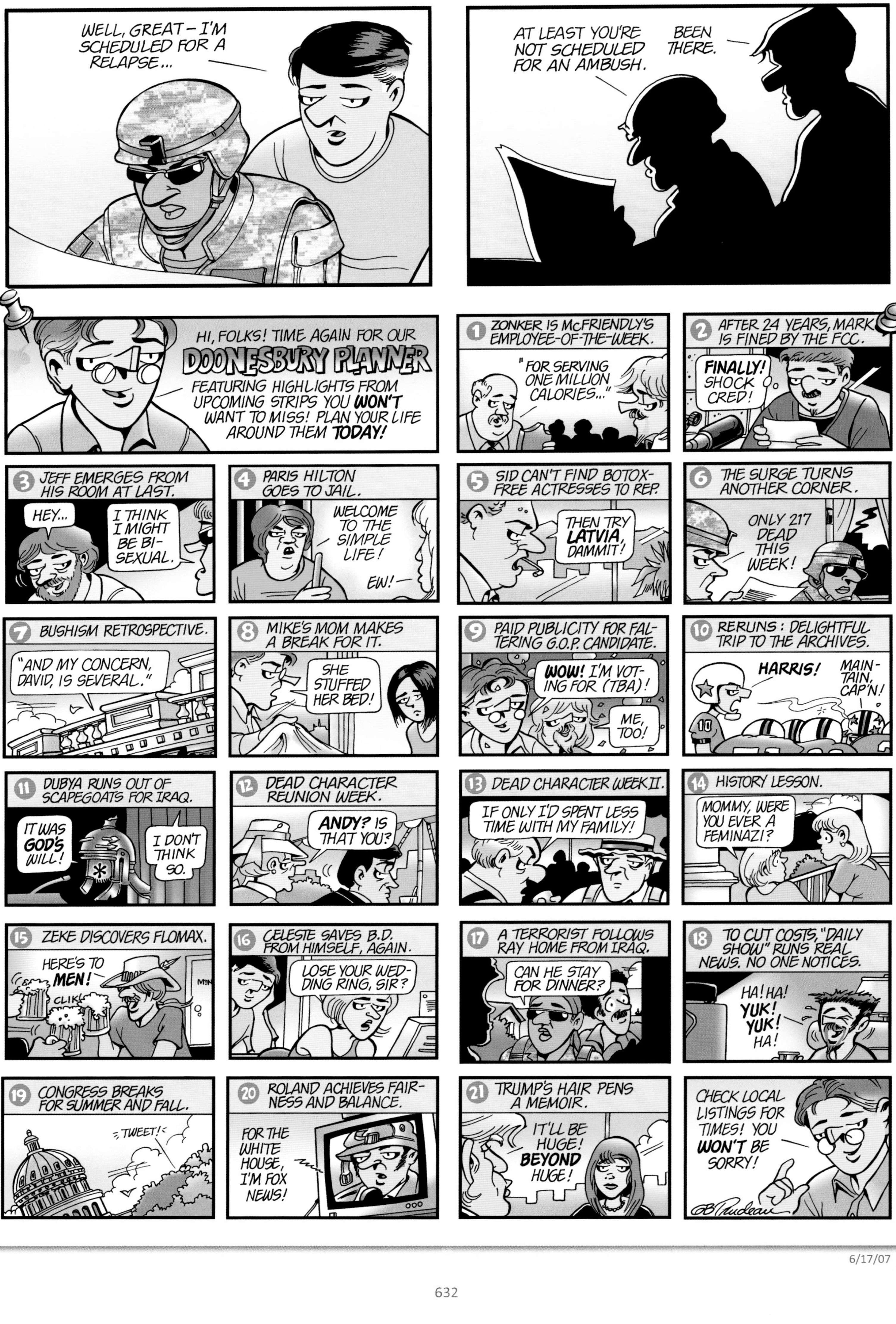
WELL, GREAT – I'M SCHEDULED FOR A RELAPSE...
AT LEAST YOU'RE NOT SCHEDULED FOR AN AMBUSH.
BEEN THERE.
HI, FOLKS! TIME AGAIN FOR OUR
DOONESBURY PLANNER
FEATURING HIGHLIGHTS FROM UPCOMING STRIPS YOU WON'T WANT TO MISS! PLAN YOUR LIFE AROUND THEM TODAY!
1 ZONKER IS McFRIENDLY'S EMPLOYEE-OF-THE-WEEK.
"FOR SERVING ONE MILLION CALORIES..."
2 AFTER 24 YEARS, MARK IS FINED BY THE FCC.
FINALLY! SHOCK CRED!
3 JEFF EMERGES FROM HIS ROOM AT LAST.
HEY...
I THINK I MIGHT BE BI-SEXUAL.
4 PARIS HILTON GOES TO JAIL.
WELCOME TO THE SIMPLE LIFE!
EW!
5 SID CAN'T FIND BOTOX-FREE ACTRESSES TO REP.
THEN TRY LATVIA, DAMMIT!
6 THE SURGE TURNS ANOTHER CORNER.
ONLY 217 DEAD THIS WEEK!
7 BUSHISM RETROSPECTIVE.
"AND MY CONCERN, DAVID, IS SEVERAL."
8 MIKE'S MOM MAKES A BREAK FOR IT.
SHE STUFFED HER BED!
9 PAID PUBLICITY FOR FALTERING G.O.P. CANDIDATE.
WOW! I'M VOTING FOR (TBA)!
ME, TOO!
10 RERUNS: DELIGHTFUL TRIP TO THE ARCHIVES.
HARRIS!
MAIN-TAIN, CAP'N!
11 DUBYA RUNS OUT OF SCAPEGOATS FOR IRAQ.
IT WAS GOD'S WILL!
I DON'T THINK SO.
12 DEAD CHARACTER REUNION WEEK.
ANDY? IS THAT YOU?
13 DEAD CHARACTER WEEK II.
IF ONLY I'D SPENT LESS TIME WITH MY FAMILY!
14 HISTORY LESSON.
MOMMY, WERE YOU EVER A FEMINAZI?
15 ZEKE DISCOVERS FLOMAX.
HERE'S TO MEN!
CLIK!
16 CELESTE SAVES B.D. FROM HIMSELF, AGAIN.
LOSE YOUR WEDDING RING, SIR?
17 A TERRORIST FOLLOWS RAY HOME FROM IRAQ.
CAN HE STAY FOR DINNER?
18 TO CUT COSTS, "DAILY SHOW" RUNS REAL NEWS. NO ONE NOTICES.
HA! HA! YUK! YUK! HA!
19 CONGRESS BREAKS FOR SUMMER AND FALL.
TWEET!
20 ROLAND ACHIEVES FAIRNESS AND BALANCE.
FOR THE WHITE HOUSE, I'M FOX NEWS!
21 TRUMP'S HAIR PENS A MEMOIR.
IT'LL BE HUGE! BEYOND HUGE!
CHECK LOCAL LISTINGS FOR TIMES! YOU WON'T BE SORRY!
GB Trudeau

6/17/07

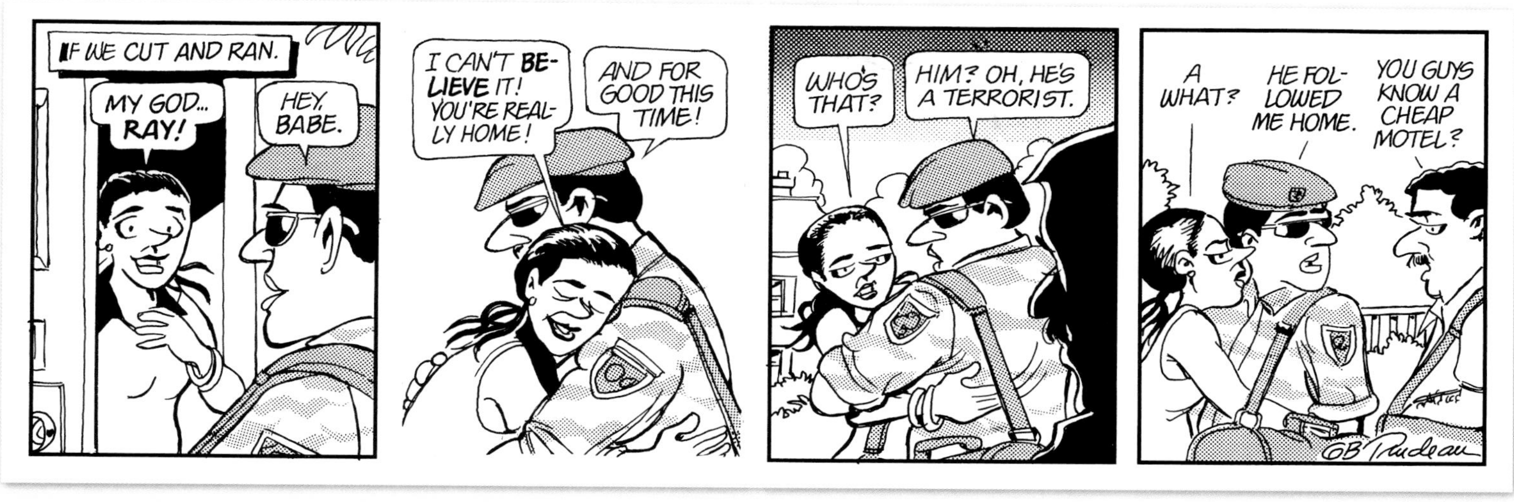
IF WE CUT AND RAN.
MY GOD... RAY!
HEY, BABE.
I CAN'T BE-LIEVE IT! YOU'RE REAL-LY HOME!
AND FOR GOOD THIS TIME!
WHO'S THAT?
HIM? OH, HE'S A TERRORIST.
A WHAT?
HE FOL-LOWED ME HOME.
YOU GUYS KNOW A CHEAP MOTEL?
©B Trudeau

8/20/07

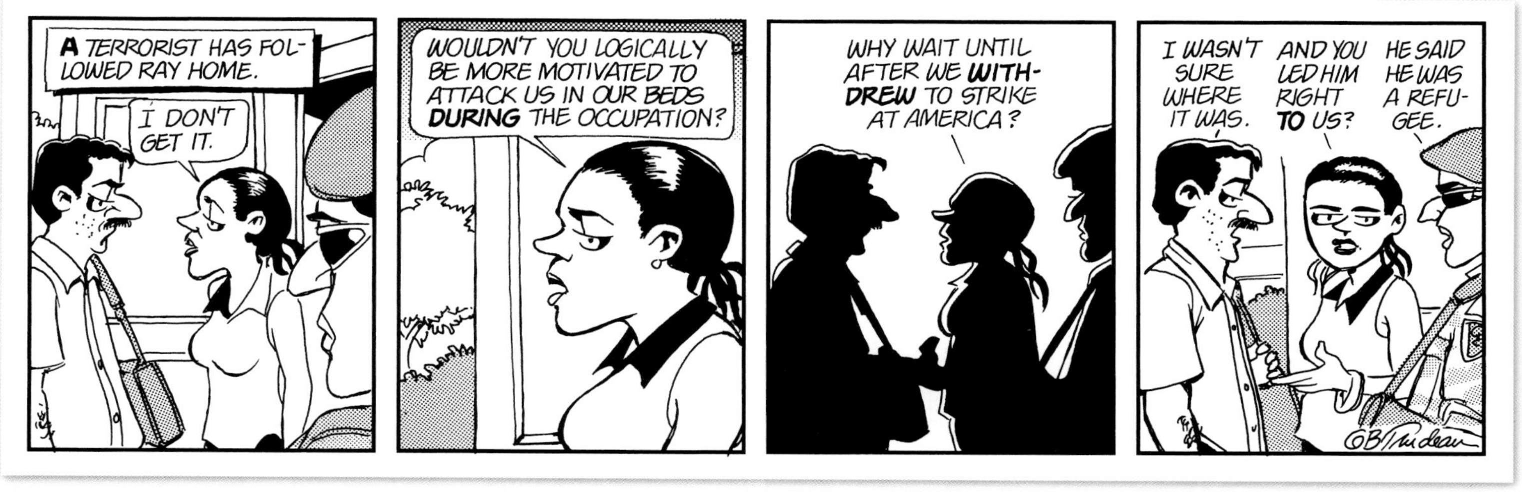
A TERRORIST HAS FOL-LOWED RAY HOME.
I DON'T GET IT.
WOULDN'T YOU LOGICALLY BE MORE MOTIVATED TO ATTACK US IN OUR BEDS DURING THE OCCUPATION?
WHY WAIT UNTIL AFTER WE WITH-DREW TO STRIKE AT AMERICA?
I WASN'T SURE WHERE IT WAS.
AND YOU LED HIM RIGHT TO US?
HE SAID HE WAS A REFU-GEE.
©B Trudeau

8/21/07

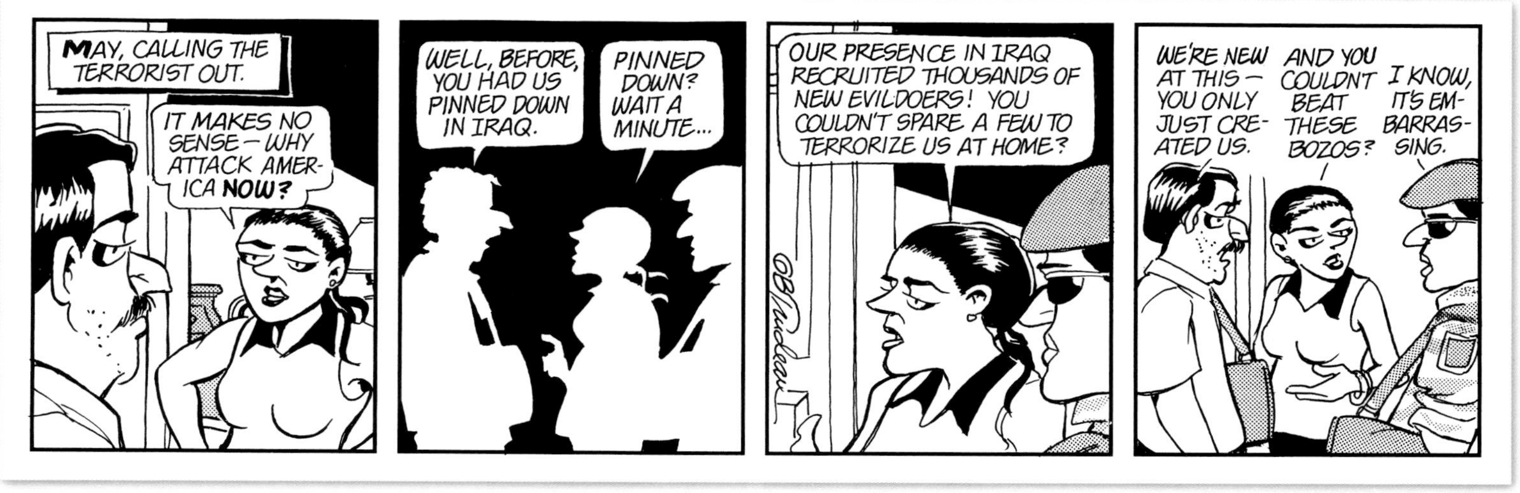
MAY, CALLING THE TERRORIST OUT.
IT MAKES NO SENSE — WHY ATTACK AMER-ICA NOW?
WELL, BEFORE, YOU HAD US PINNED DOWN IN IRAQ.
PINNED DOWN? WAIT A MINUTE...
©B Trudeau
OUR PRESENCE IN IRAQ RECRUITED THOUSANDS OF NEW EVILDOERS! YOU COULDN'T SPARE A FEW TO TERRORIZE US AT HOME?
WE'RE NEW AT THIS — YOU ONLY JUST CRE-ATED US.
AND YOU COULDN'T BEAT THESE BOZOS?
I KNOW, IT'S EM-BARRAS-SING.

8/22/07

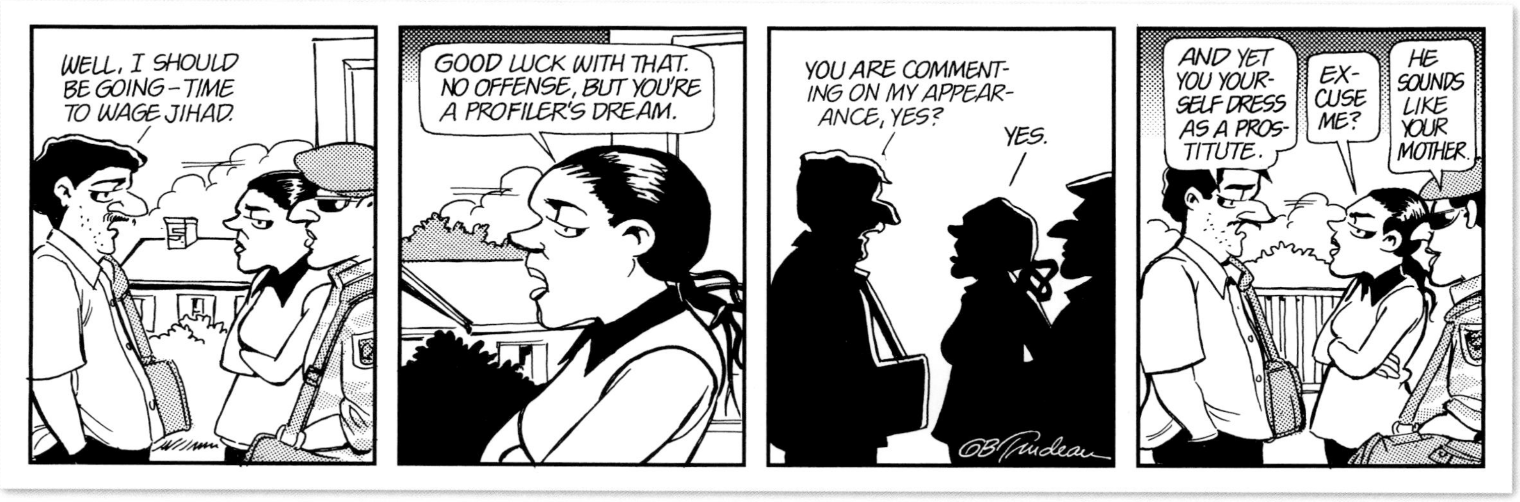
WELL, I SHOULD BE GOING — TIME TO WAGE JIHAD.
GOOD LUCK WITH THAT. NO OFFENSE, BUT YOU'RE A PROFILER'S DREAM.
YOU ARE COMMENT-ING ON MY APPEAR-ANCE, YES?
YES.
©B Trudeau
AND YET YOU YOUR-SELF DRESS AS A PROS-TITUTE.
EX-CUSE ME?
HE SOUNDS LIKE YOUR MOTHER.

8/23/07

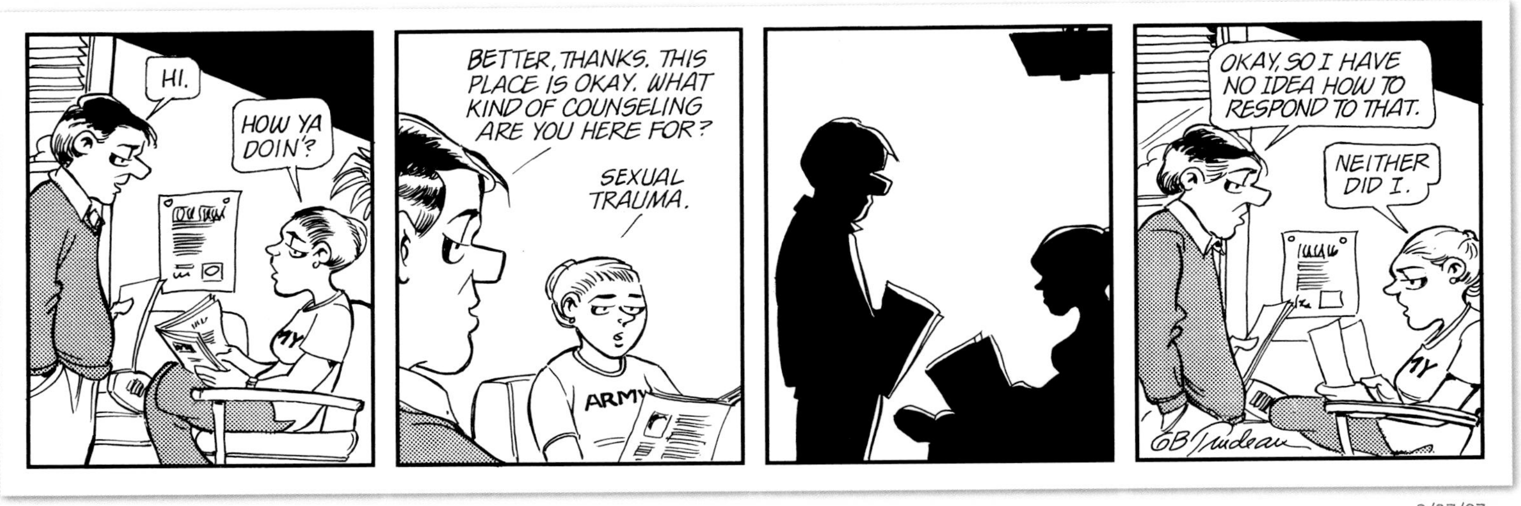
HI.
HOW YA DOIN'?
BETTER, THANKS. THIS PLACE IS OKAY. WHAT KIND OF COUNSELING ARE YOU HERE FOR?
SEXUAL TRAUMA.
OKAY, SO I HAVE NO IDEA HOW TO RESPOND TO THAT.
NEITHER DID I.
ARMY
GB Trudeau

3/27/07

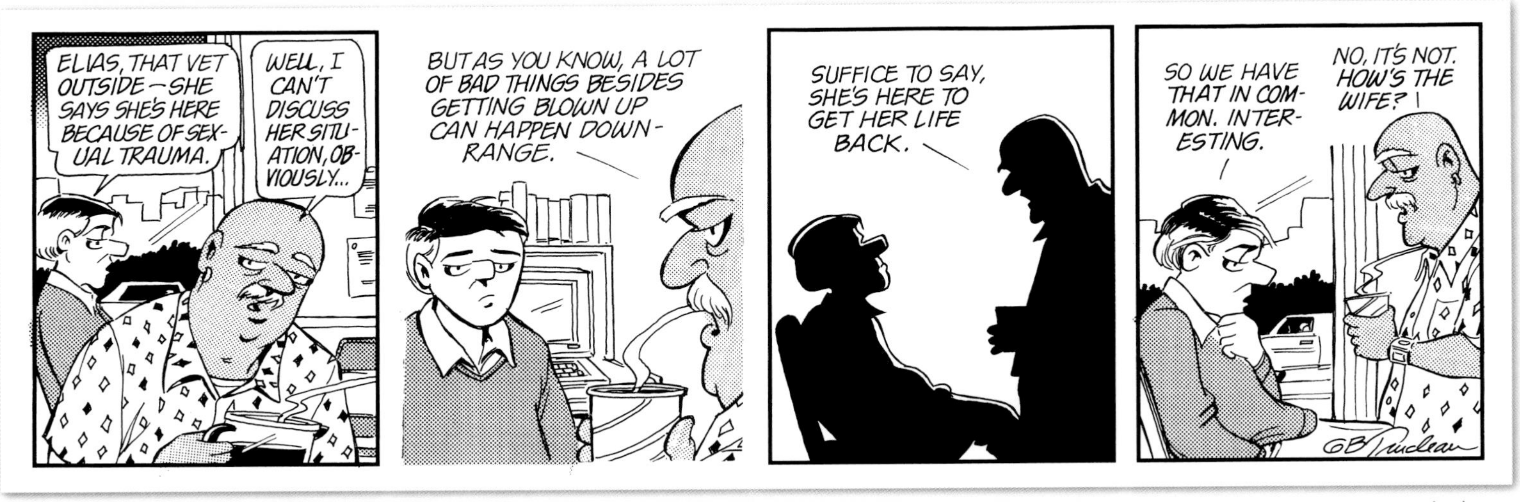
ELIAS, THAT VET OUTSIDE—SHE SAYS SHE'S HERE BECAUSE OF SEXUAL TRAUMA.
WELL, I CAN'T DISCUSS HER SITUATION, OBVIOUSLY...
BUT AS YOU KNOW, A LOT OF BAD THINGS BESIDES GETTING BLOWN UP CAN HAPPEN DOWNRANGE.
SUFFICE TO SAY, SHE'S HERE TO GET HER LIFE BACK.
SO WE HAVE THAT IN COMMON. INTERESTING.
NO, IT'S NOT. HOW'S THE WIFE?
GB Trudeau

3/28/07

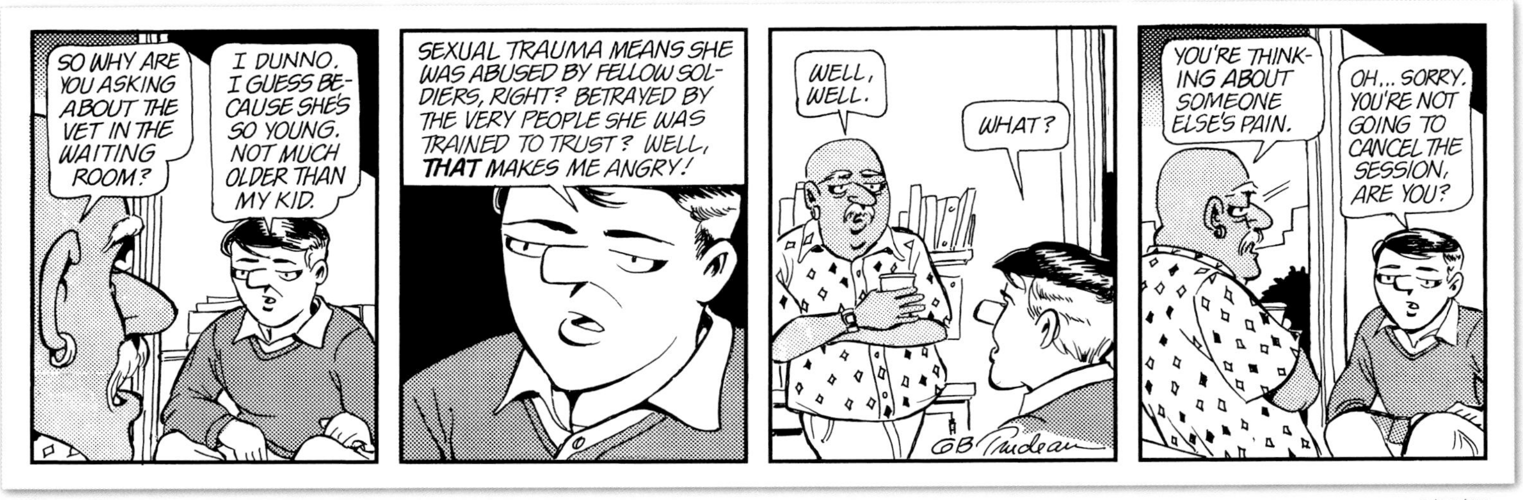
SO WHY ARE YOU ASKING ABOUT THE VET IN THE WAITING ROOM?
I DUNNO. I GUESS BECAUSE SHE'S SO YOUNG. NOT MUCH OLDER THAN MY KID.
SEXUAL TRAUMA MEANS SHE WAS ABUSED BY FELLOW SOLDIERS, RIGHT? BETRAYED BY THE VERY PEOPLE SHE WAS TRAINED TO TRUST? WELL, THAT MAKES ME ANGRY!
WELL, WELL.
WHAT?
YOU'RE THINKING ABOUT SOMEONE ELSE'S PAIN.
OH... SORRY. YOU'RE NOT GOING TO CANCEL THE SESSION, ARE YOU?
GB Trudeau

3/29/07

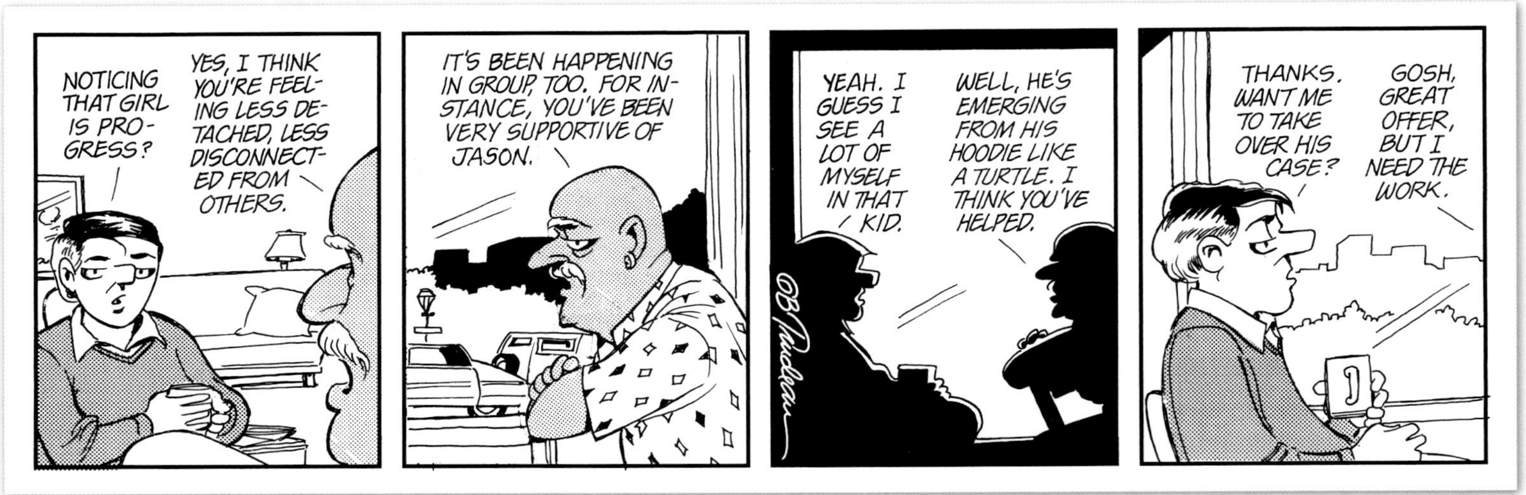
NOTICING THAT GIRL IS PROGRESS?
YES, I THINK YOU'RE FEELING LESS DETACHED, LESS DISCONNECTED FROM OTHERS.
IT'S BEEN HAPPENING IN GROUP, TOO. FOR INSTANCE, YOU'VE BEEN VERY SUPPORTIVE OF JASON.
YEAH. I GUESS I SEE A LOT OF MYSELF IN THAT KID.
WELL, HE'S EMERGING FROM HIS HOODIE LIKE A TURTLE. I THINK YOU'VE HELPED.
THANKS. WANT ME TO TAKE OVER HIS CASE?
GOSH, GREAT OFFER, BUT I NEED THE WORK.
GB Trudeau

3/30/07

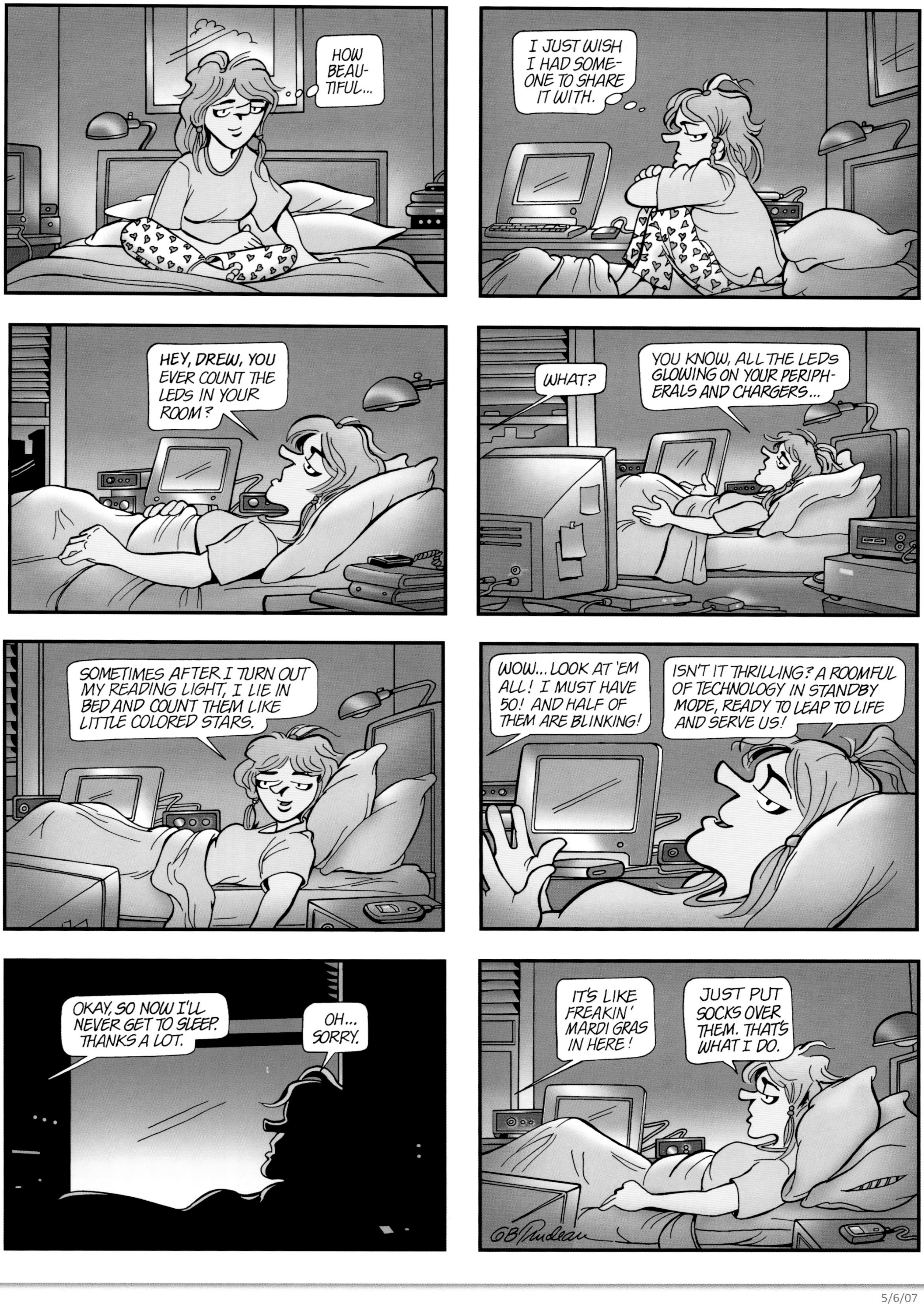
HOW BEAU- TIFUL...
I JUST WISH I HAD SOME- ONE TO SHARE IT WITH.
HEY, DREW, YOU EVER COUNT THE LEDS IN YOUR ROOM?
WHAT?
YOU KNOW, ALL THE LEDS GLOWING ON YOUR PERIPH- ERALS AND CHARGERS...
SOMETIMES AFTER I TURN OUT MY READING LIGHT, I LIE IN BED AND COUNT THEM LIKE LITTLE COLORED STARS.
WOW... LOOK AT 'EM ALL! I MUST HAVE 50! AND HALF OF THEM ARE BLINKING!
ISN'T IT THRILLING? A ROOMFUL OF TECHNOLOGY IN STANDBY MODE, READY TO LEAP TO LIFE AND SERVE US!
OKAY, SO NOW I'LL NEVER GET TO SLEEP. THANKS A LOT.
OH... SORRY.
IT'S LIKE FREAKIN' MARDI GRAS IN HERE!
JUST PUT SOCKS OVER THEM. THAT'S WHAT I DO.
GBTrudeau

5/6/07

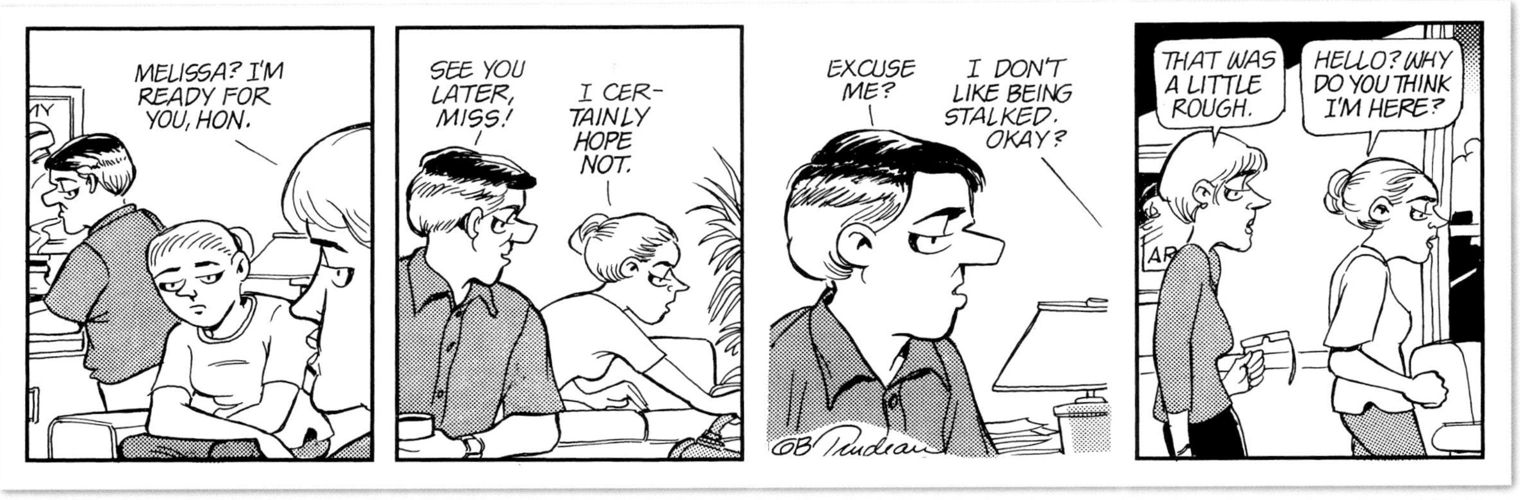
MELISSA? I'M READY FOR YOU, HON.
SEE YOU LATER, MISS!
I CERTAINLY HOPE NOT.
EXCUSE ME?
I DON'T LIKE BEING STALKED. OKAY?
THAT WAS A LITTLE ROUGH.
HELLO? WHY DO YOU THINK I'M HERE?
6/26/07

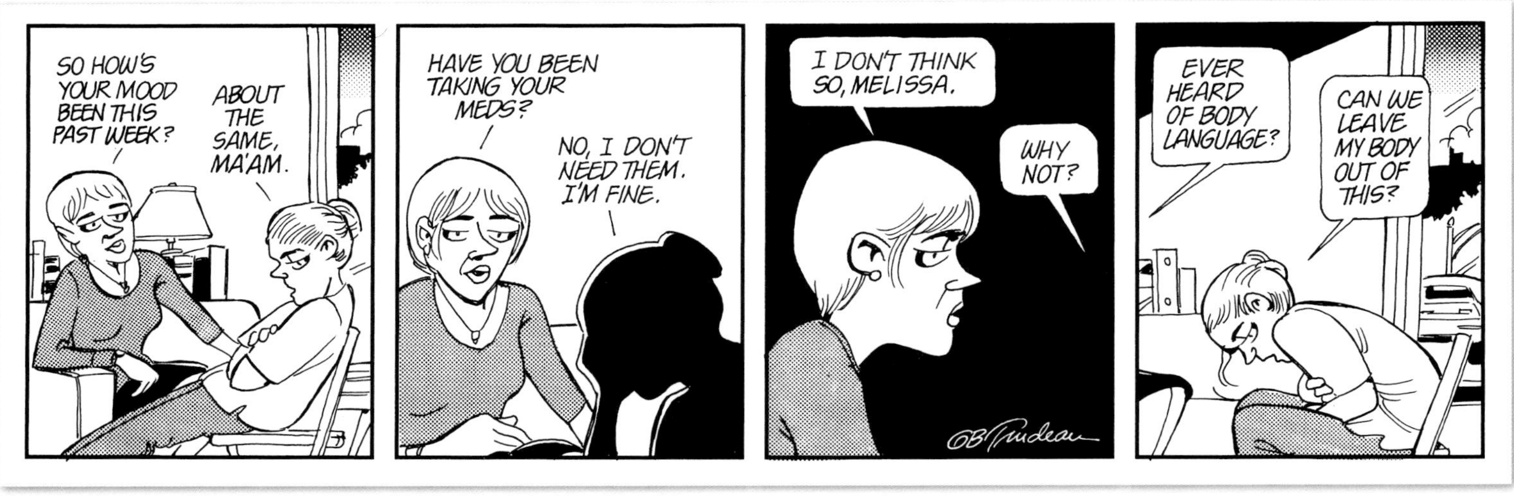
SO HOW'S YOUR MOOD BEEN THIS PAST WEEK?
ABOUT THE SAME, MA'AM.
HAVE YOU BEEN TAKING YOUR MEDS?
NO, I DON'T NEED THEM. I'M FINE.
I DON'T THINK SO, MELISSA.
WHY NOT?
EVER HEARD OF BODY LANGUAGE?
CAN WE LEAVE MY BODY OUT OF THIS?
6/27/07

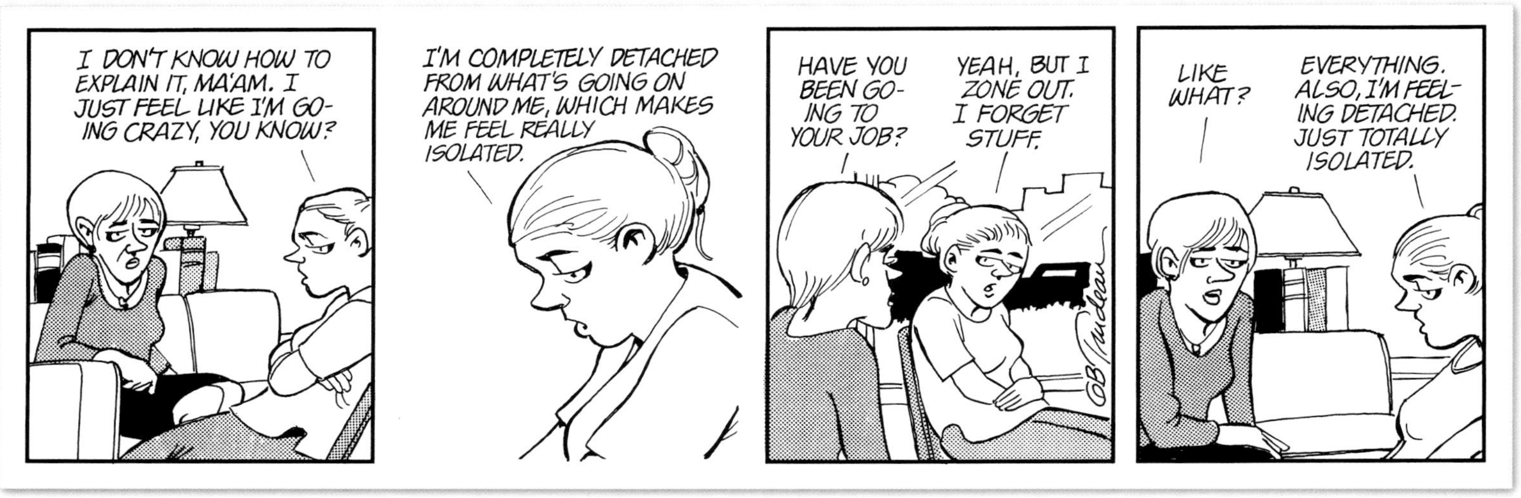
I DON'T KNOW HOW TO EXPLAIN IT, MA'AM. I JUST FEEL LIKE I'M GOING CRAZY, YOU KNOW?
I'M COMPLETELY DETACHED FROM WHAT'S GOING ON AROUND ME, WHICH MAKES ME FEEL REALLY ISOLATED.
HAVE YOU BEEN GOING TO YOUR JOB?
YEAH, BUT I ZONE OUT. I FORGET STUFF.
LIKE WHAT?
EVERYTHING. ALSO, I'M FEELING DETACHED. JUST TOTALLY ISOLATED.
6/28/07

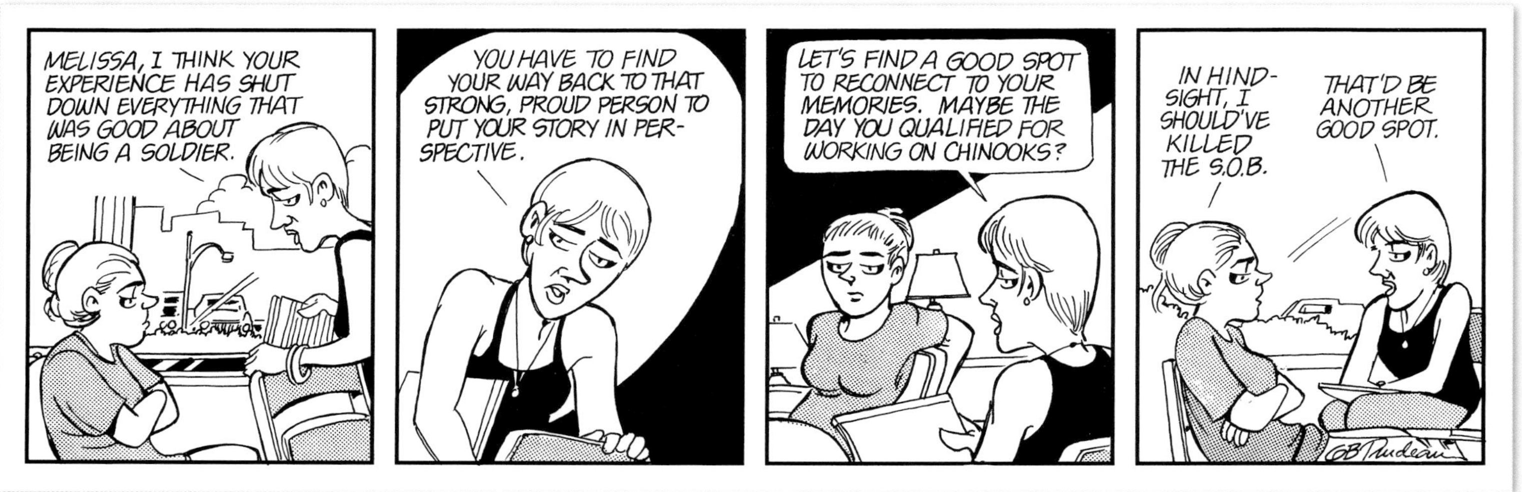
MELISSA, I THINK YOUR EXPERIENCE HAS SHUT DOWN EVERYTHING THAT WAS GOOD ABOUT BEING A SOLDIER.
YOU HAVE TO FIND YOUR WAY BACK TO THAT STRONG, PROUD PERSON TO PUT YOUR STORY IN PERSPECTIVE.
LET'S FIND A GOOD SPOT TO RECONNECT TO YOUR MEMORIES. MAYBE THE DAY YOU QUALIFIED FOR WORKING ON CHINOOKS?
IN HINDSIGHT, I SHOULD'VE KILLED THE S.O.B.
THAT'D BE ANOTHER GOOD SPOT.
7/16/07

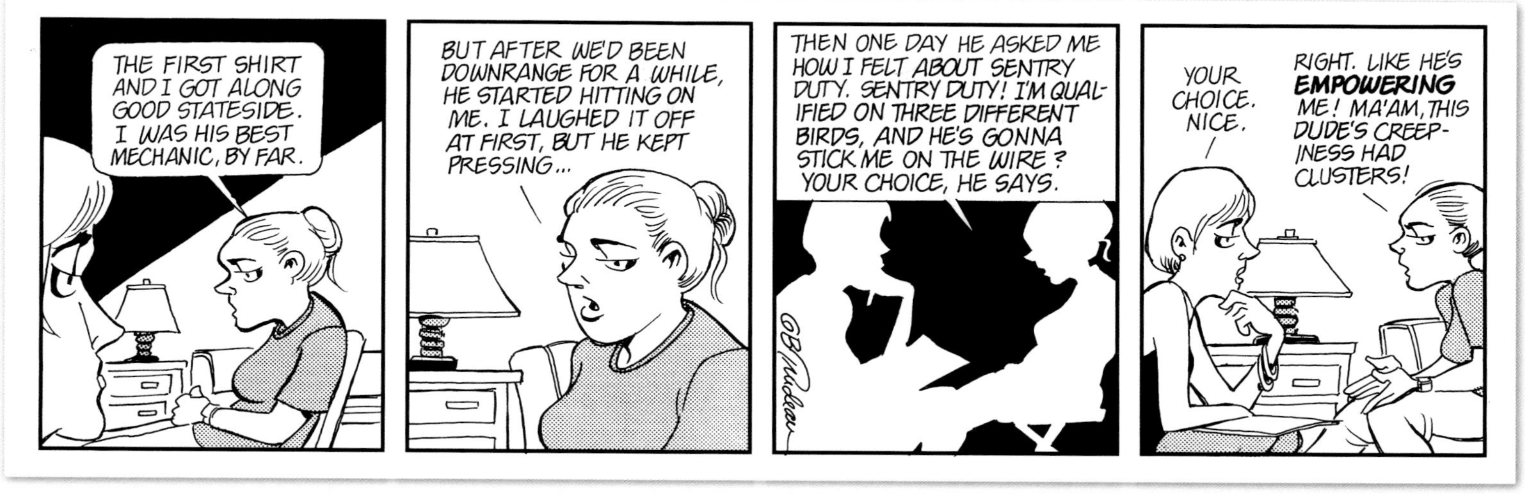
THE FIRST SHIRT AND I GOT ALONG GOOD STATESIDE. I WAS HIS BEST MECHANIC, BY FAR.
BUT AFTER WE'D BEEN DOWNRANGE FOR A WHILE, HE STARTED HITTING ON ME. I LAUGHED IT OFF AT FIRST, BUT HE KEPT PRESSING...
THEN ONE DAY HE ASKED ME HOW I FELT ABOUT SENTRY DUTY. SENTRY DUTY! I'M QUALIFIED ON THREE DIFFERENT BIRDS, AND HE'S GONNA STICK ME ON THE WIRE? YOUR CHOICE, HE SAYS.
GB Trudeau
YOUR CHOICE. NICE.
RIGHT. LIKE HE'S EMPOWERING ME! MA'AM, THIS DUDE'S CREEPINESS HAD CLUSTERS!

7/17/07

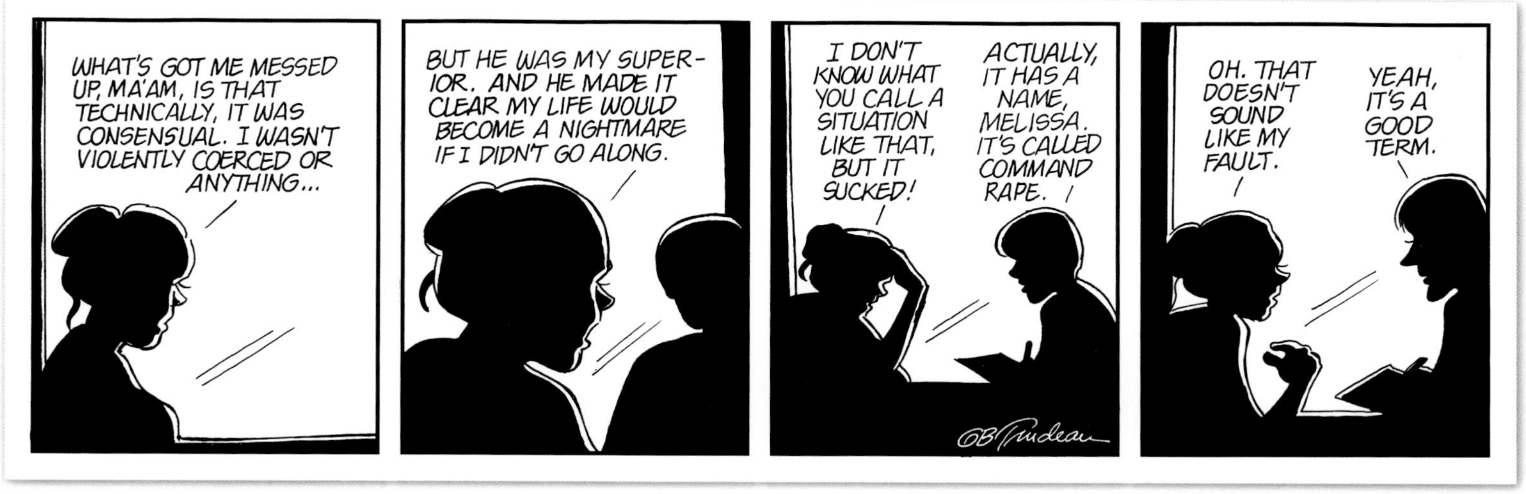
WHAT'S GOT ME MESSED UP, MA'AM, IS THAT TECHNICALLY, IT WAS CONSENSUAL. I WASN'T VIOLENTLY COERCED OR ANYTHING...
BUT HE WAS MY SUPERIOR. AND HE MADE IT CLEAR MY LIFE WOULD BECOME A NIGHTMARE IF I DIDN'T GO ALONG.
I DON'T KNOW WHAT YOU CALL A SITUATION LIKE THAT, BUT IT SUCKED!
ACTUALLY, IT HAS A NAME, MELISSA. IT'S CALLED COMMAND RAPE.
GB Trudeau
OH. THAT DOESN'T SOUND LIKE MY FAULT.
YEAH, IT'S A GOOD TERM.

7/18/07

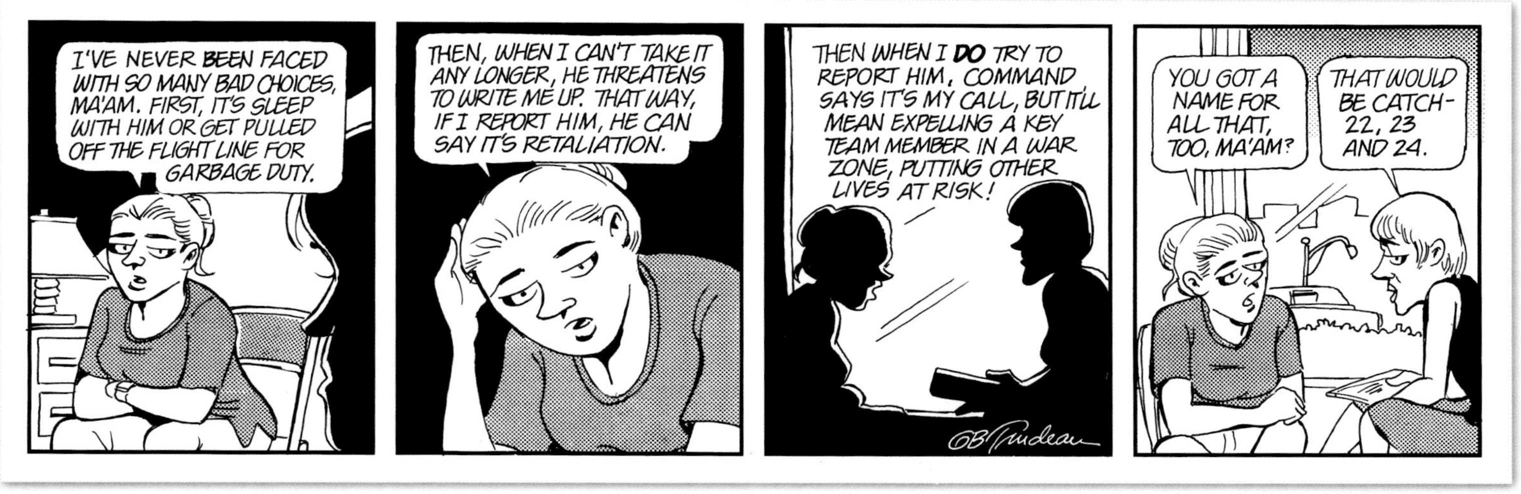
I'VE NEVER BEEN FACED WITH SO MANY BAD CHOICES, MA'AM. FIRST, IT'S SLEEP WITH HIM OR GET PULLED OFF THE FLIGHT LINE FOR GARBAGE DUTY.
THEN, WHEN I CAN'T TAKE IT ANY LONGER, HE THREATENS TO WRITE ME UP. THAT WAY, IF I REPORT HIM, HE CAN SAY IT'S RETALIATION.
THEN WHEN I DO TRY TO REPORT HIM, COMMAND SAYS IT'S MY CALL, BUT IT'LL MEAN EXPELLING A KEY TEAM MEMBER IN A WAR ZONE, PUTTING OTHER LIVES AT RISK!
GB Trudeau
YOU GOT A NAME FOR ALL THAT, TOO, MA'AM?
THAT WOULD BE CATCH-22, 23 AND 24.

7/20/07

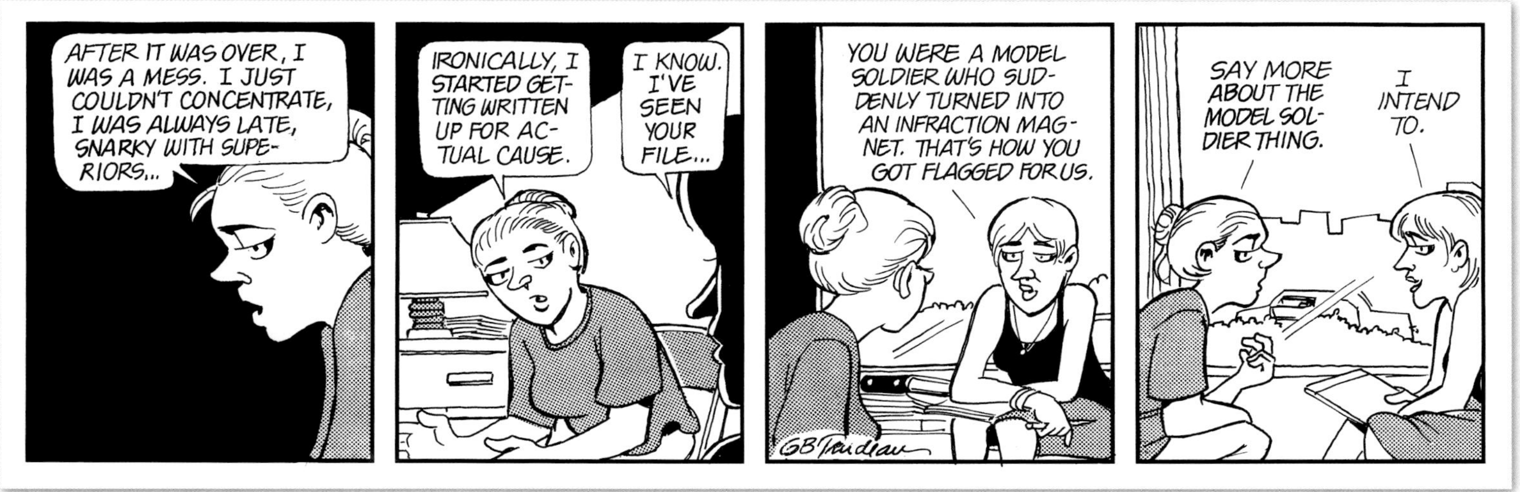
AFTER IT WAS OVER, I WAS A MESS. I JUST COULDN'T CONCENTRATE, I WAS ALWAYS LATE, SNARKY WITH SUPERIORS...
IRONICALLY, I STARTED GETTING WRITTEN UP FOR ACTUAL CAUSE.
I KNOW. I'VE SEEN YOUR FILE...
GB Trudeau
YOU WERE A MODEL SOLDIER WHO SUDDENLY TURNED INTO AN INFRACTION MAGNET. THAT'S HOW YOU GOT FLAGGED FOR US.
SAY MORE ABOUT THE MODEL SOLDIER THING.
I INTEND TO.

7/21/07

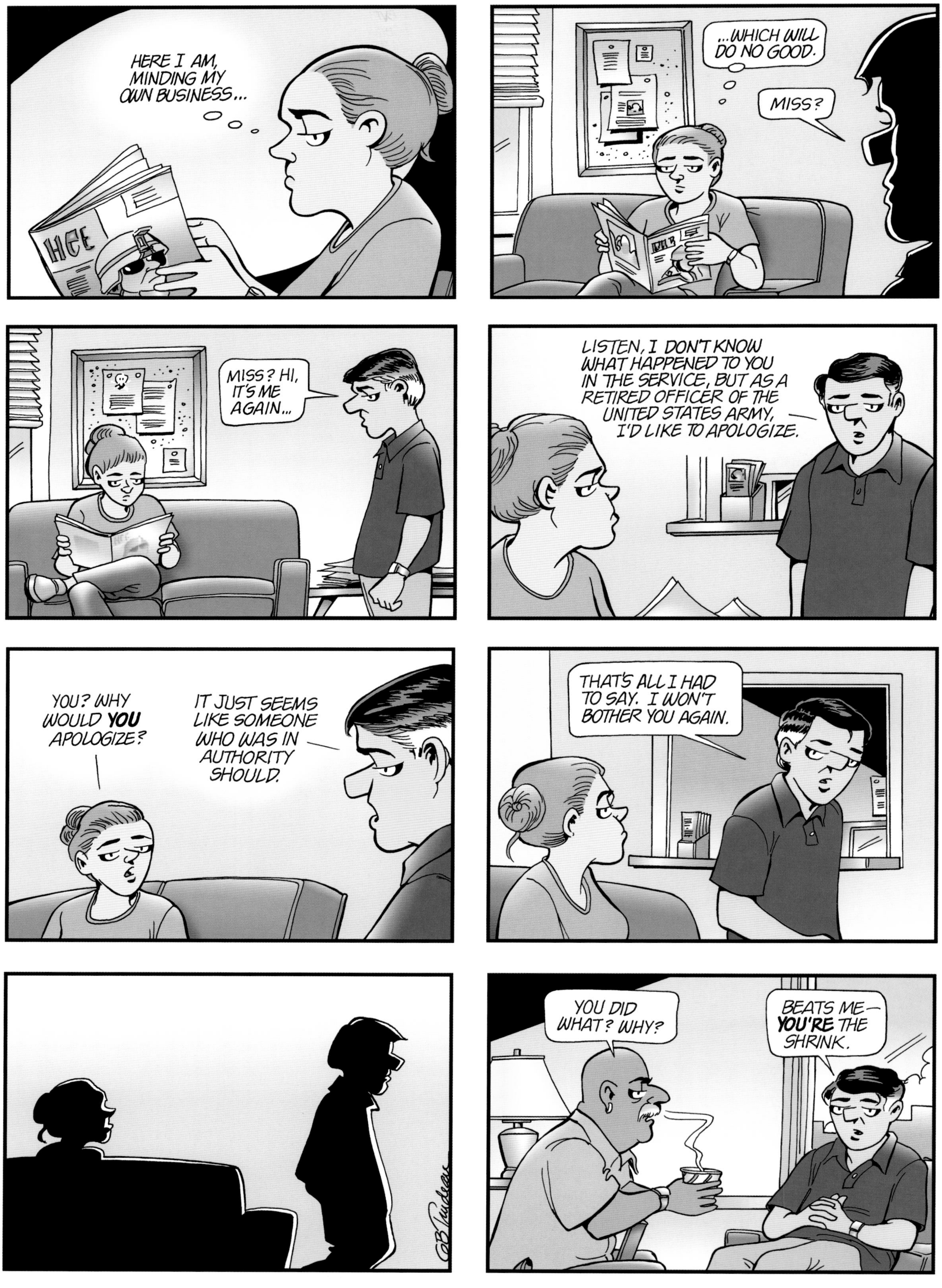
HERE I AM, MINDING MY OWN BUSINESS...
...WHICH WILL DO NO GOOD.
MISS?
MISS? HI, IT'S ME AGAIN...
LISTEN, I DON'T KNOW WHAT HAPPENED TO YOU IN THE SERVICE, BUT AS A RETIRED OFFICER OF THE UNITED STATES ARMY, I'D LIKE TO APOLOGIZE.
YOU? WHY WOULD **YOU** APOLOGIZE?
IT JUST SEEMS LIKE SOMEONE WHO WAS IN AUTHORITY SHOULD.
THAT'S ALL I HAD TO SAY. I WON'T BOTHER YOU AGAIN.
YOU DID WHAT? WHY?
BEATS ME— **YOU'RE** THE SHRINK.

8/12/07

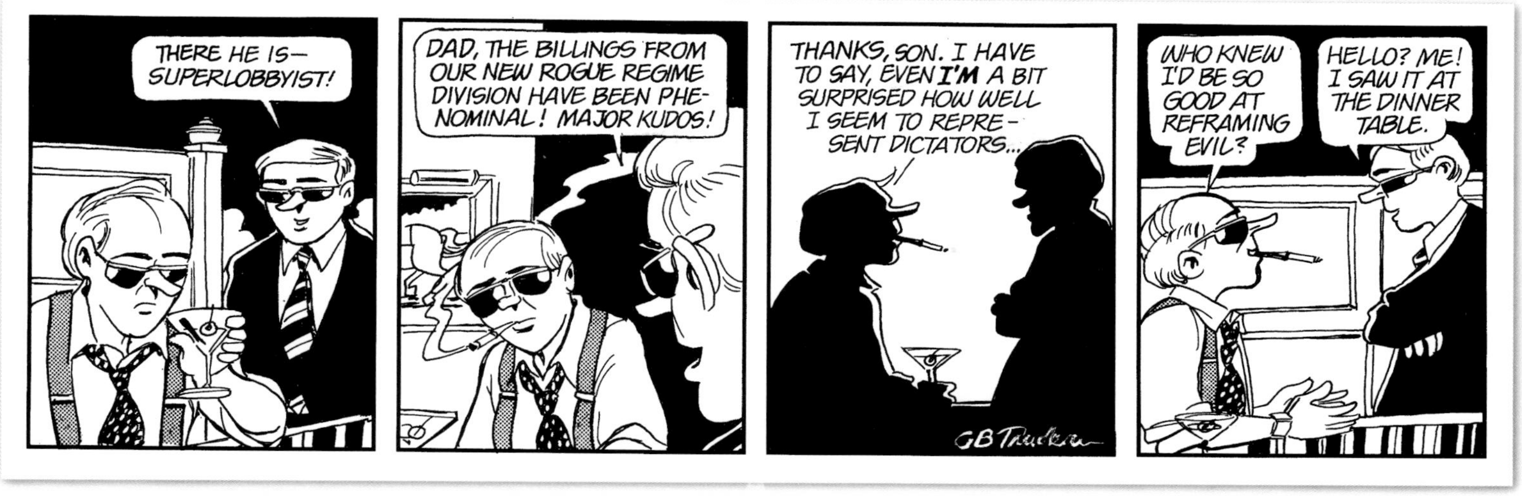
THERE HE IS—SUPERLOBBYIST!
DAD, THE BILLINGS FROM OUR NEW ROGUE REGIME DIVISION HAVE BEEN PHENOMINAL! MAJOR KUDOS!
THANKS, SON. I HAVE TO SAY, EVEN **I'M** A BIT SURPRISED HOW WELL I SEEM TO REPRESENT DICTATORS...
WHO KNEW I'D BE SO GOOD AT REFRAMING EVIL?
HELLO? ME! I SAW IT AT THE DINNER TABLE.
GB Trudeau

8/6/07

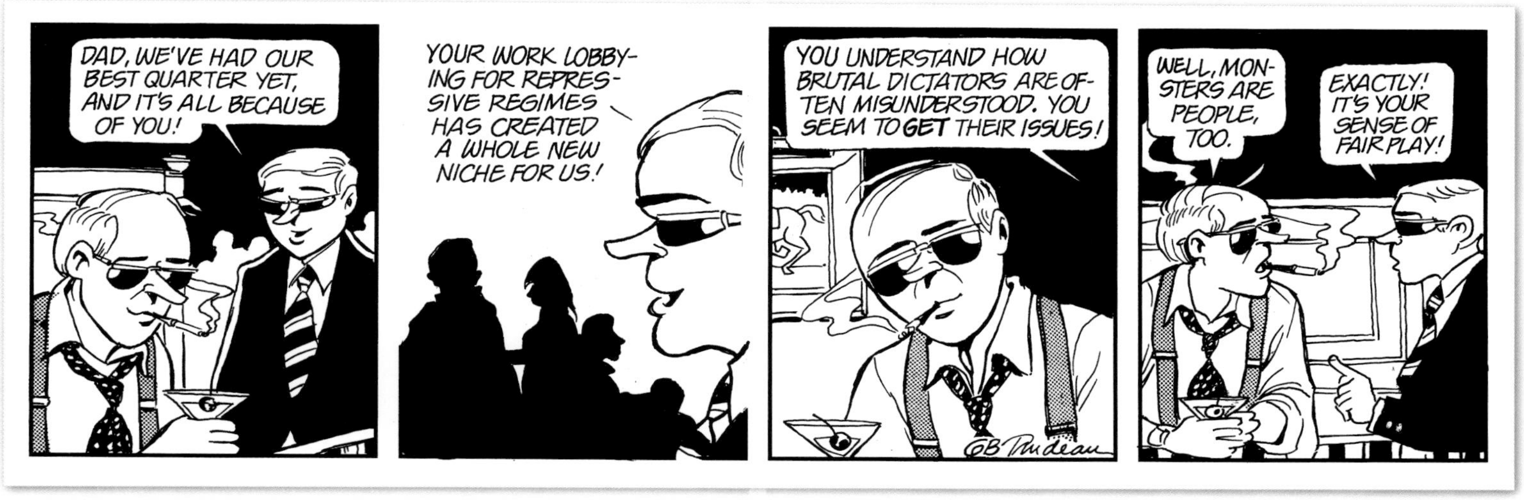
DAD, WE'VE HAD OUR BEST QUARTER YET, AND IT'S ALL BECAUSE OF YOU!
YOUR WORK LOBBYING FOR REPRESSIVE REGIMES HAS CREATED A WHOLE NEW NICHE FOR US!
YOU UNDERSTAND HOW BRUTAL DICTATORS ARE OFTEN MISUNDERSTOOD. YOU SEEM TO **GET** THEIR ISSUES!
WELL, MONSTERS ARE PEOPLE, TOO.
EXACTLY! IT'S YOUR SENSE OF FAIR PLAY!
GB Trudeau

8/7/07

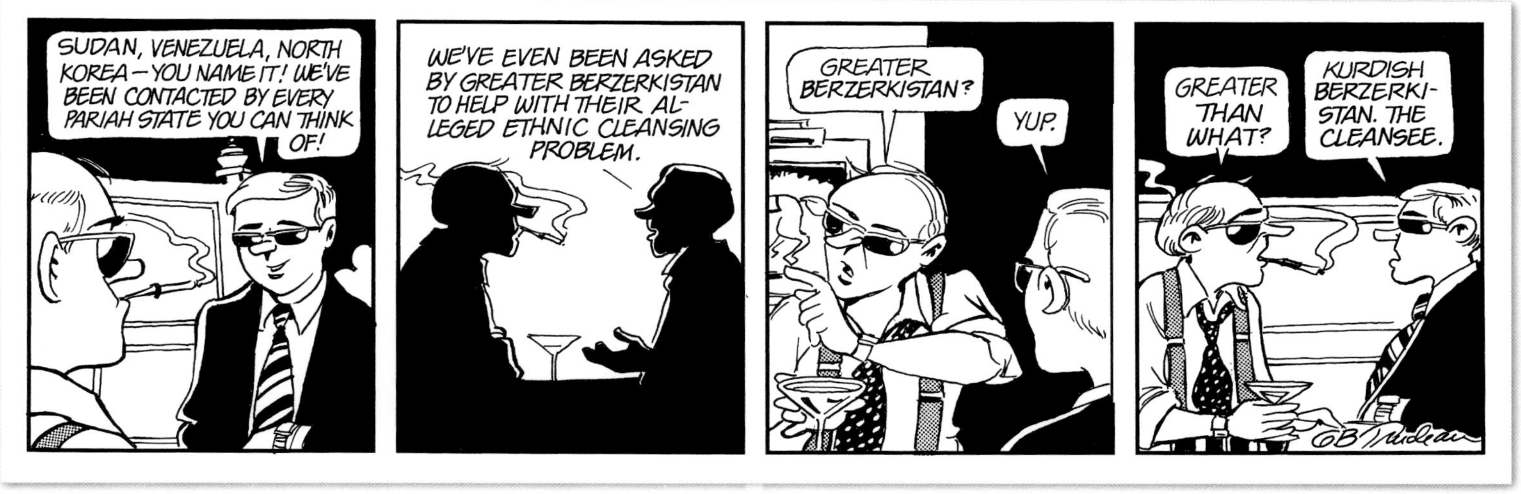
SUDAN, VENEZUELA, NORTH KOREA—YOU NAME IT! WE'VE BEEN CONTACTED BY EVERY PARIAH STATE YOU CAN THINK OF!
WE'VE EVEN BEEN ASKED BY GREATER BERZERKISTAN TO HELP WITH THEIR ALLEGED ETHNIC CLEANSING PROBLEM.
GREATER BERZERKISTAN?
YUP.
GREATER THAN WHAT?
KURDISH BERZERKISTAN. THE CLEANSEE.
GB Trudeau

8/8/07

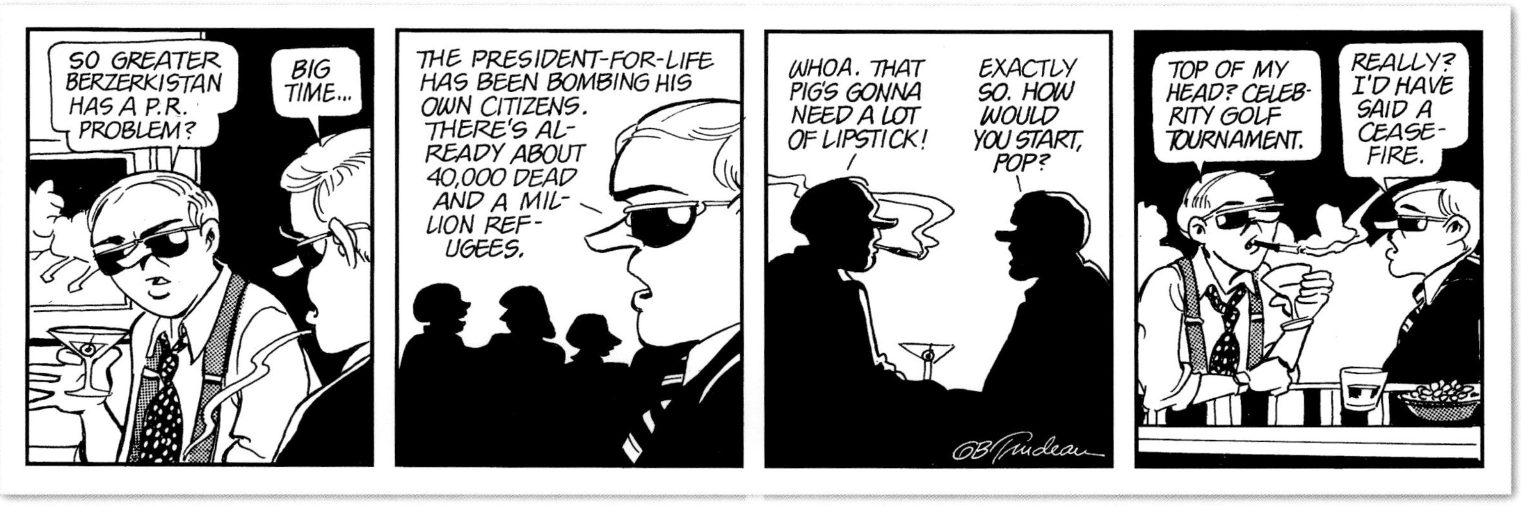
SO GREATER BERZERKISTAN HAS A P.R. PROBLEM?
BIG TIME...
THE PRESIDENT-FOR-LIFE HAS BEEN BOMBING HIS OWN CITIZENS. THERE'S ALREADY ABOUT 40,000 DEAD AND A MILLION REFUGEES.
WHOA. THAT PIG'S GONNA NEED A LOT OF LIPSTICK!
EXACTLY SO. HOW WOULD YOU START, POP?
TOP OF MY HEAD? CELEBRITY GOLF TOURNAMENT.
REALLY? I'D HAVE SAID A CEASE-FIRE.
GB Trudeau

8/9/07

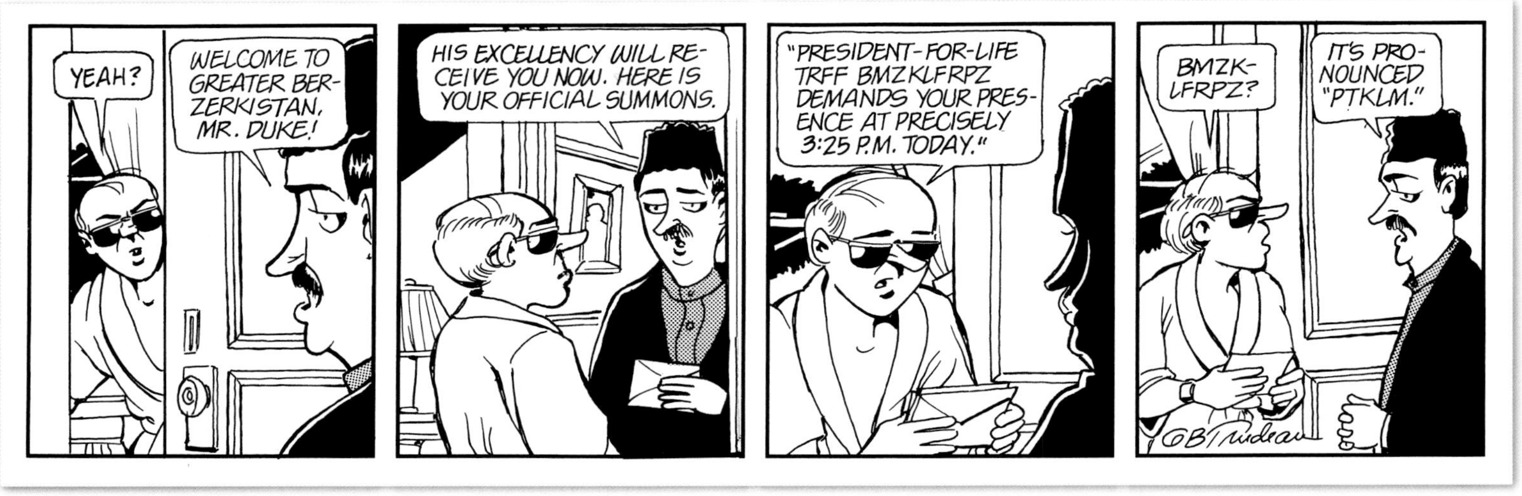
YEAH?
WELCOME TO GREATER BER-ZERKISTAN, MR. DUKE!
HIS EXCELLENCY WILL RE-CEIVE YOU NOW. HERE IS YOUR OFFICIAL SUMMONS.
"PRESIDENT-FOR-LIFE TRFF BMZKLFRPZ DEMANDS YOUR PRES-ENCE AT PRECISELY 3:25 P.M. TODAY."
BMZK-LFRPZ?
IT'S PRO-NOUNCED "PTKLM."
©B Trudeau

10/8/07

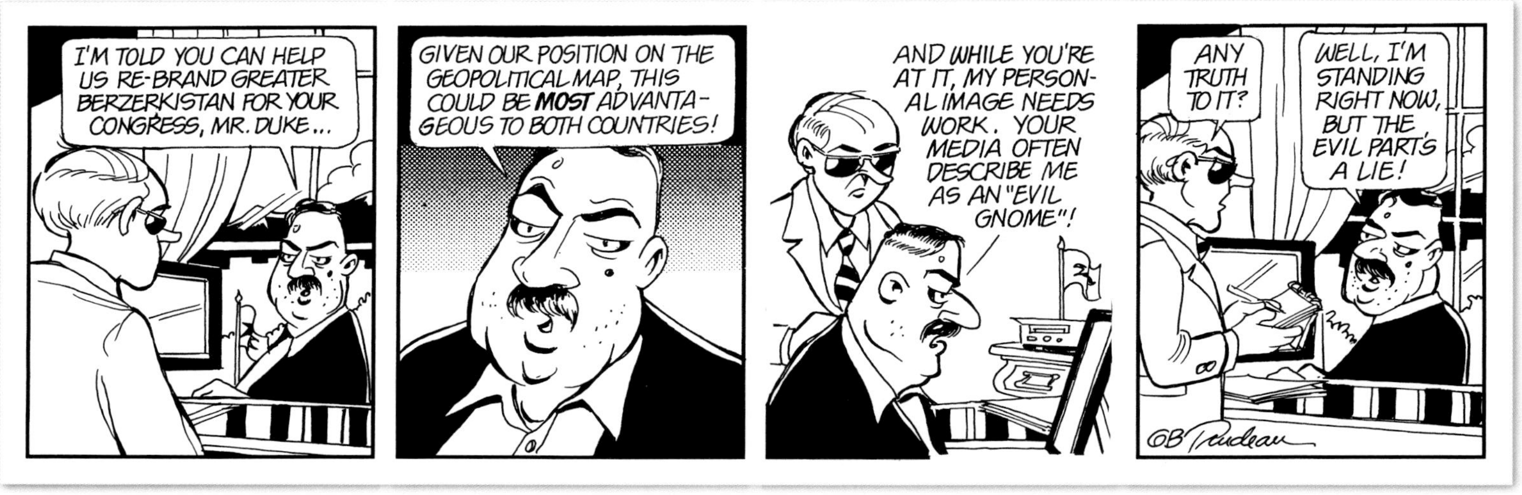
I'M TOLD YOU CAN HELP US RE-BRAND GREATER BERZERKISTAN FOR YOUR CONGRESS, MR. DUKE...
GIVEN OUR POSITION ON THE GEOPOLITICAL MAP, THIS COULD BE MOST ADVANTA-GEOUS TO BOTH COUNTRIES!
AND WHILE YOU'RE AT IT, MY PERSON-AL IMAGE NEEDS WORK. YOUR MEDIA OFTEN DESCRIBE ME AS AN "EVIL GNOME"!
ANY TRUTH TO IT?
WELL, I'M STANDING RIGHT NOW, BUT THE EVIL PART'S A LIE!
©B Trudeau

10/11/07

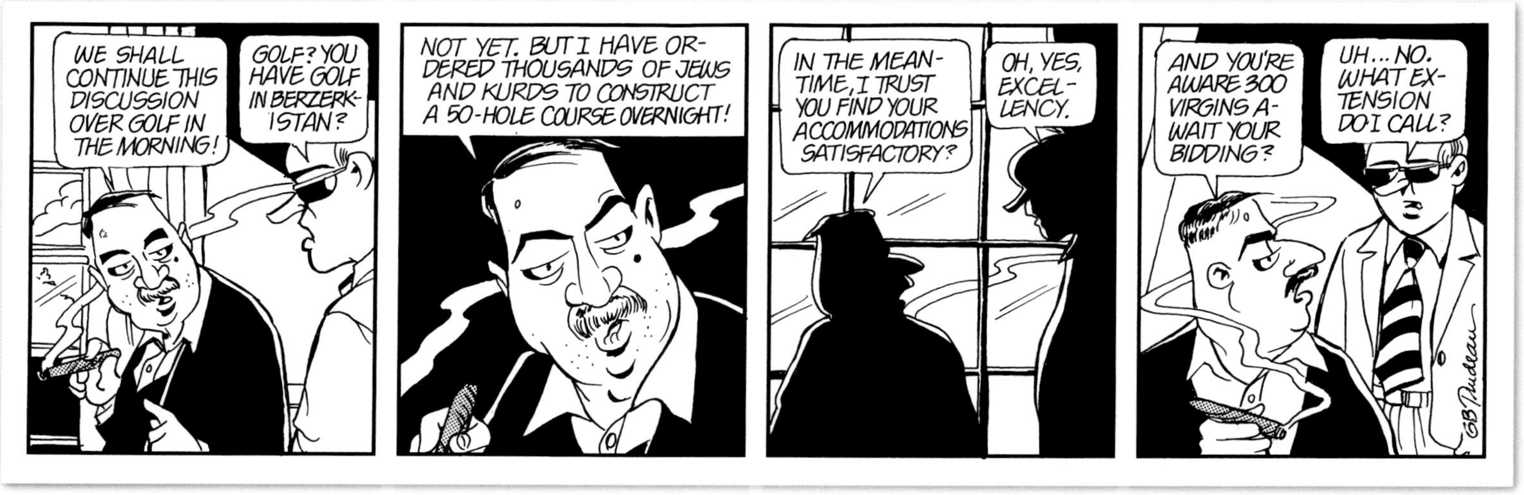
WE SHALL CONTINUE THIS DISCUSSION OVER GOLF IN THE MORNING!
GOLF? YOU HAVE GOLF IN BERZERK-ISTAN?
NOT YET. BUT I HAVE OR-DERED THOUSANDS OF JEWS AND KURDS TO CONSTRUCT A 50-HOLE COURSE OVERNIGHT!
IN THE MEAN-TIME, I TRUST YOU FIND YOUR ACCOMMODATIONS SATISFACTORY?
OH, YES, EXCEL-LENCY.
AND YOU'RE AWARE 300 VIRGINS A-WAIT YOUR BIDDING?
UH... NO. WHAT EX-TENSION DO I CALL?
©B Trudeau

10/12/07

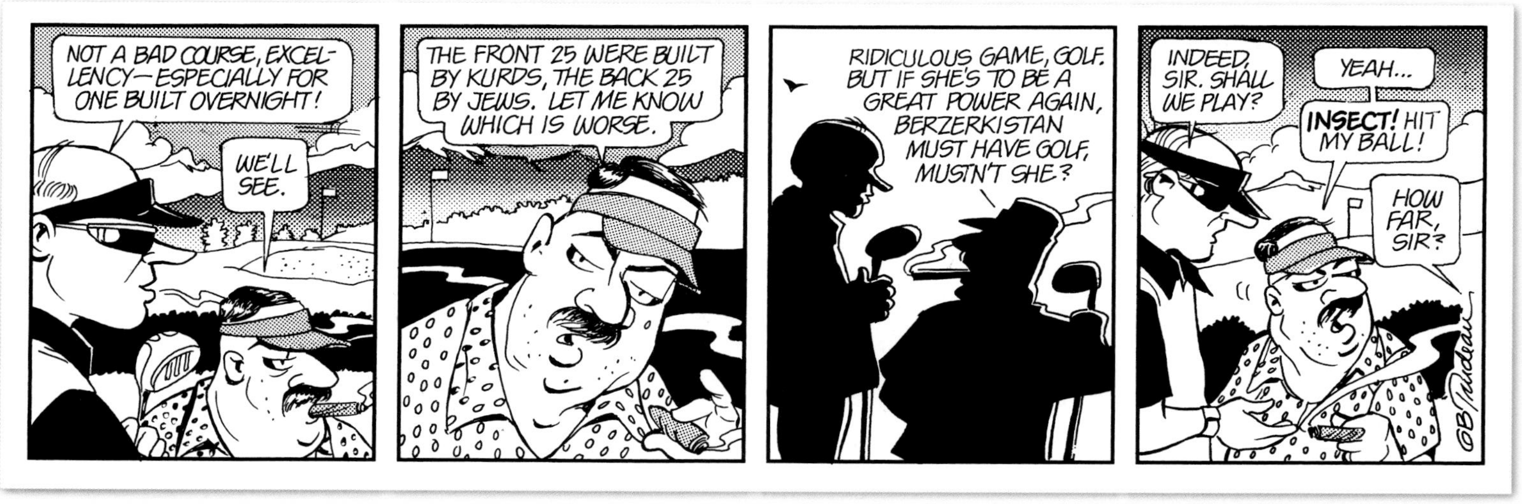
NOT A BAD COURSE, EXCEL-LENCY—ESPECIALLY FOR ONE BUILT OVERNIGHT!
WE'LL SEE.
THE FRONT 25 WERE BUILT BY KURDS, THE BACK 25 BY JEWS. LET ME KNOW WHICH IS WORSE.
RIDICULOUS GAME, GOLF. BUT IF SHE'S TO BE A GREAT POWER AGAIN, BERZERKISTAN MUST HAVE GOLF, MUSTN'T SHE?
INDEED, SIR. SHALL WE PLAY?
YEAH...
INSECT! HIT MY BALL!
HOW FAR, SIR?
©B Trudeau

10/13/07

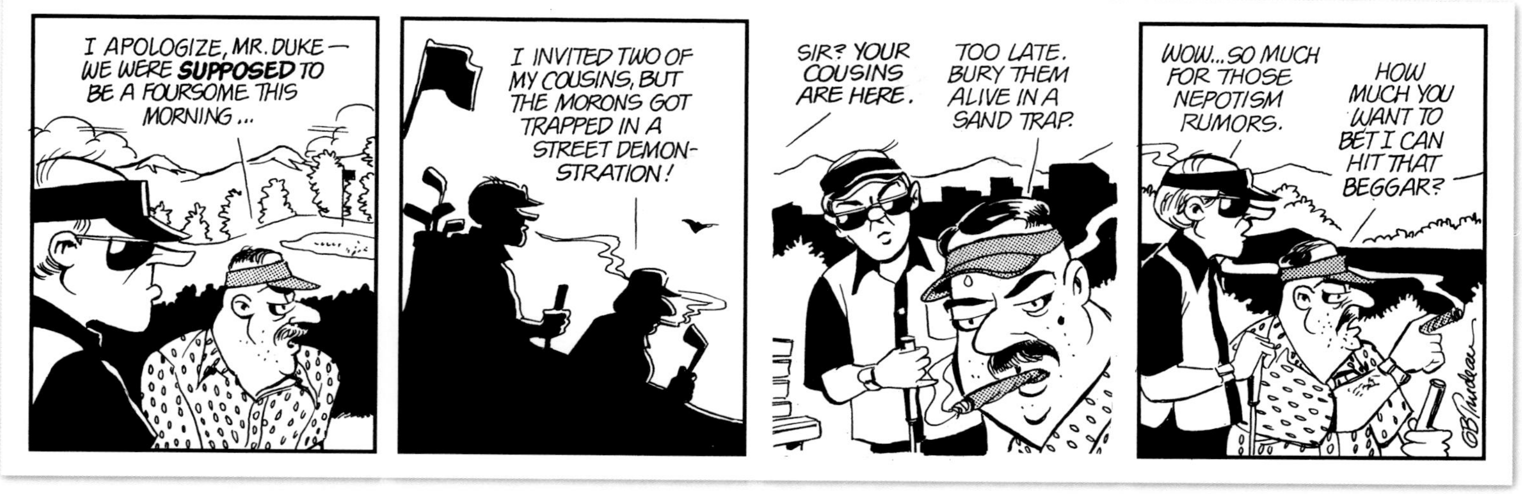
I APOLOGIZE, MR. DUKE — WE WERE **SUPPOSED** TO BE A FOURSOME THIS MORNING...
I INVITED TWO OF MY COUSINS, BUT THE MORONS GOT TRAPPED IN A STREET DEMONSTRATION!
SIR? YOUR COUSINS ARE HERE.
TOO LATE. BURY THEM ALIVE IN A SAND TRAP.
WOW...SO MUCH FOR THOSE NEPOTISM RUMORS.
HOW MUCH YOU WANT TO BET I CAN HIT THAT BEGGAR?

10/15/07

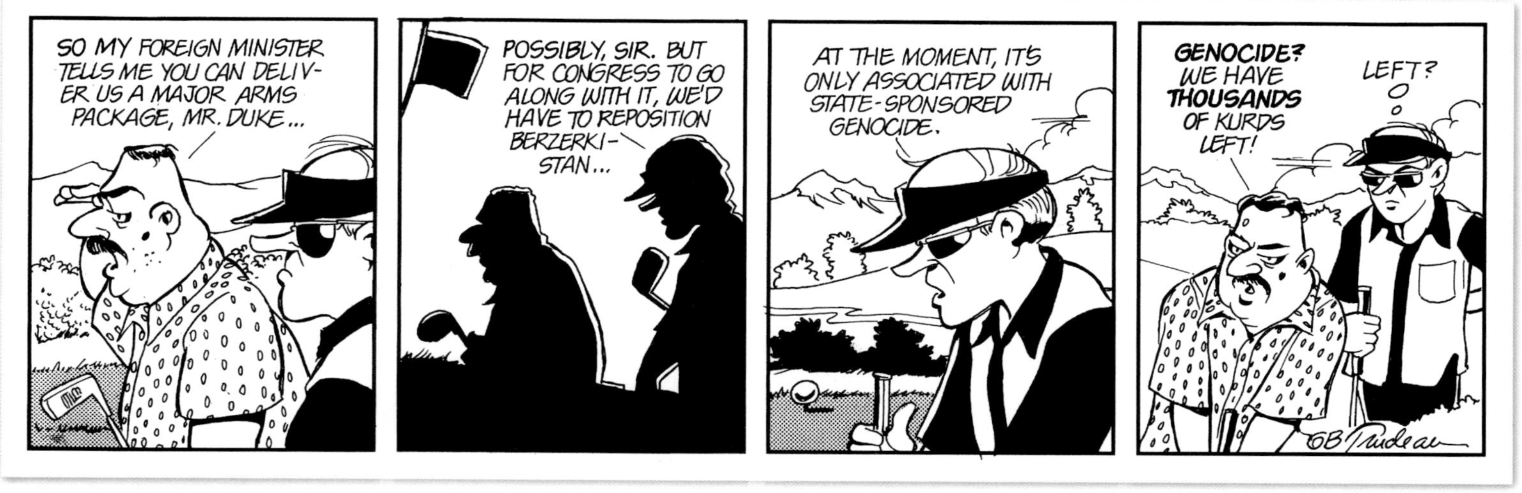
SO MY FOREIGN MINISTER TELLS ME YOU CAN DELIVER US A MAJOR ARMS PACKAGE, MR. DUKE...
POSSIBLY, SIR. BUT FOR CONGRESS TO GO ALONG WITH IT, WE'D HAVE TO REPOSITION BERZERKISTAN...
AT THE MOMENT, IT'S ONLY ASSOCIATED WITH STATE-SPONSORED GENOCIDE.
GENOCIDE? WE HAVE **THOUSANDS** OF KURDS LEFT!
LEFT?

10/16/07

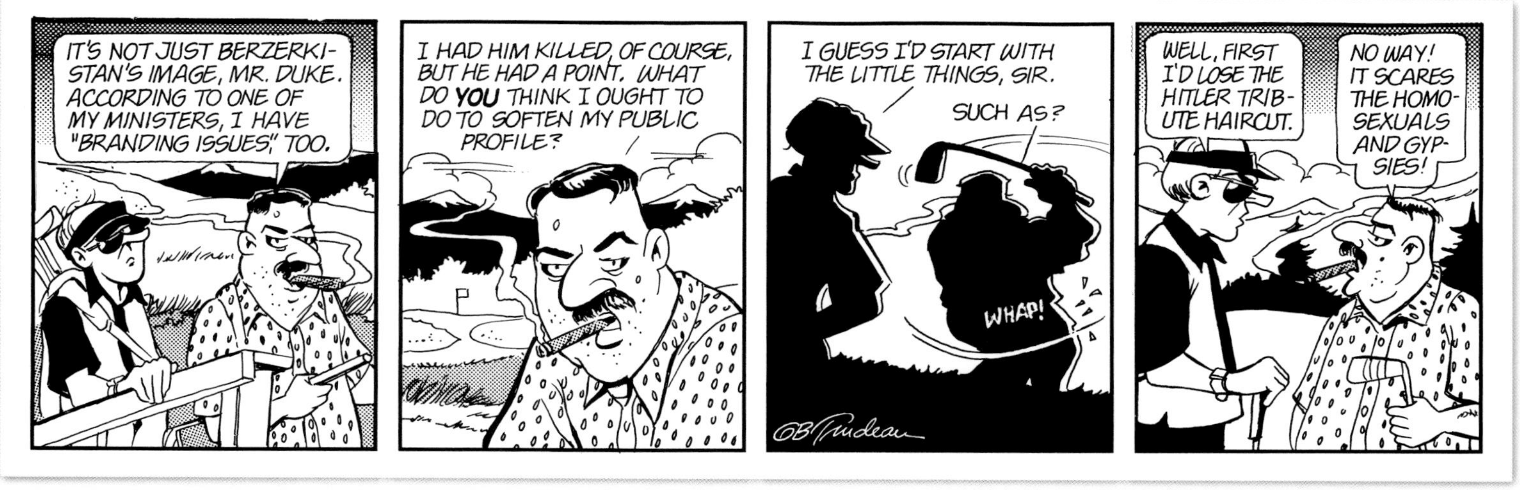
IT'S NOT JUST BERZERKISTAN'S IMAGE, MR. DUKE. ACCORDING TO ONE OF MY MINISTERS, I HAVE "BRANDING ISSUES," TOO.
I HAD HIM KILLED, OF COURSE, BUT HE HAD A POINT. WHAT DO **YOU** THINK I OUGHT TO DO TO SOFTEN MY PUBLIC PROFILE?
I GUESS I'D START WITH THE LITTLE THINGS, SIR.
SUCH AS?
WHAP!
WELL, FIRST I'D LOSE THE HITLER TRIBUTE HAIRCUT.
NO WAY! IT SCARES THE HOMOSEXUALS AND GYPSIES!

10/17/07

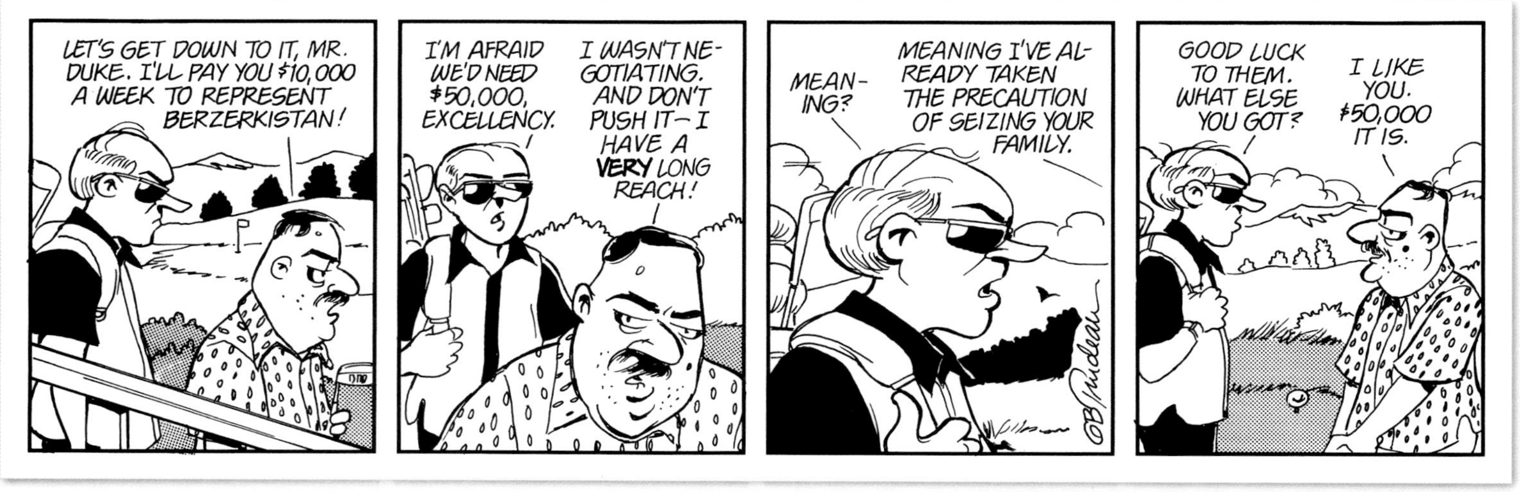
LET'S GET DOWN TO IT, MR. DUKE. I'LL PAY YOU $10,000 A WEEK TO REPRESENT BERZERKISTAN!
I'M AFRAID WE'D NEED $50,000, EXCELLENCY.
I WASN'T NEGOTIATING. AND DON'T PUSH IT — I HAVE A **VERY** LONG REACH!
MEANING?
MEANING I'VE ALREADY TAKEN THE PRECAUTION OF SEIZING YOUR FAMILY.
GOOD LUCK TO THEM. WHAT ELSE YOU GOT?
I LIKE YOU. $50,000 IT IS.

10/18/07

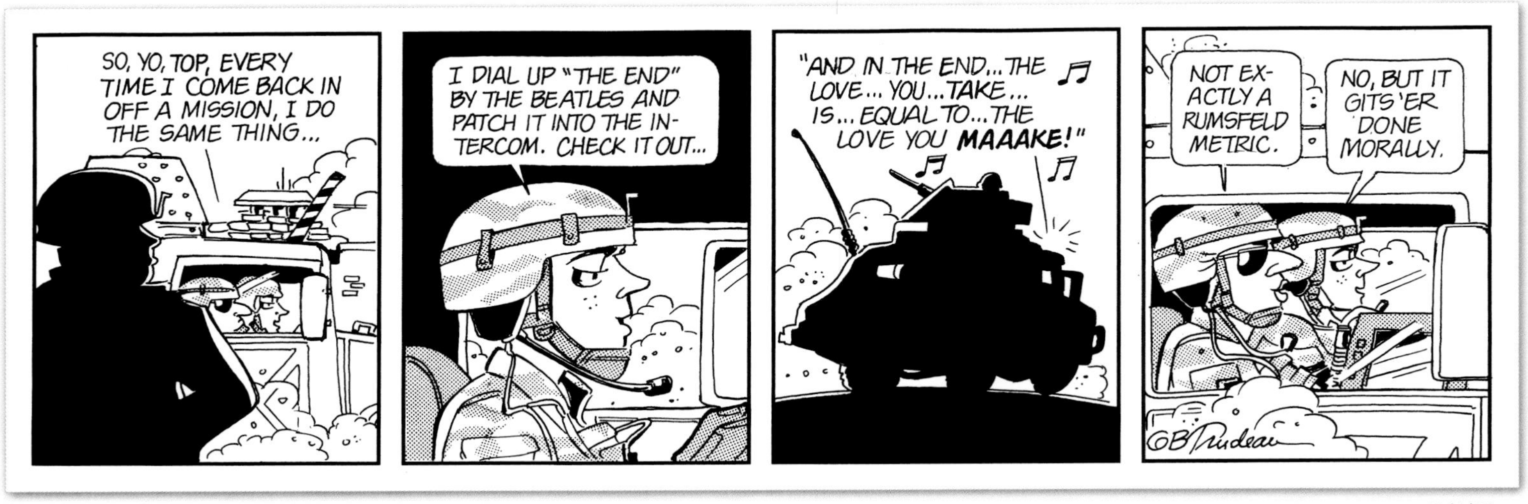
SO, YO, TOP, EVERY TIME I COME BACK IN OFF A MISSION, I DO THE SAME THING...
I DIAL UP "THE END" BY THE BEATLES AND PATCH IT INTO THE INTERCOM. CHECK IT OUT...
"AND IN THE END... THE LOVE... YOU... TAKE... IS... EQUAL TO... THE LOVE YOU **MAAAKE!**"
NOT EXACTLY A RUMSFELD METRIC.
NO, BUT IT GITS 'ER DONE MORALLY.

12/1/07

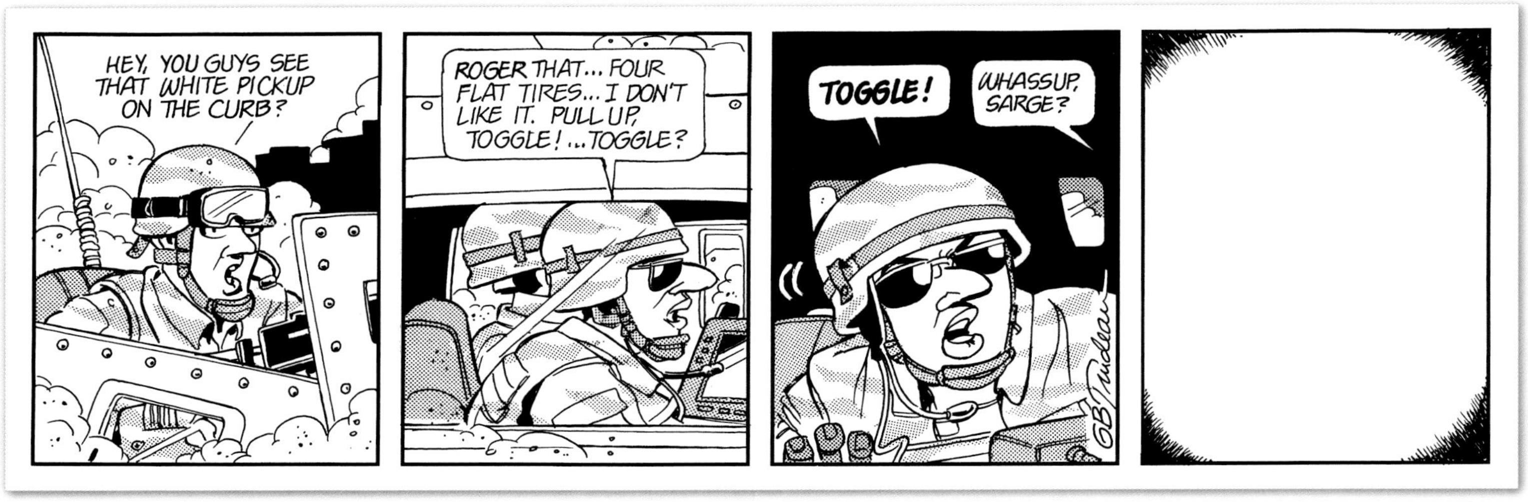
HEY, YOU GUYS SEE THAT WHITE PICKUP ON THE CURB?
ROGER THAT... FOUR FLAT TIRES... I DON'T LIKE IT. PULL UP, TOGGLE! ...TOGGLE?
TOGGLE!
WHASSUP, SARGE?

12/3/07

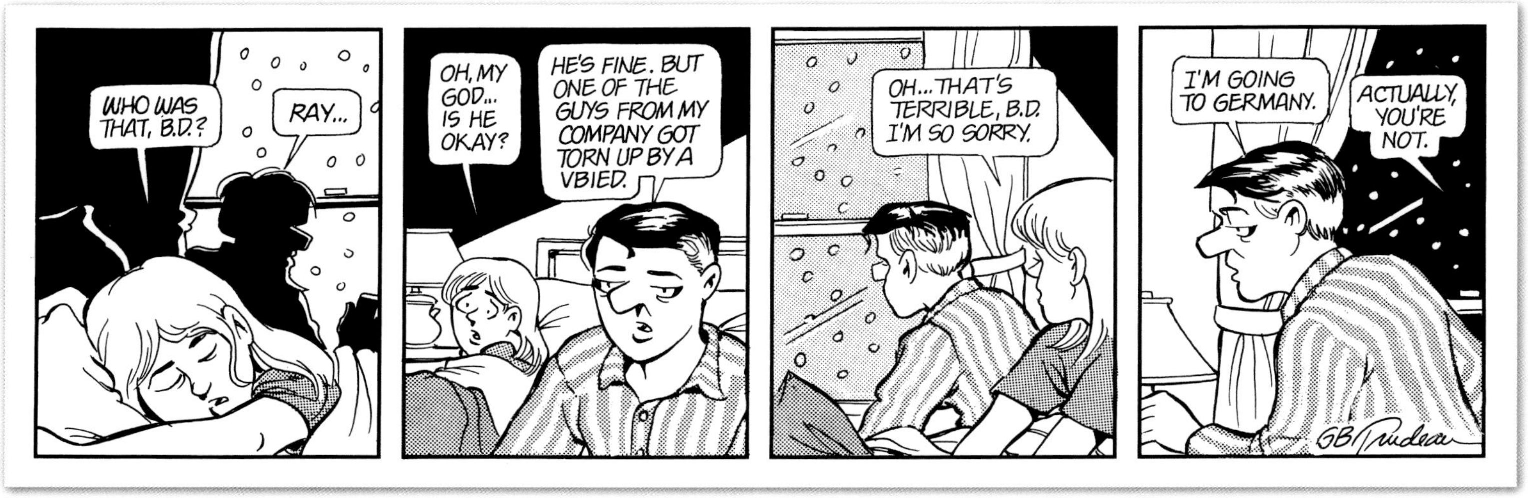
WHO WAS THAT, B.D.?
RAY...
OH, MY GOD... IS HE OKAY?
HE'S FINE. BUT ONE OF THE GUYS FROM MY COMPANY GOT TORN UP BY A VBIED.
OH... THAT'S TERRIBLE, B.D. I'M SO SORRY.
I'M GOING TO GERMANY.
ACTUALLY, YOU'RE NOT.

12/4/07

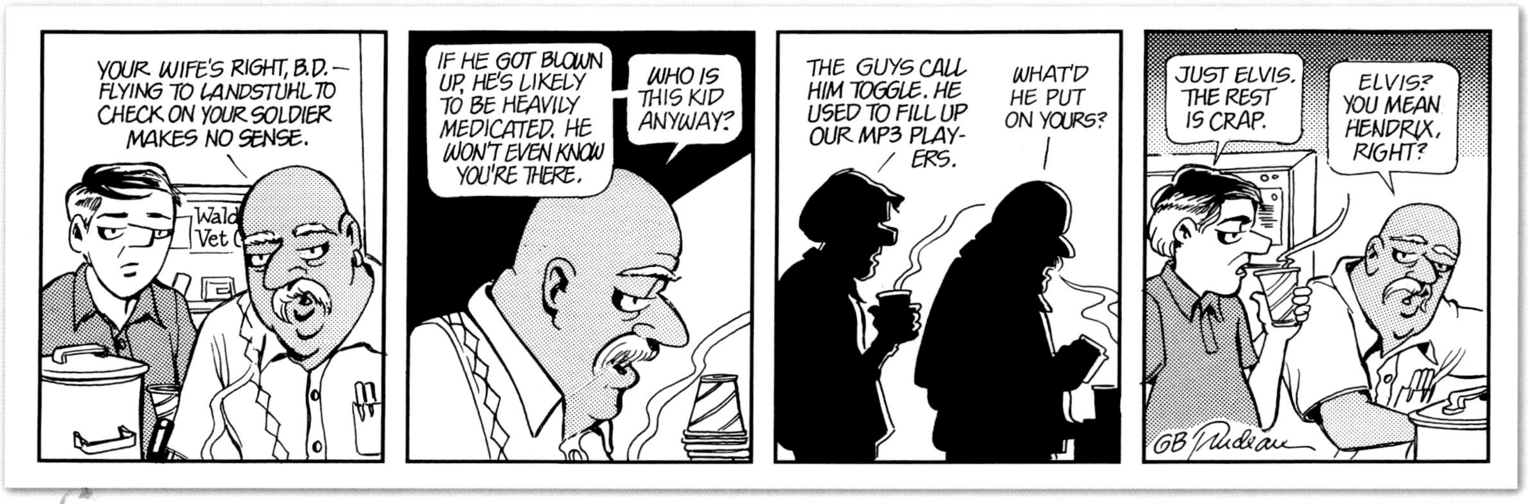
YOUR WIFE'S RIGHT, B.D.— FLYING TO LANDSTUHL TO CHECK ON YOUR SOLDIER MAKES NO SENSE.
IF HE GOT BLOWN UP, HE'S LIKELY TO BE HEAVILY MEDICATED. HE WON'T EVEN KNOW YOU'RE THERE.
WHO IS THIS KID ANYWAY?
THE GUYS CALL HIM TOGGLE. HE USED TO FILL UP OUR MP3 PLAYERS.
WHAT'D HE PUT ON YOURS?
JUST ELVIS. THE REST IS CRAP.
ELVIS? YOU MEAN HENDRIX, RIGHT?

12/5/07

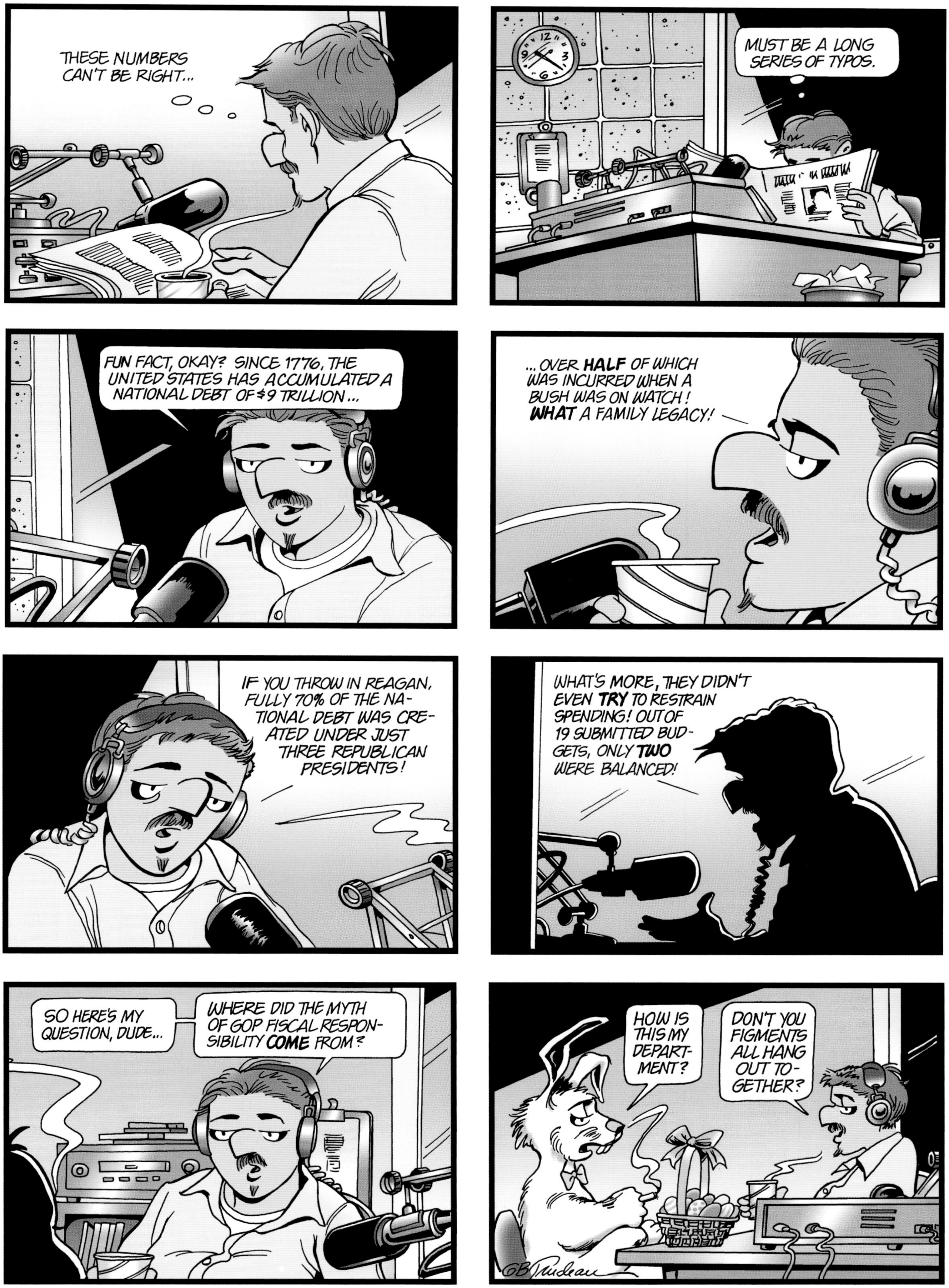
THESE NUMBERS CAN'T BE RIGHT...
MUST BE A LONG SERIES OF TYPOS.
FUN FACT, OKAY? SINCE 1776, THE UNITED STATES HAS ACCUMULATED A NATIONAL DEBT OF $9 TRILLION...
...OVER HALF OF WHICH WAS INCURRED WHEN A BUSH WAS ON WATCH! WHAT A FAMILY LEGACY!
IF YOU THROW IN REAGAN, FULLY 70% OF THE NATIONAL DEBT WAS CREATED UNDER JUST THREE REPUBLICAN PRESIDENTS!
WHAT'S MORE, THEY DIDN'T EVEN TRY TO RESTRAIN SPENDING! OUT OF 19 SUBMITTED BUDGETS, ONLY TWO WERE BALANCED!
SO HERE'S MY QUESTION, DUDE...
WHERE DID THE MYTH OF GOP FISCAL RESPONSIBILITY COME FROM?
HOW IS THIS MY DEPARTMENT?
DON'T YOU FIGMENTS ALL HANG OUT TOGETHER?
GB Trudeau

9/2/07

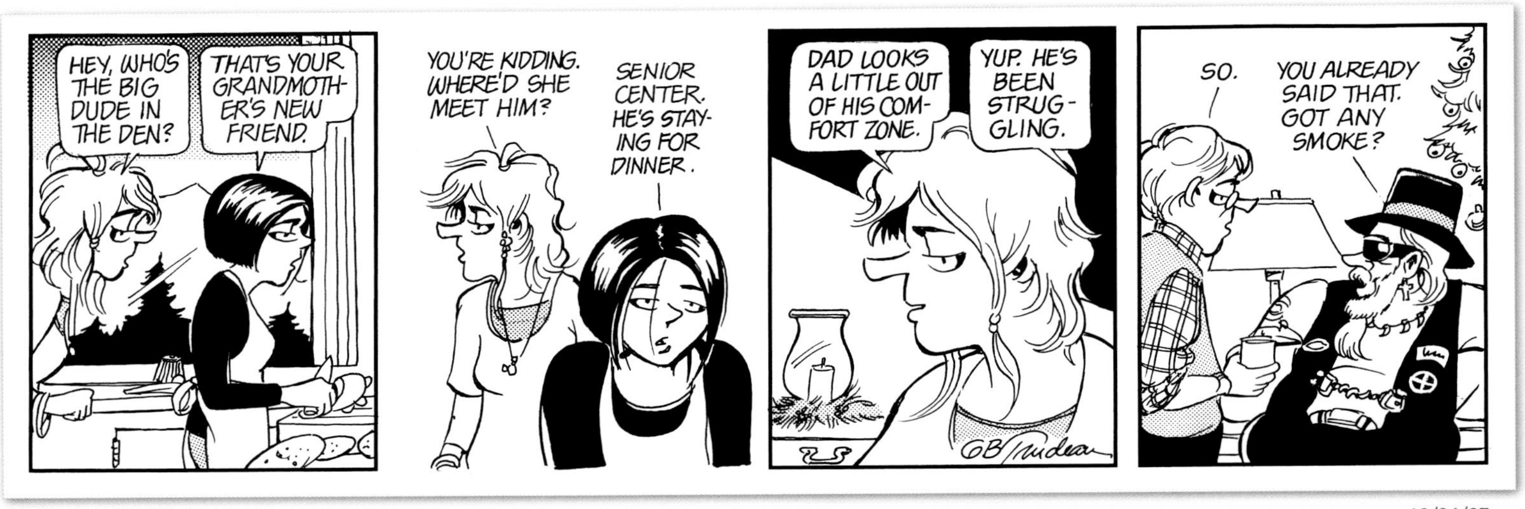
HEY, WHO'S THE BIG DUDE IN THE DEN?
THAT'S YOUR GRANDMOTHER'S NEW FRIEND.
YOU'RE KIDDING. WHERE'D SHE MEET HIM?
SENIOR CENTER. HE'S STAYING FOR DINNER.
DAD LOOKS A LITTLE OUT OF HIS COMFORT ZONE.
YUP. HE'S BEEN STRUGGLING.
GBTrudeau
SO.
YOU ALREADY SAID THAT. GOT ANY SMOKE?

12/24/07

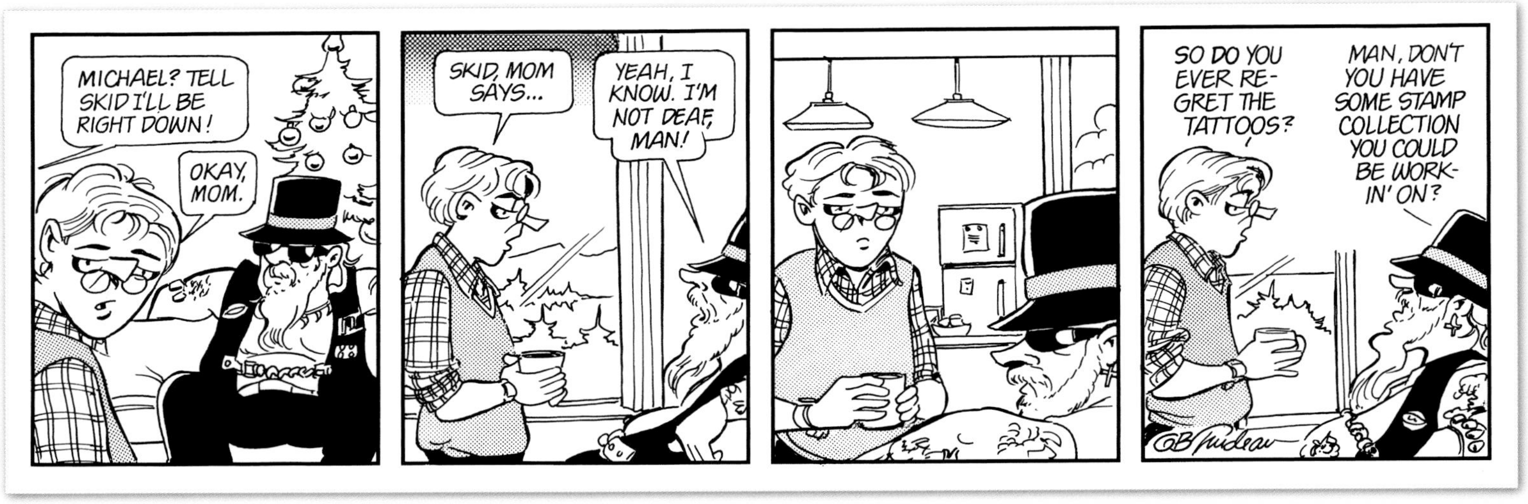
MICHAEL? TELL SKID I'LL BE RIGHT DOWN!
OKAY, MOM.
SKID, MOM SAYS...
YEAH, I KNOW. I'M NOT DEAF, MAN!
SO DO YOU EVER REGRET THE TATTOOS?
MAN, DON'T YOU HAVE SOME STAMP COLLECTION YOU COULD BE WORKIN' ON?
GBTrudeau

12/25/07

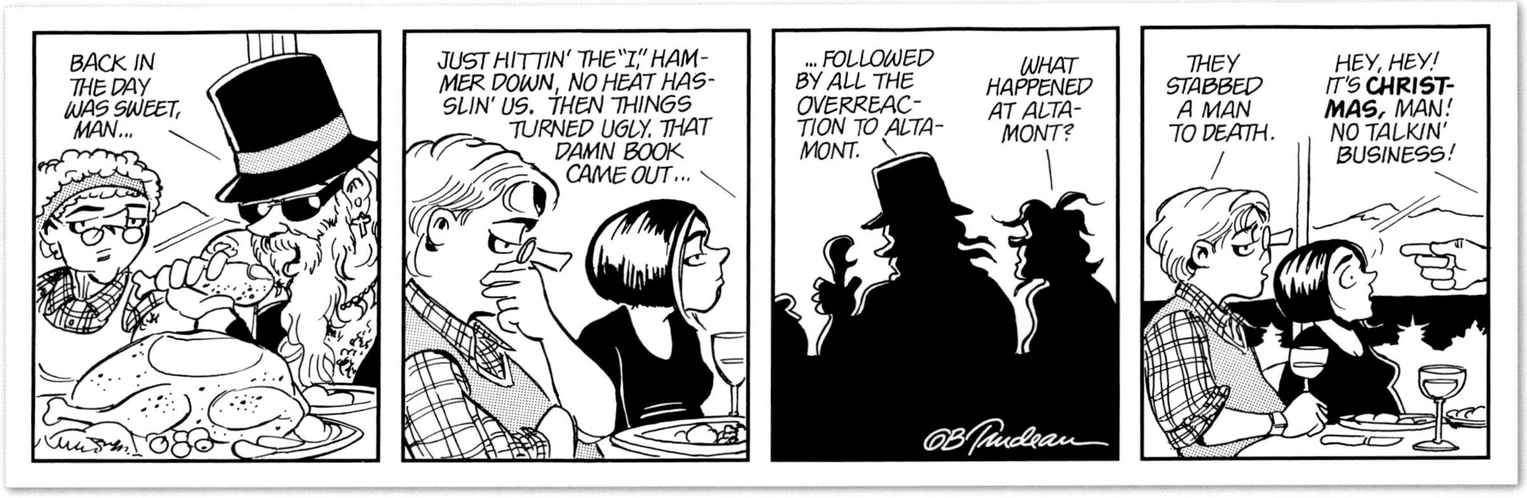
BACK IN THE DAY WAS SWEET, MAN...
JUST HITTIN' THE "I," HAMMER DOWN, NO HEAT HASSLIN' US. THEN THINGS TURNED UGLY. THAT DAMN BOOK CAME OUT...
...FOLLOWED BY ALL THE OVERREACTION TO ALTAMONT.
WHAT HAPPENED AT ALTAMONT?
GBTrudeau
THEY STABBED A MAN TO DEATH.
HEY, HEY! IT'S **CHRISTMAS,** MAN! NO TALKIN' BUSINESS!

12/26/07

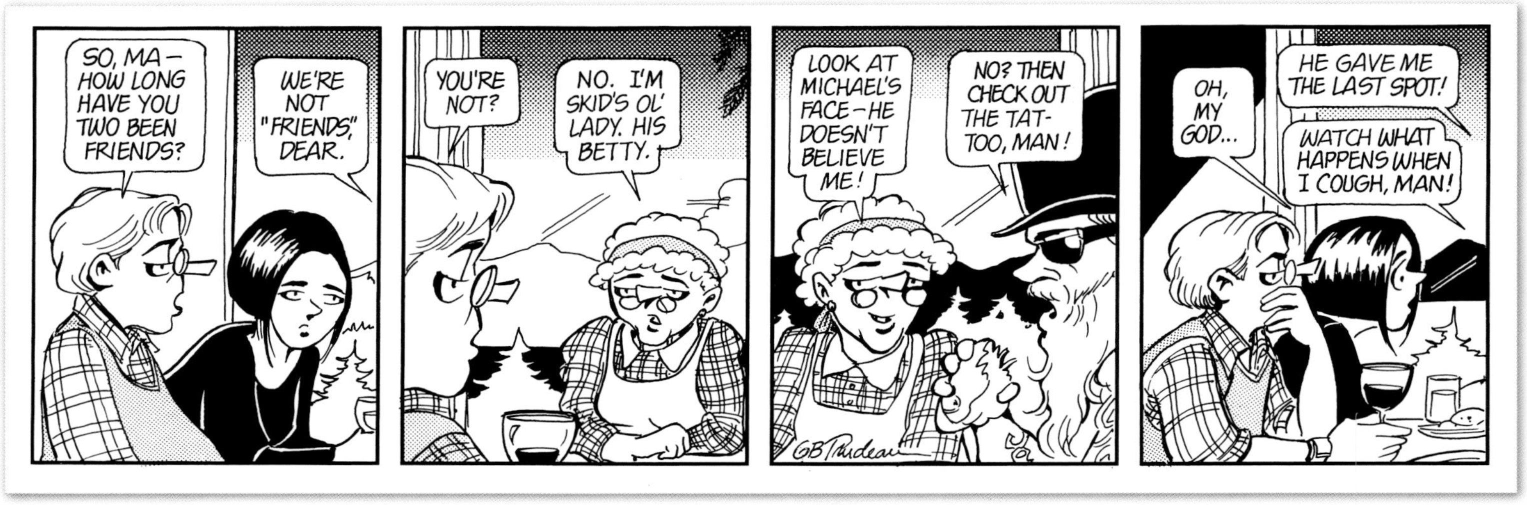
SO, MA— HOW LONG HAVE YOU TWO BEEN FRIENDS?
WE'RE NOT "FRIENDS," DEAR.
YOU'RE NOT?
NO. I'M SKID'S OL' LADY. HIS BETTY.
LOOK AT MICHAEL'S FACE—HE DOESN'T BELIEVE ME!
NO? THEN CHECK OUT THE TATTOO, MAN!
GBTrudeau
OH, MY GOD...
HE GAVE ME THE LAST SPOT!
WATCH WHAT HAPPENS WHEN I COUGH, MAN!

12/27/07

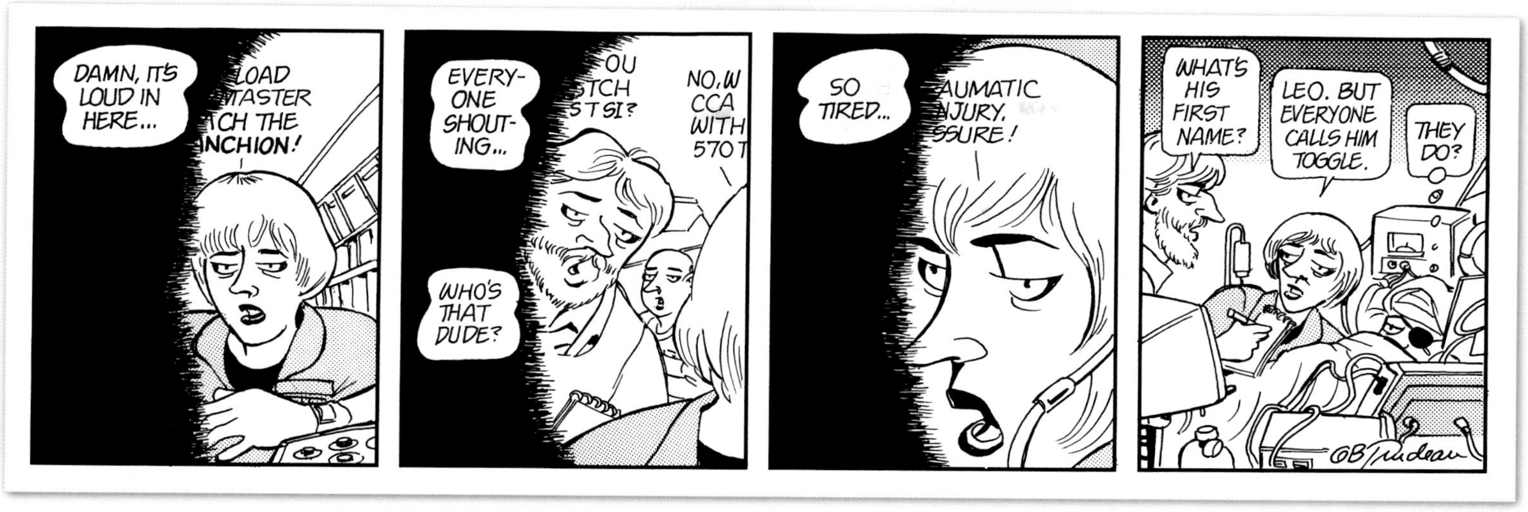

DAMN, IT'S LOUD IN HERE...
LOAD MASTER CH THE NCHION!
EVERY-ONE SHOUT-ING...
OU TCH ST SI?
NO, W CCA WITH 570 T
WHO'S THAT DUDE?
SO TIRED...
AUMATIC NJURY. SSURE!
WHAT'S HIS FIRST NAME?
LEO. BUT EVERYONE CALLS HIM TOGGLE.
THEY DO?

1/21/08

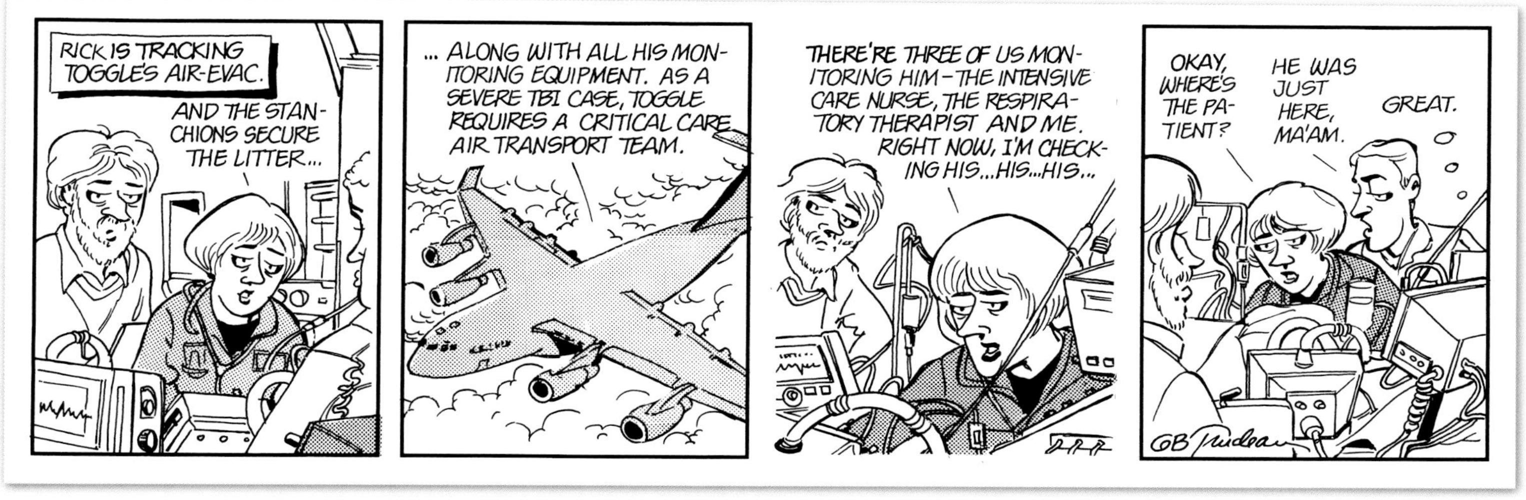

RICK IS TRACKING TOGGLE'S AIR-EVAC.
AND THE STAN-CHIONS SECURE THE LITTER...
... ALONG WITH ALL HIS MON-ITORING EQUIPMENT. AS A SEVERE TBI CASE, TOGGLE REQUIRES A CRITICAL CARE AIR TRANSPORT TEAM.
THERE'RE THREE OF US MON-ITORING HIM — THE INTENSIVE CARE NURSE, THE RESPIRA-TORY THERAPIST AND ME. RIGHT NOW, I'M CHECK-ING HIS...HIS...HIS...
OKAY, WHERE'S THE PA-TIENT?
HE WAS JUST HERE, MA'AM.
GREAT.

1/22/08

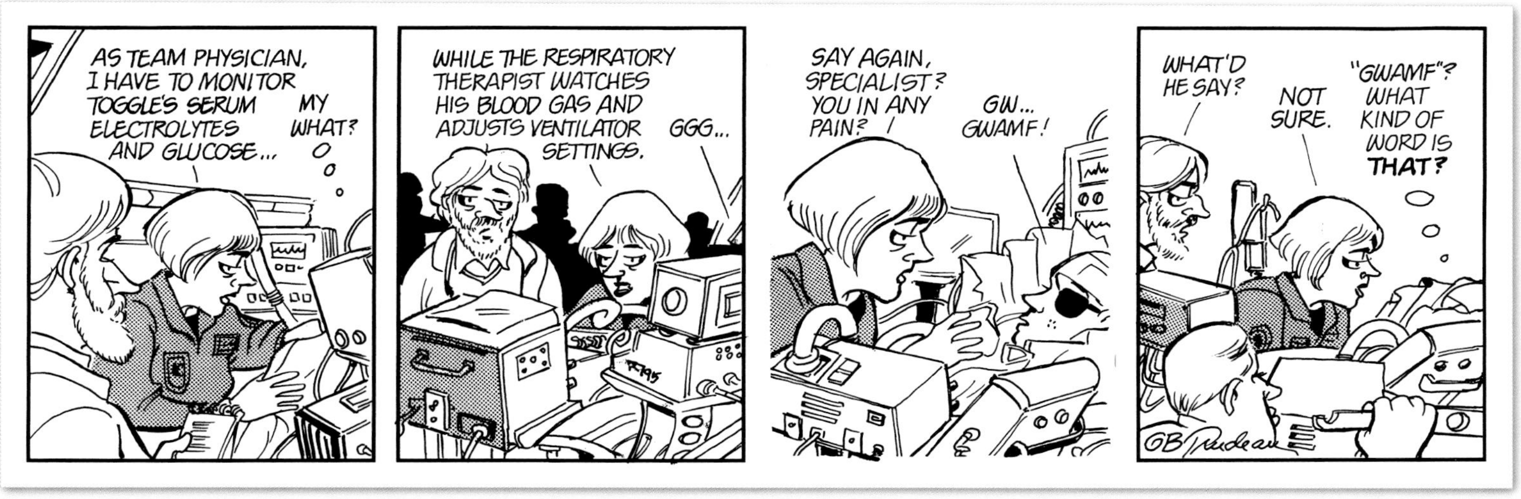

AS TEAM PHYSICIAN, I HAVE TO MONITOR TOGGLE'S SERUM ELECTROLYTES AND GLUCOSE...
MY WHAT?
WHILE THE RESPIRATORY THERAPIST WATCHES HIS BLOOD GAS AND ADJUSTS VENTILATOR SETTINGS.
GGG...
SAY AGAIN, SPECIALIST? YOU IN ANY PAIN?
GW... GWAMF!
WHAT'D HE SAY?
NOT SURE.
"GWAMF"? WHAT KIND OF WORD IS **THAT?**

1/23/08

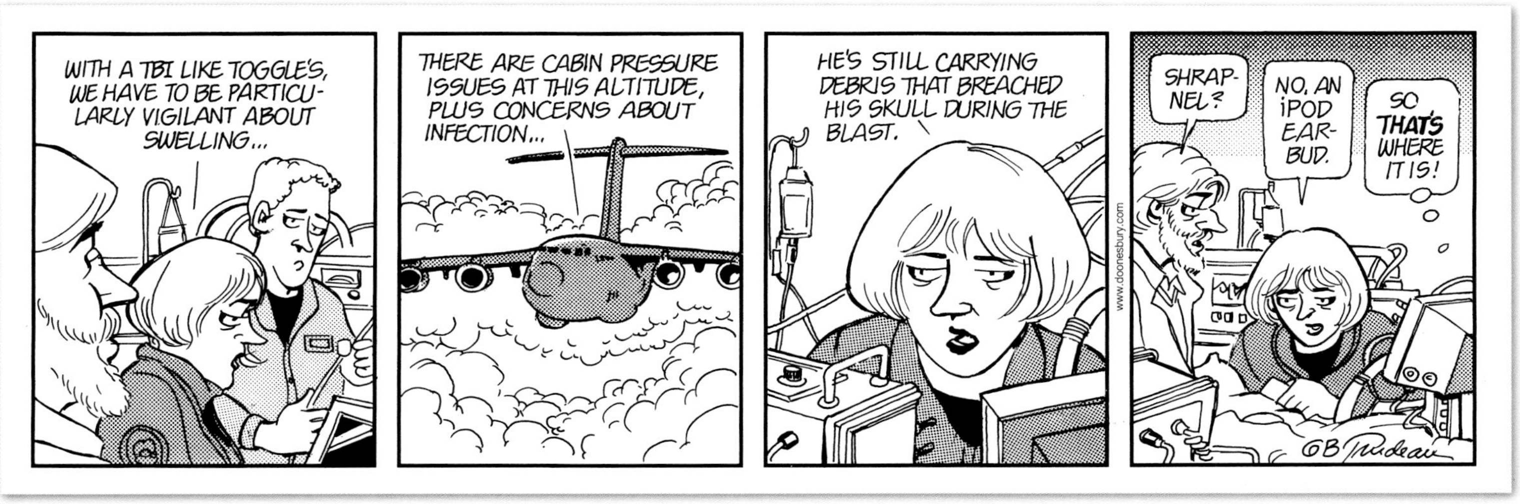

WITH A TBI LIKE TOGGLE'S, WE HAVE TO BE PARTICU-LARLY VIGILANT ABOUT SWELLING...
THERE ARE CABIN PRESSURE ISSUES AT THIS ALTITUDE, PLUS CONCERNS ABOUT INFECTION...
HE'S STILL CARRYING DEBRIS THAT BREACHED HIS SKULL DURING THE BLAST.
www.doonesbury.com
SHRAP-NEL?
NO, AN iPOD EAR-BUD.
SO **THAT'S** WHERE IT IS!

1/24/08

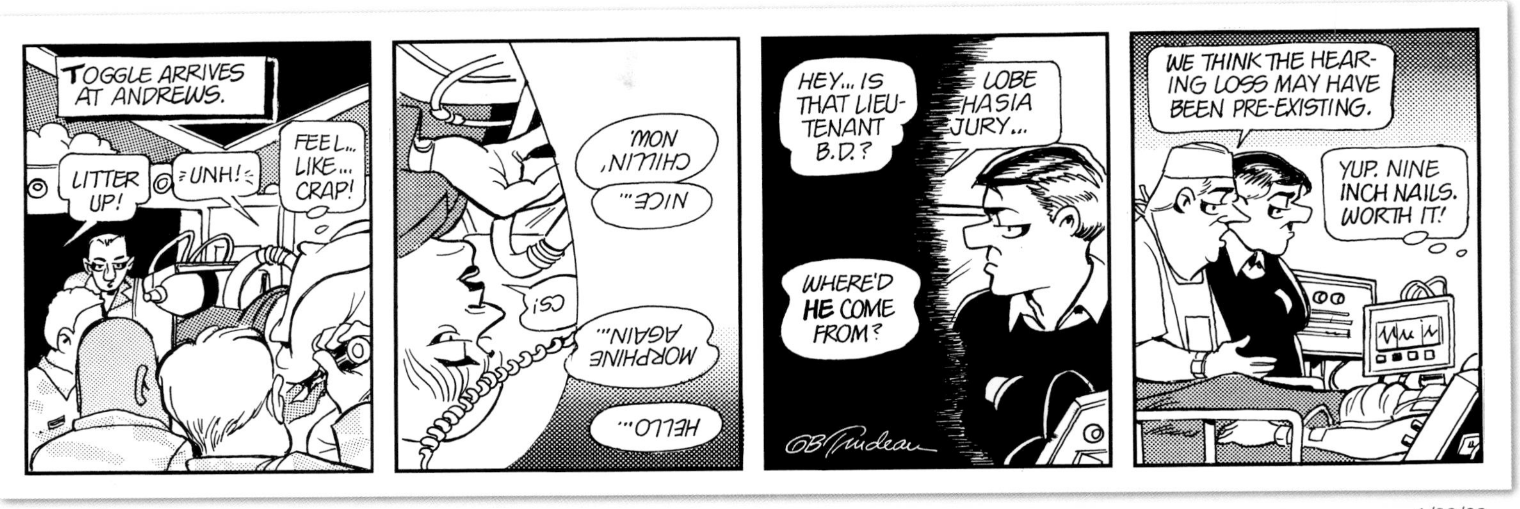
TOGGLE ARRIVES AT ANDREWS.
LITTER UP!
UNH!
FEEL... LIKE... CRAP!
HELLO...
MORPHINE AGAIN...
CSI!
NICE...
CHILLIN' NOW.
HEY... IS THAT LIEUTENANT B.D.?
LOBE HASIA JURY...
WHERE'D HE COME FROM?
WE THINK THE HEARING LOSS MAY HAVE BEEN PRE-EXISTING.
YUP. NINE INCH NAILS. WORTH IT!

1/28/08

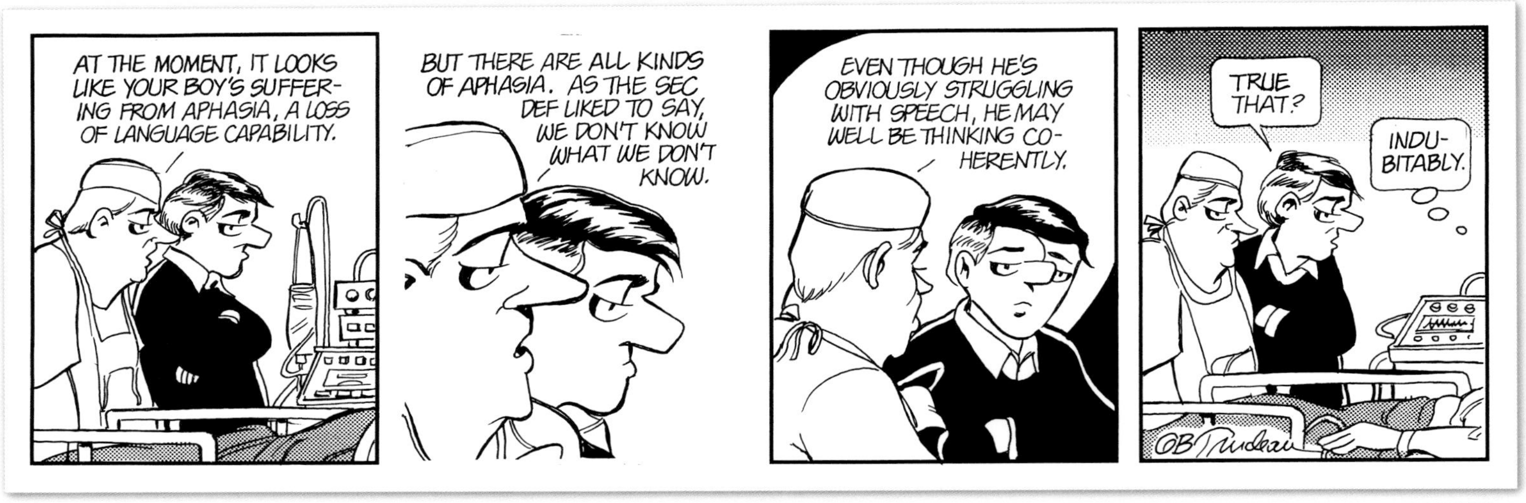
AT THE MOMENT, IT LOOKS LIKE YOUR BOY'S SUFFERING FROM APHASIA, A LOSS OF LANGUAGE CAPABILITY.
BUT THERE ARE ALL KINDS OF APHASIA. AS THE SEC DEF LIKED TO SAY, WE DON'T KNOW WHAT WE DON'T KNOW.
EVEN THOUGH HE'S OBVIOUSLY STRUGGLING WITH SPEECH, HE MAY WELL BE THINKING COHERENTLY.
TRUE THAT?
INDUBITABLY.

1/29/08

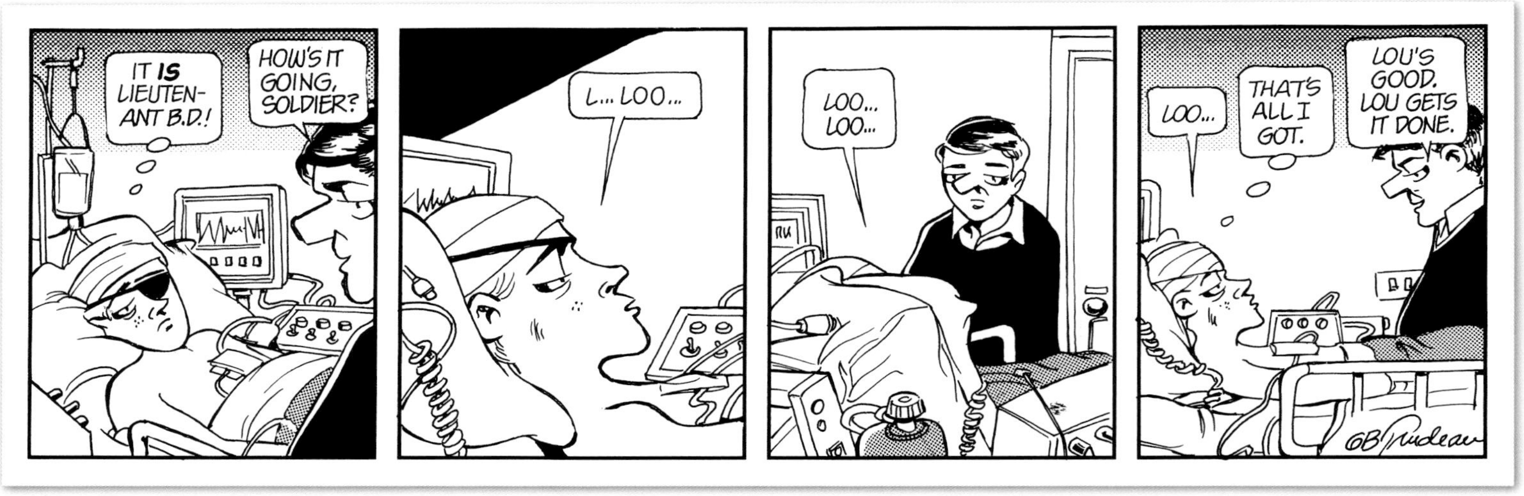
IT IS LIEUTENANT B.D.!
HOW'S IT GOING, SOLDIER?
L... LOO...
LOO... LOO...
LOO...
THAT'S ALL I GOT.
LOU'S GOOD. LOU GETS IT DONE.

1/30/08

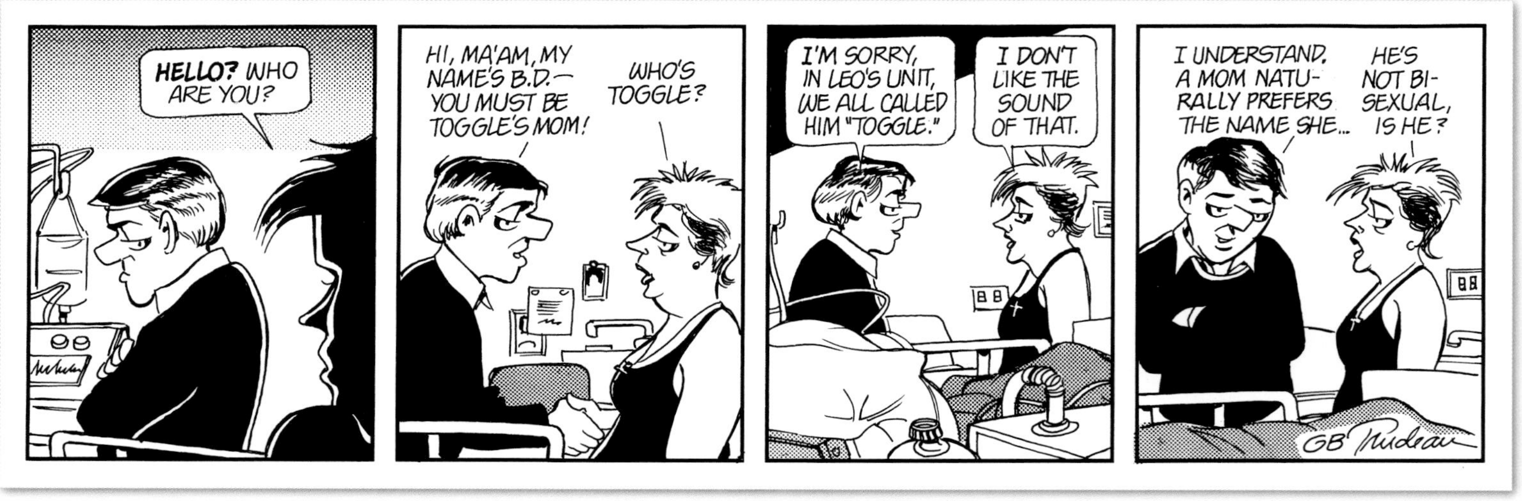
HELLO? WHO ARE YOU?
HI, MA'AM, MY NAME'S B.D.— YOU MUST BE TOGGLE'S MOM!
WHO'S TOGGLE?
I'M SORRY, IN LEO'S UNIT, WE ALL CALLED HIM "TOGGLE."
I DON'T LIKE THE SOUND OF THAT.
I UNDERSTAND. A MOM NATURALLY PREFERS THE NAME SHE...
HE'S NOT BISEXUAL, IS HE?

1/31/08

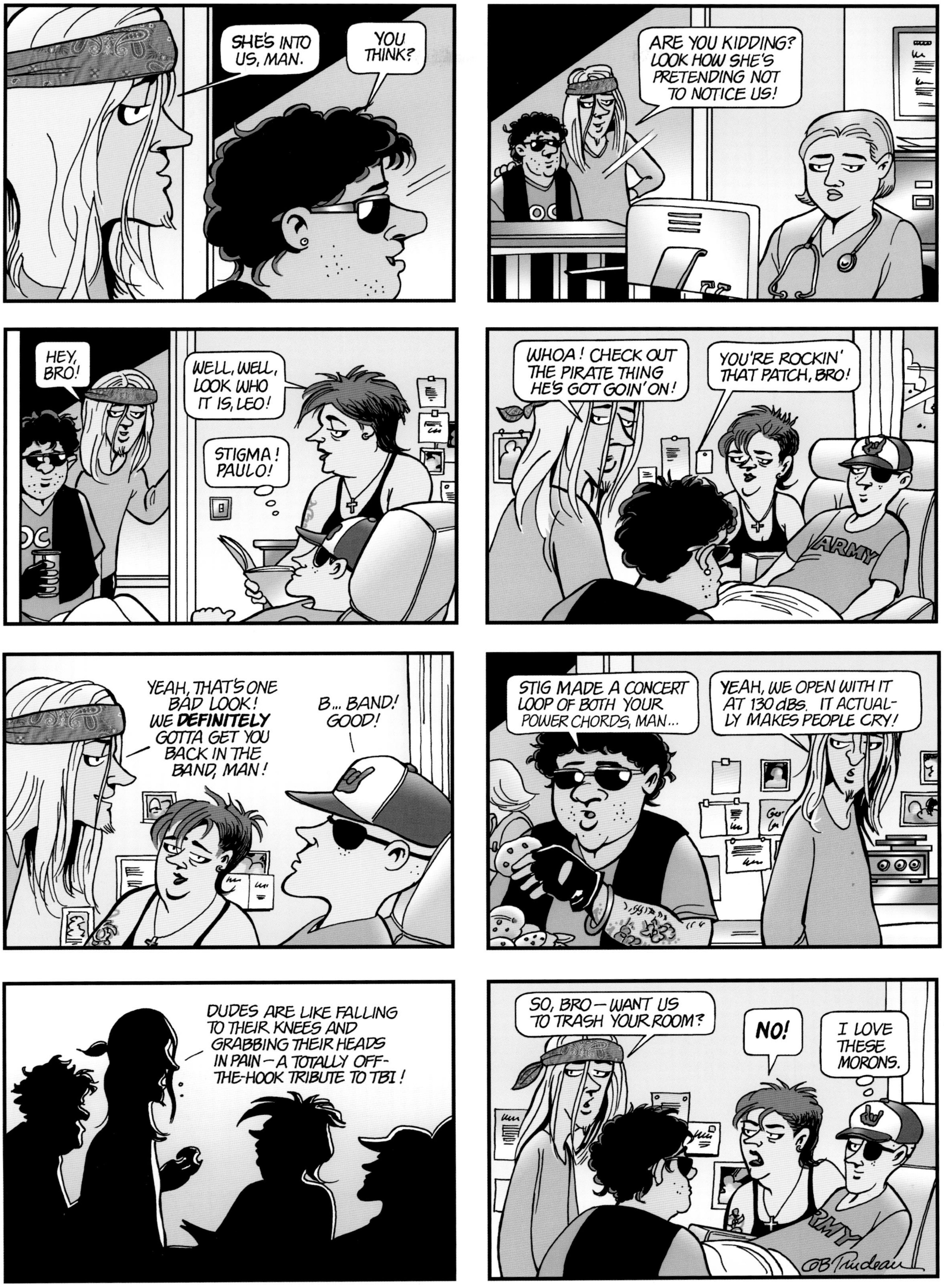

SHE'S INTO US, MAN.
YOU THINK?
ARE YOU KIDDING? LOOK HOW SHE'S PRETENDING NOT TO NOTICE US!
HEY, BRO!
WELL, WELL, LOOK WHO IT IS, LEO!
STIGMA! PAULO!
WHOA! CHECK OUT THE PIRATE THING HE'S GOT GOIN' ON!
YOU'RE ROCKIN' THAT PATCH, BRO!
YEAH, THAT'S ONE BAD LOOK! WE **DEFINITELY** GOTTA GET YOU BACK IN THE BAND, MAN!
B... BAND! GOOD!
STIG MADE A CONCERT LOOP OF BOTH YOUR POWER CHORDS, MAN...
YEAH, WE OPEN WITH IT AT 130 dBs. IT ACTUALLY MAKES PEOPLE CRY!
DUDES ARE LIKE FALLING TO THEIR KNEES AND GRABBING THEIR HEADS IN PAIN— A TOTALLY OFF-THE-HOOK TRIBUTE TO TBI!
SO, BRO— WANT US TO TRASH YOUR ROOM?
NO!
I LOVE THESE MORONS.
GBTrudeau

3/16/08

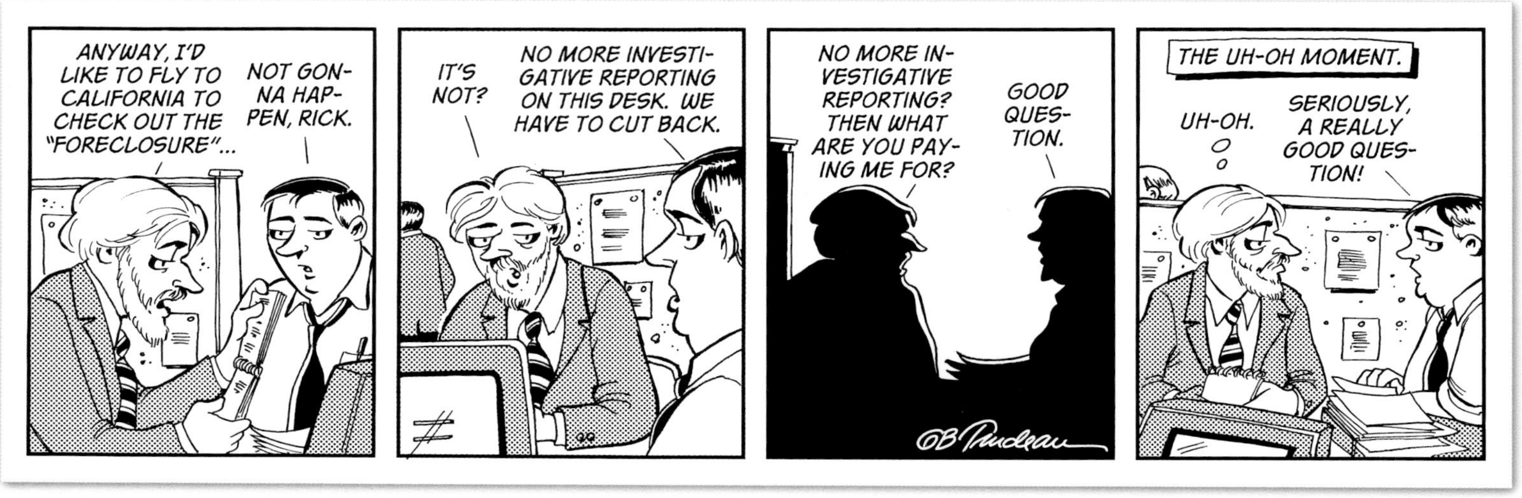
ANYWAY, I'D LIKE TO FLY TO CALIFORNIA TO CHECK OUT THE "FORECLOSURE"...
NOT GONNA HAPPEN, RICK.
IT'S NOT?
NO MORE INVESTIGATIVE REPORTING ON THIS DESK. WE HAVE TO CUT BACK.
NO MORE INVESTIGATIVE REPORTING? THEN WHAT ARE YOU PAYING ME FOR?
GOOD QUESTION.
GB Trudeau
THE UH-OH MOMENT.
UH-OH.
SERIOUSLY, A REALLY GOOD QUESTION!

9/15/08

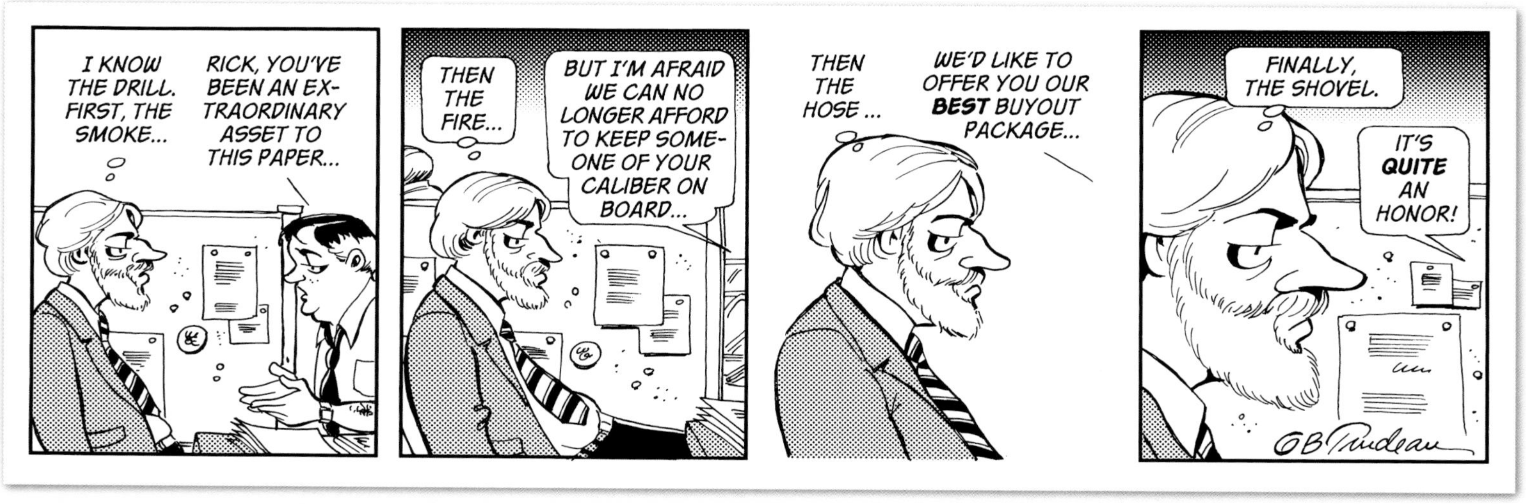
I KNOW THE DRILL. FIRST, THE SMOKE...
RICK, YOU'VE BEEN AN EXTRAORDINARY ASSET TO THIS PAPER...
THEN THE FIRE...
BUT I'M AFRAID WE CAN NO LONGER AFFORD TO KEEP SOMEONE OF YOUR CALIBER ON BOARD...
THEN THE HOSE ...
WE'D LIKE TO OFFER YOU OUR BEST BUYOUT PACKAGE...
FINALLY, THE SHOVEL.
IT'S QUITE AN HONOR!
GB Trudeau

9/16/08

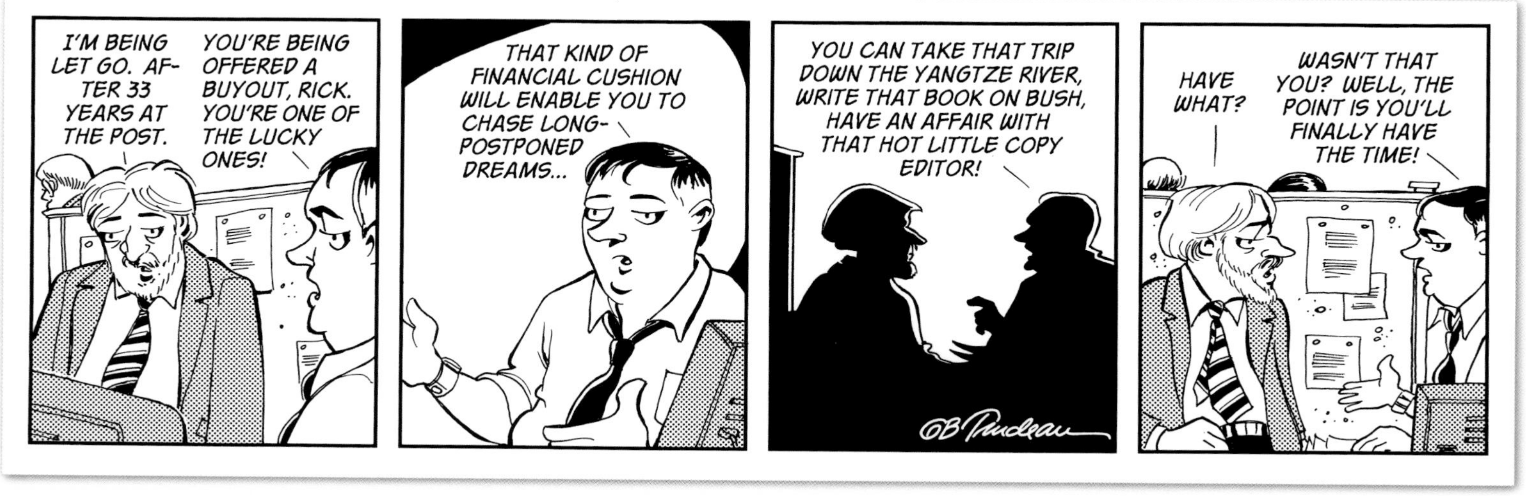
I'M BEING LET GO. AFTER 33 YEARS AT THE POST.
YOU'RE BEING OFFERED A BUYOUT, RICK. YOU'RE ONE OF THE LUCKY ONES!
THAT KIND OF FINANCIAL CUSHION WILL ENABLE YOU TO CHASE LONG-POSTPONED DREAMS...
YOU CAN TAKE THAT TRIP DOWN THE YANGTZE RIVER, WRITE THAT BOOK ON BUSH, HAVE AN AFFAIR WITH THAT HOT LITTLE COPY EDITOR!
GB Trudeau
HAVE WHAT?
WASN'T THAT YOU? WELL, THE POINT IS YOU'LL FINALLY HAVE THE TIME!

9/17/08

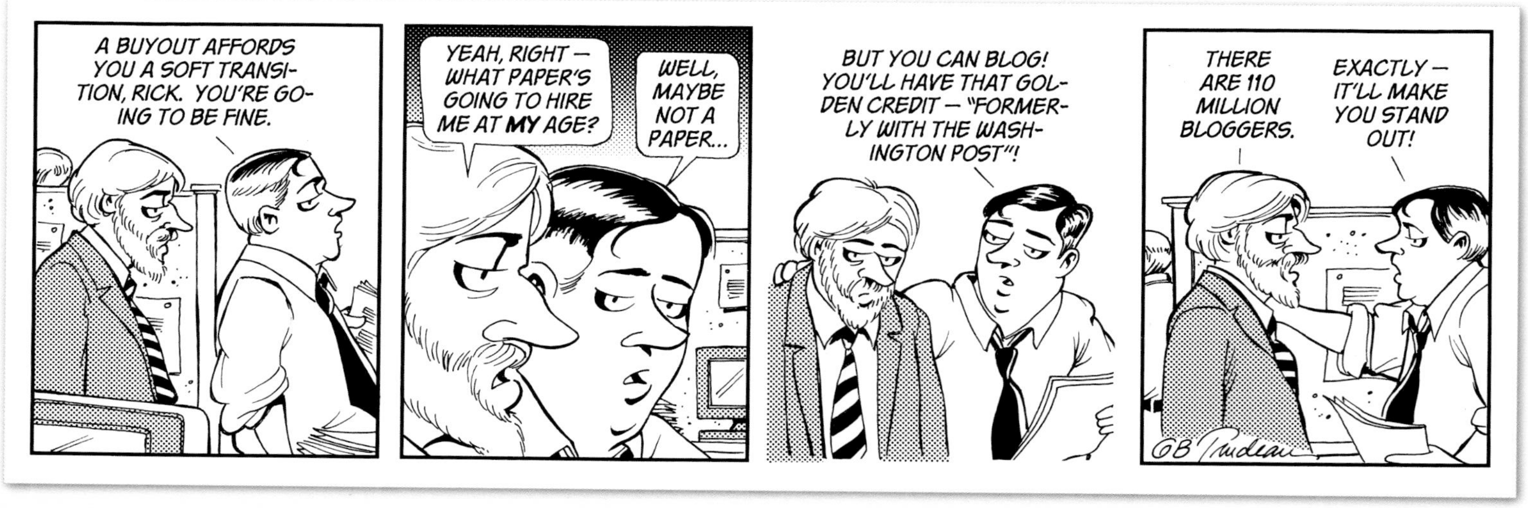
A BUYOUT AFFORDS YOU A SOFT TRANSITION, RICK. YOU'RE GOING TO BE FINE.
YEAH, RIGHT — WHAT PAPER'S GOING TO HIRE ME AT MY AGE?
WELL, MAYBE NOT A PAPER...
BUT YOU CAN BLOG! YOU'LL HAVE THAT GOLDEN CREDIT — "FORMERLY WITH THE WASHINGTON POST"!
THERE ARE 110 MILLION BLOGGERS.
EXACTLY — IT'LL MAKE YOU STAND OUT!
GB Trudeau

9/18/08

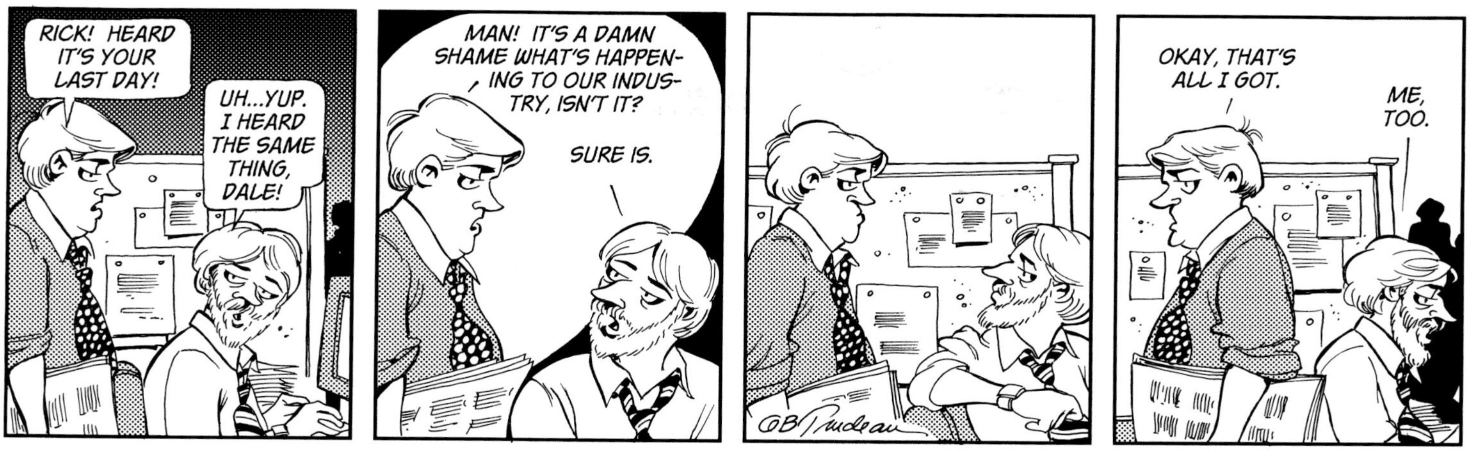
RICK! HEARD IT'S YOUR LAST DAY!
UH...YUP. I HEARD THE SAME THING, DALE!
MAN! IT'S A DAMN SHAME WHAT'S HAPPENING TO OUR INDUSTRY, ISN'T IT?
SURE IS.
OKAY, THAT'S ALL I GOT.
ME, TOO.

9/29/08

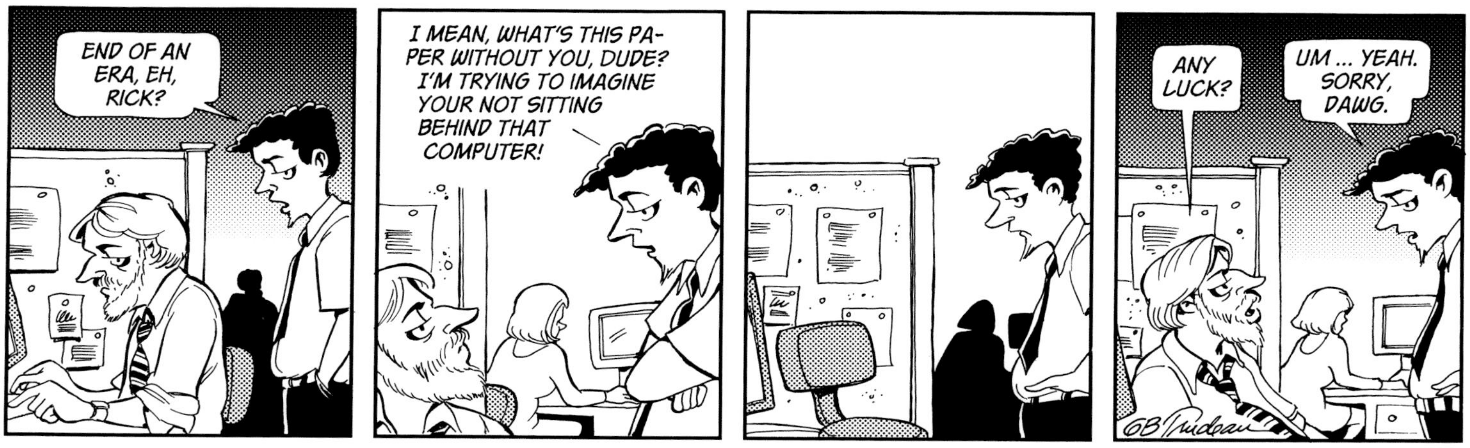
END OF AN ERA, EH, RICK?
I MEAN, WHAT'S THIS PAPER WITHOUT YOU, DUDE? I'M TRYING TO IMAGINE YOUR NOT SITTING BEHIND THAT COMPUTER!
ANY LUCK?
UM ... YEAH. SORRY, DAWG.

9/30/08

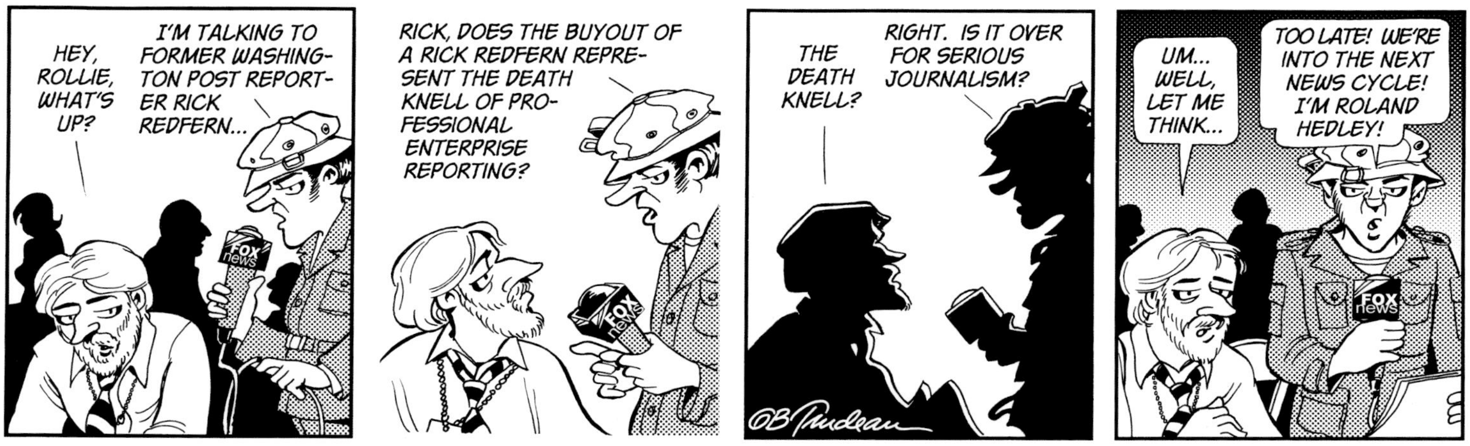
HEY, ROLLIE, WHAT'S UP?
I'M TALKING TO FORMER WASHINGTON POST REPORTER RICK REDFERN...
RICK, DOES THE BUYOUT OF A RICK REDFERN REPRESENT THE DEATH KNELL OF PROFESSIONAL ENTERPRISE REPORTING?
THE DEATH KNELL?
RIGHT. IS IT OVER FOR SERIOUS JOURNALISM?
UM... WELL, LET ME THINK...
TOO LATE! WE'RE INTO THE NEXT NEWS CYCLE! I'M ROLAND HEDLEY!

10/2/08

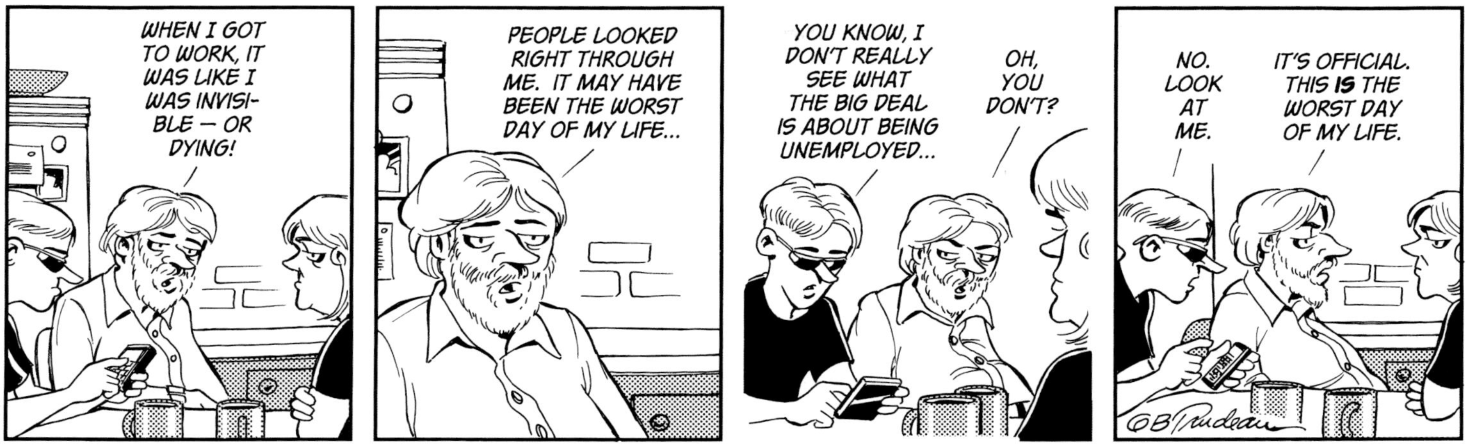
WHEN I GOT TO WORK, IT WAS LIKE I WAS INVISIBLE — OR DYING!
PEOPLE LOOKED RIGHT THROUGH ME. IT MAY HAVE BEEN THE WORST DAY OF MY LIFE...
YOU KNOW, I DON'T REALLY SEE WHAT THE BIG DEAL IS ABOUT BEING UNEMPLOYED...
OH, YOU DON'T?
NO. LOOK AT ME.
IT'S OFFICIAL. THIS **IS** THE WORST DAY OF MY LIFE.

10/3/08

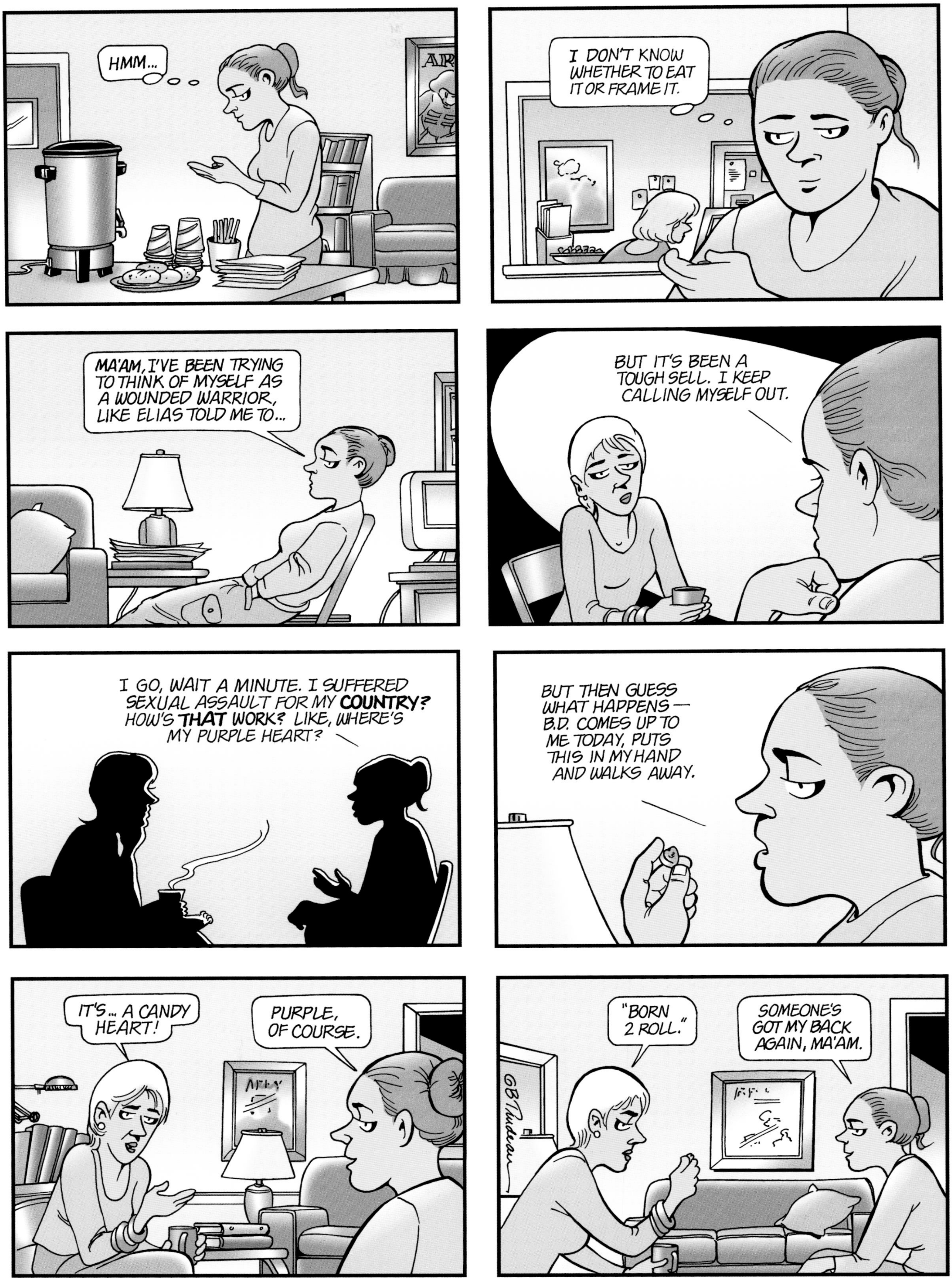
HMM...
I DON'T KNOW WHETHER TO EAT IT OR FRAME IT.
MA'AM, I'VE BEEN TRYING TO THINK OF MYSELF AS A WOUNDED WARRIOR, LIKE ELIAS TOLD ME TO...
BUT IT'S BEEN A TOUGH SELL. I KEEP CALLING MYSELF OUT.
I GO, WAIT A MINUTE. I SUFFERED SEXUAL ASSAULT FOR MY **COUNTRY?** HOW'S **THAT WORK?** LIKE, WHERE'S MY PURPLE HEART?
BUT THEN GUESS WHAT HAPPENS— B.D. COMES UP TO ME TODAY, PUTS THIS IN MY HAND AND WALKS AWAY.
IT'S... A CANDY HEART!
PURPLE, OF COURSE.
"BORN 2 ROLL."
SOMEONE'S GOT MY BACK AGAIN, MA'AM.
GB Trudeau

1/20/08

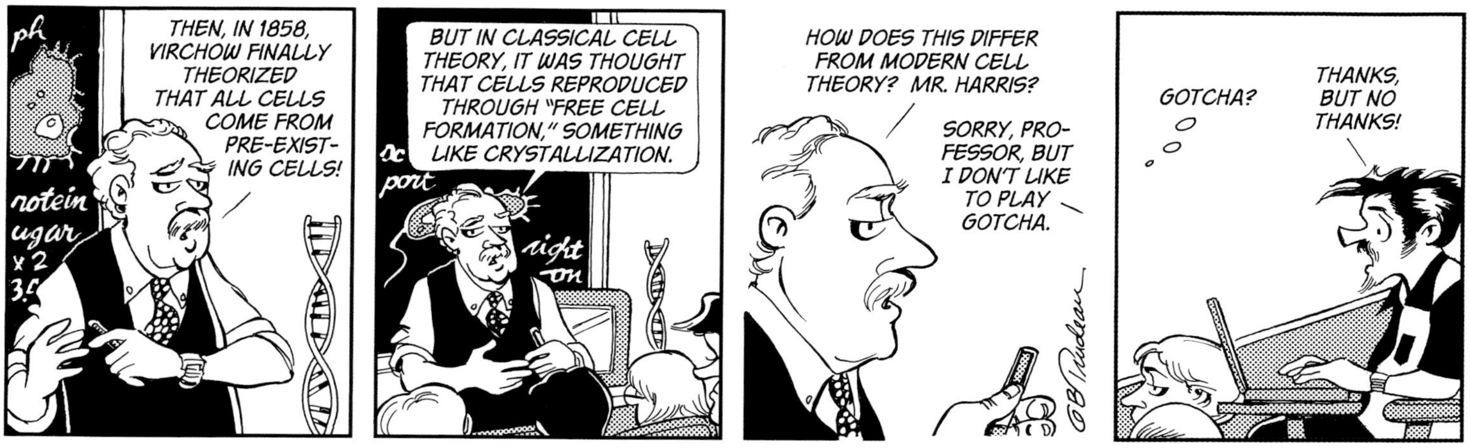
THEN, IN 1858, VIRCHOW FINALLY THEORIZED THAT ALL CELLS COME FROM PRE-EXISTING CELLS!
BUT IN CLASSICAL CELL THEORY, IT WAS THOUGHT THAT CELLS REPRODUCED THROUGH "FREE CELL FORMATION," SOMETHING LIKE CRYSTALLIZATION.
HOW DOES THIS DIFFER FROM MODERN CELL THEORY? MR. HARRIS?
SORRY, PROFESSOR, BUT I DON'T LIKE TO PLAY GOTCHA.
GOTCHA?
THANKS, BUT NO THANKS!
GB Trudeau

10/20/08

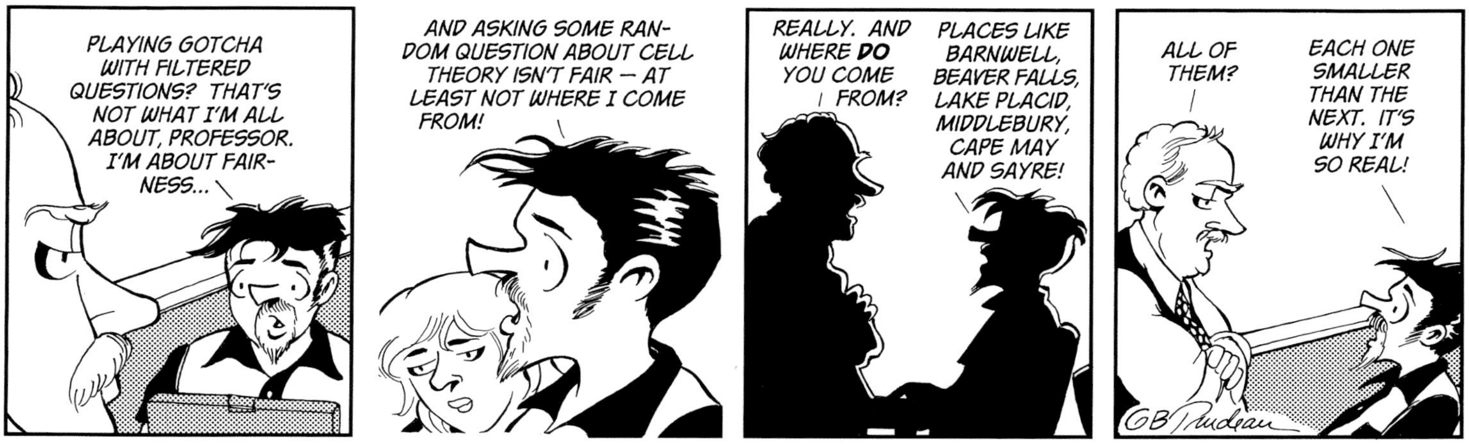
PLAYING GOTCHA WITH FILTERED QUESTIONS? THAT'S NOT WHAT I'M ALL ABOUT, PROFESSOR. I'M ABOUT FAIRNESS...
AND ASKING SOME RANDOM QUESTION ABOUT CELL THEORY ISN'T FAIR — AT LEAST NOT WHERE I COME FROM!
REALLY. AND WHERE **DO** YOU COME FROM?
PLACES LIKE BARNWELL, BEAVER FALLS, LAKE PLACID, MIDDLEBURY, CAPE MAY AND SAYRE!
ALL OF THEM?
EACH ONE SMALLER THAN THE NEXT. IT'S WHY I'M SO REAL!
GB Trudeau

10/21/08

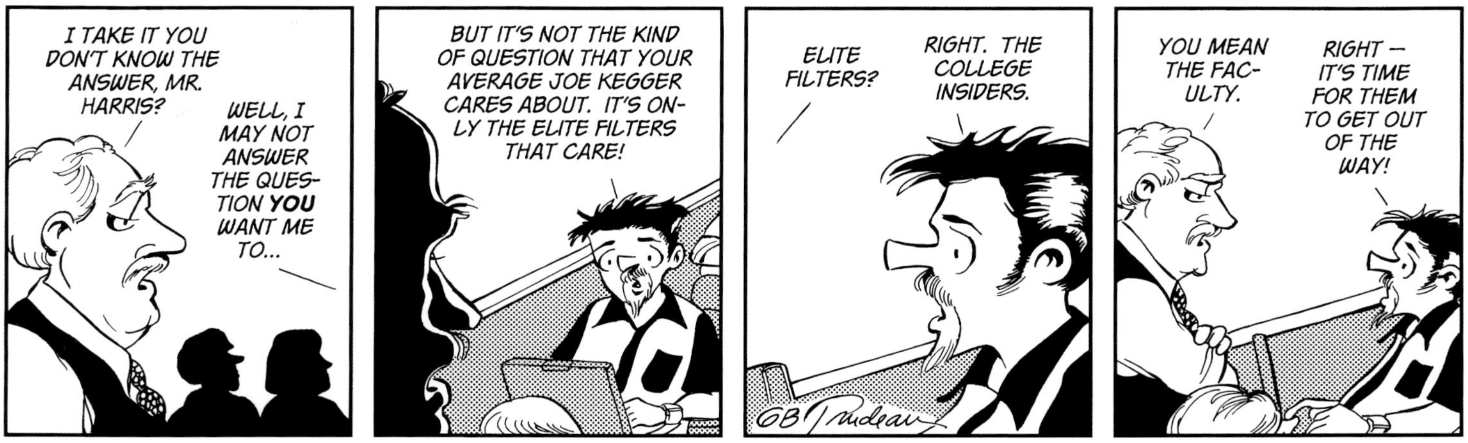
I TAKE IT YOU DON'T KNOW THE ANSWER, MR. HARRIS?
WELL, I MAY NOT ANSWER THE QUESTION **YOU** WANT ME TO...
BUT IT'S NOT THE KIND OF QUESTION THAT YOUR AVERAGE JOE KEGGER CARES ABOUT. IT'S ONLY THE ELITE FILTERS THAT CARE!
ELITE FILTERS?
RIGHT. THE COLLEGE INSIDERS.
YOU MEAN THE FACULTY.
RIGHT — IT'S TIME FOR THEM TO GET OUT OF THE WAY!
GB Trudeau

10/22/08

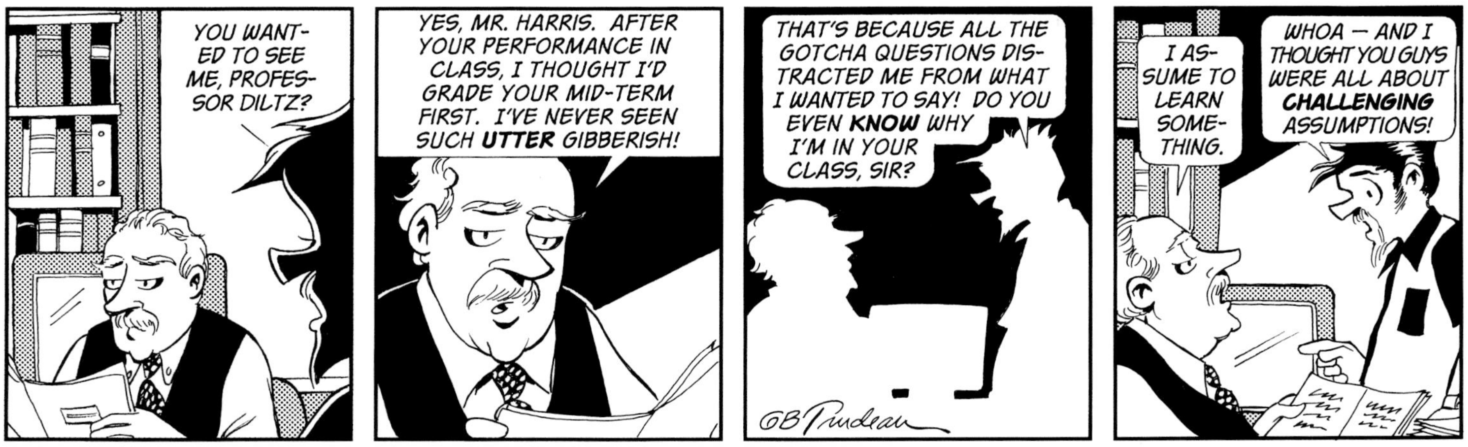
YOU WANTED TO SEE ME, PROFESSOR DILTZ?
YES, MR. HARRIS. AFTER YOUR PERFORMANCE IN CLASS, I THOUGHT I'D GRADE YOUR MID-TERM FIRST. I'VE NEVER SEEN SUCH **UTTER** GIBBERISH!
THAT'S BECAUSE ALL THE GOTCHA QUESTIONS DISTRACTED ME FROM WHAT I WANTED TO SAY! DO YOU EVEN **KNOW** WHY I'M IN YOUR CLASS, SIR?
I ASSUME TO LEARN SOMETHING.
WHOA — AND I THOUGHT YOU GUYS WERE ALL ABOUT **CHALLENGING** ASSUMPTIONS!
GB Trudeau

10/23/08

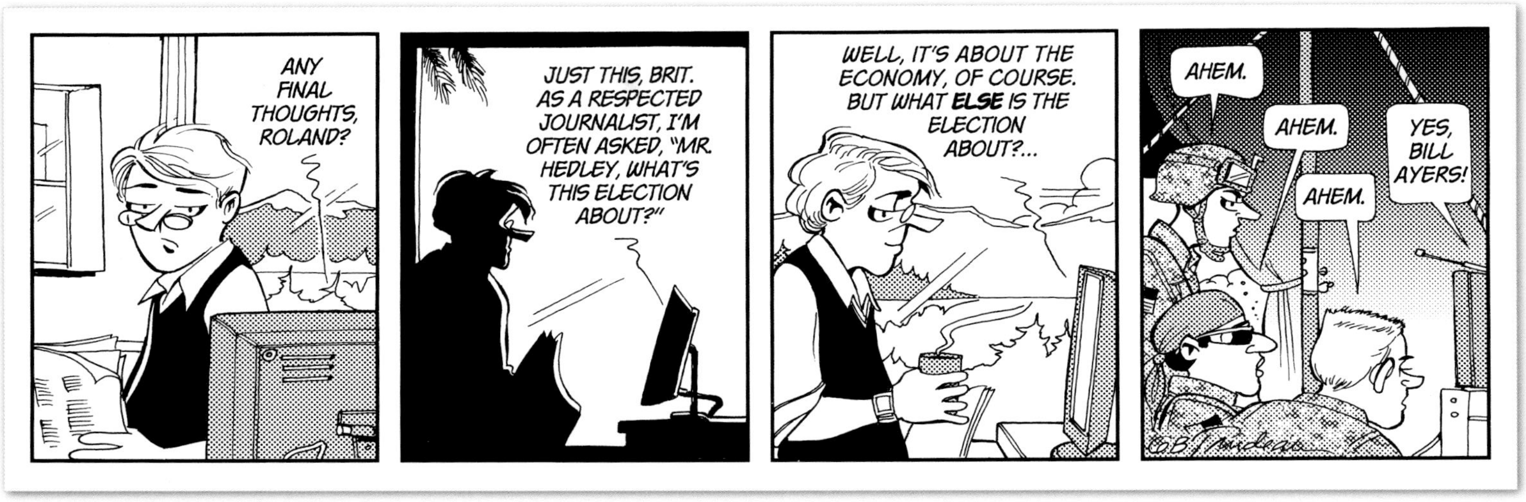

ANY FINAL THOUGHTS, ROLAND?
JUST THIS, BRIT. AS A RESPECTED JOURNALIST, I'M OFTEN ASKED, "MR. HEDLEY, WHAT'S THIS ELECTION ABOUT?"
WELL, IT'S ABOUT THE ECONOMY, OF COURSE. BUT WHAT **ELSE** IS THE ELECTION ABOUT?...
AHEM.
AHEM.
YES, BILL AYERS!
AHEM.

11/3/08

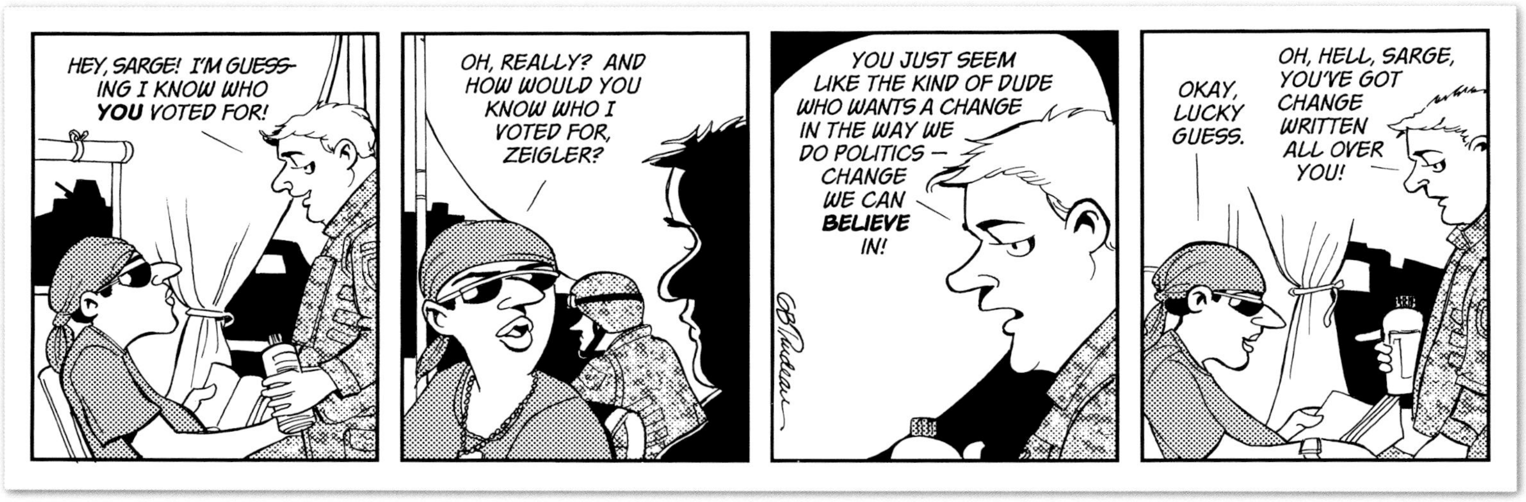

HEY, SARGE! I'M GUESSING I KNOW WHO **YOU** VOTED FOR!
OH, REALLY? AND HOW WOULD YOU KNOW WHO I VOTED FOR, ZEIGLER?
YOU JUST SEEM LIKE THE KIND OF DUDE WHO WANTS A CHANGE IN THE WAY WE DO POLITICS — CHANGE WE CAN **BELIEVE** IN!
OKAY, LUCKY GUESS.
OH, HELL, SARGE, YOU'VE GOT CHANGE WRITTEN ALL OVER YOU!

11/4/08

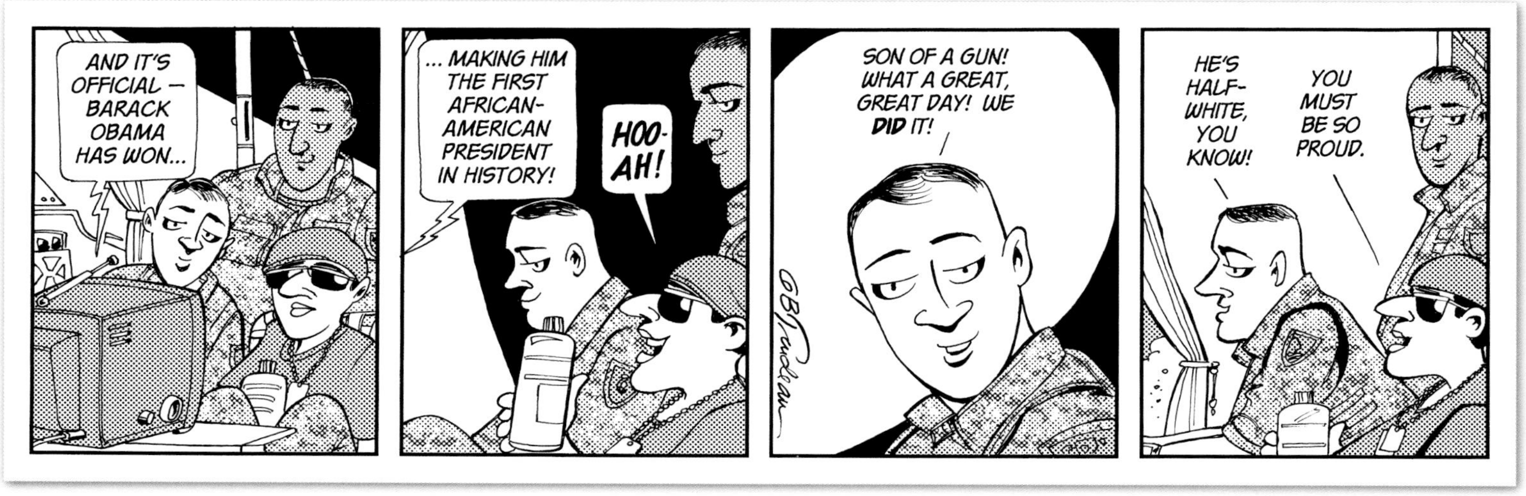

AND IT'S OFFICIAL — BARACK OBAMA HAS WON...
... MAKING HIM THE FIRST AFRICAN-AMERICAN PRESIDENT IN HISTORY!
HOO-AH!
SON OF A GUN! WHAT A GREAT, GREAT DAY! WE **DID** IT!
HE'S HALF-WHITE, YOU KNOW!
YOU MUST BE SO PROUD.

11/5/08

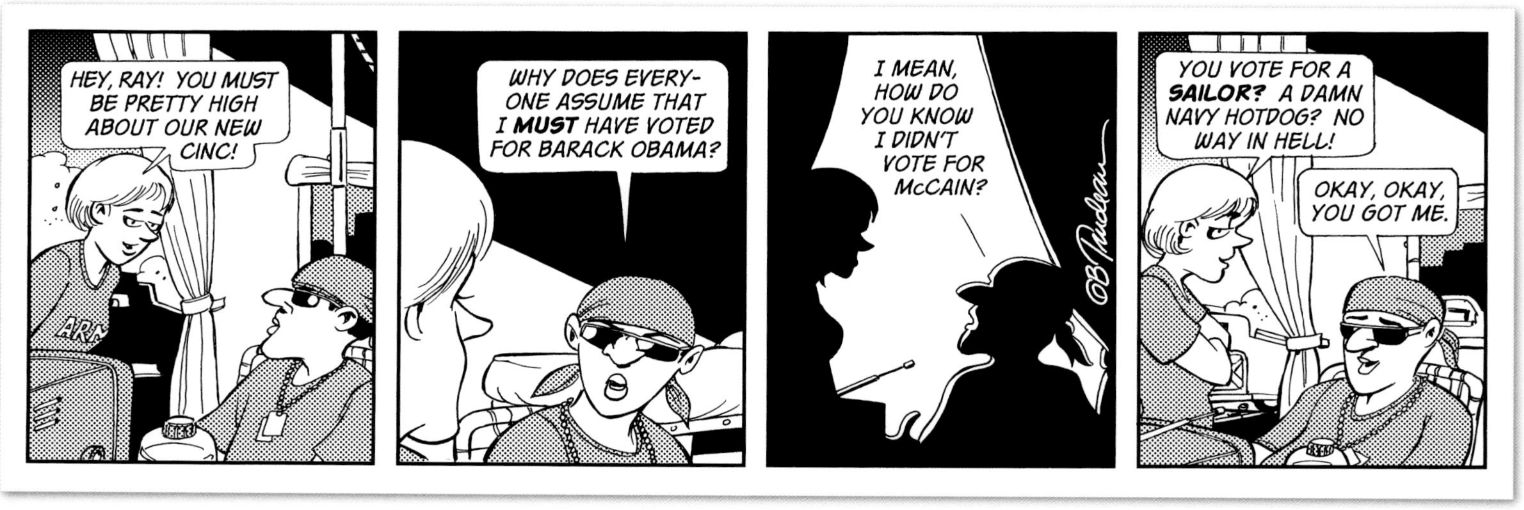

HEY, RAY! YOU MUST BE PRETTY HIGH ABOUT OUR NEW CINC!
WHY DOES EVERYONE ASSUME THAT I **MUST** HAVE VOTED FOR BARACK OBAMA?
I MEAN, HOW DO YOU KNOW I DIDN'T VOTE FOR McCAIN?
YOU VOTE FOR A **SAILOR?** A DAMN NAVY HOTDOG? NO WAY IN HELL!
OKAY, OKAY, YOU GOT ME.

11/7/08

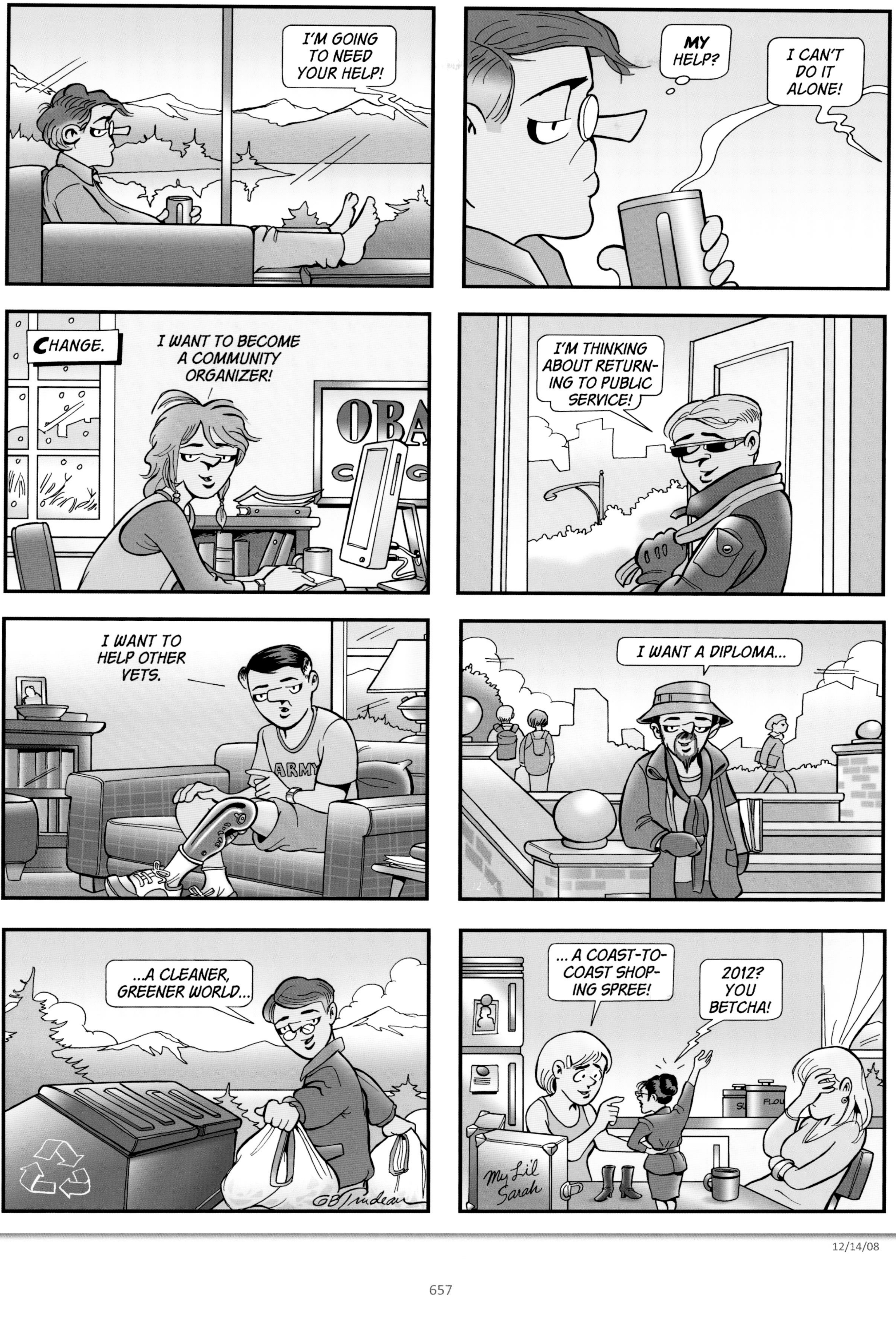
I'M GOING TO NEED YOUR HELP!
MY HELP?
I CAN'T DO IT ALONE!
CHANGE.
I WANT TO BECOME A COMMUNITY ORGANIZER!
I'M THINKING ABOUT RETURNING TO PUBLIC SERVICE!
I WANT TO HELP OTHER VETS.
ARMY
I WANT A DIPLOMA...
...A CLEANER, GREENER WORLD...
GBTrudeau
... A COAST-TO-COAST SHOPPING SPREE!
2012? YOU BETCHA!
My Lil Sarah

12/14/08

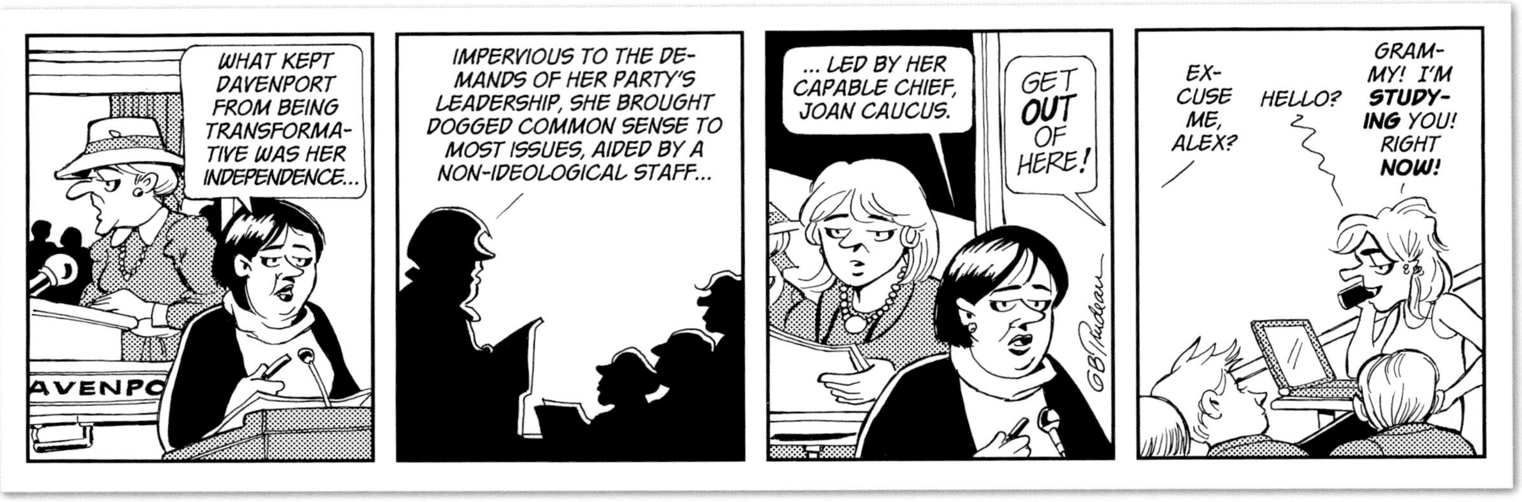
WHAT KEPT DAVENPORT FROM BEING TRANSFORMATIVE WAS HER INDEPENDENCE...
AVENPO
IMPERVIOUS TO THE DEMANDS OF HER PARTY'S LEADERSHIP, SHE BROUGHT DOGGED COMMON SENSE TO MOST ISSUES, AIDED BY A NON-IDEOLOGICAL STAFF...
... LED BY HER CAPABLE CHIEF, JOAN CAUCUS.
GET OUT OF HERE!
EXCUSE ME, ALEX?
HELLO?
GRAMMY! I'M STUDYING YOU! RIGHT NOW!

11/13/08

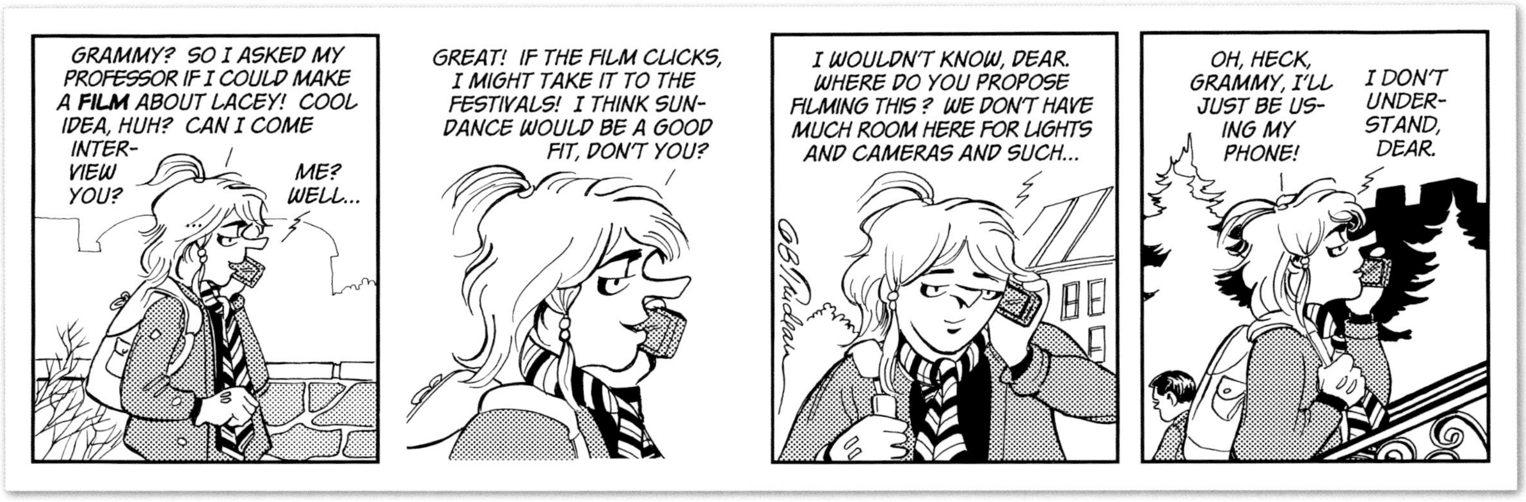
GRAMMY? SO I ASKED MY PROFESSOR IF I COULD MAKE A FILM ABOUT LACEY! COOL IDEA, HUH? CAN I COME INTERVIEW YOU?
ME? WELL...
GREAT! IF THE FILM CLICKS, I MIGHT TAKE IT TO THE FESTIVALS! I THINK SUNDANCE WOULD BE A GOOD FIT, DON'T YOU?
I WOULDN'T KNOW, DEAR. WHERE DO YOU PROPOSE FILMING THIS? WE DON'T HAVE MUCH ROOM HERE FOR LIGHTS AND CAMERAS AND SUCH...
OH, HECK, GRAMMY, I'LL JUST BE USING MY PHONE!
I DON'T UNDERSTAND, DEAR.

11/14/08

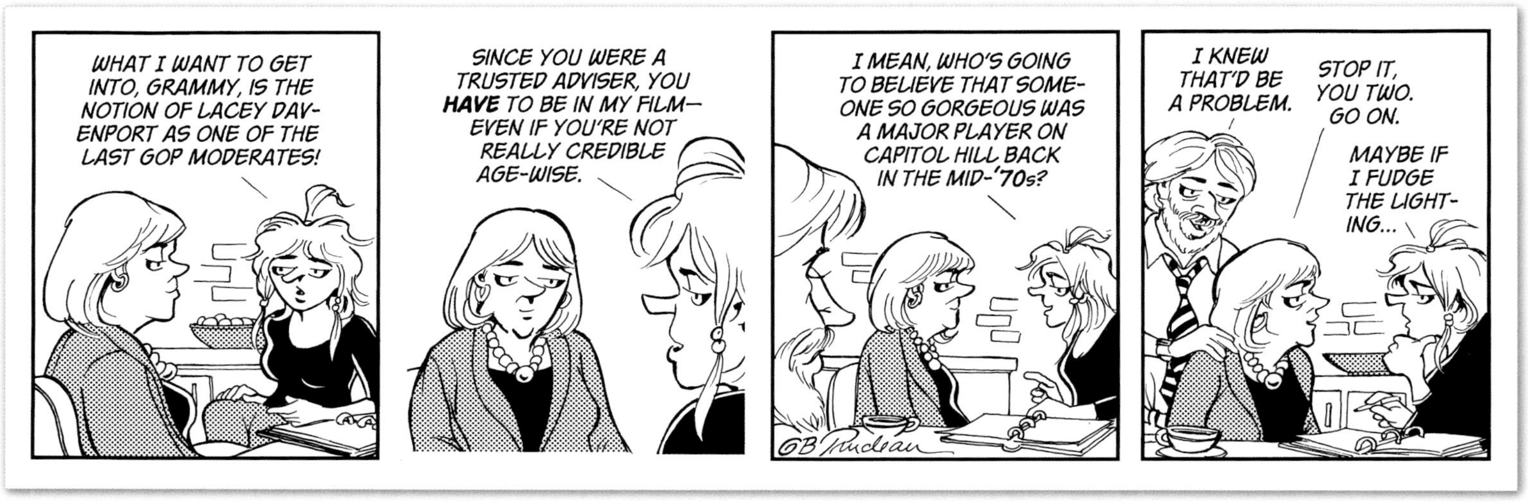
WHAT I WANT TO GET INTO, GRAMMY, IS THE NOTION OF LACEY DAVENPORT AS ONE OF THE LAST GOP MODERATES!
SINCE YOU WERE A TRUSTED ADVISER, YOU HAVE TO BE IN MY FILM— EVEN IF YOU'RE NOT REALLY CREDIBLE AGE-WISE.
I MEAN, WHO'S GOING TO BELIEVE THAT SOMEONE SO GORGEOUS WAS A MAJOR PLAYER ON CAPITOL HILL BACK IN THE MID-'70s?
I KNEW THAT'D BE A PROBLEM.
STOP IT, YOU TWO. GO ON.
MAYBE IF I FUDGE THE LIGHTING...

11/17/08

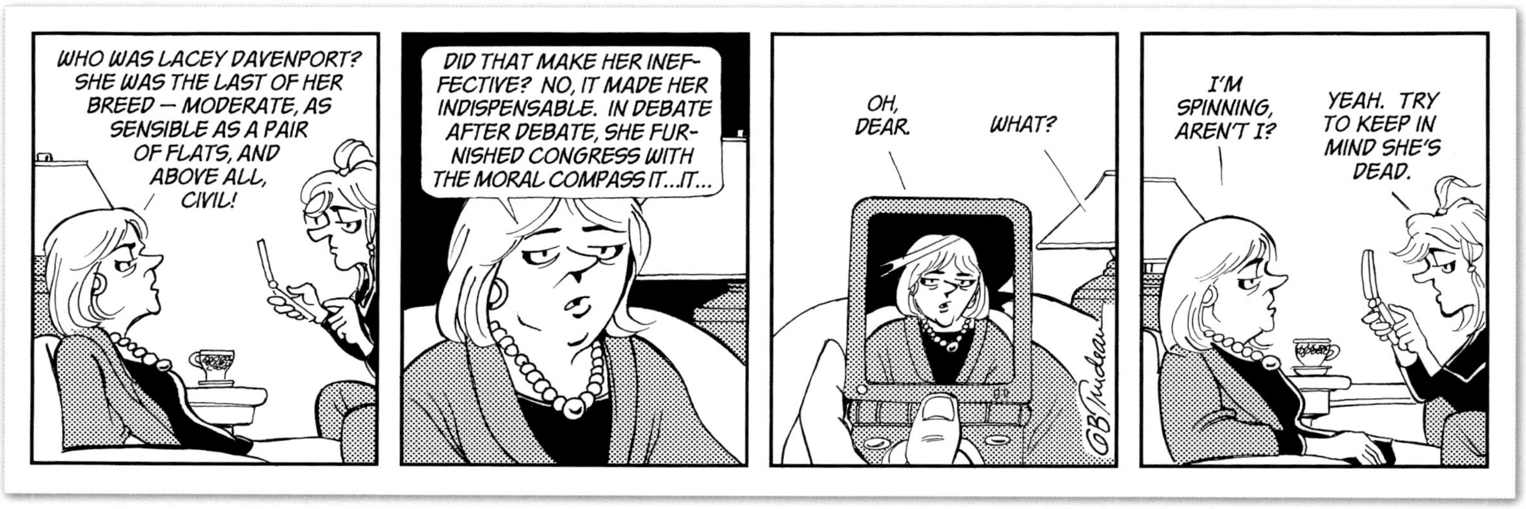
WHO WAS LACEY DAVENPORT? SHE WAS THE LAST OF HER BREED — MODERATE, AS SENSIBLE AS A PAIR OF FLATS, AND ABOVE ALL, CIVIL!
DID THAT MAKE HER INEFFECTIVE? NO, IT MADE HER INDISPENSABLE. IN DEBATE AFTER DEBATE, SHE FURNISHED CONGRESS WITH THE MORAL COMPASS IT...IT...
OH, DEAR.
WHAT?
I'M SPINNING, AREN'T I?
YEAH. TRY TO KEEP IN MIND SHE'S DEAD.

11/19/08

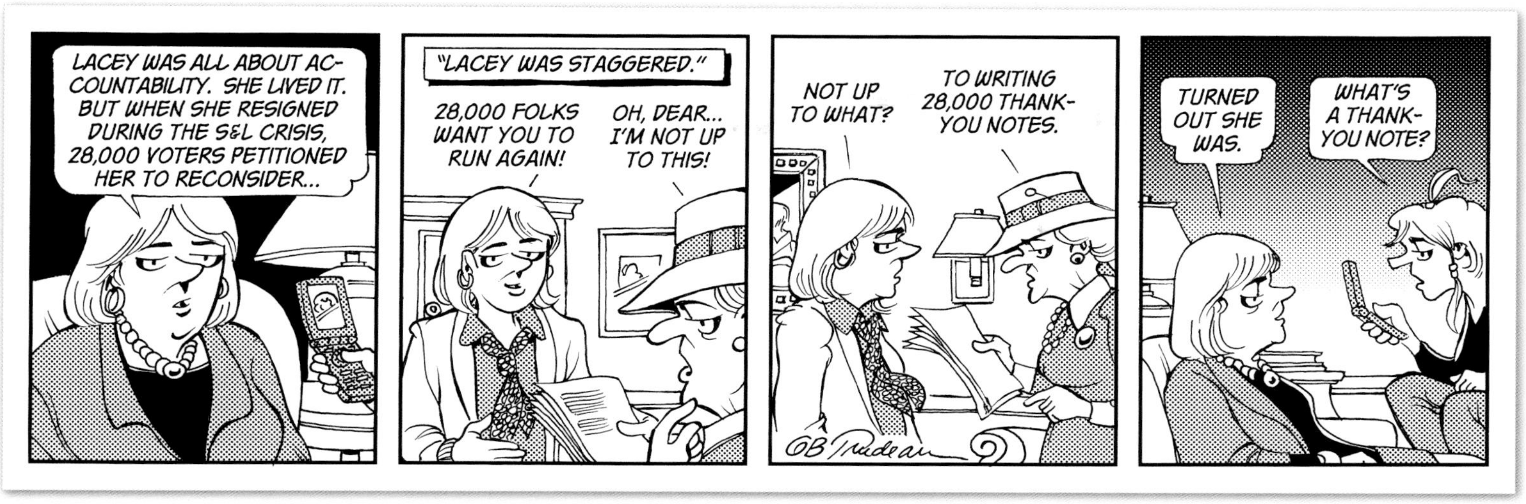
LACEY WAS ALL ABOUT ACCOUNTABILITY. SHE LIVED IT. BUT WHEN SHE RESIGNED DURING THE S&L CRISIS, 28,000 VOTERS PETITIONED HER TO RECONSIDER...
"LACEY WAS STAGGERED."
28,000 FOLKS WANT YOU TO RUN AGAIN!
OH, DEAR... I'M NOT UP TO THIS!
NOT UP TO WHAT?
TO WRITING 28,000 THANK-YOU NOTES.
TURNED OUT SHE WAS.
WHAT'S A THANK-YOU NOTE?

11/21/08

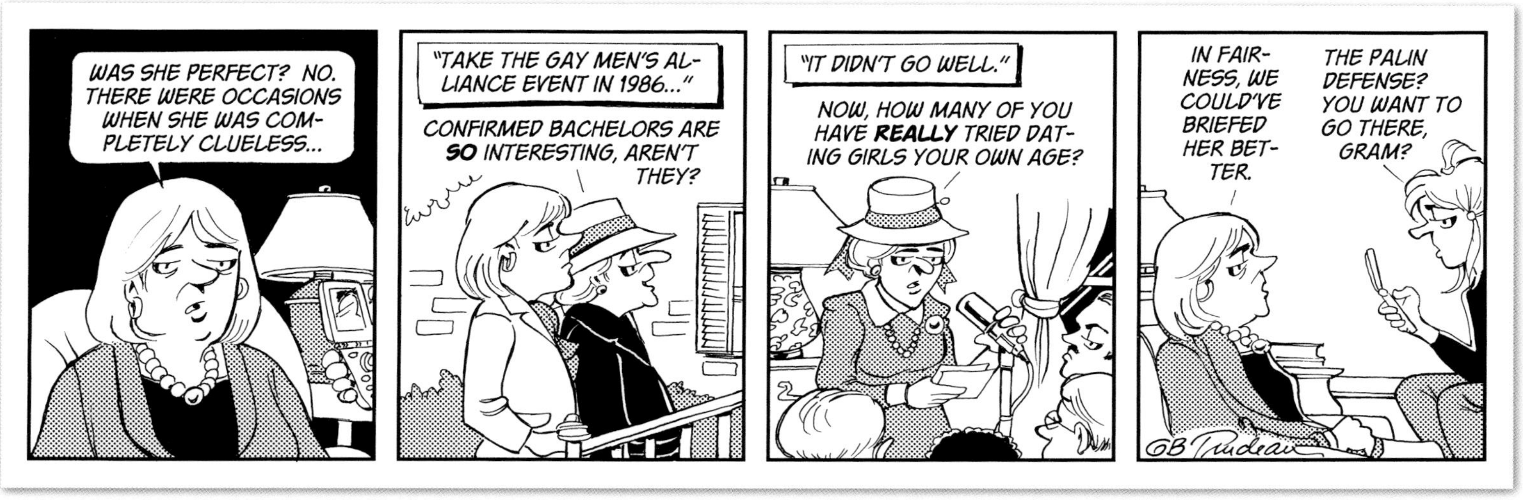
WAS SHE PERFECT? NO. THERE WERE OCCASIONS WHEN SHE WAS COMPLETELY CLUELESS...
"TAKE THE GAY MEN'S ALLIANCE EVENT IN 1986..."
CONFIRMED BACHELORS ARE **SO** INTERESTING, AREN'T THEY?
"IT DIDN'T GO WELL."
NOW, HOW MANY OF YOU HAVE **REALLY** TRIED DATING GIRLS YOUR OWN AGE?
IN FAIRNESS, WE COULD'VE BRIEFED HER BETTER.
THE PALIN DEFENSE? YOU WANT TO GO THERE, GRAM?

11/22/08

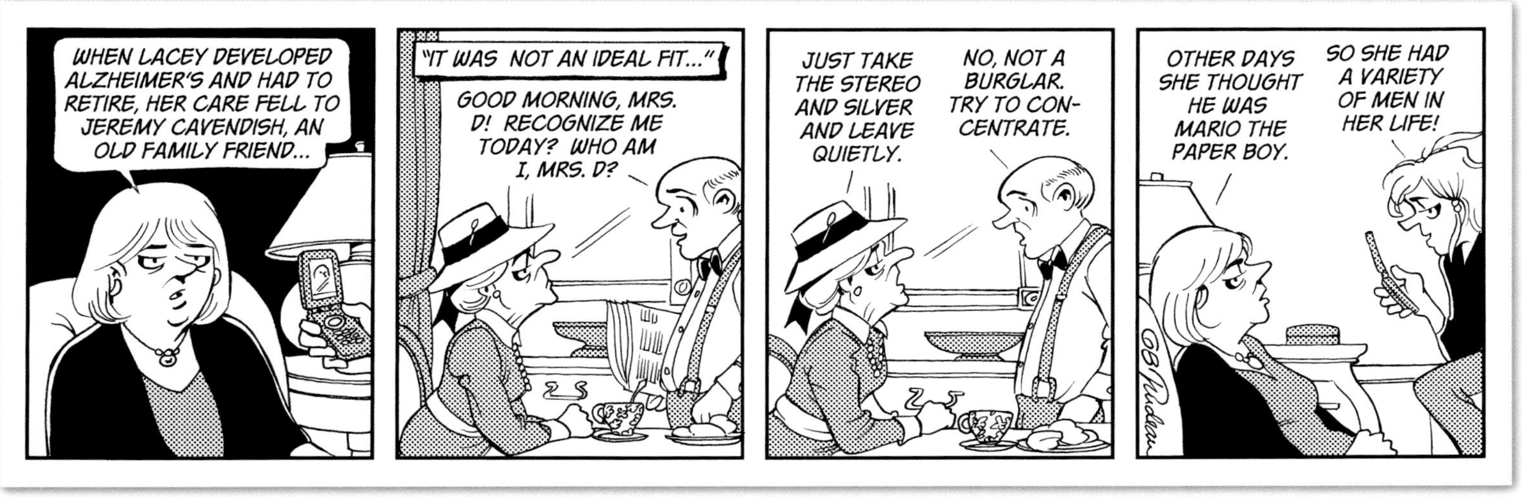
WHEN LACEY DEVELOPED ALZHEIMER'S AND HAD TO RETIRE, HER CARE FELL TO JEREMY CAVENDISH, AN OLD FAMILY FRIEND...
"IT WAS NOT AN IDEAL FIT..."
GOOD MORNING, MRS. D! RECOGNIZE ME TODAY? WHO AM I, MRS. D?
JUST TAKE THE STEREO AND SILVER AND LEAVE QUIETLY.
NO, NOT A BURGLAR. TRY TO CONCENTRATE.
OTHER DAYS SHE THOUGHT HE WAS MARIO THE PAPER BOY.
SO SHE HAD A VARIETY OF MEN IN HER LIFE!

12/11/08

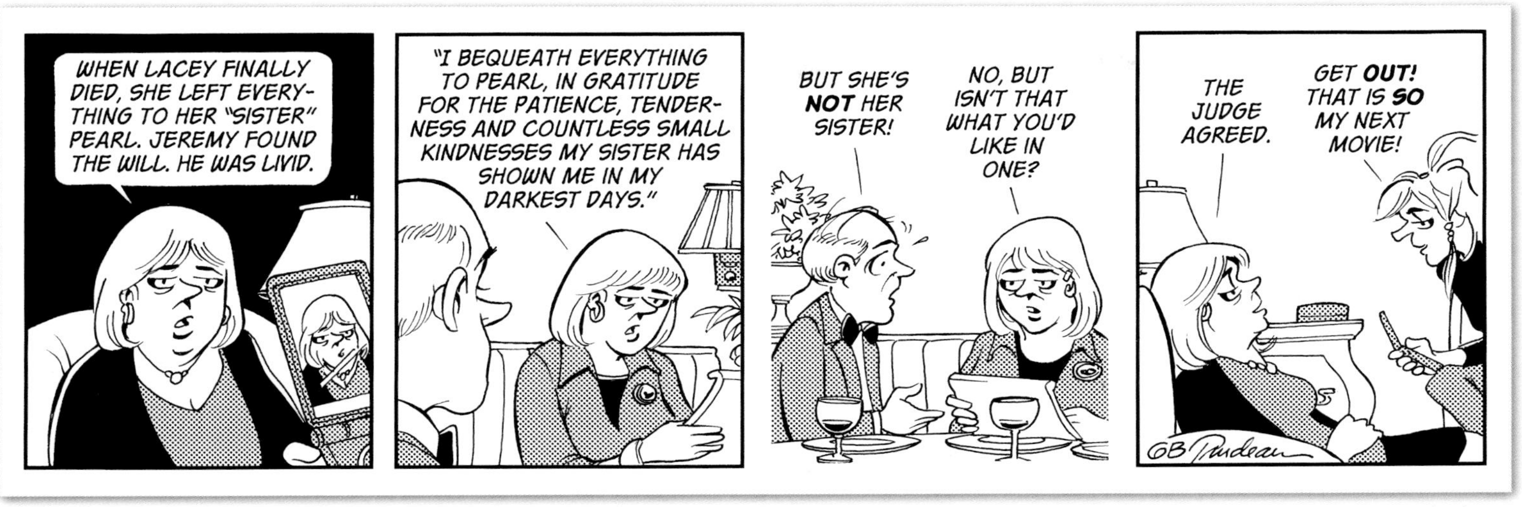
WHEN LACEY FINALLY DIED, SHE LEFT EVERYTHING TO HER "SISTER" PEARL. JEREMY FOUND THE WILL. HE WAS LIVID.
"I BEQUEATH EVERYTHING TO PEARL, IN GRATITUDE FOR THE PATIENCE, TENDERNESS AND COUNTLESS SMALL KINDNESSES MY SISTER HAS SHOWN ME IN MY DARKEST DAYS."
BUT SHE'S **NOT** HER SISTER!
NO, BUT ISN'T THAT WHAT YOU'D LIKE IN ONE?
THE JUDGE AGREED.
GET **OUT!** THAT IS **SO** MY NEXT MOVIE!

12/13/08

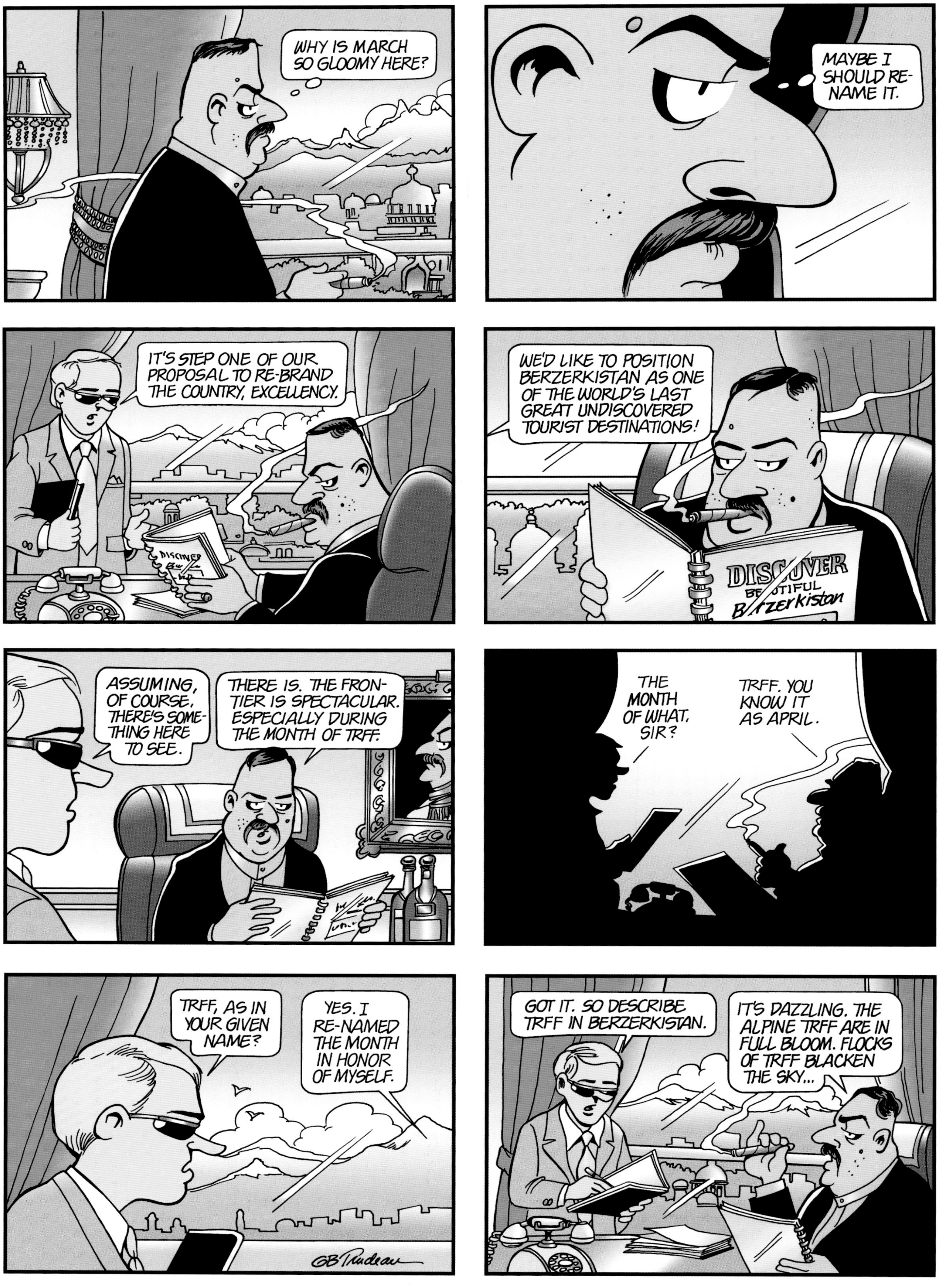

WHY IS MARCH SO GLOOMY HERE?
MAYBE I SHOULD RE-NAME IT.
IT'S STEP ONE OF OUR PROPOSAL TO RE-BRAND THE COUNTRY, EXCELLENCY.
WE'D LIKE TO POSITION BERZERKISTAN AS ONE OF THE WORLD'S LAST GREAT UNDISCOVERED TOURIST DESTINATIONS!
DISCOVER BEAUTIFUL Berzerkistan
ASSUMING, OF COURSE, THERE'S SOMETHING HERE TO SEE.
THERE IS. THE FRONTIER IS SPECTACULAR. ESPECIALLY DURING THE MONTH OF TRFF.
THE MONTH OF WHAT, SIR?
TRFF. YOU KNOW IT AS APRIL.
TRFF, AS IN YOUR GIVEN NAME?
YES. I RE-NAMED THE MONTH IN HONOR OF MYSELF.
GB Trudeau
GOT IT. SO DESCRIBE TRFF IN BERZERKISTAN.
IT'S DAZZLING. THE ALPINE TRFF ARE IN FULL BLOOM. FLOCKS OF TRFF BLACKEN THE SKY...

3/9/08

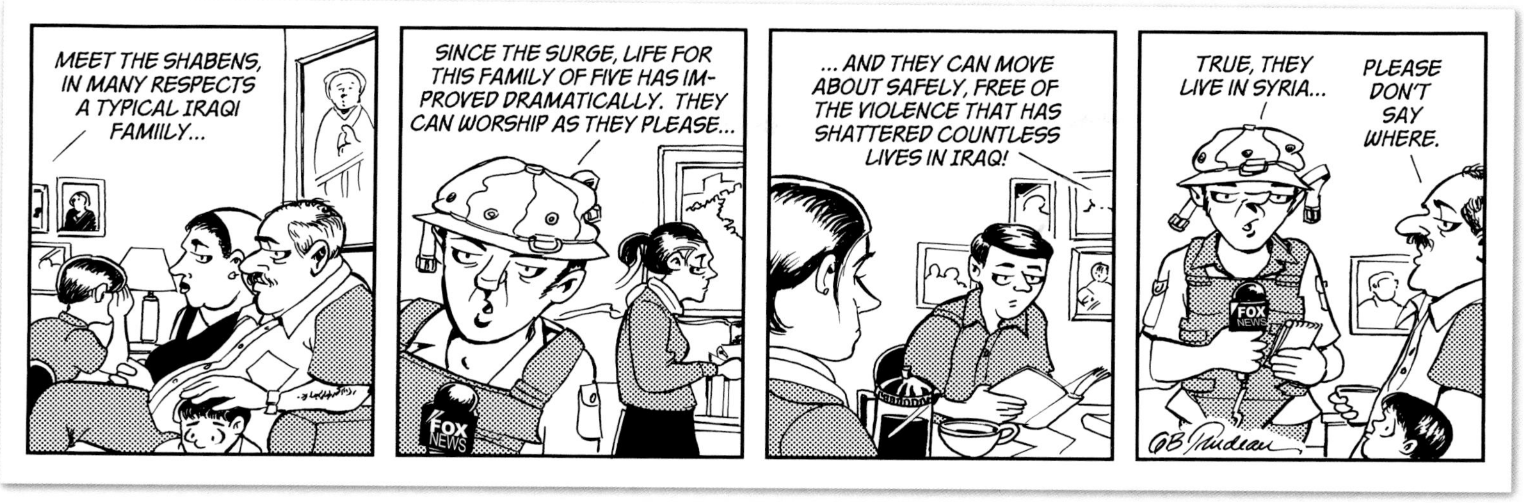
MEET THE SHABENS, IN MANY RESPECTS A TYPICAL IRAQI FAMIILY...
SINCE THE SURGE, LIFE FOR THIS FAMILY OF FIVE HAS IMPROVED DRAMATICALLY. THEY CAN WORSHIP AS THEY PLEASE...
... AND THEY CAN MOVE ABOUT SAFELY, FREE OF THE VIOLENCE THAT HAS SHATTERED COUNTLESS LIVES IN IRAQ!
TRUE, THEY LIVE IN SYRIA...
PLEASE DON'T SAY WHERE.
FOX NEWS
GB Trudeau

7/7/08

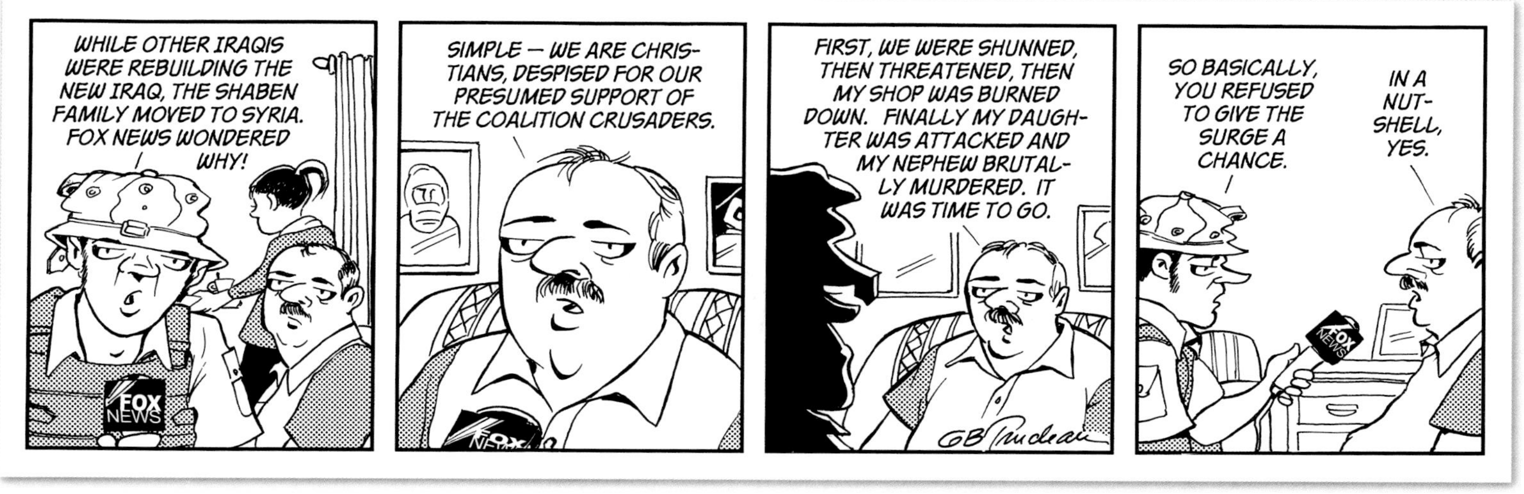
WHILE OTHER IRAQIS WERE REBUILDING THE NEW IRAQ, THE SHABEN FAMILY MOVED TO SYRIA. FOX NEWS WONDERED WHY!
SIMPLE — WE ARE CHRISTIANS, DESPISED FOR OUR PRESUMED SUPPORT OF THE COALITION CRUSADERS.
FIRST, WE WERE SHUNNED, THEN THREATENED, THEN MY SHOP WAS BURNED DOWN. FINALLY MY DAUGHTER WAS ATTACKED AND MY NEPHEW BRUTALLY MURDERED. IT WAS TIME TO GO.
SO BASICALLY, YOU REFUSED TO GIVE THE SURGE A CHANCE.
IN A NUTSHELL, YES.
FOX NEWS
GB Trudeau

7/8/08

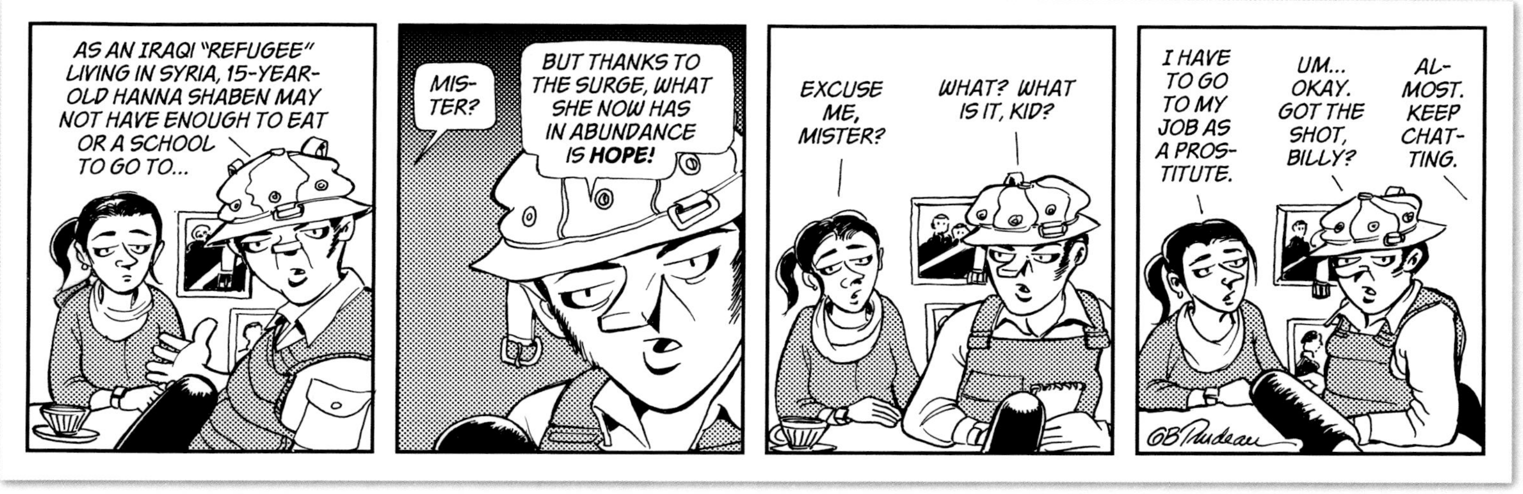
AS AN IRAQI "REFUGEE" LIVING IN SYRIA, 15-YEAR-OLD HANNA SHABEN MAY NOT HAVE ENOUGH TO EAT OR A SCHOOL TO GO TO...
MISTER?
BUT THANKS TO THE SURGE, WHAT SHE NOW HAS IN ABUNDANCE IS **HOPE!**
EXCUSE ME, MISTER?
WHAT? WHAT IS IT, KID?
I HAVE TO GO TO MY JOB AS A PROSTITUTE.
UM... OKAY. GOT THE SHOT, BILLY?
ALMOST. KEEP CHATTING.
GB Trudeau

7/9/08

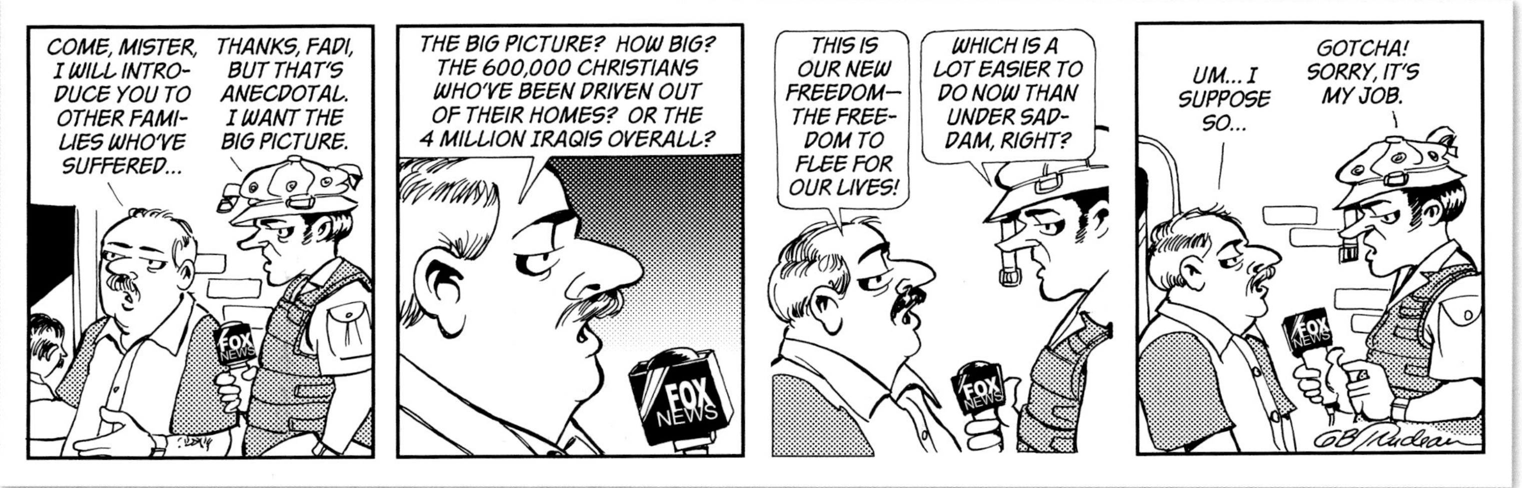
COME, MISTER, I WILL INTRODUCE YOU TO OTHER FAMILIES WHO'VE SUFFERED...
THANKS, FADI, BUT THAT'S ANECDOTAL. I WANT THE BIG PICTURE.
THE BIG PICTURE? HOW BIG? THE 600,000 CHRISTIANS WHO'VE BEEN DRIVEN OUT OF THEIR HOMES? OR THE 4 MILLION IRAQIS OVERALL?
THIS IS OUR NEW FREEDOM— THE FREEDOM TO FLEE FOR OUR LIVES!
WHICH IS A LOT EASIER TO DO NOW THAN UNDER SADDAM, RIGHT?
UM... I SUPPOSE SO...
GOTCHA! SORRY, IT'S MY JOB.
FOX NEWS
GB Trudeau

7/10/08

ELIAS

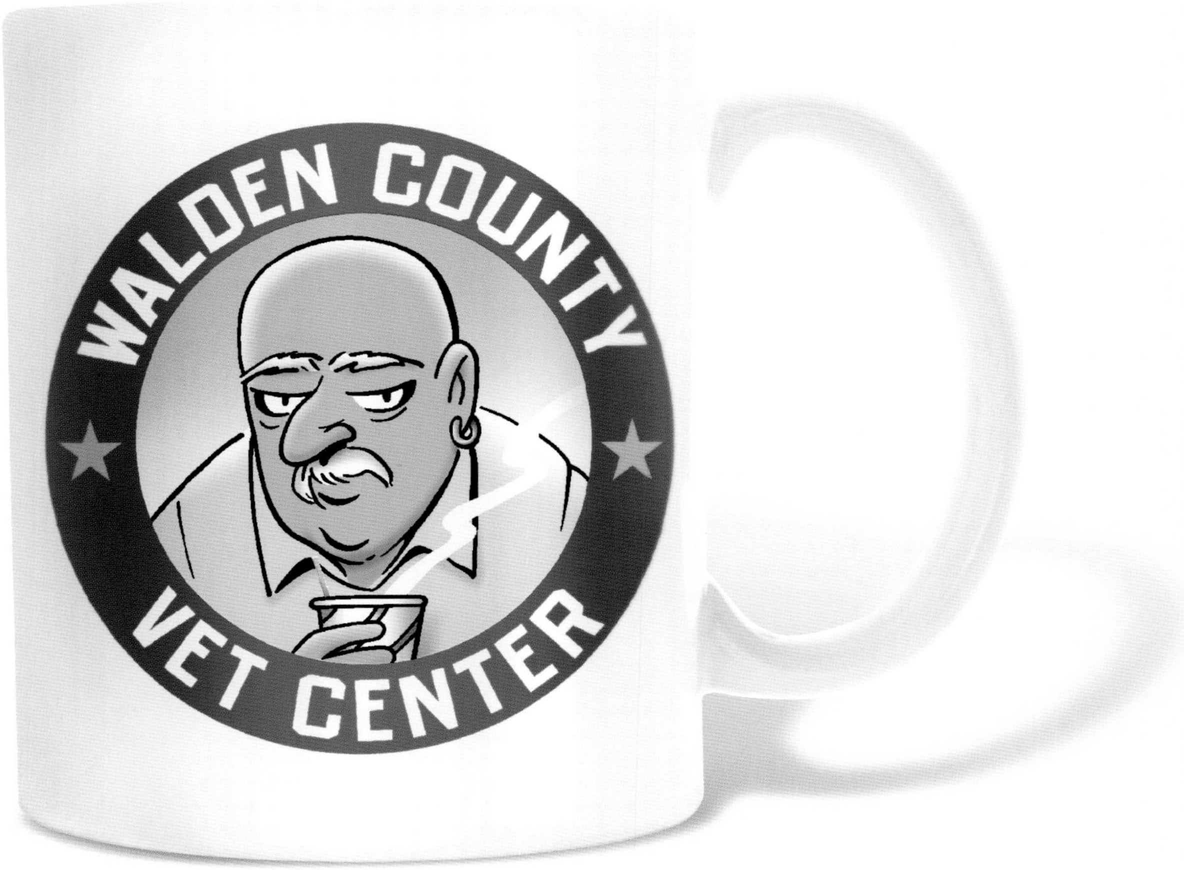
WALDEN COUNTY
VET CENTER

People I meet sometimes marvel at all the preparation they believe I do, and it is not to my credit that I let them. The truth is there's rarely time for much research, other than what I can do on the fly with Google.

Since a comic strip is not exactly a journalistic enterprise, this mostly works fine. While accuracy is nice, I can usually get by with verisimilitude, what Colbert calls truthiness. Truthiness is the satirist's stock in trade. Anyone looking for reliable information from a person who's paid to exaggerate is just not thinking clearly.

Having explained the rule, here's a big exception: the story of B.D.'s injury and recovery. The reason for proceeding with care is obvious; the last thing I wanted to do was contribute to the suffering I was trying to describe. Limb loss isn't exactly a topic anyone should be improvising on, but initially I had little information to guide me beyond what my colleague David Stanford could pull together from Web sources. I didn't personally know anyone who had been wounded in battle.

That changed quickly. Shortly after I showed B.D. being carried from the battlefield, I was contacted by the Department of Defense with an offer of assistance. Their reasoning,

“Believe it or not, your government supplies you with the services of a burned-out, gimp, bullet-headed high school dropout absolutely free!”

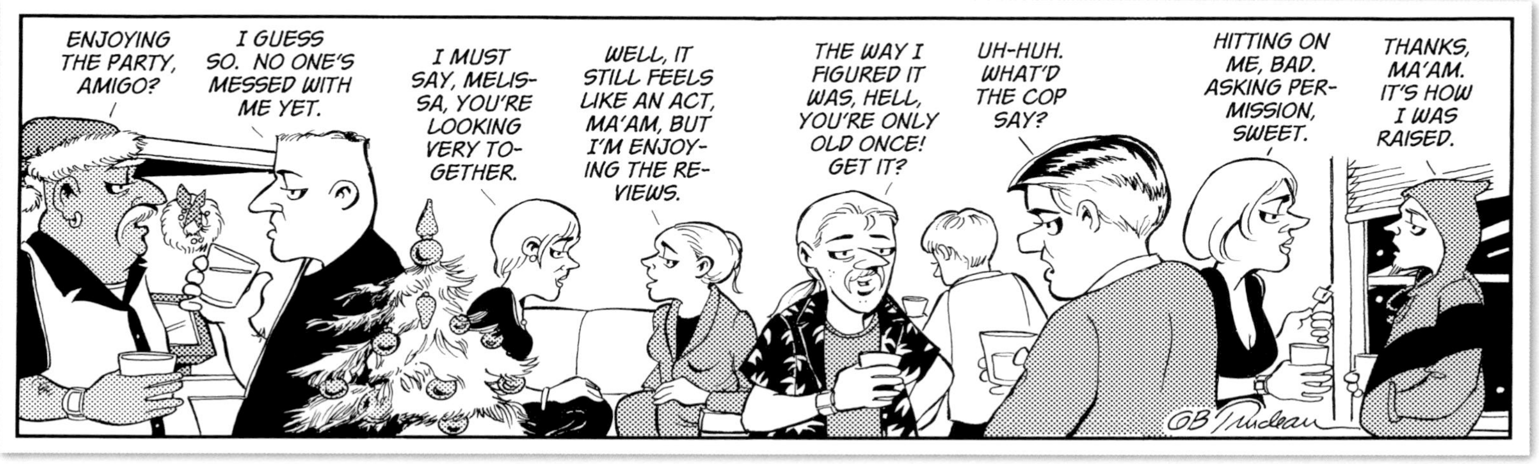
ENJOYING THE PARTY, AMIGO?
I GUESS SO. NO ONE'S MESSED WITH ME YET.
I MUST SAY, MELISSA, YOU'RE LOOKING VERY TOGETHER.
WELL, IT STILL FEELS LIKE AN ACT, MA'AM, BUT I'M ENJOYING THE REVIEWS.
THE WAY I FIGURED IT WAS, HELL, YOU'RE ONLY OLD ONCE! GET IT?
UH-HUH. WHAT'D THE COP SAY?
HITTING ON ME, BAD. ASKING PERMISSION, SWEET.
THANKS, MA'AM. IT'S HOW I WAS RAISED.

I think, was that my wounded-warrior story might have more value if I actually got it right. So I was invited to the Walter Reed Army Medical Center to talk to amputees and their doctors and all the other people that someone like B.D. might encounter during recovery.

It was the beginning of an extraordinary introduction to the world of military medicine, one I have tried to make the most of. As I've tracked B.D.'s progress over the last six years, I've been assisted by a long succession of veterans and caregivers across the country, all of whom were unstintingly generous with their time. Among them was a remarkable counselor named Wayne Miller, who first introduced me to the culture of Vet Centers. It was Miller who mapped out for me the unique Vet Center protocols, which for over thirty years have been quietly evolving in the margins of mainstream VA operations.

It was during those conversations that the character of Elias first began to take shape. Elias, like Wayne, is a Vietnam vet and amputee, and those two facts were essential to gaining the trust of the deeply resistant B.D., who had been circling the Center for some time. The bonds of common experience are powerful, and it was only after B.D. discovered the safety of peer therapy that his healing could begin.

While Elias's backstory is only lightly sketched out, I tried to convey the sense that his patience and insight were not innate, but very much hard-won. Elias is not just modeling an outcome; he's also about the struggle. He doesn't promise B.D. that he can recover the life he once had. He's simply showing him the way forward.

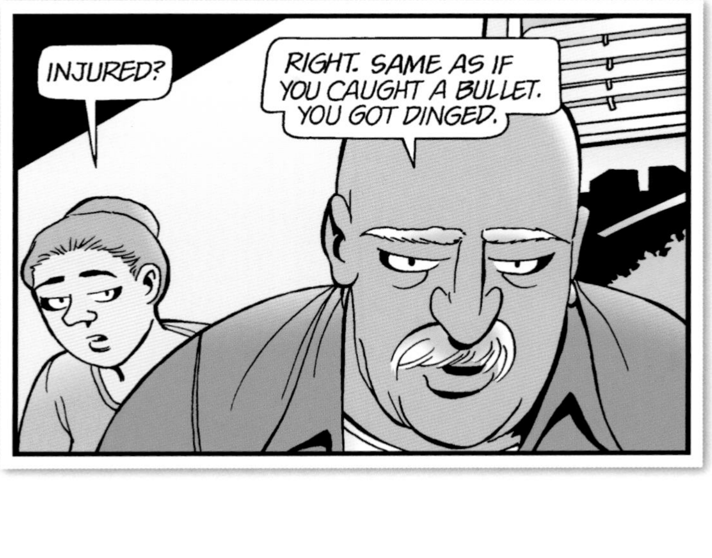
INJURED?
RIGHT. SAME AS IF YOU CAUGHT A BULLET. YOU GOT DINGED.

For a soldier with grievous physical and psychological wounds, this is no small thing. It's the beginning of hope.

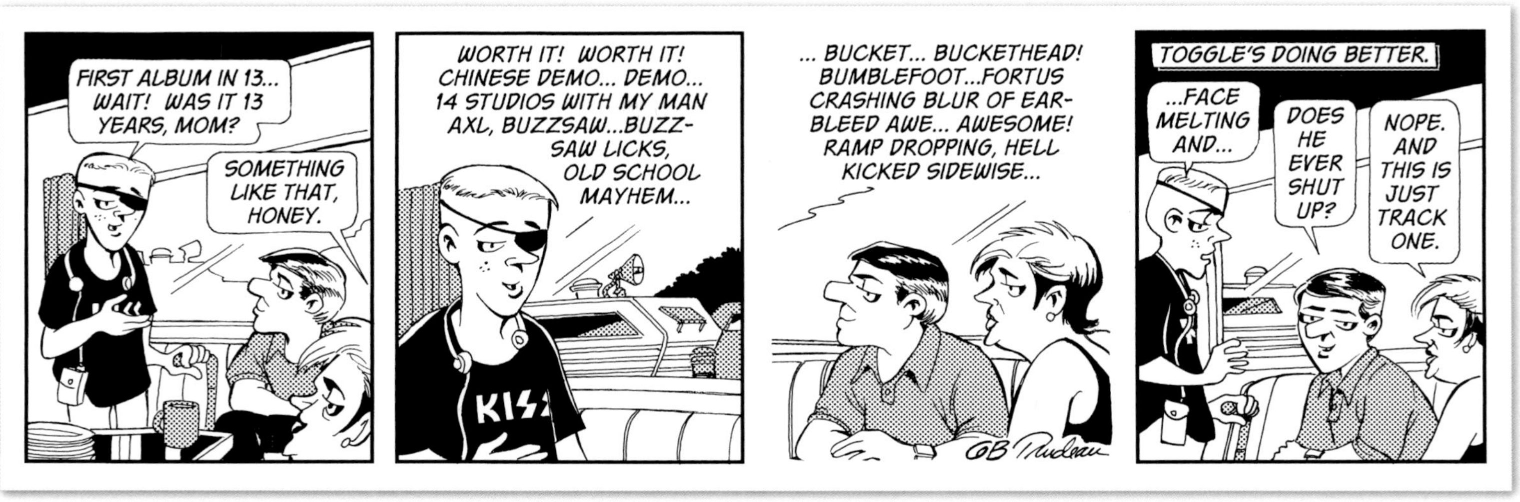
FIRST ALBUM IN 13... WAIT! WAS IT 13 YEARS, MOM?
SOMETHING LIKE THAT, HONEY.
WORTH IT! WORTH IT! CHINESE DEMO... DEMO... 14 STUDIOS WITH MY MAN AXL, BUZZSAW...BUZZSAW LICKS, OLD SCHOOL MAYHEM...
KISS
... BUCKET... BUCKETHEAD! BUMBLEFOOT...FORTUS CRASHING BLUR OF EAR-BLEED AWE... AWESOME! RAMP DROPPING, HELL KICKED SIDEWISE...
TOGGLE'S DOING BETTER.
...FACE MELTING AND...
DOES HE EVER SHUT UP?
NOPE. AND THIS IS JUST TRACK ONE.

12/15/08

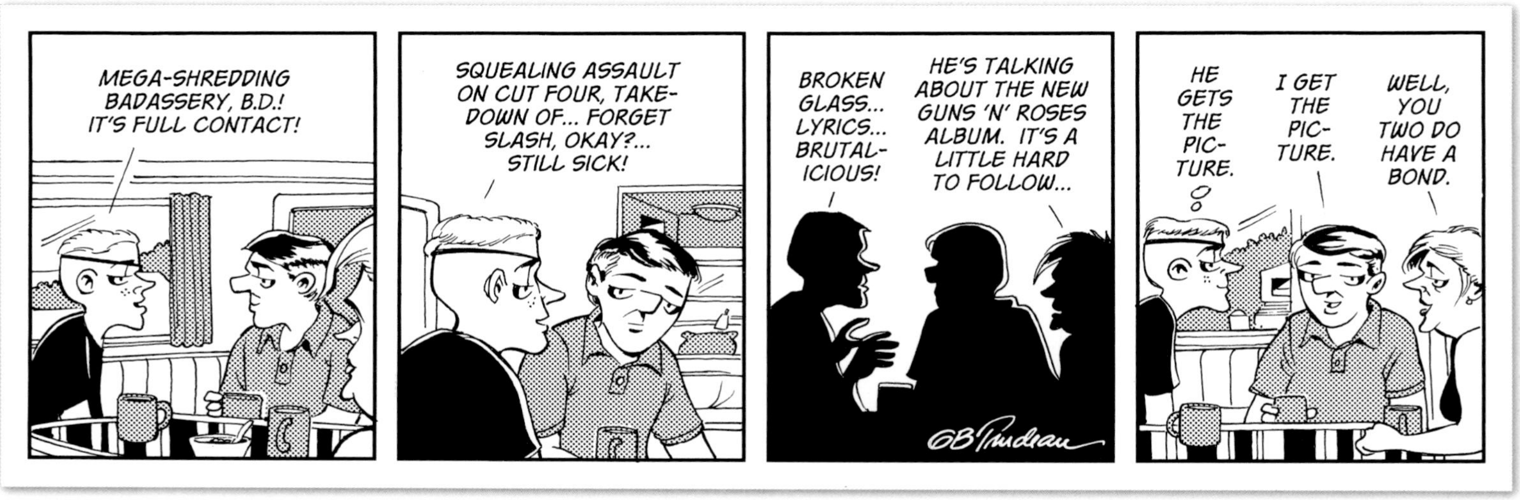
MEGA-SHREDDING BADASSERY, B.D.! IT'S FULL CONTACT!
SQUEALING ASSAULT ON CUT FOUR, TAKE-DOWN OF... FORGET SLASH, OKAY?... STILL SICK!
BROKEN GLASS... LYRICS... BRUTAL-ICIOUS!
HE'S TALKING ABOUT THE NEW GUNS 'N' ROSES ALBUM. IT'S A LITTLE HARD TO FOLLOW...
HE GETS THE PIC-TURE.
I GET THE PIC-TURE.
WELL, YOU TWO DO HAVE A BOND.

12/16/08

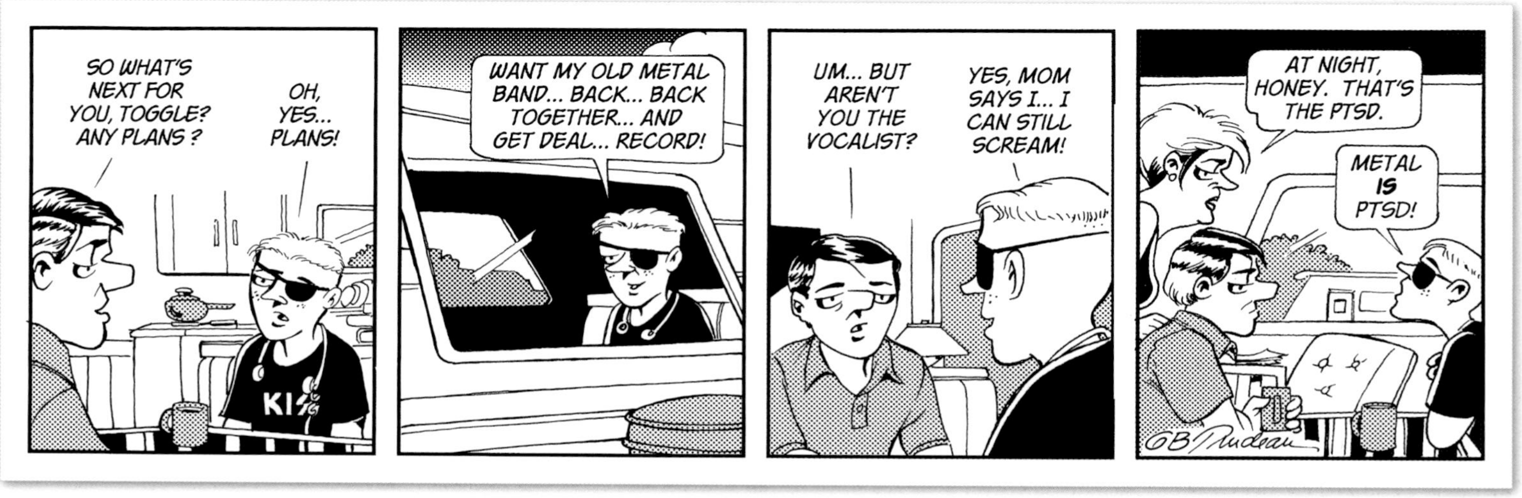
SO WHAT'S NEXT FOR YOU, TOGGLE? ANY PLANS ?
OH, YES... PLANS!
WANT MY OLD METAL BAND... BACK... BACK TOGETHER... AND GET DEAL... RECORD!
UM... BUT AREN'T YOU THE VOCALIST?
YES, MOM SAYS I... I CAN STILL SCREAM!
AT NIGHT, HONEY. THAT'S THE PTSD.
METAL IS PTSD!

12/17/08

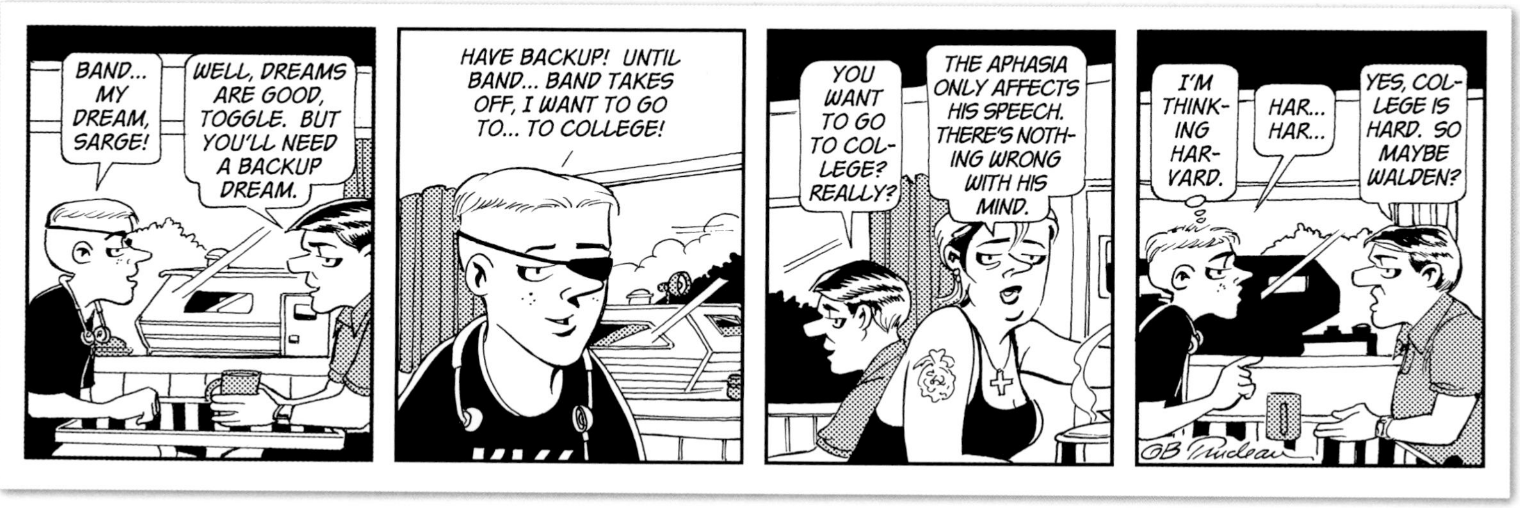
BAND... MY DREAM, SARGE!
WELL, DREAMS ARE GOOD, TOGGLE. BUT YOU'LL NEED A BACKUP DREAM.
HAVE BACKUP! UNTIL BAND... BAND TAKES OFF, I WANT TO GO TO... TO COLLEGE!
YOU WANT TO GO TO COL-LEGE? REALLY?
THE APHASIA ONLY AFFECTS HIS SPEECH. THERE'S NOTH-ING WRONG WITH HIS MIND.
I'M THINK-ING HAR-VARD.
HAR... HAR...
YES, COL-LEGE IS HARD. SO MAYBE WALDEN?

12/18/08

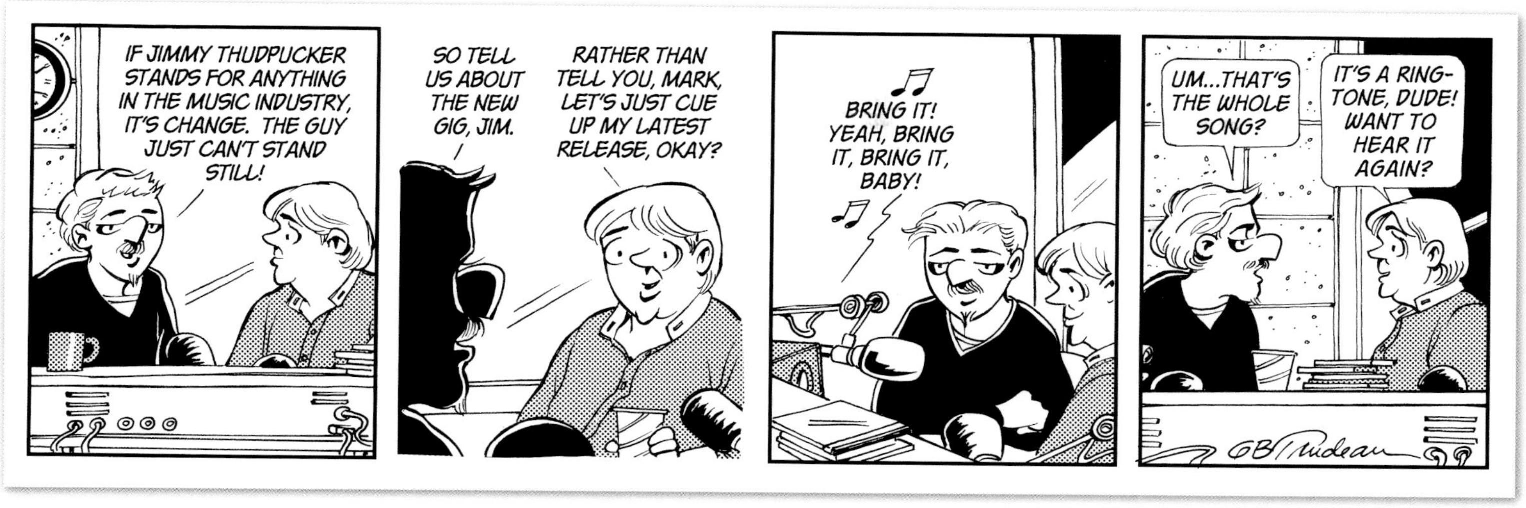
IF JIMMY THUDPUCKER STANDS FOR ANYTHING IN THE MUSIC INDUSTRY, IT'S CHANGE. THE GUY JUST CAN'T STAND STILL!
SO TELL US ABOUT THE NEW GIG, JIM.
RATHER THAN TELL YOU, MARK, LET'S JUST CUE UP MY LATEST RELEASE, OKAY?
BRING IT! YEAH, BRING IT, BRING IT, BABY!
UM...THAT'S THE WHOLE SONG?
IT'S A RING-TONE, DUDE! WANT TO HEAR IT AGAIN?
GB Trudeau

1/19/09

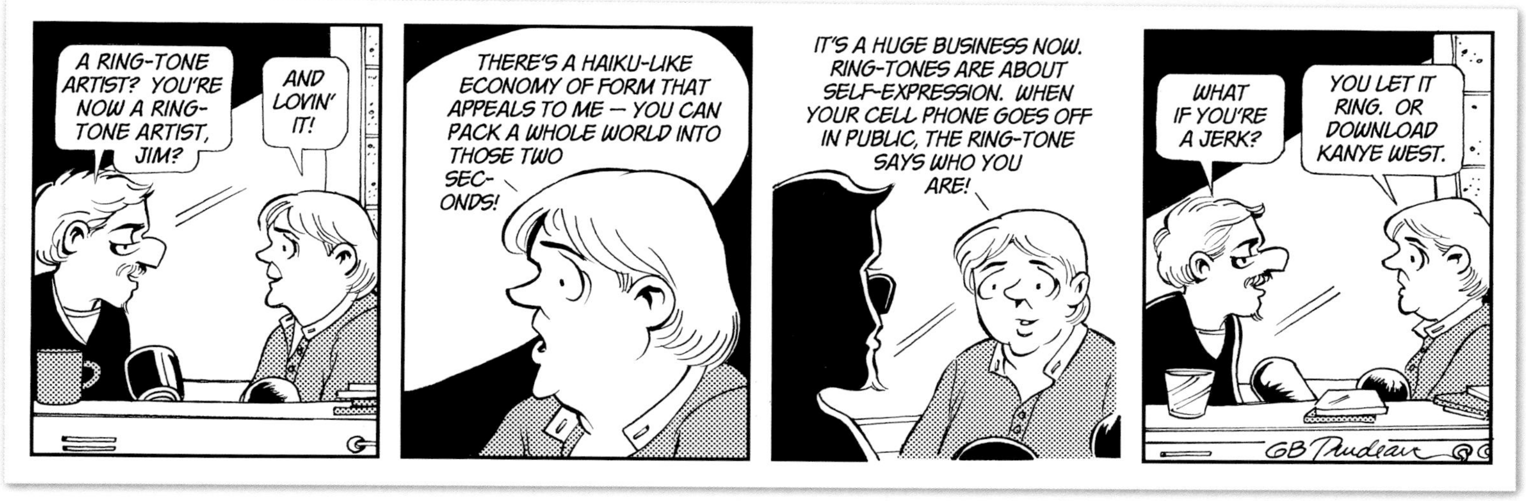
A RING-TONE ARTIST? YOU'RE NOW A RING-TONE ARTIST, JIM?
AND LOVIN' IT!
THERE'S A HAIKU-LIKE ECONOMY OF FORM THAT APPEALS TO ME — YOU CAN PACK A WHOLE WORLD INTO THOSE TWO SECONDS!
IT'S A HUGE BUSINESS NOW. RING-TONES ARE ABOUT SELF-EXPRESSION. WHEN YOUR CELL PHONE GOES OFF IN PUBLIC, THE RING-TONE SAYS WHO YOU ARE!
WHAT IF YOU'RE A JERK?
YOU LET IT RING. OR DOWNLOAD KANYE WEST.
GB Trudeau

1/20/09

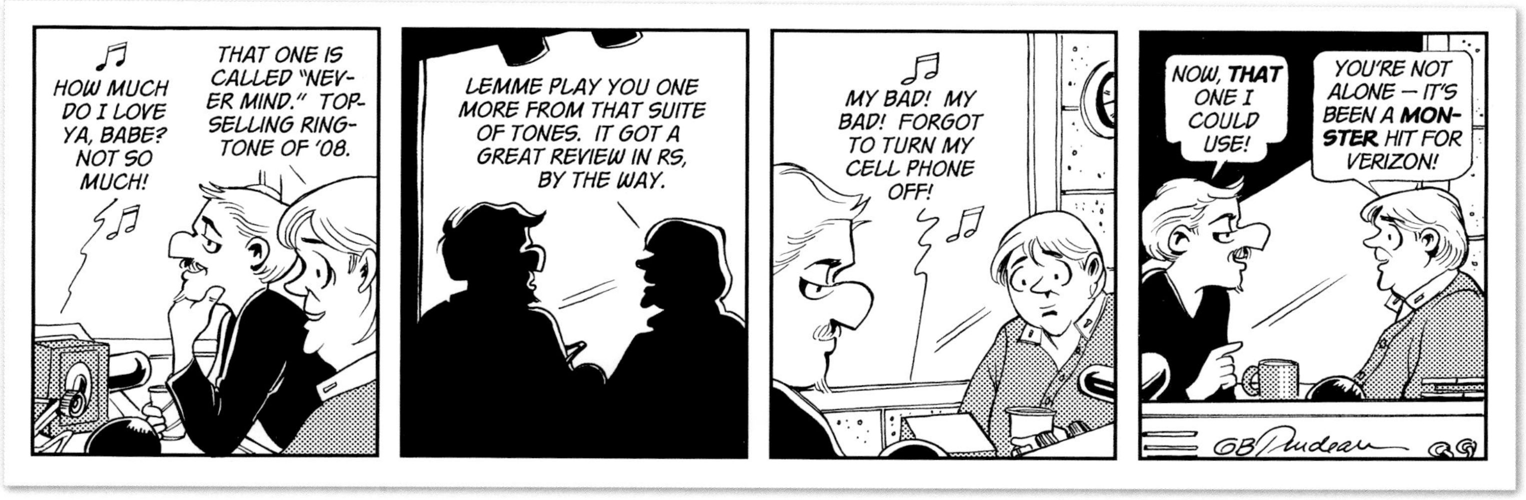
HOW MUCH DO I LOVE YA, BABE? NOT SO MUCH!
THAT ONE IS CALLED "NEVER MIND." TOP-SELLING RING-TONE OF '08.
LEMME PLAY YOU ONE MORE FROM THAT SUITE OF TONES. IT GOT A GREAT REVIEW IN RS, BY THE WAY.
MY BAD! MY BAD! FORGOT TO TURN MY CELL PHONE OFF!
NOW, THAT ONE I COULD USE!
YOU'RE NOT ALONE — IT'S BEEN A MONSTER HIT FOR VERIZON!
GB Trudeau

1/21/09

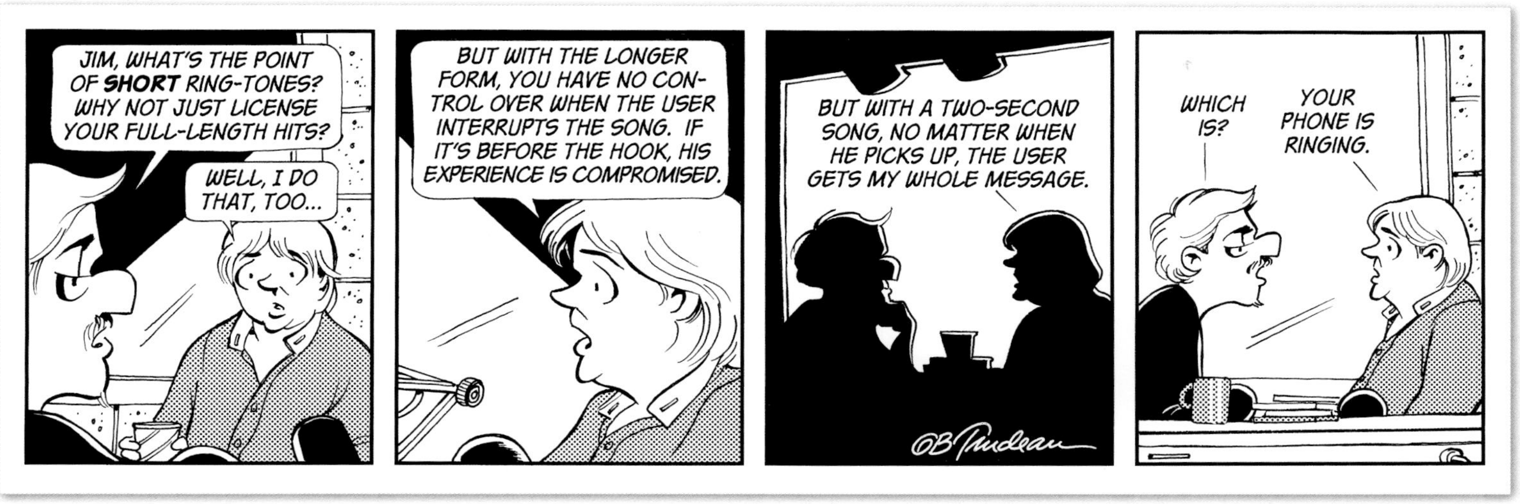
JIM, WHAT'S THE POINT OF SHORT RING-TONES? WHY NOT JUST LICENSE YOUR FULL-LENGTH HITS?
WELL, I DO THAT, TOO...
BUT WITH THE LONGER FORM, YOU HAVE NO CONTROL OVER WHEN THE USER INTERRUPTS THE SONG. IF IT'S BEFORE THE HOOK, HIS EXPERIENCE IS COMPROMISED.
BUT WITH A TWO-SECOND SONG, NO MATTER WHEN HE PICKS UP, THE USER GETS MY WHOLE MESSAGE.
GB Trudeau
WHICH IS?
YOUR PHONE IS RINGING.

1/23/09

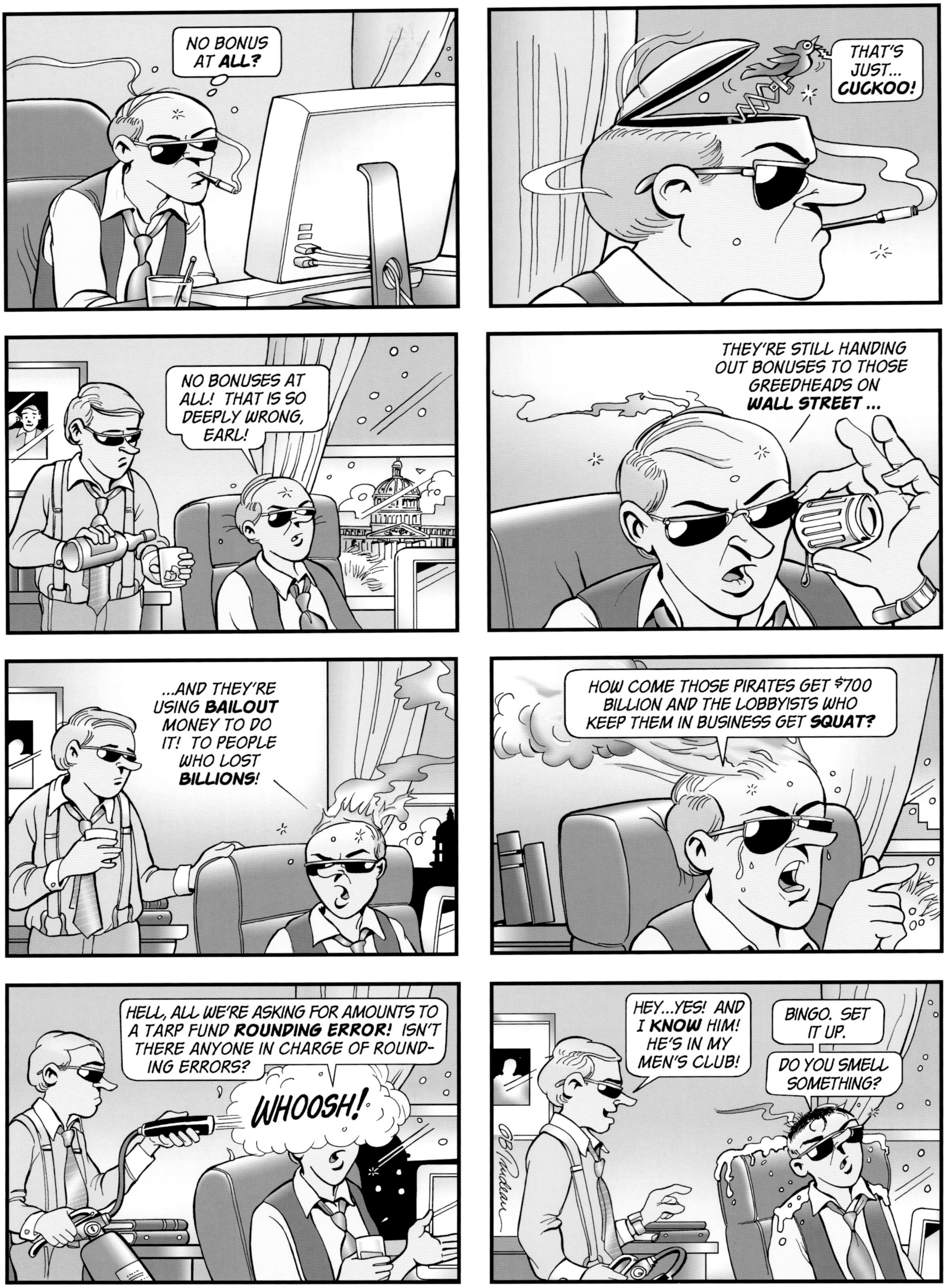
NO BONUS AT **ALL?**
THAT'S JUST... **CUCKOO!**
NO BONUSES AT ALL! THAT IS SO DEEPLY WRONG, EARL!
THEY'RE STILL HANDING OUT BONUSES TO THOSE GREEDHEADS ON **WALL STREET ...**
...AND THEY'RE USING **BAILOUT** MONEY TO DO IT! TO PEOPLE WHO LOST **BILLIONS**!
HOW COME THOSE PIRATES GET $700 BILLION AND THE LOBBYISTS WHO KEEP THEM IN BUSINESS GET **SQUAT?**
HELL, ALL WE'RE ASKING FOR AMOUNTS TO A TARP FUND **ROUNDING ERROR!** ISN'T THERE ANYONE IN CHARGE OF ROUNDING ERRORS?
WHOOSH!
HEY...YES! AND I **KNOW** HIM! HE'S IN MY MEN'S CLUB!
BINGO. SET IT UP.
DO YOU SMELL SOMETHING?

2/1/09

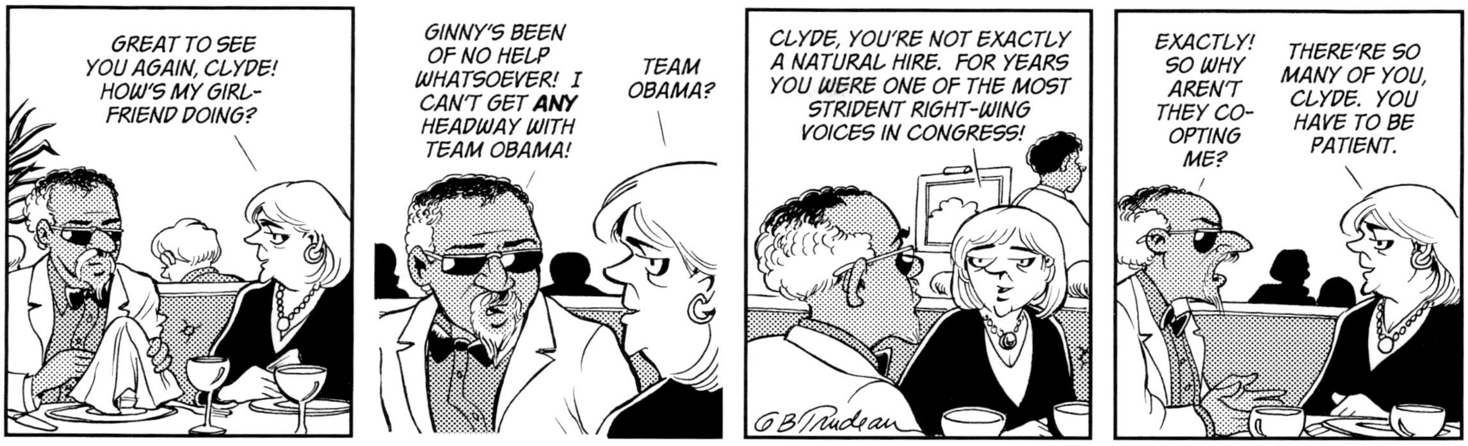
GREAT TO SEE YOU AGAIN, CLYDE! HOW'S MY GIRL-FRIEND DOING?
GINNY'S BEEN OF NO HELP WHATSOEVER! I CAN'T GET **ANY** HEADWAY WITH TEAM OBAMA!
TEAM OBAMA?
CLYDE, YOU'RE NOT EXACTLY A NATURAL HIRE. FOR YEARS YOU WERE ONE OF THE MOST STRIDENT RIGHT-WING VOICES IN CONGRESS!
GB Trudeau
EXACTLY! SO WHY AREN'T THEY CO-OPTING ME?
THERE'RE SO MANY OF YOU, CLYDE. YOU HAVE TO BE PATIENT.

1/27/09

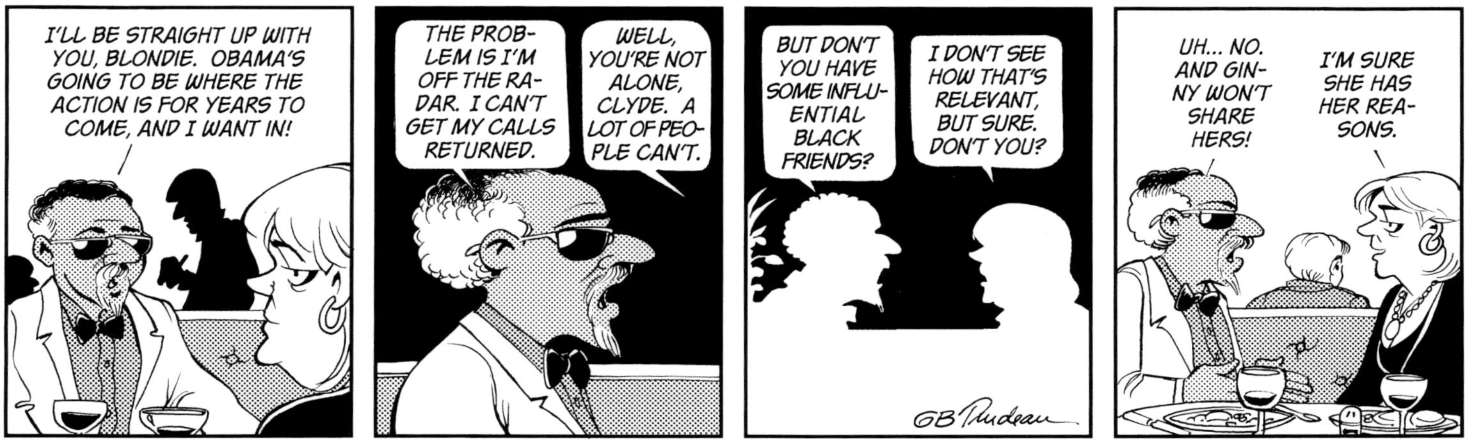
I'LL BE STRAIGHT UP WITH YOU, BLONDIE. OBAMA'S GOING TO BE WHERE THE ACTION IS FOR YEARS TO COME, AND I WANT IN!
THE PROB-LEM IS I'M OFF THE RA-DAR. I CAN'T GET MY CALLS RETURNED.
WELL, YOU'RE NOT ALONE, CLYDE. A LOT OF PEO-PLE CAN'T.
BUT DON'T YOU HAVE SOME INFLU-ENTIAL BLACK FRIENDS?
I DON'T SEE HOW THAT'S RELEVANT, BUT SURE. DON'T YOU?
GB Trudeau
UH... NO. AND GIN-NY WON'T SHARE HERS!
I'M SURE SHE HAS HER REA-SONS.

1/28/09

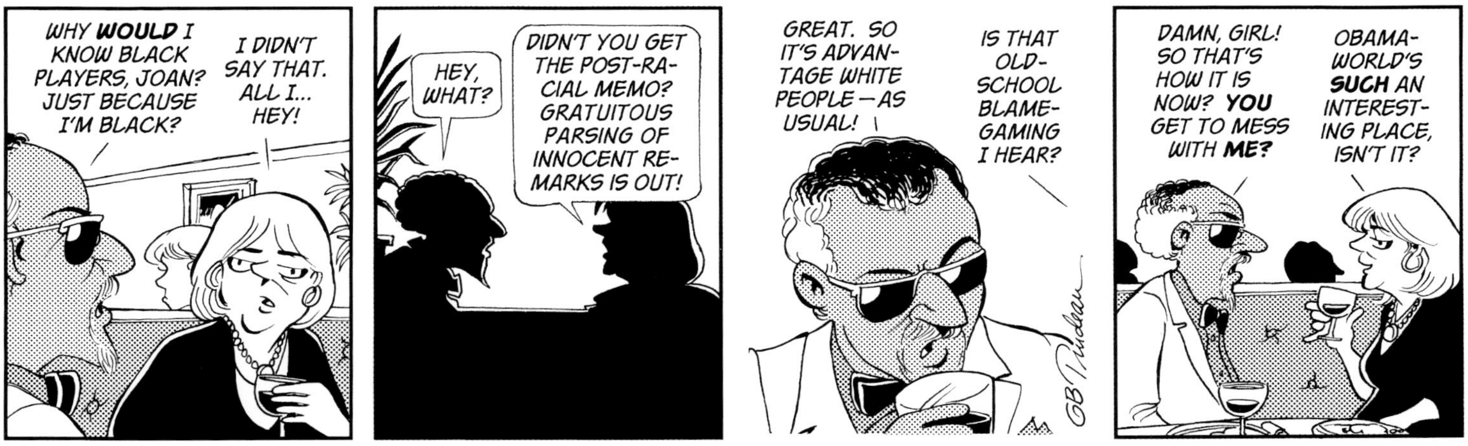
WHY **WOULD** I KNOW BLACK PLAYERS, JOAN? JUST BECAUSE I'M BLACK?
I DIDN'T SAY THAT. ALL I... HEY!
HEY, WHAT?
DIDN'T YOU GET THE POST-RA-CIAL MEMO? GRATUITOUS PARSING OF INNOCENT RE-MARKS IS OUT!
GREAT. SO IT'S ADVAN-TAGE WHITE PEOPLE — AS USUAL!
IS THAT OLD-SCHOOL BLAME-GAMING I HEAR?
GB Trudeau
DAMN, GIRL! SO THAT'S HOW IT IS NOW? **YOU** GET TO MESS WITH **ME?**
OBAMA-WORLD'S **SUCH** AN INTEREST-ING PLACE, ISN'T IT?

1/29/09

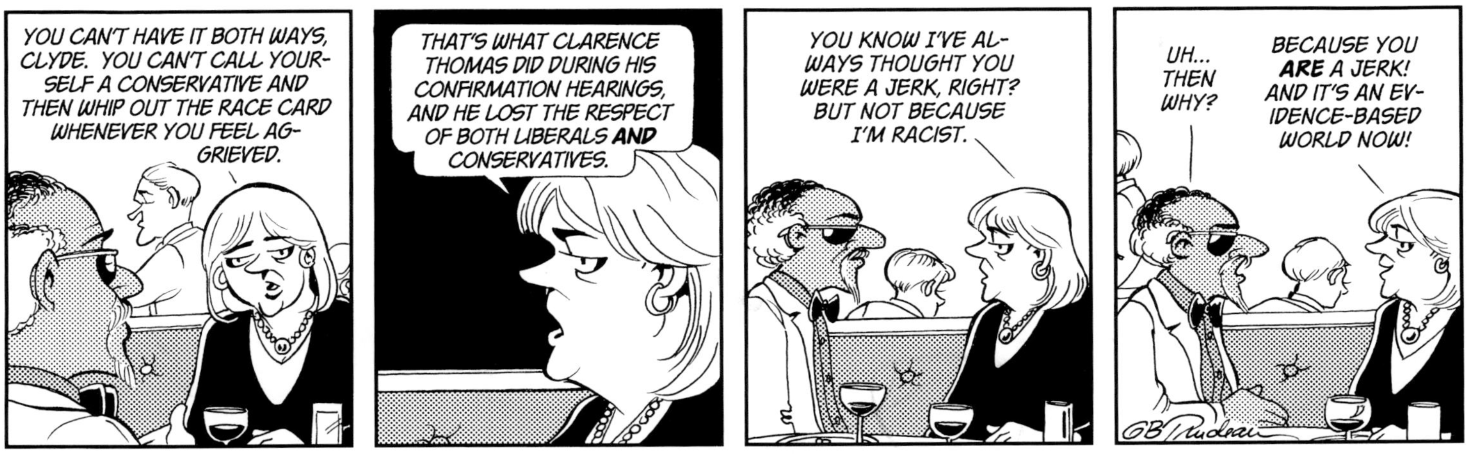
YOU CAN'T HAVE IT BOTH WAYS, CLYDE. YOU CAN'T CALL YOUR-SELF A CONSERVATIVE AND THEN WHIP OUT THE RACE CARD WHENEVER YOU FEEL AG-GRIEVED.
THAT'S WHAT CLARENCE THOMAS DID DURING HIS CONFIRMATION HEARINGS, AND HE LOST THE RESPECT OF BOTH LIBERALS **AND** CONSERVATIVES.
YOU KNOW I'VE AL-WAYS THOUGHT YOU WERE A JERK, RIGHT? BUT NOT BECAUSE I'M RACIST.
GB Trudeau
UH... THEN WHY?
BECAUSE YOU **ARE** A JERK! AND IT'S AN EV-IDENCE-BASED WORLD NOW!

1/30/09

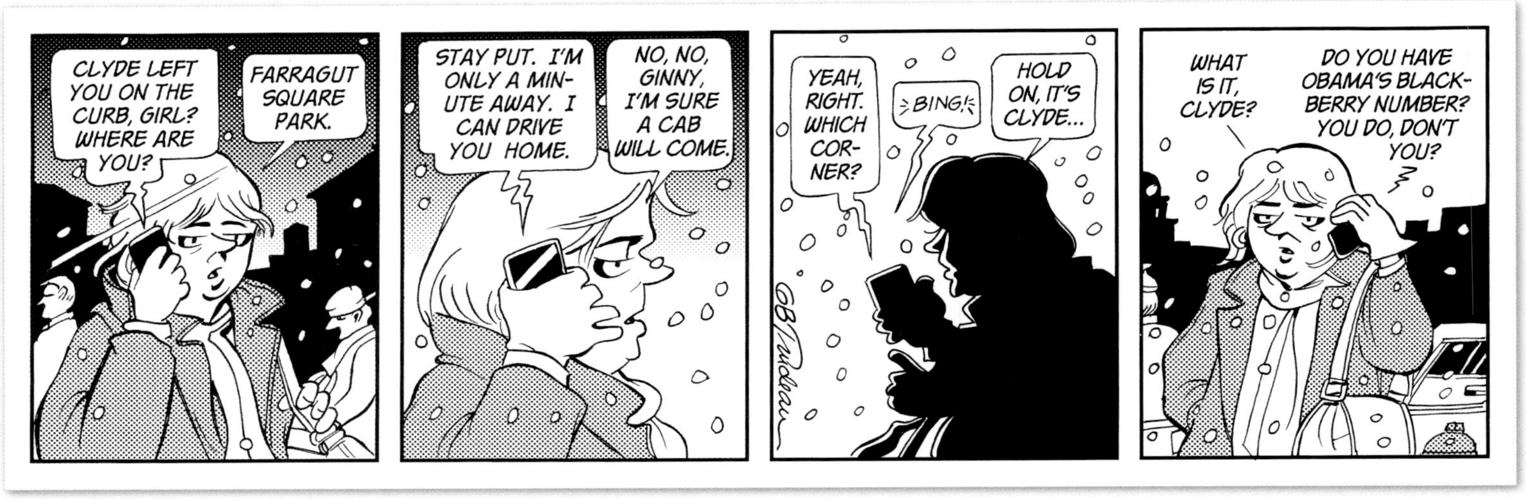
CLYDE LEFT YOU ON THE CURB, GIRL? WHERE ARE YOU?
FARRAGUT SQUARE PARK.
STAY PUT. I'M ONLY A MINUTE AWAY. I CAN DRIVE YOU HOME.
NO, NO, GINNY, I'M SURE A CAB WILL COME.
YEAH, RIGHT. WHICH CORNER?
BING!
HOLD ON, IT'S CLYDE...
WHAT IS IT, CLYDE?
DO YOU HAVE OBAMA'S BLACKBERRY NUMBER? YOU DO, DON'T YOU?

2/3/09

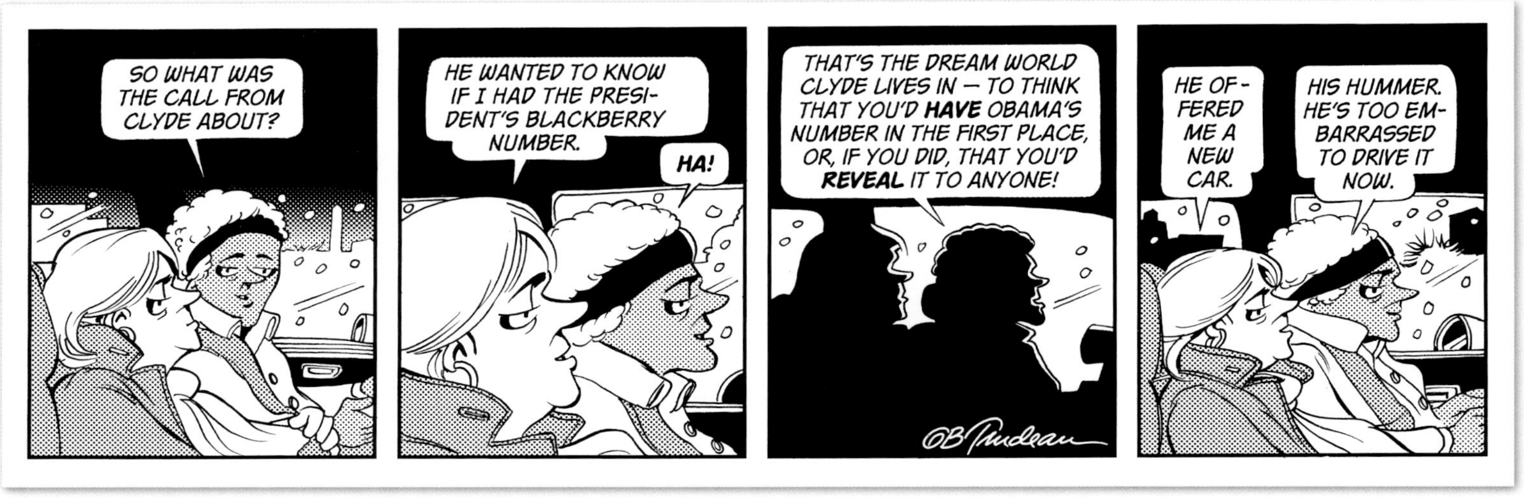
SO WHAT WAS THE CALL FROM CLYDE ABOUT?
HE WANTED TO KNOW IF I HAD THE PRESIDENT'S BLACKBERRY NUMBER.
HA!
THAT'S THE DREAM WORLD CLYDE LIVES IN — TO THINK THAT YOU'D **HAVE** OBAMA'S NUMBER IN THE FIRST PLACE, OR, IF YOU DID, THAT YOU'D **REVEAL** IT TO ANYONE!
HE OFFERED ME A NEW CAR.
HIS HUMMER. HE'S TOO EMBARRASSED TO DRIVE IT NOW.

2/4/09

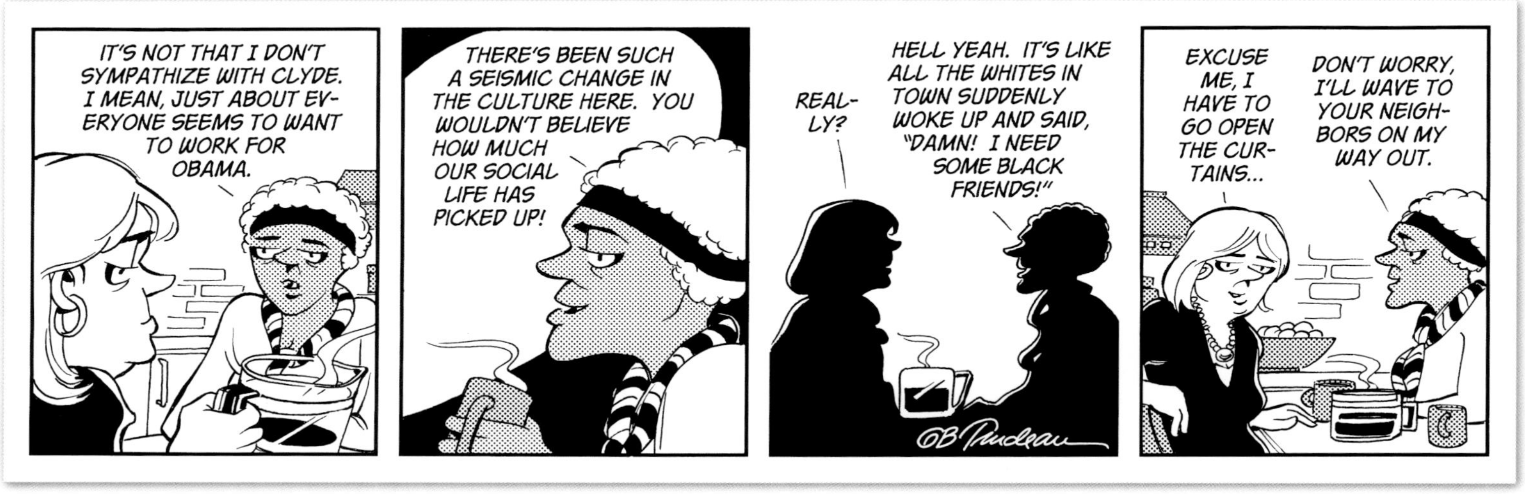
IT'S NOT THAT I DON'T SYMPATHIZE WITH CLYDE. I MEAN, JUST ABOUT EVERYONE SEEMS TO WANT TO WORK FOR OBAMA.
THERE'S BEEN SUCH A SEISMIC CHANGE IN THE CULTURE HERE. YOU WOULDN'T BELIEVE HOW MUCH OUR SOCIAL LIFE HAS PICKED UP!
REALLY?
HELL YEAH. IT'S LIKE ALL THE WHITES IN TOWN SUDDENLY WOKE UP AND SAID, "DAMN! I NEED SOME BLACK FRIENDS!"
EXCUSE ME, I HAVE TO GO OPEN THE CURTAINS...
DON'T WORRY, I'LL WAVE TO YOUR NEIGHBORS ON MY WAY OUT.

2/5/09

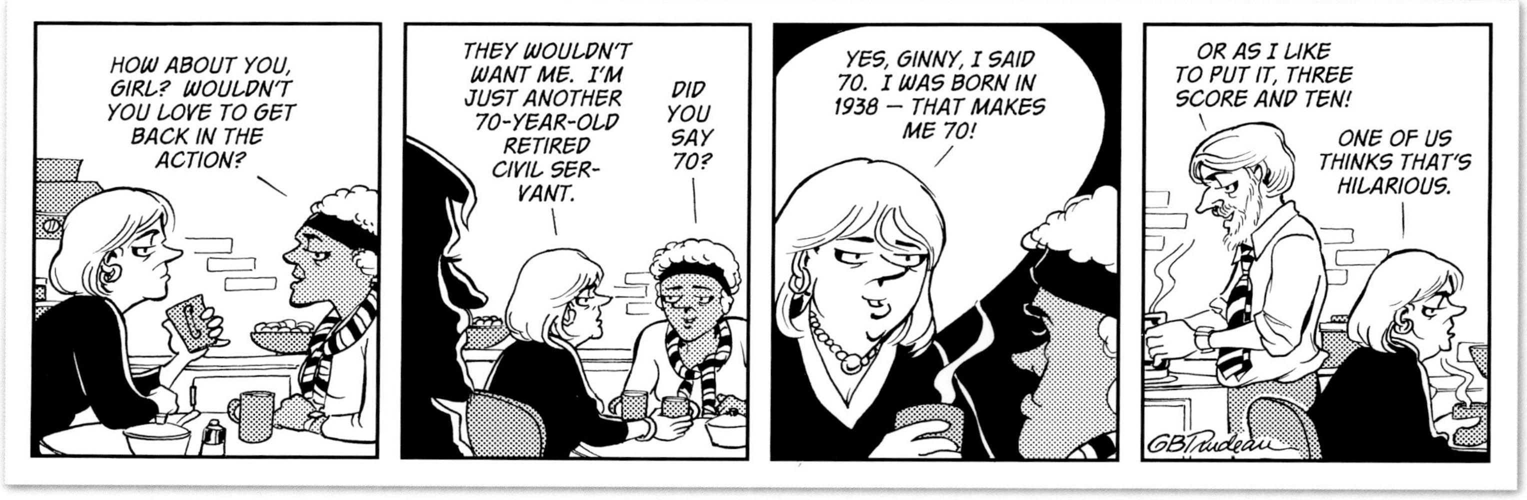
HOW ABOUT YOU, GIRL? WOULDN'T YOU LOVE TO GET BACK IN THE ACTION?
THEY WOULDN'T WANT ME. I'M JUST ANOTHER 70-YEAR-OLD RETIRED CIVIL SERVANT.
DID YOU SAY 70?
YES, GINNY, I SAID 70. I WAS BORN IN 1938 — THAT MAKES ME 70!
OR AS I LIKE TO PUT IT, THREE SCORE AND TEN!
ONE OF US THINKS THAT'S HILARIOUS.

2/6/09

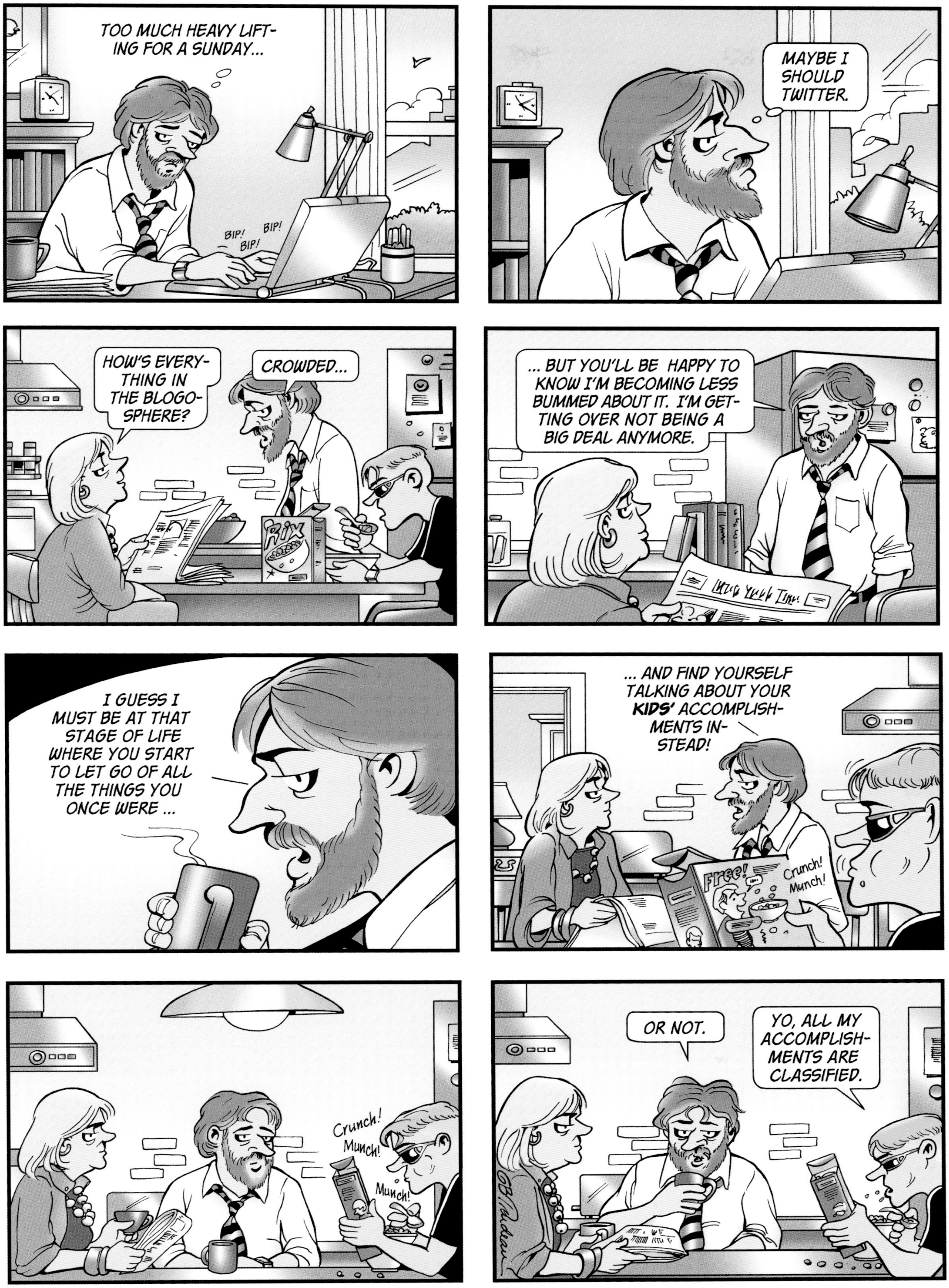

TOO MUCH HEAVY LIFTING FOR A SUNDAY...
BIP! BIP! BIP!
MAYBE I SHOULD TWITTER.
HOW'S EVERYTHING IN THE BLOGOSPHERE?
CROWDED...
RIX
... BUT YOU'LL BE HAPPY TO KNOW I'M BECOMING LESS BUMMED ABOUT IT. I'M GETTING OVER NOT BEING A BIG DEAL ANYMORE.
I GUESS I MUST BE AT THAT STAGE OF LIFE WHERE YOU START TO LET GO OF ALL THE THINGS YOU ONCE WERE ...
... AND FIND YOURSELF TALKING ABOUT YOUR KIDS' ACCOMPLISHMENTS INSTEAD!
Free!
Crunch! Munch!
Crunch! Munch!
Munch!
OR NOT.
YO, ALL MY ACCOMPLISHMENTS ARE CLASSIFIED.
GB Trudeau

4/19/09

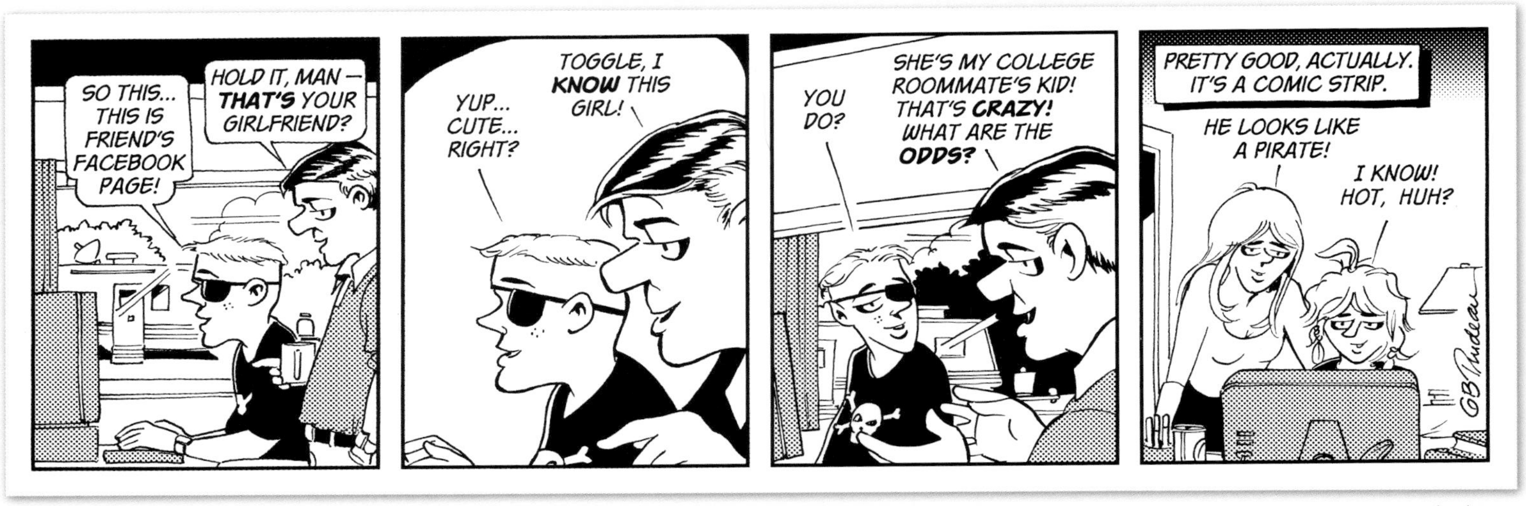
SO THIS... THIS IS FRIEND'S FACEBOOK PAGE!
HOLD IT, MAN — THAT'S YOUR GIRLFRIEND?
YUP... CUTE... RIGHT?
TOGGLE, I KNOW THIS GIRL!
YOU DO?
SHE'S MY COLLEGE ROOMMATE'S KID! THAT'S CRAZY! WHAT ARE THE ODDS?
PRETTY GOOD, ACTUALLY. IT'S A COMIC STRIP.
HE LOOKS LIKE A PIRATE!
I KNOW! HOT, HUH?

3/21/09

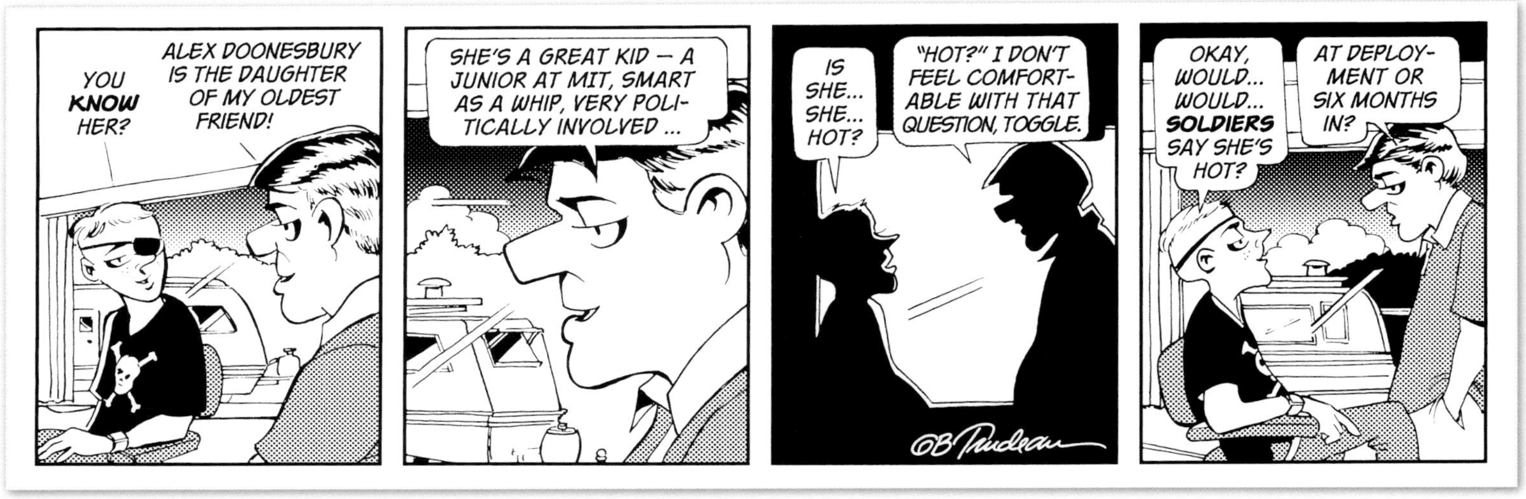
YOU KNOW HER?
ALEX DOONESBURY IS THE DAUGHTER OF MY OLDEST FRIEND!
SHE'S A GREAT KID — A JUNIOR AT MIT, SMART AS A WHIP, VERY POLITICALLY INVOLVED ...
IS SHE... SHE... HOT?
"HOT?" I DON'T FEEL COMFORTABLE WITH THAT QUESTION, TOGGLE.
OKAY, WOULD... WOULD... SOLDIERS SAY SHE'S HOT?
AT DEPLOYMENT OR SIX MONTHS IN?

3/23/09

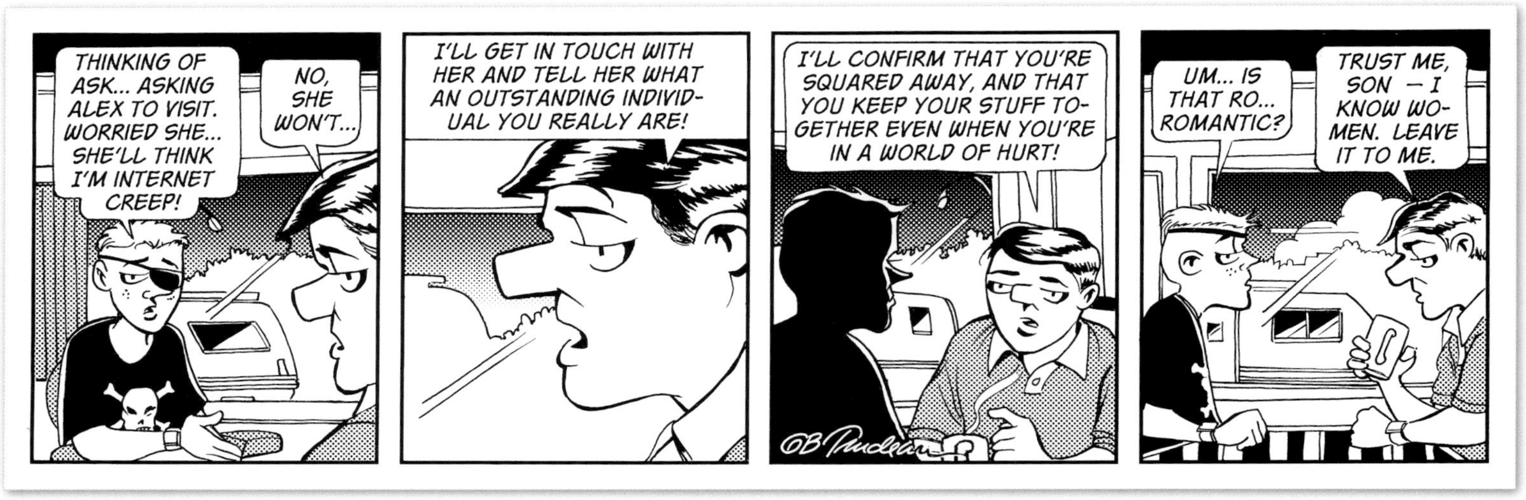
THINKING OF ASK... ASKING ALEX TO VISIT. WORRIED SHE... SHE'LL THINK I'M INTERNET CREEP!
NO, SHE WON'T...
I'LL GET IN TOUCH WITH HER AND TELL HER WHAT AN OUTSTANDING INDIVIDUAL YOU REALLY ARE!
I'LL CONFIRM THAT YOU'RE SQUARED AWAY, AND THAT YOU KEEP YOUR STUFF TOGETHER EVEN WHEN YOU'RE IN A WORLD OF HURT!
UM... IS THAT RO... ROMANTIC?
TRUST ME, SON — I KNOW WOMEN. LEAVE IT TO ME.

3/25/09

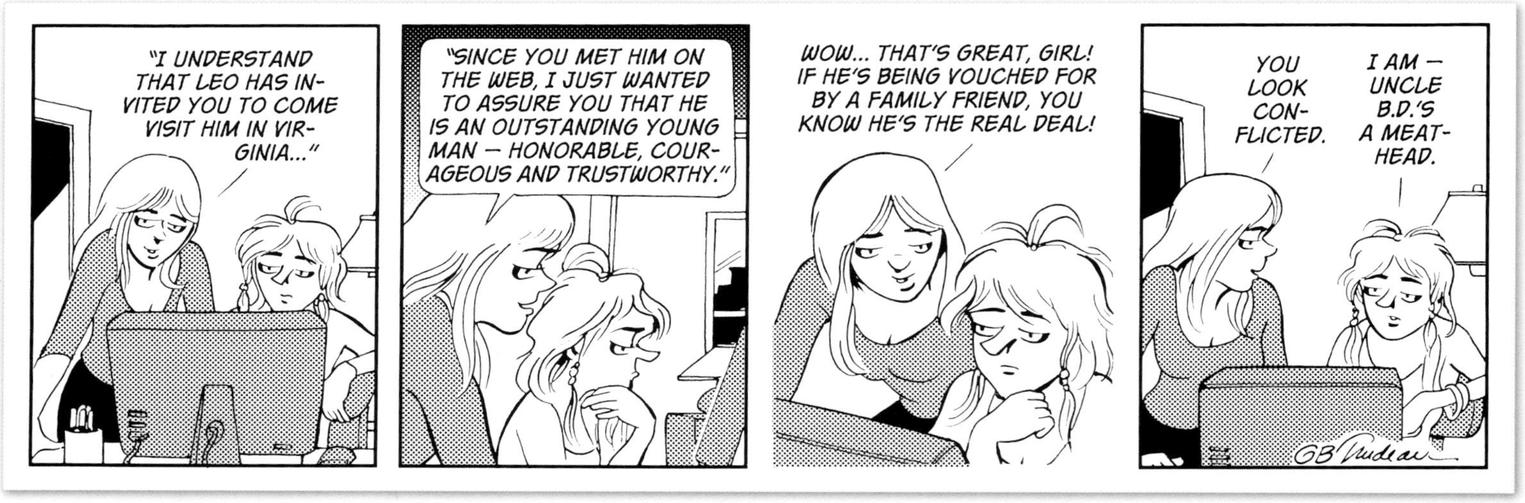
"I UNDERSTAND THAT LEO HAS INVITED YOU TO COME VISIT HIM IN VIRGINIA..."
"SINCE YOU MET HIM ON THE WEB, I JUST WANTED TO ASSURE YOU THAT HE IS AN OUTSTANDING YOUNG MAN — HONORABLE, COURAGEOUS AND TRUSTWORTHY."
WOW... THAT'S GREAT, GIRL! IF HE'S BEING VOUCHED FOR BY A FAMILY FRIEND, YOU KNOW HE'S THE REAL DEAL!
YOU LOOK CONFLICTED.
I AM — UNCLE B.D.'S A MEATHEAD.

3/26/09

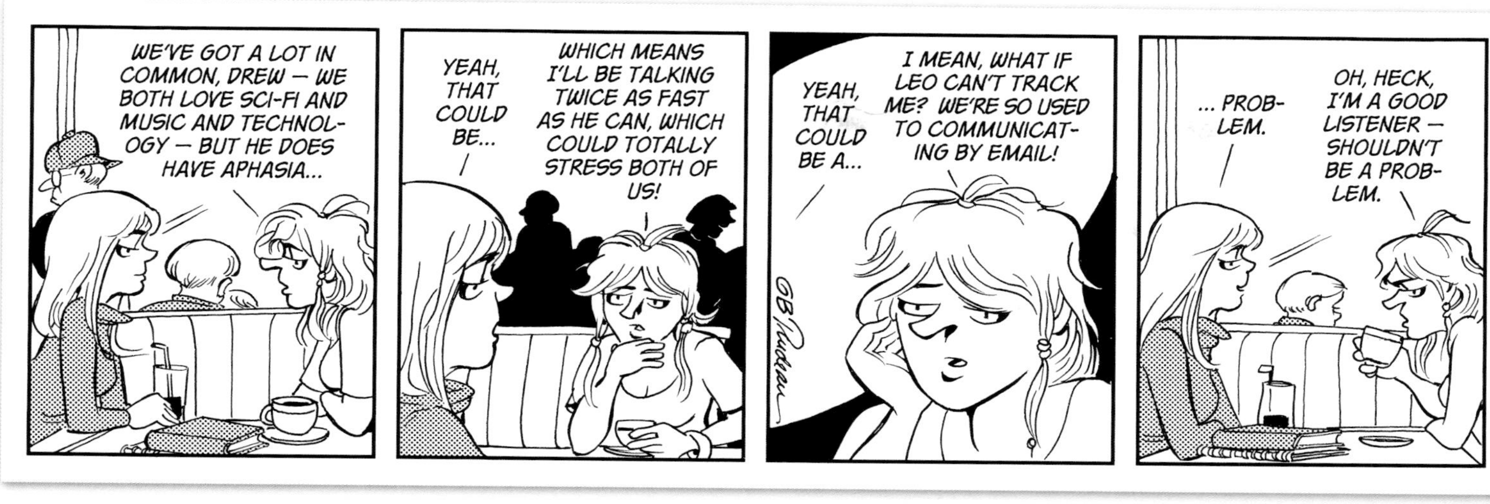
WE'VE GOT A LOT IN COMMON, DREW — WE BOTH LOVE SCI-FI AND MUSIC AND TECHNOLOGY — BUT HE DOES HAVE APHASIA...
YEAH, THAT COULD BE...
WHICH MEANS I'LL BE TALKING TWICE AS FAST AS HE CAN, WHICH COULD TOTALLY STRESS BOTH OF US!
YEAH, THAT COULD BE A...
I MEAN, WHAT IF LEO CAN'T TRACK ME? WE'RE SO USED TO COMMUNICATING BY EMAIL!
... PROB-LEM.
OH, HECK, I'M A GOOD LISTENER — SHOULDN'T BE A PROB-LEM.

3/27/09

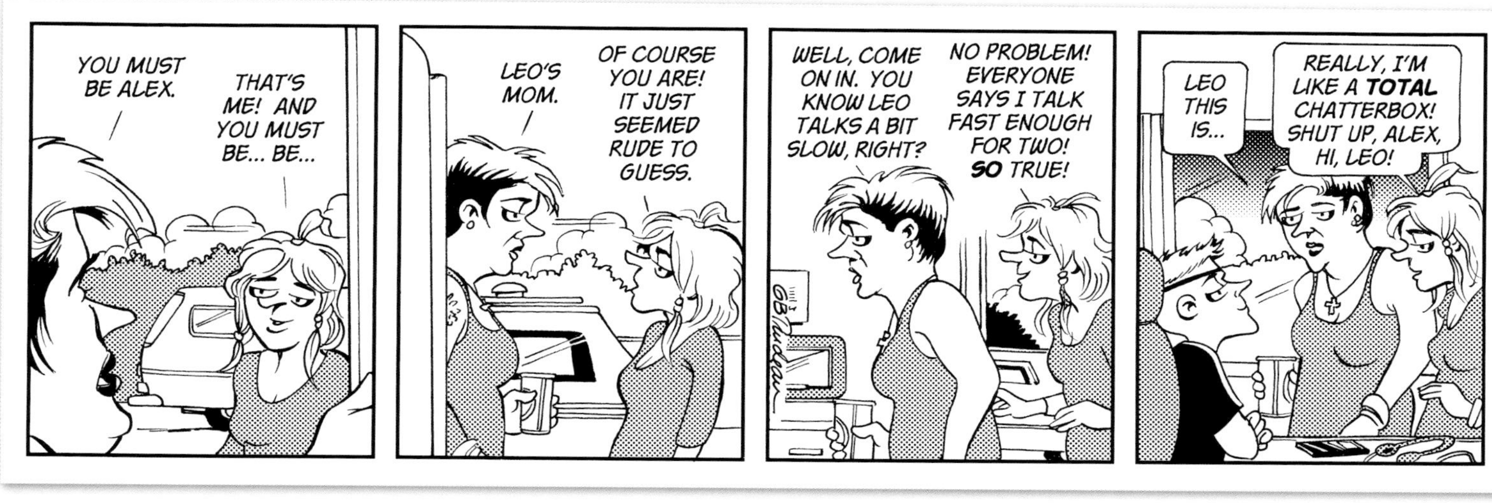
YOU MUST BE ALEX.
THAT'S ME! AND YOU MUST BE... BE...
LEO'S MOM.
OF COURSE YOU ARE! IT JUST SEEMED RUDE TO GUESS.
WELL, COME ON IN. YOU KNOW LEO TALKS A BIT SLOW, RIGHT?
NO PROBLEM! EVERYONE SAYS I TALK FAST ENOUGH FOR TWO! **SO** TRUE!
LEO THIS IS...
REALLY, I'M LIKE A **TOTAL** CHATTERBOX! SHUT UP, ALEX, HI, LEO!

4/6/09

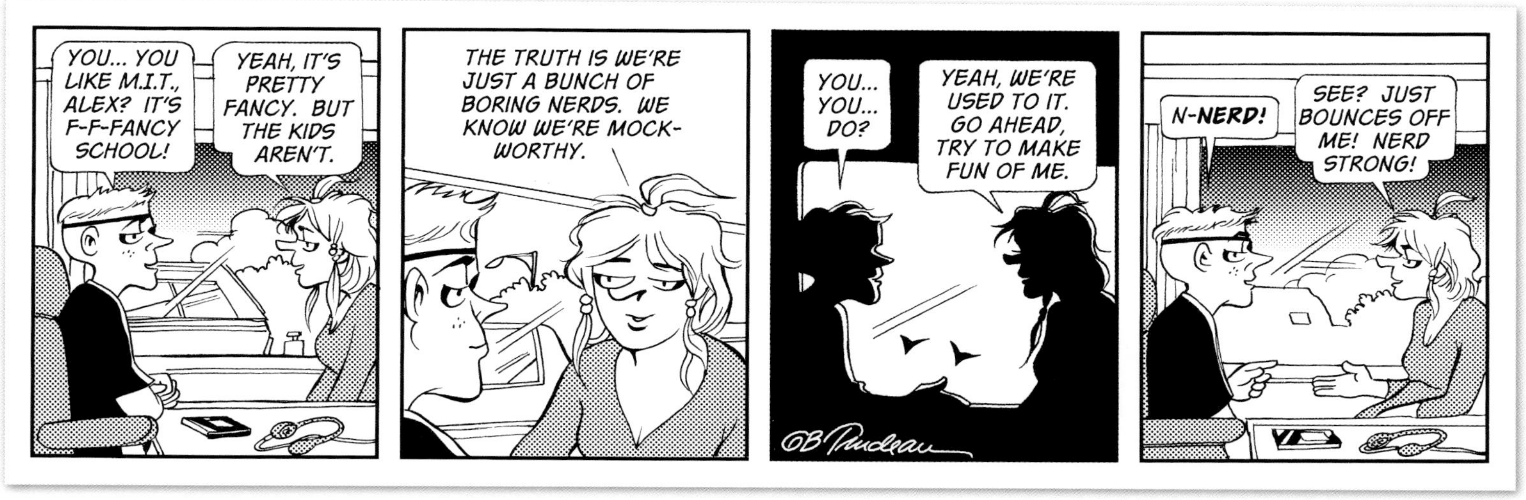
YOU... YOU LIKE M.I.T., ALEX? IT'S F-F-FANCY SCHOOL!
YEAH, IT'S PRETTY FANCY. BUT THE KIDS AREN'T.
THE TRUTH IS WE'RE JUST A BUNCH OF BORING NERDS. WE KNOW WE'RE MOCK-WORTHY.
YOU... YOU... DO?
YEAH, WE'RE USED TO IT. GO AHEAD, TRY TO MAKE FUN OF ME.
N-**NERD!**
SEE? JUST BOUNCES OFF ME! NERD STRONG!

4/8/09

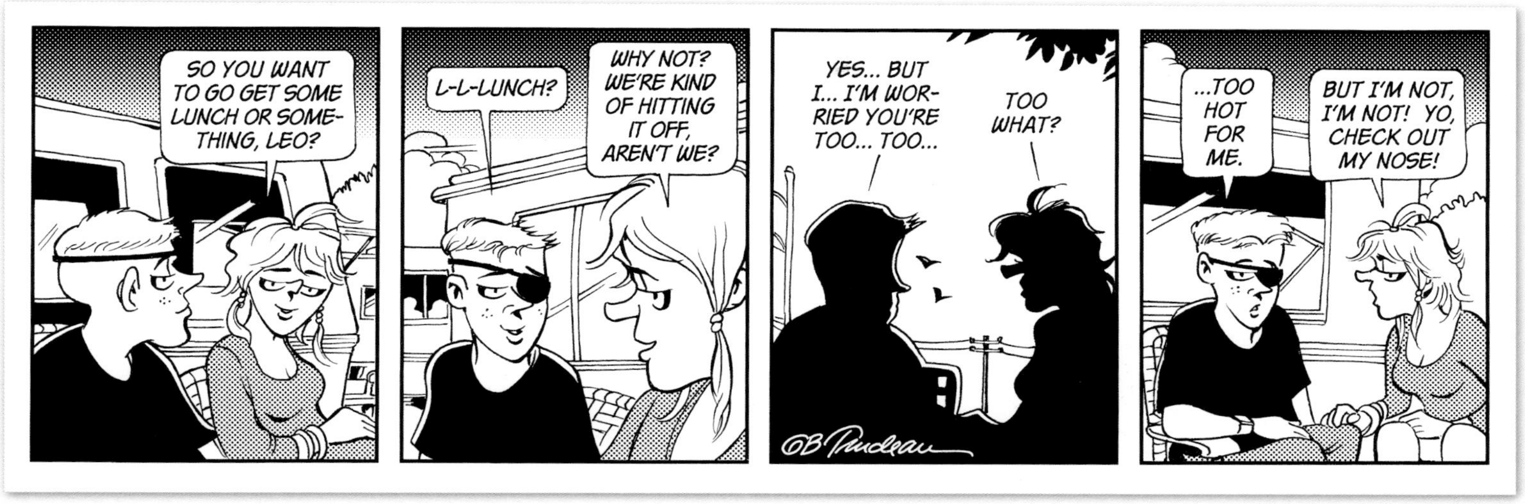
SO YOU WANT TO GO GET SOME LUNCH OR SOMETHING, LEO?
L-L-LUNCH?
WHY NOT? WE'RE KIND OF HITTING IT OFF, AREN'T WE?
YES... BUT I... I'M WORRIED YOU'RE TOO... TOO...
TOO WHAT?
...TOO HOT FOR ME.
BUT I'M NOT, I'M NOT! YO, CHECK OUT MY NOSE!

4/10/09

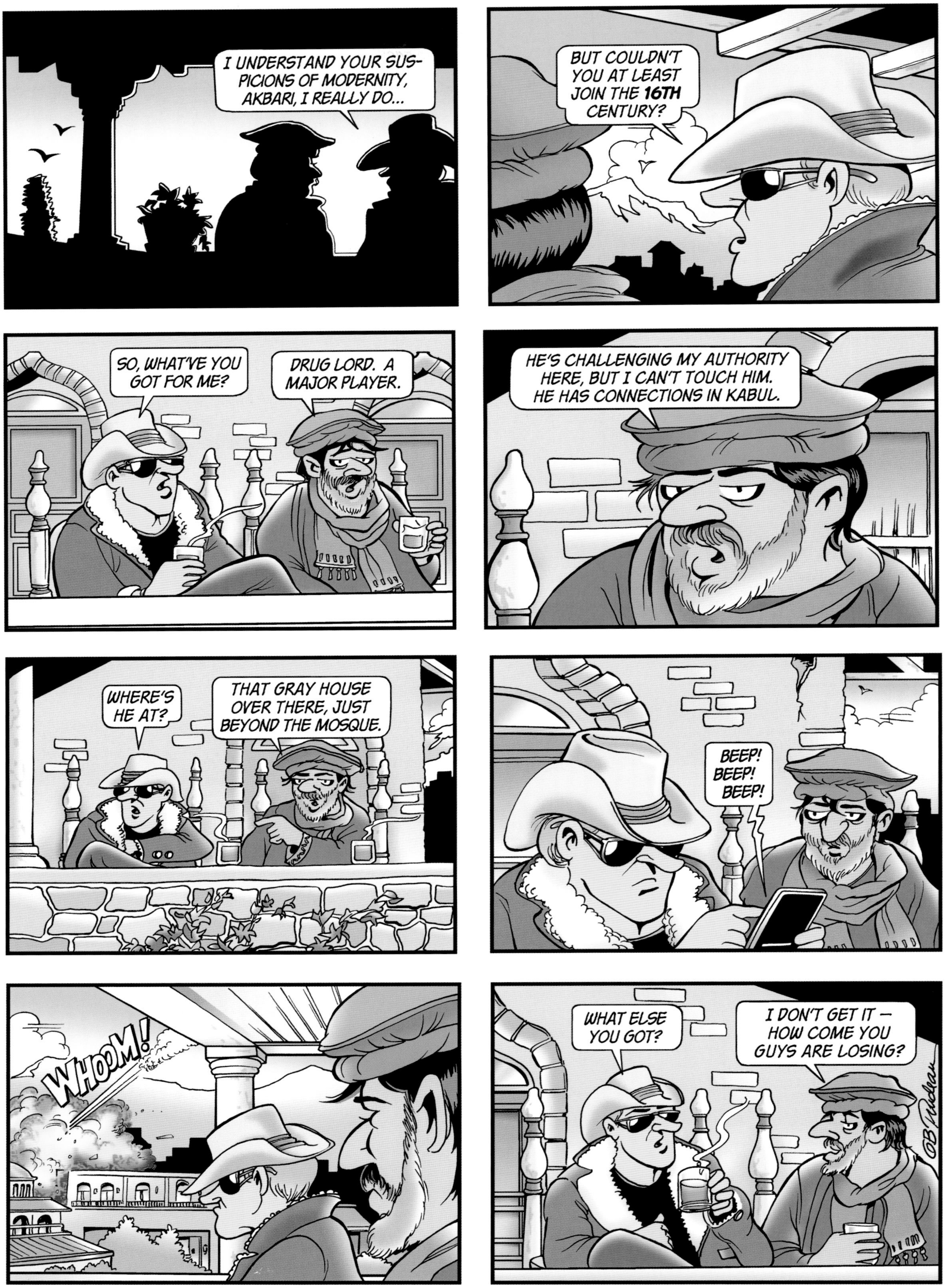
I UNDERSTAND YOUR SUSPICIONS OF MODERNITY, AKBARI, I REALLY DO...
BUT COULDN'T YOU AT LEAST JOIN THE 16TH CENTURY?
SO, WHAT'VE YOU GOT FOR ME?
DRUG LORD. A MAJOR PLAYER.
HE'S CHALLENGING MY AUTHORITY HERE, BUT I CAN'T TOUCH HIM. HE HAS CONNECTIONS IN KABUL.
WHERE'S HE AT?
THAT GRAY HOUSE OVER THERE, JUST BEYOND THE MOSQUE.
BEEP! BEEP! BEEP!
WHOOM!
WHAT ELSE YOU GOT?
I DON'T GET IT — HOW COME YOU GUYS ARE LOSING?
GBTrudeau

4/5/09

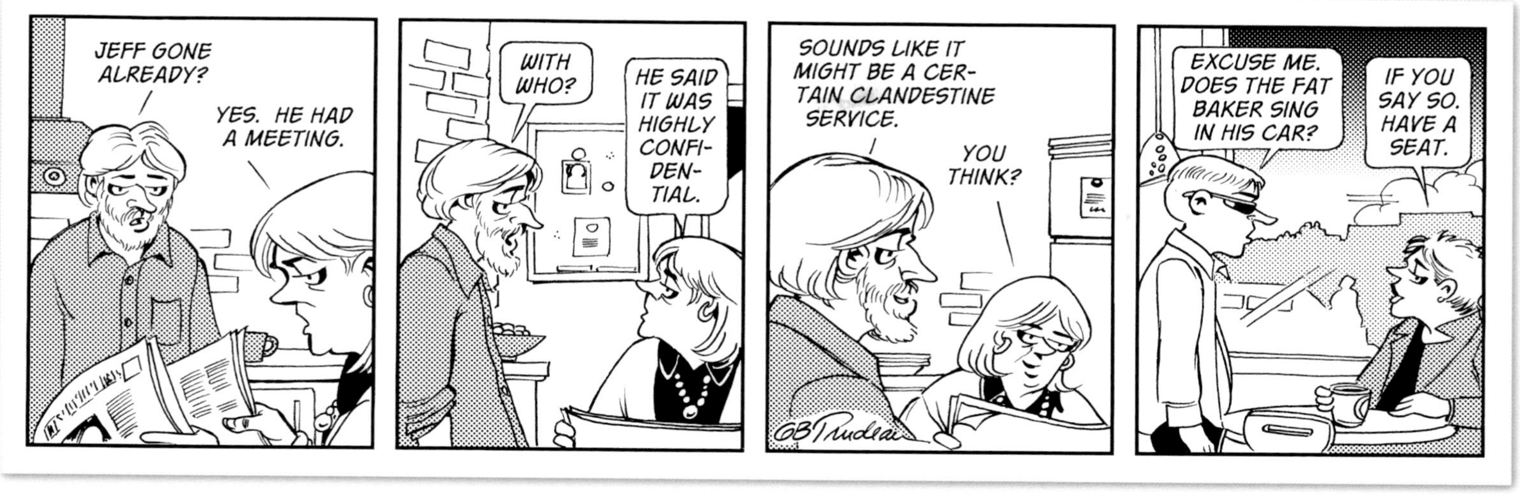
JEFF GONE ALREADY?
YES. HE HAD A MEETING.
WITH WHO?
HE SAID IT WAS HIGHLY CONFI-DEN-TIAL.
SOUNDS LIKE IT MIGHT BE A CER-TAIN CLANDESTINE SERVICE.
YOU THINK?
GB Trudeau
EXCUSE ME. DOES THE FAT BAKER SING IN HIS CAR?
IF YOU SAY SO. HAVE A SEAT.

4/13/09

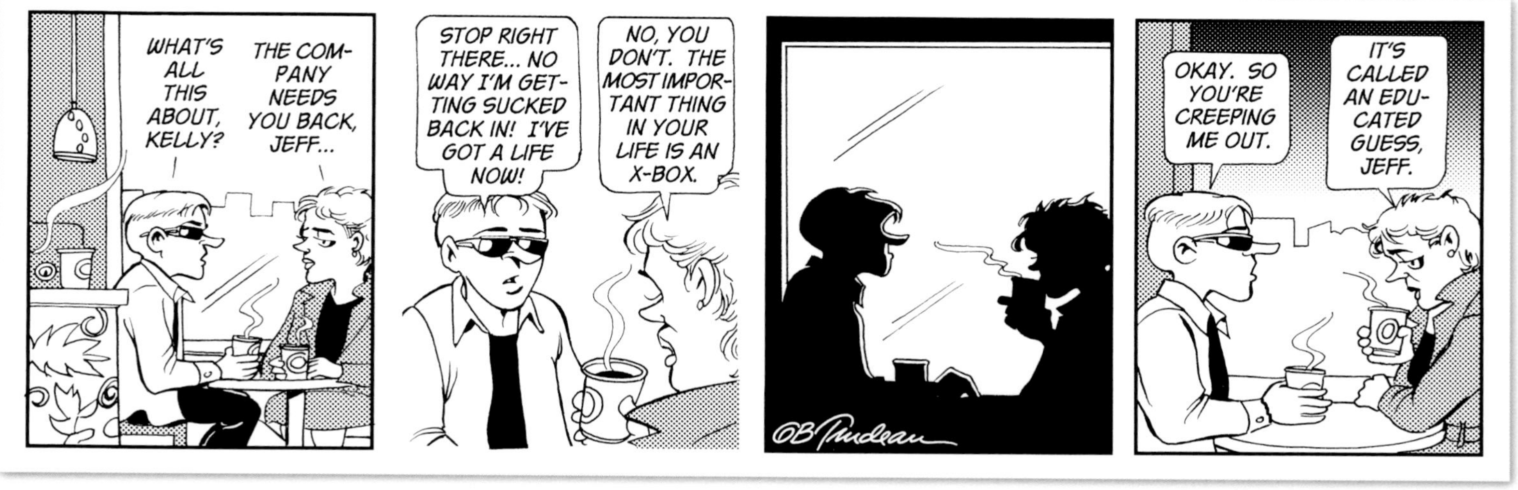
WHAT'S ALL THIS ABOUT, KELLY?
THE COM-PANY NEEDS YOU BACK, JEFF...
STOP RIGHT THERE... NO WAY I'M GET-TING SUCKED BACK IN! I'VE GOT A LIFE NOW!
NO, YOU DON'T. THE MOST IMPOR-TANT THING IN YOUR LIFE IS AN X-BOX.
GB Trudeau
OKAY. SO YOU'RE CREEPING ME OUT.
IT'S CALLED AN EDU-CATED GUESS, JEFF.

4/14/09

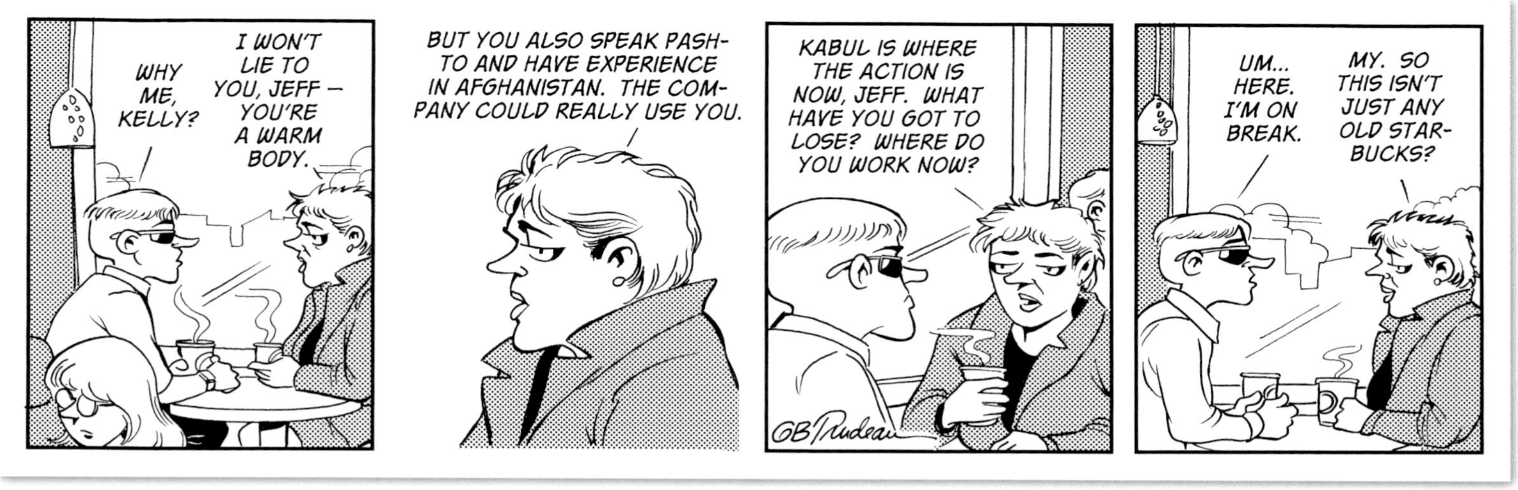
WHY ME, KELLY?
I WON'T LIE TO YOU, JEFF — YOU'RE A WARM BODY.
BUT YOU ALSO SPEAK PASH-TO AND HAVE EXPERIENCE IN AFGHANISTAN. THE COM-PANY COULD REALLY USE YOU.
KABUL IS WHERE THE ACTION IS NOW, JEFF. WHAT HAVE YOU GOT TO LOSE? WHERE DO YOU WORK NOW?
GB Trudeau
UM... HERE. I'M ON BREAK.
MY. SO THIS ISN'T JUST ANY OLD STAR-BUCKS?

4/15/09

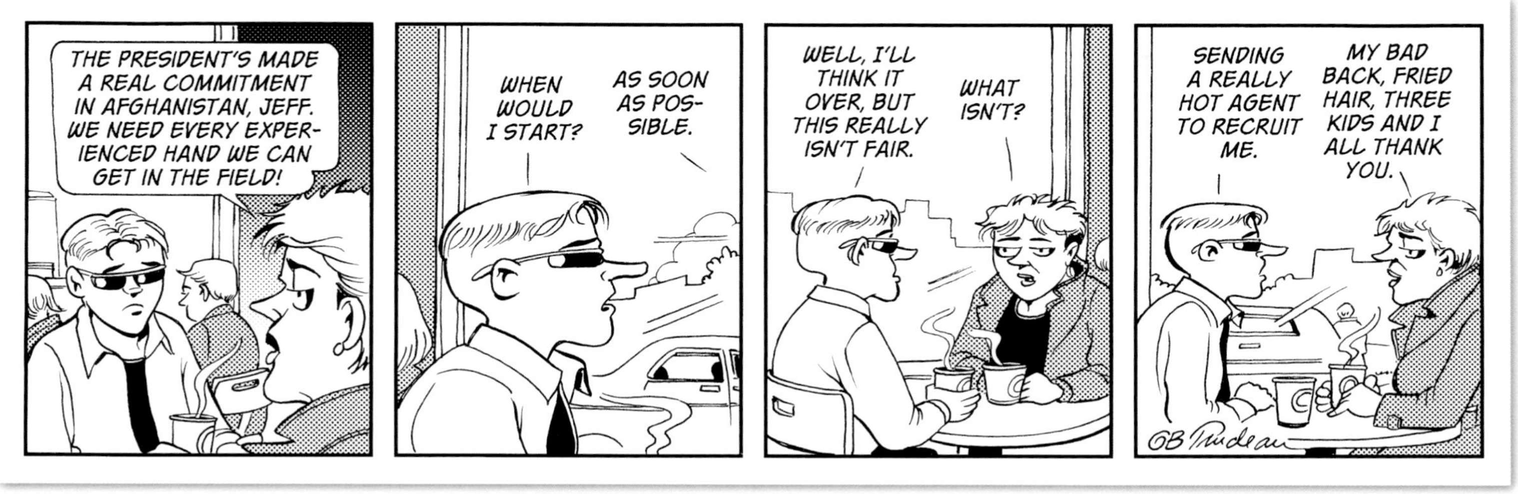
THE PRESIDENT'S MADE A REAL COMMITMENT IN AFGHANISTAN, JEFF. WE NEED EVERY EXPER-IENCED HAND WE CAN GET IN THE FIELD!
WHEN WOULD I START?
AS SOON AS POS-SIBLE.
WELL, I'LL THINK IT OVER, BUT THIS REALLY ISN'T FAIR.
WHAT ISN'T?
SENDING A REALLY HOT AGENT TO RECRUIT ME.
MY BAD BACK, FRIED HAIR, THREE KIDS AND I ALL THANK YOU.
GB Trudeau

4/17/09

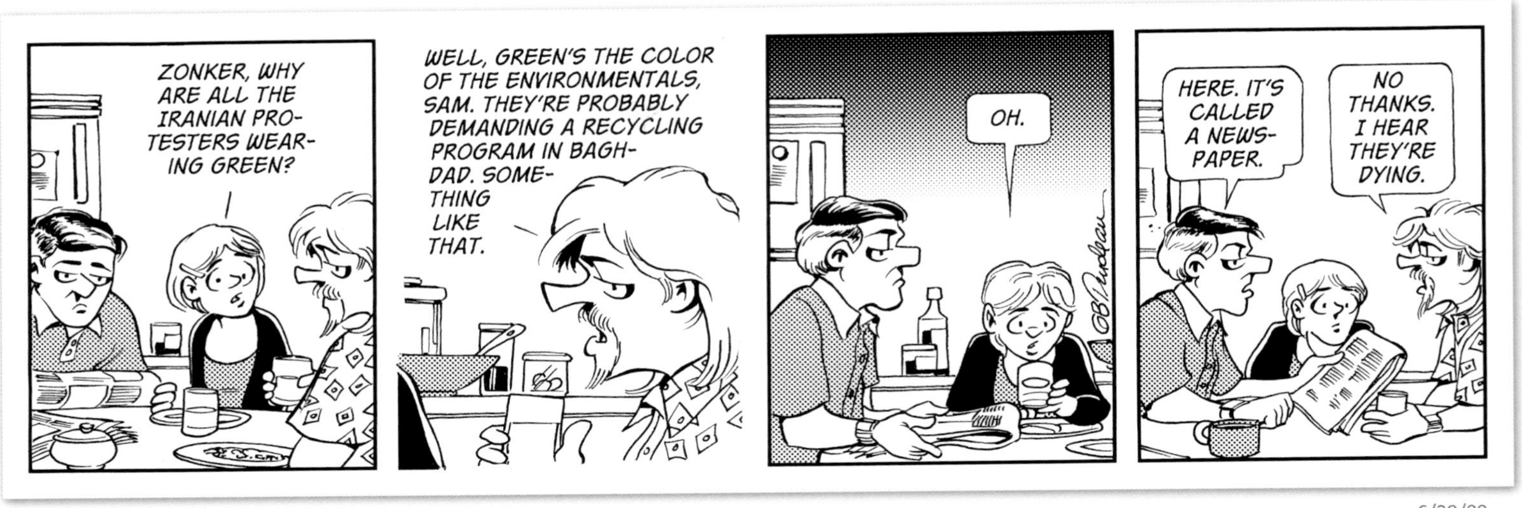
ZONKER, WHY ARE ALL THE IRANIAN PROTESTERS WEARING GREEN?
WELL, GREEN'S THE COLOR OF THE ENVIRONMENTALS, SAM. THEY'RE PROBABLY DEMANDING A RECYCLING PROGRAM IN BAGHDAD. SOMETHING LIKE THAT.
OH.
HERE. IT'S CALLED A NEWSPAPER.
NO THANKS. I HEAR THEY'RE DYING.
GBTrudeau

6/29/09

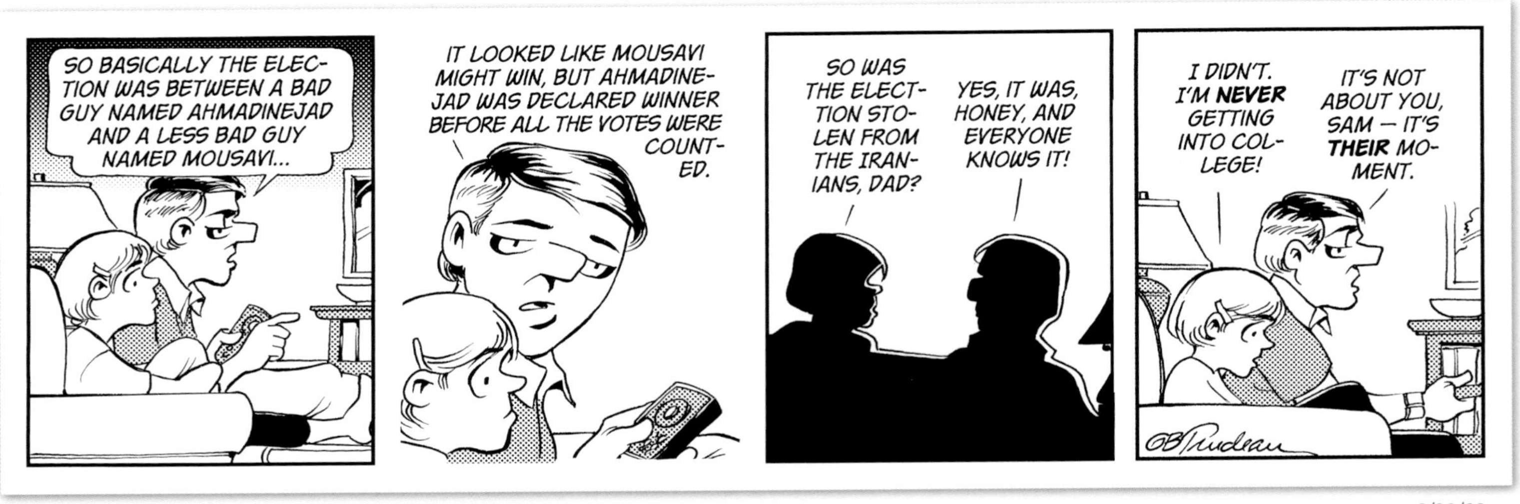
SO BASICALLY THE ELECTION WAS BETWEEN A BAD GUY NAMED AHMADINEJAD AND A LESS BAD GUY NAMED MOUSAVI...
IT LOOKED LIKE MOUSAVI MIGHT WIN, BUT AHMADINEJAD WAS DECLARED WINNER BEFORE ALL THE VOTES WERE COUNTED.
SO WAS THE ELECTION STOLEN FROM THE IRANIANS, DAD?
YES, IT WAS, HONEY, AND EVERYONE KNOWS IT!
I DIDN'T. I'M **NEVER** GETTING INTO COLLEGE!
IT'S NOT ABOUT YOU, SAM — IT'S **THEIR** MOMENT.
GBTrudeau

6/30/09

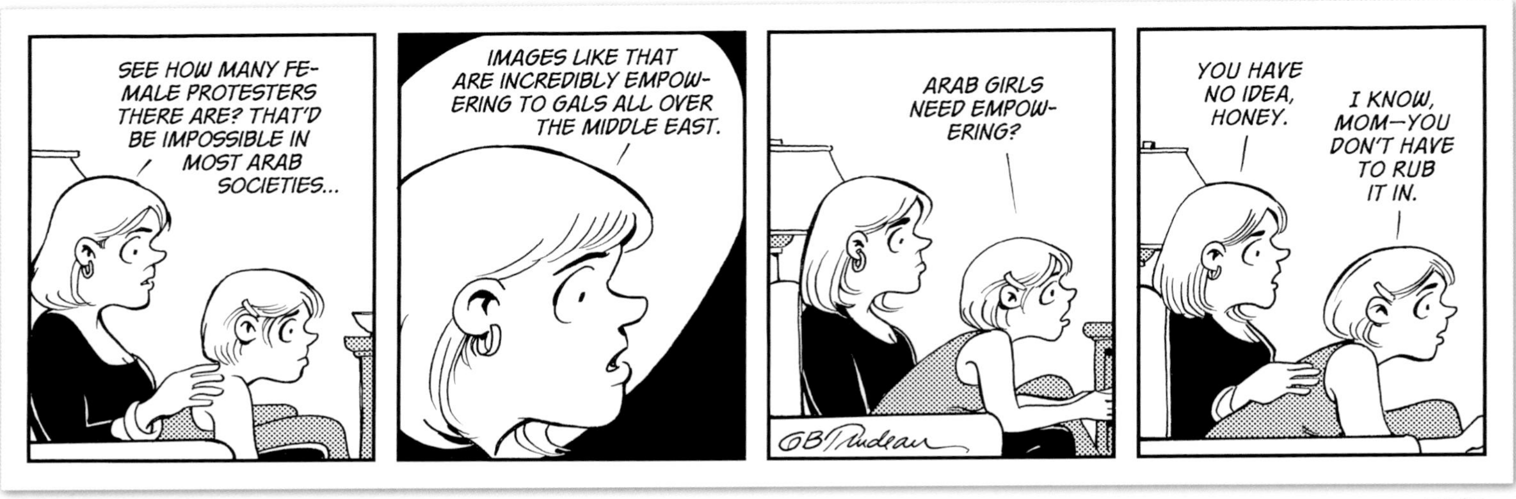
SEE HOW MANY FEMALE PROTESTERS THERE ARE? THAT'D BE IMPOSSIBLE IN MOST ARAB SOCIETIES...
IMAGES LIKE THAT ARE INCREDIBLY EMPOWERING TO GALS ALL OVER THE MIDDLE EAST.
ARAB GIRLS NEED EMPOWERING?
GBTrudeau
YOU HAVE NO IDEA, HONEY.
I KNOW, MOM—YOU DON'T HAVE TO RUB IT IN.

7/1/09

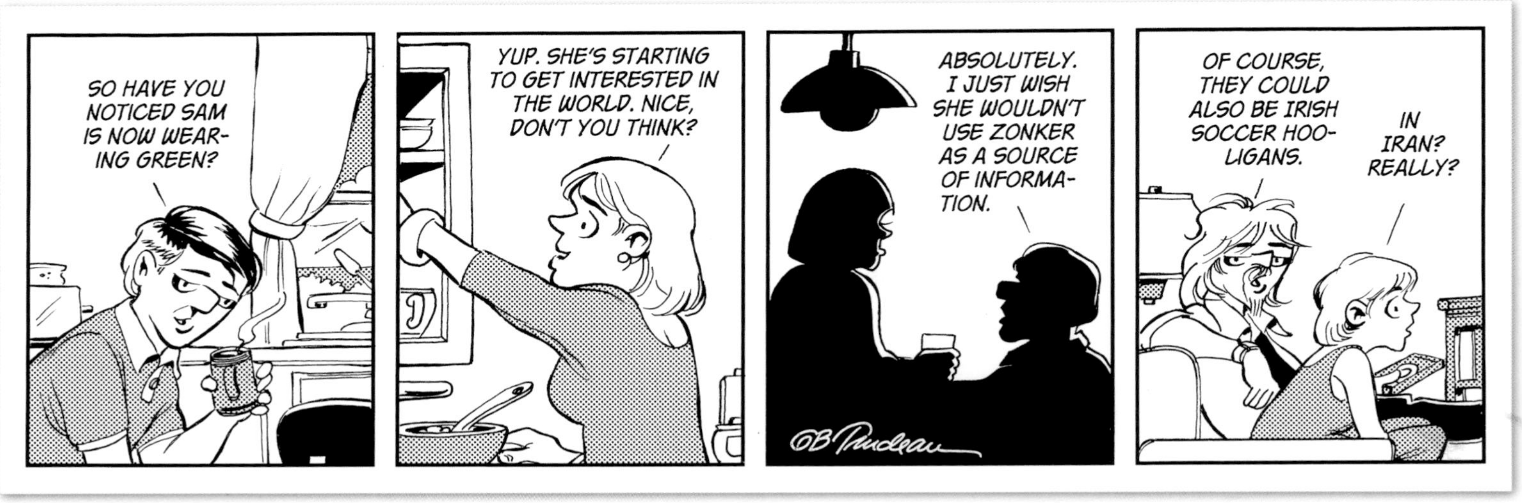
SO HAVE YOU NOTICED SAM IS NOW WEARING GREEN?
YUP. SHE'S STARTING TO GET INTERESTED IN THE WORLD. NICE, DON'T YOU THINK?
ABSOLUTELY. I JUST WISH SHE WOULDN'T USE ZONKER AS A SOURCE OF INFORMATION.
GBTrudeau
OF COURSE, THEY COULD ALSO BE IRISH SOCCER HOOLIGANS.
IN IRAN? REALLY?

7/2/09

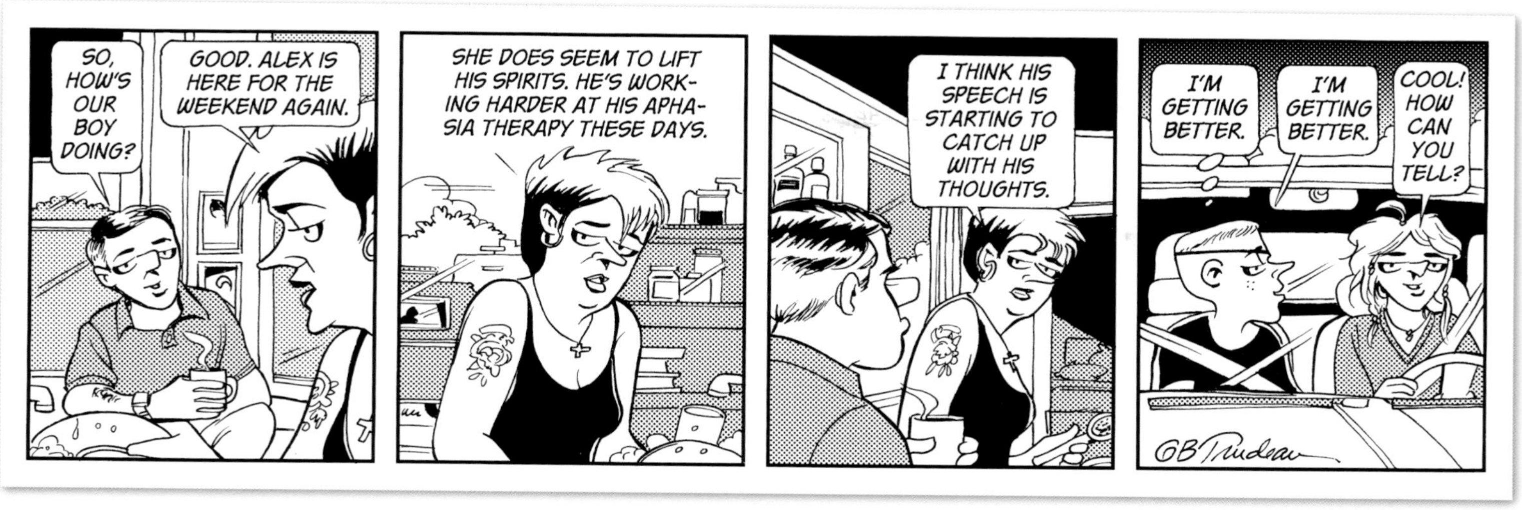
SO, HOW'S OUR BOY DOING?
GOOD. ALEX IS HERE FOR THE WEEKEND AGAIN.
SHE DOES SEEM TO LIFT HIS SPIRITS. HE'S WORKING HARDER AT HIS APHASIA THERAPY THESE DAYS.
I THINK HIS SPEECH IS STARTING TO CATCH UP WITH HIS THOUGHTS.
I'M GETTING BETTER.
I'M GETTING BETTER.
COOL! HOW CAN YOU TELL?

5/11/09

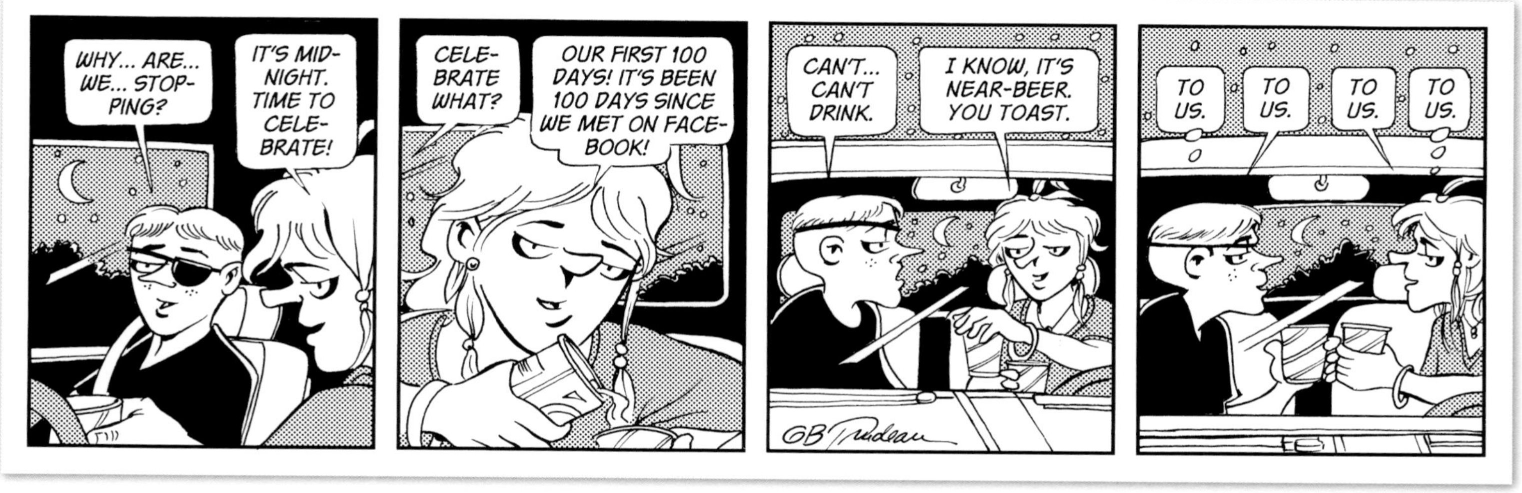
WHY... ARE... WE... STOPPING?
IT'S MIDNIGHT. TIME TO CELEBRATE!
CELEBRATE WHAT?
OUR FIRST 100 DAYS! IT'S BEEN 100 DAYS SINCE WE MET ON FACEBOOK!
CAN'T... CAN'T DRINK.
I KNOW, IT'S NEAR-BEER. YOU TOAST.
TO US.
TO US.
TO US.
TO US.

5/12/09

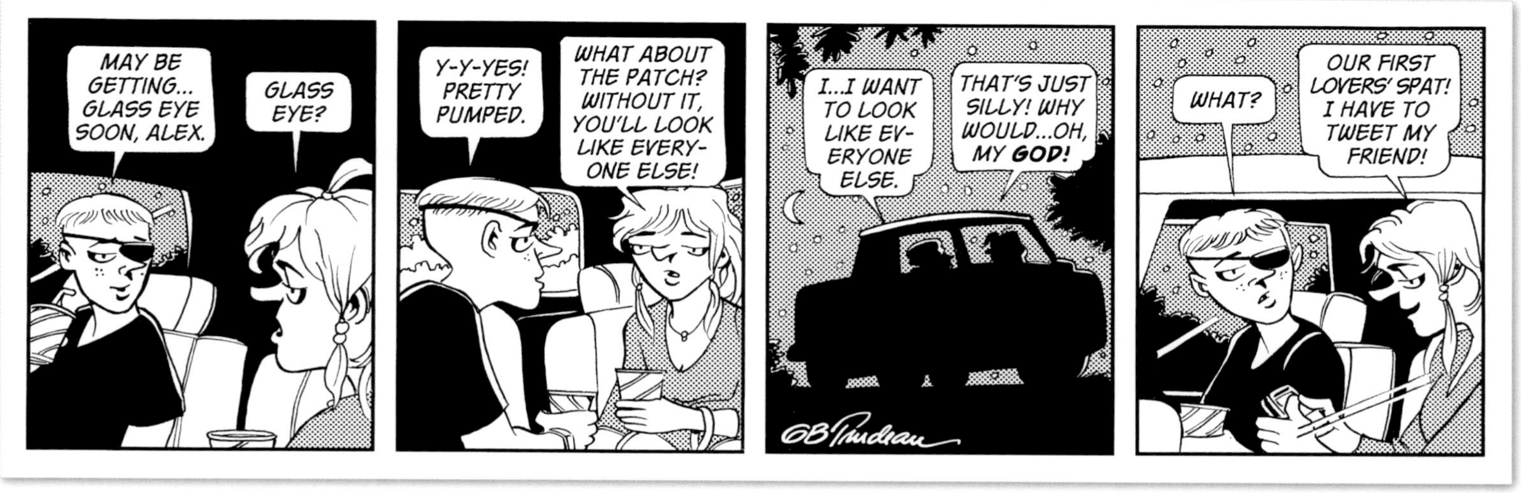
MAY BE GETTING... GLASS EYE SOON, ALEX.
GLASS EYE?
Y-Y-YES! PRETTY PUMPED.
WHAT ABOUT THE PATCH? WITHOUT IT, YOU'LL LOOK LIKE EVERYONE ELSE!
I...I WANT TO LOOK LIKE EVERYONE ELSE.
THAT'S JUST SILLY! WHY WOULD...OH, MY **GOD!**
WHAT?
OUR FIRST LOVERS' SPAT! I HAVE TO TWEET MY FRIEND!

5/14/09

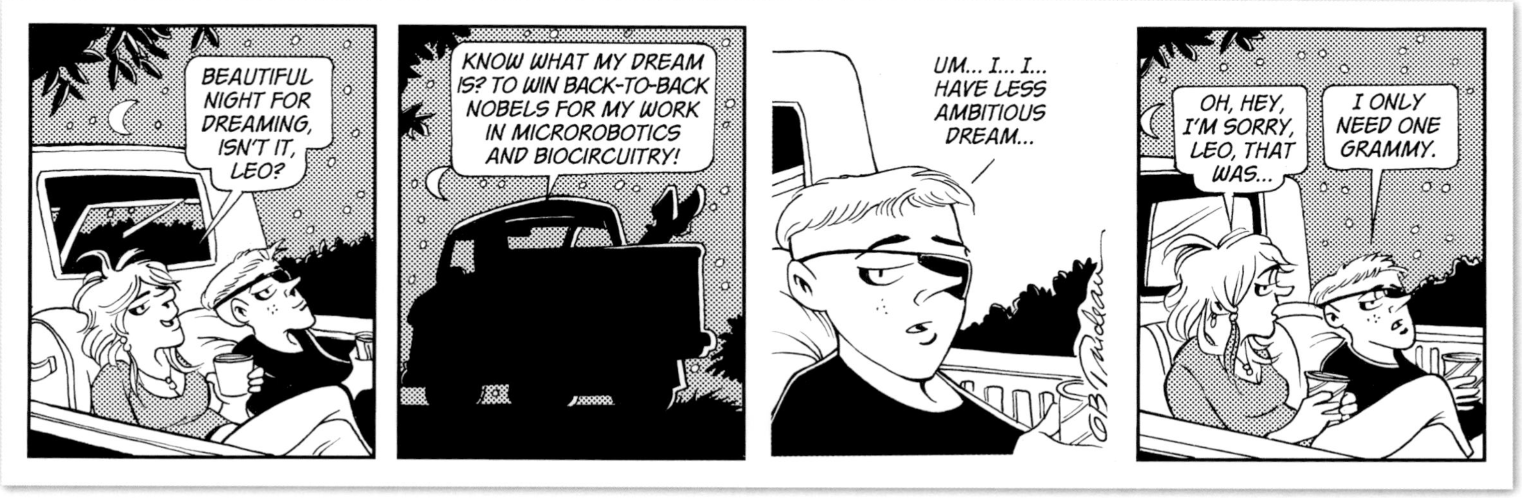
BEAUTIFUL NIGHT FOR DREAMING, ISN'T IT, LEO?
KNOW WHAT MY DREAM IS? TO WIN BACK-TO-BACK NOBELS FOR MY WORK IN MICROROBOTICS AND BIOCIRCUITRY!
UM... I... I... HAVE LESS AMBITIOUS DREAM...
OH, HEY, I'M SORRY, LEO, THAT WAS...
I ONLY NEED ONE GRAMMY.

5/15/09

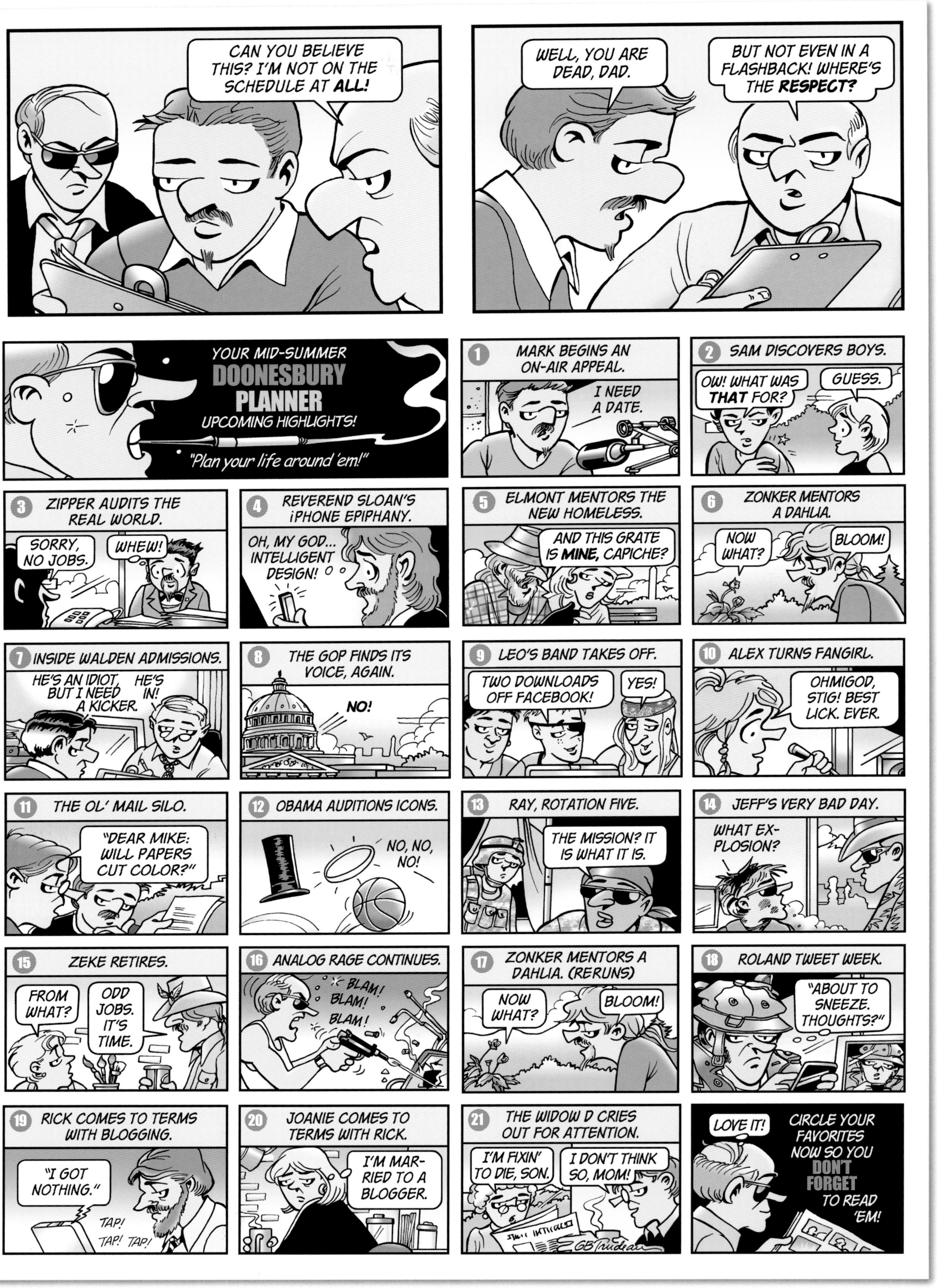
CAN YOU BELIEVE THIS? I'M NOT ON THE SCHEDULE AT ALL!
WELL, YOU ARE DEAD, DAD.
BUT NOT EVEN IN A FLASHBACK! WHERE'S THE RESPECT?
YOUR MID-SUMMER DOONESBURY PLANNER UPCOMING HIGHLIGHTS!
"Plan your life around 'em!"
1 MARK BEGINS AN ON-AIR APPEAL.
I NEED A DATE.
2 SAM DISCOVERS BOYS.
OW! WHAT WAS THAT FOR?
GUESS.
3 ZIPPER AUDITS THE REAL WORLD.
SORRY, NO JOBS.
WHEW!
4 REVEREND SLOAN'S iPHONE EPIPHANY.
OH, MY GOD... INTELLIGENT DESIGN!
5 ELMONT MENTORS THE NEW HOMELESS.
AND THIS GRATE IS MINE, CAPICHE?
6 ZONKER MENTORS A DAHLIA.
NOW WHAT?
BLOOM!
7 INSIDE WALDEN ADMISSIONS.
HE'S AN IDIOT, BUT I NEED A KICKER.
HE'S IN!
8 THE GOP FINDS ITS VOICE, AGAIN.
NO!
9 LEO'S BAND TAKES OFF.
TWO DOWNLOADS OFF FACEBOOK!
YES!
10 ALEX TURNS FANGIRL.
OHMIGOD, STIG! BEST LICK. EVER.
11 THE OL' MAIL SILO.
"DEAR MIKE: WILL PAPERS CUT COLOR?"
12 OBAMA AUDITIONS ICONS.
NO, NO, NO!
13 RAY, ROTATION FIVE.
THE MISSION? IT IS WHAT IT IS.
14 JEFF'S VERY BAD DAY.
WHAT EX-PLOSION?
15 ZEKE RETIRES.
FROM WHAT?
ODD JOBS. IT'S TIME.
16 ANALOG RAGE CONTINUES.
BLAM! BLAM! BLAM!
17 ZONKER MENTORS A DAHLIA. (RERUNS)
NOW WHAT?
BLOOM!
18 ROLAND TWEET WEEK.
"ABOUT TO SNEEZE. THOUGHTS?"
19 RICK COMES TO TERMS WITH BLOGGING.
"I GOT NOTHING."
TAP! TAP! TAP!
20 JOANIE COMES TO TERMS WITH RICK.
I'M MAR-RIED TO A BLOGGER.
21 THE WIDOW D CRIES OUT FOR ATTENTION.
I'M FIXIN' TO DIE, SON.
I DON'T THINK SO, MOM!
G.B. Trudeau
LOVE IT!
CIRCLE YOUR FAVORITES NOW SO YOU DON'T FORGET TO READ 'EM!

7/12/09

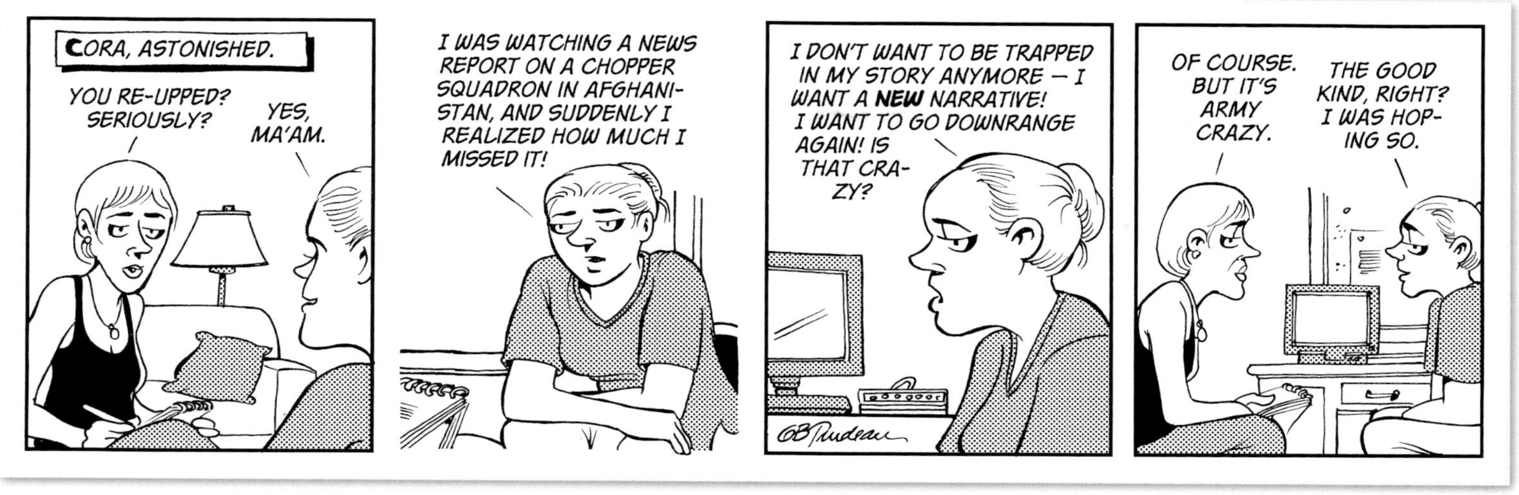
CORA, ASTONISHED.
YOU RE-UPPED? SERIOUSLY?
YES, MA'AM.
I WAS WATCHING A NEWS REPORT ON A CHOPPER SQUADRON IN AFGHANISTAN, AND SUDDENLY I REALIZED HOW MUCH I MISSED IT!
I DON'T WANT TO BE TRAPPED IN MY STORY ANYMORE — I WANT A **NEW** NARRATIVE! I WANT TO GO DOWNRANGE AGAIN! IS THAT CRAZY?
OF COURSE. BUT IT'S ARMY CRAZY.
THE GOOD KIND, RIGHT? I WAS HOPING SO.

7/27/09

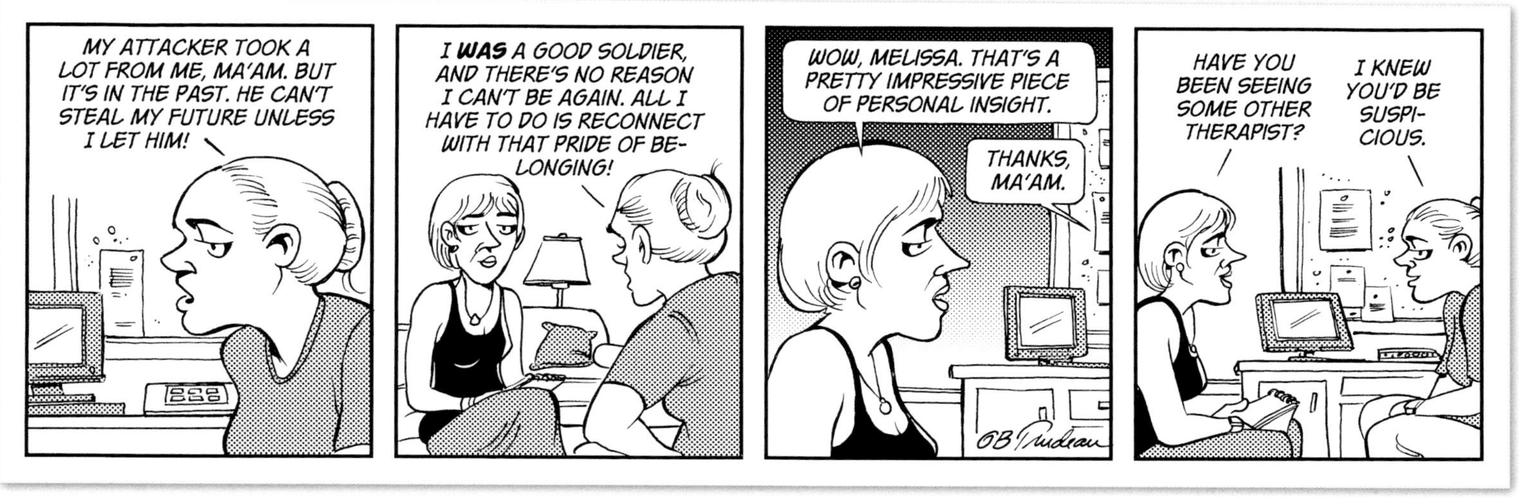
MY ATTACKER TOOK A LOT FROM ME, MA'AM. BUT IT'S IN THE PAST. HE CAN'T STEAL MY FUTURE UNLESS I LET HIM!
I **WAS** A GOOD SOLDIER, AND THERE'S NO REASON I CAN'T BE AGAIN. ALL I HAVE TO DO IS RECONNECT WITH THAT PRIDE OF BELONGING!
WOW, MELISSA. THAT'S A PRETTY IMPRESSIVE PIECE OF PERSONAL INSIGHT.
THANKS, MA'AM.
HAVE YOU BEEN SEEING SOME OTHER THERAPIST?
I KNEW YOU'D BE SUSPICIOUS.

7/28/09

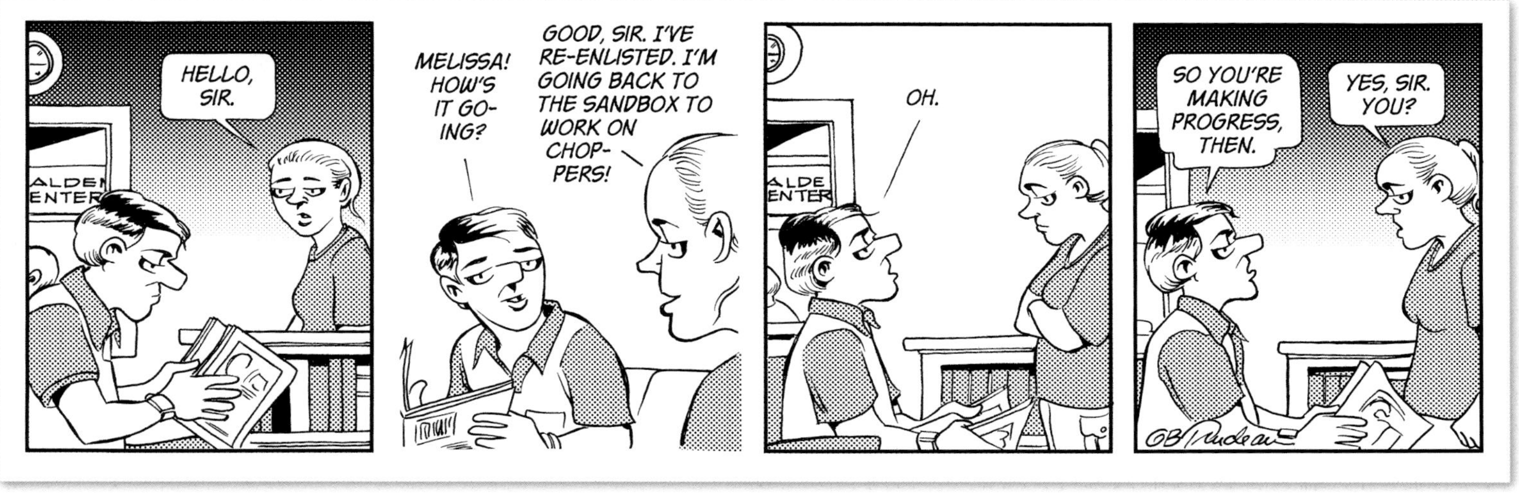
HELLO, SIR.
MELISSA! HOW'S IT GOING?
GOOD, SIR. I'VE RE-ENLISTED. I'M GOING BACK TO THE SANDBOX TO WORK ON CHOPPERS!
OH.
SO YOU'RE MAKING PROGRESS, THEN.
YES, SIR. YOU?

7/30/09

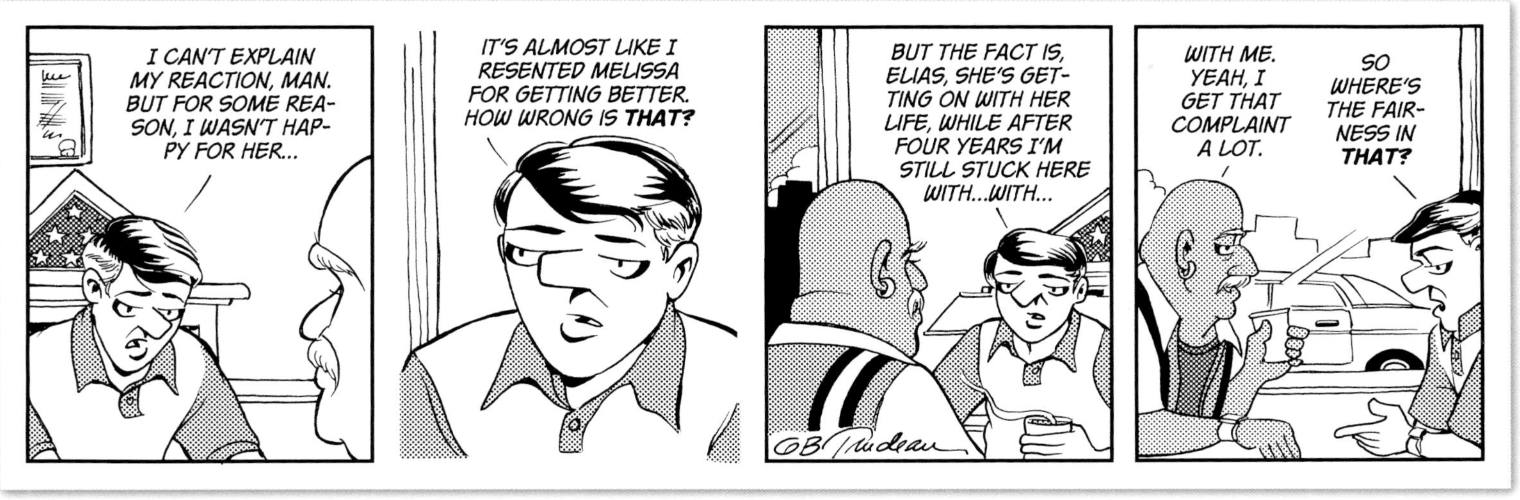
I CAN'T EXPLAIN MY REACTION, MAN. BUT FOR SOME REASON, I WASN'T HAPPY FOR HER...
IT'S ALMOST LIKE I RESENTED MELISSA FOR GETTING BETTER. HOW WRONG IS **THAT?**
BUT THE FACT IS, ELIAS, SHE'S GETTING ON WITH HER LIFE, WHILE AFTER FOUR YEARS I'M STILL STUCK HERE WITH...WITH...
WITH ME. YEAH, I GET THAT COMPLAINT A LOT.
SO WHERE'S THE FAIRNESS IN **THAT?**

8/1/09

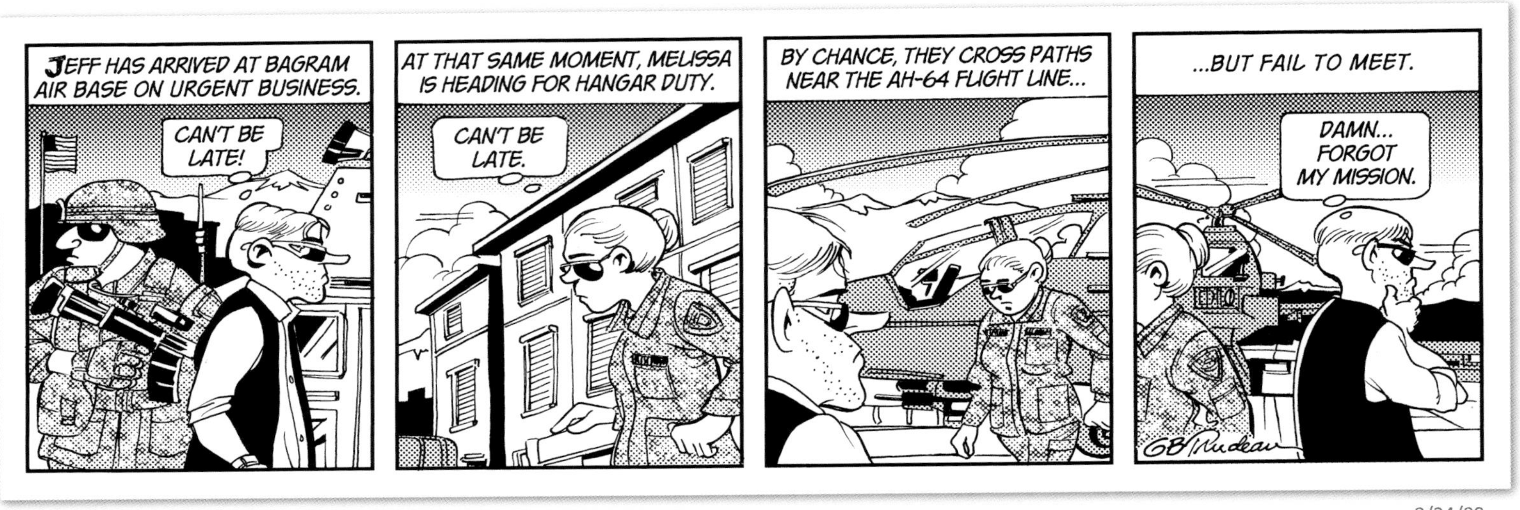
JEFF HAS ARRIVED AT BAGRAM AIR BASE ON URGENT BUSINESS.
CAN'T BE LATE!
AT THAT SAME MOMENT, MELISSA IS HEADING FOR HANGAR DUTY.
CAN'T BE LATE.
BY CHANCE, THEY CROSS PATHS NEAR THE AH-64 FLIGHT LINE...
...BUT FAIL TO MEET.
DAMN... FORGOT MY MISSION.
GB Trudeau

8/24/09

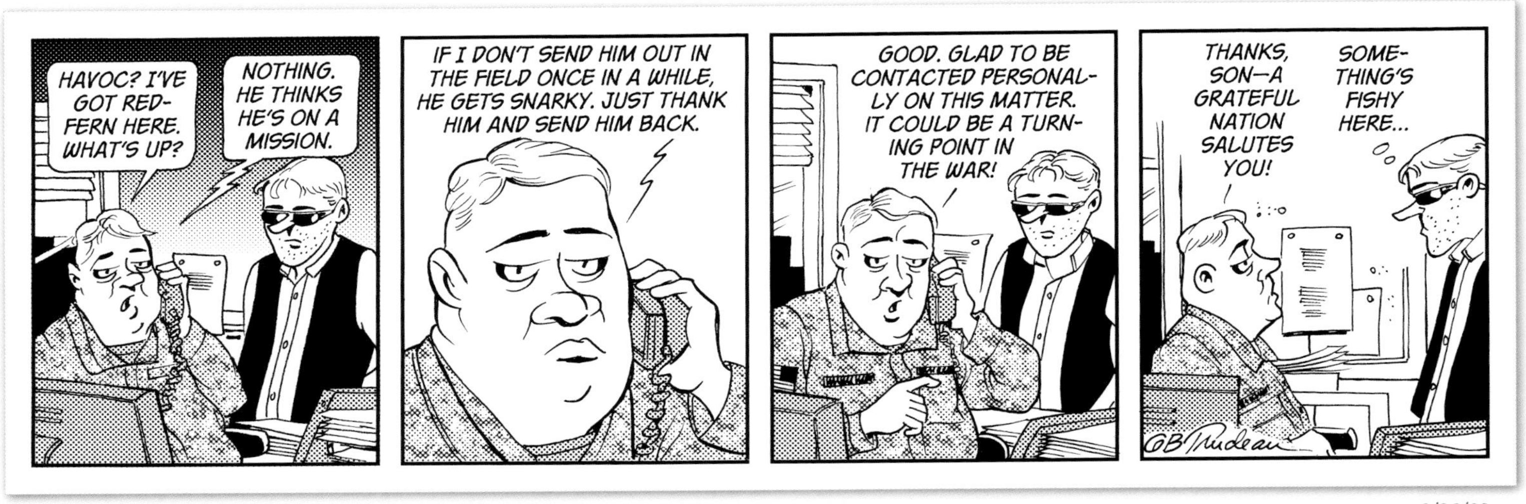
HAVOC? I'VE GOT RED-FERN HERE. WHAT'S UP?
NOTHING. HE THINKS HE'S ON A MISSION.
IF I DON'T SEND HIM OUT IN THE FIELD ONCE IN A WHILE, HE GETS SNARKY. JUST THANK HIM AND SEND HIM BACK.
GOOD. GLAD TO BE CONTACTED PERSONAL-LY ON THIS MATTER. IT COULD BE A TURN-ING POINT IN THE WAR!
THANKS, SON—A GRATEFUL NATION SALUTES YOU!
SOME-THING'S FISHY HERE...
GB Trudeau

8/26/09

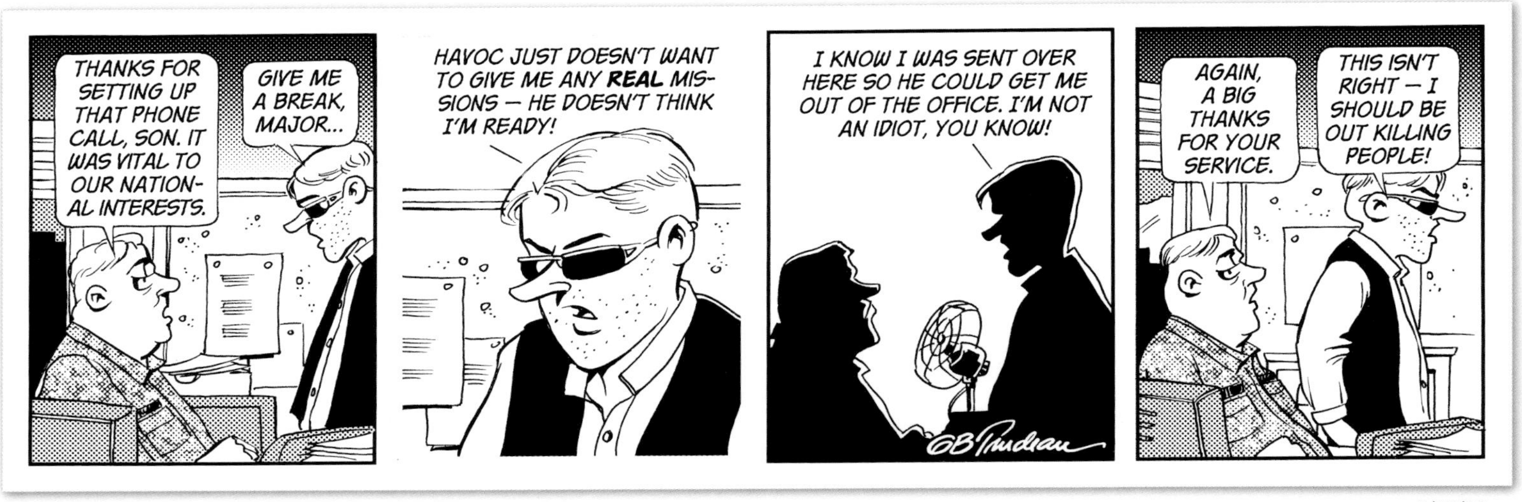
THANKS FOR SETTING UP THAT PHONE CALL, SON. IT WAS VITAL TO OUR NATION-AL INTERESTS.
GIVE ME A BREAK, MAJOR...
HAVOC JUST DOESN'T WANT TO GIVE ME ANY REAL MIS-SIONS — HE DOESN'T THINK I'M READY!
I KNOW I WAS SENT OVER HERE SO HE COULD GET ME OUT OF THE OFFICE. I'M NOT AN IDIOT, YOU KNOW!
GB Trudeau
AGAIN, A BIG THANKS FOR YOUR SERVICE.
THIS ISN'T RIGHT — I SHOULD BE OUT KILLING PEOPLE!

8/27/09

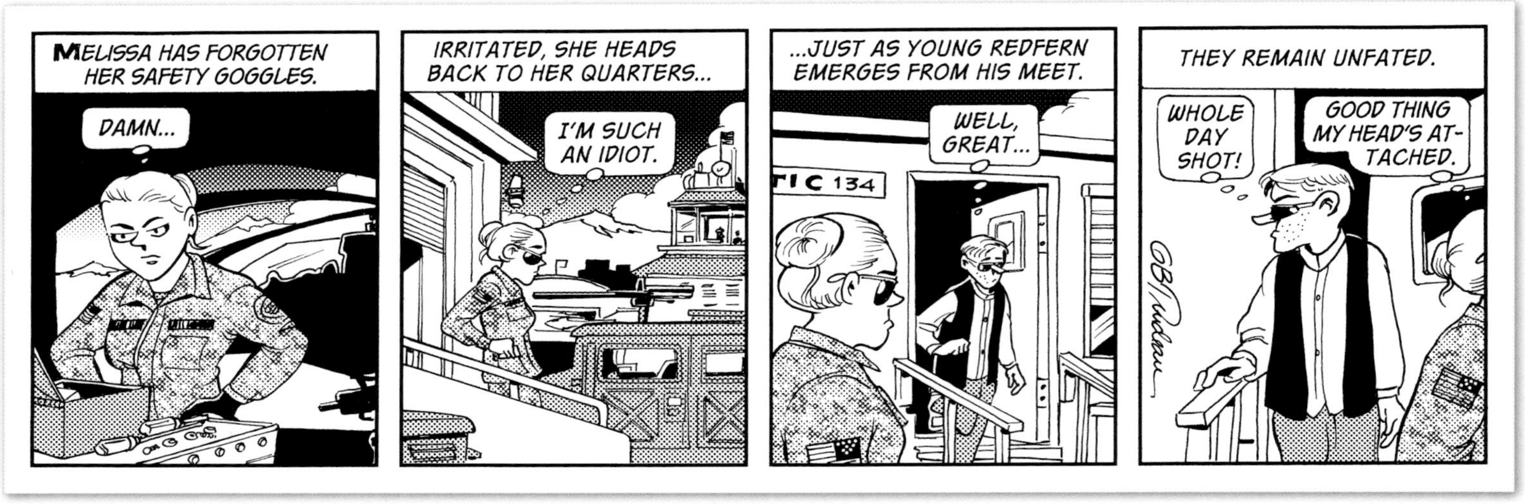
MELISSA HAS FORGOTTEN HER SAFETY GOGGLES.
DAMN...
IRRITATED, SHE HEADS BACK TO HER QUARTERS...
I'M SUCH AN IDIOT.
...JUST AS YOUNG REDFERN EMERGES FROM HIS MEET.
TIC 134
WELL, GREAT...
THEY REMAIN UNFATED.
WHOLE DAY SHOT!
GOOD THING MY HEAD'S AT-TACHED.
GB Trudeau

8/28/09

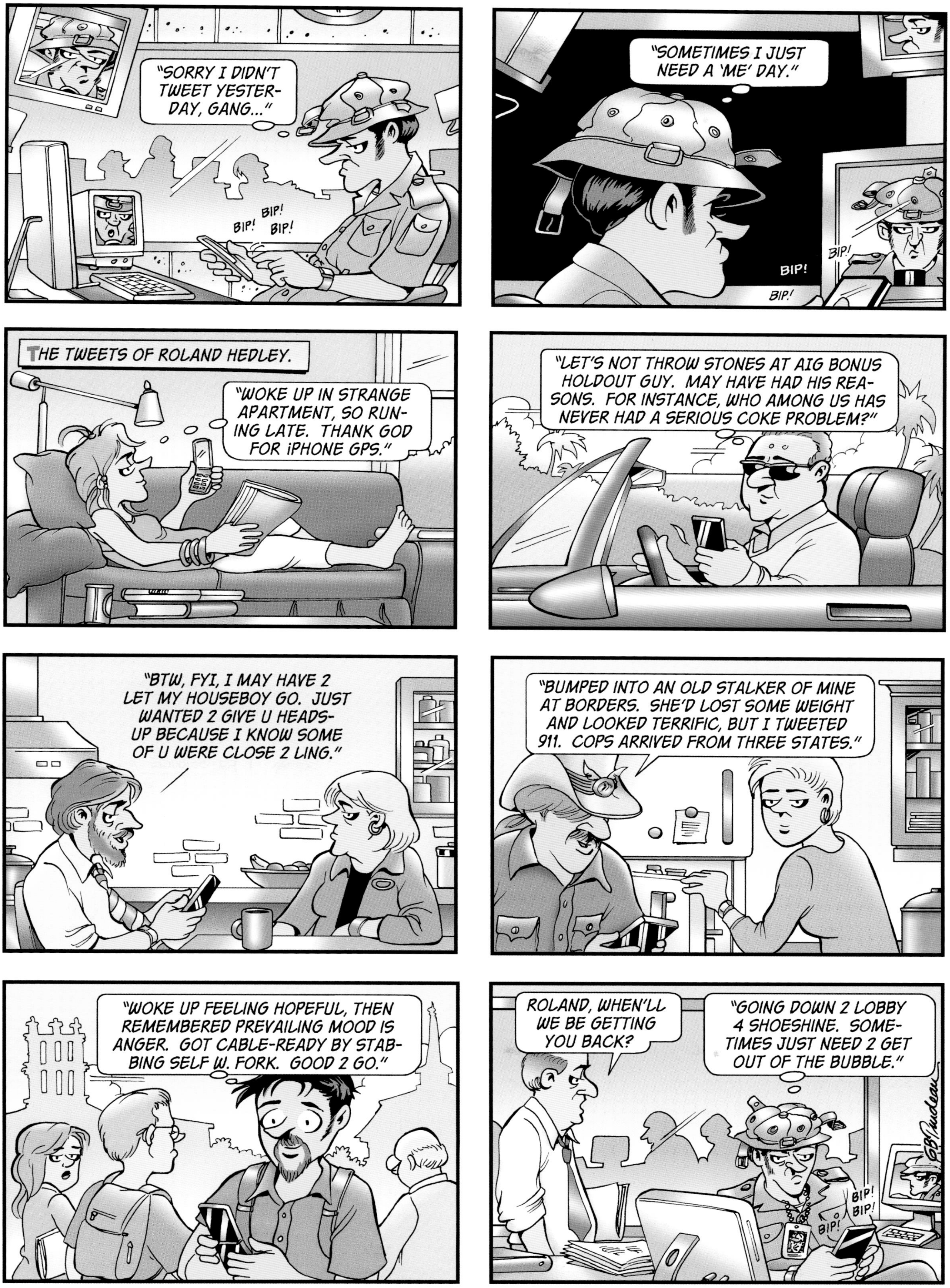
"SORRY I DIDN'T TWEET YESTERDAY, GANG..."
BIP! BIP! BIP!
"SOMETIMES I JUST NEED A 'ME' DAY."
BIP! BIP! BIP!
THE TWEETS OF ROLAND HEDLEY.
"WOKE UP IN STRANGE APARTMENT, SO RUNNING LATE. THANK GOD FOR iPHONE GPS."
"LET'S NOT THROW STONES AT AIG BONUS HOLDOUT GUY. MAY HAVE HAD HIS REASONS. FOR INSTANCE, WHO AMONG US HAS NEVER HAD A SERIOUS COKE PROBLEM?"
"BTW, FYI, I MAY HAVE 2 LET MY HOUSEBOY GO. JUST WANTED 2 GIVE U HEADS-UP BECAUSE I KNOW SOME OF U WERE CLOSE 2 LING."
"BUMPED INTO AN OLD STALKER OF MINE AT BORDERS. SHE'D LOST SOME WEIGHT AND LOOKED TERRIFIC, BUT I TWEETED 911. COPS ARRIVED FROM THREE STATES."
"WOKE UP FEELING HOPEFUL, THEN REMEMBERED PREVAILING MOOD IS ANGER. GOT CABLE-READY BY STABBING SELF W. FORK. GOOD 2 GO."
ROLAND, WHEN'LL WE BE GETTING YOU BACK?
"GOING DOWN 2 LOBBY 4 SHOESHINE. SOMETIMES JUST NEED 2 GET OUT OF THE BUBBLE."
BIP! BIP! BIP!
GBTrudeau

5/17/09

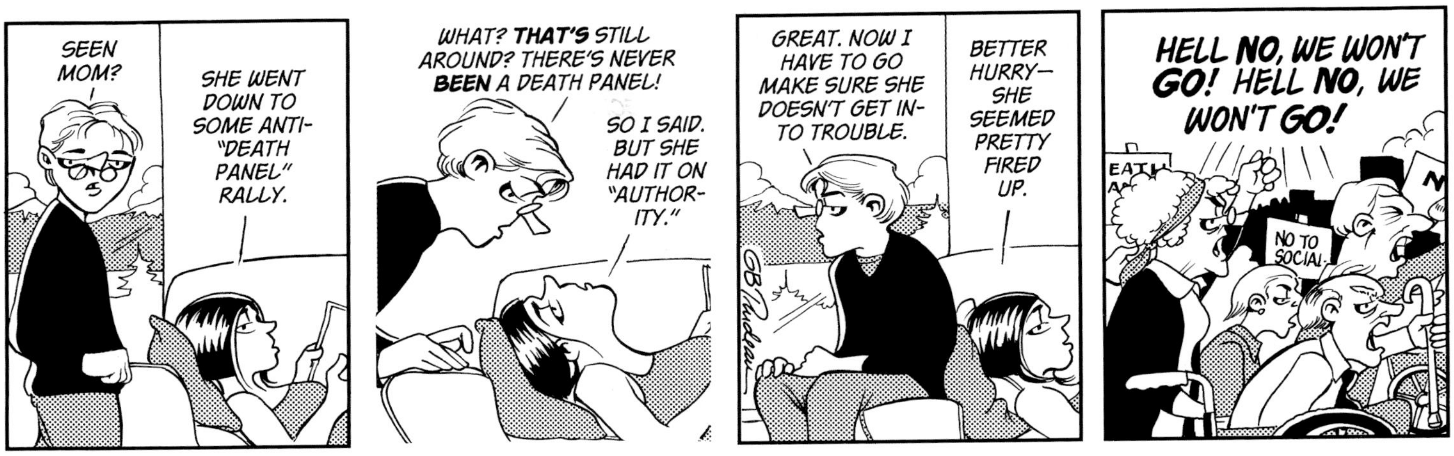
SEEN MOM?
SHE WENT DOWN TO SOME ANTI-"DEATH PANEL" RALLY.
WHAT? **THAT'S** STILL AROUND? THERE'S NEVER **BEEN** A DEATH PANEL!
SO I SAID. BUT SHE HAD IT ON "AUTHORITY."
GREAT. NOW I HAVE TO GO MAKE SURE SHE DOESN'T GET INTO TROUBLE.
BETTER HURRY—SHE SEEMED PRETTY FIRED UP.
HELL **NO**, WE WON'T **GO!** HELL **NO**, WE WON'T **GO!**
NO TO SOCIAL
GB Trudeau

9/21/09

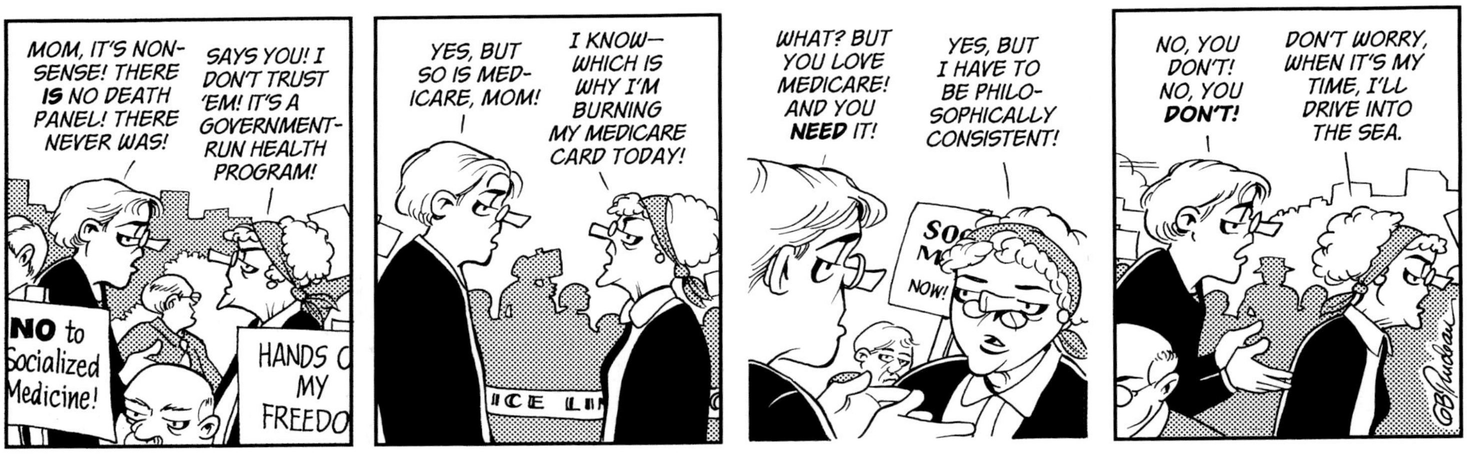
MOM, IT'S NONSENSE! THERE **IS** NO DEATH PANEL! THERE NEVER WAS!
SAYS YOU! I DON'T TRUST 'EM! IT'S A GOVERNMENT-RUN HEALTH PROGRAM!
NO to Socialized Medicine!
YES, BUT SO IS MEDICARE, MOM!
I KNOW—WHICH IS WHY I'M BURNING MY MEDICARE CARD TODAY!
WHAT? BUT YOU LOVE MEDICARE! AND YOU **NEED** IT!
YES, BUT I HAVE TO BE PHILOSOPHICALLY CONSISTENT!
NO, YOU DON'T! NO, YOU **DON'T!**
DON'T WORRY, WHEN IT'S MY TIME, I'LL DRIVE INTO THE SEA.
GB Trudeau

9/22/09

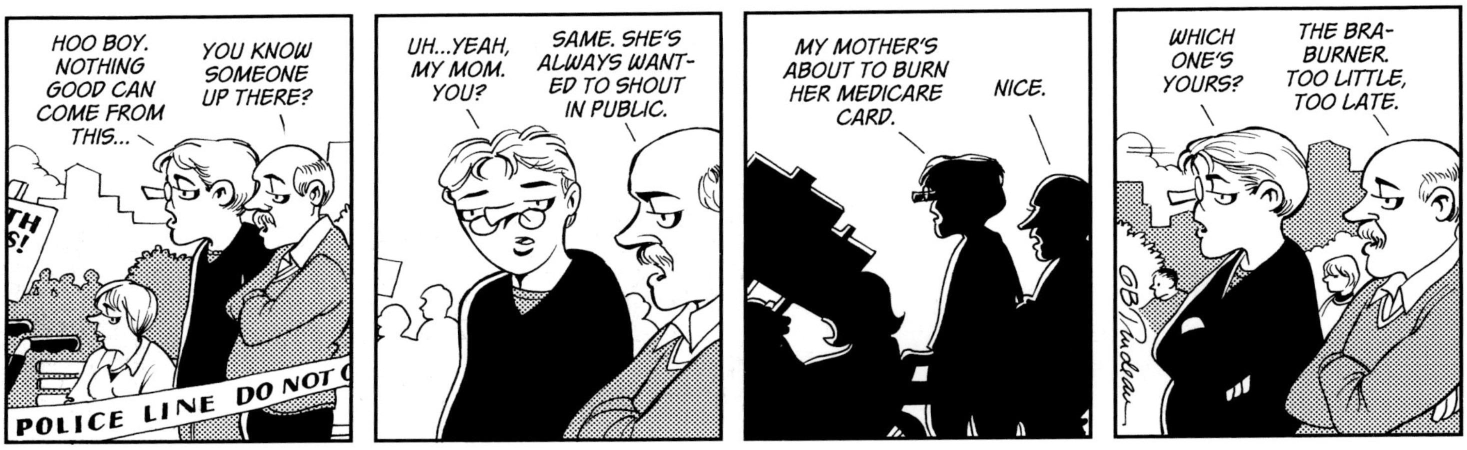
HOO BOY. NOTHING GOOD CAN COME FROM THIS...
YOU KNOW SOMEONE UP THERE?
POLICE LINE DO NOT
UH...YEAH, MY MOM. YOU?
SAME. SHE'S ALWAYS WANTED TO SHOUT IN PUBLIC.
MY MOTHER'S ABOUT TO BURN HER MEDICARE CARD.
NICE.
WHICH ONE'S YOURS?
THE BRA-BURNER. TOO LITTLE, TOO LATE.
GB Trudeau

9/23/09

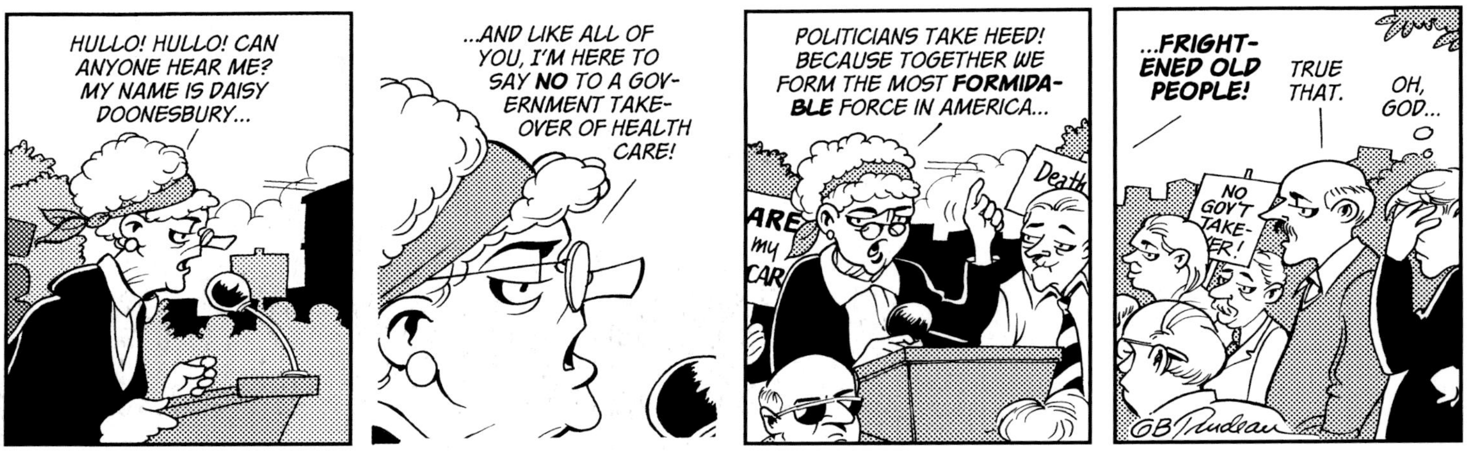
HULLO! HULLO! CAN ANYONE HEAR ME? MY NAME IS DAISY DOONESBURY...
...AND LIKE ALL OF YOU, I'M HERE TO SAY **NO** TO A GOVERNMENT TAKEOVER OF HEALTH CARE!
POLITICIANS TAKE HEED! BECAUSE TOGETHER WE FORM THE MOST **FORMIDABLE** FORCE IN AMERICA...
...FRIGHTENED OLD PEOPLE!
TRUE THAT.
OH, GOD...
GB Trudeau

9/24/09

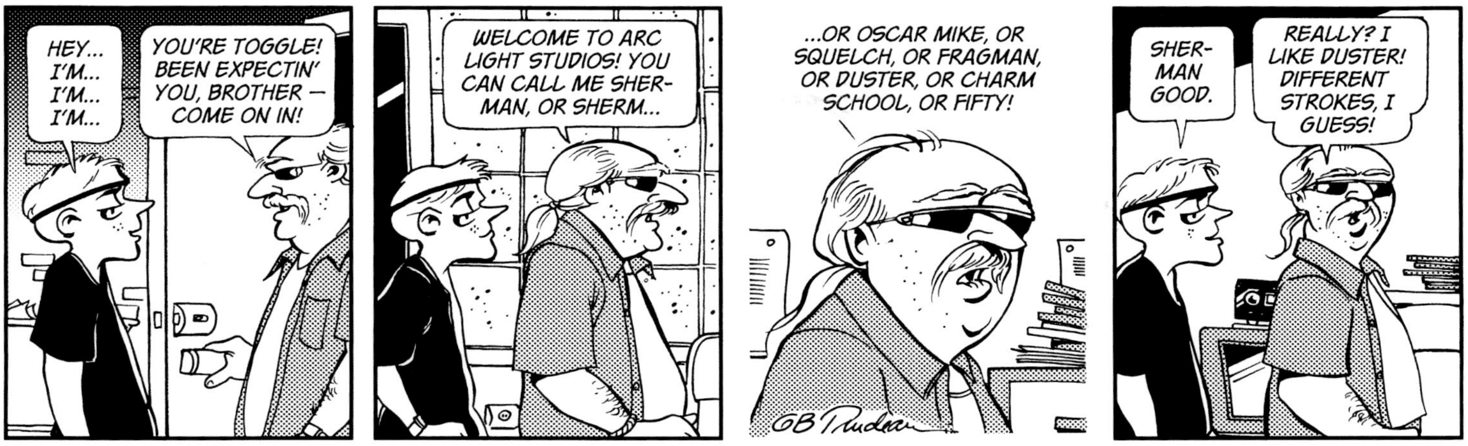
HEY... I'M... I'M... I'M...
YOU'RE TOGGLE! BEEN EXPECTIN' YOU, BROTHER — COME ON IN!
WELCOME TO ARC LIGHT STUDIOS! YOU CAN CALL ME SHERMAN, OR SHERM...
...OR OSCAR MIKE, OR SQUELCH, OR FRAGMAN, OR DUSTER, OR CHARM SCHOOL, OR FIFTY!
SHERMAN GOOD.
REALLY? I LIKE DUSTER! DIFFERENT STROKES, I GUESS!

12/2/09

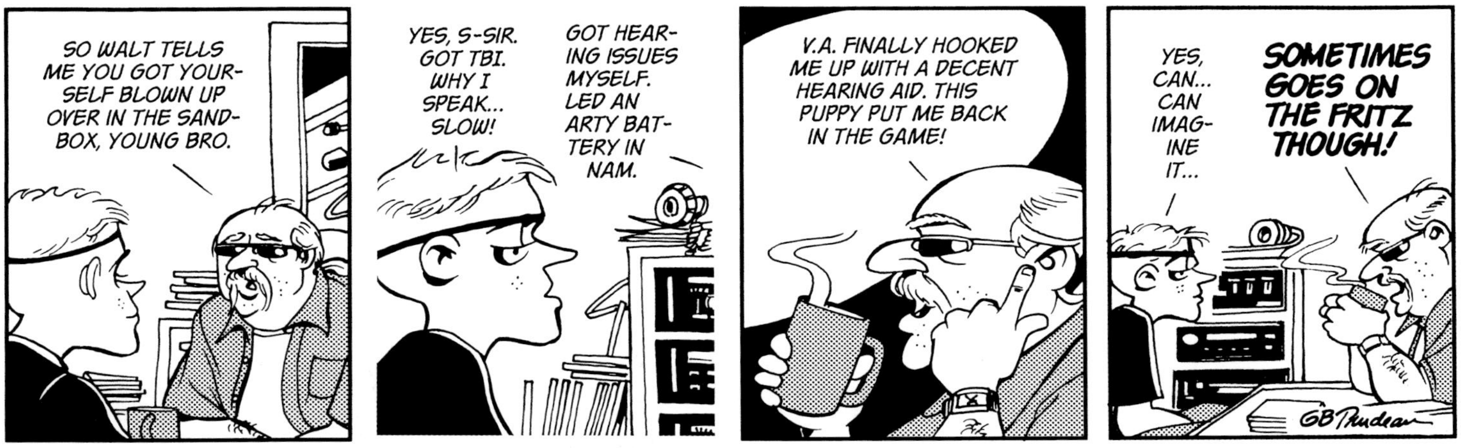
SO WALT TELLS ME YOU GOT YOURSELF BLOWN UP OVER IN THE SANDBOX, YOUNG BRO.
YES, S-SIR. GOT TBI. WHY I SPEAK... SLOW!
GOT HEARING ISSUES MYSELF. LED AN ARTY BATTERY IN NAM.
V.A. FINALLY HOOKED ME UP WITH A DECENT HEARING AID. THIS PUPPY PUT ME BACK IN THE GAME!
YES, CAN... CAN IMAGINE IT...
SOMETIMES GOES ON THE FRITZ THOUGH!

12/3/09

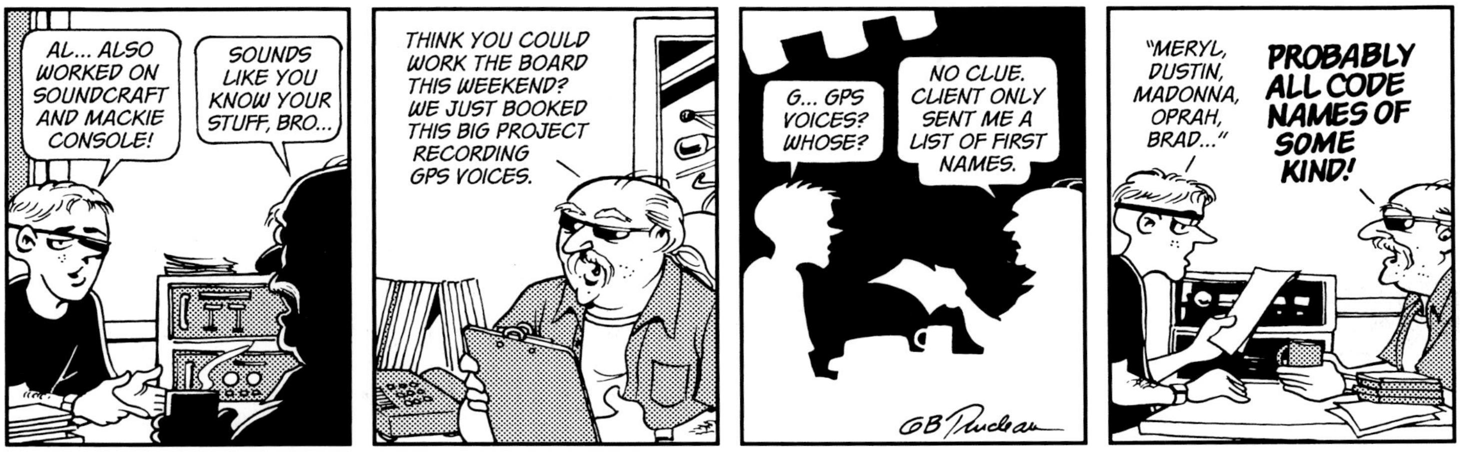
AL... ALSO WORKED ON SOUNDCRAFT AND MACKIE CONSOLE!
SOUNDS LIKE YOU KNOW YOUR STUFF, BRO...
THINK YOU COULD WORK THE BOARD THIS WEEKEND? WE JUST BOOKED THIS BIG PROJECT RECORDING GPS VOICES.
G... GPS VOICES? WHOSE?
NO CLUE. CLIENT ONLY SENT ME A LIST OF FIRST NAMES.
"MERYL, DUSTIN, MADONNA, OPRAH, BRAD..."
PROBABLY ALL CODE NAMES OF SOME KIND!

12/4/09

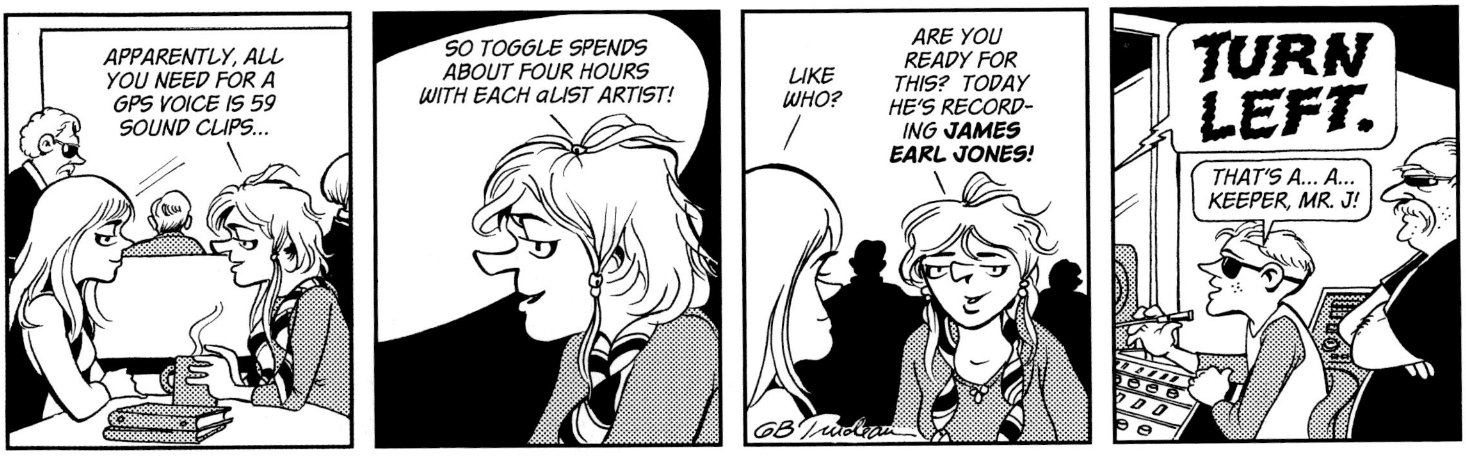
APPARENTLY, ALL YOU NEED FOR A GPS VOICE IS 59 SOUND CLIPS...
SO TOGGLE SPENDS ABOUT FOUR HOURS WITH EACH aLIST ARTIST!
LIKE WHO?
ARE YOU READY FOR THIS? TODAY HE'S RECORDING JAMES EARL JONES!
TURN LEFT.
THAT'S A... A... KEEPER, MR. J!

12/7/09

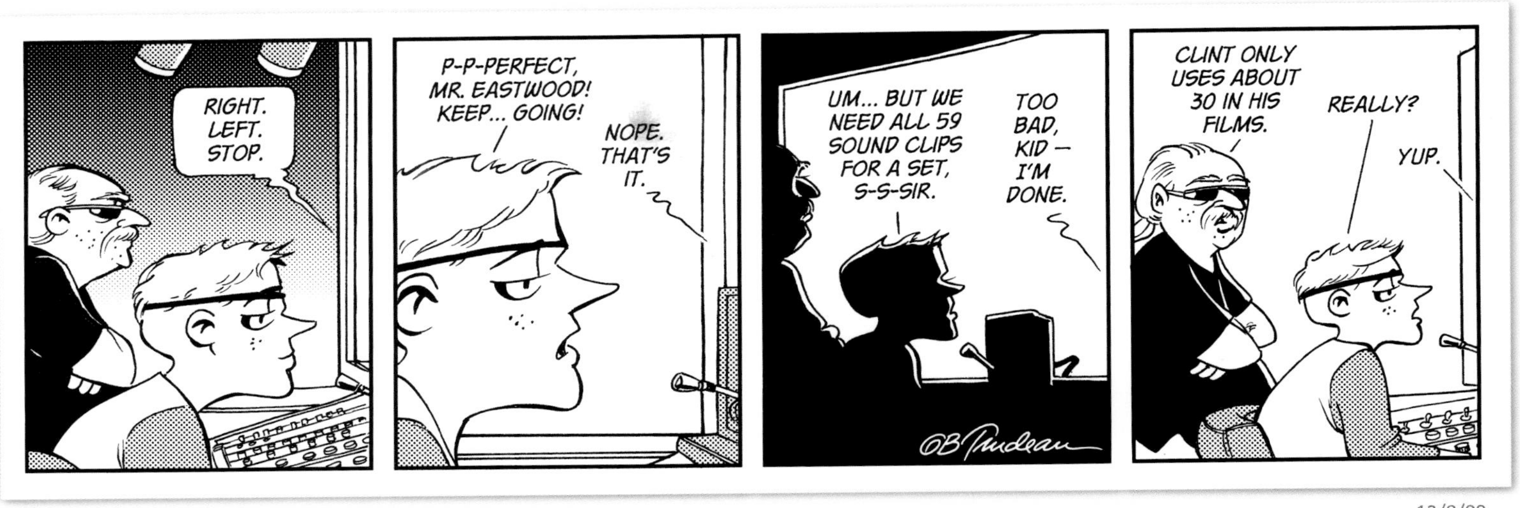
RIGHT. LEFT. STOP.
P-P-PERFECT, MR. EASTWOOD! KEEP... GOING!
NOPE. THAT'S IT.
UM... BUT WE NEED ALL 59 SOUND CLIPS FOR A SET, S-S-SIR.
TOO BAD, KID — I'M DONE.
CLINT ONLY USES ABOUT 30 IN HIS FILMS.
REALLY?
YUP.

12/8/09

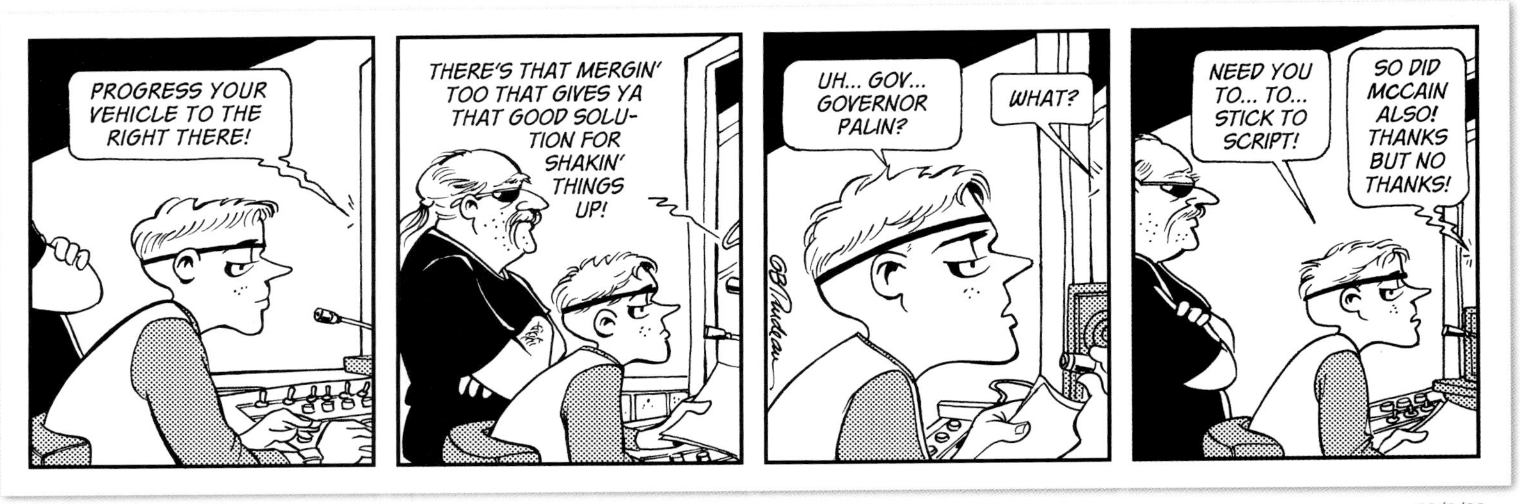
PROGRESS YOUR VEHICLE TO THE RIGHT THERE!
THERE'S THAT MERGIN' TOO THAT GIVES YA THAT GOOD SOLUTION FOR SHAKIN' THINGS UP!
UH... GOV... GOVERNOR PALIN?
WHAT?
NEED YOU TO... TO... STICK TO SCRIPT!
SO DID MCCAIN ALSO! THANKS BUT NO THANKS!

12/9/09

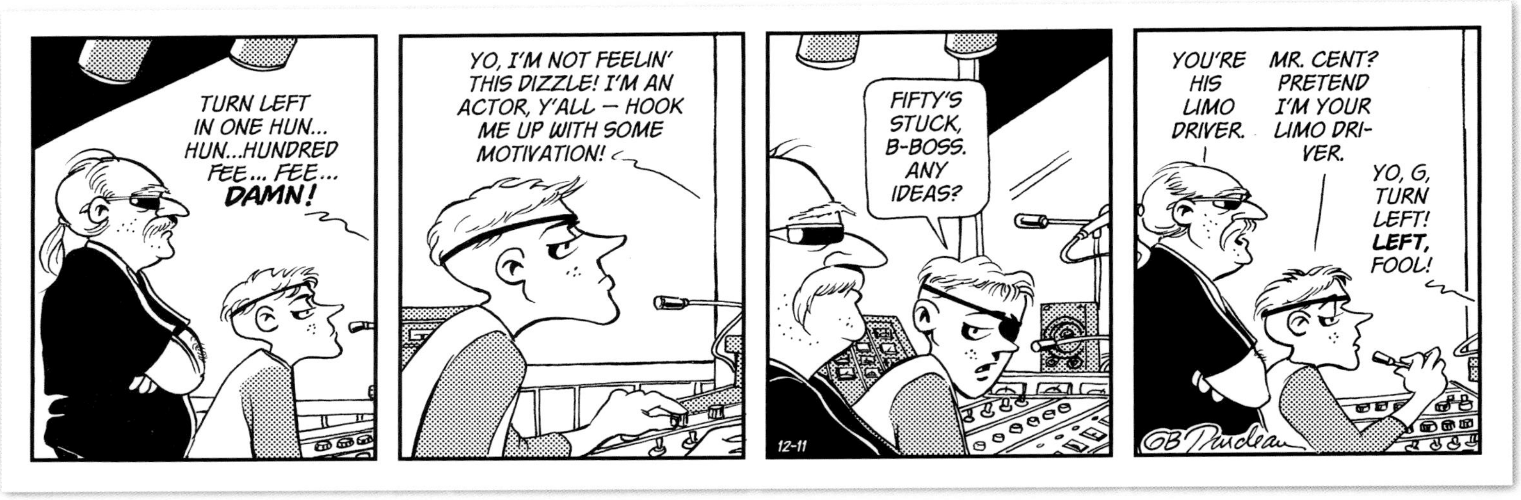
TURN LEFT IN ONE HUN... HUN...HUNDRED FEE... FEE... **DAMN!**
YO, I'M NOT FEELIN' THIS DIZZLE! I'M AN ACTOR, Y'ALL — HOOK ME UP WITH SOME MOTIVATION!
FIFTY'S STUCK, B-BOSS. ANY IDEAS?
12-11
YOU'RE HIS LIMO DRIVER.
MR. CENT? PRETEND I'M YOUR LIMO DRIVER.
YO, G, TURN LEFT! **LEFT,** FOOL!

12/11/09

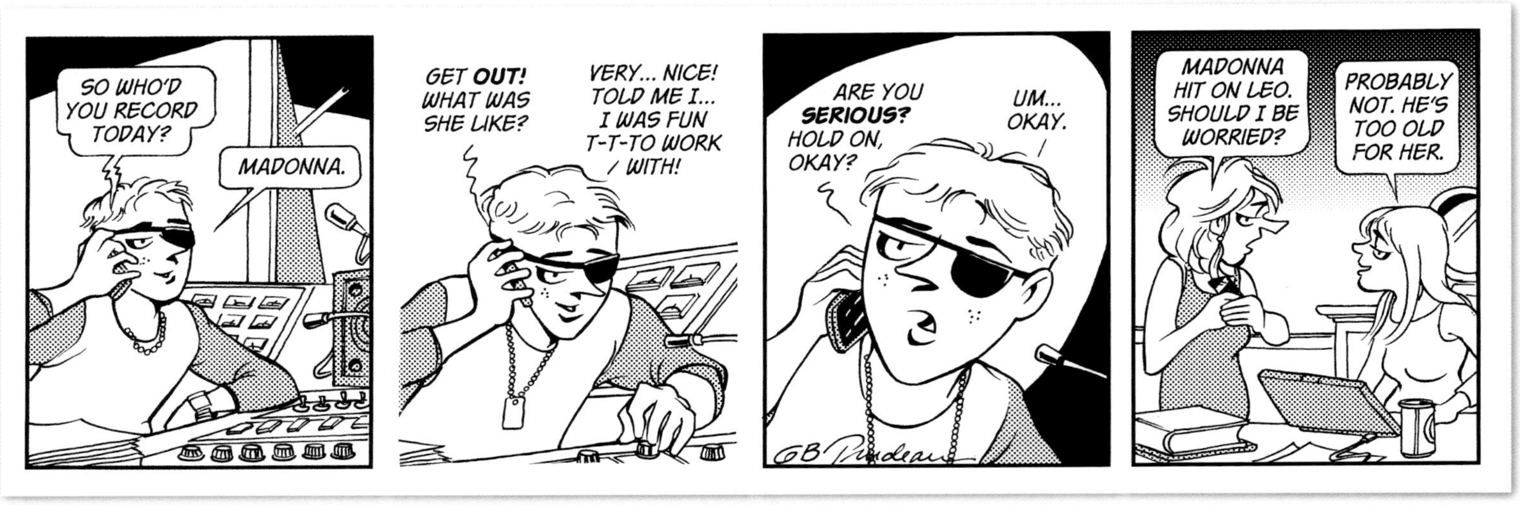
SO WHO'D YOU RECORD TODAY?
MADONNA.
GET **OUT!** WHAT WAS SHE LIKE?
VERY... NICE! TOLD ME I... I WAS FUN T-T-TO WORK WITH!
ARE YOU **SERIOUS?** HOLD ON, OKAY?
UM... OKAY.
MADONNA HIT ON LEO. SHOULD I BE WORRIED?
PROBABLY NOT. HE'S TOO OLD FOR HER.

12/12/09

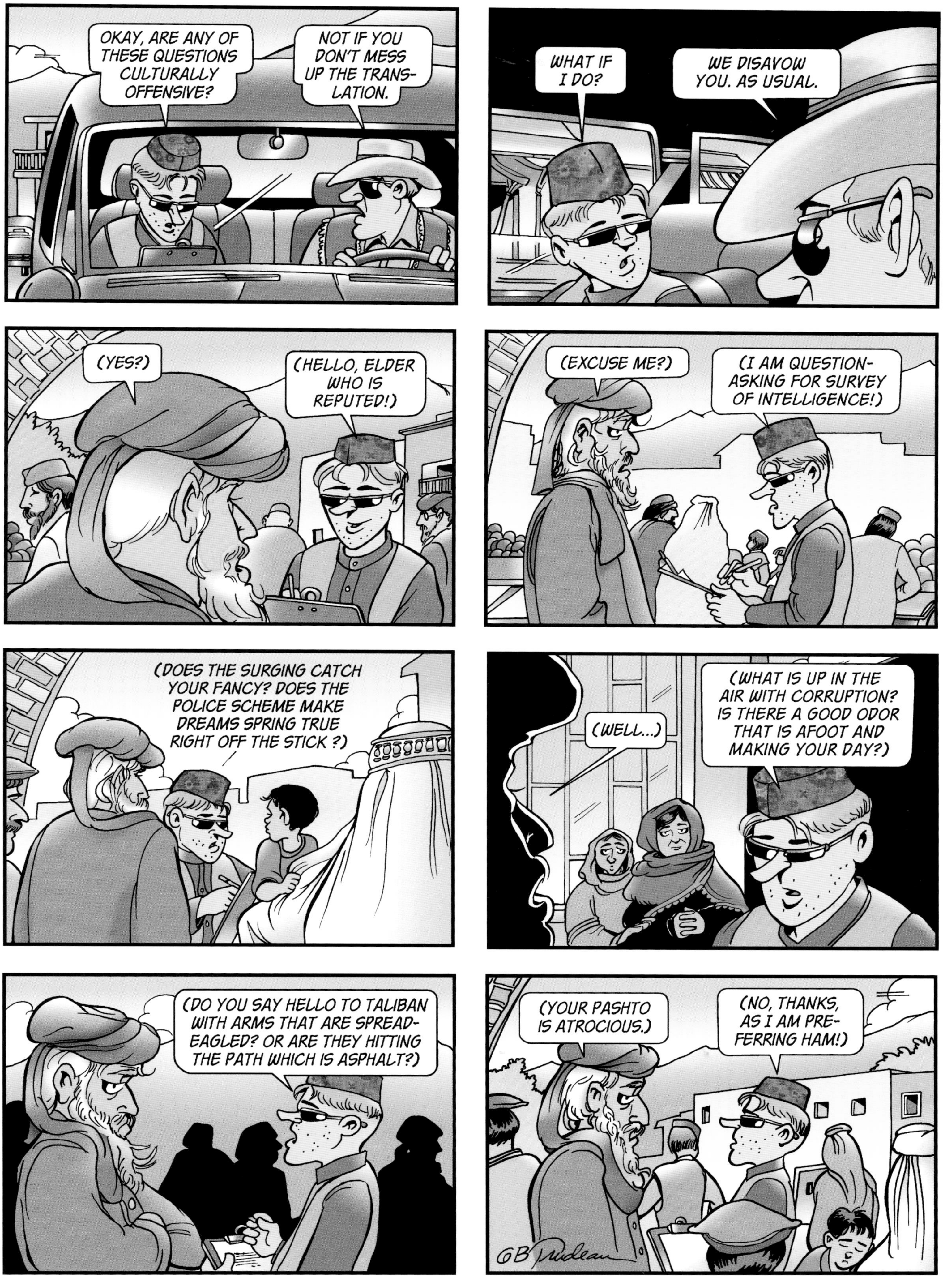
OKAY, ARE ANY OF THESE QUESTIONS CULTURALLY OFFENSIVE?
NOT IF YOU DON'T MESS UP THE TRANS-LATION.
WHAT IF I DO?
WE DISAVOW YOU. AS USUAL.
(YES?)
(HELLO, ELDER WHO IS REPUTED!)
(EXCUSE ME?)
(I AM QUESTION-ASKING FOR SURVEY OF INTELLIGENCE!)
(DOES THE SURGING CATCH YOUR FANCY? DOES THE POLICE SCHEME MAKE DREAMS SPRING TRUE RIGHT OFF THE STICK ?)
(WELL...)
(WHAT IS UP IN THE AIR WITH CORRUPTION? IS THERE A GOOD ODOR THAT IS AFOOT AND MAKING YOUR DAY?)
(DO YOU SAY HELLO TO TALIBAN WITH ARMS THAT ARE SPREAD-EAGLED? OR ARE THEY HITTING THE PATH WHICH IS ASPHALT?)
(YOUR PASHTO IS ATROCIOUS.)
(NO, THANKS, AS I AM PRE-FERRING HAM!)
GB Trudeau

3/28/10

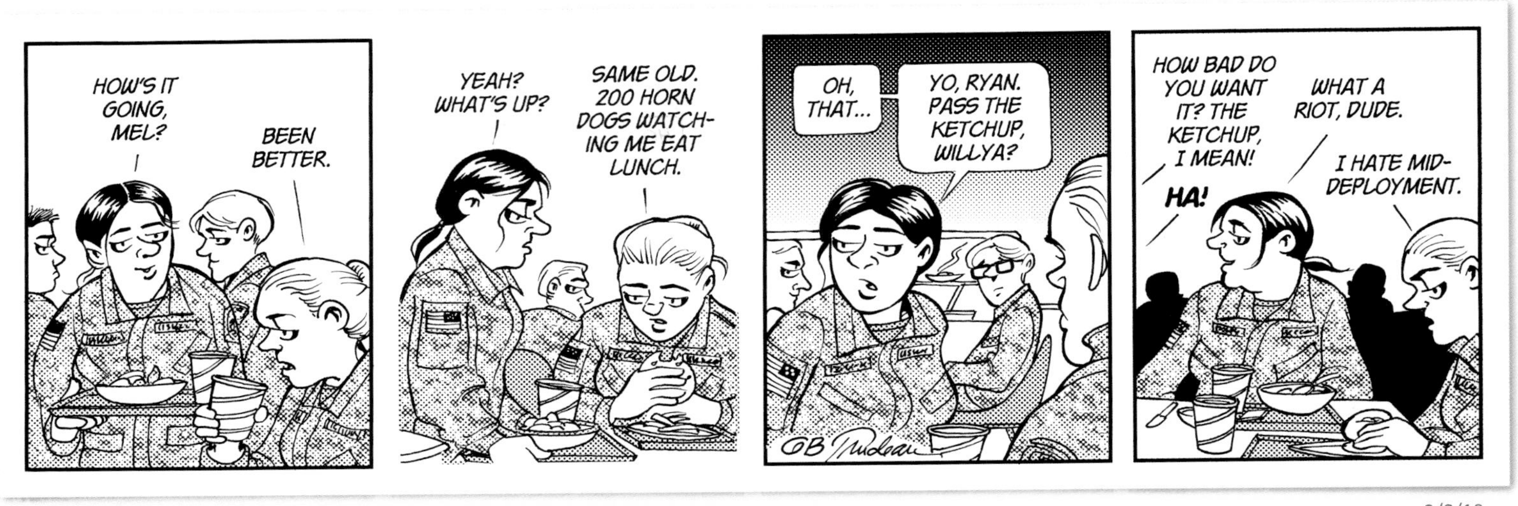
HOW'S IT GOING, MEL?
BEEN BETTER.
YEAH? WHAT'S UP?
SAME OLD. 200 HORN DOGS WATCHING ME EAT LUNCH.
OH, THAT...
YO, RYAN. PASS THE KETCHUP, WILLYA?
HOW BAD DO YOU WANT IT? THE KETCHUP, I MEAN!
HA!
WHAT A RIOT, DUDE.
I HATE MID-DEPLOYMENT.

2/8/10

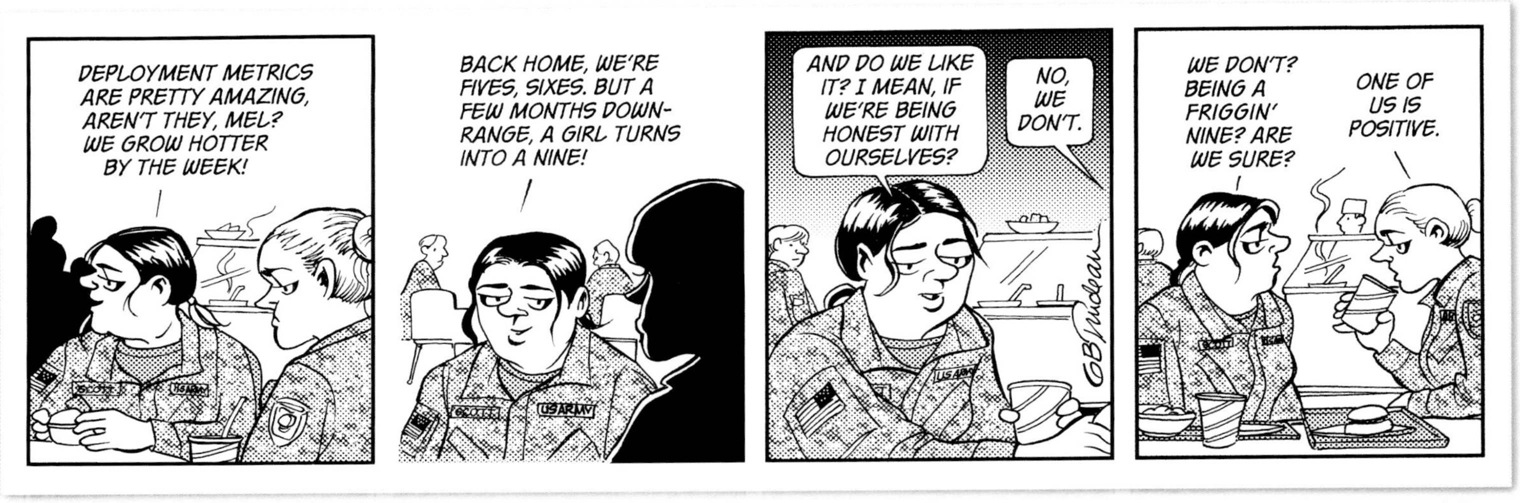
DEPLOYMENT METRICS ARE PRETTY AMAZING, AREN'T THEY, MEL? WE GROW HOTTER BY THE WEEK!
BACK HOME, WE'RE FIVES, SIXES. BUT A FEW MONTHS DOWN-RANGE, A GIRL TURNS INTO A NINE!
AND DO WE LIKE IT? I MEAN, IF WE'RE BEING HONEST WITH OURSELVES?
NO, WE DON'T.
WE DON'T? BEING A FRIGGIN' NINE? ARE WE SURE?
ONE OF US IS POSITIVE.

2/9/10

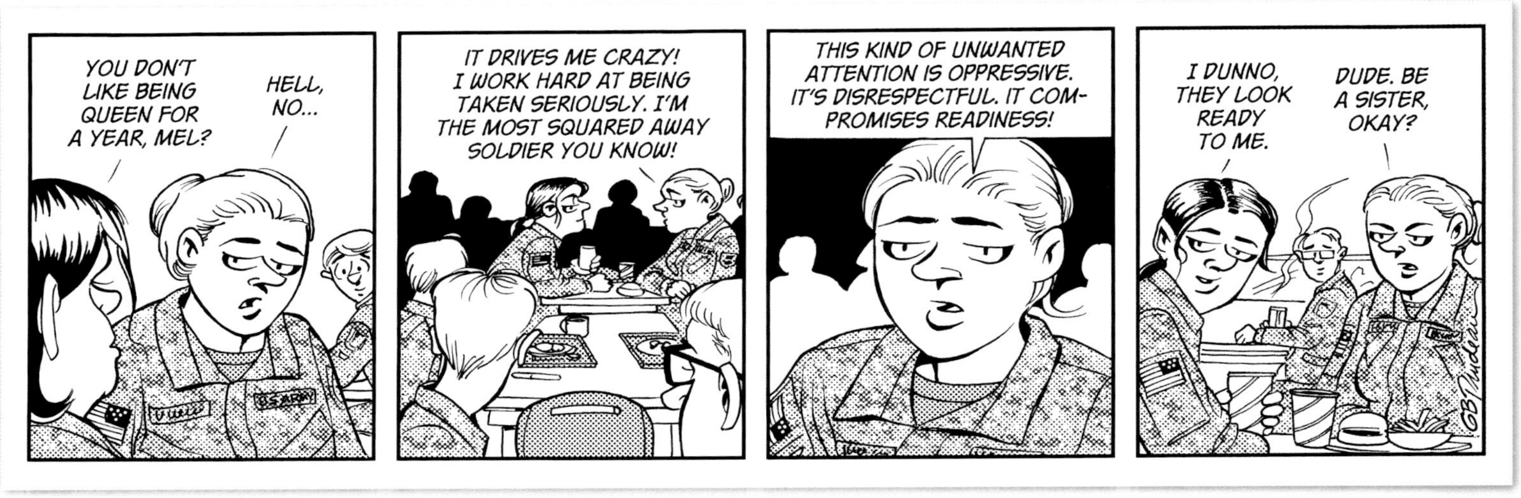
YOU DON'T LIKE BEING QUEEN FOR A YEAR, MEL?
HELL, NO...
IT DRIVES ME CRAZY! I WORK HARD AT BEING TAKEN SERIOUSLY. I'M THE MOST SQUARED AWAY SOLDIER YOU KNOW!
THIS KIND OF UNWANTED ATTENTION IS OPPRESSIVE. IT'S DISRESPECTFUL. IT COMPROMISES READINESS!
I DUNNO, THEY LOOK READY TO ME.
DUDE. BE A SISTER, OKAY?

2/10/10

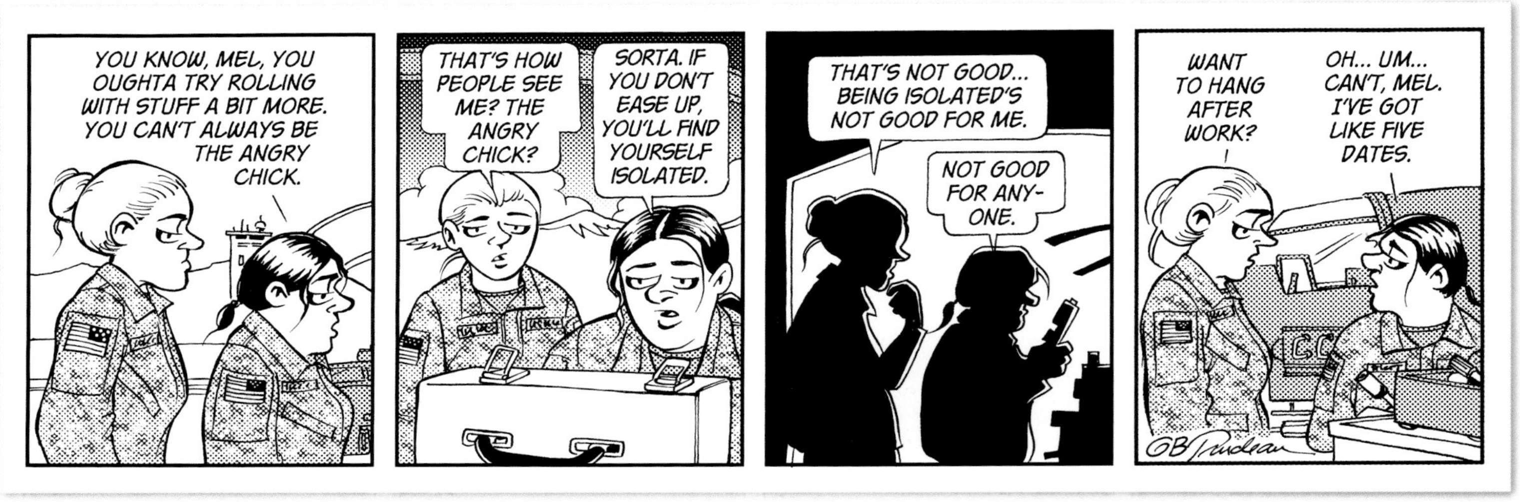
YOU KNOW, MEL, YOU OUGHTA TRY ROLLING WITH STUFF A BIT MORE. YOU CAN'T ALWAYS BE THE ANGRY CHICK.
THAT'S HOW PEOPLE SEE ME? THE ANGRY CHICK?
SORTA. IF YOU DON'T EASE UP, YOU'LL FIND YOURSELF ISOLATED.
THAT'S NOT GOOD... BEING ISOLATED'S NOT GOOD FOR ME.
NOT GOOD FOR ANY-ONE.
WANT TO HANG AFTER WORK?
OH... UM... CAN'T, MEL. I'VE GOT LIKE FIVE DATES.

2/12/10

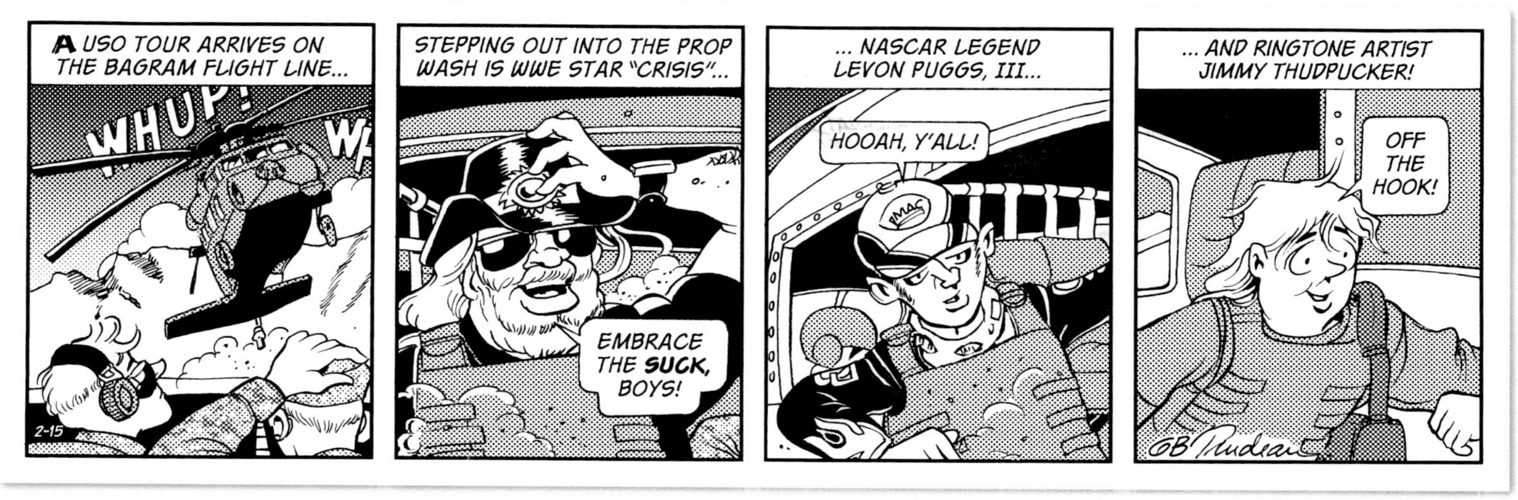
A USO TOUR ARRIVES ON THE BAGRAM FLIGHT LINE...
WHUP!
STEPPING OUT INTO THE PROP WASH IS WWE STAR "CRISIS"...
EMBRACE THE SUCK, BOYS!
... NASCAR LEGEND LEVON PUGGS, III...
HOOAH, Y'ALL!
... AND RINGTONE ARTIST JIMMY THUDPUCKER!
OFF THE HOOK!

2/15/10

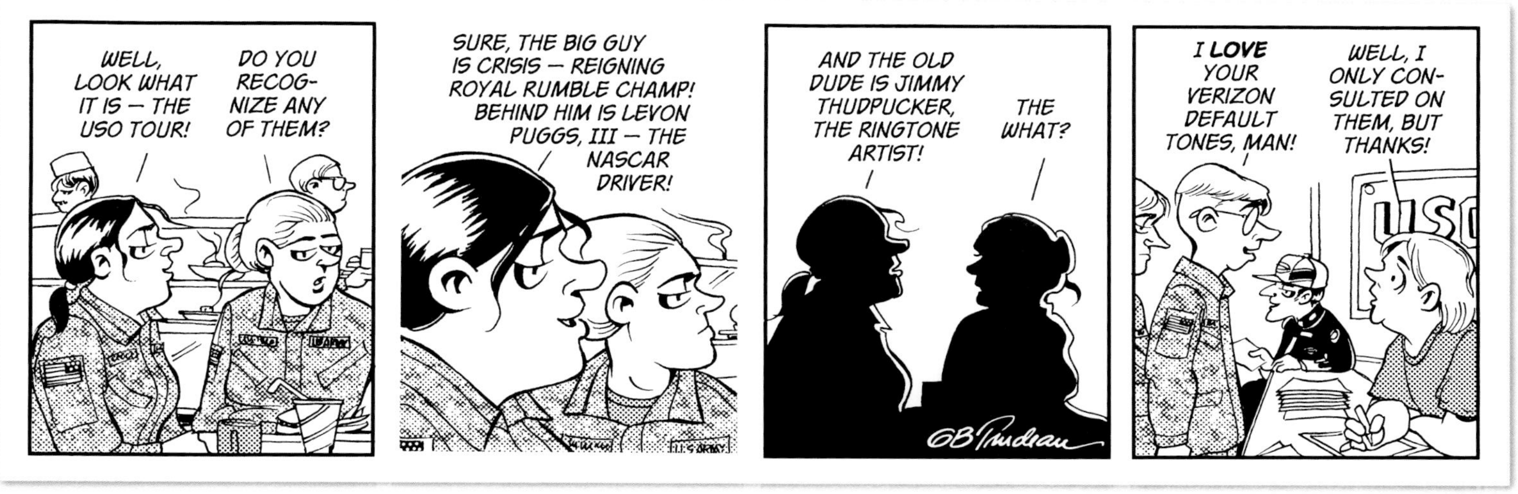
WELL, LOOK WHAT IT IS — THE USO TOUR!
DO YOU RECOG-NIZE ANY OF THEM?
SURE, THE BIG GUY IS CRISIS — REIGNING ROYAL RUMBLE CHAMP! BEHIND HIM IS LEVON PUGGS, III — THE NASCAR DRIVER!
AND THE OLD DUDE IS JIMMY THUDPUCKER, THE RINGTONE ARTIST!
THE WHAT?
I LOVE YOUR VERIZON DEFAULT TONES, MAN!
WELL, I ONLY CON-SULTED ON THEM, BUT THANKS!

2/17/10

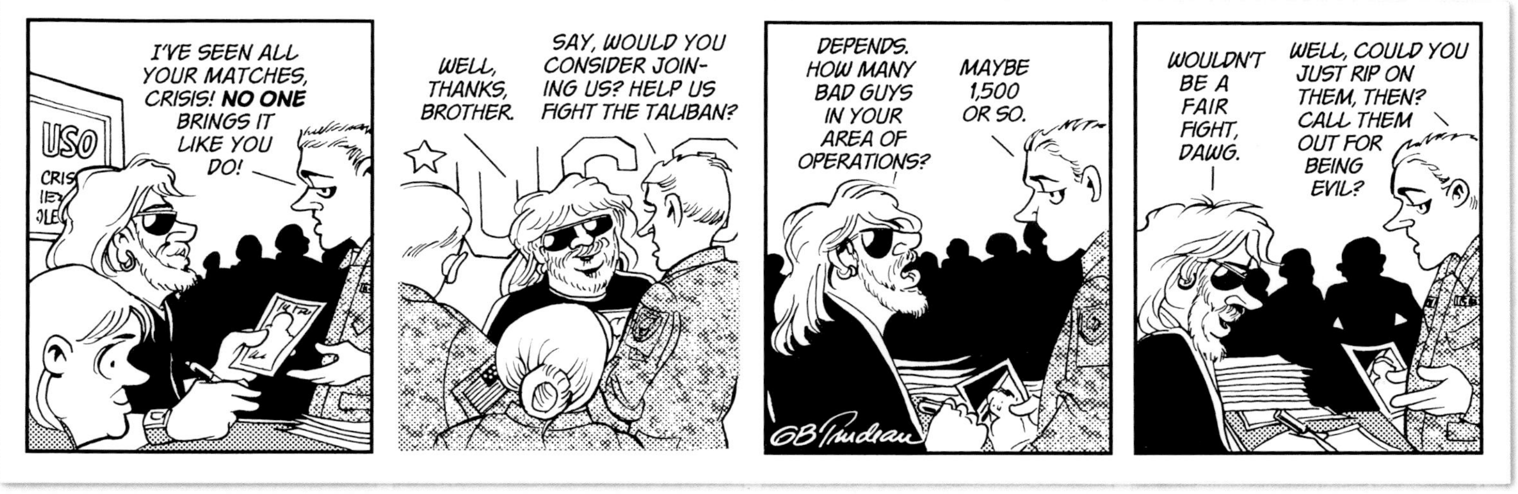
I'VE SEEN ALL YOUR MATCHES, CRISIS! NO ONE BRINGS IT LIKE YOU DO!
WELL, THANKS, BROTHER.
SAY, WOULD YOU CONSIDER JOIN-ING US? HELP US FIGHT THE TALIBAN?
DEPENDS. HOW MANY BAD GUYS IN YOUR AREA OF OPERATIONS?
MAYBE 1,500 OR SO.
WOULDN'T BE A FAIR FIGHT, DAWG.
WELL, COULD YOU JUST RIP ON THEM, THEN? CALL THEM OUT FOR BEING EVIL?

2/18/10

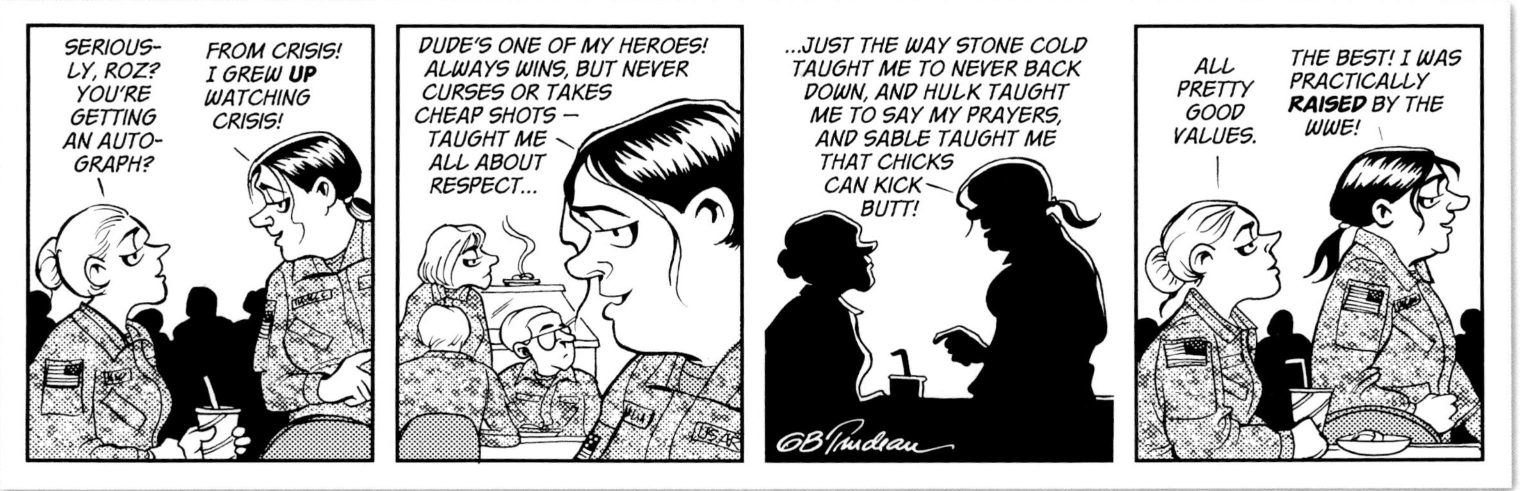
SERIOUS-LY, ROZ? YOU'RE GETTING AN AUTO-GRAPH?
FROM CRISIS! I GREW UP WATCHING CRISIS!
DUDE'S ONE OF MY HEROES! ALWAYS WINS, BUT NEVER CURSES OR TAKES CHEAP SHOTS — TAUGHT ME ALL ABOUT RESPECT...
...JUST THE WAY STONE COLD TAUGHT ME TO NEVER BACK DOWN, AND HULK TAUGHT ME TO SAY MY PRAYERS, AND SABLE TAUGHT ME THAT CHICKS CAN KICK BUTT!
ALL PRETTY GOOD VALUES.
THE BEST! I WAS PRACTICALLY RAISED BY THE WWE!

2/20/10

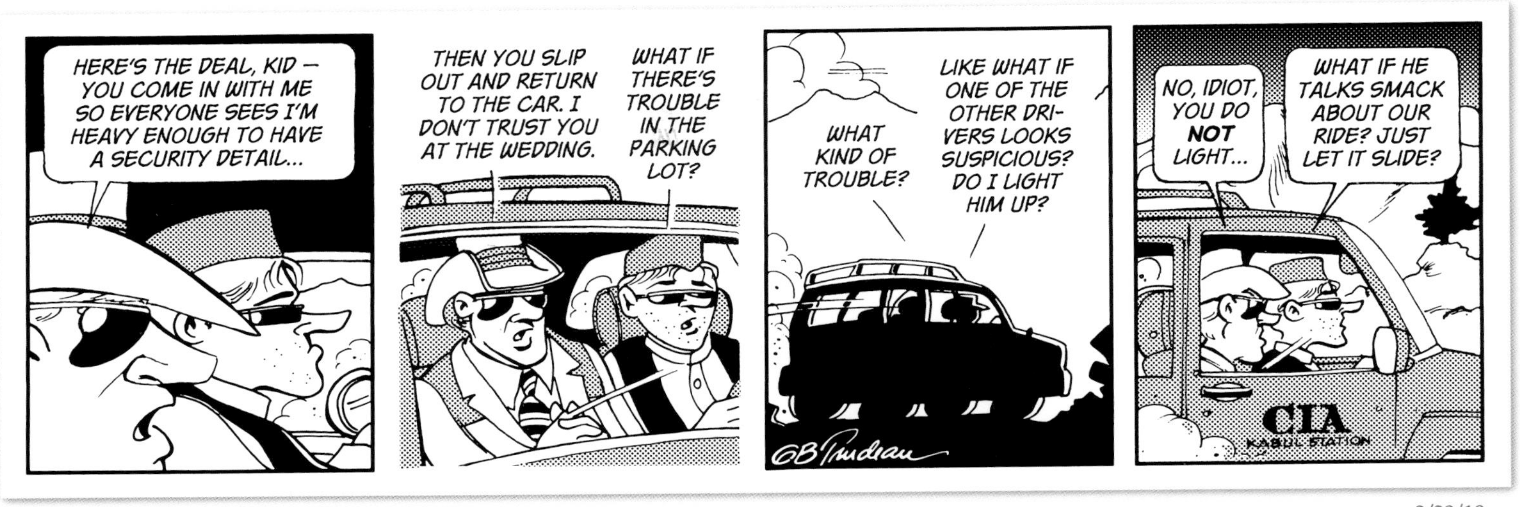
HERE'S THE DEAL, KID — YOU COME IN WITH ME SO EVERYONE SEES I'M HEAVY ENOUGH TO HAVE A SECURITY DETAIL...
THEN YOU SLIP OUT AND RETURN TO THE CAR. I DON'T TRUST YOU AT THE WEDDING.
WHAT IF THERE'S TROUBLE IN THE PARKING LOT?
WHAT KIND OF TROUBLE?
LIKE WHAT IF ONE OF THE OTHER DRIVERS LOOKS SUSPICIOUS? DO I LIGHT HIM UP?
NO, IDIOT, YOU DO **NOT** LIGHT...
WHAT IF HE TALKS SMACK ABOUT OUR RIDE? JUST LET IT SLIDE?
CIA
KABUL STATION

2/22/10

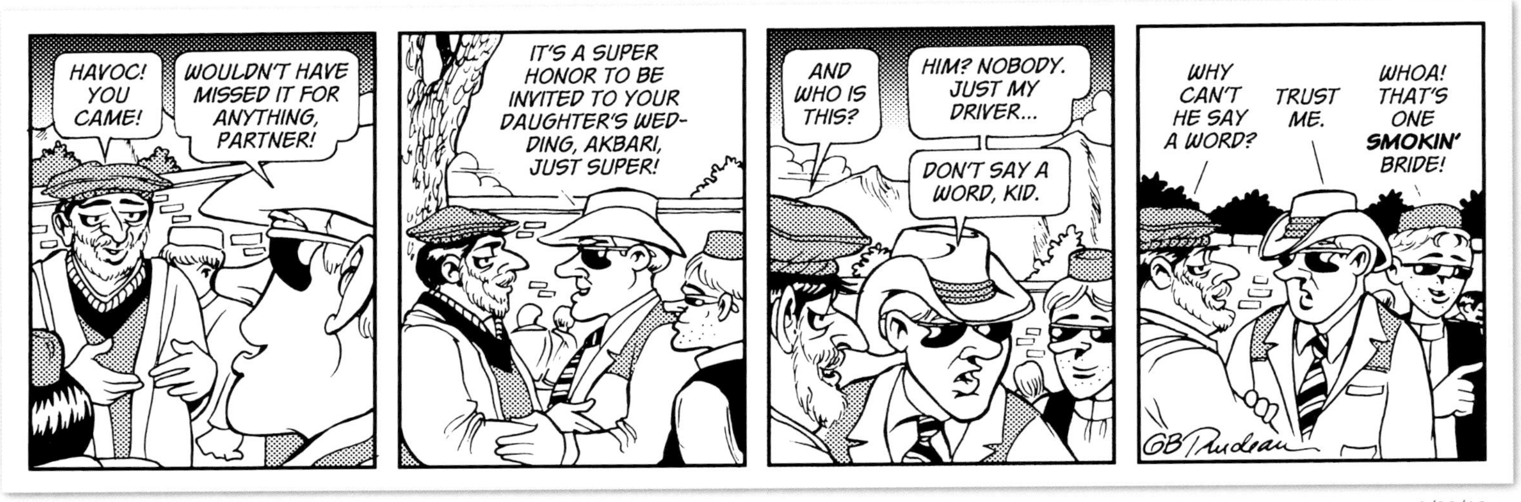
HAVOC! YOU CAME!
WOULDN'T HAVE MISSED IT FOR ANYTHING, PARTNER!
IT'S A SUPER HONOR TO BE INVITED TO YOUR DAUGHTER'S WEDDING, AKBARI, JUST SUPER!
AND WHO IS THIS?
HIM? NOBODY. JUST MY DRIVER...
DON'T SAY A WORD, KID.
WHY CAN'T HE SAY A WORD?
TRUST ME.
WHOA! THAT'S ONE **SMOKIN'** BRIDE!

2/23/10

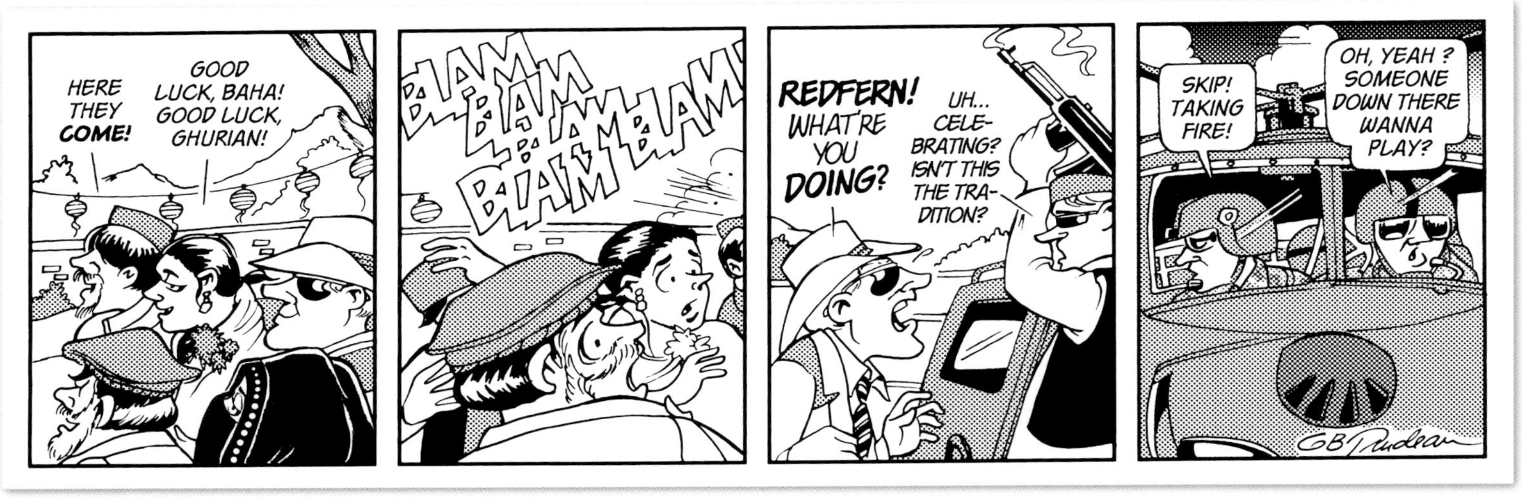
HERE THEY **COME!**
GOOD LUCK, BAHA! GOOD LUCK, GHURIAN!
BLAM BLAM BLAM BLAM!
BLAM BLAM
REDFERN! WHAT'RE YOU **DOING?**
UH... CELEBRATING? ISN'T THIS THE TRADITION?
SKIP! TAKING FIRE!
OH, YEAH? SOMEONE DOWN THERE WANNA PLAY?

2/25/10

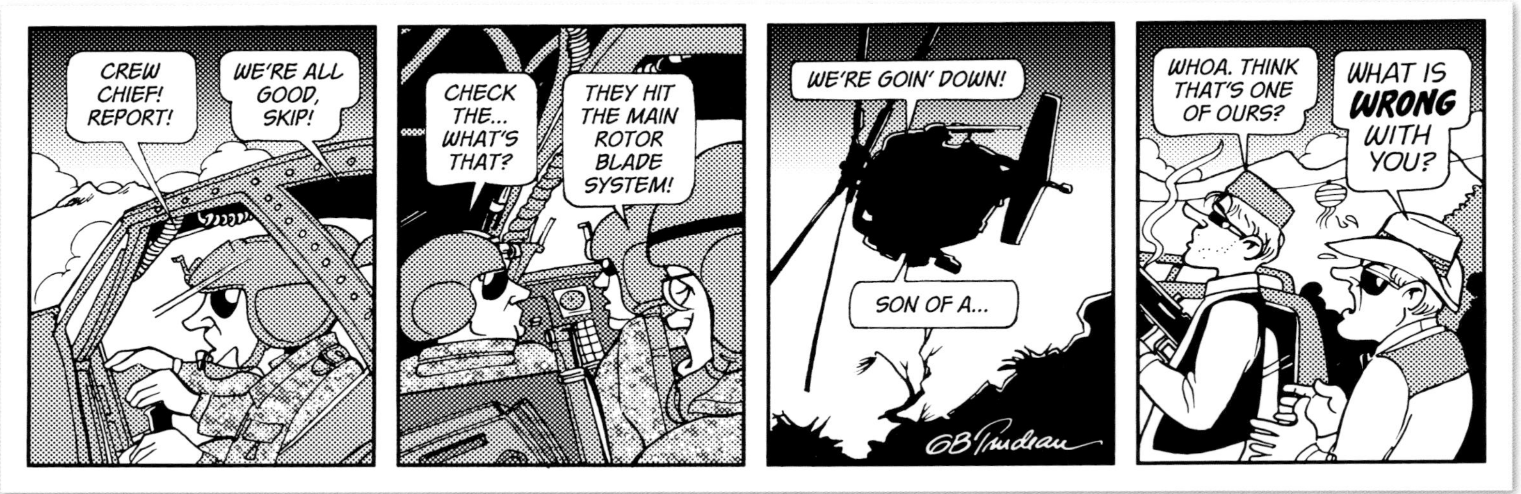
CREW CHIEF! REPORT!
WE'RE ALL GOOD, SKIP!
CHECK THE... WHAT'S THAT?
THEY HIT THE MAIN ROTOR BLADE SYSTEM!
WE'RE GOIN' DOWN!
SON OF A...
WHOA. THINK THAT'S ONE OF OURS?
WHAT IS **WRONG** WITH YOU?

2/26/10

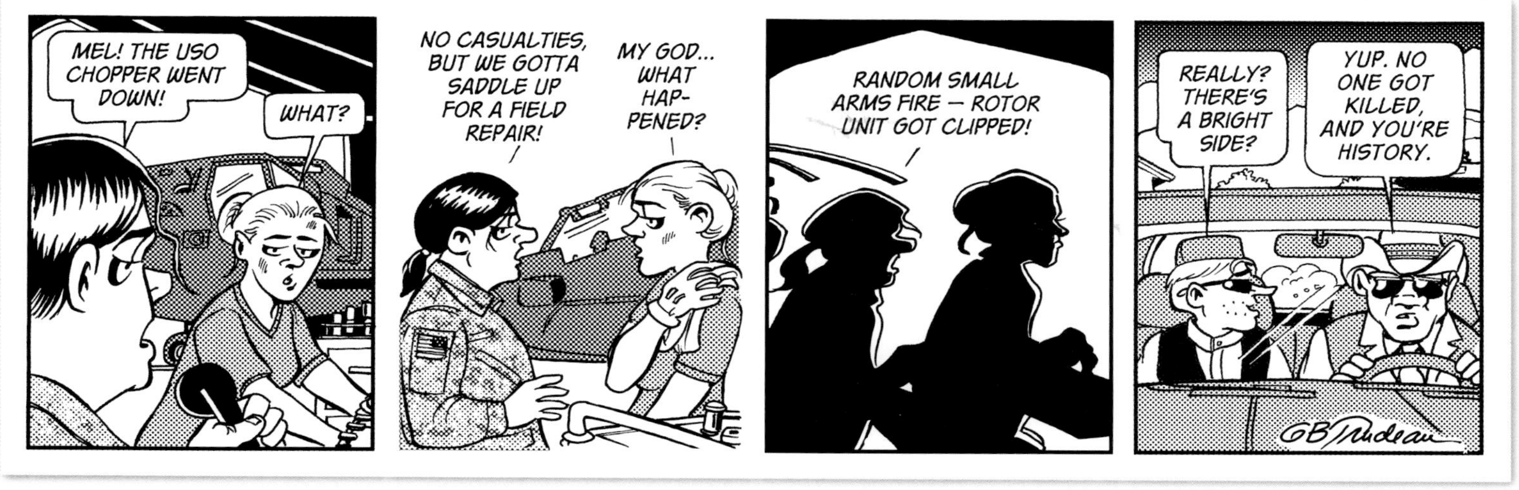
MEL! THE USO CHOPPER WENT DOWN!
WHAT?
NO CASUALTIES, BUT WE GOTTA SADDLE UP FOR A FIELD REPAIR!
MY GOD... WHAT HAP-PENED?
RANDOM SMALL ARMS FIRE — ROTOR UNIT GOT CLIPPED!
REALLY? THERE'S A BRIGHT SIDE?
YUP. NO ONE GOT KILLED, AND YOU'RE HISTORY.
GB Trudeau

3/1/10

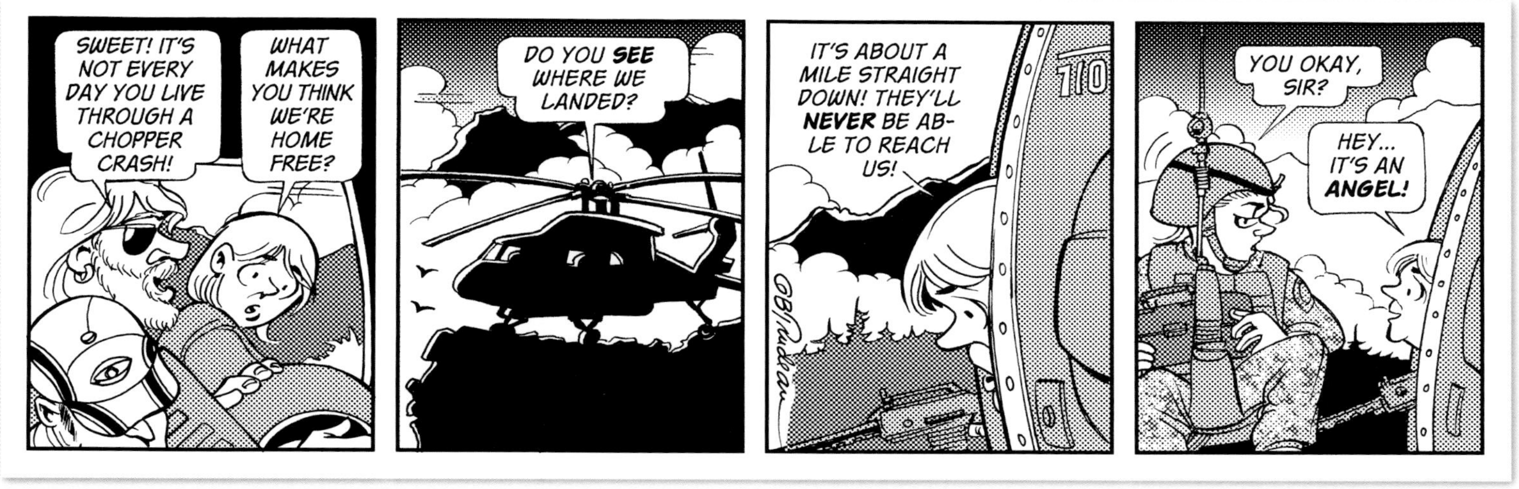
SWEET! IT'S NOT EVERY DAY YOU LIVE THROUGH A CHOPPER CRASH!
WHAT MAKES YOU THINK WE'RE HOME FREE?
DO YOU SEE WHERE WE LANDED?
IT'S ABOUT A MILE STRAIGHT DOWN! THEY'LL NEVER BE ABLE TO REACH US!
GB Trudeau
YOU OKAY, SIR?
HEY... IT'S AN ANGEL!

3/3/10

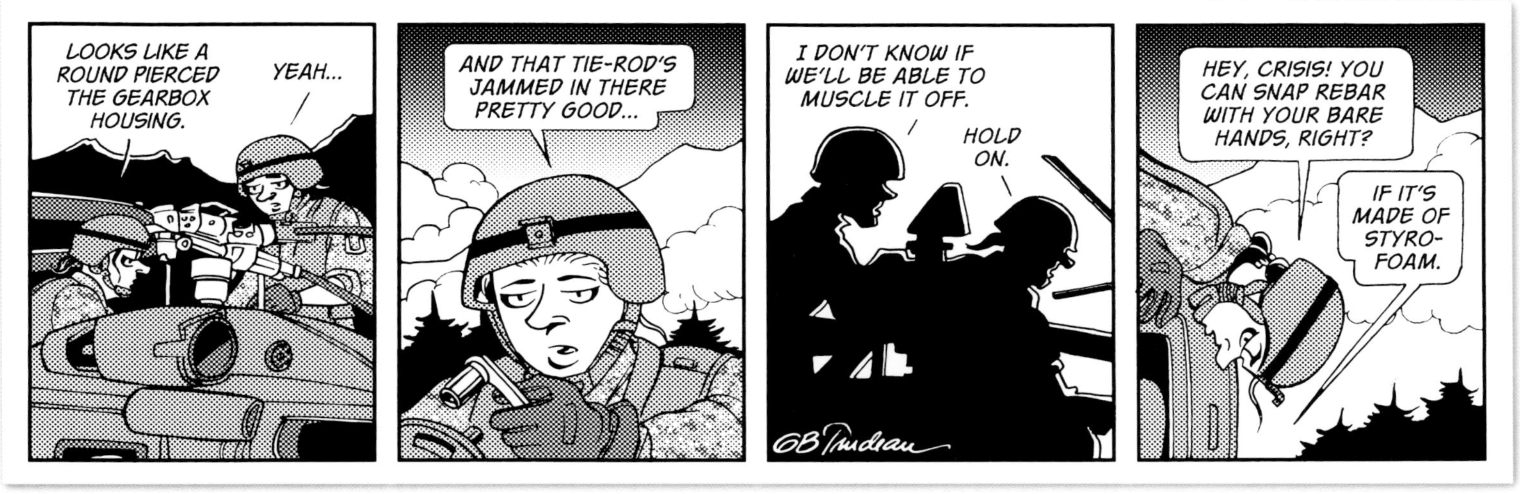
LOOKS LIKE A ROUND PIERCED THE GEARBOX HOUSING.
YEAH...
AND THAT TIE-ROD'S JAMMED IN THERE PRETTY GOOD...
I DON'T KNOW IF WE'LL BE ABLE TO MUSCLE IT OFF.
HOLD ON.
GB Trudeau
HEY, CRISIS! YOU CAN SNAP REBAR WITH YOUR BARE HANDS, RIGHT?
IF IT'S MADE OF STYRO-FOAM.

3/4/10

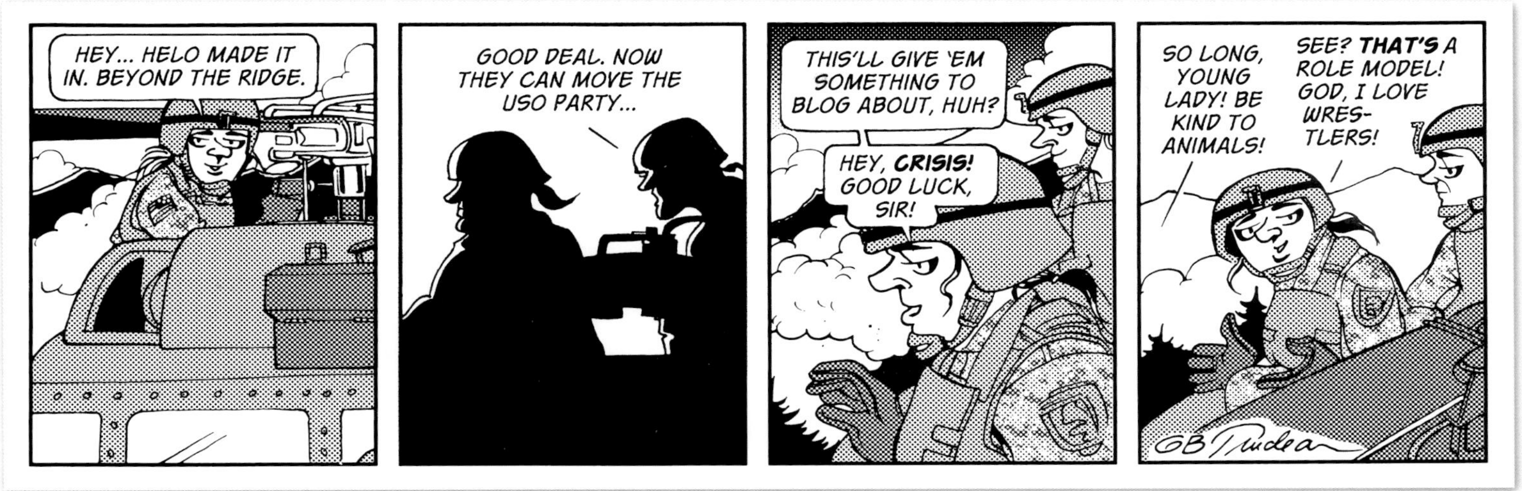
HEY... HELO MADE IT IN. BEYOND THE RIDGE.
GOOD DEAL. NOW THEY CAN MOVE THE USO PARTY...
THIS'LL GIVE 'EM SOMETHING TO BLOG ABOUT, HUH?
HEY, CRISIS! GOOD LUCK, SIR!
SO LONG, YOUNG LADY! BE KIND TO ANIMALS!
SEE? THAT'S A ROLE MODEL! GOD, I LOVE WRES-TLERS!
GB Trudeau

3/5/10

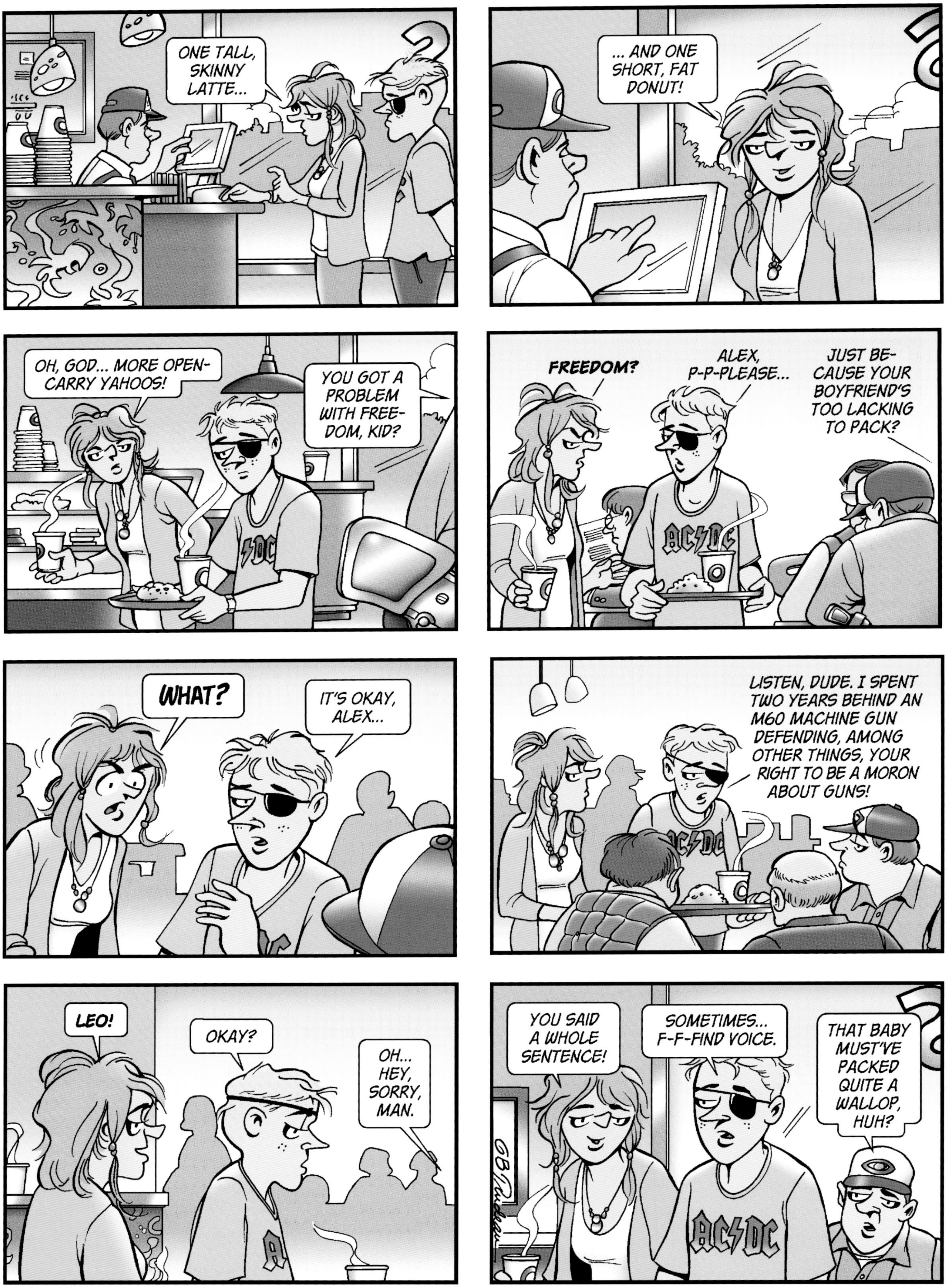
ONE TALL, SKINNY LATTE...
... AND ONE SHORT, FAT DONUT!
OH, GOD... MORE OPEN-CARRY YAHOOS!
YOU GOT A PROBLEM WITH FREE-DOM, KID?
FREEDOM?
ALEX, P-P-PLEASE...
JUST BE-CAUSE YOUR BOYFRIEND'S TOO LACKING TO PACK?
WHAT?
IT'S OKAY, ALEX...
LISTEN, DUDE. I SPENT TWO YEARS BEHIND AN M60 MACHINE GUN DEFENDING, AMONG OTHER THINGS, YOUR RIGHT TO BE A MORON ABOUT GUNS!
LEO!
OKAY?
OH... HEY, SORRY, MAN.
YOU SAID A WHOLE SENTENCE!
SOMETIMES... F-F-FIND VOICE.
THAT BABY MUST'VE PACKED QUITE A WALLOP, HUH?
AC/DC

5/2/10

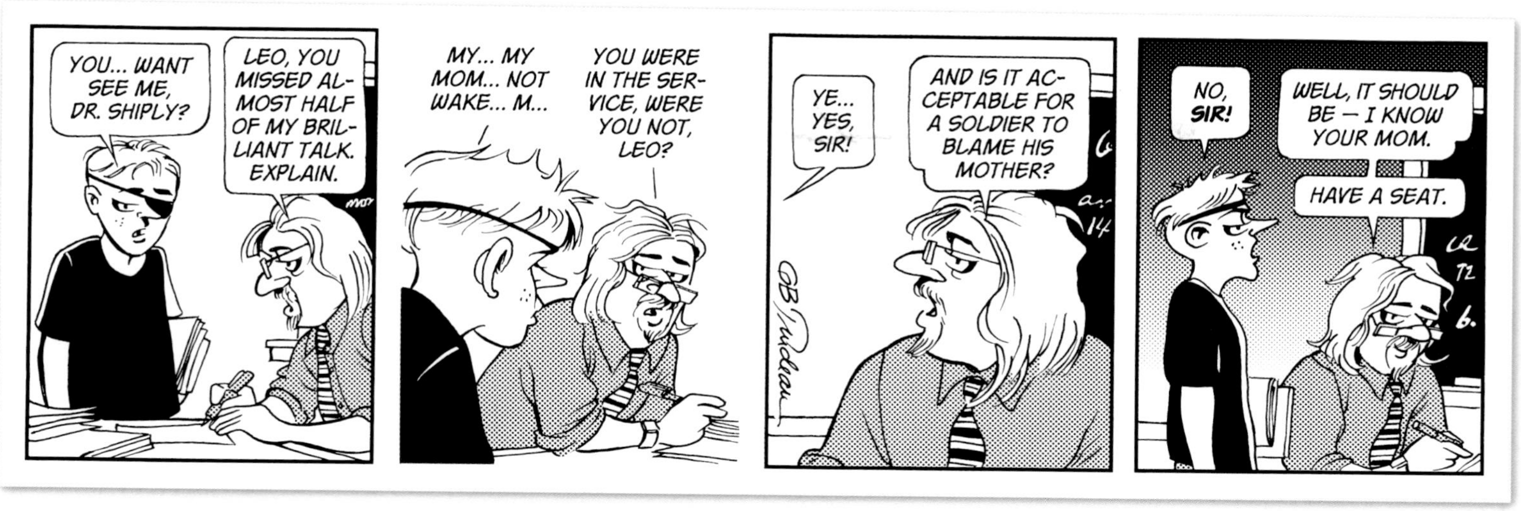
YOU... WANT SEE ME, DR. SHIPLY?
LEO, YOU MISSED ALMOST HALF OF MY BRILLIANT TALK. EXPLAIN.
MY... MY MOM... NOT WAKE... M...
YOU WERE IN THE SERVICE, WERE YOU NOT, LEO?
YE... YES, SIR!
AND IS IT ACCEPTABLE FOR A SOLDIER TO BLAME HIS MOTHER?
NO, SIR!
WELL, IT SHOULD BE — I KNOW YOUR MOM.
HAVE A SEAT.

1/18/10

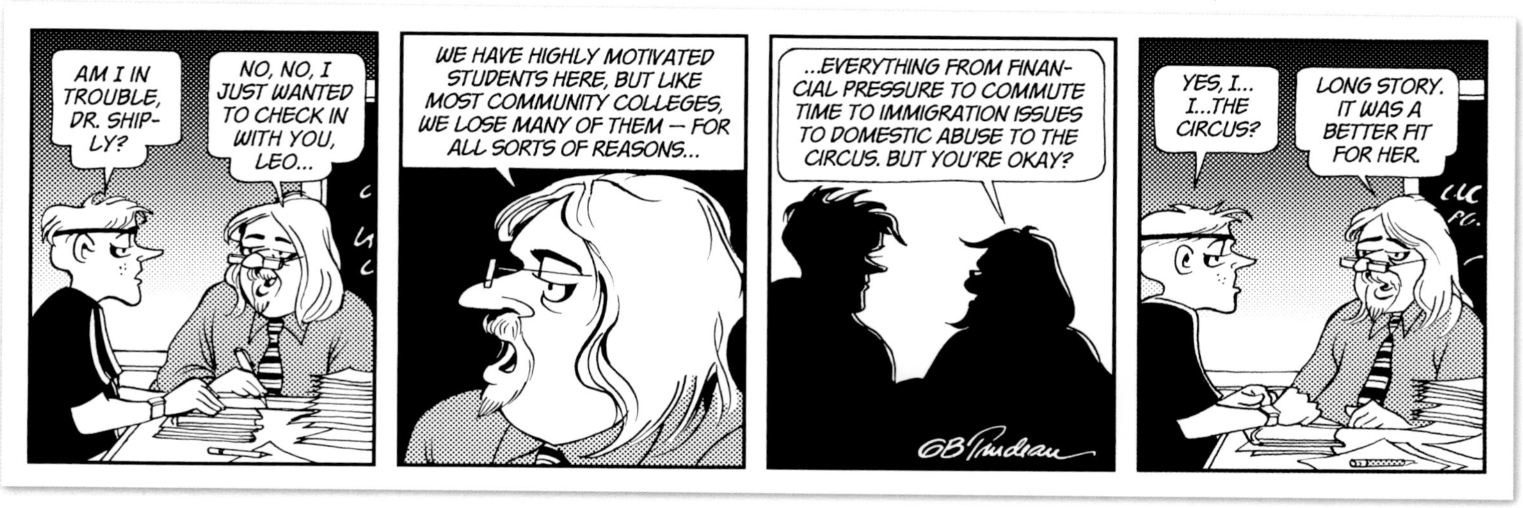
AM I IN TROUBLE, DR. SHIPLY?
NO, NO, I JUST WANTED TO CHECK IN WITH YOU, LEO...
WE HAVE HIGHLY MOTIVATED STUDENTS HERE, BUT LIKE MOST COMMUNITY COLLEGES, WE LOSE MANY OF THEM — FOR ALL SORTS OF REASONS...
...EVERYTHING FROM FINANCIAL PRESSURE TO COMMUTE TIME TO IMMIGRATION ISSUES TO DOMESTIC ABUSE TO THE CIRCUS. BUT YOU'RE OKAY?
YES, I... I...THE CIRCUS?
LONG STORY. IT WAS A BETTER FIT FOR HER.

1/19/10

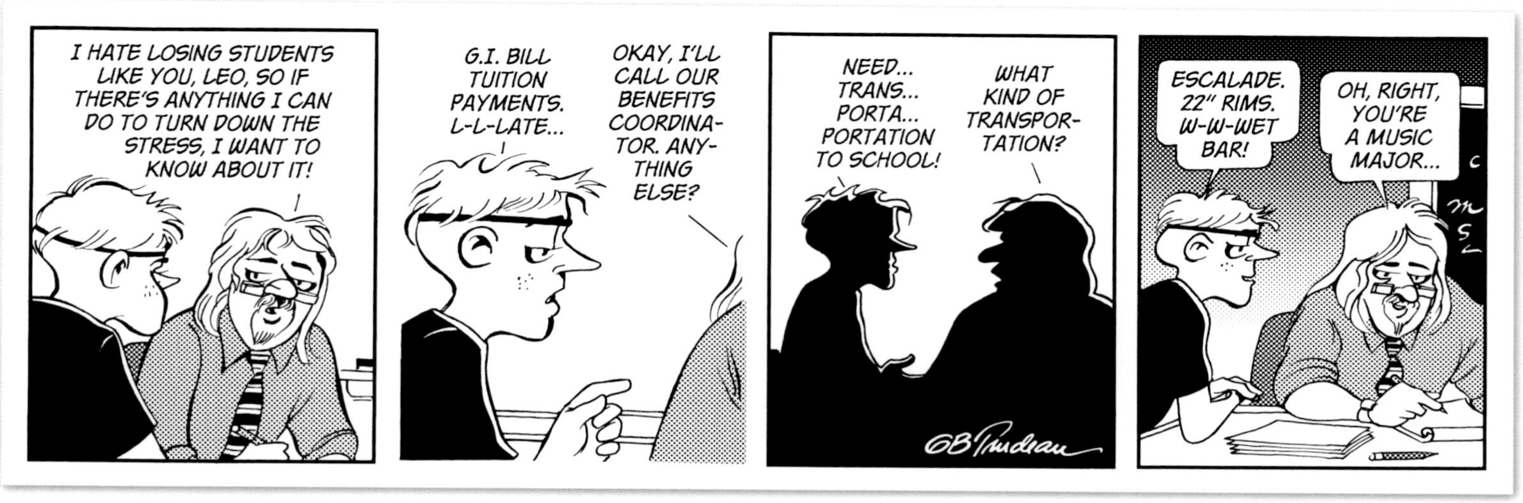
I HATE LOSING STUDENTS LIKE YOU, LEO, SO IF THERE'S ANYTHING I CAN DO TO TURN DOWN THE STRESS, I WANT TO KNOW ABOUT IT!
G.I. BILL TUITION PAYMENTS. L-L-LATE...
OKAY, I'LL CALL OUR BENEFITS COORDINATOR. ANYTHING ELSE?
NEED... TRANS... PORTA... PORTATION TO SCHOOL!
WHAT KIND OF TRANSPORTATION?
ESCALADE. 22" RIMS. W-W-WET BAR!
OH, RIGHT, YOU'RE A MUSIC MAJOR...

1/20/10

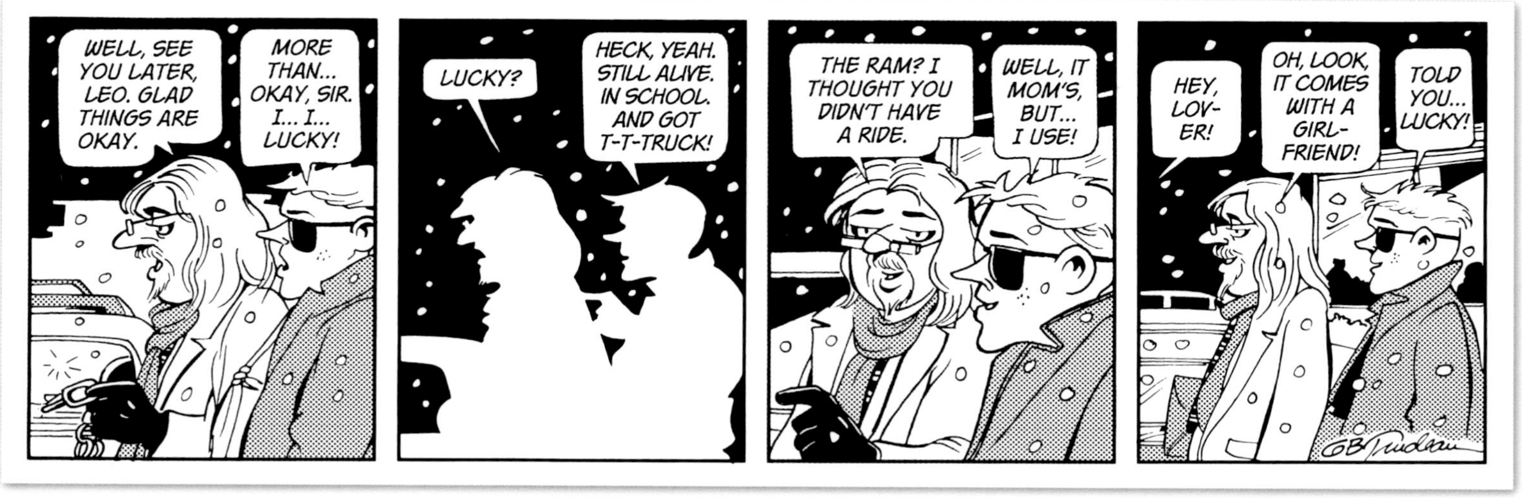
WELL, SEE YOU LATER, LEO. GLAD THINGS ARE OKAY.
MORE THAN... OKAY, SIR. I... I... LUCKY!
LUCKY?
HECK, YEAH. STILL ALIVE. IN SCHOOL. AND GOT T-T-TRUCK!
THE RAM? I THOUGHT YOU DIDN'T HAVE A RIDE.
WELL, IT MOM'S, BUT... I USE!
HEY, LOVER!
OH, LOOK, IT COMES WITH A GIRLFRIEND!
TOLD YOU... LUCKY!

1/23/10

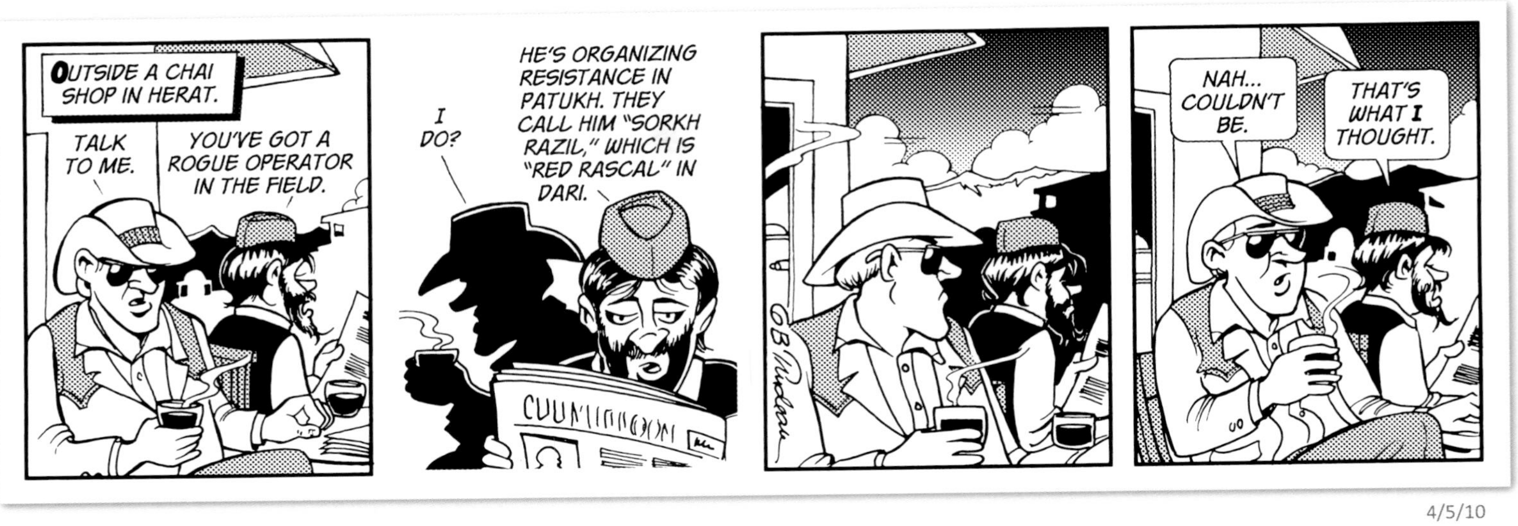
OUTSIDE A CHAI SHOP IN HERAT.
TALK TO ME.
YOU'VE GOT A ROGUE OPERATOR IN THE FIELD.
I DO?
HE'S ORGANIZING RESISTANCE IN PATUKH. THEY CALL HIM "SORKH RAZIL," WHICH IS "RED RASCAL" IN DARI.
GB Trudeau
NAH... COULDN'T BE.
THAT'S WHAT I THOUGHT.

4/5/10

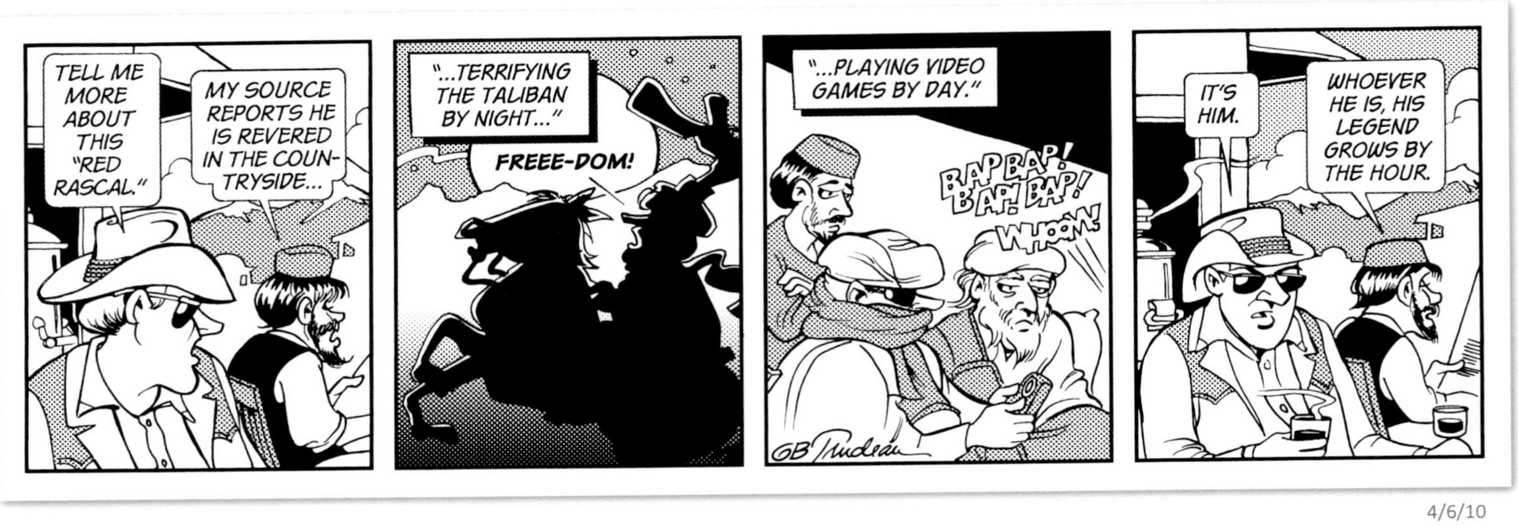
TELL ME MORE ABOUT THIS "RED RASCAL."
MY SOURCE REPORTS HE IS REVERED IN THE COUNTRYSIDE...
"...TERRIFYING THE TALIBAN BY NIGHT..."
FREEE-DOM!
"...PLAYING VIDEO GAMES BY DAY."
BAP BAP! BAP! BAP!
WHOOM!
GB Trudeau
IT'S HIM.
WHOEVER HE IS, HIS LEGEND GROWS BY THE HOUR.

4/6/10

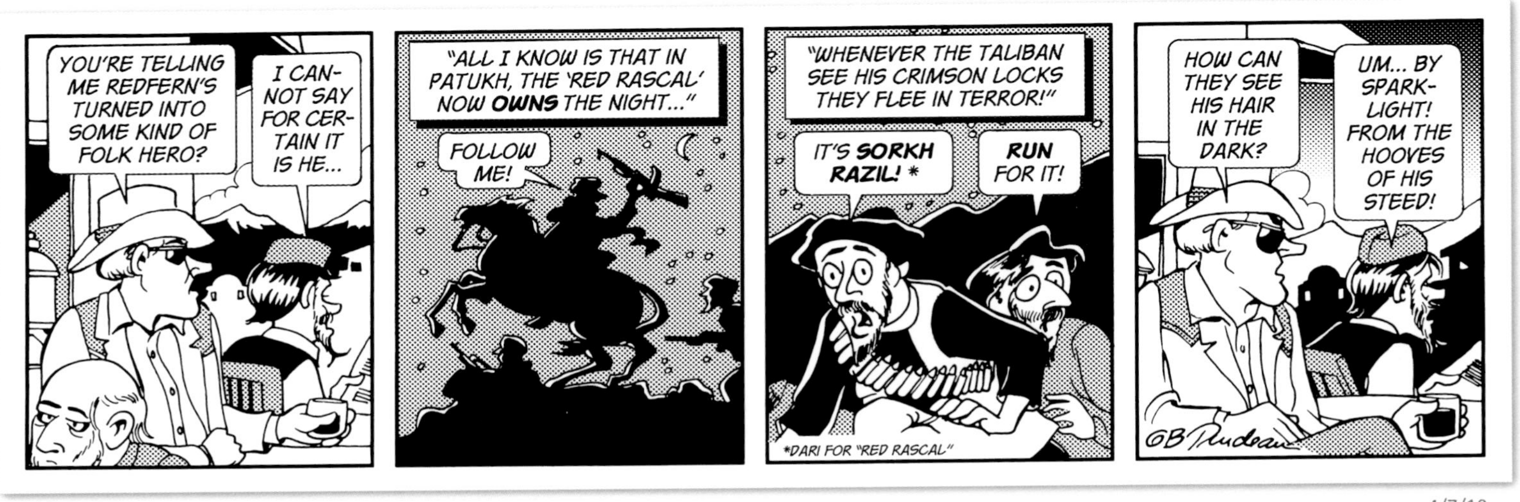
YOU'RE TELLING ME REDFERN'S TURNED INTO SOME KIND OF FOLK HERO?
I CANNOT SAY FOR CERTAIN IT IS HE...
"ALL I KNOW IS THAT IN PATUKH, THE 'RED RASCAL' NOW OWNS THE NIGHT..."
FOLLOW ME!
"WHENEVER THE TALIBAN SEE HIS CRIMSON LOCKS THEY FLEE IN TERROR!"
IT'S SORKH RAZIL! *
RUN FOR IT!
*DARI FOR "RED RASCAL"
HOW CAN THEY SEE HIS HAIR IN THE DARK?
UM... BY SPARKLIGHT! FROM THE HOOVES OF HIS STEED!
GB Trudeau

4/7/10

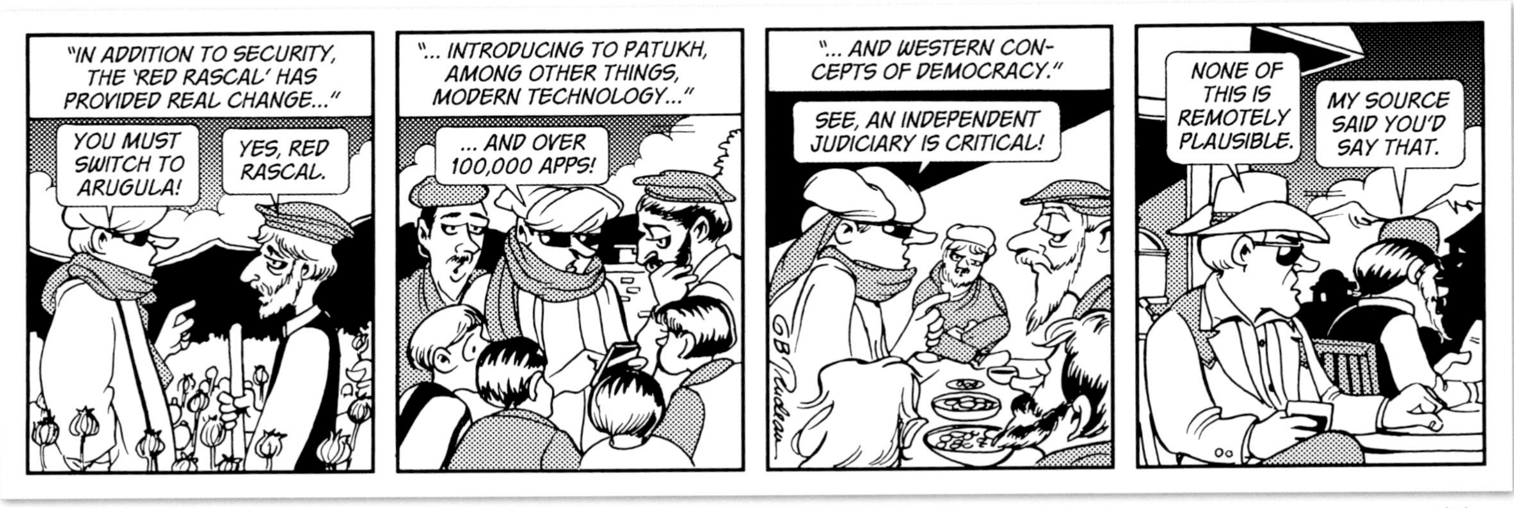
"IN ADDITION TO SECURITY, THE 'RED RASCAL' HAS PROVIDED REAL CHANGE..."
YOU MUST SWITCH TO ARUGULA!
YES, RED RASCAL.
"... INTRODUCING TO PATUKH, AMONG OTHER THINGS, MODERN TECHNOLOGY..."
... AND OVER 100,000 APPS!
"... AND WESTERN CONCEPTS OF DEMOCRACY."
SEE, AN INDEPENDENT JUDICIARY IS CRITICAL!
GB Trudeau
NONE OF THIS IS REMOTELY PLAUSIBLE.
MY SOURCE SAID YOU'D SAY THAT.

4/8/10

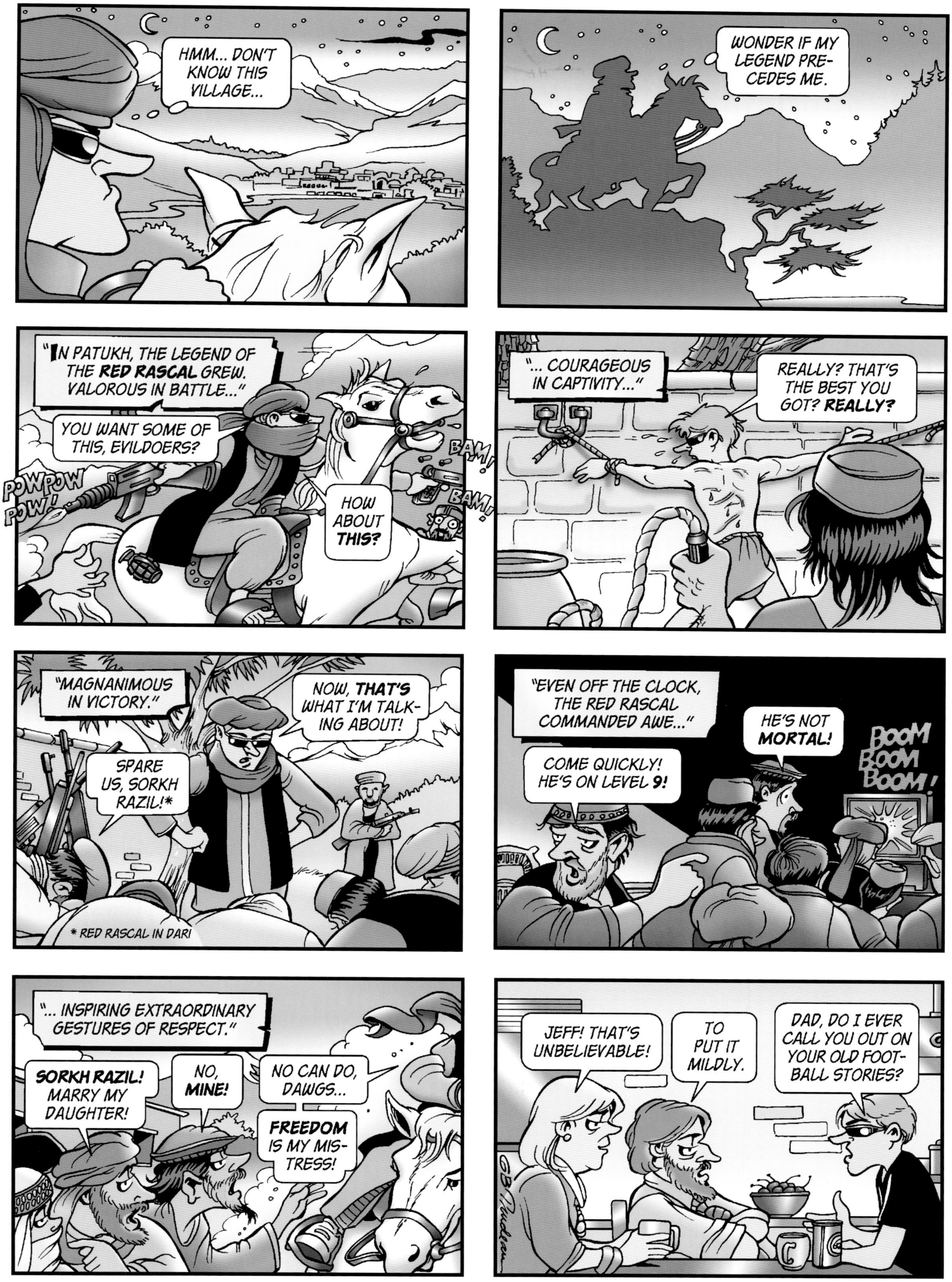
HMM... DON'T KNOW THIS VILLAGE...
WONDER IF MY LEGEND PRECEDES ME.
"IN PATUKH, THE LEGEND OF THE RED RASCAL GREW. VALOROUS IN BATTLE..."
YOU WANT SOME OF THIS, EVILDOERS?
POWPOW POW!
BAM! BAM!
HOW ABOUT THIS?
"... COURAGEOUS IN CAPTIVITY..."
REALLY? THAT'S THE BEST YOU GOT? REALLY?
"MAGNANIMOUS IN VICTORY."
NOW, THAT'S WHAT I'M TALKING ABOUT!
SPARE US, SORKH RAZIL!*
* RED RASCAL IN DARI
"EVEN OFF THE CLOCK, THE RED RASCAL COMMANDED AWE..."
HE'S NOT MORTAL!
COME QUICKLY! HE'S ON LEVEL 9!
BOOM BOOM BOOM!
"... INSPIRING EXTRAORDINARY GESTURES OF RESPECT."
SORKH RAZIL! MARRY MY DAUGHTER!
NO, MINE!
NO CAN DO, DAWGS...
FREEDOM IS MY MISTRESS!
JEFF! THAT'S UNBELIEVABLE!
TO PUT IT MILDLY.
DAD, DO I EVER CALL YOU OUT ON YOUR OLD FOOTBALL STORIES?
GBTrudeau

5/16/10

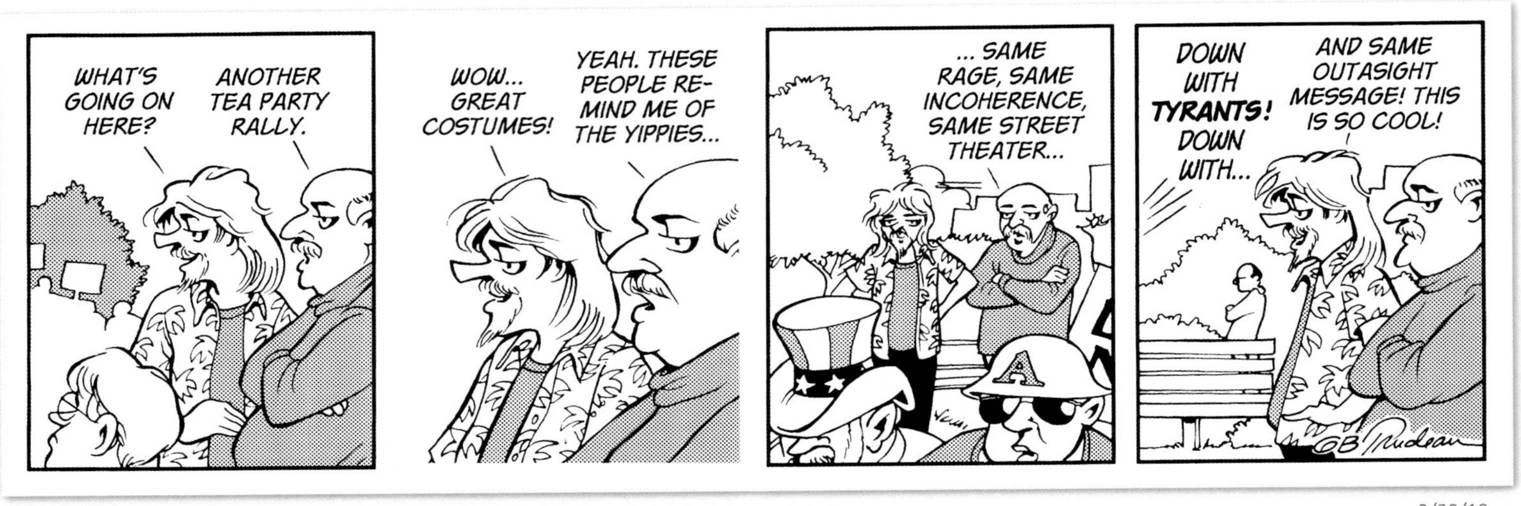
WHAT'S GOING ON HERE?
ANOTHER TEA PARTY RALLY.
WOW... GREAT COSTUMES!
YEAH. THESE PEOPLE REMIND ME OF THE YIPPIES...
... SAME RAGE, SAME INCOHERENCE, SAME STREET THEATER...
DOWN WITH TYRANTS! DOWN WITH...
AND SAME OUTASIGHT MESSAGE! THIS IS SO COOL!
GB Trudeau

3/29/10

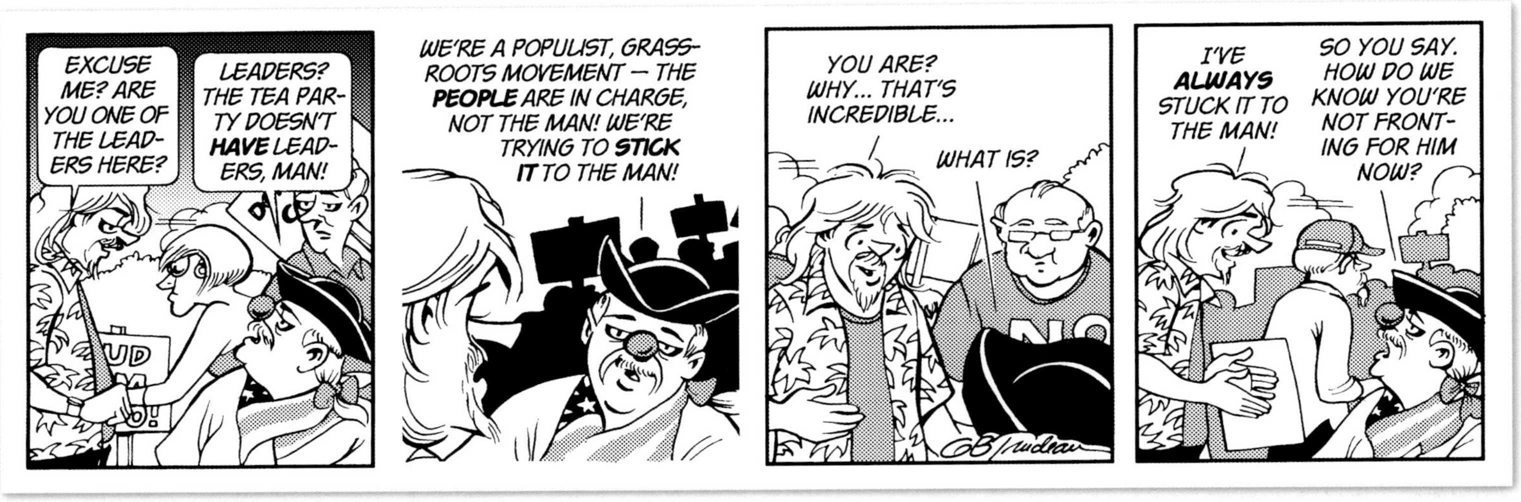
EXCUSE ME? ARE YOU ONE OF THE LEADERS HERE?
LEADERS? THE TEA PARTY DOESN'T HAVE LEADERS, MAN!
WE'RE A POPULIST, GRASSROOTS MOVEMENT — THE PEOPLE ARE IN CHARGE, NOT THE MAN! WE'RE TRYING TO STICK IT TO THE MAN!
YOU ARE? WHY... THAT'S INCREDIBLE...
WHAT IS?
I'VE ALWAYS STUCK IT TO THE MAN!
SO YOU SAY. HOW DO WE KNOW YOU'RE NOT FRONTING FOR HIM NOW?
GB Trudeau

3/30/10

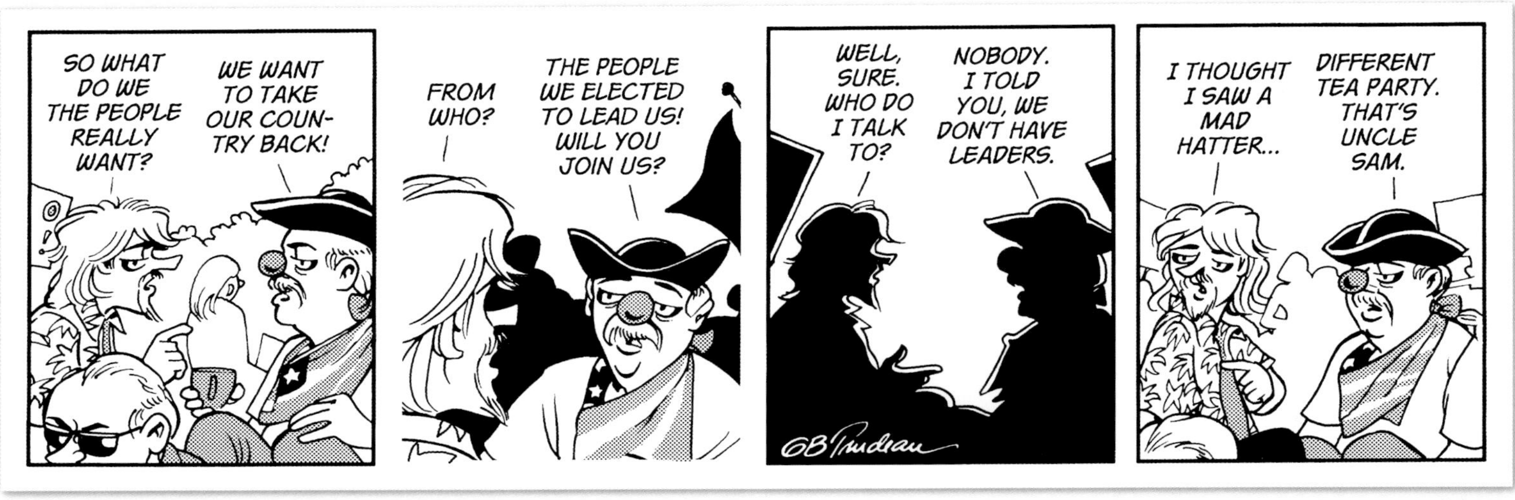
SO WHAT DO WE THE PEOPLE REALLY WANT?
WE WANT TO TAKE OUR COUNTRY BACK!
FROM WHO?
THE PEOPLE WE ELECTED TO LEAD US! WILL YOU JOIN US?
WELL, SURE. WHO DO I TALK TO?
NOBODY. I TOLD YOU, WE DON'T HAVE LEADERS.
I THOUGHT I SAW A MAD HATTER...
DIFFERENT TEA PARTY. THAT'S UNCLE SAM.
GB Trudeau

4/1/10

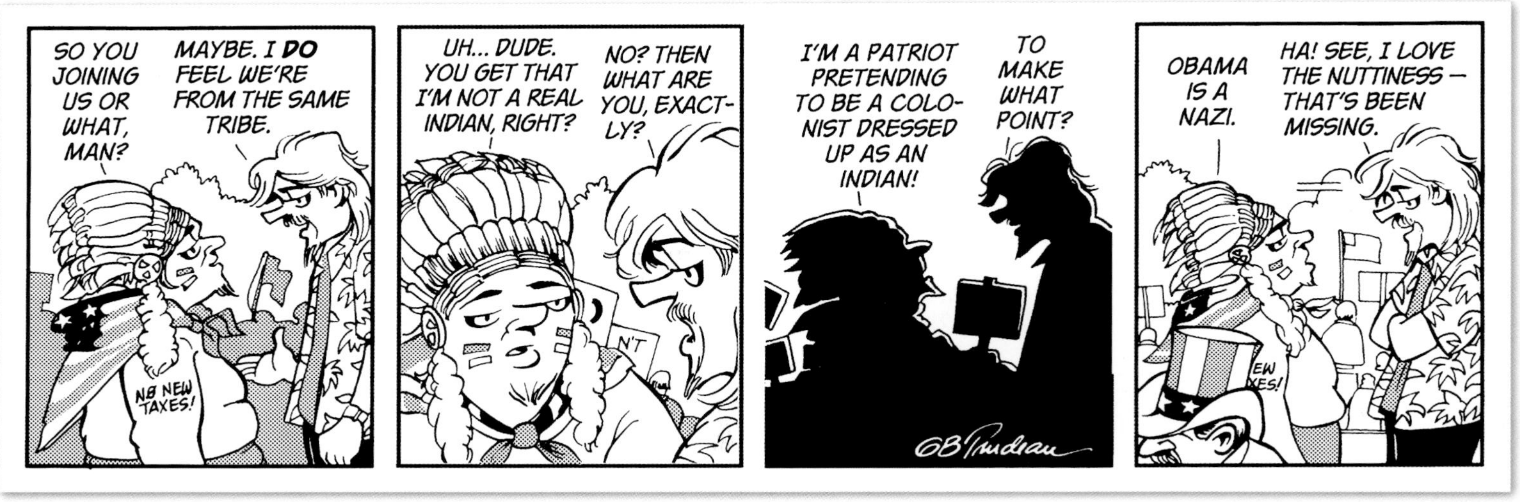
SO YOU JOINING US OR WHAT, MAN?
MAYBE. I DO FEEL WE'RE FROM THE SAME TRIBE.
UH... DUDE. YOU GET THAT I'M NOT A REAL INDIAN, RIGHT?
NO? THEN WHAT ARE YOU, EXACTLY?
I'M A PATRIOT PRETENDING TO BE A COLONIST DRESSED UP AS AN INDIAN!
TO MAKE WHAT POINT?
OBAMA IS A NAZI.
HA! SEE, I LOVE THE NUTTINESS — THAT'S BEEN MISSING.
GB Trudeau

4/2/10

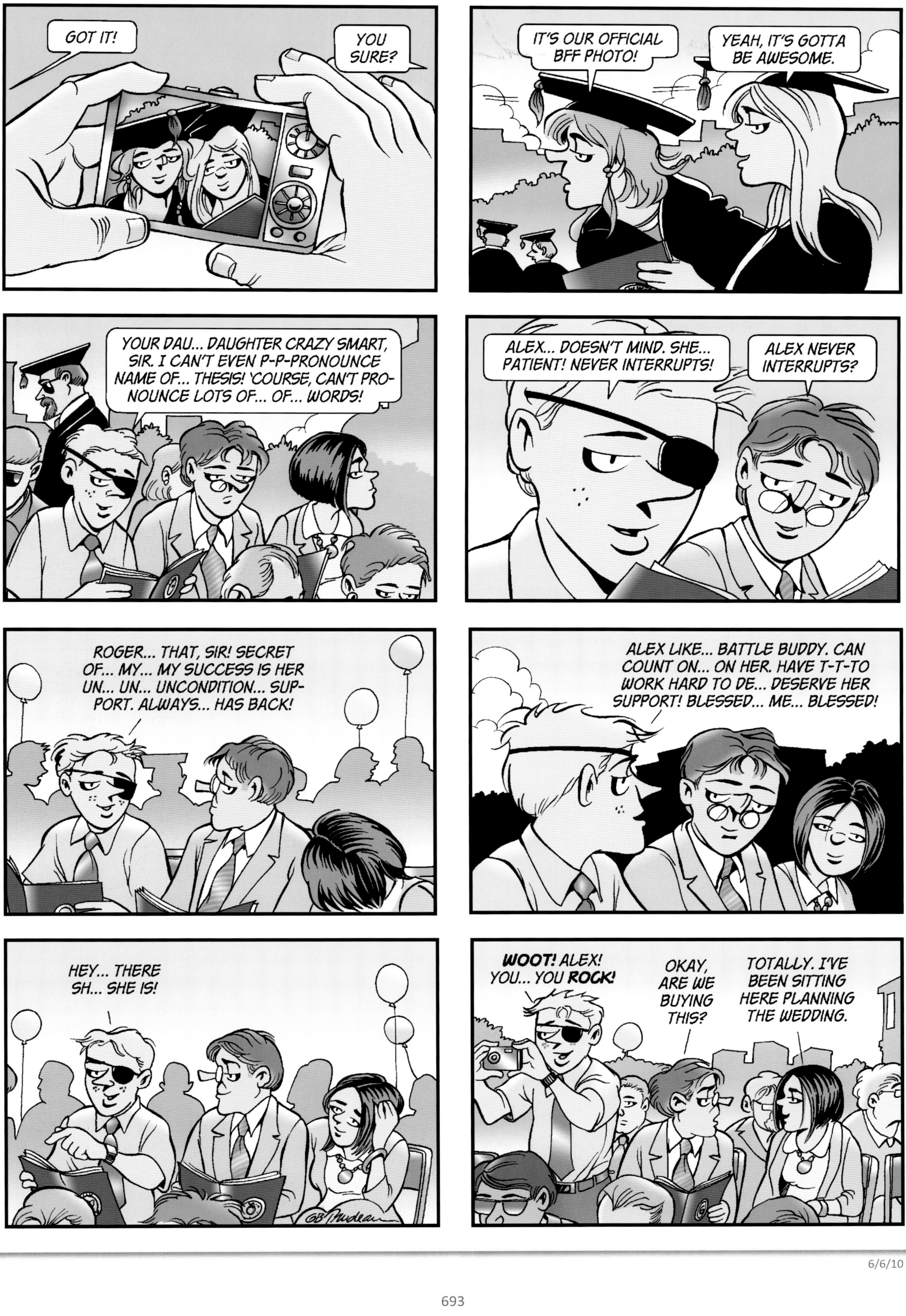
GOT IT!
YOU SURE?
IT'S OUR OFFICIAL BFF PHOTO!
YEAH, IT'S GOTTA BE AWESOME.
YOUR DAU... DAUGHTER CRAZY SMART, SIR. I CAN'T EVEN P-P-PRONOUNCE NAME OF... THESIS! 'COURSE, CAN'T PRONOUNCE LOTS OF... OF... WORDS!
ALEX... DOESN'T MIND. SHE... PATIENT! NEVER INTERRUPTS!
ALEX NEVER INTERRUPTS?
ROGER... THAT, SIR! SECRET OF... MY... MY SUCCESS IS HER UN... UN... UNCONDITION... SUPPORT. ALWAYS... HAS BACK!
ALEX LIKE... BATTLE BUDDY. CAN COUNT ON... ON HER. HAVE T-T-TO WORK HARD TO DE... DESERVE HER SUPPORT! BLESSED... ME... BLESSED!
HEY... THERE SH... SHE IS!
WOOT! ALEX! YOU... YOU **ROCK!**
OKAY, ARE WE BUYING THIS?
TOTALLY. I'VE BEEN SITTING HERE PLANNING THE WEDDING.
GB Trudeau

6/6/10

Acknowledgments

To understand just how much I owe the folks I work with, you need only learn how long each of them has put up with me.

42 years ago, John McMeel and his late partner Jim Andrews talked me into joining their fledgling syndicate, Universal Press. You wouldn't think I'd need much encouragement, but I had others plans, and who knew there was a nice living to be made as a wise guy? Jim, my brilliant editor, passed away in 1980, but John remains the most indulgent boss man on the planet and the dearest of friends.

39 years ago, Don Carlton volunteered to help me survive grad school by inking the strip, and he's been helping me survive deadlines ever since. He has never missed a week for any reason, and I am grateful beyond measure for his talent and loyalty.

33 years ago, Margaret Jane Pauley volunteered to be my girlfriend, and three years later, my wife, even though she knew about the deadline thing, which is famously murder on families. Without her unconditional support, I cannot imagine how this career could have been possible. I love her madly.

Also 33 years ago, Lee Salem, who joined UPS's skeletal staff in 1974, took over as my editor. In addition to saving me from myself, he also shielded me from countless irate publishers, taking hit after hit from clients who accused him, ironically, of not editing the strip. For his steady guidance I will always be appreciative.

30 years ago, David Stanford came on as a personal assistant, and shortly thereafter started editing the *Doonesbury* books, which he does to this day. Currently the Duty Officer at Doonesbury.com and the guiding force behind our milblog, The Sandbox, David has been sounding board, confidant, and brother. I cannot thank him enough.

25 years ago, George Corsillo was brought in to work on a *Doonesbury* desk diary. He has been my design guru and colormaster ever since. As I was originally a graphics guy myself, George's work gives me an inordinate amount of pleasure. More than anyone else, he makes me look more talented than I am, for which I am usually privately grateful.

20 years ago, Mike Seeley joined me as office manager, and he has been keeping chaos at bay ever since. Like everyone else, Mike works with me part-time, but you'd never know it to see my studio. As anyone who's ever dealt with him is aware, Mike's the nicest guy on the team, although as the newbie, he has to be.

For this 40th anniversary volume all the above hands were on deck, but additional thanks are owed to Andrews McMeel honcho Hugh Andrews and honcha Kirsty Melville, whose boundless enthusiasm pushed the book forward; Dorothy O'Brien, for calmly keeping the book on track through its long gestation; Caty Neis, for relentlessly tracking down almost-lost strips; copy chief Dave Shaw, who copyedited everything on the fly; Amy Worley and Kathy Hilliard, for beating the marketing drums softly but persistently; and Michael Reagan, who in addition to the two years he spent overseeing the design and production of the book, surely gave up a couple more anxiously waiting by the presses in China for the final signatures (including this one) to arrive. For all of their care and forbearance I am most grateful.

There are many others who have been a big part of the strip's story through the years, but among the most valued are my wonderful colleagues and friends from back in the day, Kathy Andrews, Bob Duffy, Tom Thornton, and Alan McDermott, as well as my current editor, Sue Roush. To them and all the other members of what remains the coolest family-owned business on earth, my profound thanks.